— 1998 —

INFORMATION

PLEASE®

ALMANAC

Borgna Brunner

EDITOR

information
please LLC

BOSTON

The Information Please® Almanac

Editor
Borgna Brunner

Managing Editor
Tasha M. Vincent

Senior Contributing Editor
Otto T. Johnson (the Sciences, Aerospace,
Military, Disasters, and Finance)

Contributing Editors
Thomas Nemeth (Countries)
Arthur Reed (Current Events)
Christine Frantz (Sports)

The Year in Pictures
Kelly Knauer and Anthony Kosner

Production Editor
Christine Frantz

Electronic Production Specialists
Linda Bean-Pardee, Paul Crook,
Susan Hyde, Nick Raphael

Editorial Assistants
Jessica Angell, Renée Scott

Proofreading and Factchecking
Tina Diodati, Elissa Haney, Holly Hartman,
Ann-Marie Imbornoni, Priscilla Lee,
Geraldine McGowan, Elaine Rho

Indexing
Barbara E. Cohen

The *Information Please Almanac* welcomes comments and suggestions from readers. Though the editors carefully consider each suggestion, because of the volume of correspondence we receive we cannot respond personally to each writer. Information Please does not rule on bets or wagers.

Information Please Almanac
Editorial Office
31 St. James Avenue
Boston, MA 02116-4101
Email: ipa@infoplease.com

ISBN (Paperback): 0-395-88276-1
ISBN (Hardcover): 0-395-88275-3
ISSN: 0073-7860

Previous editions of the *Information Please Almanac* were published from 1995–1996 by Inso Corporation, from 1984–1994 by Houghton Mifflin Company, in 1982 by A&W Publishing Company, from 1979–1981 by Simon & Schuster, from 1977–1978 by Information Please Publishing, Inc., and from 1947–1976 by Dan Golenpaul Associates.

Distributed by Houghton Mifflin Company.

HOW TO ORDER BY MAIL

Copies of the *Information Please Almanac* may be ordered directly by contacting

Customer Service Department
Houghton Mifflin Company
181 Ballardvale Road, Wilmington, MA 01187
phone: 800-225-3362
fax: 800-634-7568

Information Please and *Information Please Almanac* are registered trademarks of Information Please LLC.

Printed in the United States of America.
WP Pa BP Hbd 10 9 8 7 6 5 4 3 2 1

Quick Contents

Special Articles

Sections

Sports Contents

Comprehensive Index

Page numbers in **boldface** refer to main entries in the almanac. Page numbers followed by "n" indicate information in footnotes.

A

Abacus, 539
Abbreviations:
  postal, 628
  of weights and measures, 556–559
Abidjan, Côte d'Ivoire, 220
Abortion, 167, 168, 169, 171, 174, 182
ABSCAM, 168
Absolute zero, 543, 556, 563
Abu Dhabi, United Arab Emirates, 328
Abuja, Nigeria, 290
Academy Awards (Oscars), 713–717
Acadia, 151, 210
Acadia National Park, 578
Accidents. See also Disasters
  aircraft, 466–467, 593, 598–599
  deaths from, 593–602, 842
  fires and explosions, 596–597
  motor vehicle, **844**
  railroad, 600, 844
  rate of, **844**
  shipwrecks, 597–598
Accra, Ghana, 244
Aconcagua Peak, 193, 475, 487
Acre (measure), 557, 558, 560, 563
Acropolis, 143, 669
Actium, Battle of, 145
Actors and actresses:
  awards for, 713–717, 728, 730, 747–748
  famous, 677–705
Adams, John, 50, 54, 77. See also Headline history; Presidents, U.S.
Adams, John Quincy, 54, 78–79. See also Headline history; Presidents, U.S.
Addis Ababa, Ethiopia, 232
Address, forms of, 664–665
Adenauer, Konrad, 243, 677
Administration, Office of, 74–75
Administrative Conference of the U.S., 76
Admirals (U.S.), first, 53
Adrenaline, isolation of, 539
Adriatic Sea, 190, 260, 306, 342
Advent (season), 424, 425
Advertising, 113
Aegean Islands, 245
Aegean Sea, 245, 325
Aerial combat, first, 467
Aerial photographers, first, 466
Aeschylus, 143
Affirmative action, 173
Afghanistan, 168, 189, 302
AFL-CIO, 164, 633–634
Africa. See also Continents; Countries
  area and elevation of, 487
  environmental outlook in, 572
  exploration of, 487
  map of, 508
  partition of, 158
  political situation in, 1005
  population of, 179, 485
  Portuguese territory in, 299
  religions of, 407
  southernmost point of, 313
Agate (measure), 560
Age:
  arrests by, 854
  death rates by, 846
  at first marriage, 363, **837**
  life expectancy by, 846–847
  population by, 826, 829

  and poverty, 123
  school enrollment by, **862**
Age limits, driving licenses, 857
Agencies:
  U.N., 346–347
  U.S., 75–77
Aggtelek Cavern, 481
Agincourt, Battle of, 148
Aging, 630. See also Social security
Agnew, Spiro T., 55, 56n, 167
Agriculture. See also Food
  ancient, 141, 538
  animals on farms, 118
  economic statistics, 117–118
  farm employment, 130
  income from, 118
  production by state, 117
  world, 187–188
Agriculture, U.S. Dept. of (USDA):
  description, 75
  Secretaries of, 68–71, 75
AIDS, 610–612
  cases of, 611
  deaths from, 842, **843**
  reference books, 629
  treatment, 611–612
  worldwide situation, 610–611
Air (atmosphere), 433, 446–447
Air Force, U.S.:
  Secretary of, 75
Air Force Academy, U.S., 385
Airlines. See also Travel
  first scheduled passenger service, 467
  freight carried by, 114, 469
  Internet resources, 551
  passenger traffic, 469
Airmail:
  first, 53, 467
  international, **628**
  rates, **628**
Airplanes:
  accidents, 598–599
  exports and imports, 119
  invention of, 466, 539
  passenger traffic, 469
Air pollutants, 577
Airports, world's busiest, 469
Air transport company, first, 466
Akkadian civilization, 141, 143
Alabama, 753
Alabama-Coosa River, 493
Alamo, Battle of the, 155, 782
Aland Islands, 234
Alaska, 753–754
  discovery of, 151
  exploration of, 488, 754
  Gold Rush in, 754
  maps of, 501, **502**
  mountain peaks, 493
  national parks in, 578–579, 754
  natives of, 100, 103
  oil in, 754
  purchase of, 46, 156, 754
  volcanoes in, 754
Albania, 189–190, 1006
Albany, N.Y., 774
Alberta, Canada, 209
Albert Canal, 676
Albright, Madeleine, 520, 1021
Alcohol. See Liquor
Alcohol abuse, 380
Aldrin, Edwin E., Jr., 166, 459
Aleutian Islands, 153
  maps of, 500, **502**
Alexander the Great, 143, 189, 229, 255, 487, 677

Alexandria, Egypt, 228
  Pharos of, 669
Alfred the Great, 147
Algeria, 190–191, 1005
  independence of, 166
  War of Independence, 164, 235
Algiers, Algeria, 190
Alhambra, 670
Ali, Muhammad (Cassius Clay), 918, 946
Aliens. See Immigration statistics
Allende, Salvador, 213
Alliance for Progress, 165
All Saints' Day, 424
All-Star Game (baseball), 976–977
Almaty, Kazakhstan, 263
Alpha Centauri, 433
Alps, 195, 235, 260, 318
  tunnels under, 676
Altamaha-Ocmulgee River, 493
Altamira Cave, 481
Altiplano, 201
Altitude records, aircraft, 471
Altitudes. See Elevations
Aluminum, chemical properties of, 531
Amazon River, 203–204, 217, 478, 488
Amendments to Constitution, 40–44
  civil rights, 40–44
  right to bear arms, 40
  unreasonable search and seizure, 40
American Academy of Arts and Letters, 635
American Battle Monuments Commission, 76
American Cancer Society, 834
American Federation of Labor, 164, 633–634
American folklore, 57
American Heart Association, 834
American history. See United States history
American Independent Party, 62
American Indian Movement (AIM), 99
American Indians. See Indians (American)
American League. See Baseball; Football
American Red Cross, 642, 834
American Revolution. See Revolutionary War, American
American Samoa, 788–789
American's Creed, 50
American Sign Language, 668
America's Cup, 974–975
Amish. See Mennonites
Amman, Jordan, 263
Amperes, 556, 560
Amphetamines, 378
Amsterdam, Netherlands, 286
Amsterdam-Rhine Canal, 676
Amtrak, 77
Amu Darya River, 478
Amur (Heilong) River, 214, 478
Amusement. See Entertainment and culture; Leisure; Recreation
Ancient empires, 141–145
  maps of, 142, 144, 146
Ancient history, events of, 141–145
Andaman Islands, 252
Andaman Sea, 476
Andes, 193, 213, 217, 296, 475–476
Andorra, 191
Andorra la Vella, Andorra, 191
Andropov, Yuri V., 168, 169, 303

H

Q

R

T

X

Y

Z

U.S. History & Government

The Declaration of Independence

In Congress, July 4, 1776

The unanimous Declaration of the thirteen United States of America

When in the Course of human events it becomes necessary for one people to dissolve the political bands which have connected them with another, and to assume among the powers of the earth, the separate and equal station to which the Laws of Nature and of Nature's God entitle them, a decent respect to the opinions of mankind requires that they should declare the causes which impel them to the separation.

We hold these truths to be self-evident, that all men are created equal, that they are endowed by their Creator with certain unalienable Rights, that among these are Life, Liberty and the pursuit of Happiness.—That to secure these rights, Governments are instituted among Men, deriving their just powers from the consent of the governed,—That whenever any Form of Government becomes destructive of these ends, it is the Right of the People to alter or to abolish it, and to institute new Government, laying its foundation on such principles and organizing its powers in such form, as to them shall seem most likely to effect their Safety and Happiness. Prudence, indeed, will dictate that Governments long established should not be changed for light and transient causes; and accordingly all experience hath shewn that mankind are more disposed to suffer, while evils are sufferable, than to right themselves by abolishing the forms to which they are accustomed. But when a long train of abuses and usurpations, pursuing invariably the same Object evinces a design to reduce them under absolute Despotism, it is their right, it is their duty, to throw off such Government, and to provide new Guards for their future security.—Such has been the patient sufferance of these Colonies; and such is now the necessity which constrains them to alter their former Systems of Government. The history of the present King of Great Britain is a history of repeated injuries and usurpations, all having in direct object the establishment of an absolute Tyranny over these States. To prove this, let Facts be submitted to a candid world.

He has refused his Assent to Laws, the most wholesome and necessary for the public good.

He has forbidden his Governors to pass Laws of immediate and pressing importance, unless suspended in their operation till his Assent should be obtained; and when so suspended, he has utterly neglected to attend to them.

He has refused to pass other Laws for the accommodation of large districts of people, unless those people would relinquish the right of Representation in the Legislature, a right inestimable to them and formidable to tyrants only.

He has called together legislative bodies at places unusual, uncomfortable, and distant from the depository of their Public Records, for the sole purpose of fatiguing them into compliance with his measures.

He has dissolved Representative Houses repeatedly, for opposing with manly firmness his invasions on the rights of the people.

He has refused for a long time, after such dissolutions, to cause others to be elected; whereby the Legislative Powers, incapable of Annihilation, have returned to the People at large for their exercise; the State remaining in the mean time exposed to all the dangers of invasion from without, and convulsions within.

He has endeavoured to prevent the population of these States; for that purpose obstructing the Laws for Naturalization of Foreigners; refusing to pass others to encourage their migrations hither, and raising the conditions of new Appropriations of Lands.

He has obstructed the Administration of Justice, by refusing his Assent to Laws for establishing Judiciary Powers.

He has made Judges dependent on his Will alone, for the tenure of their offices, and the amount and payment of their salaries.

He has erected a multitude of New Offices, and sent hither swarms of Officers to harass our people, and eat out their substance.

He has kept among us, in times of peace, Standing Armies without the Consent of our legislatures.

He has affected to render the Military independent of and superior to the Civil Power.

He has combined with others to subject us to a jurisdiction foreign to our constitution, and unacknowledged by our laws; giving his Assent to their Acts of pretended Legislation:

For quartering large bodies of armed troops among us:

For protecting them, by a mock Trial, from punishment for any Murders which they should commit on the Inhabitants of these States:

For cutting off our Trade with all parts of the world:

For imposing Taxes on us without our Consent:

For depriving us in many cases, of the benefits of Trial by Jury:

For transporting us beyond Seas to be tried for pretended offences:

For abolishing the free System of English Laws in a neighbouring Province, establishing therein an Arbitrary

---

NOTE: On April 12, 1776, the legislature of North Carolina authorized its delegates to the Continental Congress to join with others in a declaration of separation from Great Britain; the first colony to instruct its delegates to take the actual initiative was Virginia on May 15. On June 7, 1776, Richard Henry Lee of Virginia offered a resolution to the Congress to the effect "that these United Colonies are, and of right ought to be, free and independent States. . . ." A committee, consisting of Thomas Jefferson, John Adams, Benjamin Franklin, Robert R. Livingston, and Roger Sherman was organized to "prepare a declaration to the effect of the said first resolution." The Declaration of Independence was adopted on July 4, 1776.
Most delegates signed the Declaration August 2, but George Wythe (Va.) signed August 27; Richard Henry Lee (Va.), Elbridge Gerry (Mass.), and Oliver Wolcott (Conn.) in September; Matthew Thornton (N.H.), not a delegate until September, in November; and Thomas McKean (Del.), although present on July 4, not until 1781 by special permission, having served in the army in the interim.

government, and enlarging its Boundaries so as to render it at once an example and fit instrument for introducing the same absolute rule into these Colonies:

For taking away our Charters, abolishing our most valuable Laws and altering fundamentally the Forms of our Governments:

For suspending our own Legislatures, and declaring themselves invested with power to legislate for us in all cases whatsoever.

He has abdicated Government here, by declaring us out of his Protection and waging War against us.

He has plundered our seas, ravaged our Coasts, burnt our towns, and destroyed the lives of our people.

He is at this time transporting large Armies of foreign Mercenaries to compleat the works of death, desolation, and tyranny, already begun with circumstances of Cruelty & Perfidy scarcely paralleled in the most barbarous ages, and totally unworthy the Head of a civilized nation.

He has constrained our fellow Citizens taken Captive on the high Seas to bear Arms against their Country, to become the executioners of their friends and Brethren, or to fall themselves by their Hands.

He has excited domestic insurrections amongst us, and has endeavoured to bring on the inhabitants of our frontiers, the merciless Indian Savages, whose known rule of warfare, is an undistinguished destruction of all ages, sexes and conditions.

In every stage of these Oppressions We have Petitioned for Redress in the most humble terms: Our repeated Petitions have been answered only by repeated injury. A Prince, whose character is thus marked by every act which may define a Tyrant, is unfit to be the ruler of a free people.

Nor have We been wanting in attentions to our Brittish brethren. We have warned them from time to time of attempts by their legislature to extend an unwarrantable jurisdiction over us. We have reminded them of the circumstances of our emigration and settlement here. We have appealed to their native justice and magnanimity, and we have conjured them by the ties of our common kindred to disavow these usurpations, which would inevitably interrupt our connections and correspondence. They too have been deaf to the voice of justice and of consanguinity. We must, therefore, acquiesce in the necessity, which denounces our Separation, and hold them, as we hold the rest of mankind, Enemies in War, in Peace Friends.

We, therefore, the Representatives of the United States of America, in General Congress, Assembled, appealing to the Supreme Judge of the world for the rectitude of our intentions, do, in the Name, and by Authority of the good People of these Colonies, solemnly publish and declare, That these United Colonies are, and of Right ought to be Free and Independent States; that they are Absolved from all Allegiance to the British Crown, and that all political connection between them and the State of Great Britain, is and ought to be totally dissolved; and that as Free and Independent States, they have full Power to levy War, conclude Peace, contract Alliances, establish Commerce, and to do all other Acts and Things which Independent States may of right do.—And for the support of this Declaration, with a firm reliance on the protection of Divine Providence, we mutually pledge to each other our Lives, our Fortunes and our sacred Honor.

—John Hancock

New Hampshire
Josiah Bartlett
Wm. Whipple
Matthew Thornton

Rhode Island
Step. Hopkins
William Ellery

Connecticut
Roger Sherman
Sam'el Huntington
Wm. Williams
Oliver Wolcott

New York
Wm. Floyd
Phil. Livingston
Frans. Lewis
Lewis Morris

New Jersey
Richd. Stockton
Jno. Witherspoon
Fras. Hopkinson
John Hart
Abra. Clark

Pennsylvania
Robt. Morris
Benjamin Rush
Benj. Franklin
John Morton
Geo. Clymer
Jas. Smith
Geo. Taylor
James Wilson
Geo. Ross

Massachusetts-Bay
Saml. Adams
John Adams
Robt. Treat Paine
Elbridge Gerry

Delaware
Caesar Rodney
Geo. Read
Tho. M'Kean

Maryland
Samuel Chase
Wm. Paca
Thos. Stone
Charles Carroll of Carrollton

Virginia
George Wythe
Richard Henry Lee
Th. Jefferson
Benj. Harrison
Ths. Nelson, Jr.
Francis Lightfoot Lee
Carter Braxton

North Carolina
Wm. Hooper
Joseph Hewes
John Penn

South Carolina
Edward Rutledge
Thos. Heyward, Junr.
Thomas Lynch, Junr.
Arthur Middleton

Georgia
Button Gwinnett
Lyman Hall
Geo. Walton

Constitution of the United States of America

(Historical text has been edited to conform to contemporary American usage. The bracketed words are designations for your convenience; they are not part of the Constitution.)

The oldest federal constitution in existence was framed by a convention of delegates from twelve of the thirteen original states in Philadelphia in May, 1787, Rhode Island failing to send a delegate. George Washington presided over the session, which lasted until September 17, 1787. The draft (originally a preamble and seven Articles) was submitted to all thirteen states and was to become effective when ratified by nine states. It went into effect on the first Wednesday in March, 1789, having been ratified by New Hampshire, the ninth state to approve, on June 21, 1788. The states ratified the Constitution in the following order:

Delaware	December 7, 1787	Delaware	December 7, 1787
Pennsylvania	December 12, 1787	South Carolina	May 23, 1788
New Jersey	December 18, 1787	New Hampshire	June 21, 1788
Georgia	January 2, 1788	Virginia	June 25, 1788
Connecticut	January 9, 1788	New York	July 26, 1788
Massachusetts	February 6, 1788	North Carolina	November 21, 1789
Maryland	April 28, 1788	Rhode Island	May 29, 1790

[Preamble]

We the people of the United States, in order to form a more perfect Union, establish justice, insure domestic tranquility, provide for the common defence, promote the general welfare, and secure the blessings of liberty to ourselves and our posterity, do ordain and establish this Constitution for the United States of America.

Article I

Section 1

[Legislative powers vested in Congress.] All legislative powers herein granted shall be vested in a Congress of the United States, which shall consist of a Senate and House of Representatives.

Section 2

[Composition of the House of Representatives.—1.] The House of Representatives shall be composed of members chosen every second year by the people of the several States, and the electors in each State shall have the qualifications requisite for electors of the most numerous branch of the State Legislature.

[Qualifications of Representatives.—2.] No Person shall be a Representative who shall not have attained to the age of twenty-five years, and been seven years a citizen of the United States, and who shall not, when elected, be an inhabitant of that State in which he shall be chosen.

[Apportionment of Representatives and direct taxes—census.[1]—3.] (Representatives and direct taxes shall be apportioned among the several States which may be included within this Union, according to their respective numbers, which shall be determined by adding to the whole number of free persons, including those bound to service for a term of years, and excluding Indians not taxed, three fifths of all other persons.) The actual enumeration shall be made within three years after the first meeting of the Congress of the United States, and within every subsequent term of ten years, in such manner as they shall by law direct. The number of Representatives shall not exceed one for every thirty thousand, but each State shall have at least one Representative; and until such enumeration shall be made, the State of New Hampshire shall be entitled to choose three, Massachusetts eight, Rhode-Island and Providence Plantations one, Connecticut five, New York six, New Jersey four, Pennsylvania eight, Delaware one,

Maryland six, Virginia ten, North Carolina five, South Carolina five, and Georgia three.

[Filling of vacancies in representation.—4.] When vacancies happen in the representation from any State, the Executive Authority thereof shall issue writs of election to fill such vacancies.

[Selection of officers; power of impeachment.—5.] The House of Representatives shall choose their Speaker and other officers; and shall have the sole power of impeachment.

Section 3[2]

[The Senate.—1.] The Senate of the United States shall be composed of two Senators from each State, chosen by the Legislature thereof, for six years; and each Senator shall have one vote.

[Classification of Senators; filling of vacancies.—2.] Immediately after they shall be assembled in consequence of the first election, they shall be divided as equally as may be into three classes. The seats of the Senators of the first class shall be vacated at the expiration of the second year, of the second class at the expiration of the fourth year, and of the third class at the expiration of the sixth year, so that one-third may be chosen every second year; and if vacancies happen by resignation, or otherwise, during the recess of the Legislature of any State, the Executive thereof may make temporary appointments (until the next meeting of the Legislature, which shall then fill such vacancies).

[Qualification of Senators.—3.] No person shall be a Senator who shall not have attained to the age of thirty years, and been nine years a citizen of the United States, and who shall not, when elected, be an inhabitant of that State for which he shall be chosen.

[Vice President to be President of Senate.—4.] The Vice President of the United States shall be President of the Senate, but shall have no vote, unless they be equally divided.

[Selection of Senate officers; President pro tempore.—5.] The Senate shall choose their other officers, and also a President pro tempore, in the absence of the Vice President, or when he shall exercise the office of President of the United States.

[Senate to try impeachments.—6.] The Senate shall have the sole power to try all impeachments. When sitting for that purpose, they shall be on oath or affirmation. When the President of the United States is tried,

---

1. The clause included in parentheses is amended by the 14th Amendment, Section 2.
2. The first paragraph of this section and the part of the second paragraph included in parentheses are amended by the 17th Amendment.

the Chief Justice shall preside: and no person shall be convicted without the concurrence of two thirds of the members present.

[Judgment in cases of Impeachment.—7.] Judgment in cases of impeachment shall not extend further than to removal from office, and disqualification to hold and enjoy any office of honor, trust, or profit under the United States: but the party convicted shall nevertheless be liable and subject to indictment, trial, judgment and punishment, according to Law.

Section 4

[Control of congressional elections.—1.] The times, places, and manner of holding elections for Senators and Representatives, shall be prescribed in each State by the Legislature thereof; but the Congress may at any time by law make or alter such regulations, except as to the places of choosing Senators.

[Time for assembling of Congress³—2.] The Congress shall assemble at least once in every year, and such meeting shall be on the first Monday in December, unless they shall by law appoint a different day.

Section 5

[Each house to be the judge of the election and qualifications of its members; regulations as to quorum.—1.] Each House shall be the judge of the elections, returns, and qualifications of its own members, and a majority of each shall constitute a quorum to do business; but a smaller number may adjourn from day to day, and may be authorized to compel the attendance of absent members, in such manner, and under such penalties as each House may provide.

[Each house to determine its own rules.—2.] Each House may determine the rules of its proceedings, punish its members for disorderly behavior, and, with the concurrence of two thirds, expel a member.

[Journals and yeas and nays.—3.] Each House shall keep a journal of its proceedings, and from time to time publish the same, excepting such parts as may in their judgment require secrecy; and the yeas and nays of the members of either House on any question shall, at the desire of one fifth of those present, be entered on the journal.

[Adjournment.—4.] Neither House, during the session of Congress, shall, without the consent of the other, adjourn for more than three days, nor to any other place than that in which the two Houses shall be sitting.

Section 6

[Compensation and privileges of members of Congress.—1.] The Senators and Representatives shall receive a compensation for their services, to be ascertained by law, and paid out of the Treasury of the United States. They shall in all cases, except treason, felony, and breach of the peace, be privileged from arrest during their attendance at the session of their respective Houses, and in going to and returning from the same; and for any speech or debate in either House, they shall not be questioned in any other place.

[Incompatible offices; exclusions.—2.] No Senator or Representative shall, during the time for which he was elected, be appointed to any civil office under the authority of the United States, which shall have been created, or the emoluments whereof shall have been increased during such time; and no person holding any office under the United States shall be a member of either House during his continuance in office.

Section 7

[Revenue bills to originate in House.—1.] All bills for raising revenue shall originate in the House of Rep-

resentatives; but the Senate may propose or concur with amendments as on other bills.

[Manner of passing bills; veto power of President.—2.] Every bill which shall have passed the House of Representatives and the Senate, shall, before it becomes a law, be presented to the President of the United States; if he approve he shall sign it, but if not he shall return it, with his objections to that House in which it shall have originated, who shall enter the objections at large on their journal, and proceed to reconsider it. If after such reconsideration two thirds of that House shall agree to pass the bill, it shall be sent, together with the objections, to the other House, by which it shall likewise be reconsidered, and if approved by two thirds of that House, it shall become a law. But in all such cases the votes of both Houses shall be determined by yeas and nays, and the names of the persons voting for and against the bill shall be entered on the journal of each house, respectively. If any bill shall not be returned by the President within ten days (Sundays excepted) after it shall have been presented to him, the same shall be a law, in like manner as if he had signed it, unless the Congress by their adjournment prevent its return, in which case it shall not be a law.

[Concurrent orders or resolutions, to be passed by President.—3.] Every order, resolution, or vote to which the concurrence of the Senate and House of Representatives may be necessary (except on a question of adjournment) shall be presented to the President of the United States; and before the same shall take effect, shall be approved by him, or being disapproved by him, shall be repassed by two thirds of the Senate and House of Representatives, according to the rules and limitations prescribed in the case of a bill.

Section 8

[General powers of Congress.⁴]

[Taxes, duties, imposts, and excises.—1.] The Congress shall have power to lay and collect taxes, duties, imposts and excises, to pay the debts and provide for the common defense and general welfare of the United States; but all duties, imposts and excises shall be uniform throughout the United States;

[Borrowing of money.—2.] To borrow money on the credit of the United States;

[Regulation of commerce.—3.] To regulate commerce with foreign nations, and among the several States, and with the Indian tribes;

[Naturalization and bankruptcy.—4.] To establish a uniform rule of naturalization, and uniform laws on the subject of bankruptcies throughout the United States;

[Money, weights and measures.—5.] To coin money, regulate the value thereof, and of foreign coin, and fix the standard of weights and measures;

[Counterfeiting.—6.] To provide for the punishment of counterfeiting the securities and current coin of the United States;

[Post offices.—7.] To establish post offices and post roads;

[Patents and copyrights.—8.] To promote the progress of science and useful arts, by securing for limited times to authors and inventors the exclusive right to their respective writings and discoveries;

[Inferior courts.—9.] To constitute tribunals inferior to the Supreme Court;

[Piracies and felonies.—10.] To define and punish piracies and felonies committed on the high seas, and offences against the law of nations;

---

3. Amended by the 20th Amendment, Section 2.
4. By the 16th Amendment, Congress is given the power to lay and collect taxes on income.

[**War; marque and reprisal.—11.**] To declare war, grant letters of marque and reprisal, and make rules concerning captures on land and water;

[**Armies.—12.**] To raise and support armies, but no appropriation of money to that use shall be for a longer term than two years;

[**Navy.—13.**] To provide and maintain a navy;

[**Land and naval forces.—14.**] To make rules for the government and regulation of the land and naval forces;

[**Calling out militia.—15.**] To provide for calling forth the militia to execute the laws of the Union, suppress insurrections, and repel invasions;

[**Organizing, arming, and disciplining militia.—16.**] To provide for organizing, arming, and disciplining, the militia, and for governing such part of them as may be employed in the service of the United States, reserving to the States, respectively, the appointment of the officers, and the authority of training the militia according to the discipline prescribed by Congress;

[**Exclusive legislation over District of Columbia.—17.**] To exercise exclusive legislation in all cases whatsoever, over such district (not exceeding ten miles square) as may, by cession of particular States, and the acceptance of Congress, become the seat of the Government of the United States, and to exercise like authority over all places purchased by the consent of the Legislature of the State in which the same shall be, for the erection of forts, magazines, arsenals, dock-yards, and other needful buildings;—And

[**To enact laws necessary to enforce Constitution.—18.**] To make all laws which shall be necessary and proper for carrying into execution the foregoing powers, and all other powers vested by this Constitution in the Government of the United States, or in any department or officer thereof.

Section 9

[**Migration or importation of certain persons not to be prohibited before 1808.—1.**] The migration or importation of such persons as any of the States now existing shall think proper to admit, shall not be prohibited by the Congress prior to the year one thousand eight hundred and eight, but a tax or duty may be imposed on such importation, not exceeding ten dollars for each person.

[**Writ of habeas corpus not to be suspended; exception.—2.**] The privilege of the writ of habeas corpus shall not be suspended, unless when in cases of rebellion or invasion the public safety may require it.

[**Bills of attainder and ex post facto laws prohibited.—3.**] No bill of attainder or ex post facto law shall be passed.

[**Capitation and other direct taxes.—4.**] No capitation, or other direct, tax shall be laid, unless in proportion to the census or enumeration herein before directed to be taken.[5]

5. See the 16th Amendment.

[**Exports not to be taxed.—5.**] No tax or duty shall be laid on articles exported from any State.

[**No preference to be given to ports of any States; interstate shipping.—6.**] No preference shall be given by any regulation of commerce or revenue to the ports of one State over those of another: nor shall vessels bound to, or from, one State, be obliged to enter, clear, or pay duties in another.

[**Money, how drawn from treasury; financial statements to be published.—7.**] No money shall be drawn from the Treasury, but in consequence of appropriations made by law; and a regular statement and account of the receipts and expenditures of all public money shall be published from time to time.

[**Titles of nobility not to be granted; acceptance by government officers of favors from foreign powers.—8.**] No title of nobility shall be granted by the United States: and no person holding any office of profit or trust under them, shall, without the consent of the Congress, accept of any present, emolument, office, or title, of any kind whatever, from any king, prince, or foreign state.

Section 10

[**Limitations of the powers of the several States.—1.**] No State shall enter into any treaty, alliance, or confederation; grant letters of marque and reprisal; coin money; emit bills of credit; make any thing but gold and silver coin a tender in payment of debts; pass any bill of attainder, ex post facto law, or law impairing the obligation of contracts, or grant any title of nobility.

[**State imposts and duties.—2.**] No State shall, without the consent of the Congress, lay any imposts or duties on imports or exports, except what may be absolutely necessary for executing its inspection laws; and the net produce of all duties and imposts, laid by any State on imports or exports, shall be for the use of the Treasury of the United States; and all such laws shall be subject to the revision and control of the Congress.

[**Further restrictions on powers of States.—3.**] No State shall, without the consent of Congress, lay any duty of tonnage, keep troops, or ships of war in time of peace, enter into any agreement or compact with another state, or with a foreign power, or engage in war, unless actually invaded, or in such imminent danger as will not admit of delay.

Article II

Section 1

[**The President; the executive power.—1.**] The executive power shall be vested in a President of the United States of America. He shall hold his office during the term of four years, and, together with the Vice President, chosen for the same term, be elected, as follows

[**Appointment and qualifications of presidential electors.—2.**] Each State shall appoint, in such manner as the Legislature thereof may direct, a number of electors, equal to the whole number of Senators and Representatives to which the State may be entitled in the Congress: but no Senator or Representative, or person holding an office of trust or profit under the United States, shall be appointed an elector.

[**Original method of electing the President and Vice President.[6]**] (The electors shall meet in their respective States, and vote by ballot for two persons, of whom one at least shall not be an inhabitant of the same State with themselves. And they shall make a list of all the persons voted for, and of the number of votes for each; which list they shall sign and certify, and transmit sealed to the seat of the Government of the United States, directed to the President of the Senate. The President of the Senate shall, in the presence of the Senate and House of Representatives, open all the certificates, and the votes shall then be counted. The person having the greatest number of votes shall be the President, if such number be a majority of the whole number of electors appointed; and if there be more than one who have such majority, and have an equal number of votes, then the House of Representatives shall immediately choose by ballot one of them for President; and if no person have a majority, then from the five highest on the list the said House shall in like manner choose the President. But in choosing the President, the votes shall be taken by States, the representation from each State having one vote; A quorum for this purpose shall

---

6. This clause has been superseded by the 12th Amendment.

consist of a member or members from two thirds of the States, and a majority of all the states shall be necessary to a choice. In every case, after the choice of the President, the person having the greatest number of votes of the electors shall be the Vice President. But if there should remain two or more who have equal votes, the Senate should choose from them by ballot the Vice President.)

[Congress may determine time of choosing electors and day for casting their votes.—3.] The Congress may determine the time of choosing the electors, and the day on which they shall give their votes; which day shall be the same throughout the United States.

[Qualifications for the office of President.[7]—4.] No person except a natural born citizen, or a citizen of the United States, at the time of the adoption of this Constitution, shall be eligible to the office of President; neither shall any person be eligible to that office who shall not have attained to the age of thirty-five years, and been fourteen years a resident within the United States.

[Filling vacancy in the office of President.[8]—5.] In case of the removal of the President from office, or of his death, resignation, or inability to discharge the powers and duties of the said office, the same shall devolve on the Vice President, and the Congress may by law provide for the case of removal, death, resignation or inability, both of the President and Vice President, declaring what officer shall then act as President, and such officer shall act accordingly, until the disability be removed, or a President shall be elected.

[Compensation of the President.—6.] The President shall, at stated times, receive for his services, a compensation, which shall neither be increased nor diminished during the period for which he shall have been elected, and he shall not receive within that period any other emolument from the United States, or any of them.

[Oath to be taken by the President.—7.] Before he enter on the execution of his office, he shall take the following oath or affirmation:—"I do solemnly swear (or affirm) that I will faithfully execute the office of President of the United States, and will to the best of my ability, preserve, protect, and defend the Constitution of the United States."

Section 2

[The President to be commander in chief of army and navy and head of executive departments; may grant reprieves and pardons.—1.] The President shall be Commander in Chief of the Army and Navy of the United States, and of the militia of the several States, when called into the actual service of the United States; he may require the opinion, in writing, of the principal officer in each of the executive departments, upon any subject relating to the duties of their respective offices, and he shall have power to grant reprieves and pardons for offences against the United States, except in cases of impeachment.

[President may, with concurrence of Senate, make treaties, appoint ambassadors, etc.; appointment of inferior officers, authority of Congress over.—2.] He shall have power, by and with the advice and consent of the Senate, to make treaties, provided two thirds of the Senators present concur; and he shall nominate, and by and with the advice and consent of the Senate, shall appoint ambassadors, other public ministers and consuls, judges of the Supreme Court, and all other officers of the United States, whose appointments are not herein otherwise provided for, and which shall be established by law: but the Congress may by law vest the appoint-

ment of such inferior officers, as they think proper, in the President alone, in the courts of law, or in the heads of departments.

[President may fill vacancies in office during recess of Senate.—3.] The President shall have power to fill up all vacancies that may happen during the recess of the Senate, by granting commissions which shall expire at the end of their session.

Section 3

[President to give advice to Congress; may convene or adjourn it on certain occasions; to receive ambassadors, etc.; have laws executed and commission all officers.] He shall from time to time give to the Congress information of the state of the Union, and recommend to their consideration such measures as he shall judge necessary and expedient; he may, on extraordinary occasions, convene both Houses, or either of them, and in case of disagreement between them, with respect to the time of adjournment, he may adjourn them to such time as he shall think proper; he shall receive ambassadors and other public ministers: he shall take care that the laws be faithfully executed, and shall commission all the officers of the United States.

Section 4

[All civil officers removable by impeachment.] The President, Vice President, and all civil officers of the United States shall be removed from office on impeachment for, and conviction of, treason, bribery, or other high crimes and misdemeanors.

Article III

Section 1

[Judicial powers; how vested; term of office and compensation of judges.] The judicial Power of the United States, shall be vested in one Supreme Court, and in such inferior courts as the Congress may from time to time ordain and establish. The judges, both of the supreme and inferior courts, shall hold their offices during good behavior, and shall, at stated times, receive for their services, a compensation, which shall not be diminished during their continuance in office.

Section 2

[Jurisdiction of Federal courts[9]—1.] The judicial power shall extend to all cases, in law and equity, arising under this Constitution, the laws of the United States, and treaties made, or which shall be made, under their authority; to all cases affecting ambassadors, other public ministers and consuls; to all cases of admiralty and maritime jurisdiction; to controversies to which the United States, shall be a party; to controversies between two or more States; between a State and citizens of another State; between citizens of different States; between citizens of the same State claiming lands under grants of different states, and between a State, or the citizens thereof, and foreign states, citizens, or subjects.

[Original and appellate jurisdiction of Supreme Court.—2.] In all cases affecting ambassadors, other public ministers and consuls, and those in which a State shall be party, the Supreme Court shall have original jurisdiction. In all the other cases before mentioned, the Supreme Court shall have appellate jurisdiction, both as to law and fact, with such exceptions, and under such regulations, as the Congress shall make.

[Trial of all crimes, except impeachment, to be by jury.—3.] The trial of all crimes, except in cases of impeachment, shall be by jury; and such trial shall be held in the State where the said crimes shall have been committed; but when not committed within any State,

7. For qualifications of the Vice President, see the 12th Amendment.
8. Amended by the 20th Amendment, Sections 3 and 4.
9. This section is abridged by the 11th Amendment.

the trial shall be at such place or places as the Congress may by law have directed.

Section 3

[**Treason defined; conviction of.—1.**] Treason against the United States, shall consist only in levying war against them, or, in adhering to their enemies, giving them aid and comfort. No person shall be convicted of treason unless on the testimony of two witnesses to the same overt act, or on confession in open court.

[**Congress to declare punishment for treason; proviso.—2.**] The Congress shall have power to declare the punishment of treason, but no attainder of treason shall work corruption of blood, or forfeiture except during the life of the person attained.

Article IV

Section 1

[**Each State to give full faith and credit to the public acts and records of other States.**] Full faith and credit shall be given in each State to the public acts, records, and judicial proceedings of every other State. And the Congress may by general laws prescribe the manner in which such acts, records, and proceedings shall be proved, and the effect thereof.

Section 2

[**Privileges of citizens.—1.**] The citizens of each State shall be entitled to all privileges and immunities of citizens in the several States.

[**Extradition between the several States.—2.**] A person charged in any State with treason, felony, or other crime, who shall flee from justice, and be found in another State, shall on demand of the Executive authority of the State from which he fled, be delivered up, to be removed to the State having jurisdiction of the crime.

[**Persons held to labor or service in one State, fleeing to another, to be returned.—3.**] No person held to service or labor in one State, under the laws thereof, escaping into another, shall, in consequence of any law or regulation therein, be discharged from such service or labor, but shall be delivered up on claim of the party to whom such service or labor may be due.

Section 3

[**New States.—1.**] New States may be admitted by the Congress into this Union; but no new State shall be formed or erected within the jurisdiction of any other State; nor any State be formed by the junction of two or more States, or parts of States, without the consent of the Legislatures of the States concerned as well as of the Congress.

[**Regulations concerning territory.—2.**] The Congress shall have power to dispose of and make all needful rules and regulations respecting the territory or other property belonging to the United States; and nothing in this Constitution shall be so construed as to prejudice any claims of the United States, or of any particular State.

Section 4

[**Republican form of government and protection guaranteed the several States.**] The United States shall guarantee to every State in this Union a Republican form of government, and shall protect each of them against invasion; and on application of the Legislature, or of the Executive (when the Legislature cannot be convened) against domestic violence.

Article V

[**Ways in which the Constitution can be amended.**] The Congress, whenever two thirds of both Houses shall deem it necessary, shall propose amendments to this Constitution, or, on the application of the Legislatures of two thirds of the several States shall call a convention for proposing amendments, which, in either case, shall be valid to all intents and purposes, as part of this Constitution, when ratified by the Legislatures of three fourths of the several States, or by conventions in three fourths thereof, as the one or the other mode of ratification may be proposed by the Congress; provided that no amendment which may be made prior to the year one thousand eight hundred and eight shall in any manner affect the first and fourth clauses in the ninth Section of the first Article; and that no State, without its consent, shall be deprived of its equal suffrage in the Senate.

Article VI

[**Debts contracted under the confederation secured.—1.**] All debts contracted and engagements entered into, before the adoption of this Constitution, shall be as valid against the United States under this Constitution, as under the Confederation.

[**Constitution, laws, and treaties of the United States to be supreme.—2.**] This Constitution, and the laws of the United States which shall be made in pursuance thereof; and all treaties made, or which shall be made, under the authority of the United States, shall be the supreme law of the land; and the judges in every State shall be bound thereby, any thing in the Constitution or laws of any State to the contrary notwithstanding.

[**Who shall take constitutional oath; no religious test as to official qualification.—3.**] The Senators and Representatives before mentioned, and the members of the several State Legislatures, and all executive and judicial officers, both of the United States and of the several States, shall be bound by oath or affirmation, to support this Constitution; but no religious test shall ever be required as a qualification to any office or public trust under the United States.

Article VII

[**Constitution to be considered adopted when ratified by nine States.**] The ratification of the conventions of nine States shall be sufficient for the establishment of this Constitution between the States so ratifying the same.

Done in convention by the unanimous consent of the States present the seventeenth day of September in the year of our Lord one thousand seven hundred and eighty seven and of the independence of the United States of America the Twelfth. In witness whereof we have hereunto subscribed our names.

George Washington
President and Deputy from Virginia

New Hampshire
John Langdon
Nicholas Gilman

Massachusetts
Nathaniel Gorham
Rufus King

Connecticut
Wm. Saml. Johnson
Roger Sherman

New York
Alexander Hamilton

New Jersey
Wil. Livingston

Wm. Paterson
David Brearley
Jona. Dayton

Pennsylvania
B. Franklin
Thomas Mifflin
Robt. Morris
Geo. Clymer
Thos. FitzSimons
Jared Ingersoll
James Wilson
Gouv. Morris

Delaware
Geo. Read
Gunning Bedford Jun.
John Dickinson
Richard Bassett
Jaco. Broom

Maryland
James McHenry
Dan. of St. Thos. Jenifer
Danl. Carroll

Virginia
John Blair
James Madison, Jr.

North Carolina
Wm. Blount
Richd Dobbs Spaight
Hu. Williamson

South Carolina
J. Rutledge
Charles Cotesworth Pinckney
Charles Pinckney
Pierce Butler

Georgia
William Few
Abr. Baldwin
Attest: William Jackson,
Secretary

Amendments to the Constitution of the United States

(Amendments I to X inclusive, popularly known as the Bill of Rights, were proposed and sent to the states by the first session of the First Congress. They were ratified Dec. 15, 1791.)

Amendment I

[Freedom of religion, speech, of the press, and right of petition.] Congress shall make no law respecting an establishment of religion, or prohibiting the free exercise thereof; or abridging the freedom of speech, or of the press; or the right of the people peaceably to assemble, and to petition the Government for a redress of grievances.

Amendment II

[Right of people to bear arms not to be infringed.] A well regulated militia, being necessary to the security of a free State, the right of the people to keep and bear arms, shall not be infringed.

Amendment III

[Quartering of troops.] No soldier shall, in time of peace be quartered in any house, without the consent of the owner, nor in time of war, but in a manner to be prescribed by law.

Amendment IV

[Persons and houses to be secure from unreasonable searches and seizures.] The right of the people to be secure in their persons, houses, papers, and effects, against unreasonable searches and seizures, shall not be violated, and no warrants shall issue, but upon probable cause, supported by oath or affirmation, and particularly describing the place to be searched, and the persons or things to be seized.

Amendment V

[Trials for crimes; just compensation for private property taken for public use.] No person shall be held to answer for a capital, or otherwise infamous crime, unless on a presentment or indictment of a Grand Jury, except in cases arising in the land or naval forces, or in the militia, when in actual service in time of war or public danger; nor shall any person be subject for the same offence to be twice put in jeopardy of life or limb; nor shall be compelled in any criminal case to be a witness against himself, nor be deprived of life, liberty, or property, without due process of law; nor shall private property be taken for public use, without just compensation.

Amendment VI

[Civil rights in trials for crimes enumerated.] In all criminal prosecutions, the accused shall enjoy the right to a speedy and public trial, by an impartial jury of the State and district wherein the crime shall have been committed, which district shall have been previously ascertained by law, and to be informed of the nature and cause of the accusation; to be confronted with the witnesses against him; to have compulsory process for obtaining witnesses in his favor, and to have the assistance of counsel for his defense.

Amendment VII

[Civil rights in civil suits.] In suits at common law, where the value in controversy shall exceed twenty dollars, the right of trial by jury shall be preserved, and no fact tried by a jury, shall be otherwise re-examined in any court of the United States, than according to the rules of the common law.

Amendment VIII

[Excessive bail, fines, and punishments prohibited.] Excessive bail shall not be required, nor excessive fines imposed, nor cruel and unusual punishments inflicted.

Amendment IX

[Reserved rights of people.] The enumeration in the Constitution, of certain rights, shall not be construed to deny or disparage others retained by the people.

Amendment X

[Powers not delegated, reserved to states and people respectively.] The powers not delegated to the United States by the Constitution, nor prohibited by it to the States, are reserved to the States, respectively, or to the people.

Amendment XI

(The proposed amendment was sent to the states Mar. 5, 1794, by the Third Congress. It was ratified Feb. 7, 1795.)
[Judicial power of United States not to extend to suits against a State.] The judicial power of the United States shall not be construed to extend to any suit in law or equity, commenced or prosecuted against one of the United States by citizens of another State, or by citizens or subjects of any foreign state.

Amendment XII

(The proposed amendment was sent to the states Dec. 12, 1803, by the Eighth Congress. It was ratified July 27, 1804.)

[Present mode of electing President and Vice-President by electors.[1]]

The electors shall meet in their respective states, and vote by ballot for President and Vice President, one of whom, at least, shall not be an inhabitant of the same state with themselves; they shall name in their ballots the person voted for as President, and in distinct ballots the person voted for as Vice President, and they shall make distinct lists of all persons voted for as President, and of all persons voted for as Vice President, and of the number of votes for each, which lists they shall sign and certify, and transmit sealed to the seat of the government of the United States, directed to the President of the Senate; the President of the Senate shall, in the presence of the Senate and House of Representatives, open all the certificates and the votes shall then be counted; the person having the greatest number of votes for President, shall be the President, if such number be a majority of the whole number of electors appointed; and if no person have such majority, then from the persons having the highest numbers not exceeding three on the list of those voted for as President, the House of Representatives shall choose immediately, by ballot, the President. But in choosing the President, the votes shall be taken by states, the representation from each State having one vote; a quorum for this purpose shall consist of a member or members from two thirds of the states, and a majority of all the states shall be necessary to a choice. And if the House of Representatives shall not choose a President whenever the right of choice shall devolve upon them, before the fourth day of March next following, then the Vice President shall act as President, as in the case of the death or other constitutional disability of the President. The person having the greatest number of votes as Vice President, shall be the Vice President, if such number be a majority of the whole number of electors appointed, and if no person have a majority, then from the two highest numbers on the list, the Senate shall choose the Vice President; a quorum for the purpose shall consist of two thirds of the whole number of Senators, and a majority of the whole number shall be necessary to a choice. But no person constitutionally ineligible to the office of President shall be eligible to that of Vice President of the United States.

Amendment XIII

(The proposed amendment was sent to the states Feb. 1, 1865, by the Thirty-eighth Congress. It was ratified Dec. 6, 1865.)

Section 1

[Slavery prohibited.] Neither slavery nor involuntary servitude, except as a punishment for crime whereof the party shall have been duly convicted, shall exist within the United States, or any place subject to their jurisdiction.

Section 2

[Congress given power to enforce this article.] Congress shall have power to enforce this article by appropriate legislation.

Amendment XIV

(The proposed amendment was sent to the states June 16, 1866, by the Thirty-ninth Congress. It was ratified July 9, 1868.)

Section 1

[Citizenship defined; privileges of citizens.] All persons born or naturalized in the United States, and subject to the jurisdiction thereof, are citizens of the United States and of the State wherein they reside. No State shall make or enforce any law which shall abridge the privileges or immunities of citizens of the United States; nor shall any State deprive any person of life, liberty, or property, without due process of law; nor deny to any person within its jurisdiction the equal protection of the laws.

Section 2

[Apportionment of Representatives.] Representatives shall be apportioned among the several States according to their respective numbers, counting the whole number of persons in each State, excluding Indians not taxed. But when the right to vote at any election for the choice of electors for President and Vice President of the United States, Representatives in Congress, the executive and judicial officers of a State, or the members of the Legislature thereof, is denied to any of the male inhabitants of such State, being twenty-one years of age, and citizens of the United States, or in any way abridged, except for participation in rebellion, or other crime, the basis of representation therein shall be reduced in the proportion which the number of such male citizens shall bear to the whole number of male citizens twenty-one years of age in such State.

Section 3

[Disqualification for office; removal of disability.] No person shall be a Senator or Representative in Congress, or elector of President and Vice President, or hold any office, civil or military, under the United States, or under any State, who, having previously taken an oath, as a member of Congress, or as an officer of the United States, or as a member of any State Legislature, or as an executive or judicial officer of any State, to support the Constitution of the United States, shall have engaged in insurrection or rebellion against the same, or given aid or comfort to the enemies thereof. But Congress may, by a vote of two thirds of each House, remove such disability.

Section 4

[Public debt not to be questioned; payment of debts and claims incurred in aid of rebellion forbidden.] The validity of the public debt of the United States, authorized by law, including debts incurred for payment of pensions and bounties for services in suppressing insurrection or rebellion, shall not be questioned. But neither the United States nor any State shall assume or pay any debt or obligation incurred in aid of insurrection or rebellion against the United States, or any claim for the loss or emancipation of any slave; but all such debts, obligations, and claims shall be held illegal and void.

Section 5

[Congress given power to enforce this article.] The Congress shall have power to enforce, by appropriate legislation, the provisions of this article.

Amendment XV

(The proposed amendment was sent to the states Feb. 27, 1869, by the Fortieth Congress. It was ratified Feb. 3, 1870.)

Section 1

[Right of certain citizens to vote established.] The right of citizens of the United States to vote shall not be denied or abridged by the United States or by any State on account of race, color, or previous condition of servitude.

---

1. Amended by the 20th Amendment, Sections 3 and 4.

Section 2

[Congress given power to enforce this article.] The Congress shall have power to enforce this article by appropriate legislation.

Amendment XVI

(The proposed amendment was sent to the states July 12, 1909, by the Sixty-first Congress. It was ratified Feb. 3, 1913.)

[Taxes on income; Congress given power to lay and collect.] The Congress shall have power to lay and collect taxes on incomes, from whatever source derived, without apportionment among the several States, and without regard to any census or enumeration.

Amendment XVII

(The proposed amendment was sent to the states May 16, 1912, by the Sixty-second Congress. It was ratified April 8, 1913.)

[Election of United States Senators; filling of vacancies; qualifications of electors.] The Senate of the United States shall be composed of two Senators from each State, elected by the people thereof, for six years; and each Senator shall have one vote. The electors in each State shall have the qualifications requisite for electors of the most numerous branch of the State Legislatures.

When vacancies happen in the representation of any State in the Senate, the executive authority of such State shall issue writs of election to fill such vacancies: Provided, that the legislature of any State may empower the executive thereof to make temporary appointment until the people fill the vacancies by election as the legislature may direct.

This amendment shall not be so construed as to affect the election or term of any Senator chosen before it becomes valid as part of the Constitution.

Amendment XVIII[2]

(The proposed amendment was sent to the states Dec. 18, 1917, by the Sixty-fifth Congress. It was ratified by three quarters of the states by Jan. 16, 1919, and became effective Jan. 16, 1920.)

Section 1

[Manufacture, sale, or transportation of intoxicating liquors, for beverage purposes, prohibited.] After one year from the ratification of this article the manufacture, sale, or transportation of intoxicating liquors within, the importation thereof into, or the exportation thereof from the United States and all territory subject to the jurisdiction thereof for beverage purposes is hereby prohibited.

Section 2

[Congress and the several States given concurrent power to pass appropriate legislation to enforce this article.] The Congress and the several States shall have concurrent power to enforce this article by appropriate legislation.

Section 3

[Provisions of article to become operative, when adopted by three fourths of the States.] This article shall be inoperative unless it shall have been ratified as an amendment to the Constitution by the legislatures of the several States, as provided in the Constitution, within seven years from the date of the submission hereof to the States by Congress.

Amendment XIX

(The proposed amendment was sent to the states June 4, 1919, by the Sixty-sixth Congress. It was ratified Aug. 18, 1920.)

[The right of citizens to vote shall not be denied because of sex.] The right of citizens of the United States to vote shall not be denied or abridged by the United States or by any State on account of sex.

[Congress given power to enforce this article.] Congress shall have power to enforce this article by appropriate legislation.

Amendment XX

(The proposed amendment, sometimes called the "Lame Duck Amendment," was sent to the states Mar. 3, 1932, by the Seventy-second Congress. It was ratified Jan. 23, 1933; but, in accordance with Section 5, Sections 1 and 2 did not go into effect until Oct. 15, 1933.)

Section 1

[Terms of President, Vice President, Senators, and Representatives.] The terms of the President and Vice President shall end at noon on the twentieth day of January, and the terms of Senators and Representatives at noon on the third day of January, of the years in which such terms would have ended if this article had not been ratified; and the terms of their successors shall then begin.

Section 2

[Time of assembling Congress.] The Congress shall assemble at least once in every year, and such meeting shall begin at noon on the third day of January, unless they shall by law appoint a different day.

Section 3

[Filling vacancy in office of President.] If, at the time fixed for the beginning of the term of the President, the President-elect shall have died, the Vice President-elect shall become President. If a President shall not have been chosen before the time fixed for the beginning of his term, or if the President-elect shall have failed to qualify, then the Vice President shall have qualified; and the Congress may by law provide for the case wherein neither a President-elect nor a Vice President-elect shall have qualified, declaring who shall then act as President, or the manner in which one who is to act shall be selected, and such person shall act accordingly until a President or Vice President shall have qualified.

Section 4

[Power of Congress in Presidential succession.] The Congress may by law provide for the case of the death of any of the persons from whom the House of Representatives may choose a President whenever the right of choice shall have devolved upon them, and for the case of the death of any of the persons from whom the Senate may choose a Vice President whenever the right of choice shall have devolved upon them.

Section 5

[Time of taking effect.] Sections 1 and 2 shall take effect on the 15th day of October following the ratification of this article.

Section 6

[Ratification.] This article shall be inoperative unless it shall have been ratified as an amendment to the Constitution by the legislatures of three fourths of the several States within seven years from the date of its submission.

Amendment XXI

(The proposed amendment was sent to the states Feb. 20, 1933, by the Seventy-second Congress. It was ratified Dec. 5, 1933.)

---

2. Repealed by the 21st Amendment.

Section 1

[Repeal of Prohibition Amendment.] The eighteenth article of amendment to the Constitution of the United States is hereby repealed.

Section 2

[Transportation of intoxicating liquors.] The transportation or importation into any State, territory, or possession of the United States for delivery or use therein of intoxicating liquors, in violation of the laws thereof, is hereby prohibited.

Section 3

[Ratification.] This article shall be inoperative unless it shall have been ratified as an amendment to the Constitution by convention in the several States, as provided in the Constitution, within seven years from the date of the submission thereof to the States by the Congress.

Amendment XXII

(The proposed amendment was sent to the states Mar. 21, 1947, by the Eightieth Congress. It was ratified Feb. 27, 1951.)

Section 1

[Limit to number of terms a President may serve.] No person shall be elected to the office of the President more than twice, and no person who has held the office of President, or acted as President, for more than two years of a term to which some other person was elected President shall be elected to the office of the President more than once. But this article shall not apply to any person holding the office of President when this article was proposed by the Congress, and shall not prevent any person who may be holding the office of President, or acting as President, during the term within which this article becomes operative from holding the office of President or acting as President during the remainder of such term.

Section 2

[Ratification.] This article shall be inoperative unless it shall have been ratified as an amendment to the Constitution by the legislatures of three fourths of the several States within seven years from the date of its submission to the States by the Congress.

Amendment XXIII

(The proposed amendment was sent to the states June 16, 1960, by the Eighty-sixth Congress. It was ratified March 29, 1961.)

Section 1

[Electors for the District of Columbia.] The District constituting the seat of Government of the United States shall appoint in such manner as the Congress may direct: A number of electors of President and Vice President equal to the whole number of Senators and Representatives in Congress to which the District would be entitled if it were a State, but in no event more than the least populous State; they shall be in addition to those appointed by the States, but they shall be considered, for the purposes of the election of President and Vice President, to be electors appointed by a State; and they shall meet in the District and perform such duties as provided by the twelfth article of amendment.

Section 2

[Congress given power to enforce this article.] The Congress shall have the power to enforce this article by appropriate legislation.

Amendment XXIV

(The proposed amendment was sent to the states Aug. 27, 1962, by the Eighty-seventh Congress. It was ratified Jan. 23, 1964.)

Section 1

[Payment of poll tax or other taxes not to be prerequisite for voting in federal elections.] The right of citizens of the United States to vote in any primary or other election for President or Vice President, for electors for President or Vice President, or for Senator or Representative in Congress, shall not be denied or abridged by the United States or any State by reasons of failure to pay any poll tax or other tax.

Section 2

[Congress given power to enforce this article.] The Congress shall have the power to enforce this article by appropriate legislation.

Amendment XXV

(The proposed amendment was sent to the states July 6, 1965, by the Eighty-ninth Congress. It was ratified Feb. 10, 1967.)

Section 1

[Succession of Vice President to Presidency.] In case of the removal of the President from office or of his death or resignation, the Vice President shall become President.

Section 2

[Vacancy in office of Vice President.] Whenever there is a vacancy in the office of the Vice President, the President shall nominate a Vice President who shall take office upon confirmation by a majority vote of both Houses of Congress.

Section 3

[Vice President as Acting President.] Whenever the President transmits to the President pro tempore of the Senate and the Speaker of the House of Representatives his written declaration that he is unable to discharge the powers and duties of his office, and until he transmits to them a written declaration to the contrary, such powers and duties shall be discharged by the Vice President as Acting President.

Section 4

[Vice President as Acting President.] Whenever the Vice President and a majority of either the principal officers of the executive departments or of such other body as Congress may by law provide, transmit to the President pro tempore of the Senate and the Speaker of the House of Representatives their written declaration that the President is unable to discharge the powers and duties of his office, the Vice President shall immediately assume the powers and duties of the office as Acting President.

Thereafter, when the President transmits to the President pro tempore of the Senate and the Speaker of the House of Representatives his written declaration that no inability exists, he shall resume the powers and duties of his office unless the Vice President and a majority of either the principal officers of the executive department or of such other body as Congress may by law provide, transmit within four days to the President pro tempore of the Senate and the Speaker of the House of Representatives their written declaration that the President is unable to discharge the powers and duties of his office. Thereupon Congress shall decide the issue, assembling within forty-eight hours for that purpose if not in session. If the Congress, within twenty-one days after receipt of the latter written declaration, or, if Congress is not in session, within twenty-one days after Congress is required to assemble, determines by two thirds vote of both Houses that the President is unable to discharge the powers and duties of his office, the Vice President shall continue to discharge the same as Acting President; otherwise, the President shall resume the powers and duties of his office.

Amendment XXVI

(The proposed amendment was sent to the states Mar. 23, 1971, by the Ninety-second Congress. It was ratified July 1, 1971.)

Section 1

[Voting for 18-year-olds.] The right of citizens of the United States, who are 18 years of age or older, to vote shall not be denied or abridged by the United States or by any state on account of age.

Section 2

[Congress given power to enforce this article.] The Congress shall have power to enforce this article by appropriate legislation.

Amendment XXVII

(Ratified May 7, 1992.)

[Congressional raises.] No law, varying the compensation for the services of the Senators and Representatives, shall take effect, until an election of Representatives shall have intervened.

1. Amended by the 20th Amendment, Sections 3 and 4. 2. Repealed by the 21st Amendment.

Order of Presidential Succession

1. The Vice President
2. Speaker of the House
3. President pro tempore of the Senate
4. Secretary of State
5. Secretary of the Treasury
6. Secretary of Defense
7. Attorney General
8. Secretary of the Interior
9. Secretary of Agriculture
10. Secretary of Commerce
11. Secretary of Labor
12. Secretary of Health and Human Services
13. Secretary of Housing and Urban Development
14. Secretary of Transportation
15. Secretary of Energy
16. Secretary of Education
17. Secretary of Veterans Affairs

NOTE: An official cannot succeed to the Presidency unless that person meets the Constitutional requirements.

History of the Flag

Source: Encyclopaedia Britannica.

The first official American flag, the Continental or Grand Union flag, was displayed on Prospect Hill, Jan. 1, 1776, in the American lines besieging Boston. It had 13 alternate red and white stripes, with the British Union Jack in the upper left corner.

On June 14, 1777, the Continental Congress adopted the design for a new flag, which actually was the Continental flag with the red cross of St. George and the white cross of St. Andrew replaced on the blue field by 13 stars, one for each state. No rule was made as to the arrangement of the stars, and while they were usually shown in a circle, there were various other designs. It is uncertain when the new flag was first flown, but its first official announcement is believed to have been on Sept. 3, 1777.

The first public assertion that Betsy Ross made the first Stars and Stripes appeared in a paper read before the Historical Society of Pennsylvania on March 14, 1870, by William J. Canby, a grandson. However, Mr. Canby on later investigation found no official documents of any action by Congress on the flag before June 14, 1777. Betsy Ross's own story, according to her daughter, was that Washington, Robert Morris, and George Ross, as representatives of Congress, visited her in Philadelphia in June 1776, showing her a rough draft of the flag and asking her if she could make one. However, the only actual record of the manufacture of flags by Betsy Ross is a voucher in Harrisburg, Pa., for 14 pounds and some shillings for flags for the Pennsylvania navy.

On Jan. 13, 1794, Congress voted to add two stars and two stripes to the flag in recognition of the admission of Vermont and Kentucky to the Union. By 1818, there were 20 states in the Union, and as it was obvious that the flag would soon become unwieldy, Congress voted April 18 to return to the original 13 stripes and to indicate the admission of a new state simply by the addition of a star the following July 4. The 49th star, for Alaska, was added July 4, 1959; and the 50th star, for Hawaii, was added July 4, 1960.

The first Confederate flag, adopted in 1861 by the Confederate convention in Montgomery, Ala., was called the Stars and Bars; but because of its similarity in colors to the American flag, there was much confusion in the Battle of Bull Run. To remedy this situation, Gen. G. T. Beauregard suggested a battle flag, which was used by the Southern armies throughout the war. The flag consisted of a red field on which was placed a blue cross of St. Andrew separated from the field by a white fillet and adorned with 13[1] white stars for the Confederate states. In May 1863, at Richmond, an official flag was adopted by the Confederate Congress. This flag was white and twice as long as wide; the union, two-thirds the width of the flag, contained the battle flag designed for Gen. Beauregard. A broad transverse stripe of red was added Feb. 4, 1865, so that the flag might not be mistaken for a signal of truce.

1. 11 states formally seceded, and unofficial groups in Kentucky and Missouri adopted ordinances of secession. On this basis, these two states were admitted to the Confederacy, although the official state governments remained in the Union.

The Pledge of Allegiance[1] to the Flag

"I pledge allegiance to the Flag of the United States of America, and to the Republic for which it stands, one Nation under God,[2] indivisible, with liberty and justice for all."

1. The original pledge was published in the Sept. 8, 1892, issue of The Youth's Companion in Boston. For years, the authorship was in dispute between James B. Upham and Francis Bellamy of the magazine's staff. In 1939, after a study of the controversy, the United States Flag Association decided that authorship be credited to Bellamy. 2. The phrase "under God" was added to the pledge on June 14, 1954.

The Statue of Liberty

The Statue of Liberty ("Liberty Enlightening the World") is a 225-ton, steel-reinforced copper female figure, 152 ft. in height, facing the ocean from Liberty[1] Island in New York Harbor. The right hand holds aloft a torch, and the left hand carries a tablet upon which is inscribed: "July IV MDCCLXXVI."

The statue was designed by Frédéric Auguste Bartholdi of Alsace as a gift to the United States from the people of France to memorialize the alliance of the two countries in the American Revolution and their abiding friendship. The French people contributed the $250,000 cost.

The 150-foot pedestal was designed by Richard M. Hunt and built by Gen. Charles P. Stone, both Americans. It contains steel underpinnings designed by Alexander Eiffel of France to support the statue. The $270,000 cost was borne by popular subscription in this country. President Grover Cleveland accepted the statue for the United States on Oct. 28, 1886.

On Sept. 26, 1972, President Richard M. Nixon dedicated the American Museum of Immigration, housed in structural additions to the base of the statue. In 1984

1. Called Bedloe's Island prior to 1956.

scaffolding went up for a major restoration and the torch was extinguished on July 4. It was relit with much ceremony July 4, 1986 to mark its centennial.

On a tablet inside the pedestal is engraved the following sonnet, written by Emma Lazarus (1849–1887):

The New Colossus
Not like the brazen giant of Greek fame.
With conquering limbs astride from land to land;
Here at our sea-washed, sunset gates shall stand
A mighty woman with a torch, whose flame
Is the imprisoned lightning, and her name
Mother of Exiles. From her beacon-hand
Glows world-wide welcome; her mild eyes command
The air-bridged harbor that twin cities frame.
'Keep, ancient lands, your storied pomp!' cries she
With silent lips. 'Give me your tired, your poor,
Your huddled masses yearning to breathe free,
The wretched refuse of your teeming shore.
Send these, the homeless, tempest-tost to me,
I lift my lamp beside the golden door!'

The Mayflower Compact

On Sept. 6, 1620, the *Mayflower,* a sailing vessel of about 180 tons, started her memorable voyage from Plymouth, England, with about 100[1] pilgrims aboard, bound for Virginia to establish a private permanent colony in North America. Arriving at what is now Provincetown, Mass., on Nov. 11 (Nov. 21, new style calendar), 41 of the passengers signed the famous "Mayflower Compact" as the boat lay at anchor in that Cape Cod harbor. A small detail of the pilgrims, led by William Bradford, assigned to select a place for permanent settlement landed at what is now Plymouth, Mass., on Dec. 21 (n.s.).

The text of the compact follows:

In the name of God, Amen. We, whose names are underwritten, the Loyal Subjects of our dread Sovereign Lord, King *James,* by the Grace of God, of *Great Britain, France and Ireland,* King, *Defender of the Faith,* &

Having undertaken for the Glory of God, and Advancement of the Christian Faith, and the Honour of our King and Country, a voyage to plant the first colony in the northern Parts of Virginia; do by these Presents, solemnly and mutually in the Presence of God and one of another, covenant and combine ourselves together into a civil Body Politick, for our better Ordering and Preservation, and Furtherance of the Ends aforesaid; And by Virtue hereof to enact, constitute, and frame, such just and equal Laws, Ordinances, Acts, Constitutions and Offices, from time to time, as shall be thought most meet and convenient for the General good of the Colony; unto which we promise all due Submission and Obedience.

In Witness whereof we have hereunto subscribed our names at *Cape Cod* the eleventh of *November,* in the Reign of our Sovereign Lord, King *James* of *England, France* and *Ireland,* the eighteenth, and of *Scotland* the fifty-fourth. *Anno Domini,* 1620

John Carver	William Mullins	John Billington	Peter Brown
Digery Priest	Thomas English	Thomas Tinker	John Turner
William Brewster	John Howland	Samuel Fuller	Edward Tilly
Edmund Margesson	Stephen Hopkins	Richard Clark	John Craxton
John Alden	Edward Winslow	John Allerton	Thomas Rogers
George Soule	Gilbert Winslow	Richard Warren	John Goodman
James Chilton	Miles Standish	Edward Liester	Edward Fuller
Francis Cooke	Richard Bitteridge	William Bradford	Richard Gardiner
Moses Fletcher	Francis Eaton	Thomas Williams	William White
John Ridgate	John Tilly	Isaac Allerton	Edward Doten
Christopher Martin			

1. Historians differ as to whether 100, 101, or 102 passengers were aboard.

The Monroe Doctrine

The Monroe Doctrine was announced in President James Monroe's message to Congress, during his second term on Dec. 2, 1823, in part as follows:

"In the discussions to which this interest has given rise, and in the arrangements by which they may terminate, the occasion has been deemed proper for asserting as a principle in which rights and interests of the United States are involved, that the American continents, by the free and independent condition which they have assumed and maintain, are henceforth not to be considered as subjects for future colonization by any European power. . . . We owe it, therefore, to candor and to the amicable relations existing between the United States and those powers to declare that we should consider any attempt on their part to extend their system to any portion of this hemisphere as dangerous to our peace and safety. With the existing colonies or dependencies of any European power we have not interfered and shall not interfere. But with the governments who have declared their independence and maintain it, and whose independence we have, on great consideration and on just principles, acknowledged, we could not view any interposition for the purpose of oppressing them or controlling in any other manner their destiny by any European power in any other light than as the manifestation of an unfriendly disposition toward the United States."

Territorial Expansion

Accession	Date	Area[1]	Accession	Date	Area[1]
United States	—	3,536,278	Other territory	—	4,664
Territory in 1790	—	891,364	Philippines	1898	115,600[2]
Louisiana Purchase	1803	831,321	Puerto Rico	1899	3,426
Florida	1819	69,866	Guam	1899	209
Texas	1845	384,958	American Samoa	1900	77
Oregon	1846	283,439	Canal Zone[3]	1904	553
Mexican Cession	1848	530,706	Virgin Islands of U.S.	1917	134
Gadsden Purchase	1853	29,640	Trust Territory of Pacific Islands	1947	177[4]
Alaska	1867	591,004	All other	—	14
Hawaii	1898	6,471	**Total, 1990**	—	3,540,315

1. Total land and water area in square miles. 2. Became independent in 1946. 3. Reverted to Panama. 4. Land area only; Palau only Trust Territory remaining. *Source:* U.S. Bureau of the Census, web: www.census.gov.

The Star-Spangled Banner

Francis Scott Key, 1814

O say, can you see, by the dawn's early light,
What so proudly we hail'd at the twilight's last gleaming?
Whose broad stripes and bright stars, thro' the perilous fight,
O'er the ramparts we watch'd, were so gallantly streaming?
And the rockets' red glare, the bombs bursting in air,
Gave proof thro' the night that our flag was still there.
O say, does that star-spangled banner yet wave
O'er the land of the free and the home of the brave?

On the shore dimly seen thro' the mists of the deep,
Where the foe's haughty host in dread silence reposes,
What is that which the breeze, o'er the towering steep,
As it fitfully blows, half conceals, half discloses?
Now it catches the gleam of the morning's first beam,
In full glory reflected, now shines on the stream:
'Tis the star-spangled banner: O, long may it wave
O'er the land of the free and the home of the brave!

And where is that band who so vauntingly swore
That the havoc of war and the battle's confusion,
A home and a country should leave us no more?
Their blood has wash'd out their foul footsteps' pollution.
No refuge could save the hireling and slave
From the terror of flight or the gloom of the grave:
And the star-spangled banner in triumph doth wave
O'er the land of the free and the home of the brave.

O thus be it ever when free-men shall stand
Between their lov'd home and the war's desolation;
Blest with vict'ry and peace, may the heav'n-rescued land
Praise the Pow'r that hath made and preserv'd us a nation!
Then conquer we must, when our cause it is just,
And this be our motto: "In God is our trust!"
And the star-spangled banner in triumph shall wave
O'er the land of the free and the home of the brave!

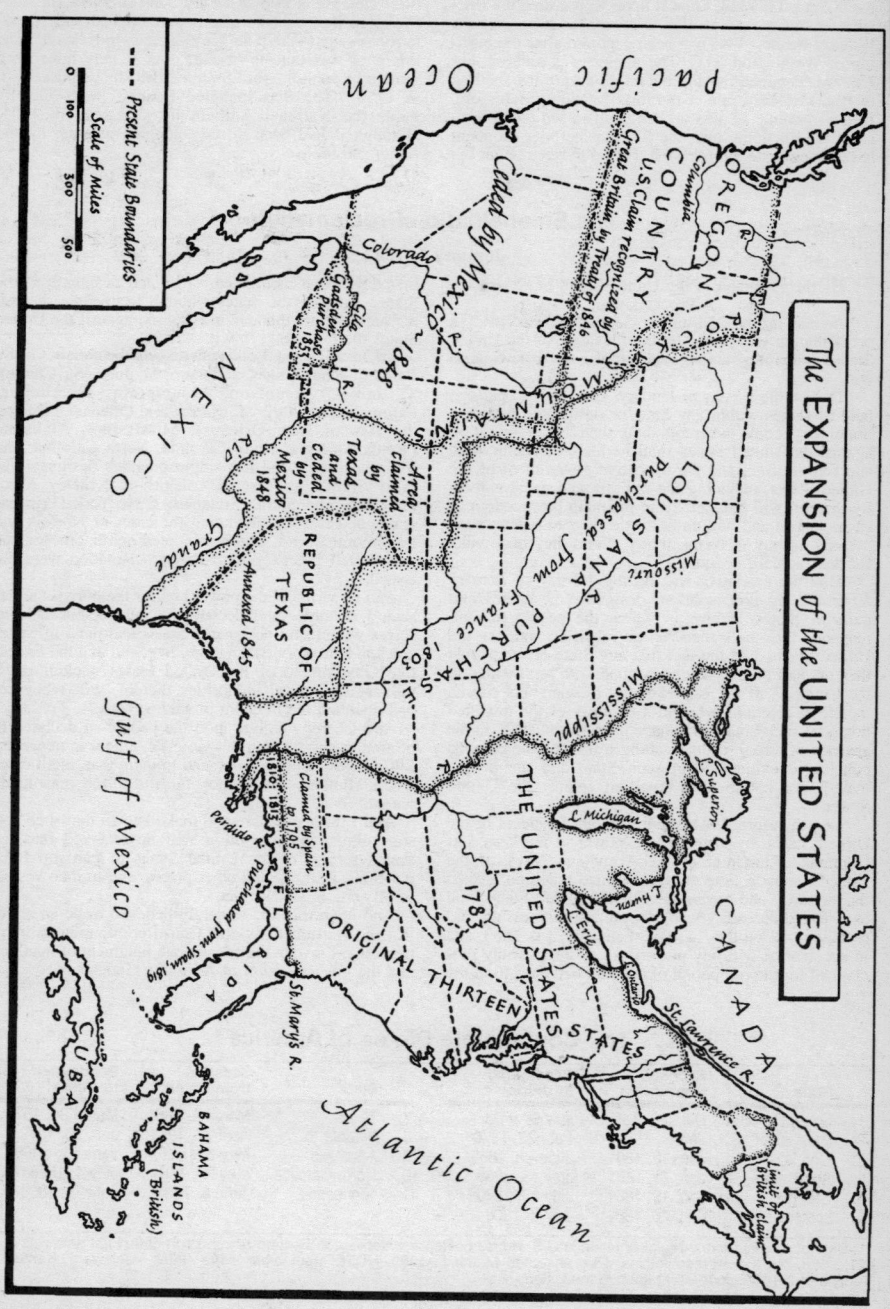

The EXPANSION of the UNITED STATES

Present State Boundaries

Scale of Miles
0   100   300   500

Pacific Ocean

OREGON COUNTRY
U.S. Claim recognized by Great Britain by Treaty of 1846
Columbia R.

Ceded by Mexico ~ 1848

Colorado R.

Gila R.
Gadsden Purchase 1853

Rio Grande

MEXICO

Area claimed by Texas and ceded by Mexico 1848

REPUBLIC OF TEXAS
Annexed 1845

LOUISIANA PURCHASE
Purchased from France 1803

Missouri R.

Mississippi R.

L. Superior

L. Michigan

L. Huron

L. Erie

L. Ontario

CANADA

St. Lawrence R.

THE UNITED STATES
1783

ORIGINAL THIRTEEN STATES

Claimed by Spain to 1795

Perdido R.

St. Mary's R.

FLORIDA
purchased from Spain 1819

Gulf of Mexico

CUBA

BAHAMA ISLANDS
(British)

Atlantic Ocean

Limit of British claim

On Sept. 13, 1814, Francis Scott Key visited the British fleet in Chesapeake Bay to secure the release of Dr. William Beanes, who had been captured after the burning of Washington, D.C. The release was secured, but Key was detained on ship overnight during the shelling of Fort McHenry, one of the forts defending Baltimore. In the morning, he was so delighted to see the American flag still flying over the fort that he began a poem to commemorate the occasion. First published under the title "Defense of Fort M'Henry," and later as "The Star-Spangled Banner," the poem soon attained wide popularity as sung to the tune "To Anacreon in Heaven." The origin of this tune is obscure, but it may have been written by John Stafford Smith, a British composer born in 1750. "The Star-Spangled Banner" was officially made the National Anthem by Congress in 1931, although it had been already adopted as such by the Army and the Navy.

The Emancipation Proclamation

January 1, 1863

By the President of the United States of America: A Proclamation.

Whereas on the 22d day of September, A.D. 1862, a proclamation was issued by the President of the United States, containing, among other things, the following, to wit:

"That on the 1st day of January, A.D. 1863, all persons held as slaves within any State or designated part of a State the people whereof shall then be in rebellion against the United States shall be then, thenceforward, and forever free; and the executive government of the United States, including the military and naval authority thereof, will recognize and maintain the freedom of such persons and will do not act or acts to repress such persons, or any of them, in any efforts they may make for their actual freedom."

"That the executive will on the 1st day of January aforesaid, by proclamation, designate the States and parts of States, if any, in which the people thereof, respectively, shall then be in rebellion against the United States; and the fact that any State or the people thereof shall on that day be in good faith represented in the Congress of the United States by members chosen thereto at elections wherein a majority of the qualified voters of such States shall have participated shall, in the absence of strong countervailing testimony, be deemed conclusive evidence that such State and the people thereof are not then in rebellion against the United States."

Now, therefore, I, Abraham Lincoln, President of the United States, by virtue of the power in me vested as Commander-in-Chief of the Army and Navy of the United States in time of actual armed rebellion against the authority and government of the United States, and as a fit and necessary war measure for suppressing said rebellion, do, on this 1st day of January, A.D. 1863, and in accordance with my purpose so to do, publicly proclaimed for the full period of one hundred days from the first day above mentioned, order and designate as the States and parts of States wherein the people thereof, respectively, are this day in rebellion against the United States the following, to wit:

Arkansas, Texas, Louisiana (except the parishes of St. Bernard, Plaquemines, Jefferson, St. John, St. Charles, St. James, Ascension, Assumption, Terrebonne, Lafourche, St. Mary, St. Martin, and Orleans, including the city of New Orleans), Mississippi, Alabama, Florida, Georgia, South Carolina, North Carolina, and Virginia (except the forty-eight counties designated as West Virginia, and also the counties of Berkeley, Accomac, Northhampton, Elizabeth City, York, Princess Anne, and Norfolk, including the cities of Norfolk and Portsmouth), and which excepted parts are for the present left precisely as if this proclamation were not issued.

And by virtue of the power and for the purpose aforesaid, I do order and declare that all persons held as slaves within said designated States and parts of States are, and henceforward shall be, free; and that the Executive Government of the United States, including the military and naval authorities thereof, will recognize and maintain the freedom of said persons.

And I hereby enjoin upon the people so declared to be free to abstain from all violence, unless in necessary self-defense; and I recommend to them that, in all cases when allowed, they labor faithfully for reasonable wages.

And I further declare and make known that such persons of suitable condition will be received into the armed service of the United States to garrison forts, positions, stations, and other places, and to man vessels of all sorts in said service.

And upon this act, sincerely believed to be an act of justice, warranted by the Constitution upon military necessity, I invoke the considerate judgment of mankind and the gracious favor of Almighty God.

The Confederate States of America

	State	Seceded from Union	Readmitted to Union[1]		State	Seceded from Union	Readmitted to Union[1]
1.	South Carolina	Dec. 20, 1860	July 9, 1868	7.	Texas	March 2, 1861	March 30, 1870
2.	Mississippi	Jan. 9, 1861	Feb. 23, 1870	8.	Virginia	April 17, 1861	Jan. 26, 1870
3.	Florida	Jan. 10, 1861	June 25, 1868	9.	Arkansas	May 6, 1861	June 22, 1868
4.	Alabama	Jan. 11, 1861	July 13, 1868	10.	North Carolina	May 20, 1861	July 4, 1868
5.	Georgia	Jan. 19, 1861	July 15, 1870[2]	11.	Tennessee	June 8, 1861	July 24, 1866
6.	Louisiana	Jan. 26, 1861	July 9, 1868				

1. Date of readmission to representation in U.S. House of Representatives. 2. Second readmission date. First date was July 21, 1868, but the representatives were unseated March 5, 1869. NOTE: Four other slave states—Delaware, Kentucky, Maryland, and Missouri—remained in the Union.

Lincoln's Gettysburg Address

The Battle of Gettysburg, one of the most noted battles of the Civil War, was fought on July 1, 2, and 3, 1863. On Nov. 19, 1863, the field was dedicated as a national cemetery by President Lincoln in a two-minute speech that was to become immortal. At the time of its delivery the speech was relegated to the inside pages of the papers, while a two-hour address by Edward Everett, the leading orator of the time, caught the headlines.

The following is the text of the address revised by President Lincoln from his own notes:

Fourscore and seven years ago our fathers brought forth on this continent a new nation conceived in liberty and dedicated to the proposition that all men are created equal. Now we are engaged in a great civil war testing whether that nation, or any nation so conceived and so dedicated, can long endure. We are met on a great battlefield of that war. We have come to dedicate a portion of that field as a final resting-place for those who here gave their lives that that nation might live. It is altogether fitting and proper that we should do this. But, in a larger sense, we cannot dedicate, we cannot consecrate, we cannot hallow this ground. The brave men, living and dead, who struggled here have consecrated it far above our poor power to add or detract. The world will little note nor long remember what we say here, but it can never forget what they did here. It is for us the living rather to be dedicated here to the unfinished work which they who fought here have thus far so nobly advanced. It is rather for us to be here dedicated to the great task remaining before us—that from these honored dead we take increased devotion to that cause for which they gave the last full measure of devotion—that we here highly resolve that these dead shall not have died in vain, that this nation under God shall have a new birth of freedom, and that government of the people, by the people, for the people shall not perish from the earth.

The Early Congresses

At the urging of Massachusetts and Virginia, the First Continental Congress met in Philadelphia on Sept. 5, 1774, and was attended by representatives of all the colonies except Georgia. Patrick Henry of Virginia declared: "The distinctions between Pennsylvanians, New Yorkers and New Englanders are no more. I am not a Virginian but an American." This Congress, which adjourned Oct. 26, 1774, passed intercolonial resolutions calling for extensive boycott by the colonies against British trade.

The following year, most of the delegates from the colonies were chosen by popular election to attend the Second Continental Congress, which assembled in Philadelphia on May 10. As war had already begun between the colonies and England, the chief problems before the Congress were the procuring of military supplies, the establishment of an army and proper defenses, the issuing of continental bills of credit, etc. On June 15, 1775, George Washington was elected to command the Continental army. Congress adjourned Dec. 12, 1776.

Other Continental Congresses were held in Baltimore (1776–77), Philadelphia (1777), Lancaster, Pa. (1777), York, Pa. (1777–78), and Philadelphia (1778–81).

In 1781, the Articles of Confederation, although establishing a league of the thirteen states rather than a strong central government, provided for the continuance of Congress. Known thereafter as the Congress of the Confederation, it held sessions in Philadelphia (1781–83), Princeton, N.J. (1783), Annapolis, Md. (1783–84), and Trenton, N.J. (1784). Five sessions were held in New York City between the years 1785 and 1789.

The Congress of the United States, established by the ratification of the Constitution, held its first meeting on March 4, 1789, in New York City. Several sessions of Congress were held in Philadelphia, and the first meeting in Washington, D.C., was on Nov. 17, 1800.

Presidents of the Continental Congresses

Name	Elected	Birth and Death Dates	Name	Elected	Birth and Death Dates
Peyton Randolph, Va.	9/5/1774	c.1721–1775	John Hanson, Md.	11/5/1781	1715–1783
Henry Middleton, S.C.	10/22/1774	1717–1784	Elias Boudinot, N.J.	11/4/1782	1740–1821
Peyton Randolph, Va.	5/10/1775	c.1721–1775	Thomas Mifflin, Pa.	11/3/1783	1744–1800
John Hancock, Mass.	5/24/1775	1737–1793	Richard Henry Lee, Va.	11/30/1784	1732–1794
Henry Laurens, S.C.	11/1/1777	1724–1792	John Hancock, Mass.[1]	11/23/1785	1737–1793
John Jay, N.Y.	12/10/1778	1745–1829	Nathaniel Gorham, Mass.	6/6/1786	1738–1796
Samuel Huntington, Conn.	9/28/1779	1731–1796	Arthur St. Clair, Pa.	2/2/1787	1734–1818
Thomas McKean, Del.	7/10/1781	1734–1817	Cyrus Griffin, Va.	1/22/1788	1748–1810

[1]. Resigned May 29, 1786, never having served, because of continued illness.

The Great Seal of the U.S.

On July 4, 1776, the Continental Congress appointed a committee consisting of Benjamin Franklin, John Adams, and Thomas Jefferson "to bring in a device for a seal of the United States of America." After many delays, a verbal description of a design by William Barton was finally approved by Congress on June 20, 1782. The seal shows an American bald eagle with a ribbon in its mouth bearing the device *E pluribus unum* (One out of many). In its talons are the arrows of war and an olive branch of peace. On the reverse side it shows an unfinished pyramid with an eye (the eye of Providence) above it. Although this description was adopted in 1782, the first drawing was not made until four years later, and no die has ever been cut.

The American's Creed

William Tyler Page

"I believe in the United States of America as a government of the people, by the people, for the people; whose just powers are derived from the consent of the governed; a democracy in a republic; a sovereign Nation of many sovereign States; a perfect union, one and inseparable; established upon those principles of freedom, equality, justice, and humanity for which American patriots sacrificed their lives and fortunes.

'I therefore believe it is my duty to my country to love it, to support its Constitution, to obey its laws, to respect its flag, and to defend it against all enemies.'

NOTE: William Tyler Page, Clerk of the U.S. House of Representatives, wrote "The American's Creed" in 1917. It was accepted by the House on behalf of the American people on April 3, 1918.

Assassinations and Attempts in U.S. Since 1865

Cermak, Anton J. (Mayor of Chicago): Shot Feb. 15, 1933, in Miami by Giuseppe Zangara, who attempted to assassinate Franklin D. Roosevelt; Cermak died March 6.

Ford, Gerald R. (President of U.S.): Escaped assassination attempt Sept. 5, 1975, in Sacramento, Calif., by Lynette Alice (Squeaky) Fromm, who pointed but did not fire .45-caliber pistol. Escaped assassination attempt in San Francisco, Calif., Sept. 22, 1975, by Sara Jane Moore, who fired one shot from a .38-caliber pistol that was deflected.

Garfield, James A. (President of U.S.): Shot July 2, 1881, in Washington, D.C., by Charles J. Guiteau; died Sept. 19.

Jordan, Vernon E., Jr. (civil rights leader): Shot and critically wounded in assassination attempt May 29, 1980, in Fort Wayne, Ind.

Kennedy, John F. (President of U.S.): Shot Nov. 22, 1963, in Dallas, Tex., allegedly by Lee Harvey Oswald; died same day. Injured was Gov. John B. Connally of Texas. Oswald was shot and killed two days later by Jack Ruby.

Kennedy, Robert F. (U.S. Senator from New York): Shot June 5, 1968, in Los Angeles by Sirhan Bishara Sirhan; died June 6.

King, Martin Luther, Jr. (civil rights leader): Shot April 4, 1968, in Memphis by James Earl Ray; died same day.

Lincoln, Abraham (President of U.S.): Shot April 14, 1865, in Washington, D.C., by John Wilkes Booth; died April 15.

Long, Huey P. (U.S. Senator from Louisiana): Shot Sept. 8, 1935, in Baton Rouge by Dr. Carl A. Weiss; died Sept. 10.

McKinley, William (President of U.S.): Shot Sept. 6, 1901, in Buffalo by Leon Czolgosz; died Sept. 14.

Reagan, Ronald (President of U.S.): Shot in left lung in Washington by John W. Hinckley, Jr., on March 30, 1981; three others also wounded.

Roosevelt, Franklin D. (President-elect of U.S.): Escaped assassination unhurt Feb. 15, 1933, in Miami.

Roosevelt, Theodore (ex-President of U.S.): Escaped assassination (though shot) Oct. 14, 1912, in Milwaukee while campaigning for President.

Seward, William H. (Secretary of State): Escaped assassination (though injured) April 14, 1865, in Washington, D.C., by Lewis Powell (or Paine), accomplice of John Wilkes Booth.

Truman, Harry S. (President of U.S.): Escaped assassination unhurt Nov. 1, 1950, in Washington, D.C., as Puerto Rican nationalists attempted to shoot their way into Blair House.

Wallace, George C. (Governor of Alabama): Shot and critically wounded in assassination attempt May 15, 1972, at Laurel, Md., by Arthur Herman Bremer. Wallace paralyzed from waist down.

Impeachments of Federal Officials

Source: Congressional Directory

The procedure for the impeachment of Federal officials is detailed in Article I, Section 3, of the Constitution. The Senate has sat as a court of impeachment in the following cases:

William Blount, Senator from Tennessee; charges dismissed for want of jurisdiction, Jan. 14, 1799.

John Pickering, Judge of the U.S. District Court for New Hampshire; removed from office March 12, 1804.

Samuel Chase, Associate Justice of the Supreme Court; acquitted March 1, 1805.

James H. Peck, Judge of the U.S. District Court for Missouri; acquitted Jan. 31, 1831.

West H. Humphreys, Judge of the U.S. District Court for the middle, eastern, and western districts of Tennessee; removed from office June 26, 1862.

Andrew Johnson, President of the United States; acquitted May 26, 1868.

William W. Belknap, Secretary of War; acquitted Aug. 1, 1876.

Charles Swayne, Judge of the U.S. District Court for the northern district of Florida; acquitted Feb. 27, 1905.

Robert W. Archbald, Associate Judge, U.S. Commerce Court; removed Jan. 13, 1913.

George W. English, Judge of the U.S. District Court for eastern district of Illinois; resigned Nov. 4, 1926; proceedings dismissed.

Harold Louderback, Judge of the U.S. District Court for the northern district of California; acquitted May 24, 1933.

Halsted L. Ritter, Judge of the U.S. District Court for the southern district of Florida; removed from office April 17, 1936.

Harry E. Claiborne, Judge of the U.S. District Court for the district of Nevada; removed from office Oct. 9, 1986.

Alcee L. Hastings, Judge of the U.S. District Court for the southern district of Florida; removed from office Oct. 20, 1989.

Walter L. Nixon, Judge of the U.S. District Court for Mississippi; removed from office Nov. 3, 1989.

The White House

Source: Department of the Interior, U.S. National Park Service.

The White House, the official residence of the President, is at 1600 Pennsylvania Avenue in Washington, D.C. 20500. The site, covering about 18 acres, was selected by President Washington and Pierre Charles L'Enfant, and the architect was James Hoban. The design appears to have been influenced by Leinster House, Dublin, and James Gibb's *Book of Architecture*. The cornerstone was laid Oct. 13, 1792, and the first residents were President and Mrs. John Adams in November 1800. The building was fired by the British in 1814.

From December 1948 to March 1952, the interior of the White House was rebuilt, and the outer walls were strengthened.

The rooms for public functions are on the first floor; the second and third floors are used as the residence of the President and First Family. The most celebrated public room is the East Room, where formal receptions take place. Other public rooms are the Red Room, the Green Room, and the Blue Room. The State Dining Room is used for formal dinners. There are 132 rooms.

U.S. Capitol

When the French architect and engineer Maj. Pierre L'Enfant first began to lay out the plans for a new Federal city (now Washington, D.C.), he noted that Jenkins' Hill, overlooking the area, seemed to be "a pedestal waiting for a monument." It was here that the U.S. Capitol would be built. The basic structure as we know today evolved over a period of more than 150 years. In 1792 a competition was held for the design of a capitol building. Dr. William Thornton, a physician and amateur architect, submitted the winning plan, a simple, low-lying structure of classical proportions with a shallow dome. Later, internal modifications were made by Benjamin Henry Latrobe. After the building was burned by the British in 1814, Latrobe and architect Charles Bulfinch were responsible for its reconstruction. Finally, under Thomas Walter, who was Architect of the Capitol from 1851 to 1865, the House and Senate wings and the imposing cast iron dome topped with the Statue of Freedom were added, and the Capitol assumed the form we see today. It was in the old Senate chamber that Daniel Webster cried out, "Liberty and Union, now and forever, one and inseparable!" In Statuary Hall, which used to be the old House chamber, a small disk on the floor marks the spot where John Quincy Adams was fatally stricken after more than 50 years of service to his country. A whisper from one side of this room can be heard across the vast space of the hall. Visitors can see the original Supreme Court chamber a floor below the Rotunda.

In addition to its historical association, the Capitol Building is also a vast artistic treasure house. The works of such famous artists as Gilbert Stuart, Rembrandt Peale, and John Trumbull are displayed on the walls. The Great Rotunda, with its 180-foot- (54.9-m-) high dome, is decorated with a massive fresco by Constantino Brumidi, which extends some 300 feet (90 m) in circumference. Throughout the building are many paintings of events in U.S. history and sculptures of outstanding Americans. The Capitol itself is situated on a 68-acre (27.5-ha) park designed by the 19th-century landscape architect Frederick Law Olmsted. There are free guided tours of the Capitol, which include admission to the House and Senate galleries. Those who wish to visit the visitors' gallery in either wing without taking the tour may obtain passes from their Senators or Congressmen. Visitors may ride on the monorail subway that joins the House and Senate wings of the Capitol with the Congressional office buildings.

Washington Monument

Construction of this magnificent Washington, D.C., monument, which draws some two million visitors a year, took nearly a century of planning, building, and controversy. Provision for a large equestrian statue of George Washington was made in the original city plan, but the project was soon dropped. After Washington's death it was taken up again, and a number of false starts and changes of design were made. Finally, in 1848, work was begun on the monument that stands today. The design, by architect Robert Mills, then featured an ornate base. In 1854, however, political squabbling and

a lack of money brought construction to a halt. Work was resumed in 1880, and the monument was completed in 1884 and opened to the public in 1888. The tapered shaft, faced with white marble and rising from walls 15 feet thick (4.6 m) at the base was modeled after the obelisks of ancient Egypt. The monument, one of the tallest masonry constructions in the world, stands just over 555 feet (169 m). Memorial stones from the 50 States, foreign countries, and organizations line the interior walls. The top, reached only by elevator, commands a panoramic view of the city.

The Liberty Bell

The Liberty Bell was cast in England in 1752 for the Pennsylvania Statehouse (now named Independence Hall) in Philadelphia. It was recast in Philadelphia in 1753. It is inscribed with the words, "Proclaim liberty throughout all the land unto all the inhabitants thereof" (Lev. 25:10). The bell was rung on July 8, 1776, for the first public reading of the Declaration of Independence.

Hidden in Allentown during the British occupation of Philadelphia, it was replaced in Independence Hall in 1778. The bell cracked on July 8, 1835, while tolling the death of Chief Justice John Marshall. In 1976 the Liberty Bell was moved to a special exhibition building near Independence Hall.

Arlington National Cemetery

Arlington National Cemetery occupies 612 acres in Virginia on the Potomac River, directly opposite Washington. This land was part of the estate of John Parke Custis, Martha Washington's son. His son, George Washington Parke Custis, built the mansion which later became the home of Robert E. Lee. In 1864, Arlington became a military cemetery. More than 240,000 service members and their dependents are buried there. Expansion of the cemetery began in 1966, using a 180-acre tract of land directly east of the present site.

In 1921, an Unknown American Soldier of World War I was buried in the cemetery; the monument at the

Tomb was opened to the public without ceremony in 1932. Two additional Unknowns, one from World War II and one from the Korean War, were buried May 30, 1958. The Unknown Serviceman of Vietnam was buried on May 28, 1984. The inscription carved on the Tomb of the Unknowns reads:

HERE RESTS IN
HONORED GLORY
AN AMERICAN
SOLDIER
KNOWN BUT TO GOD

Milestones in the Gay Rights Movement

Source: Excerpted from *The Reader's Companion to American History*. Copyright © 1991 by Houghton Mifflin Company.

Late in the [19th] century, as large cities allowed for greater anonymity, as wage labor apart from family became common, and as more women were drawn out of the home, evidence of a new pattern of homosexual expression surfaced. . . .

At first, these individuals developed ways of meeting one another and institutions to foster a sense of identity. . . . By 1915, one participant in this new gay world was referring to it as "a community distinctly organized." For the most part hidden from view because of social hostility, an urban gay subculture had come into existence by the 1920s and 1930s.

World War II served as a critical divide in the social history of homosexuality. Large numbers of the young left families, small towns, and closely knit ethnic neighborhoods to enter a sex-segregated military or to migrate to larger cities for wartime employment. . . .

After the war, many of them made choices designed to support their gay identities. Pat Bond, a woman from Iowa who first met other lesbians while in the military, decided to stay in San Francisco after her discharge. [Donald] Vining remained in New York City rather than return to his small hometown in New Jersey. They, along with countless others, sustained a vibrant gay subculture that revolved around bars and friendship net-

works. Many cities saw their first gay bars during the 1940s. . . .

This new visibility provoked latent cultural prejudices....Firings from government jobs and purges from the military intensified in the 1950s. President Dwight D. Eisenhower issued an executive order in 1953 barring gay men and lesbians from all federal jobs. Many state and local governments and private corporations followed suit. The FBI began a surveillance program against homosexuals.

The lead taken by the federal government encouraged local police forces to harass gay citizens. Vice officers regularly raided gay bars, sometimes arresting dozens of men and women on a single night....Under these conditions, some gays began to organize politically. In November 1950 in Los Angeles, a small group of men led by Harry Hay and Chuck Rowland met to form what would become the Mattachine Society. Mostly male in membership, it was joined in 1955 by a lesbian organization in San Francisco, the Daughters of Bilitis founded by Del Martin and Phyllis Lyon. In the 1950s these organizations remained small, but they established chapters in several cities and published magazines that were a beacon of hope to the readers.

In the 1960s, influenced by the model of a militant

black civil rights movement, the "homophile movement," as the participants dubbed it, became more visible. Activists, such as Franklin Kameny and Barbara Gittings, picketed government agencies in Washington to protest discriminatory employment policies. In San Francisco, Martin, Lyon, and others targeted police harassment. By 1969, perhaps fifty homophile organizations existed in the United States, with memberships of a few thousand.

Then, on Friday evening, June 27, 1969, the police in New York City raided a Greenwich Village gay bar, the Stonewall Inn. Contrary to expectations, the patrons fought back, provoking three nights of rioting in the area accompanied by the appearance of "gay power" slogans on the buildings. Almost overnight, a massive grassroots gay liberations movement was born. Owing much to the radical protest of blacks, women, and college students in the 1960s, gays challenged all forms of hostility and punishment meted out by society. Choosing to "come out of the closet" and publicly proclaim their identity, they ushered in a social change movement that has grown substantially. By 1973, there were almost eight hundred gay and lesbian organizations in the United States; by 1990, the number was several thousand. By 1970, 5,000 gay men and lesbians marched in New York City to commemorate the first anniversary of the Stonewall Riots; in October 1987, over 600,000 marched in Washington, to demand equality.

The changes were far-reaching. Over the next two decades, half the states decriminalized homosexual behavior, and police harassment was sharply contained. Many large cities included sexual orientation in their civil rights statutes, as did Wisconsin and Massachusetts, first among the states to do so....[In 1975] the Civil Service Commission eliminated the ban on the employment of homosexuals in most federal jobs. Many of the nation's religious denominations engaged in spirited debates about the morality of homosexuality, and some, like Unitarianism and Reformed Judaism, opened their doors to gay and lesbian ministers and rabbis. The lesbian and gay world was no longer an underground subculture but, in larger cities especially, a well-organized community, with businesses, political clubs, social service agencies, community centers, and religious congregations bringing people together. In a number of places, openly gay candidates ran for elective office and won.

These changes spawned opposition. In 1977 the singer Anita Bryant led a campaign to repeal a gay rights ordinance in Dade County, Florida. Her success encouraged others, and by the early 1980s, a well-organized conservative force had materialized to target the gay rights movement. Politicians, such as Senator Jesse Helms of North Carolina, and fundamentalist ministers, such as Jerry Falwell of Lynchburg, Virginia, who formed Moral Majority, Inc., joined forces to slow the progress of the gay movement.

The onset of the AIDS epidemic in the 1980s, although it intensified the antigay rhetoric of the New Right, also stimulated further organizing within the gay community. AIDS made political mobilization a matter of life and death. With a large majority of the cases striking male homosexuals, the gay community in short order created a host of organizations, such as the Gay Men's Health Crisis in New York City, to provide services and assistance to those infected. Local and national gay civil rights groups also grew in size and number, as the community sought to increase funding for research and education and to win protection against discrimination. A personal and social tragedy of immense proportions, AIDS paradoxically strengthened the political arm of the gay movement. □

Firsts in America

This selection is based on our editorial judgment. Other sources may list different firsts.

Admiral in U.S. Navy: David Glasgow Farragut, 1866.

Air-mail route, first transcontinental: Between New York City and San Francisco, 1920.

Assembly, representative: House of Burgesses, founded in Virginia, 1619.

Bank established: Bank of North America, Philadelphia, 1781.

Birth in America to English parents: Virginia Dare, born Roanoke Island, N.C., 1587.

Black newspaper: *Freedom's Journal*, 1827, edited by John B. Russworm.

Black U.S. diplomat: Ebenezer D. Bassett, 1869, minister-resident to Haiti.

Black elected governor of a state: L. Douglas Wilder, Virginia, 1990.

Black elected to U.S. Senate: Hiram Revels, 1870, Mississippi.

Black elected to U.S. House of Representatives: Jefferson Long, Georgia, 1870.

Black associate justice of U.S. Supreme Court: Thurgood Marshall, Oct. 2, 1967.

Black U.S. cabinet minister: Robert C. Weaver, 1966, Secretary of the Department of Housing and Urban Development.

Botanic garden: Established by John Bartram in Philadelphia, 1728 and is still in existence in its original location.

Cartoon, colored: "The Yellow Kid," by Richard Outcault, in *New York World*, 1895.

College: Harvard, founded 1636.

College to confer degrees on women: Oberlin (Ohio) College, 1841.

College to establish coeducation: Oberlin (Ohio) College, 1833.

Electrocution of a criminal: William Kemmler in Auburn Prison, Auburn, N.Y., Aug. 6, 1890.

Five and Dime Store: Founded by Frank Woolworth, Utica, N.Y., 1879 (moved to Lancaster, Pa., same year).

Fraternity, Greek-letter: Phi Beta Kappa; founded Dec. 5, 1776, at College of William and Mary.

Gay and lesbian civil rights advocacy organization: National Gay and Lesbian Task Force, founded in New York City, 1973.

Gay Power: Rioting following police raid on N.Y.C. gay bar, the Stonewall Inn, mobilizes gay community and leads to birth of gay liberation movement, June 27, 1969.

Homosexual, acknowledged, elected to high local office: Harvey Milk, 1977, San Francisco Board of Supervisors.

Law to be declared unconstitutional by U.S. Supreme Court: Judiciary Act of 1789. Case: *Marbury v. Madison*, 1803.

Library, circulating: Philadelphia, 1731.

Newspaper, illustrated daily: *New York Daily Graphic,* 1873.

Newspaper published daily: *Pennsylvania Packet and General Advertiser,* Philadelphia, Sept., 1784.

Newspaper published over a continuous period: *The Boston News-Letter,* April, 1704.

Newsreel: Pathé Frères of Paris, in 1910, circulated a weekly issue of their *Pathé Journal.*

Oil well, commercial: Titusville, Pa., 1859.

Panel quiz show on radio: *Information Please,* May 17, 1938.

Postage stamps issued: 1847.

Public School: Boston Latin School, Boston, 1635.

Radio station licensed: KDKA, Pittsburgh, Pa., Oct. 27, 1920.

Railroad, transcontinental: Central Pacific and Union Pacific railroads, joined at Promontory, Utah, May 10, 1869.

Savings bank: The Provident Institute for Savings, Boston, 1816.

Science museum: Founded by Charleston (S.C.) Library Society, 1773.

Skyscraper: Home Insurance Co., Chicago, 1885 (10 floors, 2 added later).

Slaves brought into America: At Jamestown, Va., 1619, from a Dutch ship.

Sorority: Kappa Alpha Theta, at De Pauw University, 1870.

State to abolish capital punishment: Michigan, 1847.

State to enter Union after original 13: Vermont, 1791.

Steam-heated building: Eastern Hotel, Boston, 1845.

Steam railroad (carried passengers and freight): Baltimore & Ohio, 1830.

Strike on record by union: Journeymen Printers, New York City, 1776.

Subway: Opened in Boston, 1897.

"Tabloid" picture newspaper: *The Illustrated Daily News* (now *The Daily News*), New York City, 1919.

Vaudeville theater: Gaiety Museum, Boston, 1883.

Woman astronaut to ride in space: Dr. Sally K. Ride, 1983.

Woman astronaut to walk in space: Dr. Kathryn D' Sullivan, 1984.

Woman cabinet member: Frances Perkins, Secretary of Labor, 1933.

Woman candidate for President: Victoria Claflin Woodhull, nominated by National Woman's Suffrage Assn. on ticket of Nation Radical Reformers, 1872.

Woman candidate for Vice-President: Geraldine A. Ferraro, nominated on a major party ticket, Democratic Party, 1984.

Woman doctor of medicine: Elizabeth Blackwell M.D. from Geneva Medical College of Western New York, 1849.

Woman elected governor of a state: Nellie Taylor Ross, Wyoming, 1925.

Woman elected to U.S. Senate: Hattie Caraway Arkansas; elected Nov., 1932.

Woman graduate of law school: Ada H. Kepley Union College of Law, Chicago, 1870.

Woman member of U.S. House of Representatives Jeannette Rankin; elected Nov., 1916.

Woman member of U.S. Senate: Rebecca Latimer Felton of Georgia; appointed Oct. 3, 1922.

Woman member of U.S. Supreme Court: Sandra Day O'Connor; appointed July 1981.

Woman Secretary of State: Madeleine Albright appointed Dec. 1996.

Woman suffrage granted: Wyoming Territory, 1869.

Written constitution: *Fundamental Orders of Connecticut,* 1639.

Presidents

	Name and (party)[1]	Term	State of birth	Born	Died	Religion	Age at inaug.	Age at death
1.	Washington (F)[2]	1789–1797	Va.	2/22/1732	12/14/1799	Episcopalian	57	67
2.	J. Adams (F)	1797–1801	Mass.	10/30/1735	7/4/1826	Unitarian	61	90
3.	Jefferson (DR)	1801–1809	Va.	4/13/1743	7/4/1826	Deist	57	83
4.	Madison (DR)	1809–1817	Va.	3/16/1751	6/28/1836	Episcopalian	57	85
5.	Monroe (DR)	1817–1825	Va.	4/28/1758	7/4/1831	Episcopalian	58	73
6.	J. Q. Adams (DR)	1825–1829	Mass.	7/11/1767	2/23/1848	Unitarian	57	80
7.	Jackson (D)	1829–1837	S.C.	3/15/1767	6/8/1845	Presbyterian	61	78
8.	Van Buren (D)	1837–1841	N.Y.	12/5/1782	7/24/1862	Reformed Dutch	54	79
9.	W. H. Harrison (W)[3]	1841	Va.	2/9/1773	4/4/1841	Episcopalian	68	68
10.	Tyler (W)	1841–1845	Va.	3/29/1790	1/18/1862	Episcopalian	51	71
11.	Polk (D)	1845–1849	N.C.	11/2/1795	6/15/1849	Methodist	49	53
12.	Taylor (W)[3]	1849–1850	Va.	11/24/1784	7/9/1850	Episcopalian	64	65
13.	Fillmore (W)	1850–1853	N.Y.	1/7/1800	3/8/1874	Unitarian	50	74
14.	Pierce (D)	1853–1857	N.H.	11/23/1804	10/8/1869	Episcopalian	48	64
15.	Buchanan (D)	1857–1861	Pa.	4/23/1791	6/1/1868	Presbyterian	65	77
16.	Lincoln (R)[4]	1861–1865	Ky.	2/12/1809	4/15/1865	Liberal	52	56
17.	A. Johnson (U)[5]	1865–1869	N.C.	12/29/1808	7/31/1875	([6])	56	66
18.	Grant (R)	1869–1877	Ohio	4/27/1822	7/23/1885	Methodist	46	63
19.	Hayes (R)	1877–1881	Ohio	10/4/1822	1/17/1893	Methodist	54	70
20.	Garfield (R)[4]	1881	Ohio	11/19/1831	9/19/1881	Disciples of Christ	49	49
21.	Arthur (R)	1881–1885	Vt.	10/5/1830	11/18/1886	Episcopalian	50	56
22.	Cleveland (D)	1885–1889	N.J.	3/18/1837	6/24/1908	Presbyterian	47	71
23.	B. Harrison (R)	1889–1893	Ohio	8/20/1833	3/13/1901	Presbyterian	55	67
24.	Cleveland (D)[7]	1893–1897	—	—	—	—	55	—
25.	McKinley (R)[4]	1897–1901	Ohio	1/29/1843	9/14/1901	Methodist	54	58
26.	T. Roosevelt (R)	1901–1909	N.Y.	10/27/1858	1/6/1919	Reformed Dutch	42	60

	Name and (party)[1]	Term	State of birth	Born	Died	Religion	Age at inaug.	Age at death
27.	Taft (R)	1909–1913	Ohio	9/15/1857	3/8/1930	Unitarian	51	72
28.	Wilson (D)	1913–1921	Va.	12/28/1856	2/3/1924	Presbyterian	56	67
29.	Harding (R)[3]	1921–1923	Ohio	11/2/1865	8/2/1923	Baptist	55	57
30.	Coolidge (R)	1923–1929	Vt.	7/4/1872	1/5/1933	Congregationalist	51	60
31.	Hoover (R)	1929–1933	Iowa	8/10/1874	10/20/1964	Quaker	54	90
32.	F. D. Roosevelt (D)[3]	1933–1945	N.Y.	1/30/1882	4/12/1945	Episcopalian	51	63
33.	Truman (D)	1945–1953	Mo.	5/8/1884	12/26/1972	Baptist	60	88
34.	Eisenhower (R)	1953–1961	Tex.	10/14/1890	3/28/1969	Presbyterian	62	78
35.	Kennedy (D)[4]	1961–1963	Mass.	5/29/1917	11/22/1963	Roman Catholic	43	46
36.	L. B. Johnson (D)	1963–1969	Tex.	8/27/1908	1/22/1973	Disciples of Christ	55	64
37.	Nixon (R)[8]	1969–1974	Calif.	1/9/1913	4/22/1994	Quaker	56	81
38.	Ford (R)	1974–1977	Neb.	7/14/1913	—	Episcopalian	61	—
39.	Carter (D)	1977–1981	Ga.	10/1/1924	—	Southern Baptist	52	—
40.	Reagan (R)	1981–1989	Ill.	2/6/1911	—	Disciples of Christ	69	—
41.	Bush (R)	1989–1993	Mass.	6/12/24	—	Episcopalian	64	—
42.	Clinton (D)	1993–	Ark.	8/19/46	—	Baptist	46	—

1. F—Federalist; DR—Democratic-Republican; D—Democratic; W—Whig; R—Republican; U—Union. 2. No party for first election. The party system in the U.S. made its appearance during Washington's first term. 3. Died in office. 4. Assassinated in office. 5. The Republican National Convention of 1864 adopted the name Union Party. It renominated Lincoln for President; for Vice President it nominated Johnson, a War Democrat. Although frequently listed as a Republican Vice President and President, Johnson undoubtedly considered himself strictly a member of the Union Party. When that party broke apart after 1868, he returned to the Democratic Party. 6. Johnson was not a professed church member; however, he admired the Baptist principles of church government. 7. Second nonconsecutive term. 8. Resigned Aug. 9, 1974.

Vice Presidents

	Name and (party)[1]	Term	State of birth	Birth and death dates	President served under
1.	John Adams (F)[2]	1789–1797	Massachusetts	1735–1826	Washington
2.	Thomas Jefferson (DR)	1797–1801	Virginia	1743–1826	J. Adams
3.	Aaron Burr (DR)	1801–1805	New Jersey	1756–1836	Jefferson
4.	George Clinton (DR)[3]	1805–1812	New York	1739–1812	Jefferson and Madison
5.	Elbridge Gerry (DR)[3]	1813–1814	Massachusetts	1744–1814	Madison
6.	Daniel D. Tompkins (DR)	1817–1825	New York	1774–1825	Monroe
7.	John C. Calhoun[4]	1825–1832	South Carolina	1782–1850	J. Q. Adams and Jackson
8.	Martin Van Buren (D)	1833–1837	New York	1782–1862	Jackson
9.	Richard M. Johnson (D)	1837–1841	Kentucky	1780–1850	Van Buren
10.	John Tyler (W)[5]	1841	Virginia	1790–1862	W. H. Harrison
11.	George M. Dallas (D)	1845–1849	Pennsylvania	1792–1864	Polk
12.	Millard Fillmore (W)[5]	1849–1850	New York	1800–1874	Taylor
13.	William R. King (D)[3]	1853	North Carolina	1786–1853	Pierce
14.	John C. Breckinridge (D)	1857–1861	Kentucky	1821–1875	Buchanan
15.	Hannibal Hamlin (R)	1861–1865	Maine	1809–1891	Lincoln
16.	Andrew Johnson (U)[5]	1865	North Carolina	1808–1875	Lincoln
17.	Schuyler Colfax (R)	1869–1873	New York	1823–1885	Grant
18.	Henry Wilson (R)[3]	1873–1875	New Hampshire	1812–1875	Grant
19.	William A. Wheeler (R)	1877–1881	New York	1819–1887	Hayes
20.	Chester A. Arthur (R)[5]	1881	Vermont	1830–1886	Garfield
21.	Thomas A. Hendricks (D)[3]	1885	Ohio	1819–1885	Cleveland
22.	Levi P. Morton (R)	1889–1893	Vermont	1824–1920	B. Harrison
23.	Adlai E. Stevenson (D)	1893–1897	Kentucky	1835–1914	Cleveland
24.	Garrett A. Hobart (R)[3]	1897–1899	New Jersey	1844–1899	McKinley
25.	Theodore Roosevelt (R)[5]	1901	New York	1858–1919	McKinley
26.	Charles W. Fairbanks (R)	1905–1909	Ohio	1852–1918	T. Roosevelt
27.	James S. Sherman (R)[3]	1909–1912	New York	1855–1912	Taft
28.	Thomas R. Marshall (D)	1913–1921	Indiana	1854–1925	Wilson
29.	Calvin Coolidge (R)[5]	1921–1923	Vermont	1872–1933	Harding
30.	Charles G. Dawes (R)	1925–1929	Ohio	1865–1951	Coolidge
31.	Charles Curtis (R)	1929–1933	Kansas	1860–1936	Hoover
32.	John N. Garner (D)	1933–1941	Texas	1868–1967	F. D. Roosevelt
33.	Henry A. Wallace (D)	1941–1945	Iowa	1888–1965	F. D. Roosevelt
34.	Harry S. Truman (D)[5]	1945	Missouri	1884–1972	F. D. Roosevelt
35.	Alben W. Barkley (D)	1949–1953	Kentucky	1877–1956	Truman
36.	Richard M. Nixon (R)	1953–1961	California	1913–1994	Eisenhower
37.	Lyndon B. Johnson (D)[5]	1961–1963	Texas	1908–1973	Kennedy
38.	Hubert H. Humphrey (D)	1965–1969	South Dakota	1911–1978	Johnson
39.	Spiro T. Agnew (R)[6]	1969–1973	Maryland	1918–1996	Nixon
40.	Gerald R. Ford (R)[7]	1973–1974	Nebraska	1913–	Nixon

	Name and (party)[1]	Term	State of birth	Birth and death dates	President served under
41.	Nelson A. Rockefeller (R)[8]	1974–1977	Maine	1908–1979	Ford
42.	Walter F. Mondale (D)	1977–1981	Minnesota	1928–	Carter
43.	George Bush (R)	1981–1989	Massachusetts	1924–	Reagan
44.	J. Danforth Quayle (R)	1989–1993	Indiana	1947–	Bush
45.	Albert A. Gore, Jr. (D)	1993–	Washington, D.C.	1948–	Clinton

1. F—Federalist; DR—Democratic-Republican; D—Democratic; W—Whig; R—Republican; U—Union. 2. No party for first election. The party system in the U.S. made its appearance during Washington's first term as President. 3. Died in office. 4. Democratic-Republican with J. Q. Adams; Democratic with Jackson. Calhoun resigned in 1832 to become a U.S. Senator. 5. Succeeded to presidency on death of President. 6. Resigned Oct. 10, 1973, after pleading no contest to Federal income tax evasion charges. 7. Nominated by Nixon on Oct. 12, 1973, under provisions of 25th Amendment. Confirmed by Congress on Dec. 6, 1973, and was sworn in same day. He became President Aug. 9, 1974, upon Nixon's resignation. 8. Nominated by Ford Aug. 20, 1974; confirmed by Congress on Dec. 19, 1974, and was sworn in same day.

Burial Places of the Presidents

President	Burial place	President	Burial place
Washington	Mt. Vernon, Va.	Hayes	Fremont, Ohio
J. Adams	Quincy, Mass.	Garfield	Cleveland, Ohio
Jefferson	Charlottesville, Va.	Arthur	Albany, N.Y.
Madison	Montpelier Station, Va.	Cleveland	Princeton, N.J.
Monroe	Richmond, Va.	B. Harrison	Indianapolis
J. Q. Adams	Quincy, Mass.	McKinley	Canton, Ohio
Jackson	The Hermitage, nr. Nashville, Tenn.	T. Roosevelt	Oyster Bay, N.Y.
		Taft	Arlington National Cemetery
Van Buren	Kinderhook, N.Y.	Wilson	Washington National Cathedral
W. H. Harrison	North Bend, Ohio	Harding	Marion, Ohio
Tyler	Richmond, Va.	Coolidge	Plymouth, Vt.
Polk	Nashville, Tenn.	Hoover	West Branch, Iowa
Taylor	Louisville, Ky.	F. D. Roosevelt	Hyde Park, N.Y.
Fillmore	Buffalo, N.Y.	Truman	Independence, Mo.
Pierce	Concord, N.H.	Eisenhower	Abilene, Kan.
Buchanan	Lancaster, Pa.	Kennedy	Arlington National Cemetery
Lincoln	Springfield, Ill.	L. B. Johnson	Stonewall, Tex.
A. Johnson	Greeneville, Tenn.	Nixon	Yorba Linda, Calif.
Grant	New York City		

"In God We Trust"

'In God We Trust' first appeared on U.S. coins after April 22, 1864, when Congress passed an act authorizing the coinage of a 2-cent piece bearing this motto. Thereafter, Congress extended its use to other coins. On July 30, 1956, it became the national motto.

Wives and Children of the Presidents

President	Wife's name	Year and place of wife's birth	Married	Wife died	Children[1] Sons	Daughters
Washington	Martha Dandridge Custis	1732, Va.	1759	1802	—	—
John Adams	Abigail Smith	1744, Mass.	1764	1818	3	2
Jefferson	Martha Wayles Skelton	1748, Va.	1772	1782	1	5
Madison	Dorothy "Dolley" Payne Todd	1768, N.C.	1794	1849	—	—
Monroe	Elizabeth "Eliza" Kortright	1768, N.Y.	1786	1830	—	2
J. Q. Adams	Louisa Catherine Johnson	1775, England	1797	1852	3	1
Jackson	Mrs. Rachel Donelson Robards	1767, Va.	1791	1828	—	—
Van Buren	Hannah Hoes	1788, N.Y.	1807	1819	4	—
W. H. Harrison	Anna Symmes	1775, N.J.	1795	1864	6	4
Tyler	Letitia Christian	1790, Va.	1813	1842	3	4
	Julia Gardiner	1820, N.Y.	1844	1889	5	2
Polk	Sarah Childress	1803, Tenn.	1824	1891	—	—
Taylor	Margaret Smith	1788, Md.	1810	1852	1	5
Fillmore	Abigail Powers	1798, N.Y.	1826	1853	1	1
	Caroline Carmichael McIntosh	1813, N.J.	1858	1881	—	—
Pierce	Jane Means Appleton	1806, N.H.	1834	1863	3	—

President	Wife's name	Year and place of wife's birth	Married	Wife died	Children[1]	
					Sons	Daughters
Buchanan	(Unmarried)	—	—	—	—	—
Lincoln	Mary Todd	1818, Ky.	1842	1882	4	—
A. Johnson	Eliza McCardle	1810, Tenn.	1827	1876	3	2
Grant	Julia Dent	1826, Mo.	1848	1902	3	1
Hayes	Lucy Ware Webb	1831, Ohio	1852	1889	7	1
Garfield	Lucretia Rudolph	1832, Ohio	1858	1918	5	2
Arthur	Ellen Lewis Herndon	1837, Va.	1859	1880	2	1
Cleveland	Frances Folsom	1864, N.Y.	1886	1947	2	3
B. Harrison	Caroline Lavinia Scott	1832, Ohio	1853	1892	1	1
	Mary Scott Lord Dimmick	1858, Pa.	1896	1948	—	1
McKinley	Ida Saxton	1847, Ohio	1871	1907	—	2
T. Roosevelt	Alice Hathaway Lee	1861, Mass.	1880	1884	—	1
	Edith Kermit Carow	1861, Conn.	1886	1948	4	1
Taft	Helen Herron	1861, Ohio	1886	1943	2	1
Wilson	Ellen Louise Axson	1860, Ga.	1885	1914	—	3
	Edith Bolling Galt	1872, Va.	1915	1961	—	—
Harding	Florence Kling DeWolfe	1860, Ohio	1891	1924	—	—
Coolidge	Grace Anna Goodhue	1879, Vt.	1905	1957	2	—
Hoover	Lou Henry	1875, Iowa	1899	1944	2	—
F. D. Roosevelt	Anna Eleanor Roosevelt	1884, N.Y.	1905	1962	5	1
Truman	Bess Wallace	1885, Mo.	1919	1982	—	1
Eisenhower	Mamie Geneva Doud	1896, Iowa	1916	1979	2	—
Kennedy	Jacqueline Lee Bouvier	1929, N.Y.	1953	1994	2	1
L. B. Johnson	Claudia Alta "Lady Bird" Taylor	1912, Tex.	1934	—	—	2
Nixon	Thelma Catherine "Pat" Ryan	1912, Nev.	1940	1993	—	2
Ford	Elizabeth "Betty" Bloomer Warren	1918, Ill.	1948	—	3	1
Carter	Rosalynn Smith	1928, Ga.	1946	—	3	1
Reagan	Jane Wyman	1914, Mo.	1940[2]	—	1[3]	1
	Nancy Davis	1921 (?)[4], N.Y.	1952	—	1	1
Bush	Barbara Pierce	1925, N.Y.	1945	—	4	2
Clinton	Hillary Rodham	1946, Ill.	1975	—	—	1

1. Includes children who died in infancy. 2. Divorced in 1948. 3. Adopted. 4. Birthday officially given as 1923 but her high school and college records show 1921 for year of birth.

Figures and Legends in American Folklore

Appleseed, Johnny (John Chapman, 1774–1847): Massachusetts-born nurseryman; reputed to have spread seeds and seedlings out of which grew the apple orchards of the Midwest.

Billy the Kid (William H. Bonney, 1859–1881): Desperado who killed his first man before he reached his teens; after short life of crime in Wild West was gunned down by Sheriff Pat Garrett; symbol of lawless West.

Boone, Daniel (1734–1820): Frontiersman and Indian fighter, about whom legends of early America have been built; figured in Byron's *Don Juan.*

Buffalo Bill (William F. Cody, 1846–1917): Buffalo hunter and Indian scout; many of legends about him stem from his own Wild West show, which he operated in late 19th century.

Bunyan, Paul: Mythical lumberjack; subject of tall tales throughout timber country (that he dug Grand Canyon, for example).

Crockett, David (1786–1836): Frontiersman, Congressman, and defender of the Alamo, his backwoods humor and larger-than-life adventured made him synonymous with the Wild West.

James, Jesse (1847–1882): Bank and train robber; often portrayed as the American Robin Hood.

Jones, Casey (John Luther Jones, 1863–1900): Example of heroic locomotive engineer given to feats of prowess; died in wreck when his Illinois Central "Cannonball" express hit freight train at Vaughan, Miss.

Ross, Betsy (1752–1836): Member of Philadelphia flag-making family; reported to have designed and sewn first American flag. (Report is without confirmation.)

Uncle Sam: Personification of U.S. and its people; origin uncertain; may be based on inspector of government supplies in Revolutionary War and War of 1812.

How a President Is Nominated and Elected

The Conventions

The National Conventions of both major parties are held during the summer of a presidential-election year. Earlier, each party selects delegates by primaries, conventions, committees, etc.

At each convention, a temporary chairman is chosen. After a credentials committee seats the delegates, a permanent chairman is elected. The convention then votes on a platform, drawn up by the platform committee.

By the third or fourth day, presidential nominations begin. The chairman calls the roll of states alphabetically. A state may place a candidate in nomination or yield to another state.

Voting, again alphabetically by roll call of states, begins after all nominations have been made and seconded. A simple majority is required in each party, although this may require many ballots.

Finally, the vice-presidential candidate is selected. Although there is no law saying that the candidates *must* come from different states, it is, practically, necessary for this to be the case. Otherwise, according to the Constitution (*see* the 12th Amendment), electors from that state could vote for only one of the candidates and would have to cast their other vote for some person of another state. This could result in a presidential candidate's receiving a majority electoral vote and his running mate's failing to.

The Electoral College

The next step in the process is the nomination of electors in each state, according to its laws. These electors must not be Federal office holders. In the November election, the voters cast their votes for electors, not for President. In some states, the ballots include only the names of the presidential and vice-presidential candidates; in others, they include only names of the electors. Nowadays, it is rare for electors to be split between parties. The last such occurrence was in North Carolina

in 1968[1]; the last before that, in Tennessee in 1948. On three occasions (1824, 1876, and 1888), the presidential candidate with the largest popular vote failed to obtain an electoral-vote majority.

Each state has as many electors as it has Senators and Representatives. For the 1992 election, the total electors were 538, based on 100 Senators, 435 Representatives, plus 3 electoral votes from the District of Columbia as a result of the 23rd Amendment to the Constitution.

On the first Monday after the second Wednesday in December, the electors cast their votes in their respective state capitols. Constitutionally they may vote for someone other than the party candidate but usually they do not since they are pledged to one party and its candidate on the ballot. Should the presidential or vice-presidential candidate die between the November election and the December meetings, the electors pledged to vote for him could vote for whomever they pleased. However, it seems certain that the national committee would attempt to get an agreement among the state party leaders for a replacement candidate.

The votes of the electors, certified by the states, are sent to Congress, where the president of the Senate opens the certificates and has them counted in the presence of both Houses on January 6. The new President is inaugurated at noon on January 20.

Should no candidate receive a majority of the electoral vote for President, the House of Representatives chooses a President from among the three highest candidates, voting, not as individuals, but as states, with a majority (now 26) needed to elect. Should no vice-presidential candidate obtain the majority, the Senate, voting as individuals, chooses from the highest two.

1. In 1956, 1 of Alabama's 11 electoral votes was cast for Walter B. Jones. In 1960, 6 of Alabama's 11 electoral votes and 1 of Oklahoma's 8 electoral votes were cast for Harry Flood Byrd. (Byrd also received all 8 of Mississippi's electoral votes.)

Electoral College List of States and Votes, 1996 Presidential Election Total: 538; Majority Needed to Elect: 270

State	Votes	State	Votes	State	Votes
Alabama	9	Kentucky	8	North Dakota	3
Alaska	3	Louisiana	9	Ohio	21
Arizona	8	Maine	4	Oklahoma	8
Arkansas	6	Maryland	10	Oregon	7
California	54	Massachusetts	12	Pennsylvania	23
Colorado	8	Michigan	18	Rhode Island	4
Connecticut	8	Minnesota	10	South Carolina	8
Delaware	3	Mississippi	7	South Dakota	3
District of Columbia	3	Missouri	11	Tennessee	11
Florida	25	Montana	3	Texas	32
Georgia	13	Nebraska	5	Utah	5
Hawaii	4	Nevada	4	Vermont	3
Idaho	4	New Hampshire	4	Virginia	13
Illinois	22	New Jersey	15	Washington	11
Indiana	12	New Mexico	5	West Virginia	5
Iowa	7	New York	33	Wisconsin	11
Kansas	6	North Carolina	14	Wyoming	3

National Political Conventions Since 1856

Opening date	Party	Where held	Opening date	Party	Where held
June 17, 1856	Republican	Philadelphia	June 26, 1928	Democratic	Houston
June 2, 1856	Democratic	Cincinnati	June 14, 1932	Republican	Chicago
May 16, 1860	Republican	Chicago	June 27, 1932	Democratic	Chicago
April 23, 1860	Democratic	Charleston and Baltimore	June 9, 1936	Republican	Cleveland
			June 23, 1936	Democratic	Philadelphia
June 7, 1864	Republican[1]	Baltimore	June 24, 1940	Republican	Philadelphia
Aug. 29, 1864	Democratic	Chicago	July 15, 1940	Democratic	Chicago
May 20, 1868	Republican	Chicago	June 26, 1944	Republican	Chicago
July 4, 1868	Democratic	New York City	July 19, 1944	Democratic	Chicago
June 5, 1872	Republican	Philadelphia	June 21, 1948	Republican	Philadelphia
June 9, 1872	Democratic	Baltimore	July 12, 1948	Democratic	Philadelphia
June 14, 1876	Republican	Cincinnati	July 17, 1948	(3)	Birmingham
June 28, 1876	Democratic	St. Louis	July 22, 1948	Progressive	Philadelphia
June 2, 1880	Republican	Chicago	July 7, 1952	Republican	Chicago
June 23, 1880	Democratic	Cincinnati	July 21, 1952	Democratic	Chicago
June 3, 1884	Republican	Chicago	Aug. 20, 1956	Republican	San Francisco
July 11, 1884	Democratic	Chicago	Aug. 13, 1956	Democratic	Chicago
June 19, 1888	Republican	Chicago	July 25, 1960	Republican	Chicago
June 6, 1888	Democratic	St. Louis	July 11, 1960	Democratic	Los Angeles
June 7, 1892	Republican	Minneapolis	July 13, 1964	Republican	San Francisco
June 21, 1892	Democratic	Chicago	Aug. 24, 1964	Democratic	Atlantic City
June 16, 1896	Republican	St. Louis	Aug. 5, 1968	Republican	Miami Beach
July 7, 1896	Democratic	Chicago	Aug. 26, 1968	Democratic	Chicago
June 19, 1900	Republican	Philadelphia	July 10, 1972	Democratic	Miami Beach
July 4, 1900	Democratic	Kansas City	Aug. 21, 1972	Republican	Miami Beach
June 21, 1904	Republican	Chicago	July 12, 1976	Democratic	New York City
July 6, 1904	Democratic	St. Louis	Aug. 16, 1976	Republican	Kansas City, Mo.
June 16, 1908	Republican	Chicago			
July 7, 1908	Democratic	Denver	Aug. 11, 1980	Democratic	New York City
June 18, 1912	Republican	Chicago	July 14, 1980	Republican	Detroit
June 25, 1912	Democratic	Baltimore	Aug. 20, 1984	Republican	Dallas
June 7, 1916	Republican	Chicago	July 16, 1984	Democratic	San Francisco
June 14, 1916	Democratic	St. Louis	July 18, 1988	Democratic	Atlanta
June 8, 1920	Republican	Chicago	Aug. 15, 1988	Republican	New Orleans
June 28, 1920	Democratic	San Francisco	July 13, 1992	Democratic	New York City
June 10, 1924	Republican	Cleveland	Aug. 17, 1992	Republican	Houston
June 24, 1924[2]	Democratic	New York City	Aug. 10, 1996	Republican	San Diego
June 12, 1928	Republican	Kansas City	Aug. 26, 1996	Democratic	Chicago

1. The Convention adopted name Union party to attract War Democrats and others favoring prosecution of war. 2. In session until July 10, 1924. 3. States' Rights delegates from 13 Southern states.

National Committee Chairmen Since 1944

Chairman and (state)	Term	Chairman and (state)	Term
Republican		Jim Nicholson (Colo.)	1997–
Herbert Brownell, Jr. (N.Y.)	1944–46	**Democratic**	
Carroll Reece (Tenn.)	1946–48	Robert E. Hannegan (Mo.)	1944–47
Hugh D. Scott, Jr. (Pa.)	1948–49	J. Howard McGrath (R.I.)	1947–49
Guy G. Gabrielson (N.J.)	1949–52	William M. Boyle, Jr. (Mo.)	1949–51
Arthur E. Summerfield (Mich.)	1952–53	Frank E. McKinney (Ind.)	1951–52
Wesley Roberts (Kan.)	1953	Stephen A. Mitchell (Ill.)	1952–54
Leonard W. Hall (N.Y.)	1953–57	Paul M. Butler (Ind.)	1955–60
Meade Alcorn (Conn.)	1957–59	Henry M. Jackson (Wash.)	1960–61
Thruston B. Morton (Ky.)	1959–61	John M. Bailey (Conn.)	1961–68
William E. Miller (N.Y.)	1961–64	Lawrence F. O'Brien (Mass.)	1968–69
Dean Burch (Ariz.)	1964–65	Fred R. Harris (Okla.)	1969–70
Ray C. Bliss (Ohio)	1965–69	Lawrence F. O'Brien (Mass.)	1970–72
Rogers C. B. Morton (Md.)	1969–71	Jean Westwood (Utah)	1972
Robert Dole (Kan.)	1971–73	Robert S. Strauss (Tex.)	1972–77
George H. Bush (Tex.)	1973–74	Kenneth M. Curtis (Me.)	1977
Mary Louise Smith (Iowa)	1974–77	John C. White (Tex.)	1977–81
William E. Brock III (Tenn.)	1977–81	Charles T. Manatt (Calif.)	1981–85
Richard Richards (Utah)	1981–83	Paul G. Kirk, Jr. (Mass.)	1985–89
Frank J. Fahrenkopf, Jr. (Nevada)	1983–89	Ronald H. Brown (D.C.)	1989–93
Lee Atwater (S.C.)	1989–91	David Wilhelm (Ill.)	1993–94
Clayton K. Yeutter (Neb.)	1991–99	Christopher J. Dodd (Conn.)	1995–96
Richard Bond (N.Y.)	1992–93	Steven Grossman (Mass.)	1996–
Haley Barbour (Miss.)	1993–97		

Republican National Committee: 310 First St., S.E., Washington, D. C. 20003. *Democratic National Committee:* 430 South Capitol St., S.E., Washington, D.C. 20003.

Presidential Elections, 1789 to 1996

For the original method of electing the President and the Vice President (elections of 1789, 1792, 1796, and 1800), *see* Article II, Section 1, of the Constitution. The election of 1804 was the first one in which the electors voted for President and Vice President on separate ballots. (See Amendment XII to the Constitution.)

Year	Presidential candidates	Party	Electoral vote	Year	Presidential candidates	Party	Electoral vote
1789[1]	George Washington	(no party)	69	1796	John Adams	Federalist	71
	John Adams	(no party)	34		Thomas Jefferson	Dem.-Rep.	68
	Scattering	(no party)	35		Thomas Pinckney	Federalist	59
	Votes not cast		8		Aaron Burr	Dem.-Rep.	30
					Scattering		48
1792	George Washington	Federalist	132				
	John Adams	Federalist	77	1800[2]	Thomas Jefferson	Dem.-Rep.	73
	George Clinton	Anti-Federalist	50		Aaron Burr	Dem.-Rep.	73
	Thomas Jefferson	Anti-Federalist	4		John Adams	Federalist	65
	Aaron Burr	Anti-Federalist	1		Charles C. Pinckney	Federalist	64
	Votes not cast		6		John Jay	Federalist	1

Year	Presidential candidates	Party	Electoral vote	Vice-presidential candidates	Party	Electoral vote
1804	Thomas Jefferson	Dem.-Rep.	162	George Clinton	Dem.-Rep.	162
	Charles C. Pinckney	Federalist	14	Rufus King	Federalist	14
1808	James Madison	Dem.-Rep.	122	George Clinton	Dem.-Rep.	113
	Charles C. Pinckney	Federalist	47	Rufus King	Federalist	47
	George Clinton	Dem.-Rep.	6	John Langdon	Ind. (no party)	9
	Votes not cast		1	James Madison	Dem.-Rep.	3
				James Monroe	Dem.-Rep.	3
				Votes not cast		1
1812	James Madison	Dem.-Rep.	128	Elbridge Gerry	Dem.-Rep.	131
	De Witt Clinton	Federalist	89	Jared Ingersoll	Federalist	86
	Votes not cast		1	Votes not cast		1
1816	James Monroe	Dem.-Rep.	183	Daniel D. Tompkins	Dem.-Rep.	183
	Rufus King	Federalist	34	John E. Howard	Federalist	22
	Votes not cast		4	James Ross	Ind. (no party)	5
				John Marshall	Federalist	4
				Robert G. Harper	Ind. (no party)	3
				Votes not cast		4
1820	James Monroe	Dem-Rep	231	Daniel D. Tompkins	Dem.-Rep.	218
	John Quincy Adams	Ind. (no party)	1	Richard Stockton	Ind. (no party)	8
	Votes not cast		3	Daniel Rodney	Ind. (no party)	4
				Richard Rush	Ind. (no party)	1
				Robert G. Harper	Ind. (no party)	1
				Votes not cast		3
1824[3]	John Quincy Adams	(no party)	84	John C. Calhoun	(no party)	182
	Andrew Jackson	(no party)	99	Nathan Sanford	(no party)	30
	William H. Crawford	(no party)	41	Nathaniel Macon	(no party)	24
	Henry Clay	(no party)	37	Andrew Jackson	(no party)	13
				Martin Van Buren	(no party)	9
				Henry Clay	(no party)	2
				Votes not cast		1
1828	Andrew Jackson	Democratic	178	John C. Calhoun	Democratic	171
	John Quincy Adams	Natl. Rep.	83	Richard Rush	Natl. Rep.	83
				William Smith	Democratic	7
1832	Andrew Jackson	Democratic	219	Martin Van Buren	Democratic	189
	Henry Clay	Natl. Rep.	49	John Sergeant	Natl. Rep.	49
	John Floyd	Ind. (no party)	11	Henry Lee	Ind. (no party)	11
	William Wirt	Antimasonic[4]	7	Amos Ellmaker	Antimasonic	7
	Votes not cast		2	William Wilkins	Ind. (no party)	30
				Votes not cast		2
1836	Martin Van Buren	Democratic	170	Richard M. Johnson[5]	Democratic	147
	William H. Harrison	Whig	73	Francis Granger	Whig	77
	Hugh L. White	Whig	26	John Tyler	Whig	47
	Daniel Webster	Whig	14	William Smith	Ind. (no party)	23
	W. P. Mangum	Ind. (no party)	11			

Year	Presidential candidates	Party	Electoral vote	Vice-presidential candidates	Party	Electoral vote
1840	William H. Harrison[6]	Whig	234	John Tyler	Whig	234
	Martin Van Buren	Democratic	60	Richard M. Johnson	Democratic	48
				L. W. Tazewell	Ind. (no party)	11
				James K. Polk	Democratic	1
1844	James K. Polk	Democratic	170	George M. Dallas	Democratic	170
	Henry Clay	Whig	105	Theo. Frelinghuysen	Whig	105
1848	Zachary Taylor[7]	Whig	163	Millard Fillmore	Whig	163
	Lewis Cass	Democratic	127	William O. Butler	Democratic	127
1852	Franklin Pierce	Democratic	254	William R. King	Democratic	254
	Winfield Scott	Whig	42	William A. Graham	Whig	42
1856	James Buchanan	Democratic	174	John C. Breckinridge	Democratic	174
	John C. Fremont	Republican	114	William L. Dayton	Republican	114
	Millard Fillmore	American[8]	8	A. J. Donelson	American[8]	8
1860	Abraham Lincoln	Republican	180	Hannibal Hamlin	Republican	180
	John C. Breckin-ridge	Democratic	72	Joseph Lane	Democratic	72
	John Bell	Const. Union	39	Edward Everett	Const. Union	39
	Stephen A. Douglas	Democratic	12	H. V. Johnson	Democratic	12
1864	Abraham Lincoln[9]	Union[10]	212	Andrew Johnson	Union[15]	212
	George B. McClel-lan	Democratic	21	G. H. Pendleton	Democratic	21
1868	Ulysses S. Grant	Republican	214	Schuyler Colfax	Republican	214
	Horatio Seymour	Democratic	80	Francis P. Blair, Jr.	Democratic	80
	Votes not counted[11]		23	Votes not counted[11]		23

Year	Presidential candidates	Party	Electoral vote	Popular vote	Vice-presidential candidates and party
1872	Ulysses S. Grant	Republican	286	3,597,132	Henry Wilson—R
	Horace Greeley	Dem., Liberal Rep.	(12)	2,834,125	B. Gratz Brown—D, LR—(47)
	Thomas A. Hendricks	Democratic	42		Scattering—(19)
	B. Gratz Brown	Dem., Liberal Rep.	18		Votes not counted—(14)
	Charles J. Jenkins	Democratic	2		
	David Davis	Democratic	1		
	Votes not counted		17		
1876[13]	Rutherford B. Hayes	Republican	185	4,033,768	William A. Wheeler—R
	Samuel J. Tilden	Democratic	184	4,285,992	Thomas A. Hendricks—D
	Peter Cooper	Greenback	0	81,737	Samuel F. Cary—G
1880	James A. Garfield[14]	Republican	214	4,449,053	Chester A. Arthur—R
	Winfield S. Hancock	Democratic	155	4,442,035	William H. English—D
	James B. Weaver	Greenback	0	308,578	B. J. Chambers—G
1884	Grover Cleveland	Democratic	219	4,911,017	Thomas A. Hendricks—D
	James G. Blaine	Republican	182	4,848,334	John A. Logan—R
	Benjamin F. Butler	Greenback	0	175,370	A. M. West—G
	John P. St. John	Prohibition	0	150,369	William Daniel—P
1888	Benjamin Harrison	Republican	233	5,440,216	Levi P. Morton—R
	Grover Cleveland	Democratic	168	5,538,233	A. G. Thurman—D
	Clinton B. Fisk	Prohibition	0	249,506	John A. Brooks—P
	Alson J. Streeter	Union Labor	0	146,935	Charles E. Cunningham—UL
1892	Grover Cleveland	Democratic	277	5,556,918	Adlai E. Stevenson—D
	Benjamin Harrison	Republican	145	5,176,108	Whitelaw Reid—R
	James B. Weaver	People's[15]	22	1,041,028	James G. Field—Peo
	John Bidwell	Prohibition	0	264,133	James B. Cranfill—P
1896	William McKinley	Republican	271	7,035,638	Garret A. Hobart—R
	William J. Bryan	Dem., People's[15]	176	6,467,946	Arthur Sewall—D—(149)
					Thomas E. Watson—Peo—(27)
	John M. Palmer	Natl. Dem.	0	133,148	Simon B. Buckner—ND
	Joshua Levering	Prohibition	0	132,007	Hale Johnson—P
1900	William McKinley[16]	Republican	292	7,219,530	Theodore Roosevelt—R
	William J. Bryan	Dem., People's[15]	155	6,358,071	Adlai E. Stevenson—D, Peo
	Eugene V. Debs	Social Democratic	0	94,768	Job Harriman—SD

Year	Presidential candidates	Party	Electoral vote	Popular vote	Vice-presidential candidates and party
1904	Theodore Roosevelt	Republican	336	7,628,834	Charles W. Fairbanks—R
	Alton B. Parker	Democratic	140	5,084,491	Henry G. Davis—D
	Eugene V. Debs	Socialist	0	402,400	Benjamin Hanford—S
1908	William H. Taft	Republican	321	7,679,006	James S. Sherman—R
	William J. Bryan	Democratic	162	6,409,106	John W. Kern—D
	Eugene V. Debs	Socialist	0	402,820	Benjamin Hanford—S
1912	Woodrow Wilson	Democratic	435	6,286,214	Thomas R. Marshall—D
	Theodore Roosevelt	Progressive	88	4,126,020	Hiram Johnson—Prog
	William H. Taft	Republican	8	3,483,922	Nicholas M. Butler—R[17]
	Eugene V. Debs	Socialist	0	897,011	Emil Seidel—S
1916	Woodrow Wilson	Democratic	277	9,129,606	Thomas R. Marshall—D
	Charles E. Hughes	Republican	254	8,538,221	Charles W. Fairbanks—R
	A. L. Benson	Socialist	0	585,113	G. R. Kirkpatrick—S
1920	Warren G. Harding[18]	Republican	404	16,152,200	Calvin Coolidge—R
	James M. Cox	Democratic	127	9,147,353	Franklin D. Roosevelt—D
	Eugene V. Debs	Socialist	0	917,799	Seymour Stedman—S
1924	Calvin Coolidge	Republican	382	15,725,016	Charles G. Dawes—R
	John W. Davis	Democratic	136	8,385,586	Charles W. Bryan—D
	Robert M. LaFollette	Progressive, Socialist	13	4,822,856	Burton K. Wheeler—Prog S
1928	Herbert Hoover	Republican	444	21,392,190	Charles Curtis—R
	Alfred E. Smith	Democratic	87	15,016,443	Joseph T. Robinson—D
	Norman Thomas	Socialist	0	267,420	James H. Maurer—S
1932	Franklin D. Roosevelt	Democratic	472	22,821,857	John N. Garner—D
	Herbert Hoover	Republican	59	15,761,841	Charles Curtis—R
	Norman Thomas	Socialist	0	884,781	James H. Maurer—S
1936	Franklin D. Roosevelt	Democratic	523	27,751,597	John N. Garner—D
	Alfred M. Landon	Republican	8	16,679,583	Frank Knox—R
	Norman Thomas	Socialist	0	187,720	George Nelson—S
1940	Franklin D. Roosevelt	Democratic	449	27,244,160	Henry A. Wallace—D
	Wendell L. Willkie	Republican	82	22,305,198	Charles L. McNary—R
	Norman Thomas	Socialist	0	99,557	Maynard C. Krueger—S
1944	Franklin D. Roosevelt[19]	Democratic	432	25,602,504	Harry S. Truman—D
	Thomas E. Dewey	Republican	99	22,006,285	John W. Bricker—R
	Norman Thomas	Socialist	0	80,518	Darlington Hoopes—S
1948	Harry S. Truman	Democratic	303	24,179,345	Alben W. Barkley—D
	Thomas E. Dewey	Republican	189	21,991,291	Earl Warren—R
	J. Strom Thurmond	States' Rights	39	1,176,125	Fielding L. Wright—SR
	Henry A. Wallace	Dem.	0	1,157,326	Glen Taylor—Prog
	Norman Thomas	Progressive Socialist	0	139,572	Tucker P. Smith—S
1952	Dwight D. Eisenhower	Republican	442	33,936,234	Richard M. Nixon—R
	Adlai E. Stevenson	Democratic	89	27,314,992	John J. Sparkman—D
1956	Dwight D. Eisenhower	Republican	457	35,590,472	Richard M. Nixon—R
	Adlai E. Stevenson	Democratic	73[20]	26,022,752	Estes Kefauver—D
1960	John F. Kennedy[22]	Democratic	303	34,226,731	Lyndon B. Johnson—D
	Richard M. Nixon	Republican	219[21]	34,108,157	Henry Cabot Lodge—R
1964	Lyndon B. Johnson	Democratic	486	43,129,484	Hubert H. Humphrey—D
	Barry M. Goldwater	Republican	52	27,178,188	William E. Miller—R
1968	Richard M. Nixon	Republican	301	31,785,480	Spiro T. Agnew—R
	Hubert H. Humphrey	Democratic	191	31,275,166	Edmund S. Muskie—D
	George C. Wallace	American Independent	46	9,906,473	Curtis F. LeMay—AI

Year	Presidential candidates	Party	Electoral vote	Popular vote	Vice-presidential candidates and party
1972	Richard M. Nixon[23]	Republican	520[24]	47,169,911	Spiro T. Agnew—R
	George McGovern	Democratic	17	29,170,383	Sargent Shriver—D
	John G. Schmitz	American	0	1,099,482	Thomas J. Anderson—A
1976	Jimmy Carter	Democratic	297	40,830,763	Walter F. Mondale—D
	Gerald R. Ford	Republican	240[25]	39,147,973	Robert J. Dole—R
	Eugene J. McCarthy	Independent	0	756,631	None
1980	Ronald Reagan	Republican	489	43,899,248	George Bush—R
	Jimmy Carter	Democratic	49	36,481,435	Walter F. Mondale—D
	John B. Anderson	Independent	0	5,719,437	Patrick J. Lucey—I
1984	Ronald Reagan	Republican	525	54,455,075	George Bush—R
	Walter F. Mondale	Democratic	13	37,577,185	Geraldine A. Ferraro—D
1988	George H. Bush	Republican	426	48,886,097	J. Danforth Quayle—R
	Michael S. Dukakis	Democratic	111[26]	41,809,074	Lloyd Bentsen—D
1992	William J. Clinton	Democratic	370	44,909,889	Albert A. Gore, Jr.—D
	George H. Bush	Republican	168	39,104,545	J. Danforth Quayle—R
	H. Ross Perot	Independent	0	19,742,267	James B. Stockdale—I
1996	William J. Clinton	Democratic	379	47,402,357	Albert A. Gore, Jr.—D
	Robert J. Dole	Republican	159	39,198,755	Jack F. Kemp—R
	H. Ross Perot	Independent	0	8,085,402	Pat Choate—I

1. Only 10 states participated in the election. The New York legislature chose no electors, and North Carolina and Rhode Island had not yet ratified the Constitution. 2. As Jefferson and Burr were tied, the House of Representatives chose the President. In a vote by states, 10 votes were cast for Jefferson, 4 for Burr; 2 votes were not cast. 3. As no candidate had an electoral-vote majority, the House of Representatives chose the President from the first three. In a vote by states, 13 votes were cast for Adams, 7 for Jackson, and 4 for Crawford. 4. The Antimasonic Party on Sept. 26, 1831, was the first party to hold a nominating convention to choose candidates for President and Vice-President. 5. As Johnson did not have an electoral-vote majority, the Senate chose him 33–14 over Granger, the others being legally out of the race. 6. Harrison died April 4, 1841, and Tyler succeeded him April 6. 7. Taylor died July 9, 1850, and Fillmore succeeded him July 10. 8. Also known as the Know-Nothing Party. 9. Lincoln died April 15, 1865, and Johnson succeeded him the same day. 10. Name adopted by the Republican National Convention of 1864. Johnson was a War Democrat. 11. 23 Southern electoral votes were excluded. 12. See Election of 1872 in Unusual Voting Results. 13. See Election of 1876 in Unusual Voting Results. 14. Garfield died Sept. 19, 1881, and Arthur succeeded him Sept. 20. 15. Members of People's Party were called Populists. 16. McKinley died Sept. 14, 1901, and Roosevelt succeeded him the same day. 17. James S. Sherman, Republican candidate for Vice President, died Oct. 30, 1912, and the Republican electoral votes were cast for Butler. 18. Harding died Aug. 2, 1923, and Coolidge succeeded him Aug. 3. 19. Roosevelt died April 12, 1945, and Truman succeeded him the same day. 20. One electoral vote from Alabama was cast for Walter B. Jones. 21. Sen. Harry F. Byrd received 15 electoral votes. 22. Kennedy died Nov. 22, 1963, and Johnson succeeded him the same day. 23. Nixon resigned Aug. 9, 1974, and Gerald R. Ford succeeded him the same day. 24. One electoral vote from Virginia was cast for John Hospers, Libertarian Party. 25. One electoral vote from Washington was cast for Ronald Reagan. 26. One electoral vote from West Virginia was cast for Lloyd Bentsen.

Gerrymander

Source: The Reader's Companion to American History, Houghton Mifflin Company.

Gerrymander refers to the drawing of boundaries of legislative districts to benefit one party or group and handicap another. Although the practice dates back to the colonial period, its name is derived from Elbridge Gerry, a signer of the Declaration of Independence, a nonsigning delegate to the Federal Convention of 1787, and a leader of the Jeffersonian Republican party.

In 1812, while Gerry was governor of Massachusetts, the Republican-dominated legislature redrew district lines to weigh representation in favor of Republicans and against Federalists. The Federalists attacked the redistricting, specifically blaming Gerry although he had nothing to do with the project and, in private, opposed it. A Federalist newspaper published a political cartoon depicting the oddly shaped district covering Essex County as a salamander; the cartoonist dubbed his creation a "Gerry-mander." The word quickly passed into common parlance.

Since the 1950s, the federal courts have been increasingly willing to examine states' defining of representative districts to determine their adherence to the principle of "one man, one vote," as enunciated in *Baker v. Carr* (1962). Ironically, in light of the term's New England origins, most gerrymanders examined by the Supreme Court have come from southern states, where local legislatures sought to dilute the representation of urban residents and African-Americans. □

Qualifications for Voting

The Supreme Court decision of March 21, 1972, declared lengthy requirements for voting in state and local elections unconstitutional and suggested that 30 days was an ample period. Most of the states have changed or eliminated their durational residency requirements to comply with the ruling, as shown.

NO DURATIONAL RESIDENCY REQUIREMENT

Alabama,[6] Arkansas, Connecticut,[13] Delaware,[12] District of Columbia,[16] Florida,[5] Georgia,[2] Hawaii,[2] Iowa,[6] Louisiana,[8] Maine, Maryland, Massachusetts,[3] Missouri,[4] Nebraska,[9] New Hampshire,[17] New Mexico,[7] Oklahoma, South Carolina,[21] South Dakota,[10] Texas,[2] Virginia, West Virginia,[2] Wyoming,[2] Tennessee[2]

30-DAY RESIDENCY REQUIREMENT

Alaska,[18] Arizona,[11] Idaho,[22] Illinois, Indiana, Michigan, Mississippi,[20] Montana, Nevada, New Jersey, New York, North Carolina, North Dakota, Ohio, Pennsylvania,[2] Rhode Island, Utah, Washington[2]

OTHER

California,[19] Colorado,[1] Minnesota[15] and Oregon,[23] 20 days; Kentucky, 28 days; Kansas, 14 days; Vermont, 10–12 days;[14] Wisconsin, 10 days

1. 25 days immediately preceding the election. 2. 30-day registration requirement. 3. No residency required to register to vote. 4. Must be registered by the fourth Wednesday prior to election. 5. 29-day registration requirement before national election; 29-day registration requirement before first and second state primary. 6. 10-day registration requirement. In-person registration by 5 PM, eleven days before election date. 7. Must register 28 days before election. 8. Register 24 days prior to any election. 9. Registration requirement, 2nd Friday prior to elections. 10. 15-day registration requirement. 11. Residency in the state 29 days next preceding the election. 12. Must reside in Delaware and register by the last day that the books are open for registration. 13. Registration deadline 14th day before election; registration and party enrollment deadline by 12 noon the day before primary. 14. Administrative cut-off date for processing applications 2nd Saturday before the election by 12 noon. 15. Permits registration and voting on election day with approved ID. 16. Registration stops 30 days before any election. Voters must inform Board of Elections of change of address within 30 days of moving. 17. Registration requirement, 10 days prior to elections. Same day registrations for Federal and State elections. 18. If otherwise qualified but has not been a resident of the election district for at least 30 days preceding the date of a presidential election, is entitled to register and vote for presidential and vice-presidential candidates. 19. Must be a registered voter 29 days before an election. 20. 30 days registration required, 60 days if registration is by mail. 21. Registration certificate not valid for 30 days but if you move within the state you can vote in old precinct during the 30 days. 22. May register 25 days prior to any election with County Clerk. If eligible to vote, an individual may register in person at the polling place on election day at the resident precinct and complete a registration card, make an oath and provide proof of residence. 23. By close of business day registering agencies (which varies) 21st day before the election.

Source: Information Please questionnaires to the states.

Facts About Elections

Candidate with highest popular vote: Reagan (1984), 54,455,075.
Candidate with highest electoral vote: Reagan (1984), 525
Candidate carrying most states: Nixon (1972) and Reagan (1984), 49.

Candidate running most times: Norman Thomas, 6 (1928, 1932, 1936, 1940, 1944, 1948).

Candidate elected, defeated, then reelected: Cleveland (1884, 1888, 1892).

Plurality and Majority

In order to win a plurality, a candidate must receive a greater number of votes than anyone running against him. If he receives 50 votes, for example, and two other candidates receive 49 and 2, he will have a plurality of one vote over his closest opponent.

However, a candidate does not have a majority unless he receives more than 50% of the total votes cast. In the example above, the candidate does not have a majority, because his 50 votes are less than 50% of the 101 votes cast.

Unusual Voting Results

Election of 1872

The presidential and vice-presidential candidates of the Liberal Republicans and the northern Democrats in 1872 were Horace Greeley and B. Gratz Brown. Greeley died Nov. 29, 1872, before his 66 electors voted. In the electoral balloting for President, 63 of Greeley's votes were scattered among four other men, including Brown.

Election of 1876

In the election of 1876 Samuel J. Tilden, the Democratic candidate, received a popular majority but lacked one undisputed electoral vote to carry a clear majority of the electoral college. The crux of the problem was in the 22 electoral votes which were in dispute because Florida, Louisiana, South Carolina, and Oregon each sent in two sets of election returns. In the three southern states, Republican election boards threw out enough Democratic votes to certify the Republican candidate, Hayes. In Oregon, the Democratic governor disqualified a Republican elector, replacing him with a Democrat. Since the Senate was Republican and the House of Representatives Democratic, it seemed useless to refer the disputed returns to the two houses for solution. Instead Congress appointed an Electoral Commission with five representatives each from the Senate, the House, and the Supreme Court. All but one Justice was named, giving the Commission seven Republican and seven Democratic members. The naming of the fifth Justice was left to the other four. He was a Republican who first favored Tilden but, under pressure from his party, switched to Hayes, ensuring his election by the Commission voting 8 to 7 on party lines.

Minority Presidents

Sixteen candidates have become President of the United States with a popular vote less than 50% of the total cast. It should be noted, however, that in elections before 1872, presidential electors were not chosen by popular vote in all states. Adams' election in 1824 was by the House of Representatives, which chose him over Jackson, who had a plurality of both electoral and popular votes, but not a majority in the electoral college.

Besides Jackson in 1824, only two other candidates receiving the largest popular vote have failed to gain a majority in the electoral college—Samuel J. Tilden (D) in 1876 and Grover Cleveland (D) in 1888. The "minority" Presidents are listed in the following table:

Vote Received by Minority Presidents

Year	President	Electoral Percent	Popular Percent	Year	President	Electoral Percent	Popular Percent
1824	John Q. Adams	31.8	29.8	1888	Benjamin Harrison (R)	58.1	47.8
1844	James K. Polk (D)	61.8	49.3	1892	Grover Cleveland (D)	62.4	46.0
1848	Zachary Taylor (W)	56.2	47.3	1912	Woodrow Wilson (D)	81.9	41.8
1856	James Buchanan (D)	58.7	45.3	1916	Woodrow Wilson (D)	52.1	49.3
1860	Abraham Lincoln (R)	59.4	39.9	1948	Harry S. Truman (D)	57.1	49.5
1876	Rutherford B. Hayes (R)	50.1	47.9	1960	John F. Kennedy (D)	56.4	49.7
1880	James A. Garfield (R)	57.9	48.3	1968	Richard M. Nixon (R)	56.1	43.4
1884	Grover Cleveland (D)	54.6	48.8	1992	William J. Clinton (D)	68.8	43.0

National Voter Turnout in Federal Elections: 1960–1996

Year	Voting Age Population	Voter Registration	Voter Turnout	% of Turnout of Voting Age Population[1]
1996	196,511,000	146,211,960	96,456,345	49.1%
1994	193,650,000	130,292,822	75,105,860	38.8
1992	189,529,000	133,821,178	104,405,155	55.1
1990	185,812,000	121,105,630	67,859,189	36.5
1988	182,778,000	126,379,628	91,594,693	50.1
1986	178,566,000	118,399,984	64,991,128	36.4
1984	174,466,000	124,150,614	92,652,680	53.1
1982	169,938,000	110,671,225	67,615,576	39.8
1980	164,597,000	113,043,734	86,515,221	52.6
1978	158,373,000	103,291,265	58,917,938	37.2
1976	152,309,190	105,037,986	81,555,789	53.6
1974	146,336,000	96,199,020[2]	55,943,834	38.2
1972	140,776,000	97,328,541	77,718,554	55.2
1970	124,498,000	82,496,747[3]	58,014,338	46.6
1968	120,328,186	81,658,180	73,211,875	60.8
1966	116,132,000	76,288,283[4]	56,188,046	48.4
1964	114,090,000	73,715,818	70,644,592	61.9
1962	112,423,000	65,393,751[5]	53,141,227	47.3
1960	109,159,000	64,833,096[6]	68,838,204	63.1

1. Definitions: % T/O of VAP=Percent Turnout of Voting Age Population 2. Registrations from Iowa not included. 3. Registrations fro Iowa and Missouri not included. 4. Registrations from Iowa, Kans., Miss., Mo., Nebr., and Wyo. not included. D.C.did not have independent status. 5. Registrations from Ala., Alaska, D.C., Iowa, Kans., Ky., Miss., Mo., Nebr., N.C., N.Dak., Okla., S.Dak., Wis., and Wyo. not included. 6. Registrations from Ala., Alaska, D.C., Iowa, Kans., Ky., Miss., Mo., Nebr., N.Mex., N.C., N.Dak., Okla., S.Dak., Wis., and Wyo. not included. *Source:* Federal Election Commission.

How a Bill Becomes a Law

When a Senator or a Representative introduces a bill, he sends it to the clerk of his house, who gives it a number and title. This is the *first reading,* and the bill is referred to the proper committee.

The committee may decide the bill is unwise or unnecessary and *table* it, thus killing it at once. Or it may decide the bill is worthwhile and hold hearings to listen to facts and opinions presented by experts and other interested persons. After members of the committee have debated the bill and perhaps offered amendments, a vote is taken; and if the vote is favorable, the bill is sent back to the floor of the house.

The clerk reads the bill sentence by sentence to the house, and this is known as the *second reading.* Members may then debate the bill and offer amendments. In the House of Representatives, the time for debate is limited by a *cloture rule,* but there is no such restriction in the Senate for cloture, where 60 votes are required. This makes possible a *filibuster,* in which one or more opponents hold the floor to defeat the bill.

The *third reading* is by title only, and the bill is put to a vote, which may be by voice or roll call, depending on the circumstances and parliamentary rules. Members who must be absent at the time but who wish to record their vote may be paired if each negative vote has a balancing affirmative one.

The bill then goes to the other house of Congress, where it may be defeated, or passed with or without amendments. If the bill is defeated, it dies. If it is passed with amendments, a joint Congressional committee must be appointed by both houses to iron out the differences.

After its final passage by both houses, the bill is sent to the President. If he approves, he signs it, and the bill becomes a law. However, if he disapproves, he *vetoes* the bill by refusing to sign it and sending it back to the house of origin with his reasons for the veto. The objections are read and debated, and a roll-call vote is taken. If the bill receives less than a two-thirds vote, it is defeated and goes no farther. But if it receives a two-thirds vote or greater, it is sent to the other house for a vote. If that house also passes it by a two-thirds vote,

the President's veto is *overridden*, and the bill becomes a law.

Should the President desire neither to sign nor to veto the bill, he may retain it for ten days, Sundays excepted, after which time it automatically becomes a law without signature. However, if Congress has adjourned within those ten days, the bill is automatically killed, that process of indirect rejection being known as a *pocket veto*.

Government Officials

Cabinet Members With Dates of Appointment

Although the Constitution made no provision for a President's advisory group, the heads of the three executive departments (State, Treasury, and War) and the Attorney General were organized by Washington into such a group; and by about 1793, the name "Cabinet" was applied to it. With the exception of the Attorney General up to 1870 and the Postmaster General from 1829 to 1872, Cabinet members have been heads of executive departments.

A Cabinet member is appointed by the President, subject to the confirmation of the Senate; and as his term is not fixed, he may be replaced at any time by the President. At a change in Administration, it is customary for him to tender his resignation, but he remains in office until a successor is appointed.

The table of Cabinet members lists only those members who actually served after being duly commissioned.

The dates shown are those of appointment. "Cont." indicates that the term continued from the previous Administration for a substantial amount of time.

With the creation of the Department of Transportation in 1966, the Cabinet consisted of 12 members. This figure was reduced to 11 when the Post Office Department became an independent agency in 1970 but, with the establishment in 1977 of a Department of Energy, became 12 again. Creation of the Department of Education in 1980 raised the number to 13. Creation of the Department of Veterans' Affairs in 1989 raised the number to 14.

Washington

Secretary of State	Thomas Jefferson, 1789
	Edmund Randolph, 1794
	Timothy Pickering, 1795
Secretary of the Treasury	Alexander Hamilton, 1789
	Oliver Wolcott, Jr., 1795
Secretary of War	Henry Knox, 1789
	Timothy Pickering, 1795
	James McHenry, 1796
Attorney General	Edmund Randolph, 1789
	William Bradford, 1794
	Charles Lee, 1795

J. Adams

Secretary of State	Timothy Pickering (Cont.)
	John Marshall, 1800
Secretary of the Treasury	Oliver Wolcott, Jr. (Cont.)
	Samuel Dexter, 1801
Secretary of War	James McHenry (Cont.)
	Samuel Dexter, 1800
Attorney General	Charles Lee (Cont.)
Secretary of the Navy	Benjamin Stoddert, 1798

Jefferson

Secretary of State	James Madison, 1801
Secretary of the Treasury	Samuel Dexter (Cont.)
	Albert Gallatin, 1801
Secretary of War	Henry Dearborn, 1801
Attorney General	Levi Lincoln, 1801
	Robert Smith, 1805
	John Breckinridge, 1805
	Caesar A. Rodney, 1807
Secretary of the Navy	Benjamin Stoddert (Cont.)
	Robert Smith, 1801

Madison

Secretary of State	Robert Smith, 1809
	James Monroe, 1811
Secretary of the Treasury	Albert Gallatin (Cont.)
	George W. Campbell, 1814
	Alexander J. Dallas, 1814
	William H. Crawford, 1816

Secretary of War	William Eustis, 1809
	John Armstrong, 1813
	James Monroe, 1814
	William H. Crawford, 1815
Attorney General	Caesar A. Rodney (Cont.)
	William Pinckney, 1811
	Richard Rush, 1814
Secretary of the Navy	Paul Hamilton, 1809
	William Jones, 1813
	B. W. Crowninshield, 1814

Monroe

Secretary of State	John Quincy Adams, 1817
Secretary of the Treasury	William H. Crawford (Cont.)
Secretary of War	John C. Calhoun, 1817
Attorney General	Richard Rush (Cont.)
	William Wirt, 1817
Secretary of the Navy	B. W. Crowninshield (Cont.)
	Smith Thompson, 1818
	Samuel L. Southard, 1823

J. Q. Adams

Secretary of State	Henry Clay, 1825
Secretary of the Treasury	Richard Rush, 1825
Secretary of War	James Barbour, 1825
	Peter B. Porter, 1828
Attorney General	William Wirt (Cont.)
Secretary of the Navy	Samuel L. Southard (Cont.)

Jackson

Secretary of State	Martin Van Buren, 1829
	Edward Livingston, 1831
	Louis McLane, 1833
	John Forsyth, 1834
Secretary of the Treasury	Samuel D. Ingham, 1829
	Louis McLane, 1831
	William J. Duane, 1833
	Roger B. Taney[2], 1833
	Levi Woodbury, 1834
Secretary of War	John H. Eaton, 1829
	Lewis Cass, 1831

Attorney General	John M. Berrien, 1829
	Roger B. Taney, 1831
	Benjamin F. Butler, 1833
Postmaster General[1]	William T. Barry, 1829
	Amos Kendall, 1835
Secretary of the Navy	John Branch, 1829
	Levi Woodbury, 1831
	Mahlon Dickerson, 1834

1. The Postmaster General did not become a Cabinet member until, 1829. Earlier Postmasters General were: Samuel Osgood (1789), Timothy Pickering (1791), Joseph Habersham (1795), Gideon Granger (1801), Return J. Meigs, Jr. (1814), and John McLean (1823). 2. Not confirmed by the Senate.

Van Buren

Secretary of State	John Forsyth (Cont.)
Secretary of the Treasury	Levi Woodbury (Cont.)
Secretary of War	Joel R. Poinsett, 1837
Attorney General	Benjamin F. Butler (Cont.)
	Felix Grundy, 1838
	Henry D. Gilpin, 1840
Postmaster General	Amos Kendall (Cont.)
	John M. Niles, 1840
Secretary of the Navy	Mahlon Dickerson (Cont.)
	James K. Paulding, 1838

W. H. Harrison

Secretary of State	Daniel Webster, 1841
Secretary of the Treasury	Thomas Ewing, 1841
Secretary of War	John Bell, 1841
Attorney General	John J. Crittenden, 1841
Postmaster General	Francis Granger, 1841
Secretary of the Navy	George E. Badger, 1841

Tyler

Secretary of State	Daniel Webster (Cont.)
	Abel P. Upshur, 1843
	John C. Calhoun, 1844
Secretary of the Treasury	Thomas Ewing (Cont.)
	Walter Forward, 1841
	John C. Spencer[1], 1843
	George M. Bibb, 1844
Secretary of War	John Bell (Cont.)
	John C. Spencer, 1841
	James M. Porter[1], 1843
	William Wilkins, 1844
Attorney General	John J. Crittenden (Cont.)
	Hugh S. Legaré, 1841
	John Nelson, 1843
Postmaster General	Francis Granger (Cont.)
	Charles A. Wickliffe, 1841
Secretary of the Navy	George E. Badger (Cont.)
	Abel P. Upshur, 1841
	David Henshaw[1], 1843
	Thomas W. Gilmer, 1844
	John Y. Mason, 1844

1. Not confirmed by the Senate.

Polk

Secretary of State	James Buchanan, 1845
Secretary of the Treasury	Robert J. Walker, 1845
Secretary of War	William L. Marcy, 1845
Attorney General	John Y. Mason, 1845
	Nathan Clifford, 1846
	Isaac Toucey, 1848
Postmaster General	Cave Johnson, 1845
Secretary of the Navy	George Bancroft, 1845
	John Y. Mason, 1846

Taylor

| Secretary of State | John M. Clayton, 1849 |

Secretary of the Treasury	William M. Meredith, 1849
Secretary of War	George W. Crawford, 1849
Attorney General	Reverdy Johnson, 1849
Postmaster General	Jacob Collamer, 1849
Secretary of the Navy	William B. Preston, 1849
Secretary of the Interior	Thomas Ewing, 1849

Fillmore

Secretary of State	Daniel Webster, 1850
	Edward Everett, 1852
Secretary of the Treasury	Thomas Corwin, 1850
Secretary of War	Charles M. Conrad, 1850
Attorney General	John J. Crittenden, 1850
Postmaster General	Nathan K. Hall, 1850
	Samuel D. Hubbard, 1852
Secretary of the Navy	William A. Graham, 1850
	John P. Kennedy, 1852
Secretary of the Interior	Thos. M. T. McKennan, 1850
	Alex. H. H. Stuart, 1850

Pierce

Secretary of State	William L. Marcy, 1853
Secretary of the Treasury	James Guthrie, 1853
Secretary of War	Jefferson Davis, 1853
Attorney General	Caleb Cushing, 1853
Postmaster General	James Campbell, 1853
Secretary of the Navy	James C. Dobbin, 1853
Secretary of the Interior	Robert McClelland, 1853

Buchanan

Secretary of State	Lewis Cass, 1857
	Jeremiah S. Black, 1860
Secretary of the Treasury	Howell Cobb, 1857
	Philip F. Thomas, 1860
	John A. Dix, 1861
Secretary of War	John B. Floyd, 1857
	Joseph Holt, 1861
Attorney General	Jeremiah S. Black, 1857
	Edwin M. Stanton, 1860
Postmaster General	Aaron V. Brown, 1857
	Joseph Holt, 1859
	Horatio King, 1861
Secretary of the Navy	Isaac Toucey, 1857
Secretary of the Interior	Jacob Thompson, 1857

Lincoln

Secretary of State	William H. Seward, 1861
Secretary of the Treasury	Salmon P. Chase, 1861
	William P. Fessenden, 1864
	Hugh McCulloch, 1865
Secretary of War	Simon Cameron, 1861
	Edwin M. Stanton, 1862
Attorney General	Edward Bates, 1861
	James Speed, 1864
Postmaster General	Montgomery Blair, 1861
	William Dennison, 1864
Secretary of the Navy	Gideon Welles, 1861
Secretary of the Interior	Caleb B. Smith, 1861
	John P. Usher, 1863

A. Johnson

Secretary of State	William H. Seward (Cont.)
Secretary of the Treasury	Hugh McCulloch (Cont.)
Secretary of War	Edwin M. Stanton (Cont.)
	John M. Schofield, 1868
Attorney General	James Speed (Cont.)
	Henry Stanbery, 1866
	William M. Evarts, 1868
Postmaster General	William Dennison (Cont.)
	Alexander W. Randall, 1866
Secretary of the Navy	Gideon Welles (Cont.)

Secretary of the Interior	John P. Usher (Cont.)
	James Harlan, 1865
	Orville H. Browning, 1866

Grant

Secretary of State	Elihu B. Washburne, 1869
	Hamilton Fish, 1869
	George S. Boutwell, 1869
	William A. Richardson, 1873
	Benjamin H. Bristow, 1874
	Lot M. Morrill, 1876
Secretary of War	John A. Rawlins, 1869
	William W. Belknap, 1869
	Alphonso Taft, 1876
	James D. Cameron, 1876
Attorney General	Ebenezer R. Hoar, 1869
	Amos T. Akerman, 1870
	George H. Williams, 1871
	Edwards Pierrepont, 1875
	Alphonso Taft, 1876
Postmaster General	John A. J. Creswell, 1869
	Marshall Jewell, 1874
	James N. Tyner, 1876
Secretary of the Navy	Adolph E. Borie, 1869
	George M. Robeson, 1869
Secretary of the Interior	Jacob D. Cox, 1869
	Columbus Delano, 1870
	Zachariah Chandler, 1875

Hayes

Secretary of State	William M. Evarts, 1877
Secretary of the Treasury	John Sherman, 1877
Secretary of War	George W. McCrary, 1877
	Alexander Ramsey, 1879
Attorney General	Charles Devens, 1877
Postmaster General	David M. Key, 1877
	Horace Maynard, 1880
	Richard W. Thompson, 1877
	Nathan Goff, Jr., 1881
Secretary of the Interior	Carl Schurz, 1877

Garfield

Secretary of State	James G. Blaine, 1881
Secretary of the Treasury	William Windom, 1881
Secretary of War	Robert T. Lincoln, 1881
Attorney General	Wayne MacVeagh, 1881
Postmaster General	Thomas L. James, 1881
Secretary of the Navy	William H. Hunt, 1881
Secretary of the Interior	Samuel J. Kirkwood, 1881

Arthur

Secretary of State	James G. Blaine (Cont.)
	F. T. Frelinghuysen, 1881
Secretary of the Treasury	William Windom (Cont.)
	Charles J. Folger, 1881
	Walter Q. Gresham, 1884
	Hugh McCulloch, 1884
Secretary of War	Robert T. Lincoln (Cont.)
Attorney General	Wayne MacVeagh (Cont.)
	Benjamin H. Brewster, 1881
Postmaster General	Thomas L. James (Cont.)
	Timothy O. Howe, 1881
	Walter Q. Gresham, 1883
	Frank Hatton, 1884
Secretary of the Navy	William H. Hunt (Cont.)
	William E. Chandler, 1882
Secretary of the Interior	Samuel J. Kirkwood (Cont.)
	Henry M. Teller, 1882

Cleveland

Secretary of State	Thomas F. Bayard, 1885
Secretary of the Treasury	Daniel Manning, 1885
	Charles S. Fairchild, 1887
Secretary of War	William C. Endicott, 1885
Attorney General	Augustus H. Garland, 1885

Postmaster General	William F. Vilas, 1885
	Don M. Dickinson, 1888
Secretary of the Navy	William C. Whitney, 1885
Secretary of the Interior	Lucius Q. C. Lamar, 1885
	William F. Vilas, 1888
Secretary of Agriculture	Norman J. Colman, 1889

B. Harrison

Secretary of State	James G. Blaine, 1889
	John W. Foster, 1892
Secretary of the Treasury	William Windom, 1889
	Charles Foster, 1891
Secretary of War	Redfield Proctor, 1889
	Stephen B. Elkins, 1891
Attorney General	William H. H. Miller, 1889
Postmaster General	John Wanamaker, 1889
Secretary of the Navy	Benjamin F. Tracy, 1889
Secretary of the Interior	John W. Noble, 1889
Secretary of Agriculture	Jeremiah M. Rusk, 1889

Cleveland

Secretary of State	Walter Q. Gresham, 1893
	Richard Olney, 1895
Secretary of the Treasury	John G. Carlisle, 1893
Secretary of War	Daniel S. Lamont, 1893
Attorney General	Richard Olney, 1893
	Judson Harmon, 1895
Postmaster General	Wilson S. Bissell, 1893
	William L. Wilson, 1895
Secretary of the Navy	Hilary A. Herbert, 1893
Secretary of the Interior	Hoke Smith, 1893
	David R. Francis, 1896
Secretary of Agriculture	Julius Sterling Morton, 1893

McKinley

Secretary of State	John Sherman, 1897
	William R. Day, 1898
	John Hay, 1898
Secretary of the Treasury	Lyman J. Gage, 1897
Secretary of War	Russell A. Alger, 1897
	Elihu Root, 1899
Attorney General	Joseph McKenna, 1897
	John W. Griggs, 1898
	Philander C. Knox, 1901
Postmaster General	James A. Gary, 1897
	Charles E. Smith, 1898
Secretary of the Navy	John D. Long, 1897
Secretary of the Interior	Cornelius N. Bliss, 1897
	Ethan A. Hitchcock, 1898
Secretary of Agriculture	James Wilson, 1897

T. Roosevelt

Secretary of State	John Hay (Cont.)
	Elihu Root, 1905
	Robert Bacon, 1909
Secretary of the Treasury	Lyman J. Gage (Cont.)
	Leslie M. Shaw, 1902
	George B. Cortelyou, 1907
Secretary of War	Elihu Root (Cont.)
	William H. Taft, 1904
	Luke E. Wright, 1908
Attorney General	Philander C. Knox (Cont.)
	William H. Moody, 1904
	Charles J. Bonaparte, 1906
Postmaster General	Charles E. Smith (Cont.)
	Henry C. Payne, 1902
	Robert J. Wynne, 1904
	George B. Cortelyou, 1905
	George von L. Meyer, 1907
Secretary of the Navy	John D. Long (Cont.)
	William H. Moody, 1902
	Paul Morton, 1904
	Charles J. Bonaparte, 1905
	Victor H. Metcalf, 1906
	Truman H. Newberry, 1908

Secretary of the Interior	Ethan A. Hitchcock (Cont.)
	James R. Garfield, 1907
Secretary of Agriculture	James Wilson (Cont.)
Secretary of Commerce and Labor	George B. Cortelyou, 1903
	Victor H. Metcalf, 1904
	Oscar S. Straus, 1906

Taft

Secretary of State	Philander C. Knox, 1909
Secretary of the Treasury	Franklin MacVeagh, 1909
Secretary of War	Jacob M. Dickinson, 1909
	Henry L. Stimson, 1911
Attorney General	George W. Wickersham, 1909
Postmaster General	Frank H. Hitchcock, 1909
Secretary of the Navy	George von L. Meyer, 1909
Secretary of the Interior	Richard A. Ballinger, 1909
	Walter L. Fisher, 1911
Secretary of Agriculture	James Wilson (Cont.)
Secretary of Commerce and Labor	Charles Nagel, 1909

Wilson

Secretary of State	William J. Bryan, 1913
	Robert Lansing, 1915
	Bainbridge Colby, 1920
Secretary of the Treasury	William G. McAdoo, 1913
	Carter Glass, 1918
	David F. Houston, 1920
Secretary of War	Lindley M. Garrison, 1913
	Newton D. Baker, 1916
Attorney General	James C. McReynolds, 1913
	Thomas W. Gregory, 1914
	A. Mitchell Palmer, 1919
Postmaster General	Albert S. Burleson, 1913
Secretary of the Navy	Josephus Daniels, 1913
Secretary of the Interior	Franklin K. Lane, 1913
	John B. Payne, 1920
Secretary of Agriculture	David F. Houston, 1913
	Edwin T. Meredith, 1920
Secretary of Commerce	William C. Redfield, 1913
	Joshua W. Alexander, 1919
Secretary of Labor	William B. Wilson, 1913

Harding

Secretary of State	Charles E. Hughes, 1921
Secretary of the Treasury	Andrew W. Mellon, 1921
Secretary of War	John W. Weeks, 1921
Attorney General	Harry M. Daugherty, 1921
Postmaster General	Will H. Hays, 1921
	Hubert Work, 1922
	Harry S. New, 1923
Secretary of the Navy	Edwin Denby, 1921
Secretary of the Interior	Albert B. Fall, 1921
	Hubert Work, 1923
Secretary of Agriculture	Henry C. Wallace, 1921
Secretary of Commerce	Herbert Hoover, 1921
Secretary of Labor	James J. Davis, 1921

Coolidge

Secretary of State	Charles E. Hughes (Cont.)
	Frank B. Kellogg, 1925
Secretary of the Treasury	Andrew W. Mellon (Cont.)
Secretary of War	John W. Weeks (Cont.)
	Dwight F. Davis, 1925
Attorney General	Harry M. Daugherty (Cont.)
	Harlan F. Stone, 1924
	John G. Sargent, 1925
Postmaster General	Harry S. New (Cont.)
Secretary of the Navy	Edwin Denby (Cont.)
	Curtis D. Wilbur, 1924
Secretary of the Interior	Hubert Work (Cont.)
	Roy O. West, 1928
Secretary of Agriculture	Henry C. Wallace (Cont.)
	Howard M. Gore, 1924
	William M. Jardine, 1925

Secretary of Commerce	Herbert Hoover (Cont.)
	William F. Whiting, 1928
Secretary of Labor	James J. Davis (Cont.)

Hoover

Secretary of State	Frank B. Kellogg (Cont.)
	Henry L. Stimson, 1929
Secretary of the Treasury	Andrew W. Mellon (Cont.)
	Ogden L. Mills, 1932
Secretary of War	James W. Good, 1929
	Patrick J. Hurley, 1929
Attorney General	William D. Mitchell, 1929
Postmaster General	Walter F. Brown, 1929
Secretary of the Navy	Charles F. Adams, 1929
Secretary of the Interior	Ray Lyman Wilbur, 1929
Secretary of Agriculture	Arthur M. Hyde, 1929
Secretary of Commerce	Robert P. Lamont, 1929
	Roy D. Chapin, 1932
Secretary of Labor	James J. Davis (Cont.)
	William N. Doak; 1930

F. D. Roosevelt

Secretary of State	Cordell Hull, 1933
	E. R. Stettinius, Jr., 1944
Secretary of the Treasury	William H. Woodin, 1933
	Henry Morgenthau, Jr., 1934
Secretary of War	George H. Dern, 1933
	Harry H. Woodring, 1936
	Henry L. Stimson, 1940
Attorney General	Homer S. Cummings, 1933
	Frank Murphy, 1939
	Robert H. Jackson, 1940
	Francis Biddle, 1941
Postmaster General	James A. Farley, 1933
	Frank C. Walker, 1940
Secretary of the Navy	Claude A. Swanson, 1933
	Charles Edison, 1940
	Frank Knox, 1940
	James Forrestal, 1944
Secretary of the Interior	Harold L. Ickes, 1933
Secretary of Agriculture	Henry A. Wallace, 1933
	Claude R. Wickard, 1940
Secretary of Commerce	Daniel C. Roper, 1933
	Harry L. Hopkins, 1938
	Jesse H. Jones, 1940
	Henry A. Wallace, 1945
Secretary of Labor	Frances Perkins, 1933

Truman

Secretary of State	E. R. Stettinius, Jr. (Cont.)
	James F. Byrnes, 1945
	George C. Marshall, 1947
	Dean Acheson, 1949
Secretary of the Treasury	Henry Morgenthau, Jr. (Cont.)
	Frederick M. Vinson, 1945
	John W. Snyder, 1946
Secretary of Defense	James Forrestal, 1947
	Louis A. Johnson, 1949
	George C. Marshall, 1950
	Robert A. Lovett, 1951
Attorney General	Francis Biddle (Cont.)
	Tom C. Clark, 1945
	J. Howard McGrath, 1949
	James P. McGranery, 1952
Postmaster General	Frank C. Walker (Cont.)
	Robert E. Hannegan, 1945
	Jesse M. Donaldson, 1947
Secretary of the Interior	Harold L. Ickes (Cont.)
	Julius A. Krug, 1946
	Oscar L. Chapman, 1949
Secretary of Agriculture	Claude R. Wickard (Cont.)
	Clinton P. Anderson, 1945
	Charles F. Brannan, 1948

Secretary of Commerce	Henry A. Wallace (Cont.)
	W. Averell Harriman, 1946
	Charles Sawyer, 1948
Secretary of Labor	Frances Perkins (Cont.)
	Lewis B. Schwellenbach, 1945
	Maurice J. Tobin, 1948
Secretary of War[1]	Henry L. Stimson (Cont.)
	Robert P. Patterson, 1945
	Kenneth C. Royall, 1947
Secretary of the Navy[1]	James Forrestal (Cont.)

1. On July 26, 1947, the Departments of War and of the Navy were incorporated into the Department of Defense.

Eisenhower

Secretary of State	John Foster Dulles, 1953
	Christian A. Herter, 1959
Secretary of the Treasury	George M. Humphrey, 1953
	Robert B. Anderson, 1957
Secretary of Defense	Charles E. Wilson, 1953
	Neil H. McElroy, 1957
	Thomas S. Gates, Jr., 1959
Attorney General	Herbert Brownell, Jr., 1953
	William P. Rogers, 1958
Postmaster General	Arthur E. Summerfield, 1953
Secretary of the Interior	Douglas McKay, 1953
	Frederick A. Seaton, 1956
Secretary of Agriculture	Ezra Taft Benson, 1953
Secretary of Commerce	Sinclair Weeks, 1953
	Lewis L. Strauss[1], 1958
	Frederick H. Mueller, 1959
Secretary of Labor	Martin P. Durkin, 1953
	James P. Mitchell, 1953
Secretary of Health, Education, and Welfare	Oveta Culp Hobby, 1953
	Marion B. Folsom, 1955
	Arthur S. Flemming, 1958

1. Not confirmed by the Senate.

Kennedy

Secretary of State	Dean Rusk, 1961
Secretary of the Treasury	C. Douglas Dillon, 1961
Secretary of Defense	Robert S. McNamara, 1961
Attorney General	Robert F. Kennedy, 1961
Postmaster General	J. Edward Day, 1961
	John A. Gronouski, 1963
Secretary of the Interior	Stewart L. Udall, 1961
Secretary of Agriculture	Orville L. Freeman, 1961
Secretary of Commerce	Luther H. Hodges, 1961
Secretary of Labor	Arthur J. Goldberg, 1961
	W. Willard Wirtz, 1962
Secretary of Health, Education, and Welfare	Abraham A. Ribicoff, 1961
	Anthony J. Celebrezze, 1962

L. B. Johnson

Secretary of State	Dean Rusk (Cont.)
Secretary of the Treasury	C. Douglas Dillon (Cont.)
	Henry H. Fowler, 1965
	Joseph W. Barr[1], 1968
Secretary of Defense	Robert S. McNamara (Cont.)
	Clark M. Clifford, 1968
Attorney General	Robert F. Kennedy (Cont.)
	N. de B. Katzenbach, 1965
	Ramsey Clark, 1967
Postmaster General	John A. Gronouski (Cont.)
	Lawrence F. O'Brien, 1965
	W. Marvin Watson, 1968
Secretary of the Interior	Stewart L. Udall (Cont.)
Secretary of Agriculture	Orville L. Freeman (Cont.)
Secretary of Commerce	Luther H. Hodges (Cont.)
	John T. Connor, 1964
	A. B. Trowbridge, 1967
	C. R. Smith, 1968
Secretary of Labor	W. Willard Wirtz (Cont.)
Secretary of Health, Education, and Welfare	Anthony J. Celebrezze (Cont.)
	John W. Gardner, 1965
	Wilbur J. Cohen, 1968

Secretary of Housing and Urban Development	Robert C. Weaver, 1966
	Robert C. Wood[1], 1969
Secretary of Transportation	Alan S. Boyd, 1966

1. Recess appointment.

Nixon

Secretary of State	William P. Rogers, 1969
	Henry A. Kissinger, 1973
Secretary of the Treasury	David M. Kennedy, 1969
	John B. Connally, 1971
	George P. Shultz, 1972
	William E. Simon, 1974
Secretary of Defense	Melvin R. Laird, 1969
	Elliot L. Richardson, 1973
	James R. Schlesinger, 1973
Attorney General	John N. Mitchell, 1969
	Richard G. Kleindienst, 1972
	Elliot L. Richardson, 1973
	William B. Saxbe, 1974
Postmaster General[1]	William M. Blount, 1969
Secretary of the Interior	Walter J. Hickel, 1969
	Rogers C. B. Morton, 1971
Secretary of Agriculture	Clifford M. Hardin, 1969
	Earl L. Butz, 1971
Secretary of Commerce	Maurice H. Stans, 1969
	Peter G. Peterson, 1972
	Frederick B. Dent, 1973
Secretary of Labor	George P. Shultz, 1969
	James D. Hodgson, 1970
	Peter J. Brennan, 1973
Secretary of Health, Education, and Welfare	Robert H. Finch, 1969
	Elliot L. Richardson, 1970
	Caspar W. Weinberger, 1973
Secretary of Housing and Urban Development	George Romney, 1969
	James T. Lynn, 1973
Secretary of Transportation	John A. Volpe, 1969
	Claude S. Brinegar, 1973

1. The Postmaster General is no longer a Cabinet member.

Ford

Secretary of State	Henry A. Kissinger (Cont.)
Secretary of the Treasury	William E. Simon (Cont.)
Secretary of Defense	James R. Schlesinger (Cont.)
	Donald H. Rumsfeld, 1975
Attorney General	William B. Saxbe (Cont.)
	Edward H. Levi, 1975
Secretary of the Interior	Rogers C. B. Morton (Cont.)
	Stanley K. Hathaway, 1975
	Thomas S. Kleppe, 1975
Secretary of Agriculture	Earl L. Butz (Cont.)
	John Knebel, 1976
Secretary of Commerce	Frederick B. Dent (Cont.)
	Rogers C. B. Morton, 1975
	Elliot L. Richardson, 1976
Secretary of Labor	Peter J. Brennan (Cont.)
	John T. Dunlop, 1975
	William J. Usery, Jr., 1976
Secretary of Health, Education, and Welfare	Caspar W. Weinberger (Cont.)
	F. David Mathews, 1975
Secretary of Housing and Urban Development	James T. Lynn (Cont.)
	Carla A. Hills, 1975
Secretary of Transportation	Claude S. Brinegar (Cont.)
	William T. Coleman, Jr., 1975

Carter

Secretary of State	Cyrus R. Vance, 1977
	Edmund S. Muskie, 1980
Secretary of the Treasury	W. Michael Blumenthal, 1977
	G. William Miller, 1979
Secretary of Defense	Harold Brown, 1977
Attorney General	Griffin B. Bell, 1977
	Benjamin R. Civiletti, 1979
Secretary of the Interior	Cecil D. Andrus, 1977
Secretary of Agriculture	Bob S. Bergland, 1977

Secretary of Commerce	Juanita M. Kreps, 1977
	Philip M. Klutznick, 1979
Secretary of Labor	F. Ray Marshall, 1977
Secretary of Health and Human Services[1]	Joseph A. Califano, Jr., 1977
	Patricia Roberts Harris, 1979
Secretary of Housing and Urban Development	Patricia Roberts Harris, 1977
	Moon Landrieu, 1979
Secretary of Transportation	Brock Adams, 1977
	Neil E. Goldschmidt, 1979
Secretary of Energy	James R. Schlesinger, 1977
	Charles W. Duncan, Jr., 1979
Secretary of Education	Shirley Mount Hufstedler, 1979

1. Known as Department of Health, Education, and Welfare until May, 1980.

Reagan

Secretary of State	Alexander M. Haig, Jr., 1981
	George P. Shultz, 1982
Secretary of the Treasury	Donald T. Regan, 1981
	James A. Baker 3rd, 1985
	Nicholas F. Brady, 1988
Secretary of Defense	Caspar W. Weinberger, 1981
	Frank C. Carlucci, 1987
Attorney General	William French Smith, 1981
	Edwin Meese 3rd, 1985
	Richard L. Thornburgh, 1988
Secretary of the Interior	James G. Watt, 1981
	William P. Clark, 1983
	Donald P. Hodel, 1985
Secretary of Agriculture	John R. Block, 1981
	Richard E. Lyng, 1986
Secretary of Commerce	Malcolm Baldrige, 1981
	C. William Verity, Jr., 1987
Secretary of Labor	Raymond J. Donovan, 1981
	William E. Brock, 1985
	Ann Dore McLaughlin, 1987
Secretary of Health and Human Services	Richard S. Schweiker, 1981
	Margaret M. Heckler, 1983
	Otis R. Bowen, 1985
Secretary of Housing and Urban Development	Samuel R. Pierce, Jr., 1981
Secretary of Transportation	Andrew L. Lewis, Jr., 1981
	Elizabeth H. Dole, 1983
	James H. Burnley 4th, 1987
Secretary of Energy	James B. Edwards, 1981
	Donald P. Hodel, 1983
	John S. Herrington, 1985
Secretary of Education	T. H. Bell, 1981
	William J. Bennett, 1985
	Lauro F. Cavazos, 1988

Bush

Secretary of State	James A. Baker 3d, 1989
	Lawrence S. Eagleburger, 1992
Secretary of the Treasury	Nicholas F. Brady (Cont.)

Secretary of Defense	Richard Cheney, 1989
Attorney General	Richard L. Thornburgh (Cont.)
	William P. Barr, 1992
Secretary of the Interior	Manuel Lujan Jr., 1989
Secretary of Agriculture	Clayton K. Yeutter, 1989
	Edward Madigan, 1991
Secretary of Commerce	Robert A. Mosbacher Sr., 1989
	Barbara H. Franklin, 1992
Secretary of Labor	Elizabeth H. Dole, 1989
	Lynn Martin, 1991
Secretary of Health and Human Services	Louis W. Sullivan, 1989
Secretary of Housing and Urban Development	Jack F. Kemp, 1989
Secretary of Transportation	Samuel K. Skinner, 1989
	Andrew Card, 1992
Secretary of Energy	James D. Watkins, 1989
Secretary of Education	Lauro F. Cavazos (Cont.)
	Lamar Alexander, 1991
Secretary of Veterans Affairs	Edward J. Derwinski, 1989

Clinton

Secretary of State	Warren M. Christopher, 1993–96
	Madeleine Albright, 1996
Secretary of the Treasury	Lloyd Bentsen, 1993–95
	Robert E. Rubin, 1995
Secretary of Defense	Les Aspin, 1993–94
	William J. Perry, 1994–96
	William S. Cohen, 1997
Attorney General	Janet Reno, 1993
Secretary of the Interior	Bruce Babbitt, 1993
Secretary of Agriculture	Mike Espy, 1993–95
	Dan Glickman, 1995
Secretary of Commerce	Ronald H. Brown, 1993–96
	Mickey Kantor, 1996-97
	William M. Daley, 1997
Secretary of Labor	Robert B. Reich, 1993–97
	Alexis Herman, 1997
Secretary of Health and Human Services	Donna E. Shalala, 1993
Secretary of Housing and Urban Development	Henry G. Cisneros, 1993–97
	Andrew M. Cuomo, 1997
Secretary of Transportation	Federico F. Pena, 1993–97
	Rodney Slater, 1997
Secretary of Energy	Hazel R. O'Leary, 1993–97
	Frederico F. Pena
Secretary of Education	Richard W. Riley, 1993
Secretary of Veterans Affairs	Jesse Brown, 1993

Members of the Supreme Court of the United States

| Name; appointed from | Service | | Birth | | | |
	Term	Yrs	Place	Date	Died	Religion
Chief Justices						
John Jay, N.Y.	1789–1795	5	N.Y.	1745	1829	Episcopal
John Rutledge, S.C.	1795	0	S.C.	1739	1800	Church of England
Oliver Ellsworth, Conn.	1796–1800	4	Conn.	1745	1807	Congregational
John Marshall, Va.	1801–1835	34	Va.	1755	1835	Episcopal
Roger B. Taney, Md.	1836–1864	28	Md.	1777	1864	Roman Catholic
Salmon P. Chase, Ohio	1864–1873	8	N.H.	1808	1873	Episcopal
Morrison R. Waite, Ohio	1874–1888	14	Conn.	1816	1888	Episcopal
Melville W. Fuller, Ill.	1888–1910	21	Maine	1833	1910	Episcopal
Edward D. White, La.	1910–1921	10	La.	1845	1921	Roman Catholic
William H. Taft, Conn.	1921–1930	8	Ohio	1857	1930	Unitarian
Charles E. Hughes, N.Y.	1930–1941	11	N.Y.	1862	1948	Baptist

Name; appointed from	Service Term	Yrs	Birth Place	Date	Died	Religion
Harlan F. Stone, N.Y.	1941–1946	4	N.H.	1872	1946	Episcopal
Frederick M. Vinson, Ky.	1946–1953	7	Ky.	1890	1953	Methodist
Earl Warren, Calif.	1953–1969	15	Calif.	1891	1974	Protestant
Warren E. Burger, Va.	1969–1986	17	Minn.	1907	1995	Presbyterian
William H. Rehnquist, Ariz.	1986–		Wis.	1924	—	Lutheran
Associate Justices						
James Wilson, Pa.	1789–1798	8	Scotland	1742	1798	Episcopal
John Rutledge, S.C.	1790–1791	1	S.C.	1739	1800	Church of England
William Cushing, Mass.	1790–1810	20	Mass.	1732	1810	Unitarian
John Blair, Va.	1790–1796	5	Va.	1732	1800	Presbyterian
James Iredell, N.C.	1790–1799	9	England	1751	1799	Episcopal
Thomas Johnson, Md.	1792–1793	0	Md.	1732	1819	Episcopal
William Paterson, N.J.	1793–1806	13	Ireland	1745	1806	Protestant
Samuel Chase, Md.	1796–1811	15	Md.	1741	1811	Episcopal
Bushrod Washington, Va.	1799–1829	30	Va.	1762	1829	Episcopal
Alfred Moore, N.C.	1800–1804	3	N.C.	1755	1810	Episcopal
William Johnson, S.C.	1804–1834	30	S.C.	1771	1834	Presbyterian
Brockholst Livingston, N.Y.	1807–1823	16	N.Y.	1757	1823	Presbyterian
Thomas Todd, Ky.	1807–1826	18	Va.	1765	1826	Presbyterian
Gabriel Duval, Md.	1811–1835	23	Md.	1752	1844	French Protestant
Joseph Story, Mass.	1812–1845	33	Mass.	1779	1845	Unitarian
Smith Thompson, N.Y.	1823–1843	20	N.Y.	1768	1843	Presbyterian
Robert Trimble, Ky.	1826–1828	2	Va.	1777	1828	Protestant
John McLean, Ohio	1830–1861	31	N.J.	1785	1861	Methodist-Epis.
Henry Baldwin, Pa.	1830–1844	14	Conn.	1780	1844	Trinity Church
James M. Wayne, Ga.	1835–1867	32	Ga.	1790	1867	Protestant
Philip P. Barbour, Va.	1836–1841	4	Va.	1783	1841	Episcopal
John Catron, Tenn.	1837–1865	28	Pa.	1786	1865	Presbyterian
John McKinley, Ala.	1837–1852	14	Va.	1780	1852	Protestant
Peter V. Daniel, Va.	1841–1860	18	Va.	1784	1860	Episcopal
Samuel Nelson, N.Y.	1845–1872	27	N.Y.	1792	1873	Protestant
Levi Woodbury, N.H.	1845–1851	5	N.H.	1789	1851	Protestant
Robert C. Grier, Pa.	1846–1870	23	Pa.	1794	1870	Presbyterian
Benjamin R. Curtis, Mass.	1851–1857	5	Mass.	1809	1874	(2)
John A. Campbell, Ala.	1853–1861	8	Ga.	1811	1889	Episcopal
Nathan Clifford, Maine	1858–1881	23	N.H.	1803	1881	(1)
Noah H. Swayne, Ohio	1862–1881	18	Va.	1804	1884	Quaker
Samuel F. Miller, Iowa	1862–1890	28	Ky.	1816	1890	Unitarian
David Davis, Ill.	1862–1877	14	Md.	1815	1886	(4)
Stephen J. Field, Calif.	1863–1897	34	Conn.	1816	1899	Episcopal
William Strong, Pa.	1870–1880	10	Conn.	1808	1895	Presbyterian
Joseph P. Bradley, N.J.	1870–1892	21	N.Y.	1813	1892	Presbyterian
Ward Hunt, N.Y.	1872–1882	9	N.Y.	1810	1886	Episcopal
John M. Harlan, Ky.	1877–1911	33	Ky.	1833	1911	Presbyterian
William B. Woods, Ga.	1880–1887	6	Ohio	1824	1887	Protestant
Stanley Matthews, Ohio	1881–1889	7	Ohio	1824	1889	Presbyterian
Horace Gray, Mass.	1882–1902	20	Mass.	1828	1902	(3)
Samuel Blatchford, N.Y.	1882–1893	11	N.Y.	1820	1893	Presbyterian
Lucius Q. C. Lamar, Miss.	1888–1893	5	Ga.	1825	1893	Methodist
David J. Brewer, Kan.	1889–1910	20	Asia Minor	1837	1910	Protestant
Henry B. Brown, Mich.	1890–1906	15	Mass.	1836	1913	Protestant
George Shiras, Jr., Pa.	1892–1903	10	Pa.	1832	1924	Presbyterian
Howell E. Jackson, Tenn.	1893–1895	2	Tenn.	1832	1895	Baptist
Edward D. White, La.*	1894–1910	16	La.	1845	1921	Roman Catholic
Rufus W. Peckham, N.Y.	1895–1909	13	N.Y.	1838	1909	Episcopal
Joseph McKenna, Calif.	1898–1925	26	Pa.	1843	1926	Roman Catholic
Oliver W. Holmes, Mass.	1902–1932	29	Mass.	1841	1935	Unitarian
William R. Day, Ohio	1903–1922	19	Ohio	1849	1923	Protestant
William H. Moody, Mass.	1906–1910	3	Mass.	1853	1917	Episcopal
Horace H. Lurton, Tenn.	1909–1914	4	Ky.	1844	1914	Episcopal
Charles E. Hughes, N.Y.*	1910–1916	5	N.Y.	1862	1948	Baptist
Willis Van Devanter, Wyo.	1910–1937	26	Ind.	1859	1941	Episcopal
Joseph R. Lamar, Ga.	1910–1916	4	Ga.	1857	1916	Ch. of Disciples
Mahlon Pitney, N.J.	1912–1922	10	N.J.	1858	1924	Presbyterian
James C. McReynolds, Tenn.	1914–1941	26	Ky.	1862	1946	Disciples of Christ
Louis D. Brandeis, Mass.	1916–1939	22	Ky.	1856	1941	Jewish
John H. Clarke, Ohio	1916–1922	5	Ohio	1857	1945	Protestant

Name; appointed from	Service Term	Yrs	Birth Place	Date	Died	Religion
George Sutherland, Utah	1922–1938	15	England	1862	1942	Episcopal
Pierce Butler, Minn.	1923–1939	16	Minn.	1866	1939	Roman Catholic
Edward T. Sanford, Tenn.	1923–1930	7	Tenn.	1865	1930	Episcopal
Harlan F. Stone, N.Y.*	1925–1941	16	N.H.	1872	1946	Episcopal
Owen J. Roberts, Pa.	1930–1945	15	Pa.	1875	1955	Episcopal
Benjamin N. Cardozo, N.Y.	1932–1938	6	N.Y.	1870	1938	Jewish
Hugo L. Black, Ala.	1937–1971	34	Ala.	1886	1971	Baptist
Stanley F. Reed, Ky.	1938–1957	19	Ky.	1884	1980	Protestant
Felix Frankfurter, Mass.	1939–1962	23	Austria	1882	1965	Jewish
William O. Douglas, Conn.	1939–1975	36	Minn.	1898	1980	Presbyterian
Frank Murphy, Mich.	1940–1949	9	Mich.	1890	1949	Roman Catholic
James F. Byrnes, S.C.	1941–1942	1	S.C.	1879	1972	Episcopal
Robert H. Jackson, Pa.	1941–1954	13	N.Y.	1892	1954	Episcopal
Wiley B. Rutledge, Iowa	1943–1949	6	Ky.	1894	1949	Unitarian
Harold H. Burton, Ohio	1945–1958	13	Mass.	1888	1964	Unitarian
Tom C. Clark, Tex.	1949–1967	17	Tex.	1899	1977	Presbyterian
Sherman Minton, Ind.	1949–1956	7	Ind.	1890	1965	Roman Catholic
John M. Harlan, N.Y.	1955–1971	16	Ill.	1899	1971	Presbyterian
William J. Brennan, Jr., N.J.	1956–1990	33	N.J.	1906	—	Roman Catholic
Charles E. Whittaker, Mo.	1957–1962	5	Kan.	1901	1973	Methodist
Potter Stewart, Ohio	1958–1981	23	Mich.	1915	1985	Episcopal
Byron R. White, Colo.	1962–	—	Colo.	1917	—	Episcopal
Arthur J. Goldberg, Ill.	1962–1965	2	Ill.	1908	1990	Jewish
Abe Fortas, Tenn.	1965–1969	3	Tenn.	1910	1982	Jewish
Thurgood Marshall, N.Y.	1967–1991	24	Md.	1908	1993	Episcopal
Harry A. Blackmun, Minn.	1970–1994	24	Ill.	1908	—	Methodist
Lewis F. Powell, Jr., Va.	1972–1987	15	Va.	1907	—	Presbyterian
William H. Rehnquist, Ariz.*	1972–1986	14	Wis.	1924	—	Lutheran
John Paul Stevens, Ill.	1975–	—	Ill.	1920	—	Protestant
Sandra Day O'Connor, Ariz.	1981–	—	Tex.	1930	—	Episcopal
Antonin Scalia, D.C.	1986–	—	N.J.	1936	—	Roman Catholic
Anthony M. Kennedy, Calif.	1988–	—	Calif.	1936	—	Roman Catholic
David H. Souter, N.H.	1990–	—	Mass.	1939	—	Episcopal
Clarence Thomas, D.C.	1991–	—	Ga.	1948	—	Roman Catholic
Ruth Bader Ginsburg, D.C.	1993–	—	N.Y.	1933	—	Jewish
Stephen G. Breyer, Mass.	1994–	—	Calif.	1938	—	n.a.

*Served as both Chief Justice and Associate Justice. 1. Congregational; later Unitarian. 2. Unitarian; then Episcopal. 3. Unitarian or Congregational. 4. Not a member of any church. NOTE: n.a. = not available.

Milestone Cases in Supreme Court History

1803 *Marbury v. Madison* was the first instance in which a law passed by Congress was declared unconstitutional. The decision greatly expanded the power of the Court by establishing its right to overturn acts of Congress, a power not explicitly granted by the Constitution.

1819 *McCulloch v. Maryland* upheld the right of Congress to create a Bank of the United States, ruling that it was a power implied but not enumerated by the Constitution. The case is significant because it advanced the doctrine of implied powers, or a loose construction of the Constitution. The Court, Chief Justice John Marshall wrote, would sanction laws reflecting "the letter and spirit" of the Constitution.

1857 *Dred Scott v. Sanford* was a highly controversial case that intensified the national debate over slavery. The case involved Dred Scott, a slave, who was taken from a slave state to a free territory. Scott filed a lawsuit claiming that because he had lived on free soil he was entitled to his freedom. Chief Justice Roger B. Taney disagreed, ruling that blacks were not citizens and therefore could not sue in Federal Court. Taney further inflamed anti-slavery forces by declaring that Congress had no right to ban slavery from U.S. territories.

1896 *Plessy v. Fergusson* was the infamous case that asserted that "equal but separate accommodations" for blacks on railroad cars did not violate the "equal protection under the laws" clause of the 14th Amendment. By defending the constitutionality of racial segregation, the Court paved the way for the repressive Jim Crow laws of the south. The lone dissenter on the Court, Justice John Marshall Harlan, protested, "The thin disguise of 'equal' accommodations . . . will not mislead anyone."

1954 *Brown v. Board of Education of Topeka* invalidated racial segregation in schools, and led to the unraveling of de jure segregation in all areas of public life. In the unanimous decision spearheaded by Chief Justice Earl Warren, the Court invalidated the Plessy ruling, declaring "in the field of public education, the doctrine of 'separate but equal' has no place," and contending that "separate educational facilities are inherently unequal." Future Supreme Court Justice Thurgood Marshall was one of the NAACP lawyers who successfully argued the case.

1973 *Roe v. Wade* legalized abortion and is at the center of the current controversy between "Pro-Life" and "Pro-Choice" advocates. The Court ruled that a woman has the right to an abortion without interference from the government in the first trimester of pregnancy, contending that it is part of her "right to privacy." The Court maintained that right to privacy is not absolute, however, and granted states the right to intervene in the second and third trimesters of pregnancy.

Major Decisions of the U.S. Supreme Court, 1996–97 Term

Police Upheld on Right to Search Cars (Nov. 18, 1996): Justices rule unanimously that when a car is stopped for a traffic violation, the driver may be asked to permit the search without further notification.

Previous Acquittals Ruled Factor in Sentencing (Jan. 6, 1997): Seven justices agree that courts may, and sometimes must, consider the defendant's record before imposing sentence.

Endangered Species Act Interpreted (March 19): The Court unanimously defends view that citizens, in addition to suing government for doing too little to protect endangered species, can also sue it for doing too much.

Drug Testing of Candidates Rejected (April 15): Justices, 8–1, overturn Georgia law requiring urine test for illegal drugs as a condition for a place on a ballot. It is the first decision to strike down as unconstitutional a government drug-testing program.

Setback is Dealt to Minor Parties (April 28): Justices rule, 6–3, that states are not constitutionally required to permit candidates to appear on more than one political party's ballot.

Special Rule for Drug Searches Rejected (April 28): Court unanimously decides that police must observe constitutional requirement for knocking and announcing their presence before entering a premise.

Justices Ease Policy on Voting Rights (May 12): In 7–2 ruling, Court restricts Justice Department's ability to insist on greater representation of minorities as requirement for approving redistricting plans.

Nonprofit Organizations Get Tax Break (May 19): Court rules 5–4, that states offering favorable treatment to charities cannot grant status based on whether the charity primarily serves in-state or out-of-state clients. Maine law ruled unconstitutional.

Clinton Rebuffed in Harassment Case (May 27): Justices rule unanimously in proceedings brought by Paula Jones, former Arkansas state employee, that a sitting President can be sued for actions outside the scope of his official duties.

Suspension Without Pay Upheld (June 9): Justices rule unanimously that Constitution does not automatically entitle public employees to a hearing before being temporarily furloughed without pay.

U.S. Loses Redistricting Challenge (June 19): Justices, 5–4, uphold court-ordered plan that leaves Georgia with only one black-majority Congressional district instead of three.

Environmentalists Upheld on Alaska Boundary (June 19): In 6–3 ruling, Court declares U.S. owns disputed offshore areas of Arctic coast that are ecologically fragile and rich in oil and gas deposits.

Curb on Parochial Schools Reversed (June 23): In sweeping 5–4 decision, Justices rule that Constitution permits public school systems to send teachers into parochial schools to teach remedial and supplemental classes for needy children.

Sex Predator Law Upheld (June 23): Justices rule, 5–4, that states may confine some offenders to mental hospitals after they have served prison sentences if they are deemed likely to continue crimes.

Private Prisons Guards Lose Immunity (June 23): In 5–4 decision, Court rules that employees of privately run institutions under contract with state or local governments are subject to prisoners' lawsuits.

Clinton Setback on Whitewater Notes (June 23): Justices decline to overturn lower court ruling requiring White House lawyers to turn over notes of conversations between the First Lady and attorneys regarding Whitewater investigation.

Court Strikes Down $1.3 Billion Asbestos Settlement (June 25): Rules against legality of class-action settlement to victims of asbestos exposure because asbestos victims are too diverse a group to be covered by a single class-action ruling. Settlement deemed unfair to future asbestos victims who may not experience the effects of exposure for several more decades—to hold them to a potentially obsolete settlement could unfairly disadvantage them.

Conviction in Securities Trading Case Upheld (June 25): In 6–3 decision, Court rules insider trading laws apply to persons having confidential information even if they have no connection with the company whose shares are being bought.

Religious Rights Law Overturned (June 25): Court decides 6–3 that Congress exceeded its authority when it passed statute giving religious practices more protection than the Justices themselves had found to be constitutionally required.

Ban on Internet Pornography Overruled (June 26): In an essentially unanimous decision (Rehnquist dissented to part of it), Court declares unconstitutional a federal law making it a crime to send or display "indecent" material that may be available to minors. Ruling is a sweeping endorsement of free speech online.

Right to Assisted Suicide Denied (June 26): In two 9–0 decisions, Court rejects constitutional challenges to New York and California laws outlawing such aid to dying. Justices leave opening for future claims.

Major Provision of Brady Bill Stricken (June 27): In 5–4 ruling, gun control measure is found to violate the "principle of state sovereignty"by requiring state officials to conduct background checks of prospective handgun buyers. Court thus continues Justices' debate about state–federal powers.

Executive Departments and Agencies

Source: United States Government Manual, 1997–1998

Unless otherwise indicated, addresses shown are in Washington, D.C.

Central Intelligence Agency (CIA)
Washington, D.C. (20505).
  Established: 1947.
  Director: George J. Tenet
Council of Economic Advisers (CEA)
Room 314, Old Executive Office Bldg. (20503).
  Members: 3.
  Established: Feb. 20, 1946.
  Chair: Janet L. Yellen
Council on Environmental Quality
Old Executive Office Bldg. (20503)

  Members: 3.
  Established: 1969.
  Chair: Kathleen A. McGinty
National Security Council (NSC)
Old Executive Office Bldg. (20503).
  Members: 4.
  Established: July 26, 1947.
  Chair: The President.
National Security Adviser: Samuel R. (Sandy) Berger
  Other members: Vice President; Secretary of State; Secretary of Defense.
Office of Administration
Old Executive Office Bldg. (20503).

Established: Dec. 12, 1977.
Director: Patsy L. Thomasson
Office of Management and Budget
Old Executive Office Bldg. (20503).
Established: July 1, 1970.
Director: Franklin D. Raines
Office of Science and Technology Policy
Executive Office Building (20500).
Established: May 11, 1976.
Director: John H. Gibbons.
Office of the United States Trade Representative
600 17th St. (20506).
Established: Jan. 15, 1963.
Trade Representative: Charlene Barshefsky.
Office of National Drug Control Policy
Executive Office of the President (20502).
Established: March 13, 1989.
Director: Barry R. McCaffrey

Executive Departments

Department of State
2201 C St., N.W. (20520).
Established: 1781 as Department of Foreign Affairs; reconstituted, 1789, following adoption of Constitution; name changed to Department of State Sept. 15, 1789.
Secretary: Madeleine Albright
Chief Delegate to U.N.: Bill Richardson
Department of the Treasury
15th St. & Pennsylvania Ave., N.W. (20220).
Established: Sept. 2, 1789
Secretary: Robert E. Rubin
Deputy Secretary: Lawrence H. Summers
Treasurer of the U.S.: Mary Ellen Withrow
Department of Defense
The Pentagon (20301).
Established: July 26, 1947, as National Department Establishment; name changed to Department of Defense on Aug. 10, 1949. Subordinate to Secretary of Defense are Secretaries of Army, Navy, Air Force.
Secretary: William S. Cohen
Deputy Secretary: John White
Secretary of Army: Togo G. West, Jr.
Secretary of Navy: John H. Dalton
Secretary of Air Force: Sheila E. Widnall
Commandant of Marine Corps: Gen. Charles C. Krulak
Joint Chiefs of Staff: Gen. Henry Shelton, Chairman; Gen. Joseph W. Ralston, Vice Chairman; Gen. Dennis J. Reimer, Army; Adm. Jay L. Johnson, Navy (acting chief); Gen. Ronald R. Fogleman, Air Force; Gen. Richard D. Hearney, Marine Corps.
Department of Justice
950 Pennsylvania Ave., N.W. (20530).
Established: Office of Attorney General was created Sept. 24, 1789. Although he was one of original Cabinet members, he was not executive department head until June 22, 1870, when Department of Justice was established.
Attorney General: Janet Reno
Deputy Attorney General: Seth P. Waxman (acting)
Solicitor General: Walter E. Dellinger
Director of FBI: Louis Joseph Freeh
Department of the Interior
1849 C St. (20240).
Established: March 3, 1849
Secretary: Bruce Babbitt
Deputy Secretary: John Garamendi
Department of Agriculture
Independence Ave.,14th St., S.W. (20250).
Established: May 15, 1862. Administered by Commissioner of Agriculture until 1889, when it was made executive department.
Secretary: Dan Glickman
Deputy Secretary: Richard Rominger

Department of Commerce
14th St. between Constitution Ave. & Constitution Ave., N.W. (20230)
Established: Department of Commerce and Labor was created Feb. 14, 1903. On March 4, 1913, all labor activities were transferred out of Department of Commerce and Labor and it was renamed Department of Commerce.
Secretary: William M. Daley
Department of Labor
Third Street and Constitution Ave., N.W. (20210).
Established: Bureau of Labor was created in 1884 under Department of the Interior; later became independent department without executive rank. Returned to bureau status in Department of Commerce and Labor, but on March 4, 1913, became independent executive department under its present name.
Secretary: Alexis Herman
Deputy Secretary: Cynthia A. Metzler (acting)
Department of Health and Human Services[1]
200 Independence Ave., S.W. (20201).
Established: April 11, 1953, replacing Federal Security Agency created in 1939.
Secretary: Donna Shalala
Surgeon General: Charles H. Roadman II (nominated)
1. Originally Department of Health, Education and Welfare. Name changed in May 1980 when Department of Education was activated.
Department of Housing and Urban Development
451 7th St., S.W. (20410)
Established: 1965, replacing Housing and Home Finance Agency created in 1947.
Secretary: Andrew M. Cuomo
Under Secretary: Dwight P. Robinson
Department of Transportation
400 7th St., S.W. (20590)
Established: Oct. 15, 1966, as result of Department of Transportation Act, which became effective April 1, 1967.
Secretary: Rodney Slater
Deputy Secretary: Mort Downey
Department of Energy
1000 Independence Ave., S.W. (20585)
Established: Aug. 1977.
Secretary: Frederico F. Pena
Deputy Secretary: Charles B. Curtis
Department of Education
600 Independence Ave., S.W. (20202).
Established: Oct. 17, 1979
Secretary: Richard Riley
Deputy Secretary: Marshall Smith (acting)
Department of Veterans' Affairs
810 Vermont Avenue, N.W. (20420).
Established: March 15, 1989, replacing Veterans Administration created in 1930.
Secretary: Jesse Brown
Deputy Secretary: Hershel Gober

Major Independent Agencies

Consumer Product Safety Commission
4330 East West Highway, Bethesda, Md. (20814)
Members: 5
Established: Oct. 27, 1972
Chairperson: Ann Brown
Corporation for National Service
1201 New York Ave., N.W. (20525)
Established: April 9, 1994
CEO: Harris Wofford
Environmental Protection Agency (EPA)
401 M St., S.W. (20460)
Established: Dec. 2, 1970
Administrator: Carol M. Browner
Equal Employment Opportunity Commission (EEOC)
1801 L St. (20507)
Members: 5
Established: July 2, 1965

Chair: Gilbert Casellas
Farm Credit Administration (FCA)
1501 Farm Credit Dr., McLean, Va. (22102)
Members: 13
Established: July 17, 1916
Chair: Marsha Pyle Martin
Federal Deposit Insurance Corporation (FDIC)
550 17th St., N.W. (20429)
Members: 3
Established: June 16, 1933
Chair: Ricki Tigert Helfer
Federal Election Commission (FEC)
999 E St., N.W. (20463)
Members: 6
Established: 1974
Chair: John Warren McGarry
Federal Maritime Commission
800 North Capitol St., N.W. (20573–0001)
Members: 5
Established: Aug. 12, 1961
Chair: Harold J. Creek
Federal Mediation and Conciliation Service (FMCS)
2100 K St., N.W. (20427)
Established: 1947
Director: John Calhoun Wells
Federal Reserve System (FRS), Board of Governors of
20th St. & Constitution Ave., N.W. (20551)
Members: 7
Established: Dec. 23, 1913
Chair: Alan Greenspan
Federal Trade Commission (FTC)
Pennsylvania Ave. at 6th St., N.W. (20580)
Members: 5
Established: Sept. 26, 1914
Chair: Robert Pitofsky
General Services Administration (GSA)
18th and F Sts., N.W. (20405)
Established: July 1, 1949
Acting Administrator: David L. Barram
National Aeronautics and Space Administration (NASA)
300 E St., S.W. (20546)
Established: 1958
Administrator: Daniel S. Goldin
National Foundation on the Arts and the Humanities
1100 Pennsylvania Ave., N.W., (20506)
Established: 1965
Chairs: National Endowment for the Arts, Chair, Jane Alexander; National Endowment for the Humanities, Chair, Sheldon Hackney.
National Labor Relations Board (NLRB)
1099 14th St., N.W. (20570)
Members: 5
Established: July 5, 1935
Chair: William Gould IV
National Mediation Board
Suite 250 East, 1301 K St. (20572)
Members: 3
Established: June 21, 1934
Chair: Kenneth B. Hipp
National Science Foundation (NSF)
4201 Wilson Blvd., Arlington, Va. (22230)
Established: 1950
Director: Neal F. Lane
National Transportation Safety Board
490 L'Enfant Plaza, S.W. (20594)
Members: 5
Established: April 1, 1975
Chair: James Hall
Nuclear Regulatory Commission (NRC)
Rockville, Md. (20852)
Members: 5
Established: Jan. 19, 1975
Chair: Shirley Jackson
Office of Personnel Management (OPM)

1900 E St., N.W. (20415)
Members: 3
Established: Jan. 1, 1979
Director: James B. King
Securities and Exchange Commission (SEC)
450 5th St., N.W. (20549)
Members: 5
Established: July 2, 1934
Chair: Arthur Levitt
Selective Service System (SSS)
National Headquarters 1515 Wilson Blvd., Arlington, Va. 22209
Established: Sept. 16, 1940
Director: Gil Coronado
Small Business Administration (SBA)
409 3rd St., S.W. (20416)
Established: July 30, 1953
Administrator: Aida Alvarez
Tennessee Valley Authority (TVA)
400 West Summit Hill Drive, Knoxville, Tenn. (37902). Washington office: One Massachusetts Ave. (20444–0001).
Members of Board of Directors: 3
Established: May 18, 1933
Chairman: Craven H. Crowell, Jr.
U.S. Arms Control and Disarmament Agency
320 21st St., N.W., (20451)
Established: Sept. 26, 1961
Director: John Holum
U.S. Commission on Civil Rights
624 9th St. (20425)
Members: 8
Established: 1957
Chair: Mary Frances Berry
U.S. Information Agency
301 Fourth St., S.W. (20547)
Established: Aug. 1, 1953. Reorganized April 1, 1978.
Director: Dr. Joseph Duffey.
U.S. International Trade Commission
500 E St., S.W. (20436)
Members: 6
Established: Sept. 8, 1916
Chair: Marcia E. Miller
U.S. Postal Service
475 L'Enfant Plaza West, S.W. (20260)
Postmaster General: Marvin T. Runyon
Deputy Postmaster General: Michael S. Coughlin
Established: In 1775 with the appointment of Benjamin Franklin as the first Postmaster General under the Continental Congress. In 1970 became independent agency headed by 11-member board of governors.

Other Independent Agencies

Administrative Conference of the United States—Suite 500, 2120 L St., N.W. (20037)
American Battle Monuments Commission—Room 5127 Pulaski Bldg. 20 Massachusetts Ave., N.W. (20314)
Appalachian Regional Commission—1666 Connecticut Ave., N.W. (20235)
Commission of Fine Arts—Pension Bldg. 441 F St., N.W. (20001)
Commodity Futures Trading Commission—1155 21 St., N.W. (20581)
Export-Import Bank of the United States—811 Vermont Ave., N.W. (20571)
Federal Emergency Management Agency—500 C St., S.W. (20472)
Federal Housing Finance Board—1777 F St., N.W. (20006)
Federal Labor Relations Authority—607 14th St., N.W. (20424)
Inter-American Foundation—901 N. Stuart St., Arlington, Va. (22203)

National Commission on Libraries and Information Science—Suite 820, 1110 Vermont Ave., N.W. (20005)

National Credit Union Administration—1775 Duke St., Alexandria, Va. (22314–3428)

Occupational Safety and Health Review Commission—1120 20th St., N.W. (20036–3419)

Panama Canal Commission—Suite 1050, 1825 I St., N.W. (20006)

Peace Corps—1990 K St., N.W. (20526)

Pension Benefit Guaranty Corporation—1200 K St.(20006)

Postal Rate Commission—Suite 300, 1333 H St., N.W. (20268–0001)

President's Committee on Employment of People With Disabilities—Suite 300, 1331 F St., N.W. (20004)

President's Council on Physical Fitness and Sports—701 Pennsylvania Ave., N.W., Suite 250 (20004)

U.S. Railroad Retirement Board (RRB)—844 Rush St., Chicago, Ill. (60611); Office of Legislative Affairs: Suite 500, 1310 G St., N.W. (20005–3004).

U.S. Parole Commission—5550 Friendship Blvd., Chevy Chase, Md. (20815)

Legislative Department

Architect of the Capitol—Room SB-15 U.S. Capitol Building (20515)

General Accounting Office (GAO)—441 G St., N.W. (20548)

Government Printing Office (GPO)—North Capitol & H Sts., N.W. (20401)

Library of Congress—101 Independence Ave., S.E. (20540)

Office of Technology Assessment—600 Pennsylvania Ave., S.E. (20510)

United States Botanic Garden—Office of Director, 245 First St., S.W. (20024)

Quasi-Official Agencies

American National Red Cross—430 Seventeenth St., N.W. (20006)

Legal Services Corporation—750 First St., N.E. (20002–4250)

National Academy of Sciences, National Academy of Engineering, National Research Council, Institute of Medicine—2101 Constitution Ave., N.W. (20418)

National Railroad Passenger Corporation (Amtrak)—60 Massachusetts Ave., N.E. (20002)

Smithsonian Institution—1000 Jefferson Dr., S.W. (20560)

Biographies of the Presidents

GEORGE WASHINGTON was born on Feb. 22, 1732 (Feb. 11, 1731/2, old style) in Westmoreland County, Va. While in his teens, he trained as a surveyor, and at the age of 20 he was appointed adjutant in the Virginia militia. For the next three years, he fought in the wars against the French and Indians, serving as Gen. Edward Braddock's aide in the disastrous campaign against Fort Duquesne. In 1759, he resigned from the militia, married Martha Dandridge Custis, a widow, and settled down as a gentleman farmer at Mount Vernon, Va.

As a militiaman, Washington had been exposed to the arrogance of the British officers, and his experience as a planter with British commercial restrictions increased his anti-British sentiment. He opposed the Stamp Act of 1765 and after 1770 became increasingly prominent in organizing resistance. A delegate to the Continental Congress, Washington was selected as commander in chief of the Continental Army and took command at Cambridge, Mass., on July 3, 1775.

Inadequately supported and sometimes covertly sabotaged by the Congress, in charge of troops who were inexperienced, badly equipped, and impatient of discipline, Washington conducted the war on the policy of avoiding major engagements with the British and wearing them down by harassing tactics. His able generalship, along with the French alliance and the growing weariness within Britain, brought the war to a conclusion with the surrender of Cornwallis at Yorktown, Va., on Oct. 19, 1781.

The chaotic years under the Articles of Confederation led Washington to return to public life in the hope of promoting the formation of a strong central government. He presided over the Constitutional Convention and yielded to the universal demand that he serve as first President. He was inaugurated on April 30, 1789, in New York, the first national capital. In office, he sought to unite the nation and establish the authority of the new government at home and abroad. Greatly distressed by the emergence of the Hamilton-Jefferson rivalry, Washington worked to maintain neutrality but actually sympathized more with Hamilton. Following his unanimous re-election in 1792, his second term was dominated by the Federalists. His Farewell Address on Sept. 17, 1796 (published but never delivered) rebuked party spirit and warned against "permanent alliances" with foreign powers.

He died at Mount Vernon on Dec. 14, 1799.

JOHN ADAMS born on Oct. 30 (Oct. 19, old style), 1735, at Braintree (now Quincy), Mass. A Harvard graduate, he considered teaching and the ministry but finally turned to law and was admitted to the bar in 1758. Six years later, he married Abigail Smith. He opposed the Stamp Act, served as lawyer for patriots indicted by the British, and by the time of the Continental Congresses, was in the vanguard of the movement for independence. In 1778, he went to France as commissioner. Subsequently he helped negotiate the peace treaty with Britain, and in 1785 became envoy to London. Resigning in 1788, he was elected Vice President under Washington and was re-elected in 1792.

Though a Federalist, Adams did not get along with Hamilton, who sought to prevent his election to the presidency in 1796 and thereafter intrigued against his administration. In 1798, Adam's independent policy averted a war with France but completed the break with Hamilton and the right-wing Federalists; at the same time, the enactment of the Alien and Sedition Acts, directed against foreigners and against critics of the government, exasperated the Jeffersonian opposition. The split between Adams and Hamilton resulted in Jefferson's becoming the next President. Adams retired to his home in Quincy. He and Jefferson died on the same day, July 4, 1826, the 50th anniversary of the signing of the Declaration of Independence.

His *Defence of the Constitutions of Government of the United States* (1787) contains original and striking, if conservative, political ideas.

THOMAS JEFFERSON was born on April 13 (April 2, old style), 1743, at Shadwell in Goochland (now Albemarle) County, Va. A William and Mary graduate, he studied law, but from the start showed an interest in science and philosophy. His literary skill and political clarity brought him to the forefront of the revolutionary movement in Virginia. As delegate to the Continental Congress, he drafted the Declaration of Independence. In 1776, he entered the Virginia House of Delegates and initiated a comprehensive reform program for the abolition of feudal survivals in land tenure and the separation of church and state.

In 1779, he became governor, but constitutional limitations on his power, combined with his own lack of executive energy, caused an unsatisfactory administration, culminating in Jefferson's virtual abdication when the British invaded Virginia in 1781. He retired to his beautiful home at Monticello, Va., to his family. His wife, Martha Wayles Skelton, whom he married in 1772, died in 1782.

Jefferson's *Notes on Virginia* (1784–85) illustrate his many-faceted interests, his limitless intellectual curiosity, his deep faith in agrarian democracy. Sent to Congress in 1783, he helped lay down the decimal system and drafted basic reports on the organization of the western lands. In 1785 he was appointed minister to France, where the Anglo-Saxon liberalism he had drawn from John Locke, the British philosopher, was stimulated by contact with the thought that would soon ferment in the French Revolution. In 1789, Washington appointed him Secretary of State. While favoring the Constitution and a strengthened central government, Jefferson came to believe that Hamilton contemplated the establishment of a monarchy. Growing differences resulted in Jefferson's resignation on Dec. 31, 1793.

Elected vice president in 1796, Jefferson continued to serve as spiritual leader of the opposition to Federalism, particularly to the repressive Alien and Sedition Acts. He was elected President in 1801 by the House of Representatives as a result of Hamilton's decision to throw the Federalist votes to him rather than to Aaron Burr, who had tied him in electoral votes. He was the first President to be inaugurated in Washington, which he had helped to design.

The purchase of Louisiana from France in 1803, though in violation of Jefferson's earlier constitutional scruples, was the most notable act of his administration. Re-elected in 1804, with the Federalist Charles C. Pinckney opposing him, Jefferson tried desperately to keep the United States out of the Napoleonic Wars in Europe, employing to this end the unpopular embargo policy.

After his retirement to Monticello in 1809, he developed his interest in education, founding the University of Virginia and watching its development with never-flagging interest. He died at Monticello on July 4, 1826. Jefferson had an enormous variety of interests and skills, ranging from education and science to architecture and music.

JAMES MADISON was born in Port Conway, Va., on March 16, 1751 (March 5, 1750/1, old style). A Princeton graduate, he joined the struggle for independence on his return to Virginia in 1771. In the 1770s and 1780s he was active in state politics, where he championed the Jefferson reform program, and in the Continental Congress. Madison was influential in the Constitutional Convention as leader of the group favoring a strong central government and as recorder of the debates; and he subsequently wrote, in collaboration with Alexander Hamilton and John Jay, the *Federalist* papers to aid the campaign for the adoption of the Constitution.

Serving in the new Congress, Madison soon emerged as the leader in the House of the men who opposed Hamilton's financial program and his pro-British leanings in foreign policy. Retiring from Congress in 1797, he continued to be active in Virginia and drafted the Virginia Resolution protesting the Alien and Sedition Acts. His intimacy with Jefferson made him the natural choice for Secretary of State in 1801.

In 1809, Madison succeeded Jefferson as President, defeating Charles C. Pinckney. His attractive wife, Dolley Payne Todd, whom he married in 1794, brought a new social sparkle to the executive mansion. In the meantime, increasing tension with Britain culminated in the War of 1812—a war for which the United States was unprepared and for which Madison lacked the executive talent to clear out incompetence and mobilize the nation's energies. Madison was re-elected in 1812, running against the Federalist De Witt Clinton. In 1814, the British actually captured Washington and forced Madison to flee to Virginia.

Madison's domestic program capitulated to the Hamiltonian policies that he had resisted 20 years before and he now signed bills to establish a United States Bank and a higher tariff.

After his presidency, he remained in retirement in Virginia until his death on June 28, 1836.

JAMES MONROE was born on April 28, 1758, in Westmoreland County, Va. A William and Mary graduate, he served in the army during the first years of the Revolution and was wounded at Trenton. He then entered Virginia politics and later national politics under the sponsorship of Jefferson. In 1786, he married Elizabeth (Eliza) Kortright.

Fearing centralization, Monroe opposed the adoption of the Constitution and, as senator from Virginia, was highly critical of the Hamiltonian program. In 1794, he was appointed minister to France, where his ardent sympathies with the Revolution exceeded the wishes of the State Department. His troubled diplomatic career ended with his recall in 1796. From 1799 to 1802, he was governor of Virginia. In 1803, Jefferson sent him to France to help negotiate the Louisiana Purchase and for the next few years he was active in various negotiations on the Continent.

In 1808, Monroe flirted with the radical wing of the Republican Party, which opposed Madison's candidacy; but the presidential boom came to naught and, after a brief term as governor of Virginia in 1811, Monroe accepted Madison's offer to become Secretary of State. During the War of 1812, he vainly sought a field command and instead served as Secretary of War from September 1814 to March 1815.

Elected President in 1816 over the Federalist Rufus King, and re-elected without opposition in 1820, Monroe, the last of the Virginia dynasty, pursued the course of systematic tranquilization that won for his administrations the name "the era of good feeling." He continued Madison's surrender to the Hamiltonian domestic program, signed the Missouri Compromise, acquired Florida, and with the able assistance of his Secretary of State, John Quincy Adams, promulgated the Monroe Doctrine in 1823, declaring against foreign colonization or intervention in the Americas. He died in New York City on July 4, 1831, the third president to die on the anniversary of Independence.

JOHN QUINCY ADAMS was born on July 11, 1767 at Braintree (now Quincy), Mass., the son of John Adams, the second President. He spent his early years in Europe with his father, graduated from Harvard, and entered law practice. His anti-Jeffersonian newspaper articles won him political attention. In 1794, he became minister to the Netherlands, the first of several diplomatic posts that occupied him until his return to Boston in 1801. In 1797, he married Louisa Catherine Johnson.

In 1803, Adams was elected to the Senate, nominally as a Federalist, but his repeated displays of independence on such issues as the Louisiana Purchase and the embargo caused his party to demand his resignation and ostracize him socially. In 1809, Madison rewarded him for his support of Jefferson by appointing him minister to St. Petersburg. He helped negotiate the Treaty of Ghent in 1814, and in 1815 became minister to London. In 1817 Monroe appointed him Secretary of State where he served with great distinction, gaining Florida from Spain without hostilities and playing an equal part with

Monroe in formulating the Monroe Doctrine.

When no presidential candidate received a majority of electoral votes in 1824, Adams, with the support of Henry Clay, was elected by the House in 1825 over Andrew Jackson, who had the original plurality. Adams had ambitious plans of government activity to foster internal improvements and promote the arts and sciences, but congressional obstructionism, combined with his own unwillingness or inability to play the role of a politician, resulted in little being accomplished. After being defeated for re-election by Jackson in 1828, he successfully ran for the House of Representatives in 1830. There though nominally a Whig, he pursued as ever an independent course. He led the fight to force Congress to receive antislavery petitions and fathered the Smithsonian Institution.

Stricken on the floor of the House, he died on Feb. 23, 1848. His long and detailed *Diary* gives a unique picture of the personalities and politics of the times.

ANDREW JACKSON was born on March 15, 1767, in what is now generally agreed to be Waxhaw, S.C. After a turbulent boyhood as an orphan and a British prisoner, he moved west to Tennessee, where he soon qualified for law practice but found time for such frontier pleasures as horse racing, cockfighting, and dueling. His marriage to Rachel Donelson Robards in 1791 was complicated by subsequent legal uncertainties about the status of her divorce. During the 1790s, Jackson served in the Tennessee Constitutional Convention, the United States House of Representatives and Senate, and on the Tennessee Supreme Court.

After some years as a country gentleman, living at the Hermitage near Nashville, Jackson in 1812 was given command of Tennessee troops sent against the Creeks. He defeated the Indians at Horseshoe Bend in 1814; subsequently he became a major general and won the Battle of New Orleans over veteran British troops, though after the treaty of peace had been signed at Ghent. In 1818, Jackson invaded Florida, captured Pensacola, and hanged two Englishmen named Arbuthnot and Ambrister, creating an international incident. A presidential boom began for him in 1821, and to foster it, he returned to the Senate (1823–25). Though he won a plurality of electoral votes in 1824, he lost in the House when Clay threw his strength to Adams. Four years later, he easily defeated Adams.

As President, Jackson greatly expanded the power and prestige of the presidential office and carried through an unprecedented program of domestic reform, vetoing the bill to extend the United States Bank, moving toward a hard-money currency policy, and checking the program of federal internal improvements. He also vindicated federal authority against South Carolina with its doctrine of nullification and against France on the question of debts. The support given his policies by the workingmen of the East as well as by the farmers of the East, West, and South resulted in his triumphant re-election in 1832 over Clay.

After watching the inauguration of his handpicked successor, Martin Van Buren, Jackson retired to the Hermitage, where he maintained a lively interest in national affairs until his death on June 8, 1845.

MARTIN VAN BUREN was born on Dec. 5, 1782, at Kinderhook, N.Y. After graduating from the village school, he became a law clerk, entered practice in 1803, and soon became active in state politics as state senator and attorney general. In 1820, he was elected to the United States Senate. He threw the support of his efficient political organization, known as the Albany Regency, to William H. Crawford in 1824 and to Jackson in 1828. After leading the opposition to Adams's administration in the Senate, he served briefly as governor of New York (1828–29) and resigned to become Jackson's Secretary of State. He was soon on close personal terms with Jackson and played an important part in the Jacksonian program.

In 1832, Van Buren became vice president; in 1836, President. The Panic of 1837 overshadowed his term. He attributed it to the overexpansion of the credit and favored the establishment of an independent treasury as repository for the federal funds. In 1840, he established a 10-hour day on public works. Defeated by Harrison in 1840, he was the leading contender for the Democratic nomination in 1844 until he publicly opposed immediate annexation of Texas, and was subsequently beaten by the Southern delegations at the Baltimore convention. This incident increased his growing misgivings about the slave power.

After working behind the scenes among the antislavery Democrats, Van Buren joined in the movement that led to the Free-Soil party and became its candidate for President in 1848. He subsequently returned to the Democratic Party while continuing to object to its pro-Southern policy. He died in Kinderhook on July 24, 1862. His *Autobiography* throws valuable sidelights on the political history of the times.

His wife, Hannah Hoes, whom he married in 1807, died in 1819.

WILLIAM HENRY HARRISON was born in Charles City County, Va., on Feb. 9, 1773. Joining the army in 1791, he was active in Indian fighting in the Northwest, became secretary of the Northwest Territory in 1798 and governor of Indiana in 1800. He married Anna Symmes in 1795. Growing discontent over white encroachments on Indian lands led to the formation of an Indian alliance under Tecumseh to resist further aggressions. In 1811, Harrison won a nominal victory over the Indians at Tippecanoe and in 1813 a more decisive one at the Battle of the Thames, where Tecumseh was killed.

After resigning from the army in 1814, Harrison had an obscure career in politics and diplomacy, ending up 20 years later as a county recorder in Ohio. Nominated for President in 1835 as a military hero whom the conservative politicians hoped to be able to control, he ran surprisingly well against Van Buren in 1836. Four years later, he defeated Van Buren but caught pneumonia and died in Washington on April 4, 1841, a month after his inauguration. Harrison was the first president to die in office.

JOHN TYLER born in Charles City County, Va., on March 29, 1790. A William and Mary graduate, he entered law practice and politics, serving in the House of Representatives (1817–21), as governor of Virginia (1825–27), and as senator (1827–36). A strict constructionist, he supported Crawford in 1824 and Jackson in 1828, but broke with Jackson over his United States Bank policy and became a member of the Southern state-rights group that cooperated with the Whigs. In 1836, he resigned from the Senate rather than follow instructions from the Virginia legislature to vote for a resolution expunging censure of Jackson from the Senate record.

Elected vice president on the Whig ticket in 1840, Tyler succeeded to the presidency on Harrison's death. His strict-constructionist views soon caused a split with the Henry Clay wing of the Whig party and a stalemate on domestic questions. Tyler's more considerable achievements were his support of the Webster-Ashburton Treaty with Britain and his success in bringing about the annexation of Texas.

After his presidency he lived in retirement in Virginia until the outbreak of the Civil War, when he emerged briefly as chairman of a peace convention and then as delegate to the provisional Congress of the Confederacy. He died on Jan. 18, 1862. He married Letitia

Christian in 1813 and, two years after her death in 1842, Julia Gardiner.

JAMES KNOX POLK was born in Mecklenburg County, N.C., on Nov. 2, 1795. A graduate of the University of North Carolina, he moved west to Tennessee, was admitted to the bar, and soon became prominent in state politics. In 1825, he was elected to the House of Representatives, where he opposed Adams and, after 1829, became Jackson's floor leader in the fight against the Bank. In 1835, he became Speaker of the House. Four years later, he was elected governor of Tennessee, but was beaten in tries for re-election in 1841 and 1843.

The supporters of Van Buren for the Democratic nomination in 1844 counted on Polk as his running mate; but, when Van Buren's stand on Texas alienated Southern support, the convention swung to Polk on the ninth ballot. He was elected over Henry Clay, the Whig candidate. Rapidly disillusioning those who thought that he would not run his own administration, Polk proceeded steadily and precisely to achieve four major objectives—the acquisition of California, the settlement of the Oregon question, the reduction of the tariff, and the establishment of the independent treasury. He also enlarged the Monroe Doctrine to exclude all non-American intervention in American affairs, whether forcible or not, and he forced Mexico into a war that he waged to a successful conclusion.

His wife, Sarah Childress, whom he married in 1824, was a woman of charm and ability. Polk died in Nashville, Tenn., on June 15, 1849.

ZACHARY TAYLOR was born at Montebello, Orange County, Va., on Nov. 24, 1784. Embarking on a military career in 1808, Taylor fought in the War of 1812, the Black Hawk War, and the Seminole War, meanwhile holding garrison jobs on the frontier or desk jobs in Washington. A brigadier general as a result of his victory over the Seminoles at Lake Okeechobee (1837), Taylor held a succession of Southwestern commands and in 1846 established a base on the Rio Grande, where his forces engaged in hostilities that precipitated the war with Mexico. He captured Monterrey in September 1846 and, disregarding Polk's orders to stay on the defensive, defeated Santa Anna at Buena Vista in February 1847, ending the war in the northern provinces.

Though Taylor had never cast a vote for president, his party affiliations were Whiggish and his availability was increased by his difficulties with Polk. He was elected president over the Democrat Lewis Cass. During the revival of the slavery controversy, which was to result in the Compromise of 1850, Taylor began to take an increasingly firm stand against appeasing the South; but he died in Washington on July 9, 1850, during the fight over the Compromise. He married Margaret Mackall Smith in 1810. His bluff and simple soldierly qualities won him the name Old Rough and Ready.

MILLARD FILLMORE was born at Locke, Cayuga County, N.Y., on Jan. 7, 1800. A lawyer, he entered politics with the Anti-Masonic Party under the sponsorship of Thurlow Weed, editor and party boss, and subsequently followed Weed into the Whig Party. He served in the House of Representatives (1833–35 and 1837–43) and played a leading role in writing the tariff of 1842. Defeated for governor of New York in 1844, he became State comptroller in 1848, was put on the Whig ticket with Taylor as a concession to the Clay wing of the party, and became president upon Taylor's death in 1850.

As president, Fillmore broke with Weed and William H. Seward and associated himself with the pro-Southern Whigs, supporting the Compromise of 1850. Defeated for the Whig nomination in 1852, he ran for president in 1856 as candidate of the American, or Know-Nothing

Party, which sought to unite the country against foreigners in the alleged hope of diverting it from the explosive slavery issue. Fillmore opposed Lincoln during the Civil War. He died in Buffalo on March 8, 1874.

He was married in 1826 to Abigail Powers, who died in 1853, and in 1858 to Caroline Carmichael McIntosh.

FRANKLIN PIERCE was born at Hillsboro, N.H., on Nov. 23, 1804. A Bowdoin graduate, lawyer, and Jacksonian Democrat, he won rapid political advancement in the party, in part because of the prestige of his father, Gov. Benjamin Pierce. By 1831 he was Speaker of the New Hampshire House of Representatives; from 1833 to 1837, he served in the federal House and from 1837 to 1842 in the Senate. His wife, Jane Means Appleton, whom he married in 1834, disliked Washington and the somewhat dissipated life led by Pierce; in 1842 Pierce resigned from the Senate and began a successful law practice in Concord, N.H. During the Mexican War, he was a brigadier general.

Thereafter Pierce continued to oppose antislavery tendencies within the Democratic Party. As a result, he was the Southern choice to break the deadlock at the Democratic convention of 1852 and was nominated on the 49th ballot. In the election, Pierce overwhelmed Gen. Winfield Scott, the Whig candidate.

As president, Pierce followed a course of appeasing the South at home and of playing with schemes of territorial expansion abroad. The failure of his foreign and domestic policies prevented his renomination; and he died in Concord on Oct. 8, 1869, in relative obscurity.

JAMES BUCHANAN was born near Mercersburg, Pa., on April 23, 1791. A Dickinson graduate and a lawyer, he entered Pennsylvania politics as a Federalist. With the disappearance of the Federalist Party, he became a Jacksonian Democrat. He served with ability in the House (1821–31), as minister to St. Petersburg (1832–33), and in the Senate (1834–45), and in 1845 became Polk's Secretary of State. In 1853, Pierce appointed Buchanan minister to Britain, where he participated with other American diplomats in Europe in drafting the expansionist Ostend Manifesto.

He was elected president in 1856, defeating John C. Frémont, the Republican candidate, and former President Millard Fillmore of the American Party. The growing crisis over slavery presented Buchanan with problems he lacked the will to tackle. His appeasement of the South alienated the Stephen Douglas wing of the Democratic Party without reducing Southern militancy on slavery issues. While denying the right of secession, Buchanan also denied that the federal government could do anything about it. He supported the administration during the Civil War and died in Lancaster, Pa., on June 1, 1868.

The only president to remain a bachelor throughout his term, Buchanan used his charming niece, Harriet Lane, as White House hostess.

ABRAHAM LINCOLN was born in Hardin (now Larue) County, Ky., on Feb. 12, 1809. His family moved to Indiana and then to Illinois, and Lincoln gained what education he could along the way. While reading law, he worked in a store, managed a mill, surveyed, and split rails. In 1834, he went to the Illinois legislature as a Whig and became the party's floor leader. For the next 20 years he practiced law in Springfield, except for a single term (1847–49) in Congress, where he denounced the Mexican War. In 1855, he was a candidate for senator and the next year he joined the new Republican Party.

A leading but unsuccessful candidate for the vice-presidential nomination with Frémont, Lincoln gained national attention in 1858 when, as Republican candidate for senator from Illinois, he engaged in a series of debates with Stephen A. Douglas, the Democratic candidate. He lost the election, but continued to prepare the way for the 1860 Republican convention and was rewarded with the presidential nomination on the third ballot. He won the election over three opponents.

From the start, Lincoln made clear that, unlike Buchanan, he believed the national government had the power to crush the rebellion. Not an abolitionist, he held the slavery issue subordinate to that of preserving the Union, but soon perceived that the war could not be brought to a successful conclusion without freeing the slaves. His administration was hampered by the incompetence of many Union generals, the inexperience of the troops, and the harassing political tactics both of the Republican Radicals, who favored a hard policy toward the South, and the Democratic Copperheads, who desired a negotiated peace. The Gettysburg Address of Nov. 19, 1863, marks the high point in the record of American eloquence. Lincoln's long search for a winning combination finally brought Generals Ulysses S. Grant and William T. Sherman on the top; and their series of victories in 1864 dispelled the mutterings from both Radicals and Peace Democrats that at one time seemed to threaten Lincoln's re-election. He was re-elected in 1864, defeating Gen. George B. McClellan, the Democratic candidate. His inaugural address urged leniency toward the South: "With malice toward none, with charity for all . . . let us strive on to finish the work we are in; to bind up the nation's wounds . . ." This policy aroused growing opposition on the part of the Republican Radicals, but before the matter could be put to the test, Lincoln was shot by the actor John Wilkes Booth at Ford's Theater, Washington, on April 14, 1865. He died the next morning.

Lincoln's marriage to Mary Todd in 1842 was often unhappy and turbulent, in part because of his wife's pronounced instability.

ANDREW JOHNSON was born at Raleigh, N.C., on Dec. 29, 1808. Self-educated, he became a tailor in Greeneville, Tenn., but soon went into politics, where he rose steadily. He served in the House of Representatives (1843–54), as governor of Tennessee (1853–57), and as a senator (1857–62). Politically he was a Jacksonian Democrat and his specialty was the fight for a more equitable land policy. Alone among the Southern Senators, he stood by the Union during the Civil War. In 1862, he became war governor of Tennessee and carried out a thankless and difficult job with great courage. Johnson became Lincoln's running mate in 1864 as a result of an attempt to give the ticket a nonpartisan and nonsectional character. Succeeding to the presidency on Lincoln's death, Johnson sought to carry out Lincoln's policy, but without his political skill. The result was a hopeless conflict with the Radical Republicans who dominated Congress, passed measures over Johnson's vetoes, and attempted to limit the power of the executive concerning appointments and removals. The conflict culminated with Johnson's impeachment for attempting to remove his disloyal Secretary of War in defiance of the Tenure of Office Act which required senatorial concurrence for such dismissals. The opposition failed by one vote to get the two thirds necessary for conviction.

After his presidency, Johnson maintained an interest in politics and in 1875 was again elected to the Senate. He died near Carter Station, Tenn., on July 31, 1875. He married Eliza McCardle in 1827.

ULYSSES SIMPSON GRANT was born (as Hiram Ulysses Grant) at Point Pleasant, Ohio, on April 27, 1822. He graduated from West Point in 1843 and served without particular distinction in the Mexican War. In 1848 he married Julia Dent. He resigned from the army in 1854, after warnings from his commanding officer about his drinking habits, and for the next six years held a wide variety of jobs in the Middle West. With the outbreak of the Civil War, he sought a command and soon, to his surprise, was made a brigadier general. His continuing successes in the western theaters, culminating in the capture of Vicksburg, Miss., in 1863, brought him national fame and soon the command of all the Union armies. Grant's dogged, implacable policy of concentrating on dividing and destroying the Confederate armies brought the war to an end in 1865. The next year, he was made full general.

In 1868, as Republican candidate for president, Grant was elected over the Democrat, Horatio Seymour. From the start, Grant showed his unfitness for the office. His Cabinet was weak, his domestic policy was confused, many of his intimate associates were corrupt. The notable achievement in foreign affairs was the settlement of controversies with Great Britain in the Treaty of London (1871), negotiated by his able Secretary of State, Hamilton Fish.

Running for re-election in 1872, he defeated Horace Greeley, the Democratic and Liberal Republican candidate. The Panic of 1873 graft scandals close to the presidency created difficulties for his second term.

After retiring from office, Grant toured Europe for two years and returned in time to accede to a third-term boom, but was beaten in the convention of 1880. Illness and bad business judgment darkened his last years, but he worked steadily at the *Personal Memoirs*, which were to be so successful when published after his death at Mount McGregor, near Saratoga, N.Y., on July 23, 1885.

RUTHERFORD BIRCHARD HAYES was born in Delaware, Ohio, on Oct. 4, 1822. A graduate of Kenyon College and the Harvard Law School, he practiced law in Lower Sandusky (now Fremont) and then in Cincinnati. In 1852 he married Lucy Webb. A Whig, he joined the Republican party in 1855. During the Civil War he rose to major general. He served in the House of Representatives from 1865 to 1867 and then confirmed a reputation for honesty and efficiency in two terms as Governor of Ohio (1868–72). His election to a third term in 1875 made him the logical candidate for those Republicans who wished to stop James G. Blaine in 1876, and he was nominated.

The result of the election was in doubt for some time and hinged upon disputed returns from South Carolina, Louisiana, Florida, and Oregon. Samuel J. Tilden, the Democrat, had the larger popular vote but was adjudged by the strictly partisan decisions of the Electoral Commission to have one fewer electoral vote, 185 to 184. The national acceptance of this result was due in part to the general understanding that Hayes would pursue a conciliatory policy toward the South. He withdrew the troops from the South, took a conservative position on financial and labor issues, and urged civil service reform.

Hayes served only one term by his own wish and spent the rest of his life in various humanitarian endeavors. He died in Fremont on Jan. 17, 1893.

JAMES ABRAM GARFIELD the last president to be born in a log cabin, was born in Cuyahoga County, Ohio, on Nov. 19, 1831. A Williams graduate, he taught school for a time and entered Republican politics in Ohio. In 1858, he married Lucretia Rudolph. During the Civil War, he had a promising career, rising to major general of volunteers; but he resigned in 1863, having been elected to the House of Representatives, where he served until 1880. His oratorical and parliamentary abilities soon made him the leading Republican in the House, though his record was marred by his unorthodox acceptance of a fee in the DeGolyer paving contract case and by suspicions of his complicity in the Crédit Mobilier scandal.

In 1880, Garfield was elected to the Senate, but instead became the presidential candidate on the 36th ballot as a result of a deadlock in the Republican convention. In the election, he defeated Gen. Winfield Scott Hancock, the Democratic candidate. Garfield's administration was barely under way when he was shot by Charles J. Guiteau, a disappointed office seeker, in Washington on July 2, 1881. He died in Elberton, N.J., on Sept. 19.

CHESTER ALAN ARTHUR was born at Fairfield, Vt., on Oct. 5, 1830. A graduate of Union College, he became a successful New York lawyer. In 1859, he married Ellen Herndon. During the Civil War, he held administrative jobs in the Republican state administration and in 1871 was appointed collector of the Port of New York by Grant. This post gave him control over considerable patronage. Though not personally corrupt, Arthur managed his power in the interests of the New York machine so openly that President Hayes in 1877 called for an investigation and the next year Arthur was suspended.

In 1880 Arthur was nominated for vice president in the hope of conciliating the followers of Grant and the powerful New York machine. As president upon Garfield's death, Arthur, stepping out of his familiar role as spoilsman, backed civil service reform, reorganized the Cabinet, and prosecuted political associates accused of post office graft. Losing machine support and failing to gain the reformers, he was not nominated for a full term in 1884. He died in New York City on Nov. 18, 1886.

STEPHEN GROVER CLEVELAND was born at Caldwell, N.J., on March 18, 1837. He was admitted to the bar in Buffalo, N.Y., in 1859 and lived there as a lawyer, with occasional incursions into Democratic politics, for more than 20 years. He did not participate in the Civil War. As mayor of Buffalo in 1881, he carried through a reform program so ably that the Democrats ran him successfully for governor in 1882. In 1884 he won the Democratic nomination for President. The campaign contrasted Cleveland's spotless public career with the uncertain record of James G. Blaine, the Republican candidate, and Cleveland received enough Mugwump (independent Republican) support to win.

As president, Cleveland pushed civil service reform, opposed the pension grab and attacked the high tariff rates. While in the White House, he married Frances Folsom in 1886. Renominated in 1888, Cleveland was defeated by Benjamin Harrison, polling more popular but fewer electoral votes. In 1892, he was elected over Harrison. When the Panic of 1893 burst upon the country, Cleveland's attempts to solve it by sound-money measures alienated the free-silver wing of the party, while his tariff policy alienated the protectionists. In 1894, he sent troops to break the Pullman strike. In foreign affairs, his firmness caused Great Britain to back down in the Venezuela border dispute.

In his last years Cleveland was an active and much-respected public figure. He died in Princeton, N.J., on June 24, 1908.

BENJAMIN HARRISON was born in North Bend, Ohio, on Aug. 20, 1833, the grandson of William Henry Harrison, the ninth president. A graduate of Miami University in Ohio, he took up the law in Indiana and became active in Republican politics. In 1853, he married Caroline Lavinia Scott. During the Civil War, he rose to brigadier general. A sound-money Republican, he was elected senator from Indiana in 1880. In 1888, he received the Republican nomination for President on the eighth ballot. Though behind on the popular vote, he

won over Grover Cleveland in the electoral college by 233 to 168.

As President, Harrison failed to please either the bosses or the reform element in the party. In foreign affairs he backed Secretary of State Blaine, whose policy foreshadowed later American imperialism. Harrison was renominated in 1892 but lost to Cleveland. His wife died in the White House in 1892 and Harrison married her niece, Mary Scott (Lord) Dimmick, in 1896. After his presidency, he resumed law practice. He died in Indianapolis on March 13, 1901.

WILLIAM McKINLEY was born in Niles, Ohio, on Jan. 29, 1843. He taught school, then served in the Civil War, rising from the ranks to become a major. Subsequently he opened a law office in Canton, Ohio, and in 1871 married Ida Saxton. Elected to Congress in 1876, he served there until 1891, except for 1883–85. His faithful advocacy of business interests culminated in the passage of the highly protective McKinley Tariff of 1890. With the support of Mark Hanna, a shrewd Cleveland businessman interested in safeguarding tariff protection, McKinley became governor of Ohio in 1892 and Republican presidential candidate in 1896. The business community, alarmed by the progressivism of William Jennings Bryan, the Democratic candidate, spent considerable money to assure McKinley's victory.

The chief event of McKinley's administration was the war with Spain, which resulted in our acquisition of the Philippines and other islands. With imperialism an issue, McKinley defeated Bryan again in 1900. On Sept. 6, 1901, he was shot at Buffalo, N.Y., by Leon F. Czolgosz, an anarchist, and he died there eight days later.

THEODORE ROOSEVELT was born in New York City on Oct. 27, 1858. A Harvard graduate, he was early interested in ranching, in politics, and in writing picturesque historical narratives. He was a Republican member of the New York Assembly in 1882–84, an unsuccessful candidate for mayor of New York in 1886, a U.S. Civil Service Commissioner under Benjamin Harrison, Police Commissioner of New York City in 1895, and Assistant Secretary of the Navy under McKinley in 1897. He resigned in 1898 to help organize a volunteer regiment, the Rough Riders, and take a more direct part in the war with Spain. He was elected governor of New York in 1898 and vice president in 1900, in spite of lack of enthusiasm on the part of the bosses.

Assuming the presidency of the assassinated McKinley in 1901, Roosevelt embarked on a wide-ranging program of government reform and conservation of natural resources. He ordered antitrust suits against several large corporations, threatened to intervene in the anthracite coal strike of 1902, which prompted the operators to accept arbitration, and, in general, championed the rights of the "little man" and fought the "malefactors of great wealth." He was also responsible for such progressive legislation as the Elkins Act of 1901, which outlawed freight rebates by railroads; the bill establishing the Department of Commerce and Labor; the Hepburn Act, which gave the I.C.C. greater control over the railroads; the Meat Inspection Act; and the Pure Food and Drug Act.

In foreign affairs, Roosevelt pursued a strong policy, permitting the instigation of a revolt in Panama to dispose of Colombian objections to the Panama Canal and helping to maintain the balance of power in the East by bringing the Russo-Japanese War to an end, for which he won the Nobel Peace Prize, the first American to achieve a Nobel prize in any category. In 1904, he decisively defeated Alton B. Parker, his conservative Democratic opponent.

Roosevelt's increasing coldness toward his successor, William Howard Taft, led him to overlook his earlier disclaimer of third-term ambitions and to re-enter politics. Defeated by the machine in the Republican convention of 1912, he organized the Progressive Party (Bull Moose) and polled more votes than Taft, though the split brought about the election of Woodrow Wilson. From 1915 on, Roosevelt strongly favored intervention in the European war. He became deeply embittered at Wilson's refusal to allow him to raise a volunteer division. He died in Oyster Bay, N.Y., on Jan. 6, 1919. He was married twice: in 1880 to Alice Hathaway Lee, who died in 1884, and in 1886 to Edith Kermit Carow.

WILLIAM HOWARD TAFT was born in Cincinnati on Sept. 15, 1857. A Yale graduate, he entered Ohio Republican politics in the 1880s. In 1886 he married Helen Herron. From 1887 to 1890, he served on the Ohio Superior Court; 1890–92, as solicitor general of the United States; 1892–1900, on the federal circuit court. In 1900 McKinley appointed him president of the Philippine Commission and in 1901 governor general. Taft had great success in pacifying the Filipinos, solving the problem of the church lands, improving economic conditions, and establishing limited self-government. His period as Secretary of War (1904–08) further demonstrated his capacity as administrator and conciliator, and he was Roosevelt's hand-picked successor in 1908. In the election, he polled 321 electoral votes to 162 for William Jennings Bryan, who was running for the presidency for the third time.

Though he carried on many of Roosevelt's policies, Taft got into increasing trouble with the progressive wing of the party and displayed mounting irritability and indecision. After his defeat in 1912, he became professor of constitutional law at Yale. In 1921 he was appointed Chief Justice of the United States. He died in Washington on March 8, 1930.

THOMAS WOODROW WILSON was born in Staunton, Va., on Dec. 28, 1856. A Princeton graduate, he turned from law practice to post-graduate work in political science at Johns Hopkins University, receiving his Ph.D. in 1886. He taught at Bryn Mawr, Wesleyan, and Princeton, and in 1902 was made president of Princeton. After an unsuccessful attempt to democratize the social life of the university, he welcomed an invitation in 1910 to be the Democratic gubernatorial candidate in New Jersey, and was elected. His success in fighting the machine and putting through a reform program attracted national attention.

In 1912, at the Democratic convention in Baltimore, Wilson won the nomination on the 46th ballot and went on to defeat Roosevelt and Taft in the election. Wilson proceeded under the standard of the New Freedom to enact a program of domestic reform, including the Federal Reserve Act, the Clayton Antitrust Act, the establishment of the Federal Trade Commission, and other measures designed to restore competition in the face of the great monopolies. In foreign affairs, while privately sympathetic with the Allies, he strove to maintain neutrality in the European war and warned both sides against encroachments on American interests.

Re-elected in 1916 as a peace candidate, he tried to mediate between the warring nations; but when the Germans resumed unrestricted submarine warfare in 1917, Wilson brought the United States into what he now believed was a war to make the world safe for democracy. He supplied the classic formulations of Allied war aims and the armistice of Nov. 11, 1918 was negotiated on the basis of Wilson's Fourteen Points. In 1919 he strove at Versailles to lay the foundations for enduring peace. He accepted the imperfections of the Versailles Treaty in the expectation that they could be remedied by action within the League of Nations. He probably could have secured ratification of the treaty by the Senate if he had adopted a more conciliatory attitude toward the mild reservationists; but his insistence on all or nothing eventually caused the diehard isolationists and diehard Wilsonites to unite in rejecting a compromise.

In September 1919 Wilson suffered a paralytic stroke that limited his activity. After leaving the presidency he lived on in retirement in Washington, dying on Feb. 3, 1924. He was married twice—in 1885 to Ellen Louise Axson, who died in 1914, and in 1915 to Edith Bolling Galt.

WARREN GAMALIEL HARDING was born in Morrow County, Ohio, on Nov. 2, 1865. After attending Ohio Central College, Harding became interested in journalism and in 1884 bought the *Marion* (Ohio) *Star.* In 1891 he married a wealthy widow, Florence Kling De Wolfe. As his paper prospered, he entered Republican politics, serving as state senator (1899–1903) and as lieutenant governor (1904–06). In 1910, he was defeated for governor, but in 1914 was elected to the Senate. His reputation as an orator made him the keynoter at the 1916 Republican convention.

When the 1920 convention was deadlocked between Leonard Wood and Frank O. Lowden, Harding became the dark-horse nominee on his solemn affirmation that there was no reason in his past that he should not be. Straddling the League question, Harding was easily elected over James M. Cox, his Democratic opponent. His Cabinet contained some able men, but also some manifestly unfit for public office. Harding's own intimates were mediocre when they were not corrupt. The impending disclosure of the Teapot Dome scandal in the Interior Department and illegal practices in the Justice Department and Veterans' Bureau, as well as political setbacks, profoundly worried him. On his return from Alaska in 1923, he died unexpectedly in San Francisco on Aug. 2.

JOHN CALVIN COOLIDGE was born in Plymouth, Vt., on July 4, 1872. An Amherst graduate, he went into law practice at Northampton, Mass., in 1897. He married Grace Anna Goodhue in 1905. He entered Republican state politics, becoming successively mayor of Northampton, state senator, lieutenant governor and, in 1919, governor. His use of the state militia to end the Boston police strike in 1919 won him a somewhat undeserved reputation for decisive action and brought him the Republican vice-presidential nomination in 1920. After Harding's death Coolidge handled the Washington scandals with care and finally managed to save the Republican Party from public blame for the widespread corruption.

In 1924, Coolidge was elected without difficulty, defeating the Democrat, John W. Davis, and Robert M. La Follette running on the Progressive ticket. His second term, like his first, was characterized by a general satisfaction with the existing economic order. He stated that he did not choose to run in 1928.

After his presidency, Coolidge lived quietly in Northampton, writing an unilluminating *Autobiography* and conducting a syndicated column. He died there on Jan. 5, 1933.

HERBERT CLARK HOOVER was born at West Branch, Iowa, on Aug. 10, 1874, the first president to be born west of the Mississippi. A Stanford graduate, he worked from 1895 to 1913 as a mining engineer and consultant throughout the world. In 1899, he married Lou Henry. During World War I, he served with distinction as chairman of the American Relief Committee in London, as chairman of the Commission for Relief in Belgium, and as U.S. Food Administrator. His political affiliations were still too indeterminate for him to be mentioned as a possibility for either the Republican or Democratic nomination in 1920, but after the election he served Harding and Coolidge as Secretary of Commerce.

In the election of 1928, Hoover overwhelmed Gov. Alfred E. Smith of New York, the Democratic candidate and the first Roman Catholic to run for the presidency. He soon faced the worst depression in the nation's history, but his attacks upon it were hampered by his devotion to the theory that the forces that brought the crisis would soon bring the revival and then by his belief that there were too many areas in which the federal government had no power to act. In a succession of vetoes, he struck down measures proposing a national employment system or national relief, he reduced income tax rates, and only at the end of his term did he yield to popular pressure and set up agencies such as the Reconstruction Finance Corporation to make emergency loans to assist business.

After his 1932 defeat, Hoover returned to private business. In 1946, President Truman charged him with various world food missions; and from 1947 to 1949 and 1953 to 1955, he was head of the Commission on Organization of the Executive Branch of the Government. He died in New York City on Oct. 20, 1964.

FRANKLIN DELANO ROOSEVELT was born in Hyde Park, N.Y., on Jan. 30, 1882. A Harvard graduate, he attended Columbia Law School and was admitted to the New York bar. In 1910, he was elected to the New York State Senate as a Democrat. Reelected in 1912, he was appointed Assistant Secretary of the Navy by Woodrow Wilson the next year. In 1920, his radiant personality and his war service resulted in his nomination for vice president as James M. Cox's running mate. After his defeat, he returned to law practice in New York. In August 1921, Roosevelt was stricken with infantile paralysis while on vacation at Campobello, New Brunswick. After a long and gallant fight, he recovered partial use of his legs. In 1924 and 1928, he led the fight at the Democratic national conventions for the nomination of Gov. Alfred E. Smith of New York, and in 1928 Roosevelt was himself induced to run for governor of New York. He was elected, and was re-elected in 1930.

In 1932, Roosevelt received the Democratic nomination for president and immediately launched a campaign that brought new spirit to a weary and discouraged nation. He defeated Hoover by a wide margin. His first term was characterized by an unfolding of the New Deal program, with greater benefits for labor, the farmers, and the unemployed, and the progressive estrangement of most of the business community.

At an early stage, Roosevelt became aware of the menace to world peace posed by totalitarian fascism, and from 1937 on he tried to focus public attention on the trend of events in Europe and Asia. As a result, he was widely denounced as a warmonger. He was re-elected in 1936 over Gov. Alfred M. Landon of Kansas by the overwhelming electoral margin of 523 to 8, and the gathering international crisis prompted him to run for an unprecedented third term in 1940. He defeated Wendell L. Willkie.

Roosevelt's program to bring maximum aid to Britain and, after June 1941, to Russia was opposed, until the Japanese attack on Pearl Harbor restored national unity. During the war, Roosevelt shelved the New Deal in the interests of conciliating the business community, both in order to get full production during the war and to prepare the way for a united acceptance of the peace settlements after the war. A series of conferences with Winston Churchill and Joseph Stalin laid down the bases for the postwar world. In 1944 he was elected to a fourth term, running against Gov. Thomas E. Dewey of New York.

On April 12, 1945, Roosevelt died of a cerebral hemorrhage at Warm Springs, Ga., shortly after his return from the Yalta Conference. His wife, Anna Eleanor Roosevelt, whom he married in 1905, was a woman of great ability who made significant contributions to her husband's policies.

HARRY S. TRUMAN was born on a farm near Lamar, Mo., on May 8, 1884. During World War I, he served in France as a captain with the 129th Field Artillery. He married Bess Wallace in 1919. After engaging briefly and unsuccessfully in the haberdashery business in Kansas City, Mo., Truman entered local politics. Under the sponsorship of Thomas Pendergast, Democratic boss of Missouri, he held a number of local offices, preserving his personal honesty in the midst of a notoriously corrupt political machine. In 1934, he was elected to the Senate and was re-elected in 1940. During his first term he was a loyal but quiet supporter of the New Deal, but in his second term, an appointment as head of a Senate committee to investigate war production brought out his special qualities of honesty, common sense, and hard work, and he won widespread respect.

Elected vice president in 1944, Truman became president upon Roosevelt's sudden death in April 1945 and was immediately faced with the problems of winding down the war against the Axis and preparing the nation for postwar adjustment.

The years 1947–48 were distinguished by civil-rights proposals, the Truman Doctrine to contain the spread of Communism, and the Marshall Plan to aid in the economic reconstruction of war-ravaged nations. Truman's general record, highlighted by a vigorous Fair Deal campaign, brought about his unexpected election in 1948 over the heavily favored Thomas E. Dewey.

Truman's second term was primarily concerned with the Cold War with the Soviet Union, the implementing of the North Atlantic Pact, the United Nations police action in Korea, and the vast rearmament program with its accompanying problems of economic stabilization.

On March 29, 1952, Truman announced that he would not run again for the presidency. After leaving the White House, he returned to his home in Independence, Mo., to write his memoirs. He further busied himself with the Harry S. Truman Library there. He died in Kansas City, Mo., on Dec. 26, 1972.

DWIGHT DAVID EISENHOWER was born in Denison, Tex., on Oct. 14, 1890. His ancestors lived in Germany and emigrated to America, settling in Pennsylvania, early in the 18th century. His father, David, had a general store in Hope, Kans., which failed. After a brief time in Texas, the family moved to Abilene, Kan.

After graduating from Abilene High School in 1909, Eisenhower did odd jobs for almost two years. He won an appointment to the Naval Academy at Annapolis, but was too old for admittance. Then he received an appointment in 1910 to West Point, from which he graduated as a second lieutenant in 1915.

He did not see service in World War I, having been stationed at Fort Sam Houston, Tex. There he met Mamie Geneva Doud, whom he married in Denver on July 1, 1916, and by whom he had two sons: Doud Dwight (died in infancy) and John Sheldon Doud.

Eisenhower served in the Philippines from 1935 to 1939 with Gen. Douglas MacArthur. Afterward, Gen. George C. Marshall, the Army Chief of Staff, brought him into the War Department's General Staff and in 1942 placed him in command of the invasion of North Africa. In 1944, he was made Supreme Allied Commander for the invasion of Europe.

After the war, Eisenhower served as Army Chief of Staff from November 1945 until February 1948, when he was appointed president of Columbia University.

In December 1950, President Truman recalled Eisenhower to active duty to command the North Atlantic Treaty Organization forces in Europe. He held his post until the end of May 1952.

At the Republican convention of 1952 in Chicago,

Eisenhower won the presidential nomination on the first ballot in a close race with Senator Robert A. Taft of Ohio. In the election, he defeated Gov. Adlai E. Stevenson of Illinois.

Through two terms, Eisenhower hewed to moderate domestic policies. He sought peace through Free World strength in an era of new nationalisms, nuclear missiles, and space exploration. He fostered alliances pledging the United States to resist Red aggression in Europe, Asia, and Latin America. The Eisenhower Doctrine of 1957 extended commitments to the Middle East.

At home, the popular president lacked Republican Congressional majorities after 1954, but he was re-elected in 1956 by 457 electoral votes to 73 for Stevenson.

While retaining most Fair Deal programs, he stressed "fiscal responsibility" in domestic affairs. A moderate in civil rights, he sent troops to Little Rock, Ark., to enforce court-ordered school integration.

With his wartime rank restored by Congress, Eisenhower returned to private life and the role of elder statesman, with his vigor hardly impaired by a heart attack, an ileitis operation, and a mild stroke suffered while in office. He died in Washington on March 28, 1969.

JOHN FITZGERALD KENNEDY

JOHN FITZGERALD KENNEDY was born in Brookline, Mass., on May 29, 1917. His father, Joseph P. Kennedy, was Ambassador to Great Britain from 1937 to 1940.

Kennedy was graduated from Harvard University in 1940 and joined the Navy the next year. He became skipper of a PT boat that was sunk in the Pacific by a Japanese destroyer. Although given up for lost, he swam to a safe island, towing an injured enlisted man.

After recovering from a war-aggravated spinal injury, Kennedy entered politics in 1946 and was elected to Congress. In 1952, he ran against Senator Henry Cabot Lodge, Jr., of Massachusetts, and won.

Kennedy was married on Sept. 12, 1953, to Jacqueline Lee Bouvier, by whom he had three children: Caroline, John Fitzgerald, Jr., and Patrick Bouvier (died in infancy).

In 1957 Kennedy won the Pulitzer Prize for a book he had written earlier, *Profiles in Courage*.

After strenuous primary battles, Kennedy won the Democratic presidential nomination on the first ballot at the 1960 Los Angeles convention. With a plurality of only 118,574 votes, he carried the election over Vice President Richard M. Nixon and became the first Roman Catholic president.

Kennedy brought to the White House the dynamic idea of a "New Frontier" approach in dealing with problems at home, abroad, and in the dimensions of space. Out of his leadership in his first few months in office came the 10-year Alliance for Progress to aid Latin America, the Peace Corps, and accelerated programs that brought the first Americans into orbit in the race in space.

Failure of the U.S.-supported Cuban invasion in April 1961 led to the entrenchment of the Communist-backed Castro regime, only 90 miles from United States soil. When it became known that Soviet offensive missiles were being installed in Cuba in 1962, Kennedy ordered a naval "quarantine" of the island and moved troops into position to eliminate this threat to U.S. security. The world seemed on the brink of a nuclear war until Soviet Premier Khrushchev ordered the removal of the missiles.

A sudden "thaw," or the appearance of one, in the cold war came with the agreement with the Soviet Union on a limited test-ban treaty signed in Moscow on Aug. 6, 1963.

In his domestic policies, Kennedy's proposals for medical care for the aged, expanded area redevelopment, and aid to education were defeated, but on minimum wage, trade legislation, and other measures he won important victories.

Widespread racial disorders and demonstrations led to Kennedy's proposing sweeping civil rights legislation. As his third year in office drew to a close, he also recommended an $11-billion tax cut to bolster the economy. Both measures were pending in Congress when Kennedy, looking forward to a second term, journeyed to Texas for a series of speeches.

While riding in a procession in Dallas on Nov. 22, 1963, he was shot to death by an assassin firing from an upper floor of a building. The alleged assassin, Lee Harvey Oswald, was killed two days later in the Dallas city jail by Jack Ruby, owner of a strip-tease place.

At 46 years of age, Kennedy became the fourth president to be assassinated and the eighth to die in office.

LYNDON BAINES JOHNSON

LYNDON BAINES JOHNSON was born in Stonewall, Tex., on Aug. 27, 1908. On both sides of his family he had a political heritage mingled with a Baptist background of preachers and teachers. Both his father and his paternal grandfather served in the Texas House of Representatives.

After his graduation from Southwest Texas State Teachers College, Johnson taught school for two years. He went to Washington in 1932 as secretary to Rep. Richard M. Kleberg. During this time, he married Claudia Alta Taylor, known as "Lady Bird." They had two children: Lynda Bird and Luci Baines.

In 1935, Johnson became Texas administrator for the National Youth Administration. Two years later, he was elected to Congress as an all-out supporter of Franklin D. Roosevelt, and served until 1949. He was the first member of Congress to enlist in the armed forces after the attack on Pearl Harbor. He served in the Navy in the Pacific and won a Silver Star.

Johnson was elected to the Senate in 1948 after he had captured the Democratic nomination by only 87 votes. He was 40 years old. He became the Senate Democratic leader in 1953. A heart attack in 1955 threatened to end his political career, but he recovered fully and resumed his duties.

At the height of his power as Senate leader, Johnson sought the Democratic nomination for president in 1960. When he lost to John F. Kennedy, he surprised even some of his closest associates by accepting second place on the ticket.

Johnson was riding in another car in the motorcade when Kennedy was assassinated in Dallas on Nov. 22, 1963. He took the oath of office in the presidential jet on the Dallas airfield.

With Johnson's insistent backing, Congress finally adopted a far-reaching civil-rights bill, a voting-rights bill, a Medicare program for the aged, and measures to improve education and conservation. Congress also began what Johnson described as "an all-out war" on poverty.

Amassing a record-breaking majority of nearly 16 million votes, Johnson was elected president in his own right in 1964, defeating Senator Barry Goldwater of Arizona.

The double tragedy of a war in Southeast Asia and urban riots at home marked Johnson's last two years in office. Faced with disunity in the nation and challenges within his own party, Johnson surprised the country on March 31, 1968, with the announcement that he would not be a candidate for re-election. He died of a heart attack suffered at his LBJ Ranch on Jan. 22, 1973.

RICHARD MILHOUS NIXON

RICHARD MILHOUS NIXON was born in Yorba Linda, Calif., on Jan. 9, 1913, to Midwestern-bred parents, Francis A. and Hannah Milhous Nixon, who raised their five sons as Quakers.

Nixon was a high school debater and was undergraduate president at Whittier College in California, where he was graduated in 1934. As a scholarship student at Duke University Law School in North Carolina, he graduated third in his class in 1937.

After five years as a lawyer, Nixon joined the Navy in August 1942. He was an air transport officer in the South Pacific and a legal officer stateside before his discharge in 1946 as a lieutenant commander.

Running for Congress in California as a Republican in 1946, Nixon defeated Rep. Jerry Voorhis. As a member of the House Un-American Activities Committee, he made a name as an investigator of Alger Hiss, a former high State Department official, who was later jailed for perjury. In 1950, Nixon defeated Rep. Helen Gahagan Douglas, a Democrat, for the Senate. He was criticized for portraying her as a Communist dupe.

Nixon's anti-Communism, his Western base, and his youth figured in his selection in 1952 to run for vice president on the ticket headed by Dwight D. Eisenhower. Demands for Nixon's withdrawal followed disclosure that California businessmen had paid some of his Senate office expenses. He televised rebuttal, known as "the Checkers speech" (named for a cocker spaniel given to the Nixons), brought him support from the public and from Eisenhower. The ticket won easily in 1952 and again in 1956.

Eisenhower gave Nixon substantive assignments, including missions to 56 countries. In Moscow in 1959, Nixon won acclaim for his defense of U.S. interests in an impromptu "kitchen debate" with Soviet Premier Nikita S. Khrushchev.

Nixon lost the 1960 race for the presidency to John F. Kennedy.

In 1962, Nixon failed in a bid for California's governorship and seemed to be finished as a national candidate. He became a Wall Street lawyer, but kept his old party ties and developed new ones through constant travels to speak for Republicans.

Nixon won the 1968 Republican presidential nomination after a shrewd primary campaign, then made Gov. Spiro T. Agnew of Maryland his surprise choice for vice president. In the election, they edged out the Democratic ticket headed by Vice President Hubert H. Humphrey by 510,314 votes out of 73,212,065 cast.

Committed to wind down the U.S. role in the Vietnamese War, Nixon pursued "Vietnamization"—training and equipping South Vietnamese to do their own fighting. American ground combat forces in Vietnam fell steadily from 540,000 when Nixon took office to none in 1973 when the military draft was ended. But there was heavy continuing use of U.S. air power.

Nixon improved relations with Moscow and reopened the long-closed door to mainland China with a goodwill trip there in February 1972. In May of that year, he visited Moscow and signed agreements on arms limitation and trade expansion and approved plans for a joint U.S.-Soviet space mission in 1975.

Inflation was a campaign issue for Nixon, but he failed to master it as president. On Aug. 15, 1971, with unemployment edging up, Nixon abruptly announced a new economic policy: a 90-day wage-price freeze, stimulative tax cuts, a temporary 10% tariff, and spending cuts. A second phase, imposing guidelines on wage, price and rent boosts, was announced October 7.

The economy responded in time for the 1972 campaign, in which Nixon played up his foreign-policy achievements. Played down was the burglary on June 17, 1972, of Democratic national headquarters in the Watergate apartment complex in Washington. The Nixon-Agnew re-election campaign cost a record $60 million and swamped the Democratic ticket headed by Senator George McGovern of South Dakota with a plurality of 17,999,528 out of 77,718,554 votes. Only Mas-

sachusetts, with 14 electoral votes, and the District of Columbia, with 3, went for McGovern.

In January 1973, hints of a cover-up emerged at the trial of six men found guilty of the Watergate burglary. With a Senate investigation under way, Nixon announced on April 30 the resignations of his top aides, H. R. Haldeman and John D. Ehrlichman, and the dismissal of White House counsel John Dean III. Dean was the star witness at televised Senate hearings that exposed both a White House cover-up of Watergate and massive illegalities in Republican fund-raising in 1972.

The hearings also disclosed that Nixon had routinely tape-recorded his office meetings and telephone conversations.

On Oct. 10, 1973, Agnew resigned as vice president, then pleaded no-contest to a negotiated federal charge of evading income taxes on alleged bribes. Two days later, Nixon nominated the House minority leader, Rep. Gerald R. Ford of Michigan, as the new vice president. Congress confirmed Ford on Dec. 6, 1973.

In June 1974, Nixon visited Israel and four Arab nations. Then he met in Moscow with Soviet leader Leonid I. Brezhnev and reached preliminary nuclear arms limitation agreements.

But, in the month after his return, Watergate ended the Nixon regime. On July 24 the Supreme Court ordered Nixon to surrender subpoenaed tapes. On July 30, the Judiciary Committee referred three impeachment articles to the full membership. On August 5, Nixon bowed to the Supreme Court and released tapes showing he halted an FBI probe of the Watergate burglary six days after it occurred. It was in effect an admission of obstruction of justice, and impeachment appeared inevitable.

Nixon resigned on Aug. 9, 1974, the first president ever to do so. A month later, President Ford issued an unconditional pardon for any offenses Nixon might have committed as president, thus forestalling possible prosecution.

In 1940, Nixon married Thelma Catherine (Pat) Ryan. They had two daughters, Patricia (Tricia) Cox and Julie, who married Dwight David Eisenhower II, grandson of the former president.

He died on April 22, 1994, in New York City of a massive stroke.

GERALD RUDOLPH FORD was born in Omaha, Neb., on July 14, 1913, the only child of Leslie and Dorothy Gardner King. His parents were divorced in 1915. His mother moved to Grand Rapids, Mich., and married Gerald R. Ford. The boy was renamed for his stepfather.

Ford captained his high school football team in Grand Rapids, and a football scholarship took him to the University of Michigan, where he starred as varsity center before his graduation in 1935. A job as assistant football coach at Yale gave him an opportunity to attend Yale Law School, from which he graduated in the top third of his class in 1941.

He returned to Grand Rapids to practice law, but entered the Navy in April 1942. He saw wartime service in the Pacific on the light aircraft carrier *Monterey* and was a lieutenant commander when he returned to Grand Rapids early in 1946 to resume law practice and dabble in politics.

Ford was elected to Congress in 1948 for the first of his 13 terms in the House. He was soon assigned to the influential Appropriations Committee and rose to become the ranking Republican on the subcommittee on Defense Department appropriations and an expert in the field.

As a legislator, Ford described himself as "a moderate on domestic issues, a conservative in fiscal affairs, and a dyed-in-the-wool internationalist." He carried the ball for Pentagon appropriations, was a hawk on the war in Vietnam, and kept a low profile on civil-rights issues.

He was also dependable and hard-working and popular with his colleagues. In 1963, he was elected chairman of the House Republican Conference. He served in 1963-64 as a member of the Warren Commission that investigated the assassination of John F. Kennedy. A revolt by dissatisfied younger Republicans in 1965 made him minority leader.

Ford shelved his hopes for the speakership on Oct. 12, 1973, when Nixon nominated him to fill the vice presidency left vacant by Agnew's resignation under fire. It was the first use of the procedures for filling vacancies in the vice presidency laid down in the 25th Amendment to the Constitution, which Ford had helped enact.

Congress confirmed Ford as vice president on Dec. 6, 1973. Once in office, he said he did not believe Nixon had been involved in the Watergate scandals, but criticized his stubborn court battle against releasing tape recordings of Watergate-related conversations for use as evidence.

The scandals led to Nixon's unprecedented resignation on Aug. 9, 1974, and Ford was sworn in immediately as the 38th president, the first to enter the White House without winning a national election.

Ford assured the nation when he took office that "our long national nightmare is over" and pledged "openness and candor" in all his actions. He won a warm response from the Democratic 93rd Congress when he said he wanted "a good marriage" rather than a honeymoon with his former colleagues. In December 1974 Congressional majorities backed his choice of former New York Gov. Nelson A. Rockefeller as his successor in the again-vacant vice presidency.

The cordiality was chilled by Ford's announcement on Sept. 8, 1974, that he had granted an unconditional pardon to Nixon for any crimes he might have committed as president. Although no formal charges were pending, Ford said he feared "ugly passions" would be aroused if Nixon were brought to trial. The pardon was widely criticized.

To fight inflation, the new president first proposed fiscal restraints and spending curbs and a 5% tax surcharge that got nowhere in the Senate and House. Congress again rebuffed Ford in the spring of 1975 when he appealed for emergency military aid to help the governments of South Vietnam and Cambodia resist massive Communist offensives.

In November 1974, Ford visited Japan, South Korea, and the Soviet Union, where he and Soviet leader Leonid I. Brezhnev conferred in Vladivostok and reached a tentative agreement to limit the number of strategic offensive nuclear weapons. It was Ford's first meeting as president with Brezhnev, who planned a return visit to Washington in the fall of 1975.

Politically, Ford's fortunes improved steadily in the first half of 1975. Badly divided Democrats in Congress were unable to muster votes to override his vetoes of spending bills that exceeded his budget. He faced some right-wing opposition in his own party, but moved to pre-empt it with an early announcement—on July 8, 1975—of his intention to be a candidate in 1976.

Early state primaries in 1976 suggested an easy victory for Ford despite Ronald Reagan's bitter attacks on administration foreign policy and defense programs. But later Reagan primary successes threatened the President's lead. At the Kansas City convention, Ford was nominated by the narrow margin of 1,187 to 1,070. But Reagan had moved the party to the right, and Ford himself was regarded as a caretaker president lacking in strength and vision. He was defeated in November by Jimmy Carter.

In 1948, Ford married Elizabeth Anne (Betty) Bloomer. They had four children, Michael Gerald, John Gardner, Steven Meigs, and Susan Elizabeth.

JAMES EARL CARTER, JR., was born in the tiny village of Plains, Ga., Oct. 1, 1924, and grew up on the family farm at nearby Archery. Both parents were fifth-generation Georgians. His father, James Earl Carter, was known as a segregationist, but treated his black and white workers equally. Carter's mother, Lillian Gordy, was a matriarchal presence in home and community and opposed the then-prevailing code of racial inequality. The future President was baptized in 1935 in the conservative Southern Baptist Church and spoke often of being a "born again" Christian, although committed to the separation of church and state.

Carter married Rosalynn Smith, a neighbor, in 1946. Their first child, John William, was born a year later in Portsmouth, Va. Their other children are James Earl III, born in Honolulu in 1950; Donnel Jeffrey, born in New London, Conn., in 1952, and Amy Lynn, born in Plains in 1967.

In 1946 Carter was graduated from the U.S. Naval Academy at Annapolis and served in the nuclear-submarine program under Adm. Hyman G. Rickover. In 1954, after his father's death, he resigned from the Navy to take over the family's flourishing warehouse and cotton gin, with several thousand acres for growing seed peanuts.

Carter was elected to the Georgia Senate in 1962. In 1966 he lost the race for Governor, but was elected in 1970. His term brought a state government reorganization, sharply reduced agencies, increased economy and efficiency, and new social programs, all with no general tax increase. In 1972 the peanut farmer-politician set his sights on the Presidency and in 1974 built a base for himself as chairman of the Democratic Campaign Committee, appealing for revival and reform. In 1975 his image as a typical Southern white was erased when he won support of most of the old Southern civil-rights coalition after endorsement by Rep. Andrew Young, black Democrat from Atlanta, who had been the closest aide to the Rev. Martin Luther King, Jr. At Carter's 1971 inauguration as Governor he had called for an end to all forms of racial discrimination.

In the 1976 spring primaries, he won 19 out of 31 with a broad appeal to conservatives and liberals, black and white, poor and well-to-do. Throughout his campaigning Carter set forth his policies in his soft Southern voice, and with his electric-blue stare faced down skeptics who joked about "Jimmy Who?" His toothy smile became his trademark. He was nominated on the first roll-call vote of the 1976 Bicentennial Democratic National Convention in New York, and defeated Gerald R. Ford in November. Likewise, in 1980 he was renominated on the first ballot after vanquishing Senator Edward M. Kennedy of Massachusetts in the primaries. At the convention he defeated the Kennedy forces in their attempt to block a party rule that bound a large majority of pledged delegates to vote for Carter. In the election campaign, Carter attacked his rivals, Ronald Reagan and John B. Anderson, independent, with the warning that a Reagan Republican victory would heighten the risk of war and impede civil rights and economic opportunity. In November Carter lost to Reagan, who won 489 Electoral College votes and 51% of the popular tally, to 49 electoral votes and 41% for Carter.

In his one term, Carter fought hard for his programs against resistance from an independent-minded Democratic Congress that frustrated many pet projects although it overrode only two vetoes. Many of his difficulties were traced to his aides' brusqueness in dealing with Capitol Hill and insensitivity to Congressional feelings and tradition. Observers generally viewed public dissatisfaction with the "stagflation" economy as a principal factor in his defeat. Others included his jittery performance in the debate Oct. 28 with Reagan and the final uncertainties in the negotiations for freeing the Iranians' hostages, along with earlier staff problems, friction with Congress, long gasoline lines, and the months-long Iranian crisis, including the abortive sally in April 1980 to free the hostages. The President, however, did deflect criticism resulting from the activities of his brother, Billy. Yet, assessments of his record noted many positive elements. There was, for one thing, peace throughout his term, with no American combat deaths and with a brake on the advocates of force. Regarded as perhaps his greatest personal achievements were the Camp David accords between Israel and Egypt and the resulting treaty—the first between Israel and an Arab neighbor. The treaty with China and the Panama Canal treaties were also major achievements. Carter worked for nuclear-arms control. His concern for international human rights was credited with saving lives and reducing torture, and he supported the British policy that ended internecine warfare in Rhodesia, now Zimbabwe. Domestically, his environmental record was a major accomplishment. His judicial appointments won acclaim; the Southerner who had forsworn racism made 265 choices for the Federal bench that included minority members and women. On energy, he ended by price decontrols the practice of holding U.S. petroleum prices far below world levels.

—*Arthur P. Reed, Jr.*

RONALD WILSON REAGAN rode to the Presidency in 1980 on a tide of resurgent right-wing sentiment among an electorate battered by winds of unwanted change, longing for a distant, simpler era.

He left office in January 1989 with two-thirds of the American people approving his performance during his two terms. It was the highest rating for any retiring President since World War II. In his farewell speech, Reagan exhorted the nation to cling to the revival of patriotism that he had fostered. And he spoke proudly of the economic recovery during his Administrations, although regretting the huge budget deficit, for which, in part, many blamed his policies.

Reagan had retained the public's affection as he applied his political magic to policy goals. His place in history will rest, perhaps, on the short- and intermediate-range missile treaty consummated on a cordial visit to the Soviet Union that he had once reviled as an "evil empire." Its provisions, including a ground-breaking agreement on verification inspection, were formulated in four days of summit talks in Moscow in May 1988 with the Soviet leader, Mikhail S. Gorbachev.

And Reagan can point to numerous domestic achievements: sharp cuts in income tax rates, sweeping tax reform; creating economic growth without inflation, reducing the unemployment rate, among others. He failed, however, to win the "Reagan Revolution" on such issues as abortion and school prayer, and he seemed aloof from "sleazy" conduct by some top officials.

In his final months Reagan campaigned aggressively to win election as President for his two-term Vice President, George Bush.

Reagan's popularity with the public dipped sharply in 1986 when the Iran-Contra scandal broke, shortly after the Democrats gained control of the Senate. Observers agreed that Reagan's presidency had been weakened, if temporarily, by the two unrelated events. Then the weeks-long Congressional hearings in the summer of 1987 heard an array of Administration officials, present and former, tell their tales of a White House riven by deceit and undercover maneuvering. Yet no breath of illegality touched the President's personal reputation; on Aug. 12, 1987, he told the nation that he had not known of questionable activities but agreed that he was "ultimately accountable."

Ronald Reagan, actor turned politician, New Dealer turned conservative, came to the films and politics from a thoroughly Middle-American background—middle class, Middle West and small town. He was born in Tampico, Ill., Feb. 6, 1911, the second son of John Edward Reagan and Nelle Wilson Reagan, and the family later moved to Dixon, Ill. The father, of Irish descent, was a shop clerk and merchant with Democratic sympathies. It was an impoverished family; young Ronald sold homemade popcorn at high school games and worked as a lifeguard to earn money for his college tuition. When the father got a New Deal WPA job, the future President became an ardent Roosevelt Democrat.

Reagan won a B.A. degree in 1932 from Eureka (Ill.) College, where a photographic memory aided in his studies and in debating and college theatricals. In a Depression year, he was making $100 a week as a sports announcer for radio station WHO in Des Moines, Iowa, from 1932 to 1937. His career as a film and TV actor stretched from 1937 to 1966, and his salary climbed to $3,500 a week. As a World War II captain in Army film studios, Reagan recoiled from what he saw as the laziness of Civil Service workers, and moved to the Right. As president of the Screen Actors Guild, he resisted what he considered a Communist plot to subvert the film industry. With advancing age, Reagan left leading-man roles and became a television spokesman for the General Electric Company at $150,000.

With oratorical skill his trademark, Reagan became an active Republican. At the behest of a small group of conservative Southern California businessmen, he ran for governor with a pledge to cut spending, and was elected by almost a million votes over the political veteran, Democratic Gov. Edmund G. Brown, father of the later governor.

In the 1980 election battle against Jimmy Carter, Reagan broadened his appeal by espousing moderate policies, gaining much of his support from disaffected Democrats and blue-collar workers. The incoming Administration immediately set out to "turn the government around" with a new economic program. Over strenuous Congressional opposition, Reagan triumphed on his "supply side" theory to stimulate production and control inflation through tax cuts and sharp reductions in government spending.

The President won high acclaim for his nomination of Sandra Day O'Connor as the first woman on the Supreme Court. His later nominations met increasing opposition but did much to tilt the Court's orientation to the Right.

In 1982, the President's popularity had slipped as the economy declined into the worst recession in 40 years, with persistent high unemployment and interest rates. Initial support for "supply side" economics faded but the President won crucial battles in Congress.

Internationally, Reagan confronted numerous critical problems in his first term. The successful invasion of Grenada accomplished much diplomatically. But the intervention in Lebanon and the withdrawal of Marines after a disastrous terrorist attack were regarded as military failures.

The popular President won reelection in the 1984 landslide, with the economy improving and inflation under control. Domestically, a tax reform bill that Reagan backed became law. But the constantly growing budget deficit remained a constant irritant, with the President and Congress persistently at odds over priorities in spending for defense and domestic programs. His foreign policy met stiffening opposition, with Congress increasingly reluctant to increase spending for the Nicarguan "Contras" and the Pentagon and to expand the development of the MX missile. But even severe critics praised Reagan's restrained but decisive handling of the crisis following the hijacking of an American plane in Beirut by Moslem extremists. The attack on Libya in April 1986 galvanized the nation, although it drew scathing disapproval from the NATO alliance.

Barely three months into his first term, Reagan was the target of an assassin's bullet; his courageous comeback won public admiration.

Reagan is devoted to his wife, Nancy, whom he married after his divorce from the screen actress Jane Wyman. The children of the first marriage are Maureen, his daughter by Miss Wyman, and Michael, an adopted son. In the present marriage the children are Patricia and Ron.

—*Arthur P. Reed, Jr.*

GEORGE HERBERT WALKER BUSH became

President on January 20, 1989, with his theme harmony and conciliation after the often-turbulent Reagan years. With his calm and unassuming manner, he emerged from his subordinate Vice-Presidential role with an air of quiet authority. His Inaugural address emphasized "A new breeze is blowing, and the old bipartisanship must be made new again."

In his first months, the President, the nation's 41st, established himself as his own man and all but erased memories of what many had regarded as his fiercely abrasive Presidential election campaign of 1988 and questionable tactics against his Democratic opponent. People liked his easy style and readiness to compromise even as he remained a staunch conservative, although that readiness had disconcerted some conservatives.

Bush's early Cabinet choices reflected a pragmatic desire for an efficient nonideological Government. And with his usual cautious instinct, in 1990 he nominated to the Supreme Court the scholarly David H. Souter, with broadly conservative views. Souter was confirmed without a bruising battle.

In his first year, Bush, a World War II hero, had won plaudits at home and abroad for his confident, competent conduct at the NATO 40th anniversary summit meeting in Brussels, the Paris economic conference, on his tour of Eastern Europe, and at the Malta conference with Gorbachev. Grave challenges in that year were the Lebanese hostage crisis and the ongoing war on the drug traffic.

Domestically, Bush had to cope with such issues as the *Exxon Valdez* oil spill in Alaska and the dispute over flag-burning restrictions, which was resolved, if only for a time, in mid-1990.

But in his second year, 1990, the President confronted a mounting array of problems, the most critical being on the domestic side. Chief among them were the staggering and mushrooming budget deficit and the savings and loan crisis. Other vexing issues were the question of cutting defense expenditures with consequent economic dislocation, the war on drugs and environmental matters.

At home, the President's popularity dipped sharply from its near-record public approval following the invasion of Panama in late 1989. This plunge followed Bush's recantation of his campaign "no new taxes" pledge as he sat down with Congressional leaders to tame the budget deficit and deal with a faltering economy.

In 1991, the 67-year-old President emerged as the leader of an international coalition of Western democracies, Japan, and even some Arab states that freed invaded Kuwait and vanquished, at least for a time, Iraq's President Saddam Hussein and his armies.

A nation grateful at feeling the end of the "Vietnam syndrome" gave the President an overall rating of 89 percent in a Gallup poll in March after the end of the war. The approval rate fell as the year went on, but a solid majority continued to approve the President's performance, although with growing concern about the faltering economy and other domestic problems. And there were nagging doubts about the Persian Gulf war, its motives and conduct, and about the ensuing refugee crisis.

A major Bush accomplishment in 1991 was the Strategic Arms Reduction Treaty (Start), signed in July with Soviet President Mikhail S. Gorbachev at their fourth summit conference, marking the end of the long weapons buildup. Succeeding events in the Soviet Union and the apparent disintegration of the Communist empire could only enhance his status.

The year also saw the President undergoing treatment for Graves' disease, a thyroid disorder, from which he suffered serious side effects.

Bush, scion of an aristocratic New England family, came to the White House after a long career in public service, in which he held top positions in national and international organizations. As Vice President, he avoided the appearance of direct involvement in the Iran-Contra affair while not seeming to shy away from the President.

Earlier, in the 1960s, Bush won two contests for a Texas Republican seat in the House of Representatives, but lost two bids for a Senate seat and one for the Presidency. After his second race for the Senate, President Nixon appointed him U.S. delegate to the United Nations with the rank of Ambassador and he later became Republican National Chairman. He headed the United States liaison office in Beijing before becoming Director of Central Intelligence.

In 1980 Bush became Reagan's running mate despite earlier criticism of Reagan "voodoo economics" and by the 1984 election had won acclaim for devotion to Reagan's conservative agenda despite his own reputation as somewhat more liberally inclined. Nevertheless, die-hard right-wingers could find satisfaction in Bush's war record and his Government service, particularly with the C.I.A. Throughout he remained influential in White House decisions, particularly in foreign affairs.

In the 1988 campaign, Bush's choice of Senator Dan Quayle of Indiana for Vice President surprised his friends and provoked criticism and ridicule that continued even after the Administration was established in office. Nonetheless Bush strongly defended his choice.

In the 1992 Presidential election, Bush was defeated by Gov. Bill Clinton of Arkansas.

The future President joined the Navy after war broke out and at 18 became the Navy's youngest commissioned pilot, serving from 1942 to 1945. The man later derided by some as a "wimp" fought the Japanese on 58 missions and was shot down once. He won the Distinguished Flying Cross.

Throughout his whole career, Bush had the backing of an established family, headed by his father, the autocratic and wealthy Prescott Bush, who was elected to the Senate from Connecticut in 1952. And his family helped the young patrician became established in his early business ventures, a rich uncle raising most of the capital required for founding a new oil company in Texas.

George Herbert Walker Bush was born June 12, 1924, in Milton, Mass., to Prescott and Dorothy Bush. The family later moved to Connecticut. The youth studied at the elite Phillips Academy in Andover, Mass., before entering the Navy.

After the war, Bush earned an economics degree and a Phi Beta Kappa key in two and a half years at Yale University. While there he captained the baseball team and was initiated into "Skull and Bones," the prestigious Yale secret society.

In 1945 Bush married Barbara Pierce of Rye, N.Y., daughter of a magazine publisher. With his bride, Bush moved to Texas instead of entering his father's investment banking business. There he founded his oil company and in 1980 reported an estimated wealth of $1.4 million.

The Bushes have lived in 17 cities and more than a score of homes and have traveled in as many countries. In her husband's frequent absences during the early years, Mrs. Bush was often matriarch of a family of four boys and a girl. Bush is close to his immediate family and to 10 grandchildren, a sister, and three brothers.

After the Clinton inauguration in January, the Bushes flew to Houston, Texas, where they had rented a home.
—*Arthur P. Reed, Jr.*

WILLIAM JEFFERSON CLINTON was born William Jefferson Blythe III in Hope, Ark., on August 19, 1946. He was named for his father, who was killed in an automobile accident before Clinton's birth. Virginia Kelley, his mother, set an example of hard work and perseverance. She eventually married Roger Clinton, a car dealer, whose name the future president later adopted.

In high school in Hot Springs, Ark., Clinton considered becoming a doctor, but politics beckoned after a meeting with President John F. Kennedy in Washington on a Boys' Nation trip. He earned a B.S. in international affairs in 1968 at Georgetown University, having spent his junior year working for Arkansas Senator J. William Fulbright. He was a Rhodes scholar at Oxford between 1968 and 1970. He then attended Yale Law School, where he met his future wife, Hillary Rodham, a Wellesley graduate. The couple has one child, Chelsea, now a freshman at Stanford.

Clinton taught at the University of Arkansas (1974–1976), was elected state attorney general (1976), and in 1979 became the nation's youngest governor. But he was defeated for re-election by voters irate at a rise in the state's automobile license fees. In 1982 he was elected again. This time he reined in liberal tendencies to accommodate the conservative bent of the voters.

Clinton became the 42nd U.S. president following a turbulent political campaign. He overcame vigorous personal attacks on his character and on his actions during the Vietnam war, which he actively opposed. The "character issue" stemmed from allegations of infidelity, which Clinton refuted in a television interview in which he and Hillary avowed their relationship was solid. Throughout his term in office, Clinton was dogged by allegations in connection with the Whitewater real estate deal in which he and Hillary were involved prior to the 1992 election. Though the Clintons were never accused of any wrongdoing, their partners in the venture, including the governor of Arkansas, Jim Guy Tucker, were convicted of fraud and conspiracy in a trial in 1996.

The problems faced by the new president were as daunting as they were varied. Almost immediately after his inauguration in January 1993 he became embroiled with the military leadership over a politically sensitive issue—his campaign pledge to allow homosexuals to serve openly in the armed services. He ultimately agreed to compromise, dubbed the "don't ask, don't tell" policy. This controversy was soon supplanted by a series of blunders in appointments to fill positions in his administration.

Early in his tenure, the new president encountered a major defeat when Congress rejected his proposed economic stimulus package. He later won approval for his budget, but it barely survived the criticism of conservatives in Congress, including Democrats, who demanded

more spending cuts, fewer taxes, and caps on entitlement programs. In his second year, Clinton faced persistent troubles on the domestic front, with acrimonious battles raging over health care, welfare reform, crime prevention, and White House personnel problems. Clinton appointed his wife to craft a health care reform package, but after months of effort the plan failed to garner sufficient support. Clinton had to reduce his objectives from massive overhaul to incremental reform. Though the health care reform was soundly defeated, Clinton won a major victory with the passage of the North American Free Trade Agreement (NAFTA) and the Global Agreement on Tariffs and Trade (GATT). Congress also approved Clinton's deficit reduction bill, rules allowing abortion counseling in federally funded clinics, a waiting period for handgun purchases (the "Brady bill," named for Reagan Press Secretary Jim Brady), and a national service program.

Foreign affairs, once a weak point for a man elected on a domestic economic agenda, became a proving ground for the former Arkansas governor. With issues erupting around the world, in places as disparate as Bosnia, Somalia, Rwanda, Haiti, and Cuba, Clinton was able to capitalize on several opportunities to improve his international image. The Israel-Jordan peace agreement was signed at the White House in the summer of 1994 by Israeli Prime Minister Yitzhak Rabin and Jordan's King Hussein. In the fall of that year, the administration succeeded in restoring Haiti's ousted president, Jean-Bertrand Aristide, to power. Clinton scored again by bolstering Russian president Boris Yeltsin's popularity with promises of economic aid.

But the problems in Eastern Europe put an end to his winning streak. Though Clinton wanted desperately to end the brutal "ethnic cleansing" in Bosnia and offer security to the 2 million refugees scrambling from one U.N. safe haven to another, he did not want to commit American ground troops to do so. A peace accord, which included provisions for American troops in a peacekeeping role, was ultimately constructed by Richard Holbrook and signed in Dayton, Ohio, in November 1995. The peace accord, however tenuous, greatly improved Clinton's standing the eyes of the international community.

Foreign affairs continued to plague Clinton's presidency in 1996. In Russia, Clinton's support for Yeltsin drew criticism as the war for Chechen independence erupted. Challenges in the Middle East resurfaced in the form of continuing Israeli-Palestinian disputes and Iraq's invasion of Kurdish territory. Clinton responded to the Iraqi aggression by ordering missile attacks on Iraqi planes and ground forces.

The Republican sweep of the 1994 elections resulted in a Republican-controlled Congress, and 1995 was largely a tug-of-war between the White House and Capitol Hill over budget-balancing and other key points of the G.O.P.'s "Contract with America," crafted by Speaker of the House Newt Gingrich. Government operations shut down repeatedly as the funds allocated in successive continuing resolutions dried up, and the President and Congress were unable to pass budget legislation.

In 1996 Clinton approved several major legislative measures, including a welfare-reform bill reversing several decades of federal policy, which Clinton signed reluctantly and for which he was sharply criticized by liberals. He also enacted measures to improve access to health care, to raise the minimum wage by 90 cents per hour to $5.15, and to impose sanctions on companies that do business with Iran and Libya. In a move to discourage teenage smoking, Clinton approved a series of curbs on cigarette advertising, and introduced plans for the FDA to regulate nicotine as a controlled substance. Clinton criticized the tobacco deal, which had emerged in 1997 from months of negotiations among state attorneys general and tobacco industry executives, for not doing enough to stop teenage smoking.

Clinton's second term saw a shift away from the budget battlefield as a stable economy made it easier for both sides to agree to balanced-budget legislation in 1997. Instead the political wrangling took place in a series of investigations aimed at uncovering irregularities in Democratic fund-raising for the 1996 election. Though Clinton and Vice President Gore both insisted their actions were within the letter of the law, the ensuing controversy highlighted the need for campaign finance reform. Ironically, Clinton had called for such reforms during his first term, but could not get the Republican-controlled Congress to cooperate. Clinton was also embarrassed when the Supreme Court ruled that a sexual harassment suit could proceed while the President was in office. Claims that the President was to busy to handle the distractions of a lawsuit while in office were not persuasive, so the claim could go forward.

—*Arthur P. Reed, Jr.*

The Hundred and Fifth Congress

Composition of the 104th and 105th Congresses

105th Congress	Rep.	Dem.	Male	Female	104th Congress	Rep.	Dem.	Male	Female
Senate	55	45	90	10	Senate	53	46	92	8
House[1]	228	206	388	47	House[1]	233	199	386	49

1. One independent member in the House.

The Senate

In the following list, the senior senator is listed first. Dates in left column indicate term in office; birthdates are given in parentheses after name and party affiliation. All terms are for six years and expire in January. Mailing address: The Senate, Washington, D.C. 20515.

Alabama
1987–99 Richard C. Shelby (R) (1934)
1997–2003 Jeff Sessions (R) (1946)
Alaska
1970–2003 Ted Stevens (R) (1923)
1981–99 Frank H. Murkowski (R) (1933)
Arizona
1987–99 John McCain (R) (1936)
1995–2001 Jon Kyl (R) (1942)
Arkansas
1975–99 Dale Bumpers (D) (1925)
1979–2003 Tim Hutchinson (R) (1949)
California
1993–2001 Dianne Feinstein (D) (1933)
1993–99 Barbara Boxer (D) (1940)
Colorado
1993–99 Ben Nighthorse Campbell (R) (1933)
1997–2003 Wayne Allard (R) (1943)
Connecticut
1981–99 Christopher J. Dodd (D) (1944)
1989–2001 Joseph I. Lieberman (D) (1942)
Delaware
1971–2001 William V. Roth, Jr. (R) (1921)
1973–2003 Joseph R. Biden, Jr. (D) (1942)
Florida
1987–99 Bob Graham (D) (1936)
1989–2001 Connie Mack III (R) (1940)
Georgia
1993–99 Paul Coverdell (R) (1939)
1997–2003 Max Cleland (D) (1942)
Hawaii
1963–99 Daniel K. Inouye (D) (1924)
1990–2001 Daniel K. Akaka (D) (1924)
Idaho
1991–2003 Larry E. Craig (R) (1945)
1993–99 Dirk Kempthorne (R) (1951)
Illinois
1993–99 Carol Mosely Braun (D) (1947)
1997–2003 Richard J. Durbin (D) (1944)
Indiana
1977–2001 Richard G. Lugar (R) (1932)
1989–99 Dan Coats (R) (1943)
Iowa
1981–99 Charles E. Grassley (R) (1933)
1985–2003 Tom Harkin (D) (1939)
Kansas
1997–2003 Sam Brownback (R) (1956)
1997–2003 Pat Roberts (R) (1936)

Kentucky
1974–99 Wendell H. Ford (D) (1924)
1985–2003 Mitch McConnell (R) (1942)
Louisiana
1987–99 John B. Breaux (D) (1944)
1997–2003 Mary L. Landrieu (D) (1955)
Maine
1995–2001 Olympia J. Snowe (R) (1947)
1997–2003 Susan M. Collins (R) (1952)
Maryland
1977–2001 Paul Sarbanes (D) (1933)
1987–99 Barbara A. Mikulski (D) (1936)
Massachusetts
1962–2001 Edward M. Kennedy (D) (1932)
1985–2003 John F. Kerry (D) (1943)
Michigan
1979–2003 Carl Levin (D) (1934)
1995–2001 Spencer Abraham (R) (1952)
Minnesota
1991–2003 Paul Wellstone (D) (1944)
1995–2001 Rod Grams (R) (1948)
Mississippi
1978–2003 Thad Cochran (R) (1937)
1989–2001 Trent Lott (R) (1941)
Missouri
1987–99 Christopher S. "Kit" Bond (R) (1939)
1995–2001 John Ashcroft (R) (1942)
Montana
1978–2003 Max Baucus (D) (1941)
1989–2001 Conrad Burns (R) (1935)
Nebraska
1989–2001 Robert Kerrey (D) (1943)
1997–2003 Chuck Hagel (R) (1946)
Nevada
1987–99 Harry M. Reid (D) (1939)
1989–2001 Dick Bryan (D) (1937)
New Hampshire
1991–2003 Robert C. Smith (R) (1941)
1993–99 Judd Gregg (R) (1947)
New Jersey
1982–2001 Frank R. Lautenberg (D) (1924)
1997–2003 Robert G. Torricelli (D) (1951)
New Mexico
1973–2003 Pete V. Domenici (R) (1932)
1983–2001 Jeff Bingaman (D) (1943)
New York
1977–2001 Daniel P. Moynihan (D) (1927)
1981–2003 Alfonse M. D'Amato (R) (1937)

North Carolina
1973–2003 Jesse Helms (R) (1921)
1993–99 Lauch Faircloth (R) (1928)
North Dakota
1993–2001 Kent Conrad (D) (1948)
1987–99 Byron Dorgan (D) (1942)
Ohio
1974–99 John H. Glenn, Jr. (D) (1921)
1995–2001 Mike DeWine (R) (1947)
Oklahoma
1989–99 Don Nickles (R) (1948)
1994–2003 James M. Inhofe (R) (1934)
Oregon
1996–99 Ron Wyden (D)
1997–2003 Gordon Smith (R) (1952)
Pennsylvania
1981–99 Arlen Specter (R) (1930)
1995–2001 Rick Santorum (R) (1958)
Rhode Island
1976–2001 John H. Chafee (R) (1922)
1997–2003 Jack Reed (D) (1949)
South Carolina
1957–2003 Strom Thurmond (R) (1902)
1966–99 Ernest F. Hollings (D) (1922)
South Dakota
1987–99 Thomas A. Daschle (D) (1947)
1997–2003 Tim Johnson (D) (1946)

Tennessee
1995–2003 Fred Thompson (R) (1942)
1995–2001 Bill Frist (R) (1952)
Texas
1985–2003 Phil Gramm (R) (1942)
1995–2001 Kay Bailey Huchison (R) (1943)
Utah
1977–2001 Orrin G. Hatch (R) (1934)
1993–99 Robert Bennett (R) (1933)
Vermont
1975–99 Patrick J. Leahy (D) (1940)
1989–2001 James M. Jeffords (R) (1934)
Virginia
1979–2003 John H. Warner (R) (1927)
1989–2001 Charles Robb (D) (1939)
Washington
1989–2001 Slade Gorton (R) (1928)
1993–99 Patty Murray (D) (1950)
West Virginia
1959–2001 Robert C. Byrd (D) (1918)
1985–2003 John D. "Jay" Rockefeller IV (D) (1937)
Wisconsin
1989–2001 Herbert Kohl (D) (1935)
1993–99 Russell D. Feingold, Jr. (D) (1953)
Wyoming
1995–2001 Craig Thomas (R) (1933)
1997–2003 Michael B. Enzi (R) (1944)

The House of Representatives

In the following lists, the numeral indicates the Congressional District represented; AL is for representatives At Large. All terms expire January 1999. Mailing address: House of Representatives, Washington, D.C. 20515. Election results as of 4 p.m., Nov. 6, 1996.

Alabama
1. Sonny Callahan (R)
2. Terry Everett (R)
3. Bob Riley (R)
4. Robert Aderholt (R)
5. Robert E. "Bud" Cramer (D)
6. Spencer Bachus (R)
7. Earl F. Hilliard (D)

Alaska
1. AL Don Young (R)

Arizona
1. Matt Salmon (R)
2. Ed Pastor (D)
3. Bob Stump (R)
4. John Shadegg (R)
5. Jim Kolbe (R)
6. J.D. Hayworth (R)

Arkansas
1. Marion Berry (D)
2. Vic Snyder (D)
3. Tim Hutchinson (R)
4. Jay Dickey (R)

California
1. Frank Riggs (R)
2. Wally Herger (R)
3. Vic Fazio (D)
4. John T. Doolittle (R)
5. Robert T. Matsui (D)
6. Lynn Woolsey (D)
7. George Miller (D)
8. Nancy Pelosi (D)
9. Ronald V. Dellums (D)
10. Ellen O. Tauscher (D)
11. Richard W. Pombo (R)
12. Tom Lantos (D)
13. Fortney Pete Stark (D)
14. Anna G. Eshoo (D)
15. Tom Campbell (R)
16. Zoe Lofgren (D)
17. Sam Farr (D)
18. Gary A. Condit (D)
19. George P. Radanovich (R)
20. Cal Dooley (D)
21. Bill Thomas (R)
22. Walter Holden Capps (D)
23. Elton Gallegly (R)
24. Brad Sherman (D)
25. Howard P. "Buck" McKeon (R)
26. Howard L. Berman (D)
27. James E. Rogan (R)
28. David Dreier (R)
29. Henry A. Waxman (D)
30. Xavier Becerra (D)
31. Matthew G. Martinez (D)
32. Julian C. Dixon (D)
33. Lucille Roybal-Allard (D)
34. Esteban E. Torres (D)
35. Maxine Waters (D)
36. Jane Harman (D)
37. Juanita Millender-McDonald (D)
38. Steve Horn (R)
39. Ed Royce (R)
40. Jerry Lewis (R)
41. Jay C. Kim (R)
42. George E. Brown, Jr. (D)
43. Ken Calvert (R)
44. Sonny Bono (R)
45. Dana Rohrabacher (R)
46. Robert K. Dornan (R)
47. Christopher Cox (R)
48. Ron Packard (R)
49. Brian P. Bilbray (R)
50. Bob Filner (D)
51. Randy "Duke" Cunningham (R)
52. Duncan Hunter (R)

Colorado
1. Diana DeGette (D)
2. David E. Skaggs (D)
3. Scott McInnis (R)
4. Bob Shaffer (R)
5. Joel Hefley (R)
6. Dan Schaefer (R)

Connecticut
1. Barbara B. Kennelly (D)
2. Sam Gejdenson (D)

3. Rosa DeLauro (D)
4. Christopher Shays (R)
5. James H. Maloney (D)
6. Nancy L. Johnson (R)

Delaware
1. AL Michael N. Castle (R)

Florida
1. Joe Scarborough (R)
2. Allen Boyd (D)
3. Corrine Brown (D)
4. Tillie Fowler (R)
5. Karen L. Thurman (D)
6. Cliff Stearns (R)
7. John L. Mica (R)
8. Bill McCollum (R)
9. Michael Bilirakis (R)
10. C.W. Bill Young (R)
11. Jim Davis (D)
12. Charles T. Canady (R)
13. Dan Miller (R)
14. Porter J. Goss (R)
15. Dave Weldon (R)
16. Mark Foley (R)
17. Carrie P. Meek (D)
18. Ileana Ros-Lehtinen (R)
19. Robert Wexler (D)
20. Peter Deutsch (D)
21. Lincoln Diaz-Balart (R)
22. E. Clay Shaw, Jr. (R)
23. Alcee L. Hastings (D)

Georgia
1. Jack Kingston (R)
2. Sanford D. Bishop, Jr. (D)
3. Mac Collins (R)
4. Cynthia A. McKinney (D)
5. John Lewis (D)
6. Newt Gingrich (R)
7. Bob Barr (R)
8. Saxby Chambliss (R)
9. Nathan Deal (R)
10. Charlie Norwood (R)
11. John Linder (R)

Hawaii
1. Neil Abercrombie (D)
2. Patsy T. Mink (D)

Idaho
1. Helen Chenoweth (R)
2. Michael D. Crapo (R)

Illinois
1. Bobby L. Rush (D)
2. Jesse Jackson, Jr. (D)
3. William O. Lipinski (D)
4. Luis V. Gutierrez (D)
5. Rod R. Blagojevich (D)
6. Henry J. Hyde (R)
7. Danny K. Davis (D)
8. Philip M. Crane (R)
9. Sidney R. Yates (D)
10. John Edward Porter (R)
11. Jerry Weller (R)
12. Jerry F. Costello (D)
13. Harris W. Fawell (R)
14. Dennis Hastert (R)
15. Thomas W. Ewing (R)
16. Donald Manzullo (R)
17. Lane Evans (D)
18. Ray LaHood (R)
19. Glenn Poshard (D)
20. John M. Shimkus (R)

Indiana
1. Peter J. Visclosky (D)
2. David M. McIntosh (R)
3. Tim Roemer (D)
4. Mark Souder (R)
5. Steve Buyer (R)
6. Dan Burton (R)
7. Edward A. Pease (R)
8. John Hostettler (R)
9. Lee H. Hamilton (D)
10. Julia M. Carson (D)

Iowa
1. Jim Leach (R)
2. Jim Nussle (R)
3. Leonard L. Boswell (R)
4. Greg Ganske (R)
5. Tom Latham (R)

Kansas
1. Jerry Moran (R)
2. Jim Ryun (R)
3. Vince Snowbarger (R)
4. Todd Tiahrt (R)

Kentucky
1. Edward Whitfield (R)
2. Ron Lewis (R)
3. Anne Meagher Northup (R)
4. Jim Bunning (R)
5. Harold Rogers (R)
6. Scotty Baesler (D)

Louisiana
1. Robert L. Livingston (R)
2. William J. Jefferson (D)
3. "Billy" Tauzin (R)
4. Jim McCrery (R)
5. John Cooksey (R)
6. Richard H. Baker (R)
7. Chris John (D)

Maine
1. Thomas H. Allen (D)
2. John Baldacci (D)

Maryland
1. Wayne T. Gilchrest (R)
2. Robert Ehrlich, Jr. (R)
3. Benjamin L. Cardin (D)
4. Albert R. Wynn (D)
5. Steny H. Hoyer (D)
6. Roscoe G. Bartlett (R)
7. Elijah E. Cummings (D)
8. Constance A. Morella (R)

Massachusetts
1. John W. Olver (D)
2. Richard E. Neal (D)
3. James P. McGovern (D)
4. Barney Frank (D)
5. Martin T. Meehan (D)
6. John F. Tierney (D)
7. Edward J. Markey (D)
8. Joseph P. Kennedy II (D)
9. Joe Moakley (D)
10. William D. Delahunt (D)

Michigan
1. Bart Stupak (D)
2. Peter Hoekstra (R)
3. Vernon J. Ehlers (R)
4. Dave Camp (R)
5. James A. Barcia (D)
6. Fred Upton (R)
7. Nick Smith (R)
8. Debbie Stabenow (D)
9. Dale E. Kildee (D)
10. David E. Bonior (D)
11. Joe Knollenberg (R)
12. Sander M. Levin (D)
13. Lynn Rivers (D)
14. John Conyers, Jr. (D)
15. Carolyn Cheeks Kilpatrick (D)
16. John D. Dingell (D)

Minnesota
1. Gil Gutknecht (R)
2. David Minge (D)
3. Jim Ramstad (R)
4. Bruce F. Vento (D)

5. Martin Olav Sabo (D)
6. William P. "Bill" Luther (D)
7. Collin C. Peterson (D)
8. James L. Oberstar (D)

Mississippi
1. Roger Wicker (R)
2. Bennie Thompson (D)
3. Charles W. "Chip" Pickering, Jr. (R)
4. Mike Parker (R)
5. Gene Taylor (D)

Missouri
1. William L. Clay (D)
2. James M. Talent (R)
3. Richard A. Gephardt (D)
4. Ike Skelton (D)
5. Karen McCarthy (D)
6. Pat Danner (D)
7. Roy Blunt (R)
8. Jo Ann Emerson (R)
9. Kenny Hulshof (R)

Montana
1. AL Rick Hill (R)

Nebraska
1. Doug Bereuter (R)
2. Jon Christensen (R)
3. Bill Barrett (R)

Nevada
1. John Ensign (R)
2. Jim Gibbons (R)

New Hampshire
1. John E. Sununu (R)
2. Charles Bass (R)

New Jersey
1. Robert E. Andrews (D)
2. Frank A. LoBiondo (R)
3. H. James Saxton (R)
4. Christopher H. Smith (R)
5. Marge Roukema (R)
6. Frank Pallone, Jr. (D)
7. Bob Franks (R)
8. William J. Pascrell, Jr. (D)
9. Steven R. Rothman (D)
10. Donald M. Payne (D)
11. Rodney Frelinghuysen (R)
12. Mike Pappas (R)
13. Robert Menendez (D)

New Mexico
1. Steven H. Schiff (R)
2. Joe Skeen (R)
3. Bill Redmond (D)

New York
1. Michael P. Forbes (R)
2. Rick A. Lazio (R)
3. Peter T. King (R)
4. Carolyn McCarthy (D)
5. Gary L. Ackerman (D)
6. Floyd H. Flake (D)
7. Thomas J. Manton (D)
8. Jerrold Nadler (D)
9. Charles E. Schumer (D)
10. Edolphus Towns (D)
11. Major R. Owens (D)
12. Nydia M. Velazquez (D)
13. (vacant)
14. Carolyn B. Maloney (D)
15. Charles B. Rangel (D)
16. Jose E. Serrano (D)
17. Eliot L. Engel (D)
18. Nita M. Lowey (D)
19. Sue W. Kelly (R)
20. Benjamin A. Gilman (R)
21. Michael R. McNulty (D)
22. Gerald B.H. Solomon (R)
23. Sherwood Boehlert (R)
24. John M. McHugh (R)
25. James T. Walsh (R)
26. Maurice D. Hinchey (D)
27. Bill Paxon (R)
28. Louise M. Slaughter (D)
29. John L. LaFalce (D)
30. Jack Quinn (R)
31. Amo Houghton (R)

North Carolina
1. Eva Clayton (D)
2. Bob Etheridge (D)
3. Walter B. Jones, Jr. (R)
4. David E. Price (D)
5. Richard M. Burr (R)
6. Howard Coble (R)
7. Mike McIntyre (D)
8. W.G. "Bill" Hefner (D)
9. Sue Myrick (R)
10. Cass Ballenger (R)
11. Charles H. Taylor (R)
12. Melvin Watt (D)

North Dakota
1. AL Earl Pomeroy (D)

Ohio
1. Steve Chabot (R)
2. Rob Portman (R)
3. Tony P. Hall (D)
4. Michael G. Oxley (R)
5. Paul E. Gillmor (R)
6. Ted Strickland (D)
7. David L. Hobson (R)
8. John A. Boehner (R)
9. Marcy Kaptur (D)
10. Dennis J. Kucinich (D)
11. Louis Stokes (D)
12. John R. Kasich (R)
13. Sherrod Brown (D)
14. Tom Sawyer (D)
15. Deborah Pryce (R)
16. Ralph Regula (R)
17. James A. Traficant, Jr. (D)
18. Bob Ney (R)
19. Steven C. LaTourette (R)

Oklahoma
1. Steve Largent (R)
2. Tom Coburn (R)
3. Wes Watkins (I)
4. J.C. Watts (R)
5. Ernest Istook (R)
6. Frank D. Lucas (R)

Oregon
1. Elizabeth Furse (D)
2. Bob Smith (R)
3. Earl Blumenauer (D)
4. Peter A. DeFazio (D)
5. Darlene Hooley (D)

Pennsylvania
1. Thomas M. Foglietta (D)
2. Chaka Fattah (D)
3. Robert A. Borski (D)
4. Ron Klink (D)
5. John E. Peterson (R)
6. Tim Holden (D)
7. Curt Weldon (R)
8. James C. Greenwood (R)
9. Bud Shuster (R)
10. Joseph M. McDade (R)
11. Paul E. Kanjorski (D)
12. John P. Murtha (D)
13. Joseph M. Hoeffel (D)[1]
14. Jon D. Fox (R)[1]
15. William J. Coyne (D)
16. Paul McHale (D)
17. Joseph R. Pitts (R)
18. George W. Gekas (R)
19. Mike Doyle (D)
20. Bill Goodling (R)
21. Frank R. Mascara (D)

22. Phil English (R)
1. Recount.

Rhode Island
1. Patrick J. Kennedy (D)
2. Robert A. Weygand (D)

South Carolina
1. Mark Sanford (R)
2. Floyd D. Spence (R)
3. Lindsey Graham (R)
4. Bob Inglis (R)
5. John M. Spratt, Jr. (D)
6. James E. Clyburn (D)

South Dakota
1. AL John R. Thune (R)

Tennessee
1. William L. "Bill" Jenkins (R)
2. John J. "Jimmy" Duncan, Jr. (R)
3. Zach Wamp (R)
4. Van Hilleary (R)
5. Bob Clement (D)
6. Bart Gordon (D)
7. Ed Bryant (R)
8. John Tanner (D)
9. Harold E. Ford (D)

Texas
1. Max Sandlin (D)
2. Jim Turner (D)
3. Sam Johnson (R)
4. Ralph M. Hall (D)
5. Pete Sessions (R)
6. Joe L. Barton (R)
7. Bill Archer (R)
8. Kevin Brady (R)
9. Steve Stockman (R)
10. Lloyd Doggett (D)
11. Chet Edwards (D)
12. Kay Granger (R)
13. William M. "Mac" Thornberry (R)
14. Ron Paul (R)
15. Ruben Hinojosa (D)
16. Silvestre Reyes (D)
17. Charles W. Stenholm (D)
18. Shelia Jackson Lee (D)
19. Larry Combest (R)
20. Henry B. Gonzalez (D)
21. Lamar Smith (R)
22. Tom DeLay (R)
23. Henry Bonilla (R)
24. Martin Frost (D)
25. Ken Bentsen (D)

26. Dick Armey (R)
27. Solomon P. Ortiz (D)
28. Ciro D. Rodriguez (D)
29. Gene Green (D)
30. Eddie Bernice Johnson (D)

Utah
1. James V. Hansen (R)
2. Merrill Cook (R)
3. Christopher B. Cannon (R)

Vermont
1. AL Bernard Sanders (I)

Virginia
1. Herbert H. Bateman (R)
2. Owen B. Pickett (D)
3. Robert C. Scott (D)
4. Norman Sisisky (D)
5. Virgil H. Goode, Jr. (D)
6. Robert W. Goodlatte (R)
7. Thomas J. Bliley, Jr. (R)
8. James P. Moran, Jr. (D)
9. Frederick C. "Rick" Boucher (D)
10. Frank R. Wolf (R)
11. Thomas M. Davis III (R)

Washington
1. Rick White (R)
2. Kevin Quigley (D)
3. Brian Baird (D)
4. Richard "Doc" Hastings (R)
5. George Nethercutt (R)
6. Norm Dicks (D)
7. Jim McDermott (D)
8. Jennifer Dunn (R)
9. Adam Smith (D)

West Virginia
1. Alan B. Mollohan (D)
2. Bob Wise (D)
3. Nick J. Rahall II (D)

Wisconsin
1. Mark W. Neumann (R)
2. Scott L. Klug (R)
3. Ron Kind (D)
4. Gerald Kleczka (D)
5. Thomas M. Barrett (D)
6. Tom Petri (R)
7. David R. Obey (D)
8. Jay Johnson (D)
9. F. James Sensenbrenner, Jr. (R)

Wyoming
1. AL Barbara Cubin (R)

The Governors of the Fifty States

State	Governor	Current term[1]	State	Governor	Current term[1]
Ala.	Fob James, Jr. (R)	1995–1999	Md.	Parris N. Glendening (D)	1995–1999
Alaska	Tony Knowles (D)	1994–1998[2]	Mass.	Paul Cellucci (R)	1995–1999
Ariz.	Fife Symington (R)	1995–1999	Mich.	John Engler (R)	1995–1999
Ark.	Mike Huckabee (R)	1996–1999	Minn.	Arne H. Carlson (R)	1995–1999
Calif.	Pete Wilson (R)	1995–1999	Miss.	Kirk Fordice (R)	1996–2000
Colo.	Roy Romer (D)	1995–1999	Mo.	Mel Carnahan (D)	1997–2001
Conn.	John Rowland (R)	1995–1999	Mont.	Marc Racicot (R)	1997–2001
Del.	Thomas R. Carper (D)	1997–2001	Neb.	E. Benjamin Nelson (D)	1995–1999
Fla.	Lawton Chiles (D)	1995–1999	Nev.	Robert J. Miller (D)	1995–1999
Ga.	Zell Miller (D)	1995–1999	N.H.	Jeanne Shaheen (D)	1997–1999
Hawaii	Benjamin J. Cayetano (D)	1994–1998[2]	N.J.	Christine Todd Whitman (R)	1994–1998
Idaho	Philip E. Batt (R)	1995–1999	N.M.	Gary E. Johnson (R)	1995–1999
Ill.	Jim Edgar (R)	1995–1999	N.Y.	George E. Pataki (R)	1995–1999
Ind.	Frank O'Bannon(D)	1997–2001	N.C.	James B. Hunt, Jr. (D)	1997–2001
Iowa	Terry Branstad (R)	1995–1999	N.D.	Edward T. Schafer (R)	1997–2001
Kan.	Bill Graves (R)	1995–1999	Ohio	George V. Voinovich (R)	1995–1999
Ky.	Paul E. Patton (D)	1995–1999[2]	Okla.	Frank Keating (R)	1995–1999
La.	Murphy J. "Mike" Murphy (D)	1996–2000	Ore.	John A. Kitzhaber (D)	1995–1999
Maine	Angus King. (I)	1995–1999	Pa.	Tom Ridge (R)	1995–1999

State	Governor	Current term[1]	State	Governor	Current term[1]
R.I.	Lincoln C. Almond (R)	1995–1999	Vt.	Howard Dean (D)	1997–1999
S.C.	David M. Beasley (R)	1995–1999	Va.	George Felix Allen (R)	1994–1998
S.D.	William J. Janklow (R)	1995–1999	Wash.	Gary Locke (D)	1997–2001
Tenn.	Don Sundquist (R)	1995–1999	W. Va.	Cecil H. Underwood (R)	1997–2001
Texas	George W. Bush (R)	1995–1999	Wis.	Tommy G. Thompson (R)	1995–1999
Utah	Michael O. Leavitt (R)	1997–2001	Wyo.	Jim Geringer (R)	1995–1999

1. Except where indicated, all terms begin in January. 2. December.

Senate and House Standing Committees, 105th Congress

Committees of the Senate

Aging (18 members)
Chairman: Charles E. Grassley (Iowa)
Ranking Dem.: John B. Breaux (La.)
Agriculture, Nutrition, and Forestry (18 members)
Chairman: Richard G. Lugar (Ind.)
Ranking Dem.: Tom Harkin (Iowa)
Appropriations (28 members)
Chairman: Ted Stevens (Alaska)
Ranking Dem.: Robert C. Byrd (W.Va.)
Armed Services (18 members)
Chairman: Strom Thurmond (S.C.)
Ranking Dem.: Carl Levin (Mich.)
Banking, Housing, and Urban Affairs (18 members)
Chairman: Alfonse D'Amato (N.Y.)
Ranking Dem.: Paul S. Sarbanes (Md.)
Budget (22 members)
Chairman: Pete V. Domenici (N.M.)
*Ranking Dem.:*Frank R. Lautenberg (N.J.)
Commerce, Science, and Transportation (20 members)
Chairman: John McCain (Ariz.)
Ranking Dem.: Ernest F. Hollings (S.C.)
Energy and Natural Resources (20 members)
Chairman: Frank H. Murkowski (Alaska)
*Ranking Dem.:*Dale Bumpers (Ark.)
Environment and Public Works (18 members)
Chairman: John H. Chafee (R.I.)
Ranking Dem.: Max Baucus (Mont.)
Ethics (6 members)
Chairman: Robert C. Smith (N.H)
Ranking Dem.: Harry Reid (Nev.)
Finance (20 members)
Chairman: William V. Roth, Jr. (Del.)
Ranking Dem.: Daniel Patrick Moynihan (N.Y.)
Foreign Relations (18 members)
Chairman: Jesse Helms (N.C.)
Ranking Dem.: Joseph R. Biden Jr. (Del.)
Governmental Affairs (18 members)
*Chairman:*Fred Thompson (Tenn.)
Ranking Dem.: John Glenn (Ohio)
Indian Affairs (14 members)
*Chairman:*Ben Nighthorse Campbell (Colo.)
Ranking Dem.: Daniel K. Inouye (Hawaii)
Intelligence (17 members)
Chairman: Richard C. Shelby (Ala.)
Ranking Dem.: Bob Kerrey (Neb.)
Judiciary (18 members)
Chairman: Orrin G. Hatch (Utah)
Ranking Dem.: Patrick J. Leahy (Vt.)
Labor and Human Resources (18 members)
Chairman: James M. Jeffords (Vt.)
Ranking Dem.: Edward M. Kennedy (Mass.)
Rules and Administration (16 members)
Chairman: John W. Warner (Va.)
Ranking Dem.: Wendell H. Ford (Ky.)
Small Business (18 members)
Chairman: Christopher S. Bond (Mo.)
Ranking Dem.: John Kerry (Mass.)
Veterans' Affairs (12 members)
Chairman: Arlen Specter (Pa.)
Ranking Dem: John D. Rockefeller IV (W.Va.)

Committees of the House

Agriculture (50 members)
Chairman: Bob Smith (Ore.)
Ranking Dem.: Charles W. Stenholm (Tex.)
Appropriations (60 members)
Chairman: Robert L. Livingston (La.)
Ranking Dem.: David R. Obey (Wis.)
Banking and Financial Services (54 members)
Chairman: Jim Leach (Iowa)
Ranking Dem.: Henry B. Gonzalez (Texas)
Budget (43 members)
Chairman: John R. Kasich (Ohio)
Ranking Dem.: John M. Spratt Jr. (S.C.)
Commerce (51 members)
Chairman: Thomas J. Bliley, Jr. (Va.)
Ranking Dem.: John D. Dingell (Mich.)
Education And the Workforce (45 members)
Chairman: Bill Goodling (Pa.)
Ranking Dem.: William L. Clay (Mo.)
Government Reform and Oversight (43 members)
Chairman: Dan Burton (Ind.)
Ranking Dem.: Henry A. Waxman (Calif.)
House Oversight (8 members)
Chairman: Bill Thomas (Calif.)
Ranking Dem.: Sam Gejdenson (Conn.)
Intelligence (16 members)
*Chairman:*Porter J. Goss (Fla.)
*Ranking Dem.:*Norm Dicks (Wash.)
International Relations (47 members)
Chairman: Benjamin A. Gilman (N.Y.)
Ranking Dem.: Lee H. Hamilton (Ind.)
Judiciary (35 members)
Chairman: Henry J. Hyde (Ill.)
Ranking Dem.: John Conyers, Jr. (Mich.)
National Security (56 members)
Chairman: Floyd D. Spence (S.C.)
Ranking Dem.: Ronald V. Dellums (Calif.)
Energy and Natural Resources (50 members)
Chairman: Don Young (Alaska)
Ranking Dem.: George Miller (Calif.)
Rules (13 members)
Chairman: Gerald B. H. Solomon (N.Y.)
Ranking Dem.: Joe Moakley (Mass.)
Science (46 members)
Chairman: F. James Sensenbrenner Jr. (Wis.)
Ranking Dem.: George E. Brown, Jr. (Calif.)
Small Business (35 members)
Chairman: James M. Talent (Mo.)
Ranking Dem.: John J. LaFalce (N.Y.)
Standards of Official Conduct (10 members)
Chairman: James V. Hansen (Utah)
Ranking Dem.: Howard L. Berman (Calif.)
Transportation and Infrastructure (73 members)
Chairman: Bud Shuster (Pa.)
Ranking Dem.: James L. Obestar (Minn.)
Veterans' Affairs (29 members)
Chairman: Bob Stump (Ariz.)
Ranking Dem.: Lane Evans (Ill.)
Ways and Means (39 members)
Chairman: Bill Archer (Texas)
Ranking Dem.: Charles B. Rangel (N.Y.)

Floor Leaders of the Senate

Democratic	Republican
Gilbert M. Hitchcock, Neb. (Min. 1919–20)	Charles Curtis, Kan. (Maj. 1925–29)
Oscar W. Underwood, Ala. (Min. 1920–23)	James E. Watson, Ind. (Maj. 1929–33)
Joseph T. Robinson, Ark. (Min. 1923–33, Maj. 1933–37)	Charles L. McNary, Ore. (Min. 1933–44)
Alben W. Barkley, Ky. (Maj. 1937–46, Min. 1947–48)	Wallace H. White, Jr., Maine (Min. 1944–47, Maj. 1947–48)
Scott W. Lucas, Ill. (Maj. 1949–50)	Kenneth S. Wherry, Neb. (Min. 1949–51)
Ernest W. McFarland, Ariz. (Maj. 1951–52)	Styles Bridges, N.H. (Min. 1951–52)
Lyndon B. Johnson, Tex. (Min. 1953–54, Maj. 1955–60)	Robert A. Taft, Ohio (Maj. 1953)
Mike Mansfield, Mont. (Maj. 1961–77)	William F. Knowland, Calif. (Maj. 1953–54, Min. 1955–58)
Robert C. Byrd, W. Va. (Maj. 1977–81, Min. 1981–86, Maj. 1987–88)	Everett M. Dirksen, Ill. (Min. 1959–69)
George John Mitchell, Maine (Maj. 1989–1994)	Hugh Scott, Pa. (Min. 1969–1977)
Thomas A. Daschle, S.D. (Min. 1995–)	Howard H. Baker, Jr., Tenn. (Min. 1977–81, Maj. 1981–84)
	Robert J. Dole, Kan. (Maj. 1985–86, Min. 1987–94, Maj. 1995–96)
	Trent Lott, Miss. (Maj. 1996–)

Source: United States Senate, Secretary for the Majority. NOTE: Min. = Minority Leader; Maj. = Majority Leader.

Speakers of the House of Representatives

Dates served	Congress	Name and State	Dates served	Congress	Name and State
1789–1791	1	Frederick A. C. Muhlenberg (Pa.)	1869–1869	40	Theodore M. Pomeroy (N.Y.)[5]
1791–1793	2	Jonathan Trumbull (Conn.)	1869–1875	41–43	James G. Blaine (Maine)
1793–1795	3	Frederick A. C. Muhlenberg (Pa.)	1875–1876	44	Michael C. Kerr (Ind.)[6]
1795–1799	4–5	Jonathan Dayton (N.J.)[1]	1876–1881	44–46	Samuel J. Randall (Pa.)
1799–1801	6	Theodore Sedgwick (Mass.)	1881–1883	47	J. Warren Keifer (Ohio)
1801–1807	7–9	Nathaniel Macon (N.C.)	1883–1889	48–50	John G. Carlisle (Ky.)
1807–1811	10–11	Joseph B. Varnum (Mass.)	1889–1891	51	Thomas B. Reed (Maine)
1811–1814	12–13	Henry Clay (Ky.)[2]	1891–1895	52–53	Charles F. Crisp (Ga.)
1814–1815	13	Langdon Cheves (S.C.)	1895–1899	54–55	Thomas B. Reed (Maine)
1815–1820	14–16	Henry Clay (Ky.)[3]	1899–1903	56–57	David B. Henderson (Iowa)
1820–1821	16	John W. Taylor (N.Y.)	1903–1911	58–61	Joseph G. Cannon (Ill.)
1821–1823	17	Philip P. Barbour (Va.)	1911–1919	62–65	Champ Clark (Mo.)
1823–1825	18	Henry Clay (Ky.)	1919–1925	66–68	Frederick H. Gillett (Mass.)
1825–1827	19	John W. Taylor (N.Y.)	1925–1931	69–71	Nicholas Longworth (Ohio)
1827–1834	20–23	Andrew Stevenson (Va.)[4]	1931–1933	72	John N. Garner (Tex.)
1834–1835	23	John Bell (Tenn.)	1933–1934	73	Henry T. Rainey (Ill.)[7]
1835–1839	24-25	James K. Polk (Tenn.)	1935–1936	74	Joseph W. Byrns (Tenn.)[8]
1839–1841	26	Robert M. T. Hunter (Va.)	1936–1940	74-76	William B. Bankhead (Ala.)[9]
1841–1843	27	John White (Ky.)	1940–1947	76–79	Sam Rayburn (Tex.)
1843–1845	28	John W. Jones (Va.)	1947–1949	80	Joseph W. Martin, Jr. (Mass.)
1845–1847	29	John W. Davis (Ind.)	1949–1953	81–82	Sam Rayburn (Tex.)
1847–1849	30	Robert C. Winthrop (Mass.)	1953–1955	83	Joseph W. Martin, Jr. (Mass.)
1849–1851	31	Howell Cobb (Ga.)	1955–1961	84–87	Sam Rayburn (Tex.)[10]
1851–1855	32–33	Linn Boyd (Ky.)	1962–1971	87–91	John W. McCormack (Mass.)[11]
1855–1857	34	Nathaniel P. Banks (Mass.)	1971–1977	92–94	Carl Albert (Okla.)[12]
1857–1859	35	James L. Orr (S.C.)	1977–1987	95–99	Thomas P. O'Neill, Jr. (Mass.)[13]
1859–1861	36	Wm. Pennington (N.J.)	1987–1989	100–101	James C. Wright, Jr. (Tex.)[14]
1861–1863	37	Galusha A. Grow (Pa.)	1989–1994	101–103	Thomas S. Foley (Wash.)
1863–1869	38-40	Schuyler Colfax (Ind.)	1995–	104–	Newt Gingrich (Ga.)

1. George Dent (Md.) was elected Speaker pro tempore for April 20 and May 28, 1798. 2. Resigned during second session of 13th Congress. 3. Resigned between first and second sessions of 16th Congress. 4. Resigned during first session of 23rd Congress. 5. Elected Speaker and served the day of adjournment. 6. Died between first and second sessions of 44th Congress. During first session, there were two Speakers pro tempore: Samuel S. Cox (N.Y.), appointed for Feb. 17, May 12, and June 19, 1876, and Milton Sayler (Ohio), appointed for June 4, 1876. 7. Died in 1934 after adjournment of second session of 73rd Congress. 8. Died during second session of 74th Congress. 9. Died during third session of 76th Congress. 10. Died between first and second sessions of 87th Congress. 11. Not a candidate in 1970 election. 12. Not a candidate in 1976 election. 13. Not a candidate in 1986 election. 14. Resigned during first session of 101st Congress. Source: Congressional Directory.

Presidential Election of 1996, Electoral and Popular Vote Summary

Principal Candidates for President and Vice President
Democratic: William J. Clinton; Albert A. Gore, Jr.
Republican: Robert J. Dole; Jack F. Kemp
Independent: H. Ross Perot; Pat Choate

	William J. Clinton		Robert J. Dole		H. Ross Perot		Electoral Votes		
	Popular Vote	%	Popular Vote	%	Popular Vote	%	D	R	I
Alabama	662,165	43	769,044	50	92,149	6		9	
Alaska	80,380	33	122,746	51	26,333	11		3	
Arizona	653,288	46	622,073	44	112,072	8	8		
Arkansas	475,171	54	325,416	37	69,884	8	6		
California	5,119,835	51	3,828,380	38	697,847	7	54		
Colorado	671,152	44	691,848	46	99,629	7		8	
Connecticut	735,740	52	483,109	35	139,523	10	8		
Delaware	140,355	52	99,062	37	28,719	11	3		
D.C.	158,220	85	17,339	9	3,611	2	3		
Florida	2,546,870	48	2,244,536	42	483,870	9	25		
Georgia	1,053,849	46	1,080,843	47	146,337	6		13	
Hawaii	205,012	57	113,943	32	27,358	7	4		
Idaho	165,443	34	256,595	52	62,518	13		4	
Illinois	2,341,744	54	1,587,021	37	346,408	8	22		
Indiana	887,424	42	1,006,499	47	224,299	10		12	
Iowa	620,258	50	492,644	40	105,159	8	7		
Kansas	387,659	36	583,245	54	92,639	9		6	
Kentucky	636,614	46	623,283	45	120,396	9	8		
Louisiana	927,837	52	712,586	40	123,293	7	9		
Maine	312,788	52	186,378	31	85,970	14	4		
Maryland	966,207	54	681,530	38	115,812	6	10		
Massachusetts	1,571,763	61	718,107	28	227,217	9	12		
Michigan	1,989,653	52	1,481,212	38	336,670	9	18		
Minnesota	1,120,438	51	766,476	35	257,704	12	10		
Mississippi	394,022	44	439,838	49	52,222	6		7	
Missouri	1,025,935	47	890,016	41	217,188	10	11		
Montana	167,922	41	179,652	44	55,229	13		3	
Nebraska	236,761	35	363,467	54	71,278	10		5	
Nevada	203,974	44	199,244	43	43,986	9	4		
New Hampshire	246,214	49	196,532	39	48,390	10	4		
New Jersey	1,652,329	54	1,103,078	36	262,134	8	15		
New Mexico	273,495	49	232,751	42	32,257	6	5		
New York	3,756,177	59	1,933,492	31	503,458	8	33		
North Carolina	1,107,849	44	1,225,938	49	168,059	7		14	
North Dakota	106,905	40	125,050	47	32,515	12		3	
Ohio	2,148,222	47	1,859,883	40	483,207	11	21		
Oklahoma	488,105	40	582,315	48	130,788	11		8	
Oregon	649,641	47	538,152	39	121,221	9	7		
Pennsylvania	2,215,819	49	1,801,169	40	430,984	10	23		
Rhode Island	233,050	60	104,683	27	43,723	11	4		
South Carolina	506,283	44	573,458	50	64,386	5		8	
South Dakota	139,333	43	150,543	46	31,250	10		3	
Tennessee	909,146	48	863,530	46	105,918	5	11		
Texas	2,459,683	44	2,736,167	49	378,537	7		32	
Utah	221,633	33	361,911	54	66,461	10		5	
Vermont	137,894	53	80,352	31	31,024	12	3		
Virginia	1,091,060	45	1,138,350	47	159,861	7		13	
Washington	1,123,323	50	840,712	37	201,003	9	11		
West Virginia	327,812	51	233,946	37	71,639	11	5		
Wisconsin	1,071,971	49	845,029	39	227,339	10	11		
Wyoming	77,934	37	105,386	50	25,928	12		3	
Total	**47,402,357**	**49%**	**39,198,755**	**41%**	**8,085,402**	**8%**	**379**	**159**	

NOTE: Total electoral votes = 538. Total electoral votes needed to win = 270. Source: Federal Election Commission.

Native Americans

Mascots and Other Public Appropriations of Indian Culture

by Philip J. Deloria, University of Colorado at Boulder

When the Florida State Seminoles football team rushes onto the field, it follows the university's mascot—a stereotyped Indian warrior with colored turkey feathers and a flaming spear, which is planted in the end zone with a whoop. Florida State's fans, many in Indian costume themselves, then proceed to chant a faux-Indian melody, swinging their arms in a synchronized "tomahawk chop." The Florida State experience is a common one. "Indians"—in a variety of flavors ranging from warriors, red men, braves, and chiefs to "Fighting Sioux" and "Apaches" have been the most consistently popular mascot in American athletic history.

The University of Wisconsin at Lacrosse first named its teams Indians in 1909. In 1912, the Boston Braves baseball team followed suit, and three years later, Cleveland's baseball club also became the Indians. During the 1920s, many college and professional teams—including teams at Stanford, Dartmouth, and the University of Illinois, as well as the Chicago Black Hawks hockey club—adopted Indian names. The practice filtered down to thousands of high schools and junior high schools seeking institutional identities. Today, professional sports boasts five major clubs that use "the Indian" as a name and mascot. In addition to Chicago and Cleveland, Atlanta has the Braves, Kansas City has the Chiefs, and Washington, D.C. has the Redskins. While some colleges and universities—including Stanford and Dartmouth—have dropped their Indian logos and mascots, many more continue to insist that their use of Indian stereotypes is harmless fun.

Primitivist Nostalgia

Americans' embrace of Indian mascots was only part of a broad, early-twentieth-century primitivist nostalgia that stamped Indian imagery on a nickel, positioned baskets and pottery in the "Indian corners" of arts-and-crafts revival homes, and permeated the rituals of Boy Scouts and Campfire Girls. At the turn of the century, many Americans perceived that the story they had been telling themselves about their origins and character—one of frontier struggle between bold adventurers and savage Indians—had lost much of its cultural power as historians and critics declared the frontier "closed." On the contemporary side of this closed frontier, Americans saw the modern world—a place of cities, immigrants, technology, lost innocence, and limited opportunity. Many Americans used a ritualized set of symbols—cowboys, Indians, scouts, and pioneers—to evoke the bygone "American" qualities of the frontier era: "authenticity," nature, community, and frontier hardiness. Through summer camp and wilderness outings in "nature," touristic contact with the "authenticity" of Indian primitivism in the southwestern deserts, and an increased emphasis on rugged, character-building athletic competition, they sought to reimagine "modern" compensatory experiences that might take the place of the now-lost "frontier struggle."

The Tomahawk Chop

Bringing Indians—potent symbols both of a nostalgic, innocent past and of the frontier struggle itself—into the athletic stadium helped evoke the mythic narrative being metaphorically replayed on the field. It was no accident that many other mascots—mustangs, pioneers, and so on—were also prominent characters in the athletic rendering of the national story. Indian chiefs and braves represented the aggressiveness and fighting spirit that was supposed to characterize good athletic teams. This racial stereotyping justified an American history in which peaceable cowboys and settlers simply defended themselves against innately aggressive Indians in a defensive conquest of the continent. As mascots celebrated "Indian" ferocity and martial (read also athletic) skill, they were at the same time trophies of Euro-American colonial superiority: "Indians were tough opponents, but 'we' prevailed. Now we 'honor' them (and in doing so, celebrate ourselves)."

The performative aspects of mascot ritual bring this American narrative to life, and demonstrate to participants that their myths, enacted both on the athletic field and in the stands, remain valid. The virulent response to Indian protests against Indian mascots demonstrates the deep emotional investment many Americans have made both in their imagining of Indian people as ahistorical symbols and in their sports affiliations. In mass society, athletic spectacles have become a deeply ingrained tradition to which many Americans turn for personal and social identities. The Florida State Seminole, then, signifies not only the frontieresque American character sought by early-twentieth-century fans, but also a more contemporary longing for the relative purity, simplicity, and tradition of the early twentieth century itself.

Harmless or Offensive?

Indian people have reacted to the use of Indian mascots differently. While many native people expressed dismay, others saw athletic rituals as truly honoring Indians. American Indian Movement (AIM) leader Dennis Banks, for example, has claimed that, until the late 1950s, Stanford and other schools promoted "positive, respectful images" of Indians. According to Banks, during the 1960s fans became more involved in a disrespectful, racist spectacle, and clubs expanded their mascot activities. In Atlanta, for example, "Chief Noc-a-homa" came out of a tipi and danced wildly each time the Braves hit a home run. So while some Indians have always found the very idea of mascots offensive, others do not find it so even today, and still others join Banks in being most concerned about the positive or negative quality of the stereotyping.

In 1972, Banks and other media-conscious Indian activists forcibly brought the mascot issue into public discussion. AIM's Russell Means threatened the Cleveland Indians and the Atlanta Braves baseball clubs with lawsuits, and delegations from AIM, Americans for Indian Opportunity, and the National Congress of American Indians met with Washington Redskins owner

William Bennett to ask him to change the team's name. Aside from cosmetic changes to mascot rituals and team songs, however, these efforts proved unsuccessful. Although Indians continued to protest, the effort to eliminate Indian mascots lost momentum for almost twenty years.

Then, in October 1991, the Atlanta Braves played the Minnesota Twins in baseball's World Series. Just a few months later, in January 1992, the Washington Redskins competed in football's Super Bowl. Both events took place in Minneapolis, a city with a high concentration of Indian people in a state that had been attempting to eliminate Indian mascots at the college and high school levels. This convergence of place, people, and issue launched a series of protests and an often rancorous national dialogue about the appropriateness of Indian mascots in American sports.

Chief Seattle and the Environmental Movement

The practice of appropriating Indians as mascots, good-luck charms, or standard-bearers for nostalgia and national anxiety has not been confined to the ballpark or football field. In the late 1960s, countercultural rebels used a primitivist, antimodern version of "the Indian" to criticize American society for its perceived lack of community, spiritual values, and ecological sensibility. Environmental activists, for example, appropriated the famous "Chief Seattle speech" ("This we know. The earth does not belong to man. Man belongs to the earth"). Many Americans took these words, despite their non-Indian origins in a Southern Baptist-sponsored film script, as a representative "Indian" statement about natural balance and harmony. A well-known 1972 antipollution campaign featuring a teary-eyed Iron Eyes Cody contemplating roadside litter worked in a similar way: as America's "first environmentalists," Indians made admirable mascots for the modern environmental movement.

Black Elk Speaks to the Sixties

Like environmentalists, communitarians also borrowed the trappings of native cultures—tipis, clothing, newly constituted "family" kinship groupings, arts and crafts, and so on—to construct and evoke closely knit communal ties. For many, taking on "Indianized" names like Moonflower and Dancing Bear seemed to be a good way to acquire premodern communal identities. Spiritual and psychedelic seekers sought out their own version of enlightened Indianness. Many followed Sun Bear, Rolling Thunder, and other shamanistic leaders who promised to teach "authentic" Indian practices. A 1972 paperback edition of *Black Elk Speaks*, for

example, aimed specifically at this market, promised an account of a "personal vision that makes an LSD trip pale by comparison." Political radicals opposed to U.S. involvement in Vietnam appropriated nineteenth-century Indian leaders as ancestral rebels against American colonialism. On many walls, one could find a popular series of posters featuring Geronimo, Sitting Bull, and Red Cloud—representational mascots who signified the same type of rebellion political activists themselves sought to foment. Just as Indian athletic mascots contain multiple, overlapping meanings, all of these different forms of countercultural activity blended together as people imagined and appropriated new meanings for "Indians."

Old Traditions for a New Age

None of these ideas about Indians originated or were contained in a historical vacuum. The use of "Indians" as mascots for a nostalgic antimodernism has a long history in American culture. One can trace the 1960s counterculture back through the 1950s primitivism of beat intellectuals to the early-twentieth-century antimodern criticism of New Mexico figures such as John Colliers, D.H. Lawrence, and Mabel Dodge Luhan. Likewise, the same set of ideas about Indian people resurfaced later, in the 1980s and 1990s, under the auspices of the New Age and men's movements.

The continual use of Indianness as an important American symbol has raised serious questions and dilemmas for native people. Some Indians, for example, have left their communities and performed for white Americans a series of "positive" antimodern roles—spiritual "teacher," eco-guru, community sage—in order to acquire political and economic power. While such performances indeed generate valuable cultural capital, they also force Indian people to define themselves around non-Indian criteria. For other native people, it has become increasingly apparent that, in an age of mass communication, Indians need to exert some control over—or, at the very least, constantly challenge—any and all ways they are represented in public discourse. As a result, many Indian people—in contrast to many non-Indians—have found struggles against the use of Indian mascots and against the activities of non-Indian countercultural and New Age spokespersons to be critical and significant in terms of social, cultural, and political survival.

Philip J. Deloria is a member of a prominent Lakota family and a coauthor of *The Native Americans*. He received his Ph.D. from Yale and teaches at the University of Colorado at Boulder. Reprinted with permission of Houghton Mifflin Company from *Encyclopedia of North American Indians*, ed. Frederick E. Hoxie, 1996.

Latest Estimates of American Indian Population

(as of July 1, 1996)

	All ages	Under 5 years	5 to 17 years	18 to 24 years	25 to 44 years	45 to 64 years	65 years and over	Median age
American Indian, Eskimo & Aleut	1,954,000	169,000	504,000	220,000	603,000	323,000	134,000	27.6
Male	961,000	85,000	256,000	111,000	298,000	154,000	57,000	26.7
Female	993,000	84,000	249,000	109,000	304,000	169,000	78,000	28.6

Source: U.S. Census Bureau, Department of Commerce, *U.S. Population Estimates by Age, Sex, Race, and Hispanic Origin: 1990 to 1996, PPL-57.*

American Indian Tribes With Populations Greater Than 10,000

(1990 U.S. Census figures)

American Indian Tribe	Number	Percent distribution	American Indian Tribe	Number	Percent distribution
American Indian population, total[1]	1,878,285	100.0	Canadian and Latin American	22,379	1.2
Cherokee	308,132	16.4	Chickasaw	20,631	1.1
Navajo	219,198	11.7	Potawatomi	16,763	0.9
Chippewa	103,826	5.5	Tohono O'Odham	16,041	0.9
Sioux	103,255	5.5	Pima	14,431	0.8
Choctaw	82,299	4.4	Tlingit	13,925	0.7
Pueblo	52,939	2.8	Seminole	13,797	0.7
Apache	50,051	2.7	Alaskan Athabaskans	13,738	0.7
Iroquois	49,038	2.6	Cheyenne	11,456	0.6
Lumbee	48,444	2.6	Comanche	11,322	0.6
Creek	43,550	2.3	Paiute	11,142	0.6
Blackfoot	32,234	1.7	Puget Sound Salish	10,246	0.5

1. Includes other American Indian tribes, not shown separately. *Source:* U.S. Bureau of the Census, *1990 Census of Population, General Population Characteristics, American Indian and Alaska Native Areas* (CP-1-1A); and press releases CB91-232 and CB92-244

Social and Economic Characteristics of the American Indian Population

(1990 Census figures)

Characteristic	American Indian, total[1]	Chero-kee	Navajo	Sioux	Chip-pewa	Choctaw	Pueblo	Apache	Iro-quois	Lumbee
Total persons	1,937,391	369,035	225,298	107,321	105,988	86,231	55,330	53,330	52,557	50,888
Percent under 5 years old	9.7	6.3	13.6	12.3	10.3	8.2	10.3	10.2	8.1	8.3
Percent 18 years old and over	65.8	73.3	57.7	60.0	64.0	68.8	64.2	64.7	71.1	66.2
Percent 65 years old and over	5.9	7.2	4.6	4.4	4.7	8.0	5.8	3.4	6.7	5.6
Educational Attainment										
Persons 25 years old and over	1,040,955	229,231	100,594	51,014	54,804	49,128	28,597	27,717	30.882	27,343
Percent high school graduates or higher	65.6	68.2	51.0	69.7	69.7	70.3	71.5	63.8	71.9	51.6
Percent bachelor's degree or higher	9.4	11.1	4.5	8.9	8.2	13.3	7.3	6.9	11.3	9.4
Family Type										
Total families	449,281	98,610	44,845	22,669	25,077	21,856	11,825	12,314	12,988	12,650
Percent distribution: Married couple	65.8	73.1	61.1	54.2	58.4	75.2	61.2	66.9	67.5	68.5
Female householder, no spouse present	26.2	20.8	28.6	36.0	33.1	20.0	29.2	24.7	25.5	23.9
Male householder, no spouse present	8.0	6.1	10.3	9.8	8.5	4.8	9.6	8.4	7.0	7.6
Income in 1989										
Median family (dol.)	21,619	24,907	13,940	16,525	20,249	24,467	19,845	19,690	27,025	23,934
Median household (dol.)	19,900	21,922	12,817	15,611	18,801	21,640	19,097	18,484	23,460	21,708
Per capita (dol.)	8,284	10,469	4,788	6,508	7,777	9,463	6,679	7,271	10,568	8,625
Families below poverty level	122,237	19,100	21,204	8,939	7,814	4,347	3,691	3,913	2,249	2,554
Percent below poverty level	27.2	19.4	47.3	39.4	31.2	19.9	31.2	31.8	17.3	20.2
Persons below poverty level	585,273	79,271	107,526	45,658	35,231	19,453	17,981	19,246	10,253	10,966
Percent below poverty level	31.2	22.0o	48.8	44.4	34.3	23.0	33.2	37.5	20.1	22.1

1. Includes other American Indian tribes not shown separately. *Source:* U.S. Bureau of the Census, *1990 Census of Population, Characteristics of American Indians by Tribe and Language,* 1990 CP-3-7.

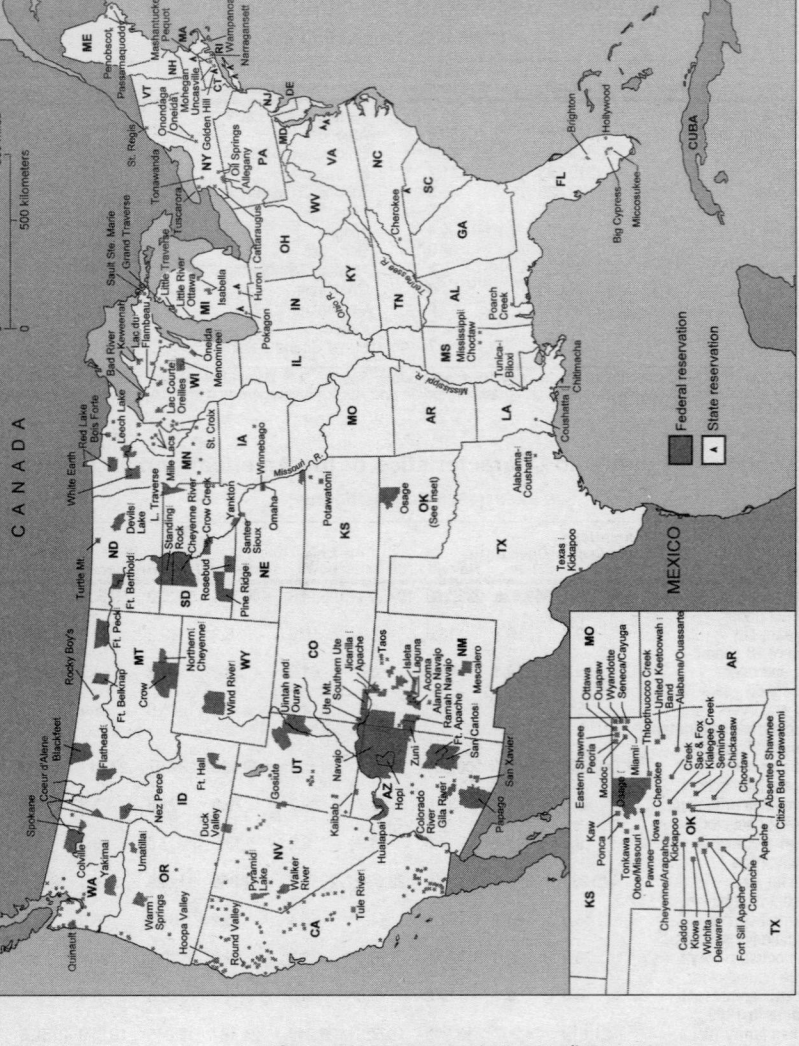

U.S. Federal and State Reservations

Populations of the Ten Largest Reservations
(1990 Census figures)

Name	Population
Navajo (Ariz., N.M., Utah)	143,405
Pine Ridge (Neb., S.D.)	11,182
Fort Apache (Ariz.)	9,825
Gila River (Ariz.)	9,116
Papago (Ariz.)	8,480
Rosebud (S.D.)	8,043
San Carlos (Ariz.)	7,110
Zuni Pueblo (Ariz., N.M.)	7,073
Hopi (Ariz.)	7,061
Blackfeet (Mont.)	7,025

The 218,320 American Indians living on these 10 reservations account for about half of all American Indians living on reservations and trust lands. *Source:* 1990 Census. *Map source:* Frederick E. Hoxie, ed., *Encyclopedia of North American Indians* (Boston: Houghton Mifflin, 1996). Reprinted with permission.

Legend:
- Federal reservation
- ▲ State reservation

Facts About American Indians Today

Source: Bureau of Indian Affairs, U.S. Department of the Interior

Who is an Indian?

No single federal or tribal criterion establishes a person's identity as an Indian. Tribal membership is determined by the enrollment criteria of the tribe from which Indian blood may be derived, and this varies with each tribe. Generally, if linkage to an identified tribal member is far removed, one would not qualify for membership.

To be eligible for Bureau of Indian Affairs services, an Indian must (1) be a member of a tribe recognized by the federal government, (2) be of one-half or more Indian blood of tribes indigenous to the United States; or (3) must, for some purposes, be of one-fourth or more Indian ancestry. By legislative and administrative decision, the Aleuts, Eskimos and Indians of Alaska are eligible for BIA services. Most of the BIA's services and programs, however, are limited to Indians living on or near Indian reservations.

The Bureau of the Census counts anyone an Indian who declares himself or herself to be an Indian. In 1990 the Census figures showed there were 1,959,234 American Indians and Alaska Natives living in the United States (1,878,285 American Indians, 57,152 Eskimos, and 23,797 Aleuts). This is a 37.9 percent increase over the 1980 recorded total of 1,420,000. The increase is attributed to improved census taking and more self-identification during the 1990 count.

How does one trace Indian ancestry and become a member of a tribe?

The first step in tracing Indian ancestry is basic genealogical research if one does not already have specific family information and documents that identify tribal ties. Some information to obtain is: names of ancestors; dates of birth, marriages and death; places where they lived; brothers and sisters, if any; and, most importantly, tribal affiliations. Among family documents to check are Bibles, wills, and other such papers. The next step is to determine whether one's ancestors are on an official tribal roll or census by contacting the tribe.

What is a federally recognized tribe?

There are more than 550 federally recognized tribes in the United States, including 223 village groups in Alaska. "Federally recognized" means these tribes and groups have a special, legal relationship with the U.S. government. This relationship is referred to as a government-to-government relationship.

A number of Indian tribes and groups in the U.S. do not have a federally recognized status, although some are state-recognized. This means they have no relations with the BIA or the programs it operates. A special program of the BIA, however, works with those groups seeking federal recognition status. Of the 150 petitions for federal recognition received by the BIA since 1978, 12 have received acknowledgment through the BIA process, two groups had their status clarified by the Department of the Interior through other means, and seven were restored or recognized by Congress.

Reservations.

In the U.S. there are only two kinds of reserved lands that are well-known: military and Indian. An Indian reservation is land reserved for a tribe when it relinquished its other land areas to the U.S. through treaties. More recently, Congressional acts, Executive Orders, and administrative acts have created reservations. Today some reservations have non-Indian residents and land owners.

There are approximately 275 Indian land areas in the U.S. administered as Indian reservations (reservations, pueblos, rancherias, communities, etc.). The largest is the Navajo Reservation of some 16 million acres of land in Arizona, New Mexico, and Utah. Many of the smaller reservations are less than 1,000 acres with the smallest less than 100 acres. On each reservation, the local governing authority is the tribal government.

Approximately 56.2 million acres of land are held in trust by the United States for various Indian tribes and individuals. Much of this is reservation land; however, not all reservation land is trust land. On behalf of the United States, the Secretary of the Interior serves as trustee for such lands with many routine trustee responsibilities delegated to BIA officials.

The states in which reservations are located have limited powers over them, and only as provided by federal law. On some reservations, however, a high percentage of the land is owned and occupied by non-Indians. Some 140 reservations have entirely tribally owned land.

Taxes.

Indians pay the same taxes as other citizens with the following exceptions: federal income taxes are not levied on income from trust lands held for them by the United States; state income taxes are not paid on income earned on an Indian reservation; state sales taxes are not paid by Indians on transactions made on an Indian reservation; and local property taxes are not paid on reservation or trust land.

Laws.

As U.S. citizens, Indians are generally subject to federal, state, and local laws. On Indian reservations, however, only federal and tribal laws apply to members of the tribe unless the Congress provides otherwise. In federal law, the Assimilative Crimes Act makes any violation of state criminal law a federal offense on reservations. Most tribes now maintain tribal court systems and facilities to detain tribal members convicted of certain offenses within the boundaries of the reservation.

Indian Gaming Regulations.

Indian land is not under state law unless a federal law places it under state law. The Supreme Court held that even if a tribe is under state law the state gaming regulations do not apply on Indian trust land. In 1988 Congress passed the Indian Gaming Regulatory Act. This law allows traditional Indian gaming as well as bingo, pull tabs, lotto, punch boards, tip jars, and certain card games on tribal land. However, it requires a tribal/state compact for other forms of gaming such as cards or slot machines. Today there are about 145 tribal-state gaming compacts. Nearly 130 tribes in 24 states are involved in some kind of gaming. The National Indian Gaming Commission was established by Congress to develop regulations for Indian gaming. For more information contact the National Indian Gaming Commission, 9th Floor, 1441 L Street, N.W., Washington, DC 20005, 202-632-7003.

Why are Indians sometimes referred to as Native Americans?

The term, "Native American," came into usage in the 1960s to denote the groups served by the Bureau of Indian Affairs: American Indians and Alaska Natives (Indians, Eskimos and Aleuts of Alaska). Later the term also included Native Hawaiians and Pacific Islanders in some federal programs. It, therefore, came into disfavor among some Indian groups. The preferred term is American Indian. The Eskimos and Aleuts in Alaska are two culturally distinct groups and are sensitive about being included under the "Indian" designation. They prefer "Alaska Native."

American Indian Languages Spoken at Home by American Indian Persons 5 Years and Over in Households: 1990

	Number of households		Number of households
All American Indian languages	281,990	Muskogean languages	13,772
Algonquian languages	12,887	Penutian languages	8,190
Athapascan Eyak languages	157,694	Siouan languages	19,693
Caddoan languages	354	Tanoan languages	8,255
Central and South American Indian languages	431	Tlingit	1,088
		Tonkawa	3
Haida	110	Uto-Aztecan languages	23,493
Hokan languages	2,430	Wakashan and Salish languages	1,105
Iroquoian languages	12,046	Yuchi	65
Keres	8,346	Unspecified American Indian languages	12,038

Source: U.S. Bureau of the Census. The American Indian languages shown above are the major languages. NOTE: Data are estimates based on a sample.

Major Pre-Columbian Indian Cultures in the United States

Date	Culture or event	Comments
c. 15,000 years ago, near the end of the Ice Age[1]	First migration of Paleo-Indians in North America by people of Beringian subcontinent.	Nomadic hunters from northeast Asia are believed to have crossed the Bering Strait land bridge (that scientists call Beringia) into present-day Alaska.
c. 11,200 years ago	Clovis Culture	Known for invention of superbly crafted grooved or fluted stone projectiles (Clovis points) first found near Clovis, New Mexico, in 1932. Clovis points have been found throughout the Americas. Hunted big game, notably mammoths.
c. 10,900 years ago	Folsom Culture	Named for site found near Folsom, New Mexico, 1926. Developed a smaller, thinner, fluted spear point than Clovis type. Hunted big game, notably the huge bison ancestor of the modern buffalo. First used a spear-throwing device called an atlatl (an Aztec word for "spear-thrower"). Discovery of Folsom point in 1927 gave first proof of Glacial Man in America.
c. 10,500 years ago	Plano or Plainview Culture	Named after the site in Plainview, Texas. They are associated primarily with the Great Plains area. Were bison hunters. Developed a delicately flaked spear point that lacked fluting. Adopted mass-hunting technique (jump-kill) to drive animal herds off a cliff. Preserved meat in the form of pemmican. First to use grinding stones to grind seeds and meat.
c. 8,500 years ago	Northwest Coast Indians. Some modern descendants are the Tlingit, Haida, Kwakiutl, Nootka, and Makah tribes.	Settled along the shores, rivers, and creeks of southeastern Alaska to northern California. A maritime culture, were expert canoe builders. Salmon fishing was important. Some tribes hunted whales and other sea mammals. Developed a high culture without the benefit of agriculture, pottery, or influence of ancient Mexican civilizations. Tribes lived in large, complex communities, constructed multifamily cedar plank houses. Evolved a caste system of chiefs, commoners, and slaves. Were highly skilled in crafts and woodworking that reached their height after European contact, which provided them steel tools. Placed an inordinate value on accumulated wealth and property. Held lavish feasts (called potlatches) to display their wealth and social status. Important site: Ozette, Wash. (a Makah village).
c. 500 B.C.E.–C.E. 200	Adena Culture	Named for the estate called Adena near Chillicothe, Ohio, where their earthwork mounds were first found. Culture was centered in present southern Ohio, but also lived in Pennsylvania, Indiana, Kentucky, and West Virginia. Were the pioneer mound builders in the U.S. and constructed spectacular burial and effigy mounds. Settled in villages of circular post-and-wattle houses. Primarily hunter-gatherers, they farmed corn, tobacco, squash, pumpkins, and sunflowers at an early date. Important sites: The Adena Mound, Ohio; Grave Creek Mound, W.V.; Monks Mound, Ill., is the largest mound. May have built the Great Serpent Mound in Ohio.

Date	Culture or event	Comments
c. c.e. 300–1300	Hohokam people (a Pima Indian word meaning "The Vanished Ones"). Believed to be ancestors of the modern Papago (Tohono O'odham) and Pima (Akimel O'odham) Indian groups.	Settled in present-day Arizona. Were desert farmers. Cultivated corn. Were first to grow cotton in the Southwest. Wove cotton fabrics. Built pit houses and later multi-storied buildings (pueblos). Constructed vast network of irrigation systems. Major canals were over 30 miles long. Built ball courts and truncated pyramids similar to those found in Middle America. First in world known to master etching (etched shells with fermented Saguaro juice). Traded with Mesoamerican Toltecs. Important sites: Pueblo Grande, Ariz.; Snaketown, Ariz; Casa Grande, Ariz.
c. 300 b.c.e.–c.e. 1100	Mogollon Culture	Were highland farmers but also hunters in what is now eastern Arizona and southwestern New Mexico. Named after cluster of mountain peaks along Arizona-New Mexico border. They developed pit houses, later dwelt in pueblos. Were accomplished stoneworkers. Famous for magnificent black on white painted pottery (Minbres Valley pottery), the finest North American native ceramics. Important settlements: Casa Malpais, Ariz. (first ancient catacombs in U.S., discovered there 1990); Gila Cliff, N.M.; Galaz, N.M. Casa Grandes in Mexico was largest settlement.
c. 300 b.c.e.–c.e. 1300	Anasazi (a Navajo word meaning "The Ancient Ones"). Their descendants are the Hopi and other Pueblo Indians.	Inhabited Colorado Plateau "four corners," where Arizona, New Mexico, Utah, and Colorado meet. An agricultural society that cultivated cotton, wove cotton fabrics. The early Anasazi are known as the Basketmaker People for their extraordinary basketwork. Were skilled workers in stone. Carved stone Kachina dolls. Built pit houses, later apartment-like pueblos. Constructed road networks. Were avid astronomers. Used a solar calendar. Traded with Mesoamerican Toltecs. Important sites: Chaco Canyon, N.M.; Mesa Verde, Colo.; Canyon de Chelly, Ariz.; Bandelier, N.M.; Betatkin, N.M. The Acoma Pueblo, N.M., built c. c.e. 1300 and still occupied, may be the oldest continuously inhabited village in the U.S.
c. 100 b.c.e.–c.e. 500	Hopewell Culture. May be ancestors of present-day Zuni Indians.	Named after site in southern Ohio. Lived in Ohio valley, central Mississippi, and Illinois River Valleys. Were both hunter-gatherers and farmers. Villages were built along rivers, characterized by large conical or dome-shaped burial mounds and elaborate earthen walls enclosing large oval or rectangular areas. Were highly skilled craftsmen in pottery, stone, sculpture, and metalworking, especially copper. Engaged in widespread trade all over northern America extending west to the Rocky Mountains. Important sites: Newark Mound, Ohio; Great Serpent Mound, Ohio; Crooks Mound, La.
c. c.e.700–European contact.	Mississippi Culture. Major tribes of the Southeast are their modern descendants.	Extended from Mississippi Valley into Alabama, Georgia, and Florida. Constructed large flat-topped earthen mounds on which were built wooden temples and meeting houses and residences of chiefs and priests. (They were also known as Temple Mound Builders.) Built huge cedar pole circles ("woodhenges") for astronomical observations. Were highly skilled hunters with bow and arrow. Practiced large-scale farming of corn, beans, and squash. Were skilled craftsmen. Falcon and Jaguar were common symbols in their art. Had clear ties with Mexico. The largest Mississippian center and largest of all mounds (Monks Mound) was at Cahokia, Ill. Other great temple centers were at Spiro, Okla.; Moundville, Ala.; and Etowah, Ga.

Dates may vary according to different sources. 1. There is no consensus when people first migrated to the Americas. Estimates vary between 12,000 and 50,000 years ago. However, archaeologists have established that humans already lived in rock shelters and other sites at the southern tip of Argentina (Tierra del Fuego) between 11,500 and 10,000 years ago.

Business & Economy

Major Business Events in 1997

January 1997

Intel Reports Doubled Profits in Fourth Quarter (Jan. 15): Booming international and corporate demand drove the chip maker's revenue to $6.44 billion, an increase of 41%. Intel's continuing strong results led some analysts to predict that it could become the world's most profitable company by 1998 or 1999.

Columbia/HCA Healthcare Signs Definitive Agreement to Acquire Value Health (Jan. 16): The transaction, valued at approximately $1.3 billion in a tax-free stock swap, will provide Columbia with specialty health care services offered by Value Health.

Pepsico Spins Off $11 Billion Restaurant Business (Jan. 23): Proposed sale of Pizza Hut and Taco Bell businesses reverses diversification strategy to return to its roots in beverage and snacks industries.

ABC Ordered to Pay $5.5 Million in Damages (Jan. 23): A federal jury awards Food Lion punitive damages for a hidden camera report accusing the grocery chain of selling tainted food. Food Lion did not dispute the facts of the story, but sued over the way in which the facts were obtained.

Wealth Distribution Gap Narrows (Jan. 24): The Federal Reserve Board releases data that finds middle income families enjoyed higher growth in net worth than wealthy families in 1995, as compared to surveys conducted in 1989 and 1992.

American Express Announces 3,300 Layoffs (Jan. 28): In its fourth round of staff cuts since 1991, American Express plans to trim another 5% of its workforce amidst reports of solid earnings that meet analyst expectations.

Barnes & Noble Teams with America Online to Sell Books Online (Jan. 28): In a bid to compete with the likes of Amazon.com, Barnes & Noble prepares to launch a major venture with AOL.

America Online Reaches Settlement with Customers (Jan. 30): Settles class-action suit by customers disgruntled at inaccessibility of the service since AOL introduced its flat-rate pricing in December. Agrees to refund up to $40 per customer to compensate for lost online time.

February 1997

Morgan Stanley and Dean Witter, Discover Agree to Merge (Feb. 5): The $8.8 billion stock swap will create the largest securities firm in the nation, with a market capitalization of $20 billion.

America Online Reports Loss (Feb. 7): AOL reports a loss of $155 million for its fiscal second quarter in the wake of refunds to angry customers who encountered busy signals when they tried to log on. AOL plans to add 50,000 modems by April to meet the surge in demand that followed their flat-rate pricing announced in December.

1996 IPOs raise $11.8 Billion (Feb. 7): VentureOne Corporation's 1996 Report of Venture-Backed Companies reports a banner year for initial public offerings. A record 260 venture-backed companies went public in 1996, most from information technology and life sciences industries.

Judge Upholds Tobacco Disclosure (Feb. 9): A Massachusetts law requiring tobacco companies to disclose ingredients in cigarettes is upheld by a federal judge. The law requires that ingredients be listed by "weight, measure, or numerical count," which tobacco companies argue would require disclosure of trade secrets.

Dow Breaks 7000 Barrier (Feb. 13): After a 103.52 gain led by technology stocks the day before, the Dow Jones Industrial Average soars 61 points to close at 7022.82. Other composite indices, Standard & Poor's and the NYSE, also set new highs.

American Strike Sparks Fare War (Feb. 18): The American Airlines pilots' strike lasted just 24 minutes before President Clinton signed an executive order mandating a 60-day cooling off period. To lure back travelers who had postponed or made plans on other carriers, American slashes its fares; rival carriers follow suit, creating deep discounts for consumers. American's pilots vow to strike again in 60 days unless demands for new contracts and higher wages are met. **Pilots Ratify Agreement (May 6):** 69.3 percent of American's pilots vote to ratify a five-year agreement, concluding months of negotiations.

Philip Morris Shredded Damning Documents (Feb. 21): A chemist who worked for Philip Morris in the 1980s says in a deposition that he was ordered to shred documents revealing high levels of carcinogens in cigarette smoke. He also testified that cigarettes sold to consumers contain more chemical additives than those used for research tests.

Raytheon to Sell Appliance Division (Feb. 24): In a bid to return to its core business in the defense industry, Raytheon hopes to raise $1 billion or more as it sells off its appliance division, which includes Amana and Speed Queen, among other brands.

3Com to Buy U.S. Robotics for $6.6 Billion (Feb. 27): In what will be the second-largest technology acquisition ever, 3Com hopes to challenge Cisco Systems, the leader in the network-equipment market.

SEC to Mutual Funds: "Simplify" (Feb. 28): If new Securities and Exchange Commission proposals are implemented, prospectuses for over 6,000 mutual funds will be simple enough for Aunt Edna to understand. The reforms are meant to address the overwhelming numbers of first-time and individual investors who have been placing their retirement savings into the stock market through mutual funds.

March 1997

Microsoft Buys Web Site Analysis Company (Mar. 4): Financial terms were not disclosed for Microsoft's purchase of Interse Corp., a developer of software that tracks the number and behavior of visitors to a web page. The acquisition continues Microsoft's trend in acquiring Internet-related technologies.

CSX to Buy Conrail for $10.5 Billion (Mar. 4): Conrail's board approves the deal, ending one of the most expensive takeovers in railroad history. CSX will sell off parts of Northeast route system, over which it now holds a monopoly.

Bank of America to Extend Health Benefits to All Domestic Partners (Mar. 11): Starting January 1, 1998, the bank plans to extend its current policy of offering health care coverage to spouses and dependent children of its U.S. employees to also cover domestic partners of the same or opposite sex. Though many high-technology companies, such as IBM and Hewlett-Packard, currently employ this policy, San Francisco-based Bank of America is believed to be the first bank to do so.

FTC Blocks Staples' Purchase of Office Depot (Mar. 11): The ruling stated that the $4 billion merger would violate antitrust laws and increase prices for office supplies.

Staples said it would fight the ruling. **(Mar. 13):** Staples agrees to sell 63 stores to OfficeMax to ensure compliance with antitrust laws. **(July 1):** Federal judge rules that the acquisition would violate antitrust laws; negotiations end.

Dow Jones Industrial Average Changes Composition (Mar. 13): Effective March 17, four companies will be replaced in the largest change in the history of the index. Travelers, Hewlett-Packard, Johnson & Johnson, and Wal-Mart will replace outgoing Westinghouse, Texaco, Bethlehem Steel, and Woolworth.

ESPNET SportZone to Allow Short-term Subscriptions (Mar. 17): In an unprecedented move among major Web sites, the company announced plans to offer subscriptions for daily use, rather than the monthly or annual models pursued by most sites.

Liggett Admits Cigarettes are Addictive (Mar. 21): In a boost to the Justice Department's investigation of the tobacco industry, the Liggett Group reached a historic settlement with the attorneys general from 22 states in which the company admitted to knowledge that cigarettes are addictive, agreed to put warnings to that effect on the package, and agreed to provide documents that could implicate other tobacco companies currently facing lawsuits. News of the settlement sent tobacco industry stocks into a tailspin.

Amazon.com Files for IPO (Mar. 25): The Seattle-based pioneer of bookselling over the Internet filed for an initial public offering, which values the firm at almost $300 million.

Fed Raises Rates (Mar. 26): In a move aimed at heading off inflation, the Federal Reserve raised the federal funds rate to 5.5%. Though Wall Street had long anticipated the move, the markets were volatile and trading was heavy.

Texaco Settlement Approved (Mar. 26): The largest settlement ever awarded in a racial discrimination suit, $176.1 million, has been approved by a federal judge, and will benefit blacks employed in salaried positions from March 1991 through November 1996.

April

Apple Computer Seeks Buyer (Apr. 3): Unable to find internal solutions to its many problems, Apple Computer is reportedly seeking a friendly merger. Oracle chairman Larry Ellison has formed a group to determine investor interest in buying Apple, while Sun Microsystems continues its direct discussions with Apple. **(Apr. 30):** Ellison announces he will not bid for Apple at this time, but may reconsider. **(July 10):** CEO Gilbert Amelio is fired as co-founder Steve Jobs's role is expanded. Jobs returned to Apple when it purchased NeXT computer in 1996.

Bankers Trust Buys Alex. Brown (Apr. 7): The stock swap, valued at around $1.7 billion, is the largest purchase of a securities firm by a U.S. commercial bank, and is the clearest indication yet of the deterioration of the Glass-Steagall law mandating the separation of commercial and investment banking enterprises.

Microsoft Buys WebTV for $425 Million (Apr. 7): The combination stock and cash deal will provide Microsoft access to low-cost Internet devices, which it plans to use to expedite the development of digital television. **Justice Department Scrutinizes the Deal (May 20):** Microsoft announces that the Justice Department has requested more information regarding the planned acquisition.

Garment Makers Sued Over Misrepresenting Origin of Clothing (Apr. 10): Limited Inc. and many of its subsidiaries (Victoria's Secret, Abercrombie & Fitch, Lane Bryant, Cacique, and Express) are being sued by a textile industry group that claims the company purchased garments manufactured in China then claimed they were made in Hong Kong, a violation of customs laws.

Tobacco Companies Discuss Settlement (Apr. 16): Philip Morris and RJR Nabisco are discussing ways to limit liability for the cigarette industry in current and future lawsuits by setting up a fund of $300 billion to pay out claims over the next 25 years. The settlement, which would require new legislation and therefore Congressional approval, may include stricter regulation of advertising and sale of tobacco products.

U.S. Budget Deficit Shrinks 13% (Apr. 22): An increase in individual tax receipts caused the deficit to decrease to $111.28 billion compared to the same six-month period a year ago.

Judge Says FDA Can Regulate Cigarettes (Apr. 28): In another blow to the embattled tobacco industry, a federal judge rules that cigarettes can be regulated. Attorneys general from 24 states are suing the industry to recover costs of treating smoking-related illnesses.

Federal Debt Declines by $65 Billion (Apr. 29): A dramatic rise in tax receipts has enabled the Treasury to pay down the deficit, only the second such cut in the debt since 1981, and the largest ever. **U.S. Government Surplus . . . ? (May 22):** The government announced that, due to record individual income tax return revenue, it posted a $93.94 billion surplus in April. The surplus oiled the wheels of budget negotiations, since all sides could attain their goals without the severe budget cutbacks needed in previous years.

May 1997

Scudder for Sale (May 1): The mutual-fund firm is expected to sell for $1 to $1.5 billion, with bids coming from U.S. and foreign financial institutions. **(June 27):** Swiss insurance firm Zurich Group agrees to purchase Scudder, Stevens & Clark in a deal that could be valued at $2 billion.

Unemployment Drops to 4.9% for April (May 2): Despite slow jobs growth, with only 142,000 non-farm jobs added to payrolls in April, unemployment fell to its lowest rate in over 23 years.

Bre-X Minerals Says Land is Worthless (May 5): In what has become the largest-scale securities fraud in mining history, Canada's Bre-X Minerals Ltd. admits that earlier claims that the Busang gold discovery was the richest this century were unfounded and based on falsified evidence. **Bre-X Stock Delisted (May 8):** The Toronto Stock Exchange halted trading of the stock as the police inquiry into the Busang property begins. **Bre-X Files for Bankruptcy (May 9):** Top officers resigned as the company seeks protection from its creditors in the latest fallout from the Busang fraud.

Dow Surpasses 7200 (May 5): Exuberant over the balanced budget agreement and settlement of a Florida tobacco suit, the Dow Jones Industrial Average surges 143.29 points to close at 7,214.49.

R.J. Reynolds Wins Wrongful Death Suit (May 5): A Florida jury found that Reynolds was not negligent and denied claims by the plaintiff's family that the company was responsible for the death of a long-time smoker.

GTE to Buy BBN (May 6): The Internet pioneer is expected to sell for well over its current market capitalization of $500 million, perhaps as much as $1 billion. **Price set at $616 Million (May 7):** GTE confirmed plans to purchase BBN for $616 million and to spend $2 billion in capital expenditures over the next four years.

PNC Bank to Buy Oppenheimer for $500 Million (May 8): The mid-sized securities firm is also receiving offers from other suitors seeking to shore up their position in the consolidating U.S. securities business.

US Air To Drop Routes (May 9): In an effort to curb its costs, the highest in the airline industry, US Airways is planning to ground 22 planes and trim 6.5% of all flights to eliminate unprofitable routes.

Sun Microsystems Skirts Security Law (May 10): In a move bound to draw government criticism, Sun plans to sell encryption technology from a Russian supplier to overseas firms. Government regulations prohibit the sale of such technologies to international markets in an effort to control the proliferation of security software, which it believes jeopardizes national security.

Digital Sues Intel (May 14): Digital Equipment Corp. filed suit against Intel Corp. claiming patent infringement. Digital claims that certain elements of the Pentium chip line were based on Digital's Alpha chip semiconductor technology, and that these elements were stolen from Digital. **Intel Sues Digital (May 28):** Intel's suit claims Digital has failed to return certain confidential documents pertaining to Intel microprocessors and other technologies. **(July 24):** Digital accuses Intel of monopolistic business practices.

GM to Make Cars in China (May 20): The leading U.S. automaker reached an agreement with the Chinese government that leaves the company poised to set up shop in China, whose emerging economy is especially promising as both a labor market and an outlet for finished goods.

AT&T to Buy Baby Bell for $50 Billion (May 27): AT&T is negotiating with SBC Communications, parent company to Southwestern Bell and Pacific Telesis, in a deal that would be the largest acquisition ever. Critics claim the combination will return AT&T to the monopolistic status it held prior to the antitrust suit, reducing competition from local (and foreign) companies. **(June 27):** Concerns about governmental opposition to the merger derail the discussions.

Bribery Outlawed as Tactic (May 27): An agreement among leading industrial nations promises to improve the chances of fair competition by making it illegal to bribe officials to gain commercial contracts.

June 1997

Sears Reaches Settlement Over Questionable Collections Practices (June 5): Sears admitted to going after consumers who had filed for bankruptcy, and will now repay them $100 million. They still face a Justice Department investigation and a lawsuit by 39 state attorneys general.

Networks Rake in Ad Revenue for Fall Line-up (June 5): NBC, CBS, ABC, and Fox project $6 billion in advance sales, up 6% over last year.

Northwest Snubs Boeing (June 6): In a boost to Airbus Industrie's lagging sales to U.S.-based airlines, Northwest plans to purchase 50 of the company's smallest aircraft. The deal would be worth around $2 billion at list prices for the planes. Airbus had recently complained that Boeing's sole-supplier agreements with American, Delta, and Continental were hindering its ability to compete.

Lowest Unemployment Since 1973 (June 9): May's unemployment rate fell to 4.8% from 4.9% in April. Wages rose slightly, but economists believe there is insufficient inflationary pressure to overheat the economy.

Chrysler Passes on the Gas (June 10): In a bid to meet federal standards for developing fuel-efficient vehicles, Chrysler plans to introduce engines that can run on ethanol as well as gasoline in a third of its future minivans.

Dow Does it Again (June 12): For the fourth time in June and the seventh time in 1997, the Dow Jones Industrial Average surpasses a 100-point milestone. It passed the 7000 mark in February, and twice broke two 100-point barriers within a single trading session, on May 5 and June 12.

Royal Caribbean Has a Little Celebrity Coming (June 18): In a deal worth $1.3 billion, Royal Caribbean agreed to acquire Celebrity Cruise Lines. Royal Caribbean will assume Celebrity's debts (some $800 million) and pay $500 million in stock and cash.

McDonald's Wins Hollow Victory (June 20): Though it won its libel suit against two vegetarian activists in Britain, the international conglomerate spent three years and mil-

lions of dollars making its case, and is unlikely to collect the $98,298 award from its penniless defendants.

Historic Tobacco Industry Agreement (June 23): In an agreement worked out between public health officials, tobacco industry leaders, and the attorneys general from several of the 39 states who had sued to recoup costs of treating smokers' health ailments, the tobacco companies would pay $368.5 billion over the next 25 years to settle future claims. The FDA would regulate the levels of nicotine in cigarettes, and the industry would be prohibited from advertising targeted to minors. The deal, which has been months in the making, now faces months of Congressional hearings

Boeing Makes Concessions to E.U. (June 25): Boeing's exclusive supplier agreements with three American airlines have drawn criticism from E.U. officials probing Boeing's proposed $14 billion acquisition of McDonnell Douglas. To mollify their concerns and win their approval of the deal, Boeing may offer to modify the agreements. **(July 18):** Clinton joins the fray, and hints at a possible trade war if the E.U. blocks the merger. **(July 24):** Boeing wins tentative E.U. approval for the merger in exchange for cancelling its sole-supplier agreements.

Dow Does It Again: 1997 Milestones

Date	Milestone	Close
Feb. 13	7000	7022.44
May 5	7100	7214.49
May 5	7200	7214.49
May 15	7300	7333.55
June 6	7400	7435.78
June 10	7500	7539.27
June 12	7600	7711.47
June 12	7700	7711.47
July 3	7800	7895.81
July 9	7900	7962.31
July 16	8000	8038.88
July 24	8100	8116.93
July 30	8200	8254.89

July 1997

Mississippi Wins Tobacco Settlement (July 7): Tobacco industry officials agreed to pay Mississippi $3.6 billion over 25 years and $136 million annually thereafter to settle a class-action lawsuit seeking to recover medical expenses for treating smoking-related illnesses. The agreement could be superseded by the industry-wide pact agreed upon in June, if it survives Washington's scrutiny. **(July 10):** Clinton announces that the deal will require modifications before it would be approved, but hopes to modify it rather than scrap it.

British Telecom Purchase of MCI Approved (July 8): The U.S. Justice Department approved the largest-ever deal in which a foreign company buys a U.S. company.

Studies Show Securities Suits Soaring (July 9): Though a 1995 law was enacted to reduce lawsuits brought by shareholders, the number of suits filed has returned to levels in the early 1990s.

Apple Fires Amelio (July 10): Apple's CEO was ousted amidst reports that the firm cannot predict when it will return to profitability. Co-founder Steve Jobs, who had been advising Amelio since rejoining the company in late 1996, is expected to take on a broader role. **(Aug. 6):** Jobs negotiates $150 million settlement from Microsoft of an old patent-infringement suit. Microsoft agrees to offer Office on the Macintosh platform, and to allow Apple to ship Microsoft's browser with the Macintosh operating system. **(Sept. 17):** Jobs is named interim CEO.

End of an Era (July 17): Woolworth announces it will close the more than 400 retail outlets that had become staples of small-town America.

America Online to Sell its Customers (July 23): Further inflaming the privacy policy debate, AOL announces plan to sell its customers' phone numbers to telemarketing firms. **(July 24):** AOL decides against its plan.

Intel Buys Graphics Chips Producer (July 28): The $420 million purchase of Chips & Technologies indicates the increasing importance of graphics in the PC industry.

Tax Deal Reduces Capital Gains (July 30): Profits from the sale of most homes will no longer be subjected to taxes, and reduced rates for stocks held longer than 18 months are expected to spur investment.

August 1997

UPS Strikes (Aug. 4): Teamsters walk off the job in a dispute over a company-sponsored pension plan and the part-time employment status of many workers. Rival carriers pick up the business left behind by the nation's leading shipping company. **(Aug. 20):** Under a new 5-year contract proposed to settle the strike, UPS labor costs could increase by over $1 billion within 3 years. The costs are associated with pay increases and new full-time jobs. Managment also agreed to support union-run pension plans. **(Aug. 22):** Seniority rules in the new Teamsters contract means layoffs for former welfare recipients who were hired recently. The company expects to trim 15,000 jobs as a result of reduced volume due to the strike.

Thai Government Faces Financial Woes (Aug. 5): After spending $16 billion to prop up financial firms, and another $20 billion to shore up the currency, the government opts to close half the country's financial companies. **(Aug. 22):** The bhat fell to a record low against the dollar in the wake of the IMF bailout plan.

Columbia/HCA Subject of Criminal Probe (Aug. 13): In a move indicating that prosecutors believe they have enough evidence to indict the entire company in addition to individual executives, the government is investigating the firm for possible fraud.

Smith Barney Does it the Old Fashioned Way: They Settle (Aug. 19): A sexual discrimination lawsuit filed by 26 current and former female employees was brought more than a year ago.

British Telecom and MCI Reduce Value of Deal (Aug. 25): British Telecom reduced the price by $5 billion, reflecting MCI's increased costs of entering the local telephone markets.

Tobacco Firms Settle with Florida (Aug. 26): The deal, in which companies will pay the state $11.3 billion, also bans billboard advertising and cigarette vending machines accessible to youths.

Hudson Foods Packs It In (Aug. 26): Hudson announced plans to sell its beef-processing plant following Burger King's announcement that it will seek another supplier for its hamburger. The announcement comes in the wake of a shut-down of Hudson's meat-packing plant and a nationwide recall of 25 million pounds of beef suspected of carrying the potentially deadly E. coli bacteria. **(Sept. 4):** Tyson Foods agrees to buy Hudson for an estimated $643 million.

Fidelity to Close Magellan (Aug. 27): The world's largest mutual fund will be closed to most new investments after Sept. 30, a move designed to simplify the management of the $62.9 billion fund.

September 1997

Hike In Minimum Wage Coincides With Labor Day (Sept. 1): The second phase of the increase in the minimum wage goes into effect today, and will affect approximately 7 million American workers. Women are the biggest winners since they comprise the largest share of the 6.8 million minimum-wage earners; they will now make $5.15 per hour, up from $4.75.

Luxury Cars Go Abroad (Sept. 1): Consumers in Japan, Hong Kong, Singapore, Sweden, and parts of the former Soviet Union will be able to buy Cadillacs from their local dealer, beginning in October. General Motors is seeking to expand its international presence, and will offer its 1998 Cadillac Seville model first overseas, then in the U.S.

Dow Takes Off (Sept. 2): In the largest single-day point gain in its history, the Dow Jones racked up 257.35 points, 37% more than the previous record of 186.84 points, set on October 21, 1987.

Apple Backs Down from Strategy on Clones (Sept. 2): Apple Computer announces plans to purchase assets of Power Computing Corp., one of the companies to which Apple had licensed rights to sell hardware and software based on the Macintosh. Apple hopes that the purchase, valued at $100 million in stock, will slow Apple's losses in market share.

Hotel Industry Consolidates (Sept. 2): The combination of Doubletree with Promus Hotel Corp. will result in one of the world's largest hotel concerns, including Doubletree, Embassy Suites, Hampton Inns, and others.

ESPN to Buy Classic Sports (Sept. 3): In a bid to expand its leading market share, ESPN has agreed to buy the provider of vintage sports programs for an estimated $150–$175 million.

Columbia HCA Probes Continue (Sept. 4): Columbia breaths a sigh of relief when Alabama Attorney General Bill Pryor concludes there was no criminal wrongdoing in the company's Medicaid billing practices. Company officials may be hyperventilating soon, however, as South Carolina, Georgia, and Arkansas all announced plans to begin their own investigations. The six state-level probes are unrelated to the federal investigation.

Tobacco Industry Documents Can't Be Used in Florida Trial (Sept. 6): Damning documents made public in the Liggett Group trial earlier this year will not be entered as evidence in a Miami class-action lawsuit. Dade County Judge Robert Kaye ruled that the documents were subject to attorney-client privilege and could not be used against other cigarette makers in the secondhand-smoke trial.

CompuServe Sold; AOL Inherits Subscribers (Sept. 8): CompuServe parent H&R Block announces it will divide the assets of the pioneering online service between America Online, Inc., who will get the 2.6 million subscribers, and WorldCom Inc., who will take over the commercial services. The deal is valued at $1.2 billion.

Campbell Returns to Its Meat and Potatoes (Sept. 9): Campbell Soup plans to combine seven of its non-core businesses into a separate spin-off company with annual revenues of $1.4 billion. The move will allow Campbell to focus its strategy on its core soups, sauces, and biscuits business, which is experiencing faster growth.

Joe Camel Pays Up (Sept. 9): R.J. Reynolds will pay $10 million to settle a California lawsuit charging the company with unfair business practices, using the Joe Camel ads to attract underage smokers.

Tobacco Tax Break Terminated (Sept. 10): A little-known provision in the budget bill passed in July called for allowing tobacco companies to deduct approximately $50 billion in increased taxes from its proposed settlement of $368 billion with state attorneys general. The Senate voted to repeal that law; a similar measure is working its way through the House.

Long-Awaited Utility Deregulation Nearly Here (Sept. 12): Consumers inundated by direct mail, telemarketing, and Internet advertising campaigns by utilities attempting to secure market share may well be more careful about what they ask for in the future.

Tobacco Deal Unacceptable (Sept. 15): President Clinton delivers his thumbs-down verdict on the proposed settlement, citing the need to do more to reduce smoking among teenagers as a larger priority than simply getting money out of the tobacco industry. ☐

The Bumpy Road from Welfare to Work

Not all welfare cases are created equal.

As the nation begins the task of moving throngs of people from dependency to jobs over the next five years, stereotypes quickly fall away. About 20 percent of all women who land on the welfare rolls are off in a year or less, according to a study by researchers at Harvard's Kennedy School of Government, and nearly half are off within three years.

The welfare caseload is as diverse as the nation itself: college-educated, recently divorced mothers are in the system along with pregnant, never-married high-school dropouts and grown men with chronic disabling ailments. The self-confident and energetic are there, too, as are those staggered by domestic violence, healthy mothers with sick children, addicts, and ex-cons. And to a large extent, the success or failure of the mammoth welfare overhaul will hinge on acknowledging these differences.

"Public services have traditionally been one-size-fits all," explains Don Thomas, top welfare administrator in Hamilton County, Ohio, home to 867,000 people in Cincinnati and its environs. "We have to start individualizing our services if we want to be really effective."

Change is well underway in Ohio. Like many other states, it anticipated federal welfare-reform mandates by passing legislation of its own last summer—placing a time limit on benefits and imposing work requirements on many recipients. In urban, Republican-leaning Hamilton County, where both Proctor & Gamble Co. and Federated Department Stores Inc. are headquartered, the combined effects of the new law and a resurgent economy are already being felt. The county's wel-

Geography of Reform

Federal law sets a five-year lifetime benefit limit. Each state gets a lump-sum grant and wide latitude to run its own welfare program. States are penalized if they don't get a required percentage of recipients to work.

Wisconsin: Probably the toughest work requirements in the country. Virtually nobody is exempt and those who don't cooperate lose all cash assistance.

Minnesota: If too many of neighboring Wisconsin's poor start arriving, pressure may grow to take a harder line. So far, there is little evidence that welfare recipients migrate based on state benefits.

Vermont: Arguably the nation's most compassionate plan. It gives single parents of young children extra time before a work requirement kicks in.

California: The largest state's caseload increased 6 percent between January 1993 and September 1996, when rolls nationwide fell 15 percent. It has yet to pass a welfare-reform law and has the nation's largest population of immigrants, who take the worst hit from the federal law.

Iowa: First state to drop large numbers of families from the rolls for refusing to comply with work requirements.

Mississippi: Low benefits, tough work requirements. Gov. Kirk Fordice urges churches to play a larger role in caring for the poor, an idea that is also catching on in the Midwest.

Calendar of Cutbacks

Federal deadlines for reducing benefits. States can impose more stringent deadlines.

July 1, 1997
- About 14 percent of 965,000 disabled children now getting Supplemental Security Income benefits will lose them under tougher criteria.
- Cutoff of disability benefits for substance abusers.
- Cutoff of federal aid to unmarried teen parents not living at home or under adult supervision, as well as to teen parents not attending school.
- States must cut benefits of mothers who refuse to cooperate in locating fathers behind in child support.

August 22, 1997
- Legal immigrants lose food stamps and disability benefits. Congress is weighing an easing of such cuts.

October 1998
- The five states showing largest percentage reductions in out-of-wedlock births receive federal bonuses.

fare caseload has tumbled to about 45,000, down by about 20,000 from its 1992 peak.

But many of those who have returned to work are the most capable welfare recipients. That leaves a harder core for social-service administrators to contend with as they enforce stiffer state work requirements that took effect April 1: only adults with children under one year old—just 15 percent of the caseload—are exempt from work.

A significant chunk of the caseload won't have much trouble complying with the stricter rules. These people need relatively little prodding to enter the labor market, and little coaching once they get there. According to caseworkers in Cincinnati, such clients typically have high-school diplomas, recent work experience, good health, and strong motivation.

A second group needs a firmer push. These clients often lack self-esteem and schooling, or have flagging health.

The rest face immense obstacles. They often have scant education and problems coping with authority. Many have histories of mental illness, addiction, or crime that make potential employers wary.

No one can say precisely how many people fall into each category. Hamilton County's Mr. Thomas figures that the easiest and toughest cases each represent about 2 percent of the caseload, while as may as 60 percent fall into the middle group.

But the categories don't give the full picture. In each case folder is a separate story of human hardship and hope, spanning the spectrum of need, and suggesting how elusive self-sufficiency can be—even for the tens of thousands who genuinely want to leave the system behind. ☐

Top Stocks by Market Value, December 31, 1996

Company Name	Market Value (millions)	Shares (millions)	Exchange	Company Name	Market Value (millions)	Shares (millions)	Exchange
General Electric Co.	183,603	1,857	NYSE	Federal National Mortgage Assn.	42,053	1,129	NYSE
Coca-Cola Co.	180,487	3,430	NYSE	American Home Products Corp.	41,675	711	NYSE
Exxon Corp.	177,656	1,813	NYSE	Eli Lilly and Co.	41,530	569	NYSE
Merck & Co., Inc.	117,601	1,484	NYSE	Cisco Systems Inc.	41,308	649	Nasdaq
Intel Corp.	107,714	823	Nasdaq	Bellsouth Corp.	40,730	1,009	NYSE
Philip Morris Co. Inc.	105,340	935	NYSE	Amoco Corp.	40,079	498	NYSE
Microsoft Corp.	98,752	1,195	Nasdaq	Abbott Laboratories	40,040	789	NYSE
International Business Machines Corp.	83,675	554	NYSE	Chase Manhattan Corp.	39,297	440	NYSE
Johnson & Johnson	76,357	1,535	NYSE	Minnesota Mining & Mfg. Co.	39,118	472	NYSE
Procter & Gamble Co.	74,595	694	NYSE	BankAmerica Corp.	38,632	387	NYSE
AT&T Co.	70,434	1,619	NYSE	McDonald's Corp.	37,572	830	NYSE
Bristol-Myers Squibb Co.	59,643	548	NYSE	Boeing Co.	37,152	349	NYSE
Pfizer Inc.	57,059	688	NYSE	Motorola, Inc.	36,394	593	NYSE
American Intl. Group, Inc.	54,782	506	NYSE	Royal Dutch Petroleum Co.	35,833	210	NYSE
du Pont de Nemours and Co.	54,647	579	NYSE	Ameritech Corp.	35,654	588	NYSE
Mobil Corp.	54,419	445	NYSE	Travelers Group Inc.	34,103	752	NYSE
Wal-Mart Stores, Inc.	52,613	2,300	NYSE	Schering-Plough Corp.	32,852	507	NYSE
Citicorp	51,472	500	NYSE	Ford Motor Co.	32,518	1,020	NYSE
Hewlett-Packard Co.	51,091	1,017	NYSE	SBC Communications Inc.	32,110	620	NYSE
PepsiCo, Inc.	50,460	1,725	NYSE	Monsanto Co.	31,954	822	NYSE
Walt Disney Co.	47,496	682	NYSE	Schlumberger Limited	30,848	309	NYSE
Berkshire Hathaway Inc.	46,951	1,377	NYSE	Eastman Kodak Co.	29,986	374	NYSE
Chevron Corp.	46,312	712	NYSE	Lucent Technologies Inc.	29,446	637	NYSE
GTE Corp.	44,601	980	NYSE	Bell Atlantic Corp.	28,349	438	NYSE
Gillette Co. (The)	43,644	561	NYSE				
General Motors Corp.	42,182	757	NYSE				

Source: New York Stock Exchange *1996 Fact Book* and The Nasdaq Stock Market *1997 Fact Book & Company Directory.*

Most Active Stocks, 1996

Company Name	Share Volume (In thousands)	Exchange	Company Name	Share Volume (In thousands)	Exchange
Intel Corp.	2,338,855	Nasdaq	Coca-Cola Co.	505,541	NYSE
Cisco Systems, Inc.	1,789,884	Nasdaq	Chase Manhattan Corp.	499,883	NYSE
Sun Microsystems Inc.	1,261,363	Nasdaq	General Electric	493,513	NYSE
Microsoft Corp.	1,205,766	Nasdaq	Apple Computer Inc.	474,634	Nasdaq
Oracle Systems Corp.	1,161,632	Nasdaq	General Motors	460,903	NYSE
Micron Technology Inc.	1,070,608	NYSE	Xilinx Inc.	458,991	Nasdaq
Applied Materials Inc.	1,028,617	Nasdaq	LSI Logic Corp.	453,454	NYSE
MCI Communications Corp.	944,600	Nasdaq	Chrysler Corp.	439,895	NYSE
Tele-Communications Inc. Cl A	934,703	Nasdaq	Cascade Communications Corp.	429,520	Nasdaq
3Com Corp.	907,541	Nasdaq	S3 Inc.	421,536	Nasdaq
Dell Computer Corp.	903,925	Nasdaq	Gateway 2000 Inc.	421,410	Nasdaq
WorldCom Inc. Cl A	878,830	Nasdaq	Texas Instruments	420,023	NYSE
Informix Corp.	852,084	Nasdaq	Citicorp	416,230	NYSE
AT&T Corp.	818,961	NYSE	Cirrus Logic Inc.	397,826	Nasdaq
Novell Inc.	791,904	Nasdaq	Digital Equipment Corp.	391,910	NYSE
PepsiCo, Inc.	757,314	NYSE	Comcast Corp. Cl A Special	390,832	Nasdaq
International Business Machines	738,603	NYSE	Telecomm Brasil Telebras	388,920	NYSE
Atmel Corp.	737,999	Nasdaq	Integrated Device Technology	384,490	Nasdaq
Wal-Mart Stores	731,486	NYSE	Imatron Inc.	383,766	Nasdaq
LM Ericsson Telephone Co. ADR	721,929	Nasdaq	Medaphis Corp.	380,287	Nasdaq
Ascend Communications Inc.	697,982	Nasdaq	McDonald's Corp.	379,766	NYSE
DSC Communications Corp.	681,502	Nasdaq	Adobe Systems Inc.	378,279	Nasdaq
US Robotics Corp.	677,018	Nasdaq	Netscape Communications Corp.	376,935	Nasdaq
K-Mart Corp.	621,617	NYSE			
Compaq Computer	610,362	NYSE	ValuJet Inc.	372,745	Nasdaq
Ford Motor Co.	609,330	NYSE	Seagate Technology Inc.	367,982	NYSE
Motorola Inc.	594,376	NYSE	MFS Communications Co.	366,183	Nasdaq
Amgen Inc.	589,563	Nasdaq	Westinghouse Electric	364,817	NYSE
Bay Networks Inc.	583,576	NYSE	IMP Inc.	361,089	Nasdaq
Federal National Mortgage Assn.	575,663	NYSE	Pharmacia Upjohn Inc.	358,500	NYSE
Telefonos de Mexico	570,226	NYSE	WMX Technologies Inc.	358,297	NYSE
Philip Morris Co. Inc.	569,998	NYSE	Read-Rite Corp.	357,513	Nasdaq
Hewlett-Packard Co.	565,972	NYSE	Arakis Energy Corp.	354,645	Nasdaq
Altera Corp.	564,442	Nasdaq	Oxford Health Plans Inc.	352,545	Nasdaq
Hanson Plc	555,065	NYSE	Johnson & Johnson	352,129	NYSE
Merck & Co., Inc.	553,598	NYSE	EMC Corp.	350,241	NYSE
Intel Corp.	525,079	Nasdaq	Adaptec Inc.	348,625	Nasdaq
Staples Inc.	520,055	Nasdaq			

Source: New York Stock Exchange *1996 Fact Book* and The Nasdaq Stock Market *1997 Fact Book & Company Directory.*

Largest U.S. Businesses of 1996

1996 rank	1995 rank	Company	Revenues $ millions	Assets $ millions	1996 rank	1995 rank	Company	Revenues $ millions	Assets $ millions
1	1	General Motors Corp.	$168,369	$22,142	48	55	Merck & Co., Inc.	19,829	24,393
					49	46	Costco	19,566	4,912
2	2	Ford Motor Co.	146,991	262,867	50	66	Home Depot	19,536	9,342
3	3	Exxon Corp.	119,434	95,527	51	41	Xerox	19,521	26,818
4	4	Wal-Mart Stores, Inc.	106,147	39,501	52	54	Atlantic Richfield	19,168	25,715
					53	49	BellSouth	19,040	32,568
5	7	General Electric Co.	79,179	272,402	54	42	CIGNA	18,950	98,932
6	6	Intl. Business Machines	75,947	81,132	55	102	Walt Disney Co.	18,739	37,306
					56	45	American Stores	18,678	7,881
7	5	AT&T Co.	74,525	55,552	57	50	Sara Lee	18,624	12,602
8	8	Mobil	72,267	46,408	58	48	Coca-Cola Co.	18,546	16,161
9	9	Chrysler Corp.	61,397	56,184	59	68	MCI Communications	18,494	22,978
10	10	Philip Morris Co. Inc.	54,553	54,871	60	72	Compaq Computer	18,109	10,526
11	14	Texaco	44,561	26,963	61	53	AMR	17,753	20,497
12	12	State Farm Insurance	42,781	93,245	62	59	NationsBank	17,509	185,794
13	11	Prudential Ins. Co. of America	40,175	219,072	63	61	New York Life Insurance	17,347	78,809
14	13	E.I. du Pont de Nemours	39,689	37,987	64	65	American Express	17,280	108,512
15	18	Chevron Corp.	38,691	34,854	65	58	Safeway	17,269	5,545
16	20	Hewlett-Packard Co.	38,420	27,699	66	64	RJR Nabisco Holdings	17,063	31,289
					67	91	Aetna	16,900	92,913
					68	63	Caterpillar	16,522	18,728
17	15	Sears, Roebuck	38,236	36,167	69	52	Fleming	16,487	4,055
18	17	Procter & Gamble Co.	35,284	27,730	70	57	Supervalu	16,486	4,184
					71	70	UAL	16,362	12,677
19	23	Amoco	32,726	32,100	72	67	Eastman Kodak	15,968	14,438
20	19	Citicorp	32,605	281,018	73	76	J.P. Morgan & Co.	15,866	222,026
21	21	PepsiCo, Inc.	31,645	24,512	74	81	Phillips Petroleum	15,807	13,548
22	16	Kmart Corp.	31,437	14,286	75	69	Federated Department Stores	15,229	14,264
23	25	American Intl. Group, Inc.	28,205	148,431	76	79	Bristol-Myers Squibb	15,065	14,685
24	24	Motorola, Inc.	27,973	24,076	77	84	Ameritech	14,917	23,707
25	71	Chase Manhattan Corp.	27,421	336,099	78	77	Digital Equipment Corp.	14,563	10,075
26	29	Lockheed Martin	26,875	29,257	79	90	Rockwell International	14,343	10,065
27	28	Dayton Hudson	25,371	13,389	80	82	Lehman Brothers Holdings	14,260	128,596
28	27	Kroger	25,171	5,825	81	62	Minnesota Mining & Mfg.	14,236	13,364
29	32	Fannie Mae	25,054	351,041	82	80	Sprint	14,235	16,953
30	33	Merrill Lynch	25,011	213,016	83	86	American Home Products	14,088	20,785
31	26	ConAgra, Inc.	24,822	11,197	84	73	AlliedSignal	13,971	12,829
32	31	Allstate	24,299	74,508	85	93	SBC Communications	13,898	23,499
33	34	J.C. Penney	23,649	22,088	86	164	College Retirement Equities Fund	13,865	98,975
34	30	United Technologies	23,512	16,745	87	74	McDonnell Douglas	13,834	11,631
35	22	Metropolitan Life Insurance	23,000	190,000	88	109	Teachers Insurance & Annuity Assn.	13,828	86,358
36	40	Boeing Co.	22,681	27,254	89	96	Albertson's, Inc.	13,777	4,715
37	35	United Parcel Service	22,368	14,954	90	87	McKesson	13,719	3,504
					91	85	NYNEX	13,454	27,659
38	37	BankAmerica Corp.	22,071	250,753	92	101	SYSCO	13,395	3,325
39	43	Johnson & Johnson	21,620	20,010	93	92	Archer Daniels Midland	13,314	10,450
40	56	Travelers Group Inc.	21,345	151,067	94	141	Enron	13,289	16,137
41	38	GTE Corp.	21,339	38,422	95	78	Kimberly-Clark	13,149	11,846
42	47	USX	21,076	16,980	96	116	Morgan Stanley Group	13,144	196,446
43	60	Intel Corp.	20,847	23,735	97	95	Alcoa	13,128	13,450
44	39	International Paper	20,143	28,252	98	88	Goodyear Tire & Rubber	13,113	9,672
45	36	Dow Chemical	20,053	24,673	99	83	Bell Atlantic Corp.	13,081	24,856
46	44	Loews	19,965	67,683	100	75	Georgia-Pacific	13,024	12,818
47	51	Columbia/HCA Healthcare	19,909	21,272					

New Business Concerns and Business Failures

Formations and failures	1994[1]	1993	1992	1991	1990	1989	1985	1980
Business formations								
Index, net formations (1967 = 100)	125.5	121.1	116.3	115.3	120.7	124.7	120.9	129.9
New incorporations (1,000)	n.a.	707	667	629	647	677	663	534
Failures, number (1,000)	71.5	86.1	97.0	88.1	60.0	50.4	57.1	11.7
Rate per 10,000 concerns	79	96	109	107	75	65	115	42

1. Preliminary. n.a. = not available. NOTE: Data are most recent available. *Sources:* U.S. Bureau of Economic Analysis and Dun & Bradstreet Corporation. From *Statistical Abstract of the United States 1996*, web: www.census.gov/stat_abstract.

Corporate Profits[1]

(in billions of dollars)

Item	1997[2]	1996	1995	1994	1990	1985	1980	1975	1970
Domestic industries	$614.5	$578.2	$511.7	$445.7	$236.4	$190.8	$161.9	$107.6	$62.4
Financial	116.5	103.5	97.6	69.4	18.7	21.0	26.9	11.8	12.1
Nonfinancial	498.0	474.7	414.1	376.3	217.7	169.7	134.9	95.8	50.2
Manufacturing	208.2	205.5	181.3	151.6	88.8	73.0	72.9	52.6	26.6
Wholesale and retail trade	104.1	87.2	68.8	75.4	41.5	49.7	23.6	21.3	9.5
Other	94.2	90.3	77.6	66.2	87.5	47.0	38.4	21.9	14.1
Rest of world	97.4	95.9	86.7	73.4	56.9	31.8	29.9	13.0	6.5
Total	**711.9**	**674.1**	**598.4**	**519.1**	**293.3**	**222.6**	**191.7**	**120.6**	**68.9**

1. Corporate profits before tax with inventory valuation adjustment. 2. First quarter (seasonally adjusted at annual rates). *Source:* U.S. Bureau of Economic Analysis, *Survey of Current Business*, June 1996, web: www.bea.doc.gov.

Shareholders in Public Corporations

Characteristic	1992	1990	1985	1980	1975	1970
Individual shareholders (thousands)	51,300	51,440	47,040	30,200	25,270	30,850
Adult shareowner incidence in population	1 in 3	1 in 4	1 in 4	1 in 5	1 in 6	1 in 4
Median household income	$52,000	$43,800	$36,800	$27,750	$19,000	$13,500
Adult shareowners with household income:						
under $10,000 (thousands)	n.a.	n.a.	2,151	1,742	3,420	8,170
$10,000 and over (thousands)	n.a.	n.a.	40,999	25,715	19,970	20,130
$15,000 and over (thousands)	48,600	42,920	39,806	22,535	15,420	12,709
$25,000 and over (thousands)	43,700	38,230	32,690	15,605	6,642	4,114
$50,000 and over (thousands)	28,500	17,910	11,321	3,982	1,216	n.a.
Adult female shareowners (thousands)	n.a.	17,750	17,547[1]	13,696	11,750	14,290
Adult male shareowners (thousands)	n.a.	30,220	27,446[1]	14,196	11,630	14,340
Median age	45	43	44	46	53	48

NOTE: 1990 results are not strictly comparable with previous studies because of differences in methodologies. 1. Revised to correspond to 1990 methodology. n.a. = not available. *Source:* New York Stock Exchange. Data are latest available as of 1997.

Life Insurance in Force

(in millions of dollars)

As of Dec. 31	Ordinary	Group	Industrial	Credit	Total
1915	$ 16,650	$ 100	$ 4,279	—	$ 21,029
1930	78,576	9,801	17,963	$ 73	106,413
1945	101,550	22,172	27,675	365	151,762
1950	149,116	47,793	33,415	3,844	234,168
1955	216,812	101,345	39,682	14,493	372,332
1960	341,881	175,903	39,563	29,101	586,448
1965	499,638	308,078	39,818	53,020	900,554
1970	734,730	551,357	38,644	77,392	1,402,123
1980	1,760,474	1,579,355	35,994	165,215	3,541,038
1985	3,247,289	2,561,595	28,250	215,973	6,053,107
1990	5,366,982	3,753,506	24,071	248,038	9,392,597
1994	6,835,239	4,608,746	20,145	209,491	11,673,621
1995	7,547,537	4,777,912	19,977	231,251	12,576,677

Source: American Council of Life Insurance.

Leading Advertising Agencies in Revenues

(in thousands of dollars)

Agency	1996 Revenues	1996 Billings
Leo Burnett Co.	$393,708	$2,649,658
J. Walter Thompson	384,700	2,688,000
Grey Advertising	352,200	2,349,200
McCann-Erickson	341,000	2,549,000
BBDO	332,269[1]	2,929,667
Young & Rubicam	296,510	2,840,000
Foote, Cone & Belding	288,400	2,999,000
DDB Needham	271,931	2,474,438
Ogilvy & Mather	233,340	2,283,096
Bozell	231,800	1,885,000

1. Estimated. *Source: Adweek*, Top 100 U.S.-Based Agency Networks, April 7, 1997, edition. © 1997 Adweek. Used with permission of *Adweek*.

World's Largest Banks

(in millions of U.S. dollars)

Rank		Total assets	Rank		Total assets
1	Bank of Tokyo-Mitsubishi Ltd., Japan	$648,161	28	Bayerische Vereinsbank, Munich, Germany	$260,848
2	Deutsche Bank AG, Frankfurt, Germany	575,072	29	Mitsui Trust & Banking Co. Ltd., Tokyo, Japan	254,189
3	Credit Agricole Mutuel, Paris, France	479,963	30	Lloyds TSB Group Inc., London, United Kingdom	252,292
4	Dai-Ichi Kangyo Bank Ltd., Tokyo, Japan	434,115	31	Sumitomo Trust & Banking Co. Ltd., Osaka, Japan	248,418
5	Fuji Bank Ltd., Tokyo, Japan	432,992			
6	Sanwa Bank Ltd., Osaka, Japan	427,689	32	BankAmerica Corp., San Francisco, United States	247,892
7	Sumitomo Bank Ltd., Osaka, Japan	426,103	33	Long-Term Credit Bank of Japan Ltd., Tokyo, Japan	231,761
8	Sakura Bank Ltd., Tokyo, Japan	423,017			
9	HSBC Holdings, Plc., London, United Kingdom	404,979	34	Asahi Bank Ltd., Tokyo, Japan	230,080
10	Norinchukin Bank, Tokyo, Japan	375,210	35	Bayerische Landesbank Girozentrale, Munich, Germany	223,496
11	Dresdner Bank, Frankfurt, Germany	358,829			
12	Banque Nationale de Paris, France	357,322	36	J.P. Morgan & Co., Inc., New York, United States	221,814
13	Industrial Bank of Japan Ltd., Tokyo, Japan	350,468	37	Bayerische Hypotheken-und Wechsel Bank, Munich, Germany	220,100
14	ABN-AMRO Bank, N.V., Amsterdam, Netherlands	341,916			
15	Societe Generale, Paris, France	341,867	38	Credit Suisse First Boston, Zurich, Switzerland	218,870
16	Chase Manhattan Corp., New York, United States	333,777	39	Bankgesellschaft Berlin, AG, Berlin, Germany	218,226
17	Union Bank of Switzerland, Zurich, Switzerland	326,190	40	Daiwa Bank Ltd., Osaka, Japan	212,967
18	NatWest Group, London, United Kingdom	317,295	41	Abbey National, Plc, London, United Kingdom	212,307
19	Credit Lyonnais, Paris, France	311,747	42	Deutsche Genossenschaftsbank, Frankfurt, Germany	212,061
20	Barclays Plc, London, United Kingdom	308,710			
21	Westdeutsche Landesbank Girozentrale, Duesseldorf, Germany	298,455	43	Yasuda Trust & Banking Co., Ltd., Tokyo, Japan	196,520
			44	Toyo Trust & Banking Co., Ltd., Tokyo, Japan	192,802
22	Compagnie Financiere de Paribas, Paris, France	292,320	45	NationsBank Corp., Charlotte, N.C., United States	184,886
23	Commerzbank, Frankfurt, Germany	290,300	46	Rabobank Nederland, Utrecht, Netherlands	180,960
24	Mitsubishi Trust & Banking Corp., Tokyo, Japan	284,528	47	ING Bank, Amsterdam, Netherlands	178,886
25	Citicorp, New York, United States	278,941	48	Halifax Building Society, Halifax, United Kingdom	175,111
26	Tokai Bank Ltd., Nagoya, Japan	273,430	49	Generale Bank, Brussels, Belgium	174,639
27	Swiss Bank Corp., Basel, Switzerland	268,519	50	Istituto Bancario San Paolo di Torino, Italy	172,540

Source: American Banker, July 29, 1997. Reprinted with permission. Copyright © American Banker/Bond Buyer.

Domestic Freight Traffic by Major Carriers

(in billions of ton-miles)[1]

Year	Railroads		Trucks		Oil pipeline		Inland waterways[2]		Air		Total
	Amt.	%	Amt.	%	Amt.	%	Amt.	%	Amt.	%	
1940	379	61.3	62	10.0	59	9.6	118	19.1	0.01	—	618
1945	691	67.3	67	6.5	127	12.3	143	13.9	0.09	—	1,028
1950	597	56.2	173	16.3	129	12.1	163	15.4	0.32	—	1,062
1955	632	49.5	223	17.5	203	16.0	217	17.0	0.48	—	1,274
1960	579	44.1	285	21.7	229	17.4	220	16.8	0.78	—	1,314
1965	709	43.3	359	21.9	306	18.7	262	16.0	1.91	0.1	1,638
1970	771	39.8	412	21.3	431	22.3	319	16.4	3.27	0.2	1,936
1975	759	36.7	454	22.0	507	24.6	342	16.5	3.73	0.2	2,066
1980	932	37.5	555	22.3	588	23.6	407	16.4	4.84	0.19	2,487
1985	895	36.4	610	24.8	564	22.9	382	15.5	6.71	0.27	2,458
1986	889	35.6	632	25.3	578	23.1	393	15.7	7.34	0.29	2,499
1987	972	36.8	663	25.1	587	22.2	411	15.6	8.67	0.33	2,642
1988	1,028	37.0	700	25.2	601	21.6	438	15.8	9.33	0.34	2,776
1989	1,070	37.8	716	25.3	584	20.6	449	15.9	10.21	0.36	2,829
1990	1,091	37.7	735	25.4	584	20.2	475	16.4	10.42	0.36	2,895
1991	1,100	37.9	758	26.1	579	19.9	459	15.8	9.96	0.34	2,906
1992	1,138	37.6	815	27.0	589	19.5	470	15.5	10.99	0.36	3,023
1993	1,183	38.1	861	27.7	593	19.1	456	14.7	11.54	0.37	3,105
1994	1,275	39.1	908	27.8	591	18.1	475	14.6	12.03	0.37	3,261
1995	1,375	40.4	921	27.1	599	17.6	497	14.6	12.72	0.37	3,405

1. Mail and express included, except railroads for 1970. 2. Rivers, canals, and domestic traffic on Great Lakes. NOTE: Data are latest available. *Source: Transportation in America by Rosalyn Wilson.*

Tonnage Handled by Principal U.S. Ports

Top 50 Ports in Total Tons

Port	1995	Port	1995
Port of South Louisiana	204,482,591	Port Plaquemine, La.	72,897,301
Houston, Tex.	135,231,322	Corpus Christi, Tex.	70,456,033
New York, N.Y. & N.J.	119,341,574	Long Beach, Calif.	53,227,490
Baton Rouge, La.	83,612,788	Tampa, Fla.	51,911,335
Valdez, Alaska	80,955,084	Mobile, Ala.	50,972,223
New Orleans, La.	76,984,036	Texas City, Tex.	50,402,938

Port	1995	Port	1995
Port Arthur, Tex.	49,799,977	Richmond, Calif.	20,839,258
Pittsburgh, Pa.	48,849,508	Freeport, Tex.	19,661,621
Norfolk Harbor, Va.	47,658,182	Detroit, Mich.	18,660,925
Lake Charles, La.	46,569,641	Port Everglades, Fla.	18,367,389
Los Angeles, Calif.	46,478,586	Savannah, Ga.	17,379,724
Duluth-Superior, Minn./Wis.	45,049,184	Boston, Mass.	16,744,386
Baltimore, Md.	44,695,812	Memphis, Tenn.	15,944,945
Philadelphia, Pa.	40,634,284	Indiana Harbor, Ind.	15,700,153
Portland, Ore.	31,255,509	Jacksonville, Fla.	15,692,999
Marcus Hook, Pa.	30,818,134	San Juan, P.R.	15,477,965
St. Louis, Mo./Ill.	30,137,632	Cleveland, Ohio	15,393,496
Huntington, W. Va.	28,265,731	Lorain, Ohio	14,964,284
Pascagoula, Miss.	26,926,582	Toledo, Ohio	14,074,499
Seattle, Wash.	26,179,838	Oakland, Calif.	13,224,118
Chicago, Ill.	25,329,030	Anacortes, Wash.	13,109,828
Paulsboro, N.J.	24,780,664	Cincinnati, Ohio	13,068,362
Newport News, Va.	23,365,005	New Castle, Del.	12,455,809
Beaumont, Tex.	20,937,132	Honolulu, Hawaii	11,545,102
Tacoma, Wash.	20,878,751	Portland, Maine	11,456,007

Source: U.S. Department of the Army, Corps of Engineers.

State Motor Vehicle Registrations, 1995

State	Autos[1]	Trucks[1]	Buses[2]	Motorcycles	Total
Alabama	1,842	1,702	8	38	3,590
Alaska	305	236	2	13	556
Arizona	1,881	988	4	69	2,942
Arkansas	807	800	6	17	1,630
California	14,850	7,539	43	519	22,951
Colorado	1,705	1,101	6	88	2,900
Connecticut [3]	2,079	534	9	49	2,671
Delaware	405	185	2	9	601
Dist. of Col.	206	34	3	2	245
Florida	7,595	2,734	40	185	10,554
Georgia	4,226	1,879	16	72	6,193
Hawaii	533	265	4	13	815
Idaho	587	453	3	33	1,076
Illinois	6,612	2,345	16	184	9,157
Indiana	3,370	1,677	24	96	5,167
Iowa	1,829	976	9	111	2,925
Kansas	1,086	995	4	43	2,128
Kentucky	1,630	990	12	33	2,665
Louisiana	1,958	1,307	20	36	3,321
Maine	624	340	3	26	993
Maryland	2,705	938	11	39	3,693
Massachusetts	3,507	984	11	74	4,576
Michigan	5,315	2,335	24	127	7,801
Minnesota	2,552	1,314	16	118	4,000
Mississippi	1,408	726	10	30	2,174
Missouri	2,747	1,496	12	55	4,310
Montana	538	427	3	21	989
Nebraska	849	612	6	19	1,486
Nevada	593	452	2	21	1,068
New Hamp-shire[3]	731	389	2	49	1,171
New Jersey[3]	4,689	1,198	20	88	5,995
New Mexico	832	648	3	31	1,514
New York[3]	7,917	2,311	46	168	10,442
North Carolina	3,685	1,962	35	67	5,749
North Dakota	372	321	2	17	712
Ohio	7,193	2,584	33	218	10,028
Oklahoma	1,629	1,212	15	55	2,911
Oregon	1,629	1,144	12	60	2,845
Pennsylvania[3]	6,014	2,433	34	170	8,651
Rhode Island[3]	545	152	2	17	716
South Carolina	1,865	953	15	34	2,867
South Dakota	380	326	3	25	734
Tennessee	3,935	1,448	17	70	5,470
Texas	8,605	5,005	72	126	13,808
Utah	800	646	1	22	1,469
Vermont	317	173	2	18	510
Virginia	3,976	1,620	17	58	5,671
Washington	2,960	1,535	8	95	4,598
West Virginia	857	565	3	18	1,443

State	Autos[1]	Trucks[1]	Buses[2]	Motorcycles	Total
Wisconsin	2,424	1,557	13	168	4,162
Wyoming	368	231	2	17	618
Total	136,066	64,778	686	3,728	205,258

NOTE: Numbers in thousands. Includes federal, state, county, and municipal vehicles, but not military vehicles. 1. Personal passenger vans, passenger minivans, and utility-type vehicles, formerly included with automobiles, are now included in the trucks. 2. Numbers reflect Federal Highway Administration estimates of buses in operation rather than the registration counts of the states. 3. The following farm trucks, registered at a nominal fee and restricted to use in the vicinity of the owner's farm, are not included in the table: Connecticut, 10,001; New Hampshire, 4,099; New Jersey, 6,347; New York, 15,631; Pennsylvania, 23,339; and Rhode Island, 1,073. *Source:* Federal Highway Administration, Sept. 1996.

Passenger Car Production by Make

Companies and models	1996	1995	1990	1985	1980	1975	1970
American Motors Corporation	—	—	—	109,919	164,725	323,704	276,127
Chrysler Corporation							
Plymouth	185,705	129,571	212,354	369,487	293,342	443,550	699,031
Dodge	280,416	331,253	361,769	482,388	263,169	354,482	405,699
Chrysler	52,071	121,022	136,339	414,193	82,463	102,940	158,614
Imperial	—	—	16,280	—	—	1,930	10,111
Total	518,192	576,846	726,742	1,266,068	638,974	902,902	1,273,455
Ford Motor Company							
Ford	1,036,048	1,012,818	933,466	1,098,627	929,627	1,301,414	1,647,918
Mercury	244,676	225,308	221,436	374,446	324,528	405,104	310,463
Lincoln	145,035	157,584	222,449	163,077	52,793	101,520	58,771
Total	1,425,759	1,395,710	1,377,351	1,636,150	1,306,948	1,808,038	2,017,152
General Motors Corporation							
Chevrolet	537,711	665,955	1,025,379	1,691,254	1,737,336	1,687,091	1,504,614
Pontiac	541,844	574,455	649,255	702,617	556,429	523,469	422,212
Oldsmobile	300,032	391,216	418,742	1,168,982	783,225	654,342	439,632
Buick	342,538	393,879	405,123	1,001,461	783,575	535,820	459,931
Cadillac	162,249	186,113	252,540	322,765	203,991	278,404	152,859
Saturn	313,937	301,540	4,245	—	—	—	—
Toyota/Cavalier	11,701	1,978	—	—	—	—	—
Total	2,210,012	2,515,136	2,755,284	4,887,079	4,064,556	3,679,126	2,979,248
Volkswagen of America	—	—	—	96,458	197,106	—	—
Honda	634,348	552,995	435,437	238,159	145,337	—	—
Nissan	277,869	333,234	95,844	43,810	—	—	—
Toyota	545,351	516,878	321,523	—	—	—	—
Diamond Star[1]	192,961	218,161	148,379	—	—	—	—
Auto Alliance[2]	129,442	148,932	184,428	—	—	—	—
Subaru Legacy	98,747	80,669	32,461	—	—	—	—
BMW	50,546	11,872	—	—	—	—	—
Industry total [3]	6,083,227	6,350,433	6,077,449	8,184,821	6,375,506	6,716,951	6,550,128

1. Produces Misubishi and Chrysler/Dodge/Eagle vehicles. 2. Formerly listed as Mazda; includes Mazda MX-6 and 626 and Ford Probe. 3. Industry total may not be the sum of models and companies listed due to timing of company reports. *Source:* American Automobile Manufacturers Association.

Domestic and Export Factory Sales of Motor Vehicles
(in thousands)

	From plants in United States								
	Passenger cars			Motor trucks and buses			Total motor vehicles		
Year	Total	Domestic	Exports	Total	Domestic	Exports	Total	Domestic	Exports
1970	6,547	6,187	360	1,692	1,566	126	8,239	7,753	486
1975	6,713	6,073	640	2,272	2,003	269	8,985	8,076	909
1980	6,400	5,840	560	1,667	1,464	203	8,067	7,304	763
1985	8,002	7,337	665	3,464	3,234	231	11,467	10,571	896
1990	6,050	5,502	548	3,725	3,455	270	9,775	8,957	818
1991	5,407	4,874	533	3,388	3,050	338	8,795	7,924	871
1992	5,685	5,165	520	4,062	3,702	360	9,747	8,847	880
1993	5,962	5,473	489	4,895	4,471	424	10,857	9,944	913
1994	6,549	5,964	585	5,640	5,139	501	12,189	11,103	1,086
1995	6,310	5,788	522	5,713	5,211	502	12,023	10,999	1,024
1996	6,141	5,617	524	5,776	5,249	527	11,917	10,866	1,051

Source: American Automobile Manufacturers Association.

Motor Vehicle Data

	1995	1994	1990	1980	1970	1960
U.S. passenger cars and taxis registered (thousands)	134,981	133,930	143,550	121,724	89,280	61,671
Total mileage of U.S. passenger cars (millions)	1,541,458	1,501,402	1,513,184	1,111,596	916,700	588,083
Total fuel consumption of U.S. passenger cars (millions of gallons)	68,317	67,517	71,989	71,883	67,820	41,169
World registration of cars, trucks, and buses (thousands)	646,759	629,077	582,982	411,113	246,368	126,955
U.S. registration of cars, trucks, and buses (thousands)	200,446	198,045	188,655	155,796	108,418	73,858
U.S. share of world registration of cars, trucks, and buses	31.0%	31.5%	32.4%	37.9%	44.0%	58.2%

Source: American Automobile Manufacturers Association.

Agricultural Output by States, 1996 Crops

State	Corn (1,000 bu)	Wheat (1,000 bu)	Cotton[2] (1,000 ba[3])	Potatoes (1,000 cwt)	Tobacco (1,000 lb)	Cattle[4] (1,000 head)	Swine[5] (1,000 head)
Alabama	22,960	3,520	810	1,309	—	1,600	—
Alaska	—	—	—	129	—	11	—
Arizona	7,000	16,090	770	2,475	—	790	—
Arkansas	28,750	66,960	1,600	—	—	1,900	860
California	35,200	51,750	2,400	15,651	—	4,550	—
Colorado	133,480	75,500	—	31,890	—	3,150	—
Connecticut[1]	—	—	—	—	3,498	71	—
Delaware	21,450	4,134	—	1,475	—	27	—
Florida	9,856	380	120	9,613	20,100	1,970	—
Georgia	49,875	16,800	2,100	—	113,620	1,490	800
Hawaii	—	—	—	—	—	166	—
Idaho	5,400	119,200	—	139,960	—	1,750	—
Illinois	1,468,800	41,800	—	1,650	—	1,680	4,400
Indiana	670,350	27,360	—	1,352	14,972	1,150	3,600
Iowa	1,718,100	1,575	—	315	—	3,900	12,100
Kansas	357,200	255,200	3	—	—	6,550	1,360
Kentucky	148,800	28,090	—	—	428,280	2,550	600
Louisiana	65,375	5,590	1,300	—	—	1,000	—
Maine[1]	—	—	—	21,175	—	116	—
Maryland	64,635	11,804	—	380	12,000	270	—
Massachusetts[1]	—	—	—	676	1,225	62	—
Michigan	216,200	23,940	—	13,800	—	1,130	950
Minnesota	868,750	102,382	—	24,600	—	2,750	5,000
Mississippi	61,710	11,270	1,850	—	—	1,340	—
Missouri	355,100	48,750	600	1,633	6,300	4,450	3,300
Montana	2,055	176,710	—	3,213	—	2,700	—
Nebraska	1,186,900	73,500	—	5,887	—	6,550	3,550
Nevada	—	1,650	—	3,160	—	520	—
New Hampshire[1]	—	—	—	—	—	41	—
New Jersey	11,844	1,748	—	663	—	68	—
New Mexico	14,700	4,070	96	3,964	—	1,490	—
New York	67,410	6,450	—	7,980	—	1,540	—
North Carolina	85,500	25,960	990	3,338	590,683	1,190	9,500
North Dakota	65,520	395,130	—	28,820	—	1,900	—
Ohio	305,250	51,870	—	1,275	14,110	1,460	1,450
Oklahoma	24,650	93,100	130	—	—	5,400	1,370
Oregon	5,445	67,605	—	31,684	—	1,450	—
Pennsylvania	127,330	9,120	—	4,208	15,464	1,750	970
Rhode Island[1]	—	—	—	212	—	7	—
South Carolina	30,020	12,150	465	—	117,810	520	—
South Dakota	370,000	139,270	—	1,596	—	3,800	1,130
Tennessee	78,880	17,600	674	—	114,046	2,400	—
Texas	201,600	75,400	4,350	3,385	—	14,100	—
Utah	2,730	7,760	—	1,176	—	930	—
Vermont[1]	—	—	—	—	—	300	—
Virginia	39,060	14,575	160	1,800	106,249	1,830	—
Washington	22,200	182,670	—	94,990	—	1,200	—
West Virginia	4,200	495	—	—	2,470	450	—
Wisconsin	333,000	5,725	—	31,590	4,620	3,700	790
Wyoming	6,150	7,110	—	224	—	1,490	—
Total U.S.	9,293,435	2,281,763	18,418	497,119	1,565,447	101,209	55,900

. Individual state estimates not always available. 2. Production ginned and to be ginned. 3. 480-lb net weight bales. 4. As of Jan. 1, 1997. 5. Individual state estimates not available for the 33 other states, which contain another 4,170 head. Source: U.S. Department of Agriculture, National Agricultural Statistics Service, web: www.usda.gov/nass.

Livestock on Farms
(in thousands)

Type	1997	1996	1995	1994	1990	1985	1980	1975	1970	1965
Cattle[1]	101,209	103,487	102,755	100,988	95,816	109,582	111,242	132,028	112,369	109,000
Dairy cows[1]	9,281	9,416	9,487	9,528	10,015	10,311	10,758	11,220	13,303	16,981
Sheep[1]	7,937	8,461	8,886	9,714	11,358	10,716	12,699	14,515	20,423	25,127
Swine[2]	56,171	58,264	59,990	57,904	53,788	54,073	67,318	54,693	57,046	56,106
Chickens[3]	386,418	384,622	383,829	379,640	357,241	347,443	400,585	384,101	422,096	401,813
Turkeys[4]	301,378	n.a.	292,856	286,605	282,445	185,427	165,243	124,165	116,139	105,914

Except as noted, these figures represent the number of animals on a given day, rather than the number produced over the year. 1. As of January 1. 2. As of December 1 of the previous year. 3. As of December 1 of previous year; excludes commercial broilers. 4. Inventory data on turkeys is not available; represents the number produced. Source: U.S. Department of Agriculture, National Agricultural Statistics Service, web: www.usda.gov/nass.

Farm Indexes

(1990–92 = 100)

Year	Prices paid by farmers[1]	Prices rec'd by farmers[2]	Ratio
1975	47	73	155
1980	75	98	137
1985	86	91	106
1990	99	104	105
1991	100	100	99
1992	101	98	98
1993	103	101	98
1994	106	100	94
1995	110	102	92
1996	115	112	98

1. Commodities, interest, and taxes and wage rates. 2. All crops and livestock. Source: U.S. Department of Agriculture, National Agricultural Statistics Service, web: www.usda.gov/nass.

Farm Income
(in millions of dollars)

Year	Cash receipts from marketings		Government payments	Total cash income[1]
	Crops	Livestock, livestock products		
1930	$ 3,868	$ 5,187	—	$ 9,055
1935	2,977	4,143	$ 573	7,693
1940	3,469	4,913	723	9,105
1945	9,655	12,008	742	22,405
1950	12,356	16,105	283	28,764
1955	13,523	15,967	229	29,842
1960	15,023	18,989	703	34,958
1965	17,479	21,886	2,463	42,215
1970	20,977	29,532	3,717	54,768
1975	45,813	43,089	807	90,707
1980	71,746	67,991	1,285	143,295
1985	74,293	69,822	7,705	157,854
1990	80,131	89,843	9,298	186,824
1993	84,497	90,555	13,402	197,215
1994	91,600	88,100	7,900	196,700
1995	98,900	86,800	7,300	203,900
1996[2]	107,900	90,500	7,300	216,900
1997[2]	103,400	93,300	7,600	215,600

1. Includes items not listed. 2. Forecast. Source: U.S. Department of Agriculture, Economic Research Service, web: www.usda.gov.

Estimated Annual Retail and Wholesale Sales by Kind of Business

(in millions of dollars)

Kind of business	1995	1996
Retail sales, total	$2,234,038	$2,445,296
Building materials stores	125,831	134,485
Automotive dealers	551,330	592,919
Furniture, home furnishings, and equipment stores	127,270	133,486
General merchandise stores	299,169	312,792
Food stores	409,617	423,318
Gasoline service stations	146,080	154,967
Apparel and accessory stores	110,429	113,668
Eating and drinking places	232,060	236,526
Drug and proprietary stores	85,554	90,682
Liquor stores	21,966	22,850
Merchant wholesale sales, total	2,265,732	2,420,679
Durable goods, total	1,179,197	1,245,781
Motor vehicles and automotive parts and supplies	202,556	211,094
Furniture and home furnishings	40,861	43,606
Lumber and other construction materials	77,139	85,809
Professional and commercial equipment and supplies	194,647	231,360

Kind of business	1995	1996
Metals and minerals except petroleum	100,514	98,441
Electrical goods	169,776	173,762
Hardware, plumbing, and heating equipment	67,622	70,516
Machinery, equipment, and supplies	182,748	187,311
Miscellaneous durable goods	143,334	143,882
Nondurable goods, total	1,086,535	1,174,898
Paper and paper products	81,976	82,655
Drugs, drug proprietaries, and druggists' sundries	95,039	102,854
Apparel, piece goods, & notions	70,583	75,507
Groceries and related products	304,695	315,383
Farm-product raw materials	113,691	130,158
Chemical and allied products	47,774	53,493
Petroleum and petroleum products	150,560	177,769
Beer, wine, distilled alcoholic beverages	54,060	56,363
Miscellaneous nondurable goods	168,157	180,716

Source: U.S. Bureau of the Census, web: www.census.gov.

Imports and Exports of Leading Commodities

by Principal SITC Groupings (in millions of dollars)

Item	Cumulative 1996 Exports	Imports	Item	Cumulative 1996 Exports	Imports
Selected commodities [1]			Meat and preparations	6,958	2,317
ADP equipment; office machines	39,666	66,499	Metal manufactures, n.e.s.	9,234	10,843
			Metal ores; scrap	4,278	4,048
Airplane parts	11,723	3,464	Metalworking machinery	5,241	6,789
Airplanes	18,962	3,943	Mineral fuels, other	3,167	1,816
Alcoholic bev., distilled	385	2,048	Natural gas	261	4,002
Aluminum	3,485	4,828	Nickel	307	1,137
Animal feeds	4,183	633	Oils/fats, vegetable	1,024	1,416
Artwork/antiques	887	2,791	Optical goods	1,378	2,327
Basketware, etc.	2,239	3,014	Paper and paperboard	9,837	11,637
Cereal flour	1,170	1,213	Petroleum preparations	3,948	13,858
Chemicals - cosmetics	4,323	2,443	Photographic equipment	3,743	5,271
Chemicals - dyeing	2,716	2,165	Plastic articles, n.e.s.	4,439	5,306
Chemicals - fertilizers	3,070	1,400	Platinum	248	1,716
Chemicals - inorganic	4,657	4,954	Pottery	95	1,569
Chemicals - medicinal	7,160	7,076	Power generating mach.	22,292	22,499
Chemicals - n.e.s.	9,651	4,568	Printed materials	4,346	2,700
Chemicals - organic	14,744	14,820	Pulp and waste paper	4,034	2,648
Chemicals - plastics	15,467	7,443	Records/magnetic media	6,555	4,078
Cigarettes	4,736	69	Rice	1,029	157
Clothing	7,285	41,559	Rubber articles, n.e.s.	972	1,465
Coal	3,849	606	Rubber tires and tubes	1,959	3,074
Coffee	4	2,491	Scientific instruments	20,599	12,385
Copper	1,553	2,953	Ships, boats	1,014	1,029
Cork, wood, lumber	5,501	7,532	Silver and bullion	638	569
Corn	8,623	116	Soybeans	7,447	31
Cotton, raw and linters	2,740	300	Spacecraft	636	232
Crude fertilizers	1,526	1,176	Specialized ind. machinery	25,659	18,509
Crude oil	460	50,582	Sugar	5	1,001
Electrical machinery	56,637	75,525	Television, VCR, etc.,	19,838	34,167
Fish and preparations	2,930	6,657	Textile yarn, fabric	7,814	10,248
Footwear	761	12,749	Tobacco, unmanufactured	1,390	1,053
Furniture and bedding	3,323	9,431	Toys/games/sporting goods	3,693	14,734
Gem diamonds	151	6,588	Travel goods	306	3,581
General industrial machinery	26,599	25,286	Vegetables and fruits	7,313	7,514
Glass	1,814	1,679	Vehicles	49,584	103,664
Glassware	680	1,413	Watches/clocks/parts	277	2,805
Gold, nonmonetary	6,641	2,737	Wheat	6,302	247
Hides and skins	1,515	133	Wood manufactures	1,685	4,037
Iron and steel mill prod	4,795	13,368	**Total, selected categories:**		
Jewelry	618	4,362	Manufactured goods [1]	483,874	659,867
Lighting, plumbing	1,358	2,579	Agricultural commodities [1]	59,311	32,565
Liquified propane/butane	302	1,263	Mineral fuels [1]	12,057	73,028
Live animals	533	1,595	**Total [2]**	624,767	791,364

1. Domestic exports 2. Total exports (domestic and foreign). Details may not equal totals due to rounding. Data not seasonally adjusted. *Source:* U.S. Bureau of the Census, Foreign Trade Division, web: www.census.gov.

Foreign Investors in U.S. Business Enterprises

	Number				Investment outlays (millions of dollars)			
	1996[1]	1994	1992	1990	1996[1]	1994	1992	1990
Investments, total	1,158	1,036	941	1,617	$80,537	$ 45,626	$15,333	$65,932
Acquisitions	707	605	463	839	72,253	38,753	10,616	55,315
Establishments	451	431	478	778	8,284	6,873	4,718	10,617
Investors, total	1,304	1,144	1,019	1,768	80,537	45,626	15,333	65,932
Foreign direct investors	351	345	350	670	35,234	13,628	4,058	14,026
U.S. affiliates	953	799	669	1,098	45,303	31,999	11,275	51,906

1. Figures are preliminary. *Source:* U.S. Department of Commerce, Bureau of Economic Analysis, web: www.bea.doc.gov.

The Job Outlook Through 2005

Every two years, the Bureau of Labor Statistics (BLS) publishes its latest projections on the structure of the economy, labor force demographics, and future job growth. The following is a summary of the most recent BLS projections that were released at the end of 1995. They focused on occupational changes over the period 1994–2005.

Labor Force

The projected growth of the labor force during the 1994–2005 period is 16 million. This is 3.5 million less than it was during the previous 11 years. Its growth is slowing because growth of the civilian non-institutional population 16 years of age and older is declining.

The number of Hispanics, Asians, and others in the labor force will continue to increase much faster than white non-Hispanics, due primarily to immigration. However, white non-Hispanics will still account for the vast majority of workers in 2005.

The number of blacks in the labor force will grow slightly faster than the labor force as a whole.

The rate at which women enter the labor force will continue to be much faster than the rate for men, and women's share of the labor force will increase to 48%.

The rapid rate of increase of women and minority groups into the labor force has been widely discussed. However, another important change in labor force activity has continued for a very long period and has received much less attention: the long-term decline in labor force participation rates of virtually all age groups of men.

Reasons behind this trend have not been fully explored, but a contributing factor includes the increase in the number of men who report that they are unable to work. Also, the structural changes in the U.S. economy have clearly left many men ill-prepared for the direction job growth has taken during the last two decades, particularly men with the least education or training who worked in manufacturing or mining industries. Consequently, many men displaced by structural adjustments in the economy left the labor force permanently because they had insufficient education or training for the available jobs.

Gross Domestic Product

Exports will grow very rapidly, but employment will grow little in most industries producing goods for export because of rising productivity. Foreign trade is expected to continue to play an increasing role in the U.S. economy. The real GDP is expected to increase 2.3% per year over the 1994–2005 period according to the BLS moderate projections. This is slower than the 2.9% annual growth over the previous period 1983–1994.

Industry and Employment Projections

Employment shows a slower growth rate than it did in the previous period. Nevertheless, it is still expected to expand by 17.7 million by 2005, of which 16.8 million are nonfarm wage and salary jobs.

Industry employment will be very concentrated. The services and retail trade industry divisions will account for 16.2 million new wage and salary jobs, about 96% of the total. Most of the growth will be in just four areas: health, education, business services, and eating and drinking places. On the other hand, manufacturing will have 1.3 million fewer workers in 2005 than in 1994.

Within retail trade, employment of salespersons, cashiers, waiters and waitresses, food preparation workers, marketing and salesworker supervisors, and food service and lodging managers is expected to grow substantially.

Although retail trade will increase by 2.7 million jobs, self-employed workers in the industry will continue to decline as small, independent retail establishments have difficulty competing with large establishments and retail chains.

Employment in transportation, communications, and utilities is projected to increase 7%, slower than average. Half of the growth will be in trucking and warehousing. Transportation is expected to add more than 476,000 jobs over the 1994–2005 period. The future shape of the communications industry is highly uncertain. Employment reached a 1.4 million peak in 1982 mostly in telecommunications (1.1 million). Since then, it has declined to 903,000.

Jobs in the financial, insurance, and real estate sector are expected to increase except in depository institutions (banks, credit unions, savings and loans) because their growth will be dampened as banks continue to consolidate and restructure. Additionally, banks will continue to extend the use of automatic tellers and other computerized means of providing services to customers, instead of hiring additional employees.

Employment for insurance carriers is expected to grow by 82,000 to slightly more than 1.6 million in 2005. Employment for agents, brokers, and service will increase slightly for a gain of only 16,000.

The real estate sector is projected to increase from 1.3 million in 1994 to 1.5 million by 2005.

Wholesale trade will grow slowly. Business consolidation and direct selling of goods from manufacturers to retail establishments will reduce growth compared to that of recent years.

In the public sector, state and local government employment (excluding education and hospitals) will increase by 450,000 jobs. Much of the projected increase is related to law enforcement. Federal government positions will decline by more than 200,000 jobs, largely due to the decline in defense-related jobs.

Total employment in all divisions in the goods-producing sector will decline, except for construction. Construction will increase at a slower rate than previously because of significant overbuilding of office buildings and other types of construction in the past.

Agriculture, forestry, fishing, and related occupations are projected to decline by 112,000 jobs. They will only account for 2.5% of all jobs by 2005.

Mining, the smallest industry division, is projected to decline by 162,200 wage and salary jobs, led by a decline of nearly 100,000 jobs in oil and gas extraction.

Because of the close relationship between industries and occupations, most health occupations, which are concentrated in the rapidly growing health services industry, will grow faster than average. Health occupations will increase by 2.7 million jobs or 15% of total employment growth, in large part because of the need to care for an aging population with a longer life expectancy.

There will be numerous opportunities for registered nurses, licensed practical nurses, nursing aides, orderlies and attendants, health-care orderlies, and personal and home-care aides.

Education-related occupations will increase by nearly 2 million and account for 11% of employment growth over the 1994–2005 period. These occupations accounted only for 6% in 1994. Public and private elementary and secondary school teachers are expected to experience the most growth and special education teachers are projected to grow fastest because of legislation emphasizing training and employment for individuals with disabilities and a growing public interest in people with special needs.

Engineers, scientists, and workers in related fields numbered 4.6 million in 1994, or 4% of total employment, but are expected to account for 7% of total employment growth over the 1994–2005 period.

Because of the continuing spread of computer technology, employment in the computer sector will account for 60% of the overall growth. Within this field, there will be slower growth for computer programmers due to improved software and programming techniques that simplify or eliminate some programming tasks.

Employment in administrative support occupations including clerical numbered 22.2 million in 1994, more than any occupational cluster, and accounted for about 18% of all workers. However, this cluster will account for only a small share of employment growth and is projected to grow by only 4% or 994,000 jobs through 2005.

Office automation is expected to have a large impact on many of the individual occupations in this group. For example, the demand for typists and bookkeeping, accounting, and auditing clerks will be held down by advances in computer technology.

Fastest Growing Occupations, 1994–2005

Occupation	Change in employment, 1994–2005	
	Percent	Numerical
Homemaker/home-health aides	107%	640,000
Computer scientists and systems analysts	91	755,000
Physical therapy assistants and aides	83	64,000
Occupational therapy assistants and aides	82	13,000
Physical therapists	80	81,000
Human services workers	75	125,000
Services sales representatives	72	441,000
Occupational therapists	72	39,000
Medical assistants	59	121,000
Paralegals	58	64,000
Medical record technicians	56	45,000
Special education teachers	53	206,000
Correctional officers	51	158,000
Operations research analysts	50	22,000
Guards	48	415,000
Speech-language pathologists and audiologists	46	39,000
Private detectives and investigators	44	24,000
Surgical technologists	43	19,000
Dental assistants	42	79,000
Dental hygienists	42	53,000
General office clerks	41	26,000
Teacher aides	39	364,000
Securities and financial services sales representatives	37	90,000
Emergency medical technicians	36	49,000
Respiratory therapists	36	26,000
Management analysts and consultants	35	82,000
Radiologic technologists	35	59,000
Employment interviewers	35	27,000
Social workers	34	187,000
Preschool teachers and child-care workers	33	358,000
Restaurant and food service managers	33	192,000

Source: U.S. Department of Labor, Bureau of Labor Statistics, *1996–97 Occupational Outlook Handbook, 1994–2005*, web: stats.bls.gov/.

Top Declining Occupations, 1994–2005

Occupation	Projected employment decline (in thousands)
Farmers	−273
Typists and word processors	−212
Bookkeeping, accounting and auditing clerks	−178
Bank tellers	−152
Sewing machine operators, garment	−140
Cleaners and servants, private household	−108
Computer operators, except peripheral equipment	−98
Billing, posting, and calculating machine operators	−64
Duplicating, mail, and other office machine operators	−56
Textile draw-out and winding machine operators and tenders	−47
File clerks	−42
Freight, stock, and material movers, hand	−36
Farm workers	−36
Machine tool cutting operators and tenders, metal and plastic	−34
Central office operators	−34
Central office and PBX installers and repairers	−33
Electrical and electronic assemblers	−30
Station installers and repairers, telephone	−26
Personnel clerks, except payroll and timekeeping	−26
Data entry keyers, except composing	−25
Bartenders	−25
Inspectors, testers, and graders, precision	−25
Directory assistance operators	−24
Lathe and turning machine tool setters and set-up operators, metal and plastic	−22
Custom tailors and sewers	−21
Machine feeders and offbearers	−20
Machinists	−20
Service station attendants	−20
Machine forming operators and tenders, metal and plastic	−19
Communication, transportation, and utilities operations managers	−19

Source: U.S. Department of Labor, Bureau of Labor Statistics, *1996–1997 Occupational Outlook Handbook, 1994–2005*, web: stats.bls.gov/.

Balance of International Payments

(in billions of dollars)

Item	1996[1]	1995	1990	1985	1980	1975	1970	1965	1960
Exports of goods, services, and income	$1,032.5	$ 969.2	$ 652.9	$ 366.0	$ 343.2	$ 157.9	$ 68.4	$ 42.7	$ 30.5
Goods, adjusted, excluding military	611.7	575.9	389.5	214.4	224.0	107.1	42.5	26.5	19.7
Transfers under U.S. military agency sales contracts	13.8	13.4	9.8	9.0	8.2	3.9	1.5	0.8	0.3
Receipts of income on U.S. investments abroad	196.9	182.7	130.0	90.0	75.9	25.4	11.8	7.4	4.6
Other services	201.1	197.2	123.3	45.0	36.5	19.3	9.9	6.4	4.3
Imports of goods and services	−1,155.1	−1,082.3	−722.7	−461.2	−333.9	−132.6	−60.0	−32.8	−23.7
Goods, adjusted, excluding military	−799.3	−749.4	−497.6	−339.0	−249.3	−98.0	−39.9	−21.5	−14.8
Direct defense expenditures	−11.0	−9.8	−17.1	−12.0	−10.7	−4.8	4.9	−3.0	−3.1
Payments of income on foreign assets in U.S.	−205.3	−190.7	−118.1	−65.0	−43.2	−12.6	−5.5	−2.1	−1.2
Other services	−139.4	−132.4	−89.8	−46.0	−30.7	−17.2	−9.8	−6.2	−4.6
Unilateral transfers, excluding military grants, net	−42.5	−35.1	−22.3	−15.0	−7.0	−4.6	−3.3	−2.9	−2.3
U.S. government assets abroad, net	−0.7	−0.3	2.9	−2.8	−5.2	−3.5	−1.6	−1.6	−1.1
U.S. private assets abroad, net	−312.8	−297.8	−58.5	−26.0	−71.5	−35.4	−10.2	−5.3	−5.1
U.S. assets abroad, net	−306.8	−307.9	−57.7	−27.7	−86.1	−39.7	−9.3	−5.7	−4.1
Foreign assets in U.S., net	525.0	424.5	86.3	127.1	50.3	15.6	6.4	0.7	2.3
Statistical discrepancy	−53.1	31.5	63.5	23.0	29.6	5.5	−0.2	−0.5	−1.0
Balance on goods, services, and income	−122.6	−113.1	−69.7	−106.8	9.5	25.2	8.5	10.0	6.9
Balance on current account	−165.1	−148.2	−92.1	−118.0	3.7	18.4	2.4	5.4	2.8

1. Preliminary. NOTE: — denotes debits. *Source:* U.S. Department of Commerce, Bureau of Economic Analysis, web: www.bea.doc.gov.

U.S. Direct Investment in Other Countries, 1996

(in millions of dollars)

	All industries	Petroleum	Manufacturing	Wholesale trade	Banking	Finance, insurance, real estate	Services	Other industries
All countries	796,494	75,479	272,564	72,462	32,504	257,213	36,673	49,600
Canada	91,587	10,997	43,817	7,764	974	15,816	4,729	7,490
Europe	399,632	28,907	134,733	37,602	14,005	146,379	23,832	14,174
Belgium	18,604	370	8,425	2,225	282	4,130	2,274	897
France	34,000	1,103	16,600	4,141	739	7,392	2,939	1,086
Germany	44,259	(*)	22,741	2,886	1,395	11,597	(*)	2,261
Ireland	11,749	(*)	7,457	470	(*)	2,780	863	74
Italy	18,687	549	11,549	2,537	320	1,900	1,474	358
Netherlands	44,667	2,564	10,472	3,910	134	23,592	2,424	1,571
Spain	11,393	191	7,109	1,023	1,572	733	517	248
Switzerland	35,751	703	4,426	10,341	2,083	16,826	1,241	131
United Kingdom	142,560	14,889	32,341	7,365	5,260	68,339	8,521	5,846
South America	52,153	4,489	26,919	2,263	3,191	6,847	688	7,756
Brazil	26,166	698	19,346	530	1,164	3,019	264	1,146
Central America	38,905	1,275	12,290	2,176	541	19,488	635	2,500
Mexico	18,747	169	11,408	764	443	2,864	515	2,585
Panama	18,256	839	150	559	80	16,527	108	7
Other Western Hemisphere	53,151	724	1,401	3,246	1,900	42,847	2,189	844
Bermuda	33,783	(*)	17	1,455	0	30,600	1,826	(*)
Asia and Pacific	140,402	19,943	49,382	18,907	10,932	23,738	4,005	13,495
Australia	28,769	1,609	9,360	2,511	3,742	3,395	1,437	6,715
Hong Kong	16,022	599	2,601	5,022	1,506	4,656	815	823
Japan	39,593	4,816	16,534	7,344	379	9,150	816	555
Singapore	14,150	2,799	5,870	1,777	507	2,521	487	189

* Suppressed to avoid disclosure of data of individual companies. *Source:* U.S. Department of Commerce, Bureau of Economic Analysis, web: www.bea.doc.gov.

U.S. Contributions to International Organizations

(for fiscal year 1996)

Organization	Amount (in millions)	Organization	Amount (in millions)
United Nations and affiliated agencies:		World Trade Organization/ General Agreement on Tariffs and Trade	13
Food and Agriculture Organization	$75	Customs Cooperation Council	4
International Atomic Energy Agency	63	International Agency for Research on Cancer	2
International Civil Aviation Organization	13	Intl. Center for Study of Preservation & Restoration of Cultural Properties	1
International Labor Organization	65		
International Maritime Organization	1	International Bureau of Weights and Measures	1
International Telecommunications Union	8		
United Nations	311	Interparliamentary Union	1
Universal Postal Union	2	Other international organizations	1
World Health Organization	97	Subtotal	23
World Intellectual Property Organization	1	**Total**	**892**
World Meteorological Organization	12	International peacekeeping activities:	
Subtotal	648	U.N. Disengagement Observer Force	8
Inter-American organizations:		U.N. Interim Force in Lebanon	16
Inter-American Institute for Cooperation on Agriculture	16	U.N. Angola Verification Mission	52
Organization of American States	52	U.N. Iraq–Kuwait Observer Mission	3
Pan American Health Organization	48	U.N. Operations in the Former Yugoslavia	122
Subtotal	116	U.N. Observer Mission in Georgia	1
Regional organizations:		U.N. Mission in Haiti	40
Asia Pacific Economic Cooperation	1	U.N. Observer Mission in Liberia	6
North Atlantic Assembly	1	U.N. Assistance Mission for Rwanda	14
North Atlantic Treaty Organization	37	U.N. Force in Cyprus	3
Organization for Economic Cooperation and Development	65	U.N. Mission in Tajikistan	2
South Pacific Commission	1	Payment of Prior Year Balances	92
Subtotal	105	**Total**	**359**
Other international organizations:			

Source: Budget of the United States Government Fiscal Year 1998.

Poverty and Income in the United States

Source: U.S. Bureau of the Census, *Poverty in the United States: 1995* and *Money Income in the United States: 1995* both issued September 1996.

The number of persons below the official government poverty level was 36.4 million in 1995, representing 13.8 percent of the nation's population. Both the number of poor and the poverty rate showed a significant decline from the 1994 figure of 38.1 million and a poverty rate of 14.5 percent. Both the number of poor and the poverty rate showed a significant decline from the 1994 figure of 38.1 million and a poverty rate of 14.5 percent.

Age

In 1995, the poverty rate for all persons under 18 years old was 20.8%. Higher than the percentage for other age groups, this was significantly lower than the 1994 rate of 21.8%. About half of the nation's poor in 1995 were either under 18 years of age or 65 and over (49%).

The elderly are under-represented in the poverty population. These persons 65 and over are approximately 12% of the total population but make up only

Poverty Thresholds

The poverty thresholds in 1996 were as follows: one person under 65: $8,163; age 65 and over: $7,525; two persons: householder under 65, $10,562; householder 65 and over, $9,491; three persons: $12,517; four persons, $16,029; five persons, $18,951; six persons, $21,418; seven persons, $24,247; eight persons, $27,012; and nine or more persons, $32,203.

9% of the poor. However, a higher proportion of elderly (7%) than nonelderly (4%) were concentrated just over their respective poverty thresholds (between 100% and 125% of their thresholds); 18% of the nation's 12.3 million "near poor" persons were elderly.

Persons under age 18 continue to represent a very large segment of the poor (40%) even though they are only a little more than one-fourth of the total population.

Children under age six have been particularly vulnerable to poverty. In 1995, the overall poverty rate for related children under six years of age was 23.7%. Of related children under six years old living in families with a female householder, no spouse present, 61.8% were poor, compared to 11.1% of such young children in married-couple families.

Race and Hispanic Origin

In 1995, the poverty rate was 11.2% for whites, 8.5% for non-Hispanic whites, and 29.3% for blacks. For persons of Hispanic origin (who may be of any race) the poverty rate was 30.3%. For Asians and Pacific Islanders, the largest component of persons of other races, the poverty rate was 14.6% in 1995.

Even though the poverty rate for whites was lower than that for the other racial and ethnic groups, the majority of poor persons in 1995 were white (67%), and 45% were non-Hispanic white.

Blacks showed a significant decrease in the poverty rate between 1994 and 1995. Whites overall and non-Hispanic whites in particular showed a decrease in both their poverty rates and the number of poor between

Persons Below the Poverty Level, 1975–1995

(in thousands)

Year	All persons	White	Black	Hispanic origin[1]	Year	All persons	White	Black	Hispanic origin[1]
1975	25,877	17,770	7,545	2,991	1986	32,370	22,183	8,983	5,117
1976	24,975	16,713	7,595	2,783	1987	32,221	21,195	9,520	5,422
1977	24,720	16,416	7,726	2,700	1988	31,745	20,715	9,356	5,357
1978	24,497	16,259	7,625	2,607	1989	31,528	20,785	9,302	5,430
1979	26,072	17,214	8,050	2,921	1990	33,585	22,326	9,837	6,006
1980	29,272	19,699	8,579	3,491	1991	35,708	23,747	10,242	6,339
1981	31,822	21,553	9,173	3,713	1992	38,014	25,259	10,827	7,592
1982	34,398	23,517	9,697	4,301	1993	39,265	26,226	10,877	8,126
1983	35,303	23,984	9,882	4,633	1994	38,059	25,379	10,196	8,416
1984	33,700	22,955	9,490	4,806	1995	36,425	24,423	9,872	8,574
1985	33,064	22,860	8,926	5,236					

1. Persons of Hispanic origin may be of any race. *Source:* U.S. Bureau of the Census, web: www.census.gov.

1994 and 1995. Persons of Hispanic origin showed no significant change in the number living in poverty, or in the poverty rate. The poverty rate for Asians and Pacific Islanders did not change significantly between 1994 and 1995.

Families

There was a significant decrease in both the number of poor families and in their poverty rate between 1994 and 1995. The poverty rate for families was 10.8% in 1995 compared with 11.6% in 1994. The decline in poverty for families was true for all family types. Married couples had a 1995 poverty rate of 5.6%, down from 6.1% in 1994.

There was no significant change for black or Hispanic-origin families overall. For families with a female householder, no spouse present, the poverty rate was 32.4%, down from 34.6% in 1994. Female-householder families were overrepresented among the poor. While 54% of all poor families had a female householder with no spouse present, only 18% of all families in the United States had a female householder. Neither of these figures was statistically different from their respective 1994 estimates.

Income

For the first time in six years, the real median income of households in the United States increased in 1995. Median household income in 1995 was $34,076. Between 1994 and 1995, median household income increased by 2.7%. .

Race and Hispanic Origin

Among the race and Hispanic origin groups, Asian and Pacific Islander households had the highest median household income in 1995 ($40,614), and black and Hispanic-origin households had the lowest ($22,393 and $22,860, respectively). Households maintained by white persons had a median income of $35,766.

White and black households experienced an increase in real income between 1994 and 1995. Black households experienced a 3.6% increase, while white households gained 2.2%. Hispanic-origin household incomes declined 5.1%. Since 1989 the median income of Hispanic-origin households has dropped 14.6%. Asian and Pacific Islander households have remained largely unchanged since 1991.

Year-Round, Full-Time Workers

The real median earnings of year-round, full-time workers 15 years old and over remained unchanged between 1994 and 1995. Though unemployment declined between 1994 and 1995, there were no increases in median earnings for full-time year-round workers. The median earnings of female, year-round full-time workers in 1995 fell by 1.5% to $22,497, decreasing the female-male earnings ratio to 0.71 from its all-time high of 0.72 reached in 1990 and 1994.

Per Capita Income

Overall, per capita income did not change in real terms between 1994 and 1995, for the total population or for race and Hispanic-origin groups. Per capita incomes were $17,611 for whites, $10,650 for blacks, $16,902 for Asian and Pacific Islanders and $9,435 for Hispanic-origin populations. The 1995 per capita income was $17,227 for the total population.

Percent of Persons in Poverty, by State: 1992–1995

State	1995 Percent	1994 Percent	1993 Percent	1992 Percent	State	1995 Percent	1994 Percent	1993 Percent	1992 Percent
Alabama	20.1	16.4	17.4	17.3	Georgia	12.1	14.0	13.5	17.7
Alaska	7.1	10.2	9.1	10.2	Hawaii	10.3	8.7	8.0	11.2
Arizona	16.1	15.9	15.4	15.8	Idaho	14.5	12.0	13.1	15.2
Arkansas	14.9	15.3	20.0	17.5	Illinois	12.4	12.4	13.6	15.6
California	16.7	17.9	18.2	16.4	Indiana	9.6	13.7	12.2	11.8
Colorado	8.8	9.0	9.9	10.8	Iowa	12.2	10.7	10.3	11.5
Connecticut	9.7	10.8	8.5	9.8	Kansas	10.8	14.9	13.1	11.1
Delaware	10.3	8.3	10.2	7.8	Kentucky	14.7	18.5	20.4	19.7
D.C.	22.2	21.2	26.4	20.3	Louisiana	19.7	25.7	26.4	24.5
Florida	16.2	14.9	17.8	15.6	Maine	11.7	9.4	15.4	13.5

State	1995 Percent	1994 Percent	1993 Percent	1992 Percent	State	1995 Percent	1994 Percent	1993 Percent	1992 Percent
Maryland	10.1	10.7	9.7	11.8	Oklahoma	17.1	16.7	19.9	18.6
Massachusetts	11.0	9.7	10.7	10.3	Oregon	11.2	11.8	11.8	11.4
Michigan	12.2	14.1	15.4	13.6	Pennsylvania	12.2	12.5	13.2	11.9
Minnesota	9.2	11.7	11.6	13.0	Rhode Island	10.6	10.3	11.2	12.4
Mississippi	23.5	19.9	24.7	24.6	South Carolina	19.9	13.8	18.7	19.0
Missouri	9.4	15.6	16.1	15.7	South Dakota	14.5	14.5	14.2	15.1
Montana	15.3	11.5	14.9	13.8	Tennessee	15.5	14.6	19.6	17.0
Nebraska	9.6	8.8	10.3	10.6	Texas	17.4	19.1	17.4	18.3
Nevada	11.1	11.1	9.8	14.7	Utah	8.4	8.0	10.7	9.4
New Hampshire	5.3	7.7	9.9	8.7	Vermont	10.3	7.6	10.0	10.5
New Jersey	7.8	9.2	10.9	10.3	Virginia	10.2	10.7	9.7	9.5
New Mexico	25.3	21.1	17.4	21.6	Washington	12.5	11.7	12.1	11.2
New York	16.5	17.0	16.4	15.7	West Virginia	16.7	18.6	22.2	22.3
North Carolina	12.6	14.2	14.4	15.8	Wisconsin	8.5	9.0	12.6	10.9
North Dakota	12.0	10.4	11.2	12.1	Wyoming	12.2	9.3	13.3	10.3
Ohio	11.5	14.1	13.0	12.5					

Source: "Poverty in the United States, 1995," *Current Population Reports*, U.S. Bureau of the Census, web: www.census.gov.

Gross Domestic Product or Expenditure[1]
(in billions)

Item	1996	1995	1994	1993	1992	1989	1987	1980	1970
Gross domestic product	7,580.0	7,245.8	6,931.4	6,343.3	6,038.5	5,244.0	4,539.9	2,708.0	1,010.7
GDP in chained (1992) dollars	6,911.0	6,739.0	6,604.2	6,383.8	6,244.4	6,060.4	5,648.4	4,611.9	3,388.2
Personal consumption expenditures	5,152.0	4,924.3	4,698.7	4,378.2	4,139.9	3,517.9	3,052.2	1,748.1	646.5
Durable goods	632.2	606.4	580.9	538.0	497.3	459.8	403.0	212.5	85.3
Nondurable goods	1,545.1	1,486.1	1,429.7	1,339.2	1,300.9	1,146.9	1,011.1	682.9	270.4
Services	2,974.7	2,831.8	2,688.1	2,501.0	2,341.6	1,911.2	1,637.4	852.7	290.8
Gross private domestic investment	1,119.8	1,065.3	1,014.4	882.0	796.5	837.6	749.3	467.6	150.3
Residential	310.2	289.8	287.7	250.6	223.6	230.9	225.2	123.3	41.4
Nonresidential	790.4	738.5	667.2	616.1	565.5	570.7	497.8	353.8	106.7
Change in business inventories	19.3	37.0	59.5	15.4	7.3	36.0	26.3	−9.5	2.3
Net export of goods and services	−99.6	−102.3	−96.4	−65.3	−29.6	−82.9	−143.1	−14.7	1.2
Government purchases	1,407.7	1,358.5	1,314.7	1,148.4	1,131.8	971.4	881.5	507.1	212.7
Federal	524.1	516.7	516.3	443.6	448.8	401.4	384.9	209.1	100.1
State and local	883.6	841.7	798.4	704.7	683.0	570.0	496.6	298.0	112.6

1. Current dollars except as noted. Source: U.S. Bureau of Economic Analysis, *Survey of Current Business*, February 1997, web: www.bea.doc.gov.

The Federal Budget—Receipts and Outlays
(in billions of dollars)

	Actual 1995	Actual 1996	Budgeted 1997		Actual 1995	Actual 1996	Budgeted 1997
Receipts by Source				Commerce and housing credit	−17.8	−10.6	−8.8
Individual income taxes	590.2	656.4	672.7	Transportation	39.4	39.6	39.3
Corporation income taxes	157	171.8	176.2	Community and regional development	10.6	10.7	12.8
Social insurance taxes and contributions	484.5	509.4	535.8	Education, training, employment, and social services	54.3	52	51.3
Excise taxes	57.5	54	57.2	Health	115.4	119.4	127.6
Estate and gift taxes	15.6	17.2	17.6	Medicare	159.9	174.2	194.3
Customs duties	20.9	18.7	17.3	Income security	220.5	226	238.9
Miscellaneous receipts	28.6	25.5	28.6	Social security	335.8	349.7	367.7
Total receipts	**1,355.2**	**1,453.1**	**1,505.4**	Veterans benefits and services	37.9	37	39.7
Outlays by Function				Administration of justice	16.2	17.5	20.8
National defense	272.1	265.7	267.2	General government	13.8	11.9	13.1
International affairs	16.4	13.5	14.8	Net interest	232.2	241.1	247.4
General science, space and technology	16.7	16.7	16.6	Undistributed offsetting receipts	−44.5	−37.6	−46.5
Energy	4.9	2.8	2.1	**Total outlays**	**1,515.7**	**1,560.3**	**1,631.0**
Natural resources and environment	22.1	21.6	22.8	**Total Deficit**	**−160.5**	**−107.3**	**−125.6**
Agriculture	9.8	9.2	10.3				

1. Estimated. NOTE: The fiscal year is from Oct. 1 to Sept. 30. Source: Budget of the United States Government, Fiscal Years 1997 and 1998.

Government Employment and Payrolls

Year and function	Employees (in thousands)				October payrolls (in millions)			
	Total	Federal[1]	State	Local	Total	Federal[1]	State	Local
1940	4,474	1,128	3,346		$ 566	177	$389	
1945	6,556	3,375	3,181		1,110	642	468	
1950	6,402	2,117	1,057	3,228	1,528	613	218	696
1955	7,432	2,378	1,199	3,855	2,265	846	326	1,093
1960	8,808	2,421	1,527	4,860	3,333	1,118	524	1,691
1965	10,589	2,588	2,028	5,973	4,884	1,484	849	2,551
1970	13,028	2,881	2,755	7,392	8,334	2,428	1,612	4,294
1975	14,973	2,890	3,271	8,813	13,224	3,584	2,653	6,987
1980	16,213	2,898	3,753	9,562	19,935	5,205	4,285	10,445
1982	15,841	2,848	3,744	9,249	23,173	5,959	5,022	12,192
1983	16,034	2,875	3,816	9,344	24,525	6,302	5,346	12,878
1984	16,436	2,942	3,898	9,595	26,904	7,137	5,815	13,952
1985	16,690	3,021	3,984	9,685	28,945	7,580	6,329	15,036
1986	16,933	3,019	4,068	9,846	30,670	7,561	6,810	16,298
1987	17,212	3,091	4,116	10,005	32,669	7,924	7,263	17,482
1988	17,588	3,112	4,236	10,240	34,203	7,976	7,842	18,385
1990	18,369	3,105	4,503	10,760	39,228	8,999	9,083	21,146
1995, total	6,866	2,895	3,971	10,120	14,090	n.a.	10,927	3,163
National defense and international relations	831	831	(2)	(2)	n.a.	n.a.	(2)	(2)
Postal service	849	849	(2)	(2)	n.a.	n.a.	(2)	(2)
Education	7,088	n.a.	1,469	5,619	18,791	n.a.	4,173	14,618
Instructional employees	4,331	n.a.	474	3,858	13,366	n.a.	1,927	11,439
Highways	547	4	253	290	1,357	n.a.	667	690
Health and hospitals	1,731	315	651	760	3,635	n.a.	1,689	1,945
Police protection	865	86	90	689	2,477	n.a.	287	2,190
Fire protection	274	(2)	(2)	274	950	(2)	(2)	950
Sewerage and solid waste management	234	(2)	3	232	608	(2)	4	604
Parks and recreation	272	26	39	207	502	n.a.	81	421
Natural resources	398	210	152	36	475	n.a.	395	80
Financial administration	486	131	164	190	916	n.a.	444	472
All other	3,412	443	1,147	1,821	8,004	n.a.	3,187	4,817

1. Civilians only. 2. Not applicable. NOTE: n.a. = not available. Detail may not add to totals because of rounding. *Source:* U.S. Bureau of the Census, web: www.census.gov.

Receipts and Outlays of the Federal Government

(in millions of dollars)

From 1789 to 1842, the federal fiscal year ended Dec. 31; from 1844 to 1976, on June 30; and beginning 1977, on Sept. 30.

	Receipts					
	Customs (including tonnage tax)[1]	Internal revenue		Miscellaneous taxes and receipts	Total receipts	Net receipts[2]
		Income and profits tax	Other			
1789–1791	$ 4	—	—	—	$ 4	$ 4
1800	9	—	$ –1	$ 1	11	11
1810	9	—	—	1	9	9
1820	15	—	—	3	18	18
1830	22	—	—	3	25	25
1840	14	—	—	6	20	20
1850	40	—	—	4	44	44
1860	53	—	—	3	56	56
1870	195	—	185	32	411	411
1880	187	—	124	23	334	334
1890	230	—	143	31	403	403
1900	233	—	295	39	567	567
1910	334	—	290	52	675	675
1915	210	$ 80	335	72	698	683
1929	602	2,331	607	493	4,033	3,862
1939	319	2,189	2,972	188	5,668	4,979
1944	431	34,655	7,030	3,325	45,441	43,563
1945	355	35,173	8,729	3,494	47,750	44,362
1950	423	28,263	11,186	1,439	41,311	36,422

	Receipts					
	Customs (including tonnage tax)[1]	Internal revenue		Miscellaneous taxes and receipts	Total receipts	Net receipts[2]
		Income and profits tax	Other			
1956	705	56,639	20,564	389	78,297	74,547
1960	1,123	67,151	28,266	1,190	97,730	92,492
1965	1,478	79,792	39,996	1,598	122,863	116,833
1970	2,494	138,689	65,276	3,424	209,883	193,743
1975	3,782	202,146	108,371	6,711	321,010	280,997
1980	7,482	359,927	192,436	12,797	572,641	520,050
1985	12,079	474,074	311,092	18,576	815,821	733,996
1988	16,198	495,376	377,469	19,909	(4)	908,953
1989	16,334	549,273	402,200	22,800	(4)	990,691
1990	16,707	560,391	426,893	27,470	(4)	1,031,462
1991	15,949	565,913	449,577	22,846	(4)	1,054,265
1992	17,359	576,234	470,401	26,459	(4)	1,090,453
1993	18,802	627,200	488,934	18,290	(4)	1,153,226
1994	20,099	683,123	531,924	22,041	(4)	1,257,187
1995	19,300	747,247	556,721	27,309	(4)	1,350,578
1996	18,670	828,241	534,948	25,534	(4)	1,407,393

	Outlays					
Year	Department of Defense (Army, 1789–1950)	Department of the Navy	Interest on public debt	All other	Net outlays[3]	Surplus (+) or deficit (—)
1789–1791	$ 1	—	$ 2	$ 1	$ 4	—
1800	3	$ 3	3	1	11	—
1810	2	2	3	1	8	$ +1
1820	3	4	5	6	18	—
1830	5	3	2	5	15	+10
1840	7	6	—	11	24	−4
1850	9	8	4	18	40	+4
1860	16	12	3	32	63	−7
1870	58	22	129	101	310	+101
1880	38	14	96	120	268	+66
1890	45	22	36	215	318	+85
1900	135	56	40	290	521	+46
1910	190	123	21	359	694	−19
1915	202	142	23	379	746	−63
1929	426	365	678	1,658	3,127	+734
1939	695	673	941	6,533	8,841	−3,862
1944	49,438	26,538	2,609	16,401	94,986	−51,423
1945	50,490	30,047	3,617	14,149	98,303	−53,941
1950	5,789	4,130	5,750	23,875	39,544	−3,122
1956	35,693	—	6,787	27,981	70,460	+4,087
1960	43,969	—	9,180	39,075	92,223	+269
1965	47,179	—	11,346	59,904	118,430	−1,596
1970	78,360	—	19,304	98,924	196,588	−2,845
1975	87,471	—	32,665	205,969	326,105	−45,108
1980	136,138	—	74,860	368,013	579,011	−58,961
1985	244,054	—	178,945	513,810	936,809	−202,813
1988	290,349	—	151,711	621,995	1,064,055	−155,102
1989	303,600	—	169,100	649,943	1,142,643	−123,785
1990	299,355	—	183,790	768,725	1,251,850	−220,388
1991	273,292	—	194,541	855,924	1,323,757	−269,492
1992	298,350	—	199,439	883,005	1,380,794	−290,340
1993	291,186	—	198,811	918,635	1,408,532	−255,306
1994	281,451	—	202,957	976,149	1,460,557	−203,370
1995	271,895	—	232,175	1,010,364	1,514,434	−163,856
1996	265,748	—	241,092	1,053,492	1,560,330	−152,937

1. Beginning 1933, tonnage tax is included in "Other receipts." 2. Net receipts equal total receipts less (a) appropriations to federal old-age and survivors' insurance trust fund beginning fiscal year 1939 and (b) refunds of receipts beginning fiscal year 1933. 3. Includes Air Force 1950–65 (in millions): 1950, $3,521; 1956, $16,750; 1960, $19,065; 1965, $18,471. 4. Net receipts are now the total receipts. Public Law 99-177 moved two social security trust funds off-budget. *Source:* Budget of the United States Government, Fiscal Year 1998.

Social Welfare Expenditures Under Public Programs

(in millions of dollars)

Year and source of funds	Social insurance	Public aid	Health and medical programs[1]	Veterans' programs	Education	Housing	Other social welfare	All health and medical care[2]	Total social welfare	Total social welfare as: Percent of gross domestic product	Percent of total govt. outlays
Federal											
1982	250,551	52,485	14,598	24,463	11,917	7,176	6,500	90,776	367,691	11.8	52.5
1984	288,743	58,480	16,622	25,970	13,010	10,226	7,349	103,927	420,399	11.4	50.2
1986	326,588	65,615	19,926	27,072	15,022	10,164	7,977	125,730	472,364	11.2	47.6
1988	358,412	74,137	22,681	28,845	16,952	14,006	8,112	149,102	523,144	11.0	49.1
1990	422,257	92,858	27,204	30,428	18,374	16,612	8,905	190,616	616,639	11.2	51.4
1991	453,534	113,235	29,668	32,331	19,084	18,696	9,831	213,811	676,380	11.9	52.8
1992	495,710	138,704	31,872	34,212	20,188	17,950	10,677	249,528	749,312	12.6	57.1
1993	534,310	151,851	35,209	36,034	20,455	18,006	10,838	275,390	804,702	12.4	60.0
State and Local											
1982	52,481	28,367	19,195	245	121,957	778	5,154	40,738	228,178	7.4	62.6
1984	52,378	32,206	20,383	301	139,046	1,306	5946	44,540	251,569	7.0	58.9
1986	63,816	37,464	24,408	373	163,495	1,872	6,728	53,884	298,158	7.3	58.2
1988	73,783	46,237	29,859	409	202,416	2,550	7,368	70,511	362,622	7.5	60.1
1990	91,565	53,953	36,263	488	240,011	2,856	9,012	85,775	434,148	7.9	68.0
1991	107,641	68,104	38,504	526	258,063	2,826	9,949	102,715	485,613	8.6	70.4
1992	121,266	69,241	39,163	555	272,011	2,668	10,855	104,559	515,758	8.7	70.6
1993	123,018	69,214	41,294	572	311,455	1,748	11,832	106,372	559,183	8.6	81.2
Total											
1982	303,033	80,852	33,793	24,708	133,874	7,954	11,654	131,514	595,869	19.2	55.7
1984	341,120	90,685	37,006	26,275	152,056	11,532	13,295	148,467	671,969	18.3	52.8
1986	390,404	103,079	44,334	27,445	178,518	12,036	14,705	179,614	770,522	18.5	47.9
1988	432,195	120,375	52,540	29,254	219,368	16,556	15,480	219,613	885,766	18.5	52.8
1990	513,823	146,811	63,467	30,916	258,385	19,468	17,918	276,391	1,050,788	19.2	56.7
1991	561,175	181,339	68,172	32,857	277,147	21,523	19,780	316,526	1,161,993	20.5	58.6
1992	616,975	207,945	71,035	34,767	292,198	20,617	21,532	354,058	1,265,070	21.3	61.6
1993	657,328	221,065	74,503	36,606	331,910	19,803	22,670	381,762	1,363,884	21.1	66.7
Percent of total, by type											
1986	50.7	13.4	5.8	3.6	23.2	1.6	1.9	23.3	100.0	(3)	(3)
1988	48.8	13.6	5.9	3.3	24.8	1.9	1.7	24.8	100.0	(3)	(3)
1990	49.0	14.0	6.0	3.0	25.0	2.0	1.0	26.0	100.0	(3)	(3)
1991	48.0	16.0	6.0	3.0	24.0	2.0	1.0	27.0	100.0	(3)	(3)
1992	48.8	16.4	5.6	2.7	23.1	1.6	1.7	28.0	100.0	(3)	(3)
1993	46.7	16.2	5.5	2.7	24.3	1.5	1.7	28.0	100.0	(3)	(3)
Federal spending as a percent of total											
1986	83.6	63.7	44.9	98.6	8.4	84.4	54.2	70.0	61.3	(3)	(3)
1988	82.9	61.6	43.2	98.6	7.7	84.6	52.4	67.9	59.1	(3)	(3)
1990	82.0	63.0	43.0	98.0	7.0	85.0	50.0	69.0	59.0	(3)	(3)
1991	81.0	62.0	44.0	98.0	7.0	87.0	50.0	68.0	58.0	(3)	(3)
1992	80.3	66.7	44.9	98.4	6.9	87.1	49.6	70.5	59.2	(3)	(3)
1993	81.3	68.7	44.6	98.4	6.2	90.9	47.8	72.4	59.0	(3)	(3)

1. Excludes program parts of social insurance, public aid, veterans, and other social welfare. 2. Combines health and medical programs with medical services provided in connection with social insurance, public aid, veterans, and other social welfare programs. 3. Not applicable. NOTE: Figures are latest available. *Source:* Social Security Administration, web: www.ssa.gov.

Distribution of Federal Funds by State and Territory, Fiscal Year 1996

(thousands of dollars)

State/Territory	Total	Grants to state and local governments	Salaries and wages	Direct payments to individuals	Procurement	Other programs
Alabama	23,548,131	3,671,049	2,897,623	13,751,879	2,936,599	290,981
Alaska	4,377,772	1,139,630	1,327,453	1,054,171	803,901	52,618
Arizona	21,951,337	3,395,691	2,523,183	12,383,572	3,485,395	163,497
Arkansas	12,164,019	2,203,342	1,037,424	8,108,779	453,019	361,455
California	31,430,901	28,965,425	18,037,723	81,135,681	27,723,583	1,768,443
Colorado	3,655,714	2,708,894	3,234,543	9,020,677	4,656,320	390,864
Connecticut	18,142,499	3,472,326	1,417,972	9,904,484	3,122,527	225,190
Delaware	3,407,556	699,666	411,168	2,115,785	153,775	27,162
District of Columbia	22,678,122	3,408,183	11,304,118	2,728,453	4,579,905	657,464
Florida	79,614,086	9,055,445	7,660,372	53,695,103	8,125,596	1,077,568
Georgia	34,856,944	5,500,636	5,904,188	18,276,375	4,741,012	434,734
Hawaii	7,990,275	1,104,527	2,408,570	3,348,461	1,027,398	101,319

State/Territory	Total	Grants to state and local governments	Salaries and wages	Direct payments to individuals	Procurement	Other programs
Idaho	5,488,748	897,142	630,056	2,918,817	945,045	97,688
Illinois	51,585,730	9,609,532	5,440,017	32,487,293	3,165,199	883,690
Indiana	24,250,211	3,746,849	1,969,920	15,283,432	2,090,255	1,159,756
Iowa	13,414,932	2,099,279	944,096	7,817,743	777,558	1,776,255
Kansas	12,359,419	1,737,041	1,700,085	7,157,452	1,109,643	655,199
Kentucky	19,742,132	3,445,335	2,441,966	11,467,719	2,004,606	382,506
Louisiana	22,048,454	4,727,673	2,083,585	12,766,873	2,086,487	383,836
Maine	6,818,678	1,348,266	722,301	3,781,545	907,359	59,206
Maryland	37,109,915	4,283,397	7,323,944	14,744,129	8,521,750	2,236,696
Massachusetts	36,135,976	7,415,495	2,856,647	19,416,262	6,080,621	366,951
Michigan	39,633,242	7,845,890	2,778,247	26,464,208	2,188,854	356,043
Minnesota	18,993,582	3,923,376	1,654,705	10,885,914	1,534,730	994,857
Mississippi	15,183,933	2,725,601	1,571,451	8,334,822	2,326,200	225,860
Missouri	35,321,108	4,439,832	3,184,746	15,966,130	10,593,615	1,136,785
Montana	4,972,344	1,002,520	631,939	2,446,687	262,931	628,268
Nebraska	7,590,600	1,234,820	1,031,443	4,295,707	584,873	443,757
Nevada	7,514,329	934,322	849,697	4,276,915	1,406,672	46,723
New Hampshire	5,049,288	933,782	447,956	2,936,384	671,585	59,581
New Jersey	38,467,353	6,529,361	3,556,418	24,355,024	3,750,337	276,212
New Mexico	12,140,579	2,126,085	1,686,421	4,508,437	3,676,231	143,406
New York	95,797,668	26,117,662	7,156,846	55,293,792	6,319,855	909,513
North Carolina	33,369,968	6,300,299	4,898,359	19,619,765	2,293,304	258,239
North Dakota	3,605,287	811,437	643,553	1,696,190	209,820	244,287
Ohio	50,600,614	9,394,074	4,611,998	31,540,664	4,583,274	470,603
Oklahoma	16,843,155	2,583,797	2,720,514	10,020,570	1,205,250	313,024
Oregon	14,245,806	3,058,001	1,409,950	8,907,536	610,417	259,902
Pennsylvania	64,609,863	11,017,142	5,625,127	41,534,652	5,530,752	902,190
Rhode Island	5,718,500	1,171,780	633,646	3,428,422	422,850	61,802
South Carolina	18,353,933	3,006,853	2,203,242	10,497,000	2,504,519	142,319
South Dakota	3,866,775	863,987	534,450	2,017,490	248,588	202,259
Tennessee	27,519,943	4,526,953	2,702,165	15,704,701	4,317,302	268,822
Texas	86,782,734	13,937,288	11,248,969	46,389,523	13,840,351	1,366,602
Utah	8,153,411	1,508,069	1,477,902	3,984,496	1,072,486	110,459
Vermont	2,783,966	664,979	269,784	1,533,893	295,096	20,215
Virginia	50,688,090	3,992,366	12,321,991	18,790,230	14,528,576	1,054,927
Washington	29,563,084	4,998,193	4,573,912	14,964,092	4,603,131	423,756
West Virginia	10,065,585	2,145,950	814,784	6,491,961	513,725	99,165
Wisconsin	20,094,794	4,023,901	1,377,481	13,122,733	1,161,640	409,039
Wyoming	2,503,838	705,602	395,363	1,215,004	153,196	34,672
Guam	829,830	139,982	384,104	179,940	112,399	13,405
Northern Mariana Islands	40,968	31,080	1,730	6,611	1,471	75
Puerto Rico	10,402,871	3,501,464	713,229	5,701,652	404,700	81,825
Virgin Islands	611,798	377,354	42,451	159,749	22,287	9,958
U.S. undistributed	20,913,946	228,253	1,297,198	298,111	19,090,384	—
Total U.S.	**1,398,228,413**	**241,474,089**	**169,731,086**	**760,958,495**	**200,543,114**	**25,521,629**

Source: Consolidated Federal Funds Report, Fiscal Year 1996.

Employed and Unemployed Workers

By Full- and Part-Time Status, Sex, and Age

(in thousands)

	1996[2]	1995[2]	1994[2]	1993[1]	1992[1]	1990[1]	1985	1980	1970
Men, 20 yr. and over									
Employed	64,897	64,085	63,294	62,335	61,496	61,678	56,562	53,101	45,581
Full time	59,543	58,707	57,707	57,010	56,274	57,055	52,425	49,699	43,138
Part time	5,354	5,377	5,587	5,345	5,223	4,623	4,137	3,403	2,444
Unemployed	3,147	3,239	3,627	4,287	4,717	3,239	3,715	3,353	1,638
Full time	2,899	2,988	3,359	4,011	4,430	3,000	3,479	3,167	1,502
Part time	248	251	269	276	287	239	236	186	137
Women, 20 yr. and over									
Employed	53,310	54,396	53,606	52,099	51,328	50,535	44,154	38,492	26,952
Full time	41,953	40,943	40,183	40,209	39,544	39,138	33,604	29,391	20,654
Part time	13,357	13,453	13,423	11,890	11,783	11,397	10,550	9,102	6,297

	1996[2]	1995[2]	1994[2]	1993[1]	1992[1]	1990[1]	1985	1980	1970
Unemployed	2,783	2,819	3,049	3,288	3,469	2,596	3,129	2,615	1,349
Full time	2,258	2,265	2,506	2,670	2,840	2,079	2,536	2,135	1,077
Part time	525	554	543	619	628	517	593	480	271
Total 16 yr. and over									
Employed	126,707	124,900	123,060	120,259	118,492	118,793	107,150	99,303	78,678
Full time	103,537	101,679	99,772	99,114	97,664	98,666	88,535	82,564	66,752
Part time	23,170	23,220	23,288	21,145	20,828	20,128	18,615	16,742	11,924
Unemployed	7,236	7,404	7,996	8,940	9,613	7,047	8,312	7,637	4,093
Full time	5,803	5,909	6,513	7,305	7,923	5,677	6,793	6,269	3,206
Part time	1,433	1,495	1,483	1,635	1,690	1,369	1,519	1,369	889
Total 16–19 yr.									
Employed	6,499	6,419	6,161	5,805	5,669	6,581	6,434	7,710	6,144
Full time	2,041	2,029	1,883	1,895	1,846	2,473	2,507	3,474	2,960
Part time	4,458	4,390	4,278	3,910	3,822	4,107	3,927	4,237	3,183
Unemployed	1,307	1,346	1,320	1,365	1,427	1,212	1,468	1,669	1,106
Full time	646	657	648	625	653	598	777	966	626
Part time	661	689	672	740	775	614	690	701	480

1. Revised; data beginning in 1990 are not directly comparable with earlier years due to the introduction of 1990 census-based population controls, adjusted for the estimated under-count. 2. Data beginning in 1994 are not directly comparable with earlier years due to the introduction of a major redesign of the Current Population Survey. *Source:* Current Population Survey, web: www.bls.census.gov/cps/pubsmain.htm.

Persons in the Labor Force

Year	Labor force[1] Number (thousands)	% Working-age population	Percent in labor force in[2] Farm occupation	Nonfarm occupation	Year	Labor force[1] Number (thousands)	% Working-age population	Percent in labor force in[2] Farm occupation	Nonfarm occupation
1840	5,420	46.6	68.6	31.4	1920	42,434	51.3	27.0	73.0
1850	7,697	46.8	63.7	36.3	1930	48,830	49.5	21.4	78.6
1860	10,533	47.0	58.9	41.1	1940	52,789	52.2	17.4	82.6
1870	12,925	45.8	53.0	47.0	1950	60,054	53.5	11.6	88.4
1880	17,392	47.3	49.4	50.6	1960	69,877	55.3	6.0	94.0
1890	23,318	49.2	42.6	57.4	1970	82,049	58.2	3.1	96.9
1900	29,073	50.2	37.5	62.5	1980	106,085	62.0	2.2	97.8
1910	37,371	52.2	31.0	69.0	1990	125,182	65.3	1.6	98.4

1. For 1830 to 1930, the data relate to the population and gainful workers at ages 10 and over. For 1940 to 1960, the data relate to the population and labor force at ages 14 and over; for 1970 and 1980, the data relate to the population and labor force at age 16 and over. For 1940 to 1980, the data include the Armed Forces. 2. The farm and nonfarm percentages relate only to the experienced civilian labor force. *Source:* U.S. Bureau of the Census, web: www.census.gov.

Employment Status of Women

(in thousands)

Labor force status	1996[2]	1995[2]	1994[2]	1993[1]	1992[1]	1991[1]	1990[1]	1989
In the labor force:	61,857	60,944	60,239	58,795	58,141	57,178	56,829	56,030
16 to 19 years of age	3,763	3,729	3,585	3,408	3,345	3,470	3,698	3,818
20 years and over	58,094	57,215	56,655	55,388	54,796	53,708	53,131	52,212
Employed	58,501	57,523	56,610	54,910	54,052	53,496	53,689	53,027
16 to 19 years of age	3,190	3,127	3,005	2,811	2,724	2,862	3,154	3,282
20 years and over	55,311	54,396	53,606	52,099	51,328	50,634	50,535	49,745
Unemployed	3,356	3,421	3,629	3,885	4,090	3,683	3,140	3,003
16 to 19 years of age	573	602	580	597	621	608	544	536
20 years and over	2,783	2,819	3,049	3,288	3,469	3,074	2,596	2,467
Not in the labor force:	42,528	42,462	42,221	42,711	42,394	42,468	41,957	41,601
Women as percent of labor force	46.2	46.1	46.0	45.5	45.4	45.3	45.2	45.2
Total civilian noninstitutional population of women	104,385	103,406	102,460	101,506	100,535	99,646	98,787	97,630

1. Revised; data beginning in 1990 are not directly comparable with earlier years due to the introduction of 1990 census-based population controls, adjusted for estimated under-count. 2. Data beginning in 1994 are not directly comparable with earlier years due to the introduction of a major redesign of the Current Population Survey. *Source:* Current Population Survey, web: www.bls.census.gov/cps/cpsmain.htm.

Unemployment Rate, 1996

Race, and age	Men 1995	Men 1996	Women 1995	Women 1996	Race, and age	Men 1995	Men 1996	Women 1995	Women 1996
Total, 16 years and over	5.6	5.4	5.6	5.4	Total, 25 years and over	4.3	4.1	4.4	4.3
White	4.9	4.7	4.8	4.7	White	3.8	3.6	3.9	3.8
Black	10.6	11.1	10.2	10.0	Black	7.5	8.0	7.3	7.4

Annual averages. *Source:* Bureau of Labor Statistics, U.S. Department of Labor, web: stats.bls.gov.

Employed Persons 16 Years and Over, by Race and Major Occupational Groups

Race and occupational group	1996 Number (in thousands)	1996 Percent distribution	1995 Number (in thousands)	1995 Percent distribution	1994 Number (in thousands)	1994 Percent distribution
White						
Managerial and professional specialty	32,127	29.8	31,323	29.4	30,045	28.6
Executive, administrative, & managerial	15,848	14.7	15,398	14.5	14,605	13.9
Professional specialty	16,279	15.1	15,924	15.0	15,439	14.7
Technical, sales, & administrative support	32,127	29.8	32,184	30.2	32,232	30.6
Technicians & related support	3,342	3.1	3,361	3.2	3,301	3.1
Sales occupations	13,476	12.5	13,366	12.6	13,235	12.6
Administrative support, including clerical	15,309	14.2	15,457	14.5	15,696	14.9
Service occupations	13,476	12.5	13,208	12.4	13,207	12.6
Precision production, craft, and repair	11,967	11.1	11,949	11.2	11,974	11.4
Operators, fabricators, and laborers	14,662	13.6	14,496	13.6	14,416	13.7
Farming, forestry, fishing	3,342	3.1	3,330	3.1	3,315	3.2
Total	**107,808**	**100.0**	**106,490**	**100.0**	**105,190**	**100.0**
Black						
Managerial and professional specialty	2,708	20.0	2,651	20.0	2,405	18.7
Executive, administrative, & managerial	1,219	9.0	1,233	9.3	1,103	8.6
Professional specialty	1,490	11.0	1,418	10.7	1,302	10.1
Technical, sales, & administrative support	3,873	28.6	3,808	28.7	3,637	28.3
Technicians & related support	366	2.7	378	2.8	376	2.9
Sales occupations	1,219	9.0	1,183	8.9	1,056	8.2
Administrative support, including clerical	2,289	16.9	2,248	16.9	2,205	17.2
Service occupations	2,966	21.9	2,880	21.7	2,890	22.5
Precision production, craft, and repair	1,070	7.9	1,073	8.1	1,040	8.1
Operators, fabricators, and laborers	2,790	20.6	2,712	20.4	2,677	20.9
Farming, forestry, and fishing	135	1.0	154	1.2	187	1.5
Total	**13,542**	**100.0**	**13,279**	**100.0**	**12,835**	**100.0**

Source: U.S. Department of Labor, Bureau of Labor Statistics, web: stats.bls.gov.

Mothers Participating in Labor Force

Year	Percentage of Mothers with children Under 18 years	Percentage of Mothers with children 6 to 17 years	Percentage of Mothers with children Under 6 years[1]	Year	Percentage of Mothers with children Under 18 years	Percentage of Mothers with children 6 to 17 years	Percentage of Mothers with children Under 6 years[1]
1955	27.0	38.4	18.2	1989	65.7	74.2	56.7
1965	35.0	45.7	25.3	1990	66.7	74.7	58.2
1975	47.4	54.8	38.9	1991	66.6	74.4	58.4
1980	56.6	64.4	46.6	1992	67.2	75.9	58.0
1985	62.1	69.9	53.5	1993	66.9	75.4	57.9
1986	62.8	70.4	54.4	1994	68.4	76.0	60.3
1987	64.7	72.0	56.7	1995	69.7	76.4	62.3
1988	65.0	73.3	56.1	1996	70.2	77.2	62.3

1. May also have older children. NOTE: 1955 data are for April; 1965 and 1975-94 data are for March. *Source:* U.S. Department of Labor, Bureau of Labor Statistics, web: stats.bls.gov.

National Labor Organizations With Membership Over 100,000

Members[1]	Union
756,538	United International Union of Automobile, Aerospace and Agricultural Implement Workers of America[2]
110,000	Bakery, Confectionery, and Tobacco Workers International Union
123,041	International Association of Bridge, Structural, Ornamental and Reinforcing Iron Workers
510,000	*United Brotherhood of Carpenters and Joiners of America
650,000	*Communications Workers of America
2,279,101	National Education Association, (Ind.)
750,000	*International Brotherhood of Electrical Workers
150,000	*International Union of Electronic, Electrical, Salaried, Machine and Furniture Workers
210,000	*International Association of Fire Fighters
1,400,000	United Food and Commercial Workers International Union
210,000	American Federation of Government Employees
175,000	*Graphic Communications International Union
300,000	*Hotel Employees and Restaurant Employees International Union
750,000	Laborers' International Union of North America
315,000	National Association of Letter Carriers
600,000	International Association of Machinists and Aerospace Workers[2]
200,000	Mine Workers of America, United
300,000	Union of Needletrades, Industrial and Textile Employees[3]

Members[1]	Union
182,000	American Nurses Association (Ind.)
130,000	Office and Professional Employees International Union
375,000	*International Union of Operating Engineers
125,000	International Brotherhood of Painters and Allied Trades
290,000	*United Paperworkers International Union
292,000	*United Association of Journeymen and Apprentices of the Plumbing and Pipe Fitting Industry of the United States and Canada
365,000	*American Postal Workers Union
100,000	Retail, Wholesale, and Department Store Union
100,000	United Rubber, Cork, Linoleum, and Plastic Workers of America[4]
1,100,000	*Service Employees International Union
140,000	Sheet Metal Workers' International Association
1,300,000	American Federation of State, County and Municipal Employees
700,000	*United Steelworkers of America[2]
925,000	American Federation of Teachers
1,500,000	*International Brotherhood of Teamsters
160,000	*Amalgamated Transit Union
125,000	Transportation • Communications International Union
135,000	United Transportation Union

1. Data are for 1997, except *, which did not respond to *Information Please* mailings. Unless otherwise noted, unions are AFL-CIO affiliated. 2. These three unions announced on July 27, 1995, they will merge over a five-year period. 3. Merger of the International Ladies Garment Workers' Union and the Amalgamated Clothing and Textile Workers Union. 4. Merged with the United Steelworkers of America, July 1, 1995.

Work Stoppages Involving 1,000 Workers or More

Year	Work stoppages	Workers involved (thousands)	Days idle (thousands)	Year	Work stoppages	Workers involved (thousands)	Days idle (thousands)
1950	424	1,698	30,390	1988	40	118	4,381
1960	222	896	13,260	1989	51	452	16,996
1970	381	2,468	52,761	1990	44	185	5,926
1975	235	965	17,563	1991	40	392	4,584
1980	187	795	20,844	1992	35	364	3,989
1983	81	909	17,461	1993	35	184	3,981
1984	68	391	8,499	1994	45	322	5,020
1985	61	584	7,079	1995	28	176	5,736
1986	72	900	11,861	1996	37	273	4,887
1987	46	174	4,456				

NOTE: Refers to stoppages that began in the year. Days idle is total for all stoppages in effect. Workers are counted more than once if they were involved in more than one stoppage during the year. *Source:* U.S. Department of Labor. Bureau of Labor Statistics, *Monthly Labor Review.* March 1997, web: stats.bls.gov.

Occupations of Employed Women

Occupations	1996	1995	1994	1993	1992	1990	1988	1986
Managerial and professional	34.1	29.4	28.7	28.3	27.4	26.2	25.2	23.7
Technical, sales, administrative support	41.3	41.9	42.4	43.0	43.8	44.4	44.6	45.6
Service occupations	12.8	17.7	17.8	18.0	17.9	17.7	17.9	18.3
Precision production, craft and repair	2.4	2.1	2.2	2.1	2.1	2.2	2.3	2.4
Operators, fabricators, laborers	8.9	7.6	7.7	7.6	7.9	8.5	8.9	8.9
Farming, forestry, fishing	0.5	1.3	1.2	0.9	1.0	1.0	1.1	1.1

NOTE: Percentage of female labor force (16 years of age and over) employed in each occupation, annual averages. Details may not add up to totals because of rounding. *Source:* U.S. Department of Labor, Bureau of Labor Statistics, web: stats.bls.gov.

Women in the Civilian Labor Force

Year	Number[1] (thousands)	% Female population aged 16 and over[1]	% of Labor force population aged 16 and over[1]	Year	Number[1] (thousands)	% Female population aged 16 and over[1]	% of Labor force population aged 16 and over[1]
1900	5,319	18.8	18.3	1970	31,543	43.3	38.1
1910	7,445	21.5	19.9	1980	45,487	51.5	42.5
1920	8,637	21.4	20.4	1990[2]	56,829	57.5	45.2
1930	10,752	22.0	22.0	1993	58,795	57.9	45.5
1940	12,845	25.4	24.3	1994[3]	60,239	58.8	46.0
1950	18,389	33.9	29.6	1995	60,944	58.9	46.1
1960	23,240	37.7	33.4	1996	61,857	59.3	46.2

1. For 1900-1930, data relate to population and labor force aged 10 and over; for 1940, to population and labor force aged 14 and over; beginning 1950, to civilian population and labor force aged 16 and over. 2. Data beginning in 1990 are not strictly comparable with data for prior years because population controls were adjusted. 3. Data beginning 1994 are not strictly comparable with data for prior years because of a major redesign of the Current Population Survey (household survey) questionnaire and collection methodology. *Sources:* U.S. Department of Labor, Women's Bureau.

Unemployment Rate in the Civilian Labor Force

Year	Unemployment rate	Year	Unemployment rate	Year	Unemployment rate	Year	Unemployment rate
1920	5.2	1956	4.1	1986	7.0	May	5.5
1928	4.2	1958	6.8	1987	6.2	June	5.3
1930	8.7	1960	5.5	1988	5.4	July	5.4
1932	23.6	1962	5.5	1989	5.3	Aug.	5.2
1934	21.7	1964	5.2	1990	5.5	Sept.	5.2
1936	16.9	1966	3.8	1991	6.7	Oct.	5.2
1938	19.0	1968	3.6	1992	7.4	Nov.	5.3
1940	14.6	1970	4.9	1993	6.8	Dec.	5.3
1942	4.7	1972	5.6	1994	6.1	1997	
1944	1.2	1974	5.6	1995	5.6	Jan.	5.4
1946	3.9	1976	7.7	1996	5.4	Feb.	5.3
1948	3.8	1978	6.0	Jan.	5.8	March	5.2
1950	5.3	1980	7.1	Feb.	5.5	April	4.9
1952	3.0	1982	9.7	March	5.6	May	5.6
1954	5.5	1984	7.5	April	5.5		

NOTE: Estimates prior to 1940 are based on sources other than direct enumeration. *Source:* U.S. Department of Labor, Bureau of Labor Statistics, web: stats.bls.gov.

Unemployment by Marital Status, Sex, and Race[1]

	Men				Women			
	Number (in thousands)		Unemployment rate		Number (in thousands)		Unemployment rate	
Marital status and race	1996	1995	1996	1995	1996	1995	1996	1995
White	2,896	2,999	4.7	4.9	2,404	2,460	4.7	4.8
Married, spouse present	1,094	1,165	2.8	3.0	1,020	1,070	3.5	3.6
Widowed, divorced, or separated	408	428	5.9	6.4	506	526	5.2	5.5
Single (never married)	1,394	1,406	8.6	8.7	878	864	7.3	7.3
Black	808	762	11.1	10.6	784	777	10.0	10.2
Married, spouse present	163	166	4.9	5.0	113	143	4.4	5.5
Widowed, divorced, or separated	117	100	10.5	9.3	169	155	7.8	7.5
Single (never married)	528	496	18.7	17.6	502	479	16.1	16.2
Total	3,880	3,983	5.4	5.6	3,356	3,421	5.4	5.6
Married, spouse present	1,322	1,424	3.0	3.3	1,211	1,296	3.6	3.9
Widowed, divorced, or separated	541	551	6.5	6.9	706	712	5.7	5.9
Single (never married)	2,016	2,007	10.0	10.1	1,439	1,413	9.1	9.1

1. Persons 16 years and over; 1996 annual averages. *Source: Employment & Earnings,* January 1997, U.S. Department of Labor, Bureau of Labor Statistics, web: stats.bls.gov.

Employment and Unemployment by Industry

(in millions of persons)

Category	1996[1]	1995[2]	1993	1990	1985	1980	1970	1950	1945	1932	1929
Employment Status[3]											
Civilian noninstitutional population	200.6	198.6	194.8	189.2	178.2	167.7	137.1	105.0	94.1	—	—
Civilian labor force	133.9	132.3	129.2	125.8	115.5	106.9	82.8	62.2	53.9	—	—
Civilian labor force participation rate	66.8	66.6	66.3	66.5	64.8	63.8	60.4	59.2	57.2	—	—
Employed	126.7	124.9	120.3	118.8	107.2	99.3	78.7	58.9	52.8	38.9	47.6
Employment-population ratio	63.2	62.9	61.7	62.8	60.1	59.2	57.4	56.1	56.1	—	—
Agriculture	3.4	3.4	3.1	3.2	3.2	3.4	3.5	7.2	8.6	10.2	10.5
Nonagricultural industries	123.3	121.5	117.1	115.6	104.0	95.9	75.2	51.8	44.2	28.8	37.2
Unemployed	7.2	7.4	8.9	7.1	8.3	7.6	4.1	3.3	1.0	12.1	1.6
Unemployment rate	5.4	5.6	6.9	5.6	7.2	7.1	4.9	5.3	1.9	23.6	3.2
Not in labor force	66.6	66.3	65.6	63.3	62.7	60.8	54.3	42.8	40.2	—	—
Industry											
Total nonfarm employment	119.5	117.2	110.7	109.4	97.4	90.4	70.9	45.2	40.4	23.6	31.3
Goods-producing industries	24.3	24.2	23.4	24.9	24.8	25.7	23.6	18.5	17.5	8.6	13.3
Mining	0.6	0.6	0.6	0.7	0.9	1.0	0.6	0.9	0.8	0.7	1.1
Construction	5.4	5.2	4.7	5.1	4.7	4.3	3.6	2.4	1.1	1.0	1.5
Manufacturing: Durable goods	10.7	10.7	10.4	10.7	11.5	12.2	11.2	8.1	9.1	—	—
Nondurable goods	7.8	7.8	7.9	7.8	7.8	8.1	8.2	7.2	6.4	—	—
Services-producing industries	95.3	93.0	87.4	84.5	72.5	64.7	47.3	26.7	22.9	15.0	18.0
Transportation and public utilities	6.3	6.2	5.8	5.8	5.2	5.1	4.5	4.0	3.9	2.8	3.9
Trade, wholesale	6.6	6.4	6.0	6.2	5.7	5.3	4.0	2.6	2.0	—	—
Retail	21.6	21.2	19.8	19.6	17.3	15.0	11.0	6.7	5.4	—	—
Finance, insurance, and real estate	7.0	6.8	6.8	6.7	5.9	5.2	3.6	1.9	1.5	—	—
Services	34.4	33.1	30.2	27.9	21.9	17.9	11.5	5.4	4.2	—	—
Federal government	2.8	2.8	2.9	2.8	2.9	2.9	2.7	1.9	2.8	—	—
State and local government	16.7	16.5	15.9	15.2	13.5	13.4	9.8	4.1	3.1	2.7	2.5

1. Preliminary. 2. Revised. 3. For 1929–45, figures on employment status relate to persons 14 years and over; beginning in 1950, 16 years and over. Data for 1990–93 have been revised. Data beginning in 1990 are not directly comparable with earlier years due to the introduction of 1990 census-based population controls, adjusted for the estimated under-count. Data beginning in 1994 are not directly comparable with earlier years because of the introduction of a major redesign of the Current Population Survey. *Source:* U.S. Department of Labor, Bureau of Labor Statistics, web: stats.bls.gov.

Full-Time Workers by Occupation and Sex, 1996

Occupation	Total		Men		Women	
	Number of workers (in thousands)	Median weekly earnings	Number of workers (in thousands)	Median weekly earnings	Number of workers (in thousands)	Median weekly earnings
Managerial and prof. specialty	27,222	$ 718	13,934	$ 852	13,288	$ 616
Executive, admin, and managerial	13,300	699	7,187	846	6,113	585
Professional specialty	13,922	730	6,747	857	7,175	647
Technical, sales, and admin. support	26,116	441	9,988	567	16,128	394
Technicians and related support	3,215	573	1,662	650	1,553	498
Sales occupations	9,041	474	5,114	589	3,927	353
Administrative support, incl. clerical	13,860	405	3,212	489	10,648	391
Service occupations	9,957	305	4,958	357	5,000	273
Private household	365	212	19	(1)	346	213
Protective service	1,902	538	1,627	562	275	439
Service, except private household and protective	7,690	285	3,312	304	4,379	272
Precision production, craft, and repair	11,020	540	10,076	560	944	373
Mechanics and repairers	3,834	568	3,672	571	162	516
Construction trades	3,563	516	3,585	518	68	389
Operators, fabricators, and laborers	15,100	391	11,613	422	3,487	307
Machine operators, assemblers, and inspectors	7,100	380	4,527	437	2,573	307
Transportation and material moving occupations	4,254	476	3,982	486	272	350

Occupation	Total		Men		Women	
	Number of workers (in thousands)	Median weekly earnings	Number of workers (in thousands)	Median weekly earnings	Number of workers (in thousands)	Median weekly earnings
Handlers, equipment cleaners, helpers, and laborers	3,747	330	3,105	343	642	295
Farming, forestry, and fishing	1,502	294	1,326	300	176	255

1. Data not shown where base is less than 50,000. *Source:* U.S. Department of Labor, Bureau of Labor Statistics, *Employment & Earnings,* January 1997, web: stats.bls.gov.

Manufacturing Industries—Gross Average Weekly Earnings and Hours Worked

Industry	1996		1990		1985		1980		1975		1970	
	Earnings	Hours worked	Earnings	Hours worked	Earnings	Hours worked	Earnings	Hours worked	Earnings	Hours worked	Earnings	Hours worked
All manufacturing	$ 531.65	41.6	$ 442.27	40.8	$ 385.56	40.5	$ 288.62	39.7	$ 189.51	39.4	$ 133.73	39.8
Durable goods	565.19	42.4	468.76	41.3	415.71	41.2	310.78	40.1	205.09	39.9	143.07	40.3
Lumber and wood products	425.95	40.8	365.82	40.2	326.36	39.8	252.18	38.5	167.35	39.1	117.51	39.7
Furniture and fixtures	399.91	39.4	333.52	39.1	283.29	39.4	209.17	38.1	142.13	37.9	108.58	39.2
Primary metal industries	662.56	44.2	550.83	42.7	484.72	41.5	391.78	40.1	246.80	40.0	159.17	40.5
Iron and steel foundries	605.22	44.6	484.99	42.1	429.62	40.8	328.00	40.0	220.99	40.4	151.03	40.6
Nonferrous foundries	504.71	42.7	413.48	40.3	388.74	41.8	291.27	39.9	190.03	39.1	138.16	39.7
Fabricated metal products	527.90	42.3	447.28	41.3	398.96	41.3	300.98	40.4	201.60	40.0	143.67	40.7
Hardware, cutlery, hand tools	525.34	42.4	440.08	40.9	396.42	40.7	275.89	39.3	187.07	39.3	132.33	40.1
Structural metal products	493.41	42.1	416.56	41.0	369.00	41.0	291.85	40.2	202.61	40.2	142.61	40.4
Electric and electronic equipment	503.42	41.4	420.65	40.8	384.48	40.6	276.21	39.8	180.91	39.5	130.54	39.8
Industrial machinery, and equipment	585.73	43.1	494.34	42.0	427.04	41.5	328.00	41.0	219.22	40.9	154.95	41.1
Transportation equipment	758.56	44.0	592.20	42.0	542.72	42.7	379.61	40.6	242.61	40.3	163.22	40.3
Motor vehicles and equipment	800.57	44.9	619.46	42.4	584.64	43.5	394.00	40.0	262.68	40.6	170.07	40.3
Nondurable goods	484.79	40.5	405.60	40.0	342.86	39.5	255.45	39.0	168.78	38.8	120.43	39.1
Textile mill products	392.04	40.5	320.40	40.0	266.39	39.7	203.31	40.1	133.28	39.2	97.76	39.9
Apparel and other textile products	294.15	37.0	239.88	36.4	208.00	36.3	161.42	35.4	111.97	35.1	84.37	35.3
Leather and leather products	326.52	38.1	258.43	37.4	217.09	37.3	169.09	36.7	120.80	37.4	92.63	37.2
Food and kindred products	460.02	41.0	392.90	40.8	341.60	40.0	271.95	39.7	184.17	40.3	127.98	40.5
Tobacco manufactures	781.60	40.0	645.23	39.2	448.26	37.2	294.89	38.1	171.38	38.0	110.00	37.8
Paper and allied products	635.64	43.3	532.59	43.3	466.34	43.1	330.85	42.2	207.58	41.6	144.14	41.9
Printing and publishing	482.85	38.2	426.38	37.9	365.31	37.7	279.36	37.1	198.32	37.0	147.78	37.7
Chemicals and allied products	699.84	43.2	576.80	42.6	484.78	41.9	344.45	41.5	219.63	40.9	153.50	41.6
Petroleum and allied products	841.48	43.6	723.86	44.6	603.72	43.0	422.18	41.8	267.07	41.6	182.76	42.7

Source: U.S. Department of Labor, Bureau of Labor Statistics *Employment & Earnings,* March 1997, web: stats.bls.gov.

Nonmanufacturing Industries—Gross Average Weekly Earnings and Hours Worked

Industry	1996 Earnings	1996 Hours worked	1990 Earnings	1990 Hours worked	1985 Earnings	1985 Hours worked	1975 Earnings	1975 Hours worked	1970 Earnings	1970 Hours worked
Bituminous coal and lignite mining	$ 871.64	45.9	$ 740.52	44.0	$ 630.77	41.4	$ 284.53	39.2	$ 186.41	40.8
Metal mining	764.28	44.0	602.07	42.7	547.24	40.9	250.72	42.3	165.68	42.7
Nonmetallic minerals	650.48	47.0	524.12	45.3	451.68	44.5	213.09	43.4	155.11	44.7
Telephone communications	703.90	42.2	578.74	40.9	512.52	41.1	221.18	38.4	131.60	39.4
Radio and TV broadcasting	558.79	35.1	438.61	34.7	381.39	37.1	214.50	39.0	147.45	38.2
Electric, gas, and sanitary services	768.46	42.2	636.76	41.7	534.59	41.7	246.79	41.2	172.64	41.5
Local and suburban transportation	437.38	38.4	376.65	38.2	309.85	38.3	196.89	40.1	142.30	42.1
Wholesale trade	491.77	38.3	411.48	38.1	358.36	38.7	188.75	38.6	137.60	40.0
Retail trade	229.82	28.8	195.26	28.8	177.31	29.7	108.22	32.4	82.47	33.8
Hotels, tourist courts, motels	251.02	30.8	214.68	30.8	176.90	30.5	89.64	31.9	68.16	34.6
Laundries and dry cleaning plants	263.50	34.0	232.22	34.0	198.70	34.2	106.05	35.0	77.47	35.7
General building contracting	560.01	38.2	487.08	37.7	414.78	37.1	254.88	36.0	184.40	36.3

Source: U.S. Department of Labor, Bureau of Labor Statistics, *Employment & Earnings*, March 1997, web: stats.bls.gov.

Earnings by Gender and Race, 1970–1995

Year	Median Earnings — All Races Men	Median Earnings — All Races Women	All Races Women	White Men	White Women	Black Men	Black Women	Hispanic Origin[1] Men	Hispanic Origin[1] Women
1995	$32,199	$23,777	73.8%	104.1%	75.4%	77.0%	65.5%	63.8%	55.5%
1994	32,508	23,924	73.6%	102.6%	75.6%	77.2%	65.3%	64.9%	58.3%
1993	32,776	23,697	72.3%	102.4%	73.9%	75.8%	65.4%	65.7%	55.1%
1992 [4]	33,491	23,998	71.7%	102.4%	72.5%	74.6%	65.7%	64.4%	57.3%
1990	33,790	24,010	71.1%	103.8%	71.9%	74.1%	64.0%	66.8%	55.8%
1989	34,928	24,136	69.1%	104.4%	69.9%	72.9%	62.9%	65.3%	56.3%
1988	35,223	23,891	67.8%	103.4%	68.8%	75.8%	61.7%	66.5%	55.6%
1986	36,006	23,420	65.0%	102.8%	66.0%	72.5%	57.8%	65.7%	54.8%
1985	35,408	23,019	65.0%	102.8%	65.9%	71.9%	58.4%	69.4%	54.1%
1984	35,209	22,621	64.2%	103.4%	64.9%	70.6%	58.5%	71.5%	54.3%
1983	34,440	22,155	64.3%	102.7%	65.2%	72.9%	57.8%	72.8%	52.8%
1982	34,521	21,781	63.1%	102.7%	63.9%	72.9%	57.2%	72.0%	52.5%
1980	35,504	21,464	60.5%	102.9%	61.0%	72.4%	56.9%	71.9%	51.6%
1979 [3]	35,997	21,688	60.2%	102.9%	60.8%	74.2%	55.7%	71.8%	49.6%
1978	36,264	21,767	60.0%	101.9%	60.6%	78.0%	56.2%	74.4%	51.9%
1976	35,557	21,326	60.0%	103.0%	60.4%	73.8%	56.5%	75.2%	51.4%
1974	35,074	20,932	59.7%	102.8%	59.8%	76.1%	57.2%	74.1%	50.8%
1972	36,171	20,777	57.4%	103.6%	58.6%	70.0%	50.1%	n.a.	n.a.
1971 [2]	34,055	20,159	59.2%	102.8%	59.9%	70.3%	52.9%	n.a.	n.a.
1970	33,890	20,074	59.2%	102.9%	60.3%	70.1%	49.4%	n.a.	n.a.

Year-round, full-time workers, aged 15 years old and over. Income in 1995 CPI-U-X1 adjusted dollars. n.a. = not available. 1. Persons of Hispanic origin may be of any race. 2. Implementation of 1970 census population controls 3. Implementation of 1980 census population controls. 4. Implementation of 1990 census population controls. *Source:* Current Population Reports, Series P60, U.S. Bureau of the Census, web: www.census.gov.

Median Four-Person Family Income

(in current dollars)

Year	Income	Percent change	Year	Income	Percent change
1995	$ 49,687	5.7	1984	31,097	6.6
1994	47,012	4.1	1983	29,184	5.7
1993	45,161	2.1	1982	27,619	5.1
1992	44,251	2.8	1981	26,274	8.0
1991	43,056	3.9	1980	24,332	8.6
1990	41,151	1.7	1979	22,395	9.6
1989	40,763	4.4	1978	20,428	9.1
1988	39,051	6.1	1977	18,723	8.1
1987	36,812	6.0	1976	17,315	9.3
1986	34,716	5.9	1975	15,848	7.5
1985	32,777	5.4			

Source: Income Statistics Branch/HHES Division, U.S. Bureau of the Census, web: www.census.gov.

Per Capita Personal Income

Year	Amount	Year	Amount	Year	Amount	Year	Amount	Year	Amount
1935	$ 474	1970	3,893	1983	12,098	1989	17,696	1995[1]	23,196
1945	1,223	1975	5,851	1984	13,114	1990	18,635	1996[2]	24,231
1950	1,501	1979	8,638	1985	13,896	1991[1]	19,638		
1955	1,881	1980	9,910	1986	14,597	1992[1]	20,582		
1960	2,219	1981	10,949	1987	15,638	1993[1]	21,223		
1965	2,773	1982	11,480	1988	16,615	1994[1]	22,045		

1. Revised. 2. Preliminary. *Source:* U.S. Department of Commerce, *Survey of Current Business*, web: www.doc.gov.

Per Capita Income and Personal Consumption Expenditures

(In current dollars)

Year	Gross national product	Personal income	Disposable personal income	Personal Consumption Expenditures			
				Durable goods	Nondurable goods	Services	Total
1950	$ 1,900	$ 1,504	$ 1,368	$ 203	$ 648	$ 416	$ 1,267
1955	2,456	1,901	1,687	235	755	570	1,560
1960	2,851	2,265	1,986	240	847	741	1,829
1965	3,268	2,840	2,505	327	987	954	2,268
1970	4,951	4,056	3,489	418	1,318	1,385	3,121
1975	7,401	6,081	5,291	627	1,927	2,135	4,689
1980	11,985	9,916	8,421	963	2,992	3,653	7,607
1985	16,776	13,895	11,861	1,555	3,807	5,622	10,985
1990	21,737	18,477	15,695	1,910	4,748	7,888	14,547
1991	22,500	19,100	16,700	1,800	5,000	8,700	15,400
1992	23,340	19,802	17,346	1,881	5,053	9,101	16,035
1993	24,576	20,810	18,153	2,083	5,185	9,683	16,951
1994	25,774	21,846	19,003	2,266	5,342	10,126	17,734
1995	27,545	23,233	20,214	2,305	5,648	10,767	18,719
1996	28,503	24,294	21,040	2,381	5,820	11,203	19,404

Source: U.S. Department of Commerce, *Survey of Current Business*, May 1997, web: www.doc.gov.

Total Household Income

Income range	White			Black			Hispanic[1]		
	1995	1980	1972	1995	1980	1972	1995	1980	1972
Number of households[2]	84,511	71,872	60,618	11,577	8,847	6,809	7,939	3,906	2,655
Percent distribution									
Under $5,000	2.9	2.9	3.9	8.6	8.5	8.7	6	5.1	3.9
$5,000 to $9,999	7.7	8.8	8.2	15.4	18.2	16.6	13.9	11.9	9.1
$10,000 to $14,999	8.4	8.1	7.7	11.5	13.2	12.7	12.2	11.6	13
$15,000 to $24,999	15.6	16.1	15.2	18.8	20.3	21.5	21.5	21.2	22.1
$25,000 to $34,999	14.4	14.8	15.7	13.6	12.9	15.0	15.4	16.2	20.7
$35,000 to $49,999	17.3	19.9	20.9	14.6	13.9	13.1	13.3	16.9	17.3
$50,000 to $74,999	17.9	18.3	18.4	11.2	9.8	9.9	11.6	12.3	10.3
$75,000 to $99,999	8.2	6.7	6.0	4.0	2.5	1.6	3.7	3.3	2.1
$100,000 and over	7.7	4.4	4.0	2.2	0.9	0.9	2.4	1.7	1.4
Median income	$35,766	$34,598	$34,918	$22,393	$19,932	$20,382	$22,860	$25,278	$26,351

NOTE: Income in 1995 CPI-U-X1 adjusted dollars. Households as of March 1 of the following year. 1. Persons of Hispanic origin may be of any race. 2. As of March of the following year. *Source:* U.S. Bureau of the Census, *Current Population Reports*, "Consumer Income, Money Income in the United States," web: www.census.gov/prod/2/pop/p60/p60-193.pdf.

Per Capita Personal Income by State

State	1996	1993	1990	1980	State	1996	1993	1990	1980
Alabama	$20,055	$17,447	$14,899	$7,465	Montana	19,047	17,614	14,743	8,342
Alaska	24,558	22,808	20,887	13,007	Nebraska	23,047	19,714	17,379	8,895
Arizona	20,989	18,442	16,262	8,854	Nevada	25,451	22,343	20,248	10,848
Arkansas	18,928	16,361	13,779	7,113	New Hampshire	26,520	22,755	20,231	9,150
California	25,144	22,389	20,656	11,021	New Jersey	31,053	27,608	24,182	10,966
Colorado	25,084	21,990	18,818	10,143	New Mexico	18,770	16,485	14,213	7,940
Connecticut	33,189	29,070	25,426	11,532	New York	28,782	25,179	22,322	10,179
Delaware	27,622	23,999	19,719	10,059	North Carolina	22,010	19,135	16,284	7,780
D.C.	34,932	30,423	24,643	12,251	North Dakota	20,710	17,052	15,320	8,642
Florida	24,104	21,152	18,785	9,246	Ohio	23,537	20,292	17,547	9,399
Georgia	22,709	19,651	17,121	8,021	Oklahoma	19,350	17,356	15,117	9,018
Hawaii	25,159	23,712	20,905	10,129	Oregon	22,668	19,486	17,201	9,309
Idaho	19,539	17,581	15,304	8,105	Pennsylvania	24,668	21,722	18,884	9,353
Illinois	26,598	22,993	20,159	10,454	Rhode Island	24,765	21,747	19,035	9,227
Indiana	22,440	19,647	16,815	8,914	South Carolina	19,755	17,136	15,101	7,392
Iowa	22,560	18,564	16,683	9,226	South Dakota	21,516	17,766	15,628	7,800
Kansas	23,281	20,243	17,639	9,880	Tennessee	21,764	18,975	15,903	7,711
Kentucky	19,687	17,167	14,751	7,679	Texas	22,045	19,451	16,747	9,439
Louisiana	19,824	17,183	14,279	8,412	Utah	19,156	16,391	14,063	7,671
Maine	20,826	18,552	17,041	7,760	Vermont	22,124	19,504	17,444	7,957
Maryland	27,221	24,295	22,088	10,394	Virginia	24,925	22,101	19,543	9,413
Massachusetts	29,439	25,348	22,248	10,103	Washington	24,838	22,014	19,268	10,256
Michigan	24,810	21,041	18,239	9,801	West Virginia	18,444	16,259	13,964	7,764
Minnesota	25,580	21,643	18,784	9,673	Wisconsin	23,269	20,169	17,399	9,364
Mississippi	17,471	14,853	12,578	6,573	Wyoming	21,245	19,608	16,905	11,018
Missouri	22,864	19,689	17,407	8,812	**United States**	**24,231**	**21,223**	**18,667**	**9,494**

Source: U.S. Department of Commerce, Bureau of Economic Analysis, *Survey of Current Business*, web: www.bea.doc.gov.

Earnings by Educational Attainment and Sex, 1995

Years of school completed	Median income		Income gap in dollars	Women's income as a percent of men's	Men's income as a percent of women's
	Women[1]	Men[1]			
Less than 9th grade	$13,577	$18,354	4,777	74%	135%
9th to 12th grade	15,825	22,185	6,360	71%	140%
High school graduate	20,463	29,510	9,047	69%	144%
Some college	23,997	33,883	9,886	71%	141%
Bachelor's degree	32,051	45,266	13,215	71%	141%
Master's degree	40,263	55,216	14,953	73%	137%

1. Persons aged 18 and over as of March 1995. *Source:* U.S. Bureau of the Census, web: www.census.gov.

Median Income of Households with Selected Characteristics, 1995

Characteristic	White		Black		Hispanic Origin[1]		All Races	
	As a % of all white households	Median income	As a % of all black households	Median income	As a % of all Hispanic households	Median income	As a % of all households	Median income
Overall		35,766		22,393		22,860		34,076
Region								
Northeast	20%	37,772	19%	21,947	17%	19,936	20%	36,111
Midwest	25%	37,220	19%	22,027	7%	27,777	24%	35,839
South	33%	32,917	53%	22,567	34%	21,907	35%	30,942
West	21%	36,390	9%	23,416	42%	24,368	21%	35,979
Type of household								
Family households	70%	43,265	70%	26,838	79%	25,491	70%	41,224
Married-couple families	57%	47,608	32%	41,362	53%	30,195	54%	47,129
Single father household	3%	35,129	5%	27,071	5%	25,053	4%	33,534
Single mother household	10%	24,431	33%	15,589	20%	14,755	13%	21,348
Nonfamily households	30%	20,585	30%	15,007	21%	13,780	30%	19,929
Male living alone	10%	23,552	11%	17,017	8%	14,181	10%	22,586
Female living alone	15%	14,667	16%	10,958	8%	8,908	15%	14,331
Size of household								
One person	25%	17,512	26%	13,229	16%	11,074	25%	17,063
Two persons	34%	36,939	26%	24,133	23%	22,127	33%	35,700
Three persons	16%	44,997	19%	26,578	19%	22,977	17%	42,244
Four persons	15%	51,611	15%	32,086	19%	27,903	15%	49,531

Characteristic	White As a % of all white households	White Median income	Black As a % of all black households	Black Median income	Hispanic Origin[1] As a % of all Hispanic households	Hispanic Origin[1] Median income	All Races As a % of all households	All Races Median income
Five persons	6%	49,073	8%	27,630	12%	26,701	7%	45,710
Six persons	2%	47,249	3%	28,028	7%	29,114	2%	44,263
Seven persons or more	1%	41,109	3%	28,908	5%	30,180	1%	39,013
Number of earners								
No earners	21%	14,267	24%	7,651	17%	7,486	21%	13,102
One	33%	29,175	40%	20,268	37%	18,062	34%	27,567
Two	36%	50,910	29%	40,357	34%	34,170	35%	50,000
Three	7%	64,311	5%	48,737	8%	43,709	7%	63,191
Four or more	3%	75,092	2%	67,415	4%	56,612	3%	74,243

1. Persons of Hispanic origin may be of any race.

National Income by Type

(in billions of dollars)

Type of income	1996	1995	1994	1990	1985	1980	1975	1970	1965	1960
National income	6,164.2	5,828.9	5,495.1	4,611.9	3,351.5	2,216.1	1,295.5	836.6	587.8	426.2
Compensation of employees	4,448.5	4,222.7	4,008.3	3,352.8	2,425.7	1,653.9	951.3	618.1	399.8	296.7
Wages and salaries	3,630.1	3,433.2	3,255.9	2,757.5	1,995.7	1,377.6	814.7	551.5	363.7	272.8
Supplements to wages and salaries	818.4	789.5	752.4	595.2	430.0	276.3	136.6	66.6	36.1	23.8
Proprietors' income[1,2]	527.3	486.1	450.9	361.0	257.4	167.9	116.5	78.0	63.5	50.5
Farm	44.7	27.9	35.0	36.3	24.5	13.8	24.2	14.8	13.0	11.5
Business and professional	482.6	458.2	415.0	324.6	232.5	154.1	92.3	63.2	50.4	39.1
Rental income[1]	115.0	111.7	116.6	61.4	49.1	35.3	26.6	24.7	22.5	19.1
Corporate profits[1,2]	670.2	604.8	526.5	369.5	282.2	167.1	121.1	75.7	80.9	48.8
Net interest	403.3	403.6	392.8	467.3	337.2	191.9	80.0	40.0	21.1	11.2

1. Includes capital consumption adjustment. 2. Includes inventory valuation adjustment. *Source:* U.S. Department of Commerce, Bureau of Economic Analysis, *Survey of Current Business,* May 1997, web: www.bea.doc.gov.

Consumer Price Index for All Urban Consumers

(1982–84 = 100)

Group	March 1997	March 1996	March 1995	Group	March 1997	March 1996	March 1995
All items	160.0	155.7	151.4	Fuel oil, coal, bottled gas	105.5	99.3	89.0
Food	156.6	151.6	147.4	House operation[1]	125.4	124.6	122.6
Alcoholic beverages	162.1	157.4	153.1	House furnishings	111.1	111.7	111.2
Apparel and upkeep	134.5	134.8	134.4	Transportation	144.9	141.2	138.0
Men's and boys' apparel	129.2	129.1	127.2	Medical care	233.4	226.6	218.4
Women's and girls' apparel	130.1	129.9	131.5	Personal care	151.8	149.4	146.0
Footwear	127.0	128.1	125.9	Tobacco products	238.2	230.8	222.5
Housing, total	155.9	151.7	147.4	Entertainment	162.1	158.4	152.6
Rent	165.1	160.6	156.7	Personal and educational expenses	255.8	244.1	232.0
Gas and electricity	123.4	118.2	117.1				

1. Combines house furnishings and operation. *Source: Monthly Labor Review,* May 1997.

Producer Price Indexes by Major Commodity Groups

(1982 = 100)

Commodity	1996	1995	1990	1985	1980	1975	1970
All commodities	129.1	124.7	116.3	103.2	89.8	58.4	38.1
Farm products	114.8	107.4	112.2	95.1	102.9	77.0	45.8
Processed foods and feeds	134.2	127.0	121.9	103.5	95.9	72.6	44.6
Textile products and apparel	122.7	120.8	114.9	102.9	89.7	67.4	52.4
Hides, skins, and leather products	154.4	153.7	141.7	108.9	94.7	56.5	42.0
Fuels and related products and power	93.3	78.0	82.2	91.4	82.8	35.4	15.3
Chemicals and allied products	143.2	142.5	123.6	103.7	89.0	62.0	35.0
Rubber and plastic products	123.7	124.3	113.6	101.9	90.1	62.2	44.9
Lumber and wood products	179.7	178.1	129.7	106.6	101.5	62.1	39.9
Pulp, paper, and allied products	167.2	172.2	141.3	113.3	86.3	59.0	37.5

Commodity	1996	1995	1990	1985	1980	1975	1970
Metals and metal products	129.9	134.5	123.0	104.4	95.0	61.5	38.7
Machinery and equipment	126.2	126.6	120.7	107.2	86.0	57.9	40.0
Furniture and household durables	130.9	128.2	119.1	107.1	90.7	67.5	51.9
Nonmetallic mineral products	131.9	129.0	114.7	108.6	88.4	54.4	35.3
Transportation equipment	142.6	139.7	121.5	107.9	82.9	56.7	41.9

Source: U.S. Department of Labor, Bureau of Labor Statistics, Division of Industrial Prices and Price Indexes, web: stats.bls.gov

Consumer Credit

(installment credit outstanding; in billions of dollars, not seasonally adjusted)

Holder	1997[4]	1996	1995	1994	1993	1992	1991	1990	1985	1980	1975
Commercial banks	518.5	529.4	507.8	427.8	367.1	331.9	340.7	347.1	245.1	147.0	82.9
Finance companies	152.3	154.5	152.6	134.8	117.0	117.1	121.9	133.3	111.7	62.3	32.7
Credit unions	147.4	144.1	131.9	119.5	114.4	97.6	92.7	93.1	72.7	44.0	25.7
Retailers[1]	74.1	79.7	85.1	38.4	47.4	42.1	39.8	43.5	43.0	28.7	18.2
Other[2]	46.6	44.7	40.1	60.9	37.5	47.8	50.3	57.0	53.8	20.1	9.2
Pools[3]	274.7	271.9	214.4	143.3	123.6	120.4	99.6	77.9	—	—	—
Total	**1,213.6**	**1,224.4**	**1,131.9**	**925.0**	**807.1**	**756.9**	**745.0**	**751.9**	**526.3**	**302.1**	**168.7**

1. Starting in 1994, source includes retailers and gasoline companies in nonfinancial business category. 2. Includes mutual savings banks, savings and loan associations, and gasoline companies (until 1994). 3. Beginning 1989, outstanding balances of pools upon which securities have been issued; these balances are no longer on the balance sheets for the loan originators. 4. Preliminary data as of May 1997. Source: Federal Reserve Board.

Per Capita Consumption of Principal Foods[1]

Food	1995	1994	1993	1992	Food	1995	1994	1993	1992
Red meat[2]	114.7	114.8	112.1	114.1	Fruits[5]	120.1	279.5	278.4	262.4
Poultry[2]	62.9	63.7	62.6	60.9	Peanuts	5.7	5.8	6.0	6.2
Fish and shellfish[2]	14.9	15.1	14.9	14.7	Vegetables	405.0	398.3	402.0	394.3
Eggs	30.2	30.6	30.3	30.3	Sugar	65.5	65.0	64.3	64.6
Fluid milk and cream[3]	223.2	225.7	226.8	230.9	Corn sweeteners	83.2	81.3	78.7	75.3
Ice cream	15.7	16.1	16.1	16.3	Flour and cereal products	192.4	198.7	195.8	190.7
Cheese	27.3	26.8	26.3	26.0	Soft drinks (gal)	n.a.	52.2	50.2	48.5
Butter	4.5	4.8	4.7	4.4	Coffee bean equivalent	20.5[6]	8.2	9.1	10.0
Margarine	9.2	9.9	11.1	11.0	Cocoa (chocolate liquor equivalent)	3.6	4.1	4.4	4.6
Total fats and oils[4]	66.8	66.9	68.4	65.7					

1. Except where noted, consumption is from commercial sources and is in pounds retail weight. 2. Boneless, trimmed equivalent. 3. Includes milk and cream produced and consumed on farms. 4. Fat-content basis. 5. Excludes wine grapes. 6. Gallons. NOTE: Data are latest available. Source: U.S. Department of Agriculture, web: www.usda.gov.

The Public Debt

Year	Gross debt Amount (in millions)	Per capita	Year	Gross debt Amount (in millions)	Per capita
1800 (Jan. 1)	$ 83	$ 15.87	1960	284,093[1]	1,572.31
1860 (June 30)	65	2.06	1965	313,819[1]	1,612.70
1865	2,678	75.01	1970	370,094[1]	1,807.09
1900	1,263	16.60	1975	533,189	2,496.90
1920	24,299	228.23	1980	907,701	3,969.55
1925	20,516	177.12	1985	1,823,103	7,598.51
1930	16,185	131.51	1990	3,233,313	12,823.28
1935	28,701	225.55	1994	4,643,711	17,805.64
1940	42,968	325.23	1995	4,973,983	18,928.53
1945	258,682	1,848.60	1996	5,217,305	19,681.26
1950	256,087[1]	1,688.30	1997	5,355,085	20,006.08
1955	272,807[1]	1,650.63			

1. Adjusted to exclude issues to the International Monetary Fund and other international lending institutions to conform to the budget presentation. Source: U.S. Department of the Treasury, Financial Management Service.

Headline History

In any broad overview of history, arbitrary compartmentalization of facts is self-defeating (and makes locating interrelated people, places, and things that much harder). Therefore, Headline History is designed as a "timeline"—a chronology that highlights both the march of time and interesting, sometimes surprising, juxtapositions. *See also* related sections of *Information Please,* particularly Inventions and Discoveries and Countries of the World.

B.C.E.

Before the Common Era (B.C.E.) or Before Christ (B.C.)

4.5 billion B.C.E.   Planet Earth formed.

3 billion B.C.E.   First signs of primeval life (bacteria and blue-green algae) appear in oceans.

600 million B.C.E.   Earliest date to which fossils can be traced.

4.4 million B.C.E.   Earliest known hominid fossils (*Australopithecus ramidis*) found in Aramis, Ethiopia, 1994.

4.2 million B.C.E.   *Australopithecus anamensis* found in Lake Turkana, Kenya, 1995.

3.2 million B.C.E.   *Australopithecus afarenis* (nicknamed "*Lucy*") found in Ethiopia, 1974.

2.5 million B.C.E.   *Homo habilis* ("Handy Man"), first brain expansion and first chipped stones.

1.8 million B.C.E.   *Homo erectus* ("Upright Man"). Brain size twice that of *Australopithecine* species.

1.7 million B.C.E.   *Homo erectus* leaves Africa.

100,000 B.C.E.   First modern *Homo eapiens* in South Africa.

70,000 B.C.E.   Neanderthal man (use of fire and advanced tools).

35,000 B.C.E.   Neanderthal man being replaced by later groups of *Homo sapiens* (i.e. Cro-Magnon man, etc.).

18,000 B.C.E.   Cro-Magnons being replaced by later cultures.

15,000 B.C.E.   Migrations across Bering Straits into the Americas.

10,000 B.C.E.   Semi-permanent agricultural settlements in Old World.

10,000–4,000 B.C.E.   Development of settlements into cities and development of skills such as the wheel, pottery and improved methods of cultivation in Mesopotamia and elsewhere.

4500–3000 B.C.E.   Sumerians in the Tigris and Euphrates valleys develop a city-state civilization; first phonetic writing (c. 3500 B.C.E.). Egyptian agriculture develops. Western Europe is neolithic, without metals or written records. Earliest recorded date in Egyptian calendar (4241 B.C.E.). First year of Jewish calendar (3760 B.C.E.). Copper used by Egyptians and Sumerians.

3000–2000 B.C.E.   Pharaonic rule begins in Egypt. Cheops, 4th dynasty (2700–2675 B.C.E.). The Great Sphinx of Giza. Earliest Egyptian mummies. Papyrus. Phoenician settlements on coast of what is now Syria and Lebanon. Semitic tribes settle in Assyria. Sargon, first Akkadian king, builds Mesopotamian empire. The Gilgamesh epic (c. 3000 B.C.E.). The Great Pyramid at Giza completed (c. 2680 B.C.E.). Abraham leaves Ur (c. 2000 B.C.E.). Systematic astronomy in Egypt, Babylon, India, China.

3000–1500 B.C.E.   The most ancient civilization on the Indian subcontinent, the sophisticated and extensive Indus Valley civilization, flourishes in what is today Pakistan.

2000–1500 B.C.E.   Hyksos invaders drive Egyptians from Lower Egypt (17th century B.C.E.). Amosis I frees Egypt from Hyksos (c. 1600 B.C.E.). Assyrians rise to power—cities of Ashur and Nineveh. Twenty-four-character alphabet in Egypt. Israelites enslaved in Egypt. Cuneiform inscriptions used by Hittites. Peak of Minoan culture on Isle of Crete—earliest form of written Greek. Hammurabi, king of Babylon, develops oldest existing code of laws (18th century B.C.E.). In Britain, Stonehenge erected on some unknown astronomical rationale.

1500–1000 B.C.E.   Ikhnaton develops monotheistic religion in Egypt (c. 1375 B.C.E.). His successor, Tutankhamen, returns to earlier gods. Moses leads Israelites out of Egypt into Canaan—Ten Commandments. Greeks destroy Troy (c. 1193 B.C.E.). End of Greek civilization in Mycenae with invasion of Dorians. Chinese civilization develops under Shang dynasty. Olmec civilization in Mexico—stone monuments; picture writing.

1000–900 B.C.E.   Solomon succeeds King David, builds Jerusalem temple. After Solomon's death, kingdom divided into Israel and Judah. Hebrew elders begin to write Old Testament books of Bible. Phoenicians colonize Spain with settlement at Cadiz.

Ra, Sun God
(3000–2000 B.C.E.)

Egyptian Pyramid
(c. 2680 B.C.E.)

Stonehenge

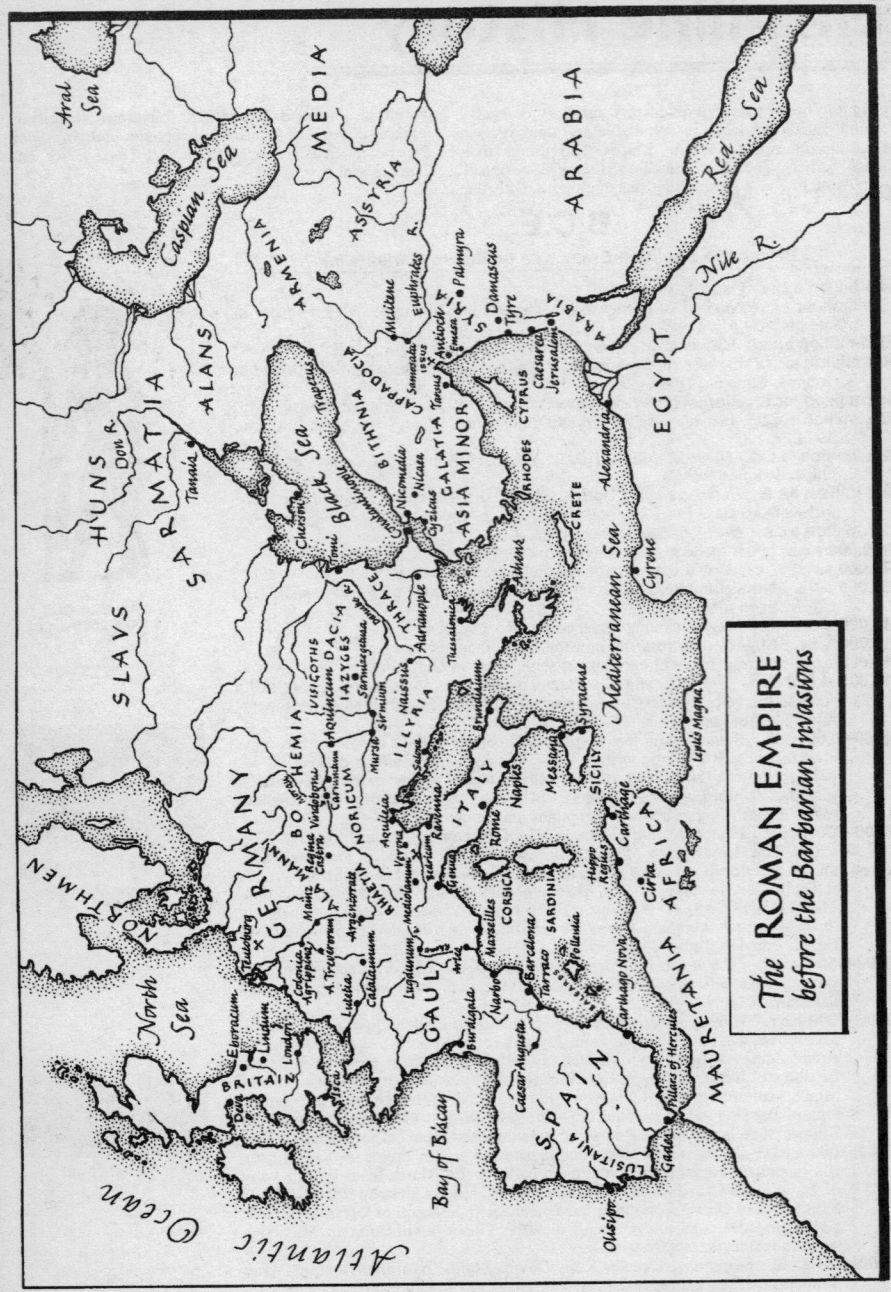

The ROMAN EMPIRE
before the Barbarian Invasions

Some Ancient Civilizations

Name	Approximate dates	Location	Major cities
Akkadian	2350-2230 B.C.E.	Mesopotamia, parts of Syria, Asia Minor, Iran	Akkad, Ur, Erich
Assyrian	1800-889 B.C.E.	Mesopotamia, Syria	Assur, Nineveh, Calah
Babylonian	1728-1686 B.C.E. (old) 625-539 B.C.E. (new)	Mesopotamia, Syria, Palestine	Babylon
Cimmerian	750-500 B.C.E.	Caucasus, northern Asia Minor	—
Egyptian	2850-715 B.C.E.	Nile valley	Thebes, Memphis, Tanis
Etruscan	900-396 B.C.E.	Northern Italy	—
Greek	900-200 B.C.E.	Greece	Athens, Sparta, Thebes, Mycenae, Corinth
Hittite	1640-1200 B.C.E.	Asia Minor, Syria	Hattusas, Nesa
Indus Valley	3000-1500 B.C.E.	Pakistan, Northwestern India	—
Lydian	700-547 B.C.E.	Western Asia Minor	Sardis, Miletus
Mede	835-550 B.C.E.	Iran	Media
Minoan	3000-1100 B.C.E.	Crete	Knossos
Persian	559-330 B.C.E.	Iran, Asia Minor, Syria	Persepolis, Pasargadae
Phoenician	1100-332 B.C.E.	Palestine (colonies: Gibraltar, Carthage, Sardinia)	Tyre, Sidon, Byblos
Phrygian	1000-547 B.C.E.	Central Asia Minor	Gordion
Roman	500 B.C.E.-C.E. 300	Italy, Mediterranean region, Asia Minor, western Europe	Rome, Byzantium
Scythian	800-300 B.C.E.	Caucasus	—
Sumerian	3200-2360 B.C.E.	Mesopotamia	Ur, Nippur

900–800 B.C.E. Phoenicians establish Carthage (c. 810 B.C.E.). The *Iliad* and the *Odyssey,* perhaps composed by Greek poet Homer.

800–700 B.C.E. Prophets Amos, Hosea, Isaiah. First recorded Olympic games (776 B.C.E.). Legendary founding of Rome by Romulus (753 B.C.E.). Assyrian king Sargon II conquers Hittites, Chaldeans, Samaria (end of Kingdom of Israel). Earliest written music. Chariots introduced into Italy by Etruscans.

700–600 B.C.E. End of Assyrian Empire (616 B.C.E.).—Nineveh destroyed by Chaldeans (Neo-Babylonians) and Medes (612 B.C.E.). Founding of Byzantium by Greeks (c. 660 B.C.E.). Building of the Acropolis in Athens. Solon, Greek lawgiver (640-560 B.C.E.). Sappho of Lesbos, Greek poetess, Lao-Tse, Chinese philosopher and founder of Taoism (born c. 604 B.C.E.).

600–500 B.C.E. Babylonian king Nebuchadnezzar builds empire, destroys Jerusalem (586 B.C.E.). Babylonian Captivity of the Jews (starting 587 B.C.E.). Hanging Gardens of Babylon. Cyrus the Great of Persia creates great empire, conquers Babylon (539 B.C.E.), frees the Jews. Athenian democracy develops. Aeschylus, Greek dramatist (525-465 B.C.E.). Pythagoras (c. 582– c. 507 B.C.E.), Greek philosopher and mathematician. Confucius (551-479 B.C.E.) develops philosophy-religion in China. Buddha (563-483 B.C.E.) founds Buddhism in India.

500–400 B.C.E. Greeks defeat Persians: battles of Marathon (490 B.C.E.), Thermopylae (480 B.C.E.), Salamis (480 B.C.E.). Peloponnesian Wars between Athens and Sparta (431-404 B.C.E.)—Sparta victorious. Pericles comes to power in Athens (462 B.C.E.). Flowering of Greek culture during the Age of Pericles (450-400 B.C.E.). Sophocles, Greek dramatist (496-c.406 B.C.E.). Hippocrates, Greek "Father of Medicine" (born 460 B.C.E.). Xerxes I, king of Persia (rules 485-465 B.C.E.).

400–300 B.C.E. Pentateuch—first five books of the Old Testament evolve in final form. Philip of Macedon assassinated (336 B.C.E.) after conquering Greece; succeeded by son, Alexander the Great (356-323 B.C.E.) who destroys Thebes (335 B.C.E.), conquers Tyre and Jerusalem (332 B.C.E.), occupies Babylon (330 B.C.E.), invades India, and dies in Babylon. His empire is divided among his generals; one of them, Seleucis I, establishes Middle East empire with capitals

**Pythagoras
(c. 582–c. 507 B.C.E.)**

**Buddha
(563–483 B.C.E.)**

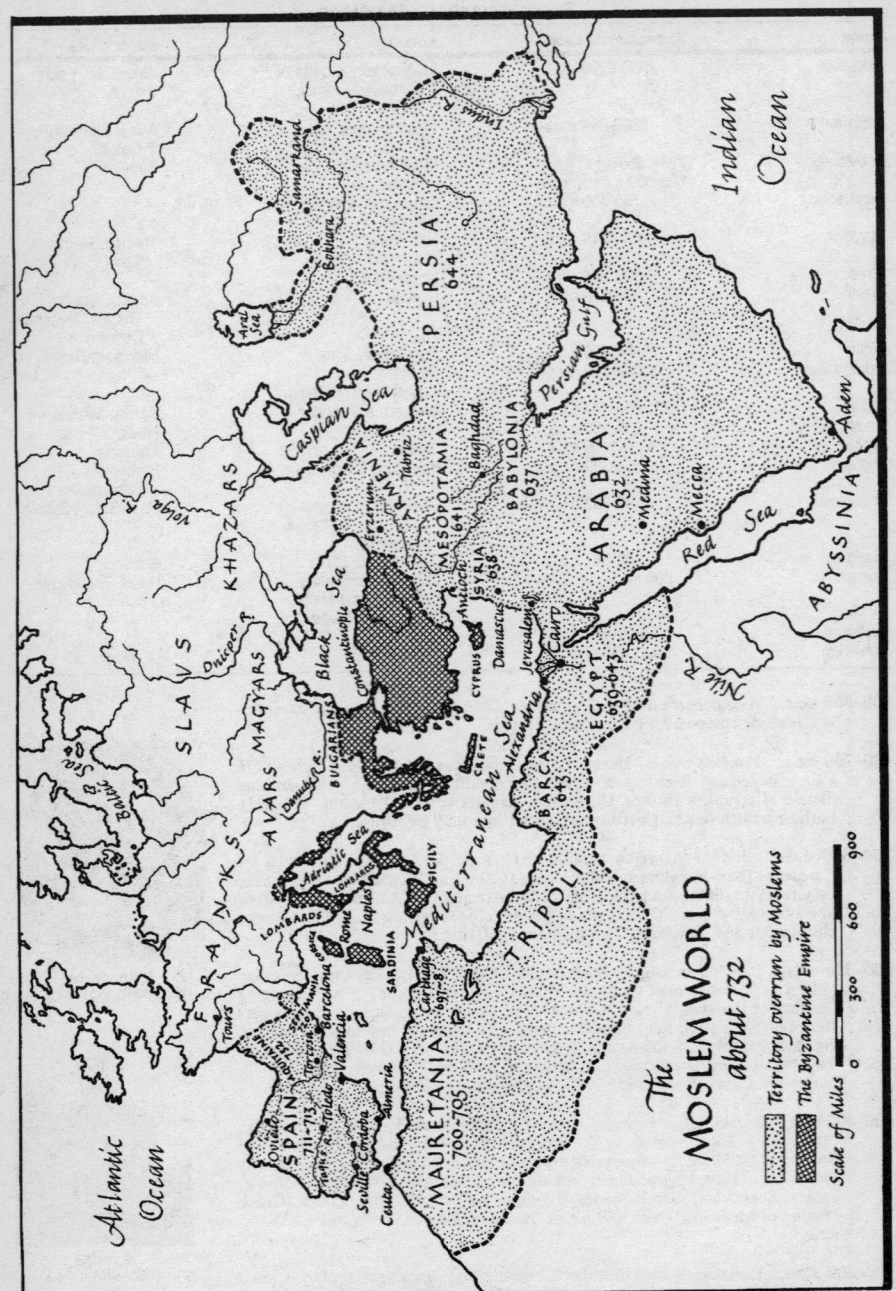

The MOSLEM WORLD about 732

Territory overrun by Moslems
The Byzantine Empire

Scale of Miles
0   300   600   900

at Antioch (Syria) and Seleucia (in Iraq). Trial and execution of Greek philosopher Socrates (399 B.C.E.). Dialogues recorded by his student, Plato. Euclid's work on geometry (323 B.C.E.). Aristotle, Greek philosopher (384-322 B.C.E.). Demosthenes, Greek orator (384-322 B.C.E.). Praxiteles, Greek sculptor (400-330 B.C.E.).

300–251 B.C.E. First Punic War (264-241 B.C.E.): Rome defeats the Carthaginians and begins its domination of the Mediterranean. Temple of the Sun at Teotihuacan, Mexico (c. 300 B.C.E.). Invention of Mayan calendar in Yucatán—more exact than older calendars. First Roman gladiatorial games (264 B.C.E.). Archimedes, Greek mathematician (287-212 B.C.E.).

250–201 B.C.E. Second Punic War (219-201 B.C.E.): Hannibal, Carthaginian general (246-142 B.C.E.), crosses the Alps (218 B.C.E.), reaches gates of Rome (211 B.C.E.), retreats, and is defeated by Scipio Africanus at Zama (202 B.C.E.). Great Wall of China built (c. 215 B.C.E.).

200–151 B.C.E. Romans defeat Seleucid King Antiochus III at Thermopylae (191 B.C.E.)— beginning of Roman world domination. Maccabean revolt against Seleucids (167 B.C.E.).

150–101 B.C.E. Third Punic War (149-146 B.C.E.): Rome destroys Carthage, killing 450,000 and enslaving the remaining 50,000 inhabitants. Roman armies conquer Macedonia, Greece, Anatolia, Balearic Islands, and southern France. Venus de Milo (c. 140 B.C.E.). Cicero, Roman orator (106-43 B.C.E.).

100–51 B.C.E. Julius Caesar (100-44 B.C.E.) invades Britain (55 B.C.E.) and conquers Gaul (France) (c. 50 B.C.E.). Spartacus leads slave revolt against Rome (71 B.C.E.). Romans conquer Seleucid empire. Roman general Pompey conquers Jerusalem (63 B.C.E.). Cleopatra on Egyptian throne (51-31 B.C.E.). Chinese develop use of paper (c. 100 B.C.E.). Virgil, Roman poet (70-19 B.C.E.). Horace, Roman poet (65-8 B.C.E.).

50–1 B.C.E. Caesar crosses Rubicon to fight Pompey (50 B.C.E.). Herod made Roman governor of Judea (47 B.C.E.). Caesar murdered (44 B.C.E.). Caesar's nephew, Octavian, defeats Mark Antony and Cleopatra at Battle of Actium (31 B.C.E.), and establishes Roman empire as Emperor Augustus—rules 27 B.C.E.-C.E. 14. Pantheon built under Agrippa, 27 B.C.E. Birth of Jesus Christ (variously given from 4 B.C.E. to C.E. 7. Ovid, Roman poet (43 B.C.E.-C.E. 18).

**Plato
(427?–347 B.C.E.)**

**Mayan Hieroglyphics
(c. 200 B.C.E.)**

C.E.

The Common Era (C.E.) or Christian Era (A.D.)

1–49 After Augustus, Tiberius becomes emperor (dies, 37), succeeded by Caligula (assassinated, 41), who is followed by Claudius. Crucifixion of Jesus (probably 30). Han dynasty in China founded by Emperor Kuang Wu Ti. Buddhism introduced to China.

50–99 Claudius poisoned (54), succeeded by Nero (commits suicide, 68). Missionary journeys of Paul the Apostle 34-60). Jews revolt against Rome; Jerusalem destroyed (70). Roman persecutions of Christians begin (64). Colosseum built in Rome (71-80). Trajan (rules 98-116); Roman empire extends to Mesopotamia, Arabia, Balkans. First Gospels of St. Mark, St. John, St. Matthew.

100–149 Hadrian rules Rome (117-138); codifies Roman law, establishes postal system, builds wall between England and Scotland. Jews revolt under Bar Kokhba (122-135); final *Diaspora* (dispersion) of Jews begins.

150–199 Marcus Aurelius (rules Rome 161-180). Oldest Mayan temples in Central America (c. 200); Mayan civilization develops writing, astronomy, mathematics.

200–249 Goths invade Asia Minor (c. 220). Roman persecutions of Christians increase. Persian (Sassanid) empire re-established. End of Chinese Han dynasty.

250–299 Increasing invasions of the Roman empire by Franks and Goths. Buddhism spreads in China.

300–349 Constantine the Great (rules 312-337) reunites eastern and western Roman empires, with new capital (Constantinople) on site of Byzantium (330); issues Edict of Milan legalizing Christianity (313); becomes a Christian on his deathbed (337). Council of Nicaea (325) defines orthodox Christian doctrine. First Gupta dynasty in India (c. 320).

350–399 Huns (Mongols) invade Europe (c. 360). Theodosius the Great (rules 392-395)—last emperor of a united Roman empire. Roman empire permanently divided in 395: western empire ruled from Rome; eastern empire ruled from Constantinople.

400–449 Western Roman empire disintegrates under weak emperors. Alaric, king of the Visigoths, sacks Rome (410). Attila, Hun chieftain, attacks Roman provinces (433). St. Patrick returns to Ireland (432). St. Augustine's *City of God* (411). The Parthenon is built in Athens as a temple of the goddess Athena.

450–499 Vandals destroy Rome (455). Western Roman empire ends as Odoacer, German chieftain, overthrows last Roman emperor, Romulus Augustulus, and becomes king of Italy (476). Ostrogothic kingdom of Italy established by Theodoric the Great (493). Clovis, ruler of the Franks, is converted to Christianity

Pantheon in Rome

Celtic Cross

Parthenon

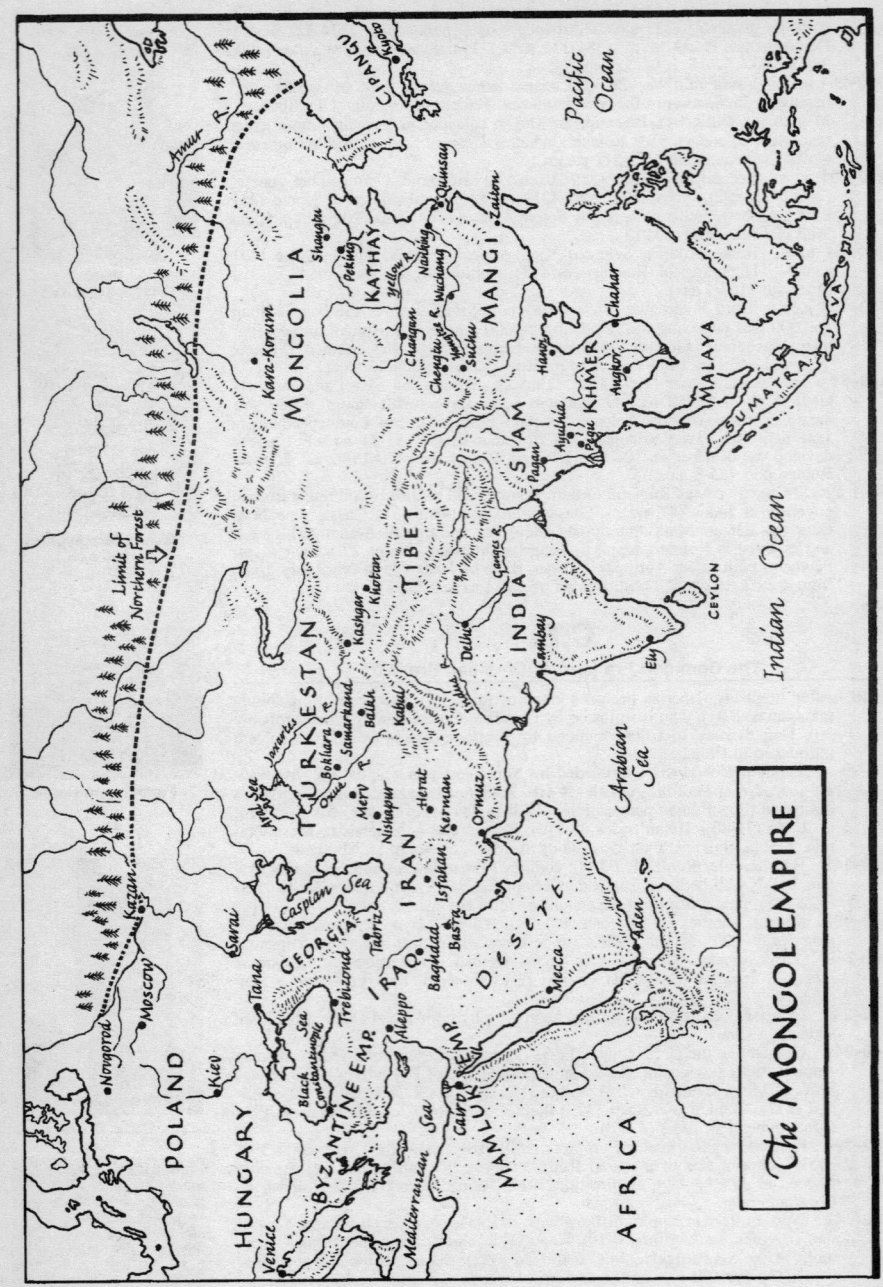

The Mongol Empire

(496). First schism between western and eastern churches (484). Peak of Mayan culture in Mexico (c. 460).

500–549 Eastern and western churches reconciled (519). Justinian I, the Great (483-565), becomes Byzantine emperor (527), issues his first code of civil laws (529), conquers North Africa, Italy, and part of Spain. Plague spreads through Europe (from 542). Arthur, semi-legendary king of the Britons (killed, c. 537). Boëthius, Roman scholar (executed, 524).

550–599 Beginnings of European silk industry after Justinian's missionaries smuggle silkworms out of China (553). Mohammed, founder of Islam (570-632). Buddhism in Japan (c. 560). St. Augustine of Canterbury brings Christianity to Britain (597). After killing about half the population, plague in Europe subsides (594).

600–649 Mohammed flees from Mecca to Medina (the *Hegira*); first year of the Muslim calendar (622). Muslim empire grows (634). Arabs conquer Jerusalem (637), destroy Alexandrian library (641), conquer Persians (641). Fatima, Mohammed's daughter (606-632).

Pagoda

650–699 Arabs attack North Africa (670), destroy Carthage (697). Venerable Bede, English monk (672-735).

700–749 Arab empire extends from Lisbon to China (by 716). Charles Martel, Frankish leader, defeats Arabs at Tours/Poitiers, halting Arab advance in Europe (732). Charlemagne (742-814). Introduction of pagodas in Japan from China.

750–799 Caliph Harun al-Rashid rules Arab empire (786-809): the "golden age" of Arab culture. Vikings begin attacks on Britain (790), land in Ireland (795). Charlemagne becomes king of the Franks (771). City of Machu Picchu flourishes in Peru.

800–849 Charlemagne (Charles the Great) crowned first Holy Roman Emperor in Rome (800). Arabs conquer Crete, Sicily, and Sardinia (826-827). Charlemagne dies (814), succeeded by his son, Louis the Pious, who divides France among his sons (817).

850–899 Norsemen attack as far south as the Mediterranean but are repulsed (859), discover Iceland (861). Alfred the Great becomes king of Britain (871), defeats Danish invaders (878). Russian nation founded by Vikings under Prince Rurik, establishing capital at Novgorod (855-879).

Viking Ship (c. 900)

900–949 Vikings discover Greenland (c. 900). Arab Spain under Abd ar-Rahman III becomes center of learning (912-961). Beginning of Mayan Post-Classical period (900–1519).

950–999 Eric the Red establishes first Viking colony in Greenland (982). Mieczyslaw I becomes first ruler of Poland (960). Hugh Capet elected King of France in 987; Capetian dynasty to rule until 1328. Musical notation systematized (c. 990). Vikings and Danes attack Britain (988-999). Holy Roman Empire founded by Otto I, King of Germany since 936, crowned by Pope John XII in 962.

1000–1099 (C.E.)

c.1000 Hungary and Scandinavia converted to Christianity. Viking raider Leif Ericson discovers North America, calls it *Vinland*. Chinese invent gunpowder. *Beowulf*, Old English epic.

1009 Moslems destroy Holy Sepulchre in Jerusalem.

1013 Danes control England. Canute takes throne (1016), conquers Norway (1028), dies (1035); kingdom divided among his sons: Harold Harefoot (England), Sweyn (Norway), Hardecanute (Denmark).

1040 Macbeth murders Duncan, king of Scotland.

1050–1300 Classic Pueblo period of Anasazi culture; cliffdwellings.

1053 Robert Guiscard, Norman invader, establishes kingdom in Italy, conquers Sicily (1072).

1054 Final separation between Eastern (Orthodox) and Western (Roman) churches.

1055 Seljuk Turks, Asian nomads, move west, capture Baghdad, Armenia (1064), Syria, and Palestine (1075).

1066 William of Normandy invades England, defeats last Saxon king, Harold II, at Battle of Hastings, crowned William I of England ("the Conqueror").

1068 Construction on the Cathedral in Pisa, Italy, begins.

Mesa Verde (cliff dwellings)

Cathedral and Tower at Pisa

The Crusades (1096–1291)

In 1095 at Council of Clermont, Pope Urban II calls for war to rescue Holy Land from Moslem infidels. *First Crusade* (1096)—about 500,000 peasants led by Peter the Hermit prove so troublesome that Byzantine Emperor Alexius ships them to Asia Minor; only 25,000 survive return after massacre by Seljuk Turks. Followed by organized army, led by nobility, which reaches Constantinople (1097), conquers Jerusalem (1099), Acre (1104), establishes Latin Kingdom protected by Knights of St. John the Hospitaller (1100), and Knights Templar (1123). Seljuk Turks start series of counterattacks (1144). *Second Crusade* (1146) led by King Louis VIII of France and Emperor Conrad III. Crusaders perish in Asia Minor (1147).

Saladin controls Egypt (1171), unites Islam in Holy War (*Jihad*) against Christians, recaptures Jerusalem (1187). *Third Crusade* (1189) under kings of France, England, and Germany fails to reduce Saladin's power. *Fourth Crusade* (1200-1204)—French knights sack Greek Christian Constantinople, establish Latin empire in Byzantium. Greeks re-establish Orthodox faith (1262).

Children's Crusade (1212)—Only 1 of 30,000 French children and about 200 of 20,000 German children survive to return home. Other Crusades—against Egypt (1217), *Sixth* (1228), *Seventh* (1248), *Eighth* (1270). Mamelukes conquer Acre; end of the Crusades (1291).

Chartres Cathedral

1073 Emergence of strong papacy when Gregory VII is elected. Conflict with English and French kings and German emperors will continue throughout medieval period.

1100–1199 (c.e.)

1100–1300 Construction of Cathedral at Chartres, France.

1150–67 Universities of Paris and Oxford founded in France and England.

1162 Thomas á Becket named Archbishop of Canterbury, murdered by Henry II's men (1170). Troubadours (wandering minstrels) glorify romantic concepts of feudalism.

1189 Richard I ("the Lionhearted") succeeds Henry II in England, killed in France (1199), succeeded by King John.

1200–1299 (c.e.)

1211 Genghis Khan invades China, captures Peking (1214), conquers Persia (1218), invades Russia (1223), dies (1227).

1215 King John forced by barons to sign Magna Carta at Runneymede, limiting royal power.

1233 The Inquisition begins as Pope Gregory IX assigns Dominicans responsibility for combating heresy. Torture used (1252). Ferdinand and Isabella establish Spanish Inquisition (1478). Tourquemada, Grand Inquisitor, forces conversion or expulsion of Spanish Jews (1492). Forced conversion of Moors (1499). Inquisition in Portugal (1531). First Protestants burned at the stake in Spain (1543). Spanish Inquisition abolished (1834).

**King John
(1167–1216)**

1241 Mongols defeat Germans in Silesia, invade Poland and Hungary, withdraw from Europe after Ughetai, Mongol leader, dies.

1251 Kublai Khan governs China, becomes ruler of Mongols (1259), establishes Yuan dynasty in China (1280), invades Burma (1287), dies (1294).

1271 Marco Polo of Venice travels to China, in court of Kublai Khan (1275-1292), returns to Genoa (1295) and writes *Travels*.

1273 Thomas Aquinas stops work on *Summa Theologica*, the basis of all Catholic theological teaching.

1295 English King Edward I summons the Model Parliament.

1300–1399 (c.e.)

1312–37 Mali Empire reaches its height in Africa under King Mansa Musa.

1337–1453 Hundred Years' War—English and French kings fight for control of France.

c.1325 The beginning of the Renaissance in Italy: writers Dante, Petrarch, Boccaccio; painter Giotto. Development of *No* drama in Japan. Aztecs establish capital on site of modern Mexico City. Peak of Moslem culture in Spain. Small cannon in use.

**Thomas Aquinas
(1225–74)**

1347–1351 At least 25 million people die in Europe's "Black Death" (bubonic plague).

1368 Ming dynasty begins in China.

1376–82 John Wycliffe, pre-Reformation religious reformer and followers translate Latin Bible into English.

1378 The Great Schism (to 1417)—rival popes in Rome and Avignon, France, fight for control of Roman Catholic Church.

c.1387 Chaucer's *Canterbury Tales*.

1400–1499 (c.e.)

1415 Henry V defeats French at Agincourt. Jan Hus, Bohemian preacher and follower of Wycliffe, burned at stake in Constance as heretic.

1418–60 Portugal's Prince Henry the Navigator sponsors exploration of Africa's coast. Brunelleschi begins work on teh duomo in Florence (1420).

**The Duomo in
Florence**

1428 Joan of Arc leads French against English, captured by Burgundians (1430) and turned over to the English, burned at the stake as a witch after ecclesiastical trial (1431).

1438 Inca rule in Peru.

1450 Florence becomes center of Renaissance arts and learning under the Medicis.

1453 Turks conquer Constantinople, end of the Byzantine empire. Hundred Years' War between France and England ends.

1455 The Wars of the Roses, civil wars between rival noble factions, begin in England (to 1485). Having invented printing with movable type at Mainz, Germany, Johann Gutenberg completes first Bible.

1462 Ivan the Great rules Russia until 1505 as first czar; ends payment of tribute to Mongols.

1492 Moors conquered in Spain by troops of Ferdinand and Isabella. Columbus becomes first European to encounter Caribbean islands, returns to Spain (1493). Second voyage to Dominica, Jamaica, Puerto Rico (1493–1496). Third voyage to Orinoco (1498). Fourth voyage to Honduras and Panama (1502–1504).

**Joan of Arc
(1412–1431)**

1497 Vasco da Gama sails around Africa and discovers sea route to India (1498). Establishes Portuguese colony in India (1502). John Cabot, employed by England, reaches and explores Canadian coast. Michelangelo's *Bacchus* sculpture.

1500–1599 (C.E.)

1501 First black slaves in America brought to Spanish colony of Santo Domingo.

c.1503 Leonardo da Vinci paints the *Mona Lisa*. Michelangelo sculpts the *David* (1504).

1506 St. Peter's Church started in Rome; designed and decorated by such artists and architects as Bramante, Michelangelo, da Vinci, Raphael, and Bernini before its completion in 1626.

1509 Henry VIII ascends English throne. Michelangelo paints the ceiling of the Sistine Chapel.

**Michelangelo's David
(1504)**

1513 Balboa becomes the first European to encounter the Pacific ocean.

1517 Turks conquer Egypt, control Arabia. Martin Luther posts his 95 theses denouncing church abuses on church door in Wittenberg—start of the Reformation in Germany.

1519 Ulrich Zwingli begins Reformation in Switzerland. Hernando Cortes conquers Mexico for Spain. Charles I of Spain is chosen Holy Roman Emperor Charles V. Portuguese explorer Fernando Magellan sets out to circumnavigate the globe.

1520 Luther excommunicated by Pope Leo X. Suleiman I ("the Magnificent") becomes Sultan of Turkey, invades Hungary (1521), Rhodes (1522), attacks Austria (1529), annexes Hungary (1541), Tripoli (1551), makes peace with Persia (1553), destroys Spanish fleet (1560), dies (1566). Magellan reaches the Pacific, is killed by Philippine natives (1521). One of his ships under Juan Sebastián del Cano continues around the world, reaches Spain (1522).

1524 Verrazano, sailing under the French flag, explores the New England coast and New York Bay.

**Martin Luther
(1483–1546)**

1527 Troops of the Holy Roman Empire attack Rome, imprison Pope Clement VII—the end of the Italian Renaissance. Castiglione writes *The Courtier*. The Medici expelled from Florence.

1532 Pizarro marches from Panama to Peru, kills the Inca chieftain, Atahualpa, of Peru (1533). Machiavelli's *Prince* published posthumously.

1535 Reformation begins as Henry VIII makes himself head of English Church after being excommunicated by Pope. Sir Thomas More executed as traitor for refusal to acknowledge king's religious authority. Jacques Cartier sails up the St. Lawrence River, basis of French claims to Canada.

1536 Henry VIII executes second wife, Anne Boleyn. John Calvin establishes Presbyterian form of Protestantism in Switzerland, writes *Institutes of the Christian Religion*. Danish and Norwegian Reformations. Michelangelo's *Last Judgment*.

1541 John Knox leads Reformation in Scotland, establishes Presbyterian church (1560).

**Queen Elizabeth I
(1533–1603)**

1543 Publication of *On the Revolution of Heavenly Bodies* by Polish scholar Nicolaus Copernicus—giving his theory that the earth revolves around the sun.

1545 Council of Trent to meet intermittently until 1563 to define Catholic dogma and doctrine, reiterate papal authority.

1547 Ivan IV ("the Terrible") crowned as Czar of Russia, begins conquest of Astrakhan and Kazan (1552), battles nobles (boyars) for power (1564), kills his son (1580), dies, and is succeeded by a son who gives power to Boris Godunov (1584).

1553 Roman Catholicism restored in England by Queen Mary I, who rules until 1558. Religious radical Michael Servetus burned as heretic in Geneva by order of John Calvin.

1554 Benvenuto Cellini completes the bronze *Perseus*.

1556 Akbar the Great becomes Mogul emperor of India, conquers Afghanistan (1581), continues wars of conquest (until 1605).

**William Shakespeare
(1564–1616)**

1558 Queen Elizabeth I ascends the throne (rules to 1603). Restores Protestantism, establishes state Church of England (Anglicanism). Renaissance will reach height in England—Shakespeare, Marlowe, Spenser.

1561 Persecution of Huguenots in France stopped by Edict of Orleans. French religious wars begin again with massacre of Huguenots at Vassy. St. Bartholomew's Day Massacre—thousands of Huguenots murdered (1572). Amnesty granted (1573). Persecution continues periodically until Edict of Nantes (1598) gives Huguenots religious freedom (until 1685).

1568 Protestant Netherlands revolts against Catholic Spain; independence will be acknowledged by Spain in 1648. High point of Dutch Renaissance—painters Rubens, Van Dyck, Hals, and Rembrandt.

1570 Japan permits visits of foreign ships. Queen Elizabeth I excommunicated by Pope. Turks attack Cyprus and war on Venice. Turkish fleet defeated at Battle of Lepanto by Spanish and Italian fleets (1571). Peace of Constantinople (1572) ends Turkish attacks on Europe.

**Rembrandt
(1606–69)**

Marie de Medici
(1573–1642)

Galileo
(1564–1642)

Pocahontas
(c. 1595–1617)

Taj Mahal

John Milton
(1608–74)

1580 Francis Drake returns to England after circumnavigating the globe. Knighted by Queen Elizabeth I (1581). Montaigne's *Essays* published.

1583 William of Orange rules The Netherlands; assassinated on orders of Philip II of Spain (1584).

1587 Mary, Queen of Scots, executed for treason by order of Queen Elizabeth I. Monteverdi's *First Book of Madrigals.*

1588 Defeat of the Spanish Armada by English. Henry, King of Navarre and Protestant leader, recognized as Henry IV, first Bourbon king of France. Converts to Roman Catholicism in 1593 in attempt to end religious wars.

1590 Henry IV enters Paris, wars on Spain (1595), marries Marie de Medici (1600), assassinated (1610). Spenser's *The Faerie Queen*, El Greco's *St. Jerome.* Galileo's experiments with falling objects.

1598 Boris Godunov becomes Russian Czar. Tycho Brahe describes his astronomical experiments.

1600–1699 (C.E.)

1600 Giordano Bruno burned as a heretic. Ieyasu rules Japan, moves capital to Edo (Tokyo). Shakespeare's *Hamlet* begins his most productive decade. English East India Company established to develop overseas trade.

1607 Jamestown, Virginia, established—first permanent English colony on American mainland. Pocahontas, daughter of Chief Powhatan, saves life of John Smith.

1609 Samuel de Champlain establishes French colony of Quebec.

1611 Gustavus Adolphus elected King of Sweden. King James Version of the Bible published in England. Rubens paints his *Descent from the Cross.*

1614 John Napier discovers logarithms.

1618 Start of the Thirty Years' War (to 1648)—Protestant revolt against Catholic oppression; Denmark, Sweden, and France will invade Germany in later phases of war. Kepler proposes his Third Law of planetary motion.

1619 A Dutch ship brings the first Africans to British North America.

1620 Pilgrims, after three-month voyage in *Mayflower*, land at Plymouth Rock. Francis Bacon's *Novum Organum.*

1633 Inquisition forces Galileo to recant his belief in Copernican theory.

1642 English Civil War. Cavaliers, supporters of Charles I, against Roundheads, parliamentary forces. Oliver Cromwell defeats Royalists (1646). Parliament demands reforms. Charles I offers concessions, brought to trial (1648), beheaded (1649). Cromwell becomes Lord Protector (1653). Rembrandt paints his *Night Watch.*

1643 Taj Mahal completed.

1644 End of Ming Dynasty in China—Manchus come to power. Descartes' *Principles of Philosophy.* John Milton's *Areopagitica* on the freedom of the press.

1648 End of the Thirty Years' War. German population about half of what it was in 1618 because of war and pestilence.

1658 Cromwell dies; his son, Richard, resigns and Puritan government collapses.

1660 English Parliament calls for the restoration of the monarchy; invites Charles II to return from France.

1661 Charles II is crowned King of England. Louis XIV begins personal rule as absolute monarch; starts to build Versailles.

1664 British take New Amsterdam from the Dutch. English limit "Nonconformity" with re-established Anglican Church. Isaac Newton's experiments with gravity.

1665 Great Plague in London kills 75,000.

1666 Great Fire of London. Molière's *Misanthrope.*

1683 War of European powers against the Turks (to 1699). Vienna withstands three-month Turkish siege; high point of Turkish advance in Europe.

1685 James II succeeds Charles II in England, calls for freedom of conscience (1687). Protestants fear restoration of Catholicism and demand "Glorious Revolution." William of Orange invited to England and James II escapes to France (1688). William III and his wife, Mary, crowned. In France, Edict of Nantes of 1598, granting freedom of worship to Huguenots (French Protestants), is revoked by Louis XIV; thousands of Protestants flee.

1689 Peter the Great becomes Czar of Russia—attempts to westernize nation and build Russia as a military power. Defeats Charles XII of Sweden at Poltava (1709). Beginning of the French and Indian Wars (to 1763), campaigns in America linked to a series of wars between France and England for domination of Europe.

1690 William III of England defeats former King James II and Irish rebels at Battle of the Boyne in Ireland. John Locke's *Human Understanding.*

1700–1799 (c.e.)

1701 War of the Spanish Succession begins—the last of Louis XIV's wars for domination of the continent. The Peace of Utrecht (1714) will end the conflict and mark the rise of the British Empire. Called Queen Anne's War in America, it ends with the British taking New Foundland, Acadia, and Hudson's Bay Territory from France, and Gibraltar and Minorca from Spain.

1704 Deerfield (Mass.) Massacre of English colonists by French and Indians. Bach's first cantata. Jonathan Swift's *Tale of a Tub. Boston News Letter*—first newspaper in America.

1707 United Kingdom of Great Britain formed—England, Wales, and Scotland joined by parliamentary Act of Union.

**Benjamin Franklin
(1706–90)**

1729 J. S. Bach's *St. Matthew Passion.* Isaac Newton's *Principia* translated from Latin into English.

1732 Benjamin Franklin begins publishing *Poor Richard's Almanack.*

1735 John Peter Zenger, New York editor, acquitted of libel in New York, establishing press freedom.

1740 Capt. Vitus Bering, Dane employed by Russia, discovers Alaska. Frederick II "the Great" crowned King of Prussia.

1746 British defeat Scots under Stuart Pretender Prince Charles at Culloden Moor. Last battle fought on British soil.

1751 Publication of the *Encyclopédie* begins in France, the "bible" of the Enlightenment.

1755 Samuel Johnson's *Dictionary* first published. Great earthquake in Lisbon, Portugal—over 60,000 die. U.S. postal service established.

**Frederick the Great
(1712–86)**

1756 Seven Years' War (French and Indian War in America) (to1763), in which Britain and Prussia defeat France, Spain, Austria, and Russia. France loses North American colonies; Spain cedes Florida to Britain in exchange for Cuba. In India, over 100 British prisoners die in "Black Hole of Calcutta."

1757 Beginning of British Empire in India as Robert Clive, British commander, defeats Nawab of Bengal at Plassey.

1759 British capture Quebec from French. Voltaire's *Candide.* Haydn's *Symphony No. 1.*

1762 Catherine II ("the Great") becomes Czarina of Russia. J. J. Rousseau's *Social Contract.* Mozart tours Europe as six-year-old prodigy.

1765 James Watt invents the steam engine.

1769 Sir William Arkwright patents a spinning machine—an early step in the Industrial Revolution.

1772 Joseph Priestley and Daniel Rutherford independently discover nitrogen. Partition of Poland—in 1772, 1793, and 1795, Austria, Prussia, and Russia divide land and people of Poland, end its independence.

**Samuel Johnson
(1709–84)**

1775 The American Revolution. Priestley discovers hydrochloric and sulfuric acids.

The Founding of the American Nation

Colonization of America begins: Jamestown, Va. (1607); Pilgrims in Plymouth (1620); Massachusetts Bay Colony (1630); New Netherland founded by Dutch West India Company (1623), captured by English (1664). Delaware established by Swedish trading company (1638), absorbed later by Penn family. Proprietorships by royal grants to Lord Baltimore (Maryland,1632); Captain John Mason (New Hampshire, 1635); Sir William Berkeley and Sir George Carteret (New Jersey,1663); friends of Charles II (the Carolinas, 1663); William Penn (Pennsylvania,1682); James Oglethorpe and others (Georgia,1732).

Increasing conflict between colonists and Britain on western frontier because of royal edict limiting western expansion (1763) and regulation of colonial trade and increased taxation of colonies (Writs of Assistance allow search for illegal shipments, 1761; Sugar Act, 1764; Currency Act, 1764; Stamp Act, 1765; Quartering Act, 1765; Duty Act, 1767.) Boston Massacre (1770). Lord North attempts conciliation (1770). Boston Tea Party (1773), followed by punitive measures passed by Parliament—the "Intolerable Acts."

First Continental Congress (1774) sends "Declaration of Rights and Grievances" to king, urges colonies to form Continental Association. Paul Revere's ride and Lexington and Concord battle between Massachusetts Minutemen and British (1775).

Second Continental Congress (1775), while sending "olive branch" to the king, begins to raise army, appoints Washington commander-in-chief, and seeks alliance with France. Some colonial legislatures urge their delegates to vote for independence. Declaration of Independence **(July 4, 1776).**

Major Battles of the Revolutionary War: *Long Island:* Howe defeats Putnam's division of Washington's Army in Brooklyn Heights, but Americans escape across East River (1776). *Trenton and Princeton:* Washington defeats Hessians at Trenton, British at Princeton. Winters at Morristown (1776-77). Howe winters in Philadelphia; Washington in Valley Forge (1777-78). Burgoyne surrenders British army to General Gates at *Saratoga* (1777).

France recognizes American independence (1778). The War moves south: Savannah captured by British (1778); Charleston occupied (1780); Americans fight successful guerrilla actions under Marion, Pickens, and Sumter. In the West, George Rogers Clark attacks Forts Kaskaskia and Vincennes (1778-1779), defeating British in the region. Cornwallis surrenders at *Yorktown,* Virginia **(Oct. 19, 1781).** By 1782, Britain is eager for peace because of conflicts with European nations. *Peace of Paris* (1783): Britain recognizes American independence.

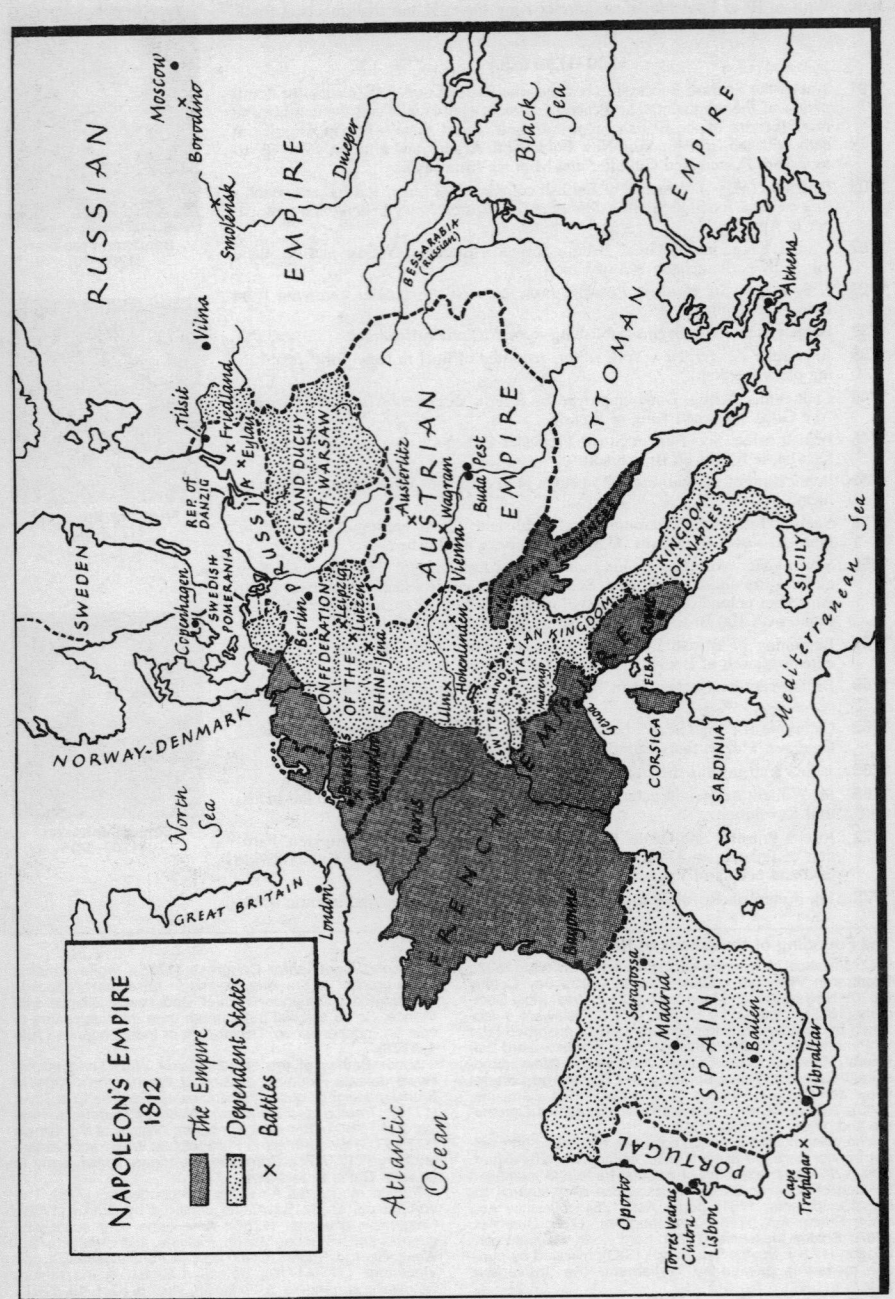

NAPOLEON'S EMPIRE
1812

The Empire
Dependent States
× Battles

1776 Adam Smith's *Wealth of Nations.* Edward Gibbon's *Decline and Fall of the Roman Empire.* Thomas Paine's *Common Sense.* Fragonard's *Washerwoman.* Mozart's *Haffner Serenade.*

1778 Capt. James Cook discovers Hawaii. Franz Mesmer uses hypnotism.

1781 Immanuel Kant's *Critique of Pure Reason.* Herschel discovers Uranus.

1783 End of Revolutionary War. William Blake's poems. Beethoven's first printed works.

1784 Crimea annexed by Russia. John Wesley's *Deed of Declaration,* the basic work of Methodism.

1785 Russians settle Aleutian Islands.

1787 The Constitution of the United States signed. Lavoisier's work on chemical nomenclature. Mozart's *Don Giovanni.*

1788 French *Parlement* presents grievances to Louis XVI who agrees to convening of Estates-General in 1789—not called since 1613. Goethe's *Egmont.* Laplace's *Laws of the Planetary System.*

1789 French Revolution. In U.S., George Washington elected President with all 69 votes of the Electoral College, takes oath of office in New York City. Vice President: John Adams. Secretary of State: Thomas Jefferson. Secretary of Treasury: Alexander Hamilton.

1790 H.M.S. *Bounty* mutineers settle on Pitcairn Island. Aloisio Galvani experiments on electrical stimulation of the muscles. Philadelphia temporary capital of U.S. as Congress votes to establish new capital on Potomac. U.S. population about 3,929,000, including 698,000 slaves. Lavoisier formulates *Table of 31 chemical elements.*

1791 U.S. Bill of Rights ratified. Boswell's *Life of Johnson.*

1794 Kosciusko's uprising in Poland quelled by the Russians. In U.S., Whiskey Rebellion in Pennsylvania as farmers object to liquor taxes.

1796 Napoleon Bonaparte, French general, defeats Austrians. In the U.S., Washington's Farewell Address **(Sept. 17)**; John Adams elected President; Thomas Jefferson, vice president. Edward Jenner introduces smallpox vaccination.

1798 Napoleon extends French conquests to Rome and Egypt. U.S. Navy Department established.

1799 Napoleon leads coup that overthrows Directory, becomes First Consul—one of three who rule France.

George Washington
(1732–99)

1800–1899 (C.E.)

1800 Napoleon conquers Italy, firmly establishes himself as First Consul in France. In the U.S., federal government moves to Washington. Robert Owen's social reforms in England. William Herschel discovers infrared rays. Alessandro Volta produces electricity.

1801 Austria makes temporary peace with France. United Kingdom of Great Britain and Ireland established with one monarch and one parliament; Catholics excluded from voting.

1803 U.S. negotiates Louisiana Purchase from France: For $15 million, U.S. doubles its domain, increasing its territory by 827,000 sq. mi. (2,144,500 sq km), from Mississippi River to Rockies and from Gulf of Mexico to British North America.

1804 Haiti declares independence from France; first black nation to gain freedom from European colonial rule. Napoleon proclaims himself emperor of France, systematizes French law under *Code Napoleon.* In the U.S., Alexander Hamilton is mortally wounded in duel with Aaron Burr. Lewis and Clark expedition begins exploration of what is now northwestern U.S.

1805 Lord Nelson defeats the French-Spanish fleets in the Battle of Trafalgar. Napoleon victorious over Austrian and Russian forces at the Battle of Austerlitz.

1807 Robert Fulton makes first successful steamboat trip on *Clermont* between New York City and Albany.

1808 French armies occupy Rome and Spain, extending Napoleon's empire. Britain begins aiding Spanish guerrillas against Napoleon in Peninsular War. In the U.S., Congress bars importation of slaves. Beethoven's *Fifth* and *Sixth Symphonies* performed.

1812 Napoleon's Grand Army invades Russia in June. Forced to retreat in winter, most of Napoleon's 600,000 men are lost. In the U.S., war with Britain declared over freedom of the seas for U.S. vessels. U.S.S. *Constitution* sinks British frigate.

Napoleon Bonaparte
(1769–1821)

Ludwig van Beethoven
(1770–1827)

Edgar Allen Poe
(1809–49)

French Revolution (1789–1799)

Revolution begins when Third Estate (Commons) delegates swear not to disband until France has a constitution. Paris mob storms Bastille, symbol of royal power **(July 14, 1789).** National Assembly votes for Constitution, Declaration of the Rights of Man, a limited monarchy, and other reforms (1789-90). Legislative Assembly elected, Revolutionary Commune formed, and French Republic proclaimed (1792). War of the First Coalition—Austria, Prussia, Britain, Netherlands, and Spain fight to restore French nobility (1792-97). Start of series of wars between France and European powers that will last, almost without interruption, for 23 years. Louis XVI and Marie Antoinette executed. Committee of Public Safety begins Reign of Terror as political control measure. Interfactional rivalry leads to mass killings. Danton and Robespierre executed. Third French Constitution sets up Directory government (1795).

Atlantic
Ocean

MEXICO

Rio Grande

Mississippi

San Francisco

Gulf of
Mexico

Mexico

CUBA

BELIZE

HAITI

PUERTO
RICO

CENTRAL AMERICA

Caribbean Sea

PANAMA

Caracas

VENEZUELA

NEW GRENADA

Bogota

COLOMBIA

GUIANA

Quito

QUITO

Amazon

BRAZIL

Pacific

Ocean

PERU

Lima

BOLIVIA

Sucre

PARAGUAY

Asuncion

R.

Rio de Janeiro

CHILE

UNITED PROVINCES
of LA PLATA

Parana

CISPLATINE
PROVINCE

Santiago

Buenos
Aires

Montevideo

LATIN
AMERICAN
STATES
after the
REVOLUTIONS

0   500   1000   1500

Scale of Miles

Atlantic
Ocean

1814 French defeated by allies (Britain, Austria, Russia, Prussia, Sweden, and Portugal) in War of Liberation. Napoleon exiled to Elba, off Italian coast. Bourbon King Louis XVIII takes French throne. George Stephenson builds first practical steam locomotive.

1815 Napoleon returns: "Hundred Days" begin. Napoleon defeated by Wellington at Waterloo, banished again to St. Helena in South Atlantic. Congress of Vienna: victorious allies change the map of Europe.

1817 Simón Bolívar establishes independent Venezuela, as Spain loses hold on South American countries. Bolívar named President of Colombia (1819). Peru, Guatemala, Panama, and Santo Domingo proclaim independence from Spain (1821).

1820 Missouri Compromise—Missouri admitted as slave state but slavery barred in rest of Louisiana Purchase north of 36°30′ N.

Frederick Douglass
(c. 1817–95)

1822 Greeks proclaim a republic and independence from Turkey. Turks invade Greece. Russia declares war on Turkey (1828). Greece also aided by France and Britain. War ends and Turks recognize Greek independence (1829). Brazil becomes independent of Portugal. Schubert's *Eighth Symphony* ("The Unfinished").

1823 U.S. Monroe Doctrine warns European nations not to interfere in Western Hemisphere.

1824 Mexico becomes a republic, three years after declaring independence from Spain. Beethoven's *Ninth Symphony*.

1825 First passenger-carrying railroad in England.

1830 French invade Algeria. Louis Philippe becomes "Citizen King" as revolution forces Charles X to abdicate. Mormon church formed in U.S. by Joseph Smith.

1831 Polish revolt against Russia fails. Belgium separates from the Netherlands. In U.S., Nat Turner leads unsuccessful slave rebellion.

1833 Slavery abolished in British Empire.

1834 Charles Babbage invents "analytical engine," precursor of computer. McCormick patents reaper.

Harriet Tubman
(c. 1820–1913)

1836 Boer farmers start "Great Trek"—Natal, Transvaal, and Orange Free State founded in South Africa. Mexican army besieges Texans in Alamo. Entire garrison, including Davy Crockett and Jim Bowie, wiped out. Texans gain independence from Mexico after winning Battle of San Jacinto. Dickens's *Pickwick Papers*.

1837 Victoria becomes Queen of Great Britain. Mob kills Elijah P. Lovejoy, Illinois abolitionist publisher.

1839 First Opium War (to1842) between Britain and China, over importation of drug into China.

1840 Lower and Upper Canada united.

1841 U.S. President Harrison dies **(April 4)** one month after inauguration; John Tyler becomes first vice president to succeed to Presidency.

1843 Wagner's opera *The Flying Dutchman.*

1844 Democratic convention calls for annexation of Texas and acquisition of Oregon ("Fifty-four-forty-or-fight"). Five Chinese ports opened to U.S. ships. Samuel F. B. Morse patents telegraph.

Harriet Beecher Stowe
(1811–96)

1845 Congress adopts joint resolution for annexation of Texas. Edgar Allen Poe publishes *The Raven and Other Poems.*

1846 Failure of potato crop causes famine in Ireland. U.S. declares war on Mexico. California and New Mexico annexed by U.S. Brigham Young leads Mormons to Great Salt Lake. W.T. Morton uses ether as anesthetic. Sewing machine patented by Elias Howe. Frederick Douglass launches abolitionist newspaper *The North Star.*

1848 Revolt in Paris: Louis Philippe abdicates; Louis Napoleon elected President of French Republic. Revolutions in Vienna, Venice, Berlin, Milan, Rome, and Warsaw. Put down by royal troops in 1848-49. U.S.-Mexico War ends; Mexico cedes claims to Texas, California, Arizona, New Mexico, Utah, Nevada. U.S. treaty with Britain sets Oregon Territory boundary at 49th parallel. Karl Marx and Friedrich Engels' *Communist Manifesto.* Harriet Tubman escapes from slavery and joins the Underground Railroad.

1849 California gold rush begins.

1850 Henry Clay opens great debate on slavery, warns South against secession.

1851 Herman Melville's *Moby Dick.* Harriet Beecher Stowe's *Uncle Tom's Cabin.*

1852 South African Republic established. Louis Napoleon proclaims himself Napoleon III ("Second Empire").

Richard Wagner
(1813–83)

War of 1812

British interference with American trade, impressment of American seamen, and "War Hawks" drive for western expansion lead to war. American attacks on Canada foiled; U.S. Commodore Perry wins battle of Lake Erie (1813). British capture and burn Washington (1814) but fail to take Fort McHenry at Baltimore. Andrew Jackson repulses assault on New Orleans after treaty of Ghent ends war (1815). War settles little but strengthens U.S. as independent nation.

**Walt Whitman
(1819–92)**

**Dred Scott
(1795?–1858)**

**Charles Darwin
(1809–82)**

**Abraham Lincoln
(1809–65)**

1853 Crimean War begins as Turkey declares war on Russia. Commodore Perry reaches Tokyo.

1854 Britain and France join Turkey in war on Russia. In U.S., Kansas-Nebraska Act permits local option on slavery; rioting and bloodshed. Japanese allow American trade. Antislavery men in Michigan form Republican Party. Tennyson's *Charge of the Light Brigade.* Thoreau's *Walden.*

1855 Armed clashes in Kansas between pro- and anti-slavery forces. Florence Nightingale nurses wounded in Crimea. Walt Whitman's *Leaves of Grass.*

1856 Flaubert's *Madame Bovary.*

1857 Supreme Court, in Dred Scott decision, rules that a slave is not a citizen. Financial crisis in Europe and U.S. Great Mutiny (Sepoy Rebellion) begins in India. India placed under crown rule as a result.

1858 Pro-slavery constitution rejected in Kansas. Abraham Lincoln makes strong antislavery speech in Springfield, Ill.: "...this Government cannot endure permanently half slave and half free." Lincoln-Douglas debates. First trans-Atlantic telegraph cable completed by Cyrus W. Field.

1859 John Brown raids Harpers Ferry; is captured and hanged. Work begins on Suez Canal. Unification of Italy starts under leadership of Count Cavour, Sardinian premier. Joined by France in war against Austria. Edward Fitzgerald's *Rubaiyat of Omar Khayyam.* Charles Darwin's *Origin of Species.* J. S. Mill's *On Liberty.*

1861 U.S. Civil War begins as attempts at compromise fail. Congress creates Colorado, Dakota, and Nevada territories; adopts income tax; Lincoln inaugurated. Serfs emancipated in Russia. Pasteur's theory of germs. Independent Kingdom of Italy proclaimed under Sardinian King Victor Emmanuel II.

1863 French capture Mexico City; proclaim Archduke Maximilian of Austria emperor.

1865 Lincoln fatally shot at Ford's Theater by John Wilkes Booth. Vice President Johnson sworn as successor. Booth caught and dies of gunshot wounds; four conspirators are hanged. Joseph Lister begins antiseptic surgery. Gregor Mendel's *Law of Heredity.* Lewis Carroll's *Alice's Adventures in Wonderland.*

1866 Alfred Nobel invents dynamite (patented in Britain 1867). Seven Weeks' War: Austria defeated by Prussia and Italy.

1867 Austria-Hungary Dual Monarchy established. French leave Mexico; Maximilian executed. Dominion of Canada established. U.S. buys Alaska from Russia for $7,200,000. South African diamond field discovered. Volume I of Marx's *Das Kapital.* Strauss's *Blue Danube.*

1868 Revolution in Spain; Queen Isabella deposed, flees to France. In U.S., Fourteenth Amendment giving civil rights to blacks is ratified. Georgia under military government after legislature expels blacks.

The Civil War (The War Between the States or the War of the Rebellion)

Apart from the matter of slavery, the Civil War arose out of both the economic and political rivalry between an agrarian South and an industrial North and the issue of the right of states to secede from the Union.

1861 After South Carolina secedes **(Dec. 20, 1860)**, Mississippi, Florida, Alabama, Georgia, Louisiana, and Texas follow, forming the Confederate States of America, with Jefferson Davis as president **(Jan.-March)**. War begins as Confederates fire on Fort Sumter **(April 12)**. Lincoln calls for 75,000 volunteers. Southern ports blockaded by superior Union naval forces. Virginia, Arkansas, Tennessee, and North Carolina secede to complete 11-state Confederacy. Union army advancing on Richmond repulsed at first Battle of Bull Run **(July)**.

1862 Edwin M. Stanton named Secretary of War **(Jan.)**. Grant wins first important Union victory in West, at Fort Donelson; Nashville falls **(Feb.)**. Ironclads, Union's *Monitor* and Confederate's *Virginia (Merrimac)* duel at Hampton Roads **(March)**. New Orleans falls to Union fleet under Farragut; city occupied **(April)**. Grant's army escapes defeat at Shiloh. Memphis falls as Union gunboats control upper Mississippi **(June)**. Confederate General Robert E. Lee victorious at second Battle of Bull Run **(Aug.)**. Union army under McClellan halts Lee's attack on Washington in the Battle of Antietam **(Sept.)**. Lincoln removes McClellan

for lack of aggressiveness. Burnside's drive on Richmond fails at Fredericksburg **(Dec.)**. Union forces under Rosecrans chase Bragg through Tennessee; battle of Murfreesboro **(Oct.-Jan. 1863)**.

1863 Lee defeats Hooker at Chancellorsville; "Stonewall" Jackson, Confederate general, dies **(May)**. Confederate invasion of Pennsylvania stopped at Gettysburg by George Meade—Lee loses 20,000 men—the greatest battle of the War **(July)**. It and the Union victory at Vicksburg mark the war's turning point. Union general George H. Thomas, the "Rock of Chickamauga," holds Bragg's forces on Georgia-Tennessee border **(Sept.)**. Sherman, Hooker, and Thomas drive Bragg back to Georgia. Tennessee restored to the Union **(Nov.)**.

1864 Ulysses S. Grant named commander-in-chief of Union forces **(March)**. In the Wilderness campaign, Grant forces Lee's Army of Northern Virginia back toward Richmond **(May-June)**. Sherman's Atlanta campaign and "march to the sea" **(May-Sept.)**. Farragut's victory at Mobile Bay **(Aug.)**. Hood's Confederate army defeated at Nashville. Sherman takes Savannah **(Dec.)**.

1865 Sheridan defeats Confederates at Five Forks; Confederates evacuate Richmond **(April)**. On April 9, Lee surrenders to Grant at Appomattox.

1869 First U.S. transcontinental rail route completed. James Fisk and Jay Gould attempt to control gold market causes Black Friday panic. Suez Canal opened. Mendeleev's periodic table of elements.

1870 Franco-Prussian War (to1871): Napoleon III capitulates at Sedan. Revolt in Paris; Third Republic proclaimed.

1871 France surrenders Alsace-Lorraine to Germany; war ends. German Empire proclaimed with Prussian King as Kaiser Wilhelm I. Fighting with Apaches begins in American West. Boss Tweed corruption exposed in New York. The Chicago Fire, with 250 deaths and $196-million damage. Stanley meets Livingston in Africa.

1872 Congress gives amnesty to most Confederates. Jules Verne's *Around the World in 80 Days.*

1873 Economic crisis in Europe. U.S. establishes gold standard.

1875 First Kentucky Derby.

1876 Sioux kill Gen. George A. Custer and 264 troopers at Little Big Horn River. Alexander Graham Bell patents the telephone.

1877 After Presidential election of 1876, Electoral Commission gives disputed Electoral College votes to Rutherford B. Hayes despite Tilden's popular majority. Russo-Turkish war (ends in 1878 with power of Turkey in Europe broken). Reconstruction ends in the American South. Thomas Edison patents phonograph. The Nez Perce leader Chief Joseph is forced to surrender. Tchaikovsky's *Swan Lake.*

1878 Congress of Berlin revises Treaty of San Stefano ending Russo-Turkish War; makes extensive redivision of southeastern Europe. First commercial telephone exchange opened in New Haven, Conn.

1880 U.S.-China treaty allows U.S. to restrict immigration of Chinese labor.

1881 President Garfield fatally shot by assassin; Vice President Arthur succeeds him. Charles J. Guiteau convicted and executed (in1882).

1882 Terrorism in Ireland after land evictions. Britain invades and conquers Egypt. Germany, Austria, and Italy form Triple Alliance. In U.S., Congress adopts Chinese Exclusion Act. Rockefeller's Standard Oil Trust is first industrial monopoly. In Berlin, Robert Koch announces discovery of tuberculosis germ.

1883 Congress creates Civil Service Commission. Brooklyn Bridge and Metropolitan Opera House completed.

1885 British Gen. Charles G. "Chinese" Gordon killed at Khartoum in Egyptian Sudan.

1886 Bombing at Haymarket Square, Chicago, kills seven policemen and injures many others. Eight alleged anarchists accused—three imprisoned, one commits suicide, four hanged. (In 1893, Illinois Governor Altgeld, critical of trial, pardons three survivors.) Statue of Liberty dedicated. Geronimo, Apache Indian chief, surrenders.

1887 Queen Victoria's Golden Jubilee. Sir Arthur Conan Doyle's first Sherlock Holmes story, *A Study in Scarlet.*

1888 Historic March blizzard in Northeast U.S.—many perish, property damage exceeds $25 million. George Eastman's box camera (the Kodak). J.B. Dunlop invents pneumatic tire. Jack the Ripper murders in London.

1889 Second (Socialist) International founded in Paris. Indian Territory in Oklahoma opened to settlement. Thousands die in Johnstown, Pa., flood. Mark Twain's *A Connecticut Yankee in King Arthur's Court.* Eiffel Tower built for the Paris exposition.

1890 Congress votes Sherman Antitrust Act. Sitting Bull killed in Sioux uprising.

1892 Battle between steel strikers and Pinkerton guards at Homestead, Pa.; union defeated after militia intervenes. Silver mine strikers in Idaho fight non-union workers; U.S. troops dispatched. Diesel engine patented.

1894 Sino-Japanese War begins (ends in1895 with China's defeat). In France, Capt. Alfred Dreyfus convicted on false treason charge (pardoned in 1906). In U.S., Jacob S. Coxey of Ohio leads "Coxey's Army" of unemployed on Washington. Eugene V. Debs calls general strike of rail workers to support Pullman Company strikers; strike broken, Debs jailed for six months. Thomas A. Edison's kinetoscope given first public showing in New York City.

1895 X-rays discovered by German physicist, Wilhelm Roentgen.

Robert E. Lee
(1807–70)

William Tecumseh
Sherman
(1820–91)

Chief Joseph
(c. 1840–1904)

Samuel Clemens
(Mark Twain)
(1835–1910)

Spanish-American War (1898–1899)

War fires stoked by "jingo journalism" as American people support Cuban rebels against Spain. American business sees economic gain in Cuban trade and resources and American power zones in Latin America. Outstanding events: Submarine mine explodes U.S. battleship *Maine* in Havana Harbor (**Feb. 15**); 260 killed; responsibility never fixed. Congress declares independence of Cuba (**Apr. 19**). Spain declares war on U.S. (**Apr. 24**); Congress (**Apr. 25**) formally declares nation has been at war with Spain since **Apr. 21.** Commodore George Dewey wins seven-hour battle of Manila Bay (**May 1**). Spanish fleet destroyed off Santiago, Cuba (**July 3**); city surrenders (**July 17**). Treaty of Paris (ratified by Senate 1899) ends war. U.S. given Guam and Puerto Rico and agrees to pay Spain $20 million for Philippines. Cuba independent of Spain; under U.S. military control for three years until **May 20, 1902.** Yellow fever is eradicated and political reforms achieved.

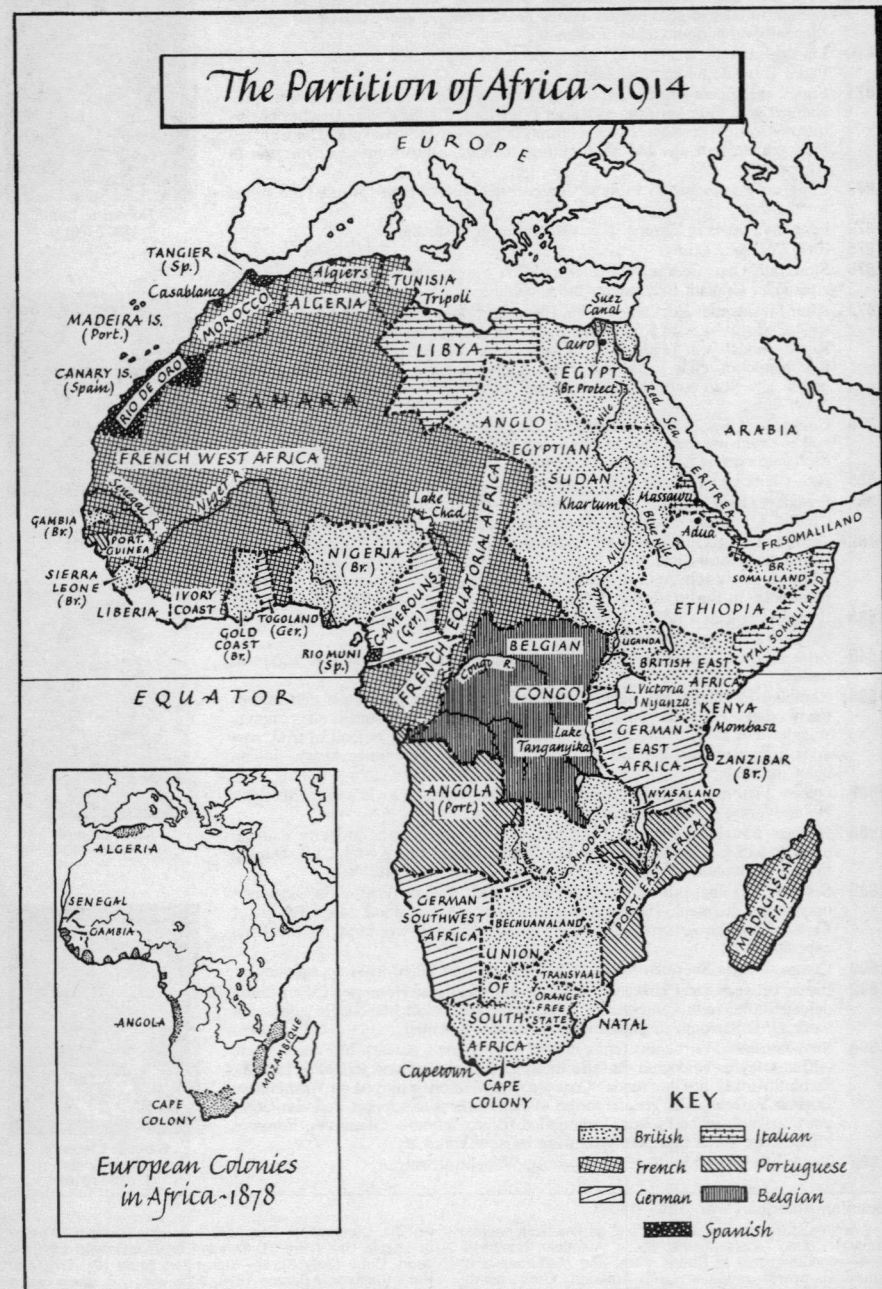

The Partition of Africa ~ 1914

EUROPE

TANGIER (Sp.)
Casablanca
MADEIRA IS. (Port.)
ALGIERS
ALGERIA
MOROCCO
TUNISIA
Tripoli
LIBYA
Suez Canal
Cairo
EGYPT (Br. Protect.)
CANARY IS. (Spain)
RIO DE ORO
SAHARA
ARABIA
FRENCH WEST AFRICA
ANGLO EGYPTIAN SUDAN
Khartum
Massawa
Red Sea
ERITREA
Adua
Lake Chad
Blue Nile
FR. SOMALILAND
GAMBIA (Br.)
PORT. GUINEA
NIGERIA (Br.)
BR. SOMALILAND
SIERRA LEONE (Br.)
IVORY COAST
LIBERIA
GOLD COAST (Br.)
TOGOLAND (Ger.)
CAMEROUNS (Ger.)
FRENCH EQUATORIAL AFRICA
RIO MUNI (Sp.)
ETHIOPIA
(ITAL. SOMALILAND)
UGANDA
BELGIAN
CONGO
L. Victoria Nyanza
BRITISH EAST AFRICA
KENYA
Mombasa
EQUATOR
Lake Tanganyika
GERMAN EAST AFRICA
ZANZIBAR (Br.)
ANGOLA (Port.)
NYASALAND
RHODESIA
PORT. EAST AFRICA
GERMAN SOUTHWEST AFRICA
BECHUANALAND
MADAGASCAR (Fr.)
UNION OF SOUTH AFRICA
TRANSVAAL
ORANGE FREE STATE
NATAL
Capetown
CAPE COLONY

KEY

British		Italian	
French		Portuguese	
German		Belgian	
Spanish			

ALGERIA
SENEGAL
GAMBIA
ANGOLA
MOZAMBIQUE
CAPE COLONY

European Colonies
in Africa ~ 1878

1896 Supreme Court's *Plessy v. Ferguson* decision—"separate but equal" doctrine. Alfred Nobel's will establishes prizes for peace, science, and literature. Marconi receives first wireless patent in Britain. William Jennings Bryan delivers "Cross of Gold" speech at Democratic Convention in Chicago. First modern Olympic games held in Athens, Greece.

1898 Chinese "Boxers," anti-foreign organization, established. They stage uprisings against Europeans in 1900; U.S. and other Western troops relieve Peking legations. Spanish-American War. Pierre and Marie Curie discover radium and polonium.

1899 Boer War (or South African War). Conflict between British and Boers (descendants of Dutch settlers of South Africa). Causes rooted in longstanding territorial disputes and in friction over political rights for English and other "uitlanders" following 1886 discovery of vast gold deposits in Transvaal. (British victorious as war ends in 1902.) Casualties: 5,774 British dead, about 4,000 Boers. Union of South Africa established in 1908 as confederation of colonies; becomes British dominion in 1910.

**Marie Curie
(1867–1934)**

1900–1999 (C.E.)

1900 Hurricane ravages Galveston, Tex.; 6,000 drown. Sigmund Freud's *The Interpretation of Dreams*. Fauvist movement in painting begins, led by Henri Matisse. Freud's *The Interpretation of Dreams*.

1901 Queen Victoria dies; succeeded by son, Edward VII. As President McKinley begins second term, he is shot fatally by anarchist Leon Czolgosz. Theodore Roosevelt sworn in as successor.

1902 Enrico Caruso's first gramophone recording.

1903 Wright brothers, Orville and Wilbur, fly first powered, controlled, heavier-than-air plane at Kitty Hawk, N.C. Henry Ford organizes Ford Motor Company.

1904 Russo-Japanese War—competition for Korea and Manchuria: In 1905, Port Arthur surrenders to Japanese and Russia suffers other defeats; President Roosevelt mediates Treaty of Portsmouth, N.H., ending war with concessions for Japan. *Entente Cordiale:* Britain and France settle their international differences. General theory of radioactivity by Rutherford and Soddy. New York City subway opened.

**Sigmund Freud
(1856–1939)**

1905 General strike in Russia; first workers' soviet set up in St. Petersburg. Sailors on battleship *Potemkin* mutiny; reforms including first Duma (parliament) established by Czar's "October Manifesto." Albert Einstein's special theory of relativity and other key theories in physics. Franz Lehar's *Merry Widow*.

1906 San Francisco earthquake and three-day fire; 500 dead. Roald Amundsen, Norwegian explorer, fixes magnetic North Pole.

1907 Second Hague Peace Conference, of 46 nations, adopts 10 conventions on rules of war. Financial panic of 1907 in U.S. Mahler begins work onm "Song of the earth."

1908 Earthquake kills 150,000 in southern Italy and Sicily. U.S. Supreme Court, in Danbury Hatters' case, outlaws secondary union boycotts.

1909 North Pole reached by American explorers Robert E. Peary and Matthew Henson. The National Association for the Advancement of Colored People is founded in New York by prominent black and white intellectuals and led by W.E.B. DuBois.

**Henri Matisse
(1869–1954)**

1910 Boy Scouts of America incorporated.

1911 First use of aircraft as offensive weapon in Turkish-Italian War. Italy defeats Turks and annexes Tripoli and Libya. Chinese Republic proclaimed after revolution overthrows Manchu dynasty. Sun Yat-sen named president. Mexican Revolution: Porfirio Diaz, president since 1877, replaced by Francisco Madero. Triangle Shirtwaist Company fire in New York; 145 killed. Richard Strauss's *Der Rosenkavalier*. Irving Berlin's *Alexander's Ragtime Band*. Amundsen reaches South Pole.

1912 Balkan Wars (1912–13) resulting from territorial disputes: Turkey defeated by alliance of Bulgaria, Serbia, Greece, and Montenegro; London peace treaty (1913) partitions most of European Turkey among the victors. In second war (1913), Bulgaria attacks Serbia and Greece and is defeated after Romania intervenes and Turks recapture Adrianople. *Titanic* sinks on maiden voyage; over 1,500 drown.

**W.E.B. DuBois
(1868–1963)**

1913 Suffragettes demonstrate in London. Garment workers strike in New York and Boston; win pay raise and shorter hours. Sixteenth Amendment (income tax) and 17th (popular election of U.S. senators) adopted. Bill creating U.S. Federal Reserve System becomes law. Stravinsky's *The Rite of Spring*.

1914 World War I begins. Panama Canal officially opened. Congress sets up Federal Trade Commission, passes Clayton Antitrust Act. U.S. Marines occupy Veracruz, Mexico, intervening in civil war to protect American interests.

1915 U.S. protests German submarine actions and British blockade of Germany. U.S. banks lend $500 million to France and Britain. D. W. Griffith's film *Birth of a Nation*. Albert Einstein's *General Theory of Relativity*.

**Albert Einstein
(1879–1955)**

**Vladimir Lenin
(1870–1924)**

**Woodrow Wilson
(1856–1924)**

**Benito Mussolini
(1883–1945)**

1916 Congress expands armed forces. Tom Mooney arrested for San Francisco bombing (pardoned in 1939). Pershing fails in raid into Mexico in quest of rebel Pancho Villa. U.S. buys Virgin Islands from Denmark for $25 million. President Wilson re-elected with "he kept us out of war" slogan. "Black Tom" explosion at munitions dock in Jersey City, N.J., $40,000,000 damages; traced to German saboteurs. Margaret Sanger opens first birth control clinic. Easter Rebellion in Ireland put down by British troops.

1917 First U.S. combat troops in France as U.S. declares war (**April 6**). Russian Revolution—climax of long unrest under czars. February Revolution—Czar forced to abdicate, liberal government created. Kerensky becomes prime minister and forms provisional government (**July**). In October Revolution, Bolsheviks seize power in armed coup d'état led by Lenin and Trotsky. Kerensky flees. Revolutionaries execute the czar and his family (1918). Reds set up Third International in Moscow (1919). Balfour Declaration promises Jewish homeland in Palestine. Sigmund Freud's *Introduction to Psychoanalysis*.

1918 Russian Civil War between Reds (Bolsheviks) and Whites (anti-Bolsheviks); Reds win in 1920. Allied troops (U.S., British, French) intervene (**March**); leave in 1919. Japanese hold Vladivostok until 1922. World-wide influenza epidemic strikes; by 1920, nearly 20 million are dead. In U.S. alone, 500,000 perish.

1919 Third International (Comintern) establishes Soviet control over international Communist movements. Paris peace conference. Versailles Treaty, incorporating Woodrow Wilson's draft Covenant of League of Nations, signed by Allies and Germany; rejected by U.S. Senate. Congress formally ends war in 1921. Eighteenth (Prohibition) Amendment adopted. Alcock and Brown make first trans-Atlantic non-stop flight.

1920 League of Nations holds first meeting at Geneva, Switzerland. U.S. Dept. of Justice "red hunt" nets thousands of radicals; aliens deported. Women's suffrage (19th) amendment ratified. First Agatha Christie mystery. Sinclair Lewis's *Main Street*.

1921 Reparations Commission fixes German liability at 132 billion gold marks. German inflation begins. Major treaties signed at Washington Disarmament Conference limit naval tonnage and pledge to respect territorial integrity of China. Irish Free State formed in southern Ireland as self-governing dominion of British Empire. In U.S., Nicola Sacco and Bartolomeo Vanzetti, Italian-born anarchists, convicted of armed robbery murder; case stirs world-wide protests; they are executed in 1927.

1922 Mussolini marches on Rome; forms Fascist government. Irish Free State officially proclaimed.

1923 Adolf Hitler's "Beer Hall Putsch" in Munich fails; in 1924 he is sentenced to five years in prison where he writes *Mein Kampf;* released after eight months. Occupation of Ruhr by French and Belgian troops to enforce reparations payments. Widespread Ku Klux Klan violence in U.S. George Gershwin's *Rhapsody in Blue*. Bessie Smith, known as "the Empress of the Blues," makes her

---

World War I (1914–1918)

Imperial, territorial, and economic rivalries lead to the "Great War" between the Central Powers (Austria-Hungary, Germany, Bulgaria, and Turkey) and the Allies (U.S., Britain, France, Russia, Belgium, Serbia, Greece, Romania, Montenegro, Portugal, Italy, Japan). About 10 million combatants killed, 20 million wounded.

1914 Austrian Archduke Francis Ferdinand and wife assassinated in Sarajevo by Serbian nationalist, Gavrilo Princip (**June 28**). Austria declares war on Serbia (**July 28**). Germany declares war on Russia (**Aug. 1**), on France (**Aug. 3**), invades Belgium (**Aug. 4**). Britain declares war on Germany (**Aug. 4**). Germans defeat Russians in Battle of Tannenberg on Eastern Front (**Aug.**). First Battle of the Marne (**Sept.**). German drive stopped 25 miles from Paris. By end of year, war on the Western Front is "positional" in the trenches.

1915 German submarine blockade of Great Britain begins (**Feb.**). Dardanelles Campaign—British land in Turkey (**April**), withdraw from Gallipoli (**Dec. to Jan. 1916**). Germans use gas at second battle of Ypres (**April–May**). *Lusitania* sunk by German submarine—1,198 lost, including 128 Americans (**May 7**). On Eastern Front, German and Austrian "great offensive" conquers all of Poland and Lithuania; Russians lose 1 million men (by **Sept. 6**) "Great Fall Offensive" by Allies results in little change from 1914 (**Sept.–Oct.**). Britain and France declare war on Bulgaria (**Oct. 14**).

1916 Battle of Verdun—Germans and French each lose about 350,000 men (**Feb.**). Extended submarine warfare begins (**March**). British-German sea battle of Jutland (**May**); British lose more ships, but German fleet never ventures forth again. On Eastern Front, the Brusilov offensive demoralizes Russians, costs them 1 million men (**June–Sept.**). Battle of the Somme—British lose over 400,000; French, 200,000; Germans, about 450,000; all with no strategic results (**July–Nov.**). Romania declares war on Austria-Hungary (**Aug. 27**). Bucharest captured (**Dec.**).

1917 U.S. declares war on Germany (**April 6**). Submarine warfare at peak (**April**). On Italian Front, Battle of Caporetto—Italians retreat, losing 600,000 prisoners and deserters (**Oct.–Dec.**). On Western Front, Battles of Arras, Champagne, Ypres (third battle), etc. First large British tank attack (**Nov.**). U.S. declares war on Austria-Hungary (**Dec. 7**). Armistice between new Russian Bolshevik government and Germans (**Dec. 15**).

1918 Great offensive by Germans (**March–June**). Americans' first important battle role at Château-Thierry—as they and French stop German advance (**June**). Second Battle of the Marne (**July-Aug.**)—start of Allied offensive at Amiens, St. Mihiel, etc. Battles of the Argonne and Ypres panic German leadership (**Sept.–Oct.**). British offensive in Palestine (**Sept.**). Germans ask for armistice (**Oct. 4**). British armistice with Turkey (**Oct.**). German Kaiser abdicates (**Nov.**). Hostilities cease on Western Front (**Nov. 11**).

first record. Irish poet William Butler Yeats, considered one of the greatest literary figures of the 20th century, wins Nobel Prize in Literature.

1924 Death of Lenin; Stalin wins power struggle, rules as Soviet dictator until death in 1953. Italian Fascists murder Socialist leader Giacomo Matteotti. Interior Secretary Albert B. Fall and oilmen Harry Sinclair and Edward L. Doheny are charged with conspiracy and bribery in the Teapot Dome scandal, involving fraudulent leases of naval oil reserves. In 1931, Fall is sentenced to year in prison; Doheny and Sinclair acquitted of bribery. Nathan Leopold and Richard Loeb convicted in "thrill killing" of Bobby Franks in Chicago; defended by Clarence Darrow; sentenced to life imprisonment. (Loeb killed by fellow convict in 1936; Leopold paroled in 1958, dies in 1971.) Robert Frost wins first of four Pulitzers.

**Joseph Stalin
(1879–1953)**

1925 Nellie Tayloe Ross elected governor of Wyoming; first woman governor elected in U.S. Locarno conferences seek to secure European peace by mutual guarantees. John T. Scopes convicted and fined for teaching evolution in a public school in Tennessee "Monkey Trial"; sentence set aside. John Logie Baird, Scottish inventor, transmits human features by television. Adolf Hitler publishes Volume I of *Mein Kampf.*

1926 General strike in Britain brings nation's activities to standstill. U.S. marines dispatched to Nicaragua during revolt; they remain until 1933. Gertrude Ederle of U.S. is first woman to swim English Channel. Ernest Hemingway's *The Sun Also Rises.*

**Bessie Smith
(1894–1937)**

1927 German economy collapses. Socialists riot in Vienna; general strike follows acquittal of Nazis for political murder. Trotsky expelled from Russian Communist Party. Charles A. Lindbergh flies first successful solo non-stop flight from New York to Paris. Ruth Snyder and Judd Gray convicted of murder of Albert Snyder; they are executed at Sing Sing prison in 1928. *The Jazz Singer,* with Al Jolson, first part-talking motion picture.

1928 Kellogg-Briand Pact, outlawing war, signed in Paris by 65 nations. Alexander Fleming discovers penicillin. Richard E. Byrd starts expedition to Antarctic; returns in 1930.

**William Butler Yeats
(1865–1939)**

1929 Trotsky expelled from U.S.S.R. Lateran Treaty establishes independent Vatican City. In U.S., stock market prices collapse, with U.S. securities losing $26 billion—first phase of Depression and world economic crisis. St. Valentine's Day gangland massacre in Chicago.

1930 Britain, U.S., Japan, France, and Italy sign naval disarmament treaty. Nazis gain in German elections. Cyclotron developed by Ernest O. Lawrence, U.S. physicist.

1931 Spain becomes a republic with overthrow of King Alfonso XIII. German industrialists finance 800,000-strong Nazi party. British parliament enacts statute of Westminster, legalizing dominion equality with Britain. Mukden Incident begins Japanese occupation of Manchuria. In U.S., Hoover proposes one-year moratorium on war debts. Harold C. Urey discovers heavy hydrogen. Gangster Al Capone sentenced to 11 years in prison for tax evasion (freed in 1939; dies in 1947).

**Dorothea Lange's photo
"Migrant Mother" (1936)
documented the Great
Depression (1929–1940)**

1932 Nazis lead in German elections with 230 Reichstag seats. Famine in U.S.S.R. In U.S., Congress sets up Reconstruction Finance Corporation to stimulate economy. Veterans march on Washington—most leave after Senate rejects payment of cash bonuses; others removed by troops under Douglas MacArthur. U.S. protests Japanese aggression in Manchuria. Amelia Earhart is first woman to fly Atlantic solo. Charles A. Lindbergh's baby son kidnapped, killed. (Bruno Richard Hauptmann arrested in 1934, convicted in 1935, executed in 1936.)

1933 Hitler appointed German chancellor, gets dictatorial powers. Reichstag fire in Berlin; Nazi terror begins. Germany and Japan withdraw from League of Nations. Giuseppe Zangara executed for attempted assassination of President-elect Roosevelt in which Chicago Mayor Cermak is fatally shot. Roosevelt inaugurated ("the only thing we have to fear is fear itself"); launches New Deal. Prohibition repealed. U.S.S.R. recognized by U.S.

**Franklin Delano
Roosevelt
(1882–1945)**

1934 Chancellor Dollfuss of Austria assassinated by Nazis. Hitler becomes Führer. U.S.S.R. admitted to League of Nations. Dionne sisters, first quintuplets to survive beyond infancy, born in Canada.

Pablo Picasso (1891–1973)

Amelia Earhart (1898–1937)

Winston Churchill (1871–1947)

1935 Saar incorporated into Germany after plebiscite. Nazis repudiate Versailles Treaty, introduce compulsory military service. Mussolini invades Ethiopia; League of Nations invokes sanctions. Roosevelt opens second phase of New Deal in U.S., calling for social security, better housing, equitable taxation, and farm assistance. Huey Long assassinated in Louisiana.

1936 Germans occupy Rhineland. Italy annexes Ethiopia. Rome-Berlin Axis proclaimed (Japan to join in 1940). Trotsky exiled to Mexico. King George V dies; succeeded by son, Edward VIII, who soon abdicated to marry American-born divorcée, and is succeeded by brother, George VI. Spanish civil war begins. (Franco's fascist forces defeat Loyalist forces by 1939, when Madrid falls.) War between China and Japan begins, to continue through World War II. Japan and Germany sign anti-Comintern pact; joined by Italy in 1937.

1937 Hitler repudiates war guilt clause of Versailles Treaty; continues to build German power. Italy withdraws from League of Nations. U.S. gunboat *Panay* sunk by Japanese in Yangtze River. Japan invades China, conquers most of coastal area. Amelia Earhart lost somewhere in Pacific on round-the-world flight. Picasso's *Guernica* mural.

1938 Hitler marches into Austria; political and geographical union of Germany and Austria proclaimed. Munich Pact—Britain, France, and Italy agree to let Germany partition Czechoslovakia. Douglas "Wrong-Way" Corrigan flies from New York to Dublin.

1939 Germany occupies Bohemia and Moravia; renounces pacts with Poland and England and concludes 10-year non-aggression pact with U.S.S.R. Russo-Finnish War begins; Finns to lose one-tenth of territory in 1940 peace treaty. World War II begins. In U.S., Roosevelt submits $1,319-million defense budget, proclaims U.S. neutrality, and declares limited emergency. Einstein writes FDR about feasibility of atomic bomb. New York World's Fair opens.

1940 Churchill becomes Britain's Prime Minister. Trotsky assassinated in Mexico. Estonia, Latvia, and Lithuania annexed by U.S.S.R. U.S. trades 50 destroyers for leases on British bases in Western Hemisphere. Selective Service Act signed.

1941 Japanese surprise attack on U.S. fleet at Pearl Harbor brings U.S. into World War II. Manhattan Project (atomic bomb research) begins. Roosevelt enunciates "four freedoms," signs lend-lease act, declares national emergency, promises aid to U.S.S.R.

1942 Declaration of United Nations signed in Washington. Women's military services established. Enrico Fermi achieves nuclear chain reaction. Japanese and persons of Japanese ancestry moved inland from Pacific Coast. Coconut Grove nightclub fire in Boston kills 491.

1943 President freezes prices, salaries, and wages to prevent inflation. Income tax withholding introduced.

1944 G.I. Bill of Rights enacted. Bretton Woods Conference creates International Monetary Fund and World Bank. Dumbarton Oaks Conference—U.S., British Commonwealth, and U.S.S.R. propose establishment of United Nations.

The Holocaust (1933–1945)

"Holocaust" is the term describing the Nazi annihilation of about 6 million Jews (two thirds of the pre-World War II European Jewish population), including 4,500,000 from Russia, Poland, and the Baltic; 750,000 from Hungary and Romania; 290,000 from Germany and Austria; 105,000 from The Netherlands; 90,000 from France; 54,000 from Greece; etc.

The Holocaust was unique in its being *genocide*—the systematic destruction of a people solely because of religion, race, ethnicity, nationality, or homosexuality—on an unmatched scale. Along with the Jews, another 9 to 10 million people—Gypsies, Slavs (Poles, Ukrainians, and Belorussians)—were exterminated.

The only comparable act of genocide in modern times was launched in April 1915, when an estimated 600,000 Armenians were massacred by the Turks.

1933 Hitler named German Chancellor **(Jan.)**. Dachau, first concentration camp, established **(March)**. Boycotts against Jews begin **(April)**.

1935 Anti-Semitic Nuremberg Laws passed by Reichstag **(Sept.)**.

1937 Buchenwald concentration camp opens **(July)**.

1938 Extension of anti-Semitic laws to Austria after annexation **(March)**. *Kristallnacht* (Night of Broken Glass)—anti-Semitic riots in Germany and Austria **(Nov. 9)**. 26,000 Jews sent to concentration camps; Jewish children expelled from schools **(Nov.)**. Expropriation of Jewish property and businesses **(Dec.)**.

1940 As war continues, Nazi acts against Jews extended to German-conquered areas.

1941 Deportation of German Jews begins; massacres of Jews in Odessa and Kiev—68,000 killed **(Nov.)**; in Riga and Vilna—almost 60,000 killed **(Dec.)**.

1942 Unified Jewish resistance in ghettos begins **(Jan.)**. 300,000 Jews from Warsaw Ghetto deported to Treblinka death camp **(July)**.

1943 Warsaw Ghetto uprisings **(Jan. and April)**; Ghetto exterminated **(May)**.

1944 476,000 Hungarian Jews sent to Auschwitz **(May-June)**. D-day **(June 6)**. Soviet Army liberates Maidanek death camp **(July)**. Nazis try to hide evidence of death camps **(Nov.)**.

1945 Americans liberate Buchenwald and British liberate Bergen-Belsen camps **(April)**. Nuremberg War Crimes Trial **(Nov. 1945 to Oct. 1946)**.

1945 Yalta Conference (Roosevelt, Churchill, Stalin) plans final defeat of Germany **(Feb.)**. Germany surrenders **(May 7)**. San Francisco Conference establishes U.N. **(April–June)**. FDR dies (April 12). Potsdam Conference (Truman, Churchill, Stalin) establishes basis of German reconstruction **(July–Aug)**. Japan signs surrender **(Sept. 2)**.

1946 First meeting of U.N. General Assembly opens in London **(Jan. 10)**. League of Nations dissolved **(April)**. Italy abolishes monarchy **(June)**. Verdict in Nuremberg war trial: 12 Nazi leaders (including 1 tried in absentia) sentenced to hang; 7 imprisoned; 3 acquitted **(Oct. 1)**. Goering commits suicide a few hours before 10 other Nazis are executed **(Oct. 15)**. Winston Churchill's "Iron Curtain" speech warns of Soviet expansion.

1947 Britain nationalizes coal mines **(Jan. 1)**. Peace treaties for Italy, Romania, Bulgaria, Hungary, Finland signed in Paris **(Feb. 10)**. Soviet Union rejects U.S. plan for U.N. atomic-energy control **(March 4)**. Truman Doctrine proposed—the first significant U.S. attempt to "contain" communist expansion **(March 12)**. Marshall Plan for European recovery proposed—a coordinated program to help European nations recover from ravages of war **(June)**. (By 1951, this "European Recovery Program" had cost $11 billion.) India and Pakistan gain independence from Britain **(Aug. 15)**. Cominform (Communist Information Bureau) founded under Soviet auspices to rebuild contacts among European Communist parties, missing since dissolution of Comintern in **1943 (Sept.)**. (Yugoslav party expelled in 1948 and Cominform disbanded in 1956.) Anne Frank's *The Diary of a Young Girl* published.

1948 Gandhi assassinated in New Delhi by Hindu fanatic **(Jan. 30)**. Communists seize power in Czechoslovakia **(Feb. 23-25)**. Burma and Ceylon granted independence by Britain. Organization of American States (OAS) Charter signed at Bogotá, Colombia **(April 30)**. Nation of Israel proclaimed; British end Mandate at midnight; Arab armies attack **(May 14)**. Berlin airlift begins **(June 21)**; ends **May 12, 1949**. Stalin and Tito break **(June 28)**. Independent Republic of Korea is proclaimed, following election supervised by U.N. **(Aug. 15)**. Verdict in Japanese war trial: Tojo and six others sentenced to hang (hanged Dec. 23); 18 imprisoned **(Nov. 12)**. United States of Indonesia established as Dutch and Indonesians settled conflict **(Dec. 27)**. Alger Hiss, former U.S. State Department official, indicted on perjury charges after denying passing secret documents to communist spy ring. Convicted in second trial (1950) and sentenced to five-year prison term. Tennessee Williams' *A Streetcar Named Desire* wins Pulitzer.

**Adolf Hitler
(1899–1945)**

Yalta Conference

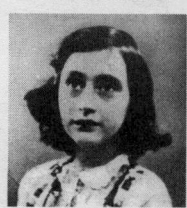

**Anne Frank
(1929–45)**

World War II (1939–1945)

Axis powers (Germany, Italy, Japan, Hungary, Romania, Bulgaria) vs. Allies (U.S., Britain, France, U.S.S.R., Australia, Belgium, Brazil, Canada, China, Denmark, Greece, Netherlands, New Zealand, Norway, Poland, South Africa, Yugoslavia).

1939 Germany invades Poland and annexes Danzig; Britain and France give Hitler ultimatum **(Sept. 1)**, declare war **(Sept. 3)**. Disabled German pocket battleship *Admiral Graf Spee* blown up off Montevideo, Uruguay, on Hitler's orders **(Dec. 17)**. Limited activity ("Sitzkrieg") on Western Front.

1940 Nazis invade Netherlands, Belgium, and Luxembourg **(May 10)**. Chamberlain resigns as Prime Minister; Churchill takes over **(May 10)**. Germans cross French frontier **(May 12)** using air/tank/infantry "Blitzkrieg" tactics. Dunkerque evacuation—about 335,000 out of 400,000 Allied soldiers rescued from Belgium by British civilian and naval craft **(May 26–June 3)**. Italy declares war on France and Britain; invades France **(June 10)**. Germans enter Paris; city undefended **(June 14)**. France and Germany sign armistice in Compiègne **(June 22)**. Nazis bomb Coventry, England **(Nov. 14)**.

1941 Germans launch attacks in Balkans. Yugoslavia surrenders—General Mihajlovic continues guerrilla warfare; Tito leads left-wing guerrillas **(April 17)**. Nazi tanks enter Athens; remnants of British Army quit Greece **(April 27)**. Hitler attacks Russia **(June 22)**. Atlantic Charter—FDR and Churchill agree on war aims **(Aug. 14)**. Japanese attacks on Pearl Harbor, Philippines, Guam force U.S. into war; U.S. Pacific fleet crippled **(Dec. 7)**. U.S. and Britain declare war on Japan. Germany and Italy declare war on U.S.; Congress declares war on those countries **(Dec. 11)**.

1942 British surrender Singapore to Japanese **(Feb. 15)**. U.S. forces on Bataan peninsula in Philippines surrender **(April 9)**. U.S. and Filipino troops on Corregidor island in Manila Bay surrender to Japanese **(May 6)**. Village of Lidice

in Czechoslovakia razed by Nazis **(June 10)**. U.S. and Britain land in French North Africa **(Nov. 8)**.

1943 Casablanca Conference—Churchill and FDR agree on unconditional surrender goal **(Jan. 14-24)**. German 6th Army surrenders at Stalingrad—turning point of war in Russia **(Feb. 1-2)**. Remnants of Nazis trapped on Cape Bon, ending war in Africa **(May 12)**. Mussolini deposed; Badoglio named premier **(July 25)**. Allied troops land on Italian mainland after conquest of Sicily **(Sept. 3)**. Italy surrenders **(Sept. 8)**. Nazis seize Rome **(Sept. 10)**. Cairo Conference: FDR, Churchill, Chiang Kai-shek pledge defeat of Japan, free Korea **(Nov. 22-26)**. Teheran Conference: FDR, Churchill, Stalin agree on invasion plans **(Nov. 28-Dec. 1)**.

1944 U.S. and British troops land at Anzio west Italian coast and hold beachhead **(Jan. 22)**. U.S. and British troops enter Rome **(June 4)**. D-Day—Allies launch Normandy invasion **(June 6)**. Hitler wounded in bomb plot **(July 20)**. Paris liberated **(Aug. 25)**. Athens freed by Allies **(Oct. 13)**. Americans invade Philippines **(Oct. 20)**. Germans launch counteroffensive in Belgium—Battle of Bulge **(Dec. 16)**.

1945 Yalta Agreement signed by FDR, Churchill, Stalin—establishes basis for occupation of Germany, returns to Soviet Union lands taken by Germany and Japan; U.S.S.R. agrees to friendship pact with China **(Feb. 11)**. Mussolini killed at Lake Como **(April 28)**. Admiral Doenitz takes command in Germany; suicide of Hitler announced **(May 1)**. Berlin falls **(May 2)**. V-E Day—Germany signs unconditional surrender terms at Rheims **(May 7)**. Potsdam Conference—Truman, Churchill, Atlee (after July 28), Stalin establish council of foreign ministers to prepare peace treaties; plan German postwar government and reparations **(July 17-Aug. 2)**. A-bomb blasts Hiroshima **(Aug. 6)**. U.S.S.R. declares war on Japan **(Aug. 8)**. Nagasaki hit by A-bomb **(Aug. 9)**. Japan surrenders **(Aug. 14)**. V-J Day—Japanese sign surrender terms aboard battleship *Missouri* **(Sept. 2)**.

**Harry S. Truman
(1884–1972)**

Atomic Bomb

**Rev. Martin Luther King, Jr.
(1929–68)**

**Woody Guthrie
(1912–67)**

1949 Cease-fire in Palestine (**Jan. 7**). Truman proposes Point Four Program to help world's backward areas (**Jan. 20**). Israel signs armistice with Egypt (**Feb. 24**). Start of North Atlantic Treaty Organization (NATO)—treaty signed by 12 nations (**April 4**). German Federal Republic (West Germany) established (**Sept. 21**). Truman discloses Soviet Union has set off atomic explosion (**Sept. 23**). Communist People's Republic of China formally proclaimed by Chairman Mao Zedong. (**Oct. 1**).

1950 Truman orders development of hydrogen bomb (**Jan. 31**). Korean War. Assassination attempt on President Truman by Puerto Rican nationalists (**Nov. 1**). Brink's robbery in Boston; almost $3 million stolen (**Jan. 17**).

1951 Six nations agree to Schuman Plan to pool European coal and steel (**March 19**)—in effect **Feb. 10, 1953**. Julius and Ethel Rosenberg sentenced to death for passing atomic secrets to Russians (**March**). Japanese peace treaty signed in San Francisco by 49 nations (**Sept. 8**). Color television introduced in U.S.

1952 George VI dies; his daughter becomes Elizabeth II (**Feb. 6**). NATO conference approves European army (**Feb.**). AEC announces "satisfactory" experiments in hydrogen-weapons research; eyewitnesses tell of blasts near Enewetak (**Nov.**).

1953 Gen. Dwight D. Eisenhower inaugurated President of United States (**Jan. 20**). Stalin dies (**March 5**). Malenkov becomes Soviet Premier; Beria, Minister of Interior; Molotov, Foreign Minister (**March 6**). Dag Hammarskjold begins term as U.N. Secretary-General (**April 10**). Edmund Hillary, of New Zealand, and Tenzing Norgay, of Nepal, reach top of Mt. Everest (**May 29**). East Berliners rise against Communist rule; quelled by tanks (**June 17**). Egypt becomes republic ruled by military junta (**June 18**). Julius and Ethel Rosenberg executed in Sing Sing prison (**June 19**). Korean armistice signed (**July 27**). Moscow announces explosion of hydrogen bomb (**Aug. 20**). Ernest Hemingway wins Pulitzer for *The Old Man and The Sea*.

1954 First atomic submarine *Nautilus*, launched (**Jan. 21**). Five U.S. Congressmen shot on floor of House as Puerto Rican nationalists fire from spectators' gallery; all five recover (**March 1**). Army *vs*. McCarthy inquiry—Senate subcommittee report blames both sides (**Apr. 22-June 17**). Dien Bien Phu, French military outpost in Vietnam, falls to Vietminh army (**May 7**). U.S. Supreme Court (in*Brown* v. *Board of Education of Topeka*) unanimously bans racial segregation in public schools (**May 17**). Eisenhower launches world atomic pool without Soviet Union (**Sept. 6**). Eight-nation Southeast Asia defense treaty (SEATO) signed at Manila (**Sept. 8**). West Germany is granted sovereignty, admitted to NATO and Western European Union (**Oct. 23**). Dr. Jonas Salk starts inoculating children against polio. Algerian War of Independence against France begins (**Nov.**); France struggles to maintain colonial rule until 1962 when it agrees to Algeria's independence. William Faulkner's *A Fable* wins Pulitzer.

1955 Nikolai A. Bulganin becomes Soviet Premier, replacing Malenkov (**Feb. 8**). Churchill resigns; Anthony Eden succeeds him (**April 6**). Federal Republic of West Germany becomes a sovereign state (**May 5**). Warsaw Pact, east European mutual defense agreement, signed (**May 14**). Argentina ousts Perón (**Sept. 19**). President Eisenhower suffers coronary thrombosis in Denver (**Sept. 24**). Martin Luther King, Jr., leads black boycott of Montgomery, Ala., bus system (**Dec. 1**); desegregated service begun (**Dec. 21**). AFL and CIO become one organization—AFL-CIO (**Dec. 5**). Tennessee Williams's *Cat on a Hot Tin Roof* wins Pulitzer.

1956 Nikita Khrushchev, First Secretary of U.S.S.R. Communist Party, denounces Stalin's excesses (**Feb. 24**). First aerial H-bomb tested over Namu islet, Bikini Atoll—10 million tons TNT equivalent (**May 21**). Worker's uprising against Communist rule in Poznan, Poland, is crushed (**June 28-30**). Egypt takes control of Suez Canal (**July 26**). Israel launches attack on Egypt's Sinai peninsula and drives toward Suez Canal (**Oct. 29**). British and French invade Egypt at Port Said (**Nov. 5**). Cease-fire forced by U.S. pressure stops British, French, and Israeli advance (**Nov. 6**). Revolt starts in Hungary—Soviet troops and tanks crush anti-Communist rebellion (**Nov.**). Ingmar Bergman's *The Seventh Seal*. Woody Guthrie composes "This Land is Your Land."

1957 Eisenhower Doctrine calls for aid to Mideast countries which resist armed aggression from Communist-controlled nations (**Jan. 5**). Eisenhower sends troops to Little Rock, Ark., to quell mob and protect school integration (**Sept.**

Korean War (1950–1953)

1950 North Korean Communist forces invade South Korea (**June 25**). U.N. calls for cease-fire and asks U.N. members to assist South Korea (**June 27**). Truman orders U.S. forces into Korea (**June 27**). North Koreans capture Seoul (**June 28**). Gen. Douglas MacArthur designated commander of unified U.N. forces (**July 8**). Pusan Beachhead—U.N. forces counterattack and capture Seoul (**Aug.-Sept.**), capture Pyongyang, North Korean capital (**Oct.**). Chinese Communists enter war (**Oct. 26**), force

U.N. retreat toward 39th parallel (**Dec.**).

1951 Gen. Matthew B. Ridgeway replaces MacArthur after he threatens Chinese with massive retaliation (**April 11**). Armistice negotiations (**July**) continue with interruptions until **June 1953**.

1953 Armistice signed (**July 27**). Chinese troops withdraw from North Korea (**Oct. 26, 1958**), but over 200 violations of armistice noted to **1959**.

24). Russians launch *Sputnik I,* first earth-orbiting satellite—the Space Age begins **(Oct. 4).**

1958 Army's Jupiter-C rocket fires first U.S. earth satellite, *Explorer I,* into orbit **(Jan. 31).** Egypt and Syria merge into United Arab Republic **(Feb. 1).** European Economic Community (Common Market) established by Rome Treaty becomes effective **Jan. 1, 1958.** Khrushchev becomes Premier of Soviet Union as Bulganin resigns **(Mar. 27).** Gen. Charles de Gaulle becomes French premier **(June 1),** remaining in power until 1969. New French constitution adopted **(Sept. 28),** de Gaulle elected president of 5th Republic **(Dec. 21).** Eisenhower orders U.S. Marines into Lebanon at request of President Chamoun, who fears overthrow **(July 15).**

1959 Cuban President Batista resigns and flees—Castro takes over **(Jan. 1).** Tibet's Dalai Lama escapes to India **(Mar. 31).** St. Lawrence Seaway opens, allowing ocean ships to reach Midwest **(April 25).**

1960 American U-2 spy plane, piloted by Francis Gary Powers, shot down over Russia **(May 1).** Khrushchev kills Paris summit conference because of U-2 **(May 16).** Powers sentenced to prison for 10 years **(Aug. 19)**—freed in **February 1962** in exchange for Soviet spy. Top Nazi murderer of Jews, Adolf Eichmann, captured by Israelis in Argentina **(May 23)**—executed in Israel in 1962. Communist China and Soviet Union split in conflict over Communist ideology. Belgium starts to break up its African colonial empire, gives independence to Belgian Congo (Zaire) on **June 30.** Cuba begins confiscation of $770 million of U.S. property **(Aug. 7).**

1961 U.S. breaks diplomatic relations with Cuba **(Jan. 3).** Robert Frost recites "The Gift Outright" at John F. Kennedy's inauguration as President of U.S. **(Jan. 20).** Kennedy proclaims Alliance for Progress—10-year plan to raise Latin American living standards **(Mar. 13).** Moscow announces putting first man in orbit around earth, Maj. Yuri A. Gagarin **(April 12).** Cuba invaded at Bay of Pigs by an estimated 1,200 anti-Castro exiles aided by U.S.; invasion crushed **(April 17).** First U.S. spaceman, Navy Cmdr. Alan B. Shepard, Jr., rockets 116.5 miles up in 302-mile trip **(May 5).** Virgil Grissom becomes second American astronaut, making 118-mile-high, 303-mile-long rocket flight over Atlantic **(July 21).** Gherman Stepanovich Titov is launched in Soviet spaceship *Vostok II:* makes 17 1/2 orbits in 25 hours, covering 434,960 miles before landing safely **(Aug. 6).** East Germans erect Berlin Wall between East and West Berlin to halt flood of refugees **(Aug. 13).** U.S.S.R. fires 50-megaton hydrogen

Dwight D. Eisenhower
(1890–1969)

Fidel Castro
(1926–)

Robert Frost
(1914–63)

Vietnam War (1950–1975)

U.S., South Vietnam, and Allies versus North Vietnam and National Liberation Front (Viet Cong). Outstanding events:

1950 President Truman sends 35-man military advisory group to aid French fighting to maintain colonial power in Vietnam.

1954 After defeat of French at Dienbienphu, Geneva Agreements (July) provide for withdrawal of French and Vietminh to either side of demarcation zone (DMZ) pending reunification elections, which are never held. Presidents Eisenhower and Kennedy (from 1954 onward) send civilian advisors and, later, military personnel to train South Vietnamese.

1960 Communists from National Liberation Front in South.

1963 Ngo Dinh Diem, South Vietnam's premier, slain in coup (Nov. 1).

1961-1963 U.S. military advisors rise from 2,000 to 15,000.

1964 North Vietnamese torpedo boats reportedly attack U.S. destroyers in Gulf of Tonkin (Aug. 2). President Johnson orders retaliatory air strikes. Congress approves Gulf of Tonkin resolution (Aug. 7) authorizing President to take necessary steps to "maintain peace."

1965 U.S. planes begin combat missions over South Vietnam. In June, 23,000 American advisors committed to combat. By end of year over 184,000 U.S. troops in area.

1966 B-52s bomb DMZ, reportedly used by North Vietnam for entry into South (July 31).

1967 South Vietnam National Assembly approves election of Nguyen Van Thieu as President (Oct. 21).

1968 U.S. has almost 525,000 men in Vietnam. In Tet offensive (Jan.-Feb.), Viet Cong guerrillas attack Saigon, Hue, and some provincial capitals. President Johnson orders halt to U.S. bombardment of North Vietnam (Oct. 31). Saigon and N.L.F. join U.S. and North Vietnam in Paris peace talks.

1969 President Nixon announces Vietnam peace offer **(May 14)**—begins troop withdrawals (June). Viet Cong

forms Provisional Revolutionary Government. U.S. Senate calls for curb on commitments (June 25). Ho Chi Minh, 79, North Vietnam president, dies (Sept. 3); collective leadership chosen. Some 6,000 U.S. troops pulled back from Thailand and 1,000 marines from Vietnam (announced Sept. 30). Massive demonstrations in U.S. protest or support war policies (Oct. 15).

1970 Nixon announces sending of troops to Cambodia (April 30). Last U.S. troops removed from Cambodia (June 29).

1971 Congress bars use of combat troops, but not air power, in Laos and Cambodia (Jan. 1). South Vietnamese troops, with U.S. air cover, fail in Laos thrust. Many American ground forces withdrawn from Vietnam combat. New York Times publishes Pentagon papers, classified material on expansion of war (June).

1972 Nixon responds to North Vietnamese drive across DMZ by ordering mining of North Vietnam ports and heavy bombing of Hanoi-Haiphong area (April 1). Nixon orders "Christmas bombing" of north to get North Vietnamese back to conference table (Dec.).

1973 President orders halt to offensive operations in North Vietnam (Jan. 15). Representatives of North and South Vietnam, U.S., and N.L.F. sign peace pacts in Paris, ending longest war in U.S. history (Jan. 27). Last American troops departed in their entirety (March 29).

1974 Both sides accuse each other of frequent violations of cease-fire agreement.

1975 Full-scale warfare resumes. Communists victorious (April 30). South Vietnam Premier Nguyen Van Thieu resigns (April 21). U.S. Marine Embassy guards and U.S. civilians and dependents evacuated (April 30). More than 140,000 Vietnamese refugees leave by air and sea, many to settle in U.S. Provisional Revolutionary Government takes control (June 6).

1976 Election of National Assembly paves way for reunification of North and South.

John H. Glenn, Jr.
(1921–)

William Faulkner
(1897–1962)

John F. Kennedy
(1917–63)

The Beatles

Thurgood Marshall
(1908–93)

bomb, biggest explosion in history (**Oct. 29**).

1962 Lt. Col. John H. Glenn, Jr., is first American to orbit earth—three times in 4 hr 55 min (**Feb. 20**). Adolf Eichmann hanged in Israel for his part in Nazi extermination of six million Jews (**May 31**). France transfers sovereignty to new republic of Algeria (**July 3**). Cuban missile crisis—U.S.S.R. to build missile bases in Cuba; Kennedy orders Cuban blockade, lifts blockade after Russians back down (**Aug.-Nov.**). James H. Meredith, escorted by federal marshals, registers in University of Mississippi (**Oct. 1**). Pope John XXIII opens Second Vatican Council (**Oct. 11**)—Council holds four sessions, finally closing **Dec. 8, 1965**. Cuba releases 1,113 prisoners of 1961 invasion attempt (**Dec. 24**). William Faulkner wins Pulitzer for *The Reivers.*

1963 France and West Germany sign treaty of cooperation ending four centuries of conflict (**Jan. 22**). Pope John XXIII dies (**June 3**)—succeeded June 21 by Cardinal Montini, who becomes Paul VI. U.S. Supreme Court rules no locality may require recitation of Lord's Prayer or Bible verses in public schools (**June 17**). Civil rights rally held by 200,000 blacks and whites in Washington, D.C. (**Aug. 28**). Washington-to-Moscow "hot line" communications link opens, designed to reduce risk of accidental war (**Aug. 30**). President Kennedy shot and killed by sniper in Dallas, Tex. Lyndon B. Johnson becomes President same day (**Nov. 22**). Lee Harvey Oswald, accused assassin of President Kennedy, is shot and killed by Jack Ruby, Dallas nightclub owner (**Nov. 24**).

1964 U.S. Supreme Court rules that Congressional districts should be roughly equal in population (**Feb. 17**). Jack Ruby convicted of murder in slaying of Lee Harvey Oswald; sentenced to death by Dallas jury (**March 14**)—conviction reversed **Oct. 5, 1966**; Ruby dies **Jan. 3, 1967**, before second trial can be held. Three civil rights workers—Schwerner, Goodman, and Cheney—murdered in Mississippi (**June**). Twenty-one arrests result in trial and conviction of seven by federal jury. President's Commission on the Assassination of President Kennedy issues Warren Report concluding that Lee Harvey Oswald acted alone. The Beatles appear on *The Ed Sullivan Show.*

1965 Rev. Dr. Martin Luther King, Jr., and more than 2,600 other blacks arrested in Selma, Ala., during three-day demonstrations against voter-registration rules (**Feb. 1**). Malcolm X, black-nationalist leader, shot to death at Harlem rally in New York City (**Feb. 21**). U.S. Marines land in Dominican Republic as fighting persists between rebels and Dominican army (**April 28**). Medicare, senior citizens' government medical assistance program, begins (**July 1**). Blacks riot for six days in Watts section of Los Angeles: 34 dead, over 1,000 injured, nearly 4,000 arrested, fire damage put at $175 million (**Aug. 11-16**). Power failure in Ontario plant blacks out parts of eight northeastern states of U.S. and two provinces of southeastern Canada (**Nov. 9**).

1966 Black teen-agers riot in Watts, Los Angeles; two men killed and at least 25 injured (**March 15**). Michael E. De Bakey implants artificial heart in human for first time at Houston hospital; plastic device functions and patient lives (**April 21**).

1967 Three Apollo astronauts—Col. Virgil I. Grissom, Col. Edward White II, and Lt. Cmdr. Roger B. Chaffee—killed in spacecraft fire during simulated launch (**Jan. 27**). Israeli and Arab forces battle; six-day war ends with Israel occupying Sinai Peninsula, Golan Heights, Gaza Strip, and east bank of Suez Canal (**June 5**). Red China announces explosion of its first hydrogen bomb (**June 17**). Racial violence in Detroit; 7,000 National Guardsmen aid police after night of rioting. Similar outbreaks occur in New York City's Spanish Harlem, Rochester, N.Y., Birmingham, Ala., and New Britain, Conn. (**July 23**). Thurgood Marshall sworn in as first black U.S. Supreme Court justice (**Oct. 2**). Dr. Christiaan N. Barnard and team of South African surgeons perform world's first successful human heart transplant (**Dec. 3**)—patient dies 18 days later.

1968 North Korea seizes U.S. Navy ship *Pueblo;* holds 83 on board as spies (**Jan. 23**). President Johnson announces he will not seek or accept presidential renomination (**March 31**). Martin Luther King, Jr., civil rights leader, is slain in Memphis (**April 4**)—James Earl Ray, indicted in murder, captured in London on **June 8**. In 1969 Ray pleads guilty and is sentenced to 99 years. Sen. Robert F. Kennedy is shot and critically wounded in Los Angeles hotel after winning California primary (**June 5**)—dies **June 6**. Sirhan B. Sirhan convicted 1969. Czechoslovakia is invaded by Russians and Warsaw Pact forces to crush liberal regime (**Aug. 20**).

1969 Richard M. Nixon is inaugurated 37th President of the U.S. (**Jan. 20**). Apollo 11 astronauts—Neil A. Armstrong, Edwin E. Aldrin, Jr., and Michael Collins—take man's first walk on moon (**July 20**). Sen. Edward M. Kennedy pleads guilty to leaving scene of fatal accident at Chappaquiddick, Mass. (**July 18**) in which Mary Jo Kopechne was drowned—gets two-month suspended sentence (**July 25**).

1970 Biafra surrenders after 32-month fight for independence from Nigeria (**Jan. 12**). Rhodesia severs last tie with British Crown and declares itself a racially segregated republic (**March 1**). Four students at Kent State University in Ohio slain by National Guardsmen at demonstration protesting April 30 incursion into Cambodia **(May 4)**. Senate repeals Gulf of Tonkin resolution **(June 24)**.

1971 Supreme Court rules unanimously that busing of students may be ordered to achieve racial desegregation **(April 20)**. Anti-war militants attempt to disrupt government business in Washington **(May 3)**—police and military units arrest as many as 12,000; most are later released. Twenty-sixth Amendment to U.S. Constitution lowers voting age to 18. U.N. seats Communist China and expels Nationalist China **(Oct. 25)**.

1972 President Nixon makes unprecedented eight-day visit to Communist China and meets with Mao Tse-tung **(Feb.)**. Britain takes over direct rule of Northern Ireland in bid for peace **(March 24)**. Gov. George C. Wallace of Alabama is shot by Arthur H. Bremer at Laurel, Md., political rally **(May 15)**. Five men are apprehended by police in attempt to bug Democratic National Committee headquarters in Washington D.C.'s Watergate complex—start of the Watergate scandal **(June 17)**. Supreme Court rules that death penalty is unconstitutional **(June 29)**. Eleven Israeli athletes at Olympic Games in Munich are killed after eight members of an Arab terrorist group invade Olympic Village; five guerrillas and one policeman are also killed **(Sept. 5)**. Ingmar Bergman's *Cries and Whispers*.

1973 Great Britain, Ireland, and Denmark enter European Common Market **(Jan. 1)**. Nixon, on national TV, accepts responsibility, but not blame, for Watergate; accepts resignations of advisers H. R. Haldeman and John D. Ehrlichman, fires John W. Dean III as counsel. **(April 30)**. Greek military junta abolishes monarchy and proclaims republic **(June 1)**. U.S. bombing of Cambodia ends, marking official halt to 12 years of combat activity in Southeast Asia **(Aug. 15)**. Fourth and biggest Arab-Israeli War begins as Egyptian and Syrian forces attack Israel as Jews mark Yom Kippur, holiest day in their calendar. **(Oct. 6)**. Spiro T. Agnew resigns as Vice President and then, in federal court in Baltimore, pleads no contest to charges of evasion of income taxes on $29,500 he received in 1967, while Governor of Maryland. He is fined $10,000 and put on three years' probation **(Oct. 10)**. In the "Saturday Night Massacre," Nixon fires special Watergate prosecutor Archibald Cox and Deputy Attorney General William D. Ruckelshaus; Attorney General Elliot L. Richardson resigns **(Oct. 20)**. Egypt and Israel sign U.S.-sponsored cease-fire accord **(Nov. 11)**. Duke Ellington's autobiography, *Music is My Mistress*, is published.

1974 Patricia Hearst, 19-year-old daughter of publisher Randolph Hearst, kidnapped by Symbionese Liberation Army. **(Feb. 5)**. House Judiciary Committee adopts three articles of impeachment charging President Nixon with obstruction of justice, failure to uphold laws, and refusal to produce material subpoenaed by the committee **(July 30)**. Richard M. Nixon announces he will resign the next day, the first President to do so **(Aug. 8)**. Vice President Gerald R. Ford of Michigan is sworn in as 38th President of the U.S. **(Aug. 9)**. Ford grants "full, free, and absolute pardon" to ex-President Nixon **(Sept. 8)**.

1975 John N. Mitchell, H. R. Haldeman, John D. Ehrlichman, and Robert C. Mardian found guilty of Watergate cover-up. Mitchell, Haldeman, and Ehrlichman are sentenced on Feb. 21 to 30 months-8 years in jail and Mardian to 10 months-3 years **(Jan. 1)**. American merchant ship *Mayaguez*, seized by Cambodian forces, is rescued in operation by U.S. Navy and Marines, 38 of whom are killed **(May 15)**. *Apollo* and *Soyuz* spacecraft take off for U.S.-Soviet link-up in space **(July 15)**. President Ford escapes assassination attempt in Sacramento, Calif., **(Sept. 5)**. President Ford escapes second assassination attempt in 17 days. **(Sept. 22)**.

1976 Supreme Court rules that blacks and other minorities are entitled to retroactive job seniority **(March 24)**. Ford signs Federal Election Campaign Act **(May 11)**. Supreme Court rules that death penalty is not inherently cruel or unusual and is a constitutionally acceptable form of punishment **(July 3)**. Nation celebrates Bicentennial **(July 4)**. Israeli airborne commandos attack Uganda's Entebbe Airport and free 103 hostages held by pro-Palestinian hijackers of Air France plane; one Israeli and several Ugandan soldiers killed in raid **(July 4)**. Mysterious disease that eventually claims 29 lives strikes American Legion convention in Philadelphia **(Aug. 4)**. Jimmy Carter elected U.S. President **(Nov. 2)**.

1977 First woman Episcopal priest ordained **(Jan. 1)**. Scientists identify previously unknown bacterium as cause of mysterious "legionnaire's disease" **(Jan. 18)**. Carter pardons Vietnam draft evaders **(Jan. 21)**. Scientists report using bacteria in lab to make insulin **(May 23)**. Supreme Court rules that states are not required to spend Medicaid funds on elective abortions **(June 20)**. Deng Xiaoping, purged Chinese leader, restored to power as "Gang of Four" is expelled from Communist Party **(July 22)**. Nuclear-proliferation pact, curbing spread of nuclear weapons, signed by 15 countries, including U.S. and U.S.S.R. **(Sept. 21)**.

1978 President chooses federal Appeals court Judge William H. Webster as F.B.I. Director **(Jan. 19)**. Rhodesia's Prime Minister Ian D. Smith and three black leaders agree on transfer to black majority rule **(Feb. 15)**. Former Italian Premier Aldo Moro kidnapped by left wing terrorists, who kill five bodyguards **(March 16)**; he is found slain **(May 9)**. U.S. Senate approves Panama Canal neutrality treaty **(March 16)**; votes treaty to turn canal over to Panama by year

Richard Nixon
(1913–94)

Mao Tse-tung
(1893–1976)

Ingmar Bergman
(1918–)

Lyndon B. Johnson
(1908–73)

Duke Ellington
(1899–1974)

Ayatollah Ruhollah Khomeini (1900–89)

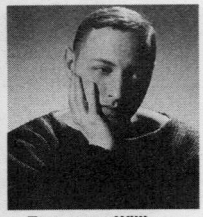

Tennessee Williams (1911–83)

Ronald Reagan (1911–)

Sandra Day O'Connor (1930–)

2000 **(April 18).** Californians in referendum approve Proposition 13 for nearly 60% slash in property tax revenues **(June 6).** Supreme Court, in Bakke case, bars quota systems in college admissions but affirms constitutionality of programs giving advantage to minorities **(June 28).** Pope Paul VI, dead at 80, mourned **(Aug. 6)**; new Pope, John Paul I, 65, dies unexpectedly after 34 days in office **(Sept. 28)**; succeeded by Karol Cardinal Wojtyla of Poland as John Paul II **(Oct. 16).** "Framework for Peace" in Middle East signed by Egypt's President Anwar el-Sadat and Israel Premier Menachem Begin after 13-day conference at Camp David led by President Carter **(Sept. 17).**

1979 Oil spills pollute ocean waters in Atlantic and Gulf of Mexico **(Jan. 1, June 8, July 21).** Ohio agrees to pay $675,000 to families of dead and injured in Kent State University shootings **(Jan. 4).** Vietnam and Cambodian insurgents in backs announce fall of Phnom Penh, Cambodian capital, and collapse of Pol Pot regime **(Jan. 7).** Shah leaves Iran after year of turmoil **(Jan. 16)**; revolutionary forces under Moslem leader, Ayatollah Ruhollah Khomeini, take over **(Feb. 1** et seq.**).** Conservatives win British election; Margaret Thatcher new Prime Minister **(March 28).** Nuclear power plant accident at Three Mile Island, Pa., releases radioactivity **(March 28).** Carter and Brezhnev sign SALT II agreement **(June 14).** Nicaraguan President Gen. Anastasio Somoza Debayle resigns and flees to Miami **(July 17)**; Sandinistas form government **(July 19).** Earl Mountbatten of Burma, 79, British World War II hero, and three others killed by blast on fishing boat off Irish coast **(Aug. 27)**; two I.R.A. members accused **(Aug. 30).** Iranian militants seize U.S. Embassy in Teheran and hold hostages **(Nov. 4).** Soviet invasion of Afghanistan stirs world protests **(Dec. 27).** Tennessee Williams receives Kennedy Center Honor.

1980 Six U.S. Embassy aides escape from Iran with Canadian help **(Jan. 29).** F.B.I.'s undercover operation "Abscam" (for Arab scam) implicates public officials **(Feb. 2).** U.S. breaks diplomatic ties with Iran **(April 7).** Eight U.S. servicemen are killed and five are injured as helicopter and cargo plane collide in abortive desert raid to rescue American hostages in Teheran **(April 25).** Supreme Court upholds limits on federal aid for abortions **(June 30).** Shah of Iran dies at 60 **(July 27).** Anastasio Somoza Debayle, ousted Nicaragua ruler, and two aides assassinated in Asunción, Paraguay capital **(Sept. 17).** Iraq troops hold 90 square miles of Iran after invasion **(Sept. 19).** Ronald Reagan elected President in Republican sweep **(Nov. 4).** Three U.S. nuns and lay worker found shot in El Salvador **(Dec. 4).** John Lennon of Beatles shot dead in New York City **(Dec. 8).** Martin Scorsese's *Raging Bull.*

1981 U.S.-Iran agreement frees 52 hostages held in Teheran since Nov. 4, 1979 **(Jan. 20)**; hostages welcomed back in U.S. **(Jan. 25).** Ronald Reagan takes oath as 40th President **(Jan. 20).** President Reagan wounded by gunman, with press secretary and two law-enforcement officers **(March 30).** Pope John Paul II wounded by gunman **(May 14).** Supreme Court rules, 4-4, that former President Nixon and three top aides may be required to pay monetary damages for unconstitutional wiretap of home telephone of former national security aide **(June 22).** Reagan nominates Judge Sandra Day O'Connor, 51, of Arizona, as first woman on Supreme Court **(July 7).** More than 110 die in collapse of aerial walkways in lobby of Hyatt Regency Hotel in Kansas City; 188 injured **(July 18).** Air controllers strike, disrupting flights **(Aug. 3)**; Government dismisses strikers **(Aug. 11).**

1982 British overcome Argentina in Falklands war **(April 2-June 15).** Israel invades Lebanon in attack on P.L.O. **(June 4).** John W. Hinckley, Jr. found not guilty because of insanity in shooting of President Reagan **(June 21).** Alexander M. Haig, Jr. resigns as Secretary of State **(June 25).** Equal rights amendment fails ratification **(June 30).** Lebanese Christian Phalangists kill hundreds of people in two Palestinian refugee camps in West Beirut **(Sept. 15).** Princess Grace, 52, dies of injuries when car plunges off mountain road; daughter, Stephanie, 17, suffers serious injuries **(Sept. 14).** Leonid I. Brezhnev, Soviet leader, dies at 75 **(Nov. 10).** Yuri V. Andropov, 68, chosen as successor **(Nov. 15).** Artificial heart implanted for first time in Dr. Barney B. Clark, 61, at University of Utah Medical Center in Salt Lake City **(Dec. 2)**; Barney Clark dies **(March 23, 1983).**

1983 Pope John Paul II signs new Roman Catholic code incorporating changes brought about by Second Vatican Council **(Jan. 25).** Second space shuttle, *Challenger,* makes successful maiden voyage, which includes the first U.S. space walk in nine years **(April 4).** U.S. Supreme Court declares many local abortion restrictions unconstitutional **(June 15).** Sally K. Ride, 32, first U.S. woman astronaut in space as a crew member aboard space shuttle *Challenger* **(June 18).** U.S. admits shielding former Nazi Gestapo chief, Klaus Barbie, 69, the "butcher of Lyons," wanted in France for war crimes **(Aug. 15).** Benigno S. Aquino, Jr., 50, political rival of Philippines President Marcos, slain in Manila **(Aug. 21).** South Korean Boeing 747 jetliner bound for Seoul apparently strays into Soviet airspace and is shot down by a Soviet SU-15 fighter after it had tracked the airliner for two hours; all 269 aboard are killed, including 61 Americans **(Aug. 30).** Terrorist explosion kills 237 U.S. Marines in

Beirut **(Oct. 23)**. U.S. and Caribbean allies invade Grenada **(Oct. 25)**.

1984 Bell System broken up **(Jan. 1)**. France gets first deliveries of Soviet natural gas **(Jan. 1)**. Syria frees captured U.S. Navy pilot, Lieut. Robert C. Goodman, Jr. **(Jan. 3)**. U.S. and Vatican exchange diplomats after 116-year hiatus **(Jan. 10)**. Reagan orders U.S. Marines withdrawn from Beirut international peace-keeping force **(Feb. 7)**. Yuri V. Andropov dies at 69; Konstantin U. Chernenko, 72, named Soviet Union leader **(Feb. 9)**. Italy and Vatican agree to end Roman Catholicism as state religion **(Feb. 18)**. Reagan ends U.S. role in Beirut by relieving Sixth Fleet from peacekeeping force **(March 30)**. Congress rebukes President Reagan on use of federal funds for mining Nicaraguan harbors **(April 10)**. Soviet Union withdraws from summer Olympic games in U.S., and other bloc nations follow **(May 7 et seq.)**. José Napoleón Duarte, moderate, elected president of El Salvador **(May 11)**. Three hundred slain as Indian Army occupies Sikh Golden Temple in Amritsar **(June 6)**. Thirty-ninth Democratic National Convention, in San Francisco, nominates Walter F. Mondale and Geraldine A. Ferraro **(July 16-19)**. Thirty-third Republican National Convention, at Dallas, renominates President Reagan and Vice President Bush **(Aug. 20-25)**. Brian Mulroney and Conservative party win Canadian election in landslide **(Sept. 4)**. Indian Prime Minister Indira Gandhi assassinated by two Sikh bodyguards; 1,000 killed in anti-Sikh riots; son Rajiv succeeds her **(Oct. 31)**. President Reagan re-elected in landslide with 59% of vote **(Nov. 7)**. Toxic gas leaks from Union Carbide plant in Bhopal, India, killing 2,000 and injuring 150,000 **(Dec. 3)**.

**Indira Gandhi
(1917–84)**

1985 Ronald Reagan, 73, takes oath for second term as 40th President **(Jan. 20)**. General Westmoreland settles libel action against CBS **(Feb. 18)**. Prime Minister Margaret Thatcher addresses Congress, endorsing Reagan's policies **(Feb. 20)**. U.S.S.R. leader Chernenko dies at 73 and is replaced by Mikhail Gorbachev, 54 **(March 11)**. Two Shiite Moslem gunmen capture TWA airliner with 133 aboard, 104 of them Americans **(June 14)**; 39 remaining hostages freed in Beirut **(June 30)**. Supreme Court, 5-4, bars public school teachers from parochial schools **(July 1)**. Arthur James Walker, 50, retired naval officer, convicted by federal judge of participating in Soviet spy ring **(Aug. 9)**. P.L.O. terrorists hijack *Achille Lauro,* Italian cruise ship, with 80 passengers, plus crew **(Oct. 7)**; American, Leon Klinghoffer, killed **(Oct. 8)**. Italian government toppled by political crisis over hijacking of *Achille Lauro* **(Oct. 16)**. John A. Walker and son, Michael I. Walker, 22, sentenced in Navy espionage case **(Oct. 28)**. Reagan and Gorbachev meet at summit **(Nov. 19)**; agree to step up arms control talks and renew cultural contacts **(Nov. 21)**. Terrorists seize Egyptian Boeing 737 airliner after takeoff from Athens **(Nov. 23)**; 59 dead as Egyptian forces storm plane on Malta **(Nov. 24)**. U.S. budget-balancing bill enacted **(Dec. 12)**.

1986 Spain and Portugal join Common Market **(Jan. 1)**. President freezes Libyan assets in U.S. **(Jan. 8)**. Supreme Court bars racial bias in trial jury selection **(Jan. 14)**. *Voyager 2* spacecraft reports secrets of Uranus **(Jan. 26)**. Space shuttle *Challenger* explodes after launch at Cape Canaveral, Fla., killing all seven aboard **(Jan. 28)**. Haiti President Jean-Claude Duvalier flees to France **(Feb. 7)**. President Marcos flees Philippines after ruling 20 years, as newly elected Corazon Aquino succeeds him **(Feb. 26)**. Prime Minister Olaf Palme of Sweden shot dead **(Feb. 28)**. Kurt Waldheim service as Nazi army officer revealed **(March 3)**. Union Carbide agrees to settlement with victims of Bhopal gas leak in India **(March 22)**. Halley's Comet yields information on return visit **(April 10)**. U.S. planes attack Libyan "terrorist centers" **(April 14)**. Desmond Tutu elected Archbishop in South Africa **(April 14)**. Major nuclear accident at Soviet Union's Chernobyl power station alarms world **(April 26 et seq.)**. Ex-Navy analyst, Jonathan Jay Pollard, 31, guilty as spy for Israel **(June 4)**. Supreme Court reaffirms abortion rights **(June 11)**. World Court rules U.S. broke international law in mining Nicaraguan waters **(June 27)**. Supreme Court voids automatic provisions of budget-balancing law **(July 7)**. Jerry A. Whitworth, ex-Navy radioman, convicted as spy **(July 24)**. Moslem captors release Rev. Lawrence Martin Jenco **(July 26)**. Senate Judiciary Committee approves William H. Rehnquist to be Chief Justice of U.S. **(Aug. 14)**. House votes arms appropriations bill rejecting Administration's "star wars" policy **(Aug. 15)**. Three Lutheran church groups in U.S. set to merge **(Aug. 29)**. Congress overrides Reagan veto of stiff sanctions against South Africa **(Sept. 29 and Oct. 2)**. Congress approves immigration bill barring hiring of illegal aliens, with amnesty provision **(Oct. 17)**. Reagan signs $11.7-billion budget reduction measure **(Oct. 21)**. He approves sweeping revision of U.S. tax code **(Oct. 22)**. Democrats triumph in elections, gaining eight seats to win Senate majority **(Nov. 4)**. Secret initiative to send arms to Iran revealed **(Nov. 6 et seq.)**; Reagan denies exchanging arms for hostages and halts arms sales **(Nov. 19)**; diversion of funds from arms sales to Nicaraguan contras revealed **(Nov. 25)**. Walkers, father and son, sentenced in naval spy ring **(Nov. 6)**. Soviet lifts ban on Andrei D. Sakharov, rights activist **(Dec. 19)**.

**Corazon Aquino
(1933–)**

Toni Morrison
(1931–)

François Mitterrand
(1916–96)

Mikhail S. Gorbachev
(1931–)

Dalai Lama
(1935–)

Hubble Space Telescope

1987 William Buckley, U.S. hostage in Lebanon, reported slain **(Jan. 20)**. U.S. puts Austrian President Kurt Waldheim on list of those banned from country **(April 27)**. Quebec accepts Canadian Constitution as "distinct society" **(May 1)**. Supreme Court rules Rotary Clubs must admit women **(May 4)**. Iraqi missiles kill 37 in attack on U.S. frigate *Stark* in Persian Gulf **(May 17)**; Iraqi president apologizes **(May 18)**. Prime Minister Thatcher wins rare third term in Britain **(June 11)**. Supreme Court Justice Lewis F. Powell, Jr., retires **(June 26)**. Klaus Barbie, 73, Gestapo wartime chief in Lyons, sentenced to life by French court for war crimes **(July 4)**. Marine Lieut. Col. Oliver North, Jr., tells Congressional inquiry higher officials approved his secret Iran-Contra operations **(July 7-10)**. Admiral John M. Poindexter, former National Security Adviser, testifies he authorized use of Iran arms sale profits to aid Contras **(July 15-22)**. George P. Shultz testifies he was deceived repeatedly on Iran-Contra affair **(July 23-24)**. Defense Secretary Caspar W. Weinberger tells inquiry of official deception and intrigue **(July 31, Aug. 3)**. Reagan says Iran arms-Contra policy went astray and accepts responsibility **(Aug 12)**. Severe earthquake strikes Los Angeles, leaving 100 injured and six dead **(Oct. 1)**. Senate, 58-42, rejects Robert H. Bork as Supreme Court Justice **(Oct. 23)**. Toni Morrison wins Pulitzer for *Beloved.*

1988 U.S. and Canada reach free trade agreement **(Jan. 2)**. Supreme Court, 5-3, backs public school officials' power to censor student activities **(Jan. 13)**. Robert C. McFarlane, former National Security Adviser, pleads guilty in Iran-Contra case **(March 11)**. Supreme Court rules against private-club membership restrictions **(June 20)**. U.S. Navy ship shoots down Iranian airliner in Persian Gulf, mistaking it for jet fighter; 290 killed **(July 3)**. Terrorists kill nine tourists on Aegean cruise **(July 11)**. Democratic convention nominates Gov. Michael Dukakis of Massachusetts for President and Texas Senator Lloyd Bentsen for Vice President **(July 17 et seq.)**. Republicans nominate George Bush for President and Indiana Senator Dan Quayle for Vice President **(Aug. 15 et seq.)**. Plane blast kills Pakistani President Mohammad Zia ul-Haq **(Aug. 17)**. Republicans sweep 40 states in election. Vice President Bush beats Gov. Dukakis **(Nov. 8)**. Soviet legislature approves political restructuring and new national legislature **(Dec. 1)**. Benazir Bhutto, first Islamic woman prime minister, chosen to lead Pakistan's government **(Dec. 1)**. Pan-Am 747 explodes from terrorist bomb and crashes in Lockerbie, Scotland, killing all 259 aboard and 11 on ground **(Dec. 21)**. François Mitterrand wins second term as France's first Socialist president.0

1989 U.S. planes shoot down two Libyan fighters over international waters in Mediterranean **(Jan. 4)**. Emperor Hirohito of Japan dead at 87 **(Jan. 7)**. George Herbert Walker Bush inaugurated as 41st U.S. President **(Jan. 20)**. Iran's Ayatollah Khomeini declares author Salman Rushdie's book *The Satanic Verses* offensive and sentences him and his publishers to death **(Feb. 14)**. Ruptured tanker *Exxon Valdez* sends 11 million gallons of crude oil into Alaska's Prince William Sound **(March 24)**. Tens of thousands of Chinese students take over Beijing's central square in rally for democracy **(April 19 et seq.)**. More than one million in Beijing demonstrate for democracy; chaos spreads across nation **(mid-May et seq.)**. Mikhail S. Gorbachev named Soviet President **(May 25)**. U.S. jury convicts Oliver L. North in Iran-Contra affair **(May 4)**. Thousands killed as Chinese leaders take hard line toward demonstrators **(June 4 et seq.)**. Army Gen. Colin R. Powell is first black to become Chairman of Joint Chiefs of Staff **(Aug. 9)**. P.W. Botha quits as South Africa's President **(Aug. 14)**. *Voyager 2* spacecraft speeds by Neptune after making startling discoveries about the planet and its moons **(Aug. 29)**. L. Douglas Wilder, Democrat, is elected as first black governor of Virginia **(Nov. 7)**. Deng Xiaoping resigns from China's leadership **(Nov. 9)**. After 28 years, Berlin Wall is open to West **(Nov. 11)**. Czech Parliament ends Communists' dominant role **(Nov. 30)**. Romanian uprising overthrows Communist government **(Dec. 15 et seq.)**; President Ceausescu and wife executed **(Dec. 25)**. U.S. troops invade Panama, seeking capture of Gen. Manuel Noriega **(Dec. 20)**; resistance to U.S. collapses **(Dec. 24)**. Dalai Lama wins Nobel Peace Prize.

1990 Gen. Manuel Noriega surrenders in Panama **(Jan. 3)**. Yugoslav Communists end 45-year monopoly of power **(Jan. 22)**. Soviet Communists relinquish sole power **(Feb. 7)**. South Africa frees Nelson Mandela, imprisoned 27 1/2 years **(Feb. 11)**. Violeta Barrios de Chamorro inaugurated as Nicaraguan President; Hubble Space Telescope launched **(April 25)**. U.S.-Soviet summit reaches accord on armaments **(June 1)**. Supreme Court upsets law banning flag burning **(June 11)**. Western Alliance ends cold war and proposes joint action with Soviet Union and Eastern Europe **(July 6)**. U.S. Appeals court overturns Oliver North's Iran-Contra conviction **(July 20)**. Iraqi troops invade Kuwait and seize petroleum reserves, setting off Persian Gulf War **(Aug. 2 et seq.)**. East and West Germany reunited **(Aug. 31 et seq.)**. Republicans set back in midterm elections **(Nov. 8)**. Gorbachev assumes emergency powers **(Nov. 17)**. Leaders of 34 nations in Europe and North America proclaim a united Europe **(Nov. 21)**. Margaret Thatcher resigns as British Prime Minister **(Nov. 22)**; John Major succeeds her **(Nov. 28)**. Lech Walesa wins Poland's runoff Presidential election **(Dec. 9)**. Haiti elects leftist priest as President in first democratic election **(Dec. 17)**.

1991 Lithuania Government resigns **(Jan. 8)**. U.S. and Allies at war with Iraq **(Jan. 15)**. U.N. forces win Persian Gulf war **(Feb. 4 et seq.)**. Liberal priest becomes Haiti president **(Feb. 7)**. Warsaw Pact dissolves military alliance **(Feb. 25)**. Supreme Court limits race in trial jury selection **(April 1)**. Cease-fire ends Persian Gulf war **(April 3)**. Europeans end sanctions on South Africa **(April 15)**. Supreme Court limits death row appeals **(April 16)**. Winnie Mandela sentenced in kidnapping **(May 13)**. William H. Webster retires as Director of Central Intelligence; Robert H. Gates succeeds him **(May 14)**. France agrees to sign 1968 treaty banning spread of atomic weapons **(June 3)**. Communist Government of Albania resigns **(June 4)**. Jiang Qing, widow of Mao, commits suicide **(June 4)**. South African Parliament repeals apartheid laws **(June 5)**. Warsaw Pact dissolved **(July 1)**. Boris N. Yeltsin inaugurated as first freely elected president of Russian Republic **(July 10)**. Bush-Gorbachev summit negotiates strategic arms reduction treaty **(July 31)**. China accepts nuclear nonproliferation treaty **(Aug. 10)**. Coup fails to unseat Gorbachev after Soviet hardliners seize him; he credits Yeltsin for rescue **(Aug. 18 et seq.)**. Gorbachev seals Communist Party doom, resigns as secretary-general **(Aug. 24)**. Three Baltic republics win independence **(Aug. 25)**; Bush recognizes them **(Sept. 2)**. New Soviet ruling council recognizes independence of Lithuania, Estonia, and Latvia **(Sept. 6)**. Charges against Oliver North dropped **(Sept. 15)**. Haitian troops seize president in uprising **(Sept. 30)**. U.S. suspends assistance to Haiti **(Oct. 1)**. Professor Anita Hill accuses Judge Clarence Thomas of sexual harassment **(Oct. 6)**; Senate, 52-48, confirms Thomas for Supreme Court after stormy hearings **(Oct. 15)**. Israel and Soviet resume relations after 24 years **(Oct. 18)**. First photo ever taken of an asteroid in space, *Gaspara* **(Oct. 29)**. U.S. indicts two Libyans in 1988 bombing of Pan Am Flight 103 over Lockerbie, Scotland **(Nov. 15)**. Anglican envoy Terry Waite and U.S. Prof. Thomas M. Sutherland freed by Lebanese **(Nov. 18)**. Last three U.S. hostages freed in Lebanon **(Dec. 2-4)**. Soviet Union breaks up after President Gorbachev's resignation; constituent republics form Commonwealth of Independent States, which U.S. and other nations move to recognize **(Dec. 25)**.

1992 Yugoslav Federation broken up **(Jan. 15)**. Bush and Yeltsin proclaim formal end to Cold War **(Feb. 1)**. U.S. lifts trade sanctions against China **(Feb. 21)**. U.S. recognizes three former Yugoslav republics **(April 7)**. Gen. Noriega, former Panama leader, convicted in U.S. court **(April 9)**. Small new Yugoslavia proclaimed **(April 27)**. Four officers acquitted in Los Angeles beating; violence erupts in Los Angeles **(April 29 et seq.)**. Caspar W. Weinberger indicted in Iran-Contra affair **(June 16)**. Last Western hostages freed in Lebanon **(June 17)**. Supreme Court reaffirms right to abortion **(June 29)**. Gen. Noriega sentenced to 40 years on drug charges **(July 10)**. Court clears *Exxon Valdez* skipper **(July 10)**. Democrats nominate Bill Clinton and Al Gore **(July 1)**. Israeli Parliament approves Yitzhak Rabin's coalition government, dominated by Labor Party **(July 13)**. Supreme Court upholds return of Haitians **(Aug. 1)**. U.S. indicts four police officers in Los Angeles beating **(Aug. 5)**. North American trade compact announced **(Aug. 12)**. Republicans renominate Bush and Quayle **(Aug. 20)**. U.N. expels Serbian-dominated Yugoslavia **(Sept. 22)**. Senate ratifies second Strategic Arms Limitation Treaty **(Oct. 1)**. U.N. Council creates Bosnian "no-fly" zone **(Oct. 9)**. Top Japanese leader, Shin Kanemaru,

**General Colin Powell
(1937–)**

**George Bush
(1924–)**

**Boris Yeltsin
(1931–)**

**Saddam Hussein
(1937–)**

The Persian Gulf War (Aug. 2, 1990–April 6, 1991)

1990: Iraq invades its tiny neighbor, Kuwait, after talks break down over oil production and debt repayment. Iraqi Pres. Saddam Hussein later annexes Kuwait and declares it a 19th province of Iraq **(Aug. 2)**. President Bush believes that Iraq intends to invade Saudi Arabia and take control of the region's oil supplies. He begins organizing a multinational coalition to seek Kuwait's freedom and restoration of its legitimate government. The U.N. Security Council authorizes economic sanctions against Iraq. Pres. Bush orders U.S. troops to protect Saudi Arabia at the Saudis' request when "Operation Desert Shield" begins **(Aug. 6)**. 230,000 American troops arrive in Saudi Arabia to take defensive action, but when Iraq continues a huge military buildup in Kuwait, the President orders an additional 200,000 troops deployed to prepare for a possible offensive action by the U.S.-led coalition forces. He subsequently obtains a U.N. Security Council resolution setting a Jan. 15, 1991, deadline for Iraq to withdraw unconditionally from Kuwait **(Nov. 8)**.

1991: Pres. Bush wins Congressional approval for his position with the most devastating air assault in history against military targets in Iraq and Kuwait **(Jan. 16)**. He rejects a Soviet-Iraq peace plan for a gradual withdrawal that does not comply with all the U.N. resolutions and gives Iraq an ultimatum to withdraw from Kuwait by noon February 23 **(Feb. 22)**. The President orders the ground war to begin **(Feb. 24)**. In a brilliant and lightning-fast campaign, U.S. and coalition forces smash through Iraq's defenses and defeat Saddam Hussein's troops in only four days of combat. Allies enter Kuwait City **(Feb. 26)**. Iraqi army sets fire to over 500 of Kuwait's oil wells as final act of destruction to Kuwait's infrastructure. Pres. Bush orders a unilateral cease-fire 100 hours after the ground offensive started **(Feb. 27)**. Allied and Iraq military leaders meet on battlefield to discuss terms for a formal cease-fire to end the Gulf War. Iraq agrees to abide by all of the U.N. resolutions **(Mar. 3)**. The first Allied prisoners of war are released **(Mar. 4)**. Official cease-fire accepted and signed **(April 6)**. 532,000 U.S. forces served in Operation Desert Storm. There were a total of 148 battle deaths during the Gulf War, 145 nonbattle deaths, and 467 wounded in action. Battle deaths by branch of service were: Army, 98; Navy, 6; Marines, 24; Air Force, 20. Nonbattle deaths: Army, 105; Navy, 8; Marines, 26; and Air Force, 6. The United States estimated that Iraqi military casualties were 100,000 killed, 300,000 wounded, and over 88,000 captured.

**Benazir Bhutto
(1953–)**

**Nelson Mandela
(1918–)**

**Jean-Bertrand Aristide
(1953–)**

resigns in scandal (**Oct. 14**). Bill Clinton elected President, Al Gore Vice President; Democrats keep control of Congress (**Nov. 3**). Russian Parliament approves START treaty (**Nov. 4**). U.S. forces leave Philippines, ending nearly a century of American military presence (**Nov. 24**). Czechoslovak Parliament approves separation into two nations (**Nov. 25**). U.N. approves U.S.-led force to guard food for Somalia (**Dec. 3**). Prince and Princess of Wales agree to separate (**Dec. 9**). Bush pardons former Reagan Administration officials involved in Iran-Contra affair (**Dec. 24**).

1993 Clinton withdraws Zoe Baird nomination as Attorney General (**Jan. 22**). Vaclav Havel elected as Czech President (**Jan. 26**). Clinton agrees to compromise on military's ban on homosexuals (**Jan. 29**). Judge Kimba M. Wood withdraws as Clinton's second choice for Attorney General (**Feb. 5**); President names Janet Reno to post (**Feb. 11**). U.S. begins airdrop of supplies to besieged Bosnia towns (**Feb. 28**). Law agents besiege Texas Davidian religious cult after six are killed in raid (**March 1** et seq.). Senate, 98-0, confirms Janet Reno as Attorney General (**March 11**). Five arrested, sixth sought in bombing of World Trade Center in New York (**March 29**). Russian Congress accepts Yeltsin call for national referendum (**March 29**). Two police officers convicted in Los Angeles on rights charges in Rodney King beating (**April 17**). Fire kills 72 as cult standoff in Texas ends with federal assault (**April 19**). President of Sri Lanka assassinated (**May 1**). British Commons approves European unity pact (**May 20**). Twenty-two U.N. troops killed in Somalia (**June 5**). Ruth Bader Ginsburg, rights advocate, appointed to Supreme Court (**June 14**). Iraq accepts U.N. weapons monitoring (**July 19**). President dismisses F.B.I. Director William S. Sessions (**July 19**); names Judge Louis J. Freeh as successor (**July 20**). Vincent W. Foster, Jr., senior White House lawyer, is apparent suicide (**July 22**). Midwest flood damage expected to exceed $10 billion (**July 24**). Two Los Angeles police officers sentenced in Rodney King beating (**Aug. 4**). Israeli-Palestinian accord reached (**Aug. 28**). South Africa agrees to share transition powers (**Sept. 7**). Yeltsin dissolves Russian Parliament (**Sept. 21**). Benazir Bhutto wins second term as Prime Minister of Pakistan (**Oct.**) U.S. agents blamed in Waco, Tex., siege (**Oct. 1**). Yeltsin's forces crush revolt in Russian Parliament (**Oct. 4** et seq.). China breaks nuclear test moratorium (**Oct. 5**). NATO offers "peace partnership" to Eastern European nations (**Oct. 20-21**). Canada's opposition Liberal Party regains power in landslide (**Oct. 25**). Europe's Maastricht Treaty takes effect, creating European Union (**Nov. 1**). Jean Chretien sworn in as Canada's 20th Prime Minister (**Nov. 4**). Yeltsin approves new draft constitution for Russia (**Nov. 8**). House of Representatives approves North American Free Trade Agreement (**Nov. 17**); Senate follows (**Nov. 21**). South Africa adopts majority rule constitution (**Nov. 18**). Clinton signs Brady bill regulating firearms purchases (**Nov. 30**).

1994 Serbs heavy weapons pound Sarajevo (**Jan. 5-6**). Olympic figure skater Nancy Kerrigan attacked (**Jan. 6**); three arrested in attack (**Jan. 13**). Major earthquake jolts Los Angeles; 51 dead (**Jan. 17** et seq.). Clinton ends trade embargo on Vietnam (**Feb. 9**). Aldrich Ames, high C.I.A. official, charged with spying for Soviet (**Feb. 22**). Four convicted in World Trade Center bombing (**March 4**). Mexican Presidential candidate assassinated (**March 23**). Nelson Mandela elected President of South Africa (**April**). Thousands dead in Rwanda tribal warfare (**April 6**). Strike halts major trucking companies (**April 6**); accord reached to end tie-up (**April 29**). South Africa holds first interracial national election (**April 29**). V.M.I. upheld on exclusion of women (**May 1**). Israel and Palestinians sign accord (**May 4**). Clinton accused of sexual harassment while Governor (**May 6**). Congress votes protection for women's health clinics (**May 12**). Jacqueline Kennedy Onassis dies of cancer (**May 20**). O.J. Simpson arrested in two killings (**June 18**). Russia and NATO agree on close military ties (**June 22**). Supreme Court approves limit on abortion protests (**June 30**). Senate confirms Stephen G. Breyer for Supreme Court (**July 29**). Women's health clinic doctor shot dead outside Florida clinic (**July 29**); U.S. indicts accused killer (**Aug. 12**). Major league baseball players strike (**Aug. 13**). Carlos, international terrorist, captured (**Aug. 15**). I.R.A. declares cease-fire in Northern Ireland (**Aug. 31**). Small plane crashes against White House (**Sept. 12**). Baseball owners end season and cancel World Series (**Sept. 14**). U.S. and Russia agree on arms reduction (**Sept. 29**). Powerful earthquake strikes Japan (**Oct. 4**). Aristide returns to joyous Haiti (**Oct. 4**). Abortion protester guilty in clinic killings (**Oct. 5**). U.S. sends forces to Persian Gulf (**Oct. 7**). Ulster Protestants declare cease-fire (**Oct. 13**). Israel and Jordan sign peace treaty (**Oct. 17**). Gunman fires at White House (**Oct. 29**). Abortion foe guilty of killing two at clinic (**Nov. 2**); Florida jury recommends death penalty (**Nov. 3**). Reagan, 83, reveals Alzheimer's disease (**Nov. 6**). G.O.P. wins control of House and Senate (**Nov. 8**). Aristide forms Haitian Government with Prime Minister and full Cabinet (**Nov. 9**). Clinton orders Bosnian arms embargo ended (**Nov. 10**). Killer of women's health doctor sentenced twice (**Dec. 2**). Newt Gingrich named

House Speaker (**Dec. 5**). Bentsen resigns as Treasury Secretary (**Dec. 6**). Russians attack secessionist Republic of Chechnya (**Dec. 11** et seq.). James Woolsey, Jr., resigns as Director of Central Intelligence (**Dec. 28**). Gunman kills two at Massachusetts women's health clinic (**Dec. 30**).

1995 Republicans take control of Congress (**Jan. 4**). Heavy rains inundate California (**Jan. 9** et seq.). More than 5,000 dead in Japanese earthquake (**Jan. 17** et seq.). Criminal trial of O.J. Simpson opens in California (**Jan. 24**). Clinton offers $20 billion aid to Mexico (**Jan. 31**). Congress votes curbs on U.S. mandates to states (**Feb. 1**). U.S. shuttle rendezvous with Russian space station (**Feb. 3**). Clinton appoints retired Air Force general as intelligence chief (**Feb. 7**). U.S. rescues Mexico's economy with $20-billion aid program (**Feb. 21**). Senate rejects balanced-budget amendment (**March 2**). Russian space station greets first Americans (**March 14**). Nerve gas attack in Tokyo subway kills eight and injures thousands (**March 20**). Selena, 23, popular Spanish-language singer, slain in Texas (**March 31**). Major league baseball strike ends (**April 2**). Appeals court upholds woman's plea to enter Citadel military academy (**April 13**). U.N. Council votes easier sanctions for Iraq (**April 14**). Scores killed as terrorist's car bomb blows up hour-long Oklahoma City federal building (**April 19**); Timothy McVeigh, 27, Army veteran, arrested as suspect (**April 21**); authorities seek second suspect, link right-wing paramilitary groups to bombing (**April 22**). Death toll 2,000 in Rwanda massacre (**April 22**). Fighting escalates in Bosnia and Croatia (**May 1**). Fiftieth anniversary of V.E. Day celebrated (**May 8**). White House imposes harsh trade sanctions on Japan (**May 16**). Japanese police seize cult leader in subway nerve gas attack (**May 18**). Supreme Court rejects term-limit laws (**May 22**). Clinton vetoes G.O.P. budget-cutting bill (**June 1**). Bosnian Serbs hold U.S. troops as hostages (**June 2**). Colombia seizes a top drug-ring leader (**June 9**). Supreme Court raises doubts on affirmative action (**June 12**). U.S. shuttle docks with Russian space station (**June 27**). U.S. indicts two in Oklahoma City bombing (**Aug. 10**). F.B.I. suspends four in Idaho siege inquiry (**Aug. 11**). NATO planes bomb Bosnian Serb targets (**Aug. 28** et seq.) . Simpson jurors allowed to hear two taped epithets (**Aug. 31**). France explodes nuclear device in Pacific; wide protests ensue (**Sept. 5**). Senator Bob Packwood of Oregon resigns under pressure for sexual and official misconduct (**Sept. 6**). Israelis and Palestinians agree on transferring West Bank to Arabs (**Sept. 24**). Los Angeles jury finds O.J. Simpson not guilty of murder charges (**Oct. 3**). A.M.A. criticizes G.O.P.'s Medicare proposals (**Oct. 3**). Pope John Paul II visits U.S. on whirlwind tour (**Oct. 4-8**). Action on term limits falters in Congress (**Oct. 4**). Warring parties agree on cease-fire in Bosnia (**Oct. 5**). Million Man March draws hundreds of thousands of black men to capital (**Oct. 16**). World leaders gather in New York for 50th anniversary of founding of United Nations (**Oct. 22-24**). Fan club founder convicted of killing Selena, popular Mexican-American singer (**Oct. 23**). Russian President Yeltsin in hospital with heart attack (**Oct. 26**). Quebec narrowly rejects independence from Canada (**Oct. 30**). Israel Prime Minister Yitzhak Rabin slain by Jewish extremist at peace rally (**Nov. 4**). U.S. servicemen admit rape of Japanese schoolgirl in Okinawa (**Nov. 7**). Nigeria hangs writer and eight other minority rights advocates (**Nov. 10**). Clinton vetoes stop-gap spending and debt-ceiling bills (**Nov. 13**). Irish voters approve end to constitutional ban on divorce (**Nov. 24**). White House defies subpoena in Senate Whitewater inquiry (**Dec. 12**). Combatants sign Bosnia peace treaty (**Dec. 14**). French rail workers end strike (**Dec. 15**). Russian voters rebuff reformers as Communists make biggest gains (**Dec. 17**). U.S. and Mexico delay trading-access provision in NAFTA (**Dec. 18**). House move stalls Congress-White House negotiations to avert Government shutdown (**Dec. 20**). Seamus Heaney wins Pulitzer.

1996 Bosnian Serbs accused of abductions (**Jan. 2**). U.S. budget crisis in fourth month (**Jan. 3.**). Global warming climbs to record (**Jan. 3**). Clinton approves resumption of many government operations (**Jan. 6**). Blizzard cripples much of East (**Jan. 7**). Chechens capture 2,000 Russians (**Jan. 9**). New Japanese prime minister chosen (**Jan. 11**). Sheik sentenced to life in U.S. bomb plot (**Jan. 17**). Senate ratifies major arms reduction treaty (**Jan. 26**). France announces end to nuclear tests (**Jan. 29**). At least 73 dead in Sri Lankan suicide bombing (**Feb. 1**). Russian coal miners strike (**Feb. 1**). I.M.F. approves loan for Russia (**Feb. 8**). Balkan leaders reaffirm commitment to peace accord (**Feb. 18**). European-Asian trade partnership pledged (**March 2**). Suicide bombers kill 59 in Israel (**March 4**). Bob Dole sweeps primaries (**March 5**). G.M. strike settled after 16 days (**March 5**). Gunman slays 16 children in Scottish school (**March 13**). Disco fire kills at least 150 in Manila (**March 19**). Britain alarmed by deadly cow disease (**March 20** et seq.). U.N. tribunal charges war crimes by Bosnian Muslims and Croats (**March 22**). Russia signs accord with three former Soviet states (**March 29**). Commerce Secretary Ronald H. Brown, 54, killed in plane crash (**April 3**). F.B.I. arrests suspected Unabomber (**April 3**). North Koreans invade buffer zone (**April 7**). Clinton signs line-item veto bill (**April 9**). President blocks ban on late-term abortions (**April 10**). Nations pledge $1.23 billion in aid to rebuild Bosnia (**April 22**). P.L.O. drops stand against a Jewish state (**April 24**). South Africa gets new constitution (**May 8**). Valujet crashes in Everglades; all 110 aboard killed (**May 11**).

Seamus Heaney
(1939–)

Margaret Thatcher
(1925–)

William J. Clinton
(1946–)

**Ella Fitzgerald
(1918–96)**

**Kofi Annan
(1938–)**

**Madeleine Albright
(1937–)**

Bob Dole announces resignation from Senate (**May 15**). Chechnya peace treaty signed (**May 27**). Clinton partners in Arkansas convicted (**May 28**). Israel elects Benjamin Netanyahu as prime minister (**May 31**). Medicare funds reported to be running low (**June 5**). China agrees to world ban on atomic testing (**June 6**). Arsonists destroy 30th black church in 18 months (**June 7**). Leaders in Balkans sign accord on arms limits (**June 14**). F.A.A. shuts down Valujet in wake of Everglades crash (**June 17**). Suspect indicted on Unabomber charges (**June 18**). Truck bomb kills 19 at U.S. base in Saudi Arabia (**June 25**). Boris Yeltsin is reelected in Russian election (**July 3**). U.S. jobless rate lowest in six years (**July 5**). Senate, 74–24, approves raise in minimum wage (**July 9**). Prince Charles and Princess Diana agree on divorce (**July 12**). 747 airliner crashes in Atlantic off Long Island; all 230 aboard perish (**July 17**). Bomb mars Summer Olympic games in Atlanta (**July 25**). Two Arkansas bankers acquitted in Whitewater trial (**Aug. 1**). Congress passes welfare reform bill (**Aug. 2**). Israel lifts freeze on settlements (**Aug. 2**). Republican convention opens in San Diego (**Aug. 12**); Bob Dole and Jack Kemp nominated (**Aug. 14**). Clinton signs bill to raise minimum wage (**Aug. 2**); approves welfare reform bill (**Aug. 22**). Death toll 160 in Himalayas storm (**Aug. 25**). Democrats convene in Chicago (**Aug. 26**); Clinton and Gore accept renomination (**Aug. 29**). Iraqis strike at Kurdish enclave (**Aug. 31**); after warning, U.S. attacks Iraq's southern air defenses (**Sept. 2–3**); Iraq halts attacks on U.S. planes enforcing flight exclusion zones in north and south (**Sept. 13**). U.S. jobless rate lowest in seven years (**Sept. 6**). Bosnians re-elect existing ethnic leaders in three-person presidency (**Sept. 10**). F.D.A. approves abortion drug for sale in U.S. (**Sept. 18**). Virginia Military Institute agrees to admit women (**Sept. 21**). Violence flares in Jerusalem over Israel opening tourist tunnel (**Sept. 24**). Muslim fundamentalists capture Afghan capital (**Sept. 27**). Clinton signs illegal-immigration measure (**Sept. 30**). Dow Jones industrial average surpasses 6,000 barrier (**Oct. 7**). Ethnic violence breaks out in Zairian refugee camps (**Oct. 13**); thousands of refugees from Rwanda and Burundi abandon camps (**Oct. 21**). Supreme Court refuses to hear challenge to Administration policy on homosexuals in armed forces (**Oct. 21**). Shooting sparks rioting in St. Petersburg, Fla. (**Oct. 24**). Hundreds of thousands of Hutu refugees stranded in Zaire (**Oct. 30**). Clinton-Gore ticket wins national election; Republicans retain control of Congress (**Nov. 5**). Pakistan's prime minister, Benazir Bhutto, dismissed on corruption charges (**Nov. 5**). Russian President Boris Yeltsin undergoes heart surgery (**Nov. 5**). U.S. Army discloses sexual harassment inquiry (**Nov. 7**). Liquor companies end ban on radio and television advertising (**Nov. 7**). Bomb kills 13 in Russian cemetery (**Nov. 10**). Mid-air collision in India kills 342 (**Nov. 12**). Clinton approves Canadian plan for U.N.-backed relief mission for 1.2 million Hutu refugees starving in eastern Zaire (**Nov. 13**). High Cabinet officials announce resignations (**Nov. 13**). Texaco settles racial bias suit (**Nov. 15**). Hundreds of thousands of Hutu refugees return to Rwanda (**Nov. 15–18**). Career C.I.A. official charged with spying for Russia (**Nov. 21**). Naming of independent counsel to sift Democratic fund-raising rejected (**Nov. 29**). Clinton appoints Madeleine Albright as first female secretary of state (**Dec. 5**). Kofi Annan, 58, of Ghana, named U.N. Secretary-General (**Dec. 13**). F.B.I. agent charged with spying for Moscow (**Dec. 18**). Russian President Boris Yeltsin returns to work after heart surgery (**Dec. 20**). House speaker Newt Gingrich apologizes for ethics violations (**Dec. 21**). Thousands march in Belgrade in continuing protest against president's annulment of election results (**Dec. 26**). Jazz great Ella Fitzgerald dies.

Picture and Map Credits

The editors wish to thank the following organizations and individuals who have contributed illustrations to Headline History. The sources are listed alphabetically, with the name of the illustrations in the order in which they appear in the book.

Agence France Press/Archive Photos: **Mao Tse-tung;** AIP Niels Bohr Library: **Marie Curie, Albert Einstein;** AMW Pressedienst/Archive Photos: **Nelson Mandela;** Archive Photos: **Richard Wagner, William Butler Yeats, Pablo Picasso, Anne Frank, Woody Guthrie, Robert Frost, William Faulkner, The Beatles, Ingmar Bergman, Duke Ellington, Tennessee Williams, Toni Morrison, Seamus Heaney, Ella Fitzgerald;** Linda J. Barnes: **the Duomo in Florence;** British Information Services: **Margaret Thatcher;** Consolidated News/Archive Photos: **Jean-Bertrand Aristide;** Tina Diodati: **Parthenon;** Embassy of the Philippines: **Corazon Aquino;** The French Consulate, Boston: **François Mitterrand;** Peter F. Harrington: **Stonehenge;** Erik Hjortshoj: **Pagoda;** Imapress/Archive Photos: **Boris Yeltsin;** INA/Reuters/Archive Photos: **Saddam Hussein;** John Fitzgerald Kennedy Library, Boston: **John F. Kennedy;** Priscilla Lee: **Dalai Lama;** Leo Baeck Inst./Archive Photos: **Sigmund Freud;** The Library of Congress Picture Collection: **Pocahontas, Taj Mahal, Edgar Allen Poe, Harriet Tubman, Walt Whitman, Dred Scott, Samuel Clemens (Mark Twain), Henri Matisse, W.E.B. DuBois, Woodrow Wilson, Bessie Smith, Dorothea Lange photo, Amelia Earhart, Harry S. Truman, John H. Glenn, Jr., Richard Nixon, Lyndon B. Johnson;** Pete Maio: **Mesa Verde;** Muzammil Paha/Reuters/Archive Photos: **Benazir Bhutto;** National Archives and Records Admin.: **Frederick Douglass, Harriet Beecher Stowe, Abraham Lincoln, Robert E. Lee, William Tecumseh Sherman, Chief Joseph, Benito Mussolini, Franklin Delano Roosevelt, Adolf Hitler, Winston Churchill, Atomic Bomb, Dwight D. Eisenhower, Rev. Martin Luther King, Jr.;** NASA: **Hubble Space Telescope;** Novosti Photos: **Vladimir Lenin, Mikhail S. Gorbachev;** Elaine Ouellette: **Pantheon in Rome;** The Permanent Mission of India to the U.N.: **Indira Gandhi;** Permanent Mission of Islamic Republic of Iran to the U.N.: **Ayatollah Ruhollah Khomeini;** Renée Scott: **Celtic Cross;** The Republican National Committee: **Ronald Reagan, George Bush;** Kim Storm: **Egyptian Pyramid;** United Nations: **Fidel Castro, Kofi Annan;** U.S. Army Photo: **Joseph Stalin, Yalta Conference, General Colin Powell;** U.S. State Department: **Madeleine Albright;** U.S. Supreme Court: **Thurgood Marshall, Sandra Day O'Connor;** Tasha Vincent: **Cathedral and Tower at Pisa, Chartres Cathedral, Michelangelo's David;** The White House: **William J. Clinton.** Maps courtesy of *An Encyclopedia of World History,* by William L. Langer, 5th Edition, © 1972 by Houghton Mifflin Company. Reprinted by permission of Houghton Mifflin Company.

World Statistics

A Profile of the World

Source: The 1996 CIA World Factbook

Geography

Total area: 510.072 million sq km (196.93 million sq mi.). **Land area:** 148.94 million sq km (57.50 sq mi.). **Water area:** 361.132 million sq km (139.43 sq mi.). **Comparative area:** land area about 15 times the size of the United States. **Note:** 70.8% of the world is water, 29.2% is land.

Land boundaries: The land boundaries in the world total 250,883.64 km (155,891.81 mi.) (not counting shared boundaries twice)

Maritime claims: *Contiguous zone:* 24 nm (nautical miles) claimed by most but can vary. *Continental shelf:* 200-m (656 ft.) depth claimed by most or to the depth of exploitation, others claim 200 nm or to the edge of the continental margin. *Exclusive fishing zone:* 200 nm claimed by most but can vary. *Exclusive economic zone:* 200 nm claimed by most but can vary. *Territorial sea:* 12 nm claimed by most but can vary.

Climate: Two large areas of polar climates are separated by two rather narrow temperate zones from a wide equatorial band of tropical to subtropical climates.

Terrain: Highest elevation is Mt. Everest at 8,848 meters (29,028 ft.) and lowest depression is the Dead Sea at 408 meters (1,286 ft.) below sea level; greatest ocean depth is the Marianas Trench at 10,924 meters (35,840 ft.).

Natural resources: The rapid consumption of nonrenewable mineral resources, the depletion of forest areas and wetlands, the extinction of animal and plant species, and the deterioration in air and water quality (especially in Eastern Europe and the former U.S.S.R.) pose serious long-term problems that governments and people are only beginning to address.

Land use: *Arable land:* 10%. *Permanent crops:* 1%. *Meadows and pastures:* 24%. *Forest and woodland:* 31%. *Other:* 34%.

Environment: Large areas are subject to severe weather (tropical cyclones), natural disasters (earthquakes, landslides, tsunamis, volcanic eruptions), overpopulation, industrial disasters, pollution (air, water, acid rain, toxic substances), loss of vegetation (overgrazing, deforestation, desertification), loss of wildlife, soil degradation, soil depletion, erosion.

People

Population: 5,868,720,793 (Sept. 1997 est. from U.S. Census Bureau)

Growth rate: 1.4% (1996 est.)

Birth rate: 23 births/1,000 population (1996 est.)

Death rate: 9 deaths/1,000 live births (1996 est.)

Infant mortality rate: 60 deaths/1,000 live births (1996 est.)

Life expectancy at birth: *Total population:* 62 years. *Male:* 61 years. *Female:* 64 years

Total fertility rate: 2.9 children born/woman (1996 est.)

Literacy: age 15 and over can read and write (1994 est.) *Combined:* 82%. *Male:* 68%. *Female:* 75%.

Labor force: 2.24 billion (1992)

Government

Administrative divisions: 266 sovereign nations, dependent areas, other, and miscellaneous entries

Legal system: Varies by individual country; 186 (not including Yugoslavia) are parties to the United Nations International Court of Justice (ICJ or World Court)

Economy

Overview: Real global output—gross world product (GWP)—again rose 3% in 1995, with the newly industrializing Third World countries setting the pace. And once more, results varied widely among regions and countries. Average growth of 2.5% in the GDP of industrialized countries (56% of GWP in 1995) and average growth of 5% in the GDP of less developed countries (38% of GWP) were partly offset by a small 1.5% drop in the GDP of the former U.S.S.R./Eastern Europe area (only 6% of GWP). With the notable exception of Japan at 3.1%, unemployment was typically 6%–12% in the industrial world. The U.S. accounted for 22% of GWP in 1995; Western Europe accounted for 21%; and Japan accounted for 8%. These are the three "economic superpowers" presumably destined to compete for mastery in international markets on into the 21st century. As for the less developed countries: China, India, and the Four Dragons—South Korea, Taiwan, Hong Kong, and Singapore—once again posted records of 5% growth or better; however, many other countries, especially in Africa, continued to suffer from drought, rapid population growth, inflation, and civil strife. Central Europe continued its progress in moving toward "market-friendly" economies. The 15 ex-Soviet countries typically experienced further declines in output, although considerably less than in 1992–94. Externally, the nation-state, as a bedrock economic-political institution, is steadily losing control over international flows of people, goods, funds, and technology. Internally, the central government in a number of cases is losing control over resources as separatist regional movements—typically based on ethnicity—gain momentum, e.g., in the successor states of the former Soviet Union, in the former Yugoslavia, in India, and in Canada. In Western Europe, governments face the difficult political problem of channeling resources away from welfare programs in order to increase investment and strengthen incentives to seek employment. The addition of nearly 100 million people each year to an already overcrowded globe is exacerbating the problems of pollution, desertification, underemployment, epidemics, and famine. Because of their own internal problems, the industrialized countries have inadequate resources to deal effectively with the poorer areas of the world, which, at least from the economic point of view, are becoming further marginalized.

National product: GWP (gross world product)—purchasing power equivalent—$33.7 trillion (1995 est.)

National product real growth rate: 3% (1995 est.)

National product per capita: $5,900 (1995 est.)

Inflation rate (consumer prices): *Developed countries:* 2%–6% typically (1995 est.). *Developing countries:* 10%–60% typically (1995 est.).

Note: these figures vary widely in individual cases

Unemployment rate: developed countries typically 6%–12%; developing countries, 30% combined unemployment and underemployment (1995 est.)

Exports: $4.3 trillion (f.o.b. 1995 est.) *Commodities:* the whole range of industrial and agricultural goods and services. *Partners:* in value, about 75% of exports from the developed countries.

Imports: $4.4 trillion (c.i.f., 1995 est.) *Commodities:* the whole range of industrial and agricultural goods and services. *Partners:* in value, about 75% of imports by the developed countries

External debt: $2 trillion for less developed countries (1995 est.)

Industrial production: growth rate 5% (1995 est.)

Electricity: 2,773,000,000 kW capacity; 11,601 trillion kWh produced, 1,937 kWh per capita (1993)

Industries: industry worldwide is dominated by the onrush of technology, especially in computers, robotics, telecommunications, and medicines and medical equipment; most of these advances take place in Organization for Economic Cooperation and Development (OECD)[1] nations; only a small portion of non-OECD countries have succeeded in rapidly adjusting to these technological forces, and the technological gap between the industrial nations and the less-developed countries continues to widen; the rapid development of new industrial (and agricultural) technology is complicating already grim environmental problems.

Agriculture: World agriculture runs the gamut of crops, livestock, forest products, and fish.

1. 24 full members: Australia, Austria, Belgium, Canada, Denmark, Finland, France, Germany, Greece, Iceland, Ireland, Italy, Japan, Luxembourg, Netherlands, New Zealand, Norway, Portugal, Spain, Sweden, Switzerland, Turkey, U.K., U.S.

Transportation

Railroads: 148,775 mi. (239,430 km) of narrow gauge track; 441,642 mi. (710,754 km) of standard gauge track; 156,059 mi. (251,153 km) of broad gauge track; includes about 118,060 to 121,167 mi. (190,000 to 195,000 km) of electrical routes of which 91,814 mi. (147,760 km) are in Europe, 15,229 mi. (24,509 km) in the Far East, 6,866 mi. (11,050 km) in Africa, 2,624 mi. (4,223 km) in South America, and only 2,585 mi. (4,160 km) in North America; fastest speed in daily service is 186 mph (300 kph) attained by France's SNCF TGV-Atlantique line

Ports: Chiba, Houston, Kawasaki, Kobe, Marseille, Mina' al Ahmadi (Kuwait), New Orleans, New York, Rotterdam, Yokohama

Merchant marine: 25,521 ships (1,000 GRT [gross register ton] or over) totaling 442,276,527 GRT/701,647,274 DWT (dead weight ton) (1995 est.)

Defense Forces

Branches: ground, maritime, and air forces at all levels of technology

Defense expenditures: A small decline is likely in 1995 to somewhat less than three-quarters of a trillion dollars, or roughly 2% of gross world product (1995 est.)

Area and Population of Countries

Mid-1997 Estimates

Country	Area (in sq km)	Population	Country	Area (in sq km)	Population
Afghanistan	647,500	23,738,085	Columbia	1,138,910	37,418,290
Albania	28,750	3,293,252	Comoros	2,170	589,797
Algeria	2,381,740	29,830,370	Congo	342,000	2,583,198
Andorra	450	74,839	Democratic Republic of	2,345,410	47,440,362
Angola	1,246,700	10,623,994	Congo (formerly Zaire)		
Antigua and Barbuda	440	66,175	Costa Rica	51,100	3,534,174
Argentina	2,766,890	35,797,536	Côte d'Ivoire	322,460	14,986,218
Armenia	29,800	3,465,611	Croatia	56,538	5,026,995
Australia	7,686,850	18,438,824	Cuba	110,860	10,999,041
Austria	83,850	8,054,078	Cyprus	9,250	752,808
Azerbaijan	86,600	7,735,918	Czech Republic	78,703	10,318,958
The Bahamas	13,940	262,034	Denmark	43,070	5,268,775
Bahrain	620	603,318	Djibouti	22,000	434,116
Bangladesh	144,000	125,340,261	Dominica	750	83,226
Barbados	430	257,731	Dominican Republic	48,730	8,228,151
Belarus	207,600	10,439,916	Ecuador	283,560	11,690,535
Belgium	30,510	10,203,683	Egypt	1,001,450	64,791,891
Belize	22,960	224,663	El Salvador	21,040	5,661,827
Benin	112,620	5,902,178	Equatorial Guinea	28,050	442,516
Bhutan	47,000	1,865,191	Eritrea	121,320	3,589,687
Bolivia	1,098,580	7,669,868	Estonia	45,100	1,444,721
Bosnia and Herzegovenia	51,233	2,607,734	Ethiopia	1,127,127	58,732,577
Botswana	600,370	1,500,765	Fiji	18,270	792,441
Brazil	8,511,965	164,511,366	Finland	337,030	5,109,148
Brunei	5,770	307,616	France	547,030	58,470,421
Bulgaria	110,910	8,652,745	Gabon	267,670	1,190,159
Burkina Faso	274,200	10,891,159	The Gambia	11,300	1,248,085
Burundi	27,830	6,052,614	Georgia	69,700	5,174,642
Cambodia	181,040	11,163,861	Germany	356,910	84,068,216
Cameroon	475,440	14,677,510	Ghana	238,540	18,100,703
Canada	9,976,140	29,123,194	Greece	131,940	10,583,126
Cape Verde	4,030	393,843	Grenada	340	95,537
Central African Republic	622,980	3,342,051	Guatemala	108,890	11,558,407
Chad	1,284,000	7,166,023	Guinea	245,860	7,405,375
Chile	756,950	14,508,168	Guinea-Bissau	36,120	1,178,584
China, People's Republic of	9,596,960	1,221,591,778	Guyana	214,970	706,116

Country	Area (in sq km)	Population	Country	Area (in sq km)	Population
Haiti	27,750	6,611,407	Paraguay	406,750	5,651,634
Honduras	112,090	5,751,384	Peru	1,285,220	24,949,512
Hungary	93,030	9,935,774	Philippines	300,000	76,103,564
Iceland	103,000	272,550	Poland	312,683	38,700,291
India	3,287,590	967,612,804	Portugal	92,080	9,867,654
Indonesia	1,919,440	209,774,138	Qatar	11,000	665,485
Iran	1,648	67,540,002	Romania	237,500	21,399,114
Iraq	437,072	22,219,289	Russia	17,075,200	147,987,101
Ireland	70,280	3,555,500	Rwanda	26,340	7,737,537
Israel	20,770	5,534,672	Saint Kitts and Nevis	269	41,803
Italy	301,230	57,534,088	Saint Lucia	620	159,639
Jamaica	10,990	2,615,582	Saint Vincent and	340	119,092
Japan	377,835	125,716,637	the Grenadines		
Jordan	89,213	4,324,638	Western Samoa	2,860	219,509
Kazakhstan	2,717,300	16,898,572	Sao Tome and Principe	960	147,865
Kenya	582,650	28,803,085	Saudi Arabia	1,960,582	20,087,965
Kiribati	717	82,449	Senegal	196,190	9,403,546
North Korea	120,540	24,317,004	Seychelles	455	78,142
South Korea	98,480	45,948,811	Sierra Leone	71,740	4,891,546
Kuwait	17,820	2,076,805	Singapore	632.6	3,461,929
Kyrgyzstan	198,500	4,540,185	Slovakia	48,845	5,393,016
Laos	236,800	5,116,959	Slovenia	20,256	1,945,998
Latvia	64,100	2,437,649	Solomon Islands	28,450	426,855
Lebanon	10,400	3,858,736	Somalia	637,660	9,940,232
Lesotho	30,350	2,007,814	South Africa	1,219,912	42,327,458
Liberia	111,370	2,602,068	Spain	504,750	39,244,195
Libya	1,759,540	5,648,359	Sri Lanka	65,610	18,762,075
Liechtenstein	160	31,461	Sudan	2,505,810	32,594,128
Lithuania	65,200	3,635,932	Suriname	163,270	443,446
Luxembourg	2,586	422,474	Swaziland	17,360	1,031,600
Macedonia	25,333	2,113,866	Sweden	449,964	8,946,193
Madagascar	587,040	14,061,627	Switzerland	41,290	7,248,984
Malawi	118,480	9,609,081	Syria	185,180	16,137,899
Malaysia	329,750	20,376,235	Taiwan	35,980	21,655,515
Maldives	300	280,391	Tajikistan	143,100	6,013,855
Mali	1,240,000	9,945,383	Tanzania	945,090	29,460,753
Malta	320	379,365	Thailand	514,000	59,450,818
Marshall Islands	181.3	60,652	Togo	56,790	4,735,610
Mauritania	1,030,700	2,411,317	Tonga	748	107,335
Mauritius	1,860	1,154,272	Trinidad and Tobago	5,130	1,273,141
Mexico	1,972,550	97,563,374	Tunisia	163,610	9,183,097
Micronesia	702	127,616	Turkey	780,580	63,528,225
Moldova	33,700	4,475,232	Turkmenistan	488,100	4,225,351
Mongolia	1,565,000	2,538,211	Uganda	236,040	20,604,874
Morocco	446,550	30,391,423	Ukraine	603,700	50,684,635
Mozambique	801,590	18,165,476	United Arab Emirates	75,581	2,262,309
Namibia	825,418	1,727,183	United Kingdom	244,820	58,610,182
Nepal	140,800	22,641,061	United States	9,372,610	267,954,767
Netherlands	37,330	15,653,091	Uruguay	176,220	3,261,707
New Zealand	268,680	3,587,275	Uzbekistan	447,400	23,860,452
Nicaragua	129,494	4,386,399	Vanuatu	14,760	181,358
Niger	1,267,000	9,388,859	Venezuela	912,050	22,396,407
Nigeria	923,770	107,129,469	Vietnam	329,560	75,123,880
Norway	324,220	4,404,456	Yemen	527,970	13,972,477
Oman	212,460	2,264,590	Yugoslavia[1]	102,350	10,655,317
Pakistan	803,940	132,185,299	Zambia	752,610	9,349,975
Panama	78,200	2,693,417	Zimbabwe	390,580	11,423,175
Papua New Guinea	461,690	4,496,221			

1. On April 27, 1992, Serbia and Montenegro formed a new state, the Federal Republic of Yugoslavia. *Source:* U.S. Bureau of the Census, International Data Base and *1996 CIA World Factbook.*

Projected World Population by Country, 1997–2022

(Countries whose 1997 population is more than 10 million)

Country	1997	2002	2012	2022
Afghanistan	23,738,085	28,029,976	35,770,296	45,007,876
Algeria	29,830,370	33,108,533	39,796,704	45,959,147
Angola	10,623,994	12,143,484	15,776,632	20,215,181
Argentina	35,797,536	38,184,118	42,908,263	47,213,357
Australia	18,438,824	19,272,163	20,703,032	21,909,112
Bangladesh	125,340,261	136,478,427	157,137,076	175,536,845
Belarus	10,439,916	10,630,366	10,970,004	11,071,740
Belgium	10,203,683	10,322,672	10,344,805	10,242,133
Brazil	164,511,366	172,577,455	186,236,303	195,887,202
Burkina Faso	10,891,159	12,201,905	14,610,501	17,115,938
Burma (Myanmar)	46,821,943	51,121,539	60,058,965	69,367,760
Cambodia	11,163,861	12,754,087	16,503,256	21,228,608
Cameroon	14,677,510	16,854,808	21,627,103	27,047,716
Canada	29,123,194	30,533,589	33,003,411	35,135,689
Chile	14,508,168	15,294,990	16,633,943	17,720,861
China	1,221,591,778	1,272,337,569	1,357,286,463	1,423,222,593
Colombia	37,418,290	40,291,398	45,510,214	50,104,071
Democratic Rep. of Congo (formerly Zaire)	47,440,362	54,554,842	73,426,055	96,505,510
Cote d'Ivoire	14,986,218	16,748,880	20,789,303	25,051,726
Cuba	10,999,041	11,207,802	11,542,971	11,708,047
Czech Republic	10,318,958	10,404,552	10,421,012	10,226,086
Ecuador	11,690,535	12,802,225	14,951,949	16,922,978
Egypt	64,791,891	70,877,062	83,110,165	94,508,723
Ethiopia	58,732,577	66,892,322	84,863,828	105,147,022
France	58,470,421	59,530,092	61,041,226	61,301,290
Germany	84,068,216	86,713,543	89,145,040	88,499,962
Ghana	18,100,703	20,026,959	23,649,573	27,202,907
Greece	10,583,126	10,842,403	11,161,220	11,015,598
Guatemala	11,558,407	12,979,289	15,859,315	18,682,780
India	967,612,804	1,042,283,247	1,183,531,797	1,314,093,764
Indonesia	209,774,138	225,562,496	255,274,111	280,890,811
Iran	67,540,002	75,222,785	91,461,203	107,378,625
Iraq	22,219,289	26,516,920	36,760,223	48,769,287
Italy	57,534,088	57,970,787	57,346,832	55,185,554
Japan	125,716,637	127,122,190	127,135,814	122,415,920
Kazakstan	16,898,572	17,031,541	17,727,908	18,589,248
Kenya	28,803,085	31,458,451	34,235,123	35,506,954
North Korea	24,317,004	26,196,918	28,994,319	31,437,063
South Korea	45,948,811	48,252,721	51,809,489	53,792,251
Madagascar	14,061,627	16,168,094	21,187,590	27,288,396
Malaysia	20,376,235	22,425,715	26,518,337	30,638,296
Mexico	97,563,374	106,441,839	123,413,405	139,113,355
Morocco	30,391,423	33,458,351	39,688,506	45,675,036
Mozambique	18,165,476	20,614,041	25,895,420	31,550,926
Nepal	22,641,061	25,576,220	32,148,469	39,203,789
Netherlands	15,653,091	16,033,351	16,426,352	16,472,180
Nigeria	107,129,469	124,583,181	166,431,601	215,498,856
Pakistan	132,185,299	147,187,327	176,495,911	203,999,424
Peru	24,949,512	26,999,336	30,681,833	33,795,626
Philippines	76,103,564	84,196,679	100,326,789	116,031,414
Poland	38,700,291	39,304,086	40,507,831	40,853,809
Romania	21,399,114	20,965,774	20,635,103	20,027,581
Russia	147,987,101	148,262,622	150,194,445	149,458,184
Saudi Arabia	20,087,965	23,800,060	33,372,897	46,013,359
Serbia	10,017,394	10,219,802	10,397,883	10,380,537
South Africa	42,327,458	44,859,376	45,549,108	45,018,879
Spain	39,244,195	39,806,386	40,384,835	39,512,885
Sri Lanka	18,762,075	19,779,665	21,687,452	23,115,515
Sudan	32,594,128	37,678,426	48,928,585	61,074,991
Syria	16,137,899	18,861,502	24,449,279	30,034,420
Taiwan	21,655,515	22,581,272	24,262,047	25,319,519
Tanzania	29,460,753	32,188,967	36,866,723	41,035,529
Thailand	59,450,818	62,243,216	66,883,880	69,745,621
Turkey	63,528,225	68,647,166	78,473,792	87,316,431
Uganda	20,604,874	22,791,886	27,218,142	31,870,641

Country	1997	2002	2012	2022
Ukraine	50,684,635	50,295,754	49,758,795	48,887,311
United Kingdom	58,610,182	59,016,187	59,164,911	59,293,744
United States	267,954,767	279,498,955	302,933,462	328,030,239
Uzbekistan	23,860,452	26,216,234	31,721,533	37,864,675
Venezuela	22,396,407	24,368,211	28,067,164	31,535,376
Vietnam	75,123,880	80,381,211	90,730,882	101,117,740
Yemen	13,972,477	16,680,533	23,272,060	31,116,897
Zimbabwe	11,423,175	11,928,567	11,777,741	11,299,413

Source: U.S. Department of Commerce, Bureau of the Census, International Database.

Estimates of World Population by Regions

Year	Estimated population in millions							
	North America[1]	Latin America[2]	Europe[3]	Former U.S.S.R.	Asia[4]	Africa	Oceania	World total
1650	1	7	103	[5]	257	100	2	470
1750	1	10	144	[5]	437	100	2	694
1850	26	33	274	[5]	656	100	2	1,091
1900	81	63	423	[5]	857	141	6	1,571
1950	166	164	392	180	1,380	219	13	2,513
1960	199	215	425	214	1,683	275	16	3,027
1970	226	283	460	244	2,091	354	19	3,678
1980	252	365	484	266	2,618	472	23	4,478
1990	276	442	501	298	3,130	625	26	5,292
1995	292	481	509	297	3,403	721	28	5,734
1996	295	488	507	293	3,428	731	29	5,772
1997	297	496	508	293	3,477	750	29	5,852

1. U.S. (including Alaska and Hawaii), Bermuda, Canada, Greenland, and St. Pierre and Miquelon. 2. Mexico, Central and South America, and Caribbean Islands. 3. Includes Russia 1650–1900. 4. Excludes Russia (U.S.S.R.). 5. Included in Europe. NOTE: From 1930 on European Turkey included in Asia not Europe. *Sources:* W.F. Willcox, 1650–1900; United Nations, 1930–70. United States Department of Commerce, Bureau of the Census, International Database, 1980–97.

World's 20 Most Populous Countries: 1997 and 2022

	1997			2022 (projected)	
Rank	Country	Population	Rank	Country	Population
1.	China	1,221,591,778	1.	China	1,423,222,593
2.	India	967,612,804	2.	India	1,314,093,764
3.	United States	267,954,767	3.	United States	328,030,239
4.	Indonesia	209,774,138	4.	Indonesia	280,890,811
5.	Brazil	164,511,366	5.	Nigeria	215,498,856
6.	Russia	147,987,101	6.	Pakistan	203,999,424
7.	Pakistan	132,185,299	7.	Brazil	195,887,202
8.	Japan	125,716,637	8.	Bangladesh	175,536,845
9.	Bangladesh	125,340,261	9.	Russia	149,458,184
10.	Nigeria	107,129,469	10.	Mexico	139,113,355
11.	Mexico	97,563,374	11.	Japan	122,415,920
12.	Germany	84,068,216	12.	Philippines	116,031,414
13.	Philippines	76,103,564	13.	Iran	107,378,625
14.	Vietnam	75,123,880	14.	Ethiopia	105,147,022
15.	Iran	67,540,002	15.	Vietnam	101,117,740
16.	Egypt	64,791,891	16.	Dem. Rep. of Congo (formerly Zaire)	96,505,510
17.	Turkey	63,528,225	17.	Egypt	94,508,723
18.	Thailand	59,450,818	18.	Germany	88,499,962
19.	Ethiopia	58,732,577	19.	Turkey	87,316,431
20.	United Kingdom	58,610,182	20.	Thailand	69,745,621

Source: U.S. Department of Commerce, Bureau of the Census, International Database.

Crude Marriage Rates for Selected Countries

(per 1,000 population)

Country	1996	1995	1994	1993	1992	1991	1990	Country	1996	1995	1994	1993	1992	1991	1990
Australia	n.a.	6.1	6.2	6.4	6.6	6.6	6.9	Japan	6.3	6.3	6.3	6.4	6.1	6.0	5.8
Austria	5.2	5.3	5.4	5.6	5.8	5.6	5.8	Luxembourg	n.a.	5.1	5.9	6.0	6.4	6.7	6.2
Belgium	n.a.	5.1	5.2	5.4	5.8	6.2	6.6	Netherlands	5.8	5.2	5.4	5.8	6.4	6.3	6.4
Bulgaria	n.a.	4.0	4.5	4.9	5.0	5.4	6.7	New Zealand	n.a.	6.2	6.3	6.4	6.5	6.8	7.0
Czech Republic[1]	5.2	5.3	5.6	6.4	n.a.	6.7	8.4	Norway	n.a.	n.a.	4.6	n.a.	4.5	4.7	5.2
Denmark	6.8	6.6	6.8	6.1	6.2	6.0	6.1	Poland	6.8	5.4	5.4	5.4	5.7	6.0	6.7
Finland	4.6	4.7	4.7	4.9	4.6	4.7	4.8	Portugal	6.5	n.a.	n.a.	6.9	7.1	6.8	7.3
France	4.8	4.4	4.4	4.4	4.7	4.9	5.1	Romania	n.a.	6.8	6.7	7.1	7.7	7.9	8.3
Germany[2]	n.a.	5.3	5.4	5.4	5.7	6.3	6.5	Russia	5.9	7.3	7.3	n.a.	7.1	8.5	8.9
Greece	4.5	6.1	5.4	5.9	4.7	6.0	5.8	Sweden	3.8	3.8	3.9	3.9	4.3	4.6	4.7
Hungary	4.9	5.2	5.3	5.3	5.5	5.9	6.4	Switzerland	5.7	5.6	6.1	6.2	6.6	7.0	6.9
Ireland	n.a.	4.4	4.6	4.5	4.5	4.8	5.0	United Kingdom	n.a.	6.4	5.7	5.9	6.0	6.1	6.8
Israel	n.a.	6.1	n.a.	6.2	6.5	6.5	7.0	United States	n.a.	8.9	9.1	9.0	9.2	9.4	9.8
Italy	n.a.	4.9	5.0	4.8	5.4	5.5	5.4	Yugoslavia[3]	5.3	5.7	5.7	5.8	6.0	n.a.	6.2

1. Data prior to 1993 pertain to the former Czechoslovakia. 2. All data pertaining to Germany prior to 1990 are for West Germany. 3. Beginning January 1992, data refer to the Federal Republic of Yugoslavia. Prior to that date, data refer to the Socialist Federal Republic of Yugoslavia. NOTE: n.a. = not available. Source: United Nations, Monthly Bulletin of Statistics, June 1996.

Divorce Rate per 1,000 Married Women

Selected Countries, 1970–1994

Country	1970	1980	1990	1992	1993	1994	Country	1970	1980	1990	1992	1993	1994
Canada	6	10	11	11	11	11	Japan	4	5	5	6	6	n.a.
Denmark	8	11	13	13	13	13	Netherlands	3	8	8	9	9	n.a.
France	3	6	8	n.a.	n.a.	n.a.	Sweden	7	11	12	13	13	n.a.
Germany[1]	5	6	8	7	7	n.a.	United Kingdom	5[2]	12[2]	13	13	13	n.a.
Italy	1	1	2	2	n.a.	n.a.	United States	15	23	21	21	21	21

NOTE: n.a. = not available. 1. Data prior to 1991 are for the former West Germany. 2. England and Wales only. Source: Statistical Abstract of the United States, 1996.

Crude Birth and Death Rates for Selected Countries

(per 1,000 population)

Country	Birth rate						Death rate					
	1997	1994	1990	1985	1980	1975	1997	1994	1990	1985	1980	1975
Australia	14.0	14.5	15.4	15.7	15.3	16.9	7.0	7.1	7.0	7.5	7.4	7.9
Austria	11.0	11.5	11.6	11.6	12.0	12.5	10.0	10.0	10.6	11.9	12.2	12.8
Belgium	12.0	11.6	12.6	11.5	12.7	12.2	10.0	10.4	10.6	11.2	11.6	12.2
Czech Republic[1]	11.0	10.3	13.4	14.5	16.4	19.6	11.0	11.3	11.7	11.8	12.1	11.5
Denmark	12.0	13.4	12.4	10.6	11.2	14.2	10.0	11.8	11.9	11.4	10.9	10.1
Finland	11.0	12.9	13.2	12.8	13.1	13.9	11.0	9.4	10.0	9.8	9.3	9.3
France	11.0	12.3	13.5	13.9	14.8	14.1	9.0	9.0	9.3	10.1	10.2	10.6
Germany[2]	9.0	9.5	11.4	9.6	10.0	9.7	11.0	10.9	11.2	11.5	11.6	12.1
Greece	10.0	9.9	10.2	11.7	15.4	15.7	10.0	9.4	9.3	9.4	9.1	8.9
Hong Kong	10.0	11.8	11.7	14.0	16.9	n.a.	5.0	4.9	4.9	4.6	5.1	n.a.
Hungary	11.0	11.3	12.1	12.2	13.9	18.4	15.0	14.3	14.1	13.9	13.6	12.4
Ireland	13.0	13.4	15.1	17.6	21.9	21.5	9.0	8.6	9.1	9.4	9.7	10.6
Israel	20.0	21.2	22.2	23.5	24.1	28.2	6.0	6.3	6.2	6.6	6.7	7.1
Italy	10.0	9.2	9.8	10.1	11.2	14.8	10.0	9.6	9.4	9.5	9.7	9.9
Japan	10.0	9.9	9.9	11.9	13.7	17.2	8.0	7.0	6.7	6.2	6.2	6.4
Luxembourg	13.0	13.6	13.3	11.2	11.5	11.2	8.0	9.5	10.1	11.0	11.5	12.2
Mauritius	19.0	19.6	21.0	18.8	27.0	25.1	7.0	6.7	6.5	6.8	7.2	8.1
Netherlands	12.0	12.7	13.3	12.3	12.8	13.0	9.0	8.7	8.6	8.5	8.1	8.3
New Zealand	15.0	16.3	18.0	15.6	n.a.	18.4	8.0	7.8	7.9	8.4	n.a.	8.1
Norway	11.0	13.6	14.3	12.3	12.5	14.1	11.0	10.1	10.7	10.7	10.1	9.9
Panama	22.0	21.7	23.9	26.6	26.8	32.3	5.0	n.a.	n.a.	n.a.	n.a.	n.a.
Poland	12.0	12.5	14.3	18.2	19.5	18.9	10.0	10.1	10.2	10.3	9.8	8.7
Portugal	11.0	10.7	11.8	12.8	16.4	19.1	10.0	9.9	10.4	9.6	9.9	10.4
Romania	10.0	11.0	13.6	15.8	n.a.	n.a.	12.0	11.6	10.6	10.9	n.a.	n.a.
Singapore	16.0	16.9	17.0	16.6	17.3	17.8	5.0	5.1	n.a.	5.2	5.2	5.1
Sweden	11.0	12.8	14.5	11.8	11.7	12.6	11.0	10.3	11.0	11.3	11.0	10.8

Country	Birth rate						Death rate					
	1997	1994	1990	1985	1980	1975	1997	1994	1990	1985	1980	1975
Switzerland	11.0	11.9	12.5	11.6	11.3	12.3	10.0	8.9	9.5	9.2	9.2	8.7
Tunisia	24.0	22.7	25.8	31.3	35.2	36.6	5.0	n.a.	n.a.	n.a.	n.a.	n.a.
United Kingdom	13.0	12.9	13.9	13.3	13.5	12.5	11.0	10.7	11.2	11.8	11.8	11.9
United States	15.0	15.2	16.7	15.7	16.2	14.0	9.0	8.8	8.6	8.7	8.9	8.9
Yugoslavia[3]	n.a.	13.2	14.0	15.9	17.0	18.2	n.a.	10.1	9.0	9.1	9.0	8.7

1. Data prior to 1994 pertain to the former Czechoslovakia. 2. All data pertaining to Germany prior to 1990 are for West Germany. 3. Beginning January 1992, data refer to the Federal Republic of Yugoslavia. Prior to that date, data refer to the Socialist Federal Republic of Yugoslavia. NOTE: n.a. = not available. *Source:* United Nations, *Monthly Bulletin of Statistics, June 1996.* Data for 1997 from the U.S. Bureau of the Census, International Database.

Births to Unmarried Women

By Country, 1970–1993

	1970		1980		1990		1993	
Country	Total live births (000s)	Percent born to unmarried women	Total live births (000s)	Percent born to unmarried women	Total live births (000s)	Percent born to unmarried women	Total live births (000s)	Percent born to unmarried women
Canada[1]	372	10	360	13	398	24	388	27
Denmark	71	11	57	33	63	46	67	47
France	850	7	800	11	762	30	n.a.	35
Germany[2]	811	6	621	8	727	11	798	15
Italy	902	2	640	4	554	6	538	7
Japan	1,932	1	1,616	1	1,240	1	1,204	1
Netherlands	239	2	181	4	198	11	196	13
Sweden	110	18	97	40	124	47	118	50
United Kingdom	904	8	754	12	799	28	762	32
United States	3,731	11	3,612	18	4,158	28	4,000	31

1. Data for 1980–90 excludes Newfoundland. After 1990, a significant number of births are not allocated according to marital status, thereby understating the proportion of births to unmarried women. 2. Prior to 1991, data are for the former West Germany. NOTE: n.a. = not available. *Source:* U.S. Bureau of Labor Statistics, *Monthly Labor Review,* and unpublished data.

Infant Mortality Rates and Life Expectancy at Birth, by Sex, for Selected Countries, 1997

	Infant deaths per 1,000 live births			Life expectancy at birth (years)		
Country	Both sexes	Male	Female	Both sexes	Male	Female
North America						
Canada	6.0	6.6	5.3	79.3	75.9	82.9
Mexico	23.9	28.9	18.7	74.0	70.4	77.8
United States	6.6	7.6	5.5	76.0	72.8	79.5
Central and South America						
Brazil	53.4	56.8	49.9	61.4	56.8	66.3
Chile	13.2	14.3	12.0	74.7	71.5	78.0
Costa Rica	13.3	14.0	12.6	75.8	73.4	78.4
Ecuador	33.4	38.1	28.5	71.4	68.8	74.2
Guatemala	49.2	53.1	45.2	65.6	63.0	68.4
Panama	24.6	27.0	22.2	74.3	71.6	77.1
Peru	50.2	52.1	48.2	69.6	67.4	71.8
Trinidad and Tobago	17.9	20.2	15.6	70.5	68.1	72.9
Uruguay	14.7	16.3	13.1	75.2	72.1	78.6
Venezuela	28.5	32.2	24.6	72.4	69.4	75.6
Europe						
Albania	47.1	49.6	44.4	68.3	65.2	71.6
Austria	6.1	6.9	5.3	76.7	73.6	80.0
Belgium	6.3	6.9	5.7	77.2	74.0	80.6
Cyprus	8.2	10.2	6.0	76.5	74.4	78.8
Czech Republic	8.3	9.3	7.2	73.9	70.2	77.8
Denmark	4.8	5.5	4.0	77.4	73.9	81.1
Finland	4.9	4.6	5.1	75.6	74.0	77.3
France	6.0	6.9	5.1	78.6	74.7	82.6
Germany	5.9	6.5	5.2	76.1	73.0	79.4
Greece	7.2	7.7	6.7	78.3	75.8	81.0

Country	Infant deaths per 1,000 live births			Life expectancy at birth (years)		
	Both sexes	Male	Female	Both sexes	Male	Female
Hungary	12.2	13.7	10.6	69.2	64.4	74.2
Ireland	6.3	7.0	5.6	75.7	73.1	78.6
Italy	6.8	7.5	6.1	78.2	75.0	81.6
Netherlands	4.8	5.4	4.3	77.9	75.1	80.8
Norway	4.9	5.5	4.2	77.7	74.8	80.7
Poland	12.3	13.7	10.8	72.2	68.1	76.6
Portugal	7.5	8.2	6.7	75.5	71.8	79.5
Russia	24.3	26.5	21.9	63.8	57.2	70.7
Slovakia	10.6	12.2	8.9	73.1	69.1	77.3
Spain	6.1	6.8	5.5	78.5	75.2	82.0
Sweden	4.5	4.9	4.1	78.2	75.7	80.7
Switzerland	5.4	6.0	4.8	77.8	74.7	80.9
United Kingdom	6.3	7.0	5.6	76.6	74.0	79.3
Asia						
Bangladesh	100.0	107.8	91.9	56.3	56.4	56.2
China	37.9	30.3	46.2	70.0	68.6	71.5
India	69.2	69.2	69.2	60.2	59.5	60.8
Iran	50.8	51.6	50.0	67.8	66.5	69.2
Israel	8.3	8.9	7.6	78.2	76.3	80.2
Japan	4.4	4.8	3.9	79.7	76.7	82.8
South Korea	8.0	8.3	7.7	73.6	70.0	77.7
Pakistan	95.1	96.6	93.6	58.8	58.0	59.6
Sri Lanka	20.3	22.1	18.4	72.6	70.0	75.3
Syria	38.8	39.8	37.7	67.4	66.2	68.7
Africa						
Egypt	71.0	72.9	69.0	61.8	59.8	63.8
Kenya	55.2	58.1	52.1	54.4	54.2	54.6
South Africa	53.2	57.9	48.3	56.3	54.4	58.2
Oceania						
Australia	5.4	6.0	4.8	79.6	76.7	82.7
New Zealand	6.5	7.6	5.4	77.3	74.2	80.6

Source: U.S. Bureau of the Census, International Data Base.

Legal Abortions in Selected Countries, 1985–1994

Country	1985	1987	1988	1989	1990	1991	1992	1993	1994
Bulgaria	132,041	133,815	—	132,021	144,644	—	132,891	107,416	—
Canada	60,956	63,585	—	70,705	71,092	70,277	59,694	—	—
Cuba	138,671	152,704	155,325	151,146	147,530	124,059	—	—	—
Denmark	19,919	20,830	21,199	21,456	20,589	19,729	18,833	18,607	17,598
Finland	13,832	13,000[1]	12,995	12,658	12,232	—	—	—	10,013
France	173,335	161,036	163,000	165,199	161,646	162,902	—	—	—
Germany[1]	—	—	—	—	—	124,377	118,609	111,236	103,586
Greece	180	—	—	—	—	11,109	11,977	—	—
Hungary	81,970	84,547	87,106	90,508	90,394	89,931	87,065	75,258	74,491
Iceland	705	691	673	670	714	658	743	—	—
India	583,704	—	534,870	582,161	596,345	581,215	—	—	—
Israel	18,406	15,290	16,181	15,216	18,000	15,767	18,444	17,164	—
Italy	210,192	187,618	175,541	166,290	161,285	157,173	149,824	144,761	124,334
Japan	550,127	497,756	486,146	466,876	456,797	436,299	413,032	386,807	364,350
Netherlands	17,300	17,760	18,014	17,996	18,384	19,568	19,422	19,804	20,811
New Zealand	7,130	8,789	10,000	10,200	—	11,594	11,460	—	—
Norway	14,599	15,422	15,852	16,208	15,551	15,528	15,164	14,909	—
Poland	135,564	122,536	105,333	80,127	59,417	30,878	11,640	1,208	874
Russia	—	4,385,627	4,608,953	4,427,713	4,103,425	3,608,412	3,436,695	3,243,957	2,481,493
Singapore	23,512	21,226	20,135	20,619	18,654	17,798	17,073	16,476	15,690
Sweden	30,838	34,707	37,585	37,920	37,489	35,788	34,849	34,169	32,293
United Kingdom	180,983	165,542	178,426	180,622	184,092	178,416	171,260	173,686	169,964
United States	1,588,600	1,353,671	1,371,285	1,396,658	1,429,577	1,388,937	—	—	—

1. Figures for Germany represent those available after the unification of the Federal Republic of Germany and the German Democratic Republic in October 1990. NOTE: Data latest available. *Source:* United Nations, *Demographic Yearbook, 1995.*

Prevalence of Contraceptive Use by Region

Region	Year(s)	No method	All methods	Pill	IUD	Condom	Sterilization Total	Sterilization Male	Sterilization Female	Other modern	Traditional
Asia	1972–1994	47.7%	52.3%	8.7%	7.3%	5.4%	18.6%	3.3%	16.1%	4.%	9.1%
Commonwealth of Independent States	1990	71.0%	29.%	5.4%	31.1%	4.8%	0.8%	n.a.	n.a.	6.2%	13.3%
Eastern Europe	1976–1993	39.8%	60.2%	12.8%	11.1%	9.4%	2.1%	0.5%	2.3%	1.6%	37.4%
Latin America and the Caribbean	1975–1994	47.4%	52.6%	15.%	6.3%	5.1%	16.8%	0.7%	16.%	4.3%	7.2%
North Africa	1988–1992	52.7%	47.3%	22.2%	12.6%	1.2%	1.1%	0.%	4.2%	0.8%	6.4%
North America	1984–1988	26.3%	73.7%	13.1%	3.7%	9.3%	39.9%	12.9%	27.%	3.6%	4.5%
Near East	1971–1993	66.1%	34.%	9.4%	7.%	2.9%	2.9%	0.2%	3.2%	0.5%	11.7%
Oceania	1976–1986	68.7%	31.3%	15.9%	6.%	7.2%	21.2%	6.5%	15.3%	1.4%	10.4%
Sub-Saharan Africa	1982–1994	79.9%	20.1%	5.9%	1.7%	1.1%	2.7%	0.2%	1.9%	2.9%	7.0%
Western Europe	1973–1993	27.1%	72.9%	29.2%	11.0%	12.4%	8.2%	3.6%	5.8%	1.8%	12.5%

NOTE: n.a. = not available. Source: U.S. Bureau of the Census, International Data Base.

Cost of Living of United Nations Personnel

in selected cities as reflected by index of retail prices

(New York City, December 1996 = 100)

Country or Area	Index	Country or Area	Index	Country or Area	Index
Afghanistan, Kabul	66	Egypt, Cairo	91	Netherlands, The Hague	104
Algeria, Algiers	90	El Salvador, San Salvador	83	Nicaragua, Managua	86
Argentina, Buenos Aires	104	Estonia, Tallinn	82	Nigeria, Lagos	88[1]
Australia, Sydney	91	Ethiopia, Addis Ababa	96[1]	Pakistan, Islamabad	75
Austria, Vienna	109	Finland, Helsinki	104	Panama, Panama City	87
Bahamas, Nassau	110	France, Paris	110	Peru, Lima	92
Bangladesh, Dhaka	86	Germany, Bonn	116[1]	Philippines, Manila	101
Belarus, Minsk	88	Greece, Athens	91	Romania, Bucharest	88[1]
Belgium, Brussels	111	Guatemala, Guatemala City	84	Russia, Moscow	103
Bolivia, La Paz	80	Haiti, Port-Au-Prince	88	Senegal, Dakar	90
Bulgaria, Sofia	83	Hong Kong, Hong Kong	192	Spain, Madrid	100
Burma (Myanmar), Rangoon (Yangon)	113	Hungary, Budapest	86	Switzerland, Geneva	118
Canada, Montreal	83	India, New Delhi	89	Thailand, Bangkok	87
Chile, Santiago	96	Italy, Rome	97	Tunisia, Tunis	89
China, Beijing	99[1]	Jamaica, Kingstown	105	Turkey, Ankara	89
Colombia, Bogota	106	Japan, Tokyo	155	Ukraine, Kiev	89
Congo, Brazzaville	102[1]	Kenya, Nairobi	83	United Arab Emirates, Abu Dhabi	93
Cuba, Havana	81[1]	South Korea, Seoul	117		
Czech Republic, Prague	93	Lebanon, Beirut	103	United Kingdom, London	109
Denmark, Copenhagen	110	Malta, Valetta	88	United States, Washington, D.C.	86
Dominican Rep., Santo Domingo	96	Mexico, Mexico City	78	Uruguay, Montevideo	115
Ecuador, Quito	85	Morocco, Rabat	91	Venezuela, Caracas	85
		Nepal, Kathmandu	81		

1. Calculated on the basis of cost of government or subsidized housing, which is normally lower than prevailing rentals.
Source: United Nations, *Monthly Bulletin of Statistics, March 1997.*

Consumer Price Indexes for All Items for Selected Countries, 1996

(1990 = 100)

Country	Index	Country	Index	Country	Index
Australia	116.1	Hong Kong	164.9	Russia[1]	286,721.0
Austria	119.4	Indonesia	169.6	Singapore	115.1
Canada	113.5	Italy	132.6	Slovakia[1]	175.7
Chile	205.2	Japan	107.1	South Africa	183.2
Czech Republic[1]	173.6	Jordan	131.2	Spain	133.2
Denmark	112.6	South Korea	141.8	Sri Lanka	189.0
Egypt	204.0	Mexico[2]	181.4	Sweden	123.3
Finland	112.7	Morocco[1]	138.0	Turkey	3,172.9
France	113.8	Netherlands	116.8	United Kingdom	121.1
Germany[1]	116.5	Norway	113.9	United States	120.1
Greece	207.0	Philippines	177.8	Uruguay	1,385.4

1. Base: 1991 = 100. 2. Base: 1994 = 100. *Source:* International Labour Office from *Monthly Bulletin of Statistics, June 1997.*

Exchange Rates For Selected Currencies, 1980–1995

Country	currency	1980	1985	1990	1995
Australia[1]	dollar	114.00	70.03	78.07	74.07
Austria	schilling	12.95	20.68	11.33	10.08
Belgium	franc	29.24	59.34	33.42	29.47
Canada	dollar	1.17	1.37	1.17	1.37
Denmark	krone	5.63	10.60	6.19	5.60
France	franc	4.23	8.98	5.45	4.99
Germany	deutschemark	1.82	2.94	1.62	1.43
Greece	drachma	42.62	138.40	158.59	231.68
Hong Kong	dollar	4.98	7.79	7.79	7.74
India	rupee	7.89	12.33	17.49	32.42
Ireland[1]	pound	205.77	106.62	165.76	160.35
Italy	lira	856.20	1,908.90	1,198.27	1,629.45
Japan	yen	226.63	238.47	145.00	93.96
South Korea	won	607.43	861.89	710.64	772.82
Malaysia	ringgit	2.18	2.48	2.71	2.51
Netherlands	guilder	1.99	3.32	1.82	1.60
New Zealand[1]	dollar	97.34	49.75	59.62	65.62
Norway	krone	4.94	8.59	6.25	6.34
Portugal	escudo	50.08	172.07	142.70	149.88
Singapore	dollar	2.14	2.20	1.81	1.42
South Africa	rand	0.78	2.23	2.59	3.63
Spain	peseta	71.76	169.98	101.96	124.64
Sweden	krone	4.23	8.60	5.92	7.14
Switzerland	franc	1.68	2.46	1.39	1.18
Taiwan	dollar	36.02	39.89	26.92	26.50
Thailand	baht	20.48	27.19	25.61	24.92
United Kingdom[1]	pound	234.43	129.74	178.41	157.85

National currency units per dollar, except as noted. Data are averages of certified noon buying rates for cable transfers. 1. Value is U.S. cents per unit of foreign currency. Source: *Statistcal Abstract of the United States, 1996,* based on data from the Board of Governors of the Federal Reserve System, *Federal Reserve Bulletin,* monthly.

Ratio of Civilian Employment to Population

Country	Females[1]				Males[1]				Females as percent of total labor force			
	1980	1985	1990	1994	1980	1985	1990	1994	1980	1985	1990	1994
Australia	41.9	42.9	49.3	48.6	75.1	70.4	71.2	67.0	36.4	38.4	41.5	42.6
Canada	46.2	48.8	54.0	51.9	73.0	68.7	70.1	65.4	39.7	42.7	44.4	45.2
France	40.3	39.6	41.5	40.6[3]	68.6	62.3	61.3	58.1[3]	39.5	41.4	43.0	43.7
Germany[4]	38.9	37.1	40.9	41.2[3]	69.9	66.4	65.6	60.0[3]	39.2	39.0	41.0	42.8[3]
Italy	27.9	27.8	29.2	28.3[3]	66.0	62.5	60.0	57.2[3]	31.7	32.8	34.7	35.1[3]
Japan	45.7	46.3	48.0	48.0	77.9	75.9	75.4	75.4	38.4	39.4	40.3	40.3
Netherlands	31.0	33.4	n.a.	n.a.	74.1	67.6	n.a.	n.a.	30.2	34.0	n.a.	n.a.
Sweden	58.0	59.7	61.8	54.5[3]	73.6	70.5	70.6	61.1[3]	45.2	47.2	47.8	48.4
United Kingdom	44.8	44.3	49.6	49.0[3]	72.8	67.1	69.7	64.7[3]	40.4	42.0	43.5	45.0[3]
United States	47.7	n.a.	54.3	55.3[3]	72.0	n.a.	72.0	70.4[2]	42.4	n.a.	45.2	46.0[2]

1. Civilian employment as a percent of the civilian working age population. 2. Break in series. Data not comparable with prior years. 3. Preliminary. 4. Prior to 1991, data are for the former West Germany. NOTE: n.a. = not available. Data are most recent available. *Source:* U.S. Bureau of Labor Statistics; *Comparative Labor Force Statistics for Ten Countries, 1959–1995, June 1996.* From *Statistical Abstract of the United States 1996.*

Unemployment Figures for Selected Countries: 1990–1996

(in thousands except for percentages)

Country	1996		1995		1994		1993		1992		1990	
	No.	%	No.	%	No.	%	No.	%	No.	%	No.	%
Australia	782.6	8.6	766.3	8.5	855.5	9.7	939.2	10.9	933.1	10.8	587.1	6.9
Austria[1]	230.5	7.0	215.7	6.6	214.9	6.5	222.3	6.8	193.1	5.9	165.8	5.4
Barbados	21.4	15.5	26.9	19.7	29.4	21.7	31.0	24.7	28.8	23.0	18.6	15.0
Belgium[1]	586.6	13.7	596.9	14.1	588.7	13.9	549.7	13.1	472.9	11.2	402.8	9.8
Canada	n.a.	n.a.	1,422.0	9.6	1,458.0	10.3	1,562.0	11.2	1,556.0	11.3	1,109.0	8.1
Chile[2]	3,020.0	5.4	248.1	4.7	311.3	5.9	223.6	4.5	n.a.	n.a.	281.3	5.6
Denmark[1]	242.0	8.6	284.7	10.1	340.4	12.1	348.8	12.4	314.7	11.3	269.1	9.6

Country	1996		1995		1994		1993		1992		1990	
	No.	%	No.	%	No.	%	No.	%	No.	%	No.	%
Finland	408.0	16.3	429.6	17.2	456.0	18.4	444.0	17.9	328.0	13.1	88.0	3.4
France	3,063.0	n.a.	2,976.2	n.a.	3,329.2	n.a.	3,172.0	10.8	2,911.2	10.0	2,504.7	9.0
Germany[1, 3]	3,980.6	11.5	3,611.9	10.4	2,556.0	9.2	2,270.9	8.2	1,820.6	6.7	1,872.0	7.2
Hong Kong	86.1	2.8	n.a.	n.a.	57.2	1.9	56.9	2.0	54.7	2.0	37.0	1.3
Ireland[4]	279.2	n.a.	276.9	14.1	282.4	n.a.	294.0	n.a.	283.1	n.a.	224.7	17.4
Israel	144.0	6.7	132.3	6.3	158.5	7.8	194.9	10.0	207.5	11.2	157.9	9.6
Italy	2,763.0	12.1	n.a.	n.a.	2,561.0	11.3	2335.0	10.2	2,799.0	11.5	2,621.0	11.0
Japan	2,250.0	3.4	2,098.3	3.1	1,920.0	2.9	1,655.8	2.5	1,420.8	2.1	1,340.0	2.1
South Korea	424.7	2.0	419.0	2.0	488.8	2.4	551.1	2.8	463.4	2.4	451.0	2.5
Netherlands[1]	n.a.	n.a.	462.0	n.a.	486.0	7.6	415.0	6.5	303.0	4.2	346.0	4.9
New Zealand[1]	109.9	6.1	109.5	6.3	138.4	8.2	212.7	n.a.	216.9	n.a.	164.0	7.7
Norway	109.0	4.9	107.0	4.9	116.5	5.4	127.0	6.0	126.0	5.9	112.0	4.3
Portugal	332.3	7.3	325.4	7.2	312.2	6.8	248.3	5.6	186.9	4.1	220.1	4.7
Russia	2,558.0	9.1	2,032.0	8.3	1,286.0	7.0	728	5.3	n.a.	n.a.	n.a.	n.a.
Sweden	346.4	8.0	332.4	7.7	340.0	8.0	326.1	8.7	214.0	4.8	69.0	1.6
Switzerland[1]	168.6	4.7	153.3	4.2	171.0	4.7	163.1	4.5	92.3	n.a.	18.1	0.6
Turkey[1]	n.a.	n.a.	n.a.	n.a.	n.a.	n.a.	682.6	n.a.	840.1	n.a.	979.5	n.a.
United Kingdom[1, 5]	2,122.2	7.6	2,325.6	8.3	2,636.5	9.4	2,919.2	10.4	2,778.6	9.8	1,664.5	5.9
United States	7,236.0	5.4	7,404.0	5.6	7,996.0	6.1	8,734.0	6.8	9,384.0	7.4	6,874.0	5.5

1. Employment office statistics. All others labor force sample surveys unless otherwise indicated. 2. Average of less than 12 months. 3. Data prior to October 3, 1990, are for West Germany. 4. Excluding agriculture, fishing and private domestic services. 5. Excluding persons temporarily laid off. Excluding adult students registered for vacation employment. NOTE: n.a.= not available. *Source:* United Nations, *Monthly Bulletin of Statistics, July 1997.*

Employment for Selected Countries (Non-Agricultural), 1988–1996

(in thousands)

Country	1996	1995	1994	1993	1992	1991	1990	1988
Australia[1, 2, 3]	n.a.	7,806.0	7,483.2	7,238.5	7,201.1	7,248.2	7,399.8	6,907.3
Canada[3, 4]	13,087.3	12,951.6	12,746.0	12,457.0	12,299.0	12,344.0	12,614.0	11,804.0
Chile[3]	4,482.3	4,236.6	4,179.4	4,160.4	3,913.2	3,674.2	3,574.6	3,401.2
Finland[3]	1,948.0	1,910.0	1,857.0	1,867.0	1,987.0	2,154.0	2,260.0	2,193.0
Germany[4]	n.a.	—	27,113.0	27,409.0	27,785.0	27,557.0	26,998.0	25,740.0
Hungary[5]	2,383.8	2,567.7	2,704.8	2,614.0	1,585.7	1,916.1	2,249.9	2,614.9
Israel	1,961.8	1,968.6	1,890.4	1,754.5	1,661.5	1,551.8	1,415.5	1,259.3
Italy[3]	n.a.	—	18,546.0	18,919.0	19,710.0	19,769.0	19,409.0	19,045.0
Japan[3, 4]	61,296.7	60,893.3	60,797.5	60,663.3	60,250.0	59,410.0	57,990.0	55,360.0
Korea, South[4]	18,358.6	17,836.4	17,138.0	16,425.0	15,970.0	15,548.0	14,848.0	13,386.0
New Caledonia	49.8	48.8	48.3	47.2	46.4	45.9	44.4	38.0
New Zealand[6]	1,528.0	1,474.3	1,397.8	1,338.1	1,307.5	1,294.6	1,315.9	1,346.7
Norway[3,7]	n.a.	1,973.0	1,928.0	1,893.0	1,894.0	1,894.0	1,901.0	1,980.0
Poland	8,359.0	8,387.0	8,290.0	8,272.5	8,465.0	9,064.0	9,669.0	10,715.0
Portugal[3]	3,732.4	3,747.6	3,761.3	3,772.9	3,850.6	3,831.8	3,700.7	3,413.8
Spain[3]	11,319.7	10,935.8	10,579.2	—	10,933.5	11,264.3	11,093.3	10,078.4
Sweden[3, 4]	3,848.0	3,862.5	3,791.0	3,827.3	4,113.0	4,226.0	4,296.0	4,231.0
Switzerland	3,434.0	3,452.0	3,465.0	3,525.0	3,636.8	104.7	106.4	103.7
United States[3, 4, 8]	123,264.0	121,460.0	119,651.0[8]	116,232.0	114,391.0	113,644.0	114,728.0	111,800.0
U.S. Virgin Islands			44.6	48.6	44.8	43.8	43.1	41.5

1. Annual averages: one month of each year. 2. Excluding armed forces. 3. Persons aged 15 years and over (except Finland: 15–74; Italy: 14; Norway and Sweden: 16–74; Spain and U.S.A.: 16; Portugal: 12). 4. Civilian labor force. 5. Socialized sector. 6. Annual averages: average of less than 12 months. 7. Revised scope. 8. Including forestry and fishing. *Source:* United Nations, *Monthly Bulletin of Statistics, July 1997.*

Energy Produced and Consumed, by Country

Country	Energy consumed[1] (coal equiv.) Total (mil. metric tons)		Per capita (kilograms)		Electric energy production[2] (bil. kwh)		Crude petroleum production[3] (mil. metric tons)		Coal production[4] (mil. metric tons)	
	1994	1990	1994	1990	1994	1990	1994	1990	1994	1990
Algeria	43	40	1,583	1,586	20	16	35	37	(Z)[6]	(Z)[6]
Argentina	74	61	2,150	1,895	66	51	34	25	(Z)	(Z)
Australia	136	127	7,614	7,442	167	155	20	25	176	159
Austria	33	32	4,162	4,128	53	50	1	1	—	—
Bahrain	10	8	17,745	16,231	5	3	2	2	n.a.	n.a.
Bangladesh[7]	11	8	94	75	10	8	(Z)	(Z)[6]	n.a.	n.a.
Belgium	69	67	6,861	6,686	72	71	(X)	(X)	n.a.	1[8]
Brazil	135	117	850	785	261	223	33	32	5	5
Bulgaria	29	37	3,257	4,170	38	42	(Z)	(Z)	(Z)	(Z)[6]
Burma (Myanmar)[9]	15	2	4,263	59	n.a.	3	1	1[6]	(Z)	(Z)[6]
Canada	327	292	11,209	10,957	554	482	86	76	37	38
Chile	n.a.	17	n.a.	1.328	n.a.	18	1	1	1	2
China	1,093	893	920	788	928	621	146	138	1,240	1,080[10]
Colombia	34	27	995	821	43	35	23	22	23	20
Cuba	n.a.	15	n.a.	1,391	n.a.	15	1	1[6]	(X)	(X)
Czechoslovakia	n.a.	96	n.a.	6,149	n.a.	87	n.a.	(Z)	n.a.	22[6,8]
Denmark	27	24	5,151	4,642	41	26	9	6	(X)	(X)
Ecuador	9	8	772	728	8	6	17	15	(X)	(X)
Egypt	41	37	658	697	48	39	45	44	(X)	(X)
Ethiopia	2	1	29	30	1	1	(X)	(X)	n.a.	n.a.
Finland	38	34	7,401	6,877	66[5]	54[5]	n.a.	4	(X)	(X)
France[4]	298	295	5,151	5,191	476[5]	420[5]	3	(Z)	8	10[8]
Germany[12]	445	383	5,475	6,241	528	452	3	4[13]	58	77[6]
Greece	34	31	3,224	3,085	41	35	1	1[13]	(X)	(X)
Hong Kong	14	10	2,358	1,769	27	29	n.a.	n.a.	(X)	(X)
Hungary[9]	n.a.	39	n.a.	3,670	n.a.	28	2	2	1	2[6]
India[9]	344	269	374	318	384	289	31	33	255	202
Indonesia	90	58	465	312	61	44	74	72	29	7
Iran[14]	124	93	1,879	1,596	79	51	179	159	Z[6]	1[6]
Iraq	35	16	1,761	887	27	29	37	101	n.a.	n.a.
Ireland	15	13	4,306	3,755	17	15	(X)	(X)	(Z)	(Z)
Israel	18	15	3,261	3,149	28	21	(Z)	(Z)	(X)	(X)
Italy[15]	226	224	3,949	3,878	232	217	5	5	—	(Z)
Japan	621	564	4,978	4,567	964	857	1	1	7	8
North Korea	99	94	4,208	4,322	37	54	(X)	(X)	72[6]	68[6]
South Korea	168	119	3,772	2,743	186	119	(X)	(X)	7	17
Kuwait[16]	16	15	9,846	6,895	23	19	101	60	n.a.	n.a.
Libya	n.a.	16	n.a.	3,508	n.a.	17	67	67	(X)	(X)
Malaysia	45	27	2,291	1,490	40	23	31	30	(Z)	(Z)
Mexico	187	157	2,031	1,863	144[5]	122[5]	140	132	9	7[6]
Morocco	n.a.	9	n.a.	378	n.a.	10	(Z)	(Z)	1	1
Netherlands	111	109	7,217	7,286	80	1	(X)	(X)	—	—
New Zealand[17]	19	18	5,466	5,411	32	30	2	2	3	2
Nigeria	23	23	209	212	15	12	91	86	(Z)[6]	(Z)[6]
Norway[18]	32	29	7,441	6,803	113	122	125	80	(Z)	(Z)
Pakistan[7]	45	34	332	292	57	44	3	3	4	3
Peru	11	11	456	495	15	14	6	7	(Z)	(Z)[6]
Philippines	28	25	426	398	26	26	(Z)	(Z)	2[6]	1
Poland	134	137	3,507	3,590	135	136	(Z)	(Z)	134[6]	148[6]
Portugal	21	19	2,134	1,947	31	29	(X)	(X)	(Z)	(Z)
Romania	58	80	2,544	3,445	55	64	7	8	1[6]	4[6]
Saudi Arabia[16]	n.a.	87	n.a.	5,859	n.a.	47	401	320	n.a.	n.a.
South Africa[19]	n.a.	112	n.a.	2,608	184	167	(X)	(X)	184	176
Soviet Union (former)	(X)	1,919	n.a.	6,631	n.a.	1,764	n.a.	553	n.a.	474
Spain	119	115	3013	2,961	162	152	1	1	14	15[8]
Sudan	2	2	60	64	1	1	(X)	(X)	n.a.	n.a.
Sweden	59	57	6,794	6,707	143	146	(Z)	(Z)	—	(Z)
Switzerland[20]	32	32	4,499	4,765	66[6]	56	(X)	(X)	(X)	(X)
Syria	18	15	1,278	1,227	15	11	29	23	n.a.	n.a.
Taiwan[21]	87	67	4,139	3,285	126	90	(Z)	(Z)	(Z)	(Z)
Tanzania	n.a.	1	n.a.	39	1	1	(X)	(X)	(Z)[6]	(Z)[6]

Country	Energy consumed[1] (coal equiv.)				Electric energy production[2] (bil. kwh)		Crude petroleum production[3] (mil. metric tons)		Coal production[4] (mil. metric tons)	
	Total (mil. metric tons)		Per capita (kilograms)							
	1994	1990	1994	1990	1994	1990	1994	1990	1994	1990
Thailand	62	42	1,073	765	74	46	1	1	(Z)	—
Trinidad and Tobago	10	10	7,530	7,946	4	4	7	8	n.a.	n.a.
Tunisia	7	6	750	791	6	6	4	5	(Z)	(X)
Turkey	70	59	1,156	1,052	78	58	4	4	3	3
United Arab Emirates	39	35	21,025	21,980	19	17	104	102	n.a.	n.a.
United Kingdom	311	307	5,333	5,335	325	319	119	88	48	94[8]
United States	2,969	2,687	11,391	10,749	3,268[5]	3,012[5]	336	371	858	854
Venezuela	80	65	3,746	3,352	73	60	143	112	5	2
Vietnam	12	9	158	137	12	9	(Z)	3	6[6]	5
Zambia	2	2	187	209	8	8	(X)	(X)	(Z)[6]	(Z)
World, total	**11,258**	**10,826**	**1,993**	**2,004**	**12,681**	**11,774**	**3,032**	**3,003**	**3,580**	**3,517**

—Represents or rounds to zero. n.a. = not available. X = Not applicable. Z = Less than 50,000 metric tons. 1. Based on apparent consumption of coal, lignite, petroleum products, natural gas, and hydro, nuclear, and geothermal electricity. 2. Comprises production by utilities generating primarily for public use, and production by industrial establishments generating primarily for own use. Relates to production at generating centers, including station use and transmission losses. 3. Includes shale oil, but excludes natural gasoline. 4. Excludes lignite and brown coal, except as noted. 5. Net production, i.e., excluding station use. 6. Provisional. 7. For year ending June of year shown. 8. Includes recovered slurries. 9. For year ending April of year shown. 10. Includes lignite. 11. Includes Monaco. 12. Prior to 1991, data for former West Germany. 13. Includes inputs other than crude petroleum and natural gas liquids. 14. For year ending March 20 of year shown. 15. Includes San Marino. 16. Includes share of production and consumption in the Neutral Zone. 17. For the year ending March 31 for year shown. 18. Includes Svalbard and Jan Mayen Islands. 19. Includes Botswana, Lesotho, Namibia, and Swaziland. 20. Includes Liechtenstein. 21. Source: U.S. Bureau of Census. Data from Republic of China publications. *Source:* Except as noted, Statistical Office of the United Nations, New York, N.Y. *Energy Statistics Yearbook* annual (copyright). From: *Statistical Abstract of the United States, 1996.* NOTE: Data are most recent available.

Wheat, Rice, and Corn Production for Selected Countries, 1990–1994

Country	Wheat			Rice			Corn		
	1990	1993	1994	1990	1993	1994	1990	1993	1994
Argentina	10,992	9,604	10,680	428	593	606	5,047	10,901	10,246
Australia	15,066	16,877	8,803	846	858	1,017	219	199	256
Bangladesh	890	1,176	1,131	26,778	26,925	27,537	3	3	3
Brazil	3,094	2,153	2,276	7,421	10,143	10,582	21,348	30,004	32,305
Burma (Myanmar)	124	139	109	13,969	16,760	19,057	187	205	271
Canada	32,098	27,232	23,350	n.a.	n.a.	n.a.	7,066	6,501	7,043
China	98,232	106,395	101,205	191,589	179,975	178,251	97,158	103,046	103,550
Egypt	4,268	4,833	4,437	3,167	4,161	4,582	4,799	5,039	4,883
France	33,346	29,252	30,652	121	128	124	9,401	14,843	13,040
Germany	15,242	15,767	16,429	n.a.	n.a.	n.a.	1,552	2,656	2,357
Hungary	6,198	3,021	4,900	39	13	14	4,500	4,044	4,920
India	49,850	56,762	59,131	111,517	117,052	118,400	8,962	9,653	10,500
Indonesia	n.a.	n.a.	n.a.	45,179	48,181	46,245	6,734	6,460	6,617
Iran	8,012	10,732	11,500	1,981	2,281	2,700	130	210	210
Italy	8,109	8,126	7,805	1,291	1,286	1,324	5,864	8,029	7,661
Japan	952	638	565	13,124	9,793	14,976	1	1	—
Kazakstan	16,197	11,585	9,052	579	403	283	442	355	233
South Korea	1	1	2	7,722	6,597	7,056	120	82	75
Mexico	3,931	3,582	3,589	394	388	375	14,635	18,648	19,193
Nigeria	50	30	30	2,500	3,759	3,857	1,832	2,300	2,000
Pakistan	14,316	16,157	15,114	4,891	5,992	5,269	1,185	1,215	1,288
Philippines	—	—	—	9,885	9,534	10,150	4,854	4,798	5,400
Romania	7,289	5,314	5,991	67	36	14	6,810	7,987	9,300
Russia	49,596	43,500	32,094	896	688	522	2,451	2,441	879
South Africa	1,730	1,984	1,850	3	3	3	8,709	9,663	11,811
Thailand	—	1	1	17,193	19,917	18,447	3,722	3,328	3,800
Turkey	20,022	21,016	17,500	230	225	200	2,100	2,500	1,850
Ukraine	30,374	21,831	13,857	118	68	79	4,737	3,786	1,539
United Kingdom	14,033	12,900	13,100	n.a.	n.a.	n.a.	—	—	—
United States	74,473	65,210	63,141	7,080	7,081	8,972	201,534	160,954	256,629
Total	**592,589**	**564,065**	**527,982**	**519,407**	**527,150**	**534,701**	**477,090**	**470,354**	**569,557**

In thousands of metric tons. NOTES: Data pertain to the calendar year in which all or most of the crop was harvested. — Represents or rounds to zero. n.a. = not available. *Source:* Food and Agriculture Organization of the United Nations, Rome, Italy, FAO AGRISTAT database. From *Statistical Abstract of the United States 1996.* NOTE: Data are most recent available.

Wheat, Rice and Corn Exports and Imports, 1990–1994

	Exports				Imports		
Leading Exporters	1990	1993	1994	**Leading Importers**	1990	1993	1994
Wheat				**Wheat**			
United States	28,749	37,141	32,110	China	13,487	7,368	8,120
France	19,337	20,954	15,033	Japan	5,474	5,814	6,353
Canada	18,166	18,415	21,683	Russia	n.a.	5,774	2,285
Australia	11,629	9,582	12,823	Brazil	1,962	5,671	6,322
Argentina	6,041	6,019	5,572	Italy	4,705	5,066	4,904
Germany	2,829	4,640	6,148	Egypt	6,439	5,038	7,125
United Kingdom	4,561	4,014	3,616	South Korea	2,516	4,939	6,057
Italy	1,777	1,902	1,823	Algeria	3,604	4,244	5,585
Belgium-Luxembourg	1,367	1,797	1,888	Uzbekistan	n.a.	4,100	—
Saudi Arabia	1,267	1,569	895	Pakistan	2,047	2,890	1,902
Rice				**Rice**			
Thailand	4,017	4,989	4,859	Iran	620	1,159	475
United States	2,474	2,680	2,822	Brazil	414	701	987
Vietnam	1,624	1,765	1,970	Iraq	380	655	200
China	405	1,507	1,630	Saudi Arabia	280	577	434
Pakistan	744	1,032	984	Malaysia	330	389	341
India	505	768	891	South Africa	306	385	431
Italy	577	574	619	Hong Kong	374	373	358
Uruguay	290	505	408	Cuba	235	370	255
Australia	424	482	585	United Arab Emirates	309	370	350
Indonesia	2	351	169	Senegal	392	363	348
Corn				**Corn**			
United States	52,172	40,365	35,877	Japan	16,008	16,863	15,930
China	3,405	11,098	8,740	South Korea	6,158	6,207	5,749
France	7,195	7,758	8,013	China	5,440	5,466	5,601
Argentina	2,998	4,871	4,154	Russia	n.a.	4,391	901
Belgium-Luxembourg	20	414	489	Spain	1,810	2,401	2,339
Canada	122	357	381	Egypt	1,900	2,148	2,021
Germany	226	219	308	Malaysia	1,480	2,058	1,969
South Africa	2,001	216	4,000	United Kingdom	1,627	1,508	1,602
Zimbabwe	742	216	150	Brazil	699	1,323	1,409
Italy	80	213	16	Belgium-Luxembourg	1,035	1,284	1,557

In thousands of metric tons. Countries listed are the 10 leading exporters or importers in 1993. — Represents or rounds to zero. n.a. = not available. *Source:* Food and Agriculture Organization of the United Nations, Rome, Italy, FAO AGRISTAT database. From *Statistical Abstract of the United States 1996*. NOTE: Data are most recent available.

Meat Production by Country

Country	1994	1993	1990	1980
Argentina	3,557	3,617	3,383	3,622
Brazil	9,434	7,545	6,439	4,550
China	46,720	40,175	30,073	n.a.
France	6,296	6,085	5,765	5,455
Germany	5,757	5,947	7,292	6,972
India	4,083	3,992	3,723	2,675
Italy	3,997	3,936	3,950	3,564
Japan	3,303	3,378	3,503	3,046
Mexico	3,475	3,628	3,478	2,540
Russia[1]	6,871	15,566	19,996	15,072
Spain	3,816	3,701	3,466	2,648
United Kingdom	3,394	2,340	3,357	3,070
United States	32,847	31,350	28,632	24,599
World[2]	194,657	185,917	178,169	135,940

1. Prior to 1994, data are for the former U.S.S.R. 2. Includes other countries not shown separately. NOTE: Data in thousands of metric tons. Covers beef and veal (incl. buffalo meat), pork (incl. bacon and ham), mutton and lamb (incl. goat meat), horsemeat, and poultry. Refers to meat from animals slaughtered within the national boundaries irrespective of origin of animals, and relates to commercial and farm slaughter. Excludes lard, tallow, and edible offals. *Source:* Food and Agriculture Organization of the United Nations, Rome, Italy. From: *Statistical Abstract of the United States, 1996*. NOTE: Data are most recent available.

Countries of the World

Major sources: Information Please Almanac questionnaires to the individual countries, C.I.A. *World Factbook,* and Center for International Research, Bureau of the Census. (As of Sept. 15, 1997. For later reports, *see* Current Events of 1996–1997.)

Definitions: Gross domestic product (GDP): The value of all goods and services produced domestically; Gross national product (GNP): the value of all goods and services produced domestically plus income earned abroad, minus income earned by foreigners from domestic production; c.i.f.: cost, insurance, and freight; f.o.b.: free on board; inflation: based on consumer prices; literacy rates are those supplied by the individual countries or else taken from the World Fact Book.

AFGHANISTAN

Islamic State of Afghanistan
National name: Dawlat Islami Afghanistan
President: Burhanuddin Rabbani (1992)
Prime Minister: Gulbuddin Hekmatyar (1997)
Area: 250,000 sq mi. (647,500 sq km)
Population (1996 est.): 22,664,136 (average annual rate of natural increase: 2.494%); birth rate: 42.72/1000; infant mortality rate: 146.70/1000; density per square mile: 90
Capital: Kabul. **Largest cities (1993 est.):** Kabul, 1,424,400; Kandahar, 225,500; Herat, 177,300; Mazare-Sharif, 131,000. **Monetary unit:** Afghani. **Languages:** Pushtu, Dari Persian, other Turkic and minor languages. **Ethnicity/Race:** Pashtun 38%, Tajik 25%, Uzbek 6%, Hazara 19%, minor ethnic groups (Chahar Aimaks, Turkmen, Baloch, and others). **Religion:** Islam (Sunni, 84%; Shiite, 15%; other 1%). **Literacy rate:** 29%
Economic summary: Gross domestic product: purchasing power parity (1995): $12.8 billion; $600 per capita. Real growth rate n.a. Inflation n.a. Arable land 12%. Labor force: 4.98 million. Principal products: wheat, corn, barley, rice, cotton, fruit, nuts, karakul pelts, wool. Labor force in industry: 10.2%; agriculture and animal husbandry, 67.8%; construction, 6.3%; services and other, 10.7%. Unemployment rate: n.a. Major industrial products: carpets, rugs, textiles, furniture, shoes, fertilizer, cement, soap. Natural resources: natural gas, oil, coal, copper, sulfur, lead, zinc, iron, salt, precious and semi-precious stones. Exports: $188.2 million (f.o.b., 1991): fresh and dried fruits, nuts, natural gas, carpets, karakul. Imports: $616.4 million (c.i.f., 1991): petroleum products, sugar, manufactured goods, tea. Major trading partners: Europe, Central Asian republics, Japan, Singapore, Malaysia, India, and Pakistan.

Geography. Afghanistan, approximately the size of Texas, is bordered on the north by Turkmenistan, Uzbekistan, and Tajikistan, on the extreme northeast by China, on the east and south by Pakistan, and by Iran in the west. The country is split east to west by the Hindu Kush mountain range, rising in the east to heights of 24,000 feet (7,315 m). With the exception of the southwest, most of the country is covered by high snow-capped mountains and is traversed by deep valleys.

Government. With the fall of the Marxist Najibullah regime in April 1992, the victorious insurgents established a 50-member ruling council of guerrillas, religious leaders and intellectuals, who announced the creation of an Islamic republic and promised free elections. Mr. Rabbani signed a peace accord May 27, 1996, with rival Hezb-i-Islami members and formed an interim administration.

History. Darius I and Alexander the Great were the first conquerors to use Afghanistan as the gateway to India. Islamic conquerors arrived in the 7th century and Genghis Khan and Tamerlane followed in the 13th and 14th centuries.

In the 19th century, Afghanistan became a battleground in the rivalry of imperial Britain and Czarist Russia for the control of Central Asia. The Afghan Wars (1838–42 and 1878–81) fought against the British by Dost Mohammed and his son and grandson ended in defeat.

Afghanistan regained autonomy by the Anglo-Russian agreement of 1907 and full independence by the Treaty of Rawalpindi in 1919. Emir Amanullah founded the Kingdom in 1926.

After a coup in 1978, Noor Taraki's attempts to create a Marxist state with Soviet aid brought armed resistance from conservative Muslim opposition.

Taraki was eventually succeeded by Babrak Karmal, who called for Soviet troops under a mutual defense treaty.

The Soviet invasion was met with unanticipated fierce resistance from the Afghan population, resulting in a bloody war. Soviet troops had to fight Afghan tribesmen who called themselves "mujahedeen," or "holy warriors". In the early fighting, many of the guerrillas were armed only with flintlock rifles, but later they acquired more modern weapons, including rockets that they used to attack Soviet installations.

In April 1988, the U.S.S.R., U.S.A., Afghanistan, and Pakistan signed accords calling for an end to outside aid to the warring factions, in return for Soviet withdrawal by 1989. This took place in February of that year.

An agreement signed in September 1991 between the U.S.S.R. and the U.S.A. called for an end to all outside military assistance to the warring factions. By mid-April 1992 then-President Najibullah was ousted as Islamic rebels advanced on the capital. Almost immediately the various rebel groups began fighting each other for control.

The Taliban, a group of former Islamic seminarians, seized control of Kabul in September 1996. By mid-1997 their control extended to virtually the entire country, imposing fanatical Islamic rule in their wake. Adulterers, for example, are stoned to death, and women are beaten for working outside the home. The former government, however, continues to retain the Afghan seat in the U.N. General Assembly.

ALBANIA

The Republic of Albania
National name: Republika E Shqiperise
President: Rexhep Mejdani (1997)
Prime Minister: Bashkim Fino (1997)
Area: 11,100 sq mi. (28,748 sq km)
Population (1996 est.): 3,249,136 (average annual rate of natural increase: 1.41%); birth rate: 21.68/1000;

infant mortality rate: 47.1/1000; density per square mile: 292.7

Capital and largest city (1991 est.): Tiranë, 300,000. **Monetary unit:** Lek. **Language:** Albanian, Greek. **Ethnicity/Race:** Albanian 95%, Greeks 3%, other 2%: Vlachs, Gypsies, Serbs, and Bulgarians (1989 est.). Note: in 1989, other estimates of the Greek population ranged from 1% (official Albanian statistics) to 12% (from a Greek organization). **Religions (1980):** Muslim, 70%; Greek Orthodox, 20%; Roman Catholic, 10%. **Literacy rate** 75%

Economic summary: Gross domestic product: purchasing power parity (1995 est.): $4.1 billion; per capita $1,210; real growth rate (1997) 14%; inflation 17.4 (1997 est.); unemployment 19%. Arable land: 21%: Labor force: 1.692 million (1994 est.). Principal agricultural products: wheat, corn, potatoes, sugar beets, cotton, tobacco. Labor force by occupation: agriculture, 49.5%; private sector, 22.2%; state sector, 28.3%. Major products: textiles, timber, construction materials, fuels, semi-processed minerals. Exports: $141 million (f.o.b., 1994 est.): asphalt, petroleum products, metals and metallic ores, electricity, crude oil, vegetables, fruits, and tobacco. Imports: $601 million (f.o.b., 1993 est.): machinery, consumer goods, grains. Major trading partners: Italy, Macedonia, Germany, Czechoslovakia, Romania, Poland, Hungary, Bulgaria, Greece.

Geography. Albania is situated on the eastern shore of the Adriatic Sea, with former Yugoslavia to the north and east and Greece to the south. Slightly larger than Maryland, it is a mountainous country, mostly over 3,000 feet (914 m) above sea level, with a narrow, marshy coastal plain crossed by several rivers. The centers of population are contained in the interior mountain plateaus and basins.

Government. A multiparty system was installed in March 1991. Election of the President is by parliamentary majority.

History. A part of Illyria in ancient times, and later, of the Roman Empire, Albania was ruled by the Byzantine Empire from c.e. 535 to 1204. An alliance (1444–1466) of Albanian chiefs failed to halt the advance of the Turks and the country remained under at least nominal Turkish rule for more than four centuries, until it proclaimed its independence on Nov. 28, 1912.

Largely agricultural, Albania is one of the poorest countries in Europe. A battlefield in World War I, after the war it became a republic in which a conservative Moslem landlord, Ahmed Zogu, proclaimed himself president in 1925, and then proclaimed himself King Zog I in 1928. He ruled until Italy annexed Albania in 1939. Communist guerrillas under Enver Hoxha seized power in 1944, near the end of World War II. Hoxha was a devotee of Stalin, and he emulated the Soviet leader's repressive tactics, imprisoning or executing landowners and others who did not conform to the socialist ideal. Hoxha eventually broke with Soviet communism in 1961 because of differences with Khrushchev, and then aligned himself with Chinese communism, which he also abandoned in 1978 after the death of Mao. From then on Albania went its own way to forge its own version of the socialist state, and became one of the most isolated countries in the world. Hoxha was succeeded by Ramiz Alia in 1982.

The elections in March 1991 gave the Communists a decisive majority. But a general strike and street demonstrations soon forced the all-Communist cabinet to resign. In June 1991 the Communist Party of Labor renamed itself the Socialist Party and renounced its past ideology. The opposition Democratic Party won a landslide victory in 1992 elections. The ruling Democratic

Party overwhelmingly won the general election of May 1996, garnishing 101 of the 140 seats in parliament.

The collapse of shady pyramid investment schemes in early 1997 brought the country to the brink of anarchy. More than a third of the population lost their savings. A multinational force arrived in April to safeguard aid shipments. The political parties agreed to hold parliamentary elections in mid-year to help ease the explosive national mood.

ALGERIA

Democratic and Popular Republic of Algeria
National name: République Algérienne Democratique et Populaire—El Djemhouria El Djazaïria Demokratia Echaabia
President: Liamine Zeroual (1995)
Prime Minister: Ahmed Ouyahia (1995)
Area: 919,595 sq mi. (2,381,751 sq km)
Population (1996 est.): 28,183,032 (average annual rate of natural increase: 2.22%); birth rate: 28/1000; infant mortality rate: 47.1/1000; density per square mile: 31
Capital: Algiers. **Largest cities (1987):** Algiers, 1,507,241; Oran, 628,558; Constantine, 440,842; Annaba, 305,526. **Monetary unit:** Dinar. **Languages:** Arabic (official), French, Berber dialects. **Ethnicity/Race:** Arab-Berber 99%, European less than 1%. **Religion:** 99% Islam (Sunni). **Literacy rate** (1990): 57%.

Economic summary: Gross domestic product: purchasing power parity (1995 est.): $108.7 billion; $3,800 per capita; real growth rate 3.5%; inflation 28%; unemployment 25%. Arable land 3%: Labor force: 6.2 million (1992 est.). Labor force by occupation: government, 29.5%; agriculture, 22%; construction and public works, 16.2%; industry, 13.6%; commerce and services, 13.5%; transportation and communication, 5.2% (1989). Principal agricultural products: wheat, barley, oats, wine, citrus fruits, olives, livestock. Major industrial products: petroleum, gas, petrochemicals, fertilizers, iron and steel, textiles, transport equipment. Natural resources: petroleum, natural gas, iron ore, phosphates, lead, zinc, mercury, uranium. Exports: $9.5 billion (f.o.b., 1995 est.): petroleum and natural gas, 97%. Imports: $10.6 billion (f.o.b., 1995 est.): capital goods, 39.7%; food and beverages, 21.7%; consumer goods, 11.8% (1990). Major trading partners: France, Germany, Italy, Spain, U.S., Japan.

Geography. Nearly four times the size of Texas, Algeria is bordered on the west by Morocco and Western Sahara and on the east by Tunisia and Libya. To the south are Mauritania, Mali, and Niger. Low plains cover small areas near the Mediterranean coast, with 68% of the country a plateau between 2,625 and 5,250 feet (800 and 1,600 m) above sea level. The highest point is Mount Tahat in the Sahara, which rises 9,850 feet (3,000 m).

Government. Headed by a Chief of Government (official title) appointed in January 1996 after the presidential elections won by President Liamine Zeroual.

History. As ancient Numidia, Algeria became a Roman colony at the close of the Punic Wars (145 b.c.e.). Conquered by the Vandals about c.e. 440, it fell from a high state of civilization to virtual barbarism, from which it partly recovered after invasion by the Moslems about 650.

In 1492 the Moors and Jews, who had been expelled from Spain, settled in Algeria. Falling under Turkish control in 1518, Algiers served for three centuries as the headquarters of the Barbary pirates. The French took Algeria in 1830 and made it a part of France in 1848.

On July 5, 1962, Algeria was proclaimed independent. In October 1963, Ahmed Ben Bella was elected president. He began to nationalize foreign holdings and aroused opposition. He was overthrown in a military coup on June 19, 1965, by Col. Houari Boumediène, who suspended the constitution and sought to restore financial stability.

Boumediène died in December 1978 after a long illness. Chadli Bendjedid, Secretary-General of the National Liberation Front, took the presidency in a smooth transition of power.

In December 1991 in the first parliamentary elections ever held in Algeria a militant Islamic fundamentalist party won. In an apparent effort to thwart the electoral results, senior army commanders arranged the resignation of President Benjedid. The government then canceled the continuation of the electoral process. In late June President Boudiaf was assassinated.

Since January 1992 when the army cancelled a general election that the fundamentalist Islamic Salvation Front (FIS) was expected to win, the country has been caught in a bloody civil war. An estimated 60,000 civilians have been massacred since 1992 by Islamic terrorists.

Parliamentary elections in June 1997 gave the relatively new National Democratic Rally, a pro-Zeroual party, 155 seats in the 38-seat assembly. The government hoped the vote would lead to a stable democracy, although opposition parties rejected the results.

ANDORRA

Principality of Andorra
National name: Valls d'Andorra
Head of Government: Marc Forné Moiné (1995)
Area: 175 sq mi. (453 sq km)
Population (1996 est.): 72,766 (average annual growth rate: 2.96%); birth rate: 10.9/1000; infant mortality rate: 2.2/1000; density per square mile: 416
Capital and largest city (1993 est.): Andorra la Vella, 22,390. **Monetary units:** French franc and Spanish peseta. **Languages:** Catalán (official); French, Spanish. **Ethnicity/Race:** Spanish 61%, Andorran 30%, French 6%, other 3%. **Religion:** Roman Catholic. **Literacy rate** 100%
Economic summary: Gross domestic product: purchasing power parity (1993 est.): $1 billion; per capita: $16,200; real growth rate n.a.; inflation rate n.a.; unemployment rate 0%. Arable land: 2%; Labor force: n.a. Principal agricultural products: oats, barley, cattle, sheep. Major industrial products: tobacco products, electric power, tourism. Natural resources: water power, mineral water. Exports: $46.2 million (f.o.b., 1993): electricity, tobacco products, furniture. Imports: $920.2 million (1993): consumer goods, food. Major trading partners: Spain, France, and U.S.

Geography. Andorra lies high in the Pyrenees Mountains on the French-Spanish border. The country is drained by the Valira River.

Government. A parliamentary democracy (since March 1993). A new constitution, their first, was approved on March 14, 1993, which redefined Andorra as a parliamentary co-principality and sharply differentiated the three branches of government.

History. An autonomous and semi-independent co-principality, Andorra has been under the joint suzerainty of the French state and the Spanish bishops of Urgel since 1278.

In 1990 Andorra approved a customs union treaty with the E.U. permitting free movement of industrial goods between the two, but Andorra would apply the E.U.'s external tariffs to third countries. This treaty went into effect on July 1, 1991.

Andorra became a member of the U.N. in 1993 and a member of the Council of Europe in 1994.

Parliamentary elections in February 1997 gave a clear victory to Forne's Liberal Union Party, winning 16 of the 28 seats.

ANGOLA

Republic of Angola
President: José Eduardo dos Santos (1979)
Prime Minister: Fernando José de Franca Dias van Dunen (1996)
Area: 481,350 sq mi. (1,246,700 sq km)
Population (1996 est.): 10,342,899 (average annual rate of natural increase: 2.68%); birth rate: 44.1/1000; infant mortality rate: 135.7/1000; density per square mile: 21.5
Capital and largest city (1993): Luanda, 2,000,000. **Other large cities (1993 est.):** Huambo, 400,000; Lubango, 105,000. **Monetary unit:** Kwanza. **Languages:** Bantu, Portuguese (official). **Ethnicity/Race:** Ovimbundu 37%, Kimbundu 25%, Bakongo 13%, mestico (mixed European and Native African) 2%, European 1%, other 22%. **Religions:** Roman Catholic, 47%; Protestant, 38%; Indigenous, 15%. **Literacy rate:** 42%
Economic summary: Gross domestic product: purchasing power parity (1995 est.): $7.4 billion; $700 per capita; real growth rate 4%; inflation 20% (per month, 1994 est.); unemployment (1993 est.) 24%. Arable land: 2%. Labor force: 2.783 million. Labor force by occupation: agriculture, 85%; industry, 15% (1985 est.). Principal agricultural products: coffee, sisal, corn, cotton, sugar, tobacco, bananas, cassava. Major industrial products: oil, diamonds, processed fish, tobacco, textiles, cement, processed food and sugar, brewing. Natural resources: diamonds, gold, iron, oil. Exports: $3 billion (f.o.b., 1993 est.): oil, coffee, diamonds, fish and fish products, iron ore, timber, corn. Imports: $1.6 billion (f.o.b., 1992 est.): machinery and electrical equipment, bulk iron, steel and metals, textiles, clothing, food, substantial military deliveries. Major trading partners: U.S., France, Germany, Netherlands, Brazil, Portugal, Spain.

Geography. Angola, more than three times the size of California, extends for more than 1,000 miles (1,609 km) along the South Atlantic in southwestern Africa. Congo is to the north and east, Zambia to the east, and South-West Africa (Namibia) to the south. A plateau averaging 6,000 feet (1,829 m) above sea level rises abruptly from the coastal lowlands. Nearly all the land is desert or savanna, with hardwood forests in the northeast.

Government. President José Eduardo dos Santos, head of the Popular Movement for the Liberation of Angola, won a U.N.-certified election in September 1992 against the guerrilla organization UNITA led by Jonas Savimbi. A coalition government with UNITA was sworn into office in April 1997.

History. Explored by the Portuguese navigator Diego Cao in 1482, Angola became a link in trade with India and the Far East. Later it was a major source of slaves for Portugal's New World colony of Brazil. Development of the interior began after the Treaty of Berlin in 1885 fixed the colony's borders, and British and Portuguese investment pushed mining, railways, and agriculture.

Following World War II, independence movements began but were sternly suppressed by military force.

The April revolution of 1974 brought about a reversal of Portugal's policy, and the next year President Francisco da Costa Gomes signed an agreement to grant independence to Angola. The plan called for election of a constituent assembly and a settlement of differences by the MPLA and the National Front for the Liberation of Angola (FNLA) and the National Union for the Total Independence of Angola (UNITA).

The Organization of African Unity recognized the MPLA government led by Agostinho Neto on Feb. 11, 1976, and the People's Republic of Angola became the 47th member of the organization.

In March 1977 and May 1978, Zairian refugees in Angola invaded Zaire's (now the Democratic Republic of the Congo) Shaba Province, bringing charges by Zaire's President Mobutu Sese Seko that the unsuccessful invasions were Soviet-backed with Angolan help. Angola, the U.S.S.R., and Cuba denied complicity.

Neto died in Moscow of cancer on Sept. 10, 1979. The Planning Minister, José Eduardo dos Santos, was named president.

The South-West Africa People's Organization, or SWAPO, the guerrillas fighting for the independence of the disputed territory south of Angola also known as Namibia, fought from bases in Angola. The South African armed forces also maintained troops there, both to fight the SWAPO guerrillas and to assist the UNITA guerrillas against Angolan and Cuban troops.

In December 1988, Angola, Cuba, and South Africa signed agreements calling for Cuban withdrawal from Angola and South African withdrawal from Namibia by July 1991 and independence for Namibia.

Elections in late September 1992 gave the MPLA the most votes with UNITA second. A runoff was set when UNITA's Savimbi withdrew, charging the election was unfair. Fighting resumed between the government and UNITA in October.

The U.N.-negotiated accord between the government and UNITA was signed in Zambia in November 1994. After three postponements, a government of national unity took office in April 1997 with Savimbi officially taking the title of opposition leader.

ANTIGUA AND BARBUDA

Sovereign: Queen Elizabeth II (1952)
Governor-General: Sir James Beethoven Carlisle (1993)
Prime Minister: Hon. Lester Bryant Bird (1994)
Land area: 171 sq mi. (442 sq km)
Population (1996 est.): 65,647 (average annual growth rate: 1.12%); birth rate: 16.56/1000; infant mortality rate: 16.7/1000; density per square mile: 383.9
Capital and largest city (1991): St. John's, 21,514; Cordrington (capital), est. pop. 1,000. . **Monetary unit:** East Caribbean dollar. **Language:** English. **Ethnicity/Race:** black, British, Portuguese, Lebanese, Syrian. **Religions:** Anglican and Roman Catholic. **Literacy rate:** 90%
Economic summary: Gross domestic product: purchasing power parity (1994 est.): $425 million; per capita $6,600; real growth rate 4.2%; inflation rate 3.5%; unemployment rate (1995 est.) 5%–10%. Arable land: 18%. Labor force: 30,000; by occupation: industry, 7%; commerce and services, 82%; agriculture, 11%. Principal products: cotton, bananas, coconuts, cucumbers, mangoes. Major industry: tourism, which accounts for 60% of economic activity and over half of the GDP. Exports: $40.9 million (f.o.b., 1994 est.): petroleum products, manufactured goods, machinery and transport equipment. Imports: $443.8 million (f.o.b., 1994 est.): fuel, food, machinery. Major trading partners: U.K., U.S., Canada, Caribbean community and Common Market members. **Member of Commonwealth of Nations**

Geography. Antigua, the larger of the two main islands located 295 miles (420 km) south-southeast of San Juan, P.R., is low-lying except for a range of hills in the south that rise to their highest point at Boggy Peak (1,330 ft.; 405 m). As a result of its relative flatness, Antigua suffers from cyclical drought, despite a mean annual rainfall of 44 inches. Barbuda (formally known as Dulcina) is a coral island, well-wooded.

Antigua is 108 sq. miles (280 sq km), and the island dependencies of Redonda (an uninhabited rocky islet) and Barbuda are 0.5 sq miles (1.30 sq km) and 62 sq miles (161 sq km), respectively.

Government. Executive power is held by the cabinet, presided over by Prime Minister Lester B. Bird. A 17-member parliament is elected by universal suffrage. The Antigua Labour Party, led by Prime Minister Bird, holds 11 seats.

History. Antigua was explored by Christopher Columbus in 1493 and named for the Church of Santa Maria la Antigua in Seville. Colonized by Britain in 1632, it joined the West Indies Federation in 1958. With the breakup of the Federation, it became one of the West Indies Associated States in 1967, self-governing in internal affairs. Full independence was granted Nov. 1, 1981. The Bird dynasty has controlled the island since Vere C. Bird founded the Antigua Labor party in the mid-1940's. Bird, the former Prime Minister, and his sons, one of whom is the current Prime Minister, have a history of corruption that includes money laundering, arms sales, drug trafficking, and extortion.

Protests in early 1995 against new taxes yielded a government concession not to add any in the 1995 budget, but recent impositions were to remain.

A September 1995 hurricane caused major damage to the infrastructure of the country.

In September 1996 the finance minister, Molwyn Joseph, resigned. His post was taken by John St. Luce.

ARGENTINA

Argentine Republic
National name: República Argentina.
President: Carlos S. Menem (1989)
Area: 1,072,067 sq mi. (2,776,654 sq km)
Population (1996 est.): 34,672,997 (average annual rate of natural increase: 1.23%); birth rate: 20/1000; infant mortality rate: 19.4/1000; density per square mile: 32.3
Capital and largest city (1991 est.): Buenos Aires, 2,961,000 (plans to move to Viedma by 1990 indefinitely postponed). **Largest cities (1991 est.):** Buenos Aires, 2,961,000; Córdoba, 1,180,000; La Matanza, 1,121,164; General Sarmiento, 646,900; Morón, 641,540 (1983); Rosario, 950,000 (1983). **Monetary unit:** Peso. **Language:** Spanish, English, Italian, German, French. **Ethnicity/Race:** white 85%, mestizo, Indian, or other nonwhite groups 15%. **Religion:** Predominantly Roman Catholic (nominally). **Literacy rate:** 95% (1990)
Economic summary: Gross domestic product: purchasing power parity (1995 est.): $278.5 billion; $8,100 per capita; real growth rate −4.4%; inflation 1.7%; unemployment 16% (1995 est.). Arable land: 9%. Principal products: grains, oilseeds, livestock products. Labor force (1985 est.): 10.9 million; industry: 31%, agriculture 12%, services 57% (1985 est.). Major products: processed foods, motor vehicles, consumer durables, textiles, chemicals. Natural resources: minerals, lead, zinc, tin, copper, iron, manganese, oil, uranium. Exports: $20.7 billion (f.o.b., 1995): meat, wheat,

corn, oilseed, hides, wool. Imports: $19.5 billion (c.i.f., 1995): machinery and equipment, chemicals, fuels and lubricants, agricultural products. Major trading partners: U.S., Brazil, Bolivia, Germany, Japan, Italy, Netherlands, Bolivia.

Geography. With an area slightly less than one-third of the United States and second in South America only to its eastern neighbor, Brazil, in size and population, Argentina is a plain, rising from the Atlantic to the Chilean border and the towering Andes peaks. Aconcagua (23,034 ft.; 7,021 m) is the highest peak in the world outside Asia. It is bordered also by Bolivia and Paraguay on the north, and by Uruguay on the east.

The northern area is the swampy and partly wooded Gran Chaco, bordering on Bolivia and Paraguay. South of that are the rolling, fertile pampas, rich for agriculture and grazing and supporting most of the population. Next southward is Patagonia, a region of cool, arid steppes with some wooded and fertile sections.

Government. Argentina is a federal union of 23 provinces and the federal district. Under the constitution of 1853, the President and Vice President are elected every six years by popular vote through an electoral college. The President appoints his cabinet. The Vice President presides over the Senate but has no other powers. The Congress consists of two houses: a 46-member senate and a 254-member Chamber of Deputies.

History. Discovered in 1516 by Juan Díaz de Solis, Argentina developed slowly under Spanish colonial rule. Buenos Aires was settled in 1580; the cattle industry was thriving as early as 1600.

Invading British forces were expelled in 1806–07, and when Napoleon conquered Spain, the Argentinians set up their own government in the name of the Spanish King in 1810. On July 9, 1816, independence was formally declared.

As in World War I, Argentina proclaimed neutrality at the outbreak of World War II, but in the closing phase declared war on the Axis on March 27, 1945, and became a founding member of the United Nations. Juan D. Perón, an army colonel, emerged as the strongman of the postwar era, winning the presidential elections of 1946 and 1951.

Opposition to Perón's increasing authoritarianism, led to a coup by the armed forces that sent Perón into exile in 1955. Argentina entered a long period of military dictatorships with brief intervals of constitutional government.

The former dictator returned to power in 1973 and his wife was elected Vice-President.

After Perón's death in 1974, his widow Isabel became the hemisphere's first woman chief of state, but was deposed in 1976 by a military junta.

In December 1981, Lt. Gen. Leopoldo Galtieri, commander of the army, was named president.

On April 2, 1982, Galtieri landed thousands of troops on the Falkland Islands and reclaimed the Malvinas, their Spanish name, as national territory. By May 21, 5,000 British marines and paratroops landed from the British armada, and regained control of the islands.

Galtieri resigned three days after the surrender of the island garrison on June 14. Maj. Gen. Reynaldo Bignone, took office as president on July 1.

In the presidential election of October 1983, Raúl Alfonsín, leader of the middle-class Radical Civic Union, handed the Peronist Party its first defeat since its founding.

Twin economic problems of growing unemployment and quadruple-digit inflation led to a Peronist victory in the elections of May 1989. Inflation of food prices led to riots that induced Alfonsín to step down in June 1989, six months early, in favor of the Peronist, Carlos Menem.

A group of army leaders and their followers attempted an uprising on December 3, 1990. Most commanders, however, stood by the legitimate government, and the insurrection was suppressed in less than 24 hours.

In 1991 President Menem hammered out a vast deregulation of the economy designed to reverse decades of state intervention and protectionism.

During the first half of 1997 the President and his ruling Peronist Party saw their popularity dramatically fall over increasing social disturbances and a scandal over presidential links to an alleged mobster. Although inflation is in check, unemployment has recently soared.

ARMENIA

President: Levon A. Ter-Petrossian (1990)
Prime Minister: Robert Kocharyan (1997)
Vice President: Gaguik G. Haroutunian (1997)
Area: 11,500 sq mi. (29,800 sq km)
Population (1996 est.): 3,463,574 (average annual rate of increase: 0.918%) (Armenian, 93%; others, Kurds, Ukrainians, and Russians); birth rate: 17/1000; infant mortality rate: 38.7/1000, density per square mile: 301.2
Capital and largest city (1994 est.): Yerevan, 1,226,000; other large cities (1994 est.): Gyumri (Leninakan), 120,000. **Monetary unit:** Dram. **Language:** Armenian. **Ethnicity/Race:** Armenian 93%, Azeri 3%, Russian 2%, other (mostly Yezidi Kurds) 2% (1989) note: as of the end of 1993, virtually all Azeris had emigrated from Armenia. **Religion:** Armenian Orthodox, 94%. **Literacy rate:** 100% (1970)
Economic summary: Gross domestic product: purchasing power parity (1995 estimate as extrapolated from the World Bank estimate for 1994): $9.1 billion; $2,560 per capita; real growth rate (1995 est.) 5.2%; inflation 32.2% (1995 est.); unemployment 8%. Labor force (1995): 1.012 million; industry and construction 46%; agriculture 2%; transportation and communication 7%; other 45% (1992). Agriculture: 49% of gross domestic product; arable land 29%; dairy farming, vineyards. Exports: $248 million (1995): gold and jewelry, aluminum, transport equipment, scrap metal. Imports: $661 million (c.i.f., 1995): from countries outside the successor states of the former U.S.S.R.: machinery, energy, consumer goods. Major trading partners: Iran, Russia, Turkmenistan, Georgia, U.S., E.U.

Geography. Armenia is located in the southern Caucasus and is the smallest of the former Soviet republics. It is bounded by Georgia on the north, Azerbaijan on the east, Iran on the south, and Turkey on the west. It is a land of rugged mountains and extinct volcanoes. Mt. Aragats, 13,435 ft. (4,095 m) is the highest point. Although the terrain is rugged and dry with few trees, it has excellent pastures. The largest lake, Sevan, 541 sq mi., is the main source of the republic's vast irrigation system and hydroelectric power.

Government. A presidential republic.

History. Armenia has been the scene of struggle throughout its long history with the Greeks, Romans, Persians, Mongols, and Turks. Russia acquired the present day Armenia S.S.R. from Persia in 1828. Armenia joined Azerbaijan and Georgia in 1917 to form the anti-Bolshevik Transcaucasian Federation, but it was dissolved in 1918. Armenia's independence was short-lived and it was annexed by the Red Army in 1920. On March 12, 1922, the Soviets joined Georgia, Armenia, and Azerbaijan to form the Transcaucasian Soviet Socialist Republic, which became part of the U.S.S.R. In 1936, after a reorganization, Armenia became a separate constituent republic of the U.S.S.R.

Since 1983, Armenia has been involved in a territorial dispute with Azerbaijan over the enclave of Nagorno-Karabakh to which both republics lay claim. The autonomous region of Nagorno-Karabakh lies entirely within Azerbaijan. The majority population of the enclave are Armenian Christians who want to secede from Azerbaijan and join with Armenia.

The political disruption in Azerbaijan in June 1993 led to significant military advances for the Armenian forces, leaving them in control of much of the disputed region as well as a corridor to Armenia proper.

In March 1995 a treaty was signed with Russia permitting the latter to maintain two military bases in the country for 25 years. The ruling Armenian National Movement handily won July parliamentary elections after most opposition groups were banned from participating. A referendum on a new constitution was also approved bestowing additional powers on the President.

To protest the parliamentary decision to eliminate deferment of military service for students in higher education, the speaker, Babken Ararktsyan, in June 1997 attempted to resign. Parliament refused to accept his decision. After lengthy talks he withdrew his resignation. Various compromises were being discussed.

AUSTRALIA

Commonwealth of Australia
Sovereign: Queen Elizabeth II (1952)
Governor-General: Sir. William Deane (1996)
Prime Minister: John Howard (1996)
Area: 2,966,150 sq mi. (7,682,300 sq km)
Population (1997 est.): 18,438,824 (average annual rate of natural increase: 0.68%); birth rate: 13.73/1000; infant mortality rate: 5.4/1000; density per square mile: 6.1
Capital (1994 est.): Canberra, 278,904. **Largest cities (1994 est.):** Sydney, 3,738,500; Melbourne, 3,198,200; Adelaide, 1,076,400; Perth, 1,239,100; Brisbane, 786,442. **Monetary unit:** Australian dollar. **Language:** English. **Ethnicity/Race:** Caucasian 95%, Asian 4%, aboriginal and other 1%. **Religions:** Anglican 26.1%, Roman Catholic 26.0%, Other Christian 24.3%. **Literacy rate:** 100%
Economic summary: Gross domestic product: purchasing power parity (1995 est.): $405.4 billion; per capita $22,100; real growth rate 3.3%; inflation 4.75%; unemployment 8.1%. Arable land: 6%. Principal products: wool, meat, cereals, sugar, sheep, cattle, dairy products. Labor force: 8.65 million (1992–93); finance and services 33.8%; public and community services 22.3%; wholesale and retail trade 20.1%; manufacturing 16.2%. Natural resources: iron ore, bauxite, zinc, lead, tin, coal, oil, gas, copper, nickel, uranium. Exports: $51.57 billion (f.o.b, 1995): coal, gold, meat, wool, aluminum, wheat, machinery, and transport equipment. Imports: $57.41 billion (f.o.b, 1995): machinery and transport equipment, computers and office machines, crude oil and petroleum products. Major trading partners: Japan, U.S., U.K., New Zealand, Germany, South Korea, Singapore. **Member of Commonwealth of Nations**

Geography. The continent of Australia, with the island state of Tasmania, is approximately equal in area to the United States (excluding Alaska and Hawaii), and is nearly 50% larger than Europe (excluding the U.S.S.R.).

Mountain ranges run from north to south along the east coast, reaching their highest point in Mount Kosciusko (7,308 ft.; 2,228 m). The western half of the continent is occupied by a desert plateau that rises into barren, rolling hills near the west coast. It includes the Great Victoria Desert to the south and the Great Sandy Desert to the north. The Great Barrier Reef, extending about 1,245 miles (2,000 km), lies along the northeast coast.

The island of Tasmania (26,178 sq mi.; 67,800 sq km) is off the southeastern coast.

Government. The federal parliament consists of a bicameral legislature. The House of Representatives has 146 members elected for three years by popular vote. The Senate has 76 members elected by popular vote for six years. One-half of the Senate is elected every three years. Voting is compulsory at 18. Supreme federal judicial power is vested in the High Court of Australia in the federal courts, and in the State Courts invested by parliament with federal jurisdiction. The High Court consists of seven justices, appointed by the Governor-General in Council. Each of the states has its own judicial system.

History. Dutch, Portuguese, and Spanish ships sighted Australia in the 17th century; the Dutch landed at the Gulf of Carpentaria in 1606. Australia was called New Holland, Botany Bay, and New South Wales until about 1820.

Captain James Cook, in 1770, claimed possession for Great Britain. A British penal colony was set up at what is now Sydney, then Port Jackson, in 1788, and about 161,000 transported English convicts were settled there until the system was suspended in 1839.

Free settlers established six colonies: New South Wales (1786), Tasmania (then Van Diemen's Land) (1825), Western Australia (1829), South Australia (1834), Victoria (1851), and Queensland (1859).

The six colonies became states and in 1901 federated into the Commonwealth of Australia with a constitution that incorporated British parliamentary tradition and U.S. federal experience. Australia became known for liberal legislation: free compulsory education, protected trade unionism with industrial conciliation and arbitration, the "Australian" ballot facilitating selection, the secret ballot, women's suffrage, maternity allowances, and sickness and old age pensions.

In the election of 1983, Robert Hawke, head of the Labour Party, became Prime Minister. The Labour government was re-elected in a federal election in December 1984.

Amid a deep recession Hawke was ousted by Paul Keating in 1991—the first time an Australian Prime Minister was removed from office by his own party.

In March 1996 the opposition Liberal Party-National Party coalition easily won the national elections, removing the Labour Party after 13 years.

Federal parliamentarians in March 1997 rescinded a highly controversial Northern Territory law, the world's only, allowing doctor-assisted suicide.

Australian External Territories

Norfolk Island (13 sq mi.; 36.3 sq km) was placed under Australian administration in 1914. Population 2,756 (July 1995); growth rate 1.69%.

The Ashmore and Cartier Islands (0.8 sq mi.) situated in the Indian Ocean off the northwest coast of Australia, came under Australian administration in 1934. In 1938 the islands were annexed to the Northern Territory. On the attainment of self-government by the Northern Territory in 1978, the islands which are uninhabited were retained as Commonwealth Territory.

The Australian Antarctic Territory (2,360,000 sq mi.; 6,112,400 sq km), comprises all the islands and territories, other than Adélie Land, situated south of lat 60°S and lying between long. 160° to 45°E. It came under Australian administration in 1936.

Heard Island and the McDonald Islands (158 sq mi.; 409.2 sq km), lying in the sub-Antarctic, were placed under Australian administration in 1947. The islands are uninhabited.

Christmas Island (52 sq mi.; 134.7 sq km) is situated in the Indian Ocean. It came under Australian administration in 1958. Population 889 (July 1995).

Coral Sea Islands (400,000 sq mi.; 1,036,000 sq km, but only a few sq mi. of land) became a territory of Australia in 1969. There is no permanent population on the islands.

Cocos (Keeling) Islands. The territory of the Cocos is composed of a group of 27 small coral islands in two separate atolls in the Indian Ocean, 1,721 miles (2,768 kilometers) northwest of Perth. West Island is the largest, about 6.2 miles (10 kilometers) long. The islands became an Australian territory in 1955. Population 604 (July 1995); growth rate –0.5%.

AUSTRIA

Republic of Austria
National name: Republik Österreich
President: Thomas Klestil (1992)
Chancellor: Viktor Klima (1997)
Area: 32,375 sq mi. (83,851 sq km)
Population (1997 est.): 8,047.000 (average annual rate of natural increase: 0.05%); birth rate 10.92/1000; infant mortality rate: 6.1/1000; density per square mile: 248.8
Capital and largest city (1991 est.): Vienna, 1,600,000. **Other large cities (1995 est.):** Graz, 237,150; Linz, 203,000; Salzburg, 144,000; Innsbruck, 118,000. **Monetary unit:** Schilling. **Languages:** German. Slovene, Croatian, Hungarian. **Religion:** Roman Catholic, 82%. **Ethnicity/Race:** German 99.4%, Croatian 0.3%, Slovene 0.2%. **Literacy rate:** 98%
Economic summary: Gross domestic product: purchasing power parity (1996): $156.3 billion; per capita $19,500; real growth rate 1.8%; inflation rate 2%; unemployment 4.1%. Arable land: 17%. Labor force (1995): 2.2 million, 56.4% in services. Principal agricultural products: livestock, forest products, grains, sugar beets, potatoes. Principal products: iron and steel, chemicals, machinery, paper, and pulp. Natural resources: iron ore, petroleum, timber, magnesite, aluminum, coal, lignite, cement, copper, hydropower. Exports: $53.7 billion (1995): iron and steel products, timber, paper, textiles, chemical products. Imports: $65.4 billion (1995): machinery, chemicals, foodstuffs, textiles and clothing, petroleum. Major trading partners: Germany and European Union (E.U.), Eastern Europe, U.S., Japan.

Geography. Slightly smaller than Maine, Austria includes much of the mountainous territory of the eastern Alps (about 75% of the area). The country contains many snowfields, glaciers, and snowcapped peaks, the highest being the Grossglockner (12,530 ft.; 3,819 m). The Danube is the principal river. Forests and woodlands cover about 40% of the land area.

Almost at the heart of Europe, Austria has as its neighbors Italy, Switzerland, Germany, Czech Republic, Hungary, Slovenia, and Liechtenstein.

Government. Austria is a federal republic composed of nine provinces (Bundesländer), including Vienna. The President is elected by the people for a term of six years. The bicameral legislature consists of the Bundesrat, with 58 members chosen by the provincial assemblies, and the Nationalrat, with 183 members popularly elected for four years. Presidency of the Bundesrat revolves every six months, going to the provinces in alphabetical order.

History. Settled in prehistoric times, the Central European land that is now Austria was overrun in pre-Roman times by various tribes, including the Celts. Charlemagne conquered the area in 788 and encouraged colonization and Christianity. In 1252, Ottokar, King of Bohemia, gained possession, only to lose the territories to Rudolf of Hapsburg in 1278. Thereafter, until World War I, Austria's history was largely that of its ruling house, the Hapsburgs.

Austria emerged from the Congress of Vienna in 1815 as the continent's dominant power. The *Ausgleich* of 1867 provided for a dual sovereignty, the empire of Austria and the Kingdom of Hungary, under Franz Joseph I, who ruled until his death on Nov. 21, 1916. His grandnephew, Charles I, succeeded him.

During World War I, Austria-Hungary was one of the Central Powers with Germany, Bulgaria, and Turkey, and the conflict left the country in political chaos and economic ruin. Austria, shorn of Hungary, was proclaimed a republic in 1918, and the monarchy was dissolved in 1919.

A parliamentary democracy was set up by the constitution of Nov. 10, 1920. To check the power of Nazis advocating union with Germany, Chancellor Engelbert Dolfuss in 1933 established a dictatorship, but was assassinated by the Nazis on July 25, 1934. Kurt von Schuschnigg, his successor, struggled to keep Austria independent but on March 12, 1938, German troops occupied the country, and Hitler proclaimed its *Anschluss* (union) with Germany, annexing it to the Third Reich.

After World War II, the U.S. and Britain declared the Austrians a "liberated" people. But the Russians prolonged the occupation. Finally Austria concluded a state treaty with the U.S.S.R. and the other occupying powers and regained its independence on May 15, 1955. The second Austrian republic, established Dec. 19, 1945, on the basis of the 1920 constitution (amended in 1929), was declared by the federal parliament to be permanently neutral.

On June 8, 1986, former U.N. Secretary-General Kurt Waldheim was elected to the ceremonial office of president in a campaign marked by controversy over his alleged links to Nazi war-crimes in Yugoslavia.

The chief of Austria's diplomatic corps, Thomas Klestil, handily won election to the Presidency, paving the way for a normalization of relations strained during Waldheim's term.

Voters in June 1994 emphatically endorsed membership in the European Union, which took effect on January 1, 1995. Despite the membership Austria retained its strict constitutional neutrality and forbade the stationing of foreign troops on its soil.

Sudden elections in December 1995 reaffirmed the strength of the country's two largest parties. In January 1997 Chancellor Vranitzky resigned, being replaced by his finance minister Viktor Klima.

AZERBAIJAN

Republic of Azerbaijan
President: Heydar Aliyev (1993)
Prime Minister: Artur Razizade (1996)
Area: 33,400 sq mi. (86,600 sq km)
Population (1997 est.): 7,735,918 (average annual rate of natural increase: 1.33%). The republic is noted for the longevity of its population. Forty-eight out of every 100,000 residents are over 100 years old. Birth rate: 21.95/1000; infant mortality rate: 73.9/1000; density per square mile: 231.6
Capital and largest city (1991): Baku, 1,713,300, a port on the Caspian Sea. Other large cities: Ganja (1989), 278,000; Sumgait, 231,000. **Monetary unit:** Manat.

Languages: Azerbaijani Turkic, 82%; Russian, 7%; Armenian, 2%. **Ethnicity/Race:** Azeri 90%, Dagestani Peoples 3.2%, Russian 2.5%, Armenian 2.3%, other 2% (1995 est.) note: almost all Armenians live in the separatist Nagorno-Karabakh region. **Religion:** Moslem, 87%; Russian Orthodox, 5.6%; Armenian Orthodox, 2%.

Economic summary: Gross domestic product: purchasing power parity (1995 estimate as extrapolated from World Bank estimate for 1994): $11.5 billion; $1,480 per capita (1995 est.); real growth rate (1995 est.) -17%; inflation 85% (1995 est.); unemployment 2.3%. Azerbaijan's Apsheron peninsula is an oil-rich area and is now being developed under a $7.4 billion contract with western oil companies. Industries: petroleum and natural gas, petroleum products, oilfield equipment, steel, iron ore, cement, chemicals, petrochemicals, and textiles. Agricultural production includes cotton, wheat, tobacco, fruit, wine grapes, potatoes, sheep and other livestock. Labor force: 2.789 million (1990): agriculture and forestry: 32%; industry and construction: 26%; other: 42%. Exports: $549.9 million (f.o.b., 1995) to outside the successor states of the former U.S.S.R. oil and gas, chemicals, textiles, cotton. Imports: $681.5 million (c.i.f., 1995) from outside the successor states of the former U.S.S.R.: machinery and parts, consumer durables, foodstuffs, textiles. Major trading partners: Mostly C.I.S. and European countries.

Geography. Azerbaijan is located on the western shore of the Caspian Sea at the southeastern extremity of the Caucasus. The region is a mountainous country. About 7% of it is arable land. The Kura River Valley is the area's major agricultural zone. The republic is bounded on the north by Russia, by the Caspian Sea in the east, by Iran in the south, by Georgia and Armenia in the west, and by a 10-mile border with Turkey.

Government. A constitutional republic with 125-seat parliament.

History. Azerbaijan was known in ancient times as Albania. The area was the site of many conflicts involving Arabs, Kazars, and the Turks. After the 11th century, the territory became dominated by the Turks and eventually became a stronghold of the Shi'ite Muslim religion and Islamic culture.

The territory of Soviet Azerbaijan was acquired by Russia from Persia through the Treaty of Gulistan in 1813 and the Treaty of Turkamanchai in 1828.

After the Bolshevik Revolution, Azerbaijan declared its independence from Russia in May 1918. The republic was reconquered by the Red Army in 1920, and was annexed into the Transcaucasian Soviet Federated Socialist Republic in 1922. It was later reestablished as a separate Soviet Republic on Dec. 5, 1936.

Since 1983, the rival republics of Azerbaijan and Armenia have been feuding over the enclave of Nagorno-Karabakh located within Azerbaijan. Both nations claim this autonomous region. The majority of the enclave's residents are both Armenians and Christians and they are agitating to secede from the predominantly Muslim Azerbaijan and join with Armenia.

Campaigning on a platform calling for the country to break from the C.I.S. and retain Nagorno-Karabakh, Popular Front leader Elchibey won the 1992 vote.

A power struggle in June 1993 sent Elchibey fleeing when rebel forces advanced on the capital. These events were set against a worsening of the economy and major reverses in the war with Armenia.

In November 1993 Aliyev received almost 99% of the vote in a presidential election.

In June 1997 the leaders of France, Russia, and the United States presented a proposal for resolving the on-going dispute over Nagorno-Karabakh to Armenia and Azerbaijan.

BAHAMAS

Commonwealth of the Bahamas

Sovereign: Queen Elizabeth II (1952)
Governor-General: Sir Orville Alton Turnquest (1995)
Prime Minister: Hubert Ingraham (1992)
Area: 5,380 sq mi. (13,939 sq km)
Population (1997 est.): 262,034 (average annual rate of natural increase: 1.25%); birth rate: 18.2/1000; infant mortality rate: 22.2/1000; density per square mile: 48.7
Capital and largest city (1991 census): Nassau, 171,542. **Monetary unit:** Bahamian dollar. **Language:** English. **Ethnicity/Race:** black 85%, white 15%. **Religions:** Baptist, 29%; Anglican, 23%; Roman Catholic, 22%, others. **Literacy rate:** 95%
Economic summary: Gross domestic product: purchasing power parity (1995 est.): $4.8 billion; $18,700 per capita; real growth rate 2% (1995 est.); inflation rate 1.5% (1996); unemployment 15% (1995 est.). Labor force: 136,900 (1993); government: 30%; tourism: 40%; business services: 10%; agriculture: 5%. Principal agricultural products: fruits, vegetables. Major industrial products: fish, refined petroleum, pharmaceutical products, tourism, banking, rum, cement, salt production, spiral welded steel pipe. Natural resources: salt, aragonite, timber. Exports: $224.257 million (f.o.b., 1994): rum, crawfish, pharmaceuticals, cement. Imports: $1.08 billion (c.i.f., 1994): foodstuffs, manufactured goods, fuels. Major trading partners: U.S., U.K., Nigeria, Japan, Norway, France, Denmark. **Member of Commonwealth of Nations**

Geography. The Bahamas are an archipelago of about 700 islands and 2,400 uninhabited islets and cays lying 50 miles off the east coast of Florida. They extend from northwest to southeast for more than 760 miles (1,223 km). Only 22 of the islands are inhabited; the most important is New Providence (80 sq mi.; 207 sq km), on which Nassau is situated. Other islands include Grand Bahama, Abaco, Eleuthera, Andros, Cat Island, San Salvador (or Watling's Island), Exuma, Long Island, Crooked Island, Acklins Island, Mayaguana, and Inagua.

The islands are mainly flat, few rising above 200 feet (61 m). There are no fresh water streams. There are large brackish lakes on several islands including Inagua and New Providence.

Government. The Bahamas moved toward greater autonomy in 1968 after the overwhelming victory in general elections of the Progressive Liberal Party, led by Prime Minister Lynden O. Pindling. The black leader's party won 29 seats in the House of Assembly to only 7 for the predominantly white United Bahamians, who had controlled the islands for decades before Pindling became Premier in 1967.

With its new mandate from the 85% black population, Pindling's government negotiated a new constitution with Britain under which the colony became the Commonwealth of the Bahama Islands in 1969. On July 10, 1973, the Bahamas became an independent nation as the Commonwealth of the Bahamas. The islands established diplomatic relations with Cuba in 1974.

Hubert A. Ingraham was sworn in as Prime Minister on Aug. 20, 1992, ending 25 years of rule by the Progressive Liberal Party.

History. The islands were reached by Columbus in October 1492, and were a favorite pirate area in the early 18th century. The Bahamas were a Crown colony from 1717 until they were granted internal self-government in 1964.

The government was elected to a second term as a result of March 1997 elections, which saw a further decline in the Progressive Liberals.

In May 1997 the Bahamas formally recognized the People's Republic of China as the legal government of China and severed diplomatic ties with Taiwan.

BAHRAIN

State of Bahrain
Emir: Sheik Isa bin-Sulman al-Khalifa (1961)
Prime Minister: Sheik Khalifa bin Sulman al-Khalifa (1970)
Area: 240 sq mi. (620 sq km)
Population (1997 est.): 603,318 (average annual rate of natural increase: 1.97%); birth rate: 23/1000; infant mortality rate: 16.4/1000; density per square mile: 2,513.8
Capital (1992 est.): Al-Manámah, 140,401. **Monetary unit:** Bahrain dinar. **Languages:** Arabic (official), English, Farsi, Urdu. **Ethnicity/Race:** Bahraini 63%, Asian 13%, other Arab 10%, Iranian 8%, other 6%. **Religion:** Islam. **Literacy rate:** 80%
Economic summary: Gross domestic product: purchasing power parity (1995 est.): $7.3 billion, $12,000 per capita; real growth rate −2%; inflation 3% (1995 est.); unemployment 25% (1994 est.). Labor force: 140,000; breakdown by industry: 85%; agriculture: 5%; services: 5%; government: 3% (1982). Principal agricultural products: eggs, vegetables, fruits. Major industries: petroleum processing and refining, aluminum smelting, offshore banking, ship repairing. Natural resources: oil, fish. Exports: $3.2 billion (f.o.b., 1995 est.): petroleum and petroleum products, 80%; aluminum, 7%. Imports: $3.29 billion (c.i.f., 1995 est.): machinery, oil-industry equipment, motor vehicles, foodstuffs. Major trading partners: Saudi Arabia, U.S., U.K., Japan, India, Germany, U.A.E.

Geography. Bahrain is an archipelago in the Persian Gulf off the coast of Saudi Arabia. The islands for the most part are level expanses of sand and rock.

Government. Traditional monarchy. Political parties prohibited.

History. A sheikdom that passed from the Persians to the al-Khalifa family from Arabia in 1782, Bahrain became, by treaty, a British protectorate in 1820. It has become a major Middle Eastern oil center and, through use of oil revenues, is one of the most developed of the Persian Gulf sheikdoms. The Emir, Sheik Isa bin-Sulman al-Khalifa, who succeeded to the post in 1961, is a member of the original ruling family. Bahrain announced its independence on Aug. 14, 1971.

In June 1996 the government arrested 29 on charges of plotting to overthrow the ruling family and establish an Iranian-style Muslim regime. In an effort to increase trade and investment, an economic agreement aimed at furthering joint projects was signed between Jordan and Bahrain in June 1997.

BANGLADESH

People's Republic of Bangladesh
President: Shahabuddin Ahmed (1996)
Prime Minister: Sheik Hasina Wazed (1996)
Area: 55,598 sq mi. (143,998 sq km)
Population (1997 est.): 125,340,261 (average annual rate of natural increase: 1.89%); birth rate: 29.8/1000; infant mortality rate: 100/1000; density per square mile: 2,254.4
Capital and largest city (mid-1994 est.): Dhaka, 7,000,000+. **Other large cities (est. mid-1994):** Chittagong, 3,000,000; Khulna, 2,000,000. **Monetary unit:** Taka. **Principal languages:** Bangla (official), English. **Ethnicity/Race:** Bengali 98%, Biharis 250,000, tribals less than 1 million. **Religions:** Islam (official) 88.3%; Hindu 10.51%. **Literacy rate:** 36%
Economic summary: Gross domestic product: purchasing power parity (1995 est.): $144.5 billion; per capita $1,130. Real growth rate 4.6%; inflation 4.5% (1995 est.); unemployment rate n.a. Arable land 67%. Agriculture accounts for 40% of gross domestic and 70% of employment. Principal agricultural products: rice, jute, tea, sugar, potatoes, beef. Labor force 50.1 million; agriculture 65%; services 21%; industry and mining 14% (1989). Major industrial products: jute goods, textiles, sugar, fertilizer, paper, processed foods. Natural resources: natural gas, uranium, timber. Exports: $2.7 billion (1995 est.): garments, jute and jute goods, leather and leather goods, seafood, tea, paper, fertilizer. Imports: $4.7 billion (1995 est.): capital goods, petroleum, food, textiles. Major trading partners: U.S., E.U., Japan, China, Hong Kong, Singapore. **Member of Commonwealth of Nations**

Geography. Bangladesh, on the northern coast of the Bay of Bengal, is surrounded by India, with a small common border with Burma in the southeast. It is approximately the size of Wisconsin. The country is low-lying riverine land traversed by the many branches and tributaries of the Ganges and Brahmaputra rivers. Elevations average less than 600 feet (183 m) above sea level. Tropical monsoons and frequent floods and cyclones inflict heavy damage in the delta region.

Government. Khaleda Zia, widow of assassinated President Ziaur Rahman, and her Bangladesh Nationalist Party won the election of late-February 1991. P.M. Zia returned Bangladesh to the parliamentary system. In a referendum in September 1991 the electorate voted to reduce the president to a figurehead.

History. The former East Pakistan was part of imperial British India until Britain withdrew in 1947. The two Pakistans were united by religion (Islam), but their peoples were separated by culture, physical features, and 1,000 miles of Indian territory. Bangladesh consists primarily of East Bengal (West Bengal is part of India and its people are primarily Hindu) plus the Sylhet district of the Indian state of Assam. For almost 25 years after independence from Britain, its history was as part of Pakistan (see Pakistan).

The East Pakistanis unsuccessfully sought greater autonomy from West Pakistan. The first general elections in Pakistani history, in December 1970, saw virtually all 171 seats of the region (out of 300 for both East and West Pakistan) go to Sheik Mujibur Rahman's Awami League.

Attempts to write an all-Pakistan constitution to replace the military regime of Gen. Yahya Khan failed. Yahya put down a revolt in March 1971. An estimated one million Bengalis were killed in the fighting or later slaughtered. Ten million more took refuge in India.

In December 1971, India invaded East Pakistan, routed the West Pakistani occupation forces, and created Bangladesh. In February 1974, Pakistan agreed to recognize the independence of Bangladesh.

On March 24, 1982, Gen. Hossain Mohammad Ershad, army chief of staff, took control in a bloodless coup. A court in April 1997 indicted 20, including 18 military officers, for conspiring in the assassination of the Prime Minister's father in 1975.

Gen. Ershad resigned on December 6, 1990 amidst protests and numerous allegations of corruption.

After years of frequently violent protests Prime Minister Khaleda Zia resigned on March 30, 1996. Parliamentary elections in June provided a win for the liberal

Awami League, whose leader, the daughter of the country's founding father, became Prime Minister later that month.

BARBADOS

Sovereign: Queen Elizabeth II (1952)
Governor-General: Sir Clifford Husbands (June 1996)
Prime Minister: Owen Arthur (1994)
Area: 166 sq mi. (431 sq km)
Population (1997 est.): 257,731; (growth rate: 0.7%); birth rate: 15.15/1000; infant mortality rate: 18.2/1000; density per square mile: 1,552.6
Capital and largest city (1990): Bridgetown, 6,700. **Monetary unit:** Barbados dollar. **Language:** English. **Ethnicity/Race:** African 80%, European 4%, other 16%. **Religions:** Anglican, 40%; Methodist, 7%; Pentecostal, 8%; Roman Catholic, 4%. **Literacy rate:** 99%
Economic summary: Gross domestic product: purchasing power parity (1995 est.): $2.5 billion; per capita $9,800; real growth rate 2%; inflation 1.7% (1995 est.); unemployment 19.9% (1995). Arable land: 77%. Principal products: sugar cane, subsistence foods. Labor force (1993): 126,000; 37% services and government. Major industrial products: light manufactures, sugar milling, tourism. Tourism industry is major employer of Labor force; services and government 41%; commerce 15%; manufacturing and construction 18%; transportation (1992 est.). Exports: $158.6 million (f.o.b., 1995 est.): sugar and molasses, chemicals, electrical components, clothing, rum, machinery and transport equipment. Imports: $693 million (c.i.f., 1995 est.): foodstuffs, consumer durables, raw materials, machinery, crude oil, construction materials, chemicals. Major trading partners: U.S., Caribbean nations, U.K., Japan. **Member of Commonwealth of Nations**

Geography. An island in the Atlantic about 300 miles (483 km) north of Venezuela, Barbados is only 21 miles long (34 km) and 14 miles across (23 km) at its widest point. It is circled by fine beaches and narrow coastal plains. The highest point is Mount Hillaby (1,105 ft.; 337 m) in the north central area.

Government. The Barbados legislature dates from 1627. It is bicameral, with a Senate of 21 appointed members and an Assembly of 28 elected members. The major political parties are the Barbados Labour Party (19 seats in Assembly), led by Prime Minister Owen Arthur, Democratic Labour Party (8 seats), led by David Thompson; and the National Democratic Party (1 seat).

History. Barbados, with a population 90% black, was settled by the British in 1627. It became a Crown colony in 1885. It was a member of the Federation of the West Indies from 1958 to 1962. Britain granted the colony independence on Nov. 30, 1966, and it became a parliamentary democracy.

Prime Minister Sandiford handily won a second five-year term as a result of parliamentary elections in January 1991.

Local anger over rulings by the final appeals court, appointed by Queen Elizabeth, led to the creation in 1997 of a constitutional commission to consider abandoning all ties to Great Britain.

BELARUS

Republic of Belarus
President: Aleksandr Lukashenko (1994)
Prime Minister: Syarhei Linh (acting 1996–97)
Area: 80,200 sq mi. (207,600 sq km)
Population (1997 est.): 10,439,916 (average annual rate of natural increase: –0.07%) (In 1989: Belarusian, 77.9%; Russian, 13.2%; Polish, 4.1%; Ukrainian, 2.9%; Jewish, 1.1%); birth rate: 12.68/1000; infant mortality rate: 12.6/1000; density per square mile: 130.2
Capital (1992 est.): Mensk (Minsk), 1,666,000. **Other large cities (1992 est.):** Gomel, 517,300; Vitebsk, 373,000; Mogilyov, 364,000; Grodno, 291,800; Brest, 284,000; Bobruysk, 224,000. **Monetary unit:** Belarusian ruble. **Language:** Belarusian (White Russian). **Ethnicity/Race:** Belarussian 77.9%, Russian 13.2%, Polish 4.1%, Ukrainian 2.9%, other 1.9%. **Religion:** Orthodoxy is predominant. **Literacy rate:** 100%
Economic summary: Gross domestic product: purchasing power parity (1995 estimate as extrapolated from the World Bank estimate for 1994): $49.2 billion; per capita $4,700; real growth rate (1995 est.) –10% ; inflation 244%; unemployment 2.6%. Labor force: 4.259 million; industry and construction, 40%; agriculture and forestry, 21%; other: 39%. Industry accounts for about two-thirds of the country's income. Major industries include tractors, trucks, agricultural machinery, textiles, timber, chemical products including fertilizers, light manufacturing including TV sets, refrigerators, and food processing. Belarus's land is not well suited for farming. One-quarter of the republic's work force is employed in agriculture. High-yield agricultural crops are potatoes and vegetables, flax, rye, oats, other grains, sugar beets, fruit, and considerable quantities of meat, milk, and eggs. Exports: $4.2 billion (f.o.b., 1995): machinery and transport equipment, chemicals, foodstuffs; to outside of the successor states of the former U.S.S.R.. Imports: $4.6 billion (c.i.f., 1995): fuel, natural gas, industrial raw materials textiles, sugar; from outside of the successor states of the former U.S.S.R.. Major trading partners: Russia, Ukraine, Poland, Germany.

Geography. Much of Belarus (formerly Byelorussia) is a hilly lowland with forests, swamps, and numerous rivers and lakes. There are wide rivers emptying into the Baltic and the Black Seas. Its forests cover over one third of the land and its peat marshes are a valuable natural resource. The largest lake is Narach, 31 sq mi (79.6 sq km). The republic borders Latvia and Lithuania on the north, Ukraine on the south, Russia on the east, and Poland on the west.

Government. A constitutional republic. The Parliament (Supreme Soviet) has 260 deputies.

History. In the 5th century, Belarus (also known as White Russia) was colonized by east Slavic tribes and was dominated by Kiev from the 9th to 12th centuries. After the destruction of Kiev by the Mongols in the 13th century, the territory was conquered by the dukes of Lithuania. Belarus became part of the Grand Duchy of Lithuania which merged with Poland in 1569.

Following the partitions of Poland in 1772, 1793, and the final partition which divided Poland between Russia, Prussia, and Austria, Belarus became part of the Russian empire.

The peace Treaty of Riga in March 1921 ending the Polish-Soviet War ceded west Belarus to Poland. The eastern part of the country was joined to the U.S.S.R. in 1922. In 1939, the Soviet Union took back West Belarus under the secret protocol of the Nazi-Soviet Nonaggression Pact and incorporated it into the Belarussian Soviet Socialist Republic.

Following the end of World War II, Belarus was given membership in the United Nations in 1945. Belarus declared its sovereignty in July 1990 and its independence in August 1991.

The Belarus President, Nikolai Dementei, a Commu-
ist hard liner, was forced to resign under pressure fol-
owing the August 1991 attempted coup, and Stanislav
. Shushkevich, First Deputy Chairman of the Parlia-
ent, assumed leadership of the country. Belarus
ecame a co-founder of the Commonwealth of Indepen-
ent States (C.I.S.) in Dec. 1991.

In January 1994 the country's parliament ousted its
eform-minded leader in protest against his support for
arket economics. In March Parliament adopted a new
onstitution, creating a presidency, and reconstructed
e 260-seat parliament. Lukashenka won, receiving
ore than 80% of the vote.

With much fanfare, Belarus and Russia signed a
eaty in April 1997 aimed at significantly increasing
ooperation between the two states, stopping just short
f union. Many of the details remained ambiguous how-
ver, as well as their implications, and critics denounced
e increasingly oppressive political atmosphere in
elarus.

BELGIUM

Kingdom of Belgium
National name: Royaume de Belgique—
Koningrijk van België
Sovereign: King Albert II (1993)
Prime Minister: Jean-Luc Dehaene (1992)
Area: 11,781 sq mi. (30,513 sq km)
Population (1997): 10,203,683 (average annual rate of
natural increase: 0.17%); birth rate: 12.01/1000; infant
mortality rate: 6.3/1000; density per square mile: 866.1
Capital and largest city (1994): Brussels, 949,070
(metro area). **Other large cities (1994):** Antwerp,
462,880; Ghent, 228,490; Charleroi, 206,898; Liege,
195,389; Bruges, 116,724; Namur, 104,610. **Monetary
Unit:** Belgian franc. **Languages:** Dutch (Flemish),
57%; French, 32%; bilingual (Brussels), 10%; German,
0.7%. **Ethnicity/Race:** Fleming 55%, Walloon 33%,
mixed or other 12%. **Religion:** Roman Catholic, 75%.
Literacy rate: 99%
Economic summary: Gross domestic product: purchasing power parity (1995 est.): $197 billion; per capita
$19,500; real growth rate 2.3% (1995 est.); infla-
tion rate 1.6% (1995 est.); unemployment rate 14%
(1995 est.). Arable land: 46%. Agricultural products:
pork, beef, milk, fruits and vegetables, ornamental
plants, meals, sugar beets, eggs, dairy products.
Labor force: 4.126 million; services: 63.6%; industry:
28%; construction 6.1%; agriculture: 2% (1988). Major
products: chemicals, mechanical, electrical and plastic equipment, textiles, nonferrous metals, iron and
steel, glass. Exports: $108 billion (f.o.b., 1994):
machinery, transportation equipment, iron and steel,
tractors, diamonds, mineral products. Imports: $140
billion (c.i.f., 1994): pharmaceuticals and chemicals,
plastics, fuels, grains, and foodstuffs. Major trading partners: Germany, France, Netherlands, U.S.

Geography. A neighbor of France, Germany, the
Netherlands, and Luxembourg, Belgium has about 40
les of seacoast on the North Sea at the Strait of
over. It is approximately the size of Maryland. The
rthern third of the country is a plain extending east-
rd from the seacoast. North of the Sambre and Meuse
vers is a low plateau; to the south lies the heavily
ooded Ardennes plateau, attaining an elevation of
out 2,300 feet (700 m).
The Schelde River, which rises in France and flows
rough Belgium, emptying into the Schelde estuaries,
ables Antwerp to be an ocean port.

Government. Belgium, a parliamentary democracy
der a constitutional monarch, consists of ten prov-
ces. Its bicameral legislature has a Senate, with its 71
members elected for four years. The 150-member
Chamber of Representatives is directly elected for four
years by proportional representation. There is universal
suffrage, and those who do not vote are fined.

Belgium joined the North Atlantic Alliance in 1949
and is a member of the European Union.. NATO and the
European Union have their headquarters in Brussels.

The late sovereign, Baudouin I, was born Sept. 7,
1930, the son of King Leopold III and Queen Astrid. He
became King on July 17, 1951, after the abdication of
his father. He married Doña Fabiola de Mora y Aragón
on Dec. 15, 1960. Since he had no children, his brother,
Prince Albert, became King upon his death in 1993.

History. Belgium occupies part of the Roman province
of Belgica, named after the Belgae, a people of ancient
Gaul. The area was conquered by Julius Caesar in
57–50 B.C.E., then was overrun by the Franks in the 5th
century. It was part of Charlemagne's empire in the 8th
century, then in the next century was absorbed into
Lotharingia and later into the Duchy of Lower Lorraine.
In the 12th century it was partitioned into the Duchies
of Brabant and Luxembourg, the Bishopric of Liège,
and the domain of the Count of Hainaut, which included
Flanders.

In the 16th century, Belgium, with most of the area of
the Low Countries, passed to the Duchy of Burgundy
and was the marriage portion of Archduke Maximilian
of Hapsburg and the inheritance of his grandson,
Charles V, who incorporated it into his empire. Then, in
1555, they were united with Spain.

By the treaty of Utrecht in 1713, the country's sovereignty passed to Austria. During the wars that followed
the French Revolution, Belgium was occupied and later
annexed to France. But with the downfall of Napoleon,
the Congress of Vienna in 1815 gave the country to the
Netherlands. The Belgians revolted in 1830 and
declared their independence.

Germany's invasion of Belgium in 1914 set off World
War I. The Treaty of Versailles (1919) gave the areas of
Eupen, Malmédy, and Moresnet to Belgium. Leopold III
succeeded Albert, King during World War I, in 1934. In
World War II, Belgium was overwhelmed by Nazi Germany, and Leopold III was made prisoner. When he
attempted to return in 1950, Socialists and Liberals
revolted. He abdicated July 16, 1951, and his son, Baudouin, became King the next day.

Despite the increasingly strong divisions between the
French- and Flemish-speaking communities, a Christian
Democrat-Liberal coalition that took office in December
1981 came close to setting a record for longevity among
the 32 governments that had ruled Belgium since World
War II. In national elections of November 1991 the
environmental and far-right parties made significant
gains. Political instability in The Democratic Republic
of Congo (now Congo) following riots there led to Belgian troops supervising an exodus of foreigners in September 1991.

In 1993 the constitution was changed, turning the
country into a federal state. Compulsory military service
was also eliminated.

The discovery of a child sex and murder gang in
1996 led to national outrage that was compounded with
disclosures that official negligence resulted in even
more child deaths.

BELIZE

Sovereign: Queen Elizabeth II (1952)
Governor-General: Colville Young (1993)
Prime Minister: Manuel Esquivel (1993)
Area: 8,867 sq mi. (22,965 sq km)
Population (1997 est.): 224,663 (average annual rate of
natural increase: 2.63%); birth rate: 31.91/1000; infant

mortality rate: 33.2/1000.; density per square mi.: 25.3
Capital (1993 est.): Belmopan, 3,852. **Largest city (1993):** Belize City, 47,724. **Monetary unit:** Belize dollar. **Languages:** English (official) and Spanish, Maya, Carib. **Ethnicity/Race:** mestizo 44%, Creole 30%, Maya 11%, Garifuna 7%, other 8%. **Religions:** Roman Catholic, 62%; Protestant, 30%. **Literacy rate:** 91% (est.)
Economic summary: Gross domestic product: purchasing power parity (1994 est.): $575 million; per capita $2,750; real growth rate 2%; inflation 2.3%; unemployment 10% (1993 est.). Principal products: sugar cane, corn, molasses, rice, bananas, livestock. Labor force: 51,500; agriculture: 30%; services: 16%; government: 15.4%; commerce: 11.2%; manufacturing: 10.3%. Major products: timber, processed foods, furniture, rum, soap. Natural resources: timber, fish. Exports: $115 million (f.o.b., 1993): sugar, molasses, clothing, lumber, citrus concentrates, fish. Imports: $281 million (c.i.f., 1993): fuels, transportation equipment, foodstuffs, machinery, chemicals, pharmaceuticals, manufactured goods. Major trading partners: European Union, Mexico, CARICOM, U.S. **Member of Commonwealth of Nations**

Geography. Belize is situated on the Caribbean Sea south of Mexico and east and north of Guatemala. In area, it is about the size of New Hampshire. Most of the country is heavily forested with various hardwoods. Mangrove swamps and cays along the coast give way to hills and mountains in the interior. The highest point is Victoria Peak, 3,681 feet (1,122 m).

Government. Formerly the colony of British Honduras, Belize became a fully independent commonwealth on Sept. 21, 1981, after having been self-governing since 1964. Executive power is nominally wielded by Queen Elizabeth II through an appointed Governor-General but effective power is held by the Prime Minister, who is responsible to a 29-member parliament elected by universal suffrage.

History. Once a part of the Mayan empire, the area was deserted until British timber cutters began exploiting valuable hardwoods in the 17th century. Efforts by Spain to dislodge British settlers, including a major naval attack in 1798, were defeated. The territory was formally named a British colony in 1862 but administered by the Governor of Jamaica until 1884.

Guatemala has long made claims to the territory. A tentative agreement was reached between Britain, Belize, and Guatemala in March 1981 that would offer access to the Caribbean through Belizean territory for Guatemala. The agreement broke down, however.

Guatemala recognized Belize's sovereignty in September 1991 and abandoned its territorial claim, although unease remains.

The general election of June 1993 saw a victory for the United Democratic Party, which won 16 of the 29 seats in the House of Representatives.

Although of increasing importance to drug trafficking, Belize received a national security waver from the U.S., permitting the continuation of official aid. In early 1997 Belizean–U.S. anti-drug forces staged two raids off the coast.

BENIN

Republic of Benin
National name: Republique du Benin
President: Mathieu Kerekou (1996)
Prime Minister: Adrien Houngbédji (1996)
Area: 43,483 sq mi. (112,622 sq km)
Population (1997 est.): 5,902,178 (average annual rate of natural increase: 3.31%); birth rate: 46.28/1000; infant mortality rate: 102.7/1000; density per square mile: 135.7
Capital and largest city (1996): Porto-Novo (official), 177,660; Cotonou (de facto capital) 33,212. **Other large city (1992):** Djougou, 132,192. **Monetary unit:** Franc CFA. **Ethnic groups:** Fons and Adjas, Baribas, Yorubas, Mahis. **Languages:** French, African languages. **Ethnicity/Race:** African 99% (42 ethnic groups, most important being Fon, Adja, Yoruba, Bariba), Europeans 5,500. **Religions:** indigenous, 70%; Christian, 15%; Islam, 15%. **Literacy rate (1990 est.):** 23%
Economic summary: Gross domestic product: purchasing power parity (1995 est.): $7.6 billion; $1,380 per capita; real growth rate 6%; inflation rate 55% (1994 est.); unemployment n.a. Arable land 12%. Principal agricultural products: palm oils, peanuts, cotton, coffee, tobacco, corn, rice, livestock, fish. Labor force: 1.9 million (1987); agriculture: 60%; transport, commerce, and public services: 38%; industry: less than 2%. Major industrial products: processed palm oil, palm kernel oil, textiles, beverages. Natural resources: limestone, some offshore oil, marble, timber. Exports: $310 million (f.o.b., 1994 est.): crude oil, cotton, palm products, cocoa. Imports: $439 million (c.i.f., 1994 est.): foodstuffs, beverages, tobacco, petroleum products, intermediate goods, capital goods, light consumer goods. Major trading partners: France and other Western European countries, Japan, U.S.

Geography. This West African nation on the Gulf of Guinea, between Togo on the west and Nigeria on the east, is about the size of Tennessee. It is bounded also by Burkina Faso and Niger on the north. The land consists of a narrow coastal strip that rises to a swampy, forested plateau and then to highlands in the north. A hot and humid climate blankets the entire country.

Government. The change in name from Dahomey to Benin was announced by President Mathieu Kerekou on November 30, 1975. Benin commemorates an African kingdom that flourished in the 17th century. Benin is a republic under a multiparty democratic rule with a unicameral legislature, the National Assembly. At the National Conference held at Cotonou, Feb. 19–28, 1990, Marxism-Leninism was abolished as the state philosophy, a multiparty system was established, and political detainees and prisoners were released.

History. One of the smallest and most densely populated states in Africa, Benin was annexed by the French in 1893. The area was incorporated into French West Africa in 1904. It became an autonomous republic within the French Community in 1958, and on Aug. 1, 1960, was granted its independence within the Community.

Gen. Christophe Soglo deposed the first president, Hubert Maga, in an army coup in 1963. He dismissed the civilian government in 1965, proclaiming himself chief of state. A group of young army officers seized power in December 1967, deposing Soglo. They promulgated a new constitution in 1968.

In December 1969, Benin had its fifth coup of the decade, with the army again taking power. In May 1970, a three-man presidential commission was created to take over the government. The commission had a six-year term. In May 1972, yet another army coup ousted the triumvirate and installed Lt. Col. Mathieu Kerekou as president.

Student protests and widespread strikes in 1989 and 1990 moved Benin toward multiparty democracy. In March 1991 Prime Minister Soglo won the first free presidential election.

Presidential elections in March 1996 resulted in a victory for former-President and Marxist military ruler

Kerekou, with 52.49%, over the incumbent Soglo.

Since 1990 the government has embarked on a vast privatization drive. The sale of SONICOG (a producer of butter, soap, and edible oils) in 1997 was contingent on the retention of the entire Labor force.

BHUTAN

Kingdom of Bhutan
National name: Druk-yul
Ruler: King Jigme Singye Wangchuck (1972)
Area: 18,000 sq mi. (46,620 sq km)
Population (1997 est.): 1,865,191 (average annual rate of natural increase: 2.29%); birth rate: 37.91/1000; infant mortality rate: 114/1000; density per square mile: 103.6
Capital and largest city (1993): Thimphu (official), 30,340. **Monetary unit:** Ngultrum. **Language:** Dzongkha (official). **Ethnicity/Race:** Bhote 50%, ethnic Nepalese 35%, indigenous or migrant tribes 15%. **Religions:** Buddhist, 75%; Hindu, 25%. **Literacy rate:** n.a.
Economic summary: Gross domestic product: purchasing power parity (1995 est.): $1.3 billion; per capita $730; real growth rate 6% (1995 est.); inflation 8.6% (FY 94/95 est.); unemployment n.a. Arable land: 16%. Labor force: n.a.; agriculture: 93%; services: 5%; industry and commerce: 2%. Principal products: wood, wood products, rice, barley, wheat, potatoes, fruit, cardamon, coal, limestone, gypsum, dolomite, graphite. Major industrial products: hydroelectricity, wood, wood products, cement, calcium carbide, ferro sillicon, fruit processing, alcoholic beverages. Natural resources: hydroelectric power, timber, minerals. Exports: $70.9 million (f.o.b., FY 94/95 est.): cardamon, gypsum, timber, handicrafts, cement, fruit, electricity (to India), precious stones, spices. Imports: $113.6 million (c.i.f., FY 94/95 est.): equipment for telecommunications, machinery, rice, fuel, vehicles, grains, consumer merchandise. Major trading partners: India, Bangladesh.

Geography. Mountainous Bhutan, half the size of Indiana, is situated on the southeast slope of the Himalayas, bordered on the north and east by Tibet and on the south and west and east by India. The landscape consists of a succession of lofty and rugged mountains running generally from north to south and separated by deep valleys. In the north, towering peaks reach a height of 24,000 feet (7,315 m).

Government. Bhutan is a monarchy. The King rules with a cabinet and a Royal Advisory Council. There is a National Assembly (parliament), which meets semiannually, but no political parties.

History. British troops invaded the country in 1865 and negotiated an agreement under which Britain undertook to pay an annual allowance to Bhutan on condition of good behavior. A treaty with India in 1949 increased this subsidy and placed Bhutan's foreign affairs under Indian control.

In the 1960s, Bhutan undertook modernization, abolishing slavery and the caste system, emancipating women and enacting land reform. In 1985, Bhutan made its first diplomatic links with non-Asian countries.

A pro-democracy campaign emerged in 1991 that the government claimed was composed largely of Nepalese immigrants. Some 70,000 Nepalese civil servants in 1992 fled the country as part of the pro-democracy campaign.

Nepalese activism and a refugee problem continue to plague the country. The International Red Cross investigated charges of human rights violations in 1993. During 1995, discussions with Nepal over the problem bore little fruit, and immigration laws were tightened.

Although the U.N. General Assembly overwhelmingly approved the Comprehensive Test Ban Treaty in a September 1996 vote, Bhutan was one of only three countries to vote against it.

BOLIVIA

Republic of Bolivia
National name: República de Bolivia
President: Hugo Banzer Suárez (1997)
Area: 424,162 sq mi. (1,098,581 sq km)
Population (1997 est.): 7,669,868 (average annual rate of natural increase: 2.19%); birth rate: 32.14/1000; infant mortality rate: 65.7/1000; density per square mile: 18
Historic and Judicial capital (1992): Sucre, 130,952
Administrative capital (1992): La Paz, 711,036. **Largest cities (1992 est.):** Santa Cruz, 694,616; El Alto, 404,367; Cochabamba, 404,102; Oruro, 183,194. **Monetary unit:** Boliviano. **Languages:** Spanish, Quechua, Aymara. **Ethnicity/Race:** Quechua 30%, Aymara 25%, mestizo (mixed European and Indian ancestry) 25%–30%, European 5%–15%. **Religion:** Roman Catholic, 85%. **Literacy rate:** 78%
Economic summary: Gross domestic product: purchasing power parity (1995 est.): $20 billion; per capita $2,530; real growth rate 3.7%; inflation rate 12%; unemployment rate (urban rate) 8%. Arable land: 3%. Principal agricultural products (1994): soybeans, timber, sugar, cotton, Brazil nuts, coffee. Major industrial products: refined petroleum, processed foods, tin, textiles, clothing. Labor force (1993): 3.54 million; agriculture: n.a.; services and utilities: 20%; manufacturing, mining, and construction: 7%. Natural resources: petroleum, natural gas, tin, lead, zinc, copper, tungsten, bismuth, antimony, gold, sulfur, silver, iron ore. Exports: $1.1 billion (f.o.b., 1994 est.): metals 39%, natural gas 9%, soybeans 11%, jewelry 11%, wood 8%. Imports: $1.21 billion (c.i.f., 1994 est.): food, petroleum, consumer goods, capital goods. Major trading partners: U.S., Argentina, U.K., Peru, Chile, Brazil, Japan, Germany.

Geography. Landlocked Bolivia, equal in size to California and Texas combined, lies to the west of Brazil. Its other neighbors are Peru and Chile on the west and Argentina and Paraguay on the south.

The country is a low alluvial plain throughout 60% of its area toward the east, drained by the Amazon and Plata river systems. The western part, enclosed by two chains of the Andes, is a great plateau—the Altiplano, with an average altitude of 12,000 feet (3,658 m). More than 43.7% of the population lives on the plateau, which also contains Oruro, Potosi, and La Paz. At an altitude of 11,910 feet (3,630 m), La Paz is the highest administrative capital city in the world.

Lake Titicaca, half the size of Lake Ontario, is one of the highest large lakes in the world, at an altitude of 12,507 feet (3,812 m). Islands in the lake hold ruins of the ancient Incas.

Government. The Bolivian constitution provides for a democratic, representative, unitary republic, with a government made up of three branches: legislative, executive, and judicial. Executive power is exercised by the president, elected by a direct vote for a five-year term. Legislative power is vested in the National Congress, consisting of the Chamber of Deputies and the Senate. Judicial power is in the hands of the Supreme Court of Justice, made up of twelve members.

History. Famous since Spanish colonial days for its mineral wealth, modern Bolivia was once a part of the ancient Incan Empire. After the Spaniards defeated the

Incas in the 16th century, Bolivia's predominantly Indian population was reduced to slavery. The country won its independence in 1825 and was named after Simón Bolívar, the famed liberator.

Harassed by internal strife, Bolivia lost great slices of territory to three neighbor nations. Several thousand square miles and its outlet to the Pacific were taken by Chile after the War of the Pacific (1879–84). In 1903 a piece of Bolivia's Acre province, rich in rubber, was ceded to Brazil. And in 1938, after a war with Paraguay, Bolivia gave up claim to nearly 100,000 square miles of the Gran Chaco.

In 1965, a guerrilla movement mounted from Cuba and headed by Maj. Ernesto (Ché) Guevara began a revolutionary war. With the aid of U.S. military advisers, the Bolivian army, helped by the peasants, smashed the guerrilla movement, wounding and capturing Guevara on Oct. 8, 1967, and shooting him to death the next day.

Faltering steps toward restoration of civilian government were halted abruptly on July 17, 1980, when Gen. Luis Garcia Meza Tejada seized power. A series of military leaders followed before the military moved, in 1982, to return the government to civilian rule. Hernán Siles Zuazo was inaugurated President on Oct. 10, 1982.

Under Siles's left-of-center government, the country was regularly shut down by work stoppages, the bulk of Bolivia's natural resources—natural gas, gold, lithium, potassium and tungsten—were either sold on the black market or left in the ground, the country had the lowest per-capita income in South America, and inflation approached 3,000 percent. In 1985, the 73-year-old Siles decided he was unable to carry on and quit a year early.

As in 1985 the inconclusive presidential election of 1989 was decided in Congress, where the second place finisher Bánzer threw his support to Paz Zamora, who finished third, in exchange for naming a majority of the new cabinet.

The presidential elections of June 1993 gave the post to a millionaire mining entrepreneur who ran on a platform calling for free market policies and privatization. A presidential proposal to privatize six state companies was passed by Congress in March 1994. Former General Banzer was elected President for the second time in August 1997.

BOSNIA AND HERZEGOVINA

The Federation of Bosnia and Herzegovina
President: Alija Izetbegovic (1996)
Co-Prime Ministers: Haris Silajdzic and Boro Bosic
Area: 19,741 sq mi. (51,129 sq km)
Population (1997 est.): 2,607,734 (official figures not available due to ethnic cleansing); (average annual rate of natural increase: –0.82%), Muslims, 44%, Serbs, 31%, Croats, 17%. Birth rate: 6.38/1000; infant mortality rate: 36.3/1000; density per square mile: 132
Capital and largest city (1994 est.): Sarajevo (Bosnia), 300,000 (unofficial). Mostar is capital of Herzegovina. **Other large city (1991, prewar est.):** Banja Luka (Bosnia), 195,139. **Monetary unit:** Dinar. **Language:** Bosnian, written in Latin and Cyrillic. **Ethnicity/Race:** Serb 40%, Muslim 38%, Croat 22% (est.). **Religions:** Slavic Muslim, 44%; Orthodox, 31%; Catholic, 15%; Protestant, 4%, other, 6%.
Economic summary: (Reliable economic statistics not available) Gross domestic product: purchasing power parity (1995 est.): $1 billion, real growth rate n.a; inflation n.a.; unemployment n.a. Labor force: 1,026,254. Industries: steel production, mining (coal, iron ore, lead, zinc, manganese, and bauxite, vehicle assembly, textiles, tobacco products, wooden furniture, domestic appliances, oil refining. Agriculture: orchards, vineyards, livestock, some wheat and corn. Exports: n.a. Imports: n.a. Major trading partners: principally the other former Yugoslav republics.

Geography. Bosnia and Herzegovina is a roughly triangular-shaped republic about one-half the size of the state of Kentucky. The Bosnian region in the north is mountainous and covered with thick forests. The Herzegovina region in the south is largely a rugged and flat farm land. The republic is bordered on the east by Serbia, the southeast by Montenegro, and in the north and west by the Republic of Croatia. It has a narrow coastline without natural harbors stretching 13 miles (20 km) along the Adriatic Sea. The Sava and Drina Rivers form much of the country's northern and eastern boundaries with Croatia and Serbia, respectively. The Sava and its tributaries are the nation's chief rivers.

Government. Democratic republic with bicameral legislature. Following the post-war general elections in 1996, a three-person multi-ethnic collective presidency was formed.

History. Bosnia and Herzegovina were once part of the Roman provinces of Illyricum and Pannonia. Serbs first settled in the land during the 7th century C.E. and by the end of the 10th century, Bosnia became an independent state. Later Bosnia came under Hungarian rule in the middle of the 12th century.

Medieval Bosnia reached the height of its power and prestige during the 14th century when it controlled many of the surrounding territories including Herzegovina. During this period, religious strife arose among the Roman Catholic, Orthodox, and Muslim populations which weakened the country and in 1463, Ottoman Turks conquered the disunited nation.

At the Congress of Berlin in 1878 following the end of the Russo-Turkish War (1877–78), Austria was given a mandate to occupy and govern Bosnia and Herzegovina. Although the provinces were still officially part of the Ottoman Empire, they were annexed into the Austro-Hungarian empire on Oct. 7, 1908. As a result, relations with Serbia, which had claims on Bosnia and Herzegovina, became embittered. The hostile tension between the two countries climaxed in the assassination of Austrian archduke Franz Ferdinand at Sarajevo on June 28, 1914, by a Serbian nationalist. This event precipitated the start of World War I (1914–1918).

Bosnia and Herzegovina were annexed to Serbia as part of the newly formed Kingdom of Serbs, Croats, and Slovenes on Oct. 26, 1918. The name was later changed to Yugoslavia in 1929.

When Germany invaded Yugoslavia in 1941, Bosnia and Herzegovina were made part of a Croatian state that was controlled by a Fascist dictatorship. During the German and Italian occupation of their land, Bosnian and Herzegovinan resistance fighters fought a fierce guerrilla warfare against the Fascist troops.

After the defeat of Germany in 1945, Bosnia and Herzegovina were reunited into a single state as one of the six republics of the newly reestablished Yugoslavia.

In December 1991, Bosnia and Herzegovina declared their independence from Yugoslavia and asked for recognition by the 12 member nations of the European Union (E.U.). The E.U. said that before it could recommend recognition, Bosnia and Herzegovina should hold a referendum on independence.

Most Bosnian voters chose independence during a referendum held in March 1992 and President Izetbegovic again declared the nation an independent state. Attempting to carve out enclaves for themselves the Serbian minority, with the help of the largely Serbian

Yugoslav army, took the offensive and laid siege, particularly on Sarajevo, resulting in countless deaths. By the end of August, rebel Bosnian Serbs had conquered over 60% of Bosnia and Herzegovina. The Serbs formally halted their siege of Sarajevo in February 1994 at the request of Russia. In March the government signed an agreement with Bosnian Croats linking their territories into a single federation.

U.S.-sponsored peace talks in Dayton, Ohio, led to an agreement, signed in Paris in December 1995, and called for a Muslim-Croat federation and a Serb entity. 60,000 NATO troops were to supervise its implementation.

Fighting abated and orderly elections were held in September 1996. The Bosnian Muslim leader, President Alija Izetbegovic, won the majority of votes to become the leader of the three-member presidency. The other two presidents of the rotating chair are Momcilo Krajisnik (Serb) and Kresimir Zubak (Croat). Much of the administrative power lies with the local authorities. Bosnia and Herzegovina is made up of the Bosnian Serb Republic (Repulika Srpska), whose president is Biljana Plavsic (1996–), and the Muslim-Croat federation (Federacija Bosne i Hercegovine), whose federal president is Vladimir Soljik (1997–) and whose federal prime minister is Edhem Bicakcic (1997–).

Municipal elections, called for in the Dayton agreement, were repeatedly delayed amid charges of irregularities in voter registration list, but finally took place in September 1997. Little progress has been made on other conditions of the Dayton accord, including the apprehension of war crimes suspects or the resettlement of the more than 1.4 million who were displaced by the war.

BOTSWANA

Republic of Botswana
President: Quett K. J. Masire (1980)
Area: 231,800 sq mi. (600,360 sq km)
Population (1997 est.): 1,500,765 (average annual rate of natural increase: 1.47%); birth rate: 32.65/1000; infant mortality rate: 54.9/1000; density per square mile: 6.5
Capital and largest city (1992 est.): Gaborone, 138,000. **Monetary unit:** Pula. **Languages:** English, Setswana. **Ethnicity/Race:** Batswana 95%, Kalanga, Basarwa, and Kgalagadi 4%, white 1%. **Religions:** indigenous beliefs, 50%; Christian, 50%. **Literacy rate:** 80%
Economic summary: Gross domestic product: purchasing power parity (1995 est.): $4.5 billion, per capita $3,200; real growth rate 1%; inflation 10% (1994 est.); unemployment 21%. Arable land: 2%. Principal agricultural products: livestock, sorghum, corn, millet, cowpeas, beans. Labor force (1992): 428,000; 220,000 formal sector employees, most others involved in cattle raising and subsistence agriculture. 14,300 employed in South African mines. Major industrial products: diamonds, copper, nickel, salt, soda ash, potash, coal, frozen beef, tourism. Natural resources: diamonds, copper, nickel, salt, soda ash, potash, coal, natural gas. Exports: $1.8 billion (f.o.b., 1994): diamonds, 78%; copper and nickel, 6%; meat, 5%. Imports: $1.8 billion (c.i.f., 1992): foodstuffs, vehicles, textiles, petroleum products. Major trading partners: Switzerland, U.K., Southern African Customs Union (SACU), U.S. **Member of Commonwealth of Nations**

Geography. Twice the size of Arizona, Botswana is in South Central Africa, bounded by Namibia, Zambia, Zimbabwe, and South Africa. Most of the country is near-desert, with the Kalahari occupying the western part of the country. The eastern part is hilly, with salt lakes in the north.

Government. A parliamentary republic. The Botswana constitution provides, in addition to the unicameral National Assembly, for a House of Chiefs, which has a voice on bills affecting tribal affairs. There is universal suffrage.

History. Botswana is the land of the Batawana tribes, which, when threatened by the Boers in Transvaal, asked Britain in 1885 to establish a protectorate over the country, then known as Bechuanaland. In 1961, Britain granted a constitution to the country. Self-government began in 1965, and on Sept. 30, 1966, the country became independent.

Owing to a land scandal the Vice President and the minister of agriculture were forced to resign in March 1992. The minister of finance was selected to be the new Vice President.

October 1994 elections for the Assembly gave 26 of the 40 contested seats to the Botswana Democratic Party.

The President reduced the voting age to 18 in April 1995.

Botswana, along with Namibia and Zimbabwe, received permission in June 1997 from a U.N. wildlife panel to sell 5.9 tons of stockpiled ivory to Japan.

BRAZIL

Federative Republic of Brazil
National name: República Federativa do Brasil
President: Fernando Henrique Cardoso (1994)
Area: 3,286,470 sq mi. (8,511,957 sq km)
Population (1997 est.): 164,511,366 (average annual rate of natural increase: 1.1%); birth rate: 20.43/1000; infant mortality rate: 53.4/1000; density per square mile: 50
Capital (1995 est.): Brasilia, 2,500,000. **Largest cities (1995 est.):** São Paulo, 15,800,000; Rio de Janeiro, 10,000,000; Porto Alegre, 3,000,000; Recife, 2,900,999; Salvador, 2,600,000; Belo Horizonte, 2,600,000. **Monetary unit:** Real. **Language:** Portuguese. **Ethnicity/Race:** white (includes Portuguese, German, Italian, Spanish, Polish) 55%, mixed white and African 38%, African 6%, other (includes Japanese, Arab, Amerindian) 1%. **Religion:** Roman Catholic, 90% (nominal). **Literacy rate:** 81%
Economic summary: Gross domestic product: purchasing power parity (1995 est.): $976.8 billion; per capita $6,100; 4.2% real growth rate; inflation 23% (1995); unemployment 5%. Arable land: 7%. Principal products: world's largest producer of coffee. Sugar cane, oranges, cocoa, soybeans, tobacco, cattle. Labor force (1989 est.): 57 million; services: 42%; agriculture: 31%; industry: 27%. Major industrial products: steel, chemicals, petrochemicals, machinery, motor vehicles, cement, lumber. Natural resources: iron ore, manganese, bauxite, nickel, other industrial metals, hydropower, timber. Exports: $46.5 billion (f.o.b., 1995): coffee, iron ore, soybeans, sugar, beef, transport equipment, footwear, orange juice. Imports: $49.7 billion (f.o.b., 1995): crude oil, capital goods, chemical products, foodstuffs, coal. Major trading partners: U.S., European Union, Japan, Latin America, Middle East.

Geography. Brazil covers nearly half of South America, extends 2,965 miles (4,772 km) north-south, 2,691 miles (4,331 km), east-west, and borders every nation on the continent except Chile and Ecuador.

More than a third of Brazil is drained by the Amazon and its more than 200 tributaries. The Amazon is navigable for ocean steamers to Iquitos, Peru, 2,300 miles

(3,700 km) upstream. Southern Brazil is drained by the Plata system—the Paraguay, Uruguay, and Paraná Rivers. The most important stream entirely within Brazil is the São Francisco, navigable for 1,000 miles (1,903 km), but broken near its mouth by the 275-foot (84 m) Paulo Afonso Falls.

Government. A federal republic. The President and Vice President are elected for a 4-year term. They cannot be re-elected for a consecutive term. The National Congress maintains a bicameral structure—a Senate, whose members serve eight-year terms, and a Chamber of Deputies, elected for four-year terms.

History. Brazil is the only Latin American nation deriving its language and culture from Portugal. Adm. Pedro Alvares Cabral claimed the territory for the Portuguese in 1500. He brought to Portugal a cargo of wood, pau-brasil, from which the land received its name. Portugal began colonization in 1532 and made the area a royal colony in 1549.

During the Napoleonic wars, King João VI, then Prince Regent, fled the country in 1807 in advance of the French armies and in 1808 set up his court in Rio de Janeiro. João was drawn home in 1820 by a revolution, leaving his son as Regent. When Portugal sought to reduce Brazil again to colonial status, the Prince declared Brazil's independence on Sept. 7, 1822, and became Pedro I, Emperor of Brazil.

Harassed by his parliament, Pedro I abdicated in 1831 in favor of his five-year-old son, who became Emperor in 1840 as Pedro II. The son was a popular monarch, but discontent built up and, in 1889, following a military revolt, he had to abdicate. Although a republic was proclaimed, Brazil was under two military dictatorships during the next four years. A revolt permitted a gradual return to stability under civilian presidents.

The President during World War I, Wenceslau Braz, cooperated with the Allies and declared war on Germany.

In World War II, Brazil cooperated with the Western Allies, welcoming Allied air bases, patrolling the South Atlantic, and joining the invasion of Italy after declaring war on the Axis.

Gen. João Baptista de Oliveira Figueiredo became president in 1979 and pledged a return to democracy in 1985.

The electoral college's choice of Tancredo Neves on Jan. 15, 1985, as the first civilian president since 1964 brought a nationwide wave of optimism, but the 75-year-old President-elect was hospitalized and underwent a series of intestinal operations. When Neves died on April 21, Vice President Sarney became president. However, he was widely distrusted because he had previously been a member of the military regime's political party.

Collor de Mello won the election of late 1989 and took office in March 1990 despite his lack of support from a major party. In the campaign he pledged to lower the chronic hyperinflation following the path of free-market economics.

On the basis of a corruption scandal, Collor faced impeachment by Congress in 1992. Just minutes after the trial began on December 29 the President resigned, and the Vice President assumed the presidency.

A former finance minister, Fernando Cordoso won the presidency in the October 1994 election with 54% of the vote. However, his party and its coalition allies failed to win a majority in either of the congressional houses.

In light of vivid revelations of police brutality, a new law was passed in April 1997 making torture a crime. A constitutional amendment protecting human rights was also drawn up and approved in a Senate committee.

BRUNEI DARUSSALAM

State of Brunei Darussalam
Sultan: Haji Hassanal Bolkiah (1967)
Area: 2,226 sq mi. (5,765 sq km)
Population (1997 est.): 307,616 (annual rate of natural increase: 2%); birth rate: 25.2/1000; infant mortality rate: 23.8/1000; density per square mile: 138.2
Capital and largest city (1991 est.): Bandar Seri Begawan, 21,484, Seria, Kuala Belait, Tutong, Bangar.
Monetary unit: Brunei Dollar. **Languages:** Malay (official), Chinese, English. **Ethnicity/Race:** Malay 69%, Chinese 18%, other 8%. **Religions:** Islam (official religion), 67%; Christian, 9%; Buddhist, 12%; indigenous beliefs and other, 12%. **Literacy rate:** 85%
Economic summary: Gross domestic product: purchasing power parity (1995 est.): $4.6 billion; per capita $15,800; real growth rate 2%; inflation 6.0% (1995 est.); unemployment 4.7% (1995 est.). Arable land: 1%; principal agricultural products: fruit, rice, pepper, buffaloes. Labor force: 135,000 (1996): social and personal service sectors, 49%; commerce and services, 14%; government and public authorities, 40%; construction, 13%. Major industrial products: crude petroleum, liquefied natural gas, timber. Natural resources: petroleum, natural gas, timber. Exports: $2.4 billion (f.o.b., 1994 est.): crude petroleum, liquefied natural gas. Imports: $1.8 billion (c.i.f., 1994 est.): machinery, transport equipment, manufactured goods, foodstuffs, chemicals. Major trading partners: Japan, Thailand, U.S., U.K., Singapore, South Korea; regional group trading partners: ASEAN, APEC, and E.U.

Geography. About the size of Delaware, Brunei is an independent sultanate on the northwest coast of the island of Borneo in the South China Sea, wedged between the Malaysian states of Sabah and Sarawak. Three quarters of the thinly populated country is covered with tropical rain forest; there are rich oil and gas deposits.

Government. Sultan Hassanal Bolkiah is ruler of the state, a former British protectorate, which became fully sovereign and independent on New Year's Day, 1984, presiding over a Privy Council and Council of Ministers appointed by himself.

History. Brunei (pronounced broon-eye) was a powerful state from the 16th to the 19th century, ruling over the northern part of Borneo and adjacent island chains. But it fell into decay and lost Sarawak in 1841, becoming a British protectorate in 1888 and a British dependency in 1905.

The Sultan regained control over internal affairs in 1959, but Britain retained responsibility for the state's defense and foreign affairs until the end of 1983, when the sultanate became fully independent.

Sultan Bolkiah was Crowned in 1968 at the age of 22, succeeding his father, Sir Omar Ali Saifuddin, who had abdicated. During his reign, exploitation of the rich Seria oilfield had made the sultanate wealthy.

Warning against opposition to his government, the Islamic religion and himself, the Sultan in 1990 said that the laws of the sultanate would be restructured into conformity with Islamic law.

In October 1995 the country joined the IMF and the World Bank.

Although well more than half of the estimated number of illegal immigrants from Indonesia and the Philippines had registered by July 1995, many had yet to do so before the cutoff at the end of August.

BULGARIA

Republic of Bulgaria
National name: Narodna Republika Bulgariya
President: Petar Stoyanov (1997)
Prime Minister: Ivan Kostov (1997)
Area: 42,823 sq mi. (110,912 sq km)
Population (1997 est.): 8,652,745 (average annual rate of natural increase: –0.5%); birth rate: 8.42/1000; infant mortality rate: 15.4/1000; density per square mile: 202
Capital and largest city (1994 est.): Sofia, 1,113,674. **Largest cities (1994 est.):** Plovdiv, 345,205; Varna, 307,200; Burgas, 198,439; Ruse, 170,209. **Monetary unit:** Lev. **Language:** Bulgarian. **Ethnicity/Race:** Bulgarian 85.3%, Turk 8.5%, Gypsy 2.6%, Macedonian 2.5%, Armenian 0.3%, Russian 0.2%, other 0.6%. **Religions:** Eastern Orthodox, 90%; Muslim, Catholic, Protestant, Judaic, Armeno-Gregorian. **Literacy rate:** 95%
Economic summary: Gross domestic product: purchasing power parity (1995 est.): $43.2 billion, per capita $4,920; real growth rate 2.4%; inflation 35%; unemployment 11.9%. Arable land: 34%. Principal products: grains, tobacco, fruits, vegetables. Labor force: 3.1 million; industry: 41%; agriculture: 18%; other: 41%. Major products: processed agricultural products, machinery, electronics, chemicals. Natural resources: metals, minerals, timber. Exports: $4.2 billion (f.o.b., 1994): machinery and transport equipment, fuels, minerals, raw materials, agricultural products. Imports: $4 billion (c.i.f., 1994): machinery and transportation equipment, fuels, raw materials, metals, agricultural raw products. Major trading partners: C.I.S., U.S., Eastern European countries, E.U.

Geography. Two mountain ranges and two great valleys mark the topography of Bulgaria, a country the size of Tennessee. Situated on the Black Sea in the eastern part of the Balkan peninsula, it shares borders with Serbia, Macedonia, Romania, Greece, and Turkey. The Balkan belt crosses the center of the country, almost due east-west, rising to a height of 6,888 feet (2,100 m). The Rhodope, Rila, and Pirin mountains straighten out along the western and southern border. Between the two ranges, is the valley of the Maritsa, Bulgaria's principal river. Between the Balkan range and the Danube, which forms most of the northern boundary with Romania, is the Danubian tableland.

Southern Dobruja, a fertile region of 2,900 square miles (7,511 sq km), below the Danube delta, is an area of low hills, fens, and sandy steppes.

Government. An emerging democracy. The National Assembly, consisting of 240 members is the legislative body.

History. The first Bulgarians, a tribe of wild horsemen akin to the Huns, crossed the Danube from the north in c.e. 679 and subjugated the Slavic population of Moesia. They adopted a Slav dialect and Slavic customs and twice conquered most of the Balkan peninsula between 893 and 1280. After the Serbs subjected their kingdom in 1330, the Bulgars gradually fell prey to the Turks, and from 1396 to 1878 Bulgaria was a Turkish province. In 1878, Russia forced Turkey to give the country its independence; but the European powers, fearing that Bulgaria might become a Russian dependency, intervened. By the Treaty of Berlin in 1878, Bulgaria became autonomous under Turkish sovereignty.

In 1887, Prince Ferdinand of Saxe-Coburg-Gotha was elected ruler of Bulgaria; on Oct. 5, 1908, he declared the country independent and took the title of Tsar.

Bulgaria joined Germany in World War I and lost. On Oct. 3, 1918, Tsar Ferdinand abdicated in favor of his son, Tsar Boris III. Boris assumed dictatorial powers in

1934–35. When Hitler awarded Bulgaria southern Dobruja, taken from Romania in 1940, Boris joined the Nazis in war the next year and occupied parts of Yugoslavia and Greece. Later the Germans tried to force Boris to send his troops against the Russians. Boris resisted and died under mysterious circumstances on Aug. 28, 1943. Simeon II, infant son of Boris, became nominal ruler under a regency. Russia declared war on Bulgaria on Sept. 5, 1944. An armistice was agreed to three days later, after Bulgaria had declared war on Germany. Russian troops streamed in the next day and under an informal armistice a coalition "Fatherland Front" cabinet was set up under Kimon Georgiev.

A Soviet-style People's Republic was established in 1947 and Bulgaria acquired the reputation of being the most slavishly loyal to Moscow of all the East European Communist countries.

The General Secretary of the Bulgarian Communist Party, Todor Zhikov, resigned in 1989 after 35 years in power. His successor, Peter Mladenov, purged the Politburo, ended the Communist monopoly on power and held free elections in May 1990 that led to a surprising victory for the Communists, renamed the Bulgarian Socialist Party. Mladenov was forced to resign in July 1990.

Parliamentary elections in October 1991 resulted in a victory for the opposition Union of Democratic Forces. In the presidential election of January 1992, UDF leader Zhelev won 53.5% of the vote.

December 1994 parliamentary elections gave an absolute majority in the Assembly to the Socialists. The economy, however, had deteriorated in recent years amid growing concern over the spread of organized crime.

Parliamentary elections in April 1997 gave 137 seats in the legislature to the pro-Western UDF with the Socialists retaining only 58 seats. The new government pledged to work toward qualifying for membership in the European Union and NATO.

BURKINA FASO

National name: Burkina Faso
President: Blaise Compaore (1991)
Prime Minister: Kadre Desire Ouedraogo (1996)
Area: 105,870 sq mi. (274,200 sq km)
Population (1997 est.): 10,891,159 (average annual rate of natural increase: 2.61%); birth rate: 46.43/1000; infant mortality rate: 116.6/1000; density per square mile: 102.9
Capital and largest city (1994 est.): Ouagadougou, 500,000. **Monetary unit:** Franc CFA. **Languages:** French, Tribal languages. **Ethnicity/Race:** Mossi (about 24%), Gurunsi, Senufo, Lobi, Bobo, Mande, Fulani. **Religions:** Muslim, 50%; Christian (mainly Roman Catholic), 10%; indigenous beliefs, 40%. **Literacy rate:** 18%
Economic summary: Gross domestic product: purchasing power parity (1995 est.): $7.4 billion, per capita $700; real growth rate 4%; inflation 5%; unemployment n.a. Arable land: 10%. Labor force: n.a.; in agriculture: 80%; industry: 15%; commerce, services, and government: 5%. Principal products: millet, sorghum, corn, rice, livestock, peanuts, sugar cane, cotton. Major industrial products: processed agricultural products, light industrial items, brick, brewed products. Natural resources: manganese, limestone, marble, gold, uranium, bauxite, copper. Exports: $273 million (f.o.b., 1993): oilseeds, cotton, live animals, gold. Imports: $636 million (f.o.b., 1993): grain, dairy products, petroleum, machinery. Major trading partners: E.U., Côte d'Ivoire, Africa, Taiwan, Japan, Thailand.

Geography. Slightly larger than Colorado, Burkina Faso, formerly known as Upper Volta, is a landlocked country in West Africa. Its neighbors are Côte d'Ivoire, Mali, Niger, Benin, Togo, and Ghana. The country consists of extensive plains, low hills, high savannas, and a desert area in the north.

Government. In June 1991 voters approved a draft constitution providing for three branches of government and presidential elections every seven years. Seventeen political parties are represented in the National Assembly.

History. The country, called Upper Volta by the French, consists chiefly of the lands of the Mossi Empire, where France established a protectorate over the Kingdom of Ouagadougou in 1897. Upper Volta became a separate colony in 1919, was partitioned among Niger, the Sudan, and Côte d'Ivoire in 1932, and was reconstituted in 1947. An autonomous republic within the French Community, it became independent on Aug. 5, 1960.

President Maurice Yameogo was deposed on Jan. 3, 1966, by a military coup led by Col. Sangoulé Lamizana, who dissolved the National Assembly and suspended the constitution. constitutional rule returned in 1978 with the election of an Assembly and a presidential vote in June in which Gen. Lamizana won by a narrow margin over three other candidates.

On Nov. 25, 1980, there was a bloodless coup which placed Gen. Lamizana under house arrest. Col. Sayé Zerbo took charge as the president of the Military Committee of Reform for National Progress. Maj. Jean-Baptiste Ouedraogo toppled Zerbo in another coup on Nov. 7, 1982. Captain Thomas Sankara, in turn, deposed Ouedraogo a year later. His government changed the country's name on Aug. 3, 1984, to Burkina Faso (the "land of upright men") to sever ties with its colonial past. He was overthrown and killed by Blaise Compaore in 1987.

For unstated reasons, Prime Minister Kabore resigned in February 1996, and was replaced by a little-known economist, Kadre Desire Ouedraogo. The ruling party, Congress for Democracy and Progress, won 101 of the 111 seats in the parliamentary election of May 1997. Three opposition parties split the remaining 10 seats.

BURMA (MYANMAR)

Union of Burma or Union of Myanmar
National name: Pyidaungsu Myanmar Naingngandau
Head of State (Chairman): Senior Gen. Than Shwe (1992)
Area: 261,220 sq mi. (676,560 sq km)
Population (1997 est.): 46,821,943 (average annual rate of natural increase: 1.81%); birth rate: 29.54/1000; infant mortality rate: 78.5/1000; density per square mile: 179.2
Capital: Rangoon. **Largest cities (est. 1983):** Rangoon (Yangon), 2,458,712; Mandalay, 532,895. **Monetary unit:** Kyat. **Language:** Burmese, minority languages. **Ethnicity/Race:** Burman 68%, Shan 9%, Karen 7%, Rakhine 4%, Chinese 3%, Mon 2%, Indian 2%, other 5%. **Religions:** Buddhist 89.5%, Christian 4.9%, Muslim 3.8%, Hindu 0.05%, Animist 1.3%. **Literacy rate:** 81%
Economic summary: Gross domestic product: purchasing power parity (1995 est.): $47 billion; $1,000 per capita; real growth rate 6.8% (1994 est.). Arable land: 15%. Principal products: oilseed, pulses, sugar cane, corn, rice. Labor force (FY89 est.): 16,036,000: 65.2% agriculture, 14.3% industry. Major products: textiles, footwear, processed agricultural

products, wood and wood products, refined petroleum. Natural resources: timber, tin, antimony, zinc, copper, precious stones, crude oil and natural gas. Exports (FY 94/95 est.): $879 million: rice, teak, oilseeds, metals, rubber, gems. Imports (FY 94/95 est.): $1.5 billion: machinery, transportation equipment, chemicals, food products. Major trading partners: Japan, E.U., China, Singapore, Thailand, India, Hong Kong, Malaysia.

Geography. Burma occupies the northwest portion of the Indochinese peninsula. India lies to the northwest and China to the northeast. Bangladesh, Laos, and Thailand are also neighbors. The Bay of Bengal touches the southwestern coast.

Slightly smaller than Texas, the country is divided into three natural regions: the Arakan Yoma, a long, narrow mountain range forming the barrier between Burma and India; the Shan Plateau in the east, extending southward into Tenasserim; and the Central Basin, running down to the flat fertile delta of the Irrawaddy in the south. This delta contains a network of intercommunicating canals and nine principal river mouths.

Government. A military regime. On March 2, 1962, the government of U Nu was overthrown and replaced by a Revolutionary Council, which assumed all power in the state. Gen. U Ne Win, as chairman of the Revolutionary Council, became the chief executive. In 1972, Ne Win and his colleagues resigned their military titles. In 1974, Ne Win dissolved the Revolutionary Council and became president under the new constitution. He voluntarily relinquished the presidency on Nov. 9, 1981. A military coup led by Gen. Saw Maung overthrew the civilian government in 1988.

In 1989, the military government changed the name of Burma to Myanmar. The U.S. State Department does not recognize the name Myanmar or the military regime that represents it since they illegally retained power after the National League of Democracy (NLD) won a 1990 election.

On April 23, 1992, Senior Gen. Saw Maung handed over the power to Senior General Than Shwe, who continued to take the responsibility of the Chairman of the State Law and Order Restoration Council. The State Law and Order Restoration Council (SLORC) is a military government and is made up of the chairman and 20 other members.

History. In 1612, the British East India Company sent agents to Burma, but the Burmese long resisted efforts of British traders, and Dutch and Portuguese as well, to establish posts on the Bay of Bengal. Through the Anglo-Burmese War in 1824–26 and two following wars, the British East India Company expanded to the whole of Burma by 1886. Burma was annexed to India. It became a separate colony in 1937.

During World War II, Burma was a key battleground; the 800-mile Burma Road was the Allies' vital supply line to China. The Japanese invaded the country in December 1941, and by May 1942 had occupied most of it, cutting off the Burma Road. After one of the most difficult campaigns of the war, Allied forces liberated most of Burma prior to the Japanese surrender in August 1945.

Burma became independent on Jan. 4, 1948. In 1951 and 1952 the Socialists achieved power.

In 1968, after the government had made headway against the Communist and separatist rebels, the military regime adopted a policy of strict nonalignment and followed "the Burmese Way" to socialism. But the insurgents continued to be active.

The civilian government was overthrown in Sept. 1988 by a military junta led by General Saw Maung, an associate of U Ne Win.

The new government held elections in May 1990 and the opposition National League for Democracy won in a landslide. The military, or SLORC (State Law and Order Restoration Council), refused to recognize the election results. The leader of the opposition, Aung San Suu Kyi, was awarded the Nobel Peace Prize in 1991, which focused world attention on SLORC's repressive policies. Daughter of the assassinated general Aung San, revered as the father of Burmese independence, Suu Kyi remained under house arrest from 1989 to July 10, 1995.

A new constitution was drafted in 1994 that called for an elected executive branch but appeared designed specifically to forbid Aung San Suu Kyi from becoming president. The Association of Southeast Asian Nations decided to admit the country despite Suu Kyi's plea to the contrary.

In April 1997 the U.S. government imposed sanctions designed to prevent U.S. private investment in Burma.

The government has subdued fifteen insurgent groups over the last several decades. The last major ethnic group to continue fighting against SLORC is the Karen rebels.

BURUNDI

Republic of Burundi
National name: Republika Y'Uburundi
President: Major Pierre Buyoya (1996)
Prime Minister: Pascal Firmin Ndmira (1996)
Area: 10,747 sq mi. (27,834 sq km)
Population (1997 est.): 6,052,614 (average annual rate of natural increase: 2.72%); birth rate: 42.33/1000; infant mortality rate: 100.5/1000; density per square mile: 563.2
Capital and largest city (1994 est.): Bujumbura, 300,000. **Other large city (est. 1982):** Gitega, 101,827. **Monetary unit:** Burundi franc. **Languages:** Kirundi and French (official), Swahili. **Ethnicity/Race:** Africans: Hutu (Bantu) 85%, Tutsi (Hamitic) 14%, Twa (Pygmy) 1%; non-Africans: Europeans 3,000, South Asians 2,000. **Religions:** Roman Catholic, 62%; Protestant, 5%; indigenous, 32%. **Literacy rate:** 50%
Economic summary: Gross domestic product: purchasing power parity (1995 est.): $4 billion, per capita $600; real growth rate 2.7%; inflation 10% (1993 est.). Arable land: 43%. Principal agricultural products: coffee, tea, cotton, bananas, sorghum. Labor force: 1.9 million (1983 est.); 93% in agriculture. Major industrial products: light consumer goods. Natural resources: nickel, uranium, rare earth oxide, peat, cobalt, copper, unexploited platinum, vanadium. Exports: $68 million (f.o.b., 1993): coffee, tea, cotton, hides and skins. Imports: $203 million (c.i.f., 1993): food, petroleum products, capital goods, consumer goods. Major trading partners: U.S., Western Europe, Asia.

Geography. Wedged between Tanzania, Congo, and Rwanda in east central Africa, Burundi occupies a high plateau divided by several deep valleys. It is equal in size to Maryland.

Government. A republic. Legislative and executive power is vested in the President.

A new constitution adopted by referendum on March 9, 1992, established a multiparty system.

History. Burundi was once part of German East Africa. An integrated society developed among the Watusi, a tall, warlike people and nomad cattle raisers, and the Bahutu, a Bantu people, who were subject farmers. Belgium won a League of Nations mandate in 1923, and subsequently Burundi, with Rwanda, was transferred to the status of a United Nations trust territory.

In 1962, Burundi gained independence and became a kingdom under Mwami Mwambutsa IV. His son deposed him in 1966 to rule as Ntaré V. He was overthrown by Premier Micombero.

One of Africa's worst tribal wars, which became genocide, occurred in Burundi in April 1972, following the return of Ntaré V. He was given a safe-conduct promise in writing by President Micombero but was "judged and immediately executed" by the Burundi leader. His return was apparently attended by an invasion of exiles of Burundi's Hutu tribe. Whether Hutus living in Burundi joined the invasion is unclear, but after it failed, the victorious Tutsis proceeded to massacre some 100,000 persons in six weeks, with possibly 100,000 more slain by summer.

On Nov. 1, 1976, Lt. Col. Jean-Baptiste Bagaza led a coup and assumed the presidency. He suspended the constitution, and announced that a 30-member Supreme Revolutionary Council would be the governing body.

The Burundi Democracy Front's candidate Melchior Ndadaye won the first democratic presidential elections held on June 2, 1993.

Ndadaye, the first Hutu to assume power in a country dominated by the Tutsi minority, was killed by Tutsi paratroopers on April 6, 1994, when his plane was shot down. The plane crash also killed the Rwandan president. As a result, Hutu youth gangs began massacring Tutsis; the Tutsi–controlled army retaliated by killing Hutus.

The frequency of ethnic clashes increased, developing into a low-intensity civil war. A six-nation regional proposal to send troops into Burundi to maintain peace and order was devised in July 1996. Distrustful of the scheme, the Tutsi-dominated army led a coup deposing the Hutu president and installed Major Pierre Buyoya, a Tutsi, that month.

An African embargo, the intent of which was to force negotiations between the Tutsis and the Hutu rebels, was eased in April 1997 after showing no evidence in achieving its political aims.

CAMBODIA

King: Prince Norodom Sihanouk (1991)
Prime Minister: Ung Huot (1997)
Area: 69,884 sq mi. (181,035 sq km)
Population (1997 est.): 11,163,861 (average annual rate of natural increase: 2.72%); birth rate: 42.63/1000; infant mortality rate: 106/1000; density per square mile: 159.7
Capital and largest city (1991 est.): Phnom Penh, 900,000. **Monetary unit:** Riel. **Ethnic groups:** Khmer, 90%; Chinese, 5%; other minorities 5%. **Languages:** Khmer (official), French, English. **Ethnicity/Race:** Khmer 90%, Vietnamese 5%, Chinese 1%, other 4%. **Religion:** Theravada Buddhist, 5% others. **Literacy rate:** 35%
Economic summary: Gross domestic product: purchasing power parity (1995 est.): $7 billion, per capita $660; real growth rate 6.7%; inflation 6%. Arable land: 16%. Principal agricultural products: rice, rubber, corn. Labor force: 2.5–3.0 million; 80% in agriculture. Major industrial products: fish, wood and wood products, milled rice, rubber, cement. Natural resources: timber, gemstones, iron ore, manganese, phosphate. Exports: $240.7 million (1995 est.): natural rubber, rice, pepper, wood. Imports: $630.5 million (1995 est.): foodstuffs, fuel, consumer goods. Major trading partners: Vietnam, Japan, India, Singapore, Malaysia, China, Thailand.

Geography. Situated on the Indochinese peninsula, Cambodia is bordered by Thailand and Laos on the north and Vietnam on the east and south. The Gulf of

Siam is off the western coast. The country, the size of Missouri, consists chiefly of a large alluvial plain ringed in by mountains and on the east by the Mekong River. The plain is centered on Lake Tonle Sap, which is a natural storage basin of the Mekong.

Government. Constitutional monarchy.

History. Cambodia came under Khmer rule about C.E. 600. Under the Khmers, magnificent temples were built at Angkor. The Khmer Kingdom once ruled over most of Southeast Asia, but attacks by the Thai and the Vietnamese almost annihilated the empire until the French joined Cambodia, Laos, and Vietnam into French Indochina.

Under Norodom Sihanouk, enthroned in 1941, and particularly under Japanese occupation during World War II, nationalism revived. After the ouster of the Japanese, the Cambodians sought independence, but the French returned in 1946, granting the country a constitution in 1947 and independence within the French Union in 1949. Sihanouk won full military control during the French-Indochinese War in 1953. He abdicated in 1955 in favor of his parents, remaining head of the government, and when his father died in 1960, became chief of state without returning to the throne. In 1963, he sought a guarantee of Cambodia's neutrality from all parties to the Vietnam War.

On March 18, 1970, while Sihanouk was abroad trying to get North Vietnamese and the Vietcong out of border sanctuaries near Vietnam, anti-Vietnamese riots occurred, and Sihanouk was overthrown.

The Vietnam peace agreement of 1973 stipulated withdrawal of foreign forces from Cambodia, but fighting continued between Hanoi-backed insurgents and U.S.-supplied government troops.

Fighting climaxed in April 1975 when the Lon Nol regime was overthrown by Pol Pot, leader of the Communist Khmer Rouge forces.

Between 1975 and 1979, from 1 to 2 million people were executed by the Khmer Rouge or died under the brutal conditions of forced labor. Border clashes with Vietnam developed into a Vietnamese invasion and Pol Pot was ousted by Vietnamese forces on Jan. 8, 1979, and a new government led by Heng Samrin was installed.

While Sihanouk remained in exile, about 9,000 non-Communist troops loyal to him and another 15,000 under Son Sann joined about 35,000 Communist Pol Pot forces fighting the 170,000 Vietnamese troops supporting the Heng Samrin government.

The Vietnamese plan originally called for them to withdraw by early 1990 and negotiate a political settlement. The talks, however, stalled through 1990 on into 1991. In 1992 a U.N. agreement was signed in Paris under which Prince Sihanouk was to be the leader of a Supreme National Council that was to run the country until free elections in 1993.

Free elections in May 1993 saw the defeat of the ruling party. In June the victors, the royalist opposition, completed a power sharing deal with the ruling party. In September the constitution was changed, restoring the monarchy. Later that month Sihanouk was formally installed.

The Khmer Rouge stronghold in the western jungles splintered in 1997, with factions warring against each other or defecting. In July 1997, the Khmer Rouge tried and sentenced their notorious leader, Pol Pot, to lifetime house arrest, dissatisfying many who felt he should have faced an international tribunal.

First Prime Minister Hun Sen deposed the First Prime Minister, Prince Norodom Ranariddh, the country's only popularly elected leader, and installed a new First Prime Minister, viewed by the international community as Hun Sen's puppet.

CAMEROON

Republic of Cameroon
National name: République du Cameroun
President: Paul Biya (1988)
Prime Minister: Peter Musonge Mafani (1996)
Area: 183,569 sq mi. (475,442 sq km)
Population (1997 est.): 14,677,510 (average annual rate of natural increase: 2.85%); birth rate: 42.22/1000; infant mortality rate: 77.6/1000; density per square mile: 80
Capital: Yaoundé. **Largest cities (1991 est.):** Douala, 908,000; Yaoundé, 730,000. **Monetary unit:** Franc CFA. **Languages:** French and English (both official); 24 major African language groups. **Ethnicity/Race:** Cameroon Highlanders 31%, Equatorial Bantu 19%, Kirdi 11%, Fulani 10%, Northwestern Bantu 8%, Eastern Nigritic 7%, other African 13%, non-African less than 1%. **Religions:** 51% indigenous beliefs, 33% Christian, 16% Muslim. **Literacy rate:** 56.2%
Economic summary: Gross domestic product: purchasing power parity (1995 est.): $16.5 billion, per capita $1,200; real growth rate 1.8%; inflation 48% (1994); unemployment n.a. Arable land: 13%. Agriculture: coffee, cocoa, timber, corn, peanuts, cotton, rubber, bananas, oilseed, grains, livestock, root starches. Labor force in agriculture: 74.4%; industry and transport: 11.4%; other services: 14.2% (1983). Industries: crude oil products, food processing, light consumer goods, textiles, sawmills. Natural resources: timber, some oil, bauxite, hydropower potential. Exports: $1.2 billion (f.o.b., 1994): cocoa, coffee, timber, petroleum, aluminum products. Imports: $810 million (f.o.b., 1994): machines and electrical equipment, transport equipment, consumer goods. Major trading partners: France, U.S., Western European nations, African countries, Japan.

Geography. Cameroon is a central African nation on the Gulf of Guinea, bordered by Nigeria, Chad, the Central African Republic, the Congo, Equatorial Guinea, and Gabon. It is nearly twice the size of Oregon.

The interior consists of a high plateau, rising to 4,500 feet (1,372 m), with the land descending to a lower, densely wooded plateau and then to swamps and plains along the coast. Mount Cameroon (13,350 ft.; 4,069 m), near the coast, is the highest elevation in the country. The main rivers are the Benue, Nyong, and Sanaga.

Government. After a 1972 plebiscite, a unitary nation was formed out of East and West Cameroon to replace the former Federal Republic. At present the country is a multiparty democracy with a one house legislative body, the National Assembly, holding 180 seats.

History. The Republic of Cameroon is inhabited by Hamitic and Semitic peoples in the north, where Islam is the principal religion, and by Bantu peoples in the central and southern regions, where native animism prevails. The tribes were conquered by many invaders.

The land escaped colonial rule until 1884, when treaties with tribal chiefs brought the area under German domination. After World War I, the League of Nations gave the French a mandate over 80% of the area, and the British 20% adjacent to Nigeria. After World War II, when the country came under a U.N. trusteeship in 1946, self-government was granted, and the Cameroon People's Union emerged as the dominant party by campaigning for reunification of French and British Cameroon and for independence. Accused of being under Communist control, it waged a campaign of revolutionary terror from 1955 to 1958, when it was crushed. In British Cameroon, unification was pressed also by the leading party, the Kamerun National Democratic Party, led by John Foncha.

France set up Cameroon as an autonomous state in 1957, and the next year its legislative assembly voted for independence by 1960. In 1959 a fully autonomous government of Cameroon was formed under Ahmadou Ahidjo. Cameroon became an independent republic on Jan. 1, 1960.

Biya won the presidential election in October 1992 but by a narrow margin.

In November 1995, the country was accepted into the Commonwealth of Nations. Although fraught with massive irregularities, parliamentary elections in May 1997 gave a majority of seats to the President's People's Democratic Movement. The voting was contested by 45 parties.

CANADA

Sovereign: Queen Elizabeth II (1952)
Governor General: Roméo LeBlanc (1995)
Prime Minister: Jean Chrétien (1993)
Area: 3,851,809 sq mi. (9,976,186 sq km)
Population (1997 est.): 29,123,194. Average annual rate of natural increase: 0.58%; birth rate: 13.06/1000; infant mortality rate: 6/1000; density per square mile: 7.6
Capital: Ottawa, Ontario. **Largest cities (1996 census; metropolitan areas):** Toronto, 4,263,757; Montreal, 3,326,510; Vancouver: 1,831,665; Ottawa/Hull, 1,010,498; Edmonton, 862,597; Calgary, 821,628; Quebec, 671,889; Winnipeg, 667,209; Hamilton, 624,360; London, 398,616; . **Monetary Unit:** Canadian dollar. **Languages:** English, French. **Ethnicity/Race:** British Isles origin 40%, French origin 27%, other European 20%, indigenous Indian and Inuit 1.5%, other, mostly Asian 11.5%. **Religions:** 46% Roman Catholic, 16% United Church, 10% Anglican. **Literacy rate:** 99%
Economic Summary: Gross domestic product: purchasing power parity (1995 est.): $694 billion, per capita $24,400; real growth rate 2.1%; inflation 2.4% (1995 est.); unemployment 9.5%. Arable land: 7.47%. Principal products: wheat, barley, oats, livestock. Labor force: 14.93 million; 75% in manufacturing. Major industrial products: transportation equipment, petroleum, chemicals, wood products. Exports: $185 billion (f.o.b., 1995 est.): newsprint, wood pulp, timber, crude petroleum, machinery, natural gas, aluminum, motor vehicles and parts, telecommunications equipment. Imports: $166.7 billion (c.i.f., 1995 est.): crude petroleum, chemicals, motor vehicles and parts, durable consumer goods, computers, telecommunications equipment and parts. Major trading partners: U.S., Japan, U.K., C.I.S. nations, Germany, Mexico, South Korea, Taiwan.

Geography. Covering most of the northern part of the North American continent and with an area larger than that of the United States, Canada has an extremely varied topography. In the east the mountainous maritime provinces have an irregular coastline on the Gulf of St. Lawrence and the Atlantic. The St. Lawrence plain, covering most of southern Quebec and Ontario, and the interior continental plain, covering southern Manitoba and Saskatchewan and most of Alberta, are the principal cultivable areas. They are separated by a forested plateau rising from Lakes Superior and Huron.

Westward toward the Pacific, most of British Columbia, Yukon, and part of western Alberta are covered by parallel mountain ranges including the Rockies. The Pacific border of the coast range is ragged with fiords and channels. The highest point in Canada is Mount Logan (19,850 ft.; 6,050 m), which is in the Yukon.

Canada has an abundance of large and small lakes. In addition to the Great Lakes on the U.S. border, there are

Population by Provinces and Territories

Province	1996 (April 1)	1991 (Census)
Alberta	2,774,512	2,545,553
British Columbia	3,835,748	3,282,061
Manitoba	1,141,727	1,091,942
New Brunswick	761,873	723,900
Newfoundland	571,192	568,474
Nova Scotia	941,235	899,942
Ontario	11,209,474	10,084,885
Prince Edward Island	137,316	129,765
Quebec	7,366,883	6,895,963
Saskatchewan	1,020,138	988,928
Northwest Territories	66,164	57,649
Yukon Territory	31,107	27,797
Total	**29,857,369**	**27,296,859**

Source: Statistics Canada.

9 others that are more than 100 miles long (161 km) and 35 that are more than 50 miles long (80 km). The two principal river systems are the Mackenzie and the St. Lawrence. The St. Lawrence, with its tributaries, is navigable for over 1,900 miles (3,058 km).

Government. Canada is a federation of 10 provinces (Alberta, British Columbia, Manitoba, New Brunswick, Newfoundland, Nova Scotia, Ontario, Prince Edward Island, Quebec, and Saskatchewan) and two territories (Northwest Territories and Yukon) whose powers were spelled out in the British North America Act of 1867. With the passing of the constitutional Act of 1981, the act and the constitutional amending power were transferred from the British Parliament to Canada so that the Canadian constitution is now entirely in the hands of Canadians.

While the Governor General is officially the representative of Queen Elizabeth II as the head of state, in reality the Governor General acts only upon the advice of the Canadian Prime Minister and the cabinet, who also sit in the federal Parliament. The Parliament has two houses: a Senate of 104 members appointed for a term ending on their 75th birthday, and a House of Commons of 295 members apportioned according to provincial population. Elections are held at least every five years or whenever the party in power is voted down in the House of Commons or considers it expedient to appeal to the people. The Prime Minister is the leader of the majority party in the House of Commons—or, if no single party holds a majority, the leader of the party able to command the support of a majority of members of the House. Laws must be passed by both houses of Parliament and signed by the Governor General in the Queen's name.

The 10 provincial governments are nominally headed by Lieutenant Governors appointed by the federal government, but the executive power in each actually is vested in a cabinet headed by a Premier, who is leader of the majority party. The provincial legislatures are composed of one-house assemblies whose members are elected for four-year terms. They are known as Legislative Assemblies, except in Newfoundland, where it is the House of Assembly, and in Quebec, where it is the National Assembly.

The judicial system consists of a Supreme Court in Ottawa (established in 1875), with appellate jurisdiction, and a Supreme Court in each province, as well as county courts with limited jurisdiction in most of the provinces. The Governor General in Council appoints these judges.

History. The Norse explorer Leif Ericson probably reached the shores of Canada (Labrador or Nova Scotia) in C.E. 1000, but the history of the white man in the

Canadian Governors General and Prime Ministers Since 1867

Term of Office	Governor General	Term	Prime Minister	Party
1867–1868	Viscount Monck[1]	1867–1873	Sir John A. Macdonald	Conservative
1869–1872	Baron Lisgar	1873–1878	Alexander Mackenzie	Liberal
1872–1878	Earl of Dufferin	1878–1891	Sir John A. Macdonald	Conservative
1878–1883	Marquess of Lorne	1891–1892	Sir John J. C. Abbott	Conservative
1883–1888	Marquess of Lansdowne	1892–1894	Sir John S. D. Thompson	Conservative
1888–1893	Baron Stanley of Preston	1894–1896	Sir Mackenzie Bowell	Conservative
1893–1898	Earl of Aberdeen	1896	Sir Charles Tupper	Conservative
1898–1904	Earl of Minto	1896–1911	Sir Wilfrid Laurier	Liberal
1904–1911	Earl Grey	1911–1917	Sir Robert L. Borden	Conservative
1911–1916	Duke of Connaught	1917–1920	Sir Robert L. Borden	Unionist
1916–1921	Duke of Devonshire	1920–1921	Arthur Meighen	Unionist
1921–1926	Baron Byng of Vimy	1921–1926	W. L. Mackenzie King	Liberal
1926–1931	Viscount Willingdon	1926	Arthur Meighen	Conservative
1931–1935	Earl of Bessborough	1926–1930	W. L. Mackenzie King	Liberal
1935–1940	Baron Tweedsmuir	1930–1935	Richard B. Bennett	Conservative
1940–1946	Earl of Athlone	1935–1948	W. L. Mackenzie King	Liberal
1946–1952	Viscount Alexander	1948–1957	Louis S. St. Laurent	Liberal
1952–1959	Vincent Massey	1957–1963	John G. Diefenbaker	Conservative
1959–1967	George P. Vanier	1963–1968	Lester B. Pearson	Liberal
1967–1973	Roland Michener	1968–1979	Pierre Elliott Trudeau	Liberal
1974–1979	Jules Léger	1979–1980	Charles Joseph Clark	Conservative
1979–1984	Edward R. Schreyer	1980–1984	Pierre Elliott Trudeau	Liberal
1984–1990	Jeanne Sauvé	1984–1984	John Turner	Liberal
1990–1995	Raymond John Hnatyshyn	1984–1993	Brian Mulroney	Conservative
1995–	Roméo LeBlanc	1993–1993	Kim Campbell	Conservative
		1993–	Jean Chrétien	Liberal

1. Became Governor General of British North America in 1861.

country actually began in 1497, when John Cabot, an Italian in the service of Henry VII of England, reached Newfoundland or Nova Scotia. Canada was taken for France in 1534 by Jacques Cartier. The actual settlement of New France, as it was then called, began in 1604 at Port Royal in what is now Nova Scotia; in 1608, Quebec was founded. France's colonization efforts were not very successful, but French explorers by the end of the 17th century had penetrated beyond the Great Lakes to the western prairies and south along the Mississippi to the Gulf of Mexico. Meanwhile, the English Hudson's Bay Company had been established in 1670. Because of the valuable fisheries and fur trade, a conflict developed between the French and English; in 1713, Newfoundland, Hudson Bay, and Nova Scotia (Acadia) were lost to England.

During the Seven Years' War (1756–63), England extended its conquest, and the British Maj. Gen. James Wolfe won his famous victory over Gen. Louis Montcalm outside Quebec on Sept. 13, 1759. The Treaty of Paris in 1763 gave England control.

At that time the population of Canada was almost entirely French, but in the next few decades, thousands of British colonists emigrated to Canada from the British Isles and from the American colonies. In 1849, the right of Canada to self-government was recognized. By the British North America Act of 1867, the Dominion of Canada was created through the confederation of Upper and Lower Canada, Nova Scotia, and New Brunswick. Prince Edward Island joined the Dominion in 1873.

In 1869 Canada purchased from the Hudson's Bay Company the vast middle west (Rupert's Land) from which the provinces of Manitoba (1870), Alberta, and Saskatchewan (1905) were later formed. In 1871, British Columbia joined the Dominion. The country was linked from coast to coast in 1885 by the Canadian Pacific Railway.

During the formative years between 1866 and 1896, the Conservative Party, led by Sir John A. Macdonald, governed the country, except during the years 1873–78. In 1896, the Liberal Party took over and, under Sir Wilfrid Laurier, an eminent French Canadian, ruled until 1911.

By the Statute of Westminster in 1931 the British Dominions, including Canada, were formally declared to be partner nations with Britain, "equal in status, in no way subordinate to each other," and bound together only by allegiance to a common Crown.

Newfoundland became Canada's 10th province on March 31, 1949, following a plebiscite. Canada includes two territories—the Yukon Territory, the area north of British Columbia and east of Alaska, and the Northwest Territories, including all of Canada north of 60° north latitude except Yukon and the northernmost sections of Quebec and Newfoundland. This area includes all of the Arctic north of the mainland, Norway having recognized Canadian sovereignty over the Svendrup Islands in the Arctic in 1931.

The Liberal Party, led by William Lyon Mackenzie King, dominated Canadian politics from 1921 until 1957, when it was succeeded by the Progressive Conservatives. The Liberals, under the leadership of Lester B. Pearson, returned to power in 1963. Pearson remained Prime Minister until 1968, when he retired and was replaced by a former law professor, Pierre Elliott Trudeau. Trudeau maintained Canada's defensive alliance with the United States, but began moving toward a more independent policy in world affairs.

Trudeau's election was considered in part a response to the most serious problem confronting the country, the division between French- and English-speaking Canadians, which had led to a separatist movement in the predominantly French province of Quebec. In 1974, the provincial government voted to make French the official language of Quebec.

Despite Trudeau's removal of price and wage controls in 1978, continuing inflation and a high rate of unemployment caused him to delay elections until May 22, 1979. The delay gave Trudeau no advantage—the Progressive Conservatives under Charles Joseph Clark defeated the Liberals everywhere except in Quebec, New Brunswick, and Newfoundland.

His government collapsed after only six months when a motion to defeat the Tory budget carried by 139–133 on Dec. 13, 1979. On the same day, the Quebec law making French the exclusive official language of the province—an issue which had been expected to provide Clark's first major internal test—was voided by the Canadian Supreme Court. In national elections Feb. 18, 1980, the resurgent Liberals under Trudeau scored an unexpectedly big victory.

Resolving a dispute that had occupied Trudeau since the beginning of his tenure, Queen Elizabeth II, in Ottawa on April 17, 1982, signed the Constitution Act, cutting the last legal tie between Canada and Britain. The constitution retains Queen Elizabeth as Queen of Canada and keeps Canada's membership in the Commonwealth.

In the national election on Sept. 4, 1984, the Progressive Conservative Party scored an overwhelming victory, fundamentally changing the country's political landscape. The Conservatives, led by Brian Mulroney, a 45-year-old corporate lawyer, won the highest political majority in Canadian history, Mulroney was sworn in as Canada's 18th Prime Minister on Sept. 17.

The dominant foreign issue was a free trade pact with the U.S., a treaty bitterly opposed by the Liberal and New Democratic parties. The conflict led to elections in Nov. 1988 that solidly re-elected Mulroney and gave him a mandate to proceed with the agreement.

The issue of separatist sentiments in French-speaking Quebec flared up again in 1990 with the failure of the Meech Lake accord. The accord was designed to ease the Quebecers' fear of losing their identity within the English-speaking majority by giving Quebec constitutional status as a "distinct society."

In an attempt to keep Canada united, the three major political parties came to an agreement in February 1992 on constitutional reforms. Voters in the Northwest Territories authorized the division of their region in two, creating a homeland for Canadian Eskimos, the Inuits.

Also in 1992 Canada announced its decision to withdraw its combat units from NATO command. The economy continued to be mired in a long recession many blamed on the free trade agreement.

A national referendum was held in October 1992 on the proposal to change the constitution to insure greater representation in Parliament for the more populous regions and thereby the French-speaking Quebecers. The referendum, however was defeated.

Brian Mulroney's popularity continued to slump in 1992 and early 1993, leading to his decision to retire prior to the required November election. The governing Progressive Conservative Party chose Defense Minister Kim Campbell as its leader in June making her the first female Prime Minister in Canadian history.

The national election in October 1993 resulted in the reemergence of the Liberal Party, which won 177 seats in the House of Commons.

The Quebec referendum on secession in October 1995 yielded a narrow rejection of the proposal. But the separatists vowed to try again.

Early parliamentary elections in June 1997 gave a reduced majority to the ruling Liberals. The Reform Party, based largely in the West, replaced the Bloc Quebecois as the official opposition.

CAPE VERDE

Republic of Cape Verde
National name: República de Cabo Verde
President: Antonio Mascarenhas Monteiro (1991)
Prime Minister: Carlos Wahnon Veiga (1991)
Area: 1,557 sq mi. (4,033 sq km)
Population: (1997 est.): 393,843 (average annual rate of natural increase: 2.81%); birth rate: 35.45/1000; infant mortality rate: 49.6/1000; density per square mile: 253
Capital (1990): Praia, 61,797. **Other large city (est. 1982):** Mindelo, 50,000. **Monetary unit:** Cape Verdean escudo. **Language:** Portuguese, Criuolo. **Ethnicity/Race:** Creole (mulatto) 71%, African 28%, European 1%. **Religion:** Roman Catholic fused with indigenous beliefs. **Literacy rate:** 66%
Economic summary: Gross domestic product: purchasing power parity (1994 est.): $440 million, per capita $1,040; real growth rate 4.6% (1994); inflation 5%; unemployment 35% (1994). Arable land: 9%. Labor force (1985 est.): 102,000; in agriculture: 57%, services: 29%, industry 14% (1981). Principal agricultural products: bananas, corn, sugar cane, beans. Major industries: fishing, salt mining. Natural resources: salt, siliceous rock. Exports: $4.4 million (f.o.b., 1992 est.): fish, bananas, salt. Imports: $173 million (f.o.b., 1992 est.): petroleum, foodstuffs, consumer goods, industrial products. Major trading partners: Portugal, Angola, Algeria, Italy, Netherlands, Spain, France, U.S., Germany, Sweden.

Geography. Cape Verde, only slightly larger than Rhode Island, is an archipelago in the Atlantic 385 miles (500 km) west of Senegal.

The islands are divided into two groups: Barlavento in the north, comprising Santo Antão (291 sq mi.; 754 sq km), Boa Vista (240 sq mi.; 622 sq km), São Nicolau (132 sq mi.; 342 sq km), São Vicente (88 sq mi.; 246 sq km), Sal (83 sq mi.; 298 sq km), and Santa Luzia (13 sq mi.; 34 sq km); and Sotavento in the south, consisting of São Tiago (383 sq mi.; 992 sq km), Fogo (184 sq mi.; 477 sq km), Maio (103 sq mi.; 267 sq km), and Brava (25 sq mi.; 65 sq km). The islands are mostly mountainous, with the land deeply scarred by erosion. There is an active volcano on Fogo.

Government. The islands became independent on July 5, 1975, under an agreement negotiated with Portugal in 1974. Elections of January 13, 1991 resulted in the ruling African Party for the Independence of Cape Verde losing its majority in the 79-seat parliament. The big winner was the Movement for Democracy, whose candidate, Antonio Monteiro, won the subsequent presidential election on February 17. These were the first free elections since independence in 1975.

History. Uninhabited upon their discovery in 1456, the Cape Verde islands became part of the Portuguese empire in 1495. A majority of their modern inhabitants are of mixed Portuguese and African ancestry.

The former opposition MPD that had won the parliamentary and the presidential elections early in 1991 also won 10 out of 14 councils in the country's first local elections.

In the presidential ballot of February 1996 Monteiro handily won re-election. The government announced in October that although economic figures were favorable, the level of imports was unacceptably widening.

CENTRAL AFRICAN REPUBLIC

National name: République Centrafricaine
Head of Government: Gen. André Kolingba (1986)
President: Ange-Félix Patassé (1993)
Prime Minister: Michel Gbezera-Bria (1997)
Area: 241,313 sq mi. (625,000 sq km)
Population (1997 est.): 3,342,051 (average annual rate of natural increase: 2.15%); birth rate: 39.52/1000; infant mortality rate: 110/1000; density per square mile: 14
Capital and largest city (1990 est.): Bangui, 706,000.

Monetary unit: Franc CFA. **Languages:** French (official), Sangho, Arabic, Hansa, Swahili. **Ethnicity/Race:** Baya 34%, Banda 27%, Sara 10%, Mandjia 21%, Mboum 4%, M'Baka 4%, Europeans 6,500 (including 3,600 French). **Religions:** 24% indigenous beliefs, 50% Protestant and Roman Catholic with animist influence, 15% Muslim, 11% other. **Literacy rate:** 33%

Economic summary: Gross domestic product: purchasing power parity (1995 est.): $2.5 billion, per capita $800; real growth rate 4.1%; inflation 45% (1994 est.); unemployment n.a. Arable land: 3%. Principal products: cotton, coffee, peanuts, food crops, livestock. Labor force (1986 est.): 775,413; 85% in agriculture. Major industrial products: timber, textiles, soap, cigarettes, diamonds, processed food, brewed beverages. Natural resources: diamonds, uranium, timber. Exports: $154 million (f.o.b., 1994): diamonds, cotton, timber, coffee, tobacco. Imports: $215 million (f.o.b., 1994): machinery and electrical equipment, petroleum products, textiles, food, motor vehicles, chemicals, pharmaceuticals, consumer goods, industrial products. Major trading partners: France, Belgium, Italy, Japan, U.S., Western Europe, Algeria, Yugoslavia.

Geography. Situated about 500 miles north (805 km) of the equator, the Central African Republic is a landlocked nation bordered by Cameroon, Chad, the Sudan, The Democratic Republic of Congo, and the Congo. Twice the size of New Mexico, it is covered by tropical forests in the south and semidesert land in the east. The Ubangi and Shari are the largest of many rivers.

Government. The Central African Republic has been ruled since 1981 by General André Kolingba who came to power in a bloodless coup and was elected to a six-year term as president in 1986. A constitution was adopted on November 21, 1987 establishing a unicameral National Assembly. The following year the Central African Democracy Party (R.D.C.) was formed as the only political party. Since April 1991 other political parties legally registered by the Ministry of the Interior are allowed to compete for legislative and presidential elections and presidential and legislative elections were held in September 1993.

History. As the colony of Ubangi-Shari, what is now the Central African Republic was united with Chad in 1905 and joined with Gabon and the Middle Congo in French Equatorial Africa in 1910. After World War II a rebellion in 1946 forced the French to grant self-government. In 1958 the territory voted to become an autonomous republic within the French Community, but on Aug. 13, 1960, President David Dacko proclaimed the republic's independence from France.

Dacko undertook to move the country into Beijing's orbit, but was overthrown in a coup on Dec. 31, 1965, by the then Col. Jean-Bédel Bokassa, Army Chief of Staff.

On Dec. 4, 1976, the Central African Republic became the Central African Empire. Marshal Jean-Bédel Bokassa, who had ruled the republic since he took power in 1965, was declared Emperor Bokassa I. He was overthrown in a coup on Sept. 20, 1979. Former President David Dacko, returned to power and changed the country's name back to the Central African Republic. An army coup on Sept. 1, 1981, deposed President Dacko again.

Although President Kolingba in 1991, under pressure, announced a move toward multiparty democracy no specifics were given, leading to further civil unrest. A general strike called for in August resulted in the legalization of three opposition parties.

Elections in August 1993 saw the defeat of Kolingba. Former Prime Minister Patassé won the presidency in the second round.

Although voters approved a referendum on a new constitution in December 1994, the turnout was relatively low.

A military revolt was crushed with the aid of French soldiers in January 1997. Later that month the President appointed Gbezera-Bria to replace the Prime Minister, who was thought to side with the rebellion.

CHAD

Republic of Chad
National name: République du Tchad
President: Gen. Idriss Deby (1991)
Prime Minister: Nassour Guelengdoussia Ouaido (1997)
Area: 495,752 sq mi. (1,284,000 sq km)
Population (1997 est.): 7,166,023 (average annual rate of natural increase, 2.67%); birth rate: 43.85/1000; infant mortality rate: 118/1000; density per square mile: 14.5
Capital and largest city (1993): N'Djamena, 529,555.
Monetary unit: Franc CFA. **Languages:** French and Arabic (official), many tribal languages. **Ethnicity/Race:** nonindigenous 150,000, of whom 1,000 are French north and center: Muslims (Arabs, Toubou, Hadjerai, Fulbe, Kotoko, Kanembou, Baguirmi, Boulala, Zaghawa, and Maba) south: non-Muslims (Sara, Ngambaye, Mbaye, Goulaye, Moundang, Moussei, Massa). **Religions:** Islam, 44%; Christian, 33%; traditional, 23%. **Literacy rate:** 17%
Economic summary: Gross domestic product: purchasing power parity (1995 est.): $3.3 billion, per capita $600; real growth rate 4%; inflation 41% (1994). Arable land: 2%; principal agricultural products: cotton, cattle, sugar, subsistence crops. Labor force: n.a.; in agriculture: 85%. Major products: livestock and livestock products, beer, food processing, textiles, cigarettes. Natural resources: petroleum, unexploited uranium, kaolin. Exports: $132 million (f.o.b., 1993): cotton, livestock and animal products, fish, textiles. Imports: $201 million (f.o.b., 1993): machinery and transportation equipment, industrial goods, petroleum products, foodstuffs. Major trading partners: France, Nigeria, U.S., Cameroon.

Geography. A landlocked country in north central Africa, Chad is about 85% the size of Alaska. Its neighbors are Niger, Libya, the Sudan, the Central African Republic, Cameroon, and Nigeria. Lake Chad, from which the country gets its name, lies on the western border with Niger and Nigeria. In the north is a desert that runs into the Sahara.

Government. Hissen Habré was overthrown by Col. Idriss Deby in December 1990. A transitional government mandate expired in April 1996 and parliamentary elections were scheduled in anticipation of complete democracy.

History. Chad was absorbed into the colony of French Equatorial Africa, as part of Ubangi-Shari, in 1910. France began the country's development after 1920, when it became a separate colony. In 1946, French Equatorial Africa was admitted to the French Union. By referendum in 1958 the Chad territory became an autonomous republic within the French Union.

A movement led by the first Premier and President, François (later Ngarta) Tombalbaye, achieved complete independence on Aug. 11, 1960.

Tombalbaye was killed in the 1975 coup and was succeeded by Gen. Félix Malloum, who faced a Libyan-financed rebel movement throughout his tenure in office. A ceasefire backed by Libya, Niger, and the Sudan early in 1978 failed to end the fighting.

Nine rival groups meeting in Lagos, Nigeria, in March 1979 agreed to form a provisional government headed by Goukouni Oueddei, a former rebel leader. Fighting broke out again in Chad in March 1980, when Defense Minister Hissen Habré challenged Goukouni and seized the capital. By the year's end, Libyan troops supporting Goukouni recaptured N'djamena, and Libyan President Muammar el-Qaddafi, in January 1981, proposed a merger of Chad with Libya.

The Libyan proposal was rejected and Libyan troops withdrew from Chad but in 1983 poured back into the northern part of the country in support of Goukouni. France, in turn, sent troops into southern Chad in support of Habré.

Government troops then launched an offensive in early 1987 that drove the Libyans out of most of the country.

After the overthrow of Habré's government, Deby, a former defense minister, declared himself President, dissolved the legislature (elected the previous July), and suspended the constitution.

In the two rounds of the parliamentary elections held in January and February 1997, the President's Patriotic Salvation Movement won 55 of the 125 seats. The foreign minister's party, the National Union for Development and Renewal, won 15 seats.

CHILE

Republic of Chile
National name: República de Chile
President: Eduardo Frei Ruiz-Tagle (1994)
Area: 292,132 sq mi. (756,622 sq km)
Population (1997 est.): 14,508,168 (average annual rate of natural increase: 1.18%); birth rate: 17.53/1000; infant mortality rate: 13.2/1000; density per square mile: 49.7
Capital and largest city (1993 est.): Santiago, 4,628,320. **Other large cities (1993 est.):** Valparaíso, 301,677; Concepción, 318,140; Viña del Mar, 319,440; Temuco, 262,624; Talcahuano, 257,767. **Monetary unit:** Peso. **Language:** Spanish. **Ethnicity/Race:** European and European-Indian 95%, Indian 3%, other 2%. **Religion:** Roman Catholic, 89%; Protestant, 11%; small Jewish and Muslim populations. **Literacy rate:** 94%
Economic summary: Gross domestic product: purchasing power parity (1995 est.): $113.2 billion; $8,000 per capita; 8.5% real growth rate; inflation 8.1%; unemployment 5.4%. Arable land: 7%. Principal agricultural products: wheat, corn, sugar beets, vegetables, wine, livestock. Labor force: 4.728 million; 38.3% in services, industry and commerce, 19.2% in agriculture, forestry and fishing. Major industrial products: processed fish, iron and steel, pulp, paper, furniture, apparel, processed food. Natural resources: copper, gold, timber, fruits and vegetables, nitrates, iron. Exports: $15.9 billion (f.o.b., 1995 est.): copper, bleached pulp, fishmeal, fresh fruit, timber, seafood, frozen and canned fruits, wine. Imports: $14.3 billion (f.o.b., 1995): oil, vehicles, computers, industrial machinery, electric and electronic equipment, chemicals. Major trading partners: U.S., European Union, Asia, Latin America.

Geography. Situated south of Peru and west of Bolivia and Argentina, Chile fills a narrow 1,800-mile (2,897 km) strip between the Andes and the Pacific. Its area is nearly twice that of Montana.

One third of Chile is covered by the towering ranges of the Andes. In the north is the mineral-rich Atacama Desert, between the coastal mountains and the Andes. In the center is a 700-mile-long (1,127 km) valley, thickly populated, between the Andes and the coastal plateau. In the south, the Andes border on the ocean.

At the southern tip of Chile's mainland is Punta Arenas, the southernmost city in the world, and beyond that lies the Strait of Magellan and Tierra del Fuego, an island divided between Chile and Argentina. The southernmost point of South America is Cape Horn, a 1,390-foot (424-m) rock on Horn Island in the Wollaston group, which belongs to Chile. Chile also claims sovereignty over 482,628 sq mi (1,250,000 sq km) of Antarctic territory.

The Juan Fernández Islands, in the South Pacific about 400 miles (644 km) west of the mainland, and Easter Island, about 2,000 miles (3,219 km) west, are Chilean possessions.

Government. The President serves a six-year term (with the exception of the 1990–1994 term). There is a bicameral legislature, the National Congress.

History. Chile was originally under the control of the Incas in the north and the fierce Araucanian people in the south. In 1541, a Spaniard, Pedro de Valdivia, founded Santiago. Chile won its independence from Spain in 1818 under Bernardo O'Higgins and an Argentinian, José de San Martin. O'Higgins, dictator until 1823, laid the foundations of the modern state with a two-party system and a centralized government.

The dictator from 1830 to 1837, Diego Portales, fought a war with Peru in 1836–39 that expanded Chilean territory. The Conservatives were in power from 1831 to 1861. Then the Liberals, winning a share of power for the next 30 years, disestablished the church and limited presidential power. Chile fought the War of the Pacific with Peru and Bolivia from 1879 to 1883, winning Antofagasta, Bolivia's only outlet to the sea, and extensive areas from Peru. A revolt in 1890 led by Jorge Montt overthrew, in 1891, José Balmaceda and established a parliamentary dictatorship that existed until a new constitution was adopted in 1925. Industrialization began before World War I and led to the formation of Marxist groups.

Juan Antonio Ríos, President during World War II, was originally pro-Nazi but in 1944 led his country into the war on the side of the U.S.

A small abortive army uprising in 1969 raised fear of military intervention to prevent a Marxist, Salvador Allende Gossens, from taking office after his election to the presidency on Sept. 4, 1970. Dr. Allende was the first president in a non-Communist country freely elected on a Marxist-Leninist program.

Allende quickly established relations with Cuba and the People's Republic of China and nationalized several American companies.

Allende's overthrow and death in an army assault on the presidential palace in September 1973 ended a 46-year era of constitutional government in Chile.

The takeover was led by a four-man junta headed by Army Chief of Staff Augusto Pinochet Ugarte, who assumed the office of President.

Committed to "exterminate Marxism," the junta embarked on a right-wing dictatorship. It suspended Parliament, banned political activity, and broke relations with Cuba.

In 1977, Pinochet, in a speech marking his fourth year in power, promised elections by 1985 if conditions warranted. Earlier, he had abolished DINA, the secret police, and decreed an amnesty for political prisoners.

Pinochet was inaugurated on March 11, 1981, for an eight-year term as president, at the end of which, according to the constitution adopted six months earlier, the junta would nominate a civilian as successor. He stepped down in January 1990 in favor of Patricio Aylwin who was elected Dec. 1989 as the head of a 17-party coalition.

The presidential election of December 1993 saw the reemergence of a member of the Frei family. Eduardo Frei, the candidate of a center-left coalition, won. His father had been president from 1964–1970.

The country signed a free trade agreement with the four-nation Mercosur block in 1996 and one with Canada in mid-1997. Chile already has such a pact with Mexico and hopes eventually to join NAFTA.

CHINA

People's Republic of China
National name: Zhonghua Renmin Gongheguo
President: Jiang Zemin (1993)
Premier: Li Peng (1987)
Area: 3,691,521 sq mi. (9,561,000 sq km)[1]
Population (1997 est.): 1,221,591,778 (average rate of natural increase: 0.96%); birth rate: 16.52/1000; infant mortality rate: 37.9/1000; density per square mile: 331. China has 56 ethnic groups. In 1991, the Han people accounted for 92% of the population
Capital: Beijing. **Largest cities (1997 est.):** Chongqing, 30,000,000; Shanghai, 14,1500,000; Beijing (Peking) 12,5100,000; Tianjin (Tientsin) 9,420,000; Canton, 2,914,000; Wuhan, 3,284,200; Shenyang (Mukden), 3,604,000; Nanjing (Nanking), 2,100,000; Harbin, 2,443,400. **Monetary unit:** Yuan. **Languages:** Chinese, Mandarin, also local dialects. **Ethnicity/Race:** Han Chinese 91.9%, Zhuang, Uygur, Hui, Yi, Tibetan, Miao, Manchu, Mongol, Buyi, Korean, and other nationalities 8.1%. **Religions:** Officially atheist but traditional religion contains elements of Confucianism, Taoism, Buddhism. **Literacy rate:** 73%
Economic summary: Gross domestic product: purchasing power parity (1995): $3.5 trillion; $2,900 per capita; 10.3% real growth rate; inflation rate (Dec. 1995 over Dec. 1994): 10.1%; unemployment rate in urban areas: 5.2%. Arable land: 10%. Principal agricultural products: rice, wheat, grains, cotton. Labor force: 583.6 million; agriculture and forestry, 60%; industry and commerce, 25%; construction and mining, 5%. Major industrial products: iron and steel, textiles, armaments, petroleum. Natural resources: coal, natural gas, limestone, marble, metals, hydropower potential. Exports: $148.8 billion (f.o.b., 1995): textiles, garments, footwear, toys, machinery and equipment, weapon systems. Imports: $132.1 billion (c.i.f., 1995): rolled steel, motor vehicles, textile machinery, oil products, aircraft. Major trading partners: Japan, Hong Kong, U.S., Germany, Taiwan and Macau, Russia.

1. Including Manchuria and Tibet.

Geography. China, which occupies the eastern part of Asia, is slightly larger in area than the U.S. Its coastline is roughly a semicircle. The greater part of the country is mountainous, and only in the lower reaches of the Yellow and Yangtze Rivers are there extensive low plains.

The principal mountain ranges are the Tien Shan, to the northwest; the Kunlun chain, running south of the Taklimakan and Gobi Deserts; and the Trans-Himalaya, connecting the Kunlun with the borders of China and Tibet. Manchuria is largely an undulating plain connected with the north China plain by a narrow lowland corridor. Inner Mongolia contains the relatively fertile southern and eastern portions of the Gobi. The large island of Taiwan (360,000 sq km) lies off the southeast coast.

China proper consists of three great river systems. The northern part of the country is drained by the Yellow River (Huang Ho), 2,109 miles long (5,464 km) and mostly unnavigable. The central part is drained by the Chang Jiang (Yangtze Kiang), the third longest river

in the world 2,432 miles (6,300 km). The Zhujiang (Si Kiang) in the south is 848 miles long (2,197 km) and navigable for a considerable distance. In addition, the Amur (1,144 sq mi.; 2,965 km) forms part of the northeastern boundary.

Government. With 2,978 deputies, elected for four-year terms by universal suffrage, the National People's Congress is the chief legislative organ. A State Council has the executive authority. All ministries are under the State Council, headed by the Premier. The Communist Party controls the government.

History. By 2000 B.C.E., the Chinese were living in the Huang Ho basin, and they had achieved an advanced stage of civilization by 1200 B.C.E. The great philosophers Lao-tse, Confucious, Mo Ti, and Mencius lived during the Chou dynasty (1122–249 B.C.E.) The warring feudal states were first united under Emperor Ch'in Shih Huang Ti, during whose reign (246–210 B.C.E.) work was begun on the Great Wall. Under the Han dynasty (206 B.C.E.–C.E. 220), China prospered and traded with the West.

In the T'ang dynasty (618–907), often called the golden age of Chinese history, painting, sculpture, and poetry flourished, and printing made its earliest known appearance.

The Mings, last of the native rulers (1368–1644), overthrew the Mongol, or Yuan, dynasty (1280–1368) established by Kublai Khan. The Mings in turn were overthrown in 1644 by invaders from the north, the Manchus.

China closely restricted foreign activities, and by the end of the 18th century only Canton and the Portuguese port of Macao were open to European merchants. Following the Anglo-Chinese War of 1839–42, however, several treaty ports were opened, and Hong Kong was ceded to Britain. Treaties signed after further hostilities (1856–60) weakened Chinese sovereignty and removed foreigners from Chinese jurisdiction. The disastrous Chinese-Japanese War of 1894–95 was followed by a scramble for Chinese concessions by European powers, leading to the Boxer Rebellion (1900), suppressed by an international force.

The death of the Empress Dowager Tzu Hsi in 1908 and the accession of the infant Emperor Hsüan T'ung (Pu-Yi) were followed by a nationwide rebellion led by Dr. Sun Yat-sen, who became first president of the Provisional Chinese Republic in 1911. The Manchus abdicated on Feb. 12, 1912. Dr. Sun resigned in favor of Yuan Shih-k'ai, who suppressed the republicans but was forced by a serious uprising in 1915–16 to abandon his intention of declaring himself Emperor. Yuan's death in June 1916 was followed by years of civil war between rival militarists and Dr. Sun's republicans.

Nationalist forces, led by Gen. Chiang Kai-shek and with the advice of Communist experts, soon occupied most of China, setting up a Kuomintang regime in 1928 Internal strife continued, however, and Chiang broke with the Communists.

An alleged explosion on the South Manchurian Railway on Sept. 18, 1931, brought invasion of Manchuria by Japanese forces, who installed the last Manchu Emperor, Henry Pu-Yi, as nominal ruler of the puppet state of "Manchukuo." Japanese efforts to take China's northern provinces in July 1937 were resisted by Chiang, who meanwhile had succeeded in uniting most of China behind him. Within two years, however, Japan seized most of the ports and railways. The Kuomintang government retreated first to Hankow and then to Chungking, while the Japanese set up a puppet government at Nanking headed by Wang Jingwei.

Japan's surrender in 1945 touched off civil war between Nationalist forces under Chiang and Communist forces led by Mao Zedong, the party chairman

Provinces and Regions of China

Name	Area (sq mi.)	Area (sq km)	Capital
Provinces			
Anhui (Anhwei)	54,015	139,900	Hefei (Hofei)
Fujian (Fukien)	47,529	123,100	Fuzhou (Fukien)
Gansu (Kansu)	137,104	355,100	Lanzhou (Lanchow)
Guangdong (Kwangtung)	76,100	197,100	Canton
Guizhou (Kweichow)	67,181	174,000	Guiyang (Kweiyang)
Hainan	13,200	34,300	Haikou
Hebei (Hopei)	81,479	211,030	Shijiazhuang (Shitikiachwang)
Heilongjiang (Heilungkiang)[1]	178,996	463,600	Harbin
Henan (Honan)	64,479	167,000	Zhengzhou (Chengchow)
Hubei (Hupeh)	72,394	187,500	Wuhan
Hunan	81,274	210,500	Changsha
Jiangsu (Kiangsu)	40,927	106,000	Nanjing (Nanking)
Jiangxi (Kiangsi)	63,629	164,800	Nanchang
Jilin (Kirin)[1]	72,201	187,000	Changchun
Liaoning[1]	53,301	138,050	Shenyang
Quinghai (Chinghai)	278,378	721,000	Xining (Sining)
Shaanxi (Shensi)	75,598	195,800	Xian (Sian)
Shandong (Shantung)	59,189	153,300	Jinan (Tsinan)
Shanxi (Shansi)	60,656	157,100	Taiyuan
Sichuan (Szechwan)	219,691	569,000	Chengdu (Chengtu)
Yunnan	168,417	436,200	Kunming
Zhejiang (Chekiang)	39,305	101,800	Hangzhou (Hangchow)
Autonomous Regions			
Guangxi Zhuang (Kwangsi Chuang)	85,096	220,400	Nanning
Nei Monggol (Inner Mongolia)[1]	454,633	1,177,500	Hohhot (Huhehot)
Ningxia Hui	30,039	77,800	Yinchuan (Yinchwan)
Xinjiang Uygur (Sinkiang Uighur)[1]	635,829	1,646,800	Urumqi (Urumchi)
Xizang (Tibet)	471,660	1,221,600	Lhasa

1. Together constitute (with Taiwan) what has been traditionally known as Outer China, the remaining territory forming the historical China Proper. NOTE: Names are in Pinyin, with conventional spelling in parentheses.

Despite U.S. aid, the Chiang forces were overcome by the Maoists, backed by the Soviet bloc, and were expelled from the mainland. The Mao regime, established in Beijing as the new capital, proclaimed the People's Republic of China on Oct. 1, 1949, with Zhou Enlai as Premier.

After the Korean War began in June 1950, China led the Communist bloc in supporting North Korea, and on Nov. 26, 1950, the Mao regime intervened openly.

In 1958, Mao undertook the "Great Leap Forward" campaign, which combined the establishment of rural communes with a crash program of village industrialization but it failed and was abandoned.

China exploded its first atomic (fission) bomb in 1964 and produced a fusion bomb in 1967.

Mao moved to Shanghai, and from that base he and his supporters waged what they called a Cultural Revolution. In the spring of 1966 the Mao group formed Red Guard units dominated by youths and students, closing the schools to free the students for agitation.

The Red Guards campaigned against "old ideas, old culture, old habits, and old customs." Often they were no more than uncontrolled mobs, and brutality was frequent. Early in 1967 efforts were made to restore control. The Red Guards were urged to return home. Schools started opening.

Persistent overtures by the Nixon Administration resulted in the dramatic announcement in July 1971 that Henry Kissinger, President Richard M. Nixon's national security adviser, had secretly visited Beijing and reached agreement on a visit by the President to China.

The movement toward reconciliation, which signaled the end of the U.S. containment policy toward China, provided irresistible momentum for Chinese admission to the U.N. Despite U.S. opposition to expelling Taiwan (Nationalist China), the world body overwhelmingly ousted Chiang in seating Beijing.

President Nixon went to Beijing for a week early in 1972, meeting Mao as well as Zhou. The summit ended with a historic communiqué on February 28, in which both nations promised to work toward improved relations. Full diplomatic relations were barred by China as long as the U.S. continued to recognize Nationalist China.

On Jan. 8, 1976, Zhou died. His successor, Vice Premier Deng Xiaoping was supplanted within a month by Hua Guofeng, former Minister of Public Security. Hua became permanent Premier in April. In October he was named successor to Mao as Chairman of the Communist Party.

After Mao died on Sept. 10, a campaign against his widow, Jiang Qing, and three of her "radical" colleagues began. The "Gang of Four" was denounced for having undermined the party, the government, and the economy. They were tried and convicted in 1981.

At the Central Committee meeting of 1977, Deng was reinstated as Deputy Premier, Chief of Staff of the Army, and member of the Central Committee of the Politburo.

At the same time, Jiang Qing, Wang Hongwen, Zhang Chunqiao, and Yao Wenyuan—the notorious "Gang of Four"—were removed from all official posts and banished from the party.

In May 1978, expulsion of ethnic Chinese by Vietnam produced an open rupture. Beijing sided with Cambodia in the border fighting that flared between Vietnam and Cambodia, charging Hanoi with aggression.

Beijing and Washington announced that they would open full diplomatic relations on Jan. 1, 1979 and the Carter Administration abrogated the Taiwan defense treaty. Deputy Premier Deng sealed the agreement with a visit to the U.S. that coincided with the opening of embassies in both capitals on March 1.

On Deng's return from the U.S. Chinese troops

invaded Vietnam to avenge alleged violations of Chinese territory. The action was seen as a reaction to Vietnam's invasion of Cambodia.

After the Central Committee meeting of June 27–29, 1981, Hu Yaobang, a Deng protégé, was elevated to the party chairmanship, replacing Hua Guofeng. Deng became chairman of the military commission of the central committee, giving him control over the army. The committee's 215 members concluded the session with a statement holding Mao Zedong responsible for the "grave blunder" of the Cultural Revolution.

Under Deng Xiaoping's leadership, meanwhile, China's Communist ideology was almost totally reinterpreted and sweeping economic changes were set in motion in the early 1980s. The Chinese scrapped the personality cult that idolized Mao Zedong, muted Mao's old call for class struggle and exportation of the Communist revolution, and imported Western technology and management techniques to replace the Marxist tenets that retarded modernization.

Also under Deng's leadership, the Chinese Communists worked out an arrangement with Britain for the future of Hong Kong after 1997. The flag of China was raised but the territory retained its social, economic and legal system.

The removal of Hu Yaobang as party chairman in January 1987 was a sign of a hard line resurgence. He was replaced by former Premier Zhao Ziyang. Conflict between hard liners and moderates continued and reached a violent climax in 1989. Student demonstrations calling for accelerated liberalization were crushed by military force in June, resulting in several hundred deaths.

The rubber-stamp National People's Congress concluded its April 1992 session with a call to guard against "leftism," widely interpreted as a sign of consolidation and a call for accelerating the drive for economic reform. Nevertheless, several hard liners remained in their conspicuous positions.

The annual session of the National People's Congress in March 1993 was widely seen as an effort by Deng Xiaoping, the paramount leader, to maintain China's moves toward a market economy while retaining political authoritarianism. Communist Party leader Jiang Zemin was elected president, while hard liner Li Peng was re-elected to another five-year term as Prime Minister despite, or perhaps because of, his politics.

The economy continued to grow rapidly in 1993. In November the Central Committee adopted a resolution envisaging the conversion of state-owned enterprises into joint-stock companies, the creation of a central bank and modern tax system.

Deng Xiaoping's death in February 1997 left a younger generation in charge of managing the enormous country. Hong Kong's reversion to Chinese rule on July 1 was watched with studied concern by the international community for signs of future developments within other parts of China.

HONG KONG

Status: Special Administrative Region of the People's Republic of China
Chief Executive: Tung Chee Hwa
Area: 416 sq mi. (1,077 sq km)
Population (1997 est.): 6,412,786 (average annual rate of natural increase: 0.5%); birth rate: 10.41/1000; infant mortality rate: 5/1000; density per square mile: 15,415.3
Capital (1995 est.): Victoria (Hong Kong Island), 6,205,300. **Monetary unit:** Hong Kong dollar. **Literacy rate:** 77%
Economic summary: Gross domestic product: purchasing power parity (1995 est.): $152.4 billion; $27,500 per capita; real growth rate 5%; inflation 8.4%; unemployment 3.5%. Arable land: 7%. Principal agricultural products: vegetables, rice, dairy products. Labor force (1994): 2,915,400: 28.5% manufacturing; 27.9%, wholesale, retail, hotels, restaurants. Major industrial products: textiles, clothing, toys, transistor radios, watches, electronic components. Exports: $177.1 billion (including re-exports) (f.o.b., 1995 est.): clothing, textiles, toys, watches, electrical appliances, footwear. Imports: $195.4 billion (c.i.f., 1995): raw materials, transport equipment, food. Major trading partners: U.S., U.K., Japan, Germany, China, Taiwan.

The territory of Hong Kong consists of the island of Hong Kong (32 sq mi.; 83 sq km), Stonecutters' Island, Kowloon Peninsula, and the New Territories on the adjoining mainland. The island of Hong Kong, located at the mouth of the Pearl River about 90 miles (145 km) southeast of Canton, was ceded to Britain in 1841.

Stonecutters' Island and Kowloon were annexed in 1860, and the New Territories, which are mainly agricultural lands, were leased from China in 1898 for 99 years. Hong Kong was attacked by Japanese troops Dec. 7, 1941, and surrendered the following Christmas. It remained under Japanese occupation until August 1945.

After two years of painstaking negotiation, authorities of Britain and the People's Republic of China agreed in 1984 that Hong Kong would return to Chinese sovereignty on July 1, 1997, when Britain's lease on the New Territories expired. They also agreed that the vibrant capitalist enclave on China's coast would retain its status as a free port and its social, economic, and its laws would remain unchanged for 50 years.

The chief executive under the new government, Tung Chee Hwa, formulated a policy agenda based upon the concept of "one country, two systems," thus preserving Hong Kong's economic freedom. Hong Kong will continue to have its own finances and issue its own travel documents, and Beijing will not levy taxes. As the British lease on Hong Kong expired on July 1, 1997, the international community anxiously eyed the Chinese takeover for signs of its commitment to uphold the region's free-market economy.

COLOMBIA

Republic of Colombia
National name: República de Colombia
President: Ernesto Samper Pizano (1994)
Area: 439,735 sq mi. (1,138,910 sq km)
Population (1997 est.): 37,418,290 (average annual rate of natural increase, 1.61%); birth rate: 20.78/1000; infant mortality rate: 24.7/1000; density per square mile: 85.1
Capital and largest city (1995 est.): Santafé de Bogotá 5,025,989. **Largest cities (1995 est.):** Cali, 1,718,871; Medellín, 1,621,356; Barranquilla, 1,064,255; Cartagena, 745,689. **Monetary unit:** Peso. **Language:** Spanish. **Ethnicity/Race:** mestizo 58%, white 20%, mulatto 14%, black 4%, mixed black-Indian 3%, Indian 1%. **Religion:** 95% Roman Catholic. **Literacy rate:** 91.3%
Economic summary: Gross domestic product: purchasing power parity (1995 est.): $192.5 billion, per capita $5,300; real growth rate 5.3%; inflation 19.5%; unemployment 9.5%. Arable land: 4%. Principal agricultural products: coffee, bananas, rice, corn, sugar cane, cotton, tobacco, oilseeds, fresh cut flowers. Labor force: 12 million (1990); 46% services; 30% agriculture; 24% industry. Major industrial products: textiles, processed food, beverages, chemicals, cement. Natural resources: petroleum, natural gas, coal, iron ore, nickel, gold, copper, emeralds. Exports: $10.5 billion (f.o.b., 1995 est.): coffee, fuel oil, coal,

bananas, fresh cut flowers, nickel, chemicals, emeralds. Imports: $13.5 billion (c.i.f., 1995 est.): machinery, paper products, aircraft, telecommunications equipment, vehicles, gasoline, wheat. Major trading partners: U.S., E.U., Japan, Venezuela, Brazil.

Geography. Colombia, in the northwestern part of South America, is the only country on that continent that borders on both the Atlantic and Pacific Oceans. It is nearly equal to the combined areas of California and Texas.

Through the western half of the country, three Andean ranges run north and south, merging into one at the Ecuadorean border. The eastern half is a low, jungle-covered plain, drained by spurs of the Amazon and Orinoco, inhabited mostly by isolated, tropical forest Indian tribes. The fertile plateau and valley of the eastern range are the most densely populated parts of the country.

Government. Colombia's President, who appoints his own cabinet, serves for a four-year term. The Senate, the upper house of Congress, has 102 members elected for four years by direct vote. The House of Representatives of 165 members is directly elected for four years. Mayor and state governors are also elected by direct vote for three-year terms.

History. Spaniards in 1510 founded Darien, the first permanent European settlement on the American mainland. In 1538 the Spaniards established the colony of New Granada, the area's name until 1861. After a 14-year struggle, in which Simón Bolívar's Venezuelan troops won the battle of Boyacá in Colombia on Aug. 7, 1819, independence was attained in 1824. Bolívar united Colombia, Venezuela, Panama, and Ecuador in the Republic of Greater Colombia (1819–30), but lost Venezuela and Ecuador to separatists. Bolívar's Vice President, Francisco de Paula Santander, founded the Liberal Party as the Federalists while Bolívar established the Conservatives as the Centralists.

Santander's presidency (1832–36) re-established order, but later periods of Liberal dominance (1849–57 and 1861–80), when the Liberals sought to disestablish the Roman Catholic Church, were marked by insurrection and even civil war. Rafael Nuñez, in a 15-year-presidency, restored the power of the central government and the church, which led in 1899 to a bloody civil war and the loss in 1903 of Panama over ratification of a lease to the U.S. of the Canal Zone. For 21 years, until 1930, the Conservatives held power as revolutionary pressures built up.

The Liberal administrations of Enrique Olaya Herrera and Alfonso López (1930–38) were marked by social reforms that failed to solve the country's problems, and in 1946, insurrection and banditry broke out, claiming hundreds of thousands of lives by 1958. Laureano Gómez (1950–53); the Army Chief of Staff, Gen. Gustavo Rojas Pinilla (1953–56), and a military junta (1956–57) sought to curb disorder by repression.

The Liberals won a solid majority in 1982, but a party split enabled Belisario Betancur Cuartas, the Conservative candidate, to win the presidency on May 31. After his inauguration, he ended the state of siege that had existed almost continuously for 34 years and renewed the general amnesty of 1981.

In an official war against drug trafficking, Colombia became a public battleground with bombs, killings and kidnapping. In 1989 a leading presidential candidate, Luis Carlos Galán, was murdered. In an effort to quell the terror President Gaviria proposed lenient punishment in exchange for surrender by the leading drug dealers. In addition in 1991 the constitutional convention voted to ban extradition. In July 1992 Pablo Escobar of the Medellin drug cartel escaped from prison in an operation that left six dead.

In the country's closest presidential contest in 24 years Mr. Samper, the candidate of the Liberal Party, won 50% of the vote in June 1994.

Amid allegations of having accepted campaign contributions from drug traffickers, Samper in May 1996 ordered emergency security measures in southern Columbia to fight leftist rebels. In June the House of Representatives absolved him of the charges by a 111-to-43 vote.

A bill allowing extradition slowly moved through Congress in the first half of 1997. In June President Samper announced that he was eliminating 3,000 government jobs and some offices in order to reduce the deficit and bureaucracy.

COMOROS

Federal Islamic Republic of the Comoros
National name: République Fédéral Islamique des Comores
President: Mohamed Taki Abdoulkarim (1996)
Prime Minister: Dismissed in September 1997.
Area: 690 sq mi. (1,787 sq km)
Population (1997 est.): 589,797 (average annual rate of natural increase: 3.54%); birth rate: 45.37/1000; infant mortality rate: 73.2/1000; density per square mile: 854.8
Capital and largest city (1990 est.): Moroni (on Grande Comoro), 23,432. **Monetary unit:** Franc CFA. **Languages:** Shaafi Islam (Swahili dialect), Malagasu, French, Arabic. **Ethnicity/Race:** Antalote, Cafre, Makoa, Oimatsaha, Sakalava. **Religions:** Sunni Muslim, 86%; Roman Catholic, 14%. **Literacy rate:** 48%
Economic summary: Gross domestic product: purchasing power parity (1994 est.): $370 million; $700 per capita; real growth rate 0.9%; inflation 15% (1993 est.); unemployment 15.8%. Arable land: 35%. Labor force: 140,000 (1982); 80% in agriculture. Principal agricultural products: perfume essences, copra, coconuts, cloves, vanilla, cassava, bananas. Major industrial products: perfume distillations. Exports: $13.7 million (f.o.b., 1993 est.): perfume essences, vanilla, copra, cloves. Imports: $40.9 million (f.o.b., 1993 est.): foodstuffs, cement, petroleum products, consumer goods. Major trading partners: France, Germany, U.S., Africa, Pakistan, China.

Geography. The Comoros Islands—Grande Comoro, Anjouan, Mohéli, and Mayotte (which retains ties to France)—are an archipelago of volcanic origin in the Indian Ocean between Mozambique and Madagascar.

Government. Democratic elections were held in March 1990. The interim President Said Djohar won from among a field of eight candidates. The constitution dates from October 1, 1978, and the country is an Islamic republic with a 42-member unicameral legislature.

History. Under French rule since 1886, the Comoros declared themselves independent July 6, 1975. However, Mayotte, with a Christian majority, voted against joining the other, mainly Islamic islands, in the move to independence. It remains a French overseas territory.

A month after independence, Justice Minister Ali Soilih staged a coup with the help of mercenaries, overthrowing the new nation's first president, Ahmed Abdallah. He was overthrown on May 13, 1978.

Voters approved a new constitution in a referendum of June 1992.

In June 1993 the President dissolved the federal assembly, appointing an interim Prime Minister. Amid widespread irregularities the President's supporters won 50% of the seats in the Assembly.

An attempted coup in September 1995 was suppressed with the aid of French forces.

Anjouan Island declared independence on August 3, 1997, after months of protests and clashes with security forces. Mohéli, the smallest island, also seceded. A failed assault by President Taki's forces in September attempted to retake the island. Taki then declared a state of emergency and dismissed his top military and civilian advisers as well as the government of Prime Minister Ahmed Abdou.

CONGO

Republic of the Congo
National name: République Populaire du Congo
President: Prof. Pascal Lissouba (1992)
Prime Minister: Bernard Kolelas (1997)
Area: 132,046 sq mi. (342,000 sq km)
Population (1997 est.): 2,583,198 (average annual rate of natural increase: 2.14%); birth rate: 38.79/1000; infant mortality rate: 106/1000; density per square mile: 19.6
Capital and largest city (1992 est.): Brazzaville, 937,580. **Other large city (1992 est.):** Pointe-Noire, 576,206. **Monetary unit:** Franc CFA. **Languages:** French, Lingala, Kikongo, others. **Ethnicity/Race:** south: Kongo 48%; north: Sangha 20%, M'Bochi 12%; center: Teke 17%, Europeans 8,500 (mostly French). **Religions:** 50% Christian, 48% animist, 2% Muslim. **Literacy rate:** 57%
Economic summary: Gross domestic product: purchasing power parity (1995 est.): $7.7 billion; per capita $3,100; real growth rate 3.3%; inflation 61% (1994 est.). Arable land: 2%. Principal agricultural products: cassava, rice, corn, peanuts, coffee, cocoa. Labor force: 79,100; 75% in agriculture, 25% in commerce, industry and government. Major industrial products: crude oil, cigarettes, cement, beverages, milled sugar. Natural resources: wood, potash, petroleum, natural gas. Exports: $1 billion (f.o.b., 1995): oil, lumber, coffee, cocoa, sugar, diamonds. Imports: $600 million (c.i.f., 1995): foodstuffs, consumer goods, intermediate manufactures, capital equipment. Major trading partners: France, Italy, Spain, Germany, other E.U. countries, Brazil, Japan, U.S.

Geography. The Congo is situated in west Central Africa astride the Equator. It borders on Gabon, Cameroon, the Central African Republic, The Democratic Republic of Congo, and the Angola exclave of Cabinda, with a short stretch of coast on the South Atlantic. Its area is nearly three times that of Pennsylvania.

Most of the inland is tropical rain forest, drained by tributaries of the Congo River, which flows south along the eastern border with The Democratic Republic of Congo to Stanley Pool. The narrow coastal plain rises to highlands separated from the inland plateaus by the 200-mile-wide Niari River Valley, which gives passage to the coast.

History. The inhabitants of the former French Congo, mainly Bantu peoples with Pygmies in the north, were subjects of several kingdoms in earlier times.

The Frenchman Pierre Savorgnan de Brazza signed a treaty with Makoko, ruler of the Bateke people, in 1880, which established French control. The area, with Gabon and Ubangi-Shari, was constituted the colony of French Equatorial Africa in 1910. It joined Chad in supporting the Free French cause in World War II. The Congo proclaimed its independence without leaving the French Community in 1960.

Maj. Marien Ngouabi, head of the National Council of the Revolution, took power as President on Jan. 1, 1969. He was sworn in for a second five-year term in 1975.

A four-man commando squad assassinated Ngouabi in Brazzaville on March 18, 1977.

Col. Joachim Yhombi-Opango, Army Chief of Staff, assumed the presidency on April 4. Yombhi-Opango resigned on Feb. 4, 1979, and was replaced by Col. Denis Sassou-Neguessou.

In July 1990 the leaders of the ruling party voted to end the one-party system. A national political conference, hailed as a model for sub-Saharan Africa, renounced Marxism in 1991, and scheduled the country's first free elections for 1992. The national conference ending in June 1991 rewrote the constitution.

Political and ethnic tensions remained high in 1993 particularly after legislative elections in May and run-offs in June.

The opposition's rejection of the results developed into violence. A peace agreement was achieved between the government and opposition in August 1994.

Fighting flared up in the capital between soldiers and an armed militia loyal to Sassau-Neguessou in June 1997. This stalled the presidential election, which had been planned for July 27. Fighting continued throughout the summer, devastating Brazzaville, the capital.

CONGO, DEMOCRATIC REPUBLIC OF

Democratic Republic of Congo
President: Laurent Kabila (1997)
Prime Minister: Likulia Bolongo (1997)
Area: 905,365 sq mi. (2,344,885 sq km)
Population (1997 est.): 47,440,362 (average annual rate of natural increase: 3.1%); birth rate: 47.66/1000; infant mortality rate: 105/1000; density per sq mi.: 52.4
Capital and largest city (1994 est.): Kinshasa, 4,655,313. **Other large cities:** Lubumbashi, 851,381; Mbuji-Mayi, 806,475; Kisangani, 417,517; Kolwezi, 417,810. **Monetary unit:** Zaire. **Languages:** French (official), English, Bantu dialects, mainly Swahili, Lingala, Ishiluba, and Kikongo. **Ethnicity/Race:** over 200 African ethnic groups, the majority are Bantu; the four largest tribes—Mongo, Luba, Kongo (all Bantu), and the Mangbetu-Azande (Hamitic)—make up about 45% of the population. **Religions:** Roman Catholic 50%, Protestant 20%, Kimbanguist 10%, Islam 10%; syncretic and traditional, 10%. **Literacy rate:** 72%
Economic summary: Gross domestic product: purchasing power parity (1994 est.): $18.8 billion; $440 per capita; 4% real growth rate; inflation 40% per mo. (1993 est.); unemployment: n.a. Arable land: 3%. Principal agricultural products: coffee, palm oil, rubber, quinine, cassava, bananas, plantains, vegetables, fruits. Labor force: 15,000,000; 13% in industry. Major industrial products: processed and unprocessed minerals, consumer goods. Natural resources: copper, cobalt, zinc, industrial diamonds, manganese, tin, gold, silver, bauxite, iron, coal, crude oil, hydroelectric potential. Exports: $362 million (f.o.b., 1993 est.): copper, cobalt, diamonds, petroleum, coffee. Imports: $356 million (f.o.b., 1993 est.): consumer goods, foodstuffs, mining and other machinery, transport equipment, and fuels. Major trading partners: Belgium, France, U.S., Germany, South Africa, Italy, Japan, U.K.

Geography. The Democratic Republic of Congo is situated in west central Africa and is bordered by the Congo Republic, the Central African Republic, the Sudan, Uganda, Rwanda, Burundi, Tanzania, Zambia, Angola, and the Atlantic Ocean. It is one quarter the size of the U.S.

The principal rivers are the Ubangi and Bomu in the north and the Congo in the west, which flows into the Atlantic. The entire length of Lake Tanganyika lies along the eastern border with Tanzania and Burundi.

Government. A republic with a multiparty unicameral legislature. The President and the legislature are elected by universal suffrage for five-year terms.

History. Formerly the Belgian Congo, this territory was inhabited by ancient Negrito peoples (Pygmies), who were pushed into the mountains by Bantu and Nilotic invaders. The American correspondent Henry M. Stanley navigated the Congo River in 1877 and opened the interior to exploration. Commissioned by King Leopold II of the Belgians, Stanley made treaties with native chiefs that enabled the King to obtain personal title to the territory at the Berlin Conference of 1885.

Criticism of forced labor under royal exploitation prompted Belgium to take over administration of the Congo, which remained a colony until agitation for independence forced Brussels to grant freedom on June 30, 1960. Moise Tshombe, Premier of the then Katanga Province seceded from the new republic on July 11, and another mining province, South Kasai, followed. Belgium sent paratroopers to quell the civil war, and with President Joseph Kasavubu and Premier Patrice Lumumba of the national government in conflict, the United Nations flew in a peacekeeping force.

Kasavubu staged an army coup in 1960 and handed Lumumba over to the Katangan forces. A U.N. investigating commission found that Lumumba had been killed by a Belgian mercenary in the presence of Tshombe. Dag Hammarskjold, U.N. Secretary-General, died in a plane crash en route to a peace conference with Tshombe on Sept. 17, 1961.

U.N. Secretary-General U Thant submitted a national reconciliation plan in 1962 that Tshombe rejected. Tshombe's troops fired on the U.N. force in December, and in the ensuing conflict Tshombe capitulated on Jan. 14, 1963. The peacekeeping force withdrew, and, in a complete about-face, Kasavubu named Tshombe Premier to fight a spreading rebellion. Tshombe used foreign mercenaries and, with the help of Belgian paratroops airlifted by U.S. planes, defeated the most serious opposition, a Communist-backed regime in the northeast.

Kasavubu abruptly dismissed Tshombe in 1965 and was himself ousted by Gen. Joseph-Desiré Mobutu, Army Chief of Staff. The new President nationalized the Union Minière, the Belgian copper mining enterprise that had been a dominant force in the Congo since colonial days. The plane carrying the exiled Tshombe was hijacked in 1967 and he was held prisoner in Algeria until his death from a heart attack was announced June 29, 1969.

Mobutu eliminated opposition to win election in 1970 to a term of seven years, which was renewed in a 1977 election. In 1975, he nationalized much of the economy, barred religious instruction in schools, and decreed the adoption of African names.

On March 8, 1977, invaders from Angola calling themselves the Congolese National Liberation Front pushed into Shaba and threatened the important mining center of Kolwezi. France and Belgium responded to Mobutu's pleas for help with weapons, but the U.S. gave only nonmilitary supplies.

In April, France flew 1,500 Moroccan troops to Shaba to defeat the invaders, who were, Mobutu charged, Soviet-inspired and Cuban-led. U.S. intelligence sources, however, confirmed Soviet and Cuban denials of any participation and identified the rebels as former Katanga gendarmes who had fled to Angola after their 1963 defeat.

In April 1990 Mobutu announced he intended to introduce multiparty democracy, but that elections in January 1991 would reduce the number of political parties to two besides his own. Opposition leaders denounced the scheme as giving Mobutu's party an unfair advantage.

A national conference was scheduled for July 1991, but in June three opposition groups announced a boycott. The conference was postponed. The conference finally convened in August, but, boycotted by the main opposition parties, it was adjourned without achieving anything. Mobutu offered the Prime Ministerial post to an opposition leader. The ensuing power struggle led to his dismissal in October.

In early 1993 Mobutu rejected Western demands that he yield power and announced plans to regroup his one-party parliament, dismissing the main opposition leader, Prime Minister Tshisekedi. In January 1994 Mobutu dissolved Parliament and dismissed his prime minister, which led to a general strike in the capital.

After a seven-month rebellion against the Mobutu regime, Laurent Kabila entered Kinshasa in mid-1997 with Mobutu fleeing into exile in Morocco, where he died of cancer in September. Kabila proclaimed himself president, renamed the country, decreed a new flag, appointed a new government, and banned political activity. Opposition figures questioned whether the country had indeed been liberated.

COSTA RICA

Republic of Costa Rica
National name: República de Costa Rica
President: José Maria Figueres Olsen (1994)
Area: 19,652 sq mi. (50,898 sq km)
Population (1997 est.): 3,534,174 (average annual rate of natural increase: 1.92%); birth rate: 23.35/1000; infant mortality rate: 13.3/1000; density per square mile: 179.8
Capital and largest city (1994 est.): San José, 315,909. **Monetary unit:** Colón. **Language:** Spanish. **Ethnicity/Race:** white (including mestizo) 96%, black 2%, Indian 1%, Chinese 1%. **Religion:** 95% Roman Catholic. **Literacy rate (1984):** 93%
Economic summary: Gross domestic product: purchasing power parity (1995 est.): $18.4 billion; per capita $5,400; real growth rate 2.5%; inflation 22.5% (1995 est.); unemployment 5.2%. Arable land: 6%. Principal products: bananas, coffee, sugar cane, rice, corn, livestock. Labor force: 868,300; 35.1% in industry and commerce, 33% in government and services, and 27% in agriculture. Major products: processed foods, textiles and clothing, construction materials, fertilizer. Natural resource: hydropower potential. Exports: $2.4 billion (f.o.b., 1995 est.): coffee, bananas, textiles, sugar. Imports: $3 billion (c.i.f., 1995 est.): raw materials, consumer goods, capital equipment, petroleum. Major trading partners: U.S., Central American countries, Germany, Japan, United Kingdom, France, Netherlands.

Geography. This Central American country lies between Nicaragua to the north and Panama to the south. Its area slightly exceeds that of Vermont and New Hampshire combined.

Most of Costa Rica is tableland, from 3,000 to 6,000 feet (914 to 1,829 m) above sea level. Cocos Island (10 sq mi.; 26 sq km), about 300 miles (483 km) off the Pacific Coast, is under Costa Rican sovereignty.

Government. Under the 1949 constitution, the President and the one-house Legislative Assembly of 57 members are elected for terms of four years.

The army was abolished in 1949. There is a civil guard and a rural guard.

History. Costa Rica was inhabited by 25,000 Indians when Columbus landed on it and probably named it in 1502. Few of the Indians survived the Spanish conquest, which began in 1563. The region was administered as a Spanish province. Costa Rica achieved independence in 1821 but was absorbed for two years by Agustín de Iturbide in his Mexican Empire. It was established as a republic in 1848.

Except for the military dictatorship of Tomás Guardia from 1870 to 1882, Costa Rica has enjoyed one of the most democratic governments in Latin America.

Rodrigo Carazo Odio, leader of a four-party coalition called the Unity Party, won the presidency in February 1978. His tenure was marked by a disastrous decline in the economy.

On Feb. 2, 1986, Oscar Arias Sanchez won the national elections on a neutralist platform. Arias initiated a policy of preventing contra usage of Costa Rican territory. Rafael Calderón won the presidential election of February 4, 1990 with 51% of the vote.

The presidential election in February 1994 was won by Maria Figueres Olsen, although the tone of the campaign shocked many Costa Ricans. Mr. Figueres proposed more government intervention in the economy. Mr. Calderon was constitutionally prevented from running for a second term.

As a result of IMF displeasure with the government's economic programs, the World Bank withheld $100 million of financing.

The security minister abruptly and unexpectedly resigned in November 1996 after being questioned by the Comptroller-General's office.

CÔTE D'IVOIRE

Republic of Côte d'Ivoire
National name: République de la Côte d'Ivoire
President: Henri Konan Bédié (1993)
Prime Minister: Daniel Kablan Duncan (1993)
Area: 124,502 sq mi. (322,462 sq km)
Population (1997 est.): 14,986,218 (average annual rate of natural increase: 2.53%); birth rate: 42.43/1000; infant mortality rate: 99.7/1000; density per square mile: 120.4
Capital (1988): Yamoussoukro[1] (since March 1983), 106,786. **Largest city (est. 1988):** Abidjan, 2,797,000.
Monetary unit: Franc CFA. **Languages:** French and African languages (Diaula esp.). **Ethnicity/Race:** Baoule 23%, Bete 18%, Senoufou 15%, Malinke 11%, Agni, foreign Africans (mostly Burkinabe and Malians, about 3 million), non-Africans 130,000 to 330,000 (French 30,000 and Lebanese 100,000 to 300,000). **Religions:** 60% indigenous, 17% Christian, 23% Islam. **Literacy rate:** 54%
Economic summary: Gross domestic product: purchasing power parity (1995 est.): $21.9 billion; per capita $1,500; real growth rate 5%; inflation 10%. Arable land: 9%; Labor force: 5.718 million; over 85% in agriculture. Unemployment rate n.a. Principal products: coffee, cocoa, corn, beans, timber. Major industrial products: food, wood, refined oil, textiles, fertilizer. Natural resources: diamonds, iron ore, crude oil, manganese, cobalt, bauxite, copper. Exports: $2.9 billion (f.o.b., 1994): cocoa 55%, coffee 12%, tropical woods 11%, petroleum, cotton, bananas, pineapples, palm oil. Imports: $1.6 billion (f.o.b., 1994 est.): food, capital goods, consumer goods, fuel. Major trading partners: France, Germany, Netherlands, Belgium, Spain, other E.U. countries, U.S., Nigeria, Japan.

1. Not recognized by U.S., which recognizes Abidjan.

Geography. Côte d'Ivoire (also known as the Ivory Coast) in western Africa on the Gulf of Guinea, is a little larger than New Mexico. Its neighbors are Liberia, Guinea, Mali, Burkina Faso, and Ghana.

The country consists of a coastal strip in the south, dense forests in the interior, and savannas in the north.

Rainfall is heavy, especially along the coast.

Government. The government is headed by a President who is elected every five years by popular vote, together with a National Assembly of 175 members.

History. Côte d'Ivoire attracted both French and Portuguese merchants in the 15th century. French traders set up establishments early in the 19th century, and in 1842, the French obtained territorial concessions from local tribes, gradually extending their influence along the coast and inland. The area was organized as a territory in 1893, became an autonomous republic in the French Union after World War II, and achieved independence on Aug. 7, 1960.

The Côte d'Ivoire formed a customs union in 1959 with Dahomey (Benin), Niger, and Burkina Faso.

Roman Catholic President Houphouët-Boigny ordered the building of the largest Christian church in the world, Notre Dame de la Pax, in the capital city, which he periodically paid for.

Falling cocoa and coffee prices made this nation the largest per capita debtor in Africa. Massive protests by students, farmers and professionals forced the president to legalize opposition parties and hold the first contested presidential election. In October 1990 Houphouët-Boigny won 81% of the vote and is currently serving his seventh consecutive five-year term. In the first multiparty legislative elections in November the President's Democratic Party won 163 of the 175 seats.

The country's long-time President Houphouët-Boigny died in December 1993, but a smooth transition ensued to Bédié.

The presidential election of October 1995, marred by violence and a boycott by the opposition, was won by the incumbent. Legislative elections in November gave the ruling party 147 seats.

In June 1997 the government announced it was lifting price controls on domestically produced tobacco products, sugar, and various spices.

CROATIA

Republic of Croatia
President: Franjo Tudjman
Prime Minister: Zlatko Matesa (1995)
Area: 21,829 sq mi. (56,537 sq km)
Population (1997 est.): 5,026,995 (average annual rate of natural increase: −0.15%), Birth rate: 9.8/1000; infant mortality rate: 10/1000; density per square mile: 230.3
Capital (1991): Zagreb, 930,753. **Other large cities (1991):** Split, 189,444; Rijeka, 167,757; Osijek, 104,553. **Monetary unit:** Kuna (May 1994). **Languages:** Croatian. **Ethnicity/Race:** Croat 78%, Serb 12%, Muslim 0.9%, Hungarian 0.5%, Slovenian 0.5%, others 8.1% (1991). **Literacy rate:** est. 90%. **Religion:** predominantly Roman Catholic
Economic summary: Gross domestic product: purchasing power parity (1996 est.): $18.5 billion; $3,800 per capita; real growth rate 6.5%; inflation 3.8%; unemployment 18.8% (1996). Industries: chemicals, plastics, machine tools, fabricated metals, electronics, rolled steel products, aluminum processing, wood products, building materials, petroleum and petroleum refining, food processing, beverages, pharmaceuticals, and shipbuilding. Agriculture: wheat, corn, oats, sugar beets, potatoes, livestock breeding, dairy farming, vineyards, and fishing. Exports: $4.6 billion (1996): machinery and transport equipment, chemicals, food and live animals, raw materials, fuels and lubricants, and beverages and tobacco. Imports: $7.8 billion (1996).

Geography. Croatia is about half the size of the state of Louisiana (or the size of West Virginia). It is bounded in the northwest by the Republic of Slovenia, in the northeast by Hungary, in the east and south by the Federal Republic of Yugoslavia (Serbia and Montenegro), in the south by the Republic of Bosnia and Herzegovina, and in the west by the Adriatic Sea. Part of Croatia is a barren, rocky region lying in the Dinaric Alps. The Zagorje region north of the capital, Zagreb, is a land of rolling hills, and the fertile agricultural region of the Pannonian Plain is bordered by the Drava, Danube, and Sava Rivers in the east. Over one-third of Croatia is forested.

Government. A parliamentary democracy with two legislative houses.

History. The original home of the Slavic Croats was in an area that was part of the Republic of Ukraine. During the 6th century C.E., other tribes arrived in the region which was then part of the Roman province of Pannonia. The Croats converted to Christianity between the 7th and 9th centuries and adopted the Roman alphabet.

In C.E. 925, the Croats defeated Byzantine and Frankish invaders and established their own independent kingdom which reached its peak during the 11th century.

A civil war ensued in 1089 which later led to the country being conquered by the Hungarians in 1091. The signing of the *Pacta Conventa* by Croatian tribal chiefs and the Hungarian King in 1102 united the two nations politically under the Hungarian monarch.

When the Hungarians were defeated by the Turks in 1526, most of Croatia fell under Ottoman rule until the end of the 17th century. The rest of Croatia elected Ferdinand of Austria as their King and became associated with the Hapsburgs of Austria.

After the establishment of the Austro-Hungarian kingdom in 1867, Croatia and Slovenia became part of Hungary until the collapse of Austria-Hungary in 1918 following their defeat in World War I.

On Oct. 29, 1918, Croatia proclaimed its independence and joined in union with Montenegro, Serbia, and Slovenia to form the Kingdom of Serbs, Croats, and Slovenes. The name was changed to Yugoslavia in 1929.

When Germany invaded Yugoslavia in 1941, an independent Croatian state was created that was controlled by a Fascist dictatorship. After Germany was defeated in 1945, Croatia was made into a republic of the newly reestablished nation of Yugoslavia.

In May 1991, Croatian voters supported a referendum calling for their republic's independence and when the Croatian parliament passed a declaration of independence from Yugoslavia in June, a six-month civil war followed with the Serbian-dominated Yugoslavian army. The war claimed thousands of lives and wrought mass destruction on the land.

A U.N. cease-fire was arranged on Jan. 2, 1992. The Security Council in February approved sending a 14,000-member peacekeeping force to monitor the ceasefire and protect the minority Serbs in Croatia.

By the end of August, rebel Serbs in Croatia still controlled a third of that republic.

In a 1993 referendum the Serb-occupied portion of Croatia (Krajina) resoundingly voted for integration with Serbs in Bosnia and Serbia proper. Although the Zagreb government and representatives of Krajina signed a ceasefire in March 1994 further negotiations broke down shortly afterward over the political status of the latter region.

In a lightning operation the Croatian army retook western Slavonia in May 1995. Similarly, in August the central Croatian region of Krajina, held by Serbs, was returned to Zagreb's control.

Elections for the upper house of parliament in April 1997 gave the ruling party 42 of 63 seats.

Tudjman easily won the presidential election of June. Outside monitors, however, criticized the campaign procedure.

CUBA

Republic of Cuba
National name: República de Cuba
President: Fidel Castro Ruz (1976)
Area: 42,843 sq mi. (110,992 sq km)
Population (1997 est.): 10,999,041 (average annual rate of natural increase: 0.57%); birth rate: 13.21/1000; infant mortality rate: 8.9/1000; density per square mile: 248.7
Capital and largest city (1994 est.): Havana, 2,241,000. **Other large cities (1994 est.):** Santiago de Cuba, 440,084; Camagüey, 293,961; Holguin, 242,085; Guantánamo, 207,796; Santa Clara, 205,400. **Monetary unit:** Peso. **Language:** Spanish. **Ethnicity/Race:** mulatto 51%, white 37%, black 11%, Chinese 1%. **Religion:** at least 85% nominally Roman Catholic before Castro assumed power. **Literacy rate:** 94%
Economic summary: Gross domestic product: purchasing power parity (1995 est.): $14.7 billion, per capita $1,300; real growth rate 2.5%, inflation rate n.a.; unemployment rate n.a. Arable land: 23%. Principal agricultural products: sugar and sugar byproducts, tobacco, coffee, rice, fruits. Labor force (1989): 4.71 million; services and government 30%; industry 22%; agriculture 20%; commerce 11%. Major industrial products: processed sugar and tobacco, refined oil products, textiles, chemicals, paper and wood products, metals, consumer products. Natural resources: metals (primarily nickel), timber. Exports: $1.6 billion (f.o.b., 1995 est.): coffee, sugar (world's largest sugar exporter), nickel, shellfish, tobacco, medical products, citrus. Imports: $2.4 billion (c.i.f., 1995 est.): petroleum, food, machinery, chemicals. Trading partners: China, Canada, Mexico, Spain, Russia.

Geography. The largest island of the West Indies group (equal in area to Pennsylvania), Cuba is also the westernmost—just west of Hispaniola (Haiti and the Dominican Republic), and 90 miles (145 km) south of Key West, Florida, at the entrance to the Gulf of Mexico. The island is mountainous in the southeast and south central area (Sierra Maestra). Elsewhere it is flat or rolling.

Government. Since 1976, elections have been held every five years to elect the National Assembly, which in turn elects the 31-member Council of States, its President, and Secretary. Fidel Castro is President of the Council of States and of the government and First Secretary of the Communist Party of Cuba, the only political party.

History. Arawak Indians inhabiting Cuba when Columbus landed on the island in 1492 died off from diseases brought by sailors and settlers. By 1511, Spaniards under Diego Velásquez were founding settlements that served as bases for Spanish exploration. Cuba soon after served as an assembly point for treasure looted by the conquistadores, attracting French and English pirates.

Black slaves and free laborers were imported to work sugar and tobacco plantations, and waves of chiefly Spanish immigrants maintained a European character in the island's culture. Early slave rebellions and conflicts between colonials and Spanish rulers laid the foundation for an independence movement that turned into open warfare from 1867 to 1878. In 1895, the poet José

Marti led the struggle that finally ended Spanish rule, thanks largely to U.S. intervention in 1898 after the sinking of the battleship *Maine* in Havana harbor.

A treaty in 1899 made Cuba an independent republic under U.S. protection. The U.S. occupation, which ended in 1902, suppressed yellow fever and brought large American investment. From 1906 to 1909, Washington invoked the Platt Amendment to the treaty, which gave it the right to intervene in order to suppress any revolt. U.S. troops came back in 1912 and again in 1917 to restore order. The Platt Amendment was abrogated in 1934.

Fulgencio Batista, an army sergeant, led a revolt in 1933 that overthrew the regime of President Gerado Machado.

Batista's Cuba was a police state. Corrupt officials took payoffs from American gamblers who operated casinos, demanded bribes from Cubans for various public services and enriched themselves with raids on the public treasury. Dissenters were murdered and their bodies dumped in gutters.

Fidel Castro Ruz, a tall, bearded attorney in his 30s, landed in Cuba on Christmas Day 1956 with a band of 12 fellow revolutionaries, evaded Batista's soldiers, and set up headquarters in the jungled hills of the Sierra Maestra range. By 1958 his force had grown to about 2,000 guerrillas, for the most part young and middle class. Castro's brother, Raul, and Ernesto (Ché) Guevara, an Argentine physician, were his top lieutenants. Businessmen and landowners who opposed the Batista regime gave financial support to the rebels. The United States, meanwhile, cut off arms shipments to Batista's army.

The beginning of the end for Batista came when the rebels routed 3,000 government troops and captured Santa Clara, capital of Las Villas province 150 miles from Havana, and a trainload of Batista reinforcements refused to get out of their railroad cars. On New Year's Day 1959, Batista flew to exile in the Dominican Republic and Castro took over the government. Crowds cheered the revolutionaries on their seven-day march to the capital.

The United States initially welcomed what looked like the prospect for a democratic Cuba, but a rude awakening came within a few months when Castro established military tribunals for political opponents, jailed hundreds, and began to veer leftward. Castro disavowed Cuba's 1952 military pact with the United States. He confiscated U.S. investments in banks and industries and seized large U.S. landholdings, turning them first into collective farms and then into Soviet-type state farms. The United States broke relations with Cuba on Jan. 3, 1961. Castro thereupon forged an alliance with the Soviet Union.

From the ranks of the Cuban exiles who had fled to the United States, the Central Intelligence Agency recruited and trained an expeditionary force, numbering less than 2,000 men, to invade Cuba, with the expectation that the invasion would spark an uprising of the Cuban populace against Castro. The invasion was planned under the Eisenhower administration and President John F. Kennedy gave the go-ahead for it in the first months of his administration, but rejected a CIA proposal for U.S. planes to provide air support. The landing at the Bay of Pigs on April 17, 1961, was a fiasco. Not only did the invaders fail to receive any support from the populace, but Castro's tanks and artillery made short work of the small force.

A Soviet attempt to change the global power balance by installing in Cuba medium-range missiles—capable of striking targets in the United States with nuclear warheads—provoked a crisis between the superpowers in 1962 that had the potential of touching off World War III. After a visit to Moscow by Cuba's war minister,

Raul Castro, work began secretly on the missile launching sites.

Denouncing the Soviets for "deliberate deception," President Kennedy on Oct. 22 announced that the U.S navy would enforce a "quarantine" of shipping to Cuba and search Soviet bloc ships to prevent the missiles themselves from reaching the island. After six days of tough public statements on both sides and secret diplomacy, Soviet Premier Nikita Khrushchev on Oct. 28 ordered the missile sites dismantled, crated and shipped back to the Soviet Union, in return for a U.S. pledge not to attack Cuba. Limited diplomatic ties were re-established on Sept. 1, 1977.

Emigration increased dramatically after April 1 1980, when Castro, irritated by the granting of asylum to would-be refugees by the Peruvian embassy in Havana, removed guards and allowed 10,000 Cubans to swarm into the embassy grounds.

As an airlift began taking the refugees to Costa Rica, Castro opened the port of Mariel to a "freedom flotilla" of ships and yachts from the United States, many of them owned or chartered by Cuban-Americans to bring out relatives. It wasn't until after they had reached the United States that it was discovered that the regime had opened prisons and mental hospitals to permit criminals, homosexuals and others unwanted in Cuba to join the refugees.

For most of President Ronald Reagan's first term U.S.-Cuban relations were frozen. But late in 1984, an agreement was reached between the two countries: Cuba would take back more than 2,700 Cubans who had come to the United States in the Mariel exodus but were not eligible to stay in the country under U.S. immigration law because of criminal or psychiatric disqualification. Castro cancelled it when the U.S. began the Radio Marti broadcasts in May 1985 to bring a non-Communist view to the Cuban people.

In the face of sweeping changes in Eastern Europe and the Soviet Union itself, Cuba has reaffirmed it adherence to Marxism-Leninism.

With the collapse of Communism in Eastern Europe, Cuba's foreign trade plummeted as did aid from Russia, producing the worst economic crisis in the island's history.

The government moved slightly toward a mixed economy in 1993 by permitting limited private enterprise in a number of trades and services and allowing Cubans to possess convertible currencies.

In April 1997 Cuba announced it would ratify a worldwide ban on chemical weapons.

CYPRUS

Republic of Cyprus
National name: Kypriaki Dimokratia—Kibris Cumhuriyeti
President: Glafcos Clerides (1993)
Area: 3,572 sq mi (9,251 sq km)
Population (1997 est.): 752,808; (average annual rate of natural increase: 0.746%[1]; birth rate: 15/1000[1]; infant mortality rate: 8.2/1000[1]; density per square mile: 210.7
Capital and largest city (1993): Lefkosia (Nicosia) (in government controlled area), 186,400. **Monetary unit:** Cyprus pound. **Languages:** Greek, Turkish (official), English is widely spoken. **Ethnicity/Race:** total: Greek 78% (99.5% of the Greeks live in the Greek area; 0.5% of the Greeks live in the Turkish area), Turkish 18% (1.3% of the Turks live in the Greek area; 98.7% of the Turks live in the Turkish area), other 4% (99.2% of the other ethnic groups live in the Greek area; 0.8% of the other ethnic groups live in the Turkish area). **Religions (1993 est.):** Greek Orthodox,

78%; Sunni Muslim, 18%; Maronite, Armenian, Apostolic, Latin and others, 4%. **Literacy rate (1993):** 94%
Economic summary: Gross domestic product: purchasing power parity (1995[1]): $7.8 billion, $13,000 per capita; 5% real growth rate; inflation 3%; unemployment 2.7%. Arable land: 46.8%. Principal agricultural products: vine products, citrus, potatoes, vegetables, olives, barley. Labor force: 294,100; 26% in industry, 61.5% in services, and 12.5% in agriculture. Major industrial products: food, beverages, footwear, clothing, metal products, pharmaceuticals, furniture. Hotels and restaurants contributed 8.6% to the gross domestic product in 1996. Natural resources: copper, asbestos, gypsum, timber, marble, clay, amber, ochre. Exports: $891.1 billion (f.o.b., 1995): citrus, potatoes, grapes, wine, cement, clothing, footwear, chemical products, paper products. Imports: $3.3 billion (c.i.f., 1995): consumer goods, petroleum and lubricants, food and feed grains, machinery. Major trading partners: U.K., Greece, Lebanon, Germany, Saudi Arabia. **Member of Commonwealth of Nations**
1. Government-controlled area only.

Geography. The third largest island in the Mediterranean (one and one-half times the size of Delaware), Cyprus lies off the southern coast of Turkey and the western shore of Syria. Most of the country consists of a wide plain lying between two mountain ranges that cross the island. The highest peak is Mount Olympus at 6,406 feet (1,953 m).

Government. The President is elected for a five-year term and exercises executive power through an appointed Council of Ministers.

Legislative power lies with the House of Representatives which is comprised of 80 members elected for five years. 56 members are Greek-Cypriots elected by the Greek-Cypriot community; 24 are Turkish-Cypriots elected by the Turkish-Cypriot community. Since the Turkish-Cypriot ministers and other officials withdrew from their posts in 1963, the 24 seats allotted to the Turkish Cypriots remain vacant. The Cypriot House assembly has been functioning with only its 56 Greek Cypriot members. Representatives from the Maronite, Armenian, and Latin minorities are also elected as observers. Mediation efforts by the U.N. seek to achieve reunification of the island under one federated system of government.

History. Cyprus was the site of early Phoenician and Greek colonies. For centuries its rule passed through many hands. It fell to the Turks in 1571, and a large Turkish colony settled on the island.

In World War I, on the outbreak of hostilities with Turkey, Britain annexed the island. It was declared a Crown colony in 1925.

For centuries the Greek population, regarding Greece as its mother country, has sought self-determination and reunion with it (enosis). The resulting quarrel with Turkey threatened NATO. Cyprus became an independent nation on Aug. 16, 1960, with Britain, Greece, and Turkey as guarantor powers.

Archbishop Makarios, President since 1959, was overthrown July 15, 1974 by a military coup led by the Cypriot National Guard. The new regime named Nikos Giorgiades Sampson as President and Bishop Gennadios as head of the Cypriot Church to replace Makarios. Diplomacy failed to resolve the crisis. Turkey invaded Cyprus by sea and air July 20, 1974, asserting its right to protect the Turkish Cypriote minority.

Geneva talks involving Greece, Turkey, Britain, and the two Cypriote factions failed in mid-August, and the Turks subsequently gained control of 40% of the island. Greece made no armed response to the superior Turkish force, but bitterly suspended military participation in the NATO alliance.

The tension continued after Makarios returned to become president on Dec. 7, 1974. He offered self-government to the Turkish minority, but rejected any solution "involving transfer of populations and amounting to partition of Cyprus."

Turkish Cypriots proclaimed a separate state under Rauf Denktas in the northern part of the island in Nov. 1983, and proposed a "biregional federation."

Makarios died on Aug. 3, 1977, and Spyros Kyprianou was elected to serve the remainder of his term. Kyprianou was subsequently re-elected in 1978, 1983, and 1985. In 1988, George Vassiliou defeated Kyprianou.

Then-President Vassiliou won a plurality in the presidential election of February 1993 but fell short of a majority. A 73-year-old conservative and critic of U.N. proposals to reunify Cyprus narrowly won the second round of elections to become president

Parliamentary elections in May 1996 resulted in the ruling conservative-center coalition retaining a seat majority ahead of the Communists.

The purchase of missiles capable of reaching the Turkish coast evoked threats of retaliation from Turkey in January 1997.

Northern Cyprus— In 1974, Turkey invaded Cyprus and has since occupied 37% of the island in the north. Some 180,000 Greek Cypriots (about 40% of the Greek Cypriot population) were forced by the Turkish troops to flee to the Government-controlled area in the south and are still prevented by the occupying forces from returning to their homes and properties.

On Nov. 15, 1983, Turkish Cypriot leader Rauf Denktas unilaterally declared the occupied area independent, naming it the "Turkish Republic of Northern Cyprus." The U.N. Security Council, in its Resolution 541 of Nov. 18, 1983, declared this action legally invalid and called for withdrawal. No country except Turkey has recognized this illegal entity. The government of the Republic of Cyprus is the only internationally recognized Government on the island.

Invitations were sent out by the U.N. in June 1997 to the leaders of the respective communities to engage in talks on the status of the island.

NORTHERN CYPRUS

Turkish Republic of Northern Cyprus
National name: Kuzey Kibris Türk Cumhuriyeti (Turkish Republic of Northern Cyprus)
President: Rauf Denktas (1990)
Prime Minister: Dervis Erogln (1996)
Area: 1,295 sq mi. (3,355 sq km)
Population (1994 est.): 175,494; Turkish Cypriots, 174,818; Greek Cypriots, 488; Maronites, 188; (average annual rate of natural increase: 1.14%); birth rate: 18/1,000; infant mortality rate: 12/1000; density per square mile: 135
Capital and largest city (1983): Nicosia North (Lefkosa), 41,815. **Monetary unit:** Turkish lira. **Official language:** Turkish. **Religions:** Moslem, 99%; others, 1%. **Literacy rate (1993):** 99%
Economic summary: Gross domestic product: purchasing power parity (1995): $520 million; per capita $3,900. Real growth rate 0.5%. Inflation 215%. Arable land (1994): 56.71%. Unemployment 1.6% (1994). Principal agricultural products: citrus, potatoes, tobacco, vegetables. Labor force (1994): 75,320;

52.9% in services; 23.6% in industry; 23.5% in agriculture. Major industrial products: concentrated citrus, hides, leathers, P.V.C. covered electric cables, footwear, clothing, consumables. Natural resources: gypsum, pyrite mine. Exports: dairy products, citrus, live animals, potatoes, ready-made clothing, tobacco, carobs, hides and leathers. Imports: consumer goods, petroleum and lubricants, food, machinery and transport equipment, chemicals. Major trading partners: E.U. countries (mainly U.K. and Germany) and Turkey.

Geography. The Turkish Republic of Northern Cyprus covers the northern part of the island of Cyprus. North Cyprus consists of the coastal plains, the Besparmak (Five-Finger) Mountains (the highest peak is Mount Selvili at 3,360 feet), and the interior plains.

Government. The constitution envisages a parliamentary democracy. The legislative power is exercised by an Assembly composed of 50 deputies elected for five years. The President is Head of State and represents the unity of the state. He appoints the Prime Minister from among the deputies.

Denktas dissolved Parliament in Ocotober 1993 with a call for new elections in December, whose results led to the formation of a coalition government.

The European Court of Justice in July 1994 ordered an embargo on exports, consisting chiefly of fruits and clothing. Although this led to some deprivations, financial assistance from Turkey helped ameliorate the situation.

Negotiations were set to begin in 1996 on a move to integrate Cyprus into the European Union, providing incentives to Turkey, as a convoluted means of resolving the political impasse in the division of the island.

CZECH REPUBLIC

President: Vaclav Havel (1993)
Prime Minister: Vaclav Klaus (1992)
Area: 30,464 sq mi. (78,902 sq km)
Population (1997 est.): 10,318,958 (average annual rate of natural increase: −0.039%); birth rate: 10.54/1000; infant mortality rate: 8.3/1000; density per square mile: 338.7
Capital and largest city (Jan. 1, 1994): Prague, 1,215,771. **Other large cities:** Brno, 389,727; Ostrava, 326,396; Plzen, 172,402; Olomouc, 106,003.
Monetary unit: Koruna. **Language:** Czech. **Ethnicity/Race:** Czech 94.4%, Slovak 3%, Polish 0.6%, German 0.5%, Gypsy 0.3%, Hungarian 0.2%, other 1%.
Religions: Roman Catholic major; other: Protestant, Orthodox. **Literacy rate:** 99%
Economic summary: Gross domestic product (1995 est.): $106.2 billion; per capita $10,200; real growth rate 5%; inflation 9.1%; unemployment 2.9%. The Czech Republic has a developed but deteriorating industrialized economy—much of its plant equipment is among the oldest in Europe. Natural resources: hard coal, kaolin, clay, graphite; Industries: fuels, ferrous metallurgy, machinery and equipment, coal, motor vehicles, glass, armaments; Agriculture: diversified crops including grains, potatoes, sugar beets, hops, fruit, hogs, cattle and poultry. Labor force (1990): 5.389 million; industry, 37.9%; agriculture, 8.1%; construction, 8.8%; communications and other 45.2%. Exports: $17.4 billion (f.o.b., 1995 est.): manufactured goods, machinery and transport equipment, chemicals, fuels, minerals, and metals. Imports: $21.3 billion (f.o.b., 1995 est.): machinery and transport equipment, fuels and lubricants, manufactured goods, raw materials, chemicals, agricultural products. Major trading partners: C.I.S., Slovakia, Germany, Hungary, Poland, Austria, and Switzerland.

Geography. The Czech Republic lies in central Europe. It is bordered on the north by Poland, on the east by Slovakia, on the south by Austria, and on the west and northwest by Germany. The two principal regions are Bohemia and Moravia. The Bohemian landscape consists of rolling hills and plateaus surrounded by low mountains to the north, west, and south. Moravia is bordered on the north by mountains and generally has more hills than Bohemia. The principal rivers are the Elbe and the Vltava which are vital to the nation's waterborne and agricultural commerce. The Czech Republic is about the size of the state of South Carolina.

Government. A parliamentary democracy headed by the President. The Parliament consists of two chambers—the 200-member House, elected for four-year terms, and the 81-member Senate, elected for six-year terms. The President is elected for a five-year term by both chambers of Parliament.

History. Probably about the 5th century C.E., Slavic tribes from the Vistula basin settled in the region of the traditional Czech lands of Bohemia, Moravia, and Silesia. The Czechs founded the Kingdom of Bohemia, the Premyslide dynasty, which ruled Bohemia and Moravia from the 10th to the 16th century.

One of the Bohemian Kings, Charles IV, Holy Roman Emperor, made Prague an imperial capital and a center of Latin scholarship. The Hussite movement founded by Jan Hus (1369?–1415) linked the Slavs to the Reformation and revived Czech nationalism, previously under German domination. A Hapsburg, Ferdinand I, ascended the throne in 1526. The Czechs rebelled in 1618. Defeated in 1620, they were ruled for the next 300 years as part of the Austrian Empire. Full independence from the Hapsburgs was not achieved until the end of World War I following the collapse of the Austrian-Hungarian Empire.

A union of the Czech lands and Slovakia was proclaimed in Prague on Nov. 14, 1918, and the Czech nation became one of the two component parts of the newly formed Czechoslovakian state.

In March 1939, German troops occupied Czechoslovakia and Czech Bohemia and Moravia became German protectorates for the duration of World War II. The former government returned in April 1945 when the war ended and the country's pre-1938 boundaries were restored.

When elections were held in 1946, the Communists became the dominant political party and gained control of the Czechoslovakian government in 1948. Thereafter, the former democracy was turned into a Soviet-style state.

Nearly 42 years of Communist rule ended when Vaclav Havel was elected president of Czechoslovakia in 1989. The return of democratic political reform saw a strong Slovak nationalist movement emerge by the end of 1991 which sought independence for Slovakia as a sovereign nation and the breakup of the two Czechoslovakian republics.

When the general elections of June 1992 failed to resolve the continuing coexistence of the two republics within the Federation, Czech and Slovak political leaders agreed to separate their states into two fully independent nations. On Aug. 26, 1992 they announced their intentions to dissolve the Czechoslovakian federation on Jan. 1, 1993.

Havel was elected for a 5-year term as president in January 1993 by the 200-member parliament.

Unexpectedly inconclusive elections in May-June 1996 stripped the ruling center-right coalition of its majority in Parliament. The Prime Minister formed a minority government under an agreement with the second-place Social Democrats.

In anticipation of its expected invitation to join NATO, critics, both domestic and foreign, questioned the government's slashing of the defense budget in April and May 1997 as part of an overall austerity package.

DENMARK

Kingdom of Denmark
National name: Kongeriget Danmark
Sovereign: Queen Margrethe II (1972)
Prime Minister: Poul Nyrup Rasmussen
Area: 16,631 sq mi. (43,075 sq km)[1]
Population (1997 est.): 5,268,775 (average annual rate of natural increase: 0.14%); birth rate: 11.85/1000; infant mortality rate: 4.8/1000; density per square mile: 316.8
Capital and largest city (1992): Copenhagen, 1,339,395. **Other large cities (1992):** Aarhus, 204,139; Odense, 140,886; Alborg, 114,970. **Monetary unit:** Krone. **Language:** Danish, Faroese, Greenlandic (an Inuit dialect), small German-speaking minority. **Ethnicity/Race:** Scandinavian, Eskimo, Faroese, German. **Religion (1992):** 88% Evangelical Lutheran. **Literacy rate:** 99%
Economic summary: Gross domestic product: purchasing power parity (1995 est.): $112.8 billion; $21,700 per capita; real growth rate 3.1%; inflation rate 2.4%; unemployment rate 9.5%. Arable land: 61%. Principal agricultural products: meat, dairy products, fish, grains. Labor force: 2,553,900: private services, 37.1%; government services, 30.4%; manufacturing and mining, 20%. Major industrial products: processed foods, machinery and equipment, textiles. Natural resources: crude oil, natural gas, fish, salt, limestone. Exports: $39.6 billion (f.o.b., 1994): meat and dairy products, fish, industrial machinery, chemical products, transportation equipment. Imports: $34 billion (c.i.f., 1994 est.): machinery and equipment, transport equipment, petroleum, chemicals, grains and foodstuffs, textiles, paper. Major trading partners: Germany, Sweden, France, U.K., U.S., Norway, Japan.

1. Excluding Faeroe Islands and Greenland.

Geography. Smallest of the Scandinavian countries (half the size of Maine), Denmark occupies the Jutland peninsula, which extends north from Germany between the tips of Norway and Sweden. To the west is the North Sea and to the east the Baltic.

The country also consists of several Baltic islands; the two largest are Sjaelland, the site of Copenhagen, and Fyn. The narrow waters off the north coast are called the Skagerrak and those off the east, the Kattegat.

Government. Denmark has been a constitutional monarchy since 1849. Legislative power is held jointly by the Sovereign and Parliament. The constitution of 1953 provides for a unicameral parliament called the Folketing, consisting of 179 popularly elected members who serve for four years. The Cabinet is presided over by the Sovereign, who formally appoints the Prime Minister, who is responsible to parliament.

The Sovereign, Queen Margrethe II, was born April 16, 1940, and became Queen—the second in Denmark's history—Jan. 15, 1972, the day after her father, King Frederik IX, died at 72 in the 25th year of his reign. Margrethe was the eldest of his three daughters (by Princess Ingrid of Sweden). The nation's constitution was amended in 1953 to permit her to succeed her father in the absence of a male heir to the throne. (Denmark was ruled six centuries ago by Margrethe I, but she was never Crowned Queen since there was no female right of succession.)

History. Denmark emerged with establishment of the Norwegian dynasty of the Ynglinger in Jutland at the end of the 8th century. Danish mariners played a major role in the raids of the Vikings, or Norsemen, on Western Europe and particularly England. The country was Christianized by St. Ansgar and Harald Blaatand (Bluetooth)—the first Christian King—in the 10th century. Harald's son, Sweyn, conquered England in 1013. His son, Canute the Great, who reigned from 1014 to 1035, united Denmark, England, and Norway under his rule; the southern tip of Sweden was part of Denmark until the 17th century. On Canute's death, civil war tore the country until Waldemar I (1157–82) re-established Danish hegemony over the north.

In 1282, the nobles won the Great Charter, and Eric V was forced to share power with Parliament and a Council of Nobles. Waldemar IV (1340–75) restored Danish power, checked only by the Hanseatic League of north German cities allied with ports from Holland to Poland. His daughter, Margrethe, in 1397 united under her rule Denmark, Norway, and Sweden. But Sweden later achieved autonomy and in 1523, under Gustavus I, independence.

Denmark supported Napoleon, for which it was punished at the Congress of Vienna in 1815 by the loss of Norway to Sweden. In 1864, Bismarck, together with the Austrians, made war on the little country as an initial step in the unification of Germany. Denmark was neutral in World War I.

In 1940, Denmark was invaded by the Nazis. King Christian X reluctantly cautioned his countrymen to accept the occupation, but there was widespread resistance against the Nazis. In 1944, Iceland declared its independence from Denmark, ending a union that had existed since 1380.

Liberated by British troops in May 1945, the country staged a fast recovery in both agriculture and manufacturing and was a leader in liberalizing trade. It joined the United Nations in 1945 and NATO in 1949.

Disputes over economic policy led to elections in 1981 that led to Poul Schlüter coming to power in early 1982. Further disputes over his pro-NATO posture led to elections in May, 1988 that marginally confirmed his position.

A second referendum on the Maastricht accord in May 1993 passed with 56.8 percent of the vote but confidence in European monetary and political unity was waning in other European community countries.

The Social Democratic Party took over the reins of government at the head of a four-party slightly left leaning coalition in 1993.

A Danish court in June 1997 upheld the constitutionality of the Maastricht treaty, which paves the way for greater European integration. Critics have charged that the treaty would surrender Denmark's sovereignty.

Outlying Territories of Denmark

FAEROE ISLANDS

Status: Autonomous part of Denmark
Chief of State: Queen Margrethe II (1972)
High Commissioner: Bent Klinte
Prime Minister: Edmund Joensen (1994)
Lagmand (President): Jogran Sundstein (1989)
Area: 540 sq mi. (1,399 sq km)
Population (1997 est.): 43,057 (average annual growth rate: 0.42%); birth rate: 13.12/1000; infant mortality rate: 7.1/1000; density per square mile: 79.7
Capital and largest city (1993 est.): Thorshavn, 16,100. **Monetary unit:** Faeroese krone. **Ethnicity/Race:** Scandinavian. **Literacy rate:** 99%
Economic summary: Gross domestic product: purchasing power parity (1989 est.): $662 million, per capita

$14,000; real growth rate −10.8%; inflation (1993 est.) 6.8%; unemployment (1993) 23%. Arable land: 2%; principal agricultural products: sheep, vegetables. Labor force: 17,585, largely engaged in fishing manufacturing, transportation and commerce. Major industrial products: fish, ships, handicrafts. Exports: $345.3 million (f.o.b., 1993 est.): fish and fish products. Imports: $234.4 million (c.i.f., 1993 est.): machinery and transport equipment, foodstuffs, petroleum and petroleum products. Major trading partners: Denmark, U.S., U.K., Germany, Canada, France, Japan.

This group of 18 islands, lying in the North Atlantic about 200 miles (322 km) northwest of the Shetland Islands, joined Denmark in 1386 and has since been part of the Danish Kingdom. The islands were occupied by British troops during World War II, after the German occupation of Denmark.

The Faeroes have home rule under a bill enacted in 1948; they also have two representatives in the Danish Folketing.

GREENLAND

Status: Autonomous part of Denmark
Chief of State: Queen Margrethe II (1972)
High Commissioner: Torben Hede Pedersen (1993)
Premier: Lars Emil Johansen (1991)
Area: 840,000 sq mi. (incl. 708,069 sq mi. covered by icecap) (2,175,600 sq km)
Population (1997 est.): 58,768 (growth rate: 0.94%); birth rate:16.39/1000; infant mortality rate: 22.60/1000; density per square mile: 0.06.
Capital and largest city (1995 est.): Godthaab, 12,723.
Monetary unit: Krone. **Ethnicity/Race:** Greenlander 86% (Eskimos and Greenland-born whites), Danish 14%. **Literacy rate:** 99%
Economic summary: Gross national product (1988): $500 million, per capita $9,000; real growth rate 5%; inflation (1993 est.) 1.3%; unemployment (1993 est.) 6.6%. Arable land: 0%; principal agricultural products: hay, sheep, garden produce. Labor force: 22,800, largely engaged in fishing, hunting, sheep breeding. Major industries: fish processing, lead and zinc processing, handicrafts. Natural resources: metals, cryolite, iron ore, coal, uranium, fish. Exports: $330.5 million (f.o.b., 1993): fish and fish products, metallic ores and concentrates. Imports: $369.6 million (c.i.f., 1993 est.): petroleum and petroleum products, machinery and transport equipment, foodstuffs, manufactured goods. Major trading partners: Denmark, U.S., Germany, Sweden, Japan, Norway.

Greenland, the world's largest island, was colonized in 985–86 by Eric the Red. Danish sovereignty, which covered only the west coast, was extended over the whole island in 1917. In 1941 the U.S. signed an agreement with the Danish minister in Washington, placing it under U.S. protection during World War II but maintaining Danish sovereignty. A definitive agreement for the joint defense of Greenland within the framework of NATO was signed in 1951. A large U.S. air base at Thule in the far north was completed in 1953.

Under 1953 amendments to the Danish constitution, Greenland became part of Denmark, with two representatives in the Danish Folketing. On May 1, 1979, Greenland gained home rule, with its own local parliament (Landsting), replacing the Greenland Provincial Council.

In February 1982, Greenlanders voted to withdraw from the European Union, which they had joined as part of Denmark in 1973. Danish Premier Anker Jørgensen said he would support the request, but with reluctance.

An election in early March 1991 gave the Siumut Party 11 of the 27 available seats. The early election was called after a scandal allegedly involving overspending on entertainment by government officials.

DJIBOUTI

Republic of Djibouti
National name: Jumhouriyya Djibouti
President: Hassan Gouled Aptidon (1977)
Prime Minister: Barkat Gourad Hamadou (1978)
Area: 8,878 sq mi. (23,000 sq km)
Population (1997 est.): 434,116 (average annual rate of natural increase: 2.71%); birth rate: 42.16/1000; infant mortality rate: 104/1000; density per square mile: 51.1
Capital (1992 est.): Djibouti, 395,000. **Monetary unit:** Djibouti franc. **Languages:** Arabic, French, Afar, Somali. **Ethnicity/Race:** Somali 60%, Afar 35%, French, Arab, Ethiopian, and Italian 5%. **Religions:** Muslim, 94%; Christian, 6%. **Literacy rate:** 48%
Economic summary: Gross domestic product: purchasing power parity (1994 est.): $500 million, $1,200 per capita; real growth rate −3%; inflation 6% (1993 est.); unemployment over 30% (1994 est.). Arable land: 2%. Principal agricultural products: goats, sheep, camels. Labor force: 282,000; in agriculture, 75%; industry, 11%; services, 14%. Industries: small-scale enterprises such as dairy products and mineral-water bottling. Djibouti is a free port. Natural resources: salt, limestone, gypsum, perlite, diatoms, geothermal energy. Exports: $184 million (f.o.b., est. 1994): hides, skins, livestock. Imports: $384 million (f.o.b., 1994 est.): foodstuffs, machinery, transport equipment, consumer goods. Major trading partners: Ethiopia, Somalia, the Republic of Yemen, Saudi Arabia.

Geography. Djibouti lies in northeastern Africa on the Gulf of Aden at the southern entrance to the Red Sea. It borders on Ethiopia, Eritrea, and Somalia. The country, the size of Massachusetts, is mainly a stony desert, with scattered plateaus and highlands.

Government. A republic with a unicameral legislature. On June 27, 1977, France transferred sovereignty to the new nation of Djibouti. On Sept. 4, 1992, voters approved in referendum a new multiparty constitution. The last presidential election took place May 7, 1993, and President Aptidon was re-elected for another six-year term.

History. The territory that is now Djibouti was acquired by France between 1843 and 1886 by treaties with the Somali sultans. Small, arid, and sparsely populated, Djibouti is important chiefly because of the capital city's port, the terminal of the Djibouti-Addis Ababa railway that carries 60% of Ethiopia's foreign trade.

Originally known as French Somaliland, the colony voted in 1958 and 1967 to remain under French rule. It was renamed the Territory of the Afars and Issas in 1967 and took the name of its capital city on attaining independence.

The two principal opposition groups in exile banded to form a common front in early 1990.

A referendum in 1992 approved a new constitution permitting a multiparty system.

The President won the May 1993 election against four opponents in an election criticized for irregularities.

Feuding within the major rebel opposition led to the naming of a new leader in 1994. Two members of the major faction in the opposition and others joined the government in June 1995.

A border incident in April 1996 further strained relations with neighboring Eritrea.

DOMINICA

Commonwealth of Dominica
President: Crispin Sorhaindo (1993)
Prime Minister: Edison James (1995)
Area: 290 sq mi. (751 sq km)
Population: (1997 est.): 83,226 (average annual rate of natural increase: 1.27%); birth rate: 18.05/1000; infant mortality rate: 9.3/1000; density per square mile: 286
Capital and largest city (1991): Roseau, 15,853. **Monetary unit:** East Caribbean dollar. **Languages:** English and French patois. **Ethnicity/Race:** black, Carib Indians. **Religions:** Roman Catholic, 77%; Protestant, 15%. **Literacy rate:** 94%
Economic summary: Gross domestic product: purchasing power parity (1995 est.): $200 million, per capita $2,450; real growth rate –1%; inflation 0.4%; unemployment 15% (1992 est.). Arable land: 9%. Principal products: bananas, citrus fruits, coconuts, plantains. Labor force: 25,000; 40% in agriculture; 32% in industry and commerce; 28% in services. Major industries: agricultural processing; tourism. Exports: $48.3 million (f.o.b., 1993): bananas, coconuts, soap, vegetables, grapefruit, oranges. Imports: $98.8 million (f.o.b., 1993): manufactured goods, machinery and equipment, food, chemicals. Major trading partners: U.K., Caribbean countries, U.S., Italy, Canada. **Member of Commonwealth of Nations**

Geography. Dominica is an island of the Lesser Antilles in the Caribbean south of Guadeloupe and north of Martinique.

Government. Dominica is a republic, with a President elected by the House of Assembly as head of state and a Prime Minister appointed by the President on the advice of the Assembly. The United Workers Party (12 of 21 seats in the Assembly) is led by Prime Minister Edison James. The Freedom Party holds four seats and the United Dominica Labor Party holds five seats.

History. Visited by Columbus in 1493, Dominica was claimed by Britain and France until 1815, when Britain asserted sovereignty. Dominica, along with other Windward Isles, became a self-governing member of the West Indies Associated States in free association with Britain in 1967.

Dissatisfaction over the slow pace of reconstruction after Hurricane David struck the island in September 1979 brought a landslide victory for the Freedom Party in July 1980. The vote gave the Prime Ministership to Mary Eugenia Charles, a strong advocate of free enterprise. The Freedom Party won again in 1985 elections, giving Miss Charles a second five-year term as Prime Minister. She and her party won a third term in elections on May 28, 1990, though with a greatly reduced mandate.

The government in 1993 pursued its policy of divesting itself of state enterprises.

The opposition United Workers' Party captured the general election of June 1995. The new government planned to privatize numerous enterprises.

Prime Minister James reshuffled his cabinet in June 1996, taking on in addition to his other duties those of the Ministry of Finance.

DOMINICAN REPUBLIC

National name: República Dominicana
President: Leonel Fernández Reyna (1996)
Area: 18,704 sq mi. (48,442 sq km)
Population (1997 est.): 8,228,151 (average annual rate of natural increase: 1.73%); birth rate: 22.91/1000; infant mortality rate: 46/1000; density per square mile: 439.9

Capital and largest city (1993): Santo Domingo, 2,100,000. **Other large city (1993):** Santiago de los Caballeros, 690,000. **Monetary unit:** Peso. **Language:** Spanish, English widely spoken. **Ethnicity/Race:** white 16%, black 11%, mixed 73%. **Religion:** 90% Roman Catholic. **Literacy rate:** 74%
Economic summary: Gross domestic product: purchasing power parity (1995 est.): $26.8 billion, $3,4000 per capita, 3.5% real growth rate; inflation rate 9.5%; unemployment rate 30%. Arable land: 23%. Principal agricultural products: sugar cane, coffee, cocoa, tobacco, beef, fruit and vegetables. Agriculture accounts for 13% of gross domestic product. Labor force (1991 est.): 2.3–2.6 million; 50% in agriculture; 32% in services and government; 18% in industry. Major industries: tourism, sugar processing, ferronickel and gold mining, textiles, cement, tobacco. Natural resources: nickel, bauxite, gold, silver. Exports: $837.7 million (f.o.b., 1995): sugar, coffee, cocoa, gold, ferronickel, silver, meats, fruits and vegetables. Imports: $2.867 billion (f.o.b., 1995 est.): foodstuffs, petroleum, cotton and fabrics, chemicals and pharmaceuticals. Major trading partners: U.S., including Puerto Rico, E.U.

Geography. The Dominican Republic in the West Indies, occupies the eastern two-thirds of the island of Hispaniola, which it shares with Haiti. Its area equals that of Vermont and New Hampshire combined.

Crossed from northwest to southeast by a mountain range with elevations exceeding 10,000 feet (3,048 m), the country has fertile, well-watered land in the north and east, where nearly two thirds of the population lives. The southwest part is arid and has poor soil, except around Santo Domingo.

Government. The President is elected by direct vote every four years. Legislative powers rest with a Senate and a Chamber of Deputies, both elected by direct vote, also for four years. All citizens must vote when they reach 18 years of age, or even earlier if they are married.

History. The Dominican Republic was visited by Columbus in 1492. He named it La Española, and his son, Diego, was its first viceroy. The capital, Santo Domingo, founded in 1496, is the oldest European settlement in the Western Hemisphere. Spain ceded the colony to France in 1795, and Haitian blacks under Toussaint L'Ouverture conquered it in 1801.

In 1808 the people revolted and captured Santo Domingo the next year, setting up the first republic. Spain regained title to the colony in 1814. In 1821 the people overthrew Spanish rule, but in 1822 they were reconquered by the Haitians. They revolted again in 1844, threw out the Haitians, and established the Dominican Republic, headed by Pedro Santana. Uprisings and Haitian attacks led Santana to make the country a province of Spain from 1861 to 1865. The U.S. Senate refused to ratify a treaty of annexation. Disorder continued until the dictatorship of Ulíses Heureaux; in 1916, when disorder broke out again, the U.S. sent in a contingent of marines, who remained until 1934.

A sergeant in the Dominican army trained by the marines, Rafaél Leonides Trujillo Molina, overthrew Horacio Vásquez in 1930 and established a dictatorship that lasted until his assassination 31 years later.

Leftists rebelled April 24, 1965, and U.S. President Lyndon Johnson sent in marines and troops. After an OAS ceasefire request May 6, a compromise installed Hector Garcia-Godoy as provisional President. Joaquin Balaguer won in free elections in 1966 against Bosch, and a peacekeeping force of 9,000 U.S. troops and 2,000 from other countries withdrew. Balaguer restored political and economic stability.

In 1978, the army suspended the counting of ballots when Balaguer trailed in a fourth-term bid. After a warning from President Jimmy Carter, however, Balaguer accepted the victory of Antonio Guzmán of the opposition Dominican Revolutionary Party.

Salvador Jorge Blanco of the Dominican Revolutionary Party was elected President on May 16, 1982, defeating Balaguer and Bosch.

Balaguer was elected President in May 1986 and aimed economic policy at diversifying the economy.

In a bitter presidential contest Mr. Balaguer maintained a slim lead over his opponent in the May 1994 election before election officials stopped releasing tallies. The opposition charged widespread fraud. Eventually the crisis eased when a constitutional amendment gave the current President a two-year term with new elections scheduled for May 1996.

Opposition leader Pena Gomez obtained the most votes in the first round of that presidential election but fell short of a majority. In the runoff of June 30 U.S.-raised Leonel Fernandez secured more than 51% of the vote through an alliance with Balaguer.

The first item on the President's agenda in August 1996 was the partial sale of a number of state–owned enterprises. Fernandez signed the bill into law in June 1997. Investors are to be allowed to own a maximum of 50% of the stock in the companies.

ECUADOR

Republic of Ecuador
National name: República del Ecuador
President: Fabián Alarcón (1997)
Area: 106,822[1] sq mi (276,670 sq km)
Population (1997 est.): 11,690,535 (average annual rate of natural increase: 1.91%); birth rate: 24.58/1000; infant mortality rate: 33.4/1000; density per square mile: 109.4
Capital: Quito. **Largest cities (1992):** Guayaquil, 1,475,118; Quito, 1,094,318; Cuenca, 195,738. **Monetary unit:** Sucre. **Languages:** Spanish (by 90% of population), Quéchua. **Ethnicity/Race:** mestizo (mixed Indian and Spanish) 55%, Indian 25%, Spanish 10%, black 10%. **Religion:** Roman Catholic, 95%. **Literacy rate:** 92%
Economic summary: Gross domestic product: purchasing power parity (1995 est.): $44.6 billion, per capita $4,100; real growth rate 2.3%; inflation 25%; unemployment 7.1% (1994). Arable land: 6%; principal agricultural products: bananas, cocoa, coffee, sugar cane, manioc, plantains, potatoes, rice. Labor force (1995 est.): 2.8 million; 35% in agriculture; 21% in manufacturing; 16% in commerce. Major industries: food processing, textiles, chemicals, fishing, timber, petroleum. Exports: $4 billion (f.o.b., 1994): petroleum, coffee, bananas, cocoa products, shrimp, fish products. Imports: $3.7 billion (c.i.f., 1994): transport equipment, vehicles, machinery, chemicals. Major trading partners: U.S., Latin America, E.U., Caribbean, Japan.

1. Does not include area under dispute with Peru.

Geography. Ecuador, about equal in area to Nevada, is in the northwest part of South America fronting on the Pacific. To the north is Colombia and to the east and south is Peru. Two high and parallel ranges of the Andes, traversing the country from north to south, are topped by tall volcanic peaks. The highest is Chimborazo at 20,577 feet (6,272 m).

The Galápagos Islands (or Colón Archipelago) (3,029 sq mi.; 7,845 sq km), in the Pacific Ocean about 600 miles (966 km) west of the South American mainland, became part of Ecuador in 1832.

Government. A 1978 constitution returned Ecuador to civilian government after eight years of military rule. The President is elected to a term of four years and a House of Representatives of 71 members is popularly elected for the same period.

History. The tribes in the northern highlands of Ecuador formed the Kingdom of Quito around c.e. 1000. It was absorbed, by conquest and marriage, into the Inca Empire. Pizarro conquered the land in 1532, and through the 17th century a thriving colony was built by exploitation of the Indians. The first revolt against Spain occurred in 1809. Ecuador then joined Venezuela, Colombia, and Panama in a confederacy known as Greater Colombia.

On the collapse of this union in 1830, Ecuador became independent. Subsequent history was one of revolts and dictatorships; it had 48 presidents during the first 131 years of the republic. Conservatives ruled until the Revolution of 1895 ushered in nearly a half century of Radical Liberal rule, during which the church was disestablished and freedom of worship, speech, and press was introduced.

In 1988, Rodrigo Borja was elected president. He was also able to form a coalition in the House, confirming a leftward shift in the government and promising smoother executive-legislative relations.

Blamed for economic conditions, the governing Social Democrats were defeated in elections of May 1992 by right-wing parties promising free-market reforms.

In the runoff presidential election of July 5, 1992 Sixto Duran Ballen captured 58% of the vote.

On charges of mental incapacity, Congress voted in February 1997 to remove President Bucaram, who refused to yield, and declared its leader Fabián Alarcón president. The next day Vice President Rosalia Arteaga declared herself president. After negotiations, Ms. Arteaga was sworn in as president for a few days until Congress reappointed Alarcón president. In May a national referendum overwhelmingly approved the interim presidency.

EGYPT

Arab Republic of Egypt
President: Hosni Mubarak (1981)
Prime Minister: Dr. Kamal Al-Ganzoury (1996)
Area: 386,900 sq. mi. (1,002,000 sq km)
Population (1997 est.): 64,791,891 (average annual rate of natural increase: 1.91%); birth rate: 27.68/1000; infant mortality rate: 71/1000; density per square mile: 167.5
Capital and largest city (1992 est.): Cairo, 6,849,000. **Other large cities (1992 est.):** Alexandria, 3,382,000; Giza, 2,144,000; Shubra el Khema, 834,000; El Mahalla el Kubra, 408,000. **Monetary unit:** Egyptian pound. **Language:** Arabic. **Ethnicity/Race:** Eastern Hamitic stock (Egyptians, Bedouins, and Berbers) 99%, Greek, Nubian, Armenian, other European (primarily Italian and French) 1%. **Religions:** Islam, 94%; Christian (mostly Coptic), 6%. **Literacy rate:** 50.2%
Economic summary: Gross domestic product: purchasing power parity (1995 est.): $171 billion; $2,760 per capita; 4% real growth rate; inflation rate 9.4%; unemployment rate 20%. Arable land: 3%. Principal agricultural products: cotton, wheat, rice, corn, beans. Labor force: 16 million; 34% in agriculture; 36% in government, public sector enterprises, and armed forces; 20% in privately owned services and manufacturing. Major industries: textiles, food processing, tourism, chemicals, petroleum, construction, cement, metals. Natural resources: crude oil, natural gas,

iron ore, phosphates, manganese, limestone, gypsum, talc, asbestos, lead, zinc. Exports: $5.4 billion (f.o.b., FY 94/95 est.): cotton, petroleum, yarn, textiles, metal products, chemicals. Imports: $15.2 billion (c.i.f., FY 94/95 est.): foodstuffs, machinery, fertilizers, woods, durable consumer goods, capital goods. Major trading partners: U.S., Western Europe, Japan, Eastern Europe.

Geography. Egypt, at the northeast corner of Africa on the Mediterranean Sea, is bordered on the west by Libya, on the south by the Sudan, and on the east by the Red Sea and Israel. It is nearly one and one-half times the size of Texas.

The historic Nile flows through the eastern third of the country. On either side of the Nile valley are desert plateaus, spotted with oases. In the north, toward the Mediterranean, plateaus are low, while south of Cairo they rise to a maximum of 1,015 feet (309 m) above sea level. At the head of the Red Sea is the Sinai Peninsula, between the Suez Canal and Israel.

Navigable throughout its course in Egypt, the Nile is used largely as a means of cheap transport for heavy goods. The irrigation of the land depends mainly on water from the Nile. The Nile is one of the famous tourist spots in the country. The principal ports are Alexandria, Port Said and Damietta.

The Nile delta starts 100 miles (161 km) south of the Mediterranean and fans out to a sea front of 155 miles between the cities of Alexandria and Port Said. From Cairo north, the Nile branches into many streams, the principal ones being the Damietta and the Rosetta.

Except for a narrow belt along the Mediterranean, Egypt lies in an almost rainless area, in which high daytime temperatures fall quickly at night.

Government. Executive power is held by the President, who is elected every six years and can appoint one or more Vice Presidents.

The National Democratic Party, led by President Hosni Mubarak, is the dominant political party. Elections in Nov. 1990 confirmed its huge majority. There are also 14 opposition parties and some independents in the Parliament.

History. Egyptian history dates back to about 4000 B.C.E., when the kingdoms of upper and lower Egypt, already highly civilized, were united. Egypt's "Golden Age" coincided with the 18th and 19th dynasties (16th to 13th centuries B.C.E.), during which the empire was established. Persia conquered Egypt in 525 B.C.E., Alexander the Great subdued it in 332 B.C.E., and then the dynasty of the Ptolemies ruled the land until 30 B.C.E., when Cleopatra, last of the line, committed suicide and Egypt became a Roman province. From 641 to 1517 the Arab caliphs ruled Egypt, and then the Turks took it for their Ottoman Empire.

Napoleon's armies occupied the country from 1798 to 1801. In 1805, Mohammed Ali, leader of a band of Albanian soldiers, became Pasha of Egypt. After completion of the Suez Canal in 1869, the French and British took increasing interest in Egypt.

British troops occupied Egypt in 1882, and British resident agents became its actual administrators, though it remained under nominal Turkish sovereignty. In 1914, this fiction was ended, and Egypt became a protectorate of Britain.

Egyptian nationalism forced Britain to declare Egypt an independent, sovereign state on Feb. 28, 1922, although the British reserved rights for the protection of the Suez Canal and the defense of Egypt. In 1936, by an Anglo-Egyptian treaty of alliance, all British troops and officials were to be withdrawn, except from the Suez Canal Zone. When World War II started, Egypt remained neutral. British imperial troops finally ended the Nazi threat to Suez in 1942 in the battle of El Alamein, west of Alexandria.

In 1951, Egypt abrogated the 1936 treaty and the 1899 Anglo-Egyptian condominium of the Sudan (*See* Sudan). Rioting and attacks on British troops in the Suez Canal Zone followed, reaching a climax in January 1952. The army, led by Gen. Mohammed Naguib, seized power on July 23, 1952. Three days later, King Farouk abdicated in favor of his infant son. The monarchy was abolished and a republic proclaimed on June 18, 1953, with Naguib holding the posts of Provisional President and Premier. He relinquished the latter in 1954 to Gamal Abdel Nasser, leader of the ruling military junta. Naguib was deposed seven months later and Nasser confirmed as president in a referendum on June 23, 1956.

Nasser's policies embroiled his country in continual conflict. In 1956, the U.S. and Britain withdrew their pledges of financial aid for the building of the Aswan High Dam. In reply, Nasser nationalized the Suez Canal and expelled British oil and embassy officials. Israel, barred from the Canal and exasperated by terrorist raids, invaded the Gaza Strip and the Sinai Peninsula. Britain and France, after demanding Egyptian evacuation of the Canal Zone, attacked Egypt on Oct. 31, 1956. Worldwide pressure forced Britain, France, and Israel to halt the hostilities. A U.N. emergency force occupied the Canal Zone, and all troops were evacuated in the spring of 1957.

On June 5, 1967, Israel invaded the Sinai Peninsula, the East Bank of the Jordan River, and the zone around the Gulf of Aqaba. A U.N. ceasefire on June 10 saved the Arabs from complete rout.

Nasser declared the 1967 cease-fire void along the Canal in April 1969 and began a war of attrition. The U.S. peace plan of June 19, 1970, resulted in Egypt's agreement to reinstate the cease-fire for at least three months, (from August) and to accept Israel's existence within "recognized and secure" frontiers that might emerge from U.N.-mediated talks. In return, Israel accepted the principle of withdrawing from occupied territories.

Then, on Sept. 28, 1970, Nasser died, at 52, of a heart attack. The new president was Anwar el-Sadat, an associate of Nasser and a former newspaper editor.

In July 1972, Sadat ordered the expulsion of Soviet "advisors and experts" from Egypt because the Russians had not provided the sophisticated weapons he felt were needed to retake territory lost to Israel in 1967.

The fourth Arab-Israeli war broke out Oct. 6, 1973, while Israelis were commemorating Yom Kippur, the Jewish high holy day. Egypt swept deep into the Sinai, while Syria strove to throw Israel off the Golan Heights.

A U.N.-sponsored truce was accepted on October 22. In January 1974, both sides agreed to a settlement negotiated by U.S. Secretary of State Henry A. Kissinger that gave Egypt a narrow strip along the entire Sinai bank of the Suez Canal. In June, President Nixon made the first visit by a U.S. President to Egypt and full diplomatic relations were established. The Suez Canal was cleared and reopened on June 5, 1975.

In the most audacious act of his career, Sadat flew to Jerusalem at the invitation of Prime Minister Menachem Begin and pleaded before Israel's Knesset on Nov. 20, 1977, for a permanent peace settlement. The Arab world reacted with fury—only Morocco, Tunisia, Sudan, and Oman approved.

Egypt and Israel signed a formal peace treaty on March 26, 1979. The pact ended 30 years of war and established diplomatic and commercial relations.

Egyptian and Israeli officials met in the Sinai desert on April 26, 1979, to implement the peace treaty calling for the phased withdrawal of occupation forces from the peninsula. By mid-1980, two thirds of the Sinai was transferred, but progress here was not matched elsewhere—the negotiation of Arab autonomy in the Gaza Strip and the West Bank remained stymied.

Sadat halted further talks in August 1980 because of continued Israeli settlement of the West Bank. On October 6 1981, Sadat was assassinated by extremist Muslim soldiers at a parade in Cairo. Vice President Hosni Mubarak, a former Air Force chief of staff, was confirmed by the Parliament as president the next day.

Although feared unrest in Egypt did not occur in the wake of the assassination, and Israel completed the return of the Sinai to Egyptian control on April 25, 1982, Mubarak was unable to revive the autonomy talks. Israel's invasion of Lebanon in June imposed a new strain on him, and brought a marked cooling in Egyptian-Israeli relations, but not a disavowal of the peace treaty.

While President Mubarak's stand during the Persian Gulf war won wide praise in the West, domestically this position proved far less popular.

A presidential referendum in October 1993 supported Mubarak's bid for a third term although only a third of the population registered to vote.

The government has concentrated much of its time and attention in recent years combating Islamic extremism. In November 1995 elections took place for the People's Assembly. The ruling National Democratic Party won 416 seats and the opposition 13, with independents taking the remaining seats. The People's Assembly in February 1997 assented to the President's decree extending the state of emergency, introduced with the assassination of Anwar Sadat, into the year 2000.

Suez Canal. The Suez Canal, in Egyptian territory between the Arabian desert and the Sinai Peninsula, is an artificial waterway about 100 miles (161 km) long between Port Said on the Mediterranean and Suez on the Red Sea. Construction work, directed by the French engineer Ferdinand de Lesseps, was begun April 25, 1859, and the Canal was opened Nov. 17, 1869. The cost was 432,807,882 francs. The concession was held by an Egyptian joint stock company, Compagnie Universelle du Canal Maritime de Suez, in which the British government held 353,504 out of a total of 800,000 shares. The concession was to expire Nov. 17, 1968, but the company was nationalized July 26, 1956, by unilateral action of the Egyptian government.

The Canal was closed in June 1967 after the Arab-Israeli conflict. With the help of the U.S. Navy, work was begun on clearing the Canal in 1974, after the cease-fire ending the Arab-Israeli war. It was reopened to traffic June 5, 1975.

EL SALVADOR

Republic of El Salvador
National name: República de El Salvador
President: Armando Calderón Sol (1994)
Area: 8,260 sq mi. (21,393 sq km)
Population (1997 est.): 5,661,827 (average annual rate of natural increase: 2.07%); birth rate: 27.22/1000; infant mortality rate: 30.3/1000; density per square mile: 685.4
Capital and largest city (1993 est.): San Salvador, 972,810. **Other large cities (1993 est.):** Santa Ana, 208,322; San Miguel, 161,156; Zacatecoluca, 81,035.
Monetary unit: Colón. **Language:** Spanish. **Ethnicity/Race:** mestizo 94%, Indian 5%, white 1%. **Religion:** Roman Catholic. **Literacy rate:** 73%
Economic summary: Gross domestic product: purchasing power parity (1995 est.): $11.4 billion; $1,950 per capita; real growth rate 6.3%; inflation 11.4%; unemployment 6.7% (1993). Arable land: 27%. Principal agricultural products: coffee, cotton, corn, sugar,

rice, sorghum. Labor force: 1.7 million (1982 est.); 40% in agriculture; 16% in commerce; 15% in manufacturing; 13% in government; 9% in financial services. Major industrial products: processed foods, clothing and textiles, petroleum products. Natural resources: hydro- and geothermal power, crude oil. Exports: $1.6 billion (f.o.b., 1995 est.): coffee, cotton, sugar, shrimp. Imports: $3.3 billion (c.i.f., 1995 est.): raw materials, consumer goods, capital goods. Major trading partners: U.S., Guatemala, Germany, Mexico, Venezuela, Costa Rica.

Geography. Situated on the Pacific coast of Central America, El Salvador has Guatemala to the west and Honduras to the north and east. It is the smallest of the Central American countries, its area equal to that of Massachusetts, and the only one without an Atlantic coastline.

Most of the country is a fertile volcanic plateau about 2,000 feet (607 m) high. There are some active volcanoes and many scenic crater lakes.

Government. The President is elected for a nonrenewable, five-year term, and legislative power is in a unicameral 84-member National Assembly elected by universal suffrage and proportional representation.

History. Pedro de Alvarado, a lieutenant of Cortés, conquered El Salvador in 1525. El Salvador, with the other countries of Central America, declared its independence from Spain on Sept. 15, 1821, and was part of a federation of Central American states until that union was dissolved in 1838. Its independent career for decades thereafter was marked by numerous revolutions and wars against other Central American republics.

On Oct. 15, 1979, a junta deposed the President, Gen. Carlos Humberto Romero, seeking to halt increasingly violent clashes between leftist and rightist forces.

On Dec. 4, 1980, three American nuns and an American lay worker were killed in an ambush near San Salvador, causing the Carter Administration to suspend all aid pending an investigation. The naming of José Napoleón Duarte, a moderate civilian, as head of the governing junta brought a resumption of U.S. aid.

In an election closely monitored by U.S. and other foreign observers, Duarte was elected President in May 1984.

Duarte's Christian Democratic Party scored an unexpected electoral triumph in national legislative and municipal elections held in March 1985, a winning majority in the new National Assembly. The rightist parties that had been dominant in the previous Constituent Assembly demanded that the vote be nullified, but the army high command rejected their assertion that the voting had been fraudulent.

At the same time, U.S. officials said that while the rebels still were far from being defeated, there had been marked improvement in the effectiveness of government troops in the civil war against anti-government guerrillas that was being waged mainly in the countryside. Talks with the rebels broke down in September 1986. Duarte's inability to find solutions led to the rightwing ARENA party controlling half the seats in the National Assembly, in the elections of March, 1988. The decisive victory of Alfredo Cristiani, the ARENA candidate for president, gave the right-wing party effective control of the country, given its political control of most of the municipalities.

On January 16, 1992 the government signed a peace treaty with the guerrilla forces formally ending a 12-year civil war that had claimed 75,000 lives.

The candidate of the right-wing ARENA party, Calderón Sol won the presidential election of March 1994 on a pledge to continue the peace process.

Elections for the National Assembly in March 1997 denied a majority to either of the two major parties with

ARENA winning 28 seats and the National Liberation Front 27. A total of 13 parties participated in the legislative campaign.

EQUATORIAL GUINEA

Republic of Equatorial Guinea
National name: República de Guinea Ecuatorial
President: Col. Teodoro Obiang Nguema Mbasogo (1979)
Prime Minister: Angel Serafin Seriche Dougan (1996)
Area: 10,830 sq mi. (28,051 sq km)
Population (1997 est.): 442,516 (average annual rate of natural increase: 2.56%); birth rate: 39.33/1000; infant mortality rate: 95.7/1000; density per square mile: 40.9
Capital and largest city (1983): Malabo, 30,418. **Monetary unit:** CFA Franc. **Languages:** Spanish (official), pidgin English, Fang, Bubi, Creole. **Ethnicity/Race:** Bioko (primarily Bubi, some Fernandinos), Rio Muni (primarily Fang), Europeans less than 1,000, mostly Spanish. **Religions:** Roman Catholic, Protestant, traditional. **Literacy rate:** 50%
Economic summary: Gross domestic product: purchasing power parity (1995 est.): $18.1 billion; $1,620 per capita; real growth rate –2.4%; inflation: 25.8%; unemployment: at least 45% (1994 est). Labor force: 4.228 million (1993 est.); 70% in agriculture; 22% in transport and services; 8% in industry. Arable land: 8%. Principal products: cocoa, wood, coffee, rice, yams. Natural resources: wood, crude oil. Exports: $2.2 billion (f.o.b., 1995 est.): cocoa, wood, coffee. Imports: $1.8 billion (c.i.f., 1995 est.): petroleum, foodstuffs, textiles, machinery. Major trading partners: South Africa, U.K., Germany, and Japan.

Geography. Equatorial Guinea, formerly Spanish Guinea, consists of Rio Muni (10,045 sq mi.; 26,117 sq km), on the western coast of Africa, and several islands in the Gulf of Guinea, the largest of which is Bioko (formerly Fernando Po) (785 sq mi.; 2,033 sq km). The other islands are Annobón, Corisco, Elobey Grande, and Elobey Chico. The total area is twice that of Connecticut.

Government. A President with an 80-member House of Representatives exercises power.

History. Fernando Po and Annobón came under Spanish control in 1778. From 1827 to 1844, with Spanish consent, Britain administered Fernando Po, but in the latter year Spain reclaimed the island. Río Muni was given to Spain in 1885 by the Treaty of Berlin.

Negotiations with Spain led to independence on Oct. 12, 1968.

In 1969, anti-Spanish incidents in Río Muni, including the tearing down of a Spanish flag by national troops, caused 5,000 Spanish residents to flee for their safety, and diplomatic relations between the two nations became strained. A month later, President Masie Nguema Biyogo Negue Ndong charged that a coup had been attempted against him. He seized dictatorial powers and arrested 80 opposition politicians and even several of his cabinet ministers and the Secretary of the National Assembly.

A coup on Aug. 3, 1979, deposed Masie, and a junta led by Lieut. Col. Teodoro Obiang Nguema Mbasogo took over the government.

After delays the legislative elections of November 1993 resulted in an easy win for the governing party although turnout was low and opposition parties boycotted the process.

President Obiang handily won the presidential election of February 1996 with 99% of the vote. Outside observers and opposition members denounced the balloting as riddled with irregularities.

A military court sentenced 11 non-commissioned officers for having, among other things, participated in an alleged coup attempt in July 1996.

ERITREA

President: Isaias Afwerki (1993)
Area: 45,754 sq mi. (123,300 sq km)
Population (1997 est.): 3,589,687 (of which 0.5 million are refugees awaiting repatriation). Average annual rate of natural increase: 2.870%; birth rate: 43.96/1000; infant mortality rate: 117.2/1000; density per square mile: 78.4
Capital and largest city (1993): Asmara, 400,000. Other major cities: the ports of Massawa and Assab. **Monetary unit:** Birr. **Languages:** Afar, Bilen, Kunama, Nara, Arabic, Tobedawi, Saho, Tigre, Tigrinya. **Ethnicity/Race:** ethnic Tigrinya 50%, Tigre and Kunama 40%, Afar 4%, Saho (Red Sea coast dwellers) 3%. **Religions:** Islam and Eritrean Orthodox Christianity. **Literacy rate:** 20%
Economic summary: Gross domestic product: purchasing power parity (1995 est.): $2 billion; $570 per capita; 10% growth rate. Inflation: 10%. Unemployment: n.a. Labor force: n.a. The economy and infrastructure were severely damaged by the war for independence and natural disasters. Eritrea has inherited the entire coastline of Ethiopia and has long-term prospects for revenues from the development of offshore oil, offshore fishing, and tourism. Major manufacturing industries are textiles, leather, food products, beverages. Most Eritreans are employed in agriculture and important crops are cotton, wheat, and coffee. Major mineral resources are salt and copper. Exports: $33 million: livestock, sorghum, textiles. Imports: $420 million: processed goods, machinery, petroleum products. Important trading partners: Ethiopia, Saudi Arabia, Yemen, Italy, Germany, U.K.

Geography. Eritrea was formerly the northernmost province of Ethiopia and is about the size of Indiana. Much of the country is mountainous. Its narrow Red Sea coastal plain is one of the hottest and driest places in Africa. The cooler central highlands have fertile valleys that support agriculture. Eritrea is bordered by the Sudan on the north and west, the Red Sea on the north and east, and Ethiopia and Djibouti on the south.

Government. A transitional government committed to a democratic system.

History. Eritrea was part of the first Ethiopian kingdom of Askum until its decline in the 8th century C.E. It came under control of the Ottoman Empire in the 16th century, and later the Egyptians. The Italians captured the coastal areas in 1885, and the Treaty of Uccialli (May 2, 1889) gave Italy sovereignty over part of Eritrea. The Italians named their colony after the Roman name for the sea—*Mare Erythraeum*—and ruled it up until World War II.

The British captured Eritrea in 1941 and later administered it as a U.N. Trust Territory until it became federated with Ethiopia on Sept. 15, 1952. It was made an Ethiopian province on Nov. 14, 1962.

A civil war broke out against the Ethiopian government led by rebel groups who opposed the union and wanted independence for Eritrea. The bitter conflict raged on for 17 years against the hard line Communist regime of the Ethiopian dictator, Mengistu Haile Mariam until he was overthrown in May 1991.

The Eritrean People's Liberation Front (EPLF) took control of Eritrea and shared power in a multiparty government in Addis Ababa with the Ethiopian People's

Revolutionary Democratic Front (EPRDF). They agreed to hold a referendum on Eritrean independence within two years and on April 23–25, 1993, Eritrean voters almost unanimously opted for an independent republic. Ethiopia recognized Eritrea's sovereignty on May 3, 1993, and sought a new era of cooperation between the two countries.

While relations with Ethiopia remained good in 1995, those with the Sudan deteriorated.

In November 1996 Eritrea accused the Sudan of plotting to assassinate the President. The mission was thwarted by a Sudanese anti–government group. Sudan denied the charge, although Eritrea provided specific names and dates of those allegedly involved.

ESTONIA

Republic of Estonia
National name: Eesti
President: Lennart Meri (1992)
Prime Minister: Mart Siiman (1997)
Area: 18,370 sq mi. (47,549 sq km)
Population (1997 est.): 1,444,721 (average annual rate of natural increase: −0.25%); birth rate: 11.58/1000; infant mortality rate: 17.4/1000; density per square mile: 78.6
Capital and largest city (1992 est.): Tallinn, 471,608. Other large city (1992 est.): Tartu, 113,400. **Monetary unit:** Kroon. **Languages:** Estonian (official), Russian, Finnish, English. **Ethnicity/Race:** Estonian 61.5%, Russian 30.3%, Ukrainian 3.2%, Belarussian 1.8%, Finn 1.1%, other 2.1% (1989). **Religions:** Lutheran, 78%; Orthodox, 19%. **Literacy:** 100%
Economic summary: Gross domestic product: purchasing power parity (1996 est.): $4.5 billion/$7,600 per capita; real growth rate 4.5%; inflation 14%. Unemployment (1996 est.): 4%. Labor force (1992): 750,000; 42% in industry and construction, 20% in agriculture and forestry. The Estonian government has pursued a program of market reforms and rough stabilization measures, which is rapidly transforming the economy. There is low inflation, living standards are rising, and the private sector is growing rapidly. Exports: $2.0 billion (1996): animals, animal products, food, beverages, tobacco, textiles and textile products, machinery and electrical equipment, vehicles, base metals. Imports: $3.2 billion (1996): food, beverages, tobacco, mineral products, textiles, textile products, machinery, electrical equipment, vehicles. Major trading partners: Finland, Russia, Sweden, Germany, Holland, Latvia.

Geography. Estonia borders on the Baltic Sea in the west, the Gulfs of Riga and Finland in the southwest and north, respectively, Latvia in the south, and Russia in the east. It is mainly a lowland country with numerous lakes. Lake Peipus is the largest and is important to the fishing and shipping industries.

Government. Parliamentary democracy.

History. Born out of World War I, this small Baltic state enjoyed a mere two short decades of independence before it was absorbed again by its powerful neighbor, Russia. In the 13th century, the Estonians had been conquered by the Teutonic Knights of Germany, who reduced them to serfdom. In 1526, the Swedes took over, and the power of the German (Balt) landowning class was curbed somewhat. But after 1721, when Russia succeeded Sweden as the ruling power, the Estonians were subject to a double bondage—the Balts and the tsarist officials. The oppression lasted until the closing months of World War I, when Estonia finally achieved independence after a victorious War of Independence (1918–20).

Shortly after the start of World War II, the nation was occupied by Russian troops and was incorporated as the 16th republic of the U.S.S.R. in 1940. Germany occupied the nation from 1941 to 1944, when it was retaken by the Russians.

Soon after Lithuania's declaration of independence from the Soviet Union in March 1990, the Estonian congress renamed its country on May 8 and omitted the words "Soviet Socialist" and adopted the former (1918) Coat of Arms of the Republic of Estonia. Thereafter, the government cautiously promoted national autonomy.

After the attempted Soviet coup to remove President Gorbachev failed, Estonia formally declared its independence from the U.S.S.R. on August 20, 1991. Recognition by European and other countries followed. The Soviet Union recognized Estonia's independence on September 6 and it received U.N. membership on Sept. 17, 1991.

March 1995 elections gave 41 of the 101 seats in Parliament to two left-leaning parties. The leader of the winning alliance, however, ran on a program embracing free-market reforms.

The presidential vote in Parliament in August 1996 gave neither candidate, the incumbent Meri and former president Ruutel, the needed two–thirds majority. After two further indecisive attempts, voting shifted to an electoral college, which in September re-elected Lennart Meri in the second round.

ETHIOPIA

Federal Democratic Republic of Ethiopia
President: Negasso Gidada (1995)
Prime Minister: Meles Zenawi (1995)
Area: 446,952 sq mi. (1,157,585 sq km)
Population (1997 est.): 58,732,577 (average annual rate of natural increase: 2.8%); birth rate: 45.59/1000; infant mortality rate: 121.5/1000; density per square mile: 131.4
Capital and largest city (1993 est.): Addis Ababa, 2,200,186. **Monetary unit:** Birr. **Languages:** Amharic (official), English, Orominga, Tigrigna, over 70 languages spoken. **Ethnicity/Race:** Oromo 40%, Amhara and Tigrean 32%, Sidamo 9%, Shankella 6%, Somali 6%, Afar 4%, Gurage 2%, other 1%. **Religions:** Ethiopian Orthodox, 35–40%; Islam, 40–45%; animist, 15–20%; other, 5%. **Literacy rate:** 33%
Economic summary: Gross domestic product: purchasing power parity (1995 est.): $22.6 billion; $400 per capita; real growth rate 2.7%; inflation (1995): 8%. Unemployment rate: n.a. Arable land: 12%. Principal agricultural products: coffee, barley, wheat, corn, sugar cane, cotton, oilseeds, livestock. Major industrial products: cement, textiles, processed foods, refined oil, beverages, footwear, furniture. Natural resources: potash, gold, platinum, copper. Labor force: 18 million; 80% in agriculture and animal husbandry; 12% in government and services; 8% in industry and construction. Exports: $296 million (f.o.b., 1994 est.): coffee, leather products, gold, petroleum products. Imports: $972 million (c.i.f., 1994 est.): machinery and equipment, industrial inputs, pharmaceuticals, chemicals. Major trading partners: Japan, U.S., Djibouti, Saudi Arabia, Germany, Italy, France, Eritrea.

Geography. Ethiopia is in east central Africa, bordered on the west by the Sudan, the east by Somalia and Djibouti, the south by Kenya, and northeast by Eritrea. It is nearly three times the size of California.

Over its main plateau land, Ethiopia has several high mountains, the highest of which is Ras Dashan at 15,158 feet (4,620 m). The Blue Nile, or Abbai, rises in the northwest and flows in a great semicircle east, south, and northwest before entering the Sudan. Its chief reservoir, Lake Tana, lies in the northwestern part of the plateau.

Government. A constitution was ratified by a constituent assembly elected in June 1994. The bicameral Parliament has 548 seats (House of People's Representatives, and the federal council has one seat for each nationality plus one seat for each additional one million of the nationality.)

History. Black Africa's oldest state, Ethiopia can trace 2,000 years of recorded history. Its now deposed royal line claimed descent from King Menelik I, traditionally believed to have been the son of the Queen of Sheba and King Solomon. The present nation is a consolidation of smaller kingdoms that owed feudal allegiance to the Ethiopian Emperor.

Hamitic peoples migrated to Ethiopia from Asia Minor in prehistoric times. Semitic traders from Arabia penetrated the region in the 7th century B.C.E. Its Red Sea ports were important to the Roman and Byzantine Empires. Coptic Christianity came to the country in C.E. 341, and a variant of that communion became Ethiopia's state religion.

Ancient Ethiopia reached its peak in the 5th century, then was isolated by the rise of Islam and weakened by feudal wars. Modern Ethiopia emerged under Emperor Menelik II, who established its independence by routing an Italian invasion in 1896. He expanded Ethiopia by conquest.

Disorders that followed Menelik's death brought his daughter to the throne in 1917, with his cousin, Tafari Makonnen, as Regent, heir presumptive, and strongman. When the Empress died in 1930, Tafari was Crowned Emperor Haile Selassie I.

As Regent, Haile Selassie outlawed slavery. As Emperor, he worked for centralization of his diffuse realm, in which 70 languages are spoken, and for moderate reform. In 1931, he granted a constitution, revised in 1955, that created a parliament with an appointed Senate and an elected Chamber of Deputies, and a system of courts. But basic power remained with the Emperor.

Bent on colonial empire, fascist Italy invaded Ethiopia on Oct. 3, 1935, forcing Haile Selassie into exile in May 1936. Ethiopia was annexed to Eritrea, then an Italian colony, and Italian Somaliland to form Italian East Africa, losing its independence for the first time in recorded history. In 1941, British troops routed the Italians, and Haile Selassie returned to Addis Ababa.

In August 1974, the Armed Forces Committee nationalized Haile Selassie's palace and estates and directed him not to leave Addis Ababa. On Sept. 12, 1974, he was deposed after nearly 58 years as Regent and Emperor. The 82-year-old "Lion of Judah" was placed under guard. Parliament was dissolved, the constitution suspended and Ethiopia was proclaimed a socialist state.

Lt. Col. Mengistu Haile Mariam was named head of state, Feb. 2, 1977, and when a Communist regime was established on Sept. 10, 1984, Mengistu became party leader.

A cut-off of Soviet aid led to mass animosity, and a rebel offensive began in February 1991. Mengistu resigned and fled the country in May. A group called the Ethiopian People's Revolutionary Democratic Front seized the capital. Also in May a separatist guerrilla organization, the Eritrean People's Liberation Front, took control of the province of Eritrea. The two groups agreed in early July that Eritrea would have an internationally supervised referendum on independence. This election took place in April 1993 with an almost unanimous support for Eritrean independence. Ethiopia accepted and recognized Eritrea as an independent state within a few days.

General elections in May 1995 gave the ruling coalition a landslide victory after a boycott by most opposition groups. A new government was established in August with a 17-member Council of Ministers chosen to reflect the ethnic makeup of the country.

Sixty-eight leaders of the former military government were put on trial in April 1996 on charges including genocide and crimes against humanity.

FIJI

Republic of Fiji

President: Ratu Sir Kamisese Mara (1994)
Prime Minister: Maj. Gen. Sitiveni Rabuka (1992)
Area: 7,078 sq mi. (18,333 sq km)
Population (1997 est.): 792,441 (average annual rate of natural increase: 1.5%); birth rate: 23.12/1000; infant mortality rate: 17/1000; density per square mile: 111.9
Capital (1990 est.): Suva (on Viti Levu), 200,000. **Monetary unit:** Fiji dollar. **Languages:** Fijian, Hindustani, English (official). **Ethnicity/Race:** Fijian 49%, Indian 46%, European, other Pacific Islanders, overseas Chinese, and other 5%. **Religions:** Christian, 52%; Hindu, 38%; Islam, 8%; other, 2%. **Literacy rate:** 86%
Economic summary: Gross domestic product: purchasing power parity (1995 est.): $4.7 billion; $6,100 per capita; real growth rate 2.2%; inflation rate 3.1% (1996); unemployment rate (1996 est.): 6%. Arable land: 8%. Principal products: sugar, copra, ginger. Labor force (1996 est.): 287,000; 67% subsistence agriculture; 18% wage earners; salary earners, 15%. Major industrial products: refined sugar, gold, lumber. Natural resources: timber, fish, gold, copper. Exports: $571.8 million (f.o.b., 1995): sugar, copra, processed fish, lumber, gold, clothing. Imports: $864.3 million (c.i.f., 1995): machinery and transport equipment, food, petroleum products, consumer goods, chemicals. Major trading partners: E.U., Australia, Japan, U.S., U.K., New Zealand, Pacific Islands.

Geography. Fiji consists of 332 islands in the southwestern Pacific Ocean about 1,960 miles (3,152 km) from Sydney, Australia. About 110 of these islands are inhabited. The two largest are Viti Levu (4,109 sq mi.; 10,642 sq km) and Vanua Levu (2,242 sq mi.; 5,807 sq km). The island of Rotuma (18 sq mi.; 47 sq km), about 400 miles (644 km) to the north, is a province of Fiji. Overall, Fiji is nearly as large as New Jersey.

The largest islands in the group are mountainous and volcanic, with the tallest peak being Mount Victoria (4,341 ft.; 1,323 m) on Viti Levu. The southeastern windward sides of the main islands have dense forests, while the west and northwestern leeward sides have grasslands and scattered light forests.

Government. Military coup leader Major General Sitiveni Rabuka formerly declared Fiji a republic on Oct. 6, 1987. The Sept. 23, 1988 constitution provided for a bicameral parliament consisting of a 342-member Senate and a 70-member House of Representatives.

The new constitution of July 1990 ensured ethnic Fijians a majority of seats in the parliament as well as the presidency, Prime Ministership and other central positions. The constitution is currently under review to account for the interests of other races, notably the Indians, who make up 45% of the population.

History. In 1874, an offer of cession by the Fijian chiefs was accepted, and Fiji was proclaimed a possession and dependency of the British Crown.

During World War II, the archipelago was an important air and naval station on the route from the U.S. and Hawaii to Australia and New Zealand.

Fiji became independent on Oct. 10, 1970. The next year it joined the five-island South Pacific Forum, which intends to become a permanent regional group to promote collective diplomacy of the newly independent members.

In Oct., 1987, then Brig. Gen. Sitiveni Rabuka, the coup leader, declared Fiji a republic and removed it from the British Commonwealth.

In elections of May 1992, Rabuka, as leader of the Fijian Political Party, became Prime Minister.

Rabuka began his second term in February 1994 after his party's victory in a general election that month.

The House of Representatives overwhelmingly approved a constitution Amendment Bill in July 1997. It now goes to the Senate for approval. The Bill would eliminate the constitutional provision ensuring ethnic Fijians parliamentary seats.

FINLAND

Republic of Finland
National name: Suomen Tasavalta—Republiken Finland
President: Martti Ahtisaari (1994)
Premier: Paavo Lipponen (1995)
Area: 130,558 sq mi. (338,145 sq km)
Population (1997 est.): 5,109,148 (average annual rate of natural increase: —0.003%); birth rate: 10.79/1000; infant mortality rate: 4.9/1000; density per square mile: 39.1
Capital and largest city (1995 est.): Helsinki, 515,765. **Other large cities (1995 est.):** Espoo, 186,507; Tampere, 179,251; Vantaa, 164,376; Turku, 162,370. **Monetary unit:** Markka. **Languages:** Finnish, Swedish. **Ethnicity/Race:** Finn, Swede, Lapp, Gypsy, Tatar. **Religions:** Evangelical Lutheran, 90%; Greek Orthodox, 1.2%. **Literacy rate:** 100%
Economic summary: Gross domestic product: purchasing power parity (1995 est.): $92.4 billion; $18,200 per capita; 5% real growth rate; inflation rate: 2%; unemployment rate: 17%. Arable land: 8.3%. Principal products: dairy and meat products, cereals, sugar beets, potatoes. Labor force: 2.533 million; 30.4% in public services; 20.9% in industry; 15% in commerce; 10.2% in finance, insurance, and business services. Major products: metal manufactures, forestry and wood products, refined copper, ships, machinery, chemicals, clothing, footwear. Natural resource: timber. Exports: $29.7 billion (f.o.b., 1994): timber, paper and pulp, ships, machinery, clothing, footwear, chemicals. Imports: $23.2 billion (c.i.f., 1994): petroleum and petroleum products, chemicals, transportation equipment, machinery, textile yarns, foodstuffs, fodder grain, iron and steel. Major trading partners: Germany, Sweden, U.K., U.S., France, Russia, Denmark, Norway, Netherlands.

Geography. Finland stretches 721 miles (1,160 km) from south to north, Russia extends along the entire eastern frontier while Norway is on her northern border and Sweden lies on her western border. In area, Finland is three times the size of Ohio.

Off the southwest coast are the Aland Islands, controlling the entrance to the Gulf of Bothnia. Finland has more than 200,000 lakes.

The Swedish-populated Aland Islands (581 sq mi.; 1,505 sq km) have an autonomous status under a law passed in 1921.

Government. The President, chosen for six years by popular vote, appoints the cabinet. The one-chamber Diet, the Eduskunta, consists of 200 members elected for four-year terms by proportional representation.

History. At the end of the 7th century, the Finns came to Finland from their Volga settlements, taking the country from the Lapps, who retreated northward. The

Finns' repeated raids on the Scandinavian coast impelled Eric IX, the Swedish King, to conquer the country in 1157 and bring it into contact with Western Christendom. By 1809 the whole of Finland was conquered by Alexander I of Russia, who set up Finland as a Grand Duchy.

The first period of Russification (1809–1905) resulted in a lessening of the powers of the Finnish Diet. The Russian language was made official, and the Finnish military system was superseded by the Russian. The pace of Russification was intensified from 1908 to 1914. When Russian control was weakened as a consequence of the March Revolution of 1917, the Diet on July 20, 1917, proclaimed Finland's independence, which became complete on Dec. 6, 1917.

Finland rejected Soviet territorial demands, and the U.S.S.R. attacked on Nov. 30, 1939. The Finns made an amazing stand of three months and finally capitulated, ceding 16,000 square miles (41,440 sq km) to the U.S.S.R. Under German pressure, the Finns joined the Nazis against Russia in 1941, but were defeated again and ceded the Petsamo area to the U.S.S.R. In 1948, a 20-year treaty of friendship and mutual assistance was signed by the two nations and renewed for another 20 years in 1970.

Premier Mauno Koivisto, leader of the Social Democratic Party, was elected president on Jan. 26, 1982, winning decisively over a conservative rival with support from Finnish Communists.

Running on a platform calling to invigorate the economy, Ahtisaari, a Social Democrat, won the country's first direct presidential election in a runoff in February 1994. Previously the president had been chosen by electors.

Finland became a member of the European Union in January 1995, but made clear it would not become a full member of the Western European Union. In March elections the Social Democrats replaced the Centre Party as the largest group in parliament.

Showing concern over NATO expansion eastward, Russian President Yeltsin in March 1997 iterated his view that Finnish membership in the military alliance was unacceptable. The Finnish government has repeatedly stated its intention to continue to continue its policy of non–alignment.

FRANCE

French Republic
National name: République Française
President: Jacques Chirac (1995)
Prime Minister: Lionel Jospin (1997)
Area: 211,208 sq mi. (547,030 sq km)
Population (1997 est.): 58,470,421 (average annual rate of natural increase: 0.17%); birth rate: 10.78/1000; infant mortality rate: 6/1000; density per square mile: 276.8
Capital: Paris. **Largest cities (1990):** Paris, 2,152,000 (10,650,600, Paris region); Marseille, 801,000; Lyon, 415,000; Toulouse, 359,000; Nice, 342,000; Strasbourg, 252,000; Nantes, 245,000; Bordeaux, 201,000.
Monetary unit: French Franc. **Language:** French, declining regional dialects. **Ethnicity/Race:** Celtic and Latin with Teutonic, Slavic, North African, Indochinese, Basque minorities. **Religion:** Roman Catholic, 81%; Protestant, 1.7%; Muslim, 6.9%; Jewish, 1.3%. **Literacy rate:** 99%
Economic summary: Gross domestic product: purchasing power parity (1995 est.): $1.173 trillion; $20,200 per capita; 2.4% real growth rate; inflation 1.7%; unemployment 11.7%. Arable land: 32%. Principal products: cereals, feed grains, livestock and dairy products, wine, fruits, vegetables, potatoes. Labor

force: 24.17 million: 61.5% in services; 31.3% in industry; 7.2% in agriculture. Major products: chemicals, automobiles, processed foods, iron and steel, aircraft, textiles, clothing. Natural resources: coal, iron ore, bauxite, fish, forests. Exports: $285.4 billion (1995): textiles and clothing, chemicals, machinery and transport equipment, agricultural products, foodstuffs. Imports: $264.4 billion (1995): machinery, crude petroleum, chemicals, agricultural products, iron and steel products. Major trading partners: Germany, Italy, U.S., Belgium-Luxembourg, U.K., Netherlands, Spain, Japan.

Geography. France is about 80% the size of Texas. In the Alps near the Italian and Swiss borders is Europe's highest point—Mont Blanc (15,781 ft.; 4,810 m). The forest-covered Vosges Mountains are in the northeast, and the Pyrenees are along the Spanish border.

Except for extreme northern France, which is part of the Flanders plain, the country may be described as four river basins and a plateau. Three of the streams flow west—the Seine into the English Channel, the Loire into the Atlantic, and the Garonne into the Bay of Biscay. The Rhône flows south into the Mediterranean. For about 100 miles (161 km), the Rhine is France's eastern border.

West of the Rhône and northeast of the Garonne lies the central plateau, covering about 15% of France's area and rising to a maximum elevation of 6,188 feet (1,886 m). In the Mediterranean, about 115 miles (185 km) east-southeast of Nice, is Corsica (3,367 sq mi.; 8,721 sq km).

Government. The President is elected for seven years by universal suffrage. He appoints the Premier, and the cabinet is responsible to parliament. The President has the right to dissolve the National Assembly or to ask parliament for reconsideration of a law. The parliament consists of two houses: the National Assembly and the Senate.

History. The history of France, as distinct from ancient Gaul, begins with the Treaty of Verdun (843), dividing the territories corresponding roughly to France, Germany, and Italy among the three grandsons of Charlemagne. Julius Caesar had conquered part of Gaul in 57–52 B.C.E., and it remained Roman until Franks invaded it in the 5th century.

Charles the Bald, inheritor of *Francia Occidentalis,* founded the Carolingian dynasty, which ruled over a kingdom increasingly feudalized. By 987, the Crown passed to Hugh Capet, a Princeling who controlled only the Ile-de-France, the region surrounding Paris. For 350 years, an unbroken Capetian line added to its domain and consolidated royal authority until the accession in 1328 of Philip VI, first of the Valois line. France was then the most powerful nation in Europe, with a population of 15 million.

The missing pieces in Philip's domain were the French provinces still held by the Plantagenet Kings of England, who also claimed the French Crown. Beginning in 1338, the Hundred Years' War eventually settled the contest. English longbows defeated French armored knights at Crécy (1346) and the English also won the second landmark battle at Agincourt (1415), but the final victory went to the French at Castillon (1453).

Absolute monarchy reached its apogee in the reign of Louis XIV (1643–1715), the Sun King, whose brilliant court was the center of the Western world.

Revolution plunged France into a blood bath beginning in 1789 and ending with a new authoritarianism under Napoleon Bonaparte, who had successfully defended the infant republic from foreign attack and then made himself First Consul in 1799 and Emperor in 1804.

The Congress of Vienna (1815) sought to restore the pre-Napoleonic order in the person of Louis XVIII, but industrialization and the middle class, both fostered under Napoleon, built pressure for change, and a revolution in 1848 drove Louis Phillipe, last of the Bourbons, into exile.

A second republic elected as its president Prince Louis Napoleon, a nephew of Napoleon I, who declared the Second Empire in 1852 and took the throne as Napoleon III. His opposition to the rising power of Prussia ignited the Franco-Prussian War (1870–71), ending in his defeat and abdication.

A new France emerged from World War I as the continent's dominant power. But four years of hostile occupation had reduced northeast France to ruins. The postwar Third Republic was plagued by political instability and economic chaos.

From 1919, French foreign policy aimed at keeping Germany weak through a system of alliances, but it failed to halt the rise of Adolf Hitler and the Nazi war machine. On May 10, 1940, mechanized Nazi troops attacked, and, as they approached Paris, Italy joined with Germany. The Germans marched into an undefended Paris and Marshal Henri Philippe Pétain signed an armistice June 22. France was split into an occupied north and an unoccupied south, the latter becoming a totalitarian state with Pétain as its chief.

Allied armies liberated France in August 1944. The French Committee of National Liberation, formed in Algiers in 1943, established a provisional government in Paris headed by Gen. Charles de Gaulle. The Fourth Republic was born Dec. 24, 1946.

The Empire became the French Union; the National Assembly was strengthened and the presidency weakened; and France joined the North Atlantic Treaty Organization. A war against Communist insurgents in Indochina was abandoned after the defeat at Dien Bien Phu. A new rebellion in Algeria threatened a military coup, and on June 1, 1958, the Assembly invited de Gaulle to return as Premier with extraordinary powers. He drafted a new constitution for a Fifth Republic, adopted Sept. 28, which strengthened the presidency and reduced legislative power. He was elected president Dec. 21.

De Gaulle took France out of the NATO military command in 1967 and expelled all foreign-controlled troops from the country. He later went on to attempt to achieve a long-cherished plan of regional reform. This, however, aroused wide opposition. He decided to stake his fate on a referendum. At the voting in April 1969, the electorate defeated the plan.

His successor Georges Pompidou continued the de Gaulle policies of seeking to expand France's influence in the Mideast and Africa.

Socialist François Mitterrand attained a stunning victory in the May 10, 1981, presidential election over the Gaullist alliance that had held power since 1958.

The victors immediately moved to carry out campaign pledges to nationalize major industries, halt nuclear testing, suspend nuclear power plant construction, and impose new taxes on the rich. On Feb. 11, 1982, the nationalization bills became law.

The Socialists' policies during Mitterrand's first two years created a 12% inflation rate, a huge trade deficit, and devaluations of the franc. In early 1983, Mitterrand embarked on an austerity program to control inflation and reduce the trade deficit. He increased taxes and slashed government spending. A halt in economic growth, declining purchasing power for the average Frenchman, and an increase in unemployment to 10% followed. Mitterrand sank lower and lower in the opinion polls.

In March 1986, a center-right coalition led by Jacques Chirac won a slim majority in legislative elections.

Rulers of France

Name	Born	Ruled[1]
Carolingian Dynasty		
Pepin the Short	c. 714	751–768
Charlemagne[2]	742	768–814
Louis I the Debonair[3]	778	814–840
Charles I the Bald[4]	823	840–877
Louis II the Stammerer	846	877–879
Louis III[5]	c. 863	879–882
Carloman[5]	?	879–884
Charles II the Fat[6]	839	884–887[7]
Eudes (Odo), Count of Paris	?	888–898
Charles III the Simple[8]	879	893–923[9]
Robert I[10]	c. 865	922–923
Rudolf (Raoul), Duke of Burgundy	?	923–936
Louis IV d'Outremer	c. 921	936–954
Lothair	941	954–986
Louis V the Sluggard	c. 967	986–987
Capetian Dynasty		
Hugh Capet	c. 940	987–996
Robert II the Pious[11]	c. 970	996–1031
Henry I	1008	1031–1060
Philip I	1052	1060–1108
Louis VI the Fat	1081	1108–1137
Louis VII the Young	c.1121	1137–1180
Philip II (Philip Augustus)	1165	1180–1223
Louis VIII the Lion	1187	1223–1226
Louis IX (St. Louis)	1214	1226–1270
Philip III the Bold	1245	1270–1285
Philip IV the Fair	1268	1285–1314
Louis X the Quarreler	1289	1314–1316
John I[12]	1316	1316
Philip V the Tall	1294	1316–1322
Charles IV the Fair	1294	1322–1328
House of Valois		
Philip VI	1293	1328–1350
John II the Good	1319	1350–1364
Charles V the Wise	1337	1364–1380
Charles VI the Well-Beloved	1368	1380–1422
Charles VII	1403	1422–1461
Louis XI	1423	1461–1483
Charles VIII	1470	1483–1498
Louis XII the Father of the People	1462	1498–1515
Francis I	1494	1515–1547
Henry II	1519	1547–1559
Francis II	1544	1559–1560
Charles IX	1550	1560–1574
Henry III	1551	1574–1589
House of Bourbon		
Henry IV of Navarre	1553	1589–1610
Louis XIII	1601	1610–1643
Louis XIV the Great	1638	1643–1715

Name	Born	Ruled[1]
Louis XV the Well-Beloved	1710	1715–1774
Louis XVI	1754	1774–1792[13]
Louis XVII (Louis Charles de France)[14]	1785	1793–1795
First Republic		
National Convention	—	1792–1795
Directory (Directoire)	—	1795–1799
Consulate		
Napoleon Bonaparte[15]	1769	1799–1804
First Empire		
Napoleon I	1769	1804–1815[16]
Restoration of House of Bourbon		
Louis XVIII le Désiré	1755	1814–1824
Charles X	1757	1824–1830[17]
Bourbon-Orleans Line		
Louis Philippe ("Citizen King")	1773	1830–1848[18]
Second Republic		
Louis Napoleon[19]	1808	1848–1852
Second Empire		
Napoleon III (Louis Napoleon)	1808	1852–1870[20]
Third Republic (Presidents)		
Louis Adolphe Thiers	1797	1871–1873
Marie E. P. M. de MacMahon	1808	1873–1879
François P. J. Grévy	1807	1879–1887
Sadi Carnot	1837	1887–1894
Jean Casimir-Périer	1847	1894–1895
François Félix Faure	1841	1895–1899
Émile Loubet	1838	1899–1906
Clement Armand Fallières	1841	1906–1913
Raymond Poincaré	1860	1913–1920
Paul E. L. Deschanel	1856	1920–1920
Alexandre Millerand	1859	1920–1924
Gaston Doumergue	1863	1924–1931
Paul Doumer	1857	1931–1932
Albert Lebrun	1871	1932–1940
Vichy Government(Chief of State)		
Henri Philippe Pétain	1856	1940–1944
Provisional Government(Presidents)		
Charles de Gaulle	1890	1944–1946
Félix Gouin	1884	1946–1946
Georges Bidault	1899	1946–1947
Fourth Republic (Presidents)		
Vincent Auriol	1884	1947–1954
René Coty	1882	1954–1959
Fifth Republic (Presidents)		
Charles de Gaulle	1890	1959–1969
Georges Pompidou	1911	1969–1974
Valéry Giscard d'Estaing	1926	1974–1981
François Mitterrand	1916	1981–1995
Jacques Chirac	1932	1995–

1. For Kings and Emperors through the Second Empire, year of end of rule is also that of death, unless otherwise indicated. 2. Crowned Emperor of the West in 800. His brother, Carloman, ruled as King of the Eastern Franks from 768 until his death in 771. 3. Holy Roman Emperor 814–840. 4. Holy Roman Emperor 875–877 as Charles II. 5. Ruled jointly 879–882. 6. Holy Roman Emperor 881–887 as Charles III. 7. Died 888. 8. King 893–898 in opposition to Eudes. 9. Died 929. 10. Not counted in regular line of Kings of France by some authorities. Elected by nobles but killed in Battle of Soissons. 11. Sometimes called Robert I. 12. Posthumous son of Louis X; lived for only five days. 13. Executed 1793. 14. Titular King only. He died in prison according to official reports, but many pretenders appeared during the Bourbon restoration. 15. As First Consul, Napoleon held the power of government. In 1804, he became Emperor. 16. Abdicated first time June 1814. Re-entered Paris March 1815, after escape from Elba; Louis XVIII fled to Ghent. Abdicated second time June 1815. He named as his successor his son, Napoleon II, who was not acceptable to the Allies. He died 1821. 17. Died 1836. 18. Died 1850. 19. President; became Emperor in 1852. 20. Died 1873.

Chirac became Premier initiating a period of "cohabitation" between him and the Socialist president, Mitterrand.

Mitterrand's decisive re-election in May 1987, led to Chirac being replaced as Premier by Michel Rocard, a Socialist.

Relations, however, cooled with Rocard, and in May 1991 he was replaced with Edith Cresson, France's first female Prime Minister and, like Mitterrand, a Socialist.

On his third try Chirac won the presidency in May 1995, gaining more than 52% of the vote. He campaigned vigorously on a platform to reduce unemployment, but moved quickly to cement ties with Germany.

Elections for the National Assembly on June 1st, 1997, gave the Socialists and those close to them 273 seats, but the conservative coalition only 249. The next day Chirac asked Socialist leader Jospin to become Prime Minister. The Socialists campaigned on reducing France's 12.8% unemployment while preserving and expanding the welfare state.

Overseas Departments

Overseas Departments elect representatives to the National Assembly, and the same administrative organization as that of mainland France applies to them.

FRENCH GUIANA (INCLUDING ININI)

Status: Overseas Department
Prefect: Pierre Dartout (1995)
Area: 32,253 sq mi. (83,534 sq km)
Population (1997 est.): 156,946; growth rate: 1.96%; birth rate 24.19/1000; infant mortality rate 14/1000; density per square mile: 4.9
Capital and largest city (1995 est.): Cayenne, 41,659.
Monetary unit: Franc. **Language:** French. **Ethnicity/ Race:** black or mulatto 66%, white 12%, East Indian, Chinese, Amerindian 12%, other 10%. **Religion:** Roman Catholic. **Literacy rate:** 73%
Economic summary: Gross domestic product: purchasing power parity (1993 est.): $800 million; $6,000 per capita; inflation (1992): 2.5%; unemployment: 24.1%. Arable land: negligible; principal agricultural products: rice, cassava, bananas, sugar cane. Labor force (1993): 36,597; 60.6% in services, government and commerce, 18.2% in agriculture (1980). Major industrial products: timber, rum, rosewood essence, gold mining, processed shrimp. Natural resources: bauxite, timber, cinnabar, kaolin. Exports: $110 million (f.o.b., 1993): shrimp, timber, rum, rosewood essence. Imports: $719 million (c.i.f., 1992): food, consumer and producer goods, petroleum. Major trading partners: U.S., France, Japan.

French Guiana, lying north of Brazil and east of Suriname on the northeast coast of South America, was first settled in 1637. Penal settlements, embracing the area around the mouth of the Maroni River and the Iles du Salut (including Devil's Island), were founded in 1852; they have since been abolished.

During World War II, French Guiana at first adhered to the Vichy government, but the Free French took over in 1943. French Guiana accepted in 1958 the new constitution of the French Fifth Republic and remained an Overseas Department of the French Republic.

GUADELOUPE

Status: Overseas Department
Prefect: Michel Diefenbacher
Area: 327 sq mi. (1,848 sq km)
Population (1997 est.): 412,614 (average annual growth rate: 1.17%); birth rate: 17.36/1000; infant mortality rate: 8.1/1000; density per square mile: 1,261.8
Capital (1990): Basse-Terre, 14,000. **Largest city (1990):** Pointe-à-Pitre, over 26,029. **Monetary unit:** Franc. **Language:** French, Creole patois. **Ethnicity/ Race:** black or mulatto 90%, white 5%, East Indian, Lebanese, Chinese less than 5%. **Religions:** Roman Catholic. **Literacy rate:** over 70%
Economic summary: Gross domestic product: purchasing power parity (1995 est.): $3.7 billion; $9,200 per capita; real growth rate n.a.; inflation (1990): 3.7%; unemployment (1990): 33.1%. Arable land: 18%; principal agricultural products: sugar cane, bananas, eggplant, flowers. Labor force (1993): 129,700; 15% in agriculture; 20% in industry; 65% in services. Major industries: construction, public works, sugar, rum, tourism. Exports: $130 million (f.o.b., 1992): sugar, rum, bananas. Imports: $1.4 billion (c.i.f., 1993): foodstuffs,

clothing, consumer goods, construction materials, petroleum products, vehicles. Major trading partners: France, Martinique, Italy, Germany, U.S.

Guadeloupe, in the West Indies about 300 miles (483 km) southeast of Puerto Rico, was landed on by Columbus in 1493. It consists of the twin islands of Basse-Terre and Grande-Terre and five dependencies—Marie-Galante, Les Saintes, La Désirade, St. Barthélemy, and the northern half of St. Martin. The volcano Soufrière (4,813 ft.; 1,467 m), also called La Grande Soufrière, is the highest point on Guadeloupe. Violent activity in 1976 and 1977 caused thousands to flee their homes.

French colonization began in 1635. In 1958, Guadeloupe voted in favor of the new constitution of the French Fifth Republic and remained an Overseas Department of the French Republic.

MARTINIQUE

Status: Overseas Department
Prefect: Jean-Francois Cordet
Area: 436 sq mi. (1,128 sq km)
Population (1997 est.): 403,531 (average annual growth rate: 1.1%); birth rate: 16.9/1000; infant mortality rate: 71/1000; density per square mile: 925.5
Capital and largest city (1990): Fort-de-France, 100,072; Other cities (1990): Le Lamentin, 30,026; Schoelcher, 19,683; Sainte-Marie, 19,683. **Monetary unit:** Franc. **Languages:** French, Creole patois. **Ethnicity/Race:** African and African-white-Indian mixture 90%, white 5%, East Indian, Lebanese, Chinese less than 5%. **Religion:** Roman Catholic. **Literacy rate:** over 70%
Economic summary: Gross domestic product: purchasing power parity (1993 est.): $3.9 billion, $10,000 per capita; inflation (1990): 3.9%; unemployment (1994): 23.5%. Average annual growth rate n.a. Arable land: 10%; principal agricultural products: sugar cane, bananas, rum, pineapples. Labor force (1994): 164,877; 31.7% in service industry. Major industries: sugar, rum, refined oil, cement, tourism. Natural resources: coastal scenery and beaches. Exports: $247 million (f.o.b., 1992): bananas, refined petroleum products, rum, sugar, pineapples. Imports: $1.75 billion (c.i.f., 1992): foodstuffs, clothing and other consumer goods, petroleum, construction materials. Major trading partners: France, U.S., Guadeloupe, Germany, U.K., Italy, Japan.

Martinique, lying in the Lesser Antilles about 300 miles (483 km) northeast of Venezuela, was probably discovered by Columbus in 1502 and was taken for France in 1635. Following the Franco-German armistice of 1940, it had a semiautonomous status until 1943, when authority was relinquished to the Free French. The area, administered by a Prefect assisted by an elected council, is represented in the French parliament. In 1958, Martinique voted in favor of the new constitution of the French Fifth Republic and remained an Overseas Department of the French Republic.

RÉUNION

Status: Overseas Department
Prefect: Pierre Steinmetz (1995)
Area: 970 sq mi. (2,512 sq km)
Population (1997 est.): 692,204 (average annual growth rate: 1.86%); birth rate: 23.4/1000; infant mortality rate: 7.3/1000; density per square mile: 713.6
Capital and largest city (1993): Saint-Denis, 121,999. Other cities (est. 1993): Saint-Paul, 71,667; Saint-Pierre, 58,846; Le Tampon, 47,598; Saint-Louis, 37,420. **Monetary unit:** Franc. **Languages:** French, Creole. **Ethnicity/Race:** French, African, Malagasy, Chinese, Pakistani, Indian. **Religion:** Roman Catholic

Economic summary: Gross domestic product: purchasing power parity (1995 est.): $2.9 billion, $4,300 per capita; inflation n.a.; unemployment (Feb.1991) 35%. Arable land: 20%; principal agricultural products: rum, vanilla, bananas, perfume plants. Major industrial products: rum, cigarettes, processed sugar. Labor force: 242,169: 30% in agriculture; 21% in industry; 49% in services. Exports: $174 million (f.o.b., 1993): sugar, perfume essences, rum, molasses. Imports: $2.08 billion (c.i.f., 1993): manufactured goods, foodstuffs, beverages, machinery and transportation equipment, petroleum products. Major trading partners: France, Mauritius, Bahrain, South Africa, Italy.

First explored by Portuguese navigators in the 16th century, the island of Réunion, then uninhabited, was taken as a French possession in 1642. It is located about 450 miles (724 km) east of Madagascar, in the Indian Ocean. In 1958, Réunion approved the constitution of the Fifth French Republic and remained an Overseas Department of the French Republic.

ST. PIERRE AND MIQUELON

Status: Overseas Territory
Prefect: René Maurice
Area: 93 sq mi. (242 sq km)
Population (1997 est.): 6,862; growth rate 0.704%; birth rate 12.63/1000; infant mortality rate 9.26/1000; density per square mile: 73.8
Capital (1990): Saint Pierre, 5,683. **Ethnicity/Race:** Basques and Bretons (French fishermen)
Economic summary: Gross domestic product: purchasing power parity (1994 est.): $68 million, $10,000 per capita; unemployment 9.6%. Major industries: fishing, canneries. Labor force: 2,980. Exports: $13.74 million (f.o.b., 1994): fish, pelts. Imports: $42 million (c.i.f., 1994): meat, clothing, fuel, electrical equipment, machinery, building materials. Major trading partners: Canada, France, U.S., U.K., the Netherlands.

The sole remnant of the French colonial empire in North America, these islands were first occupied by the French in 1604. Their only importance arises from proximity to the Grand Banks, located 10 miles south of Newfoundland, making them the center of the French Atlantic cod fisheries. On July 19, 1976, the islands became an Overseas Department of the French Republic.

Overseas Territories

Overseas Territories are comparable to Departments, except that their administrative organization includes a locally elected government.

FRENCH POLYNESIA

Status: Overseas Territory
High Commissioner: Paul Ronciere
Area: 1,609 sq mi. (4,167 sq km)
Population (1997 est.): 233,488 (average annual growth rate: 1.83%); birth rate: 23.27/1000; infant mortality rate: 13.7/1000; density per square mile: 145.1
Capital (1988): Papeete (on Tahiti), 23,555. **Monetary unit:** Pacific financial community franc. **Language:** French. **Ethnicity/Race:** Polynesian 78%, Chinese 12%, local French 6%, metropolitan French 4%. **Religions:** Protestant, 55%; Roman Catholic, 32%
Economic summary: Gross domestic product: purchasing power parity (1995 est.): $1.76 billion, $8,000 per capita; inflation (1994) 1.5%; unemployment n.a. Principal agricultural product: copra. Major industries: tourism, maintenance of French nuclear test base. Exports: $230 million (f.o.b., 1994): coconut products, mother of pearl, vanilla. Imports: $912 million (c.i.f.,

1994): fuels, foodstuffs, equipment. Major trading partners: France, U.S.

The term French Polynesia is applied to the scattered French possessions in the South Pacific—Mangareva (Gambier), Makatea, the Marquesas Islands, Rapa, Rurutu, Rimatara, the Society Islands, the Tuamotu Archipelago, Tubuai, Raivavae, and the island of Clipperton—which were organized into a single colony in 1903. There are 120 islands, of which 25 are uninhabited.

The President of the Territorial Government is assisted by a Council of Government and a popularly elected Territorial Assembly. The principal and most populous island—Tahiti, in the Society group—was claimed as French in 1768. In 1958, French Polynesia voted in favor of the new constitution of the French Fifth Republic and remained an Overseas Territory of the French Republic. The natives are mostly Maoris.

The Pacific Nuclear Test Center on the atoll of Mururoa, 744 miles (1,200 km) from Tahiti, was completed in 1966.

To compensate the residents for the nuclear weapons tests in 1995–96 France offered a 10-year $194 million annual compensation package.

MAYOTTE

Status: Territorial collectivity
Prefect: Alain Weil
Area: 146 sq mi. (378 sq km)
Population (1997 est.): 104,715; average annual rate of natural increase 3.764%; birth rate 47.42/1000; infant mortality rate 73.2/1000; density per square mile: 717.2
Capital and largest city (1991): Dzaoudzi (Mamoudzou), 20,450
Economic summary: Gross domestic product: purchasing power parity (1993 est.): $54 million, $600 per capita. Exports: $2.9 million (f.o.b., 1992). Imports: $87.5 million (f.o.b., 1992). Principal products: vanilla, ylang-ylang, coffee, copra. Exports: ylang-ylang, vanilla. Imports: building materials, transportation equipment, rice, clothing, flour. Major trading partners: France, Comoros, Reunion, Kenya, South Africa, Pakistan.

The most populous of the Comoro Islands in the Indian Ocean, with a Christian majority, Mayotte voted in 1974 and 1976 against joining the other, predominantly Moslem islands, in declaring themselves independent. It continues to retain its ties to France.

NEW CALEDONIA AND DEPENDENCIES

Status: Overseas Territory
High Commissioner: Didier Cultiaux
Area: 7,374 sq mi. (19,103 sq km)[1]
Population (1997 est.): 191,003 (average annual growth rate: 1.65%); birth rate: 21.43/1000; infant mortality rate: 13.3/1000; density per square mile: 25.9
Capital (1989): Nouméa, 65,110. **Monetary unit:** Pacific financial community franc. **Languages:** French, Melanesian and Polynesian dialects. **Ethnicity/Race:** Melanesian 42.5%, European 37.1%, Wallisian 8.4%, Polynesian 3.8%, Indonesian 3.6%, Vietnamese 1.6%, other 3%. **Religion:** Roman Catholic, 60%; Protestant, 30%. **Literacy rate:** 91%
Economic summary: Gross domestic product: purchasing power parity (1995 est.): $1.5 billion, $8,000 per capita income; real growth rate n.a.; inflation (1990) 1.4%; unemployment (1994) 15%. Principal agricultural products: coffee, copra, beef, wheat, vegetables. Major industrial product: nickel. Natural resources: nickel, chromite, iron ore. Labor force: 70,044: 32% in agriculture; 20% in industry; 40% in

services; 8% in mining. Exports: $477 million (f.o.b., 1992): nickel, chrome. Imports: $926 million (c.i.f., 1992): mineral fuels, machinery, electrical equipment, foodstuffs. Major trading partners: France, Japan, U.S., Australia.

1. Including dependencies.

New Caledonia (6,466 sq mi.; 16,747 sq km), about 1,070 miles (1,722 km) northeast of Sydney, Australia, was explored by Capt. James Cook in 1774 and annexed by France in 1853. The government also administers the Isle of Pines, the Loyalty Islands (Uvéa, Lifu, and Maré), the Belep Islands, the Huon Island group, and Chesterfield Islands.

The native people are Melanesians; about one-third of the population is white and one-fifth Indochinese and Javanese. The French National Assembly on July 31, 1984, voted a bill into law that granted internal autonomy to New Caledonia and opened the way to possible eventual independence. This touched off ethnic tensions and violence between the natives and the European settlers, with the natives demanding full independence and sovereignty while the settlers wanted to remain part of France. In June 1988, France resumed direct administration of the territory and promised a referendum on self-determination in 1998. This was agreed to by organizations representing the natives and the French settlers.

SOUTHERN AND ANTARCTIC LANDS

Status: Overseas Territory
Administrator: Christian Dors
Area: 3,004 sq mi. (7,781 sq km, excluding Adélie Land)
Capital: Port-au-Français

This territory is uninhabited except for the personnel of scientific bases. It consists of Adélie Land (166,752 sq mi.; 431,888 sq km) on the Antarctic mainland and the following islands in the southern Indian Ocean: the Kerguelen and Crozet archipelagos and the islands of Saint-Paul and New Amsterdam.

WALLIS AND FUTUNA ISLANDS

Status: Overseas Territory
Administrator: Léon-Alexandre Legrand
Area: 106 sq mi. (274 sq km)
Population (1997 est.): 14,817; growth rate 1.88%; birth rate 23.7/1000; infant mortality rate 22.26/1000; density per square mile: 139.8
Capital (1983): Mata-Utu. **Lanuages:** French, Wallisian. **Ethnicity/Race:** Polynesian. **Religion:** Roman Catholic. **Literacy rate:** 50%
Economic summary: Gross domestic product: purchasing power parity (1995 est.): $28.7 million, $2,500 per capita. Exports: $370,000 (f.o.b. 1995 est.). Imports: $13.5 million (c.i.f., 1995 est.): foodstuffs, manufactured goods, transport equipment, fuel.

The two islands groups in the South Pacific between Fiji and Samoa were settled by French missionaries at the beginning of the 19th century. A protectorate was established in the 1880s. Following a referendum by the Polynesian inhabitants, the status was changed to that of an Overseas Territory in 1961.

GABON

Gabonese Republic
National name: République Gabonaise
President: Omar Bongo (1967)
Premier: Paulin Obame-Nguema (1994)
Area: 103,346 sq mi. (267,667 sq km)
Population (1997 est.): 1,190,159 (average annual rate of natural increase: 1.47%); birth rate: 28.11/1000; infant mortality rate: 87.8/1000; density per square mile: 11.5
Capital and largest city (1994): Libreville, 419,596. Other cities (1994): Port-Gentil, 80,000; Franceville, 42,000. **Monetary unit:** Franc CFA. **Languages:** French (official). **Ethnicity/Race:** (1993) Bantu tribes, including six major tribal groupings: Fang 25%, Punu 23%, Nzeiby 13%, Mbede (Obamba/Bateke) 9%, Kota 7%, and Myene 5%; Pygmies 0.7%, naturalized population 0.3%, foreigners 15% . **Religions:** Catholic 75%, Protestant 20%, Animist 4%. **Literacy rate:** 61
Economic summary: Gross domestic product: purchasing power parity (1995 est.): $6 billion; $5,200 per capita (1995); real growth rate: 2%; inflation 15%; unemployment 20% (1995). Arable land: more than 65%. Principal agricultural products: cocoa, coffee, wood, palm oil. Labor force: 120,000; 65% in agriculture; 30% in industry and commerce; 2.5% in services; 2.5% in government. Major industrial products: petroleum, natural gas, processed wood, manganese, uranium. Natural resources: wood, petroleum, iron ore, manganese, uranium. Exports: $2.1 billion (f.o.b., 1994 est.): crude oil, manganese, wood, uranium. Imports: $800 million (f.o.b., 1994 est.): foodstuffs, chemical products, petroleum products, construction materials, manufactures, machinery. Major trading partners: France, U.S., Germany, Japan, Cameroon. **Member of French Community**

Geography. This West African country with the Atlantic as its western border is also bounded by Equatorial Guinea, Cameroon, and the Congo. Its area is slightly less than Colorado's.

From mangrove swamps on the coast, the land becomes divided plateaus in the north and east and mountains in the north. Most of the country is covered by a dense tropical forest.

Government. A republic, with a multiparty presidential regime (opposition parties legalized 1990). The President is elected for a five-year term. Legislative powers are exercised by a 120-seat National Assembly, which is elected for a five-year term. After his conversion to Islam in 1973, President Bongo changed his given name, Albert Bernard, to Omar. The Rassemblement Social Démocrate Gabonais is led by President Bongo. He was re-elected without opposition in 1973, 1980, and in 1993.

History. The earliest humans in Gabon were believed to be the Babinga, or Pygmies, dating back to 7,000 B.C.E., who were later followed by Bantu groups from southern and eastern Africa. Now there are many tribal groups in the country, the largest being the Fang people who constitute 25% of the population.

Gabon was first visited by the Portuguese navigator Diego Cam in the 15th century. In 1472 the Portuguese explorers encountered the mouth of the Como river, and because its shape looks like a coat, they named it "Rio de Gabao," river of Gabon, which later became the name of the country. The Dutch began arriving in 1593, and the French in 1630. In 1839, the French founded their first settlement on the left bank of the Gabon Estuary and gradually occupied the hinterland during the second half of the 19th century. It was organized as a French territory in 1888 and became an autonomous republic within the French Union after World War II and an independent republic on Aug. 17, 1960.

Following strikes and riots the President called a national conference in March 1990. In May it adopted a transitional constitution legalizing political parties and calling for free elections.

In its first multiparty election in December 1993 the incumbent President received just over 51% of the vote while the opposition candidate refused to accept defeat charging fraud and tried to establish a rival government.

Rioting in the capital caused the issuance of a state of siege in February 1994. A university strike by students in May caused the government to close the institution for a period. Growing dissension within the army also led the President to call for a peace conference in September. As a result a coalition government was formed in November.

A referendum on a new constitution, supported by all political parties, took place in July 1995 and won approval.

The first round of parliamentary elections in December 1996 produced a big win for the President's party. In the second round the Democratic party again scored heavily, thus obtaining a total of 100 of the 120 seats in the National Assembly.

GAMBIA, THE

Republic of the Gambia
President: Colonel Yahya A. J. J. Jammeh (1997)
Area: 4,093 sq mi. (10,600 sq km)
Population (1997 est.): 1,248,085 (average annual rate of natural increase: 3.05%); birth rate: 43.86/1000; infant mortality rate: 78.8/1000; density per square mile: 304.9
Capital (1986): Banjul, 44,188. **Monetary unit:** Dalasi. **Languages:** Native tongues, English (official). **Ethnicity/Race:** African 99% (Mandinka 42%, Fula 18%, Wolof 16%, Jola 10%, Serahuli 9%, other 4%), non-Gambian 1%. **Religions:** Islam, 90%; Christian, 9%; traditional, 1%. **Literacy rate:** 27%
Economic summary: Gross domestic product: purchasing power parity (1995 est.): $1.1 billion; per capita $1,100; real growth rate 2%; inflation 1.7% (1994). Arable land: 16%. Principal products: peanuts, rice, palm kernels. Labor force: 400,000 (1986 est.); 75.0% in agriculture; 18.9% in industry, commerce and services; 6.1% in government. Major industrial products: processed peanuts, fish, and hides. Natural resources: fish. Exports: $35 million (f.o.b., 1994 est.): peanuts and peanut products, fish, cotton, lint, palm kernels. Imports: $209 million (f.o.b., 1994 est.): foodstuffs, fuel, machinery, transport equipment, manufactures, raw materials. Major trading partners: U.S., E.U., Asia. **Member of Commonwealth of Nations**

Geography. Situated on the Atlantic coast in westernmost Africa and surrounded on three sides by Senegal, Gambia is twice the size of Delaware. The Gambia River flows for 200 miles (322 km) through Gambia on its way to the Atlantic. The country, the smallest on the continent, averages only 20 miles (32 km) in width.

Government. A civilian government, following presidential and legislative elections in September 1996 and January 1997 respectively.

History. During the 17th century, Gambia was settled by various companies of English merchants. Slavery was the chief source of revenue until it was abolished in 1807. Gambia became a Crown colony in 1843 and an independent nation within the Commonwealth of Nations on Feb. 18, 1965.

Full independence was approved in a 1970 referendum, and on April 24 of that year Gambia proclaimed itself a republic.

Elections of April 29, 1992 returned Jawara for a fifth term. His People's Progressive Party won 25 of the 36 seats in the House of Representatives.

A military coup in July 1994 deposed the President, suspended the constitution, and banned political parties.

The promised election was held in September 1996. Incumbent President Jammeh won 55% of the vote against his nearest rival, Ousseynou Darboe, who received 36%. The next month Jammeh was sworn in as president.

GEORGIA

Republic of Georgia
President: Eduard Shevardnadze (1995)
Secretary of State: Niko Lekishvili (1995)
Area: 26,900 sq mi. (169,000 sq km)
Population (1997 est.): 5,174,642; average annual rate of natural increase: 0.16%; birth rate: 13.93/1000; infant mortality rate: 22.4/1000; density per square mile: 192.4
Capital and largest city (1991): Tbilisi, 1,279,000. Other cities (1989): Kutaisi, 235,000; Batumi, 136,000; and Sukhumi, 121,000. **Monetary unit:** coupon (temporary). **Language:** Georgian (official), 71%; Russian, 9%; Armenian, 7%; Azerbaijani, 6%. **Ethnicity/Race:** Georgian 70.1%, Armenian 8.1%, Russian 6.3%, Azeri 5.7%, Ossetian 3%, Abkhaz 1.8%, other 5%. **Religion:** Georgian Orthodox, 65%; Russian Orthodox, 10%; Armenian Orthodox, 8%; Muslim, 11%
Economic summary: Gross domestic product: purchasing power parity (1995 estimate as extrapolated from the World Bank estimate for 1994): $6.2 billion; $1,080 per capita; −11% real growth rate; inflation 2.2% (per month); unemployment 5%. Labor force: 2.763 million: 31% in industry and construction; 25% in agriculture and forestry. Industries: heavy industrial products include raw steel, rolled steel, cement, lumber, machine tools, foundry equipment, electric locomotives, tower cranes, welding equipment, meat packing, dairy and fishing, farm machinery. Agriculture: citrus fruits, grapes, sugar, vegetables, grains, cattle, sheep, goats, pigs, and poultry. Exports: $140 million (c.i.f., 1995): citrus fruits, tea, other agricultural products, diverse types of machinery, ferrous and nonferrous metals, textiles. Imports: $250 million (f.o.b., 1995): machinery and parts, fuel, transport equipment, textiles. Major trading partners: Russia, Turkey, Azerbaijan, Ukraine, Germany, U.S.

Geography. Georgia is a land of snow-capped mountains, turbulent rivers, dense forests, and fertile valleys. Mt. Kazbet, 16,541 ft. (5,042 m) is the country's tallest peak. Georgia's principal rivers, Kura Mtkvari and the Rioni and their tributaries are harnessed to provide an abundance of hydroelectric power for the country. Georgia is bordered by the Black Sea in the west, by Turkey and Armenia in the south, by Azerbaijan in the east, and Russia in the north. The republic also includes the Abkhaz and Adzhar autonomous republics and the Yugo-Ossetian Autonomous Oblast.

Government. A republic with a unicameral Parliament. The President and 246-member Parliament were elected on Nov. 5, 1995.

History. Georgia became a kingdom about 4 B.C.E. and reached its greatest period of expansion in the 12th century when its territory included the whole of Transcaucasia. The country was the scene of a struggle between Persia and Turkey from the 16th century on, and in the 18th century became a vassal to Russia in exchange for protection from the Turks.

Georgia joined Azerbaijan and Armenia in 1917 to establish the anti-Bolshevik Transcaucasian Federation, and upon its dissolution, proclaimed its independence in 1918. In 1922, the Red Army invaded Georgia and replaced the republic with a Soviet government. In 1922, Georgia, Armenia, and Azerbaijan were annexed and formed into the Transcaucasian Soviet Socialist Republic affiliated with the U.S.S.R. In 1936, it became a separate Soviet republic.

Zviad Gamsakhurdia won the first directly elected Soviet presidency in 1990 with 86.5% of the vote, pledging to lead Georgia toward independence. Georgia proclaimed its independence on April 9, 1990.

Gamsakhurdia was later accused of dictatorial policies, the jailing of opposition leaders, human rights abuses, and clamping down on the media. A two week civil war centered in the capital of Tbilisi ensued and Gamsakhurdia was forced to flee to Azerbaijan and later to Armenia. A ruling military council was established by the opposition until a civilian authority can be restored.

During 1993 the government continued to fight separatists in Abkhazia.

In February 1994 Russia and Georgia signed a cooperation treaty that authorized Russia to keep three military bases in Georgia and allow Russians to train and equip the Georgian army.

Parliament ratified the cooperation treaty with Russia in January 1996. In May Georgia and its breakaway region of South Ossetia agreed to a cessation of hostilities in their 6-year conflict.

With little progress in resolving the Abkhazia situation, Parliament in April 1997 voted overwhelmingly to threaten Russia with loss of its military bases should it fail to extend Russian military control of the separatist region.

GERMANY

Federal Republic of Germany
National name: Bundesrepublik Deutschland
President: Roman Herzog (1994)
Chancellor: Helmut Kohl (1982)
Area: 137,826 sq mi. (356,970 sq km): Western Germany: 96,095 sq mi, the size of Wyoming; Eastern Germany: 41,731 sq mi, the size of Virginia
Population (1997 est.): 84,068,216 (average annual growth rate: 2%); birth rate: 9.46/1000; infant mortality rate: 5.9/1000; density per square mile: 609.9
Capital and largest city (1997): Berlin (capital since Oct. 3, 1990), 3,477,900; Bonn (seat of government), 295,300. **Largest cities (1997):** Hamburg, 1,703,800; Munich, 1,251,100; Cologne, 963,300; Frankfurt, 656,200; Essen, 619,600; Dortmund, 601,500; Stuttgart, 592,000; Duesseldorf, 573,100; Bremen, 551,000; Hanover, 526,400; Duisburg, 536,500. **Monetary unit:** Deutsche Mark. **Language:** German.
Ethnicity/Race: German 95.1%, Turkish 2.3%, Italians 0.7%, Greeks 0.4%, Poles 0.4%, other 1.1% (made up largely of people fleeing the war in the former Yugoslavia). **Religions (1993):** Protestant, 35%; Roman Catholic, 34%; other or none, 31%. **Literacy rate:** 98%
Economic summary (1996): Gross domestic product: purchasing power parity: $5,308.05 billion; per capita $21,773; **Western Germany:** $2,005 billion; per capita: $31,066; **Eastern Germany:** $250 billion; per capita: $16,200; **real growth rate:** 1.4%; **West** 1.3%; **East** 2%; inflation (1994): 1.7%; **unemployment (1996):** West 9%, East 15.7%. Labor force: 34.5 million, 37% in industry, agriculture 6%. Exports: $461.35 billion (1996): manufactures 86.6% (including machines and precision tools, chemicals, motor vehicles, iron and steel products), agricultural products 4.9%, raw materials 2.3%, fuels 1.3%. Imports: $403.94 billion (1996): manufactures 68.5%, agricultural products 12%, fuels 9.7%, raw materials 1.3%.
Industries: West: among the world's largest producers of iron, steel, coal, cement, chemicals, machinery, vehicles, machine tools, electronics, food and beverages. **East:** metal fabrication, chemicals, brown coal, shipbuilding, machine building, food and beverages, textiles, petroleum refining. **West:** fishing and forestry, diversified crop and livestock farming; principal crops include potatoes, wheat, rye, barley, sugar beets, fruit, cabbage, cattle, pigs, poultry. **East:** fishing and forestry, principal crops include wheat, rye, barley, potatoes, sugar beets, fruit, pork, beef, chicken, milk, hides and skins. Natural resources: iron ore, coal, potash, timber, lignite, uranium, copper, natural gas, salt, nickel. Major trading partners: France, Netherlands, Italy, Belgium-Luxembourg, U.S., U.K.

Geography. Located in central Europe, Germany's neighbors are Denmark to the north; Netherlands, Belgium, Luxembourg, France to the west; Switzerland, Austria to the south; and Czech republic, Poland to the east.

The Federal Republic of Germany was occupied by the United States, Britain, and France after World War II, when the eastern half of prewar Germany was split roughly between a Soviet-occupied zone, which became the German Democratic Republic, and an area annexed by Poland. After being divided for more than four decades, the two Germanys were reunited on Oct. 3, 1990. The united Federal Republic is about the size of Montana.

The northern plain, the central hill country, and the southern mountain district constitute the main physical divisions of West Germany, which is slightly smaller than Oregon. The Bavarian plateau in the southwest averages 1,600 feet (488 m) above sea level, but it reaches 9,721 feet (2,962 m) in the Zugspitze Mountains, the highest point in the country.

Important navigable rivers are the Danube, rising in the Black Forest and flowing east across Bavaria into Austria, and the Rhine, which rises in Switzerland and flows across the Netherlands in two channels to the North Sea and is navigable by ocean-going and coastal vessels as far as Cologne. The Elbe, which also empties into the North Sea, is navigable within Germany for smaller vessels. The Weser, flowing into the North Sea, and the Main and Mosel (Moselle), both tributaries of the Rhine, are also important. In addition, the Oder and Neisse Rivers form the border with Poland. The rivers Danube and Rhine in the Black Sea and the North Sea were connected in 1992, with the completion of the Rhine Main-Danube canal.

Government. Under the constitution of May 23, 1949, the Federal Republic was established as a parliamentary democracy. The Parliament consists of the Bundesrat, an upper chamber representing and appointed by the Länder, or states, and the Bundestag, a lower house elected for four years by universal suffrage. A federal assembly composed of Bundestag deputies as well as deputies from the state parliaments elects the President of the Republic for a five-year term; the Bundestag alone chooses the Chancellor, or Prime Minister. Each of the 16 Länder have a legislature popularly elected for a four-year or five-year term.

The major political parties are the Christian Democratic Union-Christian Social Union, with 244 seats (CDU) and 50 seats (CSU), led by Chancellor Helmut Kohl; the Social Democratic Party (SPD) with 252 seats, led by Rudolf Scharping; the Free Democratic Party (FDP) with 47 seats, led by Klaus Kinkel; the Alliance '90/Greens with 49 seats, led by Krista Sager and Jurgen Trittin; the Party of Democratic Socialism (PDS) with 30 seats, led by Lothar Bisky. Kohl's government is a coalition with the Free Democrats.

History. Immediately before the Christian era, when the Roman Empire had pushed its frontier to the Rhine, what is now Germany was inhabited by several tribes believed to have migrated from Central Asia between

Rulers of Germany and Prussia

Name	Born	Ruled[1]	Name	Born	Ruled[1]
Kings of Prussia			**German Federal Republic (West) (Chancellors)**		
Frederick I[2]	1657	1701–1713	Konrad Adenauer	1876	1949–1963
Frederick William I	1688	1713–1740	Ludwig Erhard	1897	1963–1966
Frederick II the Great	1712	1740–1786	Kurt Georg Kiesinger	1904	1966–1969
Frederick William II	1744	1786–1797	Willy Brandt	1913	1969–1974
Frederick William III	1770	1797–1840	Helmut Schmidt	1918	1974–1984
Frederick William IV	1795	1840–1861	Helmut Kohl	1930	1984–1990
William I	1797	1861–1871[3]	**German Democratic Republic (East)**		
Emperors Of Germany			Wilhelm Pieck[5]	1876	1949–1960
William I	1797	1871–1888	Walter Ulbricht[8]	1893	1960–1973
Frederick III	1831	1888–1888	Willi Stoph[9]	1914	1973–1976
William II	1859	1888–1918[4]	Erich Honecker[9]	1912	1976–1989
Weimar Republic			Egon Krenz[9]	1937	1989–1989
Friedrich Ebert[5]	1871	1919–1925	Manfred Gerlach[9]		1989–1990
Paul von Hindenburg[5]	1847	1925–1934	Sabine Bergman-Pohl[9]		1990–1990
Third Reich			**German Federal Republic Chancellors**		
Adolf Hitler[6, 7]	1889	1934–1945	Helmut Kohl	1930	1991–
Karl Doenitz[6]	1891	1945–1945			

1. Year of end of rule is also that of death, unless otherwise indicated. 2. Was Elector of Brandenburg (1688–1701) as Frederick III. 3. Became Emperor of Germany in 1871. 4. Died 1941. 5. President. 6. Führer. 7. Named Chancellor by President von Hindenburg in 1933. 8. Chairman of Council of State. Died 1973. 9. Chairman of Council of State.

the 6th and 4th centuries B.C.E. One of those tribes, the Franks, attained supremacy in western Europe under Charlemagne, who was Crowned Holy Roman Emperor C.E. 800. By the Treaty of Verdun (843), Charlemagne's lands east of the Rhine were ceded to the German Prince Louis. Additional territory acquired by the Treaty of Mersen (870) gave Germany approximately the area it maintained throughout the Middle Ages. For several centuries after Otto the Great was Crowned King in 936, the German rulers were also usually heads of the Holy Roman Empire.

Relations between state and church were changed by the Reformation, which began with Martin Luther's 95 theses, and came to a head in 1547, when Charles V scattered the forces of the Protestant League at Mühlberg. Freedom of worship was guaranteed by the Peace of Augsburg (1555), but a Counter Reformation took place later, and a dispute over the succession to the Bohemian throne brought on the Thirty Years' War (1618–48), which devastated Germany and left the empire divided into hundreds of small principalities virtually independent of the Emperor.

Meanwhile, Prussia was developing into a state of considerable strength. Frederick the Great (1740–86) reorganized the Prussian army and defeated Maria Theresa of Austria in a struggle over Silesia. After the defeat of Napoleon at Waterloo (1815), the struggle between Austria and Prussia for supremacy in Germany continued, reaching its climax in the defeat of Austria in the Seven Weeks' War (1866) and the formation of the Prussian-dominated North German Confederation (1867).

The architect of German unity was Otto von Bismarck, a conservative, monarchist, and militaristic Prussian Junker who had no use for "empty phrase-making and constitutions." From 1862 until his retirement in 1890 he dominated not only the German but also the entire European scene. He unified all Germany in a series of three wars against Denmark (1864), Austria (1866), and France (1870–71), which many historians believe were instigated and promoted by Bismarck in his zeal to build a nation through "blood and iron."

On Jan. 18, 1871, King Wilhelm I of Prussia was proclaimed German Emperor in the Hall of Mirrors at Versailles. The North German Confederation, created in 1867, was abolished, and the Second German Reich, consisting of the North and South German states, was born. With a powerful army, an efficient bureaucracy,

and a loyal bourgeoisie, Chancellor Bismarck consolidated a powerful centralized state.

Wilhelm II dismissed Bismarck in 1890 and embarked upon a "New Course," stressing an intensified colonialism and a powerful navy. His chaotic foreign policy culminated in the diplomatic isolation of Germany and the disastrous defeat in World War I (1914–18).

The Second German Empire collapsed following the defeat of the German armies in 1918, the naval mutiny at Kiel, and the flight of the Kaiser to the Netherlands on November 10. The Social Democrats, led by Friedrich Ebert and Philipp Scheidemann, crushed the Communists and established a moderate republic with Ebert as President.

The Weimar constitution of 1919 provided for a President to be elected for seven years by universal suffrage and a bicameral legislature, consisting of the Reichsrat, representing the states, and the Reichstag, representing the people. It contained a model Bill of Rights. It was weakened, however, by a provision that enabled the President to rule by decree.

President Ebert died Feb. 28, 1925, and on April 26, Field Marshal Paul von Hindenburg was elected President.

The mass of Germans regarded the Weimar Republic as a child of defeat, imposed upon a Germany whose legitimate aspirations to world leadership had been thwarted by a world conspiracy. Added to this were a crippling currency debacle, a tremendous burden of reparations, and acute economic distress.

Adolf Hitler, an Austrian war veteran and a fanatical nationalist, fanned discontent by promising a Greater Germany, abrogation of the Treaty of Versailles, restoration of Germany's lost colonies, and destruction of the Jews. When the Social Democrats and the Communists refused to combine against the Nazi threat, President von Hindenburg made Hitler chancellor on Jan. 30, 1933.

With the death of von Hindenburg on Aug. 2, 1934, Hitler repudiated the Treaty of Versailles and began full-scale rearmament. In 1935 he withdrew Germany from the League of Nations, and the next year he reoccupied the Rhineland and signed the anti-Comintern pact with Japan, at the same time strengthening relations with Italy. Austria was annexed in March 1938. By the Munich agreement in September 1938 he gained the Czech Sudetenland, and in violation of this agreement

The Berlin Wall (1961–1990)

Major anti-Communist riots broke out in East Berlin in June 1953 and, on Aug. 13, 1961, the Soviet Sector was sealed off by a Communist-built wall, 26½ miles (43 km) long, running through the city. It was built to stem the flood of refugees seeking freedom in the West, 200,000 having fled in 1961 before the wall was erected.

On Nov. 9, 1989, several weeks after the resignation of East Germany's long-time Communist leader, Erich Honecker, the wall's designer and chief proponent, the East German government opened its borders to the West and allowed thousands of its citizens to pass freely through the Berlin Wall. They were cheered and greeted by thousands of West Berliners, and many of the jubilant newcomers celebrated their new freedom by climbing on top of the hated wall.

The following day, East German troops began dismantling parts of the wall. It was ironic that this wall was built to keep the citizens from leaving and, 28 years later, it was being dismantled for the same reason.

On Nov. 22, new passages were opened at the north and south of the Brandenburg Gate in an emotional ceremony attended by Chancellor Helmut Kohl of West Germany and Chancellor Hans Modrow of East Germany. The opening of the Brandenburg Gate climaxed the ending of the barriers that had divided the German people since the end of World War II. By the end of 1990, the entire wall had been removed.

---

he completed the dismemberment of Czechoslovakia in March 1939. His invasion of Poland on Sept. 1, 1939, precipitated World War II.

Hitler established the death camps to carry out "the final solution to the Jewish question." By the end of the war, Hitler's holocaust had killed 6 million Jews, as well as Gypsies, homosexuals, the handicapped, and others not fitting the Aryan ideal.

On May 8, 1945, Germany surrendered unconditionally to Allied and Soviet military commanders, and on June 5 the four-nation Allied Control Council became the *de facto* government of Germany.

(For details of World War II and the Holocaust, *see* Headline History, World War II.)

At the Berlin (or Potsdam) Conference (July 17–Aug. 2, 1945) President Truman, Premier Stalin, and Prime Minister Clement Attlee of Britain set forth the guiding principles of the Allied Control Council. They were Germany's complete disarmament and demilitarization, destruction of its war potential, rigid control of industry, and decentralization of the political and economic structure. Pending final determination of territorial questions at a peace conference, the three victors agreed in principle to the ultimate transfer of the city of Königsberg (now Kaliningrad) and its adjacent area to the U.S.S.R. and to the administration by Poland of former German territories lying generally east of the Oder-Neisse Line.

For purposes of control Germany was divided in 1945 into four national occupation zones, each headed by a Military Governor.

The Western powers were unable to agree with the U.S.S.R. on any fundamental issue. Work of the Allied Control Council was hamstrung by repeated Soviet vetoes; and finally, on March 20, 1948, Russia walked out of the Council. Meanwhile, the U.S. and Britain had taken steps to merge their zones economically (Bizone); and on May 31, 1948, the U.S., Britain, France, and the Benelux countries agreed to set up a German state comprising the three Western Zones.

The U.S.S.R. reacted by clamping a blockade on all ground communications between the Western Zones and Berlin, an enclave in the Soviet Zone. The Western Allies countered by organizing a gigantic airlift to fly supplies into the beleaguered city, assigning 60,000 men to it. The U.S.S.R. was finally forced to lift the blockade on May 12, 1949.

The Federal Republic of Germany was proclaimed on May 23, 1949, with its capital at Bonn. In free elections, West German voters gave a majority in the Constituent Assembly to the Christian Democrats, with the Social Democrats largely making up the opposition. Konrad Adenauer became chancellor, and Theodor Heuss of the Free Democrats was elected first president.

When the Federal Republic of Germany was established in West Germany, the East German states adopted a more centralized constitution for the Democratic Republic of Germany, and it was put into effect on Oct. 7, 1949. The U.S.S.R. thereupon dissolved its occupation zone but Soviet troops remained. The Western Allies declared that the East German Republic was a Soviet creation undertaken without self-determination and refused to recognize it. It was recognized only within the Soviet bloc.

The area that was occupied by East Germany, as well as adjacent areas in Eastern Europe, consists of Mecklenburg, Brandenburg, Lusatia, Saxony, and Thuringia. Soviet armies conquered the five territories by 1945. In the division of 1945 they were allotted to the U.S.S.R. Soviet forces, creating a State controlled by the secret police with a single party, the Socialist Unity (Communist) Party. The Russians appropriated East German plants to restore their war-ravaged industry.

The 25-year diplomatic hiatus between East Germany and the U.S. ended Sept. 4, 1974, with the establishment of formal relations.

Agreements in Paris in 1954 giving the Federal Republic full independence and complete sovereignty came into force on May 5, 1955. Under it, West Germany and Italy became members of the Brussels treaty organization created in 1948 and renamed the Western European Union. West Germany also became a member of NATO. In 1955 the U.S.S.R. recognized the Federal Republic. The Saar territory, under an agreement between France and West Germany, held a plebiscite and despite economic links to France, voted to rejoin West Germany. It became a state of West Germany on Jan. 1, 1957.

In 1963, Chancellor Adenauer concluded a treaty of mutual cooperation and friendship with France and then retired. He was succeeded by his chief inner-party critic, Ludwig Erhard, who was followed in 1966 by Kurt Georg Kiesinger. He, in turn, was succeeded in 1969 by Willy Brandt, former mayor of West Berlin.

The division between West Germany and East Germany was intensified when the Communists erected the Berlin Wall in 1961. In 1968, the East German Communist leader, Walter Ulbricht, imposed restrictions on West German movements into West Berlin. The Soviet-bloc invasion of Czechoslovakia in August 1968 added to the tension.

West Germany in 1970 signed a treaty with Poland, renouncing force and setting Poland's western border as the Oder-Neisse Line. It subsequently resumed formal relations with Czechoslovakia in a pact that "voided" the Munich treaty that gave Nazi Germany the Sudetenland.

By 1973, normal relations were established between

East and West Germany and the two states entered the United Nations.

Brandt, winner of a Nobel Peace Prize for his foreign policies, was forced to resign in 1974 when an East German spy was discovered to be one of his top staff members. Succeeding him was a moderate Social Democrat, Helmut Schmidt.

Helmut Schmidt, Brandt's successor as chancellor, staunchly backed U.S. military strategy in Europe nevertheless, staking his political fate on the strategy of placing U.S. nuclear missiles in Germany unless the Soviet Union reduced its arsenal of intermediate missiles.

The chancellor also strongly opposed nuclear freeze proposals and won 2–1 support for his stand at the convention of Social Democrats in April. The Free Democrats then deserted the Socialists after losing ground in local elections and joined with the Christian Democrats to unseat Schmidt and install Helmut Kohl as chancellor in 1982. An economic upswing in 1986 led to Kohl's re-election.

The fall of the Communist government in East Germany left only Soviet objections to German reunification to be dealt with. This was resolved in July 1990. Soviet objections to a reunified Germany belonging to NATO were dropped in return for German promises to reduce their military and engage in wide-ranging economic cooperation with the Soviet Union.

In ceremonies beginning the evening of Tuesday, Oct. 2, 1990, and continuing throughout the next day, the German Democratic Republic acceded to the Federal Republic and Germany became a united and sovereign state for the first time since 1945. Some one million people gathered at midnight Oct. 2 at the Reichstag in Berlin. At midnight, a replica of the Liberty Bell, a gift from the United States, rang, and unity was officially proclaimed.

Following unification, the Federal Republic became the second largest country in Europe, after the Soviet Union. A reunited Berlin serves as the official capital, although the government will initially remain in Bonn.

During the national election campaign of late 1990 the central issue remained the cost of unification, including the modernization of the former East German economy.

In the December 2 election the Christian Democrats emerged as the strongest group, taking 43.8% of the vote. Analysts generally considered the vote to be an expression of thanks and support to the Chancellor for his forceful drive for political unity. The Party of Democratic Socialism, formerly the Communist Party, won 17 seats in Parliament.

The new Parliament convened in January 1991 re-electing Helmut Kohl chancellor. Nevertheless it soon became clear that previous official estimates of the cost and time required to absorb eastern Germany were considerably understated.

On June 20, 1991 the German Parliament officially voted in favor of moving the seat of the federal government to Berlin, although given the huge expense of such a move it would be done slowly and require 12 years before Berlin would be a fully functional federal capital.

Germany ratified the Maastricht Treaty in October 1993, being the last of the 12 E.U. members to do so.

The federal constitutional court in July 1994 ruled in favor of the use of German military forces outside the country if parliamentary approval is received first.

General elections in October 1994 gave the ruling coalition a majority in the Bundestag. In November Kohl received formal re-election in that body.

Voters in the relatively new state of Brandenburg in the east rejected in May 1996 a proposal to merge with Berlin, dramatizing a lingering psychological division between eastern and western Germany.

Owing to a budget deficit that threatened the country's eligibility for introducing the future common European currency, the government in June 1997 proposed to revalue its foreign exchange holdings. The plan met with sneers both domestically and in international circles as a bookkeeping trick.

GHANA

Republic of Ghana
President: Jerry John Rawlings
Area: 92,100 sq mi. (238,537 sq km)
Population (1997 est.): 18,100,703 (average annual rate of natural increase: 2.29%; birth rate: 33.88/1000; infant mortality rate: 78.9/1000; density per square mile: 196.5
Capital: Accra. **Largest cities (est. 1988):** Accra, 949,100; Kumasi, 385,200; Tamale, 151,100. **Monetary unit:** Cedi. **Languages:** English (official), Native tongues (Brong Ahafo, Twi, Fanti, Ga, Ewe, Dagbani). **Ethnicity/Race:** black African 99.8% (major tribes: Akan 44%, Moshi-Dagomba 16%, Ewe 13%, Ga 8%), European and other 0.2%. **Religions:** indigenous belief, 38%; Islam, 30%; Christian, 24%. **Literacy rate:** 60%
Economic summary: Gross domestic product: purchasing power parity (1995 est.): $25.1 billion; per capita $1,400; real growth rate 5%; inflation 69%; unemployment (1993 est.) 10%. Arable land: 5%. Principal products: cocoa, coconuts, coffee, cassava, yams, rice, rubber. Labor force (1983): 3,700,000; 54.7% in agriculture and fishing; 18.7% in industry. Major products: mining products, cocoa products, aluminum. Natural resources: gold, industrial diamonds, bauxite, manganese, timber, fish. Exports: $1 billion (f.o.b., 1993 est.): cocoa beans and products, gold, timber, tuna, bauxite, and aluminum. Imports: $1.7 billion (f.o.b., 1993 est.): petroleum, consumer goods, foods, intermediate goods, capital equipment. Major trading partners: U.K., U.S., Germany, France, Japan, South Korea. **Member of Commonwealth of Nations**

Geography. A West African country bordering on the Gulf of Guinea, Ghana is bounded by Côte d'Ivoire to the west, Burkina Faso to the north, Togo to the east and the Atlantic Ocean to the south. It compares in size to Oregon.

The coastal belt, extending about 270 miles (435 km), is sandy, marshy, and generally exposed. Behind it is a gradually widening grass strip. The forested plateau region to the north is broken by ridges and hills. The largest river is the Volta.

Government. A republic. presidential and parliamentary elections were held Nov. 3, 1992 and ushered in the Fourth Republic on Jan. 7, 1993.

History. Created as an independent country on March 6, 1957, Ghana is the former British colony of the Gold Coast. The area was first seen by Portuguese traders in 1470. They were followed by the English (1553), the Dutch (1595), and the Swedes (1640). British rule over the Gold Coast began in 1820, but it was not until after quelling the severe resistance of the Ashanti in 1901 that it was firmly established. British Togoland, formerly a colony of Germany, was incorporated into Ghana by referendum in 1956. As the result of a plebiscite, Ghana became a republic on July 1, 1960.

Premier Kwame Nkrumah attempted to take leadership of the Pan-African Movement, holding the All-African People's Congress in his capital, Accra, in 1958 and organizing the Union of African States with Guinea and Mali in 1961. But he oriented his country toward the Soviet Union and China and built an autocratic rule over all aspects of Ghanaian life.

In February 1966, while Nkrumah was visiting Beijing and Hanoi, he was deposed by a military coup led by Gen. Emmanuel K. Kotoka.

A series of military coups followed and on June 4, 1979, Flight Lieutenant Jerry Rawlings overthrew Lt. Gen. Frederick Akuffo's military rule. Rawlings permitted the election of a civilian president to go ahead as scheduled the following month, and Hilla Limann, candidate of the People's National Party, took office. Charging the civilian government with corruption and repression, Rawlings staged another coup on Dec. 31, 1981. As chairman of the Provisional National Defense Council, Rawlings instituted an austerity program and reduced budget deficits.

In a referendum of May 1992, over 92% of the voters approved a new constitution, which provided for a multiparty system.

In the elections of late 1992 Rawlings won a majority of the votes for president.

Despite consistent economic growth, almost daily demonstrations occurred largely in protest against the introduction of a 17.5% value-added tax in March 1995. In June it was removed, and the finance minister resigned in July.

Elections in December 1996 saw the re-election of Rawlings as president with 57% of the vote. His party also secured 133 of the 200 seats in Parliament. The opposition New Patriotic Party won 60 seats.

GREECE

Hellenic Republic
National name: Elliniki Dimokratia
President: Costis Stephanopoulos (1995)
Prime Minister: Costas Simitis (1996)
Area: 50,961 sq mi. (131,990 sq km)
Population (1997 est.): 10,583,126 (average annual rate of natural increase: 0.02%); birth rate: 9.74/1000; infant mortality rate: 7.2/1000; density per square mile: 207.7
Capital: Athens. **Largest cities (1991 est.):** Athens, 3,000,000; Salonika, 720,000; Piraeus, 170,000; Patras, 155,000; Heraklion, 117,000; Larissa, 113,500.
Monetary unit: Drachma. **Language:** Greek.
Ethnicity/Race: Greek 98%, other 2% note: the Greek Government states there are no other divisions in Greece. **Religion:** Greek Orthodox, 98%; Muslim, 1.3%. **Literacy rate:** 93%
Economic summary: Gross domestic product: purchasing power parity (1996 est.): $122.8 billion; $11,668 per capita; 2.6% real growth rate; inflation 6.6%; unemployment 9.8%. Arable land: 23%. Principal agricultural products: grains, fruits, vegetables, olives, olive oil, tobacco, cotton, livestock, dairy products. Labor force (1994): 4.077 million; 54% services, 21% agriculture, 25% industry. Major industrial products: textiles, chemicals, food processing. Natural resources: bauxite, lignite, magnesite, crude oil, marble. Exports: $5.8 billion (1995): manufactured goods, food and live animals, fuels and lubricants, raw materials. Imports: $23 billion (1995): machinery and automotive equipment, petroleum, consumer goods, chemicals, foodstuffs. Major trading partners: Germany, Italy, France, U.S., U.K., Netherlands.

Geography. Greece, on the Mediterranean Sea, is the southernmost country on the Balkan Peninsula in southern Europe. It is bordered on the north by Albania, Yugoslavia, and Bulgaria; on the west by the Ionian Sea; and on the east by the Aegean Sea and Turkey. It is slightly smaller than Alabama.

North central Greece, Epirus, and western Macedonia all are mountainous. The main chain of the Pindus Mountains rises to 10,256 feet (3,126 m) in places, separating Epirus from the plains of Thessaly. Mt. Olympus, rising to 9,570 feet (2,909 m) in the north near the Aegean Sea, is the highest point in the country. Greek Thrace is mostly a lowland region separated from European Turkey by the lower Evros River.

Among the many islands are the Ionian group off the west coast; the Cyclades group to the southeast; other islands in the eastern Aegean, including the Dodecanese Islands, Euboea, Lesbos, Samos, and Chios; and Crete, the fourth largest Mediterranean island.

Government. A referendum in December 1974, five months after the collapse of a military dictatorship, ended the Greek monarchy and established a republic. Ceremonial executive power is held by the President; the Prime Minister heads the government and is responsible to a 300-member unicameral Parliament.

History. Greece, with a recorded history going back to 766 B.C.E., reached the peak of its glory in the 5th century B.C.E., and by the middle of the 2nd century B.C.E. it had declined to the status of a Roman province. It remained within the Eastern Roman Empire until Constantinople fell to the Crusaders in 1204.

In 1453, the Turks took Constantinople, and by 1460 Greece was a Turkish province. The insurrection made famous by the poet Lord Byron broke out in 1821, and in 1827 Greece won independence with sovereignty guaranteed by Britain, France, and Russia.

The protecting powers chose Prince Otto of Bavaria as the first King of modern Greece in 1832 to reign over an area only slightly larger than the Peloponnese Peninsula. Chiefly under the next King, George I, chosen by the protecting powers in 1863, Greece acquired much of its present territory. During his 57-year reign, a period in which he encouraged parliamentary democracy, Thessaly, Epirus, Macedonia, Crete, and most of the Aegean islands were added from the disintegrating Turkish empire. An unsuccessful war against Turkey after World War I brought down the monarchy, to be replaced by a republic in 1923.

Two military dictatorships and a financial crisis brought George II back from exile, but only until 1941, when Italian and German invaders defeated tough Greek resistance. After British and Greek troops liberated the country in October 1944, Communist guerrillas staged a long campaign in which the government received U.S. aid under the Truman Doctrine, the predecessor of the Marshall Plan.

A military junta seized power in April 1967, sending young King Constantine II into exile December 14. Col. George Papadopoulos, as Prime Minister, converted the government to republican form in 1973 and as president, ended martial law. He was moving to restore democracy when he was ousted in November of that year by his military colleagues. The regime of the "colonels," which had tortured its opponents and scoffed at human rights, resigned July 23, 1974, after having bungled an attempt to seize Cyprus.

Former Premier Karamanlis returned from exile to become Premier of Greece's first civilian government since 1967.

On Jan. 1, 1981, Greece became the 10th member of the European Union.

Double-digit inflation and scandals in the Socialist government led to them losing their majority in the elections of June 1989. Elections in April 1990 finally gave the conservative New Democracy Party a one-seat majority in Parliament. Soon afterwards Karamanlis, the founder of that party, was elected president by Parliament.

An election in October 1993 saw the return to power of Mr. Papandreou, who two years earlier had been acquitted of criminal charges.

A January 1996 vote among socialist lawmakers to replace Papandreou as Prime Minister gave a victory to his rival Costas Simitis. Later that month tensions rose with Turkey over a disputed unpopulated 10-acre island.

In September 1996 parliamentary elections the Prime Minister's Socialist Party captured 162 seats and the conservatives 108 seats. A cabinet reshuffle followed later that month.

None of the four main parties won a clear victory in the election of March 1990. Negotiations led to the National Democratic Congress forming a government with the support of several members from other parties.

Parliamentary elections in June 1995 gave the opposition New National Party a majority of seats and allowed its leader to form a new government.

The Prime Minister flew to Cuba in April 1997 to meet with Castro on a trip characterized by the former as an attempt to bridge the gap. Opposition politicians in Grenada denounced the journey.

GRENADA

State of Grenada
Sovereign: Queen Elizabeth II (1952)
Governor General: Sir Daniel Williams (1996)
Prime Minister: Hon. Dr. Keith C. Mitchell (June 1995)
Area: 133 sq mi. (344 sq km)
Population (1997 est.): 95,537 (average annual growth rate 2.3%); birth rate: 28.61/1000; infant mortality rate: 11.6/1000; density per square mile: 718.3
Capital and largest city (1991): St. George's, 4,439.
Monetary unit: East Caribbean dollar. **Ethnic groups (1991):** Black African descent 85%, mixed 11%, white, other 0.3%. **Language:** English. **Ethnicity/Race:** black African. **Religions:** Roman Catholic, 64%; Anglican, 21%. **Literacy rate:** 98%
Economic summary: Gross domestic product: purchasing power parity (1995): $284 million; $3,000 per capita; 3% real growth rate; inflation rate 3%; unemployment rate 14% (1995 est.). Labor force: 36,000; 31% in services; 24% in agriculture; 8% in construction; 5% in manufacturing. Arable land: 15%. Principal products: spices, cocoa, bananas. Tourism is the leading foreign exchange earner followed by agricultural exports. Exports: $24.2 million (f.o.b., 1995 est.): nutmeg, cocoa beans, bananas, mace, textiles. Imports: $162.2 million (f.o.b., 1995 est.): foodstuffs, machinery, manufactured goods, petroleum, chemicals, fuel. Major trading partners: U.K., Trinidad and Tobago, U.S., Japan, Canada. **Member of Commonwealth of Nations**

Geography. Grenada (the first "a" is pronounced as in "gray") is the most southerly of the Windward Islands, about 100 miles (161 km) from the South American coast. It is a volcanic island traversed by a mountain range, the highest peak of which is Mount St. Catherine (2,756 ft.; 840 m).

Government. A Governor-General represents the sovereign, Elizabeth II. The Prime Minister is the head of government, chosen by a 15-member House of Representatives elected by universal suffrage every five years.

History. Grenada was visited by Columbus in 1498. After more than 200 years of British rule, most recently as part of the West Indies Associated States, it became independent Feb. 7, 1974, with Eric M. Gairy as Prime Minister.

Prime Minister Maurice Bishop, a protégé of Cuba's President Castro, was killed in a military coup on Oct. 19, 1983. At the request of five members of the Organization of Eastern Caribbean States, President Reagan ordered an invasion of Grenada on Oct. 25 involving over 1,900 U.S. troops and a small military force from Barbados, Dominica, Jamaica, St. Lucia, and St. Vincent. The troops met strong resistance from Cuban military personnel on the island.

A centrist coalition led by Herbert A. Blaize, a 66-year-old lawyer, won 14 of the 15 seats in Parliament in an election in December 1984.

GUATEMALA

Republic of Guatemala
National name: República de Guatemala
President: Alvaro Arzú Irigoyen (1996)
Area: 42,042 sq mi. (108,889 sq km)
Population (1997 est.): 11,558,407 (average annual rate of natural increase: 2.62%); birth rate: 33.27/1000; infant mortality rate: 49.2/1000; density per square mile: 247.9
Capital and largest city (1994 est.): Guatemala City, 1,150,452. **Other large cities (1994 est.):** Mixco, 413,002; Villa Nueva, 154,508. **Monetary unit:** Quetzal. **Languages:** Spanish, Indian languages. **Ethnicity/Race:** Mestizo—mixed Amerindian-Spanish ancestry (in local Spanish called Ladino) 56%, Amerindian or predominantly Amerindian 44%. **Religion:** Roman Catholic, Protestant, Mayan. **Literacy rate:** 55%
Economic summary: Gross domestic product: purchasing power parity (1995 est.): $36.7 billion; per capita $3,300; real growth rate 4.9%; inflation 9%; unemployment 4.9%. Arable land: 12%. Principal products: corn, beans, coffee, cotton, cattle, sugar, bananas, fruits and vegetables. Labor force: 3.2 million (1994 est.); 60% in agriculture; 13% in services; 12% in manufacturing; 7% in commerce; 4% in construction. Principal products: sugar, textiles and clothing, furniture, chemicals, petroleum, metals, rubber. Natural resources: nickel, crude oil, rare woods, fish, chicle. Exports: $2.3 billion (f.o.b., 1995 est.): coffee, sugar, bananas, beef. Imports: $2.85 billion (c.i.f., 1995 est.): fuel and petroleum products, machinery, grain, fertilizers, motor vehicles. Major trading partners: U.S., Central-American nations, Caribbean, Mexico, Germany.

Geography. The northernmost of the Central American nations, Guatemala is the size of Tennessee. Its neighbors are Mexico on the north and west, and Belize, Honduras, and El Salvador on the east. The country consists of three main regions—the cool highlands with the heaviest population, the tropical area along the Pacific and Caribbean coasts, and the tropical jungle in the northern lowlands. The principal mountain range rises to the highest elevation in Central America and contains many volcanic peaks. Volcanic eruptions are frequent.

The Petén region in the north contains important resources and archaeological sites of the Mayan civilization.

Government. A republic with a unicameral legislative branch, the Congress of the Republic.

History. Once the site of the ancient Mayan civilization, Guatemala, conquered by Spain in 1524, set itself up as a republic in 1839. From 1898 to 1920, the dictator Manuel Estrada Cabrera ran the country, and from 1931 to 1944, Gen. Jorge Ubico Castaneda was the strongman.

Jacobo Arbenz Guzmán won the 1950 election. He expropriated the large estates, including plantations of the United Fruit Company. With covert U.S. backing, a revolt was led by Col. Carlos Castillo Armas, and Arbenz took refuge in Mexico. Castillo Armas became president but was assassinated in 1957. Gen. Miguel Ydigoras Fuentes was elected president in 1957.

A wave of terrorism, by left and right, began in 1967. Fear of anarchy led to the election in 1970 of Army Chief of Staff Carlos Araña Osorio. Araña, surprisingly, pledged social reforms when he took office. Another military candidate, Gen. Kjell Laugerud, won the presidency in 1974 amid renewed political violence.

The administration of Gen. Romeo Lucas Garcia, elected president in 1978, ended in a coup by a three-man military junta on March 23, 1982. Lucas Garcia was charged by Amnesty International with responsibility for at least 5,000 political murders in a reign of brutality and corruption that brought a cutoff of U.S. military aid in 1978. Hopes for improvement under the junta faded when Gen. José Efraín Ríos Montt took sole power in June.

President Oscar Mejía Victores, another general, seized power from Rios Montt in an August 1983 coup.

Jorge Serrano Elias presided over seven years of democratic rule until in May 1993 he moved to dissolve congress and the supreme court and suspend constitutional rights. Under strong foreign and domestic pressure the military deposed Serrano on June 1 and allowed the inauguration of de Leon Carpio, the former Attorney General of Human Rights and no particular friend of the military.

The basis for new negotiations to end a long-standing leftist rebellion was reached in January 1994. In the January 1996 runoff presidential election Alvaro Arzú Irigoyen of the National Advancement Party defeated the far-right candidate.

A peace agreement was signed in December 1996 ending a 36-year civil war. In June 1997 President Arzu and the guerrilla movement leader Ricardo Ramirez were awarded the UNESCO Houphouet—Boigny peace prize.

GUINEA

Republic of Guinea
National name: République de Guinée
President: Brig. Gen. Lansana Conté (1984)
Premier: Sidia Touré (1996)
Area: 94,925 sq mi. (245,857 sq km)
Population (1997 est.): 7,405,375 (average annual rate of natural increase: 2.37%); birth rate: 41.95/1000; infant mortality rate: 131.5/1000; density per square mile: 78
Capital and largest city (1995 est.): Conakry, 1,508,000. **Monetary unit:** Guinean franc. **Languages:** French (official), native tongues (Malinké, Susu, Fulani). **Ethnicity/Race:** Peuhl 40%, Malinke 30%, Soussou 20%, smaller tribes 10%. **Religions:** Islam, 85%; 7% indigenous, 8% Christian. **Literacy rate:** 24% in French; 48% in local languages
Economic summary: Gross domestic product: purchasing power parity (1995 est.): $6.5 billion; per capita $1,020; real growth rate 4%; inflation 4.1% (1994 est.). Arable land: 6%. Principal agricultural products: rice, cassava, millet, corn, coffee, bananas, pineapples. Labor force: 2.4 million (1983); 80% in agriculture; 11% in industry and commerce; 5.4% in services; 3.6% in civil service. Major industrial products: bauxite, aluminum, light manufactured and processed goods, diamonds. Natural resources: bauxite, iron ore, diamonds, gold, water power. Exports: $562 million (1994 est.): bauxite, aluminum, diamonds, pineapples, bananas, coffee. Imports: $688 million (1994 est.): petroleum, machinery, transport equipment, foodstuffs,

textiles. Major trading partners: U.S., France, Brazil, Germany, Belgium, Ireland, Spain, Côte d'Ivoire, Hong Kong.

Geography. Guinea, in West Africa on the Atlantic, is also bordered by Guinea-Bissau, Senegal, Mali, Côte d'Ivoire, Liberia, and Sierra Leone. Slightly smaller than Oregon, the country consists of a coastal plain, a mountainous region, a savanna interior, and a forest area in the Guinea Highlands. The highest peak is Mount Nimba at 5,748 ft. (1,752 m).

Government. Military government headed by President Lansana Conté, who promoted himself from colonel to brigadier general after a 1984 coup. In 1989, President Conté announced that Guinea would move to a multiparty democracy.

A new constitution approved in a nationwide referendum, December 1990, provided for the establishment of a directly elected multiparty Parliament (five-year terms) and a popularly elected President for a maximum of two five-year terms, and a judiciary to be independent of either the presidency or the legislature. A transitional Committee for National Recovery (CTRN) replaced the military committee to guide implementation of the new constitution.

History. Previously part of French West Africa, Guinea achieved independence by rejecting the new French constitution, and on Oct. 2, 1958, became an independent state with Sékou Touré as president. Touré led the country into being the first avowedly Marxist state in Africa. Diplomatic relations with France were suspended in 1965, with the Soviet Union replacing France as the country's chief source of economic and technical assistance.

Prosperity came in 1960 after the start of exploitation of bauxite deposits. Touré was re-elected to a seven-year term in 1974 and again in 1981.

After 26 years as president, Touré died in the United States in March 1984, following surgery. A week later, a military regime headed by Col. Lansana Conté took power with a promise not to shed any more blood after Touré's harsh rule. Conté became president and his co-conspirator in the coup, Col. Diara Traoré, became Prime Minister, but Conté later demoted Traoré to Education Minister. Traoré tried to seize power on July 4, 1985, while Conté was out of the country, but his attempted coup was crushed by troops loyal to Conté.

In 1991 voters approved a new constitution that would lead the country to democracy. Under mounting popular pressure Conté declared in April 1992 that constitutional rule would begin.

In December 1993 elections the President's Unity and Progress Party took almost 51% of the vote cast.

In February 1996 rebellious soldiers demanding pay in arrears besieged the presidential palace. Loyal troops repulsed the attacks.

The President appointed Sidia Toure to the newly created position of Premier in July 1996.

GUINEA-BISSAU

Republic of Guinea-Bissau
National name: Républica da Guiné-Bissau
President: João Bernardo Vieira (1980)
Prime Minister: Carlos Correia (1997)
Area: 13,948 sq mi. (36,125 sq km)
Population (1997 est.): 1,178,584 (average annual rate of natural increase: 2.33%); birth rate: 39.17/1000; infant mortality rate: 113.7/1000; density per square mile: 84.5
Capital and largest city (1991 est.): Bissau, 200,000.
Monetary unit: Guinea-Bissau peso. **Language:**

Portugese Criolo, African languages. **Ethnicity/Race:** African 99% (Balanta 30%, Fula 20%, Manjaca 14%, Mandinga 13%, Papel 7%), European and mulatto less than 1%. **Religions:** traditional, 65%; Islam, 30%; Christian, 5%. **Literacy rate:** 36% (1991 est.)
Economic summary: Gross domestic product: purchasing power parity (1994 est.): $1 billion; $900 per capita; real growth rate n.a.; inflation: 15%. Arable land: 9%. Principal products: palm kernels, cotton, cashew nuts, peanuts. Labor force: 403,000 (est.): agriculture, 90%; industry, services, and commerce, 5%; government, 5%. Major industries: food processing, beer, soft drinks. Natural resources: unexploited deposits of bauxite, petroleum, phosphates; fish and timber. Exports: $32 million (f.o.b., 1994): peanuts, cashews, fish, palm kernels. Imports: $63 million (f.o.b., 1994): capital equipment, consumer goods, semiprocessed goods, foods, petroleum. Major trading partners: Portugal, Spain, and other European countries, Senegal, U.S., China, India, Nigeria.

Geography. A neighbor of Senegal and Guinea in West Africa, on the Atlantic coast, Guinea-Bissau is about half the size of South Carolina.

The country is a low-lying coastal region of swamps, rain forests, and mangrove-covered wetlands, with about 25 islands off the coast. The Bijagos archipelago extends 30 miles (48 km) out to sea. Internal communications depend mainly on deep estuaries and meandering rivers, since there are no railroads. Bissau, the capital, is the main port.

Government. After the overthrow of Louis Cabral in November 1980, the nine-member Council of the Revolution formed an interim government. At present the government consists of a President and a single 100-member legislative body.

History. Guinea-Bissau was discovered in 1446 by the Portuguese Nuno Tristao, and colonists in the Cape Verde Islands obtained trading rights in the territory. In 1879 the connection with the Cape Verde Islands was broken. Early in the 1900s the Portuguese managed to pacify some tribesmen, although resistance to colonial rule remained.

The African Party for the Independence of Guinea-Bissau and Cape Verde was founded in 1956 and several years later began guerrilla warfare that grew increasingly effective. By 1974 the rebels controlled most of the countryside, where they formed a government that was soon recognized by scores of countries. The military coup in Portugal in April 1974 brightened the prospects for freedom, and in August the Lisbon government signed an agreement granting independence to the province as of Sept. 10. The new republic took the name Guinea-Bissau.

In November 1980, Prémier João Bernardo Vieira headed a coup that deposed Luis Cabral, President since 1974. A Revolutionary Council assumed the powers of government, with Vieira as its head. An extraordinary congress of the ruling party in January 1991 approved a multiparty system. In June the constitution was amended to allow for opposition parties.

July 1994 multiparty presidential and legislative elections gave the President's party 64 seats in the Assembly although Vieira himself less than a majority. In the runoff election Vieira officially received 52% of the vote.

Citing continuing economic problems, President Viera dissolved the government of Prime Minister Manuel Saturnino Costa in May 1997, and in June named Carlos Correia the new Prime Minister.

GUYANA

Cooperative Republic of Guyana
President: Samuel Hinds (1997)
Prime Minister: Janet Jagan (1997)
Area: 83,000 sq mi. (214,969 sq km)
Population (1997 est.): 706,116 (average annual rate of natural increase: 0.86%); birth rate: 18.71/1000; infant mortality rate: 51.4/1000; density per square mile: 8.5
Capital and largest city (1992 est.): Georgetown, 248,500. **Monetary unit:** Guyana dollar. **Languages:** English (official), Amerindian dialects. **Ethnicity/Race:** East Indian 51%, black and mixed 43%, Amerindian 4%, European and Chinese 2%. **Religions:** Hindu, 34%; Protestant, 18%; Islam, 9%; Roman Catholic, 18%; Anglican, 16%. **Literacy rate:** 95%
Economic summary: Gross domestic product: purchasing power parity (1995 est.): $1.6 billion; $2,200 per capita; real growth rate 5.1%; inflation: 8.1%; unemployment (1994 est.): 8–10%. Arable land: 3%. Principal products: sugar, rice. Labor force (1995): 300,000; 44.5% industry and commerce. Major products: bauxite, aluminum. Natural resources: bauxite, gold, diamonds, hardwood timber, shrimp. Exports: $550 million (f.o.b., 1995 est.): sugar, bauxite, rice, timber, shrimp, gold, molasses, rum. Imports: $620 million (c.i.f., 1995 est.): petroleum, food, machinery, manufactured goods. Major trading partners: U.K., U.S., Canada, Japan, Trinidad and Tobago, Germany.
Member of Commonwealth of Nations

Geography. Guyana is situated on the northern coast of South America east of Venezuela, west of Suriname, and north of Brazil. The country consists of a low coastal area and the Guiana Highlands in the south. There is an extensive north-south network of rivers. Guyana is the size of Idaho.

Government. Guyana, formerly British Guiana, proclaimed itself a republic on Feb. 23, 1970, ending its tie with Britain while remaining in the Commonwealth.

Guyana has a unicameral legislature, the National Assembly, with 53 members directly elected for five-year terms and 12 elected by local councils. A 13-member cabinet is headed by the President.

History. British Guiana won internal self-government in 1952. The next year the People's Progressive Party, headed by Cheddi B. Jagan, an East Indian dentist, won the elections and Jagan became Prime Minister. British authorities deposed him for alleged Communist connections. A coalition ousted Jagan in 1964, installing a moderate Socialist, Forbes Burnham, a black, as Prime Minister. On May 26, 1966, the country became an independent member of the Commonwealth and resumed its traditional name, Guyana.

After ruling Guyana for 21 years, Burnham died on Aug. 6, 1985, in a Guyana hospital after a throat operation.

Jagan's People's Progressive Party won a majority in the general election of October 1992.

Upon President Jagan's death in March 1997, Prime Minister Samuel Hinds assumed the presidency. Nine days later Janet Jagan, the late President's widow, became Prime Minister, becoming the nation's first female in that office.

HAITI

Republic of Haiti
National name: République d'Haïti
President: René García Préval (1996)
Prime Minister: Eric Pierre (1997)

Area: 10,714 sq mi. (27,750 sq km)
Population (1997 est.): 6,611,407 (average annual rate of natural increase: 1.78%); birth rate: 33.12/1000; infant mortality rate: 102.4/1000; density per square mile: 617.1
Capital and largest city (1993 est.): Port-au-Prince, 1.5 million. **Monetary unit:** Gourde. **Languages:** Creole, French. **Ethnicity/Race:** black 95%, mulatto and European 5%. **Religion:** Roman Catholic, 80%; Protestant, 16%; Vaudou, 95%. **Literacy rate:** 25%
Economic summary: Gross domestic product: purchasing power parity (1995 est.): $6.5 billion; $1,000 per capita; 4.5% real growth rate; inflation 14.5% (FY 94/95 est.); unemployment 60%. Arable land: 50%. Principal agricultural products: coffee, sugar cane, rice, corn, sorghum. Labor force: 2.3 million; 66% in agriculture; 25% in services; 9% in industry. Major industrial products: refined sugar, textiles, flour, cement, light assembly products. Natural resource: bauxite. Exports: $161 million (f.o.b., 1995 est.): coffee, light industrial products, agricultural products. Imports: $537 million (f.o.b., 1995 est.): machines and manufactures, food and beverages, petroleum products, fats and oils, chemicals. Major trading partners: U.S., Europe, Latin America.

Geography. Haiti, in the West Indies, occupies the western third of the island of Hispaniola, which it shares with the Dominican Republic. About the size of Maryland, Haiti is two-thirds mountainous, with the rest of the country marked by great valleys, extensive plateaus, and small plains. The most densely populated region is the Cul-de-Sac plain near Port-au-Prince.

Government. A republic with a bicameral assembly consisting of an upper house or Senate and a lower house, the House of Deputies. The National Assembly consists of 27 senate seats and 83 deputies.

Democratically elected President Aristide was replaced by a de facto regime in October 1991 following a military coup on Sept. 30, 1991. He was reinstated in October 1993 by a U.S.-led multinational force appointed by U.N. Resolution 940. A U.S. peace mission in September 1994 reached a compromise with the military leaders, avoiding a U.S. invasion. Acting as peacekeepers, U.S. troops landed in Haiti, allowing Aristide to return in mid-October. President René Préval was elected Dec. 17, 1995, and was inaugurated on Feb. 7, 1996.

History. Visited by Columbus, who landed at Môle Saint Nicolas on Dec. 6, 1492, Haiti in 1697 became a French possession known as Saint Domingue. An insurrection among a slave population of 500,000 in 1791 ended with a declaration of independence by Pierre-Dominique Toussaint l'Ouverture in 1801. Napoleon Bonaparte suppressed the independence movement, but it eventually triumphed in 1804 under Jean-Jacques Dessalines, who gave the new nation the aboriginal name Haiti.

Its prosperity dissipated by internal strife as well as disputes with neighboring Santo Domingo during a succession of 19th-century dictatorships, a bankrupt Haiti accepted a U.S. customs receivership from 1905 to 1941. Direct U.S. rule from 1915 to 1934 brought a measure of stability and a population growth that made Haiti the most densely populated nation in the hemisphere.

In 1949, after four years of democratic rule by President Dumarsais Estimé, dictatorship returned under Gen. Paul Magloire, who was succeeded by François Duvalier in 1957.

Duvalier established a dictatorship based on secret police, known as the "Ton-ton Macoutes," who gunned down opponents of the regime. Duvalier's son, Jean-Claude, or "Baby Doc," succeeded his father in 1971 as ruler of the poorest nation in the Western Hemisphere. Duvalier fled the country in 1986 after strong unrest.

Following the election of December 6, 1990, Jean-Bertrand Aristide, a Roman Catholic priest, was sworn in as president on February 7, 1991—the country's first freely elected chief executive.

In September 1991 elements of the military seized the President and took control of the government. Although the OAS attempted to have Aristide reinstated the army forced the Assembly officially to depose him. The OAS call for economic blockade led to a sharp downturn in an already poor economy.

The population largely ignored parliamentary elections the following January. In July Aristide and the army signed an accord to return the exiled President to power. When the military leaders failed to resign, the U.N. reimposed an embargo.

The winner of the second free election in the country's history was René Préval, who was sworn into office in February 1996.

Former President Aristide's new opposition Lavalas Family party scored well in the legislative elections of April 1997, but voter turnout was minuscule amid charges of fraud. The pro-government party then threatened to boycott the second round of voting originally scheduled for May in which Aristide's party looked sure to win. In early June the Prime Minister, with a deteriorating economy, announced his resignation, and Préval nominated Eric Pierre as Prime Minister.

HONDURAS

Republic of Honduras
National name: República de Honduras
President: Carlos Roberto Reina Idiáquez (1994)
Area: 43,872 sq mi. (112,492 sq km)
Population (1997 est.): 5,751,384 (average annual rate of natural increase: 2.69%); birth rate: 32.63/1000; infant mortality rate: 40.2/1000; density per square mile: 131
Capital and largest city (1995): Tegucigalpa, 1,500,000. **Monetary unit:** Lempira. **Languages:** Spanish (official), English widely spoken in business. **Ethnicity/Race:** mestizo (mixed Indian and European) 90%, Indian 7%, black 2%, white 1%. **Religion:** Roman Catholic, 94%, Protestant minority. **Literacy rate:** 73%
Economic summary: Gross domestic product: purchasing power parity (1995 est.): $10.8 billion; $1,980 per capita; real growth rate 4%; inflation 30%; unemployment 10%. Arable land: 14%. Principal products: bananas, coffee, timber, beef, shrimp, citrus. Labor force (1985): 1.3 million; agriculture 62%; services 20%; manufacturing 9%; construction 3%. Major industrial products: processed agricultural products, textiles and clothing, wood products. Natural resources: timber, gold, silver, copper, lead, zinc, iron ore, antimony. Exports: $843 million (f.o.b., 1994): bananas, coffee, lumber, shrimp and lobster, minerals. Imports: $1.1 billion (c.i.f., 1994): manufactured goods, machinery, transportation equipment, chemicals, petroleum. Major trading partners: U.S., Caribbean countries, Western Europe, Japan, Latin America.

Geography. Honduras, in the north central part of Central America, has a 400-mile (644-km) Caribbean coastline and a 40-mile (64-km) Pacific frontage. Its neighbors are Guatemala to the west, El Salvador to the south, and Nicaragua to the east. Honduras is slightly larger than Tennessee. Generally mountainous, the country is marked by fertile plateaus, river valleys, and narrow coastal plains.

Government. The President serves a four-year term. There is a 128-member National Congress.

History. Columbus explored Honduras on his last voyage in 1502. Honduras, with four other countries of Central America, declared its independence from Spain in 1821 and was part of a federation of Central American states until 1838. In that year it seceded from the federation and became a completely independent country.

In July 1969, El Salvador invaded Honduras after Honduran landowners had deported several thousand Salvadorans. The fighting left 1,000 dead and tens of thousands homeless. By threatening economic sanctions and military intervention, the OAS induced El Salvador to withdraw.

Although parliamentary democracy returned with the election of Roberto Suazo Córdova as president in 1982 after a decade of military rule, Honduras faced severe economic problems and tensions along its border with Nicaragua. "Contra" rebels, waging a guerrilla war against the Sandinista regime in Nicaragua, used Honduras as a training and staging area. At the same time, the United States used Honduras as a site for military exercises and built bases to train both Honduran and Salvadoran troops.

In the first democratic transition of power since 1932 Rafael Callejas became President in January 1990. The immediate task was to deal with a deficit caused in part by reduced U.S. aid and the previous government's fiscal policies.

Running on a platform attacking governmental corruption and military influence the candidate of the Liberal Party, Carlos Reina, won the general election of November 1993 against the ruling National Party.

The lack of a final resolution of a maritime border dispute with Nicaragua led to incidents in 1997 in which Honduran fishermen were detained and fined in Nicaragua.

HUNGARY

Republic of Hungary
National name: Magyar Köztársaság
President: Á rpád Göncz (1990)
Premier: Gyula Horn (1994)
Area: 35,919 sq mi. (93,030 sq km)
Population (1997 est.): 9,935,774 (average annual rate of natural increase: –0.4%); birth rate: 10.9/1000; infant mortality rate: 12.2/1000; density per square mile: 276.6
Capital and largest city (1995 est.): Budapest, 1,9306,000. **Other large cities (1995 est.):** Debrecen, 210,000; Miskolc, 182,000; Szeged, 169,000; Gyor, 127,000, Pécs, 163,000. **Monetary unit:** Forint. **Language:** Magyar. **Ethnicity/Race:** Hungarian 89.9%, Gypsy 4%, German 2.6%, Serb 2%, Slovak 0.8%, Romanian 0.7%. **Religions:** Roman Catholic, 67.5%; Protestant, 25%; atheist and others, 7.5%. **Literacy rate:** 99%
Economic summary: Gross domestic product: purchasing power parity (1995 est.): $72.5 billion; $7,000 per capita; 1.5% real growth rate; inflation rate 28.3%; unemployment rate 10.4% (1995). Arable land: 54%. Principal agricultural products: corn, wheat, potatoes, sugar beets, sun flowers, livestock, dairy products. Labor force: 4.8 million; 47.2% in services, trade and government; 29.7% in industry; 16.1% in agriculture; 7.0% in construction. Major industrial products: steel, chemicals, pharmaceuticals, textiles, transport equipment. Natural resources: bauxite, coal, natural gas. Exports: $13 billion (f.o.b., 1995 est.): raw materials, semi-finished goods, chemicals, machinery, light industry, food and agricultural, fuels and energy. Imports: $15 billion (f.o.b., 1995 est.): fuels and energy, raw materials, semi-finished goods, chemicals,

machinery, light industry, food and agriculture. Major trading partners: Germany, Austria, Italy, C.I.S. countries, Eastern Europe.

Geography. This central European country the size of Indiana is bordered by Austria to the west, Slovakia to the north, Ukraine and Romania to the east, and Yugoslavia to the south.

Most of Hungary is a fertile, rolling plain lying east of the Danube River and drained by the Danube and Tisza rivers. In the extreme northwest is the Little Hungarian Plain. South of that area is Lake Balaton (250 sq mi.; 648 sq km).

Government. Hungary is a Republic with legislative power vested in the unicameral National Assembly, whose 386 members are elected directly for four-year terms. The National Assembly elects the President.

The major political parties are the Socialist Party, the Hungarian Democratic Forum, the Alliance of Free Democrats, the Independent Socialist Party, and the Young Democrats (FIDESZ).

History. About 2,000 years ago, Hungary was part of the Roman provinces of Pannonia and Dacia. In C.E. 896 it was invaded by the Magyars, who founded a kingdom. Christianity was accepted during the reign of Stephen I (St. Stephen) (997–1038).

The peak of Hungary's great period of medieval power came during the reign of Louis I the Great (1342–82), whose dominions touched the Baltic, Black, and Mediterranean seas.

War with the Turks broke out in 1389, and for more than 100 years the Turks advanced through the Balkans. When the Turks smashed a Hungarian army in 1526, western and northern Hungary accepted Hapsburg rule to escape Turkish occupation. Transylvania became independent under Hungarian Princes. Intermittent war with the Turks was waged until a peace treaty was signed in 1699.

After the suppression of the 1848 revolt against Hapsburg rule, led by Louis Kossuth, the dual monarchy of Austria-Hungary was set up in 1867.

The dual monarchy was defeated with the other Central Powers in World War I. After a short-lived republic in 1918, the chaotic Communist rule of 1919 under Béla Kun ended with the Romanians occupying Budapest on Aug. 4, 1919. When the Romanians left, Adm. Nicholas Horthy entered the capital with a national army. The Treaty of Trianon of June 4, 1920, cost Hungary 68% of its land and 58% of its population. Meanwhile, the National Assembly had restored the legal continuity of the old monarchy; and, on March 1, 1920, Horthy was elected Regent.

Following the German invasion of Russia on June 22, 1941, Hungary joined the attack against the Soviet Union, but the war was not popular and Hungarian troops were almost entirely withdrawn from the eastern front by May 1943. German occupation troops set up a puppet government after Horthy's appeal for an armistice with advancing Soviet troops on Oct. 15, 1944, had resulted in his overthrow. The German regime soon fled the capital, however, and on December 23 a provisional government was formed in Soviet-occupied eastern Hungary. On Jan. 20, 1945, it signed an armistice in Moscow. Early the next year, the National Assembly approved a constitutional law abolishing the thousand-year-old monarchy and establishing a republic.

By the Treaty of Paris (1947), Hungary had to give up all territory it had acquired since 1937 and to pay $300 million reparations to the U.S.S.R., Czechoslovakia, and Yugoslavia. In 1948 the Communist Party, with the support of Soviet troops seized control. Hungary was proclaimed a People's Republic and one-party state in 1949. Industry was nationalized, the land collectivized into state farms, and the opposition terrorized by the secret police.

The terror, modeled after that of the U.S.S.R., reached its height with the trial of József Cardinal Mindszenty, Roman Catholic primate. He confessed to fantastic charges under duress of drugs or brainwashing and was sentenced to life imprisonment in 1949. Protests were voiced in all parts of the world.

On Oct. 23, 1956, anti-Communist revolution broke out in Budapest. To cope with it, the Communists set up a coalition government and called former Premier Imre Nagy back to head it. But he and most of his ministers were swept by the logic of events into the anti-Communist opposition, and he declared Hungary a neutral power, withdrawing from the Warsaw Treaty and appealing to the United Nations for help.

One of his ministers, János Kádár, established a counter-regime and asked the U.S.S.R. to send in military power. Soviet troops and tanks suppressed the revolution in bloody fighting after 190,000 people had fled the country and Mindszenty, freed from jail, had taken refuge in the U.S. Embassy.

Kádár was succeeded as Premier, but not party secretary, by Gyula Kallai in 1965. Continuing his program of national reconciliation, Kádár emptied prisons, reformed the secret police, and eased travel restrictions.

Following local and parliamentary elections in October 1990, József Antall's Hungarian Democratic Forum and its conservative coalition parties held 60% of the parliamentary seats. The last Soviet troops left Hungary in June 1991, thereby ending almost 47 years of military presence.

The transition to a market economy proved difficult. Hungary strengthened its ties with Poland and Czechoslovakia but grew concerned about the fate of ethnic Hungarians in neighboring countries. Hungary cautiously watched the birth of Slovakia and its treatment of a large ethnic Hungarian minority.

Parliamentary elections in May 1994 gave the Socialists, formerly the Communists, a 15-seat majority. A coalition government with the Free Democrats was formed in July.

Prime Minister Horn signed an agreement with the Vatican in June 1997 concerning restitution or compensation for property seized during the Communist era. Critics charged that the pact favors the Catholic Church over other religions.

ICELAND

Republic of Iceland
National name: Lydveldid Island
President: Ólafur Ragnar Grimsson (1996)
Prime Minister: David Oddsson (1991)
Area: 39,709 sq mi. (102,846 sq km)[1]
Population (1997 est.): 272,550 (average annual rate of natural increase: 1.06%); birth rate: 16.71/1000; infant mortality rate: 4.2/1000; density per square mile: 6.8
Capital and largest city (1994 est.): Reykjavik, 103,036. **Monetary unit:** M.N. króna. **Language:** Icelandic. **Ethnicity/Race:** homogeneous mixture of descendants of Norwegians and Celts. **Religion:** Church of Iceland (Lutheran) 95%, other Lutherans 5%, Roman Catholic, 10%.. **Literacy rate:** 100%
Economic summary: Gross domestic product: purchasing power parity (1996 est.): $4.5 billion; $19,905 per capita; real growth rate 2.4%; inflation 1.3%; unemployment 7%. Arable land: 1%; principal agricultural products: livestock, potatoes and turnips. Labor force: 127,900; 60% in commerce, transportation, and services; 12.5% in manufacturing; 11.8% in fishing and fish processing. Major products: processed aluminum,

fish. Natural resources: fish, diatomite, hydroelectric and geothermal power. Exports: $1.6 billion (f.o.b., 1994): fish, animal products, aluminum, diatomite, ferrosilicon. Imports: $1.5 billion (c.i.f., 1994): petroleum products, machinery and transportation equipment, food, textiles. Major trading partners: European Union (E.U.) countries, European Free Trade Association (EFTA) countries, U.S., Japan, and Denmark.
1. Including some offshore islands.

Geography. Iceland, an island about the size of Kentucky, lies in the north Atlantic Ocean east of Greenland and just touches the Arctic Circle. It is one of the most volcanic regions in the world.

Small fresh-water lakes are to be found throughout the island, and there are many natural phenomena, including hot springs, geysers, sulfur beds, canyons, waterfalls, and swift rivers. More than 13% of the area is covered by snowfields and glaciers, and most of the people live in the 7% of the island comprising fertile coastlands.

Government. The President is elected for four years by popular vote. Executive power resides in the Prime Minister and his cabinet. The Althing (Parliament) is composed of 63 members.

History. Iceland was first settled shortly before 900, mainly by Norse. A constitution drawn up about 930 created a form of democracy and provided for an Althing, the world's oldest practicing legislative assembly.

In 1262–64, Iceland came under Norwegian rule and passed to ultimate Danish control through the formation of the Union of Kalmar in 1483. In 1874, Icelanders obtained their own constitution. In 1918, Denmark recognized Iceland as a separate state with unlimited sovereignty but still nominally under the Danish King.

On June 17, 1944, after a popular referendum, the Althing proclaimed Iceland an independent republic.

The British occupied Iceland in 1940, immediately after the German invasion of Denmark. In 1942, the U.S. took over the burden of protection. Iceland refused to abandon its neutrality in World War II and thus forfeited charter membership in the United Nations, but it cooperated with the Allies throughout the conflict. Iceland joined the North Atlantic Treaty Organization in 1949.

Iceland unilaterally extended its territorial waters from 12 to 50 nautical miles in 1972, precipitating a running dispute with Britain known as the "cod war."

Elections to the Althing in April 1991 gave the opposition Independence Party 26 of the 63 seats, up from 18. Prime Minister Hermannson resigned allowing David Oddsson of the Independence Party to enter into talks with the Social Democrats about a coalition government.

General election results in April 1995 gave the former coalition Independence Party and Social Democrats what would have been only a one-seat majority. A new coalition was formed between the Independence Party and the centrist Progressives, who also oppose Iceland seeking membership in the European Union.

Government projections in mid–1997 showed that the country would have a large budget surplus for the year owing to fiscal management and a healthy economy. The government hoped to cut public spending further and boost the surplus even more.

INDIA

Republic of India
National name: Bharat
President: K. R. Narayanan (1997)
Prime Minister: Inder Kumar Gujral (1997)

Area: 1,229,737 sq mi. (3,185,019 sq km)
Population (1997 est.): 967,612,804 (average annual rate of natural increase: 1.59%); birth rate: 25.33/1000; infant mortality rate: 69.2/1000; density per square mile: 786.8
Capital (1991): New Delhi, 294,149. **Largest cities (1992):** Greater Bombay (Mumbai), 12,916,272; Calcutta, 10,916,272; Delhi, 8,375,188; Madras (Chennai), 5,361,468; Ahmedabad, 4,775,670; Bangalore, 4,807,019; Kanpur, 2,284,000. **Monetary unit:** Rupee.
Principal languages: Hindi (official), English (official), Bengali, Gujarati, Kashmiri, Malayalam, Marathi, Oriya, Punjabi, Tamil, Telugu, Urdu, Kannada, Assamese, Sanskrit, Sindhi (all recognized by the constitution). Dialects, 1,652. **Ethnicity/Race:** Indo-Aryan 72%, Dravidian 25%, Mongoloid and other 3%. **Religions:** Hindu, 82.6%; Islam, 11.3%; Christian, 2.4%; Sikh, 2%; Buddhists, 0.71%; Jains, 0.48%. **Literacy rate:** 52.11%
Economic summary: Gross domestic product: purchasing power parity (1995 est.): $1.4087 trillion; $1,500 per capita; 5.5% real growth rate; inflation 9%; unemployment: n.a. Arable land: 55%. Principal products: rice, wheat, oilseeds, cotton, tea, opium poppy (for pharmaceuticals). Labor force (1990): 314.751 million; 65% in agriculture (1993 est.). Major industrial products: jute, processed food, steel, machinery, transport machinery, cement. Natural resources: iron ore, coal, manganese, mica, bauxite, limestone, textiles. Exports: $29.96 billion (f.o.b., 1995): gems and jewelry, clothing, engineering goods, leather manufactures, cotton yarn and fabric. Imports: $33.5 billion (c.i.f., 1995): crude oil and petroleum products, gems, fertilizer, chemicals, machinery. Major trading partners: U.S., C.I.S. nations, Germany, Italy, Belgium.
Member of Commonwealth of Nations

Geography. One third the area of the United States, the Republic of India occupies most of the subcontinent of India in south Asia. It borders on China in the northeast. Other neighbors are Pakistan on the west, Nepal and Bhutan on the north, and Burma and Bangladesh on the east.

The country contains a large part of the great Indo-Gangetic plain, which extends from the Bay of Bengal on the east to the Afghan frontier and the Arabian Sea on the west. This plain is the richest and most densely settled part of the subcontinent. Another distinct natural region is the Deccan, a plateau of 2,000 to 3,000 feet (610 to 914 m) in elevation, occupying the southern portion of the subcontinent.

Forming a part of the republic are several groups of islands—the Laccadives (14 islands) in the Arabian Sea and the Andamans (204 islands) and the Nicobars (19 islands) in the Bay of Bengal.

India's three great river systems, all rising in the Himalayas, have extensive deltas. The Ganges flows south and then east for 1,540 miles (2,478 km) across the northern plain to the Bay of Bengal; part of its delta, which begins 220 miles (354 km) from the sea, is within the republic. The Indus, starting in Tibet, flows northwest for several hundred miles in the Kashmir before turning southwest toward the Arabian Sea; it is important for irrigation in Pakistan. The Brahmaputra, also rising in Tibet, flows eastward, first through India and then south into Bangladesh and the Bay of Bengal.

Government. India is a federal republic. It is also a member of the Commonwealth of Nations, a status defined at the 1949 London Conference of Prime Ministers, by which India recognizes the Queen as head of the Commonwealth. Under the constitution effective Jan. 26, 1950, India has a parliamentary type of government.

The constitutional head of the state is the President, who is elected every five years. He is advised by the Prime Minister and a cabinet based on a majority of the bicameral Parliament, which consists of a Council of States (Rajya Sabha), representing the constituent units of the republic and a House of the People (Lok Sabha), elected every five years by universal suffrage.

History. The Aryans who invaded India between 2400 and 1500 B.C.E. from the northwest found a land already well civilized. Buddhism was founded in the 6th century B.C.E. and spread throughout northern India, most notably by one of the great ancient Kings, Asoka (c. 269–232 B.C.E.), who also unified most of the Indian subcontinent.

In 1526, Moslem invaders founded the great Mogul empire, centered on Delhi, which lasted, at least in name, until 1857. Akbar the Great (1542–1605) strengthened and consolidated this empire. The long reign of his great-grandson, Aurangzeb (1658–1707), represents both the greatest extent of the Mogul empire and the beginning of its decay.

Vasco da Gama, the Portuguese explorer, visited India first in 1498, and for the next 100 years the Portuguese had a virtual monopoly on trade with the subcontinent. Meanwhile, the English founded the East India Company, which set up its first factory at Surat in 1612 and began expanding its influence, fighting the Indian rulers and the French, Dutch, and Portuguese traders simultaneously.

Bombay, taken from the Portuguese, became the seat of English rule in 1687. The defeat of French and Islamic armies by Lord Clive in the decade ending in 1760 laid the foundation of the British Empire in India. From then until 1858, when the administration of India was formally transferred to the British Crown following the Sepoy Mutiny of native troops in 1857, the East India Company suppressed native uprisings and extended British rule.

After World War I, in which the Indian states sent more than 6 million troops to fight beside the Allies, Indian nationalist unrest rose to new heights under the leadership of a Hindu lawyer, Mohandas K. Gandhi, called Mahatma Gandhi. His tactics called for nonviolent revolts against British authority. He soon became the leading spirit of the All-India Congress Party, which was the spearhead of revolt. In 1919 the British gave added responsibility to Indian officials, and in 1935 India was given a federal form of government and a measure of self-rule.

In 1942, with the Japanese pressing hard on the eastern borders of India, the British War Cabinet tried and failed to reach a political settlement with nationalist leaders. The Congress Party took the position that the British must quit India. In 1942, fearing mass civil disobedience, the government of India carried out widespread arrests of Congress leaders, including Gandhi.

Gandhi was released in 1944 and negotiations for a settlement were resumed. Finally, in February 1947, the Labor government announced its determination to transfer power to "responsible Indian hands" by June 1948 even if a constitution had not been worked out.

Lord Mountbatten as Viceroy, by June 1947, achieved agreement on the partitioning of India along religious lines and on the splitting of the provinces of Bengal and the Punjab, which the Moslems had claimed.

The Indian Independence Act, passed quickly by the British Parliament, received royal assent on July 18, 1947, and on August 15 the Indian Empire passed into history.

Jawaharlal Nehru, leader of the Congress Party, was made Prime Minister. Before an exchange of populations could be arranged, bloody riots occurred among the communal groups, and armed conflict broke out over rival claims to the princely state of Jammu and

Kashmir. Peace was restored only with the greatest difficulty. In 1949 a constitution, along the lines of the U.S. Constitution, was approved making India a sovereign republic. Under a federal structure the states were organized on linguistic lines.

The dominance of the Congress Party contributed to stability. In 1956 the republic absorbed the former French settlements. Five years later, it forcibly annexed the Portuguese enclaves of Goa, Damao, and Diu.

Nehru died in 1964. His successor, Lal Bahadur Shastri, died on Jan. 10, 1966. Nehru's daughter, Indira Gandhi, became Prime Minister, and she continued his policy of nonalignment.

In 1971 the Pakistani army moved in to quash the independence movement in East Pakistan that was supported by clandestine aid from India, and some 10 million Bengali refugees poured across the border into India, creating social, economic, and health problems. After numerous border incidents, India invaded East Pakistan and in two weeks forced the surrender of the Pakistani army. East Pakistan was established as an independent state and renamed Bangladesh.

In the summer of 1975, the world's largest democracy veered suddenly toward authoritarianism when a judge in Allahabad, Mrs. Gandhi's home constituency, found her landslide victory in the 1971 elections invalid because civil servants had illegally aided her campaign. Amid demands for her resignation, Mrs. Gandhi decreed a state of emergency on June 26 and ordered mass arrests of her critics, including all opposition party leaders except the Communists.

In 1976, India and Pakistan formally renewed diplomatic relations.

Despite strong opposition to her repressive measures and particularly the resentment against compulsory birth control programs, Mrs. Gandhi in 1977 announced parliamentary elections for March. At the same time, she freed most political prisoners. The landslide victory of Morarji R. Desai unseated Mrs. Gandhi.

Mrs. Gandhi staged a spectacular comeback in the elections of January 1980.

In 1984, Mrs. Gandhi ordered the Indian army to root out a band of Sikh holy men and gunmen who were using the holiest shrine of the Sikh religion, the Golden Temple in Amritsar, as a base for terrorist raids in a violent campaign for greater political autonomy in the strategic Punjab border state. The perceived sacrilege to the Golden Temple kindled outrage among many of India's 14 million Sikhs and brought a spasm of mutinies and desertions by Sikh officers and soldiers in the army.

On Oct. 31, 1984, Mrs. Gandhi was assassinated by two men identified by police as Sikh members of her bodyguard. The ruling Congress Party chose her older son, Rajiv Gandhi, to succeed her as Prime Minister.

One week after the resignation of Prime Minister Shekhar, India's President in March 1991 called for national elections. While at an election rally on May 22 former Prime Minister Rajiv Gandhi was assassinated. Final phases of the election were postponed a month. When they were resumed the Congress Party and its allies won 236 seats in the lower house, 20 short of a majority. P.V. Narasimha Rao was chosen to form a new government.

The ruling Congress Party lost the parliamentary elections of May 1996. The Hindu nationalist Bharatiya Janata Party's leader, Atal Bihari Vajpayee, became Prime Minister a week later. His government, however, lasted only 13 days. Deve Gowda of the United Front coalition, next became Prime Minister.

Losing the support of the Congress party, Prime Minister Gowda lost a confidence vote in April 1997. Congress then said it would support the government if Gowda were replaced. Foreign Minister Gujral was sworn in later that month.

Native States. Most of the 560-odd native states and subdivisions of pre-1947 India acceded to the new nation, and the central government pursued a vigorous policy of integration. This took three forms: merger into adjacent provinces, conversion into centrally administered areas, and grouping into unions of states. Finally, under a controversial reorganization plan effective Nov. 1, 1956, the unions of states were abolished and merged into adjacent states, and India became a union of 15 states and 8 centrally administered areas. A 16th state was added in 1962, and in 1966, the Punjab was partitioned into two states. Today India consists of 25 states and 7 Union Territories.

Resolution of the territorial dispute over Kashmir grew out of peace negotiations following the two-week India-Pakistan war of 1971. After sporadic skirmishing, an accord reached July 3, 1972, committed both powers to withdraw troops from a temporary cease-fire line after the border was fixed. Agreement on the border was reached Dec. 7, 1972.

In April 1975, the Indian Parliament voted to make the 300-year-old Kingdom of Sikkim a full-fledged Indian state, and the annexation took effect May 16. Situated in the Himalayas, Sikkim was a virtual dependency of Tibet until the early 19th century. Under an 1890 treaty between China and Great Britain, it became a British protectorate, and was made an Indian protectorate after Britain quit the subcontinent.

INDONESIA

Republic of Indonesia
National name: Republik Indonesia
President: Suharto (1993)[1]
Area: 735,268 sq mi. (1,904,344 sq km)[2]
Population (1997 est.): 209,774,138 (average annual rate of natural increase: 1.5%; birth rate: 23.39/1000; infant mortality rate: 61.2/1000; density per square mile: 285.3
Capital and largest city (1990): Jakarta, 8,259,266.
  Other large cities (1990): Surabaya, 2,421,000; Medan, 1,685,972; Bandung, 2,026,893; Semarang, 1,005,316. **Monetary unit:** Rupiah. **Languages:** Bahasa Indonesia (official), Dutch, English, and more than 583 languages, and dialects. **Ethnicity/Race:** Javanese 45%, Sundanese 14%, Madurese 7.5%, coastal Malays 7.5%, other 26%. **Religions:** Islam, 87%; Christian, 9%; Hindu, 2%; other, 2%. **Literacy rate:** 86.3%
Economic summary: Gross domestic product: purchasing power parity (1995 est.): $710.9 billion; $3,500 per capita; real growth rate 7.5%; inflation 8.6%; unemployment 3%. Arable land: 8%. Principal agricultural products: rice, cassava, peanuts, rubber, coffee. Labor force: 67 million; 55% in agriculture; 10% in manufacturing; 4% in construction; 3% in transport and communications (1985 est.). Major industrial products: petroleum, timber, textiles, cement, fertilizer, rubber. Natural resources: oil, timber, nickel, natural gas, tin, bauxite, copper. Exports: $39.9 billion (f.o.b., 1994): petroleum and liquid natural gas, timber, rubber, coffee, textiles. Imports: $32 billion (f.o.b., 1994): chemicals, machinery, manufactured goods. Major trading partners: Japan, U.S., Singapore, Germany.

---

1. Re-elected President for the 6th five-year term in office.
2. Includes West Irian (former Netherlands New Guinea), renamed Irian Jaya in March 1973 (159,355 sq mi.; 421,981 sq km), and former Portuguese Timor (5,763 sq mi.; 14,874 sq km), annexed in 1976.

Geography. Indonesia is part of the Malay archipelago in Southeast Asia with an area nearly three times that of Texas. It consists of the islands of Sumatra, Java, Bali, Kalimantan (Indonesia's part of Borneo), Sulawesi (Celebes), the Nusa Tenggara islands, the Maluku Islands. Iranian Java (eastern part of New Guinea), and about 30 smaller archipelagos, totaling 17,508 islands, of which about 6,000 are inhabited. Its neighbor to the north is Malaysia and to the east Papua New Guinea.

A backbone of mountain ranges extends throughout the main islands of the archipelago. Earthquakes are frequent, and there are many active volcanoes.

The "Wallace Line," a zoological demarcation between Asian and Australian flora and fauna, divides Indonesia.

Government. The President is elected by the People's Consultative Assembly, whose 1,000 members include the functioning legislative arm, the 500-member House of Representatives. Meeting at least once every five years, the Assembly has broad policy functions. The House, 100 of whose members are appointed from the armed forces, meets at least annually. General Suharto was elected unopposed to a sixth five-year term in 1993.

History. Indonesia is inhabited by Javanese (45%), Sudanese (14%), Madurese (7.5%), and Malays (7.5%), as well as a host of other ethnic groups.

During the first few centuries of the Christian era, most of the islands came under the influence of Hindu priests and traders, who spread their culture and religion. Moslem invasions began in the 13th century, and most of the area was Moslem by the 15th. Portuguese traders arrived early in the 16th century but were ousted by the Dutch about 1595. After Napoleon subjugated the Netherlands homeland in 1811, the British seized the islands but returned them to the Dutch in 1816. In 1922 the islands were made an integral part of the Netherlands Kingdom.

During World War II, Indonesia was under Japanese military occupation with nominal native self-government. When the Japanese surrendered to the Allies, President Sukarno and Mohammed Hatta, his Vice President, proclaimed Indonesian independence from the Dutch on Aug. 17, 1945. Allied troops—mostly British Indian troops—fought the nationalists until the arrival of Dutch troops. In November 1946, the Dutch and the Indonesians reached a draft agreement contemplating formation of a Netherlands-Indonesian Union, but differences in interpretation resulted in more fighting between Dutch and Indonesian forces.

On Nov. 2, 1949, Dutch and Indonesian leaders agreed upon the terms of union. The transfer of sovereignty took place at Amsterdam on Dec. 27, 1949. In February 1956 Indonesia abrogated the Union with the Netherlands and in August 1956 repudiated its debt to the Netherlands. In 1963, Netherlands New Guinea was transferred to Indonesia and renamed West Irian. In 1973 it became Irian Jaya.

Hatta and Sukarno, the co-fathers of Indonesian independence, split after it was achieved over Sukarno's concept of "guided democracy." Under Sukarno, the country's leading political figure for almost a half century, the Indonesian Communist Party gradually gained increasing influence.

After an attempted coup was put down by General Suharto, the army chief of staff, and officers loyal to him, thousands of Communist suspects were sought out and killed all over the country. Suharto took over the reins of government, gradually eased Sukarno out of office, and took full power in 1967.

Suharto permitted national elections, which moved the nation back to representative government. He also ended hostilities with Malaysia. Under President Suharto, Indonesia has been strongly antiCommunist. It also has been politically stable and has made progress in economic development.

Indonesia invaded the former Portuguese half of the island of Timor in 1975, and annexed the territory in 1976. More than 100,000 Timorese, a sixth of the mostly Catholic population, were reported to have died from famine, disease, and fighting since the annexation.

In March 1993 the 1,000 member People's Consultative Assembly, a body which meets every five years for the express purpose of choosing a President, re-elected Suharto, who ran unopposed.

Elections for the country's mostly ceremonial parliament in May 1997 gave the ruling Golkar party an overwhelming victory with approximately 74 percent of the vote. Only three parties were allowed to compete.

IRAN

Islamic Republic of Iran
President: Mohammad Khatami (1997)
Area: 636,293 sq mi. (1,648,000 sq km)
Population (1997 est.): 67,540,002 (average annual rate of natural increase: 2.61%); birth rate: 32.51/1000; infant mortality rate: 50.8/1000; density per square mile: 106.1
Capital: Teheran. **Largest cities (1991 est.):** Teheran, 6,450,500; Mashad, 1,500,000; Isfahan, 1,100,000; Tabriz, 1,090,000. **Monetary unit:** Rial. **Languages:** Farsi (Persian), Azari, Kurdish, Arabic. **Ethnicity/Race:** Persian 51%, Azerbaijani 24%, Gilaki and Mazandarani 8%, Kurd 7%, Arab 3%, Lur 2%, Baloch 2%, Turkmen 2%, other 1%. **Religions:** Shi'ite Moslem, 95%; Sunni Moslem, 4%. **Literacy rate:** 79.3% (1996)
Economic summary: Gross domestic product: purchasing power parity (1995 est.-): $323.5 billion; $4,700 per capita; real growth rate –2%; inflation 60%; unemployment over 30%. Arable land: 8%. Principal agricultural products: wheat, barley, rice, sugar beets, cotton, dates, raisins, sheep, goats. Labor force: 15.4 million; 33% in agriculture; 21% in manufacturing. Major industrial products: crude and refined oil, textiles, petrochemicals, cement, processed foods, steel and copper fabrication. Natural resources: oil, gas, iron, copper. Exports: $16 billion (f.o.b., 1994 est.): petroleum, carpets, fruits, nuts, hides. Imports: $13 billion (c.i.f., 1994 est.): machinery, military supplies, foodstuffs, pharmaceuticals, metal works, technical services. Major trading partners: Japan, Germany, Netherlands, U.K., Italy, Spain, Turkey, France.

Geography. Iran, a Middle Eastern country south of the Caspian Sea and north of the Persian Gulf, is three times the size of Arizona. It shares borders with Iraq, Turkey, Azerbaijan, Turkmenistan, Armenia, Afghanistan, and Pakistan.

In general, the country is a plateau averaging 4,000 feet (1,219 m) in elevation. There are also maritime lowlands along the Persian Gulf and the Caspian Sea. The Elburz Mountains in the north rise to 18,603 feet (5,670 m) at Mt. Damavend. From northwest to southeast, the country is crossed by a desert 800 miles (1,287 km) long.

Government. The Pahlavi monarchy regime was overthrown on Feb. 11, 1979. The Islamic Republic of Iran was established and endorsed by a universal referendum on March 30, the same year. A new constitution was drafted by the Assembly of Experts and was approved in a national referendum in Dec. 1979.

The constitution recognizes the executive, legislative, and judiciary, as independent branches. The President is elected by direct vote for a four years term. He runs the government and is accountable for the implementation of the constitution before the Parliament (*Majles*), which consists of 270 representatives popularly elected for a period of four years.

In the course of the Islamic Revolution, Ayatollah Khomeini emerged as the leader of Iran. After his death on July 3, 1989, the Assembly of Experts elected Ayatollah Ali Khameneie as his successor. The Assembly itself consists of experts elected directly by the nation.

History. Oil-rich Iran was called Persia before 1935. Its key location blocks the lower land gate to Asia and also stands in the way of traditional Russian ambitions for access to the Indian Ocean. After periods of Assyrian, Median, and Achaemenidian rule, Persia became a powerful empire under Cyrus the Great, reaching from the Indus to the Nile at its zenith in 525 B.C.E. It fell to Alexander in 331–330 B.C.E. and to the Seleucids in 312–302 B.C.E., and a native Persian regime arose about 130 B.C.E. Another Persian regime arose about 224, but it fell to the Arabs in 637. In the 12th century, the Mongols took their turn ruling Persia, and in the early part of the 18th century, the Turks occupied the country.

An Anglo-Russian convention of 1907 divided Persia into two spheres of influence. British attempts to impose a protectorate over the entire country were defeated in 1919. Two years later, Gen. Reza Pahlavi seized the government and was elected hereditary Shah in 1925. Subsequently he did much to modernize the country and abolished all foreign extraterritorial rights.

Increased pro-Axis activity led to Anglo-Russian occupation of Iran in 1941 and deposition of the Shah in favor of his son, Mohammed Reza Pahlavi.

Ali Razmara became Premier in 1950 and pledged to restore efficient and honest government, but he was assassinated after less than nine months in office and Mohammed Mossadegh took over. Mossadegh was ousted in August 1953, by Fazollah Zahedi, whom the Shah had named Premier.

Opposition to the Shah spread, despite the imposition of martial law in September 1978, and massive demonstrations demanded the return of the exiled Ayatollah Ruhollah Khomeini. Riots and strikes continued despite the appointment of an opposition leader, Shahpur Bakhtiar, as Premier on Dec. 29. The Shah and his family left Iran on Jan. 16, 1979, for a "vacation," leaving power in the hands of a regency council.

Khomeini returned on Feb. 1 to a nation in turmoil as military units loyal to the Shah continued to support Bakhtiar and clashed with revolutionaries. Khomeini appointed Mehdi Bazargan as Premier of the provisional government and in two days of fighting, revolutionaries forced the military to capitulate on Feb. 11.

The new government began a program of nationalization of insurance companies, banks, and industries both locally and foreign-owned. Oil production fell amid the political confusion.

Khomeini, ignoring opposition, proceeded with his plans for revitalizing Islamic traditions. He urged women to return to the veil, or chador; banned alcohol and mixed bathing, and prohibited music from radio and television broadcasting, declaring it to be "no different from opium."

Revolutionary militants invaded the U.S. Embassy in Teheran on Nov. 4, 1979, seized staff members as hostages, and precipitated an international crisis.

Khomeini refused all appeals, even a unanimous vote by the U.N. Security Council demanding immediate release of the hostages.

Iranian hostility toward Washington was reinforced by the Carter administration's economic boycott and deportation order against Iranian students in the U.S., the break in diplomatic relations and ultimately an aborted U.S. raid in April aimed at rescuing the hostages.

As the first anniversary of the embassy seizure neared, Khomeini and his followers insisted on their original conditions: guarantee by the U.S. not to interfere in Iran's affairs, cancellation of U.S. damage claims against Iran, release of $8 billion in frozen Iranian assets, an apology, and the return of the assets held by the former imperial family.

These conditions were largely met and the 52 American hostages were released on Jan. 20, ending 444 days in captivity.

From the release of the hostages onward, President Bani-Sadr and the conservative clerics of the dominant Islamic Republican Party clashed with growing frequency. He was stripped of his command of the armed forces by Khomeini on June 6 and ousted as president on June 22. On July 24, Prime Minister Mohammed Ali Rajai was elected overwhelmingly to the Presidency.

Rajai and Prime Minister Mohammed Javad Bahonar were killed on Aug. 30 by a bomb in Bahonar's office. Hojatolislam Mohammed Ali Khamenei, a clergyman, leader of the Islamic Republican Party and spokesman for Khomeini, was elected president on Oct. 2, 1981.

The sporadic war with Iraq regained momentum in 1982, as Iran launched an offensive in March and regained much of the border area occupied by Iraq in late 1980.

Iran continued to be at war with Iraq well into 1988. Although Iraq expressed its willingness to cease fighting, Iran stated that it would not stop the war until Iraq agreed to make payment for war damages to Iran, and punish the Iraqi government leaders involved in the conflict.

On July 20, 1988, Khomeini, after a series of Iranian military reverses, agreed to cease-fire negotiations with Iraq. A cease-fire went into effect Aug. 20, 1988. Khomeini died in June 1989.

By early 1991 the Islamic Revolution appeared to have lost much of its militancy. Attempting to revive a stagnant economy, President Rafsanjani took measures to decentralize the command system and introduce free-market mechanisms.

In June 1996 Ali Akbar Nateq-Nouri, a hard liner, was re-elected for one year as speaker of Parliament.

Mohammad Khatami, a moderate cleric and former culture minister, won the presidential balloting with 69% of the vote in May 1997. His principal opponent, Nateq–Nouri, accused Khatami during the campaign of pro-Western sympathies.

IRAQ

Republic of Iraq
National name: Jumhouriyat Al Iraq
President: Saddam Hussein (1979)
Area: 167,920 sq mi. (434,913 sq km)
Population (1997 est.): 22,219,289 (average annual rate of natural increase: 3.61%); birth rate: 42.52/1000; infant mortality rate: 57.5/1000; density per square mile: 132.3
Capital: Baghdad. **Largest cities (est. 1985):** Baghdad, 4,648,609; Basra, 616,700; Mosul, 570,926. **Monetary unit:** Iraqi dinar. **Languages:** Arabic (official) and Kurdish. **Ethnicity/Race:** Arab 75%–80%, Kurdish 15%–20%, Turkoman, Assyrian or other 5%. **Religions:** Islam, 95%; Christian or other, 5%. **Literacy rate:** 60%
Economic summary: Gross domestic product: purchasing power parity (1995 est.): $41.1 billion, $2,000 per

capita; real growth rate n.a.; inflation: n.a. Unemployment rate: n.a. Arable land: 12%. Principal products: dates, livestock, wheat, barley, cotton, rice. Labor force: 4.4 million (1989); services, 48%; agriculture, 30%; industry, 22%. Major products: petroleum, chemicals, textiles, construction materials. Natural resources: oil, natural gas, phosphates, sulfur. Exports: petroleum and refined products, machinery, chemicals, dates. Imports: manufactured goods, food. Major trading partners: France, Italy, Japan, Germany, Brazil, U.K., U.S., Turkey, C.I.S. countries.

Geography. Iraq, a triangle of mountains, desert, and fertile river valley, is bounded on the east by Iran, on the north by Turkey, the west by Syria and Jordan, and the south by Saudi Arabia and Kuwait. It is twice the size of Idaho.

The country has arid desertland west of the Euphrates, a broad central valley between the Euphrates and Tigris, and mountains in the northeast. The fertile lower valley is formed by the delta of the two rivers, which join about 120 miles (193 km) from the head of the Persian Gulf. The gulf coastline is 26 miles (42 km) long. The only port for seagoing vessels is Basra, which is on the Shatt-al-Arab River near the head of the Persian Gulf.

Government. Since the coup d'état of July 1968, Iraq has been governed by the Arab Ba'ath Socialist Party through a Council of Command of the Revolution headed by the President. There is also a Council of Ministers headed by the President and a National Council (parliament).

History. From earliest times Iraq was known as Mesopotamia—the land between the rivers—for it embraces a large part of the alluvial plains of the Tigris and Euphrates.

An advanced civilization existed by 4000 B.C.E. Sometime after 2000 B.C.E. the land became the center of the ancient Babylonian and Assyrian empires. It was conquered by Cyrus the Great of Persia in 538 B.C.E., and by Alexander in 331 B.C.E. After an Arab conquest in 637–40, Baghdad became capital of the ruling caliphate. The country was cruelly pillaged by the Mongols in 1258, and during the 16th, 17th, and 18th centuries was the object of repeated Turkish-Persian competition.

Nominal Turkish suzerainty imposed in 1638 was replaced by direct Turkish rule in 1831. In World War I, an Anglo-Indian force occupied most of the country, and Britain was given a mandate over the area in 1920. The British recognized Iraq as a kingdom in 1922 and terminated the mandate in 1932 when Iraq was admitted to the League of Nations. In World War II, Iraq generally adhered to its 1930 treaty of alliance with Britain, but in 1941, British troops were compelled to put down a pro-Axis revolt led by Premier Rashid Ali.

Iraq became a charter member of the Arab League in 1945, and Iraqi troops took part in the Arab invasion of Palestine in 1948.

Faisal II, born on May 2, 1935, succeeded his father, Ghazi I, who was killed in an automobile accident on April 4, 1939. Faisal and his uncle, Crown Prince Abdul-Illah, were assassinated in July 1958 in a swift revolutionary coup that brought to power a military junta headed by Abdul Karem Kassim. Kassim, in turn, was overthrown and killed in a coup staged March 8, 1963, by the Ba'ath Socialist Party.

Abdel Salam Arif, a leader in the 1958 coup, staged another coup in November 1963, driving the Ba'ath members of the revolutionary council from power. He adopted a new constitution in 1964. In 1966, he, two cabinet members, and other supporters died in a helicopter crash. His brother, Gen. Abdel Rahman Arif, assumed the presidency, crushed the opposition, and won an indefinite extension of his term in 1967. His regime was ousted in July 1968 by a junta led by Maj. Gen. Ahmed Hassan al-Bakr.

A long-standing dispute over control of the Shatt al-Arab waterway between Iraq and Iran broke into full-scale war on Sept. 20, 1980. Iraqi planes attacked Iranian airfields and the Abadan refinery, and Iraqi ground forces moved into Iran.

Despite the smaller size of its armed forces, Iraq took and held the initiative by seizing Abadan and Khurramshahr together with substantial Iranian territory by December and beating back Iranian counterattacks in January. Peace efforts by the Islamic nations, the non-aligned, and the United Nations failed as 1981 wore on and the war stagnated.

In 1982, the Iraqis fell back to their own country and dug themselves in behind sandbagged defensive fortifications. From the beginning of the war in September 1980 to September 1984, foreign military analysts estimated that more than 100,000 Iranians and perhaps 50,000 Iraqis had been killed. The Iraqis clearly wanted to end the war, but the Iranians refused.

In February 1986, Iranian forces gained on two fronts; but Iraq retook most of the lost ground in 1988 and the war continued as a stalemate. In August, Iraq and Iran agreed they would hold direct talks after a cease-fire took effect.

In July 1990, President Hussein claimed that Kuwait was flooding world markets with oil and forcing down prices. A mediation attempt by Arab leaders failed, and on Aug. 2, 1990, over this and territorial claims, Iraqi troops invaded Kuwait and set up a puppet government. On January 18, 1991, U.N. forces, under the leadership of U.S. General Norman Schwarzkopf, launched Operation Desert Storm, liberating Kuwait in less than a week.

After the Gulf War, Saddam Hussein was still in power. The U.N. Security Council affirmed an embargo against military supplies to that country and a trade embargo was still in place.

In May 1996 the country was permitted to sell $2 billion of oil over an initial six-month period so as to buy much-needed food and medicine. In June 1997 the U.N. Security Council agreed to extend the plan. Shortly after, however, Iraq temporarily suspended its oil exports to protest what it felt were slow deliveries of food and medicine.

IRELAND

National name: Ireland, or Eire in the Irish language
President: vacant as of Sept. 1997
Taoiseach (Prime Minister): Bertie Ahern (1997)
Area: 27,136 sq mi. (70,282 sq km)
Population (1997 est.): 3,555,500 (average annual rate of natural increase: 0.36%); birth rate: 13.5/1000; infant mortality rate: 6.3/1000; density per square mile: 12.56
Capital: Dublin. **Largest cities (1991):** Dublin, 1,056,666; Cork, 293,254; Galway, 131,503; Limerick, 112,975. **Monetary unit:** Irish pound (punt). **Languages:** Irish, English. **Ethnicity/Race:** Celtic, English. **Religions:** Roman Catholic, 92%; others, 8%. **Literacy rate:** 99%
Economic summary: Gross domestic product: purchasing power parity (1996): $58.4 billion; $16,128 per capita; real growth rate 7.25%; inflation 1.6%; unemployment 11.6%. Arable land: 14%. Principal products: cattle and dairy products, pigs, poultry and eggs, sheep and wool, horses, barley, sugar beets. Labor force (1996): 1,424,000; 28% in manufacturing and construction. Major products: processed foods, brews,

textiles, clothing, chemicals, pharmaceuticals, machinery, transportation equipment, glass and crystal. Natural resources: zinc, lead, natural gas, crude oil, barite, copper, gypsum, limestone, dolomite, peat, silver. Exports: $53.49 billion (1996): livestock, dairy products, machinery, chemicals, data processing equipment. Imports: $46.09 billion (1996): food, animal feed, chemicals, petroleum products, machinery, textile clothing. Major trading partners: U.K., Western European countries, U.S.

Geography. Ireland is situated in the Atlantic Ocean and separated from Britain by the Irish Sea. Half the size of Arkansas, it occupies the entire island except for the six counties which make up Northern Ireland.

Ireland resembles a basin—a central plain rimmed with mountains, except in the Dublin region. The mountains are low, with the highest peak, Carrantuohill in County Kerry, rising to 3,415 feet (1,041 m).

The principal river is the Shannon, which begins in the north central area, flows south and southwest for about 240 miles (386 km), and empties into the Atlantic.

Government. Ireland is a parliamentary democracy. The National Parliament (Oireachtas) consists of the President and two Houses, the House of Representatives (Dáil éireann) and the Senate (Seanad éireann), whose members serve for a maximum term of five years. The House of Representatives has 166 members elected by proportional representation; the Senate has 60 members, 11 of whom are nominated by the Prime Minister, 6 by the universities and the remaining 43 from five vocational panels. The Prime Minister (Taoiseach), who is the head of government, is appointed by the President on the nomination of the House of Representatives, to which he is responsible.

History. In the Stone and Bronze Ages, Ireland was inhabited by Picts in the north and a people called the Erainn in the south, the same stock, apparently, as in all the isles before the Anglo-Saxon invasion of Britain. About the fourth century B.C.E., tall, red-haired Celts arrived from Gaul or Galicia. They subdued and assimilated the inhabitants and established a Gaelic civilization.

By the beginning of the Christian Era, Ireland was divided into five kingdoms—Ulster, Connacht, Leinster, Meath, and Munster. St. Patrick introduced Christianity in 432 and the country developed into a center of Gaelic and Latin learning. Irish monasteries, the equivalent of universities, attracted intellectuals as well as the pious and sent out missionaries to many parts of Europe and, some believe, to North America.

Norse depredations along the coasts, starting in 795, ended in 1014 with Norse defeat at the Battle of Clontarf by forces under Brian Boru. In the 12th century, the Pope gave all Ireland to the English Crown as a papal fief. In 1171, Henry II of England was acknowledged "Lord of Ireland," but local sectional rule continued for centuries, and English control over the whole island was not reasonably absolute until the 17th century. By the Act of Union (1801), England and Ireland became the "United Kingdom of Great Britain and Ireland."

A steady decline in the Irish economy followed in the next decades. The population had reached 8.25 million when the great potato famine of 1846–48 took many lives and drove millions to emigrate to America. By 1921 it was down to 4.3 million.

In the meantime, anti-British agitation continued along with demands for Irish home rule. The advent of World War I delayed the institution of home rule and resulted in the Easter Rebellion in Dublin (April 24–29, 1916), in which Irish nationalists unsuccessfully attempted to throw off British rule. Guerrilla warfare against British forces followed proclamation of a republic by the rebels in 1919.

The Irish Free State was established as a dominion on Dec. 6, 1922, with the six northern counties as part of the United Kingdom. Ireland was neutral in World War II.

In 1948, Eamon de Valera, American-born leader of the Sinn Fein, who had won establishment of the Free State in 1921 in negotiations with Britain's David Lloyd George, was defeated by John A. Costello, who demanded final independence from Britain. The Republic of Ireland was proclaimed on April 18, 1949. It withdrew from the Commonwealth but in 1955 entered the United Nations.

Through the 1960s, two antagonistic currents dominated Irish politics. One sought to bind the wounds of the rebellion and civil war. The other was the effort of the outlawed extremist Irish Republican Army to bring Northern Ireland into the republic.

In the elections of June 11, 1981, Garret M. D. FitzGerald, leader of the Fine Gael, was elected Prime Minister. FitzGerald resigned Jan. 27, 1982, after his presentation of an austerity budget aroused the opposition of independents who had backed him previously.

Three candidates vied in the November 1990 presidential election. Although Brian Lenihan of Fianna Fail led in the first round, Mary Robinson, supported by the Labour Party and the Workers Party, won the second round with 52.8% of the vote, becoming the first non-Fianna Fail president since 1945.

Amid allegations of scandal Prime Minister Haughey resigned in early 1992. Albert Reynolds was chosen by a majority of his Fianna Fail party to become the next Prime Minister. The general election of November 1992 saw Reynolds's Fianna Fail receive a plurality.

Reynolds's government fell in January 1995 over a scandal involving the handling of the extradition of a priest convicted of child molestation in the North.

A referendum on divorce, under certain conditions, which hitherto had been constitutionally forbidden, was held in November 1995 and narrowly passed.

National elections in June 1997 gave the opposition Fianna Fail, the country's largest party, a plurality of seats in the 166 seat Dail. However, failing a majority, a coalition had to be arranged.

ISRAEL

State of Israel
National name: Medinat Yisra'el
President: Ezer Weizman (1993)
Prime Minister: Benjamin Netanyahu (1996)
Area: 8,020 sq mi. (20,772 sq km)
Population (1997 est.): 5,534,672[1] (average annual rate of natural increase: 1.39%); birth rate: 20.16/1000; infant mortality rate: 8.3/1000; density per square mile: 690.1
Capital and largest city (1993 est.): Jerusalem[2], 550,500. **Other large cities (1993 est.):** Tel Aviv, 355,900; Haifa, 250,000. **Monetary unit:** Shekel. **Languages:** Hebrew, Arabic, English. **Ethnicity/Race:** Jewish 82% (Israel-born 50%, Europe/Americas/Oceania-born 20%, Africa-born 7%, Asia-born 5%), non-Jewish 18% (mostly Arab) (1993 est.). **Religions:** Judaism, 82%; Islam, 14%; Christian, 2%; others, 2%. **Literacy rate:** 92%
Economic summary: Gross domestic product: purchasing power parity (1995 est.): $80.1 billion; $15,500 per capita; real growth rate 7.1%; inflation 10.1%; unemployment 6.3%. Arable land: 17%. Principal agricultural products: citrus and other fruits, vegetables, beef, dairy and poultry products. Labor force (1992): 1.9 million; 29.3% in public services, industry 21.2%, commerce 13.9%; finance and business 10.4%. Major

industrial products: processed foods, cut diamonds, clothing and textiles, chemicals, metal products, transport and electrical equipment, high-technology electronics. Natural resources: sulfur, copper, phosphates, potash, bromine. Exports: $28.4 billion (f.o.b., 1995 est.): polished diamonds, citrus and other fruits, clothing and textiles, processed foods, electronics, military hardware, fertilizer and chemical products. Imports: $40.1 billion (c.i.f., 1995 est.): rough diamonds, chemicals, oil, machinery, iron and steel, cereals, textiles, vehicles, ships, aircraft. Major trading partners: U.S., E.U., Japan.

1. Includes West Bank, Gaza Strip, East Jerusalem. 2. Not recognized by U.S. which recognizes Tel Aviv.

Geography. Israel, slightly smaller than Massachusetts, lies at the eastern end of the Mediterranean Sea. It is bordered by Egypt on the west, Syria and Jordan on the east, and Lebanon on the north. Northern Israel is largely a plateau traversed from north to south by mountains and broken by great depressions, also running from north to south.

The maritime plain of Israel is remarkably fertile. The southern Negev region, which comprises almost half the total area, is largely a wide desert steppe area. The National Water Project irrigation scheme is now transforming it into fertile land. The Jordan, the only important river, flows from the north through Lake Hule (Waters of Merom) and Lake Kinneret (Sea of Galilee or Sea of Tiberias), finally entering the Dead Sea, 1,290 feet (393 m) below sea level. This "sea," which is actually a salt lake (394 sq mi.; 1,020 sq km), has no outlet, its water balance being maintained by evaporation.

Government. Israel, which does not have a written constitution, has a republican form of government headed by a President elected for a five-year term by the Knesset. The President may serve no more than two terms. The Knesset has 120 members elected by universal suffrage under proportional representation for four years. The government is administered by the cabinet, which is headed by the Prime Minister.

The Knesset decided in June 1950 that Israel would acquire a constitution gradually through the years by the enactment of fundamental laws. Israel grants automatic citizenship to every Jew who desires to settle within its borders, subject to control of the Knesset.

History. Palestine, cradle of two great religions and homeland of the modern state of Israel, was known to the ancient Hebrews as the "Land of Canaan." Palestine's name derives from the Philistines, a people who occupied the southern coastal part of the country in the 12th century B.C.E.

A Hebrew kingdom established in 1000 B.C.E. was later split into the kingdoms of Judah and Israel; they were subsequently invaded by Assyrians, Babylonians, Egyptians, Persians, Macedonians, Romans, and Byzantines. The Arabs took Palestine from the Byzantine empire C.E. 634–40. With the exception of a Frankish Crusader Kingdom from 1099 to 1187, Palestine remained under Moslem rule until the 20th century (Turkish rule from 1516), when British forces under Gen. Sir Edmund Allenby defeated the Turks and captured Jerusalem Dec. 9, 1917. The League of Nations granted Britain a mandate to govern Palestine, effective in 1923.

Jewish colonies—Jews from Russia established one as early as 1882—multiplied after Theodor Herzl's 1897 call for a Jewish state. The Zionist movement received official approval with the publication of a letter Nov. 2, 1917, from Arthur Balfour, British Foreign Secretary, to Lord Rothschild, a British Jewish leader. Balfour promised support for the establishment of a Jewish homeland in Palestine on the understanding that the civil and religious rights of non-Jewish Palestinians

would be safeguarded.

A 1937 British proposal called for an Arab and a Jewish state separated by a mandated area incorporating Jerusalem and Nazareth. Arabs opposed this, demanding a single state with minority rights for Jews, and a 1939 British White Paper retreated, offering instead a single state with further Jewish immigration to be limited to 75,000. Although the White Paper satisfied neither side, further discussion ended on the outbreak of World War II, when the Jewish population stood at nearly 500,000—mostly the result of Hitler's persecution of European Jews—or 30% of the total. The war allowed Hitler to carry out his "final solution" for the Jews—the genocide of six million Jews at the hands of the Nazis and their collaborators, known as the Holocaust. Illegal and legal immigration during the war brought the Jewish population to 678,000 in 1946, compared with 1,269,000 Arabs. Unable to reach a compromise, Britain turned the problem over to the United Nations in 1947, which on November 29 voted for partition—despite strong Arab opposition.

Britain did not help implement the U.N. decision and withdrew on expiration of its mandate May 14, 1948. Zionists had already seized control of areas designated as Jewish, and, on the day of British departure, the Jewish National Council proclaimed the State of Israel.

U.S. recognition came within hours. The next day, Jordanian and Egyptian forces invaded the new nation. At the cease-fire Jan. 7, 1949, Israel increased its original territory by 50%, taking western Galilee, a broad corridor through central Palestine to Jerusalem, and part of modern Jerusalem. (In April 1950, Jordan annexed areas of eastern and central Palestine that had been designated for an Arab state, together with the old city of Jerusalem.) Chaim Weizmann and David Ben-Gurion became Israel's first President and Prime Minister. The new government was admitted to the U.N. May 11, 1949.

The next clash with Arab neighbors came when Egypt nationalized the Suez Canal in 1956 and barred Israeli shipping. Coordinating with an Anglo-French force, Israeli troops seized the Gaza Strip and drove through the Sinai to the east bank of the Suez Canal, but withdrew under U.S. and U.N. pressure. In 1967, Israel threatened retaliation against Syrian border raids, and Syria asked Egyptian aid. Egypt demanded the removal of U.N. peace-keeping forces from Suez, staged a national mobilization, closed the Gulf of Aqaba, and moved troops into the Sinai. Starting with simultaneous air attacks against Syrian, Jordanian, and Egyptian air bases on June 5, Israel during a six-day war totally defeated its Arab enemies. Expanding its territory by 200%, Israel at the cease-fire held the Golan Heights, the West Bank of the Jordan River, the Old City, and all of the Sinai and the east bank of the Suez Canal.

Israel insisted that Jerusalem remain a unified city and that peace negotiations be conducted directly, something the Arab states had refused to do because it would constitute a recognition of their Jewish neighbor.

Egypt's President Gamal Abdel Nasser renounced the 1967 cease-fire in 1969 and began a "war of attrition" against Israel, firing Soviet artillery at Israeli forces on the east bank of the canal. Nasser died of a heart attack on Sept. 28, 1970, and was succeeded by Anwar el-Sadat.

In the face of Israeli reluctance even to discuss the return of occupied territories, the fourth Mideast war erupted Oct. 6, 1973, with a surprise Egyptian and Syrian assault on the Jewish high holy day of Yom Kippur. Initial Arab gains were reversed when a cease-fire took effect two weeks later, but Israel suffered heavy losses in manpower.

U.S. Secretary of State Henry A. Kissinger arranged a disengagement of forces on both the Egyptian and

Syrian fronts. Geneva talks, aimed at a lasting peace, foundered, however, when Israel balked at inclusion of the Palestine Liberation Organization.

A second-stage Sinai withdrawal signed by Israel and Egypt in September 1975 required Israel to give up the strategic Mitla and Gidi passes and to return the captured Abu Rudeis oil fields. Egypt guaranteed passage of Israeli cargoes through the reopened Suez Canal, and both sides renounced force in the settlement of disputes. Two hundred U.S. civilian technicians were stationed in a widened U.N. buffer zone to monitor and warn either side of truce violations.

A dramatic breakthrough in the tortuous history of Mideast peace efforts occurred Nov. 9, 1977, when Egypt's President Sadat declared his willingness to go anywhere to talk peace. Prime Minister Menachem Begin on Nov. 15 extended an invitation to the Egyptian leader to address the Knesset. Sadat's arrival in Israel four days later raised worldwide hopes. But optimism ebbed even before Begin was invited to Ismailia by Sadat, December 25–26.

An Israeli peace plan unveiled by Begin on his return, and approved by the Knesset, offered to end military administration in the West Bank and the Gaza Strip, with a degree of Arab self-rule but no relinquishment of sovereignty by Israel. Sadat severed talks on Jan. 18 and, despite U.S. condemnation, Begin approved new West Bank settlements by Israelis.

On March 14, 1979, after a visit by President Carter, the Knesset approved a final peace treaty, and 12 days later Begin and Sadat signed the document, together with Carter, in a White House ceremony. Israel began its withdrawal from the Sinai on May 25 by handing over the coastal town of El Arish and the two countries opened their border on May 29.

One of the most difficult periods in Israel's history began with a confrontation with Syria over the placing by Syria of Soviet surface-to-air missiles in the Bekaa Valley of Lebanon in April 1981. President Reagan dispatched Philip C. Habib to prevent a clash. While Habib was seeking a settlement, Begin ordered a bombing raid against an Iraqi nuclear reactor on June 7, invoking the theory of preemptive self-defense because he said Iraq was planning to make nuclear weapons to attack Israel.

Although Israel withdrew its last settlers from the Sinai in April 1982 and agreed to a Sinai "peace patrol" composed of troops from four West European nations, the fragile peace engineered by Habib in Lebanon was shattered on June 9 by a massive Israeli assault on southern Lebanon. The attack was in retaliation for what Israel charged was a PLO attack that had critically wounded the Israeli ambassador to London six days earlier.

Israeli armor swept through UNIFIL lines in southern Lebanon, destroyed PLO strongholds in Tyre and Sidon, and reached the suburbs of Beirut on June 10. As Israeli troops ringed Moslem East Beirut, where 5,000 PLO guerrillas were believed trapped, Habib sought to negotiate a safe exit for them.

A U.S.-mediated accord between Lebanon and Israel, signed on May 17, 1983, provided for Israeli withdrawal from Lebanon. Israeli withdrawal was conditioned on withdrawal of Syrian troops from the Bekaa Valley, however, and the Syrians refused to leave. Israel eventually withdrew its troops from the Beirut area, but kept them in southern Lebanon. Lebanon, under pressure from Syria, canceled the accord in March 1984.

Prime Minister Begin resigned on Sept. 15, 1983. On Oct. 10, Likud Party stalwart Yitzhak Shamir was elected Prime Minister.

After a close election, the two major parties worked out a carefully balanced power-sharing agreement and the Knesset, on Sept. 14, 1984 approved a national unity government including both the Labor Alignment and the Likud bloc.

In one hopeful development, the coalition government declared an economic emergency on July 1 and imposed sweeping austerity measures intended to break the country's 260% inflation. By the end of Peres' term in October, 1986, the shekel had been revalued and stabilized and inflation was down to less than 20%.

In Dec. 1987, riots by Gazan Palestinians led to the current general uprising throughout the occupied territories which consists of low-level violence and civil disobedience.

A deadlock in the elections of Dec. 1988 led to a continuation of the Likud-Labor national unity government. This collapsed in 1990, leading to Shamir forming a right-wing coalition that included the religious parties.

The relaxation of Soviet emigration rules resulted in a massive wave of Jews entering Israel. Citing for one the severe housing shortage, but probably owing as much to political considerations, Israel embarked on constructing new settlements in the West Bank.

Elections in late June 1992 scored a major victory for Rabin's Labor Party but without a parliamentary majority, forcing the new Prime Minister to search for coalition partners.

In highly secretive Norwegian-sponsored talks Israel and the PLO hammered out an agreement for limited Palestinian self-rule and measured Israeli withdrawal from the West Bank. The accord itself was signed in Cairo in May 1994.

On November 4, 1995, Prime Minister Rabin was slain by a Jewish extremist, jeopardizing the tenuous progress toward peace. Shimon Peres succeeded him until May 1996 elections for the Knesset gave Israel a new hard line Prime Minister by a razor-thin margin.

Elections for seats on the Palestinian Council and for its president took place in January 1996. A number of independent candidates won a position, but Yasser Arafat obtained an easy victory as president.

The Prime Minister narrowly escaped indictment in an influence–peddling scandal in early 1997, and his political stock eroded in light of the charges. Yet despite opposition calls for his resignation, Netanyahu retained his position.

The peace process in the meantime largely slowed. However, in January 1997 Israel and the Palestinian Authority agreed on an accord for Israeli withdrawal from Hebron.

ITALY

Italian Republic
National name: Repubblica Italiana
President: Oscar Luigi Scalfaro (1992)
Prime Minister: Romano Prodi (1996)
Area: 116,500 sq mi. (301,278 sq km)
Population (1997 est.): 57,534,088 (average annual rate of natural increase: –0.01%); birth rate: 9.8/1000; infant mortality rate: 6.8/1000; density per square mile: 493.8
Capital and largest city (1994 est.): Rome, 2,687,881. **Other large cities:** Milan, 1,334,171; Naples, 1,061,583; Turin, 945,551; Palermo, 694,749; Genoa, 659,754; Bologna, 394,969; Florence, 392,800; Bari, 338,949; Catania, 327,163; Venice, 306,439. **Monetary unit:** Lira. **Language:** Italian. **Ethnicity/Race:** Italian (includes small clusters of German-, French-, and Slovene-Italians in the north and Albanian-Italians and Greek-Italians in the south), Sicilians, Sardinians. **Religion:** Roman Catholic, almost 100%. **Literacy rate:** 97%
Economic summary: Gross domestic product: purchasing power parity (1995 est.): $1.0886 trillion, $18,700

per capita; 3.2% real growth rate; inflation rate 5.4%; unemployment rate 12.2% (Jan. 95). Arable land: 32%. Principal agricultural products: grapes, olives, citrus fruits, vegetables, wheat, corn. Labor force: 23.988 million; 58% in services; 32.2% in industry; 9.8% in agriculture. Major industrial products: machinery, iron and steel, autos, textiles, shoes, chemicals. Natural resources: mercury, potash, sulfur, fish, gas, marble. Exports: $190.8 billion (f.o.b., 1994): textiles, apparel, metals, transport equipment, chemicals. Imports: $168.7 billion (c.i.f., 1994): petroleum, industrial machinery, chemicals, food, metals. Major trading partners: United States, E.U., OPEC.

Geography. Italy is a long peninsula shaped like a boot bounded on the west by the Tyrrhenian Sea and on the east by the Adriatic. Slightly larger than Arizona, it has for neighbors France, Switzerland, Austria, and Yugoslavia.

Approximately 600 of Italy's 708 miles (1,139 km) of length are in the long peninsula that projects into the Mediterranean from the fertile basin of the Po River. The Apennine Mountains, branching off from the Alps between Nice and Genoa, form the peninsula's backbone, and rise to a maximum height of 9,560 feet (2,912 m) at the Gran Sasso d'Italia (Corno). The Alps form Italy's northern boundary.

Several islands form part of Italy. Sicily (9,926 sq mi.; 25,708 sq km) lies off the toe of the boot, across the Strait of Messina, with a steep and rockbound northern coast and gentler slopes to the sea in the west and south. Mount Etna, an active volcano, rises to 10,741 feet (3,274 m), and most of Sicily is more than 500 feet (3,274 m) in elevation. Sixty-two miles (100 km) southwest of Sicily lies Pantelleria (45 sq mi.; 117 sq km), and south of that are Lampedusa and Linosa. Sardinia (9,301 sq mi.; 24,090 sq km), which is just south of Corsica and about 125 miles (200 km) west of the mainland, is mountainous, stony, and unproductive.

Italy has many northern lakes, lying below the snow-covered peaks of the Alps. The largest are Garda (143 sq mi.; 370 sq km), Maggiore (83 sq mi.; 215 sq km), and Como (55 sq mi.; 142 sq km).

The Po, the principal river, flows from the Alps on Italy's western border and crosses the Lombard plain to the Adriatic.

Government. The President is elected for a term of seven years by Parliament in joint session with regional representatives. The President nominates the Premier and, upon the Premier's recommendations, the members of the cabinet. Parliament is composed of two houses: a Senate with 315 elective members and a Chamber of Deputies of 630 members elected by the people for a five-year term.

History. Until C.E. 476, when the German Odoacer became head of the Roman Empire in the west, the history of Italy was largely the history of Rome. From C.E. 800 on, the Holy Roman Emperors, Popes, Normans, and Saracens all vied for control over various segments of the Italian peninsula. Numerous city states, such as Venice and Genoa, and many small principalities flourished in the late Middle Ages.

In 1713, after the War of the Spanish Succession, Milan, Naples, and Sardinia were handed over to Austria, which lost some of its Italian territories in 1735. After 1800, Italy was unified by Napoleon, who Crowned himself King of Italy in 1805; but with the Congress of Vienna in 1815, Austria once again became the dominant power in Italy.

Austrian armies crushed Italian uprisings in 1820–1821, and 1831. In the 1830s Giuseppe Mazzini, brilliant liberal nationalist, organized the Risorgimento (Resurrection), which laid the foundation for Italian unity.

Disappointed Italian patriots looked to the House of Savoy for leadership. Count Camille di Cavour (1810–61), Premier of Sardinia in 1852 and the architect of a united Italy, joined England and France in the Crimean War (1853–56), and in 1859, helped France in a war against Austria, thereby obtaining Lombardy. By plebiscite in 1860, Modena, Parma, Tuscany, and the Romagna voted to join Sardinia. In 1860, Giuseppe Garibaldi conquered Sicily and Naples and turned them over to Sardinia. Victor Emmanuel II, King of Sardinia, was proclaimed King of Italy in 1861.

Allied with Germany and Austria-Hungary in the Triple Alliance of 1882, Italy declared its neutrality upon the outbreak of World War I on the ground that Germany had embarked upon an offensive war. In 1915, Italy entered the war on the side of the Allies.

Benito (Il Duce) Mussolini, a former Socialist, organized discontented Italians in 1919 into the Fascist Party to "rescue Italy from Bolshevism." He led his Black Shirts in a march on Rome and, on Oct. 28, 1922, became Premier. He transformed Italy into a dictatorship, embarking on an expansionist foreign policy with the invasion and annexation of Ethiopia in 1935 and allying himself with Adolf Hitler in the Rome-Berlin Axis in 1936. He was executed by Partisans on April 28, 1945 at Dongo on Lake Como.

Following the overthrow of Mussolini's dictatorship and the armistice with the Allies (Sept. 3, 1943), Italy joined the war against Germany as a co-belligerent. King Victor Emmanuel III abdicated May 9, 1946, and left the country after having installed his son as King Humbert II. A plebiscite rejected monarchy, however, and on June 13, King Humbert followed his father into exile.

The peace treaty of Sept. 15, 1947, required Italian renunciation of all claims in Ethiopia and Greece and the cession of the Dodecanese to Greece and of five small Alpine areas to France. Much of the Istrian Peninsula, including Fiume and Pola, went to Yugoslavia.

The Trieste area west of the new Yugoslav territory was made a free territory (until 1954, when the city and a 90-square-mile zone were transferred to Italy and the rest to Yugoslavia).

Scandal brought the long reign of the Christian Democrats to an end when Italy's 40th Premier since World War II, Arnaldo Forlani, was forced to resign in the wake of disclosure that many high-ranking Christian Democrats and civil servants belonged to a secret Masonic lodge known as "P-2."

In elections of April 1992 the Christian Democrats obtained less than one-third of the vote, their lowest ever but still making them the largest party. Andreotti routinely handed in his resignation but to compound matters President Cossiga also did so shortly afterwards.

During the early months of 1993 the nation was riveted by a political scandal of a seemingly ever-growing size involving the Mafia and many government leaders. In a referendum in mid-April voters approved changing the current proportional system of representation in the Senate for one utilizing majority voting.

As a result of March 1994 elections an alliance between the Forza Italia party and two other parties dislodged the Christian Democrats.

In the face of a gradual erosion of support during the year, Berlusconi was forced to resign in December. The Dini government nominated in January 1995 was seen as a reprieve from the ongoing corruption inquiries.

Just as Prime Minister Dini was to start as president of the European Union, he failed to win support in Parliament for his government. He submitted his resignation in January 1996.

Italian forces in early 1997 assumed leadership of a military mission to protect international aid reaching strife–torn Albania. The Communists refused to support the operation but refrained from withdrawing support from the government.

JAMAICA

Sovereign: Queen Elizabeth II (1952)
Governor-General: H.E. The Most Hon. Sir Howard F. H. Cooke (1991)
Prime Minister: The Rt. Hon. Percival J. Patterson (1992)
Area: 4,411 sq mi. (11,424 sq km)
Population (1997 est.): 2,615,582 (average annual rate of natural increase: 1.6%); birth rate: 21.56/1000; infant mortality rate: 15/1000; density per square mile: 593
Capital and largest city (1991 est.): Kingston, 104,000.
Monetary unit: Jamaican dollar. **Language:** English, Jamaican Creole. **Ethnicity/Race:** African 76.3%, Afro-European 15.1%, East Indian and Afro-East Indian 3%, white 3.2%, Chinese and Afro-Chinese 1.2%, other 1.2%. **Religions:** Protestant, 55.9%; Roman Catholic, 5%; other, 39.1%. **Literacy rate:** 98%
Economic summary: Gross domestic product: purchasing power parity (1995 est.): $8.2 billion; $3,200 per capita; real growth rate 0.8%; inflation 25.5%; unemployment 15.4% (1994 est.). Arable land: 19%. Principal products: sugar cane, citrus fruits, bananas, coffee, potatoes, livestock. Labor force: 1,062,100; services, 41%; agriculture, 22.5%; industry, 19%. Industries: tourism, bauxite mining, textiles, processed foods, light manufactures. Natural resources: bauxite, gypsum. Exports: $2 billion (f.o.b., 1995 est.): alumina, bauxite, sugar, bananas. Imports: $2.7 billion (f.o.b., 1995 est.): fuels, machinery, consumer goods, construction goods, food. Major trading partners: U.S., U.K., Canada, Norway, Trinidad and Tobago, Venezuela, Japan. **Member of Commonwealth of Nations**

Geography. Jamaica is an island in the West Indies, 90 miles (145 km) south of Cuba and 100 miles (161 km) west of Haiti. It is a little smaller than Connecticut.

The island is made up of a plateau and the Blue Mountains, a group of volcanic hills, in the east. Blue Mountain (7,402 ft.; 2,256 m) is the tallest peak.

Government. The legislature is a 60-member House of Representatives elected by universal suffrage and an appointed Senate of 21 members. The Prime Minister is appointed by the Governor-General and must, in the Governor-General's opinion, be the person best able to command the confidence of a majority of the members of the House of Representatives.

History. Jamaica was inhabited by Arawak Indians when Columbus visited it in 1494 and named it St. Iago. It remained under Spanish rule until 1655, then became a British possession. The island prospered from wealth brought by buccaneers to their base, Port Royal, the capital, until the city disappeared in the sea in 1692 after an earthquake. The Arawaks died off from disease and exploitation, and slaves, mostly black, were imported to work sugar plantations. Abolition of the slave trade (1807), emancipation of the slaves (1833), and a gradual drop in sugar prices led to depressed economic conditions that resulted in an uprising in 1865.

The following year Jamaica's status was changed to that of a colony, and conditions improved considerably. Introduction of banana cultivation made the island less dependent on the sugar crop for its well-being.

On May 5, 1953, Jamaica attained internal autonomy, and in 1958 it led in organizing the West Indies Federation. This effort at Caribbean unification failed. A nationalist labor leader, Sir Alexander Bustamente, led a campaign for withdrawal from the Federation. As the result of a popular referendum in 1961, Jamaica became independent on Aug. 6, 1962.

Michael Manley became Prime Minister in 1972 and initiated a socialist program.

The Labour Party defeated Manley's People's National Party in 1980 and its capitalist-oriented leader, Edward P. G. Seaga, became Prime Minister. He instituted measures to encourage private investment.

Like other Caribbean countries, Jamaica was hard-hit by the 1981–82 recession. By 1984, austerity measures that Seaga instituted in the hope of bringing the economy back into balance included elimination of government subsidies. Devaluation of the Jamaican dollar made Jamaican products more competitive on the world market and Jamaica achieved record growth in tourism and agriculture. Manufacturing also grew. But at the same time, the cost of many foods went up 50% to 75% and thousands of Jamaicans fell deeper into poverty.

The PNP decisively won local elections in mid-July, 1987, signaling a weakening in Seaga's position. In 1989, Manley swept back into power with a clear-cut victory. He indicated that he would pursue more centrist policies than he did in his previous administration.

Manley stepped down in 1992 for reasons of health, being replaced by P. J. Patterson.

Parliamentary elections in March 1993 were marred by violence in which 11 died. The PNP received 53 of the 60 seats in Parliament.

In May 1997 the government signed an agreement with the U.S. allowing authorities from the latter to enter Jamaican waters and search vessels with the government's permission.

JAPAN

National name: Nippon
Emperor: Akihito (1989)
Prime Minister: Ryutaro Hashimoto
Area: 145,874 sq mi. (377,815 sq km)
Population (1997): 125,716,637; average annual rate of natural increase: 0.248% (1990 census); birth rate: 10.38/1000; infant mortality rate: 4.4/1000; density per square mile: 861.8
Capital: Tokyo. **Largest cities (Jan. 1993):** Tokyo, 8,122,000; Yokohama, 3,276,000; Osaka, 2,601,000; Nagoya, 2,162,000; Sapporo, 1,719,000; Kobe, 1,501,000; Kyoto, 1,456,000; Fukuoka, 1,263,000; Kawasaki, 1,196,000; Hiroshima, 1,099,000. **Monetary unit:** Yen. **Language:** Japanese. **Ethnicity/Race:** Japanese 99.4%, other 0.6% (mostly Korean). **Religions:** Shintoist, 111.8 million; Buddhist, 93.1 million; Christian, 1.4 million; other, 11.4 million. **Literacy rate:** 99.9%
Economic summary: Gross domestic product: purchasing power parity (1995 est.): $2.6792 trillion; $21,300 per capita; real growth rate 0.3%; inflation –0.1%; unemployment 3.1%. Arable land: 14%. Principal agricultural products: rice, vegetables, fruits, meat and dairy products. Labor force (1995): 66.7 million; 54% in trade and services; 33% in manufacturing, mining, and construction; 7% in agriculture, forestry, and fishing. Major industrial products: machinery and equipment, metals and metal products, autos, consumer electronics, chemicals, electrical and electronic equipment. Natural resource: fish. Exports: $442.84 billion (f.o.b, 1995): machinery and equipment, automobiles, metals and metal products, consumer electronics, semiconductors. Imports: $336.09 billion (c.i.f.,1995): fossil fuels, raw materials, foodstuffs, machinery and equipment. Major trading partners: U.S., Southeast Asia, European Union.

Geography. An archipelago extending in an arc more than 1,744 miles (2,790 km) from northeast to southwest in the Pacific, Japan is separated from the east coast of Asia by the Sea of Japan. It is approximately the size of Montana.

Japan's four main islands are Honshu, Hokkaido, Kyushu, and Shikoku. The Ryukyu chain to the southwest was U.S.-occupied and the Kuriles to the northeast are Russian-occupied. The surface of the main islands consists largely of mountains separated by narrow valleys. There are about 60 more or less active volcanoes, of which the best-known is Mount Aso. Mount Fuji, seen on postcards, is not active.

Government. Japan's constitution, promulgated on Nov. 3, 1946, replaced the Meiji constitution of 1889. The 1946 constitution, sponsored by the U.S. during its occupation of Japan, brought fundamental changes to the Japanese political system, including the abandonment of the Emperor's divine rights. The Diet (Parliament) consists of a House of Representatives of 500 members, elected for four years, and a House of Councilors of 252 members, half of whom are elected every three years for six-year terms. Executive power is vested in the cabinet, which is headed by a Prime Minister, nominated by the Diet from its members.

On Jan. 7, 1989, Emperor Hirohito, Japan's longest-reigning monarch died and was succeeded by his son, Akihito (born 1933). He was married in 1959 to Michiko Shoda (the first time a Crown Prince married a commoner).

History. A series of legends attributes creation of Japan to the sun goddess, from whom the later emperors were allegedly descended. The first of them was Jimmu Tenno, supposed to have ascended the throne in 660 B.C.E.

Recorded Japanese history begins with the first contact with China in the 5th century C.E. Japan was then divided into strong feudal states, all nominally under the Emperor, but with real power often held by a court minister or clan. In 1185, Yoritomo, chief of the Minamoto clan, was designated Shogun (Generalissimo) with the administration of the islands under his control. A dual government system—Shogun and Emperor—continued until 1867.

First contact with the West came about 1542, when a Portuguese ship off course arrived in Japanese waters. Portuguese traders, Jesuit missionaries, and Spanish, Dutch, and English traders followed. Suspicious of Christianity and of Portuguese support of a local Japanese revolt, the shoguns prohibited all trade with foreign countries; only a Dutch trading post at Nagasaki was permitted. Western attempts to renew trading relations failed until 1853, when Commodore Matthew Perry sailed an American fleet into Tokyo Bay.

Japan now quickly made the transition from a medieval to a modern power. Feudalism was abolished and industrialization was speeded. An imperial army was established with conscription. The shogun system was abolished in 1868 by Emperor Meiji, and parliamentary government was established in 1889. After a brief war with China in 1894–95, Japan acquired Formosa (Taiwan), the Pescadores Islands, and part of southern Manchuria. China also recognized the independence of Korea (Chosen), which Japan later annexed (1910).

In 1904–05, Japan defeated Russia in the Russo-Japanese War, gaining the territory of southern Sakhalin (Karafuto) and Russia's port and rail rights in Manchuria. In World War I Japan seized Germany's Pacific islands and leased areas in China. The Treaty of Versailles then awarded it a mandate over the islands.

At the Washington Conference of 1921–22, Japan agreed to respect Chinese national integrity. The series of Japanese aggressions that was to lead to the nation's downfall began in 1931 with the invasion of Manchuria. The following year, Japan set up this area as a puppet state, "Manchukuo," under Emperor Henry Pu-Yi, last of China's Manchu dynasty. On Nov. 25, 1936, Japan joined the Axis by signing the anti-Comintern pact. The invasion of China came the next year and the Pearl Harbor attack on the U.S. on Dec. 7, 1941.

(For details of World War II (1939–45), *see* Headline History, World War II.)

Japan surrendered formally on Sept. 2, 1945, aboard the battleship *Missouri* in Tokyo Bay after atomic bombs had devastated Hiroshima and Nagasaki. Southern Sakhalin and the Kurile Islands reverted to the U.S.S.R., and Formosa (Taiwan) and Manchuria to China. The Pacific islands remained under U.S. occupation. General Douglas MacArthur was appointed Supreme Commander for the Allied Powers on Aug. 14, 1945.

A new Japanese constitution went into effect in 1947. In 1949, many of the responsibilities of government were returned to the Japanese. Full sovereignty was granted to Japan by the Japanese Peace Treaty in 1951.

Following the visit of Prime Minister Eisaku Sato to Washington in 1969, the U.S. agreed to return Okinawa and other Ryukyu Islands to Japan in 1972, and both nations renewed the security treaty in 1970.

The general election of July 1989 for the upper house of Parliament scored a loss for the ruling Liberal Democratic Party, the first in 35 years. The following month, however, the party's president, Toshiki Kaifu, was elected Prime Minister.

Kaifu pledged to provide $9 billion to the U.S. to help defray the expense of the latter's operations in the Persian Gulf. The government attempted to push legislation that would have permitted Japan to send a military contingent to the Gulf in noncombat roles. This was defeated amid public outcry against it.

During Soviet President Gorbachev's visit to Tokyo in April 1991 he and Prime Minister Kaifu attempted to resolve a territorial dispute arising out of the last days of World War II. No breakthrough resulted, and the issue still remained at an impasse.

Rebellious legislators in June 1993 joined with the opposition to force a vote of no confidence in the government. In its wake Prime Minister Miyazawa dissolved Parliament. Many of the rebels quit the ruling Liberal Democrats to form three new parties.

The elections of July saw the largest loss for the Liberal Democrats since the party's creation. Yet it managed to retain 223 of the 511 seats, making it the largest single party.

An odd partnership was formed in June 1994 when the Liberal Democrats were instrumental in electing the Socialist Party head as Prime Minister. Fears were immediately raised that all progress toward deregulating the economy and reforming the political system would grind to a halt.

A devastating earthquake shook on October 4, 1994. Particularly hard hit was the city of Hokkaido.

Parliamentary elections in October 1996 gave 239 seats in the Diet to Liberal Democrats, although voter turnout was at a record low. In November the Prime Minister won re-election in the lower house, winning the support of former coalition partners.

JORDAN

The Hashemite Kingdom of Jordan
National name: Al Mamlaka al Urduniya al Hashemiyah
Ruler: King Hussein I (1952)
Prime Minister: Abdul Salam al-Majali (1997)
Area: 34,573 sq mi (89,544 sq km) excludes West Bank

Population (1997 est.): 4,324,638 (average annual rate of natural increase: 3.2%); birth rate: 35.95/1000; infant mortality rate: 30.7/1000; density per square mile: 125.1
Capital and largest city (1994 est.): Amman, 963,490. **Largest cities (1994 est.):** Zarka, 420,900 (1990); Irbid, 208,201; As-Salt, 187,014. **Monetary unit:** Jordanian dinar. **Languages:** Arabic (official), English. **Ethnicity/Race:** Arab 98%, Circassian 1%, Armenian 1%. **Religions:** Islam, 92%; Christian, 6%; Other, 2%. **Literacy rate:** 82%
Economic summary: Gross domestic product: purchasing power parity (1995 est.): $19.3 billion; $4,700 per capita; 6.5% real growth rate; inflation: 3%; unemployment: 16% (1994 est.). Arable land: 4%. Principal products: wheat, fruits, vegetables, olive oil. Labor force (1995): 860,000: industry 11.4%; commerce, restaurants, and hotels 10.5%; construction 10%; transport and communications 8.7%; agriculture 7.4%. Major products: phosphate, refined petroleum products, cement. Natural resources: phosphate, potash. Exports: $1.7 billion (f.o.b., 1994): phosphates, fruits, and vegetables, shale oil, fertilizer, manufactures. Imports: $3.8 billion (c.i.f., 1994): petroleum products, textiles, capital goods, motor vehicles, foodstuffs. Major trading partners: U.S., Japan, Saudi Arabia, Iraq, E.U., China, India.

Geography. The Middle East Kingdom of Jordan is bordered on the west by Israel and the Dead Sea, on the north by Syria, on the east by Iraq, and on the south Saudi Arabia. It is comparable in size to Indiana.

Arid hills and mountains make up most of the country. The southern section of the Jordan River flows through the country.

Government. Jordan is a constitutional monarchy with a bicameral Parliament. The upper house consists of 40 members appointed by the King and the lower house is composed of 80 members elected by popular vote. The constitution guarantees freedom of religion, speech, press, association, and private property. Political parties were legalized in 1991.

History. In biblical times, the country that is now Jordan contained the lands of Edom, Moab, Ammon, and Bashan. In C.E. 106 it became part of the Roman province of Arabia and in 633–36 was conquered by the Arabs.

Taken from the Turks by the British in World War I, Jordan (formerly known as Transjordan) was separated from the Palestine mandate in 1920, and in 1921, placed under the rule of Abdullah ibn Hussein.

In 1923, Britain recognized Jordan's independence, subject to the mandate. In 1946, grateful for Jordan's loyalty in World War II, Britain abolished the mandate. That part of Palestine occupied by Jordanian troops was formally incorporated by action of the Jordanian Parliament in 1950.

King Abdullah was assassinated in 1951. His son Talal was deposed as mentally ill the next year. Talal's son Hussein, born Nov. 14, 1935, succeeded him.

From the beginning of his reign, Hussein had to steer a careful course between his powerful neighbor to the west, Israel, and rising Arab nationalism, frequently a direct threat to this throne. Riots erupted when he joined the Central Treaty Organization (the Baghdad Pact) in 1955, and he incurred further unpopularity when Britain, France, and Israel attacked the Suez Canal in 1956, forcing him to place his army under nominal command of the United Arab Republic of Egypt and Syria.

The 1961 breakup of the UAR eased Arab national pressure on Hussein, who was the first to recognize Syria after it reclaimed its independence. Jordan was swept into the 1967 Arab-Israeli war, however, and lost the old city of Jerusalem and all of its territory west of the Jordan river, the West Bank. Embittered Palestinian guerrilla forces virtually took over sections of Jordan in the aftermath of defeat, and open warfare broke out between the Palestinians and government forces in 1970.

Despite intervention of Syrian tanks, Hussein's Bedouin army defeated the Palestinians, suffering heavy casualties. A U.S. military alert and Israeli armor massed on the Golan Heights contributed psychological weight, but the Jordanians alone drove out the Syrians and invited the departure of 12,000 Iraqi troops who had been in the country since the 1967 war. Ignoring protests from other Arab states, Hussein by mid-1971 crushed Palestinian strength in Jordan and shifted the problem to Lebanon, where many of the guerrillas had fled.

As Egypt and Israel neared final agreement on a peace treaty early in 1979, Hussein met with Yassir Arafat, the PLO leader, on March 17 and issued a joint statement of opposition. Although the U.S. pressed Jordan to break Arab ranks on the issue, Hussein elected to side with the great majority, cutting ties with Cairo and joining the boycott against Egypt.

In September 1980, Jordan declared itself with Iraq in its conflict with Iran and, despite threats from Syria, opened ports to war shipments for Iraq.

Jordan's stance during the Persian Gulf war strained relations with the U.S. and led to the termination of U.S. aid. The signing of a national charter by King Hussein and leaders of the main political groups in June 1991 meant political parties were permitted in exchange for acceptance of the constitution and the monarchy.

King Hussein's decision to join the Middle East peace talks in mid-1991 helped his country's relations with the U.S.

In July 1994 King Hussein and the Israeli Prime Minister signed a declaration ending the state of belligerency between the two countries. A peace between the two countries was signed on October 26, 1994, although a clause in it calling the King the "custodian" of Islamic holy shrines in Jerusalem angered the PLO. In the wake of the agreement Jordan's relations with the U.S. and with the moderate Arab states warmed. Normal relations with Saudi Arabia resumed.

The resignation of the Prime Minister and his cabinet for unstated reasons in March 1997 led the King to ask Majali, a former Prime Minister and confidant to form a new government.

KAZAKHSTAN

Republic of Kazakhstan
President: Nursultan A. Nazarbaev (1990)
Prime Minister: Arkezhan Kazhgeldin (1994)
Area: 1,049,000 sq mi. (2,717,300 sq km)
Population (1997 est.): 16,898,572; average annual rate of natural increase: 0.923%; birth rate: 18.91/1000; infant mortality rate, 62.3/1000; density per square mile: 16.1
Capital and largest city (1991 est.): Almaty, 1,200,000. **Other large cities (1991 est.):** Karaganda, 608,600; Shymkent, 438,000; Ust-Kamenogorsk, 332,900; Aktyubinsk (Aktobe), 266,600; Taraz, 312,300. **Monetary unit:** Tenge. **Language:** Kazakh (Qazaq).
Ethnicity/Race: Kazak (Qazaq) 41.9% Russian 37%, Ukrainian 5.2%, German 4.7%, Uzbek 2.1%, Tatar 2%, other 7.1% (1991). **Religion:** Muslim, 47%; Russian Orthodox; Lutheran. **Literacy rate:** 100%
Economic summary: Gross domestic product: purchasing power parity (1995 estimate as extrapolated from the World Bank estimate for 1994): $46.9 billion; $2,700 per capita; real growth rate –8.9%; inflation

28.7% (1996); unemployment 1.4%. Labor force: 7.356 million: industry and construction 31%; agriculture and forestry 26%. Industries: extractive industries (oil, coal, iron ore, manganese, bauxite, gold, silver, phosphates, sulfur), iron and steel, nonferrous metals, tractors and other agricultural machinery, electric motors, construction materials. Agriculture: grains, meat, cotton, and wool. Exports: $5.1 (1995): oil, ferrous and nonferrous metals, chemicals, wool, grain, meat. Imports: $3.9 billion (1995): from outside the successor states of the former U.S.S.R.: machinery and parts, industrial materials. Trading partners: Russia, Ukraine, Uzbekistan, and other former Soviet republics, China.

Geography. Kazakhstan lies in the north of the central Asian republics and is bounded by Russia in the north, China in the east, the Kyrgyzstan and Uzbekistan in the south, and the Caspian Sea and part of Turkmenistan in the west. It has almost 15,000 miles of coastline on the Caspian Sea. Kazakhstan is the second largest republic of the Commonwealth of Independent States in area and is slightly more than twice the size of Texas. The territory is mostly steppe land with hilly plains and plateaus.

Government. The Republic of Kazakhstan is a unitary state with a presidential form of government.

History. The indigenous Kazakhs were a nomadic Turkic people who belonged to several divisions of Kazakh hordes. They grouped together in settlements and lived in dome-shaped tents made of felt called "yurts." Their tribes migrated seasonally to find pastures for their herds of sheep, horses, and goats. Although they had chiefs, the Kazakhs were rarely united as a single nation under one great leader. Their tribes fell under Mongol rule in the 13th century and they were dominated by Tartar Khanates until the area was conquered by Russia in the 18th century.

Kazakhstan became a constituent republic of the Soviet Union in 1936 and collective farming and modern industrial production methods were instituted.

The world's first fast-breeder nuclear reactor was built in the republic and the main space center for the Commonwealth of Independent States is located in Baikonur.

Kazakhstan sought greater political autonomy but delayed seeking independence from the former Soviet Union. Kazakhstan proclaimed its membership in the Commonwealth of Independent States on Dec. 21, 1991, along with ten other former Soviet republics.

In 1993 the country overwhelmingly approved the Nuclear Non-Proliferation Treaty.

In a referendum held on April 29, 1995, the electorate voted in support of extending the President's term to December 2000. Nazarbaev introduced a draft constitution in the summer that gave the President expanded powers. Although attacked from various quarters, it won the approval of 89% in a referendum held in August.

The President restructured and consolidated many operations of the government in March 1997. Eliminated were a third of the government ministries and agencies.

KENYA

Republic of Kenya
National name: Jamhuri ya Kenya
President: H. E. Daniel Toroitch arap Moi (1978)
Area: 224,960 sq mi. (582,646 sq km)
Population (1997 est.): 28,803,085 (average annual rate of natural increase: 2.16%); birth rate: 32.44/1000; infant mortality rate: 55.2/1000; density

per square mile: 128
Capital and largest city (1991 est.): Nairobi, 2,000,000. **Other large city:** Mombasa, 600,000. **Monetary unit:** Kenyan shilling. **Languages:** English (official), Swahili (national), and several other languages spoken by 25 ethnic groups. **Ethnicity/Race:** Kikuyu 22%, Luhya 14%, Luo 13%, Kalenjin 12%, Kamba 11%, Kisii 6%, Meru 6%, Asian, European, and Arab 1%, other 15%. **Religions:** Protestant, 40%; Roman Catholic, 28%; traditional, 6%; Islam, 16%, others, 2%. **Literacy rate:** 69%

Economic summary: Gross domestic product: purchasing power parity (1995 est.): $36.8 billion; $1,300 per capita; real growth rate 5%; inflation 1.7%; unemployment: 35% (1994 urban est.). Arable land: 3%. Principal agricultural products: coffee, sisal, tea, pineapples, livestock. Labor force: n.a.; agriculture, 75–80% (1993 est). Major industrial products: textiles, processed foods, consumer goods, refined oil. Natural resources: gold, limestone, minerals, wildlife. Exports: $1.6 billion (f.o.b., 1994): tourism, tea, coffee, horticulture, petroleum products, cement, soda ash, and pyrethrum extracts. Imports: $2.2 billion (f.o.b., 1994): crude oil, pharmaceuticals, industrial supplies, machinery, other capital equipment. Major trading partners: Uganda, U.K., Tanzania, Germany, Netherlands, France, Italy, Saudi Arabia, United Arab Emirates, U.S., Japan, India. **Member of Commonwealth of Nations**

Geography. Kenya lies across the equator in east central Africa on the coast of the Indian Ocean. It is twice the size of Nevada. Kenya borders Somalia to the east, Ethiopia to the north, Tanzania to the south, Uganda to the west, and Sudan to the northwest.

In the north, the land is arid; the southwestern corner is in the fertile Lake Victoria Basin; and a length of the eastern depression of Great Rift Valley separates western highlands from those that rise from the lowland coastal strip. Large game reserves have been developed.

Government. Under its constitution Kenya has a one-house National Assembly of 188 members elected for five years by universal suffrage and 12 nominated and 2 ex-officio, for a total of 202. Since 1992, the President has been elected in a presidential and parliamentary election.

History. Kenya, formerly a British colony and protectorate, was made a Crown colony in 1920. The whites' domination of the rich plateau area, the White Highlands, long regarded by indigenous Kenyans as their territory, was a factor leading to native terrorism, called the Mau Mau movement, in 1952. In 1954 the British began preparing the territory for African rule and independence. In 1961 Jomo Kenyatta was freed from banishment to become leader of the Kenya African National Union (KANU).

Internal self-government was granted in 1963; Kenya became independent on Dec. 12, 1963, with Kenyatta the first President. The opposition boycotted the opening of parliament in protest.

From 1964 to 1992 Kenya was ruled by the Kenya African National Union (KANU) under its leaders, Jomo Kenyatta, followed by Daniel arap Moi. Moi allowed for multiparty elections in 1992.

The government reimposed price controls and broke with the IMF and World Bank in March 1993, risking a break in Western aid.

President Moi in early 1995 moved against the opposition, ordering the arrest of anyone who insulted him. In June the renowned paleontologist Richard Leakey registered a new political party.

In anticipation of general elections a number of Christian clergymen in May 1997 joined together to demand greater political freedom. In June the government approved the sale of state holdings in eight firms.

KIRIBATI

Republic of Kiribati
President: Teburoro Tito (1994)
Area: 280 sq mi. (726 sq km)
Population (1997 est.): 82,449 (average annual growth rate: 1.9%); birth rate: 26.79/1000; infant mortality rate: 51.15/1000; density per square mile: 294.4
Capital (1990): Tarawa, 25,154. **Monetary unit:** Australian dollar. **Language:** English. **Ethnicity/Race:** Micronesian. **Religions:** Roman Catholic, 52.6%; Protestant, 40.9%. **Literacy rate:** 90%
Economic summary: Gross domestic product: purchasing power parity (1995 est.): $68 million; $860 per capita; 2.6% real growth rate; inflation 5.5%, unemployment 2% (1992 est.). Arable land: negligible. Principal agricultural products: copra, vegetables. Exports: $6.3 million (f.o.b, 1995 est.): fish, copra. Imports: $38.6 million (c.i.f, 1995 est.): foodstuffs, fuel, transportation equipment. Major trading partners: New Zealand, Australia, Japan, American Samoa, U.K., U.S., Fiji. **Member of Commonwealth of Nations**

Geography. Kiribati, formerly the Gilbert Islands, consists of three widely separated main groups of Southwest Pacific islands, the Gilberts on the equator, the Phoenix Islands to the east, and the Line Islands further east. Ocean Island, producer of phosphates until it was mined out in 1981, is also included in the two million square miles of ocean, which give Kiribati an important fishery resource.

Government. The President holds executive power. The legislature consists of a House Assembly with 39 members.

History. A British protectorate since 1892, the Gilbert and Ellice Islands became a colony in 1915–16. The two island groups were separated in 1975 and given internal self-government.

Tarawa and others of the Gilbert group were occupied by Japan during World War II. Tarawa was the site of one of the bloodiest battles in U.S. Marine Corps history when Marines landed in November 1943 to dislodge the Japanese defenders.

Princess Anne, representing Queen Elizabeth II, presented the independence documents to the new government on July 12, 1979.

President Tabai resigned in July 1991 after the maximum 12 years in office, being succeeded by his Vice President.

The government continued its moves in 1993–94 to privatize the public sector with its plans to sell off several major enterprises.

A no-confidence vote in the Assembly in May 1994 led to general elections in July. A coalition of opposition parties won a majority.

A trial for corruption of President Tito, which had started in 1995, ended in early 1996. The charges were dismissed, and the plaintiffs ordered to pay the President's legal fees.

KOREA, NORTH

Democratic People's Republic of Korea
National name: Choson Minjujuui Inmin Konghwaguk
Head of State: Kim Jong Il (1994)
Premier: Hong Song Nam (acting 1997)
Area: 46,768 sq mi. (121,129 sq km)
Population (1997 est.): 24,317,004 (average annual rate of natural increase: 1.68%); birth rate: 22.27/1000; infant mortality rate: 25/1000; density per square mile: 519.9
Capital and largest city (est. 1987): Pyongyang, 2,355,000. **Monetary unit:** Won. **Language:** Korean. **Ethnicity/Race:** racially homogeneous. **Religions:** Buddhism and Confucianism, religious activities almost nonexistent. **Literacy rate:** 99%
Economic summary: Gross domestic product: purchasing power parity (1995 est.): $21.5 billion; $920 per capita; real growth rate –5%. Arable land: 18%. Unemployment n.a. Principal agricultural products: corn, rice, vegetables. Labor force: 9.615 million; 36% agricultural; 64% nonagricultural. Major industrial products: machines, electric power, chemicals, textiles, processed food, metallurgical products. Natural resources: coal, iron ore, hydroelectric power. Exports: $840 million (f.o.b, 1994 est.): minerals, metallurgical products, agricultural products, manufactures (including armaments). Imports: $1.27 billion (f.o.b, 1994 est.): machinery and equipment, petroleum, grain, coking coal. Major trading partners: C.I.S. countries, China, Japan, Hong Kong, Germany, Singapore.

Geography. Korea is a 600-mile (966 km) peninsula jutting from Manchuria and China (and a small portion of the U.S.S.R.) into the Sea of Japan and the Yellow Sea off eastern Asia. North Korea occupies an area slightly smaller than Pennsylvania north of the 38th parallel.

The country is almost completely covered by a series of north-south mountain ranges separated by narrow valleys. The Yalu River forms part of the northern border with Manchuria.

Government. The elected Supreme People's Assembly, as the chief organ of government, chooses a Presidium and a cabinet. The cabinet, which exercises executive authority, is subject to approval by the Assembly and the Presidium.

The Korean Workers (Communist) Party is the only political party.

History. According to myth, Korea was founded in 2333 B.C.E. by Tangun. In the 17th century, it became a vassal of China and was isolated from all but Chinese influence and contact until 1876, when Japan forced Korea to negotiate a commercial treaty, opening the land to the U.S. and Europe. Japan achieved control as the result of its war with China (1894–95) and with Russia (1904–05) and annexed Korea in 1910. Japan developed the country but never won over the Korean nationalists.

After the Japanese surrender in 1945, the country was divided into two occupation zones, the U.S.S.R. north of and the U.S. south of the 38th parallel. When the cold war developed between the U.S. and U.S.S.R., trade between the zones was cut off. In 1948, the division between the zones was made permanent with the establishment of separate regimes in the north and south. By mid-1949, the U.S. and U.S.S.R. withdrew all troops. The Democratic People's Republic of Korea (North Korea) was established on May 1, 1948. The Communist Party, headed by Kim Il Sung, was established in power.

On June 25, 1950, the North Korean army launched a surprise attack on South Korea. On June 26, the U.N. Security Council condemned the invasion as aggression and ordered withdrawal of the invading forces. On June 27, President Harry S. Truman ordered air and naval units into action to enforce the U.N. order. The British government did the same, and soon a multinational U.N. command was set up to aid the South Koreans. The North Korean invaders took Seoul and pushed the

South Koreans into the southeast corner of their country.

Gen. Douglas MacArthur, U.N. commander, made an amphibious landing at Inchon on September 15 behind the North Korean lines, which resulted in the complete rout of the North Korean army. The U.N. forces drove north across the 38th parallel, approaching the Yalu River. Then Communist China entered the war, forcing the U.N. forces into headlong retreat. Seoul was lost again, then regained; ultimately the war stabilized near the 38th parallel but dragged on for two years while the billigerents negotiated. An armistice was agreed to on July 27, 1953.

Tensions continued to build in early 1994 over international inspection of North Korea's nuclear sites.

Kim Il Sung's death on July 8, 1994, introduced a period of uncertainty. Negotiations over the country's suspected atomic weapons program proved lengthy and thorny, but an agreement was reached in June 1995 which included providing the North with a South Korean nuclear reactor.

Ominous signs of a dire economic situation in the country continued to mount in 1996, and a widespread food shortage was believed to be occurring. In March 1997 South Korea lifted a ban on civilian shipments of rice to the north.

Premier Kang Song San was replaced in February 1997 for health reasons just one day before his death.

KOREA, SOUTH

Republic of Korea
National name: Taehan Min'guk
President: Kim Young Sam (1993)
Prime Minister: Koh Kun (1997)
Area: 38,031 sq mi. (99,392 sq km)
Population (1997 est.): 45,948,811 (average annual rate of natural increase: 1.05%); birth rate: 16.17/ 1000; infant mortality rate: 8/1000; density per square mile: 1,208
Capital and largest city: Seoul, 10,229,000. **Other cities:** Pusan, 3,814,000; Taegu, 2,449,000; Inchon, 2,308,000. **Monetary unit:** Won. **Language:** Korean. **Ethnicity/Race:** homogeneous (except for about 20,000 Chinese). **Religions (est. mid-1996):** Christian, 48.2%; Buddhist, 48.8%; Confucianist, 0.8%; Chondogyo (religion of the Heavenly Way), 0.2%; Other, 2%. **Literacy rate:** 96%
Economic summary: Gross domestic product: purchasing power parity (1996): $508.3 billion; $11,270 per capita; 9.0% real growth rate; inflation 4.5% (1996); unemployment 2% (1996). Arable land: 21%. Principal agricultural products: rice, soybeans, corn, barley. Labor force (April '96 est.): 21,168,000; 23% in mining and manufacturing. Major products: clothing, textiles, automobiles, steel, electronics equipment. Natural resources: coal, iron, zinc, lead, tungsten, hydropower. Exports: $11.3 billion (May 1996 est.): agricultural products, electronics, machinery, textiles, steel and metal products, chemicals. Imports: $12.8 billion (May 1996 est.): machinery, mineral fuels, electronic parts, agricultural products, iron and steel products, raw materials. Major trading partners: U.S., Japan.

Geography. Slightly larger than Indiana, South Korea lies below the 38th parallel on the Korean peninsula, bordering the East sea and the Yellow sea. It is mountainous in the east; in the west and south are many harbors on the mainland and offshore islands.

Government. Constitutional amendments enacted in Sept. 1987 called for direct election of a President, who would be limited to a single five-year term, and increased the powers of the National Assembly vis à vis the President.

The National Assembly was expanded from 276 to 299 seats, filled by proportional representation.

History. South Korea came into being in the aftermath of World War II as the result of a 1945 agreement making the 38th parallel the boundary between a northern zone occupied by the U.S.S.R. and a southern zone occupied by U.S. forces. (For details, see Korea, North.)

Elections were held in the U.S. zone in 1948 for a national assembly, which adopted a republican constitution and elected Syngman Rhee president. The new republic was proclaimed on August 15 and was recognized as the legal government of Korea by the U.N. on Dec. 12, 1948.

On June 25, 1950, South Korea was attacked by North Korean Communist forces. U.S. armed intervention was ordered on June 27 by President Harry S. Truman, and on the same day the U.N. invoked military sanctions against North Korea. Gen. Douglas MacArthur was named commander of the U.N. forces. U.S. and South Korean troops fought a heroic holding action but, by the first week of August, they had been forced back to a 4,000-square-mile beachhead in southeast Korea.

There they stood off superior North Korean forces until September 15, when a major U.N. amphibious attack was launched far behind the Communist lines at Inchon, port of Seoul. By September 30, U.N. forces were in complete control of South Korea. They then invaded North Korea and were nearing the Manchurian and Siberian borders when several hundred thousand Chinese Communist troops entered the conflict in late October. U.N. forces were then forced to retreat below the 38th parallel.

On May 24, 1951, U.N. forces recrossed the parallel and had made important new inroads into North Korea when truce negotiations began on July 10. An armistice was finally signed at Panmunjom on July 27, 1953, leaving a devastated Korea in need of large-scale rehabilitation.

The U.S. and South Korea signed a mutual-defense treaty on Oct. 1, 1953.

Rhee, President since 1948, resigned in 1960 in the face of rising disorders. Po Sun Yun was elected to succeed him, but political instability continued. In 1961, Gen. Park Chung Hee took power and subsequently built up the country. The U.S. stepped up military aid, building up South Korea's armed forces to 600,000 men. The South Koreans sent 50,000 troops to Vietnam, at U.S. expense.

Park's assassination on Oct. 26, 1979, by Kim Jae Kyu, head of the Korean Central Intelligence Agency, brought a liberalizing trend as Choi Kyu Hah, the new president, freed imprisoned dissidents. The release of opposition leader Kim Dae Jung in February 1980 generated anti-government demonstrations that turned into riots by May. Choi resigned on Aug. 16. Chun Doo Wha, head of a military Special Committee for National Security Measures, was the sole candidate as the electoral college confirmed him as president on Aug. 27.

Debate over the presidential succession in 1988 was the main dispute in 1986–87 with Chun wanting election by the electoral college and the opposition demanding a direct popular vote, charging that Chun could manipulate the college. On April 13, 1987, Chun declared a close on the debate but when, in June, he appointed Roh Tae Woo, the DJP chairman as his successor, violent protests broke out. Roh, and later, Chun, agreed that direct elections should be held. A split in the opposition led to Roh's election on Dec. 16, 1987, with 36.6% of the vote.

Weeks of anti-government protests in May 1991 led to the resignation of then-Prime Minister Ro Ja Bong.

In early 1991 the Soviet Union announced it would

not oppose South Korea's application for U.N. membership.

In his first year in office President Kim began a massive anticorruption campaign, purging thousands of military men with links to previous regimes, bureaucrats and businessmen.

As part of the GATT South Korea in December 1993 announced it would allow foreign rice imports, a move that led to a major cabinet reshuffle.

During 1995 two past presidents were indicted for their role in a 1979 coup. Later one of them was also accused of accepting substantial bribes.

As part of the government shakeup in the aftermath of the scandal, the President appointed a former Seoul mayor as Prime Minister.

KUWAIT

State of Kuwait
National name: Dawlat al Kuwayt
Emir: Sheik Jaber al-Ahmad al-Sabah (1977)
Prime Minister: Sheik Sa'ad Abdullah al-Salim (1978)
Area: 6,880 sq mi. (17,820 sq km)
Population (1997 est.): 2,076,805 (average annual rate of natural increase: 1.73%); birth rate: 19.56/1000; infant mortality rate: 10.6/1000; density per square mile: 301.9
Capital (1990 est.): Kuwait, 151,060. **Other large city (1993 est.):** as-Salimiyah, 116,104. **Monetary unit:** Kuwaiti dinar. **Languages:** Arabic and English. **Ethnicity/Race:** Kuwaiti 45%, other Arab 35%, South Asian 9%, Iranian 4%, other 7%. **Religions:** Islam 85% (Shi'a 30%, Sunni 45%, other 10%); Christian, Hindu, Parsi, and other 15%. **Literacy rate:** 74%
Economic summary: Gross domestic product: purchasing power parity (1995 est.): $30.8 billion; $17,000 per capita; real growth rate 3%; inflation 5% (1994 est.). Labor force: 1 million (1995 est.); 25% in industry and agriculture; 25% in services; 50% in government and social services. Major products: crude and refined oil, petrochemicals, building materials, salt. Natural resources: petroleum, fish, shrimp. Exports: $11.9 billion (f.o.b., 1994): oil. Imports: $6.7 billion (f.o.b., 1994): foodstuffs, automobiles, building materials, machinery, textiles. Major trading partners: U.S., Japan, Italy, U.K., Canada, France.

Geography. Kuwait is situated northeast of Saudi Arabia at the northern end of the Persian Gulf, south of Iraq. It is slightly larger than Hawaii. The low-lying land is mainly sandy and barren.

Government. Sheik Jaber al-Ahmad al-Sabah rules as Emir of Kuwait and appoints the Prime Minister, who appoints his cabinet (Council of Ministers). National elections were held in 1992 and the National Assembly (legislative branch), dissolved in 1986 was reinstated. There are no political parties in Kuwait.

History. Kuwait obtained British protection in 1897 when the Sheik feared that the Turks would take over the area. In 1961, Britain ended the protectorate, giving Kuwait independence, but agreed to give military aid on request. Iraq immediately threatened to occupy the area and Sheik Sabah al-Salem al-Sabah called in British troops in 1961. Soon afterward the Arab League sent in troops, replacing the British. The prize was oil.

Oil was discovered in the 1930s. Kuwait proved to have 20% of the world's known oil resources. It has been a major producer since 1946, the world's second largest oil exporter. The Sheik, who gets half the profits, devotes most of them to the education, welfare, and modernization of his kingdom. In 1966, Sheik Sabah designated a relative, Jaber al-Ahmad al-Sabah, as his successor.

By 1968, the sheikdom had established a model welfare state, and it sought to establish dominance among the sheikdoms and Emirates of the Persian Gulf.

In July 1990, Iraq President Hussein blamed Kuwait for falling oil prices. After a failed Arab mediation attempt to solve the dispute peacefully, Iraq invaded Kuwait on Aug. 2, 1990, and set up a pro-Iraqi provisional government.

A coalition of Arab and Western military forces drove Iraqi troops from Kuwait in February 1991. The Emir returned to his country from Saudi Arabia in mid-March. Martial law, in effect since the end of the Gulf war, ended in late June.

The U.S. sent 2,400 troops to the country in August 1992 as part of a training exercise but this was widely interpreted as a show of strength to Saddam Hussein.

The general election of October 1992 was widely interpreted as a success for supporters of a return to Islamic law. A political independent was named speaker of the Parliament, and the opposition held 31 of the 50 seats.

Iraqi "training" maneuvers near the Kuwaiti border in October 1994 renewed fears of aggression in the country. A Kuwaiti appeal brought the quick deployment of U.S. and British troops and equipment.

In the wake of October 1996 parliamentary elections the Emir reappointed the Prime Minister. The results of the election are seen as producing a plurality of pro-government MPs.

KYRGYZSTAN

The Kyrgyz Republic
President: Askar Akaev (1990)
Prime Minister: Apas Jumagulov (1993)
Area: 76,000 sq mi. (198,500 sq km)
Population (1997 est.): 4,540,185; (Kyrgyz, 52%; Russian, 21%; Uzbek, 13%, other, 14%); average annual rate of natural increase: 1.7%; birth rate: 25.81/1000; infant mortality rate: 76.6/1000; density per square mile: 59.7
Capital and largest city (1994): Bishkek (Frunze), 631,000. Other (1994): Osh 213,000. **Monetary unit:** Som. **Language:** Kyrgyz (official); Russian is de facto second language of communication. **Ethnicity/Race:** Kirghiz 52.4%, Russian 21.5%, Uzbek 12.9%, Ukrainian 2.5%, German 2.4%, other 8.3%. **Religion:** Muslim, 70%; Russian Orthodox, n.a. **Literacy rate:** 100%
Economic summary: Gross domestic product: purchasing power parity (1995 estimate as extrapolated from the World Bank estimate for 1994): $5.4 billion, $1,140 per capita; –6% real growth rate; inflation 32%; unemployment 4.8%. Important natural resources: rare earth metals, gold, coal. Industrial production: electrical engineering, hydroelectric power, agricultural machine building, washing machines, furniture, cement, paper, and brick. Agricultural products are food crops: vegetables, grains, fruit. Also cotton, hemp, tobacco, livestock: cattle, sheep, goats. Labor force: 1.836 million; agriculture and forestry, 38%; industry and construction, 21%. Exports: $380 million (1995): wool, chemicals, cotton, ferrous and nonferrous metals, shoes, machinery, tobacco. Imports: $439 million (1995): grain, lumber, industrial products, ferrous metals, fuel, machinery, textiles, footwear. Trading partners: Russia, Ukraine, Uzbekistan, Kazakhstan.

Geography. Kyrgyzstan (formerly Kirghizia) is a rugged country with the Tien Shan mountain range covering approximately 95 percent of the whole territory. The mountain tops are covered with perennial snow and glaciers. Kyrgyzstan borders Kazakhstan on the north and northwest, Uzbekistan in the southwest, Tajikistan in the south, and China in the southeast. The republic is the same size in area as the state of Nebraska.

Government. A constitutional republic.

History. The native Kyrgyz are a Turkic people who in ancient times first settled in the Tien Shan mountains. They were traditionally pastoral nomads. There was extensive Russian colonization in the 1900s and Russian settlers were given much of the best agricultural land. This led to an unsuccessful and disastrous revolt by the Kyrgyz people in 1916. Kyrgyzstan became part of the Soviet Federated Socialist Republic in 1924, and was made an autonomous republic in 1926. Kyrgyzstan became a constituent republic of the U.S.S.R. in 1936. The Soviets forced the Kyrgyz to abandon their nomadic culture and brought modern farming and industrial production techniques into their society. It has greatly changed their traditional way of life.

President Askar Akaev supported Soviet President Gorbachev's reform programs and promoted them in his country.

Kyrgyzstan proclaimed its independence from the Soviet Union on Aug. 31, 1991. On Dec. 21, 1991, Kyrgyzstan joined the Commonwealth of Independent States.

The country joined the U.N. and the IMF in 1992 and adopted a shock-therapy economic program.

Voters formally overwhelmingly endorsed market reforms in a referendum held in January 1994.

Incumbent President Akaev won the contested election of December 1995 with about 60% of the vote. In February 1996 referendum voters overwhelmingly endorsed proposed constitutional changes that enhanced the power of the president. The government resigned later that month, although it remained in place in a caretaker role.

Representatives of the country along with those of Russia, China, Kazakhstan, and Tajikistan signed a non–aggression agreement in April 1996. In March 1997 Russian border control was extended until the end of the year.

LAOS

~~Lao People's Democratic Republic~~
President: Nouhak Phoumsavanh (1992)
Premier: Khamtai Siphandon (1991)
Area: 91,429 sq mi. (236,800 sq km)
Population (1997 est.): 5,116,959 (average annual rate of natural increase: 2.78%); birth rate: 41.25/1000; infant mortality rate: 94.3/1000; density per square mile: 56
Capital and largest city (1990): Vientiane, 442,000.
Monetary unit: Kip. **Languages:** Lao (official), French, English. **Ethnicity/Race:** Lao Loum (lowland) 68%, Lao Theung (upland) 22%, Lao Soung (highland) including the Hmong ("Meo") and the Yao (Mien) 9%, ethnic Vietnamese/Chinese 1%. **Religions:** Buddhist, 85%; animist and other, 15%. **Literacy rate:** 50%
Economic summary: Gross domestic product: purchasing power parity (1995 est.): $5.2 billion; $1,100 per capita; 8% real growth rate; inflation rate: 20%; unemployment rate (1992 est.): 21%. Arable land: 4%. Principal agricultural products: rice, corn, vegetables. Labor force: 1–1.5 million; 80% in agriculture. Major industrial products: tin, timber, electric power, gypsum. Natural resources: tin, timber, hydroelectric power. Exports: $278 million (f.o.b., 1994): electric power, forest products, tin concentrates, coffee, gypsum, cardamon, rattan, clothing and textiles. Imports: $486 million (c.i.f., 1994): rice, foodstuffs, petroleum products, machinery, transport equipment. Major trading partners: Thailand, Malaysia, Vietnam, C.I.S. countries, Japan, France, U.S., Hong Kong, Singapore.

Geography. A landlocked nation in Southeast Asia occupying the northwestern portion of the Indochinese peninsula, Laos is surrounded by China, Vietnam, Cambodia, Thailand, and Burma. It is twice the size of Pennsylvania.

Laos is a mountainous country, especially in the north, where peaks rise above 9,000 feet (2,800 m). Dense forests cover the northern and eastern areas. The Mekong River, which forms the boundary with Burma and Thailand, flows entirely through the country for 932 miles (1,500 km) of its course.

Government. Laos is a people's democratic republic with executive power in the hands of the Premier. The monarchy was abolished Dec. 2, 1975, when the Pathet Lao ousted a coalition government and King Sisavang Vatthana abdicated. The King was appointed "Supreme Adviser" to the President, the former Prince Souphanouvong. Former Prince Souvanna Phouma, Premier since 1962, was made an "adviser" to the government. The Lao People's Revolutionary Party (Pathet Lao) is the only political party.

History. Laos became a French protectorate in 1893, and the territory was incorporated into the union of Indochina. A strong nationalist movement developed during World War II, but France reestablished control in 1946 and made the King of Luang Prabang constitutional monarch of all Laos. France granted semiautonomy in 1949 and then, spurred by the Viet Minh rebellion in Vietnam, full independence within the French Union in 1950. In 1951, Prince Souphanouvong organized the Pathet Lao, a Communist independence movement, in North Vietnam. The Viet Minh in 1953 established the Pathet Lao in power at Samneua. Viet Minh and Pathet Lao forces invaded central Laos, and civil war resulted.

By the Geneva agreements of 1954 and an armistice of 1955, two northern provinces were given the Pathet Lao, the royal regime the rest. Full sovereignty was given the kingdom by the Paris agreements of Dec. 29, 1954. In 1957, Prince Souvanna Phouma, the royal Premier, and the Pathet Lao leader, Prince Souphanouvong, the Premier's half-brother, agreed to reestablishment of a unified government, with Pathet Lao participation and integration of Pathet Lao forces into the royal army. The agreement broke down in 1959, and armed conflict broke out again.

In 1960, the struggle became three-way as Gen. Phoumi Nosavan, controlling the bulk of the royal army, set up in the south a pro-Western revolutionary government headed by Prince Boun Gum. General Phoumi took Vientiane in December, driving Souvanna Phouma into exile in Cambodia. The Soviet bloc supported Souvanna Phouma. In 1961, a cease-fire was arranged and the three Princes agreed to a coalition government headed by Souvanna Phouma.

But North Vietnam, the U.S. (in the form of Central Intelligence Agency personnel), and China remained active in Laos after the settlement. North Vietnam used a supply line (Ho Chi Minh trail) running down the mountain valleys of eastern Laos into Cambodia and South Vietnam, particularly after the U.S–South Vietnamese incursion into Cambodia in 1970 stopped supplies via Cambodian seaports.

An agreement, reached in 1973 revived coalition government. The Communist Pathet Lao seized complete power in 1975, installing Souphanouvong as president and Kaysone Phomvihane as Premier. Since then other parties and political groups have been moribund and most of their leaders have fled the country.

The Supreme People's Assembly in August 1991 adopted a new constitution that dropped all references to socialism but retained the one-party state. In addition to implementing market-oriented policies, the country has passed laws governing property, inheritance and contracts. Laos agreed to trade with Moscow and Hanoi in hard currency.

While the Pathet Lao's political control in 1993 remained firm, they proceeded apace in the creation of a market economy. Despite the rush to a free-market, the Communists retained tight political control.

During 1995 the country continued to relax tensions with its neighbors. Economic agreements were reached with Burma, and the U.S. announced a lifting of its ban on aid.

The sixth congress of the ruling People's Revolutionary Party took place in March 1996. Later that month Laos formally applied for full leadership in ASEAN.

LATVIA

The Republic of Latvia
National name: Latvija
President: Guntis Ulmanis (1993)
Prime Minister: Andris Skele (1995)
Area: 25,400 sq mi. (65,786 sq km)
Population (1997 est.): 2,437,649; average annual rate of natural increase: −0.35%; birth rate: 11.62/1000; infant mortality rate: 20.7/1000; density per square mile: 96
Capital and largest city (1993 est.): Riga, 874,000.
Other large cities: Daugavpils, 125,000; Liepaja, 108,000. **Monetary unit:** Lats. **Language:** Latvian.
Ethnicity/Race: Latvian 51.8%, Russian 33.8%, Belarussian 4.5%, Ukrainian 3.4%, Polish 2.3%, other 4.2%. **Religions:** Lutheran, Catholic, and Baptist.
Literacy: 100%
Economic summary: Most industrialized of the Baltic states. Gross domestic product: purchasing power parity (1995 est.): $14.7 billion; per capita $5,300; real growth rate −1.5%; inflation rate 20%; unemployment (1995): 6.5%. Labor force: 1.407 million: industry and construction 41%; agriculture and forestry 16% (1990). Latvia's major industries are: forestry, wood products, building materials, and metals. Agriculture is principally dairy farming and livestock raising. Natural resources: peat, sapropel, timber, limestone, dolomite, and clay. Exports: $1.3 billion (f.o.b., 1995 est.): timber and wood products, ferrous metals and products, electrical machinery and equipment, fish, furniture, apparel, pharmaceuticals, appliances, buses. Imports: $1.7 billion (c.i.f., 1995 est.): machinery and appliances, electrical equipment, natural gas, fuels, pharmaceuticals, electricity, cars, apparel. Major trading partners: European Union, C.I.S. countries, Lithuania, Poland, Estonia, U.S., Czech Republic, Australia, Hungary, Japan.

Geography. Latvia borders Estonia on the north, Lithuania in the south, the Baltic Sea with the Gulf of Riga in the west, Russia in the east, and Belarus in the southeast. Latvia is largely a fertile lowland with numerous lakes and hills to the east.

Government. Latvia is a parliamentary democracy.

History. Descended from Aryan stock, the Latvians were early tribesmen who settled along the Baltic Sea and, lacking a central government, fell an easy prey to more powerful peoples. The German Teutonic knights first conquered them in the 13th century and ruled the area, consisting of Livonia and Courland, until 1562.

Poland conquered the territory in 1562 and ruled until 1795 in Courland; control of Livonia was disputed between Sweden and Poland from 1562 to 1629. Sweden controlled Livonia from 1629 to 1721. Russia took over Livonia in the latter year and Courland after the third partition of Poland in 1795.

From that time until 1918, the Latvians remained Russian subjects, although they preserved their language, customs, and folklore. The Russian Revolution of 1917 gave them their opportunity for freedom, and the Latvian republic was proclaimed on Nov. 18, 1918.

The republic lasted little more than 20 years. It was occupied by Russian troops in 1939 and incorporated into the Soviet Union in 1940. German armies occupied the nation from 1941 to 1943–44, when they were driven out by the Russians. Most countries, including the United States, refused to recognize the Soviet annexation of Latvia.

When the coup against Soviet President Mikhail Gorbachev failed, the Baltic nations saw a historic opportunity to free themselves from Soviet domination and, following the actions of Lithuania and Estonia, Latvia declared its independence on Aug. 21, 1991.

European and most other nations quickly recognized their independence, and on Sept. 2, 1991, President Bush announced full diplomatic recognition for Latvia, Estonia, and Lithuania. The Soviet Union recognized Latvia's independence on September 6, and U.N. membership followed on Sept. 17, 1991.

In addition to severe economic problems the issue of citizenship loomed explosive as almost half the population is non-Latvian.

In the first post-Soviet parliamentary elections in June 1993 an alliance of former Communists and emigres made a strong showing. The franchise, however, was by and large not extended to the non-ethnic-Latvian minority.

In August Latvia celebrated the official withdrawal of Russian troops from the country, although Russia was allowed to retain control of its radar station in Skrunda until mid-1998.

The citizenship law was amended in August in accordance with the wishes of the Council of Europe.

Latvia's parliament, the Saeima, re-elected Ulmanis president in June 1996 over several other candidates.

The resignation of the finance minister in January 1997 led the Prime Minister to resign that post to become acting finance minister. However, in February Andris Skele again won approval of the Parliament as Prime Minister.

LEBANON

Republic of Lebanon
National name: Al-Joumhouriya al-Lubnaniya
President: Elias Hrawi (1989)
Premier: Rafiq al-Hariri (1992)
Area: 4,015 sq mi. (10,400 sq km)
Population (1997 est.): 3,858,736 (average annual rate of natural increase: 2.16%); birth rate: 27.86/1000; infant mortality rate: 35.4/1000; density per square mile: 961
Capital and largest city (1991 est.): Beirut, 1,100,000.
Other large cities: Tripoli, 240,000; Sidon, 100,000.
Monetary unit: Lebanese pound. **Languages:** Arabic (official), French, English. **Ethnicity/Race:** Arab 95%, Armenian 4%, other 1%. **Religions:** Islam, 60%; Christian, 40% (17 recognized sects); Judaism negl. (1 sect). **Literacy rate:** 80%
Economic summary: Gross domestic product: purchasing power parity (1995 est.): $18.3 billion; $4,900 per capita; real growth rate 6.5%; inflation: 9%; unemployment 30%. Arable land: 21%; principal agricultural products: citrus fruits, vegetables, potatoes, tobacco, olives, shrimp. Labor force: 650,000; 60% in services;

28% in industry; 12% in agriculture. Major industrial products: processed foods, textiles, cement, chemicals, refined oil. Exports: $1 billion (f.o.b., 1995 est.): fruits, vegetables, textiles, chemicals, semiprecious metals and jewelry, metals and metal products. Imports: $7.3 billion (c.i.f., 1995 est.): consumer goods, machinery and transport equipment, petroleum products. Major trading partners: U.S., Western European and Arab countries.

Geography. Lebanon lies at the eastern end of the Mediterranean Sea north of Israel and west of Syria. It is four fifths the size of Connecticut.

The Lebanon Mountains, which parallel the coast on the west, cover most of the country, while on the eastern border is the Anti-Lebanon range. Between the two lies the Bekaa Valley, the principal agricultural area.

Government. Lebanon is governed by a President, elected by Parliament for a six-year term, and a cabinet of Ministers appointed by the President but responsible to Parliament.

The unicameral Parliament has 108 members elected for a four-year term by universal suffrage and chosen by proportional division of religious groups.

History. After World War I, France was given a League of Nations mandate over Lebanon and its neighbor Syria, which together had previously been a single political unit in the Ottoman Empire. France divided them in 1920 into separate colonial administrations, drawing a border that separated predominantly Moslem Syria from the kaleidoscope of religious communities in Lebanon in which Maronite Christians were then dominant. After 20 years of the French mandate regime, Lebanon's independence was proclaimed on Nov. 26, 1941, but full independence came in stages. Under an agreement between representatives of Lebanon and the French National Committee of Liberation, most of the powers exercised by France were transferred to the Lebanese government on Jan. 1, 1944. The evacuation of French troops was completed in 1946.

Civil war broke out in 1958, with Moslem factions led by Kamal Jumblat and Saeb Salam rising in insurrection against the Lebanese government headed by President Camille Chamoun, a Maronite Christian. At Chamoun's request, President Eisenhower on July 15 sent U.S. troops to reestablish the government's authority.

Clan warfare between various factions in Lebanon goes back centuries. The hodgepodge includes Maronite Christians, who since independence have dominated the government; Sunni Moslems, who have prospered in business and shared political power; the Druse, a secretive Islamic splinter group; and at the bottom of the heap until recently, Shiite Moslems.

A new—and bloodier—Lebanese civil war that broke out in 1975 resulted in the addition of still another ingredient in the brew—the Syrians. In the fighting between Lebanese factions, 40,000 Lebanese were estimated to have been killed and 100,000 wounded between March 1975 and November 1976. At that point, a Syrian-dominated Arab Deterrent Force intervened and brought large-scale fighting to a halt.

Palestinian guerrillas staging raids on Israel from Lebanese territory drew punitive Israeli raids on Lebanon, and two large-scale Israeli invasions. The Israelis withdrew in June after the U.N. Security Council created a 6,000-man peacekeeping force for the area, called UNIFIL. As they departed, the Israelis turned their strong points over to a Christian militia that they had organized, instead of to the U.N. force.

The second Israeli invasion came on June 6, 1982, and this time it was a total one. It was in response to an assassination attempt by Palestinian terrorists on the Israeli ambassador in London.

A U.S. special envoy, Philip C. Habib, negotiated the dispersal of most of the PLO to other Arab nations and Israel pulled back some of its forces. The violence seemed to have come to an end when, on Sept. 14, Bashir Gemayel, the 34-year-old President-elect, was killed by a bomb that destroyed the headquarters of his Christian Phalangist Party.

The day after Gemayel's assassination, Israeli troops moved into west Beirut in force. On Sept. 17 it was revealed that Christian militiamen had massacred hundreds of Palestinians in two refugee camps, but Israel denied responsibility.

On Sept. 20, Amin Gemayel, older brother of Bashir Gemayel, was elected president by the Parliament.

The massacre in the refugee camps prompted the return of a multinational peacekeeping force composed of U.S. Marines and British, French, and Italian soldiers. Their mandate was to support the central Lebanese government, but they soon found themselves drawn into the struggle for power between different Lebanese factions. During their stay in Lebanon, 260 U.S. Marines and about 60 French soldiers were killed, most of them in suicide bombings of the Marine and French army compounds on Oct. 23, 1983. The multinational force left in the spring of 1984.

In July 1986, Syrian observers took position in Beirut to monitor a peacekeeping agreement. The agreement broke down and fighting between Shiite and Druze militia in West Beirut became so intense that Syrian troops moved in force in February 1987, suppressing militia resistance.

Amin Gemayel's Presidency expired on Sept. 23, 1988. The impossibility of setting up elections led Gemayel to designate a government under army chief Gen. Michael Aoun. Aoun's government was rejected by Prime Minister Selim al-Hoss who established a rival government in Muslim West Beirut.

In October 1989, Lebanese Christian and Moslem deputies approved a tentative peace accord and the new National Assembly selected a president.

In early 1991 the Lebanese government, backed by Syria, attempted to regain control over the south and disband all private militias, thereby ending the 16-year civil war.

In the general elections of August 1992 most Christians abstained from voting demanding that Syrian forces first leave the country. The new legislature consisted of mostly pro-Syrian members. The largest Christian party was further weakened when in January 1993 it appeared to split into two factions.

In May 1995 the Prime Minister asked for a constitutional amendment to allow the presidential term to be extended by three years in the interests of stability. Despite some opposition, the amendment was passed in October. In the multi-round parliamentary elections in September 1996, pro-Syrian candidates and those favored by the government won a major victory for the 128-member body.

LESOTHO

Kingdom of Lesotho
Sovereign: King Letsie III (1990)
Prime Minister: Dr. Ntsu Mokhehle
Area: 11,720 sq mi. (30,355 sq km)
Population (1997 est.): 2,007,814 (average annual rate of natural increase: 1.82%); birth rate: 32.19/1000; infant mortality rate: 80.3/1000; density per square mile: 171.3
Capital and largest city (1992): Maseru (1992), 170,000. **Monetary unit:** Loti. **Languages:** English and Sesotho (official); also Zulu and Xhosa. **Ethnicity/Race:** Sotho 99.7%, Europeans 1,600, Asians 800.

Religions: Christian, 80%; indigenous beliefs; Muslim; and Bahai. **Literacy rate:** 59% (1989)
Economic summary: Gross domestic product: purchasing power parity (1994 est.): $2.8 billion; $1,430 per capita; 13.5% real growth rate; inflation 9.5% (1995); unemployment: exact figures n.a. Arable land: 10%. Principal products: corn, wheat, sorghum, barley. Labor force: 689,000; 86.2% in subsistence agriculture. Natural resources: diamonds. Exports: $142 million (f.o.b., 1994 est.): wool, mohair, wheat, cattle, hides and skins, peas, beans, corn, baskets. Imports: $1 billion (c.i.f., 1994 est.): foodstuffs, building materials, clothing, vehicles, machinery, corn, medicines. Major trading partners: Asia, South Africa, E.U., North and South America. **Member of Commonwealth of Nations**

Geography. Mountainous Lesotho, the size of Maryland, is surrounded by the Republic of South Africa in the east central part of that country except for short borders on the east and south with two discontinuous units of the Republic of Transkei. The Drakensberg Mountains in the east are Lesotho's principal chain. Elsewhere the region consists of rocky tableland.

Government. A constitutional monarchy. The executive power is with the Prime Minister and the cabinet (Council of Ministers).

History. Lesotho (formerly Basutoland) was constituted a native state under British protection by a treaty signed with the native chief Moshesh in 1843. It was annexed to Cape Colony in 1871, but in 1884 it was restored to direct control by the Crown.

The colony of Basutoland became the independent nation of Lesotho on Oct. 4, 1966, with King Moshoeshoe II as sovereign.

In the 1970 elections, Ntsu Mokhehle, head of the Basutoland Congress Party, claimed a victory, but Prime Minister Leabua Jonathan declared a state of emergency, suspended the constitution, and arrested Mokhehle.

King Moshoeshoe returned after a compromise with Jonathan in which the new constitution would name him head of state but forbid his participation in politics.

After the King refused to approve the replacements in February 1990 of individuals dismissed by Justin Metsino Lekhanya, the chairman of the Military Council, the latter stripped the King of his executive power. Then in early March Lekhanya sent the King into exile. In November the King was dethroned, and his son was sworn in as King Letsie III.

Lekhanya was himself forced to resign in April 1991. Col. Ramaema became the new chairman in May.

In January 1995 the Crown reverted to the father of Letsie III, Moshoeshoe II. Letsie again became Crown Prince. In 1996, however, King Moshoeshoe died in an automobile accident and Letsie again assumed the throne.

In June 1997 the Prime Minister and several cabinet members formed a new political party. Earlier in the year the Prime Minister was removed from the leadership of the Basotholand Congress Party by a rival faction.

LIBERIA

Republic of Liberia
President: Charles Taylor (1997)
Area: 43,000 sq mi. (111,370 sq km)
Population (1997 est.): 2,602,068 (average annual rate of natural increase: 3.07%); birth rate: 42.3/1000; infant mortality rate: 105.6/1000; density per square mile: 60.5

Capital and largest city (1993 est.): Monrovia, 1,000,000. **Monetary unit:** Liberian dollar. **Languages:** English (official) and tribal dialects. **Ethnicity/Race:** indigenous African tribes 95% (including Kpelle, Bassa, Gio, Kru, Grebo, Mano, Krahn, Gola, Gbandi, Loma, Kissi, Vai, and Bella), Americo-Liberians 5% (descendants of former slaves). **Religions:** traditional, 70%; Christian, 10%; Islam, 20%. **Literacy rate:** 50%
Economic summary: Civil war since 1990 has destroyed much of Liberia's economy. Gross domestic product: purchasing power parity (1994 est.): $2.3 billion; $770 per capita; 0% real growth rate; inflation: 50%; unemployment: n.a. Arable land: 1%. Principal agricultural products: rubber, rice, palm oil, cassava, coffee, cocoa. Labor force: 510,000; 70.5% in agriculture; 10.8% in services; 4.5% in industry and commerce. Major industrial products: iron ore, diamonds, processed rubber, processed food, construction materials. Natural resources: iron ore, gold, timber, diamonds. Exports: $530 million (f.o.b., 1994 est.): iron ore, rubber, timber, coffee. Imports: machinery, petroleum products, transport equipment, foodstuffs. Major trading partners: U.S., E.U., Netherlands, Japan, China.

Geography. Lying on the Atlantic in the southern part of West Africa, Liberia is bordered by Sierra Leone, Guinea, and Côte d'Ivoire. It is comparable in size to Tennessee.

Most of the country is a plateau covered by dense tropical forests, which thrive under an annual rainfall of about 160 inches a year.

Government. A dual system of statutory law based on Anglo-American common law for the modern sector and customary law based on tribal practice for the indigenous sector.

History. Liberia was founded in 1822 as a result of the efforts of the American Colonization Society to settle freed American slaves in West Africa. In 1847, it became the Free and Independent Republic of Liberia.

The government of Africa's first republic was modeled after that of the United States, and Joseph J. Roberts of Virginia was elected the first President. He laid the foundations of a modern state. The English-speaking descendants of U.S. blacks, known as Americo-Liberians, were the intellectual and ruling class. The indigenous inhabitants, divided, constitute 99% of the population.

After 1920, considerable progress was made toward opening up the interior, a process that was spurred in 1951 by the establishment of a 43-mile (69-km) railroad to the Bomi Hills from Monrovia.

In July 1971, while serving his sixth term as president, William V. S. Tubman died following surgery and was succeeded by his long-time associate, Vice President William R. Tolbert, Jr.

Tolbert was ousted in a military coup carried out April 12, 1980, by army enlisted men led by Master Sgt. Samuel K. Doe.

A rebellion led by Charles Taylor, a former Doe aide, started in December 1989 and, by mid-July 1990, had taken most of Liberia's key population and economic centers and surrounded the capital.

A West African peacekeeping force intervened in Liberia and effectively partitioned the country into two zones. A national conference in March 1991 failed to reach an agreement but re-elected Amos Sawyer as interim president.

Despite a 1991 peace, factional fighting continued at times in the country's civil war.

The various feuding parties met in May 1994 to form a government. Fighting, however, continued at various levels both then and in subsequent months. A coup attempt in September was quelled the following day. In late December another ceasefire was proclaimed. This, in turn, broke down in March 1995.

A peace agreement among six warlords took effect in 1995. After a few months, however, it began unraveling first in the rural areas, then in the capital. By mid-April 1996 the civil war destroyed any last vestige of normality and civil society.

In November 1996 another peace agreement was reached with the help of the Economic Community of West African States.

Charles Taylor won 75.3% of the presidential vote in July 1997, defeating Ellen Johnson–Sirleaf. Taylor's National Patriotic Party won 21 of 26 seats in the senate.

LIBYA

Socialist People's Libyan Arab Jamahiriya
National name: Socialist People's Libyan Arab Jamahiriya
Head of State: Col. Muammar el-Qaddafi (1969)
Secretary of the General People's Committee: Abd al-Majid al-Qa'ud (1994)
Area: 679,536 sq mi. (1,759,998 sq km)
Population (1997 est.): 5,648,359 (average annual rate of natural increase: 3.64%); birth rate: 43.94/1000; infant mortality rate: 57.7/1000; density per square mile: 8.3
Capital: Tripoli. **Largest cities (est. 1988):** Tripoli, 591,062; Benghazi, 446,250. **Monetary unit:** Libyan dinar. **Language:** Arabic, Italian and English widely understood in major cities. **Ethnicity/Race:** Berber and Arab 97%, Greeks, Maltese, Italians, Egyptians, Pakistanis, Turks, Indians, Tunisians. **Religion:** Islam. **Literacy rate:** 64%
Economic summary: Gross domestic product: purchasing power parity (1994 est.): $32.9 billion; $6,510 per capita; real growth rate -0.9%; inflation 25% (1993 est.); unemployment n.a. Arable land: 1%. Principal products: wheat, barley, olives, dates, citrus fruits, peanuts. Labor force: 1 million (includes about 280,000 resident foreigners); 31% in industry; services 27%; government 24%; agriculture 18%. Major products: petroleum, processed foods, textiles, handicrafts, cement. Natural resources: petroleum, natural gas. Exports: $7.2 billion (f.o.b., 1994 est.): petroleum, peanuts, hides, natural gas. Imports: $6.9 billion (f.o.b., 1994 est.): machinery, foodstuffs, manufactured goods. Major trading partners: Italy, Germany, U.K., France, Spain, Japan, Turkey, former U.S.S.R., Korea, Belgium/Luxembourg.

Geography. Libya stretches along the northeastern coast of Africa between Tunisia and Algeria on the west and Egypt on the east; to the south are the Sudan, Chad, and Niger. It is one-sixth larger than Alaska.

A greater part of the country lies within the Sahara. Along the Mediterranean coast and farther inland is arable plateau land.

Government. In a bloodless coup d'état on Sept. 1, 1969, the military seized power in Libya. King Idris I, who had ruled since 1951, was deposed and the Libyan Arab Republic proclaimed. The official name was changed in 1977 to the Socialist People's Libyan Arab Jamahiriya—Jamahiriya (a state of the masses): in theory, governed by the populace through local councils; in fact, a military dictatorship. The Revolutionary Council that had governed since the coup was renamed the General Secretariat of the General People's Congress. The Arab Socialist Union Organization is the only political party.

History. Libya was a part of the Turkish dominions from the 16th century until 1911. Following the outbreak of hostilities between Italy and Turkey in that year, Italian troops occupied Tripoli; Italian sovereignty was recognized in 1912.

Libya was the scene of much desert fighting during World War II. After the fall of Tripoli on Jan. 23, 1943, it came under Allied administration. In 1949, the U.N. voted that Libya should become independent by 1952.

Discovery of oil in the Libyan Desert promised financial stability and funds for economic development.

On Aug. 19, 1981, two U.S. Navy F-14's shot down two Soviet-made SU-22's of the Libyan air force that had attacked them in air space above the Gulf of Sidra, claimed by Libya but held to be international by the U.S. In December, Washington asserted that Libyan "hit squads" had been dispatched to the U.S. and security was drastically tightened around President Reagan and other officials. When the Mobil Oil Company abandoned its operations in April 1982, only four U.S. firms were still in Libya, using Libyan or third-country personnel.

On March 24, 1986, U.S. and Libyan forces skirmished in the Gulf of Sidra, with two Libyan patrol boats being sunk. Qaddafi's troops also supported rebels in Chad but suffered major military reverses in 1987.

A two-year-old U.S. covert policy to destabilize the Libyan government with U.S.-trained Libyan ex-P.O.W.s ended in failure in December 1990 when a Libyan-supplied guerrilla force assumed power in Chad, where the commandos were based, and asked the band to leave.

For its refusal to extradite two Libyans accused of U.N. approved trade and air traffic embargoes in April 1992, seriously affecting the Libyan economy.

The U.S. attempted in March 1995 to get a total international embargo of Libyan oil.

Against the wishes of the United States, the Vatican in March 1997 established diplomatic ties with Libya in the hope of protecting its small Catholic population and to promote peace in the region.

LIECHTENSTEIN

Principality of Liechtenstein
Ruler: Prince Hans Adam (1989)
Prime Minister: Dr. Mario Frick (1994)
Area: 61 sq mi. (157 sq km)
Population (1997 est.): 31,461 (average annual growth rate: 0.45%); birth rate: 11.32/1000; infant mortality rate: 5.2/1000; density per square mile: 515.7
Capital and largest city (1994): Vaduz, 5,067. **Monetary unit:** Swiss franc. **Language:** German. **Ethnicity/Race:** Alemannic 95%, Italian and other 5%. **Religions:** Roman Catholic, 80.36%; Protestant, 7.1%; other 12.5%. **Literacy rate:** 100%
Economic summary: Gross domestic product: purchasing power parity (1990 est.): $630 million; $22,300 per capita; inflation (1994) 0.9%; growth rate n.a.; unemployment 0.9% (1995). Arable land: 25%. Principal agricultural products: livestock, vegetables, corn, wheat, potatoes, grapes. Labor force (1994): 21,109 (including 12,971 foreigners); industry, trade and building, 48.1%; service, 50.2%. Major industrial products: electronics, metal products, textiles, ceramics, pharmaceuticals, food products, precision instruments. Natural resource: hydroelectric power. Exports: $2.6 billion (c.i.f., 1994): small specialty machinery, dental products, stamps, hardware, pottery. Imports: machinery, processed foods, metal goods, textiles, motor vehicles. Major trading partners: Switzerland and other Western European countries.

Geography. Tiny Liechtenstein, not quite as large as Washington, D.C., lies on the east bank of the Rhine River south of Lake Constance between Austria and Switzerland. It consists of low valley land and Alpine peaks. Falknis (8,401 ft.; 2,561 m) and Naafkopf (8,432 ft.; 2,570 m) are the tallest.

Government. The constitution of 1921 provides for a legislature, the Landtag, of 25 members elected by direct suffrage.

History. Founded in 1719, Liechtenstein was a member of the German Confederation from 1815 to 1866, when it became an independent principality. It abolished its army in 1868 and has managed to stay neutral and undamaged in all European wars since then. In a referendum on July 1, 1984, male voters granted women the right to vote, a victory for Prince Hans Adam.

A treaty negotiated between EFTA and the then European Union was ratified in a December 1993 vote, but in Switzerland it was rejected. The treaty was under revision during 1994 so as to maintain the country's traditional link with Switzerland. After renegotiation the treaty was again subjected to a referendum in April 1995 and approved.

February 1997 parliamentary elections gave the dominant centrist party, the Fatherland Union, 13 seats with 49% of the vote and the Progressive Citizen's Party 10 seats taking 39% of the vote.

LITHUANIA

Republic of Lithuania
National name: Lietuva
President: Algirdas Mykolas Brazauskas (1993)
Prime Minister: Gediminas Vagnorius (1996)
Area: 25,212 sq mi. (65,300 sq km)
Population (1997 est.): 3,635,932; (average annual rate of natural increase: 0.05%); birth rate: 13.68/1000; infant mortality rate: 16.3/1000; density per square mi: 144.2
Capital and largest city (1993 est.): Vilnius, 590,100.
  Other large cities: Kaunas, 429,000; Klaipėda, 206,400. **Monetary unit:** Litas. **Languages:** Lithuanian. **Ethnicity/Race:** Lithuanian 80.1%, Russian 8.6%, Polish 7.7%, Belarussian 1.5%, other 2.1%. **Religion:** Catholic, 85%. **Literacy:** very high
Economic summary: Gross domestic product: purchasing power parity (1995 estimate as extrapolated from the World Bank estimate for 1994): $13.3 billion; $3,400 per capita; real growth rate 1% (1995 est.); inflation 35% (1995 est.). Labor force: 1.836 million; 42% in industry and construction; 18% in agriculture in forestry. Natural resources: peat, sand and gravel, quartz, gypsum, dolomite, clay, limestone, mineral water. Amber found on Baltic Sea coast. Industries: metal cutting, electric motors, TV sets, refrigerators and freezers, petroleum refining, shipbuilding, furniture, textiles, food processing, electronic components, computers. Agriculture (36% of Labor force): Most developed are the livestock and dairy branches. Lithuania is a net exporter of meat, milk, and eggs. Exports: $2.2 billion (1994): textiles, chemical products and related industries, mineral products, mechanical goods and electrical equipment. Imports: $2.7 billion (1994): mineral products (incl. oil and gas), machinery, electrical equipment, metals, transport equipment. Major trading partners: C.I.S. nations, E.U. including Germany, the Netherlands, and Italy.

Geography. Lithuania is situated on the eastern shore of the Baltic Sea and borders Latvia on the north, Belarus on the east and south, Poland and the Kalinin-grad region of Russia on the southwest. It is a country of gently rolling hills, many forests, rivers and streams, and lakes. Its principal natural resource is agricultural land.

Government. Lithuania is a parliamentary democracy. The head of state is the directly elected President. The President nominates the Prime Minister who is then approved by the Parliament (Seimas).

History. Southernmost of the three Baltic states, Lithuania in the Middle Ages was a grand duchy joined to Poland through royal marriage. Poles and Lithuanians merged forces to defeat the Teutonic knights of Germany at Tannenberg in 1410 and extended their power far into Russian territory. In 1795, however, following the third partition of Poland, Lithuania fell into Russian hands and did not regain its independence until 1918, toward the end of the first World War.

The republic was occupied by the Soviet Union in June 1940 and annexed in August 1940. From June 1941 to 1944 it was occupied by German troops and then was retaken by Russia. Western countries, including the United States, never recognized the Russian annexation of Lithuania.

Nineteen eighty-eight saw a re-emergence of the Lithuanian independence movement. Elections were held on Feb. 24, 1990, and Vytautas Landsbergis, the non-Communist head of the largest Lithuanian popular movement (Sajudis) was elected to Parliament that day, and on March 11, 1990, the Parliament elected him as its president. On the same day, the Supreme Council rejected Soviet rule and declared the restoration of Lithuania's independence, the first Baltic republic to take this action.

Confrontation with the Soviet Union ensued along with economic sanctions, but they were lifted after both sides agreed to a face-saving compromise.

Lithuania's independence was quickly recognized by major European and other nations, and on Sept. 2, 1991, President Bush announced full diplomatic recognition for the Baltic republics. The Soviet Union finally recognized the independence of the Baltic states on September 6. U.N. admittance followed on Sept. 17, 1991.

Elections in February 1993 made Algirdas Brazauskas, a former Communist Party leader, president.

As a result of a banking scandal and his handling of it, Adolfas Slezevicius was fired from the post of Prime Minister. The Seimas approved Mindaugas Stankevicius, a prominent figure in the Democratic Labor Party, as a replacement.

The ruling Democratic Labor Party suffered severe losses in the two round parliamentary elections held in October and November 1996. In its wake a conservative coalition government was formed.

LUXEMBOURG

Grand Duchy of Luxembourg
National name: Grand-Duché de Luxembourg
Ruler: Grand Duke Jean (1964)
Premier: Jean-Claude Juncker (1994)
Area: 999 sq mi. (2,586 sq km)
Population (1997 est.): 422,474 (average annual rate of natural increase: 0.47%); birth rate: 12.85/1000; infant mortality rate: 4.6/1000; density per square mile: 422.9
Capital and largest city (1991): Luxembourg, 75,622.
  Monetary unit: Luxembourg franc. **Languages:** Luxembourgish, French, German. **Ethnicity/Race:** Celtic base (with French and German blend), Portuguese, Italian, and European (guest and worker residents). **Religion:** Mainly Roman Catholic. **Literacy rate:** 100%

Economic summary: Gross domestic product: purchasing power parity (1995 est.): $10 billion; $24,800 per capita; real growth rate 2.6%; inflation: 3.6% (1992); unemployment: 2.5% (1995). Arable land: 24%. Principal agricultural products: livestock, dairy products, wine. Labor force (1994): 203,200; one-third are foreign workers. Services, 65%; industry, 31.6%; agriculture, 3.4%. Major industrial products: banking, steel, processed food, chemicals, metal products, tires, glass. Natural resource: Iron ore. Exports: $5.9 billion (f.o.b., 1993 est.): steel, chemicals, rubber products, glass, aluminum. Imports: $7.5 million (c.i.f., 1993 est.): minerals, metals, foodstuffs, consumer goods. Major trading partners: European Union.

Geography. Luxembourg is a neighbor of Belgium on the west, Germany on the east, and France on the south. The Ardennes Mountains extend from Belgium into the northern section of Luxembourg.

Government. Luxembourg's unicameral legislature, the Chamber of Deputies, consists of 60 members elected for five years.

History. Sigefroi, Count of Ardennes, an offspring of Charlemagne, was Luxembourg's first sovereign ruler. In 1060, the country came under the rule of the House of Luxembourg. From the 15th to the 18th century, Spain, France, and Austria held it in turn. The Congress of Vienna in 1815 made it a Grand Duchy and gave it to William I, King of the Netherlands. In 1839 the Treaty of London ceded the western part of Luxembourg to Belgium.

The eastern part, continuing in personal union with the Netherlands and a member of the German Confederation, became autonomous in 1848 and a neutral territory by decision of the London Conference of 1867, governed by its Grand Duke. Germany occupied the duchy in World Wars I and II. Allied troops liberated the enclave in 1944.

In 1961, Prince Jean, son and heir of Grand Duchess Charlotte, was made head of state, acting for his mother. She abdicated in 1964, and Prince Jean became Grand Duke. Grand Duchess Charlotte died in 1985.

By a customs union between Belgium and Luxembourg, which came into force on May 1, 1922, to last for 50 years, customs frontiers between the two countries were abolished. On Jan. 1, 1948, a customs union with Belgium and the Netherlands (Benelux) came into existence. On Feb. 3, 1958, it became an economic union.

Luxembourg's parliament approved the "Maastricht Accord" in July 1992, with the proviso that the country negotiate an exemption to the clause granting foreigners the vote.

In July 1997 Luxembourg assumed the rotating presidency of the European Union for the second time.

MACEDONIA

Republic of Macedonia[1]
National Name: Republica Makedonija
President: Kiro Gilgorov (1991)
Prime Minister: Branko Crvenkovski (1992)
Area: 9,928 sq mi. (25,713 sq km)
Population (1997 est.): 2,113,866 (average annual rate of natural increase: 0.48%); birth rate: 13.34/1000; infant mortality rate: 29.2/1000; density per square mile: 212.9
Capital and largest city (1994 est.): Skopje, 444,229. Other large cities: Bitola, 84,002; Kumanovo, 68,148; Prelep, 70,152; Tetovo, 50,344; Titov Veles, 42,826; Ohrid, 42,903; Sitip, 42,826. **Monetary unit:** Dinar.
Languages: Macedonian, which uses the Cyrillic alphabet, 70%; Albanian, 21%; Turkish, 3%; other, 6%.
Ethnicity/Race: Macedonian 65%, Albanian 22%, Turkish 4%, Serb 2%, Gypsies 3%, other 4%. **Religions (1994):** Eastern Orthodox, 67%; Muslim, 30%
Economic summary: Gross domestic product: purchasing power parity (1995 est.): $1.9 billion; $880 per capita; real growth rate, 4%; inflation: 14.8%; unemployment: 37%. Labor force: 591,773 (1994): manufacturing and mining, 40% (1992). Industries: low-level technology (basic fuels) mining, basic textiles, wood products, and tobacco. Agriculture: rice, tobacco, wheat, corn, millet, cotton, citrus fruits, and vegetables. Exports (1995): $916.2 million: manufactured goods, 40%; machinery and transport equipment, 14%; miscellaneous manufactured articles, 23%; raw materials, 7.6%; food (rice) and live animals, 5.7%; beverages and tobacco, 4.5%; chemicals, 4.7% (1990). Imports (1995): $199 million: fuel and lubricants, 19%; manufactured goods, 18%; machinery and transport equipment, 15%; food and live animals, 14%; chemicals, 11.4%; raw materials, 10%. Major trading partners: Germany, Albania, Bulgaria, former Yugoslav republics, Greece.

1. The U.N. recognized the Republic of Macedonia on April 8, 1993 under the temporary name the Former Yugoslav Republic of Macedonia. The U.S. recognized Macedonia as a state in February 1994.

Geography. Macedonia is a landlocked state in the heart of the Balkans and is slightly smaller than the state of Vermont. It is a mountainous country with small basins of agricultural land linked by rivers. It borders the Yugoslavian republic of Serbia in the north, Bulgaria in the east, Greece in the south, and Albania in the west. The three major rivers are the Aliakmon, the Vardar, and the Strymon. The Vardar is the largest and most important river.

Government. A democratic republic with a legislative house consisting of 120 deputies, each elected for a four-year term. The Assembly's President and Vice Presidents are elected from among its members.

History. The Republic of Macedonia occupies the western half of the ancient Kingdom of Macedonia. Historic Macedonia was defeated by Rome and became a Roman province in 148 B.C.E.

After the Roman Empire was divided in C.E. 395, Macedonia was intermittently ruled by the Byzantine Empire until Turkey took possession of the land in 1389. The Ottoman Turks dominated Macedonia for the next five centuries, up until 1913.

During the 19th and 20th centuries, there was a constant struggle by the Balkan powers to possess Macedonia for its economic and strategic military corridors. The Treaty of San Stefano in 1878 ending the Russo-Turkish War gave the largest part of Macedonia to Bulgaria. Bulgaria lost much of its Macedonian territory when it was defeated by the Greeks and Serbs in the Second Balkan War of 1913. Most of Macedonia went to Serbia and the remainder was divided among Greece and Bulgaria.

In 1914, Serbia, which included Macedonia, joined in union with Croatia, Slovenia, and Montenegro to form the Kingdom of Serbs, Croats, and Slovenes, which was renamed Yugoslavia in 1929.

Bulgaria joined the Axis powers in World War II and occupied parts of Yugoslavia including Macedonia in 1941. During the occupation of their country, Macedonian resistance fighters fought a guerrilla warfare against the invading troops.

The Yugoslavian Republic was reestablished after the defeat of Germany in 1945, and in 1946, the government removed Macedonia from Serbian control and made it an autonomous Yugoslavian republic. Later, when President Tito recognized the Macedonian people as a separate nation, the Macedonians strove to develop their own culture and language separate from Bulgaria and Serbia.

In January 1992, Macedonia declared its independence from Yugoslavia and asked for recognition from the European Union nations. In December 1993 six European nations recognized Macedonia.

The President won re-election in October 1994. As a result of that voting, a coalition government was created from the Social Democratic Alliance, the Liberals, the Socialists, and a mainly ethnic-Albanian party.

In October 1995 Greece lifted its trade embargo as a result of an agreement reached in New York the previous month. In September the country was admitted into the Council of Europe.

The government in 1997 urged NATO to extend its peacekeeping role in the Balkans beyond its mid-1998 mandate, saying NATO troops provided a stabilizing role.

MADAGASCAR

Republic of Madagascar
National name: Repoblikan'i Madagasikara
President and Head of State: Didier Ratsiraka (1997)
Prime Minister: Pascal Rakotomavo (1997)
Area: 226,660 sq mi. (587,050 sq km)
Population (1997 est.): 14,061,627 (average annual rate of natural increase: 2.81%); birth rate: 42.26/1000; infant mortality rate: 92/1000; density per square mile: 62
Capital and largest city (1993 est.): Antananarivo, 1,000,000. **Monetary unit:** Malagasy franc. **Languages:** Malagasy, French. **Ethnicity/Race:** Malayo-Indonesian (Merina and related Betsileo), Cotiers (mixed African, Malayo-Indonesian, and Arab ancestry—Betsimisaraka, Tsimihety, Antaisaka, Sakalava), French, Indian, Creole, Comoran. **Religions:** traditional, 52%; Christian, 41%; Islam, 7%. **Literacy rate:** 80%
Economic summary: Gross domestic product: purchasing power parity (1995 est.): $11.4 billion; $820 per capita; 2.7% real growth rate; inflation 35% (1994 est.). Arable land: 4%. Principal agricultural products: rice, livestock, coffee, vanilla, sugar, cloves, cardamom, beans, bananas. Labor force: 4.3 million in subsistence agriculture (96% of total labor force not receiving money wages). Major industrial products: processed food, textiles, assembled automobiles, soap, cement. Natural resources: graphite, chromium, bauxite, semiprecious stones. Exports: $240 million (f.o.b., 1993 est.): coffee, cloves, vanilla, sugar, petroleum products. Imports: $510 million (f.o.b., 1993 est.): consumer goods, foodstuffs, crude petroleum. Major trading partners: France, U.S., Japan, Italy, Germany, U.K., and other E.U.

Geography. Madagascar lies in the Indian Ocean off the southeast coast of Africa opposite Mozambique. The world's fourth-largest island, it is twice the size of Arizona. The country's low-lying coastal area gives way to a central plateau. The once densely wooded interior has largely been cut down.

Government. A republic. Under the new constitution of the Third Republic, August 19, 1992, Albert Zafy was elected President, February 1993, for a 5-year term. The prime minister, Francisque Ravony, was elected by the Unicameral National Assembly, composed of 19 political parties, which voted in August 1993.

History. The present population is of black and Malay stock, with perhaps some Polynesian, called Malagasy. The French took over a protectorate in 1885, and then

in 1894–95 ended the monarchy, exiling Queen Rànavàlona III to Algiers. A colonial administration was set up, to which the Comoro Islands were attached in 1908, and other territories later. In World War II, the British occupied Madagascar, which retained ties to Vichy France.

An autonomous republic within the French Community since 1958, Madagascar became an independent member of the Community in 1960. In May 1973, an army coup led by Maj. Gen. Gabriel Ramanantsoa ousted Philibert Tsiranana, President since 1959.

On June 15, 1975, Comdr. Didier Ratsiraka was named President. He announced that he would follow a socialist course and, after nationalizing banks and insurance companies, declared all mineral resources nationalized.

In July 1991 opposition leaders named an alternative government. After a 15-day strike the President offered a referendum on a multiparty constitution and named a new Prime Minister. An interim government was formed in May that included the opposition and would prepare constitutional changes.

Albert Zafy decidedly won the second round of the presidential election in February 1993.

As a result of a referendum held in September 1995, the President was given the power to appoint and fire the Prime Minister. The then Prime Minister, who was frequently at odds with the President, resigned in October, being replaced by the agriculture minister.

In February 1997 Ratsiraka again took office as President. Within two weeks, he named his Prime Minister and cabinet.

MALAWI

Republic of Malawi
President: Bakili Muluzi (1994)
Area: 45,747 sq mi. (118,484 sq km)
Population (1997 est.): 9,609,081 (average annual rate of natural increase: 1.57%); birth rate: 40.79/1000; infant mortality rate: 138.9/1000; density per square mile: 210
Capital (1993 est.): Lilongwe, 260,000. **Largest city (1993 est.):** Blantyre, 399,000. **Monetary unit:** Kwacha. **Languages:** English and Chichewa (National). **Ethnicity/Race:** Chewa, Nyanja, Tumbuko, Yao, Lomwe, Sena, Tonga, Ngoni, Ngonde, Asian, European. **Religions:** Christian, 75%; Islam, 20%. **Literacy rate:** 41.2%
Economic summary: Gross domestic product: purchasing power parity (1995 est.): $6.9 billion; $700 per capita; growth rate 9.9%; inflation rate 83.3%. Arable land: 25%. Agriculture accounts for 40% of GDP and 90% of export revenues. Principal agricultural products: tobacco, tea, sugar, corn, cotton. Labor force: 428,000 wage earners; 43% in agriculture; 16% in manufacturing; 15% in personal services; 9% in commerce; 7% in construction; other permanently employed 6% (1986). Major industrial products: food, tobacco, cement, processed wood, consumer goods. Natural resources: limestone, uranium, coal, bauxite. Exports: $365 million (f.o.b., 1994): tobacco, sugar, tea, coffee, peanuts. Imports: $240 million (c.i.f., 1994): transport equipment, food, petroleum, consumer goods. Major trading partners: U.K., U.S., Japan, Germany, South Africa, Zambia, Zimbabwe.
Member of Commonwealth of Nations

Geography. Malawi is a landlocked country the size of Pennsylvania in southeastern Africa, surrounded by Mozambique, Zambia, and Tanzania. Lake Malawi, formerly Lake Nyasa, occupies most of the country's eastern border. The north-south Rift Valley is flanked by mountain ranges and high plateau areas.

Government. Under a provisional constitution which came into effect on May 17, 1994, the President is the head of state and government. There is a Vice President. The National Assembly (parliament) is composed of 177 members. There are eight registered parties and the ruling party since May 17, 1994 is the United Democratic Front (UDF) of President Bakili Muluzi.

History. The first European to make extensive explorations in the area was David Livingstone in the 1850s and 1860s. In 1884, Cecil Rhodes's British South African Company received a charter to develop the country. The company came into conflict with the Arab slavers in 1887–89. After Britain annexed the Nyasaland territory in 1891, making it a protectorate in 1892, Sir Harry Johnstone, the first high commissioner, using Royal Navy gunboats, wiped out the slavers.

Nyasaland became the independent nation of Malawi on July 6, 1964. Two years later, it became a republic within the Commonwealth of Nations.

Dr. Hastings K. Banda, Malawi's first prime minister, became its first President. He pledged to follow a policy of "discretionary nonalignment." Banda alienated much of black Africa by maintaining good relations with South Africa.

The results of a referendum in June 1993 on Banda's one-party rule gave 63% in favor of a multiparty democracy.

Bakili Muluzi won the country's first free election in May 1994. He was sworn in a few days later and quickly released the remaining political prisoners. Budget trimming was the order of the day in 1995, which received commendation from the IMF.

Banda, charged with misuse of state funds during his reign, was found incompetent to stand trial by a judge in May 1997. Three associates, however, were scheduled to be tried in October.

MALAYSIA

Paramount Ruler: His Majesty Tuanku Ja'afar ibni Al-Marhum Tuanku Abdul Rahman (1994)
Prime Minister: Dato' Seri Dr. Mahathir bin Mohamad (1981)
Area: 128,328 sq mi. (332,370 sq km)
Population (1997 est.): 20,376,235 (average annual rate of natural increase: 2.02%); birth rate: 25.7/1000; infant mortality rate: 23.2/1000; density per square mile: 158.8
Capital and largest city (1991 est.): Kuala Lumpur, 1,145,000. **Largest cities (1991 est.):** Georgetown (Pinang), 220,000; Ipoh, 382,600. **Monetary unit:** Ringgit. **Languages:** Malay (official), Chinese, Tamil, English. **Ethnicity/Race:** Malay and other indigenous 59%, Chinese 32%, Indian 9%. **Ethnic divisions:** 59% Malay and other indigenous; 32% Chinese; 9% Indian. **Religions:** Malays (all Muslims), Chinese (predominantly Buddhists), Indians (predominantly Hindus). **Literacy rate:** 78%
Economic summary: Gross domestic product: purchasing power parity (1995 est.): $193.6 billion; $9,800 per capita; real growth rate 9.5%; inflation: 5.3%; unemployment 2.8%. Arable land: 3%. Principal agricultural products: rice, rubber, palm products. Labor force (1995): 8 million. Major industrial products: processed rubber, timber, and palm oil, tin, petroleum, light manufactures, electronics equipment. Natural resources: tin, oil, copper, timber. Exports: $72 billion: natural rubber, palm oil, tin, timber, petroleum, electronics, textiles. Imports: $72.2 billion: food, crude oil, capital equipment, chemicals, consumer goods. Major trading partners: Japan, Singapore, U.S., Western European countries, Taiwan. **Member of Commonwealth of Nations**

Geography. Malaysia is on the Malay Peninsula in southeast Asia. The nation also includes Sabah and Sarawak on the island of Borneo to the east. Its area slightly exceeds that of New Mexico.

Most of Malaysia is covered by forest, with a mountain range running the length of the peninsula. Extensive forests provide ebony, sandalwood, teak, and other woods.

Government. Malaysia is a sovereign constitutional monarchy practicing parliamentary democracy based on universal suffrage. The Paramount Ruler is elected for a five-year term by the hereditary rulers of the states from among themselves. He is advised by the Prime Minister and his cabinet. There is a bicameral legislature. The Senate, whose role is comparable more to that of the British House of Lords than to the U.S. Senate, has 69 members, partly appointed by the Paramount Ruler to represent minority and special interests, and partly elected by the legislative assemblies of the various states.

The House of Representatives, is made up of 192 members, who are elected for five-year terms.

History. Malaysia came into existence on Sept. 16, 1963, as a federation of Malaya, Singapore, Sabah (North Borneo), and Sarawak. In 1965, Singapore withdrew from the federation. Since 1966, the 11 states of former Malaya have been known as West Malaysia, and Sabah and Sarawak have been known as East Malaysia.

The Union of Malaya was established April 1, 1946, being formed from the Federated Malay States of Negri Sembilan, Pahang, Perak, and Selangor; the Unfederated Malay States of Johore, Kedah, Kelantan, Perlis, and Trengganu; and two of the Straits Settlements—Malacca and Penang. The Malay states had been brought under British administration during the late 19th and early 20th centuries.

It became the Federation of Malaya on Feb. 1, 1948, and the Federation attained full independence within the Commonwealth of Nations in 1957.

Sabah, constituting the extreme northern portion of the island of Borneo, was a British protectorate administered under charter by the British North Borneo Company from 1881 to 1946, when it assumed the status of a colony. It was occupied by Japanese troops from 1942 to 1945.

Sarawak extends along the northwestern coast of Borneo for about 500 miles (805 km). In 1841, part of the present territory was granted by the Sultan of Brunei to Sir James Brooke. Sarawak continued to be ruled by members of the Brooke family until the Japanese occupation.

From 1963, it was the target of guerrilla infiltration from Indonesia, but beat off invasion attempts. In 1966, when Sukarno fell and the Communist Party was liquidated in Indonesia, hostilities ended.

In the late 1960s, the country was torn by communal rioting directed against Chinese and Indians, who controlled a disproportionate share of the country's wealth. Beginning in 1968, the government moved to achieve greater economic balance through a national economic policy.

Malaysia felt the impact of the "boat people" fleeing Vietnam early in 1978. Because the refugees were mostly ethnic Chinese, the government was apprehensive about any increase of a minority that previously had been the source of internal conflict in the country. In April 1988, it announced that starting in April 1989 it would accept no more refugees.

General elections were held in October 1990 producing another victory for Prime Minister Mahathir and his Barisan National Coalition, which won 127 of the 180 parliamentary seats.

In 1994 the constitution was amended to state that the monarch had to obey the government's advice and that any bill not signed by him within 30 days became law automatically.

The Prime Minister's party scored a massive victory in parliamentary elections in 1995.

The U.S. and Malaysia agreed in 1997 to permit unrestricted commercial airline service between the two countries. The U.S. already had four such agreements with Pacific Rim countries.

MALDIVES

Republic of Maldives
President: Maumoon Abdul Gayoom (1978)
Area: 115 sq mi. (298 sq km)
Population (1997 est.): 280,391 (average annual rate of natural increase: 3.46%); birth rate: 40.9/1000; infant mortality rate: 44.1/1000 (1994 est.); density per square mile: 2,438.2
Capital and largest city (1995 census): Malé, 62,973. **Monetary unit:** Maldivian Rufiyaa. **Language:** Dhivehi. **Ethnicity/Race:** Sinhalese, Dravidian, Arab, African. **Religion:** Islam (Sunni Muslim). **Literacy rate:** 98%
Economic summary: Gross domestic product (1994 est.): $390 million; $1,560 per capita; 6.6% real growth rate; inflation: 16.5%; unemployment negl. Arable land: 10%. Principal agricultural products: maize, sorghum, finger millet, alocasia, cassava, sweet potato, onion, coconuts. Labor force: 66,000; 25% in fishing. Major products: fish, processed coconut, handicraft. Natural resource: fish. Tourism is also an important sector of the economy. Exports: $75.3 million (f.o.b., 1994 est.): fish, clothing. Imports: $195.1 million (c.i.f., 1994 est.): intermediate and capital goods, consumer goods, petroleum products. Major trading partners: Thailand, U.S., Singapore, U.K., Germany, India.

Geography. The Republic of Maldives is a group of atolls in the Indian Ocean about 417 miles (671 km) southwest of Sri Lanka. Its 1,190 coral islets stretch over an area of 35,200 square miles (90,000 sq km). With concerns over global warming and the shrinking of the polar ice caps, Maldives feels directly threatened, as none of its islands rises more than six feet above sea level.

Government. The 15-member cabinet is headed by the President. The Majlis (parliament) is a unicameral legislature consisting of 48 members. Eight of these are appointed by the President. The others are elected for five-year terms, 2 from the capital island of Malé and 2 from each of the 19 administrative atolls. There are no political parties in the Maldives.

History. The Maldives (formerly called the Maldive Islands) are inhabited by an Islamic seafaring people. Originally the islands were under the suzerainty of Ceylon. They came under British protection in 1887 and were a dependency of the then-colony of Ceylon until 1948. The independence agreement with Britain was signed July 26, 1965.

For centuries a Sultanate, the islands adopted a republican form of government in 1952, but the Sultanate was restored in 1954. In 1968, however, as the result of a referendum, a republic was again established in the islands.

Ibrahim Nasir, President since 1968, was removed from office by the Majlis in November 1978 and replaced by Maumoon Abdul Gayoom. The President was elected to a fourth five-year term in October 1993.

Ever concerned with the possibility of rising sea levels, the country has constructed with Japanese aid a line of concrete breakwaters along the capital's southern coast.

MALI

Republic of Mali
National name: République de Mali
President of the Republic: Alpha Oumar Konaré (1992)
Prime Minister: Ibrahima Boubacar Keita (1994)
Area: 478,819 sq mi. (1,240,142 sq km)
Population (1997 est.): 9,945,383 (average annual rate of natural increase: 3.18%); birth rate: 50.89/1000; infant mortality rate: 101/1000; density per square mile: 20.8
Capital and largest city (1992 est.): Bamako, 746,000. **Monetary unit:** Franc CFA. **Ethnic groups:** Bambara, Peul, Soninke, Malinke, Songhai, Dogon, Senoufo, Minianka, Berbers, and Moors. **Languages:** French (official), African languages. **Ethnicity/Race:** Mande 50% (Bambara, Malinke, Sarakole), Peul 17%, Voltaic 12%, Songhai 6%, Tuareg and Moor 10%, other 5%. **Religions:** Islam, 90%; traditional, 9%; Christian, 1%. **Literacy rate:** 32%
Economic summary: Gross domestic product: purchasing power parity (1994 est.): $5.4 billion; $600 per capita; real growth rate 2.4%; inflation 8% (1995 est.). Arable land: 2%; Principal agricultural products: millet, corn, rice, cotton, peanuts, livestock. Labor force: 2.666 million (1986 est.); 80% in agriculture; 19% in services; 1% in industry and commerce (1981). Major industrial products: consumer goods, phosphates, gold, fish. Natural resources: bauxite, iron ore, manganese, phosphate, salt, limestone, gold. Exports: $415 million (f.o.b., 1993): cotton, livestock, gold. Imports: $842 million (f.o.b., 1993): machinery and equipment, foodstuffs, construction materials, petroleum, textiles. Major trading partners: Western Europe.

Geography. Most of Mali, in West Africa, lies in the Sahara. A landlocked country four-fifths the size of Alaska, it is bordered by Guinea, Senegal, Mauritania, Algeria, Niger, Burkina Faso, and the Cote D'Ivoire.

The only fertile area is in the south, where the Niger and Senegal Rivers provide irrigation.

Government. The army overthrew the government on Nov. 19, 1968, and formed a provisional government. The Military Committee of National Liberation consists of 14 members and forms the decision-making body.

Soldiers promising a multiparty democracy overthrew the Dictatorship of General Traoré in March 1991.

The present government is a multiparty democracy with one parliamentary house of 129 seats, 13 of which are designated for Malians abroad.

History. Subjugated by France by the end of the 19th century, this area became a colony in 1904 (named French Sudan in 1920) and in 1946 became part of the French Union. On June 20, 1960, it became independent and, under the name of Sudanese Republic, was federated with the Republic of Senegal in the Mali Federation. However, Senegal seceded from the Federation on Aug. 20, 1960, and the Sudanese Republic then changed its name to the Republic of Mali on September 22.

In the 1960s, Mali concentrated on economic development, continuing to accept aid from both Soviet bloc and Western nations, as well as international agencies. In the late 1960s, it began retreating from close ties with China. But a purge of conservative opponents brought greater power to President Modibo Keita, and in 1968 the influence of the Chinese and their Malian sympathizers increased.

Mali, with Mauritania, Côte D'Ivoire, Senegal, Dahomey (Benin), Niger, and Burkina Faso signed a treaty establishing the Economic Community for West Africa.

Mali and Burkina Faso fought a brief border war from December 25 to 29, 1985.

The leader of the March 1991 coup, Lieut. Col. Amadou Toumani Touré, promised the army would return to the barracks. There were at least 59 casualties after the overnight coup, which France welcomed.

Multiparty elections in 1992 gave the Alliance for Democracy in Mali 76 of the 116 parliamentary seats, and the presidency went to that party's candidate, Alpha Oumar Konaré with 70% of the vote.

Following large demonstrations and riots in early 1993 the Prime Minister resigned, being replaced by the minister of defense, Abdoulaye Sekou Sow.

Prime Minister Sow in turn resigned in February 1994 claiming political differences with the governing party. He was replaced with the foreign minister, Ibrahima Boubacar Keita.

The first round of legislative elections in April 1997 was declared invalid two weeks later by a constitutional court owing to irregularities, and the second round was cancelled. The presidential election in May was boycotted by many opposition groups. President Konaré easily won a second term.

MALTA

Malta
President: Dr. Ugo Mifsud Bonnicí (1994)
Prime Minister: Alfred Sant (1996)
Area: 122 sq mi. (316 sq km)
Population (1997 est.): 379,365 (average annual rate of natural increase: 0.8%); birth rate: 14.71/1000; infant mortality rate: 6.4/1000; density per square mile: 3,109.5
Capital (1992 est.): Valletta, 9,183. **Largest city (est. 1987):** Sliema. **Monetary unit:** Maltese lira. **Languages:** Maltese and English. **Ethnicity/Race:** Arab, Sicilian, Norman, Spanish, Italian, English. **Religion:** Roman Catholic. **Literacy rate:** 84%
Economic summary: Gross domestic product: purchasing power parity (1995 est.): $4.4 billion; $12,000 per capita; real growth rate 5%; inflation 5%; unemployment 3.4%. Arable land: 38%. Principal agricultural products: potatoes, wheat, barley, citrus, vegetables, hogs, poultry. Labor force: 139,600; 37% in government; 26% in services; 22% in manufacturing; 9% in training programs. Major manufacturing products are high-tech semiconductors, electrical switch gear, gold and silver items, rubber products, and textiles. The same products are exported. Tourism is also important to the economy. Exports: $1.5 billion (f.o.b., 1994): clothing, textiles, footwear, ships. Imports: $2.5 billion (c.i.f., 1994): food, petroleum, machinery, and semi-manufactured goods. Major trading partners: Germany, Italy, U.K., U.S. **Member of Commonwealth of Nations**

Geography. The five Maltese islands—with a combined land area smaller than Philadelphia—are in the Mediterranean about 60 miles (97 km) south of the southeastern tip of Sicily.

Government. The government is headed by a Prime Minister, responsible to a 65-member House of Representatives elected by universal suffrage.

The major political parties are the Nationalists (34 of 65 seats in the House), led by Prime Minister Dr. Edward Fenech-Adami; Malta Labor Party (31 seats), led by Dr. Alfred Sant.

History. The strategic importance of Malta was recognized by the Phoenicians, who occupied it, as did in their turn the Greeks, Carthaginians, and Romans. The apostle Paul was shipwrecked there in c.e. 58.

The Knights of St. John (Malta), who obtained the three habitable Maltese islands of Malta, Gozo, and Comino from Charles V in 1530, reached their highest fame when they withstood an attack by superior Turkish forces in 1565.

Napoleon seized Malta in 1798, but the French forces were ousted by British troops the next year, and British rule was confirmed by the Treaty of Paris in 1814.

Malta was heavily attacked by German and Italian aircraft during World War II, but was never invaded by the Axis.

Malta became an independent nation on Sept. 21, 1964, and a republic Dec. 13, 1974, but remained in the British Commonwealth. The Governor-General, Sir Anthony Mamo, was sworn in as the first President and Dom Mintoff became prime minister.

Fenech Adami won re-election as prime minister in February 1992 when his party won an absolute majority of three seats in the parliament.

The European Council indicated in 1994 that Malta's application for membership in the European Union would be accepted in the next expansion phase.

parliamentary elections in October 1996 gave a victory to the Labour Party with slightly over 50% of the vote. Labour leader Alfred Sant was sworn into office as prime minister along with his cabinet later that month.

MARSHALL ISLANDS

Republic of the Marshall Islands
President: Imata Kabua (1997)
Total land area: 70 sq mi (181.3 sq km), includes the atolls of Bikini, Eniwetok, and Kwajalein
Population (1997 est.): 60,652; growth rate 3.85%; birth rate 45.54/1000; infant mortality rate 45.7/1000; density per square mile: 866.4
Capital and largest city (1990 est.): Majuro, 20,000. **Ethnicity/Race:** Micronesian. **Religion:** predominantly Christian, mostly Protestant. **Literacy rate:** 93%. **Language:** Both Marshallese and English are official languages. Marshallese is a dialect of the Malayo-Polynesian family
Economic summary: Gross domestic product: purchasing power parity (1995 est.): $94 million; per capita, $1,680; real growth rate, 1.5%; inflation, 4%; unemployment, 16%. Labor force (1986): 4,800. Exports: $21.3 million (f.o.b., 1995 est.): coconut oil, fish, live animals, trichus shells. Imports: $69.9 million (c.i.f., 1995 est.): foodstuffs, machinery and equipment, beverages and tobacco, fuels. Agriculture, marine resources, and tourism are the top development priorities for the Republic of the Marshall Islands (RMI). The government of the RMI is the largest employer with some 2,000 workers. Direct U.S. aid under the Compact of Free Association, the U.S. is to provide approximately $40 million annually in aid. Major trading partners: U.S., Japan, Australia.

Geography. The Marshall Islands, east of the Carolines, are divided into two chains: the western, or Ralik, group, including the atolls Jaluit, Kwajalein, Wotho, Bikini, and Eniwetok; and the eastern, or Ratak, group, including the atolls Mili, Majuro, Maloelap, Wotje, and Likiep. The islands are of the coral-reef type and rise only a few feet above sea level. The Marshall Islands comprise an area slightly larger than Washington, D.C.

Government. Constitutional government in free association with the United States.

History. The United States and the RMI signed a Compact of Free Association on October 15, 1986, which became effective as of October 21, 1986. The termination of the Trusteeship Agreement became effective on November 3, 1986. The Marshall Islands were admitted to the U.N. on Sept. 17, 1991.

The government in 1994 again considered allowing the dumping of nuclear waste on such islands as Bikini and Eniwetok, which are already uninhabitable owing to nuclear tests decades ago.

Although parliament approved a 10% wage cut for public sector employees in 1995, it was not put into effect due to public opposition.

President Kabua died in office in December 1996 and Kunio Lemari became acting President.

MAURITANIA

Islamic Republic of Mauritania
National name: République Islamique de Mauritanie
Chief of State and Head of Government: Pres. Maaouye Ould Sidi Ahmed Taya (1984)
Prime Minister: Cheikh El Afia Ould Mohamed Khouna (1996)
Area: 397,953 sq mi. (1,030,700 sq km)
Population (1997 est.): 2,411,317 (average annual rate of natural increase: 3.17%); birth rate: 46.55/1000; infant mortality rate: 80/1000; density per square mile: 6.1
Capital and largest city (1992 est.): Nouakchott, 480,000. **Monetary unit:** Ouguiya. **Languages:** Arabic (official) and French. **Ethnicity/Race:** mixed Maur/black 40%, Maur 30%, black 30%. **Religion:** Islam. **Literacy rate:** 34%
Economic summary: Gross domestic product: purchasing power parity (1995 est.): $2.8 billion; $1,200 per capita; real growth rate 4%; inflation 3.5%; unemployment (1991 est.) 20%. Arable land: 1%; Principal agricultural products: livestock, millet, maize, wheat, dates, rice. Labor force: 465,000 (1981 est.); 45,000 wage earners; 47% in agriculture; 29% in services; 14% in industry and commerce; 10% in government. Major industrial products: iron ore, processed fish. Natural resources: copper, iron ore, gypsum, fish. Exports: $390 million (f.o.b., 1994 est.): iron ore, fish, gum arabic, gypsum. Imports: $355 million (c.i.f., 1994 est.): foodstuffs, petroleum, capital goods. Major trading partners: E.U., Japan, Côte d'Ivoire, Algeria, China, U.S.

Geography. Mauritania, three times the size of Arizona, is situated in northwest Africa with about 350 miles (592 km) of coastline on the Atlantic Ocean. It is bordered by Morocco on the north, Algeria and Mali on the east, and Senegal on the south.

The country is mostly desert, with the exception of the fertile Senegal River valley in the south and grazing land in the north.

Government. An army coup on July 10, 1978, deposed Moktar Ould Daddah, who had been President since Mauritania's independence in 1960. President Mohammed Khouna Ould Haldala, who seized power in the 1978 coup, was in turn deposed in a Dec. 12, 1984, coup by army chief of staff Maaouye Ould Sidi Ahmed Taya, who assumed the title of President.

In the January 1992 elections President Taya won 62% of the electorate vote.

The constitution guarantees freedom of press, opinion, and assembly among others to all Mauritanian citizens. There are about 20 political parties. There is a bicameral legislature Senate (Majlis Al-Shuyukh) and a National Assembly (Majlis Al-Watani).

History. Mauritania was first explored by the Portuguese. The French organized the area as a territory in 1904.

Mauritania became an independent nation on Nov. 28, 1960, and was admitted to the United Nations in 1961 over the strenuous opposition of Morocco, which claimed the territory. With Moors, Arabs, Berbers, and blacks frequently in conflict, the government in the late 1960s sought to make Arab culture dominant to unify the country.

Mauritania acquired administrative control of the southern part of the former Spanish Sahara when the colonial administration withdrew in 1975, under an agreement with Morocco and Spain.

Increased military spending and rising casualties in Western Sahara helped bring down the civilian government of Ould Daddah in 1978. A succession of military rulers followed.

In 1989 Mauritania fought a border war with Senegal. Although the country voted in the U.N. to support the embargo against Iraq, the government actually leaned the other way.

The government in April 1991 announced a transition to a multiparty system. A constitutional reform embodying these changes won approval in a referendum in July.

The opposition's call for a boycott of the March parliamentary elections reduced turnout to no more than 40%. Yet Taya's party won 67 of the 79 available seats.

Six opposition parties in July 1995 banded together in a new coalition to fight for democracy. The ruling party won 71 seats in the parliamentary elections held in October 1996. Voter turnout was very low in the capital, but higher in other areas.

MAURITIUS

President: Cassam Uteem (1992)
Prime Minister: Navinchandra Ramgoolam (1995)
Area: 787 sq mi. (2,040 sq km)
Population (1997 est.): 1,154,272 (average annual rate of natural increase: 1.21%); birth rate: 18.81/1000; infant mortality rate: 16.9/1000; density per square mile: 1,466.7
Capital and largest city (1993 est.): Port Louis, 134,516. **Monetary unit:** Mauritian rupee. **Languages:** English (official), French, Creole, Hindi, Urdu, Hakka, Bojpoori. **Ethnicity/Race:** Indo-Mauritian 68%, Creole 27%, Sino-Mauritian 3%, Franco-Mauritian 2%. **Religions:** Hindu, 52%, Christian, 28.3%; Islam, 16.6%; other, 3.1%. **Literacy rate:** 82.8%
Economic summary: Gross domestic product: purchasing power parity (1995 est.): $10.9 billion; $9,600 per capita; real growth rate 2.7%; inflation 9.4%; unemployment 2.4% (1991 est.). Arable land: 54%. Principal products: sugar cane, tea. Labor force: 335,000; 22% in manufacturing; 29% in government services; 27% in agriculture and fishing. Major products: processed sugar, wearing apparel, chemical products, textiles. Natural resources: fish. Exports: $1.3 billion (f.o.b., 1994): sugar, light manufactures, textiles. Imports: $1.9 billion (f.o.b., 1994): foodstuffs, manufactured goods. Major trading partners: E.U., South Africa, U.S.
Member of Commonwealth of Nations

Geography. Mauritius is a mountainous island in the Indian Ocean east of Madagascar.

Government. Mauritius is a republic within the British Commonwealth. The unicameral Legislative Assembly has 70 members, 62 of whom are elected by direct suffrage. The remaining 8 are chosen from among the unsuccessful candidates.

History. After a brief Dutch settlement, French immigrants who came in 1715 gave the name of Isle de France to the island and established the first road and harbor infrastructure, as well as the sugar industry, under the leadership of Gov. Mahe de Labourdonnais. Blacks from Africa and Madagascar came as slaves to work in the cane fields. In 1810, the British captured the island and in 1814, by the Treaty of Paris, it was ceded to Great Britain along with its dependencies.

Indian immigration, which followed the abolition of slavery in 1835, rapidly changed the fabric of Mauritian society, and the country flourished with the increased cultivation of sugar cane.

Mauritius became independent on March 12, 1968. The Labor Party government of Sir Seewoosagur Ramgoolam, who had ruled Mauritius since independence, was toppled in a 1982 election by the Movement Militant Mauricien, which had campaigned for recovery of Diego Garcia island, separated from Mauritius during the colonial period and leased by Britain to the United States for a naval base. But an Alliance Party coalition, including the Labor Party, regained power at the end of 1983 and brought back Ramgoolam as prime minister. He was succeeded by Aneerood Jugnauth of his party in 1982.

A transformation of the nation from a constitutional monarchy into a republic was attempted in mid-1990. Public dissent, however, arose, and the required parliamentary vote was never taken.

The country formally broke ties with the British crown in March 1992 becoming a republic. The President was elected by the Legislative Assembly on June 30.

An alliance of opposition parties emerged victorious in December 1995 elections to the Assembly, capturing all the seats.

The budget for 1997–98, announced in June, called for eliminating a levy introduced in 1996 on the sugar industry. In return, the government asked sugar growers to initiate a number of social programs for employees and their families.

MEXICO

United Mexican States
Official name: Estados Unidos Mexicanos
President: Ernesto Zedillo Ponce de Léon (1994)
Area: 761,600 sq mi. (1,967,183 sq km)
Population (1997 est.): 97,563,374 (average annual rate of natural increase: 2.12%); birth rate: 25.8/1000; infant mortality rate: 23.9/1000; density per square mile: 128.1
Capital and largest city (1995): Mexico City, 8,483,623.
Largest cities (1995): Guadalajara, 1,632,521; Ecatepic, 1,456,438 (part of Mexico City metropolitan area); Nezahualcóyotl, 1,133,680; Puebla, 1,222,177; Monterrey, 1,088,041. **Monetary unit:** Peso. **Languages:** Spanish, Indian languages. **Ethnicity/Race:** mestizo (Indian-Spanish) 60%, Amerindian or predominantly Amerindian 30%, Caucasian or predominantly Caucasian 9%, other 1%. **Religion:** nominally Roman Catholic, 97%; Protestant, 3%. **Literacy rate:** 88%
Economic summary: Gross domestic product: purchasing power parity (1995 est.): $721.4 billion; $7,700 per capita; real growth rate –6.9%; inflation 52%; unemployment 10%. Arable land: 12%; principal products: corn, cotton, fruits, wheat, beans, coffee, tomatoes, rice. Labor force (1994): 33.6 million; in commerce; 11.1% in manufacturing; 28% in agriculture, forestry, hunting and fishing; 31.7% in services. Major products: processed foods, chemicals, basic metals and metal products, petroleum. Natural resources: petroleum, silver, copper, gold, lead, zinc, natural gas, timber. Exports: $80 billion (f.o.b., 1995 est.): motor vehicles, consumer electronics, cotton, shrimp, coffee, petroleum, petroleum products, engines. Imports:

$72 billion (f.o.b., 1995 est.): grain, metal manufactures, agricultural machinery, electrical equipment, car parts for assembly, motor vehicle repair parts, aircraft and aircraft parts. Major trading partners: U.S., Japan, Western European countries.

Geography. The United States' neighbor to the south, Mexico is about one-fifth its size. Baja California in the west, an 800-mile (1,287-km) peninsula, forms the Gulf of California. In the east are the Gulf of Mexico and the Bay of Campeche, which is formed by Mexico's other peninsula, the Yucatán.

The center of Mexico is a great, high plateau, open to the north, with mountain chains on east and west and with ocean-front lowlands lying outside of them.

Government. The President, who is popularly elected for six years and is ineligible to succeed himself, governs with a cabinet of secretaries. Congress has two houses—a 500-member Chamber of Deputies, elected for three years, and a 64-member Senate, elected for six years, half of which is renewed every three years. Popularly elected officials (President, members of Congress, mayors, etc.) cannot seek re-election.

Each of the 31 states has considerable autonomy, with a popularly elected governor, a legislature, and a local judiciary.

History. At least two civilized races—the Mayas and later the Toltecs—preceded the wealthy Aztec empire, conquered in 1519–21 by the Spanish under Hernando Cortés. Spain ruled for the next 300 years until 1810 (the date was Sept. 16 and is now celebrated as Independence Day), when the Mexicans first revolted. They continued the struggle and finally won independence in 1821.

From 1821 to 1877, there were two emperors, several Dictators, and enough Presidents and provisional executives to make a new government on the average of every nine months. Mexico lost Texas (1836), and after defeat in the war with the U.S. (1846–48) it lost the area comprising the present states of California, Nevada, and Utah, most of Arizona and New Mexico, and parts of Wyoming and Colorado.

In 1855, the Indian patriot Benito Juárez began a series of liberal reforms, including the disestablishment of the Catholic Church, which had acquired vast property. A subsequent civil war was interrupted by the French invasion of Mexico (1861), the crowning of Maximilian of Austria as Emperor (1864), and then his overthrow and execution by forces under Juárez, who again became President in 1867.

The years after the fall of the Dictator Porfirio Diaz (1877–80 and 1884–1911) were marked by bloody political-military strife and trouble with the U.S., culminating in the punitive U.S. expedition into northern Mexico (1916–17) in unsuccessful pursuit of the revolutionary Pancho Villa. Since a brief period of civil war in 1920, Mexico has enjoyed a period of gradual agricultural, political, and social reforms. Relations with the U.S. were again disturbed in 1938 when all foreign oil wells were expropriated. Agreement on compensation was finally reached in 1941.

During 1983 and 1984, Mexico suffered its worst financial crisis in 50 years, leading to critically high unemployment and an inability to pay its foreign debt. The collapse of oil prices in 1986 cut into Mexico's export earnings and worsened the situation.

Although the ruling Institutional Revolutionary Party's candidate, Carlos Salinas de Gortari, won the presidential election of 1988, the opposition parties on the left and the right showed unprecedented strength.

At the start of 1994 peasant rebels seized a colonial city and declared war on the state. Negotiations and a cease-fire began in mid-January. In March the leading presidential candidate was shot and killed in Tijuana.

The campaign manager was then selected to be the party's presidential candidate. Zedillo won the election by more than 20% and the governing party retained its majority in both legislative houses.

In February 1995 agreement was reached with the U.S. to prevent the collapse of Mexico's private banks. The strict provisions, however, gave the U.S. virtual veto power over key elements in Mexico's economic policy.

Elections in July 1997 brought a stunning upset for the long ruling PRI, which lost control of the lower legislative house and the mayoralty of Mexico City. An opposition party also took two key governorships in what observers called the freest election in the country's history.

MICRONESIA

Federated States of Micronesia
President: Jacob Nena (1997)
Total area: 271 sq mi (703 sq km). Land area, same (includes islands of Pohnpei, Yap, Chuuk, and Kosrae)
Population (1997 est.): 106,000 (average annual rate of natural increase: 2.17%); birth rate: 27.9/1000; infant mortality rate: 35.8/1000; density per square mile: 462
Capital: Palikir. **Language:** English is the official and common language; major indigenous languages are Chukese, Pohnpeian, Yapase, and Kosrean.
Ethnicity/Race: nine ethnic Micronesian and Polynesian groups. **Literacy rate:** 90%
Government: A constitutional government in free association with the United States since November 1986
Economic summary: Gross domestic product: purchasing power parity (1994 est.): $205 million (note: GDP is supplemented by grant aid, averaging perhaps $100 million annually), per capita, $1,700; 1.4% growth rate; 4% inflation rate (1994 est.). Labor force: n.a. Unemployment rate: 27%. Exports: $29.1 million (f.o.b., 1994 est.): fish, garments, bananas, black pepper. Imports: $141.1 million (c.i.f., 1994 est.): food, manufactured goods, machinery and equipment, beverages. Financial assistance from the U.S. is the primary source of revenue, with the U.S. pledged to spend $1 billion in the islands in the 1990s. Micronesia also earns about $4 million a year in fees from foreign fishing concerns. Economic activity consists primarily of subsistence farming and fishing. Unemployment rate: 80% **Aid:** Under the terms of the Compact of Free Association, the U.S. will provide $1.3 billion in grand aid during the period 1986–2001.

Geography. The Micronesian islands vary geologically from high mountainous islands to low, coral atolls, with volcanic outcroppings on Pohnpei, Kosrae, and Chuuk. The climate is tropical, with heavy, year-round rainfall. The islands are located 3,200 miles (5,150 km) west-southwest of the Honolulu in the North Pacific Ocean, about three-quarters of the way between Hawaii and Indonesia.

Government. A constitutional government in free association with the United States since November 1986.

History. On April 2, 1947, the United Nations Security Council created the Trust Territory of the Pacific Islands under which the Northern Mariana, Caroline, and Marshall Islands were placed under the administration of the United States. These islands comprised what is now called the Federated States of Micronesia, and only the Republic of Palau is still administered as a Trust Territory. Micronesia was admitted to the United Nations on September 17, 1991. In July 1993 the country became a member of the International Monetary Fund.

In July 1996, President Olter suffered a stroke. The Vice President assumed his duties in November. Legislative elections were held in March and April 1997. In April Nena officially became President.

MOLDOVA

Republic of Moldova
President: Petru Lucinschi (1997)
Prime Minister: Ion Chebuk (1997)
Area: 13,000 sq mi. (33,700 sq km)
Population (1997 est.): 4,475,232 (average annual rate of natural increase: 0.54%); birth rate: 17.22/1000; infant mortality rate: 46.2/1000; density per square mile: 344.2
Capital and largest city (1991): Chisinau, 676,700. **Other large cities (1991 est.):** Tiraspol, 186,000; Beltsy, 165,000; Bendery (Tighina), 141,500. **Monetary unit:** Moldovan Lem. **Language:** Romanian official language since 1989. **Ethnicity/Race:** Moldavian/Romanian 64.5%, Ukrainian 13.8%, Russian 13%, Gagauz 3.5%, Jewish 1.5%, Bulgarian 2%, other 1.7% (1989 figures)
Economic summary: Gross domestic product: purchasing power parity (1995 estimate extrapolated from the World Bank estimate for 1994): $10.4 billion; $2,310 per capita; real growth rate –3%; inflation: 24%; unemployment: 1.2% (includes only officially registered unemployed; large numbers of underemployed workers). Labor force: 2.03 million (January 1994); 34.4% in agriculture, 20.1% in industry; other 45.5%. Others include power engineering, textiles, metalworking, building materials, machine-building, TV sets, washing machines and other consumer goods, and manufacturing of electrical equipment. Agricultural products are wheat, corn, barley, sugar beets, fruits, and wine grapes, soybeans, tobacco, and animal husbandry. Eighty-five percent of all the land is cultivated. Exports: $720 million: foodstuffs, wine, tobacco, textiles and footwear, machinery, chemicals (1991). Imports: $822 million: oil, gas, coal, steel machinery, foodstuffs, automobiles and other consumer durables. Major trading partners: Russia, Kazakhstan, Ukraine, Uzbekistan, Romania, Germany.

Geography. Moldova (formerly Moldavia) is a landlocked republic of hilly plains lying in the southwestern part of the former Soviet Union between the Prut and Dnestr (Dneister) Rivers. The Prut River separates it from Romania in the west and Ukraine borders it in the north, east, and south. The area is a very fertile region with rich black soil (chernozem) covering three-quarters of the territory.

Government. A democratic republic in transition with a parliament made up of 101 deputies. The working body of the parliament is the presidium.

History. Most of Moldova was an independent principality in the 14th century. In the 16th century it came under Ottoman Turkish rule. Russia acquired Moldovan territory in 1791, and in 1812 (The Treaty of Bucharest) when Turkey gave up the province of Bessarabia[1] to Russia. Turkey held the rest of Moldova but it was passed to Romania in 1918. Russia did not recognize the cession of this territory.

In 1924, the U.S.S.R. established Moldova as an Autonomous Soviet Socialist Republic of the Ukraine. As a result of the Nazi-Soviet Nonaggression Pact of 1939, Romania was forced to cede all of Bessarabia to the Soviet Union in 1940 and the Moldovan A.S.S.R. was merged with the Romanian-speaking districts of Bessarabia to form the Moldovan Soviet Socialist Republic.

During World War II, Romania joined Germany in the attack on the Soviet Union and reconquered Bessarabia. Soviet troops retook the territory in 1944 and reestablished the Moldovan S.S.R.

For many years, a controversy existed between Romania and the U.S.S.R. over Bessarabia. Following the aborted coup against Soviet President Mikhail Gorbachev, Moldova proclaimed its independence in September 1991.

Conflict between ethnic Romanians and Slavs in Trans-Dniester erupted upon independence. The Prime Minister and most of his cabinet resigned in early June 1992 because of the continued strife. Russia and Moldova agreed in July 1992 to send a joint peacekeeping force to the region and outlined guarantees for its future.

The first parliamentary elections in February 1994 saw a victory for the former Communist establishment.

A new government formed in January 1997, received parliamentary approval a week later. In May Moldova and Trans-Dniester signed a document in Moscow agreeing to the integrity of the country and calling for the removal of Russian troops upon the conclusion of a definite peace settlement.

1. The area between the Prut and Dnestr Rivers.

MONACO

Principality of Monaco
National name: Principauté de Monaco
Ruler: Prince Rainier III (1949)
Minister of State: Michel Lévêque (1997)
Area: 0.73 sq mi. (465 acres)
Population (1997 est.): 31,892 (average annual growth rate: –0.14%); birth rate 10.66/1000; infant mortality rate: 6.7/1000; density per square mile: 43,687.7
Capital and largest city (1995 est.): Monaco, 30,400.
  Monetary unit: French franc. **Languages:** French, Monégasque, Italian. **Ethnicity/Race:** French 47%, Monegasque 16%, Italian 16%, other 21%. **Religion:** Roman Catholic, 95%. **Literacy rate:** 99%
Economic summary: Gross domestic product: purchasing power parity (1994 est.): $788 million; $25,000 per capita; real growth rate, n.a. Labor force; n.a.; unemployment rate 3.1%. About 50% of Monaco's revenues come from value-added taxes on hotels, banks, and industrial sector. About 25% of revenues comes from tourism. Exports n.a. Imports n.a. Full customs integration with France, which collects and rebates Monacan trade duties; also participates in E.U.

Geography. Monaco is a tiny, hilly wedge driven into the French Mediterranean coast nine miles east of Nice.

Government. Prince Albert of Monaco gave the principality a constitution in 1911, creating a National Council of 18 members popularly elected for five years. The head of government is the Minister of State.

Prince Rainier III, born May 31, 1923, succeeded his grandfather, Louis II, on the latter's death, May 9, 1949. Rainier was married April 18, 1956, to Grace Kelly, U.S. actress. A daughter, Princess Caroline Louise Margueritte, was born on Jan. 23, 1957 (married to Philippe Junot June 28, 1978 and divorced in 1980; married to Stefano Casiraghi Dec. 29, 1983, and gave birth to a son, Andrea Albert, June 9, 1984; a daughter, Charlotte, Aug. 3, 1986; a son, Pierre, Sept. 4, 1987. Stefano Casiraghi died Oct. 3, 1990); a son, Prince Albert Louis Pierre, on March 14, 1958; and Princess Stéphanie Marie Elisabeth, on Feb. 1, 1965. Princess Grace died Sept. 14, 1982, of injuries received the day before when the car she was driving went off the road near Monte Carlo. She was 52.

The special significance attached to the birth of descendants to Prince Rainier stems from a clause in the Treaty of July 17, 1919, between France and Monaco stipulating that in the event of vacancy of the Crown, the Monégasque territory would become an autonomous state under a French protectorate.

The National and Democratic Union (all 18 seats in National Council), led by Jean Louis Campora, is the only political party.

History. The Phoenicians, and after them the Greeks, had a temple on the Monacan headland honoring Hercules. From *Monoikos,* the Greek surname for this mythological strong man, the principality took its name. After being independent for 800 years, Monaco was annexed to France in 1793 and was placed under Sardinia's protection in 1815. In 1861, it went under French guardianship but continued to be independent.

By a treaty in 1918, France stipulated that the French government be given a veto over the succession to the throne.

Monaco is a little land of pleasure with a tourist business that runs as high as 1.5 million visitors a year. It had popular gaming tables as early as 1856. Five years later, a 50-year concession to operate the games was granted to François Blanc, of Bad Homburg. This concession passed into the hands of a private company in 1898.

Monaco's practice of providing a tax shelter for French businessmen resulted in a dispute between the countries. When Rainier refused to end the practice, France retaliated with a customs tax. In 1967, Rainier took control of the Société des Bains de Mer, operator of the famous Monte Carlo gambling casino, in a program to increase hotel and convention space.

The country was admitted to the U.N. in May 1993, making it the smallest country represented there.

The country celebrated the 700th anniversary of the Grimaldi reign during 1997. Although events were planned throughout the year, the major ceremony took place in January.

MONGOLIA

Mongolia
President: Ntsaagiyn Bagabandi (1997)
Prime Minister: Mendsayhany Enkhsaikhan (1996)
Area: 604,250 sq mi. (1,565,000 sq km)
Population (1997 est.): 2,538,211 (average annual rate of natural increase: 1.61%); birth rate: 24.57/1000; infant mortality rate: 68/1000; density per square mile: 4.2
Capital and largest city (1993 est.): Ulan Bator, 619,000. **Monetary unit:** Tugrik. **Language:** Mongolian, 90%; also Turkic, Russian, and Chinese. **Ethnicity/Race:** Mongol 90%, Kazak 4%, Chinese 2%, Russian 2%, other 2%. **Religion:** predominantly Tibetan Buddhist; Islam about 4%. **Literacy rate:** 90% (est.)
Economic summary: Gross domestic product: purchasing power parity (1995 est.): $4.9 billion; $1,970 per capita; real growth rate 6%; inflation 53%; unemployment 15% (1991 est.). Labor force: 1.115 million (mid-1993 estimate); involved in primarily herding and agricultural work. Arable land: 1%. Principal agricultural products: livestock, wheat, potatoes, forage, barley. Mongolia has the highest number of livestock per person in the world. Major industrial products: coal, copper and molybdenum concentrate. Natural resources: coal, copper, molybdenum, iron, oil, lead, gold, and tungsten. Exports: $400 million (f.o.b., 1995 est.): copper, cashmere, livestock, animal products, wool, nonferrous metals. Imports: $223 million (f.o.b., 1994): fuels, food products, industrial consumer

goods, chemicals, building materials, machinery and equipment. Major trading partners: C.I.S. nations, China, Japan, Austria.

Geography. Mongolia lies in central Asia between Siberia on the north and China on the south. It is slightly larger than Alaska.

The productive regions of Mongolia—a tableland ranging from 3,000 to 5,000 feet (914 to 1,524 m) in elevation—are in the north, which is well drained by numerous rivers, including the Hovd, Onon, Selenga, and Tula. Much of the Gobi Desert falls within Mongolia.

Government. In January 1992, the Great People's Hural (parliament) approved a new constitution that became effective Feb. 12, 1992, and changed the name of the former communist state to Mongolia. Mongolia became an independent sovereign republic now in transition from communism. The highest organ of state power is the State Great Hural (SGH). The SGH has one chamber consisting of 76 members. Its chairman and vice-chairman are elected for a term of four years.

History. The State of Mongolia was formerly known as Outer Mongolia. It contains the original homeland of the historic Mongols, whose power reached its zenith during the 13th century under Kublai Khan. The area accepted Manchu rule in 1689, but after the Chinese Revolution of 1911 and the fall of the Manchus in 1912, the northern Mongol Princes expelled the Chinese officials and declared independence under the Khutukhtu, or "Living Buddha."

In 1921, Soviet troops entered the country and facilitated the establishment of a republic by Mongolian revolutionaries in 1924 after the death of the last Living Buddha. China, meanwhile, continued to claim Outer Mongolia but was unable to back the claim with any strength. Under the 1945 Chinese-Russian Treaty, China agreed to give up Outer Mongolia, which, after a plebiscite, became a nominally independent country.

Allied with the U.S.S.R. in its dispute with China, Mongolia has mobilized troops along its borders since 1968 when the two powers became involved in border clashes on the Kazakh-Sinkiang frontier to the west and on the Amur and Ussuri Rivers. A 20-year treaty of friendship and cooperation, signed in 1966, entitled Mongolia to call upon the U.S.S.R. for military aid in the event of invasion.

Free elections were held in August 1990 that produced a multiparty government, though still largely Communist. As a result Mongolia has decided to move toward a market economy.

The former Communist Party won a landslide victory in parliamentary elections of June 1992, causing considerable consternation in the democratic forces.

During the spring of 1996 immense grass fires blazed across the country. parliamentary elections were held in June and gave 50 of the 76 seats to the non-Communist opposition coalition.

The presidential election of May 1997 produced a landslide vote for a former communist and chairman of the People's Revolutionary Party. The balloting was generally interpreted as a reaction to the rapid pace of economic reforms and not a rejection of democracy.

MOROCCO

Kingdom of Morocco
National name: al-Mamlaka al-Maghrebia
Ruler: King Hassan II (1961)
Prime Minister: Abd al-Latif Filali (1995)
Area: 172,413 sq mi. (446,550 sq km)
Population (1997 est.): 30,391,423 (average annual

rate of natural increase: 2.12%); birth rate: 26.83/1000; infant mortality rate: 40.7/1000; density per square mile: 176.3
Capital (1993 est.): Rabat, 1,220,000. **Largest cities:** Casablanca, 2,943,000; Marrakech, 602,000; Fez, 564,000; Salé, 521,000. **Monetary unit:** Dirham. **Languages:** Arabic, French, Berber dialects, Spanish. **Ethnicity/Race:** Arab-Berber 99.1%, other 0.7%, Jewish 0.2%. **Religions:** Islam, 98.7%, Christian, 1.1%; Jewish, 0.2%. **Literacy rate:** 50%
Economic summary: Gross domestic product: purchasing power parity (1995 est.): $87.4 billion; $3,000 per capita; real growth rate –6.5%; inflation 5.4%; unemployment 16% (1994 est.). Arable land: 20%. Products: barley, wheat, citrus fruits, vegetables. Labor force: 7.4 million: agriculture 50%; services 26%; industry 15% (1985). Major products: textiles, processed food, phosphates, leather goods. Natural resources: phosphates, lead, manganese, fisheries. Exports: $4 billion (f.o.b., 1994): food and beverages, semiprocessed goods, consumer goods, phosphates. Imports: $7.2 billion (c.i.f., 1994): capital goods, fuels, foodstuffs, raw materials, consumer goods. Major trading partners: E.U., C.I.S. nations, Japan, U.S., India, Iraq.

Geography. Morocco, about one-tenth larger than California, is just south of Spain across the Strait of Gibraltar and looks out on the Atlantic from the northwest shoulder of Africa. Algeria to the east and Mauritania to the south.

On the Atlantic coast there is a fertile plain. The Mediterranean coast is mountainous. The Atlas Mountains, running northeastward from the south to the Algerian frontier, average 11,000 feet (3,353 m) in elevation.

Government. A constitutional monarchy. The King, after suspending parliament in 1965, promulgated a new constitution in 1972. He continued to rule by decree until June 3, 1977, when the first free elections since 1962 took place. The constitution was revised and approved by referendum in 1992, and again in 1996. The National Assembly has 306 seats. Morocco has 14 political parties.

History. Morocco was once the home of the Berbers, who helped the Arabs invade Spain in c.e. 711 and then revolted against them and gradually won control of large areas of Spain for a time after 739.

The country was ruled successively by various native dynasties and maintained regular commercial relations with Europe, even during the 17th and 18th centuries when it was the headquarters of the famous Salé pirates. In the 19th century, there were frequent clashes with the French and Spanish. Finally, in 1904, France and Spain divided Morocco into zones of French and Spanish influence, and these were established as protectorates in 1912.

Meanwhile, Morocco had become the object of bigpower rivalry, which almost led to a European war in 1905 when Germany attempted to gain a foothold in the rich mineral country. By terms of the Algeciras Conference (1906), Morocco was internationalized economically, and France's privileges were limited.

The Tangier Statute, concluded by Britain, France, and Spain in 1923, created an international zone at the port of Tangier, permanently neutralized and demilitarized. In World War II, Spain occupied the zone, ostensibly to ensure order, but was forced to withdraw in 1945.

Sultan Mohammed V was deposed by the French in 1953 and replaced by his uncle, but nationalist agitation forced his return in 1955. On his death on Feb. 26, 1961, his son, Hassan, became King.

France and Spain recognized the independence and sovereignty of Morocco in 1956.

In 1975, tens of thousands of Moroccans crossed the border into Spanish Sahara to back their government's contention that the northern part of the territory was historically part of Morocco. At the same time, Mauritania occupied the southern half of the territory in defiance of Spanish threats to resist such a takeover. Abandoning its commitment to self-determination for the territory, Spain withdrew, and only Algeria protested.

When Mauritania signed a peace treaty with the Algerian-backed Polisario Front in August 1979, Morocco occupied the southern part of the Western Sahara, in addition to the northern part, which it already occupied. Under pressure from other African leaders, Hassan agreed in mid-1981 to a cease-fire with a referendum under international supervision to decide the fate of the Sahara territory, but the referendum was never carried out.

King Hassan became the second Arab leader to meet with an Israeli leader when, on July 21, 1986, Israeli Prime Minister Shimon Peres came to Morocco.

Morocco became the first Arab state to condemn the 1990 Iraqi invasion of Kuwait and promised to send an 1,100-men contingent to Saudi Arabia. Public opinion, however, as evidenced by sanctioned marches in Rabat, mounted against Moroccan involvement and demanded withdrawal from the U.S.-led alliance.

The opposition was victorious in June 1993 parliamentary elections, although observers believed King Hassan's rule was secure owing to the need for a coalition and the limited powers of the Assembly.

In May 1995 the U.N. Security Council extended the mandate for U.N. forces in the Western Sahara by one month. In late June the Polisario rebels pulled out of a U.N.-sponsored voter registration program.

Representatives of the government and of the Polisario discussed the status of Western Sahara in the presence of U.N. mediators for the first time in June 1997.

MOZAMBIQUE

Republic of Mozambique
National name: República de Moçambique
President: Joaquim Chissanó (1986)
Prime Minister: Dr. Pascoal Mocumbi (1994)
Area: 303,073 sq mi. (799,380 sq km)
Population (1997 est.): 18,165,476 (average annual rate of natural increase: 2.6%); birth rate: 44.33/1000; infant mortality rate: 122.9/1000; density per square mile: 59.9
Capital and largest city (1996 est.): Maputo, 1,095,300.
Monetary unit: Metical. **Languages:** Portuguese (official), Bantu languages. **Ethnicity/Race:** indigenous tribal groups 99.66% (Shangaan, Chokwe, Manyika, Sena, Makua, and others), Europeans 0.06%, Euro-Africans 0.2%, Indians 0.08%. **Religions:** traditional, 60%; Christian, 30%; Islam, 10%. **Literacy rate:** 33%
Economic summary: Gross domestic product: purchasing power parity (1995 est.): $12.2 billion; $700 per capita; real growth rate –2.5%; inflation 50%; unemployment (1989 est.) 50%. Arable land: 4%. Principal agricultural products: cotton, cashew nuts, sugar, tea, shrimp. Labor force: n.a.; 90% in agriculture. Major industrial products: processed foods, petroleum products, beverages, textiles, tobacco. Natural resources: coal, titanium. Exports: $170 million (f.o.b., 1995 est.): cashew nuts, sugar, shrimp, copra, citrus. Imports: $1.14 billion (c.i.f., 1994 est.) incl. aid: food, clothing, farm equipment, petroleum. Major trading partners: Spain, South Africa, Portugal, U.S., France, U.K., Japan.

Geography. Mozambique stretches for 1,535 miles (2,470 km) along Africa's southeast coast. It is nearly twice the size of California. Tanzania is to the north; Malawi, Zambia, and Zimbabwe to the west; and South Africa and Swaziland to the south.

The country is generally a low-lying plateau broken up by 25 sizable rivers that flow into the Indian Ocean. The largest is the Zambezi, which provides access to central Africa. The principal ports are Maputo, Beira, and Nacala.

Government. After having been under Portuguese colonial rule for 470 years, Mozambique became independent on June 25, 1975. The first President, Samora Moises Machel, headed the National Front for the Liberation of Mozambique (FRELIMO) in its 10-year guerrilla war for independence. He died in a plane crash on Oct. 19, 1986, and was succeeded by his Foreign Minister, Joaquim Chissano.

History. Mozambique was explored by Vasco da Gama in 1498, although the Arabs had penetrated into the area as early as the 10th century. It was first colonized in 1505, and by 1510, the Portuguese had control of all the former Arab Sultanates on the east African coast.

FRELIMO was organized in 1963. Guerrilla activity had become so extensive by 1973 that Portugal was forced to dispatch 40,000 troops to fight the rebels. A cease-fire was signed in September 1974, when Portugal agreed to grant Mozambique independence.

On Jan. 25, 1985, after a decade of independence, the government was locked in a five-year-old, stalemated, paralyzing war with anti-government guerrillas, known as the MNR, backed by the white minority government in South Africa.

President Chissano decided to abandon Marxism-Leninism in 1989. A new constitution was drafted calling for three branches of government and granting civil liberties.

A cease-fire agreement was signed in October 1992 between the government and the MNR to end 16 years of civil war.

In April 1994 the President announced that a multiparty general election would be held in late October. On the first day of balloting the opposition leader declared that he and his party would boycott the process, but he changed his mind the next day. Although it lost the presidency to the incumbent, the main opposition party made a very respectable showing.

In November 1995 the country became the first non-former-British colony to become a member of the British Commonwealth.

During the first half of 1997 the main opposition political party RENAMO disputed with the government's setting of December 27th for the first municipal elections and for instigating riots while duplicitously blaming them on RENAMO.

MYANMAR

See Burma.

NAMIBIA

Republic of Namibia
President: Sam Nujoma (1990)
Prime Minister: Hage Geingob (1990)
Status: Independent Country
Area: 318,261 sq mi. (824,296 sq km)
Population (1997 est.): 1,727,183 (average annual growth rate: 2.93%); birth rate: 37.08/1000; infant mortality rate:

45.6/1000; density per square mile: 5.4
Capital and largest city (1992 est.): Windhoek, 161,000
Summer capital (est. 1980): Swakopmund, 17,500.
Monetary unit: Namibian dollars. **Languages:** Afrikaans, German, English (official), several indigenous. **Ethnicity/Race:** black 86%, white 6.6%, mixed 7.4% note: about 50% of the population belong to the Ovambo tribe and 9% to the Kavangos tribe; other ethnic groups are: Herero 7%, Damara 7%, Nama 5%, Caprivian 4%, Bushmen 3%, Baster 2%, Tswana 0.5%. **Religion:** Predominantly Christian. **Literacy rate:** 58%
Economic summary: Gross domestic product: purchasing power parity (1994 est.): $5.8 billion; $3,600 per capita; real growth rate 6.6%; inflation 11%; unemployment (urban areas) 35% (1993 est.). Arable land: 1%. Principal products: corn, millet, sorghum, livestock. Labor force: 500,000; 60% in agriculture, 19% in industry and commerce, 8% in services, 7% in government, 6% in mining (1981 est). Major products: canned meat, dairy products, tanned leather, textiles, clothing. Natural resources: diamonds, copper, lead, zinc, uranium, fish. Exports: $1.3 billion (f.o.b., 1993): diamonds, copper, lead, zinc, beef cattle, karakul pelts, marble, semi-precious stones, uranium, beef, gold. Imports: $1.2 billion (f.o.b., 1993): construction materials, fertilizer, grain, foodstuffs, petroleum products and fuel. Major trading partners: Australia, U.K., South Africa, France, Germany, Switzerland, U.S., Japan.

Geography. Namibia, bounded on the north by Angola and Zambia and on the east by Botswana and South Africa in the south. The Portuguese explorer Bartholomius Diaz was the first European to visit Namibia in the late 15th century. It is for the most part a portion of the high plateau of southern Africa with a general elevation of from 3,000 to 4,000 feet.

Government. Namibia became independent in 1990 after its new constitution was ratified. A multiparty democracy with an independent judiciary was established. There is a bicameral legislature consisting of a 26 seat National Council and a 72-seat National Assembly.

History. Formerly called South West Africa, the territory became a German colony in 1884 but was taken by South African forces in 1915, becoming a South African mandate by the terms of the Treaty of Versailles in 1920.

South Africa's application for incorporation of the territory was rejected by the U.N. General Assembly in 1946 and South Africa was invited to prepare a trusteeship agreement instead. By a law passed in 1949, however, the territory was brought into much closer association with South Africa—including representation in its parliament.

In 1969, South Africa extended its laws to the mandate over the objection of the U.N., particularly its black African members. When South Africa refused to withdraw them, the Security Council condemned it.

Under a 1974 Security Council resolution, South Africa was required to begin the transfer of power to the Namibians by May 30, 1975, or face U.N. action, but 10 days before the deadline Prime Minister Balthazar J. Vorster rejected U.N. supervision. He said, however, that his government was prepared to negotiate Namibian independence, but not with the South-West African People's Organization, the principal black separatist group. Meanwhile, the all-white legislature of South-West Africa eased several laws on apartheid in public places.

Despite international opposition, the Turnhalle Conference in Windhoek drafted a constitution to organize an interim government based on racial divisions, a proposal overwhelmingly endorsed by white voters in the territory in 1977. At the urging of ambassadors of the five Western members of the Security Council—the U.S., Britain, France, West Germany, and Canada—South Africa on June 11 announced rejection of the Turnhalle constitution and acceptance of the Western proposal to include the South-West Africa People's Organization (SWAPO) in negotiations.

Although negotiations continued between South Africa, the western powers, neighboring black African states, and internal political groups, there was still no agreement on a final independence plan. A new round of talks aimed at resolving the 18-year-old conflict ended in a stalemate on July 25, 1984.

As policemen wielding riot sticks charged demonstrators in a black, South-West Africa township, South Africa handed over limited powers to a new, multiracial administration in the former German colony on June 17, 1985. Installation of the new government ended South Africa's direct rule, but South Africa retained an effective veto over the new government's decisions along with responsibility for the territory's defense and foreign policy.

An agreement between South Africa, Angola, and Cuba arranged for elections for a Constituent Assembly in Nov. 1989 to establish a new government. SWAPO won 57% of the vote, a majority but not enough to dictate a constitution unilaterally. In February 1990, SWAPO leader Sam Nujoma was elected President and took office when Namibia became independent on March 21, 1990.

In December 1994 elections SWAPO obtained an overwhelming mandate winning not only the presidency again for the incumbent but also absolute control of the parliament. Dissidents within SWAPO in May 1995 broke away to found a new party.

As a result of exceptionally dry weather, electricity production from the country's main hydroelectric plant was greatly reduced during the first half of 1997, at a time when demand because of the cold winter was higher than usual. A proposal for an additional plant along the Kunene River is opposed by residents of the area, who would be uprooted.

NAURU

Republic of Nauru
President: Kinza Godfrey Clodumar (1997)
Area: 8.2 sq mi. (21 sq km)
Population (1997 est.): 10,390; average annual growth rate: 1.29%; birth rate 18.03/1000; infant mortality rate 40.6/1000 (1995 est.); density per square mile: 1,267.1
Capital (1983): Yaren, 559. **Monetary unit:** Australian dollar. **Languages:** Nauruan and English. **Ethnicity/Race:** Nauruan 58%, other Pacific Islander 26%, Chinese 8%, European 8%. **Religions:** Protestant, 58%; Roman Catholic, 24%; Confucian and Taoist, 8%. **Literacy rate:** 99%
Economic summary: Gross national product: purchasing power parity (1993 est.): $100 million; $10,000 per capita. Real growth rate: n.a.; unemployment: 0%. Major industrial products: phosphates. Natural resources: phosphates. Exports: $25.3 million (f.o.b., 1991): phosphates. Imports: $21.1 million (c.i.f., 1991): foodstuffs, fuel, machinery. Major trading partners: Australia, New Zealand, U.K., Japan. **Special relationship within the Commonwealth of Nations**

Geography. Nauru (pronounced NAH-oo-roo) is an island in the Pacific just south of the equator, about 2,500 miles (4,023 km) southwest of Honolulu.

Government. Legislative power is invested in a popularly elected 18-member parliament, which elects the President from among its members. Executive power rests with the President, who is assisted by a five-member cabinet.

History. Nauru was annexed by Germany in 1888. It was placed under joint Australian, New Zealand, and British mandate after World War I, and in 1947 it became a U.N. trusteeship administered by the same three powers. On Jan. 31, 1968, Nauru became an independent republic.

In 1993 Australia offered an out-of-court settlement for damages Nauru presented to the International Court of Justice because of phosphate mining. Australia agreed to pay $2.5 million Australian dollars for 20 years, and New Zealand and the U.K. additionally agreed to pay a one-time settlement of $12 million each.

Elections in February 1997 returned the last four Presidents to their parliamentary seats. A few days later Kinza Clodumar was appointed President amid an expected sharp decline in national income.

NEPAL

Kingdom of Nepal
Ruler: King Birendra Bir Bikram Shah Dev (1972)
Prime Minister: Lokendra Bahadur Chand (1997)
Area: 54,463 sq mi. (141,059 sq km)
Population (1997 est.): 22,641,061 (average annual rate of natural growth: 2.44%); birth rate: 36.68/1000; infant mortality rate: 76.8/1000; density per square mile: 415.7
Capital and largest city (1993): Kathmandu, 535,000. **Other large cities:** Lalitpur, 190,000; Biratnagar, 132,000. **Monetary unit:** Nepalese rupee. **Languages:** Nepali (official), Newari, Bhutia, Maithali. **Ethnicity/Race:** Newars, Indians, Tibetans, Gurungs, Magars, Tamangs, Bhotias, Rais, Limbus, Sherpas. **Religions:** Hindu, 90%; Buddhist, 5%; Islam, 3%. **Literacy rate:** 36%
Economic summary: Gross domestic product: purchasing power parity (1995 est.): $25.2 billion; $1,200 per capita; real growth rate 2.3%; inflation: 6.7% (FY 94/95); unemployment n.a. Arable land: 17%. Labor force: 8.5 million; 93% in agriculture; 5% in services; 2% in industry (note: severe lack of skilled labor). Principal products: rice, maize, wheat, millet, jute, sugar cane, oilseed, potatoes. Agriculture is the mainstay of the economy accounting for 60% of the GDP and 90% of the work force. Major products: sugar, textiles, jute, cigarettes, cement. Natural resources: water, timber, hydroelectric potential. Exports: $430 million (f.o.b., 1995 est., does not include unrecorded border trade with India): clothing, carpets, leather goods, grain. Imports: $1.4 billion (c.i.f., 1995 est.): petroleum products, fertilizer, machinery. Major trading partners: India, U.S., Germany, Singapore, U.K., Japan.

Geography. A landlocked country the size of Arkansas, lying between India and the Tibetan Autonomous Region of China, Nepal contains Mount Everest (29,108 ft.; 8,872 m), the tallest mountain in the world. Along its southern border, Nepal has a strip of level land that is partly forested, partly cultivated. North of that is the slope of the main section of the Himalayan range, including Everest and many other peaks higher than 20,000 feet (6,096 m).

Government. In November, 1990, King Birendra promulgated a new constitution and introduced a multiparty democracy in Nepal. In the general elections held in November 1994, the Nepal Communist Party (NML) emerged as the single largest party with 88 seats and formed a minority government headed by Prime Minister Man Mohan Adhikari on November 30, 1994. Parliament consists of two houses: the higher with 60 members and a lower house with 205.

History. The Kingdom of Nepal was unified in 1768 by King Prithwi Narayan Shah. A commercial treaty was signed with Britain in 1792, and in 1816, after more than a year's hostilities, the Nepalese agreed to allow British residents to live in Katmandu, the capital. In 1923, Britain recognized the absolute independence of Nepal. Between 1846 and 1951, the country was ruled by the Rana family, which always held the office of prime minister. In 1951, however, the King took over all power and proclaimed a constitutional monarchy.

Mahendra Bir Bikram Shah became king in 1955. After Mahendra, who had ruled since 1955, died of a heart attack in 1972, Prince Birendra, at 26, succeeded to the throne.

In 1990, pro-democracy movement forced King Birendra to lift the ban on political parties and appoint an opposition leader to head an interim government as prime minister.

The first free election in three decades provided a victory for the liberal Nepali Congress Party in 1991, although the Communists made a strong showing.

Parliamentary elections held in November 1994 placed the Communists in control of 88 seats in the House of Representatives. The Communist leader became prime minister later that month.

In June 1995 the King dissolved Parliament and ordered new elections. Two opposition parties contested that decision, and the Supreme Court agreed. The leader of the Congress Party became prime minister, forming a coalition government with the National Democratic Party.

Prime Minister Sher Bahadur Deuba narrowly lost a vote of confidence in March 1997. Despite their efforts to diminish the power of the monarchy, the Communists supported a royalist for prime minister in return for his support for their coalition.

THE NETHERLANDS

Kingdom of the Netherlands
National name: Koninkrijk der Nederlanden
Sovereign: Queen Beatrix (1980)
Premier: Wim Kok (1994)
Area: 16,033 sq mi. (41,526 sq km)
Population (1997 est.): 15,653,091 (average annual rate of natural increase: 0.3%); birth rate: 11.79/1000; infant mortality rate: 4.8/1000; density per square mile: 976.3
Capital and largest city (1994 est.): Amsterdam, 724,096. **Other large cities (1994 est.):** Rotterdam, 598,521; The Hague (seat of government), 445,279; Utrecht, 234,106; Eindhoven, 196,130. **Monetary unit:** Guilder. **Language:** Dutch. **Ethnicity/Race:** Dutch 96%, Moroccans, Turks, and other 4% (1988). **Religions:** Roman Catholic, 36%; Protestant, 27%; other, 4%; unaffiliated, 33%. **Literacy rate:** 99%
Economic summary: Gross domestic product: purchasing power parity (1995 est.): $301.9 billion; $19,500 per capita; real growth rate 2.5%; inflation 2.25%; unemployment 7.1%. Arable land: 25%. Principal products: wheat, barley, sugar beets, potatoes, meat and dairy products. Labor force: 6.4 million (1993); 73% in services, 23% in manufacturing and construction; 4% in agriculture (1994). Major products: metal fabrication, electrical machinery and equipment, chemicals, electronic equipment, petroleum, fishing. Exports: $146 billion (f.o.b., 1995): foodstuffs, natural gas, chemicals, metal products, textiles, tobacco, agricultural products. Imports: $133 billion (c.i.f., 1995): raw

materials, consumer goods, transportation equipment, food products, crude petroleum. Major trading partners: Germany, Belgium-Luxembourg, France, U.K., U.S.

Geography. The Netherlands, on the coast of the North Sea, has Germany to the east and Belgium to the south. It is twice the size of New Jersey.

Part of the great plain of north and west Europe, the Netherlands has maximum dimensions of 190 by 160 miles (360 by 257 km) and is low and flat except in Limburg in the southeast, where some hills rise to 300 feet (92 m). About half the country's area is below sea level, making the famous Dutch dikes a requisite to the use of much land. Reclamation of land from the sea through dikes has continued through recent times.

All drainage reaches the North Sea, and the principal rivers—Rhine, Maas (Meuse), and Schelde— have their sources outside the country. The Rhine is the most heavily used waterway in Europe.

Government. The Netherlands and its former colony, the Netherlands Antilles form the Kingdom of the Netherlands.

The Netherlands is a constitutional monarchy with a bicameral parliament. The Upper Chamber has 75 members elected for six years by representative bodies of the provinces, half of the members retiring every three years. The Lower Chamber has 150 members elected by universal suffrage for four years. The two Chambers have the right of investigation and interpellation; the Lower Chamber can initiate legislation and amend bills.

The Sovereign, Queen Beatrix Wilhelmina Armgard, born Jan. 31, 1938, was married on March 10, 1966, to Claus von Amsberg, a former West German diplomat. The marriage drew public criticism because of the bridegroom's service in the German army during World War II. In 1967, Beatrix gave birth to a son, Willem-Alexander Claus George Ferdinand, the first male heir to the throne since 1884. She also has two other sons, Johan Friso Bernhard Christian David, born in 1968, and Constantijn Christof Frederik Aschwin, born the next year.

History. Julius Caesar found the low-lying Netherlands inhabited by Germanic tribes—the Nervii, Frisii, and Batavi. The Batavi on the Roman frontier did not submit to Rome's rule until 13 B.C.E., and then only as allies.

A part of Charlemagne's empire in the 8th and 9th centuries C.E., the area later passed into the hands of Burgundy and the Austrian Hapsburgs, and finally in the 16th century came under Spanish rule.

When Philip II of Spain suppressed political liberties and the growing Protestant movement in the Netherlands, a revolt led by William of Orange broke out in 1568. Under the Union of Utrecht (1579), the seven northern provinces became the Republic of the United Netherlands.

The Dutch East India Company was established in 1602, and by the end of the 17th century Holland was one of the great sea and colonial powers of Europe.

The nation's independence was not completely established until after the Thirty Years' War (1618–48), after which the country's rise as a commercial and maritime power began. In 1814, all the provinces of Holland and Belgium were merged into one Kingdom, but in 1830 the southern provinces broke away to form the Kingdom of Belgium. A liberal constitution was adopted by the Netherlands in 1848.

In spite of its neutrality in World War II, the Netherlands was invaded by the Nazis in May 1940, and the East Indies were later taken by the Japanese. The nation was liberated in May 1945. In 1948, after a reign of 50 years, Queen Wilhelmina resigned and was succeeded by her daughter Juliana.

In 1949, after a four-year war, the Netherlands granted independence to the East Indies, which became the Republic of Indonesia. In 1963, it turned over the western half of New Guinea to the new nation, ending 300 years of Dutch presence in Asia. Attainment of independence by Suriname on Nov. 25, 1975, left the Dutch Antilles as the Netherlands' only overseas territory.

Prime Minister Van Agt lost his narrow majority in elections on May 26, 1981, in which the major issue was the deployment of U.S. cruise missiles on Dutch soil. Van Agt lost his centrist coalition in May 1982 in a dispute over economic policy, and was succeeded by Ruud Lubbers as Premier.

A general election in May 1994 resulted in the ruling coalition of the Christian Democratic and Labor Parties losing a third of its legislative seats. Nevertheless Labor became the largest party in parliament. The Christian Democratic Party leader attempted in vain to form a government. In August the Laborite leader succeeded in forming a cabinet without a single Christian Democratic member.

Provincial legislative elections in May 1995 saw a further decline in the fortunes of the Christian Democrats.

Although prostitution is legal, the government moved in July 1997 to permit the operation of brothels as a means of regulating the former. Only those with a valid resident's permit would be permitted to be employed in the brothels.

Netherlands Autonomous Countries

NETHERLANDS ANTILLES

Status: Part of the Kingdom of the Netherlands
Governor: Mr. J.M. Saleh (1990)
Premier: Mingull A. Pourier
Area: 313 sq mi. (800 sq km)
Population (1997 est.): 211,093 (average annual growth rate: 1.02%); birth rate: 15.61/1000; infant mortality rate: 8.8/1000; density per square mile: 674.4.
   Ethnicity/Race: mixed African 85%, Carib Indian, European, Latin, Asian
Capital and largest city (1993 est.): Willemstad, 197,019.. **Literacy rate:** 95%
Economic summary: Gross domestic product: purchasing power parity (1994 est.): $1.92 billion; $10,400 per capita; real growth rate 1.8%; inflation 1.5%; unemployment 13.4%. Arable land: 8%. Principal agricultural products: aloes, sorghum, peanuts. Labor force: 89,000; 28% in industry and commerce, 65% in government (1983). Major industries: oil refining, tourism. Natural resource: phosphate. Exports: $1.3 billion (f.o.b., 1993): petroleum products. Imports: $1.8 billion (f.o.b., 1993): crude petroleum, food. Major trading partners: U.S., Venezuela, Netherlands, U.K., Guadeloupe.

Geography. The Netherlands Antilles comprise two groups of Caribbean islands 500 miles (805 km) apart: one, about 40 miles (64 km) off the Venezuelan coast, consists of Curaçao (173 sq mi.; 448 sq km), Bonaire (95 sq mi.; 246 sq km), the other, lying to the northeast, consists of three small islands with a total area of 34 square miles (88 sq km).

Government. There is a constitutional government formed by the Governor and cabinet and an elected Legislative Council. The area has complete autonomy in domestic affairs.

ARUBA

Status: Part of the Kingdom of the Netherlands
Governor: Olindo Koolman (1992)

Prime Minister: Henny Eman (1994)
Area: 75 sq mi. (193 sq km)
Population (1996 est.): 66,404; growth rate 0.79%; birth rate: 14.2/1000; infant mortality rate: 8.1/1000; density per square mile: 885
Capital and largest city (1991 est.): Oranjestad, 20,050. **Ethnicity/Race:** mixed European/Caribbean Indian 80%. **Literacy rate:** 95%
Economic summary: Gross domestic product (1993 est.): $1.2 billion; $17,400 per capita; real growth rate 5%; inflation 6.5%; unemployment 0.6.% (1992). Little agriculture. Major industries: tourism, light manufacturing (tobacco, beverages, consumer goods). Exports: $1.3 billion (f.o.b., 1993): mostly petroleum products. Imports: $1.6 billion (f.o.b., 1993): food, consumer goods, manufacturers. Major trading partners: U.S., E.U.

Geography. Aruba, an island slightly larger than Washington D.C., lies 18 miles (28.9 km) off the coast of Venezuela in the southern Caribbean.

Government. The governmental structure comprises the Governor, appointed by the Queen for a term of six years; the Legislature consisting of 21 members elected by universal suffrage for terms not exceeding four years; and the Council of Ministers, presided over by the Prime Minister, who holds executive power.

NEW ZEALAND

Sovereign: Queen Elizabeth II (1952)
Governor-General: Sir Michael Hardie Boyes (1996)
Prime Minister: Rt. Hon. James Brendan Bolger (1990)
Area: 103,884 sq mi. (270,534 sq km) (excluding dependencies)
Population (1997 est.): 3,587,275 (average annual growth rate: 0.76%); birth rate: 15.35/1000; infant mortality rate: 6.5/1000; density per square mile: 34.5
Capital: Wellington. **Largest cities (est. 1995):** Auckland, 952,600; Wellington, 331,100; Christchurch, 324,400. **Monetary unit:** New Zealand dollar. **Languages:** English, Maori. **Ethnicity/Race:** European 88%, Maori 8.9%, Pacific Islander 2.9%, other 0.2%. **Religions:** Christian, 81%; none or unspecified, 18%; Hindu, Confucian, and other, 1%. **Literacy rate:** 99%
Economic summary: Gross domestic product: purchasing power parity (1995): $62.3 billion; $18,300 per capita; real growth rate 5.5%; inflation 2%; unemployment 6.1%. Arable land: 2%. Principal products: wool, meat, dairy products, livestock. Labor force (1995): 1,634,500; services 64.6%; industry 25%; agriculture 10.4%. Major products: processed foods, textiles, machinery, transport equipment, wood and paper products, financial services. Natural resources: forests, natural gas, iron ore, coal, gold. Exports: $13.41 billion (1995): meat, dairy products, wool. Imports: $13.62 billion (1995): consumer goods, petroleum, motor vehicles, industrial equipment. Major trading partners: Japan, Australia, E.U., U.S., China, South Korea, Taiwan. **Member of Commonwealth of Nations**

Geography. New Zealand, about 1,250 miles (2,012 km) southeast of Australia, consists of two main islands and a number of smaller, outlying islands so scattered that they range from the tropical to the antarctic. The country is the size of Colorado.

New Zealand's two main components are North Island and South Island, separated by Cook Strait, which varies from 16 to 190 miles (26 to 396 km) in width. North Island (44,281 sq mi.; 115,777 sq km) is 515 miles (829 km) long and volcanic in its southcentral part. This area contains many hot springs and beautiful geysers. South Island (58,093 sq mi.; 151,215

sq km) has the Southern Alps along its west coast, with Mount Cook (12,283.3 ft.; 3,754 m) the highest point.

The largest of the outlying islands are the Auckland Islands (234 sq mi.; 606 sq km), Campbell Island (44 sq mi.; 114 sq km), the Antipodes Islands (24 sq mi.; 62 sq km), and the Kermadec Islands (13 sq mi.; 34 sq km).

Government. New Zealand was granted self-government in 1852, a full parliamentary system and ministries in 1856, and dominion status in 1907. The Queen is represented by a Governor-General, and the cabinet is responsible to a unicameral parliament of 99 members, who are elected by popular vote for three years.

New Zealand voted in a referendum (1993) for the mixed member system of proportional representation which replaced the former system in the 1996 general election.

History. New Zealand was visited and named in 1642 by Abel Tasman, a Dutch navigator. Captain James Cook explored the islands in 1769. In 1840, Britain formally annexed them.

From the first, the country has been in the forefront in instituting social welfare legislation. It adopted old age pensions (1898); a national child welfare program (1907); social security for the aged, widows, and orphans, along with family benefit payments; minimum wages; a 40-hour week and unemployment and health insurance (1938); and socialized medicine (1941).

The outcome of the November 1993 general election resulted in the governing National Party winning a bare majority of 50 seats to Labour's 45. Political maneuvering in 1994 kept the National Party with a majority despite anxious by-elections.

In the general election of October 1996, the first under the new system of proportional representation, the National Party received 34% of the vote and Labour 28%.

Cook Islands and Overseas Territories

The Cook Islands (93 sq mi.; 241 sq km) were placed under New Zealand administration in 1901. They achieved self-governing status in association with New Zealand in 1965. **Population (1997 est.):** 19,776; growth rate 1.75%; birth rate: 22.7/1000; infant mortality rate: 24.7/1000; density per square mile: 212.6. The seat of government is on Rarotonga Island.

Economic summary: Gross domestic product (1993 est.): $57 million; $3,000 per capita. Exports: $3.4 million (f.o.b., 1990): citrus juice, clothing, canned fruit, and pineapple juice. Imports: $50 million (c.i.f., 1990): foodstuffs, textiles, fuels, timber. Nearly all of the trade is with New Zealand, some with Japan, Australia, and U.S.

Niue (100 sq mi.; 259 sq km) was formerly administered as part of the Cook Islands. It was placed under separate New Zealand administration in 1901 and achieved self-governing status in association with New Zealand in 1974. The capital is Alofi. **Population (July 1995 est.):** 1,837; growth rate −3.66%.

Economic summary: Gross national product (1993 est.): $2.4 million; per capita, $1,200. Exports: $117,500 (f.o.b., 1989): canned coconut cream, copra, honey, passion fruit products, pawpaw, root crops, limes, footballs, stamps, handicrafts. Imports: $4.1 million (c.i.f., 1989): food, live animals, manufactured goods, machinery, fuels, chemicals, lubricants, drugs. Major trading partners: New Zealand, 59%; Fiji, 20%; Japan, 13%.

The Ross Dependency (160,000 sq mi.; 414,400 sq km), an Antarctic region, was placed under New Zealand administration in 1923.

Tokelau (4 sq mi.; 10 sq km) was formerly administered as part of the Gilbert and Ellice Islands colony. It was placed under New Zealand administration in 1925. Its population is about 1,503 (July 1995 est.).

NICARAGUA

Republic of Nicaragua
National name: República de Nicaragua
President: Arnoldo Alemán (1997)
Area: 50,180 sq mi. (130,000 sq km)
Population (1997 est.): 4,386,399 (average annual rate of natural increase: 2.71%); birth rate: 33/1000; infant mortality rate: 44.1/1000; density per square mile: 87.4
Capital and largest city (1992 est.): Managua, 974,000. **Monetary unit:** Cordoba. **Language:** Spanish. **Ethnicity/Race:** mestizo (mixed Amerindian and white) 69%, white 17%, black 9%, Indian 5%. **Religion:** Roman Catholic, 95%; Protestant, 5%. **Literacy rate:** 57%
Economic summary: Gross domestic product: purchasing power parity (1995): $7.1 billion; $1,700 per capita; real growth rate 4.2%; inflation 11.4%, unemployment 20%. Arable land: 9%. Principal products: coffee, sugar cane, corn, beans, cattle. Labor force: 1.086 million (1995); 13% in industry; 43% in services; 44% in agriculture. Major products: processed foods, chemicals, metal products, clothing and textiles, beverages, footwear. Natural resources: timber, fisheries, gold, silver, copper, tungsten, lead, zinc. Exports: $525.5 million: coffee, cotton, seafood, bananas, sugar, meat, chemicals. Imports: $870 million: machinery, chemicals, food, clothing, petroleum. Major trading partners: E.U., U.S., Japan, Costa Rica, El Salvador, Mexico, Venezuela, Guatemala.

Geography. Largest but most sparsely populated of the Central American nations, Nicaragua borders on Honduras to the north and Costa Rica to the south. It is slightly larger than New York State.

Nicaragua is mountainous in the west, with fertile valleys. A plateau slopes eastward toward the Caribbean. Two big lakes—Nicaragua, about 100 miles long (161 km), and Managua, about 38 miles long (61 km)—are connected by the Tipitapa River. The Pacific coast is volcanic and very fertile. The Caribbean coast, swampy and indented, is aptly called the "Mosquito Coast."

Government. A republic. The President is chief of state and head of government. The National Assembly is the legislative branch.

History. Nicaragua, which established independence in 1838, was first visited by the Spaniards in 1522. The chief of the country's leading Indian tribe at that time was called Nicaragua, from whom the nation derived its name. A U.S. naval force intervened in 1909 after two American citizens had been executed, and a few U.S. Marines were kept in the country from 1912 to 1925. The Bryan-Chamorro Treaty of 1916 (terminated in 1970) gave the U.S. an option on a canal route through Nicaragua, and naval bases. Disorder after the 1924 elections brought in the Marines again.

A guerrilla leader, Gen. César Augusto Sandino, began fighting the occupation force in 1927. He fought the U.S. troops until their withdrawal in 1933. Gen. Anastasio Somoza García emerged and ruled as Dictator from 1936 until his assassination in 1956. He was succeeded by his son Luis, who alternated with trusted family friends in the presidency until his death in 1967. Another son, Maj. Gen. Anastasio Somoza Debayle, became President in 1967.

Sandinista guerrillas, leftists who took their name from Gen. Sandino, launched an offensive in May 1979.

After seven weeks of fighting, Somoza fled the country on July 17, 1979. The Sandinistas assumed power on July 19, promising to maintain a mixed economy, a nonaligned foreign policy, and a pluralist political system.

On Jan. 23, 1981, the Reagan Administration suspended U.S. aid, charging that Nicaragua, with the aid of Cuba and the Soviet Union, was supplying arms to rebels in El Salvador. The Sandinistas denied the charges. Later that year, Nicaraguan guerrillas known as "contras," began a war to overthrow the Sandinistas.

The elections were finally held on Nov. 4, 1984, with Daniel Ortega Saavedra, the Sandinista junta coordinator, winning 63% of the votes cast for President. He began a six-year term on Jan. 10, 1985.

The war intensified in 1986–87, with the resupplied contras establishing themselves inside the country. Negotiations sponsored by the Contadora (neutral Latin American) nations foundered, but a peace plan sponsored by Arias, the Costa Rican President, led to a treaty signed by the Central American leaders in August 1987, that called for an end to outside aid to guerrillas and negotiations between hostile parties.

In 1989, an accord established a one-year advance in general elections to Feb. 1990.

Violetta Chamorro, owner of the opposition paper *La Prensa*, led a broad anti-Sandinista coalition to victory in the presidential and legislative elections, ending 11 years of Sandinista rule.

After a year in office President Chamorro found herself besieged. Business groups were dissatisfied with the pace of reforms; Sandinistas, upset with what they regarded as the dismantling of their earlier achievements and threatened to take up arms again. In Feb. 1991 the President brought the military under her direct command.

By early 1993 relations between the President and the coalition that backed her had soured over charges of corruption and the continuing influence of the Sandinistas in the government and the army.

In February 1995 the Sandinista military leader Humberto Ortego stepped down, marking the first peaceful transfer of that position in the country's history. Nevertheless, the President and the Assembly continued their bitter quarrel, this time over rival constitutions. Finally in June the President agreed to a new package that would bolster the legislative branch at the expense of the executive.

The October 1996 presidential election gave former Managua mayor Aleman 51% of the vote. His closest rival was former President Daniel Ortega, who received 38%. In January 1997 Arnoldo Aleman took the oath of office. In April he ordered an investigation of possible frauds during the previous government's privatization programs.

NIGER

Republic of Niger
National name: République du Niger
President: Col. Ibrahim Bare Mainassara (1996)
Prime Minister: Amadou Cissé (1996)
Area: 489,206 sq mi. (1,267,044 sq km)
Population (1997 est.): 9,388,859 (average annual rate of natural increase: 2.97%); birth rate: 53.73/1000; infant mortality rate: 116/1000; density per square mile: 19.2
Capital and largest city (1988): Niamey, 398,265. **Other large cities:** Zinder, 120,900; Maradi, 112,970. **Monetary unit:** Franc CFA. **Ethnicity/Race:** Hausa 56%, Djerma 22%, Fula 8.5%, Tuareg 8%, Beri Beri (Kanouri) 4.3%, Arab, Toubou, and Gourmantche 1.2%, about 4,000 French expatriates. **Languages:** French (official); Hausa, Songhai; Arabic. **Religions:**

Islam, 80%; Animist and Christian, 20%. **Literacy rate:** 28%

Economic summary: Gross domestic product: purchasing power parity (1995 est.): $5.5 billion; $600 per capita; real growth rate 6.7%; inflation: 35.6%. Arable land: 3%. Principal products: peanuts, cotton, livestock, millet, sorghum, cassava, rice. Labor force: 2.5 million (1982); 90% in agriculture; 6% in industry and commerce; 4% in government. Major industrial products: uranium, cement, bricks, light industrial products. Natural resources: uranium, coal, iron ore, tin, phosphates. Exports: $232 million (f.o.b., 1994 est.): uranium, cowpeas, livestock, hides, skins. Imports: $234 million (c.i.f., 1994 est.): fuels, machinery, transport equipment, foodstuffs, consumer goods, pharmaceuticals, chemical products. Major trading partners: France, Nigeria, Algeria, U.S., Italy, Côte d'Ivoire, Germany.

Geography. Niger, in West Africa's Sahara region, is four-fifths the size of Alaska. It is surrounded by Mali, Algeria, Libya, Chad, Nigeria, Benin, and Burkina Faso.

The Niger River in the southwest flows through the country's only fertile area. Elsewhere the land is semiarid.

Government. Niger held its first democratic elections in April 1993 and formed a new coalition government on April 23, 1993. Political parties and the constitution were suspended after a coup on Jan. 27, 1996, led by Col. Mainassara. He promised new elections in July and a return to democratic rule. However, when he was declared winner of the new elections on July 10, he banned opposition parties.

History. Niger was incorporated into French West Africa in 1896. There were frequent rebellions, but when order was restored in 1922, the French made the area a colony. In 1958, the voters approved the French constitution and voted to make the territory an autonomous republic within the French Community. The republic adopted a constitution in 1959 and the next year withdrew from the Community, proclaiming its independence.

The 1974 army coup ousted President Hamani Diori, who had held office since 1960. An estimated 2 million people were starving in Niger, but 200,000 tons of imported food, half U.S.-supplied, substantially ended famine conditions by the year's end. The new President, Lt. Col. Seyni Kountché, Chief of Staff of the army, installed a 12-man military government. A predominantly civilian government was formed by Kountché in 1976.

The country's first multiparty election in February 1993 resulted in the need for a runoff for the presidency in March. Ousmane Mahamane, the candidate of the biggest opposition party, won.

In January 1996 a coup deposed the country's first democratically elected President. The constitution was suspended and the President arrested. In July the military leader of the coup was declared the winner of a presidential election by a commission he established after removing the independent commission during the balloting.

A cease-fire between the government and ethnic rebels of the Revolutionary Armed Forces of the Sahara went into effect in June 1997. The two sides agreed to resume negotiations in three months.

NIGERIA

Federal Republic of Nigeria
Head of State: Gen. Sani Abacha (1993)
Area: 356,700 sq mi. (923,853 sq km)

Population (1997 est.): 107,129,469; average annual rate of natural increase: 3.01%; birth rate: 42.58/1000; infant mortality rate: 70.2/1000; density per square mile: 300.3

Capital (1995 est.): Abuja, 339,000. **Other large cities:** Lagos, 1,484,000; Ibadan, 1,365,000; Ogbomosho, 711,900; Kano, 657,300. **Monetary unit:** Naira. **Languages:** English (official) Hausa, Yoruba, Ibo. **Ethnicity/Race:** non-Africans 27,000; North, Hausa and Fulani; southwest, Yoruba; southeast, Ibos. **Religions:** Islam, 50%; Christian, 40%; indigenous, 10%. **Literacy rate:** 51%

Economic summary: Gross domestic product: purchasing power parity (1995 est.): $135.9 billion; $1,300 per capita; real growth rate 2.6%; inflation 57% (1994 est.); unemployment 28% (1992 est.). Arable land: 31%. Principal products: peanuts, rubber, cocoa, grains, fish, yams, cassava, livestock. Labor force: 42.844, million, 54% in agriculture; 15% in government; 19% in industry, commerce and services. Major products: crude oil, natural gas, coal, tin, processed rubber, cotton, petroleum, hides, textiles, cement, chemicals. Natural resources: petroleum, tin, columbite, iron ore, coal, limestone, lead. Exports: $9.9 billion (f.o.b., 1993): oil, cocoa, palm products, rubber. Imports: $7.5 billion (c.i.f., 1993): consumer goods, capital equipment, raw materials, chemicals. Major trading partners: Western European countries, U.S., Japan. **Member of Commonwealth of Nations**

Geography. Nigeria, one-third larger than Texas and sub-Saharan Africa's most populous nation, is situated on the Gulf of Guinea in West Africa. Its neighbors are Benin, Niger, Cameroon, and Chad.

The lower course of the Niger River flows south through the western part of the country into the Gulf of Guinea. Swamps and mangrove forests border the southern coast; inland are hardwood forests.

Government. A military government since Dec. 31, 1983. The government annulled the results of the June 12, 1993 presidential election and suspended the return to civilian rule. Gen. Sani Abacha declared himself ruler in November 1993.

History. Between 1879 and 1914, private colonial developments by the British, with reorganizations of the Crown's interest in the region, resulted in the formation of Nigeria as it exists today. During World War I, native troops of the West African frontier force joined with French forces to defeat the German garrison in the Cameroons.

Nigeria became independent on Oct. 1, 1960. Organized as a loose federation of self-governing states, the independent nation faced an overwhelming task of unifying a country with 250 ethnic and linguistic groups.

Rioting broke out in 1966, the military commander was seized, and Col. Yakubu Gowon took power. Also in that year, the Moslem Hausas in the north massacred the predominantly Christian Ibos in the east, many of whom had been driven from the north. Thousands of Ibos took refuge in the Eastern Region, which declared its independence as the Republic of Biafra on May 30, 1967. Civil war broke out.

In January 1970, after 31 months of civil war, Biafra surrendered to the federal government.

Gowon's nine-year rule was ended in 1975 by a bloodless coup that made Army Brigadier Muritala Rufai Mohammed the new chief of state. The return of civilian leadership was established with the election of Alhaji Shehu Shagari, as President in 1979.

A coup on December 31, 1983, restored military rule. The military regime headed by Maj. Gen. Mohammed Buhari was overthrown in a bloodless coup on Aug. 27, 1985, led by Maj. Gen. Ibrahim Babangida, who proclaimed himself President.

The presidential election of June 1993 was almost immediately voided by the government. Nevertheless Babangida resigned as President in August. In November the military, headed by defense minister Sani Abacha, seized power again.

Municipal elections were held in March 1997, the first multiparty voting in four years. Only five parties, all with ties to the regime, were allowed to compete. Inconclusive balloting in three areas led the election commission to cancel elections there. At that time General Abacha granted himself the power to dismiss elected local officials who misused the public trust.

NORWAY

Kingdom of Norway
National name: Kongeriket Norge
Sovereign: King Harald V (1991)
Prime Minister: Thorbjørn Jagland (1996)
Area: 125,049 sq mi. (323,877 sq km)
Population (1997 est.): 4,404,456 (average annual growth rate: 0.07%); birth rate: 11.39/1000; infant mortality rate: 4.9/1000; density per square mile: 35.2
Capital and largest city (1995): Oslo, 483,401. **Other large cities:** Bergen, 221,717; Trondheim, 142,927; Stavanger, 103,496. **Monetary unit:** Krone. **Language:** Norwegian. **Ethnicity/Race:** Germanic (Nordic, Alpine, Baltic), Lapps (Sami) 20,000. **Religion:** Evangelical Lutheran (state), 94%; other Protestant and Roman Catholic, 4%. **Literacy rate:** 100%
Economic summary: Gross domestic product: purchasing power parity (1995 est.): $106.2 billion; $24,500 per capita; real growth rate 4.5%; inflation 2.5%; unemployment 8%. Labor force: 2.13 million; services, 71%; industry, 23%; agriculture, forestry and fishing, 6%. Arable land: 3%. Principal products: dairy products, livestock, grain, potatoes, furs, wool. Major products: oil and gas, fish, pulp and paper, ships, aluminum, iron, steel, nickel, fertilizers, transportation equipment, hydroelectric power, petrochemicals. Natural resources: fish, timber, hydroelectric power, ores, oil, gas. Exports: $34.7 billion (f.o.b., 1994): oil, natural gas, fish products, ships, pulp and paper, aluminum. Imports: $27.3 billion (c.i.f., 1994): machinery, fuels and lubricants, transportation equipment, chemicals foodstuffs, and clothing. Major trading partners: U.K., Sweden, Germany, U.S., Denmark, Netherlands, Japan.

Geography. Norway is situated in the western part of the Scandinavian peninsula. It extends about 1,100 miles (1,770 km) from the North Sea along the Norwegian Sea to more than 300 miles (483 km) above the Arctic Circle, the farthest north of any European country. It is slightly larger than New Mexico. Sweden borders on most of the eastern frontier, with Finland and the U.S.S.R. in the northeast.

Nearly 70% of Norway is uninhabitable and covered by mountains, glaciers, moors, and rivers. The hundreds of deep fiords that cut into the coastline give Norway an overall oceanfront of more than 12,000 miles (19,312 km). Nearly 50,000 islands off the coast form a breakwater and make a safe coastal shipping channel.

Government. Norway is a constitutional hereditary monarchy. Executive power is vested in the King together with a cabinet, or Council of State, consisting of a Prime Minister and at least seven other members. The Storting, or parliament, is composed of 165 members elected by the people under proportional representation. The Storting discusses and votes on political and financial questions, but divides itself into two sections (Lagting and Odelsting) to discuss and pass on legislative matters. The King cannot dissolve the Storting before the expiration of its term.

The sovereign is Harald V, born in 1937, son of Olav V and Princess Martha of Sweden. He succeeded to the throne upon the death of his father in January 1991. He married Sonja Haraldsen, a daughter of a merchant, in 1968.

History. Norwegians, like the Danes and Swedes, are of Teutonic origin. The Norsemen, also known as Vikings, ravaged the coasts of northwestern Europe from the 8th to the 11th century.

In 1815, Norway fell under the control of Sweden. The union of Norway, inhabited by fishermen, sailors, merchants, and peasants, and Sweden, an aristocratic country of large estates and tenant farmers, was not a happy one, but it lasted for nearly a century. In 1905, the Norwegian parliament arranged a peaceful separation and invited a Danish Prince to the Norwegian throne—King Haakon VII. A treaty with Sweden provided that all disputes be settled by arbitration and that no fortifications be erected on the common frontier.

When World War I broke out, Norway joined with Sweden and Denmark in a decision to remain neutral and to cooperate in the joint interest of the three countries. In World War II, Norway was invaded by the Germans on April 9, 1940. It resisted for two months before the Nazis took over complete control. King Haakon and his government fled to London, where they established a government-in-exile. Maj. Vidkun Quisling, whose name is now synonymous with traitor or fifth columnist, was the most notorious Norwegian collaborator with the Nazis. He was executed by the Norwegians on Oct. 24, 1945.

Despite severe losses in the war, Norway recovered quickly. The country led the world in social experimentation. It entered the North Atlantic Treaty Organization in 1949.

The Conservative government of Jan Syse resigned in October 1990 over the issue of Norway's future relationship to the E.U. A minority Labor government headed by Gro Brundtland was installed a few days later.

In an advisory referendum held in November 1994 voters rejected seeking membership for their nation in the European Union.

The country became the second largest net oil exporter after Saudi Arabia in 1995.

Prime Minister Brundtland resigned in October 1996. Later that month she was replaced by Thorbjørn Jagland.

Dependencies of Norway

Svalbard (24,208 sq mi,; 62,700 sq km), in the Arctic Ocean about 360 miles north of Norway, consists of the Spitsbergen group and several smaller islands, including Bear Island, Hope Island, King Charles Land and White Island (or Gillis Land). The capital is Longyearbyen. It came under Norwegian administration in 1925. Population (July 1995 est.): 2,914; growth rate –3.5%. Coal mining is major economic activity. There is also some trapping of seal, polar bear, fox, and walrus.

Bouvet Island (23 sq mi.; 60 sq km), in the South Atlantic about 1,600 miles south-southwest of the Cape of Good Hope, came under Norwegian administration in 1928. It is uninhabited.

Jan Mayen Island (147 sq mi.; 380 sq km), in the Arctic Ocean between Norway and Greenland, came under Norwegian administration in 1929. There are no permanent inhabitants.

Peter I Island (96 sq mi.; 249 sq km), lying off Antarctica in the Bellinghausen Sea, came under Norwegian administration in 1931.

Queen Maud Land, a section of Antarctica, came under Norwegian administration in 1939.

OMAN

Sultanate of Oman
National name: Saltonat Uman
Sultan: Qabus Bin Said (1970)
Area: 82,030 sq mi. (212,458 sq km)[1]
Population (1997 est.): 2,264,590 (average annual rate of natural increase: 3.34%); birth rate: 37.85/1000; infant mortality rate: 26.4/1000; density per square mile: 27.6
Capital and largest city (1991 est.): Muscat, 350,000.
Monetary unit: Omani Rial. **Language:** Arabic (official); also English and Indian languages. **Ethnicity/Race:** Arab, Baluchi, South Asian (Indian, Pakistani, Sri Lankan, Bangladeshi), African. **Religion:** Islam, 95%. **Literacy rate:** 65.8%
Economic summary: Gross domestic product: purchasing power parity (1995 est.): $19.1 billion; $10,800 per capita; real growth rate 3.5%; inflation –0.7%; unemployment n.a. Principal agricultural products: dates, fruit, cereal, livestock. Labor force: 454,000; 37% in agriculture. Major industries: petroleum drilling, fishing, construction. Natural resources: oil, marble, copper, limestone. Exports: $4.8 billion (f.o.b., 1994 est.): oil, 87%; reexports: fish, processed copper, textiles. Imports: $4 billion (c.i.f., 1994 est.): machinery and transport equipment, food, manufactured goods, livestock, lubricants. Major trading partners: U.K., U.S., Japan, U.A.E., South Korea, France.

1. Excluding the Kuria Muria Islands.

Geography. Oman is a 1,000-mile-long (1,700-km) coastal plain at the southeastern tip of the Arabian peninsula lying on the Arabian Sea and the Gulf of Oman. The interior is a plateau. The country is the size of Kansas.

Government. The Sultan of Oman, an absolute monarch, is assisted by a council of ministers, seven specialized councils, a Shura Council, and personal advisers.
There are no political parties.

History. Although Oman is an independent state under the rule of the Sultan, it has been under British protection since the early 19th century.
Muscat, the capital of the geographical area known as Oman, was occupied by the Portuguese from 1508 to 1648. Then it fell to Persian Princes and later was regained by the Sultan.
In a palace coup on July 23, 1970, the Sultan, Sa'id bin Taimur, who had ruled since 1932, was overthrown by his son, who promised to establish a modern government and use new-found wealth to aid the people of this very isolated state.
A long border dispute with Yemen ended in late October 1992 when the Sultan signed an agreement with the Yemeni President.
In the first round of voting for an expanded consultative assembly called by the Sultan in November 1994, four women were elected.
Sultan Qabus in June 1997 granted women the right to be elected to the country's consultative body the Shura Council. The Sultan has final say in deciding its 80 members.

PAKISTAN

Islamic Republic of Pakistan
President: Farooq Ahmad Khan Leghari (1993)
Prime Minister: Nawaz Sharif (1997)
Area: 310,400 sq mi. (803,936 sq km)[1]
Population (1997 est.): 132,185,299 (average annual growth rate: 2.43%); birth rate: 35.26/1000; infant mortality rate: 95.1/1000; density per square mile: 425.8

Capital (1981 census): Islamabad, 201,000. **Largest cities (1981 census for metropolitan area):** Karachi, 5,208,100; Lahore, 2,952,700; Faisalabad, (Lyallpur) 1,920,000; Rawalpindi, 920,000; Hyderabad, 795,000. **Monetary unit:** Pakistan rupee. **Principal languages:** Urdu (national), English (official), Punjabi, Sindhi, Pashtu, and Baluchi. **Ethnicity/Race:** Punjabi, Sindhi, Pashtun (Pathan), Baloch, Muhajir (immigrants from India and their descendants). **Religions:** Islam, 97%; Hindu, Christian, Buddhist, Parsi. **Literacy rate:** 35%
Economic summary: Gross national product: purchasing power parity (1995 est.): $274.2 billion; $2,100 per capita; real growth rate 4.7%; inflation 13% (1995 est.); unemployment n.a. Arable land: 26%. Principal products: wheat, rice, cotton, sugarcane. Labor force: 36 million; agriculture, 46%; mining and manufacturing, 18%; services, 17%; other, 19%. Major products: cotton textiles, processed foods, petroleum products, construction materials. Natural resources: natural gas, limited petroleum, iron ore. Exports: $8.7 billion: cotton, rice, textiles, clothing. Imports: $10.7 billion: edible oil, crude oil, machinery, chemicals, transport equipment. Major trading partners: U.S., E.U., Japan, Hong Kong.

1. Excluding Kashmir and Jammu.

Geography. Pakistan is situated in the western part of the Indian subcontinent, with Afghanistan and Iran on the west, India on the east, and the Arabian Sea on the south. The name "Pakistan" is derived from two Persian words "Pak" (meaning pure) and "stan" (meaning country).
Nearly twice the size of California, Pakistan consists of towering mountains, including the Hindu Kush in the west, a desert area in the east, the Punjab plains in the north, and an expanse of alluvial plains. The 1,000-mile-long (1,609 km) Indus River flows through the country from the Kashmir to the Arabian Sea.

Government. Pakistan is a federal republic with a bicameral legislature—a 217-member National Assembly and an 87-member Senate.

History. Pakistan was one of the two original successor states to British India. For almost 25 years following independence in 1947, it consisted of two separate regions East and West Pakistan, but now comprises only the western sector. It consists of Sind, Baluchistan, the former North-West Frontier Province, western Punjab, the Princely state of Bahawalpur, and several other smaller native states.
The British became the dominant power in the region in 1757 following Lord Clive's military victory, but rebellious tribes kept the northwest in turmoil. In the northeast, the formation of the Moslem League in 1906 estranged the Moslems from the Hindus. In 1930, the League, led by Mohammed Ali Jinnah, demanded creation of a Moslem state wherever Moslems were in the majority. He supported Britain during the war. Afterward, the League received an almost unanimous Moslem vote in 1946, and Britain agreed to the formation of Pakistan as a separate dominion.
Pakistan was proclaimed a republic March 23, 1956. The election of 1970 set the stage for civil war when Sheik Muuibur told East Pakistanis to stop paying taxes to the central government. West Pakistan troops moved in and fighting began. The independent state of Bangladesh, or Bengali nation, was proclaimed March 26, 1971. The intervention of Indian troops protected the new state and brought President Yahya Kahn down. Zulfikar Ali Bhutto took over and accepted Bangladesh as an independent entity.
Diplomatically, 1976 saw the resumption of formal relations between India and Pakistan.

Pakistan's first elections under civilian rule took place in March 1977 and provoked bitter opposition protest when Bhutto's party was declared to have won 155 of the 200 elected seats in the 216-member National Assembly. A rising tide of violent protest and political deadlock led to a military takeover on July 5. Gen. Mohammed Zia ul-Haq became Chief Martial Law Administrator.

Bhutto was tried and convicted for the 1974 murder of a political opponent, and despite worldwide protests was executed on April 4, 1979, touching off riots by his supporters. Zia declared himself President on Sept. 16, 1978, a month after Fazel Elahi Chaudhry left office upon the completion of his 5-year term.

A measure of representative government was restored with the election of a new National Assembly in February 1985, although leaders of opposition parties were banned from the election.

On December 30, 1985, Zia ended martial law.

On August 19, 1988, President Zia was killed in a mid-air explosion of a Pakistani Air Force plane. Elections at the end of 1988 brought longtime Zia opponent Benazir Bhutto, daughter of Zulfikar Bhutto, into office as prime minister.

In August 1990, Pakistan's President dismissed Prime Minister Bhutto on charges of corruption and incompetence and dissolved Parliament. Nawaz Sharif's coalition, the Islamic Democratic Alliance, won the elections of October 1990.

In April 1993 the President dismissed the Prime Minister on charges of corruption and dissolved the parliament. A month later, however, the country's Supreme Court overturned the order. The next day parliament gave the Prime Minister a vote of confidence.

October 1993 elections gave a plurality of parliamentary seats to Ms. Bhutto's Pakistan People's Party, ensuring her the prime ministry.

The President dismissed the Bhutto government in November 1996 on charges of corruption and incompetence. Parliamentary elections in January 1997 gave Ms. Bhutto's party a scant 19 seats. Nawaz Sharif's Pakistan Muslim League won 136 seats, and he assumed the office of Prime Minister in February. In April parliament amended the constitution to prevent a President from dismissing a government.

PALAU

Republic of Palau
President: Kuniwo Nakamura (1993)
Total area: 177 sq mi. (458 sq km)
Population (1997 est.): 17,240 (average rate of natural increase: 1.44%); birth rate: 21.04/1000; infant mortality rate: 25.07/1000; density per square mile: 97.4
Capital and largest city (1995): Koror, 12,299. **Monetary unit:** U.S. dollar used. **Language:** Palauan is the official language, though English is commonplace. **Ethnicity/Race:** Palauans are a composite of Polynesian, Malayan, and Melanesian races. **Religion:** Christian. About one-third of the islanders observe Modekngei religion, indigenous to Palau. **Literacy rate:** 92%
Economic summary: Gross domestic product (1994 est.): $81.8 million (note: GDP numbers reflect U.S. spending), $5,000 per capita. Unemployment rate: 20% (1986). Industries: tourism, craft items (shell, wood, pearl), some commercial fishing, and agriculture (subsistence-level production of coconut, copra, cassava, sweet potatoes). Exports: $600,000 (f.o.b., 1989) trochus (a shellfish), tuna, copra, handicrafts. Imports: $24.6 million (c.i.f., 1989). Major trading partners: U.S., Japan.

Geography. The Palau island chain consists of about 200 islands located in the western Pacific Ocean 528 mi. (650 km) southeast of the Philippines. The islands vary geologically from the high mountainous main island of Babelthuap to low, coral islands usually fringed by large barrier reefs.

Government. A republic with a bicameral Parliament. There is a 14-member Senate and a 16-member House of Delegates. Palau became a sovereign nation on October 1, 1994.

History. Spain held the islands for 300 years before selling them to Germany in 1899. Japan occupied Palau during World War I and received a mandate over them from the League of Nations in 1920. It remained in Japanese control and served as an important naval base until the U.S. seized it during World War II. After the war it became a U.N. trusteeship (1947) and was administered by the U.S. until 1994.

The presidential election in November 1996 saw the re-election of President Nakamura with 62% of the vote against his challenger Ibedul Yutaka Gibbons.

PANAMA

Republic of Panama
National name: República de Panamá
President: Ernesto Pérez Balladares (1994)
Area: 29,761 sq mi. (77,082 sq km)
Population (1997 est.): 2,693,417 (average annual rate of natural increase: 1.71%); birth rate: 22.27/1000; infant mortality rate: 24.6/1000; density per square mile: 90.5
Capital and largest city (1993 est.): Panama City, 450,668. **Other large cities:** San Miguelito, 293,564; Colón, 137,825. **Monetary unit:** Balboa. **Language:** Spanish (official); many bilingual in English. **Ethnicity/Race:** mestizo (mixed Indian and European ancestry) 70%, West Indian 14%, white 10%, Indian 6%. **Religions:** Roman Catholic, over 93%; Protestant, 6%. **Literacy rate:** 88%
Economic summary: Gross domestic product: purchasing power parity (1995 est.): $13.6 billion; $5,100 per capita; real growth rate 2.8%; inflation 1.1%; unemployment 13.8%. Arable land: 6%. Principal agricultural products: bananas, corn, sugar, rice, coffee. Labor force: 979,000 (1994 est.): government and community services 31.8%; agriculture, hunting, fishing 26.8%; commerce, restaurants, hotels 16.4%; manufacturing and mining 9.4%; construction 3.2%; transportation and communications 6.2%; finance, insurance, and real estate 4.3%. Major industrial products: refined petroleum, sugar, cement, paper products. Natural resources: copper, mahogany, shrimp. Exports: $548 million (f.o.b., 1995): bananas, sugar, shrimp, coffee, clothing. Imports: $2.45 billion (c.i.f., 1995): petroleum, manufactured goods, machinery and transportation equipment, food, chemicals. Major trading partners: U.S., E.U., Central America and Caribbean, Japan.

Geography. The southernmost of the Central American nations, Panama is south of Costa Rica and north of Colombia. The Panama Canal bisects the isthmus at its narrowest and lowest point, allowing passage from the Caribbean Sea to the Pacific Ocean.

Panama is slightly smaller than South Carolina. It is marked by a chain of mountains in the west, moderate hills in the interior, and a low range on the east coast. There are extensive forests in the fertile Caribbean area.

Government. Panama is a centralized republic. The executive power is vested in the President and two Vice Presidents who exercise power jointly with a cabinet of

12 ministers of state appointed by the President. Presidents and Vice Presidents are elected for five-year terms and may not succeed themselves. The legislative function is exercised through the National Assembly. The legislators are elected for five-year terms by direct vote and can be re-elected.

History. Visited by Columbus in 1502 on his fourth voyage and explored by Balboa in 1513, Panama was the principal transshipment point for Spanish treasure and supplies to and from South and Central America in colonial days. In 1821, when Central America revolted against Spain, Panama joined Colombia, which already had declared its independence. For the next 82 years, Panama attempted unsuccessfully to break away from Colombia. After U.S. proposals for canal rights over the narrow isthmus had been rejected by Colombia, Panama proclaimed its independence with U.S. backing in 1903.

For canal rights in perpetuity, the U.S. paid Panama $10 million and agreed to pay $250,000 each year, increased to $430,000 after devaluation of the U.S. dollar in 1933 and was further increased under a revised treaty signed in 1955. In exchange, the U.S. got the Canal Zone—a 10-mile-wide strip across the isthmus—and a considerable degree of influence in Panama's affairs.

Panama and the U.S. agreed in 1974 to negotiate the eventual reversion of the canal to Panama, despite strongly expressed opposition in the U.S. Congress. The texts of two treaties—one governing the transfer of the canal and the other guaranteeing its neutrality after transfer—were negotiated by August 1977 and were signed by Pres. Omar Torrijos Herara and President Carter in Washington on September 7. A Panamanian referendum approved the treaties by more than two-thirds on October 23, but further changes were insisted upon by the U.S. Senate.

The principal change was a reservation specifying that despite the neutrality treaty's specification that only Panama shall maintain forces in its territory after transfer of the canal Dec. 31, 1999, the U.S. should have the right to use military force to keep the canal operating if it should become obstructed. The Senate approved the treaties in March–April 1978.

Nicolas Ardito Barletta, Panama's first directly elected President in 16 years, was inaugurated on Oct. 11, 1984, for a five-year term. He lacked the necessary support to solve the country's economic crisis and resigned September 28, 1985. He was replaced by Vice President Eric Arturo Delvalle.

In June 1986, reports surfaced that the behind-the-scenes strongman, Gen. Manuel Noriega, was involved in drug trafficking and the murder of an opposition leader. In 1987, Noriega was accused by his ex-Chief of Staff of assassinating Torrijos in 1981. He was indicted in the U.S. for drug trafficking but when Delvalle attempted to fire him, he forced the National Assembly to replace Delvalle with Manuel Solis Palma.

The crisis continued when Noriega called presidential elections for when the current term expired. Despite massive fraud by Noriega, the opposition seemed headed to a landslide. Noriega annulled the elections and suppressed protests by the opposition.

In December 1989, the Assembly named Noriega the "maximum leader" and declared the U.S. and Panama to be in a state of war. A further series of incidents led to a U.S. invasion overthrowing Noriega, who was brought to the U.S. to stand trial for drug trafficking. Guillermo Endara, who probably would have won the election suppressed by Noriega, was instated as President.

In elections of May 1994 a left-of-center businessman won the country's presidential election.

In June 1997 a new law created an autonomous Canal Authority to administer the Panama Canal after the U.S.

relinquishes its last controls over the waterway.

Panama Canal. First conceived by the Spaniards in 1524, when King Charles V of Spain ordered a survey of a waterway across the Isthmus, a construction concession was granted by the Colombian government in 1878 to St. Lucien N. B. Wyse, representing a French company. Two years later, the French Canal Company, inspired by Ferdinand de Lesseps, began construction of what was to have been a sea-level canal. The effort ended in bankruptcy nine years later and the United States ultimately paid the French $40 million for their rights and assets.

The U.S. project, built on territory controlled by the United States, and calling for the creation of an interior lake connected to both oceans by locks, got under way in 1904. Completed in 1914, the Canal is 50.7 miles long and lifts ships 85 feet above sea level through a series of three locks on the Pacific and Atlantic sides. Enlarged in later years, each lock now measures 1,000 feet in length, 110 feet in width, and 40 feet in depth of water.

PAPUA NEW GUINEA

Sovereign: Queen Elizabeth II (1952)
Governor General: Wiwa Korowi (1991)
Prime Minister: Bill Skate (1997)
Area: 178,704 sq mi. (462,840 sq km)
Population (1997 est.): 4,496,221 (average annual rate of natural increase: 2.28%); birth rate: 32.65/1000; infant mortality rate: 58.6/1000; density per square mile: 25.2
Capital and largest city (1994): Port Moresby, 250,000.
Monetary unit: Kina. **Languages:** English, Melanesian pidgin, Hiri Motu, and 717 distinct native languages. **Ethnicity/Race:** Melanesian, Papuan, Negrito, Micronesian, Polynesian. **Religions:** over half Christian, remainder indigenous. **Literacy rate:** 52%
Economic summary: Gross domestic product: purchasing power parity (1995 est.): $10.2 billion; $2,400 per capita; –3% real growth rate; inflation 15%; unemployment n.a. Labor force: 1.941 million; 64% in agriculture. Principal products: coffee, copra, palm oil, cocoa, tea, coconuts. Major industrial products: coconut oil, plywood, wood chips, gold, silver. Natural resources: copper, gold, silver, timber, natural gas. Exports: $2.4 billion (f.o.b., 1995 est.): gold, copper, coffee, palm oil, copra, timber, lobster. Imports: $1.4 billion (c.i.f., 1995 est.): food, machinery, transport equipment, fuels, chemicals, consumer goods. Major trading partners: Australia, U.K., Japan, Singapore, New Zealand, U.S., South Korea, Germany. **Member of Commonwealth of Nations**

Geography. Papua New Guinea occupies the eastern half of the island of New Guinea, just north of Australia, and many outlying islands. The Indonesian province of Irian Jaya is to the west. To the north and east are the islands of Manus, New Britain, New Ireland, and Bougainville, all part of Papua New Guinea.

Papua New Guinea is about one-tenth larger than California. Its mountainous interior has only recently been explored. The high-plateau climate is temperate, in contrast to the tropical climate of the coastal plains. Two major rivers, the Sepik and the Fly, are navigable for shallow-draft vessels.

Government. Papua New Guinea attained independence Sept. 16, 1975, ending a United Nations trusteeship under the administration of Australia. Parliamentary democracy was established by a constitution that invests power in a 109-member national legislature.

History. The eastern half of New Guinea was first visited by Spanish and Portuguese explorers in the 16th century, but a permanent European presence was not established until 1884, when Germany declared a protectorate over the northern coast and Britain took similar action in the south. Both nations formally annexed their protectorates and, in 1901, Britain transferred its rights to a newly independent Australia. Australian troops invaded German New Guinea in World War I and retained control under a League of Nations mandate that eventually became a United Nations trusteeship, incorporating a territorial government in the southern region, known as Papua.

Australia granted limited home rule in 1951. Autonomy in internal affairs came nine years later.

In February 1990 guerrillas of the Bougainville Revolutionary Army (BRA) attacked plantations, forcing the evacuation of numerous workers. In May the BRA declared Bougainville's independence, whereupon the government blockaded the island until January 1991, when a peace treaty was signed.

Rebel guerrillas who had occupied the Bougainville copper mine withdrew to the surrounding hills in September 1994 allowing government forces to reclaim it.

South African mercenaries in the employ of the government landed on Bougainville in March 1997, although officially to train soldiers, not to fight the rebels.

PARAGUAY

Republic of Paraguay
National name: República del Paraguay
President: Juan Carlos Wasmosy (1993)
Area: 157,047 sq mi. (406,752 sq km)
Population (1997 est.): 5,651,634 (average annual rate of natural increase: 2.62%); birth rate: 30.47/1000; infant mortality rate: 22.3/1000; density per square mile: 36
Capital and largest city (1992): Asunción, 502,426.
Other large cities (1992): Ciudad del Este, 133,893; San Lorenzo, 133,311. **Monetary unit:** Guaraní. **Languages:** Spanish (official), Guaraní. **Ethnicity/Race:** mestizo (mixed Spanish and Indian) 95%, whites plus Amerindians 5%. **Religion:** Roman Catholic, 90%. **Literacy rate:** 90%
Economic summary: Gross domestic product: purchasing power parity (1995 est.): $17 billion; $3,200 per capita; real growth rate 4.2%; inflation 10.5%; unemployment 12%. Arable land: 20%. Principal agricultural products: soybeans, cotton, timber, cassava, tobacco, corn, rice, sugar cane. Labor force (1993): 1.692 million; 45% agriculture. Major industrial products: packed meats, crushed oilseeds, beverages, textiles, light consumer goods, cement. Natural resources: iron ore, timber, manganese, limestone, hydropower. Exports: $819.5 million (f.o.b., 1995): cotton, soybeans, meat products, timber, coffee, tung oil, vegetable oils. Imports: $2.871 billion (c.i.f., 1995): fuels and lubricants, beverages, tobacco, foodstuffs, capital goods, consumer goods, fuels and lubricants. Major trading partners: Argentina, Brazil, U.S., E.U., Japan.

Geography. California-size Paraguay is surrounded by Brazil, Bolivia, and Argentina in south central South America. Eastern Paraguay, between the Paraná and Paraguay Rivers, is upland country with the thickest population settled on the grassy slope that inclines toward the Paraguay River. The greater part of the Chaco region to the west is covered with marshes, lagoons, dense forests, and jungles.

Government. The President is elected by popular vote for five years. The legislature is bicameral, consisting of a Senate of 45 members and a Chamber of Representatives of 80 members. There is also a Council of State, whose members are nominated by the government.

History. In 1526 and again in 1529, Sebastian Cabot explored Paraguay when he sailed up the Paraná and Paraguay Rivers. From 1608 until their expulsion from the Spanish dominions in 1767, the Jesuits maintained an extensive establishment in the south and east of Paraguay. In 1811, Paraguay revolted against Spanish rule and became a nominal republic under two consuls.

Actually, Paraguay was governed by three Dictators during the first 60 years of independence. The third, Francisco López, waged war against Brazil and Argentina in 1865–70, a conflict in which the male population was almost wiped out. A new constitution in 1870, designed to prevent Dictatorships and internal strife, failed to do so, and not until 1912 did a period of comparative economic and political stability begin.

After World War II, politics became particularly unstable.

Alfredo Stroessner ruled under a state of siege until 1965, when the Dictatorship was relaxed and exiles returned. The constitution was revised in 1967 to permit Stroessner to be re-elected.

The Stroessner regime was criticized by the U.S. during the Carter administration as a violator of human rights, but unlike Argentina and Uruguay, Paraguay did not suffer cuts in U.S. military aid.

Stroessner was overthrown by an army leader, Gen. Andres Rodriguez, in 1989. Rodriguez won in Paraguay's first multi-candidate election in decades. The National Assembly in June 1991 approved a reform of the constitution.

The country's first democratic presidential election took place in May 1993. Juan Carlos Wasmosy, a wealthy businessman and the candidate of the governing Colorado Party won a five-year term in an election that despite irregularities was regarded as reliable.

The Colorado Party in June 1997 took the unusual step of demanding the resignation of the President, his entire government, and the Central Bank President for economic reasons.

PERU

Republic of Peru
National name: República del Perú
President: Alberto Fujimori (1990)
Premier: Alberto Pandolf (1996)
Area: 496,222 sq mi. (1,285,216 sq km)
Population (1997 est.): 24,949,512 (average annual rate of natural increase: 1.77%); birth rate: 23.75/1000; infant mortality rate: 50.2/1000; density per square mile: 50
Capital and largest city (1993): Lima, 6,479,000. **Other large cities:** Arequipa, 939,800; Callao, 648,000; Trujillo, 1,287,000; Chiclayo, 951,000. **Monetary unit:** Nuevo Sol (1991). **Languages:** Spanish, Quéchua, Aymara, and other native languages. **Ethnicity/Race:** Indian 45%, mestizo (mixed Indian and European ancestry) 37%, white 15%, black, Japanese, Chinese, and other 3%. **Religion:** Roman Catholic. **Literacy rate:** 85%
Economic summary: Gross domestic product: purchasing power parity (1995 est.): $87 billion; $3,600 (est.) per capita; real growth rate 6.8%; inflation 10.2%; unemployment 15% (1992 est.). Arable land: 3%. Principal products: wheat, potatoes, beans, rice, sugar, cotton, coffee. Labor force: 8 million (1992); government and other services, 44%; agriculture, 37%; industry, 19%. Major products: processed minerals, fish meal, refined petroleum, textiles. Natural resources: silver, gold, iron, copper, fish, petroleum, timber. Exports: $5.6 billion (f.o.b., 1995 est.): copper, fish products, cotton, sugar, coffee, lead, silver, zinc, oil. Imports: $7.4 billion (f.o.b., 1995 est.): machinery, foodstuffs, chemicals, pharmaceuticals, transport

equipment. Major trading partners: U.S., Japan, Western European, and Latin American countries.

Geography. Peru, in western South America, extends for nearly 1,500 miles (2,414 km) along the Pacific Ocean. Colombia and Ecuador are to the north, Brazil and Bolivia to the east, and Chile to the south.

Five-sixths the size of Alaska, Peru is divided by the Andes Mountains into three sharply differentiated zones. To the west is the coastline, much of it arid, extending 50 to 100 miles (80 to 160 km) inland. The mountain area, with peaks over 20,000 feet (6,096 m), lofty plateaus, and deep valleys, lies centrally. Beyond the mountains to the east is the heavily forested slope leading to the Amazonian plains.

Government. A republic. The President, Alberto Fujimori was elected in 1990 by universal suffrage for a five-year term and holds executive power. He was re-elected in April 1995 by an absolute majority for five more years. A new 120-member congress was also elected by universal suffrage.

History. Peru was once part of the great Incan empire and later the major vice-royalty of Spanish South America. It was conquered in 1531–33 by Francisco Pizarro. On July 28, 1821, Peru proclaimed its independence, but the Spanish were not finally defeated until 1824. For a hundred years thereafter, revolutions were frequent, and a new war was fought with Spain in 1864–66.

Peru emerged from 20 years of Dictatorship in 1945 with the inauguration of President José Luis Bustamente y Rivero after the first free election in many decades. But he served for only three years and was succeeded in turn by Gen. Manual A. Odria, Manuel Prado y Ugarteche, and Fernando Belaúnde Terry. On Oct. 3, 1968, Belaúnde was overthrown by Gen. Juan Velasco Alvarado.

Velasco nationalized the nation's second biggest bank and turned two large newspapers over to Marxists in 1970, but he also allowed a new agreement with a copper-mining consortium of four American firms.

In 1975, Velasco was replaced in a bloodless coup by his Premier, Gen. Francisco Morales Bermudez, who promised to restore civilian government. In elections held on May 18, 1980, Belaunde Terry, the last previous civilian President and the candidate of the conservative parties that have traditionally ruled Peru, was elected President again.

But Peru's fragile democracy survived this period of stress and when he left office in 1985 Belaunde Terry was the first elected President to turn over power to a constitutionally elected successor since 1945.

In the June run-off to the April 1990 elections Alberto Fujimori won 56.5% of the vote. Citing continuing terrorism, drug trafficking, and corruption Fujimori in April 1992 dissolved Congress, suspended the constitution and imposed censorship. A new constitution received approval in a referendum held in October 1993.

In January 1995 fighting flared once again along part of the poorly defined border with Ecuador, claiming nine lives. Peru declared a unilateral ceasefire in mid-February.

In the April elections President Fujimori was re-elected, and his party obtained a majority in the legislature.

In December 1996, Tupac Amaru rebels seized control of the diplomatic compound of the Japanese ambassador in Lima, holding 72 hostages. The standoff continued until April when government forces successfully stormed the residence, freeing the hostages. In the months that followed Fujimori came under fire for an increasingly authoritarian style.

THE PHILIPPINES

Republic of the Philippines
National name: Republika ng Pilipinas
President: Fidel V. Ramos (1992)
Prime Minister: Joseph Estrada (1992)
Area: 115,830 sq mi. (300,000 sq km)
Population (1997 est.): 76,103,564 (average annual rate of natural increase: 2.23%); birth rate: 28.97/1000; infant mortality rate: 35.2/1000; density per square mile: 657
Capital and largest city (1990): Manila, 1,601,234.
Other large cities: Quezon City, 1,669,776; Cebu, 610,415. **Monetary unit:** Peso. **Languages:** Filipino (based on Tagalog), English; regional languages: Tagalog, Ilocano, Cebuano, others. **Ethnicity/Race:** Christian Malay 91.5%, Muslim Malay 4%, Chinese 1.5%, other 3%. **Religions:** Roman Catholic, 84%; Protestant, 10%; Islam, 5%; Buddhist and other, 3%. **Literacy rate:** 93.5%
Economic summary: Gross domestic product: purchasing power parity (1995 est.): $179.7 billion; $2,530 per capita; real growth rate 4.8%; inflation 8.1%; unemployment 9.5%. Arable land: 9.8%. Principal products: rice, corn, coconuts, sugar cane, bananas, pineapple. Labor force: 24.12 million; agriculture, 46%; services, 18.5%; industry and commerce, 16%; government, 10%; other, 9.5%. Major products: textiles, pharmaceuticals, chemicals, food processing, electronics assembly. Natural resources: forests, crude oil, metallic and non-metallic minerals. Exports: $17.4 billion (f.o.b., 1995): electrical equipment, coconut products, chemicals, logs and lumber, copper concentrates, nickel. Imports: $26.5 billion (f.o.b., 1995): petroleum, industrial equipment, raw materials. Major trading partners: U.S., Japan, E.U., Taiwan, Saudi Arabia.

Geography. The Philippine Islands are an archipelago of over 7,000 islands lying about 500 miles (805 km) off the southeast coast of Asia. The overall land area is comparable to that of Arizona. The northernmost island, Y'Ami, is 65 miles (105 km) from Taiwan, while the southernmost, Saluag, is 40 miles (64 km) east of Borneo.

Only about 7% of the islands are larger than one square mile, and only one-third have names. The largest are Luzon in the north (40,420 sq mi.; 104,687 sq km), Mindanao in the south (36,537 sq mi.; 94,631 sq km), Samar (5,124 sq mi.; 13,271 sq km).

The islands are of volcanic origin, with the larger ones crossed by mountain ranges. The highest peak is Mount Apo (9,690 ft.; 2,954 m) on Mindanao.

Government. On February 2, 1987, the Filipino people voted for a new constitution that established a 24-seat Senate and a 250-seat House of Representatives and gave the President a six-year term. It limits the powers of the President, who can't be re-elected.

History. Fernando Magellan, the Portuguese navigator in the service of Spain, explored the Philippines in 1521. Twenty-one years later, a Spanish exploration party named the group of islands in honor of Prince Philip, later Philip II of Spain. Spain retained possession of the islands for the next 350 years.

The Philippines were ceded to the U.S. in 1899 by the Treaty of Paris after the Spanish-American War. Meanwhile, the Filipinos, led by Emilio Aguinaldo, had declared their independence. They continued guerrilla warfare against U.S. troops until the capture of Aguinaldo in 1901. By 1902, peace was established except among the Moros.

The first U.S. civilian governor-general was William Howard Taft (1901–04). The Jones Law (1916) provided for the establishment of a Philippine Legislature composed of an elective Senate and House of Representatives. The Tydings-McDuffie Act (1934) provided for a transitional period until 1946, at which time the Philippines would become completely independent.

Under a constitution approved by the people of the Philippines in 1935, the Commonwealth of the Philippines came into being, with Manuel Quezon y Molina as President.

On Dec. 8, 1941, the Philippines were invaded by Japanese troops. Following the fall of Bataan and Corregidor, Quezon established a government-in-exile, which he headed until his death in 1944. He was succeeded by Vice President Sergio Osmeña.

U.S. forces led by Gen. Douglas MacArthur reinvaded the Philippines in October 1944 and, after the liberation of Manila in February 1945, Osmeña reestablished the government.

The Philippines achieved full independence on July 4, 1946. Manual A. Roxas y Acuña was elected first President. Subsequent Presidents have been Elpidio Quirino (1948–53), Ramón Magsaysay (1953–57), Carlos P. García (1957–61), Diosdado Macapagal (1961–65), Ferdinand E. Marcos (1965–86).

Marcos, who had freed the last of the national leaders still in detention, former Senator Benigno S. Aquino, Jr., in 1980 and permitted him to go to the United States, ended eight years of martial law on January 17, 1981.

Despite having been warned by First Lady Imelda Marcos that he risked being killed if he came back, opposition leader Aquino returned to the Philippines from self-exile on Aug. 21, 1983. He was shot to death as he was being escorted from his plane by military police at Manila International Airport. There was widespread suspicion that the Marcos government was involved in the murder.

In an attempt to re-secure American support, Marcos set presidential elections for Feb. 7, 1986. With the support of the Catholic church, Corazon Aquino, widow of Benigno Aquino, declared her candidacy. Marcos was declared the winner, but the vote was widely considered to be rigged and anti-Marcos protests continued. The defection of Defense Minister Juan Enrile and Lt. Gen. Fidel Ramos signaled an end of military support for Marcos, who fled into exile in the U.S. on Feb. 25, 1986.

The Aquino government survived coup attempts by Marcos supporters and other right-wing elements including one, in November, by Enrile. Legislative elections on May 11, 1987, gave pro-Aquino candidates a large majority.

Negotiations on renewal of leases for U.S. military bases threatened to sour relations between the two countries. The volcanic eruptions from Mount Pinatubo, however, severely damaged Clark Air Base. In July 1991 the U.S. decided simply to abandon the base.

In elections of May 1992 Gen. Fidel Ramos, who had the support of outgoing Corazon Aquino, won the presidency in a seven-way race.

The U.S. Navy turned over the Subic Bay naval base to the Philippines in September, ending a long U.S. military presence.

After protracted negotiations the Moro National Liberation Front agreed in 1996 to a government plan leading to more political autonomy in the south.

An administrative body, headed by the former rebel chief, was established to oversee development on the southern islands. Although frequent and violent clashes between the army and another rebel group, the Moro Islamic Liberation Front, continued, by mid-1997 separate peace talks had begun.

POLAND

Republic of Poland
National name: Rzeczpospolita Polska
President: Aleksander Kwasniewski (1995)
Prime Minister: Wlodzimierz Cimoszewicz (1996)
Area: 120,727 sq mi. (312,683 sq km)
Population (1997 est.): 38,700,291 (average annual rate of natural increase: 0.19%); birth rate: 12.04/1000; infant mortality rate: 12.3/1000; density per square mile: 320.6
Capital and largest city (1994 est.): Warsaw, 1,642,700. **Other large cities:** Lodz, 833,700; Krakow, 745,100; Wroclaw, 642,300; Poznan, 582,800; Gdansk, 463,100; Szczecin, 417,700. **Monetary unit:** Zloty. **Language:** Polish. **Ethnicity/Race:** Polish 97.6%, German 1.3%, Ukrainian 0.6%, Belarussian 0.5% (1990 est.). **Religions:** Roman Catholic, 95%; Russian Orthodox, Protestant, and other, 5%. **Literacy rate:** 98%
Economic summary: Gross domestic product: purchasing power parity (1995 est.): $226.7 billion; $5,800 per capita; real growth rate 6.5%; inflation 21.6%; unemployment 14.9%. Arable land: 59%. Principal products: rye, rapeseed, potatoes, hogs and other livestock. Labor force: 17.743 million (1994): industry and construction 32%, agriculture and food products 27.6%; trade, transport and communications 14.7%. Major products: iron and steel, chemicals, textiles, processed foods, machine building. Natural resources: coal, sulfur, copper, natural gas. Exports: $22.2 billion (f.o.b., 1995 est.): coal, machinery and equipment, industrial products, chemicals, metals. Imports: $23.4 billion (f.o.b., 1995 est.): machinery and equipment, fuels, agricultural and food products, chemicals. Major trading partners: Germany, former U.S.S.R., Italy, U.K., the Netherlands, U.S.

Geography. Poland, a country the size of New Mexico in north central Europe, borders on Germany to the west, Czech and Slovak Republics to the south, and Ukraine, Balarus, Lithuania, and Russia to the east. In the north is the Baltic Sea.

Most of the country is a plain with no natural boundaries except the Carpathian Mountains in the south and the Oder and Neisse Rivers in the west. Other major rivers, which are important to commerce, are the Vistula, Warta, and Bug.

Government. Voters approved a new constitution in May 1997 that upholds a market economy, private ownership of land, personal freedoms, and clear divisions of power within the branches of the government. The supreme organ of state authority is the Sejm (parliament), which is composed of 460 members elected for four years and a 100–member senate (Senat).

History. Little is known about Polish history before the 11th century, when King Boleslaus I (the Brave) ruled over Bohemia, Saxony, and Moravia. Meanwhile, the Teutonic knights of Prussia conquered part of Poland and barred the latter's access to the Baltic. The knights were defeated by Wladislaus II at Tannenberg in 1410 and became Polish vassals, and Poland regained a Baltic shoreline. Poland reached the peak of power between the 14th and 16th centuries, scoring military successes against the Russians and Turks. In 1683, John III (John Sobieski) turned back the Turkish tide at Vienna.

An elective monarchy failed to produce strong central authority, and Prussia and Austria were able to carry out a first partition of the country in 1772, a second in 1792, and a third in 1795. For more than a century thereafter, there was no Polish state, but the Poles never ceased their efforts to regain their independence.

Poland was formally reconstituted in November 1918, with Marshal Josef Pilsudski as Chief of State. In 1919, Ignace Paderewski, the famous pianist and patriot, became the first Premier. In 1926, Pilsudski seized complete power in a coup and ruled dictatorially until his death on May 12, 1935, when he was succeeded by Marshal Edward Smigly-Rydz.

Despite a 10-year nonaggression pact signed in 1934, Hitler attacked Poland on Sept. 1, 1939. Russian troops invaded from the east on September 17, and on September 28 a German-Russian agreement divided Poland between Russia and Germany. Wladyslaw Raczkiewicz formed a government-in-exile in France, which moved to London after France's defeat in 1940.

All of Poland was occupied by Germany after the Nazi attack on the U.S.S.R. in June 1941.

The legal Polish government soon fell out with the Russians, and, in 1944, a Communist-dominated Polish Committee of National Liberation received Soviet recognition. Moving to Lublin after that city's liberation, it proclaimed itself the Provisional Government of Poland. Some former members of the Polish government in London joined with the Lublin government to form the Polish Government of National Unity, which Britain and the U.S. recognized.

On Aug. 2, 1945, in Berlin, President Harry S. Truman, Joseph Stalin, and Prime Minister Clement Attlee of Britain established a new *de facto* western frontier for Poland along the Oder and Neisse Rivers. (The border was finally agreed to by West Germany in a nonaggression pact signed Dec. 7, 1970.) On Aug. 16, 1945, the U.S.S.R. and Poland signed a treaty delimiting the Soviet-Polish frontier. Under these agreements, Poland was shifted westward. In the east it lost 69,860 square miles (180,934 sq km) with 10,772,000 inhabitants; in the west it gained (subject to final peace-conference approval) 38,986 square miles (100,973 sq km) with a prewar population of 8,621,000.

A New constitution in 1952 made Poland a "people's democracy" of the Soviet type. In 1955, Poland became a member of the Warsaw Treaty Organization, and its foreign policy became identical with that of the U.S.S.R. The government undertook persecution of the Roman Catholic Church as a remaining source of opposition.

Wladyslaw Gomulka was elected leader of the United Workers (Communist) Party in 1956. He denounced the Stalinist terror, ousted many Stalinists, and improved relations with the church. Most collective farms were dissolved, and the press became freer.

A strike that began in shipyards and spread to other industries in August 1980 produced a stunning victory for workers when the economically hard-pressed government accepted for the first time in a Marxist state the right of workers to organize in independent unions.

Led by Solidarity, a free union founded by Lech Walesa, workers launched a drive for liberty and improved conditions. A national strike for a five-day week in January 1981 led to the dismissal of Premier Pinkowski and the naming of the fourth Premier in less than a year, Gen. Wojciech Jaruzelski.

Martial law was declared on Dec. 13, when Walesa and other Solidarity leaders were arrested. It formally ended in 1984 but the government retained emergency powers.

Increasing opposition to the government because of the failing economy led to a new wave of strikes in 1988. Unable to totally quell the dissent, the government relegalized Solidarity and allowed it to compete in elections.

Solidarity members won a stunning victory in 1989, taking almost all the seats in the Senate and all of the 169 seats they were allowed to contest in the Sejm. This gave them substantial influence in the new government.

Taduesz Mazowiecki was appointed Prime Minister.

The presidential election of 1990 was essentially a three-way race between Mazowiecki, Solidarity-leader Lech Walesa and an almost unknown businessman Stanislaw Tyminski. In the second round Walesa received 74% of the vote.

In 1991, the first fully free parliamentary election since World War II resulted in representation for 29 political parties.

In the second democratic parliamentary election of September 1993 voters returned power to ex-Communists and their allies.

The second round of the presidential election in November 1995 pitted Walesa against Aleksander Kwasniewski, leader of the successor to the Communist Party. The latter won despite strong support for Walesa from the Church.

In May 1997 the country's highest court overturned portions of a law that liberalized previous abortion measures. Parliament in June rejected the ruling party's plan to hold a referendum in September on the issue. Parliament also voted to abolish the death penalty in June.

PORTUGAL

Republic of Portugal
National name: República Portuguesa
President: Jorge Sampaio (1996)
Prime Minister: Antonio Guterres (1995)
Area: 35,550 sq mi. (92,075 sq km)
Population (1997 est.): 9,867,654 (average annual rate of natural increase: 0.03%); birth rate: 10.59/1000; infant mortality rate: 7.5/1000; density per square mile: 277.6
Capital and largest city (1991): Lisbon, 677,790. **Other large city (1991):** Oporto, 350,000. **Monetary unit:** Escudo. **Language:** Portuguese. **Ethnicity/Race:** homogeneous Mediterranean stock in mainland, Azores, Madeira Islands; citizens of black African descent who immigrated to mainland during decolonization number less than 100,000. **Religion:** Roman Catholic 97%, 1% Protestant, 2% other. **Literacy rate:** 85%
Economic summary: Gross domestic product: purchasing power parity (1995 est.): $116.2 billion; $11,000 per capita; real growth rate 2.8%; inflation 3.4% (1996); unemployment: 7.5% (1996). Arable land: 32%. Principal products: grains, potatoes, olives, wine grapes. Labor force (1994 est.): 4.24 million; services 54.5%; manufacturing 24.4%; agriculture, forestry and fisheries 11.2%; construction 8.3%; utilities 1.0%; mining 0.5% (1992). Major products: textiles, footwear, wood pulp, paper, cork, metal products, refined oil, chemicals, canned fish, wine. Natural resources: fish, cork, tungsten, iron ore. Exports: $18.9 billion (f.o.b., 1995): cotton, textiles, cork and cork products, canned fish, wine, timber and timber products, resin, machinery, appliances. Imports: $24.1 billion (c.i.f., 1995): machinery and transport equipment, agricultural products, chemicals, petroleum, textiles. Major trading partners: Western European countries, U.S.

Geography. Portugal occupies the western part of the Iberian Peninsula, bordering on the Atlantic Ocean to the west and Spain to the north and east. It is slightly smaller than Indiana.

The country is crossed by many small rivers, and also by three large ones that rise in Spain, flow into the Atlantic, and divide the country into three geographic areas. The Minho River, part of the northern boundary, cuts through a mountainous area that extends south to the vicinity of the Douro River. South of the Douro, the mountains slope to the plains about the Tejo River. The remaining division is the southern one of Alentejo.

The Azores, stretching over 340 miles (547 km) in the Atlantic, consist of nine islands divided into three groups, with a total area of 902 square miles (2,335 sq km). The nearest continental land is Cape da Roca, Portugal, about 900 miles (1,448 km) to the east. The Azores are an important station on Atlantic air routes, and Britain and the U.S. established airbases there during World War II. Madeira, consisting of two inhabited islands, Madeira and Porto Santo, and two groups of uninhabited islands, lie in the Atlantic about 535 miles (861 km) southwest of Lisbon. The Madeiras are 307 square miles (796 sq km) in area.

Government. A republic. The President is elected for a five-year term, the unicameral legislature (the Assembly of the Republic), for four years.

History. Portugal was a part of Spain until it won its independence in the middle of the 12th century. King John I (1385–1433) unified his country at the expense of the Castilians and the Moors of Morocco. The expansion of Portugal was brilliantly coordinated by John's son, Prince Henry the Navigator. In 1488, Bartolomew Diaz reached the Cape of Good Hope, proving that the Far East was accessible by sea. In 1498, Vasco da Gama reached the west coast of India. By the middle of the 16th century, the Portuguese Empire extended to West and East Africa, Brazil, Persia, Indochina, and Malaya.

In 1581, Philip II of Spain invaded Portugal and held it for 60 years, precipitating a catastrophic decline of Portuguese commerce. Courageous and shrewd explorers, the Portuguese proved to be inefficient and corrupt colonizers. By the time the Portuguese dynasty was restored in 1640, Dutch, English, and French competitors began to seize the lion's share of the world's colonies and commerce. Portugal retained Angola and Mozambique in Africa, and Brazil (until 1822).

The corrupt King Carlos, who ascended the throne in 1889, made Joao Franco the Premier with dictatorial power in 1906. In 1908, Carlos and his heir were shot dead on the streets of Lisbon. The new King, Manoel II, was driven from the throne in the Revolution of 1910 and Portugal became a French-style republic.

Traditionally friendly to Britain, Portugal fought in World War I on the Allied side in Africa as well as on the Western Front. Weak postwar governments and a revolution in 1926 brought Antonio Oliveira Salazar to power. He kept Portugal neutral in World War II but gave the Allies naval and air bases after 1943.

Portugal lost the tiny remnants of its Indian empire—Goa, Daman, and Diu—to Indian military occupation in 1961, the year an insurrection broke out in Angola. For the next 13 years, Salazar, who died in 1970, and his successor, Marcello Caetano, fought independence movements amid growing world criticism. Leftists in the armed forces, weary of a losing battle, launched a successful revolution on April 25, 1974.

In late 1985, a PSP-PSD split ended Mario Soare's coalition government. Cavaco Silva, an advocate of free-market economics and the Social Democratic candidate, was elected as Prime Minister.

In July 1987, the governing Social Democratic Party was swept back into office with 50.22% of the popular vote, giving Portugal its first majority Government since democracy was restored in 1974.

Mario Soares easily won a second five-year term as President in January 1991 elections.

General elections in October 1995 went to the Socialist Party, which fell just short of an absolute majority in the Assembly. Lisbon mayor Jorge Sampaio, a Socialist, won the race for President in January 1996.

The European Union started legal proceedings in April 1997 against the country for failure to implement directives from Brussels concerning the adoption and implementation of law for veterinary medication.

Portuguese Overseas Territory

After the April 1974 revolution, the military junta moved to grant independence to the territories, beginning with Portuguese Guinea in September 1974, which became the Republic of Guinea-Bissau.

Mozambique and Angola followed, leaving only Portuguese Timor and Macau of the former empire. Despite Lisbon's objections, Indonesia annexed Timor.

MACAU

Status: Territory
Governor: Vasco Rocha Vieira (1991)
Area: 6 sq mi. (15.5 sq km)
Population (1991 est.): 502,325 (average annual growth rate: 0.93%); birth rate: 13.78/1000; infant mortality rate: 5.3/1000; density per square mile: 83,705.8
Capital (1991): Macao, 326,460. **Monetary unit:** Pataca. **Languages:** Portuguese and Chinese are both official languages (1991). Cantonese is most common, English is also spoken in business. **Religions:** Buddhist 17%, Roman Catholic 7%, Protestant 7%. **Literacy rate (1981):** almost 100% among Portuguese and Macanese, no data on Chinese
Economic summary: Gross domestic product (1993 est.): $4.8 billion; $10,000 per capita; real growth rate 5%; inflation 6.3%. Major industrial products: clothing, textiles, plastics, furniture. Exports: $1.8 billion (1992 est.): textiles, clothing, toys. Imports: $2 billion (1992 est.): raw materials, foodstuffs, capital goods. Major trading partners: Hong Kong, China, U.S., Germany, France, Japan.

Macau comprises the peninsula of Macau and the two small islands of Taipa and Colôane on the South China coast, about 35 miles (53 km) from Hong Kong. Established by the Portuguese in 1557, it is the oldest European outpost in the China trade, but Portugal's sovereign rights to the port were not recognized by China until 1887. The port has been eclipsed in importance by Hong Kong, but it is still a busy distribution center and also has an important fishing industry. Portugal will return Macau to China in 1999.

QATAR

State of Qatar
Emir: Sheikh Hamad bin Khalifa al-Thani (1995)
Area: 4,000 sq mi. (11,437 sq km)
Population (1997 est.): 665,485 (average annual rate of natural increase: 1.67%); birth rate: 20.25/1000; infant mortality rate: 18.9/1000; density per square mile: 166.4
Capital (1990 est.): Doha, 300,000. **Monetary unit:** Qatari riyal. **Language:** Arabic; English is also widely spoken. **Ethnicity/Race:** Arab 40%, Pakistani 18%, Indian 18%, Iranian 10%, other 14%. **Religion:** Islam, 95%. **Literacy rate:** 76%
Economic summary: Gross domestic product: purchasing power parity (1994 est.): $10.7 billion; $20,820 per capita; −1% real growth rate; inflation: 3% (1993); unemployment n.a. Labor force: 233,000. Major industrial product: oil. While Qatar depends on oil for much of its revenue, the government is increasing the development of its natural gas production. Qatar is one of the five leading gas producers in the world. Natural resources: oil, gas. Exports: $2.9 billion (f.o.b., 1994 est.): petroleum products 85%; steel, fertilizers. Imports: $2 billion (c.i.f., 1994 est.): machinery and equipment, consumer goods, food, chemicals. Major

trading partners: France, U.K., U.S., Germany, Japan, Brazil, South Korea, U.A.E.

Geography. Qatar occupies a small peninsula that extends into the Persian Gulf from the east side of the Arabian Peninsula. Saudi Arabia is to the west and the United Arab Emirates to the south. The country is mainly barren.

Government. For a long time, Qatar was under Turkish protection, but in 1916, the Emir accepted British protection. After the discovery of oil in the 1940s and its exploitation in the 1950s and 1960s, political unrest spread to the sheikhdoms. Qatar declared its independence in 1971.

History. The Emir agreed to the deployment of Arab and Western forces in Qatar following the Iraqi invasion of Kuwait in 1991.

A border dispute erupted with Saudi Arabia that was settled in December 1992. A territorial dispute with Bahrain over the Hawar Islands remains unresolved, however.

In June Qatar signed a defense pact with the U.S., becoming the third Gulf state to do so.

In June 1995 Crown Prince Hamad bin Khalifa al-Thani asked his father, the Emir, to leave the country.

The Emir was not stripped of his title, and much of the power was already in the son's hands. In December Qatar announced it was reviewing its membership in the Gulf Cooperation Council.

The Emir in October 1996 appointed his brother Sheikh Abdullah bin Khalifa al-Thani, Prime Minister.

ROMANIA

Republic of Romania
President: Emil Constantinescu (1996)
Prime Minister: Victor Ciorbea (1996)
Area: 91,700 sq mi. (237,500 sq km)
Population (1997 est.): 21,399,114 (average annual rate of natural increase: −0.25%); birth rate: 9.86/1000; infant mortality rate: 22.9/1000; density per square mile: 233.4
Capital and largest city (1992): Bucharest, 2,351,000.
Largest cities (1992): Constanta, 350,476; Iasi, 342,994; Timisoara, 334,278; Cluj-Napoca, 328,008; Galati, 325,788; Brasov, 323,835. **Monetary unit:** Leu.
Languages: Romanian (official). **Ethnicity/Race:** Romanian 89.1%, Hungarian 8.9%, German 0.4%, Ukrainian, Serb, Croat, Russian, Turk, and Gypsy 1.6%. **Religions:** Christian Orthodox, 86.8%; Roman Catholic, 5%, Protestant, 3.5%. **Literacy rate:** 98%
Economic summary: Gross national product: purchasing power parity (1995 est.): $105.7 billion; $4,600 per capita; real growth rate 5.4%; inflation 25%; unemployment 8.9% (Dec. 95). Arable land: 43%. Principal products: corn, wheat, livestock, sunflowers, potatoes. Labor force, 11.3 million (1992): industry 38%, agriculture 28%, other 34% (1989). Major products: timber, metal production and processing, chemicals, food processing, petroleum. Natural resources: oil, timber, natural gas, coal, iron ore. Exports: $6.2 billion (f.o.b., 1995): machinery, metals, chemicals, timber, furniture, textiles, foodstuffs. Imports: $7.1 billion (c.i.f., 1995): minerals, fuel, machinery, consumer goods. Major trading partners: Germany, Italy, Russia, France, U.K., U.S.

Geography. A country in southeastern Europe slightly smaller than Oregon, Romania is bordered on the west by Hungary and Yugoslavia, on the north and east by Moldova and Ukraine, on the east by the Black Sea, and on the south by Bulgaria.

The Carpathian Mountains divide Romania's upper half from north to south and connect near the center of the country with the Transylvanian Alps, running east and west.

North and west of these ranges lies the Transylvanian plateau, and to the south and east are the plains of Moldavia and Walachia. In its last 190 miles (306 km), the Danube River flows through Romania only. It enters the Black Sea in northern Dobruja, just south of the border with the Ukraine.

Government. A multiparty republic with a bicameral Parliament consisting of an upper house or Senate and a lower house, the Chamber of Deputies.

History. Most of Romania was the Roman province of Dacia from about C.E. 100 to 271. From the 6th to the 12th century, wave after wave of barbarian conquerors overran the native Daco-Roman population. By the 16th century, the main Romanian principalities of Moldavia and Walachia had become satellites within the Ottoman Empire, although they retained much independence. After the Russo-Turkish War of 1828–29, they became Russian protectorates. The nation became a Kingdom in 1881 after the Congress of Berlin.

King Ferdinand ascended the throne in 1914. At the start of World War I, Romania proclaimed its neutrality, but later joined the Allied side and in 1916 declared war on the Central Powers. The armistice of Nov. 11, 1918, gave Romania vast territories from Russia and the Austro-Hungarian Empire.

The gains of World War I, making Romania the largest Balkan state, included Bessarabia, Transylvania, and Bukovina. The Banat, a Hungarian area, was divided with Yugoslavia.

In 1925, Crown Prince Carol renounced his rights to the throne, and when King Ferdinand died in 1927, Carol's son, Michael (Mihai) became King under a regency. However, Carol returned from exile in 1930, was crowned King Carol II, and gradually became a powerful political force in the country. In 1938, he abolished the democratic constitution of 1923.

In 1940, the country was reorganized along Fascist lines, and the Fascist Iron Guard became the nucleus of the new totalitarian party. On June 27, the Soviet Union occupied Bessarabia and northern Bukovina. By the Axis-dictated Vienna Award of 1940, two-fifths of Transylvania went to Hungary, after which Carol dissolved Parliament and granted the new Premier, Ion Antonescu, full power. He abdicated and again went into exile.

Romania subsequently signed the Axis Pact on Nov. 23, 1940, and the following June joined in Germany's attack on the Soviet Union, reoccupying Bessarabia. Following the invasion of Romania by the Red Army in August 1944, King Michael led a coup that ousted the Antonescu government. An armistice with the Soviet Union was signed in Moscow on Sept. 12, 1944.

A Communist-dominated government bloc won elections in 1946, Michael abdicated on Dec. 30, 1947, and Romania became a "people's republic." In 1955, Romania joined the Warsaw Treaty Organization and the United Nations.

Nikolae Ceausescu ruled from 1965 to 1989, when he was overthrown by a coup rising from opposition to his repressive domestic policies.

An army-assisted rebellion in Dec. 1989 led to Ceausescu's overthrow. He was tried and executed. Elections in May 1990 led to the head of the interim government, Ion Iliescu, being elected President.

The government remained torn between introducing free-market reforms and its pledges to hold down unemployment and reduce shortages. The opposition remained weak and fragmented.

General elections in September 1992 saw the President returned for a second term, and his party became the largest single party in Parliament.

The country applied for membership in the E.U. in June 1995 and much legislation that year was crafted in hopes of meeting that objective. Nevertheless, the reform process proceeded slowly.

In the first round of the presidential elections in November 1996 incumbent Ion Iliescu received the most votes, followed by Emil Constantinescu of the Romanian Democratic Convention. The second round later that month produced a victory for Constantinescu with 54% of the votes.

RUSSIA

Russian Federation
President: Boris N. Yeltsin (1991)
Prime Minister: Viktor Chernomyrdin (1992)
Area: 6,592,800 sq mi. (17,075,400 sq km)
Population (1997 est.): 147,987,101 (average annual rate of natural increase: –0.48%); birth rate: 10.89/1000; infant mortality rate: 24.3/1000; density per square mile: 22.4
Capital and largest city (1994 est.): Moscow, 8,792,000. **Other large cities:** St. Petersburg, 4,882,600; Novosibirsk, 1,418,200; Samara, 1,222,500; Chelyabinsk, 1,124,500; Yekaterinburg, 1,347,000; Nizhny Novgorod, 1,424,600; Kazau, 1,092,300; Perm, 1,086,100; Ufa, 1,091,800; Volgograd, 1,000,400.
Monetary unit: Ruble. **Religion:** Mainly Eastern Orthodox. **Ethnicity/Race:** Russian 81.5%, Tatar 3.8%, Ukrainian 3%, Chuvash 1.2%, Bashkir 0.9%, Belarussian 0.8%, Moldavian 0.7%, other 8.1%. **Language:** Russian. **Literacy rate:** 100%
Economic summary: Russia is a highly industrialized-agrarian republic. Its vast mineral resources include oil and natural gas, coal, iron, zinc, lead, nickel, aluminum, molybdenum, gold, platinum, and other nonferrous metals. Russia has the world's largest oil and natural gas reserves. Three-quarters of the republic's mineral wealth is concentrated in Siberia and the Far East. Approximately ten million people are engaged in agriculture and they produce half of the region's grain, meat, milk, and other dairy products. The largest granaries are located in the North Caucasus and the Volga and Amur regions. Gross domestic product: purchasing power parity (1995 estimate as extrapolated from the World Bank estimate for 1994): $796 billion; $5,300 per capita; –4% real growth rate; inflation 7% (per mo. avg.); unemployment: 8.2% (Dec. 95). Labor force (1993 est.): 85 million; production and economic services 83.9%; government 16.1%. Exports: $77.8 billion (f.o.b., 1995): petroleum and petroleum products, natural gas, wood and wood products, coal, nonferrous metals, chemicals, civilian and military manufacturers. Imports: $57.9 billion (c.i.f., 1995): machinery and equipment, chemicals, consumer goods, grain, meat, semifinished metal products. Foreign investment in Russia (1993 est.): $500 million. Major trading partners: Europe, N. America, Japan, Cuba.

Geography. The Russian Federation is the largest republic of the Commonwealth of Independent States. It occupies an area about one- and four-fifths the size of the United States and occupies most of eastern Europe and north Asia. Russia stretches from the Baltic Sea in the west to the Pacific Ocean in the east and from the Arctic Ocean in the north to the Black Sea and the Caucasus, the Altai, and Sayan Mountains, and the Amur and Ussuri Rivers in the south. It is bordered by Norway and Finland in the northwest, Estonia, Latvia, Belarus and Ukraine in the west, Georgia and Azerbaijan in the southwest, and Kazakhstan, Mongolia, and China along the southern border. The federation is composed of 21 republics.

Government. A constitutional republic. A new constitution adopted Dec. 12, 1993 gave the President considerable power to rule independently of the Parliament. The upper house or Federation Council has 176 elected members, two from each of Russia's 88 constituent regions. The State Duma or lower house has 450 elected members. The President and the Parliament are elected for four-year terms.

History. Tradition says the Viking Rurik came to Russia in C.E. 862 and founded the first Russian dynasty in Novgorod. The various tribes were united by the spread of Christianity in the 10th and 11th centuries; Vladimir "the Saint" was converted in 988. During the 11th century, the grand dukes of Kiev held such centralizing power as existed. In 1240, Kiev was destroyed by the Mongols, and the Russian territory was split into numerous smaller dukedoms. Early dukes of Moscow extended their dominions through their office of tribute collector for the Mongols.

In the late 15th century, Duke Ivan III acquired Novgorod and Tver and threw off the Mongol yoke. Ivan IV, the Terrible (1533–84), first Muscovite Tsar, is considered to have founded the Russian state. He crushed the power of rival Princes and boyars (great landowners), but Russia remained largely medieval until the reign of Peter the Great (1689–1725), grandson of the first Romanov Tsar, Michael (1613–45). Peter made extensive reforms aimed at westernization and, through his defeat of Charles XII of Sweden at the Battle of Poltava in 1709, he extended Russia's boundaries to the west.

Catherine the Great (1762–96) continued Peter's westernization program and also expanded Russian territory, acquiring the Crimea and part of Poland. During the reign of Alexander I (1801–25), Napoleon's attempt to subdue Russia was defeated (1812–13), and new territory was gained, including Finland (1809) and Bessarabia (1812). Alexander originated the Holy Alliance, which for a time crushed Europe's rising liberal movement.

Alexander II (1855–81) pushed Russia's borders to the Pacific and into central Asia. Serfdom was abolished in 1861, but heavy restrictions were imposed on the emancipated class. Revolutionary strikes following Russia's defeat in the war with Japan forced Nicholas II (1894–1917) to grant a representative national body (Duma), elected by narrowly limited suffrage. It met for the first time in 1906, little influencing Nicholas in his reactionary course.

World War I demonstrated tsarist corruption and inefficiency and only patriotism held the poorly equipped army together for a time. Disorders broke out in Petrograd (renamed Leningrad now St. Petersburg) in March 1917, and defection of the Petrograd garrison launched the revolution. Nicholas II was forced to abdicate on March 15, 1917, and he and his family were killed by revolutionists on July 16, 1918.

A provisional government under the successive Premierships of Prince Lvov and a moderate, Alexander Kerensky, lost ground to the radical, or Bolshevik, wing of the Socialist Democratic Labor Party. On Nov. 7, 1917, the Bolshevik revolution, engineered by N. Lenin[1] and Leon Trotsky, overthrew the Kerensky government and authority was vested in a Council of People's Commissars, with Lenin as Premier.

The humiliating Treaty of Brest-Litovsk (March 3, 1918) concluded the war with Germany, but civil war and foreign intervention delayed Communist control of all Russia until 1920. A brief war with Poland in 1920

Rulers of Russia Since 1533

Name	Born	Ruled [1]	Name	Born	Ruled [1]
Ivan IV the Terrible	1530	1533–1584	Nicholas I	1796	1825–1855
Theodore I	1557	1584–1598	Alexander II	1818	1855–1881
Boris Godunov	c.1551	1598–1605	Alexander III	1845	1881–1894
Theodore II	1589	1605–1605	Nicholas II	1868	1894–1917[7]
Demetrius I[2]	?	1605–1606	PROVISIONAL GOVERNMENT (PREMIERS)		
Basil IV Shuiski	?	1606–1610[3]	Prince Georgi Lvov	1861	1917–1917
"Time of Troubles"	—	1610–1613	Alexander Kerensky	1881	1917–1917
Michael Romanov	1596	1613–1645	POLITICAL LEADERS OF U.S.S.R.		
Alexis I	1629	1645–1676	N. Lenin	1870	1917–1924
Theodore III	1656	1676–1682	Aleksei Rykov	1881	1924–1930
Ivan V[4]	1666	1682–1689[5]	Vyacheslav Molotov	1890	1930–1941
Peter I the Great[4]	1672	1682–1725	Joseph Stalin[8]	1879	1941–1953
Catherine I	c.1684	1725–1727	Georgi M. Malenkov	1902	1953–1955
Peter II	1715	1727–1730	Nikolai A. Bulganin	1895	1955–1958
Anna	1693	1730–1740	Nikita S. Khrushchev	1894	1958–1964
Ivan VI	1740	1740–1741[6]	Leonid I. Brezhnev	1906	1964–1982
Elizabeth	1709	1741–1762	Yuri V. Andropov	1914	1982–1984
Peter III	1728	1762–1762	Konstantin U. Chernenko	1912	1984–1985
Catherine II the Great	1729	1762–1796	Mikhail S. Gorbachev	1931	1985–1991
Paul I	1754	1796–1801	PRESIDENT OF RUSSIA		
Alexander I	1777	1801–1825	Boris Yeltsin	1931	1991–

1. For Tsars through Nicholas II, year of end of rule is also that of death, unless otherwise indicated. 2. Also known as Pseudo-Demetrius. 3. Died 1612. 4. Ruled jointly until 1689, when Ivan was deposed. 5. Died 1696. 6. Died 1764. 7. Killed 1918. 8. General Secretary of Communist Party, 1924–53.

resulted in Russian defeat.

1. N. Lenin was the pseudonym taken by Vladimir Ilich Ulyanov. It is sometimes given as Nikolai Lenin or V. Lenin.

Emergence of the U.S.S.R. The Union of Soviet Socialist Republics was established as a federation on Dec. 30, 1922.

The death of Lenin on Jan. 21, 1924, precipitated an intraparty struggle between Joseph Stalin, General Secretary of the party, and Trotsky, who favored swifter socialization at home and fomentation of revolution abroad. Trotsky was dismissed as Commissar of War in 1925 and banished from the Soviet Union in 1929. He was murdered in Mexico City on Aug. 21, 1940, by a political agent.

Stalin further consolidated his power by a series of purges in the late 1930s, liquidating prominent party leaders and military officers. Stalin assumed the Premiership May 6, 1941.

Soviet foreign policy, at first friendly toward Germany and antagonistic toward Britain and France and then, after Hitler's rise to power in 1933, becoming anti-Fascist and pro-League of Nations, took an abrupt turn on Aug. 24, 1939, with the signing of a nonaggression pact with Nazi Germany. The next month, Moscow joined in the German attack on Poland, seizing territory later incorporated into the Ukrainian and Belarussian S.S.R.'s. The war with Finland, 1939–40, added territory to the Karelian S.S.R. set up March 31, 1940; the annexation of Bessarabia and Bukovina from Romania became part of the new Moldavian S.S.R. on Aug. 2, 1940; and the annexation of the Baltic republics of Estonia, Latvia, and Lithuania in June 1940 created the 14th, 15th, and 16th Soviet Republics. The illegal annexation of the Baltic republics was never recognized by the U.S. for the 51 years leading up to Soviet recognition of Estonia, Latvia and Lithuania's independence on September 6, 1991.

The Soviet-German collaboration ended abruptly with a lightning attack by Hitler on June 22, 1941, which seized 500,000 square miles of Russian territory before Soviet defenses, aided by U.S. and British arms, could halt it. The Soviet resurgence at Stalingrad from November 1942 to February 1943 marked the turning point in a long battle, ending in the final offensive of January 1945.

Then, after denouncing a 1941 nonaggression pact with Japan in April 1945, when Allied forces were nearing victory in the Pacific, the Soviet Union declared war on Japan on Aug. 8, 1945, and quickly occupied Manchuria, Karafuto, and the Kurile islands.

The U.S.S.R. built a cordon of Communist states running from Poland in the north to Albania and Bulgaria in the south, including East Germany, Czechoslovakia, Hungary, and Romania, composed of the territories Soviet troops occupied at the war's end. With its Eastern front solidified, the Soviet Union launched a political offensive against the non-Communist West, moving first to block the Western access to Berlin. The Western powers countered with an airlift, completed unification of West Germany, and organized the defense of Western Europe in the North Atlantic Treaty Organization.

Stalin died on March 6, 1953, and was succeeded the next day by G. M. Malenkov as Premier.

The new power in the Kremlin was Nikita S. Khrushchev, First Secretary of the party. Khrushchev formalized the Eastern European system into a Council for Mutual Economic Assistance (Comecon) and a Warsaw Pact Treaty Organization as a counterweight to NATO.

The Soviet Union exploded a hydrogen bomb in 1953, developed an intercontinental ballistic missile by 1957, sent the first satellite into space (Sputnik I) in 1957, and put Yuri Gagarin in the first orbital flight around the earth in 1961.

Khrushchev's downfall stemmed from his decision to place Soviet nuclear missiles in Cuba and then, when challenged by the U.S., backing down and removing the weapons. He was also blamed for the ideological break with China after 1963.

Khrushchev was forced into retirement on Oct. 15, 1964, and was replaced by Leonid I. Brezhnev as First Secretary of the Party and Aleksei N. Kosygin as Premier.

Carter and the ailing Brezhnev signed the SALT II treaty in Vienna on June 18, 1979, setting ceilings on each nation's arsenal of intercontinental ballistic missiles. Doubts about U.S. Senate ratification grew, and became a certainty on Dec. 27, when Soviet troops invaded Afghanistan.

On November 10, 1982, Soviet radio and television

announced the death of Leonid Brezhnev. Yuri V. Andropov, who had formerly headed the K.G.B., was chosen to succeed Brezhnev as General Secretary. By mid-June 1983, Andropov had assumed all of Brezhnev's three titles.

After months of illness, Andropov died in February 1984. Konstantin U. Chernenko, a 72-year-old party stalwart who had been close to Brezhnev, succeeded him as General Secretary and, by mid-April, had also assumed the title of President. In the months following Chernenko's assumption of power, the Kremlin took on a hostile mood toward the West of a kind rarely seen since the height of the cold war 30 years before. Led by Moscow, all the Soviet bloc countries except Romania boycotted the 1984 Summer Olympic Games in Los Angeles—tit-for-tat for the U.S.-led boycott of the 1980 Moscow Games, in the view of most observers.

After 13 months in office, Chernenko died on March 10, 1985. He had been ill much of the time and left only a minor imprint on Soviet history.

Chosen to succeed him as Soviet leader was Mikhail S. Gorbachev, at 54 the youngest man to take charge of the Soviet Union since Stalin. Under Gorbachev, the Soviet Union began its long-awaited shift to a new generation of leadership. Unlike his immediate predecessors, Gorbachev did not also assume the title of President but wielded power from the post of party General Secretary. In a surprise move, Gorbachev elevated Andrei Gromyko, 75, for 28 years the Soviet Union's stony-faced Foreign Minister, to the largely ceremonial post of President. He installed a younger man with no experience in foreign affairs, Eduard Shevardnadze, 57, as Foreign Minister.

The Soviet Union took much criticism in early 1986 over the April 24 meltdown at the Chernobyl nuclear plant and its reluctance to give out any information on the accident.

In June 1987, Gorbachev obtained the support of the Central Committee for proposals that would loosen some government controls over the economy and in June 1988, an unusually open party conference approved several resolutions for changes in the structure of the Soviet system. These included a shift of some power from the Party to local soviets, and a ten-year limit on the terms of elected government and party officials. Gorbachev was elected President in 1989. The elections to the Congress were the first competitive elections in the Soviet Union since 1917. Dissident candidates won a surprisingly large minority although pro-Government deputies maintained a strong lock on the Supreme Soviet.

The possible beginning of the fragmentation of the Communist party took place when Boris Yeltsin, leader of the Russian S.S.R. who urges faster reform, left the Communist party along with other radicals.

In March 1991 the Soviet people were asked to vote on a referendum on national unity engineered by President Gorbachev. The resultant victory for the federal government was tempered by the separate approval in Russia for the creation of a popularly elected republic presidency. In addition, six republics boycotted the vote.

The bitter election contest for the Russian presidency principally between Yeltsin and a Communist loyalist resulted in a major victory for Yeltsin. He took the oath of office for the new position on July 10.

Reversing his relative hard-line position adopted in the autumn of 1990, Gorbachev together with leaders of nine Soviet republics signed an accord, called the Union Treaty, which was meant to preserve the unity of the nation. In exchange the federal government would have turned over control of industrial and natural resources to the individual republics.

An attempted coup d'état took place on August 19 orchestrated by a group of eight senior officials calling itself the State Committee on the State of Emergency. Boris Yeltsin, barricaded in the Russian Parliament building, defiantly called for a general strike. The next day huge crowds demonstrated in Leningrad, and Yeltsin supporters fortified barricades surrounding the parliament building. On August 21 the coup committee disbanded, and at least some of its members attempted to flee Moscow. The Soviet Parliament formally reinstated Gorbachev as President. Two days later he resigned from his position as General-Secretary of the Communist Party and recommended that its Central Committee be disbanded. On August 29 the Parliament approved the suspension of all Communist Party activities pending an investigation of its role in the failed coup.

At the time of the attempted coup, the republic's President Boris Yeltsin was the most popular political figure in the lands comprising the former Soviet Union. A leading reformer, he became the first directly elected leader in Russian history and received 60% of the vote for President of the Russian Republic.

During the attempted coup in August 1991 by hardline Communists to dislodge Mikhail Gorbachev, Yeltsin risked his life and rallied the opposition against the coup leaders. His heroism won him worldwide acclaim when the coup failed and he gained new stature and influence.

Yeltsin championed the cause for national reconstruction and the adoption of a Union Treaty with the other republics to create a free-market economic association.

Dissolution of the U.S.S.R. On Dec. 12, 1991, the Russian Parliament ratified Yeltsin's plea to establish a new commonwealth of independent nations open to all former members of the Soviet Union. The new union was created with the governments of Ukraine and Belarus who along with Russia were the three original cofounders of the Soviet Union in 1922.

After the end of the Soviet Union, Russia and ten other Soviet republics joined in a Commonwealth of Independent States on Dec. 21, 1991.

At the start of 1992, Russia embarked on a series of dramatic economic reforms, including the freeing of prices on most goods, which led to an immediate downturn.

A national referendum on confidence in Yeltsin and his economic program took place in April 1993. To the surprise of many the President and his shock-therapy program won by a resounding margin. Yeltsin convened a constitutional conference in June, which adopted a draft document in July. In September Yeltsin dissolved the legislative bodies left over from the Soviet era. The impasse between the executive and the legislature resulted in an armed conflict on October 3. Yeltsin prevailed largely through the support of the military and other forces.

The constitutional referendum on December 12 was a victory for Yeltsin, but the parliamentary election on the same day saw the rise of the extreme nationalist Vladimir Zhirinovsky, with western-oriented parties performing relatively poorly.

The southern republic of Chechnya's President accelerated his region's drive for independence in 1994. In December Russian troops closed the borders and sought to squelch the independence drive. The Russian military forces met firm and costly resistance.

Shortly before the scheduled presidential election of June 1996 a ceasefire was arranged in Chechnya. Yeltsin started the year with slim chances for re-election. But bolstered by favorable media attention, fear of a Communist resurgence, and vigorous campaigning he won the second round of voting in July against a Communist opponent.

In May 1997 the two-year war formally ended with

the signing of a peace treaty that adroitly avoided the issue of Chechen independence.

Soon afterward, Yeltsin underwent bypass surgery, recuperation from which prevented him from working in the Kremlin. Opposition grumbling was compounded by Yeltsin's catching pneumonia that further delayed his return to daily work until January 1997.

RWANDA

Rwandese Republic
National name: Republika y'u Rwanda
President: Pasteur Bizimungu (1994)
Prime Minister: Pierre-Céléstin Rwigema (1995)
Area: 10,169 sq mi. (26,338 sq km)
Population (1997 est.): 7,737,537 (average annual rate of natural increase: 1.76%); birth rate: 38.73/1000; infant mortality rate: 118/1000; density per square mile: 760.9
Capital and largest city (1991): Kigali, 232,733. **Monetary unit:** Rwanda franc. **Languages:** Kinyarwanda, French, Swahili, English. **Ethnicity/Race:** Hutu 80%, Tutsi 19%, Twa (Pygmoid) 1%. **Religions:** Roman Catholic, 56%; Protestant, 18%; Islam, 1%; Animist, 25%. **Literacy rate:** 5%
Economic summary: Gross domestic product: purchasing power parity (1995 est.): $3.8 billion; $400 per capita; real growth rate –2.7%; inflation 64% (1994 est.); unemployment n.a. Arable land: 29%. Principal products: coffee, tea, bananas, yams, beans. Labor force: 3.6 million; 93% in agriculture; 5% in government and services; 2% in industry and commerce. Major products: processed foods, light consumer goods, minerals. Natural resources: gold, cassiterite, wolfram. Exports: $52 million (f.o.b., 1994 est.): coffee, tea, tungsten, tin, pyrethrum. Imports: $37 million (1994 est.): textiles, foodstuffs, machinery, and equipment, capital goods, steel. Major trading partners: Belgium, Germany, Kenya, Japan, France, U.S., Italy, U.K.

Geography. Rwanda, in east central Africa, is surrounded by Congo, Uganda, Tanzania, and Burundi. It is slightly smaller than Maryland.

Steep mountains and deep valleys cover most of the country. Lake Kivu in the northwest, at an altitude of 4,829 feet (1,472 m) is the highest lake in Africa. Extending north of it are the Virunga Mountains, which include Volcan Karisimbi (14,187 ft.; 4,324 m), Rwanda's highest point.

Government. A republic. A National Unity government was installed by the Rwandan Patriotic Front on July 19, 1994. Former President Gen. Juvénal Habyarimana was killed on April 6, 1994, in a mysterious plane crash over the capital Kigali. The new cabinet is composed of 22 members. Maj. Gen. Paul Kagame, the victorious Tutsi rebel leader, is both Vice President and defense minister.

History. Rwanda, which was part of German East Africa, was first visited by European explorers in 1854. During World War I, it was occupied in 1916 by Belgian troops. After the war, it became a Belgian League of Nations mandate, along with Burundi, under the name of Ruanda-Urundi. The mandate was made a U.N. trust territory in 1946. Until the Belgian Congo achieved independence in 1960, Ruanda-Urundi was administered as part of that colony.

Ruanda became the independent nation of Rwanda on July 1, 1962. In August 1992 a formal agreement was signed ending the civil war between the government and the Rwandan Patriotic Front.

After the downing of an aircraft in April 1994 carrying the Presidents of Rwanda and Burundi, both of whom died in the crash, deep-seated ethnic hatred erupted and Hutus slaughtered an estimated 800,000 minority Tutsis. Tutsi rebels then swept across the country in a 14-week civil war, routing the largely Hutu government. In the immediate aftermath an estimated 1.7 million Hutus fled across the border into neighboring Zaire (now called The Democratic Republic of Congo), creating an international humanitarian problem.

The tragic ethnic war continued into and through 1995. With the war many fled into neighboring Democratic Republic of Congo. In November 1996 a massive repatriation began, but an estimated half million fled into the forests. In 1997 with the deteriorating situation in the Democratic Republic of Congo, another repatriation operation began.

ST. KITTS AND NEVIS

Federation of St. Kitts and Nevis
Sovereign: Queen Elizabeth II (1952)
Governor General: Sir Cuthbert Montroville Sebastian (1996)
Prime Minister: Dr. Denzil Douglas (1995)
Area: St. Kitts 65 sq mi. (169 sq km); Nevis 35 sq mi. (100 sq km)
Population (1997 est.): 41,803 (average annual rate of natural increase: 1.42%); birth rate: 23.08/1000; infant mortality rate: 18.4/1000; density per square mile: 418
Capital: Basseterre (on St. Kitts), 19,000. **Largest town on Nevis:** Charlestown, 1,771. **Monetary unit:** East Caribbean dollar. **Ethnicity/Race:** black African. **Literacy rate:** 98%
Economic summary: Gross domestic product: purchasing power parity (1995 est.): $220 million; per capita $5,380; real growth rate 3%; inflation –0.9%; unemployment 4.3%. Arable land: 22%. Principal agricultural products: sugar, rice, yams. Labor force: 18,172; 69% in services; 31% in manufacturing. Major industries: tourism, sugar processing, salt extraction. Exports: $35.4 million (f.o.b., 1994 est.): sugar, manufactures, postage stamps. Imports: $112.4 million (f.o.b., 1994 est.): foodstuffs, manufactured goods, machinery, fuels. Major trading partners: U.S., U.K., Japan, Trinidad and Tobago, Canada.

St. Christopher-Nevis, preferably St. Kitts and Nevis, was formerly part of the West Indies Associated States which were established in 1967 and consisted of Antigua and St. Kitts-Nevis-Anguilla of the Leeward Islands, and Dominica, Grenada, St. Lucia, and St. Vincent of the Windward Islands. Statehood for St. Vincent was held up until 1969 because of local political uncertainties. Anguilla's association with St. Christopher-Nevis ended in 1980.

St. Christopher-Nevis, now St. Kitts and Nevis, became independent on September 19, 1983.

The Premier of Nevis in 1990 announced that he intended to seek an end to the federation with St. Kitts by the end of 1992, but a local election in June 1992 removed the threat of succession for the time being.

Parliamentary elections held on July 3, 1995, for the 11 seats resulted in a victory for the opposition Labour Party.

Three trials for murder, the last beginning in May 1997, involving large amounts of cocaine, drew international attention. Each of the trials resulted in a hung jury, and the issue of jury tampering was raised in each case.

ST. LUCIA

Sovereign: Queen Elizabeth II (1952)
Governor-General: H.E. William George Mallet (1996)

Prime Minister: Kenny D. Anthony (1997)
Area: 238 sq mi. (616 sq km)
Population (1997 est.): 159,639 (average annual rate of natural increase: 1.55%); birth rate: 21.54/1000; infant mortality rate: 19.6/1000; density per square mile: 670.7
Capital and largest city (1992 est.): Castries, 13,600.
Monetary unit: East Caribbean dollar. **Languages:** English and patois. **Ethnicity/Race:** African descent 90.3%, mixed 5.5%, East Indian 3.2%, white 0.8%. **Religions:** Roman Catholic, 90%; Protestant, 7%; Anglican, 3%. **Literacy rate:** 90%
Economic summary: Gross domestic product: purchasing power parity (1995 est.): $640 million; $4,080 per capita; real growth rate 2%; inflation 0.8% (1993); unemployment (1993 est.): 25%. Labor force: 43,800; 43.4% in agriculture; 38.9% in services; 17.7% in industry and commerce. Arable land: 8%. Principal products: bananas, coconuts, cocoa, citrus fruit. Major industrial products: clothing, assembled electronics, beverages. Exports: $122.8 million (f.o.b., 1992): bananas, cocoa, clothing, vegetables, fruits, coconut oil. Imports: $276 million (f.o.b., 1992): foodstuffs, machinery and equipment, fertilizers, petroleum products. Major trading partners: U.K., U.S., Caribbean countries, Japan, Canada. **Member of Commonwealth of Nations**

Geography. One of the Windward Isles of the Eastern Caribbean, St. Lucia lies just south of Martinique. It is of volcanic origin. A chain of wooded mountains runs from north to south, and from them flow many streams into fertile valleys.

Government. A governor-general represents the sovereign, Queen Elizabeth II. A Prime Minister is head of government, chosen by a 17-member House of Assembly elected by universal suffrage for a maximum term of five years.

History. Explored by Spain in 1503, and ruled by Spain and then France, St. Lucia became a British territory in 1803. With other Windward Isles, St. Lucia was granted home rule in 1967 as one of the West Indies Associated States. On Feb. 22, 1979, St. Lucia achieved full independence in ceremonies boycotted by the opposition St. Lucia Labor Party, which had advocated a referendum before cutting ties with Britain.

Unrest and a strike by civil servants forced Prime Minister John Compton to hold elections in July, 1979, in which his United Workers Party lost its majority for the first time in 15 years.

A Labor Party government was ousted in turn by Compton and his followers, in elections in May 1982.

Formerly dependent on a single crop, bananas, St. Lucia has sought to lower its chronic unemployment and payments deficit.

Elections of April 1982 returned the Prime Minister and his party once again to office.

Parliamentary elections in May 1997 gave the opposition Labour Party 16 of the 17 seats. Labour had stressed economic issues and corruption. The United Workers Party denied the corruption charges.

ST. VINCENT AND THE GRENADINES

Sovereign: Queen Elizabeth II (1952)
Governor-General: Sir Charles Antrobus (1996)
Prime Minister: James Mitchell (1984)
Area: 150 sq mi. (389 sq km)
Population (1997 est.): 119,092 (average annual rate of natural increase: 1.37%); birth rate: 19.07/1000; infant mortality rate: 16.2/1000; density per square mile: 793.9
Capital and largest city (1992 est.): Kingstown, 15,466.
Monetary unit: East Caribbean dollar. **Language:** English, some French patois. **Ethnicity/Race:** African descent, white, East Indian, Carib Indian. **Religions:** Anglican, 47%; Methodist, 28%; Roman Catholic, 13%. **Literacy rate:** 96%
Economic summary: Gross domestic product: purchasing power parity (1995 est.): $240 million; $2,060 per capita; 0.4% real growth rate; inflation: –0.2%; unemployment: 35–40% (1994 est.). Arable land: 38%. Principal products: bananas, arrowroot, coconuts. Labor Force: 67,000 (1984 est.); in agriculture, industry, services, other. Major industry: food processing. Exports: $57.1 million (f.o.b., 1993): bananas, arrowroot, eddos and dasheen (taro), tennis racquets. Imports: $134.6 million (f.o.b., 1993): foodstuffs, machinery and equipment, chemicals, fuels, minerals. Major trading partners: U.K., U.S., Caribbean nations. **Member of Commonwealth of Nations**

Geography. St. Vincent, chief island of the chain, is 18 miles (29 km) long and 11 miles (18 km) wide. One of the Windward Islands in the Lesser Antilles, it is 100 miles (161 km) west of Barbados. The island is mountainous and well forested. The Grenadines, a chain of nearly 600 islets with a total area of only 17 square miles (27 sq km), extend for 60 miles (96 km) from northeast to southwest between St. Vincent and Grenada, southernmost of the Windwards.

St. Vincent is dominated by the volcano La Soufrière, part of a volcanic range running north and south, which rises to 4,048 feet (1,234 m). The volcano erupted over a 10-day period in April 1979, causing the evacuation of the northern two-thirds of the island. (There is also a volcano of the same name on Basse-Terre, Guadeloupe, which became violently active in 1976 and 1977.)

Government. A governor-general represents the sovereign, Queen Elizabeth II. A Prime Minister, elected by a 15-member unicameral legislature, holds executive power.

History. Explored by Columbus in 1498, and alternately claimed by Britain and France, St. Vincent became a British colony by the Treaty of Paris in 1783. The islands won home rule in 1969 as part of the West Indies Associated States and achieved full independence Oct. 26, 1979. Prime Minister Milton Cato's government quelled a brief rebellion Dec. 8, 1979, attributed to economic problems following the eruption of La Soufrière in April 1979. Unlike the 1902 eruption which killed 2,000, there was no loss of life but widespread losses to agriculture.

The election of February 1994 provided a victory for the Prime Minister and his party albeit with a reduced majority in Parliament. The deputy Prime Minister resigned in September 1995 due to a "financial impropriety."

The country's permanent representative to the Organization of American States assumed the chairmanship of that body's Permanent Council in 1997.

SAN MARINO

Most Serene Republic of San Marino
National name: Repubblica di San Marino
Captains Regent: Paride Andreoli and Pier Marino Mularoni (1997)
Area: 23.6 sq mi. (62 sq km)
Population (1997 est.): 24,714 (average annual growth rate 0.27%); birth rate: 10.68/1000; infant mortality rate: 5.5/1000; density per square mile: 1,047.2

Capital and largest city (1992 est.): San Marino, 2,397. **Monetary unit:** Italian lira. **Language:** Italian. **Ethnicity/Race:** SamMarinese, Italian. **Religion:** Roman Catholic. **Literacy rate:** 96%

Economic summary: Gross domestic product: purchasing power parity (1993 est.): $380 million; $15,800 per capita; 2.4% growth rate; inflation: 5.5%; unemployment: 4.9% (Dec. 93). Arable land: 17%. Principal products: wheat and other grains, grapes, olives, cheese. Labor force: 14,874 (1993 est.); 40% in industry; 2% in agriculture. The tourist sector contributed over 50% of GDP. Key industries are apparel, electronics, and ceramics. Other industrial products: textiles, leather, cement, wine, olive oil. Exports: building stone, lime, chestnuts, wheat, hides, baked goods. Imports: manufactured consumer goods, food. Major trading partner: Italy.

Geography. One-tenth the size of New York City, San Marino is surrounded by Italy. It is situated in the Apennines, a little inland from the Adriatic Sea near Rimini.

Government. The country is governed by two Captains Regent. Executive power is exercised by ten ministers. In 1959, the Grand Council granted women the vote. San Marino is a member of the Conference on Security and Cooperation in Europe.

History. According to tradition, San Marino was founded about C.E. 350 and had good luck for centuries in staying out of the many wars and feuds on the Italian peninsula. It is the oldest republic in the world.

Those born in San Marino remain citizens and can vote no matter where they live.

Spring 1993 elections for the Great and General Council gave a majority to the Christian Democrats and Socialists.

In April 1997 a Socialist, Paride Andreoli, and a Christian Democrat, Pier Mularoni, took office as the Co-Regents.

SÃO TOMÉ AND PRÍNCIPE

Democratic Republic of São Tomé and Príncipe
President: Miguel Trovoada (1991)
Prime Minister: Raul Neto (1997)
Area: 370 sq mi. (958 sq km)
Population (1997 est.): 147,865 (average annual growth rate: 2.53%); birth rate: 33.77/1000; infant mortality rate: 60.2/1000; density per square mile: 399.6
Capital and largest city (1990 est.): São Tomé, 43,420.
Monetary unit: Dobra. **Language:** Portuguese.
Ethnicity/Race: mestico, angolares (descendants of Angolan slaves), forros (descendants of freed slaves), servicais (contract laborers from Angola, Mozambique, and Cape Verde), tongas (children of servicais born on the islands), Europeans (primarily Portuguese).
Religions: Roman Catholic, Evangelical Protestant, Seventh-Day Adventist. **Literacy rate:** 57% (est.)
Economic summary: Gross domestic product: purchasing power parity (1994 est.): $138 million; $1,000 per capita; 1.5% real growth rate; inflation: 38%; unemployment: n.a. Arable land: 1%. Principal agricultural products: cocoa, copra, coconuts, palm oil, coffee, bananas. Labor force: 21,096 (1981): mostly in subsistence agriculture and fishing. Shortages of plantation labor and of skilled workers. Major industrial products: shirts, soap, beer, processed fish and shrimp. Exports: $7.1 million (f.o.b., 1994 est.): cocoa, coffee, copra, palm oil. Imports: $23.8 million (c.i.f., 1994 est.): textiles, machinery, electrical equipment, fuels, food products. Major trading partners: Netherlands, Portugal, Germany, China, Angola.

Geography. The tiny volcanic islands of São Tomé and Príncipe lie in the Gulf of Guinea about 150 miles (240 km) off West Africa. São Tomé (about 330 sq mi.; 859 sq km) is covered by a dense mountainous jungle, out of which have been carved large plantations. Príncipe (about 40 sq mi.; 142 sq km) consists of jagged mountains. Other islands in the republic are Pedras Tinhosas and Rolas.

Government. The constitution grants supreme power to a 55-seat People's Assembly composed of members elected for four years. In 1990 a referendum approved a new constitution paving the way for a multiparty democracy.

History. São Tomé and Príncipe were explored by Portuguese navigators in 1471 and settled by the end of the century. Intensive cultivation by slave labor made the islands a major producer of sugar during the 17th century but output declined until the introduction of coffee and cacao in the 19th century brought new prosperity. The island of São Tomé was the world's largest producer of cacao in 1908 and the crop is still the most important. An exile liberation movement was formed in 1953 after Portuguese landowners quelled labor riots by killing several hundred African workers.

The Portuguese revolution of 1974 brought the end of the overseas empire and the new Lisbon government transferred power to the liberation movement on July 12, 1975.

A former Prime Minister and dissident Miguel Trovoada was elected President in March 1991 after the withdrawal of the two other candidates.

In April 1995 Príncipe became autonomous. In August a bloodless military coup was reversed through Angolan mediation. In December an agreement was struck on forming a coalition government.

President Trovoada won re-election in July 1996 against challenger and former President Pinto da Costa.

Protests erupted in April 1997 when the government, in response to its inability to pay for imported oil, raised gasoline prices 140% in order to stem demand.

SAUDI ARABIA

Kingdom of Saudi Arabia
National name: Al-Mamlaka al-'Arabiya as-Sa'udiya
King and Prime Minister: King Fahd bin 'Abdulaziz (1982)
Area: 865,000 sq mi. (2,250,070 sq km)
Population (1997 est.): 20,087,965 (average annual rate of natural increase: 3.26%); birth rate: 37.94/1000; infant mortality rate: 43.9/1000; density per square mile: 23.2
Capital: Riyadh. **Largest cities (1993):** Riyadh, 3,000,000; Jeddah, 2,500,000; Makkah (Mecca) (1994 est.) 550,000. **Monetary unit:** Riyal. **Language:** Arabic, English widely spoken. **Ethnicity/Race:** Arab 90%, Afro-Asian 10%. **Religion:** Islam, 100%. **Literacy rate:** 65%
Economic summary: Gross domestic product: purchasing power parity (1995 est.): $189.3 billion; $10,100 per capita; real growth rate: 0%; inflation 5%; unemployment: 6.5% (1992 est.). Arable land: 5%. Principal agricultural products: dates, grains, livestock, wheat, fish, flowers. Labor force: 6–7 million; 40% in government; 25% in industry and oil; 30% in services; 5% in agriculture. Major industrial products: petroleum, cement, plastic products, steel, packaged goods. Natural resources: oil, natural gas, iron ore. Exports: $41.7 billion (f.o.b., 1994 est.): petroleum and petroleum products. Imports: $21.3 billion (f.o.b., 1994

est.): manufactured goods, transport equipment, construction materials, processed food. Major trading partners: U.S., Germany, U.K. and other Western European countries, South Korea, Taiwan, Japan.

Geography. Saudi Arabia occupies most of the Arabian Peninsula, with the Red Sea and the Gulf of Aqaba to the west, the Arabian Gulf to the east. Neighboring countries are Jordan, Iraq, Kuwait, Qatar, the United Arab Emirates, the Sultanate of Oman, Yemen, and Bahrain, connected to the Saudi mainland by a causeway.

A narrow coastal plain on the Red Sea rims a mountain range that spans the length of the western coastline. These mountains gradually rise in elevation from north to south. East of these mountains is a massive plateau that slopes gently downward toward the Arabian Gulf. Part of this plateau is covered by the world's largest continuous sand desert, the Rub Al-Khali, or Empty Quarter. Saudi Arabia's oil region lies primarily in the eastern province along the Arabian Gulf, but significant recent discoveries have also been made in the interior south of Riyadh.

Government. Saudi Arabia is a monarchy based on the Sharia (Islamic law), as revealed in the Koran (the holy book) and the Hadith (teachings and sayings of the prophet Mohammed). A Council of Ministers was formed in 1953, which acts as a cabinet under the leadership of the King. There are 21 ministries.

Royal and ministerial decrees account for most of the promulgated legislation, treaties, and conventions. There are no political parties.

In March 1992 King Fahd announced new bylaws for the Consultative Council to propose and review laws. The cabinet, composed of 21 members (four are members of the Saudi royal family) passes laws.

History. Mohammed united the Arabs in the 7th century, and his followers, led by the caliphs, founded a great empire, with its capital at Medina. Later, the caliphate capital was transferred to Damascus and then Baghdad, but Arabia retained its importance because of the holy cities of Mecca and Medina. In the 16th and 17th centuries, the Turks established at least nominal rule over much of Arabia, and in the middle of the 18th century, it was divided into separate principalities.

The Kingdom of Saudi Arabia is almost entirely the creation of King Ibn Saud (1882–1953). A descendant of earlier Wahabi rulers, he seized Riyadh, the capital of Nejd, in 1901 and set himself up as leader of the Arab nationalist movement. By 1906 he had established Wahabi dominance in Nejd. He conquered Hejaz in 1924–25, consolidating it and Nejd into a dual Kingdom in 1926. In 1932, Hejaz and Nejd became a single Kingdom, which was officially named Saudi Arabia. A year later the region of Asir was incorporated into the Kingdom.

Oil was discovered in 1936, and commercial production began during World War II. Saudi Arabia was neutral until nearly the end of the war, but it was permitted to be a charter member of the United Nations. The country joined the Arab League in 1945 and took part in the 1948–49 war against Israel.

On Ibn Saud's death in 1953, his eldest son, Saud, began an 11-year reign marked by an increasing hostility toward the radical Arabism of Egypt's Gamal Abdel Nasser. In 1964, the ailing Saud was deposed and replaced by the Premier, Crown Prince Faisal, who gave vocal support but no military help to Egypt in the 1967 Mideast war.

Faisal's assassination by a deranged kinsman in 1975 shook the Middle East, but failed to alter his Kingdom's course. His successor was his brother, Prince Khalid. Khalid gave influential support to Egypt during negotiations on Israeli withdrawal from the Sinai desert.

King Khalid died of a heart attack June 13, 1982, and was succeeded by his half-brother, Prince Fahd bin 'Abdulaziz, 60, who had exercised the real power throughout Khalid's reign. King Fahd, a pro-Western modernist, chose his 58-year-old half-brother, Abdullah, as Crown Prince.

Saudi Arabia and the smaller, oil-rich Arab states on the Persian Gulf, fearful that they might become Ayatollah Ruhollah Khomeini's next targets if Iran conquered Iraq, made large financial contributions to the Iraqi war effort. They began being dragged into the conflict themselves in the spring of 1984, when Iraq and Iran extended their ground war to attacks on Gulf shipping. First, Iraq attacked tankers loading at Iran's Kharg Island terminal with air-to-ground missiles, then Iran struck back at tankers calling at Saudi Arabia and other Arab countries.

At the same time, cheating by other members of the Organization of Petroleum Exporting Countries, competition from nonmember oil producers, and conservation efforts by consuming nations combined to drive down the world price of oil. Saudi Arabia has one-third of all known oil reserves, but falling demand and rising production outside OPEC combined to reduce its oil revenues from $120 billion in 1980 to $43 billion in 1984 to less the $25 billion in 1985, threatening the country with domestic unrest and undermining its influence in the Gulf area.

At the start of 1996 King Faud passed authority to his half-brother Abdullah, saying he needed rest. Although not an abdication, it was unclear how long the King would be absent.

A fire and the accompanying stampede in a crowded tent killed more than 300 in April 1997. The victims were on a pilgrimage to Mecca.

SENEGAL

Republic of Senegal
National name: République du Sénégal
President: Abdou Diouf (1981)
Prime Minister: Habib Thiam (1991)
Area: 75,954 sq mi. (196,722 sq km)
Population (1997 est.): 9,403,546 (average annual rate of natural increase: 3.35%); birth rate: 44.91/1000; infant mortality rate: 62.6/1000; density per square mile: 123.8
Capital and largest city (1994 est.): Dakar, 1,729,823.
Monetary unit: Franc CFA. **Ethnicity/Race:** Wolof 36%, Fulani 17%, Serer 17%, Toucouleur 9%, Diola 9%, Mandingo 9%, European and Lebanese 1%, other 2%. **Languages:** French (official); Wolof, Serer, other ethnic dialects. **Religions:** Islam, 92%; indigenous, 6%; Christian, 2%. **Literacy rate:** 38%
Economic summary: Gross domestic product: purchasing power parity (1995 est.): $14.5 billion; $1,600 per capita; real growth rate 4.5%; inflation 6.1%; unemployment n.a. Arable land: 27%. Principal agricultural products: peanuts, millet, corn, rice, sorghum. Labor force: 2.509 million; 77% subsistence-level agriculture workers; less than 1% wage earners (private sector 40%; government and parapublic 60%). Major industrial products: processed food, phosphates, refined petroleum, cement, and fish. Natural resources: fish, phosphate, iron ore. Exports: $940 million (f.o.b., 1994 est.): peanuts, phosphate rock, canned fish, petroleum products. Imports: $1.1 billion (c.i.f., 1994 est.): foodstuffs, consumer goods, machinery, transport equipment, petroleum. Major trading partners: U.S., Western European countries, African neighbors, Japan, China, India.

Geography. The capital of Senegal, Dakar, is the westernmost point in Africa. The country, slightly smaller than South Dakota, surrounds Gambia on three sides and is bordered on the north by Mauritania, on the east by Mali, and on the south by Guinea and Guinea-Bissau.

Senegal is mainly a low-lying country, with a semi-desert area in the north and northeast and forests in the southwest. The largest rivers include the Senegal in the north and the Casamance in the south tropical climate region.

Government. There is a National Assembly of 120 members, elected every five years. There is universal suffrage and a constitutional guarantee of equality before the law.

History. The Portuguese had some stations on the banks of the Senegal River in the 15th century, and the first French settlement was made at Saint-Louis about 1650. The British took parts of Senegal at various times, but the French gained possession in 1840 and organized the Sudan as a territory in 1904. In 1946, together with other parts of French West Africa, Senegal became part of the French Union. On June 20, 1960, it became an independent republic federated with the Sudanese Republic in the Mali Federation, from which it withdrew two months later.

In 1973, Senegal joined with six other states to create the West African Economic Community.

In elections of February 21, 1993, President Diouf was re-elected. In May legislative elections the President's Socialist Party captured 84 of the 120 seats.

An opposition leader became a member of a new coalition government in March 1995.

In June 1997 the government announced its intended sale of 49% of the state-owned, highly profitable electric company SENELEC to a private firm. The government would retain the majority share.

SEYCHELLES

Republic of Seychelles
President: France-Albert René (1977)
Area: 175 sq mi. (453 sq km)
Population (1997 est.): 78,142 (average annual rate of natural increase: 1.39%); birth rate: 20.53/1000; infant mortality rate: 12.1/1000; density per square mile: 446.5
Capital and largest city (1993 est.): Victoria, 25,000.
Monetary unit: Seychelles rupee. **Languages:** English and French (official); Creole. **Ethnicity/Race:** Seychellois (mixture of Asians, Africans, Europeans). **Religions:** Roman Catholic, 90%; Anglican, 8%. **Literacy rate:** 58%
Economic summary: Gross domestic product: purchasing power parity (1993 est.): $430 million; $6,000 per capita; real growth rate –2%; inflation: 3.9%; unemployment 9%. Arable land: 4%. Principal agricultural products: vanilla, coconuts, cinnamon. Labor force: 27,700; 31% in industry and commerce; 21% in services; 20% in government; 12% in agriculture, forestry, and fishing. Major industrial products: processed coconut and vanilla, coir rope. Exports: $50 million (f.o.b., 1993 est.): fish, canned tuna, copra, cinnamon bark. Imports: $261 million (f.o.b., 1993 est.): food, tobacco, manufactured goods, machinery, petroleum products, transport equipment. Major trading partners: U.K., France, Japan, Pakistan, Reunion, South Africa. **Member of Commonwealth of Nations**

Geography. Seychelles consists of an archipelago of about 100 islands in the Indian Ocean northeast of Madagascar. The principal islands are Mahé (55 sq mi.; 142 sq km), Praslin (15 sq mi.; 38 sq km), and La Digue (4 sq mi.; 10 sq km). The Aldabra, Farquhar, and Desroches groups are included in the territory of the republic.

Government. A multiparty republic with one legislative house, the National Assembly. Seized from France by Britain in 1810, the Seychelles Islands remained a colony until June 29, 1976. The state is an independent republic within the Commonwealth.

On June 5, 1977, Prime Minister Albert René ousted the islands' first President, James Mancham, suspending the constitution and the 25-member National Assembly. Mancham, whose "lavish spending" and flamboyance were cited by René in seizing power, charged that Soviet influence was at work. The new President denied this and, while more left than his predecessor, pledged to keep the Seychelles in the nonaligned group of countries.

An unsuccessful attempted coup against René attracted international attention when a group of 50 South African mercenaries posing as rugby players attacked the Victoria airport on Nov. 25, 1981.

An election was held in July 1992 for members of a commission to write a new constitution. Fourteen of the 23 seats went to the President's Seychelles People's Progressive Party. The draft constitution that emerged, however, was defeated in a referendum in November, failing to get the 60% of the vote needed for adoption.

The commission reconvened in January 1993 with the participation of the opposition Democratic Party. In May a draft constitution, institutionalizing a multiparty system and a 33-member National Assembly, was ready. In the June referendum more than 73% of the votes approved it. The presidential election in July under the new terms affirmed René's position and that of his party.

To increase revenue the government in 1996 quietly initiated an Economic Citizenship Program that provides foreigners with the opportunity to obtain a Seychelles passport upon payment of $25,000. A new law in late 1995 granted immunity from criminal prosecution to anyone investing $10 million in the country.

SIERRA LEONE

Republic of Sierra Leone
President: Johnny Paul Koroma (1997)
Area: 27,925 sq mi (73,326 sq km)
Population (1997 est.): 4,891,546 (average annual rate of natural increase: 2.89%); birth rate: 46.67/1000; infant mortality rate: 132.5/1000; density per square mile: 175.2
Capital and largest city (1994 est.): Freetown, 1,300,000. **Monetary unit:** Leone. **Languages:** English (official), Mende, Temne, Krio. **Ethnicity/Race:** 13 native African tribes 99% (Temne 30%, Mende 30%, other 39%), Creole, European, Lebanese, and Asian 1%. **Religions:** Islam, 40%, Christian, 35%; Indigenous, 20%. **Literacy rate:** 21%
Economic summary: Gross domestic product: purchasing power parity (1994 est.): $4.4 billion; $960 per capita; real growth rate –4%; inflation 24%; unemployment n.a. Arable land: 25%; principal agricultural products: coffee, cocoa, palm kernels, rice. Labor force: 1.369 million; 65% in agriculture; 19% in industry; 16% in services. Major industrial products: diamonds, bauxite, rutile, beverages, cigarettes, textiles, footwear. Natural resources: diamonds, bauxite, iron ore. Exports: $115 million (f.o.b., 1994): diamonds, rutile, bauxite, cocoa, coffee. Imports: $150 million (c.i.f., 1994): food, petroleum, products, capital goods. Major trading partners: U.K., U.S., Western European countries, Japan, China, Nigeria. **Member of Commonwealth of Nations**

Geography. Sierra Leone, on the Atlantic Ocean in West Africa, is half the size of Illinois. Guinea, in the north and east, and Liberia, in the south, are its neighbors.

Mangrove swamps lie along the coast, with wooded hills and a plateau in the interior. The eastern region is mountainous.

Government. Sierra Leone became an independent nation on April 27, 1961, and declared itself a republic on April 19, 1971.

Sierra Leone became a one party state under the aegis of the All People's Congress Party in April 1978.

A military government came into power in April 1992 but was replaced by a democratically elected President and an independent parliament in March 1996.

History. The coastal area of Sierra Leone was ceded to English settlers in 1788 as a home for blacks discharged from the British armed forces and also for runaway slaves who had found asylum in London. The British protectorate over the hinterland was proclaimed in 1896.

After elections in 1967, the British governor-general replaced Sir Albert Margai, head of the Sierra Leone People's Party (SLPP), which had held power since independence, with Siaka Stevens, head of All People's Congress (APC), as Prime Minister. The army took over the government; then another coup in April 1968 restored civilian rule and put the military leaders in jail.

A coup attempt early in 1971 by the army commander was apparently foiled by loyal army officers, but the then Prime Minister Stevens called in troops of neighboring Guinea's army, under a 1970 mutual defense pact, to guard his residence. After perfunctorily blaming the U.S. for the coup attempt, Stevens switched Governors-General, changed the constitution, and ended up with a republic, of which he was first President. Dr. Stevens's picked successor, Major-General Joseph Saidu Momoh was elected unopposed on Oct. 1, 1985.

Rebel soldiers in April 1992 toppled the government, voicing support for democracy. A few days later the ruling junta arrested their leader, placing in charge their second-in-command.

The government in December 1993 announced a timetable for a return to civilian rule and a multiparty democracy. Nevertheless, rebels continued to reject a government they considered corrupt.

A military coup ousted the country's military leader and President in January 1996. Nevertheless, a multi-party presidential election proceeded in February, despite being marred by violence. As no one received a majority, a runoff was necessary. As the second-round votes were counted in March a ceasefire with the rebels was announced. People's Party candidate Ahmed Tejan Kabbah won with 59.4% of the votes. In November 1996, a peace treaty was signed by the government and the Revolutionary United Front, ending a civil rebellion.

A military coup ousted President Kabbah's civilian government in May 1997 and successfully battled Nigerian soldiers poised in the capital to prevent such and event. In June the leader of the coup, Major Johnny Paul Koroma, became Head of State, promising to return the country eventually to democratic rule.

SINGAPORE

Republic of Singapore
President: Ong Teng Cheong (1993)
Prime Minister: Goh Chok Tong (1990)
Area: 246.7 sq mi. (639 sq km)
Population (1997 est.): 3,461,929 (average annual rate of natural increase: 1.16%); birth rate: 16.25/1000; infant mortality rate: 4.7/1000; density per square mile: 14,032.9

Capital (1992 est.): Singapore, 2,792,000. **Monetary unit:** Singapore dollar. **Languages:** Malay, Chinese (Mandarin), Tamil, English. **Ethnicity/Race:** Chinese 76.4%, Malay 14.9%, Indian 6.4%, other 2.3%. **Religions:** Islam, Christian, Buddhist, Hindu, Taoist. **Literacy rate:** 91.3%

Economic summary: Gross domestic product: purchasing power parity (1995 est.): $66.1 billion; $22,900 per capita; real growth rate 8.9%; inflation 1.7%; unemployment 2.6%. Arable land: 4%. Principal agricultural products: poultry, rubber, copra, vegetables, fruits. Labor force: (1994): 1.649 million; 25.6% in manufacturing; 22.9% in commerce; 33.5% in financial and business services; 6.6% in construction; other 11.4%. Major industries: petroleum refining, ship repair, electronics, financial and business services, biotechnology. Exports: $119.6 billion (1995 est.): petroleum products, rubber, manufactured goods, electrical and electronics, computers and computer peripherals. Imports: $125.9 billion (1995): aircraft, petroleum, chemicals, foodstuffs. Major trading partners: U.S., E.U., Hong Kong, Japan, Malaysia. **Member of Commonwealth of Nations**

Geography. The Republic of Singapore consists of the main island of Singapore, off the southern tip of the Malay Peninsula between the South China Sea and the Indian Ocean, and 58 nearby islands.

There are extensive mangrove swamps extending inland from the coast, which is broken by many inlets.

Government. There is a cabinet, headed by the Prime Minister, and a Parliament of 81 members elected by universal suffrage.

History. Singapore, founded in 1819 by Sir Stamford Raffles, became a separate crown colony of Britain in 1946, when the former colony of the Straits Settlements was dissolved. The other two settlements—Penang and Malacca—were transferred to the Union of Malaya, and the small island of Labuan was transferred to North Borneo. The Cocos (or Keeling) Islands and Christmas Island were transferred to Australia in 1955 and in 1958, respectively.

Singapore attained full internal self-government in 1959. On Sept. 16, 1963, it joined Malaya, Sabah (North Borneo), and Sarawak in the Federation of Malaysia. It withdrew from the Federation on Aug. 9, 1965, and proclaimed itself a republic the next month.

A law of January 1991 expanded the powers of the presidency. In August the ruling People's Action Party won 36 of the 40 contested parliamentary seats.

The first direct presidential election took place in August 1993. Ong Teng Cheong faced what initially appeared to be only token opposition but which took 40% of the vote.

The government announced in August 1994 that unwed mothers could no longer receive subsidized housing.

parliamentary elections on New Year's Day, 1997 gave the ruling People's Action Party 34 of the 36 contested seats. For the other 47 seats the PAP ran unopposed.

SLOVAKIA

Republic of Slovakia
President: Michal Kovác (1993)
Prime Minister: Vladimir Meciar (1994)
Area: 18,917 sq mi. (48,995 sq km)
Population (1997 est.): 5,393,016. (Average annual rate

of natural increase: 0.34%); birth rate: 12.78/1000; infant mortality rate: 10.6/1000; density per square mile: 285.1

Capital and largest city (1993 est.): Bratislava, 446,600. **Other large city (1993 est.):** Kosice, 237,300. **Monetary unit:** Koruna. **Language:** Slovak (official), Hungarian. **Ethnicity/Race:** Slovak 85.7%, Hungarian 10.7%, Gypsy 1.5%, Czech 1%, Ruthenian 0.3%, Ukrainian 0.3%, German 0.1%, Polish 0.1%. **Religions:** Roman Catholic 60.3%, atheist 9.7%, Protestant 8.4%, Orthodox 4.1%, other 17.5%. **Literacy rate:** 99%

Economic summary: Gross domestic product: purchasing power parity (1995 est.): $39 billion; $7,200 per capita; real growth rate: 6%; inflation: 7.5%; unemployment: 13%. Industries: iron and nonferrous mining, metal processing, shipbuilding, construction materials, consumer appliances, and leather goods. Labor force: 2.484 million; 33.2% in industry; 12.2% in agriculture; 10.3% in construction; 44.3% in communication and other. Major agricultural products: grains, potatoes, sugar beets, fruit, vegetables, forestry. Livestock: pigs, cattle, poultry, sheep. Land use: 37% forest and woodland, 13% meadows and pastures, 1% permanent crops, 9% other. Exports: $8.8 billion (f.o.b., Jan.–Nov. 95): machinery and transport equipment, chemicals, fuels, minerals, metals, agricultural products. Imports: $8.7 billion (f.o.b., Jan.–Nov. 95): machinery, transport equipment, fuels and lubricants, manufactured goods, raw materials, chemicals, agricultural products. Major trading partners: Czech Republic, C.I.S. republics, Germany, Poland, Austria, Hungary, Italy, U.K., U.S., Switzerland.

Geography. Slovakia is bordered by Poland in the north, Ukraine in the east, Hungary in the south, Austria in the southwest, and the Czech Republic in the west. The land has rugged mountains, rich in mineral resources, with vast forests and pastures. Southern Slovakia includes a river island called "Zitny Ostrov," with fertile soil. Slovakia is about twice the size of the state of Maryland.

Government. A parliamentary democracy. The President is elected to a five-year term by the unicameral National Council (legislative branch). The 150 members of the National Council are elected for a four-year term.

History. Present day Slovakia was settled by Slavic Slovaks about the 5th century C.E. They were politically united in the Moravian empire in the 9th century. In 907, the Germans and the Magyars conquered the Moravian state and the Slovaks fell under Hungarian control from the 10th century up until 1918.

When the Hapsburg state collapsed in 1918 following World War I, the Slovaks joined the Czech lands of Bohemia, Moravia, and part of Silesia to form the new joint state of Czechoslovakia.

In March 1939, Germany occupied Czechoslovakia, established a German "protectorate," and created a puppet state out of Slovakia with Monsignor Josef Tiso as Premier. The country was liberated from the Germans by the Soviet army in the spring of 1945, and Slovakia was restored to its pre-war status and rejoined to a new Czechoslovakian state.

After the Communist party took power in February 1948, Slovakia was again subjected to a centralized Czech-dominated government and antagonism between the two republics developed. On January 1969, the nation became the Slovak Socialist Republic of Czechoslovakia.

Nearly 42 years of Communist rule for Slovakia ended when Vaclav Havel became President of Czechoslovakia in 1989 and democratic political reform began. However, with the demise of Communist power, a

strong Slovak nationalist movement resurfaced and the rival relationship between the two states increased.

By the end of 1991, tensions heightened between Slovak and Czech political leaders following a debate over a Declaration of Slovak Sovereignty proclaimed by the Slovak parliament. Various attempts to resolve the issue by both parties failed. A crisis developed over whether the Czech and Slovak republics should continue to coexist within the federal structure or divide into two independent states.

The results of the general election in June 1992 failed to affirm the continuing coexistence of the Czech and Slovak Republics within a federal state and resulted in the Czech and Slovak political leaders agreeing to separate their nations into two fully independent republics. The Republic of Slovakia came into existence on January 1, 1993. The Parliament in February elected Michael Kovac President.

Nationalist Prime Minister Vladimir Meciar lost a vote of confidence in March 1994. A coalition of 5 parties chose the more moderate Josef Moravcik to form a new government.

General elections later that year produced an unexpectedly strong showing for Meciar's party, thrusting him again into the premiership.

Meciar signed a bilateral treaty with Hungary in March 1995, but it failed to end concern for ethnic minorities.

A referendum in May 1997 on whether the country should join NATO was boycotted by 90% of the electorate after it turned into a showdown between the Prime Minister and the President, who wanted a question about direct election of the President placed on the ballot.

SLOVENIA

Republic of Slovenia
President: Milan Kucan (1990)
Prime Minister: Janez Drnovsek (1992)
Area: 7,819 sq mi. (20,256 sq km)
Population (1997 est.): 1,945,998. Birth rate: 8.24/1000; infant mortality rate: 7.3/1000; density per square mile: 248.9
Capital and largest city (1996 est.): Ljubljana, 330,000. **Other large city:** Maribor, 103,512. **Monetary unit:** Slovenian Tolar. **Languages:** Slovenian; most can also speak Serbo-Croatian. **Ethnicity/Race:** Slovene 91%, Serbo-Croation, 7%; other, 2%. **Religions:** predominantly Roman Catholic. **Literacy rate:** 99%
Economic summary: Gross domestic product: purchasing power parity (1995 est.): $22.6 billion; $11,000 per capita; real growth rate 4.8%; inflation 8%; unemployment: 8%. Labor force: 786,036; 2% in agriculture; 46% in manufacturing and mining. Principal products are corn, rye, oats, potatoes, fruit, livestock raising, and forestry. Mineral resources include coal, timber, and natural gas. Major manufactured products are automobiles, iron and steel, cement, chemicals, textiles, furniture, shoes, electrical machinery, pharmaceuticals. Exports: $8.3 billion (f.o.b., 1995 est.): machinery and transport equipment, 38%; other manufactured goods, 44%; chemicals, 9%; food and live animals, 4.6%; raw materials, 3%. Imports: $9.1 billion (f.o.b., 1995 est.): machinery and transport equipment, 35%; other manufactured goods, 26.7%; chemicals, 14.5%; raw materials, 9.4%; fuels and lubricants, 7%. Trading partners: Germany, Italy, France, Croatia, Austria, Russia, Macedonia, U.S.

Geography. Slovenia occupies an area about the size of the state of Massachusetts. It borders Austria on the north, Hungary in the northeast, the Republic of Croatia in the south, and Italy and the Adriatic Sea in the west. It is largely a mountainous republic and almost half of the land is forested, with hilly plains spread across the central and eastern regions. Mount Triglav, the highest peak, rises to 9,393 ft. (2,864 m).

Government. A parliamentary democracy with two legislative houses consisting of an 90-member National Assembly and 40-member State Council.

History. The Slovenes were a south-Slavic group that settled in the region during the 6th century C.E. During the 7th century, they established the Slavic state of Samu, which owed its allegiance to the Avars, who dominated the Hungarian plain until Charlemagne defeated them in the late 8th century.

In the 11th century, Slovenia was a separate province of the Kingdom of Hungary. When the Hungarians were defeated by the Turks in 1526, Hungary accepted Austrian Hapsburg rule in order to escape Turkish domination. Thus, Slovenia and Croatia became part of the Austro-Hungarian Kingdom when the dual-monarchy was established in 1857.

After 1848, nationalism was revived in Slovenia and following the defeat and collapse of Austria-Hungary in World War I, Slovenia declared its independence. It formally joined with Montenegro, Serbia, and Croatia on Dec. 4, 1918, to form the new nation called the Kingdom of the Serbs, Croats, and Slovenes. The name was later changed to Yugoslavia in 1929.

During World War II, Germany occupied Yugoslavia and Slovenia was divided among Germany, Italy, and Hungary. For the duration of the war many Slovenes fought a guerrilla warfare against the Nazis under the leadership of the Croatian-born communist resistance leader, Marshal Tito. After the final defeat of the Axis powers in 1945, Slovenia was again made into a republic of the newly established nation of Yugoslavia.

Slovenia declared its independence from Yugoslavia on June 25, 1991. The Serbian-dominated Yugoslavian army tried to keep Slovenia in line and some brief fighting took place, but the Yugoslavian army withdrew its forces and, unlike neighboring Croatia, Slovenia was able to maintain a peaceful status.

A coalition government of the Liberal Democrats and the Christian Democrats was formed in January 1993 in the wake of the December 1992 election.

The Prime Minister won re-election by parliament to that post in January 1997, but in early February his proposed government was rebuffed. Later in the month parliament approved a new government.

In April 1997 all of the country's political parties declared their support for membership in NATO.

SOLOMON ISLANDS

Sovereign: Queen Elizabeth II (1952)
Governor-General: Sir Moses Pitakaka (1994)
Prime Minister: Hon. Solomon Mamaloni (1994)
Area: 11,500 sq mi. (29,785 sq km)
Population (1997 est.): 426,855 (average annual rate of natural increase: 3.29%); birth rate: 37.28/1000; infant mortality rate: 24.9/1000; density per square mile: 37.1
Capital and largest city (1990 est.): Honiara (on Guadalcanal), 35,288. **Monetary unit:** Solomon Islands dollar. **Languages:** English, Solomon Pijin, 80 other languages and dialects. **Ethnicity/Race:** Melanesian 93%, Polynesian 4%, Micronesian 1.5%, European 0.8%, Chinese 0.3%, other 0.4%. **Religions:** Anglican; Roman Catholic; South Seas Evangelical; Seventh-Day Adventist, United (Methodist) Church, other Protestant. **Literacy rate:** 30%
Economic summary: Gross domestic product: purchasing power parity (1992 est.): $1 billion; $2,590 per capita; real growth rate 8%; inflation 13%. Arable land: 1%. Principal agricultural products: coconuts, palm oil, rice, cocoa, yams, pigs. Labor force: 26,842; 23.7% in agriculture, forestry, fishing; 41.5% in services; 21.7% in commerce, transport and finance; 13.1% in construction, manufacturing and mining. Major industrial products: processed fish, copra. Natural resources: fish, timber, gold, bauxite. Exports: $94 million (f.o.b., 1993): fish, timber, copra, palm oil. Imports: $101 million (c.i.f., 1993): machinery and transport equipment, foodstuffs, fuel. Major trading partners: Japan, E.U., Australia, Thailand, Singapore, Hong Kong, China. **Member of British Commonwealth**

Geography. A scattered archipelago of mountainous islands and low-lying coral atolls, the Solomon Islands lie east of Papua New Guinea and northeast of Australia in the south Pacific. The islands include: Guadalcanal, Malaita, Santa Isabel, San Cristóbal, Choiseul, New Georgia, Santa Cruz group, and numerous smaller islands.

Government. After 85 years of British rule, the Solomons achieved independence July 7, 1978. The crown is represented by a governor-general and legislative power is vested in a unicameral legislature of 47 members, led by the Prime Minister.

History. Explored in 1567 by Alvaro de Mendana, the Solomons were not visited again for about 200 years. In 1886, Great Britain and Germany divided the islands between them. In 1914, Australian forces took over the German islands and the Solomons became an Australian mandate in 1920. In World War II, most of the islands were occupied by the Japanese. American forces landed on Guadalcanal on Aug. 7, 1942.

The general election in May 1993 resulted in a loss of parliamentary majority for Prime Minister Mamaloni. The National Coalition Partners, an alliance of 7 groups, formed a new government.

Francis Billy Hilly served as Prime Minister in 1993–94, but in early November Mamalonie assumed the post for the third time. The new government promised to urge the privatization of the public sector.

The civil war in nearby Papua New Guinea threatened to involve the Solomon Islands in mid-1997 when suspicions arose that hit-men from PNG had arrived to assassinate rebel leaders who were staying in Honiara.

SOMALIA

Somali Democratic Republic
National name: Al Jumhouriya As-Somalya al-Dimocradia
President: Vacant, no functioning government in place
Prime Minister: Vacant
Area: 246,199 sq mi. (637,655 sq km)
Population (1997 est.): 9,940,232 (average annual rate of natural increase: 3.05%); birth rate: 43.53/1000; infant mortality rate: 118/1000; density per square mile: 40.4
Capital and largest city (1990 est.): Mogadishu, 900,000. **Monetary unit:** Somali shilling. **Language:** Somali (official), Arabic, English, Italian. **Ethnicity/Race:** Somali 85%, Bantu, Arabs. **Religion:** Islam (Sunni). **Literacy rate:** 24%
Economic summary: Political turmoil in 1991–92 resulted in widespread famine and a substantial drop in economic output. Much of the economy has been devastated by the civil war. Agriculture is most important sector with livestock accounting for about 40% of GDP and about 65% of export earnings. Gross

domestic product: purchasing power parity (1995 est.): $3.6 billion; $500 per capita; real growth rate: 2%. Arable land: 2%. Principal agricultural products: livestock, bananas, sorghum, cereals, sugar cane, maize. Labor force: 3.7 million (1993 est.); very few are skilled laborers. A few small industries: sugar refining, textiles, petroleum refining. Natural resources: uranium. Exports: $100 million (1995 est.): livestock, skins and hides, bananas. Imports: $249 million (1990 est.): textiles, foodstuffs, construction materials and equipment, petroleum products. Major trading partners: Saudi Arabia, Italy, U.S., U.K., Germany.

Geography. Somalia, situated in the Horn of Africa, lies along the Gulf of Aden and the Indian Ocean. It is bounded by Djibouti in the northwest, Ethiopia in the west, and Kenya in the southwest. In area it is slightly smaller than Texas. Generally arid and barren, Somalia has two chief rivers, the Shebelle and the Juba.

Government. None. Last President was overthrown in January 1991 and Somalia was plunged into anarchy.

History. From the 7th to the 10th century, Arab and Persian trading posts were established along the coast of present-day Somalia. Nomadic tribes occupied the interior, occasionally pushing into Ethiopian territory. In the 16th century, Turkish rule extended to the northern coast and the Sultans of Zanzibar gained control in the south.

After British occupation of Aden in 1839, the Somali coast became its source of food. The French established a coaling station in 1862 at the site of Djibouti and the Italians planted a settlement in Eritrea. Egypt, which for a time claimed Turkish rights in the area, was succeeded by Britain. By 1920, a British protectorate and an Italian protectorate occupied what is now Somalia. The British ruled the entire area after 1941, with Italy returning in 1950 to serve as United Nations trustee for its former territory.

In mid-1960, Britain and Italy granted independence to their respective sectors, enabling the two to join as the Republic of Somalia on July 1. Somalia broke diplomatic relations with Britain in 1963 when the British granted the Somali-populated Northern Frontier District of Kenya to the Republic of Kenya.

On Oct. 15, 1969, President Abdi Rashid Ali Shermarke was assassinated and the army seized power, dissolving the legislature and arresting all government leaders. Maj. Gen. Mohamed Siad Barre, as President of a renamed Somali Democratic Republic, leaned heavily toward the U.S.S.R.

In 1977, Somalia openly backed rebels in the easternmost area of Ethiopia, the Ogaden desert, which had been seized by Ethiopia at the turn of the century.

Somalia acknowledged defeat in an eight-month war against the Ethiopians that year, having lost much of its 32,000-man army and most of its tanks and planes.

President Siad Barre fled the country in late January 1991. His departure left Somalia in the hands of a number of clan-based guerrilla groups, none of which trusted each other.

U.S. troops were sent in to protect the delivery of food in December 1992. In May the U.N. took control of the relief efforts from the U.S. The warlord Mohammed Farah Aidid ambushed U.N. troops and dragged American bodies through the streets, causing an about-face in America's willingness to involve itself in the fate of this anarchic country. Peace talks in Kenya appeared to be moving slowly but steadily toward an agreement on an interim government, at least in principle, when on March 23, 1994, they collapsed. The last of the U.S. troops left in late March, leaving 19,000 U.N. troops behind.

In January 1997 leaders of 26 factions agreed to establish a National Salvation Council to provide a central government. Notably, Hussein Aidid, son of the late Mohammed Aidid and self-appointed President, boycotted the meeting. In May Aidid and Ali Mahdi Mohamed announced a cease-fire between their factions and the start of peace talks. This was their third agreed cease-fire.

SOUTH AFRICA

Republic of South Africa
National name: Republic of South Africa
President: Nelson Mandela (1994)
Deputy President: Thabo Mbeki
Area: 471,440 sq mi. (1,221,030 sq km)
Population (1997 est.): 42,327,458 (average annual rate of natural increase: 1.5%); birth rate: 26.89/1000; infant mortality rate: 53.2/1000; density per square mile: 89.8
Administrative capital: Pretoria
Legislative capital: Cape Town
Judicial capital: Bloemfontein. No decision has been made to relocate the seat of government. South Africa is demarcated into nine provinces, consisting of the Gauteng, Northern Province, Mpumalanga, North West, KwaZulu/Natal, Eastern Cape, Western Cape, Northern Cape, and Free State. Each province has its own capital. **Largest metropolitan areas (1995):** Cape Peninsula, 2,350,157; Johannesburg, 1,916,063; East Rand, 1,378,792; Durban/Pinetown, 1,137,378; Pretoria, 1,080,187. **Monetary unit:** Rand. **Languages:** English, Afrikaans, Ndebele, Sesotho sa Leboa, Sesotho, Swati, Xitsonga, Setswana, Tshivenda, Xhosa and Zulu are the official languages of the interim period. **Ethnicity/Race:** black 75.2%, white 13.6%, Colored 8.6%, Indian 2.6%. **Religions:** Christian; Hindu; Islam. **Literacy rate:** 76%
Economic summary: Gross domestic product: purchasing power parity (1995 est.): $215 billion; $4,800 per capita; 3.3% real growth rate; inflation 8.7%. Arable land: 11.59%. Principal agricultural products: corn, wool, wheat, sugar cane, fruits, vegetables. Labor force: 14.2 million economically active (1996); by occupation: services 35%, agriculture 30%, industry 20%, mining 9%, other 6%. Major industrial products: gold, chromium, diamonds, assembled automobiles, machinery, textiles, iron and steel, chemicals, fertilizer. Natural resources: gold, diamonds, platinum, uranium, coal, iron ore, phosphates, manganese. Exports: $27.9 billion (f.o.b 1995): gold, diamonds, minerals and metals, food, chemicals. Imports: $27 billion (f.o.b.1995): motor vehicle parts, machinery, metals, chemicals, textiles, scientific instruments. Major trading partners: Germany, U.S., other E.U., Japan, U.K., Hong Kong, Italy, Taiwan.

Geography. South Africa, on the continent's southern tip, is washed by the Atlantic Ocean on the west and by the Indian Ocean on the south and east. Its neighbors are Namibia in the northwest, Zimbabwe and Botswana in the north, and Mozambique and Swaziland in the northeast. The Kingdom of Lesotho forms an enclave within the southeastern part of South Africa. Bophuthatswana, Transkei, Ciskei, and Venda are independent states within South Africa, which occupies an area nearly three times that of California.

The country has a high interior plateau, or veld, nearly half of which averages 4,000 feet (1,219 m) in elevation.

There are no important mountain ranges, although the Great Escarpment, separating the veld from the coastal plain, rises to over 11,000 feet (3,350 m) in the Drakensberg Mountains in the east. The principal river is the Orange, rising in Lesotho and flowing westward for 1,300 miles (2,092 km) to the Atlantic.

The southernmost point of Africa is Cape Agulhas, located in the Western Cape Province about 100 miles (161 km) southeast of the Cape of Good Hope.

Government. South Africa is a constitutional state with three tiers of government, and a chapter for fundamental human rights. A schedule in the bill sets out binding and justiciable constitutional principles.

Parliament consists of a 400-member National Assembly and a 90-person Council of Provinces. The National Assembly consists of 200 members from the provincial ballot. Election to these bodies takes place on the basis of proportional representation.

Each of the nine provinces has its own constitution that is in accordance with the national constitution. A constitutional court has final jurisdiction on matters pertaining to the interpretation, protection, and enforcement of the constitution.

A new constitution was adopted in May 1996 guaranteeing equal rights for everyone. The constitution is to come into effect slowly over a three-year period.

History. The San people were the first settlers. The Dutch East India Company landed the first European settlers on the Cape of Good Hope in 1652, launching a colony that by the end of the 18th century numbered only about 15,000. Known as Boers or Afrikaners, speaking a Dutch dialect known as Afrikaans, the settlers as early as 1795 tried to establish an independent republic.

After occupying the Cape Colony in that year, Britain took permanent possession in 1814 at the end of the Napoleonic wars, bringing in 5,000 settlers. Anglicization of government and the freeing of slaves in 1833 drove about 12,000 Afrikaners to make the "great trek" north and east into African tribal territory, where they established the republics of the Transvaal and the Orange Free State.

The discovery of diamonds in 1867 and gold nine years later brought an influx of "outlanders" into the republics and spurred Cecil Rhodes to plot annexation. Rhodes's scheme of sparking an "outlander" rebellion to which an armed party under Leander Starr Jameson would ride to the rescue misfired in 1895, forcing Rhodes to resign as Prime Minister of the Cape colony. What British expansionists called the "inevitable" war with the Boers eventually broke out on Oct. 11, 1899.

The defeat of the Boers in 1902 led in 1910 to the Union of South Africa, composed of four provinces, the two former republics and the old Cape and Natal colonies. Louis Botha, a Boer, became the first Prime Minister. Organized political activity among Africans started with the establishment of the African National Congress in 1912.

Jan Christiaan Smuts brought the nation into World War II on the Allied side against Nationalist opposition, and South Africa became a charter member of the United Nations in 1945, but refused to sign the Universal Declaration of Human Rights. Apartheid—racial separation—dominated domestic politics as the Nationalists gained power and imposed greater restrictions on Bantus, Coloreds, and Asians. African voters were removed form the voter rolls in 1936.

Afrikaner hostility to Britain triumphed in 1961 with the declaration on May 31 of the Republic of South Africa and the severing of ties with the Commonwealth. Nationalist Prime Minister H. F. Verwoerd's government in 1963 asserted the power to restrict freedom of those who opposed rigid racial laws. Three years later, amid increasing racial tension and criticism from the outside world, Verwoerd was assassinated. His Nationalist successor, Balthazar J. Vorster, launched a campaign of conciliation toward conservative black African states, offering development loans and trade concessions.

Elections on May 7, 1987, increased the power of President Botha's Nationalist party while enabling the far-right Conservative Party to replace the liberal Progressives as the official opposition. The results of the whites-only vote indicated a strong conservative reaction against Botha's policy of limited reform.

A stroke led Botha to step down as leader of his party in 1989 in favor of F. W. de Klerk. De Klerk accelerated the pace of reform. He unbanned the African National Congress, the principal anti-apartheid organization, and released Nelson Mandela, the ANC deputy President and all other anti-apartheid movements/organizations after 27½ years imprisonment. Negotiations between the government and the ANC commenced.

On June 5, 1991 the parliament scrapped the country's apartheid laws concerning property ownership. On June 17 the parliament did the same for the Population Registration Act of 1950, which classified all South Africans at birth by race.

In February 1993 the ANC approved a plan that would allow minority parties to participate in the government for five years after the end of white rule. Also in February the first nonwhites entered the cabinet in an apparent bid to broaden the base of the ruling National Party.

The 1994 election, as expected, resulted in a massive victory for Mandela and his ANC. The new government included six ministers from the Nation Party and three from the Inkatha Freedom Party.

The government announced that as of July 1997 South Africans would be allowed to invest a limited amount abroad or in foreign currency accounts domestically. The ceiling might later be raised if economic conditions permit.

SPAIN

Kingdom of Spain
National name: Reino de España
Ruler: King Juan Carlos I (1975)
Prime Minister: Joeé María Aznar (1996)
Area: 195,364.5 sq mi. (505,992 sq km)[1]
Population (1997 est.): 39,244,195 (average annual growth rate: 0.11%); birth rate: 10.07/1000; infant mortality rate: 6.1/1000; density per square mile: 200.9
Capital and largest city (1994 est.): Madrid, 3,041,101.
Largest cities: Barcelona, 1,630,867; Valencia, 764,293; Seville, 714,148. **Monetary unit:** Peseta.
Languages: Spanish, Basque, Catalan, Galician.
Ethnicity/Race: composite of Mediterranean and Nordic types. **Religion:** Roman Catholic, 99%. **Literacy rate:** 97%
Economic summary: Gross domestic product: purchasing power parity (1995 est.): $565 billion; $14,300 per capita; real growth rate 3%; inflation 4.3%; unemployment (1995): 22.8%. Arable land: 31%. Principal agricultural products: cereals, vegetables, citrus fruits, wine, olives and olive oil, livestock. Labor force: 11.837 million: 59% in services; 21% in industry; 11% in agriculture; 9% in construction. Major industrial products: processed foods, textiles, footwear, petrochemicals, steel, automobiles, ships. Natural resources: coal, lignite, water power, uranium, mercury, pyrites, fluorospar, gypsum, iron ore, zinc, lead, tungsten, copper. Exports: $85 billion (f.o.b., 1995): cars and trucks, semifinished manufactured goods, foodstuffs, machinery and electrical equipment. Imports: $110 billion (c.i.f., 1995): machinery and transportation equipment, chemicals, petroleum, semifinished goods, consumer goods, machines and electrical equipment. Major trading partners: Germany, Italy, France, U.S., U.K.

1. Including the Balearic and Canary Islands.

Geography. Spain occupies 85% of the Iberian Peninsula in southwestern Europe, which it shares with Portugal; France is to the northeast, separated by the Pyrenees. The Bay of Biscay lies to the north, the Atlantic Ocean to the west, and the Mediterranean Sea to the south and east: Africa is less than 10 miles (16 km) south at the Strait of Gibraltar.

A broad central plateau slopes to the south and east, crossed by a series of mountain ranges and river valleys.

Principal rivers are the Ebro in the northeast, the Tajo in the central region, and the Guadalquivir in the south.

Off Spain's east coast in the Mediterranean are the Balearic Islands (1,936 sq mi.; 5,014 sq km), the largest of which is Majorca. Sixty miles (97 km) west of Africa are the Canary Islands (2,808 sq mi.; 7,273 sq km).

Government. A parliamentary monarchy. The Cortes, or Parliament, consists of a Chamber of Deputies of 350 members and a Senate of 208, all elected by universal suffrage.

History. Spain, originally inhabited by Celts, Iberians, and Basques, became a part of the Roman Empire in 206 B.C.E., when it was conquered by Scipio Africanus. In C.E. 412, the barbarian Visigothic leader Ataulf crossed the Pyrenees and ruled Spain, first in the name of the Roman emperor and then independently. In 711, the Moslems under Tariq entered Spain from Africa and within a few years completed the subjugation of the country. In 732, the Franks, led by Charles Martel, defeated the Moslems near Poitiers, thus preventing the further expansion of Islam in southern Europe. Internal dissension of Spanish Islam invited a steady Christian conquest from the north.

Aragon and Castile were the most important Spanish states from the 12th to the 15th century, consolidated by the marriage of Ferdinand II and Isabella I in 1469. The last Moslem stronghold, Granada, was captured in 1492. Roman Catholicism was established as the official state religion and the Jews (1492) and the Moslems (1502) expelled.

In the era of exploration, discovery, and colonization, Spain amassed tremendous wealth and a vast colonial empire through the conquest of Peru by Pizarro (1532–33) and of Mexico by Cortés (1519–21). The Spanish Hapsburg monarchy became for a time the most powerful in the world.

In 1588, Philip II sent his Invincible Armada to invade England, but its destruction cost Spain its supremacy on the seas and paved the way for England's colonization of America. Spain then sank rapidly to the status of a second-rate power and never again played a major role in European politics. Its colonial empire in the Americas and the Philippines vanished in wars and revolutions during the 18th and 19th centuries.

In World War I, Spain maintained a position of neutrality. In 1923, Gen. Miguel Primo de Rivera became Dictator. In 1930, King Alfonso XIII revoked the Dictatorship, but a strong antimonarchist and republican movement led to his leaving Spain in 1931. The new constitution declared Spain a workers' republic, broke up the large estates, separated church and state, and secularized the schools. The elections held in 1936 returned a strong Popular Front majority, with Manuel Azaña as President.

On July 18, 1936, a conservative army officer in Morocco, Francisco Franco Bahamonde, led a mutiny against the government. The civil war that followed lasted three years and cost the lives of nearly a million people. Franco was aided by Fascist Italy and Nazi Germany, while Soviet Russia helped the Loyalist side. Several hundred leftist Americans served in the Abraham Lincoln Brigade on the side of the republic. The

war ended when Franco took Madrid on March 28, 1939.

Franco became head of the state, national chief of the Falange Party (the governing party), and Premier and caudillo (leader). In a referendum in 1947, the Spanish people approved a Franco-drafted succession law declaring Spain a monarchy again. Franco, however, continued as chief of state.

In 1969, Franco and the Cortes designated Prince Juan Carlos Alfonso Victor María de Borbón (who married Princess Sophia of Greece on May 14, 1962) to become King of Spain when the provisional government headed by Franco came to an end.

Franco died of a heart attack on Nov. 20, 1975, after more than a year of ill health, and Juan Carlos was proclaimed King seven days later.

Under pressure from Catalonian and Basque nationalists, Premier Adolfo Suárez granted home rule to these regions in 1979. Basque separatists (ETA) committed hundreds of terrorist bombings and kidnappings that continue through the present.

With the overwhelming election of Prime Minister Felipe González Márquez and his Spanish Socialist Workers Party in the Oct. 20, 1982, parliamentary elections, the Franco past was finally buried.

A treaty admitting Spain, along with Portugal, to the European Economic Community took effect on Jan. 1, 1986. Later that year, in June, Spain voted to remain in NATO, but outside of its military command.

General elections of June 1993 returned the Socialist Party to power through the assistance of Catalonia's main nationalist party, which increasingly pressed in 1994 for greater self-government for the region as the price for that support.

General elections in March 1996 produced a victory for the conservative Popular Party, which, although lacking an absolute majority in the Cortes, received the backing of regional parties for a coalition government with Aznar as Prime Minister.

In June 1997 Socialist leader Gonzales stepped aside, providing the opportunity for his party to choose a new head at its 34th Congress. Joaquin Almunia, Socialist Party spokesman, was chosen to lead the party.

SRI LANKA

Democratic Socialist Republic of Sri Lanka
President: Chandrika B. Kumaratunga (1994)
Prime Minister: Sirimao R. D. Bandaranayake
Area: 25,332 sq mi. (65,610 sq km)
Population (1997 est.): 18,762,075 (average annual rate of natural increase: 1.18%); birth rate: 17.64/1000; infant mortality rate: 20.3/1000; density per square mile: 740.6
Capital and largest city (1992 est.): Sri Jayewardenepura Kotte (Colombo), 1,994,000. **Other large cities (1992 est.):** Gampaha, 1,543,000; Kurunegala, 1,445,000; Kandy, 1,257,000. **Monetary unit:** Sri Lanka rupee. **Languages:** Sinhala, Tamil, English. **Ethnicity/Race:** Sinhalese 74%, Tamil 18%, Moor 7%, Burgher, Malay, and Vedda 1%. **Religions:** Buddhist, 69%; Hindu, 15%; Islam, 8%; Christian, 8%. **Literacy rate:** 89%
Economic summary: Gross domestic product: purchasing power parity (1995 est.): $65.6 billion; $3,600 per capita; 5% real growth rate; 8.4% inflation (1994 est.);13% unemployment (1994 est.). Arable land: 16%. Principal products: tea, coconuts, rubber, rice, spices. Labor force: 6.1 million; 45% in agriculture; 37% in services; 18% in industry (1993 est.). Major products: processed rubber, tea, coconuts, textiles, cement, refined petroleum. Natural resources: limestone, graphite, gems. Exports: $3.2 billion (f.o.b.),

1994): textiles, tea, rubber, petroleum products, gems and jewelry. Imports: $4.8 billion (c.i.f., 1994): petroleum, machinery, transport equipment, sugar. Major trading partners: U.S., U.K., Germany, Japan, Singapore, India, Iran, Taiwan, Belgium, Hong Kong, China. **Member of Commonwealth of Nations**

Geography. An island in the Indian Ocean off the southeast tip of India, Sri Lanka is about half the size of Alabama. Most of the land is flat and rolling; mountains in the south central region rise to over 8,000 feet (2,438 m).

Government. Ceylon became an independent country in 1948 after British rule and reverted to the traditional name ("resplendent island") on May 22, 1972. A new constitution adopted in 1978 set up the National State Assembly, a 225-member unicameral legislature that serves for six years unless dissolved earlier.

History. Following Portuguese and Dutch rule, Ceylon became an English crown colony in 1798. The British developed coffee, tea, and rubber plantations and granted six Constitutions between 1798 and 1924. The constitution of 1931 gave a large measure of self-government. Ceylon became a self-governing dominion of the Commonwealth of Nations in 1948.

Presidential elections were held in December 1982, and won by J. R. Jayewardene.

Tension between the Tamil minority and the Sinhalese majority continued to build and erupted in bloody violence in 1983 that has grown worse since. There are about 2.6 million Tamils in Sri Lanka, while the Sinhalese make up about three-quarters of the 17-million population. Tamil extremists are fighting for a separate nation.

The civil war continued during 1990 after a 13-month cease-fire collapsed. The President ruled month to month. The Tamil guerrillas announced a unilateral cease-fire to take effect on January 1, 1991, and the government, too, suspended operations.

India had sent soldiers in July 1987 to help enforce an accord granting the Tamil minority limited autonomy. The agreement failed, and Indian troops withdrew at the end of 1989.

President Ranasinghe Premadasa was assassinated at a May Day political rally in 1993 when a Tamil rebel detonated explosives strapped to himself.

A general election in August 1994 gave a coalition of left-of-center opposition parties 105 seats in the state assembly. A November presidential election was won by the coalition's head running on a peace platform and support for a free-market economy.

The war with Tamil rebels continued unabated through mid-1996. In April the President extended the state of emergency to the entire country.

The government launched an offensive in May 1997 against the Tamil rebel stronghold in the Wanni region. Heavy fighting ensued with significant losses on both sides reported.

SUDAN

Republic of the Sudan
National name: Jamhuryat es-Sudan
President: Lt. Gen. Omar Hassam Ahmed Bashir (1993)
Area: 967,491 sq mi. (2,505,802 sq km)
Population (1997 est.): 32,594,128 (average annual rate of natural increase: 2.93%); birth rate: 40.54/1000; infant mortality rate: 74.3/1000; density per square mile: 33.7
Capital (1993 est.): Khartoum, 924,505. **Largest cities:** Omdurman, 1,267,077; Port Sudan, 305,385. **Monetary unit:** Sudanese pound. **Languages:** Arabic,

English, tribal dialects. **Ethnicity/Race:** black 52%, Arab 39%, Beja 6%, foreigners 2%, other 1%. **Religions:** Islam, 70% (Sunni); indigenous, 20%; Christian, 5%. **Literacy rate:** 32%
Economic summary: Gross domestic product: purchasing power parity (1995 est.): $25 billion; $800 per capita; real growth rate 0%; inflation 66%; unemployment 30% (FY 1992–93 est.). Arable land: 5%. Principal agricultural products: cotton, oil seeds, gum arabic, sorghum, wheat, millet, sheep. Labor force: 8.9 million; 80% in agriculture; 10% in industry and commerce; 6% in government (note: labor shortages for almost all categories of skilled employment) (1993 est.). Major industrial products: cement, textiles, pharmaceuticals, shoes, soap, refined petroleum, gold. Natural resources: crude oil, some iron ore, copper, chrome, industrial metals. Exports: $535 million (f.o.b., 1995 est.): cotton, peanuts, gum arabic, sesame. Imports: $1.1 billion (c.i.f., 1995 est.): petroleum products, machinery and equipment, medicines and chemicals. Major trading partners: Western Europe, Saudi Arabia, Eastern Europe, Japan.

Geography. The Sudan, in northeast Africa, is the largest country on the continent, measuring about one-fourth the size of the United States. Its neighbors are Chad and the Central African Republic on the west, Egypt and Libya on the north, Ethiopia and Eritrea on the east, and Kenya, Uganda, and Congo on the south. The Red Sea washes about 500 miles of the eastern coast.

The country extends from north to south about 1,200 miles (1,931 km) and west to east about 1,000 miles (1,609 km). The northern region is a continuation of the Libyan Desert. The southern region is fertile, abundantly watered, and, in places, heavily forested. It is traversed from north to south by the Nile, all of whose great tributaries are partly or entirely within its borders.

Government. On January 31, 1991, a criminal code became law that applied Islamic law in the predominantly Moslem north. The ruling military council passed a decree in 1993 dividing the country into 26 states each administered by a governor and a cabinet of ministers.

History. The early history of the Sudan (known as the Anglo-Egyptian Sudan between 1898 and 1955) is linked with that of Nubia, where a powerful local Kingdom was formed in Roman times with its capital at Dongola. After conversion to Christianity in the 6th century, the Sudan joined with Ethiopia and resisted Mohammedanization until the 14th century. Thereafter the area was broken up into many small states until 1820–22, when it was conquered by Mohammed Ali, Pasha of Egypt. Egyptian forces were evacuated during the Mahdist revolt (1881–98), but the Sudan was reconquered by the Anglo-Egyptian expeditions of 1896–98, and in 1899 became an Anglo-Egyptian condominium, which was reaffirmed by the Anglo-Egyptian treaty of 1936.

Egypt and Britain agreed in 1953 to grant self-government to the Sudan under an appointed governor-general. An all-Sudanese parliament was elected in November–December 1953, and an all-Sudanese government was formed. In December 1955, the Parliament declared the independence of the Sudan, which, with the approval of Britain and Egypt, was proclaimed on Jan. 1, 1956.

In October 1969, Maj. Gen. Gaafar Mohamed Nimeiri, the President of the Council for the Revolution, took over as Prime Minister. He was elected the nation's first President in 1971.

On April 6, 1985, while out of the country on visits to the United States and Egypt, Nimeiri lost power by a military coup headed by his Defense Minister, Gen. Abdel Rahman Siwar el-Dahab.

Among the problems that the new government faced were a debilitating civil war with rebels in the south of the country, other sectarian and tribal conflicts, and a famine.

During 1992 the government attempted to impose militant Islam throughout the nation as well as initiate capitalistic economic reforms, including the lifting of subsidies on basic commodities.

March 1996 elections gave an easy victory to the incumbent President, who faced largely unknown opponents. His supporters also did well in the parliamentary voting.

A peace treaty between the government and four rebel factions was signed in April 1997 that permitted southerners to keep their weapons and provided for a referendum on southern independence in four years. Yet the largest faction refused to sign the pact.

SURINAME

Republic of Suriname

President: Jules Wijdenbosch (1996)
Prime Minister: Pretaapnarian Radhakishun (1996)
Area: 63,251 sq mi. (163,820 sq km)
Population (1997 est.): 443,446 (average annual rate of natural increase: 1.77%); birth rate: 23.52/1000; infant mortality rate: 28.4/1000; density per square mile: 7
Capital and largest city (1993 est.): Paramaribo, 200,970. **Monetary unit:** Suriname guilder. **Languages:** Dutch, Surinamese (lingua franca), English widely spoken. **Ethnicity/Race:** Hindustani (also known locally as "East" Indians; their ancestors emigrated from northern India in the latter part of the 19th century) 37%, Creole (mixed European and African ancestry) 31%, Javanese 15.3%, "Bush Black" (also known as "Bush Creole" whose ancestors were brought to the country in the 17th and 18th centuries as slaves) 10.3%, Amerindian 2.6%, Chinese 1.7%, Europeans 1%, other 1.1%. **Religions:** Protestant, 25.2%; Roman Catholic, 22.8%; Hindu, 27.4%; Islam, 19.6%; indigenous, about 5%. **Literacy rate:** 95%
Economic summary: Gross domestic product: purchasing power parity (1995 est.): $1.3 billion; $2,950 per capita; real growth rate 0.7%; inflation 62%; unemployment: n.a. Arable land: negl. Principal product: rice. Labor force: 98,240 in agriculture, industry, services. Major products: aluminum, alumina, processed foods, lumber. Natural resources: bauxite, iron ore, timber, fish, shrimp. Exports: $293.6 million (f.o.b, 1994 est.): bauxite, alumina, aluminum, rice, shrimp and fish, bananas. Imports: $194.3 million (f.o.b., 1994 est.): capital equipment, petroleum, cotton, foodstuffs, consumer goods. Major trading partners: U.S., Trinidad, Netherlands, Norway, Germany, Brazil, U.K., Japan, Netherlands Antilles.

Geography. Suriname lies on the northeast coast of South America, with Guyana to the west, French Guiana to the east, and Brazil to the south. It is about one-tenth larger than Michigan. The principal rivers are the Corantijn on the Guyana border, the Marowijne in the east, and the Suriname, on which the capital city of Paramaribo is situated. The Tumuc-Humac Mountains are on the border with Brazil.

Government. Suriname, formerly known as Dutch Guiana, became an independent republic on Nov. 25, 1975. The executive branch consists of the President and Prime Minister, Cabinet of Ministers, and Council of State. The legislative branch consists of a unicameral National Assembly with 51 members.

History. England established the first European settlement on the Suriname River in 1650 but transferred sovereignty to the Dutch in 1667 in the Treaty of Breda, by which the British acquired New York. Colonization was confined to a narrow coastal strip, and until the abolition of slavery in 1863, African slaves furnished the labor for the plantation economy. After 1870, laborers were imported from British India and the Dutch East Indies.

In 1948, the colony was integrated into the Kingdom of the Netherlands and two years later was granted full home rule in other than foreign affairs and defense. After race rioting over unemployment and inflation, the Netherlands offered complete independence in 1973.

During much of the 1980s Suriname was under the control of Lieut. Col. Dési Bouterse, who in late December 1990 resigned as commander of the armed forces. The following night President Ramsewak Shankar was ousted in a bloodless coup. A few days later interim President Johan Krug acted to reinstate Bouterse.

A deadlocked parliament in 1991 gave way to an assembly, consisting of members of parliament and elected representatives of local councils, convened to select Venetiaan as President.

In 1992 a draft peace treaty was signed between the government and several guerrilla groups.

In March 1997 the President announced new economic measures including eliminating import tariffs on most basic goods coupled with strict price controls. Suspicious investment funds, paying interest rates of 10% per month drew increasing attention early in the year. In June the largest of these collapsed, sending thousands of common investors into poverty.

SWAZILAND

Kingdom of Swaziland

Ruler: King Mswati III (1986)
Prime Minister: Barnabas Sibusiso Dlamini (July 1996)
Area: 6,704 sq mi. (17,363 sq km)
Population (1997 est.): 1,031,600 (average annual rate of natural increase: 3.24%); birth rate: 42.71/1000; infant mortality rate: 86.1/1000; density per square mile: 153.9
Capital and largest city (1990 est.): Mbabane 47,020.
Monetary unit: Lilangeni. **Languages:** English and Swazi (official). **Ethnicity/Race:** African 97%, European 3%. **Religions:** Christian, 60%; indigenous, 40%. **Literacy rate:** 55%
Economic summary: Gross domestic product: purchasing power parity (1995 est.): $3.6 billion; $3,700 per capita; 2.6% real growth rate; inflation 14.7%; unemployment 15%. Arable land: 8%. The economy is based on subsistence agriculture, which occupies more than 60% of the population and contributes nearly 25% to GDP. Manufacturing, which includes a number of agroprocessing factories, accounts for another quarter of GDP. Principal agricultural products: corn, livestock, sugar cane, citrus fruits, cotton, sorghum, peanuts. Labor force: 160,355; 65% in the private sector; 35% in the public sector. Major industrial products: milled sugar, ginned cotton, processed meat and wood. Natural resources: asbestos, diamonds. Exports: $798 million (f.o.b., 1994 est.): sugar, wood pulp, asbestos, citrus fruits. Imports: $827 million (f.o.b., 1994 est.): motor vehicles, transport equipment, petroleum products, foodstuffs, chemicals. Major trading partners: South Africa, U.K., U.S. **Member of Commonwealth of Nations**

Geography. Swaziland, 85% the size of New Jersey, is surrounded by South Africa and Mozambique. The country consists of a high veld in the west and a series of plateaus descending from 6,000 feet (1,829 m) to a low veld of 1,500 feet (457 m).

Government. In 1967, a new constitution established King Sobhuza II as head of state and provided for an Assembly of 24 members elected by universal suffrage, together with a Senate of 12 members—half appointed by the Assembly and half by the King. In 1973, the King renounced the constitution, suspended political parties, and took total power for himself. In 1977, he replaced the parliament with an assembly of tribal leaders. The parliament reconvened in 1979.

History. Bantu peoples migrated southwest to the area of Mozambique in the 16th century. A number of clans broke away from the main body in the 18th century and settled in Swaziland. In the 19th century they organized as a tribe, partly because they were in constant conflict with the Zulu. Their ruler, Mswazi, applied to the British in the 1840s for help against the Zulu. The British and the Transvaal governments guaranteed the independence of Swaziland in 1881.

South Africa held Swaziland as a protectorate from 1894 to 1899, but after the Boer War, in 1902, Swaziland was transferred to British administration. The Paramount Chief was recognized as the native authority in 1941.

In 1963, the territory was constituted a protectorate, and on Sept. 6, 1968, it became the independent nation of Swaziland.

The King in October 1992 dissolved Parliament and announced plans for a new constitution allowing a multiparty democracy. The first democratic elections took place in September 1993.

The government presented a tax reform plan in June 1997 intended to broaden the tax base and thereby increase revenues by at least 38%. Since 1992 the budget has gone from a surplus to a considerable deficit.

SWEDEN

Kingdom of Sweden
National name: Konungariket Sverige
Sovereign: King Carl XVI Gustaf (1973)
Prime Minister: Göran Persson (1996)
Area: 173,800 sq mi. (449,964 sq km)
Population (1997 est.): 8,946,193 (average annual rate of natural increase –0.03%); birth rate: 10.81/1000; infant mortality rate: 4.5/1000; density per sq mi.: 51.5
Capital and largest city (1994): Stockholm, 703,627. **Largest cities:** Göteborg, 444,553; Malmö, 242,706; Uppsala, 181,191. **Monetary unit:** Krona. **Language:** Swedish. **Ethnicity/Race:** white, Lapp (Sami), foreign-born or first-generation immigrants 12% (Finns, Yugoslavs, Danes, Norwegians, Greeks, Turks). **Religions:** Evangelical Lutheran, 93.5%; Roman Catholic, 1%; other, 5.5%. **Literacy rate:** 99%
Economic summary: Gross domestic product: purchasing power parity (1995 est.): $177.3 billion; $20,100 per capita; real growth rate 3.5%; inflation 2.6%; unemployment 7.8% (December 1995). Arable land: 7%. Principal agricultural products: dairy products, grains, sugar beets, potatoes. Labor force: 4.552 million (almost 50% are women); 38.3% in community, social, and personal services; 21.2% in mining and manufacturing; 14.1% in commerce, hotels and restaurants; 9% in banking and insurance; 7.2% in communications; 7% in construction; 3.2% in agriculture, fishing and forestry. Major products: iron and steel, precision equipment, wood pulp and paper products, automobiles. Natural resources: forests, iron ore, hydroelectric power, zinc, uranium. Exports: $61.2 billion (f.o.b., 1994): machinery, motor vehicles, wood pulp, paper products, chemicals, petroleum and petroleum products, iron and steel products. Imports: $51.8 billion (c.i.f., 1994): machinery, clothing, petroleum and petroleum products, foodstuffs, iron and steel,

chemicals. Major trading partners: Norway, Germany, U.K., Denmark, U.S., France, Finland, Netherlands.

Geography. Sweden occupies the eastern part of the Scandinavian peninsula, with Norway to the west, Finland and the Gulf of Bothnia to the east, and Denmark and the Baltic Sea in the south. Sweden is the fourth largest country in Europe and is one-tenth larger than California.

The country slopes eastward and southward from the Kjölen Mountains along the Norwegian border, where the peak elevation is Kebnekaise at 6,965 feet (2,123 m) in Lapland. In the north are mountains and many lakes. To the south and east are central lowlands and south of them are fertile areas of forest, valley, and plain.

Along Sweden's rocky coast, chopped up by bays and inlets, are many islands, the largest of which are Gotland and Öland.

Government. Sweden is a constitutional monarchy. Under the 1975 constitution, the Riksdag is the sole governing body. The Prime Minister is the political chief executive.

In 1967, agreement was reached on part of a new constitution after 13 years of work. It provided for a single-house Riksdag of 350 members (later amended to 349 seats) to replace the 104-year old bicameral Riksdag. The members are popularly elected for three years. One hundred fifteen present members of the Riksdag are women.

The King, Carl XVI Gustaf, was born April 30, 1946, and succeeded to the throne Sept. 19, 1973, on the death at 90 of his grandfather, Gustaf VI Adolf. Carl Gustaf was married on June 19, 1976, to Silvia Sommerlath, a West German commoner. They have three children: Princess Victoria, born July 14, 1977; Prince Carl Philip, born May 13, 1979; and Princess Madeleine, born June 10, 1982. Under the new Act of Succession, effective Jan. 1, 1980, the first child of the reigning monarch, regardless of sex, is heir to the throne.

History. The earliest historical mention of Sweden is found in Tacitus's *Germania*, where reference is made to the powerful king and strong fleet of the Suiones. Toward the end of the 10th century, Olaf Sköttkonung established a Christian stronghold in Sweden. Around 1400, an attempt was made to unite the northern nations into one kingdom, but this led to bitter strife between the Danes and the Swedes.

In 1520, the Danish King, Christian II, conquered Sweden and in the "Stockholm Bloodbath" put leading Swedish personages to death. Gustavus Vasa (1523–60) broke away from Denmark and fashioned the modern Swedish state.

Sweden played a leading role in the second phase (1630–35) of the Thirty Years' War (1618–48). By the Treaty of Westphalia (1648), Sweden obtained western Pomerania and some neighboring territory on the Baltic. In 1700, a coalition of Russia, Poland, and Denmark united against Sweden and by the Peace of Nystad (1721) forced it to relinquish Livonia, Ingria, Estonia, and parts of Finland.

Sweden emerged from the Napoleonic Wars with the acquisition of Norway from Denmark and with a new royal dynasty stemming from Marshal Jean Bernadotte of France, who became King Charles XIV (1818–44). The artificial union between Sweden and Norway led to an uneasy relationship, and the union was finally dissolved in 1905.

Sweden maintained a position of neutrality in both World Wars.

An elaborate structure of welfare legislation, imitated by many larger nations, began with the establishment of old-age pensions in 1911. Economic prosperity based on its neutralist policy enabled Sweden, together with Norway, to pioneer in public health, housing, and job security programs.

Forty-four years of Socialist government were ended in 1976 with the election of a conservative coalition headed by Thorbjörn Fälldin, a 50-year-old sheep farmer.

Fälldin resigned on Oct. 5, 1978, when his conservative coalition partners demanded fewer restrictions on nuclear power, and his successor, Ola Ullsten, resigned a year later after failing to achieve a consensus on the issue.

Olaf Palme and the Socialists were returned to power in the election of 1982. In February 1986, Palme was killed by an unknown assailant.

Elections in September 1991 ousted the Social Democrats from power. The new coalition of four conservative parties pledged to cut taxes and cut back on the welfare state but not alter Sweden's traditional neutrality.

General elections in September 1994 saw the emergence again of the Social Democrats after three years of being in opposition. Short of a majority by 13 seats in the Riksdag they decided to establish a minority government.

In a referendum held in November 1994 voters approved joining the European Union.

Ingvar Carlsson retired as Prime Minister in March 1996, as promised. The Social Democrats chose Finance Minister Persson, a technocrat, to succeed him.

Although supportive of a European monetary union, Persson in June 1997 announced that Sweden would not adopt the European single currency when it debuted in 1999 owing to public opinion against such a move.

SWITZERLAND

Swiss Confederation
National name: Schweiz/Suisse/Svizzera/Svizra
President: Arnold Koller (1997)
Vice President: Delamuraz Jean-Pascal (1995)
Area: 15,941 sq mi. (41,288 sq km)
Population (1997 est.): 7,248,984 (average annual rate of natural increase: 0.16%); birth rate: 11.16/1000; infant mortality rate: 5.4/1000; density per square mile: 454.7
Capital (1994 est.): Bern, 129,423. **Largest cities:** Zurich, 343,045; Basel, 176,220; Geneva, 171,744; Lausanne, 117,153. **Monetary unit:** Swiss franc. **Languages:** German, 65%; French, 18%; Italian, 10%; Romansch, 1%. **Ethnicity/Race:** total population: German 65%, French 18%, Italian 10%, Romansch 1%, other 6%. Swiss nationals: German 74%, French 20%, Italian 4%, Romansch 1%, other 1%. **Religions:** Roman Catholic, 49%; Protestant, 48%. **Literacy rate:** 99%
Economic summary: Gross domestic product: purchasing power parity (1995 est.): $158.5 billion; $22,400 per capita; real growth rate 1.2%; inflation 1.8%; unemployment 3.3%. Arable land: 10%. Principal products: cheese and other dairy products, livestock. Labor force: 3.48 million (900,000 foreign workers); 50% in services; 34% in industry and crafts; 10% in government; 6% in agriculture and forestry (1992). Major products: watches and clocks, precision instruments, machinery, chemicals, pharmaceuticals, textiles. Natural resources: water power, timber, salt. Exports: $69.6 billion (f.o.b., 1994 est.): machinery and equipment, precision instruments, textiles, foodstuffs, metal products. Imports: $68.2 billion (c.i.f., 1994 est.): transport equipment, foodstuffs, chemicals, textiles, construction material. Major trading partners: U.S., Japan, Western Europe.

Geography. Switzerland, in central Europe, is the land of the Alps. Its tallest peak is the Dufourspitze at 15,203 feet (4,634 m) on the Swiss side of the Italian border, one of 10 summits of the Monte Rose massif in the Apennines. The tallest peak in all of the Alps, Mont Blanc (15,771 ft.; 4,807 m), is actually in France.

Most of Switzerland comprises a mountainous plateau bordered by the great bulk of the Alps on the south and by the Jura Mountains on the northwest. About one-fourth of the total area is covered by mountains and glaciers.

The country's largest lakes—Geneva, Constance (Bodensee), and Maggiore—straddle the French, German-Austrian, and Italian borders, respectively.

The Rhine, navigable from Basel to the North Sea, is the principal inland waterway. Other rivers are the Aare and the Rhône.

Switzerland, twice the size of New Jersey, is surrounded by France, West Germany, Austria, Liechtenstein, and Italy.

Government. The Swiss Confederation consists of 23 sovereign cantons, of which three are divided into six half-cantons. Federal authority is vested in a bicameral legislature. The Ständerat, or State Council, consists of 46 members, two from each canton. The lower house, the Nationalrat, or National Council, has 200 deputies, elected for four-year terms.

Executive authority rests with the Bundesrat, or federal council, consisting of seven members chosen by parliament. The parliament elects the President, who serves for one year and is succeeded by the Vice President. The federal government regulates foreign policy, railroads, postal service, and the national mint. Each canton reserves for itself important local powers.

History. Called Helvetia in ancient times, Switzerland in the Middle Ages was a league of cantons of the Holy Roman Empire. Fashioned around the nucleus of three German forest districts of Schwyz, Uri, and Unterwalden, the Swiss Confederation slowly added new cantons. In 1648 the Treaty of Westphalia gave Switzerland its independence from the Holy Roman Empire.

French revolutionary troops occupied the country in 1798 and named it the Helvetic Republic, but Napoleon in 1803 restored its federal government. By 1815, the French- and Italian-speaking peoples of Switzerland had been granted political equality.

In 1815, the Congress of Vienna guaranteed the neutrality and recognized the independence of Switzerland. In the revolutionary period of 1847, the Catholic cantons seceded and organized a separate union called the *Sonderbund.* In 1848 the new Swiss constitution established a union modeled upon that of the U.S. The federal constitution of 1874 established a strong central government while maintaining large powers of control in each canton.

National unity and political conservatism grew as the country prospered from its neutrality. Its banking system became the world's leading repository for international accounts. Strict neutrality was its policy in World Wars I and II. Geneva was the seat of the League of Nations (later the European headquarters of the United Nations) and of a number of international organizations.

Voters in a national referendum in June 1994 rejected the creation of a volunteer military force for deployment as part of U.N. peacekeeping operations.

Allegations concerning secret assets of Jewish Holocaust victims deposited in Swiss banks led to international criticism and the establishment of a fund to reimburse them and their families.

SYRIA

Syrian Arab Republic
National name: Al-Jamhouriya al Arabiya As-Souriya
President: Hafez al-Assad (1971)
Premier: Mahmoud al-Zubi (1987)
Area: 71,498 sq mi. (185,180 sq km)
Population (1997 est.): 16,137,899 (average annual rate of natural increase: 3.3%); birth rate: 38.7/1000; infant mortality rate: 38.8/1000; density per sq mi.: 225.7
Capital (1994 est.): Damascus, 1,549,932. **Largest cities:** Aleppo, 1,591,400; Homs, 644,204; Latakia, 306,535; Hama, 229,000. **Monetary unit:** Syrian pound. **Language:** Arabic (official), French and English widely understood.. **Ethnicity/Race:** Arab 90.3%, Kurds, Armenians, and other 9.7%. **Religions:** Islam, 90%; Christian, 10%. **Literacy rate:** 64%
Economic summary: Gross domestic product: purchasing power parity (1995 est.): $91.2 billion; $5,900 per capita; real growth rate 4.4%; inflation 15.1%; unemployment: 8%. Arable land: 28%. Principal agricultural products: cotton, wheat, barley, lentils, sheep, goats. Labor force: 4.7 million: 42% in services; 36% in industry; 22% in agriculture. Major industrial products: textiles, phosphate, petroleum, processed food. Natural resources: chrome, manganese, asphalt, iron ore, rock salt, phosphate, oil, gypsum. Exports: $3.5 billion (f.o.b., 1994): petroleum, textiles, cotton, fruits and vegetables, phosphates. Imports: $5.4 billion (c.i.f., 1994): petroleum, machinery, base metals, foodstuffs and beverages. Major trading partners: E.U. countries, U.S., Canada, Arab countries, former U.S.S.R. nations.

Geography. Slightly larger than North Dakota, Syria lies at the eastern end of the Mediterranean Sea. It is bordered by Lebanon and Israel on the west, Turkey on the north, Iraq on the east, and Jordan on the south.

Coastal Syria is a narrow plain, in back of which is a range of coastal mountains, and still farther inland a steppe area. In the east is the Syrian Desert, and in the south is the Jebel Druze Range. The highest point in Syria is Mount Hermon (9,232 ft.; 2,814 m) on the Lebanese border.

Government. A republic under a military regime since March 1963 with a unicameral legislature, the People's Council. The ruling party is the Arab Socialist Resurrectionist (Ba'th) Party.

History. Ancient Syria was conquered by Egypt about 1500 B.C.E., and after that by Hebrews, Assyrians, Chaldeans, Persians, and Greeks. From 64 B.C.E. until the Arab conquest in C.E. 636, it was part of the Roman Empire except during brief periods. The Arabs made it a trade center for their extensive empire, but it suffered severely from the Mongol invasion in 1260 and fell to the Ottoman Turks in 1516. Syria remained a Turkish province until World War I.

A secret Anglo-French pact of 1916 put Syria in the French zone of influence. The League of Nations gave France a mandate over Syria after World War I, but the French were forced to put down several nationalist uprisings. In 1930, France recognized Syria as an independent republic, but still subject to the mandate. After nationalist demonstrations in 1939, the French High Commissioner suspended the Syrian constitution. In 1941, British and Free French forces invaded Syria to eliminate Vichy control. During the rest of World War II, Syria was an Allied base.

Again in 1945, nationalist demonstrations broke into actual fighting, and British troops had to restore order. Syrian forces met a series of reverses while participating in the Arab invasion of Palestine in 1948. In 1958, Egypt and Syria formed the United Arab Republic, with Gamal Abdel Nasser of Egypt as President. However, Syria became independent again on Sept. 29, 1961, following a revolution.

In the war of 1967, Israel quickly vanquished the Syrian army. Before acceding to the U.N. cease-fire, the Israeli forces took over control of the fortified Golan Heights commanding the Sea of Galilee.

Syria joined Egypt in attacking Israel in October 1973 in the fourth Arab-Israeli war, but was pushed back from initial successes on the Golan Heights to end up losing more land. However, in the settlement worked out by U.S. Secretary of State Henry A. Kissinger in 1974, the Syrians recovered all the territory lost in 1973 and a token amount of territory, including the deserted town of Quneitra, lost in 1967.

Syrian troops, in Lebanon since 1976 as part of an Arab peacekeeping force whose other members subsequently departed, intervened increasingly during 1980 and 1981 on the side of Moslem Lebanese in their clashes with Christian militants supported by Israel. When Israeli jets shot down Syrian helicopters operating in Lebanon in April 1981, Syria moved Soviet-built surface-to-air (SAM 6) missiles into Lebanon's Bekaa Valley. Israel demanded that the missiles be removed because they violated a 1976 understanding between the governments. The demand, backed up by bombing raids, prompted the Reagan Administration to send veteran diplomat Philip C. Habib as a special envoy to avert a new conflict between the nations.

Habib's carefully engineered cease-fire was shattered by a new Israeli invasion in June 1982, when Israeli aircraft bombed Bekaa Valley missile sites.

Nevertheless, while the Israelis overran most of the rest of Lebanon, the Syrians retained their positions in the Bekaa Valley. As the various Lebanese factions fought each other, the Syrians became the dominant force in the country, both militarily and politically.

The first Arab country to condemn Iraq's invasion of Kuwait, Syria sent troops to help defend Saudi Arabia from possible Iraqi attack. After the Gulf war hope for peace negotiations between Israel and Arab states, particularly Syria, rose then foundered.

In 1990 President Assad ruled out any possibility of legalizing opposition political parties. According to official sources, voters in December 1991 approved Assad staying on for a fourth term in office, giving him 99.98% of the vote.

An August general election saw another victory for the ruling party and its allies, albeit with a relatively low voter turnout.

The slowdown in the Israeli-Palestinian peace process brought with it no progress or improvement in Israeli-Syrian relations during 1996. A government spokesman blamed a January 1997 bomb attack in central Damascus on Israeli agents. Israel denied the charge.

TAIWAN

Republic of China
President: Lee Teng-hui (1988)
Premier: Lien Chan (1993)
Area: 13,895 sq mi. (35,988 sq km)
Population (1997): 21,655,515 (average annual rate of natural increase: 0.92%); birth rate: 14.83/1000; infant mortality rate: 6.9/1000; density per square mile: 1,558.5
Capital and largest city (1995): Taipei, 2,643,439. **Largest cities:** Kaohsiung, 1,423,163; Tai Chung, 848,320; Tainan, 705,565; Keelung, 367,668. **Monetary unit:** New Taiwan dollar. **Languages:** Chinese

(Mandarin). **Ethnicity/Race:** Taiwanese 84%, mainland Chinese 14%, aborigine 2%. **Religions:** Buddhist, 4.86 million; Taoist, 3.3 million; Protestant, 422,000; Catholic, 304,000. **Literacy rate:** 93.4%

Economic summary: Gross national product: purchasing power parity (1995 est.): $290.5 billion; per capita income $13,510; real growth rate 6%; inflation 4%; unemployment 1.6%. Arable land: 25%; principal products: rice, yams, sugar cane, bananas, pineapples, citrus fruits. Labor force: 8.874 million: 39% in industry; 11% in agriculture; 49% in services. Major products: textiles, clothing, chemicals, processed foods, electronic equipment, cement, ships, plywood. Natural resources: coal, natural gas, limestone, marble. Exports: $93 billion (f.o.b., 1994): textiles, electronic products, information and commercial products, plywood. Imports: $85.1 billion (c.i.f.,1994): machinery, basic metals, crude oil, chemicals. Major trading partners: U.S., Hong Kong, Japan, Germany.

Geography. The Republic of China today consists of the island of Taiwan, an island 100 miles (161 km) off the Asian mainland in the Pacific; two off-shore islands, Kinmen (Quemoy) and Matsu; and the nearby islets of the Pescadores chain. It is slightly larger than the combined areas of Massachusetts and Connecticut.

Taiwan is divided by a central mountain range that runs from north to south, rising sharply on the east coast and descending gradually to a broad western plain, where cultivation is concentrated.

Government. The central government consists of five major branches called Yuans: Executive, Legislative, Judicial, Control, and Examination. The President and Vice President are popularly elected for a term of four years. The role of parliament is jointly filled by the National Assembly, the members of which are elected for four-year terms, and the Legislative Yuan, to which members are elected for three-year terms. Taiwan's internal affairs are administered by the Taiwan Provincial Government, led by the Provincial Governor under the supervision of the Provincial Assembly, both popularly elected.

The majority and ruling party is the Kuomintang (KMT; Nationalist Party) led by President Lee Teng-hui. The main opposition parties are the Democratic Progressive Party (DPP) and the New Party.

History. Taiwan was inhabited by aborigines of Malayan descent when Chinese from the areas now designated as Fukien and Kwangtung began settling it beginning in the 7th century, becoming the majority.

The Portuguese explored the area in 1590, naming it The Beautiful (Formosa). In 1624 the Dutch set up forts in the south, the Spanish in the North. The Dutch threw out the Spanish in 1641 and controlled the island until 1661, when the Chinese General Koxinga took it over, established an independent kingdom, and expelled the Dutch. The Manchus seized the island in 1683 and held it until 1895, when it passed to Japan after the first Sino-Japanese War. Japan developed and exploited it, and it was heavily bombed by American planes during World War II, after which it was restored to China.

After the defeat of its armies on the mainland, the Nationalist Government of Generalissimo Chiang Kai-shek retreated to Taiwan in December 1949. With only 15% of the population consisting of the 1949 immigrants, Chiang dominated the island, maintaining a 600,000-man army in the hope of eventually recovering the mainland. Japan renounced its claim to the island by the San Francisco Peace Treaty of 1951.

By stationing a fleet in the Strait of Formosa the U.S. prevented a mainland invasion in 1953.

The "China seat" in the U.N., which the Nationalists held with U.S. help for over two decades was lost in October 1971, when the People's Republic of China was admitted and Taiwan ousted by the UN.

Chiang died at 87 of a heart attack on April 5, 1975. His son, Chiang Ching-kuo, continued as Premier and dominant power in the Taipei regime.

Martial law was lifted in 1987. In April 1991 President Lee Teng-Hui formally declared an end to emergency rule, yet without abandoning his government's claim to be the sole legitimate government of China.

In the first full election in many decades the governing Kuomintang in December 1991 won 71% of the vote, affirming the party's opposition to independence in principle from China.

In February 1993 the President, himself a native Taiwanese, nominated Lien Chan, another native to be Prime Minister, marking a further generational shift away from mainland exiles.

In the island's first free presidential election voters defied mainland intimidation and gave 54% of the vote to incumbent President Lee Teng-hui. The second-place finisher, with 21%, advocated complete independence from China.

The ruling Nationalists successfully defeated repeated no-confidence motions raised in response to a crime wave in May 1997. The President made a public apology and promised a new cabinet would be formed.

TAJIKISTAN

Republic of Tajikistan
President: Imomali Rakhmonov (1993)
Prime Minister: Yakhyo Azimov (1996)
Area: 55,300 sq mi. (143,100 sq km)
Population (1997 est.): 6,013,855 (average annual rate of natural increase: 2.55%); birth rate, 33.95/1000; infant mortality rate: 110.9/1000; density per square mile: 108.7
Capital and largest city (1994 est.): Dushanbe, 524,000;. **Other large city:** Khodzhent (Leninabad), 164,500. **Monetary unit:** Tajik ruble. **Religion:** Sunni Moslem, 80%. **Ethnicity/Race:** Tajik 64.9%, Uzbek 25%, Russian 3.5% (declining because of emigration), other 6.6%. **Language:** Tajik. **Literacy rate:** 98% (1989)
Economic summary: Gross national product: purchasing power parity (1995 estimate as extrapolated from the World Bank estimate for 1994): $6.4 billion; per capita $1,040; real growth rate −12.4%; inflation 28% (monthly average); unemployment 3.3%. Arable land: 6%. Labor force: 1.95 million (1992): agriculture and forestry 43%, government services 24%, industry 14%, trade and communications 11%, construction 8% (1990). Industries: aluminum, zinc, lead, cement, vegetable oil, metal cutting machine tools, refrigerators and freezers. Agriculture: cotton, grain, fruits, and grapes. Exports: $707 million (1995): aluminum, cotton, fruits, vegetable oil, textiles. Imports: $690 million (1995): chemicals, machinery and transport equipment, textiles, foodstuffs. Major trading partners: Russia, Kazakhstan, Ukraine, Uzbekistan, Turkmenistan.

Geography. Ninety-three percent of Tajikistan's territory is mountainous and the mountain glaciers are the source of its rivers. Tajikistan is an earthquake-prone area. The republic is bounded by China in the east, Afghanistan to the south, Uzbekistan and Kirghizia to the west and north. The central Asian republic also includes the Gorno-Badakh Shan Autonomous region. Tajikistan is slightly larger than the state of Illinois in area.

Government. A parliamentary democracy. The Assembly (parliament) is the Majlis.

History. The name Tadzhikstan (now Tajikistan) dates from the 1920s when the territory became an official Russian administrative area. The Tajiks had an ancient nomadic culture and were ruled at different times by Afghanistan and Persia.

Tajikistan declared its sovereignty in August 1990. In 1991, the republic's Communist leadership supported the attempted coup against Soviet President Mikhail Gorbachev. Shortly afterward pro-Communist President Makhkamov was forced to resign by mounting pressure from pro-democracy groups and the Tajikistan parliament restored an earlier ban on the Communist Party. The ban was rescinded in late September but again restored. The election of November 24 went to Rakhmon Nabiyev, former head of the local Communist Party.

Tajikistan joined with ten other former Soviet republics in the Commonwealth of Independent States on Dec. 21, 1991. A parliamentary republic was proclaimed and presidential rule abolished on November 1992. Former Communists dominated the government.

The new government immediately set out to destroy the anti-Communist coalition, consisting principally of Western-oriented intellectuals and Muslims.

Despite international efforts to end a three-year civil war, periodic fighting continued into 1996. In December the two sides signed a cease-fire and in March 1997 an agreement was reached in Moscow calling for reintegration of rebel troops into the regular armed forces. The continuing talks, however, broke down in April. Later that month the President was wounded in an assassination attempt. In May the two sides agreed on political reforms that included recognition of opposition parties.

TANZANIA

United Republic of Tanzania
President: Benjamin William Mkapa (1995)
Prime Minister: Frederick Tluway Sumaye (1995)
Area: 364,879 sq mi. (945,037 sq km)[1]
Population (1997 est.): 29,460,753 (average annual rate of natural increase: 2.18%); birth rate: 40.92/1000; infant mortality rate: 104.8/1000; density per square mile: 80.7
Capital and largest city (1988): Dar es Salaam, 1,360,850[2]. **Monetary unit:** Tanzanian shilling. **Languages:** Swahili, English, local languages. **Ethnicity/Race:** mainland: native African (95% Bantu, consisting of well over 100 tribes) 99%, Asian, European, and Arab 1%. Zanzibar: Arab, mixed Arab and native African, native African. **Religions:** Christian, 40%; Muslim, 33%. **Literacy rate:** 46%
Economic summary: Gross domestic product: purchasing power parity (1995 est.): $23.1 billion; $800 per capita; 2.7% real growth rate; inflation 25% (1994 est.); unemployment n.a. Arable land: 5%. Principal agricultural products: tobacco, corn, cassava, wheat, cotton, coffee, sisal, cashew nuts, pyrethrum, cloves. Labor force: 13.495 million; 90% in agriculture; 10% in industry and commerce (1996 est.). Major industrial products: textiles, wood products, refined oil, processed agricultural products, diamonds, cement, fertilizer. Natural resources: hydroelectric potential, phosphates, iron and coal. Exports: $462 million (f.o.b., 1994): coffee, cotton, sisal, cloves, cashew nuts, tobacco, tea. Imports: $1.4 billion (c.i.f., 1994): manufactured goods, machinery and transport equipment, crude oil, foodstuffs, cotton piece goods. Major trading partners: Germany, U.K., U.S., Japan, Italy, Denmark, Kenya, Netherlands, Hong Kong. **Member of Commonwealth of Nations**

1. Including Zanzibar. 2. Some government offices have been transferred to Dodoma, which is planned as the new national capital by the end of the 1990s.

Geography. Tanzania is in East Africa on the Indian Ocean. To the north are Uganda and Kenya; to the west, Burundi, Rwanda, and Congo; and to the south, Mozambique, Zambia, and Malawi. Its area is three times that of New Mexico.

Tanzania contains three of Africa's best-known lakes—Victoria in the north, Tanganyika in the west, and Nyasa in the south. Mount Kilimanjaro in the north, 19,340 feet (5,895 m), is the highest point on the continent.

Government. Under the republican form of government, Tanzania has a President elected by universal suffrage who appoints the cabinet ministers. The 275 members of the National Assembly are composed of 252 elected members from the mainland, 50 elected from Zanzibar, 10 members appointed by the President (from both Tanganyika and Zanzibar), 5 national members (elected by the National Assembly after nomination by various national institutions), 20 members elected by Zanzibar's House of Representatives, 25 Regional Commissioners sitting as *ex officio* members, and 15 seats reserved for women (elected by the National Assembly).

The Tanganyika African National Union, the only authorized party on the mainland, and the Afro-Shirazi Party, the only party in Zanzibar and Pemba, merged in 1977 as the Revolutionary Party (Chama Cha Mapinduzi) and elected Julius K. Nyerere as its head.

History. Arab traders first began to colonize the area in c.e. 700. Portuguese explorers reached the coastal regions in 1500 and held some control until the 17th century, when the Sultan of Oman took power. With what are now Burundi and Rwanda, Tanganyika became the colony of German East Africa in 1885. After World War I, it was administered by Britain under a League of Nations mandate and later as a U.N. trust territory.

Although not mentioned in old histories until the 12th century, Zanzibar was believed always to have had connections with southern Arabia. The Portuguese made it one of their tributaries in 1503 and later established a trading post, but they were driven out by Arabs from Oman in 1698. Zanzibar was declared independent of Oman in 1861 and, in 1890, it became a British protectorate.

Tanganyika became independent on Dec. 9, 1961; Zanzibar, on Dec. 10, 1963. On April 26, 1964, the two nations merged into the United Republic of Tanganyika and Zanzibar. The name was changed to Tanzania six months later.

An invasion by Ugandan troops in November 1978 was followed by a counterattack in January 1979, in which 5,000 Tanzanian troops were joined by 3,000 Ugandan exiles opposed to President Idi Amin. Within a month, full-scale war developed.

Tanzanian President Julius Nyerere kept troops in Uganda in open support of former Ugandan President Milton Obote, despite protests from opposition groups, until the national elections in December 1980.

In November 1985, Nyerere stepped down as President. Ali Hassan Mwinyi, his Vice-President, succeeded him. Running unopposed Mwinyi was elected President in October. Shortly thereafter plans were announced to study the benefits of instituting a multiparty democracy.

The crisis in Rwanda in 1994 sent hundreds of thousands of refugees fleeing into Tanzania, taxing the already-meager resources of the country. The government immediately appealed for international aid.

In October 1995 the country's first multiparty elections since independence took place. Although the opposition claimed irregularities had occurred, it came just short of victory in both the presidential voting and that for the legislature.

The presidential election in October 1996 on Zanzibar was won by Salmin Armour, but the main opposition party boycotted parliament since claiming irregularities in the voting.

THAILAND

Kingdom of Thailand

Ruler: King Bhumibol Adulyadej (1946)
Prime Minister: Chaovalit Yongchaiyuth (1996)
Area: 198,455 sq mi. (514,000 sq km)
Population (1997 est.): 59,450,818 (average annual rate of natural increase 0.99%); birth rate: 17.03/1000; infant mortality rate: 32.1/1000; density per square mile: 299.6
Capital and largest city (1993 est.): Bangkok, 5,572,712. **Other large cities:** Nonthanburi, 261,335; Chiang Mai, 170,397. **Monetary unit:** Baht. **Languages:** Thai (Siamese), Chinese, English. **Ethnicity/Race:** Thai 75%, Chinese 14%, other 11%. **Religions:** Buddhist, 94.4%; Islam, 4%; Hinduism, 1.1%; Christian, 0.5%. **Literacy rate:** 93%
Economic summary: Gross national product: purchasing power parity (1995 est.): $416.7 billion; $6,900 per capita; real growth rate 8.6%; inflation 5.8%; unemployment 2.7%. Arable land: 34%. Principal agricultural products: rice, rubber, corn, tapioca, sugar, coconuts. Labor force: 32,152,600; 57% in agriculture; 17% in industry; 11% in commerce; 15% in services, including government. Major industries: tourism (largest source of foreign exchange), textiles and garments, agricultural processing, beverages, tobacco, cement, light manufacturing, electric appliances and components, integrated circuits, furniture, plastics, tungsten and tin. Natural resources: fish, natural gas, forests, fluorite, tin, tungsten. Exports: $45.1 billion (f.o.b., 1994): machinery and manufactures, 76.9%; agricultural products, 14.9%; fisheries products, 5.9%. Imports: $53.9 billion (c.i.f., 1994): capital goods, 41.4%; intermediate goods and raw materials, 32.8%; consumer goods, 10.4%; oil, 8.2%. Major trading partners: Japan, U.S., Singapore, Germany, Taiwan, Malaysia, Hong Kong, South Korea, U.K., France.

Geography. Thailand occupies the western half of the Indochinese peninsula and the northern two-thirds of the Malay peninsula in southeast Asia. Its neighbors are Burma (Myanmar) on the north and west, Laos on the north and northeast, Cambodia on the east, and Malaysia on the south. Thailand is about the size of France.

Most of the population is supported in the fertile central alluvial plain, which is drained by the Chao Phraya River and its tributaries.

Government. A constitutional monarchy. The government is run by an elected civilian coalition of political parties. King Bhumibol Adulyadej, who was born Dec. 5, 1927, second son of Prince Mahidol of Songkhla, succeeded to the throne on June 9, 1946. He was married on April 28, 1950, to Queen Sirikit; their son, Vajiralongkorn, born July 28, 1952, is the crown Prince.

History. The Thais first began moving down into their present homeland from the Asian continent in the 6th century C.E. and by the end of the 13th century ruled most of the western portion. During the next 400 years, the Thais fought sporadically with the Cambodians and the Burmese. The British obtained recognition of paramount interest in Thailand in 1824, and in 1896 an Anglo-French accord guaranteed the independence of Thailand.

A coup in 1932 changed the absolute monarchy into a representative government with universal suffrage.

After five hours of token resistance on Dec. 8, 1941, Thailand yielded to Japanese occupation and became one of the springboards in World War II for the Japanese campaign against Malaya.

After the fall of its pro-Japanese puppet government in July 1944, Thailand pursued a policy of passive resistance against the Japanese, and after the Japanese surrender, Thailand repudiated the declaration of war it had been forced to make against Britain and the U.S. in 1942.

Thailand's major problem in the late 1960s was suppressing guerrilla action by Communist invaders in the north.

Although Thailand had received $2 billion in U.S. economic and military aid since 1950 and had sent troops (paid by the U.S.) to Vietnam while permitting U.S. bomber bases on its territory, the collapse of South Vietnam and Cambodia in the spring of 1975 brought rapid changes in the country's diplomatic posture.

At the Thai government's insistence, the U.S. agreed to withdraw all 23,000 U.S. military personnel remaining in Thailand by March 1976. Diplomatic relations with China were established in 1975.

After three years of civilian government ended with a military coup on Oct. 6, 1976, Thailand reverted to military rule. Political parties, banned after the coup, gained limited freedom in 1980. The same year, the National Assembly elected Gen. Prem Tinsulanonda as prime minister. General elections on April 18, 1983, and July 27, 1986, resulted in Prem continuing as prime minister over a coalition government.

Refugees from Laos, Cambodia, and Vietnam flooded into Thailand in 1978 and 1979, and despite efforts by the United States and other Western countries to resettle them, a total of 130,000 Laotian and Vietnamese refugees were living in camps along the Cambodian border in mid-1980. A drive by Vietnamese occupation forces on western Cambodian areas loyal to the Pol Pot government, culminating in invasions of Thai territory in late June, drove an estimated 100,000 Cambodians across the line as refugees, adding to the 200,000 of their countrymen already in Thailand.

On April 3, 1981, a military coup against the Prem government failed. Another coup attempt on Sept. 9, 1985, was crushed by loyal troops after 10 hours of fighting in Bangkok. Four persons were killed and about 60 wounded.

In February 1991 a nonviolent military coup led by Gen. Suchinda Kraprayoon overthrew the democratic government charging corruption. The junta leaders declared a state of emergency and martial law dismissed the houses of parliament and abolished the constitution.

Parliamentary elections in March 1992 gave more than half the seats at stake to pro-military parties. In April the top military commander was appointed prime minister.

A scandal over a land-reform program caused the fall of the government in May 1995. The Prime Minister dissolved parliament and set a date for new elections. The results of the early July voting gave the largest number of seats in parliament to the Thai Nation Party, whose leader moved quickly to form a coalition government.

A new draft constitution, calling for cabinet ministers to relinquish their parliamentary seats, came under fire in the early months of 1997 from a number of politicians.

In 1997, Thailand's economy, once one of the strongest in the region, collapsed under economic mismanagement and corruption.

TOGO

Republic of Togo
National name: République Togolaise
President: Gen. Gnassingbe Eyadema (1967)
Prime Minister: Kwassi Klutse (1996)
Area: 21,925 sq mi. (56,785 sq km)
Population (1997 est.): 4,735,610 (average annual rate of natural increase: 3.53%); birth rate: 45.71/1000; infant mortality rate: 82.1/1000; density per sq mi.: 216
Capital and largest city (1983): Lomé, 366,476.
Monetary unit: Franc CFA. **Languages:** Ewé, Mina (south), Kabyé, Cotocoli (north), French (official), and many dialects. **Ethnicity/Race:** native African (37 tribes; largest and most important are Ewe, Mina, and Kabre) 99%, European and Syrian-Lebanese less than 1%. **Religions:** Indigenous beliefs, 70%; Christian, 20%; Islam, 10%. **Literacy rate:** 43%
Economic summary: Gross domestic product: purchasing power parity (1995 est.): $4.1 billion; $900 per capita; real growth rate 6%; inflation 8.8%; unemployment: n.a. Arable land: 25%. Principal agricultural products: yams, cotton, millet, sorghum, cocoa, coffee, rice. Labor force (1993 est.): 1.538 million; 64% in agriculture; 9% in industry; 21% in services (1981 est.). Major industrial products: phosphate, textiles, processed food. Natural resources: marble, phosphate, limestone. Exports: $162.2 million (f.o.b., 1994): phosphate, cocoa, coffee, cotton. Imports: $212 million (c.i.f., 1994): consumer goods, fuels, machinery, foodstuffs, chemical products. Major trading partners: E.U., Japan, U.S., Africa.

Geography. Togo, twice the size of Maryland, is on the south coast of West Africa bordering on Ghana to the west, Burkina Faso to the north and Benin to the east. The Gulf of Guinea coastline, only 32 miles long (51 km), is low and sandy. The only port is at Lomé. The Togo hills traverse the central section.

Government. The government of Nicolas Grunitzky was overthrown in a bloodless coup on Jan. 13, 1967, led by Lt. Col. Etienne Eyadema (now Gen. Gnassingbé Eyadema). A National Reconciliation Committee was set up to rule the country. In April, however, Eyadema dissolved the Committee and took over as President. In December 1979, a 67-member National Assembly was voted in by national referendum. The Assembly of the Togolese People is the only political party.

History. Freed slaves from Brazil were the first traders to settle in Togo. Established as a German colony (Togoland) in 1884, the area was split between the British and the French as League of Nations mandates after World War I and subsequently administered as U.N. trusteeships. The British portion voted for incorporation with Ghana. Togo became independent on April 27, 1960.

The presidential election held in August 1993 gave Eyadema more than 96% of the vote, but only 36% of the electorate went to the polls. Many of the major opposition candidates withdrew prior to the election.

Elections to the National Assembly in February 1994 gave opposition parties a majority of seats. A coalition government was formed in June, although the President's party was allotted a disproportionately large number of ministries. As a result the principal opposition party boycotted the Assembly. The impasse ended in August when the government announced that an independent electoral commission would oversee future balloting.

In August 1996 Prime Minister Edem Kodjo resigned. The Planning Minister, Kwassi Klutse, was then appointed prime minister. In a few days he formed a government.

TONGA

Kingdom of Tonga
Sovereign: King Taufa'ahau Tupou IV (1965)
Prime Minister: Baron Vaea (1991)
Area: 290 sq mi. (751 sq km)
Population (1997 est.): 107,335 (average annual growth rate: 2.08%); birth rate: 26.95/1000; infant mortality rate: 39.2/1000; density per square mile: 370.1
Capital and largest city (1990 est.): Nuku'alofa, 34,000. **Monetary unit:** Pa'anga. **Languages:** Tongan, English. **Ethnicity/Race:** Polynesian, Europeans about 300. **Religions:** Christian; Free Wesleyan Church claims over 30,000 adherents. **Literacy rate:** 57%
Economic summary: Gross domestic product: purchasing power parity (1995 est.): $228 million; $2,160 per capita; real growth rate 4%; inflation 3% (1993). Arable land: 25%. Principal agricultural products: vanilla, coffee, ginger, black pepper, coconuts, bananas, copra. Labor force (1990 est.): 32,013; 70% in agriculture (1995 est.). Natural resources: fish, copra. Exports: $20.3 million (f.o.b., FY 93/94): copra, coconut products, bananas, fruits, vegetables, fish, vanilla. Imports: $57.8 million (c.i.f., FY 93/94): foodstuffs, machinery and transport equipment, fuels, chemicals, building materials. Major trading partners: New Zealand, Australia, Fiji, U.S., Japan, E.U. **Member of Commonwealth of Nations**

Geography. Situated east of the Fiji Islands in the South Pacific, Tonga (also called the Friendly Islands) consists of some 150 islands, of which 36 are inhabited. Most of the islands contain active volcanic craters; others are coral atolls.

Government. Tonga is a constitutional monarchy. Executive authority is vested in the sovereign, a privy council, and a cabinet headed by the prime minister. Legislative authority is vested in the Legislative Assembly. Nine seats are reserved for commoners; the others filled by appointees of the king.

History. The present dynasty of Tonga was founded in 1831 by Taufa'ahau Tupou, who took the name George I. He consolidated the Kingdom by conquest and in 1875 granted a constitution.

In 1900, his great-grandson, George II, signed a treaty of friendship with Britain, and the country became a British protected state. The treaty was revised in 1959. Tonga became independent on June 4, 1970.

Moves were made in 1992 to form a political party independent of the hereditary nobility that dominates the parliament.

A general election in February 1993 gave six of the nine contested parliamentary seats to pro-democracy candidates. The King, however, refused major changes in the system of government.

The European Union in April 1997 offered millions of dollars in aid grants. In addition, the international community provided emergency assistance in the wake of Cyclone Hina's damage.

TRINIDAD AND TOBAGO

Republic of Trinidad and Tobago
President: A.N.R. Robinson (1997)
Prime Minister: Basdeo Panday (1995)
Area: 1,980 sq mi. (5,128 sq km)
Population (1997 est.): 1,273,141 (average annual rate of natural increase: 0.89%); birth rate: 15.92/1000; infant mortality rate: 17.9/1000; density per square mile: 643
Capital and largest city (1995): Port-of-Spain, 52,451.

Monetary unit: Trinidad and Tobago dollar. **Languages:** English (official); Hindi, French, Spanish. **Ethnicity/Race:** black 43%, East Indian (a local term—primarily immigrants from northern India) 40%, mixed 14%, white 1%, Chinese 1%, other 1%. **Religions:** Roman Catholic, 33%; Hindu, 25%; Anglican, 15%; other Christian, 14%; Muslim, 6%. **Literacy rate:** 98% **Economic summary:** Gross domestic product: purchasing power parity (1995 est.): $16.2 billion; $12,100 per capita; real growth rate 3.5%; inflation 5.4%; unemployment 17.8%. Arable land: 14%. Principal products: sugar cane, cocoa, coffee, citrus. Labor force: 404,500; 14% in manufacturing, mining, and quarrying; 13% in construction and utilities; 11% in agriculture; 62% in services. Major industrial products: petroleum, processed food, cement; tourism. Natural resources: petroleum, natural gas, asphalt. Exports: $2.2 billion (f.o.b., 1995): including reexports—petroleum and petroleum products, steel products, fertilizer, sugar, cocoa, coffee, citrus fruits (1988). Imports: $996 million (c.i.f., 1994): raw materials, capital goods, consumer goods. Major trading partners: U.S., Caribbean, Latin America, Western Europe, U.K., Canada. **Member of Commonwealth of Nations**

Geography. Trinidad and Tobago lies in the Caribbean Sea off the northeast coast of Venezuela. The area of the two islands is slightly less than that of Delaware. Trinidad, the larger, is mainly flat and rolling, with mountains in the north that reach a height of 3,085 feet (940 m) at Mount Aripo. Tobago is heavily forested with hardwood trees.

Government. A parliamentary democracy. The legislature consists of a 24-member Senate and a 36-member House of Representatives. The political parties are the People's National Movement led by Prime Minister Mr. Patrick Manning (21 seats in the House of Representatives); the United National Congress led by Mr. Basdeo Panday (19 seats); and the National Alliance for Reconstruction led by Mr. Selby Wilson (2 seats).

History. Trinidad was explored by Columbus in 1498 and remained in Spanish possession, despite raids by other European nations, until it capitulated to the British in 1797 during a war between Britain and Spain.

Trinidad was ceded to Britain in 1802, and in 1899 it was united with Tobago as a colony. From 1958 to 1962, Trinidad and Tobago was a part of the West Indies Federation, and on Aug, 31, 1962, it became independent.

On Aug. 1, 1976, Trinidad and Tobago cut its ties with Britain and became a republic, remaining within the Commonwealth and recognizing Queen Elizabeth II only as head of that organization.

The People's National Movement won a landslide victory in elections of December 1991, making Manning prime minister.

Manning called an early election in November 1995. His party lost seats and he would not enter into a coalition, which the opposition was willing to do with the National Alliance for Reconstruction.

Robinson was sworn into office as President in March 1997 having received 46 votes in the Electoral College against the opposition candidate who polled 18.

TUNISIA

Republic of Tunisia
National name: Al-Joumhouria Attunisia
President: Mr. Zine El Abidine Ben Ali (1987)
Prime Minister: Hamed Karoui (1989)
Area: 63,170 sq mi. (163,610 sq km)
Population (1997 est.): 9,183,097 (average annual rate of natural increase: 1.84%); birth rate: 23.68/1000; infant mortality rate: 33.9/1000; density per sq mi.: 145.4
Capital and largest city (1994): Tunis, 887,800. **Monetary unit:** Tunisian dinar. **Languages:** Arabic, French. **Ethnicity/Race:** Arab-Berber 98%, European 1%, Jewish less than 1%. **Religion:** Islam (Sunni), 98%; Christian, 1%; Jewish, less than 1%. **Literacy rate:** 65%
Economic summary: Gross domestic product: purchasing power parity (1994 est.): $37.1 billion; $4,250 per capita; real growth rate 4.4%; inflation 5.5% (1995 est.); unemployment 16.2% (1993 est.). Arable land: 20%. Principal agricultural products: wheat, olives, oranges, grapes, dates. Labor force: 2.917 million (1993 est.); 55% in services; 23% in industry; 22% in agriculture (1995 est.). Manufacturing 21% of GDP, agriculture 15%, Tourism 7% of GDP. Major industrial products: textiles and leather, chemical fertilizers, petroleum, phosphate, iron ore. Tourism is an important industry. Natural resources: oil, phosphates, iron ore, lead, zinc. Exports: $4.7 billion (f.o.b., 1994): textiles, crude oil, olive oil, phosphoric acid, chemical fertilizers, triple superphosphate, fish, dates. Imports: $6.6 billion (c.i.f., 1994): raw materials, consumer goods, machinery and equipment, foodstuffs. Major trading partners: France, Italy, Germany, U.S., Belgium and Luxembourg, Spain, the Netherlands.

Geography. Tunisia, at the northernmost bulge of Africa, thrusts out toward Sicily to mark the division between the eastern and western Mediterranean Sea. Twice the size of South Carolina, it is bordered on the west by Algeria and by Libya on the south.

Coastal plains on the east rise to a north-south escarpment which slopes gently to the west. Saharan in the south, Tunisia is more mountainous in the north, where the Atlas range continues from Algeria.

Government. Executive power is vested by the constitution in the President, elected for five years and eligible for re-election to two additional terms. Legislative power is vested in a Chamber of Deputies elected by universal suffrage.

In 1975, the Chamber of Deputies amended the constitution to make Habib Bourguiba President for life. At 71, Bourguiba was re-elected to a fourth five-year term when he ran unopposed in 1974. He was deposed by Gen. Zine Ben Ali in 1987. Ben Ali was re-elected in 1989, and again for another five year term in 1994. Opposition parties entered the Chamber of Deputies for the first time (19 seats out of 163).

History. Tunisia was settled by the Phoenicians and Carthaginians in ancient times. Except for an interval of Vandal conquest in C.E. 439–533, it was part of the Roman Empire until the Arab conquest of 648–69. It was ruled by various Arab and Berber dynasties until the Turks took it in 1570–74. French troops occupied the country in 1881, and the Bey signed a treaty acknowledging a French protectorate.

Nationalist agitation forced France to grant internal autonomy to Tunisia in 1955 and to recognize Tunisian independence and sovereignty in 1956. The Constituent Assembly deposed the Bey on July 25, 1957, declared Tunisia a republic, and elected Habib Bourguiba as President. Bourguiba maintained a pro-Western foreign policy that earned him enemies. Tunisia refused to break relations with the U.S. during the Israeli-Arab war in June 1967.

Concerned with Islamic fundamentalist plots against the state, the government stepped up efforts to eradicate the movement including censorship and frequent detention of suspects.

Elections in March 1994 gave a vast majority of seats to the ruling party. The President ran unopposed as no other candidate was able to qualify.

An Association Agreement was signed in July 1995 with the E.U. that after 12 years would make the country a part of a free-trade area around the Mediterranean, called the European Economic Area.

The government in June 1997 penned an agreement with Japan's Export–Import Bank for a loan of 10 billion yen that is earmarked to support Tunisia's private sector.

TURKEY

Republic of Turkey
National name: Türkiye Cumhuriyeti
President: Süleyman Demirel (1993)
Prime Minister: Mesut Yilmaz (1997)
Area: 300,947 sq mi. (incl. 9,121 in Europe) (779,452 sq km)
Population (1997 est.): 63,528,225; average annual rate of natural increase 1.64%; birth rate: 21.83/1000; infant mortality rate: 40.7/1000; density per square mile: 211.1
Capital: Ankara (2,719,981). **Largest cities (1993):** Istanbul, 7,331,927; Izmir, 1,920,807; Adana, 1,010,363; Bursa, 949,810; Gaziantep, 683,557. **Monetary unit:** Turkish Lira. **Language:** Turkish. **Ethnicity/Race:** Turkish 80%, Kurdish 20%. **Religion:** Islam (mostly Sunni), 98%. **Literacy rate:** 90.7%
Economic summary: Gross domestic product: purchasing power parity (1995 est.): $345.7 billion; $5,500 per capita; real growth rate 6.8%; inflation: 94%; unemployment: 10.2%. Arable land: 20%. Principal agricultural products: cotton, tobacco, cereals, sugar beets, fruits, olives. Labor force: 20.9 million; 46% in agriculture; 31% in services; 23% in industry (note: in 1994 about 1.5 million Turks worked abroad). Major industrial products: textiles, coal, minerals, processed foods, steel, petroleum. Natural resources: coal, chromite, copper, borate, sulfur, petroleum. Exports: $20.7 billion (1995 est.): agricultural products, textiles, leather, glass. Imports: $32.6 billion (f.o.b., 1995 est.): crude oil, machinery, motor vehicles, metals, mineral fuels, fertilizer, chemicals. Major trading partners: Germany, France, Italy, U.S., U.K., Iran, Japan, Russia.

Geography. Turkey is at the northeastern end of the Mediterranean Sea in southeast Europe and southwest Asia. To the north is the Black Sea and to the west the Aegean Sea. Its neighbors are Greece and Bulgaria to the west, Russia and Ukraine to the north (through the Black Sea), Georgia, Armenia, Azerbaijain, and Iran to the east, and Syria and Iraq to the south. The Dardanelles, the Sea of Marmara, and the Bosporus divide the country.

Turkey in Europe comprises an area about equal to the state of Massachusetts. It is hilly country drained by the Maritsa River and its tributaries.

Turkey in Asia, or Anatolia, about the size of Texas, is roughly a rectangle in shape with its short sides on the east and west. Its center is a treeless plateau rimmed by mountains.

Government. The President is elected by the Grand National Assembly for a seven-year term and is not eligible for re-election. The Prime Minister and the Council of Ministers hold the executive power although the President has the right to veto legislation.

History. The Ottoman Turks first appeared in the early 13th century in Anatolia, subjugating Turkish and Mongol bands pressing against the eastern borders of Byzantium. They gradually spread through the Near East and Balkans, capturing Constantinople in 1453 and storming the gates of Vienna two centuries later. At its height, the Ottoman Empire stretched from the Persian Gulf to western Algeria.

Defeat of the Turkish navy at Lepanto by the Holy League in 1571 and failure of the siege of Vienna heralded the decline of Turkish power. By the 18th century, Russia was seeking to establish itself as the protector of Christians in Turkey's Balkan territories. Russian ambitions were checked by Britain and France in the Crimean War (1854–56), but the Russo-Turkish War (1877–78) gave Bulgaria virtual independence and Romania and Serbia liberation from their nominal allegiance to the Sultan.

Turkish weakness stimulated a revolt of young liberals known as the Young Turks in 1909. They forced Sultan Abdul Hamid to grant a constitution and install a liberal government. Reforms were no barrier to further defeats, however, in a war with Italy (1911–12) and the Balkan Wars (1912–13). Under the influence of German military advisors, Turkey signed a secret alliance with Germany on Aug. 2, 1914, that led to a declaration of war by the Allied powers and the ultimate humiliation of the occupation of Turkish territory by Greek and other Allied troops.

In 1919, the new Nationalist movement, headed by Mustafa Kemal, was organized to resist the Allied occupation and, in 1920, a National Assembly elected him President of both the Assembly and the government. Under his leadership, the Greeks were driven out of Smyrna, and other Allied forces were withdrawn.

The present Turkish boundaries (with the exception of Alexandretta, ceded to Turkey by France in 1939) were fixed by the Treaty of Lausanne (1923) and later negotiations. The caliphate and Sultanate were separated, and the Sultanate was abolished in 1922. On Oct. 29, 1923, Turkey formally became a republic, with Mustafa Kemal, who took the name Kemal Atatürk, as its first President. The caliphate was abolished in 1924, and Atatürk proceeded to carry out an extensive program of reform, modernization, and industrialization.

Gen. Ismet Inönü was elected to succeed Atatürk in 1938 and was re-elected in 1939, 1943, and 1946. Defeated in 1950, he was succeeded by Celâl Bayar. In 1939, a mutual assistance pact was concluded with Britain and France. Neutral during most of World War II Turkey, on Feb. 23, 1945, declared war on Germany and Japan, but took no active part in the conflict.

Turkey became a full member of NATO in 1952.

Turkey invaded Cyprus by sea and air July 20, 1974, following the failure of diplomatic efforts to resolve the crisis caused by the ouster of Archbishop Makarios.

Talks in Geneva involving Greece, Turkey, Britain, and Greek Cypriot and Turkish Cypriot leaders broke down in mid-August. Turkey unilaterally announced a cease-fire August 16, after having gained control of 40% of the island. Turkish Cypriots established their own state in the north on Feb. 13, 1975.

In July 1975, after a 30-day warning, Turkey took over control of all the U.S. installations except the big joint defense base at Incirlik, which it reserved for "NATO tasks alone."

The establishment of military government in September 1980 stopped the slide toward anarchy and brought some improvement in the economy.

A Constituent Assembly, consisting of the six-member National Security Council and members appointed by them, drafted a new constitution that was approved by an overwhelming (91.5%) majority of the voters in a Nov. 6, 1982, referendum. Prime Minister Turgut Özal's Motherland Party came to power in parliamentary elections held in late 1983. Özal was re-elected in November 1987.

The sudden death of Turgut Özal in April 1993 led to Suleyman Demirel assuming the presidency in May. In June the True Path Party chose Tansu Ciller as its new leader leading to her appointment as Turkey's first female prime minister.

In March 1995 as many as 35,000 Turkish troops moved into northern Iraq seeking to root out Kurdish rebels, who had used Iraq as a base.

Inconclusive elections in December 1995 resulted in a six-month power struggle. In June 1996 an agreement was reached with the Welfare Party (RP).

The army, alarmed at the government's failures to rein in radical Islamic groups and practices, warned in February 1997 of the possibility of military intervention. In May the prime minister pledged not to follow the path of Iran.

TURKMENISTAN

Turkmenistan
President: Saparmurad A. Niyazov (1990)
Prime Minister: Khan Akhmedov (1992)
Area: 188,500 sq mi. (488,100 sq km)
Population (1997 est.): 4,225,351 (average annual rate of natural increase: 2%); birth rate: 28.78/1000; infant mortality rate: 80.6/1000; density per square mile: 22.4
Capital and largest city (1994 est.): Ashgabat, 518,000. **Largest cities:** Chardzhou, 166,400; Tashauz, 117,000. **Monetary unit:** Manat. **Languages:** Turkmen, 72%; Russian, 12%; Uzbek, 9%.
Ethnicity/Race: Turkmen 73.3%, Russian 9.8%, Uzbek 9%, Kazak 2%, other 5.9%. **Religions:** Islam, 85%; Eastern Orthodox, 10%. **Literacy rate:** 98%
Economic summary: Gross domestic product: purchasing power parity (1995 estimate as extrapolated form the World Bank estimate for 1994): $11.5 billion; $2,820 per capita; real growth rate –10%; inflation 25% (1994, per mo.); unemployment: n.a. Labor force: 1.642 million (Jan. 1994): agriculture and forestry, 44%; industry and construction, 20%; other 36% (1992). Industries: oil and gas, petrochemicals, fertilizers, food processing, textiles. Agriculture: cotton, fruits, vegetables. Exports: $1.9 billion to outside former U.S.S.R. countries (1995): natural gas, oil, chemicals, cotton, textiles, carpets. Imports: $777 million from outside the former U.S.S.R. countries (1995): machinery and parts, plastics and rubber, consumer durables, textiles, grain, foodstuffs. Major trading partners: Ukraine, Russia, Kazakhstan, Uzbekistan, Georgia, Azerbaijan, Eastern Europe, Turkey, Argentina.

Geography. Turkmenistan (formerly Turkmenia) is bounded by the Caspian Sea in the west, Kazakhstan in the north, Uzbekistan in the east, and Iran and Afghanistan in the south. Eighty percent of the republic's territory is desert. The largest desert is the Kara-Kum (Black Sand) approximately 138,966 sq mi. (360,000 sq km) in area. A 684-mile-long (1,100km) canal runs across the Kara-Kum Desert and it supplies water from the Amu Darya River for irrigation and hydroelectric power.

Government. A republic. The constitution allows for a strong presidential rule. The President heads the Cabinet of Ministers, whose members he appoints with the consent of the Meglis (parliament). There are two parliamentary bodies, the unicameral People's Council (Halk Maslahaty) with over 100 members and the 50-member unicameral Assembly (Majlis).

History. Turkmenistan was once part of the ancient Persian empire. The Turkmen people were originally pastoral nomads and some of them continued their unsettled way of life up into the 20th century, living in transportable dome-shaped felt tents. The territory was ruled by the Seljuk Turks in the 11th century. The Mongols of Ghenghis Khan conquered the land in the 13th century and dominated the area for the next two centuries until they were deposed in the late 15th century by invading Uzbeks.

Prior to the 19th century, Turkmenia was divided into two lands, one belonging to the Khanate of Khiva and the other belonging to the Khanate of Bukhara. In 1868, the Khanate of Khiva was made part of the Russian empire and Turkmenia became known as the Transcaspia Region of Russian Turkistan. Turkmenistan was later formed out of the Turkistan Autonomous Soviet Socialist Republic, founded in 1922, and was made an independent Soviet Socialist Republic on May 13, 1925.

Turkmenistan declared its sovereignty in August 1990 and became a member of the Commonwealth of Independent States on Dec. 21, 1991 together with ten other former Soviet republics.

In the presidential election of June 1992 voters re-elected President Niyazov in a one-candidate race.

The country left the ruble zone in November 1993, introducing its own currency emblazoned with the President's image. Protests both domestic and foreign against his authoritarian rule and practices notwithstanding, the President extended his term into the next century.

A referendum held in January 1994 produced a resounding vote in favor of the ruling party's proposal to postpone presidential elections until 1997.

The government signed a cooperation agreement with Iran and Armenia in April 1997 concerning trade, transport, banking, energy, and tourism. In May an agreement was reached with Pakistan and the Unocal oil company, a U.S. firm, on the construction of a pipeline to transport natural gas.

TUVALU

Sovereign: Queen Elizabeth II (1952)
Governor-General: Tulaga Manuella (1994)
Prime Minister: Bikenibeu Paeniu (1996)
Area: 10 sq mi. (26 sq km)
Population (1997 est.): 10,297; growth rate: 1.45%; birth rate: 23.31/1000; infant mortality rate: 26.9/1000; density per square mile: 1,029.7
Capital and largest city (1991): Funafuti, 3,839. **Monetary unit:** Tuvaluan dollar, Australian dollar. **Languages:** Tuvaluan, English. **Ethnicity/Race:** Polynesian 96%. **Religion:** Church of Tuvalu (Congregationalist), 97%. **Literacy rate:** less than 50%
Economic summary: Gross domestic product: purchasing power parity (1995 est.): $7.8 million; per capita income: $800; real growth rate n.a.; inflation 2.9%; unemployment n.a. Principal agricultural products: copra and coconuts. Exports: $165,000 (f.o.b., 1989): copra. Imports: $4.4 million (c.i.f., 1989) food, fuels, machinery, animals, manufactured goods. Major trading partners: Australia, Fiji, New Zealand. **Member of Commonwealth of Nations**

Geography. Formerly the Ellice Islands, Tuvalu consists of nine small islands scattered over 500,000 square miles of the western Pacific, just south of the equator.

Government. Official executive power is vested in a governor-general, representing the Queen, who is appointed by her on the recommendation of the Tuvalu government. Actual executive power lies with a prime minister, who is responsible to a House of Assembly composed of eight elected members.

History. The Ellice Islands became a British protectorate in 1892 and were annexed by Britain in 1915–16 as part of the Gilbert and Ellice Islands Colony. The Ellice Islands were separated in 1975, given home rule, and renamed Tuvalu. Full independence was granted on Sept. 30, 1978.

Unable to select a prime minister after a mid-1993 election the Governor-General dissolved parliament in September. A new election in November led ultimately to a new prime minister in December.

A new flag that did not bear the British Union Jack was unfurled publicly in October 1995.

In December 1996 a no-confidence motion in parliament against the government passed with the minimum votes needed. A new prime minister, Bikenibeu Paeniu, was elected.

UGANDA

Republic of Uganda
President: Yoweri Museveni (1986)
Prime Minister: Kintu Musoke (1994)
Area: 91,459 sq mi. (236,880 sq km)
Population (1997 est.): 20,604,874 (average annual rate of natural increase: 2.41%); birth rate: 45.08/1000; infant mortality rate: 98.4/1000; density per square mile: 225.3
Capital and largest city (1991 est.): Kampala, 773,463.
Monetary unit: Ugandan shilling. **Languages:** English (official), Swahili, Luganda, Ateso, Luo. **Ethnicity/Race:** Baganda 17%, Karamojong 12%, Basogo 8%, Iteso 8%, Langi 6%, Rwanda 6%, Bagisu 5%, Acholi 4%, Lugbara 4%, Bunyoro 3%, Batobo 3%, European, Asian, Arab 1%, other 23%. **Religions:** Christian, 66%; Islam, 16%. **Literacy rate:** 48%
Economic summary: Gross domestic product: purchasing power parity (1995 est.): $16.8 billion; $900 per capita; real growth rate 7.1%; inflation 6.1%. Arable land: 23%. Principal agricultural products: coffee, tea, cotton, sugar. Labor force: 8.361 million (1993 est.); 86% in agriculture; 4% in industry; 10% in services. Major industrial products: refined sugar, beer, tobacco, cotton textiles, cement. Natural resources: copper, cobalt, limestone, salt. Exports: $424 million (f.o.b., 1994): coffee 97%, cotton, tea. Imports: $870 million (c.i.f., 1994): petroleum products, machinery, transport equipment, metals, food. Major trading partners: U.S., U.K., Kenya, Italy, France, Spain, South Africa.
Member of the Commonwealth of Nations

Geography. Uganda, twice the size of Pennsylvania, is in east Africa. It is bordered on the west by Congo, on the north by the Sudan, on the east by Kenya, and on the south by Tanzania and Rwanda. The country, which lies across the Equator, is divided into three main areas—swampy lowlands, a fertile plateau with wooded hills, and a desert region. Lake Victoria forms part of the southern border.

Government. The country has been run by the National Resistance Movement (NRM) since January, 1986.

History. Uganda was first visited by European explorers as well as Arab traders in 1844. An Anglo-German agreement of 1890 declared it to be in the British sphere of influence in Africa, and the Imperial British East Africa Company was chartered to develop the area. The company did not prosper financially, and in 1894 a British protectorate was proclaimed.

Uganda became independent on Oct. 9, 1962.

Sir Edward Mutesa was elected the first President and Milton Obote the first prime minister of the newly independent country. With the help of a young army officer, Col. Idi Amin, Prime Minister Obote seized control of the government from President Mutesa four years later.

On Jan. 25, 1971, Col. Amin deposed President Obote. Obote went into exile in Tanzania. Amin expelled Asian residents and launched a reign of terror against Ugandan opponents, torturing and killing tens of thousands. In 1976, he had himself proclaimed President for Life. In 1977, Amnesty International estimated that 300,000 may have died under his rule, including church leaders and recalcitrant cabinet ministers.

After Amin held military exercises on the Tanzanian border, angering Tanzania's President Julius Nyerere, a combined force of Tanzanian troops and Ugandan exiles loyal to former President Obote invaded Uganda and chased Amin into exile.

After a series of interim administrations, President Obote led his People's Congress Party to victory in 1980 elections that opponents charged were rigged.

On July, 27, 1985, army troops staged a coup taking over the government. Obote fled into exile. The military regime installed Gen. Tito Okello as Chief of State.

The National Resistance Army (NRA), an anti-Obote group led by Yoweri Musevni, kept fighting after being excluded from the new regime. They seized Kampala on January 29, 1986, and Musevni was declared President.

In October 1995 a constituent assembly produced a constitution that provided for a ban on political parties but that still called for elections in 1996.

In the presidential balloting of May 1996 the incumbent won 72% of the vote, reflecting his popularity due to the country's economic recovery.

The government instituted many major reforms in currency and trade in June 1997. Residents would now be allowed foreign accounts and to use foreign credit cards. As of April 1998 beer, soft drinks, and batteries will be allowed to be brought into the country. Cigarette imports are to be permitted as of April 1999.

UKRAINE

Ukraine
President: Leonid D. Kuchma (1994)
Prime Minister: Vasyl Durdinets (1997)
Area: 233,000 sq mi. (603,700 sq km)
Population (1997 est.): 50,684,635 (average annual rate of natural increase: –0.33%): birth rate: 11.77/1000; infant mortality rate: 22.2/1000; density per square mile: 217.5
Capital: Kyiv (Kiev). **Largest cities:** Kyiv, 2,637,000; Kharkiv, 1,622,000; Donetske, 1,121,000; Odessa, 1,104,000; Lviv, 803,000. **Monetary unit:** Karbovanets. **Language:** Ukrainian. **Ethnicity/Race:** Ukrainian 73%, Russian 22%, Jewish 1%, other 4%. **Religion:** Orthodox, 76%; Ukrainian Catholic, 13.5%; Jewish, 2.3%; Baptist, Mennonite, Protestant, and Moslem, 8.2%. **Literacy rate (1992):** 99%
Economic summary: Gross domestic product: purchasing power parity (1995 estimate as extrapolated from the World Bank estimate for 1994): $174.6 billion; per capita: $3,370; real growth rate: –4%; inflation (per mo.): 9%; unemployment: 0.7%. Labor force (Jan. 1994): 23.55 million; industry and construction, 33%; agriculture and forestry, 21%; health, education, and culture, 16%; trade and distribution, 7%; transport and communication, 7%; other, 16%. Mineral resources are iron ore, coal, manganese, natural gas, oil, salt, sulfur, graphite, titanium, magnesium, kaolin, nickel, mercury, and timber. Important agricultural crops are grain, vegetables, meat, and milk. Exports: $11.3 billion (1995): coal, electric power, ferrous and nonferrous metals, chemicals, machinery and transportation equipment, grain and meat. Imports: $10.7 billion (1995): machinery and parts, transportation equipment, chemicals, and textiles. Major trading partners: C.I.S. countries, Germany, Poland, Czech Republic, China, Italy, Switzerland.

Geography. Located in southeastern Europe, the country consists largely of fertile black soil steppes. Mountainous areas include the Carpathians in the southwest and the Crimean chain in the south. There are forest lakes in the north. It is bordered by Belarus on the north and the Russian Federation on the northeast and east, by Poland on the west, by Romania, and Moldova in the southwest, by Hungary, Slovakia, and Poland on the west, and the Black Sea and the Sea of Azov in the south.

Government. A constitutional republic. The unicameral parliament, or Supreme Council, has 450 members.

History. Ukraine was known as "Rus" (from which Russia is a derivative) up until the 16th century. In the 9th century, Kiev was the major political and cultural center in eastern Europe. Kievian Rus reached the height of its power in the 10th century and adopted Byzantine Christianity and the Cyrillic alphabet during that period.

The Mongol conquest in 1240 ended Kievian power. From the 13th to the 16th century, Kiev was under the influence of Poland and western Europe. In 1654, Ukraine asked the czar of Moscovy for protection against Poland and the Treaty of Pereyasav signed that year recognized the suzerainty of Moscow. The agreement was interpreted by Moscow as an invitation to take over Kiev and the Ukrainian state was eventually absorbed into the Russian empire.

After the Russian revolution, Ukraine declared its independence from Russia on Jan. 28, 1918 and several years of warfare ensued with several groups. The Red Army finally was victorious over Kiev and in 1920, Ukraine became a Soviet republic. In 1922, Ukraine became one of the founders of the United Soviet Socialist Republics.

Ukraine was one of the most devastated Soviet republics during World War II. For details on World War II, *see* Headline History, World War II.

On April 15, 1986, the nation's nuclear power plant at Chernobyl was the site of the world's worst nuclear accident. On Oct. 29, 1991, the Ukrainian parliament voted to shut down the reactor within two years' time and asked for international assistance in dismantling it.

When President Leonid Kravchuk was elected by the Ukrainian parliament in 1990, he vowed to seek Ukrainian sovereignty. Ukraine declared its independence on Aug. 24, 1991.

New elections were held Dec. 1, 1991 and Mr. Kravchuk was elected President with 61.5% of the vote. Voters also overwhelmingly approved a referendum to establish full independence from the Soviet Union.

On December 8, 1991, Ukrainian, Russian, and Belarus leaders cofounded a new Commonwealth of Independent States with the new capital to be situated in Minsk, Belarus. The Commonwealth was formally established on Dec. 21, 1991 with ten other former Soviet republics.

After independence Ukraine sought to affirm and exercise its territorial claim on the Crimea, which had been legally transferred from Russian jurisdiction in 1954.

The U.S. announced in January 1994 that an agreement had been reached with Russia and Ukraine for the destruction of Ukraine's entire nuclear arsenal. A presidential election in July saw the surprise ascent of Leonid Kuchma to the presidency of Ukraine. His campaign called for closer ties to Moscow.

His promises notwithstanding, Kuchma in October 1994 began a program of economic liberalization and moved to re-establish central authority over Crimea. In March 1995 the region's separatist leader was removed and the Crimean constitution revoked. In June parliament approved legislation that expanded presidential powers.

In June 1996 the last strategic nuclear warhead was removed to Russia. Also that month parliament approved a new constitution that allows for private ownership of land.

Three agreements were signed in May 1997 on the future of the Black Sea Fleet by which Ukrainian and Russian ships will share the port of Sevastopol for 20 years.

The removal of Prime Minister Lazarenko in June was widely interpreted as needed to boost economic reforms.

UNITED ARAB EMIRATES

President: Sheikh Zayed Bin Sultan Al-Nahyan (1971)
Prime Minister: Sheikh Maktoum Bin Rashid Al-Maktoum (1990)
Area: 32,000 sq mi. (82,880 sq km)
Population (1997 est.): 2,262,309 (average annual rate of natural increase: 1.55%); birth rate: 18.46/1000; infant mortality rate: 15.5/1000; density per square mile: 70.7
Capital and largest city (1989 est.): Abu Dhabi, 363,432. **Monetary unit:** U.A.E. Dirham. **Language:** Arabic. English as a second language. **Ethnicity/ Race:** Emiri 19%, other Arab and Iranian 23%, South Asian 50%, other expatriates (includes Westerners and East Asians) 8% (1982). **Religions:** Islam (Sunni 80%, Shiite 16%), others 4%. **Literacy rate:** 83.3% (1993)
Economic summary: Gross domestic product: purchasing power parity (1995 est.): $70.1 billion; $24,000 per capita; real growth rate 3.3%; inflation 4.6%. Arable land: 0%, irrigated land, 19.3 square miles. Principal agricultural products: vegetables, dates, poultry, fish. Labor force: 794,400 (1993 est.); 56% in industry and commerce; 38% in services; 6% in agriculture (note: 80% of the labor force is foreign). Major industrial products: light manufactures, petroleum, construction materials. Natural resource: oil. Exports: $25.3 billion (f.o.b., 1994 est.): oil and gas exports: $12.3 billion; non-oil exports and re-exports: $13.5 billion. Imports: $21.7 billion (f.o.b, 1994): consumer goods, food, capital goods. Major trading partners: Japan, Western Europe, U.S., Singapore, Korea, India, Iran, China, Taiwan.

Geography. The United Arab Emirates, in the eastern part of the Arabian Peninsula, extends along part of the Gulf of Oman and the southern coast of the Persian Gulf. The nation is the size of Maine. Its neighbors are Saudi Arabia in the west and south, Qatar in the north, and Oman in the east. Most of the land is barren and sandy.

Government. The United Arab Emirates was formed in 1971 by seven Emirates known as the Trucial States—Abu Dhabi (the largest), Dubai, Sharjah, Ajman, Fujairah, Ras al Khaimah and Umm al-Qaiwain.

The loose federation allows joint policies in foreign relations, defense, and development, with each member state keeping its internal local system of government headed by its own ruler. A 40-member legislature consists of eight seats each for Abu Dhabi and Dubai, six seats each for Ras al Khaimah and Sharjah, and four each for the others. It is a member of the Arab League.

History. Originally the area was inhabited by a seafaring people who were converted to Islam in the seventh century. Later, a dissident sect, the Carmathians, established a powerful sheikdom, and its army conquered Mecca. After the sheikdom disintegrated, its people became pirates.

Threatening the Sultanate of Muscat and Oman early in the 19th century, the pirates provoked the intervention of the British, who in 1820 enforced a partial truce and in 1853 a permanent truce. Thus what had been called the Pirate Coast was renamed the Trucial Coast.

A crisis with Iran over sovereignty of three islands near the Strait of Hormuz arose in 1992.

The country signed a military defense agreement with the U.S. in 1994 and one with France in 1995.

In 1997 the government attempted to increase the role of the private sector in the country's economy through state-backed companies. It also relaxed rules on foreign investments.

UNITED KINGDOM

United Kingdom of Great Britain and Northern Ireland

Sovereign: Queen Elizabeth II (1952)
Prime Minister: Tony Blair (1997)
Area: 94,247 sq mi. (244,100 sq km)
Population (1997 est.): 58,610,182 (average annual rate of natural increase: 0.16%; birth rate: 12.84/1000; infant mortality rate: 6.3/1000; density per square mile: 621.9
Capital and largest city (1992 est.): London, 6,679,699. **Other large cities:** Birmingham, 1,009,100; Leeds, 721,800; Glasgow, 681,470; Liverpool, 479,000; Bradford, 477,500; Edinburgh, 439,880; Manchester, 434,600; Bristol, 396,600. **Monetary unit:** Pound sterling (£). **Languages:** English, Welsh, Scots Gaelic. **Ethnicity/Race:** English 81.5%; Scottish 9.6%; Irish 2.4%; Welsh 1.9%; Ulster 1.8%; West Indian, Indian, Pakistani, and other 2.8%. **Religions:** Church of England (established church); Church of Wales (disestablished); Church of Scotland (established church—Presbyterian); Church of Ireland (disestablished); Roman Catholic; Methodist; Congregational; Baptist; Jewish. **Literacy rate:** 99%
Economic summary: Gross domestic product: purchasing power parity (1995 est.): $1.1384 trillion; $19,500 per capita; real growth rate 2.7%; inflation 3.1%; unemployment 8%. Arable land: 29%. Principal agricultural products: wheat, barley, potatoes, sugar beets, livestock, dairy products. Labor force: 28.048 million: services, 62.8%; manufacturing and construction, 25.0%; government 9.1%; energy 1.9%; agriculture 1.2%. Major industrial products: machinery and transport equipment, metals, processed food, paper, textiles, chemicals, clothing, aircraft, shipbuilding, electronics and communications. Natural resources: coal, oil, gas. Exports: $200.4 billion (f.o.b., 1994): machinery, transport equipment, chemicals, petroleum, manufactured goods, semifinished goods. Imports: $221.9 billion (c.i.f., 1994): foodstuffs, machinery, manufactured goods, semifinished goods, consumer goods. Major trading partners: Western European nations, U.S.

Geography. The United Kingdom, consisting of England, Wales, Scotland, and Northern Ireland, is twice the size of New York State. England, in the southeast part of the British Isles, is separated from Scotland on the north by the granite Cheviot Hills; from them the Pennine chain of uplands extends south through the center of England, reaching its highest point in the Lake District in the northwest. To the west along the border of Wales—a land of steep hills and valleys—are the Cambrian Mountains, while the Cotswolds, a range of hills in Gloucestershire, extend into the surrounding shires.

The remainder of England is plain land, though not necessarily flat, with the rocky sand-topped moors in the southwest, the rolling downs in the south and southeast, and the reclaimed marshes of the low-lying fens in the east central districts.

Scotland is divided into three physical regions—the Highlands, the Central Lowlands, containing two-thirds of the population, and the Southern Uplands. The western Highland coast is intersected throughout by long, narrow sea-lochs, or fiords. Scotland also includes the Outer and Inner Hebrides and other islands off the west coast and the Orkney and Shetland Islands off the north coast.

Wales is generally hilly; the Snowdon range in the northern part culminates in Mount Snowdon (3,560 ft., 1,085 m), highest in both England and Wales.

Important rivers flowing into the North Sea are the Thames, Humber, Tees, and Tyne. In the west are the Severn and Wye, which empty into the Bristol Channel and are navigable, as are the Mersey and Ribble.

Government. The United Kingdom is a constitutional monarchy, with a Queen and a parliament that has two houses: the House of Lords with about 830 hereditary peers, 26 spiritual peers, about 270 life peers and peeresses, and 9 law-lords, who are hereditary, or life, peers, and the House of Commons, which has 650 popularly elected members. Supreme legislative power is vested in parliament, which sits for five years unless sooner dissolved.

The executive power of the Crown is exercised by the cabinet, headed by the Prime Minister. The latter, normally the head of the party commanding a majority in the House of Commons, is appointed by the Sovereign, with whose consent he or she in turn appoints the rest of the cabinet. All ministers must be members of one or the other house of parliament; they are individually and collectively responsible to the Crown and Parliament. The cabinet proposes bills and arranges the business of Parliament, but it depends entirely on the votes in the House of Commons. The Lords cannot hold up "money" bills, but they can delay other bills for a maximum of one year.

By the Act of Union (1707), the Scottish Parliament was assimilated with that of England, and Scotland is now represented in Commons by 71 members. The Secretary of State for Scotland, a member of the cabinet, is responsible for the administration of Scottish affairs.

Ruler. Queen Elizabeth II, born April 21, 1926, elder daughter of King George VI and Queen Elizabeth, succeeded to the throne on the death of her father on Feb. 6, 1952; married Nov. 20, 1947, to Prince Philip, Duke of Edinburgh, born June 10, 1921, their children are Prince Charles[1] (heir presumptive), born Nov. 14, 1948; Princess Anne, born Aug. 15, 1950; Prince Andrew, born Feb. 19, 1960; and Prince Edward, born March 10, 1964. The Queen's sister is Princess Margaret, born Aug. 21, 1930. Prince William Arthur Philip Louis, son of the Prince and Princess of Wales and second in line to the throne, was born June 21, 1982. A second son, Prince Henry Charles Albert David, was born Sept. 15, 1984, and is third in line.

History. Roman invasions of the 1st century B.C.E. brought Britain into contact with the Continent. When the Roman legions withdrew in the 5th century C.E., Britain fell easy prey to the invading hordes of Angles, Saxons, and Jutes from Scandinavia and the Low Countries. Seven large Kingdoms were established, and the original Britons were forced into Wales and Scotland. It

---

1. The title Prince of Wales, which is not inherited, was conferred on Prince Charles by his mother on July 26, 1958. The investiture ceremony took place on July 1, 1969. The previous Prince of Wales was Prince Edward Albert, who held the title from 1911 to 1936 before he became Edward VIII.

Rulers of England and Great Britain

Name	Born	Ruled [1]	Name	Born	Ruled [1]
SAXONS[2]			Henry VI	1421	1422–1461[5]
Egbert[3]	c.775	828–839	**HOUSE OF YORK**		
Ethelwulf	?	839–858	Edward IV	1442	1461–1483[5]
Ethelbald	?	858–860	Edward V	1470	1483–1483
Ethelbert	?	860–866	Richard III	1452	1483–1485
Ethelred I	?	866–871	**HOUSE OF TUDOR**		
Alfred the Great	849	871–899	Henry VII	1457	1485–1509
Edward the Elder	c.870	899–924	Henry VIII	1491	1509–1547
Athelstan	895	924–939	Edward VI	1537	1547–1553
Edmund I the Deed-doer	921	939–946	Jane (Lady Jane Grey)[6]	1537	1553–1553
Edred	c.925	946–955	Mary I ("Bloody Mary")	1516	1553–1558
Edwy the Fair	c.943	955–959	Elizabeth I	1533	1558–1603
Edgar the Peaceful	943	959–975	**HOUSE OF STUART**		
Edward the Martyr	c.962	75–979	James I[7]	1566	1603–1625
Ethelred II the Unready	968	979–1016	Charles I	1600	1625–1649
Edmund II Ironside	c.993	1016–1016	**COMMONWEALTH**		
DANES			Council of State	—	1649–1653
Canute	995	1016–1035	Oliver Cromwell[8]	1599	1653–1658
Harold I Harefoot	c.1016	1035–1040	Richard Cromwell[8]	1626	1658–1659[9]
Hardecanute	c.1018	1040–1042	**RESTORATION OF HOUSE OF STUART**		
SAXONS			Charles II	1630	1660–1685
Edward the Confessor	c.1004	1042–1066	James II	1633	1685–
Harold II	c.1020	1066–1066			1688[10]
HOUSE OF NORMANDY			William III[11]	1650	1689–1702
William I the Conqueror	1027	1066–1087	Mary II[11]	1662	1689–1694
William II Rufus	c.1056	1087–1100	Anne	1665	1702–1714
Henry I Beauclerc	1068	1100–1135	**HOUSE OF HANOVER**		
Stephen of Boulogne	c.1100	1135–1154	George I	1660	1714–1727
HOUSE OF PLANTAGENET			George II	1683	1727–1760
Henry II	1133	1154–1189	George III	1738	1760–1820
Richard I Coeur de Lion	1157	1189–1199	George IV	1762	1820–1830
John Lackland	1167	1199–1216	William IV	1765	1830–1837
Henry III	1207	1216–1272	Victoria	1819	1837–1901
Edward I Longshanks	1239	1272–1307	**HOUSE OF SAXE-COBURG**[12]		
Edward II	1284	1307–1327	Edward VII	1841	1901–1910
Edward III	1312	1327–1377	**HOUSE OF WINDSOR**[12]		
Richard II	1367	1377–1399[4]	George V	1865	1910–1936
HOUSE OF LANCASTER			Edward VIII	1894	1936–
Henry IV Bolingbroke	1367	1399–1413			1936[13]
Henry V	1387	1413–1422	George VI	1895	1936–1952
			Elizabeth II	1926	1952–

1. Year of end of rule is also that of death, unless otherwise indicated. 2. Dates for Saxon Kings are still subject of controversy. 3. Became King of West Saxons in 802; considered (from 828) first King of all England. 4. Died 1400. 5. Henry VI reigned again briefly 1470–71. 6. Nominal Queen for 9 days; not counted as Queen by some authorities. She was beheaded in 1554. 7. Ruled in Scotland as James VI (1567–1625). 8. Lord Protector. 9. Died 1712. 10. Died 1701. 11. Joint rulers (1689–1694). 12. Name changed from Saxe-Coburg to Windsor in 1917. 13. Was known after his abdication as the Duke of Windsor, died 1972.

was not until the 10th century that the country finally became united under the Kings of Wessex. Following the death of Edward the Confessor (1066), a dispute about the succession arose, and William, Duke of Normandy, invaded England, defeating the Saxon King, Harold II, at the Battle of Hastings (1066). The Norman conquest introduced Norman law and feudalism.

The reign of Henry II (1154–89), first of the Plantagenets, saw an increasing centralization of royal power at the expense of the nobles, but in 1215 John (1199–1216) was forced to sign the Magna Carta, which awarded the people, especially the nobles, certain basic rights. Edward I (1272–1307) continued the conquest of Ireland, reduced Wales to subjection, and made some gains in Scotland. In 1314, however, English forces led by Edward II were ousted from Scotland after the Battle of Bannockburn. The late 13th and early 14th centuries saw the development of a separate House of Commons with tax-raising powers.

Edward III's claim to the throne of France led to the Hundred Years' War (1338–1453) and the loss of almost all the large English territory in France. In England, the

great poverty and discontent caused by the war were intensified by the Black Death, a plague that reduced the population by about one-third. The Wars of the Roses (1455–85), a struggle for the throne between the House of York and the House of Lancaster, ended in the victory of Henry Tudor (Henry VII) at Bosworth Field (1485).

During the reign of Henry VIII (1509–47), the Church in England asserted its independence from the Roman Catholic Church. Under Edward VI and Mary, the two extremes of religious fanaticism were reached, and it remained for Henry's daughter, Elizabeth I (1558–1603), to set up the Church of England on a moderate basis. In 1588, the Spanish Armada, a fleet sent out by Catholic King Philip II of Spain, was defeated by the English and destroyed during a storm. During Elizabeth's reign, England became a world power.

Elizabeth's heir was a Stuart—James VI of Scotland—who joined the two crowns as James I (1603–25). The Stuart Kings incurred large debts and were forced either to depend on parliament for taxes or

British Prime Ministers Since 1770

Name	Term	Name	Term
Lord North (Tory)	1770–1782	William E. Gladstone (Liberal)	1886–1886
Marquis of Rockingham (Whig)	1782–1782	Marquis of Salisbury (Conservative)	1886–1892
Earl of Shelburne (Whig)	1782–1783	William E. Gladstone (Liberal)	1892–1894
Duke of Portland (Coalition)	1783–1783	Earl of Rosebery (Liberal)	1894–1895
William Pitt, the Younger (Tory)	1783–1801	Marquis of Salisbury (Conservative)	1895–1902
Henry Addington (Tory)	1801–1804	Arthur James Balfour (Conservative)	1902–1905
William Pitt, the Younger (Tory)	1804–1806	Sir H. Campbell-Bannerman (Liberal)	1905–1908
Baron Grenville (Whig)	1806–1807	Herbert H. Asquith (Liberal)	1908–1915
Duke of Portland (Tory)	1807–1809	Herbert H. Asquith (Coalition)	1915–1916
Spencer Perceval (Tory)	1809–1812	David Lloyd George (Coalition)	1916–1922
Earl of Liverpool (Tory)	1812–1827	Andrew Bonar Law (Conservative)	1922–1923
George Canning (Tory)	1827–1827	Stanley Baldwin (Conservative)	1923–1924
Viscount Goderich (Tory)	1827–1828	James Ramsay MacDonald (Labor)	1924–1924
Duke of Wellington (Tory)	1828–1830	Stanley Baldwin (Conservative)	1924–1929
Earl Grey (Whig)	1830–1834	James Ramsay MacDonald (Labor)	1929–1931
Viscount Melbourne (Whig)	1834–1834	James Ramsay MacDonald (Coalition)	1931–1935
Sir Robert Peel (Tory)	1834–1835	Stanley Baldwin (Coalition)	1935–1937
Viscount Melbourne (Whig)	1835–1841	Neville Chamberlain (Coalition)	1937–1940
Sir Robert Peel (Tory)	1841–1846	Winston Churchill (Coalition)	1940–1945
Earl Russell (Whig)	1846–1852	Clement R. Attlee (Labor)	1945–1951
Earl of Derby (Tory)	1852–1852	Sir Winston Churchill (Conservative)	1951–1955
Earl of Aberdeen (Coalition)	1852–1855	Sir Anthony Eden (Conservative)	1955–1957
Viscount Palmerston (Liberal)	1855–1858	Harold Macmillan (Conservative)	1957–1963
Earl of Derby (Conservative)	1858–1859	Sir Alec Frederick Douglas-Home (Conservative)	1963–1964
Viscount Palmerston (Liberal)	1859–1865		
Earl Russell (Liberal)	1865–1866	Harold Wilson (Labor)	1964–1970
Earl of Derby (Conservative)	1866–1868	Edward Heath (Conservative)	1970–1974
Benjamin Disraeli (Conservative)	1868–1868	Harold Wilson (Labor)	1974–1976
William E. Gladstone (Liberal)	1868–1874	James Callaghan (Labor)	1976–1979
Benjamin Disraeli (Conservative)	1874–1880	Margaret Thatcher (Conservative)	1979–1990
William E. Gladstone (Liberal)	1880–1885	John Major (Conservative)	1990–1997
Marquis of Salisbury (Conservative)	1885–1886	Tony Blair (Labor)	1997–

to raise money by illegal means. In 1642, war broke out between Charles I and a large segment of the parliament; Charles was defeated and executed in 1649, and the monarchy was then abolished. After the death in 1658 of Oliver Cromwell, the Lord Protector, the Puritan Commonwealth fell to pieces and Charles II was placed on the throne in 1660. The struggle between the King and Parliament continued, but Charles II knew when to compromise. His brother, James II (1685–88), possessed none of his ability and was ousted by the Revolution of 1688, which confirmed the primacy of Parliament. James's daughter, Mary, and her husband, William of Orange, were now the rulers.

Queen Anne's reign (1702–14) was marked by the Duke of Marlborough's victories over France at Blenheim, Oudenarde, and Malplaquet in the War of the Spanish Succession. England and Scotland meanwhile were joined by the Act of Union (1707). Upon the death of Anne, the distant claims of the elector of Hanover were recognized, and he became King of Great Britain and Ireland as George I.

The unwillingness of the Hanoverian Kings to rule resulted in the formation by the royal ministers of a cabinet, headed by a prime minister, which directed all public business. Abroad, the constant wars with France expanded the British Empire all over the globe, particularly in North America and India. This imperial growth was checked by the revolt of the American colonies (1775–81).

Struggles with France broke out again in 1793 and during the Napoleonic Wars, which ended at Waterloo in (1815).

The Victorian era, named after Queen Victoria (1837–1901), saw the growth of a democratic system of government that had begun with the Reform Bill of 1832.

The two important wars in Victoria's reign were the Crimean War against Russia (1853–56) and the Boer War (1899–1902), the latter enormously extending Britain's influence in Africa.

Increasing uneasiness at home and abroad marked the reign of Edward VII (1901–10). Within four years after the accession of George V in 1910, Britain entered World War I when Germany invaded Belgium. The nation was led by coalition Cabinets, headed first by Herbert Asquith and then, starting in 1916, by the Welsh statesman David Lloyd George. Postwar labor unrest culminated in the general strike of 1926.

King Edward VIII succeeded to the throne on Jan. 20, 1936, at his father's death, but abdicated on Dec. 11, 1936 (in order to marry an American divorcee, Wallis Warfield Simpson) in favor of his brother, who became George VI.

The efforts of Prime Minister Neville Chamberlain to stem the rising threat of Nazism in Germany failed with the German invasion of Poland on Sept. 1, 1939, which was followed by Britain's entry into World War II on September 3. Allied reverses in the spring of 1940 led to Chamberlain's resignation and the formation of another coalition war cabinet by the Conservative leader, Winston Churchill, who led Britain through most of World War II. Churchill resigned shortly after V-E Day, May 7, 1945, but then formed a "caretaker" government that remained in office until after the parliamentary elections in July, which the Labor Party won overwhelmingly. The government formed by Clement R. Attlee began a moderate socialist program.

For details of World War II (1939–45), see Headline History.World War II.

In 1951, Churchill again became prime minister at the head of a Conservative government. George VI died

Feb. 6, 1952, and was succeeded by his daughter Elizabeth II.

Churchill stepped down in 1955 in favor of Sir Anthony Eden, who resigned on grounds of ill health in 1957, and was succeeded by Harold Macmillan and Sir Alec Douglas-Home. In 1964, Harold Wilson led the Labor Party to victory.

A lagging economy brought the Conservatives back to power in 1970. Prime Minister Edward Heath won Britain's admission to the European Community.

Margaret Thatcher became Britain's first woman prime minister as the Conservatives won 339 seats on May 3, 1979.

An Argentine invasion of the Falkland Islands on April 2, 1982, involved Britain in a war 8,000 miles from the home islands. Although Argentina had long claimed the Falklands, known as the Malvinas in Spanish, negotiations were in progress until a month before the invasion.

When more than 11,000 Argentine troops on the Falklands surrendered on June 14, 1982, Mrs. Thatcher declared her intention to garrison the islands indefinitely, together with a naval presence.

Although there were continuing economic problems and foreign policy disputes, an upswing in the economy in 1986–87 led Thatcher to call elections for June 11 in which she won a near-unprecedented third consecutive term.

Through much, if not all, of 1990 the Conservatives were losing the confidence of the electorate. The unpopularity of her poll tax together with an uncompromising position toward further European integration eroded support within her own party. When John Major won the Conservative Party leadership in November, Mrs. Thatcher resigned, paving the way for the Queen to ask Mr. Major to form a government.

In the middle of a long recession John Major called a national election for April 1992. Confounding many political observers the Conservatives won but by a far narrower margin than previously.

After months of political maneuvering the U.K. ratified the Maastrict treaty in August 1993.

Parliamentary elections in May 1997 gave Labour a resounding victory, winning 419 seats to the Tories 165. The new Prime Minister promised not to raise income taxes for 5 years and to adhere to Tory spending plans for that period.

Britain turned over its colony Hong Kong to China in July 1997.

NORTHERN IRELAND

Status: Part of United Kingdom
Secretary of State: Sir Patrick Mayhew (1992)
Area: 5,452 sq mi. (14,121 sq km)
Population (1993 est.): 1,631,800; density per square mile: 300
Capital and largest city (June 30, 1992): Belfast, 287,500. **Monetary unit:** British pound sterling. **Languages:** English, Gaelic. **Religions:** Roman Catholic, Presbyterian, Church of Ireland, Methodist.

Geography. Northern Ireland comprises the counties of Antrim, Armagh, Down, Fermanagh, Londonderry, and Tyrone, which make up predominantly Protestant Ulster and form the northern part of the island of Ireland, westernmost of the British Isles. It is slightly larger than Connecticut.

Government. Northern Ireland is an integral part of the United Kingdom (it has 12 representatives in the British House of Commons), but under the terms of the government of Ireland Act in 1920, it had a semiautonomous government. But in 1972, after three years of internal strife which resulted in more than 400 dead and thousands injured, Britain suspended the Ulster Parliament. The Ulster counties became governed directly from London after an attempt to return certain powers to an elected Assembly in Belfast.

The Northern Ireland Assembly was dissolved in 1975 and a Constitutional Convention was elected to write a constitution acceptable to Protestants and Catholics. The convention failed to reach agreement and closed down the next year.

History. Ulster was part of Catholic Ireland until the reign of Elizabeth I (1558–1603) when, after crushing three Irish rebellions, the crown confiscated lands in Ireland and settled in Ulster the Scot Presbyterians who became rooted there. Another rebellion in 1641–51, crushed as brutally by Oliver Cromwell, resulted in the settlement of Anglican Englishmen in Ulster. Subsequent political policy favoring Protestants and disadvantaging Catholics encouraged further settlement in Northern Ireland.

But the North did not separate from the South until William Gladstone presented in 1886 his proposal for home rule in Ireland as a means of settling the Irish Question. The Protestants in the North, although they had grievances like the Catholics in the South, feared domination by the Catholic majority. Industry, moreover, was concentrated in the north and dependent on the British market.

When World War I began, civil war threatened between the regions. Northern Ireland, however, did not become a political entity until the six counties accepted the Home Rule Bill of 1920. This set up a semiautonomous parliament in Belfast and a Crown-appointed Governor advised by a cabinet of the prime minister and eight ministers, as well as a 12-member representation in the House of Commons in London.

As the Republic of Ireland gained its sovereignty, relations improved between North and South, although the Irish Republican Army, outlawed in recent years, continued the struggle to end the partition of Ireland. In 1966–69, communal rioting and street fighting between Protestants and Catholics occurred in Londonderry, fomented by extremist nationalist Protestants, who feared the Catholics might attain a local majority, and by Catholics demonstrating for civil rights.

Rioting, terrorism, and sniping killed more than 2,200 people from 1969 through 1984 and the religious communities, Catholic and Protestant, became hostile armed camps. British troops were brought in to separate them but themselves became a target of Catholics.

In 1973, a new British charter created a 78-member Assembly elected by proportional representation that gave more weight to Catholic strength. It created a Province Executive with committee chairmen of the Assembly heading all government departments except law enforcement, which remained under London's control. Assembly elections in 1973 produced a majority for the new constitution that included Catholic assemblymen.

Ulster's leaders agreed in 1973 to create an 11-member Executive Body with six seats assigned to Unionists (Protestants) and four to members of Catholic parties. Unionist leader Brian Faulkner headed the Executive. Also agreed to was a Council of Ireland, with 14 seats evenly divided between Dublin and Belfast, which could act only by unanimous vote.

Although the Council lacked real authority, its creation sparked a general strike by Protestant extremists in 1974. The two-week strike caused Faulkner's resignation from the Executive and resumption of direct rule from London.

In April 1974, London instituted a new program that responded to some Catholic grievances, but assigned more British troops to cut off movement of arms and munitions to Ulster's violence-racked cities.

Violence continued unabated, with new heights reached early in 1976 when the British government announced the end of special privileges for political prisoners in Northern Ireland. British Prime Minister James Callaghan visited Belfast in July and pledged that Ulster would remain part of the United Kingdom unless a clear majority wished to separate.

In October 1977, the 1976 Nobel Prize for Peace was awarded to Mairead Corrigan and Betty Williams for their campaign for peace in Northern Ireland. Intermittent violence continued, however, and on Aug. 27, 1979, an I.R.A. bomb killed Earl Mountbatten as he was sailing off southern Ireland.

New talks aimed at a restoration of home rule in Northern Ireland began and quickly ended in 1980.

On November 15, 1985, Mrs. Thatcher signed an agreement with Irish Prime Minister Garrett Fitzgerald giving Ireland a consultative role in the affairs of Northern Ireland. It was met with intense disapproval by the Ulster Unionists.

In November 1995, a new agreement was reached that established a 3-member international commission. The British and Irish governments in February 1995 announced an approved framework within which a settlement of the status of Northern Ireland could eventually be reached.

The resumption of violence led to the stagnation of peace negotiation in 1997.

Dependencies of the United Kingdom

ANGUILLA

Status: Dependency
Governor: Alan Hoole (1995)
Area: 35 sq mi. (91 sq km)
Population (1996 est.): 10,424; average annual rate of natural increase: 1.19%; birth rate: 17.43/1000; infant mortality rate: 21.6/1000; density per square mile: 298
Capital (1992): The Valley, 1,400. **Monetary unit:** East Caribbean dollar. **Ethnicity/Race:** black African. **Literacy:** 95%
Economic summary: Gross domestic product: purchasing power parity (1994 est.): $53 million; $7,600 per capita; real growth rate: 6.5%. Unemployment (1992): 7%. Major industries: tourism, boat building, salt, lobster fishing. Labor force (1992): 4,400; 36% in commerce; 29% in services; 18% in construction; 10% in transportation and utilities; 3% in manufacturing; 4% in agriculture, fishing, forestry and mining. Exports: $556,000 (f.o.b., 1992). Imports: $33.5 million (f.o.b., 1992).

Anguilla was originally part of the West Indies Associated States as a component of St. Kitts-Nevis-Anguilla.

In 1967, Anguilla declared its independence from the St. Kitts-Nevis-Anguilla federation. Britain however, did not recognize this action. In February 1969, Anguilla voted to cut all ties with Britain and become an independent republic. In March, Britain landed troops on the island and, on March 30, a truce was signed. In July 1971, Anguilla became a dependency of Britain and two months later Britain ordered the withdrawal of all its troops.

A new constitution for Anguilla, effective in February 1976, provides for separate administration and a government of elected representatives. The Associated State of St. Kitts-Nevis-Anguilla ended Dec. 19, 1980.

BERMUDA

Status: Self-governing dependency
Governor: Thorold Masefield (1997)
Premier: Pamela Gordon (1997)
Area: 20 sq mi. (52 sq km)
Population (1997 est.): 62,569; average annual rate of natural increase: 0.76%; birth rate: 14.92/1000; infant mortality rate: 13.16/1000; density per square mile: 3,128.4
Capital (1994 est.): Hamilton, 1,100. **Monetary unit:** Bermuda dollar. **Literacy rate:** 98%
Economic summary: Gross domestic product (1994 est.): $1.7 billion; $28,000 per capita; 2.5% real growth rate; unemployment: negl. Arable land: 0%. Principal agricultural products: bananas, vegetables, citrus fruits, dairy products. Labor force: 33,650; 45% clerical; 22% in services; 21% are laborers; 13% in technical and professional; 10% in administrative and managerial; 7% are in sales; 2% in agriculture and fishing. Major industrial products: structural concrete, paints, pharmaceuticals. Natural resource: limestone. Exports: $60 million (f.o.b., 1991): semi-tropical produce, light manufactures. Imports: $519 million (f.o.b., 1993): foodstuffs, fuel, machinery. Major trading partners: U.S., U.K., Canada, Venezuela, Japan.

Bermuda is an archipelago of about 360 small islands, 580 miles (934 km) east of North Carolina. The largest is (Great) Bermuda, or Long Island. Explored by Juan de Bermúdez, a shipwrecked Spaniard, early in the 16th century, the islands were settled in 1612 by an offshoot of the Virginia Company and became a crown colony in 1684.

In 1940, sites on the islands were leased for 99 years to the U.S. for air and navy bases. Bermuda is also the headquarters of the West Indies and Atlantic squadron of the Royal Navy.

In 1968, Bermuda was granted a new constitution, its first prime minister, and autonomy, except for foreign relations, defense, and internal security. The predominantly white United Bermuda Party has retained power in four elections against the opposition—the black-led Progressive Laborites—although Bermuda's population is 60% black.

The Prime Minister's unexpected resignation in March 1997 led the ruling United Bermuda Party to name Pamela Gordon the country's first female and youngest Premier.

BRITISH ANTARCTIC TERRITORY

Status: Dependency
Commissioner: Peter M. Newton (1992)
Area: 500,000 sq mi. (1,395,000 sq km)
Population: no permanent residents

The British Antarctic Territory consists of the South Shetland Islands, South Orkney Islands, and nearby Graham Land on the Antarctic continent, largely uninhabited. They are dependencies of the British crown colony of the Falkland Islands but received a separate administration in 1962, being governed by a British-appointed High Commissioner who is governor of the Falklands.

BRITISH INDIAN OCEAN TERRITORY

Status: Dependency
Commissioner: David Ross MacLennan (1994)
Administrative headquarters: Victoria, Seychelles
Area: 85 sq mi. (220 sq km)

This dependency, consisting of the Chagos Archipelago and other small island groups, was formed in 1965 by agreement with Mauritius and the Seychelles. There is no permanent civilian population in the territory.

BRITISH VIRGIN ISLANDS

Virgin Islands

Status: Dependency
Governor: David Mackilligin (1995)
Area: 59 sq mi. (153 sq km)
Population (1997 est.): 13,368; average annual rate of natural increase: 1.41%; birth rate: 20.13/1000; infant mortality rate: 18.99/1000; density per square mile: 226.5
Capital (1991 census): Road Town (on Tortola): 3,983. **Monetary unit:** U.S. dollar
Economic summary: Gross domestic product (1991): $133 million; $10,600 per capita; 2% real growth rate. Inflation (1990 est.): 2.5%; unemployment: negl. Labor force: 4,911. Exports (f.o.b., 1988): $2.7 million: rum, fresh fish, gravel, sand, fruits, animals. Imports (c.i.f., 1988): $11.5 million: building materials, automobiles, foodstuffs, machinery.

Some 36 islands in the Caribbean Sea northeast of Puerto Rico and west of the Leeward Islands, the British Virgin Islands are economically interdependent with the U.S. Virgin Islands to the south. They were formerly part of the administration of the Leeward Islands. They received a separate administration in 1956 as a crown colony. In 1967 a new constitution was promulgated that provided for a ministerial system of government headed by the governor. The principal islands are Tortola, Virgin Gorda, Anegada, and Jost Van Dyke.

CAYMAN ISLANDS

Status: Dependency
Governor: John Wynne Owen (1995)
Area: 100 sq mi. (259 sq km)
Population (1997 est.): 36,153; average annual rate of natural increase: 0.92%; birth rate: 14.24/1000; infant mortality rate: 8.4/1000; density per square mile: 361.5
Capital (1992 est.): George Town (on Grand Cayman), 15,000. **Monetary unit:** Cayman Islands dollar
Economic Summary: Gross domestic product (1993 est.): $700 million; $23,000 per capita; inflation: 2.5% (1993 est.); unemployment: 7% (1992). Exports: $10 million (f.o.b., 1993 est.): turtle products, manufactured goods. Imports: $312 million (c.i.f., 1993 est.): foodstuffs, manufactured goods. Major trading partners: U.S., Trinidad and Tobago, U.K., Netherland Antilles, Japan.

This dependency consists of three islands—Grand Cayman (76 sq mi.; 197 sq km), Cayman Brac (22 sq mi.; 57 sq km), and Little Cayman (20 sq mi.; 52 sq km)—situated about 180 miles (290 km) northwest of Jamaica. They were dependencies of Jamaica until 1959, when they became a unit territory within the Federation of the West Indies. In 1962, upon the dissolution of the Federation, the Cayman Islands became a British dependency.

CHANNEL ISLANDS

Status: Crown dependencies
Lieutenant Governor of Jersey: Air Marshall Sir John Sutton (1990)
Lieutenant Governor of Guernsey: Vice Adm. Sir John Coward (1994)
Area: 120 sq mi. (311 sq km)
Populations (1997 est.): Jersey, 88,510; Guernsey, 63,731
Capital of Jersey (1986): St. Helier, 27,083
Capital of Guernsey (1986): St. Peter Port, 16,085.
Monetary units: Guernsey pound; Jersey pound
This group of islands, lying in the English Channel off the northwest coast of France, is the only portion of the Duchy of Normandy belonging to the English Crown, to which it has been attached since the conquest of 1066. It was the only British possession occupied by Germany during World War II.

For purposes of government, the islands are divided into the Bailiwick of Jersey (45 sq mi.; 117 sq km) and the Bailiwick of Guernsey (30 sq mi.; 78 sq km), including Alderney (3 sq mi.; 7.8 sq km); Sark (2 sq mi.; 5.2 sq km), Herm, Jethou, etc. The islands are administered according to their own laws and customs by local governments. Acts of parliament in London are not binding on the islands unless they are specifically mentioned. The Queen is represented in each Bailiwick by a lieutenant governor.

FALKLAND ISLANDS AND DEPENDENCIES

Status: Dependency
Governor: Richard Ralph (1996)
Chief Executive: R. Sampson
Area: 4,700 sq mi. (12,173 sq km)
Population (1996 est.): 2,374; density per sq mi.: 0.5
Capital (1991): Stanley (on East Falkland), 1,643. **Monetary unit:** Falkland Island pound
This sparsely inhabited dependency consists of a group of islands in the South Atlantic, about 250 miles (402 km) east of the South American mainland. The largest islands are East Falkland and West Falkland. Dependencies are South Georgia Island (1,450 sq mi.; 3,756 sq km), the South Sandwich Islands, and other islets. Three former dependencies—Graham Land, the South Shetland Islands, and the South Orkney Islands—were established as a new British dependency, the British Antarctic Territory, in 1962.

The chief industry is sheep raising and, apart from the production of wool, hides and skins, and tallow, there are no known resources. The whaling industry is carried on from South Georgia Island.

The chief export is wool.

GIBRALTAR

Status: Self-governing dependency
Governor: Sir Richard Luce (1997)
Chief Minister: Peter Caruana (1996)
Area: 2.25 sq mi. (5.8 sq km)
Population (1997 est.): 28,913; average annual rate of natural increase: 0.46%; birth rate: 13.45/1000; infant mortality rate: 6.8/1000; density per square mile: 12,850.2. **Monetary unit:** Gibraltar pound. **Literacy rate:** 99% (est.)
Economic summary: Gross national product (1993 est.): $205 million; $6,600 per capita. Exports: $57 million (f.o.b., 1992): re-exports of tobacco, petroleum, wine. Imports: $420 million (c.i.f., 1992): manufactured goods, fuels, foodstuffs. Major trading partners: U.K, Morocco, Portugal, Netherlands, Spain, U.S.

Gibraltar, at the south end of the Iberian Peninsula, is a rocky promontory commanding the western entrance to the Mediterranean. Aside from its strategic importance, it is also a free port, naval base, and coaling station. It was captured by the Arabs crossing from Africa into Spain in C.E. 711. In the 15th century, it passed to the Moorish ruler of Granada and later became Spanish. It was captured by an Anglo-Dutch force in 1704 during the War of the Spanish Succession and passed to Great Britain by the Treaty of Utrecht in 1713. Most of the inhabitants of Gibraltar are of Spanish, Italian, and Maltese descent.

Spanish efforts to recover Gibraltar culminated in a referendum in 1967 in which the residents voted overwhelmingly to retain their link with Britain. Spain sealed Gibraltar's land border in 1969 and did not open communications until April 1980, after the two governments had agreed to resolve their dispute in keeping with a United Nations resolution calling for restoration of the "Rock" to Spain.

The last British military battalion on the "Rock" was withdrawn in March 1991. Spain suggested a form of joint control, but the U.K. refused.

HONG KONG

See China.

ISLE OF MAN

Status: Self-Governing Crown Dependency
Lieutenant Governor: Air Marshall Sir Laurence Jones
Area: 221 sq mi. (572 sq km)
Population (1997 est.): 7,504; average annual rate of natural increase: 0.06%; birth rate: 12.48/1000; infant mortality rate: 2.4/1000; density per square mile: 337.1
Capital (1991): Douglas, 22,214. **Monetary unit:** Isle of Man pound

Situated in the Irish Sea, equidistant from Scotland, Ireland, and England, the Isle of Man is administered according to its own laws by a government composed of the Lieutenant Governor, a Legislative Council, and a House of Keys, one of the most ancient legislative assemblies in the world.

The chief exports are beef and lamb, fish, and livestock.

LEEWARD ISLANDS

See British Virgin Islands; Montserrat.

MONTSERRAT

Status: Dependency
Governor: Frank Savage (1993)
Chief Minister: David Brandt (1997)
Area: 38 sq mi. (98 sq km)
Population (1997 est.): 12,800; average annual rate of natural increase: 0.42%; birth rate: 14.47/1000; infant mortality rate: 11.87/1000; density per square mile: 336.8
Capital (1991 est.): Plymouth, 2,500. **Monetary unit:** East Caribbean dollar
Economic summary: Gross domestic product: purchasing power parity (1994 est.): $55.6 million; $4,500 per capita; 0.5% real growth rate (1994 est.); inflation: 9.6%. Labor force: 5,100. Exports: $2.3 million (f.o.b., 1994): electric parts, plastic bags, apparel, hot peppers, live plants, cattle. Imports: $80.6 million (f.o.b., 1992): machinery and transportation equipment, foodstuffs, cattle, potatoes, cotton, lint, recapped tires, mangoes, tomatoes, manufactured goods, fuels, lubricants and related materials.

The island of Montserrat is in the Lesser Antilles of the West Indies. Until 1956, it was a division of the Leeward Islands. Eruptions of the Soufriere Hills volcano intensified in 1997, and more than half the population has evacuated the island.

PITCAIRN ISLAND

Status: Dependency
Governor: Robert John Alston (nonresident)
Island Magistrate: Jay Warren
Area: 1.75 sq mi. (4.5 sq km)
Population (July 1995 est.): 73; density per square mile: 42
Capital: Adamstown

Pitcairn Island, in the South Pacific about midway between Australia and South America, consists of the island of Pitcairn and the three uninhabited islands of Henderson, Duicie, and Oeno. The island of Pitcairn was settled in 1790 by British mutineers from the ship *Bounty,* commanded by Capt. William Bligh. It was annexed as a British colony in 1838. Overpopulation forced removal of the settlement to Norfolk Island in 1856, but about 40 persons soon returned.

The colony is governed by a 10-member Council presided over by the Island Magistrate, who is elected for a three-year term.

ST. HELENA

Status: Dependency
Governor: David Smallman (1995)
Area: 120 sq mi. (310 sq km)
Population (1997 est.): 6,803; average annual rate of natural increase: 0.37%; birth rate: 9.3/1000; infant mortality rate: 34.19/1000; density per square mile: 56.7
Capital (1987): Jamestown, 1,332. **Monetary unit:** Pound sterling

St. Helena is a volcanic island in the South Atlantic about 1,100 miles (1,770 km) from the west coast of Africa. It is famous as the place of exile of Napoleon (1815–21).

It was taken for England in 1659 by the East India Company and was brought under the direct government of the Crown in 1834.

St. Helena has two dependencies: Ascension (34 sq mi.; 88 sq km), an island about 700 miles (1,127 km) northwest of St. Helena; and Tristan da Cunha (40 sq mi.; 104 sq km), a group of six islands about 1,500 miles (2,414 km) south-southwest of St. Helena.

TURKS AND CAICOS ISLANDS

Status: Dependency
Governor: Martin Bourk (1993)
Area: 193 sq mi. (500 sq km)
Population (1997 est.): 14,631; average annual rate of natural increase: 0.71%; birth rate: 12.3/1000; infant mortality rate: 12.5/1000; density per square mile: 75.8
Capital (1990): Cockburn Town, 3,720. **Monetary unit:** U.S. dollar
Economic summary: Gross domestic product: purchasing power parity (1992 est.): $80.8 million; $6,000 per capita; real growth rate: –1.5%. Labor force: 4,848: majority engaged in fishing and tourist industries. Exports: $6.8 million (f.o.b., 1993): lobster, dried and fresh conch, conch shells. Imports: $42.8 million (1993): food and beverages, tobacco, clothing, manufactures, construction materials. Major trading partners: U.S., U.K.

These two groups of islands are situated at the southeast end of the Bahamas. The principal islands in the Turks group are Grand Turk and Salt Cay; the principal ones in the Caicos group are South Caicos, East Caicos, Middle (or Grand) Caicos, North Caicos, Providenciales, and West Caicos.

The Turks and Caicos Islands were dependencies of Jamaica until 1959, when they became a unit territory within the Federation of the West Indies. In 1962, when Jamaica became independent, the Turks and Caicos became a British crown colony. The present constitution has been in force since 1969.

UNITED STATES

The United States of America
President: William J. Clinton (1993)
Vice President: Albert A. Gore, Jr. (1993)
Land area: 3,536,341 sq mi. (9,159,123 sq km)

Resident population (est. Sept. 13, 1997): 268,103,439; **(1990 census):** 248,709,873 (change 1980–1990: 9.8%). White: 199,686,070 (80.3%); Black: 29,986,060 (12.1%); American Indian, Eskimo, or Aleut: 1,959,234 (0.8%); Asian or Pacific Islander: 7,273,662 (2.9%); Other Race: 9,804,847 (3.9%); Hispanic Origin[1]: 22,354,059 (9.0%); (average annual rate of natural increase: 0.58%); birth rate: 14.6/1000; infant mortality rate: 6.55/1000; density per square mile: 78

Capital (1990 census.): Washington, D.C., 606,900. **Largest cities (1990 census):** New York, 7,322,564; Los Angeles, 3,485,398; Chicago, 2,783,726; Houston, 1,630,553; Philadelphia, 1,585,577; San Diego, 1,110,549; Detroit, 1,027,974; Dallas, 1,006,877; Phoenix, 983,403; San Antonio, 935,933. **Monetary unit:** Dollar. **Languages:** predominantly English, sizable Spanish-speaking minority. **Ethnicity/Race:** white 83.4%, black 12.4%, Asian 3.3%, Native American 0.8% (1992). **Religions:** Protestant, 61%; Roman Catholic, 25%; Jewish, 2%; other, 5%; none, 7%. **Literacy rate:** Age 15 and over having completed 5 or more years of schooling (1991): 97.9%

Economic summary: Gross domestic product: purchasing power parity (1995 est.): $7.248 trillion; per capita personal income (1995 est.): $27,500. Inflation rate: 2.5%; unemployment: 5.6%. Civilian labor force (July 1996): 126.9 million. Arable land: 20%. Principal products: corn, wheat, barley, oats, sugar, potatoes, soybeans, fruits, beef, veal, pork. Labor force: 132.304 million: managerial and professional 28.3%; technical, sales and administrative support: 30%; services; 13.5; manufacturing, mining, transportation and crafts 25.3%; farming, forestry and fishing 2.8%. Major industrial products: petroleum products, fertilizers, cement, pig iron and steel, plastics and resins, newsprint, motor vehicles, machinery, natural gas, electricity. Natural resources: coal, oil, copper, gold, silver, minerals, timber. Exports: $578 billion: machinery, chemicals, aircraft, military equipment, cereals, motor vehicles, grains. Illicit drugs: illicit producer of cannabis for domestic consumption. Ongoing eradication program aimed at small plots and greenhouses unsuccessful. Imports: $751 billion: crude and partly refined petroleum, machinery, automobiles. Major trading partners: Canada, Japan, Western Europe.

1. Persons of Hispanic origin can be of any race.

Government. The President is elected for a four-year term and may be re-elected only once. The bicameral Congress consists of the 100-member Senate, elected to a six-year term with one-third of the seats becoming vacant every two years, and the 435-member House of Representatives, elected every two years. The minimum voting age is 18.

(*See also* Profile of the United States, U.S. States, U.S Cities, U.S. Statistics, and U.S. History.)

URUGUAY

Oriental Republic of Uruguay
National name: Republica Oriental del Uruguay
President: Julio Sanguinetti Cairolo
Area: 68,040 sq mi. (176,224 sq km)
Population (1997 est.): 3,261,707 (average annual rate of natural increase: 0.8%); birth rate: 16.98/1000; infant mortality rate: 14.7/1000; density per square mile: 47.9

Capital and largest city (1992 est.): Montevideo, 1,500,000. **Monetary unit:** Peso. **Language:** Spanish.

Ethnicity/Race: white 88%, mestizo 8%, black 4%. **Religion:** Roman Catholic, 66%; Protestant, 2%; Jewish, 2%. **Literacy rate:** 94%

Economic summary: Gross domestic product: purchasing power parity (1995 est.): $24.4 billion: $7,600 per capita; real growth rate –2.4%; inflation 35.4% (1995 est.); unemployment 11%. Arable land: 8%. Principal products: livestock, grains. Labor force (1991 est.): 1.355 million: government, 25%; manufacturing, 19%; commerce, 12%; agriculture, 11%. Major products: processed meats, wool and hides, textiles, shoes, handbags and leather wearing apparel, cement, refined petroleum. Natural resources: hydroelectric power potential. Exports: $2.3 billion (f.o.b., 1995 est.): meat, hides, wool, fish. Imports: $3.1 billion (c.i.f., 1995 est.): transportation equipment, chemicals, machinery, plastics, minerals. Major trading partners: U.S., Brazil, Argentina, Germany, China, Italy, Nigeria.

Geography. Uruguay, on the east coast of South America south of Brazil and east of Argentina, is comparable in size to the State of Oklahoma.

The country consists of a low, rolling plain in the south and a low plateau in the north. It has a 120-mile (193 km) Atlantic shore line, a 235-mile (378 km) frontage on the Rio de la Plata, and 270 miles (435 km) on the Uruguay River, its western boundary.

Government. A republic. Presidents serve a single five-year term. The bicameral Congress, the General Assembly, consists of the Chamber of Senators and the Chamber of Representatives.

History. Juan Díaz de Solis, a Spaniard, visited Uruguay in 1516, but the Portuguese were first to settle it when they founded Colonia in 1680. After a long struggle, Spain wrested the country from Portugal in 1778. Uruguay revolted against Spain in 1811, only to be conquered in 1817 by the Portuguese from Brazil. Independence was reasserted with Argentine help in 1825, and the republic was set up in 1828.

Independence, however, did not restore order, and a revolt in 1836 touched off nearly 50 years of factional strife, with occasional armed intervention from Argentina and Brazil.

Uruguay, made prosperous by meat and wool exports, founded a welfare state early in the 20th century. A decline began in the 1950s as successive governments struggled to maintain a large bureaucracy and costly social benefits. Economic stagnation and political frustration followed.

A military coup ousted the civilian government in 1973. The military Dictatorship that followed used fear and terror to demoralize the population, taking thousands of political prisoners.

After ruling for 12 years, the military regime permitted election of a civilian government in November 1984 and relinquished rule in March 1985.

Luis Lacalle became President in March 1990, becoming the first Blanco Party member to assume that office in 23 years.

The President's continuing attempts in 1993 at economic reform met much resistance.

Presidential and legislative elections in November 1994 resulted in a narrow victory for the Colorado Party and its presidential candidate Julio Sanguinetti Cairolo, who assumed office in March 1995.

The new President pushed for constitutional and economic reforms aimed at reducing inflation and the size of the public sector, partially through tax increases and privatization.

UZBEKISTAN

Republic of Uzbekistan
National Name: Uzbekiston Respublikasi
President: Islam A. Karimov (1991)
Prime Minister: Otkir Sultonov (1995)
Area: 172,700 sq mi. (447,400 sq km)
Population (est. 1997): 23,860,452; (average annual rate of natural increase: 2.156%); birth rate: 29.49/1000; infant mortality rate: 79.10/1000; density per square mile: 138.2
Capital and largest city (1992 est.): Tashkent, 2,106,000. **Other large cities:** Samarkand, 372,000; Andijon, 302,000. **Language:** Uzbek, 85%; Russian, 5%. **Ethnicity/Race:** Uzbek 71.4%, Russian 8.3%, Tajik 4.7%, Kazak 4.1%, Tatar 2.4%, Karakalpak 2.1%, other 7%. **Religion:** Muslim (mostly Sunnis), 88%; Eastern Orthodox, 9%; other, 3%. **Literacy rate:** 97%
Economic summary: Gross domestic product (U.N., World Bank 1994 est.): $54.7 billion; $2,370 per capita: -1% real growth rate; inflation: 7.7% (per mo.); unemployment: 0.4% (1995). Labor force (1995): 8.234 million: agriculture and forestry, 43%; industry and construction, 22%. Natural resources: natural gas, petroleum, coal, gold, uranium, silver, copper, lead and zinc, tungsten, molybdenum. Agriculture: major crop is cotton. Exports (1995): $3.1 billion to outside the former U.S.S.R. countries: cotton, gold, textiles, chemicals, mineral fertilizers, vegetable oil. Imports (1995): $2.9 billion: from outside the former U.S.S.R. countries: machinery and parts, consumer durables, grain, and other food. Trading partners: Russia, Ukraine, Eastern Europe, U.S., Czech Republic.

Geography. Uzbekistan is situated in the former Soviet Central Asia between the Amu Darya and Syr Darya Rivers, the Aral Sea, and the slopes of the Tien Shan Mountains. It is bounded by Kazakhstan in the north and northwest, Kyrgyzstan and Tajikistan in the east and southeast, and Turkmenistan in the southwest. The republic also includes the Kara-Kalpak Autonomous S.S.R. since 1936 with its capital, Nukus, 1987 population, 152,000. The land is made up of deserts, oases, and mountains with valleys. Two-thirds of the territory are occupied by deserts and semi-deserts. The country is about one-tenth larger in area than the state of California.

Government. A constitutional republic.

History. The Uzbekistan land was once part of the ancient Persian empire and was later conquered by Alexander the Great in 4 B.C.E. During the 8th century, the nomadic Turkic tribes living there were converted to Islam by invading Arab forces who dominated the area. The Mongols under Ghengis Khan took over the region from the Seljuk Turks in the 13th century and it later became part of Tamerlane the Great's empire and his successors until the 16th century.

The Uzbeks invaded the territory in the early 16th century and merged with the other inhabitants in the area. Their empire broke up into separate Uzbek principalities, the khanates of Khiva, Bukhara, and Kokand. These city-states resisted Russian expansion into the area, but were conquered by the Russian forces in the mid-19th century.

The territory was made into the Uzbek Republic in 1924 and became the independent Uzbekistan Soviet Socialist Republic in 1925.

Uzbekistan joined with ten other former Soviet republics on Dec. 21, 1991, in the Commonwealth of Independent States.

In February 1992, President Karimov, a former Communist Party boss, affirmed his commitment to democracy and human rights. An election in December 1991 had given him 85% of the vote, but the main opposition parties were not allowed to field candidates.

Opposition forces in mid-1993 formed a coalition. However the government closed their headquarters and arrested the leaders. The criminal code was amended to impose stricter penalties for antigovernment activity.

Parliamentary elections in December 1994 produced a huge victory for the ruling party and an allied party. Opposition groups were largely excluded.

In March 1995 a referendum produced a big win for extending the president's term until 2000 in the name of political stability.

In April 1997 President Karimov signed a decree to stimulate the creation of private commercial banks. Under its terms Uzbekistan citizens can deposit without a declaration of their incomes. The bank profits are to be tax exempt for two years.

VANUATU

Republic of Vanuatu
President: Jean-Marie Leye (1994)
Prime Minister: Serge Vohor (1996)
Area: 5,700 sq mi. (14,760 sq km)
Population (est. 1997): 181,358 (average annual rate of natural increase: 2.124%); birth rate: 29.87/1000; infant mortality rate: 62.90/1000; density per square mile: 31.8
Capital and largest city (est. 1993): Port Vila, 26,100. **Monetary unit:** Vatu. **Languages:** English (official), French (official), pidgin. **Ethnicity/Race:** indigenous Melanesian 94%, French 4%, Vietnamese, Chinese, Pacific Islanders. **Religions:** Presbyterian, 36.7%; Roman Catholic, 15%; Anglican, 15%; other Christian, 10%; indigenous beliefs, 7.6%; other, 15.7%. **Literacy rate:** 55%
Economic Summary: GDP purchasing power parity (1994 estimate): $210 million, $1,220 per capita; real growth rate: 2%.; inflation (1995 est.) 7%. Labor force 66,597 (1989 est.); by occupation: agriculture, 65%; services, 32%; industry, 5%. Arable land: 1%. Principal agricultural products: copra, cocoa, coffee. Agriculture accounts for 40% of GDP. Exports: $24.6 million (1994): copra, cocoa, coffee, frozen fish, timber, beef. Imports: $78.6 million (1994): machines and vehicles, food, raw materials, fuel, chemicals. Major trading partners: France, New Zealand, Japan, Australia, Netherlands, Belgium, New Caledonia.

Geography. Formerly known as the New Hebrides, Vanuatu is an archipelago of some 80 islands lying between New Caledonia and Fiji in the South Pacific. Largest of the islands is Espiritu Santo (875 sq mi.; 2,266 sq km); others are Efate, Malekula, Malo, Pentecost, and Tanna.

Government. The constitution by which Vanuatu achieved independence on July 30, 1980, vests executive authority in a president, elected by an electoral college for a five-year term. A unicameral legislature of 46 members exercises legislative power.

History. The islands were discovered by Pedro Fernandes de Queiros of Portugal in 1606 and were charted and named by the British navigator James Cook in 1774. Conflicting British and French interests were resolved by a joint naval commission that administered the islands from 1887. A condominium government was established in 1906.

The islands' plantation economy, based on imported Vietnamese labor, was prosperous until the 1920s, when markets for its products declined. The New Hebrides escaped Japanese occupation in World War II and the French population was among the first to support the Gaullist Free French movement.

A brief rebellion by French settlers and plantation workers on Espiritu Santo in May 1980 threatened the scheduled independence of the islands. Britain sent a company of Royal Marines and France a contingent of 50 policemen to quell the revolt, which the new government said was financed by the Phoenix Foundation, a right-wing U.S. group. With the British and French forces replaced by soldiers from Papua New Guinea, independence ceremonies took place on July 30. The next month it was reported that the revolt had been quelled.

Disaffection with Prime Minister Lini in August 1991 led to his dismissal as head of his party. Lini formed another to contest the November general elections. The Union of Moderate Parties won and formed an alliance with Lini's. Lini's party, however, withdrew from the coalition in August 1993. While the prime minister's party retained a parliamentary majority, its position became precarious.

A parliamentary vote of no-confidence in Prime Minister Korman in September 1996 resulted in his predecessor being reinstated.

VATICAN CITY (HOLY SEE)

National name: Stato della Città del Vaticano
Ruler: Pope John Paul II (1978)
Area: 0.17 sq mi. (0.44 sq km)
Population (1995 est.): 1,000; population growth rate: 1.15%; density per square mile: 4,883. **Monetary unit:** Lira. **Languages:** Latin, Italian, and various other languages. **Ethnicity/Race:** Italians, Swiss. **Religion:** Roman Catholic
Labor force: High dignitaries, priests, nuns, guards, and 3,000 lay workers who live outside the Vatican
Budget (1996): Revenues: $198,462.00 million; Expenditures: $198,199.00 million, including capital expenditures.

Geography. The Vatican City State is situated on the Vatican hill, on the right bank of the Tiber River, within the city of Rome.

Government. The Pope has full legal, executive, and judicial powers. Executive power over the area is in the hands of a Commission of Cardinals appointed by the Pope. The College of Cardinals is the Pope's chief advisory body, and upon his death the cardinals elect his successor for life. The cardinals themselves are created for life by the Pope.

In the Vatican the central administration of the Roman Catholic Church throughout the world (Holy See) is carried on by the Secretariat of State, nine Congregations, six commissions, three tribunals, eleven councils, and five offices. In its diplomatic relations, the Holy See is represented by the Papal Secretary of State.

History. The Vatican City State, sovereign and independent, is the survivor of the papal states that in 1859 comprised an area of some 17,000 square miles (44,030 sq km). During the struggle for Italian unification, from 1860 to 1870, most of this area became part of Italy.

By an Italian law of May 13, 1871, the temporal power of the Pope was abrogated, and the territory of the Papacy was confined to the Vatican and Lateran palaces and the villa of Castel Gandolfo. The Popes consistently refused to recognize this arrangement and, by the Lateran Treaty of Feb. 11, 1929, between the Vatican and the Kingdom of Italy, the exclusive dominion and sovereign jurisdiction of the Holy See over the city of the Vatican was again recognized, thus restoring the Pope's temporal authority over the area.

The first session of Ecumenical Council Vatican II was opened by John XXIII on Oct. 11, 1962, to plan and set policies for the modernization of the Roman Catholic Church. Pope Paul VI continued the Council, opening the second session on Sept. 29, 1963.

On Aug. 26, 1978, Cardinal Albino Luciani was chosen by the College of Cardinals to succeed Paul VI, who had died of a heart attack on Aug. 6. The new Pope, who took the name John Paul I, was born on Oct. 17, 1912, at Forno di Canale in Italy.

(For a listing of all the Popes, *see* the table in Religion.)

Only 34 days after his election, John Paul I died of a heart attack, ending the shortest reign in 373 years. On Oct. 16, Cardinal Karol Wojtyla, 58, was chosen Pope and took the name John Paul II.

On May 13, 1981, a Turkish terrorist shot the Pope in St. Peter's Square, the first assassination attempt against the Pontiff in modern times.

On June 3, 1985, the Vatican and Italy ratified a new church-state treaty, known as a concordat, replacing the Lateran Pact of 1929. The new accord affirmed the independence of Vatican City but ended a number of privileges the Catholic Church had in Italy, including its status as the state religion. The treaty ended Rome's status as a "sacred city."

Relations, diplomatic and ecclesiastical, with Eastern Europe have improved dramatically with the fall of communism. Relations with Russia, while improving, have not yet reached the ambassadorial level.

Diplomatic relations were established in 1992 with a host of new countries.

Diplomatic ties were established in March 1994 with Jordan and full relations established with Israel in June. Six months earlier the two nations had accorded each other mutual recognition.

The Holy See, calling for closer relations with Orthodoxy, was scheduled to meet with Russian Patriarch Alexy II in June 1997, but differences prevented the encounter from taking place.

VENEZUELA

Republic of Venezuela
National name: Republica de Venezuela
President: Rafael Caldera (1994)
Area: 352,143 sq mi. (912,050 sq km)
Population (est. 1997): 22,396,407 (average annual rate of natural increase: 1.864%); birth rate: 23.67/1000; infant mortality rate: 28.50/1000; density per sq mi.: 63.6
Capital: Caracas. **Largest cities (est. 1990):** Caracas, 1,290,087; Maracaibo, 1,206,726; Valencia, 616,000; Barquisimento, 723,587. **Monetary unit:** Bolivar. **Language:** Spanish, Indian dialects in interior. **Ethnicity/Race:** mestizo 67%, white 21%, black 10%, Amerindian 2%. **Religion:** Roman Catholic, 96%; Protestant, 2%. **Literacy rate:** 90.7%
Economic summary: Gross domestic product (1995 est.): $195.5 billion, $9,300 per capita; real growth rate –1.6% (1997 est.); inflation 103% (1997 est.); unemployment 11.7%. Arable land: 3%. Principal agricultural products: rice, coffee, corn, cacao, sugar, bananas, dairy and meat products. Labor force: 7.6 million (1995): 63% in services, 25% in industry. Principal industrial products: refined petroleum products, aluminum, iron and steel, cement, textiles, transport equipment. Natural resources: petroleum, natural gas, iron ore, hydroelectric power. Exports: $18.3 billion (1995 est.): petroleum, iron ore, bauxite. Imports: $11.6 billion (1995 est.): industrial machinery and equipment, manufactures, chemicals, foodstuffs. Major trading partners: U.S., Japan, Germany, Italy, Netherlands, Canada.

Geography. Venezuela, a third larger than Texas, occupies most of the northern coast of South America on the Caribbean Sea. It is bordered by Colombia to the west, Guyana to the east, and Brazil to the south.

Mountain systems break Venezuela into four distinct areas: (1) the Maracaibo lowlands; (2) the mountainous region in the north and northwest; (3) the Orinoco basin, with the llanos (vast grass-covered plains) on its northern border and great forest areas in the south and southeast; (4) the Guiana Highlands, south of the Orinoco, accounting for nearly half the national territory. About 80% of Venezuela is drained by the Orinoco and its tributaries.

Government. Venezuela is a federal republic consisting of 22 states, the Federal District, and 72 islands in the Caribbean. There is a bicameral Congress, the 50 members of the Senate and the 199 members of the Chamber of Deputies being elected by popular vote to five-year terms. The President is also elected for five years. He must be a Venezuelan by birth and over 30 years old. He is not eligible for re-election until 10 years after the end of his term.

History. Columbus explored Venezuela on his third voyage in 1498. A subsequent Spanish explorer gave the country its name, meaning "Little Venice." There were no important settlements until Caracas was founded in 1567. Simón Bolívar, who led the liberation of much of the continent from Spain, was born in Caracas in 1783. With Bolívar taking part, Venezuela was one of the first South American colonies to revolt against Spain, in 1810, but it was not until 1821 that independence was won. Federated at first with Colombia and Ecuador, the country set up a republic in 1830 and then sank for many decades into a condition of revolt, dictatorship, and corruption.

From 1908 to 1935, Gen. Juan Vicente Gómez was an absolute dictator. A military junta ruled after his death in 1935. Dr. Rómulo Betancourt and the liberal Acción Democrática Party won a majority of seats in a constituent assembly to draft a new Constitution in 1946. A well-known writer, Rómulo Gallegos, candidate of Betancourt's party, easily won the presidential election of 1947. But, the army ousted Gallegos the next year and instituted a military junta.

The country overthrew the dictatorship in 1958 and thereafter enjoyed democratic government. Rafael Caldera Rodríguez, President from 1969 to 1974, legalized the Communist Party and established diplomatic relations with Moscow.

In 1974, President Carlos Andrés Pérez took office. In 1976, Venezuela nationalized 21 oil companies, mostly subsidiaries of U.S. firms, offering compensation of $1.28 billion.

Despite difficulties at home, Pérez continued to play an active foreign role in extending economic aid to Latin neighbors, in backing the human-rights policy of President Carter, and in supporting Carter's return of the Panama Canal to Panama.

Opposition Christian Democrats capitalized on Pérez's domestic problems to elect Luis Herrera Campíns President in Venezuela's fifth consecutive free election, on Dec. 3, 1978.

When the Falklands war broke out, Venezuela became one of the most vigorous advocates of the Argentine cause and one one of the sharpest critics of the U.S. decision to back Britain.

In the presidential election of December 1988 former president Carlos Andres Pérez of the Democratic Action party easily won.

President Pérez surrendered his powers in May 1993 in order to defend himself in impeachment proceedings arising out of corruption charges. Ramon Velasquez was elected by Congress to serve as acting president pending the outcome of the impeachment proceedings.

In the presidential election of December 1993 Mr. Velasquez came in fourth. After a partial recount Rafael Caldera, a former president, was declared the winner with 30 percent of the vote in January 1994.

In June 1994 approximately half of the country's banking sector collapsed. Price increases of 20 percent were announced in February 1995, and the president's popularity fell during the year.

On the other hand, the government's efforts to create a market-oriented economy won the approval of the IMF, which granted Venezuela a large credit in July 1996.

In mid-1997 the government announced it planned to permit large-scale gold and diamond mining in the Imataca reserve. The government hopes to reap large tax revenues and create new, badly needed jobs from the proposal.

VIETNAM

Socialist Republic of Vietnam

National name: Công Hòa Xa Hôi Chú Nghia Viêt Nam

President: Le Duc Anh (1992)
Premier: Vo Van Kiet (1991)
Area: 127,246 sq mi. (329,566 sq km)
Population (est. 1997): 75,123,880 (average annual rate of natural increase: 1.550%); birth rate: 22.30/1000; infant mortality rate: 37.20/1000; Density per square mile: 590.4
Capital: Hanoi. **Largest cities (1992):** Ho Chi Minh City (Saigon),[1] 4,000,000; Hanoi, 2,961,000. Other large cities (1989): Haiphong, 456,049; Da Nang, 370,670; Nha Trang, 213,687; Qui Nho'n, 160,091; Hué 211,085. **Monetary unit:** Dong. **Languages:** Vietnamese (official), French, English, Khmer, Chinese. **Ethnicity/Race:** Vietnamese 85%-90%, Chinese 3%, Muong, Thai, Meo, Khmer, Man, Cham. **Religions:** Buddhist, Roman Catholic, Islam, Taoist, Confucian, Animist. **Literacy rate:** 88%
Economic summary: GDP purchasing power parity (1995 est.): $97 billion; $1,300 per capita; 9.5% real growth rate; inflation 14%; unemployment 25%. Arable land: 22%. Principal agricultural products: rice, rubber, fruits and vegetables, corn, sugar cane, fish. Labor force: 32,700,000; 65% in agriculture. Major industrial products: processed foods, textiles, cement, chemical fertilizers, glass, tires. Natural resources: phosphates, forests, coal. Exports: $5.3 billion (1995 est.): agricultural products, minerals, marine products, coffee, petroleum, rice. Imports: $7.5 billion (1995 est.): petroleum, steel products, railroad equipment, chemicals, medicines, raw cotton, fertilizer, grain. Major trading partners: Singapore, Japan, Hong Kong, Thailand, Germany, Indonesia, South Korea, Taiwan.

1. Includes suburb of Cholon.

Geography. Vietnam occupies the eastern and southern part of the Indochinese peninsula in Southeast Asia, with the South China Sea along its entire coast. China is to the north and Laos and Cambodia to the west. Long and narrow on a north-south axis, Vietnam is about twice the size of Arizona.

The Mekong River delta lies in the south and the Red River delta in the north. Heavily forested mountain and plateau regions make up most of the country.

Government. On April 30, 1975, a joint National Assembly convened with 249 deputies representing the North and 243 representing the South. The Assembly set July 2, 1976, as the official reunification date. Hanoi became the capital.

A new constitution was adopted in April 1992 which

called for the creation of a presidency and a prime ministry. The document affirmed the free-market economy and the role of the Communist Party is limited to that of guidance. Foreign assets are guaranteed against nationalization. The assembly has 395 members.

History. The Vietnamese are descendants of Mongoloid nomads from China and migrants from Indonesia. They recognized Chinese suzerainty until the 15th century, an era of nationalistic expansion, when Cambodians were pushed out of the southern area of what is now Vietnam.

A century later, the Portuguese were the first Europeans to enter the area. France established its influence early in the 19th century and within 80 years conquered the three regions into which the country was then divided—Cochin-China in the south, Annam in the center, and Tonkin in the north.

France first unified Vietnam in 1887, when a single governor-generalship was created, followed by the first physical links between north and south—a rail and road system. Even at the beginning of World War II, however, there were internal differences among the three regions.

Japan took over military bases in Vietnam in 1940 and a pro-Vichy French administration remained until 1945. A veteran Communist leader, Ho Chi Minh, organized an independence movement known as the Vietminh to exploit a confused situation. At the end of the war, Ho's followers seized Hanoi and declared a short-lived republic, which ended with the arrival of French forces in 1946.

Paris proposed a unified government within the French Union under the former Annamite emperor, Bao Dai. Cochin-China and Annam accepted the proposal, and Bao Dai was proclaimed emperor of all Vietnam in 1949. Ho and the Vietminh withheld support, and the revolution in China gave them the outside help needed for a war of resistance against French and Vietnamese troops armed largely by the U.S.

A bitter defeat at Dien Bien Phu in northwest Vietnam on May 5, 1954, broke the French military campaign and brought the division of Vietnam at the conference of Geneva that year.

In the new South, Ngo Dinh Diem, Premier under Bao Dai, deposed the monarch in 1955 and established a republic with himself as President. Diem used strong U.S. backing to create an authoritarian regime that suppressed all opposition but could not eradicate the Northern-supplied Communist Viet Cong.

Skirmishing grew into a full-scale war, with escalating U.S. involvement. A military coup, U.S.-inspired in the view of many, ousted Diem Nov. 1, 1963, and a kaleidoscope of military governments followed. The most savage fighting of the war occurred in early 1968, during the Tet holidays.

Although the Viet Cong failed to overthrow the Saigon government, U.S. public reaction to the apparently endless war forced a limitation of U.S. troops to 550,000 and a new emphasis on shifting the burden of further combat to the South Vietnamese. Ho Chi Minh's death on Sept. 3, 1969, brought a quadrumvirate to replace him but no flagging in Northern will to fight.

U.S. bombing and invasion of Cambodia in the summer of 1970—an effort to destroy Viet Cong bases in the neighboring state—marked the end of major U.S. participation in the fighting. Most American ground troops were withdrawn from combat by mid-1971 as heavy bombing of the Ho Chi Minh trail from North Vietnam appeared to cut the supply of men and matériel to the South.

Secret negotiations for peace by Secretary of State Henry A. Kissinger with North Vietnamese officials during 1972 after heavy bombing of Hanoi and Haiphong brought the two sides near agreement in October. When the Northerners demanded the removal of the South's President Nguyen Van Thieu as their price, President Nixon ordered the "Christmas bombing" of the North. The conference resumed and a peace settlement was signed in Paris on Jan. 27, 1973. It called for release of all U.S. prisoners, withdrawal of U.S. forces, limitation of both sides' forces inside South Vietnam, and a commitment to peaceful reunification.

An armored attack across the 17th parallel in January 1975 panicked the South Vietnamese army and brought the invasion within 40 miles of Saigon by April 9. Thieu resigned on April 21 and fled, to be replaced by Vice President Tran Van Huong, who quit a week later, turning over the office to Gen. Duong Van Minh. "Big Minh" surrendered Saigon on April 30, ending a war that took 1.3 million Vietnamese and 58,000 American lives, at the cost of $141 billion in U.S. aid.

On May 3, 1977, the U.S. and Vietnam opened negotiations in Paris to normalize relations. One of the first results was the withdrawal of U.S. opposition to Vietnamese membership in the United Nations, formalized in the Security Council on July 20. Two major issues remained to be settled, however: the return of the bodies of some 2,500 U.S. servicemen missing in the war and the claim by Hanoi that former President Nixon had promised reconstruction aid under the 1973 agreement. Negotiations failed to resolve these issues.

The new year also brought an intensification of border clashes between Vietnam and Cambodia and accusations by China that Chinese residents of Vietnam were being subjected to persecution. Peking cut off all aid and withdrew 800 technicians.

Hanoi was undoubtedly preoccupied with a continuing war in Cambodia, where 60,000 Vietnamese troops were aiding the Heng Samrin regime in suppressing the last forces of the pro-Chinese Pol Pot regime. In early 1979, Vietnam was conducting a two-front war, defending its northern border against a Chinese invasion and at the same time supporting its army in Cambodia.

Economic troubles continued, with the government seeking to reschedule its $1.4-billion foreign hard-currency debt, owed mainly to Japan and the International Monetary Fund. In 1986, Vietnam's economy began to improve under *doi moi* (economic renovation).

In 1988, Vietnam also began limited troop withdrawals from Laos and Cambodia. Vietnam supported the Cambodian peace agreement signed in October 1991.

General elections in July 1992 saw 601 candidates competing for the 395 seats in the assembly.

The U.S. trade embargo was lifted in February 1994 although the Party reiterated its opposition to political reform throughout the year despite its continued pursuit of major economic reforms. Full diplomatic relations were announced between the U.S. and Vietnam in July 1995.

Reform-minded officials were named in May 1996 to head the Hanoi and Ho Chi Minh City Community Party organizations.

The government in April 1997 signed a pact with the U.S. concerning repayment of the $146 million wartime debt incurred by the South Vietnamese government.

(For a Vietnam War chronology, *see* Headline History.)

WESTERN SAMOA

Independent State of Western Samoa
Head of State: Malietoa Tanumafili II (1962)
Prime Minister: Tofilau Eti Alesana (1988)
Area: 1,093 sq mi. (2,831 sq km)
Population (est. 1997): 219,509 (average annual growth rate: 2.447%); birth rate: 30.40/1000; infant

mortality rate: 33.0/1000; density per square mile: 200.8

Capital and largest city (1991): Apia, 32,859. **Monetary unit:** Tala. **Languages:** Samoan and English. **Ethnicity/Race:** Samoan 92.6%, Euronesians 7% (persons of European and Polynesian blood), Europeans 0.4%. **Religions:** Christian, 99.7%. **Literacy rate:** 98.3%

Economic summary: Gross domestic product (1995 est.): $415 million; $1,900 per capita; 5% real growth rate; inflation 18%. Arable land: 19%. Principal agricultural products: copra, coconuts, cocoa, bananas, taro, yams. Labor force (1987): 38,000; 65% employed in agriculture. Agriculture accounts for 50% of GDP. Major industrial products: timber, processed food, fish. Natural resource: timber. Exports: $6.4 million (f.o.b., 1993): copra, cocoa, coconut oil and cream, timber. Imports: $11.5 million (c.i.f., 1992 est.): food, manufactured goods, machinery. Major trading partners: New Zealand, EC, Australia, U.S., Fiji, Japan. Member of Commonwealth of Nations.

Geography. Western Samoa, the size of Rhode Island, is in the South Pacific Ocean about 2,200 miles (3,540 km) south of Hawaii midway to Sydney, Australia, and about 800 miles (1,287 km) northeast of Fiji. The larger islands in the Samoan chain are mountainous and of volcanic origin. There is little level land except in the coastal areas, where most cultivation takes place.

Government. Western Samoa has a 49-member Legislature, consisting mainly of the titleholders (chiefs) of family groups, with two non-title members. All members are elected by universal suffrage. When the present Head of State dies, successors will be elected by the Legislature for five-year terms.

History. The Samoan islands were explored by Dutch and French traders in the 18th century. Toward the end of the 19th century, conflicting interests of the U.S., Britain, and Germany resulted in a treaty signed in 1899. It recognized the paramount interests of the U.S. in those islands east of 171° west longitude (American Samoa) and Germany's interests in the other islands (Western Samoa).

New Zealand occupied Western Samoa in 1914, and was granted a League of Nations mandate. In 1947, the islands became a U.N. trust territory administered by New Zealand. Western Samoa became independent on Jan. 1, 1962.

A referendum of 1990 gave most women the right to vote for the first time. The April 1991 election gave the ruling Human Rights Protection Party a narrow victory.

A value-added tax was introduced at the start of 1994 that produced widespread dissatisfaction and resistance. Government attempts to ameliorate the impact of the tax failed to soothe public opposition.

In March 1997 the prime minister proposed a constitutional amendment to change the country's name to Samoa.

REPUBLIC OF YEMEN

National name: Al Jumhuriyahal Yamaniyah
President: Ali Abdullah Saleh
Prime Minister: Faraj Said Bin Ghanem (1997)
Area: 203,850 sq mi. (527,970 sq km)
Population (est. 1997): 13,972,477 (average annual rate of natural increase: 3.566%); birth rate: 44.83/1000; infant mortality rate: 68.10/1000; density per square mile: 68.5
Capital (1995): Sanaá 972,011. **Largest cities (1995):** Tiaz, 2,205,947; Hodiedah, 1,749,944; Aden, 562,162.
Monetary unit: Rial. **Language:** Arabic. **Ethnicity/**

Race: predominantly Arab; Afro-Arab concentrations in western coastal locations; South Asians in southern regions; small European communities in major metropolitan areas. **Religion:** Islam (Sunni and Shiite). **Literacy rate:** 38%

Economic summary: Gross domestic product (1995 est.): $37.1 billion; $2,520 per capita; real growth rate 3.6%; inflation: 71.3% (1994 est.); unemployment: 30% (1995). Principal agricultural products: wheat, sorghum, cattle, sheep, cotton, fruits, coffee, dates. Principal industrial products: crude and refined oil, textiles, leather goods, handicrafts, fish. Exports: $1.1 billion (1995 est.): cotton, coffee, hides, vegetables, dried fish. Imports: $1.8 billion (1994 est.): textiles, manufactured consumer goods, foodstuffs, sugar, grain, flour. Major trading partners: U.K., Japan, Saudi Arabia, Australia, U.S.

Geography. Formerly known as the states of People's Democratic Republic of Yemen and the Yemen Arab Republic, the Republic of Yemen occupies the southwestern tip of the Arabian Peninsula on the Red Sea opposite Ethiopia, and extends along the southern part of the Arabian Peninsula on the Gulf of Aden and the Indian Ocean. Saudi Arabia is to the north and Oman is to the east. The country is about the size of France. A 700-mile (1,130-km) narrow coastal plain in the south gives way to a mountainous region and then a plateau area. Some of the interior highlands in the west attain a height of 12,000 feet (3,660 m).

Government. Parliamentary. The Presidential Council was abolished by a new constitution approved in September 1994.

History. The history of Yemen dates back to the Minaean kingdom (1200–650 B.C.E.). It accepted Islam in C.E. 628, and in the 10th century came under the control of the Rassite dynasty of the Zaidi sect. The Turks occupied the area from 1538 to 1630 and from 1849 to 1918. The sovereign status of Yemen was confirmed by treaties signed with Saudi Arabia and Britain in 1934.

In 1962, a military revolt of elements favoring President Gamal Abdel Nasser of Egypt broke out. A ruling junta proclaimed a republic, and Yemen became an international battleground, with Egypt and the U.S.S.R. supporting the revolutionaries, and King Saud of Saudi Arabia and King Hussein of Jordan the royalists. The civil war continued until the war between the Arab states and Israel broke out in June 1967. Nasser had to pull out many of his troops and agree to a cease-fire and withdrawal of foreign forces. The war finally ended with the defeat of the royalists in mid-1969.

The People's Republic of Southern Yemen was established Nov. 30, 1967, when Britain granted independence to the Federation of South Arabia. This Federation consisted of the state (once the colony) of Aden and 16 of the 20 states of the Protectorate of South Arabia (once the Aden Protectorate). The four states of the Protectorate that did not join the Federation later became part of Southern Yemen.

The Republic of Yemen was established on May 23, 1990, when pro-western Yemen and Marxist Yemen Arab Republic merged after 300 years of separation to form the new nation. The union had been approved by both governments in November 1989.

The new president, Ali Abdullah Saleh of Yemen, was elected by the parliaments of both countries.

In the Gulf War, Yemen favored Iraq. Consequently, many expatriates in Saudi Arabia were forced to return. A referendum in May 1992 on a constitution resulted in a landslide in favor of it.

Differences over power-sharing and the pace of integration between the north and the south came to a head in 1994, resulting in a civil war. The north's superior forces quickly overwhelmed the south in May and early June despite the south's brief declaration of succession. The victorious north presented a reconciliation plan providing for a general amnesty and pledges to protect political democracy.

Border clashes occurred periodically with Saudi Arabia during 1995 despite ongoing talks.

The president's party, the General People's Congress, won an enormous victory in the April 1997 parliamentary elections, the first since the civil war. A new government pledged to continue the economic reforms agreed to with the World Bank and the IMF.

YUGOSLAVIA

Federal Republic of Yugoslavia
National name: Federativna Republika Jugoslavijá
President: Slobodan Milosevic (1997)
Prime Minister: Radoje Kontic (1993)
Area: 39,449 sq mi. (102,169 sq km)
Population (est. 1996): 10,611,558 (average annual rate of natural increase: 1.0%); birth rate: 13/1000; infant mortality rate: 26/1000; density per square mile: 269
Capital and largest city (1994 est): Belgrade, 1,168,454. **Other large cities:** Novi Sad, 179,626; Nis, 175,391; Pristina, 155,499. **Monetary unit:** Yugoslav new Dinar. **Languages:** Serbo-Croatian 100%. **Ethnicity/Race:** Serbs 63%, Albanians 14%, Montenegrins 6%, Hungarians 4%, other 13%. **Religions:** Orthodox, 65%; Muslim, 19%; Christian religions, 5%. **Literacy rate:** 90.5%
Economic summary Gross domestic product (1995 est.): $20.6 billion; per capita $2,000; growth rate 4%; inflation 20% (1995): unemployment more than 40%. Labor force (1990): 2,640,909; industry and mining, 40%; agriculture, 5%. Industries: machine building (incl. aircraft, trucks, automobiles), nonferrous metallurgy, consumer goods, electronics, chemicals, petroleum products, pharmaceuticals. Exports: n.a.: machinery and transportation equipment, manufactured goods and articles, chemicals, food, and live animals. Imports: n.a.: machinery and transport equipment, fuels and lubricants, other manufacturers, chemicals, raw materials, food, and animals. Trading partners: C.I.S. countries, E.U., U.S., Eastern European countries.

Geography. Yugoslavia consists of the two states of Serbia and Montenegro. The nation is bordered by Hungary in the north, Romania and Bulgaria in the east, Macedonia in the south, Albania and the Adriatic Sea in the west, and the former Yugoslavian republics of Bosnia-Herzegovina and Croatia in the west. Yugoslavia is about the size of the state of Kentucky.

Yugoslavia is largely a mountainous country. The northeastern section of Serbia is part of the rich, fertile Danubian Plain drained by the Danube, Tisa, Sava, and Morava River systems. Montenegro is a jumbled mass of mountains, containing also some grassy slopes and fertile river valleys.

Government. Yugoslavia (Serbia and Montenegro) is a federal republic. The bicameral Federal Assembly consists of an upper house or Chamber of Republics and a lower house or Chamber of Deputies. The current Federation is the third state to be referred to by the name Yugoslavia.

History. Yugoslavia was formed Dec. 4, 1918, from the patchwork of Balkan states and territories where World War I began with the assassination of Archduke Ferdinand of Austria at Sarajevo on June 28, 1914. The new Kingdom of Serbs, Croats, and Slovenes included the former kingdoms of Serbia and Montenegro; Bosnia-Herzegovina, previously administered jointly by Austria and Hungary; Croatia-Slavonia, a semi-autonomous region of Hungary, and Dalmatia, formerly administered by Austria. King Peter I of Serbia became the first monarch, his son acting as Regent until his accession as Alexander I on Aug. 16, 1921.

Croatian demands for a federal state forced Alexander to assume dictatorial powers in 1929 and to change the country's name to Yugoslavia. Serbian dominance continued despite his efforts, amid the resentment of other regions. A Macedonian associated with Croatian dissidents assassinated Alexander in Marseilles, France, on Oct. 9, 1934, and his cousin, Prince Paul, became Regent for the King's son, Prince Peter.

Paul's pro-Axis policy brought Yugoslavia to sign the Axis Pact on March 25, 1941, and opponents overthrew the government two days later. On April 6 the Nazis occupied the country, and the young King and his government fled. Two guerrilla armies—the Chetniks under Draza Mihajlovic supporting the monarchy and the Partisans under Tito (Josip Broz) leaning toward the U.S.S.R.—fought the Nazis for the duration of the war. In 1943, Tito established an Executive National Committee of Liberation to function as a provisional government.

Tito won the election held in the fall of 1945, as monarchists boycotted the vote. A new Assembly abolished the monarchy and proclaimed the Federal People's Republic of Yugoslavia, with Tito as Prime Minister. Ruthlessly eliminating opposition, the Tito government executed Mihajlovic in 1946.

Tito broke with the Soviet bloc in 1948 and Yugoslavia followed a middle road, combining orthodox Communist control of politics and general overall economic policy with a varying degree of freedom in the arts, travel, and individual enterprise. Tito became President in 1953 and President for life under a revised Constitution adopted in 1963.

After Tito's death on May 4, 1980, a rotating presidency designed to avoid internal dissension was put into effect immediately, and the feared clash of Yugoslavia's multiple nationalities and regions appeared to have been averted.

In May 1991 Croatian voters supported a referendum calling for their republic to become an independent nation. A similar referendum passed in December in Slovenia. In June the respective parliaments in both republics passed declarations of independence. Ethnic violence flared almost immediately. The largely Serbian-led Yugoslav military pounded break-away Bosnia and Herzegovina, leading the U.N. Security Council in May 1992 to impose economic sanctions on the Belgrade government.

Despite rampant inflation reaching approximately 3000% per month in December 1993, the Serbian government of Slobodan Milosevic maintained its effective control over the rump Yugoslavia. Final results of the late year parliamentary elections gave the Socialist Party the largest number of seats, just three short of a majority.

Trade sanctions were lifted in December 1995 following the signing of the Dayton Accords. In June 1996 the UN Security Council lifted its heavy weapons embargo.

Large groups of demonstrators in 1996–97 engaged in several months of daily protests after Slobodan Milosevic refused to recognize opposition victories in local elections.

Constitutionally barred from a third term as Serbian president, Milosevic turned his sights in mid-1997 on the largely ceremonial federal Yugoslav presidency. Speculation was rife that he would seek to enhance the powers of that office. To that end he called for a constitutional change for direct presidential election.

ZAIRE

See Congo, Democratic Rebublic of.

ZAMBIA

Republic of Zambia
President: Frederick T. J. Chiluba (1991)
Area: 290,586 sq mi. (752,610 sq km)
Population (est. 1997): 9,349,975 (average annual rate of natural increase: 2.019%); birth rate: 44.37/1000; infant mortality rate: 96.50/1000; density per square mile: 32.2
Capital: Lusaka. **Largest cities (1997):** Lusaka, 1.6 million; (1990 est.) Kitwe, 338,207; Ndola, 376,311; Chingola, 167,954. **Monetary unit:** Kwacha. **Languages:** English and local dialects. **Ethnicity/Race:** African 98.7%, European 1.1%, other 0.2%. **Religions:** Christian, 50–75%; Islam and Hindu, 24–49%; remainder indigenous beliefs. **Literacy rate:** 75.7%
Economic summary: Gross domestic product (1995 est.): $8.9 billion; $900 per capita; real growth rate n.a.; inflation 535%; unemployment n.a. Arable land: 7%. Principal agricultural products: corn, tobacco, rice, sugar cane. Labor force: 3.4 million; Agriculture 85%. Major industrial products: copper, textiles, chemicals, zinc, fertilizers. Natural resources: copper, zinc, lead, cobalt, coal. Exports: $1.190 billion (1995 est.): copper, zinc, lead, cobalt, tobacco. Imports: $1.278 billion (1995 est.): manufactured goods, machinery and transport equipment, foodstuffs, fuels. Major trading partners: Western Europe, Japan, South Africa, U.S., Saudi Arabia, India. Member of Commonwealth of Nations.

Geography. Zambia, a landlocked country in south central Africa, is about one-tenth larger than Texas. It is surrounded by Angola, Zaire, Tanzania, Malawi, Mozambique, Zimbabwe, Botswana, and Namibia (formerly South-West Africa). The country is mostly a plateau that rises to 8,000 feet (2,434 m) in the east.

Government. A multiparty system. Zambia (formerly Northern Rhodesia) is governed by a president, elected by universal suffrage, and a unicameral Legislative Assembly, consisting of 150 members elected by universal suffrage every five years.

History. Empire builder Cecil Rhodes obtained mining concessions in 1889 from King Lewanika of the Barotse and sent settlers to the area soon thereafter. It was ruled by the British South Africa Company, which he established, until 1924, when the British government took over the administration.

From 1953 to 1964, Northern Rhodesia was federated with Southern Rhodesia and Nyasaland in the Federation of Rhodesia and Nyasaland. On Oct. 24, 1964, Northern Rhodesia became the independent nation of Zambia.

Kenneth Kaunda, the first president, kept Zambia within the Commonwealth of Nations. The country's economy, dependent on copper exports, was threatened when Rhodesia declared its independence from British rule in 1965 and defied U.N. sanctions, which Zambia supported, an action that deprived Zambia of its trade route through Rhodesia. The U.S., Britain, and Canada organized an airlift in 1966 to ship gasoline into Zambia. In 1967, Britain agreed to finance new trade routes for Zambia.

Kaunda visited China in 1967, and China later agreed to finance a 1,000-mile railroad from the copper fields to Dar es Salaam in Tanzania. A pipeline was opened in 1968 from Ndola in Zambia's copper belt to the Indian Ocean at Dar es Salaam, ending the three-year oil drought.

In 1969, Kaunda announced the nationalization of the foreign copper-mining industry, with Zambia to take 51% (over $1 billion, estimated), and an agreement was reached with the companies on payment. He then announced a similar takeover of foreign oil producers.

With a soaring debt and inflation rate the government in 1990 turned to the International Monetary Fund and the World Bank, with whom an agreement was reached in exchange for economic reforms. Soaring prices in June 1990 led to riots in Lusaka, resulting in a number of killings. Mounting domestic pressure forced Kaunda to move Zambia toward multiparty democracy.

National elections on October 31, 1991 brought a stunning defeat to the long-serving President Kaunda and a repudiation of his long belief in a one-party state. The newly-elected chief executive, Frederick Chiluba, called for sweeping economic reforms including privatization and the establishing of a stock market.

The president declared a state of emergency in March 1993 after the uncovering of a plot to overthrow the government. The state of emergency was lifted in May.

Parliament passed a bill in May 1996 that stated a president may serve only two terms, thus preventing any possible political return of Kenneth Kaunda.

With low voter turnout, general elections in November 1996 saw the reelection of President Chiluba with 70% of the vote. The president's party also won approximately 130 parliamentary seats.

ZIMBABWE

Republic of Zimbabwe
Executive President: Robert Mugabe (1987)
Area: 150,698 sq mi. (390,308 sq km)
Population (est. 1997): 11,423,175 (average annual rate of natural increase: 1.263%); birth rate: 31.65/1000; infant mortality rate: 72.60/1000; density per square mile: 75.8
Capital and largest city (1992): Harare, 1,184,169.. **Other large cities:** Bulawayo, 621,000; Chitungwiza, 274,035. **Monetary unit:** Zimbabwean dollar. **Languages:** English (official), Ndebele, Shona (85%). **Ethnicity/Race:** African 98% (Shona 71%, Ndebele 16%, other 11%), white 1%, mixed and Asian 1%. **Religions:** Christian, 25%; Animist, 24%; Syncretic, 50%. **Literacy rate:** 85%
Economic summary: Gross domestic product (1995 est.): $18.1 billion; $1,620 per capita; real growth rate -2.4%; inflation 25.8% (1995); unemployment: at least 45%. Arable land: 7%. Principal agricultural products: tobacco, corn, sugar, cotton, livestock. Labor force: 4.228 million; 70% in agriculture; 22%, transport and services. Major industrial products: steel, textiles, chemicals, vehicles, gold, copper. Natural resources: gold, copper, chrome, nickel, tin, asbestos. Exports: $2.2 billion (f.o.b., 1995 est.): gold, tobacco, asbestos, copper, meat, chrome, nickel, corn, sugar. Imports: $1.8 billion (c.i.f., 1995 est.): machinery, petroleum products, transport equipment. Major trading partners: U.K., South Africa, Germany, Japan, U.S.

Geography. Zimbabwe, a landlocked country in south central Africa, is slightly smaller than California. It is bordered by Botswana on the west, Zambia on the north, Mozambique on the east, and South Africa on the south.

A high veld up to 6,000 feet (1,829 m) crosses the country from northeast to southwest. This is flanked by a somewhat lower veld that contains ranching country. Tropical forests that yield hardwoods lie in the southeast.

Government. A parliamentary democracy with a 150-seat unicameral legislature, the House of Assembly. The Executive President is chief of state and head of government. There are two co-vice presidents.

History. The land's earliest settlers, the Khoisan, date back to 200 B.C.E. After a period of Bantu domination, the Shona people ruled, followed by the Nguni and Zulu peoples. By the mid-nineteenth century the descendents of the Nguni and Zulu, the Ndebele, had established a powerful warrior kingdom.

The first British explorers, colonists, and missionaries arrived in the 1850s, and the massive influx of foreigners led to the establishment of the territory Rhodesia, named after Cecil Rhodes of the British South Africa Company. In 1923, European settlers voted to become the self-governing British colony of Southern Rhodesia rather than merge with the Union of South Africa. After a brief federation with Northern Rhodesia and Nyasaland in the post-World War II period, Southern Rhodesia (also known as Rhodesia) chose to remain a colony when its two partners voted for independence in 1963.

On Nov. 11, 1965, the white-minority government of Rhodesia unilaterally declared its independence from Britain.

In 1967, the U.N. imposed mandatory sanctions against Rhodesia. The country moved slowly toward meeting the demands of black Africans. The white-minority regime of Prime Minister Ian Smith withstood British pressure, economic sanctions, guerrilla attacks, and a right-wing assault.

On March 1, 1970, Rhodesia formally proclaimed itself a republic, and within the month nine nations, including the U.S., closed their consulates there.

Heightened guerrilla war and a withdrawal of South African military aid marked the beginning of the collapse of Smith's 11 years of resistance in the spring of 1976. Under pressure from South Africa, Smith agreed with the U.S. that majority rule should come within two years.

In the fall, Smith met with black nationalist leaders in Geneva. The meeting broke up when the Rhodesian Premier insisted that whites must retain control of the police and armed forces during the transition to majority rule.

Divisions between Rhodesian blacks—Bishop Abel Muzorewa of the African National Congress and Ndabaningi Sithole as moderates versus Robert Mugabe and Joshua Nkomo of the Patriotic Front as advocates of guerrilla force—sharpened in 1977 and no agreement was reached. In July, with white residents leaving in increasing numbers and the economy showing the strain of war, Smith rejected outside mediation and called for general elections in order to work out an "internal solution" of the transfer of power.

On March 3, 1978, Smith, Muzorewa, Sithole, and Chief Jeremiah Chirau signed an agreement to transfer power to the black majority by Dec. 31, 1978. They constituted themselves an Executive Council, with chairmanship rotating but Smith retaining the title of Prime Minister. Blacks were named to each cabinet ministry, serving as co-ministers with the whites already holding these posts. African nations and the Patriotic Front leaders immediately denounced the action, but Western governments were more reserved, although none granted recognition to the new regime.

White voters ratified a new constitution on Jan. 30, 1979, enfranchising all blacks, establishing a black majority Senate and Assembly, and changing the country's name to Zimbabwe Rhodesia.

Muzorewa agreed to negotiate with Mugabe and Nkomo in British-sponsored talks beginning Sept. 9. By December, all parties accepted a new draft constitution, a cease-fire, and a period of British administration pending a general election.

In voting completed on Feb. 29, 1980, Mugabe's ZANU-Patriotic Front party won 57 of the 80 Assembly seats reserved for blacks. In an earlier vote on Feb. 14, the Rhodesian Front won all 20 seats reserved for whites in the Assembly.

On April 18, 1980, Britain formally recognized the independence of Zimbabwe.

In April 1990, Mugabe was re-elected and his ZANU(PF) party given virtual unanimity in the Assembly.

In December 1990 the parliament voted to amend the original 1980 constitution to allow the compulsory acquisition of white-owned farmland at government-set prices. Indeed, white farmers would have no judiciary recourse. Britain and the U.S. warned that forceful land acquisitions would deter foreign investments and further depress the country.

A split in the opposition Zimbabwe Unity Movement in June 1991 reduced pressure on the ruling ZANU(PF). At that time the latter deleted all references to Marxism-Leninism and scientific socialism from its constitution.

The Land Acquisition Act was amended in 1992 to permit compensation for compulsorily acquired land.

Parliamentary elections in April 1995 gave Mugabe's party a stunning victory with 63 of the 65 contested seats. Mugabe won another six-year term as president in a March 1996 election. He ran unopposed as the only other candidate withdrew just prior to the voting.

The agriculture minister, one of the two white members of the Cabinet, resigned in April 1997 for personal reasons. Although it accepted a privatization program 6 years ago, little progress had been made until June, when the government announced the first public sale of a state-owned farm.

(For late reports, *see* Current Events, What Happened in 1996–97)

International Relations

Preamble of the United Nations Charter

The Charter of the United Nations was adopted at the San Francisco Conference of 1945. The complete text may be obtained by writing to the United Nations Sales Section, United Nations, New York, N.Y. 10017, and enclosing $1.

We the peoples of the United Nations determined to save succeeding generations from the scourge of war, which twice in our lifetime has brought untold sorrow to mankind, and

To reaffirm faith in fundamental human rights, in the dignity and worth of the human person, in the equal rights of men and women and of nations large and small, and

To establish conditions under which justice and respect for the obligations arising from treaties and other sources of international law can be maintained, and

To promote social progress and better standards of life in larger freedom, and for these ends

To practice tolerance and live together in peace with one another as good neighbors, and

To unite our strength to maintain international peace and security, and

To insure, by the acceptance of principles and the institution of methods, that armed force shall not be used, save in the common interest, and

To employ international machinery for the promotion of the economic and social advancement of all peoples, have resolved to combine our efforts to accomplish these aims.

Accordingly, our respective Governments, through representatives assembled in the city of San Francisco, who have exhibited their full powers found to be in good and due form, have agreed to the present Charter of the United Nations and do hereby establish an international organization to be known as the United Nations.

Principal Organs of the United Nations

Secretariat

This is the directorate on U.N. operations, apart from political decisions. All members contribute to its upkeep. Its headquarters staff of about 4,730 specialists is recruited from member nations on the basis of as wide a geographical distribution as possible. The staff works under the Secretary-General, whom it assists and advises.

Secretaries-General

Kofi Annan, Ghana, Jan. 1, 1997.
Boutros Boutros-Ghali, Egypt, Jan. 1, 1992 to Dec. 31, 1996.
Javier Pérez de Cuéllar, Peru, Jan. 1, 1982, to Dec. 31, 1991.
Kurt Waldheim, Austria, Jan. 1, 1972, to Dec. 31, 1981.
U Thant, Burma (Myanmar), Nov. 3, 1961, to Dec. 31, 1971.
Dag Hammarskjöld, Sweden, April 11, 1953, to Sept. 17, 1961.
Trygve Lie, Norway, Feb. 1, 1946, to April 10, 1953.

General Assembly

The General Assembly is the world's forum for discussing matters affecting world peace and security, and for making recommendations concerning them. It has no power of its own to enforce decisions.

The Assembly is composed of the 51 original member nations and those admitted since, a total of 185. Each nation has one vote. On important questions including international peace and security, a two-thirds majority of those present and voting is required. Decisions on other questions are made by a simple majority.

The Assembly's agenda can be as broad as the Charter. It can make recommendations to member nations, the Security Council, or both. Emphasis is given on questions relating to international peace and security brought before it by any member, the Security Council, or nonmembers.

The Assembly also maintains a broad program of international cooperation in economic, social, cultural, educational, and health fields, and for assisting in human rights and freedoms.

Among other duties, the Assembly has functions relating to the trusteeship system, and considers and approves the U.N. Budget. Every member contributes to operating expenses according to its means.

Security Council

The Security Council is the primary instrument for establishing and maintaining international peace. Its main purpose is to prevent war by settling disputes between nations.

Under the Charter, the Council is permitted to dispatch a U.N. force to stop aggression. All member nations undertake to make available armed forces, assistance, and facilities to maintain international peace and security.

Any member may bring a dispute before the Security Council or the General Assembly. Any nonmember may do so if it accepts the charter obligations of pacific settlement.

The Security Council has 15 members. There are five permanent members: the United States, the Russian Federation, Britain, France, and China; and 10 temporary members elected by the General Assembly for two-year terms, from five different regions of the world.

Voting on procedural matters requires a nine-vote majority to carry. However, on questions of substance, the vote of each of the five permanent members is required.

The ten non-permanent members of the Council in 1997 are Chile (1997), Costa Rica (1998), Egypt (1997), Guinea-Bissau (1997), Japan (1998), Kenya (1998), Republic of Korea (1997), Poland (1997), Portugal (1998), and Sweden (1998).

Economic and Social Council

This council is composed of 54 members elected by the General Assembly to 3-year terms. It works closely with the General Assembly as a link with groups formed within the U.N. to help peoples in such fields as education, health, and human rights. It insures that there is no overlapping and sets up commissions to deal with economic conditions and collect facts and figures on conditions over the world. It issues studies and reports and may make recommendations to the Assembly and specialized agencies.

Functional Commissions

Commission on Population and Development; Commission for Social Development; Commission on Human Rights; Commission on the Status of Women; Statistical Commission; Commission on Narcotic Drugs; Commission on Sustainable Development; Commission on Crime Prevention and Criminal Justice; Commission on Science and Technology for Development.

Regional Commissions

Economic Commission for Europe (ECE); Economic and Social Commission for Asia and the Pacific (ESCAP); Economic Commission for Latin America and the Caribbean (ECLAC); Economic Commission for Africa (ECA); Economic and Social Commission for Western Asia (ESCWA).

Trusteeship Council

The Trusteeship Council has five members: China, France, Russian Federation, United Kingdom, and the United States. With the independence of Palau, the last remaining United Nations trust territory, the Council formally suspended operation on November 1, 1994. By a resolution adopted on that day, the Council amended its rules of procedure to drop the obligation to meet annually and agreed to meet as occasion required—by its decision or the decision of its President, or at the request of a majority of its members or the General Assembly or the Security Council.

International Court of Justice

The International Court of Justice sits at The Hague, the Netherlands. Its 15-judge bench was established to hear disputes among states, which must agree to accept its verdicts. Its judges, charged with administering justice under international law, deal with cases ranging from disputes over territory to those concerning rights of passage.

Following are the members of the Court and the years in which their terms expire on Feb. 5:

President: Stephen M. Schwebel, United States (2000 as president, 2006 term)
Vice President: Christopher Gregory Weeramantry, Sri Lanka (2000)
Mohammed Bedjaoui, Algeria (2006)
Carl-August Fleischauer, Germany (2003)
Gilbert Guillaume, France (2000)
Géza Herczegh, Hungary (2003)
Rosalyn Higgins, United Kingdom (2000)
Jiuyong Shi, China (2003)
Pieter H. Kooijmans, Netherlands (2006)
Abdul G. Koroma, Sierra Leone (2003)
Shigeru Oda, Japan (2003)
Gonzalo Parra-Aranguren, Venezuela (2000)
Raymond Ranjeva, Madagascar (2000)
José Francisco Rezek, Brazil (2006)
Vladlen S. Vereshchetin, Russian Federation (2006)

Agencies of the United Nations

Intl. Atomic Energy Agency (IAEA)

Established: Statute for IAEA, approved on Oct. 26, 1956, at a conference held at U.N. Headquarters, New York, came into force on July 29, 1957. The Agency is under the aegis of the U.N., but unlike the following, it is not a specialized agency.

Purpose: To promote the peaceful uses of atomic energy; to ensure that assistance provided by it or at its request or under its supervision or control is not used in such a way as to further any military purpose.

Headquarters: Vienna International Center, P.O. Box 100, Wagramer Strasse 5, A-1400 Vienna, Austria.

Food and Agriculture Organization of the United Nations (FAO)

Established: October 16, 1945, when constitution became effective.

Purpose: To raise nutrition levels and living standards; to secure improvements in production and distribution of food and agricultural products.

Headquarters: Via delle Terme di Caracalla, 00100, Rome, Italy.

World Trade Organization (WTO)

Established: Jan. 1, 1995.

Purpose: The World Trade Organization (WTO) replaced the General Agreement on Tariffs and Trade (GATT) as the major entity overseeing international trade. Unlike GATT, which was a treaty serviced by an ad hoc Secretariat, the WTO is a full-fledged organization in its own right.

Headquarters: Geneva, Switzerland.

International Bank for Reconstruction and Development (IBRD) (World Bank)

Established: December 27, 1945, when Articles of Agreement drawn up at Bretton Woods Conference in July 1944 came into force. Began operations on June 25, 1946.

Purpose: To assist in reconstruction and development of economies of members by facilitating capital investment and by making loans to governments and furnishing technical advice.

Headquarters: 1818 H St., N.W., Washington, D.C. 20433.

Intl. Civil Aviation Organization (ICAO)

Established: April 4, 1947, after working as a provisional organization since June 1945.

Purpose: To study problems of international civil aviation; to establish international standards and regulations; to promote safety measures, uniform regulations for operation, simpler procedures at international borders, and the use of new technical methods and equipment. It has evolved standards for meteorological services, traffic control, communications, radio beacons and ranges, search and rescue organization, and other facilities. It has brought about much simplification of customs, immigration, and public health regulations as they apply to international air transport. It drafts international air law conventions, and is concerned with economic aspects of air travel.

Headquarters: 1000 Sherbrooke St. West, Montreal, Quebec, H3A 2R2, Canada.

Intl. Development Association (IDA)

Established: Sept. 24, 1960. An affiliate of the World Bank, IDA has the same officers and staff as the Bank.

Purpose: To further economic development of its members by providing finance on terms which bear less heavily on balance of payments of members than those of conventional loans.

Headquarters: 1818 H St., N.W., Washington, D.C. 20433.

International Finance Corporation (IFC)

Established: Charter of IFC came into force on July 20, 1956. Although IFC is affiliated with the World Bank, it is a separate legal entity, and its funds are entirely separate from those of the Bank. However, membership in the Corporation is open only to Bank members.

Purpose: To further economic development by encouraging the growth of productive private enterprise in its member countries, particularly in the less developed areas; to invest in productive private enterprises in association with private investors, without government guarantee of repayment where sufficient private capital is not available on reasonable terms; to serve as a clearing house to bring together investment opportunities, private capital (both foreign and domestic), and experienced management.

Headquarters: 1818 H St., N.W., Washington, D.C. 20433.

International Fund for Agricultural Development (IFAD)

Established: June 18, 1976. Began operations in December 1977.

Purpose: To mobilize additional funds for agricultural and rural development in developing countries through projects and programs directly benefiting the poorest rural populations.

Headquarters: 107 Via del Serafico, 00142, Rome, Italy.

International Labor Organization (ILO)

Established: April 11, 1919, when constitution was adopted as Part XIII of Treaty of Versailles. Became specialized agency of U.N. in 1946.

Purpose: To contribute to establishment of lasting peace by promoting social justice; to improve labor conditions and living standards through international action; to promote economic and social stability. The U.S. withdrew from the ILO in 1977 and resumed membership in 1980.

Headquarters: 4, Route des Morillons, CH-1211 Geneva 22, Switzerland.

International Maritime Organization (IMO)

Established: March 17, 1958.

Purpose: To give advisory and consultative help to promote international cooperation in maritime navigation and to encourage the highest standards of safety and navigation. Its aim is to bring about a uniform system of measuring ship tonnage; systems now vary widely in different parts of the world. Other activities include cooperation with other U.N. agencies on matters affecting the maritime field.

Headquarters: 4 Albert Embankment, London SE 1 7SR England.

International Monetary Fund (IMF)

Established: Dec. 27, 1945, when Articles of Agreement drawn up at Bretton Woods Conference in July 1944 came into force. Fund began operations on March 1, 1947.

Purpose: To promote international monetary cooperation and expansion of international trade; to promote exchange stability; to assist in establishment of multilateral system of payments in respect of currency transactions between members.

Headquarters: 700 19th St., N.W., Washington, D.C. 20431.

International Telecommunication Union (ITU)

Established: 1865. Became specialized agency of U.N. in 1947.

Purpose: To extend technical assistance to help members keep up with present day telecommunication needs; to standardize communications equipment and procedures; to lower costs. It also works for orderly sharing of radio frequencies and makes studies and recommendations to benefit its members.

Headquarters: Place des Nations, 1211 Geneva 20, Switzerland.

United Nations Educational, Scientific, and Cultural Organization (UNESCO)

Established: Nov. 4, 1946, when twentieth signatory to constitution deposited instrument of acceptance with government of U.K.

Purpose: To promote collaboration among nations through education, science, and culture in order to further justice, rule of law, and human rights and freedoms without distinction of race, sex, language, or religion.

Headquarters: UNESCO House. 7, Place de Fontenoy, 75007 Paris, France.

United Nations Industrial Development Organization (UNIDO)

Established: Nov. 17, 1966. Became specialized agency of the U.N. in 1986.

Purpose: To promote and accelerate the industrialization of the developing countries.

Headquarters: UNIDO, Vienna International Centre, P.O. Box 300, A-1400 Vienna, Austria.

Universal Postal Union (UPU)

Established: Oct. 9, 1874. Became specialized agency of U.N. in 1947.

Purpose: To facilitate reciprocal exchange of correspondence by uniform procedures by all UPU members; to help governments modernize and speed up mailing procedures.

Headquarters: Weltpoststrasse 4, Berne, Switzerland.

World Health Organization (WHO)

Established: April 7, 1948, when 26 members of the U.N. had accepted its constitution, adopted July 22, 1946, by the International Health Conference in New York City.

Purpose: To aid attainment by all people of highest possible level of health.

Headquarters: 20 Avenue Appia, 1211 Geneva 27, Switzerland.

World Intellectual Property Organization (WIPO)

Established: April 26, 1970, when its Convention came into force. Originated as International Bureau of Paris Union (1883) and Berne Union (1886), later succeeded by United International Bureau for the Protection of Intellectual Property (BIRPI). Became a specialized agency of the U.N. in December 1974.

Purpose: To promote legal protection of intellectual property, including artistic and scientific works, artistic performances, sound recordings, broadcasts, inventions, trademarks, industrial designs, and commercial names.

Headquarters: 34 Chemin des Colombettes, CH-1211 Geneva 20, Switzerland.

World Meteorological Organization (WMO)

Established: March 23, 1950, succeeding the International Meteorological Organization, a nongovernmental organization founded in 1873.

Purpose: To promote international exchange of weather reports and maximum standardization of observations; to help developing countries establish weather services for their own economic needs; to fill gaps in observation stations; to promote meteorological investigations affecting jet aircraft, satellites, energy resources, etc.

Headquarters: 41, Avenue Giuseppe-Motta, CH-1211 Geneva 2, Switzerland.

The 185 Members of the United Nations and Their Gross Contributions to the 1997 Budget

Country	Joined U.N.[1]	1997 Budget Assessment	Country	Joined U.N.[1]	1997 Budget Assessment
Afghanistan	1946	124,820	Germany	1973	113,087,023
Albania	1955	124,820	Ghana	1957	124,820
Algeria	1962	1,997,122	Greece	1945	4,743,164
Andorra	1993	124,820	Grenada	1974	124,820
Angola	1976	124,820	Guatemala	1945	249,640
Antigua and Barbuda	1981	124,820	Guinea	1958	124,820
Argentina	1945	5,991,366	Guinea-Bissau	1974	124,820
Armenia	1992	624,101	Guyana	1966	124,820
Australia	1945	18,473,377	Haiti	1945	124,820
Austria	1955	10,859,350	Honduras	1945	124,820
Azerbaijan	1992	1,373,021	Hungary	1955	1,747,482
Bahamas	1973	249,640	Iceland	1946	374,460
Bahrain	1971	249,640	India	1945	3,869,424
Bangladesh	1974	124,820	Indonesia	1950	1,747,482
Barbados	1966	124,820	Iran	1945	5,616,905
Belarus	1945	3,494,963	Iraq	1945	1,747,482
Belgium	1945	12,606,832	Ireland	1955	2,621,223
Belize	1981	124,820	Israel	1949	3,370,143
Benin	1960	124,820	Italy	1955	65,530,560
Bhutan	1971	124,820	Jamaica	1962	124,820
Bolivia	1945	124,820	Japan	1956	195,343,478
Bosnia and Herzegovina	1992	124,820	Jordan	1955	124,820
Botswana	1966	124,820	Kazakhstan	1992	2,371,582
Brazil	1945	20,220,859	Kenya	1963	124,820
Brunei Darussalam	1984	249,640	North Korea		
Bulgaria	1955	998,561	(Democratic People's		
Burkina Faso	1960	124,820	Republic of Korea)	1991	624,101
Burma (Myanmar)	1948	124,820	South Korea (Republic of		
Burundi	1962	124,820	Korea)	1991	10,235,250
Cambodia	1955	124,820	Kuwait	1963	2,371,582
Cameroon	1960	124,820	Kyrgyzstan	1992	374,460
Canada	1945	38,819,056	Laos	1955	124,820
Cape Verde	1975	124,820	Latvia	1991	998,561
Central African Republic	1960	124,820	Lebanon	1945	124,820
Chad	1960	124,820	Lesotho	1966	124,820
Chile	1945	998,561	Liberia	1945	124,820
China[2]	1945	9,236,689	Libya	1955	2,496,402
Colombia	1945	1,248,201	Liechtenstein	1990	124,820
Comoros	1975	124,820	Lithuania	1991	998,561
Congo	1960	124,820	Luxembourg	1945	873,741
Congo, Democratic Republic of			Macedonia[4]	1993	124,820
the (formerly Zaire)	1960	124,820	Madagascar	1960	124,820
Costa Rica	1945	124,820	Malawi	1964	124,820
Côte d'Ivoire	1960	124,820	Malaysia	1957	1,747,482
Croatia	1992	1,123,381	Maldives	1965	124,820
Cuba	1945	624,101	Mali	1960	124,820
Cyprus	1960	374,460	Malta	1964	124,820
Czech Republic[3]	1993	3,120,503	Marshall Islands	1991	124,820
Denmark	1945	8,987,048	Mauritania	1961	124,820
Djibouti	1977	124,820	Mauritius	1968	124,820
Dominica	1978	124,820	Mexico	1945	9,860,789
Dominican Republic	1945	124,820	Micronesia	1991	124,820
Ecuador	1945	249,640	Moldova	1992	998,561
Egypt	1945	998,561	Monaco	1993	124,820
El Salvador	1945	124,820	Mongolia	1961	124,820
Equatorial Guinea	1968	124,820	Morocco	1956	374,460
Eritrea	1993	124,820	Mozambique	1975	124,820
Estonia	1991	499,281	Namibia	1990	124,820
Ethiopia	1945	124,820	Nepal	1955	124,820
Fiji	1970	124,820	Netherlands	1945	19,846,398
Finland	1955	7,738,847	New Zealand	1945	2,995,683
France	1945	80,134,513	Nicaragua	1945	124,820
Gabon	1960	124,820	Niger	1960	124,820
Gambia	1965	124,820	Nigeria	1960	1,373,021
Georgia	1992	1,373,021	Norway	1945	6,989,927

Country	Joined U.N.[1]	1997 Budget Assessment	Country	Joined U.N.[1]	1997 Budget Assessment
Oman	1971	499,281	South Africa	1945	3,994,244
Pakistan	1947	748,921	Spain	1955	29,707,187
Palau	1994	124,820	Sri Lanka	1955	124,820
Panama	1945	124,820	Sudan	1956	124,820
Papua New Guinea	1975	124,820	Suriname	1975	124,820
Paraguay	1945	124,820	Swaziland	1968	124,820
Peru	1945	748,921	Sweden	1946	15,352,874
Philippines	1945	748,921	Syria	1945	624,101
Poland	1945	4,119,064	Tajikistan	1992	249,640
Portugal	1955	3,494,963	Tanzania	1961	124,820
Qatar	1971	499,281	Thailand	1946	1,622,662
Romania	1955	1,872,302	Togo	1960	124,820
Russian Federation	1945	53,298,189	Trinidad and Tobago	1962	374,460
Rwanda	1962	124,820	Tunisia	1956	374,460
St. Kitts and Nevis	1983	124,820	Turkey	1945	4,743,164
St. Lucia	1979	124,820	Turkmenistan	1992	374,460
St. Vincent and the Grena-			Uganda	1962	124,820
dines	1980	124,820	Ukraine	1945	13,605,393
Samoa, Western	1976	124,820	United Arab Emirates	1971	2,371,582
San Marino	1992	124,820	United Kingdom	1945	66,404,301
São Tomé and Príncipe	1975	124,820	United States	1945	312,050,284
Saudi Arabia	1945	8,862,228	Uruguay	1945	499,281
Senegal	1960	124,820	Uzbekistan	1992	1,622,662
Seychelles	1976	124,820	Vanuatu	1981	124,820
Sierra Leone	1961	124,820	Venezuela	1945	4,119,064
Singapore	1965	1,747,482	Viet Nam	1977	124,820
Slovakia[3]	1993	998,561	Yemen, Republic of	1947	124,820
Slovenia	1992	873,741	Yugoslavia	1945	1,248,201
Solomon Islands	1978	124,820	Zambia	1964	124,820
Somalia	1960	124,820	Zimbabwe	1980	124,820

1. The U.N. officially came into existence on Oct. 24, 1945. 2. On Oct. 25, 1971, the U.N. voted membership to the People's Republic of China, which replaced the Republic of China (Taiwan) in the world body. 3. Czechoslovakia was an original member of the United Nations from Oct. 24, 1945. As of December 31, 1992 it ceased to exist and the Czech Republic and Slovakia as successor states were admitted January 19, 1993. 4. The General Assembly on April 8, 1993 decided to admit the state provisionally being referred to as "The Former Yugoslav Republic of Macedonia" pending settlement of the difference that has arisen over its name.

Foreign Embassies in the United States

Source: U.S. Department of State.

Embassy of the Republic of Afghanistan, 2341 Wyoming Ave., N.W., Washington, D.C. 20008. Phone: 202-234-3770, 3771. Fax: 202-328-3516.

Embassy of the Republic of Albania, 1511 K St., N.W., Suite 1000, Washington, D.C. 20005. Phone: 202-223-4942, 8187. Fax: 202-628-7342.

Embassy of the Democratic & Popular Republic of Algeria, 2118 Kalorama Rd., N.W., Washington, D.C. 20008. Phone: 202-265-2800. Fax: 202-667-2174.

Embassy of the Republic of Angola, 1050 Connecticut Ave., N.W., Suite 760, Washington, D.C. 20036. Phone: 202-785-1156. Fax: 202-785-1258.

Embassy of Antigua & Barbuda, 3216 New Mexico Ave., N.W., Washington, D.C. 20016. Phone: 202-362-5211, 5166, 5122. Fax: 202-362-5225.

Embassy of the Argentine Republic, 1600 New Hampshire Ave., N.W., Washington, D.C. 20009. Phone: 202-939-6400 to 6403, inclusive. Fax: 202-332-3171.

Embassy of the Republic of Armenia, 2225 R Street, N.W., Washington, D.C. 20008. Phone: 202-319-1976. Fax: 202-319-2982.

Embassy of Australia, 1601 Massachusetts Ave., N.W., Washington, D.C. 20036. Phone: 202-797-3000. Fax: 202-797-3168.

Embassy of Austria, 3524 International Court, N.W., Washington, D.C. 20008. Phone: 202-895-6700. Fax: 202-895-6750.

Embassy of the Republic of Azerbaijan, 927-15th St., N.W., Suite 700, P.O. Box 27839, Washington, D.C. 20038–7839. Phone: 202-842-0001. Fax: 202-842-0004.

Embassy of The Commonwealth of The Bahamas, 2220 Massachusetts Ave., N.W., Washington, D.C. 20008. Phone: 202-319-2660. Fax: 202-319-2668.

Embassy of the State of Bahrain, 3502 International Dr., N.W., Washington, D.C. 20008. Phone: 202-342-0741, 0742. Fax: 202-362-2192.

Embassy of the People's Republic of Bangladesh, 2201 Wisconsin Ave., N.W., Washington, D.C. 20007. Phone: 202-342-8372 to 8376.

Embassy of Barbados, 2144 Wyoming Ave., N.W., Washington, D.C. 20008. Phone: 202-939-9200 to 9202.

Embassy of the Republic of Belarus, 1619 New Hampshire Ave., N.W., Washington, D.C. 20009. Phone: 202-986-1640. Fax: 202-986-1805.

Embassy of Belgium, 3330 Garfield St., N.W., Washington, D.C. 20008. Phone: 202-333-6900. Fax: 202-333-3079.

Embassy of Belize, 2535 Massachusetts Ave., N.W., Washington, D.C. 20008. Phone: 202-332-9636. Fax: 202-332-6888.

Embassy of the Republic of Benin, 2737 Cathedral Ave., N.W., Washington, D.C. 20008. Phone: 202-232-6656 to 6658. Fax: 202-265-1996.

Embassy of the Republic of Bolivia, 3014 Massachusetts Ave., N.W., Washington, D.C. 20008. Phone: 202-483-4410 to 4412. Fax: 202-328-3712.

Embassy of the Republic of Bosnia and Herzegovina, 1707 L St., N.W., Suite 760, Washington, D.C. 20036. Phone: 202-833-3612, 3613, and 3615. Fax: 202-833-2061.

Embassy of the Republic of Botswana, 3400 International Dr., N.W., Suite 7M, Washington, D.C. 20008. Phone: 202-244-4990, 4991. Fax: 202-244-4164.

Brazilian Embassy, 3006 Massachusetts Ave., N.W., Washington, D.C. 20008. Phone: 202-745-2700. Fax: 202-745-2827.

Embassy of the State of Brunei Darussalam, Watergate, 2600 Virginia Ave., N.W., Suite 300, 3rd floor, Washington, D.C. 20037. Phone: 202-342-0159. Fax: 202-342-0158.

Embassy of the Republic of Bulgaria, 1621-22nd St., N.W., Washington, D.C. 20008. Phone: 202-387-7969. Fax: 202-234-7973.

Embassy of Burkina Faso, 2340 Massachusetts Ave., N.W., Washington, D.C. 20008. Phone: 202-332-5577, 6895.

Embassy of the Union of Burma, 2300 5th St., N.W., Washington, D.C. 20008. Phone: 202-332-9044, 9045. Fax: 202-332-9046.

Embassy of the Republic of Burundi, 2233 Wisconsin Ave., N.W., Suite 212, Washington, D.C. 20007. Phone: 202-342-2574.

Embassy of the Republic of Cambodia, 4500 16th St., N.W., Washington, D.C. 20011. Phone: 202-726-7742. Fax: 202-726-8381.

Embassy of the Republic of Cameroon, 2349 Massachusetts Ave., N.W., Washington, D.C. 20008. Phone: 202-265-8790 to 8794.

Embassy of Canada, 501 Pennsylvania Ave., N.W., Washington, D.C. 20001. Phone: 202-682-1740. Fax: 202-682-7726.

Embassy of the Republic of Cape Verde, 3415 Massachusetts Ave., N.W., Washington, D.C. 20007. Phone: 202-965-6820. Fax: 202-965-1207.

Embassy of Central African Republic, 1618-22nd St. N.W., Washington, D.C. 20008. Phone: 202-483-7800, 7801. Fax: 202-332-9893.

Embassy of the Republic of Chad, 2002 R St., N.W., Washington, D.C. 20009. Phone: 202-462-4009. Fax: 202-265-1937.

Embassy of Chile, 1732 Massachusetts Ave., N.W., Washington, D.C. 20036. Phone: 202-785-1746. Fax: 202-887-5579.

Embassy of the People's Republic of China, 2300 Connecticut Ave., N.W., Washington, D.C. 20008. Phone: 202-328-2500 to 2502.

Embassy of Colombia, 2118 Leroy Pl., N.W., Washington, D.C. 20008. Phone: 202-387-8338. Fax: 202-232-8643.

Embassy of the Federal and Islamic Republic of Comoros, c/o Permanent Mission of the Federal and Islamic Republic of Comoros to the United Nations, 336 E. 45th St., 2nd floor, New York, N.Y. 10017. Phone: 212-972-8010.

Embassy of the Democratic Republic of Congo, 1800 New Hampshire Ave., N.W., Washington, D.C. 20009. Phone: 202-234-7690, 7691. Fax: 202-6863631.

Embassy of the Republic of Congo, 4891 Colorado Ave., N.W., Washington, D.C. 20011. Phone: 202-726-5500. Fax: 202-726-1860.

Embassy of Costa Rica, 2114 S St., N.W., Washington, D.C. 20008. Phone: 202-234-2945. Fax: 202-265-4795.

Embassy of the Republic of Cote d'Ivoire, 2424 Massachusetts Ave., N.W., Washington, D.C. 20008. Phone: 202-797-0300.

Embassy of the Republic of Croatia, 2343 Massachusetts Ave., N.W., Washington, D.C. 20008.

Phone: 202-588-5899. Fax: 202-588-8936.

Cuban Interests Section, 2630 16th St., N.W., Washington, D.C. 20009. Phone: 202-797-8518 to 8520.

Embassy of the Republic of Cyprus, 2211 R St. N.W., Washington, D.C. 20008. Phone: 202-462-5772. Fax: 202-483-6710.

Embassy of the Czech Republic, 3900 Spring of Freedom St., N.W., Washington, D.C. 20008. Phone: 202-274-9101, 9102. Fax: 202-966-8540.

Royal Danish Embassy, 3200 Whitehaven St., N.W., Washington, D.C. 20008. Phone: 202-234-4300. Fax: 202-328-1470.

Embassy of the Republic of Djibouti, 1156-15th St., N.W., Suite 515, Washington, D.C. 20005. Phone: 202-331-0270. Fax: 202-331-0302.

Embassy of the Commonwealth of Dominica, 3216 New Mexico Ave., N.W., Washington, D.C. 20016. Phone: 202-364-6781. Fax: 202-364-6791.

Embassy of the Dominican Republic, 1715-22nd St., N.W., Washington, D.C. 20008. Phone: 202-332-6280, 6281. Fax: 202-265-8057.

Embassy of Ecuador, 2535-15th St., N.W., Washington, D.C. 20009. Phone: 202-234-7200.

Embassy of the Arab Republic of Egypt, 3521 International Court, N.W., Washington, D.C. 20008. Phone: 202-895-5400. Fax: 202-244-4319/5131.

Embassy of El Salvador, 2308 California St., N.W., Washington, D.C. 20008. Phone: 202-265-9671, 9672.

Embassy of Equatorial Guinea, 1511 K St., N.W., Suite 405, Washington, D.C. 20005. Phone: 202-393-0525. Fax: 202-393-0348.

Embassy of the State of Eritrea, 1708 New Hampshire Ave., N.W., Washington, D.C., 20009. Phone: 202-319-1991. Fax: 202-319-1304.

Embassy of Estonia, 2131 Massachusetts Ave., Washington, D.C. 20008. Phone: 202-588-0101. Fax: 202-588-0108.

Embassy of Ethiopia, 2134 Kalorama Rd., N.W., Washington, D.C. 20008. Phone: 202-234-2281, 2282. Fax: 202-328-7950.

Embassy of The Republic of Fiji, 2233 Wisconsin Ave., N.W., Suite 240, Washington, D.C. 20007. Phone: 202-337-8320. Fax: 202-337-1996.

Embassy of Finland, 3301 Massachusetts Ave., N.W., Washington, D.C. 20008. Phone: 202-298-5800. Fax: 202-298-6030.

Embassy of France, 4101 Reservoir Rd., N.W., Washington, D.C. 20007. Phone: 202-944-6000. Fax: 202-944-6166.

Embassy of the Gabonese Republic, 2034-20th St., N.W., Washington, D.C. 20009. Phone: 202-797-1000. Fax: 202-332-0668.

Embassy of The Gambia, 1155-15th St., N.W., Suite 1000, Washington, D.C. 20005. Phone: 202-785-1399, 1379, 1425. Fax: 202-785-1430.

Embassy of the Republic of Georgia, 1511 K St., N.W., Suite 424, Washington, D.C. 20005. Phone: 202-393-5959. Fax: 202-393-4537.

Embassy of the Federal Republic of Germany, 4645 Reservoir Rd., N.W., Washington, D.C. 20007. Phone: 202-298-4000. Fax: 202-298-4249.

Embassy of Ghana, 3512 International Dr., N.W., Washington, D.C. 20008. Phone: 202-686-4520. Fax: 202-686-4527.

Embassy of Greece, 2221 Massachusetts Ave., N.W., Washington, D.C. 20008. Phone: 202-939-5800. Fax: 202-939-5824.

Embassy of Grenada, 1701 New Hampshire Ave., N.W., Washington, D.C. 20009. Phone: 202-265-2561.

Embassy of Guatemala, 2220 R St., N.W., Washington, D.C. 20008. Phone: 202-745-4952 to 4954. Fax: 202-745-1908.

Embassy of the Republic of Guinea, 2112 Leroy Pl., N.W., Washington, D.C. 20008. Phone: 202-483-9420. Fax: 202-483-8688.

Embassy of the Republic of Guinea-Bissau, 918 16th St., N.W., Mezzanine Suite, Washington, D.C. 20006. Phone: 202-872-4222. Fax: 202-872-4226.

Embassy of Guyana, 2490 Tracy Pl., N.W., Washington, D.C. 20008. Phone: 202-265-6900, 6901.

Embassy of the Republic of Haiti, 2311 Massachusetts Ave., N.W., Washington, D.C. 20008. Phone: 202-332-4090 to 4092. Fax: 202-745-7215.

Apostolic Nunciature of the Holy See, 3339 Massachusetts Ave., N.W., Washington, D.C. 20008. Phone: 202-333-7121.

Embassy of Honduras, 3007 Tilden St., N.W., Washington, D.C. 20008. Phone: 202-966-7702, 2604, 5008, 4596. Fax: 202-966-9751.

Embassy of the Republic of Hungary, 3910 Shoemaker St., N.W., Washington, D.C. 20008. Phone: 202-362-6730. Fax: 202-966-8135.

Embassy of Iceland, 1156-15th St., N.W., Suite 1200, Washington, D.C. 20005. Phone: 202-265-6653 to 6655. Fax: 202-265-6656.

Embassy of India, 2107 Massachusetts Ave., N.W., Washington, D.C. 20008. Phone: 202-939-7000. Fax: 202-483-3972.

Embassy of the Republic of Indonesia, 2020 Massachusetts Ave., N.W., Washington, D.C. 20036. Phone: 202-775-5200. Fax: 202-775-5365.

Iranian Interests Section, 2209 Wisconsin Ave., N.W., Washington, D.C. 20007. Phone: 202-965-4990.

Iraqi Interests Section, 1801 P St., N.W., Washington, D.C. 20036. Phone: 202-483-7500.

Embassy of Ireland, 2234 Massachusetts Ave., N.W., Washington, D.C. 20008. Phone: 202-462-3939. Fax: 202-232-5993.

Embassy of Israel, 3514 International Dr., N.W., Washington, D.C. 20008. Phone: 202-364-5500. Fax: 202-364-5610.

Embassy of Italy, 1601 Fuller St., N.W., Washington, D.C. 20009. Phone: 202-328-5500. Fax: 202-483-2187.

Embassy of Jamaica, 1520 New Hampshire Ave., N.W., Washington, D.C. 20036. Phone: 202-452-0660. Fax: 202-452-0081.

Embassy of Japan, 2520 Massachusetts Ave., N.W., Washington, D.C. 20008. Phone: 202-939-6700. Fax: 202-328-2187.

Embassy of the Hashemite Kingdom of Jordan, 3504 International Dr., N.W., Washington, D.C. 20008. Phone: 202-966-2664. Fax: 202-966-3110.

Embassy of the Republic of Kazakhstan, (temporary) 3421 Massachusetts Ave., N.W., Washington, D.C. 20008. Phone: 202-333-4504. Fax: 202-333-4509.

Embassy of the Republic of Kenya, 2249 R St., N.W., Washington, D.C. 20008. Phone: 202-387-6101. Fax: 202-462-3829.

Embassy of the Republic of Korea, 2450 Massachusetts Ave., N.W., Washington, D.C. 20008. Phone: 202-939-5600.

Embassy of the State of Kuwait, 2940 Tilden St., N.W., Washington, D.C. 20008. Phone: 202-966-0702. Fax: 202-966-0517.

Embassy of the Kyrgyz Republic, 1732 Wisconsin Ave., Washington, D.C. 20007. Phone: 202-338-5141. Fax: 202-338-5139.

Embassy of the Lao People's Democratic Republic, 2222 S St., N.W., Washington, D.C. 20008. Phone: 202-332-6416. Fax: 202-332-4923.

Embassy of Latvia, 4325-17th St., N.W., Washington, D.C. 20011. Phone: 202-726-8213, 8214. Fax: 202-726-6785.

Embassy of Lebanon, 2560-28th St., N.W., Washington, D.C. 20008. Phone: 202-939-6300. Fax: 202-939-6324.

Embassy of the Kingdom of Lesotho, 2511 Massachusetts Ave., N.W., Washington, D.C. 20008. Phone: 202-797-5533 to 5536. Fax: 202-234-6815.

Embassy of the Republic of Liberia, 5201 16th St., N.W., Washington, D.C. 20011. Phone: 202-291-0761. Fax: 202-723-0437.

Embassy of the Republic of Lithuania, 2622 16th St., N.W., Washington, D.C. 20009. Phone: 202-234-5860. Fax: 202-328-0466.

Embassy of the Grand Duchy of Luxembourg, 2200 Massachusetts Ave., N.W., Washington, D.C. 20008. Phone: 202-265-4171. Fax: 202-328-8270.

Embassy of the Former Yugoslav Republic of Macedonia, 3050 K St., N.W., Suite 210, Washington, D.C. 20007. Phone: 202-337-3063.

Embassy of the Republic of Madagascar, 2374 Massachusetts Ave., N.W., Washington, D.C. 20008. Phone: 202-265-5525, 5526.

Embassy of Malawi , 2408 Massachusetts Ave., N.W., Washington, D.C. 20008. Phone: 202-797-1007.

Embassy of Malaysia, 2401 Massachusetts Ave., N.W., Washington, D.C. 20008. Phone: 202-328-2700. Fax: 202-483-7661.

Embassy of the Republic of Mali, 2130 R St., N.W., Washington, D.C. 20008. Phone: 202-332-2249; 202-939-8950. Fax: 202-332-6603.

Embassy of Malta, 2017 Connecticut Ave., N.W., Washington, D.C. 20008. Phone: 202-462-3611, 3612. Fax: 202-387-5470.

Embassy of the Republic of the Marshall Islands, 2433 Massachusetts Ave., N.W., Washington, D.C. 20008. Phone: 202-234-5414. Fax: 202-232-3236.

Embassy of the Islamic Republic of Mauritania, 2129 Leroy Pl., N.W., Washington, D.C. 20008. Phone: 202-232-5700.

Embassy of the Republic of Mauritius, 4301 Connecticut Ave., N.W., Suite 441, Washington, D.C. 20008. Phone: 202-244-1491, 1492. Fax: 202-966-0983.

Embassy of Mexico, 1911 Pennsylvania Ave., N.W.,, Washington, D.C. 20006. Phone: 202-728-1600.

Embassy of the Federated States of Micronesia, 1725 N St., N.W., Washington, D.C. 20036. Phone: 202-223-4383. Fax: 202-223-4391.

Embassy of the Republic of Moldova, 2101 S St., N.W., Washington, D.C. 20008. Phone: 202-667-1130. Fax: 202-667-1204.

Embassy of Mongolia, 2833 M St., N.W., Washington, D.C. 20007. Phone: 202-333-7117. Fax: 202-298-9227.

Embassy of the Kingdom of Morocco, 1601 21st St., N.W., Washington, D.C. 20009. Phone: 202-462-7979 to 7982, inclusive. Fax: 202-265-0161.

Embassy of the Republic of Mozambique, 1990 M St., N.W., Suite 570, Washington, D.C. 20036. Phone: 202-293-7146. Fax: 202-835-0245.

Embassy of the Union of Myanmar, 2300 S St., N.W., Washington, D.C. 20008. Phone: 202-332-9044, 9045.

Embassy of the Republic of Namibia, 1605 New Hampshire Ave., N.W., Washington, D.C. 20009. Phone: 202-986-0540. Fax: 202-986-0443.

Royal Nepalese Embassy, 2131 Leroy Pl., N.W., Washington, D.C. 20008. Phone: 202-667-4550. Fax: 202-667-5534.

Royal Netherlands Embassy, 4200 Linnean Ave., N.W., Washington, D.C. 20008. Phone: 202-244-5300; after 6 p.m. 202-494-8594. Fax: 202-362-3430.

Embassy of New Zealand, 37 Observatory Circle, N.W., Washington, D.C. 20008. Phone: 202-328-4800.

Embassy of Nicaragua, 1627 New Hampshire Ave., N.W., Washington, D.C. 20009. Phone: 202-939-6570.

Embassy of the Republic of Niger, 2204 R St., N.W., Washington, D.C. 20008. Phone: 202-483-4224 to 4227, inclusive.

Embassy of the Federal Republic of Nigeria, 1333 16th St., N.W., Washington, D.C. 20036. Phone: 202-986-8400.

Royal Norwegian Embassy, 2720 34th St., N.W., Washington, D.C. 20008. Phone: 202-333-6000. Fax: 202-337-0870.

Embassy of the Sultanate of Oman, 2535 Belmont Rd., N.W., Washington, D.C. 20008. Phone: 202-387-1980 to 1982. Fax: 202-745-4933.

Embassy of Pakistan, 2315 Massachusetts Ave., N.W., Washington, D.C. 20008. Phone: 202-939-6200. Fax: 202-387-0484.

Embassy of the Republic of Palau, 2000 L St., N.W., Suite 407, Washington, D.C. 20036. Phone: 202-452-6814. Fax: 202-452-6281.

Embassy of the Republic of Panama, 2862 McGill Terrace, N.W., Washington, D.C. 20008. Phone: 202-483-1407.

Embassy of Papua New Guinea, 1615 New Hampshire Ave., N.W., 3rd floor, Washington, D.C. 20009. Phone: 202-745-3680. Fax: 202-745-3679.

Embassy of Paraguay, 2400 Massachusetts Ave., N.W., Washington, D.C. 20008. Phone: 202-483-6960 to 6962. Fax: 202-234-4508.

Embassy of Peru, 1700 Massachusetts Ave., N.W., Washington, D.C. 20036. Phone: 202-833-9860 to 9869. Fax: 202-659-8124.

Embassy of the Philippines, 1600 Massachusetts Ave., N.W., Washington, D.C. 20036. Phone: 202-467-9300. Fax: 202-328-7614.

Embassy of the Republic of Poland, 2640 16th St., N.W., Washington, D.C. 20009. Phone: 202-234-3800 to 3802. Fax: 202-328-6271.

Embassy of Portugal, 2125 Kalorama Rd., N.W., Washington, D.C. 20008. Phone: 202-328-8610. Fax: 202-462-3726.

Embassy of the State of Qatar, 4200 Wisconsin Ave., N.W., Washington, D.C. 20016. Phone: 202-274-1600.

Embassy of Romania, 1607 23rd St., N.W., Washington, D.C. 20008. Phone: 202-332-4846, 4848, 4851; after hours 332-4846. Fax: 202-232-4748.

Embassy of the Russian Federation, 2650 Wisconsin Ave., N.W., Washington, D.C. 20007. Phone: 202-298-5700 to 5704 inclusive. Fax: 202-298-5735.

Embassy of the Republic of Rwanda, (temporary) 2141 Wisconsin Ave., Suites C1, C2, N.W., Washington, D.C. 20007. Phone: 202-232-2882. Fax: 202-232-4544.

Embassy of Saint Kitts and Nevis, 3216 New Mexico Ave., N.W., Washington, D.C. 20016. Phone: 202-686-2636. Fax: 202-686-5740.

Embassy of Saint Lucia, 3216 New Mexico Ave., N.W., Washington, D.C. 20016. Phone: 202-364-6792 to 6795. Fax: 202-364-6728.

Embassy of Saint Vincent and the Grenadines, 3216 New Mexico Ave., N.W., Washington, D.C. 20016. Phone: 202-364-6730. Fax: 202-364-6736.

Embassy of Saudi Arabia, 601 New Hampshire Ave., N.W., Washington, D.C. 20037. Phone: 202-342-3800.

Embassy of the Republic of Senegal, 2112 Wyoming Ave., N.W., Washington, D.C. 20008. Phone: 202-234-0540, 0541.

Embassy of the Republic of Seychelles, c/o Permanent Mission of Seychelles to the United Nations, 820 Second Ave., Suite 900F, New York, N.Y. 10017. Phone: 212-972-1785. Fax: 202-972-1786.

Embassy of Sierra Leone, 1701 19th St., N.W., Washington, D.C. 20009. Phone: 202-939-9261–63. Fax: 202-483-1793.

Embassy of the Republic of Singapore, 3501 International Pl., N.W., Washington, D.C. 20008. Phone: 202-537-3100. Fax: 202-537-0876.

Embassy of the Slovak Republic, 2201 Wisconsin Ave., N.W., Suite 250, Washington, D.C. 20007. Phone: 202-965-5161. Fax: 202-965-5166.

Embassy of the Republic of Slovenia, 1525 New Hampshire Ave., N.W., Washington, D.C. 20036. Phone: 202-667-5363. Fax: 202-667-4563.

Embassy of the Republic of South Africa, 3051 Massachusetts Ave., N.W., Washington, D.C. 20008. Phone: 202-232-4400. Fax: 202-265-1607.

Embassy of Spain, 2375 Pennsylvania Ave., N.W., Washington, D.C. 20037. Phone: 202-452-0100 and 728-2340. Fax: 202-833-5670.

Embassy of the Democratic Socialist Republic of Sri Lanka, 2148 Wyoming Ave., N.W., Washington, D.C. 20008. Phone: 202-483-4025 to 4028. Fax: 202-232-7181.

Embassy of the Republic of the Sudan, 2210 Massachusetts Ave., N.W., Washington, D.C. 20008. Phone: 202-338-8565 to 8570. Fax: 202-667-2406.

Embassy of the Republic of Suriname, 4301 Connecticut Ave., N.W., Suite 108, Washington, D.C. 20008. Phone: 202-244-7488, 7590 to 7592. Fax: 202-244-5878.

Embassy of the Kingdom of Swaziland, 3400 International Drive, N.W., Washington, D.C. 20008. Phone: 202-362-6683, 6685. Fax: 202-244-8059.

Embassy of Sweden, 1501 M St., N.W., Washington, D.C. 20005. Phone: 202-467-2600. Fax: 202-467-2699.

Embassy of Switzerland, 2900 Cathedral Ave., N.W., Washington, D.C. 20008. Phone: 202-745-7900. Fax: 202-387-2564.

Embassy of the Syrian Arab Republic, 2215 Wyoming Ave., N.W., Washington, D.C. 20008. Phone: 202-232-6313. Fax: 202-234-9548.

Embassy of the United Republic of Tanzania, 2139 R St., N.W., Washington, D.C. 20008. Phone: 202-939-6125. Fax: 202-797-7408.

Royal Thai Embassy, 1024 Wisconsin Ave., N.W., Washington, D.C. 20007. Phone: 202-944-3600. Fax: 202-944-3611.

Embassy of the Republic of Togo, 2208 Massachusetts Ave., N.W., Washington, D.C. 20008. Phone: 202-234-4212, 4213. Fax: 202-232-3190.

Embassy of Trinidad and Tobago, 1708 Massachusetts Ave., N.W., Washington, D.C. 20036. Phone: 202-467-6490. Fax: 202-785-3130.

Embassy of Tunisia, 1515 Massachusetts Ave., N.W., Washington, D.C. 20005. Phone: 202-862-1850.

Embassy of the Republic of Turkey, 1714 Massachusetts Ave., N.W., Washington, D.C. 20036. Phone: 202-659-8200.

Embassy of Turkmenistan, 2207 Massachusetts Ave., N.W., Washington, D.C. 20008. Phone: 202-588-1500. Fax: 202-588-0697.

Embassy of the Republic of Uganda, 5911-16th St., N.W., Washington, D.C. 20011. Phone: 202-726-7100 to 7102, 0416. Fax: 202-726-1727.

Embassy of Ukraine, 3350 M St., N.W., Washington, D.C. 20007. Phone: 202-333-0606. Fax: 202-333-0817.

Embassy of the United Arab Emirates, 3000 K St., N.W., Suite 600, Washington, D.C. 20007. Phone: 202-338-6500. Fax: 202-338-6500.

United Kingdom of Great Britain & Northern Ireland— British Embassy, 3100 Massachusetts Ave., N.W., Washington, D.C. 20008. Phone: 202-588-6500. Fax: 202-588-7870.

Embassy of Uruguay, 2715 M St., N.W., Washington, D.C. 20007. Phone: 202-331-1313 to 1316. Fax: 202-331-8147.

Embassy of the Republic of Uzbekistan, 1746 Massachusetts Ave., N.W., Washington, D.C. 20036. Phone: 202-887-5300. Fax: 202-293-6804.

Embassy of the Republic of Venezuela, 1099 30th St., N.W., Washington D.C. 20007. Phone: 202-342-2214. Fax: 202-342-6820.

Embassy of Vietnam, 1233 20th St., N.W., Washington, D.C. 20036. Phone: 202-861-0737. Fax: 202-861-0917.

Embassy of the Independent State of Western Samoa, 820 Second Ave., Suite 800D, New York, N.Y. 10017. Phone: 212-599-6196, 6197. Fax: 212-599-0797.

Embassy of the Republic of Yemen, 2600 Virginia Ave., N.W., Suite 705, Washington, D.C. 20037. Phone: 202-965-4760, 4761.

Embassy of the former Socialist Federal Republic of Yugoslavia, 2410 California St., N.W., Washington, D.C. 20008. Phone: 202-462-6566.

Embassy of the Republic of Zambia, 2419 Massachusetts Ave., N.W., Washington, D.C. 20008. Phone: 202-265-9717 to 9719. Fax: 202-332-0826.

Embassy of the Republic of Zimbabwe, 1608 New Hampshire Ave., N.W., Washington, D.C. 20009. Phone: 202-332-7100. Fax: 202-483-9326.

Diplomatic Personnel To and From the U.S.

Country	U.S. Representative to[1]	Rank	Representative from[2]	Rank
Afghanistan	—	—	Yar Mohammad Mohabbat	Cd'A.
Albania	Joseph E. Lake	Amb.	Lublin Dilja	Amb.
Algeria	Ronald E. Neumann	Amb.	Ramtane Lamamra	Amb.
Angola	Edmund T. DeJarnette	Dir.	Antonio dos Santos Franca	Amb.
Antigua and Barbuda	(Post closed)	—	Lionel A. Hurst	Amb.
Argentina	James R. Cheek	Amb.	Raul Enrique Granillo Ocampo	Amb.
Armenia	Harry J. Gilmore	Amb.	Rouben Robert Shugarian	Amb.
Australia	Edward Perkins	Amb.	Andrew Sharp Peacock	Amb.
Austria	Swanee G. Hunt	Amb.	Helmut Tuerk	Amb.
Azerbaijan	Richard D. Kauzlarich	Cd'A.	Hafiz Mir Jalal Pashayev	Amb.
Bahamas	Sidney Williams	Amb.	Sir Arlington Griffith Butler	Amb.
Bahrain	David M. Ransom	Amb.	Muhammad Abdul Ghaffar	Amb.
Bangladesh	John C. Holzman	Amb.	K. M. Shehabuddin	Amb.
Barbados	Jeanette W. Hyde	Amb.	Dr. Courtney N. Blackman	Amb.
Belarus	Daniel V. Speckhard	Amb.	Valery V. Tsepkalo	Amb.
Belgium	Alan J. Blinken	Amb.	Andre Adam	Amb.
Belize	George Charles Bruno	Amb.	James S. Murphy	Amb.
Benin	Ruth A. Davis	Amb.	Lucien Edgar Tonoukouin	Amb.
Bermuda	Robert A. Farmer	Cons. Gen.	—	—
Bolivia	Curt Warren Kamman	Amb.	Fernando Cossio	Amb.
Bosnia-Herzegovina	Richard Dale Kauzlarich	Amb.	Sven Alkalaj	Amb.
Botswana	Howard F. Jeter	Amb.	Archibald Mooketsa Mogwe	Cd'A.
Brazil	Melvyn Levitsky	Amb.	Paulo-Tarso Flecha de Lima	Amb.
Brunei	Theresa A. Tull	Amb.	Pengiran Anak Dato Puteh	Amb.
Bulgaria	William D. Montgomery	Amb.	Dr. Snejana Damianova Botoucharova	Amb.
Burkina Faso	Donald J. McConnell	Amb.	Gaetan R. Ouedraogo	Amb.
Burma (Myanmar)	(Vacancy)	Amb.	Tin Winn	Amb.
Burundi	Robert C. Krueger	Amb.	Severin Ntahomvukiye	Amb.
Cambodia	Charles H. Twining	Dir.	Huoth Var	Amb.
Cameroon	Harriet W. Isom	Amb.	Jerome Mendouga	Amb.
Canada	Gordon D. Giffin	Amb.	Raymond A. J. Chretien	Amb.
Cape Verde	Joseph M. Segars	Amb.	Corentino Virgilio Santos	Amb.
Central African Republic	Robert E. Gribbin III	Amb.	Henry Koba	Amb.
Chad	Lawrence E. Pope II	Amb.	Ahmat Mahamat-Saleh	Amb.
Chile	Curtis W. Kamman	Amb.	John Biehl	Amb.
China	J. Stapleton Roy	Amb.	Li Daoyu	Amb.
Colombia	Myles R.R. Frechette	Amb.	Juan Carlos Esguerra	Amb.
Comoros	(Post closed)	—	—	—
Congo	William C. Ramsay	Amb.	Dieudonne Antoine Ganga	Amb.
Congo, Democratic Republic of	(Vacancy)	Amb.	Tambo A. Kabila	Min.-Consl.
Costa Rica	(Vacancy)	—	Sonia Picado	Amb.
Côte d'Ivoire	Hume A. Horan	Amb.	Koffi Moise Koumoue	Amb.
Croatia	Peter W. Galbraith	Amb.	Miomir Zuzul	Amb.
Cyprus	Richard A. Boucher	Amb.	Andros A. Nicolaides	Amb.
Czech Republic	Adrian A. Basora	Amb.	Alexandr Vondrova	Amb.
Denmark	Edward E. Elson	Amb.	K. Erik Tygesen	Amb.
Djibouti	Martin L. Cheshes	Amb.	Roble Olhaye	Amb.
Dominica	—	—	Edward I. Watty	Amb.

Country	U.S. Representative to[1]	Rank	Representative from[2]	Rank
Dominican Republic	Donna Jean Hrinak	Amb.	Bernardo Vega	Amb.
Ecuador	Peter F. Romero	Amb.	Fernando Flores	Min.
Egypt	Edward S. Walker, Jr.	Amb.	Ahmed Maher El Sayed	Amb.
El Salvador	Alan H. Flanigan	Amb.	Ana Cristina Sol	Amb.
Equatorial Guinea	John E. Bennett	Amb.	Pastor Micha Ondo Bile	Amb.
Eritrea	Robert G. Houdek	Amb.	Berhane Asresahei Kidane	Cd'A.
Estonia	(Vacancy)	Amb.	Grigore-Kalev Stoicescu	Amb.
Ethiopia	Irvin Hicks	Cd'A.	Berhane Gebre-Christos	Amb.
Fiji	(Vacancy)	Amb.	Napolioni Masirewa	Amb.
Finland	Derek N. Shearer	Amb.	Jaakko Tapani Laajava	Amb.
France	Felix Rohatyn	Amb.	François V. Bujon	Amb.
Gabon	Joseph C. Wilson IV	Amb.	Paul Boundoukou-Latha	Amb.
Gambia	Andrew J. Winter	Amb.	Malamin K. Juwara	Cd'A.
Georgia	Kent N. Brown	Cd'A.	Dr. Tedo Japaridze	Amb.
Germany	John Christian Kornblum	Amb.	Juergen Chrobog	Amb.
Ghana	Kenneth L. Brown	Amb.	Ekwow Spio-Garbrah	Amb.
Greece	Thomas M.T. Niles	Amb.	Loucas Tsilas	Amb.
Grenada	(Vacancy)	Amb.	Denis G. Antoine	Amb.
Guatemala	Marilyn McAfee	Amb.	Pedro Miguel Lamport	Amb.
Guinea	Joseph A. Saloom III	Amb.	Mohamed Aly Thiam	Amb.
Guinea-Bissau	Roger A. McGuire	Amb.	Rufino Jose Mendes	Amb.
Guyana	James F. Mack	Amb.	Dr. Mohammed Ali Odeen Ishmael	Amb.
Haiti	William Lacy Swing	Amb.	Jean Casimir	Amb.
Holy See	Raymond L. Flynn	Amb.	Most Rev. Agostino Cacciavillan	Pro-Nuncio
Honduras	William T. Pryce	Amb.	Roberto Flores Bermudez	Amb.
Hong Kong	Richard W. Mueller	Cons. Gen.	—	—
Hungary	Donald M. Blinken	Amb.	Gyorgy Banlaki	Amb.
Iceland	Parker W. Borg	Amb.	Einar Benediktsson	Amb.
India	Frank G. Wisner	Amb.	Naresh Chandra	Amb.
Indonesia	Robert L. Barry	Amb.	Arifin Mohamad Siregar	Amb.
Ireland	Jean Kennedy Smith	Amb.	Dermot A. Gallagher	Amb.
Israel	(Vacancy)	Amb.	Eliahu Ben-Elissar	Amb.
Italy	Reginald Bartholomew	Amb.	Ferdinando Salleo	Amb.
Jamaica	(Vacancy)	Amb.	Richard Leighton Bernal	Amb.
Japan	(Vacancy)	Amb.	Kunihiko Saito	Amb.
Jordan	Wesley E. Egan, Jr.	Amb.	Marwan Jamil Muasher	Amb.
Kazakhstan	William H. Courtney	Amb.	Bolat K. Nurgaliyev	Amb.
Kenya	Aurelia Brazeal	Amb.	Benjamin Edgar Kipkorir	Amb.
South Korea	(Vacancy)	Amb.	Kun Woo Park	Amb.
Kuwait	Ryan C. Crocker	Amb.	Mohammed Sabah Al-Salim Al-Sabah	Amb.
Kyrgyzstan	Anne Marie Sigmund	Amb.	Baktybek Abdrissaev	Amb.
Laos	Victor L. Tomseth	Amb.	Hiem Phommachanh	Amb.
Latvia	Ints M. Silins	Amb.	Ojars Eriks Kalnins	Amb.
Lebanon	Mark G. Hambley	Amb.	Mohamad Baha Chatah	Amb.
Lesotho	(Vacancy)	Amb.	Dr. Eunice M. Bulane	Amb.
Liberia	William P. Twaddell	Cd'A.	Konah K. Blackett	Cd'A.
Lithuania	Keith C. Smith	Amb.	Alfonsas Eidintas	Amb.
Luxembourg	Clay Constantinou	Amb.	Alphonse Berns	Amb.
Macedonia	Victor R. Conras	P.O.	Lubica Z. Acevska	Amb.
Madagascar	Dennis P. Barrett	Amb.	Pierrot J. Rajaonarivelo	Amb.
Malawi	Peter R. Chaveas	Amb.	Willie Chokani	Amb.
Malaysia	John S. Wolf	Amb.	Dato Dali Mahmud Hashim	Amb.
Mali	William H. Dameron III	Amb.	Cheick Oumar Diarrah	Amb.
Malta	Joseph R. Paolino, Jr.	Amb.	Mark Anthony Micallef	Amb.
Marshall Islands	David C. Fields	Amb.	Banny De Brum	Amb.
Mauritania	Dorothy Myers Sanpas	Amb.	Ahmed Ould Sid Ahmed	Amb.
Mauritius	Leslie M. Alexander	Amb.	Chitmansing Jesseramsing	Amb.
Mexico	James R. Jones	Amb.	Jesus Silva Herzog	Amb.
Micronesia	March Fong Eu	Amb.	Jesse B. Marehalau	Amb.
Moldova	Mary C. Pendleton	Amb.	Nicolae Tau	Amb.
Mongolia	Donald C. Johnson	Amb.	Jalbuu Choinhor	Amb.
Morocco	Marc C. Ginsberg	Amb.	Mohamed Benaissa	Amb.
Mozambique	Dennis Coleman Jett	Amb.	Marcus Geraldo Namashulua	Amb.
Namibia	Marshall F. McCallie	Amb.	Veiccoh Nghiwete	Amb.
Nepal	Ralph Frank	Amb.	Bhekh Bahadur Thapa	Amb.
Netherlands	K. Terry Dornbush	Amb.	Adriaan Pieter Roetert Jacobovits de Szeged	Amb.
New Zealand	Josiah Horton Beeman	Amb.	L. John Wood	Amb.
Nicaragua	John F. Maisto	Amb.	Francisco Aguirre Sacasa	Amb.

Country	U.S. Representative to[1]	Rank	Representative from[2]	Rank
Niger	John S. Davison	Amb.	Joseph Diatta	Amb.
Nigeria	Walter C. Carrington	Amb.	Dato Walkili Hassan Adamu	Amb.
Norway	Thomas A. Loftus	Amb.	Tom Eric Vraalsen	Amb.
Oman	David J. Dunford	Amb.	Abdulla Moh'd Aqueel Al-Dhahab	Amb.
Pakistan	John C. Monjo	Amb.	Zamir Akram	Cd'A.
Palau	Ihjod W. Moss	USLO	Riaz Khokhar	Amb.
Panama	(Vacancy)	Amb.	Eduardo Gonzalez Morgan	Amb.
Papua New Guinea	Richard W. Teare	Amb.	Nagora Y. Bogan	Amb.
Paraguay	Maura Harty	Amb.	Jorge G. Prieto	Amb.
Peru	Alvin P. Adams, Jr.	Amb.	Ricardo V. Luna	Amb.
Philippines	John D. Negroponte	Amb.	Raul Chaves Rabe	Amb.
Poland	Nicholas Andrew Rey	Amb.	Jerzy Koźminski	Amb.
Portugal	Elizabeth Frawley Bagley	Amb.	Fernando Andresen Guimaraes	Amb.
Qatar	Kenton W. Keith	Amb.	Saad Mohamed Al Kiobaisi	Amb.
Romania	Alfred H. Moses	Amb.	Mircea Geoana	Amb.
Russia	James Franklin Collins	Amb.	Yuli M. Vorontsov	Amb.
Rwanda	David P. Rawson	Amb.	Theogene N. Rudasingwa	Amb.
Saint Kitts and Nevis	—	—	Osbert W. Liburd	Amb.
Saint Lucia	—	—	Dr. Joseph Edsel Edmunds	Amb.
Saint Vincent and the Grenadines	—	—	Kingsley C.A. Layne	Amb.
Samoa, Western	Josiah Horton Beeman	Amb.	Tuiloma Neroni Slade	Amb.
Saudi Arabia	Raymond E. Mabus, Jr.	Amb.	Prince Bandar Bin Sultan	Amb.
Senegal	Mark Johnson	Amb.	Mamadou Mansour Seck	Amb.
Seychelles	Carl Burton Stokes	Amb.	Claude Morel	Cd'A.
Sierra Leone	Lauralee M. Peters	Amb.	John Ernest Leigh	Amb.
Singapore	Timothy A. Chorba	Amb.	Heng-Chee Chan	Amb.
Slovakia	Theodore E. Russell	Amb.	Branislav Lichardus	Amb.
Slovenia	E. Allan Wendt	Amb.	Dr. Ernest Petric	Amb.
Somalia	Richard W. Bogosian	Amb.	(Closed operations)	
South Africa	Princeton N. Lyman	Amb.	Franklin Sonn	Amb.
Spain	Richard N. Gardner	Amb.	Antonio Oyarzabal	Amb.
Sri Lanka	Teresita C. Schaffer	Amb.	M. Neetha Geethangani de Silva	Cd'A.
Sudan	Donald K. Petterson	Amb.	Mahdi Ibrahim Mohamed	Amb.
Suriname	Roger R. Gamble	Amb.	Arnold T. Halfhide	Amb.
Swaziland	John T. Sprott	Amb.	Mary M. Kanya	Amb.
Sweden	Thomas L. Siebert	Amb.	Carl Henrik Sihver Liljegren	Amb.
Switzerland	M. Larry Lawrence	Amb.	Alfred Defago	Amb.
Syria	Christopher W.S. Ross	Amb.	Walid Al-Moualem	Amb.
Tajikistan	Stanley T. Escudero	Amb.	—	—
Tanzania	Steven A. Browning	Amb.	Mustafa Salim Nyang'anyi	Amb.
Thailand	David F. Lambertson	Amb.	Nitya Pibulsonggram	Amb.
Togo	Johnny Young	Amb.	Kossivi Osseyi	Amb.
Trinidad and Tobago	Sally G. Cowal	Amb.	Corinne Averille McKnight	Amb.
Tunisia	Mary Ann Casey	Amb.	Azouz Ennifar	Amb.
Turkey	Marc Grossman	Amb.	Nuzhet Kandemir	Amb.
Turkmenistan	Joseph S. Hulings III	Amb.	Halil Ugur	Amb.
Uganda	E. Michael Southwick	Amb.	Edith Ssempala	Amb.
Ukraine	William Green Miller	Amb.	Yuriy Mikolayevych Shcherbak	Amb.
United Arab Emirates	William A. Rugh	Amb.	Mohammad bin Hussein Al-Shaali	Amb.
United Kingdom	Philip Lader	Amb.	Sir John Olav Kerr	Amb.
Uruguay	Thomas J. Dodd	Amb.	Dr. Alvaro Diez de Medina	Amb.
Uzbekistan	Henry L. Clarke	Amb.	Sadiq Safaev	Amb.
Venezuela	Jeffrey Davidow	Amb.	Pedro Luis Echeverria	Amb.
Vietnam	James H. Hall	USLO	Bang Van Le	Cd'A.
Yemen	Arthur H. Hughes	Amb.	Abdulwahab Alhajjri	Cd'A.
Yugoslavia (former)	(vacancy)	—	Nebojsa Vujovic	Cd'A.
Zambia	Roland K. Kuchel	Amb.	Dunstan Weston Kamana	Amb.
Zimbabwe	E. Gibson Lanpher	Amb.	Amos Bernard Muvengwa Midzi	Amb.

1. As of Fall 1995. 2. As of June 1997. NOTE: Amb.=Ambassador; Cd'A.=Charge d'Affaires; Secy.=Secretary; Cons. Gen.=Consul General; Consl.=Counselor; Min.=Minister; P.O.=Principal Officer; Dir.=Director; USLO=U.S. Liaison Office. *Source:* U.S. Department of State.

Travel

Chasing Value in Fliers' Miles

by David Cay Johnston, *The New York Times*

Some people will go to absurd lengths to collect frequent flier miles, traveling from New York to Seattle by way of Charlotte, Atlanta, or even Miami, or staying in a pricey hotel on the company tab to take advantage of a double miles offer. But how much value you get for your miles can be even more important than how you earn them.

As demand for air travel has grown with the economy, the airlines have in the last couple of years trimmed back on miles they give out, raised the number of miles for some awards, added blackout dates, tightened up on the availability of seats that can be purchased with frequent flier miles, and added new fees. But there are ways to get more bang for your miles.

The rule of thumb is that a frequent flier mile is worth 2 cents, based on the notion that a domestic ticket typically costs $500 and such a ticket requires 25,000 miles on most airlines. With some smart moves, frequent flier miles can be worth a nickel or even close to a dime each. But the airlines are perfectly happy to let you redeem 25,000 miles for a ticket you could have bought for $100, valuing your miles at less than a half cent each.

Flexibility Is a Major Plus

What you can get for your miles depends on your travel plans, your tastes and knowing how to spot a chance to get a good deal from the airlines.

It also helps to be flexible, and to know the signals that an airline has seats going begging. And you might consider using miles for benefits you might otherwise regard as extravagances, such as first class or even a ride on the Concorde.

The first rule of cashing in miles is flexibility. "Go off peak," advises Karen Goodwin, editor of *Frequent Flyer Magazine*. "Don't expect to find the seat you want at the busiest season. The airlines can easily sell seats to London in July and August so they don't make as many free ones available."

Joe Chapline, Delta Air Lines' frequent flier director, says it also pays "to be flexible about which days you travel. Going one or two days earlier or later will truly make a difference," he continued, "and remember that flying Thursdays and Saturdays you are more likely to get frequent flier award seats."

Being flexible about which airport, or changing planes, can help, too. If you want to fly from New York to Los Angeles and are told no seats are available, ask about a seat to nearby Orange County, said John McDonald, a spokesman for T.W.A. Flights to Orlando may not be available, but the amusement parks are only an hour or so drive from Tampa, Daytona Beach, and other Central Florida cities whose flights may have plenty of seats.

Likewise, if you want to spend high season in Paris, London, or Rome but cannot find a seat, you might have better luck asking about a seat to Brussels, Nice, Milan, or Manchester, assuming you want to visit one of those cities and like European trains.

Changing planes instead of going nonstop can also help at busy times, said Richard Metzner, a vice president for marketing at Continental. "If the agent tells you nothing is available nonstop, ask, 'Is there anything available via Cleveland or Houston?'"

If you want to stop over in a connecting city, say in Pittsburgh on your way from Boston to New Orleans, most airlines will charge you a much higher fare, but many reward tickets allow stopovers, according to Mark Seltzer, a Toronto dealer in rare travel books. Likewise, tickets bought on deep discounts often prohibit an "open jaw," in which you fly to one city, but fly home from another, while many reward tickets allow this option.

The second rule is to watch for signs that an airline has unsold seats. Last summer, when most airlines offered fewer frequent flier seats across the North Atlantic because they had a surge of paying customers, Continental increased the number of frequent flier seats to Europe by 68 percent. The reason? The airline had added more flights, increasing its capacity by 30 percent. If the airlines are offering incredibly inexpensive seats or bonus miles, they may well have seats available for reward travel.

Airlines often offer deals to new destinations or when they are trying to get fliers to associate their name with a destination. When United bought Pan American's Asian route system a decade ago, for example, it offered travel to Japan or Tokyo for half the usual number of miles, a program that packed its planes and soaked up a lot of frequent flier miles, which are a liability on the company's books. Cathay Pacific recently offered round-trip coach travel to Hong Kong for 40,000 American Airlines miles from any city in the United States. In the recent past, it has offered trips to Australia, Thailand, India and South Africa for similar amounts.

"If you see a destination on sale, it's a good bet that there are plenty of frequent flier seats on those flights," said David Castleveter, a spokesman for US Airways.

Airlines will sometimes offer brief frequent flier sales. Continental sometimes has trips to Europe for 25,000 miles, half the usual requirement. And United and some other airlines also sometimes offer a combination cash and miles deal, such as Europe from the East Coast for 20,000 miles and $100.

High-Value Upgrades

Some of the best deals come from using frequent flier miles for business class or first class. US Airways frequent fliers can go round trip to Europe on five carriers—Air France, Alitalia, Sabena, Swissair and US Airways in coach for 60,000 miles during the warm months, when an advance purchase ticket is often around $1,000. But business class requires only slightly more at 80,000 miles. First class is 100,000 miles, while a first-class ticket costs about $8,000, making miles worth about 8 cents each.

Greg Lyon, 25, a computer consultant in St. Louis, used 85,000 miles last May to fly T.W.A. business class to New York and first class on to London and return the same way. "For 50,000 miles I could have flown coach from St. Louis to London, a ticket worth maybe $500." Mr. Lyon said. "But for 70 percent more miles I got a ticket that would have cost five to eight times that much. To me that's an excellent value."

Tony Todd, 44, a software developer in Tampa, figures he got $24,000 worth of tickets for 240,000 miles and $1,000. He used 160,000 miles for two round-trip first-class tickets to London and another 80,000 miles to upgrade two round-trip coach tickets, which had cost $500 each, to business class. "I figure I got close to a dime per mile," he said.

His trip also illustrates two additional ways to get more value for your miles: plan and travel in pairs. American Airlines requires 200,000 miles for an "anytime" first-class ticket to Europe good on any flight. But by planning your trip well in advance and avoiding the blackout dates, you only need 100,000 miles. If you travel with a companion, however, two first-class plan ahead tickets bought well ahead of time require only 160,000 miles, a 20 percent discount.

But sometimes, you can get more value for your money with a last-minute trip, if seats are available. Airlines often charge a fee of $50 to $75 for arranging tickets within three weeks or less of flying. But some will let you redeem miles at the airport—Delta Air Lines, for example, charges $60 for last-second mile redemption—and take the next flight with an open seat.

Frequent Flyer Magazine, in an annual reader poll, found that the availability of first-class upgrades was the most desired perk for people who participate in frequent flier programs, but that 66 percent of those responding said it was getting harder to get into first class.

Airlines typically offer three ways to fly up front without buying a first-class ticket: an upgrade certificate given as a bonus to its most frequent fliers; a fee, typically $30 for short flights and $90 cross-country or an upgrade bought with miles. If you choose the last option, be careful which miles are deducted because miles in old programs can often be more valuable.

On Delta Air Lines, for example, to upgrade from coach to business or first class from most fares, including a deeply discounted ticket, you need only 2,500 miles from its old program. But if you use miles from its current Sky Miles program, the upgrade costs 10,000 miles.

The worst way to get value for your miles is to let them expire. Continental, T.W.A., and US Airways miles never expire. But American Airlines miles expire after three years, as have United and Northwest miles. Delta Air Lines miles also expire after three years if you have not flown on the airline in that time.

Source: Copyright © 1997 by The New York Times Co. Reprinted with permission.

Current Travel Warnings

Source: U.S. Department of State (travel.state.gov)

Country	Most Recent Warning Issued	Country	Most Recent Warning Issued
Afghanistan	6/10/97	Iran	7/8/97
Albania*	6/10/97	Iraq	6/25/97
Algeria	1/31/97	Lebanon	7/15/96
Angola	4/18/97	Liberia	9/13/96
Bosnia and Herzegovina	6/5/96	Libya	6/3/97
Burundi	8/23/96	Nigeria	11/19/96
Cambodia*	7/9/97	Rwanda	2/14/97
Central African Republic	3/28/97	Sierra Leone	6/1/97
Colombia	2/11/97	Somalia	6/28/96
Congo Republic*	6/17/97	Sudan	1/31/96
Dem. Rep. of Congo* (formerly Zaire)	6/4/97		

*Travel warnings issued for the first time in 1997.

Tips on Tipping

Source: American Society of Travel Agents, Alexandria, Va.

Who do you tip? When? How much?

These are the questions that have nagged at consumers since the first service transaction. The practice of tipping is meant as a form of thank-you for services rendered, or beforehand as a subtle bribe for special treatment.

Tipping need not be considered mandatory or automatic. Too often, tips are taken for granted or expected regardless of the quality of service. Tipping should be done at your discretion and as a reward for good or superlative service.

Below are some tipping suggestions for travelers. At nearly every step of the traveling process, there are professionals waiting to "lighten your load" or provide assistance. So remember to carry a lot of change and small bills for tips.

1. **Taxi/Limo Drivers:** A $2 to $3 tip is usually satisfactory; more if he helps you with your bags and/or takes special steps to get you to your destination on time.

2. **Porters:** A standard tip for airport and train porters is $1 per bag; more if your luggage is very heavy.

3. **Hotel Bellman:** Again, $1 per bag is standard. Tip when he shows you to your room and again if he assists you upon checkout. Tip more if he provides any additional service. Note: A $5 tip upon arrival can usually guarantee you special attention should you require it.

4. **Doorman:** Typically, a $1 tip for hailing a taxi is appropriate. However, you may want to tip more for special service, such as carrying your bags or shielding you with an umbrella.

5. **Concierge:** Tip for special services such as making restaurant or theater reservations, arranging sightseeing tours, etc. The amount of the tip is generally dependent on the type and complexity of service(s) provided—$2 to $10 is a standard range. You may elect to tip for each service, or in one sum upon departure. If you want to ensure special treatment from the concierge, you might consider a $10–$20 tip upon arrival.

6. **Hotel Maid:** Maids are often forgotten about when it comes to tipping because they typically do their work when you are not around. For stays of more than one

night, $1 per night is standard. The tip should be left in the hotel room in a marked envelope.

7. **Parking Attendants:** Tip $1 to $2 when your car is delivered.

8. **Waiters:** 15–20% of your pre-tax check is considered standard. The same applies for room service waiters. Some restaurants will automatically add a 15% gratuity to your bill, especially for large parties—look for it before tipping. If the 15% is added, you need only tip up to another 5% for superlative service.

9. **Cloakroom Attendants:** If there is a charge for the service, a tip is not necessary. However, if there is no charge, or extra care is taken with your coat and/or bags, a $1 to $2 tip is appropriate.

10. **Tour Guides/Charter Bus Drivers:** If a tip is not automatically included, tip $1 for a half-day tour, $2 for full-day tour, and anywhere from $5 to $10 for a week-long tour. Tip a private guide more.

These are some of the people you are most likely to encounter while traveling. Undoubtedly there will be others. If there is one standard rule in tipping it is this: If someone renders special service to you along the way, show your appreciation with a tip.

Tourism by Region of the World, 1996

	Arrivals	% Change 95/96	Receipts (in millions of U.S. dollars)	% Change 95/96
WORLD	592,122,000	4.6	423,116	7.6
Europe	347,437,000	3.6	214,474	5.9
Americas	115,511,000	4.3	106,378	6.1
East Asia/Pacific	90,091,000	8.3	82,436	13.3
Africa	19,454,000	2.3	7,622	9.2
Middle East	15,144,000	10.5	8,243	14.7
South Asia	4,485,000	4.3	3,963	8.8

Preliminary estimates. *Source:* World Tourism Organization (WTO). Reprinted with permission.

Americans' Favorite Summer Destinations in the U.S., 1997

Destination	Percent of travelers	Destination	Percent of travelers
Florida	34%	Colorado	9%
California	28	Arizona	7
Hawaii	17	Texas	7
Nevada	12	Washington, D.C.	6
New York	12	Alaska	6

Source: Travel Industry Association of America, April 1997.

The World's Top 40 Tourism Destinations, 1996

International Tourist Arrivals (excluding same-day visitors)

Rank 1990	1996	Countries	Arrivals 1996	Rank 1990	1996	Countries	Arrivals 1996
1	1	France	61,500,000	23	22	Singapore	6,608,000
2	2	United States	44,791,000	20	23	Netherlands	6,546,000
3	3	Spain	41,295,000	22	24	Belgium	5,753,000
4	4	Italy	32,853,000	27	25	Ireland	5,280,000
7	5	United Kingdom	26,025,000	38	26	Indonesia	5,034,000
12	6	China	22,765,000	54	27	South Africa	4,944,000
8	7	Mexico	21,428,000	34	28	Macau	4,890,000
5	8	Hungary	20,670,000	32	29	Argentina	4,286,000
28	9	Poland	19,420,000	36	30	Australia	4,167,000
10	10	Canada	17,386,000	29	31	Tunisia	3,885,000
6	11	Austria	17,090,000	31	32	Korea Republic	3,684,000
16[1]	12	Czech Republic	17,000,000	35	33	Egypt	3,675,000
9	13	Germany	15,205,000	37	34	Saudi Arabia	3,458,000
17[2]	14	Russian Federation	14,587,000	33	35	Puerto Rico	3,065,000
19	15	Hong Kong	11,703,000	30	36	Romania	2,834,000
11	16	Switzerland	11,097,000	25	37	Bulgaria	2,795,000
14	17	Portugal	9,900,000	39	38	Norway	2,746,000
13	18	Greece	8,987,000	26	39	Morocco	2,693,000
24	19	Turkey	7,966,000	46	40	Bahrain	2,669,000
21	20	Thailand	7,192,000			Total 1–40	515,010,000
15	21	Malaysia	7,138,000			**World Total**	**593,638,000**

1. Former Czechslovakia. 2. Former USSR. *Source:* World Tourism Organization (WTO). Reprinted with permission.

Consumer Complaints Against U.S. Airlines: 1987 to 1995

Complaint Category	1987	1988	1989	1990	1991	1992	1993	1994	1995
TOTAL	40,985	21,493	10,553	7,703	6,106	5,639	4,438	5,179	4,629
Flight problems[1]	18,019	8,831	4,111	3,034	1,877	1,624	1,211	1,586	1,133
Customer Service[2]	3,888	2,120	1,002	758	714	695	599	805	667
Ticketing/boarding[3]	2,458	1,445	821	624	659	680	577	598	666
Baggage	7,438	3,938	1,702	1,329	883	752	627	761	628
Refunds	3,313	1,667	1,023	701	783	721	482	393	576
Oversales[4]	2,122	1,353	607	399	301	265	257	301	263
Fares[5]	937	455	341	312	388	573	398	267	185
Advertising	344	141	89	96	96	54	51	94	66
Tours	90	37	22	29	23	12	16	127	18
Smoking	888	546	232	74	30	25	30	20	15
Credit	101	35	19	5	10	10	4	2	4
Other	1,387	925	584	342	342	228	186	225	408

1. Cancellations, delays, etc. from schedule. 2. Unhelpful employees, inadequate meals or cabin service, treatment of delayed passengers. 3. Errors in reservations and ticketing; problems in making reservations and obtaining tickets. 4. All bumping problems, whether or not airline complied with DOT regulations. 5. Incorrect or incomplete information about fares, discount fare conditions, and availability, etc. *Source:* U.S. Dept. of Transportation, Office of Consumer Affairs, *Air Travel Consumer Report.*

U.S. Passport Information

Source: Department of State, Bureau of Consular Affairs and Department of the Treasury, Customs Service.

With a few exceptions, a passport is required for all U.S. citizens to depart and enter the United States and to enter most foreign countries. A valid U.S. passport is the best documentation of U.S. citizenship available. Persons who travel to a country where a U.S. passport is not required should be in possession of documentary evidence of their U.S. citizenship and identity to facilitate reentry into the United States. Travelers should check passport and visa requirements with consular officials of the countries to be visited well in advance of their departure date.

Application for a passport may be made at a passport agency; to a clerk of any federal court or state court of record; or a judge or clerk of any probate court accepting applications; or at a post office selected to accept passport applications. Passport agencies are located in Boston, Chicago, Honolulu, Houston, Los Angeles, Miami, New Orleans, New York, Philadelphia, San Francisco, Seattle, Stamford, Conn., and Washington, D.C.

All persons are required to obtain individual passports in their own names. Neither spouses nor children may be included in each others' passports. Applicants age 13 years and older must appear in person before the clerk or agent executing the application. For children under the age of 13, a parent or legal guardian may execute an application for them.

First time passport applicants must apply in person. Applicants must present evidence of citizenship (e.g., a certified copy of birth certificate), personal identification (e.g., a valid driver's license), two identical black and white or color photographs taken within six months (2×2 inches, with the image size measured from the bottom of the chin to the top of the head [including hair] not less than 1 inch nor more than 1 3/8 inches on a plain white or off-white background, vending machine photographs not acceptable), plus a completed passport application (DSP-11). If you were born abroad, you may also use as proof of citizenship: a Certificate of Naturalization, a Certificate of Citizenship, a Report of Birth Abroad of a Citizen of the United States of America, or a Certification of Birth. A fee of $65 plus a $10 execution fee is charged for adults 18 years and older for a passport valid for ten years from the date of issue. The fee for minor children under 18 years of age

is $30 for a five-year passport plus $10 for the execution of the application.

You may apply for a passport by mail if you have been the bearer of a passport issued within 12 years prior to the date of a new application, are able to submit your most recent U.S. passport with your new application, and your previous passport was not issued before your 18th birthday. If you are eligible to apply by mail, include your previous passport, a completed, signed, and dated DSP-82 "Application for Passport by Mail," new photographs, and the passport fee of $55. The $10 execution fee is not required when renewing your passport. Mail the application and attachments in accordance with the instructions on the form.

Passports may be presented for amendment to show a married name or legal change of name or to correct descriptive data. Any alterations to the passport by the bearer other than in the spaces provided for change of address and next of kin data are forbidden.

If you **must** have your passport within 10 days, you will need to pay an additional $30 expedite fee and provide proof of the need for this service.

Loss, theft or destruction of a passport should be reported to Passport Services, 1111 19th Street, N.W., Washington, D.C. 20522-1705 immediately, or to the nearest passport agency. If you are overseas, report loss to the nearest U.S. embassy or consulate and to local police authorities. Your passport is a valuable citizenship and identity document. It should be carefully safeguarded. Its loss could cause you unnecessary travel complications as well as significant expense. It is advisable to photocopy the data page of your passport and keep it in a place separate from your passport to facilitate the issuance of a replacement passport should one be necessary.

Portsmouth National Passport Center

The Department of State has opened the largest passport processing center in the United States at Portsmouth, New Hampshire. Known as the National Passport Center, the facility is capable of issuing 6,000 passports per day but can be expanded to issue 9,000 passports per day.

The Center is processing passport mail renewal applications from around the United States. Passport fees are deposited in Pittsburgh, with the applications subsequently express mailed to Portsmouth for processing. The other passport agencies will process first-time applications and any other requests for passport services presented in person.

To renew a passport by mail, applicants must:

1. Obtain an "Application for Passport by Mail" (Form DSP-82) from a passport acceptance facility (post office, court house or passport agency).

2. Complete and sign the application and attach the most recent passport issued not more than 12 years ago but after the applicant's 18th birthday, two identical 2″ × 2″ passport photographs, and a check or money order for $55 payable to Passport Services.

3. Mail the above items to the National Passport Center, Post Office Box 371971, Pittsburgh, Pennsylvania 15250-7971.

State and City Tourism Offices

The following is a selected list of state tourism offices. Where a toll-free 800 or 888 number is available, it is given. However, the numbers are subject to change.

Alabama
Bureau of Tourism & Travel
P.O. Box 4927
Montgomery, AL 36103-4927
334-242-4169 or
   1-888-520-3434

Alaska
Alaska Division of Tourism
P.O. Box 110801
Juneau, AK 99811-0801
907-465-2010

Arizona
Arizona Office of Tourism
2702 N. 3rd St., Ste. 4015
Phoenix, AZ 85004
602-230-7733 or
   1-800-842-8257

Arkansas
Arkansas Department of
   Parks and Tourism
1 Capitol Mall
Little Rock, AR 72201
501-682-7777 or
   1-800-NATURAL (to receive
   literature both in and out of
   state)

California
California Division of Tourism
P.O. Box 1499
Sacramento, CA 95812-1499
1-800-862-2543

Colorado
No longer has a tourism board.
Tourists need to contact individual cities.

Connecticut
Tourism Promotion Service
CT Dept. of Economic
   Development
865 Brook St.
Rocky Hill, CT 06067-3405
203-258-4355 or
   800-CTBOUND
   (nationwide)

Delaware
Delaware Tourism Office
Delaware Economic
   Development Office
99 Kings Highway
P.O. Box 1401

Dover, DE 19903
302-739-4271 or
   1-800-441-8846 (both in
   and out of state)

**District of Columbia
(Washington, D.C.)**
Washington Convention and
   Visitors Association
717 14th St., NW
Washington, D.C. 20005-3992
202-789-7000

Florida
Visitor Services
Florida Tourism Industry
   Marketing Corp.
P.O. Box 1100
Tallahassee, FL 32302-1100
904-488-5607

Georgia
Tourist Division
P.O. Box 1776
Atlanta, GA 30301-1776
404-656-3590, 1-800-VISIT
   GA or 1-800-847-4842

Hawaii
Hawaii Visitors Bureau
2270 Kalakaua Ave., Ste. 801
Honolulu, HI 96815
808-923-1811

Idaho
Department of Commerce,
   Tourism Development
700 W. State St.
P.O. Box 83720
Boise, ID 83720-0093
208-334-2470 or
   1-800-635-7820

Illinois
Illinois Bureau of Tourism
100 W. Randolph, Ste. 3-400
Chicago, IL 60601
800-2CONNECT
www.enjoyillinois.com

Indiana
Indiana Department of
   Commerce
Tourism & Film Development
   Division
1 North Capitol, Ste. 700

Indianapolis, IN 46204-2288
1-800-289-6646

Iowa
Iowa Department of Economic
   Development
Division of Tourism
200 East Grand Ave.
Des Moines, IA 50309
515-242-4705 or
   1-800-345-IOWA

Kansas
Kansas Department of
   Commerce & Housing
Travel & Tourism
   Development Division
700 SW Harrison St., Ste.
   1300
Topeka, KS 66603-3712
913-296-2009 or
   1-800-2KANSAS

Kentucky
Department of Travel
   Development
Dept. MR
P.O. Box 2011
Frankfort, KY 40602
1-800-225-TRIP Ext. 67 (from
   the United States and
   Canada)

Louisiana
Office of Tourism
P.O. Box 94291
Baton Rouge, LA 70804-9291
504-342-8119 or
   1-800-33GUMBO

Maine
Maine Publicity Bureau
P.O. Box 2300
Hallowell, ME 04347-2300
207-623-0363

Maryland
Office of Tourism
   Development
217 E. Redwood St., 9th
   Floor
Baltimore, MD 21202
410-767-3400 (business office
   only)
1-800-543-1036 (Maryland
   Travel Kit)

Average Daily Temperatures (°F) in Tourist Cities

Location	January High	January Low	April High	April Low	July High	July Low	October High	October Low
Acapulco (Mexico)	87	72	87	73	90	76	89	76
Amsterdam (Netherlands)	40	34	52	43	68	59	56	48
Athens (Greece)	54	42	67	52	90	72	74	60
Auckland (New Zealand)	73	60	67	56	56	46	63	52
Bangkok (Thailand)	89	68	95	77	90	76	88	75
Beijing (China)	34	15	69	44	89	72	66	44
Belgrade (Yugoslavia)	37	27	64	45	84	61	65	47
Berlin (Germany)	35	26	55	38	74	55	55	41
Bombay (India)	83	67	89	76	85	77	89	76
Cairo (Egypt)	65	47	83	57	96	70	86	65
Calcutta (India)	80	55	97	75	89	79	89	74
Cape Town (South Africa)	69	56	66	54	60	50	65	53
Caracas (Venezuela)	75	56	81	60	78	61	79	61
Copenhagen (Denmark)	36	29	50	37	72	55	53	42
Dublin (Ireland)	47	35	54	38	67	51	57	43
Glasgow (Scotland)	43	34	53	38	66	52	54	43
Hamilton (Bermuda)	68	58	71	59	85	73	79	69
Helsinki (Finland)	27	17	43	31	71	57	45	37
Hong Kong (China)	64	56	75	67	87	78	81	73
Istanbul (Turkey)	45	36	61	45	81	65	67	54
Jerusalem (Israel)	55	41	73	50	87	63	81	59
Kingston (Jamaica)	86	67	87	70	90	73	88	73
Lagos (Nigeria)	88	74	89	77	83	74	85	74
Lisbon (Portugal)	56	46	64	52	79	63	69	57
London (United Kingdom)	44	35	56	40	73	55	58	44
Madrid (Spain)	47	33	64	44	87	62	66	48
Mexico City (Mexico)	66	42	77	51	73	53	70	50
Montreal (Canada)	21	6	50	33	78	61	54	40
Moscow (Russia)	21	9	47	31	76	55	46	34
Nairobi (Kenya)	77	54	75	58	69	51	76	55
Nassau (Bahamas)	77	65	81	69	88	75	85	73
Oslo (Norway)	30	20	50	34	73	56	49	37
Paris (France)	42	32	60	41	76	55	59	44
Prague (Czech Republic)	34	25	55	40	74	58	54	44
Quebec (Canada)	18	2	45	29	76	57	51	37
Rio de Janeiro (Brazil)	84	73	80	69	75	63	77	66
Rome (Italy)	54	39	68	46	88	64	73	53
San José (Costa Rica)	75	58	79	62	77	62	77	60
San Juan (Puerto Rico)	80	70	82	72	85	75	85	75
Seoul (Korea)	32	15	62	41	84	70	67	45
Singapore	86	73	88	75	88	75	87	74
Stockholm (Sweden)	31	23	45	32	70	55	48	39
Sydney (Australia)	78	65	71	58	60	46	71	56
Taipei (Taiwan)	66	54	77	63	92	76	81	67
Tokyo (Japan)	47	29	63	46	83	70	69	55
Toronto (Canada)	30	16	50	34	79	59	56	40
Vancouver (Canada)	41	32	58	40	74	54	57	44
Vienna (Austria)	34	26	57	41	75	59	55	44
Zurich (Switzerland)	36	26	60	41	77	56	57	43

U.S. Cities (*See* Climate of 100 Selected U.S. Cities).

Massachusetts
Office of Travel and Tourism
100 Cambridge St., 13th
   Floor
Boston, MA 02202
617-727-3201
800-447-MASS (6277) (Mass
   Getaway Guide)

Michigan
Michigan Jobs Commission
Travel Michigan
P.O. Box 3393
Livonia, MI 48151

1-800-5432-YES
www.travel-michigan.state.mi.us

Minnesota
Minnesota Office of Tourism
100 Metro Square
121 7th Place E
St. Paul, MN 55101-2112
612-296-5029 or
   1-800-657-3700

Mississippi
Department of Economic and
   Community Development
Tourism Development

P.O. Box 1705
Ocean Springs, MS
   39566-1705
601-359-3297 or
   1-800-927-6378

Missouri
Missouri Division of Tourism
Truman State Office Bldg.
301 W. High St.
P.O. Box 1055
Jefferson City, MO 65102
573-751-4133 or
   1-800-877-1234

Montana
Department of Commerce
Travel Montana
P.O. Box 200533
Helena, MT 59620-0533
406-444-2654 or 1-800-VISIT
MT

Nebraska
Department of Economic
Development
Division of Travel and Tourism
301 Centennial Mall South
P.O. Box 98913
Lincoln, NE 68509
402-471-3796 or
1-800-228-4307 (in-state or
out-of-state)

Nevada
Commission on Tourism
5151 S. Carson St.
Carson City, NV 89701
1-800-NEVADA-8

New Hampshire
Office of Travel and Tourism
P.O. Box 1856
Concord, NH 03302-1856
603-271-2666 or for recorded
weekly events, ski
conditions, foliage reports
1-800-258-3608

New Jersey
Division of Travel and Tourism
CN 826
Trenton, NJ 08625
1-800-JERSEY-7

New Mexico
New Mexico Department of
Tourism
491 Old Santa Fe Trail
Lamy Bldg.
Santa Fe, NM 87503
505-827-7400 or
1-800-733-6396

New York
Division of Tourism
1 Commerce Plaza
Albany, NY 12245
Toll free from anywhere in the
U.S. and its territorial
possessions
1-800-225-5697. From
Canada, call 518-474-4116

North Carolina
Travel and Tourism Division
Department of Commerce
430 North Salisbury St.
Raleigh, NC 27603
919-733-4171 or 1-800-VISIT
NC

North Dakota
North Dakota Tourism
604 E. Boulevard
Bismarck, ND 58505

701-328-2525 or
1-800-HELLO ND
www.ndtourism.com

Ohio
Ohio Division of Travel and
Tourism
P.O. Box 1001
Columbus, OH 43266-1010
614-466-8844 (business
office)
1-800-BUCKEYE (in U.S. and
Canada)

Oklahoma
Oklahoma Tourism and
Recreation Department
Literature Distribution Center
P.O. Box 60789
Oklahoma City, OK
73146-9910
405-521-2409 (in Oklahoma
City area) or nationwide at
1-800-652-6552

Oregon
Tourism Commission
775 Summer St., NE
Salem, OR 97310
503-373-1270 (Business
Office)
1-800-547-7842 (Travel
Information)

Pennsylvania
Office of Travel, Tourism, and
Film Promotion
Room 456, Forum Building
Harrisburg, PA 17120
717-787-5453 (business
office) or 1-800-VISIT PA,
ext. 257 (To order single
free copy of Pa. Travel
Guide)

Rhode Island
Rhode Island Economic
Development Corporation
1 West Exchange St.
Providence, RI 02903
401-277-2601 or
1-800-556-2484 (in U.S.
and Canada)

South Carolina
South Carolina Division of
Tourism
Box 71
Columbia, SC 29202
803-734-0122

South Dakota
Department of Tourism
711 E. Wells Ave.
Pierre, SD 57501
1-800-S-DAKOTA

Tennessee
Department of Tourist
Development
P.O. Box 23170
Nashville, TN 37243

615-741-2159 or
1-800-491-TENN

Texas
Travel Information Division
Texas Department of
Transportation
P.O. Box 5064
Austin, TX 78763-5064
1-800-452-9292

Utah
Utah Travel Council
Council Hall, Capitol Hill
Salt Lake City, UT 84114
801-538-1030
801-538-1399 (fax)
www.utah.com

Vermont
Department of Tourism and
Marketing
134 State St.
P.O. Box 1471
Montpelier, VT 05601-1471
1-800-VERMONT
www.Travel-Vermont.com

Virginia
Virginia Tourism Corporation
901 East Byrd St.
Richmond, VA 23219
804-786-4484 or
1-800-932-5827
www.virginia.org

Washington
Washington State Department
of Community, Trade and
Economic Development
906 Columbia St., SW
P.O. Box 48300
Olympia, WA 98504-8300
360-753-2200

Washington, D.C.
See District of Columbia

West Virginia
Division of Tourism
2101 Washington St., E.
Charleston, WV 25305
304-558-2286 or
1-800-CALL-WVA

Wisconsin
Travel Information
Department of Tourism
Box 7606
Madison, WI 53707-7606
Toll free in WI and neighbor
states 1-800-372-2737;
others: 608-266-2161;
nationally 1-800-432-TRIP
tourism.state.wi.us

Wyoming
Wyoming Division of Tourism
I-25 at College Dr.
Cheyenne, WY 82002
307-777-7777 or
1-800-225-5996

Family Trends

Marital Status

Men and women are marrying later than ever before. The estimated median age at first marriage is higher than ever before. In 1994, the median age at first marriage was 26.7 years for men and 24.5 years for women, approximately 3½ years higher than the median age in 1970 (23.2 years for men and 20.8 years for women). Another indication of delayed marriage is the significant increase of the proportion of young adults who have not yet married.

Since 1970, the proportions of men and women who had never married have at least doubled or in some cases tripled for the age groups between 25 and 44 years. For example, the proportion of persons 30 to 34 years old who had never married tripled from 6 to 20 percent for women and from 9 to 30 percent for men between 1970 and 1994. Among persons 35 to 39 years old, the proportions never married doubled from 5 to 13 percent for women and nearly tripled from 7 to 19 percent for men during this period.

One in every nine adults lives alone. In 1994, 23.6 million persons lived alone or 12 percent of all adults. While women accounted for the larger share of persons living alone in 1994 (6 of 10), the number of men living alone increased at a faster pace. Between 1970 and 1994, the number of women living alone increased 94 percent (from 7.3 to 14.2 million). During the same period, there was a 167 percent increase in the number of men living alone (from 3.5 to 9.4 million).

Living alone is more common among the elderly, especially among women. Of adults under 35 years old, only 5 percent of women and 7 percent of men lived alone in 1994. For persons 75 years old and over, the proportion living alone was 52 percent for women and 21 percent for men. Since 1970, there has been virtually no change in the proportion of elderly men living alone, while the proportion of elderly women living alone has grown significantly (from 19 to 21 percent for men and from 37 to 52 percent of women between 1970 and 1994).

There has been a sevenfold increase in unmarried-couple households since 1970. An unmarried-couple household is composed of two adults of the opposite sex (one of whom is the householder) who share a housing unit with or without the presence of children under 15 years old. The count of unmarried-couple households is intended mainly to estimate the number of cohabiting couples, but it may also include households with a roommate, boarder, or paid employee of the opposite sex. Since 1970, the number of unmarried-couple households has grown from 523,000 to 3.7 million in 1994. There were 7 unmarried couples for every 100 married couples in 1994, compared with only 1 for every 100 in 1970. About one-third had children under 15 years old present in the home.

The number of children living with never-married parents is on the rise. Children living with one parent (18.6 million) represented 27 percent of all children under 18 years old in 1994, up from 12 percent in 1970. The majority lived with their mother, but an increasing proportion lived with their father. In 1994, 12 percent of the children in a one-parent situation lived with their father, up from 9 percent in 1970. Of the children who lived with one parent, the proportion who lived with a parent who has never married has grown by one-half in the past decade (from 24 to 36 percent) while the proportion who lived with a divorced parent has declined (from 42 to 37 percent). In 1983, a child in a one-parent situation was almost twice as likely to be living with a divorced parent as with a never-married parent; whereas today, the child is just as likely to be living with a divorced parent as with a never-married parent (37 percent compared with 36 percent, respectively). The proportion of children living with a separated parent decreased from 23 to 18 percent between 1983 and 1994. □

Source: U. S. Bureau of the Census, Current Population Reports, Series P23–189, *Population Profile of the United States: 1995.*

Estimated Median Age at First Marriage, by Sex: 1970 to 1994

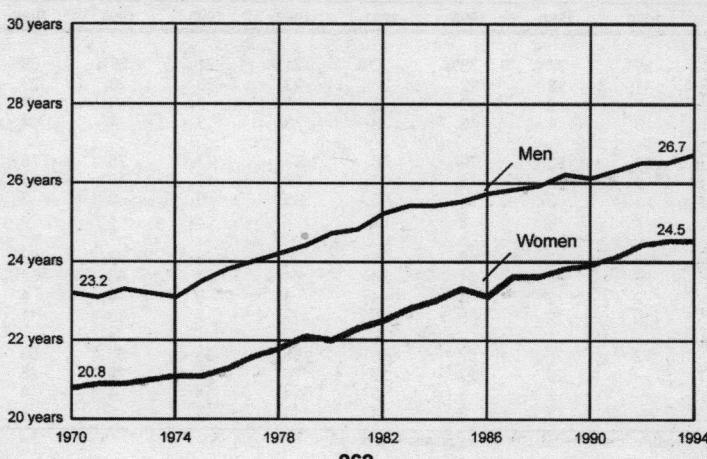

Marriage and Divorce Rates: United States, 1950–94

Source: Monthly Vital Statistics Report, Vol. 43, No. 13, October 23, 1995.

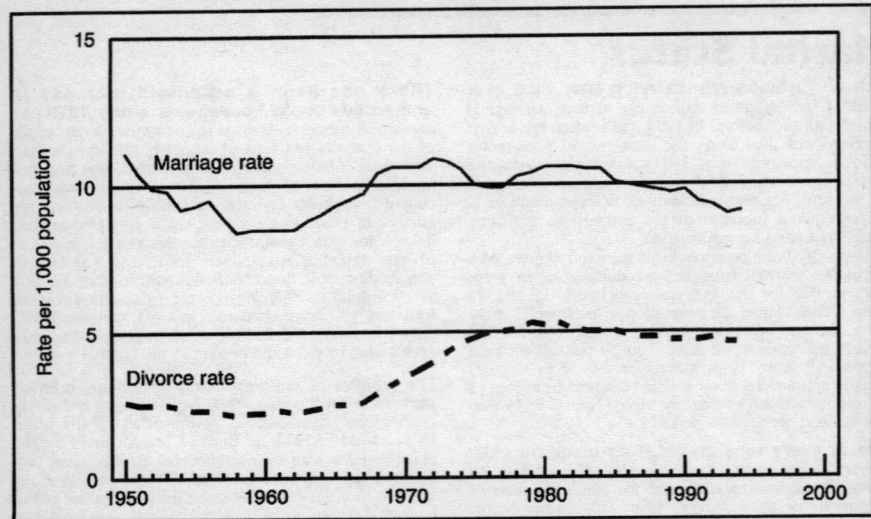

Marriage and Divorce, 1996

The marriage rate for 1996 was 8.8 per 1000 people in the United States, which was 1 percent lower than the 1995 marriage rate of 8.9 per 1000 people. The rate has generally declined since the early 1980s and is currently the lowest annual rate since 1963.

The estimated total number of marriages for the year was 2,344,000.

Marriages in 1996 exhibited the typical seasonal pattern, with the peak number of weddings in June (242,000) and the lowest number in January (100,000).

The divorce rate per 1,000 married women in the United States for 1996 was 19.5, 2 percent lower that for 1995 (19.8). It is the lowest annual divorce rate since 1974. The estimated number of divorces for the year was 1,150,000. □

Source: Monthly Vital Statistics Report, Vol. 45, No. 12. July 17, 1997.

Family Structure

(Under age 18, by race and Hispanic origin, for selected years 1970–96.)

Family type	1970	1980	1990	1991	1992	1993	1994	1995	1996
Total									
Two parents	85%	77%	73%	72%	71%	71%	69%	69%	68%
Mother only	11	18	22	22	23	23	23	23	24
Father only	1	2	3	3	3	3	3	4	4
No parent	3	4	3	3	3	3	4	4	4
White									
Two parents	90	83	79	78	77	77	76	76	75
Mother only	8	14	16	17	18	17	18	18	18
Father only	1	2	3	3	3	3	3	3	4
No parent	2	2	2	2	2	2	3	3	3
Black									
Two parents	58	42	38	36	36	36	33	33	33
Mother only	30	44	51	54	54	54	53	52	53
Father only	2	2	4	4	3	3	4	4	4
No parent	10	12	8	6	7	7	10	11	9
Hispanic									
Two parents	78	75	67	66	65	65	63	63	62
Mother only	—	20	27	27	28	28	28	28	29
Father only	—	2	3	3	4	4	4	4	4
No parent	—	3	3	4	3	4	5	4	5

Source: U. S. Bureau of the Census, Current Population Reports.

Family Structure

The number of parents living with a child is generally linked to the amount and quality of human and economic resources available to that child. Children who live with one parent are substantially more likely to have family incomes below the poverty line than are children who grow up in a household with two adults. Research indicates that poverty, in turn, increases the risk that a child will experience significant difficulties.

• In 1996, 68 percent of American children lived with two parents: down from 85 percent in 1970.

• In 1996, almost a quarter (24 percent) of children lived with only their mothers; 4 percent lived with only their fathers; and 4 percent lived with neither of their parents.

• The percentage of children living with two parents has been declining among all major racial and ethnic groups.

• White children are much more likely than black children and somewhat more likely than Hispanic children to live with two parents. In 1996, 75 percent of white children lived with two parents, compared to 33 percent of black children and 62 percent of Hispanic children.

• Among the factors contributing to the increase in the percentage of children living with just one parent is the sharp rise in the percentage of all births that were to unmarried mothers: from 5 percent in 1960 to 32 percent in 1995. Almost two-thirds of those children living with only their mothers in 1995, however, were living with formerly married mothers (divorced, separated, widowed), while a little over one-third lived with never-married mothers. □

Blended Families[1]

Characteristics of women	Number	Any child	Stepchild	Child of relative, friend, or partner	Foster child	Adopted child
Age						
18–19 years	3,508,000	1.9	—	1.6	—	—
20–24 years	9,041,000	4.3	0.8	2.4	0.1	0.1
25–29 years	9,693,000	8.2	1.6	5.2	0.8	0.3
30–34 years	11,065,000	11.1	3.4	6.7	0.6	0.5
35–39 years	11,211,000	16.0	5.7	7.3	1.7	1.7
40–44 years	10,230,000	17.5	5.7	7.8	1.2	2.0
Marital status						
Never married	17,300,000	5.2	0.0	4.1	0.3	0.1
Currently married	29,600,000	13.5	5.3	5.7	1.1	1.2
Formerly married	7,849,000	14.9	3.2	9.2	1.1	1.2
Parity						
0 birth	19,998,000	8.0	2.3	4.1	0.3	1.2
1 birth	10,502,000	12.2	4.9	5.5	0.7	0.6
2 births	13,871,000	12.9	3.7	6.9	1.1	0.8
3 or more births	10,377,000	13.5	3.3	7.4	1.7	0.5
Education at interview						
No high school diploma or GED	5,424,000	14.2	3.2	9.0	1.5	0.7
High school diploma or GED	18,169,000	14.1	4.3	7.4	0.9	0.9
Some college, no bachelor's degree	12,399,000	13.7	4.3	7.2	1.1	1.1
Bachelor's degree or higher	11,748,000	7.4	2.8	2.6	0.7	1.1
Poverty level income at interview						
0–149 percent	10,080,000	12.7	2.7	8.0	1.3	0.4
0–99 percent	5,992,000	12.8	1.9	9.0	1.4	0.4
150–299 percent	14,932,000	13.0	4.0	6.9	1.3	0.8
300 percent or higher	22,736,000	11.8	4.2	5.3	0.6	1.4
Race and Hispanic origin						
Hispanic	6,015,000	11.5	2.5	6.3	0.8	0.6
Non–Hispanic white	38,987,000	10.8	3.8	4.9	1.3	0.9
Non–Hispanic black	7,357,000	12.9	1.9	9.1	0.8	1.0
Non–Hispanic other	2,390,000	9.3	2.1	6.5	0.4	0.5

NOTE: Percents may not add to "Any child" total because some women lived and cared for more than one child not born to them. 1. Number of women 18–44 years of age and percent who have ever lived with and cared for a child to whom they did not give birth, by the child's relationship to them and selected characteristics: in the United States in 1995. *Source: Health, United States, 1995.*

Young Adults Living at Home 1960–1995

	Male			Female		
	Total pop., 25–34 years old	Number living at home	Percent	Total pop,. 25–34 years old	Number living at home	Percent
1960	10,896,000	1,185,000	11%	11,587,000	853,000	7%
1970	11,929,000	1,129,000	9	12,637,000	829,000	7
1980	18,107,000	1,894,000	10	18,689,000	1,300,000	7
1985	20,184,000	2,685,000	13	20,673,000	1,661,000	8
1990	21,462,000	3,213,000	15	21,779,000	1,774,000	8
1995	20,589,000	3,166,000	15	20,800,000	1,759,000	8

NOTE: Unmarried college students living in dorms are counted as living at home. *Source: U.S. Bureau of the Census, Current Population Reports.*

Percentage of Babies Breast-fed

Breast-feeding, which has gone in and out of fashion over the decades, more than doubled between 1970 and 1987 and continues to be on the rise. Breast milk contains antibodies that help protect babies against illnesses and allergies, and is considered by doctors to be more beneficial than formula.

Selected characteristics of mother	Percent of Babies Breast-fed								
	1970–71	1972–73	1974–75	1976–77	1978–79	1980–81	1982–83	1984–85	1986–87
Total	24.9	29.1	34.2	42.0	44.4	52.5	57.3	55.5	55.0
Race									
White	26.4	30.4	37.3	45.9	48.1	57.2	62.3	59.9	60.3
Black	10.8	14.6	17.1	19.5	24.5	24.5	27.0	22.9	23.5
Education									
Less than 12 years	15.0	23.4	18.4	25.6	25.8	34.0	30.5	32.9	33.8
12 years	20.8	27.6	30.2	34.8	41.6	45.8	53.6	46.8	51.2
13 years or more	38.5	35.1	49.5	62.3	58.9	73.5	73.6	74.7	73.0
Geographic region									
Northeast	31.8	24.3	31.4	38.5	37.7	46.6	67.7	65.3	64.6
Midwest	23.7	23.8	29.3	43.6	48.1	54.6	46.7	44.2	44.8
South	11.7	22.0	22.9	32.1	31.8	41.8	56.4	54.3	46.2
West	39.5	55.5	61.6	61.3	66.5	70.1	67.7	67.4	72.5
Age									
20–24 years	—	—	22.0	27.8	30.4	45.4	31.8	31.9	42.4
25–44 years	24.9	29.3	34.6	44.1	47.9	58.1	60.5	61.8	62.1
25–29 years	13.9	24.1	25.6	35.5	45.0	55.0	48.4	54.8	57.5
30–44 years	25.8	30.7	38.8	50.2	50.4	61.8	66.2	66.9	67.0

Source: National Center for Health Statistics. *Health, United States, 1995*. Hyattsville, Maryland: Public Health Service, p. 98, 1996.

Childcare

Most preschoolers receive care in a home environment. The choice of childcare arrangements for preschool-age children is one of the most important daily decisions parents make. It is an age when children are most dependent on a care provider's supervisory skills and often marks the time when children make their first prolonged social contacts with persons outside the immediate family. In 1991, there were 9.9 million children under the age of 5 who were in need of care while their mothers were at work.

About two-thirds of preschool-age children were cared for in either their own home (36 percent) or another home (31 percent) for the majority of time their mothers were away at work. Most of the children taken care of in their own homes were cared for by their fathers. In comparison, among those taken care of outside of the home, most were cared for by family daycare providers—nonrelatives in the provider's home. Nearly one quarter (23 percent) received care in an organized facility, such as a nursery school or a daycare center. Virtually all the remaining kids (9 percent) were cared for by their mothers while they worked; most of these moms worked at home.

Grandparents and fathers often play a significant role in preschooler care. Sixteen percent of preschool children were cared for by their grandparents during their mothers' working hours and about 20 percent were cared for by their fathers. Relatives other than grandparents and fathers played a smaller role in providing childcare services, amounting to about 8 percent of all arrangements for preschoolers.

Preschoolers' childcare arrangements have changed dramatically over the past few years. A noteworthy change in the type of childcare arrangements used by preschoolers between 1988 and 1991 was in the proportion of children cared for by family daycare providers. The proportion of children cared for by these providers sharply fell from 24 percent in 1988 to 18 percent in 1991. This marked the first substantial decline in the use of family daycare providers since the mid-1980s. Between 1988 and 1991 the proportion of preschoolers who were cared for by organized childcare facilities also declined from 26 to 23 percent. Recent declines in these services may reflect the desires of parents to cut down on childcare costs and move to more parental supervision of their children whenever possible, or they may indicate more difficulties in securing licensed family daycare providers.

In contrast to declines in the usage of family daycare providers and organized childcare facilities, father care, while remaining at about the 15 percent level between 1977 and 1988, sharply increased to 20 percent by fall 1991. In the 1988–1991 period, father-provided childcare increased for children whose fathers worked at full-time jobs, even if their fathers worked day shifts. Father care, however, was greatest among children whose fathers experienced long-term joblessness: 56 percent of preschoolers whose fathers were out of work for 4 or more months in 1991 were cared for by Dad while Mom was at work.

Mothers working evening or night shifts have an easier time arranging for in-home care. The type of shift that a mother works makes a big difference in the kind of primary care arrangement that she uses. Children whose mothers work day shifts are more likely to be cared for away from home than children whose mothers work nonday shifts. For example, among preschoolers whose mothers worked a day shift at their

Recent Changes in Selected Childcare Arrangements: 1988–1991

(Percent of preschoolers whose mothers used childcare arrangements)

	1988	1990	1991
Father care	15%	17%	20%
Family day care	24	20	18
Organized facility	26	28	23

principal job, 34 percent were cared for in another home, compared with 27 percent of children whose mothers worked a nonday shift. Use of organized child-care facilities was also more prevalent for children of women working day shifts, accounting for 30 percent of all childcare arrangements. Children of women working nonday shifts used these facilities less frequently, amounting to 14 percent of all childcare arrangements.

Working nonday rather than day shifts may offer more opportunities for women with preschoolers to secure care for their children at home, especially by the children's fathers. Overall, 47 percent of the preschool-age children of women working nonday shifts were cared for in their own home, compared with 27 percent of the children of women working day shifts. In-home childcare of preschoolers by fathers accounted for 31 percent of all arrangements used by women working nonday shifts compared with only 12 percent used by women working day shifts.

Mothers working part-time have an easier time arranging for in-home care. Patterns by the number of hours worked are similar—preschool children of mothers employed full-time were less likely to be cared for in the child's home (30 percent) than were children of mothers employed part-time (44 percent). On the other hand, full-time working mothers relied more heavily on childcare in either someone else's home or in

organized childcare facilities (64 percent) than did part-time working mothers (41 percent).

Preschool children of part-time working mothers were more likely to be cared for by their mothers while at work (15 percent), than were children of mothers who worked full-time (4 percent). In addition, childcare provided by the father was also more frequent when the mother worked part-time (27 percent) than full-time (15 percent). More preschoolers with mothers who worked part-time had mothers who worked nonday schedules (66 percent) than did children with mothers who worked full-time (27 percent). This potentially enabled fathers who worked on a "9 to 5" schedule the opportunity to look after the children.

For many families, childcare is a costly expense. In 1991, half as many poor families paid for childcare as did nonpoor families (32 percent versus 64 percent). Poor families with only preschoolers paid less for child-care than their nonpoor counterparts: $52 compared with $70 per week. However, poor families spent a larger percentage of their family income on childcare (20 percent) than similar nonpoor families (8 percent).   □

Source: U.S. Bureau of the Census, Current Population Reports, Series P23–189, *Population Profile of the United States: 1995.*

Births to Unmarried Women

Increases in births to unmarried women are among the many changes in American society that have affected family structure and the economic security of children. Children of unmarried mothers are at higher risk of having adverse birth outcomes, because their mothers are less likely to have received adequate prenatal care, less likely

to have gained adequate weight during pregnancy, and more likely to have smoked during pregnancy, even when differences in age and educational level are taken into account. They are also more likely to live in poverty than children of married mothers.   □

Birth Rates for Unmarried Women by Age of Mother 1980–94

(Births per 1,000 unmarried women in each age group.)

Year	Total: 15–44	15–17	18–19	20–24	25–29	30–34	35–39	40–44
1980	29.4	20.6	39.0	40.9	34.0	21.1	9.7	2.6
1981	29.5	20.9	39.0	41.1	34.5	20.8	9.8	2.6
1982	30.0	21.5	39.6	41.5	35.1	21.9	10.0	2.7
1983	30.3	22.0	40.7	41.8	35.5	22.4	10.2	2.6
1984	31.0	21.9	42.5	43.0	37.1	23.3	10.9	2.5
1985	32.8	22.4	45.9	46.5	39.9	25.2	11.6	2.5
1986	34.2	22.8	48.0	49.3	42.2	27.2	12.2	2.7
1987	36.0	24.5	48.9	52.6	44.5	29.6	13.5	2.9
1988	38.5	26.4	51.5	56.0	48.5	32.0	15.0	3.2
1989	41.6	28.7	56.0	61.2	52.8	34.9	16.0	3.4
1990	43.8	29.6	60.7	65.1	56.0	37.6	17.3	3.6
1991	45.2	30.9	65.7	68.0	56.5	38.1	18.0	3.8
1992	45.2	30.4	67.3	68.5	56.5	37.9	18.8	4.1
1993	45.3	30.6	66.9	69.2	57.1	38.5	19.0	4.4
1994	46.9	32.0	70.1	72.2	59.0	40.1	19.8	4.7

Source: Centers for Disease Control and Prevention, National Center of Health Statistics, 1996.

Teen Births

Research indicates that for a young woman, bearing a child during adolescence is associated with long-term difficulties for herself, her child, and society. These consequences are often attributable to the poverty and other adverse socioeconomic circumstances that frequently accompany early childbearing. Compared with babies born to older mothers, babies born to adolescent mothers, particularly young adolescent mothers, are at higher risk of low birth weight and infant mortality. They are

more likely to grow up in homes that offer lower levels of emotional support and cognitive stimulation, and they are less likely to earn a high school diploma. For the mothers, giving birth during adolescence is associated with limited educational attainment, which in turn can reduce future employment prospects and earnings potential. The birth rate for young women ages 15 to 17 is one measure of adolescent childbearing.   □

Teen Birth Rates by Age, Race, and Hispanic Origin, Selected Years

Age	1980	1985	1990	1991	1992	1993	1994
All races							
10–14 years	1.1	1.2	1.4	1.4	1.4	1.4	1.4
15–19 years	53.0	51.0	59.9	62.1	60.7	59.6	58.9
White, non–Hispanic							
10–14 years	0.4	—	0.5	0.5	0.5	0.5	0.5
15–19 years	41.2	—	42.5	43.4	41.7	40.7	40.4
Black							
10–14 years	4.3	4.5	4.9	4.8	4.7	4.6	4.6
15–19 years	97.8	95.4	112.8	115.5	112.4	108.6	104.5
American Indian/ Alaskan Native							
10–14 years	1.9	1.7	1.6	1.6	1.6	1.4	1.9
15–19 years	82.2	79.2	81.9	85.0	84.4	83.1	80.8
Asian/ Pacific Islander							
10–14 years	0.3	0.4	0.7	0.8	0.7	0.6	0.7
15–19 years	26.2	23.8	26.4	27.4	26.6	27.0	27.1
Hispanic							
10–14 years	1.7	—	2.4	2.4	2.6	2.7	2.7
15–19 years	82.2	—	100.3	106.7	107.1	106.8	107.7

Source: Centers for Disease Control and Prevention, National Center for Health Statistics, National Vital Statistics System.

Child Abuse and Neglect

Research on the effects of child abuse and neglect document both immediate and long-term harm to children. In extreme cases, the physical consequence of abuse and neglect is death; in many other cases, the outcome is serious injury, permanent disability, and/or a range of social, psychological, and cognitive problems. The incidence of child abuse and neglect is very difficult to measure. Presented here is the best current estimate available, from a survey conducted in 1993. Despite the importance of consistent monitoring over time, trend data from a survey administered at frequent intervals on this subject are unavailable.

• In 1993, professionals reported approximately 1.6 million children to be victims of maltreatment, either abuse or neglect. This number is a rate of 23.1 per 1,000 children under age 18.

• Of these children, approximately 734,2000 suffered physical, sexual, or emotional abuse. This is a rate of 11.1 per 1,000 children.

• Approximately 879,000 suffered physical, emotional, or educational neglect. This is a rate of 13.1 per 1,000 (the numbers of victims of abuse and neglect overlap to some extent, since some children suffer both forms of maltreatment).

• Girls were sexually abused three times more often than boys.

• Boys were at greater risk of serious injury than girls.

• Children of single parents were at a much greater risk of abuse or neglect than were children living with both parents.

• Children from families with incomes below $15,000 were twenty-two times more likely to experience some form of maltreatment than children from families with incomes above $30,000. □

Child Abuse and Neglect

	Number	Rate (per 1,000 children)								
			Family structure			Family income (in $1,000s)			Gender	
Type of maltreatment	Total	Total	Both parents	Single parent	No parent	Under $15	$15–30	$30 or more	Male	Female
All maltreatment	1,553,800	23.1	15.5	27.3	22.9	47.0	20.0	2.1	21.7	24.5
All abuse	743,200	11.1	8.4	11.4	13.7	22.2	9.7	1.6	9.5	12.6
Physical	381,700	5.7	3.9	6.9	7.0	11.0	5.0	0.7	5.8	5.6
Sexual	217,700	3.2	2.6	2.5	6.3	7.0	2.8	0.4	1.6	4.9
Emotional	204,500	3.0	2.6	2.5	5.4	6.5	2.5	0.5	2.9	3.1
Neglect	879,000	13.1	7.9	17.3	10.3	27.2	11.3	0.6	13.3	12.9
Physical	338,900	5.0	3.1	5.8	4.3	12.0	2.9	0.3	5.5	4.5
Emotional	212,800	3.2	2.3	4.0	3.1	5.9	4.3	0.2	3.5	2.8
Educational	397,300	5.9	3.0	9.6	3.1	11.1	4.8	0.2	5.5	6.4
Severity of injury										
Fatal	—	—	0.019	0.015	0.016	0.060	0.002	0.001	0.04	0.01
Serious	—	—	5.8	10.5	8.0	17.9	7.8	0.8	9.3	7.5
Moderate	—	—	8.1	15.4	10.1	23.3	10.5	1.3	11.3	13.3
Inferred	—	—	1.6	1.4	4.8	5.7	1.6	0.1	1.1	3.8

Source: National Center on Child Abuse and Neglect, Third National Incidence Study of Child Abuse and Neglect (NIS–3).

Gender Issues

A Harsh Rite of Passage

The abolition of female genital mutilation has become a worldwide human rights cause.

In 1994, when a 17-year-old girl from Togo sought asylum in the United States to escape genital mutilation, few Americans understood the brutal nature of this ancient and widespread African ritual. Fauziya Kassindja ran away from home the day she would have been forced to have her genitals severed in preparation for an arranged marriage to an old man, becoming one of his four wives. She eventually made her way to the United States, but instead of granting her asylum, immigration officials arrested her for illegal entry and sent her to prison for a year and a half, where she was sometimes shackled and placed in solitary confinement. Although human rights advocates sought her release, the courts found her story "not credible." Only when the media exposed her plight was she freed.

Legislation and Media Awareness

Fauziya's case became a lightning rod for growing legislative and media attention, awakening the nation to a dangerous and painful practice that is the social norm for women in many central African countries. Representative Patricia Schroeder (D-Colo.), now retired, advocated banning the practice for twenty years before getting a bill through Congress, and remarked that some members of Congress simply could not believe such a practice actually existed. Senator Harry Reid (D-Nev.) fought for a ban although "all my staff advised me to stay away from it," considering it a squeamish subject for a male politician. When Stephanie Walsh was awarded the Pulitzer Prize in 1996 for her photographs of a genital mutilation rite in Kenya, the inhumanity of the procedure was exposed to the general public, helping to legitimize a subject that many found uncomfortable to discuss.

Genital mutilation, also referred to as female circumcision, genital cutting, or excision, is a coming-of-age ritual that signifies a girl's entry into womanhood. It is accompanied by public celebrations and is often a source of pride for the girl. For some it also carries religious significance. Usually performed on girls between the ages of 4 and 12, but also on teenagers, it involves the partial or total excision of the external female genitalia. It is performed by a female elder using a razor, knife, or piece of glass, usually without anesthetic, while several women hold the girl down. Agonizingly painful, it robs her of sexual pleasure and frequently causes medical problems, including hemorrhaging, infection, urinary incontinence, infertility, and complications in childbirth.

Genital mutilation is practiced in 28 countries in central Africa, ranging from Somalia in the east coast and stretching westward to Senegal on the Atlantic. The rite is believed to have originated more than two thousand years ago in Egypt or the Horn of Africa (what is now Eritrea, Djibouti, Ethiopia, and Somalia). The World Health Organization estimates that more than 130 million women have undergone the procedure. Although it is most often associated with Islam, it is also practiced by Christians, adherents to traditional African religions, and one Jewish sect.

Three Types, Varying in Severity

There are generally three different types of circumcision: clitoridectomy, the amputation of the clitoris; excision of the labia minora as well as the clitoris; and infibulation, the removal all external genitalia including the labia majora, after which the edges of the wound are stitched together, allowing for only a tiny opening. The risk of infection and problematic childbirth are naturally greatly exacerbated by infibulation, and it is estimated that 20% to 25% of sterility cases in the Sudan have resulted from the procedure. The prevalence of circumcision and the type of procedure vary enormously from country to country. According to a study by Demographic and Health Survey, 93% of women in Mali and 98% in Djibouti and Somalia undergo genital cutting, whereas in Uganda and the Congo the number drops to 5%. Clitoridectomy is the most common procedure. Infibulation accounts for about 15% of women, with an estimated 80% to 90% of all infibulations occurring in Djibouti, Somalia, and the Sudan. The only country where the genital mutilation is noticeably decreasing is the Central African Republic, where the practice was not widespread to begin with.

"We have done it, we do it, and we will continue to do it."

Genital cutting is seen as a way of ensuring that a woman is clean, chaste, and ready for marriage; uncut women are associated with promiscuity and lack of social respectability. Deadening the woman's sexual pleasure is a way of guaranteeing her virginity and fidelity. Because it is a valued social rite, most girls are willing to succumb to the pain and the subsequent health problems. But whether they wish to be excised or not, the choice is not theirs. Living in a staunchly patriarchal world, they are dependent on men for social and economic survival. As a father from the Ivory Coast told the *New York Times,* " If your daughter has not been excised. . . . No man in the village will marry her. It is an obligation. We have done it, we do it, and we will continue to do it. . . . She has no choice. I decide. Her viewpoint is not important."

Countries Practicing Genital Mutilation

Benin	Ivory Coast
Burkina Faso	Kenya
Cameroon	Liberia
Central African Republic	Mali
Chad	Mauritania
Djibouti	Niger
Egypt	Nigeria
Eritrea	Senegal
Ethiopia	Sierra Leone
Gambia	Somalia
Ghana	Sudan
Guinea	Tanzania
Guinea-Bissau	Togo
Ghana	Uganda

An Ancient Tradition Resists Reform

For the past ten to fifteen years, France has criminally prosecuted immigrant parents who have had their daughters excised, and in October 1996 the U.S. Congress outlawed female genital mutilation in this country. The U.N. announced a global campaign in 1997 to eradicate the practice, and a growing number of refugee, women's, and human rights organizations in Africa and around the world have called for its prohibition. But progress has been slow. Western reform movements are sometimes counterproductive, with Africans resisting the dictates of patronizing outsiders. Outlawing the practice had already been attempted by colonial governments in Africa during the first half of the century, provoking only resistance and protests. African governments have also been ineffective. Kenya, Sudan, Burkino Faso, the Ivory Coast, and Egypt have passed laws limiting the practice, but they are not enforced.

The World Health Organization estimates it will take a minimum of ten years to reduce the prevalence of genital mutilation, and three generations to eradicate it. It will take time to transform awareness of a firmly entrenched ritual that is valued by the local culture but considered dangerous and demeaning by outsiders. —BB　　　□

Beyond the Glass Ceiling: Pay Equity

Women may perform different jobs than men in a company, but if their jobs are equally valuable to an organization, women should be paid comparably.

Three out of four American working women, including full-time and part-time workers, are paid less than $25,000 a year. About half of all women work in traditionally female jobs, such as nursing, clerical work, childcare, cooking, cleaning, and library work, all of which are relatively low-paying. Although progress has been made in reducing the wage gap between men and women, women still earn 71 cents on average for each dollar that men earn. According to a recent Department of Labor survey, few women think that their wages reflect the real value of their work or what they need to support their families. Over a woman's lifetime, unequal pay has big consequences. It directly affects her social security or pension benefits. Women retirees receive only half the average pension received by men, in part because of their wage gap.

In April of 1997, the White House took a symbolic first step in addressing the problem of unfair pay practices in the workplace by proclaiming a "National Pay Inequity Awareness Day." President Clinton called upon employers to review their wage-setting practices and to see that their employees, particularly women and people of color, are paid fairly for their work.

In his proclamation the President stated:

'. . . unfair pay practices exist at all education levels and in every occupation. Last year, women physicians and lawyers earned substantially less than their male counterparts. The problem is particularly acute in female-dominated professions and in jobs where minority groups are disproportionately represented. Though changing technologies and a growing demand for services have made their positions increasingly vital, America's child-care providers, secretaries, textile workers, telephone operators, social workers, and maintenance people are among those who bear the greatest wage discrepancies.'

Fairness in the Workforce

Many women still work in jobs that are different from those that men do, even though the work may be of equal or equivalent value. Fair pay or pay equity means equal pay for work of equal value even when the work is different. Most Americans agree with this concept. Polls consistently show that 70% of Americans would support a law requiring the same pay for men and women in jobs requiring similar skills and responsibilities.

More progress toward fair pay has been made in the public rather than the private sector, partly because the wages and job descriptions of government employees are public information. Job evaluation studies that compare and measure actual job responsibilities can easily fit civil service systems. Also, laws governing collective bargaining and the civil service often refer to the importance of fair and equitable pay.

For nearly two decades, the state of Minnesota has led pay equity efforts in the nation. Minnesota was the first to provide pay equity for state government employees and the first to require pay equity for local government and school district employees. For some workers, it has meant the difference between being on the edge of

---

What is "Equal Value"?

The following text is excerpted from the Canadian Human Rights Commission's booklet for employers, *Equal Dollars Make Good Sense.*

Pay equity legislation defines value as a composite of four factors—skill, responsibility, effort, and working conditions. Job evaluation plans are used to determine the value of each job in a consistent, equitable manner. The principle is simple. Each job must be rated in a way which is fair, unbiased, and uniform. The content of jobs is broken down by the job evaluation plan into a standardized set of elements which fall under the four factors mentioned above. Points are awarded to jobs being evaluated, element by element, according to a standard scoring system. Evaluators must be careful not to overlook elements of work done by women that have been ignored or undervalued, in the past, elements such as manual dexterity, record-keeping, and exposure to illness.

After jobs are rated on each factor, the evaluator totals the scores. Jobs that appear quite different may still receive the same final score. Let's say, for example, that the male-dominated job of hospital research technician receives 125 points for skill, 55 for responsibility, 50 for effort, and 20 for working conditions. That job is "worth" a total of 250 points. Now let's say that the female-dominated job of nutritionist working in the same hospital receives 145 points for skill, 65 for responsibility, 30 for effort, and 10 for working conditions. Overall, it also scores 250 points. Therefore, the nutritionist should be paid the same salary as the technician.

Source: Equal Dollars Make Good Sense. Excerpted with permission of the Minister of Supply and Services, Canada, 1991.

poverty and being self-supporting. For example, a single mother earning $8,600 as a clerk/typist saw her wages rise to $23,000 and no longer had to depend on government assistance.

In another case preceding the institution of pay equity, general maintenance workers were paid more than the clerical staff, who were required to have more skills and training. When pay equity was implemented, it did not penalize the maintenance workers, and they continued to get raises. In fact, it is illegal to reduce pay for employees to remedy past imbalances.

A 1992 study of Los Angeles Children's Social Service workers (mostly women) indicated that they were getting paid 34% less than county probation officers (mostly men) even though their jobs required similar skill, effort, responsibility, and had similar working conditions. Social workers were being paid about $35,000 a year; the probation officers received $55,000. The social workers' union pushed for and was awarded a 20% wage increase.

Pay Equity is the Law

Under Title VII of the Civil Rights Act, employers who have at least 15 workers cannot:

• Pay women less for work similar to that performed by men when they share the same employer;

• Withhold training opportunities from women workers that are offered to men;

• Refuse to consider promoting women to higher paid managerial or professional positions;

• Set lower wages for "women's jobs" than for "men's jobs" that require equal skill, effort, responsibility, and working conditions because women "will work for less" or because the job market allows lower wages for women.

For More Information

In 1996, the U.S. Department of Labor Women's Bureau launched the Fair Pay Clearinghouse to provide information and resources for working women and men, employers, and other organizations concerned about fair pay. Improving pay scales is a top priority for the Bureau. —*OTJ*

Women's Bureau, U.S. Department of Labor
200 Constitution Avenue, NW
Washington, DC 20036
(800) 347-3741
www.dol.gov/dol.wb

National Committee on Pay Equity
1126 Sixteenth Street, NW
Washington, DC 20036
(202) 331-7406
www.feminist.com/fairpay.htm

Institute for Women's Policy Research
1400 20th Street, NW, Suite 104
Washington, DC 20036
(202) 785-5100
www.iwpr.org

1995 Median Annual Earnings Year-Round, Full-Time Workers

Men	$31,496
Women	$22,497
Wage gap:	71.4%

1995 Median Annual Earnings by Race and Sex

Race/Gender	Earnings	Wage Ratio
White Men	$32,172	100.0%
White Women	$22,911	71.2%
Black Men	$24,428	75.9%
Black Women	$20,665	64.2%
Hispanic Men	$20,379	63.3%
Hispanic Women	$17,178	53.4%

Gender Issues Web Sites

WWWomen: www.wwwomen.com
Women's Bureau: www.dol.gov/dol/wb/
Abortion and Reproductive Rights:
www.caral.org/abortion.html
Women's International Center: www.wic.org/
Violence Against Women: www.usdoj.vawo/
The Allan Guttmacher Institute (reproductive
health): www.agi-usa.org
National Organization for Women: www.now.org/
Independent Women's Forum: www.iwf.org
Institute for Women's Policy Research:
www.iwpr.org
National Committee on Pay Equity:
feminist.com/fairpay.htm

Women's Earnings as a Percent of Men's, 1979–1992

Year	Hourly	Weekly	Annual
1979	64.1	62.5	59.7
1980	64.8	64.4	60.2
1981	65.1	64.6	59.2
1982	67.3	65.4	61.7
1983	69.4	66.7	63.6
1984	69.8	67.8	63.7
1985	70.0	68.2	64.6
1986	70.2	69.2	64.3
1987	72.1	70.0	65.2
1988	73.8	70.2	66.0
1989	75.4	70.1	68.7
1990	76.8	71.8	71.6
1991	77.5	74.0	69.9
1992	79.4	75.4	70.6

Source: U.S. Women's Bureau.

The National Women's Hall of Fame

The National Women's Hall of Fame is the only national membership organization that honors and celebrates the achievements of American women. Founded in 1969 in Seneca Falls, New York, where in 1848 the first Women's Rights Convention was held, the Hall inducts distinguished women and offers programs and exhibits in Seneca Falls, the Finger Lakes area, Washington, D.C., and elsewhere.

Women are chosen for inclusion in the Hall of Fame on the basis of:

• The value of their contribution to society, to significant groups within society, or to the progress and freedom of women.

• Their contributions to art, athletics, business, government, philanthropy, humanities, science, and education.

• The enduring value of their achievements.

For further information, contact The National Women's Hall of Fame, 76 Fall Street, Seneca Falls, N.Y. 13148. Phone: (315) 568-8060.

Honorees

Bella Abzug	Dorothea Dix	Barbara Jordan	Wilma Rudolph
Abigail Adams	Elizabeth Hanford Dole	Helen Keller	Josephine St. Pierre Ruffin
Jane Addams	Anne Dallas Dudley	Nannerl O. Keohane	Florence Sabin
Louisa May Alcott	Amelia Earhart	Billie Jean King	Margaret Sanger
Ethel Percy Andrus	Catherine East	Maggie Kuhn	Katherine Siva Saubel
Marian Anderson	Mary Baker Eddy	Suzette La Flesche	Betty Bone Schiess
Susan B. Anthony	Marian Wright Edelman	Anne Morrow Lindbergh	Patricia Schroeder
Virginia Apgar	Gertrude Belle Elion	Belva Lockwood	Florence Seibert
Ella Baker	Alie Evans	Juliette Gordon Low	Elizabeth Seton
Ann Bancroft	Geraldine Ferraro	Mary Lyon	Muriel Siebert
Clara Barton	Ella Fitzgerald	Mary Mahoney	Bessie Smith
Mary McLeod Bethune	Betty Friedan	Wilma Mankiller	Margaret Chase Smith
Antoinette Blackwell	Margaret Fuller	Maria Goeppert Mayer	Hannah Greenebaum
Elizabeth Blackwell	Matilda Joslyn Gage	Barbara McClintock	Solomon
Emily Blackwell	Lillian Moller Gilbreth	Louise McManus	Elizabeth Cady Stanton
Amelia Bloomer	Charlotte Perkins Gilman	Margaret Mead	Gloria Steinem
Margaret Bourke-White	Ella Grasso	Maria Mitchell	Nettie Stevens
Myra Bradwell	Martha Griffiths	Constance Baker Motley	Lucy Stone
Mary Breckinridge	Mary A. Hallaren	Lucretia Mott	Harriet Beecher Stowe
Gwendolyn Brooks	Fannie Lou Hamer	Antonio Novello	Maria Tallchief
Pearl S. Buck	Alice Hamilton	Annie Oakley	Helen Brook Taussig
Charlotte Anne Bunch	Helen Hayes	Sandra Day O'Connor	Sojourner Truth
Francis Xavier Cabrini	Mary Harris, "Mother Jones"	Georgia O'Keeffe	Harriet Tubman
Annie Jump Cannon	Dorothy Height	Rosa Parks	Lillian D. Wald
Rachel Carson	Oveta Culp Hobby	Alice Paul	Madam C. J. Walker
Mary Cassatt	Wilhelmina Cole Holladay	Frances Perkins	Faye Wattleton
Willa Cather	Grace Hopper	Esther Peterson	Ida B. Wells-Barnett
Carrie Chapman Catt	Dolores Huerta	Jeannette Rankin	Edith Wharton
Shirley Chisholm	Helen Hunt	Ellen Swallow Richards	Oprah Winfrey
Jacqueline Cochran	Zora Neale Hurston	Linda Richards	Sarah Winnemucca
Eileen Collins	Anne Hutchinson	Sally Ride	Fanny Wright
Ruth Colvin	Mary Jacobi	Eleanor Roosevelt	Rosalyn Yalow
Jane Cunningham Croly	Frances Wisebart Jacobs	Ernestine Potowski Rose	Gloria Yerkovich
Emily Dickinson	Mae Jemison	Sister Elaine Roulet	"Babe" Didrikson Zaharias

Societal Attitudes About Rape

Teenagers

In a survey of high school students, 56% of girls and 76% of the boys believed forced sex was acceptable under some circumstances.

A survey of 11-to-14 year-olds found:

51% of the boys and 41% of the girls said forced sex was acceptable if the boy "spent a lot of money" on the girl;

31% of the boys and 32% of the girls said it was acceptable for a man to rape a woman with past sexual experience;

87% of the boys and 79% of the girls said sexual assault was acceptable if the man and woman were married;

65% of the boys and 47% of the girls said it was acceptable for a boy to rape a girl if they had been dating for more than six months.

College Students

A survey of 6,159 college students enrolled at 32 institutions in the U.S. found:

54% of the women surveyed had been victims of some form of sexual abuse;

More than one in four college-aged women had been the victim of rape or attempted rape;

57% of the assaults occurred on dates;

42% of the victims told no one.

In a survey of male college students, 35% anonymously admitted that, under certain circumstances, they would commit rape if they believed they could get away with it.

One in 12 admitted to committing acts that met the legal definitions of rape, and 84% of men who committed rape did not label it as rape.

In another survey of college males, 43% admitted to using coercive behavior to have sex, including ignoring a woman's protest, using physical aggression, and forcing intercourse.

15% acknowledged that they had committed acquaintance rape, and 11% acknowledged using physical restraints to force a woman to have sex.

Source: The American Medical Association (AMA).

Race and Ethnicity

The Tuskegee Syphilis Experiment

> The United States government did something that was wrong—deeply, profoundly, morally wrong. It was an outrage to our commitment to integrity and equality for all our citizens. . . . clearly racist.
>
> —President Clinton's apology for the Tuskegee Syphilis Experiment to the eight remaining survivors, May 16, 1997

For forty years between 1932 and 1972, the U.S. Public Health Service (PHS) conducted an experiment on 399 black men in the late stages of syphilis. These men, for the most part illiterate sharecroppers from one of the poorest counties in Alabama, were never told what disease they were suffering from or of its seriousness. Informed that they were being treated for "bad blood,"[1] their doctors had no intention of curing them of syphilis at all. The data for the experiment was to be collected from autopsies of the men, and they were thus deliberately left to degenerate under the ravages of tertiary syphilis—which can include tumors, heart disease, paralysis, blindness, insanity, and death. "As I see it," one of the doctors involved explained, "we have no further interest in these patients until they die."

Using Human Beings as Laboratory Animals

The true nature of the experiment had to be kept from the subjects to ensure their cooperation. The sharecroppers' grossly disadvantaged lot in life made them easy to manipulate. Pleased at the prospect of free medical care—almost none of them had ever seen a doctor before—these unsophisticated and trusting men became the pawns in what James Jones, author of the excellent history on the subject, *Bad Blood,* identified as "the longest nontherapeutic experiment on human beings in medical history."

The study was meant to discover how syphilis affected blacks as opposed to whites—the theory being that whites experienced more neurological complications from syphilis whereas blacks were more susceptible to cardiovascular damage. How this knowledge would have changed clinical treatment of syphilis is uncertain. Although the PHS touted the study as one of great scientific merit, from the outset its actual benefits were hazy. It took almost forty years before someone involved in the study took a hard and honest look at the end results, reporting that "nothing learned will prevent, find, or cure a single case of infectious syphilis or bring us closer to our basic mission of controlling venereal disease in the United States." When the experiment was was brought to the attention of the media in 1972, news anchor Harry Reasoner described it as an experiment that "used human beings as laboratory animals in a long and inefficient study of how long it takes syphilis to kill someone."

A Heavy Price in the Name of Bad Science

By the end of the experiment, 28 of the men had died directly of syphilis, 100 were dead of related complications, 40 of their wives had been infected, and 19 of their children had been born with congenital syphilis. How had these men been induced to endure a fatal disease in the name of science? To persuade the community to support the experiment, one of the original doctors admitted it "was necessary to carry on this study under the guise of a demonstration and provide treatment." At first, the men were prescribed the syphilis remedies of the day—bismuth, neoarsphenamine, and mercury—but in such small amounts that only 3 percent showed any improvement. These token doses of medicine were good public relations and did not interfere with the true aims of the study. Eventually, all syphilis treatment was replaced with "pink medicine"—aspirin. To ensure that the men would show up for a painful and potentially dangerous spinal tap, the PHS doctors misled them with a letter full of promotional hype: "Last Chance for Special Free Treatment." The fact that autopsies would eventually be required was also concealed. As a doctor explained, "If the colored population becomes aware that accepting free hospital care means a post-mortem, every darky will leave Macon County. . . " Even the Surgeon General of the United States participated in enticing the men to remain in the experiment, sending them certificates of appreciation after 25 years in the study.

Following Doctors' Orders

It takes little imagination to ascribe racist attitudes to the white government officials who ran the experiment, but what can one make of the numerous African Americans who collaborated with them? The experiment's name comes from the Tuskegee Institute, the black university founded by Booker T. Washington. Its affiliated hospital lent the PHS its medical facilities for the study, and other predominantly black institutions as well as local black doctors also participated. A black nurse, Eunice Rivers, was a central figure in the experiment for most of its forty years. The promise of recognition by a prestigious government agency may have obscured the troubling aspects of the study for some. A Tuskegee doctor, for example, praised "the educational advantages offered our interns and nurses as well as the added standing it will give the hospital." Nurse Rivers explained her role as one of passive obedience: "we were taught that we never diagnosed, we never prescribed; we followed the doctor's instructions!" It is clear that the men in the experiment trusted her and that she sincerely cared about their well-being, but her unquestioning submission to authority eclipsed her moral judgment. Even after the experiment was exposed to public scrutiny, she genuinely felt nothing ethical had been amiss.

One of the most chilling aspects of the experiment was how zealously the PHS kept these men from receiving treatment. When several nationwide campaigns to eradicate venereal disease came to Macon County, the men were prevented from participating. Even when penicillin was discovered in the 1940s—the first real cure for syphilis—the Tuskegee men were deliberately denied the medication. During World War II, 250 of the men registered for the draft and were consequently ordered to get treatment for syphilis, only to have the PHS exempt them. Pleased at their success, the PHS representative announced: "So far, we are keeping the known positive patients from getting treatment." The experiment continued in spite of the Henderson Act (1943), a public health law requiring testing and treatment for venereal disease, and in spite of the World Health Organization's Declaration of Helsinki (1964), which specified that "informed consent" was needed for experiment involving human beings.

Blowing the Whistle

The story finally broke in the *Washington Star* on July 25, 1972, in an article by Jean Heller of the Associated Press. Her source was Peter Buxtun, a former PHS venereal disease interviewer and one of the few whistle blowers over the years. The PHS, however, remained unrepentant, claiming the men had been "volunteers" and "were always happy to see the doctors," and an Alabama state health officer who had been involved claimed "somebody is trying to make a mountain out of a molehill."

Under the glare of publicity, the government ended their experiment, and for the first time provided the men with effective medical treatment for syphilis. Fred Gray, a lawyer who had previously defended Rosa Parks and Martin Luther King, filed a class action suit that provided a $10 million out-of-court settlement for the men and their families. Gray, however, named only whites and white organizations in the suit, portraying Tuskegee as a black and white case when it was in fact more complex than that—black doctors and institutions had been involved from beginning to end.

The PHS did not accept the media's comparison of Tuskegee with the appalling experiments performed by Nazi doctors on their Jewish victims during World War II. Yet in addition to the medical and racist parallels, the PHS offered the same morally bankrupt defense offered at the Nuremberg trials: they claimed they were just carrying out orders, mere cogs in the wheel of the PHS bureaucracy, exempt from personal responsibility.

The study's other justification—for the greater good of science—is equally spurious. Scientific protocol had been shoddy from the start. Since the men had in fact received some medication for syphilis in the beginning of the study, however inadequate, it thereby corrupted the outcome of a study of "untreated syphilis."

In 1990, a survey found that 10 percent of African Americans believed that the U.S. government created AIDS as a plot to exterminate blacks, and another 20 percent could not rule out the possibility that this might be true. As preposterous and paranoid as this may sound, at one time the Tuskegee experiment must have seemed equally farfetched. Who could imagine the government, all the way up to the Surgeon General of the United States, deliberately allowing a group of its citizens to die from a terrible disease for the sake of an ill-conceived experiment? In light of this and many other shameful episodes in our history, African Americans' widespread mistrust of the government and white society in general should not be a surprise to anyone. —*BB* ☐

1. All quotations in the article are from *Bad Blood: The Tuskegee Syphilis Experiment*, James H. Jones, expanded edition (New York: Free Press, 1993).

Interracial Married Couples: 1960 to the Present

(Includes all interracial married couples with at least one spouse of white or black race.)

		Interracial married couples					
			Black/white				
Year	Total married couples	Total	Total	Black husband, white wife	White husband, black wife	White/ other race*	Black/ other race*
1960	40,491,000	149,000	51,000	25,000	26,000	90,000	7,000
1970	44,598,000	310,000	65,000	41,000	24,000	233,000	12,000
1980	49,514,000	953,000	121,000	94,000	27,000	785,000	47,000
1990	51,718,000	1,461,000	213,000	159,000	54,000	1,173,000	75,000
1995	54,937,000	1,392,000	328,000	206,000	122,000	988,000	76,000

*"Other race," is any race other than white or black, such as American Indian, Japanese, Chinese, etc. *Source:* U. S. Bureau of the Census, Current Population Reports, Series, "Household and Family Characteristics: March 1994," and earlier reports.

Ancestry of U.S. Population by Rank, 1990 Census

(Over one million)

1990 Rank	Ancestry group	Number	Percent	1990 Rank	Ancestry group	Number	Percent
	Total population	248,709,873	100.0	13	Scottish	5,393,581	2.2
1	German	57,947,873	23.3	14	Swedish	4,680,863	1.9
2	Irish	38,735,539	15.6	15	Norwegian	3,869,395	1.6
3	English	32,651,788	13.1	16	Russian	2,952,987	1.2
4	African American	23,777,098	9.6	17	French Canadian	2,167,127	0.9
5	Italian	14,664,550	5.9	18	Welsh	2,033,893	0.8
6	American	12,395,999	5.0	19	Spanish	2,024,004	0.8
7	Mexican	11,586,983	4.7	20	Puerto Rican	1,955,323	0.8
8	French	10,320,935	4.1	21	Slovak	1,882,897	0.8
9	Polish	9,366,106	3.8	22	White	1,799,711	0.7
10	American Indian	8,708,220	3.5	23	Danish	1,634,669	0.7
11	Dutch	6,227,089	2.5	24	Hungarian	1,582,302	0.6
12	Scotch-Irish	5,617,773	2.3	25	Chinese	1,505,245	0.6

1990 Rank	Ancestry group	Number	Percent	1990 Rank	Ancestry group	Number	Percent
26	Filipino	1,450,512	0.6	30	Hispanic	1,113,259	0.4
27	Czech	1,296,411	0.5	31	Greek	1,110,373	0.4
28	Portuguese	1,153,351	0.5	32	Swiss	1,045,495	0.4
29	British	1,119,154	0.4	33	Japanese	1,004,645	0.4

Note: Data are based on a sample and subject to sampling variability. Since persons who reported multiple ancestries were included in more than one group, the sum of the persons reporting the ancestry is greater than the total; for example, a person reporting "English-French" was tabulated in both the "English" and "French" categories. Ancestry groups with fewer than 2,000 persons were not included in this report. *Source:* U.S. Bureau of the Census, 1993.

Ethnic Concentrations in the U.S.

Ancestry groups show striking differences in where they choose to settle in the United States. These differences often reflect initial settlement patterns, especially for the newer immigrant groups. Of the largest European ancestries, French, Scottish, and Welsh are distributed fairly evenly throughout the country. Other large European groups were more concentrated. For example, more than half of the nation's Italians live in the Northeast, and over half of the Norwegians and Czechs were clustered in the Midwest. About 47 percent of the Scotch-Irish were concentrated in the South, while 45 percent of the Danish lived in the West.

The regional concentration of persons of Hispanic ancestry depended on their specific country of origin. For instance, the Northeast contained 86 percent of the country's Dominicans, 66 percent of Puerto Ricans, and 63 percent of Ecuadorians. The South was home to 69 percent of Cubans and 51 percent of Nicaraguans. About 62 percent of Salvadorans and Guatemalans and 57 percent of Mexicans lived in the West.

Persons of West Indian ancestry were concentrated in the Northeast: 59 percent of the nation's Jamaicans and 55 percent of Haitians live there.

Among the larger Southwest Asian ancestry groups, over half of the Armenians and Iranians resided in the West, and 43 percent of the Syrians lived in the Northeast.

People of Asian and Pacific Islander ancestry are found largely in the West. The West is home to 87 percent of the country's Hawaiians, 72 percent of Japanese, 59 percent of Cambodians, and 55 percent of Chinese and Vietnamese.

California—the perennial destination of many migrants—had the largest number of persons of German, Irish, English, African American, Mexican, French, American Indian, Dutch Scotch-Irish, Scottish, and Swedish ancestry of any state, according to the 1990 census. New York—the traditional port of entry for large numbers of immigrant—had more Italians and Polish than any other state, and Minnesota ranked first for Norwegians.

About 5 percent of respondents to the 1990 census reported their ancestry as "American." Texas had the largest number of persons who considered this to be their ethnic identity.

Population, by Selected Ancestry Group and Region: 1990

Ancestry Group	Total	North-east	Mid-west	South	West
European:					
Austrian	865,000	38	21	19	22
British	1,119,000	17	18	39	26
Croatian	544,000	21	43	20	16
Czech	1,296,000	10	52	22	16
Danish	1,635,000	9	34	12	45
Dutch	6,227,000	16	34	29	21
English	32,652,000	18	22	35	25
European	467,000	14	17	31	39
Finnish	659,000	14	47	11	27
French	10,321,000	26	26	29	20
German	57,947,000	17	39	25	19
Greek	1,110,000	37	23	21	19
Hungarian	1,582,000	36	32	17	16
Irish	38,736,000	24	25	33	17
Italian	14,665,000	51	17	17	15
Lithuanian	812,000	43	28	16	13
Norwegian	3,869,000	6	52	10	33
Polish	9,366,000	37	37	15	11
Portuguese	1,153,000	49	3	8	41
Russian	2,953,000	44	16	18	22
Scandinavian	679,000	8	33	15	45
Scotch-Irish	5,618,000	14	19	47	20
Scottish	5,394,000	20	21	33	26

Ancestry Group	Total	North-east	Mid-west	South	West
Slovak	1,883,000	40	34	14	11
Swedish	4,681,000	14	40	14	32
Swiss	1,045,000	16	36	17	30
Ukrainian	741,000	51	22	14	13
Welsh	2,034,000	22	24	27	27
Yugoslavian	258,000	23	28	12	37
Central and South America and Spain:					
Cuban	860,000	18	3	69	9
Dominican	506,000	86	1	10	2
Hispanic	1,113,000	13	6	31	50
Mexican	11,587,000	1	9	33	57
Puerto Rican	1,955,000	66	11	15	8
Salvadoran	499,000	13	2	23	62
Spanish	2,024,000	16	8	30	45
West Indian:					
Jamaican	435,000	59	5	31	6
Asia:					
Asian Indian	570,000	32	19	26	24
Chinese	1,505,000	25	8	12	55
Filipino	1,451,000	10	9	13	68
Japanese	1,005,000	9	8	11	72
Korean	837,000	22	14	20	44
Vietnamese	536,000	9	8	28	54

Source: U.S. Bureau of the Census, 1990. (As of April 1. Covers persons who reported single and multiple ancestry groups. Persons who reported multiple ancestry group may be included in more than one category. Major classifications of ancestry groups do not represent strict geographic or cultural definitions.)

For more information on race and ethnicity, *see* U.S. Statistics.

Drug Use and Abuse

Drug Use, by Type of Drug and Age Group: 1974 to 1994

Age and Type of Drug	Ever Used			Current User		
	1974	1985	1994	1974	1985	1994
12 to 17 years old						
Marijuana	23.0	23.2	16.0	12.0	11.9	7.3
Cocaine	3.6	4.8	1.3	1.0	1.4	0.4
Hallucinogens	6.0	3.2	4.0	1.3	1.2	1.2
Heroin	.0	0.4	0.4	(B)	0.1	(B)
Alcohol	54.0	55.4	41.2	34.0	31.0	16.3
Cigarettes	52.0	45.3	33.5	25.0	15.3	9.8
18 to 25 years old						
Marijuana	52.7	59.4	43.4	25.2	21.9	12.2
Cocaine	12.7	24.4	9.6	3.1	7.5	1.0
Hallucinogens	16.6	11.6	11.7	2.5	1.8	1.5
Heroin	4.5	1.3	0.2	(B)	0.3	0.1
Alcohol	81.6	92.0	86.8	69.3	70.7	63.8
Cigarettes	68.8	75.2	68.6	48.8	36.6	26.5
26 years old and over						
Marijuana	9.9	26.6	35.0	2.0	6.0	3.0
Cocaine	0.9	9.2	10.9	(B)	1.9	0.6
Hallucinogens	1.3	6.0	8.0	(B)	(B)	—
Heroin	0.5	1.1	1.3	(B)	(B)	(B)
Alcohol	73.2	89.2	91.0	54.5	59.8	55.6
Cigarettes	65.4	80.6	76.8	39.1	32.7	24.7

B = Base too small to meet statistical standards for reliability of a derived figure. *Source:* U.S. Substance Abuse and Mental Health Services Administration, *National Household Survey on Drug Abuse,* annual.

Commonly Abused Drugs

Narcotics of Natural Origin

Opium

There were no legal restrictions on the importation or use of opium until the early 1900s. In those days, patent medicines often contained opium without any warning label. Today, there are state, federal, and international laws governing the production and distribution of narcotics substances, and there is little abuse of opium in the United States.

Although a small amount of opium is used to make antidiarrheal preparations, such as paregoric, virtually all the opium imported into this country is broken down into its alkaloid constituents, principally morphine and codeine.

Morphine

The principal constituent of opium, ranging in concentration from 4 to 21 percent, morphine is one of the most effective drugs known for the relief of pain. It is marketed in the form of white crystals, hypodermic tablets, and injectable preparations. Its licit use is restricted primarily to hospitals. Morphine is odorless, tastes bitter, and darkens with age. It may be administered subcutaneously, intramuscularly, or intravenously, the latter method being the one most frequently resorted to by addicts.

Codeine

This alkaloid is found in raw opium in concentrations ranging from 0.7 to 2.5 percent. It was first isolated in 1832 as an impurity in a batch of morphine. Although it occurs naturally, most codeine is produced from morphine.

Semi-Synthetic Narcotics

Heroin

First synthesized from morphine in 1874, heroin was not extensively used in medicine until the beginning of this century. While it received widespread acceptance, the medical profession for years remained unaware of its potential for addiction. The first comprehensive control of heroin in the United States was established with the Harrison Narcotic Act of 1914.

Pure heroin is a white powder with a bitter taste. Illicit heroin may vary in both form and color. Most illicit heroin is a powder which may vary in color from white to dark brown because of impurities left from the manufacturing process or the presence of additives, such as food coloring, cocoa, or brown sugar.

Pure heroin is rarely sold on the street. A "bag"—slang for a single dosage unit of heroin—may weigh about 100 mg, usually containing about five percent heroin. To increase the bulk of the material sold to the addict, diluents are mixed with the heroin in ratios ranging from 9 to 1 to as much as 99 to 1. Sugars, starch, powdered milk, and quinine are among the diluents used.

Hydromorphone

Most commonly sold as Dilaudid, hydromorphone is the second oldest semi-synthetic narcotic analgesic. Marketed both in tablet and injectable form, it is shorter acting and more sedating than morphine, but its potency is from two to eight times as great. It is, therefore, a highly abusable drug, much sought after by narcotic addicts, who usually obtain it through fraudulent prescription or theft.

376

Oxycodone

Oxycodone is synthesized from thebaine. It is similar to codeine, but more potent and with a higher dependence potential. It is effective orally and is marketed in combination with aspirin as Percodan for the relief of pain. Addicts take Percodan orally or dissolve tablets in water, filter out the insoluble material, and "mainline" the active drug.

Synthetic Narcotics

In contrast to pharmaceutical products derived directly or indirectly from narcotics of natural origin, synthetic narcotics are produced entirely within the laboratory. A continuing search for a product that will retain the analgesic properties of morphine without the consequent dangers of tolerance and dependence has yet to yield a drug that is not susceptible to abuse. The two that are most widely available are meperidine and methadone.

Meperidine (Pethidine)

The first synthetic narcotic, meperidine, is chemically dissimilar to morphine but resembles it in its analgesic effect. It is probably the most widely used drug for the relief of moderate to severe pain. Available in pure form as well as in products containing other medicinal ingredients, it is administered either orally or by injection, the latter method being the most widely abused. Tolerance and dependence develop with chronic use, and large doses can result in convulsions or death.

Methadone

German scientists synthesized methadone during World War II because of a shortage of morphine. Although chemically unlike morphine or heroin, it produces many of the same effects. Introduced into the United States in 1947, it became widely used in the 1960s in the treatment of narcotic addicts. The effects of methadone differ from morphine-based drugs in that they have a longer duration of action, lasting up to 24 hours, thereby permitting administration only once a day in heroin detoxification and maintenance programs. Moreover, methadone is almost as effective when administered orally as it is by injection. But tolerance and dependence may develop, and withdrawal symptoms, though they develop more slowly and are less severe, are more prolonged. Ironically, methadone, designed to control narcotic addiction, has emerged in some metropolitan areas as a major cause of overdose deaths.

Depressants

Depressants have a potential for abuse associated with both physical and psychological dependence. Taken as prescribed by a physician, depressants may be beneficial for the relief of anxiety, irritability, and tension, and for the symptomatic treatment of insomnia. In excessive amounts, however, they produce a state of intoxication that is remarkably similar to that of alcohol.

Tolerance to the intoxicating effects develops rapidly, leading to a progressive narrowing of the margin of safety between an intoxicating and lethal dose. The person who is unaware of the dangers of increasing dependence will often increase the daily dose up to 10 or 20 times the recommended therapeutic level. The source of supply may be no farther than the family medicine cabinet. Depressants are also frequently obtained by theft, illegal prescription, or purchase on the illicit market.

In the world of illicit drug use, depressants often are used as self-medication to soothe jangled nerves brought on by the use of stimulants, to quell the anxiety of "flashbacks" resulting from prior use of hallucinogens, or to ease withdrawal from heroin. The dangers, it should be stressed, are compounded when depressants are used in combination with alcohol or other drugs. Chronic intoxication, though it affects every age group, is not common in middle age. The problem often remains unrecognized until the user exhibits recurrent confusion or an obvious inability to function.

Barbiturates

Among the drugs most frequently prescribed to induce sedation and sleep by both physicians and veterinarians are the barbiturates. About 2,500 derivatives of barbituric acid have been synthesized, but of these only about 15 remain in medical use. Small therapeutic doses tend to calm nervous conditions, and larger dozes cause sleep 20 to 60 minutes after oral administration. As in the case of alcohol, some individuals may experience a sense of excitement before sedation takes effect. If dosage is increased, however, the effects of the barbiturates may progress through successive stages of sedation, sleep, and coma to death from respiratory arrest and cardiovascular complications.

Stimulants

Cocaine

The most potent stimulant of natural origin, cocaine is extracted from the leaves of the coca plant (Erythroxylon coca), which has been grown in the Andean highlands of South America since prehistoric times. The leaves of the plant are chewed in the region for refreshment and relief from fatigue.

Pure cocaine, the principal psychoactive ingredient, was first isolated in the 1880s. It was used as an anesthetic in eye surgery for which no previously known drug had been suitable. It became particularly useful in surgery of the nose and throat because of its ability to anesthetize tissue while simultaneously constricting blood vessels and limiting bleeding. Many of its therapeutic applications are now obsolete because of the development of safer drugs as local anesthetics.

Illicit cocaine is usually distributed as a white crystalline powder, often diluted by a variety of other ingredients, the most common of which are sugars such as lactose, inositol, mannitol, and local anesthetics such as lidocaine. The frequent adulteration is to increase volume and thus to multiply profits.

The drug is most commonly administered by being "snorted" through the nasal passages. Symptoms of repeated use in this manner may resemble the congested nose of a common cold.

The intensity of the psychological effects of cocaine, as with many psychoactive drugs, depends on the rate of entry into the blood. Intravenous injection or smoking produces an almost immediate intense experience. Cocaine hydrochloride, the usual form in which cocaine is sold, while soluble in water and sometimes injected, is fairly insensitive to heat. Conversion of cocaine hydrochloride to cocaine base yields a substance that will become volatile when heated. "Crack," or cocaine base in the form of chips, chunks or "rocks," is usually vaporized in a pipe or smoked with plant material in a cigarette or a "joint." Inhalation of the cocaine fumes produces effects that are very fast in onset, very intense, and are quickly over. These intense effects are often followed within minutes by a dysphoric "crash," leading to frequently repeated doses and rapid addiction.

Excessive doses of cocaine may cause seizures and death from, for example, respiratory failure, stroke, cerebral hemorrhage, or heart failure. There is no specific treatment for cocaine overdose. Nor does tolerance develop to the toxic effects of cocaine. In fact, there are studies which indicate that repeated use lowers the dose at which toxicity occurs. There is no "safe" dose of cocaine.

Amphetamines

Amphetamine, dextroamphetamine, and methamphetamine are so similar in the effects they induce that they can be differentiated from one another only by laboratory analysis. Amphetamine was first used clinically in the mid-1930s to treat narcolepsy, a rare disorder resulting in an uncontrollable tendency to sleep. After the introduction of the amphetamines into medical practice, the number of conditions for which they were prescribed multiplied, as did the quantities made available.

For a time, they were sold without prescription in inhalers and other over-the-counter preparations. Abuse became popular. Many segments of the population, especially those concerned with extensive or irregular hours, were among those who used amphetamines orally in excessive amounts. "Speed freaks," who injected amphetamines, became known for their bizarre and often violent behavior. Over-the-counter availability (except inhalers) was terminated and amphetamines now are available only by prescription. Inhalers still are available over-the-counter.

Their illicit use closely parallels that of cocaine in the range of its short-term and long-term effects. Despite broad recognition of the risks, clandestine laboratories produce vast quantities of amphetamines, particularly methamphetamine, for distribution on the illicit market.

Methamphetamine Abusers

Abuse patterns suggest an estimated two- to four-year latency period from first use to full addiction. Most treatment clients interviewed initiated use by intranasal snorting, but then turned to intravenous (IV) administration. Compulsive abuse accelerates with IV use because of the drug's rapid onset of action in a pattern similar to crack cocaine abuse. Although crack is not injected, inhalation of its vapors provides a rapid pulmonary delivery of the drug in concentrated dose to the brain promoting an intensified onset of action. This method, like IV methamphetamine use, triggers an initial, short-term jolt which compels the user to repeat drug use again and again in a futile attempt to re-experience the drug's exhilarating effects.

Cannabis

Cannabis sativa L., the hemp plant, grows wild throughout most of the tropic and temperate regions of the world. It is a single species. This plant has long been cultivated for the tough fiber of the stem, the seed used in feed mixtures, and the oil as an ingredient of paint, as well as for its biologically active substances, most highly concentrated in the leaves and resinous flowering tops.

The plant material has been used as a drug for centuries. In 1839, it entered the annals of western medicine with the publication of an article surveying its therapeutic potential, including possible uses as an analgesic and anticonvulsant agent. It was alleged to be effective in treating a wide range of physical and mental ailments during the remainder of the 19th century. With the introduction of many new synthetic drugs in the 20th century, interest in it as a medication waned.

The controls imposed with the passage of the Marihuana Tax Act of 1937 further curtailed its use in treatment, and by 1941 it had been deleted from the *U.S. Pharmacopeia* and the *National Formulary,* the official compendia of drugs.

Cannabis products are usually smoked in the form of loosely rolled cigarettes ("joints"). They may be used alone or in combination with other substances. They may also be administered orally, but are reported to be about three times more potent when smoked. The effects are felt within minutes, reach their peak in 10 to 30 minutes, and may linger for 2 or 3 hours.

A condensed description of these effects is apt to be inadequate or even misleading. So much depends upon the experience and expectations of the individual as well as the activity of the drug itself. Low doses tend to induce restlessness and an increasing sense of wellbeing, followed by a dreamy state of relaxation, and frequently hunger, especially a craving for sweets. Changes of sensory perception—a more vivid sense of sight, smell, touch, taste, and hearing—may be accompanied by subtle alterations in thought formation and expression. Stronger doses intensify reactions. The individual may experience shifting sensory imagery, rapidly fluctuating emotions, a flight of fragmentary thoughts with disturbed associations, an altered sense of self-identity, impaired memory, and a dulling of attention despite an illusion of heightened insight. This state of intoxication may not be noticeable to an observer. High doses may result in image distortion, a loss of personal identity, and fantasies and hallucination. Very high doses may result in a toxic psychosis.

Marijuana

The term marijuana is used in this country to refer to the cannabis plant and to any part or extract of it that produces somatic or psychic changes in humans. A tobacco-like substance produced by drying the leaves and flowering tops of the plant, marijuana varies significantly in its potency, depending on the source and selectivity of plant materials used.

Marijuana use by adolescents has continued to rise in recent years after many years of decline. The resurgence is due in part to "inter-generational forgetting"—meaning that new generations fail to learn the same dangers about drugs that former generations knew.

Hallucinogens

Hallucinogenic drugs, both natural and synthetic, are substances that distort the perception of objective reality. They induce a state of excitation of the central nervous system, manifested by alterations of mood, usually euphoric, but sometimes severely depressive. Under the influence of hallucinogens, the senses of direction, distance, and time become disoriented. A user may speak of "seeing" sounds and "hearing" colors. If taken in a large enough dose, the drug produces delusions and visual hallucinations. Occasionally, depersonalization and depression are so severe that suicide is possible, but the most common danger is impaired judgment, leading to rash decisions and accidents. Persons in hallucinogenic states should, therefore, be closely supervised and upset as little as possible to keep them from harming themselves and others. Acute anxiety, restlessness, and sleeplessness are common until the drug wears off.

Long after hallucinogens are eliminated from the body, users may experience flashbacks—fragmentary recurrences of psychedelic effects—such as the intensification of a perceived color, the apparent motion of a fixed object, or the mistaking of one object for another. Recurrent use produces tolerance, which tends to encourage resorting to greater amounts. Although no evidence of physical dependence is detectable when the drugs are withdrawn, recurrent use tends to produce psychic dependence, varying according to the drug, the dose, and the individual user. It should be stressed that the hallucinogens are unpredictable in their effects each time they are used.

LSD (LSD-25, lysergide)

LSD is an abbreviation of the German expression for lysergic acid diethylamide. It is produced from lysergic acid, a substance derived from the ergot fungus which grows on rye or from lysergic acid amide, a chemical found in morning glory seeds.

LSD was first synthesized in 1938. Its psychotomimetic effects were discovered in 1943 when a chemist accidentally took some LSD. As he began to experience the effects now known as a "trip," he was aware of vertigo and an intensification of light. Closing his eyes, he saw a stream of fantastic images of extraordinary vividness accompanied by a kaleidoscopic play of colors. This condition lasted for about two hours.

Because of the extremely high potency of LSD, its structural relationship to a chemical which is present in the brain, and its similarity in effects to certain aspects of psychosis, LSD was used as a tool of research to study the mechanism of mental illness.

LSD is usually sold in the form of tablets, thin squares of gelatin ("window panes"), or impregnated paper ("blotter acid"). The average effective oral dose is from 30 to 50 micrograms, but the amount per dosage unit varies greatly. The effects of higher doses persist for 10 to 12 hours. Tolerance develops rapidly.

Phencyclidine (PCP)

PCP is sold under at least 50 other names, including Angel Dust, Crystal, Supergrass, Killer Weed, Embalming Fluid, and Rocket Fuel, that reflect the range of its bizarre and volatile effects. It is also frequently misrepresented as mescaline, LSD, or THC. In its pure form, it is a white crystalline powder that readily dissolves in water. Most PCP now contains contaminants resulting from its makeshift manufacture, causing the color to range from tan to brown and the consistency from a powder to a gummy mass. Although sold in tablets and capsules, as well as in powder and liquid form, it is commonly applied to a leafy material, such as parsley, mint, oregano, or marijuana, and smoked.

The drug is as variable in its effects as it is in its appearance. A moderate amount often produces in the user a sense of detachment, distance, and estrangement from the surroundings. Numbness, slurred or blocked speech, and a loss of coordination may be accompanied by a sense of strength and invulnerability. A blank stare, rapid and involuntary eye movements, and an exaggerated gait are among the more common observable effects. Auditory hallucinations, image distortion as in a fun-house mirror, and severe mood disorders may also occur, producing in some acute anxiety and a feeling of impending doom, in others paranoia and violent hostility. PCP is unique among popular drugs of abuse in its power to produce psychoses indistinguishable from schizophrenia.

Smoking-Related Mortality

Cigarette smoking is the single most preventable cause of premature death in the United States. Each year, more than 400,000 Americans die from cigarette smoking. In fact, one in every five deaths in the United States is smoking related.

• About 10 million people in the United States have died from causes attributed to smoking (including heart disease, emphysema, and other respiratory diseases) since the first Surgeon General's report on smoking and health in 1964—2 million of these deaths were the result of lung cancer alone.

• Between 1960 and 1990, deaths from lung cancer among women have increased by more than 400%—exceeding breast cancer deaths in the mid-1980s. The American Cancer Society estimated that in 1994, 64,300 women died from lung cancer and 44,300 died from breast cancer.

• Men who smoke increase their risk of death from lung cancer by more than 22 times and from bronchitis and emphysema by nearly 10 times. Women who smoke increase their risk of dying from lung cancer by nearly 12 times and the risk of dying from bronchitis and emphysema by more than 10 times. Smoking triples the risk of dying from heart disease among middle-aged men and women.

• On average, smokers die nearly seven years earlier than nonsmokers.

• Annually, exposure to secondhand smoke (or environmental tobacco smoke) causes an estimated 3,000 deaths from lung cancer among American adults. Scientific studies also link secondhand smoke with heart disease.

• Approximately 80% of adult smokers started smoking before the age of 18. Every day, nearly 3,000 young people under the age of 18 become regular smokers.

Smoking Prevalence Among U.S. Adults, 1955–1994

(As a percent of population, 18 years of age and older)

Year	Overall Population	Males	Females	Whites	Blacks
1955	—	56.9	28.4	—	—
1965	42.4	51.9	33.9	42.1	45.8
1966	42.6	52.5	33.9	42.4	45.9
1970	37.4	44.1	31.5	37.0	41.4
1974	37.1	43.1	32.1	36.4	44.0
1978	34.1	38.1	30.7	33.9	37.7
1979	33.5	37.5	29.9	33.3	36.9
1980	33.2	37.6	29.3	32.9	36.9
1983	32.1	35.1	29.5	31.8	35.9
1985	30.1	32.6	27.9	29.6	34.9
1987	28.8	31.2	26.5	28.5	32.9
1988	28.1	30.8	25.7	27.8	31.7
1990	25.5	28.4	22.8	25.6	26.2
1991	25.7	28.1	23.5	25.5	29.1
1992	26.5	28.6	24.6	26.6	27.8
1993	25.0	27.7	22.5	24.9	26.1
1994	25.5	28.2	23.1	26.3	27.2

Source: Office on Smoking and Health, Centers for Disease Control and Prevention.

Alcoholism

A Widespread Problem

Currently, nearly 14 million Americans—1 in every 13 adults-abuse alcohol or are alcoholic. Several million more adults engage in risky drinking patterns that could lead to alcohol problems. In addition, approximately 53 percent of men and women in the United States report that one or more of their close relatives have a drinking problem.

What Is Alcoholism?

Alcoholism is a disease that is characterized by the following:
• Craving: A strong need, or compulsion, to drink.
• Loss of control: The frequent inability to stop drinking once a person has begun.
• Physical dependence: The occurrence of withdrawal symptoms, such as nausea, sweating, shakiness, and anxiety, when alcohol use is stopped after a period of heavy drinking. These symptoms are usually relieved by drinking alcohol or by taking another sedative drug.
• Tolerance: The need for increasing amounts of alcohol in order to get "high."

Alcoholism has little to do with what kind of alcohol one drinks, how long one has been drinking, or even exactly how much alcohol one consumes. But it has a great deal to do with a person's uncontrollable need for alcohol. This description of alcoholism helps us understand why most alcoholics can't just "use a little willpower" to stop drinking. He or she is frequently in the grip of a powerful craving for alcohol, a need that can feel as strong as the need for food or water. While some people are able to recover without help, the majority of alcoholic individuals need outside assistance to recover from their disease. With support and treatment, many individuals are able to stop drinking and rebuild their lives. Many people wonder: why can some individuals use alcohol without problems, while others are utterly unable to control their drinking? Recent research has demonstrated that for many people a vulnerability to alcoholism is inherited. Yet it is important to recognize that aspects of a person's environment, such as peer pressure and the availability of alcohol, also are significant influences. Both inherited and environmental influences are called "risk factors." But risk is not destiny. Just because alcoholism tends to run in families doesn't mean that a child of an alcoholic parent will automatically develop alcoholism.

What Is Alcohol Abuse?

Alcohol abuse differs from alcoholism in that it does not include an extremely strong craving for alcohol, loss of control, or physical dependence. In addition, alcohol abuse is less likely than alcoholism to include tolerance (the need for increasing amounts of alcohol to get "high"). Alcohol abuse is defined as a pattern of drinking that is accompanied by one or more of the following situations within a 12-month period:
• failure to fulfill major work, school, or home responsibilities;
• drinking in situations that are physically dangerous, such as while driving a car or operating machinery;
• recurring alcohol-related legal problems, such as being arrested for driving under the influence of alcohol or for physically hurting someone while drunk;
• continued drinking despite having ongoing relationship problems that are caused or worsened by the effects of alcohol.

While alcohol abuse is basically different from alcoholism, it is important to note that many effects of alcohol abuse are also experienced by alcoholics.

Alcoholism Treatment

The nature of treatment depends on the severity of an individual's alcoholism and the resources that are available in his or her community. Treatment may include detoxification (the process of safely getting alcohol out of one's system); taking doctor-prescribed medications, such as disulfiram (Antabuse) or naltrexone (ReVia™) to help prevent a return to drinking once drinking has stopped; and individual and/or group counseling. There are promising types of counseling that teach recovering alcoholics to identify situations and feelings that trigger the urge to drink and to find new ways to cope that do not include alcohol use. Any of these treatments may be provided in a hospital or residential treatment setting or on an outpatient basis.

Because the involvement of family members is important to the recovery process, many programs also offer brief marital counseling and family therapy as part of the treatment process. Some programs also link up individuals with vital community resources, such as legal assistance, job training, child care, and parenting classes.

Alcoholics Anonymous

Virtually all alcoholism treatment programs also include meetings of Alcoholics Anonymous (AA), which describes itself as a "worldwide fellowship of men and women who help each other to stay sober." While AA is generally recognized as an effective mutual help program for recovering alcoholics, not everyone responds to AA's style and message, and other recovery approaches are available. Even those who are helped by AA usually find that AA works best in combination with other elements of treatment, including counseling and medical care.

Can Alcoholism Be Cured?

While alcoholism is a treatable disease, a cure is not yet available. That means that even if an alcoholic has been sober for a long while and has regained health, he or she remains susceptible to relapse and must continue to avoid all alcoholic beverages. "Cutting down" on drinking doesn't work; cutting out alcohol is necessary for a successful recovery.

However, even individuals who are determined to stay sober may suffer one or several "slips," or relapses, before achieving long-term sobriety. Relapses are very common and do not mean that a person has failed or cannot eventually recover from alcoholism. Keep in mind, too, that every day that a recovering alcoholic has stayed sober prior to a relapse is extremely valuable time, both to the individual and to his or her family. If a relapse occurs, it is very important to try to stop drinking once again and to get whatever additional support is needed to abstain from drinking.

Resources

For more information on alcohol abuse and alcoholism, contact the following organizations:
Al-Anon Family Group Headquarters
1600 Corporate Landing Parkway
Virginia Beach, VA 23454-5617
800-356-9996
www.al-anon.alateen.org

Alcoholics Anonymous (AA) World Services
475 Riverside Drive, 11th Floor
New York, NY 10115
212-870-3400
www.alcoholics-anonymous.org

Source: The National Institute on Alcohol Abuse and Alcoholism (NIAAA).

Military and Veterans' Affairs

Gulf War Syndrome: Culprit Remains a Mystery Six Years Later

Although the Persian Gulf conflict ended in 1991, some eighty thousand veterans of the war are still suffering from unexplained health problems including chronic fatigue, joint aches, memory loss, rashes, bleeding gums, tumors, and intestinal and respiratory illnesses. They attribute their suffering to wartime service in the Gulf, though past Pentagon investigations concluded that there was no evidence to link their ailments to wartime risks such as oil-well fire smoke, vaccines, or chemical agents. Originally, the cause of these various symptoms was assumed to be post-traumatic stress, but the pervasive and varied nature of the symptoms resisted that label. Veterans groups, dissatisfied with this dismissive conclusion, have continued to focus attention on the illnesses, which have collectively become known as Gulf War Syndrome. Pressure from veterans has prompted the government to investigate further the possible causes of the syndrome: were the troops exposed to Iraqi chemical and biological weapons? Or were experimental drugs the cause? Is the government cooperating or covering up? The results so far are surprising and often conflicting.

Conflicting Claims

To begin with, very little is known about the long-term consequences of exposure to low doses of nerve gas, so it is difficult to trace a cause-and-effect relationship between possible exposure and the symptoms many veterans are now experiencing. Typical reactions to chemical weapons would include widespread and immediate illness, rather than the sporadic and delayed response experienced by many—but not all—veterans. The position maintained by the Department of Defense is that there is no conclusive evidence that any Americans were exposed to Iraqi chemical weapons, yet the Pentagon has also admitted that some soldiers may have been exposed to low-level toxic vapors of chemical or biological agents released when an ammunition dump was demolished. A separate report released in June 1997 by the General Accounting Office says the possibility that soldiers were exposed to Iraqi chemical weapons cannot be ruled out. Regardless of which U.S. governmental agency report you believe, there is outside evidence of the presence of chemicals. Czech chemical specialists recorded the presence of low-level Sarin gas several times during the fighting, and several instances were reported in which nerve gas was present at levels believed to be nonthreatening to humans. The latter reports were subsequently ignored by military commanders as false alarms.

Khamisiyah Controversy

As evidence unfolds in the ongoing investigations, government agencies have been criticized for withholding information, possibly in some widespread cover-up. In June 1996, the Pentagon admitted after years of denial that hundreds of American troops may have been exposed to mustard gas and the deadly nerve agent Sarin during the demolition of an ammunition depot near the southern Iraqi village of Khamisiyah in March

1991. Although the CIA informed the Army in 1992 that U.N. investigators, visiting the ruins of the depot in October 1991, had confirmed that it contained chemical weapons, the Pentagon did not make this information public until 1996.

In April 1997, the CIA admitted that it had evidence as far back as 1986 verifying that thousands of chemical weapons were stored in the depot. Yet they had failed to include it on a list of suspected chemical-weapon sites supplied to the Pentagon before the war. Reports now declassified show that the intelligence agency had warned the military again before the dump was destroyed, but this knowledge was never passed down to those who carried out the demolition.

Initially, the Pentagon reported that 1,100 Americans may have been exposed to chemical weapon fallout at Khamisiyah. Three months later, the figure was upgraded to as many as 5,000, then 20,000, and in July 1997 the Pentagon's latest estimate was that as many as 100,000 may have been exposed. Incredibly, all the records detailing the Khamisiyah demolition vanished with the other missing pages of the lost chemical-detection logs, further fueling the suspicion of a cover-up. The Pentagon denies that it intentionally suppressed the Khamisiyah findings, and is continuing its investigation.

Still, the fact that the CIA recognized that dangerous chemicals were stored in a depot later destroyed by U.S. troops does not link these chemicals to the health problems of many veterans. Furthermore, none of the troops in the vicinity of the chemical weapons depot when it was destroyed have reported symptoms of Gulf War Syndrome. The investigation of Khamishiyah may be just a red herring, irrelevant to discovering the cause of Gulf War Syndrome.

Would You Believe?

Adding to the controversy surrounding the ongoing investigations, in February 1997 the Pentagon made the shocking disclosure that it had lost most of its paper and computer copies of the crucial chemical warfare logs kept by the military during the Persian Gulf War. The records were kept in locked safes in two different U.S. military locations—in Aberdeen, Maryland, and Tampa,

Florida—and were supposed to record all battlefield incidents in which chemical and biological weapons were detected. Only 36 of the estimated total of 200 pages were located. Incredulous veterans point to this missing data as proof that the Pentagon is covering up the evidence that soldiers were exposed to toxic weapons. The Pentagon denied any wrongdoing but could not explain the mysterious disappearance.

Another theory suggests that symptoms of Gulf War Syndrome could be side-effects of experimental medications intentionally distributed to troops. The anti-nerve gas drug pyridostigmine was given to more than 400,000 military personnel during the conflict to protect them against possible nerve gas attacks. The drug is considered experimental—it has never been tested on humans who had been exposed to nerve gas—but the Defense Department obtained the Food and Drug Administration's permission to administer it to the troops.

Scientists are divided about whether very low exposures to nerve gas could produce the symptoms of Gulf War Syndrome, but research continues. Pentagon-sponsored research on rats suggests that low-level exposure to nerve gas could lead to memory loss, one of the symptoms exhibited by Gulf War veterans, and the U.S. government has undertaken a $2.5-million study to learn the long-term effect of low-level chemical agents on humans. In the meantime, Gulf War veterans continue to search for answers to their serious health problems.—*OTJ*

Highest Ranking Officers in U.S. History

General and Commander-in-Chief[1]

George Washington (1739–1799), b. Westmoreland County, Va., unanimously voted by Congress on June 15, 1775, to the rank of General and Commander-in-Chief (of the Continental Army).

General of the Armies[2]

John Joseph Pershing (1860–1948), b. Linn County, Mo., made permanent general of the armies, 1919.

General of the Army, General of the Air Force (5-Stars)

George Catlett Marshall (1880–1959), b. Uniontown, Pa., promoted December 1944.

Douglas MacArthur (1880–1964), b. Little Rock, Ark., promoted December 1944.

Dwight David Eisenhower (1890–1969), b. Denison, Texas, promoted December 1944.

Henry Harley Arnold (1866–1950), b. Gladwyne, Pa. General Arnold had the unique distinction of being a five-star general twice—first conferred on him in 1944 as general of the army, and later in June 1949 as general of the air force. He is the only air force general to have held the five-star rank.

Omar Nelson Bradley (1893–1981), b. Clark, Mo., promoted September 1950.

Fleet Admiral (5-Star)

William Daniel Leahy (1875–1959), b. Hampton, Iowa, promoted December 1944.

Ernest Joseph King (1878–1956), b. Lorain, Ohio, promoted December 1944.

Chester William Nimitz (1885–1966), b. Fredericksburg, Texas, promoted December 1944.

William Frederick Halsey (1882–1959), b. Elizabeth, N.J., promoted December 1945.

1. On March 15, 1978, George Washington was promoted posthumously to the newly created rank of General of the Armies of the United States. Congress authorized this title to make it clear that Washington was the Army's senior general. 2. General Pershing was given the option of 5 stars but he declined. *Source:* Department of Defense and U.S. Army Historian, Research and Analysis Center.

The Joint Chiefs of Staff (JCS)

The Joint Chiefs of Staff consist of the Chairman, the Vice Chairman, the Chief of Staff of the Army, the Chief of Naval Operations, the Chief of Staff of the Air Force, and the Commandant of the Marine Corps.

The collective body of the JCS is headed by the Chairman (or Vice Chairman in the Chairman's absence), who sets the agenda and presides over JCS meetings. Their responsibilities take precedence over their duties as the Chiefs of Military Services. The Chairman is the principal military advisor to the President, Secretary of Defense, and the National Security Council (NSC); however, all JCS members are by law military advisors, and they may respond to a request or voluntarily submit, through the Chairman, advice or opinions to the President, the Secretary of State, or the NSC. The Joint Chiefs of Staff have no executive authority to commit combatant forces.

The Department of Defense Reorganization Act of 1986 created the position of Vice Chairman of the Joint Chiefs of Staff, who performs duties as the Chief of the JCS may prescribe. By law, the Vice Chairman is the second highest ranking member of the Armed Forces and replaces the Chairman in his absence or disability. He or she is a full voting member of JCS.

In addition to their responsibilities on the JCS, the military Service Chiefs are responsible to the Secretaries of their Military Departments for management of the services. The Service Chiefs serve for four years. By custom the Vice Chiefs of the Services act for their chiefs in most matters having to do with day-to-day operation of the services.

Joint Chiefs of Staff, mid-1997

Chairman of the Joint Chiefs of Staff, General John M. Shalikashvili, U.S. Army (due to retire Sept. 30, 1997); Vice Chairman of the Joint Chiefs of Staff, General Joseph W. Ralston, U.S. Air Force (the fourth officer to hold the position); General Dennis J. Reimer, Chief of Staff of the Army; Admiral Jay L. Johnson, Chief of Naval Operations; General Ronald R. Fogleman, Chief of Staff of the U.S. Air Force (retired Sept. 1997); and Gen. Charles C. Krulak, Commandant of the Marine Corps.

Past Chairmen of the JCS

General of the Army, Omar N. Bradley, 1949–1953; Adm. Arthur W. Radford, U.S. Navy, 1953–1957; Gen. Nathan F. Twining, U.S. Air Force, 1957–1960; Gen. Lyman L. Lemnitzer, U.S. Army, 1960–1962; Gen. Maxwell D. Taylor, U.S. Army, 1962–1964; Gen. Earle G. Wheeler, U.S. Air Force, 1964–1970; Adm. Thomas H. Moorer, U.S. Navy, 1970–1974; Gen. George S. Brown, U.S. Air Force, 1974–1978; Gen. David C. Jones, U.S. Air Force, 1978–1982; Gen. John W. Vessey, Jr., U.S. Army, 1982–1985; Adm. William J. Crowe, U.S. Navy, 1985–1989; Gen. Colin L. Powell, U.S. Army, 1989–1993. □

U.S. Military Pay Grades

Source: U.S. Department of Defense.

Pay Grade	Army	Navy	Marines	Air Force
Commissioned Officers				
0-1	Second Lieutenant	Ensign	Second Lieutenant	Second Lieutenant
0-2	First Lieutenant	Lieutenant Junior Grade	First Lieutenant	First Lieutenant
0-3	Captain	Lieutenant	Captain	Captain
0-4	Major	Lieutenant Commander	Major	Major
0-5	Lieutenant Colonel	Commander	Lieutenant Colonel	Lieutenant Colonel
0-6	Colonel	Captain	Colonel	Colonel
0-7	Brigadier General	Rear Admiral (L)	Brigadier General	Brigadier General
0-8	Major General	Rear Admiral	Major General	Major General
0-9	Lieutenant General	Vice Admiral	Lieutenant General	Lieutenant General
0-10	General	Admiral	General	General
Special Grades[1]				
(5 stars)	General of The Army	Fleet Admiral	(none)	General of the Air Force
Warrant Officers (all services)				
W-1	Warrant Officer. Grades W-2 to W-5 Chief Warrant Officer			
Enlisted Personnel				
E-1	Private	Seaman Recruit	Private	Airman Basic
E-2	Private	Seaman Apprentice	Private First Class	Airman
E-3	Private First Class	Seaman	Lance Corporal	Airman First Class
E-4	Corporal Specialist 4	Petty Officer, Third Class	Corporal	Sergeant Senior Airman
E-5	Sergeant Specialist 5	Petty Officer, Second Class	Sergeant	Staff Sergeant
E-6	Staff Sergeant Specialist 6	Petty Officer, First Class	Staff Sergeant	Technical Sergeant
E-7	Sergeant First Class Specialist 7	Chief Petty Officer	Gunnery Sergeant	Master Sergeant
E-8	First Sergeant Master Sergeant	Senior Chief Petty Officer	First Sergeant Master Sergeant	Senior Master Sergeant
E-9	Command Sergeant Major Sergeant Major	Master Chief Petty Officer	Sergeant Major Master Gunnery Sergeant	Chief Master Sergeant
Special Grades[2]				
	Sergeant Major of the Army	Master Chief Petty Officer of the Navy	Sergeant Major of the Marine Corps	Chief Master Sergeant of the Air Force

1. There are no living 5-star commissioned officers. 2. Senior enlisted advisors. There is only one for each branch of service.

Monthly Basic Pay Rates by Grade Effective 1997

Grade	Years of Service									
	<2	2	4	6	10	14	16	18	20	26
Commissioned Officers										
0-10	7,360.20	7,619.10	7,619.10	7,619.10	7,911.60	8,349.90	8,947.20	8,947.20	9,546.30	10,140.90
0-9	6,522.90	6,693.90	6,836.70	6,836.70	7,010.40	7,302.00	7,911.60	7,911.60	8,349.90	8,947.20
0-8	5,908.20	6,085.50	6,229.80	6,229.80	6,693.90	7,010.40	7,302.00	7,619.10	7,911.60	8,106.60
0-7	4,909.20	5,243.10	5,243.10	5,478.30	5,795.70	6,085.50	6,693.90	7,154.40	7,154.40	7,154.40
0-6	3,638.40	3,997.50	4,259.70	4,259.70	4,259.70	4,404.60	5,100.90	5,361.30	5,478.30	6,285.60
0-5	2,910.30	3,417.00	3,653.40	3,653.40	3,763.50	4,232.40	4,549.20	4,809.60	4,955.70	5,128.80
0-4	2,452.80	2,987.10	3,186.30	3,245.40	3,619.80	3,997.50	4,173.30	4,287.90	4,287.90	4,287.90
0-3	2,279.40	2,548.50	3,014.70	3,159.00	3,449.40	3,708.60	3,708.60	3,708.60	3,708.60	3,708.60
0-2	1,987.80	2,170.80	2,695.80	2,751.60	2,751.60	2,751.60	2,751.60	2,751.60	2,751.60	2,751.60
0-1	1,725.90	1,796.10	2,170.80	2,170.80	2,170.80	2,170.80	2,170.80	2,170.80	2,170.80	2,170.80
Warrant Officers										
W-5	0.00	0.00	0.00	0.00	0.00	0.00	0.00	0.00	3,963.60	4,410.90
W-4	2,322.30	2,491.80	2,548.50	2,664.60	2,898.60	3,245.40	3,359.40	3,449.40	3,560.70	3,966.60
W-3	2,110.80	2,289.60	2,319.30	2,346.30	2,664.60	2,838.90	2,923.80	3,014.70	3,132.30	3,359.40
W-2	1,848.60	2,000.10	2,058.30	2,170.80	2,376.60	2,548.50	2,638.20	2,724.90	2,810.40	2,923.80
W-1	1,540.20	1,765.80	1,913.40	2,000.10	2,170.80	2,346.30	2,433.60	2,517.90	2,608.20	2,608.20

Grade	<2	2	4	6	10	14	16	18	20	26
					Years of Service					
Enlisted Members										
E-9	0.00	0.00	0.00	0.00	2,701.80	2,824.80	2,889.90	2,954.70	3,011.70	3,478.50
E-8	0.00	0.00	0.00	0.00	2,330.70	2,454.00	2,519.10	2,576.40	2,639.70	3,106.50
E-7	1,581.90	1,707.90	1,833.00	1,895.40	2,018.40	2,175.30	2,237.10	2,298.90	2,329.20	2,794.80
E-6	1,360.80	1,483.50	1,610.70	1,671.30	1,794.90	1,946.70	2,009.40	2,040.00	2,040.00	2,040.00
E-5	1,194.30	1,299.90	1,422.30	1,515.90	1,639.80	1,731.30	1,731.30	1,731.30	1,731.30	1,731.30
E-4	1,113.60	1,176.30	1,341.60	1,394.70	1,394.70	1,394.70	1,394.70	1,394.70	1,394.70	1,394.70
E-3	1,049.70	1,107.00	1,196.70	1,196.70	1,196.70	1,196.70	1,196.70	1,196.70	1,196.70	1,196.70
E-2	1,010.10	1,010.10	1,010.10	1,010.10	1,010.10	1,010.10	1,010.10	1,010.10	1,010.10	1,010.10
E-1>4	900.90	900.90	900.90	900.90	900.90	900.90	900.90	900.90	900.90	900.90

NOTE: E-1 with less than 4 months: $833.40. Basic allowance for quarters ranges from $202.50 per month for an enlisted E-1 with no dependents and less than 4 months service and up to $1,015.20 per month for an officer with dependents in grade 0-10.

Service Academies

U.S. Military Academy

Source: U.S. Military Academy.

Established in 1802 by an act of Congress, the U.S. Military Academy is located on the west bank of the Hudson River some 50 miles north of New York City. To gain admission a candidate must first secure a nomination from an authorized source. These sources are:

Congressional Sources

Representatives
Senators
Other: Vice Presidential
District of Columbia
Puerto Rico
Am. Samoa, Guam, Virgin Is., Northern Mariana Islands

Military-Service-Connected Sources

Presidential—Sons or daughters of active duty or retired service members
Enlisted members of Army
Enlisted members of Army Reserve/National Guard
Sons and daughters of deceased and disabled veterans
Honor military, naval schools and ROTC
Sons and daughters of persons awarded the Medal of Honor

Any number of applicants can meet the requirements for a *nomination* in these categories. *Appointments* (offers of admission), however, can only be made to a much smaller number, about 1,200 each year.

Candidates may be nominated for vacancies during the year preceding the day of admission, which occurs in late June or early July. The best time to apply is during the spring of the junior year in high school.

Candidates must be citizens of the U.S., be unmarried, be at least 17 but not yet 23 years old on July 1 of the year admitted, have a secondary-school education or its equivalent, and be able to meet the academic, medical, and physical aptitude requirements. Academic qualification is determined by an analysis of entire scholastic record, and performance on either the American College Testing (ACT) Assessment Program Test or the College Entrance Examination Board Scholastic Assessment Tests (SAT). Entrance requirements and procedures for appointment are described in the Admissions Bulletin and the Admissions Prospectus, available without charge from Admissions, U.S. Military Academy, West Point, NY 10996-1797. Phone: 914-938-4041.

Cadets are members of the U.S. Army. As such they receive annual salaries from which they pay for their uniforms, textbooks, and incidental expenses. There is no tuition and room and board are provided. Upon successful completion of the four-year course, the graduate receives the degree of Bachelor of Science and is com-

Service Academies Web Sites

U.S. Military Academy: www.usma.edu/
U.S. Air Force Academy: www.usafa.af.mil/
U.S. Naval Academy: www.nadn.navy.mil
U.S. Coast Guard Academy:
 www.dot.gov/dotinfo/uscg/hq/uscga/uscga.html
U.S. Merchant Marine Academy: www.usmma.edu/

missioned a second lieutenant in the U.S. Army with a requirement to serve as an officer on active duty for a minimum of five years.

U.S. Naval Academy

Source: U.S. Naval Academy.

The Naval School, established in 1845 at Fort Severn, Annapolis, Md., was renamed the U.S. Naval Academy in 1850. A four-year course was adopted a year later. The "Yard" as the campus is referred to, blends French Renaissance and modern architecture with many new academic, athletics, and laboratory facilities.

The Superintendent is a Navy admiral. A civilian academic dean heads the academic program. A captain heads the 4,000 members of the Brigade of Midshipmen and military, professional, and physical training. The faculty is half military and half civilian, with 650 members; 95% of the civilian faculty hold Ph.Ds. The faculty-student ratio at 1:7 is one of the lowest in the nation and provides for classes that rarely exceed seventeen.

Eighteen majors are offered, including chemistry, math, computer science, economics, general engineering, history, English, ocean engineering, aerospace engineering, electrical engineering, oceanography, political science, mechanical engineering, marine engineering, physics, and naval architecture. Graduates are awarded the Bachelor of Science or Bachelor of Science in Engineering and are commissioned as officers in the U.S. Navy or Marine Corps.

To have basic eligibility for admission, candidates must be citizens of the U.S., of good moral character, at least 17 and not more than 23 years of age on July 1 of their entering year, unmarried, not pregnant, and without legal obligation for dependents.

The Admissions Board at the Naval Academy examines each candidate's school record, College Board or ACT scores, recommendations from school officials, extracurricular activities, and evidence from other sources concerning his or her character, leadership potential, academic preparation, and physical fitness. Qualification for admission is based on all of the above factors.

Tuition, board, lodging, and medical and dental care are provided. Midshipmen receive over $540 a month for books, uniforms, and personal needs.

For general information or answers to specific questions, write: Director of Candidate Guidance, U.S. Naval Academy, Annapolis, MD 21402-5018, or call 1-800-638-9156.

U.S. Air Force Academy

Source: U.S. Air Force Academy.

The bill establishing the Air Force Academy was signed by President Eisenhower on April 1, 1954. The first class of 306 cadets was sworn in on July 11, 1955, at Lowry Air Force Base, Denver, the Academy's temporary location. The Cadet Wing moved into the Academy's permanent home north of Colorado Springs, Colorado, in 1958.

Cadets receive four years of academic, military, and physical education to prepare them for leadership as officers in the Air Force. The Academy is authorized a total of 4,000 cadets. Each new class averages 1,200. The candidates for the Academy must be at least 17 and not have passed their 23rd birthday on July 1 of the year for which they enter the Academy, must be a United States citizen, never married, and be able to meet the mental and physical requirements. International students authorized admission are exempt from the U.S. citizenship requirement. A candidate is required to take the following examinations and tests: (1) the Service Academies' Qualifying Medical Examination; (2) either the American College Testing (ACT) Assessment Program test or the College Entrance Examination Board Scholastic Aptitude Test (SAT); and (3) a Candidate Fitness Test.

Cadets receive their entire education at government expense and, in addition, are paid more than $558 per month base pay. From this sum, they pay for their uniforms, textbooks, tailoring, laundry, entertainment tickets, etc. Upon completion of the four-year program, leading to a Bachelor of Science degree, a cadet who meets the qualifications is commissioned a second lieutenant in the U.S. Air Force. For details on admissions, write: HQ USAFA/RRS, 2304 Cadet Drive, Suite 200, USAF Academy, CO 80840-5025.

U.S. Coast Guard Academy

Source: U.S. Coast Guard Academy.

The U.S. Coast Guard Academy is the only one of the four Armed Forces service academies that offers appointments based solely on the basis of an annual nationwide competition, with no congressional appointments or geographical quotas. Competition is open to all American citizens who have reached their seventeenth but not their twenty-second birthday by July 1 of the entering year.

In selecting students for admission, the Academy prohibits discrimination based on gender, race, color, national origin, or religion. Factors considered in the competition include SAT 1 or ACT scores, high school standing, and leadership potential as demonstrated by participation in high school extracurricular activities, community affairs, or part-time employment. All candidates must pass a rigid medical and physical fitness examination.

A viewbook or video can be obtained by writing to: Director of Admission, U.S. Coast Guard Academy, 15 Mohegan Avenue, New London, CT 06320, or by calling 1-800-883-8724.

U.S. Merchant Marine Academy

Source: U.S. Merchant Marine Academy.

The U.S. Merchant Marine Academy, situated at Kings Point, N.Y., on the north shore of Long Island, was dedicated Sept. 30, 1943. It is maintained by the Department of Transportation under direction of the Maritime Administration.

The Academy has a complement of approximately 950 men and women representing every state, D.C., the Canal Zone, Puerto Rico, Guam, American Samoa, and the Virgin Islands. It is also authorized to admit up to 12 candidates from the Western Hemisphere and 30 other foreign students at any one time.

Candidates are nominated by Senators and members of the House of Representatives. Nominations to the Academy are governed by a state and territory quota system based on population and the results of the College Entrance Examination Board tests.

A candidate must be a citizen not less than 17 and not yet 25 years of age by July 1 of the year in which admission is sought. Fifteen high school credits, including 3 units in mathematics (from algebra, geometry and/or trigonometry), 1 unit in science (physics or chemistry) and 3 in English are required.

The course is four years and includes one year of practical training aboard a merchant ship. Study includes marine engineering, navigation, satellite navigation and communications, electricity, ship construction, naval science and tactics, economics, business, languages, history, etc.

Upon completion of the course of study, a graduate receives a Bachelor of Science degree, a license as a merchant marine deck or engineering officer, and a commission as an Ensign in the Naval Reserve.

The National Guard

Source: Departments of the Army and the Air Force, National Guard Bureau.

Dual Role

The National Guard is unique among the United States reserve military forces, filling both federal and state missions. In peacetime, the National Guard is commanded by the governors of the states and territories and may be called to state active duty by the governor in response to natural disasters, civil disturbances, or other state emergencies. During a war or national emergency, the National Guard may be called to active duty by the President or Congress, and serves as the primary source of augmentation for the active Army and active Air Force.

The men and women of the National Guard are described as citizen soldiers and airmen. They have full-time civilian careers, but, each month they meet with their unit for military training. National Guard members receive the same training, use the same equipment, and wear the same uniform as their active duty counterparts.

The foundation for the National Guard's dual state and federal mission can be traced to the earliest militias of the 13 original colonies. The oldest units were organized in the Massachusetts Bay Colony in 1636, and have been in continuous existence ever since. Framers of the U.S. Constitution provided for the continuation of the militia, a principle that has been further developed through subsequent legislation.

Historic Origins

From its colonial beginnings, the militia system has evolved into today's Army National Guard and Air National Guard, our nation's community-based defense force of modern military units that serve their respective states and are part of the nation's overall military forces. In addition to countless call-ups for state duty, the National Guard has fought in every American war, from the Pequot War in 1637 to Operation Desert Storm in which 75,000 members of the National Guard volunteered or were called to active duty.

As a reserve component of the U.S. military, the National Guard makes up a significant part of what is called the Total Force—active duty service members, the reserve components, and the civilians who are employed by the Department of Defense. The other federal reserve components include the Army Reserve, Naval Reserve, Marine Corps Reserve, Air Force Reserve, and Coast Guard Reserve. Members in all of these organizations are trained and equipped in units which are available for full-time duty in case of war or national emergency. However, the other federal reserve components of the military services, unlike the National Guard, are legally and operationally linked only to the active duty services, not the states. This distinction of having both federal and state missions makes the National Guard unique.

Geographically Diverse

The Army National Guard is made up of more than 3,360 units located in 2,200 communities throughout the 50 states, Puerto Rico, Guam, the Virgin Islands, and the District of Columbia. The U.S. Army's largest reserve force, the Army National Guard provides roughly 55 percent of the Army's total combat capability, and approximately 35% of its combat support and 35% of its combat service support units. Units are provided modern military equipment including M-1 tanks, Bradley Fighting Vehicles, and Blackhawk helicopters.

The Air National Guard has 89 flying units and 1,534 support units at 177 locations. This represents approximately one-third of the U.S. Air Force's fighter and air transport assets. Air National Guard units fly F-16 fighters, KC-135 tankers, B-1B bombers, and C-130 transports, among other aircraft.

Same Benefits and Training as Active Duty

As part of the nation's total military force, Army and Air National Guard units are trained and equipped to mesh with active duty and other federal reserve component forces. Typically, members of the National Guard report for training duty one weekend per month, along with a minimum of 15 days of continuous unit training each year. Weekend training usually is performed at the unit's community armory or nearby military training facility. The annual training usually is performed at a large military training base or overseas location, frequently in cooperation with active duty and other reserve units. In recent years, Army National Guard units have trained in more than 30 nations, including locations in Central America, Europe, Asia, and Africa. Air National Guard units train with active Air Force and Air Force Reserve units on a regular basis at worldwide locations.

Approximately one-half of the National Guard's members join their units with no previous military experience. They complete basic military training and a technical school at an active duty training base and then return to their unit. The balance of the National Guard's membership consists of personnel who have had prior active duty in any U.S. military service.

National Guard members receive a full day's pay at their military rank for each unit training assembly they attend, for the 15 days of annual training, and for any military school or special assignment they may complete. All such training counts toward retirement. A member who has 20 or more years of qualifying military service begins to collect retired pay at age 60.

The National Guard offers its members a broad range of educational opportunities beyond the training and on-the-job experiences they receive for their military specialties. These benefits include participation in the Montgomery GI Bill and additional enlistment incentives for select military career fields. Members of the National Guard have access to active duty military shopping centers in addition to participation in many other active duty military benefit programs. Many states offer additional benefits and civilian educational incentives.

For 1996, the mission strength of the Army National Guard was 373,000, and the Air National Guard 109,178. The 1996 federal budget for the Army National Guard was $5.8 billion, the Air National Guard $4.0 billion. States and territories provide additional funds to support state missions, recruiting and training administration, armory construction, and funding for state-salaried employees.

Additional information about the National Guard may be obtained from local units or from the National Guard Bureau, 2500 Army Pentagon, Washington, DC 20310-2500.

Veterans' Benefits

Veterans have been provided for by the individual states and the federal government since Colonial days. In 1944, federal benefits for veterans were broadened in scope and value under the GI Bill. On March 15, 1989, the Veterans Administration, the federal agency that administers benefits for veterans, became the Department of Veterans Affairs.

The following benefits available to veterans generally require certain minimum periods of active duty during qualifying periods of service. Certain types of discharges are subject to special adjudication to determine eligibility.

For information or assistance in applying for veterans benefits, write, call, or visit a VA Regional Office. Consult your local telephone directory under United States Government, Department of Veterans Affairs (VA) for the address and telephone number. Toll-free telephone service is available in all 50 States: 1-800-827-1000.

Unemployment Allowances. Veterans are provided special job referral assistance through state employment agencies. Disabled veterans are provided a full range of assistance, including training and education.

Loan Guaranty. VA will guarantee loans to buy or build a home; to purchase a manufactured home with or without a lot; and to refinance a home presently owned and occupied by the veteran. VA will guarantee the lender against loss of between 40% and 50% on loans of $22,500 to $144,000, and 25% on loans of more than $144,000. On manufactured home loans, the amount of the guarantee is 40% of the loan to a maximum of $20,000.

Disability Compensation. Veterans with permanent service-connected disabilities are provided allowances set each year by Congress, depending upon the extent of disability. For special conditions, additional payments may be paid, plus allowances for dependents when the disability is 30 percent or more.

Vocational Rehabilitation. VA provides professional counseling, training and other assistance to help service-disabled veterans, rated 10 percent or more who have an employment handicap, to achieve maximum independence in daily living and, to the extent possible, to obtain and maintain suitable employment. Generally, a veteran may receive up to 48 months of this assistance within 12 years from the date he or she is notified of entitlement to VA compensation. All the expenses of a veteran's rehabilitation program are paid by VA. In addition, the veteran receives a subsistence allowance which varies based on the rate of training and number of dependents. For example, a single veteran training full time would receive $396.22 monthly in 1997.

Vocational Training for VA Pension Recipients. Veterans who are awarded pension may participate in a program of vocational training similar to that provided in VA's vocational rehabilitation program. A veteran continues to receive pension while receiving training.

Medical and Dental Care. Free medical care may be provided in VA and, in certain instances, in non-VA hospitals to disabled and low-income veterans. This includes outpatient treatment at a VA field facility or, in some cases, by an approved private physician or dentist. Full domiciliary care also may be provided to veterans with low incomes. Nursing home care may be provided at certain VA medical facilities or in approved private nursing homes. Hospital and other medical care may also be provided for the spouse and child dependents of a veteran who is permanently and totally disabled due to a service-connected disability; or for survivors of a veteran who dies from a service-connected disability; or for survivors of a veteran who at the time of death had a total disability, permanent in nature, resulting from a service-connected disability. Dependent treatment is usually provided in nonfederal facilities. Veterans must agree to make a copayment for the care they receive from VA if their incomes exceed levels that vary with number of dependents and they do not have a service-connected disability or service in certain early war periods. Contact the nearest VA medical facility for eligibility.

Readjustment Counseling. VA provides readjustment counseling to veterans of the Vietnam Era or the war or conflict zones of Lebanon, Grenada, Panama, or the Somalia or Persian Gulf theaters in need of assistance in resolving post-war readjustment problems in the areas of employment, family, education, and personal readjustment including post-traumatic stress disorder. Services are provided at community-based Vet Centers and at VA Medical Centers in certain locations. Services include individual, family and group counseling, employment and educational counseling, and assistance in obtaining referrals to various governmental and nongovernmental agencies. Contact the nearest Vet Center or VA facility.

Dependents Compensation. Payments are made to surviving dependents of veterans who died while on active duty or, after discharge, of a service-connected injury or disease. (Amount changed regularly by Congress.) An additional amount per month is added if the deceased veteran was 100 percent disabled for eight years before death. Parents and children may be eligible for additional payments.

Dependents' Educational Assistance. VA makes a monthly payment for up to 45 months of schooling to spouses and children of veterans who died of service-connected causes or who were permanently and totally disabled from service-connected causes or died while permanently and totally disabled or who are currently missing in action, captured in the line of duty, or forcibly detained or interned in line of duty by a foreign power for more than 90 days.

Montgomery GI Bill. This Act provides education benefits for individuals entering the military after June 30, 1985. Servicepersons entering active duty after that date will have their basic pay reduced by $100 per month for the first 12 months of their service, unless they specifically elect not to participate in the program.

Active duty for three years (two years, if the initial obligated period of active duty is less than three years), or two years active duty plus four years in the Selected Reserve or National Guard will entitle an individual to a monthly payment for 36 months. Those who enlist for less than three years will receive a lesser amount per month for 36 months. VA pays an additional amount, commonly called a "kicker," if directed by the Defense Department.

An educational entitlement program is also available for members of the Selected Reserve. Eligibility applies to individuals who, after June 30, 1985 enlist, re-enlist, or extend an enlistment for a six-year period. Benefits may be paid to eligible members of the Selected Reserve who complete their initial period of active duty training. Full-time monthly payments are for 36 months.

Pensions. Pension benefits may be payable to wartime veterans permanently and totally disabled from non-service-connected causes. These benefits are limited to low-income veterans. Surviving spouses and children of wartime veterans are eligible for Nonservice-Connected Death Pensions that are based on the veteran's honorable wartime service and income of the survivors.

Insurance. The VA life insurance programs each year pay millions of dollars to veterans who kept their insurance in force. Detailed information may be obtained by calling 1-800-669-8477.

Burial Benefits. Burial is provided in any VA national cemetery with available grave space to deceased veterans who were discharged under conditions other than

dishonorable. Also eligible for burial in a national cemetery are the veteran's spouse, widow, widower, minor children, and under certain conditions, unmarried adult children. Arlington Cemetery is administered by the Army and has different eligibility requirements.

Headstone or Marker. A government headstone or marker is furnished for the grave of a veteran anywhere in the world who was discharged under conditions other than dishonorable and is interred in a national, state veterans', military, or private cemetery. VA also will furnish markers to veterans' eligible dependents interred in a national, military, or state veterans' cemetery. To apply, write to NCS, Department of Veterans Affairs, Washington, DC 20420.

Veterans' Beneficiaries: A Long Gray Line

As of July 1, 1993—the latest data available—there were an estimated 26.7 million living veterans. Nearly 80 percent served during defined periods of armed hostilities. Altogether, almost one-third of the nation's population—approximately 70 million persons—are veterans, dependents, and survivors of deceased veterans who are potentially eligible for Veterans Administration (VA) benefits and services.

Care for veterans and their dependents spans centu-

ries. The last dependent of a Revolutionary War veteran died in 1911; the War of 1812's last dependent died in 1949; the Mexican War's in 1962. At last count, there were widows and children of Civil War and Indian War veterans who still draw VA benefits. In 1993, some 2,190 children and widows of Spanish-American War veterans were receiving VA compensation or pension benefits. □

Active Military Duty Personnel, 1940–1996[1]

As of September 30, 1996, there were 1,471,722 active duty military personnel. This is a decrease of 46,502 (5,178 officers; 41,379 enlisted; and 55 cadets and midshipmen) from the FY 1995 figure. The "U.S., Territories, and Special Locations" region accounted for 48,859 of the total force reduction. For the last five years, the officer/enlisted ratio has been between 5.3 and

6.0. The largest decrease of officer personnel was in the Captain-Lieutenant category, while the largest decrease among enlisted personnel was in pay grade E-4. The number of female officers, cadets, and enlisted personnel showed an increase of 1,577 from the FY 1995 figure, and the percentage of female active duty military personnel rose from 12.9 to 13.4 percent.

Year	Army[2]	Air Force[2, 3]	Navy	Marine Corps	Total
1940	269,023		160,997	28,345	458,365
1945	8,266,373		3,319,586	469,925	12,055,884
1950	593,167	411,277	380,739	74,279	1,459,462
1955	1,109,296	959,946	660,695	205,170	2,935,107
1960	873,078	814,752	616,987	170,621	2,475,438
1965	969,066	824,662	669,985	190,213	2,653,926
1970	1,322,548	791,349	691,126	259,737	3,064,760
1975	784,333	612,751	535,085	195,951	2,128,120
1980	777,036	557,969	527,153	188,469	2,050,627
1985	780,787	601,515	570,705	198,025	2,151,032
1990	732,403	535,233	579,417	196,652	2,043,705
1991	710,821	510,432	570,262	194,040	1,985,555
1992	610,450	470,315	541,883	184,529	1,807,177
1993	572,423	444,351	509,950	178,379	1,705,103
1994	541,343	426,327	468,662	174,158	1,610,490
1995	508,559	400,409	434,617	174,639	1,518,224
1996	491,103	389,001	416,735	174,883	1,471,722

1. Military personnel on extended or continuous active duty. Excludes reserves on active duty for training. Prior year totals have been corrected. 2. Represents "Command Strength" prior to June 30, 1956. 3. Army Air Forces and its predecessors for period prior to September 18, 1947. *Source:* Department of Defense.

Women and the Draft

Women have never had to register with the Selective Service system. Although unlikely, it is possible that this could change during a national emergency once women are fully integrated into the armed services and allowed to fight in direct, close-combat with an enemy.

Since the draft ended in 1973, all men ages 18 to 25 are still required to register with the Selective Service. Women are excluded because the Selective Service law as it is now written specifically states that "male persons" must register. For women to be required to register, Congress would have to amend the law.

The constitutionality of excluding women was tested in the courts. A Supreme Court decision in 1981, *Rostker v. Goldberg*, held that registering only men did not violate the due process clause of the Constitution.

The Department of Defense (DOD) reviewed this issue in 1994 at President Clinton's request. It was noted that America's prior drafts supplied adequate numbers of Army ground combat troops. Because women are excluded by policy from front line combat positions, excluding them from the draft process remains justifiable in the DOD's view. Although no conclusions were reached, DOD recognized that policies regarding women need to be reviewed periodically because the role of women in the military continues to expand.

The Selective Service system, if given the mission and additional funding, is capable of registering and drafting women with its current infrastructure. □

The Medal of Honor

Often called the Congressional Medal of Honor, it is the nation's highest military award for "uncommon valor" by men and women in the armed forces. It is given for actions that are above and beyond the call of duty in combat against an armed enemy. The medal was first awarded by the Army on March 25, 1863. In April 1991, President Bush awarded posthumously the Medal of Honor to World War I veteran, Army Cpl. Freddie Stowers. He was the first black soldier to receive the nation's highest honor for valor in either World War.

The only conscientious objector to be awarded the medal was PFC Desmond Doss, a Seventh-Day Adventist who served as a medic in the Pacific Theater during WWII.

Recipients of the medal receive $400 per month for life, a right to burial at Arlington National Cemetery,

admission for them or their children to a service academy (if they qualify and quotas permit), and free travel on government aircraft to almost anywhere in the world, on a space-available basis.

President Clinton awarded the last medals to seven black World War II veterans (six posthumously) on Jan. 13, 1997. The long overdue recognition was denied them earlier because ther were African-Americans. In order to recognize their extraordinary heroism now, Congress authorized a special statute of limitations waiver that expired for them in 1952.

Former 1st Lieut. Vernon Joseph Baker, of St. Maries, Idaho, was the only one of the seven recipients still living to receive the coveted medal.

Medal of Honor Recipients

	Total[1]	Army	Navy	Marines	Air Force	Coast Guard
Civil War	1,520	1,195	308	17	—	—
Indian Wars (1861–1898)	428	428	—	—	—	—
Korea (1871)	15	—	9	6	—	—
Spanish-American War	109	30	64	15	—	—
Philippines/Samoa	91	70	12	9	—	—
Boxer Rebellion	59	4	22	33	—	—
Veracruz (1914)	55	—	46	9	—	—
Haiti (1915)	6	—	—	6	—	—
Dominican Republic	3	—	—	3	—	—
Haiti (1919–1920)	2	—	—	2	—	—
Nicaragua (1927–1933)	2	—	—	2	—	—
Peacetime (1865–1870)	12	—	12	—	—	—
Peacetime (1871–1898)	103	—	101	2	—	—
Peacetime (1899–1911)	51	1	48	2	—	—
Peacetime (1915–1916)	8	—	8	—	—	—
Peacetime (1920–1940)	18	2	15	1	—	—
World War I	124	96	21	7	—	—
World War II	440	301	57	81	—	1
Korean War	131	78	7	42	4	—
Vietnam War	239	155	15	57	12	—
Somalia (1993)	2	2	—	—	—	—
Unknown Soldiers	9	—	—	—	—	—
Total	**3,427**	**2,362**	**745**	**294**	**16**	**1**

1. These totals reflect the total number of Medals of Honor awarded. Twenty (20) men received a second award. The total number of Medal of Honor recipients is 3,407. As of April 17, 1997, there are 169 living Medal of Honor recipients. *Source:* The Congressional Medal of Honor Society, Mt. Pleasant, S.C.

Female Military Personnel on Active Duty by Grade

Rank/Grade	Army	Air Force	Navy	Marine Corps	Total DoD
Total officers	10,584	12,047	7,825	750	31,206
Total enlisted	59,039	52,767	46,687	7,814	166,307
Cadets & midshipmen	530	638	619[1]	—	1,787
Grand total	70,153	65,452	55,131	8,564	199,307

1. Excludes other naval officer candidates. Date as of September 30, 1995.

U.S. Casualties in the Major Wars

War	Branch of Service	Numbers engaged	Battle deaths	Other deaths	Total deaths	Wounds not mortal	Total casualties[1]
Revolutionary War	Army	n.a.	4,044	n.a.	n.a.	6,004	n.a.
(1775 to 1783)	Navy	n.a.	342	n.a.	n.a.	114	n.a.
	Marines	n.a.	49	n.a.	n.a.	70	n.a.
	Total	**n.a.**	**4,435**	**n.a.**	**n.a.**	**6,188**	**n.a.**
War of 1812	Army	n.a.	1,950	n.a.	n.a.	4,000	n.a.
(1812 to 1815)	Navy	n.a.	265	n.a.	n.a.	439	n.a.
	Marines	n.a.	45	n.a.	n.a.	66	n.a.
	Total	**286,730**	**2,260**	**n.a.**	**n.a.**	**4,505**	**n.a.**
Mexican War	Army	n.a.	1,721	11,550	13,271	4,102	17,373
(1846 to 1848)	Navy	n.a.	1	n.a.	n.a.	3	n.a.
	Marines	n.a.	11	n.a.	n.a.	47	n.a.
	Total	**78,718**	**1,733**	**n.a.**	**n.a.**	**4,152**	**n.a.**
Civil War	Army	2,128,948	138,154	221,374	359,528	280,040	639,568
(1861 to 1865)[2]	Navy	84,415	2,112	2,411	4,523	1,710	6,233
	Marines		148	312	460	131	591
	Total	**2,213,363**	**140,414**	**224,097**	**364,511**	**281,881**	**646,392**
Spanish-American War	Army	280,564	369	2,061	2,430	1,594	4,024
(1898)	Navy	22,875	10	0	10	47	57
	Marines	3,321	6	0	6	21	27
	Total	**306,760**	**385**	**2,061**	**2,446**	**1,662**	**4,108**
World War I	Army	4,057,101	50,510	55,868	106,378	193,663	300,041
(1917 to 1918)	Navy	599,051	431	6,856	7,287	819	8,106
	Marines	78,839	2,461	390	2,851	9,520	12,371
	Total	**4,734,991**	**53,402**	**63,114**	**116,516**	**204,002**	**320,518**
World War II	Army[3]	11,260,000	234,874	83,400	318,274	565,861	884,135
(1941 to 1946)	Navy	4,183,466	36,950	25,664	62,614	37,778	100,392
	Marines	669,100	19,733	4,778	24,511	67,207	91,718
	Total	**16,112,566**	**291,557**	**113,842**	**405,399**	**670,846**	**1,076,245**
Korean War	Army	2,834,000	27,709	2,452	30,161	77,596	107,757
(1950 to 1953)	Navy	1,177,000	475	173	648	1,576	2,224
	Marines	424,000	4,270	339	4,609	23,744	28,353
	Air Force	1,285,000	1,198	298	1,496	368	1,864
	Total	**5,720,000**	**33,652**	**3,262**	**36,914**	**103,284**	**140,198**
War in Southeast Asia[4]	Army	4,368,000	30,914	7,275	38,189	96,802	134,991
	Navy	1,842,000	1,631	928	2,559	4,178	6,737
	Marines	794,000	13,082	1,754	14,836	51,392	66,228
	Air Force	1,740,000	1,739	844	2,583	931	3,514
	Total	**8,744,000**	**47,366**	**10,801**	**58,167**	**153,303**	**211,470**

1. Excludes captured or interned and missing in action who were subsequently returned to military control. 2. Union forces only. Totals should probably be somewhat larger as data or disposition of prisoners are far from complete. Final Confederate deaths, based on incomplete returns, were 133,821, to which should be added 26,000-31,000 personnel who died in Union prisons. 178,975 blacks served in the Union Army. 2,894 were killed in battle or mortally wounded, 33,953 died from other causes including 29,658 deaths from disease. 3. Army data include Air Force. 4. Vietnam figures provided by the U.S. Center of Military History, Reference Division, Washington, D.C., February 1994. Navy figures exclude Coast Guard of which there were 5 battle deaths. NOTE: All data are subject to revision. For wars before World War I, information represents best data from available records. However, due to incomplete records and possible difference in usage of terminology, reporting systems, etc., figures should be considered estimates. n.a. = not available. *Source:* Department of Defense.

Casualties in World War I

Country	Total mobilized forces	Killed or died[1]	Wounded	Prisoners or missing	Total Casualties
Austria-Hungary	7,800,000	1,200,000	3,620,000	2,200,000	7,020,000
Belgium	267,000	13,716	44,686	34,659	93,061
British Empire[2]	8,904,467	908,371	2,090,212	191,652	3,190,235
Bulgaria	1,200,000	87,500	152,390	27,029	266,919
France[2]	8,410,000	1,357,800	4,266,000	537,000	6,160,800
Germany	11,000,000	1,773,700	4,216,058	1,152,800	7,142,558
Greece	230,000	5,000	21,000	1,000	27,000
Italy	5,615,000	650,000	947,000	600,000	2,197,000
Japan	800,000	300	907	3	1,210
Montenegro	50,000	3,000	10,000	7,000	20,000
Portugal	100,000	7,222	13,751	12,318	33,291
Romania	750,000	335,706	120,000	80,000	535,706
Russia	12,000,000	1,700,000	4,950,000	2,500,000	9,150,000
Serbia	707,343	45,000	133,148	152,958	331,106
Turkey	2,850,000	325,000	400,000	250,000	975,000
United States	4,734,991	116,516	204,002	—	320,518

1. Includes deaths from all causes. 2. Official figures. NOTE: For additional U.S. figures, *see* the table U.S. Casualties in the Major Wars.

Casualties in World War II

Country	Men in war	Battle deaths	Wounded
Australia	1,000,000	26,976	180,864
Austria	800,000	280,000	350,117
Belgium	625,000	8,460	55,513[1]
Brazil[2]	40,334	943	4,222
Bulgaria	339,760	6,671	21,878
Canada	1,086,343[7]	42,042[7]	53,145
China[3]	17,250,521	1,324,516	1,762,006
Czechoslovakia	—	6,683[4]	8,017
Denmark	—	4,339	—
Finland	500,000	79,047	50,000
France	—	201,568	400,000
Germany	20,000,000	3,250,000[4]	7,250,000
Greece	—	17,024	47,290
Hungary	—	147,435	89,313
India	2,393,891	32,121	64,354
Italy	3,100,000	149,496[4]	66,716
Japan	9,700,000	1,270,000	140,000
Netherlands	280,000	6,500	2,860
New Zealand	194,000	11,625[4]	17,000
Norway	75,000	2,000	—
Poland	—	664,000	530,000
Romania	650,000[5]	350,000[6]	—
South Africa	410,056	2,473	—
U.S.S.R.	—	6,115,000[4]	14,012,000
United Kingdom	5,896,000	357,116[4]	369,267
United States	16,112,566	291,557	670,846
Yugoslavia	3,741,000	305,000	425,000

1. Civilians only. 2. Army and Navy figures. 3. Figures cover period July 7, 1937-Sept. 2, 1945, and concern only Chinese regular troops. They do not include casualties suffered by guerrillas and local military corps. 4. Deaths from all causes. 5. Against Soviet Russia; 385,847 against Nazi Germany. 6. Against Soviet Russia; 169,822 against Nazi Germany. 7. National Defense Ctr., Canadian Forces Hq., Director of History. NOTE: The figures in this table are unofficial estimates obtained from various sources.

Merchant Marine Casualties in World War II

In 1988, the U.S. Government conferred official veterans status on those who served aboard oceangoing merchant ships in World War II. The officers and crews played a key role in transporting the troops and war material that enabled the United States and its allies to defeat the Axis powers.

During the war, merchant seamen died as a result of enemy attacks at a rate that proportionally exceeded all branches of the armed services, with the exception of the U.S. Marine Corps.

Enemy action sank more than 700 U.S.-flag merchant ships and claimed the lives of over 6,000 civilian seafarers. Untold thousands of additional seamen were wounded or injured during these attacks, and nearly 600 were made prisoners of war. □

Personal Finance

The articles and opinions in this section are for general information only and are not intended to provide specific advice or recommendations for any individual.

What is a 401(k) Retirement Plan?

By R. Theodore Benna, President of the 401(k) Association

A 401(k) plan is a retirement plan that employers may set up to help their employees save for retirement. The first 401(k) savings plan was started on January 1, 1981, by Ted Benna at the Johnson Companies, and there were only 68 participants. There are now approximately 250,000 plans covering over 25 million participants with approximately $750 billion of assets. These plans are very popular because they provide the following advantages:

• **Tax Breaks.** The money that employees contribute goes into the plan before federal income tax is taken out, and the money in the plan grows with its dividends and earnings untaxed until the money is withdrawn.

• **Employer Contributions.** Though employers are not required to make contributions to employees' 401(k) accounts, many do so. Employers commonly add $0.25 or $0.50 to each $1.00 an employee contributes.

• **Professional Management.** Employee contributions may be invested in a variety of ways, but the most common is a professionally managed mutual fund. Company stock is another common investment.

• **Forced Savings.** The biggest advantage of 401(k) plans is that saving occurs automatically each pay period, making saving the first priority rather than the last.

Several factors have contributed to making 401(k) plans more appealing in recent years. Government regulations impose limits on tax-deductible contributions to IRAs based on the availability of company-sponsored retirement plans and income levels, while contributions to a 401(k) plan are limited to 15% of an individual's salary, regardless of income level or other available retirement plans. At the same time, the future of Social Security has become more uncertain, so workers are less confident that they will receive appreciable government assistance during their retirement. While the cost of retirement has increased dramatically because workers are retiring earlier and living longer, cost-conscious companies have pared down pension plans, shifting responsibility for retirement planning to employees.

Employer's Role

To ensure a comfortable retirement, approximately 10% of an employee's salary must be set aside for retirement beginning at age 25, assuming that Social Security survives. Very few employers are able to contribute 10% of each employee's pay to a retirement plan, so 401(k) plans depend heavily on employee contributions. The employer's role is still critical, however, because employes can only reap the benefits of a 401(k) plan if the employer agrees to adopt one.

Fortunately, the prevalence of 401(k) plans makes it likely that employers will want to offer one to employees. Recruiting and retaining skilled workers requires that similar benefit packages be widely available, and not adopting a 401(k) plan can hinder efforts to hire talented employees. Furthermore, since business owners also need to fund a retirement account, offering a 401(k) plan makes good business sense for the company, its principals, and its employees.

Other 401(k) Features

The specific design of each 401(k) plan is determined by the employer, within guidelines established by the government. The following are some common tenets underlying 401(k) plans:

Eligibility. It is permissible to exclude employees who are under age 21 and those who have been employed for less than 12 months. It is also permissible to permanently exclude part-time employyees who never work more than 1,000 hours per year, and employees who are union members. (Union members have the right to negotiate 401(k) benefits through collective bargaining.)

Hardship Withdrawals. Most plans permit employees to withdraw money from the plan while still employed if they have an IRS-approved financial hardship, such as post-secondary education, medical expenses, purchase of a primary residence, or to prevent eviction from one's home. Withdrawals are taxable, and penalty taxes may be imposed.

Vesting. This term means ownership of the money in the plan. Your contributions always belong to you, so you are "100% vested" in your contributions. Employer contributions may vest over a period of time, so you may be required to stay with your employer for a number of years before you will receive the employer contribution.

Loans. At the option of your employer, your plan may permit you to borrow a portion of the amount you have in the plan. Loans are not subject to tax, and any interest you pay when repaying the loan is interest paid to yourself.

The Future of 401(k) Plans

Despite the large number of employees currently contributing to 401(k) plans, there is much to be done. Approximately half of the U.S. workforce is not covered by any employer retirement plan because many of them work for small employers. Most employers with less than 25 employees do not offer any retirement plans, and because 401(k) plans are subject to some of our most complex tax laws, they are costly and difficult for small employers to implement. Employees without

---

The 401(k) Association was founded by Ted Benna, creator of the first 401(k) savings plan. The Association is a 401(k) advocacy group whose broad mission is to protect and promote 401(k) plans. Membership in the Association is $35.00 for the first year and $25.00 per year thereafter. Members receive two quarterly newsletters and a retirement planning workbook.

The 401(k) Association also offers a low-cost 401(k) Starter Plan to help employers with less than 25 employees set up a plan. More information may be obtained from the Association at 201 Corporate Drive East, Langhorne, PA 19047 or by calling 215-579-8830.

retirement plans are dependent upon Social Security and personal savings, which may not be sufficient.

Fortunately, Congress has enacted changes that will make it easier for small employers to adopt a 401(k) type of retirement plan called Savings Incentive Plans for Employees, or SIMPLE. SIMPLE plans are exempt from many of the complex regulations governing traditional 401(k) plans, which should make them more attractive to smaller firms. Also, firms specializing in retirement investments have begun to recognize the sizeable small-business market, and are developing lower-cost plans targeted to businesses with fewer than 25 employees. As it becomes easier and less costly to offer retirement savings plans regardless of the size of the firm, the government may require all employers to offer a payroll-deduction retirement savings plan. □

ABC's of Mutual Funds

Sound advice from the U.S. Securities and Exchange Commission

Buying and Selling Shares

You can buy some mutual fund shares by contacting the investment firm directly. Others are sold mainly through brokers, banks, financial planners, or insurance agents. All mutual funds will redeem (buy back) your shares on any business day and must send you the payment within seven days.

You can find out the value of your shares in the financial pages of major newspapers; after the funds name, look for the column marked "NAV."

What is NAV?

The NAV or Net Asset Value per share is the value of one share in a fund. When you buy shares, you pay the current NAV per shares, plus any sales charge (also called a sales load). When you sell your shares, the fund will pay you NAV less any other sales load. A fund's NAV goes up or down daily as its holdings change in value. For example: You invest $1,000 in a mutual fund with an NAV of $10.00. You will therefore own 100 shares of the fund. If the NAV drops to $9.00 (because the value of the fund's portfolio has dropped), you will still own 100 shares, but your investment is now worth $900.00. If the NAV goes up to $11.00, your investment is worth $1,100. (This example assumes no sales charge.)

How Funds Work and Earn Money

A mutual fund brings together money from many people and invests it in stocks, bonds, or other securities. (The combined holdings of stocks, bonds, or other securities and assets the fund owns are known as its *portfolio*.) Each investor owns shares, which represent a part of these holdings.

You can earn money from your investment in three ways:

First, a fund may receive income in the form of dividends and interest on the securities it owns. A fund will pay its shareholders nearly all of the income it has earned in the form of *dividends*.

Second, the price of the securities a fund owns may increase. When a fund sells a security that has increased in price, the fund has a *capital gain*. At the end of the year, most funds distribute these capital gains (minus any capital losses) to investors.

Third, if a fund does not sell but holds on to securities that have increased in price, the value of its shares (NAV) increases. The higher NAV reflects the higher value of your investment. If you sell your shares, you make a profit (this is also a capital gain).

Usually funds will give you a choice: the fund can send you payment for distributions and dividends, or you can have them *reinvested* in the fund to buy more shares, often without paying an additional sales load.

Taxes

You still owe taxes on any distributions and dividends in the year you receive them (or reinvest them).

You will also owe taxes on any capital gains you receive when you sell your shares. *Keep your account statements in order to figure out your taxes at the end of the year.*

If you invest in a *tax-exempt fund* (such as a municipal bond fund), some or all of your dividends will be exempt from federal (and sometimes state and local) income tax. You will, however, owe taxes on any capital gains.

Kinds of Mutual Funds

The three main categories of mutual funds are money market funds, bond funds, and stock funds. There are a variety of types within each category.

Money Market Funds have relatively low risks, compared to other mutual funds. They are limited by law to certain high-quality, short-term investments. Money market funds try to keep their value (NAV) at a stable $1.00 per share, but NAV may fall below $1.00 if

---

Terms To Know

Front-end Load: A front-end load is a sales charge you pay when you buy shares. This type of load, which by law cannot be higher than 8.5% of your investment, reduces the amount of your investment in the fund. *Example:* If you have $1,000 to invest in a mutual fund with a 5% front-end load, $50 will go to pay the sales charge, and $950 will be invested in the fund.

Back-end Load: A back-end load (also called a *deferred load*), is a sales charge you pay when you sell your shares. It usually starts out at 5% or 6% for the first year and gets smaller each year after that until it reaches zero (say, in year six or seven of your investment). *Example:* You invest $1,000 in a mutual fund with a back-end load that decreases to zero in the seventh year. Assume that the value of your investment remains at $1,000 for seven years. If you sell your shares during the first year, you will only get back $940 (ignoring any gains or losses). $60 will go to pay the sales charge. If you sell your shares during the seventh year, you will get back $1,000.

The 12b-1 Fee: One type of ongoing fee that is taken out of fund assets has come to be known as a rule 12b-1 fee. It most often is used to pay commissions to brokers and other salespersons, and occasionally to pay for advertising and other costs of promoting the fund to investors. It usually is between 0.25% and 1.00% of assets annually.

Funds with back-end loads usually have higher rule 12b-1 fees. If you are considering whether to pay a front-end load or a back-end load, think about how long you intend to stay in a fund. If you plan to stay in for six years or more, a front-end load may cost less than a back-end load. Even if your back-end load has fallen to zero, over time you could pay more in rule 12b-1 fees than if you paid a front-end load.

their investments perform poorly. Investor losses have been rare, but they are possible.

Bond Funds (also called **Fixed Income Funds**) have higher risks than money market funds, but seek to pay higher yields. Unlike money market funds, bond funds are not restricted to high-quality or short-term investments. Because there are many different types of bonds, bond funds can vary dramatically in their risks and rewards.

Most bond funds have credit risk, which is the risk that companies or other issuers whose bonds are owned by the fund may fail to pay their debts (including the debt owed to the holder of their bonds). Some funds have little credit risk, such as those that invest in insured bonds or U.S. Treasury bonds. But be careful: nearly all bond funds have interest rate risk, which means that the market value of the bonds they hold will go down when interest rates go up. Because of this, you can lose money in any bond fund, including those that invest only in insured bonds or Treasury bonds.

Stock Funds (also called **Equity Funds**) generally involve more risk than money market or bond funds, but they also can offer the highest returns. A stock fund's value (NAV) can rise and fall quickly over the short term, but historically stocks have performed better over the long term than other types of investments.

Not all stock funds are the same. There are classifications based on the fund's goals. For example, *growth* funds focus on stocks that may not pay a regular dividend but have the potential for a large capital gain, while *income* funds focus on corporate bonds, which pay dividends but have lower capital appreciation. Other classifications are based on the markets in which the funds invest; for example, a fund may specialize in a particular industry such as technology stocks.

A Word About Banks and Mutual Funds

Banks now sell mutual funds, some of which carry the bank's name. **But mutual funds sold in banks, including money market funds, are not bank deposits.** Don't confuse a "money market fund" with a "money market deposit account." Their names are similar, but they are completely different:

• A money market fund is a type of mutual fund. It is *not* guaranteed, and comes with a prospectus.

• A money market deposit account is a bank deposit. It *is* guaranteed, and comes with a Truth in Savings form.

• To reiterate, even if you buy a fund through a bank and the fund carries the bank name, there is no guarantee. You can lose your money.

A Word About Derivatives

Some funds may face special risks if they invest in derivatives. Derivatives are financial instruments whose performance is derived, at least in part, from the performance of an underlying asset, security, or index. Their value can be affected dramatically by even small market movements, sometimes in unpredictable ways.

There are many types of derivatives with many different uses. They do not necessarily increase risk, and may in fact reduce risk. A fund's prospectus will disclose how it may use derivatives. You may also want to call a fund and ask how it uses these instruments.

Comparing Different Funds

Once you identify the types of funds that interest you, it is time to look at particular funds in those categories.

Past Performance

A fund's past performance is not as important as you

might think. Advertisements, rankings, and ratings tell you how well a fund has performed in the past. But studies show that the future is often different. This year's "number one" fund can easily become next year's below average fund. (NOTE: Although past performance is not a reliable indicator of future performance, volatility of past returns is a good indicator of a fund's future volatility).

Tips For Comparing Performance

• Check the fund's *total return*. You will find it in the Financial Highlights, near the front of the prospectus. Total return measures increases and decreases in the value of your investment over time, after subtracting costs.

• See how total return has varied over the years. The Financial Highlights in the prospectus show yearly total return for the most recent 10-year period. An impressive 10-year total return may be based on one spectacular year followed by many average years. *Looking at year-to-year changes in total return is a good way to see how stable the fund's returns have been.*

Comparing Costs

Costs are important because they lower your returns. A fund that has a sales load and high expenses will have to perform better than a low-cost fund, just to stay even with the low-cost fund.

Find the *fee table* near the front of the fund's prospectus, where the fund's costs are laid out. You can use the fee table to compare the costs of different funds. The fee table breaks costs into two main categories:

1. sales loads and transaction fees (paid when you buy, sell, or exchange your shares), and
2. ongoing expenses (paid while you remain invested in the fund).

Tips on Comparing Costs

• Beware of a salesperson who tells you, "This is just like a no-load fund." Even if there is no front-end load, check the fee table in the prospectus to see what other loads or fees you may have to pay.

• Check the fee table to see if any part of a fund's fees or expenses have been waived. If so, the fees and expenses may increase suddenly when the waiver ends (the part of the prospectus after the fee table will tell you how much).

• Many funds allow you to exchange your shares of another fund managed by the same adviser. The first part of the fee table will tell you if there is an exchange fee.

Sales Loads

No-Load funds do not charge sales loads. When you buy no-load funds, you make your own choices, without the assistance of a financial professional. There are no-load funds in every major fund category. Even no-load funds have ongoing expenses, however, such as management fees.

When a mutual fund charges a sales-load, it usually pays for commissions to people who sell the fund's shares to you, as well as other marketing costs. Sales loads buy you a broker's services and advice; they do not ensure superior performance. In fact, funds that charge sales loads have not performed better on average (ignoring the loads) than those that do not charge sales loads.

Ongoing Expenses

The second part of the fee table tells you the kinds of ongoing expenses you will pay while you remain invested in the fund. The table shows expenses as a percentage of the fund's assets, generally for the most recent fiscal year. Here, the table will tell you the *management fee* (which pays for managing the fund's portfolio), along with any other fees and expenses.

Financial Web Sites

FinanceNet www.financenet.gov
The Syndicate
   www.moneypages.com/syndicate/index.html
Invest-o-Rama www.investorama.com/
American Association of Individual Investors
   www.aaii.org
Mutual Funds Homepage
   www.fundsinteractive.com
Foreign Exchange Rates
   www.cnnfn.com/markets/currencies.html
U.S. Securities and Exchange Commission
   www.sec.gov
Federal Deposit Insurance Corporation
   www.fdic.gov/
FannieMae www.fanniemae.com/
United States Treasury www.ustreas.gov/
U.S. Savings Bonds
   www.publicdebt.treas.gov/sav/sav.html
Debt Counselors of America www.dca.org
**Department of Labor, Pension, and Welfare
   Benefits** www.dol.gov/dol/pwba/
MetLife Online (Annuities, etc.)
   www.lifeadvice.com
American Express (financial information)
   www.americanexpress.com
American Consumer Credit Counseling
   www.consumercredit.com/
New York Stock Exchange www.nyse.com
American Stock Exchange www.amex.com
NASDAQ www.nasdaq.com
Chicago Mercantile Exhange www.cme.com
Council on Economic Priorities (social and envi-
   ronmental concerns)
   www.accesspt.com/cep

High expenses do not assure superior performance. Higher expense funds do not, on average, perform better than lower expense funds. But there may be circumstances in which you decide it is appropriate for you to pay higher expenses. For example, you can expect to pay higher expenses for certain types of funds that require extra work by its managers, such as international stock funds, which require sophisticated research. You may also pay higher expenses for funds that provide special services, like toll-free numbers, check-writing, and automatic investment programs.

A difference in expenses that may look small to you can make a big difference in the value of your investment over time. *Example:* Say you invest $1,000 in a fund. Assume that you receive a flat rate of return of 5% before expenses. If the fund has expenses of 1.5%, after 20 years you would end up with roughly $2,410. If the fund has expenses of 0.5%, you would end up with more than $2,410. This is a 22% difference.

Additional Sources of Information

Read the sections of the prospectus that discuss the risks, investment goals, and investment policies of any fund that you are considering. Funds of the same type can have significantly different risks, objectives, and policies.

All mutual funds must prepare a Statement of Additional Information (SAI, also called Part B of the prospectus). It explains a fund's operations in greater detail than the prospectus. If you ask, the fund must send you an SAI.

You can get a clearer picture of a fund's investment goals and policies by reading its annual and semi-annual reports to shareholders.

You can also research funds at most libraries. Helpful resources include fund investment books, investor magazines, and newspapers. The fund companies themselves can also provide information.

How to Measure the Shrinking Value of the Dollar

Source: Martin Lefkowitz, Economist, U.S. Chamber of Commerce.

How to use this table. This table provides a method for translating dollar values from the past 51 years into 1997 dollars. For example: What weekly salary would you need to earn in 1997 to equal the purchasing power of a weekly salary of $100 in 1960? Take the 1960 multiplier, 5.43, times $100 and you would need to earn $543 a week in 1997 to achieve the same salary.

Year	Value of dollar in 1997 dollars	Year	Value of dollar in 1997 dollars	Year	Value of dollar in 1997 dollars
1946	8.25	1964	5.19	1982	1.67
1947	6.90	1965	5.11	1983	1.61
1948	6.67	1966	4.96	1984	1.55
1949	6.76	1967	4.81	1985	1.49
1950	6.67	1968	4.62	1986	1.47
1951	6.19	1969	4.38	1987	1.42
1952	6.07	1970	4.14	1988	1.36
1953	6.02	1971	3.97	1989	1.30
1954	5.98	1972	3.85	1990	1.23
1955	6.00	1973	3.62	1991	1.18
1956	5.91	1974	3.26	1992	1.15
1957	5.72	1975	2.99	1993	1.11
1958	5.56	1976	2.83	1994	1.09
1959	5.53	1977	2.65	1995	1.06
1960	5.43	1978	2.47	1996	1.02
1961	5.38	1979	2.22	1997	1.00
1962	5.33	1980	1.95		
1963	5.26	1981	1.77		

NOTE: These figures are based on projected consumer price increases of 2.5% in 1997.

50 Largest Mutual Funds, 1996

Fund name	Total 1996 return	Annualized returns[1]		Minimum initial purchase	Net assets (millions)	Loads and fees	
		3 year	5 year			Front/ back load[2]	12b-1 fee[3]
Large-cap growth							
American Cent. 20th C Growth	15.0%	10.9%	6.3%	2,500	4,667	0.00%	0.00%
American Cent. 20th C Ultra	13.9%	14.7%	13.3%	2,500	18,419	0.00%	0.00%
Fidelity Growth Company	16.8%	16.8%	14.9%	2,500	9,603	3.00%	0.00%
Growth Fund of America	14.8%	14.2%	12.9%	1,000	9,846	5.75%	0.25%
IDS New Dimensions A	24.4%	17.8%	14.5%	2,000	6,785	5.00%	0.00%
Vanguard U.S. Growth	26.1%	21.9%	12.9%	3,000	5,591	0.00%	0.00%
Large-cap blend							
Dean Witter Dividend Growth	19.3%	15.9%	13.5%	1,000	12,354	5.00%	0.00%
Fidelity Adv. Grow. Opport. T	17.7%	17.2%	17.8%	2,500	15,528	3.50%	0.65%
Fidelity Growth & Income	20.0%	18.5%	17.2%	2,500	23,992	0.00%	0.00%
Fundamental Investors	20.0%	17.7%	16.3%	250	7,182	5.75%	0.25%
Investment Co. of America	19.4%	16.0%	13.3%	250	31,521	5.75%	0.25%
Janus	19.6%	15.3%	12.7%	2,500	15,890	0.00%	0.00%
Putnam Fund for Grth. & Inc. A	21.8%	18.4%	16.2%	500	12,354	5.75%	0.25%
Putnam Fund for Grth. & Inc. B	20.8%	17.5%	0.0%	500	9,511	5.00%	1.00%
T. Rowe Price Equity-Income	20.4%	18.8%	17.1%	2,500	7,733	0.00%	0.00%
United Income A	20.5%	15.3%	14.5%	500	4,990	5.75%	0.25%
Vanguard Index 500	22.9%	19.6%	15.1%	3,000	30,312	0.00%	0.00%
Large-cap value							
American Mutual	16.2%	15.3%	13.6%	250	8,129	5.75%	0.25%
Fidelity Destiny	18.6%	19.2%	19.8%	50	5,089	8.24%	0.00%
Fidelity Equity-Income	21.0%	16.9%	17.3%	2,500	14,355	0.00%	0.00%
Fidelity Equity-Income II	18.7%	15.7%	17.0%	2,500	15,598	0.00%	0.00%
Lord Abbett Affiliated A	20.1%	18.0%	15.9%	250	6,410	5.75%	0.50%
Neuberger & Berman Guardian	17.9%	16.1%	16.4%	1,000	5,608	0.00%	0.00%
Vanguard/Windsor II	24.2%	19.4%	16.7%	3,000	15,871	0.00%	0.00%
Washington Mutual	20.2%	19.5%	16.0%	250	25,757	5.75%	0.25%
Mid-cap growth							
AIM Constellation A	16.3%	16.9%	16.6%	500	11,915	5.50%	0.30%
Fidelity Blue Chip Growth	15.4%	17.6%	16.6%	2,500	9,838	3.00%	0.00%
PBHG Growth	9.8%	20.0%	26.6%	2,500	5,931	0.00%	0.00%
Putnam New Opportunities A	10.8%	18.8%	22.8%	500	6,036	5.75%	0.35%
Putnam New Opportunities B	10.0%	17.9%	0.0%	500	5,473	5.00%	1.00%
Putnam Voyager A	12.8%	16.7%	15.6%	500	8,953	5.75%	0.25%
Mid-cap blend							
AIM Value A	14.5%	16.8%	17.1%	500	5,128	5.50%	0.25%
AIM Value B	13.6%	15.9%	0.0%	500	4,874	5.00%	1.00%
AIM Weingarten A	17.7%	16.5%	9.6%	500	5,110	5.50%	0.30%
Fidelity Contrafund	21.9%	18.0%	18.3%	2,500	23,921	3.00%	0.00%
Fidelity Magellan	11.7%	14.5%	14.9%	2,500	55,851	3.00%	0.00%
Mid-cap value							
Fidelity Value	16.9%	16.9%	19.0%	2,500	7,285	0.00%	0.00%
Pioneer II A	22.0%	15.1%	14.7%	50	6,050	5.75%	0.25%
Small-cap growth							
Smallcap World	19.8%	12.6%	14.6%	1,000	6,970	5.75%	0.30%
Kaufmann	20.9%	21.7%	18.9%	1,500	5,274	0.00%	0.75%
Small-cap value							
Fidelity Low-Priced Stock	26.9%	18.4%	20.8%	2,500	5,298	3.00%	0.00%
International stock funds							
Capital World Growth & Inc.	21.6%	14.3%	0.0%	1,000	5,140	5.75%	0.30%
EuroPacific Growth	18.6%	10.6%	13.4%	250	15,424	5.75%	0.25%
Janus Worldwide	26.4%	16.9%	17.5%	2,500	5,046	0.00%	0.00%
New Perspective	17.3%	13.3%	13.9%	250	12,858	5.75%	0.25%
T. Rowe Price Intl. Stock	16.0%	8.6%	11.6%	2,500	9,239	0.00%	0.00%
Templeton Foreign I	18.0%	9.6%	12.5%	100	10,140	5.75%	0.25%
Templeton Growth I	20.6%	13.4%	15.0%	100	8,835	5.75%	0.25%
Templeton World I	21.5%	14.2%	15.5%	100	6,685	5.75%	0.25%
Vanguard Intl. Growth	14.7%	9.9%	12.6%	3,000	5,521	0.00%	0.00%

NOTE: Although data are gathered from reliable sources, Morningstar cannot guarantee completeness or accuracy. 1. Expressed in percentage terms, Morningstar's calculation of total return is computed each month by taking the change in monthly *net asset value*, reinvesting all income and *capital gains* distributions during that month, and dividing by the starting NAV. Reinvestments are made on the reinvestment date, and daily payoffs are also reinvested daily. Morningstar does not adjust the total returns in this section for sales charges (such as *front-end*, *deferred*, and *redemption fees*), preferring to give a clear picture of the fund's performance. The total returns do account for management, administrative, and 12b-1 fees, and other costs automatically taken out of fund assets. For ease of use, total returns for periods longer than one year are expressed in terms of compounded average annual returns (also known as geometric total return). 2. Front-end loads are the initial, one-time, sales charge deducted from an investment made into the fund. The amount is generally relative to the amount of the investment, so that larger investments incur smaller rates of charge. The sales chare serves as a commission for the broker who sold the fund. Back-end, or deferred, fees are imposed when the investor removes money from the fund. The percentage charged generally declines the longer shares are held. This charge, often coupled with 12b-1 fees as an alternative to a traditional front-end load, diminishes over time. 3. The maximum annual charge cdeducted from fund assets to pay for distribution and marketing costs. Although usually set on a percentage basis, this amount will occasionally be a flat figure. Only active 12b-1 plans are represented here. This information is taken directly from the fund's prospectus. (Morningstar lists the maximum amount.) *Source:* Data provided by Morningstar, Inc. www.morningstar.net

Mortgage Qualifications for Buying a Home

Source: Fannie Mae.

Your History

Your job history is important and it will be a major factor in whether you qualify for a loan. If you have been working continuously for two years or more, you are considered to have steady employment. However, you do not have to have held the same job for two years in order to be approved for a loan. Job moves that result in equal or more pay and continue to use proven skills are a plus for you. If there are good reasons why you haven't worked continuously for the last two years, you can explain them to the mortgage lender.

How you paid your bills in the past also gives a lender some indication of how you can be expected to pay them in the future. You will be asked to list all your debts, the amount of your monthly payments, and the number of months or years left to pay on the debts. Your lender will order a credit report to verify the information that you give.

Payment Options

When you buy a home, you need money for a down payment and "closing costs." The amount of the down payment may vary, but generally you must make a down payment that equals at least five percent of the purchase price. You will also need money for closing costs. These costs can be expensive, depending upon where you live.

The mortgage lender will want proof that you have saved the funds that you will use for a down payment and part or all of the closing costs. If the funds are in a savings account, the lender will ask the financial institution to verify the amount and the length of time that the funds have been in your account. The lender wants to make sure that you are not borrowing all the money you will use for the down payment and closing costs.

The amount of your monthly payment depends upon the amount you borrow, the interest rate, and the repayment period or "term." The shorter the term, the higher your monthly payment. For that reason, most home buyers repay their mortgage over the longest term possible, usually 30 years.

Housing Expense Guideline

When you first approach a lender about financing a mortgage for you, they will use the following two commonly accepted guidelines to help determine your ability to make mortgage payments:

1. Your monthly housing costs (including mortgage payments, property taxes, homeowner and mortgage insurance, and homeowner's fees) should total no more than 28 percent of your monthly gross (before taxes) income. In addition to your regular pay, your income can include funds you receive from overtime work, a part-time job or second job; retirement, VA, and Social Security benefits; disability; welfare and unemployment benefits; alimony; and child support.

2. Your monthly housing costs plus other long-term debts such as payments on car loans, student loans, or other installment debt (debts with more than ten months left to repay) should total no more than 36 percent of your monthly gross income. Depending upon your household income, you may be eligible for special assistance programs. These programs may make it easier for you to get a larger mortgage loan than you normally would be able to using the above qualifying rules.

How Large a Mortgage Do You Qualify For?

Source: Fannie Mae.

Interest Rates	Annual Income					
	$15,000	**$20,000**	**$25,000**	**$30,000**	**$35,000**	**$40,000**
6.5%	$49,400	$65,900	$82,400	$98,800	$115,300	$131,800
7.0%	47,000	62,600	78,300	93,900	109,600	125,300
7.5%	44,600	59,600	74,500	89,400	104,300	119,200
8.0%	45,000	56,700	70,900	85,100	99,300	113,500
8.5%	40,600	54,100	67,700	81,200	94,800	108,300
9.0%	38,800	51,700	64,700	77,700	90,600	103,500
9.5%	37,200	49,500	61,900	74,300	86,700	99,100
10.0%	35,600	47,400	59,300	71,200	83,000	94,900
10.5%	34,200	45,500	56,900	68,300	79,700	91,100
	$45,000	**$50,000**	**$55,000**	**$60,000**	**$65,000**	**$70,000**
6.5%	$148,300	$164,800	$181,300	$197,700	$214,200	$230,000
7.0%	140,900	156,600	172,300	187,900	203,600	219,200
7.5%	134,100	149,000	163,900	178,800	193,700	208,600
8.0%	127,700	141,900	156,100	170,300	184,500	198,700
8.5%	121,900	135,400	149,000	162,500	176,100	189,600
9.0%	116,500	129,400	142,400	155,300	168,200	181,200
9.5%	111,400	123,800	136,200	148,600	161,000	173,400
10.0%	106,800	118,600	130,500	142,400	154,300	166,100
10.5%	102,400	113,800	125,200	136,600	148,000	159,400

The above chart can help you find out how large a mortgage you might qualify for based on your annual income and the interest rate currently being quoted for 30-year fixed-rate mortgages. Rather than using the normal 28 percent ratio, this chart uses a 25 percent ratio and assumes that the amount you need to set aside to pay for taxes and insurance would amount to approximately the 3 percent difference. This simplified approach should give you a fairly accurate answer.

Calculate Your Mortgage Payment
Source: Fannie Mae.

Loan Amount	Interest Rates								
	6.5%	7%	7.5%	8%	8.5%	9%	9.5%	10%	10.5%
$20,000	$126	$133	$140	$147	$154	$161	$168	$176	$183
25,000	158	166	175	183	192	201	210	219	229
30,000	190	200	210	220	231	241	252	263	274
35,000	221	233	245	257	269	282	294	307	320
40,000	253	266	280	294	308	322	336	351	366
45,000	284	299	315	330	346	362	378	395	412
50,000	316	333	350	367	384	402	420	439	457
55,000	348	366	385	404	423	443	462	483	503
60,000	380	399	420	440	461	483	505	527	549
65,000	411	432	454	477	500	523	547	570	595
70,000	442	466	489	514	538	563	589	614	640
75,000	474	499	524	550	577	603	631	658	686
80,000	506	532	559	587	615	644	673	702	732
85,000	537	566	594	624	654	684	715	746	778
90,000	569	599	629	660	692	724	757	790	823
95,000	600	632	664	697	730	764	799	834	869
100,000	632	665	699	734	769	805	841	878	915

Use the chart above to calculate how much your monthly mortgage payment might be. Let's suppose that you want to purchase a house that costs $50,000. If you make a $5,000 down payment, you would need a $45,000 mortgage. As you can see on the chart, the monthly payment on a $45,000 mortgage at 8 percent interest is $330. The $330 monthly payment only covers the principal, or a portion of the amount you borrowed, and interest on the mortgage loan. There are other expenses that will be added to your monthly payment. These include taxes and homeowner's insurance. If your down payment is less than 20 percent, you may need to pay private mortgage insurance. These costs vary depending upon where you live and the cost of your home, but they can add a hundred dollars or more to your monthly payment. In addition, if you are thinking about buying a unit in a condo or cooperative building, or a house in a planned unit development, you may also need to pay monthly homeowner's fees to cover maintenance expenses or special assessments related to the common areas.

Financial Planners
Source: Consumer Federation of American and National Institute for Consumer Education.

The way in which a financial planner is compensated can directly affect the advice he or she gives clients. A relatively small percentage of the individuals offering financial advice actually get paid exclusively for giving such advice. The majority earn some or all of their income selling mutual funds, annuities, insurance, and other financial products to implement their recommendations. "Advisers" who are also salespeople, however, inevitably face a conflict of interest and will almost certainly be tempted to steer clients into products in which they have a financial interest. The greater the adviser's dependence on commission income, the greater the conflict. In the end, that conflict could cost you both in out-of-pocket expenses and in the quality of advice you receive.

Long-Term Cost

One of the chief attractions of commission-based financial planning is that it appears affordable. Typically, commission-based planners charge a relatively low fee or no fee, for the "advice," expecting to earn the real money on the back end, when they sell the products to implement their recommendations. When you buy a product to implement that plan, however, a percentage of the money you spend goes to pay a commission to the planner. Ultimately, the price you pay includes not just the commission itself, but the money it would have earned over time had it been invested. In assessing the costs of financial planning, therefore, you have to include the cost of implementation.

Quality of Advice

The increase in implementation costs is not the only price you pay for commission-based planning. You may also pay in the form of poor advice. After all, when a financial "adviser" earns most of his or her money as a financial salesperson, the product sales tend to drive the process. In the worst case scenario, the planning becomes nothing more than window dressing to attract clients for the real money-making business of selling

Additional Information

A variety of useful information can be obtained from state financial regulatory agencies, particularly the securities agencies that can be found in the blue pages of your phone book.

You can call the North American Securities Administrators Association at (202) 737-0900 for the phone number of your state security agency or the National Association of Insurance Commissioners at (816) 842-3600 for the phone number of your state insurance department.

Your planner may not be registered at the state level because the firm has more than $25 million in assets under management and is required to register with the Securities and Exchange Commission (SEC). You can call the SEC at (202) 942-8088. Their web site is www.sec.gov.

Many fee-only financial planners are members of the National Association of Personal Financial advisers (NAPFA). For a list of fee-only financial planners in your area, call NAPFA at 1-800-FEE-ONLY or visit their homepage at www.feeonly.org

products. Clients are offered one-size-fits-all plans that inevitably lead to the purchase of a handful of high-commission products.

Even those commission-based advisers who attempt to offer comprehensive financial advice still can find themselves biased by compensation considerations when it comes time to implement their recommendations. After all, the more the adviser lowers the initial fees to attract business, and the more time he or she spends on the planning process, the more he or she must earn in the implementation phase to make that investment of time pay off.

Under such circumstances, even the best of commission-based planners is unlikely to recommend no-load or low-load products, for example. Other less scrupulous planners may recommend an investment, such as a particular mutual fund or annuity, simply because of the special incentives or higher commissions they receive.

The temptation for planners to recommend higher commission products carries another risk for clients. Product sponsors tend to offer higher commissions on those products that are more difficult to sell, because they are riskier. Thus, in pushing higher commission products, the planner may encourage you to take unnecessary risks with your money.

"Fee-Only" May Be Your Best Choice

So, if you are looking for objective financial advice, a fee-only financial planner is probably your best bet. Fee-only financial planners are compensated solely by fees paid by their clients. They can be paid in a variety of ways—a flat fee or retainer, an hourly fee, a percentage of assets under management, or a percentage of income from investments. The key is that they do not accept commissions or compensation from any other source.

Fee-only financial planning does not necessarily eliminate every conceivable form of conflict-of-interest. When fee-only planners "sell" portfolio management services, for example, they may have a financial incentive to recommend those services to clients. The fee-only approach is, however, subject to fewer conflicts than any other form of financial advice. Furthermore, because fee-only planners are compensated solely by the client, there are no hidden third parties in the relationship and thus, no divided loyalties.

The Financial Planning "Name Game"

If a fee-only financial planner is probably your best bet, what about all those other planners out there? As consumers have started to wake up to the conflicts of interest that result from commission-based compensation, more and more financial planners have adopted confusing terminology designed to obscure how they are compensated. Here are a few of the most common that you should be on the look-out for:

Fee-and-commission. This is the now somewhat out of fashion term for a planner who earns a fee for developing a financial plan, then earns commissions selling the products to implement that plan. For years, planners were able to sell this arrangement as being in their client's best interests on the grounds that they were more objective than commission-only salespeople and more affordable and convenient than fee-only planners.

Since consumers have become more conscious of the total costs of fee-and-commission planning and the incentives commission-dependent planners have to steer them into costly and possibly inappropriate products, few planners now use this relatively candid terminology, though the majority continue to practice in this fashion.

Fee-based. This is today's more fashionable terminology for fee-and-commission financial planning. The conflicts are the same, but the candor is gone. Some "fee-based" financial planners will tell clients they can work either on a fee-only basis or on a fee-and-commission basis if the client wants to implement the plan through them. Somehow, however, the bulk of their clients end up as fee-and-commission clients. The term "fee-based" is misleading, so you should be wary of those who use it.

Fee-offset. Under a fee-offset arrangement, a planner imposes a fee for drawing up a strategy, then reduces up to 100 percent of that fee to account for any commissions that may be earned in implementing the plan. The problem of commission bias is less obvious, but it remains. After all, if a financial plan costs $2,000 and the planner earns $10,000 in commissions for selling the needed products, he or she will be able to pocket $8,000 in conflict-producing commissions . . . even after totally offsetting the cost of the original plan.

Excerpted from *Don't Get Burned by the Financial Planner "Name Game,"* a publication of the Consumer Federation of America and National Institute for Consumer Education. Reprinted with their permission. The Consumer Federation of America, 1424 16th Street NW, Suite 604, Washington DC 20036, (202) 387-6120, is a non-profit association of some 240 pro-consumer groups, with a combined membership of 50 million, that was founded in 1968 to advance the consumer interest through advocacy and education. The National Institute for Consumer Education at Eastern Michigan University is a professional development center for educators in consumer, economic, and personal finance education.

State Unemployment Compensation

Average Benefit, February 1997

State	Avg. Wkly. Benefit	State	Avg. Wkly. Benefit	State	Avg. Wkly. Benefit
Alabama	$146.47	Louisiana	$130.39	Oklahoma	$181.13
Alaska	$172.89	Maine	$172.79	Oregon	$193.96
Arizona	$155.37	Maryland	$202.82	Pennsylvania	$227.18
Arkansas	$168.99	Massachusetts	$266.89	Puerto Rico	$95.03
California	$152.20	Michigan	$203.30	Rhode Island	$231.51
Colorado	$211.44	Minnesota	$242.31	South Carolina	$166.66
Connecticut	$232.27	Mississippi	$145.90	South Dakota	$159.25
Delaware	$236.73	Missouri	$156.56	Tennessee	$154.94
District of Columbia	$241.33	Montana	$174.20	Texas	$189.12
Florida	$184.18	Nebraska	$167.65	Utah	$202.76
Georgia	$166.59	Nevada	$198.08	Vermont	$175.95
Hawaii	$274.76	New Hampshire	$154.36	Virgin Islands	$146.12
Idaho	$190.30	New Jersey	$259.98	Virginia	$173.83
Illinois	$227.58	New Mexico	$156.26	Washington	$208.49
Indiana	$199.21	New York	$204.46	West Virginia	$175.70
Iowa	$209.06	North Carolina	$191.97	Wisconsin	$214.69
Kansas	$208.18	North Dakota	$187.15	Wyoming	$183.49
Kentucky	$170.94	Ohio	$210.58	United States	$195.32

Average Weekly Benefit for weeks of total unemployment. *Source:* Department of Labor, Employment and Training Administration.

Social Security

Quo Vadis Social Security?

The Debate Escalates Over Social Security Reform

In 1935 when the Social Security system was created, the employed workforce paid into a fund to ensure the income of retirees. The pool of funds available seemed generous at the time, since the workforce far outnumbered retirees collecting benefits. Even in 1950 there were 15 workers for every beneficiary. But in recent years better medical technology, enabling people to live longer, and an aging baby-boom population have dramatically altered this balance. This shift has brought to the fore a debate long kept in the backs of the minds of the plan's administrators: how can the pay-as-you-go system sustain itself in the face of an aging population?

The system's original framework is crumbling under the weight of a rapidly growing retirement population; each beneficiary in the system today is supported by just over three workers. According to a June 1996 government report, the current trust fund will have been depleted by 2029 and the system will be running at a deficit.

The imminent insolvency of the Social Security system is troubling all segments of the American population. Current beneficiaries worry that their benefits may be cut; baby boomers are concerned that the system will be dismantled before they begin collecting benefits in 2011; younger workers see their taxes going to a fund from which they are unlikely to ever receive benefits.

Three Solutions Proposed

To solve the long-term financial problems of the program, Secretary of Health and Human Services Donna E. Shalala appointed a 13-member Advisory Council on Social Security in 1994. Their final report, delivered in January 1997, recommended that revenue be increased and that part of the trust fund be invested in the stock market. Currently, the entire trust fund is invested in low-yield government bonds, which, though low-risk, have historically provided lower returns than the stock market. The report theorizes that if this equity premium persists, the increased returns should prolong the life of the current system.

The report also recommended distributing the cost of these changes across all segments of the population so that no one age group is penalized while others are spared. Individual members disagreed on sources of revenue increases and on the extent of government involvement, and so proposed three separate solutions:

1. Leave the current system largely unchanged, allowing the government to continue managing the trust fund's portfolio but diversifying its investments to include stocks.
2. Preserve the existing trust fund by scaling back benefits and adding new revenue with the creation of Individual Savings Accounts, managed by the government.
3. Create a new system with a flat federal benefit and supplemental benefits provided by mandatory Personal Security Accounts, managed by individual investors.

Plan Highlights

Maintain Benefits Plan The primary tenet of this plan is that revenue increases would make it possible to maintain Social Security benefits at current levels.

Revenue increases come from:
• New taxes on Social Security benefits in excess of original contributions.
• Increased payroll tax rate; combined employee-employer rate increases by 1.6% starting in 2045.
• Enlarged contributor base, including state and local government employees hired after 1997.
• Improved return on investments through diversification into the stock market.

Government involvement: Government controls investment of a portion of the funds assets (approximately 40% by 2014) in common stocks, increasing the value of the trust fund without incurring the risks that could accompany individual investment.

The potential hazards of this approach are:
• Because of the large sums under its control, the government could alter the performance of the market, in effect reducing or eliminating the equity premium.
• Conflict of interest: should there be restrictions on the types or amounts of stock the government can own, and if so, how will this affect the returns on the portfolio?
• Policy decisions could be driven by possible effect on the fund's portfolio.
• When the market performs poorly, would the government be expected to bail out the fund?

Individual Accounts Plan The primary tenet of this plan is to create government-administered retirement accounts to supplement decreased Social Security benefits.

Revenue increases come from:
• New 1.6% payroll tax to fund Individual Accounts, similar to a 401(k) plan. Workers would have a limited choice on how they can invest these funds and they would have to choose from government-approved options.
• Reduced benefits for dependent spouses. Benefits paid to a dependent spouse would be lowered from 50% to 33% of the worker's benefit while the working spouse is alive.
• Delayed benefits for dependent spouses. If the working spouse dies before becoming eligible for retirement benefits, payment of the survivor's benefits (75% of the combined benefits) would be delayed to the date on which the deceased would have become eligible.
• New federal income tax on all benefits paid in excess of contributions.
• Slower growth rate for future benefits of middle- and high-wage earners.
• Delay in payment of benefits by increasing retirement age to 67 years old by 2011; adjusted thereafter to reflect changes in life expectancy.
• Enlarged contributor base, including state and local government employees hired after 1997.

Government involvement: Government manages the Individual Accounts and approves investment options.

Other provisions:
• Funds accumulated from the Individual Accounts would automatically be converted to annuities when individuals retire. The annuities would contain a minimum guarantee provision to assure a minimum payout to the individual or his or her heirs.

• Survivor benefits for two-earner couples would be increased. A surviving spouse's benefit would be determined as the highest of (1) his or her own basic benefit, (2) the deceased spouse's benefit, or (3) 75% of the couple's combined basic benefits.

The potential hazards of this approach are:

• Low-wage earners will have less to invest and lower standards of living in retirement.

• To the extent that they are allowed to choose among investment options, experienced investors will be at an advantage.

Personal Security Accounts (PSAs) The primary tenet of this plan is to create retirement accounts administered by individuals to supplement flat-rate federal benefits.

Revenue increases come from:

• New 1.5% payroll tax for the next 75 years (primarily to fund the accrued obligations of retirees, since current workers will be funding their own retirements).

• New tax on the portion of benefits derived from employer contributions.

• Delay in payment of benefits by increasing retirement age to 67-years-old by 2011; adjusted thereafter to reflect changes in life expectancy.

• Enlarged contributor base, including state and local government employees hired after 1997.

Government involvement: Transition the current system into a two-tiered approach: flat-rate federal benefits, and supplemental income through IRA-type individual accounts funded through payroll deductions. The PSAs will not be held by the government. Workers will be solely responsible for investing them in stocks and bonds.

Other provisions:

• PSAs funded by diverting 5% of current Social Security taxes into individual accounts.

• Safety-net provision for retirees so that they would not slip into poverty.

• Workers not required to annuitize their funds at retirement; fewer restrictions on investment options.

• Current retirees and workers age 55 and older would receive benefits under the existing Social Security system; others would receive benefits from a combination of Social Security and their PSAs.

• Over the 1998–2002 year period, the retirement earnings test which reduces benefits account of earnings above an exempt amount, would be eliminated at the age of eligibility for full retirement benefits.

The potential hazard of this approach is:

• Greater flexibility in choosing investment options leads to a greater risk that inexperienced investors can lose their nest egg through poor investments.

By offering a range of potential solutions, the council may have been attempting to avoid the political fallout of prescribing a single solution. The effect, however, was to offer a view into the possibilities, both good and bad, that diversification offers. Though the recommendations made by the council are not binding, they have succeeded in focusing attention on the dire plight of Social Security, and the need for near-term reform to ensure the long-term survival of the program.

Social Security

The original Social Security Act was passed in 1935 and is administered by the Social Security Administration and other agencies within the Department of Health and Human Services.

Old Age, Disability, and Survivors Insurance

Nine out of ten workers in the U.S. are in employment or self-employment covered by the retirement, survivors, disability, and hospital insurance programs. The major groups not covered are:

A. Federal civilian employees hired before 1984.

B. Employees of state and local governments who are members of their employer's retirement system and who have not been covered by a voluntary Federal/State Social Security Agreement.

C. Certain agricultural and domestic workers.

Cash tips count for Social Security if they amount to $20 or more in a month from employment with a single employer.

To qualify for benefits or make payments possible for your survivors, you must be in work covered by the law for a certain number of "quarters of coverage," or credits. Before 1978, a credit was earned if a worker was paid $50 or more in wages in a 3-month calendar quarter. A self-employed person got 4 credits for a year in which his or her net earnings were $400 or more.

In 1978, a worker, whether employed or self-employed, received one credit for each $250 of covered annual earnings up to a maximum of four for a year. The credit measure was increased as shown above, and will increase automatically in future years to keep pace with increases in average wages.

The number of credits needed differs for different persons and depends on the date of your birth; in general, it is related to the number of years after 1950, or after the year you reach 21, if later, and up to the year you reach 62, become disabled, or die. One credit is

Year	Credit Measure ($)	Year	Credit Measure ($)	Year	Credit Measure ($)
1979	$260	1986	$440	1993	$590
1980	290	1987	460	1994	620
1981	310	1988	470	1995	630
1982	340	1989	500	1996	640
1983	370	1990	520	1997	670
1984	390	1991	540		
1985	410	1992	570		

required for each such year in order for you or your family to get benefits. Credits earned at any time are used to decide if you have the number needed to qualify. No one will need more than 40 credits. Your local Social Security office can tell you how long you need to work.

Who Pays for the Insurance?

Both workers and their employers pay for the workers' insurance. Self-employed persons pay their own social security contributions annually along with their income tax. The rates include the cost of Medicare hospital insurance. The contribution and benefit base is $57,600 for 1993 for retirement, survivor and disability coverage, and $135,000 for 1993 for Medicare coverage, and will increase automatically in future years as earnings levels rise. The contribution rate schedules under present law are shown in the table in this section.

The separate payroll contribution to finance hospital insurance is placed in a separate trust fund in the U.S. Treasury. In addition, the medical insurance premiums, currently $46.10 a month in 1995, and the government's shares go into another separate trust fund.

How to Apply for Benefits

You apply for benefits by filing a claim either in person, by mail, or by telephone at any Social Security office. You can get the address of your nearest office either from the post office, from the phone book under the listing, United States Government—Social Security Administration, or by calling Social Security's toll-free number 1-800-772-1213. You will need certain kinds of proof, depending upon the type of benefit you are claiming. If it is a retirement benefit, you should provide your social security number and a birth certificate or religious record (preferably recorded before age 5). If you are unable to get these documents, other old documents showing your age or date of birth—such as census records, school records, early naturalization certificate, etc.—may be acceptable. A widow, or widower, 60 or older, who is claiming widow's benefits based on his/her spouse's earnings should have his/her own social security number, his/her spouse's social security number, proof of age and a copy of the marriage certificate. A child claiming child's benefits should provide a birth certificate, his/her own social security number, and the social security number of the parent on whose record benefits are being claimed. If formal proof is not available, the Social Security office will tell you what kinds of information will be acceptable. Do not delay applying even if you do not have the necessary information or proofs.

What Does Social Security Offer?

The Social Security contribution you pay gives you four different kinds of protection: (1) retirement benefits, (2) survivors' benefits, (3) disability benefits, and (4) Medicare hospital insurance protection.

Social Security Contribution and Rate Schedule

(percent of covered earnings)

Year	Retirement survivors, and disability insurance	Hospital insurance (%)	Total
Employers and Employees			
1978	4.95%	1.10%	6.05%
1979–80	5.08	1.05	6.13
1981	5.35	1.30	6.65
1982–83	5.40	1.30	6.70
1984	5.70	1.30	7.00
1985	5.70	1.35	7.05
1986–87	5.70	1.45	7.15
1988–89	6.06	1.45	7.51
1990 & later	6.20	1.45	7.65
Self-employed			
1978	7.00%	1.10%	8.10%
1979–80	7.05	1.05	8.10
1981	8.00	1.30	9.30
1982	8.05	1.30	9.35
1983	8.05	1.30	9.35
1984	11.40	2.60	*14.00
1985	11.40	2.70	*14.10
1986–87	11.40	2.90	*14.30
1988–89	12.12	2.90	*15.02
1990 & later	12.40	2.90	*15.30

* The law provides credit against self-employment tax liability in the following manner: 2.7% in 1984; 2.3% in 1985; 2.09% 1986–1989 and, beginning with the 1990 taxable year, the credit is replaced with two special provisions. First, self-employed persons will be allowed a 7.65% deduction from net profit before computing their SECA tax and second, an income tax deduction equal to one-half of the SECA tax.

Delayed Retirement Credit Rates

Age 65	Monthly percentage (%)	Yearly percentage (%)
Prior to 1982	1/12 of 1%	1 %
1982–1989	1/4 of 1%	3
1990–1991	7/24 of 1%	3.5
1992–1993	1/3 of 1%	4
1994–1995	3/8 of 1%	4.5
1996–1997	5/12 of 1%	5
1998–1999	11/24 of 1%	5.5
2000–2001	1/2 of 1%	6
2002–2003	13/24 of 1%	6.5
2004–2005	7/12 of 1%	7
2006–2007	5/8 of 1%	7.5
2008 or later	2/3 of 1%	8

Retirement and Dependents' Benefits

Currently, a worker becomes eligible for the full amount of his retirement benefits at age 65, if he has retired under the definition in the law. A worker may retire at 62 and get 80% of his full benefit. The closer he is to age 65, when he starts collecting his benefit, the larger is the fraction of his full benefit that he will get. Once the worker receives a reduced benefit, the reduction continues after age 65.

The amount of the retirement benefit you are entitled to at 65 is the key to all other benefits under the program. The retirement benefit is based on covered earnings, which will be updated (indexed) to the second year before you reach age 62, become disabled, or die, and will reflect the increases in average wages that have occurred since the earnings were paid. The largest 35 years of adjusted earnings are averaged together and a formula is applied to the adjusted average to figure the benefit rate.

A worker who delays his retirement past age 65, or who does not receive a benefit for some months after age 65 because of high earnings, will get a special credit that can mean a larger benefit. The credit adds to a worker's benefits 1% (3% for workers age 62 from 1979–1986) for each year ($\frac{1}{12}$ of 1% for each month) from age 65 to age 70 for which he did not get benefits.

If a worker receives a pension from work not covered by Social Security, a different formula, which yields a smaller benefit, applies to eliminate the weighting in the Social Security formula which applies to workers whose careers were spent in lower paying jobs.

The law provides a special minimum benefit at retirement for people who worked under Social Security for many years. The provision will help people who had low incomes but above a specific level, during their working years. The amount of the special minimum depends on the number of years above a specific earnings level called "years of coverage." For a worker retiring at 65 in January 1997 with 30 or more years of coverage, the special minimum benefit would be $548.30. These benefits are reduced if a worker is under 65 and are increased automatically for increases in the cost of living.

If you retired at age 65 in January 1997 with average earnings, you would get a benefit of $933. If your spouse is also 65, then he or she will get a spouse's benefit that is equal to half your benefit. So if your benefit is $933, your spouse gets $466.

If your spouse is between ages 62 and 65, he or she can draw a reduced benefit; the amount depends on the number of months before 65 that he or she starts getting checks. If he or she draws his or her benefit when he or she is 62, he or she will get about ⅜ of your basic benefit, or $349. (He or she will get this amount for the rest of his or her life, unless you should die first; then he or she can start getting widow's or widower's benefits, described below.)

If the spouse is entitled to a worker's retirement benefit on his or her own earnings, he or she can draw whichever amount is larger. If the spouse is entitled to a retirement benefit which is less than the spouse's benefit, he or she will receive his or her own retirement benefit plus the difference between the retirement benefit and the spouse's benefit.

If you have children under 18 or a child under age 19 and in full-time attendance at an elementary or secondary school or a son or daughter who became totally disabled prior to reaching age 22, when you retire they will get a benefit equal to half your full retirement benefits (subject to maximum monthly payment that can be made to a family). Children who can qualify for benefits include your biological or legally adopted child, or dependent stepchild or grandchild. If your spouse is caring for your child who is under 16 or who became disabled before 22 (and getting benefits too), he or she is eligible for benefits, even if he or she is under 62.

In general, the highest retirement check that can be paid to a worker who retired at 65 in January 1997 is about $1,327.60 a month. Maximum payment to the family of this retired worker is about $2,324.40 in January 1997. When your children reach age 18, their benefits will stop except for children age 19 and under attending an elementary or secondary school full time and except for a benefit that is going to a son or daughter who became totally disabled before attaining age 22. Such a person can continue to get his benefits as long as his disability meets the definition in the law.

If you are divorced, you can get Social Security benefits (the same as a spouse or widow, or widower), based on your ex-spouse's earnings record if you were married at least 10 years and if your ex-spouse has retired, or become disabled. If a divorced spouse has been divorced for at least 2 years, the spouse may be eligible for benefits even if the worker is not receiving benefits. However, both the worker and spouse must be age 62 or over and the worker must be fully insured. In either case, the divorced spouse must be unmarried.

Survivor Benefits

This feature of the Social Security program gives your family valuable life insurance protection—in some cases benefits to a family could amount to $100,000 or more over a period of years. The amount of protection is again geared to what the worker would be entitled to if he had been age 65 when he died. Your survivors could get:

1. A one-time cash payment. [NOTE: There is no restriction on the use of the lump-sum death payment.] This "lump-sum death payment" is $255.

2. A benefit for each child until he reaches 18, or 19 if the child is in full-time attendance at an elementary or secondary school, or at any age if disabled before 22. "Child" includes biological or legally adopted child, or dependent stepchild or grandchild. Each eligible child receives 75% of the basic benefit (subject to reduction for the family maximum). (A disabled child can continue to collect benefits after age 22.)

3. A benefit for your widow(er), including your surviving divorced spouse, at any age, if she/he has your entitled children under 16 or disabled in care. These are called mother/father benefits. "Your children" includes your biological or legally adopted children, dependent stepchildren or grandchildren. In the case of a surviving divorced spouse, the child must also be the divorced spouse's biological or legally adopted child. Her/his benefit is also 75% of the basic benefit. She/he can collect this as long as she/he has an entitled child under 16 or disabled

Work Credits Required for Living Persons To Be Fully Insured at Age 62

Individual's date of birth	Number of credits		Individual's date of birth	Number of credits (men & women)
	Men	Women		
1/1/1893 or earlier	6	6	1/2/13–1/1/14	24
1/2/93–1/1/94	7	6	1/2/14–1/1/15	25
1/2/94–1/1/95	8	6	1/2/15–1/1/16	26
1/2/95–1/1/96	9	6	1/2/16–1/1/17	27
1/2/96–1/1/97	10	7	1/2/17–1/1/18	28
1/2/97–1/1/98	11	8	1/2/18–1/1/19	29
1/2/98–1/1/99	12	9	1/2/19–1/1/20	30
1/2/1899–1/1/1900	13	10	1/2/20–1/1/21	31
1/2/00–1/1/01	14	11	1/2/21–1/1/22	32
1/2/01–1/1/02	15	12	1/2/22–1/1/23	33
1/2/02–1/1/03	16	13	1/2/23–1/1/24	34
1/2/03–1/1/04	17	14	1/2/24–1/1/25	35
1/2/04–1/1/05	18	15	1/2/25–1/1/26	36
1/2/05–1/1/06	19	16	1/2/26–1/1/27	37
1/2/06–1/1/07	20	17	1/2/27–1/1/28	38
1/2/07–1/1/08	21	18	1/2/28–1/1/29	39
1/2/08–1/1/09	22	19	1/2/29 or later	40
1/2/09–1/1/10	23	20		
1/2/10–1/1/11	24	21		
1/2/11–1/1/12	24	22		
1/2/12–1/1/13	24	23		

now "in care." If payments terminate they will start again upon application when she/he is 60 at a slightly lower amount.

Total family survivor benefits are estimated to be as high as $2,534.00 a month if the worker dies in 1995.

1. Your spouse or divorced spouse can get a widow's, widower's, or surviving divorced spouse's benefit starting at age 60. This benefit equals 71½% of the basic amount at age 60. A widow, or widower, who first becomes entitled at 65 or later will get 100% of his or her deceased spouse's basic amount (or the amount of the deceased spouse's reduced benefits). A widow(er) or surviving divorced spouse, including those who are disabled, must be unmarried. However, a marriage occurring after age 60, or after age 50 if disabled at the time of the remarriage, is disregarded.

2. Dependent parents can sometimes collect survivors' benefits. They are usually eligible if: (a) they were getting at least half their support from the deceased worker at (1) the time of the worker's death if the worker did not qualify for disability benefits before death, or (2) if the worker had been entitled to disability benefits which had not been terminated before death either at the beginning of the period of disability or at the time of death; (b) they have reached 62; (c) they are not eligible for a greater retirement benefit based on their own earnings; and (d) they have not married since the worker's death. One surviving parent can then get 82½% of the basic benefit. If two parents are eligible, each would get 75%.

If in addition to your Social Security benefit as a wife, husband, divorced spouse, widow, widower, or surviving divorced spouse you receive a pension based on your work in employment not covered by Social Security, your benefit as a spouse or survivor will be reduced by ⅔rds of the amount of that pension. Under an exception in the law, your government pension will not affect your spouse's or survivor's benefit if you became eligible for that pension before December 1982 and if, at the time you apply or become entitled to your

Social Security benefit as a spouse or survivor, you could have qualified for that benefit if the law in effect in January 1977 had remained in effect (*e.g.*, at that time, men had to prove they were dependent upon their wives for ½ support to be eligible for benefits as a spouse or survivor.) There are also several other exceptions in the law. Your government pension may also affect Social Security benefits based on your own work covered by Social Security. (*See* Retirement and Dependents' Benefits).

Disability Benefits

Disability benefits can be paid to several groups of people:

- Disabled workers under 65 and their families.
- Persons disabled before 22 who continue to be disabled. These benefits are payable as early as 18 when a parent (or step-parent or grandparent under certain circumstances) receives Social Security retirement or disability benefits or when an insured parent dies.
- Disabled widows and widowers and (under certain conditions) disabled surviving divorced spouses of workers who were insured at death. These benefits are payable as early as 50. Consult your local Social Security office for the latest disability information.

You Can Earn Income without Losing Benefits

If you are 70 or over you can earn any amount and still get all your benefits. If you are under 70, you can receive all benefits if your earnings do not exceed the annual exempt amount. The annual amount for 1997 is $13,500 for people 65 or over and $8,640 for people under 65.

If your earnings go over the annual amount, $1 in benefits is withheld for each $2 ($3 if age 65–69) of earnings above the limit. In 1996, Congress enacted legislation that will incrementally increase the annual exempt amount for beneficiaries age 65–69 to $30,000 in the year 2002. The legislated exempt amounts are as follows: $12,500 in 1996, $13,500 in 1997, $14,500 in 1998, $15,500 in 1999, $17,000 in 2000, $25,000 in 2001, and $30,000 in 2002. The annual exempt amount for beneficiaries under age 65 will increase in future years in accordance with increases in average wages.

Beneficiaries under age 70 who earn more than the annual exempt amount and receive some benefits during the year are required by law to report their earnings to the Social Security Administration. For years 1996 and later, SSA will accept the information reported on the form W-2 and the self-employment tax return to be the annual report required by law. This change was made to provide better service and reduce the reporting burden on the public. Beneficiaries will only need to report directly to the SSA if the information on those reports is not correct for purposes of the earnings test. If you continue to work after you have applied for Social Security, your additional earnings may increase the amount of your monthly payment. This will be done automatically by the Social Security Administration. You need not ask for it.

Supplemental Security Income

The supplemental security income (SSI) program is a federally funded program administered by the Social Security Administration. Its basic purpose is to assure a minimum level of income to people who are elderly (65 or over), blind or disabled, and who have limited income and resources.

In 1997, the maximum federal SSI payment was $484 a month for an individual and $726 a month for a couple. But in many states, SSI payments are much higher because the state adds to the federal payment.

Countable resources must be valued at $2,000 or less for an individual or $3,000 or less for a couple. But not all the things people own count for SSI. For instance, the house a person lives in and the land around it, and, usually, one car does not count.

Generally, depending on the state, people who get SSI can also get Medicaid to pay for their health care costs as well as food stamps and other social services. And in many states an application for SSI is an application for Medicaid, so people do not have to make separate applications. Certain people can also apply for food stamps at the same Social Security office where they apply for SSI.

Social Security representatives will need information about the income and resources and the citizenship or alien status of people applying for benefits. If the person is living with a spouse, or the application is for a disabled child living with parents, the same information is needed about the spouse/parents.

People who are age 65 or over will need proof of their age, while the disabled or blind will need information about the impairment and its treatment history.

It helps to have this information and evidence when you talk to a Social Security representative, but you do not need to have **any** of these things to **start** an application. All you need to do is to call Social Security to find out if you are eligible for SSI payments and the other benefits that come with it. Benefits are not retroactive, so delay can cost money.

The Social Security representative will explain just what information/evidence is needed for the SSI claim, and will provide help in getting it, if help is needed. Most Social Security offices will make an appointment for an office visit or for a telephone interview, if that is more convenient. Or people can just walk in, and wait until someone is free to help them.

Over 6 million people receive SSI benefits now. Many receive both SSI and Social Security. Do not wait. Call 1-800-772-1213, and find out more about SSI. Even the call is free!

How to Protect Your Social Security Record

Always show your Social Security card when you start a new job. In that way you will be sure that your earnings will be credited to *your* Social Security record and not someone else's. If you lose your Social Security card, contact Social Security to find out how to apply for a new one. Married persons may need to get an updated card with the married name (and the same number).

Medicare Program

The Medicare program is a federal health-insurance program for persons 65 and over, and certain disabled people under 65. Enacted under the Social Security Amendments of 1965, Medicare's official name is Title XVIII of the Social Security Act. These amendments also carried Title XIX, providing federal assistance to state medical-aid programs, which has come to be known as Medicaid.

Medicare Facts

• The federal health-insurance program does not offer medical services. It helps pay hospital, doctor, and other medical bills. You should always make sure that health care facilities or persons who provide you with treatment or services are participating in Medicare. Usually, Medicare cannot pay for care from non-participating health care organizations.

• If you live in an area served by a managed care plan, you can get your Medicare benefits either through the fee-for-service system or through a managed care plan such as a health maintenance organization (HMO). Under fee-for-service, you can choose your doctor, hospital, or other health care provider. A fee is generally charged for each service and Medicare pays its share of the bill. Under managed care, you usually must get all of your care from the doctors, hospitals, and other health care providers that are part of the plan. Medicare pays the HMO for your care. Depending on the plan, you may have to pay a monthly premium and a co-payment each time you go to the doctor or use other services.

• There are two parts of the program: (1) The hospital insurance part for the payment of most of the cost of covered care provided by participating hospitals, skilled nursing facilities, home health agencies, and hospices. (2) The medical insurance part which helps pay doctors' bills and certain other expenses.

• While Medicare pays the major share of the costs of many illnesses requiring hospitalization, it does not offer adequate protection for long-term illness or mental illness and Medicare does not pay for custodial care, so you may wish to consider supplemental insurance.

• For help in deciding whether to buy private supplemental insurance, ask at any Social Security office for the pamphlet, *Guide to Health Insurance for People with Medicare*. This free pamphlet describes the various types of supplemental insurance available.

Do You Qualify for Hospital Insurance?

If you're entitled to monthly Social Security or railroad retirement checks (as a worker, dependent, or survivor), you have hospital insurance protection automatically when you're 65. People 65 or older who are not entitled to monthly benefits must have worked long enough under Social Security or the railroad retirement system or in covered Federal, state, and local employment to get hospital insurance without paying a monthly premium. If they do not have enough work, they can get hospital insurance by paying a monthly premium. Disabled people under 65 will have hospital insurance automatically after they have been entitled to Social Security disability benefits for 24 months. Effective July 1, 1990, former disability beneficiaries will be able to purchase hospital insurance if their premium-free coverage stops due to work activity. federal, state, or local employees who are disabled before 65 may be eligible on the basis of their government employment. People are eligible at any age if they need maintenance dialysis or a kidney transplant for permanent kidney failure and are getting monthly Social Security, railroad retirement benefits, or have worked long enough.

To be sure your protection will start the month you reach 65, apply for Medicare insurance 3 months before reaching 65, even if you don't plan to retire.

Do You Qualify for Medicare Medical Insurance?

The medical insurance plan is a vital supplement to the hospital plan. It helps pay for doctors' and other medical services. Many people have not been able to obtain such insurance from private companies because they could not afford it or because of their medical histories.

Any person who can get premium-free hospital insurance benefits based on work as described above can enroll in the medical insurance plan and get medical insurance benefits. In addition, most United States residents age 65 or over can enroll in the medical insurance plan.

People who get Social Security benefits or retirement benefits under the railroad retirement system will be enrolled automatically for medical insurance—unless they say they don't want it—when they become entitled to hospital insurance. Automatic enrollment does not apply to people who have not applied for Social Security or railroad retirement benefits, who have permanent kidney failure, who are eligible for Medicare on the basis of government employment, or people who have not worked long enough to be eligible for hospital insurance. These people have to apply for medical insurance if they want it. People who have medical insurance pay a monthly premium covering part of the cost of this protection. They should enroll for Part B as soon as they are eligible, to avoid paying premium surcharges for delayed enrollment. The basic premium for enrollees is $43.50 a month in 1997.

Is Other Insurance Necessary?

As already indicated, Medicare provides only partial reimbursement. Therefore, you should know how much medical cost you can bear and perhaps arrange for other insurance.

In 1997, for the first 60 days of in-patient hospital care in each benefit period, hospital insurance pays for all covered services except for the first $760. For the 61st through 90th day of a covered in-patient hospital stay, hospital insurance pays for all covered services except for $190 a day. People who need to be in a hospital for more than 90 days in a benefit period can use some or all of their 60 lifetime reserve days. Hospital insurance pays for all covered services except for $380 a day for each reserve day used. Hospital insurance pays the full cost of the first 20 days of an in-patient stay in a skilled nursing facility per benefit period.

Under medical insurance, the patient must meet an annual deductible. In 1996, the annual deductible is $100. After the patient has met the deductible, each year, medical insurance generally pays 80% of the approved amounts for any additional covered services the patient receives during the rest of the year.

How You Obtain Coverage

If you are receiving Social Security or railroad retirement monthly benefits, you will receive from the government information concerning Medicare about 3 months before you become eligible for hospital insurance.

All other eligible people have to file an application for Medicare. They should contact a Social Security office to apply for Medicare.

Medicare Benefits

Breast Cancer Screening (Mammography): Medicare medical insurance now helps pay for X-ray screenings to detect breast cancer. Women 65 or older can use the benefit every other year. Younger disabled women covered by Medicare can use it more frequently.

Physician Payment Reforms: In 1996, physicians who do not accept assignment may not charge you more than 115% of the Medicare approved amount. Physicians who knowingly charge more than these amounts are subject to sanctions.

You no longer have to file claims to Medicare for covered medical insurance services. Doctors, suppliers, and other providers of services must submit the claims to Medicare within one year of providing the service to you or be subject to certain penalties. □

Religion

The Dead Sea Scrolls

On the fiftieth anniversary of their discovery, the scrolls remain a mystery.

Discovery of the Scrolls

The first of the Dead Sea Scroll discoveries occurred in 1947 in Qumran, a village situated about twenty miles east of Jerusalem on the northwest shore of the Dead Sea. A young Bedouin shepherd, following a goat that had gone astray, tossed a rock into one of the caves along the seacliffs and heard a cracking sound: the rock had hit a ceramic pot containing leather and papyrus scrolls that were later determined to be nearly twenty centuries old. Ten years and many searches later, eleven caves around the Dead Sea were found to contain tens of thousands of scroll fragments dating from the third century B.C.E. to C.E. 68 and representing an estimated eight hundred separate works.

The Dead Sea Scrolls comprise a vast collection of Jewish documents written in Hebrew, Aramaic, and Greek, and encompassing many subjects and literary styles. They include manuscripts or fragments of every book in the Hebrew Bible except the Book of Esther, all of them created nearly one thousand years earlier than any previously known biblical manuscripts. The scrolls also contain the earliest existing biblical commentary, on the Book of Habakkuk, and many other writings, among them religious works pertaining to Jewish sects of the time.

The Controversy Begins

The shepherd who made the discovery at Qumran brought the seven intact scrolls he found there to an antique dealer. Three were sold to a scholar at Hebrew University and four were sold to the Archbishop of Syria, who tried for years to place them with a reputable academic institution and ultimately sold them in 1954 through a classified ad in *The Wall Street Journal.* The ad was answered by Israeli archaeologist Yigael Yadin, who donated these scrolls to the state of Israel and established a museum for them, The Shrine of the Book, at Hebrew University.

Control of the remaining tens of thousands of scroll fragments, however, was not soon resolved. One year after the discovery at Qumran, the United Nations partitioned Palestine and war began. Meanwhile, a U.N.-appointed, Jesuit-trained official had summoned Roland de Vaux, director of the Ecole Biblique, a French Catholic Theological School in Arab East Jerusalem, to oversee research on the scrolls. The slow pace of publication and the extreme secrecy of de Vaux's almost entirely Catholic group fueled the theory that the Vatican wished to suppress information in the scrolls.

Then, in 1967, Zionists seized East Jerusalem and the Israel Antiquities Authority took control of the scrolls. Access, however, was merely transferred to yet another small group that seemed determined to hide them from the rest of the world. Israeli officials told prominent visiting scholars that they "would not see the scrolls in [their] lifetimes." The building media frenzy was furthered by the 1990 dismissal of the project's editor-in-chief, Harvard Divinity School professor Dr. John Strugnell, after he publicly criticized Judaism and the Israeli state. A breakthrough came in September 1990, when the Huntington Library in California made available unauthorized photographs of the scrolls. The fol-lowing year, text and translations of fifty scrolls were published in book form.

Judaism, Christianity, and the Scrolls

The Dead Sea Scrolls offer unprecedented information about Jewish religious and political life in Palestine during the turbulent late Second Temple Period (200 B.C.E. to C.E. 70), a time of great corruption and conflict under Roman rule in Palestine. Scholars estimate that the Dead Sea Scrolls were hidden in C.E. 68, when Roman legions reached the Dead Sea during the emperor Vespasian's campaign to Jericho. The discovery of the scrolls established that Jewish culture was far richer and more diverse at this time than scholars had previously believed. Three main groups of Jews were prominent during the late Second Temple Period: the Pharisees, the Sadducees, and the Essenes. Many other sects and political parties also flourished. This pluralism ended in C.E. 70 when, six years after the start of the First Jewish Rebellion, the Romans sieged Jerusalem, killing or enslaving half the Jewish population and destroying Herod's Temple. The capitol fell to the Romans, and only the Judaism of the dominant Pharisees survived.

The scrolls also shed light on the time when Jesus and John the Baptist lived and early Christians began to organize. Specifically, they offer evidence that early Christian beliefs and practices had precedents in the Jewish sects of the time. Sectarian scrolls tell of people who, like the early Christians, did not believe in the Temple worship of the Pharisees, people who had their own literature, their own rituals—including baptism—and their own beliefs, most significantly beliefs in a messiah, a divine judgment, and an apocalypse. Three different scrolls depict a sacred meal of bread and wine. These similarities as well as parallels between the literary style of certain scrolls and that of the New Testament have led some scholars to claim that Jesus and John the Baptist were either part of or strongly influenced by a sect at the Dead Sea. But no direct link has been established, and it is likely that similarities can be attributed to each being derived from a like strain of Judaism. Still, this debate has furthered speculation about the historical Jesus, such as the claim that he was a Zealot rather than a pacifist, a theory that does not fit with New Testament tradition but does fit with the history of this period. And one of the most important discoveries in the scrolls has been the use of the name Son of God to refer to someone other than Jesus, implying a cultural use of the term that was not itself synonymous with God.

Who Hid the Scrolls?

Debate continues about who actually wrote, copied, and stored the scrolls. The most prevalent theory is that this was done by an ascetic group of Essenes who had retreated to the desert to await a Messiah, and who lived at Qumran in a community guided by the Manual of Discipline, or Community Rule, a scroll detailing the beliefs and practices of a messianic sect. In the 1950s,

Roland de Vaux excavated a site between the Qumran caves and the Dead Sea that he claimed was a monastic library where Essenes had copied the scrolls. Recent archaeologists, however, think that what de Vaux believed to be the remains of desks and ink bottles are in fact remains of dining tables and perfume bottles, suggesting that the site was a Roman-style villa whose occupants were engaged in the lucrative perfume trade. Furthermore, not a single manuscript fragment has ever been found on this site. Some scholars believe that Sadducees lived at the Qumran site. Others believe that the scrolls were kept not by a religious sect but by a militant, nationalistic group, and that the Qumran site was in fact a fortress. It has been argued also that the people who lived at the Qumran site were not the same people who hid the scrolls in the caves. Still other scholars reject the idea that the scrolls can be identified with a single group, suggesting instead that the scrolls describe the beliefs and rituals of the many Jewish sects of the time. These scholars propose that the scrolls are copies of manuscripts from libraries throughout Jerusalem that Jews sought to preserve as the Romans encroached upon the capitol. One scroll, called the Copper Scroll, offers a detailed description of efforts to hide documents.

The Scrolls Today

More than fifty years after their discovery, no one can claim to know the absolute truth about the Dead Sea Scrolls, although academics and amateurs alike generate ever more intriguing theories, wild claims, and media attention. It is a complicating factor that almost all the scrolls are copies of other manuscripts—some perhaps historical, others certainly fictitious, and all together, transcribed over the course of nearly three hundred years. It will probably never be possible to know for sure what among the scrolls is fact, when exactly it was recorded, and why: their origins, scribes, keepers, and meanings will likely remain a mystery.
—*Holly Hartman* □

Worldwide Adherents of Religions

(Figures are for mid-1995.)

Statistics of the world's religions are only very rough approximations. Aside from Christianity, few religions, if any, attempt to keep statistical records; and even Protestants and Catholics employ different methods of counting members. All persons of whatever age who have received baptism in the Catholic Church are counted as members, while in most Protestant Churches only those who "join" the church are numbered. The compiling of statistics is further complicated by the fact that in China one may be at the same time a Confucian, a Taoist, and a Buddhist. In Japan, one may be both a Buddhist and a Shintoist.

Religion	Africa	Asia[1]	Europe[2]	Latin America	Northern America	Oceania	World
Baha'ists	1,851,000	3,010,000	93,000	719,000	356,000	75,000	6,104,000
Buddhists[3]	36,000	320,691,000	1,478,000	569,000	920,000	200,000	323,894,000
Chinese folk religionists[4]	12,000	224,828,000	116,000	66,000	98,000	17,000	225,137,000
Christians	348,176,000	306,762,000	551,892,000	448,006,000	249,277,000	23,840,000	1,927,953,000
Roman Catholics	122,108,000	90,041,000	270,677,000	402,691,000	74,243,000	8,265,000	968,025,000
Protestants	135,088,000	435,430,000	110,625,000	328,370,000	130,076,000	14,228,000	466,397,000
Orthodox	29,645,000	14,881,000	165,795,000	481,000	6,480,000	666,000	217,948,000
Other Christians	61,335,000	158,297,000	4,795,000	11,997,000	38,478,000	681,000	275,583,000
Confucians	1,000	5,220,000	4,000	2,000	26,000	1,000	5,254,000
Ethnic religionists	72,777,000	36,579,000	1,200,000	1,061,000	47,000	113,000	111,777,000
Hindus[5]	1,535,000	775,252,000	1,522,000	748,000	1,185,000	305,000	780,547,000
Jains	58,000	4,804,000	15,000	4,000	4,000	1,000	4,886,000
Jews	163,000	4,294,000	2,529,000	1,098,000	5,942,000	91,000	14,117,000
Muslims[6]	300,317,000	760,181,000	31,975,000	1,329,000	5,450,000	382,000	1,099,634,000
New-Religionists[7]	19,000	118,591,000	808,000	913,000	956,000	10,000	121,297,000
Shintoists	0	2,840,000	1,000	1,000	1,000	1,000	2,844,000
Sikhs	36,000	18,130,000	490,000	8,000	490,000	7,000	19,161,000
Spiritists	4,000	1,100,000	17,000	8,768,000	300,000	1,000	10,190,000
Other religionists[8]	89,000	296,000	444,000	185,000	1,069,000	43,000	2,156,000
Nonreligious[9]	2,573,000	701,175,000	94,330,000	15,551,000	25,050,000	2,870,000	841,549,000
Atheists[10]	427,000	174,174,000	40,085,000	2,977,000	1,670,000	592,000	219,925,000
Total Population[11]	**728,074,000**	**3,457,957,000**	**728,999,000**	**482,005,000**	**292,841,000**	**28,549,000**	**5,716,425,000**

1. Asia includes the former U.S.S.R. central Asian republics. 2. Europe includes the Russian Federation, extending to its easternmost boundaries. 3. Buddhists: 56% Mahayana, 38% Theravada (Hinayana), and 6% Tantrayana (Lamaism). 4. Followers of the traditional Chinese religion (local deities, ancestor veneration, Confucian ethics, Taoism, universism, divination, some Buddhist elements). 5. Hindus: including 70% Vaishnavites, 25% Shaivites, 2% neo-Hindus and antireligious Hindus. 6. Muslims: 83% Sunnites, 16% Shi'ites, 1% other. 7. Followers of Asian 20th-century New Religions, New Religious movements, radical new crisis religions, and non-Christian syncretistic mass religions, all founded since 1800 and most since 1945. 8. Including 70 minor world religions and a large number of spiritist religions, New Age religions, quasi-religions, and religious or mystic belief systems. 9. Persons professing no religion, nonbelievers, agnostics, freethinkers, and formerly religious secularists. 10. Persons professing atheism, skepticism, disbelief, or antireligion (opposed to all religion). 11. Total population figures are the U.N. medium variant figures for mid-1995 as given in *World Population Prospects: The 1994 Revision* (1995). Reprinted with permission from *1996 Britannica Book of the Year.* © 1996 Encyclopaedia Britannica, Inc.

Non-Christian Religious Adherents in the United States

Adherents	Year 1900	% of total pop.	mid-1970	% of total pop.	mid-1990	% of total pop.	mid-1995	% of total pop.	(Projected) mid-2000	% of total pop.
Total	2,724,800	3.6	18,928,000	9.2	34,942,000	14.0	38,791,000	14.7	41,644,000	15.1
Atheists	1,000	0.0	200,000	0.1	750,000	0.3	870,000	0.3	947,000	0.3
Baha'ists	2,800	0.0	138,000	0.1	250,000	0.1	300,000	0.1	365,000	0.1
Buddhists	30,000	0.0	200,000	0.1	700,000	0.3	780,000	0.3	1,070,000	0.4
Chinese folk religionists	70,000	0.1	90,000	0.0	80,000	0.0	76,000	0.0	70,000	0.0
Hindus	1,000	0.0	100,000	0.0	500,000	0.2	910,000	0.3	1,200,000	0.4
Jews	1,500,000	2.0	6,700,000	3.3	5,515,000	2.2	5,602,000	2.1	5,702,000	2.1
Muslims	10,000	0.0	800,000	0.4	4,500,000	1.8	5,100,000	1.9	5,730,000	2.1
Black Muslims	0	0.0	200,000	0.1	1,250,000	0.5	1,400,000	0.5	1,650,000	0.6
New-Religionists	0	0.0	110,000	0.1	750,000	0.3	947,000	0.4	1,074,000	0.4
Nonreligious	1,000,000	1.3	10,069,000	4.9	20,702,000	8.3	22,928,000	8.7	24,126,000	8.8
Sikhs	0	0.0	1,000	0.0	150,000	0.1	190,000	0.1	240,000	0.1
Tribal religionists	100,000	0.1	70,000	0.0	45,000	0.0	38,000	0.0	30,000	0.0
Other religionists	10,000	0.0	450,000	0.2	1,000,000	0.4	1,050,000	0.4	1,090,000	0.4

Non-Christians: Followers of non-Christian religions or of no religion; the 12 largest such varieties are listed. Jews: Core Jewish population relating to Judaism, excluding Jewish persons professing a different religion but including immigrants from the former U.S.S.R., Eastern Europe, Israel, and other areas. Figures for c.e. 2000 are projections based on current long-term trends. Source: Reprinted with permission from *1996 Britannica Book of the Year.* © 1996 Encyclopedia Britannica, Inc.

Major Religions of the World

Judaism

The determining factors of Judaism are: descendance from Israel, the *Torah*, and Tradition.

The name Israel (Jacob, a patriarch) also signifies his descendants as a people. During the 15th–13th centuries B.C.E., Israelite tribes, coming from South and East, gradually settled in Palestine, then inhabited by Canaanites. They were held together by Moses, who gave them religious unity in the worship of *Jahweh,* the God who had chosen Israel to be his people.

Under Judges, the 12 tribes at first formed an amphictyonic covenant. Saul established kingship (c. 1050 B.C.E.), and under David, his successor (1000–960 B.C.E.), the State of Israel comprised all of Palestine with Jerusalem as religio-political center. A golden era followed under Solomon (965–926 B.C.E.), who built *Jahweh* a temple.

After Solomon's death, the kingdom separated into Israel in the North and Judah in the South. A period of conflicts ensued, which ended with the conquest of Israel by Assyria in 722 B.C.E. The Babylonians defeated Judah in 586 B.C.E., destroying Jerusalem and its temple, and deporting many to Babylon.

The era of the kings is significant also in that the great prophets worked in that time, emphasizing faith in *Jahweh* as both God of Israel and God of the universe, and stressing social justice.

When the Persians permitted the Jews to return from exile (539 B.C.E.), temple and cult were restored in Jerusalem. The Persian rulers were succeeded by the Seleucides. The Maccabaean revolt against these Hellenistic kings gave independence to the Jews in 128 B.C.E., which lasted till the Romans occupied the country.

Important groups that exerted influence during these times were the Sadducees, priests in the temple in Jerusalem; the Pharisees, teachers of the Law in the synagogues; Essenes, a religious order; Apocalyptists, who were expecting the heavenly Messiah; and Zealots, who were prepared to fight for national independence.

When the latter turned against Rome in C.E. 66, Roman armies under Titus suppressed the revolt, destroying Jerusalem and its temple in C.E. 70. The Jews were scattered in the *diaspora* (Dispersion), subject to oppressions until the Age of the Enlightenment (18th century) brought their emancipation, although persecutions did not end entirely.

The fall of the Jerusalem temple was an important event in the religious life of the Jews, which now developed around *Torah* (Law) and synagogue. Around C.E. 100 the Sacred Scriptures were codified. Synagogue worship became central, with readings from *Torah* and prophets. Most important prayers are the *Shema* (Hear) and the Prayer of the 18 Benedictions.

Religious life is guided by the commandments contained in the *Torah,* such as circumcision and *Sabbath,* as well as other ethical and ceremonial commandments.

The *Talmud,* based on the *Mishnah* and its interpretations, took shape over many centuries in the Babylonian and Palestinian Schools. It was a strong binding force of Judaism in the Dispersion.

In the 12th century, Maimonides formulated his "13 Articles of Faith," which carried great authority. Fundamental in this creed are: belief in God and his oneness *(Sherma),* belief in the changeless *Torah,* in the words of Moses and the prophets, belief in reward and punishment, the coming of the Messiah, and the resurrection of the dead.

Judaism is divided into theological schools, the main divisions of which are Orthodox, Conservative, and Reform.

Christianity

Christianity is founded upon Jesus Christ, to whose life the New Testament writings testify. Jesus, a Jew, was born in about 7 B.C.E. and assumed his public life, after his 30th year, in Galilee. The Gospels tell of many extraordinary deeds that accompanied his ministry. He proclaimed the Kingdom of God, a future reality that is at the same time already present. Nationalistic-Jewish expectations of the Messiah he rejected. Rather, he referred to himself as the "Son of Man," the Christ, who has power to forgive sins now and who shall also come as Judge at the end of time. Jesus set forth the religio-ethical demands for participation in the Kingdom of God as change of heart and love of God and neighbor.

At the Last Supper he signified his death as a sacrifice, which would inaugurate the New Covenant, by which many would be saved. Circa C.E. 30 he died on a cross in Jerusalem. The early Church carried on Jesus' proclamation, the apostle Paul emphasizing his death and resurrection.

The person of Jesus is fundamental to the Christian faith since it is believed that in his life, death, and resurrection, God's revelation became historically tangible. He is seen as the turning point in history, and man's relationship to God as determined by his attitude to Jesus.

Historically, Christianity arose out of Judaism, claiming fulfillment of the promises of the Old Testament in Jesus. The early Church designated itself as "the true Israel," which expected the speedy return of Jesus. The mother church was at Jerusalem, but churches were soon founded in many other places. The apostle Paul was instrumental in founding and extending a Gentile Christianity that was free from Jewish legalism.

The new religion spread rapidly throughout the eastern and western parts of the Roman Empire. In coming to terms with other religious movements within the Empire, Christianity began to take definite shape as an organization in its doctrine, liturgy, and ministry circa C.E. 200. In the 4th century the Catholic Church had taken root in countries stretching from Spain in the West to Persia and India in the East. Christians had been repeatedly subject to persecution by the Roman state, but finally gained tolerance under Constantine the Great (C.E. 313). Since that time, the Church became favored under his successors and in 380 the Emperor Theodosius proclaimed Christianity the State religion. Paganism was suppressed and public life was gradually molded in accordance with Christian ethical demands.

It was in these years also that the Church was able to achieve a certain unity of doctrine. Due to differences of interpretation of basic doctrines concerning Christ that threatened to divide the Catholic Church, a standard Christian Creed was formulated by bishops at successive Ecumenical Councils, the first of which was held in C.E. 325 (Nicaea). The chief doctrines formulated concerned the doctrine of the Trinity, i.e., that there is one God in three persons: Father, Son, and Holy Spirit (Constantinople, C.E. 381); and the nature of Christ as both divine and human (Chalcedon, C.E. 541).

Through differences and rivalry between East and West, the unity of the Church was broken by schism in 1054. In 1517 a separation occurred in the Western Church with the Reformation. From the major Protestant denominations (Lutheran, Presbyterian, and Anglican [Episcopalian]), many Free Churches separated themselves in an age of individualism.

In the 20th century, however, the direction is toward unity. The Ecumenical Movement led to the formation of the World Council of Churches in 1948 (Amsterdam), which has since been joined by many Protestant and Orthodox Churches.

Through its missionary activity Christianity has spread to most parts of the globe.

Eastern Orthodoxy

Eastern Orthodoxy comprises the faith and practice of Churches stemming from ancient Churches in the eastern part of the Roman Empire. The term covers Orthodox Churches in communion with the See of Constantinople and Nestorian and Monophysite Churches.

The Orthodox, Catholic, Apostolic Church is the direct descendant of the Byzantine State Church and consists of a series of independent national churches that are united by Doctrine, Liturgy, and Hierarchical organization (deacons and priests, who may either be married or be monks before ordination, and bishops, who must be celibates). The heads of these Churches are patriarchs or metropolitans; the Patriarch of Con-

U.S. Religious Bodies with Members Over 1,000,000

Religious body	Members
Roman Catholic Church	60,280,454
Southern Baptist Convention	15,663,296
United Methodist Church	8,538,662
National Baptist Convention, U.S.A., Inc.	8,200,000
Church of God in Christ	5,499,875
Evangelical Lutheran Church in America	5,190,489
Church of Jesus Christ of Latter-day Saints	4,711,500
Presbyterian Church (U.S.A.)	3,669,489
National Baptist Convention of America, Inc.	3,500,000
African Methodist Episcopal Church	3,500,000
Lutheran Church—Missouri Synod	2,594,555
Episcopal Church	2,536,550
Progressive National Baptist Convention, Inc.	2,500,000
National Missionary Baptist Convention of America	2,500,000
Assemblies of God	2,387,982
Orthodox Church in America	2,000,000
Churches of Christ	1,655,000
American Baptist Churches in the U.S.A.	1,517,400
Baptist Bible Fellowship International	1,500,000
United Church of Christ	1,472,213
African Methodist Episcopal Zion Church	1,230,842
Christian Churches and Churches of Christ	1,070,616
Pentecostal Assemblies of the World	1,000,000

Source: Yearbook of American & Canadian Churches, 1997.

stantinople is only "first among equals." Rivalry between the Pope of Rome and the Patriarch of Constantinople, aided by differences and misunderstandings that existed for centuries between the eastern and western parts of the Empire, led to a schism in 1054. Repeated attempts at reunion have failed in past centuries. The mutual excommunication pronounced in that year was lifted in 1965, however, and because of greater interaction in theology between Orthodox Churches and those in the West, a climate of better understanding has been created in the 20th century. First contacts were with Anglicans and Old Catholics. Orthodox Churches belong to the World Council of Churches.

The Eastern Orthodox Churches recognize only the canons of the seven Ecumenical Councils (325-787) as binding for faith and they reject doctrines that have been added in the West.

The central worship service is called the Liturgy, which is understood as representation of God's acts of salvation. Its center is the celebration of the Eucharist, or Lord's Supper.

In their worship icons (sacred pictures) are used that have a sacramental meaning as representation. The Mother of Christ, angels, and saints are highly venerated.

The number of sacraments in the Orthodox Church is the same as in the Western Catholic Church.

Orthodox Churches are found in the Balkans and the Soviet Union also, since the 20th century, in Western Europe and other parts of the world, particularly in America.

Eastern Rite Churches

These include the Uniate Churches that recognize the authority of the Pope but keep their own traditional liturgies and those Churches dating back to the 5th century that emancipated themselves from the Byzantine State Church: the Nestorian Church in the Near East and India and the Monophysite Churches (Coptic, Ethiopian, Syrian, Armenian, and the Mar Thoma Church in India).

Roman Catholicism

Roman Catholicism comprises the belief and practice of the Roman Catholic Church. The Church stands under the authority of the Bishop of Rome, the Pope, and is ruled by him and bishops who are held to be, through ordination, successors of Peter and the Apostles, respectively. Fundamental to the structure of the Church is the juridical aspect: doctrine and sacraments are bound to the power of jurisdiction and consecration of the hierarchy. The Pope, as the head of the hierarchy of archbishops, bishops, priests, and deacons, has full ecclesiastical power, granted him by Christ, through Peter. As successor to Peter, he is the Vicar of Christ. The powers that others in the hierarchy possess are delegated.

Roman Catholics believe their Church to be the one, holy, catholic, and apostolic Church, possessing all the properties of the one, true Church of Christ.

The faith of the Church is understood to be identical with that taught by Christ and his Apostles and contained in Bible and Tradition, in other words, the original deposit of faith, to which nothing new may be added. New definitions of doctrines, such as the Immaculate Conception of Mary (1854) and the bodily Assumption of Mary (1950), have been declared by Popes, however, in accordance with the principle of development (implicit-explicit doctrine).

At Vatican Council I (1870) the Pope was proclaimed "endowed with infallibility, *ex cathedra,* i.e., when exercising the office of Pastor and Teacher of all Christians."

The center of Roman Catholic worship is the celebration of the Mass, the Eucharist, which is the commemoration of Christ's sacrificial death and of his resurrection. Other sacraments are baptism, confirmation, penance, matrimony, annointing of the sick, and holy orders. The Virgin Mary and saints, and their relics, are highly venerated and prayers are made to them to intercede with God, in whose presence they are believed to dwell.

The Roman Catholic Church is the largest Christian organization in the world, found in most countries.

Since Vatican Council II (1962–65), and the effort to "update" the Church, many interesting changes and developments have been taking place.

Protestantism

Protestantism comprises the Christian churches that separated from Rome during the Reformation in the 16th century, initiated by an Augustinian monk, Martin Luther. "Protestant" was originally applied to followers of Luther, who protested at the Diet of Spires (1529) against the decree which prohibited all further ecclesiastical reforms. Subsequently, Protestantism came to mean rejection of attempts to tie God's revelation to earthly institutions, and a return to the Gospel and the Word of God as sole authority in matters of faith and practice. Central in the biblical message is the justification of the sinner by faith alone. The Church is understood as a fellowship and the priesthood of all believers stressed.

The Augsburg Confession (1530) was the principal statement of Lutheran faith and practice. It became a model for other Confessions of Faith, which in their turn had decisive influence on Church policy. Major Protestant denominations are the Lutheran, Reformed (Calvinist), Presbyterian, and Anglican (Episcopal). Smaller ones are the Mennonite, Schwenkfeldians, and Unitarians. In the U.K. and the U.S. there are the Congregationalists, Baptists, Quakers, Methodists, and other free church types of communities. (In regarding themselves as being faithful to original biblical Christianity, these Churches differ from such religious bodies as Unitarians, Mormons, Jehovah's Witnesses, and Christian Scientists, who either teach new doctrines or reject old ones.)

Since the latter part of the 19th century, national councils of churches have been established in many countries, e.g. the Federal Council of Churches of Christ in America in 1908. Denominations across countries joined in federations and world alliances, beginning with the Anglican Lambeth Conference in 1867.

Protestant missionary activity, particularly strong in the last century, resulted in the founding of many younger churches in Asia and Africa. The Ecumenical Movement, which originated with Protestant missions, aims at unity among Christians and churches.

Islam

Islam is the religion founded in Arabia by Mohammed between 610 and 632. There are an estimated 5.4 million Muslims in Northern America and 1 billion Muslims worldwide.

Mohammed was born in C.E. 570 at Mecca and belonged to the Quraysh tribe, which was active in caravan trade. At the age of 25 he joined the caravan trade from Mecca to Syria in the employment of a rich widow, Khadiji, whom he married. Critical of the idolatry of the inhabitants of Mecca, he began to lead a contemplative life in the deserts. There he received a series of revelations. Encouraged by Khadiji, he gradually became convinced that he was given a God-appointed task to devote himself to the reform of religion and society. Idolatry was to be abandoned.

The *Hegira (Hijra)* (migration) of Mohammed from Mecca, where he was not honored, to Medina, where he was well received, occurred in 622 and marks the beginning of the Muslim era. In 630 he marched on Mecca and conquered it. He died at Medina in 632. His grave there has since been a place of pilgrimage.

Mohammed's followers, called Muslims, revered him as the prophet of *Allah* (God), beside whom there is no other God. Although he had no close knowledge of Judaism and Christianity, he considered himself succeeding and completing them as the seal of the Prophets. Sources of the Islamic faith are the *Qur'an,* regarded as the uncreated, eternal Word of God, and Tradition *(hadith)* regarding sayings and deeds of the prophet.

Islam means surrender to the will of *Allah.* He is the all-powerful, whose will is supreme and determines man's fate. Good deeds will be rewarded at the Last Judgment in paradise and evil deeds will be punished in hell.

The Five Pillars, primary duties, of Islam are: profession of faith; prayer, to be performed five times a day; almsgiving to the poor and the mosque (house of worship); fasting during daylight hours in the month of Ramadan; and pilgrimage to Mecca at least once in the Muslim's lifetime.

Islam, upholding the law of brotherhood, succeeded in uniting an Arab world that had disintegrated into tribes and castes. Disagreements concerning the succession of the prophet caused a great division in Islam between *Sunnis* and *Shias.* Among these, other sects arose *(Wahhabi).* Doctrinal issues also led to the rise of different schools of thought in theology. Nevertheless, since Arab armies turned against Syria and Palestine in

635, Islam has expanded successfully under Mohammed's successors. Its rapid conquests in Asia and Africa are unsurpassed in history. Turning against Europe, Muslims conquered Spain in 713. In 1453 Constantinople fell into their hands and in 1529 Muslim armies besieged Vienna. Since then, Islam has lost its foothold in Europe. In modern times it has made great gains in Africa.

Hinduism

Hinduism is the major religion of India where there are more than 7.6 million adherents. In contrast to other religions, it has no founder. Considered the oldest religion in the world, it dates back, perhaps, to prehistoric times.

Hinduism is hard to define, there being no common creed, no one doctrine to bind Hindus together. Intellectually there is complete freedom of belief, and one can be monotheist, polytheist, or atheist.

The most important sacred texts of the Hindu religion are written in Sanskrit and called the *Vedas* (*Veda*-knowledge). There are four Vedic books, of which the *Rig-Veda* is the oldest. It speaks of many gods and also deals with questions concerning the universe and creation. The dates of these works are unknown (1000 B.C.E.?).

The *Upanishads* (dated 1000–300 B.C.E.), commentaries on the Vedic texts, have philosophical speculations on the origin of the universe, the nature of deity, of *atman* (the human soul), and its relationship to *Brahman* (the universal soul).

Brahman is the principle and source of the universe who can be indicated only by negatives. As the divine intelligence, he is the ground of the visible world, a presence that pervades all beings. Thus the many Hindu deities came to be understood as manifestations of the one *Brahman* from whom everything proceeds and to whom everything ultimately returns. The religio-social system of Hinduism is based on the concept of reincarnation and transmigration in which all living beings, from plants below to gods above, are caught in a cosmic system that is an everlasting cycle of becoming and perishing.

Life is determined by the law of *karma,* according to which rebirth is dependent on moral behavior in a previous phase of existence. In this view, life on earth is regarded as transient (*maya*) and a burden. The goal of existence is liberation from the cycle of rebirth and redeath and entrance into the indescribable state of what in Buddhism is called *nirvana* (extinction of passion).

Further important sacred writings are the Epics (*ithasas*), which contain legendary stories about gods and men. They are the *Mahabharata* (composed between 200 B.C.E. and C.E. 200) and the *Ramayana*. The former includes the poem *Bhagavad-Gita* (Song of the Lord).

The practice of Hinduism consists of rites and ceremonies centering on the main socio-religious occasions of birth, marriage, and death. There are many Hindu temples, which are dwelling places of the deities and to which people bring offerings. There are also places of pilgrimages, the chief one being Benares on the Ganges, most sacred among the rivers in India.

Orthodox Hindu society in India was divided into four major hereditary castes: (1) Brahmans (priestly and learned class); (2) Kshatriyas (military, professional, ruling, and governing occupations); (3) Vaisyas (landowners, merchants, and business occupations); and (4) Sudras (artisans, laborers, and peasants). Below the Sudras was a fifth group, the Untouchables (lowest menial occupations and no social standing). The Indian government banned discrimination against the Untouchables in 1949.

In modern times work has been done to reform and revive Hinduism. One of the outstanding reformers was Ramakrishna (1836–86), who inspired many followers, one of whom founded the Ramakrishna mission. The mission is active both in India and in other countries and is known for its scholarly and humanitarian works.

Buddhism

Buddhism was founded in the 6th century B.C.E. in northern India by Siddhartha Gautama, who was born in southern Nepal as son to a king. His birth is surrounded by many legends, but western scholars agree that he lived from 563 to 483 B.C.E. The king, warned by a sage that his son would become an ascetic or a universal monarch, confined Siddhartha to his home. Siddhartha was able to escape and began the life of a homeless wanderer in search of peace, passing through many disappointments until he finally came to the Tree of Enlightenment, under which he lived in meditation till enlightenment came to him and he became a Buddha (enlightened one).

Now Siddhartha Gautama understood the origin of suffering, summarized in the *Four Noble Truths*, which constitutes the foundation of Buddhism. The four are the truth of suffering, which all living beings must endure; the origin of suffering, which is craving and which leads to rebirth; the belief that craving can be destroyed; and the way that leads to cessation of pain, in other words, the *Noble Eightfold Way*. This is the rule of practical Buddhism: right views, right intention, right speech, right action, right livelihood, right effort, right concentration, and right ecstasy.

Nirvana is the goal of all existence, the state of complete redemption, into which the redeemed enters. Buddha's insight can free every man from the law of reincarnation through complete emptying of the self.

The nucleus of Buddha's church or association was originally formed by monks and lay-brothers, whose houses gradually became monasteries used as places for religious instruction. The worship service consisted of a sermon, expounding of scripture, meditation, and confession. At a later stage pilgrimages to the holy places associated with the Buddha came into being, as well as veneration of relics.

In the 3rd century B.C.E., King Ashoka made Buddhism the State religion of India but, as centuries passed, it gradually fell into decay through splits, persecutions, and the hostile Brahmans. Buddhism spread to countries outside India, however.

At the beginning of the Christian era, there occurred a split that gave rise to two main types: *Hinayana* (Lesser Vehicle), or southern Buddhism, and *Mahayana* (Greater Vehicle), or northern Buddhism. The former type, more individualistic, survived in Sri Lanka and Southeast Asia. *Hinayana* retained more closely the original teachings of the Buddha, which did not know of a personal god or soul. *Mahayana*, more social, polytheistic, and developing a pluralistic cult, was strong in the Himalayas, Tibet, Mongolia, China, Korea, and Japan.

In the present century, Buddhism has found believers also in the West and there are an estimated 920,000 Buddhists in North America.

Confucianism

Confucius (K'ung Fu-tzu), born in the state of Lu (northern China), lived from 551 to 479 B.C.E. Tradition, exaggerating the importance of Confucius in life, has depicted him as a great statesman but, in fact, he seems to have been a private teacher. Anthologies of ancient Chinese classics, along with his own Analects (*Lun Yu*), became the basis of Confucianism. These Analects were transmitted as a collection of his sayings as recorded by his students, with whom he discussed ethical and social problems. They developed into men of high moral standing, who served the state as administrators.

In his teachings, Confucius emphasized the importance of an old Chinese concept *(li),* which has the connotation of proper conduct. There is some disagreement as to the religious ideas of Confucius, but he held high the concepts handed down from centuries before him. Thus he believed in Heaven *(T'ien)* and sacrificed to his ancestors. He encouraged ancestor worship as an expression of filial piety, which he considered the loftiest of virtues.

Piety to Confucius was the foundation of the family as well as the state. The family is the nucleus of the state, and the "five relations," between king and subject, father and son, man and wife, older and younger brother, and friend and friend, are determined by the virtues of love of fellow men, righteousness, and respect.

An extension of ancestor worship may be seen in the worship of Confucius, which became official in the 2nd century B.C.E. when the emperor, in recognition of Confucius's teachings as supporting the imperial rule, offered sacrifices at his tomb.

Mencius (Meng Tse), who lived around 400 B.C.E., did much to propagate and elaborate Confucianism in its concern with ordering society. Thus, for two millennia, Confucius's doctrine of state, with its emphasis on ethics and social morality, rooted in ancient Chinese tradition and developed and continued by his disciples, has been standard in China and the Far East.

With the revolution of 1911 in China, however, students, burning Confucius in effigy, called for the removal of "the old curiosity shop."

Shintoism

Shinto, the Chinese term for the Japanese *Kami no Michi,* i.e., the Way of the Gods, comprises the religious ideas and cults indigenous to Japan. *Kami,* or gods, considered divine forces of nature that are worshipped, may reside in rivers, trees, rocks, mountains, certain animals, or, particularly, in the sun and moon. The worship of ancestors, heroes, and deceased emperors was incorporated later.

After Buddhism had come from Korea, Japan's native religion at first resisted it. Then there followed a period of compromise and amalgamation with Buddhist beliefs and ceremonies, resulting, since the 9th century C.E., in a syncretistic religion, a Twofold Shinto. Buddhist deities came to be regarded as manifestations of Japanese deities and Buddhist priests took over most of the Shinto shrines.

In modern times Shinto regained independence from Buddhism. Under the reign of the Emperor Meiji (1868–1912) it became the official State religion, in which loyalty to the emperor was emphasized. The line of succession of emperors is traced back to the first Emperor Jimmu (660 B.C.E.) and beyond him to the Sun-goddess *Amaterasuomikami.*

The centers of worship are the shrines and temples in which the deities are believed to dwell and believers approach them through *torii* (gateways). Most important among the shrines is the imperial shrine of the Sun Goddess at Ise, where state ceremonies were once held in June and December. The *Yasukuni* shrine of the war dead in Tokyo is also well known.

Acts of worship consist of prayers, clapping of hands, acts of purification, and offerings. On feast days processions and performances of music and dancing take place and priests read prayers before the gods in the shrines, asking for good harvest, the well-being of people and emperor, etc. In Japanese homes there is a god-shelf, a small wooden shrine that contains the tablets bearing the names of ancestors. Offerings are made and candles lit before it.

After World War II the Allied Command ordered the disestablishment of State Shinto. To be distinguished from State Shinto is Sect Shinto, consisting of 13 recognized sects. These have arisen in modern times. Most important among them is *Tenrikyo* in Tenri City (Nara), in which healing by faith plays a central role.

Taoism

Taoism, a religion of China, was, according to tradition, founded by Lao Tse, a Chinese philosopher, long considered one of the prominent religious leaders from the 6th century B.C.E.

Information about him is for the most part legendary, however, and the *Tao Te Ching* (the classic of the Way and of its Power), traditionally ascribed to him, is now believed by many scholars to have originated in the 3rd century B.C.E. The book is composed in short chapters, written in aphoristic rhymes. Central are the word *Tao,* which means way or path and, in a deeper sense, signifies the principle that underlies the reality of this world and manifests itself in nature and in the lives of men, and the word *Te* (power).

The virtuous man draws power from being absorbed in *Tao,* the ultimate reality within an everchanging world. By non-action and keeping away from human striving, it is possible for man to live in harmony with the principles that underlie and govern the universe. *Tao* cannot be comprehended by reason and knowledge, but only by inward quiet.

Besides the *Tao Te Ching,* dating from approximately the same period, there are two other Taoist works, written by Chuang Tse and Lieh Tse.

Theoretical Taoism of this classical philosophical movement of the 4th and 3rd centuries B.C.E. in China differed from popular Taoism, into which it gradually degenerated. The standard of theoretical Taoism was maintained in the classics, of course, and among the upper classes it continued to be alive until modern times.

Religious Taoism is a form of religion dealing with deities and spirits, magic and soothsaying. In the 2nd century C.E. it was organized with temples, cult, priests, and monasteries and was able to hold its own in the competition with Buddhism that came up at the same time.

After the 7th century C.E., however, Taoist religion further declined. Split into numerous sects, which often operate like secret societies, it has become a syncretistic folk religion in which some of the old deities and saints live on.

Roman Catholic Pontiffs

St. Peter, of Bethsaida in Galilee, Prince of the Apostles, was the first Pope. He lived first in Antioch and then in Rome for 25 years. In c.e. 64 or 67, he was martyred. St. Linus became the second Pope.

Name	Birthplace	From	To	Name	Birthplace	From	To
		Reigned				Reigned	
St. Linus	Tuscia	67	76	St. Gregory I	Rome	590	604
St. Anacletus (Cletus)	Rome	76	88	(the Great)			
				Sabinianus	Tuscany	604	606
St. Clement	Rome	88	97	Boniface III	Rome	607	607
St. Evaristus	Greece	97	105	St. Boniface IV	Marsi	608	615
St. Alexander I	Rome	105	115	St. Deusdedit	Rome	615	618
St. Sixtus I	Rome	115	125	(Adeodatus I)			
St. Telesphorus	Greece	125	136	Boniface V	Naples	619	625
St. Hyginus	Greece	136	140	Honorius I	Campania	625	638
St. Pius I	Aquileia	140	155	Severinus	Rome	640	640
St. Anicetus	Syria	155	166	John IV	Dalmatia	640	642
St. Soter	Campania	166	175	Theodore I	Greece	642	649
St. Eleutherius	Epirus	175	189	St. Martin I	Todi	649	655
St. Victor I	Africa	189	199	St. Eugene I[3]	Rome	654	657
St. Zephyrinus	Rome	199	217	St. Vitalian	Segni	657	672
St. Callistus I	Rome	217	222	Adeodatus II	Rome	672	676
St. Urban I	Rome	222	230	Donus	Rome	676	678
St. Pontian	Rome	230	235	St. Agatho	Sicily	678	681
St. Anterus	Greece	235	236	St. Leo II	Sicily	682	683
St. Fabian	Rome	236	250	St. Benedict II	Rome	684	685
St. Cornelius	Rome	251	253	John V	Syria	685	686
St. Lucius I	Rome	253	254	Conon	Unknown	686	687
St. Stephen I	Rome	254	257	St. Sergius I	Syria	687	701
St. Sixtus II	Greece	257	258	John VI	Greece	701	705
St. Dionysius	Unknown	259	268	John VII	Greece	705	707
St. Felix I	Rome	269	274	Sisinnius	Syria	708	708
St. Eutychian	Luni	275	283	Constantine	Syria	708	715
St. Caius	Dalmatia	283	296	St. Gregory II	Rome	715	731
St. Marcellinus	Rome	296	304	St. Gregory III	Syria	731	741
St. Marcellus I	Rome	308	309	St. Zachary	Greece	741	752
St. Eusebius	Greece	309[1]	309[1]	Stephen II (III)[4]	Rome	752	757
St. Meltiades	Africa	311	314	St. Paul I	Rome	757	767
St. Sylvester I	Rome	314	335	Stephen III (IV)	Sicily	768	772
St. Marcus	Rome	336	336	Adrian I	Rome	772	795
St. Julius I	Rome	337	352	St. Leo III	Rome	795	816
Liberius	Rome	352	366	Stephen IV (V)	Rome	816	817
St. Damasus I	Spain	366	384	St. Paschal I	Rome	817	824
St. Siricius	Rome	384	399	Eugene II	Rome	824	827
St. Anastasius I	Rome	399	401	Valentine	Rome	827	827
St. Innocent I	Albano	401	417	Gregory IV	Rome	827	844
St. Zozimus	Greece	417	418	Sergius II	Rome	844	847
St. Boniface I	Rome	418	422	St. Leo IV	Rome	847	855
St. Celestine I	Campania	422	432	Benedict III	Rome	855	858
St. Sixtus III	Rome	432	440	St. Nicholas I	Rome	858	867
St. Leo I (the Great)	Tuscany	440	461	(the Great)			
				Adrian II	Rome	867	872
St. Hilary	Sardinia	461	468	John VIII	Rome	872	882
St. Simplicius	Tivoli	468	483	Marinus I	Gallese	882	884
St. Felix III (II)[2]	Rome	483	492	St. Adrian III	Rome	884	885
St. Gelasius I	Africa	492	496	Stephen V (VI)	Rome	885	891
Anastasius II	Rome	496	498	Formosus	Portus	891	896
St. Symmachus	Sardinia	498	514	Boniface VI	Rome	896	896
St. Hormisdas	Frosinone	514	523	Stephen VI (VII)	Rome	896	897
St. John I	Tuscany	523	526	Romanus	Gallese	897	897
St. Felix IV (III)	Samnium	526	530	Theodore II	Rome	897	897
Boniface II	Rome	530	532	John IX	Tivoli	898	900
John II	Rome	533	535	Benedict IV	Rome	900	903
St. Agapitus I	Rome	535	536	Leo V	Ardea	903	903
St. Silverius	Campania	536	537	Sergius III	Rome	904	911
Vigilius	Rome	537	555	Anastasius III	Rome	911	913
Pelagius I	Rome	556	561	Landus	Sabina	913	914
John III	Rome	561	574	John X	Tossignano	914	928
Benedict I	Rome	575	579	Leo VI	Rome	928	928
Pelagius II	Rome	579	590	Stephen VII (VIII)	Rome	928	931

Name	Birthplace	Reigned		Name	Birthplace	Reigned	
		From	To			From	To
John XI	Rome	931	935	Nicholas IV	Ascoli	1288	1292
Leo VII	Rome	936	939	St. Celestine V	Isernia	1294	1294
Stephen VIII (IX)	Rome	939	942	Boniface VIII	Anagni	1294	1303
Marinus II	Rome	942	946	Bl. Benedict XI	Treviso	1303	1304
Agapitus II	Rome	946	955	Clement V	France	1305	1314
John XII	Tusculum	955	964	John XXII	Cahors	1316	1334
Leo VIII[5]	Rome	963	965	Benedict XII	France	1334	1342
Benedict V[5]	Rome	964	966	Clement VI	France	1342	1352
John XIII	Rome	965	972	Innocent VI	France	1352	1362
Benedict VI	Rome	973	974	Bl. Urban V	France	1362	1370
Benedict VII	Rome	974	983	Gregory XI	France	1370	1378
John XIV	Pavia	983	984	Urban VI	Naples	1378	1389
John XV	Rome	985	996	Boniface IX	Naples	1389	1404
Gregory V	Saxony	996	999	Innocent VII	Sul mona	1404	1406
Sylvester II	Auvergne	999	1003	Gregory XII	Venice	1406	1415
John XVII	Rome	1003	1003	Martin V	Rome	1417	1431
John XVIII	Rome	1004	1009	Eugene IV	Venice	1431	1447
Sergius IV	Rome	1009	1012	Nicholas V	Sarzana	1447	1455
Benedict VIII	Tusculum	1012	1024	Callistus III	Jativa	1455	1458
John XIX	Tusculum	1024	1032	Pius II	Siena	1458	1464
Benedict IX[6]	Tusculum	1032	1044	Paul II	Venice	1464	1471
Sylvester III	Rome	1045	1045	Sixtus IV	Savona	1471	1484
Benedict IX	Tusculum	1045	1045	Innocent VIII	Genoa	1484	1492
(2nd time)				Alexander VI	Jativa	1492	1503
Gregory VI	Rome	1045	1046	Pius III	Siena	1503	1503
Clement II	Saxony	1046	1047	Julius II	Savona	1503	1513
Benedict IX	Tusculum	1047	1048	Leo X	Florence	1513	1521
(3rd time)				Adrian VI	Utrecht	1522	1523
Damasus II	Bavaria	1048	1048	Clement VII	Florence	1523	1534
St. Leo IX	Alsace	1049	1054	Paul III	Rome	1534	1549
Victor II	Germany	1055	1057	Julius III	Rome	1550	1555
Stephen IX (X)	Lorraine	1057	1058	Marcellus II	Montepulciano	1555	1555
Nicholas II	Burgundy	1059	1061	Paul IV	Naples	1555	1559
Alexander II	Milan	1061	1073	Pius IV	Milan	1559	1565
St. Gregory VII	Tuscany	1073	1085	St. Pius V	Bosco	1566	1572
Bl. Victor III	Benevento	1086	1087	Gregory XIII	Bologna	1572	1585
Bl. Urban II	France	1088	1099	Sixtus V	Grottammare	1585	1590
Paschal II	Ravenna	1099	1118	Urban VII	Rome	1590	1590
Gelasius II	Gaeta	1118	1119	Gregory XIV	Cremona	1590	1591
Callistus II	Burgundy	1119	1124	Innocent IX	Bologna	1591	1591
Honorius II	Flagnano	1124	1130	Clement VIII	Florence	1592	1605
Innocent II	Rome	1130	1143	Leo XI	Florence	1605	1605
Celestine II	Città di Castello	1143	1144	Paul V	Rome	1605	1621
Lucius II	Bologna	1144	1145	Gregory XV	Bologna	1621	1623
Bl. Eugene III	Pisa	1145	1153	Urban VIII	Florence	1623	1644
Anastasius IV	Rome	1153	1154	Innocent X	Rome	1644	1655
Adrian IV	England	1154	1159	Alexander VII	Siena	1655	1667
Alexander III	Siena	1159	1181	Clement IX	Pistoia	1667	1669
Lucius III	Lucca	1181	1185	Clement X	Rome	1670	1676
Urban III	Milan	1185	1187	Bl. Innocent XI	Como	1676	1689
Gregory VIII	Benevento	1187	1187	Alexander VIII	Venice	1689	1691
Clement III	Rome	1187	1191	Innocent XII	Spinazzola	1691	1700
Celestine III	Rome	1191	1198	Clement XI	Urbino	1700	1721
Innocent III	Anagni	1198	1216	Innocent XIII	Rome	1721	1724
Honorius III	Rome	1216	1227	Benedict XIII	Gravina	1724	1730
Gregory IX	Anagni	1227	1241	Clement XII	Florence	1730	1740
Celestine IV	Milan	1241	1241	Benedict XIV	Bologna	1740	1758
Innocent IV	Genoa	1243	1254	Clement XIII	Venice	1758	1769
Alexander IV	Anagni	1254	1261	Clement XIV	Rimini	1769	1774
Urban IV	Troyes	1261	1264	Pius VI	Cesena	1775	1799
Clement IV	France	1265	1268	Pius VII	Cesena	1800	1823
Bl. Gregory X	Piacenza	1271	1276	Leo XII	Genga	1823	1829
Bl. Innocent V	Savoy	1276	1276	Pius VIII	Cingoli	1829	1830
Adrian V	Genoa	1276	1276	Gregory XVI	Belluno	1831	1846
John XXI[7]	Portugal	1276	1277	Pius IX	Senegallia	1846	1878
Nicholas III	Rome	1277	1280	Leo XIII	Carpineto	1878	1903
Martin IV[8]	France	1281	1285	St. Pius X	Riese	1903	1914
Honorius IV	Rome	1285	1287	Benedict XV	Genoa	1914	1922

Name	Birthplace	Reigned From	To	Name	Birthplace	Reigned From	To
Pius XI	Desio	1922	1939	Paul VI	Concesio	1963	1978
Pius XII	Rome	1939	1958	John Paul I	Forno di Canale	1978	1978
John XXIII	Sotto il Monte	1958	1963	John Paul II	Wadowice, Poland	1978	

1. Or 310. 2. He should be called Felix II, and his successors of the same name should be numbered accordingly. The discrepancy was caused by the erroneous insertion in some lists of the name of St. Felix of Rome, Martyr. 3. He was elected during the exile of St. Martin I, who endorsed him as Pope. 4. After St. Zachary died, a Roman priest named Stephen was elected but died before his consecration as Bishop of Rome. His name is not included in all lists for this reason. In view of this historical confusion, the *National Catholic Almanac* lists the true Stephen II as Stephen II (III), the true Stephen III as Stephen III (IV), etc. 5. Confusion exists concerning the legitimacy of claims. If the deposition of John was invalid, Leo was an antipope until after the end of Benedict's reign. If the deposition of John was valid, Leo was the legitimate Pope and Benedict an antipope. 6. If the triple removal of Benedict IX was not valid, Sylvester III, Gregory VI, and Clement II were antipopes. 7. Elimination was made of the name of John XX in an effort to rectify the numerical designation of Popes named John. The error dates back to the time of John XV. 8. The names of Marinus I and Marinus II were construed as Martin. In view of these two pontificates and the earlier reign of St. Martin I, this pontiff was called Martin IV. *Source: National Catholic Almanac*, from *Annuarto Pontificio*.

The Ten Commandments

The Ten Commandments, also called the Decalogue (Greek, "ten words"), were divine laws revealed to Moses by God on Mt. Sinai. Appearing in both Exodus (Ex. 20: 2–17) and Deuteronomy (Deut. 5:6–21), the commandments are numbered differently depending on whether they appear in a Catholic, Protestant, or Hebrew Bible.

You shall have no other gods before me.

You shall not make for yourself a graven image, or any likeness of anything that is in heaven above, or that is in the earth beneath, or that is in the water under the earth; you shall not bow down to them or serve them; for I the Lord your God am a jealous God, visiting the iniquity of the fathers upon the children to the third and the fourth generation of those who hate me, but showing steadfast love to thousands of those who love me and keep my commandments.

You shall not take the name of the Lord your God in vain; for the Lord will not hold him guiltless who takes his name in vain.

Remember the Sabbath day, to keep it holy. Six days you shall labor, and do all your work; but the seventh day is a Sabbath to the Lord your God; in it you shall not do any work, you, or your son, or your daughter, your manservant, or your maidservant, or your cattle, or the sojourner who is within your gates; for in six days the Lord made heaven and earth, the sea, and all that is in them, and rested the seventh day; therefore the Lord blessed the Sabbath day and hallowed it.

Honor your father and your mother, that your days may be long in the land which the Lord your God gives you.

You shall not kill.

You shall not commit adultery.

You shall not steal.

You shall not bear false witness against your neighbor.

You shall not covet your neighbor's wife, or his manservant, or his maidservant, or his ox, or his ass, or anything that is your neighbor's.

Source: Revised Standard Version of the Bible (Ex.20: 2–17)

The Books of the Bible

Below is the Protestant canon of the Bible (New Revised Standard Version). The Roman Catholic canon also includes the Deuterocanonical books as part of the Old Testament (these are considered apocryphal by most Protestants). The Hebrew Bible recognizes the books referred to as the Old Testament in the Protestant Bible, but not the Apocryphal/Deuterocononical books or the New Testament.

The Old Testament with the Apocryphal/ Deuterocanonical Books

The Hebrew Scriptures

Genesis
Exodus
Leviticus
Numbers
Deuteronomy
Joshua
Judges
Ruth
1 Samuel
2 Samuel
1 Kings
2 Kings
1 Chronicles
2 Chronicles
Ezra
Nehemiah
Esther
Job
Psalms
Proverbs

Ecclesiastes
Song of Solomon
Isaiah
Jeremiah
Lamentations
Ezekiel
Daniel
Hosea
Joel
Amos
Obadiah
Jonah
Micah
Nahum
Habakkuk
Zephaniah
Haggai
Zechariah
Malachi

The Apocryphal/ Deuterocanonical Books

Tobit
Judith
Additions to the Book of Esther

Wisdom of Solomon
Ecclesiasticus, or the Wisdom of Jesus Son of Sirach
Baruch
The Letter of Jeremiah
The Prayer of Azariah and the Song of the Three Jews
Susanna
Bel and the Dragon
1 Maccabees
2 Maccabees
1 Esdras
Prayer of Manasseh
Psalm 151
3 Maccabees
2 Esdras
4 Maccabees

The New Testament

Matthew
Mark
Luke
John

Acts of the Apostles
Romans
1 Corinthians
2 Corinthians
Galatians
Ephesians
Philippians
Colossians
1 Thessalonians
2 Thessalonians
1 Timothy
2 Timothy
Titus
Philemon
Hebrews
James
1 Peter
2 Peter
1 John
2 John
3 John
Jude
Revelation

See Calendar and Holidays for listings of religious holidays.

Calendar & Holidays

1998

January
S	M	T	W	T	F	S
				1	2	3
4	5	6	7	8	9	10
11	12	13	14	15	16	17
18	19	20	21	22	23	24
25	26	27	28	29	30	31

February
S	M	T	W	T	F	S
1	2	3	4	5	6	7
8	9	10	11	12	13	14
15	16	17	18	19	20	21
22	23	24	25	26	27	28

March
S	M	T	W	T	F	S
1	2	3	4	5	6	7
8	9	10	11	12	13	14
15	16	17	18	19	20	21
22	23	24	25	26	27	28
29	30	31				

April
S	M	T	W	T	F	S
			1	2	3	4
5	6	7	8	9	10	11
12	13	14	15	16	17	18
19	20	21	22	23	24	25
26	27	28	29	30		

January
1—New Year's Day
6—Epiphany
15—Martin Luther King, Jr.'s Birthday
19—Martin Luther King, Jr. Day
30—End of Ramadan

February
2—Ground Hog Day
12—Lincoln's Birthday
14—Valentine's Day
16—Presidents' Day
22—Washington's Birthday
25—Ash Wednesday

March
12—Purim
17—St. Patrick's Day

April
5—Palm Sunday
5—Daylight Saving Time begins
10—Good Friday
11—1st Day of Passover
12—Easter Sunday

May
S	M	T	W	T	F	S
					1	2
3	4	5	6	7	8	9
10	11	12	13	14	15	16
17	18	19	20	21	22	23
24	25	26	27	28	29	30
31						

June
S	M	T	W	T	F	S
	1	2	3	4	5	6
7	8	9	10	11	12	13
14	15	16	17	18	19	20
21	22	23	24	25	26	27
28	29	30				

July
S	M	T	W	T	F	S
			1	2	3	4
5	6	7	8	9	10	11
12	13	14	15	16	17	18
19	20	21	22	23	24	25
26	27	28	29	30	31	

August
S	M	T	W	T	F	S
						1
2	3	4	5	6	7	8
9	10	11	12	13	14	15
16	17	18	19	20	21	22
23	24	25	26	27	28	29
30	31					

May
10—Mother's Day
21—Ascension Day
25—Memorial Day Observed
30—Memorial Day
31—1st Day of Shavuot
31—Pentecost

June
14—Flag Day
21—Father's Day

July
1—Canada Day
4—Independence Day

September
S	M	T	W	T	F	S
		1	2	3	4	5
6	7	8	9	10	11	12
13	14	15	16	17	18	19
20	21	22	23	24	25	26
27	28	29	30			

October
S	M	T	W	T	F	S
				1	2	3
4	5	6	7	8	9	10
11	12	13	14	15	16	17
18	19	20	21	22	23	24
25	26	27	28	29	30	31

November
S	M	T	W	T	F	S
1	2	3	4	5	6	7
8	9	10	11	12	13	14
15	16	17	18	19	20	21
22	23	24	25	26	27	28
29	30					

December
S	M	T	W	T	F	S
		1	2	3	4	5
6	7	8	9	10	11	12
13	14	15	16	17	18	19
20	21	22	23	24	25	26
27	28	29	30	31		

September
7—Labor Day
21—Rosh Hashanah
30—Yom Kippur

October
12—Columbus Day
12—Thanksgiving Day (Canada)
25—Daylight Saving Time ends
31—Halloween

November
1—All Saints Day
3—Election Day
11—Veterans Day
26—Thanksgiving Day
29—1st Sunday of Advent

December
14—1st Day of Hanukkah
20—Ramadan
25—Christmas Day

Seasons for the Northern Hemisphere, 1998

March 20, 2:55 P.M. EST (19:55 UT*), sun enters sign of Aries; spring begins
June 21, 10:03 A.M. EDT (14:03 UT), sun enters sign of Cancer; summer begins

Sept. 23, 1:37 A.M. EDT (05:37 UT), sun enters sign of Libra; fall begins
Dec. 21, 8:56 P.M. EST (Dec. 22, 01:56 UT), sun enters sign of Capricorn; winter begins

*Universal Time (UT), also known as Greenwich Mean Time (GMT). See p. 450 for a conversion table of Universal Time.

1997

	January					
S	M	T	W	T	F	S
			1	2	3	4
5	6	7	8	9	10	11
12	13	14	15	16	17	18
19	20	21	22	23	24	25
26	27	28	29	30	31	

	February					
S	M	T	W	T	F	S
						1
2	3	4	5	6	7	8
9	10	11	12	13	14	15
16	17	18	19	20	21	22
23	24	25	26	27	28	

	March					
S	M	T	W	T	F	S
						1
2	3	4	5	6	7	8
9	10	11	12	13	14	15
16	17	18	19	20	21	22
23	24	25	26	27	28	29
30	31					

	April					
S	M	T	W	T	F	S
		1	2	3	4	5
6	7	8	9	10	11	12
13	14	15	16	17	18	19
20	21	22	23	24	25	26
27	28	29	30			

	May					
S	M	T	W	T	F	S
				1	2	3
4	5	6	7	8	9	10
11	12	13	14	15	16	17
18	19	20	21	22	23	24
25	26	27	28	29	30	31

	June					
S	M	T	W	T	F	S
1	2	3	4	5	6	7
8	9	10	11	12	13	14
15	16	17	18	19	20	21
22	23	24	25	26	27	28
29	30					

	July					
S	M	T	W	T	F	S
		1	2	3	4	5
6	7	8	9	10	11	12
13	14	15	16	17	18	19
20	21	22	23	24	25	26
27	28	29	30	31		

	August					
S	M	T	W	T	F	S
					1	2
3	4	5	6	7	8	9
10	11	12	13	14	15	16
17	18	19	20	21	22	23
24	25	26	27	28	29	30
31						

	September					
S	M	T	W	T	F	S
	1	2	3	4	5	6
7	8	9	10	11	12	13
14	15	16	17	18	19	20
21	22	23	24	25	26	27
28	29	30				

	October					
S	M	T	W	T	F	S
			1	2	3	4
5	6	7	8	9	10	11
12	13	14	15	16	17	18
19	20	21	22	23	24	25
26	27	28	29	30	31	

	November					
S	M	T	W	T	F	S
						1
2	3	4	5	6	7	8
9	10	11	12	13	14	15
16	17	18	19	20	21	22
23	24	25	26	27	28	29
30						

	December					
S	M	T	W	T	F	S
	1	2	3	4	5	6
7	8	9	10	11	12	13
14	15	16	17	18	19	20
21	22	23	24	25	26	27
28	29	30	31			

1999

	January					
S	M	T	W	T	F	S
					1	2
3	4	5	6	7	8	9
10	11	12	13	14	15	16
17	18	19	20	21	22	23
24	25	26	27	28	29	30
31						

	February					
S	M	T	W	T	F	S
	1	2	3	4	5	6
7	8	9	10	11	12	13
14	15	16	17	18	19	20
21	22	23	24	25	26	27
28						

	March					
S	M	T	W	T	F	S
	1	2	3	4	5	6
7	8	9	10	11	12	13
14	15	16	17	18	19	20
21	22	23	24	25	26	27
28	29	30	31			

	April					
S	M	T	W	T	F	S
				1	2	3
4	5	6	7	8	9	10
11	12	13	14	15	16	17
18	19	20	21	22	23	24
25	26	27	28	29	30	

	May					
S	M	T	W	T	F	S
						1
2	3	4	5	6	7	8
9	10	11	12	13	14	15
16	17	18	19	20	21	22
23	24	25	26	27	28	29
30	31					

	June					
S	M	T	W	T	F	S
		1	2	3	4	5
6	7	8	9	10	11	12
13	14	15	16	17	18	19
20	21	22	23	24	25	26
27	28	29	30			

	July					
S	M	T	W	T	F	S
				1	2	3
4	5	6	7	8	9	10
11	12	13	14	15	16	17
18	19	20	21	22	23	24
25	26	27	28	29	30	31

	August					
S	M	T	W	T	F	S
1	2	3	4	5	6	7
8	9	10	11	12	13	14
15	16	17	18	19	20	21
22	23	24	25	26	27	28
29	30	31				

	September					
S	M	T	W	T	F	S
			1	2	3	4
5	6	7	8	9	10	11
12	13	14	15	16	17	18
19	20	21	22	23	24	25
26	27	28	29	30		

	October					
S	M	T	W	T	F	S
					1	2
3	4	5	6	7	8	9
10	11	12	13	14	15	16
17	18	19	20	21	22	23
24	25	26	27	28	29	30
31						

	November					
S	M	T	W	T	F	S
	1	2	3	4	5	6
7	8	9	10	11	12	13
14	15	16	17	18	19	20
21	22	23	24	25	26	27
28	29	30				

	December					
S	M	T	W	T	F	S
			1	2	3	4
5	6	7	8	9	10	11
12	13	14	15	16	17	18
19	20	21	22	23	24	25
26	27	28	29	30	31	

Astrological Signs

♈	**Aries (Ram):** March 21–April 19
♉	**Taurus (Bull):** April 20–May 20
♊	**Gemini (Twins):** May 21–June 20
⊗	**Cancer (Crab):** June 21–July 22
♌	**Leo (Lion):** July 23–Aug. 22
♍	**Virgo (Virgin):** Aug. 23–Sept. 22
♎	**Libra (Scales):** Sept. 23–Oct. 22
♏	**Scorpio (Scorpion):** Oct. 23–Nov. 21
♐	**Sagittarius (Archer):** Nov. 22–Dec. 21
♑	**Capricorn (Goat):** Dec. 22–Jan. 19
♒	**Aquarius (Water Bearer):** Jan. 20–Feb. 18
♓	**Pisces (Fish):** Feb. 19–March 20

PERPETUAL CALENDAR

1800...4	1844...9	1888...8	1932.13	1976.12	2020.11
1801...5	1845...4	1889...3	1933...1	1977...7	2021...6
1802...6	1846...5	1890...4	1934...2	1978...1	2022...7
1803...7	1847...6	1891...5	1935...3	1979...2	2023...1
1804...8	1848.14	1892.13	1936.11	1980.10	2024...9
1805...9	1849...2	1893...1	1937...6	1981...5	2025...4
1806...4	1850...3	1894...2	1938...7	1982...6	2026...5
1807...5	1851...4	1895...3	1939...1	1983...7	2027...6
1808.13	1852.12	1896.11	1940...9	1984...8	2028.14
1809...1	1853...7	1897...6	1941...4	1985...3	2029...2
1810...2	1854...1	1898...7	1942...5	1986...4	2030...3
1811...3	1855...2	1899...1	1943...6	1987...5	2031...4
1812.11	1856.10	1900...2	1944.14	1988.13	2032.12
1813...6	1857...5	1901...3	1945...2	1989...1	2033...7
1814...7	1858...6	1902...4	1946...3	1990...2	2034...1
1815...1	1859...7	1903...5	1947...4	1991...3	2035...2
1816...9	1860...8	1904.13	1948.12	1992.11	2036.10
1817...4	1861...3	1905...1	1949...7	1993...6	2037...5
1818...5	1862...4	1906...2	1950...1	1994...7	2038...6
1819...6	1863...5	1907...3	1951...2	1995...1	2039...7
1820.14	1864.13	1908.11	1952.10	1996...9	2040...8
1821...2	1865...1	1909...6	1953...5	1997...4	2041...3
1822...3	1866...2	1910...7	1954...6	1998...5	2042...4
1823...4	1867...3	1911...1	1955...7	1999...6	2043...5
1824.12	1868.11	1912...9	1956...8	2000.14	2044.13
1825...7	1869...6	1913...4	1957...3	2001...2	2045...1
1826...1	1870...7	1914...5	1958...4	2002...3	2046...2
1827...2	1871...1	1915...6	1959...5	2003...4	2047...3
1828.10	1872...9	1916.14	1960.13	2004.12	2048.11
1829...5	1873...4	1917...2	1961...1	2005...7	2049...6
1830...6	1874...5	1918...3	1962...2	2006...1	2050...7
1831...7	1875...6	1919...4	1963...3	2007...2	2051...1
1832...8	1876.14	1920.12	1964.11	2008.10	2052...9
1833...3	1877...2	1921...7	1965...6	2009...5	2053...4
1834...4	1878...3	1922...1	1966...7	2010...6	2054...5
1835...5	1879...4	1923...2	1967...1	2011...7	2055...6
1836.13	1880.12	1924.10	1968...9	2012...8	2056.14
1837...1	1881...7	1925...5	1969...4	2013...3	2057...2
1838...2	1882...1	1926...6	1970...5	2014...4	2058...3
1839...3	1883...2	1927...7	1971...6	2015...5	2059...4
1840.11	1884.10	1928...8	1972.14	2016.13	2060.12
1841...6	1885...5	1929...3	1973...2	2017...1	2061...7
1842...7	1886...6	1930...4	1974...3	2018...2	2062...1
1843...1	1887...7	1931...5	1975...4	2019...3	2063...2

DIRECTIONS: The number given with each year in the key above is number of calendar to use for that year.

1

```
        JANUARY                FEBRUARY                 MARCH                  APRIL
 S  M  T  W  T  F  S     S  M  T  W  T  F  S     S  M  T  W  T  F  S     S  M  T  W  T  F  S
    1  2  3  4  5  6  7                  1  2  3  4                  1  2  3  4                  1  2  3
 8  9 10 11 12 13 14     5  6  7  8  9 10 11     5  6  7  8  9 10 11     4  5  6  7  8  9 10
15 16 17 18 19 20 21    12 13 14 15 16 17 18    12 13 14 15 16 17 18    11 12 13 14 15 16 17
22 23 24 25 26 27 28    19 20 21 22 23 24 25    19 20 21 22 23 24 25    18 19 20 21 22 23 24
29 30 31                26 27 28                26 27 28 29 30 31       25 26 27 28 29 30

          MAY                    JUNE                   JULY                  AUGUST
 S  M  T  W  T  F  S     S  M  T  W  T  F  S     S  M  T  W  T  F  S     S  M  T  W  T  F  S
    1  2  3  4  5  6              1  2  3                       1        1  2  3  4  5
 7  8  9 10 11 12 13     4  5  6  7  8  9 10     2  3  4  5  6  7  8     6  7  8  9 10 11 12
14 15 16 17 18 19 20    11 12 13 14 15 16 17     9 10 11 12 13 14 15    13 14 15 16 17 18 19
21 22 23 24 25 26 27    18 19 20 21 22 23 24    16 17 18 19 20 21 22    20 21 22 23 24 25 26
28 29 30 31             25 26 27 28 29 30       23 24 25 26 27 28 29    27 28 29 30 31
                                                30 31

       SEPTEMBER               OCTOBER                NOVEMBER               DECEMBER
 S  M  T  W  T  F  S     S  M  T  W  T  F  S     S  M  T  W  T  F  S     S  M  T  W  T  F  S
                1  2     1  2  3  4  5  6  7                 1  2  3  4                 1  2
 3  4  5  6  7  8  9     8  9 10 11 12 13 14     5  6  7  8  9 10 11     3  4  5  6  7  8  9
10 11 12 13 14 15 16    15 16 17 18 19 20 21    12 13 14 15 16 17 18    10 11 12 13 14 15 16
17 18 19 20 21 22 23    22 23 24 25 26 27 28    19 20 21 22 23 24 25    17 18 19 20 21 22 23
24 25 26 27 28 29 30    29 30 31                26 27 28 29 30          24 25 26 27 28 29 30
                                                                        31
```

2

```
        JANUARY                FEBRUARY                 MARCH                  APRIL
 S  M  T  W  T  F  S     S  M  T  W  T  F  S     S  M  T  W  T  F  S     S  M  T  W  T  F  S
    1  2  3  4  5  6                 1  2  3                 1  2  3                 1  2  3
 7  8  9 10 11 12 13     4  5  6  7  8  9 10     4  5  6  7  8  9 10     4  5  6  7  8  9 10
14 15 16 17 18 19 20    11 12 13 14 15 16 17    11 12 13 14 15 16 17    11 12 13 14 15 16 17
21 22 23 24 25 26 27    18 19 20 21 22 23 24    18 19 20 21 22 23 24    18 19 20 21 22 23 24
28 29 30 31             25 26 27 28             25 26 27 28 29 30 31    25 26 27 28 29 30

          MAY                    JUNE                   JULY                  AUGUST
 S  M  T  W  T  F  S     S  M  T  W  T  F  S     S  M  T  W  T  F  S     S  M  T  W  T  F  S
       1  2  3  4  5              1  2              1  2  3  4  5                 1  2  3  4
 6  7  8  9 10 11 12     3  4  5  6  7  8  9     6  7  8  9 10 11 12     5  6  7  8  9 10 11
13 14 15 16 17 18 19    10 11 12 13 14 15 16    13 14 15 16 17 18 19    12 13 14 15 16 17 18
20 21 22 23 24 25 26    17 18 19 20 21 22 23    20 21 22 23 24 25 26    19 20 21 22 23 24 25
27 28 29 30 31          24 25 26 27 28 29 30    27 28 29 30 31          26 27 28 29 30 31

       SEPTEMBER               OCTOBER                NOVEMBER               DECEMBER
 S  M  T  W  T  F  S     S  M  T  W  T  F  S     S  M  T  W  T  F  S     S  M  T  W  T  F  S
                   1        1  2  3  4  5  6                 1  2  3                 1  2  3
 2  3  4  5  6  7  8     7  8  9 10 11 12 13     4  5  6  7  8  9 10     4  5  6  7  8  9 10
 9 10 11 12 13 14 15    14 15 16 17 18 19 20    11 12 13 14 15 16 17    11 12 13 14 15 16 17
16 17 18 19 20 21 22    21 22 23 24 25 26 27    18 19 20 21 22 23 24    18 19 20 21 22 23 24
23 24 25 26 27 28 29    28 29 30 31             25 26 27 28 29 30       25 26 27 28 29 30 31
30
```

3

```
        JANUARY                FEBRUARY                 MARCH                  APRIL
 S  M  T  W  T  F  S     S  M  T  W  T  F  S     S  M  T  W  T  F  S     S  M  T  W  T  F  S
       1  2  3  4  5                 1  2                 1  2                 1  2  3  4  5
 6  7  8  9 10 11 12     3  4  5  6  7  8  9     3  4  5  6  7  8  9     6  7  8  9 10 11 12
13 14 15 16 17 18 19    10 11 12 13 14 15 16    10 11 12 13 14 15 16    13 14 15 16 17 18 19
20 21 22 23 24 25 26    17 18 19 20 21 22 23    17 18 19 20 21 22 23    20 21 22 23 24 25 26
27 28 29 30 31          24 25 26 27 28          24 25 26 27 28 29 30    27 28 29 30
                                                31

          MAY                    JUNE                   JULY                  AUGUST
 S  M  T  W  T  F  S     S  M  T  W  T  F  S     S  M  T  W  T  F  S     S  M  T  W  T  F  S
          1  2  3  4                    1        1  2  3  4  5  6                 1  2  3
 5  6  7  8  9 10 11     2  3  4  5  6  7  8     7  8  9 10 11 12 13     4  5  6  7  8  9 10
12 13 14 15 16 17 18     9 10 11 12 13 14 15    14 15 16 17 18 19 20    11 12 13 14 15 16 17
19 20 21 22 23 24 25    16 17 18 19 20 21 22    21 22 23 24 25 26 27    18 19 20 21 22 23 24
26 27 28 29 30 31       23 24 25 26 27 28 29    28 29 30 31             25 26 27 28 29 30 31
                        30

       SEPTEMBER               OCTOBER                NOVEMBER               DECEMBER
 S  M  T  W  T  F  S     S  M  T  W  T  F  S     S  M  T  W  T  F  S     S  M  T  W  T  F  S
 1  2  3  4  5  6  7        1  2  3  4  5                    1  2        1  2  3  4  5  6  7
 8  9 10 11 12 13 14     6  7  8  9 10 11 12     3  4  5  6  7  8  9     8  9 10 11 12 13 14
15 16 17 18 19 20 21    13 14 15 16 17 18 19    10 11 12 13 14 15 16    15 16 17 18 19 20 21
22 23 24 25 26 27 28    20 21 22 23 24 25 26    17 18 19 20 21 22 23    22 23 24 25 26 27 28
29 30                   27 28 29 30 31          24 25 26 27 28 29 30    29 30 31
```

4

```
        JANUARY                FEBRUARY                 MARCH                  APRIL
 S  M  T  W  T  F  S     S  M  T  W  T  F  S     S  M  T  W  T  F  S     S  M  T  W  T  F  S
          1  2  3  4                       1                       1        1  2  3  4  5
 5  6  7  8  9 10 11     2  3  4  5  6  7  8     2  3  4  5  6  7  8     6  7  8  9 10 11 12
12 13 14 15 16 17 18     9 10 11 12 13 14 15     9 10 11 12 13 14 15    13 14 15 16 17 18 19
19 20 21 22 23 24 25    16 17 18 19 20 21 22    16 17 18 19 20 21 22    20 21 22 23 24 25 26
26 27 28 29 30 31       23 24 25 26 27 28       23 24 25 26 27 28 29    27 28 29 30
                                                30 31

          MAY                    JUNE                   JULY                  AUGUST
 S  M  T  W  T  F  S     S  M  T  W  T  F  S     S  M  T  W  T  F  S     S  M  T  W  T  F  S
             1  2  3     1  2  3  4  5  6  7           1  2  3  4  5                    1  2
 4  5  6  7  8  9 10     8  9 10 11 12 13 14     6  7  8  9 10 11 12     3  4  5  6  7  8  9
11 12 13 14 15 16 17    15 16 17 18 19 20 21    13 14 15 16 17 18 19    10 11 12 13 14 15 16
18 19 20 21 22 23 24    22 23 24 25 26 27 28    20 21 22 23 24 25 26    17 18 19 20 21 22 23
25 26 27 28 29 30 31    29 30                   27 28 29 30 31          24 25 26 27 28 29 30
                                                                        31

       SEPTEMBER               OCTOBER                NOVEMBER               DECEMBER
 S  M  T  W  T  F  S     S  M  T  W  T  F  S     S  M  T  W  T  F  S     S  M  T  W  T  F  S
    1  2  3  4  5  6              1  2  3  4                       1        1  2  3  4  5  6
 7  8  9 10 11 12 13     5  6  7  8  9 10 11     2  3  4  5  6  7  8     7  8  9 10 11 12 13
14 15 16 17 18 19 20    12 13 14 15 16 17 18     9 10 11 12 13 14 15    14 15 16 17 18 19 20
21 22 23 24 25 26 27    19 20 21 22 23 24 25    16 17 18 19 20 21 22    21 22 23 24 25 26 27
28 29 30                26 27 28 29 30 31       23 24 25 26 27 28 29    28 29 30 31
                                                30
```

5

```
        JANUARY                FEBRUARY                 MARCH                  APRIL
 S  M  T  W  T  F  S     S  M  T  W  T  F  S     S  M  T  W  T  F  S     S  M  T  W  T  F  S
             1  2  3     1  2  3  4  5  6  7     1  2  3  4  5  6  7                 1  2  3  4
 4  5  6  7  8  9 10     8  9 10 11 12 13 14     8  9 10 11 12 13 14     5  6  7  8  9 10 11
11 12 13 14 15 16 17    15 16 17 18 19 20 21    15 16 17 18 19 20 21    12 13 14 15 16 17 18
18 19 20 21 22 23 24    22 23 24 25 26 27 28    22 23 24 25 26 27 28    19 20 21 22 23 24 25
25 26 27 28 29 30 31                            29 30 31                26 27 28 29 30

          MAY                    JUNE                   JULY                  AUGUST
 S  M  T  W  T  F  S     S  M  T  W  T  F  S     S  M  T  W  T  F  S     S  M  T  W  T  F  S
             1  2        1  2  3  4  5  6              1  2  3  4                       1
 3  4  5  6  7  8  9     7  8  9 10 11 12 13     5  6  7  8  9 10 11     2  3  4  5  6  7  8
10 11 12 13 14 15 16    14 15 16 17 18 19 20    12 13 14 15 16 17 18     9 10 11 12 13 14 15
17 18 19 20 21 22 23    21 22 23 24 25 26 27    19 20 21 22 23 24 25    16 17 18 19 20 21 22
24 25 26 27 28 29 30    28 29 30                26 27 28 29 30 31       23 24 25 26 27 28 29
31                                                                      30 31

       SEPTEMBER               OCTOBER                NOVEMBER               DECEMBER
 S  M  T  W  T  F  S     S  M  T  W  T  F  S     S  M  T  W  T  F  S     S  M  T  W  T  F  S
       1  2  3  4  5                 1  2  3     1  2  3  4  5  6  7        1  2  3  4  5
 6  7  8  9 10 11 12     4  5  6  7  8  9 10     8  9 10 11 12 13 14     6  7  8  9 10 11 12
13 14 15 16 17 18 19    11 12 13 14 15 16 17    15 16 17 18 19 20 21    13 14 15 16 17 18 19
20 21 22 23 24 25 26    18 19 20 21 22 23 24    22 23 24 25 26 27 28    20 21 22 23 24 25 26
27 28 29 30             25 26 27 28 29 30 31    29 30                   27 28 29 30 31
```

6

```
        JANUARY                FEBRUARY                 MARCH                  APRIL
 S  M  T  W  T  F  S     S  M  T  W  T  F  S     S  M  T  W  T  F  S     S  M  T  W  T  F  S
                1  2        1  2  3  4  5  6        1  2  3  4  5  6                    1  2  3
 3  4  5  6  7  8  9     7  8  9 10 11 12 13     7  8  9 10 11 12 13     4  5  6  7  8  9 10
10 11 12 13 14 15 16    14 15 16 17 18 19 20    14 15 16 17 18 19 20    11 12 13 14 15 16 17
17 18 19 20 21 22 23    21 22 23 24 25 26 27    21 22 23 24 25 26 27    18 19 20 21 22 23 24
24 25 26 27 28 29 30    28                      28 29 30 31             25 26 27 28 29 30
31

          MAY                    JUNE                   JULY                  AUGUST
 S  M  T  W  T  F  S     S  M  T  W  T  F  S     S  M  T  W  T  F  S     S  M  T  W  T  F  S
                   1        1  2  3  4  5              1  2  3        1  2  3  4  5  6  7
 2  3  4  5  6  7  8     6  7  8  9 10 11 12     4  5  6  7  8  9 10     8  9 10 11 12 13 14
 9 10 11 12 13 14 15    13 14 15 16 17 18 19    11 12 13 14 15 16 17    15 16 17 18 19 20 21
16 17 18 19 20 21 22    20 21 22 23 24 25 26    18 19 20 21 22 23 24    22 23 24 25 26 27 28
23 24 25 26 27 28 29    27 28 29 30             25 26 27 28 29 30 31    29 30 31
30 31

       SEPTEMBER               OCTOBER                NOVEMBER               DECEMBER
 S  M  T  W  T  F  S     S  M  T  W  T  F  S     S  M  T  W  T  F  S     S  M  T  W  T  F  S
          1  2  3  4                 1  2           1  2  3  4  5  6                 1  2  3  4
 5  6  7  8  9 10 11     3  4  5  6  7  8  9     7  8  9 10 11 12 13     5  6  7  8  9 10 11
12 13 14 15 16 17 18    10 11 12 13 14 15 16    14 15 16 17 18 19 20    12 13 14 15 16 17 18
19 20 21 22 23 24 25    17 18 19 20 21 22 23    21 22 23 24 25 26 27    19 20 21 22 23 24 25
26 27 28 29 30          24 25 26 27 28 29 30    28 29 30                26 27 28 29 30 31
                        31
```

7

JANUARY	FEBRUARY	MARCH	APRIL
MAY	JUNE	JULY	AUGUST
SEPTEMBER	OCTOBER	NOVEMBER	DECEMBER

8

JANUARY	FEBRUARY	MARCH	APRIL
MAY	JUNE	JULY	AUGUST
SEPTEMBER	OCTOBER	NOVEMBER	DECEMBER

9

JANUARY	FEBRUARY	MARCH	APRIL
MAY	JUNE	JULY	AUGUST
SEPTEMBER	OCTOBER	NOVEMBER	DECEMBER

10

JANUARY	FEBRUARY	MARCH	APRIL
MAY	JUNE	JULY	AUGUST
SEPTEMBER	OCTOBER	NOVEMBER	DECEMBER

11

JANUARY	FEBRUARY	MARCH	APRIL
MAY	JUNE	JULY	AUGUST
SEPTEMBER	OCTOBER	NOVEMBER	DECEMBER

12

JANUARY	FEBRUARY	MARCH	APRIL
MAY	JUNE	JULY	AUGUST
SEPTEMBER	OCTOBER	NOVEMBER	DECEMBER

13

JANUARY	FEBRUARY	MARCH	APRIL
MAY	JUNE	JULY	AUGUST
SEPTEMBER	OCTOBER	NOVEMBER	DECEMBER

14

JANUARY	FEBRUARY	MARCH	APRIL
MAY	JUNE	JULY	AUGUST
SEPTEMBER	OCTOBER	NOVEMBER	DECEMBER

The Calendar

History of the Calendar

The purpose of a calendar is to reckon time in advance, to show how many days have to elapse until a certain event takes place—the harvest, a religious festival, or whatever. The earliest calendars, naturally, were crude, and they must have been strongly influenced by the geographical location of the people who made them. In the Scandinavian countries, for example, where the seasons are pronounced, the concept of the year was determined by the seasons, specifically by the end of winter. The Norsemen, before becoming Christians, are said to have had a calendar consisting of ten months of 30 days each.

But in warmer countries, where the seasons are less pronounced, the moon became the basic unit for time reckoning; an old Jewish book actually makes the statement that "the moon was created for the counting of the days." All the oldest calendars of which we have reliable information were lunar calendars, based on the time interval from one new moon to the next—a so-called "lunation." But even in a warm climate there are annual events that pay no attention to the phases of the moon. In some areas it was a rainy season; in Egypt it was the annual flooding of the Nile. It was, therefore, necessary to regulate daily life and religious festivals by lunations, but to take care of the annual event in some other manner.

The calendar of the Assyrians was based on the phases of the moon. The month began with the first appearance of the lunar crescent, and since this can best be observed in the evening, the day began with sunset. They knew that a lunation was 29½ days long, so their lunar year had a duration of 354 days, falling eleven days short of the solar year.[1] After three years such a lunar calendar would be off by 33 days, or more than one lunation. We know that the Assyrians added an extra month from time to time, but we do not know whether they had developed a special rule for doing so or whether the priests proclaimed the necessity for an extra month from observation. If they made every third year a year of 13 lunations, their three-year period would cover 1,091½ days (using their value of 29½ days for one lunation), or just about four days too short. In one century this mistake would add up to 133 days by their reckoning (in reality closer to 134 days), requiring four extra lunations per century.

We now know that an eight-year period, consisting of five years with 12 months and three years with 13 months would lead to a difference of only 20 days per century, but we do not know whether such a calendar was actually used.

The best approximation that was possible in antiquity was a 19-year period, with seven of these 19 years having 13 months. This means that the period contained 235 months. This, still using the old value for a lunation, made a total of 6,932½ days, while 19 solar years added up to 6,939.7 days, a difference of just one week per period and about five weeks per century. Even the 19-year period required constant adjustment, but it was the period that became the basis of the religious calendar of the Jews. The Arabs used the same calendar at first, but Mohammed forbade shifting from 12 months to 13 months, so that the Islamic religious calendar, even today, has a lunar year of 354 days. As a result the Islamic religious festivals run through all the seasons of the year three times per century.

The Egyptians had a traditional calendar with 12 months of 30 days each. At one time they added five extra days at the end of every year. These turned into a five-day festival because it was thought to be unlucky to work during that time.

When Rome emerged as a world power, the difficulties of making a calendar were well known, but the Romans complicated their lives because of their superstition that even numbers were unlucky. Hence their months were 29 or 31 days long, with the exception of February, which had 28 days. However, four months of 31 days, seven months of 29 days, and one month of 28 days added up to only 355 days. Therefore, the Romans invented an extra month called Mercedonius of 22 or 23 days. It was added every second year.

Even with Mercedonius, the Roman calendar was so far off that Caesar, advised by the astronomer Sosigenes, ordered a sweeping reform in 45 B.C.E. One year, made 445 days long by imperial decree, brought the calendar back in step with the seasons. Then the solar year (with the value of 365 days and 6 hours) was made the basis of the calendar. The months were 30 or 31 days in length, and to take care of the six hours, every fourth year was made a 366-day year. Moreover, Caesar decreed, the year began with the first of January, not with the vernal equinox in late March.

This was the Julian calendar, named after Julius Caesar. It is still the calendar of the Eastern Orthodox churches.

However, the year is 11½ minutes shorter than the figure written into Caesar's calendar by Sosigenes, and after a number of centuries, even 11½ minutes add up. While Caesar could decree that the vernal equinox should not be used as the first day of the new year, the vernal equinox is still a fact of Nature that could not be disregarded. One of the first (as far as we know) to become alarmed about this was Roger Bacon. He sent a memorandum to Pope Clement IV, who apparently was not impressed. But Pope Sixtus IV (reigned 1471 to 1484) decided that another reform was needed and called the German astronomer Regiomontanus to Rome to advise him. Regiomontanus arrived in 1475, but one year later he died in an epidemic, one of the recurrent outbreaks of the plague. The Pope himself survived, but his reform plans died with Regiomontanus.

Less than a hundred years later, in 1545, the Council of Trent authorized the then Pope, Paul III, to reform the calendar once more. Most of the mathematical and astronomical work was done by Father Christopher Clavius, S.J. The immediate correction, advised by Father Clavius and ordered by Pope Gregory XIII, was that Thursday, Oct. 4, 1582, was to be the last day of the Julian calendar. The next day was Friday, with the date of October 15. For long-range accuracy, a formula suggested by the Vatican librarian Aloysius Giglio (latinized into Lilius) was adopted: every fourth year is a leap year unless it is a century year like 1700 or 1800. Century years can be leap years only when they are divisible by 400 (e.g., 1600). This rule eliminates three leap years in four centuries, making the calendar sufficiently correct for all ordinary purposes.

Unfortunately, all the Protestant princes in 1582 chose to ignore the papal bull; they continued with the Julian calendar. It was not until 1698 that the German professor Erhard Weigel persuaded the Protestant rulers of Germany and of the Netherlands to change to the new calendar. In England the shift took place in 1752, and in Russia it needed the revolution to introduce the Gregorian calendar in 1918.

---

1. The correct figures are: lunation: 29 d, 12 h, 44 min, 2.8 sec (29.530585 d); solar year: 365 d, 5 h, 48 min, 46 sec (365.242216 d); 12 lunations: 354 d, 8 h, 48 min, 34 sec (354.3671 d).

Drift of the Vernal Equinox in the Julian Calendar

Date	Julian year	Date	Julian year	Date	Julian year
March 21	C.E. 325	March 17	C.E. 837	March 13	C.E. 1349
March 20	C.E. 453	March 16	C.E. 965	March 12	C.E. 1477
March 19	C.E. 581	March 15	C.E. 1093	March 11	C.E. 1605
March 18	C.E. 709	March 14	C.E. 1221		

The average year of the Gregorian calendar, in spite of the leap year rule, is about 26 seconds longer than the earth's orbital period. But this discrepancy will need 3,323 years to build up to a single day.

Modern proposals for calendar reform do not aim at a "better" calendar, but at one that is more convenient to use, especially for commercial purposes. A 365-day year cannot be divided into equal halves or quarters; the number of days per month is haphazard; the months begin or end in the middle of a week; a holiday fixed by date (e.g., the Fourth of July) will wander through a week; a holiday fixed in another manner (e.g., Easter) can fall on thirty-five possible dates. The Gregorian calendar, admittedly, keeps the calendar dates in reasonable unison with astronomical events, but it still is full of minor annoyances. Moreover, you need a calendar every year to look up dates; an ideal calendar should be one that you can memorize for one year and that is valid for all other years, too.

In 1834 an Italian priest, Marco Mastrofini, suggested taking one day out of every year. It would be made a holiday and *not* be given the name of a weekday. That would make every year begin with January 1 as a Sunday. The leap-year day would be treated the same way, so that in leap years there would be two unnamed holidays at the end of the year.

About a decade later the philosopher Auguste Comte also suggested a 364-day calendar with an extra day, which he called Year Day.

Since then there have been other unsuccessful attempts at calendar reform.

Time and Calendar

The two natural cycles on which time measurements are based are the year and the day. The year is defined as the time required for the Earth to complete one revolution around the sun, while the day is the time required for the Earth to complete one turn upon its axis. Unfortunately the Earth needs 365 days plus about six hours to go around the sun once, so that the year does not consist of so and so many days; the fractional day has to be taken care of by an extra day every fourth year.

But because the Earth, while turning upon its axis, also moves around the sun there are two kinds of days. A day may be defined as the interval between the highest point of the sun in the sky on two successive days. This, averaged out over the year, produces the customary 24-hour day. But one might also define a day as the time interval between the moments when a certain point in the sky, say a conveniently located star, is directly overhead. This is called:

Sidereal time. Astronomers use a point which they call the "vernal equinox" for the actual determination. Such a sidereal day is somewhat shorter than the "solar day," namely by about 3 minutes and 56 seconds of so-called "mean solar time."

Apparent solar time is the time based directly on the sun's position in the sky. In ordinary life the day runs from midnight to midnight. It begins when the sun is invisible by being 12 hours from its zenith. Astronomers use the so-called "Julian Day," which runs from noon to noon; the concept was invented by the astronomer Joseph Scaliger, who named it after his father Julius. To avoid the problems caused by leap-year days

and so forth, Scaliger picked a conveniently remote date in the past and suggested just counting days without regard to weeks, months, and years. The Julian Day for 0^h Jan. 31, 1996 is 245 0082.5. The reason for having the Julian Day run from noon to noon is the practical one that astronomical observations usually extend across the midnight hour, which would require a change in date (or in the Julian Day number) if the astronomical day, like the civil day, ran from midnight to midnight.

Mean solar time, rather than apparent solar time, is what is actually used most of the time. The mean solar time is based on the position of a fictitious "mean sun." The reason why this fictitious sun has to be introduced is the following: the Earth turns on its axis regularly; it needs the same number of seconds regardless of the season. But the movement of the Earth around the sun is not regular because the Earth's orbit is an ellipse. This has the result (as explained in the section The Seasons) that the Earth moves faster in January and slower in July. Though it is the Earth that changes velocity, it looks to us as if the sun did. In January, when the Earth moves faster, the *apparent* movement of the sun looks faster. The "mean sun" of time measurements, then, is a sun that moves regularly all year round; the real sun will be either ahead of or behind the "mean sun." The difference between the real sun and the fictitious mean sun is called the *equation of time.*

When the real sun is west of the mean sun we have the "sun fast" condition, with the real sun crossing the meridian ahead of the mean sun. The opposite is the "sun slow" situation when the real sun crosses the meridian after the mean sun. Of course, what is observed is the real sun. The equation of time is needed to establish mean solar time, kept by the reference clocks.

But if all clocks were actually set by mean solar time we would be plagued by a welter of time differences that would be "correct" but a major nuisance. A clock on Long Island, correctly showing mean solar time for its location (this would be *local civil time*), would be slightly ahead of a clock in Newark, N.J. The Newark clock would be slightly ahead of a clock in Trenton, N.J., which, in turn, would be ahead of a clock in Philadelphia. This condition prevailed until 1884, when a system of standard time was adopted by the International Meridian Conference. The Earth's surface was divided into 24 zones. The standard time of each zone is the mean astronomical time of one of 24 meridians, 15 degrees apart, beginning at the Greenwich, England, meridian and extending east and west around the globe to the international dateline, (This system was actually put into use a year earlier by the railroad companies of the U.S. and Canada who, until then, had to contend with some 100 conflicting local sun times observed in terminals across the land.)

For practical purposes, this convention is sometimes altered. For example, Alaska, for a time, consisted of four of the eight U.S. time zones: the Pacific Standard Time zone (east of Juneau) and the 6th (Juneau), 7th (Anchorage), and 8th (Nome) zones, encompassing the 135°, 150°, and 165° meridians, respectively. In 1983, by Act of Congress, the entire state (except the westward-most Aleutians) was united into the 6th zone, Alaska Standard Time.

The Names of Days

Latin	Old English	English	German	French	Italian	Spanish
Dies Solis	Sun's Day	Sunday	Sonntag	dimanche	domenica	domingo
Dies Lunae	Moon's Day	Monday	Montag	lundi	lunedì	lunes
Dies Martis	Tiw's Day	Tuesday	Dienstag	mardi	martedì	martes
Dies Mercurii	Woden's Day	Wednesday	Mittwoch	mercredi	mercoledì	miércoles
Dies Jovis	Thor's Day	Thursday	Donnerstag	jeudi	giovedì	jueves
Dies Veneris	Frigg's Day	Friday	Freitag	vendredi	venerdì	viernes
Dies Saturni	Seterne's Day	Saturday	Samstag	samedi	sabato	sábado

NOTE: The seven-day week originated in ancient Mesopotamia and became part of the Roman calendar in c.e. 321. The names of the days are based on the seven celestial bodies (the sun, the moon, Mars, Mercury, Jupiter, Venus, and Saturn), believed at that time to revolve around the earth and influence its events. Most of Western Europe adopted the Roman nomenclature. The Germanic languages substituted the names of four of the Roman gods for their Germanic equivalents: Tiw, the god of war, replaced Mars; Woden, the god of wisdom, replaced Mercury; Thor, the god of thunder, replaced Jupiter; and Frigg, the goddess of love, replaced Venus.

The eight U.S. Standard Time Zones are: Atlantic (includes Puerto Rico and the Virgin Islands), Eastern, Central, Mountain, Pacific, Alaska, Hawaii-Aleutian (includes all of Hawaii and those Aleutians west of the Fox Islands), and Samoa Standard Time.

The date line. While the time zones are based on the natural event of the sun crossing the meridian, the date must be an arbitrary decision. The meridians are traditionally counted from the meridian of the observatory of Greenwich in England, which is called the zero meridian. The logical place for changing the date is 12 hours, or 180° from Greenwich. Fortunately, the 180th meridian runs mostly through the open Pacific. The date line makes a zigzag in the north to incorporate the eastern tip of Siberia into the Siberian time system and then another one to incorporate a number of islands into the Hawaii-Aleutian time zone. In the south there is a similar zigzag for the purpose of tying a number of British-owned islands to the New Zealand time system. Otherwise the date line is the same as 180° from Greenwich. At points to the east of the date line the calendar is one day earlier than at points to the west of it. A traveller going eastward across the date line from one island to another would not have to re-set his watch because he would stay inside the time zone (provided he does so where the date line does *not* coincide with the 180° meridian), but it would be the same time of the previous day.

The Seasons

The seasons are caused by the tilt of the Earth's axis (23.4°) and not by the fact that the Earth's orbit around the sun is an ellipse. The average distance of the Earth from the sun is 93 million miles; the difference between aphelion (farthest away) and perihelion (closest to the sun) is 3 million miles, so that perihelion is about 91.4 million miles from the sun. The Earth goes through the perihelion point a few days after New Year, just when the northern hemisphere has winter. Aphelion is passed during the first days in July. This by itself shows that the distance from the sun is not important within these limits. What is important is that when the Earth passes through perihelion, the northern end of the Earth's axis happens to tilt away from the sun, so that the areas beyond the Tropic of Cancer receive only slanting rays from a sun low in the sky.

The tilt of the Earth's axis is responsible for four lines you find on every globe. When, say, the North Pole is tilted away from the sun as much as possible, the farthest points in the North which can still be reached by the sun's rays are 23½° from the pole. This is the Arctic Circle. The Antarctic Circle is the corresponding limit 23.4° from the South Pole; the sun's rays cannot reach beyond this point when we have mid-summer in the North.

When the sun is vertically above the equator, the day is of equal length all over the Earth. This happens twice a year, and these are the "equinoxes" in March and in September. After having been over the equator in March, the sun will seem to move northward. The northernmost point where the sun can be straight overhead is 23.4° north of the equator. This is the Tropic of Cancer; the sun can never be vertically overhead to the north of this line. Similarly the sun cannot be vertically overhead to the south of a line 23.4° south of the equator—the Tropic of Capricorn.

This explains the climatic zones. In the belt (the Greek word *zone* means "belt") between the Tropic of Cancer and the Tropic of Capricorn, the sun can be straight overhead; this is the tropical zone. The two zones where the sun cannot be overhead but will be above the horizon every day of the year are the two temperate zones; the two areas where the sun will not rise at all for varying lengths of time are the two polar areas, Arctic and Antarctic.

The Names of the Months

January: named after Janus, protector of the gateway to heaven

February: named after Februalia, a time period when sacrifices were made to atone for sins

March: named after Mars, the god of war, presumably signifying that the campaigns interrupted by the winter could be resumed

April: from *aperire,* Latin for "to open" (buds)

May: named after Maia, the goddess of growth of plants

June: from *junius,* Latin for the goddess Juno

July: named after Julius Caesar

August: named after Augustus, the first Roman Emperor

September: from *septem,* Latin for "seven"

October: from *octo,* Latin for "eight"

November: from *novem,* Latin for "nine"

December: from *decem,* Latin for "ten"

NOTE: The earliest Latin calendar was a 10-month one; thus September was the seventh month, October, the eighth, etc. July was originally called Quintilis, as the fifth month; August was originally called Sextilis, as the sixth month.

Holidays

Religious and Secular, 1998

Since 1971, by federal law, Washington's Birthday, Memorial Day, Columbus Day, and Veterans' Day have been celebrated on Mondays to create three-day weekends for federal employees. Many states now observe these holidays on the same Mondays. The dates given for the holidays listed below are the traditional ones.

First Day of Ramadan, Wednesday, Dec. 31, 1997. This day marks the beginning of a month-long fast which all Muslims must keep during the daylight hours. It commemorates the first revelation of the Koran. The last day of Ramadan, Eid al-Fitr, is celebrated on Jan. 30, 1998. The next Ramadan will begin on Dec. 20, 1998.

New Year's Day, Thursday, Jan. 1. A legal holiday in all states and the District of Columbia, New Year's Day has its origin in Roman Times, when sacrifices were offered to Janus, the two-faced Roman deity who looked back on the past and forward to the future.

Epiphany, Tuesday, Jan. 6. Falls the twelfth day after Christmas and commemorates the manifestation of Jesus as the Son of God, as represented by the adoration of the Magi, the baptism of Jesus, and the miracle of the wine at the marriage feast at Cana. Epiphany originally marked the beginning of the carnival season preceding Lent, and the evening (sometimes the eve) is known as Twelfth Night.

Martin Luther King, Jr.'s Birthday, Thursday, Jan. 15. Honors the late civil rights leader. Became a legal public holiday in 1986.

Ground-hog Day, Monday, Feb. 2. Legend has it that if the ground-hog sees his shadow, he'll return to his hole, and winter will last another six weeks.

Lincoln's Birthday, Thursday, Feb. 12. A legal holiday in many states, this day was first formally observed in Washington, D.C., in 1866, when both houses of Congress gathered for a memorial address in tribute to the assassinated President.

St. Valentine's Day, Saturday, Feb. 14. This day is the festival of two third-century martyrs, both named St. Valentine. It is not known why this day is associated with lovers. It may derive from an old pagan festival about this time of year, or it may have been inspired by the belief that birds mate on this day.

Washington's Birthday, Sunday, Feb. 22. The birthday of George Washington is celebrated as a legal holiday in every state of the Union, the District of Columbia, and all territories. The observance began in 1796.

Shrove Tuesday, Feb. 24. Falls the day before Ash Wednesday and marks the end of the carnival season, which once began on Epiphany but is now usually celebrated the last three days before Lent. In France, the day is known as Mardi Gras (Fat Tuesday), and Mardi Gras celebrations are also held in several American cities, particularly in New Orleans. The day is sometimes called Pancake Tuesday by the English because fats, which were prohibited during Lent, had to be used up.

Ash Wednesday, Feb. 25. The first day of the Lenten season, which lasts 40 days. Having its origin sometime before C.E. 1000, it is a day of public penance and is marked in the Roman Catholic Church by the burning of the palms blessed on the previous year's Palm Sun-

day. With his thumb, the priest then marks a cross upon the forehead of each worshipper. The Anglican Church and a few Protestant groups in the United States also observe the day, but generally without the use of ashes.

Purim (Feast of Lots), Thursday, March 12. A day of joy and feasting celebrating deliverance of the Jews from a massacre planned by the Persian Minister Haman. The Jewish Queen Esther interceded with her husband, King Ahasuerus, to spare the life of her uncle, Mordecai, and Haman was hanged on the same gallows he had built for Mordecai. The holiday is marked by the reading of the Book of Esther (megillah), and by the exchange of gifts, donations to the poor, and the presentation of Purim plays.

St. Patrick's Day, Tuesday, March 17. St. Patrick, patron saint of Ireland, has been honored in America since the first days of the nation. There are many dinners and meetings but perhaps the most notable part of the observance is the annual St. Patrick's Day parade on Fifth Avenue in New York City.

Palm Sunday, April 5. Is observed the Sunday before Easter to commemorate the entry of Jesus into Jerusalem. The procession and the ceremonies introducing the benediction of palms probably had their origin in Jerusalem.

Good Friday, April 10. This day commemorates the Crucifixion, which is retold during services from the Gospel according to St. John. A feature in Roman Catholic churches is the Liturgy of the Passion; there is no Consecration, the Host having been consecrated the previous day. The eating of hot cross buns on this day is said to have started in England.

First Day of Passover (Pesach), Saturday, April 11. The Feast of the Passover, also called the Feast of Unleavened Bread, commemorates the escape of the Jews from Egypt. As the Jews fled they ate unleavened bread, and from that time the Jews have allowed no leavening in the houses during Passover, bread being replaced by matzoh.

Easter Sunday, April 12. Observed in all Christian churches, Easter commemorates the Resurrection of Jesus. It is celebrated on the first Sunday after the full moon which occurs on or next after March 21 and is therefore celebrated between March 22 and April 25 inclusive. This date was fixed by the Council of Nicaea in C.E. 325. The Orthodox Church celebrates Easter (Paschal) on April 19.

Mother's Day, Sunday, May 10. Observed the second Sunday in May, as proposed by Anna Járvis of Philadelphia in 1907.

Ascension Day, Thursday, May 21. Took place in the presence of His apostles 40 days after the Resurrection of Jesus. It is traditionally held to have occurred on Mount Olivet in Bethany.

Memorial Day, Saturday, May 30. Also known as Decoration Day, Memorial Day is a legal holiday in most of the states and in the territories, and is also observed by the armed forces. In 1868, Gen. John A. Logan (Retired), Commander in Chief of the Grand Army of the Republic, issued an order designating the day as one in which the graves of soldiers would be decorated. The holiday was originally devoted to honoring the memory of those who fell in the Civil War, but is now also dedicated to the memory of all war dead.

Pentecost (Whitsunday), Sunday, May 31. This day commemorates the descent of the Holy Ghost upon the apostles 50 days after the Resurrection. The sermon by the Apostle Peter, which led to the baptism of 3,000 who professed belief, originated the ceremonies that have since been followed. "Whitsunday" is believed to have come from "white Sunday" when, among the English, white robes were worn by those baptized on the day.

First Day of Shavuot (Hebrew Pentecost), Sunday, May 31. This festival, sometimes called the Feast of Weeks, or of Harvest, or of the First Fruits, falls 50 days after Passover and originally celebrated the end of the seven-week grain harvesting season. In later tradition, it also celebrated the giving of the Law to Moses on Mount Sinai.

Flag Day, Sunday, June 14. This day commemorates the adoption by the Continental Congress on June 14, 1777, of the Stars and Stripes as the U.S. flag. Although it is a legal holiday only in Pennsylvania, President Truman, on Aug. 3, 1949, signed a bill requesting the President to call for its observance each year by proclamation.

Father's Day, Sunday, June 21. Observed the third Sunday in June. First celebrated June 19, 1910.

Independence Day, Saturday, July 4. The day of the adoption of the Declaration of Independence in 1776, celebrated in all states and territories. The observance began the next year in Philadelphia.

Labor Day, Monday, Sept. 7. Observed the first Monday in September in all states and territories, Labor Day was first celebrated in New York in 1882 under the sponsorship of the Central Labor Union, following the suggestion of Peter J. McGuire, of the Knights of Labor, that the day be set aside in honor of labor.

First Day of Rosh Hashana (Jewish New Year), Monday, Sept. 21. This day marks the beginning of the Jewish year 5758 and opens the Ten Days of Penitence closing with Yom Kippur.

Yom Kippur (Day of Atonement), Wednesday, Sept. 30. This day marks the end of the Ten Days of Penitence that began with Rosh Hashana. It is described in *Leviticus* as a "Sabbath of rest," and synagogue services begin the preceding sundown, resume the following morning, and continue to sundown.

First Day of Sukkot (Feast of Tabernacles) Monday, Oct. 5. This festival, also known as the Feast of the Ingathering, originally celebrated the fruit harvest, and the name comes from the booths or tabernacles in which the Jews lived during the harvest, although one tradition traces it to the shelters used by the Jews in their wandering through the wilderness. During the festival many Jews build small huts in their back yards or on the roofs of their houses.

Columbus Day, Monday, Oct. 12. A legal holiday in many states, commemorating the discovery of America by Columbus in 1492. Quite likely the first celebration of Columbus Day was that organized in 1792 by the Society of St. Tammany, or Columbian Order, widely known as Tammany Hall.

Simhat Torah (Rejoicing of the Law), Tuesday, Oct. 13. This joyous holiday falls on the eighth day of Sukkot. It marks the end of the year's reading of the Torah (Five Books of Moses) in the synagogue every Saturday and the beginning of the new cycle of reading.

Halloween, Saturday, Oct. 31. Eve of All Saints Day, formerly called All Hallows and Hallowmass. Halloween is traditionally associated in some countries with old customs such as bonfires, masquerading, and the telling of ghost stories. These are old Celtic practices marking the beginning of winter.

All Saints Day, Sunday, Nov. 1. A Roman Catholic and Anglican holiday celebrating all saints, known and unknown.

Election Day, (legal holiday in certain states), Tuesday, Nov. 3. Since 1845, by Act of Congress, the first Tuesday after the first Monday in November is the date for choosing Presidential electors. State elections are also generally held on this day.

Veterans Day, Wednesday, Nov. 11. Armistice Day was established in 1926 to commemorate the signing in 1918 of the Armistice ending World War I. On June 1, 1954, the name was changed to Veterans Day to honor all men and women who have served America in its armed forces.

Thanksgiving, Thursday, Nov. 26. Observed nationally on the fourth Thursday in November by Act of Congress (1941), the first such national proclamation having been issued by President Lincoln in 1863, on the urging of Mrs. Sarah J. Hale, editor of *Godey's Lady's Book.* Most Americans believe that the holiday dates back to the day of thanks ordered by Governor Bradford of Plymouth Colony in New England in 1621, but scholars point out that days of thanks stem from ancient times.

First Sunday of Advent, Nov. 29. Advent is the season in which the faithful must prepare themselves for the advent of the Saviour on Christmas. The four Sundays before Christmas are marked by special church services.

First Day of Hanukkah (Festival of Lights), Monday, Dec. 14. This festival was instituted by Judas Maccabaeus in 165 B.C.E. to celebrate the purification of the Temple of Jerusalem, which had been desecrated three years earlier by Antiochus Epiphanes, who set up a pagan altar and offered sacrifices to Zeus Olympius. In Jewish homes, a light is lighted on each night of the eight-day festival.

Christmas (Feast of the Nativity), Friday, Dec. 25. The most widely celebrated holiday of the Christian year, Christmas is observed as the anniversary of the birth of Jesus. Christmas customs are centuries old. The mistletoe, for example, comes from the Druids, who, in hanging the mistletoe, hoped for peace and good fortune. Use of such plants as holly comes from the ancient belief that such plants blossomed at Christmas. Comparatively recent is the Christmas tree, first set up in Germany in the 17th century, and the use of candles on trees developed from the belief that candles appeared by miracle on the trees at Christmas. Colonial Manhattan Islanders introduced the name Santa Claus, a corruption of the Dutch name for the 4th-century Asia Minor St. Nicholas.

Movable Holidays, 1998–2001

Christian and Secular

Year	Ash Wednesday	Easter	Pentecost	Labor Day	Election Day	Thanksgiving	1st Sun. Advent
1998	Feb. 25	April 12	May 31	Sept. 7	Nov. 3	Nov. 26	Nov. 29
1999	Feb. 17	April 4	May 23	Sept. 6	Nov. 2	Nov. 25	Nov. 28
2000	March 8	April 23	June 11	Sept. 4	Nov. 7	Nov. 23	Dec. 3
2001	Feb. 28	April 15	June 3	Sept. 3	Nov. 6	Nov. 22	Dec. 2

Shrove Tuesday: 1 day before Ash Wednesday
Palm Sunday: 7 days before Easter
Maundy Thursday: 3 days before Easter
Good Friday: 2 days before Easter

Holy Saturday: 1 day before Easter
Ascension Day: 10 days before Pentecost
Trinity Sunday: 7 days after Pentecost
Corpus Christi: 11 days after Pentecost

NOTE: Easter is celebrated on April 19, 1998, by the Orthodox Church.

Jewish Holidays

Year	Purim[1]	1st day Passover[2]	1st day Shavuot[3]	1st day Rosh Hashana[4]	Yom Kippur[5]	1st day Sukkot[6]	Simhat Torah[7]	1st day Hanukkah[8]
1998	March 12	April 11	May 31	Sept. 21	Sept. 30	Oct. 5	Oct. 12	Dec. 14
1999	March 2	April 1	May 21	Sept. 11	Sept. 20	Sept. 25	Oct. 2	Dec. 4
2000	March 21	April 20	June 9	Sept. 30	Oct. 9	Oct. 14	Oct. 21	Dec. 22
2001	March 9	April 8	May 28	Sept. 18	Sept. 27	Oct. 2	Oct. 9	Dec. 10

1. Feast of Lots. 2. Feast of Unleavened Bread. 3. Hebrew Pentecost; or Feast of Weeks, or of Harvest, or of First Fruits. 4. Jewish New Year. 5. Day of Atonement. 6. Feast of Tabernacles, or of the Ingathering. 7. Rejoicing of the Law. 8. Festival of Lights. Length of Jewish holidays (O=Orthodox, C=Conservative, R=Reform):

Passover: O & C, 8 days (holy days: first 2 and last 2); R, 7 days (holy days: first and last)
Shavuot: O & C, 2 days; R, 1 day
Rosh Hashana: O & C, 2 days; R, 1 day
Yom Kippur: All groups, 1 day

Sukkot: All groups, 7 days (holy days: O & C, first 2; R, first only) O & C observe two additional days: Shemini Atseret (Eighth Day of the Feast) and Simhat Torah. R observes Shemini Atseret but not Simhat Torah
Hanukkah: All groups, 8 days

NOTE: All holidays begin at sundown on the evening before the date given.

Islamic Holidays 1997–1999 (A.H. 1418–1419)

In the Year of the Hegira	Muharram (Islamic New Year)	Mawlid an-Nabi (Mohammed's Birthday)	Ramadan begins	Eid al-Fitr (end of Ramadan)	Eid al-Adha (Fest. of Sacrifice)
A.H. 1418	May 8, 1997	July 17, 1997	Dec. 31, 1997	Jan. 30, 1998	April 8, 1998
A.H. 1419	April 28, 1998	July 7, 1998	Dec. 20, 1998	Jan. 19, 1999	March 28, 1999

NOTE: All holidays begin at sundown on the evening before the date given. Islamic holidays are based on the lunar calendar and thus may vary by one or two days.

Chinese New Year

1998	Jan. 28	2001	Jan. 24	2004	Jan. 22	2007	Feb. 18
1999	Feb. 16	2002	Feb. 12	2005	Feb. 9	2008	Feb. 7
2000	Feb. 5	2003	Feb. 1	2006	Jan. 29	2009	Jan. 26

Birthstones

Month	Stone	Month	Stone
January	Garnet	August	Peridot or Sardonyx
February	Amethyst	September	Sapphire or Star Sapphire
March	Aquamarine or Bloodstone	October	Opal or Tourmaline
April	Diamond	November	Topaz or Citrine
May	Emerald	December	Turquoise, Lapis Lazuli, Blue Zircon or Blue Topaz
June	Pearl, Alexandrite or Moonstone		
July	Ruby or Star Ruby		

Source: Jewelry Industry Council.

Hindu Festival Dates, 1998

Source: Jantri 500, by Pal Singh Purewal.

Jan. 14	Makar Sankranti	Aug. 8	Raksha Bandhan
Feb. 1	Vasant Panchami	Aug. 14	Sri Krishna Jayanti
Feb. 25	Maha Shivaratri Vrat (fast)	Aug. 26	Ganesh Chaturathi
March 13	Holi (last day)	Sept. 6	Saradhas begin
March 28	Chetra Navratras begin	Sept. 21	Asuj Navratras begin
March 28	Bikarami Samvat begins	Sept. 30	Dassehra
April 5	Rama Navmi	Oct. 8	Karva Chauth Vrat (fast)
April 13	Vaisakhi (solar new year)	Oct. 19	Diwali (Festival of Lights)

Sikh Festival Dates, 1998

Source: Jantri 500, by Pal Singh Purewal.

Jan. 5	Birthday Guru Gobind Singh Ji	Oct. 19	Diwali
Jan. 14	Maghi	Oct. 22	Installation of Holy Scriptures as Guru Granth Sahibi Ji
March 14	Hola Muhalla		
April 13	Vaisakhi (Khalsa era begins)	Nov. 4	Birthday of Guru Nanak Dev Ji
May 29	Martyrdom Guru Arjan Dev Ji	Nov. 24	Martyrdom Guru Tegh Bahadur Ji
Aug. 23	First Parkash Granth Sahib Ji		

NOTE: Dates for Sikh and Hindu holidays are determined according to the date of their observance in India. There has been, however, a gradual change in opinion, especially for Hindu festivals, that the dates should be calculated according to a North American location. If this is done, then some holidays will differ by one day.

Chinese Calendar

The Chinese lunar year is divided into 12 months of 29 or 30 days. The calendar is adjusted to the length of the solar year by the addition of extra months at regular intervals. The years are arranged in major cycles of 60 years. Each successive year is named after one of 12 animals. These 12-year cycles are continuously repeated. The Chinese New Year is celebrated at the second new moon after the winter solstice and falls between January 21 and February 19 on the Gregorian calendar.

Rat	Ox	Tiger	Cat (Rabbit)	Dragon	Snake	Horse	Sheep (Goat)	Monkey	Rooster	Dog	Pig
1900	1901	1902	1903	1904	1905	1906	1907	1908	1909	1910	1911
1912	1913	1914	1915	1916	1917	1918	1919	1920	1921	1922	1923
1924	1925	1926	1927	1928	1929	1930	1931	1932	1933	1934	1935
1936	1937	1938	1939	1940	1941	1942	1943	1944	1945	1946	1947
1948	1949	1950	1951	1952	1953	1954	1955	1956	1957	1958	1959
1960	1961	1962	1963	1964	1965	1966	1967	1968	1969	1970	1971
1972	1973	1974	1975	1976	1977	1978	1979	1980	1981	1982	1983
1984	1985	1986	1987	1988	1989	1990	1991	1992	1993	1994	1995
1996	1997	1998	1999	2000	2001	2002	2003	2004	2005	2006	2007

Modern Wedding Anniversary Gift List

Anniversary	Gift	Anniversary	Gift	Anniversary	Gift
1st	Gold jewelry	10th	Diamond jewelry	19th	Aquamarine
2nd	Garnet	11th	Turquoise	20th	Emerald
3rd	Pearls	12th	Jade	25th	Silver jubilee
4th	Blue topaz	13th	Citrine	30th	Pearl jubilee
5th	Sapphire	14th	Opal	35th	Emerald
6th	Amethyst	15th	Ruby	40th	Ruby
7th	Onyx	16th	Peridot	45th	Sapphire
8th	Tourmaline	17th	Watches	50th	Golden jubilee
9th	Lapis	18th	Cat's-eye	60th	Diamond jubilee

Source: Jewelry Industry Council

Pacific Braces for Millennium Storm Over Matter of Degrees

By Quentin Letts, The Times (London)

Pacific islanders are squabbling over the International Date Line. They cannot agree which far-flung piece of land will be first to see the sunrise of the next millennium. The argument, which has involved the United Nations, the Royal Greenwich Observatory, and much flexing of beach-side palm trees, might not have happened but for entrepreneurial schemes for New Year's Eve, 1999. Travel agents have detected a market for "we-were-first-to-see-in-the-new-millennium" parties and are scouring the Pacific for the first landfall west of the date line. The agreed venue will make a fortune.

The search has been complicated by the decision of some islanders to "move" the date line. The tiny nation of Kiribati, formerly the Gilbert, Phoenix and Line island groups, has angered its Pacific neighbors by moving part of the line to its eastern extremity, Caroline Island. The little-noticed move was a key item in the 1993 political manifesto of President Teburoro Tito and solved the problems which beset Kiribati when it was split by the date line. It was, formerly, a bold man who used the word "today" in Kiribatian society.

Nearby Tonga, which was happily expecting to be venue for the lucrative parties, thinks that Kiribati has pulled a fast one. The King of Tonga is not happy. The International Date Line Hotel in the Tongan town of Nukualofa not only faces an unwanted name change, it may also lose the bookings it has taken for the turn of the millennium. There is similar dismay in the Chatham Islands, and on New Zealand's North Island, where the town of Gisborne was limbering up for the big night with the argument that west of the line it is the first place with good bars. Gisborne District Council was planning a party atop a mountain which has early views of the sunrise.

As a result of the presidential maneuver, however, Kiribati will now see the millennium's dawn 22 minutes before the Chathams, and a humiliating 80 minutes before Tonga. The Royal Greenwich Observatory and cartographers have accepted Kiribati's line change, and appeals to the United Nations have met with the response that the date line, decided by an international conference in 1884, is beyond its control.

Reprinted with permission of *The Times* (London), January 25th, 1996.

When is the Next Millennium?

Although January 1, 2000, has a millennial ring to it, the new age actually begins on a less resounding date: January 1, 2001. Common sense might suggest that the year 2000 is the dawning of the third millennium, but it is in fact the waning of the second. The explanation is clear cut. The sequence of years from B.C.E. to C.E. passes from B.C.E. 1 to 1 C.E.—there is no year zero.

Thus the first millennium began in 1 C.E., the second began a thousand years later in 1001 C.E., and the next will start on January 1, 2001. There is no doubt that both New Year's 2000 and 2001 will spark huge celebrations, one New Year's because it is the true millennial milestone, and the other because there is nothing quite like the numerical elegance of January 1, 2000.

Holidays

State Observances

January 6, Three Kings' Day: Puerto Rico.
January 8, Battle of New Orleans Day: Louisiana.
January 11, De Hostos' Birthday: Puerto Rico.
January 19, Robert E. Lee's Birthday: Arkansas, Florida, Kentucky, Louisiana, South Carolina, **(third Monday)** Alabama, Mississippi.
January 19, Confederate Heroes Day: Texas.
January (third Monday): Lee-Jackson-King Day: Virginia.
January 30, F.D. Roosevelt's Birthday: Kentucky.
February 15, Susan B. Anthony's Birthday: Florida, Minnesota.
March (first Tuesday), Town Meeting Day: Vermont.
March 2, Texas Independence Day: Texas.
March (first Monday), Casimir Pulaski's Birthday: Illinois.
March 17, Evacuation Day: Massachusetts (in Suffolk County).
March 20 (First Day of Spring), Youth Day: Oklahoma.
March 22, Abolition Day: Puerto Rico.
March 25, Maryland Day: Maryland.
March 26, Prince Jonah Kuhio Kalanianaole Day: Hawaii.
March (last Monday), Seward's Day: Alaska.
April 2, Pascua Florida Day: Florida
April 13, Thomas Jefferson's Birthday: Alabama, Oklahoma.
April 16, De Diego's Birthday: Puerto Rico.
April (third Monday), Patriots' Day: Maine, Massachusetts.
April 21, San Jacinto Day: Texas.
April 22, Arbor Day: Nebraska.
April 22, Oklahoma Day: Oklahoma.
April 26, Confederate Memorial Day: Florida, Georgia.
April (fourth Monday), Fast Day: New Hampshire.

April (last Monday), Confederate Memorial Day: Alabama, Mississippi.
May 1, Bird Day: Oklahoma.
May 8, Truman Day: Missouri.
May 11, Minnesota Day: Minnesota.
May 20, Mecklenburg Independence Day: North Carolina.
June (first Monday), Jefferson Davis's Birthday: Alabama, Mississippi.
June 3, Jefferson Davis's Birthday: Florida, South Carolina.
June 3, Confederate Memorial Day: Kentucky, Louisiana.
June 9, Senior Citizens Day: Oklahoma.
June 11, King Kamehameha I Day: Hawaii.
June 15, Separation Day: Delaware.
June 17, Bunker Hill Day: Massachusetts (in Suffolk County).
June 19, Emancipation Day: Texas.
June 20, West Virginia Day: West Virginia.
July 17, Muñoz Rivera's Birthday: Puerto Rico.
July 24, Pioneer Day: Utah.
July 25, Constitution Day: Puerto Rico.
July 27, Barbosa's Birthday: Puerto Rico.
August (first Sunday), American Family Day: Arizona.
August (first Monday), Colorado Day: Colorado.
August (second Monday), Victory Day: Rhode Island.
August 16, Bennington Battle Day: Vermont.
August (third Friday), Admission Day: Hawaii.
August 27, Lyndon B. Johnson's Birthday: Texas.
August 30, Huey P. Long Day: Louisiana.
September 9, Admission Day: California.
September 12, Defenders' Day: Maryland.

September 16, Cherokee Strip Day: Oklahoma.
September (first Saturday after full moon), Indian Day: Oklahoma.
October 10, Leif Erickson Day: Minnesota.
October 10, Oklahoma Historical Day: Oklahoma.
October 18, Alaska Day: Alaska.

October 31, Nevada Day: Nevada.
November 4, Will Rogers Day: Oklahoma.
November (week of the 16th), Oklahoma Heritage Week: Oklahoma.
November 19, Discovery Day: Puerto Rico.
December 7, Delaware Day: Delaware.

National Holidays Around the World, 1998

Afghanistan	Aug. 19	Germany	Oct. 3	Niger	Dec. 18
Albania	Nov. 28	Ghana	March 6	Nigeria	Oct. 1
Algeria	Nov. 1	Greece	March 25	Norway	May 17
Andorra	Sept. 8	Grenada	Feb. 7	Oman	Nov. 18
Angola	Nov. 11	Guatemala	Sept. 15	Pakistan	March 23
Antigua and Barbuda	Nov. 1	Guinea	Oct. 2	Panama	Nov. 3
Argentina	May 25	Guinea-Bissau	Sept. 24	Papua New Guinea	Sept. 16
Armenia	Sept. 21	Guyana	Feb. 23	Paraguay	May 15
Australia	Jan. 26	Haiti	Jan. 1	Peru	July 28
Austria	Oct. 26	Honduras	Sept. 15	Philippines	June 12
Azerbaijan	May 28	Hungary	Aug. 20	Poland	May 3
Bahamas	July 10	Iceland	June 17	Portugal	June 10
Bahrain	Dec. 16	India	Jan. 26	Qatar	Sept. 3
Bangladesh	March 26	Indonesia	Aug. 17	Romania	Dec. 1
Barbados	Nov. 30	Iran	Feb. 11	Rwanda	July 1
Belarus	July 27	Iraq	July 17	St. Kitts and Nevis	Sept. 19
Belgium	July 21	Ireland	March 17	St. Lucia	Feb. 22
Belize	Sept. 21	Israel	May 11[1]	St. Vincent and the	Oct. 27
Benin	Aug. 1	Italy	June 2	Grenadines	
Bhutan	Dec. 17	Jamaica	Aug. 3[2]	San Marino	Sept. 3
Bolivia	Aug. 6	Japan	Dec. 23	São Tomé and Príncipe	July 12
Botswana	Sept. 30	Jordan	May 25	Saudi Arabia	Sept. 23
Brazil	Sept. 7	Kazakhstan	Oct. 25	Senegal	April 4
Brunei Darussalam	Feb. 23	Kenya	Dec. 12	Seychelles	June 18
Bulgaria	March 3	North Korea (Dem.	Sept. 9	Sierra Leone	April 27
Burkina Faso	Aug. 4	People's Rep. of		Singapore	Aug. 9
Burma (Myanmar)	Jan. 4	Korea)		Slovakia	Sept. 1
Burundi	July 1	South Korea	Aug. 15	Slovenia	June 25
Cambodia	Nov. 9	(Rep. of Korea)		Solomon Islands	July 7
Cameroon	May 20	Kuwait	Feb. 25	Somalia	Oct. 21
Canada	July 1	Kyrgyzstan	Aug. 31	South Africa	May 31
Cape Verde	Sept. 12	Laos	Dec. 2	Spain	Oct. 12
Central African Republic	Dec. 1	Latvia	Nov. 18	Sri Lanka	Feb. 4
Chad	Aug. 11	Lebanon	Nov. 22	Sudan	Jan. 1
Chile	Sept. 18	Lesotho	Oct. 4	Suriname	Nov. 25
China	Oct. 1	Liberia	July 26	Swaziland	Sept. 6
Colombia	July 20	Libya	Sept. 1	Sweden	June 6
Comoros	July 6	Liechtenstein	Aug. 15	Switzerland	Aug. 1
Congo	Aug. 15	Lithuania	Feb. 16	Syria	April 17
Costa Rica	Sept. 15	Luxembourg	June 23	Tajikistan	Sept. 9
Côte d'Ivoire	Dec. 7	Macedonia	Aug. 2	Tanzania	April 26
Croatia	May 30	Madagascar	June 26	Thailand	Dec. 5
Cuba	Jan. 1	Malawi	July 6	Togo	Jan. 13
Cyprus	Oct. 1	Malaysia	Aug. 31	Tonga	June 4
Czech Republic	Oct. 28	Maldives	July 26	Trinidad and Tobago	Aug. 31
Denmark	April 16	Mali	Sept. 22	Tunisia	March 20
Djibouti	June 27	Malta	Sept. 21	Turkey	Oct. 29
Dominica	Nov. 3	Marshall Islands	May 1	Turkmenistan	Oct. 27
Dominican Republic	Feb. 27	Mauritania	Nov. 28	Uganda	Oct. 9
Ecuador	Aug. 10	Mauritius	March 12	Ukraine	Aug. 24
Egypt	July 23	Mexico	Sept. 16	United Arab Emirates	Dec. 2
El Salvador	Sept. 15	Micronesia	Nov. 3	United Kingdom	June 13[3]
Equatorial Guinea	Oct. 12	Moldova	Aug. 27	United States	July 4
Eritrea	May 24	Monaco	Nov. 19	Uruguay	Aug. 25
Estonia	Feb. 24	Mongolia	July 11	Uzbekistan	Sept. 1
Ethiopia	May 28	Morocco	March 3	Vanuatu	July 30
Fiji	Oct. 10	Mozambique	June 25	Venezuela	July 5
Finland	Dec. 6	Namibia	March 21	Vietnam	Sept. 2
France	July 14	Nepal	Dec. 28	Western Samoa	June 1
Gabon	Aug. 17	Netherlands	April 30	Yemen, Republic of	May 22
Gambia	Feb. 18	New Zealand	Feb. 6	Zambia	Oct. 24
Georgia	May 26	Nicaragua	Sept. 15	Zimbabwe	April 18

1. Changes yearly according to Hebrew calendar. 2. Celebrated on first Monday in August. 3. Celebrated the second Saturday in June.

Astronomy

THE GREAT COMET OF 1997. Above, the bright head of comet Hale-Bopp, called the coma, is pointed towards the sun. The coma is composed of dust and gas, masking the solid nucleus of the comet made up of rock, dust and ice. *Photo taken by Jim Young at NASA's Jet Propulsion Laboratories Table Mountain Observatory in March 1997.*

Comet Hale-Bopp

The most spectacular celestial viewing event of 1997 was the arrival of comet Hale-Bopp in the northern hemisphere. Its closest approach to Earth was on March 22nd, and its closest approach to the sun (when it was at its brightest) was on April 1st—not to return to Earth again until the year 4397. The comet, designated C/1995 O1, was discovered independently on July 23, 1995, by Alan Hale, New Mexico, and Thomas Bopp, Arizona. It was the farthest comet ever discovered by amateurs, and appeared 1,000 times brighter than comet Halley did at the same distance.

An unprecedented year-long study was made of Hale-Bopp by two NASA observatories—the Hubble Space Telescope and the International Ultraviolet Explorer. Astronomers estimated that it had a monstrous nucleus about 19 to 25 miles in diameter. The average comet is thought to have a nucleus of about three miles in diameter, or even smaller. By comparison, the comet or asteroid that struck the Earth 65 million years ago, possibly causing the extinction of the dinosaurs, was probably six to nine miles across.

Scientists were surprised to find that the different ices in its complex nucleus seemed to be isolated from each other. They reported seeing unexpectedly brief and intense bursts of activity from the nucleus during the monitoring period, suggesting that the nucleus must be an incredibly dynamic place. Astronomers using spectroscopic instruments were also amazed to discover that the comet had a thin, third tail composed of sodium atoms, a type never seen before.

Although Hale-Bopp faded from view in the Northern Hemisphere by late fall 1997, it will become visible to skywatchers in the Southern Hemisphere throughout 1998. □

Astronomical Terms

Planet is the term used for a body in orbit around the sun. Its origin is Greek; even in antiquity it was known that a number of "stars" did not stay in the same relative positions to the others. There were five such restless "stars" known—Mercury, Venus, Mars, Jupiter, and Saturn—and the Greeks referred to them as *planetes,* a word which means "wanderers." That the Earth is one of the planets was realized later. The additional planets were discovered after the invention of the telescope.

In 1994, Dr. Alexander Wolszcan, an astronomer at Pennsylvania State University, presented convincing evidence of the first known planets to exist outside our solar system. They circle a pulsar or exploded star in the constellation *Virgo.* Two of the planets are two to three times the size of the Earth and a third is about the size of our moon.

In 1995, several of these *extrasolar planets* were discovered orbiting ordinary stars similar to our sun as a result of observing gravitational variations of the stars. Swiss astronomers found a planet orbiting star 57 in the constellation *Pegasus,* about 40 light-years away. It is the first planet ever discovered to circle a normal sunlike star. The new planet's mass is about half that of Jupiter. It orbits 51 Pegasi every 4.2 days and is closer to the parent star than Mercury is to the sun. Because its surface temperature is about 1,300°C (2,756°F), it is too hot to support life.

Over the last several years, at least ten more extrasolar planets have been discovered.

Satellite (or *moon*) is the term for a body in orbit around a planet. As long as our own moon was the only moon known, there was no need for a general term for the moons of planets. But when Galileo Galilei discovered the four main moons of the planet Jupiter, Johannes Kepler (in a letter to Galileo) suggested "satellite" (from the Latin *satelles*, which means attendant) as a general term for such bodies. The word is used interchangeably with "moons": astronomers speak and write about the moons of Neptune, Saturn, etc. A satellite may be any size.

Orbit is the term for the path traveled by a body in space. It comes from the Latin *orbis*, which means circle, circuit, etc., and *orbita*, which means a rut or a wheel track. Theoretically, four mathematical figures are possible orbits: two are open (hyperbola and parabola) and two are closed (ellipse and circle), but in reality all closed orbits are ellipses. These ellipses can be nearly circular, as are the orbits of most planets, or very elongated, as are the orbits of most comets. In these orbits, the sun is in one focal point of the ellipse, and the other focal point is empty. In the orbits of satellites, the planet stands in one focal point of the orbit. The *primary* of an orbit is the body in the focal point. For planets, the point of the orbit closest to the sun is the *perihelion*, and the point farthest from the sun is the *aphelion*. For orbits around the Earth, the corresponding terms are *perigee* and *apogee*; for orbits around other planets, corresponding terms are coined when necessary.

Two heavenly bodies are in *inferior* or *superior conjunction* when they have the same *right ascension*, or are in the same meridian; that is, when one is due north or south of the other. If the bodies appear near each other as seen from the Earth, they will rise and set at the same time. They are in *opposition* when they are opposite each other in the heavens: when one rises as the other is setting. *Greatest elongation* is the greatest apparent angular distance from the sun, when a planet is most favorably suited for observation. Mercury can be seen with the naked eye only at about this time. An *occultation* of a planet or star is an eclipse of it by some other body, usually the moon.

Stars are the basic units of population in the universe. Our sun is the nearest star. Stars are very large (our sun has a diameter of 865,400 miles—a comparatively small star). Stars are composed of intensely hot gasses, deriving their energy from nuclear reactions going on in their interiors.

Galaxies are immense systems containing billions of stars. All that you can see in the sky (with a very few exceptions) belongs to our galaxy—a system of roughly 200 billion stars. The few exceptions are other galaxies. Our own galaxy, the rim of which we see as the "Milky Way," is about 100,000 light-years in diameter and about 10,000 light-years in thickness. Its shape is roughly that of a thick lens; more precisely it is a "spiral nebula," a term first used for other galaxies when they were discovered and before it was realized that these were separate and distinct galaxies. The spiral galaxy nearest to ours is in the constellation *Andromeda*. It is somewhat larger than our own galaxy and is visible to the naked eye. Astronomers have estimated that the universe could contain 40 to 50 billion galaxies.

In 1997, an international team of astronomers using the combined observations of the Hubble Space Telescope and the Keck telescope in Hawaii detected a galaxy about 13 billion light-years away from Earth. Its red shift is 4.92, the largest ever recorded, making it the most distant galaxy observed so far.

A *black hole* is the theoretical end-product of the total gravitational collapse of a massive star or group of stars. Crushed even smaller than an incredibly dense neutron star, such a body may become so dense that not even light can escape its gravitational field. It has been suggested that black holes may be detectable in proximity to normal stars when they draw matter away from their visible neighbors. Strong sources of X-rays in our galaxy and beyond may also indicate the presence of black holes.

Quasars ("quasi-stellar" objects), originally thought to be peculiar stars in our own galaxy, are now believed to be the most remote objects in the universe. Spectral studies of quasars indicate that some are 9 billion light-years away and moving away from us at the incredible rate of 150,000 miles per second. Quasars emit tremendous amounts of light and microwave radiation. Recent Hubble Space Telescope images suggest that there may be a variety of mechanisms for "turning on" quasars. Although a number of images show collisions between pairs of galaxies, which could trigger the birth of quasars, some pictures reveal apparently normal, undisturbed galaxies possessing quasars.

Quasars are among the most baffling objects in the universe because of their small size and prodigious energy output. Quasars are not much bigger than the Earth's solar system but pour out 100 to 1,000 times as much light as an entire galaxy containing a hundred billion stars.

A super massive black hole, gobbling up stars, gas, and dust, is theorized to be the "engine" powering a quasar. Most astronomers agree that an active black hole is the only credible possibility that explains how quasars can be so compact, variable, and powerful. However, no conclusive evidence supports this assumption.

Pulsars are believed to be rapidly spinning neutron stars, so crushed by their own gravity that a million tons of their matter would hardly fill a thimble. Pulsars are so named because they emit bursts of radio waves at regular intervals.

In 1996, astronomers found strong evidence for a massive black hole at the center of the Milky Way and recent evidence suggests that black holes are so common that they probably exist at the core of nearly all galaxies.

The existence of brown dwarfs, also called failed stars, was confirmed in November 1995 when astronomers at Palomar Observatory in California took the first photograph of this mysterious object. Brown dwarfs lack the mass to generate nuclear fission like true stars but are also too massive and hot to be a planet.

Origin of the Universe

Evidence tends to confirm that the universe began its existence about 15 billion years ago as a dense, hot globule of gas expanding rapidly outward. At that time, the universe contained nothing but hydrogen and a small amount of helium. There were no stars and no planets. The first stars probably began to condense out of the primordial hydrogen when the universe was about 100 million years old and continued to form as the universe aged. The sun arose in this way 4.6 billion years ago. Many stars came into being before the sun was formed; many others formed after the sun appeared. This process continues, and through telescopes we can now see stars forming out of compressed pockets of hydrogen in outer space.

In 1992, instruments aboard the Cosmic Background Explorer (COBE) satellite, launched in 1989, showed that 99.97% of the radiant energy of the universe was released within the first year of the primeval explosion. This evidence seems to confirm the Big Bang theory which holds that the universe originated from a single violent explosion (a *big bang*) of a very small agglomeration of matter of extremely high density and temperatures. Astronomers also theorize that 99% of the

Astronomical Constants

Light-year (distance traveled by light in one year)	5,880,000,000,000 mi.
Parsec (parallax of one second, or stellar distances)	3.259 light-yrs.
Velocity of light	186,281.7 mi./sec.
Astronomical unit (A.U.), or mean distance Earth-to-sun	ca. 93,000,000 mi.[1]
Mean distance, Earth to moon	238,860 mi.
General precession	50".26
Obliquity of the ecliptic	23° 27'8".26-0".4684(t-1900)[2]
Equatorial radius of the Earth	3963.34 statute mi.
Polar radius of the Earth	3949.99 statute mi.
Earth's mean radius	3958.89 statute mi.
Oblateness of the Earth	1/297
Equatorial horizontal parallax of the moon	57'2".70
Earth's mean velocity in orbit	18.5 mi./sec.
Sidereal year	365d.2564
Tropical year	365d.2422
Sidereal month	27d.3217
Synodic month	29d.5306
Mean sidereal day	23h56m4s.091 of mean solar time
Mean solar day	24h3m56s.555 of sidereal time

1. Actual mean distance derived from radar bounces: 92,935,700 mi. The value of 92,897,400 mi. (based on parallax of 8".80) is used in calculations. 2. *t* refers to the year in question, for example, 1997.

matter in the universe is invisible or *dark matter* composed of some kind of matter that they cannot yet detect.

In March 1995, astronomers found supporting evidence for the Big Bang when they concluded data obtained from the space shuttle's *Astro 2* observatory showed that helium was widespread in the early universe. The theory holds that hydrogen and helium were the first elements created when the universe was formed.

Birth and Death of a Star

When a star begins to form as a dense cloud of gas, the individual hydrogen atoms fall toward the center of the cloud under the force of the star's gravity. As it falls, it picks up speed, and its energy increases. The increase in energy heats the gas. When this process has continued for some millions of years, the temperature reaches about 20 million degrees Fahrenheit. At this temperature, the hydrogen within the star ignites and burns in a continuing series of nuclear reactions in which all the elements in the universe are manufactured from hydrogen and helium. The onset of these reactions marks the birth of a star. When a star begins to exhaust its hydrogen supply, its life nears an end. The first sign of old age is a swelling and reddening of its outer regions. Such an aging, swollen star is called a red giant. The sun, a middle-aged star, will probably swell to a red giant in 5 billion years, vaporizing the Earth and any creatures that may be left on its surface. When all its fuel has been exhausted, a star cannot generate sufficient pressure at its center to balance the crushing force of gravity. The star collapses under the force of its own weight; if it is a small star, it collapses gently and remains collapsed. Such a collapsed star, at its life's end, is called a white dwarf. The sun will probably end its life in this way. A different fate awaits a large star. Its final collapse generates a violent explosion, blowing the innards of the star out into space. There, the materials of the exploded star mix with the primeval hydrogen of the universe. Later in the history of the galaxy, other stars are formed out of this mixture. The sun is one of these stars. It contains the debris of countless other stars that exploded before the sun was born.

Supernovas

On Feb. 24, 1987, Canadian astronomer Ian Shelter at the Las Campanas Observatory in Chile discovered a supernova—an exploding star—from a photograph taken on Feb. 23 of the Large Magellanic Cloud, a galaxy some 160,000 light-years away from Earth. Astronomers believe that the dying star was Sanduleak −69°202, a 10-million-year-old blue supergiant.

Supernova 1987A was the closest and best studied supernova in almost 400 years. One was previously observed by Johannes Kepler in 1604, four years before the telescope was invented.

Formation of the Solar System

The sun's age was calculated in 1989 to be 4.49 billion years old, less than the 4.7 billion years previously believed. It was formed from a cloud of hydrogen mixed with small amounts of other substances that had been manufactured in the bodies of other stars before the sun was born. This was the parent cloud of the solar system. The dense hot gas at the center of the cloud gave rise to the sun; the outer regions of the cloud—cooler and less dense—gave birth to the planets.

Our solar system consists of one star (the sun), nine planets and all their moons, several thousand minor planets called asteroids or planetoids, and an equally large number of comets.

The Sun

All the stars, including our sun, are gigantic balls of superheated gas, kept hot by atomic reactions in their centers. In our sun, this atomic reaction is hydrogen fusion: four hydrogen atoms are combined to form one helium atom. The temperature at the core of our sun must be 20 million degrees centigrade, the surface temperature averages 6,000°C, or about 11,000°F. The diameter of the sun is 865,400 miles, and its surface area is approximately 12,000 times that of the Earth. Compared with other stars, our sun is just a bit below average in size and temperature, and is a yellow dwarf star. Its fuel supply (hydrogen) is estimated to be sufficient for another 5 billion years.

Our sun is not motionless in space; in fact it has two proper motions. One is a seemingly straight-line motion in the direction of the constellation Hercules at the rate of about 12 miles per second. But since the sun is a part of the Milky Way system and since the whole system rotates slowly around its own center, the sun also moves at the rate of 175 miles per second as part of the rotating Milky Way system.

In addition to this motion, the sun rotates on its axis. Observing the motion of sun spots (darkish areas which look like enormous whirling storms) and solar flares, which are usually associated with sun spots, has shown that the rotational period of the sun is just short of 25 days. But this figure is valid for the sun's equator only; the sections near the sun's poles seem to have a rotational period of 34 days. Naturally, since the sun generates its own heat and light, there is no temperature difference between poles and equator.

What we call the sun's "surface" is technically known as the photosphere. Since the whole sun is a ball of very hot gas, there is really no such thing as a surface; it is a question of visual impression. The next layer outside the photosphere is known as the chromosphere, which extends several thousand miles beyond the photosphere. It is in steady motion, and often enormous prominences can be seen to burst from it, extending as much as 100,000 miles into space. Outside the chromosphere is the corona. The corona consists of very tenuous gases (essentially hydrogen) and makes a magnificent sight when the sun is eclipsed.

As the sun ages, it gradually expands and heats. In 1994, American astrophysicists studying the eventual fate of the sun estimated that its brilliancy will increase by 10% over the next 1.1 billion years or more and, in about 6.5 billion years hence, our aging star will have doubled its present luminosity. The extreme heat generated will cause a catastrophic greenhouse effect on Earth and our oceans will boil away, and life on Earth as we know it will end.

The sun will eventually expand enormously to 166 times its present size and become over 2,000 times as bright. Eight billion years from now, the sun's radius will engulf the planet Mercury and extend beyond the present orbit of Venus.

However, as the sun expands, it will also lose considerable mass (as much as one-half) and weaken its gravitational pull on Venus and the other lifeless planets, causing them to orbit further away from the sun and escape total destruction.

The Moon

Mercury and Venus do not have any moons. Therefore, the Earth is the planet nearest the sun to be orbited by a moon.

The next planet farther out, Mars, has two very small moons. Jupiter has four major moons and twelve minor ones. Saturn, the ringed planet, has 19 known moons (and possibly more), of which one (Titan) is larger than the planet Mercury. Uranus has fifteen moons (four of them large) as well as rings, while Neptune has one large and seven small moons. Pluto has one moon, discovered in 1978. Some astronomers still consider Pluto to be a "runaway moon" of Neptune.

Our moon, with a diameter of 2,160 miles, is one of the larger moons in our solar system and is especially large when compared with the planet that it orbits. In fact, the common center of gravity of the Earth-moon system is only about 1,000 miles below the Earth's surface. The closest the moon can come to us (its perigee) is 221,463 miles; the farthest it can go away (its apogee) is 252,710 miles. The period of rotation of the moon is equal to its period of revolution around the Earth. Hence from Earth we can see only one hemisphere of the moon. Both periods are 27 days, 7 hours, 43 minutes and 11.47 seconds. But while the rotation of the moon is constant, its velocity in its orbit is not, since it moves more slowly in apogee than in perigee. Consequently, some portions near the rim which are not normally visible will appear briefly. This phenomenon is called "libration," and by taking advantage of the librations, astronomers have succeeded in mapping approximately 59% of the lunar surface. The other 41% can never be seen from the Earth but has been mapped by American and Russian moon-orbiting spacecraft.

Though the moon goes around the Earth in the time mentioned, the interval from new moon to new moon is 29 days, 12 hours, 44 minutes and 2.78 seconds. This delay of nearly two days is due to the fact that the Earth is moving around the sun, so that the moon needs two extra days to reach a spot in its orbit where no part is illuminated by the sun, as seen from Earth.

If the plane of the Earth's orbit around the sun (the ecliptic) and the plane of the moon's orbit around the Earth were the same, the moon would be eclipsed by the Earth every time it is full, and the sun would be eclipsed by the moon every time the moon is "new" (it would be better to call it the "black moon" when it is in this position). But because the two orbits do not coincide, the moon's shadow normally misses the Earth and the Earth's shadow misses the moon. The inclination of the two orbital planes to each other is 5°. The tides are, of course, caused by the moon with the help of the sun, but in the open ocean they are surprisingly low, amounting to about one yard. The very high tides which can be observed near the shore in some places are due to funnelling effects of the shorelines. At new moon and at full moon the tides raised by the moon are reinforced by the sun; these are the "spring tides." If the sun's tidal power acts at right angles to that of the moon (quarter moons) we get the low "neap tides."

The Pentagon announced in December 1994, that analysis of radio signals from the *Clementine* spacecraft sent to orbit the moon in 1994 suggests that there is probably ice in a dark basin near the moon's south pole. The *Lunar Prospector* spacecraft, to be launched in September 1997, will be able to confirm the presence of lunar ice if it exists

Earth

The Earth, circling the sun at an average distance of 93 million miles, is the fifth largest planet and the third from the sun. It orbits the sun at a speed of 67,000 miles per hour, making one revolution in 365 days, 5 hours, 48 minutes, and 45.51 seconds. The Earth completes one rotation on its axis every 23 hours, 56 minutes, and 4.09 seconds. Actually a bit pear-shaped rather than a true sphere, the Earth has a diameter of 7,927 miles at the Equator and a few miles less at the poles. It has an estimated mass of about 6.6 sextillion tons, with an average density of 5.52 grams per cubic centimeter. The Earth's surface area encompasses 196,949,970 square miles of which about three-fourths is water.

Origin of the Earth

The Earth, along with the other planets, is believed to have been born 4.5 billion years ago as a solidified cloud of dust and gases left over from the creation of the sun. For perhaps 500 million years, the interior of the Earth stayed solid and relatively cool, perhaps 2000°F. The main ingredients, according to the best available evidence, were iron and silicates, with small amounts of other elements, some of them radioactive. As millions of years passed, energy released by radioactive decay—mostly of uranium, thorium, and potassium—gradually heated the Earth, melting some of its constituents. The iron melted before the silicates and, being heavier, sank toward the center. This forced up the silicates that it found there. After many years, the iron reached the center, almost 4,000 miles deep, and began to accumulate. No eyes were around at that time to view the turmoil which must have taken place on the face of the Earth—gigantic heaves and bubblings on the surface, exploding volcanoes, and flowing lava covering everything in sight. Finally, the iron in the center accumulated as the core. Around it, a thin but fairly stable

The Brightest Stars

Star	Constellation	Mag.	Dist (l.-y.)	Star	Constellation	Mag.	Dist (l.-y.)
Sirius	Canis Major	-1.6	8	Antares	Scorpius	1.2	170
Canopus	Carina	-0.9	650	Fomalhaut	Piscis Austrinus	1.3	27
Alpha Centauri	Centaurus	+0.1	4	Deneb	Cygnus	1.3	465
Vega	Lyra	0.1	23	Regulus	Leo	1.3	70
Capella	Auriga	0.2	42	Beta Crucis	Crux	1.5	465
Arcturus	Boötes	0.2	32	Eta Carinae	Carina	1-7	—
Rigel	Orion	0.3	545	Alpha-one Crucis	Crux	1.6	150
Procyon	Canis Minor	0.5	10	Castor	Gemini	1.6	44
Achernar	Eridanus	0.6	70	Gamma Crucis	Crux	1.6	—
Beta Centauri	Centaurus	0.9	130	Epsilon Canis Majoris	Canis Major	1.6	325
Altair	Aquila	0.9	18	Epsilon Ursae Majoris	Ursa Major	1.7	50
Betelgeuse	Orion	0.9	600	Bellatrix	Orion	1.7	215
Aldebaran	Taurus	1.1	54	Lambda Scorpii	Scorpius	1.7	205
Spica	Virgo	1.2	190	Epsilon Carinae	Carina	1.7	325
Pollux	Gemini	1.2	31	Mira	Cetus	2-10	250

crust of solid rock formed as the Earth cooled. Depressions in the crust were natural basins in which water, rising from the interior of the planet through volcanoes and fissures, collected to form the oceans. Slowly, Earth acquired its present appearance.

Earth Today

As a result of radioactive heating over millions of years, the Earth's molten *core* is probably fairly hot today, around 11,000°F. By comparison, lead melts at around 800°F. Most of the Earth's 2,100-mile-thick core is liquid, but there is evidence that the center of the core is solid. The liquid outer portion, about 95% of the core, is constantly in motion, causing the Earth to have a magnetic field that makes compass needles point north and south. The details are not known, but the latest evidence suggests that planets that have a magnetic field probably have a solid core or a partially liquid one.

Outside the core is the Earth's *mantle,* 1,800 miles thick, and extending nearly to the surface. The mantle is composed of heavy silicate rock, similar to that brought up by volcanic eruptions. It is somewhere between liquid and solid, slightly yielding, and therefore contributing to an active, moving Earth. Most of the Earth's radioactive material is in the thin *crust* that covers the mantle, but some is in the mantle and continues to give off heat. The crust's thickness ranges from 5 to 25 miles.

Scientists recently discovered that the Earth's core is not a perfect sphere. X-ray like images of inside the Earth show that there are vast mountains six to seven miles high and deep valleys on the core. These features are in an upside-down relationship to the Earth's surface.

In 1996, geophysicists discovered that the Earth's solid-iron inner core rotates slightly faster than the rest of the planet and gains a quarter-turn every century. The finding may help explain how the Earth's magnetic field periodically reverses its polarity.

Continental Drift

A great deal of recent evidence confirms the theory that the continents of the Earth, made mostly of relatively light granite, float in the slightly yielding mantle, like logs in a pond. For many years it had been noticed that if North and South America could be pushed toward western and southern Europe and western Africa, they would fit like pieces in a jigsaw puzzle. Today, there is little question—the continents have drifted widely and continue to do so.

In 10 million years, the world as we know it may be unrecognizable, with California drifting out to sea, Florida joining South America, and Africa moving farther away from Europe and Asia.

The Earth's Atmosphere

The thin blanket of atmosphere that envelops the Earth extends several hundred miles into space. From sea level—the very bottom of the ocean of air—to a height of about 60 miles, the air in the atmosphere is made up of the same gases in the same ratio: about 78% nitrogen, 21% oxygen, and the remaining 1% being a mixture of argon, carbon dioxide, and tiny amounts of neon, helium, krypton, xenon, and other gases. The atmosphere becomes less dense with increasing altitude: more than three-fourths of the Earth's huge envelope is concentrated in the first 5 to 10 miles above the surface. At sea level, a cubic foot of atmosphere weighs about an ounce and a quarter. The entire atmosphere weighs 5,700 trillion tons, and the force with which gravity holds it in place causes it to exert a pressure of nearly 15 pounds per square inch. Going out from the Earth's surface, the atmosphere is divided into five regions. The regions, and the heights to which they extend, are: *Troposphere,* 0 to 7 miles (at middle latitudes); *stratosphere,* 7 to 30 miles; *mesosphere,* 30 to 50 miles; *thermosphere,* 50 to 400 miles; and *exosphere,* above 400 miles. The boundaries between each of the regions are known respectively as the *tropopause, stratopause, mesopause,* and *thermopause.* Alternative terms often used for the layers above the troposphere are *ozonosphere* (for stratosphere) and *ionosphere* for the remaining upper layers.

The Seasons

Seasons are caused by the 23.4-degree tilt of the Earth's axis, which alternately turns the North and South Poles toward the sun. Times when the sun's apparent path crosses the equator are known as *equinoxes.* Times when the sun's apparent path is at the greatest distance from the equator are known as *solstices.* The lengths of the days are most extreme at each solstice. If the Earth's axis were perpendicular to the plane of the Earth's orbit around the sun, there would be no seasons, and the days always would be equal in length. Since the Earth's axis is at an angle, the sun strikes the Earth directly at the equator only twice a year: in March (vernal equinox) and September (autumnal equinox). In the Northern Hemisphere, spring begins at the vernal equinox, summer at the summer solstice, fall at the autumnal equinox, and winter at the winter solstice. The situation is reversed in the Southern Hemisphere.

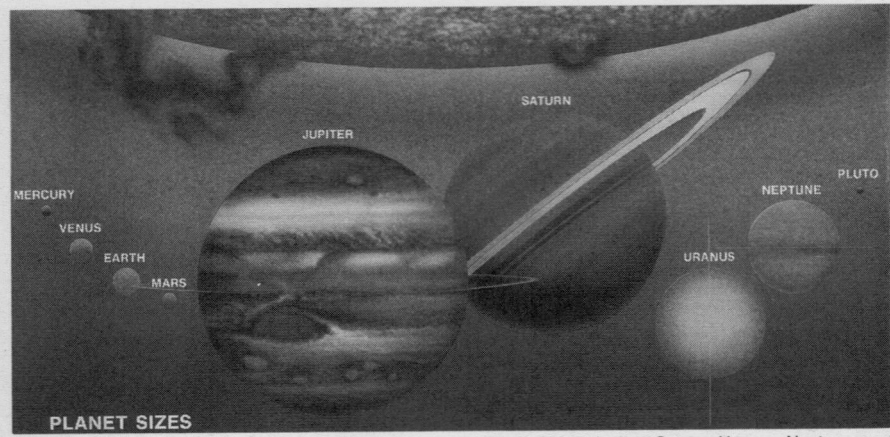

PLANET SIZES. Shown from left to right: Mercury, Venus, Earth, Mars, Jupiter, Saturn, Uranus, Neptune, and Pluto. *Copyright 1990 Hansen Planetarium, Salt Lake City, Utah. Reproduced with permission.*

Basic Planetary Data

	Mercury	Venus	Earth	Mars	Jupiter
Mean distance from sun (millions of kilometers)	57.9	108.2	149.6	227.9	778.3
Mean distance from sun (millions of miles)	36.0	67.24	92.9	141.71	483.88
Period of revolution	88 days	224.7 days	365.2 days	687 days	11.86 yrs
Rotation period	59 days	243 days retrograde	23 hr 56 min 4 sec	24 hr 37 min	9 hr 55 min 30 sec
Inclination of axis	Near 0°	3°	23°27′	25° 12′	3° 5′
Inclination of orbit to ecliptic	7°	3.4°	0°	1.9°	1.3°
Eccentricity of orbit	.206	.007	.017	.093	.048
Equatorial diameter (kilometers)	4,880	12,100	12,756	6,794	142,800
(miles)	3,032.4	7,519	7,926.2	4,194	88,736
Atmosphere (main components)	Virtually none	Carbon dioxide	Nitrogen oxygen	Carbon dioxide	Hydrogen helium
Satellites	0	0	1	2	16
Rings	0	0	0	0	1

	Saturn	Uranus	Neptune	Pluto
Mean distance from sun (millions of kilometers)	1,427	2,870	4,497	5,900
Mean distance from sun (millions of miles)	887.14	1,783.98	2,796.46	3,666
Period of revolution	29.46 yrs	84 yrs	165 yrs	248 yrs
Rotation period	10 hr 40 min 24 sec	16.8 hr(?) retrograde	16 hr 11 min(?)	6 days 9 hr 18 mins retrograde
Inclination of axis	26°44′	97°55′	28°48′	60° (?)
Inclination of orbit to ecliptic	2.5°	0.8°	1.8°	17.2°
Eccentricity of orbit	.056	.047	.009	.254
Equatorial diameter (kilometers)	120,660	51,810	49,528	2,290 (?)
(miles)	74,978	32,193	30,775	1,423 (?)
Atmosphere (main components)	Hydrogen helium	Helium hydrogen methane	Hydrogen helium methane	None detected
Satellites	19	15	8	1
Rings	1,000 (?)	11	4	?

Source: Basic NASA data and other sources.

Mercury

Mercury is the planet nearest the sun. Appropriately named for the wing-footed Roman messenger of the gods, Mercury whizzes around the sun at a speed of 30 miles per second completing one circuit in 88 days. The days and nights are long on Mercury. It takes 59 Earth days for Mercury to make a single rotation. It spins at a rate of about 10 kilometers (about 6 miles) per hour, measured at the equator, as compared to the Earth's spin of about 1,600 kilometers (about 1,000 miles) per hour at the equator.

The photographs *Mariner 10* (1974–75) radioed back to Earth revealed an ancient, heavily cratered surface on Mercury, closely resembling our own moon. The pictures showed huge cliffs, or scarps, crisscrossing the planet. These apparently were created when Mercury's interior cooled and shrank, compressing the planet's crust. The cliffs are as high as two kilometers (1.2 miles) and as long as 1,500 kilometers (932 miles). Another unique feature is the Caloris Basin, a large impact crater about 1,300 kilometers (808 miles) in diameter.

Mercury, like the Earth, appears to have a crust of light silicate rock. Scientists believe it has a heavy iron-rich core that makes up about half of its volume.

Instruments onboard *Mariner 10* discovered that the planet has a weak magnetic field and a trace of atmosphere—a trillionth the density of the Earth's and is composed chiefly of argon, neon, and helium. The spacecraft reported temperatures ranging from 510°C (950°F) on Mercury's sunlit side to –210°C (–346°F) on the dark side. Mercury literally bakes in daylight and freezes at night.

Until the *Mariner 10* probe, little was known about the planet. Even the best telescopic views from Earth showed Mercury as an indistinct object lacking any surface detail. The planet is so close to the sun that it is usually lost in the sun's glare.

Radar images taken by astronomers at Jet Propulsion Laboratories and California Institute of Technology during the summer of 1991 suggest that the polar regions of Mercury may be covered with patches of water ice. Although this seems impossible due to the planet's sizzling heat, the polar regions receive very little sunlight and may get as cold as –235°F. The radar images showed bright patterns at the poles which are characteristic of ice reflecting radar signals. Other explanations may be offered for this unexpected discovery.

Mercury is a naked eye object at morning or evening twilight when it is at greatest elongation.

Venus

Although Venus is Earth's closest neighbor, very little is known about the planet because it is permanently covered by thick clouds. In 1962, Soviet and American space probes, coupled with Earth-based radar and infrared spectroscopy, began slowly unraveling some of the mystery surrounding Venus. Twenty-eight years later, the *Magellan* spacecraft, sent by the United State,s arrived at Venus in August 1990 and began radar-mapping the planet's surface in greater detail.

According to the latest results, Venus's atmosphere exerts a pressure at the surface 94.5 times greater than Earth's. Walking on Venus would be as difficult as walking a half-mile beneath the ocean. Because of a thick blanket of carbon dioxide, a "greenhouse effect" exists on Venus. Venus intercepts twice as much of the sun's light as does Earth. The light enters freely through the carbon dioxide gas and is changed to heat radiation in molecular collisions. But carbon dioxide prevents the heat from escaping. Consequently, the temperature of the surface of Venus is over 800°F, hot enough to melt lead.

The atmospheric composition of Venus is about 96% carbon dioxide, 4% nitrogen, and minor amounts of water, oxygen, and sulfur compounds. There are at least four distinct cloud and haze layers that exist at different altitudes above the planet's surface. The haze layers contain small aerosol particles, possibly droplets of sulfuric acid. A concentration of sulfur dioxide above the cloud tops has been observed to be decreasing since 1978. The source of sulfur dioxide at this altitude is unknown; it may be injected by volcanic explosions or atmospheric overturning.

Measurements of the Venusian atmosphere and its cloud patterns reveal nearly constant high-speed zonal winds, about 100 meters per second (220 miles per hour) at the equator. The winds decrease toward the poles so that the atmosphere at cloud-top level rotates almost like a solid body. The wind speeds at the equator correspond to Venus's rotation period of four to five days at most latitudes. The circulation is always in the same direction—east to west—as Venus's slow retrograde motion. Earth's winds blow from west to east, the same direction as its rotation.

Venus is quite round, very different from the other planets and from the moon. Venus has neither polar flattening nor an equatorial bulge. The diameter of Venus is 12,100 kilometers (7,519 miles). Venus has a retrograde axial rotation period of 243.1 Earth days. The surface atmospheric pressure is 1,396 pounds per square inch (95 Earth atmospheres). The planet's mean distance from the sun is 108.2 million kilometers (67.2 million miles). The period of its revolution around the sun is 224.7 days.

The highest point on Venus is the summit of Maxwell Montes, 10.8 kilometers (6.71 miles) above the mean level, more than a mile higher than Mount Everest. There is some evidence that this huge mountain is an active volcano. The lowest point is in the rift valley, Diana Chasma, 2.9 kilometers (1.8 miles) below the mean level. This point is about one-fifth the greatest depth on Earth in the Marianas Trench.

Venus has an extreme lowland basin, Atalanta Planitia, which is about the size of Earth's North Atlantic Ocean basin. The smooth surface of the Atalanta Planitia resembles the mare basins of the moon.

There are only two highland or continental masses on Venus: Ishtar Terra and Aphrodite Terra. Ishtar Terra is 11 kilometers (6.8 miles) at its highest points (the highest peaks on Venus) and those of Aphrodite Terra rise to about 5 kilometers (3.10 miles) above the planet. Ishtar Terra is about the size of the continental United States and Aphrodite Terra is about the size of Africa.

The unmanned NASA spacecraft *Magellan* was launched on May 4, 1989, from the shuttle *Atlantis* and arrived at Venus Aug. 10, 1990, to map most of the planet. Despite some problems with its radio transmissions, the results of the radar mapping delighted scientists and provided them with the sharpest images ever taken of the planet's surface. Images taken from *Magellan* show ten times more detail than ever seen before.

The radar images provided scientists with compelling evidence that the planet has been dominated by volcanism on a global scale. The photos also showed that the planet's second-highest mountain, Maat Mons, rising five miles (eight kilometers) above the Venusian plains, appears to be covered with fresh lava and is possibly an active volcano.

Magellan discovered the longest known channel in the solar system on Venus. It is 4,200 miles (6,800 kilometers) long and averages slightly over a mile (1.8 kilometers) wide. Its origin is puzzling to scientists because high-temperature lava is unlikely to have caused such a long-distance flow on the surface and there are no known substances that could remain liquid long enough under the planet's atmospheric pressure and temperature

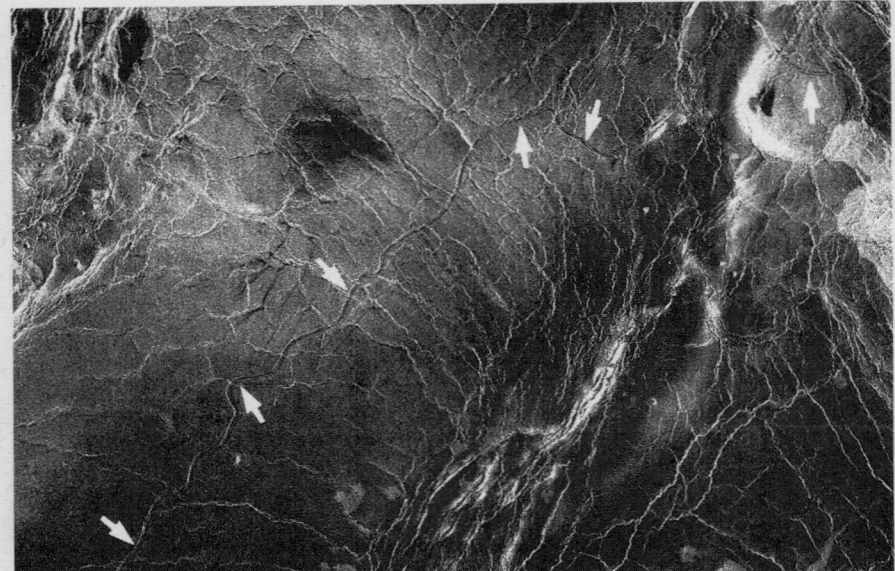

Largest Channel in Solar System. *Magellan* took the above image of the largest known channel on Venus. At 4,200 miles (6,880 kilometers) long and an average of 1.1 miles (1.8 kilometers) wide, it is longer than the Nile River, Earth's longest river, making it the longest known channel in the solar system. The channel was originally discovered by the Soviet *Venery 15* and *16* spacecraft orbiters. *Source:* NASA.

to have carved out this snake-like feature. The channel is slightly longer than the Nile River, the longest river on Earth. *Magellan* ended its radar and emissions mapping in September 1992 after covering 98% of the planet's surface.

Venus is the brightest of all the planets and is often visible in the morning or evening, when it is frequently referred to as the Morning Star or Evening Star. At its brightest, it can sometimes be seen in full daylight with the naked eye, if one knows where to look.

Mars

Mars, on the other side of the Earth from Venus, is Venus's direct opposite in terms of physical properties. Its atmosphere is cold, thin, and transparent, and readily permits observation of the planet's features. We know more about Mars than any other planet except Earth. Mars is a forbidding, rugged planet with huge volcanoes and deep chasms. The largest volcano, Olympus Mons (Olympic Mountain) rises 78,000 feet above the surface, higher than Mount Everest. The plains of Mars are pockmarked by the hits of thousands of meteors over the years.

Until the arrival of *Mars Pathfinder* in 1997, most of our information about Mars came from the *Mariner* and *Viking* spacecrafts. *Mariner 9* orbited the planet in 1971 and photographed 100% of the planet, uncovered spectacular geological formations, including a Martian "Grand Canyon" that dwarfs the one on Earth. Called Valles Marineris (Mariner Valley) it stretches more than 3,000 miles along the equatorial region of Mars and is over 4 kilometers (2.5 miles) deep in places and 80 to 100 kilometers (50–62 miles) wide. The spacecraft's cameras also recorded what appeared to be dried riverbeds, suggesting the one-time presence of water on the planet. The latter idea gives encouragement to scientists looking for life on Mars, for where there is water, there may be life. However, to date, no evidence of life has

been found. Temperatures near the equator range from –17°F in the daytime to –130°F at night.

The landing of two robot *Viking* spacecraft on the surface of Mars in 1976 provided more information about Mars in a few months than in all the previous missions.

Mars rotates upon its axis in nearly the same period as Earth—24 hours, 37 minutes—so that a Mars day is almost identical to an Earth day. Mars takes 687 days to make one trip around the sun. Because of its eccentric orbit, Mars's distance from the sun can vary by about 36 million miles. Its distance from Earth can vary by as much as 200 million miles. The atmosphere of Mars is much thinner than Earth's; atmospheric pressure is about 1% that of our planet. Its gravity is one-third of Earth's. Major constituents are carbon dioxide and nitrogen. Water vapor and oxygen are minor constituents. Mars's polar caps, composed mostly of frozen carbon dioxide (dry ice), recede and advance according to the Martian seasons.

Scientists have not yet determined if the Martian snow (as water ice or carbon dioxide particles) actually crystallizes on the polar caps or whether it falls from the clouds over them.

Mars has four seasons like Earth, but they are much longer. For example, in the northern hemisphere, the Martian spring is 198 days, and the winter season lasts 158 days.

Images taken by the Hubble Space Telescope in 1995 showed that the Martian climate has become cooler and drier since the *Viking* spacecraft visited the planet in the 1970s. NASA researchers believe that the planet's cooling may be due to diminished dust storms.

NASA has scheduled ten missions to Mars, which began with the launching of *Mars Surveyor* in November 1996, and will end in 2005 with a mission to return Martian rock and soil samples to Earth.

The *Mars Pathfinder* lander and its rover, *Sojourner*, set down on the edge of a boulder-strewn outflow channel known as *Ares Vallis* on July 4, 1997, and provided scientists with a wealth of information on the rocks, soils, and atmosphere of Mars. The lander sent back the first live pictures of the planet's topography and its tiny rover explored a variety of rocks and analyzed their mineral composition with its cameras and on-board X-ray spectrometer.

The first target *Sojourner* examined, a small roughly textured rock nicknamed *Barnacle Bill*, appeared to be rich in silica, and the analysis indicated that it could be a type of volcanic rock (called *andesites*) similar to ones found in the Andes Mountains. The second rock observed, called *Yogi*, was low in quartz and resembled basalt, which is the Earth's most common lava rock. Spectroscopic analysis of several rocks also gave additional proof that the 12 suspected Martian meteorites found on Earth did indeed come from the Red Planet. Studies of additional rocks and soils identified by NASA science teams for their interesting features will continue for as long as the lander and rover remain operational.

Analysis of the reddish surface soil pointed to the presence of oxidized iron, indicating that the planet's surface is rusting. *Sojourner* samples of soil taken from several sites found their composition similar to those analyzed by the two *Viking* landers in 1976, indicating that the Martian winds have distributed the soil evenly over the planet. Soil abrasion experiments have shown that one type of Martian soil is similar to very fine-grained silt. Its particles are less than 50 microns in diameter, which is finer than talcum powder.

Scientists were surprised to learn how rapidly the Martian temperature fluctuates due to atmospheric turbulence. It can change by as much as 30°–40°F (17°–22°C) in a matter of minutes, possibly due to strong, gusty winds bringing warm air from one region or cold air from another.

There is also a rapid fall-off of temperature in relation to altitude. In late July, during the northern Martian summer, for example, a temperature reading taken in the early afternoon at the landing site found that it was a warm 60°–70°F (16°–21°C) on the ground. Yet just 5½ feet above the lander, the temperature had dropped to a freezing −10° to −15°F (−23° to −27°C).

Pictures and subsequent data from *Pathfinder* give the strongest evidence that Mars had an abundance of water millions of years ago. Scientists have inferred from the variety of rocks and sediments found in the *Ares* basin that the spacecraft landed in a channel that was once awash with torrential floods greater than any known on Earth. The diversity of rocks deposited there suggest their different origins, and it appears that they were washed down from the highlands at a time when great floods moved over the surface of Mars. (*See* Space section for additional details.)

Mars was named for the Roman god of war, because when seen from Earth its distinct red color reminded the ancient people of blood. We know now that the reddish hue reflects the oxidized (rusted) iron in the surface material.

The Martian Moons

Mars has two very small elliptical-shaped moons, Deimos and Phobos—the Greek names for the companions of the God Mars: Deimos (Terror) and Phobos (Fear). They were discovered in August 1877 by the American astronomer Asaph Hall (1829–1907) at the U.S. Naval Observatory in Washington, D.C.

The inner satellite, Phobos, is 27 kilometers (16.78 miles) long and it revolves around the planet in 7.6 hours. The outer moon, Deimos, is 15 kilometers (9.32 miles) long and it circles the planet in 30.35 hours. The short orbital period of Phobos means that the satellite

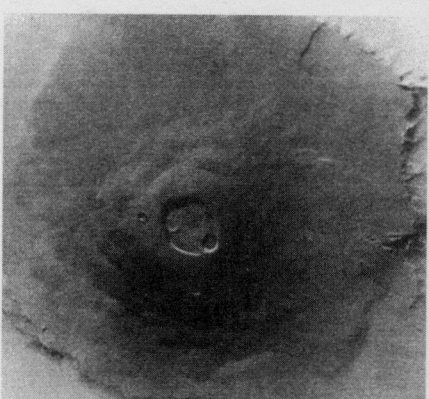

Giant Olympus Mons. The tallest volcano on Mars, is also the highest mountain in the solar system. It is 540 kilometers (336 miles) across and rises 10 miles higher than Mount Everest. *Source:* NASA.

travels around Mars twice in a Martian day. If an observer were suitably situated on the planet, he would see Phobos rise and set twice in a day.

Recent studies of Phobos indicate that its orbit is slowly decreasing downward and that in approximately 40 million years, it will crash into the planet's surface.

Meteorites from Mars

Recent research showed that a group of eight meteorites, labeled SNC[1] (named for towns where they were found: Shergotty, India, in 1865; Nakhla, Egypt, in 1911; and Chassigny, France, in 1815), are probably samples of Mars. This hypothesis was based largely on the composition of noble gases (particularly argon and xenon) trapped in the meteorites, and the shergottites in particular, which resemble measurements of the Martian atmosphere made by the *Viking* spacecraft. Major element compositions of the SNCs are also similar to Martian soil analyses made by *Viking*. *Pathfinder* rover studies of the planet's rocks also provided strong evidence of the Martian origin.

The relatively young isotopic ages of the SNC meteorites (1.3 billion years or less) suggest that Mars has been volcanically active during its recent past.

In 1991, a ninth meteorite, LEW 88516, was identified as having reached Earth from Mars some 180 million years ago. It was discovered in December 1988 near Lewis Cliff in Antarctica. The meteorite is very small with a dark pitted surface and weighs 13.2 grams (less than half an ounce).

A 4-pound, 7-ounce (1.9 kilograms) meteorite, ALH84001, found in the Allen Hills of Antarctica in 1984 was reclassified in 1993 as coming from the Red Planet, making it the tenth meteorite known to have originated from Mars. In 1996, NASA announced that meteorite ALH 84001 contained fossils of ancient Martian life forms.

A 40-pound meteorite that crashed to Earth in Nigeria in 1962 has been classified as coming from Mars. It was named Zagami for the region it was found in.

A 0.38-ounce (12-gram) meteorite (QUE94201) found in Antarctica in 1995 became the 12th meteorite identified as having a Martian origin.

Scientists do not know how the meteorites were thrown off the Martian surface.

(*See* Space section for additional information.)

---

1. Pronounced "snick."

Jupiter

Jupiter is the largest planet in the solar system—a gaseous world as large as 1,300 Earths. Its equatorial diameter is 142,800 kilometers (88,736 miles), while from pole to pole, Jupiter measures only 133,500 kilometers (84,201 miles). For comparison, the diameter of the Earth is 12,756 kilometers (7,926.2 miles). The massive planet rotates at a dizzying speed—once every 9 hours and 55 minutes. It takes Jupiter almost 12 Earth years to complete a journey around the sun.

The giant planet appears as a banded disk of turbulent clouds with all of its stripes running parallel to its bulging equator. Large dusky gray regions surround each pole. Darker gray or brown stripes called belts intermingle with lighter, yellow-white stripes called zones. The belts are regions of descending air masses and the zones are rising cloudy air masses. The strongest winds—up to 400 kilometers (250 miles) per hour—are found at boundaries between the belts and zones.

This uniquely colorful atmosphere is mainly 89% molecular hydrogen and 11% helium. It contains small amounts of methane, ammonia, ethane, and water.

Cloud-type lightning bolts similar to those on Earth have been found in the Jovian atmosphere. At the polar regions, auroras have been observed. A very thin ring of material less than one kilometer (0.6 mile) in thickness and about 6,000 kilometers (4,000 miles) in radial extent has been observed circling the planet about 55,000 kilometers (35,000 miles) above the cloud tops.

The most prominent feature on Jupiter is its "Great Red Spot," an oval larger than the planet Earth. It is a tremendous atmospheric storm that rotates counterclockwise with one revolution every six days at the outer edge, while at the center almost no motion can be seen. The spot is about 25,000 kilometers (16,000 miles) on its long axis, and would cover three Earths. The outer rim shows streamline shapes of 360-kilometer (225-mile) winds. Jupiter also has several faint rings like Saturn.

Jupiter emits 67% more heat than it absorbs from the sun. This heat is thought to be accumulated during the planet's formation several billion years ago.

Twenty-one fragments of comet Shoemaker-Levy 9 bombarded the cloud-covered surface of Jupiter, July 16–22, 1994. It was the most violent event in the recorded history of our solar system. The cometary explosions caused towering plumes of debris and hot gas to rise from the darkened impact sites.

On Dec. 7, 1995, the *Galileo* spacecraft released a probe into Jupiter's atmosphere to study the planet's physical and chemical properties. The probe lasted 57 minutes and early results indicated a lower abundance of water than was expected.

The latest *Galileo* data, released in June 1997, showed that Jupiter has both wet and dry regions, just as Earth has tropics and deserts. This could explain why the probe found less water than anticipated. These dry spots cover less than 1% of the Jovian atmosphere.

Jovian moons

The four great moons of Jupiter were discovered by Galileo Galilei (1564–1642) in January 1610, and are called the Galilean satellites after their discoverer. Their names are Io, Europa, Ganymede, and Callisto. Like our moon, the satellites always keep the same face turned toward the Earth. Jupiter has 16 known satellites.

Ganymede

Ganymede, 5,270 kilometers (3,275 miles) in diameter, is Jupiter's largest moon, and also it is the largest satellite in the solar system. Ganymede is about one and one-half times the size of our moon. It is heavily cratered and probably has the greatest variety of geologic process recorded on its surface. Ganymede is half water

and half rock, resulting in a density about two-thirds that of Europa, an ice-coated satellite. No atmosphere has been detected on it.

The first close-up photos of Ganymede taken by the *Galileo* spacecraft, during its June 1996 flyby, revealed a surface pockmarked with ancient craters and a landscape wrinkled and torn by the same forces that make mountains and move continents on Earth. *Galileo*'s findings also indicated that Ganymede is enveloped in its own magnetic field, possibly created by a molten iron core or even a thin layer of conducting salty water underneath its icy crust.

Ganymede is the first known moon with its own magnetosphere.

Europa

Europa, the brightest of Jupiter's satellites, is about 1,950 miles (3,160 kilometers) in diameter or about the size of Earth's moon. It density is about three times that of water. The moon is covered with a thin ice crust and is crisscrossed with an amazingly complex network of ridges. Some of the fractures on its crust are more than 1,850 miles (3,000 kilometers) long. Very few impact craters are visible on the surface.

Galileo spacecraft photos taken at its closest flyby on February 20, 1997, at a distance of 363 miles (586 kilometers), showed the existence of ice flows on the surface that strongly suggest that the moon has a hidden subsurface ocean of water or ice-slush. The photos revealed chunky ice rafts that appear to be floating, comparable to icebergs on Earth. The presence of water and enough heat to keep water in a liquid state on Europa enhances the possibility that it could provide an environment for some form of extraterresial ocean life. Some researchers think that Europa may have active subsurface volcanoes. Oceanographers have found life near volcanic vents on the Earth's sea floors.

Scientists hope to find more answers about Europa's likely oceans and possible evidence of erupting geysers when the spacecraft returns for another look at the moon on November 6, 1997. Eight additional Europa flybys are planned as part of *Galileo's* new two-year extended mission.

NASA scientists have proposed to send a spacecraft called the *Europa Ice Clipper* to the moon in 2001 to determine if it has a global ocean and active volcanoes below its frozen crust. The spacecraft could send an impactor into Europa's surface with such a force that fragments of the moon would be injected into space, to be collected by the *Clipper* and returned to Earth for study.

Callisto

Callisto, 2,400 miles (4,800 kilometers) in diameter, is the outermost and, apparently, the least geologically active of Jupiter's four major satellites. Its density is less than twice that of water. Callisto has the oldest body and most cratered face of any body yet observed in the solar system. Like Ganymede, it seems to have a rocky core surrounded by ice. Unlike Ganymede, the surface of Callisto is completely covered with scars left by tens of thousands of meteoric impacts. Scientist estimate that it would take several billion years to accumulate the number of craters found there. So Callisto is believed to be inactive for at least that long. Although it is the darkest of the Galilean satellites, it is twice as bright as Earth's moon.

Io

Io, 3,640 kilometers (2,262 miles) in diameter, is the most spectacular of the Galilean moons. Its brilliant colors of red, orange, and yellow set it apart from any other planet. Eight active volcanoes have been detected on Io, with some plumes extending up to 320 kilometers (200 miles) above the surface. The relative smoothness of

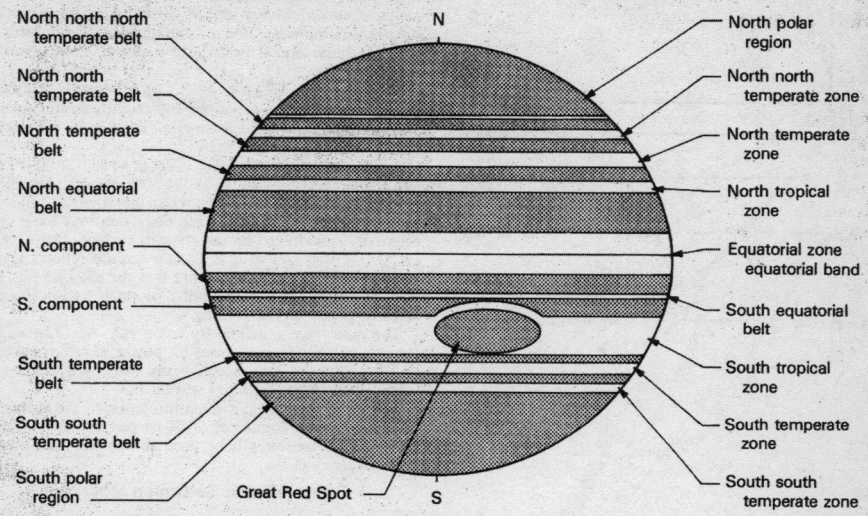

Schematic diagram of Jupiter's major features. *Source:* NASA.

Io's surface and its volcanic activity suggest that it has the youngest surface of Jupiter's moons. Its surface is composed of large amounts of sulfur and sulfur-dioxide frost, which account for the primarily yellow-orange surface color.

The volcanoes seem to eject a sufficient amount of sulfur dioxide to form a doughnut-shaped ring (torus) of ionized sulfur and oxygen atoms around Jupiter near Io's orbit. *Galileo* images taken in June 1996 revealed that Io's landscape undergoes constant change due to the numerous sulfur volcanoes that continuously erupt on its surface.

In 1996, the *Galileo* spacecraft detected a huge iron core within Io that occupies half the moon's diameter. *Galileo* also discovered evidence that Io has its own magnetic field.

Amalthea

Amalthea, Jupiter's innermost satellite, was discovered in 1892. It is so small—265 kilometers (165 miles) long and 150 kilometers (90 miles) wide—that it is extremely difficult to observe from Earth. Amalthea is an elongated, irregularly shaped satellite of reddish color. It orbits the planet every 12 hours and is in synchronous rotation, with its long axis always oriented toward Jupiter.

Jupiter's other moons are named Adrasta, Metis, Thebe, Leda, Himalia, Lysithea, Elara, Ananke, Carne, Pasiphae, and Sinope.

The Magnetosphere

Perhaps the largest structure in the solar system is the magnetosphere of Jupiter. This is the region of space that is filled with Jupiter's magnetic field and is bounded by the interaction of that magnetic field with the solar wind, which is the sun's outward flow of charged particles. The plasma of electrically charged particles that exists in the magnetosphere is flattened into a large disk more than 4.8 million kilometers (3 million miles) in diameter, is coupled to the magnetic field, and rotates around Jupiter. The Galilean satellites are located in the inner regions of the magnetosphere and are subjected to intense radiation bombardment.

The intense radiation field that surrounds Jupiter is fatal to humans. If astronauts were one day able to approach the planet as close as the *Voyager 1* spacecraft did, they would receive a dose of 400,000 rads or roughly 1,000 times the lethal dose for humans.

Even when nearest the Earth, Jupiter is still almost 400 million miles away. However, because of its size, it may rival Venus in brilliance when near. Jupiter's four large moons may be seen through field glasses, moving rapidly around Jupiter and changing their positions from night to night.

Saturn

Saturn, the second largest planet in the solar system, is the least dense. Its mass is 95 times the mass of the Earth and its density is 0.70 gram per cubic centimeter, so that it would float in an ocean if there were one big enough to hold it.

Saturn radiates about 80% more energy than it receives from the sun. However, the excess thermal energy cannot be primarily attributed to Saturn's primordial heat loss, as is speculated for Jupiter.

Saturn's diameter is 120,660 kilometers (74,978 miles) but 10% less at the poles, a consequence of its rapid rotation. Its axis of rotation is tilted by 27 degrees and the length of its day is 10 hours, 39 minutes, and 24 seconds.

Saturn is composed primarily of liquid metallic hydrogen (about 80%) and the second most common element is believed to be helium.

Saturn's atmospheric appearance is very similar to Jupiter's with dark and light cloud markings and swirls, eddies, and curling ribbons; the belts and zones are more numerous and a thick haze mutes the markings. The temperature ranges from 80°K to 90°K (176°F to −203°F).

Winds blow at extremely high speeds on Saturn. Near the equator, the *Voyagers* measured winds of about 500 meters per second (1,100 miles per hour). The winds blow primarily in an eastward direction.

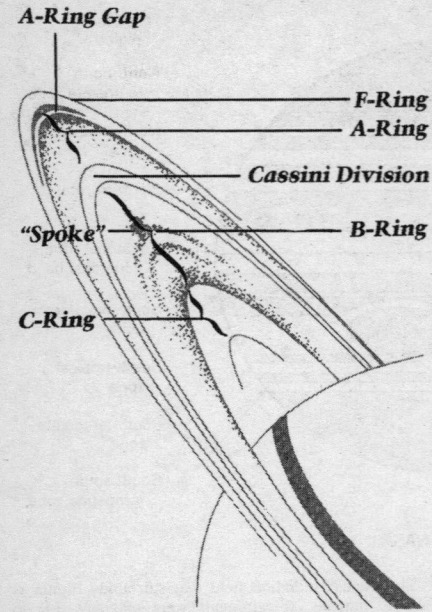

A-Ring Gap

F-Ring
A-Ring

Cassini Division

"Spoke"

B-Ring

C-Ring

NASA illustration of the divisions in Saturn's ring system.

Saturn's Rings

Saturn's spectacular ring system is unique in the solar system, with uncountable billions of tiny particles of water ice (with traces of other material) in orbit around the planet. The ring particles range in size from smaller than grains of sugar to as large as a house. The main rings stretch out from about 7,000 kilometers (4,350 miles) to above the atmosphere of the planet out to the F ring, a total span of 74,000 kilometers (45,984 miles). Saturn's rings can be likened to a phonograph, rings within rings numbering in the hundreds, and spokes in the B rings, and shepherding satellites controlling the F ring.

The main rings are called the A, B, and C rings moving from outside to inside. The gap between the A and B rings is called the Cassini Division and is named for the Italian-French astronomer, Gian Domenico Cassini, who discovered four of Saturn's major moons and the dark, narrow gap, "Cassini's Division," splitting the planet's rings.

Saturn's magnetic field has well-defined north and south magnetic poles, and is aligned with Saturn's axis of rotation to within one degree.

Saturn's moons

Saturn has 19 known moons. In May 1995, American astronomers using the Hubble Space Telescope, reported discovering several new satellites of Saturn bringing the total to 20 or more. However, it was later determined that only one of them is a moon. The five largest moons, Tethys, Dione, Rhea, Titan, and Iapetus, range from 1060 to 5150 kilometers (650 to 3,200 miles) in diameter. The planet's outstanding satellite is Titan, first discovered by the Dutch astronomer Christiaan Huygens in 1656.

Titan

Titan is remarkable because it is the only known moon in the solar system that has a substantial atmosphere—largely nitrogen with a minor amount of methane and a rich variety of other hydrocarbons. Its surface is completely hidden from view (except at infrared and radio wavelengths) by a dense, hazy atmosphere.

The diameter of Titan is 5,150 kilometers (3,200 miles) and it is the second largest satellite in the solar system after Jupiter's Ganymede. Titan is larger than the planet Mercury.

Titan's surface temperature is about –175°C (–280°F) and its surface pressure is about 50% greater than the surface pressure of the Earth. After the *Voyager I* flyby in 1980, scientists hypothesized that Titan may have an ocean of liquid hydrogen covering its surface. However, in 1990 it was shown that Titan's surface reflects and scatters radio waves, suggesting that the satellite has a solid surface with the possibility of small hydrocarbon lakes or ponds on the surface.

The data were obtained by using NASA's 70-meter antenna in California to transmit powerful radio waves to Titan, and the Very Large Array in New Mexico as the receiver of the reflected waves.

NASA plans to send a scientific probe to the surface of Titan in the summer of 2004 as part of its Cassini Mission. The probe will be provided by the European Space Agency (ESA).

Other Notable Saturnian Moons

The other four largest moons of Saturn are: Tethys, Dione, Rhea, and Iapetus.

Tethys is 1,060 kilometers (650 miles) in diameter. Its surface is heavily cratered and it has a huge, globe-girdling canyon, Ithaca Chasma. Part of the canyon stretches over three-quarters of the satellite's surface. Ithaca Chasma is about 2,500 kilometers (1,550 miles) long. It has an average width of about 100 kilometers (62 miles) and a depth of 3 to 5 kilometers (1.8 to 3.1 miles).

Tethys also has a huge impact crater named Odysseus, 4400 kilometers (244 miles) in diameter, or more than one-third its diameter.

Dione is slightly larger than Tethys, 1,120 kilometers (696 miles) and is more than half composed of water ice. It has bright, wispy markings resembling thin veils covering its features.

Rhea, the largest of the inner satellites, is 1,530 kilometers (951 miles) in diameter. It is composed mainly of water ice, causing its reflective surface to present an almost uniform white appearance.

Iapetus is the outermost of Saturn's icy satellites. Its appearance is unique because it has one dark and one bright hemisphere. The origin of the black coating of its dark face is unknown. Iapetus has a diameter of 1,460 kilometers (907 miles).

Other notable moons of Saturn are Mimas, Enceladus, Hyperion, and Phoebe.

Mimas is small, only 329 kilometers (244 miles) in diameter. It has a huge impact crater, Herschel, nearly one-third of its diameter. The crater is about 130 kilometers (81 miles) wide and its icy peak rises almost 10 kilometers (6.2 miles) above the floor.

Mimas is believed to be composed mainly of water and ice and to contain between 20 to 50% rock.

Enceladus is remarkable in that its surface shows signs of extensive and recent geological activity. There may be active water volcanism. The surface is extremely bright, reflecting more than 90% of incident sunlight. This suggests that its surface is composed of extremely pure ice without dust or rocks to contaminate it. Enceladus has a diameter of 500 kilometers (310 miles).

Hyperion orbits between Iapetus and Titan. It is irregular in shape, measuring about 400 by 250 by 200 kilometers (248 by 155 by 124 miles). It may be a remnant of a much larger object which was shattered by impact with another space body. It appears that Hyperion is composed primarily of water ice.

Hyperion orbits Saturn in a random-like motion ("chaotic tumbling").

Phoebe is Saturn's outermost satellite. It travels in a retrograde orbit at a distance of over 10 million kilometers (6.2 million miles) away from the planet. It is the darkest moon of Saturn and is the planet's only known satellite that does not keep the same face always turned to Saturn. It has been speculated that it is an asteroid that was captured by the planet. Phoebe rotates in about nine hours and orbits Saturn in 406 days. It has a diameter of 200 kilometers (124 miles).

Pan was discovered in 1990 from *Voyager 2* photos taken in 1981. An official name, Pan, is to be approved by the International Astronomical Union. The satellite is estimated to be about 20 kilometers (12.43 miles) in diameter, which makes it the planet's smallest known moon. It orbits within the Encke Gap, a 325-kilometer (202-mile) division in Saturn's A ring. It was identified by Johann Franz Encke (1791–1865) in 1837.

The remaining eight moons range from 25 to 190 kilometers (15–120 miles) in diameter. They are all non-spherical in shape. Their names are Atlas, Prometheus, Pandora, Epimetheus, Janus, Telesto, Calypso, and Helene.

NASA's planned Cassini Mission to Saturn in October 1997 will shed more light on the planet's mysteries.

Saturn is the last of the planets visible to the naked eye. Saturn is never an object of overwhelming brilliance, but it looks like a bright star. The rings can be seen with a small telescope.

Uranus

Uranus, the first planet discovered in modern times by Sir William Herschel in 1781, is the seventh planet from the sun, twice as far out as Saturn. Its mean distance from the sun is 2,869 million kilometers (1,783 million miles). Uranus's equatorial diameter is 51,810 kilometers (32,200 miles). The axis of Uranus is tilted at 97 degrees, so it goes around the sun nearly lying on its side.

Due to Uranus's unusual inclination, the polar regions receive more sunlight during a Uranus year of 84 Earth years. Scientists had thought that the temperature of its poles would be warmer than that at its equator, but *Voyager 2* discovered that the equatorial temperatures were similar to the temperatures at the poles, $-209°C$ ($-344°F$), implying that some redistribution of heat toward the equatorial region must occur within the atmosphere. The wind patterns are much like Saturn's, flowing parallel to the equator in the direction of the planet's rotation.

Ninety-eight percent of the upper atmosphere is composed of hydrogen and helium; the remaining two percent is methane. Scientists speculate that the bulk of the lower atmosphere is composed of water (perhaps as much as 50%), methane, and ammonia. Methane is responsible for Uranus's blue-green color because it selectively absorbs red sunlight and condenses to form clouds of ice crystals in the cooler, higher regions of Uranus's atmosphere.

It was also discovered that the planet's magnetic field was 60 degrees tilted from the planet's axis of rotation and offset from the planet's center by one-third of Uranus's radius. It may be generated at a depth where water is under sufficient pressure to be electrically conductive.

The Uranian Rings

Voyager 2 also expanded the body of information pertaining to the rings and moons of Uranus. *Voyager's* cameras obtained the first images of 9 previously known narrow rings and discovered at least 2 new rings, one narrow and one broadly diffused, bringing the total known rings to 11. It was found that a highly structured distribution of fine dust exists throughout the ring system.

The outermost (epsilon) ring contains nothing smaller than fist-sized particles. It is flanked by two small moons discovered interior to the orbit of the Uranian moon Miranda. The moons exert a shepherding influence on the epsilon ring and on the outer edges of the gamma and delta rings.

All of the rings lie within one planetary radius[1] of Uranus's cloud tops. Most of Uranus's rings are narrow, ranging in width from 1 to 93 kilometers (0.6 to 58 miles) and are only a few kilometers thick. The Uranian rings are colorless and extremely dark. The dark material may be either irradiated methane ice or organic-rich minerals mixed with water-impregnated, silicon-based compounds. There is evidence that incomplete rings, or "ring arcs," exist at Uranus.

The Uranian Moons

There are 15 known moons of Uranus. In order of decreasing distance from the planet, the moons are Oberon, Titania, Umbriel, Ariel, Miranda, Puck, Belinda, Cressida, Portia, Rosalind, Desdemona, Juliet, Bianca, Ophelia, and Cordelia. Nine of the new moons range in size from 26 to 108 kilometers (16–67 miles) in diameter and, being closer to the planet, have faster periods of revolution (8–15 hours) than their more distant relatives.

Oberon and Titania

The two largest moons, Oberon, 1,516 kilometers (942 miles) in diameter, and Titania, 1,580 kilometers (982 miles) in diameter, are less than half the diameter of Earth's moon. Titania, the reddest of Uranus's moons, may have endured global tectonics as evidenced by complex valleys and fault lines etched into its surface. Smooth sections indicate that volcanic resurfacing has taken place.

Umbriel and Ariel

Umbriel and Ariel are roughly three-fourths the size of Oberon and Titania. Umbriel is the darkest of the large moons with huge craters peppering its surface. Umbriel has a paucity of what are known as bright ray craters, which are formed on an older darker surface when bright submerged ice is excavated and sprayed by meteoroid impacts.

In contrast, the surface of Ariel, the brightest of the Uranian moons, is relatively free of pockmarks due to volcanism which periodically erases the damage done by foreign projectiles. However, there are several extremely deep cuts on Ariel's surface.

Miranda

The smallest of Uranus's large moons, Miranda, 472 kilometers (293 miles) in diameter, has been described as "the most bizarre body in the solar system," with the most geologically complex surface. Miranda's remarkable terrain consists of rolling, heavily cratered plains (the oldest known in the Uranian system) adjoined by three huge, 200- to 300-kilometer (120–180 mile) oval-to-trapezoidal regions known as coronae, which are characterized by networks of concentric canyons.

Puck

Puck was the first new moon discovered by *Voyager,* and is 154 kilometers (96 miles) in diameter and makes a trip around Uranus every 18 hours. Puck is shaped somewhat like a potato with a huge impact crater marring roughly one-fourth of its surface.

---

1. The equatorial radius of Uranus is 25,560 kilometers (15,880 miles) at a pressure of 1 bar.

Uranus can—on rare occasions—become bright enough to be seen with the naked eye, if one knows exactly where to look; normally, a good set of field glasses or a small portable telescope is required.

Neptune

Little was known about Neptune until August 1989, when NASA's *Voyager 2* became the first spacecraft to observe the planet. Passing about 4,950 kilometers (3,000 miles) above Neptune's north pole, *Voyager 2* made its closest approach to any planet since leaving Earth 12 years prior. The spacecraft passed about 40,000 kilometers (25,000 miles) from Neptune's largest moon, Triton, the last solid body that *Voyager 2* will have studied.

Nearly 4.5 billion kilometers (3 billion miles) from the sun, Neptune orbits the sun once in 165 years, and therefore has made not quite a full circle around the sun since it was discovered.[1]

With an equatorial diameter of 49,528 kilometers (30,775 miles), Neptune is the smallest of our solar system's four gas giants.[2] Even so, its volume could hold nearly 60 Earths. Neptune is also denser than the other gas giants (Jupiter, Saturn, and Uranus), and about 64% heavier than if it were composed entirely of water.

Neptune has a blue color as a result of methane in its atmosphere. Methane preferentially absorbs the longer wavelengths of sunlight (those near the red end of the spectrum). What are left to be reflected are colors at the blue end of the spectrum. The atmosphere of Neptune is mainly composed of hydrogen, with helium and traces of methane and ammonia.

Neptune is a dynamic planet even though it receives only 3% as much sunlight as Jupiter does. *Voyager 2* discovered several large, dark spots that were prominent features on the planet. The largest spot was about the size of the Earth and was designated the "Great Dark Spot" by its discoverers. It appeared to be an anticyclone similar to Jupiter's Great Red Spot. While Neptune's Great Dark Spot is comparable in size, relative to the planet, and at the same latitude (22°S latitude) as Jupiter's Great Red Spot, it was far more variable in size and shape than its Jovian counterpart. Bright, wispy "cirrus-type" clouds overlaid the Great Dark Spot at its southern and northeastern boundaries.

At about 42° south, a bright, irregularly shaped, eastward-moving cloud circles much faster than did the Great Dark Spot, "scooting" around Neptune in about 16 hours. This "scooter" may have been a cloud plume rising between cloud decks.

Another spot, designated "D2," was located far to the south of the Great Dark Spot at 55°S latitude. It is almond-shaped, with a bright central core, and moves eastward around the planet in about 16 hours.

In 1995, images taken by the Hubble Space Telescope showed that the Great Dark Spot has vanished. The great storm center has either dissipated or is obscured by other atmospheric conditions.

The atmosphere above Neptune's clouds is hotter near the equator, cooler in the mid-latitudes, and warm again at the south pole. Temperatures in the stratosphere were measured to be 750°K (900°F), while at the 100 millibar pressure level, they were measured to be 55°K (−360°F).

Long, bright clouds, reminiscent of cirrus clouds on Earth, were seen high in Neptune's atmosphere. They appear to form above most of the methane, and consequently are not blue.

At northern low latitudes (27°N), *Voyager* captured images of cloud streaks casting their shadows on cloud decks estimated to be about 50 to 100 kilometers (30–60 miles) below. The widths of these cloud streaks range from 50 to 200 kilometers (30–125 miles). Cloud streaks were also seen in the southern polar regions (71°S) where the cloud heights were about 50 kilometers (30 miles).

Most of the winds on Neptune blow in a westward direction, which is retrograde, or opposite to the rotation of the planet. Near the Great Dark Spot, there are retrograde winds blowing up to 1,500 miles an hour—the strongest winds measured on any planet.

The Magnetic Field

Neptune's magnetic field is tilted 47 degrees from the planet's rotation axis, and is offset at least 0.55 radii (about 13,500 kilometers or 8,500 miles) from the physical center. The dynamo electric currents produced within the planet, therefore, must be relatively closer to the surface than for Earth, Jupiter, or Saturn. Because of its unusual orientation, and the tilt of the planet's rotation axis, Neptune's magnetic field goes through dramatic changes as the planet rotates in the solar wind.

Voyager's planetary radio astronomy instrument measured the periodic radio waves generated by the magnetic field and determined that the rotation rate of the interior of Neptune is 16 hours 7 minutes.

Voyager also detected auroras, similar to the northern and southern lights on Earth, in Neptune's atmosphere. Unlike those on Earth, due to Neptune's complex magnetic field, the auroras are extremely complicated processes that occur over wide regions of the planet, not just near the planet's magnetic poles.

Neptune's Moons

Triton

The largest of Neptune's eight known satellites, Triton is different from all other icy moons that *Voyager* has studied. Triton circles Neptune in a tilted, circular, retrograde orbit, completing an orbit in 5.875 days at an average distance of 330,000 kilometers (205,000 miles) above the planet's cloud tops.

Triton shows evidence of a remarkable geologic history, and *Voyager 2* images show active geyser-like eruptions spewing invisible nitrogen gas and dark dust particles 2 to 8 kilometers (1–5 miles) into space.

Triton is about three-quarters the size of Earth's moon and has a diameter of about 2,705 kilometers (1,680 miles), and a mean density of about 2.066 grams per cubic centimeter. (The density of water is 1.0 grams per cubic centimeter.) This means that Triton contains more rock in its interior than the icy satellites of Saturn and Uranus.

The relatively high density and the retrograde orbit offer strong evidence that Triton did not originate near Neptune, but is a captured object.

An extremely thin atmosphere extends as much as 800 kilometers (500 miles) above the satellite's surface. Tiny nitrogen ice particles may form thin clouds a few kilometers above the surface. Triton is very bright, reflecting 60% to 95% of the sunlight that strikes it. (By comparison, Earth's moon reflects only 11%.)

The atmospheric pressure at Triton's surface is about 14 microbars, a mere 1/70,000th the surface pressure on Earth. Temperature at the surface is about 38°K (−391°F), making it the coldest surface of any body yet visited in the solar system.

---

1. Astronomers have studied Neptune since Sept. 23, 1846, when Johann Gottfried Galle, of the Berlin Observatory, and Louis d'Arrest, an astronomy student, discovered the eighth planet on the basis of mathematical predictions by Urbain Jean Joseph Le Verrier. Similar predictions were made independently by John Couch Adams. Galileo Galilei had seen Neptune during several nights of observing Jupiter, in January 1613, but didn't realize he was seeing a new planet.
2. These four planets are about 4 to 12 times greater in diameter than Earth. They have no solid surfaces, but possess massive atmospheres that contain substantial amounts of hydrogen and helium with traces of other gases.

Nereid

Nereid was discovered in 1948 through Earth-based telescopes. Little is known about Nereid, which is slightly smaller than Proteus, having a diameter of 340 kilometers (211 miles). The satellite's surface reflects about 14% of the sunlight that strikes it. Nereid's orbit is the most eccentric in the solar system, ranging from about 1,353,600 kilometers (841,100 miles) to 9,623,700 kilometers (5,980,200 miles).

The Smaller Satellites

In addition to the previously known moons, Triton and Nereid, *Voyager 2* found six more satellites, making the total eight.

Proteus

Like all six of Neptune's recently discovered small satellites, it is one of the darkest objects in the solar system—"as dark as soot" is a good description. It reflects only 6% of the sunlight that strikes it. Proteus is an ellipsoid about 258 kilometers (415 miles) in diameter, larger than Nereid. It circles Neptune at a distance of about 92,800 kilometers (57,700 miles) above the cloud tops, and completes one orbit in 26 hours 54 minutes. Scientists say that it is about as large as a satellite can be without being pulled into a spherical shape by its own gravity.

Proteus and its tiny companions are cratered and irregularly shaped—they are not round—and show no signs of any geologic modifications. All circle the planet in the same direction as Neptune rotates, and remain close to Neptune's equatorial plane.

Larissa

This object is only about 48,800 kilometers (30,300 miles) from Neptune and circles the planet in 13 hours 18 minutes. Its diameter is 190 kilometers (120 miles).

Despina

The satellite is 27,700 kilometers (17,200 miles) from Neptune's clouds and makes one orbit every 8 hours. Its diameter is about 150 kilometers (90 miles).

Galatea

It lies 37,200 kilometers (23,100 miles) from Neptune. Its diameter is 180 kilometers (110 miles) and it completes an orbit in 10 hours 18 minutes.

Thalassa

The satellite appears to be about 80 kilometers (50 miles) in diameter. It orbits Neptune in 7 hours 30 minutes some 25,200 kilometers (15,700 miles) above the cloud tops.

Naiad

The last satellite discovered, it is about 60 kilometers (37 miles) in diameter and orbits Neptune about 23,200 kilometers (14,400 miles) above the clouds in 7 hours 6 minutes.

Neptune's Rings

Voyager found four rings and evidence of ring *arcs* or incomplete rings. The "Main Ring" orbits Neptune at about 38,100 kilometers (23,700 miles) above the cloud tops. The "Inner Ring" is about 28,400 kilometers (17,700 miles) from Neptune's cloud tops. An "Inside Diffuse Ring"—a complete ring—is located about 17,100 kilometers (10,600 miles) from the planet's cloud tops. Some scientists suspect that this ring may extend all the way down to Neptune's cloud tops. An area called "the Plateau" is a broad, diffuse sheet of fine material just outside the so-called "Inner Ring." The fine material is approximately the size of smoke particles. All other rings contain a greater proportion of larger material.

Pluto

Pluto, the outermost and smallest planet in the solar system, is the only planet not visited by an exploring spacecraft. So little is known about it, that it is difficult to classify. Its distance is so great that the Hubble Space Telescope cannot reveal its surface features. Appropriately named for the Roman god of the underworld, it must be frozen, dark, and dead. Pluto's mean distance from the sun is 5,900 million kilometers (3,666 million miles).

In 1978, light-curve studies gave evidence of a moon revolving around Pluto within the same period as Pluto's rotation. Therefore, it stays over the same point on Pluto's surface. In addition, it keeps the same face toward the planet. The satellite was later named Charon and is estimated to be about 789 miles (1,270 kilometers) in diameter. Recent estimates indicate Pluto's diameter is about 1,441.6 miles (2,220 kilometers), making the pair more like a double planet than any other in the solar system. Previously, the Earth-moon system held this distinction. The density of Pluto is slightly greater than that of water.

There is evidence that Pluto has an atmosphere containing methane and polar ice caps that increase and decrease in size with the planet's seasons. It is not known to have water. The Hubble Space Telescope's faint-object camera revealed light and dark regions on Pluto indicating an ice cap at the planet's north pole. It is not known if there is an ice cap at Pluto's south pole.

Pluto was predicted by calculation when Percival Lowell (1855–1916) noticed irregularities in the orbits of Uranus and Neptune. Clyde Tombaugh (1906–) discovered the planet in 1930, precisely where Lowell predicted it would be. The name Pluto was chosen because the first two letters represent the initials of Percival Lowell.

Pluto has the most eccentric orbit in the solar system, bringing it at times closer to the sun than Neptune. Pluto approached the perihelion of its orbit on Sept. 5, 1989, and for the rest of this century will be closer to the sun than Neptune. Even then, it can be seen only with a large telescope.

The Asteroids

Between the orbits of Mars and Jupiter are an estimated 30,000 pieces of rocky debris, known collectively as the asteroids, or planetoids. The first and, incidentally, the largest (Ceres) was discovered during the New Year's night of 1801 by the Italian astronomer Father Piazzi (1746–1826), and its orbit was calculated by the German mathematician Karl Friedrich Gauss (1777–1855). Gauss invented a new method of calculating orbits on that occasion. A German amateur astronomer, the physician Olbers (1748–1840), discovered the second asteroid, Pallas. The number now known, catalogued, and named is over 6,000 and could reach 10,000 by the end of the 20th century. A few asteroids do not move in orbits beyond the orbit of Mars, but in orbits which cross the orbit of Mars. The first of them was named Eros because of this peculiar orbit. It had become the rule to bestow female names on the asteroids, but when it was found that Eros crossed the orbit of a major planet, it received a male name. Since then around two dozen orbit-crossers have been discovered, and they are often referred to as the "male asteroids." A few of them—Albert, Adonis, Apollo, Amor, and Icarus—cross the orbit of the Earth, and two of them may come closer than our moon; but the crossing is like a bridge crossing a highway, not like two highways intersecting. Hence there is very little danger of collision from these bodies. They are all small, 3 to 5 miles in diameter,

The First Ten Minor Planets (Asteroids)

Name	Year of discovery	Mean distance from sun (millions of miles)	Orbital period (years)	Diameter (miles)	Magnitude
1. Ceres	1801	257.0	4.60	485	7.4
2. Pallas	1802	257.4	4.61	304	8.0
3. Juno	1804	247.8	4.36	118	8.7
4. Vesta	1807	219.3	3.63	243	6.5
5. Astraea	1845	239.3	4.14	50	9.9
6. Hebe	1847	225.2	3.78	121	8.5
7. Iris	1847	221.4	3.68	121	8.4
8. Flora	1847	204.4	3.27	56	8.9
9. Metis	1848	221.7	3.69	78	8.9
10. Hygeia	1849	222.6	5.59	40(?)	9.5

and therefore very difficult objects to identify, even when quite close. Some scientists believe the asteroids represent the remains of an exploded planet.

On Oct. 29, 1991, the *Galileo* spacecraft took a historic photograph of asteroid 951 Gaspra from a distance of 10,000 miles (16,200 kilometers) away. It was the first close-up photo ever taken of an asteroid in space.

Gaspra is an irregular, potato-shaped object about 12.5 miles (20 kilometers) by 7.5 miles (12 kilometers) by 7 miles (11 kilometers) in size. Its surface is covered with a layer of loose rubble and its terrain is covered with several dozen small craters.

Close-up photos of Asteroid 243 Ida taken by the *Galileo* spacecraft on Aug. 28, 1993, revealed that Ida had a tiny egg-shaped moon measuring 0.9 miles by 0.7 miles (1.6 by 1.2 kilometers). The moon has been named Dactyl.

NASA's *Near-Earth Asteroid Rendezvous* spacecraft was launched on Feb.17, 1996. It flew within 750 miles (282 kilometers) of minor planet 253 Mathilde on June 27, 1997, and took spectacular images of the dark, crater-battered world. The asteroid's mean diameter was found to be 33 miles (52 kilometers). The *NEAR* spacecraft discovered that the carbon-rich Mathilde is one of the darkest objects in the solar system, only reflecting about 3% of the sun's light, making it twice as dark as a chunk of charcoal. The asteroid is almost completely cratered, and at least five of its craters just on the lighted side are larger than 12 miles (20 kilometers). The spacecraft will reach asteroid 433 Eros in February 1999 and orbit it for almost one year.

Comets

Comets, according to the noted astronomer, Fred L. Whipple (1906–), are enormous "snowballs" of frozen gases (mostly carbon dioxide, methane, and water vapor) and contain very little solid material. The whole behavior of comets can then be explained as the behavior of frozen gas being heated by the sun. When the comet Kohoutek made its first appearance to man in 1973, its behavior seemed to confirm this theory and later, the international study by five spacecraft that encountered Halley's comet in March 1986 confirmed Whipple's idea of the make-up of comets.

Since comets appear in the sky without any warning, people in classical times and especially during the Middle Ages believed that they had a special meaning, which, of course, was bad. Since a natural catastrophe of some sort of a military conflict occurs every year, it was quite simple to blame the comet that happened to be visible. But even in the past, there were some people who used logical reasoning. When, in Roman times, a comet was blamed for the loss of a battle and hence was called a "bad omen," a Roman writer observed that the victors in the battle probably did not think so.

Up until the middle of the 16th century, comets were believed to be phenomena of the upper atmosphere; they were usually "explained" as "burning vapors" which had risen from "distant swamps." That nobody had ever actually seen burning vapors rise from a swamp did not matter.

But a large comet which appeared in 1577 was carefully observed by Tycho Brahe (1546–1601), a Danish astronomer who is often, and with the best of reasons, called "eccentric," but who insisted on precise measurements for everything. But it was Tycho Brahe's accumulation of literally thousands of precise measurements which later enabled his younger collaborator, Johannes Kepler (1571–1630), to discover the laws of planetary motion. Measuring the motion of the comet of 1577, Tycho Brahe could show that it had been far beyond the atmosphere, even though he could not give figures for the distance. Tycho Brahe's work proved that comets were astronomical and not meteorological phenomena.

In 1682, the second Astronomer Royal of Great Britain, Dr. Edmond Halley (1656–1742), checked the orbit of a bright comet that was in the sky then and compared it with earlier comet orbits which were known in part. Halley found that the comet of 1682 was the third to move through what appeared to be the same orbit. And the three appearances were roughly 76 years apart. Halley concluded that this was the same comet, moving around the sun in a closed orbit, like the planets. He predicted that it would reappear in 1758 or 1759. Halley himself died in 1742, but a large comet appeared 16 years after his death as predicted and was immediately referred to as "Halley's comet."

Halley's comet appeared again in 1986, sparking a worldwide effort to study it up close. Five satellites in all took readings from the comet at various distances. Two Soviet craft, *Vega 1* and *Vega 2,* went in close to provide detailed pictures of the comet, including the first of the comet's core. The European Space Agency's craft, *Giotto,* entered the comet itself, coming to within 450 miles of the comet's center and successfully passing through its tail. In addition, two Japanese craft, the *Suisei* and the *Sakigake,* passed at a longer distance and analyzed the cloud and tail of the comet and the effect of solar radiation upon it.

Astronomers refer to comets as "periodic" or as "non-periodic" comets, but the latter term does not mean that these comets have no period; it merely means that their period is not known. The actual periods of comets run from 3.3 years (the shortest known) to many thousands of years. Their orbits are elliptical, like those of the planets, but they are very eccentric, long and narrow ellipses. Only comet Schwassmann-Wachmann has an orbit which has such a low eccentricity (for a cometary orbit) that it could be the orbit of a minor planet.

When a comet, coming from deep space, approaches the sun, it is at first indistinguishable from a minor planet. Somewhere between the orbits of Mars and Jupiter, its outline becomes fuzzy; it is said to develop a "coma" (the word used here is the Latin word *coma*, which means "hair," not the phonetically identical Greek word which means "deep sleep"). Then, near the orbit of Mars, the comet develops its tail, which at first trails behind. This grows steadily as the comet comes closer and closer to the sun. As it rounds the sun (as first noticed by Girolamo Fracastoro, 1483–1553) the tail always points away from the sun so that the comet, when moving away from the sun, points its tail ahead like the landing lights of an airplane.

The reason for this behavior is that the tail is pushed in these directions by the radiation pressure of the sun. It sometimes happens that a comet loses its tail at perihelion; it then grows another one. Although the tail is clearly visible against the black of the sky, it is very tenuous. It has been said that if the tail of Halley's comet could be compressed to the density of iron, it would fit into a small suitcase.

Although very low in mass, comets are among the largest members of the solar system. The nucleus of a comet may be up to 10,000 miles in diameter; its coma between 10,000 and 50,000 miles in diameter; and its tail as long as 28 million miles.

Comet Shoemaker-Levy 9 broke up into 21 fragments in July 1992 and crashed into the surface of Jupiter, July 16–22, 1994, in the most violent event in the recorded history of the solar system.

In 1951, Dutch astronomer Gerard Kuiper first suggested the existence of a disk-shaped swarm of short-period comets that begin beyond the orbit of Neptune and extend past Pluto. In 1995, the Hubble Space Telescope detected the long-sought Kuiper Belt and an estimated 200 million comets were discovered orbiting it.

Meteors and Meteorites

The term *meteor* for what is usually called a *shooting star* bears an unfortunate resemblance to the term *meteorology,* the science of weather and weather forecasting. This resemblance is due to an ancient misunderstanding that wrongly considered meteors an atmospheric phenomenon. Actually, the streak of light in the sky that scientists call a meteor is essentially an astronomical phenomenon: the entry of a small piece of cosmic matter into our atmosphere.

The distinction between *meteors* and *fireballs* (formerly also called *bolides*) is merely one of convenience; a fireball is an unusually bright meteor. Incidentally, it also means that a fireball is larger than a faint meteor.

Bodies that enter our atmosphere become visible when they are about 60 miles above the ground. The fact that they grow hot enough to emit light is not due to the "friction" of the atmosphere, as one can often read. The phenomenon responsible for the heating is one of compression. Unconfined air cannot move faster than the speed of sound. Since the entering meteorite moves with 30 to 60 times the speed of sound, the air simply cannot get out of the way. Therefore, it is compressed like the air in the cylinder of a diesel engine and is heated by compression. This heat—or part of it—is transferred to the moving body. The details of this process are now fairly well understood as a result of re-entry tests with ballistic-missile nose cones.

The average weight of a body producing a faint *shooting star* is only a small fraction of an ounce. Even a bright fireball may not weigh more than 2 or 3 pounds. Naturally, the smaller bodies are worn to dust by the passage through the atmosphere; only rather large ones reach the ground. Those that are found are called meteorites. (The *meteor,* to repeat, is the term for the light streak in the sky.) About 1,000 meteorites fall to the Earth each year.

The largest meteorite known is still imbedded in the ground near Grootfontein in southwest Africa and is estimated to weigh 70 tons. The second largest known is the 34-ton Anighito (on exhibit in the Hayden Planetarium, New York), which was found by Admiral Peary in 1892 at Cape York in Greenland. The largest meteorite found in the United States is the Willamette meteorite (found in Oregon, weight ca. 15 tons), but large portions of this meteorite weathered away before it was found. Its weight as it struck the ground may have been 20 tons.

All these are iron meteorites (an iron meteorite normally contains about 7% nickel), which form one class of meteorites. The other class consists of the stony meteorites, and between them there are the so-called "stony irons." The so-called "tektites" consist of glass similar to our volcanic glass obsidian, and because of the similarity, there is doubt in a number of cases whether the glass is of terrestrial or of extraterrestrial origin.

Though no meteorite larger than the Grootfontein is actually known, we do know that the Earth has, on occasion, been struck by much larger bodies. Evidence for such hits are the meteorite craters, of which an especially good example is located near the Cañon Diablo in Arizona. Another meteor crater in the United States is a rather old crater near Odessa, Texas. A large number of others are known, especially in eastern Canada; and for many "probables," meteoric origin has now been proved.

The 13th known lunar meteorite was found in December 1993 by a team from the Antarctic Search for Meteorites project. It is approximately 2 inches long and weighs 0.75 of an ounce.

Some scientists theorize that the mass extermination of dinosaurs from the face of the Earth 65 million years ago was due to a large meteor that struck our planet at that time.

Meteor showers are caused by multitudes of very small bodies travelling in swarms. The Earth travels in its orbit through these swarms like a car driving through falling snow. The point from which the meteors seem to emanate is called the *radiant* and is named for the constellation in that area. The Perseid meteor shower in August is the most spectacular of the year, boasting, at peak, roughly 60 meteors per hour under good atmospheric conditions. The presence of a bright moon diminishes the number of visible meteors.

The Constellations

Constellations are groupings of stars that form easily recognized and remembered patterns, such as Orion and the Big Dipper. The Big Dipper is actually as asterism, not a constellation, because it is only part of the constellation Ursa Major (the Big Bear). Actually, the stars in the majority of all constellations do not "belong together." Usually they are at greatly varying distances from the Earth and just happen to lie more or less in the same line of sight as seen from our solar system. But in a few cases, the stars of a constellation are actually associated; most of the bright stars of the Big Dipper travel together and form what astronomers call an *open cluster.*

If you observe a planet, say Mars, for one complete revolution, you will see that it passes successively through 12 constellations. All planets (except Pluto at certain times) can be observed only in these 12 constellations, which form the so-called zodiac, and the sun also moves through the zodiacal signs, though the sun's apparent movement is actually caused by the movement of the Earth.

Although the constellations are due mainly to the optical accident of line of sight and have no real significance, astronomers have retained them as reference

The 88 Recognized Constellations

In astronomical works, the Latin names of the constellations are used. The letter N or S following the Latin name indicates whether the constellation is located to the north or south of the Zodiac. The letter Z indicates that the constellation is within the Zodiac.

Latin name	Letter	English version	Latin name	Letter	English version	Latin name	Letter	English version
Andromeda	N	Andromeda	Delphinus	N	Dolphin	Pegasus	N	Pegasus
Antlia	S	Airpump	Dorado	S	Swordfish (Gold-fish)	Perseus	N	Perseus
Apus	S	Bird of Paradise				Phoenix	S	Phoenix
Aquarius	Z	Water Bearer	Draco	N	Dragon	Pictor	S	Painter (or his Easel)
Aquila	N	Eagle	Equuleus	N	Filly			
Ara	S	Altar	Eridanus	S	Eridanus (river)	Pisces	Z	Fishes
Aries	Z	Ram	Fornax	S	Furnace	Piscis Austrinus	S	Southern Fish
Auriga	N	Charioteer	Gemini	Z	Twins	Puppis	S	Poop (of Argo)[1]
Boötes	N	Herdsmen	Grus	S	Crane	Pyxis	S	Mariner's Com-pass
Caelum	S	Sculptor's Tool	Hercules	N	Hercules			
Camelopardalis	N	Giraffe	Horologium	S	Clock	Reticulum	S	Net
Cancer	Z	Crab	Hydra	N	Sea Serpent	Sagitta	N	Arrow
Canes Venatici	N	Hunting Dogs	Hydrus	S	Water Snake	Sagittarius	Z	Archer
Canis Major	S	Great Dog	Indus	S	Indian	Scorpius	Z	Scorpion
Canis Minor	S	Little Dog	Lacerta	N	Lizard	Sculptor	S	Sculptor
Capricornus	Z	Goat (or Sea-Goat)	Leo	Z	Lion	Scutum	N	Shield
			Leo Minor	N	Little Lion	Serpens	N	Serpent
Carina	S	Keel (of Argo)[1]	Lepus	S	Hare	Sextans	S	Sextant
Cassiopeia	N	Cassiopeia	Libra	Z	Scales	Taurus	Z	Bull
Centaurus	S	Centaur	Lupus	S	Wolf	Telescopium	S	Telescope
Cepheus	N	Cepheus	Lynx	N	Lynx	Triangulum	N	Triangle
Cetus	S	Whale	Lyra	N	Lyre (Harp)	Triangulum Aus-trale	S	Southern Triangle
Chameleon	S	Chameleon	Mensa	S	Table (mountain)			
Circinus	S	Compasses	Microscopium	S	Microscope	Tucana	S	Toucan
Columba	S	Dove	Monoceros	S	Unicorn	Ursa Major	N	Big Dipper
Coma Berenices	N	Berenice's Hair	Musca	S	Southern Fly	Ursa Minor	N	Little Dipper
Corona Australis	S	Southern Crown	Norma	S	Rule (straight-edge)	Vela	S	Sail (of Argo)[1]
Corona Borealis	N	Northern Crown				Virgo	Z	Virgin
Corvus	S	Crow (Raven)	Octans	S	Octant	Volans	S	Flying Fish
Crater	S	Cup	Ophiuchus	N	Serpent-Bearer	Vulpecula	N	Fox
Crux	S	Southern Cross	Orion	S	Orion			
Cygnus	N	Swan	Pavo	S	Peacock			

1. The original constellation Argo Navis (the Ship Argo) has been divided into Carina, Puppis, and Vela. Normally the brightest star in each constellation is designated by alpha, the first letter of the Greek alphabet, the second brightest by beta, the second letter of the Greek alphabet, and so forth. But the Greek letters run through Carina, Puppis, and Vela as if it were still one constellation.

areas. It is much easier to speak of a star in Orion than to give its geometrical position in the sky. During the Astronomical Congress of 1928, it was decided to recognize 88 constellations. A description of their agreed-upon boundaries was published at Cambridge, England, in 1930, under the title *Atlas Céleste.*

The Auroras

The "northern lights" *(Aurora borealis)* as well as the "southern lights" *(Aurora australis)* are upper-atmosphere phenomena of astronomical origin. The auroras center around the magnetic (not the geographical) poles of the Earth, which explains why in the Western Hemisphere, they have been seen as far to the south as New Orleans and Florida, while the equivalent latitude in the Eastern Hemisphere never sees an aurora. The northern magnetic pole happens to be in the Western Hemisphere.

The lower limit of an aurora is at about 50 miles. Upper limits have been estimated to be as high as 400 miles. Since about 1880, a connection between the auroras on Earth and sun spots has been suspected and has gradually come to be accepted. It was said that the sun spots probably eject "particles" (later the word *electrons* was substituted) which on striking the Earth's atmosphere, cause the auroras. But this explanation suffered from certain difficulties. Sometimes a very large sun spot group on the sun, with individual spots bigger than the Earth itself, would not cause an aurora. Moreover, even if a sun spot caused an aurora, the time that passed

between the appearance of the one and the occurrence of the other was highly unpredictable.

This problem of the time lag is, in all probability, solved by the discovery of the Van Allen layer by artificial satellite *Explorer I.* The Van Allen layer[1] is a double layer of charged sub-atomic particles around the Earth. The inner layer, with its center some 1,500 miles from the ground, reaches from about 40°N to about 40°S and does not touch the atmosphere. The outer layer, much larger and with its center several thousand miles from the ground, does touch the atmosphere in the vicinity of the magnetic poles.

It seems probable that the "leakage" of electrons from the outer Van Allen layer causes the auroras. A new burst of electrons from the sun seems to be caught in the outer layer first. Under the assumption that all electrons are first caught in the outer layer, the time lag can be understood. There has to be an "overflow" from the outer layer to produce an aurora.

The Atmosphere

Though reasonably transparent to visible light, the atmosphere may absorb as much as 60% of the visible and near-visible light. It is opaque to most other wavelengths, except certain fairly short radio waves. In addition to absorbing much light, our atmosphere bends

1. Named after the American physicist, James Alfred Van Allen (1914–) who discovered the broad bands of intense radiation surrounding the Earth in 1958.

light rays entering at a slant (for a given observer) so that the true position of a star close to the horizon is not what it seems to be. One effect is that we see the sun above the horizon before it actually is. And the unsteady movement of the atmosphere causes the "twinkling" of the stars, which may be romantic, but is a nuisance when it comes to observing.

The composition of our atmosphere near the ground is 78% nitrogen and 21% oxygen, the remaining 1% consisting of other gases, most of it argon. The composition stays the same to an altitude of at least 70 miles (except that higher up two impurities, carbon dioxide and water vapor, are missing), but the pressure drops very fast. At 18,000 feet, half of the total mass of the atmosphere is below, and at 100,000 feet, 99% of the mass of the atmosphere is below. The upper limit of the atmosphere is usually given as 120 miles; no definitive figure is possible, since there is no boundary line between the incredibly attenuated gases 120 miles up and space.

Some Giant Telescopes

• The world's largest fixed-dish radio telescope (1963) is located near Arecibo, Puerto Rico. It is 1,000 ft. (35 m) in diameter and spans some 25 acres.
• The Very Large Array (VLA) telescope (1980) near Socorro, N.M. is the world's most powerful radio telescope. It is Y-shaped and has 27 separate mobile antennas (each 82 ft. in diameter) and is spread out over about a 25-mile area.
• The world's largest fully-steerable radio telescope (1972) located at Effelsberg, Germany, has 100-meter (328 ft.) antenna.
• The 200-inch (5-meter) Hale telescope at Mount Palomar, Calif. (1948), is the second largest reflector in use.
• The 236-inch Special Astrophysical Observatory (1976) at Zelenchukskaya, on the northern slopes of the Caucasus Mountains in the Russian Federation, is the world's largest reflector telescope in use. However, problems with it make it less useful than the 200-inch Hale.
• The W.M. Keck Telescope (1991) at Mauna Kea, Hawaii, is the world's most powerful reflector telescope. It has a primary mirror composed of 36 hexagonal segments, each 1.8 meters in size. The Keck Telescope has a light gathering power four times greater than the 200-inch Hale.
• The 40-inch (1.01 meter) telescope at Yerkes Observatory (1897) at Williams Bay, Wisc., is the world's largest refracting telescope.

Hubble Space Telescope

The $2 billion Edwin P. Hubble Space Telescope (HST) is the most complex and sensitive space observatory ever constructed. Over three times larger and heavier than any unmanned satellite launched before by NASA, it was placed into orbit by the space shuttle *Discovery* on April 25, 1990. It has a primary mirror of 94 inches (2.4 m) in diameter. HST is 43.3 ft. (13 m) long and 14 ft. (4 m) wide, about the size of a bus or truck. Standing upright, it looks like a five-story building. Hubble weighs 25,500 pounds (11,000 kg) and orbits 335 nautical miles (620 km) above the Earth.

Since being lifted into orbit, HST has become the principal tool for exploring the universe through this decade and the next. Its light gathering power is so sensitive that it can detect the light from a typical two-battery flashlight from a quarter of a million miles away—the distance from the Earth to the moon.

Hubble is able to peer far out in space and back in time, producing imagery of unprecedented clarity of galaxies, star systems, and some of the universe's more intriguing objects: quasars, pulsars, and exploding galaxies. The space telescope can view galaxies and quasars billions of light years away, thus showing us the universe as it was early in its lifetime and revealing how matter has evolved over the eons. It has also taught us more about the large structure of the universe and provided clues as to whether the universe will continue to expand.

Astronomers discovered in June 1990 that there was a spherical aberration in one of the telescope's mirrors. In 1991, two of the craft's six gyroscopes failed, and a third failed on Nov. 18, 1993, causing additional problems. NASA successfully repaired the space telescope during the Dec. 2–13, 1993, mission of the *Endeavour*.

Crew members of the space shuttle *Discovery* made fresh repairs to the telescope during an upgrade mission in February 1997, and installed two powerful new scientific instruments—the Near Infrared Camera (NICMOS) and Multi-Object Spectrometer—giving HST still sharper and more distant views of the universe.

The Near Infrared Camera can see the universe at near infrared wavelengths more sensitively than any other existing or planned telescope. Developed at the University of Arizona, NICMOS is both a camera and a spectrometer.

Hubble's new Space Telescope Imagery Spectrograph (STIS) is sensitive to light in ultraviolet wavelengths and employs two-dimensional detectors that allow the instrument to gather 30 times more spectral data than the first-generation Hubble spectrographs. STIS is considered to be the most complex scientific instrument built for space science.

In June 1997, an international team of astronomers discovered the most distant galaxy found in the universe to date, by combining the unique sharpness of the images from the orbiting Hubble with the light-collecting power of the W.M. Keck Telescopes, with an added boost from a gravitational lens in space.

The results show that the young galaxy is as far as 13 billion light-years from us, based on an estimated age of the universe as approximately 14 billion years old. This would place the galaxy far back in time during the "formative" years after the birth of the universe in the Big Bang.

Although the Hubble Space Telescope's planned mission is scheduled to end in 2005, some NASA officials would like to extend its life for several more years until it can be replaced. Astronomers are debating what will be needed to replace Hubble when it is deactivated. □

Phenomena, 1998

Configurations of Sun, Moon, and Planets

NOTE: The hour listings are in Universal Time. For conversion to United States time zones, *see* Conversion of Universal Time to Civil Time.

JANUARY

d	h	
1	03	Mars 4° S of moon
1	23	Jupiter 3° S of moon
3	09	Moon at perigee
4	21	Earth at perihelion
5	12	Saturn 0°2 N of moon (occn.)
5	14	FIRST QUARTER
6	15	Mercury greatest elong. W (23°)
9	13	Aldebaran 0°4 S of moon (occn.)
9	17	Venus 4° N of Neptune
12	17	FULL MOON
17	11	Venus in inferior conjunction
18	21	Moon at apogee
19	23	Neptune in conjunction with sun
20	20	LAST QUARTER
21	01	Mars 0°2 S of Jupiter
26	17	Mercury 8° S of Venus
27	00	Venus 3° N of moon
27	01	Mercury 5° S of moon
28	06	NEW MOON
28	20	Uranus in conjunction with sun
29	12	Juno stationary
29	17	Jupiter 2° S of moon
30	01	Mars 1°7 S of moon
30	14	Moon at perigee

FEBRUARY

d	h	
1	21	Saturn 0°6 N of moon (occn.)
2	11	Mercury 2° S of Neptune
3	23	FIRST QUARTER
5	18	Aldebaran 0°2 S of moon (occn.)
5	18	Venus stationary
8	05	Mercury 1°4 S of Uranus
11	10	FULL MOON
14	12	Pallas in conjunction with sun
15	15	Moon at apogee
19	15	LAST QUARTER
20	02	Venus greatest brilliancy
22	08	Mercury in superior conjunction
23	09	Jupiter in conjunction with sun
23	17	Venus 1°6 N of moon
24	06	Neptune 3° S of moon
24	22	Uranus 3° S of moon
26	17	NEW MOON (eclipse)
27	20	Moon at perigee
27	22	Mars 0°7 N of moon (occn.)

MARCH

d	h	
1	09	Saturn 1°0 N of moon (Occn.)
2	17	Vesta 0°1 S of moon (Occn.)
5	00	Aldebaran 0°2 S of moon (Occn.)
5	09	FIRST QUARTER
7	10	Venus 4° N of Neptune

d	h	
11	15	Mercury 1°2 N of Mars
12	16	Pluto stationary
13	05	FULL MOON (penumbral eclipse)
13	20	Juno 0°9 N of moon (occn.)
15	01	Moon at apogee
19	07	Venus 3° N of Uranus
19	09	Juno at opposition
20	04	Mercury greatest elong. E (19°)
20	20	Equinox
21	08	LAST QUARTER
23	17	Neptune 3° S of moon
24	10	Uranus 3° S of moon
24	19	Venus 0°09 S of moon (occn.)
26	12	Jupiter 0°8 S of moon (occn.)
27	15	Mercury stationary
27	19	Venus greatest elong. W (47°)
28	03	NEW MOON
28	07	Moon at perigee
30	05	Mercury 4° N of moon (occn.)
30	20	Vesta 1°2 N of moon (occn.)

APRIL

d	h	
1	08	Aldebaran 0°2 S of moon (occn.)
3	20	FIRST QUARTER
6	17	Mercury in inferior conjunction
8	23	Ceres in conjunction with sun
11	02	Moon at apogee
11	22	FULL MOON
13	12	Saturn in conjunction with sun
19	02	Mercury stationary
19	20	LAST QUARTER
20	02	Neptune 3° S of moon
20	20	Uranus 3° S of moon
23	02	Venus 0°3 N of Jupiter
23	07	Jupiter 0°2 S of moon (occn.)
23	08	Venus 0°08 N of moon (occn.)
24	19	Mercury 0°9 N of moon (occn.)
25	18	Moon at perigee
26	12	NEW MOON
28	18	Aldebaran 0°4 S of moon (occn.)

MAY

d	h	
3	10	FIRST QUARTER
4	17	Mercury greatest elong. W (27°)
8	09	Moon at apogee
8	18	Juno stationary
11	14	FULL MOON
12	16	Mercury 0°8 S of Saturn
12	20	Mars in conjunction with sun
17	07	Neptune 3° S of moon
17	20	Uranus stationary
18	03	Uranus 3° S of moon
19	05	LAST QUARTER
20	23	Jupiter 0°4 N of moon (occn.)

d	h	
22	22	Venus 1°7 N of moon
23	08	Saturn 1°7 N of moon
24	00	Moon at perigee
24	11	Mercury 3° N of moon
25	20	NEW MOON
28	05	Pluto at opposition
29	02	Venus 0°3 N of Saturn

JUNE

d	h	
1	04	Regulus 1°0 N of moon (occn.)
2	02	FIRST QUARTER
5	00	Moon at apogee
9	19	Vesta in conjunction with sun
10	04	FULL MOON
10	07	Mercury in superior conjunction
13	12	Neptune 2° S of moon
14	08	Uranus 3° S of moon
17	11	Jupiter 0°8 N of moon (occn.)
17	11	LAST QUARTER
19	20	Saturn 2° N of moon
20	17	Moon at perigee
21	14	Solstice
21	14	Venus 3° N of moon
22	14	Aldebaran 0°4 S of moon (occn.)
24	04	NEW MOON
25	13	Mercury 5° N of moon
27	11	Mercury 5° S of Pollux
28	12	Regulus 0°8 N of moon

JULY

d	h	
1	19	FIRST QUARTER
2	17	Moon at apogee
3	05	Venus 4° N of Aldebaran
4	00	Earth at aphelion
9	16	FULL MOON
10	18	Neptune 2° S of moon
11	13	Uranus 3° S of moon
14	19	Jupiter 1°0 N of moon (occn.)
16	14	Moon at perigee
16	15	LAST QUARTER
17	03	Mercury greatest elong. E (27°)
17	05	Saturn 2° N of moon
18	18	Jupiter stationary
18	23	Ceres 1°1 S of moon (occn.)
19	21	Aldebaran 0°3 S of moon (occn.)
21	12	Venus 4° N of moon
22	03	Mars 5° N of moon
23	14	NEW MOON
23	20	Neptune at opposition
25	14	Mercury 2° S of moon
25	21	Regulus 0°7 N of moon (occn.)
26	13	Pallas stationary
30	12	Moon at apogee
31	12	FIRST QUARTER

AUGUST

d	h	
3	07	Uranus at opposition
5	03	Venus 0.8 S of Mars
7	01	Neptune 2° S of moon
7	19	Uranus 3° S of moon
8	02	FULL MOON (penumbral eclipse)
8	18	Venus 7° S of Pollux
11	00	Jupiter 0.9 N of moon (occn.)
11	12	Moon at perigee
11	21	Mars 6° S of Pollux
13	12	Saturn 2° N of moon
14	00	Mercury in inferior conjunction
14	20	LAST QUARTER
15	19	Ceres 0.9 S of moon (occn.)
16	03	Aldebaran 0.2 S of moon (occn.)
16	16	Saturn stationary
18	19	Pluto stationary
19	20	Mars 4° N of moon
20	14	Venus 3° N of moon
22	02	NEW MOON
23	05	Mercury stationary
25	23	Mercury 3° S of Venus
27	06	Moon at apogee
30	05	FIRST QUARTER
31	09	Mercury greatest elong. W (18°)

SEPTEMBER

d	h	
3	10	Neptune 2° S of moon
4	03	Uranus 3° S of moon
6	10	Venus 0.8 N of Regulus
6	11	FULL MOON (penumbral eclipse)
7	04	Jupiter 0.5 N of moon (occn.)
7	19	Mercury 0.8 N of Regulus
8	06	Moon at perigee
9	18	Saturn 2° N of moon
11	00	Mercury 0.4 N of Venus
12	08	Aldebaran 0.3 S of moon (occn.)
12	11	Ceres 0.9 S of moon (occn.)
13	02	LAST QUARTER
16	03	Jupiter at opposition
16	05	Pallas at opposition
17	12	Mars 2° N of moon

d	h	
18	11	Regulus 0.6 N of moon (occn.)
20	17	NEW MOON
23	06	Equinox
23	22	Moon at apogee
25	20	Mercury in superior conjunction
28	21	FIRST QUARTER
30	19	Neptune 2° S of moon

OCTOBER

d	h	
1	12	Uranus 3° S of moon
4	07	Pallas 1.0 S of moon (occn.)
4	09	Jupiter 0.2 S of moon (occn.)
5	20	FULL MOON
6	13	Moon at perigee
6	16	Mars 0.9 N of Regulus
7	01	Saturn 1.8 N of moon
9	16	Aldebaran 0.4 S of moon (occn.)
9	22	Ceres 0.9 S of moon (occn.)
10	17	Ceres stationary
11	11	Neptune stationary
12	11	LAST QUARTER
15	17	Regulus 0.5 N of moon (occn.)
16	04	Mars 1.0 N of moon (occn.)
19	01	Uranus stationary
20	10	NEW MOON
21	05	Moon at apogee
21	18	Mercury 7° S of moon
23	19	Saturn at opposition
28	01	Juno in conjunction with sun
28	03	Neptune 2° S of moon
28	12	FIRST QUARTER
28	20	Uranus 2° S of moon
30	04	Venus in superior conjunction
31	16	Jupiter 0.2 N of moon (occn.)

NOVEMBER

d	h	
3	09	Saturn 1.7 N of moon
4	01	Moon at perigee
4	05	FULL MOON
6	02	Aldebaran 0.6 S of moon (occn.)
6	04	Ceres 0.3 S of moon (occn.)
6	23	Pallas stationary

d	h	
9	09	Mercury 1.9 N of Antares
11	00	LAST QUARTER
11	09	Mercury greatest elong. E (23°)
11	22	Regulus 0.3 N of moon (occn.)
13	18	Mars 0.5 S of moon (occn.)
14	01	Jupiter stationary
17	06	Moon at apogee
19	04	NEW MOON
20	21	Mercury 7° S of moon
21	14	Mercury stationary
24	09	Neptune 1.9 S of moon
25	03	Uranus 2° S of moon
27	00	FIRST QUARTER
28	01	Jupiter 0.6 S of moon
28	22	Ceres at opposition
30	08	Pluto in conjunction with sun
30	17	Saturn 1.8 N of moon

DECEMBER

d	h	
1	15	Mercury in inferior conjunction
2	12	Moon at perigee
3	06	Ceres 1.2 N of moon (occn.)
3	13	Aldebaran 0.6 S of moon (occn.)
3	15	FULL MOON
9	06	Regulus 0.01 N of moon (occn.)
10	18	LAST QUARTER
11	06	Mercury stationary
12	08	Mars 1.8 S of moon
14	17	Moon at apogee
17	00	Mercury 3° S of moon
18	23	NEW MOON
20	04	Mercury greatest elong. W (22°)
21	16	Neptune 1.7 S of moon
22	02	Solstice
22	06	Mercury 7° N of Antares
22	11	Uranus 1.8 S of moon
22	23	Vesta stationary
25	11	Jupiter 1.2 N of moon (occn.)
26	11	FIRST QUARTER
27	23	Saturn 2° N of moon
30	16	Saturn stationary
30	18	Moon at perigee
30	23	Aldebaran 0.6 S of moon (occn.)

Hercules, We Are Here!

On Nov. 16, 1974, astronomers beamed up a three-minute radio message about the planet Earth to a globular cluster of stars in the northern constellation *Hercules* on the theory that 300,000 closely packed stars would increase the chances that Earth's signal might be detected by intelligent life near one of them. *Hercules* contains the spectacular star cluster called M13. We told anyone that might be listening out there about the solar system we live in, about the population of the world at the time, and about the atomic elements we're made of.

There was to be no chance at conversation any time soon. It would take the radio signals, traveling at the speed of light, 50,000 years to make a round-trip journey. The *Milky Way* is 100,000 light years in diameter. The known universe extends outwards to about 15 bil-

lion light years. These astronomers would get no return call in their lifetime.

The November 1974 experiment was Earth's first purposeful message to outer space. Unfortunately, traveling at the speed of light (about 186,000 miles per second), it will still be 27,000 years before anyone, or thing, in the vicinity of star cluster M13 sees our sun's radio brightness increase for a brief three minutes.

Until recently, the thought of life on other planets or anywhere else in the universe has been viewed as suspect. Discovering that intelligent life exists elsewhere in our universe would perhaps be the greatest event in all of human history. Humanity's view of itself would change irrevocably. □

Source: U.S. Naval Observatory.

Conversion of Universal Time (U.T.) to Civil Time

U.T.	E.D.T.[1]	E.S.T.[2]	C.S.T.[3]	M.S.T.[4]	P.S.T.[5]
00	*8P	*7P	*6P	*5P	*4P
01	*9P	*8P	*7P	*6P	*5P
02	*10P	*9P	*8P	*7P	*6P
03	*11P	*10P	*9P	*8P	*7P
04	M	*11P	*10P	*9P	*8P
05	1A	M	*11P	*10P	*9P
06	2A	1A	M	*11P	*10P
07	3A	2A	1A	M	*11P
08	4A	3A	2A	1A	M
09	5A	4A	3A	2A	1A
10	6A	5A	4A	3A	2A
11	7A	6A	5A	4A	3A
12	8A	7A	6A	5A	4A
13	9A	8A	7A	6A	5A
14	10A	9A	8A	7A	6A
15	11A	10A	9A	8A	7A
16	N	11A	10A	9A	8A
17	1P	N	11A	10A	9A
18	2P	1P	N	11A	10A
19	3P	2P	1P	N	11A
20	4P	3P	2P	1P	N
21	5P	4P	3P	2P	1P
22	6P	5P	4P	3P	2P
23	7P	6P	5P	4P	3P

1. Eastern Daylight Time. 2. Eastern Standard Time, same as Central Daylight Time. 3. Central Standard Time, same as Mountain Daylight Time. 4. Mountain Standard Time, same as Pacific Daylight Time. 5. Pacific Standard Time. NOTES: * denotes previous day. N = noon. M = midnight.

Eclipses of the Sun and Moon, 1998

Note: The day of an eclipse is given in Universal Time (U.T.) and may start a day earlier or later depending on your time zone. (*See* Phenomena, 1998 table to find time of eclipse in your area.)

February 26. Total eclipse of the sun. Visible in the Pacific Ocean, extreme southwest and eastern parts of the United States, southeast Canada, Mexico, Central America, the northern half of South America, the West Indies, the Atlantic Ocean, the southern tip of Greenland, the extreme western part of Iceland, Portugal, and West Africa.

March 13. Penumbral eclipse of the moon. The beginning phase visible in North America except Alaska and northwestern Canada, Central America, South America, Europe, Africa, western Asia, Greenland, the North polar region, parts of Antarctica (including the Palmer Peninsula, part of Marie Byrd Land, and part of Queen Maud Land), the eastern South Pacific Ocean, the southeastern North Pacific Ocean, the Atlantic Ocean, and the western Indian Ocean; the end visible in extreme eastern Asia, North America, Central America, South America, Greenland, the North polar region, parts of Antarctica (the Palmer Peninsula and Marie Byrd Land), extreme western Africa, the Iberian Peninsula, western France, the British isles, the eastern half of the Pacific Ocean, the North Atlantic Ocean, and the western South Atlantic Ocean.

August 8. Penumbral eclipse of the moon. The beginning phase visible in eastern North America, Central America, South America, southern Greenland, Africa, Europe, extreme western Asia, most of Antarctica, the eastern South Pacific Ocean, the southeastern North Pacific Ocean, the Atlantic Ocean, and the western Indian Ocean; the end visible in North America except northern and western Canada and Alaska, Central America, South America, southern Greenland, Africa except the extreme east, most of Europe, most of Antarctica, the eastern South Pacific Ocean, the southeastern North Pacific Ocean, and the Atlantic Ocean.

August 21–22. Annular eclipse of the sun. Visible in the North Indian Ocean, India, southeast Asia, southern China, Indonesia, Malaysia, Philippine Republic, southern Japan, Australasia, and the South Pacific Ocean.

September 6. Penumbral eclipse of the moon. The beginning phase visible in North America except the extreme east, Central America, South America except the extreme east, Australia except the extreme west, New Zealand, most of Antarctica, extreme eastern Asia, most of the Pacific Ocean, and the extreme western Atlantic Ocean; the end visible in western North America, Australia, New Zealand, the eastern half of Asia, most of Antarctica, the Pacific Ocean except the extreme eastern South Pacific Ocean, and the eastern half of the Indian Ocean. □

Visibility of Planets, 1998

DECLINATION OF SUN AND PLANETS, 1998

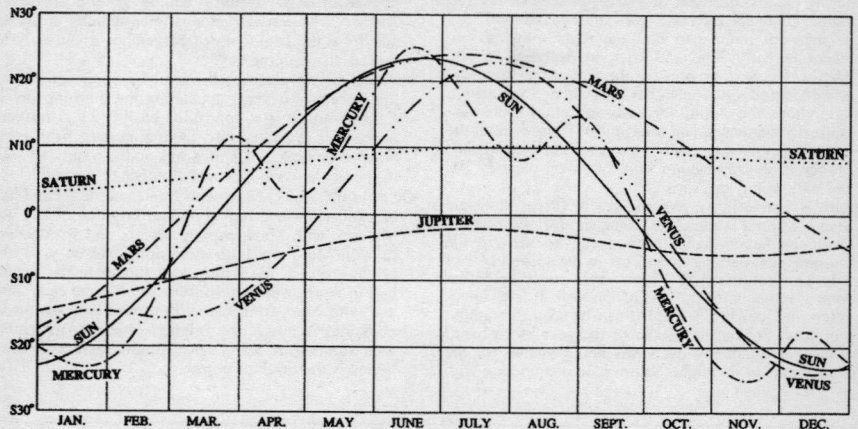

The planet diagram on page 453 shows, in graphical form for any date during the year, the local mean times of meridian passage of the sun, of the five planets, Mercury, Venus, Mars, Jupiter, and Saturn, and of every 2^h right ascension. Intermediate lines, corresponding to particular stars, may be drawn in by the user if desired. The diagram is intended to provide a general picture of the availability of planets and stars for observation during the year.

On each side of the line marking the time of meridian passage of the sun, a band 45^m wide is shaded to indicate that planets and most stars crossing the meridian within 45^m of the sun are generally too close to the sun for observation.

For any date the diagram provides immediately the local mean time of meridian passage of the sun, planets and stars, and thus the following information:

(a) whether a planet or star is too close to the sun for observation;

(b) visibility of a planet or star in the morning or evening;

(c) location of a planet or star during twilight;

(d) proximity of planets to stars or other planets.

When the meridian passage of a body occurs at midnight, it is close to opposition to the sun and is visible all night, and may be observed in both morning and evening twilights. As the time of meridian passage decreases, the body ceases to be observable in the morning, but its altitude above the eastern horizon during evening twilight gradually increases until it is on the meridian at evening twilight. From then on the body is observable above the western horizon, its altitude at evening twilight gradually decreasing, until it becomes too close to the sun for observation. When it again becomes visible, it is seen in the morning twilight, low in the east. Its altitude at morning twilight gradually increases until meridian passage occurs at the time of morning twilight, then as the time of meridian passage decreases to 0^h, the body is observable in the west in the morning twilight with a gradually decreasing altitude, until it once again reaches opposition.

Notes on the visibility of the principal planets, except Pluto, are given in the table Visibility of Planets in Morning Twilight. Further information on the visibility of planets may be obtained from the diagram above

which shows, in graphical form for any date during the year, the declinations of the bodies plotted on the planet diagram on page 453.

Mercury can only be seen low in the east before sunrise, or low in the west after sunset (about the time of the beginning or end of civil twilight). It is visible in the mornings between the following approximate dates: January 1 to February 10, April 15 to June 3, August 22 to September 16, and December 7 to December 31. The planet is brighter at the end of each period (the best conditions in northern latitudes occur during mid-December, and in southern latitudes from the end of April to mid-May). It is visible in the evenings between the following approximate dates: March 4 to March 30, June 18 to August 6, and October 9 to November 26. The planet is brighter at the beginning of each period (the best conditions in northern latitudes occur during mid-March, and in southern latitudes in July).

Venus is a brilliant object in the evening sky until midway through the second week of January when it is too close to the sun for observation. It reappears at the beginning of the third week of January as a morning star and can be seen in the morning sky until the end of the third week of September when it again is too close to the sun for observation; from mid-December until the end of the year it is visible in the evening sky. Venus is in conjunction with Mercury on January 26, August 25, and September 11, with Jupiter on April 23, with Saturn on May 29, and with Mars on August 5.

Mars can be seen in the evening sky in Capricornus, then Aquarius from the last week of January and passing into Pisces at the end of February until just after the first week of March when it is too close to the sun for observation. It reappears in the morning sky during the second week of July in Gemini (passing 6°S of *Pollux* on August 11). It remains in the morning sky for the rest of the year moving into Cancer in mid-August, Leo in mid-September (passing 0°.9 N of *Regulus* on October 6) and Virgo from the second half of November. Mars is in conjunction with Jupiter on January 21, with Mercury on March 11 and March 30, and with Venus on August 5.

Jupiter can be seen in the evening sky in Capricornus passing into Aquarius in the last week of January. It is too close to the sun for observation after the first week of February and reappears in the morning sky during the second week of March. Its westward elongation gradually increases until after mid-June it can be seen for more than half the night, passing into Pisces in early June and back to Aquarius in late August, where it remains for the rest of the year. It is at opposition on September 16 when it is visible throughout the night. Its eastward elongation then gradually decreases, and after mid-December until the end of the year it can only be seen in the evening sky. Jupiter is in conjunction with Mars on January 21, and with Venus on April 23.

Saturn is visible in the evening sky in Pisces until late March when it is too close to the sun for observation. From the beginning of May it can be seen in the morning sky, passing into Cetus in the second half of July and returning to Pisces from mid-September were it remains for the rest of the year. It is at opposition on October 23 when it can be seen throughout the night. For the remainder of the year its eastward elongation gradually decreases being visible for the greater part of the night. Saturn is in conjunction with

Mercury on May 12 and Venus on May 29.

Uranus is visible in the evening sky at the beginning of the year in Capricornus and remains in this constellation throughout the year. It appears in the morning sky from mid-February and is at opposition on August 3. Its eastward elongation gradually decreases and from the beginning of November it can only be seen in the evening sky.

Neptune is too close to the sun for observation until mid-February when it appears in the morning sky in Capricornus. It is at opposition on July 23. After mid-September it passes into Sagittarius and from early November back to Capricornus and can only be seen in the evning sky after mid-October.

Do not confuse (1) Mars with Jupiter in the second half of January when Jupiter is the brighter object. (2) Mercury with Mars in early March, and with Saturn in mid-May; on both occasions Mercury is the brighter object. (3) Venus with Jupiter in the second half of April, with Saturn from late May to early June and with Mars from late July to mid-August; on all occasions Venus is the brighter object; (4) Mercury with Venus from late August to mid-September when Venus is the brighter object. ☐

Visibility of Planets in Morning and Evening Twilight

	Morning		Evening
Venus	January 22–September 22	Venus	January 1–January 10 December 10–December 31
Mars	July 10–December 31	Mars	January 1–March 9
Jupiter	March 9–September 16	Jupiter	January 1–February 10 September 16–December 31
Saturn	May 1–October 23	Saturn	January 1–March 27 October 23–December 31

How Bright Is Bright?

You will often hear astronomers refer to the brightness of an object in terms of an objects *apparent magnitude.*

The term *apparent magnitude* refers to a star's apparent brightness, or how bright the star looks to observers on Earth. Apparent stellar brightness is a combination of two things: how bright the star actually is, and how far the star is from Earth. A dim star close to Earth could appear brighter than a bright star far away.

Back in the second century B.C.E., the Greek astronomer Hipparchus created the first known star catalog, listing star positions and brightnesses. This catalog contained about a thousand stars. The brightest stars were called first magnitude, and the faintest were called sixth magnitude, with the rest being given intermediate magnitudes. This was a crude method of classification, for his observations were made with the unaided eye. His sixth magnitude stars were the faintest naked-eye objects, and man's view at that time was that the extent of the universe was limited to what could be seen by the naked eye.

Today, magnitude classifications are made using highly precise instruments, but Hipparchus's general classification of magnitudes remains. The branch of astronomy that deals with an objects brightness is called photometry, and towards the end of the 1700s, astronomer William Herschel devised a simple method of photometry. While Herschel's methods worked, they were only approximations. One key point that arose from his

work was the determination that a first magnitude star delivers about 100 times as much light to Earth as that of a sixth magnitude star.

In 1856, after more precise methods of photometry had been invented, British astronomer Norman Pogson proposed a quantitative scale of stellar magnitudes, which was adopted by the astronomical community. He noted, like Herschel, that we receive 100 times more light from a first magnitude star as from a sixth; thus, with a difference of five magnitudes, there is a 100:1 ratio of incoming light energy, which is called *luminous flux.*

Because of the nature of human perception, equal intervals of brightness are actually equal ratios of luminous flux. Pogson's proposal was that one increment in magnitude be the fifth root of 100. This means that each increment in magnitude corresponds to an increase in the amount of energy by 2.512, approximately. A fifth magnitude star is 2.512 times as bright as a sixth, and a fourth magnitude star is 6.310 times as bright as a sixth, and so on. The naked eye, under optimum conditions, can see down to around the sixth magnitude, that is +6. Under the Pogson system, a few of the brighter stars now have negative magnitudes. For example, Sirius is –1.5. The lower the magnitude number, the brighter the object. The full moon has a magnitude of about –12.5, and the sun is a bright –26.5! ☐

Source: U.S. Naval Observatory.

LOCAL MEAN TIME OF MERIDIAN PASSAGE

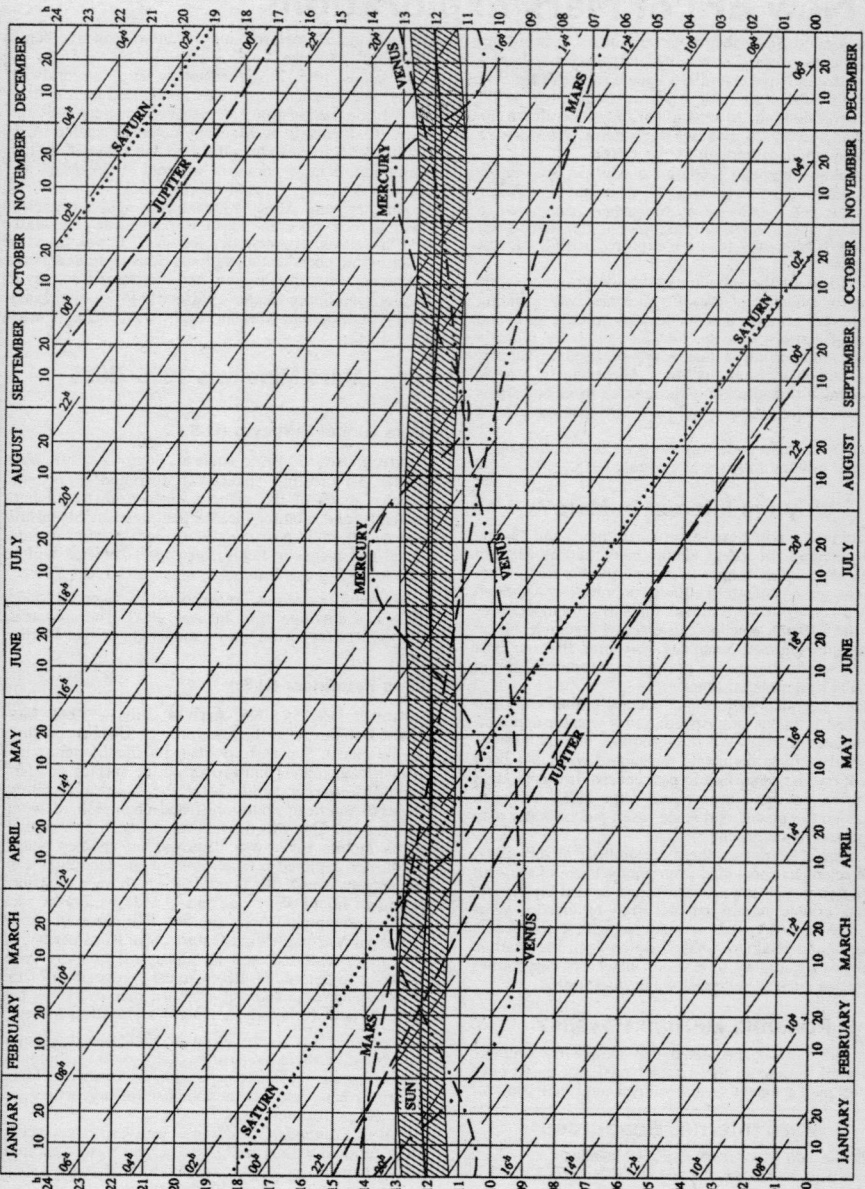

Space

A New Era of Mars Explorations

The United States began an ambitious decade-long investigation of the Earth's planetary neighbor beginning with the November 1996 launch of the *Mars Surveyor*, scheduled to orbit Mars in September 1997. NASA will continue to send a pair of spacecrafts to the Red Planet every 26 months (when Earth and Mars are favorably aligned) through the year 2005.

The first American landing on Martian soil in 21 years occurred on July 4, 1997 when the *Pathfinder* spacecraft and its tiny rover, *Sojourner*, parachuted to the Red Planet's surface. *Pathfinder* is the first of ten planned NASA missions to explore Earth's closest neighbor.

The focus of the robotic exploration program is the search for evidence of past life on Mars, understanding the Martian climate and its lessons for the past and future of Earth's climate, and assessing the planet's geology and resources that could be used to support future human missions to Mars. According to NASA, the common thread running through all these objectives is to search for water, which is a key requirement for life.

Studies are also underway for activities leading up to a human mission to Mars as early as 2018.

Why the Interest in Mars?

Mars is the most Earth-like planet known and has the most potential for future human habitation. A Martian day is just slightly longer than ours and the Red Planet has four seasons much like Earth, only longer. Although it has a very cold, dry climate, the surface temperatures near the Martian equator can reach a favorable 80° F during mid-summer. Scientists also think that our best chances for finding past or present extraterrestrial life in our solar system is on Mars.

Many scientists believe that about 4 billion years ago Mars had a thicker atmosphere and a warmer and wetter climate. *Mariner 9* and subsequent *Viking* missions observed features indicating that liquid water has been present on Mars's surface in past epochs. It was thought that there may have been rivers, large lakes, and even oceans on the planet, and some reservoirs of water may still remain underground.

Pathfinder confirmed these possibilities in July 1997, when scientists concluded from photos taken of the *Ares Vallis* terrain that the spacecraft had landed on the site of catastrophic floods that occurred billions of years ago. The bone-dry plain is scattered with a cornucopia of rocks and boulders washed down from the Martian highlands by mighty torrents of water. No one knows why these ancient bodies of water disappeared.

Possible Martian Fossils?

Scientists have speculated that simple bacteria-like organisms similar to those found on Earth could have existed in the planet's early climate and that some of these Martian life forms may even still survive below the planet's surface.

In August 1996, NASA scientists set off a worldwide flurry of excitement when they announced their discovery of compelling fossil evidence of ancient bacteria-like life forms in a Martian meteorite called ALH 84001. NASA researchers theorize that some 16 million years ago, a huge comet or asteroid struck Mars and ejected a piece of fossil-bearing rock into an orbit around the sun. About 13,000 years ago, the ancient Martian rock fell to the Earth as a meteorite (AL84001) and landed on an Antarctica ice shelf. It was found in 1984 by members of the National Science Foundation's Antarctic Meteorite Program and preserved for study in the Johnson Space Center's Meteorite Processing Laboratory. Its possible Martian origin was not recognized until 1993.

Mars Missions 1996–2005

Mars Global Surveyor (U.S.)

Launch: Nov. 7, 1996. **Arrival:** Sept. 12, 1997. **Mission:** An orbiting spacecraft designed to provide detailed maps of the planet's surface, distribution of minerals, and monitor the Martian weather. Six instruments will study Martian surface, atmosphere, gravitational and magnetic fields. *Surveyor*'s cameras will be able to distinguish features as small as 10 feet across.

Mapping operations are expected to begin in March 1998 and continue until January 2000. The spacecraft will orbit Mars for 687 days, the length of one Martian year.

Mars Pathfinder (U.S.)

Launch: Dec. 5, 1996. **Arrival:** July 4, 1997. **Mission:** Demonstrated the feasibility of low-cost landings on the planet. Successfully placed a small lander and a six-wheeled robotic mini-rover on the surface of Mars, named *Sojourner Truth* (after the nineteenth-century African-American abolitionist and champion of women's rights). This was the first time ever that an autonomous mobile rover was deployed on another planet. *Sojourner* explored a small area of the landing site in the ancient *Ares Vallis* floodplain which once contained abundant liquid water and has a wide variety of rock and soil samples. It took the first live close-up photographs of Martian surface features with its cameras. The tiny rover also deployed an alpha-proton X-ray spectrometer to determine the chemical composition of the surrounding rocks and soil—another first, as a rover had never been used before to analyze a planet's geology.

Sojourner was controlled by an Earth-based operator, but because there is a time delay 6 to 41 minutes depending on the relative position of Earth and Mars, the rover has some autonomous control in reaching targets and performing tasks.

All of *Pathfinder*'s mission objectives were successfully fulfilled within the first week and further exploration continues as long as the lander and rover remain operational in the severe Martian climate.

The day after *Pathfinder* arrived on Mars, NASA renamed the lander the Carl Sagan Memorial Station in honor of the famous astronomer who died in 1996.

Mars Internet Resources

The Martian Chronicles. A JPL Newsletter:
www.jpl.nasa.gov/mars/MARTIANCHRONICLE/index.html
The Planetary Society: www.planetary.org
The National Space Society: www.nss.org
Mars Meteorite Page: www.jpl.nasa.gov/snc/

Sojourner (U.S.)

Height: 10.9 inches (280 mm) with a ground clearance of 5 inches. **Length:** 24.5 inches (630 mm). **Width:** 18.7 inches (480 mm). **Weight:** 22 pounds (10 kg). **Power:** Three solar panels, but has back-up batteries. **Maximum Speed:** About two feet (61 cm) per minute. **Range:** About 1,600 feet (500 m) from landing site. **Cameras:** Two black and white stereo cameras in the front and one color camera in the rear. **Computer:** Has an 8-bit Intel 80 C 85 processor. **Navigation:** Follows instructions sent to it via the lander. **Mission:** Although designed to take pictures and deploy alpha-proton X-ray spectrometer, it primarily serves as an experimental vehicle to test microrover performance in the poorly understood Martian terrain and gain information for improving the design of future rovers.

Planet-B (Japan)

Launch: August 1998 from Kagoshima Space Center. **Arrival:** October 1999. **Mission:** To send an orbiter around Mars to study the effect of the solar wind on the planet's atmosphere for one Martian year (687 days). Its cameras will provide photographic data on cloud distribution, polar haze, dust storms, polar ice, and the planet's surface.

Mars Surveyor '98 (U.S.)

Launch: *Orbiter*—Dec. 10, 1998; *Lander*—January 1999. Two spacecraft will be launched separately but will comprise a single mission. **Arrival:** *(Mars Surveyor Orbiter)*—Sept. 24, 1999; *(Mars Surveyor Lander)*—Dec. 3, 1999. **Mission:** Dual spacecraft will study the planet's weather-related changes in the atmosphere and on the surface. The *Mars Surveyor Lander* will be the first probe to land in the polar region of Mars. It will photograph the surface of the south polar region as it descends. After landing, it will deploy a package of stereo cameras, and analyze soil samples with a robotic arm.

The lander will carry two microprobes that will plunge into the Martian surface prior to the spacecraft's entry into the planet's atmosphere. The probes can detect subsurface water.

Mars Surveyor 2001 (U.S.)

Launch: *Orbiter*—March 2001; *Lander*—April 2001. Two spacecraft are to be launched separately but will comprise a single mission. **Arrival:** *(Mars Surveyor Orbiter)*—December 2001; *(Mars Lander)*—January 2002. **Mission:** Analysis of Martian dust and soil and radiation environment of space and the planet's surface. The *Mars Surveyor 2001 Lander* will deliver a small rover that can travel several tens of miles across the Martian highlands. It will collect rock and soil samples for later return to Earth by a future robotic mission. Hardware on the *Lander* will be used for an in-situ demonstration test to produce rocket fuel and oxygen from gases in the Martian atmosphere. Other equipment will characterize the planet's soil and surface radiation. The *Mars Surveyor 2001 Orbiter* will conduct mineralogical mapping of the entire planet and characterize its orbital radiation environment.

Future Mars Surveyors

Launch: 2003, 2005. **Missions:** Small orbiters will capitalize on the experience of the Mars *Pathfinder* lander mssion and will serve as relay stations for international missions of the future.

A search for water is being considered in 2001 on the *Mars Surveyor 2001 Orbiter* and another planned mission will have a rover investigate an ancient highland bed to study the climate history of the planet. One of the 2001 missions may be conducted in partnership with the Russians. For the 2003 mission, NASA is exploring a partnership with the European Space Agency (ESA) to place three landers on the surface. And finally, the *Mars Surveyor 2005* mission will be an attempt to bring back a sample of Martian rocks and soil. □

Other Major Space Missions

Ulysses (U.S. and European Space Agency)

Destination: The sun. **Launch:** Oct. 6, 1990. **Flew by Jupiter, released probe:** Feb. 8, 1992. **Achieved Orbit at South Pole:** September 1994. **Achieved Orbit at North Pole:** October 1995. **Mission:** An international project to study the sun and interstellar space above and below its poles. The spacecraft was put into orbit at right angles to the solar system's ecliptic plane. This special orbit enabled *Ulysses* to examine for the first time the sun's north and south polar regions. Besides investigating the sun, the spacecraft is also studying phenomena from the Milky Way and beyond. *Ulysses* will continue to orbit the sun and will pass over the north and south poles again in 2000 and 2001.

Cassini (U.S. and the European Space Agency)

Destination: Saturn. **Launch:** Oct. 6, 1997. **Arrival:** June 2004. **Mission:** Will orbit Saturn for four years. Before reaching Saturn, *Cassini* will encounter Jupiter and fly down the giant planet's magnetotail, performing studies complementing the Galileo Mission. While orbiting Saturn, *Cassini* will send a small probe named *Huygens* (after the Dutch astronomer Christiaan Huygens, who discovered Titan) to the surface of Saturn's largest moon, Titan, to learn more about its dense atmosphere and its surface state and composition. After relaying data to the Earth from Titan, *Cassini* will continue with orbits of Saturn and flybys of the planet's 16 or more moons. The spacecraft will also examine Sat-

urn's equatorial zone and study the planet's polar regions. The Cassini mission is named for the Italian-French astronomer Gian Domenico Cassini who discovered four of Saturn's major moons.

Galileo (U.S.)

Destination: Jupiter. **Launch:** Oct. 18, 1989. **Achieved Orbit:** Dec. 7, 1995. **Mission:** To study the chemical composition and physical state of the largest planet in the solar system, its atmosphere, and four of its moons, for almost two years. The spacecraft encountered the asteroid 951 Gaspera on Oct. 29, 1991 and took the first close-up photographs ever of an asteroid in space. On Aug. 28, 1993, it passed by asteroid 243 Ida and took close-up photographs which revealed that Ida has a tiny moon. Upon arrival at Jupiter, *Galileo* released a probe into the planet's atmosphere which descended for 57 minutes before it was destroyed by the planet's extreme temperature and pressure. In 1996, *Galileo* visited and photographed Jupiter's large moons Io, Callisto and Europa and made flybys of Io, Ganymede, Europa, and Callisto in 1997. *Galileo* was named for the Italian astronomer Galileo Galilei who discovered Jupiter's four great moons that were the major targets of this mission.

Galileo Europa Mission (GEM): This is a two-year continuation of the original Galileo Mission that will be completed at the end of 1997. GEM will include eight more flybys of Europa and one or two flybys of Io, as long as the spacecraft remains healthy.

Near-Earth Asteroid Rendezvous (NEAR) (U.S.):

Destination: Asteroid 433 Eros. **Launched:** Feb. 17, 1996. **Arrival:** February 1999. **Mission:** To rendezvous with Eros and orbit the asteroid for almost one year. It will take comprehensive measurements of its surface, size, volume, mass, spin, and magnetic field. *NEAR* passed by and photographed minor planet 253 Mathilde on June 27, 1997.

Lunar Prospector (U.S.)

Destination: Earth's moon. **Launch:** Sept. 24, 1997. **Arrival:** Sept. 29, 1997. **Mission:** To fly in a low-polar orbit around the moon for at least one year and map the chemical composition of the lunar surface, possible polar ice deposits, and its global magnetic and gravity fields. The spacecraft can also locate any significant quantities of frozen water that may exist in shadowed craters. □

Space Station Alpha

Due to delays arising from financial difficulties at the Russian Space Agency, the construction of the $60-billion international space station *Alpha* has been rescheduled to begin in June 1998 instead of November 1997. Assembly will continue through 2003.

The NASA-financed core module, the Functional Cargo Block, is to be launched on a *Proton* rocket from the Baikonur Cosmodrome in Kazakhstan, and placed into orbit in June 1998. This component will supply early power and propulsion systems for the station. Two weeks later, in July, the space shuttle *Endeavour* will carry aloft a six-port docking module called Node 1 and join it to one end of the cargo block. After the two components are linked together, three spacewalks will be performed from the shuttle to connect power, data, and utility lines and install exterior equipment.

When completed, *Alpha* will be 356 feet across and 290 feet long. It will weigh about 940,000 pounds (470 tons). A crew of up to seven will live on it. In orbit 220 miles above the Earth, the space station will circle the globe at an inclination of 51.6 degrees to the equator.

Space Web Sites

NASA homepage: www.nasa.com
Space Shuttle homepage: shuttle.nasa.gov/
International Space Station: issa-www.jsc.nasa.gov
Mir Space Station:
  www.osf.hq.nasa.gov/mir/Welcome.html
National Space Science Data Center (NSSDC):
  nssdc.gsfc.nasa/gov/
National Space Society OnLine:
  www.nss.org/home.html
The Planetary Society:
  www.transatlantictech.com/tps/
European Space Agency (ESA): www.esrin.esa.it/
UN Office for Outer Space Affairs (UNOOSA):
  ecf.hq.eso.org/~ralbrech/un/un-homepage.html
SETI Intitute: www.seti-inst.edu/
Near-Earth Asteroid Tracking (NEAT):
  huey.jpl.nasa.gov/~spravdo/neat.html
Virtual Satellite Observer's Homepage:
  www.rzg.mpg.de/~/bpd/vsohp/satintro.html
Satellite Observing Resources:
  www-leland.stanford.edu/~iburrell/sat/sattrack.html
NASA Q&A on Aliens and UFOs: www.nasa.gov/
  hqpao/new_FAQ_answers2.html#ufos
Mutual UFO Network: (for believers):
  www.rutgers.edu/~mcgrew/mufon/index.html
**Committee for the Scientific Investigation of Claims
  of the Paranormal (for skeptics):** www.csicop.org/

First U.S. Satellite

The first successful U.S. satellite, *Explorer I*, was launched into Earth orbit by the Army on Jan. 31, 1958, at Cape Canaveral, Florida, four months after Russia orbited *Sputnik*. The 18-pound satellite had a cylindrical shape and was 80 inches long and six inches in diameter.

Explorer I's small package of instruments produced the first major discovery of the Space Age—The Van Allen radiation belts surrounding the Earth. *Explorer I* burned up in the atmosphere on March 30, 1970.

This orbit can be reached by the launch vehicles of all international partners and will provide an excellent Earth observation of 85 percent of the globe.

The inaugural crew, composed of two Russians and one American, are now training for a five-month tour of duty aboard *Alpha*. NASA astronaut William Shepherd will be the space station commander, Russian cosmonaut Yuri Gidzenko, the *Soyuz* commander, and Russian cosmonaut Sergei Krikalev, the flight engineer.

U.S. Unmanned Planetary and Lunar Programs

Lunar Orbiter. Series of spacecraft designed to orbit the moon, taking pictures and obtaining data in support of the subsequent manned *Apollo* landings. The U.S. launched five *Lunar Orbiters* between Aug. 10, 1966 and Aug. 2, 1967.

Mariner. Designation for a series of spacecraft designed to fly past or orbit the planets, particularly Mercury, Venus, and Mars. *Mariners* provided the early information on Venus and Mars. *Mariner 9*, orbiting Mars in 1971, returned the most startling photographs of that planet and helped pave the way for a *Viking* landing in 1976. *Mariner 10* explored Venus and Mercury in 1973 and was the first probe to use a planet's gravity to whip it toward another.

Pioneer. Designation for the United States' first series of sophisticated interplanetary spacecraft. *Pioneers 10* and *11* reached Jupiter in 1973 and 1974 and continued on to explore Saturn and the other outer planets. *Pioneer 11*, renamed *Pioneer Saturn*, examined the Saturn system in September 1979. Significant discoveries were the finding of a small new moon and a narrow new ring. In 1986, *Pioneer 10* was the first man-made object to escape the solar system. *Pioneer Venus 1* and *2* reached Venus in 1978 and provided detailed information about that planet's surface and atmosphere.

Ranger. NASA's earliest moon exploration program. Spacecraft were designed for a crash landing on the moon, taking pictures and returning scientific data up to the moment of impact. Provided the first closeup views of the lunar surface. The *Rangers* provided more than 17,000 closeup pictures, giving us more information about the moon in a few years than in all the time that had gone before.

Surveyor. Series of unmanned spacecraft designed to land gently on the moon and provide information on the surface in preparation for the manned lunar landings. Their legs were instrumented to return data on the surface hardness of the moon. *Surveyor* dispelled the fear that *Apollo* spacecraft might sink several feet or more into the lunar dust.

Viking. Designation for two spacecraft designed to conduct detailed scientific examination of the planet Mars, including a search for life. *Viking 1* landed on

July 20, 1976; *Viking 2*, Sept. 3, 1976. More was learned about the Red Planet in a few short months than in all previous missions, but the question of whether there is life on Mars remains unresolved.

Voyager. Designation for two spacecraft designed to explore Jupiter and the other outer planets. *Voyager 1* and *Voyager 2* passed Jupiter in 1979 and sent back surprising color TV images of that planet and its moons. They took a total of about 33,000 pictures. *Voyager 1* passed Saturn November 1980. *Voyager 2* passed Saturn August 1981 and Uranus in January 1986.

It encountered Neptune on Aug. 29, 1989 and made many discoveries. It found four rings around the planet, six new moons, a Giant Spot, and evidence of volcanic-like activity on its largest moon, Triton. The spacecraft sent back over 9,000 pictures of the planet and its system.

On Feb. 13, 1990, at a distance of 3.7 billion miles, *Voyager 1* took its final pictures—the sun and six of its planets as seen from deep space. NASA released the extraordinary images to the public on June 6, 1990. Only Mercury, Mars, and Pluto were not seen.

Notable Unmanned Lunar and Interplanetary Probes

Spacecraft	Launch date	Destination	Remarks
Pioneer 3 (U.S.)	Dec. 6, 1958	Moon	Max. alt.: 66,654 mi. Discovered outer Van Allen layer.
Luna 2 (U.S.S.R.)	Sept. 12, 1959	Moon	Impacted on Sept. 14. First space vehicle to reach moon.
Luna 3 (U.S.S.R.)	Oct. 4, 1959	Moon	Flew around Moon and transmitted first pictures of lunar far side, Oct. 7.
Mariner 2 (U.S.)	Aug. 27, 1962	Venus	Venus probe. Successful mid-course correction. Passed 21,648 mi. from Venus Dec. 14, 1962. Reported 800°F. surface temp. Contact lost Jan. 3, 1963 at 54 million mi.
Mariner 4 (U.S.)	Nov. 28, 1964	Mars	Transmitted first close-up pictures on June 14, 1965, from altitude of 6,000 mi.
Ranger 7 (U.S.)	July 28, 1964	Moon	Impacted near Crater Guericke 68.5 h after launch. Sent 4,316 pictures during last 15 min of flight as close as 1,000 ft. above lunar surface.
Luna 9 (U.S.S.R.)	Jan. 31, 1966	Moon	3,428 lb. Instrument capsule of 220 lb. soft-landed Feb. 3, 1966. Sent back about 30 pictures.
Surveyor 1 (U.S.)	May 30, 1966	Moon	Landed June 2, 1966. Sent almost 10,400 pictures, a number after surviving the 14-day lunar night.
Lunar Orbiter 1 (U.S.)	Aug. 10, 1966	Moon	Orbited Moon Aug. 14. 21 pictures sent.
Surveyor 3 (U.S.)	April 17, 1967	Moon	Soft-landed 65 h after launch on Oceanus Procellarum. Scooped and tested lunar soil.
Venera 4 (U.S.S.R.)	June 12, 1967	Venus	Arrived Oct. 17. Instrument capsule sent temperature and chemical data.
Surveyor 5 (U.S.)	Sept. 8, 1967	Moon	Landed near lunar equator Sept. 10. Radiological analysis of lunar soil. Mechanical claw for digging soil.
Surveyor 7 (U.S.)	Jan. 6, 1968	Moon	Landed near Crater Tycho Jan. 10. Soil analysis. Sent 3,343 pictures.
Pioneer 9 (U.S.)	Nov. 8, 1968	Sun Orbit	Achieved orbit. Six experiments returned solar radiation data.
Venera 5 (U.S.S.R.)	Jan. 5, 1969	Venus	Landed May 16, 1969. Returned atmospheric data.
Mariner 6 (U.S.)	Feb. 24, 1969	Mars	Came within 2000 mi. of Mars July 31, 1969. Sent back data & TV pictures.
Luna 16 (U.S.S.R.)	Sept. 12, 1970	Moon	Soft-landed Sept. 20, scooped up rock, returned to Earth Sept. 24.
Luna 17 (U.S.S.R.)	Nov. 10, 1970	Moon	Soft-landed on Sea of Rains Nov. 17. *Lunokhod 1*, self-propelled vehicle, used for first time. Sent TV photos, made soil analysis, etc.
Mariner 9 (U.S.)	May 30, 1971	Mars	First craft to orbit Mars, Nov. 13. 7,300 pictures, 1st close-ups of Mars's moon. Transmission ended Oct. 27, 1972.
Luna 20 (U.S.S.R.)	Feb. 14, 1972	Moon	Soft-landed Feb. 21 in Sea of Fertility. Returned Feb. 25 with rock samples.
Pioneer 10 (U.S.)	March 3, 1972	Jupiter	620-million-mile flight path through asteroid belt passed Jupiter Dec. 3, 1973, to give man first closeup of planet. In 1986, it became first man-made object to escape solar system.
Luna 21 (U.S.S.R.)	Jan. 8, 1973	Moon	Soft-landed Jan. 16. *Lunokhod 2* (moon-car) scooped up soil samples, returned them to Earth Jan. 27.
Mariner 10 (U.S.)	Nov. 3, 1973	Venus, Mercury	Passed Venus Feb. 5, 1974. Arrived Mercury March 29, 1974, for man's first closeup look at planet. First time gravity of one planet (Venus) used to whip spacecraft toward another (Mercury).
Viking 1 (U.S.)	Aug. 20, 1975	Mars	Carrying life-detection labs. Landed July 20, 1976, for detailed scientific research, including pictures. Designed to work for only 90 days, it operated for almost 6½ years before it went silent in November 1982.
Viking 2 (U.S.)	Sept. 9, 1975	Mars	Like Viking 1. Landed Sept. 3, 1976. Functioned 3½ years.

Spacecraft	Launch date	Destination	Remarks
Luna 24 (U.S.S.R.)	Aug. 9, 1976	Moon	Soft-landed Aug. 18, 1976. Returned soil samples Aug. 22, 1976.
Voyager 1 (U.S.)	Sept. 5, 1977	Jupiter, Saturn	Fly-by mission. Reached Jupiter in March 1979; passed Saturn November 1980; passed Uranus 1986.
Voyager 2 (U.S.)	Aug. 20, 1977	Jupiter, Saturn, Uranus	Launched before Voyager 1. Encountered Jupiter in July 1979; flew by Saturn Aug. 1981; passed Uranus January 1986; and passed Neptune in August 1989.
Pioneer Venus 1 (U.S.)	May 20, 1978	Venus	Arrived Dec. 4 and orbited Venus, photographing surface and atmosphere. Crashed into planet's surface mid-October 1992 after circling Venus for 14 years.
Pioneer Venus 2 (U.S.)	Aug. 8, 1978	Venus	Four-part multi-probe, landed Dec. 9.
Venera 13 (U.S.S.R.)	Oct. 30, 1981	Venus	Landed March 1, 1982. Took first X-ray fluorescence analysis of the planet's surface. Transmitted data 2 hours 7 minutes.
VEGA 1 (U.S.S.R.)	Deployed on Venus, June 10, 1985	Encounter with Halley's Comet	In flyby over Venus while en route to encounter with Halley's Comet, VEGA 1 and 2 dropped scientific capsules onto Venus to study atmosphere and surface material. Encountered Halley's Comet on March 6 and March 9, 1986. Took TV pictures and studied comet's dust particles.
VEGA 2 (U.S.S.R.)	Deployed on Venus, June 14, 1985	Encounter with Halley's Comet	See VEGA 1 above.
Suisei (Japan)	Encountered Halley's Comet March 8, 1986	Halley's Comet	Spacecraft made flyby of comet and studied atmosphere with ultraviolet camera. Observed rotation nucleus.
Sakigake (Japan)	Encountered Halley's Comet March 10, 1986	Halley's Comet	Spacecraft made flyby to study solar wind and magnetic fields. Detected plasma waves.
Giotto (E.S.A.)	Encountered Halley's Comet March 13, 1986	Halley's Comet	European Space Agency spacecraft made closest approach to comet. Studied atmosphere and magnetic fields. Sent back best pictures of nucleus. Flew by comet Grigg-Skjellerup July 10, 1992. Unable to send pictures.
Phobos Mission (U.S.S.R.)	July 7 and July 12, 1988	Mars and Phobos	Two spacecraft to probe Martian moon Phobos starting April 1989. Were to study orbit, soil chemistry, send TV pictures and data of planet. Contact was lost with Phobos 1 in August 1988 and later with Phobos 2 in March 1989 after it reached the Martian moon.
Magellan (U.S.)	May 4, 1989	Venus	Arrived at Venus on Aug. 10, 1990 and made a geologic map of planet with a powerful radar. Crashed into Venus Oct. 12, 1994.
Galileo (U.S.)	Oct. 18, 1989	Jupiter	To study Jupiter's atmosphere and its moons during 22-month mission.
Hubble Space Telescope (U.S., E.S.A.)	April 25, 1990	Earth Orbit	Studies distant stars and galaxies and searches for evidence of planets in other solar systems. The telescope was repaired by space shuttle crews in December 1993 and February 1997.
Ulysses (U.S., E.S.A.)	Oct. 6, 1990	The sun	To study the poles of the sun and interstellar space above and below the poles. First solar encounter was in 1994, second encounter in 1995.
Gamma-Ray Observatory (U.S.)	April 7, 1991	Earth Orbit	To make first survey of gamma ray sources across the whole sky, studying explosive energic sources such as supernovae, quasars, neutron stars, pulsars, and black holes.
Mars Observer (U.S.)	Sept. 25, 1992	Mars	Spacecraft was to arrive at Mars August 1993 and orbit the planet for one full Martian year to study atmosphere and surface change during the planet's seasons. Mission failed after communications with Observer lost Aug. 21, 1993.
Clementine (U.S.)	Jan. 25, 1994	Moon and asteroid Geographos 1620	Entered lunar orbit February 21 and took close-up photos of lunar surface for two months. Computer malfunction prevented planned rendezvous with Geographos.

U.S. Manned Space Flights

Mercury. *Project Mercury,* initiated in 1958 and completed in 1963, was the United States' first man-in-space program. It was designed to further knowledge about man's capabilities in space.

In April 1959, seven military jet test pilots were introduced to the public as America's first astronauts. They were: Lt. M. Scott Carpenter, USN; Capt. L. Gordon Cooper, Jr., USAF; Lt. Col. John H. Glenn, Jr., USMC; Cap. Virgil I. Grissom, USAF; Lt. Cdr. Walter M. Shirra, Jr., USN; Lt. Cdr. Alan B. Shepard, Jr., USN; and Capt. Donald K. Slayton, USAF. Six of the original seven would make a Mercury flight. Slayton was grounded for medical reasons, but remained a director of the astronaut office. He returned to flight status in 1975 as Docking Module Pilot on the Apollo-Soyuz flight.

Flight Summary

Each astronaut named his capsule and added the numeral 7 to denote the teamwork of the original astronauts.

May 5, 1961. Alan B. Shepard, Jr., makes a suborbital flight in *Freedom 7* and becomes the first American in space. Time: 15 minutes, 22 seconds.

July 21, 1961. Virgil I. Grissom makes the second successful suborbital flight in *Liberty Bell 7,* but spacecraft sank shortly after splashdown. Time: 15 minutes, 37 seconds. Grissom was later killed in *Apollo 1* fire, Jan. 27, 1967.

February 20, 1962. John H. Glenn, Jr., makes a three-orbit flight and becomes the first American in orbit. Time: 4 hours, 55 minutes.

May 24, 1962. M. Scott Carpenter duplicates Glenn's flight in *Aurora 7.* Time: 4 hours, 56 minutes.

October 3, 1962. Walter M. Schirra, Jr., makes a six-orbit engineering test flight in *Sigma 7.* Time: 9 hours, 13 minutes.

May 15-16, 1963. L. Gordon Cooper, Jr., performs the last *Mercury* mission and completes 22 orbits in *Faith 7* to evaluate effects of one day in space. Time: 34 hours, 19 minutes.

Gemini. *Gemini* was an extension of *Project Mercury,* to determine the effects of prolonged space flight on man—two weeks or longer—the time it takes to reach the moon and return. "Walks in space" provided invaluable information for astronauts' later walks on the moon. The *Gemini* spacecraft, twice as large as the *Mercury* capsule, accommodated two astronauts. Its crew named the project *Gemini* for the third constellation of the Zodiac and its twin stars, Castor and Pollux. The capsule differed from the *Mercury* spacecrafts in that it had hatches above the capsules so that the astronauts could leave the spacecraft and perform spacewalks or extra vehicular activities (EVAs).

There were ten manned flights in the *Gemini* program, starting with *Gemini 3* on March 23, 1965, and ending with the *Gemini 12* mission on Nov. 15, 1966. *Gemini 1* and 2 were unmanned test flights of the equipment.

When the *Gemini* program ended, U.S. astronauts had perfected rendezvous and docking maneuvers with other orbiting vehicles.

Apollo. *Apollo* was the designation for the United States' effort to land a man on the moon and return him safely to Earth. The goal was successfully accomplished with *Apollo 11* on July 20, 1969, culminating eight years of rehearsal and centuries of dreaming. Astronauts Neil A. Armstrong and Col. Edwin E. Aldrin, Jr., scooped up and brought back the first lunar rocks ever seen on Earth—about 47 pounds.

Tragedy struck Jan. 27, 1967, on the launch pad during a preflight test of what would become *Apollo 1,* the first manned mission. Astronauts Lt. Col. Virgil "Gus" Grissom, Lt. Col. Edward H. White, and Lt. Cdr. Roger Chafee lost their lives when a fire swept through the command module.

Six *Apollo* flights followed, ending with *Apollo 17* in December 1972. The last three *Apollos* carried mechanized vehicles called lunar rovers for wide-ranging surface exploration of the moon by astronauts. The rendezvous and docking of an *Apollo* spacecraft with a Russian *Soyuz* craft in Earth orbit on July 18, 1975, closed out the *Apollo* program.

During the Apollo project, the following 12 astronauts explored the lunar terrain: Col. Edwin E. "Buzz" Aldrin, Jr., and Neil A. Armstrong, *Apollo 11;* Cdr. Alan L. Bean and Cdr. Charles Conrad, Jr., *Apollo 12;* Edgar D. Mitchell and Alan B. Shepard, *Apollo 14;* Lt. Col. James B. Irwin (1930-1991) and Col. David R. Scott, *Apollo 15;* Col. Charles M. Duke, Jr., and Capt. John W. Young, *Apollo 16;* and Capt. Eugene A. Cernan and Dr. Harrison H. Schmitt, *Apollo 17.*

Apollo was a three-part spacecraft: the command module (CM), the crew's quarters and flight control section; the service modules (SM) for the propulsion and spacecraft support systems (when together, the two modules were called CSM); and the lunar module (LM) to take two of the crew to the lunar surface, support them on the moon, and return them to the CSM in orbit. The crews that made the lunar flights where both command modules and lunar modules were involved selected call names for the vehicles. The call names for the spacecraft in the six lunar landing missions with the command module and lunar module designations respectively were:

Apollo 11, Columbia and *Eagle; Apollo 12, Yankee Clipper* and *Intrepid;* (NOTE: The third lunar attempt, *Apollo 13,* April 11-17, 1970, 5 days, 22.9 hours, was aborted after the service module oxygen tank ruptured. The *Apollo 13* crew members were James A. Lovell, Jr., John L. Swigert, Jr., and Fred W. Haise, Jr. The mission was classified as a "successful failure," because the crew was rescued. The call names for their spacecraft were *Odyssey* (CM) and *Aquarius* (LM).) *Apollo 14, Kitty Hawk* and *Antares; Apollo 15, Endeavor* and *Falcon; Apollo 16, Casper* and *Orion;* and *Apollo 17, America* and *Challenger.*

Skylab. America's first Earth-orbiting space station. *Project Skylab* was designed to demonstrate that men can work and live in space for prolonged periods without ill effects. Originally the spent third stage of a *Saturn 5* moon rocket, *Skylab* measured 118 feet from stem to stern, and carried the most varied assortment of experimental equipment ever assembled in a single spacecraft. Three three-man crews visited the space stations, spending more than 740 hours observing the sun and bringing home more than 175,000 solar pictures. These were the first recordings of solar activity above Earth's obscuring atmosphere. *Skylab* also evaluated systems designed to gather information on Earth's resources and environmental conditions. *Skylab's* biomedical findings indicated that man adapts well to space for at least a period of three months, provided he has a proper diet and adequately programmed exercise, sleep, work, and recreation periods. *Skylab* orbited Earth at a distance of about 300 miles. Five years after the last *Skylab* mission, the 77-ton space station's orbit began to deteriorate faster than expected, owing to unexpectedly high sunspot activity. On July 11, 1979, the parts of *Skylab* that did not burn up in the atmosphere came crashing down on parts of Australia and the Indian Ocean. No one was hurt.

Space Shuttle. The Space Shuttle *Columbia* was successfully launched on April 12, 1981. It made five flights (the first four were test runs), the last completed on Nov. 16, 1982. The second shuttle, *Challenger*, made its maiden flight on April 4, 1983. In April 1984, crew members of the *Challenger* captured, repaired, and returned the *Solar Max* satellite to orbit, making it the first time a disabled satellite had been repaired in space. The third shuttle, *Discovery*, made its first flight on Aug. 30, 1984. The fourth space shuttle, *Atlantis*, made its maiden flight on Oct. 3, 1985.

A tragedy occurred on Jan. 28, 1986, when the shuttle *Challenger* exploded, killing the crew of seven 73 seconds after takeoff. It was the world's worst space flight disaster.

The dead crew members were: Francis R. Scobee, shuttle commander; Cdr. Michael J. Smith, pilot; mission specialists: Judith A. Resnik, Lt. Col. Ellison S. Onizuka, Ronald E. McNair; payload specialists: Gregory B. Jarvis and Christa McAuliffe (who was to be the first civilian schoolteacher in space).

The cause of the explosion was a rupture in a seal on one of the booster rockets that let a jet of flame escape, igniting the fuel. The weakness in the seal was caused by the cold air temperature when the shuttle was launched.

NASA has estimated that the risk of a catastrophic failure is about 1 in 145 for each shuttle flight. Eventually, another disaster could occur.

The first U.S. space mission since the *Challenger* disaster was launched 32 months later on Sept. 29, 1988, with the flight of *Discovery*. It had a crew of five and deployed a communications satellite.

The fifth and last orbiter, *Endeavor*, was built as a replacement for *Challenger*. It was named after the British Explorer James Cook's first ship. *Endeavor* was launched on its maiden voyage on May 7, 1992 with a crew of seven astronauts. They made four spacewalks and retrieved a disabled *Intelsat-6* communications satellite. During the mission, Dr. Kathryn Thornton became the second American woman to walk in space.

The shuttle *Columbia* set a record 17 days, 15 hours in space, Nov. 19–Dec. 7, 1996.

The crew of the 50th mission aboard the *Endeavor*, launched Sept. 12, 1992, included the first black woman astronaut, Dr. Mae C. Jemison, and the first married couple to fly together in space, Air Force Lt. Col. Mark C. Lee and Dr. N. Jan Davis.

Lt. Col. Eileen M. Collins became the first woman to pilot a shuttle, *Discovery*, during the spacecraft's historic rendezvous with the Russian space station *Mir* on Feb. 6, 1995. The shuttle *Atlantis* made the first linkup with the *Mir* on June 29, 1995.

Soviet Manned Space Flight Programs

Vostok. The Soviets' first manned capsule, roughly spherical, used to place the first six cosmonauts in Earth orbit (1961–65).

Voskhod. Adaptation of the *Vostok* capsule to accommodate two and three cosmonauts. *Voskhod 1* orbited three persons, and *Voskhod 2* orbited two persons performing the world's first manned extra-vehicular activity.

Soyuz. Late-model manned spacecraft with provisions for three cosmonauts and a "working compartment" accessible through a hatch. Soyuz is the Russian word for "union." The *Soyuz* spacecraft can carry three cosmonauts, and routinely brings cosmonauts and their foreign "guests" to the *Mir* space station. *Soyuz 19*, launched July 15, 1975, docked with the American *Apollo* spacecraft.

Salyut. Earth-orbiting space station intended for prolonged occupancy and re-visitation by cosmonauts. They are usually launched by Soviet Proton rockets. *Salyut 1* was launched April 19, 1971. *Salyut 2*, launched April 3, 1973, malfunctioned in orbit and was never occupied. *Salyut 3* was launched June 25, 1974. *Salyut 4* was launched Dec. 26, 1974. *Salyut 5* was launched June 22, 1976. *Salyut 6* was launched on Sept. 29, 1977. *Salyut 7* was launched on April 19, 1982. A record breaking Russian endurance flight was set (Feb. 8, 1984–Oct. 2, 1985) when Soviet astronauts spent 237 days in orbit aboard *Salyut-7*. *Salyut-7* re-entered the atmosphere and crashed into the Atlantic Ocean on Feb. 6, 1991.

Mir. The former Soviet Union's space station was launched into orbit on Feb. 20, 1986. Since that time, several space endurance records have been set in the *Mir*. On Dec. 29, 1987, Col. Yuri Romanenko set a single-mission record of 326.5 days in space. On Dec. 21, 1989, Col. Vladimir Titov and Musa Manarov returned to Earth after spending 366 days aboard the orbiting space station. On March 22, 1995, Russian cosmonaut Valeriy Polyakov set a new record for the longest human flight in space—439 days. U.S. astronaut, Dr. Shannon W. Lucid set the American and women's space endurance records of 188 days and five hours aboard the *Mir* before returning to Earth on Sept. 26, 1996.

Over the past year, the aging *Mir* has had a series of mishaps. The worst occurred on June 25, 1997, when an unmanned cargo ship collided with the station during docking tests. A solar array was damaged and the *Spektr* research module was punctured and lost its pressure. The *Spektr's* electric cables prevented the module's hatch from closing and they were disconnected in order to close the hatch and seal off the depressurized *Spektr* from the rest of the station. This action caused the *Mir* to lose almost half its power.

The Russian Space Agency considered the *Mir* crew to be too exhausted from their ordeal to attempt the risky repair work, so cosmonauts Nasily Tsibliyev and Aleksandr Lazutkin returned to earth on Aug. 14, 1997, after six troubled months in space. They were replaced by a fresh crew on August 7: *Mir-25* commander Anatoly Solovyov and flight engineer Pavel Vinogradov. American astronaut Michael Foale remained on the space station to finish his four-and-a-half-month tour. Foale is due to return home on the shuttle *Atlantis* in early October, and U.S. astronaut David Wolf is scheduled to take his place on the Russian outpost for a four-month stay.

The new Russian team and astronaut Foale traveled briefly outside the *Spektr* in the resident *Soyuz* spacecraft on August 15, and videotaped the module for signs of damage, though they were unable to identify the source of the pressure leaks.

A successful fix-it mission took place on August 22, when the two cosmonauts reopened and entered *Spektr*, replaced its hatch with a modified one, and reconnected the eleven solar panel cables. Power lines from the new hatch will be connected to batteries inside the *Mir*. During the repairs, astronaut Foale stayed inside the *Soyuz* escape pod in case an emergency arose and it became necessary for him and his Russian crew members to abandon the station. On Sept. 3, 1997, both cosmonauts are scheduled to take the first of several critical spacewalks to closely inspect the damage to *Spektr* and plan how to repair it. (*See* Current Events for follow-up information.) □

Notable Manned Space Flights

Designation and country	Date	Astronauts	Flight time (h/min)	Remarks
Vostok 1 (U.S.S.R.)	April 12, 1961	Yuri A. Gagarin	1/48	First manned orbital flight.
MR III (U.S.)	May 5, 1961	Alan B. Shepard, Jr.	0/15	Range 486 km (302 mi.), peak 187 km (116.5 mi); capsule recovered. First American in space.
Vostok 2 (U.S.S.R.)	Aug. 6–7, 1961	Gherman S. Titov	25/18	First long-duration flight.
MA VI (U.S.)	Feb. 20, 1962	John H. Glenn, Jr.	4/55	First American in orbit.
MA IX (U.S.)	May 15–16, 1963	L. Gordon Cooper, Jr.	34/20	Longest *Mercury* flight.
Vostok 6 (U.S.S.R.)	June 16–19, 1963	Valentina V. Tereshkova	70/50	First orbital flight by female cosmonaut.
Voskhod 1 (U.S.S.R.)	Oct. 12, 1964	Vladimir M. Komarov; Konstantin P. Feoktistov; Boris G. Yegorov	24/17	First 3-man orbital flight; also first flight without space suits.
Voskhod 2 (U.S.S.R.)	March 18, 1965	Alexei A. Leonov; Pavel I. Belyayev	26/2	First "space walk" (by Leonov), 10 min.
GT III (U.S.)	March 23, 1965	Virgil I. Grissom; John W. Young	4/53	First manned test of *Gemini* spacecraft.
GT IV (U.S.)	June 3–7, 1965	James A. McDivitt; Edward H. White, 2d	97/48	First American "space walk" (by White), lasting slightly over 20 min.
GT VIII (U.S.)	March 16–17, 1966	Neil A. Armstrong; David R. Scott	10/42	First docking between manned spacecraft and an unmanned space vehicle (an orbiting *Agena* rocket).
Apollo 7 (U.S.)	Oct. 11–22, 1968	Walter A. Schirra, Jr.; Donn F. Eisele; R. Walter Cunningham	260/9	First manned test of *Apollo* command module; first live TV transmissions from orbit.
Soyuz 3 (U.S.S.R.)	Oct. 26–30, 1968	Georgi T. Bergeovoi	94/51	First manned rendezvous and possible docking by Soviet cosmonaut.
Apollo 8 (U.S.)	Dec. 21–27, 1968	Frank Borman; James A. Lovell, Jr.; William A. Anders	147/00	First spacecraft in circumlunar orbit; TV transmissions from this orbit. The three astronauts were also the first men to view the Earth whole.
Apollo 9 (U.S.)	Mar. 3–13, 1969	James A. McDivitt; David R. Scott; Russell L. Schweikart	241/1	First manned flight of Lunar Module.
Apollo 10 (U.S.)	May 18–26, 1969	Thomas P. Stafford; Eugene A. Cernan; John W. Young	192/3	First descent to within 9 miles of moon's surface by manned craft.
Apollo 11 (U.S.)	July 16–24, 1969	Neil A. Armstrong; Edwin E. Aldrin, Jr.; Michael Collins	195/18	First manned landing and EVA on moon; soil and rock samples collected; experiments left on lunar surface.
Soyuz 6 (U.S.S.R.)	Oct. 11–16, 1969	Gorgiy Shonin; Valriy Kabasov	118/42	Three spacecraft and seven men put into Earth orbit simultaneously for first time.
Apollo 12 (U.S.)	Nov. 14–24, 1969	Charles Conrad, Jr.; Richard F. Gordon, Jr.; Alan Bean	244/36	Manned lunar landing mission; investigated *Surveyor 3* spacecraft; collected lunar samples. EVA time: 15 h 30 min.
Apollo 13 (U.S.)	April 11–17, 1970	James A. Lovell, Jr.; Fred W. Haise, Jr.; John L. Swigert, Jr.	142/54	Third manned lunar landing attempt; aborted due to pressure loss in liquid oxygen in service module and failure of fuel cells.
Apollo 14 (U.S.)	Jan. 31–Feb. 9, 1971	Alan B. Shepard; Stuart A. Roosa; Edgar D. Mitchell	216/42	Third manned lunar landing: returned largest amount of lunar material.
Soyuz 11 (U.S.S.R.)	June 6–30, 1971	Georgiy Tomofeyevich Dobrovolskiy; Vladislav Nikolayevich Volkov; Viktor Ivanovich Patsyev	569/40	Linked up with first space station, *Salyut 1*. Astronauts died just before re-entry due to loss of pressurization in spacecraft.
Apollo 15 (U.S.)	July 26–Aug. 7, 1971	David R. Scott; James B. Irwin; Alfred M. Worden	295/12	Fourth manned lunar landing; first use of Lunar Rover propelled by Scott and Irwin; first live pictures of LM lift-off from moon; exploration time: 18 hours.
Apollo 16 (U.S.)	April 16–27, 1972	John W. Young; Thomas K. Mattingly; Charles M. Duke, Jr.	265/51	Fifth manned lunar landing; second use of Lunar Rover Vehicle, propelled by Young and Duke. Total exploration time on the moon was 20 h 14 min, setting new record. Mattingly's in-flight "walk in space" was 1 h 23 min. Approximately 213 lb of lunar rock returned.
Apollo 17 (U.S.)	Dec. 7–19, 1972	Eugene A. Cernan; Ronald E. Evans; Harrison H. Schmitt	301/51	Sixth and last manned lunar landing; third to carry lunar rover. Cernan and Schmitt, during three EVA's, completed total of 22 h 05 min 3 sec. USS Ticonderoga recovered crew and about 250 lbs of lunar samples.

Designation and country	Date	Astronauts	Flight time (h/min)	Remarks
Skylab SL-2 (U.S.)	May 25–June 22, 1973	Charles Conrad, Jr.; Joseph P. Kerwin; Paul J. Weitz	672/50	First manned Skylab launch. Established Skylab Orbital Assembly and conducted scientific and medical experiments.
Skylab SL-3 (U.S.)	July 28–Sept. 25, 1973	Alan L. Bean, Jr.; Jack R. Lousma; Owen K. Garriott	1427/9	Second manned Skylab launch. New crew remained in space for 59 days continuing scientific and medical experiments and earth observations from orbit.
Skylab SL-4 (U.S.)	Nov. 16, 1973–Feb. 8, 1974	Gerald Carr; Edward Gibson; William Pogue	2017/16	Third manned Skylab launch; obtained medical data on crew for use in extending the duration of manned space flight; crews "walked in space" 4 times, totaling 44 h 40 min. Longest space mission yet—84 d 1 h 16 min. Splashdown in Pacific, Feb. 9, 1974.
Apollo/Soyuz Test Project (U.S. and U.S.S.R.)	July 15–24, 1975 (U.S.)	U.S.: Brig. Gen. Thomas P. Stafford, Vance D. Brand, Donald K. Slayton	216/05	World's first international manned rendezvous and docking in space; aimed at developing a space rescue capability.
Apollo/Soyuz Test Project (U.S. and U.S.S.R.)	July 15–21, 1975 (U.S.S.R.)	U.S.S.R.: Col. A. A. Leonov, V. N.Kubasov	223/35	Apollo and Soyuz docked and crewmen exchanged visits on July 17, 1975. Mission duration for Soyuz: 142 h 31 min. For Apollo: 217 h, 28 min.
Columbia (U.S.)	April 12–14, 1981	Capt. Robert L. Crippen; John W. Young	54/20	Maiden voyage of Space Shuttle, the first spacecraft designed specifically for re-use up to 100 times.
Salyut 7 (U.S.S.R.)	Feb. 8, 1984–Oct. 2, 1985	Leonid Kizim; Vladimir Solovyov; Oleg Atkov	237 days	Set a record for Soviet team endurance flight in orbiting space station.
Mir (U.S.S.R.)	Feb. 8, 1987–Dec. 29, 1987	Yuri V. Romanenko[1]	326.5 days	Set a record for Soviet single endurance flight in orbiting space station.
Mir (U.S.S.R.)	Dec. 21, 1987–Dec. 21, 1988	Col. Vladimir Titov and Musa Manarov	366 days	Set current record for Soviet team endurance flight in orbiting space station.
Endeavour (U.S.)	May 7–13, 1992	Richard J. Hieb; Maj. Thomas D. Akers; Cdr. Pierre J. Thugt	—	The three mission specialists remained free of the Endeavour for 8 hours and 20 minutes on May 13 during the repair of communications satellite, setting an absolute record for extravehicular duration in space. First capture of a satellite using hands only.
Endeavour (U.S.)	Dec. 2–13, 1993	Col. Richard O. Covey; Cdr. Kenneth D. Bowersox; Lt. Col. Tom Akers*; Dr. Jeffrey A. Hoffman**; Dr. Story Musgrave**; Claude Nicollier**; Dr. Kathryn C. Thornton* (*two space walks, **three space walks)	10 days, 19 hr., 59 min.	Repaired Hubble Space Telescope. Replaced gyroscopes, solar arrays, camera, electronics and hardware. Installed COSTAR corrective optics to compensate for flaw in Hubble's primary mirror. Record five space walks in a single mission.
Discovery (U.S.)	Feb. 3–11, 1994	Col. Charles F. Bolden; Capt. Kenneth S. Reightier, Jr.; Dr. N. Jan Davis; Dr. Franklin R. Chang-Diaz; Dr. Ronald M. Sega; Russian cosmonaut, Sergei K. Krikalev	8 days 7 hr., 22 sec.	Test flight of Wake Shield Facility, an experimental, retrievable, free-flying satellite for use in developing exotic materials. Cargo bay carried a private, commercial pressurized-laboratory, Spacehab, for experimental use, leased by NASA. Crew member Sergei K. Krikalev was first Russian cosmonaut to be launched in an American spacecraft.
Columbia (U.S.)	July 8–23, 1994	Col. Robert D. Cabana; Lieut. Col. James D. Halsell, Jr.; Richard J. Heib; Lieut. Col. Carl E. Walz; Dr. Leroy Chiao; Dr. Donald A. Thomas; and Dr. Chiaki Naito-Mukai, the first Japanese woman astronaut.	14 days 17 hr., 55 min.	Studied the effects of limited gravity of orbital flight on materials and living things including goldfish, killifish, jellyfish, sea urchins, and Japanese red-bellied newts.
Mir-17 (Russia)	Jan. 8, 1994–Mar. 22, 1995	Dr. Valery Polyakov	439[2] days	Record single endurance flight in orbiting space station. Returned to earth with crewmates cosmonaut Helena Kondakova and commander Alexander Viktorenko who spent 169 days each in the Mir.

Designation and country	Date	Astronauts	Flight time (h/min)	Remarks
Discovery (U.S.)	Feb. 3–11, 1995	Cdr. James D. Wetherbee; Lt. Col. Eileen M. Collins; Dr. Janice Voss; Dr. Bernard A. Harris, Jr.*; Dr. C. Michael Foale*; Russian cosmonaut Co. Vladimir G. Titov. *performed spacewalks.	8 days 6 hr., 29 min.	First rendezvous of U.S. spacecraft with a Russian space station (Mir), Feb. 6. Lt. Col. Collins was first female shuttle pilot. Deployed and retrieved solar observatory satellite. Extra-vehicular activity to test new space suit modifications and practice space station assembly techniques. EVA time: 4 h, 35 min.
Soyuz TM-21 (Russia)	March 14–16, 1995	Russian cosmonauts: Lieut. Col. Vladimir N. Dezhurov; Gennady M. Strekalov; and U.S. astronaut Dr. Norman E. Thagard.	—	Dr. Thagard became the first American astronaut to fly aboard a Soyuz spacecraft with a Russian crew launched from Baikonur Space Center in Kazakhstan. He also became the first American to enter the Mir space station on March 16.
Atlantis (U.S.)	June 27–July 7, 1995	Lt. Col. Charles J. Precourt; Capt. Robert L. (Hoot) Gibson; Dr. Eileen S. Baker; Gregory J. Harbaugh; Dr. Bonnie Dunbar; Russian cosmonauts: Mir-19 commander, Anatoly Y. Solovyev; Nikolai M. Budarin	10 days	Marked 100th human mission in U.S. space program and first shuttle linkup with the Mir: docked June 29, undocked July 4. Joined spacecraft held a record 10 people: 6 Americans and 4 Russians. Three Mir crew: cosmonauts: Mir-18 commander, Lieut. Col. Vladimir N. Dezhurov, Grennady M. Strekalov, and U.S. astronaut Dr. Norman E. Thagard returned to earth aboard the Atlantis. Dr. Thagard set a U.S. space record of 112 days in space aboard Mir. Cosmonauts Solovyev and Budarin remained aboard the Mir.
Atlantis (U.S.)	Nov. 12–20, 1995	Col. Kenneth D. Cameron; Lieut. Col. James D. Halsell, Jr.; Col. Jerry L. Ross; Lieut. Col. William S. McArthur, Jr.; Canadian Major Chris A. Hadfield who operated the robot arm.	8 days, 4 hr., 31 min.	Second docking with Mir. Carried 15-foot-long Russian-made docking module and attached it to the Mir. Brought two new solar-powered panels for Mir and also supplies and scientific equipment. U.S. and Russian astronauts spent 3 days together on Mir conducting experiments.
Endeavour (U.S.)	Jan. 11–20, 1996	Col. Brian Duffy; Brent Jett; Dr. Leroy Chiao**; Capt. Winston E. Scott;* Dr. Daniel T. Berry;* and Japanese astronaut Koichi Wakata, who operated robot arm. (*one spacewalk. **two spacewalks)	8 days, 22 hr., 01 min.	Deployed and retrieved NASA satellite, retrieved Japanese satellite. Two spacewalks performed to test space-suit components and practice space station construction, tools, and techniques. Total EVA time: 13 hours.
Columbia (U.S.)	Feb. 22–March 9, 1996	Lieut. Col. Andrew M. Allen; Lt. Col. Scott J. Horowitz; Dr. Franklin R. Chang-Diaz; Dr. Jeffrey A. Hoffman; Italian astronauts Maurizio Cheli and Dr. Umberto Guidoni; and Swiss astronaut Nicollier Claude.	15 days, 17 hr., 40 min.	Microgravity research flight. Second attempt to deploy Italian-built electricity-conducting satellite failed when metallic debris punctured insulation and broke tether after it was unreeled to almost its 12.5 mile length.
Atlantis (U.S.)	March 22–31, 1996	Col. Kevin P. Chilton; Lieut. Col. Richard A. Searfoss; Dr. Ronald M. Sega; Dr. Linda M. Goodwin; Lieut. Col. Michael R. Clifford; and Dr. Shannon W. Lucid.	9 days, 5 hr., 15 min.	Third linkup with Mir. (March 22–27). Clifford and Goodwin conducted 6-hour spacewalk in shuttle cargo bay while docked with Mir. Dr. Lucid remained on board Mir for scheduled 140-day tour to conduct biomedical and material science experiments. Booster problems delayed her return until mid-September. Lucid is first American woman to live on Mir. On July 15, 1996, she broke the previous record for the longest U.S. manned space flight.
Endeavour (U.S.)	May 19–29, 1996	Col. John H. Casper; Lieut. Col. Curtis L. Brown, Jr.; Cdr. Daniel W. Bursch; Mario Runco, Jr.; Dr. Andrew S.W. Thomas; and Canadian astronaut Dr. Marc Garneau.	10 days, 0 hr., 40 min.	Made record four satellite rendezvous, including three with small PAMS satellite to test the concept of a self-stabilizing satellite in orbit. Deployed and retrieved a Spartan satellite that carried an experimental inflatable antenna.

Designation and country	Date	Astronauts	Flight time (h/min)	Remarks
Columbia (U.S.)	June 20–July 7, 1996	Col. Terence T. Henricks; Kevin R. Kregel; Lieut. Col. Susan J. Helms; Richard M. Linnehan; Cdr. Charles E. Brady, Jr.; French astronaut Dr. Jean-Jacques Favier; and Canadian astronaut Dr. Robert Brent Thirsk.	16 days, 21 hr., 48 min.	Second-longest mission to date. Studied the effects of weightlessness on people, plants, and animals, and material manufacturing in near-zero gravity.
Atlantis (U.S.)	Sept.16–26, 1996	William F. Readdy; Terrence W. Wilcutt; Thomas D. Akers; John E. Blaha; Jerome Apt; Carl E. Waltz. Download: Dr. Shannon W. Lucid	10 days, 3hr.,19 min	Fourth Mir docking. Carried a Spacehab module. Transferred supplies and equipment to Mir. After breaking all American and women's space endurance records (188 days, 5 hr., 0 min), Dr. Shannon W. Lucid returned with Atlantis crew. John E. Blaha remained on Mir for a four-month stay.
Columbia (U.S.)	Nov.19–Dec.7,1996	Kenneth D. Cockrell; Cdr. Kent V. Romingel; Tamara E. Jernigan; Thomas D. Jones; Dr. F. Story Musgrave	17 days, 15 hr., 53 min	Deployed and recovered two free-flying satellites during mission: an ultraviolet telescope and Wake Shield (semiconductor processing) Facility. A jammed airlock hatch canceled two scheduled spacewalks. Is longest mission to date. Dr. Musgrave, 61, became oldest person ever in space and first to fly on all five space shuttles.
Atlantis (U.S.)	Jan.12–22, 1997	Capt. Michael A. Baker; Cdr. Brent W. Jett, Jr.; John M. Grunsfeld; Marsha S. Ivins; Peter J.K. Wiscoff; Dr. Jerry L. Linenger. Download: John E. Blaha	10 days, 04 hr., 56 min	Fifth Mir docking (Jan.14–19). Carried Spacehab double module. Transferred supplies to Mir. Conducted experiments in Spacehab and Mir. John E. Blaha returned with Atlantis crew after 128 days in space, 118 aboard the Mir. Jerry Linenger remained aboard Mir for 4.5-month stay.
Discovery (U.S.)	Feb.11–21,1997	Cdr. Kenneth Bowersox; Lt. Col. Scott J. Harowitz; Col. Mark C. Lee*; Steven A. Hawley; Gregory J. Harbaugh*; Steven L. Smith*; Joseph R. Tanner* (*spacewalks)	9 days, 23 hr., 38 min	Second Space Telescope servicing mission. Installed new imaging spectrograph and infrared camera. Also patched torn telescope insulating cover. Deployed telescope at higher altitude: 335 x 321 nautical mile orbit. Mission required five spacewalks totaling 33 hr., 11 min.
Columbia (U.S.)	April 4–8, 1997	Lt. Col. James D. Halsell, Jr.; Lt. Cdr. Susan L. Still; Janice E.Voss; Michael L. Gernhardt; Donald A. Thomas; Roger K. Crouch; Gregory T. Linteris	3 days, 23 hr., 13 min.	Planned 12-day mission to study behavior of metals, materials, and fluids in the absence of gravity and microgravity effects on fires. Was cut short due to a fuel-cell generator problem. Susan Still is second female shuttle pilot.
Atlantis (U.S.)	May 15–24,1997	Col. Charles J. Precourt; Lt. Col. Eileen M. Collins; Edward T. Lu; Maj. Carlos I. Noriega; Jean-Francois Clervoy (France); Elena V. Kondakova (Russia); C. Michael Foale. Download: Dr. Jerry M. Lineger	9 days, 5 hr., 20 min.	Sixth Mir docking (May 16–21). Carried a Spacehab double module. Transferred supplies and equipment. Jerry M. Lineger returned with Atlantis after 132 days in space. Michael Foale remained on Mir for a 4.5-month stay.
Columbia (U.S.)	July 1–17, 1997	Lt. Col. James D. Halsell, Jr.; Lt. Cdr. Susan L. Still; Janice E.Voss; Donald A. Thomas; Michael L. Gernhard; Roger K. Crouch; Gregory T. Linteris	15 days, 16 hr., 45 min	Successful reflight of the uncompleted Microgravity Science Mission (See April 4–8, 1997). Is first time the same crew flies together again to complete a previous mission.
Discovery (U.S.)	Aug. 7–19, 1997	Lt. Col. Curtis L. Brown, Jr.; Cdr. Kent V. Rominger; N. Jan Davis; Lt. Cdr. Robert L. Curbeam, Jr.; Stephen K. Robinson; Bjarni Tryggvason (Canada)	11 days, 20 hr., 28 min.	Deployed Shuttle Pallet Satellite with scientific instruments to study changes in Earth's atmosphere. Also conducted experiments with shuttle's robot arm for possible applications in Japanese experimental module of space station.

1. Returned to earth with two fellow cosmonauts, Aleksandr P. Aleksandrov and Anatoly Levchenko, who had spent a shorter stay aboard the Mir. 2. From launch to landing. NOTE: The letters MR stand for Mercury (capsule) and Redstone (rocket); MA, for Mercury and Atlas (rocket); GT, for Gemini (capsule) and Titan-II (rocket). The first astronaut listed in the Gemini and Apollo flights is the command pilot. The Mercury capsules had names: MR-III was Freedom 7, MR-IV was Liberty Bell 7, MA-VI was Friendship 7, MA-VII was Aurora 7, MA-VIII was Sigma 7, and MA-IX was Faith 7. The figure 7 referred to the fact that the first group of U.S. astronauts numbered seven men. Only one Gemini capsule had a name: GT-III was called Molly Brown (after the Broadway musical The Unsinkable Molly Brown); thereafter the practice of naming the capsules was discontinued.

Aviation

Amelia Earhart's Legacy Remembered

1997 marked the centennial of the legendary pilot's birth and the 60th anniversary of her unsolved disappearance

Linda Finch, pilot of World Flight 1997
(John Dyer, 1996)

Amelia Earhart and her Lockheed Electra

Sixty years after Amelia Earhart vanished mysteriously in the Pacific during her attempt to become the first person to circumnavigate the world along the equator, Linda Finch, a San Antonio businesswoman, accomplished pilot, and aviation historian, recreated and completed her idol's last flight as a tribute to the aviation pioneer's spirit and vision.

On March 17, 1997, Ms. Finch and a navigator took off from Oakland International Airport, California, in a restored Lockheed Electra 10E, the same make and model aircraft that Earhart used on her last journey. The mission to fulfill Amelia Earhart's dream was called "World Flight 1997." Although Ms. Finch was not the first to attempt Earhart's around-the-world journey, she was the first to do it in a historic airplane. Linda Finch closely followed the same route that Earhart flew, stopping in 18 countries before finishing the trip two and a half months later when she landed back at the Oakland Airport on May 28.

Over a million school children and others were able to follow the flight daily through an interactive web site (www.worldflight.org), part of a free multimedia educational program called "You Can Soar," provided by the project's sponsor.

Linda Finch acquired a vintage Lockheed Electra in 1994 for this adventure. Using original drawings and photographs, the 1935 aircraft was meticulously and accurately restored, right down to its rivets. The classic plane is one of only two in existence capable of flight. The only exception to the original is that Finch's Elec-

tra was equipped with modern navigation and communication equipment whereas Earhart had rudimentary radio communications by today's standards.

World Flight, Inc., is a non-profit organization founded by Linda Finch. "World Flight 1997" was sponsored by Pratt & Whitney, a unit of United Technologies Corporation. Pratt & Whitney created the original Wasp engines used to power Amelia Earhart's Lockheed Electra.

An American Heroine

Amelia Earhart is the most celebrated aviatrix in history and was one of the most famous women of her time. As America's charismatic "Lady of the Air," she set many aviation records, including becoming the first woman to fly across the Atlantic in 1928 as a passenger, the first woman (and second person after Lindbergh) to fly solo across the Atlantic in 1932, and the first person to fly alone across the Pacific, from Honolulu, Hawaii, to Oakland, California, in 1935. In an era when men dominated aviation, she was truly a pioneer.

Amelia Mary Earhart was born on July 24, 1897 in Atchison, Kansas. During her early years, she was constantly hampered by lack of funds and worked at a variety of jobs to fulfill her desire to fly. She held positions as a teacher, nursing assistant, photographer, secretary, and social worker. Earhart even bought a truck and hauled gravel to earn money to buy a plane.

AE, as she was called by her friends, was a modern woman. She was courageous, independent, and had a strong social conscience. She fought for international peace, equality for women, the advancement of women in aviation, and the viability of commercial aviation. During her lifetime, she was a role model to millions of people whom she motivated and encouraged through her actions.

In 1937, Earhart attempted to become the first person ever to fly around the world at its longest point—the equator—a challenging trip of 29,000 miles. She intended this feat to be the last record-setting flight of her legendary career. It was to be her swan song. Amelia was accompanied on the trip by a highly experienced navigator, Frederick J. Noonan.

On July 2, 1937, after successfully completing 22,000 miles of the journey in her silver twin-engine Electra, she took off from Lae, New Guinea, on the longest and most dangerous leg of her flight, some 18 hours and 2,556 miles across the vast ocean to Howland Island where the U.S. government had constructed an airfield and stored fuel supplies for her use.

Howland Island is uninhabited, a tiny island in the North Pacific about one and a half miles long and a half mile wide. The United States Coast Guard had stationed the cutter, *Itasca,* off Howland to maintain radio communications with the Electra and assist Earhart in locating the minuscule atoll.

When the plane was due to reach its destination, Earhart reported to the *Itasca* that she thought that she was flying over Howland, but couldn't see it below. Evidently lost and confused, with her plane running low on fuel, she asked for help in "homing in" by radio to the tiny island. Her last words were, "We are running north and south," presumably flying in a search pattern in hope of seeing the island. She lost critical radio communications with the *Itasca* and the cutter's radio operators could not get a bearing on her position. Repeated efforts by the *Itasca* to contact the fliers were unsuccessful and they were presumed out of fuel and lost at sea. An extensive land, air, and sea search lasting over two weeks failed to find them and no trace of the world's most famous female pilot, her navigator, or their plane has ever been found.—*OTJ* □

Famous Firsts in Aviation

1782 **First balloon flight.** Jacques and Joseph Montgolfier of Annonay, France, sent up a small smoke-filled balloon about mid-November.

1783 **First hydrogen-filled balloon flight.** Jacques A. C. Charles, Paris physicist, supervised construction by A. J. and M. N. Robert of a 13-ft. diameter balloon that was filled with hydrogen. It got up to about 3,000 ft. and traveled about 16 mi. in a 45-min flight (Aug. 27).
First human balloon flights. A Frenchman, Jean Pilâtre de Rozier made the first captive-balloon ascension (Oct. 15). With the Marquis d'Arlandes, Pilâtre de Rozier made the first free flight, reaching a peak altitude of about 500 ft., and traveling about 5½ mi. in 20 min (Nov. 21).

1784 **First powered balloon.** Gen. Jean Baptiste Marie Meusnier developed the first propeller-driven and elliptically-shaped balloon—the crew cranking three propellers on a common shaft to give the craft a speed of about 3 mph.
First woman to fly. Mme. Thible, a French opera singer (June 4).

1793 **First balloon flight in America.** Jean Pierre Blanchard, a French pilot, made it from Philadelphia to near Woodbury, Gloucester County, N.J., in a little over 45 min (Jan. 9).

1794 **First military use of the balloon.** Jean Marie Coutelle, using a balloon built for the French Army, made two 4-hr observation ascents. The military purpose of the ascents seems to have been to damage the enemy's morale.

1797 **First parachute jump.** André-Jacques Garnerin dropped from about 6,500 ft. over Monceau Park in Paris in a 23-ft. diameter parachute made of white canvas with a basket attached (Oct. 22).

1843 **First air transport company.** In London, William S. Henson and John Stringfellow filed articles of incorporation for the Aerial Transit Company (March 24). It failed.

1852 **First dirigible.** Henri Giffard, a French engineer, flew in a controllable (more or less) steam-engine powered balloon, 144 ft. long and 39 ft. in diameter, inflated with 88,000 cubic ft. of coal gas. It reached 6.7 mph on a flight from Paris to Trappe (Sept. 24).

1860 **First aerial photographers.** Samuel Archer King and William Black made two photos of Boston, still in existence.

1872 **First gas-engine powered dirigible.** Paul Haenlein, a German engineer, flew in a semi-rigid-frame dirigible, powered by a 4-cylinder internal-combustion engine running on coal gas drawn from the supporting bag.

1873 **First transatlantic attempt.** *The New York Daily Graphic* sponsored the attempt with a 400,000 cu ft. balloon carrying a lifeboat. A rip in the bag during inflation brought collapse of the balloon and the project.

1897 **First successful metal dirigible.** An all-metal dirigible, designed by David Schwarz, a Hungarian, took off from Berlin's Tempelhof Field and, powered by a 16-hp Daimler engine, got several miles before leaking gas caused it to crash (Nov. 13).

1900 **First Zeppelin flight.** Germany's Count Ferdinand von Zeppelin flew the first of his long series of rigid-frame airships. It attained a speed of 18 mph and got 3½ mi. before its steering gear failed (July 2).

1903 **First successful heavier-than-air machine flight.** Aviation was really born on the sand dunes at Kitty Hawk, N.C., when Orville Wright crawled to his prone position between the wings of the biplane he and his brother Wilbur had built, opened the throttle of their homemade 12-hp engine and took to the air. He covered 120 ft. in 12 sec. Later that day, in one of four flights, Wilbur stayed up 59 sec and covered 852 ft. (Dec. 17).

1904 **First airplane maneuvers.** Orville Wright made the first turn with an airplane (Sept. 15); 5 days later his brother Wilbur made the first complete circle.

1905 **First airplane flight over half an hour.** Orville Wright kept his craft up 33 min, 17 sec (Oct. 4).

1906 **First European airplane flight.** Alberto Santos-Dumont, a Brazilian, flew a heavier-than-air machine at Bagatelle Field, Paris (Sept. 13).

1908 **First airplane fatality.** Lt. Thomas E. Selfridge, U.S. Army Signal Corps, was in a group of officers evaluating the Wright plane at Fort Myer, Va. He was up about 75 ft. with Orville

Wright when the propeller hit a bracing wire and was broken, throwing the plane out of control, killing Selfridge and seriously injuring Wright (Sept. 17).

1909 **First cross-Channel flight.** Louis Blériot flew in a 25-hp Blériot VI monoplane from Les Baraques near Calais, France, and landed near Dover Castle, England, in a 26.61-mi. (38-km) 37-min flight across the English Channel (July 25).

First International Aviation Competition Meeting. American Glenn Curtis narrowly beat France's Louis Blériot in main event and won the Gordon Bennett Cup. Meet held at Rheims, France (Aug. 22–28).

1910 **First licensed woman pilot.** Baroness Raymonde de la Roche of France, who learned to fly in 1909, received ticket No. 36 on March 8.

First flight from shipboard. Lt. Eugene Ely, USN, took a Curtiss plane off from the deck of cruiser *Birmingham* at Hampton Roads, Va., and flew to Norfolk (Nov. 14). The following January, he reversed the process, flying from Camp Selfridge to the deck of the armored cruiser *Pennsylvania* in San Francisco Bay (Jan. 18).

First aircraft to take off from water. Henri Fabrer in Gnome-powered floatplane, at Martigues, France (March 28).

1911 **First U.S. woman pilot.** Harriet Quimby, a magazine writer, got ticket No. 37, making her the second licensed female pilot in the world.

1912 **First woman's cross-Channel flight.** Harriet Quimby flew from Dover, England, across the English Channel and landed at Hardelot, France (25 mi. south of Calais), in a Blériot monoplane loaned to her by Louis Blériot (April 16). She was later killed in a flying accident over Dorchester Bay during a Harvard–Boston aviation meet on July 1, 1912.

First parachute jump from a powered airplane. Albert Berry jumped in a test over Jefferson Barracks military post, St. Louis (March 1). Some sources credit Grant Morton as making first jump in 1911.

1913 **First multi-engined aircraft.** Built and flown by Igor Ivan Sikorsky while still in his native Russia.

1914 **First aerial combat.** In August, Allied and German pilots and observers started shooting at each other with pistols and rifles—with negligible results.

1915 **First air raids on England.** German Zeppelins started dropping bombs on four English communities (Jan. 19).

1918 **First U.S. air squadron.** The U.S. Army Air Corps made its first independent raids over enemy lines, in DH-4 planes (British-designed) powered with 400-hp American-designed Liberty engines (April 8).

First regular airmail service. Operated for the Post Office Department by the Army, the first regular service was inaugurated with one round trip a day (except Sunday) between Washington, D.C., and New York City (May 15).

1919 **First transatlantic flight.** The NC-4, one of four Curtiss flying boats commanded by Lt. Comdr. Albert C. Read, reached Lisbon, Portugal (May 27), after hops from Trepassy Bay, Newfoundland, to Horta, Azores (May 16–17), to Ponta Delgada (May 20). The Liberty-powered craft was piloted by Walter Hinton.

First nonstop transatlantic flight. Capt. John

Alcock and Lt. Arthur Whitten Brown, British World War I flyers, made the 1,900 mi. from St. John's, Newfoundland, to Clifden, Ireland, in 16 h 12 min in a Vickers-Vimy bomber with two 350-hp Rolls-Royce engines (June 15–16).

First lighter-than-air transatlantic flight. The British dirigible R-34, commanded by Maj. George H. Scott, left Firth of Forth, Scotland (July 2), and touched down at Mineola, L.I., 108 hours later. The eastbound trip was made in 75 hours (completed July 13).

First scheduled London-Paris passenger service (using airplanes). Aircraft Travel and Transport inaugurated London-Paris service (Aug. 25). Later the company started the first transchannel mail service on the same route (Nov. 10).

First free-fall parachute jump. Leslie Irvin jumped over McCook Field, Dayton, Ohio, to prove that one won't lose consciousness during a delayed free-fall using a manually-operated parachute (April 28).

1921 **First U.S. black female pilot.** Bessie Coleman received license June 15. Was killed April 30, 1926, in flying accident.

First naval vessel sunk by aircraft. Two battleships being scrapped by treaty were sunk by bombs dropped from Army planes in demonstration put on by Brig. Gen. William S. Mitchell (July 21).

First helium balloon. The C-7, non-rigid Navy dirigible was first to use non-inflammable helium as lifting gas, making a flight from Hampton Roads, Va., to Washington, D.C. (Dec. 1).

1922 **First member of Caterpillar Club.** Lt. (later Maj. Gen.) Harold Harris bailed out of a crippled plane he was testing at McCook Field, Dayton, Ohio (Oct. 20), and became the first man to join the Caterpillar Club—those whose lives have been saved by parachute.

1923 **First nonstop transcontinental flight.** Lts. John A. Macready and Oakley Kelly flew a single-engine Fokker T-2 nonstop from New York to San Diego, a distance of just over 2,500 mi. in 26 hours, 50 min (May 2–3).

First autogyro flight. Juan de la Cierva, a brilliant Spanish mathematician, made the first successful flight in a rotary wing aircraft in Madrid (June 9).

1924 First round-the-world flight. Four Douglas Cruiser biplanes of the U.S. Army Air Corps took off from Seattle under command of Maj. Frederick Martin (April 6). 175 days later, two of the planes (Lt. Lowell Smith's and Lt. Erik Nelson's) landed in Seattle after a circuitous route—one source saying 26,345 mi., another saying 27,553 mi.

1926 First polar flight. Then–Lt. Cmdr. Richard E. Byrd, acting as navigator, and Floyd Bennett as pilot, flew a trimotor Fokker from Kings Bay, Spitsbergen, over the North Pole and back in 15 ½ hours (May 8–9).

1927 First solo, nonstop transatlantic flight. Charles Augustus Lindbergh lifted his Wright-powered Ryan monoplane, *Spirit of St. Louis*, from Roosevelt Field, L.I., to stay aloft 33 hours 39 min and travel 3,600 mi. to Le Bourget Field outside Paris (May 20–21). Although 91 persons in 13 separate flights crossed the Atlantic before him, he flew directly between two great world cities and did it alone.

First transatlantic passenger. Charles A. Levine was piloted by Clarence D. Chamberlin from Roosevelt Field, L.I., to Eisleben, Germany, in a Wright-powered Bellanca (June 4–5).

1928 First east-west transatlantic crossing. Baron Guenther von Huenefeld, piloted by German Capt. Hermann Koehl and Irish Capt. James Fitzmaurice, left Dublin for New York City (April 12) in a single-engine all-metal Junkers-monoplane. Some 37 hours later, they crashed on Greely Island, Labrador. Rescued.

First U.S.–Australia flight. Sir Charles Kingsford-Smith and Capt. Charles T. P. Ulm, Australians, and two American navigators, Harry W. Lyon and James Warner, crossed the Pacific from Oakland to Brisbane. They went via Hawaii and the Fiji Islands in a trimotor Fokker (May 31–June 8).

First transarctic flight. Sir Hubert Wilkins, an Australian explorer and Carl Ben Eielson, who served as pilot, flew from Point Barrow, Alaska, to Spitsbergen (mid-April).

1929 First of the endurance records. With Air Corps Maj. Carl Spaatz in command and Capt. Ira Eaker as chief pilot, an Army Fokker, aided by refueling in the air, remained aloft 150 hours 40 min at Los Angeles (Jan. 1–7).

First round-the-world airship flight. The LZ-127, known as the *Graf Zeppelin*, flew 21,300 miles in 20 days and 4 hours. Also set distance record (August).

First blind flight. James H. Doolittle proved the feasibility of instrument-guided flying when he took off and landed entirely on instruments (Sept. 24).

First rocket-engine flight. Fritz von Opel, a German auto maker, stayed aloft in his small rocket-powered craft for 75 sec, covering nearly 2 mi. (Sept. 30).

First South Pole flight. Comdr. Richard E. Byrd, with Bernt Balchen as pilot, Harold I. June, radio operator, and Capt. A. C. McKinley, photographer, flew a trimotor Fokker from the Bay of Whales, Little America, over the South Pole and back (Nov. 28–29).

1930 First Paris–New York nonstop flight. Dieudonné Coste and Maurice Bellonte, French pilots, flew a Hispano-powered Breguet biplane from Le Bourget Field to Valley Stream, L.I., in 37 hours, 18 min. (Sept. 2–3).

1931 First flight into the stratosphere. Auguste Piccard, a Swiss physicist, and Charles Knipfer ascended in a balloon from Augsburg, Germany, and reached a height of 51,793 ft. in a 17-h flight that terminated on a glacier near Innsbruck, Austria (May 27).

First nonstop transpacific flight. Hugh Herndon and Clyde Pangborn took off from Sabishiro Beach, Japan, dropped their landing gear, and flew 4,860 mi. to near Wenatchee, Wash., in 41 hours 13 min. (Oct. 4–5).

1932 First woman's transatlantic solo. Amelia Earhart, flying a Pratt & Whitney Wasp-powered Lockheed Vega, flew alone from Harbor Grace, Newfoundland, to Ireland in approximately 15 hours (May 20–21).

First westbound transatlantic solo. James A. Mollison, a British pilot, took a de Havilland Puss Moth from Portmarnock, Ireland, to Pennfield, N.B. (Aug. 18).

First woman airline pilot. Ruth Rowland Nichols, first woman to hold three international records at the same time—speed, distance, altitude—was employed by N.Y.–New England Airways.

1933 First round-the-world solo. Wiley Post took a Lockheed Vega, *Winnie Mae*, 15,596 mi. around the world in 7 days, 18 hours, 49½ min (July 15–22).

1937 First successful helicopter. Hanna Reitsch, a German pilot, flew Dr. Heinrich Focke's FW-61 in free, fully controlled flight at Bremen (July 4). Ms. Reitsch was also the first woman civil and military aviation test pilot.

1939 First turbojet flight. Just before their invasion of Poland, the Germans flew a Heinkel He-178 plane powered by a Heinkel S3B turbojet (Aug. 27).

1940 First wartime use of military gliders. German commandos make successful glider assault on Belgium's Fort Eben-Emael during WWII (May 10).

1941–1945 Most combat missions flown by a pilot in any war. Captain Hans-Ulrich Rudel of Germany flew 2,530 combat missions during WWII while flying a JU-87 Stuka dive bomber. He survived the war.

1942–1945 Top scoring fighter pilot of any war. German Luftwaffe ace Maj. Erich Hartmann scored 352 victories all while flying a Messerschmitt BF 109 during WWII. He was involved in 800 dogfights, and flew 1,425 missions. Maj. Hartmann survived the war.

1942 First and only enemy bombing of U.S. mainland. During World War II, a floatplane launched from a Japanese submarine off Cape Blanco, Oregon, dropped incendiary bombs on the Oregon forest in two attempts to start forest fires and terrorize American civilians, but the bombs did little damage (Sept. 9 and 29).

First American jet plane flight. Robert Stanley, chief pilot for Bell Aircraft Corp., flew the Bell XP-59 *Airacomet* at Muroc Army Base, Calif. (Oct. 1).

First woman fighter pilot to shoot down an enemy aircraft. Soviet Lieutenant, Lilya Litvyak, flying a Yak-1 fighter of the women's 586th Fighter Aviation Regiment, shoots down two German planes over Stalingrad on Sept. 13, 1942.

World's 25 Busiest Airports in 1996

	Airport	Total passengers	% Chg	Airport	Total cargo	% Chg
1.	Chicago, O'Hare (ORD)	69,133,189	2.8	Memphis (MEM)	1,932,607	12.9
2.	Atlanta, Hartsfield (ATL)	63,344,730	9.7	Los Angeles (LAX)	1,719,502	7.7
3.	Dallas/Ft. Worth Airport (DFW)	58,034,503	2.7	Miami (MIA)	1,709,935	7.9
4.	Los Angeles, Ca. (LAX)	57,974,559	7.5	New York, Kennedy (JFK)	1,631,073	2.9
5.	London, Heathrow (LHR)	56,037,813	2.9	Tokyo, Narita (NRT)	1,625,840	-2.5
6.	Tokyo, Haneda (HND)	46,631,475	2.5	Hong Kong (HKG)	1,590,772	7.1
7.	San Francisco (SFO)	39,247,308	8.2	Frankfurt/Main (FRA)	1,497,354	2.5
8.	Frankfurt/Main (FRA)	38,761,174	1.5	Louisville (SDF)	1,368,701	1.3
9.	Seoul (SEL)	34,707,549	12.3	Seoul (SEL)	1,361,510	12.0
10.	Miami (MIA)	33,504,579	0.8	Anchorage, Ak. (ANC)	1,269,283	29.7
11.	Denver, Stapleton (DEN)	32,264,312	3.9	Chicago, O'Hare (ORD)	1,254,789	1.5
12.	Paris, Charles de Gaulle (CDG)	31,823,741	12.2	Singapore (SIN)	1,211,411	7.7
13.	New York, Kennedy (JFK)	31,015,239	2.1	London, Heathrow (LHR)	1,140,768	1.3
14.	Detroit (DTW)	30,014,038	5.5	Amsterdam, Schiphol (AMS)	1,124,649	10.3
15.	Las Vegas (LAS)	30,470,957	8.8	Paris, Charles de Gaulle (CDG)	978,722	5.3
16.	Phoenix, Sky Harbor (PHX)	30,376,584	9.0	Newark (EWR)	957,782	1.6'
17.	Hong Kong (HKG)	30,212,327	7.7	Atlanta, Hartsfield (ATL)	800,378	3.9
18.	Minneapolis/St. Paul (MSP)	29,612,167	10.6	Taipei (TPE)	796,155	5.8
19.	Newark (EWR)	29,072,591	9.2	Dallas/Ft. Worth Airport (DFW)	785,694	1.1
20.	Amsterdam, Schiphol (AMS)	27,753,088	9.5	Dayton, Oh. (DAY)	727,165	14.9
21.	Paris, Orly (ORY)	27,364,985	2.7	San Francisco (SFO)	715,102	2.6
22.	St. Louis (STL)	27,274,846	6.0	Bangkok (BKK)	703,077	6.1
23.	Houston (IAH)	26,475,801	7.1	Tokyo, Haneda (HND)	670,689	3.6
24.	Orlando (MCO)	25,548,773	13.7	Oakland (OAK)	613,909	11.4
25.	Tokyo, Narita (NRT)	25,408,196	4.9	Indianapolis (IND)	609,365	14.7

Top 50 ACI airports, January–December 1996. Total Passengers: enplaned and deplaned, passengers in transit counted once. Cargo: load and unloaded freight and mail (in metric tons). *Source:* Airport Council International, Geneva, Switzerland.

1944 **The first production stage rocket-engine fighter plane,** the German Messerschmitt Me 163B *Komet* (test flown 1941) becomes operational in June 1944. Some 350 of these delta-wing fighters were built before WWII in Europe ended.

1947 **First piloted supersonic flight in an airplane.** Capt. Charles E. Yeager, U.S. Air Force, flew the X-1 rocket-powered research plane built by Bell Aircraft Corp., faster than the speed of sound at Muroc Air Force Base, California (Oct. 14).

1949 **First round-the-world nonstop flight.** Capt. James Gallagher and USAF crew of 13 flew a Boeing B-50A Superfortress around the world nonstop from Ft. Worth, returning to same point: 23,452 mi. in 94 hours, 1 min, with 4 aerial refuelings enroute (Feb. 27–March 2).

1950 **First nonstop transatlantic jet flight.** Col. David C. Schilling (USAF) flew 3,300 mi. from England to Limestone, Maine, in 10 hours, 1 min (Sept. 22).

1951 **First solo across North Pole.** Charles F. Blair, Jr., flew a converted P-51 (May 29).

1952 **First jetliner service.** De Havilland Comet flight inaugurated by BOAC between London and Johannesburg, South Africa (May 2). Flight, including stops, took 23 hours, 38 min.
First transatlantic helicopter flight. Capt. Vincent H. McGovern and 1st Lt. Harold W. Moore piloted 2 Sikorsky H-19s from Westover, Mass., to Prestwick, Scotland (3,410 mi.). Trip was made in 5 steps, with flying time of 42 hours, 25 min (July 15–31).
First transatlantic round trip in same day. British Canberra twin-jet bomber flew from Aldergrove, Northern Ireland, to Gander, Newfoundland, and back in 7 hours, 59 min flying time (Aug. 26).

1955 **First transcontinental round trip in same day.** Lt. John M. Conroy piloted F-86 Sabrejet across U.S. (Los Angeles–New York) and back—5,085 mi.—in 11 hours, 33 min, 27 sec (May 21).

1957 **First round-the-world, nonstop jet plane flight.** Maj. Gen. Archie J. Old, Jr., USAF, led a flight of 3 Boeing B-52 bombers, powered with 8 10,000-lb. thrust Pratt & Whitney Aircraft J57 engines around the world in 45 hours 19 min; distance 24,325 mi.; average speed 525 mph. (Completed Jan. 18.)

1958 **First transatlantic jet passenger service.** BOAC, New York to London (Oct. 4). Pan American started daily service, New York to Paris (Oct. 26).
First domestic jet passenger service. National Airlines inaugurated service between New York and Miami (Dec. 10).

1968 **Prototype of world's first supersonic airliner,** the Soviet-designed Tupolev Tu-144 made first flight, Dec. 31. It first achieved supersonic speed on June 5, 1969.

1973 **First female pilot of a U.S. major scheduled airline.** Emily H. Warner became employed by Frontier Airlines on January 29 as second officer on a Boeing 737.

1976 **First regularly-scheduled commercial supersonic transport (SST) flights begin.** Air France and British Airways inaugurate service (January 21). Air France flies the Paris–Rio de Janeiro route; B.A., the London–Bahrain. Both airlines begin SST service to Washington, D.C. (May 24).

1977 **First successful man-powered aircraft.** Paul MacCready, an aeronautical engineer from Pasadena, Calif., was awarded the Kremer Prize for creating the world's first successful man-powered aircraft. The *Gossamer Condor* was flown by Bryan Allen over the required 3-mile course on Aug. 23.

1978 **First successful transatlantic balloon flight.** Three Albuquerque, N.M., men, Ben Abruzzo, Larry Newman, and Maxie Anderson, completed the crossing (Aug. 16.; landed, Aug. 17) in their helium-filled balloon, *Double Eagle II.*

Active Pilot Certificates Held

Year	Total	Airline transport	Commercial	Private
1970	720,028	31,442	176,585	299,491
1980	814,667	63,652	182,097	343,276
1985	722,376	79,192	155,929	320,086
1990	702,659	107,732	149,666	299,111
1993	665,069	117,070	143,014	283,700
1994	654,088	117,434	138,728	284,236
1995	639,184	123,877	133,980	261,399
1996	622,261	127,486	129,187	254,002

NOTE: Includes other pilot categories—student 94,947, helicopter 6,961, glider 9,413, and recreational 255. Also nonpilot, i.e., mechanic, parachute rigger, etc. (Nonpilot total, 534,427). Data as of Dec. 31, 1996. *Source:* Department of Transportation, Federal Aviation Administration.

1979 **First man-powered aircraft to fly across the English Channel.** The Kremer Prize for the Channel crossing was won by Bryan Allen who flew the *Gossamer Albatross* from Folkestone, England to Cap Gris-Nez, France, in 2 hours, 55 min (June 12).

1980 **First successful balloon flight over the North Pole.** Sidney Conn and his wife Eleanor, in hot-air balloon *Joy of Sound* (April 11).

First nonstop transcontinental balloon flight, and also record for longest overland voyage in a balloon. Maxie Anderson and his son, Kris, completed four-day flight from Fort Baker, Calif., to successful landing outside Matane, Quebec, on May 12 in their helium-filled balloon, *Kitty Hawk*.

First long-distance solar-powered flight. Janice Brown, 98-lb former teacher, flew tiny experimental solar-powered aircraft, *Solar Challenger* six miles in 22 min near Marana, Ariz. (Dec. 3). The craft was powered by a 2.75-hp engine.

First solar-powered aircraft to fly across the English Channel. Stephen R. Ptacek flew the 210-lb *Solar Challenger* at the average speed of 30 mph from Cormeilles-en-Vexin near Paris to the Royal Manston Air Force Base on England's southeastern coast in 5 hours, 30 min (July 7).

1984 **First solo transatlantic balloon flight.** Joe W. Kittinger landed Sept. 18 near Savona, Italy, in his helium-filled balloon *Rosie O'Grady's Balloon of Peace* after a flight of 3,535 miles from Caribou, Me.

1986 **First nonstop flight around the world without refueling.** From Edwards AFB, Calif., Dick Rutan and Jeana Yeager flew in *Voyager* around the world (24,986.727 mi.), returning to Edwards in 216 hours, 3 min, 44 sec (Dec. 14–23).

1987 **First transatlantic hot-air balloon flight.** Richard Branson and Per Lindstrand flew 2,789.6 miles from Sugarloaf Mt., Maine, to Ireland in the hot-air balloon *Virgin Atlantic Flyer* (July 2–4).

1991 **First transpacific hot-air balloon flight.** Richard Branson and Per Lindstrand flew about 6,700 miles from Miyakonyo, Japan, to 150 miles west of Yellowknife, Northwest Territories, Canada (Jan. 15–17). Record pending verification.

1992 **World's longest balloon flight.** Americans Richard Abruzzo and Troy Bradley made a flight of 3,318.23 miles from Bangor, Maine to Sidi Amar El Kadmiri, Ben Slimane, Morocco in 144 hours and 16 minutes in Cameron R-77 (Sept. 16–22).

1993 **First woman to co-pilot a commercial supersonic plane.** Barbara Harmer, British Airways, flew as first officer on the Concorde from London to New York City (March 25).

1995 **First solo transpacific balloon flight.** Steve Fossett made a flight of more than 5,430 miles from Seoul, South Korea, to Leader, Saskatchewan, Canada, in a helium-filled balloon. Also set record for distance (Feb. 18–21, 1995). Record pending verification.

1997 **World distance and duration record balloon flight.** Steve Fossett made a flight of 9,672 miles lasting 146 hours, 54 minutes from St. Louis to Sultanpur, India, in the balloon *Spirit* (Jan. 13–20). Record pending verification.

World Class Helicopter Records

Selected records. *Source:* National Aeronautic Association.

Great Circle Distance Without Landing
International: 2,213.04 mi.; 3,561.55 km.
Robert G. Ferry (U.S.) in Hughes YOH-6A helicopter powered by Allison T-63-A-5 engine; from Culver City, Calif., to Ormond Beach, Fla., April 6–7, 1966.

Distance, Closed Circuit
International: 1,739.96 mi.; 2,800.20 km.
Jack Schweibold (U.S.) in Hughes YOH-6A helicopter powered by Allison T-62-A-5 engine; Edwards Air Force Base, Calif., March 26, 1966.

Altitude Without Payload
International: 40,820 ft.; 12,442 m.
Jean Boulet (France) in Alouette SA 315-001 "Lama" powered by Artouste IIIB 735 KW engine; Istres, France, June 21, 1972.

Altitude in Horizontal Flight
International: 36,122 ft.; 11,010 m.
CWO James K. Church, (U.S.) in Sikorsky CH-54B helicopter powered by 2 P&W JFTD-12 engines; Stratford, Conn., Nov. 4, 1971.

Speed Around the World, Eastbound
40.99 mph; 65.97 kph.
Joe Ronald Bower (U.S.) pilot, in Bell JetRanger III, powered by one Allison 250-C20J of 317 shp., covered 23,800 miles in 24 days, 4 hours, 36 minutes. June 28–July 22, 1994.

Speed Around the World, Westbound
57.1 mph; 91.75 kph.
Joe Ronald Bower (U.S.) pilot, John W. Williams (U.S.), co-pilot in Bell 430 powered by 2 Allison 250-C40, 811 shp., August 17–September 3, 1996 (pending FAI approval).

Absolute World Records, Balloons

Selected records. *Source:* National Aeronautic Association.

Altitude (USA)
113,739.9 ft.; 34,668 km.
Cmdr. M.D. Ross (USNR) and Lt. Cmdr. V.A. Prather, *Lee Lewis Memorial*, Gulf of Mexico, May 4, 1961.

Distance (USA)
5,435.82 mi; 8,748.11 km
J. Stephen Fossett, *Cameron R-150*. Seoul, Korea, to Mendham, SK, Canada, February 17–22, 1995.

Duration (USA)
144 hours, 16 minutes
Richard Abruzzo and Troy Bradley, *Cameron R-77*, Bangor, Maine, USA, to Ben Slimane, Morocco, Sept. 16–22, 1992.

Absolute World Records

(Maximum Performance in Any Class)

Source: National Aeronautic Association

These official absolute world records are the supreme achievements of all the hundreds of records open to flying machines. They are the most outstanding of all the major types, and thus warrant the highest respect.

All types of airplanes are eligible for these few very special records. Airplanes may be powered by piston, turboprop, turbojet, rocket engines or a combination. They may be landplanes, seaplanes or amphibians; they may be lightplanes, business planes, military or commercial airplanes.

Over the years, many different categories of aircraft have held these records. In the past, the cost of developing high-performance aircraft has been so great that only airplanes created for military purposes have held these records. There have been two exceptions to this situation.

Most recently and most dramatically, the Rutan designed "Voyager" shattered the theory that only a complicated military behemoth could hold an absolute world record. The Voyager team and its nonstop, nonrefueled flight around the world proved that the dreams of dedicated individuals, combined with creative engineering, new technology, and hard work, could conquer the world.

The other exception was the X-15 rocket-powered research airplane. Holder of one record, it was used for both civilian and military research during its highly productive lifetime.

Speed Around the World, Nonstop, Nonrefueled

Speed (mph)	Date	Type Plane	Pilots	Place
115.65	Dec. 14-23, 1986	*Voyager*	Dick Rutan & Jeana Yeager (U.S.)	Edwards AFB, Calif.—Edwards AFB, Calif.

Distance, Great Circle Without Landing, also Distance, Closed Circuit Without Landing

Distance (mi.)	Date	Pilots	Place
24,986.727	Dec. 14-23, 1986	Dick Rutan & Jeana Yeager (U.S.)	Edwards AFB, Calif.—Edwards AFB, Calif.

Speed Over a Straight Course

Speed (mph)	Date	Type Plane	Pilot	Place
2,193.16	July 28, 1976	Lockheed SR-71A	Capt. Eldon W. Joersz (USAF)	Beale AFB, Calif.

Speed Over A Closed Circuit

Speed (mph)	Date	Type Plane	Pilot	Place
2,092.294	July 27, 1976	Lockheed SR-71A	Maj. Adolphus H. Bledsoe, Jr. (USAF)	Beale, AFB, Calif.

Altitude

Height (ft)	Date	Type Plane	Pilot	Place
123,523.58	Aug. 31, 1977	MIG-25, E-266M	Alexander Fedotov (U.S.S.R.)	U.S.S.R.

Altitude in Horizontal Flight

Height (ft)	Date	Pilot	Place
85,068.997	July 28, 1976	Capt. Robert C. Helt (USAF)	Beale AFB, Calif.

Altitude, Aircraft Launched From A Carrier Airplane

Height (ft)	Date	Type Plane	Pilot	Place
314,750.00	July 17, 1962	N. American X-15-1	Maj. Robert White (USAF)	Edwards AFB, Calif.

The Speed of Sound

Source: Air & Space/Smithsonian.

The speed of sound varies with temperature. At sea level Mach 1 is around 742 mph. It decreases with altitude until it reaches about 661 mph at 36,000 feet, then remains at that speed in a band of steady temperature up to 60,000 feet. Because of the variation, it is possible for an airplane flying supersonic at high altitude to be slower than a subsonic flight at sea level. The transonic band extends from around Mach .8—when the first supersonic shock waves form on the wing—to Mach 1.2, when the entire wing has gone supersonic.

The National Aviation Hall of Fame

Dedicated to honoring and preserving the history of outstanding air and space pioneers, the Aviation Hall of Fame was established in Dayton, Ohio on October 5, 1962, with five Daytonians as its founding fathers: James W. Jacobs, Gregory C. Karas, John A. Lombard, Larry E. O'Neil, and Gerald E. Weller. The first annual enshrinement ceremonies were held in December that same year. The United States Congress passed Public Law 88-372 in July 1964 granting the NAHF a national charter.

For additional information, contact the National Aviation Hall of Fame, Dayton Convention Center, Dayton, Ohio, 45402, (513) 226-0800.

(With Year of Enshrinement)

Allen, William McPherson (1971)
Andrews, Frank M. (1986)
Armstrong, Neil Alden (1979)
Arnold, Henry Harley (1967)
Atwood, J. Leland (1984)
Balchen, Bernt (1973)
Baldwin, Thomas Scott (1964)
Beachey, Lincoln (1966)
Beech, Olive Ann (1981)
Beech, Walter Herschel (1977)
Bell, Alexander Graham (1965)
Bell, Lawrence Dale (1977)
Bellanca, Giuseppe Mario (1993)
Bendix, Vincent Hugo (1991)
Boeing, William Edward (1966)
Bong, Richard L. (1986)
Borman, Frank (1982)
Boyd, Albert (1984)
Bradley, Mark E. (1992)
Brown, George Scratchley (1985)
Brukner, Clayton J. (1997)
Byrd, Richard Evelyn (1968)
Cessna, Clyde Vernon (1978)
Chamberlin, Clarence Duncan (1976)
Chanute, Octave (1963)
Chennault, Claire Lee (1972)
Cochran, Jacqueline (1972)
Collins, Michael (1985)
Combs, Harry B. (1996)
Conrad, Charles, Jr. (1980)
Crawford, Frederick C. (1993)
Crossfield, A. Scott (1983)
Cunningham, Alfred Austell (1965)
Curtiss, Glenn Hammond (1964)
Dargue, Herbert A. (1997)
Davis, Jr. Benjamin O. (1994)
deSeversky, Alexander P. (1970)
Doolittle, James Harold (1967)
Douglas, Donald Wills (1969)
Draper, Charles Stark (1981)
Eaker, Ira Clarence (1970)
Eielson, Carl Benjamin (1985)
Ellyson, Theodore Gordon (1964)
Ely, Eugene Burton (1965)
Everest, Frank K. (1989)
Fairchild, Sherman Mills (1979)
Fleet, Rueben Hollis (1975)
Fokker, Anthony Herman Gerard (1980)
Ford, Henry (1984)
Foss, Joseph Jacob (1984)
Foulois, Benjamin Delahauf (1963)
Frye, William John (1992)

Gabreski, Francis Stanley (1978)
Gentile, Dominic S. (1995)
Gilruth, Robert R. (1994)
Glenn, John Herschel, Jr. (1976)
Goddard, George William (1976)
Goddard, Robert Hutchings (1966)
Godfrey, Arthur (1987)
Goldwater, Barry Morris (1982)
Grissom, Virgil I. (1987)
Gross, Robert Ellsworth (1970)
Grumman, Leroy Randle (1972)
Guggenheim, Harry Frank (1971)
Haughton, Daniel J. (1987)
Hegenberger, Albert Francis (1976)
Heinemann, Edward Henry (1981)
Hoover, Robert A. (1988)
Ingalls, David Sinton (1983)
James, Daniel, Jr. (1993)
Jeppesen, Elrey B. (1990)
Johnson, Clarence Leonard (1974)
Johnston, Alvin M. (1993)
Jones, Thomas V. (1992)
Kenney, George Churchill (1971)
Kettering, Charles Franklin (1979)
Kindelberger, James Howard (1972)
Kittinger, Jr., Joe W. (1997)
Knabenshue, A. Roy (1965)
Knight, William J. (1988)
Lahm, Frank Purdy (1963)
Langley, Samuel Pierpont (1963)
Lear, William Powerll, Sr. (1978)
LeMay, Curtis Emerson (1972)
LeVier, Anthony William (1978)
Lindbergh, Anne Morrow (1979)
Lindbergh, Charles Augustus (1967)
Link, Edwin Albert (1976)
Lockheed, Allan H. (1986)
Loening, Grover (1969)
Luke, Frank, Jr. (1975)
Macready, John Arthur (1968)
Macready, Paul B. (1991)
Martin, Glenn Luther (1966)
McCampbell, David (1996)
McDonnell, James Smith (1977)
Meyer, John C. (1988)
Mitchell, William (1966)
Mitscher, Marc A. (1988)
Montgomery, John Joseph (1964)
Moorer, Thomas H. (1987)
Moss, Sanford Alexander (1976)
Neumann, Gerhard (1986)
Nichols, Ruth Rowland (1992)
Norden, Carl L. (1994)

Northrop, John Knudsen (1974)
Pangborn, Clyde Edward (1995)
Patterson, William Allan (1976)
Piper, William Thomas, Sr. (1980)
Pitcairn, Harold Frederick (1995)
Post, Wiley Hardeman (1969)
Putnam, Amelia Earhart (1968)
Read, Albert Cushing (1965)
Reeve, Robert Campbell (1965)
Rentschler, Frederick Brant (1982)
Richardson, Holden Chester (1978)
Rickenbacker, Edward Vernon (1965)
Rodgers, Calbraith Perry (1964)
Rogers, Will (1977)
Rushworth, Robert A. (1990)
Rutan, Elbert L. (1995)
Ryan, T. Claude (1974)
Schirra, Walter M., Jr. (1986)
Schriever, Bernard Adolf (1980)
Selfridge, Thomas Etholen (1965)
Shepard, Alan Bartlett, Jr. (1977)
Sikorsky, Igor Ivan (1968)
Six, Robert Forman (1980)
Slayton, Donald K. "Deke" (1996)
Smith, C.R. (1974)
Spaatz, Carl Andrew (1967)
Sperry, Elmert Ambrose, Sr. (1973)
Sperry, Lawrence Burst, Sr. (1981)
Stafford, Thomas P. (1997)
Stanley, Robert M. (1990)
Stapp, John Paul (1985)
Stearman, Lloyd C. (1989)
Taylor, Charles Edward (1965)
Thomas, Lowell (1992)
Tibbets, Paul W., Jr. (1996)
Towers, John Henry (1966)
Trippe, Juan Terry (1970)
Turner, Roscoe (1975)
Twining, Nathan Farragut (1976)
Vandenberg, Hoyt S. (1991)
von Braun, Wernher (1982)
von Karman, Theodore (1983)
von Ohain, Hans P. (1990)
Vought, Chance M. (1989)
Wade, Leigh (1974)
Walden, Henry W. (1964)
Wells, Edward Curtis (1991)
Wilson, Thornton Arnold (1983)
Woolman, Collett Everman (1994)
Wright, Orville (1962)
Wright, Wilbur (1962)
Yeager, Charles Elwood (1973)
Young, John W. (1988)

Geography

Mortals on Mount Parnassus:
A History of Climbing Everest

Called Chomolungma ("goddess mother of the world") in Tibet and Sagarmatha ("goddess of the sky") in Nepal, Mount Everest once went by the pedestrian name of Peak XV among Westerners. That was before surveyors established that it was the highest mountain on Earth, a fact that came as something of a surprise—Peak XV had seemed lost in the crowd of other formidable Himalayan peaks, many of which gave the illusion of greater height.

In 1852 the Great Trigonometrical Survey of India measured Everest's elevation as 29,002 feet above sea level. This remarkably accurate figure remained the officially accepted height for more than one hundred years. In 1955 it was adjusted by a mere 26 feet to 29,028 (8,848 m). The mountain received its official name in 1865 in honor of Sir George Everest, the British Surveyor General from 1830–1843 who had mapped the Indian subcontinent. He had some reservations about having his name bestowed on the peak, arguing that the mountain should retain its local appellation, the standard policy of geographical societies.

Pretenders to the Throne

Before the Survey of India, a number of other mountains ranked supreme in the eyes of the world. In the seventeenth and eighteenth centuries, the Andean peak Chimboraso was considered the highest. At a relatively unremarkable 20,561 feet (6,267 m), it is in fact nowhere near the highest, surpassed by about thirty other Andean peaks and several dozen in the Himalayas. In 1809, the Himalayan peak Dhaulagiri (26,810 ft.; 8,172 m) was declared the ultimate, only to be shunted aside in 1840 by Kanchenjunga (28,208 ft.; 8,598 m), which today ranks third. Everest's status has been unrivaled for the last century-and-a-half, but not without a few threats.

The most recent challenge came from a 1986 American expedition climbing K2 (28,250 ft., 8,611 m) in the Karakoram range. According to their measurements, K2 was actually 29,284 feet, beating Everest by a cool 256 feet. Had this figure been accepted, mountaineering history would have required drastic revision: Everest would have taken a back seat to K2, no longer the *ne plus ultra* of geographical extremes.

The Third Pole

Once the North and South Poles had been reached by explorers, the next geographical feat to capture the international imagination was Everest, often called the Third Pole. Attempts to climb Everest began in the 1921, when the forbidden kingdom of Tibet opened its borders to outsiders. On June 8, 1924, two members of a British expedition, George Mallory and Andrew Irvine, attempted the summit. Famous for his retort to the press—"because it's there"—when asked why he wanted to climb Everest, Mallory had already failed twice at reaching the summit. The two men were last spotted "going strong" for the top until the clouds perpetually swirling around Everest engulfed them. They vanished for good. Whether they made it to the top before the mountain killed them is unknown but believed unlikely.

Ten expeditions over a period of thirty years failed to conquer Everest, with 13 losing their lives. Then, on May 29, 1953, Edmund Hillary, a New Zealand bee-keeper, and Tenzing Norgay, an acclaimed Sherpa climber, became the first to reach the roof of the world. Their climb was made from the Nepalese side, which had eased its restrictions on foreigners at about the same time that Tibet, invaded in 1950 by China, shut its borders. World famous overnight, Hillary became a hero of the British empire—the news reached London just in time for Elizabeth II's coronation—and Norgay was touted as a symbol of national pride by three separate nations: Nepal, Tibet, and India.

Into the Death Zone

Although not considered one of the most technically challenging mountains to climb (K2 is more difficult), the dangers of Everest include avalanches, crevasses, ferocious winds up to 125 mph, sudden storms, temperatures of 40°F below zero, and oxygen deprivation. In the "death zone"—above 25,000 feet—the air holds only a third as much oxygen as at sea level, heightening the chances of hypothermia, frostbite, high-altitude pulmonary edema (when the lungs fatally fill with fluid) and high-altitude cerebral edema (when the oxygen-starved brain swells up). Even when breathing bottled oxygen, climbers experience extreme fatigue, impaired judgment and coordination, headaches, nausea, double vision, and sometimes hallucinations. Expeditions spend weeks, sometimes months, acclimatizing, and usually attempt Everest only in May and October, avoiding the winter snows and the summer monsoons.

After Hillary and Norgay's ascent of Everest, other records were broken, including the first ascent by a woman, the first solo ascent, the first to traverse up one route and down another, and the first descent on skis. Yet none of these records compared to the next true milestone: climbing Everest without supplemental oxygen. As far back as Mallory, who called the use of bottled oxygen "unsporting," climbers found they had no alternative. Yet on May 8, 1978, two Tyrolean mountaineers, Reinhold Messner and Peter Habeler, achieved the impossible. Messner had resolved that nothing would come between him and the mountain; he would climb Everest without supplemental oxygen or not at all. At the summit he described himself as "nothing more than a single narrow gasping lung." Incredulous, some disputed the veracity of an oxygenless climb. Yet two years later Messner quelled all skepticism when on August 20, 1980, he again ascended Everest without oxygen, this time solo. Climbing without oxygen has now become *de rigueur* among the climbing elite, and by 1996 more than 60 men and women had reached the top relying on their own gasping lungs.

An Icy Graveyard

Between 1921 and 1997, Everest has been climbed by more than 700 people from twenty countries. More than 150 have lost their lives, the odds being one-in-four of not making it down alive. The dead are left where they perish because the effects of the altitude make it nearly impossible to drag bodies off the mountain. Those ascending Everest pass through an icy graveyard littered with remnants of old tents and equipment, empty oxygen canisters, and frozen corpses.

In the past few years, media access to Everest has mushroomed: live Internet reports have been sent from the mountain (using solar energy); an Imax film crew has documented a climb, returning two years in a row before attaining the summit; and Jon Krakauer's best-selling account about an Everest ascent gone wrong, *Into Thin Air,* has introduced *cwm, col, sirdar, short-rope,* and *Hillary Step* into the vocabulary of mainstream America. There are now guided trips up the mountain, fanning debate about the commercialization of Everest. Purists like Hillary lament the lack of respect for the mountain and Young Turks boast they can get nearly anyone up the mountain as long as they're in decent physical shape and have $65,000 to spare. One reason for the recent media attention is the novelty of comparatively ordinary people venturing up a Mount Parnassus formerly limited to gods like Messner and Hillary. Pathologists and postal workers now follow in their footsteps. Another reason is the appalling waste of human life. In May 1996, eight lost their lives in the single greatest disaster on the mountain—yet it did not stop others from attempting the climb just weeks later, resulting in four more deaths. The total for the year was fifteen. The following May, another eight mountaineers died. As the number of climbers grow, so does the death toll, with Everest taking down world-class climbers and novice adventurers alike. —*BB* □

World Geography
Highest Mountain Peaks of the World

(*See* p. 493 for U.S. peaks).

Mountain peak	Range	Location	Height feet	meters
Everest	Himalayas	Nepal/Tibet	29,028	8,848
K2 (Godwin Austen)	Karakoram	Kashmir [1]	28,250	8,611
Kanchenjunga	Himalayas	Nepal/Sikkim	28,208	8,598
Lhotse I	Himalayas	Nepal/Tibet	27,923	8,511
Makalu I	Himalayas	Tibet/Nepal	27,824	8,481
Lhotse II	Himalayas	Nepal/Tibet	27,560	8,400
Dhaulagiri	Himalayas	Nepal	26,810	8,172
Manaslu I	Himalayas	Nepal	26,760	8,156
Cho Oyu	Himalayas	Nepal	26,750	8,153
Nanga Parbat	Himalayas	Kashmir	26,660	8,126
Annapurna	Himalayas	Nepal	26,504	8,078
Gasherbrum	Karakoram	Kashmir	26,470	8,068
Broad Peak	Karakoram	Kashmir	26,400	8,047
Gosainthan (Shishma Pangma)	Himalayas	Tibet	26,287	8,012
Annapurna II	Himalayas	Nepal	26,041	7,937
Gyachung Kang	Himalayas	Nepal	25,910	7,897
Disteghil Sar	Karakoram	Kashmir	25,858	7,882
Himalchuli	Himalayas	Nepal	25,801	7,864
Nuptse	Himalayas	Nepal	25,726	7,841
Masherbrum	Karakoram	Kashmir	25,660	7,821
Nanda Devi	Himalayas	India	25,645	7,817
Rakaposhi	Karakoram	Kashmir	25,550	7,788
Kanjut Sar	Karakoram	Kashmir	25,461	7,761
Kamet	Himalayas	India/Tibet	25,447	7,756
Namcha Barwa	Himalayas	Tibet	25,445	7,756
Gurla Mandhata	Himalayas	Tibet	25,355	7,728
Ulugh Muztagh	Kunlun	Tibet	25,340	7,724
Kungur	Muztagh Ata	China	25,325	7,719
Tirich Mir	Hindu Kush	Pakistan	25,230	7,690
Saser Kangri	Karakoram	Kashmir	25,172	7,672
Makalu II	Himalayas	Nepal	25,120	7,657
Minya Konka	Daxue Shan	China	24,900	7,590
Kula Kangri	Himalayas	Bhutan	24,784	7,554
Chang-tzu	Himalayas	Tibet	24,780	7,553
Muztagh Ata	Muztagh Ata	China	24,757	7,546
Skyang Kangri	Himalayas	Kashmir	24,750	7,544
Communism Peak	Pamirs	Tajikistan	24,590	7,495
Jongsong Peak	Himalayas	Nepal	24,472	7,459
Pobeda Peak	Tien Shan	Kyrgyzstan	24,406	7,439
Sia Kangri	Himalayas	Kashmir	24,350	7,422
Haramosh Peak	Karakoram	Kashmir	24,270	7,397
Istoro Nal	Hindu Kush	Pakistan	24,240	7,388

Mountain peak	Range	Location	Height	
			feet	meters
Tent Peak	Himalayas	Nepal	24,165	7,365
Chomo Lhari	Himalayas	Tibet/Bhutan	24,040	7,327
Chamlang	Himalayas	Nepal	24,012	7,319
Kabru	Himalayas	Nepal	24,002	7,316
Alung Gangri	Himalayas	Tibet	24,000	7,315
Baltoro Kangri	Himalayas	Kashmir	23,990	7,312
Muztagh Ata (K-5)	Kunlun	China	23,890	7,282
Mana	Himalayas	India	23,860	7,273
Baruntse	Himalayas	Nepal	23,688	7,220
Nepal Peak	Himalayas	Nepal	23,500	7,163
Amne Machin	Kunlun	China	23,490	7,160
Gauri Sankar	Himalayas	Nepal/Tibet	23,440	7,145
Badrinath	Himalayas	India	23,420	7,138
Nunkun	Himalayas	Kashmir	23,410	7,135
Lenin Peak	Pamirs	Tajikistan/Kyrgyzstan	23,405	7,134
Pyramid	Himalayas	Nepal	23,400	7,132
Api	Himalayas	Nepal	23,399	7,132
Pauhunri	Himalayas	India/China	23,385	7,128
Trisul	Himalayas	India	23,360	7,120
Korzhenevski Peak	Pamirs	Tajikistan	23,310	7,105
Kangto	Himalayas	Tibet	23,260	7,090
Nyainqentanglha	Nyainqentanglha Shan	China	23,255	7,088
Trisuli	Himalayas	India	23,210	7,074
Dunagiri	Himalayas	India	23,184	7,066
Revolution Peak	Pamirs	Tajikistan	22,880	6,974
Aconcagua	Andes	Argentina	22,834	6,960
Ojos del Salado	Andes	Argentina/Chile	22,572	6,880
Bonete	Andes	Argentina/Chile	22,546	6,872
Tupungato	Andes	Argentina /Chile	22,310	6,800
Moscow Peak	Pamirs	Tajikistan	22,260	6,785
Pissis	Andes	Argentina	22,241	6,779
Mercedario	Andes	Argentina/Chile	22,211	6,770
Huascarán	Andes	Peru	22,205	6,768
Llullaillaco	Andes	Argentina/Chile	22,057	6,723
El Libertador	Andes	Argentina	22,047	6,720
Cachi	Andes	Argentina	22,047	6,720
Kailas	Himalayas	Tibet	22,027	6,714
Incahuasi	Andes	Argentina/Chile	21,720	6,620
Yerupaja	Andes	Peru	21,709	6,617
Kurumda	Pamirs	Tajikistan	21,686	6,610
Galan	Andes	Argentina	21,654	6,600
El Muerto	Andes	Argentina/Chile	21,457	6,540
Sajama	Andes	Bolivia	21,391	6,520
Nacimiento	Andes	Argentina	21,302	6,493
Illimani	Andes	Bolivia	21,201	6,462
Coropuna	Andes	Peru	21,083	6,426
Laudo	Andes	Argentina	20,997	6,400
Ancohuma	Andes	Bolivia	20,958	6,388
Cuzco (Ausangate)	Andes	Peru	20,945	6,384
Toro	Andes	Argentina/Chile	20,932	6,380
Illampu	Andes	Bolivia	20,873	6,362
Tres Cruces	Andes	Argentina/Chile	20,853	6,356
Huandoy	Andes	Peru	20,852	6,356
Parinacota	Andes	Bolivia/Chile	20,768	6,330
Tortolas	Andes	Argentina/Chile	20,745	6,323
Ampato	Andes	Peru	20,702	6,310
El Condor	Andes	Argentina	20,669	6,300
Salcantay	Andes	Peru	20,574	6,271
Chimborazo	Andes	Ecuador	20,561	6,267
Huancarhuas	Andes	Peru	20,531	6,258
Famatina	Andes	Argentina	20,505	6,250
Pumasillo	Andes	Peru	20,492	6,246
Solo	Andes	Argentina	20,492	6,246
Polleras	Andes	Argentina	20,456	6,235
Pular	Andes	Chile	20,423	6,225
Chañi	Andes	Argentina	20,341	6,200
McKinley (Denali)	Alaska	Alaska	20,320	6,194

Mountain peak	Range	Location	Height feet	Height meters
Aucanquilcha	Andes	Chile	20,295	6,186
Juncal	Andes	Argentina/Chile	20,276	6,180
Negro	Andes	Argentina	20,184	6,152
Quela	Andes	Argentina	20,128	6,135
Condoriri	Andes	Bolivia	20,095	6,125
Palermo	Andes	Argentina	20,079	6,120
Solimana	Andes	Peru	20,068	6,117
San Juan	Andes	Argentina/Chile	20,049	6,111
Sierra Nevada	Andes	Argentina	20,023	6,103
Antofalla	Andes	Argentina	20,013	6,100
Marmolejo	Andes	Argentina/Chile	20,013	6,100

1. Kashmir is divided between India and Pakistan, with both countries disputing the boundaries. *Source:* National Geographic Society.

Oceans and Seas

Name	Area sq mi.	Area sq km	Average depth feet	Average depth meters	Greatest known depth feet	Greatest known depth meters	Place greatest known depth
Pacific Ocean	64,000,000	165,760,000	13,215	4,028	36,198	11,033	Mariana Trench
Atlantic Ocean	31,815,000	82,400,000	12,880	3,926	30,246	9,219	Puerto Rico Trench
Indian Ocean	25,300,000	65,526,700	13,002	3,963	24,460	7,455	Sunda Trench
Arctic Ocean	5,440,200	14,090,000	3,953	1,205	18,456	5,625	77° 45'N; 175°W
Mediterranean Sea[1]	1,145,100	2,965,800	4,688	1,429	15,197	4,632	Off Cape Matapan, Greece
Caribbean Sea	1,049,500	2,718,200	8,685	2,647	22,788	6,946	Off Cayman Islands
South China Sea	895,400	2,319,000	5,419	1,652	16,456	5,016	West of Luzon
Bering Sea	884,900	2,291,900	5,075	1,547	15,659	4,773	Off Buldir Island
Gulf of Mexico	615,000	1,592,800	4,874	1,486	12,425	3,787	Sigsbee Deep
Okhotsk Sea	613,800	1,589,700	2,749	838	12,001	3,658	146°10'E; 46°50'N
East China Sea	482,300	1,249,200	617	188	9,126	2,782	25°16'N; 125°E
Hudson Bay	475,800	1,232,300	420	128	600	183	Near entrance
Japan Sea	389,100	1,007,800	4,429	1,350	12,276	3,742	Central Basin
Andaman Sea	308,100	797,700	2,854	870	12,392	3,777	Off Car Nicobar Island
North Sea	222,100	575,200	308	94	2,165	660	Skagerrak
Red Sea	169,100	438,000	1,611	491	7,254	2,211	Off Port Sudan
Baltic Sea	163,000	422,200	180	55	1,380	421	Off Gotland

1. Includes Black Sea and Sea of Azov. NOTE: For Caspian Sea, *see* Large Lakes of the World.

World's Greatest Man-Made Lakes[1]

Name of dam	Location	Millions of cubic meters	Thousands of acre-feet	Year completed
Owen Falls	Uganda	204,800	166,000	1954
Kariba	Zimbabwe	181,592	147,218	1959
Bratsk	Siberia	169,270	137,220	1964
High Aswan (Sadd-el-Aali)	Egypt	168,000	136,200	1970
Akosombo	Ghana	148,000	120,000	1965
Daniel Johnson	Canada	141,852	115,000	1968
Guri (Raul Leoni)	Venezuela	136,000	110,256	1986
Krasnoyarsk	Siberia	73,300	59,425	1967
Bennett W.A.C.	Canada	70,309	57,006	1967
Zeya	Russia	68,400	55,452	1978
Cabora Bassa	Mozambique	63,000	51,075	1974
LaGrande 2	Canada	61,720	50,037	1982
LaGrande 3	Canada	60,020	48,659	1982
Ust'-Ilimsk	Russia	59,300	48,075	1980
Volga-V.I. Lenin	Russia	58,000	47,020	1955
Caniapiscau	Canada	53,790	43,608	1981
Pati (Chapetón)	Argentina	53,700	43,535	UC
Upper Wainganga	India	50,700	41,103	1987
Sáo Felix	Brazil	50,600	41,022	1986
Bukhtarma	Former U.S.S.R.	49,740	40,325	1960
Atatürk (Karababa)	Turkey	48,700	39,482	1990
Cerros Colorados	Argentina	48,000	38,914	1973

Name of dam	Location	Millions of cubic meters	Thousands of acre-feet	Year completed
Irkutsk	Russia	46,000	37,290	1956
Tucuruí	Brazil	36,375	29,489	1984
Vilyuy	Russia	35,900	29,104	1967
Sanmenxia	China	35,400	28,700	1960
Hoover	Nevada/Arizona	35,154	28,500	1936
Sobridinho	Brazil	34,200	27,726	1981
Glen Canyon	Arizona	33,304	27,000	1964
Jenpeg	Canada	31,790	25,772	1975

1. Formed by construction of dams. NOTE: UC = under construction. *Source:* Department of the Interior, Bureau of Reclamation and *International Water Power and Dam Construction.*

Large Lakes of the World

(Area more than 1,600 sq miles)

Name and location	Area		Length		Maximum depth	
	sq mi.	km	mi.	km	feet	meters
Caspian Sea, Azerbaijan-Russia-Kazakhstan-Turkmenistan-Iran[1]	152,239	394,299	745	1,199	3,104	946
Superior, U.S.-Canada	31,820	82,414	383	616	1,333	406
Victoria, Tanzania-Uganda	26,828	69,485	200	322	270	82
Aral, Kazakhstan-Uzbekistan	25,659	66,457	266	428	223	68
Huron, U.S.-Canada	23,010	59,596	247	397	750	229
Michigan, U.S.	22,400	58,016	321	517	923	281
Tanganyika, Tanzania-Congo	12,700	32,893	420	676	4,708	1,435
Baikal, Russia	12,162	31,500	395	636	5,712	1,741
Great Bear, Canada	12,000	31,080	232	373	270	82
Nyasa, Malawi-Mozambique-Tanzania	11,600	30,044	360	579	2,316	706
Great Slave, Canada	11,170	28,930	298	480	2,015	614
Chad,[2] Chad-Niger-Nigeria	9,946	25,760	—	—	23	7
Erie, U.S.-Canada	9,930	25,719	241	388	210	64
Winnipeg, Canada	9,094	23,553	264	425	204	62
Ontario, U.S.-Canada	7,520	19,477	193	311	778	237
Balkhash, Kazakhstan	7,115	18,428	376	605	87	27
Ladoga, Russia	7,000	18,130	124	200	738	225
Onega, Russia	3,819	9,891	154	248	361	110
Titicaca, Bolivia-Peru	3,141	8,135	110	177	1,214	370
Nicaragua, Nicaragua	3,089	8,001	110	177	230	70
Athabaska, Canada	3,058	7,920	208	335	407	124
Rudolf, Kenya	2,473	6,405	154	248	—	—
Reindeer, Canada	2,444	6,330	152	245	—	—
Eyre, South Australia	2,400[3]	6,216	130	209	varies	varies
Issyk-Kul, Kyrgyzstan	2,394	6,200	113	182	2,297	700
Urmia,[2] Iran	2,317	6,001	81	130	49	15
Torrens, South Australia	2,200	5,698	130	209	—	—
Vänern, Sweden	2,141	5,545	87	140	322	98
Winnipegosis, Canada	2,086	5,403	152	245	59	18
Mobutu Sese Seko, Uganda	2,046	5,299	100	161	180	55
Nettilling, Baffin Island, Canada	1,950	5,051	70	113	—	—
Nipigon, Canada	1,870	4,843	72	116	—	—
Manitoba, Canada	1,817	4,706	140	225	22	7
Great Salt, U.S.	1,800	4,662	75	121	15/25	5/8
Kioga, Uganda	1,700	4,403	50	80	about 30	9
Koko-Nor, China	1,630	4,222	66	106	—	—

1. The Caspian Sea is called "sea" because the Romans, finding it salty, named it *Mare Caspium.* Many geographers, however, consider it a lake because it is land-locked. 2. Figures represent high-water data. 3. Varies with the rainfall of the wet season. It has been reported to dry up almost completely on occasion.

Principal Rivers of the World

(For other U.S. rivers, *see* Rivers of the United States.)

River	Source	Outflow	Approx. length	
			miles	km
Nile	Tributaries of Lake Victoria, Africa	Mediterranean Sea	4,180	6,690
Amazon	Glacier-fed lakes, Peru	Atlantic Ocean	3,912	6,296
Mississippi-Missouri-Red Rock	Source of Red Rock, Montana	Gulf of Mexico	3,710	5,970
Yangtze Kiang	Tibetan plateau, China	China Sea	3,602	5,797
Ob	Altai Mts., Russia	Gulf of Ob	3,459	5,567
Huang Ho (Yellow)	Eastern part of Kunlan Mts., west China	Gulf of Chihli	2,900	4,667
Yenisei	Tannu-Ola Mts., western Tuva, Russia	Arctic Ocean	2,800	4,506
Paraná	Confluence of Paranaiba and Grande rivers	Río de la Plata	2,795	4,498
Irtish	Altai Mts., Russia	Ob River	2,758	4,438
Zaire (Congo)	Confluence of Lualab and Luapula rivers, Congo	Atlantic Ocean	2,716	4,371
Heilong (Amur)	Confluence of Shilka (Russia) and Argun (Manchuria) rivers	Tatar Strait	2,704	4,352
Lena	Baikal Mts., Russia	Arctic Ocean	2,652	4,268
Mackenzie	Head of Finlay River, British Columbia, Canada	Beaufort Sea (Arctic Ocean)	2,635	4,241
Niger	Guinea	Gulf of Guinea	2,600	4,184
Mekong	Tibetan highlands	South China Sea	2,500	4,023
Mississippi	Lake Itasca, Minnesota	Gulf of Mexico	2,348	3,779
Missouri	Confluence of Jefferson, Gallatin, and Madison rivers, Montana	Mississippi River	2,315	3,726
Volga	Valdai plateau, Russia	Caspian Sea	2,291	3,687
Madeira	Confluence of Beni and Maumoré rivers, Bolivia-Brazil boundary	Amazon River	2,012	3,238
Purus	Peruvian Andes	Amazon River	1,993	3,207
São Francisco	Southwest Minas Gerais, Brazil	Atlantic Ocean	1,987	3,198
Yukon	Junction of Lewes and Pelly rivers, Yukon Territory, Canada	Bering Sea	1,979	3,185
St. Lawrence	Lake Ontario	Gulf of St. Lawrence	1,900	3,058
Rio Grande	San Juan Mts., Colorado	Gulf of Mexico	1,885	3,034
Brahmaputra	Himalayas	Ganges River	1,800	2,897
Indus	Himalayas	Arabian Sea	1,800	2,897
Danube	Black Forest, Germany	Black Sea	1,766	2,842
Euphrates	Confluence of Murat Nehri and Kara Su rivers, Turkey	Shatt-al-Arab	1,739	2,799
Darling	Central part of Eastern Highlands, Australia	Murray River	1,702	2,739
Zambezi	11°21′S, 24°22′E, Zambia	Mozambique Channel	1,700	2,736
Tocantins	Goiás, Brazil	Pará River	1,677	2,699
Murray	Australian Alps, New South Wales	Indian Ocean	1,609	2,589
Nelson	Head of Bow River, western Alberta, Canada	Hudson Bay	1,600	2,575
Paraguay	Mato Grosso, Brazil	Paraná River	1,584	2,549
Ural	Southern Ural Mts., Russia	Caspian Sea	1,574	2,533
Ganges	Himalayas	Bay of Bengal	1,557	2,506
Amu Darya (Oxus)	Nicholas Range, Pamir Mts., Turkmenistan	Aral Sea	1,500	2,414
Japurá	Andes, Colombia	Amazon River	1,500	2,414
Salween	Tibet, south of Kunlun Mts.	Gulf of Martaban	1,500	2,414
Arkansas	Central Colorado	Mississippi River	1,459	2,348
Colorado	Grand County, Colorado	Gulf of California	1,450	2,333
Dnieper	Valdai Hills, Russia	Black Sea	1,419	2,284
Ohio-Allegheny	Potter County, Pennsylvania	Mississippi River	1,306	2,102

River	Source	Outflow	Approx. length	
			miles	km
Irrawaddy	Confluence of Nmai and Mali rivers, northeast Burma	Bay of Bengal	1,300	2,092
Orange	Lesotho	Atlantic Ocean	1,300	2,092
Orinoco	Serra Parima Mts., Venezuela	Atlantic Ocean	1,281	2,062
Pilcomayo	Andes Mts., Bolivia	Paraguay River	1,242	1,999
Xi Jiang (Si Kiang)	Eastern Yunnan Province, China	China Sea	1,236	1,989
Columbia	Columbia Lake, British Columbia, Canada	Pacific Ocean	1,232	1,983
Don	Tula, Russia	Sea of Azov	1,223	1,968
Sungari	China-North Korea boundary	Amur River	1,215	1,955
Saskatchewan	Canadian Rocky Mts.	Lake Winnipeg	1,205	1,939
Peace	Stikine Mts., British Columbia, Canada	Great Slave River	1,195	1,923
Tigris	Taurus Mts., Turkey	Shatt-al-Arab	1,180	1,899

Highest Waterfalls of the World

Waterfall	Location	River	Height	
			feet	m
Angel	Venezuela	Tributary of Caroni	3,281	1,000
Tugela	Natal, South Africa	Tugela	3,000	914
Cuquenán	Venezuela	Cuquenán	2,000	610
Sutherland	South Island, N.Z.	Arthur	1,904	580
Takkakaw	British Columbia	Tributary of Yoho	1,650	503
Ribbon (Yosemite)	California	Creek flowing into Yosemite	1,612	491
Upper Yosemite	California	Yosemite Creek, tributary of Merced	1,430	436
Gavarnie	Southwest France	Gave de Pau	1,384	422
Vettisfoss	Norway	Mörkedola	1,200	366
Widows' Tears (Yosemite)	California	Tributary of Merced	1,170	357
Staubbach	Switzerland	Staubbach (Lauterbrunnen Valley)	984	300
Middle Cascade (Yosemite)	California	Yosemite Creek, tributary of Merced	909	277
King Edward VIII	Guyana	Courantyne	850	259
Gersoppa	India	Sharavati	829	253
Kaieteur	Guyana	Potaro	822	251
Skykje	Norway	In Skykjedal (valley of Inner Hardinger Fjord)	820	250
Kalambo	Tanzania-Zambia	—	720	219
Fairy (Mt. Rainier Park)	Washington	Stevens Creek	700	213
Trummelbach	Switzerland	Trummelbach (Lauterbrunnen Valley)	700	213
Aniene (Teverone)	Italy	Tiber	680	207
Cascata delle Marmore	Italy	Velino, tributary of Nera	650	198
Maradalsfos	Norway	Stream flowing into Ejkisdalsvand (lake)	643	196
Feather	California	Fall River	640	195
Maletsunyane	Lesotho	Maletsunyane	630	192
Bridalveil (Yosemite)	California	Yosemite Creek	620	189
Multnomah	Oregon	Multnomah Creek, tributary of Columbia	620	189
Vøringsfos	Norway	Bjoreia	597	182
Nevada (Yosemite)	California	Merced	594	181
Skjeggedal	Norway	Tysso	525	160
Marina	Guyana	Tributary of Kuribrong, tributary of Potaro	500	152
Tequendama	Colombia	Funza, tributary of Magdalena	425	130
King George's	Cape of Good Hope, South Africa	Orange	400	122
Illilouette (Yosemite)	California	Illilouette Creek, tributary of Merced	370	113

Waterfall	Location	River	Height feet	Height m
Victoria	Zimbabwe-Zambia boundary	Zambezi	355	108
Handöl	Sweden	Handöl Creek	345	105
Lower Yosemite	California	Yosemite	320	98
Comet (Mt. Rainier Park)	Washington	Van Trump Creek	320	98
Vernal (Yosemite)	California	Merced	317	97
Virginia	Northwest Territories, Canada	South Nahanni, tributary of Mackenzie	315	96
Lower Yellowstone	Wyoming	Yellowstone	310	94

NOTE: Niagara Falls (New York-Ontario), though of great volume, has parallel drops of only 158 and 167 feet.

Large Islands of the World

Island	Location and political affiliation	Area sq mi.	Area sq km
Greenland	North Atlantic (Danish)	839,999	2,175,597
New Guinea	Southwest Pacific (Irian Jaya, Indonesian, west part; Papua New Guinea, east part)	316,615	820,033
Borneo	West mid-Pacific (Indonesian, south part, Brunei and Malaysian, north part)	286,914	743,107
Madagascar	Indian Ocean (Malagasy Republic)	226,657	587,042
Baffin	North Atlantic (Canadian)	183,810	476,068
Sumatra	Northeast Indian Ocean (Indonesian)	182,859	473,605
Honshu	Sea of Japan-Pacific (Japanese)	88,925	230,316
Great Britain	Off coast of NW Europe (England, Scotland, and Wales)	88,758	229,883
Ellesmere	Arctic Ocean (Canadian)	82,119	212,688
Victoria	Arctic Ocean (Canadian)	81,930	212,199
Sulawesi (Celebes)	West mid-Pacific (Indonesian)	72,986	189,034
South Island	South Pacific (New Zealand)	58,093	150,461
Java	Indian Ocean (Indonesian)	48,990	126,884
North Island	South Pacific (New Zealand)	44,281	114,688
Cuba	Caribbean Sea (republic)	44,218	114,525
Newfoundland	North Atlantic (Canadian)	42,734	110,681
Luzon	West mid-Pacific (Philippines)	40,420	104,688
Iceland	North Atlantic (republic)	39,768	102,999
Mindanao	West mid-Pacific (Philippines)	36,537	94,631
Ireland	West of Great Britain (republic, south part; United Kingdom, north part)	32,597	84,426
Hokkaido	Sea of Japan—Pacific (Japanese)	30,372	78,663
Hispaniola	Caribbean Sea (Dominican Republic, east part; Haiti, west part)	29,355	76,029
Tasmania	South of Australia (Australian)	26,215	67,897
Sri Lanka (Ceylon)	Indian Ocean (republic)	25,332	65,610
Sakhalin (Karafuto)	North of Japan (Russia)	24,560	63,610
Banks	Arctic Ocean (Canadian)	23,230	60,166
Devon	Arctic Ocean (Canadian)	20,861	54,030
Tierra del Fuego	Southern tip of South America (Argentinian, east part; Chilean, west part)	18,605	48,187
Kyushu	Sea of Japan—Pacific (Japanese)	16,223	42,018
Melville	Arctic Ocean (Canadian)	16,141	41,805
Axel Heiberg	Arctic Ocean (Canadian)	15,779	40,868
Southampton	Hudson Bay (Canadian)	15,700	40,663

Principal Deserts of the World

Desert	Location	Approximate size	Approx. elevation, ft.
Atacama	North Chile	400 mi. long	7,000–13,500
Black Rock	Northwest Nevada	About 1,000 sq mi.	2,000–8,500
Colorado	Southeast California from San Gorgonio Pass to Gulf of California	200 mi. long and a maximum width of 50 mi.	Few feet above to 250 below sea level
Dasht-e-Kavir	Southeast of Caspian Sea, Iran	—	2,000
Dasht-e-Lut	Northeast of Kerman, Iran	—	1,000
Gobi (Shamo)	Covers most of Mongolia	500,000 sq mi.	3,000–5,000

Desert	Location	Approximate size	Approx. elevation, ft.
Great Arabian	Most of Arabia	1,500 mi. long	—
An Nafud (Red Desert)	South of Jauf	400 mi. by avg of 140 mi.	3,000
Dahna	Northeast of Nejd	400 mi. by 30 mi.	—
Rub' al-Khali	South portion of Nejd	Over 200,000 sq. mi.	—
Syrian (Al-Hamad)	North of lat. 30°N	—	1,850
Great Australian	Western portion of Australia	About one half the continent	600–1,000
Great Salt Lake	West of Great Salt Lake to Nevada—Utah boundary	About 110 mi. by 50 mi.	4,500
Kalahari	South Africa— South-West Africa	About 120,000 sq mi.	Over 3,000
Kara Kum (Desert of Kiva)	Southwest Turkmenistan	115,000 sq mi.	—
Kyzyl Kum	Uzbekistan and Kazakhstan	Over 100,000 sq. mi.	160 near Lake Aral to 2,000 in southeast
Libyan	Libya, Egypt, Sudan	Over 500,000 sq mi.	—
Mojave	North of Colorado Desert and south of Death Valley, southeast California	15,000 sq mi.	2,000
Nubian	From Red Sea to great west bend of the Nile, Sudan	—	2,500
Painted Desert	Northeast Arizona	Over 7,000 sq mi.	High plateau, 5,000
Sahara	North Africa to about lat. 15°N and from Red Sea to Atlantic Ocean	3,200 mi. greatest length along lat. 20°N; area over 3,500,000 sq mi.	440 below sea level to 11,000 above; avg. elevation, 1,400–1,600
Sonoran	Southwestern Arizona, southeastern California, and northwestern Mexico	120,000 sq mi.	—
Takla Makan	Southcentral Sinkiang, China	Over 100,000 sq mi.	—
Thar (Indian)	Pakistan-India	Nearly 100,000 sq mi.	Over 1,000

Interesting Caves and Caverns of the World

Aggtelek. In village of same name, northern Hungary. Large stalactitic cavern about 5 miles long.

Altamira Cave. Near Santander, Spain. Contains animal paintings (Old Stone Age art) on roof and walls.

Antiparos. On island of same name in the Grecian Archipelago. Some stalactites are 20 ft. long. Brilliant colors and fantastic shapes.

Blue Grotto. On island of Capri, Italy. Cavern hollowed out in limestone by constant wave action. Now half filled with water because of sinking coast. Name derived from unusual blue light permeating the cave. Source of light is a submerged opening, light passing through the water.

Carlsbad Caverns. Southeast New Mexico. Largest underground labyrinth yet discovered. Three levels: 754-, 900-, and 1,320 ft. below the surface.

Fingal's Cave. On island of Staffa off coast of western Scotland. Penetrates about 200 ft. inland. Contains basaltic columns almost 40 ft. high.

Jenolan Caves. In Blue Mountain plateau, New South Wales, Australia. Beautiful stalactitic formations.

Kent's Cavern. Near Torquay, England. Source of much information on Paleolithic man.

Luray Cavern. Near Luray, Va. Has large stalactitic and stalagmitic columns of many colors.

Mammoth Cave. Limestone cavern in central Kentucky. Cave area is about 10 miles in diameter but has over 300 miles of irregular subterranean passageways at various levels. Temperature remains fairly constant at 54°F.

Peak Cavern or Devil's Hole. Derbyshire, England. About 2,250 ft. into a mountain. Lowest part is about 600 ft. below the surface.

Postojna (Postumia) Grotto. Near Postumia in Julian Alps, about 25 miles northeast of Trieste. Stalactitic cavern, largest in Europe. Piuca (Pivka) River flows through part of it. Caves have numerous beautiful stalactites.

Singing Cave. Iceland. A lava cave; name derived from echoes of people singing in it.

Wind Cave. In Black Hills of South Dakota. Limestone caverns with stalactites and stalagmites almost entirely missing. Variety of crystal formations called "boxwork."

Wyandotte Cave. In Crawford County, southern Indiana. A limestone cavern with five levels of passages; one of the largest in North America. "Monumental Mountain," approximately 135 ft. high, is believed to be one of the world's largest underground "mountains."

Plate-Tectonics Theory—The Lithosphere Plates of the Earth

Source: U.S. Department of the Interior, U.S. Geological Survey.

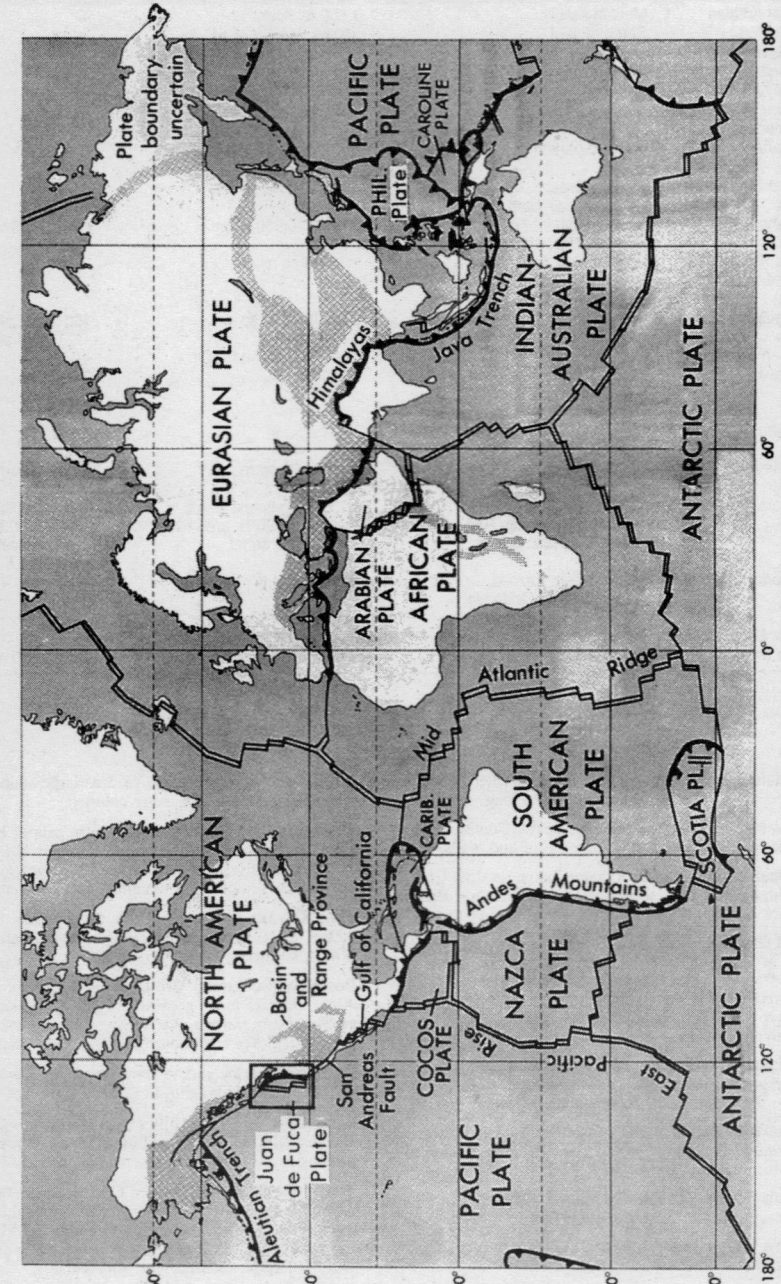

Plate-Tectonics Theory

Source: U.S. Dept. of the Interior, Geological Survey.

According to the generally accepted "plate-tectonics" theory, scientists believe that the Earth's surface is broken into a number of shifting slabs or plates, which average about 50 miles in thickness. These plates move relative to one another above a hotter, deeper, more mobile zone at average rates as great as a few inches per year. Most of the world's active volcanoes are located along or near the boundaries between shifting plates and are called "plate-boundary" volcanoes. However, some active volcanoes are not associated with plate boundaries, and many of these so-called "intra-plate" volca-

noes form roughly linear chains in the interior of some oceanic plates. The Hawaiian Islands provide perhaps the best example of an "intra-plate" volcanic chain, developed by the northwest-moving Pacific plate passing over an inferred "hot spot" that initiates the magma-generation and volcano-formation process. The peripheral areas of the Pacific Ocean Basin, containing the boundaries of several plates, are dotted by many active volcanoes that form the so-called "Ring of Fire." The "Ring" provides excellent examples of "plate-boundary" volcanoes, including Mt. St. Helens.

Volcanoes of the World

About 500 volcanoes have had recorded eruptions within historical times. Almost two thirds of these are in the Northern Hemisphere. Most volcanoes occur at the boundaries of the Earth's crustal plates, such as the famous "Ring of Fire" that surrounds the Pacific Ocean plate. Of the world's active volcanoes, about 60% are

along the perimeter of the Pacific, about 17% on mid-oceanic islands, about 14% in an arc along the south of the Indonesian islands, and about 9% in the Mediterranean area, Africa, and Asia Minor. Many of the world's volcanoes are submarine and have unrecorded eruptions.

Recent Volcanic Activity (through August 1997)

Volcano	Month of most recent eruption or activity	Volcano	Month of most recent eruption or activity
Montserrat, West Indies	Aug. 1997	Amukta, Alaska	Sept. 1996
Karymsky, Kamchatka, Russia	Aug. 1997	Loihi Seamount, Hawaii	July 1996
Sheveluch, Kamchatka	July 1997	Ruapehu, New Zealand	June 1996
Etna, Sicily, Italy	July 1997	Momotombo, Nicaragua	April 1996
Hakkoda, Japan	July 1997	Krakatau, Indonesia	April 1996
Popocatepetl, Mexico	June 1997	Long Valley Caldera, Calif.	April 1996
Shishaldin, Alaska	June 1997	Akutan, Alaska	March 1996
Pavlof, Alaska	June 1997	Komaga-take, Hokkaido, Japan	March 1996
Manam, Papua New Guinea	May 1997	Northern Gorda Ridge, Pacific Ocean	Feb. 1996
Rabaul, Papua New Guinea	May 1997	Eastern Gemini Seamount, Vanuatu	Feb.1996
San Cristobal, Nicaragua	May 1997	Fernandina, Galapagos	Jan. 1996
Mount Hili Aludo	May 1997	Metis Shoal, Tonga	June 1995
Bezymianny, Kamchatka, Russia	May1997	Fogo, Cape Verde	April 1995
Okmok, Alaska	May 1997	Cerro Negro, Nicaragua	Nov. 1995
Mount Karangetang, Indonesia	April 1997	Rincon de la Vieja, Costa Rica	Nov. 1995
Piparo, Trinidad	Feb. 1997	Ruby Seamount, Mariana Islands	Oct. 1995
Kliuchevskoi, Russia	Jan. 1997	Hosho, Kyushu, Japan	Oct. 1995
Pacaya, Guatemala	Oct. 1996	Mount St. Helens, Washington	Jan.–Sept. 1995
Grimsvotn, Iceland	Sept. 1996	Barren Island, Indian Ocean	Dec. 1994
Maderas, Nicaragua	Sept. 1996	Merapi, Indonesia	Nov. 1994
Monowai Seamount, Kermadec Islands, French Polynesia	Sept. 1996	Kilauea, Hawaii	1983, continuing

Source: Volcano World, University of North Dakota (www.volcano.und.edu).

Indonesian Volcanoes

Indonesia has 130 active volcanoes, more than any other country.

Mt. Merapi, Java (9,554 ft.; 2,912 m), is the most active, and has had at least twelve eruptions causing fatalities. The last eruption began on November 22, 1994.

Mt. Bromo, Java (7,639 ft.; 2,329 m), has erupted 53 times since 1804, most recently in 1984.

Mt. Semeru, Java (12,060 ft.; 3,339 m), the highest mountain on the island, was active in 1996.

The most famous of Indonesian volcanoes is Krakatau, a small volcanic island in the Sunda Strait between

Sumatra and Java. Its eruption in 1883 was one of the world's most violent. Giant forty-meter tidal waves hurled ashore blocks of coral weighing as much as 600 tons. More than 36,000 people were killed. Three months after the eruption a volcanic dust veil surrounded the Earth, acting as a solar filter that lowered the global temperature as much as 1.2°C in the year following the eruption. The most recent volcanic activity took place on the island of Anak Krakatau ("Child of Krakatau"—a remnant of the main island) in March 1995.

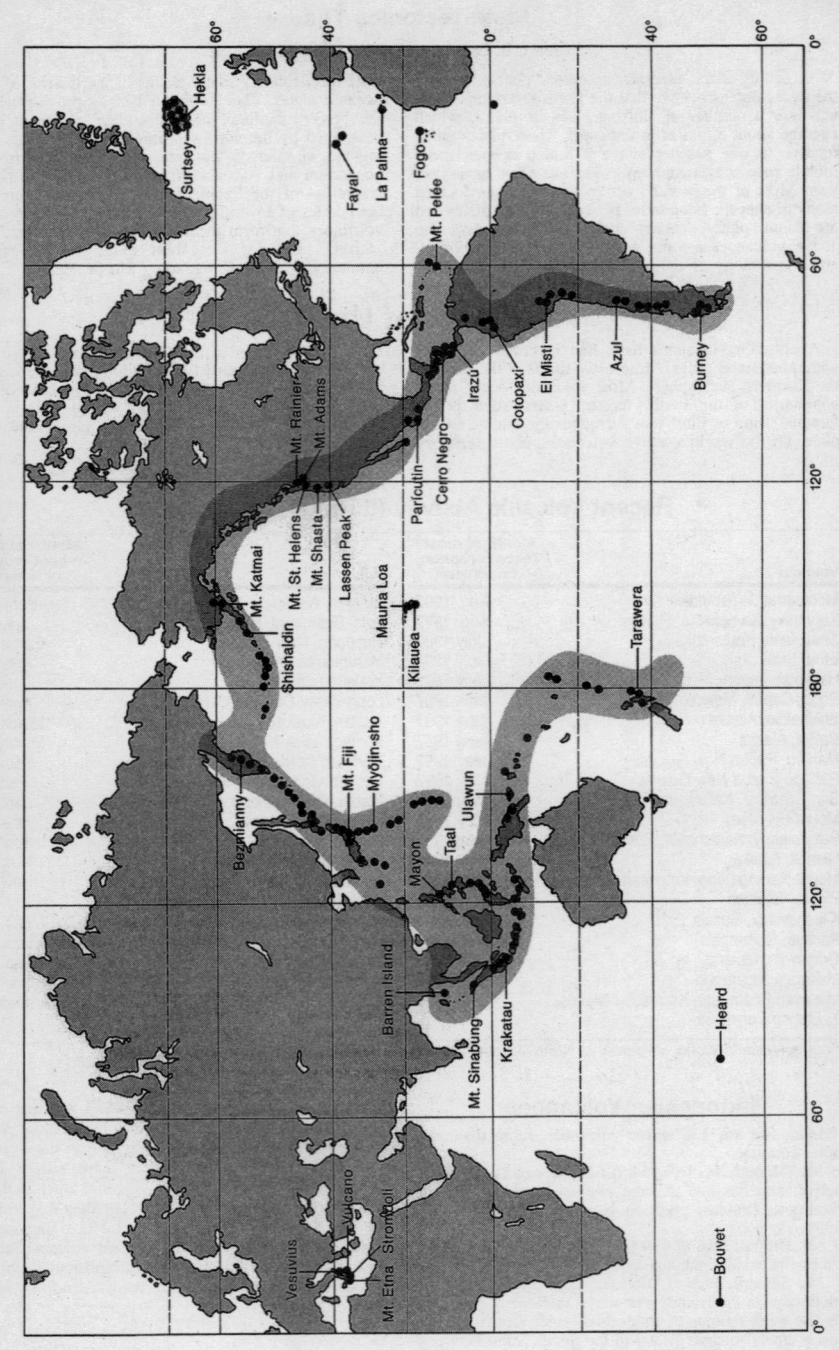

The Pacific Ocean "Ring of Fire"
Source: U.S. Department of the Interior, U.S. Geological Survey.

The Deadliest Volcanic Eruptions

Deaths	Volcano	Year	Major cause of deaths
92,000	Tambora, Indonesia	1815	Starvation
36,417	Krakatau, Indonesia	1883	Tsunami
29,025	Mt. Pelee, Martinique	1902	Ash flows
25,000	Ruiz, Colombia	1985	Mudflows
14,300	Unzen, Japan	1792	Volcano collapse, tsunami
9,350	Laki, Iceland	1783	Starvation
5,110	Kelut, Indonesia	1919	Mudflows
4,011	Galunggung, Indonesia	1882	Mudflows
3,500	Vesuvius, Italy	1631	Mudflows, lava flows
3,360	Vesuvius, Italy	C.E. 79	Ash flows and falls
2,957	Papandayan, Indonesia	1772	Ash flows
2,942	Lamington, Papua New Guinea	1951	Ash flows
2,000	El Chichon, Mexico	1982	Ash flows
1,680	Soufriere, St. Vincent	1902	Ash flows
1,475	Oshima, Japan	1741	Tsunami
1,377	Asama, Japan	1783	Ash flows, mudflows
1,335	Taal, Philipines	1911	Ash flows
1,200	Mayon, Philipines	1814	Mudflows
1,184	Agung, Indonesia	1963	Ash Flows
1,000	Cotopaxi, Ecuador	1877	Mudflows
800	Pinatubo, Philippines	1991	Roof collapses and disease
700	Komagatake, Japan	1640	Tsunami
700	Ruiz, Colombia	1845	Mudflows
500	Hibok-Hibok, Philippines	1951	Ash flows

Source: Volcano World, University of North Dakota (www.volcano.und.edu).

Principal Types of Volcanoes

Source: U.S. Dept. of Interior, Geological Survey.

Geologists generally group volcanoes into four main kinds—cinder cones, composite volcanoes, shield volcanoes, and lava domes.

Cinder Cones

Cinder cones are the simplest type of volcano. They are built from particles and blobs of congealed lava ejected from a single vent. As the gas-charged lava is blown violently into the air, it breaks into small fragments that solidify and fall as cinders around the vent to form a circular or oval cone. Most cinder cones have a bowl-shaped crater at the summit and rarely rise more than a thousand feet or so above their surroundings. Cinder cones are numerous in western North America as well as throughout other volcanic terrains of the world.

Composite Volcanoes

Some of the Earth's grandest mountains are composite volcanoes—sometimes called *stratovolcanoes*. They are typically deep-sided, symmetrical cones of large dimension built of alternating layers of lava flows, volcanic ash, cinders, blocks, and bombs and may rise as much as 8,000 feet above their bases. Some of the most conspicuous and beautiful mountains in the world are composite volcanoes, including Mt. Fuji in Japan, Mt. Cotopaxi in Ecuador, Mt. Shasta in California, Mt. Hood in Oregon, and Mt. St. Helens and Mt. Rainier in Washington.

Most composite volcanoes have a crater at the summit that contains a central vent or a clustered group of vents. Lavas either flow through breaks in the crater wall or issue from fissures on the flanks of the cone. Lava, solidified within the fissures, forms *dikes* that act as ribs which greatly strengthen the cone.

The essential feature of a composite volcano is a conduit system through which magma from a reservoir deep in the Earth's crust rises to the surface. The volcano is built up by the accumulation of material erupted through the conduit and increases in size as lava, cinders, ash, etc., are added to its slopes.

Shield Volcanoes

Shield volcanoes, the third type of volcano, are built almost entirely of fluid lava flows. Flow after flow pours out in all directions from a central summit vent, or group of vents, building a broad, gently sloping cone of flat, domical shape, with a profile much like that of a warrior's shield. They are built up slowly by the accretion of thousands of flows of highly fluid basaltic (from *basalt,* a hard, dense dark volcanic rock) lava that spread widely over great distances, and then cool as thin, gently dipping sheets. Lavas also commonly erupt from vents along fractures (rift zones) that develop on the flanks of the cone. Some of the largest volcanoes in the world are shield volcanoes. In northern California and Oregon, many shield volcanoes have diameters of 3 or 4 miles and heights of 1,500 to 2,000 feet. The Hawaiian Islands are composed of linear chains of these volcanoes, including Kilauea and Mauna Loa on the island of Hawaii.

In some shield volcano eruptions, basaltic lava pours out quietly from long fissures instead of central vents and floods the surrounding countryside with lava flow upon lava flow, forming broad plateaus. Lava plateaus of this type can be seen in Iceland, southeastern Washington, eastern Oregon, and southern Idaho.

Lava Domes

Volcanic or lava domes are formed by relatively small, bulbous masses of lava too viscous to flow any great distance; consequently, on extrusion, the lava piles over and around its vent. A dome grows largely by expansion from within. As it grows its outer surface cools and hardens, then shatters, spilling loose fragments down its sides. Some domes form craggy knobs or spines over the volcanic vent, whereas others form short, steep-sided lava flows known as *coulees.* Volcanic domes commonly occur within the craters or on the flanks of large composite volcanoes. The nearly circular Novarupta Dome that formed during the 1912 eruption of Katmai Volcano, Alaska, measures 800 feet across and 200 feet high. The internal structure of this dome—defined by layering of lava fanning upward and outward from the center—indicates that it grew largely by expansion from within. Mt. Pelée in Martinique, West Indies, and Lassen Peak and Mono domes in California, are examples of lava domes.

Submarine Volcanoes

Submarine volcanoes and volcanic vents are common features on certain zones of the ocean floor. Some are active at the present time and, in shallow water, disclose their presence by blasting steam and rock-debris high above the surface of the sea. Many others lie at such great depths that the tremendous weight of the water above them results in high, confining pressure and prevents the formation and release of steam and gases. Even very large, deepwater eruptions may not disturb the ocean floor.

The famous black sand beaches of Hawaii were created virtually instantaneously by the violent interaction between hot lava and sea water.

Earth's Greatest Volcanic Field

The largest known concentration of active volcanoes on earth was discovered by scientists aboard the research vessel *Melville* during the period November 1992 to January 1993. The vast volcanic cluster is situated under the South Pacific Ocean, 600 miles northwest of Easter Island.

A total of 1,133 seamounts and volcanic cones were found in the area which is about the size of New York State. Some of them rise to a height of almost 7,000 feet and their peaks are 2,500 to 5,000 feet below the ocean's surface.

Earthquakes

(*Source*: U.S. Dept. of the Interior, Geological Survey.)

The Richter Magnitude Scale

The Richter magnitude scale was developed in 1935 by Charles F. Richter of the California Institute of Technology as a mathematical device to compare the size of earthquakes. The magnitude of an earthquake is determined from the logarithm of the amplitude of waves recorded by seismographs. Adjustments are included in the magnitude formula to compensate for the variation in the distance between the various seismographs and the epicenter of the earthquakes. On the Richter Scale, magnitude is expressed in whole numbers and decimal fractions. For example, a magnitude of 5.3 might be computed for a moderate earthquake, and a strong earthquake might be rated as magnitude 6.3. Great earthquakes, such as the 1906 earthquake in San Francisco, have magnitudes of 8.0 or higher. Although the Richter Scale has no upper limit, the largest known shocks have had magnitudes in the 8.8 to 8.9 range.

The Richter Scale is not used to express damage. An earthquake in a densely populated area that results in many deaths and considerable damage may have the same magnitude as a shock in a remote area that does nothing more than frighten the wildlife. Large-magnitude earthquakes that occur beneath the oceans may not even be felt by humans.

The Richter scale has been largely abandoned by seismologists because it isn't very accurate for the biggest earthquakes, those in the range of 8 or 9. Because it is based on readings taken close to quakes, 100 miles or so, it is less precise in other parts of the world where the nearest seismograph may be many hundreds of miles away.

New ways have been developed to rate the magnitude of the quake in numbers similar to the familiar Richter scale. The U.S. Geological Survey's National Earthquake Information Center in Golden, Colorado, uses surface-wave magnitude, which measures the seismic waves crackling around the Earth's surface. Other seismologists use a measure known as the moment magnitude, which is based on the size of the fault on which an earthquake occurs and the amount the earth slips. So nowadays, when most seismologists announce a magnitude number, they no longer say "on the Richter scale."

Frequency of Earthquakes Worldwide[1]

Descriptor	Magnitude	Annual Average	Descriptor	Magnitude	Annual Average
Great	8 or higher	1	Light	4–4.9	6,200
Major	7–7.9	18	Minor	3–3.9	49,000
Strong	6–6.9	120	Very Minor	2–3	c.1,000
Moderate	5–5.9	800	" "	1–2	c.8,000

1. Since 1900. *Source*: United States Geological Survey.

Number of Earthquakes Worldwide, 1987–1996

Magnitude	1987	1988	1989	1990	1991	1992	1993	1994	1995	1996
8.0–9.9	0	0	1	0	0	0	1	2	3	1
7.0–7.9	11	8	6	12	11	23	15	13	22	20
6.0–6.9	112	93	79	115	105	104	141	161	185	150
5.0–5.9	1437	1485	1444	1635	1469	1541	1449	1542	1327	1126
4.0–4.9	4146	4018	4090	4493	4372	5196	5034	4544	8140	8558
3.0–3.9	1806	1932	2452	2457	2952	4643	4263	5000	5002	4521
2.0–2.9	1037	1479	1906	2364	2927	3068	5390	5369	3838	2065
1.0–1.9	102	118	418	474	801	887	1177	779	645	267
0.1–0.9	0	3	0	0	1	2	9	17	19	1
No Magnitude	2,639	3,575	4,189	5,062	3,878	4,084	3,997	1,944	1,826	2,155
Total	11,290	12,711	14,585	16,612	16,516	19,548	21,476	19,371	21,007	18,864

Source: United States Geological Survey.

See also p. 496 for largest U.S. earthquakes.

The Continents

A continent is defined as a large unbroken land mass completely surrounded by water, although in some cases continents are (or were in part) connected by land bridges.

The hypothesis first suggested late in the 19th century was that the continents consist of lighter rocks that rest on heavier crustal material in about the same manner that icebergs float on water. That the rocks forming the continents are lighter than the material below them and under the ocean bottoms is now established. As a consequence of this fact, Alfred Wegener (for the first time in 1912) suggested that the continents are slowly moving, at a rate of about one yard per century, so that their relative positions are not rigidly fixed. Many geologists that were originally skeptical have come to accept this theory of Continental Drift.

When describing a continent, it is important to remember that there is a fundamental difference between a deep ocean, like the Atlantic, and shallow seas, like the Baltic and most of the North Sea, which are merely flooded portions of a continent. Another and entirely different point to remember is that political considerations have often overridden geographical facts when it came to naming continents.

World Population, Land Areas, and Elevations

Area	Estimated population, mid-1996	Approximate land area sq mi.	Percent of total land area	Population density per sq mi.	Elevation, feet Highest	Lowest
WORLD	5,772,351,000	57,308,757	100.0	100.7	Mt. Everest, Asia, 29,028 ft.	Dead Sea, Asia, 1,312 ft. below sea level
ASIA (includes the Near East)	3,428,277,000	17,176,102	30.0	199.6	Mt. Everest, Tibet-Nepal, 29,028 ft.	Dead Sea, Israel-Jordan, 1,312 ft. below sea level
AFRICA	731,538,000	11,687,188	20.4	62.6	Mt. Kilimanjaro, Tanzania, 19,340 ft.	Lake Assal, Djibouti, 512 ft. below sea level
NORTH AMERICA	295,424,000	24,235,280	16.3	12.2	Mt. McKinley, Alaska, 20,320 ft.	Death Valley, Calif., 282 ft. below sea level
SOUTH AMERICA (includes Central America and the Caribbean)	488,608,000	6,880,638	8.9	71.0	Mt. Aconcagua, Arg.-Chile, 22,834 ft.	Valdes Peninsula, Argentina 131 ft. below sea level
ANTARCTICA	—	5,100,023	8.9	—	Vinson Massif, Sentinel Range, 16,864 ft.	Antarctica, (ice covered) 8,327 ft. below sea level
EUROPE, (includes the newly independent states of the former Soviet Union)	799,589,000	4,065,945	7.1	196.6	Elbrus, Russia, 18,510 ft.	Caspian Sea, Russia, 92 ft. below sea level
AUSTRALIA (includes Oceania)	28,915,000	3,035,651	5.2	9.5	Kosciusko, Australia 7,316 ft.	Lake Eyre, Australia, 52 ft. below sea level

Source: U.S. Bureau of the Census, International Data Base, for population figures; National Geographic Society.

Explorations

(All years are C.E. unless B.C.E. is specified.)

Country or place	Event	Explorer or discoverer	Date
AFRICA			
Sierra Leone	Visited	Hanno, Carthaginian seaman	c. 520 B.C.E.
Zaire River (Congo)	Mouth visited[1]	Diogo Cão, Portuguese explorer	c. 1484
Cape of Good Hope	Rounded	Bartolomeu Diaz, Portuguese explorer	1488
Gambia River	Explored	Mungo Park, Scottish explorer	1795
Sahara	Crossed	Dixon Denham and Hugh Clapperton, English explorers	1822–23
Zambezi River	Visited[1]	David Livingstone, Scottish explorer	1851
Sudan	Explored	Heinrich Barth, German explorer	1852–55
Victoria Falls	Visited[1]	Livingstone	1855
Lake Tanganyika	Visited[1]	Richard Burton and John Speke, British explorers	1858
Zaire River (Congo)	Traced	Sir Henry M. Stanley, British explorer	1877
ASIA			
Punjab (India)	Visited	Alexander the Great	327 B.C.E.
China	Visited	Marco Polo, Italian traveler	c. 1272

Country or place	Event	Explorer or discoverer	Date
Tibet	Visited	Odoric of Pordenone, Italian monk	c. 1325
Southern China	Explored	Niccolò dei Conti, Venetian traveler	c. 1440
India	Visited (Cape route)	Vasco da Gama, Portuguese navigator	1498
Japan	Visited	St. Francis Xavier of Spain	1549
Arabia	Explored	Carsten Niebuhr, German explorer	1762
China	Explored	Ferdinand Richthofen, German scientist	1868
Mongolia	Explored	Nikolai M. Przhevalsky, Russian explorer	1870–73
Central Asia	Explored	Sven Hedin, Swedish scientist	1890–1908
EUROPE			
Shetland Islands	Visited	Pytheas of Massilia (Marseille)	c. 325 B.C.E.
North Cape	Rounded	Ottar, Norwegian explorer	c. 870
Iceland	Colonized	Norwegian noblemen	c. 890–900
NORTH AMERICA			
Greenland	Colonized	Eric the Red, Norwegian	c. 985
Labrador; Nova Scotia (?)	Visited[1]	Leif Ericson, Norse explorer	1000
West Indies	Visited[1]	Christopher Columbus, Italian	1492
North America	Coast visited[1]	Giovanni Caboto (John Cabot), for British	1497
Pacific Ocean	Sighted[1]	Vasco Núñez de Balboa, Spanish explorer	1513
Florida	Explored	Ponce de León, Spanish explorer	1513
Mexico	Conquered	Hernando Cortés, Spanish adventurer	1519–21
St. Lawrence River	Visited[1]	Jacques Cartier, French navigator	1534
Southwest U.S.	Explored	Francisco Coronado, Spanish explorer	1540–42
Colorado River	Visited[1]	Hernando de Alarcón, Spanish explorer	1540
Mississippi River	Visited[1]	Hernando de Soto, Spanish explorer	1541
Frobisher Bay	Visited[1]	Martin Frobisher, English seaman	1576
Maine Coast	Explored	Samuel de Champlain, French explorer	1604
Jamestown, Va.	Settled	John Smith, English colonist	1607
Hudson River	Explored	Henry Hudson, English navigator	1609
Hudson Bay (Canada)	Visited[1]	Henry Hudson	1610
Baffin Bay	Visited[1]	William Baffin, English navigator	1616
Lake Michigan	Navigated	Jean Nicolet, French explorer	1634
Arkansas River	Visited[1]	Jacques Marquette and Louis Jolliet, French explorers	1673
Mississippi River	Explored	Sieur de La Salle, French explorer	1682
Bering Strait	Visited[1]	Vitus Bering, Danish explorer	1728
Alaska	Visited[1]	Vitus Bering	1741
Mackenzie River (Canada)	Visited[1]	Sir Alexander Mackenzie, Scottish-Canadian explorer	1789
Northwest U.S.	Explored	Meriwether Lewis and William Clark	1804–06
Northeast Passage (Arctic Ocean)	Navigated	Nils Nordenskjöld, Swedish explorer	1879
Greenland	Explored	Robert Peary, American explorer	1892
Northwest Passage	Navigated	Roald Amundsen, Norwegian explorer	1906
SOUTH AMERICA			
Continent	Visited	Christopher Columbus, Italian	1498
Brazil	Visited[1]	Pedro Alvarez Cabral, Portuguese	1500
Peru	Conquered	Francisco Pizarro, Spanish explorer	1532–33
Amazon River	Explored	Francisco Orellana, Spanish explorer	1541
Cape Horn	Visited[1]	Willem C. Schouten, Dutch navigator	1615
OCEANIA			
Papua New Guinea	Visited	Jorge de Menezes, Portuguese explorer	1526
Australia	Visited	Abel Janszoon Tasman, Dutch navigator	1642
Tasmania	Visited[1]	Abel Janszoon Tasman, Dutch navigator	1642
Australia	Explored	John McDouall Stuart, English explorer	1828
Australia	Explored	Robert Burke and William Wills, Australian explorers	1861

Country or place	Event	Explorer or discoverer	Date
New Zealand	Sighted (and named)	Abel Janszoon Tasman	1642
New Zealand	Visited	James Cook, English navigator	1769
ARCTIC, ANTARCTIC, AND MISCELLANEOUS			
Africa, Middle East, South and Southeast Asia, Europe	Visited	Ibn Batuta, greatest Arab traveler	1325–49
Ocean exploration	Expedition	Magellan's ships circled globe	1519–22
Galápagos Islands	Visited	Diego de Rivadeneira, Spanish captain	1535
Spitsbergen	Visited	Willem Barents, Dutch navigator	1596
Antarctic Circle	Crossed	James Cook, English navigator	1773
Antarctica	Visited[1]	Nathaniel Palmer, U.S. whaler (archipelago) and Fabian Gottlieb von Bellingshausen, Russian admiral (mainland)	1820–21
Antarctica	Explored	Charles Wilkes, American explorer	1840
North Pole	Reached	Robert E. Peary, American explorer	1909
South Pole	Reached	Roald Amundsen, Norwegian explorer	1911

1. First European to reach the area.

Latitude and Longitude of World Cities

(and time corresponding to 12:00 noon, eastern standard time)

City	Latitude °	'	Longitude °	'	Time	City	Latitude °	'	Longitude °	'	Time
Aberdeen, Scotland	57	9 n	2	9 w	5:00 p.m.	Dublin	53	20 n	6	15 w	5:00 p.m.
Adelaide, Australia	34	55 s	138	36 e	2:30 a.m.[1]	Durban, South Africa	29	53 s	30	53 e	7:00 p.m.
Algiers	36	50 n	3	0 e	6:00 p.m.	Edinburgh, Scotland	55	55 n	3	10 w	5:00 p.m.
Amsterdam	52	22 n	4	53 e	6:00 p.m.	Frankfurt	50	7 n	8	41 e	6:00 p.m.
Ankara, Turkey	39	55 n	32	55 e	7:00 p.m.	Georgetown, Guyana	6	45 n	58	15 w	1:15 p.m.
Asunción, Paraguay	25	15 s	57	40 w	1:00 p.m.	Glasgow, Scotland	55	50 n	4	15 w	5:00 p.m.
Athens	37	58 n	23	43 e	7:00 p.m.	Guatemala City, Guatemala	14	37 n	90	31 w	11:00 a.m.
Auckland, New Zealand	36	52 s	174	45 e	5:00 a.m.[1]						
Bangkok, Thailand	13	45 n	100	30 e	midnight	Guayaquil, Ecuador	2	10 s	79	56 w	12:00 noon
Barcelona	41	23 n	2	9 e	6:00 p.m.	Hamburg	53	33 n	10	2 e	6:00 p.m.
Belém, Brazil	1	28 s	48	29 w	2:00 p.m.	Hammerfest, Norway	70	38 n	23	38 e	6:00 p.m.
Belfast, Northern Ireland	54	37 n	5	56 w	5:00 p.m.	Havana	23	8 n	82	23 w	12:00 noon
Belgrade, Yugoslavia	44	52 n	20	32 e	6:00 p.m.	Helsinki, Finland	60	10 n	25	0 e	7:00 p.m.
Berlin	52	30 n	13	25 e	6:00 p.m.	Hobart, Tasmania	42	52 s	147	19 e	3:00 a.m.[1]
Birmingham, England	52	25 n	1	55 w	5:00 p.m.	Iquique, Chile	20	10 s	70	7 w	1:00 p.m.
Bogotá, Colombia	4	32 n	74	15 w	12:00 noon	Irkutsk, Russia	52	30 n	104	20 e	1:00 a.m.
Bombay	19	0 n	72	48 e	10:30 p.m.	Jakarta, Indonesia	6	16 s	106	48 e	0:30 a.m.[1]
Bordeaux, France	44	50 n	0	31 w	6:00 p.m.	Johannesburg, South Africa	26	12 s	28	4 e	7:00 p.m.
Bremen, Germany	53	5 n	8	49 e	6:00 p.m.						
Brisbane, Australia	27	29 s	153	8 e	3:00 a.m.[1]	Kingston, Jamaica	17	59 n	76	49 w	12:00 noon
Bristol, England	51	28 n	2	35 w	5:00 p.m.	Kinshasa, Congo	4	18 s	15	17 e	6:00 p.m.
Brussels	50	52 n	4	22 e	6:00 p.m.	La Paz, Bolivia	16	27 s	68	22 w	1:00 p.m.
Bucharest	44	25 n	26	7 e	7:00 p.m.	Leeds, England	53	45 n	1	30 w	5:00 p.m.
Budapest	47	30 n	19	5 e	6:00 p.m.	Lima, Peru	12	0 s	77	2 w	2:00 noon
Buenos Aires	34	35 s	58	22 w	2:00 p.m.	Lisbon	38	44 n	9	9 w	5:00 p.m.
Cairo	30	2 n	31	21 e	7:00 p.m.	Liverpool, England	53	25 n	3	0 w	5:00 p.m.
Calcutta	22	34 n	88	24 e	10:30 p.m.	London	51	32 n	0	5 w	5:00 p.m.
Canton, China	23	7 n	113	15 e	1:00 a.m.[1]	Lyons, France	45	45 n	4	50 e	6:00 p.m.
Cape Town, South Africa	33	55 s	18	22 e	7:00 p.m.	Madrid	40	26 n	3	42 w	6:00 p.m.
Caracas, Venezuela	10	28 n	67	2 w	1:00 p.m.	Manchester, England	53	30 n	2	15 w	5:00 p.m.
Cayenne, French Guiana	4	49 n	52	18 w	1:00 p.m.	Manila	14	35 n	120	57 e	1:00 a.m.[1]
						Marseilles, France	43	20 n	5	20 e	6:00 p.m.
Chihuahua, Mexico	28	37 n	106	5 w	11:00 a.m.	Mazatlán, Mexico	23	12 n	106	25 w	10:00 a.m.
Chongqing, China	29	46 n	106	34 e	1:00 a.m.[1]	Mecca, Saudi Arabia	21	29 n	39	45 e	8:00 p.m.
Copenhagen	55	40 n	12	34 e	6:00 p.m.	Melbourne	37	47 s	144	58 e	3:00 a.m.[1]
Córdoba, Argentina	31	28 s	64	10 w	2:00 p.m.	Mexico City	19	26 n	99	7 w	11:00 a.m.
Dakar, Senegal	14	40 n	17	28 w	5:00 p.m.	Milan, Italy	45	27 n	9	10 e	6:00 p.m.
Darwin, Australia	12	28 s	130	51 e	2:30 a.m.[1]	Montevideo, Uruguay	34	53 s	56	10 w	2:00 p.m.
						Moscow	55	45 n	37	36 e	8:00 p.m.
Djibouti	11	30 n	43	3 e	8:00 p.m.	Munich, Germany	48	8 n	11	35 e	6:00 p.m.

City	Latitude °	'	Longitude °	'	Time	City	Latitude °	'	Longitude °	'	Time
Nagasaki, Japan	32	48 n	129	57 e	2:00 a.m.[1]	Rome	41	54 n	12	27 e	6:00 p.m.
Nagoya, Japan	35	7 n	136	56 e	2:00 a.m.[1]	Salvador, Brazil	12	56 s	38	27 w	2:00 p.m.
Nairobi, Kenya	1	25 s	36	55 e	8:00 p.m.	Santiago, Chile	33	28 s	70	45 w	1:00 p.m.
Nanjing (Nanking), China	32	3 n	118	53 e	1:00 a.m.[1]	St. Petersburg	59	56 n	30	18 e	8:00 p.m.
						Sao Paulo, Brazil	23	31 s	46	31 w	2:00 p.m.
Naples, Italy	40	50 n	14	15 e	6:00 p.m.	Shanghai, China	31	10 n	121	28 e	1:00 a.m.[1]
Newcastle-on-Tyne, England	54	58 n	1	37 w	5:00 p.m.	Singapore	1	14 n	103	55 e	0:30 a.m.[1]
Odessa, Ukraine	46	27 n	30	48 e	8:00 p.m.	Sofia, Bulgaria	42	40 n	23	20 e	7:00 p.m.
Osaka, Japan	34	32 n	135	30 e	2:00 a.m.[1]	Stockholm	59	17 n	18	3 e	6:00 p.m.
Oslo	59	57 n	10	42 e	6:00 p.m.	Sydney, Australia	34	0 s	151	0 e	3:00 a.m.[1]
Panama City, Panama	8	58 n	79	32 w	12:00 noon	Tananarive, Madagascar	18	50 s	47	33 e	8:00 p.m.
Paramaribo, Surinam	5	45 n	55	15 w	1:30 p.m.	Teheran, Iran	35	45 n	51	45 e	8:30 p.m.
Paris	48	48 n	2	20 e	6:00 p.m.	Tokyo	35	40 n	139	45 e	2:00 a.m.[1]
Peking	39	55 n	116	25 e	1:00 a.m.[1]	Tripoli, Libya	32	57 n	13	12 e	7:00 p.m.
Perth, Australia	31	57 s	115	52 e	1:00 a.m.[1]	Venice	45	26 n	12	20 e	6:00 p.m.
Plymouth, England	50	25 n	4	5 w	5:00 p.m.	Veracruz, Mexico	19	10 n	96	10 w	11:00 a.m.
Port Moresby, Papua New Guinea	9	25 s	147	8 e	3:00 a.m.[1]	Vienna	48	14 n	16	20 e	6:00 p.m.
						Vladivostok, Russia	43	10 n	132	0 e	3:00 a.m.[1]
Prague	50	5 n	14	26 e	6:00 p.m.	Warsaw	52	14 n	21	0 e	6:00 p.m.
Rangoon, Burma	16	50 n	96	0 e	11:30 p.m.	Wellington, New Zealand	41	17 s	174	47 e	5:00 a.m.[1]
Reykjavik, Iceland	64	4 n	21	58 w	4:00 p.m.	Zürich	47	21 n	8	31 e	6:00 p.m.
Rio de Janeiro	22	57 s	43	12 w	2:00 p.m.						

1. On the following day.

U.S. Geography
Miscellaneous Data for the United States

Highest point: Mt. McKinley, Alaska — 20,320 ft. (6,198 m)
Lowest point: Death Valley, Calif. — 282 ft. (86 m) below sea level
Approximate mean elevation — 2,500 ft. (763 m)
Points farthest apart (50 states): — 5,859 mi. (9,429 km)
  Log Point, Elliot Key, Fla.,
  and Kure Island, Hawaii
Geographic center (50 states): — 44°58'N lat. 103°46'W long.
  In Butte County, S.D. (west of Castle Rock)
Geographic center (48 conterminous states): — 39°50'N lat. 98°35'W long.
  In Smith County, Kan. (near Lebanon)
Boundaries:
  Between Alaska and Canada — 1,538 mi. (2,475 km)
  Between the 48 conterminous states
  and Canada (incl. Great Lakes) — 3,987 mi. (6,416 km)
  Between the United States and Mexico — 1,933 mi. (3,111 km)
Source: Department of the Interior, U.S. Geological Survey.

Extreme Points of the United States (50 States)

Extreme point	Latitude	Longitude	Distance[1] mi.	km
Northernmost point: Point Barrow, Alaska	71°23' N	156°29' W	2,507	4,034
Easternmost point: West Quoddy Head, Me.	44°49' N	66°57' W	1,788	2,997
Southernmost point: Ka Lae (South Cape), Hawaii	18°55' N	155°41' W	3,463	5,573
Westernmost point: Cape Wrangell, Alaska (Attu Island)	52°55' N	172°27' E	3,625	5,833

1. From geographic center of United States (incl. Alaska and Hawaii), west of Castle Rock, S.D., 44°58' lat., 103°46' W long. If measured from the prime meridian in Greenwich, England, Cape Wrangell, Attu Island, Alaska would be the easternmost point.

The Continental Divide

The Continental Divide is a ridge of high ground that runs irregularly north and south through the Rocky Mountains and separates eastward-flowing from westward-flowing streams. The waters that flow east- ward empty into the Atlantic Ocean, chiefly by way of the Gulf of Mexico; those that flow westward empty into the Pacific.

Highest, Lowest, and Mean Elevations in the United States

State	Elevation ft.[1]	Highest point	Elevation ft.	Lowest point	Elevation ft.
Alabama	500	Cheaha Mountain	2,405	Gulf of Mexico	Sea level
Alaska	1,900	Mt. McKinley	20,320	Pacific Ocean	Sea level
Arizona	4,100	Humphreys Peak	12,633	Colorado River	70
Arkansas	650	Magazine Mountain	2,753	Ouachita River	55
California	2,900	Mt. Whitney	14,494	Death Valley	−282[2]
Colorado	6,800	Mt. Elbert	14,433	Arkansas River	3,350
Connecticut	500	Mt. Frissell, on south slope	2,380	Long Island Sound	Sea level
Delaware	60	Ebright Road, Del.–Pa. state line	448	Atlantic Ocean	Sea level
D.C.	150	Tenleytown, at Reno Reservoir	410	Potomac River	1
Florida	100	Sec. 30, T6N, R20W, Walton County [4]	345	Atlantic Ocean	Sea level
Georgia	600	Brasstown Bald	4,784	Atlantic Ocean	Sea level
Hawaii	3,030	Puu Wekiu, Mauna Kea	13,796	Pacific Ocean	Sea level
Idaho	5,000	Borah Peak	12,662	Snake River	710
Illinois	600	Charles Mound	1,235	Mississippi River	279
Indiana	700	Franklin Township, Wayne County	1,257	Ohio River	320
Iowa	1,100	Sec. 29, T100N, R41W, Osceola County	1,670	Mississippi River	480
Kansas	2,000	Mt. Sunflower	4,039	Verdigris River	679
Kentucky	750	Black Mountain	4,139	Mississippi River	257
Louisiana	100	Driskill Mountain	535	New Orleans	−8[2]
Maine	600	Mt. Katahdin	5,267	Atlantic Ocean	Sea level
Maryland	350	Backbone Mountain	3,360	Atlantic Ocean	Sea level
Massachusetts	500	Mt. Greylock	3,487	Atlantic Ocean	Sea level
Michigan	900	Mt. Arvon	1,979	Lake Erie	572
Minnesota	1,200	Eagle Mountain	2,301	Lake Superior	600
Mississippi	300	Woodall Mountain	806	Gulf of Mexico	Sea level
Missouri	800	Taum Sauk Mountain	1,772	St. Francis River	230
Montana	3,400	Granite Peak	12,799	Kootenai River	1,800
Nebraska	2,600	Johnson Township, Kimball County	5,424	Missouri River	840
Nevada	5,500	Boundary Peak	13,140	Colorado River	479
New Hampshire	1,000	Mt. Washington	6,288	Atlantic Ocean	Sea level
New Jersey	250	High Point	1,803	Atlantic Ocean	Sea level
New Mexico	5,700	Wheeler Peak	13,161	Red Bluff Reservoir	2,842
New York	1,000	Mt. Marcy	5,344	Atlantic Ocean	Sea level
North Carolina	700	Mt. Mitchell	6,684	Atlantic Ocean	Sea level
North Dakota	1,900	White Butte	3,506	Red River	750
Ohio	850	Campbell Hill	1,549	Ohio River	455
Oklahoma	1,300	Black Mesa	4,973	Little River	289
Oregon	3,300	Mt. Hood	11,239	Pacific Ocean	Sea level
Pennsylvania	1,100	Mt. Davis	3,213	Delaware River	Sea level
Rhode Island	200	Jerimoth Hill	812	Atlantic Ocean	Sea level
South Carolina	350	Sassafras Mountain	3,560	Atlantic Ocean	Sea level
South Dakota	2,200	Harney Peak	7,242	Big Stone Lake	966
Tennessee	900	Clingmans Dome	6,643	Mississippi River	178
Texas	1,700	Guadalupe Peak	8,749	Gulf of Mexico	Sea level
Utah	6,100	Kings Peak	13,528	Beaverdam Wash	2,000
Vermont	1,000	Mt. Mansfield	4,393	Lake Champlain	95
Virginia	950	Mt. Rogers	5,729	Atlantic Ocean	Sea level
Washington	1,700	Mt. Rainier	14,410	Pacific Ocean	Sea level
West Virginia	1,500	Spruce Knob	4,861	Potomac River	240
Wisconsin	1,050	Timms Hill	1,951	Lake Michigan	579
Wyoming	6,700	Gannett Peak	13,804	Belle Fourche River	3,099
United States	2,500	Mt. McKinley (Alaska)	20,320	Death Valley (California)	−282[2]

1. Approximate mean elevation. 2. Below sea level. *Source:* Department of the Interior, U.S. Geological Survey.

Latitude and Longitude of U.S. and Canadian Cities

(and time corresponding to 12:00 noon, eastern standard time)

City	Lat. °	Lat. ′	Long. °	Long. ′	Time
Albany, N.Y.	42	40	73	45	12:00 noon
Albuquerque, N.M.	35	05	106	39	10:00 a.m.
Amarillo, Tex.	35	11	101	50	11:00 a.m.
Anchorage, Alaska	61	13	149	54	8:00 a.m.
Atlanta	33	45	84	23	12:00 noon
Austin, Tex.	30	16	97	44	11:00 a.m.
Baker, Ore.	44	47	117	50	9:00 a.m.
Baltimore	39	18	76	38	12:00 noon
Bangor, Me.	44	48	68	47	12:00 noon
Birmingham, Ala.	33	30	86	50	11:00 a.m.
Bismarck, N.D.	46	48	100	47	11:00 a.m.
Boise, Idaho	43	36	116	13	10:00 a.m.
Boston	42	21	71	5	12:00 noon
Buffalo, N.Y.	42	55	78	50	12:00 noon
Calgary, Alberta	51	1	114	1	10:00 a.m.
Carlsbad, N.M.	32	26	104	15	10:00 a.m.
Charleston, S.C.	32	47	79	56	12:00 noon
Charleston, W. Va.	38	21	81	38	12:00 noon
Charlotte, N.C.	35	14	80	50	12:00 noon
Cheyenne, Wyo.	41	9	104	52	10:00 a.m.
Chicago	41	50	87	37	11:00 a.m.
Cincinnati	39	8	84	30	12:00 noon
Cleveland	41	28	81	37	12:00 noon
Columbia, S.C.	34	0	81	2	12:00 noon
Columbus, Ohio	40	0	83	1	12:00 noon
Dallas	32	46	96	46	11:00 a.m.
Denver	39	45	105	0	10:00 a.m.
Des Moines, Iowa	41	35	93	37	11:00 a.m.
Detroit	42	20	83	3	12:00 noon
Dubuque, Iowa	42	31	90	40	11:00 a.m.
Duluth, Minn.	46	49	92	5	11:00 a.m.
Eastport, Me.	44	54	67	0	12:00 noon
El Centro, Calif.	32	38	115	33	9:00 a.m.
El Paso	31	46	106	29	10:00 a.m.
Eugene, Ore.	44	3	123	5	9:00 a.m.
Fargo, N.D.	46	52	96	48	11:00 a.m.
Flagstaff, Ariz.	35	13	111	41	10:00 a.m.
Fort Worth, Tex.	32	43	97	19	11:00 a.m.
Fresno, Calif.	36	44	119	48	9:00 a.m.
Grand Junction, Colo.	39	5	108	33	10:00 a.m.
Grand Rapids, Mich.	42	58	85	40	12:00 noon
Havre, Mont.	48	33	109	43	10:00 a.m.
Helena, Mont.	46	35	112	2	10:00 a.m.
Honolulu	21	18	157	50	7:00 a.m.
Hot Springs, Ark.	34	31	93	3	11:00 a.m.
Houston, Tex.	29	45	95	21	11:00 a.m.
Idaho Falls, Idaho	43	30	112	1	10:00 a.m.
Indianapolis	39	46	86	10	12:00 noon
Jackson, Miss.	32	20	90	12	11:00 a.m.
Jacksonville, Fla.	30	22	81	40	12:00 noon
Juneau, Alaska	58	18	134	24	8:00 a.m.
Kansas City, Mo.	39	6	94	35	11:00 a.m.
Key West, Fla.	24	33	81	48	12:00 noon
Kingston, Ont.	44	15	76	30	12:00 noon
Klamath Falls, Ore.	42	10	121	44	9:00 a.m.
Knoxville, Tenn.	35	57	83	56	12:00 noon
Las Vegas, Nev.	36	10	115	12	9:00 a.m.
Lewiston, Idaho	46	24	117	2	9:00 a.m.
Lincoln, Neb.	40	50	96	40	11:00 a.m.
London, Ont.	43	2	81	34	12:00 noon
Long Beach, Calif.	33	46	118	11	9:00 a.m.
Los Angeles	34	3	118	15	9:00 a.m.
Louisville, Ky.	38	15	85	46	12:00 noon
Manchester, N.H.	43	0	71	30	12:00 noon
Memphis, Tenn.	35	9	90	3	11:00 a.m.
Miami, Fla.	25	46	80	12	12:00 noon
Milwaukee	43	2	87	55	11:00 a.m.
Minneapolis	44	59	93	14	11:00 a.m.
Mobile, Ala.	30	42	88	3	11:00 a.m.
Montgomery, Ala.	32	21	86	18	11:00 a.m.
Montpelier, Vt.	44	15	72	32	12:00 noon
Montreal, Que.	45	30	73	35	12:00 noon
Moose Jaw, Sask.	50	37	105	31	10:00 a.m.
Nashville, Tenn.	36	10	86	47	11:00 a.m.
Nelson, B.C.	49	30	117	17	9:00 a.m.
Newark, N.J.	40	44	74	10	12:00 noon
New Haven, Conn.	41	19	72	55	12:00 noon
New Orleans	29	57	90	4	11:00 a.m.
New York	40	47	73	58	12:00 noon
Nome, Alaska	64	25	165	30	8:00 a.m.
Oakland, Calif.	37	48	122	16	9:00 a.m.
Oklahoma City	35	26	97	28	11:00 a.m.
Omaha, Neb.	41	15	95	56	11:00 a.m.
Ottawa, Ont.	45	24	75	43	12:00 noon
Philadelphia	39	57	75	10	12:00 noon
Phoenix, Ariz.	33	29	112	4	10:00 a.m.
Pierre, S.D.	44	22	100	21	11:00 a.m.
Pittsburgh	40	27	79	57	12:00 noon
Port Arthur, Ont.	48	30	89	17	12:00 noon
Portland, Maine	43	40	70	15	12:00 noon
Portland, Ore.	45	31	122	41	9:00 a.m.
Providence, R.I.	41	50	71	24	12:00 noon
Quebec, Que.	46	49	71	11	12:00 noon
Raleigh, N.C.	35	46	78	39	12:00 noon
Reno, Nev.	39	30	119	49	9:00 a.m.
Richfield, Utah	38	46	112	5	10:00 a.m.
Richmond, Va.	37	33	77	29	12:00 noon
Roanoke, Va.	37	17	79	57	12:00 noon
Sacramento, Calif.	38	35	121	30	9:00 a.m.
St. John, N.B.	45	18	66	10	1:00 p.m.
St. Louis	38	35	90	12	11:00 a.m.
Salt Lake City, Utah	40	46	111	54	10:00 a.m.
San Antonio	29	23	98	33	11:00 a.m.
San Diego, Calif.	32	42	117	10	9:00 a.m.
San Francisco	37	47	122	26	9:00 a.m.
San Jose, Calif.	37	20	121	53	9:00 a.m.
San Juan, P.R.	18	30	66	10	1:00 p.m.
Santa Fe, N.M.	35	41	105	57	10:00 a.m.
Savannah, Ga.	32	5	81	5	12:00 noon
Seattle	47	37	122	20	9:00 a.m.
Shreveport, La.	32	28	93	42	11:00 a.m.
Sioux Falls, S.D.	43	33	96	44	11:00 a.m.
Sitka, Alaska	57	10	135	15	9:00 a.m.
Spokane, Wash.	47	40	117	26	9:00 a.m.
Springfield, Ill.	39	48	89	38	11:00 a.m.
Springfield, Mass.	42	6	72	34	12:00 noon
Springfield, Mo.	37	13	93	17	11:00 a.m.
Syracuse, N.Y.	43	2	76	8	12:00 noon
Tampa, Fla.	27	57	82	27	12:00 noon
Toledo, Ohio	41	39	83	33	12:00 noon
Toronto, Ont.	43	40	79	24	12:00 noon
Tulsa, Okla.	36	09	95	59	11:00 a.m.
Victoria, B.C.	48	25	123	21	9:00 a.m.
Virginia Beach, Va.	36	51	75	58	12:00 noon
Washington, D.C.	38	53	77	02	12:00 noon
Wichita, Kan.	37	43	97	17	11:00 a.m.
Wilmington, N.C.	34	14	77	57	12:00 noon
Winnipeg, Man.	49	54	97	7	11:00 a.m.

Named Summits in the U.S. Over 14,000 Feet Above Sea Level

Name	State	Height (ft.)	Name	State	Height (ft.)	Name	State	Height (ft.)
Mt. McKinley	Alaska	20,320	Castle Peak	Colo.	14,265	Mt. Eolus	Colo.	14,083
Mt. St. Elias	Alaska	18,008	Quandary Peak	Colo.	14,265	Windom Peak	Colo.	14,082
Mt. Foraker	Alaska	17,400	Mt. Evans	Colo.	14,264	Mt. Columbia	Colo.	14,073
Mt. Bona	Alaska	16,500	Longs Peak	Colo.	14,255	Mt. Augusta	Alaska	14,070
Mt. Blackburn	Alaska	16,390	Mt. Wilson	Colo.	14,246	Missouri Mtn.	Colo.	14,067
Mt. Sanford	Alaska	16,237	White Mtn.	Calif.	14,246	Humboldt Peak	Colo.	14,064
Mt. Vancouver	Alaska	15,979	North Palisade	Calif.	14,242	Mt. Bierstadt	Colo.	14,060
South Buttress	Alaska	15,885	Mt. Cameron	Colo.	14,238	Sunlight Peak	Colo.	14,059
Mt. Churchill	Alaska	15,638	Mt. Shavano	Colo.	14,229	Split Mtn.	Calif.	14,058
Mt. Fairweather	Alaska	15,300	Crestone Needle	Colo.	14,197	Handies Peak	Colo.	14,048
Mt. Hubbard	Alaska	14,950	Mt. Belford	Colo.	14,197	Culebra Peak	Colo.	14,047
Mt. Bear	Alaska	14,831	Mt. Princeton	Colo.	14,197	Mt. Lindsey	Colo.	14,042
East Buttress	Alaska	14,730	Mt. Yale	Colo.	14,196	Ellingwood Point	Colo.	14,042
Mt. Hunter	Alaska	14,573	Mt. Bross	Colo.	14,172	Middle Palisade	Calif.	14,040
Browne Tower	Alaska	14,530	Kit Carson Mtn.	Colo.	14,165	Little Bear Peak	Colo.	14,037
Mt. Alverstone	Alaska	14,500	Mt. Wrangell	Alaska	14,163	Mt. Sherman	Colo.	14,036
Mt. Whitney	Calif.	14,494[1]	Mt. Sill	Calif.	14,163	Redcloud Peak	Colo.	14,034
University Peak	Alaska	14,470	Mt. Shasta	Calif.	14,162	Mt. Langley	Calif.	14,027
Mt. Elbert	Colo.	14,433	El Diente Peak	Colo.	14,159	Conundrum Peak	Colo.	14,022
Mt. Massive	Colo.	14,421	Point Success	Wash.	14,158	Mt. Tyndall	Calif.	14,019
Mt. Harvard	Colo.	14,420	Maroon Peak	Colo.	14,156	Pyramid Peak	Colo.	14,018
Mt. Rainier	Wash.	14,410	Tabeguache Mtn.	Colo.	14,155	Wilson Peak	Colo.	14,017
Mt. Williamson	Calif.	14,370	Mt. Oxford	Colo.	14,153	Wetterhorn Peak	Colo.	14,015
La Plata Peak	Colo.	14,361	Mt. Sill	Calif.	14,153	North Maroon Peak	Colo.	14,014
Blanca Peak	Colo.	14,345	Mt. Sneffels	Colo.	14,150	San Luis Peak	Colo.	14,014
Uncompahgre Peak	Colo.	14,309	Mt. Democrat	Colo.	14,148	Middle Palisade	Calif.	14,012
Crestone Peak	Colo.	14,294	Capitol Peak	Colo.	14,130	Mt. Muir	Calif.	14,012
Mt. Lincoln	Colo.	14,286	Liberty Cap	Wash.	14,112	Mt. of the Holy Cross	Colo.	14,005
Grays Peak	Colo.	14,270	Pikes Peak	Colo.	14,110	Huron Peak	Colo.	14,003
Mt. Antero	Colo.	14,269	Snowmass Mtn.	Colo.	14,092	Thunderbolt Peak	Calif.	14,003
Torreys Peak	Colo.	14,267	Mt. Russell	Calif.	14,088	Sunshine Peak	Colo.	14,001

1. National Geodetic Survey. *Source:* Department of the Interior, U.S. Geological Survey.

Rivers of the United States

(350 or more miles long)

Alabama-Coosa (600 mi.; 966 km): From junction of Oostanula and Etowah R. in Georgia to Mobile R.

Altamaha-Ocmulgee (392 mi.; 631 km): From junction of Yellow R. and South R., Newton Co. in Georgia to Atlantic Ocean.

Apalachicola-Chattahoochee (524 mi.; 843 km): From Towns Co. in Georgia to Gulf of Mexico in Florida.

Arkansas (1,459 mi.; 2,348 km): From Lake Co. in Colorado to Mississippi R. in Arkansas.

Brazos (923 mi.; 1,490 km): From junction of Salt Fork and Double Mountain Fork in Texas to Gulf of Mexico.

Canadian (906 mi.; 1,458 km): From Las Animas Co. in Colorado to Arkansas R. in Oklahoma.

Cimarron (600 mi.; 966 km): From Colfax Co. in New Mexico to Arkansas R. in Oklahoma.

Colorado (1,450 mi.; 2,333 km): From Rocky Mountain National Park in Colorado to Gulf of California in Mexico.

Colorado (862 mi.; 1,387 km): From Dawson Co. in Texas to Matagorda Bay.

Columbia (1,243 mi.; 2,000 km): From Columbia Lake in British Columbia to Pacific Ocean (entering between Oregon and Washington).

Colville (350 mi.; 563 km): From Brooks Range in Alaska to Beaufort Sea.

Connecticut (407 mi.; 655 km): From Third Connecticut Lake in New Hampshire to Long Island Sound in Connecticut.

Cumberland (720 mi.; 1,159 km): From junction of Poor and Clover Forks in Harlan Co. in Kentucky to Ohio R.

Delaware (390 mi.; 628 km): From Schoharie Co. in New York to Liston Point, Delaware Bay.

Gila (649 mi.; 1,044 km): From Catron Co. in New Mexico to Colorado R. in Arizona.

Green (360 mi.; 579 km): From Lincoln Co. in Kentucky to Ohio R. in Kentucky.

Green (730 mi.; 1,175 km): From Sublette Co. in Wyoming to Colorado R. in Utah.

Illinois (420 mi.; 676 km): From St. Joseph Co. in Indiana to Mississippi R. at Grafton in Illinois.

James (sometimes called *Dakota*) (710 mi.; 1,143 km): From Wells Co. in North Dakota to Missouri R. in South Dakota.

Kanawha-New (352 mi.; 566 km): From junction of North and South Forks of New R. in North Carolina, through Virginia and West Virginia (New River becoming Kanawha River), to Ohio River.

Kansas (743 mi.; 1,196 km): From source of Arikaree R. in Elbert Co., Colorado, to Missouri R. at Kansas City, Kansas.

Koyukuk (470 mi.; 756 km): From Brooks Range in Alaska to Yukon R.

Kuskokwim (724 mi.; 1,165 km): From Alaska Range in Alaska to Kuskokwim Bay.

Licking (350 mi.; 563 km): From Magoffin Co. in Kentucky to Ohio R. at Cincinnati in Ohio.

Coastline of the United States

State	Lengths, statute miles General coastline[1]	Lengths, statute miles Tidal shoreline[2]	State	Lengths, statute miles General coastline[1]	Lengths, statute miles Tidal shoreline[2]
Atlantic Coast:			**Gulf Coast:**		
Maine	228	3,478	Florida (Gulf)	770	5,095
New Hampshire	13	131	Alabama	53	607
Massachusetts	192	1,519	Mississippi	44	359
Rhode Island	40	384	Louisiana	397	7,721
Connecticut	—	618	Texas	367	3,359
New York	127	1,850	Total Gulf coast	1,631	17,141
New Jersey	130	1,792	**Pacific Coast:**		
Pennsylvania	—	89	California	840	3,427
Delaware	28	381	Oregon	296	1,410
Maryland	31	3,190	Washington	157	3,026
Virginia	112	3,315	Hawaii	750	1,052
North Carolina	301	3,375	Alaska (Pacific)	5,580	31,383
South Carolina	187	2,876	Total Pacific coast	7,623	40,298
Georgia	100	2,344	**Arctic Coast:**		
Florida (Atlantic)	580	3,331	Alaska (Arctic)	1,060	2,521
Total Atlantic coast	2,069	28,673	Total Arctic coast	1,060	2,521
			States Total	**12,383**	**88,633**

1. Figures are lengths of general outline of seacoast. Measurements made with unit measure of 30 minutes of latitude on charts as near scale of 1:1,200,000 as possible. Coastline of bays and sounds is included to point where they narrow to width of unit measure, and distance across at such point is included. 2. Figures obtained in 1939-40 with recording instrument on largest-scale maps and charts then available. Shoreline of outer coast, offshore islands, sounds, bays, rivers, and creeks is included to head of tidewater, or to point where tidal waters narrow to width of 100 feet. *Source:* Department of Commerce, National Oceanic and Atmospheric Administration, National Ocean Service.

Little Missouri (560 mi.; 901 km): From Crook Co. in Wyoming to Missouri R. in North Dakota.

Milk (625 mi.; 1,006 km): From junction of forks in Alberta Province to Missouri R.

Mississippi (2,340 mi.; 3,766 km): From Lake Itasca in Minnesota to mouth of Southwest Pass in Louisiana.

Mississippi-Missouri-Red Rock (3,710 mi.; 5,970 km): From source of Red Rock R. in Montana to mouth of Southwest Pass in Louisiana.

Missouri (2,315 mi.; 3,726 km): From junction of Jefferson R., Gallatin R., and Madison R. in Montana to Mississippi R. near St. Louis.

Missouri-Red Rock (2,540 mi.; 4,090 km): From source of Red Rock R. in Montana to Mississippi R. near St. Louis.

Mobile-Alabama-Coosa (645 mi.; 1,040 km): From junction of Etowah R. and Oostanula R. in Georgia to Mobile Bay.

Neosho (460 mi.; 740 km): From Morris Co. in Kansas to Arkansas R. in Oklahoma.

Niobrara (431 mi.; 694 km): From Niobrara Co. in Wyoming to Missouri R. in Nebraska.

Noatak (350 mi.; 563 km): From Brooks Range in Alaska to Kotzebue Sound.

North Canadian (800 mi.; 1,290 km): From Union Co. in New Mexico to Canadian R. in Oklahoma.

North Platte (618 mi.; 995 km): From Jackson Co. in Colorado to junction with So. Platte R. in Nebraska to form Platte R.

Ohio (981 mi.; 1,579 km): From junction of Allegheny R. and Monongahela R. at Pittsburgh to Mississippi R. between Illinois and Kentucky.

Ohio-Allegheny (1,306 mi.; 2,102 km): From Potter Co. in Pennsylvania to Mississippi R. at Cairo in Illinois.

Osage (500 mi.; 805 km): From east-central Kansas to Missouri R. near Jefferson City in Missouri.

Ouachita (605 mi.; 974 km): From Polk Co. in Arkansas to Red R. in Louisiana.

Pearl (411 mi.; 661 km): From Neshoba County in Mississippi to Gulf of Mexico (Mississippi-Louisiana).

Pecos (926 mi.; 1,490 km): From Mora Co. in New Mexico to Rio Grande in Texas.

Pee Dee-Yadkin (435 mi.; 700 km): From Watauga Co. in North Carolina to Winyah Bay in South Carolina.

Pend Oreille-Clark Fork (531 mi.; 855 km): Near Butte in Montana to Columbia R. on Washington-Canada border.

Platte (990 mi.; 1593 km): From source of Grizzly Creek in Jackson Co., Colorado, to Missouri R. south of Omaha, Nebraska.

Porcupine (569 mi.; 916 km): From Yukon Territory, Canada, to Yukon R. in Alaska.

Potomac (383 mi.; 616 km): From Garrett Co. in Maryland to Chesapeake Bay at Point Lookout in Maryland.

Powder (375 mi.; 603 km): From junction of forks in Johnson Co. in Wyoming to Yellowstone R. in Montana.

Red (1,290 mi.; 2,080 km): From source of Tierra Blanca Creek in Curry County, New Mexico to Mississippi R. in Louisiana.

Red (also called *Red River of the North*) (545 mi.; 877 km): From junction of Otter Tail R. and Bois de Sioux R. in Minnesota to Lake Winnipeg in Manitoba.

Republican (445 mi.; 716 km): From junction of North Fork and Arikaree R. in Nebraska to junction with Smoky Hill R. in Kansas to form the Kansas R.

Rio Grande (1,900 mi.; 3,060 km): From San Juan Co. in Colorado to Gulf of Mexico.

Roanoke (380 mi.; 612 km): From junction of forks in Montgomery Co. in Virginia to Albemarle Sound in North Carolina.

Sabine (380 mi.; 612 km): From junction of forks in Hunt Co. in Texas to Sabine Lake between Texas and Louisiana.

Sacramento (377 mi.; 607 km): From Siskiyou Co. in California to Suisun Bay.

Saint Francis (425 mi.; 684 km): From Iron Co. in Missouri to Mississippi R. in Arkansas.

Salmon (420 mi.; 676 km): From Custer Co. in Idaho to Snake R.

San Joaquin (350 mi.; 563 km): From junction of forks in Madera Co. in California to Suisun Bay.

San Juan (360 mi.; 579 km): From Archuleta Co. in Colorado to Colorado R. in Utah.

Santee-Wateree-Catawba (538 mi.; 866 km): From McDowell Co. in North Carolina to Atlantic Ocean in South Carolina.

Smoky Hill (540 mi.; 869 km): From Cheyenne Co. in Colorado to junction with Republican R. in Kansas to form Kansas R.

Snake (1,038 mi.; 1,670 km): From Ocean Plateau in Wyoming to Columbia R. in Washington.

South Platte (424 mi.; 682 km): From Park Co. in Colorado to junction with North Platte R. in Nebraska to form Platte R.

Stikine (379 mi.; 610 km): From British Columbia in Canada to Stikine Strait near Wrangell, Alaska.

Susquehanna (444 mi.; 715 km): From Otsego Lake in New York to Chesapeake Bay in Maryland.

Tanana (659 mi.; 1,060 km): From Wrangell Mts. in Yukon Territory, Canada, to Yukon R. in Alaska.

Tennessee (652 mi.; 1,049 km): From junction of Holston R. and French Broad R. in Tennessee to Ohio R. in Kentucky.

Tennessee-French Broad (886 mi.; 1,417 km): From Transylvania Co. in North Carolina to Ohio R. at Paducah in Kentucky.

Tombigbee (525 mi.; 845 km): From junction of forks in Itawamba Co. in Mississippi to Mobile R. in Alabama.

Trinity (360 mi.; 579 km): From junction of forks in Dallas Co. in Texas to Galveston Bay.

Wabash (512 mi.; 824 km): From Darke Co. in Ohio to Ohio R. between Illinois and Indiana.

Washita (500 mi.; 805 km): From Hemphill Co. in Texas to Red R. in Oklahoma.

White (722 mi.; 1,160 km): From Madison Co. in Arkansas to Mississippi R.

Wisconsin (430 mi.; 692 km): From Vilas Co. in Wisconsin to Mississippi R.

Yellowstone (692 mi.; 1,110 km): From Park Co. in Wyoming to Missouri R. in North Dakota.

Yukon (1,979 mi.; 3,185 km): From source of McNeil R. in Yukon Territory, Canada, to Bering Sea in Alaska.

Geysers in the United States

Geysers are natural hot springs that intermittently eject a column of water and steam into the air. They exist in many parts of the volcanic regions of the world such as Japan and South America but their greatest development is in Iceland, New Zealand, and Yellowstone National Park.

There are 120 named geysers in Yellowstone National Park, Wyoming, and perhaps half that number unnamed. Most of the geysers and the 4,000 or more hot springs are located in the western portion of the park. The most important are the following:

Norris Geyser Basin has 24 or more active geysers; the number varies. There are scores of steam vents and hot springs. *Steamboat* is the largest active geyser in the world, sending water more than 300 ft. into the air for 3 to 20 minutes. It emits water every few minutes, but its major eruptions are infrequent and erratic. *Valentine* erupts 50–75 ft. at intervals varying from 18 hr to 3 days or more. *Minuté* erupts 15–20 ft. high, several hours apart. Others include: *Fearless, Veteran, Vixen, Corporal, Whirligig, Little Whirligig,* and *Pinwheel.*

Lower Geyser Basin has at least 18 active geysers. *Fountain* throws water 50–75 ft. in all directions at unpredictable intervals. *Clepsydra* erupts violently from four vents up to 30 ft. *Great Fountain* plays every 8 to 15 hr in spurts from 30 to 90 ft. high.

Midway Geyser Basin has vast steaming terraces of red, orange, pink and other colors; there are pools and springs, including the beautiful *Grand Prismatic Spring. Excelsior* crater discharges boiling water into Firehole River at the rate of 6 cu ft. per second.

Giant erupts up to 200 ft. at intervals of 2½ days to 3 mo; eruptions last about 1½ hr. *Daisy* sends water up to 75 ft. but is irregular and frequently inactive.

Old Faithful, the most famous geyser in the park, sends up a column varying from 116 to 175 ft. at intervals of about 65 min, varying from 33 to 90 min. Eruptions last about 4 min, during which time about 12,000 gal are discharged.

Giantess seldom erupts, but during its active period sends up streams 150–200 ft.

Lion Group: *Lion* plays up to 60 ft. every 2–4 days when active; *Little Cub* up to 10 ft. every 1–2 hr. *Big Cub* and *Lioness* seldom erupt.

Mammoth Hot Springs: There are no geysers in this area. The formation is travertine. Sides of a hill are steps and terraces over which flow the steaming waters of hot springs laden with minerals. Each step is tinted by algae to many shades of orange, pink, yellow, brown, green, and blue. Terraces are white where no water flows.

One Lake or Two?

It is a widely accepted fact that Lake Superior, with an area of 31,820 square miles is the world's largest freshwater lake. However, this fact is based on a historical inaccuracy in the naming of Lake Huron and Lake Michigan. What should have been considered one body of water, Lake Michigan-Huron with an area of 45,410 square miles, was mistakenly given two names, one for each lobe. The explorers in colonial times incorrectly believed each lobe to be a separate lake because of its great size.

Why should the two lakes be considered one? The Huron Lobe and the Michigan Lobe are at the same elevation and are connected by the 120-foot deep Mackinac Strait, also at the same elevation. Lakes are separated from each other by streams and rivers. The

Strait of Mackinac is not a river. It is 3.6 to 5 miles wide, wider than most lakes are long. In essence, it is just a narrowing, not a separation of the two lobes of Lake Michigan-Huron.

The flow between the two lakes can reverse. Because of the large connecting channel, the two can equalize rapidly whenever a water level imbalance occurs. Gauge records for the lakes clearly show them to have identical water level regimes and mean long-term behavior; that is, Lake Michigan and Lake Huron act as one lake for many purposes. Hydrologically they are considered one lake.

Historical names are not easily changed. The separate names for the lake are a part of history and are also legally institutionalized since Lake Michigan is treated as American and Lake Huron is bisected by the international boundary between the United States and Canada.

Of all the world's freshwater lakes, North America's Great Lakes are unique. Their five basins combine to form a single watershed with one common outlet to the ocean. The total volume of the lakes is about 5,475 cubic miles, more than 6,000 trillion gallons.

The Great Lakes are: Superior with an area of 31,820 square miles (82,414 km) shared by the United States and Canada; Huron with an area of 23,010 square miles (59,596 sq km) shared by the United States and Canada; Michigan with an area of 22,400 square miles (58,016 sq km) entirely in the United States; Erie with an area of 9,930 square miles (25,719 km) shared by the United States and Canada; and Ontario with an area of 7,520 square miles (19,477 km) shared by the United States and Canada.

The United States also has another large lake, Great Salt Lake in Utah with an area of 1,800 square miles (4,662 sq km). However it is not a freshwater lake.

The Ten Largest Earthquakes in the United States

Magnitude		Date	Location
1.	9.2	March 28, 1964	Prince William Sound, Alaska
2.	8.8	March 9, 1957	Andreanof Islands, Alaska
3.	8.7	February 4, 1965	Rat Islands, Alaska
4.	8.3	November 10, 1938	East of Shumagin Islands, Alaska
	8.3	July 10, 1958	Lituya Bay, Alaska
6.	8.2	September 10, 1899	Yakutat Bay, Alaska
	8.2	September 4, 1899	near Cape Yakataga, Alaska
8.	8.0	May 7, 1986	Andreanof Islands, Alaska
9.	7.9	February 7, 1812	New Madrid, Missouri
	7.9	January 9, 1857	Fort Tejon, California
	7.9	April 3, 1868	Ka'u District, Island of Hawaii
	7.9	October 9, 1900	Kodiak Island, Alaska
	7.9	November 30, 1987	Gulf of Alaska

Source: National Earthquake Information Center, U.S. Geological Survey.

The Ten Largest Earthquakes in the Contiguous United States

Magnitude		Date	Location
1.	7.9	February 7, 1812	New Madrid, Missouri
	7.9	January 9, 1857	Fort Tejon, California
3.	7.8	March 26, 1872	Owens Valley, California
	7.8	February 24, 1892	Imperial Valley, California
5.	7.7	December 16, 1811	New Madrid, Missouri area
	7.7	April 18, 1906	San Francisco, California
	7.7	October 3, 1915	Pleasant Valley, Nevada
8.	7.6	January 23, 1812	New Madrid, Missouri
9.	7.5	July 21, 1952	Kern County, California
10.	7.3	November 4, 1927	West of Lompoc, California
	7.3	December 16, 1954	Dixie Valley, Nevada
	7.3	August 18, 1959	Hebgen Lake, Montana
	7.3	October 28, 1983	Borah Peak, Idaho

Source: National Earthquake Information Center, U.S. Geological Survey. Note: Widely differing magnitudes have been computed for some of these earthquakes; the values differ according to the methods and data used. For example, some sources list the magnitude of the 8.7 Rat Islands earthquake as low as 7.7. On the other hand, some sources list the magnitude of the February 7, 1812, New Madrid quake as high as 8.8. Similar variations exist for most events on this list, although generally not so large as for the examples given.

Mason and Dixon's Line

Mason and Dixon's Line (often called the Mason-Dixon Line) is the boundary between Pennsylvania and Maryland, running at a north latitude of 39°43'19.11". The greater part of it was surveyed from 1763–67 by Charles Mason and Jeremiah Dixon, English astronomers who had been appointed to settle a dispute between the colonies. As the line was partly the boundary between the free and the slave states, it has come to signify the division between the North and the South.

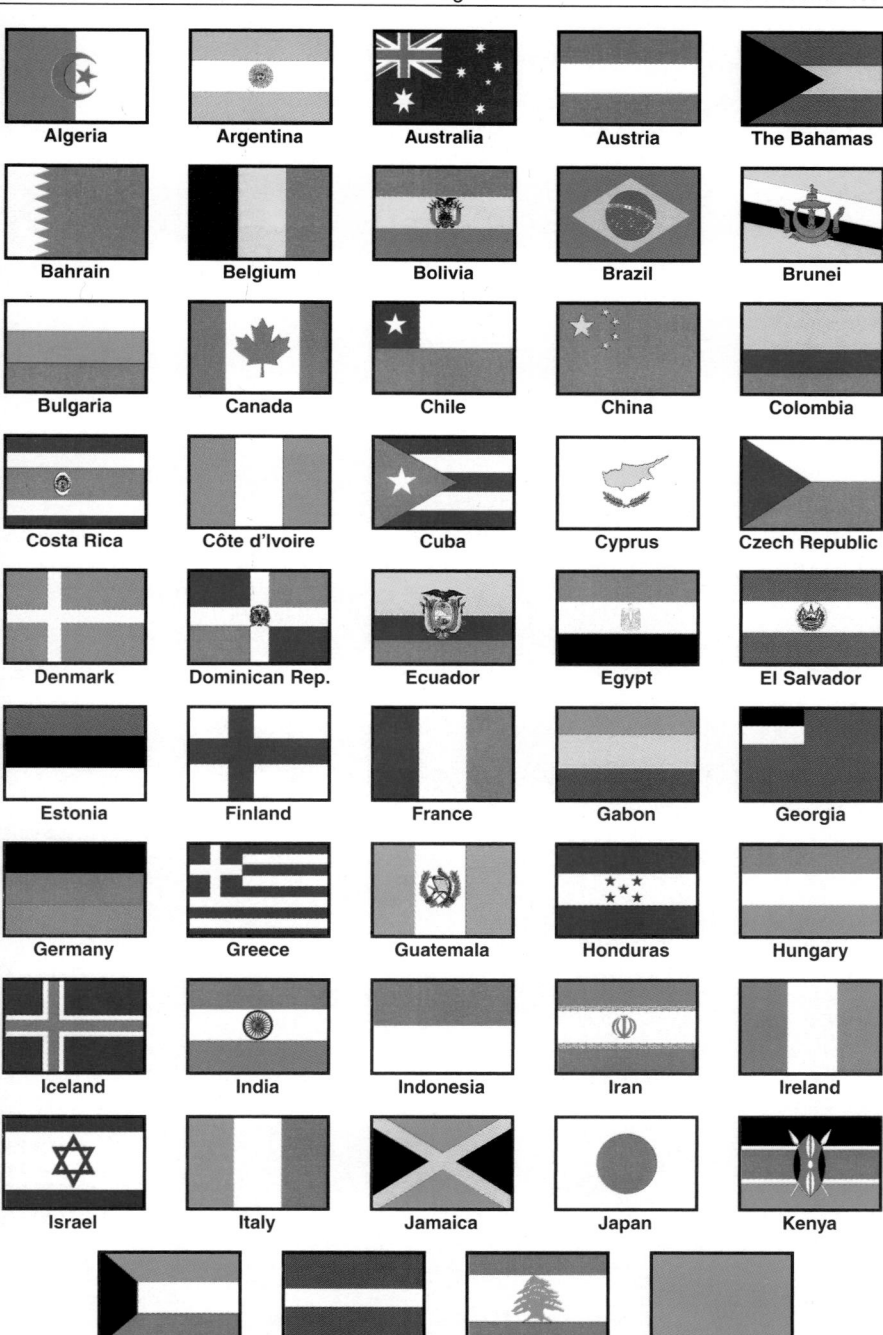

Algeria

Argentina

Australia

Austria

The Bahamas

Bahrain

Belgium

Bolivia

Brazil

Brunei

Bulgaria

Canada

Chile

China

Colombia

Costa Rica

Côte d'Ivoire

Cuba

Cyprus

Czech Republic

Denmark

Dominican Rep.

Ecuador

Egypt

El Salvador

Estonia

Finland

France

Gabon

Georgia

Germany

Greece

Guatemala

Honduras

Hungary

Iceland

India

Indonesia

Iran

Ireland

Israel

Italy

Jamaica

Japan

Kenya

Kuwait

Latvia

Lebanon

Libya

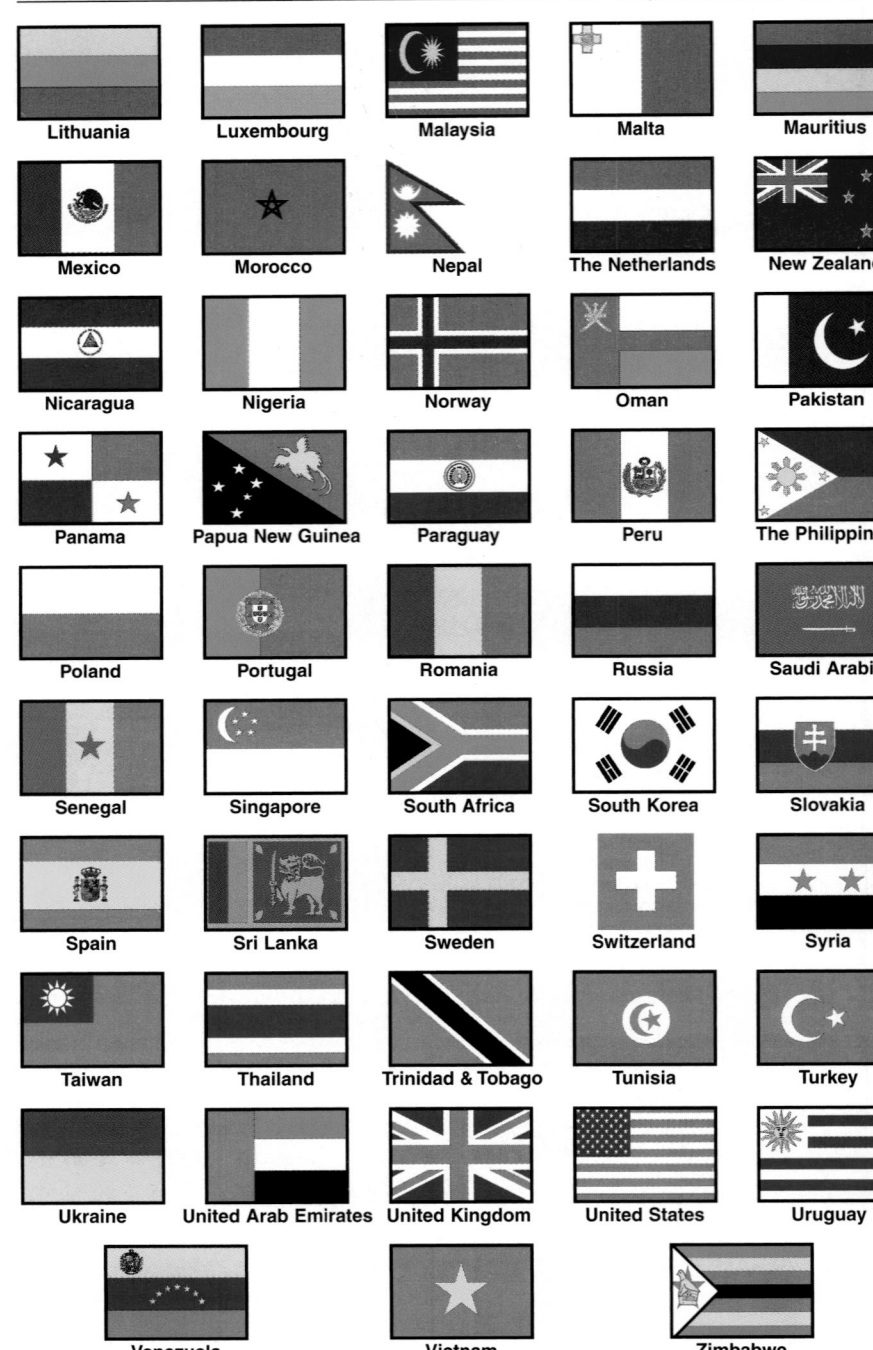

Lithuania · Luxembourg · Malaysia · Malta · Mauritius

Mexico · Morocco · Nepal · The Netherlands · New Zealand

Nicaragua · Nigeria · Norway · Oman · Pakistan

Panama · Papua New Guinea · Paraguay · Peru · The Philippines

Poland · Portugal · Romania · Russia · Saudi Arabia

Senegal · Singapore · South Africa · South Korea · Slovakia

Spain · Sri Lanka · Sweden · Switzerland · Syria

Taiwan · Thailand · Trinidad & Tobago · Tunisia · Turkey

Ukraine · United Arab Emirates · United Kingdom · United States · Uruguay

Venezuela · Vietnam · Zimbabwe

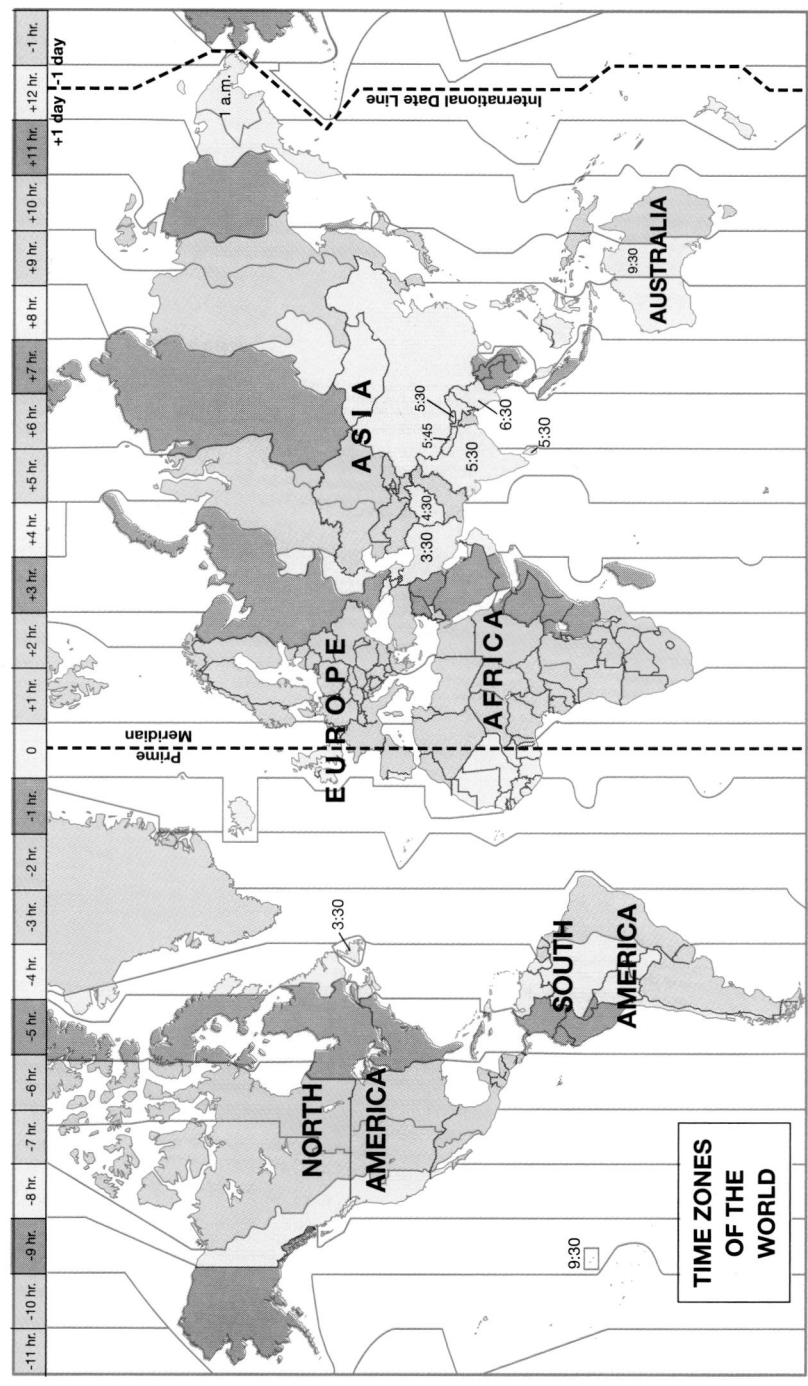

TIME ZONES OF THE WORLD

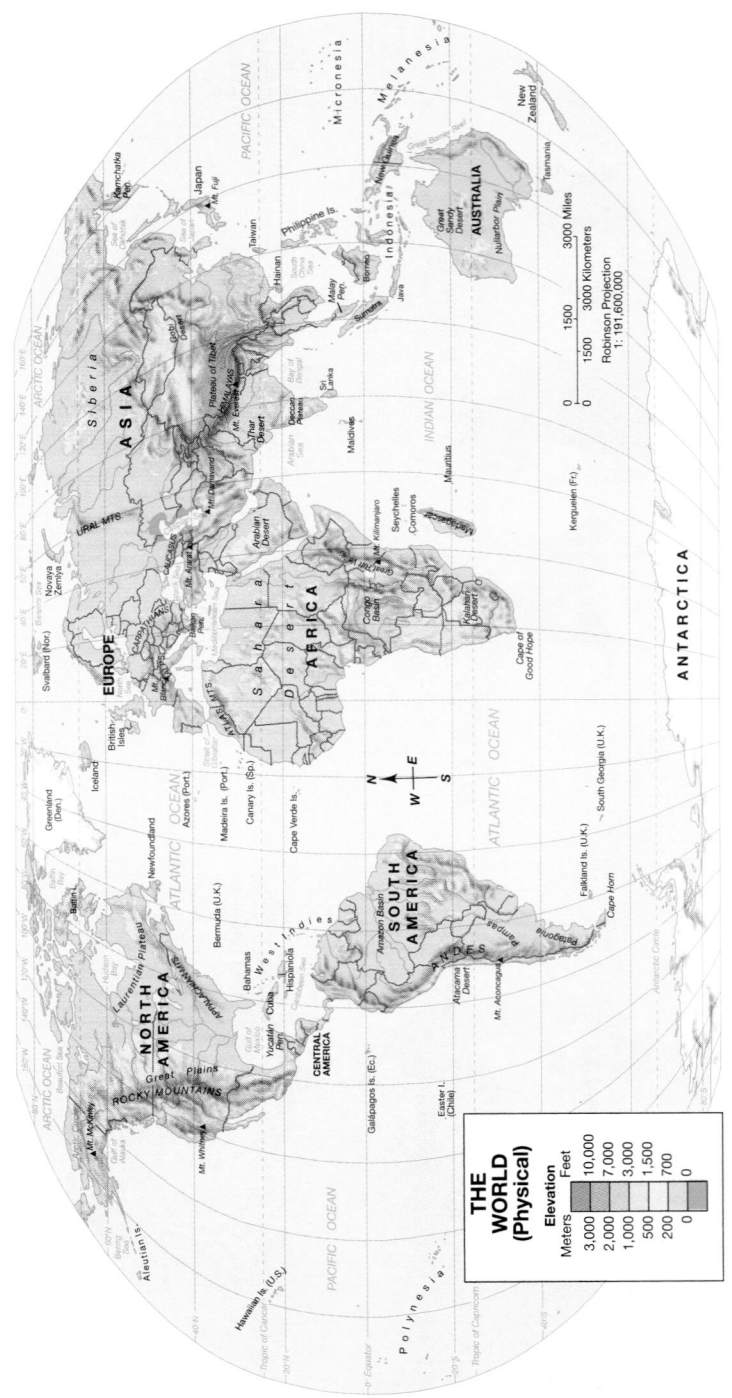

THE
WORLD
(Physical)

Elevation
Meters Feet
3,000 10,000
2,000 7,000
1,000 3,000
500 1,500
200 700
0 0

Robinson Projection
1: 191,600,000

0   1500   3000 Kilometers
0   1500   3000 Miles

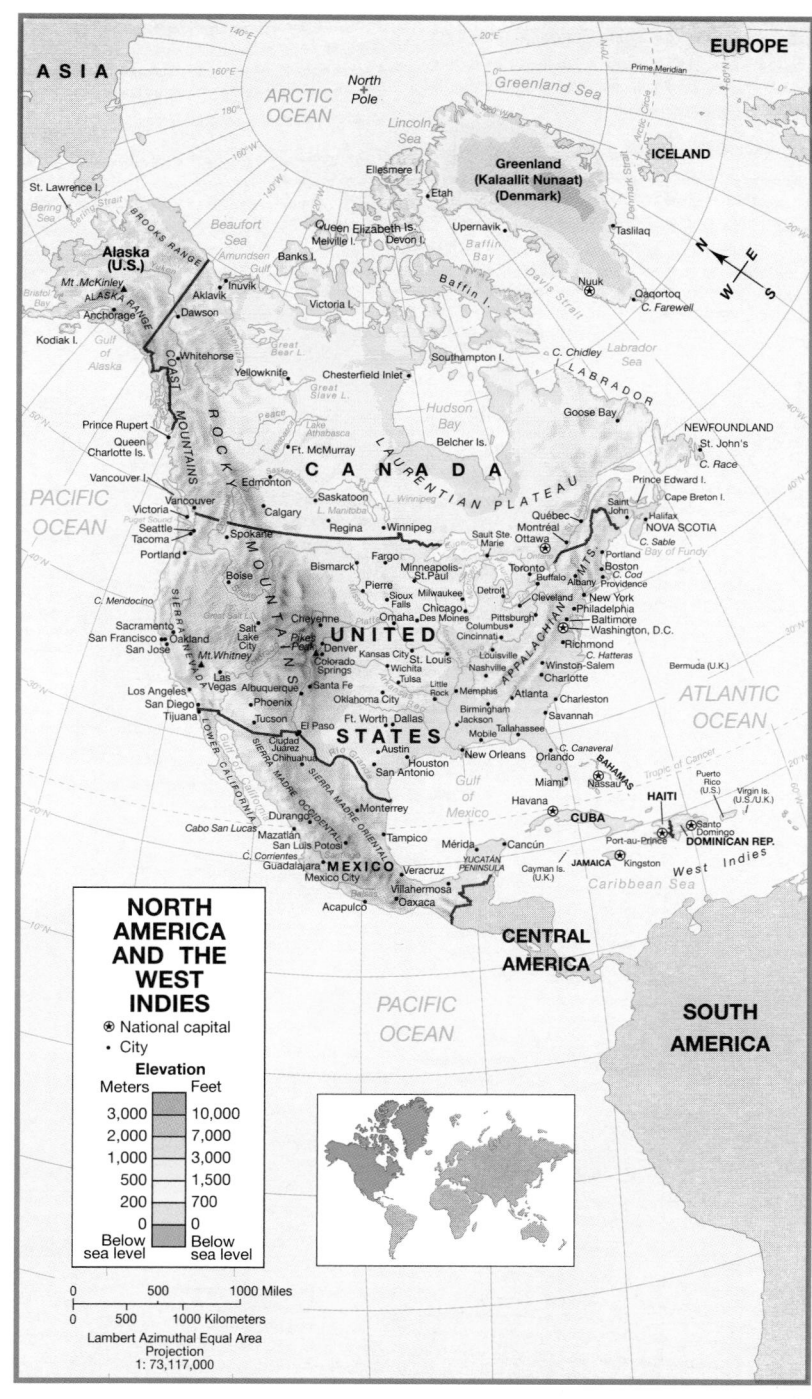

NORTH AMERICA AND THE WEST INDIES

⊛ National capital
• City

Elevation

Meters	Feet
3,000	10,000
2,000	7,000
1,000	3,000
500	1,500
200	700
0	0
Below sea level	Below sea level

0   500   1000 Miles
0   500   1000 Kilometers

Lambert Azimuthal Equal Area Projection
1: 73,117,000

UNITED STATES

⊛ National capital
★ State capital
● City

Elevation

Meters	Feet
3,000	10,000
2,000	7,000
1,000	3,000
500	1,500
200	700
0	0

0   200   400 Miles
0   200   400 Kilometers
Albers Equal-Area Projection
1: 26,044,000

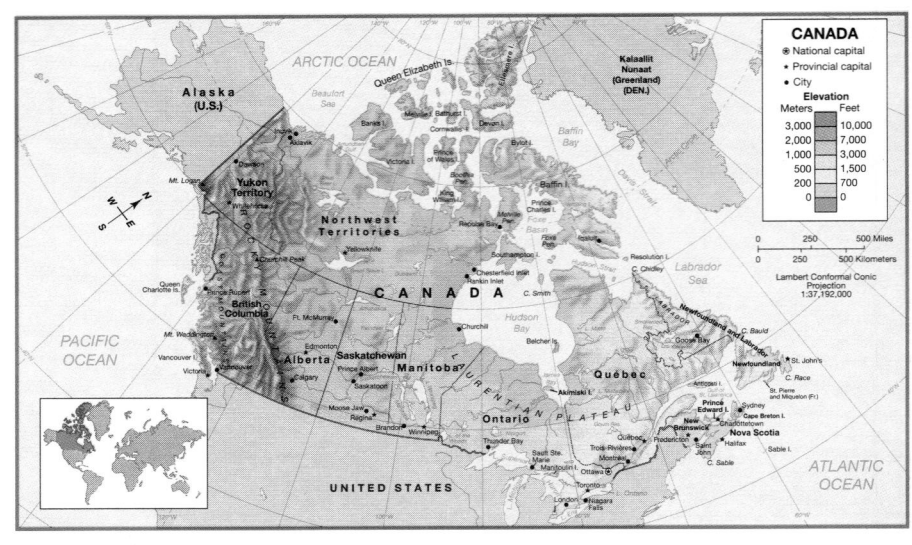

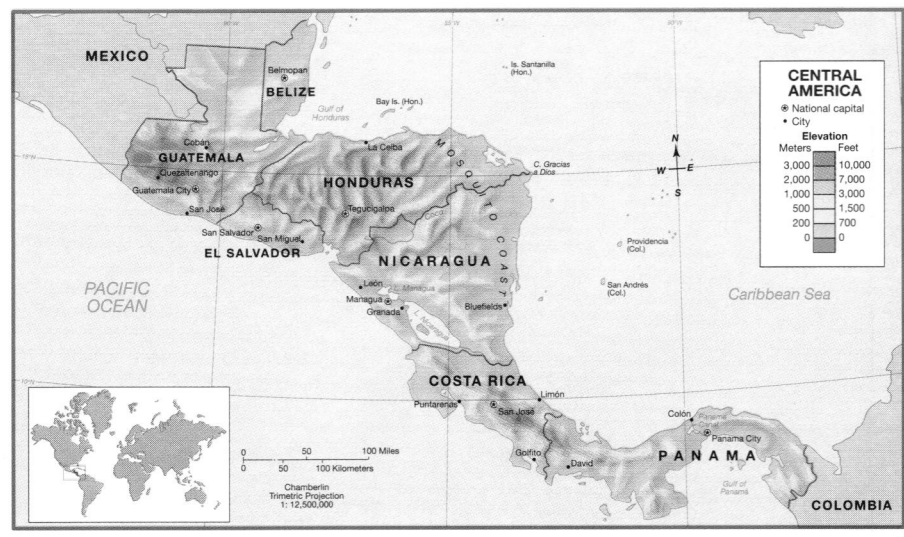

SOUTH AMERICA

⊛ National capital
• City

Elevation

Meters		Feet
3,000		10,000
2,000		7,000
1,000		3,000
500		1,500
200		700
0		0

Galápagos Is. (Ecuador)

I. Marchena
I. San Salvador
I. Isabella
I. Santa Cruz
I. Fernandina
I. San Cristóbal
I. Sta. Maria
I. Española

WEST INDIES

Tropic of Cancer

Caribbean Sea

CENTRAL AMERICA

Neth. Antilles (Neth.)
Curaçao
I. de Margarita
Gulf of Venezuela
Gulf of Paria
Barranquilla
Cartagena
Maracaibo
Caracas
VENEZUELA
Morawhanna
Georgetown
New Amsterdam
Paramaribo
GUYANA
SURINAME
Devil's I.
Cayenne
French Guiana (Fr.)

Monteria
Cúcuta
Medellín
Bucaramanga
San Cristóbal
Ciudad Bolívar
Manizales
Alto Pitacuva
COLOMBIA
Bogotá
C. Corrientes
Mt. Tolima
Buenaventura
Cali
Mt. Huila
I. Malpelo (Colombia)
I. de Maracá
I. Caviana

ATLANTIC OCEAN

ECUADOR
Mt. Cotópaxi
Mt. Chimborazo
Quito
Ambato
Guayaquil
Cuenca
Gulf of Guayaquil
Iquitos
PERU
Piura
Trujillo
Mt. Huascarán
Manaus
Belém
I. São Luis
Equator
Fortaleza
C. São Roque
Recife

Callao
Lima
Cuzco
BRAZIL
El Misti
La Paz
Trinidad
Arequipa
Cochabamba
BOLIVIA
Santa Cruz
Potosí
Sucre
Brasília
Belo Horizonte
Salvador
C. São Tomé

Iquique
PARAGUAY
São Paulo
Rio de Janeiro
Tropic of Capricorn
Antofagasta
San Miguel de Tucumán
Asunción
Santos
San Felix (Chile)
San Ambrosio (Chile)
Mt. Ojos del Salado
Curitiba
I. de Santa Catarina
Córdoba
Porto Alegre
CHILE
Viña del Mar
Valparaíso
Mt. Aconcagua
Rivera
Salto
Paysandú
URUGUAY
Santiago
Mendoza
Rosario
Juan Fernández Is. (Chile)
I. Robinson Crusoe
Vol. Maipo
Buenos Aires
Montevideo
I. Alejandro Selkirk
La Plata
Río de la Plata
L. dos Patos
L. Miri
Concepción
ARGENTINA
C. San Antonio
Mar del Plata
Bahía Blanca

PACIFIC OCEAN

Gulf of San Matías
I. de Chiloé
Pen. Valdés
Archipiélago de los Chonos
Gulf of Corcovado
Pen. Taitao
Gulf of San Jorge
C. Tres Montes
Gulf of Penas

ATLANTIC OCEAN

Falkland Islands
(U.K.; claimed by Arg.)
Stanley
Strait of Magellan
Tierra del Fuego
I. Sta. Inés
Cape Horn
I. de los Estados

South Georgia (U.K.)

Antarctic Circle

0	300	600 Miles
0	300	600 Kilometers

Lambert Azimuthal
Equal-Area Projection
1: 43,697,000

N
W — E
S

ARCTIC OCEAN

Barents
Sea

Denmark Strait

Jan Mayen
(Norway)

North
Cape

Hammerfest

Vardø

Akureyri

Arctic Circle

Norwegian
Sea

LAPLAND

Reykjavik ⊗ ICELAND

Seydhisfjördhur

Kiruna

S
W
E
D
E
N

Oulu

L. Oulu

Faroe Is. (Den.)

Trondheimsfjorden

Trondheim

Kuopio

Vaasa

FINLAND

Rockall
(U.K.)

Shetland Is. (U.K.)

Kristiansund

Ålesund

Sundsvall

Tampere

Helsinki

Hebrides

C.Wrath

Orkney Is.

Sognefjorden

Bergen

Hardanger-
fjorden

Lillehammer

Gävle

Ahvenanmaa
(Finland)

Turku

Espoo

Kotka

ATLANTIC

OCEAN

Moray
Firth

Inverness

UNITED
KINGDOM

SCOTLAND

North
Channel

Glasgow

Edinburgh

N. IRELAND

Belfast

Galway

IRELAND

Manchester

Leeds

Dublin

Liverpool

Limerick

Cork

C.Clear

WALES

Cardiff

ENGLAND

Sheffield

Birmingham

NETHERLANDS

The Wash

Frisian Is.

Kiel

Lübeck

Bornholm (Den.)

Oland

JUTLAND

Århus

DENMARK

Odense

Copenhagen

Malmö

Alborg

Göteborg

Visby

Gotland (Sw.)

Stockholm

Öland

Baltic Sea

Oslo

Drammen

Arendal

Kristiansand

NORWAY

Stavanger

Vänern

Vättern

St George's
Channel

Donegal
Bay

Irish Sea

Bradford

Newcastle-
upon-Tyne

North
Sea

Land's End

Bristol

London

The Hague

Amsterdam

Bremen

Hamburg

Southampton

Portsmouth

Rotterdam

Utrecht

Dortmund

Hannover

Berlin

Channel Is. (U.K.)

Cherbourg

Calais

Antwerp

Essen

Düsseldorf

Magdeburg

English Channel

Le Havre

Lille

Brussels

Cologne

Leipzig

Dresden

Brest

Rouen

Reims

BELGIUM

Bonn

GERMANY

Frankfurt

Nantes

Versailles

Paris

LUX.

Mannheim

Nuremberg

EASTERN
EUROPE

Orléans

FRANCE

Strasbourg

Stuttgart

Munich

Bay
of
Biscay

Loire

Vichy

MASSIF
CENTRAL

Lyon

Freiburg

Basel

Bern

Zürich

LIECHTENSTEIN

Innsbruck

Linz

Salzburg

AUSTRIA

Vienna

Bordeaux

Dordogne

Geneva

SWITZ.

Graz

C. Ortegal

CANTABRIAN MTS.

Bilbao

Biarritz

Grenoble

Mt. Blanc

Turin

Milan

Venice

Trieste

Porto

Braga

Duero

PYRENEES

Toulouse

Nîmes

Nice

Genoa

Bologna

Ravenna

Adriatic Sea

Coimbra

Salamanca

ANDORRA

Marseille

MONACO

G. of Lions

Pisa

Florence

SAN
MARINO

APENNINES

Lisbon

PORTUGAL

SIERRA DE
GUADARRAMA

Madrid

Saragossa

Corsica
(Fr.)

Ligurian
Sea

Siena

Perugia

VATICAN
CITY

Rome

Naples

Bari

Brindisi

Setúbal

Évora

Tagus

Toledo

Barcelona

Ajaccio

Guadiana

SPAIN

Valencia

Majorca

Minorca

Sardinia
(It.)

Mt. Vesuvius

C. St.
Vincent

Seville

SIERRA MORENA

Córdoba

Granada

Palma

Ibiza

C. Nao

Balearic Is.

Cagliari

Tyrrhenian
Sea

Reggio di
Calabria

G. of
Taranto

Gulf of
Cádiz

Cádiz

Málaga

Almería

C. Palos

Str. of Bonifacio

Palermo

Messina

G. of
Squillace

Gibraltar (U.K.)

C. Gata

Messina

Ionian
Sea

Strait of
Gibraltar

Cueta (Sp.)

Sicily

Catania

Mt. Etna

C. Passero

Mediterranean Sea

Valletta

MALTA

AFRICA

WESTERN
EUROPE

⊗ National capital

• City

Elevation

Meters		Feet
3,000		10,000
2,000		7,000
1,000		3,000
500		1,500
200		700
0		0

0   200   400 Miles

0   200   400 Kilometers

Azimuthal Equal-Area Projection
1: 31,019,000

EASTERN EUROPE

⊛ National capital
• City

Elevation

Meters		Feet
3,000		10,000
2,000		7,000
1,000		3,000
500		1,500
200		700
0		0

0   200   400 Miles

0   200   400 Kilometers

Azimuthal Equal-Area Projection
1 : 31,019,000

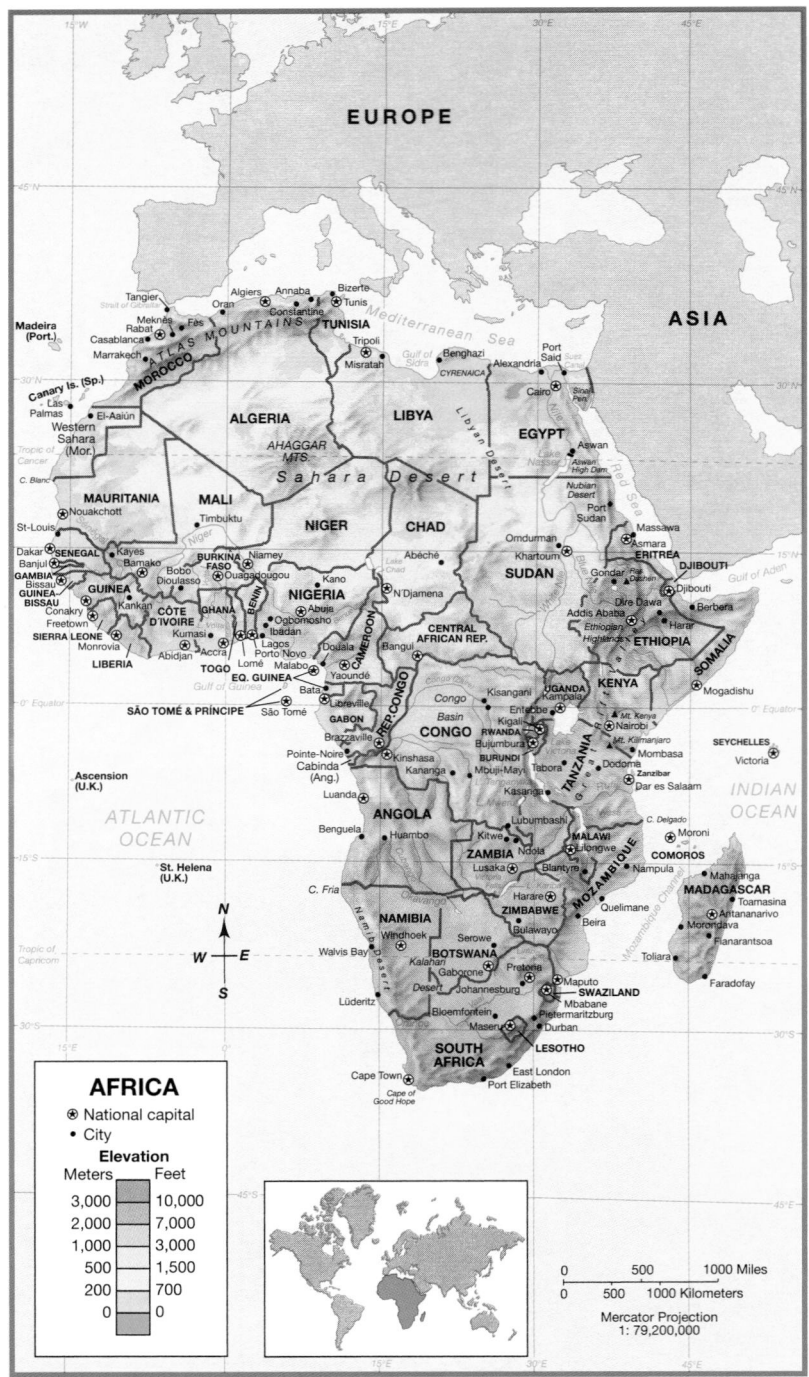

AFFRICA

⊛ National capital
• City

Elevation

Meters	Feet
3,000	10,000
2,000	7,000
1,000	3,000
500	1,500
200	700
0	0

0   500   1000 Miles

0   500   1000 Kilometers

Mercator Projection
1: 79,200,000

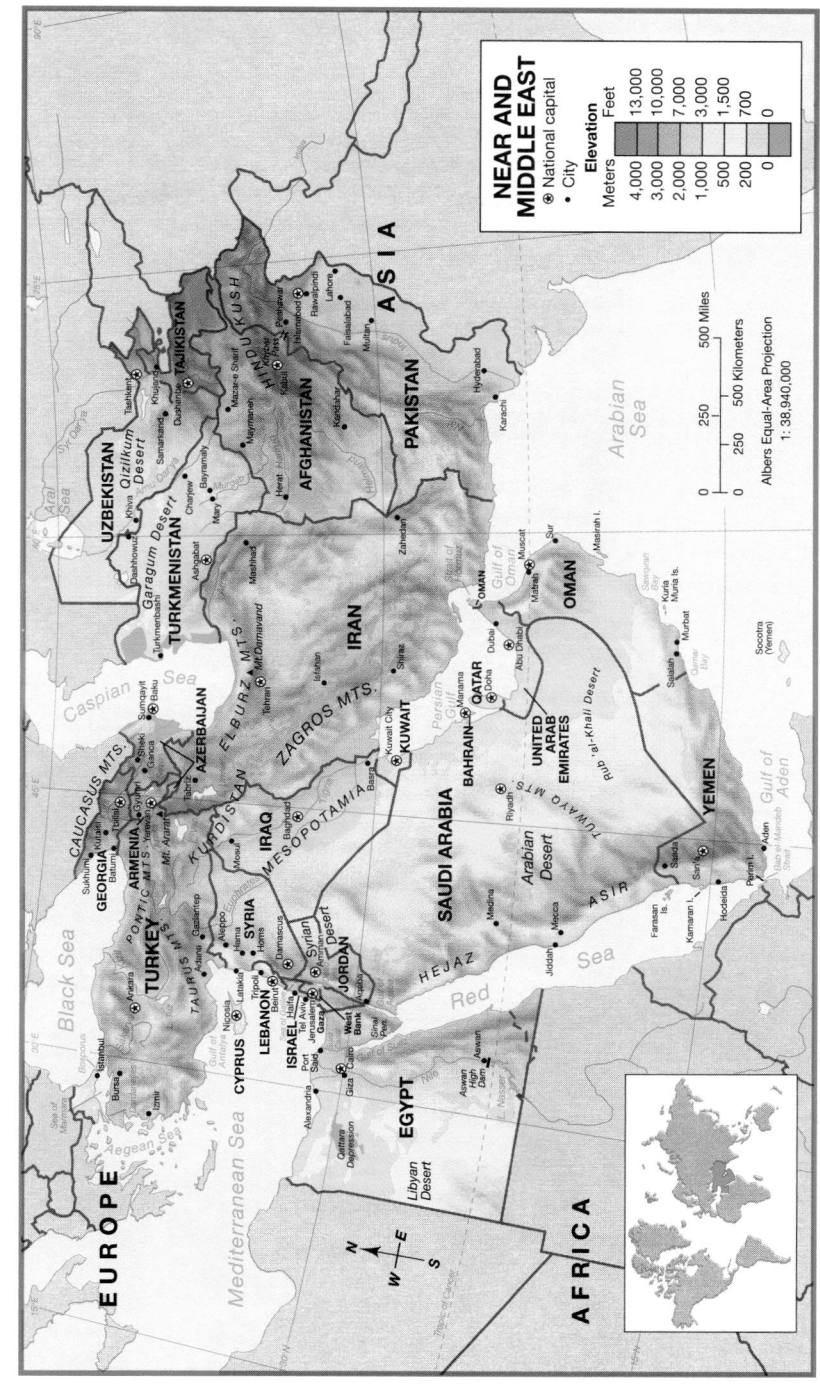

NEAR AND MIDDLE EAST

⊛ National capital
• City

Elevation

Meters	Feet
4,000	13,000
3,000	10,000
2,000	7,000
1,000	3,000
500	1,500
200	700
0	0

0   250   500 Miles

0   250   500 Kilometers

Albers Equal-Area Projection
1:38,940,000

EUROPE

ASIA

AFRICA

UZBEKISTAN

TURKMENISTAN

TAJIKISTAN

HINDU KUSH

AFGHANISTAN

PAKISTAN

Qizilkum Desert

Garagum Desert

Aral Sea

Caspian Sea

Black Sea

GEORGIA

ARMENIA

AZERBAIJAN

CAUCASUS MTS.

PONTIC MTS.

TURKEY

TAURUS MTS.

CYPRUS

KURDISTAN

IRAN

IRAQ

ELBURZ MTS.

ZAGROS MTS.

Mt. Damavand

MESOPOTAMIA

SYRIA

LEBANON

ISRAEL

JORDAN

West Bank

Syrian Desert

Mt. Ararat

KUWAIT

BAHRAIN

QATAR

UNITED ARAB EMIRATES

OMAN

Gulf of Oman

Arabian Sea

Masirah I.

Kuria Muria Is.

Socotra (Yemen)

Gulf of Aden

YEMEN

ASIR

TUWAYQ MTS.

SAUDI ARABIA

Arabian Desert

Rub' al-Khali Desert

HEJAZ

Red Sea

Mediterranean Sea

Aegean Sea

EGYPT

Libyan Desert

Qattara Depression

Tropic of Cancer

N
W — E
S

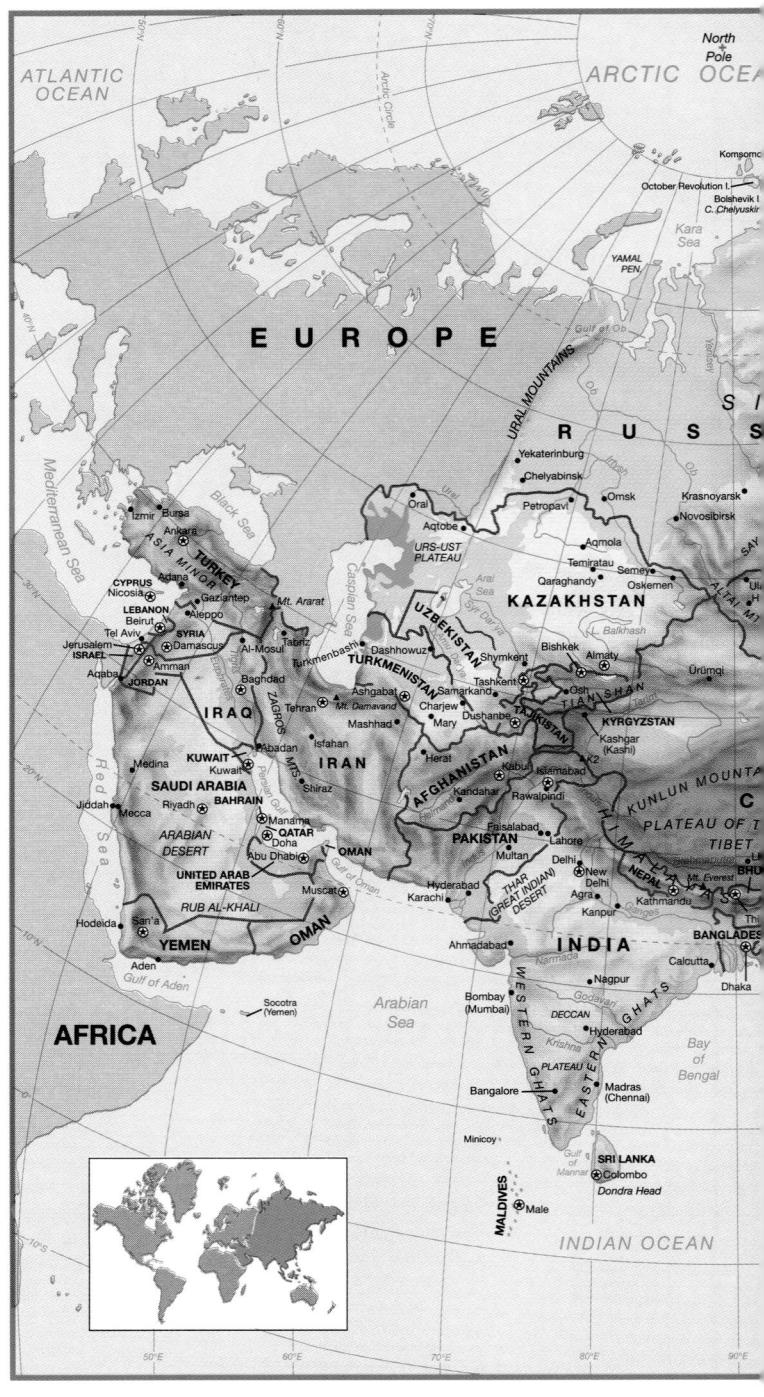

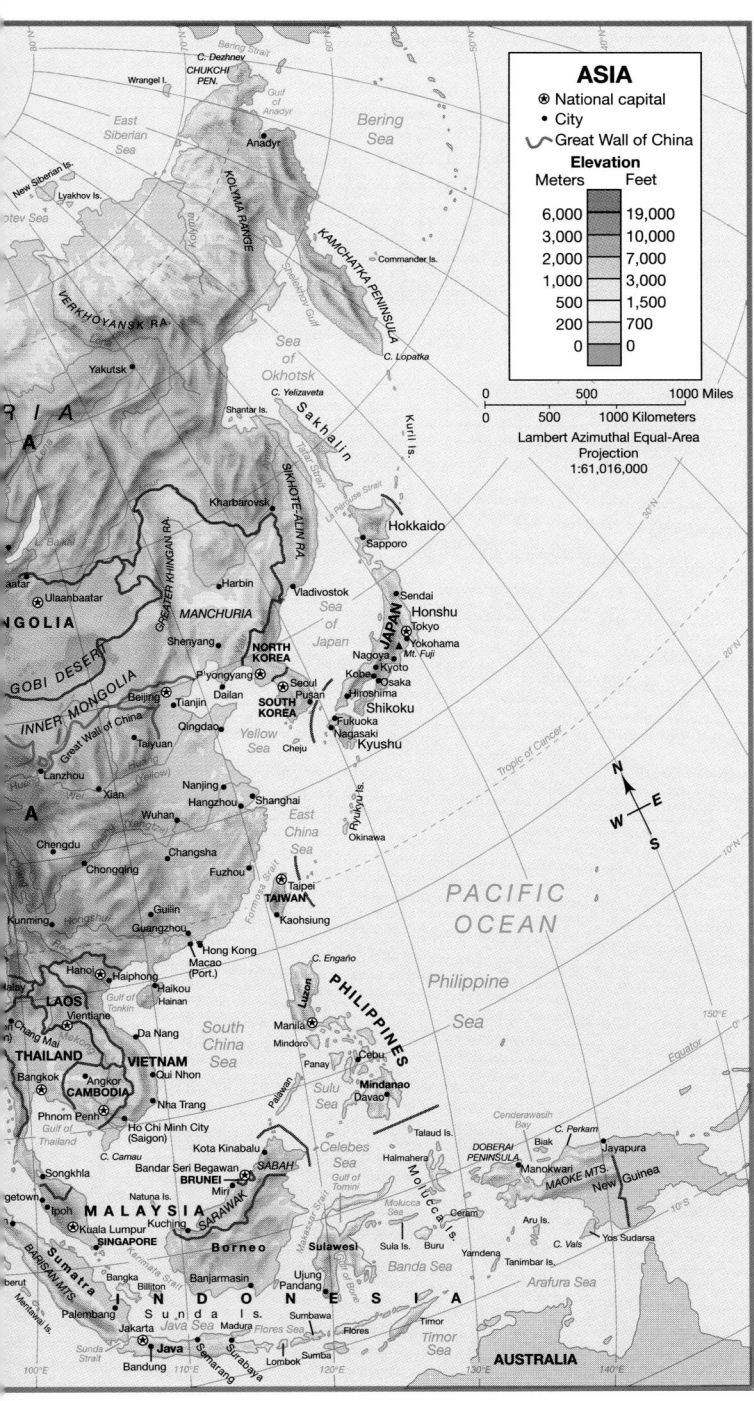

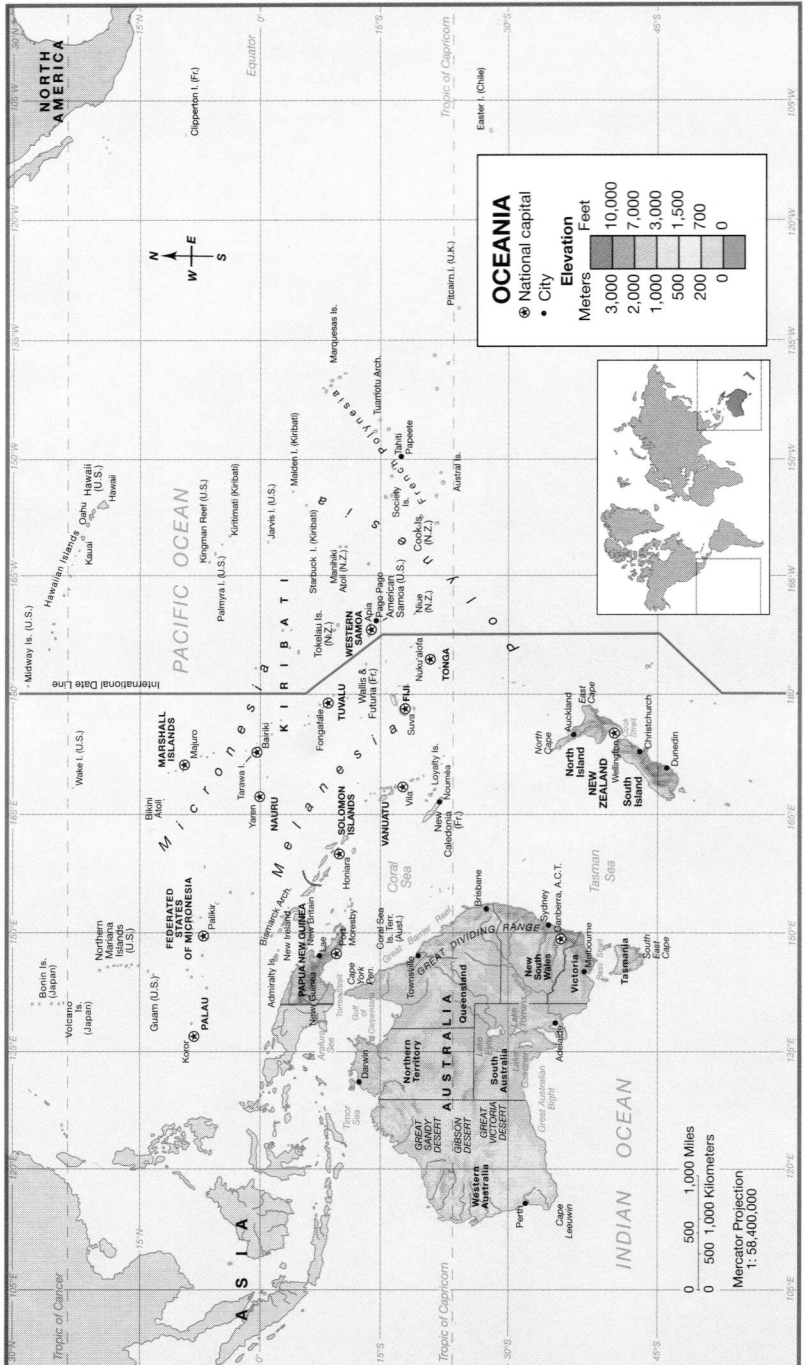

OCEANIA
⊛ National capital
● City

Elevation
Meters	Feet
3,000	10,000
2,000	7,000
1,000	3,000
500	1,500
200	700
0	0

Mercator Projection
1:58,400,000

0   500   1,000 Miles
0   500 1,000 Kilometers

ARCHIVE PHOTOS/EXPRESS NEWSPAPERS

HEAVENLY VISITOR—Comet Hale-Bopp, discovered by amateur U.S. astronomers Alan Hale and Thomas Bopp, blazed its trail over England's Stonehenge on April 1. Passing Earth at a distance of 120 million miles, the 20-mile-wide comet was among the brightest of the century.

REUTERS/GARY HERSHORN/ARCHIVE PHOTOS

SECOND WIND—On Jan. 20, William Jefferson Clinton, 50, was sworn in as President for the second time at the U.S. Capitol by Chief Justice William Rehnquist. Clinton's 1996 election victory over Sen. Robert Dole and Reform Party candidate Ross Perot made him the first Democrat to win a second term in the White House since Franklin Delano Roosevelt in 1936.

REUTERS/POOL/ARCHIVE PHOTOS

DEFICIT BUSTERS—In July President Clinton and Republican leaders Newt Gingrich and Trent Lott celebrated passage of legislation intended to balance the federal budget by 2002.

REUTERS/RICK WILKING/ARCHIVE PHOTOS

"DONORGATE" HEARINGS—Sen. Fred Thompson (R., Tenn., right), with Sen. John Glenn (D., Oh.), led a Senate committee inquiring into illegal campaign donations in the 1996 election.

ARCHIVE PHOTOS/CBS EVENING NEWS/ REUTERS

APOCALYPSE NOW—In late March, longtime UFO fanatic Marshall Applewhite, 65, led 38 members of his Heaven's Gate cult in a carefully choreographed group suicide spurred by the appearance of the Hale-Bopp comet, which he claimed was beckoning them to a higher level.

ARCHIVE PHOTOS/SD SHERIFF/REUTERS

SUICIDE PACT—The bodies of the 39 Heaven's Gate cultists were found in a spacious mansion in Rancho Santa Fe, California, each dressed in black clothing and black Nike sneakers and covered in a purple shroud. The suicide potion was phenobarbital, applesauce and vodka.

VERSACE MURDERED—The flamboyant career of trendsetting Italian fashion designer Gianni Versace was cut short when he was murdered on the front steps of his Miami Beach mansion on July 15. The chief suspect—gay con man Andrew Cunanan (inset), wanted by the FBI in four other murder cases—killed himself on a Miami Beach houseboat eight days later.

KENSINGTON PALACE: REUTERS/JASPER JUINEN/ARCHIVE PHOTOS. INSET: REUTERS/MIKE SEGAR/ARCHIVE PHOTOS

SISTERS OF MERCY—Memorial flowers surround London's Kensington Palace, home of Diana, Princess of Wales, 36, who was killed on Aug. 31 with boyfriend Dodi al Fayed when their speeding car, pursued by paparazzi, crashed in a Paris tunnel. Days later, a second noted humanitarian, Roman Catholic nun Mother Teresa (inset, with Diana in June, 1997) died at 87.

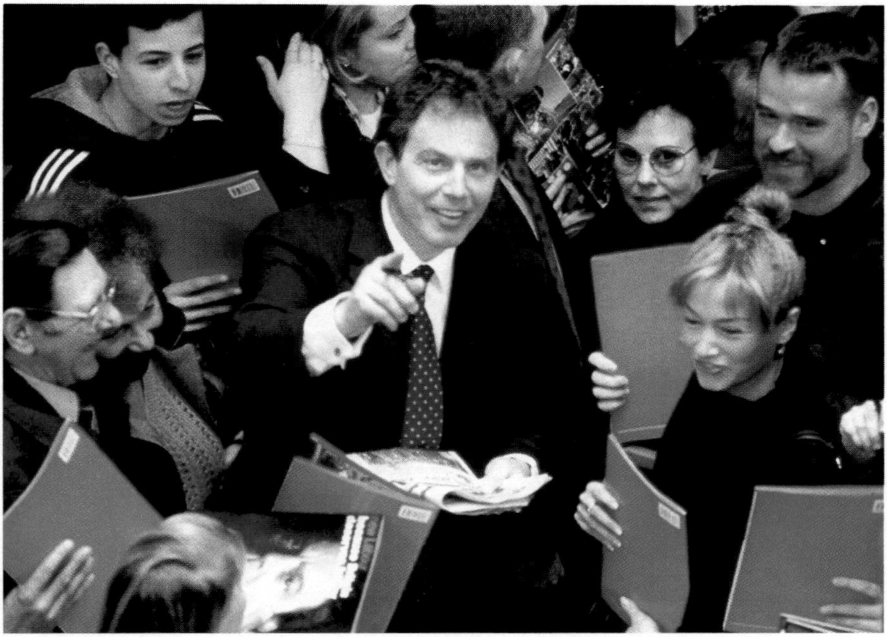

ARCHIVE PHOTOS/CHRIS HELGREN/REUTERS

LABOUR'S DAY—Dynamic new leader Tony Blair steered his Labour Party back to the political center, then crushed John Major's Tories in a May election to take power in the U.K.

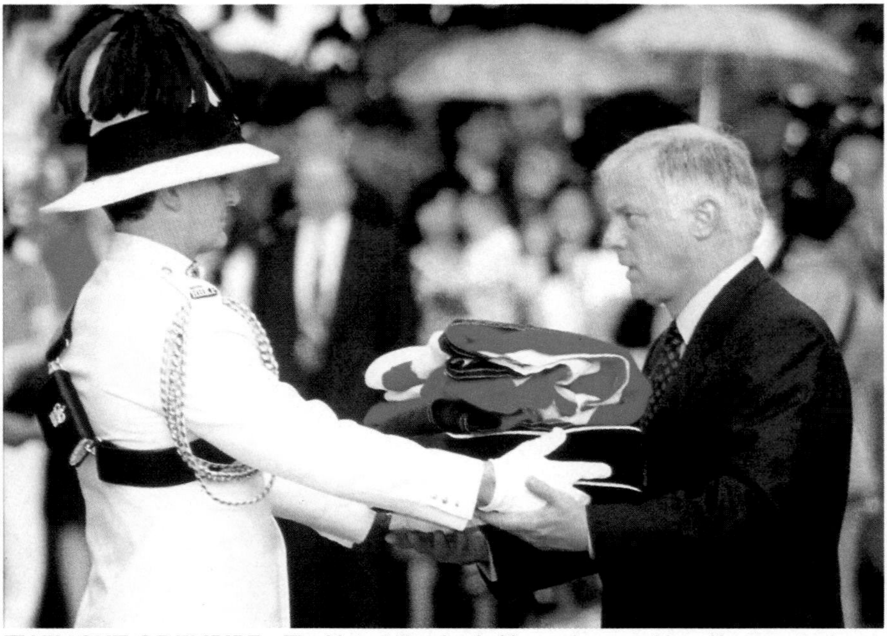

ARCHIVE PHOTOS/REUTERS

TWILIGHT OF EMPIRE—The United Kingdom's 99-year lease on Hong Kong expired on June 30, and the British formally handed over control of Asia's vibrant financial capital to China.

REUTERS/RONEN KEDEM/ARCHIVE PHOTOS

CARNAGE IN JERUSALEM—Two suicidal terrorists from the radical Islamist group Hamas set off bombs in Jersualem's main food market on July 30, killing 15 and wounding 170. On Sept. 4, three more suicide bombs killed four Israelis, seriously straining the peace process.

ARCHIVE PHOTOS/WILL BURGESS/REUTERS

ON THE ROAD—In January Madeleine Albright became the first woman to serve as U.S. Secretary of State; in February she met with China's Foreign Minister Qian Qichen in Beijing.

A TYRANT'S FALL—Cambodia's Pol Pot—notorious leader of the radical Khmer Rouge government that killed at least 1 million of its own citizens in the 1970s—was himself expelled from the far-left movement in a July show trial in the group's jungle stronghold of Anlong Veng.

"STRIKE!"—Led by Teamsters Union president Ron Carey, 185,000 United Parcel Service workers walked off their jobs on August 4. After a crippling 15-day strike, UPS management agreed to create more full-time jobs and to continue union control of employee pension funds.

REUTERS/MIKE THEILER/ARCHIVE PHOTOS

STEADY HAND—Federal Reserve chairman Alan Greenspan speaks to a Senate committee. As the U.S. economy surged through the summer, the Dow Jones average topped 8,000 in July.

REUTERS/JIM BOURG/ARCHIVE PHOTOS

ODD COUPLE—Returning to troubled Apple Computer, founder Steve Jobs (left) unveiled a surprise alliance with Apple's longtime nemesis, Microsoft czar Bill Gates (onscreen), in August.

ARCHIVE PHOTOS/NASA/REUTERS

TRIUMPH ON MARS—On July 4, NASA's 3-ft.-high Pathfinder spacecraft, swaddled in airbags, bounced to a landing on the surface of Mars and relayed this picture of the Martian landscape and the wheeled robot rover, Sojourner, which investigated rocks in the vicinity.

REUTERS/RTV/ARCHIVE PHOTOS

TROUBLE ON MIR—The 11-year-old Russian space station—now used jointly by U.S. and Russian astronauts—suffered a series of crises, including a June collision with an unmanned cargo ship that damaged its solar panels (right), leaving sections of the station without power.

REUTERS/JEFF MITCHELL/ARCHIVE PHOTOS

MY MOTHER, MYSELF—In February Dr. Ian Wilmut and his research team at the Roslin Institute near Edinburgh, Scotland, announced that they had succeeded in creating a frisky lamb, Dolly (above), by a process of cloning. The team fused cells from two adult ewes to form a new embryo that was implanted in the uterus of a third ewe, who then gave birth to Dolly.

ARCHIVE PHOTOS/M. ANSELL/TOUCHSTONE/REUTERS

"YEP, I'M GAY"—As homosexual culture continued to win mainstream acceptance in the U.S., TV star Ellen DeGeneres (left) "came out" as a lesbian twice: fictionally, in her leading role on the ABC sitcom *Ellen* with guest Laura Dern (right); and in real life on the cover of TIME.

TIGER!—Charismatic Tiger Woods, only 21, electrified the world of golf when he turned pro and proceeded to win two tournaments in three weeks. The multiracial star then dominated the venerable Masters (above), winning by 12 strokes and setting a new tournament record.

ARCHIVE PHOTOS/REUTERS

DISASTER IN DAKOTA—Some 4.5 million acres of the upper Midwest were inundated by the Red River in late April as spring floods roared through the region. Hardest hit was Grand Forks, N.D., where 50,000 fled as fire destroyed much of the city's historic business district.

Science

Cloning Humans: Facts and Fallacies

Tinkering with Mother Nature

Trepidation over humans creating duplicate people began in February 1997 when Dr. Ian Wilmut and his team of scientists in Scotland astonished the world by announcing that they had successfully cloned an adult sheep. Animals had been cloned before using the cells of developing embryos soon after they begin to form in the egg, but this was the first time ever that a mammal had been cloned from the cells of an adult animal. This major scientific breakthrough was accomplished by researchers in Edinburgh at the Roslin Institute, a center for genetic research of farm animals and PPL Therapeutics, a biotechnology company. The goal of their joint effort is to improve conventional animal breeding and create new health products for the biopharmaceutical industry.

In a process called "nuclear transplantation," researchers took an udder cell of a six-year-old ewe and transplanted the nucleus (which contains the genetic material or DNA) into an unfertilized egg of a second sheep from which its nucleus had previously been removed. The cell and the egg were fused with electric pulses. The egg began to divide normally and developed into an embryo. It was then implanted into a third, surrogate sheep who gave birth to a lamb that is genetically identical twin of the sheep from which the mammary cells were taken. The lamb named Dolly seems normal and healthy.

Should We Play God?

Because the same procedure used to make a carbon copy of the sheep is also theoretically applicable to cloning human beings, many ethical and philosophical questions have been raised. The thought of replicating humans is frightening and most scientists, including Dr. Wilmut and his coworkers, believe that it would be unethical to try to clone humans. Cloning people is banned in Britain, Belgium, Denmark, Germany, The Netherlands, and Spain. Federal funding for human cloning research is prohibited in the United States and President Clinton requested the private sector to voluntarily ban the research. Exploitation of this technology, however, cannot be prevented. Even though laws are passed forbidding research on replicating people, it would still be possible to continue these experiments secretly in private laboratories or in countries with no laws against such research.

Clones Aren't Exact Copies

There is some misunderstanding about what constitutes a clone. A human clone would be the genetic identical twin, a generation or more younger, of the donor (not the surrogate mother) who provided the nucleus. But because people are more than a product of their genes, a clone would have its own personality, character, intelligence, and talents exactly as identical twins do (who are natural clones stemming from the same egg). You cannot clone a person's brain or mind, and chance factors, the environment, and a person's experiences contribute to individual traits.

This means that even if you wanted to, you cannot duplicate your identical self. Even if you were to clone yourself several times, you would not be able to create the same person each time because every human life, no matter how conceived, is unique. A cloned Hitler would not necessarily grow up to be a mass murderer nor would a twin of Mother Teresa become a humanitarian.

It is also impossible to copy a deceased family member or a past historical figure through cloning the cells

Cloning Milestones

1938 Cloning envisioned. Dr. Hans Spemann (Germany) proposed an experiment to remove the nucleus from an unfertilized egg and replace it with the nucleus from a differentiated cell.

1953 Structure of DNA (deoxyribonucleic acid) discovered by Francis C. Crick (U.K.) and James D. Watson (U.S.).

1970 Dr. John B. Gurdon (U.K.) clones a frog by transplanting the intestinal cell of a tadpole into an enucleated frog egg, which develops into an adult frog.

1973 First successful gene splicing (recombinant DNA) by Paul Berg and Stanley N. Cohen (U.S.). A major breakthrough in genetic engineering.

1978 Birth of first child, conceived by in vitro (literally "in glass") fertilization to Leslie Brown (U.K.).

1980 U.S. Supreme Court rules that a genetically created new bacterium (a non-natural manmade microorganism) may be patented.

1984 Dr. Steen M. Willadsen (Denmark) clones a lamb from a developing sheep embryo cell. His experiment is repeated by other scientists who clone a variety of animals.

1993 First humans cloned (U.S.). Cells taken from defective human embryos that were to be discarded in infertility clinic are grown in vitro and develop up to 32-cell stage and then are destroyed.

1994 Dr. Ned First (U.S.) clones calves from cells of early embryos.

1995 Drs. Ian Wilmut and Keith Campbell (U.K.) create the world's first cloned sheep, Megan and Morag, from embryo cells.

1996 Dr. Ian Wilmut and his team clone the world's the first sheep from adult cells. The lamb born in July 1996 is named Dolly.

1997 Scientists at Oregon Regional Primate Research Center (U.S.) create first primates—two rhesus monkeys named Neti and Ditto—from DNA taken from cells of developing monkey embryos. They are not genetically identical because two different embryos were used.

1997 A team led by Drs. Ian Wilmut and Keith Campbell (U.K.) create the first sheep with a human gene in every cell of its body. The genetically engineered lamb is named Polly.

from their corpses. The same applies to dead persons that have been frozen, because you need live DNA to make a clone.

Although some scientists believe that human cloning is only 10 or 20 years around the corner, the process would be far more difficult than cloning a sheep. Researchers began by attempting to fuse 277 adult sheep cells with an equal number of eggs. This yielded only 29 embryos, which in turn resulted in only 10 pregnant sheep, only one of which successfully made it to term and gave birth to Dolly. Given these odds, it would take dozens of surrogate mothers just to give birth to one human clone.

The biggest question over cloning animals is how the clone will age. Dolly was cloned from a six-year-old ewe and therefore the nucleus of all her cells were already six years old when she was born. No one knows how this will affect her longevity or other factors in her life.

The Cloning Quandary

The debate surrounding what constitutes a "life" is sure to intensify as the issue of cloning enters the discussion. As a technology in its infancy, there will no doubt be unintended consequences, and we would need safeguards to prevent accidents from happening. Should cloning be made a personal decision? Should women have the same reproductive rights with their cells and genes that they have in choosing whether to give birth? Lesbian couples could exchange genes and nuclei with their partners and create their own children. Is it wrong for an infertile couple to clone one partner if it is their only chance to have a baby? Do grieving parents have the right to clone a child that is dying? Would it be unethical to replicate someone to serve as a compatible organ donor? Could we have gene banks of elite donors similar to sperm banks? These are just a few of the troubling questions that remain to be answered.

Society has always been alarmed by the appearance of new reproductive technologies. In the early 1970s, scientists discovered how to clone a gene from one organism and transplant it into the DNA of a different species where it would replicate along with the host DNA. The technique, called recombinant DNA, or "gene splicing," created a furor at the time, and people feared that scientists would create dangerous microorganisms that might escape from the laboratories and destroy us.

Today, pregnancy by *in vitro* fertilization is widely accepted. But back in 1978 when "test tube baby" Louise Brown was born—the first human conceived outside the body of a woman—it caused a storm of ethical debate. A similar outcry was heard when children were conceived by artificial insemination.

In June 1997, the President's 18-member National Bioethics Advisory Committee recommended that research on cloning humans should be banned for the present and the technology be re-evaluated several years from now. In the meantime, Congress may pass laws that make creating a child by cloning a criminal offense.

Certainly no one wants this new science to be misused. But like other scientific advances that we at first viewed with fear and suspicion, over time and applied ethically, cloning may serve humanity in a useful and benevolent way. —*OTJ* □

The Elements

Elements are the building blocks of nature. Water, for example, is a compound consisting of the elements hydrogen and oxygen. Each element is a pure substance that cannot be split up into any simpler pure substance.

The smallest particle of an element that can exist is an atom. An atom consists of sub-atomic particles. The most important of these are protons, which have positive electrical charges; electrons, which have negative electrical charges; and neutrons, which are electrically neutral.

The atomic number of an element is the number of protons in one atom of the element. Each element has a different electronic number. For example, the atomic numbers of hydrogen and oxygen are 1 and 8, respectively.

Elements with atomic numbers 1 (hydrogen) to 92 (uranium) occur naturally on Earth. Those with atomic numbers 93 (neptunium) onwards are artificial. They have to be synthesized from elements with lower atomic numbers. Element 100 is named fermium. Elements with atomic numbers 101 onwards are known as the transfermium elements. They are also known as heavy elements because their atoms have very large masses compared with atoms of hydrogen, the lightest of all elements.

The heaviest element synthesized to date is element 112. One atom of this element was synthesized by scientists at the Heavy-Ion Research Center (Gesellschaft für Schwerionenforschung [GSI]) in Darmstadt, Germany, in February 1996. They made it by bombarding the element lead (atomic number 82) with a high-energy beam of atoms of the element zinc (atomic number 30). The atom existed for a fraction of a second before splitting up. Elements 110 and 111 were discovered by the same group of scientists in 1994.

Names for the six new heavy elements at the end of the periodic table were approved on August 31, 1997, by the International Union of Pure and Applied Chemistry (IUPAC) in Geneva.

Approved Names for Elements 104 to 109

Atomic number	International Union of Pure and Applied Chemistry slate (1997)
104	Rutherfordium (Rf)
105	Dubnium (Db)
106	Seaborgium (Sg)
107	Bohrium (Bh)
108	Hassium (Hs)
109	Meitnerium (Mt)

To date, no names have been proposed for elements 110 to 112.

Chemical Elements

Element	Symbol	Atomic no.	Atomic wt.	Specific gravity	Melting point °C	Boiling point °C	No. of isotopes[1]	Discoverer	Year
Actinium	Ac	89	227[2]	10.07[2]	1050	3200±300	11	Debierne	1899
Aluminum	Al	13	26.9815	2.6989	660.37	2467	8	Wöhler	1827
Americium	Am	95	243[6]	13.67	994±4	2607	13[3]	Seaborg et al.	1944
Antimony	Sb	51	121.75	6.61	630.74	1750	29	Early historic times	—
Argon	Ar	18	39.948	1.7837[4]	-189.2	-185.7	8	Rayleigh and Ramsay	1894
Arsenic (gray)	As	33	74.9216	5.73	817 (28 atm.)	613[5]	14	Albertus Magnus	1250?
Astatine	At	85	-210	—	302	337	21	Corson et al.	1940
Barium	Ba	56	137.34	3.5	725	1640	25	Davy	1808
Berkelium	Bk	97	247[6]	14.00[7]	—	—	8[3]	Seaborg et al.	1949
Berylium	Be	4	9.01218	1.848	1278±5	2970 (5 mm.)	6	Vauquelin	1798
Bismuth	Bi	83	208.9806	9.747	271.3	1560±5	19	Geoffroy	1753
Boron	B	5	10.81	2.37[8]	2300	2550[5]	6	Gay-Lussac and Thénard; Davy	1808
Bromine	Br	35	79.904	3.12[4]	-7.2	58.78	19	Balard	1826
Cadmium	Cd	48	112.40	8.65	320.9	765	22	Stromeyer	1817
Calcium	Ca	20	40.08	1.55	839±2	1484	14	Davy	1808
Californium	Cf	98	251[6]	—	—	—	12[3]	Seaborg et al.	1950
Carbon	C	6	12.011	1.8-3.5[9]	-3550	4827	7	Prehistoric	—
Cerium	Ce	58	140.12	6.771	798±3	3257	19	Berzelius and Hisinger; Klaproth	1803
Cesium	Cs	55	132.9055	1.873	28.40	678.4	22	Bunsen and Kirchoff	1860
Chlorine	Cl	17	35.453	1.56[4]	-100.98	-34.6	11	Scheele	1774
Chromium	Cr	24	51.996	7.18-7.20	1857±20	2672	9	Vauquelin	1797
Cobalt	Co	27	58.9332	8.9	1495	2870	14	Brandt	c.1735
Copper	Cu	29	63.546	8.96	1083.4±0.2	2567	11	Preshistoric	—
Curium	Cm	96	247[6]	13.51[2]	1340±40	—	13[3]	Seaborg et al.	1944
Dysprosium	Dy	66	162.50	8.540	1409	2335	21	Boisbaudran	1886
Einsteinium	Es	99	254[6]	—	—	—	12[3]	Ghiorso et al.	1952
Erbium	Er	68	167.26	9.045	1522	2510	16	Mosander	1843
Europium	Eu	63	151.96	5.283	822±5	1597	21	Demarcay	1896
Fermium	Fm	100	257[6]	—	—	—	10[3]	Ghiorso et al.	1953
Fluorine	F	9	18.9984	1.108[4]	-219.62	-188.14	6	Moissan	1886
Francium	Fr	87	223[6]	—	27[2]	677[2]	21	Perey	1938
Gadolinium	Gd	64	157.25	7.898	1311±1	3233	17	Marignac	1880
Gallium	Ga	31	69.72	5.904	29.78	2403	14	Boisbaudran	1875
Germanium	Ge	32	72.59	5.323	937.4	2830	17	Winkler	1886
Gold	Au	79	196.9665	19.32	1064.43	2807	21	Prehistoric	—
Hafnium	Hf	72	178.49	13.31	2227±20	4602	17	Coster and von Hevesy	1923
Hahnium	Ha	105	262	—	—	—	—	Ghiorso et al.	1970
Helium	He	2	4.00260	0.1785[4]	-272.2 (26 atm.)	-268.934	5	Janssen	1868
Holmium	Ho	67	164.9303	8.781	1470	2720	29	Delafontaine and Soret	1878
Hydrogen	H	1	1.0080	0.070[4]	-259.14	-252.87	3	Cavendish	1766
Indium	In	49	114.82	7.31	156.61	2080	34	Reich and Richter	1863
Iodine	I	53	126.9045	4.93	113.5	184.35	24	Cortois	1811
Iridium	Ir	77	192.22	22.42	2410	4130	25	Tennant	1803
Iron	Fe	26	55.847	7.894	1535	2750	10	Prehistoric	—
Krypton	Kr	36	83.80	3.733[4]	-156.6	-152.30±0.10	23	Ramsay and Travers	1898
Lanthanum	La	57	138.9055	6.166	920±5	3454	19	Mosander	1839
Lawrenceium	Lr	103	257[6]	—	—	—	20[3]	Ghiorso et al.	1961
Lead	Pb	82	207.2	11.35	327.502	1740	29	Prehistoric	—
Lithium	Li	3	6.941	0.534	180.54	1347	5	Arfvedson	1817
Lutetium	Lu	71	174.97	9.835	1656±5	3315	22	Urbain	1907
Magnesium	Mg	12	24.305	1.738	648.8±0.5	1090	8	Black	1755
Manganese	Mn	25	54.9380	7.21-7.44[10]	1244±3	1962	11	Gahn, Scheele, and Bergman	1774
Mendelevium	Md	101	256[6]	—	—	—	3[3]	Chiorso et al.	1955
Mercury	Hg	80	200.59	13.546	-38.87	356.58	26	Prehistoric	—
Molybdenum	Mo	42	95.94	10.22	2617	4612	20	Scheele	1778
Neodymium	Nd	60	144.24	6.80 & 7.004[10]	1010	3127	16	von Welsbach	1885
Neon	Ne	10	20.179	0.89990 (g/10°C/1 atm)	-248.67	-246.048	8	Ramsay and Travers	1898
Neptunium	Np	93	237.0482	20.25	6400±1	3902	15[3]	McMillan and Abelson	1940
Nickel	Ni	28	58.71	8.902	1453	2732	11	Cronstedt	1751
Niobium (Columbium)	Nb	41	92.9064	8.57	2468±10	4742	24	Hatchett	1801
Nitrogen	N	7	14.0067	0.808[4]	-209.86	-195.8	8	Rutherford	1772
Nobelium	No	102	254[6]	—	—	—	7[3]	Ghiorso et al.	1957
Osmium	Os	76	190.2	22.57	3045±30	5027±100	19	Tennant	1803
Oxygen	O	8	15.9994	1.14[4]	-218.4	-182.962	8	Preistley	1774
Palladium	Pd	46	106.4	12.02	1552	3140	21	Wollaston	1803

Element	Symbol	Atomic no.	Atomic wt.	Specific gravity	Melting point °C	Boiling point °C	No. of isotopes[1]	Discoverer	Year
Phosphorous	P	15	30.9738	1.82 (white)	44.1	280	7	Brand	1669
Platinum	Pt	78	195.09	21.45	1772	3827±100	32	Ulloa	1735
Plutonium	Pu	94	244[6]	19.84	641	3232	16[3]	Seaborg et al.	1940
Poionium	Po	84	210[6]	9.32	254	962	34	Curie	1898
Potassium	K	19	39.102	0.862	63.65	774	10	Davy	1807
Praseodymium	Pr	59	140.9077	6.772	931±4	3212	15	von Weisbach	1885
Promethium	Pm	61	145[6]	—	≈1080	2460?	14	Marinsky et al.	1945
Protactinium	Pa	91	231.0359	15.37[2]	<1600	—	14	Hahn and Meitner	1917
Radium	Ra	88	226.0254	5.0[?]	700	1140	15	P. and M. Curie	1898
Radon	Rn	86	222[6]	4.4[4]	-71	-61.8	20	Dorn	1900
Rhenium	Re	75	186.2	21.02	3180	5627[7]	21	Noddack, Berg, and Tacke	1925
Rhodium	Rh	45	102.9055	12.41	1966±3	3727±100	20	Wollaston	1803
Rubidium	Rb	37	85.4678	1.532	38.89	688	20	Bunsen and Kirchoff	1861
Rutherfordium	Rf	104	261	—	—	—	—	Ghiorso et al.	1969
Ruthenium	Ru	44	101.07	12.44	2310	3900	16	Klaus	1844
Samarium	Sm	62	150.4	7.536	1072±5	1778	17	Boisbaudran	1879
Scandium	Sc	21	44.9559	2.989	1539	2832	15	Nilson	1879
Seaborgium	Sg	106	263	—	—	—	—	Ghiorso et al.	1974
Selenium	Se	34	78.96	4.79 (gray)	217	684.9±1	20	Berzelius	1817
Silicon	Si	14	28.086	2.33	1410	2355	8	Berzelius	1824
Silver	Ag	47	107.868	10.5	961.93	2212	27	Prehistoric	—
Sodium	Na	11	22.9898	0.971	97.81±0.03	882.9	7	Davy	1807
Strontium	Sr	38	87.62	2.54	769	1384	18	Davy	1808
Sulfur	S	16	32.06	2.07[11]	112.8	444.674	10	Prehistoric	—
Tantalum	Ta	73	180.9479	16.654	2996	5425±100	19	Ekeberg	1801
Technetium	Tc	43	98.062	11.50[2]	2172	4877	23	Perrier and Segré	1937
Tellurium	Te	52	127.60	6.24	449.5±0.3	989.8±3.8	29	von Reichenstein	1782
Terbium	Tb	65	158.9254	8.234	1360±4	3041	24	Mosander	1843
Thallium	Tl	81	204.37	11.85	303.5	1457±10	28	Crookes	1861
Thorium	Th	90	232.0381	11.72	1750	4790	12	Berzelius	1828
Thulium	Tm	69	168.9342	9.314	1545±15	1727	18	Cleve	1879
Tin	Sn	50	118.69	7.31 (white)	231.9681	2270	28	Prehistoric	—
Titanium	Ti	22	47.90	4.55	1660±10	3287	9	Gregor	1791
Tungsten (Wolfram)	W	74	183.85	19.3	3410±20	5660	22	J. and F. d'Elhuyar	1783
Uranium	U	92	238.029	-18.95	1132.3±0.8	3818	15	Peligot	1841
Vanadium	V	23	50.9414	6.11	1890±10	3380	9	del Rio	1801
Xenon	Xe	54	131.30	3.52[4]	-111.9	-107.1±3	31	Ramsay and Travers	1898
Ytterbium	Yb	70	173.04	6.972	824±5	1193	16	Marignac	1878
Yttrium	Y	39	88.9059	4.457	1523±8	3337	21	Gadolin	1794
Zinc	Zn	30	65.38	7.133	419.58	907	15	Prehistoric	—
Zirconium	Zr	40	91.22	6.506[2]	1852±2	4377	20	Klaproth	1789

1. Isotopes are different forms of the same element having the same atomic number but different atomic weights. 2. Calculated figure. 3. Artificially produced. 4. Liquid. 5. Sublimation point. 6. Mass number of the isotope of longest known life. 7. Estimated. 8. Amorphous. 9. Depending on whether amorphous, graphite or diamond. 10. Depending on allotropic form. 11. Rhombic. ≈ Is approximately. < Is less than. NOTE: In November 1994, German physicists at the Heavy Ion Research Center (GSI), Darmstadt, Germany reported creating element 110, atomic mass 269. In December 1994, they announced they had produced element 111. Creating new elements is becoming old hat at Darmstadt. On February 21, 1996, an international team at the physics research center announced that they had created element number 112. The new element, a "relative" of zinc, cadmium, and mercury that is 227 times heavier than hydrogen, was produced by bombarding lead foil with highly accelerated zinc atoms. The new atom has a nucleus of 112 protons and 165 neutrons, giving it an atomic mass of 227 and making it the heaviest nucleus created in a laboratory. At GSI, researchers are now seeking to create elements 113 and 114.

Table of Geological Periods

It is now generally assumed that planets are formed by the accretion of gas and dust in a cosmic cloud, but there is no way of estimating the length of this process. Our Earth acquired its present size, more or less, between 4,000 and 5,000 million years ago. Life on Earth originated about 2,000 million years ago, but there are no good fossil remains from periods earlier than the Cambrian, which began about 550 million years ago. The largely unknown past before the Cambrian Period is referred to as the Pre-Cambrian and is subdivided into the Lower (or older) and Upper (or younger) Pre-Cambrian—also called the Archaeozoic and Proterozoic Eras.

The known geological history of the Earth since the beginning of the Cambrian Period is subdivided into three "eras," each of which includes a number of "periods." They, in turn, are subdivided into "subperiods." In a subperiod, a certain section may be especially well known because of rich fossil finds. Such a section is called a "formation," and it is usually identified by a place name.

Paleozoic Era

This era began 550 million years ago and lasted for 355 million years. The name was compounded from Greek *palaios* (old) and *zoön* (animal).

Period	Duration[1]	Subperiods	Events
Cambrian (from *Cambria*, Latin name for Wales)	70	Lower Cambrian Middle Cambrian Upper Cambrian	Invertebrate sea life of many types, proliferating during this and the following period
Ordovician (from Latin *Ordovices*, people of early Britain)	85	Lower Ordovician Upper Ordovician	
Silurian (from Latin *Silures*, people of early Wales)	40	Lower Silurian Upper Silurian	First known fishes; gigantic sea scorpions
Devonian (from Devonshire in England)	50	Lower Devonian Upper Devonian	Proliferation of fishes and other forms of sea life, land still largely lifeless
Carboniferous (from Latin *carbo* = coal + *fero* = to bear)	85	Lower or Mississippian Upper or Pennsylvanian	Period of maximum coal formation in swampy forests; early insects and first known amphibians
Permian (from district of Perm in Russia)	25	Lower Permian Upper Permian	Early reptiles and mammals; earliest form of turtles

1. In millions of years.

Mesozoic Era

This era began 195 million years ago and lasted for 135 million years. The name was compounded from Greek *mesos* (middle) and *zoön* (animal). Popular name: Age of Reptiles.

Period	Duration[1]	Subperiods	Events
Triassic (from *trias* = triad)	35	Lower or Buntsandstein (from German *bunt* = colorful + *sandstein* = sandstone). Middle or Muschelkalk (from German *muschel* = clam + *kalk* = limestone). Upper or keuper (old miner's term)	Early saurians
Jurassic (from Jura Mountains)	35	Lower or Black Jurassic, or Lias (from French *liais* = hard stone) Middle or Brown Jurassic, or Dogger (old provincial English for ironstone) Upper or White Jurassic, or Malm (Middle English for sand)	Many sea-going reptiles; early large dinosaurs; somewhat later, flying reptile (pterosaurs), earliest known birds
Cretaceous (from Latin *creta* = chalk)	65	Lower Cretaceous Upper Cretaceous	Maximum development of dinosaurs; birds proliferating; opossum-like mammals

1. In millions of years.

Cenozoic Era

This era began 60 million years ago and includes the geological present. The name was compounded from Greek *kainos* (new) and *zoön* (animal). Popular name: Age of Mammals.

Period	Duration[1]	Subperiods	Events
Tertiary (originally thought to be the third of only three periods)	c. 60	Palecene (from Greek *palaios* = old + *kainos* = new). Eocene (from Greek *eos* = dawn + *kainos* = new). Oligocene (from Greek *oligos* = few + *kainos* = new). Miocene (from Greek *meios* = less + *kainos* = new). Pliocene (from Greek *pleios* = more + *kainos* = new)	First mammals other than marsupials. Formation of amber; rich insect fauna; early bats; steady increase of large mammals. Mammals closely resembling present types; protohumans
Pleistocene (from Greek *pleistos* = most + *kainos* = new) (popular name: Ice Age)	1	Four major glaciations, named Günz, Mindel, Riss, and Würm originally the name of rivers. Last glaciation ended 10,000 to 15,000 years ago	Various forms of early man
Holocene (from Greek *holos* = entire + *kainos* = new)		The present	The last 3,000 years are called "history"

1. In millions of years.

Major Discoveries About Human Ancestors

Living and extinct human beings and their near human ancestors are called "Hominids," and belong to the family *Hominidae* of primates. They are not to be confused with "Hominoids," which belong to the family *Hominoidea* of primates that include apes and humans. Scientists theorize that the human and ape lines branched off from a common ancestor 8 to 6 million years ago.

Years Ago	Species	Discovered	Remarks
c. 4.4 million	*Ardipithecus ramidus*	1994 in Ethiopia	Oldest known human ancestor. Had chipanzee-like skull.
c. 4.2 million	*Australopithecus anamensis*	1955, two sites at Lake Turkana, Kanapoi, and Allia Bay, Kenya	Possible ancestor of *A. afarensis* (Lucy). Walked upright.
c. 3.2 million	*Australopithecus afarensis*	1974 at Hadar in the Afar triangle of eastern Ethiopia	Nicknamed "Lucy." Her skeleton was 3.5 feet (100 cm.) tall. Had ape-like skull. Walked fully upright. Lived in family groups throughout eastern Africa.
c. 2.5 million	*Australopithecus africanus*	1924 at Taung, northern Cape Province, South Africa	Descendant of "Lucy." Lived in social groups.
c. 2 million	*Australopithecus robustus*	1938 in Kromdraai, South Africa	Was related to *A. africanus*
c. 2 million	*Homo habilis* ("skillful man")	1960 in Olduvai Gorge, Tanzania	First brain expansion; is believed to have used stone tools
c. 1.8 million	*Homo erectus* ("upright man")	1891 at Trinil, Java	Brain size twice that of *Australopithecine* species. Regarded as ancestor of *Homo sapiens*. Invented the hand ax. Could probably make fires. Was first to migrate out of Africa.
c. 100,000(?)	*Homo sapien* ("knowing or wise man")	1868, Cro-Magnon, France	Anatomically modern humans

Neanderthals and Cro-Magnons Coexisted

The Neanderthals (*Homo sapiens neanderthalensis*), c. 150,000–35,000 years ago, are the best known of all extinct human sub-species. They first appeared in Europe and their fossil remains, the first anatomically human forms to be discovered, were found in 1856 in the Neander Valley, Germany. They spread throughout Europe and Western Asia. There is recent evidence that they coexisted with modern humans and no one knows why they suddenly vanished.

The Cro-Magnon (*Homo sapiens sapiens*), c. 100,000(?) years ago, completely resembled modern humans. Although usage of the term *Cro-Magnon* strictly applies only to those who lived in southwestern France, it has been used by many to generally describe *Homo sapiens sapiens* that lived everywhere else. Their skeletons were discovered in a rock shelter in the Cro-Magnon valley, Lez Eyzies, southwestern France, in 1868.

There is evidence obtained through thermoluminescent (TL) dating and electron-spin resonance (ESR) dating at sites of modern hominids in Mount Carmel, Israel, that modern humans existed in Israel c. 100,000 years ago, long before the Neanderthal peoples arrived there. If these dates are correct, they imply that these two distinct human ancestors coexisted for many thousands of years.

More evidence emerged in 1996 when researchers announced that Neanderthals living about 34,000 years ago near Auxerre in central France may have had cultural contacts with Cro-Magnons. Their conclusion was based on stone and bone tools and jewelry-like ornaments discovered in rock shelters occupied by Neanderthals that were similar to those made by Cro-Magnons. This evidence implies that some Neanderthals may have traded with Cro-Magnons rather than learned how to make the more sophisticated artifacts themselves. A third extinct human species, *Homo erectus*, may have also lived during the same period. (*See* "Roundup of Recent Discoveries," page 537.)

The Nation's Highest Science and Technology Honors

The National Medal of Science

The National Medal of Science, established by Congress in 1959, is administered by the National Science Foundation. The medal honors the contributions made by outstanding individuals who have significantly advanced knowledge in the following fields: physics, biology, chemistry, mathematics, engineering, and sociology and other behavioral sciences.

1997 Medal of Science Recipients

William K. Estes, Emeritus Professor of Psychology at Harvard University in Cambridge, Mass., for fundamental theories of cognition and learning that transformed the field of experimental psychology and led to the development of quantitative cognitive science. His pioneering methods of quantitative modeling and insistence on rigor and precision established the standard for modern psychological science.

Darieane C. Hoffman, Director of the Glenn T. Seaborg Institute for Transactinium Science at Lawrence Berkeley National Laboratory in Berkeley, Calif., for her discovery of plutonium in nature and for her numerous contributions to our understanding of radioactive decay, notably of heavy nuclei. She is an internationally recognized leader in nuclear chemistry, particularly the topics of nuclear fission, properties of actinide elements, and reactions of heavy ions.

Harold S. Johnston, Emeritus Professor of Chemistry at the University of California in Berkeley, Calif., for understanding the chemistry of nitrogen compounds and their role and reactions in the Earth's stratosphere and in urban areas. His chemical and environmental research, along with his commitment to science in the service of society have resulted in pivotal contributions to the understanding and conservation of the Earth's atmosphere.

Marshall N. Rosenbluth, Professor of Physics at the University of California in San Diego, Calif., for his fundamental contributions to plasma physics, his leadership in the quest to develop controlled thermonuclear fusion, and his wide-ranging technical contributions to national security. His theoretical studies of the behavior of plasmas and their instabilities provided a significant foundation for the design and development of prototype devices for fusion power.

Martin Schwarzschild, Emeritus Higgins Professor of Astronomy (recently deceased) at Princeton University in Princeton, N.J., for his seminal contributions to the theory of the evolution of stars and his creative insights into the dynamics of galaxies. His research forms the basis of much of contemporary astrophysics, and the many students he trained are among today's leaders in the field.

James D. Watson, President of Cold Spring Harbor Laboratory in Cold Spring Harbor, N.Y., for five decades of scientific and intellectual leadership in molecular biology, starting with his co-discovery of the double-helix structure of DNA. He was a forceful advocate for the Human Genome Project and shaped that effort as the founding Director of the National Center for Human Genome Research.

Robert A. Weinberg, Member of the Whitehead Institute for Biomedical Research and Professor of Biology at the Massachusetts Institute of Technology in Cambridge, Mass., for crucial discoveries that clarified the genetic basis of human cancers. His work has influenced virtually all major aspects of our current understanding of the origins of cancer, from mutations affecting certain cellular genes, to the development of diagnostic tests for such mutations, to the description of the combination of events that produce cancer.

George W. Wetherill, Member of the Department of Terrestrial Magnetism of the Carnegie Institute of Washington in Washington, D.C., for his fundamental contributions to measuring astronomical time scales and understanding how Earth-like planets may be created in evolving solar systems. His pioneering achievements include developing precise radiometric techniques for dating the age of meteorites, and creating conceptual models and computer algorithms for the accretion of a few solid, terrestrial planets by collision with smaller neighbors.

Shing-Tung Yau, Professor of Mathematics at Harvard University in Cambridge, Mass., for profound contributions to mathematics that have had great impact on fields as diverse as topology, algebraic geometry, general relativity, and string theory. His work insightfully combines two different mathematical approaches and has resulted in the solution of several long-standing and important problems in mathematics.

The National Medal of Technology

The National Medal of Technology, established by Congress in 1980, is administered by the U.S. Department of Commerce. The medal is awarded for technological innovation and the advancement of U.S. global competitiveness. The medal also recognizes ground breaking contributions that commercialize a technology, create jobs, improve productivity, or stimulate the nation's growth and development in other ways.

1997 Medal of Technology Recipients

Norman R. Augustine, Chairman and CEO of Lockheed Martin Corp. in Bethesda, Md., for visionary leadership in maintaining the United States' pre-eminence in the aerospace industry, and for championing technical and managerial solutions to the challenges in civil and defense systems. **Category:** Technology Management.

Ray M. Dolby, Founder and Chairman, Dolby Laboratories, Inc., in San Francisco, Calif., for inventing technologies that have dramatically improved sound recording and reproduction, fostering their adoption worldwide, and maintaining a vision that has kept the world listening for more than 30 years. **Category:** General Product and Process Innovation; Technology Transfer.

Robert S. Ledley, Director of Medical Computing and Biophysics and Professor of Radiology, Physiology, and Biophysics at Georgetown University Medical Center in Washington, D.C., for pioneering contributions to biomedical computing and engineering, including the invention of the whole-body CT scanner, and his role in developing automated chromosome analysis for prenatal diagnosis of birth defects. **Category:** General Product and Process Innovation.

Team Award (Jointly): Vinton Cray, Senior Vice President of Data Architecture at MCI in Reston, Va., and **Robert E. Kahn,** President of the Corporation for National Research Initiatives in Reston, Va., for creating and sustaining development of Internet protocols and continuing to provide leadership in the emerging industry of internetworking. **Category:** Technology Transfer.

1997 Westinghouse Science Talent Search Winners

The Westinghouse Science Talent Search, now in its 56th year, is the nation's oldest and most prestigious science competition for high school students. The contest is sponsored by the Westinghouse Electric Corporation's Westinghouse Foundation and Science Service. Winners were announced at the National Academy of Sciences, March 10, 1997, in Washington, D.C. Awards are given to 40 finalists. The remaining 30 winners receive awards of $1,000 each.

Top Ten Winners

First Place: $40,000 scholarship, Adam Ezra Cohen, 17, Hunter College H.S., New York City, for developing a new method of photolithography, the means by which information-packed patterns are electrochemically etched onto microchips.

Second Place: $30,000 scholarship, Carrie Shilyansky, 15, San Marino (Calif.) H.S., for her study of "habituation," the lessening of an animal's response to repeated stimulations of fixed strength.

Third Place: $20,000 scholarship, mathematician Nicholas Karl Eriksson, 18, Sentinel H.S., Missoula, Mont., for his paper on the "partition function," the method for counting the ways a whole number can be divided into parts.

Fourth Place: $15,000 scholarship, mathematician Davesh Maulik, 17, Roslin High School, N.Y. for his algebra project that delved into symmetries of polynomial equations.

Fifth Place: $15,000 scholarship, Emily Beth Levy, 17, North Miami Beach (Fla.) Senior H.S., for devising a teaching method she calls "Brain Imagery," for improving reading comprehension in dyslexic children.

Sixth Place: $15,000 scholarship, Dev Edward Kumar, 17, Texas Academy of Math & Science, Denton, Tex., for his invention of an electric monitor that instantaneously measures the power efficiency of radio frequency devices such as pagers and cellular telephones.

Seventh Place: $10,000 scholarship, Ann Clair Seiferle-Valencia, 17, Farmington (N.M.) H.S., for her four-year archeological study of the Chacoan Anasazi people in Chaco Canyon.

Eighth Place: $10,000 scholarship, Dylan Micah Schwindt, 18, Montezuma-Cortez H.S., Cortez, Colo., for his analysis of trace elements in trees for a study of 13th-century Pueblo construction.

Ninth Place: $10,000 scholarship, Rose J. Payyapilli, 18, Midwood H.S. at Brooklyn College, Brooklyn, N.Y., for her four-year study of the mechanisms of blood platelet aggregation.

Tenth Place: $10,000 scholarship, Whitney Paige Bowe, 18, Lawrence H.S., Cedarhurst, N.Y. , for a study using jellyfish and algae to examine how symbiosis can be established.

Digital TV: The Good News and Bad News

Digital, or high-definition, TVs are the next generation of home entertainment technology. They offer large, extra-wide screens, similar to the proportions of movie screens, allowing viewers to see movies in their original format. They are not yet available.

For at least the next seven years, broadcasters will beam programs in both the new digital version and the conventional (analog) version we now use. The images received by your old sets will probably be in letterbox format, with dark borders at the top and bottom of the screen.

The bad news is that your present home TV will go the way of the tube radio and vinyl records. The FCC tentatively set 2006 as the date broadcasting analog signals end and only digital TV signals will be sent. This means that all the older sets will become obsolete. So will all the current VCRs. At least 95 percent of U.S.

households will eventually have to invest in new televisions if they want to continue seeing their programs and some 80 percent will eventually have to buy digital VCRs. Presumably, most people will try to keep their old sets in working order so that they can continue to view their collections of video tapes.

In all probability, consumers can continue to enjoy TV shows with their old sets by purchasing converter boxes that are expected to become available after the transition period. No one knows what the converters will cost because none have been manufactured yet. They may set you back as much as several hundred dollars.

The first digital sets should be on the market in 1998 and will cost somewhere between $1,000 to $3,000. However, it is expected that prices will drop to lower levels as sales of the new TVs rise.

Scientific Classification

Classification, or taxonomy, is a system of categorizing living things. There are seven divisions in the system:

(1) Kingdom
(2) Phylum or Division
(3) Class
(4) Order
(5) Family
(6) Genus
(7) Species

Kingdom is the broadest division. There is no consensus about the number of kingdoms, though most scientists support a four-kingdom (Animalia, Plantae, Protista, and Monera) or five-kingdom (Animalia, Plantae, Protista, Monera, and Fungi) system. The lowest, most basic division is species, which consists of organisms that resemble each other and are capable of interbreeding to produce fertile offspring. Species are identified by two names (binomial nomenclature). The first is the genus, the second is the species. For example, a leopard is *Panthera pardus*, a tiger is *Panthera tigris*. The first word is always capitalized, the second is not, and both should be italicized. Humans, of course, are *Homo sapiens*. □

Inventions and Discoveries

Roundup of Recent Discoveries

Was Three Company?

Past evidence uncovered in Israel and France has shown that Neanderthals lived on Earth at the same time as modern *Homo sapiens*. Neanderthals were found to have lived about 34,000 years ago near Auxerre in central France, and thus overlapped with modern humans, who have existed since c.100,000 years ago, according to excavations at Mount Carmel, Israel. Now the latest data suggests that the primitive *Homo erectus,* believed to have died out about 300,000 years ago, lived on the Indonesian island of Java until 27,000 to 53,000 years ago. It is not known if this surviving population of *H. erectus* actually had any contact with any of the other human species or could have interbred with them.

A team of scientists announced that their re-examination of *Homo erectus* skulls found at two sites on Java during the 1930s resulted in revised age estimates for these archaic humans. If their findings are verified, it means that the three human species once walked the Earth at the same time. It would also mean that *Homo sapiens* did not evolve from *Homo erectus* in Southeast Asia.

Stone Age High-Tech

German archeologists have found evidence that early humans were hunting big game at a much earlier date than thought possible. In early 1997, excavators in an open-pit mine site at Schoeningen found three intact heavy wooden spears about six-feet long that they believe are about 400,000 years old. The spears are balanced for javelin-like throwing to kill large animals. It was previously assumed that early humans were probably scavengers and foragers who lacked the sophistication and weapon-making know-how to hunt big game until some 40,000 years ago.

Paleolithic Nimrods

Recent evidence observed from studies of butchery marks on unearthed animal bones at a South African cave site indicates that *Homo sapiens* living there some 100,000 years ago were active hunters who probably coordinated their animal hunts and killed their prey in groups with primitive weapons.

Neanderthal Music Makers

The latest in the wave of intriguing discoveries about early humans is that the Neanderthals probably made music. Excavators at a cave near Idrija in northwestern Slovenia found a piece of a young cave bear's thighbone with four artificial holes drilled into it that were aligned in a straight line on one side. It appears to be a bone flute. Similar flute-type bone instruments have been found in Europe and Asia at modern human *(Homo sapien)* sites. It is not known if the hollow-bone object was ever used to make sounds or even music. Preliminary estimates date the artifact at between 43,000 and 82,000 years old. If the dating proves correct, it could be the oldest known musical instrument in the world.

Also in 1996, a 50,000 year-old mastodon tusk was found in the Neander Valley, Germany, that had sixteen aligned holes drilled into it, also suggesting that it might have been a Neanderthal musical instrument.

A Family Tree Grows in Ethiopia

The partial upper jaw of a 2.3 million-year old fossil of the genus *Homo*—the same lineage that humans belong to—was found in 1994 at a site in Hadar, Ethiopia. It was discovered in sediments containing nearby stone flakes and chopping tools dating from the same age. The prehistoric jawbone was dated 400,000 years older than the oldest known *Homo* fossil. The exciting find also marked the first time that a fossil *Homo* was unearthed in association with stone artifacts. Although the discovery was made two years earlier, it was not announced until 1996.

Even though the fossil has teeth similar in appearance to *H. habilis,* scientists cannot determine its genus unless its skull or more of its bones are found. It could be an unknown species of hominid.

No Family Ties

Analysis of ancient DNA extracted from the original Neanderthal skeletal remains found in the Neander Valley, Germany, in 1856, indicates that Neanderthals did not interbreed with modern humans. This remarkable achievement—the oldest DNA ever extracted from a hominid remains—was accomplished in 1997 by scientists at the University of Munich in Germany. Their unprecedented genetic findings imply that Neanderthals were not our ancestors but a distinct species who split off from the hominid line at a much earlier date than modern humans and reached their evolutionary end about 35,000 years ago.

Made in Siberia

A possible link between the Old World and the migration of Paleoindians to the New World has been found in Siberia. In 1966, American and Russian archaeologists discovered a two-inch fluted point—a pre-Columbian projectile found across North American and South America thought to be an invention of the Clovis culture—at a site called Uptar about 25 miles north of the Siberian city of Magadan. It was discovered with other artifacts that date to 8,300 years ago. Tools found at the site could be older, perhaps 11,000 to 12,000 years past.

Archaeologists agree that the earliest human inhabitants of the Americas crossed the Bering land bridge that connected Siberia and Alaska before rising sea levels submerged it about 11,000 years ago. If the Uptar point is older than 12,000 years, it may be a precursor to the technology used by the earliest inhabitants of the New World.

The important question is whether the fluted point was invented independently on both continents or whether the Clovis people brought the technology with them when they crossed the land bridge from Siberia into America.

Neolithic Neurosurgeons

A skull found at a site dating from c.5000 B.C.E. near the Alsatian town of Ensisheim shows the earliest known evidence of an attempt to operate on the brain. Prior to this discovery, the earliest evidence of successful trepanation dates from about 3000 B.C.E. The Ensisheim skull is that of a 50-year-old man who had twice undergone rudimentary surgery. At least the first operation was successful because the wound in his skull had healed before his death.

More Bird-like Dinosaurs

Two important archeological finds have added new evidence to the theory that birds are the direct descendants of dinosaurs.

In late 1996, scientists announced the discovery of a three-foot-long, 120-million-year-old fossil dinosaur in Liaoning province, northeastern China, with traces of a feathery down running from its head and down along its back and tail that suggest it could be a possible ancestor of birds. It is the first specimen of a dinosaur fossil with down-type feathers.

And more recently, a 90-million-year-old, seven-foot-long, meat-eating dinosaur that had bird-like arms was found in an ancient riverbed in Patagonia, Argentina. The dinosaur, was named *Unenlagia* ("half bird") *comahuensis* in the Mapuche Indian tongue by its discoverer. *Unenlagia* didn't actually fly, but could apparently fold its arms wing-like against its body and flap them like a bird. Its pelvis resembles that of the *Archaeopteryx*, the oldest known fossil bird dating from the Jurassic period about 145 million years ago.

T. Rex Dethroned

Researchers found more fossil bones belonging to the skull of the world's largest meat-eating dinosaur— *Giganotosaurus carolinii*—discovered in southern Argentina during 1993—and were able to determine that the huge creature was some 45-feet long and may have weighed almost 10 tons. It is larger than the long-time record holder, the *Tyrannosaurus rex*.

Giganotosaurus lived about 100 million years ago during the upper Cretaceous period and is not closely related to *T. rex*, who roamed the Earth 65 million years ago at the end of the Cretaceous period. The new predator is named after its discoverer, Rubin Carolini.

In addition to losing the honor of being the largest known flesh-eating dinosaur, scientists have found indications that the *Tyrannosaurus rex* occasionally suffered from painful bouts of gout.

Another contender for the largest carnivorous dinosaur is *Carcharodontosaurus* (shark-toothed) whose remains were uncovered in the Moroccan Sahara. Its skull measured over 5-feet long and it was estimated to be about 45-feet long.

An Earlier Origin For Life

The age of the Earth is generally accepted to be about 4.5 billion years old and some of the earliest known signs of life are fossilized bacteria found in a South African rock formation dating about 3.2 billion years ago. New research has detected evidence in rocks from southwestern Greenland, that suggests life on Earth began about 3.8 billion years ago, millions of years earlier than previously imagined.

Although no fossils were found in the Greenland rocks, researchers found chemical-biological evidence in them that could only have been produced by ancient life forms.

Rain from Space

Controversial data resulting from images taken by NASA's Polar spacecraft, launched in 1996, suggest that the Earth is bombarded by tens of thousands small icy comets every day. These house-size cosmic snowballs breakup upon entering the upper atmosphere, vaporize into clouds, and fall to Earth as rain. It is estimated that they add about one inch of water to the oceans every 10,000 years.

Some scientists even speculate that during the Earth's early violent history, giant comets bombarded the planet over millions of years, delivering enough water to form the oceans and possibly brought the simple organic compounds that developed into primal Earth life.

Antimatter Cloudburst

In 1997, astrophysicists announced their finding of an enormous cloud of antimatter, some 4,000-light years across and rising up some 3,500 light-years from someplace near the center of our Milky Way galaxy. (A light year is roughly 5.9 trillion miles.) The surprising discovery was made from observations using the Compton Gamma Ray Observatory that was launched from the space shuttle *Atlantis* on April 7, 1991.

Antimatter particles have the same characteristics as normal matter but have the opposite electrical charge of their ordinary matter counterparts. When antimatter collides with normal matter they annihilate each other, producing gamma rays. Not to worry, it is quite unlikely that particles of the antimatter cloud would ever reach the Earth.

Earliest New World Agriculture

The date for the first domestication of plants in ancient America has been moved back by several thousand years. New radiocarbon dating of squash seeds found in a Mexican cave once occupied by pre-Columbian humans in Guila Naquitz indicate that they are 10,000 years old. Corn (maize) and beans weren't cultivated in Mexico until about 4,000 years later.

Fido the Wolf

It was generally accepted that humans first tamed dogs about 14,000 years ago. However, new controversial evidence based on genetic analysis of material in wolf and dog breeds suggest that humans domesticated wolves as far back as 135,000 years ago and that modern dogs are the evolutionary descendants of these ancestral wolves.

Like Father, Like Daughter

Some scientists now think that girls get their woman's intuition and adept social skills from their father's genes whereas boys inherit their social ineptitude from their mothers. Boys only get one X chromosome from their mother and one Y from their father. Girls receive two X chromosomes, one from each parent. Researchers studying Turner's syndrome, a genetic disorder, found that those women who only get a single X chromosome from their mother as opposed to those who only received a single X from their father, tend to have more problems in social interactions. □

Inventions & Discoveries

See also Famous Firsts in Aviation, Nobel Prizes.

Adrenaline: (isolation of) John Jacob Abel, U.S., 1897

Aerosol can: Erik Rotheim, Norway, 1926

Air brake: George Westinghouse, U.S., 1868

Air conditioning: Willis Carrier, U.S., 1911

Airship: (non-rigid) Henri Giffard, France, 1852; (rigid) Ferdinand von Zeppelin, Germany, 1900

Aluminum manufacture: (by electrolytic action) Charles M. Hall, U.S., 1866

Anatomy, human: (*De fabrica corporis humani*, an illustrated systematic study of the human body) Andreas Vesalius, 1543; (comparative: parts of an organism are correlated to the functioning whole) Georges Cuvier, 1799–1805

Anesthetic: (first use of anesthetic—ether—on humans) Crawford W. Long, U.S., 1842

Antibiotics: (first demonstration of antibiotic effect) Louis Pasteur, Jules-François Joubert, France, 1887; (discovery of penicillin, first modern antibiotic) Alexander Fleming, England, 1928; (penicillin's infection-fighting properties) Howard Florey, Ernst Chain, England, 1940

Antiseptic: (surgery) Joseph Lister, England, 1867

Antitoxin, diphtheria: Emil von Behring, Germany, 1890

Appliances, electric: (fan) Schuyler Wheeler, U.S., 1882; (flatiron) Henry W. Seely, U.S., 1882; (stove) Hadaway, U.S., 1896; (washing machine) Alva Fisher, U.S., 1906

Aqualung: Jacques-Yves Cousteau, Emile Gagnan, France, 1943

Aspirin: Dr. Felix Hoffman, Germany, 1899

Astronomical calculator: The Antikythera device, first century B.C.E., Greece. Found off island of Antikythera in 1900

Atom: (nuclear model of) Ernest Rutherford, 1911

Atomic theory: (ancient) Leucippus, Democritus, Greece, c.500 B.C.E.; Lucretius, Rome c.100 B.C.E.; (modern) John Dalton, England, 1808

Automobile: (first with internal combustion engine, 250 rpm) Karl Benz, Germany, 1885; (first with practical high-speed internal combustion engine, 900 rpm) Gottlieb Daimler, Germany, 1885; (first true automobile, not carriage with motor) René Panhard, Emile Lavassor, France, 1891; (carburetor, spray) Charles E. Duryea, U.S., 1892

Autopilot: (for aircraft) Elmer A. Sperry, U.S., c.1910, first successful test, 1912, in a Curtiss flying boat

Avogadro's law: (equal volumes of all gases at the same temperature and pressure contain equal number of molecules) Amedeo Avogadro, 1811

Bacteria: Anton van Leeuwenhoek, The Netherlands, 1683

Balloon, hot-air: Joseph and Jacques Montgolfier, France, 1783

Barbed wire: (most popular) Joseph E. Glidden, U.S., 1873

Bar codes: (computer-scanned binary signal code): (retail trade use) Monarch Marking, U.S. 1970; (industrial use) Plessey Telecommunications, England, 1970

Barometer: Evangelista Torricelli, Italy, 1643

Bicycle: Karl D. von Sauerbronn, Germany, 1816; (first modern model) James Starley, England, 1884

Big Bang theory: (the universe originated with a huge explosion) Edwin Hubble, U.S., 1929; (confirmed) Arno Penzias, Robert Wilson, 1965

Blood, circulation of: William Harvey, England, 1628

Boyle's law: (relation between pressure and volume in gases) Robert Boyle, Ireland, 1662

Braille: Louis Braille, France, 1829

Bridges: (suspension, iron chains) James Finley, Pa., 1800; (wire suspension) Marc Seguin, Lyons, 1825; (truss) Ithiel Town, U.S., 1820

Bullet: (conical) Claude Minié, France, 1849

Calculating machine: (Abacus) China, c.190; (logarithms: made multiplying easier and thus calculators practical) John Napier, Scotland, 1614; (slide rule) William Oughtred, England, 1632; (digital calculator) Blaise Pascal, 1642; (multiplication machine) Gottfried Leibniz, Germany, 1671; (important 19th-century contributors to modern machine) Frank S. Baldwin, Jay R. Monroe, Dorr E. Felt, W. T. Ohdner, William Burroughs, all U.S.; ("analytical engine" design, included concepts of programming, taping) Charles Babbage, England, 1835.

Calculus: Isaac Newton, England, 1669; (differential calculus) Gottfried Leibniz, Germany, 1684

Camera: (hand-held) George Eastman, U.S., 1888; (Polaroid Land) Edwin Land, U.S., 1948.

"Canals" of Mars: Giovanni Schiaparelli, 1877

Carpet sweeper: Melville R. Bissell, U.S., 1876

Car radio: William Lear, Elmer Wavering, U.S., 1929, manufactured by Galvin Manufacturing Co., "Motorola"

Cells: (word used to describe microscopic examination of cork) Robert Hooke, 1665; (theory: cells are common structural and functional unit of all living organisms) Theodor Schwann, Matthias Schleiden, 1838–39

Cement, Portland: Joseph Aspdin, England, 1724

Chewing gum: (spruce-based) John Curtis, U.S., 1848; (chicle-based) Thomas Adams, U.S., 1870

Cholera bacterium: Robert Koch, Germany, 1883

Circuit, integrated: (theoretical) G.W.A. Dummer, England, 1952; (phase-shift oscillator) Jack S. Kilby, Texas Instruments, U.S., 1959

Classification of plants: (first modern, based on comparative study of forms) Andrea Cesalpino, 1583; (classification of plants and animals by genera and species) Carolus Linnaeus, Sweden, 1737–53

Clock, pendulum: Christian Huygens, The Netherlands, 1656

Coca-Cola: John Pemberton, U.S., 1886

Combustion: (nature of) Antoine Lavoisier, France, 1777

Compact disk: RCA, U.S., 1972

Computer: (differential analyzer, mechanically operated) Vannevar Bush, U.S., 1928; (Mark I, first information-processing digital computer) Howard Aiken, U.S., 1944; (ENIAC, Electronic Numerical Integrator and Calculator, first all-electronic) J. Presper Eckert, John W. Mauchly,

---

Science Web Sites

National Science Foundation: www.nsf.gov

National Academy of Science: www2.nas.edu/nas/

American Association for the Advancement of Science: www.aaas.org/

Federation of American Scientists: www.fas.org

The Franklin Institute of Science Museum: sln.fi.edu/tfi/welcome.html

Bio Online: www.bio.com

Science News Online: www.sciencenews.org

Popular Science: www.popsci.com

Periodic Table of Elements: mwanal.lanl.gov/cst/imagemap/periodic/periodic.html

Dinosauria Online: www.dinosauria.com/

Discovery Channel Online: www.discovery.com

Fermilab: www.fnal.gov/

Argonne National Laboratory: www.anl.gov/

American Geophysical Union: earth.agu.org/kosmos/homepage.html

Artificial Life Online: alife.santafe.edu/

Newton (for K–12 teachers and students): www.newton.dep.anl.gov

Field Museum (Chicago): www.bvis.uic.edu/museum/home.html

Santa Barbara Museum of Natural History: www.rain.org/~inverts/

Inventors Hall of Fame: www.invent.org/

The Smithsonian Web: www.si.edu/newstart.htm

U.S., 1946; (stored-program concept) John von Neumann, U.S., 1947

Concrete: (reinforced) Joseph Monier, 1877

Condensed milk: Gail Borden, U.S., 1853

Conditioned reflex: Ivan Pavlov, Russia, c.1910

Conservation of electric charge: (the total electric charge of the universe or any closed system is constant) Benjamin Franklin, U.S., 1751–54

Contagion theory: (infectious diseases caused by living agent transmitted from person to person) Girolamo Fracastoro, 1546

Continental drift theory: Antonio Snider-Pellegrini, 1858

Contraceptive, oral: Gregory Pincus, Min Chuch Chang, John Rock, Carl Djerassi, U.S., 1951

Converter, Bessemer: William Kelly, U.S., 1851

Cosmetics: Egypt, c.4000 B.C.E.

Cotton gin: Eli Whitney, U.S., 1793

Crossbow: China, c.300 B.C.E.

Cyclotron: Ernest O. Lawrence, U.S., 1931

Deuterium: (heavy hydrogen) Harold Urey, U.S., 1931

Disease: (chemicals in treatment of) crusaded by Philippus Paracelsus, 1527–1541; (germ theory) Louis Pasteur, 1862–77

DNA: (deoxyribonucleic acid) Friedrich Meischer, Germany, 1869; (determination of double-helical structure) F. H. Crick, England, James D. Watson, U.S., 1953

Dyes: (aniline, start of synthetic dye industry) William H. Perkin, 1856

Dynamite: Alfred Nobel, Sweden, 1867

Electric cooking utensil: (first) patented by St. George Lane-Fox, England, 1874

Electric generator (dynamo): (laboratory model) Michael Faraday, England, 1832; Joseph Henry, U.S., c.1832; (hand-driven model) Hippolyte Pixii, France, 1833; (alternating-current generator) Nikola Tesla, U.S., 1892

Electric lamp: (arc lamp) Sir Humphrey Davy, England, 1801; (fluorescent lamp) A.E. Becquerel, France, 1867; (incandescent lamp) Sir Joseph Swann, England, Thomas A. Edison, U.S., contemporaneously, 1870s; (carbon arc street lamp) Charles F. Brush, U.S., 1879; (first widely marketed incandescent lamp) Thomas A. Edison, U.S., 1879; (mercury vapor lamp) Peter Cooper Hewitt, U.S., 1903; (neon lamp) Georges Claude, France, 1911; (tungsten filament) Irving Langmuir, U.S., 1915

Thomas Alva Edison
(1847–1931) *Library of Congress*

Electrocardiography: demonstrated by Augustus Waller, 1887; (first practical device for recording activity of heart) Willem Einthoven, 1903, Dutch physiologist

Electromagnet: William Sturgeon, England, 1823

Electron: Sir Joseph J. Thompson, England, 1897

Elevator, passenger: (safety device permitting use by passengers) Elisha G. Otis, U.S., 1852; (elevator utilizing safety device) 1857

E = mc²: (equivalence of mass and energy) Albert Einstein, Switzerland, 1907

Engine, internal combustion: No single inventor. Fundamental theory established by Sadi Carnot, France, 1824; (two-stroke) Etienne Lenoir, France, 1860; (ideal operating cycle for four-stroke) Alphonse Beau de Roche, France, 1862; (operating four-stroke) Nikolaus Otto, Germany, 1876; (diesel) Rudolf Diesel, Germany, 1892; (rotary) Felix Wankel, Germany, 1956.

Evolution: (organic) Jean-Baptiste Lamarck, 1809; (by natural selection) Charles Darwin, England, 1859

Exclusion principle: (no two electrons in an atom can occupy the same energy level) Wolfgang Pauli, 1925

Expanding universe theory: (galaxies are receding from each other at speeds proportionate to their distance) George Lemaître, 1927

Falling bodies, law of: Galileo Galilei, Italy, 1590

Fermentation: (micro-organisms as cause of) Louis Pasteur, France, c.1860

Fiber optics: Narinder Kapany, England, 1955

Fibers, man-made: (nitrocellulose fibers treated to change flammable nitrocellulose to harmless cellulose, precursor of rayon) Sir Joseph Swann, England, 1883; (rayon) Count Hilaire de Chardonnet, France, 1889; (Celanese) Henry and Camille Dreyfuss, U.S., England, 1921; (research on polyesters and polyamides, basis for modern man-made fibers) U.S., England, Germany, 1930s; (nylon) Wallace H. Carothers, U.S., 1935

Frozen food: Clarence Birdseye, U.S. (1924)

Gene transfer: (human) Steven Rosenberg, R. Michael Blaese, W. French Anderson, U.S., 1989

Geometry, elements of: Euclid, Alexandria, Egypt, c.300 B.C.E.; (analytic) René Descartes, France; and Pierre de Fermat, Switzerland, 1637

Gravitation, law of: Sir Isaac Newton, England, c.1665 (published 1687)

Gunpowder: China, c.700

Gyrocompass: Elmer A. Sperry, U.S., 1905

Gyroscope: Léon Foucault, France, 1852

Halley's Comet: Edmund Halley, 1705

Heart, artificial: Dr. Robert Jarvik, U.S., 1982

Helicopter: (double rotor) Heinrich Focke, Germany, 1936; (single rotor) Igor Sikorsky, U.S., 1939

Helium first observed on sun: Sir Joseph Lockyer, England, 1868

Heredity, laws of: Gregor Mendel, Austria, 1865

Holograph: Dennis Gabor, England, 1947

Home videotape systems (VCR): (Betamax) Sony, Japan, 1975; (VHS) Matsushita, Japan, 1975

Ice age theory: Louis Agassiz, 1840

Induction, electric: Joseph Henry, U.S., 1828

Insulin: Sir Frederick G. Banting, J. J. R. MacLeod, Canada, 1922

Intelligence testing: Alfred Binet, Theodore Simon, France, 1905

Interferon: Alick Isaacs, Jean Lindemann, England, Switzerland, 1957

Isotopes: (concept of) Frederick Soddy, England, 1912; (stable isotopes) J. J. Thompson, England, 1913; (existence demonstrated by mass spectrography) Francis W. Ashton, 1919

Jet propulsion: (engine) Sir Frank Whittle, England, Hans von Ohain, Germany, 1936; (aircraft) *Heinkel He 178*, 1939

Kinetic theory of gases: (molecules of a gas are in a state of rapid motion) Daniel Bernoulli, 1738

Laser: (theoretical work on) Charles H. Townes, Arthur L. Schawlow, U.S., N. Basov, A. Prokhorov, U.S.S.R., 1958; (first working model) T. H. Maiman, U.S., 1960

Lawn mower: Edwin Budding, John Ferrabee, England, 1830 (31)

LCD (liquid crystal display): Hoffmann-La Roche, Switzerland, 1970

Lens, bifocal: Benjamin Franklin, U.S., c.1760

Leyden jar: (prototype electrical condenser) Canon E. G. von Kleist of Kamin, Pomerania, 1745; independently evolved by Cunaeus and P. van Musschenbroek, University of Leyden, Holland, 1746, from where name originated

Light, nature of: (wave theory) Christian Huygens, The Netherlands, 1678; (electromagnetic theory) James Clerk Maxwell, England, 1873

Light, speed of: (theory that light has finite velocity) Olaus Roemer, Denmark, 1675

Lightning rod: Benjamin Franklin, U.S., 1752

Locomotive: (steam powered) Richard Trevithick, England, 1804; (first practical, due to multiple-fire-tube boiler) George Stephenson, England, 1829; (largest steam-powered) Union Pacific's "Big Boy," U.S., 1941

Lock, cylinder: Linus Yale, U.S., 1851

Loom: (horizontal, two-beamed) Egypt, c.4400 B.C.E.;(Jacquard drawloom, pattern controlled by punch cards) Jacques de Vaucanson, France, 1745, Joseph-Marie Jacquard, 1801; (flying shuttle) John Kay, England, 1733; (power-driven loom) Edmund Cartwright, England, 1785

Machine gun: James Puckle, England, 1718; Richard J. Gatling, U.S., 1861

Magnet, Earth is: William Gilbert, 1600

Match: (phosphorus) François Derosne, France, 1816; (friction) Charles Sauria, France, 1831; (safety) J. E. Lundstrom, Sweden, 1855

Measles vaccine: John F. Enders, Thomas Peebles, U.S., 1953

Metric system: revolutionary government of France, 1790–1801

Microphone: Charles Wheatstone, England, 1827

Microscope: (compound) Zacharias Janssen, The Netherlands, 1590; (electron) Vladimir Zworykin et al., U.S., Canada, Germany, 1932–1939

Microwave oven: Percy Spencer, U.S., 1947

Motion, laws of: Isaac Newton, England, 1687

Motion pictures: Thomas A. Edison, U.S., 1893

Motion pictures, sound: Product of various inventions. First picture with synchronized musical score: *Don Juan*, 1926; with spoken dialogue: *The Jazz Singer*, 1927; both Warner Bros.

Motor, electric: Michael Faraday, England, 1822; (alternating-current) Nikola Tesla, U.S., 1892

Motorcycle: (motor tricycle) Edward Butler, England, 1884; (gasoline-engine motorcycle) Gottlieb Daimler, Germany, 1885

National Science Foundation: established by U.S. Congress, 1950 based on report by Vannevar Bush, 1945

Neptune: (discovery of) Johann Galle, 1846

Neptunium: (first transuranic element, synthesis of) Edward M. McMillan, Philip H. Abelson, U.S., 1940

Neutron: James Chadwick, England, 1932

Neutron-induced radiation: Enrico Fermi et al., Italy, 1934

Nitroglycerin: Ascanio Sobrero, Italy, 1846

Nuclear fission: Otto Hahn, Fritz Strassmann, Germany, 1938

Nuclear reactor: Enrico Fermi, et al., 1942

Ohm's law: (relationship between strength of electric current, electromotive force, and circuit resistance) Georg S. Ohm, Germany, 1827

Oil well: Edwin L. Drake, Titusville, Pa., 1859

Oxygen: (isolation of) Joseph Priestley, 1774; Carl Scheele, 1773

Ozone: Christian Schöonbein, Germany, 1839

Pacemaker: (internal) Clarence W. Lillehie, Earl Bakk, U.S., 1957

Paper China, c.100 B.C.E.

Parachute: Louis S. Lenormand, France, 1783

Pen: (fountain) Lewis E. Waterman, U.S., 1884; (ball-point, for marking on rough surfaces) John H. Loud, U.S., 1888; (ball-point, for handwriting) Lazlo Biro, Argentina, 1944

Periodic law: (that properties of elements are functions of their atomic weights) Dmitri Mendeleev, Russia, 1869

Periodic table: (arrangement of chemical elements based on periodic law) Dmitri Mendeleev, Russia, 1869

Phonograph: Thomas A. Edison, U.S., 1877

Photography: (first paper negative, first photograph, on metal) Joseph Nicéphore Niepce, France, 1816–1827; (discovery of fixative powers of hyposulfite of soda) Sir John Herschel, England, 1819; (first direct positive image on silver plate, the daguerreotype) Louis Daguerre, based on work with Niepce, France, 1839; (first paper negative from which a number of positive prints could be made) William Talbot, England, 1841. Work of these four men, taken together, forms basis for all modern photography. (First color images) Alexandre Becquerel, Claude Niepce de Saint-Victor, France, 1848–60; (commercial color film with three emulsion layers, Kodachrome) U.S., 1935.

Photovoltaic effect: (light falling on certain materials can produce electricity) Edmund Becquerel, France, 1839

Piano: (Hammerklavier) Bartolommeo Cristofori, Italy, 1709; (pianoforte with sustaining and damper pedals) John Broadwood, England, 1873

Planetary motion, laws of: Johannes Kepler, Germany, 1609, 1619

Plant respiration and photosynthesis: Jan Ingenhousz, 1779

Plastics: (first material, nitrocellulose softened by vegetable oil, camphor, precursor to Celluloid) Alexander Parkes, England, 1855; (Celluloid, involving recognition of vital effect of camphor) John W. Hyatt, U.S., 1869; (Bakelite, first completely synthetic plastic) Leo H. Baekeland, U.S., 1910; (theoretical background of macromolecules and process of polymerization on which modern plastics industry rests) Hermann Staudinger, Germany, 1922.

Plate tectonics: Alfred Wegener, Germany, 1912–15

Plow, forked: Mesopotamia, before 3000 B.C.E.

Plutonium, synthesis of: Glenn T. Seaborg, Edwin M. McMillan, Arthur C. Wahl, Joseph W. Kennedy, U.S., 1941

Polio, vaccine against: (vaccine made from dead virus strains) Jonas E. Salk, U.S., 1954; (vaccine made from live virus strains) Albert Sabin, U.S., 1960

Positron: Carl D. Anderson, U.S., 1932

Pressure cooker: (early version) Denis Papin, France, 1679

Printing: (block) Japan, c.700; (movable type) Korea, c.1400; Johann Gutenberg, Germany, c.1450 (lithography, offset) Aloys Senefelder, Germany, 1796; (rotary press) Richard Hoe, U.S., 1844; (linotype) Ottmar Mergenthaler, U.S., 1884

Probability theory: René Descartes, France; and Pierre de Fermat, Switzerland, 1654

Johann Gutenberg (c. 1400–1468)

Proton: Ernest Rutherford, England, 1919

Psychoanalysis: Sigmund Freud, Austria, c.1904

Pulsars: Jocelyn Bell Bunnell, England, 1968

Quantum theory: (general) Max Planck, Germany, 1900; (sub-atomic) Niels Bohr, Denmark, 1913; (quantum mechanics) Werner Heisenberg, Erwin Schrödinger, Germany, 1925

Quarks: Jerome Friedman, Henry Kendall, Richard Taylor, U.S. (1967)

Quasars: Marten Schmidt, U.S., 1963

Rabies immunization: Louis Pasteur, France, 1885

Radar: (limited to one-mile range) Christian Hulsmeyer, Germany, 1904; (pulse modulation, used for measuring height of ionosphere) Gregory Breit, Merle Tuve, U.S., 1925; (first practical radar—radio detection and ranging) Sir Robert Watson-Watt, England, 1934–35

Radio: (electromagnetism, theory of) James Clerk Maxwell, England, 1873; (spark coil, generator of electromagnetic waves) Henrich Hertz, Germany, 1886; (first practical system of wireless telegraphy) Guglielmo Marconi, Italy, 1895; (vacuum electron tube, basis for radio telephony) Sir John Fleming, England, 1904; (triode amplifying tube) Lee de Forest, U.S., 1906; (regenerative circuit, allowing long-distance sound reception) Edwin H. Armstrong, U.S., 1912; (frequency modulation—FM) Edwin H. Armstrong, U.S., 1933

Radioactivity: (X-rays) Wilhelm K. Roentgen, Germany, 1895; (radioactivity of uranium) Henri Becquerel, France, 1896; (radioactive elements, radium and polonium in uranium ore) Marie Sklodowska-Curie, Pierre Curie, France, 1898; (classification of alpha and beta particle radiation) Pierre Curie, France, 1900; (gamma radiation) Paul-Ulrich Villard, France, 1900; (carbon dating) Willard F. Libby et al., U.S., 1955

Radio signals, extraterrestrial: first known radio noise signals were received by U.S. engineer, Karl Jansky, originating from the Galactic Center, 1931.

Radio waves: (cosmic sources, led to radio astronomy) Karl Jansky, 1932

Razor: (safety, successfully marketed) King Gillette, U.S., 1901; (electric) Jacob Schick, U.S., 1928(31)

Reaper: Cyrus McCormick, U.S., 1834

Refrigerator: Alexander Twining, U.S., James Harrison, Australia, 1850; (first with a compressor device) the Domelse, Chicago, U.S., 1913

Refrigerator ship: (first) the *Frigorifique*, 1877, cooling unit designed by Charles Teller, France

Relativity: (special and general theories of) Albert Einstein, Switzerland, Germany, U.S., 1905–53

Revolver: Samuel Colt, U.S., 1835

Richter scale: Charles F. Richter, U.S., 1935

Rifle: (muzzle-loaded) Italy, Germany, c1475; (breech-loaded) England, France, Germany, U.S., c.1866; (bolt-action) Paul von Mauser, Germany, 1889; (automatic) John Browning, U.S., 1918

Rocket: (liquid-fueled) Robert Goddard, U.S., 1926

Roller bearing: (wooden for cartwheel) Germany or France, c.100 B.C.E.

Rotation of earth: Jean Bernard Foucault, 1851

Royal Observatory, Greenwich: established by Charles II of England, John Flamsteed first Astronomer Royal

Rubber: (vulcanization process) Charles Goodyear, U.S., 1839

Saccharin: Constantine Fuhlberg, Ira Remsen, U.S., 1879

Safety pin: Walter Hunt, U.S., 1849

Saturn, ring around: Christian Huygens, The Netherlands, 1659

"Scotch" tape: Richard Drew, U.S., 1929

Screw propeller: Sir Francis P. Smith, England, 1836; John Ericsson, England, worked independently of and simultaneously with Smith, 1837

Seismograph: (first accurate) John Milne, 1880

Sewing machine: Elias Howe, U.S., 1846; (continuous stitch) Isaac Singer, U.S., 1851

Solar energy: first realistic application of solar energy using parabolic solar reflector to drive caloric engine on steam boiler, Jon Ericsson, 1860s

Solar system, universe: (sun-centered universe) Nicolaus Copernicus, Warsaw, 1543; (establishment of planetary orbits as elliptical) Johannes Kepler, Germany, 1609; (infinity of universe) Giordano Bruno, Italian monk, 1584

Spectrum: (heterogeneity of light) Sir Isaac Newton, England, 1665–66

Spectrum analysis: Gustav Kirchoff, Robert Bunsen, 1859

Spermatozoa: Anton van Leeuwenhoek, The Netherlands, 1683

Spinning: (spinning wheel) India, introduced to Europe in Middle Ages; (Saxony wheel, continuous spinning of wool or cotton yarn) England, c.1500–1600; (spinning jenny) James Hargreaves, England, 1764; (spinning frame) Sir Richard Arkwright, England, 1769; (spinning mule, completed mechanization of spinning, permitting production of yarn to keep up with demands of modern looms) Samuel Crompton, England, 1779

Star catalog: (first modern) Tycho Brahe, 1572

Steam engine: (first commercial version based on principles of French physicist Denis Papin) Thomas Savery, England, 1639; (atmospheric steam engine) Thomas Newcomen, England, 1705; (steam engine for pumping water from collieries) Savery, Newcomen, 1725; (modern condensing, doubleacting) James Watt, England, 1782

Steamship: Claude de Jouffroy d'Abbans, France, 1783; James Rumsey, U.S., 1787; John Fitch, U.S., 1790. All preceded Robert Fulton, U.S., 1807, credited with launching first commercially successful steamship

Stethoscope: René Laënnec, 1819

Sulfa drugs: (parent compound, para-aminobenzenesulfanomide) Paul Gelmo, Austria, 1908; (antibacterial activity) Gerhard Domagk, Germany, 1935

Superconductivity: (theory) Bardeen, Cooper, Scheiffer, U.S., 1957

Symbolic logic: George Boole, 1854; (modern) Bertrand Russell, Alfred North Whitehead, 1910–13

Tank, military: Sir Ernest Swinton, England, 1914

Tape recorder: (magnetic steel tape) Valdemar Poulsen, Denmark, 1899

Teflon: DuPont, U.S., 1943

Samuel F.B. Morse (1791–1872)
Library of Congress

Telegraph: Samuel F. B. Morse, U.S., 1837

Telephone: Alexander Graham Bell, U.S., 1876

Telescope: Hans Lippershey, The Netherlands, 1608; (astronomical) Galileo Galilei, Italy, 1609; (reflecting) Isaac Newton, England, 1668

Television: (Iconoscope—T.V. camera table), Vladimir Zworkin, U.S., 1923, and also kinescope (cathode ray tube), 1928; (mechanical disk-scanning method) successfully demonstrated by J.K. Baird, England, C.F. Jenkins, U.S., 1926; (first all-electric television image), 1927, Philo T. Farnsworth, U.S; (color, mechanical disk) Baird, 1928; (color, compatible with black and white) George Valensi, France, 1938; (color, sequential rotating filter) Peter Goldmark, U.S., first introduced, 1951; (color, compatible with black and white) commercially introduced in U.S., National Television Systems Committee, 1953

Thermodynamics: (first law: energy cannot be created or destroyed, only converted from one form to another) Julius von Mayer, Germany, 1842; James Joule, England, 1843; (second law: heat cannot of itself pass from a colder to a warmer body) Rudolph Clausius, Germany, 1850; (third law: the entropy of ordered solids reaches zero at the absolute zero of temperature) Walter Nernst, Germany, 1918

Thermometer: (open-column) Galileo Galilei, c.1593; (clinical) Santorio Santorio, Padua, c.1615; (mercury, also Fahrenheit scale) Gabriel D. Fahrenheit, Germany, 1714; (centigrade scale) Anders Celsius, Sweden, 1742; (absolute-temperature, or Kelvin, scale) William Thompson, Lord Kelvin, England, 1848

Tire, pneumatic: Robert W. Thompson, England, 1845; (bicycle tire) John B. Dunlop, Northern Ireland, 1888

Toilet, flush: Product of Minoan civilization, Crete, c.2000 B.C.E. Alleged invention by "Thomas Crapper" is untrue.

Tractor: Benjamin Holt, U.S., 1900

Transformer, electric: William Stanley, U.S., 1885

Transistor: John Bardeen, William Shockley, Walter Brattain, U.S., 1948

Tuberculosis bacterium: Robert Koch, Germany, 1882

Typewriter: Christopher Sholes, Carlos Glidden, U.S., 1867

Uncertainty principle: (that position and velocity of an object cannot both be measured exactly, at the same time) Werner Heisenberg, Germany, 1927

Uranus: (first planet discovered in recorded history) William Herschel, 1781

Vaccination: Edward Jenner, England, 1796

Vacuum cleaner: (manually operated) Ives W. McGaffey, 1869; (electric) Hubert C. Booth, England, 1901; (upright) J. Murray Spangler, U.S., 1907

Van Allen (radiation) Belt: (around the earth) James Van Allen, U.S., 1958

Video disk: Philips Co., The Netherlands, 1972

Vitamins: (hypothesis of disease deficiency) Sir F. G. Hopkins, Casimir Funk, England, 1912; (vitamin A) Elmer V. McCollum, M. Davis, U.S., 1912–14; (vitamin B) Elmer V. McCollum, U.S., 1915–16; (thiamin, B_1) Casimir Funk, England, 1912; (riboflavin, B_2) D. T. Smith, E. G. Hendrick, U.S., 1926; (niacin) Conrad Elvehjem, U.S., 1937; (B_6) Paul Gyorgy, U.S., 1934; (vitamin C) C. A. Hoist, T. Froelich, Norway, 1912; (vitamin D) Elmer V. McCollum, U.S., 1922; (folic acid) Lucy Wills, England, 1933

Voltaic pile: (forerunner of modern battery, first source of continuous electric current) Alessandro Volta, 1800

Wallpaper: Europe, 16th and 17th century

Wassermann test: (for syphilis) August von Wassermann, Germany, 1906

Wheel: (cart, solid wood) Mesopotamia, c.3800–3600 B.C.E.

Windmill: Persia, c.600

Xerography: Chester Carlson, U.S., 1938

Zero: India, c.600; (absolute zero temperature, cessation of all molecular energy) William Thompson, Lord Kelvin, England, 1848

Zipper: W.L. Judson, U.S., 1891

The National Inventors Hall of Fame

The Inventors Hall of Fame, located in Akron, Ohio, was established in 1973 by the National Council of Patent Law Associations, now the National Council of Intellectual Property Law Associations, and the Patent and Trademark Office of the U.S. Department of Commerce. The year of induction is in parentheses at the end of the entry

The 1997 Class of Inductees

Acheson, Goodrich Richard, 1856–1931 (Washington, Penn.) CARBORUNDUM. Carborundum is the hardest surface made by humans and is second only to the diamond's hardness. Acheson created carborundum (silicon-carbide) by electronically fusing clay and carbon. His invention resulted in a search for a highly effective and durable abrasive needed by industry to manufacture precision-ground interchangeable metal parts. A by-product of carborundum was graphite, which proved to be useful as a lubricant. The U.S. Patent Office once named this discovery as one of the inventions most responsible for the industrial age.

Babcock, George H., 1832–1893 and **Wilcox, Stephen**, 1830–1893 WATER TUBE STEAM BOILER. Thomas Addison once proclaimed it to be ". . . the best boiler God has permitted man yet to make." Even today, nearly half of the electricity produced in the United States is produced from water tube boilers that are based on the original Babcock and Wilcox design.

Bower, Robert W., 1936– (Santa Monica, Calif.) FIELD-EFFECT DEVICE WITH INSULATED GATES. Also known as the Self-Aligned Gate MOS-FET (metal oxide semiconductor field effect transmitter). Patented in 1969, Bower's invention made possible the fast electronic circuits that are now commonplace in computer and other electronic products. He patented the device while working at the Hughes Research Laboratories in Malibu, California. Bower is currently a professor at the University of California at Davis, where he is focused on making three-dimensional microelectronics a reality.

Cray, Seymour, 1925–1996 (Chippewa Falls, Wis.) COMPUTER VECTOR REGISTER PROCESSING. Known as the supercomputer. Supercomputers are defined as computers that have extraordinary high numbers of integrated chips that allow them to process information at much higher speeds than other computers. The first Cray supercomputer, the Cray-1, was unveiled in 1976. In 1985, it was followed by the Cray-2 which was 10 times faster and featured circuits of gallium arsenide instead of silicon chips. Cray was a co-founder of Control Data Corporation in 1957 and later started Cray Research in 1972. His desire to develop the Cray 3 led him to start Cray Computer in 1988.

Dennard, Robert Heath, 1932– (Terrell, Tex.) ONE-TRANSISTOR DYNAMIC RANDOM ACCESS MEMORY. Dr. Dennard's invention of DRAM, most often called RAM, was a core development in today's computer industry and is one of the most commonly used devices in the world. RAM is the system which has supplied the memory needs of all computers since the early 1970s. Before his invention, computers were too large and heavy to be installed in private homes or desk tops. In fact, they required separate storage space and air conditioning to cool them. The device was patented in 1968 by Dennard who was a computer engineer with IBM. Since 1963, he has been a fellow at IBM's Thomas Watson Research Center in Yorktown Heights, New York.

Dean, Mark, 1957– (Jefferson City, Tenn.) and **Moeller, Dennis** 1950– (St. Louis, Mo.) MICRO-COMPUTER WITH BUS CONTROL MEANS FOR PERIPHERAL DEVICES. The work of these IBM scientists is what allows IBM and IBM-compatible computer components to communicate with each other very rapidly. This development made personal computers fast and efficient for the first time. The first commercial use of their development was marketed in 1984 in the IBM PC/AT, and is currently being used in 40 million personal computers each year. Dr. Dean was the first African-American with an IBM fellowship and is Vice President of Performance for the RS/6000 Division in Austin, Texas. Moller is a senior technical staff member of the IBM Consumer Division. □

Patents and Trademarks, 1980 to 1994

(in thousands)

Covers patents issued to citizens of the United States and residents of foreign countries.

Items	1980	1985	1990	1991	1992	1993	1994
Patent applications filed	113.0	127.1	176.7	178.4	187.2	189.4	206.9
Inventions	104.3	117.0	164.5	164.3	173.1	174.7	189.9
Designs	7.8	9.6	11.3	13.1	13.1	13.6	15.8
Botanical plants	0.2	0.2	0.4	0.4	0.4	0.4	0.5
Reissues	0.6	0.3	0.5	0.6	0.6	0.6	0.7
Patents issued	66.2	77.3	99.2	106.8	107.4	109.7	113.6
Inventions	61.8	71.7	90.4	96.5	97.4	98.3	101.7
Individuals	13.8	12.9	17.3	18.1	17.3	16.5	17.3
Corporations:							
United States	27.7	31.2	36.1	39.2	40.3	41.8	44.0
Foreign[1]	19.1	26.4	36.0	38.1	38.7	38.8	38.8
U.S. Government	1.2	1.1	1.0	1.2	1.2	1.2	1.3
Designs	3.9	5.1	8.0	9.6	9.3	10.6	11.1
Botanical plants	0.1	0.2	0.3	0.4	0.3	0.4	0.5
Reissues	0.3	0.3	0.4	0.3	0.4	0.3	0.3
U.S. residents[2]	40.8	43.3	52.8	57.7	58.7	61.1	64.2
Foreign country residents[2]	25.4	33.9	46.2	49.0	48.7	48.7	49.3
Percent of total	38.4	43.9	46.7	46.0	45.3	44.3	43.4
Other published documents[3]	(z)	(z)	0.1	0.1	0.1	0.1	0.1
Trademarks:							
Applications filed	46.8	65.1	127.3	123.3	127.8	150.4	161.1
Issued	24.7	71.7	60.8	52.4	85.8	86.9	70.1
Trademarks	18.9	65.8	53.6	46.6	80.2	80.6	63.9
Trademark renewals	5.9	5.9	7.2	5.8	5.6	6.3	6.2

1. Includes patents to foreign governments. 2. Includes patents for inventions, designs, botanical plants, and reissues. 3. Includes Defensive Publications, a practice which began in November 1968 and ended in July 1986; and Statutory Invention Registrations, the current practice, which began May 1985. These documents are patent applications, which are published to provide the defensive properties of a patent, but do not have the enforceable rights of a patent. *Source:* U.S. Patent and Trademark Office. Fiscal-year figures are published in the *Commissioner of Patents and Trademarks Annual Report.*

Top Patent Earners in 1996

Source: U.S. Patent and Trademark Office

Listed below are the organizations that received the most patents for inventions (i.e., utility patents) during the 1996 calendar year. Utility patents, the most common type, are granted for any new and useful process, machine, article of manufacture, or composition of matter. For the fourth straight year, International Business Machines Corporation (IBM) received more utility patents that any other non-federal organization. IBM's 1,867 patents in 1996 represent a 35-percent increase over its patent total for the previous year and is a new record for the most patents ever granted to an non-government organization in a single year.

Canon Kabushiki Kaisha was second with 1,541 utility patents, a 42-percent increase in its patent total over the previous year. Motorola, Inc., ranked third with 1,064 patents. The remaining organizations in the top eleven, given in order of rank, were: NEC Corporation (1,043), Hitachi, Ltd. (963), Mitsubishi Denki Kabushiki Kaisha (934); U.S. Government (923), Toshiba Corporation (914), Fujitsu Limited (869), Sony Corporation (855), and Matsushita Electric Industrial Co. Ltd. (841).

The U.S. Patent Office granted a total of 121,806 patents in 1996, of which 66,716 patents were issued to residents of the United States and 50,159 patents were issued to residents of foreign countries.

In 1996, Japan led the list of top 10 foreign countries whose residents received the most U.S. patents with 22,979 granted. Germany was second with 6,898, and France ranked third (2,972). The others in order of ranking were United Kingdom (2,668), Canada (2,444), Taiwan (2,300), Italy (1,338), South Korea (1,428), Switzerland (1,141), and Sweden (904) □

Roses Are Inventions

A small fraction of all the patents issued in 1996 were for plants—362 of them. The first plant patent awarded by the U.S. Patent and Trademark Office was issued to New Jersey resident Harry Bosenberg on August 18, 1931, for "New Dawn," a plant which bears champagne-colored roses. Red-colored roses came much later; the first one was not patented until 1950. Since that time, over 1,870 rose patents have been issued, of which 400 mention the word red.

Plant patents can be granted to anyone who invents or discovers and reproduces any distinct and new variety of plant. Two individuals at the Patent Office devote their professional expertise to examining plant patent applications. And, yes, both of them have New Dawn Roses, inherited from a predecessor, planted in their backyards. □

Computers

"Bug Hunting" Emerges as Hot Campus Sport

By Don Clark, *The Wall Street Journal*

When three Massachusetts college students became instant celebrities in March 1997 by discovering a nasty security hole in Microsoft Corp.'s Internet software, the news got David Ross's competitive juices flowing. "I was a little bit annoyed with myself that I hadn't figured out the same bug," says Mr. Ross, a 20-year-old computer science major at the University of Maryland. Two days later, Mr. Ross found a similar flaw in the same Microsoft program, bringing a wave of headlines and two job offers. "It's worked out pretty well," Mr. Ross says.

Finding a flaw in a popular software system is fast becoming a route to fame, academic distinction, and even offers of employment. The new bug hunters are mostly college or university students. Many are motivated by intellectual curiosity and a desire to protect consumers against computer crooks and hackers. But the discoveries also make good copy for the national media and are turning out to be a great way for students to get noticed in academia and the industry.

Of course, students aren't the only ones finding bugs. Also in March, David de Vitry, a software developer at the advertising agency Poppe Tyson Interactive, posted a warning on the Internet about an apparent flaw that could allow unscrupulous people to read electronic mail of Web surfers who use Netscape Communications Corp.'s browser along with Macromedia Inc. software called Shockwave. Netscape said the next day that new versions will fix the problem.

For the most part, Microsoft and other software makers say they welcome the outside help in finding flaws. Their main gripe is the sheer volume of bug claims,

many of which don't turn out to be serious problems. "I get all kinds of e-mail saying I've found a security issue, but 99 times out of 100, it's error or confusion," says Marianne Mueller, a staff engineer for Sun Microsystems Inc. One recent Web posting by British students, she claims, publicized a problem that was fixed a long time ago. "It was fairly pointless, but they made it sound like civilization as we know it would come to an end," she says.

For college students and their advisers, publicity can raise tricky questions. They must decide how to disclose security gaps without helping pranksters and saboteurs. They also want to build cooperative relationships with companies, without jeopardizing their reputations as objective, independent researchers. A research group at Princeton University, for example, publicizes flaws associated with Sun Microsystems' hit Java programming language and Microsoft software, while getting funding from both.

"I've had a bunch of talks with ethicists at Princeton," says Edward Felten, a computer science professor in charge of the Princeton group. "We have to find our own rules," he says. Prof. Felten won't disclose the companies' financial contributions. He says the group typically informs them before publishing news about bugs, but that the companies have no right to censor the group's research.

The issues aren't only academic. Web sites are becoming engines of commerce as well as amusement, and browser programs now run small programs that bring many new possibilities for misuse. In January, a group of young German hackers demonstrated how a Microsoft technology called ActiveX and Intuit Inc.'s Quicken software theoretically could be misused to make unauthorized bank transfers. (Microsoft says safeguards in its browser software usually block this type of malicious software activity.)

Paul Greene, one of the students at Worcester Polytechnic Institute who found the Microsoft flaw in February, wasn't looking for trouble when he stumbled across his bug. The 28-year-old senior, a Navy veteran, was working on a class project, using a feature in Windows 95 called "shortcuts" that works with Microsoft's Internet Explorer browser. He discovered that hackers could use this feature to booby-trap a Web page; when an unsuspecting Web surfer visited the page, the shortcut could start a program running on the surfer's own computer.

Mr. Greene and two other students, Geoffrey Elliott and Brian Morin, quickly demonstrated that the flaw could be used to wipe out the Web surfer's hard drive, among other malicious tricks. "We were up till 4 in the morning just going over what could be done," Mr. Greene recalls.

On Thursday, February 26, the students sent e-mail messages about the problem to Microsoft Chairman Bill Gates, and to the company's bug-reporting service. They got no response; they later learned that Mr. Gates was traveling.

Finding Flaws

Recent software security discoveries[*]

February 1996: Princeton's Drew Dean, Ed Felten, and Dan Wallach describe a way of attacking Sun Microsystems' Java technology by spoofing the identity of computers on the Internet.

March 1996: The Princeton team describes a different Java attack, which could allow someone to booby-trap a Web page so that it would read or delete files of anyone visiting the page.

September 1996: Berkeley graduate students Ian Goldberg and David Wagner discover a flaw in the technology of Netscape's Web browser software that protects the privacy of credit-card purchases.

January 1997: Mr. Goldberg takes just 3½ hours to crack the encryption code that the U.S. government lets companies export.

January 1997: German computer hackers show how a Microsoft Internet technology could be used to make unauthorized bank transfers.

March 1997: Students at Worcester Polytechnic Institute find a major security flaw in Microsoft's World Wide Web software, prompting similar discoveries at the University of Maryland and Massachusetts Institute of Technology.

[*] In most cases, the companies issued modified software to fix the problems.

So the students went public on a Web site they dubbed Cybersnot Industries, using the name for a kids' software company that Mr. Elliott once dreamed of starting. By the following Monday, the news was racing around Web-based news services. By Tuesday, national media had picked up the story.

The small Worcester campus was assaulted by interview requests from newspapers, radio, and TV networks. MSNBC, the joint venture of General Electric Co.'s NBC and Microsoft, offered to pick the students up in a limousine and take them to a Watertown, Mass., studio to broadcast an interview nationwide. Because the operation is related to Microsoft, "I thought they might be sending a car to dump me off in the middle of the woods," Mr. Greene jokes.

In fact, Microsoft posted software to correct the flaw, and gave the Worcester students an opportunity to test it before releasing it world-wide. Mr. Greene says one Microsoft executive mentioned internship possibilities at the company. The incident generated two other potential job offers, as well.

The news also reverberated in computer science departments and dorm rooms around the country. Maryland's Mr. Ross and two colleagues found a similar way to run a program without warning on some PCs and some versions of Microsoft's Internet Explorer. Two Massachusetts Institute of Technology students, Chris Rioux and Tim Macinta, used the same principles to find a third bug the same week that could also damage a system that called up a booby-trapped Web page. Microsoft has since posted software to fix all three.

Java also has spawned swarms of security watchdogs, partly because it has been promoted as particularly safe for distributing small Internet programs called applets. Princeton's Secure Internet Programming group has found numerous flaws since Java was released in 1995. "There have been instances when I've received more than 1,000 e-mails a day, after we find a flaw," says Prof. Felten, who has co-authored a book called *Java Security: Hostile Applets, Holes & Antidotes*.

Despite generating bad press for Netscape, Dan Wallach, co-founder of the Princeton group, was bold enough to ask the software company for an internship. He spent the summer helping Netscape develop a scheme for digitally authenticating software delivered over the Internet.

"In the beginning we didn't know anybody at the companies, so we just released our technical papers," Mr. Wallach says. "Now we call up people we know and say 'Hey, we broke it again.'" ☐

Connecting to the Internet: A Beginner's Guide

As if actually buying the computer and getting it out of the box weren't enough, now you have to sort through the myriad of disks and flyers offering to make your computer an onramp to the information superhighway. Most computers purchased today come with offers from Internet service providers, and have preinstalled software to connect you with online services such as America Online, CompuServe, Microsoft Network, and Prodigy. Which should you choose?

Though it is easy to get intimidated by all the decisions required to get online, it's really not all that difficult. Really. Once you get over your reservations you will find yourself keeping in touch with college roommates who were always "too busy to write letters;" finding out what's playing at the movies or what's happening in the news without checking the newspaper; researching airline flight schedules without the aid of a travel agent; or swapping opinions on the latest political issues with people across the country and around the world. (*See* Internet Resource Guide for a selection of information to be found online.)

First you need to get connected, for which you will need a modem and an analog phone line. If you recently purchased your computer, it probably came standard with a modem; if not, you can purchase an external one that plugs into the back of your computer. When choosing a modem, keep in mind faster is better since it will take less time to download data or send faxes and, especially in the world of online services, time is money. Modem speeds are measured in bps ("bits per second"), referring to the amount of data that can be transferred in a second. Speeds currently range from 14,400 bps to 33,600 bps. In most cases, the phone line you already have will be analog; if you have an ISDN or digital line, however, you will need an adapter to plug it into the analog modem.

Okay, so now the car has wheels; how do you get to the highway? You basically have two choices: a commercial online service, which includes forums (or discussion groups) with other members, as well as access to certain reference and information sources often not available elsewhere on the Internet; or an Internet service provider, which provides you with direct access to the Internet, but no services. Commercial services, such as America Online, CompuServe, Microsoft Network, or Prodigy, offer "one-stop shopping" for a variety of features and services. Depending on the service, you may have access to online newspapers or magazines, shopping services, and chat groups (restricted to members of that service), which are devoted to particular hobbies or interests ranging from real estate to bull fighting. Each service provider chooses a set of services and features that will appeal to its users. By presenting users with only a few of the options in each category, online services simplify the process of finding what you need, but that can also limit your choices.

To meet the growing demand of more experienced users for more choices, all the commercial online services now offer access to the Internet—the infamous Information Superhighway whose number of sites doubles every 57 days. Here users can send e-mail anywhere in the world, and find an endless list of sites in every category imaginable, with the quality ranging from the truly spectacular to the merely useless. Internet service providers, unlike online services, provide only access to the Internet. In short, the online services provide a user-friendly way to get information online, sort of like swimming in the kiddie pool with a lifeguard nearby.

The truly adventurous will sign up for the direct Internet access through an Internet service provider. This is like heading straight out into the Pacific; lifeguards may or may not be present, depending on where you choose to swim. Many of the same newspapers and magazines offered via online services can also be found here, but users need to know where to look. You can still find out the weather in Moscow, or the current leader in Malawi, but if often takes a tenacious user to track down the site with the sought-after information.

The cost of connecting to the world at large ranges from about $5 to $30 per month, depending on the type of service you choose and the amount of time you spend logged in. Some people are perfectly content in the swimming pool, and prefer the ease of use of the online service. For those who wish to spend hours surfing the 'Net, however, the hourly charges can add up. Also, subscribers to online services pay for all the features provided, regardless of how rarely they are used. If you

don't think you'll use all the features of an online service, or plan to swim more than 20 hours a month in the Pacific, the direct Internet connection may be more cost-effective since there is usually a flat monthly fee, regardless of amount of time spent logged in.

Whether you choose to swim in the pool or the ocean, it's the perfect time to get your feet wet and join the 30 million others who can connect to the Internet today. *–TMV*

Internet Timeline

1969 ARPA (Advanced Research Projects Agency) goes online in December, connecting four major U.S. universities. Designed for research, education, and government organizations, it provided a communications network linking the country in the event that a military attack destroyed conventional communications systems.

1972 Electronic mail is introduced. Queen Elizabeth sends her first e-mail in 1976.

1973 Transmission Control Protocol/Internet Protocol (TCP/IP) is designed and in 1983 it becomes the standard for communicating between computers over the Internet. One of these protocols, FTP (file transfer protocol), allows users to log onto a remote computer, list the files on that computer, and download files from that computer.

1989 The first effort to index the Internet is created by Peter Deutsch at McGill University in Montreal, who devises Archie, an archive of FTP sites. Another indexing system, WAIS (Wide Area Information Server), is developed by Brewster Kahle of Thinking Machines Corp. Tim Berners-Lee of CERN (European Laboratory for Particle Physics) develops a new technique for distributing information on the Internet, which eventually is called the World Wide Web. The Web is based on hypertext, which permits the user to connect from one document to another at different sites on the Internet via hyperlinks (specially

programmed words, phrases, buttons, or graphics). Unlike other Internet protocols, such as FTP and e-mail, the Web is accessible through a graphical user interface.

1991 Gopher, the first user-friendly interface, was created at the University of Miami and named after the school mascot. Gopher becomes the most popular interface for several years.

1993 Mosaic is developed by Marc Andreeson at the National Center for Supercomputing Applications (NCSA). It becomes the dominant navigating system for the World Wide Web, which at this time accounts for merely 1% of all Internet traffic.

1994 U.S. White House launches Web page. Initial commerce sites are established and mass marketing campaigns are launched via e-mail, introducing the term "spamming" to the Internet vocabulary.

1996 Approximately 45 million people are using the Internet, with roughly 30 million of those in North America (United States and Canada), 9 million in Europe, and 6 million in Asia/Pacific (Australia, Japan, etc.). 43.2 million (44%) of U.S. households own a personal computer, and 14 million of them are online.

Sources for this timeline include International Data Corporation, the W3C Consortium, and the Internet Society.

Internet Resource Guide

So you've just called AOL or CompuServe or MSN and signed yourself up for an Internet account. Now what? Where do you go? What do you see? What is all this hype about, anyway?

If you're like most 'Net neophytes, you're a bit overwhelmed by the possibility of accessing a worldwide network of information, and probably also frustrated that it's not better organized and easier to find what you're looking for. Here are a few tips to finding your way around the Internet, as well as some addresses that should serve as a starting place for you to explore this brave new world.

Generally, you can determine the "genre" of a site based on a 3-character extension in the address. If it ends in ".gov" it is a government site (e.g., www.whitehouse.gov); ".edu" is an educational institution (e.g., www.harvard.edu); ".com" is a company (e.g., www.cnn.com); and ".org" is an organization (e.g., www.un.org)—likely non-profit, or it would appear as a ".com." The default is for addresses in the U.S., so international addresses usually also include a 2-character country code (e.g., "uk" for United Kingdom, "de" for Germany, "fr" for France, "nl" for the

Netherlands, etc.). Chances are, if you are looking for information on a company or a college, you could access a "home page" of data over the internet by typing "www.[name of company].com" or "www.[name of institution].edu."

Not all addresses are that simple, though. If you can't find what you need, go to a search engine, many of which are available at home.netscape.com/escapes/search/. Search engines maintain an index of words that appear on Internet sites within their stated scope (some are worldwide, others are industry- or topic-specific). The engine will return you a list of sites containing your search terms. You may go to those sites by simply clicking on the address (all underlined terms on the Internet are "links" that provide direct access to other information simply by clicking on the term).

To get you started, here are a few topically arranged addresses. Many of these sites also offer links to other sites with more information. Each is rated according to content quality and ease of use with "5" being the highest rating. Though the Internet may at first appear to be a labyrinth full of dead ends and wrong turns, the journey itself is almost always interesting.

Leisure

Museums

The National Museum of American Art
www.nmaa.si.edu:80/
Content Quality: 5   Ease of Use: 5

A Web-friendly site that creatively melds technology and art to provide innovative and interactive tours of several exhibitions. Sensitive to the range of technology that visits, the site offers graphics-reduced pages and Java-enabled tours. The site is updated regularly, and with content from America's art gallery, it is worth visiting often.

Boston's Museum of Fine Art
www.mfa.org/
Content Quality: 4   Ease of Use: 5

Well-organized and easily navigable, this site's latest incarnation is surprisingly more focused on providing background and contextual information about art rather than images of the art itself. Check out the "past exhibitions" section for more images (along with the supporting text) and a somewhat more ambitious scope.

The Louvre
www.paris.org/Musees/Louvre
Content Quality: 3   Ease of Use: 3

Though the site contains some of the world's most famous art, it's not exactly modem-friendly. The images take a long time to download and there are remarkably few of them to look at once the page has loaded. Still, it's cool to tell your friends you went to see the Mona Lisa at the Louvre today.

Movies

Internet Movie Database
us.imdb.com/
Content Quality: 5   Ease of Use: 5

This exceptionally valuable resource offers biographical and professional information on just about anyone you can think of who ever had anything to do with the movies or television. Links to merchandising information, where available, and links among entries make this site invaluable to any movie trivia buff.

Mr. Showbiz
www.mrshowbiz.com
Content Quality: 4   Ease of Use: 4

Whether your 'Biz is music, television, or movies, this site has some insider info for you. With features, chat rooms, biographies, news items, and polls on current events, this is the place to keep up with all the folks who keep you up.

Disney
www.disney.com
Content Quality: 4   Ease of Use: 5

Want to find out what goes on behind the scenes of the latest Disney film? Plan a vacation to Disneyland? Or chat with the stars of an upcoming movie? This is the place to do it, with content to suit adults and kids (and the kids in all of us).

Sony
www.sony.com
Content Quality: 5   Ease of Use: 5

Sony's sprawling empire, from music, to television, to movies, to home video, are all represented here with lots of photos and glitzy graphics. Find out about the latest movie release, or plans for a new television show, or play in the online arcade. There are even links to plugins to enhance your visit to the site.

MGM/United Artists
www.mgmua.com
Content Quality: 5   Ease of Use: 4

These movie folks sure do make a pretty site; problem is, it takes forever to download all those pretty pictures. To its credit, however, the site does have a listing of top-ten web sites related to a particular production, updated weekly. Visitors can download movie clips and photos, too, which makes the site worth the wait.

Books

New York Times Books
www.nytimes.com/books/
Content Quality: 5   Ease of Use: 4

Updated daily with book-related news and reviews, it includes the complete *Sunday Book Review,* an archive of more than 50,000 *New York Times* book reviews (searchable by author and title), the first chapters from a selection of best sellers and recently reviewed books, expanded best seller lists, forums, and RealAudio presentations of world-class authors reading from their own works.

Entertainment

The Dilbert Zone
www.unitedmedia.com/comics/dilbert/
Content Quality: 5   Ease of Use: 5

While United Media is making its best efforts to capitalize on the merchandizing possibilities of Dilbert, the best features of this site are its two-week archive of comic strips, and its Daily Mental Workout. Naturally, there is a separate (easier) workout for managers, so don't be intimidated by this site, ostensibly favored only by the technically adept.

Interesting Places for Kids
www.crc.ricoh.com/people/steve/kids.html
Content Quality: 4   Ease of Use: 4

This site is a collection of links of interest to children. Many contain art or writing by children, others gear their content toward children. Though not all links are still valid, most are, and will ease parents' fears about their children surfing the 'Net.

Shopping

Amazon.com
www.amazon.com
Content Quality: 5   Ease of Use: 5

This Seattle-based bookseller offers over a million titles. Visitors can browse the shelves, search for a specific book by title, author, and subject, write a review, and purchase books for delivery within a week or so. Editors keep visitors apprised of new books within their interest categories via e-mail messages.

American Greetings
www.americangreetings.com
Content Quality: 5   Ease of Use: 5

With a calendar of card-worthy holidays and the ability to order all your cards for the year in a single visit, there's really no longer any excuse for forgetting your mother-in-law's birthday. Customized cards are moderately more expensive, but since you can choose the date on which they are sent, you can buy ahead and save several trips to the card store. Also available are the usual selection of gift ideas, all of which can be purchased and shipped from the comfort of home.

AutoWeb
www.autoweb.com
Content Quality: 5   Ease of Use: 5

Ever wanted to know what your car was worth *before* heading into the dealership? Now you can find out everything you need to know about your car and its potential replacements by visiting a single Web site. The Kelley guide will provide a benchmark price for your current car, while AutoWeb provides you with all the facts, figures, and photos you'll need to pick out a new car. You can post autos for sale, and browse other postings from around the U.S.

Egghead
www.egghead.com
Content Quality: 5   Ease of Use: 5

It only makes sense that one should be able to order software online, and Egghead's site offers a compelling reason to stop by their site. Not only can shoppers search to find the software of their dreams, they can even download certain titles and start using them right away. Now that's instant gratification.

HomeScout
www.homescout.com
Content Quality: 4   Ease of Use: 5

Searching for a new home is an arduous process, but HomeScout can make it a lot easier. With listings of over 300,000 homes available for sale nationwide, this should be the first stop for anyone seeking summary information on homes in their old (or new) neighborhood. Links to local real estate brokers provide detailed listings. Other features include a mortgage calculator, home-buying FAQs, and discounts on home-related purchases.

Imall
www.imall.com
Content Quality: 5   Ease of Use: 5

Dozens of vendors offer products, from audio to automotive, and tools to toys. To those who hate wandering around a sprawling mall in search of a particular item, the search capability will seem a godsend. Those looking to save more than their energy will like the Daily Deals, which can be e-mailed directly to visitors, if they choose, and which offer deep discounts on a chosen set of items. Transactions are secured through a secure commerce server.

Media

Online Magazines

Salon Magazine
www.salonmagazine.com
Content Quality: 5   Ease of Use: 5

Updated every weekday with snappy graphics and pointed articles, this is one site that recognizes its medium. Its mission is to provide content that can't be found elsewhere. Its daily columns, travel section, and reviews of music and books to games and comics have become a "daily fix" for many visitors. With columnists that include Camile Paglia, James Corville, and Susie Bright, *Salon* is risqué, funny, on-the-mark, and no doubt the most original magazine online.

Suck
www.suck.com
Content Quality: 4   Ease of Use: 5

Launched by staff at Wired Ventures, this satirical magazine is targeted exclusively to online readers. The 15,000 daily visitors to the site attest to the popularity of its content ("things that suck") and its format (a single column of double-spaced text that you would never find in print). And besides, it's free.

Slate
www.slate.com
Content Quality: 5   Ease of Use: 5

For a magazine designed for the Web community, this Microsoft-sponsored site does very little to take advantage of its medium. Most links are within the site, for example, and there are surprisingly few graphics and photos. Its content, however, makes up for its lack of web pyrotechnics. As the brain child of Michael Kinsley, it features incisive commentary and reviews as well as a stellar cast of contributors.

Magazines

Discover
www.enews.com/magazines/discover/
Content Quality: 5   Ease of Use: 5

Complete text of *Discover* magazine current issue, as well as ability to search archives; listings for television counterpart "Discovery" channel; directory of other science-related web sites; marketplace for Discovery-related items (videos, books, etc.).

Entertainment Weekly
pathfinder.com/ew/
Content Quality: 5   Ease of Use: 5

This glitzy online counterpart to the weekly magazine edition is enhanced with archives of previous movie reviews, interviews, photos, and a slick interface that should appeal to anyone wishing to keep up with the movers and shakers in the 'Biz.

Fortune
pathfinder.com/fortune/
Content Quality: 5   Ease of Use: 5

Features all you'd expect to find in the magazine, accessible through an attractive interface, plus a stock quote service, searchable archives, and Web-only offers for free gifts and trial copies.

Money Magazine
pathfinder.com/money/
Content Quality: 5   Ease of Use: 5

The content echoes its print counterpart, plus it includes a stock quote service (including personal portfolio tracking), links to other Web sites, and tips on goal-oriented saving and investing (for home, college, retirement, etc.).

People Magazine
people.com
Content Quality: 5   Ease of Use: 5

Features all the catty, behind-the-scenes scoop of the print magazine, but goes much further to include daily feeds (Rosie Report, horoscopes, what happened in the lives of celebrities on this date) and weekly features found only on the online site.

Time Magazine
pathfinder.com/time
Content Quality: 5   Ease of Use: 5

Accessible via a clear, crisp interface that features intelligent use of color and photographs, the content is everything in the print counterpart plus online-only features such as daily newsfeeds, searching, and a multimedia section featuring Shockwave and Java-enabled pages.

News

Networks

CNN Interactive
www.cnn.com
Content Quality: 5   Ease of Use: 4

Whether you need up-to-the-minute information about breaking news, or a resource to help you pinpoint the date of a recent event, this is the site to find it. Most stories include photos, audio, or QuickTime video clips, and links to other sites, with content ranging from world events, travel, and finance, to sports, weather, and trivia. A recent upgrade to its search engine has greatly reduced the ease of use and quality of the search capability, however.

MSNBC
www.msnbc.com
Content Quality: 5   Ease of Use: 5

A cooperative venture between Microsoft Corp. and NBC has produced this news-and-information-driven site, with instant access to top stories, current events, and online discussions. Visitors may customize the information they receive to filter out infrequently viewed material and focus on only what is of greatest interest. Search capability is simple to use and provides just what users would expect.

Yahoo! News
www.yahoo.com/headlines
Content Quality: 5   Ease of Use: 5

Though Yahoo! was first known as a search engine, it is also a great resource for timely and authoritative news information, covering domestic, international, business, high tech, entertainment, and sports categories, and it's free, too! A good entry point for business information before diving into more expensive resources, since you'll find PR Newswire and Businesswire press releases, plus a seven-day searchable archive, stock quotes, Hoover's Profiles on companies, Morningstar mutual fund reports, company news, and links to their home pages.

Newspapers

New York Times www.nytimes.com/
Content Quality: 5 Ease of Use: 4

Everything you find inside the inky pages of the paper edition can be found here, plus a few extra features especially for the Web edition. The one drawback to this site is its lack of a good search engine (or perhaps a good index) to search recent editions.

San Jose Mercury News www.sjmercury.com/
Content Quality: 5 Ease of Use: 4

With all the usual newspaper sections, plus "Good Morning Silicon Valley," Mortgage Watch, and customizable comics, it's easy to see why this site is so popular. Offering a savvy combination of content and technology, the Mercury News is a prime example of what a well-conceived and executed Web site can offer. Its only drawback is its flaky search feature, which seems to function only sporadically.

Wall Street Journal Interactive Edition www.wsj.com
Content Quality: 5 Ease of Use: 5

The online *Journal* offers all the news and analysis of its print counterpart, plus a whole lot more: continuously updated news from the regional U.S., European, and Asian editions, plus a Personal Journal clipping service to catch what you missed. An added bonus are Briefing Books—9000 companies discussed in depth, and links to audio files. The first two weeks are free, and the subscription price is lower for subscribers to the print *Journal*.

U.S. News and World Report www.usnews.com
Content Quality: 5 Ease of Use: 5

In addition to all the news items you'd expect to find, this site also includes an entire section devoted to education, with pages on finding the right college or graduate school, financial aid, campus chat rooms, career advice, and interest surveys. Of course, the main attraction of the site continues to be its "News You Can Use" section, with news on health, gardening, taxes, and advice on travel and finances, complete with color photos and chat rooms.

Health & Medicine Resources

Resources

New England Journal of Medicine www.nejm.org
Content Quality: 4 Ease of Use: 5

Confused about whether hormone replacement therapy does more harm than good? Turn here for an expert opinion, backed by authoritative research. Full-text articles published in the weekly journal are provided here, with a searching capability. The professional focus and lack of images may make the site seem intimidating, but the content is authoritative and valuable.

The National Library of Medicine www.nlm.nih.gov/
Content Quality: 5 Ease of Use: 5

A wealth of information for both health professionals and patients, this site offers published data sheets, symposia proceedings, and results of studies. Visitors can search the index, and order reprints for educational and professional uses. The focus is on the data, though, not on how pretty it is or how well the site is displayed, so it helps if you know what you're looking for.

Good Health Web www.social.com/health/
Content Quality: 5 Ease of Use: 5

This site brings together a variety of health information in one place. There's a searchable library of documents on topics such as Nutrition, Food, Drugs, and Mental Health; most are written by government agencies, and have therefore been thoroughly researched. In addition to the library there are newsgroups, health journals, FAQs, a directory of health organizations, and pointers to selected health-related web sites.

Health Risk Assessment www.youfirst.com
Content Quality: 5 Ease of Use: 5

This site provides a free, in-depth personal health profile that assesses your current health and habits versus others in your age group. The report is confidential, and covers areas ranging from clinical statistics (blood pressure, chlorestorol levels) and daily intake of major food groups, to exercise and automobile habits. You may choose to set up your own personal health "ticker"—a confidential profile that is automatically updated with research or publications in your indicated areas of interest.

**Natural Medicine and
Alternative Therapies** www.teleport.com/~amrta
Content Quality: 4 Ease of Use: 3

Though it's not pretty, the content on this page is interesting and informative, with introductory articles on such topics as acupuncture and herbal medicines, and more focused articles on vegetarian diets and nutritional food substitutes.

Reference

General Information

Britannica On-Line www.eb.com
Content Quality: 5 Ease of Use: 3

For subscribers, the entire contents of the *Encyclopedia Britannica* are available online. This authoritative source is invaluable, but its search capability is somewhat frustrating.

Virtual Reference Desk www.refdesk.com
Content Quality: 4 Ease of Use: 4

A collection of links to free reference resources on the Web, ranging in content from biographies to weights and measures. Includes links to references, including encyclopedias (*Britannica* and *Grolier*), Roget's thesaurus, and WWWebster's, as well as to networks (A&E Biography) and other vertical-information sites. Good starting place for research, but you will ultimately bookmark your chosen resources and bypass this page.

Government Information

Central Intelligence Agency www.odci.gov/cia
Content Quality: 5 Ease of Use: 5

Somehow, you just feel like you're getting away with something when you can download satellite photographs of former Soviet states, but it's all legal. The real resource here, though, is the *World Factbook*, which provides valuable information on all the countries of the world, as well as worldwide aggregate statistics. You can find the population of Afghanistan and the literacy rate of Zimbabwe, and everything in between.

**Statistical Abstract of the
United States** www.census.gov/stat_abstract
Content Quality: 5 Ease of Use: 5

Excellent and authoritative information about the U.S. is available from this site, via HTML or PDF files. Topics include education, economy, law enforcement, births, deaths, income, poverty, law enforcement, and agriculture. All information is available free of charge.

Geological Information

Volcano World   volcano.und.edu
Content Quality: 5   Ease of Use: 5

If you think a volcanologist is a guy with pointy ears from "Star Trek," then you'd better visit Volcano World, where you can ask a very Earth-bound volcanologist what makes volcanos tick. Want to see an active volcano in mid-eruption? This is the site for you, providing valuable information in an intuitive and graphically savvy interface.

History

The History Net   thehistorynet.com
Content Quality: 5   Ease of Use: 3

Bookmark this one for students of all ages. The National Historic Society sponsors this site, which includes information on world and U.S. history, a daily quiz, personality profiles, and selected magazines. This site has valuable information, though finding it with the site search is somewhat stupefying.

Company Information

Hoover's Online   www.hoovers.com/
Content Quality: 3   Ease of Use: 4

Allows users to search for information on 2,700+ public and private companies, but you can only see the profiles if you subscribe to the service (though there are sample profiles provided free at the site).

Travel

Agencies

Business Travel Resource   www.thetrip.com
Content Quality: 5   Ease of Use: 5

Full-service site for business travel. Users can define a profile that automatically applies your preferences regarding airlines, meals, hotels, and car rentals to any reservations you make. Offers electronic ticketing (where available from suppliers).

Expedia   expedia.msn.com
Content Quality: 5   Ease of Use: 5

Research and reserve your travel plans online using Expedia's travel agent, with step by step instructions for booking flights, hotels, and rental cars. The site includes forums for chatting with fellow travel enthusiasts, tips for getting cheaper fares or rates, and even a currency converter.

Guides

Fodor's   www.fodors.com
Content Quality: 5   Ease of Use: 5

An excellent resource for planning a trip or just thinking about being somewhere else, this site offers trip-planning resources, including restaurant and hotel indices, currency converter, travel advisories, and language preparation with useful phrases (including pronunciations) in four languages. The icing on the cake is that this incredibly useful content is also attractively displayed and logically arranged.

Airlines

Flyte Trax   www.weatherconcepts.com/FlyteTrax/
Content Quality: 4   Ease of Use: 4

This free service of American Weather Concepts provides up-to-the-minute information on flights in the contiguous 48 states, including where it is on its route, and its expected arrival time. Visitors must know the airline and flight number for which they are searching. The site is often very busy, which means a reply is not always available.

Weather

IntelliCast   www.intellicast.com
Content Quality: 4   Ease of Use: 5

For those interested in current weather conditions at home or abroad, this site provides instant access to local forecasts around the world. Travelers can plan ahead with the regional forecasts arranged by month.

Women

Women In Technology International   www.witi.com
Content Quality: 4   Ease of Use: 5

Welcome to the International Network of Women in Technology Web site. Founded in 1989 by Carolyn Leighton in response to growing concerns about the glass ceiling, WITI strives to enhance the status of women in science and technology. At the same time, women in all professional fields can acquire the knowledge needed to keep up in today's ever-changing world of technology.

Women's Wire   www.womenswire.com
Content Quality: 4   Ease of Use: 5

This hip magazine has sections devoted to the topics women care about: news, health, stock market, career advice, managing your money, fashion, celebrities, and horoscopes. The editors comb the online news sources daily to find stories their readers will find interesting, and their choices are right on target.

Computer Glossary

ASCII American Standard Code for Information Interchange, an encoding system for converting keyboard characters and instructions into the binary number code that the computer understands.

Baud rate The speed at which data is transmitted over a modem, measured in bits per second.

Bit (short for binary digit). It is the smallest piece of computer information and is either the number 0 or 1. Through "machine language," the computer interprets a series of 0's and 1's to form numbers, letters, punctuation marks, and symbols.

Boot To start up a computer.

Browser Software used to navigate the Internet. Netscape Navigator and Microsoft Internet Explorer are today's most popular browsers for accessing the World Wide Web.

Bug A malfunction due to an error in the program or a defect in the equipment.

Byte Most computers use combinations of eight bits, called bytes, to represent one character of data or instructions. For example, the word "cat" has three characters, and it would be represented by three bytes.

CD-ROM Compact Disc Read-Only Memory. Similar to a CD music disc, but designed for computers, a single disc can hold an entire library of books such as encyclopedias or other reference works, and multimedia programs for quick, convenient viewing.

Chip A tiny wafer of silicon containing miniature electric circuits that can store millions of bits of information.

Client A single user of a network application run off a server. A client/server architecture allows many people to use the same data simultaneously; the program's main component (the data) resides on a centralized server, with smaller components (user interface) on each client.

CPU Central Processing Unit. The "brains" or part of a computer where all the incoming information is processed and commands are executed.

Cursor A moving position-indicator displayed on the computer monitor that shows the computer operator where he or she is working.

Cyberspace Slang for the Internet.

Database A collection of similar information stored in a file, for example, a database of addresses. This information may be created and stored in a database management system (DBMS).

Debug Computer slang for finding and correcting equipment defects or malfunctions in the program.

Desktop publishing Use of a personal computer in combination with text, graphics, and page layout programs to produce publication-quality documents.

Directory A list of files stored in the computer.

Disk Two distinct types: the so-called "hard disk" that is inside the computer and stores vast amounts of data (new computers currently come standard with 1–2 gigabyte hard drives); and the "floppy" disk, which is portable, 3.5″ square, and can store about 1.4 megabytes of data (the name is a vestige of early 5.25″ disks, which were flexible).

Disk drive The equipment that a floppy disk is inserted into so that information may be stored on or retrieved from the disk.

Documentation The instruction manual for a piece of hardware or software.

Domain The name of a network or computer linked to the Internet. It is found in an e-mail address after an @ sign. The e-mail address of this almanac, for example, is ipa@infoplease.com, "infoplease.com" being its domain. A domain ends with an abbreviation indicating its type (e.g., ".com" stands for company, ".gov" for government, ".org" for organization, and ".edu" for educational institution).

DOS Disk Operating System. An operating system designed for early IBM-compatible PCs.

E-mail Electronic mail; messages, including memos or letters, sent electronically between networked computers that may be across the office or around the world.

File A set of data that is stored in the computer.

Flame An inflammatory message sent electronically.

Fonts Sets of typefaces (or characters) that come in different styles and sizes.

Forum A discussion group offered by certain online services; allows users to post messages on a given topic and solicit responses from other users. Also referred to as a "chat group" or "news group."

FTP File Transfer Protocol. The format and rules for transferring files from a host to a remote computer.

Gigabyte (GB) One thousand megabytes.

Glitch The cause of an unexpected malfunction.

Graphics Images such as charts, graphs, and diagrams that can be displayed on a computer.

Gopher An Internet search tool that allows users to access textual information through a series of menus.

GUI Graphical User Interface. A system that simplifies selecting computer commands by enabling the user to point to symbols or illustrations (called "icons") on the computer screen with a mouse.

Groupware Software that allows networked individuals to form groups and collaborate on documents, programs, or databases.

Hacker A person with technical expertise who enjoys tinkering with computer systems to produce additional features. Also one who intentionally accesses all or part of a computer or a computer system without authorization to do so (a crime in some states).

Hard copy A paper printout of what you have prepared on the computer.

Hardware The physical and mechanical components of a computer system. They include electronic circuitry, chips, screens, disk drives, keyboards, modems, and printers.

Home page The main page of a Web site used to greet visitors, provide information about the site, or to direct the viewer to other pages on the site.

HTML Hypertext Markup Language. A standard of text markup conventions used for documents on the World Wide Web. Browsers interpret the codes to give the text formatting (such as bold, blue, or italic).

HTTP Hypertext Transfer Protocol. A common system used to request and send HTML documents on the World Wide Web. It is the first portion of all URL addresses on the World Wide Web (e.g., http://www.whitehouse.gov).

Hypermedia Integrates audio, graphics, and/or video through links embedded in the main application.

Hypertext A system for organizing text through links, as opposed to a menu-driven hierarchy such as Gopher. Most Web pages include hypertext links to other pages at that site, or to other sites on the World Wide Web.

Icons Symbols or illustrations appearing on the computer screen that indicate program files or other computer functions.

Input Data that goes into a computer device.

Interface The interconnections that allow a device, a program, or a person to interact. Hardware interfaces are the cables that connect the device to its power source and to other devices. Software interfaces allow the program to communicate with other programs (such as the operating system), and user interfaces allow the user to communicate with the program (e.g., via mouse, menu commands, icons, voice commands, etc.).

Internet An international conglomeration of interconnected computer networks. Developed in the 1970s to allow government and university researchers to share information, the Internet is not controlled by any single source. Its original focus was research and communications, but it continues to expand, offering a wide array of resources for business and home users.

Java An object-oriented programming language; allows users to create small programs or applications ("applets") to enhance Web sites. Java was designed specifically for programs (particularly multimedia) to be used over the Internet.

Kilobyte (K or KB) Equal to 1,024 bytes.

Laptop and Notebook Small, lightweight, portable battery-powered computers that can fit onto your lap. They have a thin, flat, liquid crystal display screen.

Megabyte (MB) Equal to 1,048,576 bytes, usually rounded off to one million bytes.

Memory A computer device or series of devices that store information. Computer memory is measured in terms of the amount of information it can store, commonly in megabytes or gigabytes.

Menu A list of options that users can choose from.

Merge To combine two or more files into a single file.

Mhz An abbreviation for Megahertz. One million Hertz. One million cycles per second. Unit of measure for band and bandwidth, or for processor speed of a computer CPU, in millions of computer clock cycles per second. For example, the Pentium is currently available in 133 Mhz, 166 Mhz, and 200 Mhz models.

Microprocessor A complete central processing unit (CPU) contained on a single silicon chip.

Modem A device that connects two computers together over a telephone line by converting the computer's data into an audio signal.

Monitor A video display terminal.

Mouse A small hand-held device, similar to a "trackball," used to control the position of the cursor on the video display; movements of the mouse on a desktop correspond to movements of the cursor on the screen.

Multimedia Software programs that combine text and graphics with sound, video, and animation. A **multimedia PC** contains the hardware to support these capabilities.

MS-DOS An early operating system developed by Microsoft Corporation.

Network Computers that are connected to other computers.

OS/2 An operating system with a graphical user interface, developed by IBM for IBM PCs and compatible computers.

Output Data that come out of a computer device.

PC Personal computer.

Pen computer A type of PC, typically laptop or handheld, that uses a stylus (pen) to write directly on the screen rather than using a keyboard.

Pentium chip Intel's fifth generation of sophisticated high-speed microprocessors. Pentium means "the fifth element."

Personal computer A single-user computer containing a central processing unit (CPU) and one or more memory circuits.

Power PC A competitor to the Pentium chip. It is a new generation of powerful sophisticated microprocessors produced from an Apple-IBM-Motorola alliance.

Printer A mechanical device for printing your computer's output on paper. The three major types of printers are **Dot Matrix,** in which individual letters are made up of a series of tiny ink dots. The dots are formed by punching a ribbon with the ends of tiny wires; **Ink Jet,** which sprays tiny droplets of ink particles onto paper; and **Laser,** which uses a beam of light to reproduce the image of each page, then dry toner is applied to the image and transferred to paper.

Program A precise series of instructions written in a computer language that tells the computer what to do and how to do it. Programs are also called "software" or "applications."

Programming language A series of instructions written by a programmer according to a given set of rules or conventions ("syntax"). High-level programming languages are independent of the device on which the application (or program) will eventually run; low-level languages are specific to each program or platform. Programming language instructions are converted into programs in language specific to a particular machine or operating system ("machine language") so that the computer can interpret and carry out the instructions. Some common programming languages are BASIC, C, C++, dBASE, FORTRAN, and PERL.

Push technology Internet tool that delivers specific information directly to a user's desktop, eliminating the need to surf for it. PointCast, which delivers news in user-defined categories, is a popular example of this technology.

RAM Random Access Memory. One of two basic types of memory. Portions of programs are stored in RAM when the program is launched so that the program will run faster. Though a PC has a fixed amount of RAM, only portions of it will be accessed by the computer at any given time.

ROM Read-Only Memory. One of the two basic types of memory. ROM contains only permanent information put there by the manufacturer; information in ROM cannot be altered, nor can the memory be dynamically allocated by the computer or its operator.

Scanner An electronic device that uses light-sensing equipment to scan paper images such as text, photos, and illustrations and translate the images into signals that the computer can then store, modify, or distribute.

Search engine Software that makes it possible to look for and retrieve material on the Internet, particularly the Web. Some popular search engines are Alta Vista, Yahoo!, Web Crawler, and Lycos.

Server A computer that shares its resources and information with other computers, called clients, on a network.

Software Computer programs; also called "applications."

Spreadsheet Software that allows one to calculate numbers in a format that is similar to pages in a conventional ledger.

Surfing Exploring the Internet.

Trackball Input device that controls the position of the cursor on the screen; the unit is mounted near the keyboard, and movement is controlled by moving a ball.

URL Uniform Resource Locator. The protocol for identifying a document on the Web; the Web address (e.g., www.census.gov).

USENET A large unmoderated and unedited bulletin board on the Internet that offers thousands of forums, called newsgroups. These range from newsgroups exchanging information on scientific advances to celebrity fan clubs.

User friendly A program or device whose use is intuitive to people with a nontechnical background.

Virtual Reality (VR) A technology that allows you to experience and interact with images in a simulated three-dimensional environment. For example, you could design a room in a house on your computer and actually feel that you are walking around in it even though it was never built. (The holodeck in the science-fiction TV series "Star Trek: The Next Generation" would be the ultimate virtual reality.) Current technology requires the user to wear a special helmet, viewing goggles, gloves, and other equipment that is wired to the computer.

Virus An unauthorized piece of computer code attached to a computer program or portions of a computer system that secretly spreads from one computer to another by shared disks and over telephone lines.

Windows A graphical environment developed by Microsoft Corp. that enables users to select commands by pointing to illustrations or symbols with a mouse.

World Wide Web ("WWW" or "The Web") A network of servers on the Internet that use hypertext-linked databases and files. It was developed in 1989 by Tim Berners-Lee, a British computer scientist, and is now the primary platform of the Internet. The feature that distinguishes the Web from other Internet applications is its ability to display graphics in addition to text.

Word processor A computer system or program for setting, editing, revising, correcting, storing, and printing text.

Worm An unauthorized independent program that penetrates computers and replicates itself, thereby affecting computers and computer networks. In 1988, Robert T. Morris, a Cornell University graduate student, shut down a nationwide computer network with the best-known computer worm in history.

Countries With the Most Computers

(in millions)

Country[1]	Computers in use	1985	1988	1989	1991	1992	1993	1994	1995	2000[2]
United States	Total computers	21.5	40.8	47.6	62.0	68.2	76.5	85.8	96.2	160.5
	Total PCs	19.1	37.9	44.5	58.6	64.6	72.6	81.5	91.5	154.0
Japan	Total computers	2.1	5.1	6.4	9.2	10.8	12.6	14.9	18.3	46.8
	Total PCs	1.8	4.7	5.9	8.7	10.2	12.0	14.2	17.4	45.0
Germany	Total computers	1.9	4.2	5.2	7.3	8.7	10.4	12.3	14.2	29.8
	Total PCs	1.6	3.9	4.9	6.9	8.3	9.9	11.7	13.5	28.6
United Kingdom	Total computers	2.1	4.3	5.2	7.2	8.4	9.6	10.9	12.6	26.0
	Total PCs	1.8	3.9	4.8	6.8	7.9	9.1	10.4	12.0	25.0
France	Total computers	1.3	3.1	4.0	5.7	6.5	7.5	8.6	10.0	21.8
	Total PCs	1.1	2.9	3.7	5.4	6.2	7.1	8.2	9.5	21.0
Canada	Total computers	0.9	2.0	2.5	3.7	4.3	5.2	6.2	7.2	15.3
	Total PCs	0.8	1.9	2.4	3.5	4.1	5.0	5.9	6.9	14.7
Italy	Total computers	0.9	2.1	2.6	3.7	4.3	5.0	5.9	6.7	17.5
	Total PCs	0.8	1.9	2.4	3.5	4.1	4.8	5.6	6.4	16.8
Australia	Total computers	0.34	0.95	1.24	2.1	2.7	3.4	4.0	4.8	10.2
	Total PCs	0.28	0.87	1.15	1.96	2.6	3.2	3.8	4.6	9.8
South Korea	Total computers	0.13	0.28	0.43	1.0	1.4	1.9	2.6	3.5	10.6
	Total PCs	0.10	0.26	0.40	0.9	1.3	1.8	2.5	3.4	10.2
Spain	Total computers	0.20	0.50	0.79	1.44	1.8	2.3	2.9	3.5	8.1
	Total PCs	0.17	0.46	0.73	1.35	1.7	2.2	2.7	3.3	7.8
Netherlands	Total computers	0.32	0.76	1.02	1.65	2.0	2.4	2.8	3.3	7.1
	Total PCs	0.27	0.70	0.95	1.55	1.9	2.3	2.7	3.2	6.8
China	Total computers	0.12	0.28	0.40	0.67	0.92	1.34	2.0	2.9	13.3
	Total PCs	0.09	0.25	0.36	0.63	0.87	1.26	1.9	2.8	12.7
Russia	Total computers	0.10	0.23	0.34	0.65	0.93	1.37	1.9	2.7	9.2
	Total PCs	0.08	0.20	0.31	0.61	0.88	1.29	1.8	2.6	8.8
Mexico	Total computers	0.15	0.37	0.49	0.87	1.21	1.61	2.05	2.6	6.3
	Total PCs	0.12	0.34	0.46	0.82	1.14	1.52	1.94	2.4	6.0
Brazil	Total computers	0.10	0.24	0.31	0.62	0.91	1.27	1.76	2.4	7.8
	Total PCs	0.08	0.22	0.29	0.59	0.86	1.20	1.67	2.3	7.5
Worldwide Total	Total computers	38.1	79.4	97.0	136.9	159.2	186.9	218.8	257.2	556.9
	Total PCs	33.2	73.4	90.6	129.4	150.8	177.4	208.0	245.0	535.6

1. List represents the fifteen countries with the most computers. 2. Projected. *Source:* Karen Petska-Juliussen and Egil Juilussen, *8th Annual Computer Industry Almanac,* Copyright © 1996 by Computer Industry Almanac Inc., 702-749-5053; 800-377-6810 (U.S. only).

Computers Per Capita

Rank	Computers/1000 People	1985	1988	1989	1991	1992	1993	1994	1995	2000[1]
1.	United States	90.1	166.0	191.7	245.4	266.9	296.6	329.2	364.7	580.0
2.	Australia	21.5	58.4	75.3	120.5	155.0	191.9	222.7	264.3	525.7
3.	Norway	28.4	61.2	77.7	120.7	148.2	180.5	218.5	259.5	515.4
4.	Canada	36.4	77.4	96.2	136.6	157.5	189.0	219.2	254.8	511.9
5.	Denmark	25.9	58.6	76.7	127.3	153.8	184.6	217.2	252.5	510.2
6.	Finland	25.4	56.2	76.0	119.3	146.2	178.8	211.0	245.5	505.0
7.	Sweden	24.5	58.5	77.0	114.2	139.6	169.9	204.0	244.1	508.9
8.	New Zealand	25.7	57.2	73.5	115.6	136.4	159.8	191.2	224.8	499.2
9.	United Kingdom	36.4	74.8	90.7	125.7	144.8	164.8	187.4	216.5	441.1
10.	Netherlands	22.4	51.9	69.2	109.7	131.1	156.9	184.3	214.8	450.3
11.	Switzerland	24.2	53.0	70.2	109.0	126.6	149.5	174.3	201.6	443.7
12.	Singapore	17.8	46.5	59.7	84.7	104.8	126.9	153.8	188.8	412.0
13.	Belgium	20.1	47.0	63.2	100.2	117.3	138.3	161.2	188.6	405.2
14.	Ireland	23.8	54.1	68.3	102.0	117.4	136.1	159.1	186.4	404.1
15.	Germany	24.0	54.2	67.6	91.5	108.6	129.2	151.3	174.6	361.8
	Europe	14.3	31.7	40.8	60.2	71.0	83.5	97.3	113.4	248.9
	Worldwide	7.8	15.4	18.5	25.2	29.1	33.6	38.8	44.9	90.3

1. Projected. *Source:* Karen Petska-Juliussen and Egil Juliussen, *8th Annual Computer Industry Almanac,* Copyright © 1996 by Computer Industry Almanac Inc., 702-749-5053; 800-377-6810 (U.S. only).

World Wide Web Users by Segment, 1996

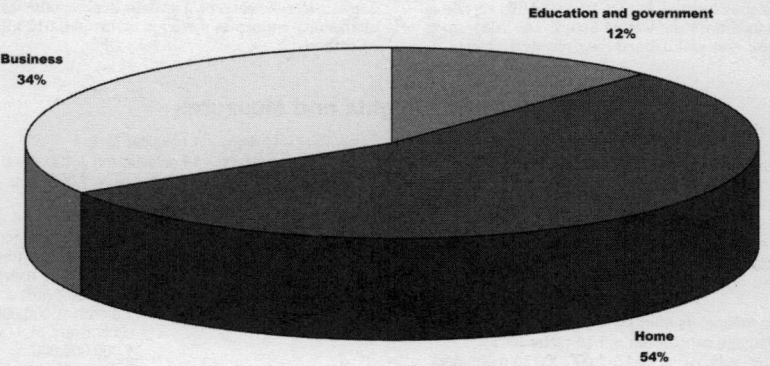

Education and government
12%

Business
34%

Home
54%

Source: Internet Program, International Data Corporation, 1996.

Weights & Measures

Kelvin Scale

Absolute zero, −273.16° on the Celsius (Centigrade) scale, is 0° Kelvin. Thus, degrees Kelvin are equivalent to degrees Celsius plus 273.16. The freezing point of water, 0°C and 32°F, is 273.16°K. The conversion formula is K° = C° + 273.16.

The International System (Metric)

Source: Department of Commerce, National Bureau of Standards.

The International System of Units is a modernized version of the metric system, established by international agreement, that provides a logical and interconnected framework for all measurements in science, industry, and commerce. The system is built on a foundation of seven basic units, and all other units are derived from them. (Use of metric weights and measures was legalized in the United States in 1866, and our customary units of weights and measures are defined in terms of the meter and kilogram.)

Length. Meter. Up until 1983, the meter was defined as 1,650,763.73 wavelengths in vacuum of the orange-red line of the spectrum of krypton-86. Since then, it is equal to the distance traveled by light in a vacuum in 1/299,792,458 of a second.

Time. Second. The second is defined as the duration of 9,192,631,770 cycles of the radiation associated with a specified transition of the cesium 133 atom.

Mass. Kilogram. The standard for the kilogram is a cylinder of platinum-iridium alloy kept by the International Bureau of Weights and Measures at Paris. A duplicate at the National Bureau of Standards serves as the mass standard for the United States. The kilogram is the only base unit still defined by a physical object.

Temperature. Kelvin. The kelvin is defined as the fraction 1/273.16 of the thermodynamic temperature of the triple point of water; that is, the point at which water forms an interface of solid, liquid and vapor. This is defined as 0.01°C on the Centigrade or Celsius scale and 32.02°F on the Fahrenheit scale. The temperature 0°K is called "absolute zero."

Electric Current. Electric current. The ampere is defined as that current that, if maintained in each of two long parallel wires separated by one meter in free space, would produce a force between the two wires (due to their magnetic fields) of 2×10^{-7} newton for each meter of length. (A newton is the unit of force that when applied to one kilogram mass would experience an acceleration of one meter per second per second.)

Luminous Intensity. Candela. The candela is defined as the luminous intensity of 1/600,000 of a square meter of a cavity at the temperature of freezing platinum (2,042K).

Amount of Substance. Mole. The mole is the amount of substance of a system that contains as many elementary entities as there are atoms in 0.012 kilogram of carbon-12.

Tables of Metric Weights and Measures

Linear Measure

10 millimeters (mm) = 1 centimeter (cm)
10 centimeters = 1 decimeter (dm) = 100 millimeters
10 decimeters = 1 meter (m) = 1,000 millimeters
10 meters = 1 dekameter (dam)
10 dekameters = 1 hectometer (hm) = 100 meters
10 hectometers = 1 kilometer (km) = 1,000 meters

Area Measure

100 square millimeters (mm²) = 1 sq centimeter (cm²)
10,000 square centimeters = 1 sq meter (m²) = 1,000,000 sq millimeters
100 square meters = 1 are (a)
100 ares = 1 hectare (ha) = 10,000 sq meters
100 hectares = 1 sq kilometer (km²) = 1,000,000 sq meters

Volume Measure

10 milliliters (ml) = 1 centiliter (cl)
10 centiliters = 1 deciliter (dl) = 100 milliliters
10 deciliters = 1 liter (l) = 1,000 milliliters

10 liters = 1 dekaliter (dal)
10 dekaliters = 1 hectoliter (hl) = 100 liters
10 hectoliters = 1 kiloliter (kl) = 1,000 liters

Cubic Measure

1,000 cubic millimeters (mm³) = 1 cu centimeter (cm³)
1,000 cubic centimeters = 1 cu decimeter (dm³) = 1,000,000 cu millimeters
1,000 cubic decimeters = 1 cu meter (m³) = 1 stere = 1,000,000 cu centimeters = 1,000,000,000 cu millimeters

Weight

10 milligrams (mg) = 1 centigram (cg)
10 centigrams = 1 decigram (dg) = 100 milligrams
10 decigrams = 1 gram (g) = 1,000 milligrams
10 grams = 1 dekagram (dag)
10 dekagrams = 1 hectogram (hg) = 100 grams
10 hectograms = 1 kilogram (kg) = 1,000 grams
1,000 kilograms = 1 metric ton (t)

Tables of Customary U.S. Weights and Measures

Linear Measure

12 inches (in.) = 1 foot (ft.)
3 feet = 1 yard (yd)
5½ yards = 1 rod (rd), pole, or perch (16½ ft.)
40 rods = 1 furlong (fur) = 220 yds = 660 ft
8 furlongs = 1 statute mile (mi.) = 1,760 yds
= 5,280 ft.
3 land miles = 1 league
5,280 feet = 1 statute or land mile
6,076.11549 feet = 1 international nautical mile

Area Measure

144 square inches = 1 sq ft.
9 square feet = 1 sq yd = 1,296 sq in.
30 1/4 square yards = 1 sq rd = 272¼ sq ft.
160 square rods = 1 acre = 4,840 sq yds =
43,560 sq ft.
640 acres = 1 sq mi.
1 mile square = 1 section (of land)
6 miles square = 1 township = 36 sections
= 36 sq mi.

Cubic Measure

1,728 cubic inches = 1 cu ft.
27 cubic feet = 1 cu yd

Liquid Measure

When necessary to distinguish the liquid pint or quart from the dry pint or quart, the word "liquid" or the abbreviation "liq" should be used in combination with the name or abbreviation of the liquid unit.

4 gills (gi) = 1 pint (pt) (= 28.875 cu in.)
2 pints = 1 quart (qt) (= 57.75 cu in.)
4 quarts = 1 gallon (gal) (= 231 cu in.) =
8 pts = 32 gills

Apothecaries' Fluid Measure

60 minims (min.) = 1 fluid dram (fl dr) (= 0.2256 cu in.)
8 fluid drams = 1 fluid ounce (fl oz) (= 1.8047 cu in.)
16 fluid ounces = 1 pt (= 28.875 cu in.) = 128 fl drs
2 pints = 1 qt (= 57.75 cu in.) = 32 fl oz = 256 fl drs
4 quarts = 1 gal (= 231 cu in.) = 128 fl oz =
1,024 fl drs

Dry Measure

When necessary to distinguish the dry pint or quart from the liquid pint or quart; the word "dry" should be used in combination with the name or abbreviation of the dry unit.

2 pints = 1 qt (=67.2006 cu in.)
8 quarts = 1 peck (pk) (=537.605 cu in.) = 16 pts
4 pecks = 1 bushel (bu) (= 2,150.42 cu in.) = 32 qts

Avoirdupois Weight

When necessary to distinguish the avoirdupois dram from the apothecaries' dram, or to distinguish the avoirdupois dram or ounce from the fluid dram or ounce, or to distinguish the avoirdupois ounce or pound from the troy or apothecaries' ounce or pound, the word "avoirdupois" or the abbreviation "avdp" should be used in combination with the name or abbreviation of the avoirdupois unit. (The "grain" is the same in avoirdupois, troy, and apothecaries' weights.)

27¹¹/₃₄ grains = 1 dram (dr)
16 drams = 1 oz = 437½ grains
16 ounces = 1 lb = 256 drams = 7,000 grains
100 pounds = 1 hundredweight (cwt)[1]
20 hundredweights = 1 ton (tn) = 2,000 lbs[1]

In "gross" or "long" measure, the following values are recognized:

112 pounds = 1 gross or long cwt[1]
20 gross or long 1 gross or long ton = 2,240 lbs[1]
hundredweights =

1. When the terms "hundredweight" and "ton" are used unmodified, they are commonly understood to mean the 100-pound hundredweight and the 2,000-pound ton, respectively; these units may be designated "net" or "short" when necessary to distinguish them from the corresponding units in gross or long measure.

Units of Circular Measure

Second (') = —
Minute (') = 60 seconds
Degree (°) = 60 minutes
Right angle = 90 degrees
Straight angle = 180 degrees
Circle = 360 degrees

Troy Weight

24 grains = 1 pennyweight (dwt)
20 pennyweights = 1 ounce troy (oz t) = 480 grains
12 ounces troy = 1 pound troy (lb t) = 240
pennyweights = 5,760 grains

Apothecaries' Weight

20 grains = 1 scruple (s ap)
3 scruples = 1 dram apothecaries' (dr ap)
= 60 grains
8 drams apothecaries' = 1 ounce apothecaries' (oz ap)
= 24 scruples = 480 grains
12 ounces apothecaries' = 1 pound apothecaries' (lb ap)
= 96 drams apothecaries' =
288 scruples = 5,760 grains

Gunter's or Surveyor's Chain Measure

7.92 inches = 1 link (li)
100 links = 1 chain (ch) = 4 rods = 66 ft.
80 chains = 1 statute mile = 320 rods = 5,280 ft.

Metric and U.S. Equivalents

1 angstrom[1] (light wave measurement)	0.1 millimicron 0.000 1 micron 0.000 000 1 millimeter 0.000 000 004 inch	1 centimeter	0.3937 inch
		1 chain (Gunter's or surveyor's)	66 feet 20.1168 meters
1 cable's length	120 fathoms 720 feet 219.456 meters	1 decimeter	3.937 inches
		1 dekameter	32.808 feet

1 fathom	6 feet 1.8288 meters
1 foot	0.3048 meter
1 furlong	10 chains (surveyor's) 660 feet 220 yards 1/8 statute mile 201.168 meters
1 inch	2.54 centimeters
1 kilometer	0.621 mile
1 league (land)	3 statute miles 4.828 kilometers
1 link (Gunter's or surveyor's)	7.92 inches 0.201 168 meter
1 meter	39.37 inches 1.094 yards
1 micron	0.001 millimeter 0.000 039 37 inch
1 mil	0.001 inch 0.025 4 millimeter
1 mile (statute or land)	5,280 feet 1.609 kilometers
1 mile (nautical international)	1.852 kilometers 1.151 statute miles 0.999 U.S. nautical miles
1 millimeter	0.03937 inch
1 millimicron (m+GRKm)	0.001 micron 0.000 000 039 37 inch
1 nanometer	0.001 micrometer or 0.000 000 039 37 inch
1 point (typography)	0.013 837 inch 1/72 inch (approximately) 0.351 millimeter
1 rod, pole, or perch	16½ feet 5.0292 meters
1 yard	0.9144 meter

AREAS OR SURFACES

1 acre	43,560 square feet 4,840 square yards 0.405 hectare
1 are	119.599 square yards 0.025 acre
1 hectare	2.471 acres
1 square centimeter	0.155 square inch
1 square decimeter	15.5 square inches

1 square foot	929.030 square centimeters
1 square inch	6.4516 square centimeters
1 square kilometer	0.386 square mile 247.105 acres
1 square meter	1.196 square yards 10.764 square feet
1 square mile	258.999 hectares
1 square millimeter	0.002 square inch
1 square rod, square pole or square perch	25.293 square meters
1 square yard	0.836 square meters

CAPACITIES OR VOLUMES

1 barrel, liquid	31 to 42 gallons[2]
1 barrel, standard for fruits, vegetables, and other dry commodities except cranberries	7,056 cubic inches 105 dry quarts 3.281 bushels, struck mea- sure
1 barrel, standard, cranberry	5,286 cubic inches 86 45/64 dry quarts 2.709 bushels, struck mea- sure
1 bushel (U.S.) struck measure	2,150.42 cubic inches 35.238 liters
1 bushel, heaped (U.S.)	2,747.715 cubic inches 1.278 bushels, struck mea- sure[3]
1 cord (firewood)	128 cubic feet
1 cubic centimeter	0.061 cubic inch
1 cubic decimeter	61.024 cubic inches
1 cubic foot	7.481 gallons 28.316 cubic decimeters
1 cubic inch	0.554 fluid ounce 4.433 fluid drams 16.387 cubic centimeters
1 cubic meter	1.308 cubic yards
1 cubic yard	0.765 cubic meter
1 cup, measuring	8 fluid ounces ½ liquid pint
1 dram, fluid or liquid (U.S.)	1/8 fluid ounces 0.226 cubic inch 3.697 milliliters 1.041 British fluid drachms
1 dekaliter	2.642 gallons 1.135 pecks

1 gallon (U.S.)	231 cubic inches 3.785 liters 0.833 British gallon 128 U.S. fluid ounces	1 dram, apothecaries'	60 grains 3.888 grams
1 gallon (British Imperial)	277.42 cubic inches 1.201 U.S. gallons 4.546 liters 160 British fluid ounces	1 dram, avoirdupois	27¹¹⁄₃₂ (=27.344) grains 1.772 grams
		1 grain	64.798 91 milligrams
1 gill	7.219 cubic inches 4 fluid ounces 0.118 liter	1 gram	15.432 grains 0.035 ounce, avoirdupois
1 hectoliter	26.418 gallons 2.838 bushels	1 hundredweight, gross or long[5]	112 pounds 50.802 kilograms
1 liter	1.057 liquid quarts 0.908 dry quart 61.024 cubic inches	1 hundredweight, net or short	100 pounds 45.359 kilograms
		1 kilogram	2.205 pounds
1 milliliter	0.271 fluid dram 16.231 minims 0.061 cubic inch	1 microgram (μg— the Greek letter mu in combination with the letter g)	0.000 001 gram
1 ounce, fluid or liquid (U.S.)	1.805 cubic inch 29.574 milliliters 1.041 British fluid ounces	1 milligram	0.015 grain
1 peck	8.810 liters	1 ounce, avoirdupois	437.5 grains 0.911 troy or apothecaries', ounce 28.350 grams
1 pint, dry	33.600 cubic inches 0.551 liter	1 ounce, troy or apothecaries'	480 grains 1.097 avoirdupois ounces 31.103 grams
1 pint, liquid	28.875 cubic inches 0.473 liter	1 pennyweight	1.555 grams
1 quart, dry (U.S.)	67.201 cubic inches 1.101 liters 0.969 British quart	1 point	0.01 carat 2 milligrams
1 quart, liquid (U.S.)	57.75 cubic inches 0.946 liter 0.833 British quart	1 pound, avoirdupois	7,000 grains 1.215 troy or apothecaries' pounds 453.592 37 grams
1 quart (British)	69.354 cubic inches 1.032 U.S. dry quarts 1.201 U.S. liquid quarts	1 pound, troy or apothecaries'	5,760 grains 0.823 avoirdupois pound 373.242 grams
1 tablespoon, measuring	3 teaspoons 4 fluid drams ½ fluid ounce	1 ton, gross or long[5]	2,240 pounds 1.12 net tons 1.016 metric tons
1 teaspoon, measuring	⅓ tablespoon 1⅓ fluid drams	1 ton, metric	2,204.623 pounds 0.984 gross ton 1.102 net tons
1 assay ton[4]	29.167 grams	1 ton, net or short	2,000 pounds 0.893 gross ton 0.907 metric ton
1 carat	200 milligrams 3.086 grains		

1. The angstrom is basically defined as 10^{-10} meter. 2. There is a variety of "barrels" established by law or usage. For example, federal taxes on fermented liquors are based on a barrel of 31 gallons; many state laws fix the "barrel for liquids" at 31½ gallons; one state fixes a 36-gallon barrel for cistern measurement; federal law recognizes a 40-gallon barrel for "proof spirits"; by custom, 42 gallons comprise a barrel of crude oil or petroleum products for statistical purposes, and this equivalent is recognized "for liquids" by four states. 3. Frequently recognized as 1¼ bushels, struck measure. 4. Used in assaying. The assay ton bears the same relation to the milligram that a ton of 2,000 pounds avoirdupois bears to the ounce troy; hence the weight in milligrams of precious metal obtained from one assay ton of ore gives directly the number of troy ounces to the net ton. 5. The gross or long ton and hundredweight are used commercially in the United States to only a limited extent, usually in restricted industrial fields. These units are the same as the British "ton" and "hundredweight."

Miscellaneous Units of Measure

Acre An area of 43,560 square feet. Originally, the area a yoke of oxen could plow in one day.

Agate Originally a measurement of type size (5½ points). Now equal to ¹⁄₁₄ inch. Used in printing for measuring column length.

Ampere Unit of electric current. A potential difference of one volt across a resistance of one ohm produces a current of one ampere.

Astronomical Unit (A.U.) 93,000,000 miles, the average distance of the earth from the sun. Used for astronomy.

Bale A large bundle of goods. In the U.S., the approximate weight of a bale of cotton is 500 pounds. The weight varies in other countries.

Board Foot (fbm) 144 cubic inches (12 in. × 12 in. × 1 in.). Used for lumber.

Bolt 40 yards. Used for measuring cloth.

Btu British thermal unit. Amount of heat needed to increase the temperature of one pound of water by one degree Fahrenheit (252 calories).

Carat (c) 200 milligrams or 3.086 grains troy. Originally the weight of a seed of the carob tree in the Mediterranean region. Used for weighing precious stones.

Chain (ch) A chain 66 feet or one-tenth of a furlong in length, divided into 100 parts called links. One mile is equal to 80 chains. Used in surveying and sometimes called Gunter's or surveyor's chain.

Cubit 18 inches or 45.72 cm. Derived from distance between elbow and tip of middle finger.

Decibel Unit of relative loudness. One decibel is the smallest amount of change detectable by the human ear.

Ell, English 1¼ yards or ¹⁄₃₂ bolt. Used for measuring cloth.

Freight, Ton (also called Measurement Ton) 40 cubic feet of merchandise. Used for cargo freight.

Great Gross 12 gross or 1728.

Gross 12 dozen or 144.

Hand 4 inches or 10.16 cm. Derived from the width of the hand. Used for measuring the height of horses at withers.

Hertz Modern unit for measurement of electromagnetic wave frequencies (equivalent to "cycles per second").

Hogshead (hhd) 2 liquid barrels or 14,653 cubic inches.

Horsepower The power needed to lift 33,000 pounds a distance of one foot in one minute (about 1½ times the power an average horse can exert). Used for measuring power of steam engines, etc.

Karat (kt) A measure of the purity of gold, indicating how many parts out of 24 are pure. For example: 18 karat gold is ¾ pure. Sometimes spelled *carat*.

Knot Not a distance, but the rate of speed of one nautical mile per hour. Used for measuring speed of ships.

League Rather indefinite and varying measure, but usually estimated at 3 miles in English-speaking countries.

Light-Year 5,880,000,000,000 miles, the distance light travels in a vacuum in a year at the rate of 186,281.7 miles (299,792 kilometers) per second. (If an astronomical unit were represented by one inch, a light-year would be represented by about one mile.) Used for measurements in interstellar space.

Magnum Two-quart bottle. Used for measuring wine, etc.

Ohm Unit of electrical resistance. A circuit in which a potential difference of one volt produces a current of one ampere has a resistance of one ohm.

Parsec Approximately 3.26 light-years of 19.2 million miles. Term is combination of first syllables of *par*allax and *sec*ond, and distance is that of imaginary star when lines drawn from it to both earth and sun form a maximum angle or parallax of one second (1/3600 degree). Used for measuring interstellar distances.

Pi (π) 3.14159265+. The ratio of the circumference of a circle to its diameter. For practical purposes, the value is used to four decimal places: 3.1416.

Pica ⅙ inch or 12 points. Used in printing for measuring column width, etc.

Pipe 2 hogsheads. Used for measuring wine and other liquids.

Point .013837 (approximately ¹⁄₇₂) inch or ¹⁄₁₂ pica. Used in printing for measuring type size.

Quintal 100,000 grams or 220.46 pounds avoirdupois.

Quire Used for measuring paper. Sometimes 24 sheets but more often 25. There are 20 quires to a ream.

Ream Used for measuring paper. Sometimes 480 sheets, but more often 500 sheets.

Roentgen International Unit of radiation exposure produced by X-rays.

Score 20 units.

Sound, Speed of Usually placed at 1,088 ft. per second at 32°F at sea level. It varies at other temperatures and in different media.

Span 9 inches or 22.86 cm. Derived from the distance between the end of the thumb and the end of the little finger when both are outstretched.

Square 100 square feet. Used in building.

Stone Legally 14 pounds avoirdupois in the U.K.

Therm 100,000 Btu's.

Township U.S. land measurement of almost 36 square miles. The south border is 6 miles long. The east and west borders, also 6 miles long, follow the meridians, making the north border slightly less than 6 miles long. Used in surveying.

Tun 252 gallons, but often larger. Used for measuring wine and other liquids.

Watt Unit of power. The power used by a current of one ampere across a potential difference of one volt equals one watt.

Conversion of Miles to Kilometers and Kilometers to Miles

Miles	Kilometers	Miles	Kilometers	Miles	Kilometers	Kilometers	Miles	Kilometers	Miles	Kilometers	Miles
1	1.6	8	12.8	60	96.5	1	0.6	8	4.9	60	37.2
2	3.2	9	14.4	70	112.6	2	1.2	9	5.5	70	43.4
3	4.8	10	16.0	80	128.7	3	1.8	10	6.2	80	49.7
4	6.4	20	32.1	90	144.8	4	2.4	20	12.4	90	55.9
5	8.0	30	48.2	100	160.9	5	3.1	30	18.6	100	62.1
6	9.6	40	64.3	1,000	1609	6	3.7	40	24.8	1,000	621
7	11.2	50	80.4			7	4.3	50	31.0		

Bolts and Screws: Conversion from Fractions of an Inch to Millimeters

Inch	mm	Inch	mm	Inch	mm	Inch	mm
1/64	0.40	17/64	6.75	33/64	13.10	49/64	19.45
1/32	0.79	9/32	7.14	17/32	13.50	25/32	19.84
3/64	1.19	19/64	7.54	35/64	13.90	51/64	20.24
1/16	1.59	5/16	7.94	9/16	14.29	13/16	20.64
5/64	1.98	21/64	8.33	37/64	14.69	53/64	21.03
3/32	2.38	11/32	8.73	19/32	15.08	27/32	21.43
7/64	2.78	23/64	9.13	39/64	15.48	55/64	21.83
1/8	3.18	3/8	9.53	5/8	15.88	7/8	22.23
9/64	3.57	25/64	9.92	41/64	16.27	57/64	22.62
5/32	3.97	13/32	10.32	21/32	16.67	29/32	23.02
11/64	4.37	27/64	10.72	43/64	17.06	59/64	23.42
3/16	4.76	7/16	11.11	11/16	17.46	15/16	23.81
13/64	5.16	29/64	11.51	45/64	17.86	61/64	24.21
7/32	5.56	15/32	11.91	23/32	18.26	31/32	24.61
15/64	5.95	31/64	12.30	47/64	18.65	63/64	25.00
1/4	6.35	1/2	12.70	3/4	19.05	1	25.40

Cooking Measurement Equivalents

16 tablespoons = 1 cup
12 tablespoons = 3/4 cup
10 tablespoons + 2 teaspoons = 2/3 cup
8 tablespoons = 1/2 cup
6 tablespoons = 3/8 cup
5 tablespoons + 1 teaspoon = 1/3 cup
4 tablespoons = 1/4 cup

2 tablespoons = 1/8 cup
2 tablespoons + 2 teaspoons = 1/6 cup
1 tablespoon = 1/16 cup
2 cups = 1 pint
2 pints = 1 quart
3 teaspoons = 1 tablespoon
48 teaspoons = 1 cup

U.S.—Metric Cooking Conversions

U.S. to Metric

Capacity		Weight	
1/5 teaspoon	1 milliliter	1 fluid oz	30 milliliters
			28 grams
1 teaspoon	5 ml	1 pound	454 grams
1 tablespoon	15 ml		
1/5 cup	50 ml		
1 cup	240 ml		
2 cups (1 pint)	470 ml		
4 cups (1 quart)	.95 liter		
4 quarts (1 gal.)	3.8 liters		

Metric to U.S.

Capacity		Weight	
1 milliliter	1/5 teaspoon	1 gram	.035 ounce
5 ml	1 teaspoon	100 grams	3.5 ounces
15 ml	1 tablespoon	500 grams	1.10 pounds
34 ml	1 fluid oz	1 kilogram	2.205 pounds
			35 oz
100 ml	3.4 fluid oz		
240 ml	1 cup		
1 liter	34 fluid oz		
	4.2 cups		
	2.1 pints		
	1.06 quarts		
	0.26 gallon		

Prefixes and Multiples

Prefix	Suffix	Equivalent	Multiple/submultiple	Prefix	Suffix	Equivalent	Multiple/submultiple
atto	a	quintillionth part	10^{-18}	deci	d	tenth part	10^{-1}
femto	f	quadrillionth part	10^{-15}	deka	da	tenfold	10
pico	p	trillionth part	10^{-12}	hecto	h	hundredfold	10^{2}
nano	n	billionth part	10^{-9}	kilo	k	thousandfold	10^{3}
micro	μ	millionth part	10^{-6}	mega	M	millionfold	10^{6}
milli	m	thousandth part	10^{-3}	giga	G	billionfold	10^{9}
centi	c	hundredth part	10^{-2}	tera	T	trillionfold	10^{12}

Common Formulas

Circumference

Circle: $C = \pi d$, in which π is 3.1416 and d the diameter.

Area

Triangle: $A = \frac{ab}{2}$, in which a is the base and b the height.

Square: $A = a^2$, in which a is one of the sides.

Rectangle: $A = ab$, in which a is the base and b the height.

Trapezoid: $A = \frac{h(a+b)}{2}$, in which h is the height, a the longer parallel side, and b the shorter.

Regular pentagon: $A = 1.720a^2$, in which a is one of the sides.

Regular hexagon: $A = 2.598a^2$, in which a is one of the sides.

Regular octagon: $A = 4.828a^2$, in which a is one of the sides.

Circle: $A = \pi r^2$, in which π is 3.1416 and r the radius.

Volume

Cube: $V = a^3$, in which a is one of the edges.

Rectangular prism: $V = abc$, in which a is the length, b is the width, and c the depth.

Pyramid: $V = \frac{Ah}{3}$, in which A is the area of the base and h the height.

Cylinder: $V = \pi r^2 h$, in which π is 3.1416, r the radius of the base, and h the height.

Cone: $V = \frac{\pi r^2 h}{3}$, in which π is 3.1416, r the radius of the base, and h the height.

Sphere: $V = \frac{4 \pi r^3}{3}$, in which π is 3.1416 and r the radius.

Miscellaneous

Distance in feet traveled by falling body: $d = 16t^2$, in which t is the time in seconds.

Speed of sound in feet per second through any given temperature of air:

$$V = \frac{1087 \sqrt{273 + t}}{16.52}$$

, in which t is the temperature Centigrade.

Cost in cents of operation of electrical device:

$$C = \frac{Wtc}{1000}$$

, in which W is the number of watts, t the time in hours, and c the cost in cents per kilowatt-hour.

Conversion of matter into energy (Einstein's Theorem): $E = mc^2$, in which E is the energy in ergs, m the mass of the matter in grams, and c the speed of light in centimeters per second ($c^2 = 9 \times 10^{20}$).

Decimal Equivalents of Common Fractions

1/2	.5000	1/10	.1000	2/7	.2857	3/11	.2727	5/9	.5556	7/11	.6364
1/3	.3333	1/11	.0909	2/9	.2222	4/5	.8000	5/11	.4545	7/12	.5833
1/4	.2500	1/12	.0833	2/11	.1818	4/7	.5714	5/12	.4167	8/9	.8889
1/5	.2000	1/16	.0625	3/4	.7500	4/9	.4444	6/7	.8571	8/11	.7273
1/6	.1667	1/32	.0313	3/5	.6000	4/11	.3636	6/11	.5455	9/10	.9000
1/7	.1429	1/64	.0156	3/7	.4286	5/6	.8333	7/8	.8750	9/11	.8182
1/8	.1250	2/3	.6667	3/8	.3750	5/7	.7143	7/9	.7778	10/11	.9091
1/9	.1111	2/5	.4000	3/10	.3000	5/8	.6250	7/10	.7000	11/12	.9167

Conversion Factors

To change	To	Multiply by	To change	To	Multiply by
acres	hectares	.4047	liters	pints (liquid)	2.1134
acres	square feet	43,560	liters	quarts (dry)	.9081
acres	square miles	.001562	liters	quarts (liquid)	1.0567
atmospheres	cms. of mercury	76	meters	feet	3.2808
BTU	horsepower-hour	.0003931	meters	miles	.0006214
BTU	kilowatt-hour	.0002928	meters	yards	1.0936
BTU/hour	watts	.2931	metric tons	tons (long)	.9842
bushels	cubic inches	2150.4	metric tons	tons (short)	1.1023
bushels (U.S.)	hectoliters	.3524	miles	kilometers	1.6093
centimeters	inches	.3937	miles	feet	5280
centimeters	feet	.03281	miles (nautical)	miles (statute)	1.1516
circumference	radians	6.283	miles (statute)	miles (nautical)	.8684
cubic feet	cubic meters	.0283	miles/hour	feet/minute	88
cubic meters	cubic feet	35.3145	millimeters	inches	.0394
cubic meters	cubic yards	1.3079	ounces avdp.	grams	28.3495
cubic yards	cubic meters	.7646	ounces	pounds	.0625
degrees	radians	.01745	ounces (troy)	ounces (avdp)	1.09714
dynes	grams	.00102	pecks	liters	8.8096
fathoms	feet	6.0	pints (dry)	liters	.5506
feet	meters	.3048	pints (liquid)	liters	.4732
feet	miles (nautical)	.0001645	pounds ap or t	kilograms	.3782
feet	miles (statute)	.0001894	pounds avdp	kilograms	.4536
feet/second	miles/hour	.6818	pounds	ounces	16
furlongs	feet	660.0	quarts (dry)	liters	1.1012
furlongs	miles	.125	quarts (liquid)	liters	.9463
gallons (U.S.)	liters	3.7853	radians	degrees	57.30
grains	grams	.0648	rods	meters	5.029
grams	grains	15.4324	rods	feet	16.5
grams	ounces avdp	.0353	square feet	square meters	.0929
grams	pounds	.002205	square kilometers	square miles	.3861
hectares	acres	2.4710	square meters	square feet	10.7639
hectoliters	bushels (U.S.)	2.8378	square meters	square yards	1.1960
horsepower	watts	745.7	square miles	square kilometers	2.5900
hours	days	.04167	square yards	square meters	.8361
inches	millimeters	25.4000	tons (long)	metric tons	1.016
inches	centimeters	2.5400	tons (short)	metric tons	.9072
kilograms	pounds avdp or t	2.2046	tons (long)	pounds	2240
kilometers	miles	.6214	tons (short)	pounds	2000
kilowatts	horsepower	1.341	watts	Btu/hour	3.4129
knots	nautical miles/hour	1.0	watts	horsepower	.001341
knots	statute miles/hour	1.151	yards	meters	.9144
liters	gallons (U.S.)	.2642	yards	miles	.0005682
liters	pecks	.1135			
liters	pints (dry)	1.8162			

Fahrenheit and Celsius (Centigrade) Scales

°Celsius	°Farenheit	°Celsius	°Farenheit
-273.1	-459.6	30	86
-250	-418	35	95
-200	-328	40	104
-150	-238	45	113
-100	-148	50	122
-50	-58	55	131
-40	-40	60	140
-30	-22	65	149
-20	-4	70	158
-10	14	75	167
0	32	80	176
5	41	85	185
10	50	90	194
15	59	95	203
20	68	100	212
25	77		

Zero on the Fahrenheit scale represents the temperature produced by the mixing of equal weights of snow and common salt.

	°Fahrenheit	°Celsius
Boiling point of water	212°	100°
Freezing point of water	32°	0°
Absolute zero	-459.6°	-273.1°

Absolute zero is theoretically the lowest possible temperature, the point at which all molecular motion would cease.

To convert Fahrenheit to Celsius (Centigrade), subtract 32 and multiply by ⅝.

To convert Celsius (Centigrade) to Fahrenheit, multiply by ⅖ and add 32.

Roman Numerals

Roman numerals are expressed by letters of the alphabet and are rarely used today except for formality or variety.

There are three basic principles for reading Roman numerals:

1. A letter repeated once or twice repeats its value that many times (XXX = 30, CC = 200, etc.).

2. One or more letters placed after another letter of greater value increases the greater value by the amount of the smaller. (VI = 6, LXX = 70, MCC = 1200, etc.).

3. A letter placed before another letter of greater value decreases the greater value by the amount of the smaller. (IV = 4, XC = 90, CM = 900, etc.).

Letter	Value	Letter	Value	Letter	Value	Letter	Value	Letter	Value
I	1	VI	6	XX	20	LXX	70	M	1,000
II	2	VII	7	XXX	30	LXXX	80	$\bar{V}$	5,000
III	3	VIII	8	XL	40	XC	90	$\bar{X}$	10,000
IV	4	IX	9	L	50	C	100	$\bar{L}$	50,000
V	5	X	10	LX	60	D	500	$\bar{C}$	100,000
								$\bar{D}$	500,000
								$\bar{M}$	1,000,000

Mean and Median

The arithmetic mean, also called the average, of a series of quantities is obtained by finding the sum of the quantities and dividing by the number of quantities. In the series 1, 3, 5, 18, 19, 20, 25, the mean or average is 13—in other words, 91 divided by 7.

The median of a series is that point which so divides it that half the quantities are on one side, half on the other. In the above series, the median is 18.

The median often better expresses the common-run, since it is not, as is the mean, affected by an excessively high or low figure. In the series 1, 3, 4, 7, 55, the median of 4 is a truer expression of the common-run than is the mean of 14.

Prime Numbers Between 1 and 1,000

2	3	5	7	11	13	17	19	23
29	31	37	41	43	47	53	59	61	67
71	73	79	83	89	97	101	103	107	109
113	127	131	137	139	149	151	157	163	167
173	179	181	191	193	197	199	211	223	227
229	233	239	241	251	257	263	269	271	277
281	283	293	307	311	313	317	331	337	347
349	353	359	367	373	379	383	389	397	401
409	419	421	431	433	439	443	449	457	461
463	467	479	487	491	499	503	509	521	523
541	547	557	563	569	571	577	587	593	599
601	607	613	617	619	631	641	643	647	653
659	661	673	677	683	691	701	709	719	727
733	739	743	751	757	761	769	773	787	797
809	811	821	823	827	829	839	853	857	859
863	877	881	883	887	907	911	919	929	937
941	947	953	967	971	977	983	991	997	(1009)

Definitions of Gold Terminology

The term "fineness" defines a gold content in parts per thousand. For example, a gold nugget containing 885 parts of pure gold, 100 parts of silver, and 15 parts of copper would be considered 885-fine.

The word "karat" indicates the proportion of solid gold in an alloy based on a total of 24 parts. Thus, 14-karat (14K) gold indicates a composition of 14 parts of gold and 10 parts of other metals.

The term "gold-filled" is used to describe articles of jewelry made of base metal which are covered on one or more surfaces with a layer of gold alloy. No article having a gold alloy portion of less than one twentieth by weight may be marked "gold-filled." Articles may be marked "rolled gold plate" provided the proportional fraction and fineness designations are also shown.

Electroplated jewelry items carrying at least 7 millionths of an inch of gold on significant surfaces may be labeled "electroplate." Plate thicknesses less than this may be marked "gold-flashed" or "gold-washed."

Portraits and Designs of U.S. Paper Currency

Currency[1]	Portrait	Design on back	Currency[1]	Portrait	Design on back
$1	Washington	ONE between obverse and reverse of Great Seal of U.S.	$50[4]	Grant	U.S. Capitol
			$100[5]	Franklin	Independence Hall
$2[2]	Jefferson	Monticello	$500	McKinley	Ornate FIVE HUNDRED
$2[3]	Jefferson	"The Signing of the Declaration of Independence"	$1,000	Cleveland	Ornate ONE THOUSAND
			$5,000	Madison	Ornate FIVE THOUSAND
$5	Lincoln	Lincoln Memorial	$10,000	Chase	Ornate TEN THOUSAND
$10	Hamilton	U.S. Treasury Building	$100,000[6]	Wilson	Ornate ONE HUNDRED THOUSAND
$20	Jackson	White House			

1. Denominations of $500 and higher were discontinued in 1969. 2. Discontinued in 1966. 3. New issue, April 1976. 4. New issue, Fall 1997. 5. New issue, March 1996. 6. For use only in transactions between Federal Reserve System and Treasury Department.

Energy

Electric Cars Powered By Gasoline?

Gasoline at the pump may power fuel cells in the family electric car

Rethinking Old Technology

Electric cars are by no means new: Americans began constructing efficient "electric carriages" as far back as 1890 when William Morrison built one in Des Moines that could travel for 13 hours at a speed of 14 mph (22.5 kph). As early as 1899, electric taxis, trams, and omnibuses were commonly seen in major cities, and electric and steam-powered cars outsold gasoline buggies. Between 1900 and 1915, more than 60 American companies were building electric vehicles, including the Andrew Riker Company (1896–1901), which offered a wide range of styles and models. In 1901, the company's electric-powered racer, the Riker Torpedo, set a record run for the mile at 57.14 mph (92 kph). Another firm, the Walker Baker Company (1899–1914), created an electric-powered racer that could go over 75 mph (120.7 kph) and was the first car to have passenger seat belts. Although electric cars were clean, quiet, and simple to operate, their drawback then, as now, was their limited range and long charging time. After 1915, they fell out of vogue as cars powered by internal-combustion engines and fueled with cheap gasoline gained favor.

As concerns in recent years have grown about global warming caused by carbon-dioxide emissions, scientists have begun to reconsider electricity as a fuel for vehicles. But today's drivers expect a vehicle that is fuel efficient, and a fuel that is readily available in numerous locations and allows "instant" refueling. Though electric cars are fairly efficient, they require frequent refueling, and the process is far from instantaneous. They're expensive, too, since normal use causes their $2,000 lead-acid batteries to wear out in just a few years. And, ironically, electric cars do very little to reduce carbon dioxide emissions because most electricity in the U.S. is generated by burning coal and other fossil fuels. To gain consumer acceptance, the car of the future will need to balance the benefits of electric cars with consumer demands for distance and dynamo. The hybrid electric vehicle holds promise as a solution to both these needs.

What Is a Hybrid Electric Vehicle?

A hybrid electric vehicle combines two sources of energy such as a battery-powered electric motor and a conventional internal combustion engine, enabling the driver to decide which source of power is appropriate for the travel requirements of given journey. Short jaunts to the grocery store or the post office could use the electric motor, while weekends in the country may require the internal combustion engine. Major American auto manufacturers are now developing production-feasible hybrid electric vehicles, and some are exploring fuel-cell technology for their electric cars.

An Extraordinary Approach

Chrysler Corporation and Delphi Automotive Systems are collaborating to build a prototype car that would use fuel cells to produce electricity to run the automobile's electric motor. Chrysler has been working with Arthur D. Little, the technology-based consulting firm, to develop this technology. Their goal is to design a fuel-cell system in which the fuel cell, batteries and electric motor are all packaged to fit into a mid-size car. The fuel cell will use an on-board fuel processor in a multi-stage, chemical reactive process to convert gasoline to water, carbon dioxide, and hydrogen, which will then be used to create electricity to power the car. The fuel cells would thereby deliver the same range as conventional gasoline-powered cars and could significantly improve fuel economy.

Current fuel cells are impractical for a number of reasons. First is the cost; current fuel cells would need to be one-tenth of their current price to be a practical alternative. There is hope, however. Prices have fallen dramatically over the past ten years, and are now only about one percent of 1987 costs.

Another obstacle is technology. Current fuel cells require hydrogen or methanol, which are not readily available to consumers (when is the last time you saw hydrogen for sale at the local filling station?). Furthermore, these fuels are required large quantities so space limitations make it difficult to store sufficient amounts onboard the vehicle. Fuel cells designed to use gasoline offer obvious advantages (one could "fill-up" an electric car at the pump with a standard-sized tank), but they do not yet exist. Another technological hurdle involves start-up time. Fuel cells need about five minutes to warm up before they can be used, so additional batteries may be needed to heat the system to operating temperatures.

Despite these challenges, fuel cells are regarded as one of the most promising future technologies. If the prototype development succeeds, it will revolutionize the automobile industry, offering affordable, environmentally friendly cars with the range, rapid refueling, and performance of conventional vehicles.—*OTJ*

Fuel Cell FAQs

The following frequently asked questions about fuel cells were provided courtesy of Fuel Cells 2000, a non-profit advocacy organization.

What is a fuel cell? In principle, a fuel cell operates like a battery. It supplies electricity by combining hydrogen and oxygen electrochemically without combustion. Unlike a battery, a fuel cell does not run down or require recharging. It will produce energy in the form of electricity and heat as long as fuel is supplied. The only "waste" is pure, drinkable water. A fuel cell consists of two electrodes sandwiched around an electrolyte. Oxygen passes over one electrode and hydrogen over the other, generating electricity, water, and heat.

Where did fuel cells come from? The first fuel cell was built in 1839 by Sir William Grove, a Welsh judge and gentleman scientist. Serious interest in the fuel cell as a practical generator did not begin until the 1960s, when they were chosen as the fuel of choice for the U.S. space program over nuclear power, considered too risky, and solar energy, considered too expensive. Fuel cells furnished power for the Gemini and Apollo spacecrafts, and provide electricity and water for the space shuttle.

What sort of fuels can be used in a fuel cell? Fuel cells can run on a variety of fuels, including hydrogen, methanol, ethanol, natural gas, and liquefied petroleum gas. Energy from biomass, wind, and solar sources can also be used. Because they function on such diverse input, fuel cells are a logical choice to transition from current technologies to renewable energy sources.

Which type of fuel cell is best? According to a recent study by Arthur D. Little, Inc., there is no single "winner" that will eclipse other types of fuel cells because the market for fuel cells is so diverse, ranging from large utility power plants to automobiles. The attributes of each fuel cell make it particularly suited to certain applications; for example, the gasoline fuel cell (when it is developed) will be most useful in electric cars. Though the hydrogen fuel cell is not suited to this application, it does not mean that the gasoline fuel cell is "better." No single type of fuel cell is best; each is suited to a particular purpose.

Where were fuel cells developed? The first commercial fuel cell to run on renewable fuel was dedicated in June 1996 at a landfill in Groton, Connecticut, ushering in a new era in energy generation. The 200 KW fuel cell system is used to clean up landfill gas and convert its methane to electricity, which is fed into a nearby power grid.

Additional information about fuel cells. Readers may write to Fuel Cells 2000, an activity of the Breakthrough Technologies Institute at 1625 "K" Street NW, Suite 790, Washington, DC 20006. Phone: 202-785-9620, Fax: 202-785-9629, or visit their web site at: www.fuelcells.org.

Fuel Cells 2000 provides information to policy makers and the public; supports the early utilization of fuel cells through pilot projects and government purchases; fosters education and training for the legal and regulatory communities for fuel cells and related technologies.

Energy Overview

Source: Annual Energy Review, 1996.

Production

Historically, three fossil fuels have accounted for the bulk of domestic energy production, which by 1996 totaled 72.6 quadrillion Btu. Coal accounted for the largest share of domestic energy production in 1949–1951 and, after a long hiatus, again in 1982 and in 1984 through 1996. In the interim, first crude oil and then natural gas dominated domestic production. In 1996, coal production totaled 22.6 quadrillion Btu. Dry natural gas production totaled 19.5 quadrillion Btu and crude oil production totaled 13.7 quadrillion Btu. Natural gas plant liquids accounted for another 2.5 quadrillion Btu.

Net generation of electricity by electric utilities increased throughout the 1949–1996 period, registering only two year-to-year declines (during the 1982 recession and again in 1992). However, the rate of growth of electricity net generation slowed during the 48-year period. From 1949 through 1979, the annual growth rate averaged 7.1 percent, whereas from 1980 through 1996, the annual growth rate averaged 1.9 percent. After the mid-1970s, coal and nuclear fuels provided increasing shares of fuel input for electricity generation, displacing substantial quantities of petroleum and, to a lesser extent, natural gas.

Hydroelectric generation (conventional and pumped storage) accounted for over 1.4 quadrillion Btu of electricity in 1949, and from the 1970s through 1995 usually provided about 3 quadrillion Btu per year. In 1988, the second year of drought, hydroelectric generation totaled only 2.3 quadrillion Btu, but it reached a record high in 1996 of 3.6 quadrillion Btu.

Other renewable energy sources also contributed to the domestic energy supply. Biofuels, a category which includes wood and waste, contributed 3.0 quadrillion Btu to the 1996 total. Geothermal, solar, and wind energy combined contributed 0.5 quadrillion Btu. Renewable energy production (including conventional hydroelectric power and excluding hydroelectric pumped storage) totaled 7.1 quadrillion Btu, 9.7 percent of U.S. total energy production.

Consumption

Energy consumption more than doubled during the 1949–1973 period, increasing from 30.5 quadrillion Btu in 1949 to 74.3 quadrillion Btu in 1973, and the U.S. economy grew at about the same rate. The domestic energy market was dominated by rapid growth in petroleum and natural gas consumption, which more than tripled during the period. After the 1973 oil shock, energy consumption fluctuated, influenced by dramatic changes in oil prices, changes in the rate of growth of the domestic economy, and such factors as concerns about the effect of energy use on the environment. The post-1973 low point of energy consumption, 70.5 quadrillion Btu, occurred in 1983 following a period of very high oil prices. The highest level of energy consumption, 93.8 quadrillion Btu, occurred in 1996, following several years when oil prices were low.

The composition of demand after 1973 reflected an increasing emphasis on electricity generated by coal, nuclear, and renewable energy sources and on non-electric utility use of renewable sources. In 1973, petroleum and natural gas accounted for 77 percent of total energy consumption; by 1995, their share had declined to 63 percent.

Changing Patterns of Trade

From 1958 forward, the United States consumed more energy than it produced, and the difference was met by energy imports. Net imports of energy (primarily petroleum) grew rapidly through 1973, as demand for cheap foreign oil eroded quotas on petroleum imports. The oil embargo of 1973–1974, coupled with the increase in the price of crude oil, interrupted growth in petroleum net imports; nevertheless, they climbed to a peak of 18 quadrillion Btu in 1977. That year, U.S. dependence on foreign sources of petroleum reached an all-time high of 47 percent. A second round of price increases in 1979 through 1981 suppressed demand for foreign oil. In 1985, petroleum net imports totaled 9.0 quadrillion Btu, and U.S. dependence fell to 27 percent of consumption. Subsequently, petroleum net imports increased every year through 1989, when U.S. dependence on foreign sources of petroleum reached 42 percent of consumption. In 1996, petroleum net imports rose to 18 quadrillion Btu and U.S. dependence on them equaled 46 percent—the second highest level in 19 years.

Natural gas trade was limited to border countries until the advent of shipping natural gas in liquefied form in the late 1960s. In 1996, natural gas net imports reached the record level of 2.8 quadrillion Btu.

Throughout the 1949–1996 period, the United States was a net exporter of coal. In 1996, coal net exports totaled 2.2 quadrillion Btu. □

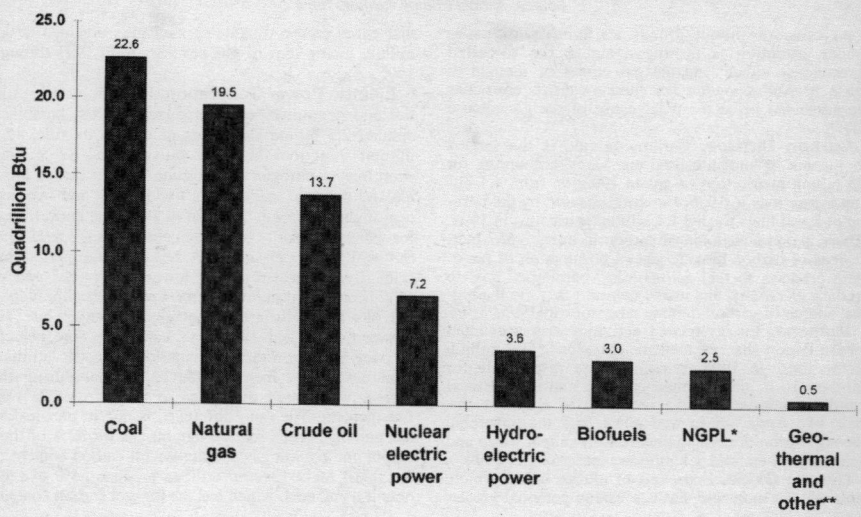

Energy Production by Source, 1996

*Natural gas plant liquids. **Conventional and pumped-storage hydroelectric power. *Source:* Energy Information Administration, *Annual Energy Review, 1996*.

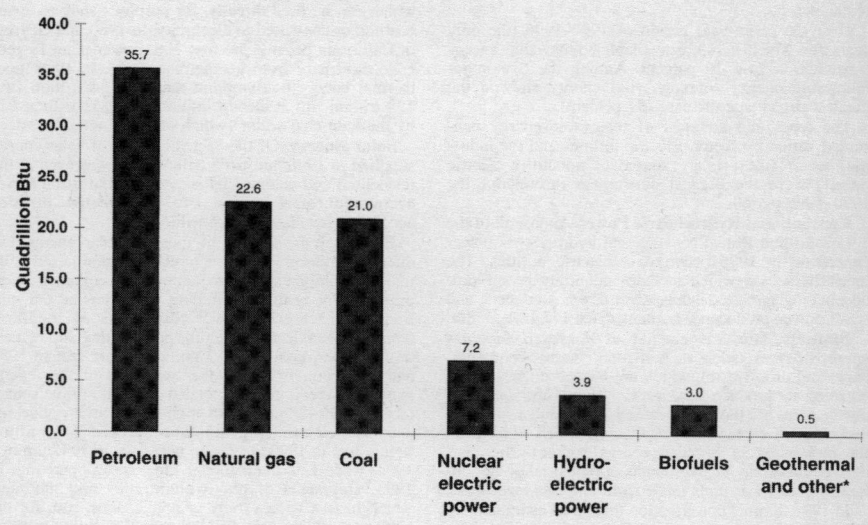

Energy Consumption by Source, 1996

*Conventional and pumped-storage hydroelectric power. *Source:* Energy Information Administration, *Annual Energy Review, 1996*.

World Greenhouse Gas Emissions

Source: Annual Energy Review, 1996.

As concerns about global warming continue to mount, attention is turning again to the so-called "greenhouse effect" and the gas emissions thought to cause it. Anthropogenic, or human-caused, emissions are suspected to be the chief cause of the greenhouse effect.

Carbon Dioxide. Carbon dioxide is the largest component of human-caused emissions, accounting for 5.3 billion metric tons of gas in 1995, up from 4.7 billion metric tons in 1985. Emissions caused by the burning of fossil fuels totaled 1.4 billion metric tons in 1995. (There is one metric ton of carbon in every 3.667 metric tons of carbon dioxide gas.) Consumption of petroleum products to fuel automobiles, burning of coal to produce electricity, and use of natural gas, were the biggest source of carbon dioxide emissions in 1995.

Methane. Energy-related activities also accounted for the largest share of methane emissions (11.4 million metric tons) in 1994. Landfills were responsible for another 10.2 million metric tons, and agricultural sources (such as digestive processes in ruminant animals like cattle, sheep and goats, and the anaerobic decomposition of organic materials in animal waste and rice paddies) emitted 9.1 million metric tons in 1994.

Nitrous Oxide. Emissions of nitrous oxide, which, molecule for molecule, has a warming potential greater

that either carbon dioxide or methane, remained at 0.5 million metric tons of gas per year from 1991 through 1995.

Electric Power Generation. In 1995, electric utilities and nonutility power producers (NPPs) combined emitted 2.5 billion short tons of carbon dioxide, 12.9 million short tons of sulfur dioxide, and 8.7 million short tons of nitrogen oxides. Emissions of carbon dioxide and nitrogen oxides were five percent and two percent higher, respectively, than in 1992, the earliest year for which data for both utilities and NPPs are available. Sulfur dioxide emissions fell 22% over the period due primarily to greater use of lower sulfur coal and of scrubbers at electric utility coal-fired generating units.

NPPs raised their total net electric output by 27% between 1992 and 1995 at a cost of a nine percent increase in carbon dioxide emissions. Electric utilities' total net output increased seven percent during the period, while their emissions of carbon dioxide rose four percent. The ratio difference is due in part to fuel use patterns: NPPs rely on natural gas for 52% of their output and natural gas has the lowest carbon content of the fossil fuels. Electric utilities produce 54% of their output using coal, which has the highest carbon content.

Renewable Energy Consumption

Source: Annual Energy Review, 1996.

In 1996, the United States consumed an estimated 7.4 quadrillion Btu of renewable energy. Conventional hydroelectric power and biofuels accounted for the largest shares (53 percent and 41 percent, respectively). Geothermal, solar, and wind energy accounted for the remainder.

Over the seven-year period of 1990–1996 (the only years for which data are available), renewable energy consumption rose 20 percent. Among the five major renewable energy sources, wind energy showed the greatest percentage increase (57 percent).

The types and amounts of renewable energy consumed varied by sector. Electric utilities and the industrial sector (the primary source of nonutility electric power) were the biggest consumers throughout the 1990–1996 period.

Conventional Hydroelectric Power. Almost all of the 3.9 quadrillion Btu of conventional hydroelectric power generation in 1996 occurred at electric utilities. The industrial sector, which includes nonutility power producers (cogenerators, independent power producers, and small power producers), accounted for 172 trillion Btu.

Biofuels. Biofuels consist of *nonfossil biomass energy sources* (such as fuelwood, waste wood, garbage, and crop waste), which are burned or gasified as received to produce heat or electricity, and *biomass-derived fuels* (including wood byproducts, refuse-derived fuel, ethanol, and methanol), which result from the processing of biomass energy sources. Biomass-derived fuels may be byproducts of industrial or agricultural processes or fuels made from biomass feedstocks.

In 1996, biofuel consumption totaled an estimated 3.0 quadrillion Btu, most of which (2.4 quadrillion Btu) was wood energy. Some industries, such as the paper and lumber industries, have ready access to wood and wood byproducts and rely heavily on wood as an energy source. Consumption of municipal solid waste and other wastes totaled 503 trillion Btu in 1996. Consumption of

alcohol fuels (ethanol) fell 29% to 74 trillion Btu, due to sharply higher prices for corn, the primary ethanol feedstock.

Geothermal Energy. The third biggest source of renewable energy in 1996 was geothermal energy, which can be used directly, for purposes such as space heating, or converted to electricity. In 1960, the Geysers in California became the first U.S. power plant to generate electricity from geothermal steam. In 1996, geothermal energy consumption reached 354 trillion Btu, 123 trillion Btu at electric utilities and 231 trillion Btu by the industrial sector (which includes nonutilities).

Solar Energy. Of the 75 trillion Btu of solar energy supplied in 1996, most (65 trillion Btu) was used in the residential and commercial sector. The industrial sector accounted for 9 trillion Btu and electric utilities accounted for less than 0.5 trillion Btu.

Because it is difficult to measure solar energy use directly, producer shipments of equipment are used as an indicator. Shipments of low-temperature collectors, used primarily for heating swimming pools, totaled 6.8 million square feet in 1995. Shipments of medium-temperature collectors, used for pool heating and domestic hot water, peaked at 12 million square feet in 1983 and 1984 but, following the expiration of the federal energy tax credit in 1985, totaled only 0.8 million square feet in 1995. Shipments of high-temperature collectors, used for electricity generation, reached 5.2 million square feet in 1990 but fell to near zero in 1991 through 1994, when Luz International Ltd. ceased operating. In 1995, shipments of photovoltaic cells and modules, which have a wide variety of applications, rose for the tenth consecutive year, to 31 thousand peak kilowatts.

Wind Energy. An estimated 36 trillion Btu of wind energy was consumed in 1996, virtually all in the industrial sector (which includes nonutilities). Very small amounts (less than 0.5 trillion Btu) were consumed at electric utilities. ☐

Nuclear Power Generation Status

Source: Annual Energy Review, 1996.

Nuclear electric power production in 1996 totaled 675 billion kilowatt-hours, up less than one percent from the 1995 level. At the end of 1996, there were 110 licensed operable nuclear generating units in the United States, most of them located east of the Mississippi River. Six other facilities had been granted construction permits, but construction on all six units had been halted or canceled. No new plants had been ordered or announced in 1996; the 1996 total of 116 plants is well below the peak total of 226 in 1974. After 1974, many planned units were canceled; after 1997, no orders for new units were announced.

The Three Mile Island accident in 1979 greatly increased concerns about the safety of nuclear power plants. In response to these concerns, new regulations governing the operation and construction of nuclear facilities were implemented. The new guidelines made nuclear plants even more expensive to build and run, which has also contributed to the decline in the number of planned nuclear units. ☐

Energy Web Sites

U.S. Department of Energy: www.doe.gov/
Energy Efficiency and Renewable Energy Network (EREN): www.eren.doe.gov
Federal Energy Regulatory Commission: www.ferc.fed.us
Energy Information Administration (EIA): www.eia.doe.gov
Nuclear Regulatory Commission (NRC): www.nrc.gov
National Renewable Energy Laboratories (NREL): www.nrel.gov
Alliance to Save Energy: www.ase.org/index.htm
Natural Resources Defense Council: www.nrdc.org/
Alternative Energy: www.webdirectory.com/Science/Energy/Alternative_Energy/
American Council for an Energy-Efficient Economy: aceee.org
The Center for Renewable Energy and Sustainable Technology (Solstice): solstice.crest.org

Largest Nuclear Power Plants in the United States

(over a million kilowatts)

Plant	Operating utility	Capacity (kilowatts)	Year operative
South Texas 1, TX	Houston Lighting & Power	1,250,000	1988
South Texas 2	Houston Lighting	1,250,000	1989
Palo Verde 1, AZ	Arizona Public Service	1,221,000	1986
Palo Verde 2, AZ	Arizona Public Service	1,221,000	1986
Palo Verde 3, AZ	Arizona Public Service	1,221,000	1988
Perry 1, OH	Cleveland Electric Illumination	1,205,000	1987
Sequoyah 1, TN	Tennessee Valley Authority	1,148,000	1981
Sequoyah 2, TN	Tennessee Valley Authority	1,148,000	1982
Callaway, MO	Union Electric	1,145,000	1984
Grand Gulf 1, MS	System Energy Resources	1,142,000	1985
Millstone 3, CT	Northeast Nuclear Energy	1,142,000	1986
Catawba 1, SC	Duke Power Co.	1,129,000	1985
Catawba 2, SC	Duke Power Co.	1,129,000	1986
McGuire 1, NC	Duke Power Co.	1,129,000	1981
McGuire 2, NC	Duke Power Co.	1,129,000	1984
Wolf Creek 1, KS	Wolf Creek Nuclear Operating	1,128,000	1985
Braidwood 1, IL	Commonwealth Edison	1,120,000	1988
Braidwood 2, IL	Commonwealth Edison	1,120,000	1988
Salem 1, DE	Public Service Electric & Gas	1,106,000	1977
Salem 2, DE	Public Service Electric & Gas	1,106,000	1981
Byron 1, IL	Commonwealth Edison	1,105,000	1985
Byron 2, IL	Commonwealth Edison	1,105,000	1987
Vogtle 2	Georgia Power	1,083,000	1989
Trojan, OR	Portland General Electric	1,095,000	1976
Fermi 2, OH	Detroit Edison	1,093,000	1988
Diablo Canyon 2	Pacific Gas & Electric	1,087,000	1986
Nine Mile Point 2, NY	Niagara Mohawk Power	1,080,000	1988
San Onofre 3, CA	Southern California Edison	1,080,000	1984
Vogtle 1, GA	Georgia Power	1,079,000	1987
Waterford 3, LA	Louisiana Power & Light	1,075,000	1985
Diablo Canyon 1, CA	Pacific Gas & Electric	1,073,000	1985
San Onofre 2, CA	Southern California Edison	1,070,000	1983
Hope Creek 1, DE	Public Service Electric & Gas	1,067,000	1986
Browns Ferry 1, AL	Tennessee Valley Authority	1,065,000	1974
Browns Ferry 2, AL	Tennessee Valley Authority	1,065,000	1975
Browns Ferry 3, AL	Tennessee Valley Authority	1,065,000	1977
Limerick 2	Philadelphia Electric	1,065,000	1990
Cook 2, MI	Indiana & Michigan Power	1,060,000	1978
Limerick 1, PA	Philadelphia Electric	1,055,000	1986
Peach Bottom 2, PA	Philadelphia Electric	1,051,000	1974
Zion 1, IL	Commonwealth Edison	1,040,000	1973
Zion 2, IL	Commonwealth Edison	1,040,000	1974

Plant	Operating utility	Capacity (kilowatts)	Year operative
La Salle 1, IL	Commonwealth Edison	1,036,000	1984
La Salle 2, IL	Commonwealth Edison	1,036,000	1984
Peach Bottom 3, PA	Philadelphia Gas & Electric	1,035,000	1974
Susquehanna 1, PA	Pennsylvania Power & Light	1,032,000	1983
Susquehanna 2, PA	Pennsylvania Power & Light	1,032,000	1985
Comanche Peak 1, TX	Texas Utilities	1,159,000	1990
Seabrook 1, NH	Public Service of N.H.	1,150,000	1990
Comanche Peak 2, TX	Texas Utilities	1,150,000	1993
Watts Bar I	Tennessee Valley Authority	1,160,000	1996

Source: Nuclear Regulatory Commission.

Estimated Number of Alternative-Fueled Vehicles in Use by Type, 1992–1996

Year	Liquefied petroleum gases[1]	Compressed natural gas	Liquefied natural gas	Methanol, 85%[2]	Ethanol, neat	Ethanol, 85%[2]	Ethanol, 95%[2]	Electricity	Total
1992	221,000	23,191	90	4,850	404	172	38	1,607	251,352
1993	269,000	32,714	299	10,263	414	441	27	1,690	314,848
1994	264,000	41,227	484	15,484	415	605	33	2,224	324,472
1995	259,000	50,218	603	18,319	386	1,527	136	2,860	333,049
1996	266,000	62,805	715	19,636	155	3,575	341	3,306	356,533

1. Vehicles in use represent lower bound estimates, rounded to the nearest thousand. 2. Remaining portion is motor gasoline. *Sources:* Energy Information Administration, *Alternatives to Traditional Transportation Fuels 1995* (December 1996), Tables 1 and 7.

Motor Vehicle Efficiency

Year	Passenger cars			All motor vehicles[1]		
	Miles per car	Gallons per car	Miles per gallon	Miles per vehicle	Gallons per vehicle	Miles per gallon
1990	10,548	502	21.02	11,107	677	16.40
1991	10,757	496	21.69	11,294	668	16.90
1992	11,100	512	21.68	11,558	683	16.91
1993	11,759[R]	559[R]	21.04[R]	11,597[R]	693	16.73[R]
1994	11,210[R]	504[R]	22.24	11,683[R]	698[R]	16.74
1995[P]	11,329	502	22.56[R]	11,801	698	16.91[R]

1. Passenger cars, motorcycles, buses, and trucks. R = Revised data. P = Preliminary data. *Source:* 1986 forward—Federal Highway Administration, *Highway Statistics,* annual, Table VM-1M.

Motor Vehicle Registrations and Motor Fuel Consumption

Year	Motor vehicle registrations (millions)					Motor fuel consumption[1] (thousand barrels per day)		
	Passenger Cars	Motorcycles	Buses	Trucks	Total	Gasoline[2]	Other Fuels[3]	Total[4]
1990	143.5	4.3	(5)	45.1	192.9	7,454	1,396	8,849
1991	143.0	4.2	(5)	45.4	192.5	7,323	1,349	8,672
1992	144.2	4.1	(5)	46.1	194.4	7,472	1,430	8,902
1993	146.3	4.0	(5)	47.7	198.0	7,607	1,534	9,141
1994	133.9[R,6]	3.7[R]	(5)	64.1[R,6]	201.8[R]	7,807[R]	1,639[R]	9,446[R]
1995	136.1	3.7	(5)	64.8	204.6	7,844	1,709	9,554

1. Includes only motor fuel taxed at the prevailing tax rates in each state. Excludes motor fuel exempt from tax payment, subject to tax refund, or taxed at rates other than the prevailing tax rate. Experience has shown that the total motor fuel consumption quantity cited here equals more than 99.0% of gross reported motor fuel consumption. 2. Motor gasoline, aviation gasoline, and gasohol. 3. Distillate fuel oil (diesel oil), liquefied gases, and kerosene when they are used to operate vehicles on highways. Excludes jet fuel beginning in 1962. 4. Excludes losses allowed for evaporation, handling, etc. 5. Included in trucks. 6. Beginning with 1994, personal passenger vans, passenger minivans, and utility-type vehicles are included in "Trucks" instead of "Automobiles." R = Revised data. E = Estimate. NOTE: Sum of components may not equal total due to independent rounding. *Source:* Federal Highway Administration, *Selected Highway Statistics and Charts 1995.*

International Energy

World Leaders

Worldwide energy production of 363 quadrillion Btu in 1995 was 49 quadrillion Btu greater than in 1985. The relative contributions of the four leading energy producers changed markedly over the ten-year period.

In 1986, the former U.S.S.R. was the leading producer of energy and its production of 65 quadrillion Btu accounted for 20.8 percent of the world total. The United States, the second leading producer, accounted for 64 quadrillion Btu, a 20.5 percent share.

As of December 31, 1991, the U.S.S.R. ceased to exist as a political entity. Three of the U.S.S.R.'s constituent republics (Russia, Ukraine, and Kazakhstan) together produced 46 quadrillion Btu of energy in 1994. That year the United States produced 71 quadrillion Btu.

Energy production in China, the third largest producer of energy in 1986, increased throughout the 10-year period. In 1986, China produced 25 quadrillion Btu of energy, much of which was coal. By 1995, Chinese production had reached 35 quadrillion Btu.

At 12 quadrillion Btu, Saudi Arabia was the fourth largest producer of energy in 1986. During the remainder of the 10-year period, Saudi Arabia energy production expanded nearly 70 percent. By 1995, it had risen to 20 quadrillion Btu.

Crude Oil Production in 1996

World production of crude oil totaled 64.0 million barrels per day in 1996, up 2.5 percent from the 1995 level. The most noticeable production increases occurred in Norway (up 12%), Venezuela (up 11%), and Nigeria (up 10%). Production declined 1.4% in the United States to 6.5 million barrels per day, and 2.0% in Russia to 5.9 million barrels per day. In Saudi Arabia, the largest producer of crude oil in 1996, production was essentially unchanged at 8.2 million barrels per day. Crude oil production by all members of the Organization of Petroleum Exporting Countries (OPEC) combined rose to 26.8 million barrels per day and accounted for 42% of the world total in 1996.

Natural Gas Production in 1995

World production of dry natural gas totaled 78 trillion cubic feet and, on a Btu basis, equaled 21 percent of world energy production in 1995. Natural gas production in 1995 was 171 percent above the 1993 level. Russia was the major producer of natural gas in 1995 and accounted for 21 trillion cubic feet, a 27 percent share of the world total. The United States was the second largest producer and accounted for 19 trillion cubic feet, a 24 percent share.

Coal Production in 1995

World production of coal totaled 5.1 billion short tons and, on a Btu basis, equaled 25 percent of world energy production in 1995. China, the leading producer, accounted for 1.5 billion short tons in 1995. Coal production in the United States, the second leading producer, totaled 1.0 billion short tons. India accounted for 311 million short tons and Russia for 310 million short tons.

Electricity Generation

As of January 1, 1995, world electricity installed capacity at all sites (including nonutility power producers) totaled 2.9 billion kilowatts. Most of the capacity (65 percent) was fossil fuel-fired. Hydroelectric generating capacity accounted for 22 percent and nuclear electric generating capacity accounted for 12 percent.

Renewable sources, such as biofuels and geothermal, solar, and wind energy, accounted for less than 1 percent of the world total.

World net electricity generation totaled 12.1 trillion kilowatthours in 1994. Fossil fuel-fired net generation totaled 7.6 trillion kilowatthours. The United States, with 2.3 trillion kilowatthours, was by far the largest producer of fossil fuel-fired net generation. China's net generation totaled 684 billion kilowatthours and Japan's totaled 580 billion kilowatthours. World hydroelectric power net generation in 1995 totaled 2.5 trillion kilowatthours, up 5 percent from the 1994 level. The top five countries in hydroelectric power net generation (Canada, the United States, Brazil, Russia, and China) together accounted for half of the world's total. In 1995, nuclear-based electricity gross generation totaled 2.4 trillion kilowatthours. The U.S. share of the world total was 30 percent. France accounted for 17% and Japan for 12% of the world total.

Petroleum Prices and Demand

Following Iraq's invasion of Kuwait in August 1990, the average price of crude oil rose to $22.22 per barrel, the highest in five years, and year-to-year growth in world petroleum consumption of only one percent was the lowest in those years. In 1991, following the resolution of the war in the Persian Gulf, the average price of crude oil fell to $19.06 per barrel. World consumption of petroleum rose 0.9 percent to 67 million barrels per day. In 1992 through 1994, the average price of crude oil fell further, reaching $15.59 per barrel. In real terms, the 1994 price was the lowest in 21 years. In 1995, the price rose 11% to $17.23 per barrel, while world consumption increased to 70 million barrels per day.

From 1960 through 1995, the United States consumed more petroleum by far than any other country. In 1995, U.S. consumption accounted for 42 percent of the 42 million barrels per day consumed by the Organization for Economic Cooperation and Development (OECD) countries. Japan consumed 5.7 million barrels per day. Of the non-OECD countries, China and Russia were the biggest consumers, accounting for 3.3 million barrels per day and 2.9 million barrels per day, respectively.

Dry Natural Gas Consumption in 1995

Although natural gas can be transported across borders in pipelines and some natural gas is shipped as liquefied natural gas, in general, natural gas tends to be consumed closer to its site of production than does petroleum. Not surprisingly, the two top producers of dry natural gas in 1995 were also the top consumers. U.S. consumption of dry natural gas totaled 22 trillion cubic feet, equal to 116 percent of its production. Russia consumed 15 trillion cubic feet, an amount equal to 69 percent of its production of dry natural gas. Germany, the third largest consumer of natural gas, consumed 3.2 trillion cubic feet and Ukraine consumed 3.0 trillion cubic feet.

Coal Consumption in 1995

World coal consumption in 1995 totaled 5.1 billion short tons, up for the fifth year in a row. China, the United States, and India, the leading producers of coal, were also the leading consumers. China consumed 1.5 billion short tons, the United States consumed 962 million short tons, India consumed 327 million short tons, and Russia consumed 306 million short tons of coal in 1995. □

Environment

The Global Environment Outlook: An Overview

Africa

• Half a billion hectares of African land are moderately to severely degraded.

• African forests are the most depleted of all the tropical regions, with only 30 percent of historical stands remaining.

• African savannahs are the richest grasslands in the world, supporting many indigenous plants and animals, including the world's greatest concentration of large mammals.

• Africa has 19 of the 25 countries that have the highest percentage of populations without access to drinking water.

• For many countries, particularly in West Africa, fish is the main source of protein.

Asia and the Pacific

• Asian timber reserves may last for no more than a further 40 years.

• Rapid growth in energy demand has led to a significant increase in air pollution. Acidification is also an emerging problem.

• Some 70 percent of the waste discharged into the Pacific receives no treatment.

• The disposal of liquid and solid wastes is increasingly problematic in a region with such high population density.

• The largest portion of the world's land affected by soil degradation is in Asia and the Pacific.

Asia, West

• West Asia lost 11 percent of its remaining natural forest during the 1980s.

• Many countries in West Asia suffer from water scarcity, with Bahrain having less than 18 percent of the minimum threshold; yet, levels of water consumption are now very high, ranging from 300 to 1,500 litres a day per capita.

• Some 1.2 million barrels of oil are spilled into the Persian Gulf annually.

• The region's coastal zone, an invaluable economic resource for development and tourism, is one of the most fragile and endangered ecosystems in the world.

Europe and the Commonwealth of Independent States

• Emissions of sulphur and nitrogen oxides are largely responsible for the 30–50 percent of the forests that are damaged or dying in Central and Eastern Europe.

• Europe has added 10 million hectares of protected areas since 1982, but 52 percent of its fish, 45 percent of its reptiles, and 42 percent of its mammals are under threat.

• Groundwater is overexploited near 60 percent of Europe's industrial and urban centers.

• Europe contributes 36 percent of world chlorofluorocarbon emissions, 30 percent of carbon dioxide emissions, and 25 percent of sulphur dioxide emissions; air quality is the top environmental priority for countries in Central and Eastern Europe.

• The average European produces 150 to 600 kilograms of municipal waste a year—but this has led to the adoption of alternative methods of waste disposal, cleaner production technologies, and more recycling.

Latin America

• Five of the 10 most species-rich countries in the world are in Latin America, but biodiversity in the region is highly threatened—with an estimated potential loss of at least 100,000 species from forested areas alone over the next 40 years.

• Some 47 percent of the region's grazing lands have lost their soil fertility as a result of erosion, overgrazing, salinization, and alkalinization.

• Large quantities of agricultural and other contaminants are discharged to streams that flow into the Caribbean, resulting in pollution from phosphorus, nitrates, and pesticides.

• Many Caribbean beaches now have average tar level 10 times higher than those estimated to adversely affect the use of beaches by tourists.

• Argentina, Brazil, Chile, Paraguay, and Uruguay experience the effects of increased ultraviolet-B radiation due to ozone depletion more acutely than any other inhabited region.

North America

• In 1996 in the United States, 728 species were endangered or threatened; in Canada, 254 species were endangered or threatened, and a further 21 species were already nationally or globally extinct.

• North American households use twice as much water as European households, but pay half as much for it.

• 2.4 million rural Americans are badly in need of a source of safe drinking water; 1 million are without piped water at all; and supplies to a further 5.6 million do not meet safe drinking water standards.

• Declining fish stocks have resulted in the collapse of East Coast fisheries, with a devastating impact on people living in the area, especially in the Canadian Maritime Provinces.

• Throughout North America, urban centers are having increasing problems finding sites for new landfills; as a result, campaigns to save resources, encourage recycling, and separate wastes have led to stricter rules in some communities.

Polar Regions: The Arctic and the Antarctic

• Melting of the Greenland ice sheet has made a positive contribution to the sea-level rise of 10–25 cm. observed over the past 100 years.

• In 1995, the Arctic contained 285 protected areas covering 2.1 million km.

• If the Antarctic ice sheet melted, it would produce a sea-level rise of at least 60 meters.

• The Antarctic ozone hole is expected to remain for many more decades.

Source: United Nations Environment Program, 1997.

Threatened and Endangered Species

(as of June 30, 1997)

Source: U.S. Fish and Wildlife Service, Dept. of the Interior.

Group	Endangered[1] U.S.	Endangered[1] Foreign	Threatened[2] U.S.	Threatened[2] Foreign	Total listings[3]	Species with recovery plans[4]
Mammals	56	252	7	16	331	39
Birds	75	178	15	6	274	72
Reptiles	14	65	18	14	111	30
Amphibians	9	8	7	1	25	11
Fishes	65	11	40	0	119	74
Snails	15	1	7	0	23	18
Clams	56	2	6	0	64	44
Crustaceans	15	0	3	0	18	6
Insects	24	4	9	0	37	21
Arachnids	5	0	0	0	5	4
Flowering plants	500	1	111	0	612	313
Conifers	2	0	0	2	4	1
Ferns & others	26	0	2	0	28	19
Total	**864**	**522**	**226**	**39**	**1,651**	**652**

1. *Endangered species* are those in danger of extinction. 2. *Threatened species* are those likely to become an endangered species within the forseeable future. 3. Separate populations of a species listed both as endangered and threatened are tallied twice. Those species are the argali, leopard, gray wolf, piping plover, roseate tern, chimpanzee, green sea turtle, and olive ridley sea turtle. 4. There are 424 approved recovery plans sponsored by the endangered species program of the U.S. Fish and Wildlife Service. They are dedicated to restoring species to a secure status in the wild. Some recovery plans cover more than one species, and a few species have separate plans covering different parts of their ranges. Recovery plans are drawn up only for species in the United States.

Some Endangered Species of the World

Common Name	Scientific Name	Range
Mammals		
Bat, gray	*Myotis grisescens*	U.S. (Central and Southeastern)
Bear, brown	*Ursus arctos pruinosus*	China (Tibet)
Cheetah	*Acinonyx jubatus*	Africa, Middle East, South Asia
Chimpanzee	*Pan troglodytes*	Africa (Western and Central)
Deer, Key	*Odocoileus virginianus*	U.S. (Florida Keys)
Dolphin, Chinese River	*Lipotes vexillifer*	China
Elephant, Asian	*Elephas maximus*	South and Southeast Asia
Ferret, black-footed	*Mustela nigripes*	U.S. and Canada
Gazelle, slender-horned	*Gazella leptoceros*	Saharan Africa
Gorilla	*Gorilla gorilla*	Africa (Western and Central)
Ibex, Walia	*Capra walie*	Ethiopia
Kangaroo, Tasmanian forester	*Macropus giganteus tasmaniensis*	Australia (Tasmania)
Leopard, snow	*Panthera uncia*	Central Asia
Lion, Asiatic	*Panthera leo persica*	Middle East, South Asia
Manatee, West Indian	*Trichechus manatus*	U.S, Mexico, Caribbean, South America
Monkey, spider	*Ateles geoffroyi frontatus*	Costa Rica, Nicaragua
Orangutan	*Pongo pygmaeus*	Sumatra, Borneo
Otter, marine	*Lutra felina*	South America
Panda, ginat	*Ailuropoda melanoleuca*	China
Panther, Florida	*Felis concolor coryi*	U.S. (Southeast)
Pronghorn, Sonoran	*Antilocapra americana sonoriensis*	Mexico, U.S.
Puma, Costa Rican	*Felis concolor costaricensis*	Nicaragua, Panama, Costa Rica
Rhinoceros, black	*Diceros bicornis*	Africa
Tiger	*Panthera tigris*	Asia
Wallaby, brindled nail-tailed	*Onycholgalea fraenata*	Australia
Whale, blue	*Balaenoptera musculus*	All oceans
Whale, humpback	*Megaptera novaeangliae*	All oceans
Wolf, gray	*Canis lupus*	Holarctic
Yak, wild	*Bos grunniens mutus*	China (Tibet), India
Zebra, mountain	*Equus zebra zebra*	South Africa
Birds		
Albatross, short-tailed	*Diomedea albatrus*	Japan, Russia, U.S., North Pacific
Condor, Andean	*Vultur gryphus*	South America
Crane, whooping	*Grus americana*	Canada, U.S., Mexico
Eagle, Philippine	*Pithecophaga jefferyi*	Philippines
Falcon, American peregrine	*Falco peregrinus anatum*	U.S., Canada, Mexico, South America
Ostrich, Arabian	*Struthio camelus syriacus*	Jordan, Saudi Arabia

Common Name	Scientific Name	Range
Parrot, red-browed	*Amazona rhodocorytha*	Brazil
Pelican, brown	*pelecanus occidentalis*	U.S, Central and South America, Caribbean
Plover, piping	*Charadrius melodus*	U.S., Canada, Mexico, Caribbean
Stork, Oriental white	*Ciconia ciconia boyciana*	China, Japan, Korea, Russia
Woodpecker, ivory-billed	*Campephilus principalis*	Cuba, U.S.
Reptiles		
Crocodile, American	*Crocodylus acutus*	U.S., Mexico, Caribbean, Central and South America
Gecko, Day	*Phelsuma edwardnewtoni*	Mauritius
Iguana, Allen's Cay	*Cyclura cychlura inornata*	Bahamas
Python, Indian	*Python molurus molurus*	India, Sri Lanka
Snake, San Francisco garter	*Thamnophis sirtalis tetrataenia*	U.S. (California)
Tortoise, Galapagos	*Geochelone elephantopus*	Ecuador (Galapagos Islands)
Turtle, aquatic box	*Terrapene coahuila*	Mexico
Amphibians		
Frog, Israel Painted	*Discoglossus nigriventer*	Israel
Salamander, Texas blind	*Typhlomolge rathbuni*	U.S. (Texas)
Toad, Puerto Rican crested	*Peltophryne lemur*	Puerto Rico, British Virgin Islands
Fishes		
Catfish, giant	*Pangasianodon gigas*	Thailand
Salmon, Sockeye	*Oncorhynchus nerka*	Pacific North Basin
Trout, Gila	*Oncorhynchus gilae*	U.S. (Arizona, New Mexico)

U.S. Zoos and Aquariums

Source: The facilities listed are members of, and accredited by, the American Zoo and Aquarium Association (AZA) to ensure that they are maintaining professional standards. It also accredits facilities outside of the United States. Their website is www.aza.org.

Abilene Zoological Gardens, Texas
African Safari Wildlife Park, Port Clinton, Texas
Akron Zoological Park, Ohio
Alameda Park Zoo, Alamogordo, N.M.
Albuquerque Biological Park, N.M.
Alexandria Zoological Park, La.
Aquarium for Wildlife Conservation, The, Brooklyn, N.Y.
Aquarium of the Americas, New Orleans, La.
Arizona-Sonora Desert Museum, Tucson
Audubon Park and Zoological Garden, New Orleans
John Ball Zoological Garden, Grand Rapids, Mich.
Baltimore Zoo, The, Md.
Beardsley Zoological Gardens, Bridgeport, Conn.
Belle Isle Aquarium, Royal Oak, Minn.
Belle Isle Zoo, Detroit
Bergen County Zoological Park, Paramus, N.J.
Bermuda Aquarium, Museum, and Zoo, Flatts, Fla.
Binder Park Zoo, Battle Creek, Mich.
Birmingham Zoo, Ala.
Blank Park Zoo, Des Moines, Iowa
Bramble Park Zoo, Watertown, S.D.
Brandywine Zoo, Wilmington, Del.
Brevard Zoo, Melbourne, Fla.
Bronx Zoo/Wildlife Conservation Park, N.Y.
Brookfield Zoo, Ill.
Brookgreen Gardens, Murrells Inlet, S.C.
Buffalo Zoological Gardens, N.Y.
Burnet Park Zoo, Syracuse, N.Y.
Busch Gardens, Tampa, Fla.
Caldwell Zoo, Tyler, Texas
Cameron Park Zoo, Waco, Texas
Cape May County Park Zoo, Cape May Court House, N.J.
Central Florida Zoological Park, Lake Monroe, Fla.
Central Park Wildlife Center, New York, N.Y.
Chaffee Zoological Gardens of Fresno, Calif.
Chahinkapa Zoo, Wahpeton, N.D.
Chehaw Wild Animal Park, Albany, Ga.
Cheyenne Mountain Zoological Park, Colorado Springs
Cincinnati Zoo and Botanical Garden, Ohio
Cleveland Metroparks Zoo, Ohio

Columbus Zoological Gardens, Ohio
Dakota Zoo, Bismarck, N.D.
Dallas Aquarium at Fair Park, Texas
Dallas World Aquarium, Texas
Dallas Zoo, Texas
Denver Zoological Gardens, Colo.
Detroit Zoological Park, Mich.
Dickerson Park Zoo, Springfield, Mo.
Discovery Island Zoological Park, Lake Buena Vista, Fla.
Dreher Park Zoo, West Palm Beach, Fla.
El Paso Zoo, Texas
Emporia Zoo, Kan.
Erie Zoo, Pa.
Florida Aquarium, Tampa, Fla.
Folsom Children's Zoo & Botanical Garden, Lincoln, Neb.
Fort Wayne Children's Zoo, Ind.
Fort Worth Zoological Park, Texas
Fossil Rim Wildlife Center, Glen Rose, Texas
Franklin Park Zoo, Boston, Mass.
Glen Oak Zoo, Peoria, Ill.
Grassmere Wildlife Park, Nashville, Tenn.
Great Plains Zoo & Museum, Sioux Falls, S.D.
Greater Baton Rouge Zoo, La.
Greenville Zoo, S.C.
Happy Hollow Park and Zoo, San Jose, Calif.
Honolulu Zoo, Hawaii
Houston Zoological Gardens, Texas
Indianapolis Zoo, Ind.
International Crane Foundation, Baraboo, Wis.
Jackson Zoological Park, Miss.
Jacksonville Zoological Park, Fla.
Kansas City Zoological Gardens, Mo.
Knoxville Zoological Gardens, Tenn.
Lake Superior Zoological Gardens, Duluth, Minn.
Lincoln Park Zoological Gardens, Chicago
Little Rock Zoological Garden, Ark.
Living Desert, The, Palm Desert, Calif.
Living Seas, The, Lake Buena Vista, Fla.
Los Angeles Zoo, Calif.

Louisville Zoological Garden, Ky.
Lowry Park Zoological Garden, Tampa, Fla.
Marine World Africa USA, Vallejo, Calif.
Memphis Zoological Garden and Aquarium, Tenn.
Mesker Park Zoo, Evansville, Ind.
Metro Washington Park Zoo, Portland, Ore.
Miami Metrozoo, Fla.
Micke Grove Zoo, Lodi, Calif.
Miller Park Zoo, Bloomington, Ill.
Mill Mountain Zoo, Roanoke, Va.
Milwaukee County Zoological Gardens, Wis.
Minnesota Zoological Garden, Apple Valley, Minn.
Monterey Bay Aquarium, Calif.
Montgomery Zoo, Ala.
Mystic Marinelife Aquarium, Mystic, Conn.
National Aquarium in Baltimore, Md.
National Aviary in Pittsburgh, Pa.
National Zoological Park, Washington, D.C.
New England Aquarium, Boston
New Jersey State Aquarium at Camden
North Carolina Aquarium at Fort Fisher, Kure Beach
North Carolina Aquarium at Pine Knoll Shores, Atlantic Beach
North Carolina Aquarium on Roanoke Island, Manteo
North Carolina Zoological Park, Asheboro
North Eastern Wisconsin Zoo, Green Bay, Wis.
Northwest Trek Wildlife Park, Eatonville, Wash.
NZP Conservation Research Center, Front Royal, Va.
Oakland Zoo, The Calif.
Oglebay's Good Children's Zoo, Wheeling, W.Va.
Oklahoma City Zoological Park, Okla.
Omaha's Henry Doorly Zoo, Neb.
Charles Paddock Zoo, Atascadero, Calif.
Palm Beach Zoo at Dreher Park, West Palm Beach, Fla.
Parrot Jungle and Gardens, Miami, Fla.
Clyde Peeling's Reptiland Ltd., Allenwood, Pa.
Philadelphia Zoological Garden, Pa.
Phoenix Zoo, The Ariz.
Pittsburgh Zoo, Pa.
Point Defiance Zoo and Aquarium, Tacoma, Wash.
Gladys Porter Zoo, Brownsville, Texas
Potawatomi Zoo, South Bend, Ind.
Potter Park Zoological Gardens, Lansing, Mich.
Prospect Park Wildlife Center, Brooklyn, N.Y.
Pueblo Zoo, Colo.
Queens Wildlife Center, Flushing, N.Y.
Racine Zoological Gardens, Wis.
Rainforest at Moody Gardens, Inc., Galveston, Texas
Reid Park Zoo, Tucson, Ariz.
Lee Richardson Zoo, Garden City, Kan.
Riverbanks Zoological Park and Botanical Garden, Columbia, S.C.

Riverside Zoo, Scottsbluff, Neb.
Henson Robinson Zoo, Springfield, Ill.
Roosevelt Zoo, Minot, N.D.
Ross Park Zoo, Binghamton, N.Y.
Sacramento Zoo, Calif.
St. Augustine Alligator Farm, Fla.
St. Catherine's Wildlife Conservation Center, Midway, Ga.
St. Louis Zoological Park, Mo.
St. Paul's Como Zoo, Minn.
Salisbury Zoological Park, Md.
San Antonio Zoological Gardens and Aquarium, Texas
San Diego Wild Animal Park, Calif.
San Diego Zoo, Calif.
San Francisco Zoological Gardens, Calif.
Santa Ana Zoo, Calif.
Santa Barbara Zoological Gardens, Calif.
Sea Life Park Hawaii, Waimanalo
Sea World of California, San Diego
Sea World of Florida, Orlando
Sea World of Ohio, Aurora
Sea World of Texas, San Antonio
Seattle Aquarium, The Wash.
Sedgwick County Zoo, Wichita, Kan.
Seneca Park Zoo, Rochester, N.Y.
Sequoia Park Zoo, Eureka, Calif.
John G. Shedd Aquarium, Chicago
Staten Island Zoo, N.Y.
Steinhart Aquarium, San Francisco, Calif.
Sunset Zoological Park, Manhattan, Kan.
Tennessee Aquarium, Chattanooga, Tenn.
Texas State Aquarium, Corpus Christi
Texas Zoo, The Victoria, Texas
Toledo Zoological Gardens, Ohio
Topeka Zoological Park, Kan.
Tracy Aviary, Salt Lake City, Utah
Trevor Zoo, Millbrook, N.Y.
Ellen Trout Zoo, Lufkin, Texas
Tulsa Zoo and Living Museum, Okla.
Utah's Hogle Zoo, Salt Lake City
Utica Zoo, N.Y.
Henry Vilas Zoo, Madison, Wis.
Virginia Zoological Park, Norfolk, Va.
Waikiki Aquarium, Hawaii
Wildlife Safari, Winston, Ore.
Wildlife World Zoo, Litchfield Park, Ariz.
The Wilds, Cumberland, Ohio
Roger Williams Park Zoo, Providence, R.I.
Woodland Park Zoological Gardens, Seattle
Zoo Atlanta, Ga.
ZOOAMERICA North American Wildlife Park, Hershey, Pa.

Animal Names: Male, Female, and Young

Animal	Male	Female	Young	Animal	Male	Female	Young	Animal	Male	Female	Young
Ass	Jack	Jenny	Foal	Duck	Drake	Duck	Duckling	Lion	Lion	Lioness	Cub
Bear	Boar	Sow	Cub					Rabbit	Buck	Doe	Bunny
Cat	Tom	Queen	Kitten	Elephant	Bull	Cow	Calf	Sheep	Ram	Ewe	Lamb
Cattle	Bull	Cow	Calf	Fox	Dog	Vixen	Cub	Swan	Cob	Pen	Cygnet
Chicken	Rooster	Hen	Chick	Goose	Gander	Goose	Gosling	Swine	Boar	Sow	Piglet
Deer	Buck	Doe	Fawn					Tiger	Tiger	Tigress	Cub
Dog	Dog	Bitch	Pup	Horse	Stallion	Mare	Foal	Whale	Bull	Cow	Calf
								Wolf	Dog	Bitch	Pup

Source: James G. Doherty, General Curator, The Wildlife Conservation Society.

Gestation, Incubation, and Longevity of Certain Animals

Animal	Gestation or incubation, in days & (average)	Longevity, in years & (record exceptions)	Animal	Gestation or incubation, in days & (average)	Longevity, in years & (record exceptions)
Ass	365	18-20 (63)	Horse	329-345 (336)	20-25 (50+)
Bear	180-240[1]	15-30 (47)	Kangaroo	32-39[1]	4-6 (23)
Cat	52-69 (63)	10-12 (26+)	Lion	105-113 (108)	10 (29)
Chicken	22	7-8 (14)	Man	253-303	([2])
Cow	c. 280	9-12 (39)	Monkey	139-270[1]	12-15[1] (29)
Deer	197-300[1]	10-15 (26)	Mouse	19-31[1]	1-3 (4)
Dog	53-71 (63)	10-12 (24)	Parakeet (Budgerigar)	17-20 (18)	8 (12+)
Duck	21-35[1] (28)	10 (15)	Pig	101-130 (115)	10 (22)
Elephant	510-730 (624)[1]	30-40 (71)	Pigeon	11-19	10-12 (39)
Fox	51-63[1]	8-10 (14)	Rabbit	30-35 (31)	6-8 (15)
Goat	136-160 (151)	12 (17)	Rat	21	3 (5)
Groundhog	31-32	4-9	Sheep	144-152 (151)[1]	12 (16)
Guinea pig	58-75 (68)	3 (6)	Squirrel	44	8-9 (15)
Hamster, golden	15-17	2 (8)	Whale	365-547[1]	—
Hippopotamus	220-255 (240)	30 (49+)	Wolf	60-63	10-12 (16)

1. Depending on kind. 2. For life expectancy charts, *see* Expectation of Life in the United States. *Source:* James G. Doherty, General Curator, The Wildlife Conservation Society.

Animal Group Terminology

Source: James G. Doherty, General Curator, The Wildlife Conservation Society and *Information Please* data.

ants: colony
bears: sleuth, sloth
bees: grist, hive, swarm
birds: flight, volery
cattle: drove
cats: clutter, clowder
chicks: brood, clutch
clams: bed
cranes: sedge, seige
crows: murder
doves: dule
ducks: brace, team
elephants: herd
elks: gang
finches: charm
fish: school, shoal, draught
foxes: leash, skulk
geese: flock, gaggle, skein
gnats: cloud, horde
goats: trip

gorillas: band
hares: down, husk
hawks: cast
hens: brood
hogs: drift
horses: pair, team
hounds: cry, mute, pack
kangaroos: troop
kittens: kindle, litter
larks: exaltation
lions: pride
locusts: plague
magpies: tidings
mules: span
nightingales: watch
oxen: yoke
oysters: bed
parrots: company
partridges: covey

peacocks: muster, ostentation
pheasants: nest, bouquet
pigs: litter
ponies: string
quail: bevy, covey
rabbits: nest
seals: pod
sheep: drove, flock
sparrows: host
storks: mustering
swans: bevy, wedge
swine: sounder
toads: knot
turkeys: rafter
turtles: bale
vipers: nest
whales: gam, pod
wolves: pack, route
woodcocks: fall

Speed of Animals

Most of the following measurements are for maximum speeds over approximate quarter-mile distances. Exceptions—which are included to give a wide range of animals—are the lion and elephant, whose speeds were clocked in the act of charging; the whippet, which was timed over a 200-yard course; the cheetah over a 100-yard distance; man for a 15-yard segment of a 100-yard run; and the black mamba, six-lined race runner, spider, giant tortoise, three-toed sloth, and garden snail, which were measured over various small distances.

Animal	Speed mph	Animal	Speed mph	Animal	Speed mph
Cheetah	70	Mongolian wild ass	40	Man	27.89
Pronghorn antelope	61	Greyhound	39.35	Elephant	25
Wildebeest	50	Whippet	35.5	Black mamba snake	20
Lion	50	Rabbit (domestic)	35	Six-lined race runner	18
Thomson's gazelle	50	Mule deer	35	Squirrel	12
Quarter horse	47.5	Jackal	35	Pig (domestic)	11
Elk	45	Reindeer	32	Chicken	9
Cape hunting dog	45	Giraffe	32	Spider (Tegenearia atrica)	1.17
Coyote	43	White-tailed deer	30	Giant Tortoise	0.17
Gray fox	42	Wart hog	30	Three-toed sloth	0.15
Hyena	40	Grizzly bear	30	Garden snail	0.03
Zebra	40	Cat (domestic)	30		

Source: Natural History Magazine, March 1974, copyright 1974. The American Museum of Natural History; and James G. Doherty, General Curator, The Wildlife Conservation Society.

Major Air Pollutants

Pollutant	Sources	Effects
Ozone. A colorless gas that is the major constituent of photochemical smog at the Earth's surface. In the upper atmosphere (stratosphere), however, ozone is beneficial, protecting us from the sun's harmful rays.	Ozone is formed in the lower atmosphere as a result of chemical reactions between oxygen, volatile organic compounds, and nitrogen oxides in the presence of sunlight, especially during hot weather. Sources of such harmful pollutants include vehicles, factories, landfills, industrial solvents, and numerous small sources such as gas stations, and farm and lawn equipment.	Ozone causes significant health and environmental problems at the Earth's surface. It can irritate the respiratory tract, produce impaired lung function and cause throat irritation, chest pain, cough, and lung inflammation. It can also reduce the yield of agricultural crops and injure forests and other vegetation. Ozone is the most injurious pollutant to plant life.
Carbon Monoxide. Odorless and colorless gas emitted in the exhaust of motor vehicles and other kinds of engines where there is incomplete fossil fuel combustion.	Automobiles, buses, trucks, small engines, and some industrial processes. High concentrations can be found in confined spaces like parking garages, poorly ventilated tunnels, or along roadsides during periods of heavy traffic.	Reduces the ability of blood to deliver oxygen to vital tissues, affecting primarily the cardiovascular and nervous systems. Lower concentrations have been shown to adversely affect individuals with heart disease; higher concentrations can cause dizziness, headaches, and fatigue.
Nitrogen Dioxide. Light brown gas at lower concentrations; in higher concentrations becomes an important component of unpleasant-looking brown, urban haze.	Result of burning fuels in utilities, industrial boilers, cars, and trucks.	One of the major pollutants that causes smog and acid rain. Can harm humans and vegetation when concentrations are sufficiently high.
Particulate Matter. Solid matter or liquid droplets from smoke, dust, fly ash and condensing vapors that can be suspended in the air for long periods of time.	Industrial processes, smelters, automobiles, burning industrial fuels, woodsmoke, dust from paved and unpaved roads, construction, and agricultural ground breaking.	These microscopic particles can affect breathing and respiratory symptoms, causing increased respiratory disease and lung damage, and possibly premature death.
Sulfur Dioxide. Colorless gas, odorless at low concentrations but pungent at very high concentrations.	Emitted largely from industrial, institutional, utility and apartment-house furnaces and boilers, as well as petroleum refineries, smelters, paper mills, and chemical plants.	One of the major pollutants that causes smog. Can, at high concentrations, affect human health, especially among asthmatics, and acidify lakes and streams.
Lead. Lead and lead compounds can adversely affect human health through either ingestion of lead-contaminated soil, dust, paint, or direct inhalation.	Transportation sources using lead in their fuels, coal combustion, smelters, car battery plants, and combustion of garbage containing lead products.	Elevated lead levels can adversely affect mental development, kidney function, and blood chemistry. Young children are particularly at risk.
Toxic Air Pollutants. Includes pollutants such as arsenic, asbestos, and benzenes.	Chemical plants, industrial processes, motor vehicle emissions and fuels, and building materials.	Known or suspected to cause cancer, respiratory effects, birth defects, and reproductive and other serious health effects.
Stratospheric Ozone Depleters. Chemicals such as chlorofluorocarbons (CFCs), halons, carbon tetrachloride, and methyl chloroform. These chemicals rise to the upper atmosphere where they destroy the protective ozone layer.	Industrial household refrigeration, cooling and cleaning processes, car and home air conditioners, some fire extinguishers, and plastic foam products.	Increased exposure to UV radiation could potentially cause an increase in skin cancer, cataracts, suppression of the human immune response system, and environmental damage.
Greenhouse gases. Gases that build up in the atmosphere that may induce global climate change or the "greenhouse effect." They include carbon dioxide, methane, and nitrous oxide.	The main man-made source of carbon dioxide emissions is fossil fuel combustion for energy-use and transportation. Methane comes from landfills, cud-chewing livestock, coal mines, and rice paddies. Nitrous oxide results from industrial processes, such as nylon fabrication.	The extent of the effects of climate change on human health and the environment is still uncertain, but could include increased global temperature, increased severity and frequency of storms and other "weather extremes," melting of the polar ice cap, and sea-level rise.

Source: Environmental Protection Agency, EPA 450–K–92–002, October 1992.

Top Twenty Most Visited National Park Sites, 1996

Rank	Name and location	Number of visitors
1.	Blue Ridge Parkway, National Va.	17,169,062
2.	Golden Gate National Recreation Area, Calif.	14,043,984
3.	Lake Mead National Recreation Area, Nev.	9,350,847
4.	Great Smoky Mountains National Park, Tenn.	9,265,667
5.	Gateway National Recreation Area, N.Y.	6,381,502
6.	George Washington Memorial Parkway, Va.	6,126,490
7.	National Capital Parks, D.C.	6,094,875
8.	Natchez Trace Parkway, Miss.	6,088,610
9.	Cape Cod National Seashore, Mass.	4,901,782
10.	Delaware Water Gap National Recreation Area, Pa. & N.J.	4,657,735
11.	Grand Canyon National Park, Ariz.	4,537,703
12.	Statue of Liberty National Monument, N.Y.	4,494,076
13.	Yosemite National Park, Calif.	4,046,207
14.	Castle Clinton National Monument, N.Y.	3,753,944
15.	San Francisco Maritime National Historic Park, Calif.	3,670,972
16.	Jefferson National Expansion Memorial, Mo.	3,649,308
17.	Chattahoochee River National Recreation Area, Ga.	3,540,375
18.	Cuyahoga Valley National Recreation Area, Ohio	3,455,878
19.	Olympic National Park, Wash.	3,348,723
20.	Colonial National Historic Park, Va.	3,145,039

Source: Department of the Interior, National Park Service. www.nps.gov

The National Park System

Source: Department of the Interior, National Park Service.

The National Park System of the United States is administered by the National Park Service, a bureau of the Department of the Interior. Started with the establishment of Yellowstone National Park on March 1, 1872, the system includes not only the most extraordinary and spectacular scenic exhibits in the United States, but also a large number of sites distinguished either for their historic or prehistoric importance or scientific interest, or for their superior recreational assets. The National Park System is made up of 374 areas covering more than 83 million acres in every state except Delaware. It also includes areas in the District of Columbia, American Samoa, Guam, Peuerto Rico, and the Virgin Islands. A comprehensive list of the areas follows. See also the excellent Web site of the Park Service: www.nps.gov.

Name, location, and year authorized	Acreage	Outstanding characteristics
Acadia (Maine), 1919	46,998.43	Rugged seashore on Mt. Desert Island and adjacent mainland
Arches (Utah), 1971	73,378.98	Unusual stone arches, windows, pedestals caused by erosion
Badlands (S.D.), 1978	242,755.94	Arid land of fossils, prairie, bison, deer, bighorn, antelope
Big Bend (Tex.), 1935	801,163.21	Mountains and desert bordering the Rio Grande
Biscayne (Fla.), 1980	172,924.07	Aquatic, coral reef park south of Miami was a national monument, 1968–80
Bryce Canyon (Utah), 1924	35,835.08	Area of grotesque eroded rocks brilliantly colored
Canyonlands (Utah), 1964	337,570.43	Colorful wilderness with impressive red-rock canyons, spires, arches
Capitol Reef (Utah), 1971	241,904.26	Highly colored sedimentary rock formations in high, narrow gorges
Carlsbad Caverns (N.M.), 1930	46,766.45	The world's largest known caves
Channel Islands (Calif.) 1980	249,353.77	Area is rich in marine mammals, sea birds, endangered species and archeology
Crater Lake (Ore.), 1902	183,224.05	Deep blue lake in heart of inactive volcano
Death Valley (Calif.-Nev.), 1994	3,367,627.68	Largest desert, surrounded by high mountains, containing the lowest point in the Western hemisphere.
Denali (Alaska), 1917	4,741,800.00	Mt. McKinley National Park was renamed and enlarged by Act of Dec. 2, 1980. Contains Mt. McKinley, N. America's highest mountain (20,320 ft.)
Dry Tortugas (Fla.), 1992	64,700.00	Formerly Ft. Jefferson National Monument. Located 70 miles off Key West. Features an underwater nature trail.
Everglades (Fla.), 1934	1,507,850.00	Subtropical area with abundant bird and animal life
Gates of the Arctic (Alaska), 1980	7,523,898.00	Diverse north central wilderness contains part of Brooks Range
Glacier (Mont.), 1910	1,013,572.42	Rocky Mountain scenery with many glaciers and lakes
Glacier Bay (Alaska), 1980	3,224,794.00	Park was a national monument (1925–1980) popular for wildlife, whale-watching, glacier-calving, and scenery
Grand Canyon (Ariz.), 1919	1,217,158.32	Mile-deep gorge, 4 to 18 miles wide, 217 miles long
Grand Teton (Wyo.), 1929	309,994.72	Picturesque range of high mountain peaks
Great Basin (Nev.), 1986	77,180.00	Exceptional scenic, biologic, and geologic attractions
Great Smoky Mts. (N.C.-Tenn.), 1926	521,621.00	Highest mountain range east of Black Hills; luxuriant plant life
Guadalupe Mountains (Tex.), 1966	86,415.97	Contains highest point in Texas: Guadalupe Peak (8,751 ft.)

Name, location, and year authorized	Acreage	Outstanding characteristics
Haleakala (Hawaii), 1960	28,091.14	World-famous 10,023-ft. Haleakala volcano (dormant)
Hawaii Volcanoes (Hawaii), 1916	209,695.38	Spectacular volcanic area; luxuriant vegetation at lower levels
Hot Springs (Ark.), 1921	5,549.46	47 mineral hot springs said to have therapeutic value
Isle Royale (Mich.), 1931	571,790.11	Largest wilderness island in Lake Superior; moose, wolves, lakes
Joshua Tree (Calif.), 1936	792,749.87	Desert region featuring Joshua trees and a great variety of plants and animals.
Katmai (Alaska), 1980	3,674,540.87	Expansion may assure brown bear's preservation. Park was national monument 1918–80; is known for fishing, 1912 eruption, bears
Kenai Fjords (Alaska), 1980	670,642.79	Mountain goats, marine mammals, wildlife are features at this seacoast park near Seward
Kings Canyon (Calif.), 1940	461,901.20	Huge canyons; high mountains; giant sequoias
Kobuk Valley (Alaska), 1980	1,750,736.86	Native culture and anthropology center around the broad Kobuk River in northwest Alaska
Lake Clark (Alaska), 1980	2,636,839.00	Park provides scenic and wilderness recreation across Cook Inlet from Anchorage
Lassen Volcanic (Calif.), 1916	106,372.36	Exhibits of impressive volcanic phenomena
Mammoth Cave (Ky.), 1926	52,830.19	Vast limestone labyrinth with underground river
Mesa Verde (Colo.), 1906	52,121.93	Best-preserved prehistoric cliff dwellings in United States
Mount Rainier (Wash.), 1899	235,612.50	Single-peak glacial system; dense forests, flowered meadows
National Park of American Samoa	9,000.00	Samoa National Park, American Samoa: two rain forest preserves and a coral reef on the island of Ofu are home to unique tropical animals. The park also includes several thousand acres on the islands of Tutuila and Ta'u.
North Cascades (Wash.), 1968	504,780.94	Roadless Alpine landscape; jagged peaks; mountain lakes; glaciers
Olympic (Wash.), 1938	922,651.01	Finest Pacific Northwest rain forest; scenic mountain park
Petrified Forest (Ariz.), 1962	93,532.57	Extensive natural exhibit of petrified wood
Redwood (Calif.), 1968	110,232.40	Coastal redwood forests; contains world's tallest known tree (369.2 ft.)
Rocky Mountain (Colo.), 1915	265,727.15	Section of the Rocky Mountains; 107 named peaks over 10,000 ft.
Saguaro (Ariz.), 1994	91,452.95	Giant saguaro cacti, unique to the Sonoran Desert, sometimes reach a height of 50 ft. in this cactus forest.
Sequoia (Calif.), 1890	402,482.38	Giant sequoias; magnificent High Sierra scenery, including Mt. Whitney
Shenandoah (Va.), 1926	197,388.98	Tree-covered mountains; scenic Skyline Drive
Theodore Roosevelt (N.D.), 1978	70,446.89	Scenic valley of Little Missouri River; T.R. Ranch; Wildlife
Virgin Islands (U.S. V.I.), 1956	14,688.87	Beaches; lush hills; prehistoric Carib Indian relics
Voyageurs (Minn.), 1971	218,035.33	Wildlife, canoeing, fishing, and hiking
Wind Cave (S.D.), 1903	28,295.03	Limestone caverns in Black Hills; buffalo herd
Wrangell-St. Elias (Alaska), 1980	8,323,617.68	Largest Park System area has abundant wildlife, second highest peak in U.S. (Mt. St. Elias); adjoins Canadian park
Yellowstone (Wyo.-Mont.-Idaho), 1872	2,219,790.71	World's greatest geyser area; abundant falls, wildlife, and canyons
Yosemite (Calif.), 1890	761,236.20	Mountains; inspiring gorges and waterfalls; giant sequoias
Zion (Utah), 1919	146,597.61	Multicolored gorge in heart of southern Utah desert

NATIONAL HISTORICAL PARKS

Name and location	Total acreage
Appomattox Court House (Va.)	1,774.81
Boston (Mass.)	41.03
Chaco Culture (N.M.)	33,974.29
Chesapeake and Ohio Canal (Md.-W.Va.-D.C.)	19,236.60
Colonial (Va.)	9,352.60
Cumberland Gap (Ky.-Tenn.-Va.)	20,454.02
Dayton Aviation Heritage (Oh.)	85.65
George Rogers Clark (Ind.)	26.17
Harpers Ferry (W.Va.-Md.)	2,287.48
Hopewell Culture (Oh.)	1,134.44
Independence (Pa.)	44.88
Jean Lafitte (La.)	20,020.00
Kalaupapa (Hawaii)	10,778.88

Name and location	Total acreage
Kaloko-Honokohau (Hawaii)	1,160.91
Keeweenaw (Mich.)	1,870.00
Klondike Goldrush (Alaska, Wash.)	13,191.35
Lowell (Mass.)	136.86
Lyndon B. Johnson (Tex.)	1,570.15
Marsh-Billings	643.07
Minuteman (Mass.)	935.55
Morristown (N.J.)	1,683.61
Natchez (Miss.)	108.26
Nez Perce (Idaho)	2,122.75
Pecos (N.M.)	6,670.65
Púuchonua o Honaunau (Hawaii)	181.80
Salt River Bay (U.S. V.I.)	945.00
San Antonio Missions (Tex.)	819.19
San Francisco Maritime (Calif.)	31.18

Name and location	Total acreage
San Juan Island (Wash.)	1,751.99
Saratoga (N.Y.)	3,392.42
Sitka (Alaska)	106.83
Tumacacori (Ariz.)	46.52
Valley Forge (Pa.)	3,466.47
War in the Pacific (Guam)	1,960.07
Women's Rights (N.Y.)	6.80
Yorktown National Cemetery (Va.)	2.91
Zuni-Cibola (N.M.)	800.00

NATIONAL MONUMENTS

Name and location	Total acreage
Agate Fossil Beds (Neb.)	3,055.22
Alibates Flint Quarries (Tex.)	1,370.97
Aniakchak (Alaska)	137,176.00
Aztec Ruins (N.M.)	319.73
Bandelier (N.M.)	32,737.20
Black Canyon (Colo.)	20,766.14
Booker T. Washington (Va.)	223.92
Buck Island Reef (U.S. V.I.)	880.00
Cabrillo (Calif.)	137.06
Canyon de Chelly (Ariz.)	83,840.00
Cape Krusenstern (Alaska)	659,807.00
Capulin Volcano (N.M.)	792.84
Casa Grande (Ariz.)	472.50
Castillo de San Marcos (Fla.)	20.51
Castle Clinton (N.Y.)	1.00
Cedar Breaks (Utah)	6,154.60
Chiricahua (Ariz.)	11,984.73
Colorado (Colo.)	20,453.93
Congaree Swamp (S.C.)	22,200.00
Craters of the Moon (Idaho)	53,440.05
Devils Postpile (Calif.)	798.46
Devils Tower (Wyo.)	1,346.91
Dinosaur (Utah-Colo.)	210,844.02
Effigy Mounds (Iowa)	1,481.39
El Malpais (N.M.)	114,275.95
El Morro (N.M.)	1,278.72
Florissant Fossil Beds (Colo.)	5,998.09
Fort Frederica (Ga.)	241.42
Fort Matanzas (Fla.)	227.76
Fort McHenry (Md.)	43.26
Fort Pulaski (Ga.)	5,623.10
Fort Stanwix (N.Y.)	15.52
Fort Sumter (S.C.)	194.60
Fort Union (N.M.)	720.60
Fossil Butte (Wyo.)	8,198.00
George Washington Birthplace (Va.)	553.23
George Washington Carver (Mo.)	210.00
Gila Cliff Dwellings (N.M.)	533.13
Grand Portage (Minn.)	709.97
Great Sand Dunes (Colo.)	38,662.18
Hagerman Fossil Beds (Idaho)	4,345.59
Hohokam Pima (Ariz.)	1,690.00
Homestead (Neb.)	195.11
Hovenweep (Utah-Colo.)	784.93
Jewel Cave (S.D.)	1,273.51
John Day Fossil Beds (Ore.)	14,014.58
Lava Beds (Calif.)	46,559.87
Little Big Horn Battlefield (Mont.)	765.34
Montezuma Castle (Ariz.)	857.69
Muir Woods (Calif.)	553.55
Natural Bridges (Utah)	7,636.49
Navajo (Ariz.)	360.00
Ocmulgee (Ga.)	701.54
Oregon Caves (Ore.)	487.98
Organ Pipe Cactus (Ariz.)	330,688.86
Petroglyph (N.M.)	7,240.33
Pinnacles (Calif.)	16,265.44
Pipe Spring (Ariz.)	40.00

Name and location	Total acreage
Pipestone (Minn.)	281.78
Poverty Point (La.)	910.85
Rainbow Bridge (Utah)	160.00
Russell Cave (Ala.)	310.45
Salinas (N.M.)	1,071.42
Scotts Bluff (Neb.)	3,003.03
Statue of Liberty (N.Y.-N.J.)	58.38
Sunset Crater (Ariz.)	3,040.00
Timpanogos Cave (Utah)	250.00
Tonto (Ariz.)	1,120.00
Tuzigoot (Ariz.)	800.62
Walnut Canyon (Ariz.)	3,541.46
White Sands (N.M.)	143,732.92
Wupatki (Ariz.)	35,442.13
Yucca House (Colo.)	33.87

NATIONAL PRESERVES

	Total acreage
Aniakchak (Alaska)	465,603.00
Bering Land Bridge (Alaska)	2,698,000.00
Big Cypress (Fla.)	716,000.00
Big Thicket (Tex.)	96,679.68
Denali (Alaska)	1,334,200.00
Gates of the Arctic (Alaska)	948,629.00
Glacier Bay (Alaska)	58,406.00
Katmai (Alaska)	418,699.30
Lake Clark (Alaska)	1,407,293.00
Little River Canyon (Ala.)	13,669.00
Mojave (Calif.)	1,450,000.00
Noatak (Alaska)	6,570,000
Timucuan Ecological and Historic Preserve (Fla.)	46,000.00
Wrangell-St. Elias (Alaska)	4,852,773.31
Yukon-Charley (Alaska)	2,526,509.46

NATIONAL RESERVES

	Total acreage
City of Rocks (Idaho)	14.407.19
Ebey's Landing (Wash.)	19,000.00

NATIONAL MILITARY PARKS

	Total acreage
Chickamauga and Chattanooga (Ga.-Tenn.)	8,119.11
Fredericksburg and Spotsylvania (Va.)	7,787.26
Fredericksburg National Cemetery	12.00
Gettysburg Nat. Mil. Park (Pa.)	5,906.30
Gettysburg Nat. Cemetery (Pa.)	20.58
Guilford Courthouse (N.C.)	220.25
Horseshoe Bend (Ala.)	2,040.00
Kings Mountain (S.C.)	3,945.29
Pea Ridge (Ark.)	4,300.35
Shiloh Nat. Cemetery (Tenn.)	10.05
Shiloh Nat. Park (Tenn.)	3,972.87
Vicksburg Nat. Cemetery (Miss.)	116.28
Vicksburg Nat. Mil. Park (Miss.)	1,736.47

NATIONAL BATTLEFIELDS

	Total acreage
Antietam (Md.)	3,255.89
Big Hole (Mont.)	655.61
Cowpens (S.C.)	841.56
Fort Donelson (Tenn.)	551.69
Fort Necessity (Pa.)	902.80
Monocacy (Md.)	1,647.01
Moores Creek (N.C.)	86.52
Petersburg (Va.)	2,744.10
Stones River (Tenn.)	708.32
Tupelo (Miss.)	1.00
Wilson's Creek (Mo.)	1,749.91

NATIONAL BATTLEFIELD PARKS

Name and location	Total acreage
Kennesaw Mountain (Ga.)	2,884.14
Manassas (Va.)	5,071.62
Richmond (Va.)	820.59

NATIONAL BATTLEFIELD SITE

Brices Cross Roads (Miss.)	1.00

NATIONAL HISTORIC SITES

Abraham Lincoln Birthplace (Ky.)	116.50
Adams (Mass.)	13.54
Allegheny Portage Railroad (Pa.)	1,249.20
Andersonville (Ga.)	494.61
Andrew Johnson (Tenn.)	16.68
Bent's Old Fort (Colo.)	799.80
Boston African American (Mass.)	0.00
Brown v. Board of Education (Kans.)	1.85
Carl Sandburg Home (N.C.)	263.52
Charles Pinckney (S.C.)	28.45
Christiansted (V.I.)	27.15
Clara Barton (Md.)	8.59
Edgar Allan Poe (Pa.)	0.52
Edison (N.J.)	21.25
Eisenhower (Pa.)	690.46
Eleanor Roosevelt (N.Y.)	180.50
Eugene O'Neill (Calif.)	13.19
Ford's Theatre (Lincoln Museum) (D.C.)	0.29
Fort Bowie (Ariz.)	1,000.00
Fort Davis (Tex.)	460.00
Fort Laramie (Wyo.)	832.85
Fort Larned (Kan.)	718.39
Fort Point (Calif.)	29.00
Fort Raleigh (N.C.)	152.93
Fort Scott (Kan.)	16.69
Fort Smith (Ark.-Okla.)	75.00
Fort Union Trading Post (N.D.-Mont.)	443.80
Fort Vancouver (Wash.)	208.89
Frederick Douglass Home (D.C.)	8.53
Frederick Law Olmsted (Mass.)	1.75
Friendship Hill (Pa.)	674.56
Golden Spike (Utah)	2,735.28
Grant-Kohrs Ranch (Mont.)	1,498.38
Hampton (Md.)	62.04
Harry S. Truman (Mo.)	6.67
Herbert Hoover (Iowa)	186.80
Home of F. D. Roosevelt (N.Y.)	290.34
Hopewell Furnace (Pa.)	848.06
Hubbell Trading Post (Ariz.)	160.09
James A. Garfield (Ohio)	7.82
Jimmy Carter (Ga.)	70.54
John F. Kennedy (Mass.)	0.09
John Muir (Calif.)	344.73
Knife River Indian Villages (N.D.)	1,758.35
Lincoln Home (Ill.)	12.24
Longfellow (Mass.)	1.98
Maggie L. Walker (Va.)	1.29
Manzanar National Historic Site (Calif.)	800.00
Martin Luther King, Jr. (Ga.)	36.95
Martin Van Buren (N.Y.)	39.58
Mary McLeod Bethune Council House National Historic Site (D.C.)	0.07
Ninety Six (S.C.)	989.14
Palo Alto Battlefield (Tex.)	3,357.42
Pennsylvania Avenue (D.C.)	0.00
Puukohola Heiau (Hawaii)	86.24
Sagamore Hill (N.Y.)	83.02
Saint-Gaudens (N.H.)	148.23
Saint Paul's Church (N.Y.)	6.13
Salem Maritime (Mass.)	9.02
San Juan (P.R.)	75.13
Saugus Iron Works (Mass.)	8.51
Springfield Armory (Mass.)	54.93
Steamtown (Pa.)	62.48
Theodore Roosevelt Birthplace (N.Y.)	0.11
Theodore Roosevelt Inaugural (N.Y.)	1.03
Thomas Stone (Md.)	328.25
Tuskegee Institute (Ala.)	57.92
Ulysses S. Grant (Mo.)	9.60
Vanderbilt Mansion (N.Y.)	211.65
Washita Battlefield (Okla.)	330.28
Weir Farm (Conn.)	60.76
Whitman Mission (Wash.)	98.15
William Howard Taft (Ohio)	3.07

NATIONAL MEMORIALS

Arkansas Post (Ark.)	389.18
Arlington House, the Robert E. Lee Memorial (Va.)	27.91
Chamizal (Tex.)	54.90
Coronado (Ariz.)	4,750.22
De Soto (Fla.)	26.84
Federal Hall (N.Y.)	0.45
Fort Caroline (Fla.)	138.39
Fort Clatsop (Ore.)	125.20
General Grant (N.Y.)	0.76
Hamilton Grange (N.Y.)	0.11
Jefferson National Expansion Memorial (Mo.)	90.96
Johnstown Flood (Pa.)	164.12
Korean War Veterans (D.C.)	2.2
Lincoln Boyhood (Ind.)	199.65
Lincoln Memorial (D.C.)	107.43
Lyndon Baines Johnson Memorial Grove on the Potomac (D.C.)	17.00
Mount Rushmore (S.D.)	1,278.45
Perry's Victory and International Peace Memorial (Ohio)	25.38
Roger Williams (R.I.)	4.56
Thaddeus Kosciuszko (Pa.)	0.02
Theodore Roosevelt Island (D.C.)	88.50
Thomas Jefferson Memorial (D.C.)	18.36
USS Arizona Memorial (Hawaii)	10.50
Vietnam Veterans Memorial (D.C.)	2.00
Washington Monument (D.C.)	106.01
Wright Brothers (N.C.)	428.44

NATIONAL CEMETERIES[1]

Antietam (Md.)	11.36
Battleground (D.C.)	1.03
Fort Donelson (Tenn.)	15.30
Poplar Grove (Va.)	8.72
Stones River (Tenn.)	719.81
Yorktown (Va.)	2.91

1. The National Cemeteries are not independent areas of the National Park System; each is part of a military area, battlefield, etc., except Battleground. Their acreage is kept separately. Arlington National Cemetery is under the Department of the Army.

NATIONAL SEASHORES

Assateague Island (Md.-Va.)	39,721.85
Canaveral (Fla.)	57,661.69
Cape Cod (Mass.)	43,569.09
Cape Hatteras (N.C.)	30,319.43
Cape Lookout (N.C.)	28,243.36
Cumberland Island (Ga.)	36,415.39
Fire Island (N.Y.)	19,578.55

Name and location	Total acreage
Gulf Islands (Fla.-Miss.)	135,607.15
Padre Island (Tex.)	130,434.27
Point Reyes (Calif.)	71,057.03

NATIONAL PARKWAYS

Blue Ridge (Va.-N.C.)	87,992.21
George Washington Memorial (Va.-Md.)	7,247.63
John D. Rockefeller, Jr., Memorial (Wyo.)	23,777.22
Natchez Trace (Miss.-Tenn.-Ala.)	51,747.59

NATIONAL LAKESHORES

Apostle Islands (Wis.)	69,371.89
Indiana Dunes (Ind.)	15,139.02
Pictured Rocks (Mich)	73,235.53
Sleeping Bear Dunes (Mich.)	71,189.40

NATIONAL WILD AND SCENIC RIVERS

Alagnak Wild River (Alaska)	30,800.00
Bluestone National Scenic River (W. Va.)	4,309.51
Delaware (N.Y.-N.J.-Pa.)	1,973.33
Great Egg Harbor River (N.J.)	n.a.
Missouri National Recreational River (Neb., S.D.)	n.a.
Obed Wild & Scenic River (Tenn.)	5,121.78
Rio Grande Wild & Scenic (Tex.)	9,600.00
St. Croix (Minn.-Wis.)	67,456.27
Upper Delaware (N.Y., N.J.-Pa.)	75,000.00

NATIONAL RIVERS

Big South Fork National River &Recreation Area (Ky.-Tenn.)	125,000.00
Buffalo (Ark.)	94,309.49
Mississippi National River & Recreation Area (Minn.)	53,775.00
New River Gorge (W.Va.)	70,911.69
Niobrara/Missouri National Scenic Riverways (Neb.-S.D.)	n.a.
Ozark (Mo.)	80,790.04

OTHER PARKS

Catoctin Mountain (Md.)	5,770.22
Constitution Gardens, (D.C.)	52.00
Fort Washington Park (Md.)	341.00
Greenbelt (Md.)	1,175.99
National Capital Parks (D.C.)	6,546.92
National Mall (D.C.)	146.35
Piscataway (Md.)	4,440.52
Prince William Forest (Va.)	18,571.55
Rock Creek Park (D.C.)	1,754.37
White House (D.C.)	18.07
Wolf Trap Farm Park for the Performing Arts (Va.)	130.28

NATIONAL RECREATION AREAS

Amistad (Tex.)	58,500.00
Bighorn Canyon (Wyo.-Mont.)	120,296.22
Boston Harbor Islands (Mass.)	1,482.25
Chattahoochee River (Ga.)	9,238.81
Chickasaw (Okla.)	9,888.83
Coulee Dam (Wash.)	100,390.31
Curecanti (Colo.)	41,972.42
Cuyahoga Valley (Ohio)	32,524.76
Delaware Water Gap (Pa.-N.J.)	67,191.66
Gateway (N.Y.-N.J.)	26,601.27
Gauley River (W. Va.)	11,145.07
Glen Canyon (Ariz.-Utah)	1,236,880.00

Name and location	Total acreage
Golden Gate (Calif.)	74,441.36
Lake Chelan (Wash.)	61,886.98
Lake Mead (Ariz.-Nev.)	1,495,665.52
Lake Meredith (Tex.)	44,977.63
Ross Lake (Wash.)	117,574.59
Santa Monica Mountains (Calif.)	150,050.00
Whiskeytown-Shasta-Trinity (Calif.)	42,503.46

NATIONAL SCENIC TRAIL

Appalachian (Maine, N.H., Vt., Mass., Conn., N.Y., N.J., Pa., Md., W.Va., Va., N.C., Tenn., Ga.)	172,109.93
Natchez Trace (Ga.-Ala.-Tenn.)	10,995.00
Potomac Heritage (D.C.-Md.-Va.-Pa.)	0.00

INTERNATIONAL HISTORIC SITE

Saint Croix Island (Maine)	35.39

AFFILIATED AREAS

(National Historic Sites unless otherwise noted.)

American Memorial Park (N. Mariana Is.)	133
Benjamin Franklin (Pa.)[1]	0.00
Blackstone River Valley National Heritage Corridor (Mass., R.I.)	0.00
Chicago Portage (Ill.)	91.20
Chimney Rock (Neb.)	83.36
David Berger (Ohio)[1]	0.00
Delaware and Lehigh Navigation Canal National Heritage Corridor (Pa.)	0.00
Father Marquette (Mich.)[1]	52.00
Gloria Dei Church (Pa.)	3.71
Green Springs Historic District (Va.)	5,490.59
Historic Camden (S.C.)	0.00
Ice Age Scenic Trail (Wis.)	0.00
Ice Age (Wis.)[2]	32,500.00
Iditarod National Historic Trail (Alaska)	0.00
Illinois and Michigan Canal National Heritage Corridor	0.00
International Peace Garden (N.D.)	2,330.30
Jamestown (Va.)	20.63
Lewis & Clark Natl. Historic Trail (Ill., Mo., Kan., Neb., Iowa, Idaho, S.D., N.D., Mont., Ore., Wash.)	39.11
Mary McLeod Bethune Council House (D.C.)	0.00
McLoughlin House (Ore.)	0.63
Mormon Pioneer Natl. Historic Trail (Ill., Iowa, Neb., Wyo., Utah)	0.00
North Country Nat'l Scenic Trail (N.Y., Pa., Ohio, Mich., Wis., Minn., N.D.)	0.00
Oregon Natl. Historic Trail (Mo., Kan., Neb., Wyo., Idaho, Ore., Wash.)	0.00
Overmountain Victory Trail (Mo. to Ore.)	0.00
Pinelands Natl. Reserve (N.J.)	0.00
Red Hill Patrick Henry (Va.)[1]	0.00
Roosevelt-Campobello International Park (Canada)	2,721.50
Santa Fe National Historic Trail (Mo. to N.M.)	0.00
Sewell-Belmont House National Historic Site (D.C.)	0.35
Touro Synagogue (R.I.)	0.23
Trail of Tears National Historic Trail (N.C. to Okla.)	0.00

1. National Memorial. 2. National Scientific Reserve.

Weather and Climate

What's Wrong With Our Weather?

By Storm Phillips

What is causing the meteorological misery this decade? Climatologists are blaming global warming. Scientists say its El Niño. No one knows for sure; it could be both.

In the United States, 26 states and half of the nation's population were affected by the March 1993 blizzard. It was a Category 3 winter hurricane and was called the "Storm of the Century" until the Blizzard of 1996 stole the title. On the Saffir-Simpson Scale of hurricane strength and damage potential, Category 3 represents winds between 111–130 mph (177–208 kph) and barometric pressure in inches of mercury of 27.91 to 28.47 (945–964 mb). The March 1993 blizzard was considered a Category 3 winter hurricane because of record low pressure readings at various observation stations in the eastern United States.

The winter of '94 and spring of '95 brought devastating floods to California from relentless Pacific storms steered by a jet stream flowing farther south of its normal position.

The 1995 Atlantic hurricane season was the second busiest since 1871 with 19 named storms. Only the 1993 season was more active with 21.

Nineteen-ninety five was the second most active midwest tornado season on record and was also the Earth's hottest year ever. Simultaneous floods and droughts were experienced worldwide during 1995. Nineteen-ninety six was no better. The January "Blizzard of '96" dumped snow from Mississippi to Maine, followed by a sudden warm-up that produced flooding as damaging as the blizzard. February 1996 brought severe arctic cold that gripped two-thirds of the United States. The 1996 Atlantic hurricane season delivered a one-two punch to North Carolina with Bertha in July and then Fran in September. The relentless winter of 1996–97 brought tremendous rain and snow to the western U.S. for the third year in a row.

Nineteen-ninety seven was highlighted by unusually strong March tornadoes in Arkansas, Mississippi, and Tennessee, accompanied by severe flooding from Texas to West Virginia. Measures taken by many of the states after the "Great Flood of 1937," prevented even worse devastation. The spring of '97 saw a deadly combination of deep snow, heavy rain, a rapid snowmelt, and ice jams on North Dakota's Red River. The resulting floods broke 100-year records in the northern plains. A rare and powerful F5 tornado hit suburban Jarrell, Texas, during an outbreak of severe thunderstorms in central Texas on May 27, 1997. (On the Fujita Scale measurement of the strength of a tornado, F5 category represents winds in excess of 261 mph [418 kph] with incredible damage.)

Not since the 30-year period between 1930 and 1960 has the United States seen such extreme weather events. Back then, scientists theorized that a strong El Niño in 1925–26 was to blame for weather extremes that followed into the 1930s. Today El Niño and the more elusive concept of "global warming" are being studied as the causes of the world's weird weather. □

Storm Phillips is a consulting meteorologist and historian with the firm STORMFAX, INC. His internet web site is www.stormfax.com.

El Niño

The climatic phenomenon called El Niño involves the periodic warming of the waters of the eastern and central Pacific Ocean along with a weakening of the equatorial trade winds. It's a naturally recurring event that causes a large mass of warm water, normally situated off Australia's coast, to move east toward South America.

The warm water displaces the cold Humboldt Current that flows north along the coast of Chile and Peru. The name was coined by Peruvian fishermen in Spanish for "the Child" when the effects of warm El Niño water were noticed around Christmas in the late 1980s. A reciprocal phase of strong trade winds and cooler eastern Pacific waters has been named "La Niña" (the little girl).

The effects of El Niño are felt worldwide in changing weather patterns and in the resulting economic consequences. International scientists say meteorological and oceanographic readings from the tropical Pacific during the summer of 1997 indicated the beginning of an El Niño that could equal or exceed this century's strongest one, which took place in 1982–83. That El Niño caused approximately $13 billion in damages around the world. Water temperatures off the coast of South America peaked at 14 degrees above normal. Fifteen-hundred deaths were blamed on that El Niño episode. General effects include droughts in Latin America, Africa, and Australia, and extraordinary typhoons in Polynesia. In the United States, severe winter storms usually occur in California and the Gulf States during El Niño conditions.

Global Warming

Many climatologists believe that increasing atmospheric concentrations of carbon dioxide and other "greenhouse gasses" released by human activities, such as burning fossil fuels and deforestation, are warming the Earth. The mechanism commonly known as the "greenhouse effect" is what makes the Earth habitable. These gasses in the atmosphere act like the glass of a greenhouse, letting sunlight in and preventing heat from escaping.

Climatic modeling studies generally estimate that global temperatures will rise a few degrees Celsius in the next century. Such a warming is likely to raise sea levels by expanding ocean water and melting glaciers and the polar ice cap. A 1995 E.P.A. report confirmed the possibility of a sea-level rise due to global warming and in that same year, the American Medical Association warned that changes in global temperatures could introduce new infectious diseases.

No one knows for certain what the consequences of this predicted climate change will be on the quality of human life, ecosystems, and loss of arable land. Some scientists disagree with the conclusions drawn from global climate models because the effects of clouds have not been factored into the current models.

Climate of 100 Selected U.S. Cities

| City | Average monthly temperature (°F)[1] | | | | Precipitation | | Snowfall | |
	Jan.	April	July	Oct.	Average (in.)[1]	annual (days)[2]	Average annual (in.)[2]	Years[2]
Albany, N.Y.	21.1	46.6	71.4	50.5	35.74	134	65.5	38
Albuquerque, N.M.	34.8	55.1	78.8	57.4	8.12	59	10.6	45
Anchorage, Alaska	13.0	35.4	58.1	34.6	15.20	115	69.2	41[3]
Asheville, N.C.	36.8	55.7	73.2	56.0	47.71	124	17.5	20
Atlanta, Ga.	41.9	61.8	78.6	62.2	48.61	115	1.9	50
Atlantic City, N.J.	31.8	51.0	74.4	55.5	41.93	112	16.4	40[3]
Austin, Texas	49.1	68.7	84.7	69.8	31.50	83	0.9	43
Baltimore, Md.	32.7	54.0	76.8	56.9	41.84	113	21.8	34
Baton Rouge, La.	50.8	68.4	82.1	68.2	55.77	108	0.1	34[3]
Billings, Mont.	20.9	44.6	72.3	49.3	15.09	96	57.2	50
Birmingham, Ala.	42.9	62.8	80.1	62.6	54.52	117	1.3	41
Bismark, N.D.	6.7	42.5	70.4	46.1	15.36	96	40.3	45
Boise, Idaho	29.9	48.6	74.6	51.9	11.71	92	21.4	45
Boston, Mass.	29.6	48.7	73.5	54.8	43.81	127	41.8	49[3]
Bridgeport, Conn.	29.5	48.6	74.0	56.0	41.56	117	26.0	36
Buffalo, N.Y.	23.5	45.4	70.7	51.5	37.52	169	92.2	41
Burlington, Vt.	16.6	42.7	69.6	47.9	33.69	153	78.2	41
Caribou, Maine	10.7	37.3	65.1	43.1	36.59	160	113.3	45
Casper, Wyom.	22.2	42.1	70.9	47.1	11.43	95	80.5	34
Charleston, S.C.	47.9	64.3	80.5	65.8	51.59	113	0.6	42
Charleston, W.Va.	32.9	55.3	74.5	55.9	42.43	151	31.5	37
Charlotte, N.C.	40.5	60.3	78.5	60.7	43.16	111	6.1	45
Cheyenne, Wyom.	26.1	41.8	68.9	47.5	13.31	98	54.1	49
Chicago, Ill.	21.4	48.8	73.0	53.5	33.34	127	40.3	26
Cleveland, Ohio	25.5	48.1	71.6	53.2	35.40	156	53.6	43
Columbia, S.C.	44.7	63.8	81.0	63.4	49.12	109	1.9	37
Columbus, Ohio	27.1	51.4	73.8	53.9	36.97	137	28.3	37[3]
Concord, N.H.	19.9	44.1	69.5	48.3	36.53	125	64.5	43
Dallas-Ft. Worth, Texas	44.0	65.9	86.3	67.9	29.46	78	3.1	31
Denver, Colo.	29.5	47.4	73.4	51.9	15.31	88	59.8	50
Des Moines, Iowa	18.6	50.5	76.3	54.2	30.83	107	34.7	45
Detroit, Mich.	23.4	47.3	71.9	51.9	30.97	133	40.4	26
Dodge City, Kan.	29.5	54.3	80.0	57.7	20.66	78	19.5	42
Duluth, Minn.	6.3	38.3	65.4	44.2	29.68	135	77.4	41[3]
El Paso, Texas	44.2	63.6	82.5	63.6	7.82	47	5.2	45
Fairbanks, Alaska	-12.7	30.2	61.5	25.1	10.37	106	67.5	33
Fargo, N.D.	4.3	42.1	70.6	46.3	19.59	100	35.9	42
Grand Junction, Colo.	25.5	51.7	78.9	54.9	8.00	72	26.1	38
Grand Rapids, Mich.	22.0	46.3	71.4	50.9	34.35	143	72.4	21
Hartford, Conn.	25.2	48.8	73.4	52.4	44.39	127	50.0	30
Helena, Mont.	18.1	42.3	67.9	45.1	11.37	96	47.9	44
Honolulu, Hawaii	72.6	75.7	80.1	79.5	23.47	100	0.0	38[3]
Houston, Texas	51.4	68.7	83.1	69.7	44.76	105	0.4	50
Indianapolis, Ind.	26.0	52.4	75.1	54.8	39.12	125	23.1	53[3]
Jackson, Miss.	45.7	65.1	81.9	65.0	52.82	109	1.2	21
Jacksonville, Fla.	53.2	67.7	81.3	69.5	52.76	116	T	43
Juneau, Alaska	21.8	39.1	55.7	41.8	53.15	220	102.8	41
Kansas City, Mo.	28.4	56.9	80.9	59.6	29.27	98	20.0	43
Knoxville, Tenn .	38.2	59.6	77.6	59.5	47.29	127	12.3	42
Las Vegas, Nev.	44.5	63.5	90.2	67.5	4.19	26	1.4	36
Lexington, Ky.	31.5	55.1	75.9	56.8	45.68	131	16.3	40
Little Rock, Ark.	39.9	62.4	82.1	63.1	49.20	104	5.4	42
Long Beach, Calif.	55.2	60.9	72.8	67.5	11.54	32	T	41[3]
Los Angeles, Calif.	56.0	59.5	69.0	66.3	12.08	36	T	49
Louisville, Ky.	32.5	56.6	77.6	57.7	43.56	125	17.5	37
Madison, Wisc.	15.6	45.8	70.6	49.5	30.84	118	40.8	36
Memphis, Tenn.	39.6	62.6	82.1	62.9	51.57	107	5.5	34
Miami, Fla.	67.1	75.3	82.5	77.9	57.55	129	0.0	42
Milwaukee, Wisc.	18.7	44.6	70.5	50.9	30.94	125	47.0	44
Minneapolis-St. Paul, Minn.	11.2	46.0	73.1	49.6	26.36	115	48.9	46
Mobile, Ala.	50.8	68.0	82.2	68.5	64.64	123	0.3	43
Montgomery, Ala.	46.7	65.2	81.7	65.3	49.16	108	0.3	40
Mt. Washington, N.H.	5.1	22.4	48.7	30.5	89.92	209	246.8	52
Nashville, Tenn.	37.1	59.7	79.4	60.2	48.49	119	11.1	43
Newark, N.J.	31.2	52.1	76.8	57.2	42.34	122	28.2	43

City	Average monthly temperature (°F)[1]				Precipitation		Snowfall	
	Jan.	April	July	Oct.	Average annual (in.)[1]	annual (days)[2]	Average annual (in.)[2]	Years[2]
New Orleans, La.	52.4	68.7	82.1	69.2	59.74	114	0.2	38[3]
New York, N.Y.	31.8	51.9	76.4	57.5	42.82	119	26.1	40[3]
Norfolk, Va.	39.9	58.2	78.4	61.3	45.22	115	7.9	36
Oklahoma City, Okla.	35.9	60.2	82.1	62.3	30.89	82	9.0	45
Olympia, Wash.	37.2	47.3	63.0	50.1	50.96	164	18.0	43
Omaha, Neb.	20.2	52.2	77.7	54.5	30.34	98	31.1	49[3]
Philadelphia, Pa.	31.2	52.9	76.5	56.5	41.42	117	21.9	42[3]
Phoenix, Ariz.	52.3	68.1	92.3	73.4	7.11	36	T	47[3]
Pittsburgh, Pa.	26.7	50.1	72.0	52.5	36.30	154	44.6	32
Portland, Maine	21.5	42.8	68.1	48.5	43.52	128	72.4	44
Portland, Ore.	38.9	50.4	67.7	54.3	37.39	154	6.8	44
Providence, R.I.	28.2	47.9	72.5	53.2	45.32	124	37.1	31
Raleigh, N.C.	39.6	59.4	77.7	59.7	41.76	112	7.7	40
Reno, Nev.	32.2	46.4	69.5	50.3	7.49	51	25.3	42
Richmond, Va.	36.6	57.9	77.8	58.6	44.07	113	14.6	47
Roswell, N.M.	41.4	61.9	81.4	61.7	9.70	52	11.4	37[3]
Sacramento, Calif.	45.3	58.2	75.6	63.9	17.10	58	0.1	36[3]
Salt Lake City, Utah	28.6	49.2	77.5	53.0	15.31	90	59.1	56
San Antonio, Texas	50.4	69.6	84.6	70.2	29.13	81	0.4	42
San Diego, Calif.	56.8	61.2	70.3	67.5	9.32	43	T	44
San Francisco, Calif.	48.5	54.8	62.2	60.6	19.71	63	T	57
Savannah, Ga.	49.1	66.0	81.2	66.9	49.70	111	0.3	34
Seattle-Tacoma, Wash.	39.1	48.7	64.8	52.4	38.60	158	12.8	40
Sioux Falls, S.D.	12.4	46.4	74.0	49.4	24.12	96	39.9	39
Spokane, Wash.	25.7	45.8	69.7	47.5	16.71	114	51.5	37
Springfield, Ill.	24.6	53.3	76.5	56.0	33.78	114	24.5	37
St. Louis, Mo.	28.8	56.1	78.9	57.9	33.91	111	19.8	48[3]
Tampa, Fla.	59.8	71.5	82.1	74.4	46.73	107	T	38
Toledo, Ohio	23.1	47.8	71.8	51.7	31.78	137	38.3	29
Tucson, Ariz.	51.1	64.9	86.2	70.4	11.14	52	1.2	44
Tulsa, Okla.	35.2	61.0	83.2	62.6	38.77	89	9.0	46
Vero Beach, Fla.	61.9	71.7	81.1	75.2	51.41	n.a.	n.a.	0
Washington, D.C.	35.2	56.7	78.9	59.3	39.00	112	17.0	41[3]
Wilmington, Del.	31.2	52.4	76.0	56.3	41.38	117	20.9	37
Wichita, Kan.	29.6	56.3	81.4	59.1	28.61	85	16.4	31

1. Based on 30-year period 1951–80. Data latest available. 2. Data through 1984 based on number of years as indicated in Years column. 3. For snowfall data where number of years differ from that for precipitation data. T = trace. n.a. = not available. *Source:* National Oceanic and Atmospheric Administration.

Wind Chill Factors

Wind speed (mph)	Thermometer reading (°F)															
	35	30	25	20	15	10	5	0	-5	-10	-15	-20	-25	-30	-35	-40	-45
5	33	27	21	19	12	7	0	-5	-10	-15	-21	-26	-31	-36	-42	-47	-52
10	22	16	10	3	-3	-9	-15	-22	-27	-34	-40	-46	-52	-58	-64	-71	-77
15	16	9	2	-5	-11	-18	-25	-31	-38	-45	-51	-58	-65	-72	-78	-85	-92
20	12	4	-3	-10	-17	-24	-31	-39	-46	-53	-60	-67	-74	-81	-88	-95	-103
25	8	1	-7	-15	-22	-29	-36	-44	-51	-59	-66	-74	-81	-88	-96	-103	-110
30	6	-2	-10	-18	-25	-33	-41	-49	-56	-64	-71	-79	-86	-93	-101	-109	-116
35	4	-4	-12	-20	-27	-35	-43	-52	-58	-67	-74	-82	-89	-97	-105	-113	-120
40	3	-5	-13	-21	-29	-37	-45	-53	-60	-69	-76	-84	-92	-100	-107	-115	-123
45	2	-6	-14	-22	-30	-38	-46	-54	-62	-70	-78	-85	-93	-102	-109	-117	-125

NOTES: This chart gives equivalent temperatures for combinations of wind speed and temperatures. For example, the combination of a temperature of 10° Fahrenheit and a wind blowing at 10 mph has a cooling power equal to -9° F. Wind speeds of higher than 45 mph have little additional cooling effect.

Tropical Storms and Hurricanes, 1886–1996

	Jan.-April	May	June	July	Aug.	Sept.	Oct.	Nov.	Dec.	Total
Number of tropical storms (incl. hurricanes)	4	4	59	75	234	318	196	45	6	951
Number of tropical storms that reached hurricane intensity	1	3	24	38	160	201	100	24	3	554

World and U.S. Extremes of Climate

Highest Recorded Temperature

	Place	Date	Degree Fahrenheit	Degree Centigrade
World (Africa)	El Azizia, Libya	Sept. 13, 1922	136	58
North America (U.S.)	Death Valley, Calif.	July 10, 1913	134	57
Asia	Tirat Tsvi, Israel	June 21, 1942	129	54
Australia	Cloncurry, Queensland	Jan. 16, 1889	128	53
Europe	Seville, Spain	Aug. 4, 1881	122	50
South America	Rivadavia, Argentina	Dec. 11, 1905	120	49
Canada	Midale and Yellow Grass, Saskatchewan	July 5, 1937	113	45
Persian Gulf (sea-surface)		August 5, 1924	96	36
South Pole		Dec. 27, 1978	7.5	-14
Antarctica	Vanda Station	Jan. 5, 1974	59	15

Lowest Recorded Temperature

	Place	Date	Degree Fahrenheit	Degree Centigrade
World (Antarctica)	Vostok	July 21, 1983	-129	-89
Asia	Verkhoyansk/Oimekon	Feb. 6, 1933	-90	-68
Greenland	Northice	Jan. 9, 1954	-87	-66
North America (excl. Greenland)	Snag, Yukon, Canada	Feb. 3, 1947	-81	-63
Alaska	Prospect Creek, Endicott Mts.	Jan. 23, 1971	-80	-62
U.S., excluding Alaska	Rogers Pass, Mont.	Jan. 20, 1954	-70	-56.5
Europe	Ust 'Shchugor, U.S.S.R.	n.a.	-67	-55
South America	Sarmiento, Argentina	Jan. 1, 1907	-27	-33
Africa	Ifrane, Morocco	Feb. 11, 1935	-11	-24
Australia	Charlotte Pass, N.S.W.	July 22, 1947	-8	-22
United States	Prospect Creek, Alaska	Jan. 23, 1971	-80	-62

Greatest Rainfalls

	Place	Date	Inches	Centimeters
1 minute (World)	Unionville, Md.	July 4, 1956	1.23	3.1
20 minutes (World)	Curtea-de-Arges, Romania	July 7, 1889	8.1	20.5
42 minutes (World)	Holt, Mo.	June 22, 1947	12	30.5
12 hours (World)	Foc-Foc, La Réunion	Jan. 7-8, 1966	45	114
24 hours (World)	Foc-Foc, La Réeunion	Jan. 7-8, 1966	72	182.5
24 hours (N. Hemisphere)	Paishih, Taiwan	Sept. 10-11, 1963	49	125
24 hours (Australia)	Bellenden Ker, Queensland	Jan. 4, 1979	44	114
24 hours (U.S.)	Alvin, Texas	July 25-26, 1979	43	109
24 hours (Canada)	Ucluelet Brynnor Mines, British Columbia	Oct. 6, 1967	19	49
5 days (World)	Commerson, La Réunion	Jan. 23-28, 1980	156	395
1 month (World)	Cherrapunji, India	July 1861	366	930
12 months (World)	Cherrapunji, India	Aug. 1860-Aug. 1861	1,042	2,647
12 months (U.S.)	Kukui, Maui, Hawaii	Dec. 1981-Dec. 1982	739	1878

Greatest Snowfalls

	Place	Date	Inches	Centimeters
1 month (U.S.)	Tamarack, Calif.	Jan. 1911	390	991
24 hours (N. America)	Montague, N.Y.	Jan. 11-12, 1997	77	195.6
24 hours (Alaska)	Thompson Pass	Dec. 29, 1955	62	157.5
19 hours (France)	Bessans	April 5-6, 1969	68	173
1 storm (N. America)	Mt. Shasta Ski Bowl, Calif.	Feb. 13-19, 1959	189	480
1 storm (Alaska)	Thompson Pass	Dec. 26-31, 1955	175	445.5
1 season (N. America)	Paradise Ranger Sta., Wash.	1971-1972	1,122	2,850
1 season (Alaska)	Thompson Pass	1952-1953	974.5	2,475
1 season (Canada)	Revelstoke Mt. Copeland, British Columbia	1971-1972	964	2,446.5

Source: U.S. Army Corps of Engineers, Engineer Topographic Laboratories.

Other Recorded Extremes

Highest average annual mean temperature (World): Dallol, Ethiopia (Oct. 1960-Dec. 1966), 94° F (35° C). **(U.S.):** Key West, Fla. (30-year normal), 78.2° F (25.7° C).
Lowest average annual mean temperature (Antarctica): Plateau Station -70° F (-57° C). **(U.S.):** Barrow, Alaska (30-year normal), 9.3°F (-13° C).
Greatest average yearly rainfall (U.S.): Mt. Waialeale, Kauai, Hawaii (32-year avg), 460 in. (1,168 cm). **(India):** Cherrapunji (74-year avg), 450 in. (1,143 cm).
Minimum average yearly rainfall (Chile): Arica (59-year avg), 0.03 in. (0.08 cm) (no rainfall for 14 consecutive years). **(U.S.):** Death Valley, Calif. (42-year avg), 1.63 in. (4.14 cm).

Bagdad, Calif., holds the U.S. record for the longest period with no measurable rain, 767 days, from Oct. 3, 1912 to Nov. 8, 1914.
Hottest summer average in Western Hemisphere (U.S.): Death Valley, Calif., 98° F (36.7° C).
Longest hot spell (W. Australia): Marble Bar, 100° F (38° C) (or above) for 162 consecutive days, Oct. 30, 1923–Apr. 7, 1924.
Largest hailstone (U.S.): Coffeyville, Kans., 17.5 in. (44.5 cm), Sept. 3, 1979.

Billion-Dollar U.S. Weather Disasters, 1991–1997

Source: National Climatic Data Center, data as of June 17, 1997. (No billion-dollar weather disasters occured in 1990.)

Northern Plains Flooding. April–May 1997, severe flooding in Dakotas and Minnesota due to heavy spring snowmelt; at least $1–$2 billion in damage/costs, 11 deaths.
Mississippi and Ohio Valleys Flooding and Tornadoes. March 1997, tornadoes and severe flooding in the states of Arkansas, Missouri, Mississippi, Tennessee, Illinois, Indiana, Kentucky, Ohio, and West Virginia; estimated $1 billion in damage/costs, 67 deaths.
West Coast Flooding. December 1996-January 1997, torrential rains and snowmelt produce severe flooding over portions of California, Washington, Oregon, Idaho, Nevada, and Montana; estimated $2-$3 billion in damage/costs, 36 deaths.
Hurricane Fran. September 1996, hurricane strikes North Carolina and Virginia; more than $5 billion in damage/costs, 37 deaths.
Southern Plains Severe Drought. Fall 1995 through summer 1996, severe drought in agricultural regions of southern Texas—Texas and Oklahoma most severely affected; more than $4 billion in estimated damage/costs, no deaths.
Pacific Northwest Severe Flooding. February 1996, very heavy, persistent rains and melting snow over Oregon, Washington, Idaho, and western Montana; approximately $1 billion in damage/costs, 9 deaths.
Blizzard of '96 Followed by Flooding. January 1996, very heavy snowstorm over Appalachians, mid-Atlantic, and Northeast, followed by severe flooding in parts of same areas due to rain and snowmelt; approximately $3 billion in damage/costs, 187 deaths.

Hurricane Opal. October 1995, hurricane strikes Florida panhandle, Alabama, western Georgia, eastern Tennessee, and the western Carolinas; more than $3 billion in damage/costs, 27 deaths.
Hurricane Marilyn. September 1995, hurricane devastates U.S. Virgin Islands; estimated $2.1 billion in damage/costs, 13 deaths.
Texas-Oklahoma-Louisiana-Mississippi Severe Weather and Flooding. May 1995, torrential rains, hail, and tornadoes across Texas—Oklahoma and southeast Louisiana-southern Mississippi, with Dallas and New Orleans areas hardest hit; $5-$6 billion in damage/costs, 32 deaths.
California Flooding. January-March 1995, frequent winter storms caused periodic flooding across much of California; more than $3 billion in damage/costs, 27 deaths.
Texas Flooding. October 1994, torrential rain and thunderstorms caused flooding across much of southeast Texas; approximately $1 billion in damage/costs, 19 deaths.
Tropical Storm Alberto. July 1994, remnants of slow-moving Alberto brought torrential 10-25 inch rains, widespread flooding in parts of Georgia, Alabama, and panhandle of Florida; approximately $1 billion in damage/costs, 32 deaths.
Southeast Ice Storm. February 1994, intense ice storm with extensive damage in portions of Texas, Oklahoma, Arkansas, Louisiana, Mississippi, Alabama, Tennessee, Georgia, South Carolina, North Carolina, and Virginia; approximately $3 billion in damage/costs, 9 deaths.
California Wildfires. Fall 1993, Southern California, approximately $1 billion in damage/costs, 4 deaths .
Midwest Flooding. Summer 1993, Central U.S.; $15–$20 billion in damage/costs, 48 deaths.
Drought/Heat Wave. Summer 1993, southeastern U.S.; about $1 billion in damage/costs, death toll undetermined.
Storm/Blizzard. March 1993, Eastern U.S.; $3–$6 billion damage/costs, approximately 270 deaths.
Nor'easter of 1992. December 1992, slow-moving storm batters northeast U.S. coast, New England hardest hit; $1-$2 billion in damage/costs, 19 deaths.
Hurricane Iniki. September 1992, hurricane hits Hawaiian Island of Kauai, about $1.8 billion in damage/costs, 7 deaths.
Hurricane Andrew. August 1992, hurricane hits Florida and Louisiana; approximately $27 billion in damage/costs, 58 deaths.
Oakland Firestorm. October 1991, Oakland, California firestorm due to low humidities and high winds; approximately $1.5 billion in damage/costs, 25 deaths.
Hurricane Bob. August 1991, mainly coastal North Carolina, Long Island, and New England; $1.5 billion in damage/costs, 18 deaths.

Weather & Climate Web Sites

National Oceanic and Atmospheric Administration: www.noaa.gov
National Weather Service: www.nws.noaa.gov
Center for Atmospheric Research: www.ucar.edu
National Climatic Data Center: www.ncdc.noaa.gov
National Hurricane Center: www.nhc.noaa.gov
The Weather Channel: www.weather.com
EPA's Global Warming Site: www.epa.gov/globalwarming/
Greenpeace Atmospheric Page: www.greenpeace.org/catm.html
Stormfax Weather Services: www.stormfax.com
Intellicast: www.intellicast.com
Storm Prediction Center: www.nssl.noaa.gov/~spc
Storm Chaser Homepage: taiga.geog.niu.edu/chaser/chaser2.html

Record Highest Temperatures by State

State	Temp. °F	Temp. °C	Date	Station	Elevation, feet
Alabama	112	44	Sept. 5, 1925	Centerville	345
Alaska	100	38	June 27, 1915	Fort Yukon	est. 420
Arizona	128	53	June 29, 1994	Lake Havasu	785
Arkansas	120	49	Aug. 10, 1936	Ozark	396
California	134	57	July 10, 1913	Greenland Ranch	-178
Colorado	118	48	July 11, 1888	Bennett	5,484
Connecticut	106	41	July 15, 1995	Danbury	457
Delaware	110	43	July 21, 1930	Millsboro	20
D.C.	106	41	July 20, 1930	Washington	410
Florida	109	43	June 29, 1931	Monticello	207
Georgia	113	45	May 27, 1978	Greenville	860
Hawaii	100	38	Apr. 27, 1931	Pahala	850
Idaho	118	48	July 28, 1934	Orofino	1,027
Illinois	117	47	July 14, 1954	E. St. Louis	410
Indiana	116	47	July 14, 1936	Collegeville	672
Iowa	118	48	July 20, 1934	Keokuk	614
Kansas	121	49	July 24, 1936*	Alton (near)	1,651
Kentucky	114	46	July 28, 1930	Greensburg	581
Louisiana	114	46	Aug. 10, 1936	Plain Dealing	268
Maine	105	41	July 10, 1911*	North Bridgton	450
Maryland	109	43	July 10, 1936*	Cumberland & Frederick	623; 325
Massachusetts	107	42	Aug. 2, 1975	New Bedford & Chester	120; 640
Michigan	112	44	July 13, 1936	Mio	963
Minnesota	114	46	July 6, 1936*	Moorhead	904
Mississippi	115	46	July 29, 1930	Holly Springs	600
Missouri	118	48	July 14, 1954*	Warsaw & Union	687; 560
Montana	117	47	July 5, 1937	Medicine Lake	1,950
Nebraska	118	48	July 24, 1936*	Minden	2,169
Nevada	125	52	June 29, 1994	Laughlin	680
New Hampshire	106	41	July 4, 1911	Nashua	125
New Jersey	110	43	July 10, 1936	Runyon	18
New Mexico	122	50	June 27, 1994	Lakewood	3,418
New York	108	42	July 22, 1926	Troy	35
North Carolina	110	43	Aug. 21, 1983	Fayetteville	81
North Dakota	121	49	July 6, 1936	Steele	1,857
Ohio	113	45	July 21, 1934*	Gallipolis (near)	673
Oklahoma	120	49	June 29, 1994*	Tipton	1,251
Oregon	119	48	Aug. 10, 1898	Pendleton	1,074
Pennsylvania	111	44	July 10, 1936*	Phoenixville	100
Rhode Island	104	40	Aug. 2, 1975	Providence	51
South Carolina	111	44	June 28, 1954*	Camden	170
South Dakota	120	49	July 5, 1936	Gannvalley	1,750
Tennessee	113	45	Aug. 9, 1930*	Perryville	377
Texas	120	49	Aug. 12, 1936	Seymour	1,291
Utah	117	47	July 5, 1895	Saint George	2,880
Vermont	105	41	July 4, 1911	Vernon	310
Virginia	110	43	July 15, 1954	Balcony Falls	725
Washington	118	48	Aug. 5, 1961*	Ice Harbor Dam	475
West Virginia	112	44	July 10, 1936*	Martinsburg	435
Wisconsin	114	46	July 13, 1936	Wisconsin Dells	900
Wyoming	114	46	July 12, 1900	Basin	3,500

* Also on earlier dates at the same or other places. *Source:* National Climatic Data Center, Asheville, N.C., and Storm Phillips, STORMFAX, INC.

Record Lowest Temperatures by State

State	Temp. °F	Temp. °C	Date	Station	Elevation, feet
Alabama	-27	-33	Jan. 30, 1966	New Market	760
Alaska	-80	-62	Jan. 23, 1971	Prospect Creek	1,100
Arizona	-40	-40	Jan. 7, 1971	Hawley Lake	8,180
Arkansas	-29	-34	Feb. 13, 1905	Pond	1,250
California	-45	-43	Jan. 20, 1937	Boca	5,532
Colorado	-61	-52	Feb. 1, 1985	Maybell	5,920
Connecticut	-32	-36	Feb. 16, 1943	Falls Village	585
Delaware	-17	-27	Jan. 17, 1893	Millsboro	20
D.C.	-15	-26	Feb. 11, 1899	Washington	410
Florida	-2	-19	Feb. 13, 1899	Tallahassee	193
Georgia	-17	-27	Jan. 27, 1940	CCC Camp F-16	est. 1,000
Hawaii	7	-14	Jan. 23, 1997	Mauna Kea	13,770
Idaho	-60	-51	Jan. 18, 1943	Island Park Dam	6,285
Illinois	-35	-37	Feb. 3, 1996	Elizabeth	880
Indiana	-36	-38	Jan. 19, 1994	New Whiteland	785
Iowa	-47	-44	Feb. 3, 1996	Elkader	745
Kansas	-40	-40	Feb. 13, 1905	Lebanon	1,812
Kentucky	-37	-38	Jan. 19, 1994	Shelbyville	730
Louisiana	-16	-27	Feb. 13, 1899	Minden	194
Maine	-48	-44	Jan. 19, 1925	Van Buren	510
Maryland	-40	-40	Jan. 13, 1912	Oakland	2,461
Massachusetts	-35	-37	Jan. 12, 1981	Chester	640
Michigan	-51	-46	Feb. 9, 1934	Vanderbilt	785
Minnesota	-60	-51	Feb. 2, 1996	Tower	1,400
Mississippi	-19	-28	Jan. 30, 1966	Corinth	420
Missouri	-40	-40	Feb. 13, 1905	Warsaw	700
Montana	-70	-57	Jan. 20, 1954	Rogers Pass	5,470
Nebraska	-47	-44	Feb. 12, 1899	Camp Clarke	3,700
Nevada	-50	-46	Jan. 8, 1937	San Jacinto	5,200
New Hampshire	-46	-43	Jan. 28, 1925	Pittsburg	1,575
New Jersey	-34	-37	Jan. 5, 1904	River Vale	70
New Mexico	-50	-46	Feb. 1, 1951	Gavilan	7,350
New York	-52	-47	Feb. 18, 1979*	Old Forge	1,720
North Carolina	-34	-37	Jan. 21, 1985	Mt. Mitchell	6,525
North Dakota	-60	-51	Feb. 15, 1936	Parshall	1,929
Ohio	-39	-39	Feb. 10, 1899	Milligan	800
Oklahoma	-27	-33	Jan. 18, 1930	Watts	958
Oregon	-54	-48	Feb. 10, 1933*	Seneca	4,700
Pennsylvania	-42	-41	Jan. 5, 1904	Smethport	est. 1,500
Rhode Island	-25	-32	Feb. 5, 1996	Greene	425
South Carolina	-20	-28	Jan. 18, 1977	Caesars Head	3,100
South Dakota	-58	-50	Feb. 17, 1936	McIntosh	2,277
Tennessee	-32	-36	Dec. 30, 1917	Mountain City	2,471
Texas	-23	-31	Feb. 8, 1933*	Seminole	3,275
Utah	-69	-56	Feb. 1, 1985	Peters Sink	8,095
Vermont	-50	-46	Dec. 30, 1933	Bloomfield	915
Virginia	-30	-34	Jan. 22, 1985	Mountain Lake	3,870
Washington	-48	-44	Dec. 30, 1968	Mazama & Winthrop	2,120; 1,765
West Virginia	-37	-38	Dec. 30, 1917	Lewisburg	2,200
Wisconsin	-54	-48	Jan. 24, 1922	Danbury	908
Wyoming	-63	-53	Feb. 9, 1933	Moran	6,770

* Also on earlier dates at the same or other places. *Source:* National Climatic Data Center, Asheville, N.C., and Storm Phillips, STORMFAX, INC.

Record High and Low Temperature in U.S. for Each Month

Source: National Climatic Data Center, Asheville, N.C., and Storm Phillips, STORMFAX, Inc.

January

The highest temperature ever recorded for the month of January occurred on January 17, 1936, and again in 1954, in Laredo, Tex. (elevation 421 ft.) where the temperature reached 98° F.

The lowest temperature ever recorded for the month of January occurred on January 20, 1954, in Rogers Pass, Mont. (elevation 5,470 ft.) where the temperature fell to -70° F.

February

The highest temperature ever recorded for the month of February occurred on February 3, 1963, in Montezuma, Ariz. (elevation 735 ft.) where the temperature reached 105° F.

The lowest temperature ever recorded for the month of February occurred on February 1, 1985, at the Peters Sink station in Utah (elevation 8,095 ft.) where the temperature fell to -69° F.

March

The highest temperature ever recorded for the month of March occurred on March 31, 1954, in Rio Grande City, Tex. (elevation 168 ft.) where the temperature reached 108° F.

The lowest temperature ever recorded for the month of March occurred on March 17, 1906, in Snake River, Wyo. (elevation 6,862 ft.) where the temperature dropped to -50° F.

April

The highest temperature ever recorded for the month of April occurred on April 25, 1898, at Volcano Springs, Calif. (elevation -220 ft.) where the temperature reached 118° F.

The lowest temperature ever recorded for the month of April occurred on April 5, 1945, in Eagle Nest, N. Mex. (elevation 8,250 ft.) where the temperature dropped to -36° F.

May

The highest temperature ever recorded for the month of May occurred on May 27, 1896, in Salton, Calif. (elevation -263 ft.) where the temperature reached 124° F.

The lowest temperature ever recorded for the month of May occurred on May 7, 1964, in White Mountain 2, Calif. (elevation 12,470 ft.) where the temperature dropped to -15° F.

June

The highest temperature ever recorded for the month of June occurred on June 23, 1902, at Volcano Springs, Calif. (elevation -220 ft.) where the temperature reached 129°F.

The lowest temperature ever recorded for the month of June occurred on June 13, 1907, in Tamarack, Calif. (elevation 8,000 ft.) where the temperature dropped to 2° F.

July

The highest temperature ever recorded for the month of July occurred on July 10, 1913, at Greenland Ranch, Calif. (elevation -178 ft.) where the temperature reached 134° F.

The lowest temperature ever recorded for the month of July occurred on July 21, 1911, at Painter, Wyo. (elevation 6,800 ft.) where the temperature fell to 10° F.

August

The highest temperature ever recorded for the month of August occurred on August 12, 1933, at Greenland Ranch, Calif. (elevation -178 ft.) where the temperature reached 127° F.

The lowest temperature ever recorded for the month of August occurred on August 25, 1910, in Bowen, Mont. (elevation 6,080 ft.) where the temperature fell to 5° F.

September

The highest temperature ever recorded for the month of September occurred on September 2, 1950, in Mecca, Calif. (elevation -175 ft.) where the temperature reached 126° F.

The lowest temperature ever recorded for the month of September occurred on September 24, 1926, at Riverside Ranger Station, Mont. (elevation 6,700 ft.) where the temperature fell to -9 F.

October

The highest temperature ever recorded for the month of October occurred on October 5, 1917, in Sentinel, Ariz. (elevation 685 ft.) where the temperature reached 116° F.

The lowest temperature ever recorded for the month of October occurred on October 29, 1917, in Soda Butte, Wyo. (elevation 6,600 ft.) where the temperature fell to -33° F.

November

The highest temperature ever recorded for the month of November occurred on November 12, 1906, in Craftonville, Calif. (elevation 1,759 ft.) where the temperature reached 105° F.

The lowest temperature ever recorded for the month of November occurred on November 16, 1959, at Lincoln, Mont. (elevation 5,130 ft.) where the temperature fell to -53° F.

December

The highest temperature ever recorded for the month of December occurred on December 8, 1938, in La Mesa, Calif. (elevation 539 ft.) where the temperature reached 100° F.

The lowest temperature ever recorded for the month of December occurred on December 19, 1924, at Riverside Ranger Station, Mont. (elevation 6,700 ft.) where the temperature fell to -59° F.

Temperature Extremes in the United States

Source: National Oceanic and Atmospheric Administration, Environmental Data and Information Service, and National Climatic Center

The Highest Temperature Extremes

Greenland Ranch, California, with 134° F on July 10, 1913, holds the record for the highest temperature ever officially observed in the United States. This station was located in barren Death Valley, 178 feet below sea level. Death Valley is about 140 miles long, four to six miles wide, and oriented north to south in southwestern California. Much of the valley is below sea level and is flanked by towering mountain ranges with Mt. Whitney, the highest landmark in the 48 conterminous states, rising to 14,495 feet above sea level, less than 100 miles to the west. Death Valley has the hottest summers in the western hemisphere, and is the only known place in the United States where nighttime temperatures sometimes remain above 100° F.

The highest annual normal (1941-70 mean) temperature in the United States, 78.2° F, and the highest summer (June-August) normal temperature, 92.8° F, are for Death Valley, California. The highest winter (December-February) normal temperature is 72.8° F for Honolulu, Hawaii.

Amazing temperature rises of 40° to 50° F in a few minutes occasionally may be brought about by chinook winds.[1]

Some Outstanding Temperature Rises

In 12 hours: 83° F, Granville, N.D., Feb. 21, 1918, from -33° F to 50° F from early morning to late afternoon.

In 15 minutes: 42° F, Fort Assiniboine, Mont., Jan. 19, 1892, from -5° F to 37°F.

In seven minutes: 34° F, Kipp, Mont., Dec. 1, 1896. The observer also reported that a total rise of 80° F occurred in a few hours and that 30 inches of snow disappeared in one-half day.

In two minutes: 49° F, Spearfish, S.D., Jan. 22, 1943, from -4° F at 7:30 a.m. to 45° F at 7:32 a.m.

The Lowest Temperature Extremes

The lowest temperature on record in the United States, -79.8° F, was observed at Prospect Creek Camp

in the Endicott Mountains of northern Alaska (latitude 66° 48'N, longitude 150° 40'W) on Jan. 23, 1971. The lowest ever recorded in the conterminous 48 states, -69.7° F, occurred at Rogers Pass, in Lewis and Clark County, Mont., on Jan. 20, 1954. Rogers Pass is in mountainous and heavily forested terrain about one-half mile east of and 140 feet below the summit of the Continental Divide.

The lowest annual normal (1941-70 mean) temperature in the United States is 9.3° F for Barrow, Alaska, which lies on the Arctic coast. Barrow also has the coolest summers (June–August) with a normal temperature of 36.4° F. The lowest winter (December–February) normal temperature, is -15.7° F for Barter Island on the arctic coast of northeast Alaska.

In the 48 conterminous states, Mt. Washington, N.H. (elevation 6,262 feet) has the lowest annual normal temperature 26.9° F and the lowest normal summer temperature, 46.8° F. A few stations in the northeastern United States and in the upper Rocky Mountains have normal annual temperatures in the 30s; summer normal temperatures at these stations are in the low 50s. Winter normal temperatures are lowest in northeastern North Dakota, 5.6° F for Langdon Experiment Farm, and in northwestern Minnesota, 5.3° F for Hallock.

Some Outstanding Temperature Falls

In 24 hours: 100° F, Browing, Mont., Jan. 23–24, 1916, from 44° to -56° F.

In 12 hours: 84° F, Fairfield, Mont., Dec. 24, 1924, from 63° at noon to -21° F at midnight.

In 2 hours: 62° F, Rapid City, S.D., Jan. 12, 1911, from 49° F at 6:00 a.m. to -13° F at 8:00 a.m.

In 27 minutes: 58° F, Spearfish, S.D., Jan. 22, 1943, from 54° F at 9:00 a.m. to -4° F at 9:27 a.m.

In 15 minutes: 47° F, Rapid City, S.D., Jan. 10, 1911, from 55° F at 7:00 a.m. to 8° F. at 7:15 a.m.

1. A warm, dry wind that descends from the eastern slopes of the Rocky Mountains, causing a rapid rise in temperature.

Winter Indoor Comfort and Relative Humidity

Compared to summer when the moisture content of the air (relative humidity) is an important factor of body discomfort, air moisture has a lesser effect on the human body during outdoor winter activities. But it is a big factor for winter indoor comfort because it has a direct bearing on health and energy consumption.

The colder the outdoor temperature, the more heat must be added indoors for body comfort. However, the heat that is added will cause a drying effect and lower the indoor relative humidity, unless an indoor moisture source is present.

While a room temperature between 71° and 77° F may be comfortable for short periods of time under very dry conditions, prolonged exposure to dry air has varying effects on the human body and usually causes discomfort. The moisture content of the air is important, and by increasing the relative humidity to above 50% within the above temperature range, 80% or more of all

average dressed persons would feel comfortable.

The following table gives apparent temperatures for various combinations of room temperature and relative humidity. As an example of how to read the table, a room temperature of 70° F combined with a relative humidity of 10% feels like 64° F, but at 80% it feels like 71° F.

Although degrees of comfort vary with age, health, activity, clothing, and body characteristics, the table on the following page can be used as a general guideline when raising the apparent temperature and the level of comfort through an increase in room moisture, rather than by an addition of heat to the room. This method of changing the apparent temperature can give the direct benefit of reducing heating costs because comfort can be maintained with a lower thermostat setting if moisture is added. □

Apparent Temperature for Values of Room Temperature and Relative Humidity

Relative Humidity (%)

Room Temperature (°F)	0	10	20	30	40	50	60	70	80	90	100
75	68	69	71	72	74	75	76	76	77	78	79
74	66	68	69	71	72	73	74	75	76	77	78
73	65	67	68	70	71	72	73	74	75	76	77
72	64	65	67	68	70	71	72	73	74	75	76
71	63	64	66	67	68	70	71	72	73	74	75
70	63	64	65	66	67	68	69	70	71	72	73
69	62	63	64	65	66	67	68	69	70	71	72
68	61	62	63	64	65	66	67	68	69	70	71
67	60	61	62	63	64	65	66	67	68	68	69
66	59	60	61	62	63	64	65	66	67	67	68
65	59	60	61	61	62	63	64	65	65	66	67
64	58	59	60	60	61	62	63	64	64	65	66
63	57	58	59	59	60	61	62	62	63	64	64
62	56	57	58	58	59	60	61	61	62	63	63
61	56	57	57	58	59	59	60	60	61	61	62
60	55	56	56	57	58	58	59	59	60	60	61

Source: National Oceanic and Atmospheric Administration, Environmental Data and Information Service and National Climatic Center.

Great Disasters

The following lists are not all-inclusive due to space limitations. Only disasters involving great loss of life and/or property, historical interest, or unusual circumstances are listed. Data as of Aug. 1, 1997. For later disasters *see* Current Events: What Happened in 1996–97.

Worst United States Disasters

Aircraft
1979 **May 25, Chicago:** American Airlines DC-10 lost left engine upon take-off and crashed seconds later, killing all 272 persons aboard and three on the ground in worst U.S. air disaster.

Dam
1928 **March 12, Santa Paula, Calif.:** collapse of St. Francis Dam left 450 dead.

Drought
1930s **Many states:** longest drought of the 20th century. Peak periods were 1930, 1934, 1936, 1939, and 1940. During 1934, dry regions stretched solidly from New York and Pennsylvania across the Great Plains to the California coast. A great "dust bowl" covered some 50 million acres in the south central plains during the winter of 1935-1936.

Earthquake
1906 **April 18, San Francisco:** earthquake accompanied by fire razed more than 4 sq mi.; more than 500 dead or missing.

Epidemic
1918 **Nationwide:** Spanish influenza killed over 500,000 Americans.

Explosion
1947 **April 16–18, Texas City, Texas:** most of the city destroyed by a fire and subsequent explosion on the French freighter *Grandcamp* carrying a cargo of ammonium nitrate. At least 516 were killed and over 3,000 injured.

Fire
1871 **Oct. 8, Peshtigo, Wis.:** over 1,200 lives lost and 2 billion trees burned in forest fire.

Flood
1889 **May 31, Johnstown, Pa.:** more than 2,200 died in flood.

Hurricane
1900 **Aug. 27–Sept. 15, Galveston, Tex.:** over 6,000 died from devastation due to both winds and tidal wave.

Marine
1865 **April 27, Mississippi River, Tenn.:** boiler explosion on Mississippi River steamboat, *Sultana,* near Memphis, 1,547 killed.

Mine
1907 **Dec. 6, Monongha, W. Va.:** coal mine explosion killed 361.

Oil Spill
1989 **Mar. 24, Prince William Sound, Alaska:** tanker, *Exxon Valdez,* hit an undersea reef and released 10 million plus gallons of oil into the waters, causing the worst oil spill in U.S. history.

Railroad
1918 **July 9, Nashville, Tenn.:** 101 killed in a two-train collision near Nashville.

Submarine
1963 **April 10, North Atlantic:** atomic-powered submarine, *Thresher,* sank: 129 dead.

Terrorist Attack
1995 **April 19, Oklahoma City:** terrorist car bomb exploded outside Federal office building, collapsing wall and floors. 168 persons were killed, including 19 children and one person who died in rescue effort. Over 220 buildings sustained damage. Bombing motive believed to be in revenge for the deaths of Branch Davidians in the Waco, Texas, compound, April 19, 1993, resulting from a botched assault by government agents. It is worst terrorist bombing on U.S. soil. *See also* Miscellaneous Disasters, 1993, April 19, Waco, Texas.

Tornado
1925 **March 18, Missouri, Illinois, and Indiana:** great tri-state tornado. 695 deaths. Eight additional tornadoes in Kentucky, Tennessee, and Alabama raised day's toll to 792 dead.

Winter Storm
1888 **March 11–14, East Coast:** The Blizzard of 1888. 400 people died, as much as 5 feet of snow. Damage was estimated at $20 million.

Earthquakes and Volcanic Eruptions

C.E. 79 **Aug. 24, Italy:** eruption of Mt. Vesuvius buried cities of Pompeii and Herculaneum, killing thousands.

1556 **Jan. 24, Shaanxi (Shensi) Province, China:** most deadly earthquake in history; 830,000 killed.

1755 **Nov. 1, Portugal:** one of the most severe of recorded earthquakes leveled Lisbon and was felt as far away as southern France and North Africa; 10,000–20,000 killed in Lisbon.

1811 **Dec. 16, Mississippi Valley near New Madrid, Missouri:** the quake reversed the course of the Mississippi River. Fatalities unknown due to the sparse population in the area. Aftershocks and tremors continued into 1812. It has been estimated that three of the series of earthquakes had surface-wave magnitudes of 8.6, 8.4, and 8.8 on the Richter Scale. It is the largest series of earthquakes known to have occurred in North America.

1883 **Aug. 26–28, Netherlands Indies:** eruption of Krakatau; violent explosions destroyed two thirds of island. Sea waves occurred as far away as Cape Horn, and possibly England. Estimated 36,000 dead.

1886 **Aug. 31, Charleston, S.C.:** sixty persons killed and damage to city extensive. The magnitude was 7.7 on the Richter Scale.

1902 **May 8, Martinique, West Indies:** Mt. Pelée erupted and wiped out city of St. Pierre; 40,000 dead.

1908 **Dec. 28, Messina, Sicily:** about 85,000 killed and city totally destroyed.

1915 **Jan. 13, Avezzano, Italy:** earthquake left 29,980 dead.

1920 **Dec. 16, Gansu (Kansu) Province, China:** earthquake killed 200,000.

1923 **Sept. 1, Japan:** earthquake destroyed third of Tokyo and most of Yokohama; more than 140,000 killed.

1933 **March 10, Long Beach, Calif.:** 117 left dead by earthquake.

1935 **May 31, India:** earthquake at Quetta killed an estimated 50,000.

1939 **Jan. 24, Chile:** earthquake razed 50,000 sq mi.; about 30,000 killed.
Dec. 27, Northern Turkey: severe quakes destroyed city of Erzingan; about 100,000 casualties.

1950 **Aug. 15, India:** earthquake affected 30,000 sq mi. in Assam; 20,000–30,000 believed killed.

1964 **March 27, Alaska:** strongest earthquake ever to strike North America hit 80 miles east of Anchorage; followed by seismic wave 50 feet high that traveled 8,445 miles at 450 miles per hour; 117 killed.

1970 **May 31, Peru:** earthquake left 50,000 dead, 17,000 missing.

1972 **Dec. 22, Managua, Nicaragua:** earthquake devastated city, leaving up to 6,000 dead.

1976 **Feb. 4, Guatemala:** earthquake left over 23,000 dead.
July 28, Tangshan, China: earthquake devastated 20-sq-mi. area of city leaving estimated 242,000 dead.
Aug. 17, Mindanao, Philippines: earthquake and tidal wave left up to 8,000 dead or missing.

1978 **Sept. 16, Tabas, Iran:** earthquake destroyed city in eastern Iran, leaving 25,000 dead.

1985 **Sept. 19–20, Mexico:** earthquake registering 8.1 on Richter scale struck central and southwestern regions, devastating part of Mexico City and three coastal states. An estimated 25,000 killed.
Nov. 14–16, Colombia: eruption of Nevada del Ruiz, 85 miles northwest of Bogotá, caused mud slides which buried most of the town of Armero and devastated Chinchiná. An estimated 25,000 were killed.

1988 **Dec. 7, Armenia:** an earthquake measuring 6.9 on the Richter scale killed nearly 25,000, injured 15,000, and left at least 400,000 homeless.

1989 **Oct. 17, San Francisco Bay Area:** an earthquake measuring 7.1 on the Richter Scale killed 67 and injured over 3,000. The quake damaged or destroyed over 100,000 buildings and caused billions of dollars of damage.

1990 **June 21, Northwestern Iran:** an earthquake measuring 7.7 on the Richter Scale destroyed cities, towns, and villages in Caspian Sea area. At least 50,000 dead, over 60,000 injured, and 400,000 homeless.

1994 **Jan. 17, San Fernando Valley, Calif.:** an earthquake measuring 6.6 on the Richter Scale killed 61 persons and injured over 8,000. Damage estimated at $13-20 billion.

1995 **Jan.17, Osaka, Kyoto, Kobe, Japan:** 5,100 killed and 26,800 injured, estimated damage $100 billion. Epicenter 12 miles under Awaji Island in the Inland Sea. Magnitude: 7.2.

1997 **May 12, Northeastern Iran:** severe earthquake measuring 7.1 on Richter Scale leaves more than 1,500 people dead and at least 4,460 injured.

Major U.S. Epidemics

1793 **Philadelphia:** more than 4,000 residents died from yellow fever.

1832 **July–August, New York City:** over 3,000 people killed in a cholera epidemic.
October, New Orleans: cholera took the lives of 4,340 persons.

1848 **New York City:** more than 5,000 deaths caused by cholera.

1853 **New Orleans:** yellow fever killed 7,790 residents.

1867 **New Orleans:** 3,093 persons perished from yellow fever.

1878 **Southern States:** over 13,000 people died from yellow fever in lower Mississippi Valley.

1916 **Nationwide:** over 7,000 deaths occurred and 27,363 cases were reported of polio (infantile paralysis) in America's worst polio epidemic.

1918 **March–November, Nationwide:** outbreak of influenza killed over 500,000 people in the worst single U.S. epidemic.

1949 **Nationwide:** 2,720 deaths occurred from polio and 42,173 cases were reported.

1952 **Nationwide:** polio killed 3,300; 57,628 cases reported; worst epidemic since 1916.

1981 **To present:** the World Health Organization estimates that 8.4 million cases of AIDS have occurred, resulting in 6.4 million deaths as of Dec. 31, 1996.

Floods, Avalanches, and Tidal Waves

1228 **Holland:** 100,000 persons reputedly drowned by sea flood in Friesland.

1642 **China:** rebels destroyed Kaifeng seawall; 300,000 drowned.

1896 **June 15, Sanriku, Japan:** earthquake and tidal wave killed 27,000.

1953 **Northwest Europe:** storm followed by floods devastated North Sea coastal areas. Netherlands was hardest hit with 1,794 dead.

1959 **Dec. 2, Frejus, France:** flood caused by collapse of Malpasset Dam left 412 dead.

1960 **Agadir, Morocco:** 10,000-12,000 dead as earthquake set off tidal wave and fire, destroying most of city.

1962 **Jan. 10, Peru:** avalanche down Huascaran, extinct Andean volcano, killed more than 3,000 persons.

1963 **Oct. 9, Italy:** landslide into the Vaiont Dam; flood killed about 2,000.

1966 **Oct. 21, Aberfan, Wales:** avalanche of coal, waste, mud, and rocks killed 144 persons, including 116 children in school.

1969 **Jan. 18–26, Southern California:** floods and mudslides from heavy rains caused widespread property damage; at least 100 dead. Another downpour (Feb. 23–26) caused further floods and mudslides; at least 18 dead.

1970 **Nov. 13, East Pakistan:** 200,000 killed by cyclone-driven tidal wave from Bay of Bengal. Over 100,000 missing.

1972 **Feb. 26, Man, W. Va.:** more than 118 died when slag-pile dam collapsed under pressure of torrential rains and flooded 17-mile valley.
June 9–10, Rapid City, S.D.: flash flood caused 237 deaths and $160 million in damage.

June 20, Eastern Seaboard: tropical storm Agnes, in 10-day rampage, caused widespread flash floods. Death toll was 129, 115,000 were left homeless, and damage estimated at $3.5 billion.

1976 **Aug. 1, Loveland, Colo.:** flash flood along Route 34 in Big Thompson Canyon left 139 dead.

1988 **August–September, Bangladesh:** heaviest monsoon in 70 years inundates three-fourths of country, killing more than 1,300 people and leaving 30 million homeless. Damage is estimated at over $1 billion.

1993 **June–August, Ill., Iowa, Kan., Ky., Minn., Mo., Neb., N.D., S.D., Wis.:** two months of heavy rain caused Mississippi River and its tributaries to flood in ten states, causing almost 50 deaths and an estimated $12 billion in damage to property and agriculture in the Midwest. Almost 70,000 people left homeless.

1997 **December 1996–January 1997, U.S. West Coast:** torrential rains and snowmelt produced severe floods in portions of California, Oregon, Washington, Idaho, Nevada, and Montana, causing 36 deaths and an estimated $2-3 billion in damage.

Tropical Storms

Cyclones, typhoons, and hurricanes are the same kind of tropical storms but are called by different names in different areas of the world. For example: a typhoon is a severe tropical hurricane that occurs in the western Pacific and China Sea.

Cyclones

1864 **Oct. 5, India:** most of Calcutta denuded by cyclone; 70,000 killed.

1942 **Oct. 16, India:** cyclone devastated Bengal; about 40,000 lives lost.

1960 **Oct. 10, East Pakistan:** cyclone and tidal wave killed about 6,000.

1963 **May 28–29, East Pakistan:** cyclone killed about 22,000 along coast.

1965 **May 11–12 and June 1–2, East Pakistan:** cyclones killed about 47,000.

Dec. 15, Karachi, Pakistan: cyclone killed about 10,000.

1970 **Nov. 12–13, East Pakistan:** cyclone and tidal waves killed 200,000 and another 100,000 were reported missing.

1971 **Sept. 29, Orissa State, India:** cyclone and tidal wave off Bay of Bengal killed as many as 10,000.

1974 **Dec. 25, Darwin, Australia:** cyclone destroyed nearly the entire city, causing mass evacuation; 50 reported dead.

1977 **Nov. 19, Andhra Pradesh, India:** cyclone and tidal wave claimed lives of 20,000.

1991 **April 30, Southeastern Bangladesh:** cyclone killed over 131,000 and left as many as 9 million homeless. Thousands of survivors died from hunger and water borne disease.

U.S. Hurricanes

(U.S. deaths only, except where noted)

1775 **Sept. 2–Sept. 9, North Carolina to Nova Scotia:** called the "Hurricane of Independence," it is believed that 4,170 in the U.S. and Canada died in the storm.

1856 **Aug. 11, Last Island, La.:** 400 died.

1893 **Aug. 28, Savannah, Ga., Charleston, S.C., Sea Islands, S.C.:** at least 1,000 died.

1900 **Aug. 27–Sept. 15, Galveston, Tex. and Texas Gulf Coast:** more than 6,000 died in hurricane and tidal wave.

1909 **Sept. 10–21, Louisiana and Mississippi:** 350 deaths.

1915 **Aug. 5–23, East Texas and Louisiana:** 275 killed.

1919 **Sept. 2–15, Florida, Louisiana and Texas:** 287 deaths, and 488 deaths at sea.

1926 **Sept. 11–22, Florida and Alabama:** 243 deaths.

1928 **Sept. 6–20, Southern Florida:** 1,836 died and 1,870 injured.

1935 **Aug. 29–Sept. 10, Southern Florida:** 408 killed.

1938 **Sept. 10–22, Long Island and Southern New England:** 600 deaths; 1,764 injured.

1944 **Sept. 9–16, North Carolina to New England:** 46 deaths, and 344 deaths at sea.

1947 **Sept. 4–21, Florida and Mid-Gulf Coast:** 51 killed.

1954 **Aug. 25–31, North Carolina to New England:** "Carol" killed 60 and injured 1,000 in Long Island-New England area.

Oct. 5–18, South Carolina to New York: "Hazel" killed 95 in U.S.; about 400-1000 in Haiti; 78 in Canada.

1955 **Aug. 7–21, North Carolina to New England:** "Diane" took 184 lives.

1957 **June 25–28. Texas to Alabama:** "Audrey" wiped out Cameron, La., causing 390 deaths.

1960 **Aug. 29–Sept. 13, Florida to New England:** "Donna" killed 50 in the United States. 115 deaths in Antilles—mostly from flash floods in Puerto Rico.

1961 **Sept. 3–15, Texas coast:** "Carla" devastated Texas gulf cities, taking 46 lives.

1965 **Aug. 27–Sept. 12, Southern Florida and Louisiana:** "Betsy" killed 75 people.

1969 **Aug. 14–22, Mississippi, Louisiana, Alabama, Virginia, W. Virginia:** 256 killed and 68 persons missing as a result of "Camille."

1972 **June 14–23, Florida to New York:** "Agnes" caused 117 deaths (50 in Pennsylvania).

1979 **Aug. 25–Sept. 7, Caribbean Islands to New England:** "David" caused 5 U.S. deaths; 1,200 in the Dominican Republic.

1980 **Aug. 3–10, Caribbean Islands to Texas Gulf:** "Allen" killed 28 in the U.S.; over 200 killed in Caribbean.

1989 **Sept. 10–22, Caribbean Sea and South and North Carolina:** "Hugo" claimed 49 U.S. lives (71 killed overall) and $4.2 billion were paid in insurance claims.

1992 **Aug. 22–26, South Florida, Louisiana, and Bahamas:** Gulf Coast hurricane "Andrew" with damage in South Florida alone estimated at $20.6 billion (est. $7.3 billion in private insurance claims) is most costly U.S. hurricane.

Other Hurricanes

1926 **Oct. 20, Cuba:** worst hurricane in 80 years, 650 reported dead.

1930 **Sept. 3 Santo Domingo:** hurricane killed about 2,000 and injured 6,000.

1934 **Sept. 21, Japan:** hurricane killed more than 4,000 on Honshu.

1955 **Sept. 19, Mexico:** hurricane "Hilda" took 200 lives.

Sept. 22–28, Caribbean: hurricane "Janet" killed 200 in Honduras and 300 in Mexico.

1961 **Oct. 31, British Honduras:** hurricane "Hattie" devastated capital Belize, killed at least 400.

1963 **Oct. 2–7, Caribbean:** hurricane "Flora" killed up to 7,000 in Haiti and Cuba.

Nuclear Power Plant Accidents

1952 **Dec. 12, Chalk River, near Ottawa, Canada:** a partial meltdown of the reactor's uranium fuel core resulted after the accidental removal of four control rods. Although millions of gallons of radioactive water accumulated inside the reactor, there were no injuries.

1957 **Oct. 7, Windscale Pile No. 1, north of Liverpool, England:** fire in a graphite-cooled reactor spewed radiation over the countryside, contaminating a 200 sq mi area.

South Ural Mountains: explosion of radioactive wastes at Soviet nuclear weapons factory 12 miles from city of Kyshtym forces the evacuation of over 10,000 people from a contaminated area. No casualties were reported by Soviet officials.

1976 **near Greifswald, East Germany:** radioactive core of reactor in the Lubmin nuclear power plant nearly melted down due to the failure of safety systems during a fire.

1979 **March 28, Three Mile Island, near Harrisburg, Pa.:** one of two reactors lost its coolant, which caused the radioactive fuel to overheat and caused a partial meltdown. Some radioactive material was released.

1986 **April 26, Chernobyl, near Kiev, U.S.S.R.:** explosion and fire in the graphite core of one of four reactors released radioactive material that spread over part of the Soviet Union, Eastern Europe, Scandinavia, and later Western Europe. 31 claimed dead. Total casualties are unknown and estimates run into the thousands. Is the worst such accident to date.

1966 **Sept. 24–30, Caribbean area:** hurricane "Inez" killed 293.

1974 **Sept. 20, Honduras:** hurricane "Fifi" struck northern section of country, leaving 8,000 dead, 100,000 homeless.

1988 **Sept. 12–17, Caribbean Sea and Gulf of Mexico:** Hhurricane "Gilbert," worst Atlantic storm ever recorded, took at least 260 lives and caused some 39 tornadoes in Texas.

Tornadoes

1884 **Feb. 19:** tornadoes in Mississippi, Alabama, North and South Carolina, Tennessee, Kentucky and Indiana caused estimated 800 deaths.

1925 **Mar. 18:** tornadoes in Missouri, Illinois, Indiana, Kentucky, Tennessee, and Alabama killed 792.

1932 **March 21:** outbreak of tornadoes in Alabama, Mississippi, Georgia, and Tennessee killed 268.

1936 **April 5–6:** series of tornadoes in Arkansas, Alabama, Tennessee, Georgia, and South Carolina killed 498.

1952 **March 21–22:** tornadoes in Arkansas, Tennessee, Missouri, Mississippi, Alabama, and Kentucky caused 343 deaths.

1953 **May 11:** a single tornado struck Waco, Texas, killing 114.

June 8: another tornado killed 116 in Flint, Michigan.

1965 **April 11:** tornadoes in Iowa, Illinois, Indiana, Ohio, Michigan, and Wisconsin caused 256 deaths.

1974 **April 3–4:** a series of tornadoes in East, South, and Midwest killed approximately 315.

Typhoons

1906 **Sept. 18, Hong Kong:** typhoon with tsunami killed an estimated 10,000 persons.

1949 **Dec. 5, off Korea:** typhoon struck fishing fleet; several thousand men reported dead.

1959 **Aug. 20, Fukien province, China:** typhoon "Iris" killed 2,334.

Sept. 27, Honshu, Japan: typhoon "Vera" killed an estimated 4,464.

1960 **June 9, Fukien province, China:** typhoon "Mary" caused at least 1,600 deaths.

1984 **Sept. 2–3, Philippines:** typhoon "Ike" hit seven major islands leaving 1,300 dead.

1991 **Nov. 5, Central Philippines:** flash floods triggered by tropical storm "Thelma" killed about 3,000 people. Leyte city of Ormoc was worst hit.

Fires and Explosions

1666 **Sept. 2, England:** "Great Fire of London" destroyed St. Paul's Church, etc. Damage £10 million.

1835 **Dec. 16, New York City:** 530 buildings destroyed by fire.

1871 **Oct. 8, Chicago:** the "Chicago Fire" burned 17,450 buildings, killed 250 persons; $196 million damage.

1872 **Nov. 9, Boston:** fire destroyed 800 buildings; $75 million damage.

1876 **Dec. 5, New York City:** fire in Brooklyn Theater killed more than 300.

1881 **Dec. 8, Vienna:** at least 620 died in fire at Ring Theatre.

1894 **Sept. 1, Minnesota:** forest fire over 480-square-mile area destroyed six towns and killed 480 people.

1900 **May 1, Scofield, Utah:** explosion of blasting powder in coal mine killed 200.

June 30, Hoboken, N.J.: piers of North German Lloyd Steamship line burned; 326 dead.

1903 **Dec. 30, Chicago:** Iroquois Theatre fire killed 602.

1906 **March 10, France:** explosion in coal mine in Courrières killed 1,060.

1907 **Dec. 19, Jacobs Creek, Pa.:** explosion in coal mine left 239 dead.

1909 **Nov. 13, Cherry, Ill.:** explosion in coal mine killed 259.

1911 **March 25, New York City:** fire in Triangle Shirtwaist Factory fatal to 145.

1913 **Oct. 22, Dawson, N.M.:** coal mine explosion left 263 dead.

1917 **April 10, Eddystone, Pa.:** explosion in munitions plant killed 133.

Dec. 6, Canada: 1,600 people died when French ammunition ship *Mont Blanc* collided with Belgium steamer in Halifax Harbor.

1930 **April 21, Columbus, Ohio:** fire in Ohio State Penitentiary killed 320 convicts.

1937 **March 18, New London, Tex.:** explosion destroyed schoolhouse; 294 killed.

1942   **April 26, Manchuria:** explosion in Honkeiko Colliery killed 1,549.

Nov. 28, Boston: Coconut Grove nightclub fire killed 491.

1944   **July 6, Hartford, Conn.:** fire and ensuing stampede in main tent of Ringling Brothers Circus killed 168, injured 487.

July 17, Port Chicago, Calif.: 322 killed as ammunition ships explode.

Oct. 20, Cleveland: liquid-gas tanks exploded, killing 130.

1946   **Dec. 7, Atlanta:** fire in Winecoff Hotel killed 119.

1948   **Dec. 3, Shanghai:** Chinese passenger ship *Kiangya*, carrying refugees fleeing Communist troops during civil war, struck an old mine, exploded, and sank off Shanghai. Over 3,000 people are believed killed.

1949   **Sept. 2, China:** fire on Chongqing (Chungking) waterfront killed 1,700.

1954   **May 26, off Quonset Point, R.I.:** explosion and fire aboard aircraft carrier *Bennington* killed 103 crewmen.

1956   **Aug. 7, Colombia:** about 1,100 reported killed when seven army ammunition trucks exploded at Cali.

Aug. 8, Belgium: 262 died in coal mine fire at Marcinelle.

1960   **Jan. 21, Coalbrook, South Africa:** coal mine explosion killed 437.

Nov. 13, Syria: 152 children killed in moviehouse fire.

1961   **Dec. 17, Niteroi, Brazil:** circus fire fatal to 323.

1962   **Feb. 7, Saarland, West Germany:** coal mine gas explosion killed 298.

1963   **Nov. 9, Japan:** explosion in coal mine at Omuta killed 447.

1965   **May 28, India:** coal mine fire in state of Bihar killed 375.

June 1, near Fukuoka, Japan: coal mine explosion killed 236.

1967   **May 22, Brussels:** fire in L'Innovation, major department store, left 322 dead.

July 29, off North Vietnam: fire on U.S. carrier *Forrestal* killed 134.

1969   **Jan. 14, Pearl Harbor, Hawaii:** nuclear aircraft carrier *Enterprise* ripped by explosions; 27 dead, 82 injured.

1970   **Nov. 1, Saint-Laurent-du-Pont, France:** fire in dance hall killed 146 young people.

1972   **May 13, Osaka, Japan:** 118 people died in fire in nightclub on top floor of Sennichi department store.

June 6, Wankie, Rhodesia: explosion in coal mine killed 427.

1973   **Nov. 29, Kumamoto, Japan:** fire in Taiyo department store killed 101.

1974   **Feb. 1, Sao Paulo, Brazil:** fire in upper stories of bank building 189 persons, many of whom leaped to death.

1975   **Dec. 27, Dhanbad, India:** explosion in coal mine followed by flooding from nearby reservoir left 372 dead.

1977   **May 28, Southgate, Ky.:** fire in Beverly Hills Supper Club; 167 dead.

1978   **July 11, Tarragona, Spain:** 140 killed at coastal campsite when tank truck carrying liquid gas overturned and exploded.

Aug. 20, Abadan, Iran: nearly 400 killed when arsonists set fire to crowded theater.

1982   **Dec. 18-21, Caracas, Venezuela:** power-plant fire leaves 128 dead.

1986   **Dec. 31, San Juan, P. R.:** arson fire in Dupont Plaza Hotel set by three hotel employees kills 96.

1989   **June 3, Ural Mountains:** liquefied petroleum gas leaking from a pipeline running alongside the Trans-Siberian railway near Uta, 72 miles east of Moscow, exploded and destroyed two passing passenger trains. About 500 travelers were killed and 723 injured of an estimated 1,200 passengers on both trains.

Oct. 23, Pasadena, Texas: a huge explosion followed by a series of others and a raging fire at a plastics manufacturing plant owned by Phillips Petroleum Co. killed 22 and injured more than 80 persons. A large leak of ethylene was presumed to be the cause.

1990   **March 25, New York City:** arson fire in illegal Happy Land Social Club, Bronx, killed 87.

1991   **Oct. 20-23, Oakland-Berkeley, Calif.:** brush fire in drought-stricken area destroyed over 3,000 homes and apartments. At least 24 persons died, damage estimated at $1.5 billion.

1993   **May 10, near Bangkok, Thailand:** Fire in doll factory killed at least 187 persons and injured 500 others. Is world's deadliest factory fire.

Shipwrecks

1833   **May 11, *Lady of the Lake:*** bound from England to Quebec, struck iceberg; 215 perished.

1853   **Sept. 29 *Annie Jane:*** emigrant vessel off coast of Scotland; 348 died.

1898   **Nov. 26, *City of Portland:*** loss of 157 off Cape Cod.

1904   **June 15, *General Slocum:*** excursion steamer burned in East River, New York; 1,021 perished.

1912   **March 5, *Principe de Asturias:*** Spanish steamer struck rock off Sebastien Point; 500 drowned.

April 15, *Titanic:* sank after colliding with iceberg; 1,513 died.

1914   **May 29, *Empress of Ireland:*** sank after collision in St. Lawrence River; 1,024 perished.

1915   **July 24, *Eastland:*** Great Lakes excursion steamer overturned in Chicago River; 812 died.

1928   **Nov. 12, *Vestris:*** British steamer sank in gale off Virginia; 110 died.

1934   **Sept. 8, *Morro Castle:*** 134 killed in fire off Asbury Park, N.J.

1939   **May 23, *Squalus:*** submarine with 59 men sank off Hampton Beach, N.H.; 33 saved.

June 1, Submarine *Thetis:* sank in Liverpool Bay, England; 99 perished.

1942   **Oct. 2, *Queen Mary:*** rammed and sank a British cruiser; 338 aboard the cruiser died.

1945   **April 9:** U.S. ship, loaded with aerial bombs, exploded at Bari, Italy; at least 360 killed.

1947   **November, Yingkow:** unidentified Chinese troopship evacuating Nationalist troops from Manchuria sank, killing an estimated 6,000 persons.

1949   **Sept. 17, *Noronic:*** Canadian Great Lakes cruise ship burned at Toronto dock; about 130 died.

1952   **April 26, *Hobson:*** minesweeper collided with aircraft carrier *Wasp* and sank during night maneuvers in mid-Atlantic; 176 persons lost.

1953   **Jan. 9, *Chang Tyong-Ho:*** South Korean ferry foundered off Pusan; 249 reported dead.

Jan. 31, *Princess Victoria:* British ferry sank in Irish Sea; 133 lost.

1956   **July 25, *Andrea Doria:*** Italian liner collided with Swedish liner *Stockholm* off Nantucket Island, Mass., sinking next day; 52, mostly passengers on Italian ship, dead or unaccounted for; over 1,600 rescued.

1962 April 8, *Dara*: British liner, exploded and sank in Persian Gulf; 236 persons dead. Caused by time bomb.

1963 May 4: U.A.R. ferry capsized and sank in upper Nile; over 200 died.

1968 Late May, *Scorpion*: nuclear submarine sank in Atlantic 400 miles S.W. of Azores; 99 dead. (Located Oct. 31.)

1970 Dec. 15: ferry in Korean Strait capsized; 261 lost.

1976 Oct. 20, Luling, La., *George Prince*: Mississippi River ferry, rammed by Norwegian tanker *Frosta*; 77 dead.

1983 May 25, *10th of Ramadan*: Nile steamer, caught fire and sank in Lake Nasser, near Aswan, Egypt; 272 dead and 75 missing.

1987 March 9, Belgium: British ferry capsized after leaving Belgian port of Zeebrugge with 500 abroad; 134 drowned. Water rushing through open bow is believed to be probable cause.

1987 Dec. 20. Manila: over 1,500 people killed when passenger ferry *Dona Paz* collided with oil tanker *Victor* off Mindoro Is., 110 miles south of Manila.

1990 April 7, Skagerrak Strait off Norway: suspected arson fire aboard Danish-owned North Sea ferry, *Scandinavian Star*, killed at least 110 passengers.
April 7, Myanmar (Burma): double-decker ferry sank in Gyaing River during a storm and 215 persons were believed drowned.

1991 Dec. 14, off coast of Safaga, Egypt: Ferry carrying 569 passengers sank in Red Sea after hitting a coral reef. Over 460 people believed drowned.

1993 Feb. 17, off southern peninsula, Haiti: triple-deck ferry *Neptune* capsized during a squall. Over 1,000 passengers believed drowned. About 300 survived the sinking.

1994 Sept. 28, off coast of Southwest Finland: Passenger ferry *Estonia* capsized and sank in a stormy Baltic Sea. Only about 140 of the estimated 1,040 passengers aboard survived.

Mysterious Disappearances

1872 The brigantine *Mary Celeste* set sail from New York harbor for Genoa, Italy, on November 5. A British brigantine, the *DeGratia*, discovered the ship derelict on December 5 and boarded her. Everyone aboard the *Mary Celeste* had vanished—her captain, his family, and its 14-man crew. The ship was in perfect order with ample supplies and there was no sign of violence or trouble. The fate of the crew remains unknown today.

1928 Dec. 22: The five-masted Danish steel barque *Köbenhavn*, a sail-training ship with a crew of 75 including 45 boy cadets, sailed from the River Plate for Melbourne, Australia, on December 14. The last radio contact with the ship was made on December 22 and all was well. The *Köbenhavn* and its crew disappeared without a trace and no one knows what happened to it.

Aircraft Accidents

(150 deaths or more, with exceptions)

1921 Aug. 24, England: *AR-2* British dirigible, broke in two on trial trip near Hull; 62 died.

1925 Sept. 3, Caldwell, Ohio: U.S. dirigible *Shenandoah* broke apart; 14 dead.

1930 Oct. 5, Beauvais, France: British dirigible *R 101* crashed, killing 47.

1933 April 4, New Jersey Coast: U.S. dirigible *Akron* crashed; 73 died.

1937 May 6, Lakehurst, N.J.: German zeppelin *Hindenburg* destroyed by fire at tower mooring; 36 killed.

1945 July 28, New York City: U.S. Army bomber crashed into Empire State Building; 13 dead.

1960 Dec. 16, New York City: United and Trans World planes collided in fog, crashed in two boroughs, killing 134 in air and on ground.

1961 Feb. 15, near Brussels: 72 on board and farmer on ground killed in crash of Sabena plane; U.S. figure skating team wiped out.

1966 Dec. 24, Binh Thai, South Vietnam: crash of military-chartered plane into village killed 129.

1971 July 30, Morioka, Japan: Japanese Boeing 727 and F-86 fighter collided in mid-air; toll was 162.

1972 Aug. 14, East Berlin, East Germany: Soviet-built East German Ilyushin plane crashed, killing 156.
Dec. 3, Santa Cruz de Tenerife, Canary Islands: Spanish charter jet carrying West German tourists crashed on take-off; all 155 aboard killed.

1973 Jan. 22, Kano, Nigeria: 171 Nigerian Moslems returning from Mecca and five crewmen died in crash.

1973 Feb. 21, Sinai: civilian Libyan Arab Airlines Boeing 727 shot down by Israeli fighters after it had strayed off course; 108 died, five survived. Officials claimed that the pilot had ignored fighters' warnings to land.

1974 March 3, Paris: Turkish DC-10 jumbo jet crashed in forest shortly after take-off; all 346 passengers and crew killed.
Dec. 4, Colombo, Sri Lanka: Dutch DC-8 carrying Moslems to Mecca crashed on landing approach, killing all 191 persons aboard.

1975 April 4, near Saigon, Vietnam: Air Force Galaxy C-5A crashed after take-off, killing 172, mostly Vietnamese children.
Aug. 3, Agadir, Morocco: Chartered Boeing 707, returning Moroccan workers home after vacation in France, plunged into mountainside; all 188 aboard killed.

1976 Sept. 10, Zagreb, Yugoslavia: midair collision between British Airways Trident and Yugoslav charter DC-9 fatal to all 176 persons aboard.

1977 March 27, Santa Cruz de Tenerife, Canary Islands: Pan American and KLM Boeing 747s collided on runway. All 249 on KLM plane and 333 of 394 aboard Pan Am jet killed. Total of 582 is highest for any type of aviation disaster.

1978 Jan. 1, Bombay: Air India 747 with 213 aboard exploded and plunged into sea minutes after takeoff.
Sept. 25, San Diego, Calif.: Pacific Southwest plane collided in midair with Cessna. All 135 on airliner, 2 in Cessna, and 7 on ground killed for total of 144.
Nov. 15, Colombo, Sri Lanka: chartered Icelandic Airlines DC-8, carrying 249 Moslem pilgrims from Mecca, crashed in thunderstorm during landing approach; 183 killed.

1979 Nov. 26, Jidda, Saudi Arabia: Pakistan International Airlines 707 carrying pilgrims returning from Mecca crashed on take-off; all 156 aboard killed.
Nov. 28, Mt. Erebus, Antarctica: Air New Zealand DC-10 crashed on sightseeing flight; 257 killed.

1980 Aug. 19, Riyadh, Saudi Arabia: all 301 aboard Saudi Arabian jet killed when burning plane made safe landing but passengers were unable to escape.

Space Accidents

1967 Jan. 27, Apollo 1: A fire aboard the space capsule on the ground at Cape Kennedy, Fla. killed astronauts Virgil I. Grissom, Edward H. White, and Roger Chaffee.

April 23–24, Soyuz 1: Vladimir M. Komarov was killed when his craft crashed after its parachute lines, released at 23,000 feet for re-entry, became snarled.

1971 June 6–30, Soyuz 11: Three cosmonauts, Georgi T. Dolrovolsky, Vladislav N. Volkov, and Viktor I. Patsayev, found dead in the craft after its automatic landing. Apparently the cause of death was loss of pressurization in the space craft during re-entry into the earth's atmosphere.

1980 March 18, U.S.S.R. A Vostok rocket exploded on its launch pad while being refueled, killing 50 at the Plesetsk Space Center.

1986 Jan 28, Challenger Space Shuttle: Exploded 73 seconds after lift off, killing all seven crew members. They were: Christa McAuliffe, Francis R. Scobee, Michael J. Smith, Judith A. Resnick, Ronald E. McNair, Ellison S. Onizuka, and Gregory B. Jarvis. A booster leak ignited the fuel, causing the explosion.

1981 Dec. 1, Ajaccio, Corsica: Yugoslav DC-9 Super 80 carrying tourists crashed into mountain on landing approach, killing all 178 aboard.

1983 Aug. 30, near island of Sakhalin off Siberia: South Korean civilian jetliner Boeing 747, flight KAL-007 shot down by Soviet fighter after it strayed off course for two hours with its navigational lights on and did not take evasive action. Its crewmembers were unaware of its location and never saw the Soviet fighter that shot them down. The Soviet fighter did not give a warning by firing tracer bullets as originally claimed. Recorded conversations indicated that the crew did not know what hit them.

Nov. 26, Madrid: a Columbian Avianca Boeing 747 crashed near Mejorada del Campó Airport killing 183 persons aboard. Eleven people survived the accident.

1985 June 23, off the coast of Ireland: Air-India Boeing 747 exploded over the Atlantic, all 329 aboard killed.

Aug. 12, Japan: Japan Air Lines Boeing 747 crashed into a mountain, killing 520 of the 524 aboard.

Dec. 12, Gander, Newfoundland: a chartered Arrow Air DC-8, bringing American soldiers home for Christmas, crashed on takeoff. All 256 aboard died.

1987 May 9, Poland: Polish airliner, Ilyushin 62M on charter flight to New York, crashes after takeoff from Warsaw killing 183.

Aug. 16, Detroit: Northwest Airlines McDonnell Douglas MD-30 plunges to heavily traveled boulevard, killing 156. Girl 4, only survivor.

Nov. 26, south of Mauritius: South African Airways Boeing 747 goes down in rough seas; 160 died.

Nov. 29, Burma: Korean Air Boeing 747 jetliner explodes from bomb planted by North Korean agents and crashes into sea, killing all 115 aboard.

1988 July 3, Persian Gulf: U.S. Navy cruiser *Vincennes* shot down Iran Air A300 Airbus, killing 290 persons, after mistaking it for an attacking jet fighter.

Aug. 28, Ramstein Air Force Base, West Germany: three jets from Italian Air Force acrobatic team collided in mid-air during air show and crashed, killing 70 persons, including the pilots and spectators on the ground. It is worst airshow disaster in history.

Dec. 21, Lockerbie, Scotland: a New-York-bound Pan-Am Boeing 747 exploded in flight from a terrorist bomb and crashed into Scottish village, killing 259 aboard and 11 persons on the ground. Passengers included 38 Syracuse University students and many U.S. military personnel.

1989 June 7, Paramaribo, Suriname: a Surinam Airways DC-8 carrying 174 passengers and nine crew members crashed into the jungle while making a third attempt to land in a thick fog, killing 168 aboard.

1991 July 11, Jedda, Saudi Arabia: Canadian-chartered DC-8 carrying pilgrims returning to Nigeria crashed after takeoff, killing 261 persons.

1994 April 14, Northern Iraq: two American F-15C fighter aircraft mistook two U.S. Army black-hawk helicopters for Russian-made Iraqi MI-24 helicopters and shot them down over no-fly zone, killing all 26 on board.

April 26, Nagoya, Japan: a China Airlines A-300 Airbus from Taiwan crash-landed and exploded on the tarmac. Only 7 of the 271 passengers aboard survived.

June 6, Xian, China: a Russian-built Tupolev-154 airliner of China Northwest Airlines crashed 10 minutes after takeoff, killing all 160 aboard.

1995 Dec. 20, near Cali, Colombia: 160 people killed when American Airlines Boeing 757 crashed in Andean Mountains.

1996 Jan. 8, Kinshasa, Zaire: a Russian-built Antonov-32 cargo plane crashed after takeoff from Kinshasa into the center of the city, killing over 350 people and injuring at least 470.

Feb. 5, off coast of Puerto Plata, Dominican Republic: a Boeing 737 crashed into Atlantic Ocean after takeoff, killing 189.

July 18, off coast of Long Island, N.Y.: a TWA Boeing 747-100 bound for Paris from New York exploded over waters of eastern L.I. and crashed into Atlantic Ocean, killing all 230 aboard.

Nov.12, near New Delhi, India: shortly after takeoff, Saudi Arabian Airlines Boeing 747 collided in midair with Kazak Airlines Ilysuhin 76 plane approaching the New Delhi airport. All 349 passengers and crew were killed; the world's worst midair collision

1997 Aug. 6, Guam: South Korean Air Boeing 747-300 from Seoul crashes into jungle near Agana International Airport killing 226 persons, 28 survive.

Railroad Accidents

NOTE: Very few passengers were killed in a single U.S. train wreck up until 1853. These early trains ran slowly, made short trips, night travel was rare, and there were not many of them in operation.

1831 June 17: the boiler exploded on America's first passenger locomotive, *The Best Friend of Charleston*, killing the fireman. He was the first person in America to be killed in a railroad accident.

1833 Nov. 8, near Heightstown, N.J.: the world's first train wreck and the first passenger fatalities recorded. A 24-passenger Camden & Amboy train was derailed due to a broken axle, killing two passengers and injuring all others. Former president, John Quincy Adams and Cornelius Vanderbilt, who later made a fortune in railroads, were aboard the train.

1853 May 6, Norwalk, Conn: a New Haven Railroad train ran through an open drawbridge and plunged into the Norwalk River. Forty-six passengers were crushed to death or drowned. This was the first major drawbridge accident.

1856 July 17, Camp Hill, Pa.: two Northern Penn trains crashed head-on. Sixty-six church school children bound for a picnic died in the flaming wreckage.

1876 Dec. 29, Ashtabula, Ohio: a Lake Shore train fell into the Ashtabula River when a bridge it was crossing collapsed during a snowstorm. Ninety-two were killed.

1887 Aug. 10, near Chatsworth, Ill.: a burning railroad trestle collapsed while a Toledo, Peoria & Western train was crossing, killing 81 and injuring 372.

1904 Aug. 7, Eden, Colo.: train derailed on bridge during flash flood; 96 killed.

1910 March 1, Wellington, Wash.: two trains swept into canyon by avalanche; 96 dead.

1915 May 22, Gretna, Scotland: two passenger trains and troop train collided; 227 killed.

1917 Dec. 12, Modane, France: nearly 550 killed in derailment of troop train near mouth of Mt. Cenis tunnel.

1918 Nov. 1, New York City: derailment of subway train in Malbone St. tunnel in Brooklyn left 92 dead.

1926 March 14, Virilla River Canyon, Costa Rica: an over-crowded train carrying pilgrims was derailed while crossing the Colima Bridge, killing over 300 people and injuring hundreds more.

1939 Dec. 22, near Magdeburg, Germany: more than 125 killed in collision; 99 killed in another wreck near Friedrichshafen.

1943 Dec. 16, near Rennert, N.C.: 72 killed in derailment and collision of two Atlantic Coast Line trains.

1944 March 2, near Salerno, Italy: 521 suffocated when Italian train stalled in tunnel.

1949 Oct. 22, near Nowy Dwor, Poland: more than 200 reported killed in derailment of Danzig-Warsaw express.

1950 Nov. 22, Richmond Hill, N.Y.: 79 died when one Long Island Rail Road commuter train crashed into rear of another.

1951 Feb. 6, Woodbridge, N.J.: 85 died when Pennsylvania Railroad commuter train plunged through temporary overpass.

1952 Oct. 8, Harrow-Wealdstone, England: two express trains crashed into commuter train; 112 dead.

1957 Sept. 1, near Kendal, Jamaica: about 175 killed when train plunged into ravine.

Sept. 29, near Montgomery, West Pakistan: express train crashed into standing oil train; nearly 300 killed.

Dec. 4, St. John's, England: 92 killed, 187 injured as one commuter train crashed into another in fog.

1960 Nov. 14, Pardubice, Czechoslovakia: two trains collided; 110 dead, 106 injured.

1962 May 3, near Tokyo: 163 killed and 400 injured when train crashed into wreckage of collision between inbound freight train and outbound commuter train.

1963 Nov. 9, near Yokohama, Japan: two passenger trains crashed into derailed freight, killing 162.

1964 July 26, Custoias, Portugal: passenger train derailed; 94 dead.

1970 Feb. 4, near Buenos Aires: 236 killed when express train crashed into standing commuter train.

1972 July 21, Seville, Spain: head-on crash of two passenger trains killed 76.

Oct. 6, near Saltillo, Mexico: train carrying religious pilgrims derailed and caught fire, killing 204 and injuring over 1,000.

Oct. 30, Chicago: two Illinois Central commuter trains collided during morning rush hour; 45 dead and over 200 injured.

1974 Aug. 30, Zagreb, Yugoslavia: train entering station derailed, killing 153 and injuring over 60.

1981 June 6, near Mansi, India: driver of train carrying over 500 passengers, braked to avoid hitting cow, causing train to plunge off a bridge into Baghmati River; 268 passengers were reported killed, but at least 300 more were missing.

1982 July 11, Tepic, Mexico: Nogales-Guadalajara train plunged down mountain gorge killing 120.

1989 Jan. 15, Maizdi Khan, Bangladesh: a train carrying Muslim pilgrims crashed head-on with a mail train killing at least 110 persons and injuring as many as 1,000. Many people were riding on the roof of the trains and between the cars.

1989 Aug. 10, near Los Mochis, Mexico: A second-class passenger train traveling from Mazatlán to Mexicali, plunged off a bridge at Puente del Rio Bamoa into the river and killed an estimated 85 people and injured 107.

1990 Jan. 4, Sangi village, Sindh province, Pakistan: An overcrowded sixteen-car passenger train was switched to the wrong track and rammed into a standing freight train. At least 210 persons were killed and 700 were believed injured in what is said to be Pakistan's worst train disaster.

1993 Sept. 22, near Mobile, Ala.: Amtrak's Sunset Limited, en route to Miami, jumped rails on weakened bridge that had been damaged by a barge, and plunges in Big Bayou Canot, killing 47 persons.

1995 Aug. 20, Firozabad, Northern India: a speeding passenger train rammed another train that had stalled after hitting a cow. About 300 persons were killed and over 400 injured.

1997 March 3, Punjab province, Pakistan: passenger train crashed due to failed brakes, killing 119 and injuring at least 80 persons.

Oil Spills

1978 March 16, off Portsall, France: wrecked supertanker *Amoco Cadiz* spilled 68 million gallons causing widespread environmental damage over 100 miles of Brittany coast—world's largest tanker disaster.

1979 **June 8, Gulf of Mexico:** exploratory oil well, Ixtoc 1, blew out, spilling an estimated 140 million gallons of crude oil into the open sea. Although it is the largest known oil spill, it had a low environmental impact.

1989 **Dec. 19, off Las Palmas, the Canary Islands:** explosion in Iranian supertanker, the *Kharg-5,* tore through its hull and caused 19 million gallons of crude oil to spill out into the Atlantic Ocean about 400 miles north of Las Palmas, forming a 100-square-mile oil slick.

1994 **Aug. 12, near Ursinsk, Russia:** huge oil spill from ruptured pipeline.
September 8, Russia: a dam built to contain oil burst and spilled oil into Kolva River tributary. U.S. Energy Department estimated spill at 2 million barrels. Russian state-owned oil company claimed spill was only 102,000 barrels.

1996 **Feb. 15, off Welsh coast:** supertanker, *Sea Empress* ran aground at port of Milford Haven, Wales, spewed out 70,000 tons of crude oil, and created a 25-mile slick.

Wartime Spills

1991 **Jan. 25, Southern Kuwait:** during the Persian Gulf War, Iraq deliberately released an estimated 460 million gallons of crude oil into the Persian Gulf from tankers at Mina al-Ahmadi and Sea Island Terminal 10 miles off Kuwait. Spill had little military significance. On Jan. 27, U.S. warplanes bombed pipe systems to stop the flow of oil.

Sports Disasters

1955 **June 11, Le Mans, France:** racing car in Grand Prix hurtled into grandstand, killing 82 spectators.

1964 **May 24, Lima, Peru:** more than 300 soccer fans killed and over 500 injured during riot and panic following unpopular ruling by referee in Peru vs. Argentina soccer game. It is worst soccer disaster on record.

1971 **Jan. 2, Glasgow, Scotland:** 66 persons killed in a crush at the Glasgow Rangers home stadium when fans trying to leave encountered fans trying to return to the stadium after hearing that a late goal had been scored.

1982 **Oct. 20, Moscow:** according to *Sovietsky Sport,* as many as 340 persons were killed at Lenin Stadium when exiting soccer fans collided with returning fans after final goal was scored. All the fans had been crowded into one section of stadium by police.

1985 **May 11, Bradford, England:** 56 persons burned to death and over 200 injured when fire engulfed the main grandstand at Bradford's soccer stadium.
May 29, Brussels, Belgium: drunken group of British soccer fans supporting Liverpool club stormed stand filled with Italian supporters of Juventus team before European Champion's Cup final. While British fans attacked rival spectators at the Heysel Stadium, concrete retaining wall collapsed and 39 persons were crushed or trampled to death, 32 of them Italians. More than 400 others were injured.

1988 **March 12, Katmandu, Nepal:** some 80 soccer fans seeking cover during a violent hail storm at the national stadium were trampled to death in a stampede because the stadium doors were locked.

1989 **April 15, Sheffield, England:** 94 people were killed and 170 injured at Hillsborough stadium when throngs of Liverpool soccer fans, many without tickets, collapsed a stadium barrier in a mad rush to see the game between Liverpool and Nottingham Forest. It is Britain's worst soccer disaster.

1996 **Oct. 16, Guatemala City:** at least 84 persons died and 147 were injured before a 1998 World Cup qualifying match between Guatemala and Peru held at the Mateo Flores National Stadium by stampeding soccer fans

Terrorist Attacks in U.S.

1920 **Sept. 16, New York City:** TNT bomb planted in unattended horse-drawn wagon exploded on Wall Street opposite House of Morgan, killing 35 persons and injuring hundreds more. Bolshevist or anarchist terrorists believed responsible but crime never solved.

1975 **Jan. 24, New York City:** bomb set off in historical Fraunces Tavern killed 4 and injured more than 50 persons. Puerto Rican nationalist group (FALN) claimed responsibility and police tied 13 other bombings to them.

1993 **Feb. 26, New York City:** bomb exploded in basement garage of World Trade Center; killed 6 persons and injured at least 1,040 others.

Miscellaneous Disasters

1958 **January–October, Austria, France, Germany, Italy, and Switzerland:** 283 people were killed in mountain climbing accidents in Alps Mountains.

1980 **Jan. 20, Sincelejo, Colombia:** bleachers at a bullring collapsed, leaving 222 dead.
March 30, Stavanger, Norway: floating hotel in North Sea collapsed, killing 123 oil workers.

1981 **July 18, Kansas City, Mo.:** suspended walkway in Hyatt Regency Hotel collapsed; 113 dead, 186 injured.

1984 **Dec. 3, Bhopal, India:** toxic gas, methyl isocyanate, seeped from Union Carbide insecticide plant, killing more than 2,000, injuring about 150,000.

1987 **Sept. 18. Goiânia, Brazil:** 244 people contaminated with cesium-137 removed from steel cylinder taken from cancer-therapy machine in abandoned clinic and sold as scrap. Four people died in worst radiation disaster in Western Hemisphere.

1988 **July 6, North Sea off Scotland:** 166 workers killed in explosion and fire on Occidental Petroleum's *Piper Alpha* rig in North Sea; 64 survivors. It is the world's worst offshore oil disaster.

1990 **July 2, Mecca, Saudi Arabia:** a stampede in a 1,800 foot-long pedestrian tunnel leading from Mecca to a tent city for pilgrims killed 1,426 pilgrims who were trampled to death.

1991 **Nov. 29, near Coalinga, Calif.:** a massive traffic accident occurred during a severe dust storm involving 104 vehicles in a pileup on Interstate 5; 17 persons killed.

1993 **April 19, Waco, Texas:** a 51-day stalemate between federal agents and members of the Christian Branch Davidian cult ended in a fiery tragedy after federal agents botched their assault on the sect's compound. Earlier, on February 28, four federal agents were shot to death in a failed attack on the heavily armed compound. About 80 Branch Davidians, including at least 17 children, died when the compound burned to the ground in a suspicious blaze. Jurors at the criminal trial of surviving cult members were unable to determine who fired the first shot on February

28. Surviving Davidians dispute the government's version of how the cult members died.

1995 **June 29, Seoul, Korea:** Five-story wing of Sampoong Department Store collapsed, killing at least 206 people, injuring 910 others.

July 12–17, U.S. Midwest and Northeast: Over 800 persons, including 560 in Chicago, die in record heat wave.

1996 **May 10–11, Mt. Everest, Nepal:** 8 climbers die near summit during storm on mountain. Is worst single loss of life to occur on Mt. Everest. Another 4 die over the remaining course of the month.

1997 **April 15, Mecca, Saudia Arabia.** Fire and stampede in pilgrim's encampment killed 217 and injured at least 1,300.

Wartime Disasters

1915 **May 6, off the coast of Ireland:** Ddespite German warnings in newspapers, the Cunard Liner *Lusitania* sailed from New York for Liverpool, England, on May 1st and was sunk by a German submarine. 1,198 passengers and crew, 128 of them Americans, died. Unknown to the passengers, the ship was carrying a cargo of small arms. The disaster contributed to the entry of the United States into World War I.

1916 **Feb. 26, Mediterranean:** 3,100 people died when the French cruiser *Provence* was sunk by a German submarine.

1940 **Sept. 13, Atlantic Ocean:** the luxury liner *S.S. City of Benares* sailed from Liverpool with over 90 British children who were being evacuated to Canada to escape harm during World War II. About 600 miles out to sea, the ship was torpedoed by a German submarine during the night and only 13 of the children survived the disaster.[1]

1941 **Dec. 7, Pearl Harbor, Hawaii:** 1,177 crewmen were killed when U.S. Battleship *Arizona* was sunk during a surprise attack on the American naval base by Japanese warplanes. The devastating air strike, which damaged or destroyed the ships of the entire battleship force of the U.S. Pacific fleet, is the worst naval catastrophe in U.S. history.

1943 **Nov. 26, Mediterranean Sea:** 1,105 U.S. soldiers died when the British troopship *HMT Rohna*, was sunk by a German air-to-surface guided missile. It is the worst U.S. troopship disaster.

Dec., Bari Harbor, Italy: U.S. ship, damaged during German bombing attack, leaked mustard gas into harbor, killing 83 U.S. servicemen and nearly 1,000 civilians.

1944 **Sept. 12, South China Sea:** U.S. submarines torpedoed and sank two Japanese troop ships[2], the *Kachidoki Maru* and the *Rakuyo Maru*. Unknown to the submarines, the Japanese, in disregard for the rules of treatment of prisoners of war, had forced 2,000 British, Australian, and American POWs into the holds of the ships which were designed to hold only 300 troops. Later, when the subs discovered the tragedy, they sought to rescue as many survivors as possible. Japanese vessels picked up most of *Kachi-*

doki Maru's prisoners but abandoned those from the *Rakuyo Maru*, taking only the Japanese survivors. Of the 1,300 POWs aboard the *Rakuyo Maru*, 159 were rescued, but only seven lived.

Oct. 24, South China Sea: the *Arisan Maru*[2] carrying 1,800 American prisoners was torpedoed by a U.S. submarine and sunk. The Japanese destroyer escort rescued Japanese military and civilian personnel and left the POWs to their fate. It is estimated that only ten prisoners survived the disaster.

Dec. 17–18, Philippine Sea: Aa typhoon struck U.S. Third Fleet's Task Force 38, sank three destroyers, damaged seven other ships, destroyed 186 aircraft, and killed 800 officers and men.

1945 **Jan. 30, Baltic Sea:** 7,700 persons died in world's largest marine disaster when the Nazi passenger ship *Wilhelm Gustoff* carrying Germans fleeing Poland was torpedoed by a Soviet submarine.

May 3: several days before World War II ended in Europe, the German passenger ship, *Cap Arcona*, carrying about 6,000, of which an estimated 5,000 were concentration camp prisoners, was sunk by British aircraft. An estimated 5,000 persons were killed, most of them prisoners who were about to gain their freedom.

May 4, Gearhart Mountain, south-central Oregon: six people on a picnic, including a mother and her unborn child, were the only persons ever killed by a balloon-carried bomb launched from Japan. During the war, Japan launched some six thousand FUGO ("windship weapons") balloons to drift across the Pacific to the U.S. and Canada, each carrying bombs and incendiaries for starting forest fires and creating death and havoc among the American people. Although over 200 of the deadly balloons floated to the U.S. before the war ended, the government kept it a secret from the American people.

July 29, near Leyte Gulf, Philippines: the heavy cruiser *Indianapolis* was torpedoed and sunk by a Japanese submarine. Of the crew of 1,199 men, only 316 survived. Due to Navy blundering, the warship was not reported missing when it did not arrive at Leyte on July 31 as scheduled and therefore no search was ever made for its crew. The survivors were discovered by a Navy patrol plane 82 hours after the ship had gone down.

1991 **February, Kuwait:** during the Persian Gulf War, Iraqi troops systematically dynamited and set fire to 650 of Kuwait's 950 oil wells, causing the world's worst man-made environmental disaster. A total of 749 wells were damaged including those set ablaze. The last of the oil fires was extinguished on Nov. 6, 1991.

---

1. During the war (1939–1945), some 10,000 children were evacuated to stay with foster parents in the United States and Canada. The sinking of the *City of Benares* ended the British government's evacuation program.
2. The ships had no identification that they were transporting prisoners of war.

First Aid

Life-Saving Skill Summary

Skill	Adult (9 years and older)	Child (1 to 8 years)	Infant (birth to 1 year)
Rescue breathing	Give 1 slow breath about every 5 seconds; about 1½ seconds per breath; 1 minute = about 10 to 12 breaths	Give 1 slow breath about every 3 seconds; about 1½ seconds per breath; 1 minute = about 20 breaths	Give 1 slow breath about every 3 seconds; about 1½ seconds per breath; 1 minute = about 20 breaths
Choking (conscious)	Determine if person is choking; stand behind person and deliver abdominal thrusts; repeat until object is expelled or victim loses consciousness	Determine if child is choking; stand or kneel behind child and deliver abdominal thrusts; repeat until object is expelled or child loses consciousness	Determine if infant is choking; give 5 back blows; give 5 chest thrusts; repeat until object is expelled or infant loses consciousness
Choking (unconscious)	Give 2 slow breaths; retilt head and give 2 slow breaths; give up to 5 abdominal thrusts; do finger sweep; give 2 slow breaths; repeat abdominal thrusts, finger sweep, and 2 slow breaths	Give 2 slow breaths; retilt head and give 2 slow breaths; give up to 5 abdominal thrusts; check for object in throat; do finger sweep if object is visible; give 2 slow breaths; repeat abdominal thrusts, foreign body check/finger sweep, and 2 slow breaths	Give 2 slow breaths; retilt head and give 2 slow breaths; give 5 back blows; give 5 chest thrusts; check for object in throat; do finger sweep if object is visible; repeat back blows, chest thrusts, foreign body check/finger sweep, and 2 slow breaths
CPR (one rescuer)	Depth of compression is about 2 inches; compressions are performed with both hands; complete 15 compressions in about 10 seconds; do cycles of 15 compressions and 2 breaths	Depth of compression is about 1½ inches; compressions are performed with 1 hand; complete 5 compressions in about 3 seconds; do cycles of 5 compressions and 1 breath	Depth of compression is about 1 inch; compressions are performed with 2 fingers; complete 5 compressions in about 3 seconds; do cycles of 5 compressions and 1 breath

Rescue Breathing

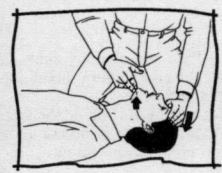

1. With head tilted back, pinch nose shut.

2. ADULT: Give 1 slow breath about every 5 seconds.

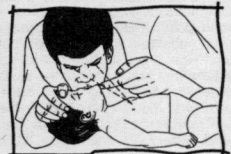

CHILD/INFANT: Give 1 slow breath about every 3 seconds.

CPR (Adult)

1. Find hand position.

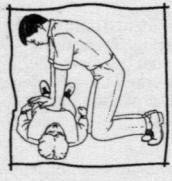

2. Position shoulders over hands. Compress chest 15 times.

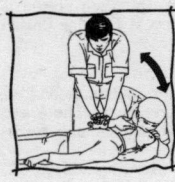

3. Give 2 slow breaths. Recheck pulse and breathing. If no pulse, continue sets of 15 compressions and 2 breaths.

Choking

If conscious but choking, give abdominal thrusts until object comes out.

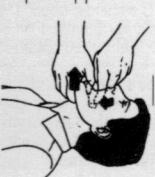

**If a person becomes unconscious:
Step 1. Clear any object from mouth.**

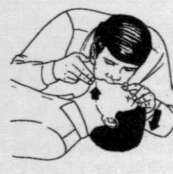

Step 2. Give 2 slow breaths.

If air won't go in, give up to 5 abdominal thrusts.

Other Emergencies

Burns

First Degree: Signs/Symptoms—reddened skin. **Treatment**—Immerse quickly in cold water or apply ice until pain stops.

Second Degree: Signs/Symptoms—reddened skin, blisters. **Treatment**—(1) Cut away loose clothing. (2) Cover with several layers of cold moist dressings or, if limb is involved, immerse in cold water for relief of pain. (3) Treat for shock.

Third Degree: Signs/Symptoms—skin destroyed, tissues damaged, charring. **Treatment**—(1) Cut away loose clothing (do not remove clothing adhered to skin). (2) Cover with several layers of sterile, cold, moist dressings for relief of pain and to stop burning action. (3) Treat for shock.

Poisons

Treatment—(1) Dilute by drinking large quantities of water. (2) Induce vomiting except when poison is corrosive or a petroleum product. (3) Call the poison control center or a doctor.

Shock

Shock may accompany any serious injury: blood loss, breathing impairment, heart failure, burns. Shock can kill—treat as soon as possible and continue until medical aid is available.

Signs/Symptoms—(1) Shallow breathing. (2) Rapid and weak pulse. (3) Nausea, collapse, vomiting. (4) Shivering. (5) Pale, moist skin. (6) Mental confusion. (7) Drooping eyelids, dilated pupils.

Treatment—(1) Establish and maintain an open airway. (2) Control bleeding. (3) Keep victim lying down. Exception: Head and chest injuries, heart attack, stroke, sun stroke. If no spine injury, victim may be more comfortable and breathe better in a semi-reclining position. If in doubt, keep the victim flat. Elevate the feet unless injury would be aggravated. Maintain normal body temperature. Place blankets under and over victim.

Frostbite

Most frequently frostbitten: toes, fingers, nose, and ears. It is caused by exposure to cold.

Signs/Symptoms—(1) Skin becomes pale or a grayish-yellow color. (2) Parts feel cold and numb. (3) Frozen parts feel doughy.

Treatment—(1) Until victim can be brought inside, the victim should be wrapped in woolen cloth and kept dry. (2) Do not rub, chafe, or manipulate frostbitten parts. (3) Bring victim indoors. (4) Place in warm water (102° to 105°) and make sure it remains warm. Test water by pouring on inner surface of your forearm. Never thaw if the victim has to go back out into the cold, which may cause the affected area to be refrozen. (5) Do not use hot water bottles or a heat lamp, and do not place victim near a hot stove. (6) Do not allow victim to walk if feet are affected. (7) Once thawed, have victim gently exercise parts. (8) For serious frostbite, seek medical aid for thawing because pain will be intense and tissue damage extensive.

Heat Cramps

Affects people who work or do strenuous exercises in a hot environment. To prevent it, such people should drink large amounts of cool water and add a pinch of salt to each glass of water.

Signs/Symptoms—(1) Painful muscle cramps in legs and abdomen. (2) Faintness. (3) Profuse perspiration.

Treatment—(1) Move victim to a cool place. (2) Give victim sips of salted drinking water (one teaspoon of salt to one quart of water). (3) Apply manual pressure to the cramped muscle.

Heat Exhaustion

Signs/Symptoms—(1) Pale and clammy skin. (2) Profuse perspiration. (3) Rapid and shallow breathing. (4) Weakness, dizziness, and headache.

Treatment—(1) Care for victim as if he or she were in shock. (2) Remove victim to a cool area, do not allow chilling. (3) If body gets too cold, cover victim.

Heat Stroke

Signs/Symptoms—(1) Face is red and flushed. (2) Victim becomes rapidly unconscious. (3) Skin is hot and dry with no perspiration.

Treatment—(1) Lay victim down with head and shoulders raised. (2) Reduce the high body temperature as quickly as possible. (3) Apply cold applications to the body and head. (4) Use ice and fan if available. (5) Watch for signs of shock and treat accordingly. (6) Get medical aid as soon as possible.

NOTE: Information Please Almanac is not responsible for actions undertaken by anyone using these first aid procedures. This information cannot substitute for a CPR or first aid course. Contact your local Red Cross to find out about a variety of community programs that teach life-saving skills and safety information. *Sources:* "Life-Saving Skills Summary" table and graphics from *First Aid First* © 1995 by the American Red Cross. "Other Emergencies" courtesy of *First Aid,* Mining Enforcement and Safety Administration, U.S. Dept. of the Interior.

Nutrition & Health

Historic Tobacco Accord Changes the Industry Forever ... Or Does It?

When negotiators emerged from three months of discussions with an agreement limiting liability claims against the tobacco industry in exchange for tighter regulation, the media heralded it as a historic achievement. No more Joe Camel ads on billboards, no more marketing targeted to minors, no more cigarette vending machines. Now the products whose industry officials have routinely denied are harmful to one's health could carry warning labels like "Use of this product will kill you." Certainly this is a great victory for public health advocates everywhere, but at what cost?

The Deal

The agreement that materialized from meetings among tobacco industry executives, state attorneys general, and public health officials calls for the following:
• $368.5 billion in payments from the tobacco industry over the next 25 years. Since the impetus for the agreement was state attorneys general suing to recover Medicare funds spent to treat smoking-related illnesses, states are hopeful that a large portion of this money will be coming their way.
• Tobacco industry admits that smoking is harmful to the health of smokers. Though public health officials have long tied smoking to mortality (some 425,000 Americans die annually of smoking-related illnesses, and around 40,000 people die annually from exposure to second-hand or environmental tobacco smoke), the industry had eschewed any responsibility until now.
• Advertising of cigarettes is severely limited. Billboards are banned, sponsorship of sporting events is outlawed, and advertisements with people or cartoon characters are eliminated. Given that the Centers for Disease Control estimate that 75 percent of smokers started before age 18, and 90 percent began before age 21, it is critical to address promotion of smoking to minors, and this accord seems to do so.
• Nicotine will be regulated. The FDA can reduce or eliminate the amount of nicotine legally sanctioned to be delivered in cigarettes. As the *Wall Street Journal* put it, until now "a product believed to be responsible for 425,000 deaths each year got less government oversight of its contents and marketing than ice cream."

The Reality

Though the deal has passed muster of those around the negotiating table, it has yet to survive the scrutiny of the White House and Congress, whose agendas will no doubt require modifications to the current accord. Some of the more hotly debated issues are likely to be:
• **Regulation of nicotine levels.** Before the tobacco accord was announced, the FDA had made history on its own by gaining the right to regulate nicotine as a drug. This authority is severely curtailed by the tobacco industry agreement, however, which sets legal standards that will make it difficult to enact any reduction in the level of nicotine present in cigarettes. Under the terms of the agreement, the FDA must prove that the reduction of legally available nicotine will not result in a market for contraband with higher-than-legally-available levels of nicotine. Even if the FDA is able to present evidence that would support reducing nicotine levels in cigarettes, the agreement provides that the industry can take the agency to court to dispute the FDA's findings. Without the "expert" status accorded the FDA in other (above-board) matters, the agency will have a difficult time meeting the burden of proof imposed by the agreement.
• **Distribution of the money.** States hoping to receive compensation for the estimated $50 billion spent annually to treat smoking-related illnesses in the U.S. may be disappointed when it comes to recovering money already spent. The accord calls for payments over 25 years as follows: $10 billion up front, followed by annual payments of $8.5 billion, rising to $15 billion by year 5. This money will fund a settlement pool from which successful litigants will draw their settlements. The money is more likely to address future claims than allow states to recover past expenditures.
• **Bans on advertising have not eliminated smoking elsewhere.** Smoking remains prevalent in other countries who have enacted bans on cigarette smoking, including Norway, Finland, New Zealand, and Canada, whose smoking rates range from 18% for Finnish women to 31% for all Canadians. A ban is unlikely to successfully eliminate smoking in the U.S. either, since 9 million American children under age five live with at least one smoker and are exposed to environmental smoke throughout the day. Children of smokers are around 1.5 times more likely to smoke than children of non-smokers, which suggests that what children see at home, not on television or T-shirts, is more likely to influence their behavior.
• **Likelihood of individual suits diminished.** Though the agreement covers only the class-action suits brought by 40 states to recover Medicaid spending, the accord makes it more difficult for individuals to sue the tobacco industry. Further class-action suits are prohibited by the agreement, so someone wishing to sue the industry will need to muster the resources to take on a multi-billion dollar conglomerate that spends an estimated $600 million annually in legal fees. Because the agreement also curtails punitive damages, the potential payoff (limited to compensation for medical expenses) is unlikely to be worth the legal fees incurred. In any case, successful litigants as a whole will be limited to $5 billion annually in settlements, which will come from the pool.
• **Volume of sales ultimately unchanged.** The most ironic provision of the accord is that, in order to receive the full annual payment from tobacco companies, the sales of cigarettes cannot fall below 1996 levels. If fewer cigarettes are sold, the industry receives a rebate on the money it has paid into the pool. Industry officials have broadly hinted that they will raise prices to offset their payments, which will cause sales to drop somewhat, particularly among teens. However, if the drop is so precipitous as to garner a rebate, the industry will again lower prices, which will stimulate demand. Sounds like not much changes in the long run.

The historic stature of the accord is undeniable. What is left of the agreement once it has been through the Washington wringer, on the other hand, has yet to be determined. — *TMV*

Ultraviolet Index: What You Need to Know

Source: American Academy of Dermatology

Did you know that overexposure to the sun can cause skin and eye injury? While some sunlight is necessary, too much is dangerous, causing sunburn, premature aging of the skin, skin cancer, cataracts, allergies, and damage to the immune system. Though the average person gets 50% of his or her lifetime sun by the age of 18, everyone needs to be aware of the dangers of exposure to sunlight.

The ill effects of sunlight are caused by ultraviolet (UV) radiation. These invisible rays from the sun come in two types, called UVA and UVB, both of which cause sun-related skin damage.

What Is the UV Index?

To help people guage sunlight exposure during outdoor activities and avoid overexposure to the damaging rays of the sun, the National Weather Service (NWS) and the Environmental Protection Agency (EPA) developed the UV Index. The index is issued daily and predicts the next day's amount of exposure to UV rays on a 0–10+ scale:

Index Number	Exposure Level
0–2	Minimal
3–4	Low
5–6	Moderate
7–9	High
10+	Very High

Always take precautions against overexposure, and take special care whenever the UV Index is 5 and above.

How Much Sun Am I Getting?

Though the amount of UV radiation to which you are exposed varies with the time of day, season, latitude, and altitude, it can also be increased depending on your immediate environment. Clouds actually provide little protection from UV rays, and clouds, water, white sand, concrete, and snow all reflect UV rays and increase exposure. Of course, exposure to the midday sun or for long periods of time is most damaging.

What Role Does Ozone-Layer Depletion Play?

The ozone layer shields the earth from the sun's harmful UV rays. Over the past ten years, scientists worldwide have recorded decreasing levels of ozone in the atmosphere. Less ozone means that more UV radiation reaches earth, increasing the danger of sun damage. The cause of the ozone depletion is under debate, but scientists agree that future levels of ozone will depend upon a combination of natural and man-made factors, including the phase-out of chlorofluorocarbons and other ozone-depleting chemicals.

Effects of Sun

Sunburn. Overexposure to the sun can happen in just a few hours. A bad reaction includes tenderness, pain, swelling, and blistering, and may include fever, chills, and nausea. While there is no cure for sunburn, wet compresses, cool tub baths, and soothing lotions may help. If you have a bad burn, see your dermatologist.

Tanning. Some people think that a tan means good health and looks. Dermatologists know that a tan does not *prevent* sun damage, it *is* sun damage. Tanning occurs when the UV rays penetrate the skin and injure the pigment cells. The effects are cumulative, and with every burn, the skin becomes more damaged.

Premature wrinkling. People who work or lay in the sun without sufficient protection get sagging cheeks and deep wrinkles that may make them look much older. The sun can also cause unsightly red, yellow, gray, or brown spots and scaly growths that may develop into skin cancer.

Skin cancer. Skin cancer is caused by too much sun, both long-term exposure and bad sunburns. More than 90 percent of all skin cancers occur on parts of the body exposed to the sun. The face, neck, ears, forearms, and hands are the most common places for skin cancer to develop.

The three main types of skin cancer are basal cell, squamous cell, and melanoma.

Basal cell carcinoma usually appears as a small, shiny, fleshy nodule on the exposed parts of the body. It grows slowly and rarely spreads to other parts of the body; but it can severely damage skin around and below it. When diagnosed and treated early, it has a high cure rate.

Squamous cell carcinoma typically develops on the face, ears, lips, and mouth, beginning as a red scaly patch. It also has a high cure rate when detected and treated early but left untreated, squamous cell carcinoma can spread to other areas of the body and can be fatal.

Melanoma is the most dangerous form of skin cancer and usually appears as a dark brown or black lump with irregular edges. Sometimes, it is multicolored with shades of red, blue, or white. If ignored, melanoma can spread or metastasize to other areas of the body, which can be fatal.

Eye damage. The sun can cause cataracts and other eye damage. Cataracts are one of the leading causes of blindness.

Immune system suppression and disease. Short periods of sun exposure can damage the human immune system and make the body more susceptible to infections and cancers. Also, some diseases can become worse with sun exposure. These include herpes simplex (cold sores), chicken pox, lupus, and certain genetic problems.

What Are Proper Precautions?

Preventing skin cancer and eye damage. Skin cancer is increasing faster than any other form of cancer, with over 1 million new cases predicted to occur in the U.S. this year.

- Listen to the UV Index reports.
- Minimize sun exposure at midday (10:00 a.m. to 4:00 p.m.)
- Avoid sunlamps, tanning beds and tanning parlors.
- Apply a broad-spectrum sunscreen with Sun Protection Factor-15 or higher and reapply every 2 hours.
- Wear protective, tightly-woven clothing, a broad-brimmed hat and sunglasses. Children who will not wear sunglasses should wear a hat with a wide brim.
- Protect children by keeping them indoors between 10:00 a.m. and 4:00 p.m., and by applying sunscreen to children older than 6 months. Children under the age of 6 months should be kept out of the sun.

Need More Information?

For more information on the UV Index, please call the **EPA Stratospheric Ozone Hotline**, 800-296-1996, or the **National Weather Service**, 301-713-0622.

Cancer Risks You Can Avoid

Source: National Cancer Institute, National Institutes of Health.

What Is Cancer?

Cancer is really a group of diseases. There are more than 100 different types of cancer, but they all are a disease of some of the body's cells.

Healthy cells that make up the body's tissues grow, divide, and replace themselves in an orderly way. This process keeps the body in good repair. Sometimes, however, normal cells lose their ability to limit and direct their growth. They divide too rapidly and grow without any order. Too much tissue is produced and *tumors* begin to form. Tumors can be either *benign* or *malignant.*

Benign tumors are not cancer. They do not spread to other parts of the body and they are seldom a threat to life. Often, benign tumors can be removed by surgery, and they are not likely to return. Malignant tumors are cancer. They can invade and destroy nearby tissue and organs. Cancer cells also can spread, or *metastasize,* to other parts of the body, and form new tumors.

Because cancer can spread, it is important for the doctor to find out as early as possible if a tumor is present and if it is cancer. As soon as a diagnosis is made, treatment can begin.

Signs and Symptoms of Cancer

Cancer and other illnesses often cause a number of problems you can watch for. The most common warning signs of cancer are:

Change in bowel or bladder habits;

A sore that does not heal;

Unusual bleeding or discharge;

Thickening or lump in the breast or elsewhere;

Indigestion or difficulty swallowing;

Obvious change in a wart or mole;

Nagging cough or hoarseness.

These signs and symptoms can be caused by cancer or by a number of other problems. They are *not* a sure sign of cancer. However, it is important to see a doctor if any problem lasts as long as two weeks. Don't wait for symptoms to become painful; pain is not an early sign of cancer.

Preventing Cancer

By choosing a lifestyle that avoids certain risks, you can help protect yourself from developing cancer. Many cancers are linked to factors that you can control.

Tobacco. Smoking and using tobacco in any form has been directly linked to cancer. Overall, smoking causes 30 percent of all cancer deaths. The risk of developing lung cancer is 10 times greater for smokers than for nonsmokers. The amount of risk from smoking depends on the number and type of cigarettes you smoke, how long you have been smoking, and how deeply you inhale. Smokers are also more likely to develop cancers of the mouth, throat, esophagus, pancreas, and bladder. And now there is emerging evidence that smoking can also cause cancer of the stomach and cervix.

The use of "smokeless" tobacco (chewing tobacco and oral snuff) increases the risk of cancer of the mouth and pharynx. Once you quit smoking or using smokeless tobacco, your risk of developing cancer begins to decrease right away.

Diet. What you eat may affect your chances of developing cancer. Scientists think there is a link between a high-fat diet and some cancers, particularly those of the breast, colon, endometrium, and prostate. Obesity is thought to be linked with increased death rates for cancers of the prostate, pancreas, breast, and ovary. Still other studies point to an increased risk of getting stomach cancer for those who frequently eat pickled, cured, and smoked foods. The National Cancer Institute believes that eating a well-balanced diet can reduce the risk of getting cancer. Americans should eat more high-fiber foods (such as whole-grain cereals and fruits and vegetables) and less fatty foods.

Sunlight. Repeated exposure to sunlight increases the risk of skin cancer, especially if you have fair skin or freckle easily. In fact, ultraviolet radiation from the sun is the main cause of skin cancer, which is the most common cancer in the United States. Ultraviolet rays are strongest from 11 a.m. to 2 p.m. during the summer, so that is when risk is greatest. Protective clothing, such as a hat and long sleeves, can help block out the sun's harmful rays. You can also use sunscreens to help protect yourself. Sunscreens with a number 15 on the label means most of the sun's harmful rays will be blocked out.

Alcohol. Drinking large amounts of alcohol (one or two drinks a day is considered moderate) is associated with cancers of the mouth, throat, esophagus, and liver. People who smoke cigarettes and drink alcohol have an especially high risk of getting cancers of the mouth and esophagus.

X-rays. Large doses of radiation increase cancer risk. Although individual x-rays expose you to very little radiation, repeated exposure can be harmful. Therefore, it is a good idea to avoid unnecessary x-rays. It's best to talk about the need for each x-ray with your doctor or dentist. If you do need an x-ray, ask if shields can be used to protect other parts of your body.

Industrial agents and chemicals. Exposure to some industrial agents or chemicals increases cancer risk. Industrial agents cause damage by acting alone or together with another cancer-causing agent found in the workplace or with cigarette smoke. For example, inhaling asbestos fibers increases the risk of lung disease and cancer. This risk is especially high for workers who smoke. You should follow work and safety rules to avoid coming in contact with such dangerous materials.

Being exposed to large amounts of household solvent cleaners, cleaning fluids, and paint thinners should be avoided. Some chemicals are especially dangerous if inhaled in high concentrations, particularly in areas that are not well ventilated. In addition, inhaling or swallowing lawn and garden chemicals increases cancer risk. Follow label instructions carefully when using pesticides, fungicides, and other chemicals. Such chemicals should not come in contact with toys or other household items.

Hormones. Taking estrogen to relieve menopausal symptoms (such as hot flashes) has been associated with higher-than-average rates of cancer of the uterus. Numerous studies also have examined the relationship between oral contraceptives (the Pill) and a variety of female cancers. Recent studies report that taking the Pill does not increase a woman's chance of getting breast cancer. Also, Pill users appear to have a lower-than-average risk of cancers of the endometrium and ovary. However, some researchers believe that there may be a higher risk of cancer of the cervix among Pill users. Women taking hormones (either estrogens or oral contraceptives) should discuss the benefits and risks with their doctor.

Leading Causes of Death for Men and Women

United States: 1995 Final Mortality

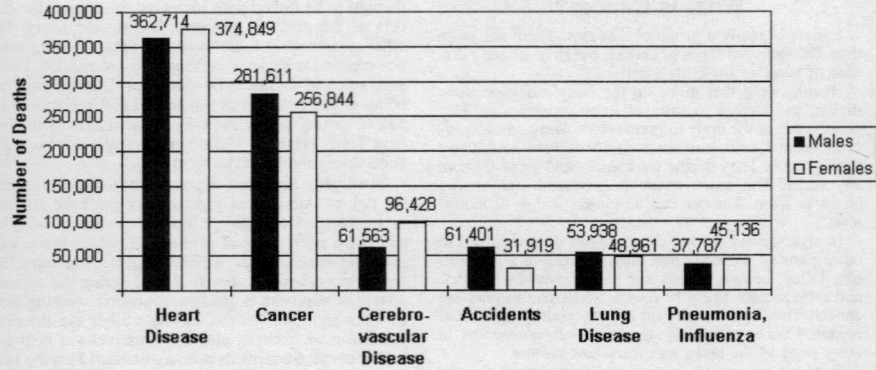

Source: Department of Health and Human Services, "Monthly Vital Statistics Report," June 12, 1997.

More Americans Of All Ages Are Overweight

Source: U.S. Department of Health and Human Services.

A growing proportion of U.S. children, adolescents, and adults are overweight, according to an article published in the "Morbidity and Mortality Weekly Report" by HHS's Centers for Disease Control and Prevention (CDC). The latest analysis from the third National Health and Nutrition Examination Survey (NHANES), conducted from 1988–94 by CDC's National Center for Health Statistics, shows that approximately 14 percent of children ages 6–11, 12 percent of adolescents ages 12–17, and 35 percent of adults ages 20 and over are overweight. This represents significant increases in all age groups since NHANES II was conducted from 1976–80.

Diet and physical activity are the two primary behavioral factors believed to be associated with overweight. NHANES III shows that calorie intakes have increased in adults since NHANES II and that recreational activity is low for many Americans. "This report tells us again that Americans need to do better in choosing a healthy diet and a sensible plan of physical activity," said HHS Secretary Donna E. Shalala. "Just last year, the Surgeon General called attention to the need for regular moderate physical activity in our lives, and for a balanced diet. It's good advice, and we all need to act on it, for the sake of our own good health."

The proportion of overweight children and adolescents has increased 6 percent between the end of NHANES II (1980) and the end of NHANES III (1994). Among adults, overweight prevalence increased approximately 9 percent between 1980 and 1994. One-third of men and 36 percent of women are overweight. The disparities by race/ethnicity are not as great for men as they are for women. Among women, one-third of non-Hispanic whites, 52 percent of non-Hispanic blacks and 50 percent of Mexican Americans are overweight.

Last July, HHS issued the first-ever Surgeon General's Report on Physical Activity and Health, recommending 30 minutes of moderate physical activity per day. Regular moderate physical activity can substantially reduce the risk of heart disease, diabetes, colon cancer, and high blood pressure, the report found. Also last year, HHS and the Department of Agriculture issued the new "Dietary Guidelines for Americans," providing easily-understood, science-based information on healthy eating. The report contains specific recommendations on good food sources for specific nutrients. For purposes of this analysis, children and adolescents were defined as overweight if their body mass index (BMI) exceeded the 95th percentile of BMI for children and adolescents of the same age and sex groups as measured in the 1960s. This differs from the definition used for adults, which was based on the 85th percentile for persons aged 20–29. A more conservative definition of overweight was used for children and adolescents to account for growth spurts and other changes that take place during youth and adolescence.

Although the National Center for Health Statistics has tracked overweight prevalence for over thirty years using these definitions, there is no universally accepted definition of overweight and using different standards would raise or lower the proportion considered overweight. However, it is clear that the overall trend towards increased overweight prevalence continues for all age groups. The Surgeon General's Report is available from CDC's Nutrition and Physical Activity information line (toll-free): 1-888-CDC-4NRG, or on the World Wide Web at www.cdc.gov. The "Dietary Guidelines" are available for 50 cents through the Consumer Information Center, Department 378-C, Pueblo, CO, 81009; or on the internet at odphp.osophs.dhhs.gov.

Overweight Persons as a Percent of the Population

	1960-62	1971-74	1976-80	1988-91
Male				
20–34	19.6	19.2	17.3	22.8
35–44	22.8	29.4	28.9	35.7
45–54	28.1	27.6	31.0	35.5
55–64	26.9	24.8	28.1	40.5
65–74	21.8	23.0	25.2	42.2
75 and over	n.a.	n.a.	n.a.	26.0
Female[1]				
20–34	13.2	14.8	16.8	24.5
35–44	24.1	27.3	27.0	35.1
45–54	30.7	32.3	32.5	39.8
55–64	43.2	38.5	37.0	48.7
65–74	42.9	38.0	38.4	39.7
75 and over	n.a.	n.a.	n.a.	31.5

1. Excludes pregnant women. NOTE: Overweight is defined as body mass index greater than or equal to 27.8 kg/m^2 for men and 27.3 kg/m^2 for women, which represent the sex-specific 85th percentiles for persons 20–29 years of age in the 1976–80 National Health and Nutrition Examination Survey. *Source:* National Center for Health Statistics, *Health, United States, 1995* Hyattsville, Md.: Public Health Service, p 183, 1996.

Fifty Facts from the World Health Report 1997

Source: The World Health Organization (WHO).

Global

• The world population reached 5.8 billion in mid-1996, an increase of more than 80 million over the previous 12 months; in 1990 the increase was 87 million.

• Between 1980 and 1995, life expectancy at birth has increased globally by 4.6 years; 4.4 years for males and 4.9 years for females.

• There are now 380 million people aged 65 years and above. By the year 2020, the over-65 population is projected to increase globally by 82 percent, to more than 690 million.

• For every baby born today in an industrialized country, there are 10 people aged 65 or over. By the year 2020 there will be 15 such elderly persons for each newborn. In developing countries, the ratio today is 2 people over 65 for every newborn, and 4 for every newborn by 2020.

• Life expectancy at birth was 48 years in 1955; 59 years in 1975; and 65 years in 1995.

• In 1960, most deaths were among people under 50. Today, most are among the over-50s.

• By 2025, more than 60 percent of all deaths will be among the over-65s, and more than 40 percent among the over-75s.

Children

• Deaths among children under 5 years declined from 19 million in 1960 to 11 million in 1996.

• About 5 million babies born in developing countries in 1995 died in the first month of life.

• Of some 140 million births a year, about 4 million babies are born with major congenital anomalies.

• Coverage of children immunized against six major childhood diseases increased from 5 percent in 1974 to 80 percent in 1995.

Deaths

• Of over 52 million deaths in 1996, over 17 million were due to infectious or parasitic diseases; more than 15 million to circulatory diseases; over 6 million to cancers; and about 3 million to respiratory diseases.

• Of over 52 million deaths in 1996, 40 million were in developing countries, including almost 9 million in the least developed countries.

• Infectious and parasitic diseases accounted for 43 percent of the 40 million deaths in developing countries; almost 40 percent were due to chronic diseases such as circulatory diseases, cancers, and respiratory diseases.

Diseases

• The leading killer among infectious diseases in 1996 was acute lower respiratory infection, which killed 3.9 million people.

• Tuberculosis killed 3 million people in 1996.

• Diarrheal diseases killed 2.5 million people in 1996.

• Malaria killed between 1.5 million and 2.7 million people in 1996.

• About 1.5 million people died of HIV/AIDS in 1996.

• By the end of 1996, a cumulative total of 29.4 million children and adults had been infected with HIV.

• Worldwide, 75–85 percent of HIV infections in adults have been transmitted through unprotected sexual intercourse, with heterosexual intercourse accounting for more than 70 percent.

• Leprosy cases fell from 2.3 to 1.7 per 10,000 population between 1995–96, and the problem has been reduced by 82 percent worldwide in the last 11 years.

• The Onchocerciasis Control Programme, which began in West Africa in 1974, has now protected an estimated 36 million people from the disease.

• More than 120 million children under 5 in India were immunized against poliomyelitis in a single day in 1996.

• Field trials in Africa in 1996 showed that insecticide-treated bed nets can reduce childhood deaths from malaria by up to 35 percent.

Chronic Illness

• Of over 15 million deaths due to circulatory diseases, 7.2 million were caused by coronary heart disease, 4.6 million by stroke, 500,000 by rheumatic fever and rheumatic heart disease, and 3 million by other forms of heart disease.

• Tobacco is calculated to cause 3 million deaths a year mainly from lung cancer and circulatory diseases.

• An estimated 691 million people have high blood pressure.

• The number of people suffering from diabetes worldwide is projected to more than double from about 135 million now to 300 million by 2025. The rise in cases will approach 200 percent in developing countries and be in the order of 45 percent in developed countries.

Cancer

• About half of the more than 6 million deaths from cancer in 1996 were due to cancers of the lung, stomach, colon-rectum, liver, and breast.

• Lung cancer killed 989,000 people in 1996 and there were an estimated 1.32 million new cases.

• Stomach cancer killed 776,000 people in 1996.

• Colorectal cancer killed 495,000 people in 1996.

• Liver cancer killed 386,000 people in 1996.

• Breast cancer killed 376,000 women in 1996.

• Worldwide, about 85 percent of lung cancers in men and 46 percent in women are tobacco-related.

• Smoking accounts for one in 7 cancer deaths worldwide.

• In 1996 there were an estimated 17.9 million persons with cancer surviving up to 5 years after diagnosis. Of these, 10.5 million were women, 5.3 million of whom had cancer either of the breast, cervix, or colon-rectum.

• The sexually-transmitted human papilloma virus is found in more than 95 percent of cervical cancer cases. A vaccine against the virus is being developed.

• At least 15 percent of all cancers worldwide are a consequence of chronic infectious disease, the most important being hepatitis B and C viruses (liver cancer); the human papilloma virus (cervical cancer) and the Helicobacter pylori bacterium (stomach cancer).

Disorders

• More than 40 million people suffer from different types of epilepsy.

• An estimated 29 million people suffer from dementia; 200,000 died of it in 1996, and there were 2.6 million new cases.

• An estimated 45 million people are affected by schizophrenia. There were 4.5 million new cases of schizophrenia and other delusional disorders last year.

• An estimated 28 million people worldwide incur significant health risks by using psychoactive substances other than alcohol, tobacco, and volatile solvents.

Occupational Hazards

• Occupational accidents account for more than 120 million injuries and at least 220,000 deaths a year.

• There are about 160 million cases a year of occupational diseases, of which 30–40 percent may lead to chronic disease and 10 percent to permanent work disability.

• Only 5–10 percent of workers in developing countries, and 20–50 percent in industrialized countries, have access to adequate occupational health services.

• Up to 40 percent of people over 70 suffer osteoarthritis of the knee.

• Almost 80 percent of patients with osteoarthritis have some degree of limitation of movement and 25 percent cannot perform their major daily activities of life.

• Rheumatoid arthritis is estimated to affect 165 million people.

The Worldwide AIDS Situation

Source: World Health Organization (WHO), December 1996

Background

Acquired immunodeficiency syndrome (AIDS) was first recognized in 1981 among homosexual men in the United States. The human immunodeficiency virus (HIV) that causes AIDS was identified in 1983. According to the World Health Organization, extensive spread of HIV appears to have begun in the late 1970s and early 1980s among men and women with multiple sexual partners in East and Central Africa and among homosexual and bisexual men in certain urban areas of the Americas, Australasia, and Western Europe.

Two major types of HIV have been recognized, HIV-1 and HIV-2. HIV-1 is the dominant type worldwide. HIV-2 is found principally in West Africa but cases have been reported from East Africa, Europe, Asia, and Latin America. There are at least 10 different genetic subtypes of HIV-1, but their biological and epidemiological significance is unclear at present. Both HIV-1 and HIV-2 are transmitted in the same ways.

Global Estimates

According to the World Health Organization, 1.5 million cases of AIDS in adults and children had been officially reported by December 1996. If one takes into account under-recognition, under-reporting, and reporting delays, it is estimated that more than 8.4 million AIDS cases have occurred since the beginning of the epidemic, and around 30 million people have been infected with HIV, some 26.8 million adults and 2.6 million children. Over 3.1 million new HIV infections occurred during 1996, which translates to more than 8,500 infected each day (7,500 adults and 1,000 children).

Today, 22.6 million people are believed to be living with AIDS—21.8 million adults and 830,000 children. Of these, an estimated 5 million adults and 1.4 million children have died.

The majority of newly infected adults are between 15 and 25 years old. Approximately 42 percent of the adults living with the HIV/AIDS are women and the proportion is growing.

Mode of Transmission

Worldwide, between 75 and 85 of every 100 adult HIV infections have been transmitted through unprotected sexual intercourse. Heterosexual (male-female) intercourse accounts for more than 70% of all infected adults to date and homosexual (male-male) intercourse for a further five to ten percent.

The sharing of HIV-infected needles by drug users accounts for 5–10 percent of all adult infections. This proportion is growing. In many parts of the world, injected drug use is the dominant mode of transmission.

Mother-to-child (vertical) transmission accounts for more than 90 percent of all infections in infants and children. Around 25–35 percent of all infants born to HIV-infected women themselves become infected with HIV before or during birth, or through breast-feeding.

Transfusion of HIV-infected blood or blood products accounts for 3–5 percent of all adult infections. In many parts of the world, HIV transmission through the transfusion of infected blood has been reduced by the use of voluntary blood donors, the routine screening of donated blood for HIV, and through a more rational use of blood aimed at reducing the number of transfusions.

Studies to date, primarily from industrialized countries, indicate that about 60 percent of adults will progress to AIDS within 12–13 years of becoming infected. Few data are available beyond 12 years but it is expected that the majority of HIV-infected people will probably develop AIDS.

Survival after the onset of AIDS has been increasing in industrialized countries from an average of less than a year to about three years at present. Survival time with AIDS in developing countries remains short and is estimated to be less than one year.

The majority of AIDS cases occur before age 35, and over 90 percent of all AIDS deaths occur in people under the age of 30. More than 90 percent of all adults with HIV infections or AIDS live in developing countries.

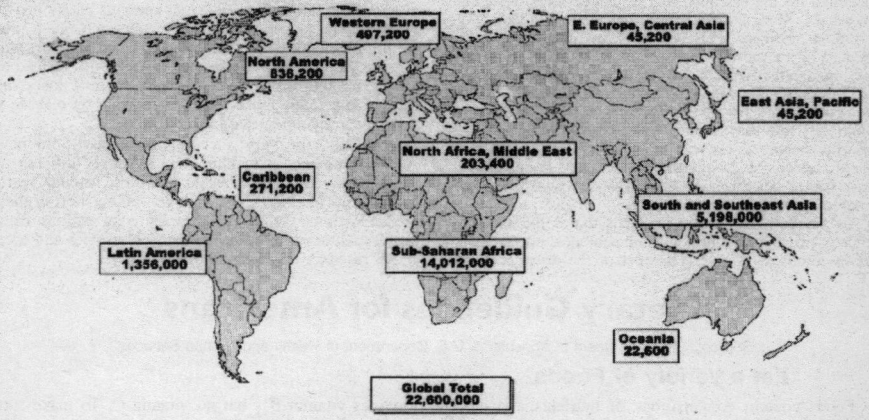

Estimated Number of Persons Living with HIV/AIDS, End 1996

New Hope for HIV and AIDS Patients

Recent scientific advances have given hope to those who suffer from HIV and AIDS. Preventing infection is still the only guaranteed method of remaining HIV- and AIDS-free, but new research also suggests that early detection of the virus may give patients a better chance of combating the virus before it develops into full-blown AIDS.

New Treatments

Research conducted by Dr. David Ho of the Aaron Diamond AIDS Research Center in New York focused on early-detection patients and treated them with a powerful combination of drugs. In a January 1997 press conference, Dr. Ho announced that the treatment was successful in eliminating all traces of HIV from the bloodstream of 20 patients. But doctors could muster only cautious optimism because the virus was still present in the patients' lymph nodes, where the virus is produced and stored. Furthermore, the treatment did not seem to benefit those whose infection had already progressed beyond the early stages.

Subsequent research provides more reason to hope. In May, Dr. Ashley Haase of the University of Minnesota and fellow researchers reported that a new three-drug "cocktail" had proven effective at eliminating 99 percent of the virus from the lymph nodes and tonsils. The findings are even more encouraging since the 10 patients in the study had moderately advanced cases of HIV, and had not been treated previously with drugs. The patients responded quickly, with HIV levels dropping dramatically in just a few days, and continuing to decline thereafter. Doctors theorized that after a heavy dosage for the first few years, patients may be able to keep the virus in check with smaller doses thereafter.

The drug cocktail approach to treatment has proven more effective than a single-drug therapy. *The New England Journal of Medicine* reported in October 1996 that deaths and complications were reduced by 50 percent in those taking a combination of drugs compared to those taking AZT alone, which formerly had been the classic method of treating HIV. In June 1997, a federal task force released new guidelines calling for early treatment of HIV-infected patients. The guidelines call

for the use of two nucleoside analogues (the category to which AZT belongs) and one protease inhibitor. Only in the case of pregnant women did the panel recommend using AZT alone.

AZT is one of the class of drugs called nucleoside analogues, which was one of the first treatments approved by the FDA to combat HIV. In December 1995, a new class of drugs called protease inhibitors was also approved. Like its predecessor, protease inhibitors inhibit replication of HIV, but do so at different points in the replication process. The protease inhibitors dramatically reduce the presence of HIV in the body, and increase the number of CD4 cells commonly annihilated by the virus and AIDS. The treatments were found to be effective alone or in combination with the nucleoside analogues. In June 1996, FDA approved Viramune (nevirapine), the first in a new class of drugs called non-nucleoside reverse transcriptase inhibitors. Viramune was approved for use in combination with nucleoside analogues to treat adults with HIV infection who have experienced clinical and/or immunological deterioration. Doctors have found that by combining these treatments, the virus can be virtually eliminated from the system. This is not a cure, but a method of managing a chronic illness, similar to the way in which diabetes and hypertension are managed through careful monitoring and medication.

A Vaccine is Possible

In a separate study also released in May, researchers at the University of Pennsylvania worked with chimpanzees to develop a vaccine. Even those animals who had been infected before receiving the vaccine showed signs of improvement. The vaccine uses no living HIV, so it cannot cause infection.

The search for an AIDS vaccine has been given a high national priority, with President Clinton issuing a challenge to the nation's scientists to find a vaccine by 2007. The challenge came as something of an unfunded mandate, however, since no additional grants were earmarked for the project. Currently, approximately 10 percent of the government's $1 billion annual research budget on HIV is allocated to the search for a vaccine.

The Cloud Over the Silver Lining

The number of deaths from AIDS and HIV infections declined for the first time in 1997, after years of regular increases. More good news comes from a federal government proposal that would allow the poor to be treated in the earlier stages of the disease, when drugs are most effective, but before the patients would normally qualify for Medicaid under the definition of disability required for assistance. It is not the higher possible cure rate that inspired the proposal, however. It is simply cheaper to prevent full-blown AIDS than to pay for the extensive hospitalization required once the disease has advanced to the stage that it would make one unable to work.

As research continues, it seems that a diagnosis of HIV-positive is no longer a death sentence, but the good news comes at a price. The cost of the drugs is astronomical, usually beyond the reach of the uninsured. Plus, patients bear a great deal of responsibility for the efficacy of the treatment. The drugs must be taken on a precise schedule and in the exact amounts prescribed to be effective, so patients who try to stretch out a prescription by taking less than the prescribed amounts will not enjoy the benefits of the drug. Worse still, instead of killing off the virus, when taken in smaller doses the drugs can actually make the virus stronger by making it resistant to treatment with these therapies.

Ironically, the very success of research into new AIDS treatments is making it increasingly difficult to raise money for AIDS-related charities. Annual charitable events like the AIDS walk are falling short of their goals. Without the steady flow of contributions from AIDS fundraisers, the future of AIDS hospices and even AIDS research may be in jeopardy.—*TMV*

Dietary Guidelines for Americans

Source: U.S. Department of Agriculture, U.S. Department of Health and Human Services.

Eat a Variety of Foods

Foods contain combinations of nutrients and other healthful substances. No single food can supply all nutrients in the amounts you need. For example, oranges provide vitamin C but no vitamin B_{12}; cheese provides vitamin B_{12} but no vitamin C. To make sure you get all of the nutrients and other substances needed for health, choose the recommended number of daily servings from each of the five major food groups.

Food Groups[1]	Daily Servings[2]	Serving Size
Grains	6–11	1 slice of bread 1 ounce of ready-to-eat cereal ½ cup of cooked cereal, rice, or pasta
Vegetables	3–5	1 cup of raw, leafy vegetables ½ cup of other vegetables—cooked or chopped raw ¾ cup of vegetable juice
Fruits	2–4	1 medium apple, banana, orange ½ cup of chopped, cooked, or canned fruit ¾ cup of fruit juice
Milk	2–3	1 cup of milk or yogurt 1 ½ ounces of natural cheese 2 ounces of processed cheese
Meat and Beans	2–3	2–3 ounces of cooked lean meat, poultry, or fish ½ cup of cooked dry beans or 1 egg counts as 1 ounce of lean meat. 2 tablespoons of peanut butter or ⅓ cup of nuts count as 1 ounce of meat.

1. Some foods fit into more than one group. Dry beans, peas, and lentils can be counted as servings in either the meat and beans group or vegetable group. These "crossover" foods can be counted as servings from either one or the other group, but not both 2. A range of servings is given for each food group. The smaller number is for people who consume about 1,600 calories a day, such as the sedentary or women. The larger number is for those who consume about 2,800 calories a day, for the very active or men.

What About Vegetarian Diets?

Some Americans eat vegetarian diets for reasons of culture, belief, or health. Most vegetarians eat milk products and eggs, and as a group, these lacto-ovo-vegetarians enjoy excellent health. Vegetarian diets are consistent with the *Dietary Guidelines for Americans* and can meet Recommended Dietary Allowances for nutrients. You can get enough protein from a vegetarian diet as long as the variety and amounts of foods consumed are adequate. Meat, fish, and poultry are major contributors of iron, zinc, and B vitamins in most American diets, and vegetarians should pay special attention to these nutrients.

Vegans eat only food of plant origin. Because animal products are the only sources of vitamin B_{12}, vegans must supplement their diets with a source of this vitamin. In addition, vegan diets, particularly those of children, require care to insure adequacy of vitamin D and calcium, which most Americans obtain from milk products.

Maintain a Healthy Weight

Many Americans believe it is normal to gain weight as we age, but doing so increases our risk for high blood pressure, heart disease, stroke, diabetes, certain types of cancer, arthritis, breathing problems, and other illnesses. To maintain a healthy body weight, people must balance the amount of calories in the foods and drinks they consume with the amount of calories the body uses. Physical activity is an important way to use food energy.

To burn calories, spend more time in activities like walking to the store or around the block. Use stairs rather than elevators. Less sedentary activity and more vigorous activity may help you reduce body fat and disease risk. Try to do 30 minutes or more of moderate physical activity on most—preferably all—days of the week.

To Decrease Calorie Intake

Eat a variety of foods that are low in calories but high in nutrients—check the Nutrition Facts Label on the foods you buy.

Eat less fat and fewer high-fat foods.

Eat smaller portions and limit second helpings of foods high in fat and calories.

Eat more vegetables and fruits without fats and sugars added in preparation or at the table.

Eat pasta, rice, breads, and cereals without fats and sugars added in preparation or at the table.

Eat less sugars and fewer sweets like candy, cookies, cakes, and soda.

Drink less or no alcohol.

Healthy Weight Ranges for Men and Women

Height*	Weight (in pounds)	Height*	Weight (in pounds)
4'10"	91-119	5'9"	129-169
4'11"	94-124	5'10"	132-174
5'0"	97-128	5'11"	136-179
5'1"	101-132	6'0"	140-184
5'2"	104-137	6'1"	144-189
5'3"	107-141	6'2"	148-195
5'4"	111-146	6'3"	152-200
5'5"	114-150	6'4"	156-205
5'6"	118-155	6'5"	160-211
5'7"	121-160	6'6"	164-216
5'8"	125-164		

* Without shoes. Without clothes. Weight *ranges* are given in the chart because people of the same height may have equal amounts of body fat but different amounts of muscle and bone. *Source:* Derived from National Research Council, 1989, for adults, p. 564.

Body Fat

Research suggests that the location of body fat also is an important factor in health risks for adults. Excess fat in the abdomen (stomach area) is a greater health risk than excess fat in the hips and thighs. Extra fat in the abdomen is linked to high blood pressure, diabetes, early heart disease, and certain types of cancer. Smoking and too much alcohol increase abdominal fat and the risk for diseases related to obesity. Vigorous exercise helps to reduce abdominal fat.

The easiest way to check your body fat distribution is to measure around your waistline with a tape measure and compare this with the measure around your hips or buttocks to see if your abdomen is larger. If you are in doubt, you may wish to seek advice from a health professional.

Although limiting fat intake may help to prevent excess weight gain in children, fat should not be restricted to children younger than two years of age. Helping overweight children to achieve a healthy weight along with normal growth requires more caution. Modest reductions in dietary fat, such as the use of lowfat milk are not hazardous. However, major efforts to change a child's diet should be accompanied by a monitoring of growth by a health professional at regular intervals.

Eat Plenty of Grains, Vegetables, and Fruits

Grain products, vegetables, and fruits are key parts of a varied diet. They are emphasized in this guideline because they provide vitamins, minerals, complex carbohydrates (starch and dietary fiber), and other substances that are important for good health. They are also generally low in fat, depending on how they are prepared and what is added to them at the table.

Fiber

Fiber is found only in plant foods like whole-grained breads and cereals, beans and peas, and other vegetables and fruits. Because there are different types of fiber in foods, choose a variety of foods daily. Eating a variety of fiber-containing plant foods is important for bowel function, can reduce symptoms of chronic constipation, diverticular disease, and hemorrhoids, and may lower the risk for heart disease and some cancers.

However, some of the health benefits associated with a high-fiber diet may come from other components present in these foods, not just the fiber itself. For this reason, fiber is best obtained from foods rather than supplements.

Choose a Diet Low in Fat, Saturated Fat, and Cholesterol

Some dietary fat is needed for good health. Fats supply energy and essential fatty acids and promote absorption of the fat-soluble vitamins A, D, E, and K. More Americans are now eating less fat, saturated fat, and cholesterol-rich goods than in the recent past. Still, many people continue to eat high-fat diets. This guideline emphasizes the continued importance of choosing a diet with less total fat, saturated fat, and cholesterol.

Avoid High-Fat Foods

Some foods and food groups are higher in fat than others. Fats and oils, and some types of desserts and snack foods that contain fat provide calories but few nutrients. Many foods in the milk group and in the meat and beans group (which includes eggs and nuts, as well as meat, poultry, and fish) are also high in fat as are some processed foods in the grain group.

Fat, whether from plant or animal sources, contains more than twice the number of calories of an equal amount of carbohydrates or protein. Choose a diet that provides no more than 30 percent of total calories from fat. The upper limit on the grams of fat in your diet will depend on the calories you need. Cutting back on fat can help you consume fewer calories. For example, at 2,000 calories per day, the suggested upper limit of calories from fat is about 600 calories (65 grams of fat x 9 calories per gram = about 600 calories).

If You Need to Lose Weight

Many people are not sure how much weight they should lose. Weight loss of only 5–10 percent of body weight may improve many of the problems associated with overweight, such as high blood pressure and diabetes. Even a smaller weight loss can make a difference.

If you are trying to lose weight, do so slowly and steadily. A generally safe rate is 1/2–1 pound a week until you reach your goal. Avoid crash weight-loss diets that severely restrict calories or the variety of foods. Extreme approaches to weight loss, such as self-induced vomiting or the use of laxatives, amphetamines, or diuretics, are not appropriate and can be dangerous to your health.

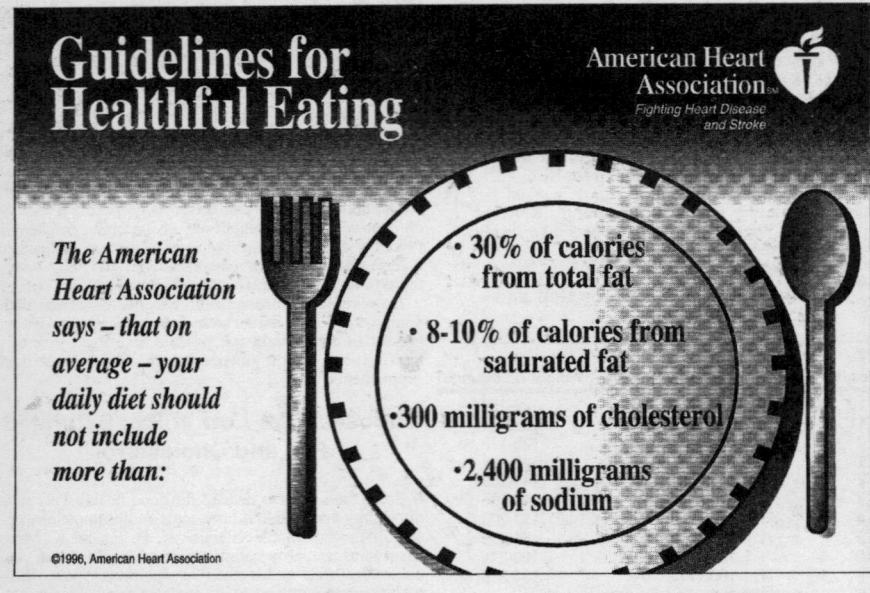

Guidelines for Healthful Eating

American Heart Association
Fighting Heart Disease and Stroke

The American Heart Association says – that on average – your daily diet should not include more than:

- 30% of calories from total fat
- 8-10% of calories from saturated fat
- 300 milligrams of cholesterol
- 2,400 milligrams of sodium

©1996, American Heart Association

Maximum Total Fat Intake at Different Calorie Levels			
Calories	1,600	2,200	2,800
Total fat (grams)	53	73	93

Saturated fat—Fats contain both saturated and unsaturated (monounsaturated and polyunsaturated) fatty acids. Saturated fat raises blood cholesterol more than other forms of fat. Reducing saturated fat to less than 10 percent of calories will help you lower your blood cholesterol level. The fats from meat, milk, and milk products are the main sources of saturated fats in most diets. Many bakery products are also sources of saturated fats. Vegetable oils supply smaller amounts of saturated fat.

Monounsaturated and polyunsaturated fat—Olive and canola oils are particularly high in monounsaturated fats; most other vegetable oils, nuts, and high-fat fish are good sources of polyunsaturated fats. Both kinds of unsaturated fats reduce blood cholesterol when they replace saturated fats in the diet. Remember that the total fat in the diet should be consumed at a moderate level—that is no more than 30 percent of calories. Mono- and polyunsaturated fat sources should replace saturated fats within this limit.

Partially hydrogenated vegetable oils, such as those used in many margarines and shortenings, contain a particular form of unsaturated fat known as trans-fatty acids that may raise blood cholesterol levels, although not as much as saturated fat.

Choose a Low Cholesterol Diet

The body makes the cholesterol it requires. In addition, cholesterol is obtained from food. Dietary cholesterol comes from animal sources such as egg yolks, meat (especially organ meats such as liver), poultry, fish, and higher fat milk products. Many of these foods are also high in saturated fat. Choosing foods with less cholesterol and saturated fat will help lower your blood pressure levels.

Avoid Too Much Sugar

Sugars are carbohydrates. Dietary carbohydrates also include the complex carbohydrates starch and fiber. During digestion all carbohydrates except fiber break down into sugars. Sugars and starches occur naturally in many foods that supply other nutrients. Examples of these foods include milk, fruits, some vegetables, breads, cereals, and grains. Some sugars are used as natural preservatives, thickeners, and baking aids in food. The body cannot tell the difference between naturally occurring and added sugars because they are identical chemically.

Because maintaining a nutritious diet and a healthy weight is very important, sugars should be used in moderation by most healthy people and sparingly by people with low calorie needs.

Avoid Too Much Sodium

Sodium and sodium chloride—known commonly as salt—occur naturally in foods, usually in small amounts. In the body, sodium plays an essential role in regulation of fluids and blood pressure. Most evidence suggests that many people at risk for high blood pressure reduce their chances of developing this condition by consuming less salt or sodium. Some questions remain, partly because other factors may interact with sodium to affect blood pressure.

Drink Alcohol in Moderation

Alcoholic beverages have been used to enhance the enjoyment of meals by many societies throughout human history. If adults choose to drink alcoholic beverages, they should do so only in moderation.

Current evidence suggests that moderate drinking is associated with a lower risk for coronary heart disease in some individuals. However, higher levels of alcohol intake raise the risk for high blood pressure, stroke, heart disease, certain cancers, accidents, violence, suicides, birth defects, and overall mortality (deaths).

Too much alcohol may cause cirrhosis of the liver, inflammation of the pancreas, and damage to the brain and heart. Heavy drinkers also are at risk of malnutrition because alcohol contains calories that may substitute for those in more nutritious foods.

What is moderation? Moderation is defined as no more than one drink per day for women and no more than two drinks per day for men.

Count as a drink:
12 ounces of regular beer (150 calories)
5 ounces of wine (100 calories)
1.5 ounces of 80-proof distilled spirits (100 calories)

Two Myths About Heart Disease

Source: "Heart and Stroke Facts: 1996 Statistical Supplement." 1995 © Copyright American Heart Association. Reproduced with permission.

Heart disease no longer represents a serious threat—Medical scientists have made tremendous progress in fighting cardiovascular diseases. Even so, every 33 seconds an American dies of CVD. That's more than 954,000 deaths annually; more than 42 percent of all deaths every year. In fact, since 1900 the number one killer in the United States has been CVD in every year but one (1918).

Deaths don't tell the whole story, either. Of the current U.S. population of about 258 million, more than 60 million people have some form of these diseases. And as the population ages, these diseases may have an even greater human and economic impact. Heart failure, for example, is becoming much more prevalent.

Cancer, AIDS, and other diseases deserve research and attention. But it's important to remember that CVD ranks far ahead of them as a cause of death. And total deaths from CVD, after years of decline, began rising in 1993.

Finally, according to the most recent computations done by the National Center for Health Statistics (NCHS), if all forms of major cardiovascular disease were eliminated, life expectancy would rise by 9.78 years. If all forms of cancer were eliminated, the gain would be three years.

If a heart attack doesn't kill you, you'll recover and be fine—People who survive the acute stage of a heart attack have a chance of illness and death that's two to nine times higher than the general population. The rates of another heart attack, sudden death, angina pectoris, heart failure, and stroke—for both men and women—are all substantial. Within six years after a heart attack:

• 23 percent of men and 31 percent of women will have another heart attack;
• 41 percent of men and 34 percent of women will develop angina;
• About 20 percent will be disabled with heart failure;
• Nine percent of men and 18 percent of women will have a stroke; and
• 13 percent of men and six percent of women will experience sudden death.

About two-thirds of heart attack patients don't make a complete recovery, but 88 percent of those under age 65 are able to return to work.

Prevalence—60,340,000 Americans—more than one in four—have one or more types of cardiovascular disease (CVD) according to current estimates.
• High blood pressure—50,000,000.
• Coronary heart disease—13,490,000.
• Stroke—3,820,000.
• Rheumatic heart disease—1,360,000.

Mortality—Cardiovascular diseases claimed 954,138 lives in the United States in 1993. This is 42.1 percent of all deaths or 1 of every 2.4 deaths.
• More than 2,600 Americans die each day from cardiovascular diseases, an average of a death every 33 seconds.
• More than one-sixth of all people killed by CVD are under age 65.
• 1992 final CVD mortality: male deaths—444,180 (48.1 percent of deaths from CVD); female deaths—479,236 (51.9 percent of deaths from CVD).
• In 1992, 38 percent of deaths from cardiovascular diseases occurred prematurely (i.e., before age 75, the average life expectancy in that year).
• 1992 death rates from CVD were 230.2 for white males and 335.6 for black males (45.8 percent higher); 128.3 for white females and 217.1 (69.2 percent higher) for black females.
• From 1983 to 1993 death rates from CVD declined 23.1 percent. Despite this decline in the death rate, in the same 10-year period the actual number of deaths declined only 3.8 percent.
• Total deaths from CVD increased significantly in 1993. One reason given for this rise is that the total U.S. population, and particularly the population of middle-aged and older people, is increasing. Another reason is that recent advances in medical treatment have allowed more people to survive previously fatal cardiovascular events, but now these people are dying of subsequent cardiovascular illnesses (e.g., heart attack victims whose lives were saved by better emergency care may now be dying of congestive heart failure).

Toll-Free Numbers for Health Information

AL-ANON Family Group Headquarters, 356-9996
Alcohol and Drug Helpline, 821-4357
Allergy Information Referral Line, 822-2762
Alzheimer's Association, 272-3900
Alzheimer's Disease Education and Referral Center, 438-4380
American Association of Kidney Patients, 749-2257
American Cancer Society Response Line, 227-2345
American Council of the Blind, 424-8666
American Council on Alcoholism, 527-5344
American Diabetes Association, 232-3472
American Dietetic Association Hotline, 366-1655
American Foundation for Urologic Disease, 242-2383
American Heart Association Stroke Connection, 553-6321
American Institute for Cancer Research, 843-8114

American Kidney Fund, 638-8299
American Leprosy Missions (Hansen's Disease), 543-3131
American Liver Foundation, 223-0179
American Paralysis Association, 225-0292
American Parkinson Disease Association, 223-2732
American Speech-Language-Hearing Association, 638-8255
APA Spinal Cord Injury Hotline, 526-3456
Arthritis Foundation Information Hotline, 283-7800
ASPO/LAMAZE, 368-4404
Asthma and Allergy Foundation of America, 727-8462
Better Hearing Institute, 327-9355.
Brain Injury Association, Family Helpline, 444-6443
Cancer Information Service, 4-CANCER; 422-6237

Health and Nutrition Web Sites

Centers for Disease Control www.cdc.gov
National Center for Infectious Diseases
www.cdc.gov/ncidod/ncid.htm
National Institutes of Health www.nih.gov
National Cancer Institute www.nci.nih.gov
National AIDS Clearinghouse www.cdcnac.gov
HIVNet www.hivnet.org
World Health Organization www.who.org
American Cancer Society www.cancer.org
American Heart Association www.amhrt.org
American Medical Association
www.ama-assn.org
Alzheimers Association www.alz.org
American Psychological Association
www.apa.org
Department of Health and Human Services
www.dhhs.gov
Allergy Information Center www.kww.com/allergy
American Academy of Pediatrics www.aap.org
U.S.D.A. Center for Nutrition and Promotion
www.usda.gov/fcs/cnpp.htm
Food and Drug Administration www.fda.gov
American Dietetic Association www.eatright.org
American Council on Science and Health
www.acsh.org
National Council Against Health Fraud, Inc.
www.ncahf.org
You First www.youfirst.com

CDC National AIDS Clearinghouse, 458-5231; 243-7012 (TDD)
CDC National HIV and AIDS Hotline, 342-2437; 344-7432 (Spanish); 243-7889 (TDD)
CDC National STD Hotline, 227-8922
Child Abuse and Neglect Clearinghouse, 394-3366
Child Find of America, Inc., 426-5678; 292-9688
CHILDHELP USA/IOF Foresters National Child Abuse Hotline, 4-A-CHILD or 422-4453; 2-A-CHILD or 222-4453 (TDD)
Children's Hospice International, 242-4453
Cleft Palate Foundation, 24-CLEFT or 242-5338
Crohn's and Colitis Foundation of America, Inc., 932-2423
Cystic Fibrosis Foundation, 344-4823
Deafness Research Foundation, 535-3323
Depression Awareness, 421-4211
Endometriosis Association, 992-3636
Epilepsy Foundation of America, 332-1000
Facial Plastic Surgery Information Service, 332-3223
Food Labeling Hotline, Meat and Poultry Hotline, 535-4555
Grief Recovery Helpline, 445-4808
Guide Dog Foundation for the Blind, Inc. 548-4337
Huntington's Disease Society of America, 345-4372
Impotence Information Center, 843-4315; 543-9632
International Childbirth Education Association, 624-4934
"Just Say No" International, 258-2766
Juvenile Diabetes Foundation International Hotline, 223-1138
La Leche League International, LA-LECHE or 525-3243
Lighthouse National Center for Vision and Aging, The, 334-5497
Living Bank, The, 528-2971
Lung Line National Jewish Center for Immunology and Respiratory Medicine, 222-5864; 552-LUNG or 552-5864 (LUNG FACTS)
Lupus Foundation of America, 558-0121
Medic Alert Foundation, 432-5378; 344-3226
Medicare Telephone Hotline, 638-6833
National Adoption Center, TO-ADOPT or 862-3678
National Center for the Blind, 638-7518

National Center for Missing and Exploited Children, 843-5678
National Center for Sight, 331-2020
National Center for Stuttering, 221-2483
National Childwatch Campaign, 222-1464
National Clearinghouse for Alcohol and Drug Information, 729-6686; 487-4889 (TTY/TDD)
National Cocaine Hotline, 262-2463
National Council on Alcoholism and Drug Dependence Hopeline Inc., 622-2255
National Down Syndrome Society Hotline, 221-4602
National Eye Care Project Hotline, 222-EYES or 222-3937
National Eye Research Foundation, 621-2258
National Foundation for Depressive Illness, 284-4344
National Headache Foundation, 843-2256
National Health Information Center, 336-4797
National Information Center for Children and Youth With Disabilities, 695-0285
National Information Center for Orphan Drugs and Rare Diseases, 300-7469
National Institute on Aging Information Center, 222-2225
National Institute on Deafness and Other Communication Disorders Information Clearinghouse, 241-1044; 241-1055 (TT)
National Kidney Foundation, 622-9010
National Lead Information Center, LEAD-FYI (Hotline) or 532-3394; 424-LEAD or 424-5323 (Clearinghouse); 526-5456 (TDD)
National Marrow Donor Program, MARROW-2 or 627-7692
National Mental Health Association Information Center, 969-6642
National Multiple Sclerosis Society, LEARN-MS or 532-7667
National Neurofibromatosis Foundation, 323-7938
National Organization for Rare Disorders, 999-6673
National Parkinson Foundation, Inc., 327-4545
National Pesticide Telecommunications Network, 858-7378
National Rehabilitation Information Center, 346-2742
National Resource Center on Child Abuse and Neglect, 227-5242
National Resource Center on Homelessness and Mental Illness, c/o Policy Research Associates, 444-7415 ext. 232
National Reye's Syndrome Foundation, 233-7393
National Runaway Switchboard, 621-4000
National Spinal Cord Injury Association, 962-9629
National Stroke Association, STROKES or 787-6537
National Tuberous Sclerosis Association, 225-6872
National Youth Crisis Hotline, 448-4663
NHTSA Auto Safety Hotline, 424-9393
Panic Disorder Information Line, 64-PANIC or 647-2642
Planned Parenthood, 230-PLAN or 230-7526
PMS Access, 222-4767
Project Inform HIV/AIDS Treatment Hotline, 822-7422
Safe Drinking Water Hotline, 426-4791
Seafood Hotline, FDA-4010 or 332-4010
Sickle Cell Disease Association of America, 421-8453
Simon Foundation for Continence, The, 237-4666
Spina Bifida Association of America, 621-3141
Stuttering Foundation of America, 992-9392
Tourette Syndrome Association, 237-0717
United Cerebral Palsy Association, 872-5827
United Network for Organ Sharing, 243-6667
United Scleroderma Foundation, 722-HOPE or 722-4673
U.S. Coast Guard Customer Information Line, 368-5647
U.S. Consumer Product Safety Commission Hotline, 638-2772; 638-8270 (TDD)
Y-ME National Organization for Breast Cancer Information Support Program, 221-2141

Consumer's Resource Guide

To Buy or Not To Buy, That Is the Question

Leasing versus Buying That New Car

With all the advertisements for snazzy new cars and low monthly payments, it is becoming increasingly difficult to resist the siren call beckoning us to our local dealership. Without exploring the compulsions that underlie the American need for constant renewal, it is nonetheless apparent that we are a society that likes to drive newer cars. The average American trades cars every three to four years. Now that competition among manufacturers has intensified, many are offering a new enticement: the short-term lease.

Since many Americans grew up with their parents telling them to "buy when you can pay for it" and "a car is an asset," it is hard to understand why leasing, which involves monthly payments for something you do not own, has caught on. The answer is twofold. For many drivers, leasing allows them to drive a nicer car than they may otherwise be able to afford. Plus, in some cases, it just makes good economic sense.

Most of us finance our triennial trades with a loan, contrary to Dad's advice, which means we're already in the habit of making monthly payments. To keep those payments as low as possible, we tend to take out a five-year loan to pay for our new purchases. The result? At the end of the five-year period we may well own the car, but chances are we really wanted to trade it in a year ago. One other point: our parents neglected to tell us that a car is a *depreciating asset,* that is, it loses value over time with some makes and models depreciating faster than others. So, the car we now own and don't really want isn't worth very much when we try to trade it in.

To Lease, Perchance To Dream . . .

The leasing alternative addresses all these desires. Because the term of the average lease is shorter than that of the average loan, it allows us to move onto the next car more quickly, and payments tend to be more affordable than loan payments. Let's look at a concrete example.

A 1997 Honda Accord retails for about $19,500, but you could probably haggle the price down to $18,500. The average interest rate on a five-year loan for a new car is approximately 8.9%, and the monthly payments will be $345 if we pay 10% of the purchase price up front. As soon as we drive the car off the lot, it becomes a used car whose value is significantly lower than the amount we have just agreed to pay back over the next sixty months. The payments made in the early part of the loan mostly cover the interest, while those in the later stages cover more principal, so it takes some time for the value we could get for the car as a trade-in to be the same as the amount we have left to pay on the loan.

If we choose to lease this car instead, we would pay $259 per month for 36 months, and at the end of that time we would have three options. First, we could buy the car at a wholesale price determined when we signed the lease and guaranteed by the terms of the lease, in this case about $13,054. Second, we could trade it in to the dealer at a (higher) average trade-in price and buy or lease another car, trade-in value being about $14,200. Third, we could decide to buy the car at the wholesale price then sell it privately (without a dealer) at a pre-

sumably still higher price, about $15,900. We could also simply choose to conclude our payments and then walk away (literally, since we would not have traded the car for a newer one or bought the one we had been leasing).

It is important to understand that the cost of the lease is really the difference in the purchase price at signing and the purchase price available to you at the end of the lease, plus some finance charges, divided by the number of months in the lease. Here's why this matters: if you plan to buy the car at the end of the lease, you want the buyout price to be as low as possible, so that when you buy it you have a lower purchase price. If, however, you plan to just lease another car, you want the buyout price to be as high as possible because the cost of the lease (i.e., the difference between the purchase prices at the beginning and end of the lease) will be smaller. Also, cars that retain their value will be cheaper to lease for the same reason: there is less depreciation between the initial value and the residual value.

Apart from the obvious benefit of leasing (instant gratification of an affordable new car every three years), leasing also offers some unique benefits that purchasing does not. For example, leasing allows you to pay for the sales tax over the period of the lease, rather than all at once when you register the car, as is required in some states when you buy a car. Leasing also provides added insurance against unexpected losses. Let's say that you drive a new car off the lot and get hit by a Mack truck, totaling the car. You consider yourself lucky to have survived the accident until you realize that you still owe the bank the full amount of the loan, but that the insurance company is going to treat the value of the car as its replacement value, which would be that for a *used* car. You would need to pay out of pocket the difference between the amount of the insurance check (for a depreciated used car) and the amount of the loan. If you had leased the car, the bank fee you would have paid goes to purchase "gap insurance," which guarantees that the leasing company will absorb any deficiency between the insurance reimbursement for a totaled or stolen car and the remaining payments on the lease.

To Buy—Aye, There's the Rub

But buying has its benefits, too. First, if you drive more than 15,000 miles per year, a lease can become quite costly. The lease agreement generally provides an allowance of 12,000 miles per year, and you must pay for every mile above the allotment, usually at $0.15 per mile. If you know up-front that you will put on more than the allotted miles, you may choose to pay for the projected excess miles ahead of time, usually at a reduced rate ($0.08 to $0.10 per mile). Also, if you tend to keep cars for more than five years, or are able to finance for shorter periods (if at all), then buying a car may be cheaper than leasing. Ultimately, you will need to balance your desire to drive a newer car with your tolerance for monthly payments to determine whether leasing is right for you. Here are a few points to keep in mind as you weigh your decision:

• Leasing is best when you plan to put less than 15,000 miles per year on the car, and when you plan to replace the car every three to four years.

• You may be able to negotiate a more favorable interest rate on a loan to purchase a car by going through a credit union, but they will require 10–20% of the purchase price as a downpayment.

• Interest rates for used cars tend to be higher than those for new cars. In general, the new car rate for which you qualify will increase by 0.5% times the age of the car (e.g., 1% more for a car that is two years old).

• Insurance payments for a financed new car should be about the same as those for leasing a new car.

• The terms of a lease for any given car are set by the leasing company, not the dealer or the manufacturer, so the same car could be leased under different terms. It is worthwhile to ask your dealer whether other leasing companies offer more favorable rates, but be sure you understand what you give up for that lower monthly payment. For example, a leasing company associated with the manufacturer (e.g., American Honda Finance Co.) may be more likely to refund the security deposit without a hassle, or may offer more favorable rates to repeat customers.

• A "zero money down" lease is a misnomer: it will usually cost at least $1,000 to drive away in your leased vehicle: first month's payment, $259; security deposit, $284 (monthly payment plus $25); "bank fee," $450–$500; "documentation/prep" fee, $75 (this is the same regardless of whether you buy or lease the car).

• You still must pay to register a leased car, and the car must be registered in the name of the leasing company with you as the co-owner. You may therefore incur added costs to register the leased car than you would to register a car you own yourself because you cannot transfer the registration from your current vehicle.

Whether you lease or buy, it is always better, economically speaking, to choose a car that retains its value over time. If you need to trade it in early, you are more likely to get back at least what you owe.—*TMV* □

Making the Best Call

How to Save Money and Avoid Problems with Your Telephone Service

Source: Federal Communications Commission and MCI.

Telephone Service Is Changing. A new federal law has opened up the telephone industry to increased competition. Many different companies may soon offer to provide you with telephone service, both long distance and local. For more than a decade, consumers have been able to choose their long distance phone company. As a result, varying types of discount plans are now available and today consumers can save money by joining the long distance calling plan that is right for them.

Similar competition may also develop for the local phone service currently offered by one company in your community. How quickly this local competition emerges depends upon several factors—including the rules laid down by your home state to manage phone service and the decisions made by individual companies on how and where to seek customers. Local competition holds the promise of lower rates and greater choice for consumers.

Companies you recognize will be offering a broader range of services, while companies unfamiliar to you may solicit you for their services also. With dozens of companies offering local service, long distance or both, consumers need to make sure they are getting the best deal.

Be a Savvy Shopper

Long Distance—Know Your Needs. The best way to save money on long distance service may be to enroll in a calling plan that fits your habits. Consider the following:

• how many calls you make a month,
• how long you talk,
• the time of day you usually make calls,
• where the calls are placed (local, domestic long distance or international),
• the rate per minute or per month, and
• any monthly fee or minimum spending limit.

A close look at your monthly bill will provide you with the information needed when choosing the right calling plan. You should request written material from companies and compare their rates to your calling patterns and make sure you fully review the details of a plan before you sign on.

Local Service Choice is Coming. The full picture of local service has yet to be completed, especially as each of the 50 states determines how it will oversee the new open market. As the local market changes, be wary of offers that commit you for a set period of time to your current local company or a new provider. While their discounts or rates may sound like a good deal, such practices can lock out competitors and limit consumer choice. For the first time in a long time, one company will be able to offer both local and long distance services to consumers. This ability to choose is convenient and can save you money. You may, however, save more money by selecting a separate company for local and long distance service. The key is: shop around among companies offering various local and long distance plans, and shop smart. This article warns you about some deceptive techniques used to sell telephone service. It can help you avoid marketing abuses today, and alert you to tactics that may be used as competition for local service develops.

CAUTION: Look Before You Leap

Slamming. You have the right to choose your primary long distance company and to change companies whenever you wish. Over the past few years, the number one consumer complaint in the telephone market involves a practice called 'slamming'—when your chosen long distance telephone service provider is switched to another company without your consent or knowledge. This practice may involve deceptive marketing tactics or outright fraud, and it could affect your local service. If your service is slammed, you could lose important service features, get lower quality service, or be charged higher rates for your long distance calls. The Federal Communications Commission's (FCC) rules and policies and the Telecommunications Act of 1996 prohibit slamming. The FCC's rules require a long distance company to obtain your authorization before changing your long distance service provider. Your state may have similar regulations. Your service may be switched through no fault of your own, or you could be misled by marketing techniques used to sign up customers for telephone service. To avoid this, you should carefully read all promotional material and all forms before signing, including sweepstakes, contests, promotional checks, or other marketing devices some companies use to induce consumers to authorize a carrier switch. FCC rules require that the forms provided by long distance companies to change long distance service be clear and not confusing, signed and dated by the consumer subscribing to the telephone line involved with the change, and easily separated from the promotional material. For instance, the form could be printed on a piece of paper that does not include any promotional material. Or, the form and promotional material could be included on a sheet of paper with perforations so that the form can be easily torn off and separated from the promotional material.

Checks in the Mail. Closely examine checks from telephone companies offering money to switch to their service. While it may be wise to take advantage of special offers, make sure you are signing up for the plan that saves you the most money. Some companies may not automatically put you on their best savings plan and you could end up paying more than the value of the check in higher monthly rates. In some cases, customers need to mark a box on the back of the check to receive the discounted service. A check must clearly state that the customer is authorizing a change in service—but read the entire offer. Look for a full explanation of the changes you are authorizing next to the signature line on the back of the check. If you do cash the check, call the customer service number provided soon after to make sure you have been placed in the best discount program for you.

Discount Plans. Carefully examine telephone or mail solicitations that offer big savings if you switch your service to a new company. These claims usually compare only the highest rates of well-known carriers. A calling plan with your current company may have lower rates and fewer restrictions than the program being offered. In any case, ask more questions and find out about any hidden costs or restrictions associated with discount plans. Do the discounts offered fit your calling habits? Will the company provide other services you need, such as 24-hour customer service and reliable billing? If you're not getting straight answers, you probably have reason to be suspicious.

Five-Digit Discount Codes. Pay close attention to mailings offering big savings if you use a so-called discount code of five digits at the start of each call you make. These offers promise not to change your long distance company, which is technically true. Dialing the five digits before the number that you are calling will connect you to a long distance company that most likely is not your primary long distance company. This company's rates may be higher or lower than the rates charged by your long distance company.

Short-Term Bargains. Watch for special offers that provide certain services at a discount or for free. These "bargains" often last for only a few weeks or months, then automatically continue at a much higher rate unless you specifically request cancellation. Also, remember that your local telephone company charges a fee to change your long distance company. Some long distance companies will pay this charge if you switch to their service.

Package Deals. Package deals can offer a good value as many companies begin to offer deep discounts to customers who buy all their telecommunications services from one source (some may include Internet, cable TV, or pager services, for instance, on top of local and long distance). Companies offer these deals because it helps them retain customers, and consumers like them because it simplifies the billing process. It could, however, be cheaper to buy separately only the services needed, rather than an entire package. Make sure you purchase what you truly want and can afford.

Selection Freeze. Your current local telephone company may tell you that you can avoid negative marketing tactics by signing up for a program that requires you to directly contact your local telephone company to change carriers. Some local companies require written permission. While written permission will help protect you from slamming, it can make it more difficult to take advantage of new competitors offering lower prices or better service.

Prepaid Calling Cards. Depending on their per-minute rate, prepaid calling cards can save money on long distance calls of short duration. If you use prepaid cards for calls from home or for local calls, however, you may pay more than if you used your regular telephone service. In addition, some companies that sold consumers calling cards have gone out of business before the customer could benefit from the full value of the card. Only prepay if you know and trust the company making an offer.

Pay Phones. Be aware that pay phones may be connected to operator service companies charging high rates and added fees. If you make calls away from home, consider getting a calling card that allows you access to the company of your choice by dialing its access code—usually an 800 number. Though illegal, some pay phones are set up to block your ability to reach your company. If you have trouble reaching your carrier or using a calling card, try to find another nearby pay phone.

Questions & Complaints: What You Can Do

Verify Your Company. If you suspect your long distance carrier has been changed without your permission, call 1-700-555-4141 from your home phone. A recording will state which carrier is connected to your home line. Its name will also be listed on your bill, which you should examine every month.

Get a Refund. If your telephone company is switched improperly, call your local telephone company and your original carrier and arrange to be switched back immediately at no charge. You have the right to demand a refund if you were charged a switching fee or were billed at higher rates than your own carrier's rates.

Get Help With a Complaint. For advice about a telephone-related problem, contact your state or local consumer protection agency, or your state Attorney General or public utilities commission. If necessary, they may take a complaint from you or refer you to another agency that can help you. Send a copy of your grievance to the company so they know you are dissatisfied. If you are unsuccessful in resolving problems about interstate or international long distance service with the company, you can write to the Federal Communications Commission. Your complaint should include: your name, address, the telephone number or numbers involved with the complaint; a telephone number where you can be reached during business hours; the names of your local and long distance companies and, where appropriate, the company that slammed you; and copies of bills or other documents related to your complaint. Be aware that complaints can take several months to process. Address your complaint to the FCC's Common Carrier Bureau, Consumer Complaints, Mail Stop 1600A2 Washington, DC 20554. □

Consumer Tips

Source: U.S. Office of Consumer Affairs.

Consumer Information Catalog

The *Consumer Information Catalog* lists approximately 200 free or low-cost federal booklets with helpful information for consumers. Topics include careers and education, cars, childcare, the environment, federal benefits, financial planning, food and nutrition, health, housing, small businesses, and more. This free catalog is published quarterly by the Consumer Information Center of the U.S. General Services Administration. Single copies of the catalog only may be ordered by sending your name and address to *Catalog,* Consumer Information Center, Pueblo, CO 81009, at www.pueblo.gsa.gov, or by calling 719-948-4000.

Non-profit groups that can distribute 25 copies or more each quarter can automatically receive copies by writing for a bulk mail card.

Consumer Web Sites

Consumer Information Center: www.pueblo.gsa.gov
Consumer World: www.consumerworld.org
National Fraud Information Center: www.fraud.org
Federal Trade Commission: www.ftc.gov
Consumer Product Safety Commission:
   www.cpsc.gov
National Highway Safety Commission:
   www.dot.gov/affairs/
Project OPEN (National Consumer League):
   www.isa.net/project-open
Council on Economic Priorities:
   www.accesspt.com/cep
Consumer Alert: www.consumeralert.org
Copyright Information: lcweb.loc.gov/copyright/
Better Business Bureau: www.bbb.org
U.S. Dept. of Justice: www.usdoj.gov

Copyrights

Source: Copyright Office, Washington, D.C.

Copyright is a form of protection provided by the laws of the United States to the creators of "original works of authorship," including literary, dramatic, musical, artistic, and certain other intellectual works. This protection is available to both published and unpublished works. The Copyright Act generally gives the owner of copyright the exclusive right to do and to authorize others to do the following:
To reproduce the copyrighted work;
To prepare derivative works based upon the copyrighted work;
To distribute copies or phonorecords of the copyrighted work to the public by sale or other transfer of ownership, or by rental, lease, or lending;
To perform the copyrighted work publicly; and
To display the copyrighted work publicly.

It is illegal for anyone to violate these rights. However, they are limited by the doctrine of "fair use," or by a "compulsory license" under which certain limited uses of copyrighted works are permitted in exchange for payment. For further information about the limitations of any of these rights, consult the Copyright Act or write to the Copyright Office.

Copyright protection exists from the time the work is created in fixed form; that is, it is an incident of the process of authorship. The copyright in the work of authorship immediately becomes the property of the author who created it. Only the author or those deriving their rights through the author can rightfully claim copyright.

In the case of works made for hire, the employer and not the employee is presumptively considered the author. The copyright statute defines a "work made for hire" as:
1. A work prepared by an employee within the scope of his or her employment; or
2. A work specially ordered or commissioned for use as a contribution to a collective work, as a part of a motion picture or other audiovisual work, as a translation, as a supplementary work, as a compilation, as an instructional text, as a test, as answer material for a test, or as an atlas, if the parties expressly agree in a written instrument signed by them that the work shall be considered a work made for hire. . . .
The authors of a joint work are co-owners of the

copyright in the work, unless there is an agreement to the contrary.

Copyright in each separate contribution to a periodical or other collective work is distinct from copyright in the collective work as a whole and vests initially with the author of the contribution.

Two General Principles:
• Mere ownership of a book, manuscript, painting, or any other copy or phonorecord does not give the possessor the copyright. The law provides that transfer of ownership of any material object that embodies a protected work does not of itself convey any rights in the copyright.
• Minors may claim copyright, but state laws may regulate the business dealings involving copyrights owned by minors. For information on relevant state laws, consult an attorney.

Copyright is secured automatically when the work is created, and a work is "created" when it is fixed in a copy or phonorecord for the first time. "Copies" are material objects from which a work can be read or visually perceived, such as books, manuscripts, sheet music, film, videotape, or microfilm. "Phonorecords" are material objects embodying fixations of sounds (excluding, by statutory definition, motion picture soundtracks), such as cassette tapes, CDs, or LPs. Thus, for example, a song (the "work") can be fixed in sheet music ("copies") or in phonograph disks ("phonorecords"), or both.

If a work is prepared over a period of time, the part of the work that is fixed on a particular date constitutes the created work as of that date.

Copyright protection is available for all unpublished works, regardless of the nationality or domicile of the author. Published works are eligible for copyright protection in the United States if any one of the several conditions regarding the nationality of the authors or place of publication is met. Check with the Copyright Office for details.

What Works Are Protected

Copyright protects "original works of authorship" including the following categories:
• literary works;
• musical works, including any accompanying words;

- dramatic works, including any accompanying music;
    - pantomimes and choreographic works;
    - pictorial, graphic, and sculptural works;
    - motion pictures and other audiovisual works;
    - sound recordings; and
    - architectural works.

These categories should be viewed quite broadly. For example, computer programs and most "compilations" are registrable as "literary works." Maps and architectural plans are registrable as "pictorial, graphic, and sculptural works."

Several categories of material are generally not eligible for statutory copyright protection. These include among others:

- Works that have not been fixed in a tangible form of expression. For example, choreographic works that have not been notated or recorded, or improvisational speeches or performances that have not been written or recorded.
- Titles, names, short phrases, and slogans; familiar symbols or designs; mere variations of typographic ornamentation, lettering, or coloring; mere listings of ingredients or contents.
- Ideas, procedures, methods, systems, processes, concepts, principles, discoveries, or devices, as distinguished from a description, explanation, or illustration.
- Works consisting entirely of information that is common property and containing no original authorship. For example, standard calendars, height and weight charts, tape measures and rulers, and lists or tables taken from public documents or other common sources.

Notice of Copyright

When a work is published, it may bear a notice of copyright to identify the year of publication and the name of the copyright owner and to inform the public that the work is protected by copyright. Use of the notice is recommended because it informs the public that the work is protected by copyright, identifies the copyright owners, and shows the year of first publication. Furthermore, in the event that a work is infringed, if the work carries a proper notice, the court will not allow a defendant to claim "innocent infringement"—that is, that he or she did not realize that the work is protected. (A successful innocent infringement claim may result in a reduction in damages that the copyright owner would otherwise receive.)

The use of the copyright notice is the responsibility of the copyright owner and does not require advance permission from, or registration with, the Copyright Office.

Form of Notice for Visually Perceptible Copies

The notice for visually perceptible copies should contain all of the following three elements:
1. The symbol © (the letter C in a circle), or the word "Copyright," or the abbreviation "Copr.";
2. The year of publication of the work; and
3. The name of the owner of copyright in the work, or an abbreviation by which the name can be recognized, or a generally known alternative designation of the owner.

Example: © 1998 John Doe

Form of Notice for Sound Recordings

The copyright notice for phonorecords of sound recordings should contain the following three elements:
1. The symbol ℗ (the letter P in a circle);
2. The year of first publication of the sound recording; and
3. The name of the owner of copyright in the sound recording, or an abbreviation by which the name can be recognized, or a generally known alternative

designation of the owner. If the producer of the sound recording is named on the phonorecord labels or containers, and if no other name appears in conjunction with the notice, the producer's name shall be considered a part of the notice.

Example: ℗ 1998 A.B.C., Inc.

NOTE: Since questions may arise from the use of variant forms of the notice, any form of the notice other than those given here should not be used without first seeking legal advice.

Position of Notice

The notice should be positioned so as to "give reasonable notice of the claim of copyright." The notice on phonorecords may appear on the surface of the phonorecord or on the phonorecord label or container, provided the manner of placement and location give reasonable notice of the claim. The Copyright Office has issued regulations concerning the form and position of the copyright notice. For more information, contact them directly.

Publications Incorporating United States Government Works

Works by the U.S. Government are not eligible for copyright protection, though portions of these works may be eligible. An example is:

© 1998 Jane Brown. Copyright claimed in Chapters 7–10, exclusive of U.S. Government maps.

Unpublished Works

To avoid an inadvertent publication without notice, the author or other owner of copyright may wish to place a copyright notice on any copies or phonorecords that leave his or her control. An appropriate notice for an unpublished work is: Unpublished work © 1998 Jane Doe.

Copyright Protection Endurance

Works Originally Created On or After Jan. 1, 1978

A work that is created on or after January 1, 1978, is automatically protected from the moment of its creation, and is ordinarily given a term of the author's life, plus 50 years. In the case of a joint work prepared by two or more authors who did not work for hire, the term lasts for 50 years after the last surviving author's death. For works made for hire, and for anonymous and pseudonymous works (unless the author's identity is revealed in Copyright Office records), the duration of copyright will be 75 years from publication or 100 years from creation, whichever is shorter.

Works Originally Created Before Jan. 1, 1978

Works that were created but not published or registered for copyright before January 1, 1978, have been automatically brought under the statute and are now given federal copyright protection. The duration of copyright in these works will generally be computed in the same way as for works created on or after January 1, 1978. The law provides that in no case will the term of copyright for works in this category expire before December 31, 2002, and for works published on or before December 31, 2002, the term of copyright will not expire before December 31, 2027. Works that were created and published or registered before January 1, 1978, generally enjoy a copyright term of 75 years from the date of publication or registration. Check with the Copyright Office for details.

International Copyright Protection

There is no "international copyright" that will automatically protect an author's work throughout the entire world. Protection against unauthorized use in a particular country depends basically on the national laws of that country. However, most countries do offer protection to foreign works under certain conditions, and these conditions have been greatly simplified by international copyright treaties and conventions. The United States belong to both global, multilateral copyright treaties— the Universal Copyright Convention (UCC) and the Berne Convention for the Protection of Literary and Artistic Works.

A U.S. author may obtain copyright protection in all countries that are members of the Berne Convention and the UCC. Some UCC countries may require formalities, which may be satisfied by the use of a UCC notice consisting of the symbol © accompanied by the name of the copyright proprietor and the year of the work.

Example: © John Smith 1998.

An author who wishes protection for his or her work in a particular country should first find out the extent of protection of foreign works in that country. If possible, this should be done before the work is published anywhere, since protection may depend on the facts existing at the time of first publication.

For a list of countries that maintain copyright relations with the United States, request Circular 38a from the Copyright Office.

Copyright Registration

Copyright registration makes a public record of the basic facts of a particular copyright. Even though registration is not a requirement for protection, the copyright law provides several incentives to encourage copyright owners to register. They include the following:

• Registration establishes a public record of the copyright claim;

• Before an infringement suit may be filed in court, registration is necessary for works of U.S. origin and for foreign works not originating in a Berne Convention country. (For more information on when a work is of U.S. origin, request Circular 93);

• If made before or within 5 years of publication, registration will establish prima facie evidence in court of the validity of the copyright and of the facts stated in the certificate; and

• If registration is made within 3 months after publication of the work or prior to an infringement of the work, statutory damages and attorney's fees will be available to the copyright owner in court actions. Otherwise, only an award of actual damages and profits is available to the copyright owner.

• Copyright registration allows the owner of the copyright to record the registration with the U.S. Customs Service for protection against the importation of infringing copies. For additional information, request Publication No. 563 from: IPR Branch, Franklin Court, Suite 4000, U.S. Customs Service, 1301 Constitution Ave., N.W., Washington, D.C. 20229.

Registration may be made at any time within the life of the copyright. When a work has been registered in unpublished form, it is not necessary to make another registration when the work becomes published (although the copyright owner may register the published edition, if desired).

To register a work, send the following three elements in the same envelope or package to the Registrar of Copyrights, Copyright Office, Library of Congress, Washington, D.C. 20559-6000:

1. A properly completed application form;

2. A nonrefundable filing fee of $20 for each application;

3. A nonreturnable deposit of the work that is being registered. Generally the deposit is two copies if the work is published and one copy if the work is unpublished. The application form details the specific deposit requirements.

A copyright registration is effective on the date the Copyright Office receives all of the required elements in acceptable form, regardless of how long it takes to process the application and mail the certificate of registration. Because of the large number of claims the Copyright Office receives, processing may take 120 days.

Although a copyright registration is not required, the Copyright Act establishes a mandatory deposit requirement for works published in the United States. In general, the owner of copyright or the owner of the exclusive right of publication in the work has a legal obligation to deposit in the Copyright Office, within 3 months of publication in the United States, 2 copies (or in the case of sound recordings, 2 phonorecords) for the use of the Library of Congress. Failure to make the deposit can result in fines and other penalties but does not affect copyright protection.

Certain categories of works are exempt entirely from the mandatory deposit requirements, and the obligation is reduced for certain other categories. For further information about mandatory deposit, request Circular 7d.

For More Information

Information on registration and application forms may be obtained free of charge by writing or calling the Copyright Office. Circular 1 contains general copyright information, including a list of application forms for copyright registration. Address inquiries to: Copyright Office, Publications Section, LM-455, Library of Congress, Washington, D.C. 20559-6000. To speak with an information specialist, call 202-707-3000 (TTY: 202-707-6737) between 8:30 a.m.–5:00 p.m., Eastern Time, Monday to Friday, except federal holidays. Requests for information may also be left on a 24-hour basis by calling 202-707-9100. To receive information via fax, call 202-707-2600. Registration forms are not available via fax.

Copyright information, including the most frequently requested circulars, is available via the Internet. Internet site addresses are: www.lcweb.loc.gov/copyright/ and gopher.marvel.loc.gov.port70.

Copyright Office records of registrations and other related documents from 1978 forward are also available over the Internet via the above addresses or telnet directly to LOCIS (Library of Congress Information System) at: locis.loc.gov

Trademarks

Source: Department of Commerce, Patent and Trademark Office.

A trademark may be defined as a word, letter, device, or symbol, as well as any combination of these, which is used in connection with merchandise and which points distinctly to the origin of the goods.

Certificates of registration of trademarks are issued under the seal of the Patent and Trademark Office and may be registered by the owner if he is engaged in interstate or foreign commerce which may lawfully be regulated by Congress since any Federal jurisdiction over trademarks arises under the commerce clause of the Constitution. Effective November 16, 1989, applications to register may also be based on a "bona fide intention to use the mark in commerce." Trademarks may be registered by foreign owners who comply with our law, as well as by citizens of foreign countries with which the U.S. has treaties relating to trademarks.

American citizens may register trademarks in foreign countries by complying with the laws of those countries. The right to registration and protection of trademarks in many foreign countries is guaranteed by treaties.

General jurisdiction in trademark cases involving Federal Registrations is given to Federal courts. Adverse decisions of examiners on applications for registration are appealable to the Trademark Trial and Appeal Board, whose affirmances, and decisions in *inter partes* proceedings, are subject to court review. Before adopting a trademark, a person should make a search of prior marks to avoid infringing unwittingly upon them.

The duration of a trademark registration is 10 years, but it may be renewed indefinitely for 10-year periods, provided the trademark is still in use at the time of expiration.

The application fee is $245 per class.

Patents

Source: Department of Commerce, Patent and Trademark Office.

A patent, in the most general sense, is a document issued by a government, conferring some special right or privilege. The term is now restricted mainly to patents for inventions; occasionally, land patents.

The grant of a patent for an invention gives the inventor the privilege, for a limited period of time, of excluding others from making, using, or selling a certain article.

In the U.S., the law provides that a patent may be granted, for a term of 20* years, to any person who has invented or discovered any new and useful art, machine, manufacture, or composition of matter, as well as any new and useful improvements thereof. A patent may also be granted to a person who has invented or discovered and asexually reproduced a new and distinct variety of plant (other than a tuber-propagated one) or has invented a new, original and ornamental design for an article of manufacture for a term of 20 years and 14 years, respectively.

A patent is granted only upon a regularly filed application, complete in all respects; upon payment of the fees; and upon determination that the disclosure is complete and that the invention is new, useful, and, in view of the prior art, unobvious to one skilled in the art. The disclosure must be of such nature as to enable others to reproduce the invention.

A complete application, which must be addressed to the Commissioner of Patents and Trademarks, Washington, D.C. 20231, consists of a specification with one or more claims; oath or declaration; drawing (whenever the nature of the case admits of it); and a basic filing fee of $385.[1] The filing fee is not returned to the applicant if the patent is refused. If the patent is allowed, another fee of $645[1] is required before the patent is issued. The fee for design patent application is $160; the issue fee is $220.[1] The fee for a plant patent application is $265; the issue fee is $325. Maintenance fees are required on utility patents at stipulated intervals.

Applications are ordinarily considered in the order in which they are received. Patents are not granted for printed matter, for methods of doing business, or for devices for which claims contrary to natural laws are made. Applications for a perpetual-motion machine have been made from time to time, but until a working model is presented that actually fulfills the claim, no patent will be issued.

* As a result of the GATT Uruguay Round implementing legislation, the term of utility and plant patents is 20 years measured from the date of filing an application in the U.S. effective June 8, 1995. 1. Fees quoted are for small entities. Fees are double for corporations.

Beware of Illegal Patent Services

It is illegal under patent law (35 USC 33) for anyone to hold himself out as qualified to prepare and prosecute patent applications unless he is registered with the Patent Office. Also, Patent Office regulations forbid registered practitioners advertising for patent business. Some inventors, unaware of this, enter into binding contracts with persons and firms which advertise their assistance in making patent searches, preparing drawings, specifications, and patent applications, only to discover much later that their applications require the services of fully qualified agents or attorneys.

National Consumer Organizations

Alliance Against Fraud In Telemarketing (AAFT), c/o National Consumers League 1701 K St., N.W., Ste. 1200, Washington, DC 20006, 202-835-3323, 202-835-0747 (fax).

The Alliance, coordinated by the National Consumers League, is an international coalition of public interest groups, trade associations, labor unions, businesses, law enforcement agencies, consumer reporters and consumer protection agencies. AAFT members promote cooperative educational efforts to alert potential victims to the threat of telemarketing fraud and steps consumers can take to protect themselves.

American Association of Retired Persons (AARP), Consumer Affairs Section, 601 E. St., N.W., Washington, DC 20049, 202-434-6030, 202-434-6466 (fax).

AARP's Consumer Affairs Section advocates on behalf of mid-life and older consumers, develops and distributes consumer information, and educates the private sector about the specific needs of older consumers. It offers programs and materials on housing, insurance, funeral practices, eligibility for public benefits, financial security, transportation and consumer protection issues, with special focus on the needs and problems of older consumers.

American Council on Consumer Interests (ACCI), 240 Stanley Hall, University of Missouri–Columbia, Columbia, MO 65211, 573-882-3817, 573-884-6571 (fax), acci@mizzou1.missouri.edu (email). Contact: Anita B. Metzen, Executive Director.

Serving the professional needs of consumer educators, researchers and policymakers, ACCI publications and educational programs foster the production, synthesis and dissemination of information in the consumer interest.

American Council on Science and Health (ACSH), 1995 Broadway, 2nd Fl., New York, NY 10023-5860, 212-362-7044, 212-362-4919 (fax).

A non-profit public education group, ACSH's goal is to provide up-to-date, sound information on the relationship among health and chemicals, foods, lifestyles and the environment. Booklets and special reports on a variety of topics are available, as is a quarterly magazine, *Priorities.*

Bankcard Holders of America (BHA), 524 Branch Dr., Salem, VA 24153, 540-389-5445, 540-389-3020 (fax).

A non-profit organization, BHA assists consumers in saving money on credit, getting out of debt and resolving credit problems. It offers lists of low-rate and secured credit cards, more than 20 guidebooks and educational brochures on credit topics, and a newsletter.

Better Business Bureau *See* Council of Better Business Bureaus, Inc. (CBBB)

Call for Action, 3400 Idaho Ave., N.W., Washington, DC 20016-3046, Network Hotline 202-362-3813, 202-537-0585.

An international non-profit hotline, Call for Action is affiliated with radio and television stations and helps consumers and small businesses through mediation of marketplace disputes. A list of the affiliated radio and television stations is available by contacting the hotline.

Center for Auto Safety (CAS), 2001 S St., N.W., Ste. 410, Washington, DC 20009, 202-328-7700.

CAS advocates on behalf of consumers in auto safety and quality, fuel efficiency, emissions and related issues. For advice on specific problems, consumers should write to CAS, including a brief statement of the problem or question, year, make and model of the vehicle, and a stamped self-addressed envelope.

Center for Science in the Public Interest (CSPI), 1875 Connecticut Ave., N.W., Ste. 300, Washington, DC 20009, 202-332-9110, 202-265-4954 (fax).

A non-profit, membership organization, CSPI conducts research, education and advocacy on nutrition, health, food safety and related issues, and publishes the monthly *Nutrition Action Healthletter,* as well as other consumer information materials.

Citizen Action, 1730 Rhode Island Ave., N.W., Ste. 403, Washington, DC 20036, 202-775-1580, 202-296-4054 (fax).

Citizen Action works on behalf of its 3 million members and 32 state organizations on health care reform, environment and energy issues.

Community Nutrition Institute (CNI), 910 17th St., N.W., Ste. 413, Washington, DC 20006, 202-776-0595, 202-776-0599 (fax).

An advocate for programs and services to enable consumers to enjoy a diet that is adequate, safe and healthy, CNI also works to increase citizen participation in the state and federal policy and administrative processes to achieve these goals. CNI publishes *Nutrition Week,* a newsletter covering nutrition and food safety issues.

Congress of Consumer Organizations (COCO), P.O. Box 158, Newton Centre, MA 02159, 617-552-8184, 617-552-2380 (fax), www.essential.org (web).

COCO publishes a monthly newsletter, the *COCO INTERCOM,* on a broad range of consumer issues.

Congress Watch, 215 Pennsylvania Ave., S.E., Washington, DC 20003, 202-546-4996, 202-547-7392 (fax).

An arm of Public Citizen, Congress Watch works for consumer-related legislation, regulation and policies in such areas as trade, health and safety, and campaign financing, and has publications available on the issues with which it deals.

Consumer Action (CA), 116 New Montgomery, Ste. 233, San Francisco, CA 94105, 415-777-9635 (consumer hotline, 10 a.m.–2 p.m., PST), 415-777-9456 (voice/ttd), 415-777-5267 (fax).

An education and advocacy organization specializing in credit, finance and telecommunications issues, Consumer Action offers a multilingual consumer complaint hotline, free information on its surveys of banks and long-distance telephone companies, and consumer education materials in as many as eight languages.

Consumer Alert, 1001 Connecticut Ave., N.W., Ste. 1128, Washington, DC 20036, 202-467-5809, 202-467-5814 (fax). www.consumeralert.org (web).

Consumer Alert is a non-profit, membership organization whose mission is to inform the public about the consumer benefits of competitive enterprise, advancing competition as the best regulator of business. A bimonthly newsletter and other materials are available.

Consumer Federation of America (CFA), 1424 16th St., Ste. 604, Washington, DC 20036, 202-387-6121, 202-265-7989 (fax).

Made up of more than 240 organizations representing 50 million consumers, CFA is a consumer advocacy and education organization. Issues on which it currently represents consumer interests before Congress and federal regulatory agencies include telephone service, insurance and financial services, product safety, indoor air pollution, health care, product liability and utility rates. It develops and distributes studies of various consumer issues, as well as consumer guides in book and pamphlet form. In addition, CFA publishes several newsletters. The National Insurance Consumer Organization (NICO) has merged with CFA and is now known as CFA Insurance Group.

Consumers for World Trade (CWT), 2000 L St., N.W., Ste. 200, Washington, DC 20036, 202-785-4835, 202-416-1734 (fax).

A non-profit organization, CWT supports trade expansion and liberalization to promote economic growth and increase consumer choice and price competition in the marketplace. Various publications are available.

Consumers Union of U.S., Inc. (CU), 101 Truman Ave., Yonkers, NY 10703-1057, 914-378-2000, 914-378-2900 (fax). Available online via CompuServe.

A non-profit, independent organization, CU researches and tests consumer goods and services and disseminates the results in its monthly magazine, *Consumer Reports,* as well as other publications and media.

Council of Better Business Bureaus, Inc. (CBBB), 4200 Wilson Blvd., Arlington, VA 22203, 703-276-0100, 703-525-8277 (fax), www.bbb.org (web).

Sponsored by national companies and the nation's Better Business Bureaus, the Council of Better Business Bureaus provides coordination and leadership to the 163 Better Business Bureaus (BBBs) in the United States, offers a national advertising review program, dispute resolution services, an advisory service that reports on national charities, consumer information services, and voluntary industry guidelines for advertising and selling products and services.

Families USA Foundation, 1334 G St., N.W., Ste. 300, Washington, DC 20005, 202-628-3030, 202-347-2417 (fax), hn0516@handsnet.org (email).

A national, non-profit membership organization committed to access to affordable health and long-term care, Families USA works to educate and mobilize consumers on health care issues. In addition to its two grassroots advocacy networks, a.s.a.p., a network of health and long-term care reform activists, and HealthLink USA, a nationwide health reform computer network for public interest groups, Families USA develops and distributes reports and other materials on health and long-term care issues.

Health Research Group (HRG), 1600 20th St., N.W., Washington, DC 20009, 202-588-1000.

A division of Public Citizen, HRG works for protection against unsafe foods, drugs, medical devices, and workplaces, and advocates for greater consumer control over personal health decisions. A monthly *Health Letter* and other publications are available.

National Association of Consumer Agency Administrators (NACAA), 1010 Vermont Ave., N.W., Ste. 514, Washington, DC 20005, 202-347-7395, 202-347-2563 (fax).

An association of the administrators of local, state and federal government consumer protection agencies, NACAA provides training programs, public policy studies and conferences, professional publications and other member services.

National Association of State Utility Consumer Advocates (NASUCA), 1133 15th St., N.W., Ste. 50, Washington, DC 20005, 202-727-3908, 202-727-3911 (fax), nacaa@essential.org (email).

A national organization of 41 utility ratepayer advocate offices in 38 states and the District of Columbia, NASUCA members represent millions of consumers served by investor-owned gas, telephone, electric, and water companies before Congress, state regulatory commissions, the courts, the Federal Energy Regulatory Commission and the Federal Communications Commission.

National Coalition for Consumer Education (NCCE), 295 Main St., Ste. 200, Madison, NJ 07940, 201-377-8987, 201-377-4828 (fax).

The coalition brings together people and resources from government, business, education, consumer organizations and the media to educate consumers about such important issues as financial management, health and safety, and the environment. The coalition develops and provides educational materials and resources to consumer educators, but does not handle requests from individuals.

National Consumers League (NCL), 1701 K St., N.W., Ste. 1200, Washington DC 20006, 202-835-3323, 202-835-0747 (fax).

Founded in 1899, NCL is America's pioneer consumer advocacy organization. The league is a non-profit, membership organization working for consumer health and safety protection and fairness in the marketplace and workplace. Current principal issue areas include consumer fraud, food and drug safety, fair labor standards, child labor, health care, the environment, financial services and telecommunications. The league develops and distributes consumer education materials and newsletters.

National Foundation For Consumer Credit, Inc. (NFCC), 8611 2nd Ave., Ste. 100, Silver Spring, MD 20910, 301-589-5600 or 800-388-2227, 301-495-5623 (fax).

A membership organization for non-profit community organizations which are often called Consumer Credit Counseling Service agencies and are in more than 1,100 locations in the United States and Canada. The agencies educate and counsel individuals and families on credit issues. Consumers are taught to budget and use credit wisely and may be helped to resolve their credit problems. The 800 number provides the location of the nearest agency.

National Fraud Information Center (NFIC), P.O. Box 65868, Washington, DC 20035, 800-876-7060 (TDD available), 202-835-0767 (fax), www.fraud.org (web).

A project of the National Consumers League, the center's toll-free hotline assists consumers with information to help them avoid becoming victims of fraud, referral to appropriate law enforcement agencies and professional associations, and assistance in filing complaints. The center also provides professionals involved in consumer fraud prevention and enforcement with telecommunications systems and data links to improve fraud regulation, prevention and law enforcement.

National Institute for Consumer Education (NICE), 207 Rackham Bldg., College of Education, Eastern Michigan University, Ypsilanti, MI 48197, 313-487-2292, 313-487-7153 (fax).

A consumer education resource and professional development center for K-12 classroom teachers, business, government, labor and community educators, NICE conducts training programs, develops teaching guides and resource lists, and manages a national clearinghouse of consumer education materials, including videos, software programs, textbooks and curriculum guides.

National Insurance Consumer Organization (NICO) *See* Consumer Federation of America (CFA)

National Senior Citizens Law Center, 1815 H St., N.W., Suite 700, Washington, DC 20006, 202-887-5280, 202-785-6792 (fax), nsclc@nsclc.org (email), www.nsclc.org (web).

The National Senior Citizens Law Center (NSCLC) was established in 1972 to help older Americans live their lives in dignity and freedom from poverty, through legal work in support of elderly poor clients, client groups, and Elder Law attorneys. NSCLC attorneys are knowledgeable in a broad range of legal issues and practice areas that affect the security and welfare of older persons of limited income.

Public Citizen, Inc., 1600 20th St., N.W., Washington, DC 20009, 202-588-1000.

A national, non-profit membership organization representing consumer interests through lobbying, litigation, research and publications, Public Citizen represents consumer interests in Congress, the courts, government agencies and the media. Primary current areas of interest include product liability, health care delivery, safe medical devices and medications, open and ethical government, and safe and sustainable energy use.

Public Voice for Food and Health Policy, 1101 14th St., N.W., Washington, DC 20005, 202-371-1840, 202-371-1910 (fax), pvoice@ix.netcom.com (email).

A national research, education and advocacy organization, Public Voice works for food and agriculture policies and practices that improve the safety, health and affordability of the food supply and protect the environment. Public Voice develops and distributes consumer information materials on pesticide reduction, nutrition labeling and seafood safety.

Society of Consumer Affairs Professionals in Business (SOCAP), 801 N. Fairfax St., Ste. 404, Alexandria, VA 22314, 703-519-3700, 703-549-4886 (fax).

An international professional organization, SOCAP provides training, conferences and publications to encourage and maintain the integrity of business in transactions with consumers; to encourage and promote effective communication and understanding among business, government and consumers; and to define and advance the consumer affairs profession.

U.S. Public Interest Research Group (U.S. PIRG), 218 D St., S.E., Washington, DC 20003-1900, 202-546-9707, pirg@pirg.org (email), www.pirg.org (web).

The group is the national lobbying office for state public interest research groups, consumer/environmental advocacy groups active in 33 states that lobby and publish reports on issues, including credit bureau errors; bank fees and services; toy, ATV and product safety; toxic chemicals in art supplies and other consumer products; and recycling, over-packaging and green consumerism. U.S. PIRG does not handle individual consumer complaints directly, but measures complaint levels to gauge the need for remedial legislation.

Postal Regulations

U.S. Postal Rates and Fees

Domestic Rates Effective July 1, 1997

First-Class Mail

Single-Piece Letter/Flat Rates

1st ounce	$0.32
Each additional ounce	0.23

Weight not over (oz.)	Rate	Weight not over (oz.)	Rate
1*	$0.32	8	$1.93
2	0.55	9	2.16
3	0.78	10	2.39
4	1.01	11	2.62
5	1.24	Over 11 ounces, see Priority Mail.	
6	1.47		
7	1.70		

*Nonstandard surcharge may apply to pieces weighing 1 ounce or less based on size.

Card Rates

Single postal card sold by USPS	$0.20
Double postal card sold by USPS	0.40
Single postcard (commercial)	0.20

Postcard Dimensions: Not larger than 4¼ by 6 inches by 0.016 inch thick. Not smaller than 3½ by 5 inches by 0.007 thick.

Periodicals

Only publishers and registered news agents approved for periodicals mailing privileges may mail at periodicals rates. Publications mailed by the public are charged at the applicable Express Mail, Priority Mail, single-piece First-Class, standard "A," or standard "B" rate.

Standard "A"

Used primarily by retailers, catalogers, and other advertisers to promote products and services. See postmaster for details. Use—For mailing certain items—circulars, books, catalogs, other printed matter, merchandise, seeds, cuttings, bulbs, and plants—weighing less than 16 ounces.

Single-Piece Rates

Weight not over (oz.)	Rate	Weight not over (oz.)	Rate
1	$0.32	8	$1.93
2	0.55	9	2.16
3	0.78	10	2.39
4	1.01	11	2.62
5	1.24	13	2.90
6	1.47	over 13 but	
7	1.70	under 16	2.95

Express Mail

Express Mail is the Post Office's fastest service. Next day delivery by 12 noon to most destinations. Delivered 365 days a year with no extra charge for Saturday, Sunday, or holiday delivery. All packages must use an Express Mail label. Items may weigh up to 70 pounds and measure up to 108 inches in combined length and girth. Call 1-800-222-1811 for delivery information between ZIP codes.

Features—Express Mail envelopes, labels, and boxes are available, at no additional charge, at post offices or by calling 1-800-222-1811.

Post Office to Addressee Service

Up to 8 ounces	$10.75
Over 8 ounces, up to 2 pounds	15.00
Up to 3 pounds	17.25
Up to 4 pounds	19.40
Up to 5 pounds	21.55
Up to 6 pounds	25.40
Up to 7 pounds	26.45
Over 7 pounds, see postmaster.	

Flat Rate Envelope—Post Office to Addressee Service

$15.00, regardless of weight or destination for matter sent in a flat rate envelope provided by the Postal Service.

Priority Mail

Priority Mail offers two-day service to most domestic destinations. Items may weigh up to 70 pounds and measure up to 108 inches in combined length and girth.

Features—Priority Mail envelopes, labels, and boxes are available, at no additional charge, at post offices or by calling 1-800-222-1811.

Single-Piece Rates[1]

Up to 2 pounds	$3.00
Up to 3 pounds	4.00
Up to 4 pounds	5.00
Up to 5 pounds	6.00
Over 5 pounds, see postmaster.	

Flat Rate Envelope

$3.00, regardless of weight or destination, for matter sent in a flat rate envelope provided by the Postal Service.

Standard "B"

For mailing circulars, books, catalogs, other printed matter, and packages weighing 16 ounces or more. Enclosed or attached First-Class Mail is charged at First-Class rates. Packages may weigh up to 70 pounds and measure up to 108 inches in combined length and girth.

1. Parcels weighing less than 15 pounds but measuring more than 84 inches in length and girth combined are chargeable with a minimum rate equal to that for a 15-pound parcel for the zone to which it is addressed.

Parcel Post Zone Rates

For rates priced by distance and weight, see postmaster.

Special Services (Domestic Mail)

Certificate of Mailing

Proves that an item was mailed. Must be purchased at time of mailing. No record kept at the post office.

Fee, in addition to postage—$0.55

Certified Mail

Provides a mailing receipt, and a record is kept at the recipient's post office. A return receipt can also be purchased for an additional fee. Available only with First-Class and Priority Mail

Fee, in addition to postage—$1.35

Insurance

Provides coverage against loss or damage. Coverage up to $600.00 for standard "A" and standard "B" mail as well as standard "A" and standard "B" matter mailed at Priority Mail or First-Class Mail rate. Insurance up to $25,000 can be purchased by using Registered Mail. Do not insure a package for more than its value.

Liability	Fee, in addition to postage
$.01 to $50.00	$ .75
$50.01 to $100.00	1.60
$100.01 to $200.00	2.50
$200.01 to $300.00	3.40
$300.01 to $400.00	4.30
$400.01 to $500.00	5.20
$500.01 to $600.00	6.10

Money Orders

Provides safe transmission of money. Available in amounts up to $700.00

Fee, in addtion to postage—$0.85

Registered Mail

Provides maximum protection and security for valuables. Available only for Priority Mail and First-Class Mail. May be combined with COD, restricted delivery, or return receipt. Additional postal insurance available.

Value	Fee, in addition to postage	
	With postal insurance	Without postal insurance
$0.00 to $100.00	$4.95	$4.85
$100.01 to $500.00	5.40	5.20
$500.01 to $1,000.00	5.85	5.55
$1,000.01 to $2,000.00	6.30	5.90

For higher values, consult your postmaster.

Restricted Delivery

Available only for Certified Mail, COD, Insured Mail for more than $50.00, or Registered Mail.

Fee, in addition to postage—$2.75

Return Receipt

Available only for Express Mail, Certified Mail, COD, Insured Mail for more than $50.00, or Registered Mail.

Requested at time of mailing:

Showing to whom (signature) and date delivered	$1.10
Showing to whom (signature), date, and addressee's address	1.50

Requested after mailing:

Showing to whom (signature) and date delivered	6.60

Special Delivery

Available for all classes except Express Mail. Provides preferential handling to the extent practicable in dispatch, transportation, and expedited delivery at the destination.

	Fee, in addition to postage		
Class of mail	2 lb. or less	Over 2 lb., but not over 10 lb.	Over 10 lb.
First-Class & Priority Mail	$ 9.95	$10.35	$11.15
Other classes	10.45	11.25	12.10

Collect on Delivery (COD)

Allows mailers to collect the price of goods and/or postage on merchandise ordered by addressee when it is delivered. Fees include insurance. Maximum amount $600.00; see postmaster for details.

Sizes for Domestic Mail

Mail must meet these standards:
• Thickness—No less than 0.007 inch thick. Pieces that are 1/4 inch thick or less must be at least 3-1/2 inches high, 5 inches long, and rectangular in shape.
• Combined length and girth—No more than 108 inches.
• Weight—No more than 70 pounds.
Keys and identification devices are exempted from these requirements.

Additional standards apply to bulk mail and mail addressed to APOs and FPOs.

The Mail Order Merchandise Rule

The mail order rule adopted by the Federal Trade Commission in October 1975 provides that when you order by mail:

You must receive the merchandise when the seller says you will.

If you are not promised delivery within a certain time period, the seller must ship the merchandise to you no later than 30 days after your order comes in.

If you don't receive it shortly after that 30-day period, you can cancel your order and get your money back.

How the Rule Works

The seller must notify you if the promised delivery date (or the 30-day limit) cannot be met. The seller must also tell you what the new shipping date will be and give you the option to cancel the order and receive a full refund or agree to the new shipping date. The seller must also give you a free way to send back your answer, such as a stamped envelope or a postage-paid postcard. *If you don't answer, it means that you agree to the shipping delay.*

The seller must tell you if the shipping delay is going to be more than 30 days. You then can agree to the delay or, if you do not agree, the seller must return your money by the end of the first 30 days of the delay.

If you cancel a prepaid order, the seller must mail you the refund within seven business days. Where there is a credit sale, the seller must adjust your account within one billing cycle.

It would be impossible, however, for one rule to apply uniformly to such a varied field as mail order merchandising. For example, the rule does not apply to mail order photo finishing, magazine subscriptions, and other serial deliveries (except for the initial shipment); to mail order seeds and growing plants; to COD orders; or to credit orders where the buyer's account is not charged prior to shipment of the merchandise.

International Postal Rates

Effective as of July 1997

Letters and Letter Packages— Airmail Rates

All countries except Canada & Mexico

Weight not over (oz.)		Weight not over (oz.)	
0.5	$0.60	9.0	7.40
1.0	1.00	9.5	7.80
1.5	1.40	10.0	8.20
2.0	1.80	10.5	8.60
2.5	2.20	11.0	9.00
3.0	2.60	11.5	9.40
3.5	3.00	12.0	9.80
4.0	3.40	12.5	10.20
4.5	3.80	13.0	10.60
5.0	4.20	13.5	11.00
5.5	4.60	14.0	11.40
6.0	5.00	14.5	11.80
6.5	5.40	15.0	12.20
7.0	5.80	15.5	12.60
7.5	6.20	16.0	13.00
8.0	6.60	16.5	13.40
8.5	7.00		

See postmaster for weights up to 4 lb. Maximum weight: 64 ounces.

Aerogrammes—All countries—$0.50.

Letters and Letter Packages— Canada and Mexico

Weight not over				Weight not over			
(lbs)	(oz.)	Can-ada[1]	Mex-ico	(lbs)	(oz.)	Can-ada[1]	Mex-ico
0	0.5	$ .46	$ .40	0	10	2.28	4.06
0	1	.52	.46	0	11	2.47	4.46
0	1.5	.64	.66	0	12	2.66	4.86
0	2	.72	.86	1	0	3.42	6.46
0	3	.95	1.26	1	8	4.30	9.66
0	4	1.14	1.66	2	0	5.18	12.86
0	5	1.33	2.06	2	8	6.06	16.06
0	6	1.52	2.46	3	0	6.94	19.26
0	7	1.71	2.86	3	8	7.82	22.46
0	8	1.90	3.26	4	0	8.70	25.66
0	9	2.09	3.66				

1. A 4-pound maximum applies except for registered items sent to Canada. Canada-bound registered items may weigh up to 66 pounds. For registered items weighing over 4 pounds, the rate is $1.76 for each additional pound up to the 66-pound limit.

Postcards and Postal Rates—Canada—$0.40; Mexico—$0.35; All others—$0.50

All Time Top 10 Most Popular Commemorative Stamps

Issue	Number of stamps saved (millions)	Issue	Number of stamps saved (millions)
Elvis '93	124.0	Legends of the West '94	46.5
Wildflowers '92	76.2	Marilyn Monroe '95	46.3
Rock and Roll '93	75.8	Summer Olympics '92	39.6
Moon Landing '94	47.9	Centennial Olympic Games '96	38.1
Civil War '95	46.6	Space Fantasy '93	36.5

State Abbreviations

Since the Post Office instituted ZIP codes and their accompanying state postal codes in 1963, the two-letter abbreviations have steadily gained popularity. Though it is usually preferable to write out the full form, space constraints often require use of an abbreviation. In this case, the preferred form should be used rather than the postal code. The postal code abbreviations should be used only in mailing addresses.

State	Preferred abbreviation	Postal code	State	Preferred abbreviation	Postal code	State	Preferred abbreviation	Postal code
Alabama	Ala.	AL	Kentucky	Ky.	KY	Ohio	Ohio	OH
Alaska	Alaska	AK	Louisiana	La.	LA	Oklahoma	Okla.	OK
Arizona	Ariz.	AZ	Maine	Maine	ME	Oregon	Ore.	OR
Arkansas	Ark.	AR	Maryland	Md.	MD	Pennsylvania	Pa.	PA
California	Calif.	CA	Massachusetts	Mass.	MA	Puerto Rico	P.R.	PR
Colorado	Colo.	CO	Michigan	Mich.	MI	Rhode Island	R.I.	RI
Connecticut	Conn.	CT	Minnesota	Minn.	MN	South Carolina	S.C.	SC
Delaware	Del.	DE	Mississippi	Miss.	MS	South Dakota	S.D.	SD
Dist. of Columbia	D.C.	DC	Missouri	Mo.	MO	Tennessee	Tenn.	TN
Florida	Fla.	FL	Montana	Mont.	MT	Texas	Tex.	TX
Georgia	Ga.	GA	Nebraska	Nebr.	NE	Utah	Utah	UT
Guam	Guam	GU	Nevada	Nev.	NV	Vermont	Vt.	VT
Hawaii	Hawaii	HI	New Hampshire	N.H.	NH	Virginia	Va.	VA
Idaho	Idaho	ID	New Jersey	N.J.	NJ	Virgin Islands	V.I.	VI
Illinois	Ill.	IL	New Mexico	N.M.	NM	Washington	Wash.	WA
Indiana	Ind.	IN	New York	N.Y.	NY	West Virginia	W.Va.	WV
Iowa	Iowa	IA	North Carolina	N.C.	NC	Wisconsin	Wis.	WI
Kansas	Kans.	KS	North Dakota	N.D.	ND	Wyoming	Wyo.	WY

Where to Find out More

Reference Books and Other Sources

While it is impossible to construct a comprehensive list of reference works in just a few pages, the editors of the *Information Please Almanac* have compiled a list of additional resources where readers can find more details on the information presented in this book.

General References

To find out a little bit of information on virtually any topic, a good place to start is a dictionary or an encyclopedia. The most authoritative dictionaries are (for American English) *The American Heritage Dictionary, Third Edition; Webster's Collegiate Dictionary, Tenth Edition;* and *Webster's Third New International Dictionary of the English Language, Unabridged.* For British English or for those interested in the history of the language, the multi-volume *Oxford English Dictionary, Second Edition,* is incomparable, providing definitions in historical order.

Encyclopedias generally present more substantive information on a variety of topics. Multivolume sets, such as the *Encyclopedia Britannica* and the *Encyclopedia Americana,* provide greater depth and breadth but are more costly and less convenient than their single-volume counterparts. Among the best single-volume encyclopedias are *The Columbia Encyclopedia, Fifth Edition,* and *The Random House Encyclopedia.* Other general references include:

Bartlett's Familiar Quotations, 16th ed., Little, Brown Books in Print, R.R. Bowker
The Cambridge Biographical Dictionary, David Crystal
Chambers's Biographical Dictionary, Cambridge University Press
Guide to Reference Books, Eugene P. Sheehy, ed.
Reader's Guide to Periodical Literature, H.W. Wilson
The Chicago Manual of Style, Univ. of Chicago Press

AIDS

And the Band Played On: Politics, People, and the AIDS Epidemic, Randy Shilts
The AIDS Directory: An Essential Guide to the 1500 Leaders in Research, Service, Policy, Advocacy and Funding/ 1995-96, Frank Baran
AIDS Sourcebook, Karen Bellenir, Peter D. Dresser

Art

American Art Directory, R.R. Bowker
Sir Bannister Fletcher's A History of Architecture, John Musgrove, ed.
Encyclopedia of Architecture: Design, Engineering and Construction, Joseph A. Wilkes and Robert T. Packard
Phaidon Dictionary of Twentieth-Century Art, 2nd ed., Dutton
Dictionary of Architecture, Nikolaus Pevsner
American Architecture Since 1780: A Guide to the Styles, Marcus Whiffen
The History of Art, H.W. Janson
The Oxford Dictionary of Art, Ian Chilvers & others, eds.
Illustrated Dictionary of Symbols in Eastern and Western Art, James Hall, Chris Puleston
Museums of the World (5th ed.), Elisabeth Richter, et al.

Associations

The Directory of Directories, James M. Ethridge, ed.
Encyclopedia of Associations, Gale Research Co.

Business

AMA Complete Guide to Marketing Research for Small Business, Holly Edmunds
Consumer Reports Buying Guide, Consumers Union
Encyclopedia of Banking & Finance, Charles J. Woelfel
Occupational Outlook Handbook, U.S. Bureau of Labor Statistics
Where to Find Business Information, 2nd ed., John Wiley & Sons
The Wall Street Journal Guide to Understanding Personal Finance, Kenneth M. Morris, Alan M. Siegel

Education

College Costs & Financial Aid Handbook, College Board Staff
American Universities and Colleges, 14th ed., Walter de Gruyter

Environment

An Environmental Agenda for the Future, John H. Adams et al.
Dictionary of the Environment, Michael Allaby
The Dictionary of Ecology and Environmental Science, Henry W. Art
The Almanac of Renewable Energy, Richard Golob, Eric Brus
Alternative Sources of Energy, Warren Brown, Russell E. Train
The Complete Guide to America's National Parks 1996– 1997: The Official Visitor's Guide, Jane Bangley McQueen, National Park Foundation

Geography

Webster's New Geographical Dictionary, Merriam-Webster
The Book of the States, Council of State Government
Pocket Data Book United States of America, U.S. Department of Commerce
Rand McNally Comprehensive World Atlas, 2nd ed., Rand McNally
The World Factbook, Central Intelligence Agency
World Geographical Encyclopedia, Sybil P. Parker

Government

America Votes, Richard M. Scammon, Alice V. McGillivray
Congressional Quarterly's Guide to Congress, Congressional Quarterly
Finding Government Information on the Internet: A How-To- Do-It Manual, John Maxymuk

Health and Medicine

Alternative Health Care Resources: A Directory and Guide, Brett Jason Sinclair
American Medical Association Family Medical Guide, Heffret R.M. Kung and Asher J. Finkel, eds.
Anatomy of the Human Body, Henry Gray, Carmine D. Clemente
Back to Reform: Values, Markets, and the Health Care System, Charles J. Dougherty
Complete Guide to Prescription & Nonprescription Drugs, H. Winter Griffith
Mosby Medical Encyclopedia, Walter D. Glanze, et al.

The U.S.P. Guide to Vitamins & Minerals, U.S. Pharmacopeia
The Wellness Encyclopedia, Staff of the University of California, Berkeley, Wellness Letter, eds.

History

The Reader's Companion to American History, Eric Foner and John A. Garraty
Famous First Facts, Joseph Nathan Kane
Encyclopedia of North American Indians, Frederick E. Hoxie, ed.
The Native Americans: An Illustrated History, Betty Ballantine and Ian Ballantine
The Times Atlas of World History, Geoffrey Barrraclough, ed.
The Illustrated Encyclopedia of World History, Donker Van Heel

Hobbies

Kovel's Antiques and Collectibles Price List, Ralph and Terry Kovel
Kovel's Know Your Collectibles, Ralph and Terry Kovel
A Field Guide to the Birds, Roger Tory Peterson, Virginia Marie Peterson
The Computer Glossary: The Complete Illustrated Desk Reference, Alan Freedman
The Encyclopedia of Computer Science, Ralston
_____ *for Dummies* (software how-to series), various authors, published by IDG
The American Horticultural Society Encyclopedia of Gardening, Christopher Brickell, *et al.*
The Essence of Herbs, An Environmental Guide to Herb Gardening, Ruth D. Wrensch

Homosexuality

The Sourcebook on Lesbian/Gay Health Care, Michael Shernoff and William A. Scott, eds.
Psychiatry, Psychology, and Homosexuality (Issues in Lesbian and Gay Life), Ellen Herman
Gay American History: Lesbians and Gay Men in the U.S.A.: A Documentary History, Jonathan Katz
A Road to Stonewall: Male Homosexuality and Homophobia in English and American Literature, 1750–1969, Byrne R.S. Fone

Literature

African-American Literature: An Anthology of Nonfiction, Fiction, Poetry, and Drama, Demetrice A. Worley, Jesse Perry
American Indian Literature: An Anthology, Alan R. Velie
The Norton Anthology of American Literature, Nina Baym
Women's Works: An Anthology of American Literature, Barbara Perkins, *et al.*
A Writer's Eye: Collected Book Reviews, Eudora Welty, Pearl Amelia McHaney
Children's Books and Their Creators, Anita Silvey, ed.
The Oxford Companion to Classical Literature, M.C. Howatson
Theater in America: 250 Years of Plays, Players, and Productions, Mary C. Henderson
The Cambridge Guide to Theater, Martin Banham
The Oxford Companion to English Literature, Margaret Drabble, Paul Harvey
Columbia Dictionary of Modern European Literature, Jean-Albert Bede
Benet's Reader's Encyclopedia, George Perkins, *et al.*
The Dictionary of Classical Mythology, Pierre Grimal, A.R. Maxwell-Hyslop
Mythology, Edith Hamilton
Tradition, Stephen Fredman

Brewer's Dictionary of Phrase & Fable, Ebenezer Cobham Brewer, *et al.*

Music

All Music Guide to Jazz, Michael Erlewine, *et al.*
Great Composers, Piero Ventura
A History of Western Music, Donald J. Grout
The La Scala Encyclopedia of the Opera, Giorgio Bagnoli, Graham Fawcett
New Harvard Dictionary of Music, Don M. Randel, ed.
The Oxford Dictionary of Music, Michael Kennedy

Performing Arts

The Concise Oxford Dictionary of Ballet, 2nd ed., Horst Koegler
The Film Encyclopedia, Ephraim Katz
The New York Public Library Performing Arts Desk Reference, Macmillan
The Oxford Companion Guide to World Theatre, 4th ed., Phyllis Hatnoll, ed.
Theatre World, Crown

References

Who's Who in African-American History, Sande Smith
Who's Who in American Art 1995–96, R.R. Bowker
Current Biography Yearbook, H.W. Wilson
Contemporary Authors, Susan M. Trotsky
American Library Directory 1996–97, R.R. Bowker Database Publishing Group
World Guide to Libraries (12th ed.)
An Etymological Dictionary of Family and Christian Names, William Arthur

Religions

Dictionary of Comparative Religions, S.G.F. Brandon, ed.
The Modern Catholic Encyclopedia, Michael Glazier, Monika K. Hellwig
The Oxford Dictionary of the Christian Church, F.L. Cross, Elizabeth A. Livingston
The New Standard Jewish Encyclopedia, Geoffrey Wigoder
Dictionary of Islam, Thomas Patrick Hughes

Science

CRC Handbook of Chemistry and Physics, David R. Lide
McGraw-Hill Encyclopedia of Science and Technology, McGraw-Hill
The Yearbook of Astronomy, Patrick Moore, ed.
Lange's Handbook of Chemistry, John A. Dean
Fundamentals of Physics, David Halliday, *et al.*

Senior Citizens

Encyclopedia of Senior Citizens Information Sources, Paul Wasserman, Barbara Koehler, Yvonne Lev (Editor)
Social Security Benefits Handbook, Stanley A. Tomkiel

Sports

ESPN Information Please Sports Almanac, John Hassan, ed.
Facts & Dates of American Sports, Gorton Carruth and Eugene Ehrlich

Women's Issues

Ending the Violence: A Guidebook Based on the Experiences of 1000 Battered Wives, Lee Bowker
Notable American Women, Edward T. James, Janet W. James

U.S. Societies & Associations

America's Strange Clubs

Americans don't just join the boy scouts or the local militia. They sign up for societies. Sometimes curious ones.

That "Americans of all ages, all conditions, and all dispositions constantly form associations" was first noticed by Alexis de Tocqueville in 1840. He saw this sociability as a cornerstone of American democracy. A century and a half has seen little change. According to the American Society of Association Executives in Washington, D.C., there are now some 100,000 associations and clubs in America. Seven out of every ten Americans belong to at least one such club; astonishingly, a quarter of the population belongs to four or more.

For the most part, these are worthy souls toiling away in their spare time for parent-teacher associations, churches, local clubs, and charities. More than 7 million American parents are active in their local PTAs; 44% of the population claims to attend a church service at least once a week. And according to the Independent Sector, also based in Washington, D.C., a hefty 89 million adults—close to half the country's grown-ups—did volunteer work in 1993.

All very altruistic. But also a bit dull. Not everybody wants to join the local PTA or volunteer for the Bid-A-Wee Home Association for unwanted animals. The local militia may be a more exciting proposition, but spending all weekend in camouflage gear stalking imaginary liberals does not appeal to everybody. What the average American really wants is a society that stands for what he most easily relates to: political mediocrity, bureaucracy, over-regulation, pessimism, indecisiveness, boredom. Fortunately, such clubs are there for the joining.

Celebrating the Mediocre

America has seen its fair share of pedestrian presidents, but few as magnificently mediocre as Millard Fillmore. A New York Whig, Vice President Fillmore became the 13th president in 1850, after a bowl of cherries and iced milk had killed Zachary Taylor, the incumbent. In an attempt to defuse tensions between North and South over slavery, Fillmore signed Henry Clay's compromise of 1850—a measure that pleased nobody. The Whigs dropped him in 1852 and, after running in vain as the Know-Nothing Party's presidential candidate in 1856, Fillmore was gone and forgotten.

Except, that is, by the Society for the Preservation and Enhancement of the Recognition of Millard Fillmore, Last of the Whigs. Based in Stratford, New Jersey, the society (motto: *E pluribus mediocritum*) was formed in 1975 to defend global standards of mediocrity. It leads by example: with a dismal 300-odd members, says Phil Arkow, the vice president (president would have sounded too ambitious), "we don't have chapters; we settled for paragraphs."

The society has been (modestly) successful in its mission to "root for the middledog," in the words of its unimpressive 13-point "Millard Carta." A Medal of Mediocrity has been awarded to such underachievers as George Bush. And thanks to the society's half-hearted efforts, Millard Fillmore Day is celebrated each year in New Mexico in recognition of a rare Fillmore triumph: he prevented Texas from annexing the state. An attempt to persuade the U.S. Postal Service to issue a stamp bearing Fillmore's image produced a more mediocre outcome. And, fittingly, the society's compromise proposal—"if not on the front of the stamp, the back"—pleased nobody.

Proliferating Red Tape

The vagaries of the postal service have helped to inspire another club, the International Association of Professional Bureaucrats (INATAPROBU). Founded in 1968, the club (motto: "when in doubt, mumble") promotes excellence in "dynamic inaction, orbital dialoguing, and creative non-responsiveness." Led by James Boren, of Northeastern State University in Tahlequah, Oklahoma, INATAPROBU's 1,700 members are dedicated to the art of obfuscation. "To deny paper to a bureaucrat is to deny canvas to the artist," says Mr. Boren.

His association holds regular events to celebrate the glory of officialdom. Using a team of canoeists, waltzers, backward-running joggers, and turtles in a 32-mile relay between Muskogee and Tahlequah, it raced mail carried by the U.S. Postal Service—and won. The association also makes awards for sustained bureaucratic excellence. Most recently, after 28 of its 29 coordinating committees had approved, this was presented to Oklahoma's Department of Environmental Quality for allowing Arkansas to pollute Oklahoma's scenic Illinois River.

Mr. Boren, who once refused to take the oath in a congressional committee because to answer Yes or No would have been unbureaucratically concise, now hopes to spread his gospel wider. In 1996 he ran unsuccessfully against James Inhofe, a Republican senator who enraged Oklahomans with a crass comment in the wake of the Oklahoma City bombing. Mr. Boren is also looking overseas. He helped to launch the Russian Academy of Bureaucratic Arts, a tribute to the country's long history of obfuscation. But he laments Russia's lack of paper, "through which the shufflistic responsibilities of bureaucrats are residuating into a low operational profile."

You Can Never Be Too Safe

Dale Lowdermilk would feel at home in Mr. Boren's association. In 1982 he formed the National Organization Taunting Safety and Fairness Everywhere, in order to lampoon America's tendency to think that legislation can right every wrong. Based in Montecito, California, NOTSAFE now has 800 members, all paid-up believers in never being too careful about anything. Take milk. A 1980s study in San Diego found that inmates of a juvenile jail drank ten times as much as their law-abiding peers, and concluded that milk could cause crime. Too cautious, reckons NOTSAFE. Why not simply ban milk and all milk-based products? Why take unnecessary risks?

As a retired air-traffic controller, Mr. Lowdermilk's deepest concerns are with air safety. But there are, he believes, simple solutions. Aircraft should taxi, rather than fly, to their destinations. If they must fly, let them do so only one at a time. Passengers should be required to fly naked: this would stop hijackings, as there would be no place to hide bombs or guns. None of this would be convenient, but safety must come first. NOTSAFE also wants safety warnings on every product sold; children kept indoors at all times; and all owners of knives or guns registered as potential criminals.

NOTSAFE greatly favors the regulation of politicians. For 12 years it has advocated a single-term limit for congressmen; it also believes each lawmaker should be allowed to introduce only one bill each year. Bills passed by a majority of less than two-thirds, reckons NOTSAFE, ought to include a five-year "sunset" provision. Voters should be allowed to decide how $1 of their yearly taxes are spent—and offered the choice of "none of the above" on ballot papers.

All these proposals should have been discussed at one of NOTSAFE's annual meetings. But mindful of the dangers posed by airborne infection at such a gathering, Mr. Lowdermilk has always postponed it.

A Long-Awaited Organization

Never doing this year what could be done next is popular at the Procrastinators Club of America (motto: We're behind you all the way). Founded in 1956 and based in Bryn Athyn, Pennsylvania, the club has yet to confirm its acting president, Les Waas. The club has 14,000 members (another 500,000 keep meaning to join). The 1976 issue of *Last Month's Newsletter,* the club journal, is hot off the presses; the 1972–73 membership drive, says Mr. Waas, is "going very nicely."

The club boasts many other achievements. Its forecasts for each year are long-awaited, partly because of their 100% record of accuracy, but mainly because they are always released a little late: 1994's were issued on January 1st 1995. The club's 1967 protest against the war of 1812 was a resounding success (a peace treaty has now been signed, notes Mr. Waas), and a sortie to put out the Great Fire of Chicago (club members took buckets of water) clearly achieved its goal: the fire is now out.

The club's most notable success concerned Philadelphia's Liberty Bell, which was manufactured by Britain's Whitechapel Foundry in the 1750s, but cracked soon afterwards. A club delegation to the London-based foundry, which is still in business, protested against this lamentable lack of quality control and demanded that the company honor the bell's 200-year guarantee (which, if it ever existed, had sadly expired). Whitechapel gave in, and offered a full refund—as long as the bell was returned in its original packaging.

Haven for the Gloomy

Members of the Benevolent and Loyal Order of Pessimists, based in Iowa City, might have predicted such a less-than-ideal outcome. Jack Duvall, a gloomy bureaucrat who founded the order 20 years ago, claims it has "several hundred members, from all crawls of life." Many others, he says dejectedly, are too pessimistic to join. After all, why bother? All they get is BLOOP's bleak reading list, which includes Orwell's "1984," Camus's "Myth of Sisyphus," and Sartre's "Being and Nothingness." And the despair of seeing optimists, such as Kurt Vonnegut, receive the order's occasional Certificates of Pessimism.

BLOOP's members have good reason to be glum. The order's annual convention, scheduled for April 15th to commemorate the sinking of the Titanic (and also the date by which Americans must file tax returns), once had to be moved because the proposed venue burned down. One Pessimist of the Year was struck by lightning. And two journalists writing stories on the order

(one from the *Wall Street Journal*) died in tragic circumstances shortly afterwards.

But the fickle lure of fame—especially to one so convinced of its pointlessness—has caught up with Mr. Duvall. In 1994 he reluctantly agreed to do a radio advertisement for MCI, a telephone company. "It was the only chance we'll ever have to sell out," grieves Mr. Duvall, "so naturally we jumped at it. And it gives the members something to grumble about."

Cutting Edge

When they finish grumbling and resign, members might switch to the Society for Basic Irreproducible Research, in Chicago Heights, Illinois. Its official organ, the *Journal of Irreproducible Results,* is published six times a year. With a 60-strong editorial board (including three Nobel laureates) and a noble mission—to blunt the cutting edge of scientific research—the journal has 10,000 subscribers. No wonder. Having published such tracts as "Calculating the Velocity of Darkness and its Possible Relevance to Lawn Maintenance" and "The Use of Patient Self-Directed Sham Liposuction Procedures as a Treatment for Anorexia Nervosa," the society is certainly on the edge of something.

It is, as George Scherr, the journal's publisher and editor, agrees, too easy to mock. But much of the society's published research has profound implications. One paper gave a warning that, with over 140 years'–worth of *National Geographic* magazines piling up in American basements (nobody, it was proved, ever throws them away), the continent is in danger of sinking. Another study found that radish seeds watered with holy water did no better than those watered from the tap. Yet another scientific landmark considered the consequences of "Psychotic Visitors to the White House." Only about half the journal's papers are spoofs—the remainder are culled from real scientific journals. The holy radishes and psychotic political groupies fall into the second category.

Fan Clubs, Cat Clubs, and the Institute for Bores

The beauty of America's clubbability is the sheer breadth of interests that it indulges. For those with no hobbies, no hobby-horses, and no hang-ups, for instance, there is the Boring Institute, based in Maplewood, New Jersey, which was set up by Alan Caruba after he concluded from a close examination of the Macy's Thanksgiving Day parade on television that each year's broadcast was in fact a tape of a single, past parade. Or there are a veritable American legion of fan clubs, ranging from Cher'd Interest to the Princess Kitty Fan Club, which celebrates "the smartest cat in the world" (sometimes rumored to be dead), whose newsletter, *Pawprints,* carries "all the mews that's fit to print."

As a last resort, you could simply get together with folk of the same name—so long as they are male. For amidst the International Forum of Alans, the Jim Smith Society, Mikes of America, and Bobs International, there does not seem to be a single association representing Janes, Jills, or Jennifers. And that shows a remarkable curiosity of American societies: most of those signing up are men. This may bode well for American women.

This article appeared in the December 23, 1995–January 5, 1996 issue of *The Economist,* and is reprinted with permission. The Economist Group, Inc. Further reproduction prohibited.

U.S. Societies and Associations

Source: Information Please questionnaires to organizations. Names are listed alphabetically according to key word in title; figure in parentheses is year of founding; other figure is membership.

The following is a partial list selected for general readership interest. A comprehensive listing of approximately 23,000 national and international organizations can be found in the *Encyclopedia of Associations,* 31st ed., 1996, published by Gale Research Company, 835 Penobscot Building, 645 Griswold St., Detroit, Mich. 48226-4049, available in most public libraries.

AARP (American Association of Retired Persons) (1958): 601 E. St. N.W., Washington, D.C. 20049. 32,000,000. Phone: (202) 434-2277.

Abortion Federation, National (1977): 1755 Mass. Ave., Suite 600, Washington, D.C. 20036. Phone: (202) 667-5881 or (800) 772-9100.

Accountants, American Institute of Certified Public (1887): 1211 Avenue of the Americas, New York, N.Y. 10036-8775. 320,000. Phone: (212) 596-6200.

Acoustical Society of America (1929): 500 Sunnyside Blvd., Woodbury, N.Y. 11797. 7,000. Phone: (516) 576-2360.

ACSM: American Congress on Surveying and Mapping (1941): 5410 Grosvenor Lane, Suite 100, Bethesda, Md. 20814. 8,000. Phone: (301) 493-0200.

Actors' Equity Association (1913): 165 W. 46th St., New York, N.Y. 10036. Phone: (212) 869-8530.

Actuaries, Society of (1949): 475 N. Martingale Rd., Suite 800, Schaumburg, Ill. 60173-2226. 16,500. Phone: (847) 706-3500.

Adirondack Mountain Club (1922): 814 Goggins Rd., Lake George, N.Y. 12845-4117. 22,000. Phone: (518) 668-4447.

ADPA/NSIA (American Defense Preparedness Assn./National Security Industrial Assn.) (1919): Two Colonial Place, Suite 400, 2101 Wilson Blvd., Arlington, Va. 22201-3061. 28,000 individual, 900 corporate. Phone: (703) 522-1820.

Aeronautic Association, National (1905): 1815 N. Fort Myer Dr., Suite 700, Arlington, Va. 22209. 300,000. Phone: (703) 527-0226.

Aerospace Industries Association of America Inc. (1919): 1250 Eye St. N.W., Washington, D.C. 20005. 52 companies. Phone: (202) 371-8400.

Aerospace Medical Association (1929): 320 S. Henry St., Alexandria, Va. 22314-3579. 4,000. Phone: (703) 739-2240.

African-American Institute, The (1953): 380 Lexington Ave., New York, N.Y. 10168-4298. Phone: (212) 949-5666.

AFS Intercultural Programs—USA (American Field Service) (1947): 198 Madison Avenue, 8th floor, New York, N.Y. 10016. 100,000. Phone: (212) 949-4242 or (800) AFS-INFO.

Aging Association, American (1970): 2129 Providence Ave., Chester, Pa. 19013. 500. Phone: (610) 874-7550.

Agricultural History Society (1919): 1301 New York Ave. N.W., Washington, D.C. 20005-4788. 1,400. Phone: (202) 219-0786.

Agronomy, American Society of (1907): 677 S. Segoe Rd., Madison, Wis. 53711-1086. 12,300. Phone: (608) 273-8080; fax: (608) 273-2021.

Air & Waste Management Association (1907): One Gateway Center, 3rd Floor, Pittsburgh, Pa. 15222. Phone: (412) 232-3444.

Aircraft Association, Experimental (1953): P.O. Box 3086, Oshkosh, Wis. 54903-3086. 165,000. Phone: (920) 426-4800.

Aircraft Owners and Pilots Association (1939): 421 Aviation Way, Frederick, Md. 21701-4798. 340,000.

Phone: (301) 695-2000; fax: (301) 695-2375; www.aopa.org.

Air Force Association (1946): 1501 Lee Highway, Arlington, Va. 22209-1198. 162,000. Phone: (703) 247-5800.

Air Line Pilots Association (1931): 1625 Massachusetts Ave. N.W., Washington, D.C. 20036 and 535 Herndon Pkwy., Herndon, Va. 20170. 43,000. Phone: (703) 689-2270.

Air Transport Association of America (1936): 1301 Pennsylvania Ave. N.W., Suite 1100, Washington, D.C. 20004-1707. 22 U.S. airlines, 3 airline foreign technical members. Phone: (202) 626-4000.

Al-Anon Family Group Headquarters, Inc. For families and friends of alcoholics. (1951): 1600 Corporate Landing Pkwy., Virginia Beach, Va. 23456-5617. 31,000 groups worldwide. Phone: (757) 563-1600.

Alateen. For children of alcoholics: 1600 Corporate Landing Pkwy., Virginia Beach, Va. 23456-5617. 4,100 groups worldwide. Phone: (800) 356-9996,fax: (757) 563-1655.

Alcoholics Anonymous (1935): General Service Office, A.A. World Services, Inc., 475 Riverside Dr., 11th Floor, New York, N.Y. 10115. 1,800,000. Phone: (212) 870-3400.

Alcoholism and Drug Dependence, National Council on (1944): 12 W. 21st St., New York, N.Y. 10010. 116 affiliates. Phone: (212) 206-6770.

Alcohol Problems, American Council on (1895): 3426 Bridgeland Dr., Bridgeton, Mo. 63044. Phone: (314) 739-5944.

Alexander Graham Bell Association for the Deaf (1890): 3417 Volta Place N.W., Washington, D.C. 20007. 6,200. Phone: (202) 337-5220 V, TTY; e-mail: agbell2@aol.com.

Alzheimer's Association (1980): 919 N. Michigan Ave., Suite 1000, Chicago, Ill. 60611-1676. More than 200 Chapters in all 50 states, over 2,000 Family Support Groups. Phone: (312) 335-8700; toll-free (800) 272-3900.

American Academy of Allergy, Asthma and Immunology (1943): 611 E. Wells St., Milwaukee, Wis. 53202. 5,000. Phone: (414) 272-6071.

American Alliance for Health, Physical Education, Recreation and Dance (1885): 1900 Association Dr., Reston, Va. 20191. 30,000. Phone: (703) 476-3400.

American Antiquarian Society (1812): 185 Salisbury St., Worcester, Mass. 01609. 650. Phone: (508) 755-5221.

American Automobile Association (1902): 1000 AAA Dr., Heathrow, Fla. 32746-5063. Phone: (407) 444-7000.

American Civil Liberties Union (1920): 125 Broad St., 18th Floor, New York, N.Y. 10004. 275,000.

American Contract Bridge League (1927): 2990 Airways Blvd., Memphis, Tenn. 38116-3847. Phone: (901) 332-5586,fax: (901) 398-7754; e-mail: 74431.3434@CompuServe.com.

American Correctional Association (1870): 4380 Forbes Boulevard, Lanham, Md. 20706-4322. 20,000. Phone: (301) 918-1800 or (800) 222-5646; fax: (301) 918-1900; www.corrections.com/aca

American Electroplaters and Surface Finishers Society (AESF) (1909): 12644 Research Pkwy., Orlando, Fla. 32826. 7,500. Phone: (407) 281-6441.

American Federation of Labor and Congress of Industrial Organizations (AFL-CIO) (1955): 815 16th St. N.W., Washington, D.C. 20006. 14,500,000.

Phone: (202) 637-5000.

American Federation of Musicians of the United States and Canada (1896): 1501 Broadway, Suite 600, Paramount Bldg., New York, N.Y. 10036. Phone: (212) 869-1330.

American Forest Foundation (1932): 1111 19th St. N.W., Suite 780, Washington, D.C. 20036. 100. Phone: (202) 463-2462.

American Forests (1875): P.O. Box 2000, Washington, D.C. 20013. 115,000. Phone: (202) 667-3300.

American Foundrymen's Society, Inc. (1896): 505 State St., Des Plaines, Ill. 60016-8399. 13,000. Phone: (847) 824-0181.

American Friends Service Committee (1917): 1501 Cherry St., Philadelphia, Pa. 19102-1479. Phone: (215) 241-7000.

American Geographical Society, The (1871): 120 Wall St., Ste. 100, New York, N.Y. 10005. 1,500. Phone: (212) 422-5456; fax: (212) 422-5480; e-mail: amgeosoc@earthlink.net.

American Geriatrics Society (1942): 770 Lexington Ave., Suite 300, New York, N.Y. 10021. 6,000. Phone: (212) 308-1414; fax: (212) 832-8646; www.americangeriatrics.org.

American Heart Association (1924): 7272 Greenville Ave., Dallas, Tex. 75231-4596. 4,200,000 volunteers. Phone: (800) AHA-USA1.

American Historical Association (1884): 400 A St. S.E., Washington, D.C. 20003. 19,000. Phone: (202) 544-2422; e-mail: aha@theaha.org; www.gmu.edu/chnm/aha.

American Hospital Association (1899): One North Franklin, Chicago, Ill. 60606. 5,000 institutions. Phone: (312) 422-3000.

American Indian Affairs, Association on (1923): Tekakwitha Complex, Agency Road #7, Box 268, Sisseton, S.D. 57262. 40,000. Phone: (605) 698-3998 or 3787.

American Jail Association (1981): 2053 Day Rd., Suite 100, Hagerstown, Md. 21740-9795. 5,000. Phone: (301) 790-3930; fax: (301) 790-2941; www.corrections.com/aja.

American Kennel Club (1884): 51 Madison Ave., New York, N.Y. 10010. 505 member clubs. Phone: (212) 696-8200 or (919) 233-9767 (customer service).

American Legion, The (1919): P.O. Box 1055, Indianapolis, Ind. 46206. 2,900,000. Phone: (317) 630-1200.

American Legion Auxiliary (1919): 777 N. Meridian St., Indianapolis, Ind. 46204. 1,000,000. Phone: (317) 635-6291.

American Mensa, Ltd. (1960): 201 Main St., Suite 1101, Fort Worth, Texas 76102. 50,000. Phone: (817) 332-2600.

American Montessori Society (1960): 281 Park Avenue South, 6th floor, New York, N.Y. 10010. Phone: (212) 358-1250; fax: (212) 358-1256.

American Museum of Natural History (1869): Central Park West at 79th St., New York, N.Y. 10024-5192. 450,000. Phone: (212) 769-5100.

American Philosophical Society (1743): 105 S. 5th St., Philadelphia, Pa. 19106-3386. 584 (resident), 126 (foreign). Phone: (215) 440-3400.

American Planning Association (1909): Administrative Offices: 122 S. Michigan Ave., Chicago, Ill. 60603. 30,000. Phone: (312) 431-9100. Administrative Offices: 1776 Massachusetts Ave. N.W., Washington, D.C. 20036 (headquarters). Phone: (202) 872-0611.

Americans for Democratic Action, Inc. (1947): 1625 K St. N.W., Suite 210, Washington, D.C. 20006. 70,000. Phone: (202) 785-5980.

American Society for Nutritional Sciences (1928): 9650 Rockville Pike, Bethesda, Md. 20814-3990.

3,600. Phone: (301) 530-7050.

American Society for Public Administration (ASPA) (1939): 1120 G St. N.W., Suite 700, Washington, D.C. 20005. 14,000. Phone: (202) 393-7878.

American Society of CLU & ChFC (1928): 270 S. Bryn Mawr Ave., Bryn Mawr, Pa. 19010-2195. Phone: (610) 526-2500.

American Universities, Association of (1900): 1200 New York Avenue NW, Suite 550, Washington, D.C. 20005. Phone: (202) 408-7500.

American Water Resources Association (1964): 950 Herndon Parkway, Ste. 300, Herndon, Va. 20170-5531. 4,000. Phone: (703) 904-1225; fax: (703) 904-1228; e-mail: awrahq@aol.com; www.awra.org/≈awra.

America's Community Bankers (1992): 900 19th St. N.W., Suite 400, Washington, D.C. 20006. Phone: (202) 857-3100.

AMIDEAST (America-Mideast Educational and Training Services) (1951): 1730 M St. N.W., Suite 1100, Washington, D.C. 20036-4505. 192 institutional members. Phone: (202) 776-9600.

Amnesty International/USA (1961): 322 Eighth Ave., New York, N.Y. 10001-4808. 300,000. Phone: (212) 807-8400.

AMVETS (American Veterans of World War II, Korea, and Vietnam) (1944): 4647 Forbes Blvd., Lanham, Md. 20706-4380. 250,000. Phone: (301) 459-9600.

Animal Protection Institute (1968): 2831 Fruitridge Rd., P.O. Box 22505, Sacramento, Calif. 95822. Phone: (916) 731-5521.

Animals, The American Society for the Prevention of Cruelty to (ASPCA) (1866): 424 E. 92nd St., New York, N.Y. 10128. 400,000+. Phone: (212) 876-7700.

Animals, The Fund For, Inc. (1967): 200 W. 57th St., New York, N.Y. 10019. 175,000. Phone: (212) 246-2096.

Animal Welfare Institute (1951): P.O. Box 3650, Washington, D.C. 20007. 4,500. Phone: (202) 337-2332.

Anthropological Association, American (1902): 4350 N. Fairfax Dr., Suite 640, Arlington, Va. 22203-1620. 11,500. Phone: (703) 528-1902.

Anti-Defamation League of B'nai B'rith (1913): 823 United Nations Plaza, New York, N.Y. 10017-3560. Phone: (212) 885-7700.

Anti-Vivisection Society, The American (1883): 801 Old York Rd., #204, Jenkintown, Pa. 19046-1685. 15,000. Phone: (215) 887-0816; fax: (215) 887-2088; e-mail: aavsonline@aol.com; www.aavs.org.

APMI International (1958): 105 College Rd. East, Princeton, N.J. 08540. 2,800. Phone: (609) 452-7700; fax: (609) 987-8523; e-mail: apmi@mpif.org.

Appraisers, American Society of (1936): P.O. Box 17265, Washington, D.C. 20041. 6,500. Phone: (800) ASA-VALU or (703) 478-2228.

Arboriculture, International Society of (1924): P.O. Box GC, Savoy, Ill. 61874-9902. 8,000. Phone: (217) 355-9411; fax (217) 355-9516.

Archaeological Institute of America (1879): 656 Beacon St., Boston, Mass. 02215-2010. 11,000. Phone: (617) 353-9361; e-mail: aia@bu.edu.; csaws.brynmawr.edu:443/aia.html.

Architects, The American Institute of (1857): 1735 New York Ave. N.W., Washington, D.C. 20006-5292. 58,000. Phone: (202) 626-7300.

Architectural Historians, Society of (1940): 1365 N. Astor St., Chicago, Ill. 60610-2144. 4,000. Phone: (312) 573-1365; fax: (312) 573-1141.

Army, Association of the United States (1950): 2425 Wilson Blvd., Arlington, Va. 22210-3385. 111,000. Phone: (703) 841-4300.

Arthritis Foundation (1948): 1330 West Peachtree St., Atlanta, Ga. 30309. 69 local chapters. Phone: (404) 872-7100; (800) 283-7800.

Arts, National Endowment for the (1965): 1100 Pennsylvania Ave. N.W., Washington, D.C. 20506. Phone: (202) 682-5400.

Arts, The American Federation of (1909): 41 E. 65th St., New York, N.Y. 10021. 525+ institutional members (museums), 500+ individual members (patrons). Phone: (212) 988-7700.

Arts and Letters, American Academy of (1898): 633 W. 155th St., New York, N.Y. 10032. 250. Phone: (212) 368-5900.

ASAE—The Society for engineering in agricultural, food, and biological systems (1907): 2950 Niles Rd., St. Joseph, Mich. 49085. 8,5 Phone: (616) 429-0300; fax: (616) 429-3852; e-mail: hq@asae.org; asae.org/

ASM International (1913): Materials Park, Ohio 44073-0002. 44,000. Phone: (216) 338-5151; fax: (216) 338-4634.

Association for Investment Management and Research (1990): 5 Boar's Head Lane, P.O. Box 3668, Charlottesville, Va. 22903. 26,000. Phone: (804) 980-3668.

Astronomical Society, American (1899): Office of Secretary, Dept. of Physics and Astronomy, Louisiana State University, Baton Rouge, La. 70803-4001. 6,300. Phone: (504) 388-1160.

Astronomical Society of the Pacific (1889): 390 Ashton Ave., San Francisco, Calif. 94112. 6,200. Phone: (415) 337-1100.

Atheists, American (1963): 7215 Cameron Rd., Austin, Tex. 78752. 40,000 Families. Phone: (512) 458-1244.

Auctioneers Association, National (1949): 8880 Ballentine, Overland Park, Kan. 66214-1985. 5,900. Phone: (913) 541-8084; fax: (913) 894-5281; e-mail: naahq@aol.com; www.auctioneers.org.

Audubon Society, National (1905): 700 Broadway, New York, N.Y. 10003-9562. 550,000. Phone: (212) 979-3000.

Authors League of America (1912): 330 W. 42nd St., 29th Floor, New York, N.Y. 10036-6902. 14,000. Phone: (212) 564-8350.

Autism Society of America (1965): 7910 Woodmont Ave., Suite 650, Bethesda, Md. 20814. Phone: (301) 657-0881; or (800) 3AUTISM; www.autism-society.org/

Automobile Club, National (1924): Bayside Plaza, 188 The Embarcadero, #300, San Francisco, Calif. 94105. 200,000. Phone: (415) 777-4000.

Automotive Hall of Fame (1939): P.O. Box 1727, Midland, Mich. 48641-1727. Phone: (517) 631-5760.

AZA (American Zoo and Aquarium Association) (1924): Exec. Office/Conservation Center, 7970-D Old Georgetown Rd., Bethesda, Md. 20814-2493. 6,000 individual members, 180 accredited zoo and aquarium facilities. Phone: (310) 907-7777.

Bar Association, American (1878): 750 N. Lake Shore Dr., Chicago, Ill. 60611-4497. 371,000. Phone: (312) 988-5000.

Barber Shop Quartet Singing in America, Society for the Preservation and Encouragement of (SPEBSQSA, Inc.) (1938): 6315 Third Ave., Kenosha, Wis., 53143-5199. 38,000. Phone: (414) 653-8440.

Better Business Bureaus, Council of (1970): 4200 Wilson Blvd., Suite 800, Arlington, Va. 22203-1838. Phone: (703) 276-0100; fax: (703) 525-8277.

Bible Society, American (1816): 1865 Broadway, New York, N.Y. 10023-9980. Phone: (212) 408-1200.

Biblical Literature, Society of (1880): 1201 Clairmont Rd., Suite 300, Decatur, Ga. 30030. 6,500 members, 1,200 subscribers. Phone: (404) 636-4744; fax: (404) 248-0815; or (404) 727-2345 for membership services.

Bibliographical Society of America (1904): P.O. Box 397, Grand Central Station, New York, N.Y. 10163. 1,200. Phone/fax: (212) 647-9171.

Big Brothers Big Sisters of America (1977): 230 N. 13th St., Philadelphia, Pa. 19107. Phone: (215) 567-7000.

Biochemistry and Molecular Biology, American Society for (1906): 9650 Rockville Pike, Bethesda, Md. 20814. 9,600. Phone: (301) 530-7145.

Biological Sciences, American Institute of (1947): 1444 Eye St. N.W., Washington, D.C. 20005. 14,000. Phone: (202) 628-1500.

Blind, American Council of the (1961): 1155 15th St. N.W., Suite 720, Washington, D.C. 20005. 40,000. Phone: (202) 467-5081.

Blind, National Federation of the (1940): 1800 Johnson St., Baltimore, Md. 21230. 50,000. Phone: (410) 659-9314.

Blindness, Research to Prevent (1960): 598 Madison Ave., New York, N.Y. 10022-1010. 1,201. Phone: (212) 752-4333.

Blue Cross and Blue Shield Association (1948 and 1946): 225 N. Michigan Avenue, Chicago, Ill. 60611. 58 Plans. Phone: (312) 297-6000; fax: (312) 297-6009; www.bluecares.com.

B'nai B'rith International (1843): 1640 Rhode Island Ave. N.W., Washington, D.C. 20036-3278. 500,000. Phone: (202) 857-6600.

Booksellers Association, American (1900): 828 So. Broadway, Tarrytown, N.Y. 10591. 8,400. Phone: (914) 591-2665, (800) 637-0037.

Boys & Girls Clubs of America (1906): 1230 West Peachtree St. N.W., Atlanta, Ga., 30309-3447. 2,599,321 youth served. Phone: (404) 815-5700; fax: (404) 815-5757.

Boy Scouts of America (1910): 1325 W. Walnut Hill Lane, P.O. Box 152079, Irving, Tex. 75015-2079. 5,628,806. Phone: (972) 580-2000.

Bridge, Tunnel, and Turnpike Association, International (1932): 2120 L St. N.W., Suite 305, Washington, D.C. 20037-1527. 250. Phone: (202) 659-4620.

Broadcasters, National Association of (1922): 1771 N St. N.W., Washington, D.C. 20036-2891. Phone: (202) 429-5300.

Brookings Institution, The (1916): 1775 Massachusetts Ave. N.W., Washington, D.C. 20036-2188. Phone: (202) 797-6000.

Brooks Bird Club, Inc., The (1932): 423 Warwood Ave., Wheeling, W. Va. 26003. 1,006. Phone: (614) 635-9246.

Business Education Association, National (1946): 1914 Association Dr., Reston, Va. 20191-1596. 16,000. Phone: (703) 860-8300; fax: (703) 620-4483; e-mail: nbea@nbea.org; www.nbea.org/nbea.html.

Business Women's Association, American (1949): 9100 Ward Parkway, P.O. Box 8728, Kansas City, Mo. 64114-0728. 80,000. Phone: (816) 361-6621; fax: (816) 361-4991; e-mail: abwa@sky.net; www.abwahq.org.

Camp Fire Boys and Girls (1910): 4601 Madison Ave., Kansas City, Mo. 64112-1278. 700,000. Phone: (816) 756-1950.

Camping Association, The American (1910): 5000 State Rd. 67 N., Martinsville, Ind. 46151-7902. 5,500. Phone: (317) 342-8456.

Cancer Society, American (1913): 1599 Clifton Rd. N.E., Atlanta, Ga. 30329. Over 2 million volunteers. Phone: (800) ACS-2345 or check local listings.

CARE, Inc. (1945): 151 Ellis St. NE, Atlanta, Ga. 30303-2439. Programs in 61 developing countries. Phone: (404) 681-2552.

Carnegie Endowment for International Peace (1910): 2400 N St. N.W., Washington, D.C. 20037. Phone: (202) 862-7900; fax: (202) 862-2610.

Catholic Charities USA (1910): 1731 King St., Alexandria, Va. 22314. 1,400 agencies and institutions. Phone: (703) 549-1390.

Catholic Daughters of the Americas (1903): 10 W. 71st St., New York, N.Y. 10023. 125,000. Phone: (212) 877-3041.

Catholic Historical Society, American (1884): 263 S. Fourth St., Philadelphia, Pa. 19106. 950. Phone: (215) 925-5752.

Catholic War Veterans of the U.S.A. Inc. (1935): 441 N. Lee St., Alexandria, Va. 22314. 25,000. Phone: (703) 549-3622.

Ceramic Society, The American (1899): P.O. Box 6136, Westerville, Ohio 43081-6136.

Cerebral Palsy Associations, Inc., United (1949): 1660 L St. N.W., Suite 700, Washington, D.C. 20036. 153 affiliates. Phone: (202) 776-0406/TT, (800) 872-5827.

Chamber of Commerce of the U.S. (1912): 1615 H St. N.W., Washington, D.C. 20062-2000. 220,000. Phone: (202) 659-6000.

Chemical Engineers, American Institute of (1908): 345 E. 47th St., New York, N.Y. 10017-2395. 55,000. Phone: (212) 705-7338 or (800) 242-4363.

Chemical Manufacturers Association, Inc. (1872): 1300 Wilson Blvd., Arlington, Va. 22209. 189 companies. Phone: (703) 741-5000.

Chemical Society, American (1876): 1155 16th St. N.W., Washington, D.C. 20036. 151,024. Phone: (202) 872-4600.

Chemists, The American Institute of (1923): 501 Wythe St., Alexandria, Va. 22314-1917. 5,000. Phone: (703) 836-2090; fax: (703) 836-2091; e-mail: TheAIC@aol.com.

Chess Federation, United States (1939): 3054 NYS Rte. 9W, New Windsor, N.Y. 12553. 85,000. Phone: (914) 562-8350/(800) 388-KING; www.uschess.org.

Child Labor Committee, National (1904): 1501 Broadway, Rm. 1111, New York, N.Y. 10036. Phone: (212) 840-1801.

Children's Aid Society, The (1853): 105 E. 22nd St., New York, N.Y. 10010. Child welfare services, community centers, camps, health services, foster care/adoption, and community schools. Phone: (212) 949-4800.

Children's Book Council (1945): 568 Broadway, Suite 404, New York, N.Y. 10012. 77 imprints. Phone: (212) 966-1990; fax: (212) 966-2073; e-mail: staff@cbcbooks.org; www.cbcbooks.org.

Child Welfare League of America (1920): 440 First St. N.W., Suite 310, Washington, D.C. 20001-2085. Phone: (202) 638-2952.

Chiropractic Association, American (1963): 1701 Clarendon Blvd., Arlington, Va. 22209. 19,000. Phone: (703) 276-8800, (800) 986-4636; fax: (703) 243-2593; e-mail: AMERICHIRO@aol.com; www.americhiro.org/ACA

Cities, National League of (1924): 1301 Pennsylvania Ave. N.W., Washington, D.C. 20004. 17,000 cities and towns. Phone: (202) 626-3000.

Civil Air Patrol, National Headquarters (1941): 105 S. Hansell St., Bldg. 714, Maxwell AFB, Ala. 36112-6332. 54,493. Phone: (334) 953-4287.

Civil Engineers, American Society of (1852): 1801 Alexander Bell Dr., Reston, Va. 20191-4400. 120,000. Phone: (800) 548–ASCE (2723).

Clinical Chemistry, Inc., American Association for (1948): 2101 L St. N.W., Suite 202, Washington, D.C. 20037. 11,000. Phone: (202) 857-0717.

Clinical Pathologists, American Society of (1922): 2100 W. Harrison St., Chicago, Ill. 60612-3798.

62,821. Phone: (312) 738-1336; fax: (312) 738-9798.

Collectors Association, American (1939): Box 39106, Minneapolis, Minn. 55439-0106. Over 3,600 debt collection agencies. Phone: (612) 926-6547.

College Board, The (1900): 45 Columbus Ave., New York, N.Y. 10023-6992. 2,900 institutions. Phone: (212) 713-8000.

The College Fund/UNCF (1944): 8260 Willow Oaks Corporate Dr., P.O. Box 10444, Fairfax, Va. 22031-4511. Phone: (703) 205-3400; fax: (703) 205-3576.

Colleges and Employers, National Association of (formerly College Placement Council) (1956): 62 E. Highland Ave., Bethlehem, Pa. 18017. 3,200. Phone: (610) 868-1421.

Common Cause (1970): 1250 Connecticut Ave. N.W., Washington, D.C. 20036. 250,000. Phone: (202) 833-1200; fax: (202) 659-3716; www.commoncause.org.

Community Colleges, American Association of (1920): One Dupont Circle N.W., Suite 410, Washington, D.C. 20036-1176. 1,100 institutions. Phone: (202) 728-0200.

Community Cultural Center Association, American (1978): 149 Cannongate III, Nashua, N.H. 03063. Phone: (603) 886-2748.

Composer/USA, National Association of (1932): P.O. Box 49256, Barrington Station, Los Angeles, Calif. 90049. 550. Phone: (310) 541-8213.

Congress of Racial Equality (CORE) (1942): 30 Cooper Square, New York, N.Y. 10003. Nationwide network of chapters. Phone: (212) 598-4000; fax: (212) 598-4000.

Conscientious Objectors, Central Committee for (1948): 1515 Cherry St., Philadelphia, Pa. 19102. Phone: (215) 563-8787; 655 Sutter St., Suite 514, San Francisco, Calif. 94102. Phone: (415) 474-3002.

Conservation Engineers, Association of (1961): Attn: Jim Price, Secretary, c/o Arkansas Game & Fish Commission, #2 Natural Resources Drive, Little Rock, Ark. 72205.

Consulting Chemists & Chemical Engineers, Inc., Association of (1928): The Chemists Club, 40 W. 45th St., New York, N.Y. 10036. 130. Phone: (212) 983-3160; fax: (212) 983-3161; e-mail: 104206.1620@compuserve.com; www.wwwprovider.com/chem/

Consumer Federation of America (1968): 1424 16th St. N.W., Suit 604, Washington, D.C. 20036. 240 member organizations. Phone: (202) 387-6121.

Consumer Interests, American Council on (1953): 240 Stanley Hall, Univ. of Missouri, Columbia, Mo. 65211. 1,500. Phone: (573) 882-3817.

Consumers League, National (1899): 1701 K St. N.W., Suite 1200, Washington, D.C. 20006. Phone: (202) 835-3323.

Consumers Union (1936): 101 Truman Ave., Yonkers, N.Y. 10703-1057. 4.6 million subscribers to *Consumer Reports Magazine.* Phone: (914) 378-2000.

Counselors, American College of (1984): 8038 Camellia Lane, Indianapolis, Ind. 46219. Phone: (317) 898-3211.

Country Music Association (1958): One Music Circle South, Nashville, Tenn. 37203. 7,000+. Phone: (615) 244-2840.

Credit Management, National Association of (1896): 8815 Centre Park Dr., Suite 200, Columbia, Md. 21045. Phone: (410) 740-5560.

Credit Union National Association (1934): P.O. Box 431, Madison, Wis. 53701. 51 state leagues representing 12,400 credit unions. Phone: (608) 231-4000.

Crime and Delinquency, National Council on (1907): 685 Market St., #620, San Francisco, Calif. 94105.

Criminal justice research, nationwide membership. Phone: (415) 896-6223.

CSA/USA, Celiac Sprue Association/United States of America, Inc., P.O. Box 31700, Omaha, Neb. 68131-0700. 6 regions in U.S., 74 chapters, 36 active resource units. Phone: (402) 558-0600; fax: (402) 558-1347.

Dairy Council, National (1915): 10255 W. Higgins Rd., Suite 900 Rosemont, Ill. 60018-5616. Phone: (847) 803-2000; fax: (847) 803-2077.

Daughters of the American Revolution, National Society (1890): 1776 D St. N.W., Washington, D.C. 20006. 200,000. Phone: (202) 628-1776.

Deaf, National Association of the (1880): 814 Thayer Ave., Silver Spring, Md. 20910. Phone: (301) 587-1788 V; (301) 587-1789 TTY.

Defenders of Wildlife (1947): 1101 14th St. N.W., #1400, Washington, D.C. 20005. 200,000 members and supporters. Phone: (202) 682-9400.

Dental Association, American (1859): 211 E. Chicago Ave., Chicago, Ill. 60611. 140,000. Phone: (312) 440-2500.

Diabetes Association, American (1940): 1660 Duke St., Alexandria, Va. 22314. Phone: (703) 549-1500.

Dignity (1969): 1500 Massachusetts Ave. N.W., Suite 11, Washington, D.C. 20005. 5,000. Phone: (202) 861-0017 and (800) 877-8797.

Disabled American Veterans (1920): 807 Maine Ave. S.W., Washington, D.C. 20024. 1,400,000. Phone: (202) 554-3501.

Dowsers, Inc., The American Society of (1961): P.O. Box 24, Danville, Vt. 05828-0024. 5,000. Phone: (802) 684-3417; fax: (802) 748-8565; e-mail: ASD@dowsers.org; www.newhampshire.com/dowsers.org.

Drug, Chemical & Allied Trades Association, Inc., The (1890): 2 Roosevelt Ave., Suite 301; Syosset, N.Y. 11791. 3,060. Phone: (516) 496-3317.

Ducks Unlimited, Inc. (1937): One Waterfowl Way, Memphis, Tenn. 38120. 600,000. Phone: (901) 758-3825.

Earthwatch (1972): 680 Mt. Auburn St., Box 403N, Watertown, Mass. 02272. 75,000. Phone: (800) 776-0188.

Eastern Star, Order of, General Grand Chapter (1876): 1618 New Hampshire Ave. N.W., Washington, D.C. 20009. 1,207,301. Phone: (202) 667-4737.

Easter Seal Society, The National (1919): 230 W. Monroe, 18th Floor, Chicago, Ill. 60606-4802. 106 state and local affiliate societies operating 409 service sites. Phone: (800) 221-6827 and (312) 726-4258 TDD.

Economic Association, American (1885): 2014 Broadway, Suite 305, Nashville, Tenn. 37203-2418. 21,000. 6,000 inst. subscribers. Phone: (615) 322-2595.

Economic Development, Committee for (1942): 477 Madison Ave., New York, N.Y. 10022. 250 trustees. Phone: (212) 688-2063.

Edison Electric Institute (1933): 701 Pennsylvania Ave. N.W., Washington, D.C. 20004-2696.

Education, American Council on (ACE), (1918): One Dupont Circle N.W., Washington, D.C. 20036-1193. Membership includes more than 1,600 accredited, degree-granting college and universities and more than 200 national and regional higher education associations. Phone: (202) 939-9300.

Education, Council for Advancement and Support of (CASE) (1974): 11 Dupont Circle N.W., Suite 400, Washington, D.C. 20036-1261. 2,950 institutions; 15,289 individuals. Phone: (202) 328-5900.

Educational Exchange, International, Council on (1947): 205 E. 42nd St., New York, N.Y. 10017. 265. Phone: (212) 822-2600.

Educational Research Association, American (1916): 1230 17th St. N.W., Washington, D.C. 20036. 22,000. Phone: (202) 223-9485.

Education Association, National (1857): 1201 16th St. N.W., Washington, D.C. 20036-3290. 2.2 million. Phone: (202) 833-4000.

Electrochemical Society, The (1902): 10 S. Main St., Pennington, N.J. 08534-2896. 7,000. Phone: (609) 737-1902; fax: (609) 737-2743; e-mail: ecs@electrochem.org; electrochem.org.

Electronic Industries Association (1924): 2500 Wilson Blvd., Arlington, Va. 22201. 1,350 member companies. Phone: (703) 907-7500.

Elks of the U.S.A., Benevolent and Protective Order of the (1868): 2750 N. Lakeview Ave., Chicago, Ill. 60614. 1,300,000. Phone: (773) 477-2750.

Energy Engineers, Association of (1977): 4025 Pleasantdale Rd., Suite 420, Atlanta, Ga. 30340. 8,500. Phone: (770) 447-5083 ext. 210; fax: (770) 446-3969; e-mail: info@aeecenter.org; www.aeecenter.org.

Engineering Science & Mechanics, Dept. of, Virginia Polytechnic Institute & State Univ., Blacksburg, Va. 24061-0219. Phone: (540) 231-6651; fax: (540) 231-4574; www.esm.vt.edu/esm.html.

English-Speaking Union of the United States (1920): 16 E. 69th St., New York, N.Y. 10021. 18,000. Phone: (212) 879-6800.

Entomological Society of America (1889): 9301 Annapolis Rd., Lanham, Md. 20706-3115. 8,500. Phone: (301) 731-4535; fax: (301) 731-4538; e-mail: esa@entsoc.org; www.entsoc.org.

Esperanto League for North America, The (1952): P.O. Box 1129, El Cerrito, Calif. 94530. Over 1,000. Phone: (800) 377-3726.

Exceptional Children, The Council for (1922): 1920 Association Dr., Reston, Va. 20191-1589. 54,000. Voice phone: (703) 620-3660; TTY: (703) 264-9446; fax: (703) 264-9494; e-mail: cec@cec.sped.org; www.cec.sped.org.

Experimental Test Pilots, The Society of (1956): 44814 Elm St., Lancaster, Calif. 93534. 1,950. Phone: (805) 942-9574.

Exploration Geophysicists, Society of (1930): P.O. Box 702740, Tulsa, Okla. 74170-2740. 14,500. Phone: (918) 497-5500.

Family and Consumer Sciences, American Association of (1909): 1555 King St., Alexandria, Va. 22314. 20,000. Phone: (703) 706-4600.

Family Campers & RVers (1949): 4804 Transit Rd., Bldg. 2, Depew, N.Y. 14043-4906. 15,000 families. Phone: (716) 668-6242; fax: (716) 668-6242.

Family Physicians, American Academy of (1947): 8880 Ward Pkwy., Kansas City, Mo. 64114-2797. 80,000. Phone: (816) 333-9700.

Family Relations, National Council on (1938): 3989 Central Ave. N.E., #550, Minneapolis, Minn. 55421-3921. 3,800. Phone: (612) 781-9331.

Family Service America, Inc. (1911): 11700 W. Lake Park Dr., Park Place, Milwaukee, Wis. 53224. Approximately 280 member agencies. Phone: (414) 359-1040 or (800) 221-2681.

Farm Bureau Federation, American (1919): 225 Touhy Ave., Park Ridge, Ill. 60068. 4.8 million member families. Phone: (847) 685-8600.

Federal Bar Association (1920): 1815 H St. N.W., Suite 408, Washington, D.C. 20006-3697. 15,000. Phone: (202) 638-0252; fax: (202) 775-0295.

Federal Employees, National Federation of (1917): 1016 16th St. N.W., Washington, D.C. 20036. Rep. 150,000. Phone: (202) 862-4400.

Feline and Canine Friends, Inc. (1973): 505 N. Bush St., Anaheim, Calif. 92805. 500. Phone: (714) 635-7975.

Fellowship of Reconciliation (1915): Box 271, Nyack, N.Y. 10960. 20,000. Phone: (914) 358-4601.

Female Executives, National Association for (1972): 30 Irving Place, New York, N.Y. 10003. 200,000. Phone: (212) 477-2200.

FFA Organization, National (1928): 5632 Mt. Vernon Memorial Hwy., P.O. Box 15160, Alexandria, Va. 22309-0160. 401,574. Phone: (703) 360-3600.

Fire Protection Association, National (1896): One Batterymarch Park, P.O. Box 9101, Quincy, Mass. 02269-9101. 68,000. Phone: (617) 770-3000.

Flag Foundation, National (1968): Flag Plaza, Pittsburgh, Pa. 15219-3630. 3,000+. Phone: (412) 261-1776.

Fleet Reserve Association (1924): 125 N. West St., Alexandria, Va. 22314-2754. 162,000. Phone: (703) 683-1400/(800) 372-1924; e-mail: news-fra@fra.org; www.fra.org/fra/

Flight Test Engineers, Society of (1968): P.O. Box 4047, Lancaster, Calif. 93539-4047. 1,000. Phone: (805) 538-9715.

Foreign Policy Association (1918): 470 Park Ave. So., New York, N.Y. 10016. Phone: (212) 481-8100/ (800) 628-5754.

Foreign Relations, Council on (1921): 58 E. 68th St., New York, N.Y. 10021. 2,600. Phone: (212) 734-0400.

Foreign Study, American Institute for (1965): 102 Greenwich Ave., Greenwich, Conn. 06830. Phone: (203) 869-9090/(800) 727-AIFS.

Foreign Trade Council, Inc., National (1914): 1270 Avenue of the Americas, New York, N.Y. 10020-1702. Over 550 companies. Phone: (212) 399-7128. Also, 1625 K St. N.W., Washington, D.C. 20006. Phone: (202) 887-0278.

Forensic Sciences, American Academy of (1948): 410 N. 21st St., Suite 203/80904, P.O. Box 669, Colorado Springs, Colo. 80901-0669. 4,315. Phone: (719) 636-1100; fax: (719) 636-1993; www.aafs.org.

Foresters, Society of American (1900): 5400 Grosvenor Lane, Bethesda, Md. 20814-2198. 19,000. Phone: (301) 897-8720.

4-H Program (early 1900s): Room 3441-S, U.S. Department of Agriculture, Washington, D.C. 20250. 5.6 million. Phone: (202) 720-2908.

Freedom of Information Center (1958): 127 Neff Annex, Univ. of Missouri, Columbia, Mo. 65211. Phone: (573) 882-4856.; e-mail: jourke@muccmail.missouri.edu; www.missouri.edu/~foiwww.

French-American Chamber of Commerce (1896): 1350 Ave. of the Americas, New York, N.Y. 10019. 605. Membership Association. Phone: (212) 765-4460.

French Institute/Alliance Française (1898): 22 E. 60th St., New York, N.Y. 10022-1077. 9,000. Phone: (212) 355-6100; www.fiaf.org.

Friendship and Good Will, International Society of (1978): 908 Hogan Way, Bakersfield, Calif. 93309. 4,117 members in 189 countries. Phone: (805) 836-0692.

Friends of Animals Inc. (1957): 777 Post Rd., Suite 205, Darien, Conn. 06820. 120,000. Phone: (203) 656-1522.

Friends of the Earth (1969): 1025 Vermont Ave. N.W., Suite 300, Washington, D.C. 20005. 35,000. Phone: (202) 783-7400.

Future Homemakers of America, Inc. (1945): 1910 Association Dr., Reston, Va. 20191. 250,000. Phone: (703) 476-4900.

Gamblers Anonymous: Box 17173, Los Angeles, Calif. 90017. Phone: (213) 386-8789.

Gay and Lesbian Task Force, National (1973): 2320 17th St. N.W., Washington, D.C. 20009-2702. 35,000 members. Phone: (202) 332-6483.

Genealogical Society, National (1903): 4527 17th St. N., Arlington, Va. 22207-2399. 18,000. Phone: (703) 525-0050; fax: (703) 525-0052; geneaology.org/ngs/

Genetic Association, American (1903): P.O. Box 257, Buckeystown, Md. 21717. 800. Phone/fax: (301) 695-9292.

Geographers, Association of American (1904): 1710 16th St. N.W., Washington, D.C. 20009-3198. 7,400. Phone: (202) 234-1450; fax: (202) 234-2744; e-mail: gaia@aag.org; www.aag.org.

Geographic Education, National Council for (1915): 16A Leonard Hall, Indiana University of Pennsylvania, Indiana, Pa. 15705. 3,700. Phone: (412) 357-6290.

Geographic Society, National (1888): 1145 17th St. N.W., Washington, D.C. 20036. 9,200,000. Phone: (202) 857-7000.

Geological Institute, American (1948): 4220 King St., Alexandria, Va. 22302-1502. 30 geoscience societies representing 100,000 geoscientists. Phone: (703) 379-2480; www.agiweb.org/.

Geological Society of America, Inc. (1888): 3300 Penrose Pl., P.O. Box 9140, Boulder, Colo. 80301. 15,000. Phone: (303) 447-2020.

German American National Congress, The (Deutsch-Amerikanischer National Kongress—D.A.N.K.) (1958): 4740 N. Western Ave., Executive Office, Chicago, Ill. 60625-2013. Phone: (773) 275-1100.

Gideons International, The (1889): 2900 Lebanon Rd., Nashville, Tenn. 37214-0800. 125,000. Phone: (615) 883-8533.

Gifted, The Association for the (1958): The Council for Exceptional Children, 1920 Association Dr., Reston, Va. 20191-1589. 2,200. Phone: (703) 620-3660.

Girl Scouts of the U.S.A. (1912): 420 Fifth Ave., New York N.Y. 10018. 3,500,000. Phone: (212) 852-8000.

Girls Incorporated (1945): 30 E. 33rd St., New York, N.Y. 10016. 350,000. Phone: (212) 689-3700; www-.girlsinc.org.

Graphoanalysis Society, International (1929): 111 N. Canal St., Chicago, Ill. 60606. 10,000. Phone: (312) 930-9446.

Gray Panthers (1970): P.O. Box 21477, Washington, D.C. 20009-9477. Over 50 chapters (networks). Phone: (202) 466-3132.

Greenpeace (1971): 1436 U St. N.W., Washington, D.C. 20009. 600,000. Phone: (202) 462-1177.

Group Psychotherapy Association, American (1942): 25 E. 21st St., 6th Floor, New York, N.Y. 10010. 4,400 Phone: (212) 477-2677, fax: (212) 979-6627.

Guide Dog Foundation for the Blind, Inc. (1946): 371 E. Jericho Turnpike, Smithtown, N.Y. 11787-2976. 100,000. Phone: (516) 265-2121; (800) 548-4337; fax: (516) 361-5192.

Hadassah, The Women's Zionist Organization of America (1912): 50 W. 58th St., New York, N.Y. 10019. 385,000. Phone: (212) 355-7900.

Handgun Control, Inc. (1974): 1225 Eye St. N.W., Washington, D.C. 20005. 400,000. Phone: (202) 898-0792.

Heating, Refrigerating and Air-Conditioning Engineers, Inc., American Society of (1894): 1791 Tullie Circle N.E., Atlanta, Ga. 30329. 50,000. Phone: (404) 636-8400; www.ashrae.org.

Helicopter Association International (1948): 1635 Prince St., Alexandria, Va. 22314. Phone: (703) 683-4646; fax: (703) 683-4745; www.rotor.com.

Hemispheric Affairs, Council on (1975): 724 9th St. N.W., Rm. 401, Washington, D.C. 20001. Phone: (202) 393-3322.

Historians, The Organization of American (1907): Indiana Univ., 112 N. Bryan St., Bloomington, Ind. 47408. 12,000. Phone: (812) 855-7311.

Historic Preservation, National Trust for (1949): 1785 Massachusetts Ave. N.W., Washington, D.C. 20036. 270,000. Phone: (202) 588-6000.

Horse Council, Inc., American (1969): 1700 K St. N.W., #300, Washington, D.C. 20006. More than 190 organizations and 2,400 individuals. Phone: (202) 296-4031.

Horse Shows Association, Inc., American (1917): 220 E. 42nd St., New York, N.Y. 10017-5876. 65,000. Phone: (212) 972-2472.

Horticultural Association, National Junior (1935): 1424 N. 8th, Durant, Okla. 74701. 12,500. Phone: (405) 924-0771.

Horticultural Society, American (1922): 7931 East Boulevard Dr., Alexandria, Va. 22308. 22,000. Phone: (703) 768-5700 or (800) 777-7931; fax: (703) 768-8700; e-mail: gardenahs@aol.com

Hostelling International—American Youth Hostels (1934): 733 15th St. N.W., Suite 840, Washington, D.C. 20005. 124,000. Phone: (202) 783-6161 for membership and reservations.

Housing Science, International Association for (1972): P.O. Box 340254, Coral Gables/Miami, Fla. 33114. 500 professionals. Member, United Nations ECOSOC, New York. Phone: (305) 446-9462.

Humane Association, American (1877): 63 Inverness Drive East, Englewood, Colo. 80112-5117. Phone: (303) 792-9900.

Humane Association, The American—Children's Division (1877): 63 Inverness Drive East, Englewood, Colo. 80112. Phone: (303) 792-9900; fax: (303) 792-5333.; e-mail: children@amerhumane.org.

Humane Society of the United States (1954): 2100 L St. N.W., Washington, D.C. 20037. 3,100,000. Phone: (202) 452-1100.

Humanities, National Endowment for the (1965): 1100 Pennsylvania Ave. N.W., Washington, D.C. 20506. Phone: (202) 606-8400.

Hydrogen Energy, International Association for (1975): P.O. Box 248266, Coral Gables, Fla. 33124. 2,500. Phone: (305) 284-4666.

Illustrators, Society of (1901): 128 E. 63rd St., New York, N.Y. 10021. 865. Phone: (212) 838-2560 .

Industrial Engineers, Institute of (1948): 25 Technology Park/Atlanta, Norcross, Ga. 30092. 24,000. Phone: (770) 449-0461.

Interfraternity Conference, National (1909): 3901 W. 86th St., Suite 390, Indianapolis, Ind. 46268-1791. 64. Phone: (317) 872-1112.

International Credit Association (ICA) (1912): P.O. Box 419057, St. Louis, Mo. 63141-1757. 7,500 members, 100 local associations. Phone: (314) 991-3030; fax: (314) 991-3029; e-mail: icahdqtrs@stlnet.com; www.ica-credit.org.

Iron and Steel Institute, American (1908): 1101 17th St. N.W., Washington, D.C. 20036-4700. 1,200. Phone: (202) 452-7100.

Izaak Walton League of America (1922): 707 Conservation Lane, Gaithersburg, Md. 20878-2983. 50,000. Phone: (301) 548-0150.

Jewish Community Centers, World Confederation of (1946): 12 Hess St., Jerusalem, Israel 94185. Phone: (02) 625-1265, fax: (02) 624-7767.

Jewish Community Centers Association (JCC) of North America (1917): 15 E. 26th St., New York, N.Y. 10010-1579. 281 affiliated Jewish Community Centers, YM-YWHAs, and camps serving 1 million+ members. Phone: (212) 532-4949; fax: (212) 481-4174; e-mail: info@jcca.org.

Jewish Congress, American (1918): 15 E. 84th St., New York, N.Y. 10028. 50,000. Phone: (212) 879-4500.

Jewish Historical Society, American (1892): 2 Thornton Rd., Waltham, Mass. 02154. 3,500. Phone: (617) 891-8110; fax: (617) 899-9208; e-mail: ajhs@ajhs.org; www.ajhs.org.

Jewish War Veterans of the U.S.A. (1896): 1811 R St. N.W., Washington, D.C. 20009-1659. Phone: (202) 265-6280.

Jewish Women, National Council of (1893): 53 W. 23rd St., New York, N.Y. 10010. 90,000. Phone: (212) 645-4048; fax: (212) 645-7466.

John Birch Society (1958): P.O. Box 8040, Appleton, Wis. 54913. Under 100,000. Phone: (414) 749-3780; fax: (414) 749-5062; www.jbs.org.

Journalists, Society of Professional, (1909): 16 S. Jackson, Greencastle, Ind. 46135. 13,500. Phone: (765) 653-3333.

Journalists and Authors, American Society of (1948): 1501 Broadway, Suite 302, New York, N.Y. 10036. 1,000+. Phone: (212) 997-0947; fax: (212) 768-7414; e-mail: ASJA@compuserve.com.

Judaism, American Council for (1943): P.O. Box 9009, Alexandria, Va. 22304. 10,000. Phone: (703) 836-2546.

Junior Achievement Inc. (1919): One Education Way, Colorado Springs, Colo. 80906-4477. 2.3 million. Phone: (719) 540-8000.

Junior Chamber of Commerce, The United States, Jaycees (1920): P.O. Box 7, Tulsa, Okla. 74102-0007. 132,000. Phone: (918) 584-2481; fax: (918) 584-4422.

Junior Leagues International, Inc., Association of (1921): 660 First Ave., New York, N.Y. 10016-3241. 293 Leagues, 200,000 members. Phone: (212) 683-1515.

Junior Statesmen of America (1934): 60 E. Third Ave., Suite 320, San Mateo, Calif. 94401. 15,000. Phone: (415) 347-1600 or (800) 334-5353.

Kiwanis International (1915): 3636 Woodview Trace, Indianapolis, Ind. 46268-3196. 316,000. Phone: (317) 875-8755; e-mail: kiwanismail@kiwanis.org.

Knights of Columbus (1882): One Columbus Plaza, New Haven, Conn. 06510-3326. 1,570,743. Phone: (203) 772-2130.

Knights Templar, Grand Encampment of (1816): 5097 N. Elston Ave., Suite 101, Chicago, Ill. 60630-2460. 220,000. Phone: (773) 777-3300.

La Leche League International (1956): 1400 N. Meacham Rd., P.O. Box 4079, Schaumburg, Ill. 60168-4079. 50,000. Phone: (847) 519-7730.

Law, American Society of International (1906): 2223 Massachusetts Ave. N.W., Washington, D.C. 20008. 4,300. Phone: (202) 939-6000.

League of Women Voters of the U.S. (1920): 1730 M St. N.W., Washington, D.C. 20036. Phone: (202) 429-1965; fax: (202) 429-0854.

Legal Aid and Defender Association, National (1911): 1625 K St. N.W., Suite 800, Washington, D.C. 20006. 2,400. Phone: (202) 452-0620.

Legal Secretaries, National Association of (1950): 2448 E. 81st St., Ste. 3400, Tulsa, Okla. 74137. 12,000. Phone: (918) 493-3540.

Leukemia Society of America (1949): 600 Third Ave., 4th Floor, New York, N.Y. 10016. Phone: (212) 573-8484.

Library Association, American (1876): 50 E. Huron St., Chicago, Ill. 60611. 56,688. Phone: (312) 944-6780; (800) 545-2433

Life Insurance, American Council of (1976): 1001 Pennsylvania Ave. N.W., Washington, D.C. 20004-2599. 606. Phone: (202) 624-2000.

Life Underwriters, National Association of (1890): 1922 F St. N.W., Washington, D.C. 20006-4387. Phone: (202) 331-6000.

Lions Clubs International (1917): 300 22nd St., Oak Brook, Ill. 60521-8842. 1,419,408. Phone: (708) 571-5466.

Lung Association, American (1904): 1740 Broadway, New York, N.Y. 10019-4374. 99 constituent and affiliate associations. Phone: (800) LUNG-USA/(800) 586-4872.

Magazine Editors, American Society of (1963): 919 Third Ave., 22nd Floor, New York, N.Y. 10022. 800. Phone: (212) 872-3700.

Magazine Publishers of America (1919): 919 Third Ave., New York, N.Y. 10022. 334 companies, 1,200+ publications. Phone: (212) 872-3700.

Management Accountants, Institute of (1919): 10 Paragon Dr., Montvale, N.J. 07645-1760. 80,000. Phone: (201) 573-9000.

Management Association, American (1923): 1601 Broadway, New York, N.Y. 10019-7420. 70,000. Phone: (212) 586-8100.

Management Consultants, Institute of (1968): 521 Fifth Ave., 35th Floor, New York, N.Y. 10175-3598. 2,600 individuals. Phone: (212) 697-8262.

Management Consulting Firms, Association of—ACME (1929): 521 Fifth Ave., 35th Floor, New York, N.Y. 10175-3598. 50 firms international. Phone: (212) 697-9693.

Manufacturers, National Association of (1895): 1331 Pennsylvania Ave. N.W., Washington, D.C. 20004-1790. Approx. 14,000. Phone: (202) 637-3000.

Manufacturers' Agents National Association (MANA) (1947): 23016 Mill Creek Rd., P.O. Box 3467, Laguna Hills, Calif. 92654-3467. 7,000. Phone: (714) 859-4040.

March of Dimes Birth Defects Foundation (1938): 1275 Mamaroneck Ave., White Plains, N.Y. 10605. 104 chapters. Phone: (914) 428-7100, (888) 663-4637; tty: (914) 997-4764; fax: (914) 997-4763; e-mail: resourcecenter@modimes.org; www-.modimes.org.

Marine Conservation, Center for (1972): 1725 De Sales St. N.W., Suite 600, Washington, D.C. 20036. 120,000. Phone: (202) 429-5609.

Marine Corps Association (1913): P.O. Box 1775, 715 Broadway, Quantico, Va. 22134. 100,723. Phone: (703) 640-6161/(800) 336-0291.

Marine Corps League (1937): 8626 Lee Hwy., Suite 201, Fairfax, Va. 22031. Correspondence address: P.O. Box 3070, Merrifield, Va. 22116-3070. 44,000. Phone: (703) 207-9588 or (703) 207-9589; fax: (703) 207-0047.

Marine Technology Society (1963): 1828 L St. N.W., Suite 906, Washington, D.C. 20036-5104. 2,700. Phone: (202) 775-5966; fax: (202) 429-9417.

Masons, Ancient and Accepted Scottish Rite, Northern Masonic Jurisdiction, Supreme Council 33 (1813): 33 Marrett Rd., Lexington, Mass. 02173. 333,709. Phone: (617) 862-4410; world.std.com/~sysmgr.

Masons, Ancient and Accepted Scottish Rite, Southern Jurisdiction, Supreme Council (1801): 1733 16th St. N.W., Washington, D.C. 20009. 500,000. Phone: (202) 232-3579.

Masons, Royal Arch, General Grand Chapter International (1797): P.O. Box 489, Danville, Ky. 40423-0489. 230,000. Phone: (606) 236-0757.

Massachusetts Audubon Society (1896): 208 South Great Rd., Lincoln, Mass. 01773. 55,000 member households, 36 wildlife sanctuaries open to the public. Phone: (800) AUDUBON.

Mathematical Association of America (1915): 1529 18th St. N.W., Washington, D.C. 20036. 29,000.

Phone: (202) 387-5200.

Mathematical Society, American (1888): P.O. Box 6248, Providence, R.I. 02940-6248. 29,350. Phone: (401) 455-4000; e-mail: ams@ams.org; www.ams.org/

Mathematical Statistics, Institute of (1935): 3401 Investment Blvd. #7, Hayward, Calif. 94545-3819. 4,000. Phone: (510) 783-8141; fax: (510) 783-4131; e-mail: ims@stat.berkeley.edu.

Mayflower Descendants, General Society of (1897): 4 Winslow St., P.O. Box 3297, Plymouth, Mass. 02361. 25,000. Phone: (508) 746-3188.

Mechanical Engineers, American Society of (1880): 345 E. 47th St., New York, N.Y. 10017. 125,000. Phone: (212) 705-7722.

Mechanics, American Academy of (1969): Dept. of Engineering Science & Mechanics, VPI & State University, Blacksburg, Va. 24061-0219. 1,600. Phone: (540) 231-6841.

Medical Association, American (1847): 515 N. State St., Chicago, Ill. 60610-4377. Phone: (312) 464-5000.

Medical Library Association (1898): Six N. Michigan Ave., Suite 300, Chicago, Ill. 60602. 5,000. Phone: (312) 419-9094.

Mental Health Association, National (1909): 1021 Prince St., Alexandria, Va., 22314-2971. 1,000,000. Phone: (703) 684-7722; 800-969-NMHA; TDD 800-433-5959; fax: (703) 684-5968; www.nmha.org, nmhainfo@aol.com.

Meteorological Society, American (1919): 45 Beacon St., Boston, Mass. 02108-3693. 11,000. Phone: (617) 227-2425.

Military Chaplains Association of the U.S.A. (1925): P.O. Box 42660, Washington, D.C. 20015-0660. 1,500. Phone: (202) 574-2423.

Mining, Metallurgical, and Petroleum Engineers, The American Institute of (1871): 345 E. 47th St., New York, N.Y. 10017. 4 Member Societies: Society for Mining, Metallurgy and Exploration, The Minerals, Metals & Materials Society, Iron & Steel Society, Society of Petroleum Engineers. Phone: (212) 705-7695; fax: (212) 371-5622; e-mail: AIME NY@aol.com; www.idis.com/aime.

Mining and Metallurgical Society of America (1910): 9 Escalle Lane, Larkspur, Calif. 94939. 370. Phone: (415) 924-7441.

Model Aeronautics, Academy of (1936): 5151 East Memorial Dr., Muncie, Ind. 47302. 160,000. Phone: (765) 287-1256.

Modern Language Association of America (1883): 10 Astor Place, New York, N.Y. 10003. 32,000. Phone: (212) 475-9500.

Modern Woodmen of America (1883): 1701 1st Ave., Rock Island, Ill. 61201. 756,392. Phone: (309) 786-6481.

Moose International, Inc. (1888): Mooseheart, Ill. 60539. 1,700,000. Phone: (630) 859-2000.

Mothers Against Drunk Driving (MADD) (1980): 511 E. John Carpenter Frwy., Suite 700, Irving, Tex. 75062-8187. 3.2 million members and supporters. Phone: (214) 744-6233; victim hotline: (800) GET-MADD.

Motion Picture & Television Engineers, Society of (1916): 595 W. Hartsdale Ave., White Plains, N.Y. 10607. 9,500. Phone: (914) 761-1100; fax: (914) 761-3115.

Motion Picture Arts & Sciences, Academy of (1927): 8949 Wilshire Blvd., Beverly Hills, Calif. 90211-1972. Phone: (310) 247-3000.

Multiple Sclerosis Society, National (1946): 733 Third Ave., New York, N.Y. 10017-3288. 400,000. Phone: (212) 986-3240/(800) FIGHT-MS (344-4867).

Muscular Dystrophy Association (1950): 3300 East Sunrise Dr., Tucson, Ariz. 85718. 2,300,000 volunteers. Phone: (520) 529-2000.

Museums, American Association of (1906): 1575 I St., NW, Suite 400, Washington, D.C. 20005. 15,000. Phone: (202) 289-1818; fax: (202) 289-6578, tty: (202) 289-8439.

Muzzle Loading Rifle Association, National (1933): P.O. Box 67, Friendship, Ind. 47021. 25,000. Phone: (812) 667-5131.

NAFSA: Association of International Educators (1948): 1875 Connecticut Ave. N.W., Suite 1000, Washington, D.C. 20009-5728. 7,500. Phone: (202) 462-4811.

National Abortion and Reproductive Rights Action League (NARAL) (1969): 1156 15th St. N.W., Washington, D.C. 20005. 250,000. Phone: (202) 973-3000

National Association for the Advancement of Colored People (1909): 4805 Mt. Hope Dr., Baltimore, Md. 21215-3297. 500,000+. Phone: (410) 358-8900.

National Audubon Society (1905): 700 Broadway, New York, N.Y. 10003-9501. 550,000. Phone: (212) 979-3000.

National Conference, The (founded as The Natl. Conf. of Christians & Jews) (1927): 71 Fifth Ave., New York, N.Y. 10003. Phone: (212) 206-0006.

National Cooperative Business Association (formerly Cooperative League of the U.S.A.) (1916): 1401 New York Ave. N.W., Suite 1100, Washington, D.C. 20005. Phone: (202) 638-6222.

National Council of the Churches of Christ in the USA (1950): 475 Riverside Drive, New York, N.Y. 10115. 33 Protestant and Orthodox communions. Phone: (212) 870-2227.

National Grange of the Order of Patrons of Husbandry, (1867): 1616 H St. N.W., Washington, D.C. 20006-4999. 300,000. Phone: (202) 628-3507 fax: (202) 347-1091.

National Press Club (1908): National Press Bldg., 529 14th St. N.W., Washington, D.C. 20045. 4,500. Phone: (202) 662-7500.

National PTA (National Congress of Parents and Teachers) (1897): 330 N. Wabash Ave., Suite 2100, Chicago, Ill. 60611-3690. 6.5 million. Phone: (312) 670-6782; e-mail: info@pta.org; www.pta.org.

National Rifle Association of America (1871): 11250 Waples Mill Rd., Fairfax, Va. 22030. 3,300,000. Phone: (703) 267-1000.

National Urban League, Inc. (1910): 120 Wall St., New York, N.Y. 10005. 115 affiliates in 34 states and D.C. Phone: (212) 558-5300.

National Wildlife Federation (1936): 8925 Leesburg Pike, Vienna, VA 22184. 4,000,000+. Phone: (703) 790-4000.

Nature Conservancy, The (1951): 1815 N. Lynn St., Arlington, Va. 22209. 830,000. Phone: (703) 841-5300.

Naturopathic Physicians, American Association of (1986): 601 Valley St. #105, Seattle, Wash. 98109. 450 ND members, 200 student; 45 corporate, 50 other. Phone: (206) 298-0126; fax: (206) 298-0129; e-mail: 75602.3715@Compuserve.com; Infinite.org/Naturopathic.Physician

Naval Architects and Marine Engineers, The Society of (1893): 601 Pavonia Ave., Suite 400, Jersey City, N.J. 07306. 11,000. Phone: (201) 798-4800.

Naval Engineers, American Society of (1888): 1452 Duke St., Alexandria, Va. 22314. 6,800. Phone: (703) 836-6727; fax: (703) 836-7491; www.jhnapl.edu/ASNE.

Naval Institute, United States (1873): 118 Maryland Ave., Annapolis, Md. 21402-5035. 90,000. Phone: (410) 268-6110.

Navigation, The Institute of (1945): 1800 Diagonal Rd., Suite 480, Alexandria, Va. 22314. 3,800. Phone: (703) 683-7101; fax: (703) 683-7105; e-mail: membership@ion.org.

Navy League of the United States (1902): 2300 Wilson Blvd., Arlington, Va. 22201-3308. 71,500. Charles L. Robinson, Capt., USN (Ret.), National Executive Director.

Neurofibromatosis Foundation, Inc., The National (1978): 95 Pine St., 16th Floor, New York, NY 10005. 38,000. Phone: (800) 323-7938; in NY State (212) 344NNFF; fax: (212) 747-0004; e-mail: nnff@aol.com; www.nf.org.

Newspaper Association of America (1887): 1921 Gallows Rd., Suite 600, Vienna, Va. 22180.

Newspaper Editors, American Society of (1922): P.O. Box 4090, Reston, Va. 20195-1700. 870. Phone: (703) 648-1144.

Nondestructive Testing, Inc., The American Society for (1941): 1711 Arlingate Lane, P.O. Box 28518, Columbus, Ohio 43228-0518. 10,240. Phone: (800) 222-ASNT.

NOT SAFE (National Organization Taunting Safety and Fairness Everywhere) (1980): P.O. Box 5743, Montecito, Calif. 93150. 975. Phone: (805) 969-6217.

Nuclear Society, American (1954): 555 N. Kensington Ave., La Grange Park, Ill. 60526. 14,700. Phone: (708) 352-6611.

Numismatic Association, American (1891): 818 N. Cascade Ave., Colorado Springs, Colo. 80903-3279. 30,000. Phone: (719) 632-2646; e-mail: ana@money.org.

Nurses Association, American (1896): 600 Maryland Ave. S.W., Suite 100, Washington, D.C. 20024-2571. 170,000. Phone: (202) 651-7000.

Odd Fellows, Sovereign Grand Lodge, Independent Order of (1819): 422 Trade St., Winston-Salem, N.C. 27101-2830. 460,000. Phone: (910) 725-5955.

Olympic Committee, United States (1921): One Olympic Plaza, Colorado Springs, Colo. 80909-5760. Phone: (719) 632-5551.

Optimist International (1919): 4494 Lindell Blvd., St. Louis, Mo. 63108. 155,000. Phone: (314) 371-6000.

Optometric Association, American (1898): 243 N. Lindbergh Blvd., St. Louis, Mo. 63141. 32,000. Phone: (314) 991-4100.

Organization of American States, General Secretariat (1890): 1889 F St. N.W., Washington, D.C. 20006. 35 member nations. Phone: (202) 458-3000.

Ornithologists' Union, American (1883): c/o National Museum of Natural History, NHB E607, MRC-116, Smithsonian Institution, Washington, D.C. 20560. 5,000. Phone: (202) 357-2051.

Overeaters Anonymous, Inc. (1960): P.O. Box 44020, Rio Rancho, N. Mex. 87174-4020. 150,000. Phone: (505) 891-2664.

Parents, Families and Friends of Lesbians and Gays (1981): 1101 14th St. N.W., Suite 1030, Washington, D.C. 20005. 67,000+ members. 400 chapters in 12 countries. Phone: (202) 638-4200.

Parents Without Partners (1957): 401 N. Michigan Ave., Chicago, Ill. 60611-4267. Phone: (312) 644-6610.

Pathology, American Society for Investigative (1976): 9650 Rockville Pike, Bethesda, Md. 20814-3993. 2,300. Phone: (301) 530-7130.

Peace Action (a merger of SANE and the Nuclear Weapons Freeze Campaign) (1957): 1819 H St. N.W., Suite 420, Washington D.C. 20006-3603. 50,000. Phone: (202) 862-9740.

People For the American Way (1980): 2000 M St. N.W., Suite 400, Washington, D.C. 20036. 300,000. Phone: (202) 467-4999.

Petroleum Geologists, American Association of (1917): P.O. Box 979, Tulsa, Okla. 74101-0979. 31,500. Phone: (918) 584-2555.

Pharmaceutical Association, American (1852): 2215 Constitution Ave. N.W., Washington, D.C. 20037. 50,000. Phone: (202) 628-4410.

Philatelic Society, American (1886): P.O. Box 8000, State College, Pa. 16803. 57,000. Phone: (814) 237-3803.

Photogrammetry and Remote Sensing, American Society for (1934): 5410 Grosvenor Lane, Suite 210, Bethesda, Md. 20814-2160. Phone: (301) 493-0290; fax: (301) 493-0208: e-mail: asprs@asprs.org.

Photographic Society of America (1934): 3000 United Founders Blvd., Suite 103, Oklahoma City, Okla. 73112. Phone: (405) 843-1437.

Photography, International Center of (1974): 1130 Fifth Ave., New York, N.Y. 10128. Midtown branch: 1133 Avenue of the Americas, New York, N.Y. 10036. Phone: (212) 860-1777.

Physical Society, The American (1899): One Physics Ellipse, College Park, Md. 20740-3844. 41,000. Phone: (301) 209-3269.

Physical Therapy Association, American (APTA) (1921): 1111 N. Fairfax St., Alexandria, Va. 22314. 70,000. Phone: (703) 684-2782.

Physics, American Institute of (1931): One Physics Ellipse, College Park, Md. 20740-3843. 125,000. Phone: (301) 209-3100.

Pilot International (1921): Pilot International Headquarters, 244 College St., P.O. Box 4844, Macon, Ga. 31208-4844. 17,000. Phone: (912) 743-7403.

Planetary Society, The (1979): 65 N. Catalina Ave., Pasadena, Calif. 91106. 100,000. Phone: (818) 793-5100.

Plan International (1937): P.O. Box 7670, 155 PLAN Way, Warwick, R.I. 02887. Phone: (401) 294-3693; fax: (401) 295-7062.

Planned Parenthood Federation of America, Inc., (1916): 810 Seventh Ave., New York, N.Y. 10019. 150 affiliates. Phone: (212) 541-7800; fax: (212) 245-1845; www.ppfa.org/ppfa.

Plastics Engineers, Society of (1942): 14 Fairfield Dr., Brookfield, Conn. 06804-0403. 37,000. Phone: (203) 775-0471. www.4spe.org.

Police, American Federation of (1966): Records Center, 3801 Biscayne Blvd., Miami, Fla. 33137. 100,000. Phone: (305) 573-0070.

Police, International Association of Chiefs of (1893): 515 N. Washington St., Alexandria Va. 22314-2357. 14,000. Phone: (703) 836-6767.

Police Hall of Fame, American (1960): 3801 Biscayne Blvd., Miami, Fla. 33137. 55,000. Phone: (305) 573-0070.

Political and Social Science, American Academy of (1889): 3937 Chestnut St., Philadelphia, Pa. 19104. Phone: (215) 386-4594.

Political Science, Academy of (1880): 475 Riverside Dr., Suite 1274, New York, N.Y. 10115-1274. 8,500. Phone: (212) 870-2500.

Prevent Blindness America (1908): 500 E. Remington Rd., Schaumburg, Ill. 60173-5611. 25 affiliates and divisions. Phone: (847) 843-2020/(800) 331-2020.

Professional Engineers, National Society of (1934): 1420 King St., Alexandria, Va. 22314. 69,000. Phone: (703) 684-2800; fax: (703) 836-4875; www.nspe.org.

Professional Photographers of America, Inc. (1880): 57 Forsyth St. N.W., Suite 1600, Atlanta, Ga. 30303. 14,000. Phone: (404) 522-8600.

Psychiatric Association, American (1844): 1400 K St. N.W., Washington, D.C. 20005. 40,537. Phone: (202) 682-6000.

Psychoanalytic Association, The American (1911): 309 E. 49th St., New York, N.Y. 10017. 3,116 psychoanalysts. Phone: (212) 752-0450; fax: (212) 593-0571; e-mail: apsaorg@compuserve.com.

Psychological Association, American (1892): 750 First St. N.E., Washington, D.C. 20002-4242. 151,000. Phone: (202) 336-5500; TDD: (202) 336-5662.

Public Health Association, American (1872): 1015 15th St. N.W., Suite 300, Washington, D.C. 20005-2600. 50,000+. Phone: (202) 789-5600.

Puppeteers of America (1937): 5 Cricklewood Path, Pasadena, Calif. 91107-1002. Phone: (818) 797-5748.

Quality Control, The American Society for (1946): 611 E. Wisconsin Ave., P.O. Box 3005, Milwaukee, Wis. 53201-3005. 135,000+. Phone: (414) 272-8575; www.asqc.org.

Railroads, Association of American (1934): 50 F St. N.W., Washington, D.C. 20001-1564. Phone: (202) 639-2100.

Recording Arts & Sciences, Inc., National Academy of (1958): 3402 Pico Blvd., Santa Monica, Calif. 90405. 10,000. Phone: (310) 392-3777.

Red Cross, American (1881): 17th and D Sts. N.W., Washington, D.C. 20006. Approx. 1,650 chapters. Phone: (202) 737-8300.

Rehabilitation Association, National (1925): 633 S. Washington St., Alexandria, Va. 22314-4193. 12,000. Phone: (703) 836-0850.

Research and Enlightenment, Association for (1931): P.O. Box 595, Virginia Beach, Va. 23451. 55,000. Phone: (757) 428-3588.

Reserve Officers Association of the United States (1922): 1 Constitution Ave. N.E., Washington, D.C. 20002. 93,000. Phone: (202) 479-2200.

Retired Federal Employees, National Association: 1533 New Hampshire Ave. N.W., Washington, D.C. 20036-1279. 500,000. Phone: (202) 234-0832.

Reye's Syndrome Foundation, National (1974): P.O. Box 829, Bryan, Ohio 43506. Phone: (800) 233-7393; fax: (419) 636-3366; e-mail: reyessyn@mail.bright.net

RID-USA (Remove Intoxicated Drivers) (1978): Box 520, Schenectady, N.Y. 12301. Over 150/41 state chapters. Phone: (518) 372-0034/(518) 393-HELP; fax: (518) 370-4917.

Right to Life, Committee, Inc., National (1973): 419 7th St. N.W., Suite 500, Washington, D.C. 20004. Phone: (202) 626-8800.

Rotary International (1905): One Rotary Center, 1560 Sherman Ave., Evanston, Ill. 60201. 1,195,500 in 155 countries and 35 geographical regions. Phone: (847) 866-3000.

SAE (Society of Automotive Engineers) (1905): 400 Commonweatlh Dr., Warrendale, Pa. 15096-0001. 71,000. Phone: (412) 776-4841.

Safety Council, National (1913): 1121 Spring Lake Dr., Itasca, IL 60143-3201. Phone: (630) 285-1121.

Salvation Army, The (1865): National Headquarters, 615 Slaters Lane, P.O. Box 269, Alexandria, Va. 22313. 453,150. Phone: (703) 684-5500.

Save-the-Redwoods League (1918): 114 Sansome St., Suite 605, San Francisco, Calif. 94104. 45,000. Phone: (415) 362-2352.

Science, American Association for the Advancement of (1848): 1200 New York Ave. N.W., Washington, D.C. 20005. 143,000. Phone: (202) 326-6400.

Science and Health, American Council on (1978): 1995 Broadway, 2nd Floor, New York, N.Y. 10023-5860. Phone: (212) 362-7044; fax: (212) 362-4919; e-mail: acsh@acsh.org; www.acsh.org.

Science Fiction Society, World (1939): c/o Southern California Institute for Fan Interests, P.O. Box 8442,

Van Nuys, Calif. 91409. 6,000. Phone: (818) 366-3827.

Science Writers, Inc., National Association of (1934): P.O. Box 294, Greenlawn, N.Y. 11740. 1,830. Phone: (516) 757-5664.

Scientists, Federation of American (FAS) (1945): 307 Massachusetts Ave. N.E., Washington, D.C. 20002. 4,000. Phone: (202) 546-3300.

SCRABBLE Association, National (1972): P.O. Box 700, Front Street Garden, Greenport, N.Y. 11944. 15,000. Phone: (516) 477-0033.

Screen Actors Guild (1933): 5757 Wilshire Blvd., 90036. 90,000. Phone: (213) 954-1600.

Sculpture Society, National (1893): 1177 Ave. of the Americas, New York, N.Y. 10036. 4,500. Phone: (212) 764-5645.

Seeing Eye Inc., The (1929): P.O. Box 375. Morristown, N.J. 07963-0375. Phone: (973) 539-4425.

Senior Citizens, National Alliance of (1974): 1744 Riggs Place, N.W., 3rd Floor, Washington, D.C. 20009. 117,000. Phone: (202) 986-0117.

Shriners of North America and Shriners Hospitals for Children, The (1872 and 1922): Box 31356, Tampa, Fla. 33631-3356. 600,000. Phone: (813) 281-0300.

Sierra Club (1892): 85 2nd Street, San Francisco, Calif. 94105-3441. 550,000. Phone: (415) 977-5500.

SIETAR INTERNATIONAL (The International Society for Intercultural Education, Training and Research) (1974): 808 17th St. N.W., Suite 200, Washington D.C. 20006-3910. 2,000+. Phone: (202) 466-7883; fax: (202) 223-9569; e-mail: SIETAR@compuserve.com.

Simon Wiesenthal Center (1978): 9786 W. Pico Blvd., Los Angeles, Calif. 90035-4792. 375,000 member families. Phone: (310) 553-9036.

Small Business United, National (1937): 1156 15th St. N.W., Washington, D.C. 20005-1711. 65,000+. Phone: (202) 293-8830; fax: (202) 872-8543; e-mail: nsbu@nsbu.org; www.nsbu.org.

SMYAL, Sexual Minority Youth Assistance League (1984): 333 1/2 Pennsylvania Ave. S.E., Washington, D.C. 20003-1148. 1,000 members. Phone: (202) 546-5940.

Social Work Education, Council on (1952): 1600 Duke St., Alexandria, Va. 22314-3421. Phone: (703) 683-8080; fax: (703) 683-8099.

Social Workers, National Association of (1955): 750 First St. N.E., Suite 700, Washington, D.C. 20002-4241. Phone: (202) 408-8600; www.nasw.org.

Society for Integrative and Comparitive Biology (formerly the American Society of Zoologists) (1890): 401 N. Michigan Ave., Chicago, Ill. 60611. 2,200. Phone: (312) 527-6697; (800) 955-1236.; fax: (312) 245-1085; e-mail: sicb@sba.com; www.sicb.org.

Soil and Water Conservation Society (1945): 7515 N.E. Ankeny Rd., Ankeny, Iowa 50021-9764. 10,000. Phone: (515) 289-2331; fax: (515) 289-1227; e-mail: swcs@swcs.org;www.swcs.org.

Songwriters Guild of America, The (1931): 1500 Harbor Blvd., Weehawken, N.J. 07087-6732. Phone: (201) 867-7603; www.songwriters.org.

Sons of Italy in America, Order (1905): 219 E St. N.E., Washington, D.C. 20002. 475,000. Phone: (202) 547-2900.

Sons of the American Revolution, National Society of the (1889): 1000 S. 4th St., Louisville, Ky. 40203. 27,000. Phone: (502) 589-1776.

Soroptimist International of the Americas (1921): Two Penn Center Plaza, Suite 1000, Philadelphia, Pa. 19102-1883. 50,000. Phone: (215) 557-9300.

Southern Early Childhood Association (formerly SACUS) (1948): P.O. Box 55930, Little Rock, Ark. 72215-5930. 19,300. Phone: (501) 663-0353; 1 (800) 304-7322; fax: (501) 663-2114; e-mail: seca@aristotle.net.

Space Education Association, U.S. (1973): Global Operations Center, 231 School Lane, P.O. Box 249, Rheems, Pa. 17570-0249. Voice/Fax: (717) 367-5196.

Space Society, National (1974): 600 Pennsylvania Ave., S.E., Suite 201, Washington, D.C. 20003-4316. Phone: (202) 543-1900; fax: (202) 546-4189; www.nss.org/.

Special Olympics International, Inc. (1968): 1325 G St. N.W., Suite 500, Washington, D.C., 20005-3104. 1,000,000. Phone: (202) 628-3630.

Speech-Language-Hearing Association, American (1925): 10801 Rockville Pike, Rockville, Md. 20852. 87,000. Phone: (301) 897-5700.

Sports Car Club of America Inc. (1944): 9033 E. Easter Place, Englewood, Colo. 80112-2105. 54,000. Phone: (303) 694-7222.

State Governments, The Council of (1933): P.O. Box 11910, Lexington, Ky. 40578-1910. All state and U.S. territories officials, all 50 states. Phone: (606) 244-8000; fax: (606) 244-8001.

Statistical Association, American (1839): 1429 Duke St., Alexandria, Va. 22314. 19,000.

Student Association, United States (1947): 1413 K Street, NW, 10th Floor, Washington, D.C. 20005. 350 schools (3.5 million students) Phone: (202) 347-8772.

Surgeons, American College of (1913): 55 E. Erie St., Chicago, Ill. 60611-2797. 58,000+. Phone: (312) 664-4050.

Symphony Orchestra League, American (1942): 1156 Fifteenth St. N.W., Suite 800, Washington, D.C. 20005-1704. 5,500. Phone: (202) 776-0212.

TASH: The Association for Persons with Severe Handicaps (1976): 29 W. Susquehanna Ave., Suite 210, Baltimore, Md. 21204. 8,500. Phone: (410) 828-TASH.

Tax Foundation (1937): 1250 H. St. N.W., Suite 750, Washington, D.C. 20005. Phone: (202) 783-2760; fax: (202) 942-7675; e-mail: taxfnd@intr.net; www.taxfoundation.org

Teachers, American Federation of (1916): 555 New Jersey Ave. N.W., Washington, D.C., 20001. 900,000+. Phone: (202) 879-4400.

Testing & Materials, American Society for (1898): 100 Barr Harbor Dr., W. Conshohocken, Pa. 19428-2959. 34,000. Phone: (610) 832-9500.

The Arc, a national organization on mental retardation (1950): 500 E. Border St., Suite 300, Arlington, Texas 76010. 140,000 members, 1,200 state and local chapters. Phone: (817) 261-6003.

Theatre Guild, Inc. (1919): 226 W. 47th St., New York, N.Y. 10036. 72,000. Phone: (212) 873-0676.

Theosophical Society in America, The (1875): P.O. Box 270, Wheaton, Ill. 60189-0270. 4,400. Phone: (630) 668-1571.

Tin Can Sailors, Inc. (1976): P.O. Box 100, Somerset, Mass. 02726-0100. 16,000+. Phone: (508) 677-0515.

Toastmasters International (1924): P.O. Box 9052, Mission Viejo, Calif. 92690-7052, and 23182 Arroyo Vista, Rancho Santa Margarita, Calif. 92688. 180,000. Phone: (714) 858-8255, club information voice mail: (800) 9WE-SPEAK; fax: (714) 858-1207; e-mail: tminfo@toastmasters.org.

TOUGHLOVE International (1977): P.O. Box 1069, Doylestown, Pa. 18901. 300 registered groups. Phone: (215) 348-7090; (800) 333-1069.

TransAfrica Forum (1981): 1744 R. St. N.W., Washington, D.C. 20009. Phone: (202) 797-2301; fax: (202) 797-2382; e-mail: transforum@igc.org.

Travel Agents, American Society of (ASTA) (1931): 1101 King St., Alexandria, Va. 22314. 28,500. Phone: (703) 739-2782.

Travelers Aid Services (1905/1982); 2 Lafayette St., New York, N.Y. 10007. Lucy N. Friedman, Executive Director. (Result of merger of Travelers Aid Society of New York and Victim Services Agency in 1982). Phone: (212) 577-7700. **Client Services:** Times Square Office, 1451 Broadway, 2nd Floor, Manhattan (212) 944-0013; JFK Airport Office, International Arrivals Bldg. 50, Jamaica, Queens (718) 656-4870; 24-Hour Crime Victims Hotline (212) 577-7777; Immigration Hotline (718) 899-4000.

Tuberous Sclerosis Association, Inc., National (1975): 8181 Professional Place, Suite 110, Landover, Md. 20785. 5,000. Phone: (301) 459-9888 or (800) 225-6872; fax: (301) 459-0394; e-mail: ntsa@aol.com; www.ntsa.org.

UFOs, National Investigations Committee on (1967): 14617 Victory Blvd., Suite 4, Van Nuys, Calif. 91411. Phone: (818) 989-5942; fax: (818) 989-2165.

UNICEF, U.S. Committee for (1947): 333 E. 38th St., New York, N.Y. 10016. 20,000 volunteers. Phone: (212) 686-5522; www.unicefusa.org.

Union of Concerned Scientists (1969): 2 Brattle Square, Cambridge, Mass. 02238-9105. 70,000. Phone: (617) 547-5552.

United Daughters of the Confederacy (1894): 328 N. Boulevard, Richmond, Va. 23220-4057. 24,000. Phone: (804) 355-1636.

United Jewish Appeal (1939): 99 Park Ave., New York, N.Y. 10016. Phone: (212) 818-9100.

United Way of America (1918): 701 N. Fairfax St., Alexandria, Va. 22314-2045. 1,800 local United Ways. Phone: (703) 836-7100; fax: (703) 683-7840; www.unitedway.org.

University Foundation, International (1973): 1301 S. Noland Rd., Independence, Mo. 64055. 67,000. Phone: (816) 461-3633.

University Women, American Association of (1881): 1111 16th St. N.W., Washington, D.C. 20036. 135,000. Phone: (202) 785-7700.

USO (United Service Organizations) (1941): World Headquarters, Washington Navy Yard, Bldg. 198, S.E., Washington, D.C. 20374-5096. Phone: (202) 610-5700.

Variety Clubs International (1927): 1560 Broadway, Suite 1209, New York, N.Y. 10036. 15,000. Phone: (212) 704-9872.

Veterans Committee, American (AVC) (1944): Bethesda, Md. 20817. 15,000. Phone & fax: (301) 320-6490.

Veterans of Foreign Wars of the U.S. (1899): 406 W. 34th St., Kansas City, Mo. 64111. VFW and Auxiliary, 2,850,000. Phone: (816) 756-3390.

Veterinary Medical Association, American (1863): 1931 N. Meacham Rd., Suite 100, Schaumburg, Ill. 60173-4360. 57,700. Phone: (847) 925-8070.

Visual Impairments, Division on (1948): The Council for Exceptional Children, 1920 Association Dr., Reston, Va. 20191-1589. 1,000. Phone: (703) 620-3660.

Volunteers of America (1896): 110 South Union Street, 2nd Floor, Alexandria, Va. 22314-3324. Provides human services in more than 400 communities. Phone: (703) 548-2288 or 1-800-899-0089.

War Resisters League (1923): 339 Lafayette St., New York, N.Y. 10012. 12,000. Phone: (212) 228-0450; fax: (212) 228-6193; e-mail: wrl@igc.apc.org; www.nonviolence.org/wrl.

Washington Legal Foundation (1977): 2009 Massachusetts Ave., N.W., Washington, D.C. 20036. 100,000. Phone: (202) 588-0302.

Water Quality Association (1974): 4151 Naperville Rd., Lisle, Ill. 60532. 2,500. Phone: (630) 505-0160; fax: (630) 505-9637.

Welding Society, American (1919): 550 N.W. LeJeune Rd., Miami, Fla. 33126. 48,000. Phone: (305) 443-9353; toll free (800) 443-9353.

Wildlife Fund, World (1961): 1250 24th St. N.W., Washington, D.C. 20037-1175. 1.2 million. Phone: (202) 293-4800.

Woman's Christian Temperance Union, National (1874): 1730 Chicago Ave., Evanston, Ill. 60201. Under 20,000. Phone: (847) 864-1396.

Women, National Organization for (NOW) (1966): 1000 16th St. N.W., Suite 700, Washington, D.C. 20036-5705. 270,000. Phone: (202) 331-0066.

Women Police, The International Association of (1915): RR1, Box 149, Deer Isle, Me. 04627. 3,000. Phone: (207) 348-6976; fax: (207) 348-6171.

Women's American ORT (1927): 315 Park Ave. South, New York, N.Y. 10010. Chapters throughout the U.S. Phone: (212) 505-7700.

Women's Educational and Industrial Union (1877): 356 Boylston St., Boston, Mass. 02116. 1,500. Phone: (617) 536-5651; fax: (617) 247-8826.

Women's International League for Peace and Freedom (1915): 1213 Race St., Philadelphia, Pa. 19107-1691. 10,000. Phone: (215) 563-7110.

World Future Society (1966): 7910 Woodmont Ave., Suite 450, Bethesda, Md. 20814. 30,000. Phone: (301) 656-8274; fax: (301) 951-0394.

World Health, American Association for (1953): 1825 K St. N.W., Washington, D.C. 20036. Phone: (202) 466-5883, fax: (202) 466-5896; e-mail: AAWHstaff@aol.com.

World Peace, International Association of Educators for (1969): P.O. Box 3282, Mastin Lake Station, Huntsville, Ala. 35810-0282. 25,000. Phone: (205) 534-5501.

World Peace Foundation (1910): One Eliot Square, Cambridge, Mass. 02138. Phone: (617) 491-5085; fax: (617) 491-8588.

Worldwatch Institute (1974): 1776 Massachusetts Ave. N.W., Washington, D.C. 20036. Global environmental research organization. Phone: (202) 452-1999; fax: (202) 296-296-7365; e-mail: world watch@worldwatch.org; www.worldwatch.org.

Writers Union, National (1983): 113 University Place, 6th Floor, New York, N.Y. 10003. 4,500. Phone: (212) 254-0279.

YMCA of the USA (1844): 101 N. Wacker Dr., Chicago, Ill. 60606. 13,500,000. Phone: (312) 977-0031.

Young Women's Christian Association of the U.S.A. (1858 in U.S.A., 1855 in England): Empire State Building, 350 Fifth Ave., 3rd floor, New York, N.Y. 10118. 1,000,000. Phone: (212) 273-7800.

Zero Population Growth (1968): 1400 Sixteenth St. N.W., Suite 320, Washington, D.C. 20036. 56,000. Phone: (202) 332-2200.

Zionist Organization of America (1897): ZOA House, 4 E. 34th St., New York, N.Y. 10016. 110,000. Phone: (212) 481-1500; fax: (212) 481-1515.

Crossword Puzzle Guide

First Aid to Crossword Puzzlers

We cannot begin to list all the odd words you might encounter in your daily and Sunday crossword puzzles, for such words run into many thousands. But we have tried to include those that turn up most frequently, as well as many others that should be of help to you when you are unable to go any further.

Also, we do not guarantee that the definitions in your puzzle will be exactly the same as ours, although we have checked every word with a standard dictionary and have followed its definition.

In nearly every case, we have used as the key word the principal noun of the definition, rather than any adjective, adjective phrase, or noun used as an adjective. And, to simplify your searching, we have grouped the words according to the number of spaces you have to fill.

Words of Two Letters

Ambary, DA
And (French, Latin), ET
Article (Arabic), AL
  (French), LA, LE, UN
  (Spanish), EL, LA, UN
At the (French), AU
  (Spanish), AL
Behold, LO
Bird: Hawaiian, OO
Birthplace: Abraham's, UR
Bone, OS
Buddha, FO
Butterfly: Peacock, IO
Champagne, AY
Chaos, NU
Chief: Burmese, BO
Coin: Roman, AS
  Siamese, AT
Concerning, RE
Dialect: Chinese, WU
Double (Egy. relig.), KA
Drama: Japanese, NO
Egg (comb. form), OO
Esker, OS
Eye (Scotch), EE
Factor: Amplification, MU
Fifty (Greek), NU
Fish: Carplike, ID
Force, OD
Forty (Greek), MU
From (French, Latin, Spanish), DE
  (Latin prefix), AB

From the (French), DU
God: Babylonian, EA, ZU
  Egyptian sun, RA
  Hindu unknown, KA
  Semitic, EL
Goddess: Babylonian, AI
  Greek earth, GE
Gold (heraldry), OR
Gulf: Arctic, OB
Heart (Egy. relig.), AB
Indian: South American, GE
King: Of Bashan, OG
Language: Artificial, RO
  Assamese, AO
Lava: Hawaiian, AA
Letter: Greek, MU, NU, PI, XI
  Hebrew, HE, PE
Lily: Palm, TI
Measure: Annamese, LY
  Chinese, HO, HU, KO, LI, MU, PU,
    TO, TU
  Japanese, GO, JO, MO, RI, SE, TO
  Metric land, AR
  Netherlands, EL
  Portuguese, PE
  Siamese, WA
  Swedish, AM
  Type, EM, EN
Monk: Buddhist, BO
Month: Jewish, AB

Mouth, OS
Mulberry: Indian, AL
Native: Burmese, WA
Note: Of Scale, DO, FA, MI, LA, RE, TI
Of (French, Latin, Spanish), DE
Of the (French), DU
One (Scotch), AE
Pagoda: Chinese, TA
Plant: East Indian fiber, DA
Ridge: Sandy, AS, OS
River: Russian, OB
Sloth: Three-toed, AI
Soul (Egy. relig.), BA
Sound: Hindu mystic, OM
Suffix: Comparative, ER
To the: French, AU
  Spanish, AL
Tree: Buddhist sacred, BO
Tribe: Assamese, AO
Type: Jumbled, PI
Weight: Annamese, TA
  Chinese, LI
  Danish, ES
  Japanese, MO
  Roman, AS
Whirlwind: Faeroe Is., OE
Yes (German), JA
  (Italian, Spanish), SI
  (Russian), DA

Words of Three Letters

Adherent: IST
Again, BIS
Age, ERA
Antelope: African, GNU, KOB
Apricot: Japanese, UME
Article (German), DAS, DEM, DEN,
  DER, DES, DIE, EIN
  (French), LES, UNE
  (Spanish), LAS, LOS, UNA
Banana: Polynesian, FEI
Barge, HOY
Bass: African, IYO
Beak, NEB, NIB
Beard: Grain, AWN
Beetle: June, DOR
Being, ENS
Berry: Hawthorn, HAW
Beverage: Hawaiian, AVA
Bird: Australian, EMU
  Crowlike, JAY
  Extinct, MOA

Fabulous, ROC
Frigate, IWA
Parson, POE, TUE, TUI
Sea, AUK
Blackbird, ANI, ANO
Born, NEE
Bronze: Roman, AES
Bugle: Yellow, IVA
By way of, VIA
Canton: Swiss, URI
Cap: Turkish, FEZ
Catnip, NEP
Character: In "Faerie Queene," UNA
Coin (Money of account): Afghan, PUL
  Albanian, LEK
  British Guiana, BIT
  Bulgarian, LEV, LEW
  French, ECU, SOU
  Indian, PIE
  Japanese, SEN, YEN
  Korean, WON
  Lithuanian, LIT

Macao, Timor, AVO
Palestinian, MIL
Persian, PUL
Peruvian, SOL
Rumanian, BAN, LEU, LEY
Scandinavian, ORE
Siamese, ATT
Collection: Facts, ANA
Commune: Belgian, ANS, ATH
  Netherlands, EDE, EPE
Community: Russian, MIR
Constellation: Southern, ARA
Contraction: Poetic, EEN, EER, OER
Covering: Apex of roof, EPI
Crab: Fiddler, UCA
Crag: Rocky, TOR
Cry: Crow, rook, raven, CAW
Cup: Wine, AMA
Cymbal, Oriental, TAL, ZEL
Disease: Silkworm, UJI
Division: Danish territorial, AMT
  Geologic, EON

Doctrine, ISM
Dowry, DOT
Dry (French), SEC
Dynasty: Chinese, CHI, HAN, SUI, WEI, YIN
Eagle: Sea, ERN
Earth (comb. form), GEO
Egg: Louse, NIT
Eggs: Fish, ROE
Emmet, ANT
Enzyme, ASE
Equal (comb. form), ISO
Extension: building, ELL
Far (comb. form), TEL
Farewell, AVE
Fiber: Palm, TAL
Finial, EPI
Fish: Carplike, IDE
    Pikelike, GAR
Flatfish, DAB
Fleur-de-lis, LIS, LYS
Food: Hawaiian, POI
Formerly, NEE
Friend (French), AMI
Game: Card, LOO
Garment: Camel-hair, ABA
Gateway, DAR
Gazelle: Tibetan, GOA
Genus: Ducks, AIX
    Grasses, POA
    Grasses (maize), ZEA
    Herbs or shrubs, IVA
    Lizards, UTA
    Rodents (incl. house mice), MUS
    Ruminants (incl. cattle), BOS
    Swine, SUS
Gibbon: Malay, LAR
God: Assyrian, SIN
    Babylonian, ABU, ANU, BEL, HEA, SIN, UTU
    Irish sea, LER
    Phrygian, MEN
    Polynesian, ORO
Goddess: Babylonian, AYA
    Etruscan, UNI
    Hindu, SRI, UMA, VAC
    Teutonic, RAN
Governor: Algerian, DEY
    Turkish, BEY
Grampus, ORC
Grape, UVA
Grass: Meadow, POA
Gypsy, ROM
Hail, AVE
Hare: Female, DOE
Hawthorn, HAW
Hay: Spread for drying, TED
Herb: Japanese, UDO
    Perennial, PIA
    Used for blue dye, WAD
Herd: Whales, GAM, POD
Hero: Spanish, CID
High (music), ALT
Honey (pharm.), MEL
Humorist: American, ADE
I (Latin), EGO
I love (Latin), AMO
Indian: Algonquian, FOX, SAC, WEA
    Chimakuan, HOH
    Keresan, SIA
    Mayan, MAM
    Shoshonean, UTE
    Siouan, KAW, OTO
    South American, ITE, ONA, URO, URU, YAO
    Tierra del Fuego, ONA
    Wakashan, AHT
Ingot, PIG
Inlet: Narrow, RIA
Island: Cyclades, IOS
    Dodecanese, COS, KOS
    (French), ILE
    River, AIT
Jackdaw, DAW
John (Gaelic), IAN
Keelbill, ANI, ANO

Kiln, OST
King: British legendary LUD
Kobold, NIS
Lace: To make, TAT
Lamprey, EEL
Language: Artificial, IDO
    Bantu, ILA
    Siamese, LAO, TAI
Leaf: Palm, OLA, OLE
Leaving, ORT
Left: Cause to turn, HAW
Letter: Greek, CHI, ETA, PHI, PSI, RHO, TAU
    Hebrew, MEM, NUN, SIN, TAV, VAU
Lettuce, COS
Life (comb. form), BIO
Lily: Palm, TOI
Lizard, EFT
Louse: Young, NIT
Love (Anglo-Irish), GRA
Lute: Oriental, TAR
Macaw: Bralizian, ARA
Marble, TAW
Match: Shooting (French), TIR
Meadow, LEA
Measure: Abyssinian, TAT
    Algerian, PIK
    Annamese, GON, MAU, NGU, VUO, SAO, TAO, TAT
    Arabian, DEN, SAA
    Belgian, VAT
    Bulgarian, OKA, OKE
    Chinese, FEN, TOU, YIN
    Cloth, ELL
    Cyprus, OKA, OKE, PIK
    Czech, LAN, SAH
    Danish, FOD, MIL, POT
    Dominican Republic, ONA
    Dutch, old, AAM
    East Indian, KIT
    Egyptian, APT, HEN, PIK, ROB
    Electric, MHO, OHM
    Energy, ERG
    English, PIN
    Estonian, TUN
    French, POT
    German, AAM
    Greek, PIK
    Hebrew, CAB, HIN, KOR, LOG
    Hungarian, AKO
    Icelandic, FET
    Indian, GAZ, GUZ, JOW, KOS
    Japanese, BOO, CHO, KEN, RIN, SHO, SUN, TAN
    Malabar, ADY
    Metric land, ARE
    Netherlands, KAN, KOP, MUD, VAT, ZAK
    Norwegian, FOT, POT
    Persian, GAZ, GUZ, MOU, ZAR, ZER
    Polish, CAL
    Rangoon, DHA, LAN
    Roman, PES, URN
    Russian, FUT, LOF
    Scotch, COP
    Siamese, KEN, NIU, RAI, SAT, SEN, SOK, WAH, YOT
    Somaliland, TOP
    Spanish, PIE
    Straits Settlements, PAU, TUN
    Swedish, ALN, FOT, MIL, REF, TUM
    Swiss, POT
    Tunisian, SAA
    Turkish, OKA, OKE, PIK
    Wire, MIL
    Württemberg, IMI
    Yarn, LEA
    Yugoslavian, OKA, RIF
Milk, LAC
Milkfish, AWA
Moccasin, PAC
Money: Yap stone, FEI
Money of Account (also Coin): Anglo-Saxon, ORA, ORE
    French, SOU
    Indian, LAC

Japanese, RIN
Oman, GAJ
Virgin Islands, BIT
Monkey: Capuchin, SAI
Morsel, ORT
Mother: Peer Gynt's, ASE
Mountain: Asia Minor, IDA
Mulberry: Indian, AAL, ACH, AWL
Muttonbird: New Zealand, OII
Nahoor, SNA
Native: Mindanao, ATA
Neckpiece, BOA
Newt, EFT
No (Scotch), NAE
Note: Guido's highest, ELA
    Of scale, SOL
Nursemaid: Oriental, AMA, IYA
Ocher: Yellow, SIL
One (Scotch), YIN
Ornament: Pagoda, TEE
Oven: Polynesian, UMU
Ox: Tibetan, YAK
Pagoda: Chinese, TAA
Parrot: Hawk, HIA
    New Zealand, KEA
Part: Footlike, PES
Particle: Electrified, ION
Pasha, DEY
Pass: Mountain, COL
Paste: Rice, AME
Pea: Indian split, DAL
Peasant: Philippine, TAO
Penpoint, NEB, NIB
Piece out, EKE
Pigeon, NUN
Pine: Textile screw, ARA
Pistol (slang), GAT
Pit: Baking, IMU
Plant: Pepper, AVA
Play: By Capek, RUR
Poem: Old French, DIT
Porgy: Japanese, TAI
Priest: Biblical high, ELI
Prince Ethiopian, RAS
Pseudonym: Dickens', BOZ
Queen: Fairy, MAB
Quince: Bengal, BEL
Record: Ship's, LOG
Refuse: Flax (Scotch), PAB, POB
Resin, LAC
Resort, SPA
Revolver (slang), GAT
Right: Cause to turn, GEE
River: Scotch or English, DEE
    (Spanish), RIO
    Swiss, AAR
Room: Harem, ODA
Rootstock: Fern, ROI
Rose (Persian), GUL
Ruff: Female, REE
Rule: Indian, RAJ
Sailor, GOB, TAR
Saint: Female (abbr.), STE
    Mohammedan, PIR
Salt, SAL
Sash: Japanese, OBI
Scrap, ORT
Seed: Poppy, MAW
    Small, PIP
Self, EGO
Serpent: Vedic sky, AHI
Sesame, TIL
Sheep: Female, EWE
    Indian, SHA
    Male, RAM
Sheepfold (Scotch), REE
Shelter, LEE
Shield, ECU
Shooting match (French), TIR
Shrew: European, ERD
Shrub: Evergreen, YEW
Silkworm, ERI
Snake, ASP, BOA
Soak, RET
Son-in-law: Mohammed's, ALI
Sorrel: Wood, OCA

Spade: Long, narrow, LOY
Spirit: Malignant, KER
Spot: Playing-card, PIP
Spread for drying, TED
Spring: Mineral, SPA
Sprite: Water, NIX
Statesman: Japanese, ITO
Stern: Toward, AFT
Stomach: Bird's, MAW
Street (French), RUE
Summer (French), ETE
Sun, SOL
Swamp, BOG, FEN
Swan: Male, COB
Tea: Chinese, CHA
Temple: Shinto, SHA
Thing (law), RES
Title: Etruscan, LAR
  Monk's, FRA
  Portuguese, DOM
  Spanish, DON
  Turkish, AGA, BEY
Tool: Cutting, ADZ, AXE
  Mining, GAD
  Piercing, AWL
Tree: Candlenut, AMA
  Central American, EBO
  East Indian, SAJ, SAL
  Evergreen, YEW
  Hawaiian, KOA, KOU
  Indian, BEL, DAR

Linden, LIN
New Zealand, AKE
Philippine, DAO, TUA, TUI
Rubber, ULE
South American, APA
Tribe: New Zealand, ATI
Turmeric, REA
Twice, BIS
Twin: Siamese, ENG
Uncle (dialect), EAM, EME
Veil: Chalice, AER, AIR
Vessel: Wine, AMA
Vestment: Ecclesiastical, ALB
Vetch: Bitter, ERS
Victorfish, AKU
Vine: New Zealand, AKA
  Philippine, IYO
Wallaba, APA
Wapiti, ELK
Water (French), EAU
Waterfall, LIN
Watering place: Prussian, EMS
Weave: Designating plain, UNI
Weight: Annamese, CAN
  Bulgarian, OKA, OKE
  Burmese, MOO, VIS
  Chinese, FEN, HAO, KIN, SSU, TAN, YIN
  Cyprus, OKA, OKE
  Danish, LOD, ORT, VOG
  East Indian, TJI

Egyptian, KAT, OKA, OKE
English, for wool, TOD
German, LOT
Greek, MNA, OKA, OKE
Indian, SER
Japanese, FUN, KIN, RIN, SHI
Korean, KON
Malacca, KIP
Mongolian, LAN
Netherlands, ONS
Norwegian, LOD
Polish, LUT
Rangoon, PAI
Roman, BES
Russian, LOT
Siamese, BAT, HAP, PAI
Swedish, ASS, ORT
Turkish, OKA, OKE
Yugoslavian, OKA, OKE
Whales: Herd, GAM, POD
Wildebeest, GNU
Wing, ALA
Witticism, MOT
Wolframite, CAL
Worm: African, LOA
Wreath: Hawaiian, LEI
Yale, ELI
Yam: Hawaiian, HOI
Yes (French), OUI
Young: Bring forth, EAN
Z (letter), ZED

Words of Four Letters

Aborigine: Borneo, DYAK
Agave, ALOE
Animal: Footless, APOD
Ant: White, ANAI, ANAY
Antelope: African, ASSE, BISA, GUIB,
  KOBA, KUDU, ORYX, POKU, PUKU,
  TOPI, TORA
Apoplexy: Plant, ESCA
Apple, POME
Apricot, ANSU
Ardor, ELAN
Armadillo, APAR, PEBA, PEVA, TATU
Ascetic: Mohammedan, SUFI
Association: Chinese, TONG
Astronomer: Persian, OMAR
Avatar: Of Vishnu, RAMA
Axillary, ALAR
Band: Horizontal (heraldry), FESS
Barracuda, SPET
Bark: Mulberry, TAPA
Base: Column, DADO
Bearing (heraldry), ORLE
Beer: Russian, KVAS
Beige, ECRU
Being, ESSE
Beverage: Japanese rice, SAKE
Bird: Asian, MINA, MYNA
  Egyptian sacred, IBIS
  Extinct, DODO, MAMO
  Flightless, KIWI
  Gull-like, TERN
  Hawaiian, IIWI, MAMO
  Parson, KOKO
  Unfledged, EYAS
Birds: As class, AVES
Black, EBON
  (French), NOIR
Blackbird: European, MERL
Boat: Flat-bottomed, DORY
Bone: Forearm, ULNA
Bones, OSSA
Box, Japanese, INRO
Bravo (rare), EUGE
Buffalo: Indian wild, ARNA
Bull (Spanish), TORO
Burden, ONUS
Cabbage: Sliced, SLAW
Caliph: Mohammedan, OMAR
Canoe: Malay, PRAU, PROA
Cap: Military, KEPI
Cape, NESS

Capital: Ancient Irish, TARA
Case: Article, ETUI
Cat: Wild, BALU, EYRA
Chalcedony, SARD
Chamber: Indian ceremonial, KIVA
Channel: Brain, ITER
Cheese: Dutch, EDAM
Chest: Sepulchral stone, CIST
Chieftain: Arab, EMIR
Church: Part of, APSE, NAVE
  (Scotch), KIRK
Claim (law), LIEN
Cluster: Flower, CYME
Coin: Chinese, TAEL, YUAN
  German, MARK
  Indian, ANNA
  Iranian, RIAL
  Italian, LIRA
  Moroccan, OKIA
  Siamese, BAHT
  South American, PESO
  Spanish, DURO, PESO
  Turkish, PARA
Commune: Belgian, AATH
Composition: Musical, OPUS
Compound: Chemical, DIOL
Constellation: Southern, PAVO
Council: Russian, DUMA
Counsel, REDE
Covering: Seed, ARIL
Cross: Egyptian, ANKH
Cry: Bacchanalian, EVOE
Cup (Scotch), TASS
Cupbearer, SAKI
Dagger, DIRK
  Malay, KRIS
Dam: River, WEIR
Dash, ELAN
Date: Roman, IDES
Dawn: Pertaining to, EOAN
Dean: English, INGE
Decay: In fruit, BLET
Deer: Sambar, MAHA
Disease: Skin, ACNE
Disk: Solar, ATEN
Dog: Hunting, ALAN
Drink: Hindu intoxicating, SOMA
Duck, SMEE, SMEW, TEAL
Dynasty: Chinese, CHEN, CHIN, CHOU,
  CHOW, HSIA, MING, SUNG, TANG,

TSIN
  Mongol, YUAN
Eagle: Biblical, GIER
  Sea, ERNE
Egyptian: Christian, COPT
Ear: Pertaining to, OTIC
Entrance: Mine, ADIT
Esau, EDOM
Escutcheon: Voided, ORLE
Eskers, OSAR
Evergreen: New Zealand, TAWA
Fairy: Persian, PERI
Family: Italian, ESTE
Far (comb. form), TELE
Farewell, VALE
Father (French), PERE
Fennel: Philippine, ANIS
Fever: Malarial, AGUE
Fiber: East Indian, JUTE
Firn, NEVE
Fish: Carplike, DACE
  Hawaiian, ULUA
  Herringlike, SHAD
  Mackerellike, CERO
  Marine, HAKE
  Sea, LING, MERO, OPAH
  Spiny-finned, GOBY
Food: Tropical, TARO
Foot: Metric, IAMB
Formerly, ERST
Founder: Of Carthage, DIDO
France: Southern, MIDI
Furze, ULEX
Gaelic, ERSE
Gaiter, SPAT
Game: Card, FARO, SKAT
Garlic: European wild, MOLY
Garment: Hindu, SARI
  Roman, TOGA
Gazelle, CORA
Gem, JADE, ONYX, OPAL, RUBY
Genus: Amphibians (incl. frogs), RANA
  Amphibians (incl. tree toads), HYLA
  Antelopes, ORYX
  Auks, ALCA, URIA
  Bees, APIS
  Birds (American ostriches), RHEA
  Birds (cranes), CRUS
  Birds (magpies), PICA
  Birds (peacocks), PAVO
  Cetaceans, INIA

Ducks (incl. mallards), ANAS
Fishes (burbots), LOTA
Fishes (incl. bowfins), AMIA
Geese (snow geese), CHEN
Gulls, XEMA
Herbs, ARUM, GEUM
Insects (water scorpions), NEPA
Lilies, ALOE
Mammals (mankind), HOMO
Orchids, DISA
Owls, ASIO, BUBO, OTUS
Palms, NIPA
Sea birds, SULA
Sheep, OVIS
Shrubs, Eurasian, ULEX
Shrubs (hollies), ILEX
Shrubs (incl. Virginia Willow), ITEA
Shrubs, tropical, EVEA
Snakes (sand snakes), ERYX
Swans, OLOR
Trees, chocolate, COLA
Trees (ebony family), MABA
Trees (incl. maples), ACER
Trees (olives), OLEA
Trees, tropical, EVEA
Turtles, EMYS
Goat: Wild, IBEX, KRAS, TAHR, TAIR, THAR
God: Assyrian, ASUR
  Babylonian, ADAD, ADDU, ENKI, ENZU, IRRA, NABU, NEBO, UTUG
  Celtic, LLEU, LLEW
  Hindu, AGNI, CIVA, DEVA, DEWA, KAMA, RAMA, SIVA, VAYU
  Phrygian, ATYS
  Semitic, BAAL
  Teutonic, HLER
Goddess: Babylonian, ERUA, GULA
  Hawaiian, PELE
  Hindu, DEVI, KALI, SHRI, VACH
Gooseberry: Hawaiian, POHA
Gourd, PEPO
Grafted (heraldry), ENTE
Grandfather (obsolete), AIEL
Grandparents: Pertaining to, AVAL
Grass: Hawaiian, HILO
Gray (French), GRIS
Green (heraldry), VERT
Groom: Indian, SYCE
Half (prefix), DEMI, HEMI, SEMI
Hamlet, DORP
Hammer-head: Part of, PEEN
Handle, ANSA
Harp: Japanese, KOTO
Hartebeest, ASSE, TORA
Hautboy, OBOE
Hawk: Taken from nest (falconry), EYAS
Hearing (law), OYER
Heater: For liquids, ETNA
Herb: Aromatic, ANET, DILL
  Fabulous, MOLY
  Perennial, GEUM, SEGO
  Pot, WORT
  Used for blue dye, WADE, WOAD
Hill: Flat-topped, MESA
  Sand, DENE, DUNE
Hoarfrost, RIME
Hog: Immature female, GILT
Holly, ILEX
House: Cow, BYRE
  (Spanish), CASA
Ice: Floating, FLOE
Image, ICON, IKON
Incarnation: Of Vishnu, RAMA
Indian: Algonquian, CREE, SAUK
  Central American, MAYA
  Iroquoian, ERIE
  Mexican, CORA
  Peruvian, CANA, INCA, MORO
  Shoshonean, HOPI
  Siouan, OTOE
  Southwestern, HOPI, PIMA, YUMA, ZUNI
Insect: Immature, PUPA
Instrument: Stringed, LUTE, LYRE
Ireland, EIRE, ERIN

Jacket: English, ETON
Jail (British), GAOL
Jar, OLLA
Judge: Mohammedan, CADI
Juniper: European, CADE
Kiln, OAST, OVEN
King: British legendary, LUDD, NUDD
Kiss, BUSS
Knife: Philippine, BOLO
Koran: Section of, SURA
Laborer: Spanish American, PEON
Lake: Mountain, TARN
  (Scotch), LOCH
Lamp: Miner's, DAVY
Landing place: Indian, GHAT
Language: Buddhist, PALI
  Japanese, AINU
Latvian, LETT
Layer: Of iris, UVEA
Leaf: Palm, OLAY, OLLA
Legislature: Ukrainian, RADA
Lemur, LORI
Leopard, PARD
Let it stand, STET
Letter: Greek, BETA, IOTA, ZETA
  Hebrew, AYIN, BETH, CAPH, KOPH, RESH, SHIN, TETH, YODH
  Papal, BULL
Lily, ALOE
Literature: Hindu sacred, VEDA
Lizard, GILA
  Monitor, URAN
Loquat, BIWA
Magistrate: Genoese or Venetian, DOGE
Man (Latin), HOMO
Mark: Omission, DELE
  armoset: South American, MICO
Meadow: Fertile, VEGA
Measure: Electric, VOLT, WATT
  Force, DYNE
  Hebrew, OMER
  Printing, PICA
  Spanish or Portuguese, VARA
  Swiss land, IMMI
Medley, OLIO
Merganser, SMEW
Milk (French), LAIT
Molding, GULA
  Curved, OGEE
Mongoose: Crab-eating, URVA
Monk: Tibetan, LAMA
Monkey: African, MONA, WAAG
  Ceylonese, MAHA
  Cochin-China, DOUC
  South American, SAKI, TITI
Monkshood, ATIS
Month: Jewish, ADAR, ELUL, IYAR
Mother (French), MERE
Mountain: Thessaly, OSSA
Mouse: Meadow, VOLE
Mythology: Norse, EDDA
Nail (French), CLOU
Native: Philippine, MORO
Nest: Of pheasants, NIDE
Network, RETE
No (German), NEIN
Noble: Mohammedan, AMIR
Notice: Death, OBIT
Novel: By Zola, NANA
Nursemaid: Oriental AMAH, AYAH, EYAH
Nut: Philippine, PILI
Oak: Holm, ILEX
Oil (comb. form), OLEO
Ostrich: American, RHEA
Oven, KILN, OAST
Owl: Barn, LULU
Ox: Celebes wild, ANOE
  Extinct wild, URUS
Palm, ATAP, NIPA, SAGO
Parliament, DIET
Parrot: New Zealand, KAKA
Pass: Indian mountain, GHAT
Passage: Closing (music), CODA
Peach: Clingstone, PAVY

Peasant: Indian, RYOT
  Old English, CARL
Pepper: Australasian, KAVA
Perfume, ATAR
Persia, IRAN
Person: Extraordinary, ONER
Pickerel or pike, ESOX
Pitcher, EWER
Plant: Aromatic, NARD
  Century, ALOE
  Indigo, ANIL
  Pepper, KAVA
Platform: Raised, DAIS
Plum: Wild, SLOE
Pods: Vegetable, OKRA, OKRO
Poem: Epic, EPOS
Poet: Persian, OMAR
  Roman, OVID
Poison, BANE
  Arrow, INEE
Porkfish, SISI
Portico: Greek, STOA
Premium, AGIO
Priest: Mohammedan, IMAM
Prima donna, DIVA
Prong: Fork, TINE
Pseudonym: Lamb's, ELIA
Queen: Carthaginian, DIDO
  Hindu, RANI
Rabbit, CONY
Race: Of Japan, AINU
Rail: Ducklike, COOT
  North American, SORA
Redshank, CLEE
Refuse: After pressing, MARC
Regiment: Turkish, ALAI
Reliquary, ARCA
Resort: Italian, LIDO
Ridges: Sandy, ASAR, OSAR
River: German, ELBE, ODER
  Italian, ADDA
  Siberian, LENA
Road: Roman, ITER
Rockfish: California, RENA
Rodent: Mouselike, VOLE
  South American, PACA
Rootstock, TARO
Salamander, NEWT
Salmon: Silver, COHO
  Young, PARR
Same (Greek), HOMO
  (Latin), IDEM
Sauce: Fish, ALEC
School: English, ETON
Seaweed, AGAR, ALGA, KELP
Secular, LAIC
Sediment, SILT
Seed: Dill, ANET
  Of vetch, TARE
Serf, ILOT
Sesame, TEEL
Settlement: Eskimo, ETAH
Shark: Atlantic, GATA
  European, TOPE
Sheep: Wild, UDAD
Sheltered, ALEE
Shield, EGIS
Ship: Jason's, ARGO
  Left side of, PORT
  Two-masted, BRIG
Shrine: Buddhist, TOPE
Shrub: New Zealand, TUTU
Sign: Magic, RUNE
Silkworm, ERIA
Skin: Beaver, PLEW
Skink: Egyptian, ADDA
Slave, ESNE
Sloth: Two-toed, UNAU
Smooth, LENE
Snow: Glacial, NEVE
Soapstone, TALC
Society: African secret, EGBO, PORO
Son: Of Seth, ENOS
Song (German), LIED
  Unaccompanied, GLEE
Sound: Lung, RALE

Sour, ACID
Sow: Young, GILT
Spike: Brad-shaped, BROB
Spirit: Buddhist evil, MARA
Stake: Poker, ANTE
Star: Temporary, NOVA
Starch: East Indian, SAGO
Stone: Precious, OPAL
Strap: Bridle, REIN
Strewn (heraldry), SEME
Sweetsop, ATES, ATTA
Sword: Fencing, EPEE, FOIL
Tambourine: African, TAAR
Tapir: Brazilian, ANTA
Tax, CESS
Tea: South American, MATE
Therefore (Latin), ERGO
Thing: Extraordinary, ONER
Three (dice, cards, etc.), TREY
Thrush: Hawaiian, OMAO
Tide, NEAP
Tipster: Racing, TOUT
Tissue, TELA
Title: Etruscan, LARS
  Hindu, BABU
  Indian, RAJA
  Mohammedan, EMIR, IMAM
  Persian, BABA
  Spanish, DONA
  Turkish, AGHA, BABA

Toad: Largest-known, AGUA
  Tree, HYLA
Tool: Cutting, ADZE
Track: Deer, SLOT
Tract: Sandy, DENE
Tree: Apple, SORB
  Central American, EBOE
  East Indian, TEAK
  Eucalyptus, YATE
  Guiana and Trinidad, MORA
  Javanese, UPAS
  Linden, LIME, LINN, TEIL, TILL
  Sandarac, ARAR
  Sassafras, AGUE
  Tamarisk salt, ATLE
Tribe: Moro, SULU
Trout, CHAR
Urchin: Street, ARAB
Vessel: Arab, DHOW
Vestment: Ecclesiastical, COPE
Vetch, TARE
Vine: East Indian, SOMA
Violinist: Famous, AUER
Vortex, EDDY
Wampum, PEAG
Wapiti, STAG
Waste: Allowance for, TRET
Watchman: Indian, MINA
Water (Spanish), AGUA

Waterfall, LINN
Wavy (heraldry), ONDE, UNDE
Wax, CERE
  Chinese, PELA
Weed: Biblical, TARE
Weight: Ancient, MINA
  Danish (pl.), ESER
  East Asian, TAEL
  Greek, MINA
  Siamese, BAHT
Well done (rare), EUGE
Whale, CETE
  Killer, ORCA
  White, HUSE, HUSO
Whirlpool, EDDY
Wife: Of Geraint, ENID
Willow: Virginia, ITEA
Wine, PORT
Winged, ALAR
  (Heraldry), AILE
Wings, ALAE
Withered, SERE
Without (French), SANS
Wool: To comb, CARD
Work, OPUS
Wrong: Civil, TORT
Young: Bring forth, YEAN

Words of Five Letters

Abode of dead: Babylonian, ARALU
Aborigine: Borneo DAYAK
Aftersong, EPODE
Aloe, AGAVE
Animal: Footless, APODE
Ant, EMMET
Antelope: African, ADDAX, BEISA, CAAMA, ELAND, GUIBA,
  ORIBI, TIANG
  Goat, GORAL, SEROW
  Indian, SASIN
  Siberian, SAIGA
Arch: Pointed, OGIVE
Armadillo, APARA, POYOU, TATOU
Arrowroot, ARARU
Artery: Trunk, AORTA
Association: Russian, ARTEL
  Secret, CABAL
Author: English, READE
Automaton, GOLEM, ROBOT
Award: Motion-picture, OSCAR
Basket: Fishing, CREEL
Beer: Russian, KVASS
Bible: Mohammedan, KORAN
Bird: Asian, MINAH, MYNAH
  Indian, SHAMA
  Larklike, PIPIT
  Loonlike, GREBE
  Oscine, VIREO
  South American, AGAMI
  Swimming, GREBE
Black: (French), NOIRE
  (Heraldry), SABLE
Blackbird: European, MERLE, OUSEL, OUZEL
Block: Glacial, SERAC
Blue (heraldry), AZURE
Boat: Eskimo, BIDAR, UMIAK
Bobwhite, COLIN, QUAIL
Bone (comb. form), OSTEO
  Leg, TIBIA
  Thigh, FEMUR
Broom: Twig, BESOM
Brother (French), FRERE
  Moses, AARON
Canoe: Eskimo, BIDAR, KAYAK
Cape: Papal, FANON, ORALE
Caravansary, SERAI
Card: Old playing, TAROT
Caterpillar: New Zealand, AWETO
Catkin, AMENT
Cavity: Stone, GEODE
Cephalopod, SQUID
Cetacean, WHALE

Chariot, ESSED
Cheek: Pertaining to, MALAR
Chieftain: Arab, EMEER
Child (Scotch), BAIRN
Cigar, CLARO
Coating: Seed, TESTA
Cockatoo: Palm, ARARA
Coin: Costa Rican, COLON
  Danish, KRONE
  Ecuadorian, SUCRE
  English, GROAT, PENCE
  French, FRANC
  German, KRONE, TALER
  Hungarian, PENGO
  Icelandic, KRONA
  Indian, RUPEE
  Iraqi, DINAR
  Norwegian, KRONE
  Polish, ZLOTY
  Russian, COPEC, KOPEK, RUBLE
  Swedish, KRONA
  Turkish, ASPER
  Yugoslav, DINAR
Collar: Papal, FANON, ORALE
  Roman, RABAT
Commune: Italian, TREIA
Composition: Choral, MOTET
Compound: Chemical, ESTER
Conceal (law), ELOIN
Council: Ecclesiastical, SYNOD
Court: Anglo-Saxon, GEMOT
  Inner, PATIO
Crest: Mountain, ARETE
Crown: Papal, TIARA
Cuttlefish, SEPIA
Date: Roman, NONES
Decree: Mohammedan, IRADE
  Russian, UKASE
Deposit: Loam, LOESS
Desert: Gobi, SHAMO
Devilfish, MANTA
Disease: Cereals, ERGOT
Disk, PATEN
Dog: Wild, DHOLE, DINGO
Dormouse, LEROT
Drum, TABOR
Duck: Sea, EIDER
Dynasty: Chinese, CHING, LIANG, SHANG
Earthquake, SEISM
Eel, ELVER, MORAY
Ermine: European, STOAT
Ether: Crystalline, APIOL

Fabric: Velvetlike, PANNE
Fabulist, AESOP
Family: Italian, CENCI
Fiber: West Indian, SISAL
Fig: Smyrna, ELEME, ELEMI
Figure: Of speech, TROPE
Finch: European, SERIN
Fish: American small, KILLY
Flower: Garden, ASTER
Friend (Spanish), AMIGO
Fruit: Tropical, MANGO
Fungus: Rye, ERGOT
Furze, GORSE
Gateway, TORAN, TORII
Gem, AGATE, BERYL, PEARL, TOPAZ
Genus: Barnacles, LEPAS
  Bears, URSUS
  Birds (loons), GAVIA
  Birds (nuthatches), SITTA
  Cats, FELIS
  Dogs, CANIS
  Fishes (chiros), ELOPS
  Fishes (perch), PERCA
  Geese, ANSER
  Grasses, STIPA
  Grasses (incl. oats), AVENA
  Gulls, LARUS
  Hares, rabbits, LEPUS
  Hawks, BUTEO
  Herbs, old world, INULA
  Herbs, trailing or climbing, APIOS
  Herbs, tropical, TACCA, URENA
  Horses, EQUUS
  Insects (olive flies), DACUS
  Lice, plant, APHIS
  Lichens, USNEA
  Lizards, AGAMA
  Moles, TALPA
  Mollusks, OLIVA
  Monkeys, CEBUS
  Palms, ARECA
  Pigeons, GOURA
  Plants (amaryllis family), AGAVE
  Ruminants (goats), CAPRA
  Shrubs, Asiatic, SABIA
  Shrubs (heath), ERICA
  Shrubs (incl. raspberry), RUBUS
  Shrubs, tropical, IXORA, TREMA; URENA
  Ticks, ARGAS
  Trees (of elm family), TREMA, ULMUS
  Trees, tropical, IXORA, TREMA
Goat: Bezoar, PASAN
God: Assyrian, ASHIR, ASHUR, ASSUR
  Babylonian, DAGAN, SIRIS
  Gaelic, DAGDA
  Hindu, BHAGA, INDRA, SHIVA
  Japanese, EBISU
  Philistine, DAGON
  Phrygian, ATTIS
  Teutonic, AEGIR, GYMIR
  Welsh, DYLAN
Goddess: Babylonian, ISTAR, NANAI
  Hindu, DURGA, GAURI, SHREE
Group: Of six, HEXAD
Grove: Sacred to Diana, NEMUS
Growing out, ENATE
Guitar: Hindu, SITAR
Gull: PEWEE, PEWIT
Hartebeest, CAAMA
Headdress: Jewish or Persian, TIARA
  Liturgical, MITER, MITRE
Heath, ERICA
Herb: Grasslike marsh, SEDGE
Heron, EGRET
Hog: Young, SHOAT, SHOTE
Image, EIKON
Indian: Cariban, ARARA
  Iroquoian, HURON
  Mexican, AZTEC, OPATA, OTOMI
  Muskhogean, CREEK
  Siouan, OSAGE, TETON
  Spanish American, ARARA, CARIB
Inflorescence: Racemose, AMENT
Insect: Immature, LARVA
Intrigue, CABAL
Iris: Yellow, SEDGE

Juniper, GORSE, RETEM
Kidneys: Pertaining to, RENAL
King: British legendary, LLUDD
Kite: European, GLEDE
Kobold, NISSE
Land: Cultivated, ARADA, ARADO
Landholder (Scotch), LAIRD, THANE
Language: Dravidian, TAMIL
Lariat, LASSO, REATA
Laughing, RIANT
Lawgiver: Athenian, DRACO, SOLON
Leaf: Calyx, SEPAL
  Fern, FROND
Lemur, LORIS
Letter: English, AITCH
  Greek, ALPHA, DELTA, GAMMA, KAPPA, OMEGA, SIGMA,
    THETA
  Hebrew, ALEPH, CHETH, GIMEL, SADHE, ZAYIN
Lichen, USNEA
Lighthouse, PHARE
Lizard: Old World, AGAMA
Loincloth, DHOTI
Louse: Plant, APHID
Macaw: Brazilian, ARARA
Mahogany: Philippine, ALMON
Mammal: Badgerlike, RATEL
  Civetlike, GENET
  Giraffelike, OKAPI
  Raccoonlike, COATI
Man (French), HOMME
Marble, AGATE
Mark: Insertion, CARET
Market place: Greek, AGORA
Marsupial: Australian, KOALA
Measure: Electric, FARAD, HENRY
  Energy, JOULE
  Metric, LITER, STERE
  Printing, AGATE
  Russian, VERST
Mixture: Smelting, MATTE
Mohicans: Last of, UNCAS
Molding: Convex, OVOLO, TORUS
Mole, TALPA
Monkey: African, PATAS
  Capuchin, SAJOU
  Howling, ARABA
Monkshood, ATEES
Month: Jewish, NISAN, SIVAN, TEBET
Museum (French), MUSEE
Musketeer, ATHOS
Native: Aleutian, ALEUT
  New Zealand, MAORI
Neckpiece: Ecclesiastical, AMICE
Nerve (comb. form), NEURO
Nest: Eagle's or hawk's, AERIE
  Insect's, NIDUS
Net: Fishing, SEINE
Newsstand, KIOSK
Nitrogen, AZOTE
Noble: Mohammedan, AMEER
Nodule: Stone, GEODE
Nostrils, NARES
Notched irregularly, EROSE
Nymph: Mohammedan, HOURI
Official: Roman, EDILE
Oleoresin, ELEMI
Opening: Mouthlike, STOMA
Oration: Funeral, ELOGE
Ostiole, STOMA
Page: Left-hand, VERSO
  Right-hand, RECTO
Palm, ARECA, BETEL
Park: Colorado, ESTES
Perfume, ATTAR
Philosopher: Greek, PLATO
Pillar: Stone, STELA, STELE
Pinnacle: Glacial, SERAC
Plain, LLANO
Plant: Century, AGAVE
  Climbing, LIANA
  Dwarf, CUMIN
  East Asian perennial, RAMIE
  Medicinal, SENNA
  Mustard family, CRESS
Plate: Communion, PATEN
Poem: Lyric, EPODE

Point: Lowest, NADIR
Poplar, ABELE, ALAMO, ASPEN
Porridge: Spanish American, ATOLE
Post: Stair, NEWEL
Priest: Mohammedan, IMAUM
Protozoan, AMEBA
Queen: (French), REINE
   Hindu, RANEE
Rabbit, CONEY
Rail, CRAKE
Red (heraldry), GULES
Religion: Moslem, ISLAM
Resin, ELEMI
Revoke (law), ADEEM
Rich man, MIDAS, NABOB
Ridge: Sandy, ESKAR, ESKER
River: French, LOIRE, SEINE
Rockfish: California, REINA
Rootstock: Fragrant, ORRIS
Ruff: Female, REEVE
Sack: Pack, KYACK
Salt: Ethereal, ESTER
Saltpeter, NITER, NITRE
Salutation: Eastern, SALAM
Sandpiper: Old World, TEREK
Scented, OLENT
School: Fish, SHOAL
   French public, LYCEE
Scriptures: Mohammedan, KORAN
Seaweeds, ALGAE
Seed: Aromatic, ANISE
Seraglio, HAREM, SERAI
Serf, HELOT
Sheep: Wild, AUDAD
Sheeplike, OVINE
Shield, AEGIS
Shoe: Wooden, SABOT
Shoots: Pickled bamboo, ACHAR
Shot: Billiard, CAROM, MASSE
Shrine: Buddhist, STUPA
Shrub: Burning bush, WAHOO
   Ornamental evergreen, TOYON
   Used in tanning, SUMAC
Silk: Watered, MOIRE
Sister (French), SOEUR
   (Latin), SOROR
Six: Group of, HEXAD
Skeleton: Marine, CORAL
Slave, HELOT
Snake, ABOMA, ADDER, COBRA, RACER
Soldier: French, POILU
   Indian, SEPOY
Sour, ACERB
Spirit: Air, ARIEL

Staff: Shepherd's, CROOK
Starwort, ASTER
Steel (German), STAHL
Stockade: Russian, ETAPE
Stop (nautical), AVAST
Storehouse, ETAPE
Subway: Parisian, METRO
Tapestry, ARRAS
Tea: Paraguayan, YERBA
Temple: Hawaiian, HEIAU
Terminal: Positive, ANODE
Theater: Greek, ODEON, ODEUM
Then (French), ALORS
Thread: Surgical, SETON
Thrush: Wilson's, VEERY
Title: Hindu, BABOO
   Indian, RAJAH, SAHEB, SAHIB
   Mohammedan, EMEER, IMAUM
Tree: Buddhist sacred, PIPAL
   East Indian cotton, SIMAL
   Hickory, PECAN
   Light-wooded, BALSA
   Malayan, TERAP
   Mediterranean, CAROB
   Mexican, ABETO
   Mexican pine, OCOTE
   New Zealand, MAIRE
   Philippine, ALMON
   Rain, SAMAN
   South American, UMBRA
   Tamarack, LARCH
   Tamarisk salt, ATLEE
   West Indian, ACANA
Trout, CHARR
Troy, ILION, ILIUM
Twin: Siamese, CHANG
Vestment: Ecclesiastical, STOLE
Violin: Famous, AMATI, STRAD
Volcano: Mud, SALSE
Wampum, PEAGE
War cry: Greek, ALALA
Wavy (heraldry), UNDEE
Weight: Jewish, GERAH
Wen, TALPA
Wheat, SPELT
Wheel: Persian water, NORIA
Whitefish, CISCO
Willow, OSIER
Window: Bay, ORIEL
Wine, MEDOC, RHINE, TINTA, TOKAY
Winged, ALATE
Woman (French), FEMME
Year: Excess of solar over lunar, EPACT
Zoroastrian, PARSI

Words of Six or More Letters

Agave, MAGUEY
Alkaloid: Crystalline, ESERIN, ESERINE
Alligator, CAYMAN
Amphibole, EDENITE, URALITE
Ant: White, TERMITE
Antelope: African, DIKDIK, DUIKER, GEMSBOK, IMPALA,
   KOODOO
   European, CHAMOIS
   Indian, NILGAI, NILGAU, NILGHAI, NILGHAU
Ape: Asian or East Indian, GIBBON
Appendage: Leaf, STIPEL, STIPULE
Armadillo, PELUDO, TATOUAY
Arrowroot, ARARAO
Ascetic: Jewish, ESSENE
Ass: Asian wild, ONAGER
Avatar: Of Vishnu, KRISHNA
Babylonian, ELAMITE
Badge: Shoulder, EPAULET
Baldness, ALOPECIA
Barracuda, SENNET
Bark: Aromatic, SINTOC
Bearlike, URSINE
Beetle, ELATER
Bible: Zoroastrian, AVESTA
Bird: Sea, PETREL
   South American, SERIEMA
   Wading, AVOCET, AVOSET

Bone: Leg, FIBULA
Branched, RAMATE
Brother (Latin), FRATER
Bunting: European, ORTOLAN
Call: Trumpet, SENNET
Canoe: Eskimo, BAIDAR, OOMIAK
Caravansary, IMARET
Cat: Asian or African, CHEETAH
   Leopardlike, OCELOT
Cenobite: Jewish, ESSENE
Centerpiece: Table, EPERGNE
Cetacean, DOLPHIN, PORPOISE
Chariot, ESSEDA, ESSEDE
Chief: Seminole, OSCEOLA
Claim: Release as (law), REMISE
Clock: Water, CLEPSYDRA
Cloud, CUMULUS, NIMBUS
Coach: French hackney, FIACRE
Coin: Czech, KORUNA
   Ethiopian, TALARI
   Finnish, MARKKA
   German, THALER
   Greek, DRACHMA
   Haitian, GOURDE
   Honduran, LEMPIRA
   Hungarian, FORINT
   Indo-Chinese, PIASTER

Netherlands, GUILDER
Panamanian, BALBOA
Paraguayan, GUARANI
Portuguese, ESCUDO
Russian, COPECK, KOPECK, ROUBLE
Spanish, PESETA
Venezuelan, BOLIVAR
Communion: Last holy, VIATICUM
Conceal (law), ELOIGN
Confection, PRALINE
Construction: Sentence, SYNTAX
Convexity: Shaft of column, ENTASIS
Court: Anglo-Saxon, GEMOTE
Cow: Sea, DUGONG, MANATEE
Cylindrical, TERETE
Dagger, STILETTO
  Malay, CREESE, KREESE
Date: Roman, CALENDS, KALENDS
Deer, CARIBOU, WAPITI
Disease: Plant, ERINOSE
Doorkeeper, OSTIARY
Dragonflies: Order of, ODANATA
Drink: Of gods, NECTAR
Drum: TABOUR
  Moorish, ATABAL, ATTABAL
Duck: Fish-eating, MERGANSER
  Sea, SCOTER
Dynasty: Chinese, MANCHU
Eel, CONGER
Edit, REDACT
Envelope: Flower, PERIANTH
Eskimo, AMERIND
Ether: Crystalline, APIOLE
Excuse (law), ESSOIN
Eyespots, OCELLI
Fabric, ESTAMENE, ESTAMIN, ETAMINE
Falcon: European, KESTREL
Figure: Used as column, CARYATID, TELAMON
Fine: For punishment, AMERCE
Fish: Asian fresh-water, GOURAMI
  Pikelike, BARRACUDA
Five: Group of, PENTAD
Fly: African, TSETSE
Foot: Metric, ANAPEST, IAMBUS
Foxlike, VULPINE
Frying pan, SPIDER
Fur, KARAKUL
Galley: Greek or Roman, BIREME, TRIREME
Game: Card, ECARTE
Garment: Greek, CHLAMYS
Gateway, GOPURA, TORANA
Genus: Birds (ravens, crows), CORVUS
  Eels, CONGER
  Fishes, ANABAS
  Foxes, VULPES
  Herbs, ANEMONE
  Insects, CICADA
  Lemurs, GALAGO
  Mints (incl. catnip), NEPETA
  Mollusks, ANOMIA, ASTARTE, TEREDO
  Mollusks (incl. oysters), OSTREA
  Monkeys (spider monkeys), ATELES
  Thrushes (incl. robins), TURDUS
  Trees (of elm family), CELTIS
  Trees (inc. dogwood), CORNUS
  Trees, tropical American, SAPOTA
  Wrens, NANNUS
Gibbon, SIAMANG, WOUWOU
Gland: Salivary, RACEMOSE
Goat: Bezoar, PASANG
Goatlike, CAPRINE
God: Assyrian, ASHSHUR, ASSHUR
  Babylonian, BABBAR, MARDUK, MERODACH, NANNAR,
    NERGAL, SHAMASH
  Hindu, BRAHMA, KRISHNA, VISHNU
  Tahitian, TAAROA
Goddess: Babylonian, ISHTAR
  Hindu, CHANDI, HAIMAVATI, LAKSHMI, PARVATI, SARAS-
    VATI, SARASWATI
Government, POLITY
Governor: Persian, SATRAP
Grandson (Scotch), NEPOTE
Group: Of five, PENTAD
  Of nine, ENNEAD
  Of seven, HEPTAD
Hare: in first year, LEVERET

Harpsichord, SPINET
Herb: Alpine, EDELWEISS
  Chinese, GINSENG
  South African, FREESIA
Hermit, EREMITE
Hero: Legendary, PALADIN
Heron, BITTERN
Horselike, EQUINE
Hound: Short-legged, BEAGLE
House (French), MAISON
Idiot, CRETIN
Implement: Stone, NEOLITH
Incarnation: Hindu, AVATAR
Indian, APACHE, COMANCHE, PAIUTE, SENECA
Inn: Turkish, IMARET
Insects: Order of, DIPTERA
Instrument: Japanese banjolike, SAMISEN
  Musical, CLAVIER, SPINET
Interstice, AREOLA
Ironwood, COLIMA
Juniper: Old Testament, RAETAM
Kettledrum, ATABAL
King: Fairy, OBERON
Kneecap, PATELLA
Knife, MACHETE
Langur: Sumatran, SIMPAI
Legislature: Spanish, CORTES
Lemur: African, GALAGO
  Madagascar, AYEAYE
Letter: Greek, EPSILON, LAMBDA, OMICRON, UPSILON
  Hebrew, DALETH, LAMEDH, SAMEKH
Lighthouse, PHAROS
Lizard, IGUANA
Llama, ALPACA
Lockjaw, TETANUS
Locust, CICADA, CICALA
Macaw: Brazilian, MARACAN
Maid: Of Astolat, ELAINE
Mammal: Madagascar, TENDRAC, TENREC
Man (Spanish), HOMBRE
Marmoset: South American, TAMARIN
Marsupial, BANDICOOT, WOMBAT
Massacre, POGROM
Mayor: Spanish, ALCALDE
Measure: Electric, AMPERE, COULOMB, KILOWATT
Medicine: Quack, NOSTRUM
Member: Religious order, CENOBITE
Molasses, TREACLE
Monkey: African, GRIVET, NISNAS
  Asian, LANGUR
  Philippine, MACHIN
  South American, PINCHE, SAIMIRI, SAMIRI, SAPAJOU
Monster, CHIMERA, GORGON
  (Comb. form), TERATO
  Cretan, MINOTAUR
Month: Jewish, HESHVAN, KISLEV, SHEBAT, TAMMUZ,
  TISHRI, VEADAR
Mountain: Asia Minor, ARARAT
Mulct, AMERCE
Musketeer, ARAMIS, PORTHOS
Nearsighted, MYOPIC
Net, TRAMMEL
New York City, GOTHAM
Nine: Group of, ENNEAD
Nobleman: Spanish, GRANDEE
Official: Roman, AEDILE
Onyx: Mexican, TECALI
Order: Dragonflies, ODANATA
  Insects, DIPTERA
Organ: Plant, PISTIL
Ornament: Shoulder, EPAULET
Overcoat: Military, CAPOTE
Ox: Wild, BANTENG
Oxidation: Bronze or copper, PATINA
Paralysis: Incomplete, PARESIS
Pear: Alligator, AVOCADO
Persimmon: Mexican, CHAPOTE
Pipe: Peace, CALUMET
Plaid (Scotch), TARTAN
Plain, PAMPAS, STEPPE, TUNDRA
Plant: Buttercup family, ANEMONE
  Century, MAGUEY
  On rocks, LICHEN
Plowing: Fit for, ARABLE
Poem: Heroic, EPOPEE
  Six-lined, SESTET

Point: Highest, ZENITH
Potion: Love, PHILTER, PHILTRE
Protozoan, AMOEBA
Punish, AMERCE
Purple (heraldry), PURPURE
Queen: Fairy, TITANIA
Race: Skiing, SLALOM
Rat, BANDICOOT, LEMMING
Retort, RIPOST, RIPOSTE
Ring: Harness, TERRET
  Little, ANNULET
Rodent: Jumping, JERBOA
  Spanish American, AGOUTI, AGOUTY
Sailor: East Indian, LASCAR
Salmon: Young, GRILSE
Salutation: Eastern, SALAAM
Sandpiper, PLOVER
Sandy, ARENOSE
Sapodilla, SAPOTA, SAPOTE
Saw: Surgical, TREPAN
Seven: Group of, HEPTAD
Sexes: Common to both, EPICENE
Shawl: Mexican, SERAPE
Sheathing: Flower, SPATHE
Sheep: Wild, AOUDAD, ARGALI
Shipworm, TEREDO
Shoes: Mercury's winged, TALARIA
Shortening: Syllable, SYSTOLE
Shrub, SPIRAEA
Sickle-shaped, FALCATE
Silver (heraldry), ARGENT
Snake, ANACONDA
Speech: Loss of, APHASIA
Spiral, HELICAL
Staff: Bishop's, CROSIER, CROZIER
Stalk: Plant, PETIOLE
State: Swiss, CANTON
Studio, ATELIER

Swan: Young, CYGNET
Swimming, NATANT
Sword-shaped, ENSATE
Terminal: Negative, CATHODE
Third (music), TIERCE
Thrust: Fencing, RIPOST, RIPOSTE
Tile: Pertaining to, TEGULAR
Tomb: Empty, CENOTAPH
Tooth (comb. form), ODONTO
Tower: Mohammedan, MINARET
Tree: African timber, BAOBAB
  Black gum, TUPELO
  East Indian, MARGOSA
  Locust, ACACIA
  Malayan, SINTOC
  Marmalade, SAPOTE
Urn: Tea, SAMOVAR
Vehicle, LANDAU, TROIKA
Verbose, PROLIX
Viceroy: Egyptian, KHEDIVE
Vulture: American, CONDOR
Warehouse (French), ENTREPOT
Whale: White, BELUGA
Whirlpool, VORTEX
Will: Addition to, CODICIL
  Having left, TESTATE
Wind, CHINOOK, MONSOON, SIMOOM, SIMOON, SI
  ROCCO
Window: In roof, DORMER
Wine, BARBERA, BURGUNDY, CABERNET, CHABLIS, CHI-
  ANTI, CLARET, MUSCATEL, RIESLING, SAUTERNE,
  SHERRY, ZINFANDEL
Wolfish, LUPINE
Woman: Boisterous, TERMAGANT
Woolly, LANATE
Workshop, ATELIER
Zoroastrian, PARSEE

Old Testament Names

We do not pretend that this list is all-inclusive. We include only those names that occur most often in crossword puzzles.

Aaron: First high priest of Jews; son of Amram; brother of Miriam and Moses; father of Abihu, Eleazer, Ithamar, and Nadab.
Abel: Son of Adam; slain by Cain.
Abigail: Wife of Nabal; later, wife of David.
Abihu: Son of Aaron.
Abimelech: King of Gerar.
Abner: Commander of army of Saul and Ishbosheth; slain by Joab.
Abraham (or Abram): Patriarch; forefather of the Jews; son of Terah; husband of Sarah; father of Isaac and Ishmael.
Absalom: Son of David and Maacah; revolted against David; slain by Joab.
Achish: King of Gath; gave refuge to David.
Achsa (or Achsah): Daughter of Caleb; wife of Othniel.
Adah: Wife of Lamech.
Adam: First man; husband of Eve; father of Cain, Abel, and Seth.
Adonijah: Son of David and Haggith.
Agag: King of Amalek; spared by Saul; slain by Samuel.
Ahasuerus: King of Persia; husband of Vashti and, later, Esther; sometimes identified with Xerxes the Great.
Ahijah: Prophet; foretold accession of Jeroboam.
Ahinoam: Wife of David.
Amasa: Commander of army of David; slain by Joab.
Amnon: Son of David and Ahinoam; ravished Tamar; slain by Absalom.
Amram: Husband of Jochebed; father of Aaron, Miriam and Moses.
Asenath: Wife of Joseph.
Asher: Son of Jacob and Zilpah.
Balaam: Prophet; rebuked by his donkey for cursing God.
Barak: Jewish captain; associated with Deborah.
Baruch: Secretary to Jeremiah.
Bathsheba: Wife of Uriah; later, wife of David.
Belshazzar: Crown prince of Babylon.
Benaiah: Warrior of David; proclaimed Solomon King.
Ben-Hadad: Name of several kings of Damascus.
Benjamin: Son of Jacob and Rachel.
Bezaleel: Chief architect of tabernacle.
Bilhah: Servant of Rachel; mistress of Jacob.

Bildad: Comforter of Job.
Boaz: Husband of Ruth; father of Obed.
Cain: Son of Adam and Eve; slayer of Abel; father of Enoch.
Cainan: Son of Enos.
Caleb: Spy sent out by Moses to visit Canaan; father of Achsa.
Canaan: Son of Ham.
Chilion: Son of Elimelech; husband of Orpah.
Cush: Son of Ham; father of Nimrod.
Dan: Son of Jacob and Bilhah.
Daniel: Prophet; saved from lions by God.
Deborah: Hebrew prophetess; helped Israelites conquer Canaanites.
Delilah: Mistress and betrayer of Samson.
Elam: Son of Shem.
Eleazar: Son of Aaron; succeeded him as high priest.
Eli: High priest and judge; teacher of Samuel; father of Hophni and Phinehas.
Eliakim: Chief minister of Hezekiah.
Eliezer: Servant of Abraham.
Elihu: Comforter of Job.
Elijah (or Elias): Prophet; went to heaven in chariot of fire.
Elimelech: Husband of Naomi; father of Chilion and Mahlon.
Eliphaz: Comforter of Job.
Elisha (or Eliseus): Prophet; successor of Elijah.
Elkanah: Husband of Hannah; father of Samuel.
Enoch: Son of Cain.
Enoch: Father of Methuselah.
Enos: Son of Seth; father of Cainan.
Ephraim: Son of Joseph.
Esau: Son of Isaac and Rebecca; sold his birthright to his brother Jacob.
Esther: Jewish wife of Ahasuerus; saved Jews from Haman's plotting.
Eve: First woman; created from rib of Adam.
Ezra (or Esdras): Hebrew scribe and priest.
Gad: Son of Jacob and Zilpah.
Gehazi: Servant of Elisha.
Gideon: Israelite hero; defeated Midianites.
Goliath: Philistine giant; slain by David.
Hagar: Handmaid of Sarah; concubine of Abraham; mother of Ishmael.

Haggith: Mother of Adonijah.
Ham: Son of Noah; father of Cush, Mizraim, Phut, and Canaan.
Haman: Chief minister of Ahasuerus; hanged on gallows prepared for Mordecai.
Hannah: Wife of Elkanah; mother of Samuel.
Hanun: King of Ammonites.
Haran: Brother of Abraham; father of Lot.
Hazael: King of Damascus.
Hephzi-Bah: Wife of Hezekiah; mother of Mannaseh.
Hiram: King of Tyre.
Holofernes: General of Nebuchadnezzar; slain by Judith.
Hophni: Son of Eli.
Isaac: Hebrew patriarch; son of Abraham and Sarah; half brother of Ishmael; husband of Rebecca; father of Esau and Jacob.
Ishmael: Son of Abraham and Hagar; half brother of Isaac.
Issachar: Son of Jacob and Leah.
Ithamar: Son of Aaron.
Jabal: Son of Lamech and Adah.
Jabin: King of Hazor.
Jacob: Hebrew patriarch; founder of Israel; son of Isaac and Rebecca; husband of Leah and Rachel; father of Asher, Benjamin, Dan, Gad, Issachar, Joseph, Judah, Levi, Naphtali, Reuben, Simeon, and Zebulun.
Jael: Slayer of Sisera.
Japheth: Son of Noah.
Jehoiada: High priest; husband of Jehoshabeath; revolted against Athaliah and made Joash King of Judah.
Jehoshabeath (or Jehosheba): Daughter of Jehoram of Judah; wife of Jehoiada.
Jephthah: Judge in Israel; sacrificed his only daughter because of vow.
Jesse: Son of Obed; father of David.
Jethro: Midianite priest; father of Zipporah.
Jezebel: Phoenician princess; wife of Ahab; mother of Ahaziah, Athaliah, and Jehoram.
Joab: Commander in chief under David; slayer of Abner, Absalom, and Amasa.
Job: Patriarch; underwent many afflictions; comforted by Bildad, Elihu, Eliphaz and Zophar.
Jochebed: Wife of Amram.
Jonah: Prophet; cast into sea and swallowed by great fish.
Jonathan: Son of Saul; friend of David.
Joseph: Son of Jacob and Rachel; sold into slavery by his brothers; husband of Asenath; father of Ephraim and Manassah.
Joshua: Successor of Moses; son of Nun.
Jubal: Son of Lamech and Adah.
Judah: Son of Jacob and Leah.
Judith: Slayer of Holofernes.
Kish: Father of Saul.
Laban: Father of Leah and Rachel.
Lamech: Son of Methuselah; father of Noah.
Lamech: Husband of Adah and Zillah; father of Jabal, Jubal, and Tubal-Cain.
Leah: Daughter of Laban; wife of Jacob.
Levi: Son of Jacob and Leah.
Lot: Son of Haran; escaped destruction of Sodom.
Maacah: Mother of Absalom and Tamar.
Mahlon: Son of Elimelech; first husband of Ruth.

Manasseh: Son of Joseph.
Melchizedek: King of Salem.
Methuselah: Patriarch; son of Enoch; father of Lamech.
Michal: Daughter of Saul; wife of David.
Miriam: Prophetess; daughter of Amram; sister of Aaron and Moses.
Mizraim: Son of Ham.
Mordecai: Uncle of Esther; with her aid, saved Jews from Haman's plotting.
Moses: Prophet and lawgiver; son of Amram; brother of Aaron and Miriam; husband of Zipporah.
Naaman: Syrian captain; cured of leprosy by Elisha.
Nabal: Husband of Abigail.
Naboth: Owner of vineyard; stoned to death because he would not sell it to Ahab.
Nadab: Son of Aaron.
Nahor: Father of Terah.
Naomi: Wife of Elimelech; mother-in-law of Ruth.
Naphtali: Son of Jacob and Bilhah.
Nathan: Prophet; reproved David for causing Uriah's death.
Nebuchadnezzar (or Nebuchadrezzar): King of Babylon; destroyer of Jerusalem.
Nehemiah: Jewish leader; empowered by Artaxerxes to rebuild Jerusalem.
Nimrod: Mighty hunter; son of Cush.
Noah: Patriarch; son of Lamech; escaped Deluge by building Ark; father of Ham, Japheth and Shem.
Nun (or Non): Father of Joshua.
Obed: Son of Boaz; father of Jesse.
Og: King of Bashan.
Orpah: Wife of Chilion.
Othniel: Kenezite; judge of Israel; husband of Achsa.
Phinehas: Son of Eleazer.
Phinehas: Son of Eli.
Phut (or Put): Son of Ham.
Potiphar: Egyptian official; bought Joseph.
Rachel: Wife of Jacob.
Rebecca (or Rebekah): Wife of Isaac.
Reuben: Son of Jacob and Leah.
Ruth: Wife of Mahlon, later of Boaz; daughter-in-law of Naomi.
Samson: Judge of Israel; famed for strength; betrayed by Delilah.
Samuel: Hebrew judge and prophet; son of Elkanah.
Sarah (or Sara, Sarai): Wife of Abraham.
Sennacherib: King of Assyria.
Seth: Son of Adam; father of Enos.
Shem: Son of Noah; father of Elam.
Simeon: Son of Jacob and Leah.
Sisera: Canaanite captain; slain by Jael.
Tamar: Daughter of David and Maachah; ravished by Amnon.
Terah: Son of Nahor; father of Abraham.
Tubal-Cain: Son of Lamech and Zillah.
Uriah: Husband of Bathsheba; sent to death in battle by David.
Vashti: Wife of Ahasuerus; set aside by him.
Zadok: High priest during David's reign.
Zebulun (or Zabulon): Son of Jacob and Leah.
Zillah: Wife of Lamech.
Zilpah: Servant of Leah; mistress of Jacob.
Zipporah: Daughter of Jethro; wife of Moses.
Zophar: Comforter of Job.

Kings of Judah and Israel

Kings Before Division of Kingdom

Saul: First King of Israel; son of Kish; father of Ish-Bosheth, Jonathan and Michal.
Ish-Bosheth (or Eshbaal): King of Israel; son of Saul.
David: King of Judah; later of Israel; son of Jesse; husband of Abigail, Ahinoam, Bathsheba, Michal, etc.; father of Absalom, Adonijah, Amnon, Solomon, Tamar, etc.
Solomon: King of Israel and Judah; son of David; father of Rehoboam.
Rehoboam: Son of Solomon; during his reign the kingdom was divided into Judah and Israel.

Kings of Judah (Southern Kingdom)

Rehoboam: First King.
Abijah (or Abijam or Abia): Son of Rehoboam.
Asa: Probably son of Abijah.
Jehoshaphat: Son of Asa.
Jehoram (or Joram): Son of Jehoshaphat; husband of Athaliah.
Ahaziah: Son of Jehoram and Athaliah.
Athaliah: Daughter of King Ahab of Israel and Jezebel; wife of Jehoram.

Joash (or Jehoash): Son of Ahaziah.
Amaziah: Son of Joash.
Uzziah (or Azariah): Son of Amaziah.
Jotham: Regent, later King; son of Uzziah.
Ahaz: Son of Jotham.
Hezekiah: Son of Ahaz; husband of Hephzi-Bah.
Manasseh: Son of Hezekiah and Hephzi-Bah.
Amon: Son of Manasseh.
Josiah (or Josias): Son of Amon.
Jehoahaz (or Joahaz): Son of Josiah.
Jehoiachin: Son of Jehoiakim.
Jehoiakim: Son of Josiah.
Zedekiah: Son of Josiah; kingdom overthrown by Babylonians under Nebuchadnezzar.

Kings of Israel (Northern Kingdom)

Jeroboam I: Led secession of Israel.
Nadab: Son of Jeroboam I.
Baasha: Overthrew Nadab.
Elah: Son of Baasha.
Zimri: Overthrew Elah.
Omri: Overthrew Zimri.

Ahab: Son of Omri; husband of Jezebel.
Ahaziah: Son of Ahab.
Jehoram (or Joram): Son of Ahab.
Jehu: Overthrew Jehoram.
Jehoahaz (or Joahaz): Son of Jehu.
Jehoash (or Joash): Son of Jehoahaz.
Jeroboam II: Son of Jehoash.
Zechariah: Son of Jeroboam II.
Shallum: Overthrew Zechariah.
Menahem: Overthrew Shallum.

Pekahiah: Son of Menahem.
Pekah: Overthrew Pekahiah.
Hoshea: Overthrew Pekah; kingdom overthrown by Assyrians under Sargon II.

Prophets

Major: Isaiah, Jeremiah, Ezekiel, Daniel.
Minor: Hosea, Obadiah, Nahum, Haggai, Joel, Jonah, Habakkuk, Zechariah, Amos, Micah, Zephaniah, Malachi.

Greek and Roman Mythology

Most of the Greek deities were adopted by the Romans, although in many cases there was a change of name. In the list below, information is given under the Greek name; the name in parentheses is the Roman equivalent. However, all Latin names are listed with cross references to the Greek ones. In addition, there are several deities that are exclusively Roman.

Acheron: One of several **Rivers of Underworld:** Acheron (woe), Cocytus (wailing), Lethe (forgetfulness), Phlegethon (fire), Styx (across which souls of dead were ferried by Charon).
Achilles: Greek warrior; slew Hector at Troy; slain by Paris, who wounded him in his vulnerable heel.
Actaeon: Hunter; surprised Artemis bathing; changed by her to stag; and killed by his dogs.
Admetus: King of Thessaly; his wife, Alcestis, offered to die in his place.
Adonis: Beautiful youth loved by Aphrodite.
Aeacus: One of three judges of dead in Hades; son of Zeus.
Aeëtes: King of Colchis; father of Medea; keeper of Golden Fleece.
Aegeus: Father of Theseus; believing Theseus killed in Crete, he drowned himself; Aegean Sea named for him.
Aegisthus: Son of Thyestes; slew Atreus; with Clytemnestra, his paramour, slew Agamemnon; slain by Orestes.
Aegyptus: Brother of Danaus; his sons, except Lynceus, slain by Danaides.
Aeneas: Trojan; son of Anchises and Aphrodite; after fall of Troy, led his followers eventually to Italy; loved and deserted Dido.
Aeolus: One of several **Winds:** Aeolus (keeper of winds), Boreas (Aquilo) (north wind), Eurus (east wind), Notus (Auster) (south wind), Zephyrus (Favonius) (west wind).
Aeson: King of Ioclus; father of Jason; overthrown by his brother Pelias; restored to youth by Medea.
Aether: Personification of sky.
Aethra: Mother of Theseus.
Agamemnon: King of Mycenae; son of Atreus; brother of Menelaus; leader of Greeks against Troy; slain on his return home by Clytemnestra and Aegisthus.
Aglaia: One of several **Graces:** Beautiful goddesses: Aglaia (Brilliance), Euphrosyne (Joy), and Thalia (Bloom); daughters of Zeus.
Ajax: Greek warrior; killed himself at Troy because Achilles's armor was awarded to Odysseus.
Alcestis: Wife of Admetus; offered to die in his place but saved from death by Hercules.
Alcmene: Wife of Amphitryon; mother by Zeus of Hercules.
Alcyone: One of several **Pleiades:** Alcyone, Celaeno, Electra, Maia, Merope, Sterope or Asterope, Taygeta; seven daughters of Atlas; transformed into heavenly constellation, of which six stars are visible (Merope is said to have hidden in shame for loving a mortal).
Alecto: One of several **Furies:** Avenging spirits; Alecto, Megaera, and Tisiphone; known also as Erinyes or Eumenides.
Alectryon: Youth changed by Ares into cock.
Althaea: Wife of Oeneus; mother of Meleager.
Amazons: Female warriors in Asia Minor; supported Troy against Greeks.
Amphion: Musician; husband of Niobe; charmed stones to build fortifications for Thebes.
Amphitrite: Sea goddess; wife of Poseidon.
Amphitryon: Husband of Alcmene.
Anchises: Father of Aeneas.
Ancile: Sacred shield that fell from heavens; palladium of Rome.
Andraemon: Husband of Dryope.
Andromache: Wife of Hector.
Andromeda: Daughter of Cepheus; chained to cliff for monster to devour; rescued by Perseus.

Anteia: Wife of Proetus; tried to induce Bellerophon to elope with her.
Anteros: God who avenged unrequited love.
Antigone: Daughter of Oedipus; accompanied him to Colonus; performed burial rite for Polynices and hanged herself.
Antinoüs: Leader of suitors of Penelope; slain by Odysseus.
Aphrodite (Venus): Goddess of love and beauty; daughter of Zeus; mother of Eros.
Apollo: God of beauty, poetry, music; later identified with Helios as Phoebus Apollo; son of Zeus and Leto.
Aquilo: One of several **Winds:** Aeolus (keeper of winds), Boreas (Aquilo) (north wind), Eurus (east wind), Notus (Auster) (south wind), Zephyrus (Favonius) (west wind).
Arachne: Maiden who challenged Athena to weaving contest; changed to spider.
Ares (Mars): God of war; son of Zeus and Hera.
Argo: Ship in which Jason and followers sailed to Colchis for Golden Fleece.
Argus: Monster with hundred eyes; slain by Hermes; his eyes placed by Hera into peacock's tail.
Ariadne: Daughter of Minos; aided Theseus in slaying Minotaur; deserted by him on island of Naxos and married to Dionysus.
Arion: Musician; thrown overboard by pirates but saved by dolphin.
Artemis (Diana): Goddess of moon; huntress; twin sister of Apollo.
Asclepius (Aesculapius): Mortal son of Apollo; slain by Zeus for raising dead; later deified as god of medicine. Also known as Asklepios.
Astarte: Phoenician goddess of love; variously identified with Aphrodite, Selene, and Artemis.
Astraea: Goddess of Justice; daughter of Zeus and Themis.
Atalanta: Princess who challenged her suitors to a foot race; Hippomenes won race and married her.
Athena (Minerva): Goddess of wisdom; known poetically as Pallas Athene; sprang fully armed from head of Zeus.
Atlas: Titan; held world on his shoulders as punishment for warring against Zeus; son of Iapetus.
Atreus: King of Mycenae; father of Menelaus and Agamemnon; brother of Thyestes, three of whose sons he slew and served to him at banquet; slain by Aegisthus.
Atropos: One of several **Fates:** Goddesses of destiny; Clotho (Spinner of thread of life), Lachesis (Determiner of length), and Atropos (Cutter of thread); also called Moirae. Identified by Romans with their goddesses of fate, Nona, Decuma, and Morta; called Parcae.
Auster: One of several **Winds:** Aeolus (keeper of winds), Boreas (Aquilo) (north wind), Eurus (east wind), Notus (Auster) (south wind), Zephyrus (Favonius) (west wind).
Avernus: Infernal regions; name derived from small vaporous lake near Vesuvius which was fabled to kill birds and vegetation.
Bellerophon: Corinthian hero; killed Chimera with aid of Pegasus; tried to reach Olympus on Pegasus and was thrown to his death.
Bellona: Roman goddess of war.
Boreas: One of several **Winds:** Aeolus (keeper of winds), Boreas (Aquilo) (north wind), Eurus (east wind), Notus (Auster) (south wind), Zephyrus (Favonius) (west wind).
Briareus: Monster of hundred hands; son of Uranus and Gaea.

Briseis: Captive maiden given to Achilles; taken by Agamemnon in exchange for loss of Chryseis, which caused Achilles to cease fighting, until death of Patroclus.

Cadmus: Brother of Europa; planter of dragon seeds from which first Thebans sprang.

Calliope: One of several **Muses,** Goddesses presiding over arts and sciences: Calliope (epic poetry), Clio (history), Erato (lyric and love poetry), Euterpe (music), Melpomene (tragedy), Polymnia or Polyhymnia (sacred poetry), Terpsichore (choral dance and song), Thalia (comedy and bucolic poetry), Urania (astronomy); daughters of Zeus and Mnemosyne.

Calypso: Sea nymph; kept Odysseus on her island Ogygia for seven years.

Cassandra: Daughter of Priam; prophetess who was never believed; slain with Agamemnon.

Castor: One of **Dioscuri,** Twins Castor and Pollux; sons of Leda by Zeus.

Celaeno: One of several **Pleiades:** Alcyone, Celaeno, Electra, Maia, Merope, Sterope or Asterope, Taygeta; seven daughters of Atlas; transformed into heavenly constellation, of which six stars are visible (Merope is said to have hidden in shame for loving a mortal).

Centaurs: Beings half man and half horse; lived in mountains of Thessaly.

Cephalus: Hunter; accidentally killed his wife Procris with his spear.

Cepheus: King of Ethiopia; father of Andromeda.

Cerberus: Three-headed dog guarding entrance to Hades.

Chaos: Formless void; personified as first of gods.

Charon: Boatman on Styx who carried souls of dead to Hades; son of Erebus.

Charybdis: Female monster; personification of whirlpool.

Chimera: Female monster with head of lion, body of goat, tail of serpent; killed by Bellerophon.

Chiron: Most famous of centaurs.

Chronos: Personification of time.

Chryseis: Captive maiden given to Agamemnon; his refusal to accept ransom from her father Chryses caused Apollo to send plague on Greeks besieging Troy.

Circe: Sorceress; daughter of Helios; changed Odysseus's men into swine.

Clio: One of several **Muses:** Goddesses presiding over arts and sciences: Calliope (epic poetry), Clio (history), Erato (lyric and love poetry), Euterpe (music), Melpomene (tragedy), Polymnia or Polyhymnia (sacred poetry), Terpsichore (choral dance and song), Thalia (comedy and bucolic poetry), Urania (astronomy); daughters of Zeus and Mnemosyne.

Clotho: One of several **Fates:** Goddesses of destiny; Clotho (Spinner of thread of life), Lachesis (Determiner of length), and Atropos (Cutter of thread); also called Moirae. Identified by Romans with their goddesses of fate; Nona, Decuma, and Morta; called Parcae.

Clytemnestra: Wife of Agamemnon, whom she slew with aid of her paramour, Aegisthus; slain by her son Orestes.

Cocytus: One of several **Rivers of Underworld:** Acheron (woe), Cocytus (wailing), Lethe (forgetfulness), Phlegethon (fire), Styx (across which souls of dead were ferried by Charon).

Creon: Father of Jocasta; forbade burial of Polynices; ordered burial alive of Antigone.

Creüsa: Princess of Corinth, for whom Jason deserted Medea; slain by Medea, who sent her poisoned robe; also known as Glaüke.

Creusa: Wife of Aeneas; died fleeing Troy.

Cronus (Saturn): Titan; god of harvests; son of Uranus and Gaea; dethroned by his son Zeus.

Cybele: Anatolian nature goddess; adopted by Greeks and identified with Rhea.

Cyclopes: Race of one-eyed giants (singular: Cyclops).

Daedalus: Athenian artificer; father of Icarus; builder of Labyrinth in Crete; devised wings attached with wax for him and Icarus to escape Crete.

Danae: Princess of Argos; mother of Perseus by Zeus, who appeared to her in form of golden shower.

Danaïdes: Daughters of Danaüs; at his command, all except Hypermnestra slew their husbands, the sons of Aegyptus.

Danaüs: Brother of Aegyptus; father of Danaïdes; slain by Lynceus.

Daphne: Nymph; pursued by Apollo; changed to laurel tree.

Decuma: One of several **Fates:** Goddesses of destiny; Clotho (Spinner of thread of life), Lachesis (Determiner of length), and Atropos (Cutter of thread); also called Moirae. Identified by Romans with their goddesses of fate; Nona, Decuma, and Morta; called Parcae.

Deino: One of several **Graeae:** Sentinels for Gorgons; Deino, Enyo, and Pephredo; had one eye among them, which passed from one to another.

Demeter (Ceres): Goddess of agriculture; mother of Persephone.

Dido: Founder and queen of Carthage; stabbed herself when deserted by Aeneas.

Diomedes: Greek hero; with Odysseus, entered Troy and carried off Palladium, sacred statue of Athena.

Diomedes: Owner of man-eating horses, which Hercules, as ninth labor, carried off.

Dione: Titan goddess; mother by Zeus of Aphrodite.

Dionysus (Bacchus): God of wine; son of Zeus and Semele.

Dioscuri: Twins Castor and Pollux; sons of Leda by Zeus.

Dryads: Wood nymphs.

Dryope: Maiden changed to Hamadryad.

Echo: Nymph who fell hopelessly in love with Narcissus; faded away except for her voice.

Electra: Daughter of Agamemnon and Clytemnestra; sister of Orestes; urged Orestes to slay Clytemnestra and Aegisthus.

Electra: One of several **Pleiades:** Alcyone, Celaeno, Electra, Maia, Merope, Sterope or Asterope, Taygeta; seven daughters of Atlas; transformed into heavenly constellation, of which six stars are visible (Merope is said to have hidden in shame for loving a mortal).

Elysium: Abode of blessed dead.

Endymion: Mortal loved by Selene.

Enyo: One of several **Graeae:** Sentinels for Gorgons; Deino, Enyo, and Pephredo; had one eye among them, which passed from one to another.

Eos (Aurora): Goddess of dawn.

Epimetheus: Brother of Prometheus; husband of Pandora.

Erato: One of several **Muses:** Goddesses presiding over arts and sciences: Calliope (epic poetry), Clio (history), Erato (lyric and love poetry), Euterpe (music), Melpomene (tragedy), Polymnia or Polyhymnia (sacred poetry), Terpsichore (choral dance and song), Thalia (comedy and bucolic poetry), Urania (astronomy); daughters of Zeus and Mnemosyne.

Erebus: Spirit of darkness; son of Chaos.

Erinyes: One of several **Furies:** Avenging spirits; Alecto, Megaera, and Tisiphone; known also as Erinyes or Eumenides.

Eris: Goddess of discord.

Eros (Amor or Cupid): God of love; son of Aphrodite.

Eteocles: Son of Oedipus, whom he succeeded to rule alternately with Polynices; refused to give up throne at end of year; he and Polynices slew each other.

Eumenides: One of several **Furies:** Avenging spirits; Alecto, Megaera, and Tisiphone; known also as Erinyes or Eumenides.

Euphrosyne: One of several **Graces:** Beautiful goddesses: Aglaia (Brilliance), Euphrosyne (Joy), and Thalia (Bloom); daughters of Zeus.

Europa: Mortal loved by Zeus, who, in form of white bull, carried her off to Crete.

Eurus: One of several **Winds:** Aeolus (keeper of winds), Boreas (Aquilo) (north wind), Eurus (east wind), Notus (Auster) (south wind), Zephyrus (Favonius) (west wind).

Euryale: One of several **Gorgons:** Female monsters; Euryale, Medusa, and Stheno; had snakes for hair; their glances turned mortals to stone.

Eurydice: Nymph; wife of Orpheus.

Eurystheus: King of Argos; imposed twelve labors on Hercules.

Euterpe: One of several **Muses:** Goddesses presiding over arts and sciences: Calliope (epic poetry), Clio (history), Erato (lyric and love poetry), Euterpe (music), Melpomene (tragedy), Polymnia or Polyhymnia (sacred poetry), Terpsichore (choral dance and song), Thalia (comedy and bucolic poetry), Urania (astronomy); daughters of Zeus and Mnemosyne.

Fates: Goddesses of destiny; Clotho (Spinner of thread of life), Lachesis (Determiner of length), and Atropos (Cutter of thread); also called Moirae. Identified by Romans with their goddesses of fate; Nona, Decuma, and Morta; called Parcae.

Fauns: Roman deities of woods and groves.

Favonius: One of several **Winds:** Aeolus (keeper of winds), Boreas (Aquilo) (north wind), Eurus (east wind), Notus (Auster) (south wind), Zephyrus (Favonius) (west wind).

Flora: Roman goddess of flowers.

Fortuna: Roman goddess of fortune.

Furies: Avenging spirits; Alecto, Megaera, and Tisiphone; known also as Erinyes or Eumenides.

Gaea: Goddess of earth; daughter of Chaos; mother of Titans; known also as Ge, Gea, Gaia, etc.

Galatea: Statue of maiden carved from ivory by Pygmalion; given life by Aphrodite.

Galatea: Sea nymph; loved by Polyphemus.

Ganymede: Beautiful boy; successor to Hebe as cupbearer of gods.

Glaucus: Mortal who became sea divinity by eating magic grass.

Golden Fleece: Fleece from ram that flew Phrixos to Colchis; Aeëtes placed it under guard of dragon; carried off by Jason.

Gorgons: Female monsters; Euryale, Medusa, and Stheno; had snakes for hair; their glances turned mortals to stone.

Graces: Beautiful goddesses: Aglaia (Brilliance), Euphrosyne (Joy), and Thalia (Bloom); daughters of Zeus.

Graeae: Sentinels for Gorgons; Deino, Enyo, and Pephredo; had one eye among them, which passed from one to another.

Hades (Dis): Name sometimes given Pluto; also, abode of dead, ruled by Pluto.

Haemon: Son of Creon; promised husband of Antigone; killed himself in her tomb.

Hamadryads: Tree nymphs.

Harpies: Monsters with heads of women and bodies of birds.

Hebe (Juventas): Goddess of youth; cupbearer of gods before Ganymede; daughter of Zeus and Hera.

Hecate: Goddess of sorcery and witchcraft.

Hector: Son of Priam; slayer of Patroclus; slain by Achilles.

Hecuba: Wife of Priam.

Helen: Fairest woman in world; daughter of Zeus and Leda; wife of Menelaus; carried to Troy by Paris, causing Trojan War.

Heliades: Daughters of Helios; mourned for Phaëthon and were changed to poplar trees.

Helios (Sol): God of sun; later identified with Apollo.

Helle: Sister of Phrixos; fell from ram of Golden Fleece; water where she fell named Hellespont.

Hephaestus (Vulcan): God of fire; celestial blacksmith; son of Zeus and Hera; husband of Aphrodite.

Hera (Juno): Queen of heaven; wife of Zeus.

Hercules: Hero and strong man; son of Zeus and Alcmene; performed twelve labors or deeds to be free from bondage under Eurystheus; after death, his mortal share was destroyed, and he became immortal. Also known as Herakles or Heracles. Labors: (1) killing Nemean lion; (2) killing Lernaean Hydra; (3) capturing Erymanthian boar; (4) capturing Cerynean hind; (5) killing man-eating Stymphalian birds; (6) procuring girdle of Hippolyte; (7) cleaning Augean stables; (8) capturing Cretan bull; (9) capturing man-eating horses of Diomedes; (10) capturing cattle of Geryon; (11) procuring golden apples of Hesperides; (12) bringing Cerberus up from Hades.

Hermes (Mercury): God of physicians and thieves; messenger of gods; son of Zeus and Maia.

Hero: Priestess of Aphrodite; Leander swam Hellespont nightly to see her; drowned herself at his death.

Hesperus: Evening star.

Hestia (Vesta): Goddess of hearth; sister of Zeus.

Hippolyte: Queen of Amazons; wife of Theseus.

Hippolytus: Son of Theseus and Hippolyte; falsely accused by Phaedra of trying to kidnap her; slain by Poseidon at request of Theseus.

Hippomenes: Husband of Atalanta, whom he beat in race by dropping golden apples, which she stopped to pick up.

Hyacinthus: Beautiful youth accidentally killed by Apollo, who caused flower to spring up from his blood.

Hydra: Nine-headed monster in marsh of Lerna; slain by Hercules.

Hygeia: Personification of health.

Hyman: God of marriage.

Hyperion: Titan; early sun god; father of Helios.

Hypermnestra: Daughter of Danaüs; refused to kill her husband Lynceus.

Hypnos (Somnus): God of sleep.

Iapetus: Titan; father of Atlas, Epimetheus, and Prometheus.

Icarus: Son of Daedalus; flew too near sun with wax-attached wings and fell into sea and was drowned.

Io: Mortal maiden loved by Zeus; changed by Hera into heifer.

Iobates: King of Lycia; sent Bellerophon to slay Chimera.

Iphigenia: Daughter of Agamemnon; offered as sacrifice to Artemis at Aulis; carried by Artemis to Tauris where she became priestess; escaped from there with Orestes.

Iris: Goddess of rainbow; messenger of Zeus and Hera.

Ismene: Daughter of Oedipus; sister of Antigone.

Iulus: Son of Aeneas.

Ixion: King of Lapithae; for making love to Hera he was bound to endlessly revolving wheel in Tartarus.

Janus: Roman god of gates and doors; represented with two opposite faces.

Jason: Son of Aeson; to gain throne of Iolcus from Pelias, went to Colchis and brought back Golden Fleece; married Medea; deserted her for Creüsa.

Jocasta: Wife of Laius; mother of Oedipus; unwittingly became wife of Oedipus; hanged herself when relationship was discovered.

Lachesis: One of several **Fates:** Goddesses of destiny; Clotho (Spinner of thread of life), Lachesis (Determiner of length), and Atropos (Cutter of thread); also called Moirae. Identified by Romans with their goddesses of fate; Nona, Decuma, and Morta; called Parcae.

Laius: Father of Oedipus, by whom he was slain.

Laocoön: Priest of Apollo at Troy; warned against bringing wooden horse into Troy; destroyed with his two sons by serpents sent by Athena.

Lares: Roman ancestral spirits protecting descendants and homes.

Lavinia: Wife of Aeneas after defeat of Turnus.

Leander: Swam Hellespont nightly to see Hero; drowned in storm.

Leda: Mortal loved by Zeus in form of Swan; mother of Helen, Clytemnestra, Dioscuri.

Lethe: One of several **Rivers of Underworld:** Acheron (woe), Cocytus (wailing), Lethe (forgetfulness), Phlegethon (fire), Styx (across which souls of dead were ferried by Charon).

Leto (Latona): Mother by Zeus of Artemis and Apollo.

Lucina: Roman goddess of childbirth; identified with Juno.

Lynceus: Son of Aegyptus; husband of Hypermnestra; slew Danaüs.

Maia: Daughter of Atlas; mother of Hermes.

Maia: One of several **Pleiades:** Alcyone, Celaeno, Electra, Maia, Merope, Sterope or Asterope, Taygeta; seven daughters of Atlas; transformed into heavenly constellation, of which six stars are visible (Merope is said to have hidden in shame for loving a mortal).

Manes: Souls of dead Romans, particularly of ancestors.

Marsyas: Shepherd; challenged Apollo to music contest and lost; flayed alive by Apollo.

Medea: Sorceress; daughter of Aeëtes; helped Jason obtain Golden Fleece; when deserted by him for Creüsa, killed her children and Creüsa.

Medusa: Gorgon; slain by Perseus, who cut off her head.

Megaera: One of several **Furies:** Avenging spirits; Alecto, Megaera, and Tisiphone; known also as Erinyes or Eumenides.

Meleager: Son of Althaea; his life would last as long as brand burning at his birth; Althaea quenched and saved it but destroyed it when Meleager slew his uncles.

Melpomene: One of several **Muses:** Goddesses presiding over arts and sciences: Calliope (epic poetry), Clio (history), Erato (lyric and love poetry), Euterpe (music), Melpomene (tragedy), Polymnia or Polyhymnia (sacred poetry), Terpsichore (choral dance and song), Thalia (comedy and bucolic poetry), Urania (astronomy); daughters of Zeus and Mnemosyne.

Memnon: Ethiopian king; made immortal by Zeus; son of Tithonus and Eos.

Menelaus: King of Sparta; son of Atreus; brother of Agamemnon; husband of Helen.

Merope: One of several **Pleiades:** Alcyone, Celaeno, Electra, Maia, Merope, Sterope or Asterope, Taygeta; seven daughters of Atlas; transformed into heavenly constellation, of which six stars are visible; said to have hidden in shame for loving a mortal.

Mezentius: Cruel Etruscan king; ally of Turnus against Aeneas; slain by Aeneas.

Midas: King of Phrygia; given gift of turning to gold all he touched.

Minos: King of Crete; after death, one of three judges of dead in Hades; son of Zeus and Europa.

Minotaur: Monster, half man and half beast, kept in Labyrinth in Crete; slain by Theseus.

Mnemosyne: Goddess of memory; mother by Zeus of Muses.

Moirae: One of several **Fates:** Goddesses of destiny; Clotho (Spinner of thread of life), Lachesis (Determiner of length), and Atropos (Cutter of thread); also called Moirae. Identified by Romans with their goddesses of fate; Nona, Decuma, and Morta; called Parcae.

Momus: God of ridicule.

Morpheus: God of dreams.

Morta: One of several **Fates:** Goddesses of destiny; Clotho (Spinner of thread of life), Lachesis (Determiner of length), and Atropos (Cutter of thread); also called Moirae. Identified by Romans with their goddesses of fate; Nona, Decuma, and Morta; called Parcae.

Muses: Goddesses presiding over arts and sciences: Calliope (epic poetry), Clio (history), Erato (lyric and love poetry), Euterpe (music), Melpomene (tragedy), Polymnia or Polyhymnia (sacred poetry), Terpsichore (choral dance and song), Thalia (comedy and bucolic poetry), Urania (astronomy); daughters of Zeus and Mnemosyne.

Naiads: Nymphs of waters, streams, and fountains.

Napaeae: Wood nymphs.

Narcissus: Beautiful youth loved by Echo; in punishment for not returning her love, he was made to fall in love with his image reflected in pool; pined away and became flower.

Nemesis: Goddess of retribution.

Neoptolemus: Son of Achilles; slew Priam; also known as Pyrrhus.

Nereids: Sea nymphs; attendants on Poseidon.

Nestor: King of Pylos; noted for wise counsel in expedition against Troy.

Nike: Goddess of victory.

Niobe: Daughter of Tantalus; wife of Amphion; her children slain by Apollo and Artemis; changed to stone but continued to weep her loss.

Nona: One of several **Fates:** Goddesses of destiny; Clotho (Spinner of thread of life), Lachesis (Determiner of length), and Atropos (Cutter of thread); also called Moirae. Identified by Romans with their goddesses of fate; Nona, Decuma, and Morta; called Parcae.

Notus: One of several **Winds:** Aeolus (keeper of winds), Boreas (Aquilo) (north wind), Eurus (east wind), Notus (Auster) (south wind), Zephyrus (Favonius) (west wind).

Nymphs: Beautiful maidens; inferior deities of nature.

Nyx (Nox): Goddess of night.

Oceanids: Ocean nymphs; daughters of Oceanus.

Oceanus: Eldest of Titans; god of waters.

Odysseus (Ulysses): King of Ithaca; husband of Penelope; wandered ten years after fall of Troy before arriving home.

Oedipus: King of Thebes; son of Laius and Jocasta; unwittingly murdered Laius and married Jocasta; tore his eyes out when relationship was discovered.

Oenone: Nymph of Mount Ida; wife of Paris, who abandoned her; refused to cure him when he was poisoned by arrow of Philoctetes at Troy.

Oreads: Mountain nymphs.

Orestes: Son of Agamemnon and Clytemnestra; brother of Electra; slew Clytemnestra and Aegisthus; pursued by Furies until his purification by Apollo.

Orion: Hunter; slain by Artemis and made heavenly constellation.

Orpheus: Famed musician; son of Apollo and Muse Calliope; husband of Eurydice.

Pales: Roman goddess of shepherds and herdsmen.

Palinurus: Aeneas' pilot; fell overboard in his sleep and was drowned.

Pan (Faunus): God of woods and fields; part goat; son of Hermes.

Pandora: Opener of box containing human ills; mortal wife of Epimetheus.

Parcae: One of several **Fates:** Goddesses of destiny; Clotho (Spinner of thread of life), Lachesis (Determiner of length), and Atropos (Cutter of thread); also called Moirae. Identified by Romans with their goddesses of fate; Nona, Decuma, and Morta; called Parcae.

Paris: Son of Priam; gave apple of discord to Aphrodite, for which she enabled him to carry off Helen; slew Achilles at Troy; slain by Philoctetes.

Patroclus: Great friend of Achilles; wore Achilles' armor and was slain by Hector.

Pegasus: Winged horse that sprang from Medusa's body at her death; ridden by Bellerophon when he slew Chimera.

Pelias: King of Ioclus; seized throne from his brother Aeson; sent Jason for Golden Fleece; slain unwittingly by his daughters at instigation of Medea.

Pelops: Son of Tantalus; his father cooked and served him to gods; restored to life; Peloponnesus named for him.

Penates: Roman household gods.

Penelope: Wife of Odysseus; waited faithfully for him for ten years while putting off numerous suitors.

Pephredo: One of several **Graeae:** Sentinels for Gorgons; Deino, Enyo, and Pephredo; had one eye among them, which passed from one to another.

Periphetes: Giant; son of Hephaestus; slain by Theseus.

Persephone (Proserpine): Queen of infernal regions; daughter of Zeus and Demeter; wife of Pluto.

Perseus: Son of Zeus and Danaë; slew Medusa; rescued Andromeda from monster and married her.

Phaedra: Daughter of Minos; wife of Theseus; caused the death of her stepson, Hippolytus.

Phaethon: Son of Helios; drove his father's sun chariot and was struck down by Zeus before he set world on fire.

Philoctetes: Greek warrior who possessed Hercules' bow and arrows; slew Paris at Troy with poisoned arrow.

Phineus: Betrothed of Andromeda; tried to slay Perseus but turned to stone by Medusa's head.

Phlegethon: One of several **Rivers of Underworld:** Acheron (woe), Cocytus (wailing), Lethe (forgetfulness), Phlegethon (fire), Styx (across which souls of dead were ferried by Charon).

Phosphor: Morning star.

Phrixos: Brother of Helle; carried by ram of Golden Fleece to Colchis.

Pirithous: Son of Ixion; friend of Theseus; tried to carry off Persephone from Hades; bound to enchanted rock by Pluto.

Pleiades: Alcyone, Celaeno, Electra, Maia, Merope, Sterope or Asterope, Taygeta; seven daughters of Atlas; transformed into heavenly constellation, of which six stars are visible (Merope is said to have hidden in shame for loving a mortal).

Pluto (Dis): God of Hades; brother of Zeus.

Plutus: God of wealth.

Pollux: One of **Dioscuri:** Twins Castor and Pollux; sons of Leda by Zeus.

Polymnia: One of several **Muses:** Goddesses presiding over arts and sciences: Calliope (epic poetry), Clio (history), Erato (lyric and love poetry), Euterpe (music), Melpomene (tragedy), Polymnia or Polyhymnia (sacred poetry), Terpsichore (choral dance and song), Thalia (comedy and bucolic poetry), Urania (astronomy); daughters of Zeus and Mnemosyne.

Polynices: Son of Oedipus; he and his brother Eteocles killed each other; burial rite, forbidden by Creon, performed by his sister Antigone.

Polyphemus: Cyclops; devoured six of Odysseus's men; blinded by Odysseus.

Polyxena: Daughter of Priam; betrothed to Achilles, whom Paris slew at their betrothal; sacrificed to shade of Achilles.

Pomona: Roman goddess of fruits.

Pontus: Sea god; son of Gaea.

Poseidon (Neptune): God of sea; brother of Zeus.

Priam: King of Troy; husband of Hecuba; ransomed Hector's body from Achilles; slain by Neoptolemus.

Priapus: God of regeneration.

Procris: Wife of Cephalus, who accidentally slew her.

Procrustes: Giant; stretched or cut off legs of victims to make them fit iron bed; slain by Theseus.

Proetus: Husband of Anteia; sent Bellerophon to Iobates to be put to death.

Prometheus: Titan; stole fire from heaven for man. Zeus punished him by chaining him to rock in Caucasus where vultures devoured his liver daily.

Proteus: Sea god; assumed various shapes when called on to prophesy.

Psyche: Beloved of Eros; punished by jealous Aphrodite; made immortal and united with Eros.

Pygmalion: King of Cyprus; carved ivory statue of maiden which Aphrodite gave life as Galatea.

Pyramus: Babylonian youth; made love to Thisbe through hole in wall; thinking Thisbe slain by lion, killed himself.

Python: Serpent born from slime left by Deluge; slain by Apollo.

Quirinus: Roman war god.

Remus: Brother of Romulus; slain by him.

Rhadamanthus: One of three judges of dead in Hades; son of Zeus and Europa.

Rhea (Ops): Daughter of Uranus and Gaea; wife of Cronus; mother of Zeus; identified with Cybele.

Rivers of Underworld: Acheron (woe), Cocytus (wailing), Lethe (forgetfulness), Phlegethon (fire), Styx (across which souls of dead were ferried by Charon).

Romulus: Founder of Rome; he and Remus suckled in infancy by she-wolf; slew Remus; deified by Romans.

Sarpedon: King of Lycia; son of Zeus and Europa; slain by Patroclus at Troy.

Satyrs: Hoofed demigods of woods and fields; companions of Dionysus.

Sciron: Robber; forced strangers to wash his feet, then hurled them into sea where tortoise devoured them; slain by Theseus.

Scylla: Female monster inhabiting rock opposite Charybdis; menaced passing sailors.

Selene: Goddess of moon.

Semele: Daughter of Cadmus; mother by Zeus of Dionysus; demanded Zeus appear before her in all his splendor and was destroyed by his lightnings.

Sibyls: Various prophetesses; most famous, Cumaean sibyl, accompanied Aeneas into Hades.

Sileni: Minor woodland deities similar to satyrs (singular: silenus). Sometimes Silenus refers to eldest of satyrs, son of Hermes or of Pan.

Silvanus: Roman god of woods and fields.

Sinis: Giant; bent pines, by which he hurled victims against side of mountain; slain by Theseus.

Sirens: Minor deities who lured sailors to destruction with their singing.

Sisyphus: King of Corinth; condemned in Tartarus to roll huge stone to top of hill; it always rolled back down again.

Sphinx: Monster of Thebes; killed those who could not answer her riddle; slain by Oedipus. Name also refers to other monsters having body of lion, wings, and head and bust of woman.

Sterope: One of several **Pleiades:** Alcyone, Celaeno, Electra, Maia, Merope, Sterope or Asterope, Taygeta; seven daughters of Atlas; transformed into heavenly constellation, of which six stars are visible (Merope is said to have hidden in shame for loving a mortal).

Stheno: One of several **Gorgons:** Female monsters; Euryale, Medusa, and Stheno; had snakes for hair; their glances turned mortals to stone.

Styx: One of several **Rivers of Underworld:** Acheron (woe), Cocytus (wailing), Lethe (forgetfulness), Phlegethon (fire), Styx (across which souls of dead were ferried by Charon).

Symplegades: Clashing rocks at entrance to Black Sea; Argo passed through, causing them to become forever fixed.

Syrinx: Nymph pursued by Pan; changed to reeds, from which he made his pipes.

Tantalus: Cruel king; father of Pelops and Niobe; condemned in Tartarus to stand chin-deep in lake surrounded by fruit branches; as he tried to eat or drink, water or fruit always receded.

Tartarus: Underworld below Hades; often refers to Hades.

Taygeta: One of several **Pleiades:** Alcyone, Celaeno, Electra, Maia, Merope, Sterope or Asterope, Taygeta; seven daughters of Atlas; transformed into heavenly constellation, of which six stars are visible (Merope is said to have hidden in shame for loving a mortal).

Telemachus: Son of Odysseus; made unsuccessful journey to find his father.

Tellus: Roman goddess of earth.

Terminus: Roman god of boundaries and landmarks.

Terpsichore: One of several **Muses:** Goddesses presiding over arts and sciences: Calliope (epic poetry), Clio (history), Erato (lyric and love poetry), Euterpe (music), Melpomene (tragedy), Polymnia or Polyhymnia (sacred poetry), Terpsichore (choral dance and song), Thalia (comedy and bucolic poetry), Urania (astronomy); daughters of Zeus and Mnemosyne.

Terra: Roman earth goddess.

Thalia: One of several **Graces:** Beautiful goddesses: Aglaia (Brilliance), Euphrosyne (Joy), and Thalia (Bloom); daughters of Zeus. Also one of several **Muses:** Goddesses presiding over arts and sciences: Calliope (epic poetry), Clio (history), Erato (lyric and love poetry), Euterpe (music), Melpomene (tragedy), Polymnia or Polyhymnia (sacred poetry), Terpsichore (choral dance and song), Thalia (comedy and bucolic poetry), Urania (astronomy); daughters of Zeus and Mnemosyne.

Thanatos (Mors): God of death.

Themis: Titan goddess of laws of physical phenomena; daughter of Uranus; mother of Prometheus.

Theseus: Son of Aegeus; slew Minotaur; married and deserted Ariadne; later married Phaedra.

Thisbe: Beloved of Pyramus; killed herself at his death.

Thyestes: Brother of Atreus; Atreus killed three of his sons and served them to him at banquet.

Tiresias: Blind soothsayer of Thebes.

Tisiphone: One of several **Furies:** Avenging spirits; Alecto, Megaera, and Tisiphone; known also as Erinyes or Eumenides.

Titans: Early gods from which Olympian gods were derived; children of Uranus and Gaea.

Tithonus: Mortal loved by Eos; changed into grasshopper.

Triton: Demigod of sea; son of Poseidon.

Turnus: King of Rutuli in Italy; betrothed to Lavinia; slain by Aeneas.

Urania: One of several **Muses:** Goddesses presiding over arts and sciences: Calliope (epic poetry), Clio (history), Erato (lyric and love poetry), Euterpe (music), Melpomene (tragedy), Polymnia or Polyhymnia (sacred poetry), Terpsichore (choral dance and song), Thalia (comedy and bucolic poetry), Urania (astronomy); daughters of Zeus and Mnemosyne.

Uranus: Personification of Heaven; husband of Gaea; father of Titans; dethroned by his son Cronus.

Vertumnus: Roman god of fruits and vegetables; husband of Pomona.

Winds: Aeolus (keeper of winds), Boreas (Aquilo) (north wind), Eurus (east wind), Notus (Auster) (south wind), Zephyrus (Favonius) (west wind).

Zephyrus: One of several **Winds:** Aeolus (keeper of winds), Boreas (Aquilo) (north wind), Eurus (east wind), Notus (Auster) (south wind), Zephyrus (Favonius) (west wind).

Zeus (Jupiter): Chief of Olympian gods; son of Cronus and Rhea; husband of Hera.

Norse Mythology

Aesir: Chief gods of Asgard.

Andvari: Dwarf; robbed of gold and magic ring by Loki.

Angerbotha (Angrbotha): Giantess; mother by Loki of Fenrir, Hel, and Midgard serpent.

Asgard (Asgarth): Abode of gods.

Ask (Aske, Askr): First man; created by Odin, Hoenir, and Lothur.

Asynjur: Goddesses of Asgard.

Atli: Second husband of Gudrun; invited Gunnar and Hogni to his court, where they were slain; slain by Gudrun.

Audhumia (Audhumbla): Cow that nourished Ymir; created Buri by licking ice cliff.

Balder (Baldr, Baldur): God of light, spring, peace, joy; son of Odin; slain by Hoth at instigation of Loki.

Bifrost: Rainbow bridge connecting Midgard and Asgard.

Bragi (Brage): God of poetry; husband of Ithunn.

Branstock: Great oak in hall of Volsungs; into it, Odin thrust Gram, which only Sigmund could draw forth.

Brynhild: Valkyrie; wakened from magic sleep by Sigurd; married Gunnar; instigated death of Sigurd; killed herself and was burned on pyre beside Sigurd.

Bur (Bor): Son of Buri; father of Odin, Hoenir, and Lothur.

Buri (Bori): Progenitor of gods; father of Bur; created by Audhumla.

Embla: First woman; created by Odin, Hoenir, and Lothur.

Fafnir: Son of Rodmar, whom he slew for gold in Otter's skin; in form of dragon, guarded gold; slain by Sigurd.

Fenrir: Wolf; offspring of Loki; swallows Odin at Ragnarok and is slain by Vitharr.

Forseti: Son of Balder.

Frey (Freyr): God of fertility and crops; son of Njorth; originally one of Vanir.

Freya (Freyja): Goddess of love and beauty; sister of Frey; originally one of Vanir.

Frigg (Frigga): Goddess of sky; wife of Odin.

Garm: Watchdog of Hel; slays, and is slain by, Tyr at Ragnarok.

Gimle: Home of blessed after Ragnarok.

Giuki: King of Nibelungs; father of Gunnar, Hogni, Guttorm, and Gudrun.

Glathsehim (Gladsheim): Hall of gods in Asgard.

Gram (meaning "Angry"): Sigmund's sword; rewelded by Regin; used by Sigurd to slay Fafnir.

Greyfell: Sigmund's horse; descended from Sleipnir.

Grimhild: Mother of Gudrun; administered magic potion to Sigurd which made him forget Brynhild.

Gudrun: Daughter of Giuki; wife of Sigurd; later wife of Atli and Jonakr.

Gunnar: Son of Giuki; in his semblance Sigurd won Brynhild for him; slain at hall of Atli.

Guttorm: Son of Giuki; slew Sigurd at Brynhild's request.

Heimdall (Heimdallr): Guardian of Asgard.

Hel: Goddess of dead and queen of underworld; daughter of Loki.

Hiordis: Wife of Sigmund; mother of Sigurd.

Hoenir: One of creators of Ask and Embla; son of Bur.

Hogni: Son of Giuki; slain at hall of Atli.

Hoth (Hoder, Hodur): Blind god of night and darkness; slayer of Balder at instigation of Loki.

Ithunn (Ithun, Iduna): Keeper of golden apples of youth; wife of Bragi.

Jonakr: Third husband of Gudrun.

Jormunrek: Slayer of Swanhild; slain by sons of Gudrun.

Jotunnheim (Jotunheim): Abode of giants.

Lif and Lifthrasir: First man and woman after Ragnarok.

Loki: God of evil and mischief; instigator of Balder's death.

Lothur (Lodur): One of creators of Ask and Embla.

Midgard (Midgarth): Abode of mankind; the earth.

Midgard Serpent: Sea monster; offspring of Loki; slays, and is slain by, Thor at Ragnarok.

Mimir: Giant; guardian of well in Jotunnheim at root of Yggdrasill; knower of past and future.

Mjollnir: Magic hammer of Thor.

Nagifar: Ship to be used by giants in attacking Asgard at Ragnarok; built from nails of dead men.

Nanna: Wife of Balder.
Nibelungs: Dwellers in northern kingdom ruled by Giuki.
Niflheim (Nifelheim): Outer region of cold and darkness; abode of Hel.
Njorth: Father of Frey and Freya; originally one of Vanir.
Norns: Demigoddesses of fate: Urth (Urdur) (past), Verthandi (Verdandi) (present), Skuld (future).
Odin (Othin): Head of Aesir; creator of world with Vili and Ve; equivalent to Woden (Wodan, Wotan) in Teutonic mythology.
Otter: Son of Rodmar; slain by Loki; his skin filled with gold hoard of Andvari to appease Rodmar.
Ragnarok: Final destruction of present world in battle between gods and giants; some minor gods will survive, and Lif and Lifthrasir will repeople world.
Regin: Blacksmith; son of Rodmar, foster-father of Sigurd.
Rerir: King of Huns; son of Sigi.
Rodmar: Father of Regin, Otter, and Fafnir; demanded Otter's skin be filled with gold; slain by Fafnir, who stole gold.
Sif: Wife of Thor.
Siggeir: King of Goths; husband of Signy; he and his sons slew Volsung and his sons, except Sigmund; slain by Sigmund and Sinflotli.
Sigi: King of Huns; son of Odin.
Sigmund: Son of Volsung; brother of Signy, who bore him Sinflotli; husband of Hiordis, who bore him Sigurd.
Signy: Daughter of Volsung; sister of Sigmund; wife of Siggeir; mother by Sigmund of Sinflotli.
Sigurd: Son of Sigmund and Hiordis; wakened Brynhild from magic sleep; married Gudrun; slain by Guttorm at instigation of Brynhild.
Sigyn: Wife of Loki.
Sinflotli: Son of Sigmund and Signy.
Skuld: One of several **Norns:** Demigoddesses of fate: Urth (Urdur) (Past), Verthandi (Verdandi) (Present), Skuld (Future).

Sleipnir (Sleipner): Eight-legged horse of Odin.
Surt (Surtr): Fire demon; slays Frey at Ragnarok.
Svartalfaheim: Abode of dwarfs.
Swanhild: Daughter of Sigurd and Gudrun; slain by Jormunrek.
Thor: God of thunder; oldest son of Odin; equivalent to Germanic deity Donar.
Tyr: God of war; son of Odin; equivalent to Tiu in Teutonic mythology.
Ull (Ullr): Son of Sif; stepson of Thor.
Urth: One of several **Norns:** Demigoddesses of fate: Urth (Urdur) (past), Verthandi (Verdandi) (present), Skuld (future).
Valhalla (Valhall): Great hall in Asgard where Odin received souls of heroes killed in battle.
Vali: Odin's son: Ragnarok survivor.
Valkyries: Virgins, messengers of Odin, who selected heroes to die in battle and took them to Valhalla; generally considered as nine in number.
Vanir: Early race of gods; three survivors, Njorth, Frey, and Freya, are associated with Aesir.
Ve: Brother of Odin; one of creators of world.
Verthandi: One of several **Norns:** Demigoddesses of fate: Urth (Urdur) (past), Verthandi (Verdandi) (present), Skuld (future).
Vili: Brother of Odin; one of creators of world.
Vingolf: Abode of goddesses in Asgard.
Vitharr (Vithar): Son of Odin; survivor of Ragnarok.
Volsung: Descendant of Odin, and father of Signy, Sigmund; his descendants were called Volsungs.
Yggdrasil: Giant ash tree springing from body of Ymir and supporting universe; its roots extended to Asgard, Jotunnheim, and Niffheim.
Ymir (Ymer): Primeval frost giant killed by Odin, Vili, and Ve; world created from his body; also, from his body sprang Yggdrasil.

Egyptian Mythology

Aaru: Abode of the blessed dead.
Amen (Amon, Ammdn): One of chief Theban deities; united with sun god under form of Amen-Ra.
Amenti: Region of dead where souls were judged by Osiris.
Anubis: Guide of souls to Amenti; son of Osiris; jackal-headed.
Apis: Sacred bull, an embodiment of Ptah; identified with Osiris as Osiris-Apis or Serapis.
Geb (Keb, Seb): Earth god; father of Osiris; represented with goose on head.
Hathor (Athor): Goddess of love and mirth; cow-headed.
Horus: God of day; son of Osiris and Isis; hawk-headed.
Isis: Goddess of motherhood and fertility; sister and wife of Osiris.
Khepera: God of morning sun.
Khnemu (Khnum, Chnuphis, Chnemu, Chnum): Ram-headed god.
Khonsu (Khensu, Khuns): Son of Amen and Mut.
Mentu (Ment): Solar deity, sometimes considered god of war; falcon-headed.

Min (Khem, Chem): Principle of physical life.
Mut (Maut): Wife of Amen.
Nephthys: Goddess of the dead; sister and wife of Set.
Nu: Chaos from which world was created, personified as a god.
Nut: Goddess of heavens; consort of Geb.
Osiris: God of underworld and judge of dead; son of Geb and Nut.
Ptah (Phtha): Chief deity of Memphis.
Ra: God of the Sun, the supreme god; son of Nut; Pharaohs claimed descent from him; represented as lion, cat, or falcon.
Serapis: God uniting attributes of Osiris and Apis.
Set (Seth): God of darkness or evil; brother and enemy of Osiris.
Shu: Solar deity; son of Ra and Hathor.
Tem (Atmu, Atum, Tum): Solar deity.
Thoth (Dhouti): God of wisdom and magic; scribe of gods; ibis-headed.

American Crossword Puzzle Tournament

March 21–23, 1997, Stamford, Connecticut

The oldest and largest crossword puzzle tournament in the United States is directed by Will Shortz, the Crossword Puzzle Editor of *The New York Times*. Competitors face eight puzzles and are scored on accuracy and speed.

Year	Winner	Year	Winner
1997	Douglas Hoylman, Chevy Chase, Md.	1987	David Rosen, New York, N.Y.
1996	Douglas Hoylman, Chevy Chase, Md.	1986	David Rosen, Buffalo, N.Y.
1995	Jon Delfin, New York, N.Y.	1985	David Rosen, Buffalo, N.Y.
1994	Douglas Hoylman, Chevy Chase, Md.	1984	John McNeill, Austin, Tex.
1993	Trip Payne, Atlanta, Ga.	1983	David Rosen, Buffalo, N.Y.
1992	Douglas Hoylman, Chevy Chase, Md.	1982	Stanley Newman, Brooklyn, N.Y.
1991	Jon Delfin, New York, N.Y.	1981	Philip Cohen, Aliquippa, Pa.
1990	Jon Delfin, New York, N.Y.	1980	Daniel Pratt, Fort Meade, Md.
1989	Jon Delfin, New York, N.Y.	1979	Miriam Raphael, Port Chester, N.Y.
1988	Douglas Hoylman, Chevy Chase, Md.	1978	Nancy Schuster, Rego Park, N.Y.

Writing and Language

A Concise Guide to Style

From *Webster's II New Riverside University Dictionary.* © 1984 by Houghton Mifflin Company.

This section discusses and illustrates the basic conventions of American capitalization, punctuation, and italicization.

Capitalization

Capitalize the following:
1. The first word of a sentence: Some spiders are poisonous; others are not. Are you my new neighbor?
2. The first word of a direct quotation, except when the quotation is split: Joyce asked, "Do you think that the lecture was interesting?" "No," I responded, "it was very boring." Tom Paine said, "The sublime and the ridiculous are often so nearly related that it is difficult to class them separately."
3. The first word of each line in a poem in traditional verse: Half a league, half a league,/Half a league onward,/All in the valley of Death/Rôde the six hundred.—Alfred, Lord Tennyson
4. The names of people, of organizations and their members, of councils and congresses, and of historical periods and events: Marie Curie, Benevolent and Protective Order of Elks, an Elk, Protestant Episcopal Church, an Episcopalian, the Democratic Party, a Democrat, the Nuclear Regulatory Commission, the U.S. Senate, the Middle Ages, World War I, the Battle of Britain.
5. The names of places and geographic divisions, districts, regions, and locales: Richmond, Vermont, Argentina, Seventh Avenue, London Bridge, Arctic Circle, Eastern Hemisphere, Continental Divide, Middle East, Far North, Gulf States, East Coast, the North, the South Shore.
   Do not capitalize words indicating compass points unless a specific region is referred to: Turn north onto Interstate 91.
6. The names of rivers, lakes, mountains, and oceans: Ohio River, Lake Como, Rocky Mountains, Atlantic Ocean.
7. The names of ships, aircraft, satellites, and space vehicles: U.S.S. *Arizona, Spirit of St. Louis,* the spy satellite Ferret-D, *Voyager II,* the space shuttle *Challenger.*
8. The names of nationalities, races, tribes, and languages: Spanish, Maori, Bantu, Russian.
9. Words derived from proper names, except in their extended senses: the Byzantine Empire. *But:* byzantine office politics.
10. Words indicating family relationships when used with a person's name as a title: Aunt Toni and Uncle Jack. *But:* my aunt and uncle, Toni and Jack Walker.
11. A title (i.e., civil, judicial, military, royal and noble, religious, and honorary) when preceding a name: Justice Marshall, General Jackson, Mayor Daley, Queen Victoria, Lord Mountbatten, Pope John Paul II, Professor Jacobson, Senator Byrd.
12. All references to the President and Vice President of the United States: The President has entered the hall. The Vice President presides over the Senate.
13. All key words in titles of literary, dramatic, artistic, and musical works: the novel *The Old Man and the Sea,* the short story "Notes from Underground," an article entitled "On Passive Verbs," James Dickey's poem "In the Tree House at Night," the play *Cat on a Hot Tin Roof,* Van Gogh's *Wheat Field and Cypress Trees,* Beethoven's *Emperor Concerto.*
14. The *The* in the title of a newspaper if it is a part of the title: *The Wall Street Journal. But:* the New York *Daily News.*
15. The first word in the salutation and in the complimentary close of a letter: My dear Carol, Yours sincerely.
16. Epithets and substitutes for the names of people and places: Old Hickory, Old Blood and Guts, The Oval Office, the Windy City.
17. Words used in personifications: When is not Death at watch/Within those secret waters?/What wants he but to catch/Earth's heedless sons and daughters?—Edmund Blunden
18. The pronoun *I: I* told them that I had heard the news.
19. Names for the Deity and sacred works: God, the Almighty, Jesus, Allah, the Supreme Being, the Bible, the Koran, the Talmud.
20. Days of the week, months of the year, holidays, and holy days: Tuesday, May, Independence Day, Passover, Ramadan, Christmas.
21. The names of specific courts: The Supreme Court of the United States, the Massachusetts Appeals Court, the United States Court of Appeals for the First Circuit.
22. The names of treaties, accords, pacts, laws, and specific amendments: Panama Canal Treaty, Treaty of Paris, Geneva Accords, Warsaw Pact countries, Sherman Antitrust Law, Labor Management Relations Act, took the Fifth Amendment.
23. Registered trademarks and service marks: Day-Glo, Comsat.
24. The names of geologic eras, periods, epochs, and strata and the names of prehistoric divisions: Paleozoic Era, Precambrian, Pleistocene, Age of Reptiles, Bronze Age, Stone Age.
25. The names of constellations, planets, and stars: Milky Way, Southern Crown, Saturn, Jupiter, Uranus, Polaris.
26. Genus but not species names in binomial nomenclature: *Rana pipiens.*
27. New Latin names of classes, families, and all groups higher than genera in botanical and zoological nomenclature: Nematoda.
   But do not capitalize derivatives from such names: nematodes.
28. Many abbreviations and acronyms: Dec., Tues., Lt. Gen., M.F.A., UNESCO, MIRV.

Italicization

Use italics to:
1. Indicate titles of books, plays, and epic poems: *War and Peace, The Importance of Being Earnest, Paradise Lost.*
2. Indicate titles of magazines and newspapers: *New York* magazine, *The Wall Street Journal,* the New York *Daily News.*
3. Set off the titles of motion pictures and radio and television programs: *Star Wars, All Things Considered, Masterpiece Theater.*

4. Indicate titles of major musical compositions: Handel's *Messiah*, Adam's *Giselle*.
5. Set off the names of paintings and sculpture: *Mona Lisa, Pietà*.
6. Indicate words, letters, or numbers that are referred to: The word *hiss* is onomatopoeic. *Can't* means *won't* in your lexicon. You form your *n*'s like *u*'s. A *6* looks like an inverted *9*.
7. Indicate foreign words and phrases not yet assimilated into English: *C'est la vie* was the response to my complaint.
8. Indicate the names of plaintiff and defendant in legal citations: *Roe* v. *Doe.*
9. Emphasize a word or phrase: When you appear on the national news, you are *somebody.*
   Use this device sparingly.
10. Distinguish New Latin names of genera, species, subspecies, and varieties in botanical and zoological nomenclature: *Homo sapiens.*
11. Set off the names of ships and aircraft: U.S.S. *Arizona, Spirit of St. Louis.*

Punctuation

Apostrophe

1. Indicates the possessive case of singular and plural nouns, indefinite pronouns, and surnames combined with designations such as *Jr., Sr.,* and *II:* my sister's husband, my three sisters' husbands, anyone's guess, They answer each other's phones, John Smith, Jr.'s car.
2. Indicates joint possession when used with the last of two or more nouns in a series: Doe and Roe's report.
3. Indicates individual possession or authorship when used with each of two or more nouns in a series: Smith's, Roe's, and Doe's reports.
4. Indicates the plurals of words, letters, and figures used as such: 60's and 70's; *x*'s, *y*'s, and *z*'s.
5. Indicates omission of letters in contractions: aren't, that's, o'clock.
6. Indicates omission of figures in dates: the class of '63.

Brackets

1. Enclose words or passages in quoted matter to indicate insertion of material written by someone other than the author: A tough but nervous, tenacious but restless race [the Yankees]; materially ambitious, yet prone to introspection. . . .—Samuel Eliot Morison
2. Enclose material inserted within matter already in parentheses: (Vancouver [B.C.] January 1, 19—).

Colon

1. Introduces words, phrases, or clauses that explain, amplify, or summarize what has gone before: Suddenly I realized where we were: Rome.
   "There are two cardinal sins from which all the others spring: impatience and laziness."—Franz Kafka
2. Introduces a long quotation: In his original draft of the *Declaration of Independence,* Jefferson wrote: "We hold these truths to be sacred and undeniable; that all men are created equal and independent, that from that equal creation they derive rights inherent and inalienable. . . ."
3. Introduces a list: We need the following items: pens, paper, pencils, blotters, and erasers.
4. Separates chapter and verse numbers in Biblical references: James 1:4.
5. Separates city from publisher in footnotes and bibliographies: Chicago: Riverside Press, 1983.
6. Separates hour and minute(s) in time designations: 9:30 a.m., a 9:30 meeting.
7. Follows the salutation in a business letter: Gentlemen:

Comma

1. Separates the clauses of a compound sentence connected by a coordinating conjunction: A difference exists between the musical works of Handel and Haydn, and it is a difference worth noting.
   The comma may be omitted in short compound sentences: I heard what you said and I am furious. I got out of the car and I walked and walked.
2. Separates *and* or *or* from the final item in a series of three or more: Red, yellow, and blue may be mixed to produce all colors.
3. Separates two or more adjectives modifying the same noun if *and* could be used between them without altering the meaning: a solid, heavy gait. *But:* a polished mahogany dresser.
4. Sets off nonrestrictive clauses or phrases (i.e., those that if eliminated would not affect the meaning of the sentences): The burglar, who had entered through the patio, went straight to the silver chest.
   The comma should not be used when a clause is restrictive (i.e., essential to the meaning of the sentence): The burglar who had entered through the patio went straight to the silver chest; the other burglar searched for the wall safe.
5. Sets off words or phrases in apposition to a noun or noun phrase: Plato, the famous Greek philosopher, was a student of Socrates.
   The comma should not be used if such words or phrases precede the noun: The Greek philosopher Plato was a student of Socrates.
6. Sets off transitional words and short expressions that require a pause in reading or speaking: Unfortunately, my friend was not well traveled. Did you, after all, find what you were looking for? I live with my family, of course.
7. Sets off words used to introduce a sentence: No, I haven't been to Paris. Well, what do you think we should do now?
8. Sets off a subordinate clause or a long phrase that precedes a principal clause: By the time we found the restaurant, we were starved. Of all the illustrations in the book, the most striking are those of the tapestries.
9. Sets off short quotations and sayings: The candidate said, "Actions speak louder than words." "Talking of axes," said the Duchess, "chop off her head."—Lewis Carroll
10. Indicates omission of a word or words: To err is human; to forgive, divine.
11. Sets off the year from the month in full dates: Nicholas II of Russia was shot on July 16, 1918.
    But note that when only the month and the year are used, no comma appears: Nicholas II of Russia was shot in July 1918.
12. Sets off city and state in geographic names: Atlanta, Georgia, is the transportation center of the South. 34 Beach Drive, Bedford, Va. 24523.
13. Separates series of four or more figures into thousands, millions, etc.: 67,000; 200,000.
14. Sets off words used in direct address: "I tell you, folks, all politics is applesauce."—Will Rogers. Thank you for your expert assistance, Dolores.
15. Separates a tag question from the rest of a sentence: You forgot your keys again, didn't you?
16. Sets off sentence elements that could be misunderstood if the comma were not used: Some time after, the actual date for the project was set.

17. Follows the salutation in a personal letter and the complimentary close in a business or personal letter: Dear Jessica, Sincerely yours, Fred.
18. Sets off titles and degrees from surnames and from the rest of a sentence: Walter T. Prescott, Jr.; Gregory A. Rossi, S.J.; Susan P. Green, M.D., presented the case.

Dash

1. Indicates a sudden break or abrupt change in continuity: "If—if you'll just let me explain—" the student stammered. And the problem—if there really is one—can then be solved.
2. Sets apart an explanatory, a defining, or an emphatic phrase: Foods rich in protein—meat, fish, and eggs—should be eaten on a daily basis.
   More important than winning the election, is governing the nation. That is the test of a political party—the acid, final test.—Adlai E. Stevenson
3. Sets apart parenthetical matter: Wolsey, for all his faults—and he had many—was a great statesman, a man of natural dignity with a generous temperament. . . .—Jasper Ridley
4. Marks an unfinished sentence: "But if my bus is late—" he began.
5. Sets off a summarizing phrase or clause: The vital measure of a newspaper is not its size but its spirit—that is its responsibility to report the news fully, accurately, and fairly.—Arthur H. Sulzberger
6. Sets off the name of an author or source, as at the end of a quotation: A poet can survive everything but a misprint.—Oscar Wilde

Ellipses

1. Indicate, by three spaced points, omission of words or sentences within quoted matter: Equipped by education to rule in the nineteenth century, . . . he lived and reigned in Russia in the twentieth century.—Robert K. Massie
2. Indicate, by four spaced points, omission of words at the end of a sentence: The timidity of bureaucrats when it comes to dealing with . . . abuses is easy to explain. . . . —New York
3. Indicate, when extended the length of a line, omission of one or more lines of poetry:
   Roll on, thou deep and dark blue ocean—roll!
   . . . .
   Man marks the earth with ruin—his control
   Stops with the shore.—Lord Byron
4. Are sometimes used as a device, as for example, in advertising copy:
   To help you Move and Grow
     with the Rigors of
   Business in the 1980's . . .
     and Beyond.—Journal of Business Strategy

Exclamation Point

1. Terminates an emphatic or exclamatory sentence: Go home at once! You've got to be kidding!
2. Terminates an emphatic interjection: Encore!

Hyphen

1. Indicates that part of a word of more than one syllable has been carried over from one line to the next:
     During the revolution, the nation was
     beset with problems—looting, fight-
     ing, and famine.
2. Joins the elements of some compounds: great-grandparent, attorney-at-law, ne'er-do-well.
3. Joins the elements of compound modifiers preceding nouns: high-school students, a fire-and-brimstone lecture, a two-hour meeting.
4. Indicates that two or more compounds share a single base: four- and six-volume sets, eight- and nine-year olds.

5. Separates the prefix and root in some combinations; check a dictionary when in doubt about the spelling: anti-Nazi, re-elect, co-author, re-form/reform, re-cover/recover, re-creation/recreation.
6. Substitutes for the word *to* between typewritten inclusive words or figures: pp. 145–155, the Boston–New York air shuttle.
7. Punctuates written-out compound numbers from 21 through 99: forty-six years of age, a person who is forty-six, two hundred fifty-nine dollars.

Parentheses

1. Enclose material that is not essential to a sentence and that if not included would not alter its meaning: After a few minutes (some say less) the blaze was extinguished.
2. Often enclose letters or figures to indicate subdivisions of a series: A movement in sonata form consists of the following elements: (1) the exposition, (2) the development, and (3) the recapitulation.
3. Enclose figures following and confirming written-out numbers, especially in legal and business documents: The fee for my services will be two thousand dollars ($2,000.00).
4. Enclose an abbreviation for a term following the written-out term, when used for the first time in a text: The patient is suffering from acquired immune deficiency syndrome (AIDS).

Period

1. Terminates a complete declarative or mild imperative sentence: There could be no turning back as war's dark shadow settled irrevocably across the continent of Europe.—W. Bruce Lincoln. Return all the books when you can. Would you kindly affix your signature here.
2. Terminates sentence fragments: Gray clouds—and what looks like a veil of rain falling behind the East German headland. A pair of ducks. A tired or dying swan, head buried in its back feathers, sits on the sand a few feet from the water's edge.—Anthony Bailey
3. Follows some abbreviations: Dec., Rev., St., Blvd., pp., Co.

Question Mark

1. Punctuates a direct question: Have you seen the new play yet? Who goes there? *But:* I wonder who said "Nothing is easy in war." I asked if they planned to leave.
2. Indicates uncertainty: Ferdinand Magellan (1480?–1521), Plato (427?–347 B.C.E.).

Quotation Marks

1. Double quotation marks enclose direct quotations: "What was Paris like in the Twenties?" our daughter asked. "Ladies and Gentlemen," the Chief Usher said, "the President of the United States." Robert Louis Stevenson said that "it is better to be a fool than to be dead." When advised not to become a lawyer because the profession was already overcrowded, Daniel Webster replied, "There is always room at the top."
2. Double quotation marks enclose words or phrases to clarify their meaning or use or to indicate that they are being used in a special way: This was the border of what we often call "the West" or "the Free World." "The Windy City" is a name for Chicago.
3. Double quotation marks set off the translation of a foreign word or phrase: *die Grenze*, "the border."
4. Double quotation marks set off the titles of series of books, of articles or chapters in publications, of essays, of short stories and poems, of individual

radio and television programs, and of songs and short musical pieces: "The Horizon Concise History" series; an article entitled "On Reflexive Verbs in English"; Chapter Nine, "The Prince and the Peasant"; Pushkin's "The Queen of Spades"; Tennyson's "Ode on the Death of the Duke of Wellington"; "The Bob Hope Special"; Schubert's "Death and the Maiden."

5. Single quotation marks enclose quotations within quotations: The blurb for the piece proclaimed, "Two years ago at Geneva, South Vietnam was virtually sold down the river to the Communists. Today the spunky little . . . country is back on its own feet, thanks to 'a mandarin in a sharkskin suit who's upsetting the Red timetable.'"—Frances FitzGerald

Put commas and periods inside quotation marks; put semicolons and colons outside. Other punctuation, such as exclamation points and question marks, should be put inside the closing quotation marks only if part of the matter quoted.

Semicolon

1. Separates the clauses of a compound sentence having no coordinating conjunction: Do not let us speak of darker days; let us rather speak of sterner days.—Winston Churchill

2. Separates the clauses of a compound sentence in which the clauses contain internal punctuation, even when the clauses are joined by conjunctions: Skis in hand, we trudged to the lodge, stowed our lunches, and donned our boots; and the rest of our party waited for us at the lifts.

3. Separates elements of a series in which items already contain commas: Among those at the diplomatic reception were the Secretary of State; the daughter of the Ambassador to the Court of St. James's, formerly of London; and two United Nations delegates.

4. Separates clauses of a compound sentence joined by a conjunctive adverb, such as *however, nonetheless,* or *hence:* We insisted upon a hearing; however, the Grievance Committee refused.

5. May be used instead of a comma to signal longer pauses for dramatic effect: But I want you to know that when I cross the river my last conscious thought will be of the Corps; and the Corps; and the Corps.—General Douglas MacArthur

Virgule

1. Separates successive divisions in an extended date: fiscal year 1983/84.

2. Represents *per:* 35 km/hr, 1,800 ft./sec.

3. Means *or* between the words *and* and *or:* Take water skis and/or fishing equipment when you visit the beach this summer.

4. Separates two or more lines of poetry that are quoted and run in on successive lines of a text: The student actress had a memory lapse when she came to the lines "Double, double, toil and trouble/Fire burn and cauldron bubble/Eye of newt and toe of frog/Wool of bat and tongue of dog" and had to leave the stage in embarrassment.

Forms of Address

Source: Webster's II New Riverside University Dictionary. © 1984 by Houghton Mifflin Company.

Academics

Dean, college or university. *Address:* Dean _____. *Salutation:* Dear Dean _____

President. *Address:* President _____ _____. *Salutation:* Dear President _____.

Professor, college or university. *Address:* Professor _____ _____. *Salutation:* Dear Professor _____.

Clerical and Religious Orders

Abbot. *Address:* The Right Reverend _____, O.S.B. Abbot of _____. *Salutation:* Right Reverend Abbot or Dear Father Abbot.

Archbishop, Eastern Orthodox. *Address:* The Most Reverend Joseph, Archbishop of _____. *Salutation:* Your Eminence.

Archbishop, Roman Catholic. *Address:* The Most Reverend _____ _____, Archbishop of _____. *Salutation:* Your Excellency.

Archdeacon, Episcopal. *Address:* The Venerable _____ _____, Archdeacon of _____. *Salutation:* Venerable Sir or Dear Archdeacon _____.

Bishop, Episcopal. *Address:* The Right Reverend _____ _____, Bishop of _____. *Salutation:* Right Reverend Sir or Dear Bishop _____.

Bishop, other Protestant. *Address:* The Reverend _____ _____. *Salutation:* Dear Bishop _____.

Bishop, Roman Catholic. *Address:* The Most Reverend _____ _____, Bishop of _____. *Salutation:* Your Excellency or Dear Bishop _____.

Brotherhood, Roman Catholic. *Address:* Brother _____ _____, C.F.C. *Salutation:* Dear Brother _____ or Dear Brother Joseph.

Brotherhood, superior of. *Address:* Brother Joseph C.F.C. Superior. *Salutation:* Dear Brother Joseph.

Cardinal. *Address:* His Eminence Joseph Cardinal Stone. *Salutation:* Your Eminence.

Clergyman/woman, Protestant. *Address:* The Reverend _____ or The Reverend _____, D.D. *Salutation:* Dear Mr./Ms. _____ or Dear Dr. _____

Dean of a cathedral, Episcopal. *Address:* The Very Reverend _____ _____, Dean of _____. *Salutation:* Dear Dean _____.

Monsignor. *Address:* The Right Reverend Monsignor _____ _____. *Salutation:* Dear Monsignor _____.

Patriarch, Greek Orthodox. *Address:* His All Holiness Patriarch Joseph. *Salutation:* Your All Holiness.

Patriarch, Russian Orthodox. *Address:* His Holiness the Patriarch of _____. *Salutation:* Your Holiness.

Pope. *Address:* His Holiness The Pope. *Salutation:* Your Holiness or Most Holy Father.

Priest, Roman Catholic. *Address:* The Reverend _____ _____, S.J. *Salutation:* Dear Reverend Father or Dear Father.

Rabbi, man or woman. *Address:* Rabbi _____ _____ or _____ _____, D.D. *Salutation:* Dear Rabbi _____ or Dear Dr. _____.

Sisterhood, Roman Catholic. *Address:* Sister _____ _____, C.S.J. *Salutation:* Dear Sister or Dear Sister _____.

Sisterhood, superior of. *Address:* The Reverend Mother Superior, S.C. *Salutation:* Reverend Mother.

Diplomats

Ambassador, U.S. *Address:* The Honorable _____ _____ The Ambassador of the United States. *Salutation:* Sir/Madam or Dear Mr./Madam Ambassador.

Ambassador to the U.S. *Address:* His/Her Excellency _____ _____, The Ambassador of _____. *Salutation:* Excellency or Dear Mr./Madam Ambassador.

Chargé d'Affaires, U.S. *Address:* The Honorable _____ _____, United States Chargé d'Affaires. *Salutation:* Dear Mr./Ms. _____.

Consul, U.S. *Address:* _____ _____, Esq., United States Consul. *Salutation:* Dear Mr./Ms. _____.

Minister, U.S. or to U.S. *Address:* The Honorable _____ _____, The Minister of _____. *Salutation:* Sir/Madam or Dear Mr./Madame Minister.

Secretary General, United Nations. *Address:* His/Her Excellency _____ _____, Secretary General of the United Nations. *Salutation:* Dear Mr./Madam/Madame Secretary General.

United Nations Representative (Foreign). *Address:* His/Her Excellency _____ _____, Representative of _____ to the United Nations. *Salutation:* Excellency or My dear Mr./Madame _____.

United Nations Representative (U.S.) *Address:* The Honorable _____ _____, United States Representative to the United Nations. *Salutation:* Sir/Madam or Dear Mr./Ms. _____.

Government Officials

Assemblyman. *Address:* The Honorable _____ _____. *Salutation:* Dear Mr./Ms.

Associate Justice, U.S. Supreme Court. *Address:* Mr./Madam Justice _____. *Salutation:* Dear Mr./Madam Justice or Sir/Madam.

Attorney General, U.S. *Address:* The Honorable _____ _____, Attorney General of the United States. *Salutation:* Dear Mr./Madam or Attorney General.

Cabinet member. *Address:* The Honorable _____ _____, Secretary of _____. *Salutation:* Sir/Madam or Dear Mr./Madam Secretary.

Chief Justice, U.S. Supreme Court. *Address:* The Chief Justice of the United States. *Salutation:* Dear Mr./Madame Chief Justice.

Commissioner (federal, state, local). *Address:* The Honorable _____ _____. *Salutation:* Dear Mr./Ms.

Governor. *Address:* The Honorable _____ _____, Governor of _____. *Salutation:* Dear Governor _____.

Judge, federal. *Address:* The Honorable _____ _____, Judge of the United States District Court for the _____, District of _____. *Salutation:* Sir/Madam or Dear Judge _____.

Judge, state or local. *Address:* The Honorable _____ _____, Judge of the Court of _____. *Salutation:* Dear Judge _____.

Lieutenant Governor. *Address:* The Honorable _____ _____, Lieutenant Governor of _____. *Salutation:* Dear Mr./Ms.

Mayor. *Address:* The Honorable _____ _____, Mayor of _____. *Salutation:* Dear Mayor _____.

President, U.S. *Address:* The President. *Salutation:* Dear Mr./Madam President.

President, U.S., former. *Address:* The Honorable _____ _____. *Salutation:* Dear Mr./Madam _____.

Representative, state. *Address:* The Honorable _____ _____. *Salutation:* Dear Mr./Ms. _____.

Representative, U.S. *Address:* The Honorable _____ _____, United States House of Representatives. *Salutation:* Dear Mr./Ms. _____.

Senator, state. *Address:* The Honorable _____ _____, The State Senate, State Capitol. *Salutation:* Dear Senator _____.

Senator, U.S. *Address:* The Honorable _____ _____, United States Senate. *Salutation:* Dear Senator _____.

Speaker, U.S. House of Representatives. *Address:* The Honorable _____ _____, Speaker of the House of Representatives. *Salutation:* Dear Mr./Madam Speaker.

Vice President, U.S. *Address:* The Vice President of the United States. *Salutation:* Sir/Madam or Dear Mr./Madam Vice President.

Military and Naval Officers

Rank. *Address:* Full rank, USN (or USCG, USAF, USA, USMC). *Salutation:* Dear (full rank) _____.

Professions

Attorney. *Address:* Mr./Ms. _____ _____, Attorney at law or _____ _____, Esq. *Salutation:* Dear Mr./Ms. _____.

Dentist. *Address:* _____ _____, D.D.S. *Salutation:* Dear Dr. _____.

Physician. *Address:* _____ _____, M.D. *Salutation:* Dear Dr. _____.

Veterinarian. *Address:* _____ _____, D.V.M. *Salutation:* Dear Dr. _____.

Foreign Words and Phrases

The English meanings given below are not necessarily literal translations. Foreign words and phrases should be set in italics (or underlined if written in long-hand) if their meanings are likely to be unknown to the reader. Whether the expression is familiar or unfamiliar, however, is a matter of judgment. Below, all foreign words have been italicized for the sake of emphasis.

ad absurdum [Lat.]: to the point of absurdity. "He tediously repeated his argument *ad absurdum.*"

ad hominem [Lat.]: attacking an opponent's character rather than answering his argument. "As usual, any attempt on my part to discuss the matter rationally was met with an *ad hominem* attack on my perceived personality flaws."

ad infinitum [Lat.]: to infinity. "The lecture seemed to drone on *ad infinitum.*"

ad nauseam [Lat.]: to a sickening degree. "The politician uttered one platitude after another *ad nauseam.*"

aficionado [Span.]: an ardent devotee. "I was surprised at what a baseball *aficionado* she had become."

annus mirabilis [Lat.]: wonderful year. "Last year was the *annus mirabilis* for my company."

au courant [Fr.]: up-to-date. "The shoes, the hair, the clothes—every last detail of her dress, in fact—was utterly *au courant.*"

beau geste [Fr.]: a fine or noble gesture, often futile. "My fellow writers supported me by writing letters of protest to the publisher, but their *beau geste* could not prevent the inevitable."

beau monde [Fr.]: high society. "Such elegant decor would impress even the *beau monde.*"

bête noire [Fr.]: something or someone particularly disliked. "Talk of the good old college days way back when had become his *bête noire,* and he began to avoid his school friends."

bona fide [Lat.]: in good faith; genuine. "For all her reticence and modesty, it was clear that she was a *bona fide* expert in her field."

bon mot [Fr.]: a witty remark or comment. "One *bon mot* after another flew out of his mouth, charming the audience."

bon vivant [Fr.]: a person who lives luxuriously and enjoys good food and drink. "It's true he's quite the *bon vivant,* but when he gets down to business he conducts himself like a Spartan."

carpe diem [Lat.]: seize the day. "So what if you have an 8:00 a.m. meeting tomorrow and a full day of appointments? *Carpe diem!*"

carte blanche [Fr.]: unrestricted power to act on one's own. "I may have *carte blanche* around the office, but at home I'm a slave to my family's demands."

caveat emptor [Lat.]: let the buyer beware. "Before you leap at that real estate deal, *caveat emptor!*"

comme ci comme ça [Fr.]: so-so. "The plans for the party strike me as *comme ci comme ça.*"

comme il faut [Fr.]: as it should be; fitting. "His end was truly *comme il faut.*"

coup de grâce [Fr.]: finishing blow. "After an already wildly successful day, the *coup de grâce* came when she won best all-around athlete."

cri de coeur [Fr.]: heartfelt appeal. "About to leave the podium, he made a final *cri de coeur* to his people to end the bloodshed."

de gustibus non est disputandum [Lat.]: there is no arguing in matters of taste. "Shaking his head at the tinsel-town ostentation of the casino, he mumbled, '*de gustibus non est disputandum.*'"

de rigueur [Fr.]: strictly required, as by etiquette, usage, or fashion. "Loudly proclaiming one's support for radical causes had become *de rigueur* among her crowd."

deus ex machina [Lat.]: a contrived device to resolve a situation. "Stretching plausibility, the movie concluded with a *deus ex machina* ending in which everyone was rescued at the last minute."

dolce vita [Ital.]: sweet life; the good life perceived as one of physical pleasure and self-indulgence. "My vacation this year is going to be two uninterrupted weeks of *dolce vita.*"

Doppelgänger [Ger.]: a ghostly double or counterpart of a living person. "I could not shake the sense that some shadowy *Doppelgänger** echoed my every move."

ecce homo [Lat.]: behold the man. "The painting depicted the common Renaissance theme, *ecco homo*—Christ wearing the crown of thorns."

éminence grise [Fr.]: gray eminence; power behind the throne. "All but the most unperceptive realized that the general was the *éminence grise* behind the puppet ruler."

enfant terrible [Fr.]: an incorrigible child; an outrageously outspoken or bold person. "Again he played the role of *enfant terrible*, jolting us with his blunt assessment; yet I was secretly thrilled that the truth had come out in such a flagrant manner."

entre nous [Fr.]: between ourselves; confidentially. "*Entre nous*, their marriage is on the rocks."

ex cathedra [Lat.]: with authority; used especially of those pronouncements of the pope that are considered infallible. "I resigned myself to obeying; my father's opinions were *ex cathedra* in our household."

ex post facto [Lat.]: retroactively. "I certainly hope that the change in policy will be honored *ex post facto.*"

fait accompli [Fr.]: an accomplished fact, presumably irreversible. "There's no use protesting—it's a *fait accompli.*"

faux pas [Fr.]: a social blunder. "Suddenly, she realized she had unwittingly committed yet another *faux pas.*"

Feinschmecker [Ger.]: gourmet. "No, I don't think McDonald's will do; he's much too much of a *Feinschmecker.*"

flagrante delicto [Lat.]: in the act. "The detective realized that without hard evidence he had no case; he would have to catch the culprit *flagrante delicto.*"

glasnost [Rus.]: open and frank discussion: initiated by Mikhail Gorbachev in 1985 in the Soviet Union.

"Once the old chairman retired, the spirit of *glasnost* pervaded the department."

hoi polloi [Gk.]: the common people. "Marie Antoinette recommended cake to the *hoi polloi.*"

in loco parentis [Lat.]: in the place of a parent. "Put those cigarettes away young man; while you're with me consider my word *in loco parentis.*"

in medias res [Lat.]: in the middle of things. "The story began *in medias res;* it was clear from the first lines that some kind of horrendous calamity had already befallen the characters."

in situ [Lat.]: situated in the original or natural position. "I prefer seeing statues *in situ* rather than in the confines of a museum."

in vino veritas [Lat.]: in wine there is truth. "By the end of drunken banquet, several of the guests had made a good deal of their private lives public, prompting the host to murmur to his wife, '*in vino veritas.*'"

ipso facto [Lat.]: by the fact itself. "An extremist, *ipso facto*, cannot become part of a coalition."

je ne sais quoi [Fr.]: I know not what; an elusive quality. "She couldn't explain it, but there was something *je ne sais quoi* about him that she found devastatingly attractive."

Kinder, Kirche, Küche [Ger.]: children, church, kitchen. "She realized that her entire life had been devoted to *Kinder, Kirche, Küche.*"

mano a mano [Span.]: a direct confrontation or conflict. "'Stay out of it,' he admonished his friends, 'I want to handle this guy *mano a mano.*'"

mea culpa [Lat.]: I am to blame. "His *mea culpa* was so offhand that I hardly think he meant it."

memento mori [Lat.]: a reminder that you must die. "The scull rested on the mantlepiece as a *memento mori.*"

modus operandi [Lat.]: a method of operating. "Her *modus operandi* is to sugar-coat the truth so thoroughly that the news almost seems welcome."

mot juste [Fr.]: the exact, appropriate word. "'Rats!' screamed the defiant three-year-old, immensely proud of his *mot juste.*"

ne plus ultra [Fr.]: the most intense degree of a quality or state. "Pulling it from the box, he realized he was face to face with the *ne plus ultra* of computers."

nom de guerre [Fr.]: pseudonym. "He went by his *nom de guerre* when frequenting trendy nightclubs."

nom de plume [Fr.]: pen name. "Deciding it was time to sit down and write novel, the would-be writer spent the first several hours deciding upon a suitably dashing *nom de plume.*"

nota bene [Ital.]: note well; take notice. "She appended her suggestions to the manuscript, underlining the words *nota bene* for added emphasis."

persona non grata [Lat.]: unacceptable or unwelcome person. "Once I was cut out of the will, I became *persona non grata* among my relatives."

pro bono [Lat.]: done or donated without charge; free. "The lawyer's *pro bono* work gave him a sense of value that his work on behalf of the corporation could not."

quid pro quo [Lat.]: something for something; an equal exchange. "She vowed that when she had the means, she would return his favors *quid pro quo.*"

sans souci [Fr.]: carefree. "Their mood was definitely *sans souci.*"

savoir faire [Fr.]: the ability to say and do the correct thing. "She presided over the gathering with impressive *savoir faire.*"

sic transit gloria mundi [Lat.]: thus passes away the glory of the world. "Watching the aging former football quarterback lumber down the street, potbellied and dissipated, his friend shook his head in disbelief and muttered, '*sic transit gloria mundi.*'"

sine qua non [Lat.]: indispensable. "Lemon is the *sine qua non* of this recipe."

terra incognita [Lat.]: unknown territory. "When the conversation suddenly switched from contemporary fiction to medieval Albanian playwrights, he felt himself entering *terra incognita.*"

tout le monde [Fr.]: everybody; everyone of importance. "Don't miss the event; it's bound to be attended by *tout le monde.*"

veni, vidi, vici [Lat.]: I came, I saw, I conquered. "After the takeover the business mogul gloated, '*veni, vidi, vici.*'"

verboten [Ger.]: forbidden, as by law; prohibited. "That topic I am afraid, is *verboten* in this household."

vox populi [Lat.]: the voice of the people. "My sentiments echo those of the *vox populi.*"

Wanderjahr [Ger.]: a year or period of travel, especially following one's schooling. "The trio took off on their *Wanderjahr* soon after they graduated, planning to circle the globe by bicycle."

Weltanschauung [Ger.]: a comprehensive conception or image of the universe and of humanity's relation to it. "His *Weltanschauung* gradually metamorphized from a grim and pessimistic one to a sunny, but no less complex, view."

Zeitgeist [Ger.]: the spirit of the time; general trend of thought or feeling characteristic of a particular period of time. "She blamed it on the *Zeitgeist,* which encouraged hedonistic excess."

*German nouns are capitalized. A familiar German expression that is not italicized, however, should be lower-cased, following the English conventions of not capitalizing common nouns. "His proclivities leaned more to the occult than to the philosophical: a poltergeist he could understand; the *Zeitgeist* he could not."

Easily Confused Words

allusion / illusion Allusion is a noun that means an indirect reference: "The speech made allusions to the final report." Illusion is a noun that means a misconception: "The policy is designed to give an illusion of reform."

alternately / alternatively Alternately is an adverb that means in turn; one after the other: "We alternately spun the wheel in the game." Alternatively is an adverb that means on the other hand; one or the other: "You can choose a large bookcase or, alternatively, you can buy two small ones."

beside / besides Beside is a preposition that means next to: "Stand here beside me. "Besides is an adverb that means also: "Besides, I need to tell you about the new products my company offers."

bimonthly / semimonthly Bimonthly is an adjective that means every two months: "I brought the cake for the bimonthly office party." Bimonthly is also a noun that means a publication issued every two months: "The bimonthly magazine will soon become a monthly publication." Semimonthly is an adjective that means happening twice a month: "We have semimonthly meetings on the 1st and the 15th."

cite / site Cite is a verb that means to quote as an authority or example: "I cited several eminent scholars in my study of water resources." It also means to recognize formally: "The public official was cited for service to the city." It can also mean to summon before a court of law: "Last year the company was cited for pollution violations." Site is a noun meaning location: "They chose a new site for the factory just outside town."

complement / compliment Complement is a noun or verb that means something that completes or makes up a whole: "The red sweater is a perfect complement to the outfit." Compliment is a noun or verb that means an expression of praise or admiration: "I received many compliments about my new outfit."

concurrent / consecutive Concurrent is an adjective that means simultaneous or happening at the same time as something else: "The concurrent strikes of several unions crippled the economy." Consecutive means successive or following one after the other: "The union called three consecutive strikes in one year."

connote / denote Connote is a verb that means to imply or suggest: "The word 'espionage 'connotes mystery and intrigue." Denote is a verb that means to indicate or refer to specifically: "The symbol for 'pi' denotes the number 3.14159."

discreet / discrete Discreet is an adjective that means prudent, circumspect, or modest: "Their discreet comments about the negotiations led the reporters to expect an early settlement." Discrete is an adjective that means separate or individually distinct: "Each company in the conglomerate operates as a discrete entity."

disinterested / uninterested Disinterested is an adjective that means unbiased or impartial: "We appealed to the disinterested mediator to facilitate the negotiations." Uninterested is an adjective that means not interested or indifferent: "They seemed uninterested in our offer."

emigrant / immigrant / migrant Emigrant is a noun that means one who leaves one's native country to settle in another: "The emigrants spent four weeks aboard ship before landing in Los Angeles." Immigrant is a noun that means one who enters and settles in a new country: "Most of the immigrants easily found jobs." Migrant is a noun that means one who travels from one region to another, especially in search of work: "The migrants worked in the strawberry fields on the west coast, then traveled east to harvest wheat."

foreword / forward Foreword is a noun that means an introductory note or preface: "In my foreword I explained my reasons for writing the book." Forward is an adjective or adverb that means toward the front: "I sat in the forward section of the bus. Please step forward when your name is called." Forward is also a verb that means to send on: "Forward the letter to the customer's new address."

further / farther Farther is an adjective and adverb that means to or at a more distant point: "We drove 50 miles today; tomorrow, we will travel 100 miles farther." Further is an adjective and adverb that means to or at a greater extent or degree: "We won't be able to suggest a solution until we are further along in our evaluation of the problem." It can also mean in addition or moreover: "They stated further that they would not change the policy."

few / less Few is an adjective that means small in number. It is used with countable objects: "This department has few employees." Less is an adjective that means small in amount or degree. It is used with objects of indivisible mass: "Which jar holds less water?"

figuratively / literally Figuratively is an adverb that means metaphorically or symbolically: "Happening upon the shadowy figure, they figuratively jumped out of their shoes." Literally is an adverb that means word for word or according to the exact meaning of the words: "I translated the Latin passage literally."

hanged / hung   Hanged is the past tense and past participle of hang when the meaning is to execute by suspending by the neck: "They hanged the prisoner for treason." "The convicted killer was hanged at dawn." Hung is the past tense and participle of hang when the meaning is to suspend from above with no support from below: "I hung the painting on the wall." "The painting was hung at a crooked angle."

it's / its   It's is a contraction for it is, whereas its is the possessive form of it: "It's a shame that we cannot talk about its size."

laid / lay / lain   Laid is the past tense and the past participle of the verb lay and not the past tense of lie. Lay is the past tense of the verb lie and lain is the past participle: "He laid his books down and lay down on the couch, where he has lain for an hour."

principal / principle   Principal is a noun that means a person who holds a high position or plays an important role: "The school principal has 20 years of teaching experience. The principals in the negotiations will meet tomorrow at 10 o'clock." It also means a sum of money on which interest accrues: "The depositors were guaranteed they would not lose their principal." Principal is also an adjective that means chief or leading: "The necessity of moving to another city was the principal reason I turned down the job offer." Principle is a noun that means a rule or standard: "They refused to compromise their principles."

stationary / stationery   Stationary is an adjective that means fixed or unmoving: "They maneuvered around the stationary barrier in the road." Stationery is a noun that means writing materials: "We printed the letters on company stationery."

American Sign Language and the Manual Alphabet

Sign language for the deaf was first systematized in France during the eighteenth century by Abbot Charles-Michel l'Epee. French Sign Language (FSL) was brought to the United States in 1816 by Thomas Gallaudet, founder of the American School for the Deaf in Hartford, Connecticut. He developed American Sign Language (ASL), a language of gestures and hand symbols that express words and concepts. It is the fourth most used language in the United States today.

Along with sign language and lip reading, many deaf people communicate with the manual alphabet, which uses finger positions that correspond to the letters of the alphabet to spell out words.

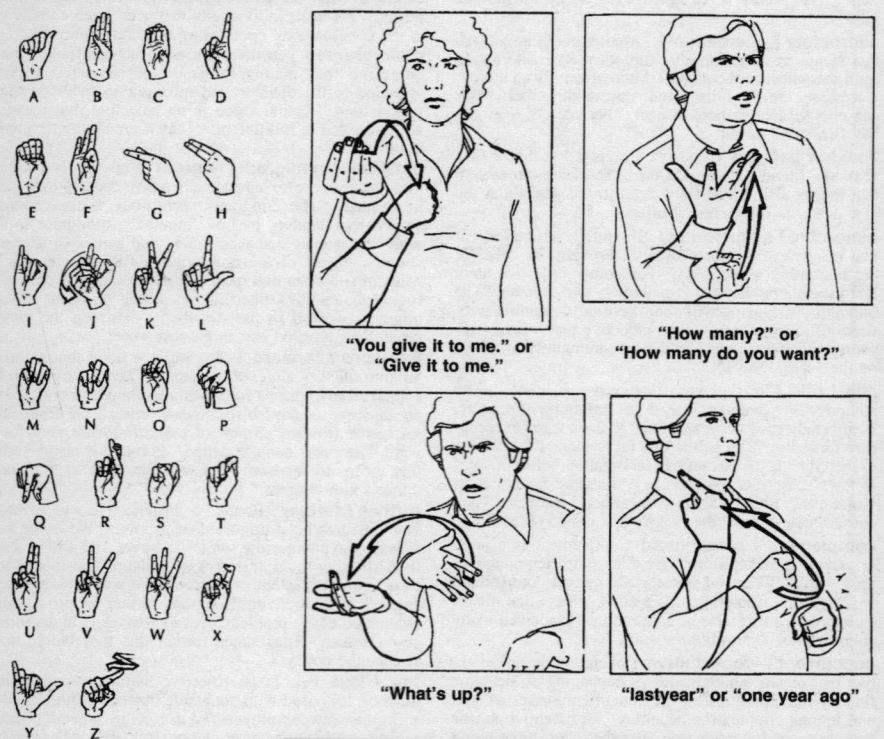

"You give it to me." or
"Give it to me."

"How many?" or
"How many do you want?"

"What's up?"

"lastyear" or "one year ago"

American Manual Alphabet

Structures

The Seven Wonders of the World

Not all classical writers list the same items as the Seven Wonders, but most of them agree on the following.

The Pyramids of Egypt. A group of three pyramids, *Khufu*, *Khafra*, and *Menkaura* at Giza, outside modern Cairo, is often called the first wonder of the world. The largest pyramid, built by Khufu (Cheops), a king of the fourth dynasty, had an original estimated height of 482 ft. (now approximately 450 ft.). The base has sides 755 ft. long. It contains 2,300,000 blocks; the average weight of each is 2.5 tons. Estimated date of construction is 2800 B.C.E. Of all the Seven Wonders, the pyramids alone survive.

Hanging Gardens of Babylon. Often listed as the second wonder, these gardens were supposedly built by Nebuchadnezzar about 600 B.C.E. to please his queen, Amuhia. They are also associated with the mythical Assyrian queen, Semiramis. Archeologists surmise that the gardens were laid out atop a vaulted building, with provisions for raising water. The terraces were said to rise from 75 to 300 ft.

The Walls of Babylon, also built by Nebuchadnezzar, are sometimes referred to as the second (or the seventh) wonder instead of the Hanging Gardens.

Statue of Zeus (Jupiter) at Olympia. The work of Phidias (5th century B.C.E.), this colossal figure in gold and ivory was reputedly 40 ft. high. All trace of it is lost, except for reproductions on coins.

Temple of Artemis (Diana) at Ephesus. A beautiful structure, begun about 350 B.C.E., in honor of a non-Hellenic goddess who later became identified with the Greek goddess of the same name. The temple, with Ionic columns 60 ft. high, was destroyed by invading Goths in C.E. 262.

Mausoleum at Halicarnassus. This famous monument was erected by Queen Artemisia in memory of her husband, King Mausolus of Caria in Asia Minor, who died in 353 B.C.E. Some remains of the structure are in the British Museum. This shrine is the source of the modern word "mausoleum."

Colossus at Rhodes. This bronze statue of Helios (Apollo), about 105 ft. high, was the work of the sculptor Chares, who reputedly labored for 12 years before completing it in 280 B.C.E. It was destroyed during an earthquake in 224 B.C.E.

Pharos of Alexandria. The seventh wonder was the Pharos (lighthouse) of Alexandria, built by Sostratus of Cnidus during the 3rd century B.C.E. on the island of Pharos off the coast of Egypt. It was destroyed by an earthquake in the 13th century.

Famous Structures

Ancient

The *Great Sphinx of Egypt,* one of the wonders of ancient Egyptian architecture, adjoins the pyramids of Giza and has a length of 240 ft. It was built in the 4th dynasty. Other Egyptian buildings of note include the *Temples of Karnak, Edfu,* and the *Tombs at Beni Hassan.*

The *Parthenon of Greece,** built on the Acropolis in Athens, was the chief temple to the goddess Athena. It was believed to have been completed by 438 B.C.E. The present temple remained intact until the 5th century C.E. Today, though the Parthenon is in ruins, its majestic proportions are still discernible.

Other great structures of ancient Greece were the *Temples at Paestum* (about 540 and 420 B.C.E.); the *Temple of Poseidon* (about 460 B.C.E.); the *Temple of Apollo* at Corinth (about 540 B.C.E.); the *Temple of Apollo* at Bassae (about 450–420 B.C.E.); the famous *Erechtheum* atop the Acropolis (about 421–405 B.C.E.); the *Temple of Athena Niké* at Athens (about 426 B.C.E.); the *Olympieum* at Athens (174 B.C.E.–C.E. 131); the *Athenian Treasury* at Delphi (about 515 B.C.E.); the *Propylaea* of the Acropolis at Athens (437–432 B.C.E.); the *Theater of Dionysus* at Athens (about 350–325 B.C.E.); the *House of Cleopatra* at Delos (138 B.C.E.) and the *Theater* at Epidaurus (about 325 B.C.E.).

The *Colosseum (Flavian Amphitheater) of Rome,* the largest and most famous of the Roman amphitheaters, was opened for use C.E. 80. Elliptical in shape, it consisted of three stories and an upper gallery, rebuilt in stone in its present form in the third century C.E. Its seats rise in tiers, which in turn are buttressed by con-

crete vaults and stone piers. It could seat between 40,000 and 50,000 spectators. It was principally used for gladiatorial combat.

The *Pantheon** at Rome, begun by Agrippa in 27 B.C.E. as a temple, was rebuilt in its present circular form by Hadrian (C.E. 110–25). Literally the Pantheon was intended as a temple of "all the gods." It is remarkable for its perfect preservation today, and it has served continuously for 20 centuries as a place of worship.

Famous Roman arches include the *Arch of Constantine* (about C.E. 315) and the *Arch of Titus* (about C.E. 80).

Later European

St. Mark's Cathedral in Venice (1063–67), one of the great examples of Byzantine architecture, was begun in the 9th century. Partly destroyed by fire in 976, it was later rebuilt as a Byzantine edifice.

Other famous Byzantine examples of architecture are *St. Sophia* in Istanbul (C.E. 532–37); *San Vitale* in Ravenna (542); *St. Paul's Outside the Walls,* Rome (5th century); *Assumption Cathedral* in the Kremlin, Moscow (begun in 1475); and *St. Lorenzo Outside the Walls,* Rome, begun in 588.

The *Cathedral Group* at Pisa (1067–1173), one of the most celebrated groups of structures built in Romanesque-style, consists of the cathedral, the cathedral's baptistery, and the *Leaning Tower.** This trio forms a group by itself in the northwest corner of the city. The cathedral and baptistery are built in varicolored marble. The campanile (*Leaning Tower*) is 179 ft.

* Photos of these structures can be found in the Headline History section.

high and leans more than 16 ft. out of the perpendicular. There is little reason to believe that the architects intended to have the tower lean.

Other examples of Romanesque architecture include the *Vézelay Abbey* in France (1130); the *Church of Notre-Dame-du-Port* at Clermont-Ferrand in France (1100); the *Church of San Zeno* (begun in 1138) at Verona; and *Durham Cathedral* in England.

The *Alhambra* (1248–1354), located in Granada, Spain, is universally esteemed as one of the greatest masterpieces of Moslem architecture. Designed as a palace and fortress for the Moorish monarchs of Granada, it is surrounded by a heavily fortified wall more than a mile in perimeter. The location of the Alhambra in the Sierra Nevada provides a magnificent setting for this jewel of Moorish Spain.

The *Tower of London* is a group of buildings and towers covering 13 acres along the north bank of the Thames. The central *White Tower*, begun in 1078 during the reign of William the Conqueror, was originally a fortress and royal residence, but was later used as a prison. The *Bloody Tower* is associated with Anne Boleyn and other notables.

Westminster Abbey, in London, was begun in 1045 and completed in 1065. It was rebuilt and enlarged in 1245–50.

Notre-Dame de Paris (begun in 1163), one of the great examples of Gothic architecture, is a twin-towered church with a steeple over the crossing and immense flying buttresses supporting the masonry at the rear of the church.

Other famous Gothic structures are *Chartres Cathedral* (12th century); *Sainte Chapelle*, Paris (1246–48); *Laon Cathedral*, France (1160–1205); *Reims Cathedral* (about 1210–50; rebuilt after its almost complete destruction in World War I); *Rouen Cathedral* (13th–16th centuries); *Amiens Cathedral* (1218–69); *Beauvais Cathedral* (begun 1247); *Salisbury Cathedral* (1220–60); *York Minster* or the *Cathedral of St. Peter* (begun in the 7th century); *Milan Cathedral* (begun 1386); and *Cologne Cathedral* (13th–19th centuries); badly damaged in World War II.

The *Duomo** (cathedral) in Florence was founded in 1298, completed by Brunelleschi and consecrated in 1436. The oval-shaped dome dominates the entire structure.

The *Vatican* is a group of buildings in Rome comprising the official residence of the Pope. The *Basilica of St. Peter*, the largest church in the Christian world, was begun in 1450. The *Sistine Chapel*, begun in 1473, is noted for the art masterpieces of Michelangelo, Botticelli, and others. The *Basilica of the Savior* (known as *St. John Lateran*) is the first-ranking Catholic Church in the world, for it is the cathedral of the Pope.

Other examples of Renaissance architecture are the *Palazzo Riccardi*, the *Palazzo Pitti*, and the *Palazzo Strozzi* in Florence; the *Farnese Palace* in Rome; *Palazzo Grimani* (completed about 1550) in Venice; the *Escorial* (1563–93) near Madrid; the *Town Hall* of Seville (1527–32); the *Louvre*, Paris; the *Château* at Blois, France; *St. Paul's Cathedral*, London (1675–1710; badly damaged in World War II); the *École Militaire*, Paris (1752); the *Pazzi Chapel*, Florence, designed by Brunelleschi (1429); the *Palace of Fontainebleau* and the *Château de Chambord* in France.

The *Palace of Versailles*, containing the famous Hall of Mirrors, was built during the reign of Louis XIV and served as the royal palace until 1793.

Outstanding European buildings of the 18th and 19th centuries are the *Superga* at Turin, the *Hôtel-Dieu* in Lyons, the *Belvedere Palace* at Vienna, the *Royal Palace* of Stockholm, the *Opera House* of Paris (1863–75); the *Bank of England*, the *British Museum*, the *University of London*, and the *Houses of Parliament*, all in London; the *Panthéon*, the *Church of the Madeleine*, the *Bourse*, and the *Palais de Justice* in Paris.

The *Eiffel Tower*, in Paris, was built for the Exposition of 1889 by Alexandre Eiffel. It is 984-ft. high (1,056 ft., including the television tower).

Asiatic and African

The *Taj Mahal** (1632–50), at Agra, India, built by Shah Jahan as a tomb for his wife, is considered by some as the most perfect example of the Mogul style and by others as the most beautiful building in the world. Four slim white minarets flank the building, which is topped by a white dome; the entire structure is of marble. Other examples of Indian architecture are the temples at Benares and Tanjore.

Among famed Moslem edifices are the *Dome of the Rock* or *Mosque of Omar*, Jerusalem (c.e. 691); the *Citadel* (1166), and the *Tombs of the Mamelukes* (15th century), in Cairo; the *Tomb of Humayun* in Delhi; the *Blue Mosque* (1468) at Tabriz; and the *Tamerlane Mausoleum* at Samarkand.

Angkor Wat, outside the city of Angkor Thom, Cambodia, is one of the most beautiful examples of Cambodian or Khmer architecture. The sanctuary was built during the 12th century.

Great Wall of China (228 b.c.e.?), designed specifically as a defense against nomadic tribes, has large watch towers which could be called buildings. It was erected by Emperor Ch'in Shih Huang Ti and is 1,400 miles long. Built mainly of earth and stone, it varies in height between 18 and 30 ft.

Typical of Chinese architecture are the pagodas or temple towers. Among some of the better-known pagodas are the *Great Pagoda of the Wild Geese* at Sian (founded in 652); *Nan t'a* (11th century) at Fang Shan; and the *Pagoda of Sung Yueh Ssu* (c.e. 523) at Sung Shan, Honan.

Other well-known Chinese buildings are the *Drum Tower* (1273), the *Three Great Halls* in the Purple Forbidden City (1627), *Buddha's Perfume Tower* (19th century), the *Porcelain Pagoda*, and the *Summer Palace*, all at Beijing.

United States

Rockefeller Center, in New York City, extends from 5th Ave. to the Avenue of the Americas between 48th and 52nd Sts. (and halfway to 7th Ave. between 47th and 51st Sts.). It occupies more than 22 acres and has 19 buildings.

The Cathedral of St. John the Divine, at 112th St. and Amsterdam Ave. in New York City, was begun in 1892 and is now in the final stages of completion. When completed, it will be the largest cathedral in the world: 601-ft. long, 146-ft. wide at the nave, 320-ft. wide at the transept. The east end is designed in Romanesque-Byzantine style, and the nave and west end are Gothic.

St. Patrick's Cathedral, at Fifth Ave. and 50th St. in New York City, has a seating capacity of 2,500. The nave was opened in 1877, and the cathedral was dedicated in 1879.

Louisiana Superdome, in New Orleans, is the largest arena in the history of mankind. The main area can accommodate up to 95,000 people. It is the world's largest steel-constructed room. Unobstructed by posts, it covers 13 acres and reaches 27 stories at its peak.

World Trade Center, in New York City, was dedicated in 1973. Its twin towers are 110 stories high (1,350 ft.), and the complex contains over 9-million sq-ft. of office space. A restaurant is on the 107th floor of the North Tower.

* Photos of these structures can be found in the Headline History section.

Notable Modern Bridges

Name	Location	Length of main span		Year completed
		feet	meters	
Suspension	**United States**			
Verrazano-Narrows	Lower New York Bay	4,260	1,298	1964
Golden Gate	San Francisco Bay	4,200	1,280	1937
Mackinac Straits	Michigan	3,800	1,158	1957
George Washington	Hudson River at New York City	3,500	1,067	1931
Tacoma Narrows II	Puget Sound at Tacoma, Wash.	2,800	853	1950
San Francisco-Oakland Bay[1]	San Francisco Bay	2,310	704	1936
Bronx-Whitestone	East River, New York City	2,300	701	1939
Delaware Memorial[1]	Delaware River near Wilmington, Del.	2,150	655	1951, 1968
Seaway Skyway	St. Lawrence River at Ogdensburg, N.Y.	2,150	655	1960
Walt Whitman	Delaware River at Philadelphia	2,000	610	1957
Ambassador International	Detroit River at Detroit	1,850	564	1929
Throgs Neck	East River, New York City	1,800	549	1961
Benjamin Franklin	Delaware River at Philadelphia	1,750	533	1926
	International			
Akashi Kaiko	Japan	6,529	1,990	1998
Storebelt	Denmark	5,328	1,624	1997
Humber	Hull, Britain	4,626	1,410	1981
Jiangyin Yangtze	China	4,543	1,385	UC99
Tsing Ma Bridge	Hong Kong	4,518	1,377	1997
Minami Bisan-Seto	Japan	3,609	1,100	1988
Second Bosporus	Istanbul, Turkey	3,576	1,090	1988
First Bosporus	Istanbul, Turkey	3,524	1,074	1973
Third Kurushima Bridge	Japan	3,379	1,030	UC99
Second Kurushima Bridge	Japan	3,346	1,020	UC99
Ponte 25 de Abril	Tagus River at Lisbon, Portugal	3,323	1,013	1966
Forth Road	Queensferry, Scotland	3,300	1,006	1964
Kita Bisan-Seto	Japan	3,248	990	1988
Severn	Severn River at Beachley, England	3,240	988	1966
Shimotsui Straits	Japan	3,084	940	1988
Ohnaruto	Japan	2,874	876	1988
Pierre Laporte	Quebec, Canada	2,190	668	1970
Cantilever	**United States**			
Commodore John Barry	Chester, Pa.	1,644	501	1974
Greater New Orleans[1]	Mississippi River, La.	1,576	480	1958
Transbay Bridge	San Francisco Bay	1,400	427	1936
	International			
Quebec Railway	St. Lawrence River at Quebec, Canada	1,800	549	1917
Forth Railway[1]	Queensferry, Scotland	1,710	521	1890
Minato Ohashi	Osaka, Japan	1,673	510	1974
Howrah	Hooghly River at Calcutta, India	1,500	457	1943
Steel Arch	**United States**			
New River Gorge	Fayetteville, W. Va.	1,700	518	1977
Bayonne	Kill Van Kull at Bayonne, N.J.	1,675	510	1931
	International			
Sydney Harbor	Sydney, Australia	1,670	509	1932
Zdákov	Vltava River, Czech Republic	1,244	380	1967
Port Mann	Fraser River at Vancouver, British Columbia	1,200	366	1964
Cable-Stayed	**United States**			
Dame Point	Jacksonville, Florida	1,300	396	1988
Houston Ship Channel	Baytown, Texas	1,250	381	1995
Hale Boggs Memorial	Luling, Louisiana	1,222	373	1983
Sunshine Skyway	Tampa, Florida	1,200	366	1987
	International			
Tatara	Ehime, Japan	2,920	890	1999
Ponte de Normandie	Le Havre, France	2,808	856	1995
Qingzhou Minjiang	Fuzhou, China	1,985	605	1996
Yang Pu	Shanghai, China	1,975	602	1993
Xupu	Shanghai, China	1,936	590	1997
Meiko Chuo	Aichi, Japan	1,936	590	1997
Skarnsundet Bridge	near Trondheim, Norway	1,739	530	1991
Tsurumi Tsubasa	Kanagawa, Japan	1,673	510	1995

Name	Location	Length of main span		Year completed
		feet	meters	
Oresund	Denmark/Sweden	1,614	492	UC2000
Ikuchi	Honshu-Shikoku, Japan	1,608	490	1991
Higashi Kobe	Hyogo, Japan	1,591	485	1994
Ting Kau	Hong Kong	1,558	475	1997
Seohae	Korea	1,542	470	UC98
Alex Fraser	Vancouver, B.C., Canada	1,525	465	1986
Yokohama-ko-odan	Kanagawa, Japan	1,509	460	1989
Second Hooghly	Calcutta, India	1,500	457	1992
Second Severn Crossing	Severn River, England	1,496	456	1996
Dartford	Thames River, Dartford, England	1,476	450	1992
Dao Kanong	Chao Phraya River, Bangkok, Thailand	1,476	450	1987
Chongqing 2nd Bridge	Sichuan Province, China	1,457	444	1996
Continuous Truss	**United States**			
Astoria	Columbia River at Astoria, Oregon	1,232	376	1966
Croton Reservoir	Croton, N.Y.	1,052	321	1970
Ravenswood	Ohio River, Ravenswood, W. Va.	902	275	1981
	International			
Oshima	Oshima Island, Japan	1,066	325	1976
Tenmon	Kumamoto, Japan	984	300	1966
Kuronoseto	Nagashima-Kyushu, Japan	984	300	1974
Graf Spee	Germany	839	256	1936
Concrete Arch	**United States**			
Natchez Trace Pkwy.	Franklin, Tenn.	582	177	1994
Westinghouse	Pittsburgh, Pa.	460	140	1931
Jack's Run	Pittsburgh, Pa.	400	120	1930
Cappelen	Minneapolis, Minn.	400	120	1923
	International			
Krk (I)	Krk, Croatia	1,280	390	1979
Gladesville	Parramatta River at Sydney, Australia	1,000	305	1964
Amizade	Paraná River at Foz do Iguassu, Brazil	951	290	1964
Arrábida	Porto, Portugal	886	270	1963
Sandö	Angerman River at Kramfors, Sweden	866	264	1943
Sibenik	Sibenik, Yugoslavia	808	246	1966
Krk (II)	Krk, Croatia	800	244	1979
Fiumarella	Catanzaro, Italy	758	231	1961
Zaporozhe	Old Dnepr River, Ukraine	748	228	1952
Northumberland Strait	(Connects Canada to Prince Edward Island)	820	250	1997
Segmental Construction	**United States**			
Jesse H. Jones Memorial	Houston Ship Channel, Texas	750	228	1982

1. Twin span. NOTE: UC = under construction. *Source:* Federal Highway Administration.

World's Highest Dams

Name	River, country, or state	Structural height		Gross reservoir capacity		Year completed
		feet	meters	thousands of acre feet	millions of cubic meters	
Rogun	Vakhsh, Tajikistan	1099	335	9,404	11,600	1985
Nurek	Vakhsh, Tajikistan	984	300	8,512	10,500	1980
Grande Dixence	Dixence, Switzerland	935	285	324	400	1962
Inguri	Inguri, Georgia	892	272	801	1,100	1984
Chicoasén	Grijalva, Mexico	869	265	1,346	1,660	1981
Vaiont	Vaiont, Italy	869	265	137	169	1961
Tehri	Bhagirathi, India	856	261	2,869	3,540	UC
Kinshau	Tons, India	830	253	1,946	2,400	1985
Guavio	Orinoco, Colombia	820	250	811	1,000	1989
Mica	Columbia, Canada	794	242	20,000	24,670	1972
Sayano-Shushensk	Yenisei, Russia	794	242	25,353	31,300	1980
Mihoesti	Aries, Romania	794	242	5	6	1983
Chivor	Batá, Colombia	778	237	661	815	1975
Mauvoisin	Drance de Bagnes, Switzerland	777	237	146	180	1957
Oroville	Feather, California	770	235	3,538	4,299	1968
Chirkey	Sulak, Ukraine	764	233	2,252	2,780	1977

Name	River, country, or state	Structural height feet	Structural height meters	Gross reservoir capacity thousands of acre feet	Gross reservoir capacity millions of cubic meters	Year completed
Bhakra	Sutlej, India	741	226	8,002	9,870	1963
El Cajón	Humuya, Honduras	741	226	4,580	5,650	1984
Hoover	Colorado, Arizona/Nevada	726	221	28,500	35,154	1936
Contra	Verzasca, Switzerland	722	220	70	86	1965
Dabaklamm	Dorferbach, Austria	722	220	191	235	UC
Mratinje	Piva, Herzegovina	722	220	713	880	1973
Dworshak	N. Fk. Clearwater, Idaho	717	219	3,453	4,259	1974
Glen Canyon	Colorado, Arizona	710	216	27,000	33,304	1964
Toktogul	Naryn, Kyrgyzstan	705	215	15,800	19,500	1978
Daniel Johnson	Manicouagan, Canada	703	214	115,000	141,852	1968
San Roque	Agno, Philippines	689	210	803	990	UC
Luzzone	Brenno di Luzzone, Switzerland	682	208	71	87	1963
Keban	Firat, Turkey	679	207	25,110	31,000	1974
Dez	Dez, Abi, Iran	666	203	2,707	3,340	1963
Almendra	Tormes, Spain	662	202	2,148	2,649	1970
Kölnbrein	Malta, Austria	656	200	166	205	1977
Karun	Karun, Iran	656	200	2,351	2,900	1976
Altinkaya	Kizil Irmak, Turkey	640	195	4,672	5,763	1986
New Bullards Bar	No. Yuba, California	637	194	960	1,184	1968
Lakhwar	Yamuna, India	630	192	470	580	1985
New Melones	Stanislaus, California	625	191	2,400	2,960	1979
Itaipu	Paraná, Brazil/Paraguay	623	190	23,510	29,000	1982
Kurobe 4	Kurobe, Japan	610	186	162	199	1964
Swift	Lewis, Washington	610	186	756	932	1958
Mossyrock	Cowlitz, Washington	607	185	1,300	1,603	1968
Oymopinar	Manavgat, Turkey	607	185	251	310	1983
Atatürk	Firat, Turkey	604	184	39,482	48,700	1990
Shasta	Sacramento, California	602	183	4,550	5,612	1945
Bennett WAC	Peace, Canada	600	183	57,006	70,309	1967
Karakaya	Firat, Turkey	591	180	7,767	9,580	1986
Tignes	Isère, France	591	180	186	230	1952
Amir Kabir (Karad)	Karadj, Iran	591	180	166	205	1962
Tachien	Tachia, Taiwan	591	180	188	232	1974
Dartmouth	Mitta-Mitta, Australia	591	180	3,243	4,000	1978
Özköy	Gediz, Turkey	591	180	762	940	1983
Emosson	Barberine, Switzerland	590	180	184	225	1974
Zillergrundl	Ziller, Austria	590	180	73	90	1986
Los Leones	Los Leones, Chile	587	179	86	106	1986
New Don Pedro	Tuolumne, California	585	178	2,030	2,504	1971
Alpa-Gera	Cormor, Italy	584	178	53	65	1965

NOTE: UC = under construction. *Source:* Department of the Interior, Bureau of Reclamation and *International Water Power and Dam Construction.*

World's Largest Dams

Dam	Location	Volume (thousands) Cubic meters	Volume (thousands) Cubic yards	Year completed
Pati (Chapetón)	Argentina	200,000	261,590	UC
Tarbela	Pakistan	121,720	159,203	1976
Fort Peck	Montana	96,049	125,628	1940
Atatürk	Turkey	84,500	110,522	1990
Yacyretá-Apipe	Paraguay/Argentina	81,000	105,944	UC
Guri (Raul Leoni)	Venezuela	78,000	102,014	1986
Rogun	Tajikistan	75,500	98,750	1985
Oahe	South Dakota	70,339	92,000	1963
Mangla	Pakistan	65,651	85,872	1967
Gardiner	Canada	65,440	85,592	1968
Afsluitdijk	Netherlands	63,400	82,927	1932
Oroville	California	59,639	78,008	1968
San Luis	California	59,405	77,700	1967
Nurek	Tajikistan	58,000	75,861	1980
Garrison	North Dakota	50,843	66,500	1956
Cochiti	New Mexico	48,052	62,850	1975
Tabka (Thawra)	Syria	46,000	60,168	1976
Bennett W.A.C.	Canada	43,733	57,201	1967

Dam	Location	Volume (thousands)		Year completed
		Cubic meters	**Cubic yards**	
Tucuruíi	Brazil	43,000	56,242	1984
Boruca	Costa Rica	43,000	56,242	UC
High Aswan (Sadd-el-Aali)	Egypt	43,000	56,242	1970
San Roque	Philippines	43,000	56,242	UC
Kiev	Ukraine	42,841	56,034	1964
Dantiwada Left Embankment	India	41,040	53,680	1965
Saratov	Russia	40,400	52,843	1967
Mission Tailings 2	Arizona	40,088	52,435	1973
Fort Randall	South Dakota	38,227	50,000	1953
Kanev	Ukraine	37,860	49,520	1976
Mosul	Iraq	36,000	47,086	1982
Kakhovka	Ukraine	35,640	46,617	1955
Itumbiara	Brazil	35,600	46,563	1980
Lauwerszee	Netherlands	35,575	46,532	1969
Beas	India	35,418	46,325	1974
Oosterschelde	Netherlands	35,000	45,778	1986

NOTE: UC = under construction. *Source:* Department of the Interior, Bureau of Reclamation and *International Water Power and Dam Construction.*

World's Largest Hydroelectric Plants

Name of Dam	Location	Rated capacity (MW)		Year of initial operation
		Present	**Ultimate**	
Itaipu	Brazil/Paraguay	1,400	12,600	1984
Grand Coulee	Washington	6,480	10,080	1942
Guri (Raul Leoni)	Venezuela	2,800	10,060	1968
Tucuruíi	Brazil	—	7,500	1985
Sayano-Shushensk	Former U.S.S.R.	—	6,400	1980
Krasnoyarsk	Russia	6,096	6,096	1968
Corpus-Posadas	Argentina/Paraguay	—	6,000	UC
LaGrande 2	Canada	5,328	5,328	1982
Churchill Falls	Canada	5,225	5,225	1971
Bratsk	Siberia	4,100	4,600	1964
Ust'-Ilimsk	Russia	3,675	4,500	1974
Cabora Bassa	Mozambique	2,075	4,150	1974
Yacyretá-Apipe	Argentina/Paraguay	—	4,050	UC98
Rogun	Tajikistan	—	3,600	1985
Paulo Afonso	Brazil	3,409	3,409	1954
Salto Santiago	Brazil	1,332	3,333	1980
Pati (Chapetón)	Argentina	—	3,300	UC
Iha Solteira	Brazil	3,200	3,200	1973
Inga I	Zaire	360	2,820	1974
Gezhouba	China	965	2,715	1981
John Day	Oregon/Washington	2,160	2,700	1969
Nurek	Tajikistan	900	2,700	1976
Revelstoke	Canada	900	2,700	1984
Sáo Simao	Brazil	2,680	2,680	1979
LaGrande 4	Canada	2,637	2,637	1984
Mica	Canada	1,736	2,610	1976
Volgograd—22nd Congress	Russia	2,560	2,560	1958
Fos do Areia	Brazil	2,511	2,511	1983
Itaparica	Brazil	—	2,500	1985
Bennett W.A.C.	Canada	2,116	2,416	1969
Chicoasén	Mexico	—	2,400	1980
Atatürk	Turkey	—	2,400	1990
Bakun	Balui, Bakun Rapids, Malaysia	—	2,400	UC2002
LaGrande 3	Canada	2,310	2,310	1982
Volga—V.I. Lenin	Russia	2,300	2,300	1955
Iron Gates I	Romania/Yugoslavia	2,300	2,300	1970
Iron Gates II	Romania/Yugoslavia	270	2,160	1983
Bath County	Virginia	—	2,100	1985
High Aswan (Saad-el-Aali)	Egypt	2,100	2,100	1967
Tarbela	Pakistan	1,400	2,100	1977
Piedra del Aquila	Argentina	—	2,100	1993
Itumbiara	Brazil	2,080	2,080	1980
Chief Joseph	Washington	2,069	2,069	1956

Name of Dam	Location	Rated capacity (MW)		Year of initial operation
		Present	Ultimate	
McNary	Oregon	980	2,030	1954
Green River	North Carolina	—	2,000	1980
Tehri	India	—	2,000	UC
Cornwall	New York	—	2,000	1978
Ludington	Michigan	1,979	1,979	1973
Robert Moses—Niagara	New York	1,950	1,950	1961

Note: MW = Megawatts, UC = under construction. *Source:* Department of the Interior, Bureau of Reclamation and *International Water Power and Dam Construction.*

World's Tallest Buildings

Building, City	Year	Stories	Height m	Height ft	Building, City	Year	Stories	Height m	Height ft
Petronas Tower 1, Kuala Lumpur	UC97	88	452	1,483	Scotia Plaza, Toronto	1989	68	275	902
Petronas Tower 2, Kuala Lumpur	UC97	88	452	1,483	Transco Tower, Houston	1983	64	275	901
Sears Tower, Chicago	1974	110	442	1,450	Renaissance Tower, Dallas	1975	56	270	886
Jin Mao Building, Shanghai	UC98	88	421	1,379	900 North Michigan Ave., Chicago	1989	66	265	871
World Trade Center One, New York	1972	110	417	1,368	NationsBank Corporate Center, Charlotte	1992	60	265	871
World Trade Center Two, New York	1973	110	415	1,362	One Peachtree Center, Atlanta	1992	60	264	867
Plaza Rakyat, Kuala Lumpur	UC98	77	382	1,254	Canada Trust Tower, Toronto	1990	51	263	863
Empire State Building, New York	1931	102	381	1,250	Water Tower Place, Chicago	1976	74	262	859
Central Plaza, Hong Kong	1992	78	374	1,227	First Interstate Tower, Los Angeles	1974	62	262	858
Bank of China Tower, Hong Kong	1989	70	369	1,209	Transamerica Pyramid, San Francisco	1972	48	260	853
T & C Tower, Kaoshiung	UC97	85	348	1,140	G.E. Rockefeller Center, New York	1933	70	259	850
Amoco Building, Chicago	1973	80	346	1,136	One First National Plaza, Chicago	1969	60	259	850
John Hancock Center, Chicago	1969	100	344	1,127	Commerzbank Tower, Frankfurt	UC97	60	259	850
Shun Hing Square, Shenzen	UC96	81	325	1,066	Two Liberty Place, Philadelphia	1990	58	258	848
Sky Central Plaza, Guangzhou	UC96	80	322	1,056	Messeturm, Frankfurt	1990	63	257	843
Chicago Beach Tower Hotel, Dubai	UC98	60	321	1,053	USX Tower, Pittsburgh	1970	64	256	841
Balyoke Tower II, Bangkok	UC97	90	320	1,050	Gate Tower, Osaka	UC96	56	254	833
Chrysler Building, New York	1930	77	319	1,046	World Trade Center, Osaka	1994	55	252	827
BDNI Center —Tower A, Jakarta	UC99	62	317	1,040	One Atlantic Center, Atlanta	1988	50	250	820
NationsBank Plaza, Atlanta	1992	55	312	1,023	BNI City Tower, Jakarta	1995	46	250	820
First Interstate World Center, Los Angeles	1989	75	310	1,018	Korea Life Insurance Company, Seoul	1985	60	249	817
AT&T Corporate Center, Chicago	1989	60	307	1,007	CitySpire, New York	1989	72	248	814
Texas Commerce Tower, Houston	1982	75	305	1,000	One Chase Manhattan Plaza, New York	1961	60	248	813
Ryugyong Hotel, Pyongyang	UC95	105	300	984	200 Park Ave., New York	1963	59	246	808
Two Prudential Plaza, Chicago	1990	64	298	978	Kompleks Tun Abdul Razak Building, Penang	1985	65	245	804
First Interstate Bank Plaza, Houston	1983	71	296	972	Shin Kong Life Tower, Taipei	1993	51	244	801
Landmark Tower, Yokohama	1993	70	296	971	Malayan Bank, Kuala Lumpur	1988	50	244	799
311 South Wacker Drive, Chicago	1990	65	292	959	Tokyo Metropolitan Govt. Bldg., Tokyo	1991	48	243	797
Jubilee Street/ Queen's Road Central, Hong Kong	UC97	69	292	958	Rialto Tower, Melbourne	1985	56	242	794
First Canadian Place, Toronto	1975	72	290	952	Woolworth Building, New York	1913	57	241	792
American International Building, New York	1932	66	290	950	Mellon Bank Center, Philadelphia	1990	54	241	792
Society Center, Cleveland	1991	57	290	950	John Hancock Tower, Boston	1976	60	240	788
One Liberty Place, Philadelphia	1987	61	287	945	BDNI Center— Tower B, Jakarta	UC99	45	240	788
Columbia Seafirst Center, Seattle	1985	76	287	943	Bank One Center, Dallas	1987	60	240	787
40 Wall Street, New York	1930	70	283	927	JR Central Towers, Nagoya	UC99	53	240	787
NationsBank Plaza, Dallas	1985	72	281	921	Commerce Court West, Toronto	1973	57	239	784
Overseas Union Bank Centre, Singapore	1986	66	280	919	Graha Kuningan, Jakarta	UC98	52	239	784
United Overseas Bank Plaza, Singapore	1992	66	280	919	Moscow State University, Moscow	1953	26	239	784
Republic Plaza, Singapore	1995	66	280	919	Empire Tower, Kuala Lumpur	1994	62	238	781
Citicorp Center, New York	1977	59	279	915	NationsBank Center, Houston	1984	56	238	780

NOTE: Height does not include TV towers and antennas. *Source:* Council on Tall Buildings and Urban Habitat, Lehigh University.

Notable Tunnels

Name	Location	Length mi.	Length km	Year completed
Railroad, excluding subways				
Seikan	Tsugara Strait, Japan	33.1	53.3	1983
Channel[1]	English Channel, England–France	31.0	49.9	1994
Simplon (I and II)	Alps, Switzerland-Italy	12.3	19.8	1906 & 1922
Apennine	Bologna-Florence, Italy	11.5	18.5	1934
St. Gotthard	Swiss Alps	9.3	14.9	1881
Lötschberg	Swiss Alps	9.1	14.6	1911
Mont Cénis	French Alps	8.5[2]	13.7	1871
New Cascade	Cascade Mountains, Washington	7.8	12.6	1929
Vosges	Vosges, France	7.0	11.3	1940
Flathead	Rocky Mountains, Montana	7.0	11.3	1970
Arlberg	Austrian Alps	6.3	10.1	1884
Moffat	Rocky Mountains, Colorado	6.2	9.9	1928
Shimuzu	Shimuzu, Japan	6.1	9.8	1931
Rimutaka	Wairarapa, New Zealand	5.5	8.9	1955
Vehicular				
St. Gotthard	Alps, Switzerland	10.2	16.4	1980
Pinglin Highway	near Taipei, Taiwan	8.0	12.9	UC99
Trans-Tokyo Bay I and II	Tokyo, Japan	5.8	9.3	1997
Store Baelt	Great Belt, Denmark	5.0	8.0	1995
Mt. Blanc	Alps, France-Italy	7.5	12.1	1965
Mt. Ena	Japan Alps, Japan	5.3	8.5	1976[3]
Great St. Bernard	Alps, Switzerland-Italy	3.4	5.5	1964
Mount Royal	Montreal, Canada	3.2	5.1	1918
Lincoln	Hudson River, New York–New Jersey	1.6	2.6	1937
Queensway Road	Mersey River, Liverpool, England	2.2	3.5	1934
Brooklyn-Battery	East River, New York City	1.7	2.7	1950
Holland	Hudson River, New York-New Jersey	1.6	2.6	1927
Fort McHenry	Baltimore, Maryland	1.7	2.7	1985
Hampton Roads	Norfolk, Virginia	1.4	2.3	1957
Queens–Midtown	East River, New York City	1.3	2.1	1940
Liberty Tubes	Pittsburgh, Pennsylvania	1.2	1.9	1923
Baltimore Harbor	Baltimore, Maryland	1.2	1.9	1957
Allegheny Tunnels	Pennsylvania Turnpike	1.2	1.9	1940[4]

1. Twin-rail. One tunnel for passenger trains, the other for shuttle trains carrying vehicles plus a central service tunnel. 2. Lengthened to its present 8.5 miles in 1881. 3. Parallel tunnel begun in 1976. 4. Parallel tunnel built in 1965, twin tunnel in 1966. *Source:* American Society of Civil Engineers and International Bridge, Tunnel & Turnpike Association, Wittiker's.

Famous Ship Canals

Name	Location	Length (miles)[1]	Width (feet)	Depth (feet)	Locks	Year opened
Albert	Belgium	80.0	53.0	16.5	6	1939
Amsterdam-Rhine	Netherlands	45.0	164.0	41.0	3	1952
Beaumont-Port Arthur	United States	40.0	200.0	34.0	—	1916
Chesapeake and Delaware	United States	19.0	250.0	27.0	—	1927
Houston	United States	50.0	[2]	40.0	—	1914
Kiel (Nord-Ostsee Kanal)	Germany	61.3	144.0	36.0	4	1895
Panama	Panama	50.7	110.0	41.0	12	1914
St. Lawrence Seaway	U.S. and Canada	2,400.0[3]	([4])	—	—	1959
Montreal to Prescott	U.S. and Canada	11.5	80.0	30.0	7	1959
Welland	Canada	27.5	80.0	27.0	8	1931
Sault Ste. Marie	Canada	1.2	60.0	16.8	1	1895
Sault Ste. Marie	United States	1.6	80.0	25.0	4	1915
Suez	Egypt	100.6[5]	197.0	36.0	—	1869

1. Statute miles. 2. 300–400 feet. 3. From Montreal to Duluth. 4. 442–550 feet; there are 11.5 miles of locks, 80-feet wide and 30-feet deep. 5. From Port Said lighthouse to entrance channel in Suez roads. *Source:* American Society of Civil Engineers.

People

Many public figures not listed here may be found elsewhere in the *Information Please Almanac*.

U.S. Presidents	British Prime Ministers
U.S. Vice Presidents	Kings of England
Families of U.S. Presidents	Kings of France
U.S. Governors	Kings of Judah and Israel
U.S. Congress	Kings of Prussia
U.S. Supreme Court Members	Kings of Russia
U.S. Government Officials	Sports Personalities

Names in parentheses indicate the original name or form of name. Locations in parentheses are the present-day name of the birthplace. Dates of birth appear as month/day/year. **Boldface** years in parentheses are dates of **(birth-death).**

Information has been gathered from many sources, including the individuals themselves. However, the *Information Please Almanac* cannot guarantee the accuracy of every item.

A

Aalto, Alvar (architect); Kuortane, Finland **(1898–1976)**
Abbado, Claudio (orchestra conductor); Milan, Italy, 1933
Abbott, Bud (William) (comedian); Asbury Park, N.J. **(1898–1974)**
Abbott, George (stage producer); Forestville, N.Y. **(1887–1995)**
Abelard, Peter (theologian); nr. Nantes, France **(1079–1142)**
Abernathy, Ralph (civil rights leader); Linden, Ala. **(1926–1990)**
Abraham, F(ahrid) Murray (actor); Pittsburgh, 10/24/39
Achebe, Chinua (writer); Ogidi, Nigeria, 11/16/30
Acheson, Dean (statesman); Middletown, Conn. **(1893–1971)**
Acuff, Roy Claxton (musician); nr. Maynardsville, Tenn. **(1903–1992)**
Adams, Abigail (First Lady, writer); Weymouth, Mass. **(1744–1818)**
Adams, Charles Francis (diplomat); Boston **(1807–1886)**
Adams, Don (actor); New York City, 4/19/26
Adams, Edie (Edie Enke) (actress); Kingston, Pa., 4/16/29
Adams, Franklin Pierce (columnist, author); Chicago **(1881–1960)**
Adams, Gerry (political leader); West Belfast, Northern Ireland, 10/6/48
Adams, Henry Brooks (historian); Boston **(1838–1918)**
Adams, Joey (comedian); New York City, 1/6/11
Adams, Maude (Maude Kiskadden) (actress); Salt Lake City **(1872–1953)**
Adams, Samuel (American Revolutionary patriot); Boston **(1722–1803)**
Adams, Scott (cartoonist); Catskill, N.Y., 6/8/57
Adamson, Joy (naturalist); Troppau, Silesia **(1910–1980)**
Addams, Charles (cartoonist); Westfield, N.J. **(1912–1988)**
Addams, Jane (social worker); Cedarville, Ill. **(1860–1935)**
Adderley, Julian "Cannonball" (jazz saxophonist); Tampa, Fla. **(1928–1975)**
Ade, George (humorist); Kentland, Ind. **(1866–1944)**
Adenauer, Konrad (statesman); Cologne, Germany **(1876–1967)**
Adler, Alfred (psychoanalyst); Vienna **(1870–1937)**
Adler, Larry (musician); Baltimore, 2/10/14
Adler, Richard (songwriter); New York City, 8/3/21
Aeschylus (dramatist); Eleusis (Greece) **(525–456 B.C.E.)**
Aesop (fabulist); Samos?, Greece, fl. c. 500 B.C.E.
Agnew, Spiro (political figure); Baltimore, Md. **(1905–1996)**
Aherne, Brian (actor); King's Norton, England **(1902–1986)**
Aiello, Danny (actor); New York City, 6/20/33
Aiken, Conrad (poet); Savannah, Ga. **(1889–1973)**
Ailey, Alvin (choreographer); Rogers, Tex. **(1931–1989)**
Akhmatova, Anna (poet); Odessa, Ukraine **(1889–1966)**
Akihito, Tsugunomiya (Emperor of Japan); Tokyo, 12/23/33
Albanese, Licia (operatic soprano); Bari, Italy, 7/22/13
Albee, Edward (playwright); Washington, D.C., 3/12/28
Albers, Josef (painter); Bottrop, Germany **(1888–1976)**
Albert, Eddie (Edward Albert Heimberger) (actor); Rock Island, Ill., 4/22/08
Albert, Edward (actor); Los Angeles, 2/20/51
Albertson, Jack (actor); Malden, Mass. **(1907–1981)**
Albright, Lola (actress); Akron, Ohio, 7/20/25
Albright, Madeleine (diplomat, U.S. Secretary of State); Prague, Czechoslovakia, 5/15/37
Alcott, Louisa May (novelist); Germantown, Pa. **(1832–1888)**
Alda, Alan (actor); New York City, 1/28/36
Alda, Robert (Alphonso d'Abruzzo) (actor); New York City **(1914–1986)**
Alden, John (American Pilgrim); England **(c. 1599–1687)**
Alexander, Jane (Quigley) (actress); Boston, 10/28/39

Alexander the Great (monarch, conqueror); Pella, Macedonia (Greece) **(356–323 B.C.E.)**
Alger, Horatio (author); Revere, Mass. **(1834–1899)**
Algren, Nelson (novelist); Detroit, Mich. **(1909–1981)**
Allen, Debbie (dancer-choreographer, actress); Houston, Tex., 1/16/50
Allen, Ethan (American Revolutionary soldier); Litchfield, Conn. **(1738–1789)**
Allen, Fred (John Florence Sullivan) (comedian); Cambridge, Mass. **(1894–1956)**
Allen, Gracie (Grace Ethel Cecile Rosalie Allen) (comedienne); San Francisco **(1906–1964)**
Allen, Mel (Melvin Israel) (sportscaster); Birmingham, Ala. **(1913–1996)**
Allen, Peter (actor, songwriter); Tenterfield, Australia **(1944–1992)**
Allen, Steve (TV entertainer); New York City, 12/26/21
Allen, Woody (Allen Stewart Konigsberg) (actor, writer, director); Brooklyn, N.Y., 12/1/35
Allende, Isabel (novelist); Lima, Peru, 8/2/42
Alley, Kirstie (actress); Wichita, Kan., 1/12/55
Allison, Fran (actress); LaPorte City, Iowa **(1908?–1989)**
Allman, Gregg (singer); Nashville, Tenn., 12/8/47
Allyson, June (Jan Allyson) (actress); New York City, 10/7/23
Alonso, Alicia (ballerina); Havana, 12/21/21?
Alpert, Herb (band leader); Los Angeles, 3/31/35?
Alsop, Joseph W., Jr. (journalist); Avon, Conn. **(1910–1989)**
Alsop, Stewart (journalist); Avon, Conn. **(1914–1974)**
Altman, Robert (film director); Kansas City, Mo., 2/20/25
Amanpour, Christiane (broadcast journalist); London, 1958
Amati, Nicola (violin maker); Cremona, Italy **(1596–1684)**
Ambler, Eric (suspense writer); London, 6/28/09
Ameche, Don (Dominic Amici) (actor); Kenosha, Wis. **(1908–1993)**
Amis, Kingsley (novelist); London **(1922–1995)**
Amory, Cleveland (writer, conservationist); Nahant, Mass., 9/2/17
Amos (Freeman F. Gosden) (radio comedian); Richmond, Va. **(1899–1982)**
Amos, John (actor); Newark, N.J., 12/27/41
Amsterdam, Morey (actor); Chicago **(1914–1996)**
Andersen, Hans Christian (author of fairy tales); Odense, Denmark **(1805–1875)**
Anderson, Gillian (actress); Chicago, 8/9/68
Anderson, Harry (actor); Newport, R.I., 10/14/52
Anderson, Ib (ballet dancer); Copenhagen, 12/14/54
Anderson, Jack (journalist); Long Beach, Calif., 10/19/22
Anderson, Dame Judith (actress); Adelaide, Australia **(1898–1992)**
Anderson, Lindsay (Gordon) (director); Bangalore, India **(1923–1994)**
Anderson, Loni (actress); St. Paul, Minn., 8/5/45
Anderson, Lynn (singer); Grand Forks, N.D., 9/26/47
Anderson, Marian (contralto); Philadelphia **(1897–1993)**
Anderson, Maxwell (dramatist); Atlantic, Pa. **(1888–1959)**
Anderson, Richard Dean (actor); Minneapolis, Minn., 1/23/50
Anderson, Robert (playwright); New York City, 4/28/17
Anderson, Sherwood (novelist); Camden, Ohio **(1876–1941)**
Andersson, Bibi (actress); Stockholm, 11/11/35
Andress, Ursula (actress); Switzerland, 3/19/38
Andrews, Dana (actor); Collins, Miss. **(1909–1992)**
Andrews, Julie (Julia Wells) (actress, singer); Walton-on-Thames, England, 10/1/35
Andrews, La Verne (singer); Minneapolis **(1916–1967)**
Andrews, Maxene (singer); Minneapolis **(1918–1995)**
Andrews, Patti (singer); Minneapolis, 2/16/20
Andy (Charles J. Correll) (radio comedian); Peoria, Ill. **(1890–1972)**

Angeles, Victoria de los (Victoria Gamez Cima) (operatic soprano); Barcelona, 11/1/24

Angelico, Fra (Guido di Pietro; Giovanni de Fiesole) (painter); nr. Florence **(c. 1400–1455)**

Angelou, Maya (poet, novelist); St. Louis, Mo., 4/4/28

Aniston, Jennifer (Anistonapoulos) (actress); Sherman Oaks, Calif., 2/11/69

Anka, Paul (singer, composer); Ottawa, 7/30/41

Annan, Kofi (diplomat, U.N. Secretary General); Kumasi, Ghana, 4/8/38

Ann-Margret (Ann-Margret Olsson) (actress); Valsjobyn, Sweden, 4/28/41

Anouilh, Jean (playwright); Bordeaux, France **(1910–1987)**

Anthony, Susan Brownell (woman suffragist); Adams, Mass. **(1820–1906)**

Antonioni, Michelangelo (director); Ferrara, Italy, 9/29/12

Antony, Mark (Marcus Antonius) (statesman); Rome **(c. 83–30 B.C.E.)**

Anuszkiewicz, Richard (painter); Erie, Pa., 5/23/30

Apollinaire, Guillaume (writer); Rome **(1880–1918)**

Aquinas, St. Thomas (philosopher); nr. Aquino (Italy) **(1225–1274)**

Arafat, Yasser (Mohammed Abdel-Raouf Arafat al Qudwa al Husseini) (Chairman of the Palestine Liberation Organization); Cairo, Egypt, 8/24/29

Arbuckle, Roscoe "Fatty" (actor, director); San Jose, Calif. **(1887–1933)**

Archimedes (physicist, mathematician); Syracuse, Sicily **(287–212 B.C.E.)**

Archipenko, Alexandre (sculptor); Kiev, Ukraine **(1887–1964)**

Arden, Elizabeth (Florence Nightingale Graham) (cosmetics executive); Woodbridge, Canada **(1891–1966)**

Arden, Eve (Eunice Quedens) (actress); Mill Valley, Calif. **(1907–1990)**

Arendt, Hannah (historian); Hannover, Germany **(1906–1975)**

Aristophanes (dramatist); Athens **(c. 448–c. 385 B.C.E.)**

Aristotle (philosopher); Stagirus, Macedonia **(384–322 B.C.E.)**

Arkin, Adam (actor); New York City, 8/19/57

Arkin, Alan (actor, director); New York City, 3/26/34

Arledge, Roone (TV executive); Forest Hills, N.Y., 7/8/31

Arlen, Harold (Hyman Arluck) (composer); Buffalo, N.Y. **(1905–1986)**

Arlen, Richard (actor); Charlottesville, Va. **(1900–1976)**

Arliss, George (actor); London **(1868–1946)**

Armstrong, Louis ("Satchmo") (musician); New Orleans **(1900–1971)**

Arnaz, Desi (Desiderio) (actor, producer); Santiago, Cuba **(1917–1986)**

Arness, James (James Aurness) (actor); Minneapolis, 5/26/23

Arno, Peter (cartoonist); New York City **(1904–1968)**

Arnold, Benedict (American Revolutionary War general, charged with treason); Norwich, Conn. **(1741–1801)**

Arnold, Eddy (singer); Henderson, Tenn., 5/15/18

Arnold, Matthew (poet, critic); Laleham, England **(1822–1888)**

Arp, Jean (sculptor, painter); Strasbourg (France) **(1887–1966)**

Arpino, Gerald (choreographer); Staten Island, N.Y., 1/14/28

Arquette ("Charley Weaver") (actor); Toledo, Ohio **(1905–1974)**

Arquette, Rosanna (actress); New York City, 8/10/59

Arrau, Claudio (pianist); Chillán, Chile **(1903–1991)**

Arroyo, Martina (soprano); New York City, 2/2/40

Arthur, Bea (Bernice Frankel) (actress); New York City, 5/13/23

Arthur, Jean (Gladys Greene) (actress); New York City **(1900–1991)**

Ashcroft, Dame Peggy (actress); Croydon, England **(1907–1991)**

Ashkenazy, Vladimir (concert pianist); Gorki, U.S.S.R., 7/6/37

Ashley, Elizabeth (actress); Ocala, Fla., 8/30/39

Ashton, Sir Frederick William Mallandaine (choreographer); Guayaquil, Ecuador **(1904–1988)**

Asimov, Isaac (author); Petrovichi, Russia **(1920–1992)**

Asner, Edward (actor); Kansas City, Mo., 11/15/29

Astaire, Fred (Frederick Austerlitz) (dancer, actor); Omaha, Neb. **(1899–1987)**

Astin, John (actor, director); Baltimore, Md., 3/30/30

Astor, Brooke (socialite, philanthropist); Portsmouth, N.H., 3/16/05

Astor, John Jacob (financier); Waldorf (Germany) **(1763–1848)**

Astor, Mary (Lucile Langhanke) (actress); Quincy, Ill. **(1906–1987)**

Ataturk, Kemal (Mustafa Kemal) (Turkish soldier, statesman); Salonika (Greece) **(1881–1938)**

Atkins, Chet (guitarist); nr. Luttrell, Tenn., 6/20/24

Atkinson, Brooks (drama critic); Melrose, Mass. **(1894–1984)**

Attenborough, Richard (actor, director); Cambridge, England, 8/29/23

Attila (King of Huns) **(406?–453)**

Attucks, Crispus (American Revolutionary Patriot); Boston **(c. 1723–1770)**

Atwill, Lionel (actor); Croydon, England **(1885–1946)**

Auberjonois, Rene (actor); New York City, 6/1/40

Auchincloss, Louis (author); Lawrence, N.Y., 9/27/17

Auden, W(ystan) H(ugh) (poet); York, England **(1907–1973)**

Audubon, John James (naturalist, painter); Haiti **(1785–1851)**

Auer, Leopold (violinist, teacher); Veszprém, Hungary **(1845–1930)**

Augustine, Saint (Aurelius Augustinus) (theologian); Tagaste, Numidia (Algeria) **(354–430)**

Augustus (Gaius Octavius) (Roman emperor); Rome **(63 B.C.E.–C.E. 14)**

Aung, San Suu Kyi (human rights activist); Rangoon, Burma, 6/19/45

Austen, Jane (novelist); Steventon, England **(1775–1817)**

Autry, Gene (singer, actor); Tioga, Tex., 9/29/07

Avalon, Frankie (singer); Philadelphia, 9/18/40

Avedon, Richard (photographer); New York City, 5/15/23

Avery, Milton (painter); Altmar, N.Y. **(1893–1965)**

Ax, Emanuel (pianist); Lvov, Ukraine, 6/8/49

Axelrod, George (playwright); New York City, 6/9/22

Ayckbourn, Alan (playwright); London, 4/12/39

Ayckroyd, Dan (actor); Ottawa, Ont., Canada, 7/1/52

Ayres, Lew (actor); Minneapolis, 12/28/08

Aznavour, Charles (singer, composer); Paris, France, 5/22/24

B

Bacall, Lauren (Betty Joan Perske) (actress); New York City, 9/16/24

Bach, Carl Phillipp Emanuel (composer); Weimar, Germany **(1714–1788)**

Bach, Johann Sebastian (composer); Eisenach, Germany **(1685–1750)**

Bacharach, Burt (songwriter); Kansas City, Mo., 5/12/29

Backus, Jim (actor); Cleveland **(1913–1989)**

Bacon, Francis (philosopher, essayist); London **(1561–1626)**

Bacon, Francis (painter); Dublin **(1910–1992)**

Bacon, Roger (philosopher, scientist); Ilchester, England **(c. 1214–1294?)**

Baez, Joan (folk singer); Staten Island, N.Y., 1/9/41

Bailey, F. Lee (lawyer); Waltham, Mass., 6/10/33

Bailey, Pearl (singer); Newport News, Va. **(1918–1990)**

Bain, Conrad (actor); Lethbridge, Alberta, Canada, 2/4/23

Baird, Bil (William B.) (puppeteer); Grand Island, Neb. **(1904–1987)**

Baker, Anita (singer); Toledo, Ohio, 1958

Baker, Carroll (actress); Johnstown, Pa., 5/28/31

Baker, Josephine (singer, dancer); St. Louis **(1906–1975)**

Baker, Russell (columnist); Loudoun County, Va., 8/14/25

Balanchine, George (choreographer); St. Petersburg, Russia **(1904–1983)**

Balboa, Vasco Nuñez de (explorer); Jerez de los Caballeros (Spain) **(1475–1517)**

Baldwin, Alec (actor); Massapequa, N.Y., 4/3/58

Baldwin, James (novelist); New York City **(1924–1987)**

Balenciaga, Cristóbal (fashion designer); Guetaria, Spain **(1895–1972)**

Ball, Lucille (Désirée) (actress, producer); Celoron (nr. Jamestown), N.Y. **(1911–1989)**

Ballard, Kaye (Catherine Gloria Balotta) (actress); Cleveland, 11/20/26

Balmain, Pierre (fashion designer); St.-Jean-de-Maurienne, France **(1914–1982)**

Balsam, Martin (actor); New York City **(1919–1996)**

Balzac, Honoré de (novelist); Tours, France **(1799–1850)**

Bancroft, Anne (Annemarie Italiano) (actress); New York City, 9/17/31

Bankhead, Tallulah (actress); Huntsville, Ala. **(1903–1968)**

Banneker, Benjamin (mathematician, astronomer); Endicott, Md. **(1731–1806)**

Banting, Fredrick Grant (physiologist); Alliston, Ont., Canada **(1891–1941)**

Bara, Theda (Theodosia Goodman) (actress); Cincinnati **(1890–1955)**

Baraka,Imamu Amiri (LeRoi Jones) (playwright); Newark, N.J., 10/7/34

Barber, Red (Walter Lanier) (sportscaster); Columbus, Miss. **(1908–1992)**

Barber, Samuel (composer); West Chester, Pa. **(1910–1981)**

Barbie, Klaus (Nazi, "The Butcher of Lyon"); Bad Godesberg, Germany **(1913–1991)**

Bardot, Brigitte (Camille Javal) (actress); Paris, 9/28/34

Barenboim, Daniel (concert pianist, conductor); Buenos Aires, 11/15/42

Barker, Bob (host); Darrington, Wash., 12/12/23

Barnard, Christiaan N. (heart surgeon); Beauford West, South Africa, 1923

Barnum, Phineas Taylor (showman); Bethel, Conn. **(1810–1891)**

Barrie, Sir James Matthew (author); Kirriemuir, Scotland **(1860–1937)**

Barrie, Wendy (actress); Hong Kong **(1913–1978)**

Barry, Gene (Eugene Klass) (actor); New York City, 6/14/21

Barry, John (naval officer); County Wexford, Ireland **(1745–1803)**

Barrymore, Diana (actress); New York City **(1921–1960)**

Barrymore, Ethel (Ethel Blythe) (actress); Philadelphia **(1879–1959)**

Barrymore, Georgiana Drew (actress); Philadelphia **(1856–1893)**

Barrymore, John (John Blythe) (actor); Philadelphia **(1882–1942)**

Barrymore, Lionel (Lionel Blythe) (actor); Philadelphia **(1878–1954)**

Barrymore, Maurice (Herbert Blythe) (actor, playwright); Agra, India **(1847–1905)**

Barth, John (novelist); Cambridge, Md., 5/27/30

Barthelme, Donald (novelist); Philadelphia **(1931 –1989)**

Barthelmess, Richard (actor); New York City **(1897–1963)**

Bartholomew, Freddie (actor); London **(1924–1992)**

Bartók, Béla (composer); Nagyszentmiklo, Hungary (Romania) **(1881–1945)**

Barton, Clara (founder of American Red Cross); Oxford, Mass. **(1821–1912)**

Baruch, Bernard Mannes (statesman); Camden, S.C. **(1870–1965)**
Baryshnikov, Mikhail Nikolayevich (ballet dancer, artistic director); Riga, Latvia, 1/27/48
Basehart, Richard (actor); Zanesville, Ohio **(1914–1984)**
Basie, Count (William) (band leader); Red Bank, N.J. **(1904–1984)**
Basinger, Kim (actress); Athens, Ga., 12/8/53
Bassett, Angela (actress); New York City, 8/16/58
Bassey, Shirley (singer); Cardiff, Wales, 1/8/37
Batchelor, Clarence Daniel (political cartoonist); Osage City, Kan. **(1888–1977)**
Bateman, Jason (actor); Rye, N.Y., 1/14/69
Bateman, Justine (actress); Rye, N.Y., 2/19/66
Bates, Alan (actor); Allestree, England, 2/17/34
Bates, Kathy (Kathleen Doyle Bates) (actress); Memphis, Tenn., 6/28/48
Battle, Kathleen (soprano); Portsmouth, Ohio, 8/13/48
Baudelaire, Charles Pierre (poet); Paris **(1821–1867)**
Baxter, Anne (actress); Michigan City, Ind. **(1923–1985)**
Baxter, Meredith (actress); Los Angeles, 6/21/47
Bean, Orson (Dallas Frederick Burrows) (actor); Burlington, Vt., 7/22/28
Beardsley, Aubrey Vincent (illustrator); Brighton, England **(1872–1898)**
Beaton, Cecil (photographer, designer); London **(1904–1980)**
Beatty, Clyde (animal trainer); Chillicothe, Ohio **(1903–1965)**
Beatty, Warren (actor, producer); Richmond, Va., 3/30/37
Beaumont, Francis (dramatist); Grace-Dieu, England **(1584–1616)**
Becket, Thomas à (Archbishop of Canterbury); London **(1118?–1170)**
Beckett, Samuel (playwright); Dublin **(1906–1989)**
Beckmann, Max (painter); Leipzig, Germany **(1884–1950)**
Bede, Saint ("The Venerable Bede") (scholar); Monkwearmouth, England **(673–735)**
Beecham, Sir Thomas (conductor); St. Helens, England **(1879–1961)**
Beecher, Henry Ward (clergyman); Litchfield, Conn. **(1813–1887)**
Beerbohm, Sir Max (author); London **(1872–1956)**
Beery, Noah (actor); Kansas City, Mo. **(1884–1946)**
Beery, Noah, Jr. (actor); New York City **(1913–1994)**
Beery, Wallace (actor); Kansas City, Mo. **(1886–1949)**
Beethoven, Ludwig von (composer); Bonn (Germany) **(1770–1827)**
Begin, Menachem (Israeli Prime Minister); Brest-Litovsk, Belarus **(1913–1992)**
Begley, Ed (actor); Hartford, Conn. **(1901–1970)**
Beiderbecke, Bix (jazz musician); Davenport, Iowa **(1903–1931)**
Belafonte, Harry (singer, actor); New York City, 3/1/27
Belafonte-Harper, Shari (actress); New York City, 9/22/54
Belasco, David (dramatist, producer); San Francisco **(1854–1931)**
Bel Geddes, Barbara (actress); New York City, 10/31/22
Bell, Alexander Graham (inventor); Edinburgh, Scotland **(1847–1922)**
Bellamy, Edward (author); Chicopee Falls, Mass. **(1850–1898)**
Bellamy, Ralph (actor); Chicago **(1904–1991)**
Bellini, Giovanni (painter); Venice **(c.1430–1516)**
Bellow, Saul (novelist); Lachine, Quebec, Canada, 6/10/15
Bellows, George Wesley (painter, lithographer); Columbus, Ohio **(1882–1925)**
Belmondo, Jean-Paul (actor); Neuilly-sur-Seine, France, 4/9/33
Belushi, Jim (actor); Chicago, 6/15/54
Belushi, John (comedian, actor); Chicago **(1949–1982)**
Benchley, Peter Bradford (novelist); New York City, 5/8/40
Benchley, Robert Charles (humorist); Worcester, Mass. **(1889–1945)**
Bendix, William (actor); New York City **(1906–1964)**
Benedict, Ruth Fulton (anthropologist); New York City **(1887–1948)**
Benes, Eduard (statesman); Kozlany, former Czechoslovakia **(1884–1948)**
Benét, Stephen Vincent (poet, story writer); Bethlehem, Pa. **(1898–1943)**
Benét, William Rose (poet, novelist); Ft. Hamilton, Brooklyn, N.Y. **(1886–1950)**
Ben-Gurion, David (David Green) (statesman); Plónsk (Poland) **(1886–1973)**
Benjamin, Richard (actor, director); New York City, 5/22/38
Bennett, Constance (actress); New York City **(1905–1965)**
Bennett, Enoch Arnold (novelist, dramatist); Hanley, England **(1867–1931)**
Bennett, James Gordon (editor); Keith, Scotland **(1795–1872)**
Bennett, Joan (actress); Palisades, N.J. **(1910–1990)**
Bennett, Robert Russell (composer); Kansas City, Mo. **(1894–1981)**
Bennett, Tony (Anthony Benedetto) (singer); Astoria, Queens, N.Y., 8/3/26
Benny, Jack (Benjamin Kubelsky) (comedian); Chicago **(1894–1974)**
Benson, Robby (actor); Dallas, Tex., 1/21/56
Bentham, Jeremy Heinrich (economist); London **(1748–1832)**
Benton, Thomas Hart (painter); Neosho, Mo. **(1889–1975)**
Berg, Alban (composer); Vienna **(1885–1935)**
Berg, Gertrude (writer, actress); New York City **(1899–1966)**
Bergen, Candice (actress); Beverly Hills, Calif., 5/9/46
Bergen, Edgar (ventriloquist); Chicago **(1903–1978)**
Bergen, Polly (actress, singer); Knoxville, Tenn., 7/14/30
Bergerac, Cyrano de (poet); Paris **(1619–1655)**

Bergman, Ingmar (film director); Uppsala, Sweden, 7/14/18
Bergman, Ingrid (actress); Stockholm **(1918–1982)**
Bergson, Henri (philosopher); Paris **(1859–1941)**
Berkeley, Busby (choreographer, director); Los Angeles **(1885–1976)**
Berle, Milton (Milton Berlinger) (comedian); New York City, 7/12/08
Berlin, Irving (Israel Baline) (songwriter); Temum, Russia **(1888–1989)**
Berlioz, Louis Hector (composer); La Côte-Saint-André, France **(1803–1869)**
Berman, Lazar (concert pianist); Leningrad, 2/26/30
Berman, Shelley (Sheldon) (comedian); Chicago, 2/3/26
Bernardi, Herschel (actor); New York City **(1922–1986)**
Bernhardt, Sarah (Rosine Bernard) (actress); Paris **(1844–1923)**
Bernini, Gian Lorenzo (sculptor, painter); Naples (Italy) **(1598–1680)**
Bernoulli, Jacques (scientist); Basel, Switzerland **(1654–1705)**
Bernsen, Corbin (actor); North Hollywood, Calif., 7/7/54
Bernstein, Leonard (conductor); Lawrence, Mass. **(1918–1990)**
Berry, Chuck (Charles Edward Berry) (singer, guitarist); San Jose, Calif., 1/15/26
Berry, Ken (actor); Moline, Ill., 11/3/30
Berryman, John (poet); McAlester, Okla. **(1914–1972)**
Bertinelli, Valerie (actress); Wilmington, Del., 4/23/60
Bethune, Mary McCleod (educator); Mayesville, S.C. **(1875–1955)**
Betjeman, Sir John (Poet Laureate); London **(1906–1984)**
Bettelheim, Bruno (psychoanalyst); Vienna **(1903–1990)**
Bickford, Charles (actor); Cambridge, Mass. **(1889–1967)**
Bierce, Ambrose Gwinnett (journalist); Meigs County, Ohio **(1842–1914?)**
Bikel, Theodore (actor, folk singer); Vienna, 5/2/24
Bing, Sir Rudolf (opera manager); Vienna, 1/9/02
Bingham, George Caleb (painter); Augusta Co., Va. **(1811–1879)**
Binoche, Juliette (actress); Paris, 3/9/65
Bishop, Joey (Joseph Gottlieb) (comedian); New York City, 2/3/19
Bismarck-Schönhausen, Prince Otto Eduard Leopold von (statesman); Schönhausen, Germany **(1815–1898)**
Bisset, Jacqueline (actress); Weybridge, England, 9/13/44
Bixby, Bill (actor); San Francisco **(1934–1993)**
Bizet, Georges (Alexandre César Léopold Bizet) (composer); Paris **(1838–1875)**
Bjoerling, Jussi (tenor); Stora Tuna, Sweden **(1911–1960)**
Black, Karen (actress); Park Ridge, Ill., 7/1/42
Black, Shirley Temple (former actress); Santa Monica, Calif., 4/23/28
Blackmer, Sidney (actor); Salisbury, N.C. **(1898–1973)**
Blackstone, Sir William (jurist); London **(1723–1780)**
Blackwell, Elizabeth (physician, educator); England **(1821–1910)**
Blaine, Vivian (actress, singer); Newark, N.J. **(1924–1995)**
Blake, Amanda (Beverly Louise Neill) (actress); Buffalo, N.Y. **(1929–1989)**
Blake, Eubie (James Hubert) (pianist); Baltimore **(1883–1983)**
Blake, Robert (Michael Gubitosi) (actor); Nutley, N.J., 9/18/33
Blake, William (poet, artist); London **(1757–1827)**
Blanc, Mel(vin Jerome) (actor, voice specialist); San Francisco **(1908–1989)**
Blass, Bill (fashion designer); Fort Wayne, Ind., 6/22/22
Bloch, Ernest (composer); Geneva **(1880–1959)**
Blondell, Joan (actress); New York City **(1909–1979)**
Bloom, Claire (actress); London, 2/15/31
Bloomgarden, Kermit (producer); Brooklyn, N.Y. **(1904–1976)**
Blume, Judy (Sussman) (young adult novelist); Elizabeth, N.J., 2/12/38
Bly, Nellie (pseud. for Elizabeth Seaman) (journalist); Cochrane Mills, Pa. **(1867–1922)**
Bly, Robert (poet, critic); Madison, Minn., 12/23/26
Boccaccio, Giovanni (author); Paris **(1313–1375)**
Boccherini, Luigi (Rodolfo) (composer); Lucca, Italy **(1743–1805)**
Boccioni, Umberto (painter, sculptor); Reggio di Calabria, Italy **(1882–1916)**
Bochco, Steven (TV producer, writer); New York City, 12/16/43
Bock, Jerry (composer); New Haven, Conn., 11/23/28
Bogarde, Dirk (Derek Van den Bogaerde) (film actor, director); London, 3/28/21
Bogart, Humphrey DeForest (actor); New York City **(1899–1957)**
Bogdanovich, Peter (producer, director); Kingston, N.Y., 7/30/39
Bohlen, Charles E. (diplomat); Clayton, N.Y. **(1904–1974)**
Bohr, Niels (atomic physicist); Copenhagen **(1885–1962)**
Bok, Sissela (Sissela Ann Myrdal) (scholar); Stockholm, 12/2/34
Bolger, Ray (dancer, actor); Dorchester, Mass **(1904–1987)**
Bolivar, Simón (South American liberator); Caracas, Venezuela **(1783–1830)**
Bologna, Giovanni da (sculptor); Douai (France) **(1529–1608)**
Bombeck, Erma (author, columnist); Dayton, Ohio **(1927–1996)**
Bonaparte, Napoleon (Emperor of the French); Ajaccio, Corsica (France) **(1769–1821)**
Bond, Julian (Georgia legislator); Nashville, Tenn., 1/14/40
Bon Jovi, Jon (musician, songwriter); Sayreville, N.J., 3/2/62
Bonnard, Pierre (painter); Fontenayaux-Roses, France **(1867–1947)**
Bono, Sonny (Salvatore) (singer, politician); Detroit, Mich., 2/16/35
Boone, Daniel (frontiersman); nr. Reading, Pa. **(1734–1820)**

Boone, Pat (Charles) (singer); Jacksonville, Fla., 6/1/34
Boone, Richard (actor); Los Angeles **(1917–1981)**
Boorstin, Daniel (historian); Atlanta, Ga., 10/1/14
Booth, Edwin Thomas (actor); Bel Air, Md. **(1833–1893)**
Booth, Evangeline Cory (religious leader); London **(1865–1950)**
Booth, John Wilkes (actor; assassin of Lincoln); Harford County, Md. **(1838–1865)**
Booth, Shirley (Thelma Booth Ford) (actress); New York City **(1907–1992)**
Borden, Lizzy (Elizabeth Andrew) (accused murderer); Fall River, Mass. **(1860–1927)**
Borge, Victor (pianist, comedian); Copenhagen, 1/3/09
Borgia, Cesare (nobleman, soldier); Rome **(1476–1507)**
Borgia, Lucrezia (Duchess of Ferrara); Rome **(1480–1519)**
Borgnine, Ernest (actor); Hamden, Conn., 1/24/17
Borromini, Francesco (architect); Bissone (Italy) **(1599–1667)**
Bosch, Hieronymus (Hieronymus van Aeken) (painter); Hertogenbosch (Netherlands) **(c.**1450–1516**)**
Bosley, Tom (actor); Chicago, 10/1/27
Bostwick, Barry (actor); San Mateo, Calif., 2/24/45
Boswell, James (diarist, biographer); Edinburgh, Scotland **(1740–1795)**
Botticelli, Sandro (Alessandro di Mariano dei Filipepi) (painter); Florence (Italy) **(1444–1510)**
Bottoms, Timothy (actor); Santa Barbara, Calif., 8/30/50
Boulez, Pierre (conductor); Montbrison, France, 3/26/25
Bourke-White, Margaret (photographer); New York City **(1906–1971)**
Boutros-Ghali, Boutros (ex-Secretary General of the U.N.); Cairo, Egypt, 11/14/22
Bow, Clara (actress); Brooklyn, N.Y. **(1905–1965)**
Bowen, Catherine Drinker (biographer); Haverford, Pa. **(1897–1973)**
Bowes, Edward (radio show director); San Francisco **(1874–1946)**
Bowie, David (David Robert Jones) (actor, musician); London, 1/8/47
Bowie, James (soldier); Burke County, Ga. **(1799–1836)**
Bowles, Chester (diplomat); Springfield, Mass. **(1901–1986)**
Boxleitner, Bruce (actor); Elgin, Ill., 5/12/50
Boyce, William (composer); London? **(1710–1779)**
Boyd, Bill ("Hopalong Cassidy") (actor); Cambridge, Ohio **(1898–1972)**
Boyd, Stephen (Stephen Millar) (actor); Belfast, Northern Ireland **(1928–1977)**
Boyer, Charles (actor); Figeac, France **(1899–1978)**
Boy George (George Alan O'Dowd) (singer); London, 1961
Boyle, Peter (actor); Philadelphia, 10/18/33
Boyle, Robert (scientist); Lismore Castle, Munster, Ireland **(1627–1691)**
Bracken, Eddie (actor); Astoria, Queens, N.Y., 2/7/20
Bradbury, Ray Douglas (science-fiction writer); Waukegan, Ill., 8/22/20
Bradlee, Benjamin C. (editor); Boston, 8/26/21
Bradley, Ed (broadcast journalist); Philadelphia, 6/22/41
Bradley, Omar N. (5-star general); Clark, Mo. **(1893–1981)**
Bradley, Thomas (mayor of Los Angeles); Calvert, Tex., 12/29/17
Brady, Matthew (early photographer); Warren Co., N.Y. **(c.** 1823–1896**)**
Brahe, Tycho (astronomer); Knudstrup, Denmark **(1546–1601)**
Brahms, Johannes (composer); Hamburg **(1833–1897)**
Braille, Louis (teacher of blind); Coupvray, France **(1809–1862)**
Brailowsky, Alexander (pianist); Kiev, Ukraine **(1896–1976)**
Bramante, Donato D'Agnolo (architect); Monte Asdrualdo (now Fermignano, Italy) **(1444–1514)**
Branagh, Kenneth (actor, director, writer, producer); Belfast, Nortern Ireland, 12/10/60
Brancusi, Constantin (sculptor); Pestisani, Romania **(1876–1957)**
Brando, Marlon (actor); Omaha, Neb., 4/3/24
Brandt, Willy (Herbert Frahm) (ex-Chancellor); Lübeck, Germany **(1913–1992)**
Braque, Georges (painter); Argenteuil, France **(1882–1963)**
Brazelton, T(homas) Berry II (pediatrician, writer); Waco, Tex., 5/10/18
Brazzi, Rossano (actor); Bologna, Italy **(1916–1994)**
Brecht, Bertolt (dramatist, poet); Augsburg, Bavaria **(1898–1956)**
Brel, Jacques (singer, composer); Brussels **(1929–1978)**
Brennan, Walter (actor); Lynn, Mass. **(1894–1974)**
Breslin, Jimmy (journalist); Jamaica, Queens, N.Y., 10/17/30
Breton, André (writer); Tinchebray, France **(1896–1966)**
Breuer, Marcel (architect, designer); Pécs, Hungary **(1902–1981)**
Brewster, Kingman, Jr. (ex-president of Yale); Longmeadow, Mass. **(1919–1988)**
Brezhnev, Leonid I. (Communist Party Secretary); Dneprodzerzhinsk, Ukraine **(1906–1982)**
Brice, Fanny (Fannie Borach) (comedienne); New York City **(1892–1951)**
Bridges, Beau (actor); Los Angeles, 12/9/41
Bridges, Jeff (actor); Los Angeles, 12/4/49
Bridges, Lloyd (actor); San Leandro, Calif., 1/15/13
Brinkley, David (TV newscaster); Wilmington, N.C., 7/10/20
Britten, Benjamin (composer); Lowestoft, England **(1913–1976)**
Brodsky, Joseph Alexandrovitch (writer); St. Petersburg, Russia **(1940–1996)**
Brody, Jane (journalist); Brooklyn, N.Y., 5/19/41
Brokaw, Tom (TV newscaster); Webster, S.D., 2/6/40

Brolin, James (actor); Los Angeles, 7/18/40
Bromfield, Louis (novelist); Mansfield, Ohio **(1896–1956)**
Bronson, Charles (Charles Buchinsky) (actor); Ehrenfield, Pa., 11/3/21
Brontë, Charlotte (novelist); Thornton, England **(1816–1855)**
Brontë, Emily Jane (novelist); Thornton, England **(1818–1848)**
Bronzino, Agnolo (painter); Monticelli (Italy) **(1503–1572)**
Brook, Peter (director); London, 3/21/25
Brooke, Rupert (poet); Rugby, England **(1887–1915)**
Brooks, Avery (actor) 4/18/49
Brooks, Geraldine (Geraldine Stroock) (actress); New York City **(1925–1977)**
Brooks, Gwendolyn (poet); Topeka, Kan., 6/7/17
Brooks, Mel (Melvin Kaminsky) (writer, film director); Brooklyn, N.Y., 6/28/26
Brosnan, Pierce (actor); County Meath, Ireland, 5/16/52
Brothers, Joyce (Bauer) (psychologist, author, radio-TV personality); New York City, 9/20/28
Broun, Matthew Heywood Campbell (journalist); Brooklyn, N.Y. **(1888–1939)**
Brown, Charles Brockden (novelist); Philadelphia **(1771–1810)**
Brown, Helen Gurley (author); Green Forest, Ark., 2/18/22
Brown, James (singer); Augusta, Ga., 5/3/34
Brown, Joe E. (comedian); Holgate, Ohio **(1892–1973)**
Brown, John (abolitionist); Torrington, Conn. **(1800–1859)**
Brown, John Mason (critic); Louisville, Ky. **(1900–1969)**
Brown, Les (band leader); Reinerton, Pa., 1912
Brown, Margaret Wise (children's author); Brooklyn, N.Y. **(1910–1962)**
Brown, Trisha (choreographer); Aberdeen, Wash., 11/25/36
Browne, Jackson (singer, guitarist); Heidelberg, Germany, 10/9/48
Browning, Elizabeth Barrett (poet); Durham, England **(1806–1861)**
Browning, Robert (poet); London **(1812–1889)**
Brubeck, Dave (musician); Concord, Calif., 12/6/20
Bruce, Lenny (comedian); Long Island, N.Y. **(1926–1966)**
Bruce, Nigel (actor); Ensenada, Mexico **(1895–1953)**
Brueghel, Pieter (painter); nr. Breda, Flanders (Netherlands) **(c.** 1520–1569**)**
Bruhn, Erik (Belton Evers) (ballet dancer); Copenhagen **(1928–1986)**
Brunelleschi, Filippo (architect); Florence (Italy) **(1377–1446)**
Bruno, Giordano (philosopher); Nola, Italy **(1548–1600)**
Brutus, Marcus Junius (Roman politician) **(85 –42 B.C.E.)**
Bryan, William Jennings (orator, politician); Salem, Ill. **(1860–1925)**
Bryant, Anita (singer); Barnsdall, Okla., 3/25/40
Bryant, William Cullen (poet, editor); Cummington, Mass. **(1794–1878)**
Brynner, Yul (Taidje Khan) (actor); Sakhalin Island, Russia **(1920–1985)**
Brzezinski, Zbigniew (ex-presidential adviser); Warsaw, 3/28/28
Buber, Martin (philosopher, theologian); Vienna **(1878–1965)**
Buchanan, Edgar (actor); Humansville, Mo. **(1903–1979)**
Buchanan, Pat (politician); Washington, D.C., 11/2/38
Buchholz, Horst (actor); Berlin, 12/4/33
Büchner, Georg (dramatist); Goddelau, Germany **(1813–1837)**
Buchwald, Art (Arthur) (columnist); Mount Vernon, N.Y., 10/20/25
Buck, Pearl S(ydenstricker) (author); Hillsboro, W. Va. **(1892–1973)**
Buckley, Christopher (writer); New York City, 1952
Buckley, William F., Jr. (journalist); New York City, 11/24/25
Buffalo Bill (William Frederick Cody) (scout); Scott County, Iowa **(1846–1917)**
Buffett, Jimmy (singer, writer); Mobile, Ala., 12/25/46
Buffett, Warren (investment expert); Omaha, Neb., 8/30/30
Bujold, Genevieve (actress); Montreal, 7/1/42
Bujones, Fernando (ballet dancer); Miami, Fla., 3/9/55
Bulgakov, Mikhail (novelist); Kiev, Ukraine **(1891–1940)**
Bullins, Ed (playwright); Philadelphia, 7/2/35
Bumbry, Grace (mezzo-soprano); St. Louis, 1/4/37
Bunche, Ralph J. (statesman); Detroit, Mich. **(1904–1971)**
Bundy, McGeorge (educator); Boston **(1919–1996)**
Bundy, William Putnam (editor); Washington, D.C., 9/24/17
Buñuel, Luis (film director); Calanda, Spain **(1900–1983)**
Bunyan, John (preacher, author); Elstow, England **(1628–1688)**
Burbank, Luther (horticulturist); Lancaster, Mass. **(1849–1926)**
Burke, Adm. Arleigh A. (ex-Chief of Naval Operations); Boulder, Colo. **(1901–1996)**
Burke, Billie (comedienne); Washington, D.C. **(1885–1970)**
Burke, Delta (actress); Orlando, Fla., 7/30/56
Burke, Edmund (statesman); Dublin **(1729–1797)**
Burne-Jones, Edward Coley (painter); Birmingham, England **(1833–1898)**
Burnett, Carol (comedienne); San Antonio, 4/26/33
Burney, Fanny (Frances) (writer); King's Lynn, England **(1752–1840)**
Burns, George (Nathan Birnbaum) (comedian); New York City **(1896–1996)**
Burns, Ken (documentary filmmaker); Brooklyn, N.Y., 7/29/53
Burns, Robert (poet); Alloway, Scotland **(1759–1796)**
Burr, Aaron (political leader); Newark, N.J. **(1756–1836)**
Burr, Raymond (William Stacey Burr) (actor); New Westminster, British Columbia, Canada **(1917–1993)**

Burroughs, Edgar Rice (novelist); Chicago **(1875–1950)**
Burrows, Abe (playwright, director); New York City **(1910–1985)**
Burstyn, Ellen (Edna Rae Gillooly) (actress); Detroit, Mich., 12/7/32
Burton, LeVar (actor, director); Landsthul, Germany, 2/16/57
Burton, Richard (Richard Jenkins) (actor); Pontrhydfen, Wales **(1925–1984)**
Burton, Tim (filmmaker); Burbank, Calif., 8/25/58
Butkus, Dick (actor); Chicago, 12/9/42
Butler, Samuel (author); Langar, England **(1835–1902)**
Butterworth, Charles (actor); South Bend, Ind. **(1896–1946)**
Buttons, Red (Aaron Chwatt) (actor); New York City, 2/5/19
Buzzi, Ruth (comedienne); Wequetequock, Conn., 7/24/36
Byrd, Richard Evelyn (polar explorer); Winchester, Va. **(1888–1957)**
Byron, George Gordon (6th Baron Byron) (poet); London **(1788–1824)**

C

Caan, James (actor); New York City, 3/26/39
Caballé, Montserrat (soprano); Barcelona, Spain, 4/12/33
Cabot, John (Giovanni Caboto) (navigator); Genoa **(1450–1498)**
Cabot, Sebastian (navigator); Venice **(c. 1476–1557)**
Cadmus, Paul (painter, etcher); New York City, 12/17/04
Caesar, Gaius Julius (statesman); Rome **(100 –44 B.C.E.)**
Caesar, Sid (comedian); Yonkers, N.Y., 9/8/22
Cage, Nicolas (Nicolas Coppola) (actor); Long Beach, Calif., 1/7/64
Cagney, James (actor); New York City **(1899–1986)**
Cahn, Sammy (songwriter); New York City **(1913–1993)**
Caine, Michael (Maurice J. Micklewhite) (actor); London, 3/14/33
Calder, Alexander (sculptor); Lawnton, Pa. **(1898–1976)**
Calderón del al Barca, Pedro (dramatist); Madrid **(1600–1681)**
Caldwell, Erskine (novelist); White Oak, Ga. **(1903–1987)**
Caldwell, Sarah (opera director, conductor); Maryville, Mo., 3/6/24
Caldwell, Taylor (novelist); Manchester, England **(1900–1985)**
Caldwell, Zoe (actress); Hawthorn, Australia, 9/14/33
Calhern, Louis (Carl Henry Vogt) (actor); Brooklyn, N.Y. **(1895–1956)**
Calhoun, John Caldwell (statesman); nr. Calhoun Mills, S.C. **(1782–1850)**
Caligula Gaius Caesar (Roman emperor); Antium, Latium **(12–41)**
Calisher, Hortense (novelist); New York City, 12/20/11
Callas, Maria (Maria Calogeropoulos) (dramatic soprano); New York City **(1923–1977)**
Calloway, Cab (Cabell) (band leader); Rochester, N.Y. **(1907–1994)**
Calvin, John (Jean Chauvin) (religious reformer); Noyon, Picardy **(1509–1564)**
Cambridge, Godfrey (comedian); New York City **(1933–1976)**
Cameron, Rod (Rod Cox) (actor); Calgary, Alberta, Canada **(1912–1983)**
Campbell, Glen (singer); nr. Delight, Ark., 4/22/38
Campbell, Mrs. Patrick (Beatrice Stella Tanner) (actress); London **(1865–1940)**
Camus, Albert (author); Mondovi, Algeria **(1913–1960)**
Canaletto, (Giovanni Antonio Canale) (painter); Venice **(1697–1768)**
Candy, John (actor, comedian); Toronto, Ont., Canada **(1950–1994)**
Caniff, Milton (cartoonist); Hillsboro, Ohio **(1907–1988)**
Cannon, Dyan (actress); Tacoma, Wash., 1/4/37
Canova, Judy (comedienne); Jacksonville, Fla. **(1916–1983)**
Cantinflas (Mario Moreno) (comedian); Mexico City, 8/12/11
Cantor, Eddie (Edward Iskowitz) (actor); New York City **(1892–1964)**
Capone, Al(fonse) (gangster); Naples, Italy **(1899–1947)**
Capote, Truman (novelist); New Orleans **(1924–1984)**
Capp, Al (Alfred Gerald Caplin) (cartoonist); New Haven, Conn. **(1909–1979)**
Capra, Frank (film producer, director); Palermo, Italy **(1897–1991)**
Caputo, Phil (Philip Joseph) (author, journalist); Chicago, 6/10/41
Caravaggio, Michelangelo Merisi da (painter); Caravaggio (Italy) **(1573–1610)**
Cardin, Pierre (fashion designer); nr. Venice, 7/7/22
Cardinale, Claudia (actress); Tunis, Tunisia, 4/15/39
Carey, Harry (actor); New York City **(1878–1947)**
Carey, Macdonald (actor); Sioux City, Iowa **(1913–1994)**
Carlin, George (comedian); Bronx, N.Y., 5/12/37
Carlisle, Kitty (singer, actress); New Orleans, 9/3/15
Carlyle, Thomas (essayist, historian); Ecclefechan, Scotland **(1795–1881)**
Carmichael, Hoagy (Hoagland Howard) (songwriter); Bloomington, Ind. **(1899–1981)**
Carne, Judy (Joyce Botterill) (singer); Northampton, England, 4/27/39
Carnegie, Andrew (industrialist); Dunfermline, Scotland **(1835–1919)**
Carney, Art (actor); Mt. Vernon, N.Y., 11/4/18
Caron, Leslie (actress); Paris, 7/1/31
Carr, Vikki (singer); El Paso, 7/19/42
Carracci, Annibale (painter); Bologna (Italy) **(1560–1609)**
Carracci, Lodovico (painter); Bologna (Italy) **(1555–1619)**
Carradine, David (actor); Hollywood, Calif., 12/8/36
Carradine, John (actor); New York City **(1906–1988)**

Carradine, Keith (actor); San Mateo, Calif., 8/8/49
Carreras, José (tenor); Barcelona, Spain, 12/5/46
Carroll, Diahann (Carol Diahann Johnson) (singer, actress); Bronx, N.Y., 7/17/35
Carroll, Leo G. (actor); Weedon, England **(1892–1972)**
Carroll, Lewis (Charles Lutwidge Dodgson) (author, mathematician); Daresbury, England **(1832–1898)**
Carson, Jack (actor); Carmen, Man., Canada **(1910–1963)**
Carson, Johnny (TV entertainer); Corning, Iowa, 10/23/25
Carson, Kit (Christopher) (scout); Madison County, Ky. **(1809–1868)**
Carson, Rachel (biologist, author); Springdale, Pa. **(1907–1964)**
Carter, Dixie (actress); McLemoresville, Tenn., 5/25/39
Carter, Jack (comedian); New York City, 1923
Carter, Lynda (actress); Phoenix, Ariz., 7/24/51
Cartier, Jacques (explorer); Saint-Malo, Brittany (France) **(1491–1557)**
Cartier-Bresson, Henri (photographer); Chanteloup, France, 8/22/08
Cartland, Barbara (author); England, 7/9/01
Caruso, Enrico (Errico) (tenor); Naples, Italy **(1873–1921)**
Carver, George Washington (botanist); Diamond Grove, Mo. **(1864–1943)**
Cary, Arthur Joyce Lunel (novelist); Londonderry, Ireland **(1888–1957)**
Casals, Pablo (cellist); Vendrell, Spain **(1876–1973)**
Casanova de Seingalt, Giovanni Jacopo (adventurer); Venice **(1725–1798)**
Cash, Johnny (singer); nr. Kingsland, Ark., 2/26/32
Cass, Peggy (comedienne); Boston, 5/21/24
Cassatt, Mary (painter); Allegheny, Pa. **(1844–1926)**
Cassavetes, John (director); New York City **(1929–1989)**
Cassidy, David (singer); New York City, 4/12/50
Cassidy, Jack (actor); Richmond Hill, Queens, N.Y. **(1927–1976)**
Cassidy, Shaun (actor); Los Angeles, 9/27/58
Cassini, Oleg (Oleg Lolewski-Cassini) (fashion designer); Paris, 4/11/13
Castagno, Andrea del (painter); San Martino a Corella (Italy) **(c.1421–1457)**
Castellano, Richard (actor); New York City **(1934–1988)**
Castle, Irene (Irene Foote) (actress, dancer); New Rochelle, N.Y. **(1893–1969)**
Castle, Vernon Blythe (dancer, aviator); Norwich, England **(1887–1918)**
Castro Ruz, Fidel (Premier); Mayari, Oriente, Cuba, 8/13/26
Cather, Willa Sibert (novelist); Winchester, Va. **(1876–1947)**
Cato, Marcus Porcius (called Cato the Elder) (statesman); Tusculum (Italy) **(234–149 B.C.E.)**
Catt, Carrie Chapman Lane (woman suffragist); Ripon, Wis. **(1859–1947)**
Catton, Bruce (historian); Petoskey, Mich. **(1899–1978)**
Catullus, Gaius Valerius (poet); Verona **(c.84–c.54 B.C.E.)**
Cavallaro, Carmen (band leader); New York City **(1913–1989)**
Cavett, Dick (Richard) (TV entertainer); Gibbon, Neb., 11/19/36
Ceausecu, Nicolae (Romanian head of state); Scornicesti, Romania **(1918–1989)**
Céline, Louis Ferdinand (pseud. of Louis Fuch Destouches) (novelist); Paris **(1894–1961)**
Cellini, Benvenuto (goldsmith, sculptor); Florence (Italy) **(1500–1571)**
Cervantes Saavedra, Miguel de (novelist); Alcalá de Henares, Spain **(1547–1616)**
Cézanne, Paul (painter); Aix-en-Provence, France **(1839–1906)**
Chagall, Marc (painter); Vitebsk, Russia **(1887–1985)**
Challapin, Feodor Ivanovitch (operatic basso); Kazan, Russia **(1873–1938)**
Chamberlain, Arthur Neville (statesman); Edgbaston, England **(1869–1940)**
Chamberlain, Richard (actor, producer); Los Angeles, 3/31/35
Champion, Gower (choreographer); Geneva, Ill. **(1921–1980)**
Champion, Marge (actress, dancer); Los Angeles, 9/2/23
Champlain, Samuel de (explorer); nr. Rochefort, France **(1567–1635)**
Chancellor, John (TV commentator); Chicago **(1927–1996)**
Chandler, Jeff (actor); Brooklyn, N.Y. **(1918–1961)**
Chandler, Raymond (writer); Chicago **(1883–1959)**
Chanel, "Coco" (Gabriel Bonheur) (fashion designer); Issoire, France **(1883–1971)**
Chaney, Lon (actor); Colorado Springs, Colo. **(1883–1930)**
Channing, Carol (actress); Seattle, 1/31/23
Channing, Stockard (actress); New York City, 2/13/44
Chaplin, Geraldine (actress); Santa Monica, Calif., 7/31/44
Chaplin, Sir Charles (actor); London **(1889–1977)**
Charisse, Cyd (Tula Finklea) (dancer, actress); Amarillo, Tex., 3/8/23
Charlemagne (Holy Roman Emperor); birthplace unknown **(742–814)**
Charles, Ray (Ray Charles Robinson) (pianist, singer, songwriter); Albany Ga., 9/23/30
Charo (Maria Rosario Pilar Martinez) (actress); Murcia, Spain, 1/15/51
Chase, Chevy (Cornelius Crane Chase) (comedian); New York City, 10/8/43
Chase, Lucia (founder Ballet Theatre [now American Ballet Theatre]); Waterbury, Conn. **(1907–1986)**
Charlemagne (Holy Roman Emperor); birthplace unknown **(742–814)**

Chateaubriand, François René de (writer, statesman); St. Malo, France **(1768–1848)**
Chaucer, Geoffrey (poet); London **(c. 1340–1400)**
Chávez, Carlos (composer); nr. Mexico City **(1899–1978)**
Chavez, Cesar (labor leader); nr. Yuma, Ariz. **(1927–1993)**
Chayefsky, Paddy (Sidney) (playwright); New York City **(1923–1981)**
Checker, Chubby (Ernest Evans) (performer); Philadelphia, 10/3/41
Cheever, John (novelist); Quincy, Mass. **(1912–1982)**
Chekhov, Anton Pavlovich (dramatist, short-story writer); Taganrog, Russia **(1860–1904)**
Cher (Cherilyn LaPiere) (actress, singer); El Centro, Calif., 5/20/46
Cherubini, Luigi (composer); Florence **(1760–1842)**
Chesterton, Gilbert Keith (author); Kensington, England **(1874–1936)**
Chestnutt, Charles Waddell (author); Cleveland, Ohio **(1858–1932)**
Chevalier, Maurice (entertainer); Paris **(1888–1972)**
Chiang Kai-shek (Chief of State); Feng-hwa, China **(1887–1975)**
Child, Julia (food expert); Pasadena, Calif., 8/15/12
Chippendale, Thomas (cabinet-maker); Otley, England **(1718–1779)**
Chirico, Giorgio de (painter); Vólos, Greece **(1888–1978)**
Chisholm, Shirley Anita St. Hill (U.S. Representative); Brooklyn, N.Y., 11/30/24
Chomsky, (Avram) Noam (linguist, educator, activist); Philadelphia, 12/7/28
Chopin, Frédéric François (composer); nr. Warsaw **(1810–1849)**
Chopin, Kate O'Flaherty (author); St. Louis, Mo. **(1851–1904)**
Christie, Agatha (mystery writer); Torquay, England **(1890–1976)**
Christie, Julie (actress); Chukua, India, 4/14/41
Chung, Connie (broadcast journalist); Washington, D.C., 8/20/46
Churchill, Sir Winston Leonard Spencer (statesman); Blenheim Palace, Oxfordshire, England **(1874–1965)**
Cicero, Marcus Tullius (orator, statesman); Arpinum (Italy) **(106–43 B.C.E.)**
Cid, El (Rodrigo [or Ruy] Diez de Bivar) (Spanish national hero); nr. Burgos, Spain **(c 1043–1099)**
Cilento, Diane (actress); Queensland, Australia, 10/5/33
Cimabue, Giovanni (painter); Florence (Italy) **(c.1240–c.1302)**
Cimino, Michael (director, writer, producer); New York City, 1943
Clair, René (René Chomette) (director); Paris **(1898–1981)**
Clapton, Eric (singer, guitarist); Ripley, England, 3/30/45
Clark, Dick (TV personality); Mt. Vernon, N.Y., 11/30/29
Clark, Mark W. (general); Madison Barracks, N.Y. **(1896–1984)**
Clark, Mary Higgins (writer); New York City, 12/24/29
Clark, Petula (singer); Epsom, England, 11/15/34
Clark, Roy (country music artist); Meherrin, Va., 4/15/33
Clark, William (explorer); Caroline County, Va. **(1770–1838)**
Clarke, Arthur C. (science fiction writer); Minehead, England, 12/16/17
Clary, Robert (actor); Paris, France, 3/1/26
Claude Lorrain (Claude Gellée) (painter); Champagne, France **(1600–1682)**
Clausewitz, Karl von (military strategist); Burg (Germany) **(1780–1831)**
Clay, Henry (statesman); Hanover County, Va. **(1777–1852)**
Clay, Lucius D. (banker, ex-general); Marietta, Ga. **(1897–1978)**
Clayburgh, Jill (actress); New York City, 4/30/44
Cleary, Beverly (Beverly Atlee Bunn) (children's author); McMinnville, Ore., 1916
Cleaver, Eldridge (Leroy) (author, activist); Wabbaseka, Ark., 1935
Cleese, John (writer, actor); Weston-super-Mare, England, 10/27/39
Clemenceau, Georges (statesman); Mouilleron-en-Pareds, Vondée, France **(1841–1929)**
Cleopatra (Queen of Egypt); Alexandria, Egypt **(69–30 B.C.E.)**
Cliburn, Van (Harvey Lavan Cliburn, Jr.) (concert pianist); Shreveport, La., 7/12/34
Clift, Montgomery (actor); Omaha, Neb. **(1920–1966)**
Cline, Patsy (singer); Winchester, Va. **(1933–1963)**
Clooney, George (actor); Lexington, Ky., 5/6/61
Clooney, Rosemary (singer); Maysville, Ky., 5/23/28
Close, Glenn (actress); Greenwich, Conn., 3/19/47
Clurman, Harold (stage producer); New York City **(1901–1980)**
Cobb, Irvin Shrewsbury (humorist); Paducah, Ky. **(1876–1944)**
Cobb, Lee J. (Leo Jacob) (actor); New York City **(1911–1976)**
Coburn, Charles Douville (actor); Savannah, Ga. **(1877–1961)**
Coburn, James (actor); Laurel, Neb., 8/31/28
Coca, Imogene (comedienne); Philadelphia, 11/18/08
Cocker, Joe (John Robert Cocker) (singer); Sheffield, England, 5/20/44
Coco, James (actor); New York City **(1929–1987)**
Cocteau, Jean (author); Maison-Lafitte, France **(1891–1963)**
Cohan, George Michael (actor, dramatist); Providence, R.I. **(1878–1942)**
Colbert, Claudette (Lily Chauchoin) (actress); Paris, 9/13/03
Cole, Nat "King" (singer); Montgomery, Ala. **(1919–1965)**
Cole, Natalie (singer); Los Angeles, 2/6/50
Cole, Thomas (painter); Lancashire, England **(1801–1848)**
Coleman, Dabney (actor); Corpus Christi, Tex., 1/2/32
Coleridge, Samuel Taylor (poet); Ottery St. Mary, England **(1772–1834)**
Colette (Sidonie-Gabrielle Colette) (novelist); St.-Sauveur, France **(c.1873–1954)**

Collingwood, Charles (TV commentator); Three Rivers, Mich. **(1917–1985)**
Collins, Joan (actress); London, 5/23/33
Collins, Judy (singer); Seattle, 5/1/39
Colman, Ronald (actor); Richmond, England **(1891–1958)**
Colonna, Jerry (comedian); Boston **(1905–1986)**
Coltrane, John (jazz musician); Hamlet, N.C. **(1926–1967)**
Columbo, Russ (singer, bandleader); San Francisco **(1908–1934)**
Columbus, Christopher (Cristoforo Colombo) (explorer); Genoa (Italy) **(1451–1506)**
Comden, Betty (writer); New York City, 5/3/19
Comenius, Johann Amos (educational reformer); Nivnice, Moravia (Czech Republic) **(1592–1670)**
Commager, Henry Steele (historian); Pittsburgh, 10/25/02
Como, Perry (Pierino) (singer); Canonsburg, Pa., 5/18/12
Compton, Karl Taylor (physicist); Wooster, Ohio **(1887–1954)**
Comte, Auguste (philosopher); Montpellier, France **(1798–1857)**
Conant, James B. (educator, statesman); Dorchester, Mass. **(1893–1978)**
Condon, Eddie (jazz musician); Goodland, Ind. **(1905–1973)**
Confucius (K'ung Fu-tzu) (philosopher); Shantung province, China **(c.551–479 B.C.E.)**
Congreve, William (dramatist); nr. Leeds, England **(1670–1729)**
Connelly, Marc (playwright); McKeesport, Pa. **(1890–1980)**
Connery, Sean (actor); Edinburgh, Scotland, 8/25/30
Conniff, Ray (band leader); Attleboro, Mass., 11/6/16
Connors, Chuck (actor); Brooklyn, N.Y. **(1921–1992)**
Connors, Mike (Krekor Ohanian) (actor); Fresno, Calif., 8/15/25
Conrad, Joseph (Teodor Jozef Konrad Korzeniowski) (novelist); Berdichev, Ukraine **(1857–1924)**
Conrad, Robert (Conrad Robert Falk) (actor); Chicago, 3/1/35
Conrad, William (actor); Louisville, Ky. **(1920–1994)**
Conried, Hans (Frank Foster) (actor); Baltimore **(1915–1982)**
Conroy, Pat (author); Atlanta, Ga., 10/26/45
Constable, John (painter); East Bergholt, Suffolk, England **(1776–1837)**
Constantine II (ex-king); Athens, 6/2/40
Constantine, Michael (actor); Reading, Pa., 5/22/27
Conte, Richard (actor); New York City **(1916–1975)**
Conti, Tom (actor); Paisley, Scotland, 11/22/41
Convy, Bert (actor, host); St. Louis, Mo. **(1933–1991)**
Conway, Tim (comedian); Chagrin Falls, Ohio, 12/15/33
Coogan, Jackie (actor); Los Angeles **(1914–1984)**
Cook, Peter (actor, writer); Torquay, England **(1937–1995)**
Cooke, Alistair (Alfred Alistair) (TV narrator, journalist); Manchester, England, 11/20/08
Cooley, Denton A(rthur) (heart surgeon); Houston, Tex., 8/22/20
Coolidge, Rita (singer); Nashville, Tenn., 5/1/45
Cooper, Alice (Vincent Furnier) (rock musician); Detroit, Mich., 2/4/48
Cooper, Gary (Frank James Cooper) (actor); Helena, Mont. **(1901–1961)**
Cooper, Dame Gladys (actress); Lewisham, England **(1898–1971)**
Cooper, Jackie (actor, director); Los Angeles, 9/15/22
Cooper, James Fenimore (novelist); Burlington, N.J. **(1789–1851)**
Cooper, Peter (industrialist, philanthropist); New York City **(1791–1883)**
Copernicus, Nicolaus (Mikolaj Kopernik) (astronomer); Thorn, Poland **(1473–1543)**
Copland, Aaron (composer); Brooklyn, N.Y. **(1900–1990)**
Copley, John Singleton (painter); Boston, Mass. **(1738–1815)**
Copperfield, David (illusionist); Metuchen, N.J., 9/16/56
Coppola, Francis Ford (film director); Detroit, Mich., 4/7/39
Corelli, Arcangelo (composer); Fusignano, Italy **(1653–1713)**
Corelli, Franco (operatic tenor); Ancona, Italy, 4/8/23
Corneille, Pierre (dramatist); Rouen, France **(1606–1684)**
Cornell, Katharine (actress); Berlin **(1893–1974)**
Corot, Jean Baptiste Camille (painter); Paris **(1796–1875)**
Correggio, Antonio Allegri da (painter); Correggio(Italy) **(1494–1534)**
Corsaro, Frank (opera director); New York harbor, 12/22/24
Cortés (or Cortez), Hernando (explorer); Medellin, Spain **(1485–1547)**
Cosby, Bill (actor); Philadelphia, 7/12/37
Cosell, Howard (Howard Cohen) (sportscaster); Winston-Salem, N.C. **(1918–1995)**
Costa-Gavras, Henri (Kostantinos Gavras) (film director); Athens, 1933
Costello, Elvis (Declan Patrick McManus) (singer, musician, songwriter); London, 1954
Costello, Lou (comedian); Paterson, N.J. **(1908–1959)**
Costner, Kevin (actor); Los Angeles, Calif., 1/18/55
Cotten, Joseph (actor); Petersburg, Va. **(1905–1994)**
Couperin, François (composer); Paris **(1668–1733)**
Courbet, Gustave (painter); Ornans, France **(1819–1877)**
Couric, Katie (TV host); Arlington, Va., 1/7/57
Courtenay, Tom (actor); Hull, England, 2/25/37
Cousins, Norman (publisher); Union Hill, N.J. **(1915–1990)**
Cousteau, Jacques-Yves (marine explorer); St. André-de-Cubzac, France **(1910–1997)**
Coward, Sir Noel (playwright, actor); Teddington, England **(1899–1973)**
Cowles, Gardner, Jr. (newspaper publisher); Algona, Iowa **(1903–1985)**

Cowper, William (poet); Great Berkhamstead, England **(1731–1800)**
Cox, Archibald (Watergate prosecutor); Plainfield, N.J., 5/17/12
Cox, Courteney (actress); Birmingham, Ala., 6/15/64
Cox, Wally (actor); Detroit, Mich. **(1924–1973)**
Cozzens, James Gould (novelist); Chicago **(1903–1978)**
Crabbe, Buster (Clarence) (actor); Oakland, Calif. **(1908–1983)**
Cranach, Lucas, the elder (painter); Kronach(Germany) **(1472–1553)**
Crane, Hart (poet); Garrettsville, Ohio **(1899–1932)**
Crane, Stephen (novelist, poet); Newark, N.J. **(1871–1900)**
Cranmer, Thomas (churchman); Aslacton, England **(1489–1556)**
Crawford, Broderick (actor); Philadelphia **(1911–1986)**
Crawford, Cheryl (stage producer); Akron, Ohio **(1902–1986)**
Crawford, Joan (Lucille LeSueur) (actress, business executive); San Antonio **(1908–1977)**
Crazy Horse (Lakota Indian leader); nr. Bear Butte, S.D. **(1840?–1877)**
Crenna, Richard (actor); Los Angeles, 11/30/27
Crespin, Régine (operatic soprano); Marseilles, France, 2/23/29
Crichton, (John) Michael (novelist); Chicago, 10/23/42
Crisp, Donald (actor); London **(1880–1974)**
Croce, Benedetto (philosopher); Peseasseroli, Aquila, Italy **(1866–1952)**
Croce, Jim (singer); Philadelphia **(1942–1973)**
Crockett, Davy (David) (frontiersman); Greene County, Tenn. **(1786–1836)**
Cromwell, Oliver (statesman); Huntingdon, England **(1599–1658)**
Cronin, A. J. (Archibald J. Cronin) (novelist); Cardross, Scotland **(1896–1981)**
Cronkite, Walter (TV newscaster); St. Joseph, Mo., 11/4/16
Cronyn, Hume (actor); London, Ontario, Canada, 7/18/11
Crosby, Bing (Harry Lillis) (singer, actor); Tacoma, Wash. **(1904–1977)**
Crosby, Bob (musician); Spokane, Wash. **(1913–1993)**
Crosby, Cathy Lee (actress); Los Angeles, 12/2/48
Crosby, Norm (comedian); Boston, 9/15/27
Cross, Ben (Bernard) (actor); Paddington, England, 12/16/47
Cross, Milton (opera commentator); New York City **(1897–1975)**
Crouse, Russel (playwright); Findlay, Ohio **(1893–1966)**
Cruise, Tom (Thomas Mapother IV) (actor, producer); Syracuse, N.Y., 7/3/62
Crystal, Billy (comedian, actor); Long Beach, L.I., N.Y., 3/14/47
Cugat, Xavier (band leader); Barcelona, Spain **(1900–1990)**
Cukor, George (film director); New York City **(1899–1983)**
Cullen, Bill (William Lawrence Cullen) (radio and TV entertainer); Pittsburgh **(1920–1990)**
Cullen, Countee (poet); New York City **(1903–1946)**
Culp, Robert (actor); Berkeley, Calif., 8/16/30
cummings, e. e. (Edward Estlin Cummings) (poet); Cambridge, Mass. **(1894–1962)**
Cummings, Robert (actor); Joplin, Mo. **(1908–1990)**
Cunningham, Merce (choreographer); Centralia, Wash., 4/16/19
Curie, Marie (Marja Sklodowska) (physical chemist); Warsaw **(1867–1934)**
Curie, Pierre (physicist); Paris **(1859–1906)**
Curtin, Jane (actress); Cambridge, Mass., 9/6/47
Curtin, Phyllis (soprano); Clarksburg, W.Va., 12/3/27
Curtis, Jamie Lee (actress); Los Angeles, 11/22/58
Curtis, Tony (Bernard Schwartz) (actor); Bronx, N.Y., 6/3/25
Curzon, Clifford (concert pianist); London **(1907–1982)**
Custer, George Armstrong (army officer); New Rumley, Ohio **(1839–1876)**

D

da Gama, Vasco (explorer); Sines, Portugal **(1460–1524)**
Daguerre, Louis (photographic pioneer); nr. Paris **(1787–1851)**
Dahl, Arlene (actress); Minneapolis, 8/11/28
Dailey, Dan (actor, dancer); New York City **(1917–1978)**
Dale, Jim (actor, singer, songwriter); Rothwell, England, 8/15/35
Daley, Richard J. (Mayor of Chicago); Chicago **(1902–1976)**
Dali, Salvador (painter); Figueras, Spain **(1904–1989)**
Dalton, John (chemist); nr. Cockermouth, England **(1766–1844)**
Daly, Tyne (actress); Madison, Wis., 2/21/46
d'Amboise, Jacques (ballet dancer); Dedham, Mass., 7/28/34
Damone, Vic (Vito Farinola) (singer); Brooklyn, N.Y., 6/12/28
Damrosch, Walter Johannes (orchestra conductor); Breslau (Poland) **(1862–1950)**
Dana, Charles Anderson (editor); Hinsdale, N.H. **(1819–1897)**
Dandridge, Dorothy (actress); Cleveland **(1923–1965)**
Dangerfield, Rodney (Jacob Cohen) (actor, comedian); Babylon, N.Y., 11/22/22
Daniels, Bebe (Virginia Daniels) (actress); Dallas **(1901–1971)**
Daniels, William (actor); Brooklyn, N.Y., 3/31/27
Danilova, Alexandra (ballerina); Peterhof, Russia **(1904–1997)**
Dannay, Frederic (novelist, pseudonym Ellery Queen); Brooklyn, N.Y. **(1905–1982)**
Danner, Blythe (actress); Philadelphia, 2/3/43

D'Annunzio, Gabriele (soldier, author); Francaville at Mare, Pescara, Italy **(1863–1938)**
Danson, Ted (actor); San Diego, Calif., 12/29/47
Dante (or Durante) Alighieri (poet); Florence (Italy) **(1265–1321)**
Danton, Georges Jacques (French Revolutionary leader); Arcis-sur-Aube, France **(1759–1794)**
Danza, Tony (actor); Brooklyn, N.Y., 4/21/51
Darnell, Linda (actress); Dallas **(1921–1965)**
Darren, James (actor); Philadelphia, 6/8/36
Darrow, Clarence Seward (lawyer); Kinsman, Ohio **(1857–1938)**
Darwell, Jane (actress); Palmyra, Mo. **(1879–1967)**
Darwin, Charles Robert (naturalist); Shrewsbury, England **(1809–1882)**
daSilva, Howard (actor); Cleveland **(1909–1986)**
Dassin, Jules (film director); Middletown, Conn., 12/18/11
Daumier, Honoré (caricaturist); Marseilles, France **(1808–1879)**
David, Jacques-Louis (painter); Paris **(1748–1825)**
David (King of Israel and Judah) died c. 973 B.C.E.
Davidson, John (singer, actor); Pittsburgh, 12/13/41
Davies, Marion (Marion Douras) (actress); New York City **(1897–1961)**
Davies, (William) Robertson (writer); Thamesville, Ontario, Canada **(1913–1996)**
da Vinci, Leonardo (painter, scientist); Vinci, Tuscany (Italy) **(1452–1519)**
Davis, Angela (social activist); Birmingham, Ala., 1/26/44
Davis, Ann B. (actress); Schenectady, N.Y., 5/5/26
Davis, Lt. Gen. Benjamin O., Jr. (Air Force general); Washington, D.C., 12/18/12
Davis, Brig. Gen. Benjamin O., Sr. (U.S. Army general); Washington, D.C. **(1877–1970)**
Davis, Bette (actress); Lowell, Mass. **(1908–1989)**
Davis, Jefferson (President of the Confederacy); Christian (now Todd) County, Ky. **(1808–1889)**
Davis, Judy (actress); Perth, Australia, 1955
Davis, Mac (singer); Lubbock, Tex., 1/21/42
Davis, Miles (jazz trumpeter); Alton, Ill. **(1926–1991)**
Davis, Ossie (actor, writer); Cogdell, Ga., 12/18/17
Davis, Sammy, Jr. (actor, singer); New York City **(1925–1990)**
Davis, Skeeter (Mary Francis Penick) (singer); Dry Ridge, Ky., 12/30/31
Davis, Stuart (painter); Philadelphia **(1894–1964)**
Dawson, Richard (actor, host); Gosport, Hampshire, England, 11/20/32
Day, Doris (Doris von Kappelhoff) (singer, actress); Cincinnati, 4/3/24
Dayan, Moshe (ex-Defense Minister of Israel); Dagania, Palestine **(1915–1981)**
Dean, James (actor); Marion, Ind. **(1931–1955)**
Dean, Jimmy (singer); Seth Ward, nr. Plainview, Tex., 8/10/28
De Bakey, Michael E. (heart surgeon); Lake Charles, La., 9/7/08
de Beauvoir, Simone (novelist, philosopher); Paris **(1908–1986)**
Debs, Eugene Victor (Socialist leader); Terre Haute, Ind. **(1855–1926)**
Debussy, Claude Achille (composer); St. Germain-en-Laye, France **(1862–1918)**
DeCamp, Rosemary (actress); Prescott, Ariz., 11/14/10
De Carlo, Yvonne (Peggy Yvonne Middleton) (actress); Vancouver, B.C., Canada, 9/1/24
de Chirico, Giorgio (painter); Volos, Greece **(1888–1978)**
Dee, Ruby Ruby Ann Wallace (actress); Cleveland, Ohio, 10/27/24
Dee, Sandra (Alexandra Zuck) (actress); Bayonne, N.J., 4/23/42
Defoe, Daniel (novelist); London **(1660–1731)**
Degas, Hilaire Germain Edgar (painter); Paris **(1834–1917)**
de Gaulle, Charles André Joseph Marie (soldier, statesman); Lille, France **(1890–1970)**
de Havilland, Olivia (actress); Tokyo, 7/1/16
de Kooning, Willem (painter); Rotterdam **(1904–1997)**
Delacroix, Eugène (painter); Charenton-St. Maurice, France **(1798–1863)**
de la Renta, Oscar (fashion designer); Santo Domingo, Dominican Republic, 7/22/32
Delaunay, Robert (painter); Paris **(1885–1941)**
De Laurentiis, Dino (film producer); Torre Annunziata, Bay of Naples, Italy, 8/8/19
della Robbia, Andrea (sculptor); Florence **(1435–1525)**
della Robbia, Luca (sculptor); Florence **(1400–1482)**
Delon, Alain (actor); Sceaux, France, 11/8/35
DeLuise, Dom (actor, comedian); Brooklyn, N.Y., 8/1/33
Demarest, William (actor); St. Paul **(1892–1983)**
de Mille, Agnes (choreographer); New York City **(1905–1993)**
De Mille, Cecil Blount (film director); Ashfield, Mass. **(1881–1959)**
Demosthenes (orator); Athens **(384?–322 B.C.E.)**
Deneuve, Catherine (actress); Paris, 10/22/43
De Niro, Robert (actor, director); New York City, 8/17/43
Dennehy, Brian (actor); Bridgeport, Conn., 7/9/40
Denning, Richard (actor); Poughkeepsie, N.Y., 3/27/14
Dennis, Sandy (actress); Hastings, Neb. **(1937–1992)**
Denny, Reginald (actor); Richmond, England **(1891–1967)**
Denver, John (Henry John Deutschendorf, Jr.) (singer); Roswell, N.M., 12/31/43
De Palma, Brian (film director); Newark, N.J., 9/11/40

Depp, Johnny (actor); Owensboro, Ky., 6/9/63
Derain, André (painter); Chatou, Seine-et-Oise, France **(1880–1954)**
Derek, John (actor, director); Los Angeles, 8/12/26
Dern, Bruce (actor); Chicago, 6/4/36
Dershowitz, Alan (lawyer); Brooklyn, N.Y., 9/1/38
Derrida, Jacques (philosopher); El-Biar, Algeria, 7/15/30
Descartes, René (philosopher, mathematician); La Haye, France **(1596–1650)**
De Seversky, Alexander P. (aviator); Tiflis (Georgia) **(1894–1974)**
De Sica, Vittorio (film director); Sora, Italy **(1901–1974)**
Desmond, Johnny (composer); Detroit, Mich. **(1921–1985)**
Desmond, William (actor); Dublin **(1878–1949)**
De Soto, Hernando (explorer); Barcarrota, Spain **(c. 1500–1542)**
De Valera, Eamon (ex-President of Ireland); New York City **(1882–1975)**
Devane, William (actor); Albany, N.Y., 9/5/39
Devine, Andy (actor); Flagstaff, Ariz. **(1905–1977)**
DeVito, Danny (Daniel Michael) (actor, director); Neptune, N.J., 11/17/44
De Vries, Peter (novelist); Chicago **(1910–1993)**
de Waart, Edo (conductor); Amsterdam, the Netherlands, 6/1/41
Dewey, George (admiral); Montpelier, Vt. **(1837–1917)**
Dewey, John (philosopher, educator); Burlington, Vt. **(1859–1952)**
Dewey, Thomas E. (politician); Owosso, Mich. **(1902–1971)**
Dewhurst, Colleen (actress); Montreal **(1924–1991)**
De Wolfe, Billy (actor); Wollaston, Mass. **(1907–1974)**
Dey, Susan (actress); Pekin, Ill., 12/10/52
Diaghilev, Sergei (ballet impressario); Novgorod, Russia **(1872–1929)**
Diamond, Neil (singer); Brooklyn, N.Y., 1/24/41
Diana (Diana Frances Spencer) (Princess of Wales); Sandringham, England **(1961–1997)**
Dichter, Misha (pianist); Shanghai, 9/27/45
Dickens, Charles John Huffam (novelist); Portsea, England **(1812–1870)**
Dickey, James (poet); Atlanta **(1923–1997)**
Dickinson, Angie (Angeline Brown) (actress); Kulm, N.D., 9/30/32
Dickinson, Emily Elizabeth (poet); Amherst, Mass. **(1830–1886)**
Diddley, Bo (Elias McDaniel) (guitarist); McComb, Miss., 12/30/28
Diderot, Denis (encyclopedist); Langres, France **(1713–1784)**
Dietrich, Marlene (Maria Magdalena von Losch) (actress); Berlin **(1901–1992)**
Diller, Phyllis (Phyllis Driver) (comedienne); Lima, Ohio, 7/17/17
Dine, Jim (painter); Cincinnati, 6/16/35
Dinesen, Isak (Karen Blixen) (author); Rungsted, Denmark **(1885–1962)**
Dinkins, David (ex-Mayor of New York City); Trenton, N.J., 7/10/27
Diogenes (philosopher); Sinope (Turkey) **(c. 412–323 B.C.E.)**
Dion (Dion DiMucci) (singer); Bronx, N.Y., 7/18/39
Dior, Christian (fashion designer); Granville, France **(1905–1957)**
Disney, Walt(er) Elias (film animator, producer); Chicago **(1901–1966)**
Disraeli, Benjamin (Earl of Beaconsfield) (statesman); London **(1804–1881)**
Dix, Dorothea (civil rights reformer); Hampden, Me. **(1802–1887)**
Dixon, Jeane (Jeane Pinckert) (seer); Medford, Wis. **(1918–1997)**
Dobbs, Mattiwilda (soprano); Atlanta, Ga., 7/11/25
Doctorow, E(dgar) L(aurence) (novelist); New York City, 1/6/31
Dole, Elizabeth (public official); Salisbury, N.C., 7/29/36
Dole, Robert (politician); Russell, Kan., 7/22/23
Dolin, Anton (dancer); Slinfold, England **(1904–1983)**
Domingo, Placido (tenor); Madrid, 1/21/41
Domino, Fats (Antoine) (musician); New Orleans, 2/26/28
Donahue, Phil (TV host); Cleveland, 12/21/35
Donahue, Troy Merle Johnson (actor); New York City, 1/27/36
Donaldson, Sam (broadcast journalist); El Paso, Tex., 3/11/34
Donat, Robert (actor); Withington, England **(1905–1958)**
Donatello (Donato Niccolò di Betto Bardi) (sculptor); Florence **(c.1386–1466)**
Donlevy, Brian (actor); Portadown, Ireland **(1899–1972)**
Donne, John (poet); London **(1573–1631)**
Donovan (Donovan Leitch) (singer, songwriter); Glasgow, Scotland, 2/10/46
Doolittle, James H. (ex-Air Force general); Alameda, Calif. **(1896–1993)**
Dorati, Antal (orchestra conductor); Budapest **(1906–1988)**
Dorris, Michael (anthropologist, writer); Louisville, Ky. **(1945–1997)**
Dorsey, Jimmy (band leader); Shenandoah, Pa. **(1904–1957)**
Dorsey, Thomas Andrew (father of gospel music); Villa Rice, Ga. **(1899–1993)**
Dorsey, Tommy (band leader); Mahanoy Plane, Pa. **(1905–1956)**
Dos Passos, John (author); Chicago **(1896–1970)**
Dostoevski, Fyodor Mikhailovich (novelist); Moscow **(1821–1881)**
Dotrice, Roy (actor); Guernsey, Channel Islands, England, 5/26/23
Douglas, Aaron (painter); Topeka, Kan. **(1900–1979)**
Douglas, Helen Gahagan (ex-Representative); Boonton, N.J. **(1900–1980)**
Douglas, Kirk (Issur Danielovitch) (actor); Amsterdam, N.Y., 12/9/16

Douglas, Melvyn (Melvyn Hesselberg) (actor); Macon, Ga. **(1901–1981)**
Douglas, Michael (actor, producer); New Brunswick, N.J., 9/25/44
Douglas, Mike (Michael D. Dowd, Jr.) (TV host); Chicago, 8/11/25
Douglas, Stephen Arnold (politician); Brandon, Vt. **(1813–1861)**
Douglass, Frederick (abolitionist, author, orator); Tuckahoe, Md. **(1817–1895)**
Dow, Charles (financier); Sterling, Conn. **(1851–1902)**
Down, Lesley-Anne (actress); London, England, 3/17/54
Downs, Hugh (broadcast journalist); Akron, Ohio, 2/14/21
Doyle, Sir Arthur Conan (novelist, spiritualist); Edinburgh, Scotland **(1859–1930)**
Doyle, David (actor); Lincoln, Neb., 12/1/29
Drake, Sir Francis (navigator); Tavistock, England **(1545–1596)**
Dreiser, Theodore (writer); Terre Haute, Ind. **(1871–1945)**
Dreyfus, Alfred (French army officer); Mulhouse, (France) **(1859–1935)**
Dreyfuss, Richard (actor); Brooklyn, N.Y., 10/29/47
Drury, Allen (novelist); Houston, 9/2/18
Dryden, John (poet); Northamptonshire, England **(1631–1700)**
Dryer, Fred (ex-NFL player, actor); Hawthorne, Calif., 7/6/46
Dubek, Alexander (ex-President of Czechoslovakia); Uhroved, former Czechoslovakia **(1921–1992)**
Dubinsky, David (David Dobnievski) (labor leader); Brest-Litovsk (Belarus) **(1892–1982)**
Du Bois, W(illiam) E(dward) B(urghardt) (scholar, activist); Great Barrington, Mass. **(1868–1963)**
Duchamp, Marcel (painter); Blainville, France **(1887–1968)**
Duchin, Eddy (pianist, bandleader); Cambridge, Mass. **(1909–1951)**
Duchin, Peter (pianist, band leader); New York City, 7/28/37
Duchovny, David (actor); New York City, 8/7/60
Dufay, Guillaume (composer); Cambrai, France **(c. 1400–1474)**
Duff, Howard (actor); Bremerton, Wash. **(1917–1990)**
Duffy, Julia (actress); Minneapolis, Minn., 6/27/50
Dufy, Raoul (painter); Le Havre, France **(1877–1953)**
Dukakis, Olympia (actress); Lowell, Mass., 6/20/31
Duke, James B. (industrialist); nr. Durham, N.C. **(1856–1925)**
Duke, Patty (Anna Marie Duke) (actress); New York City, 12/14/46
Dullea, Keir (actor); Cleveland, 5/30/36
Dulles, Allen Welsh (ex-Director of CIA); Watertown, N.Y. **(1893–1969)**
Dulles, John Foster (statesman); Washington, D.C. **(1888–1959)**
Dumas, Alexandre (called Dumas fils) (novelist); Paris **(1824–1895)**
Dumas, Alexandre (called Dumas père) (novelist); Villers-Cotterets, France **(1802–1870)**
du Maurier, Daphne (novelist); London **(1907–1989)**
du Maurier, George Louis Palmella Busson (novelist); Paris **(1834–1896)**
Dumont, Margaret (actress); Brooklyn, N.Y. **(1889–1965)**
Dunaway, Faye (actress); Bascom, Fla., 1/14/41
Dunbar, Paul Laurence (poet, novelist); Dayton, Ohio **(1872–1906)**
Duncan, Isadora (dancer); San Francisco **(1878–1927)**
Duncan, Sandy (actress); Henderson, Tex., 2/20/46
Dunham, Katherine (dancer, choreographer); Chicago, 1914
Dunne, Irene (actress); Louisville, Ky. **(1898–1990)**
Duns Scotus, John (theologian); Duns, Scotland **(1265–1303)**
Du Pont, Pierre S. (economist); Paris **(1739–1817)**
Durante, Jimmy (comedian); New York City **(1893–1980)**
Duras, Marguerite (Donnadieu) (novelist, dramatist); Gia Dinh (Vietnam) **(1914–1996)**
Durbin, Deanna (Edna Mae) (actress); Winnipeg, Canada, 12/4/22
Dürer, Albrecht (painter, engraver); Nürnberg(Germany) **(1471–1528)**
Durning, Charles (actor); Highland Falls, N.Y., 2/28/23
Durrell, Lawrence George (novelist); Julundur, India **(1912–1990)**
Duse, Eleonora (actress); Chioggia, Italy **(1859–1924)**
Dussault, Nancy (actress); Pensacola, Fla., 6/30/36
Duvall, Robert (actor, director, producer); San Diego, Calif., 1/5/31
Duvall, Shelley (actress); Houston, Tex., 1950
Dvořák, Antonin (composer); Nelahozeves (Czechoslovakia) **(1841–1904)**
Dylan, Bob (Robert Zimmerman) (folk singer, composer); Duluth, Minn., 5/24/41
Dysart, Richard (actor); Brighton, Mass., 3/30/29

E

Eakins, Thomas (painter, sculptor); Philadelphia **(1844–1916)**
Earhart, Amelia (aviator); Atchison, Kan. **(1898–1937)**
Earp, Wyatt Berry Stapp (sheriff, gunfighter); Monmouth, Ill. **(1848–1929)**
Eastman, George (inventor); Waterville, N.Y. **(1854–1932)**
Eastwood, Clint (actor, director, producer); San Francisco, 5/31/30
Ebert, Roger (film critic); Urbana, Ill., 6/18/42
Ebsen, Buddy (Christian Ebsen, Jr.) (actor); Belleville, Ill., 4/2/08
Eckstine, Billy (singer); Pittsburgh **(1914–1993)**
Eddy, Mary Baker (founder of Christian Science Church); Bow, N.H. **(1821–1910)**

Eddy, Nelson (baritone, actor); Providence, R.I. **(1901–1967)**
Edelman, Marian Wright (social activist); Bennettsville, S.C., 6/6/39
Eden, Sir Anthony (Earl of Avon) (ex-Prime Minister); Durham, England **(1897–1977)**
Eden, Barbara (actress); Tucson, Ariz., 8/23/34
Edison, Thomas Alva (inventor); Milan, Ohio **(1847–1931)**
Edwards, Anthony (actor); Santa Barbara, Calif., 7/19/62
Edwards, Blake (film writer, producer); Tulsa, Okla., 7/26/22
Edwards, Jonathan (theologian); East Windsor, Conn. **(1703–1758)**
Edwards, Ralph (TV and radio producer); Merino, Colo., 1913
Edwards, Vincent (Vincent Edward Zoino) (actor); Brooklyn, N.Y. **(1928–1996)**
Eglevsky, André (ballet dancer); Moscow **(1917–1977)**
Ehrlich, Paul (bacteriologist); Strzelin (Poland) **(1854–1915)**
Eichmann, (Karl) Adolf (Nazi, mass murderer); Solingen, Germany **(1906–1962)**
Eikenberry, Jill (actress); New Haven, Conn., 1/21/47
Einstein, Albert (physicist); Ulm, Germany **(1879–1955)**
Eisenhower, Milton S. (educator); Abilene, Kan. **(1899–1985)**
Eisenstaedt, Alfred (photographer, photojournalist); Dirschau (Prussia, now Tczew, Poland) **(1898–1995)**
Ekberg, Anita (actress); Malmö, Sweden, 9/29/31
Ekland, Britt (Britt-Marie) (actress); Stockholm, Sweden, 10/6/42
Elders, Joycelyn (Minnie Joycelyn Jones) (ex-U.S. Surgeon General); Schaal, Ark., 8/13/33
Elgar, Sir Edward (composer); Worcester, England **(1857–1934)**
Elgart, Larry (band leader); New London, Conn., 3/20/22
El Greco (Domenicos Theotocopoulos) (painter); Candia, Crete (Greece) **(c.1541–1614)**
Eliot, George (Mary Ann Evans) (novelist); Chilvers Coton, England **(1819–1880)**
Eliot, Thomas Stearns (poet); St. Louis **(1888–1965)**
Elizabeth I (Queen of England); Greenwich, England **(1533–1603)**
Elizabeth II (Queen of England); London, 4/21/26
Elizondo, Hector (actor); New York City, 12/22/36
Ellington, Duke (Edward Kennedy) (jazz musician); Washington, D.C. **(1899–1974)**
Elliot, "Mama" Cass (Ellen Naomi Cohen) (singer); Baltimore **(1941–1974)**
Elliott, Sam (actor); Sacramento, Calif., 8/9/44
Ellison, Ralph (novelist); Oklahoma City, Okla. **(1914–1994)**
Ellsberg, Daniel (activist); Chicago, 1931
Elman, Mischa (violinist); Stalnoye, Ukraine **(1891–1967)**
Emerson, Ralph Waldo (philosopher, poet); Boston **(1803–1882)**
Enesco, Georges (composer); Dorohoi, Romania **(1881–1955)**
Engels, Friedrich (Socialist writer); Barmen (Germany) **(1820–1895)**
Englund, Robert (actor); Glendale, Calif., 6/6/49
Entremont, Philippe (concert pianist); Rheims, France, 6/7/34
Ephron, Nora (writer, director); New York City, 5/19/41
Epicurus (philosopher); Samos (Greece) **(341–270 B.C.E.)**
Epstein, Sir Jacob (sculptor); New York City **(1880–1959)**
Erasmus, Desiderius (Gerhard Gerhards) (scholar); Rotterdam **(1469–1536)**
Erdrich, (Karen) Louise (writer); Little Falls, Minn., 7/6/54
Erickson, Leif (actor); Alameda, Calif. **(1911–1986)**
Erikson, Erik H. (psychoanalyst); Frankfurt, Germany **(1902–1994)**
Ernst, Max (painter); Bruhl, Germany **(1891–1976)**
Erté (Romain de Tirtoff) (artist, designer); St. Petersburg, Russia **(1892–1990)**
Euclid (mathematician); Megara (Greece), fl. 300 B.C.E.
Euler, Leonhard (mathematician); Basel, Switzerland **(1707–1783)**
Euripides (dramatist); Salamis (Greece) **(c.484–407 B.C.E.)**
Evans, Dale (Frances Butts) (actress, singer); Uvalde, Tex., 10/31/12
Evans, Dame Edith (actress); London **(1888–1976)**
Evans, Linda (actress); Hartford, Conn., 11/18/42
Evans, Maurice (actor); Dorchester, England **(1901–1989)**
Everett, Chad (Raymon Lee Cramton) (actor); South Bend, Ind., 6/11/36
Evers, Charles (civil rights leader); Decatur, Miss., 9/14/23?
Evers, Medgar (civil rights leader); Decatur, Miss. **(1925–1963)**
Evers-Williams, Myrlie (civil rights leader); Vicksburg, Miss., 3/17/33

F

Fabares, Shelley (actress); Santa Monica, Calif., 1/19/44
Fabian (Fabian Anthony Forte) (singer); Philadelphia, 2/6/43
Fabray, Nanette (Nanette Fabarés) (actress); San Diego, Calif., 10/27/22
Fadiman, Clifton (literary critic); Brooklyn, N.Y., 5/15/04
Fahrenheit, Gabriel (German physicist); Danzig (Poland) **(1686–1736)**
Fairbanks, Douglas (Douglas Ulman) (actor); Denver **(1883–1939)**
Fairbanks, Douglas, Jr. (actor); New York City, 12/9/09
Fairchild, Morgan (actress); Dallas, Tex., 2/3/50
Faith, Percy (conductor); Toronto **(1908–1976)**
Falk, Peter (actor); New York City, 9/16/27

Falla, Manuel de (composer); Cadiz, Spain **(1876–1946)**
Faludi, Susan (journalist, writer); New York City, 4/18/59
Falwell, Jerry (fundamentalist preacher); Lynchburg, Va., 8/11/33
Faraday, Michael (physicist); Newington, England **(1791–1867)**
Farentino, James (actor); Brooklyn, N.Y., 2/24/38
Farmer, Frances (actress); Seattle, Wash. **(1913–1970)**
Farmer, James (civil rights leader); Marshall, Tex., 1/12/20
Farr, Jamie (actor); Toledo, Ohio, 7/1/34
Farrar, Geraldine (soprano, actress); Melrose, Mass. **(1882–1967)**
Farrell, Eileen (operatic soprano); Willimantic, Conn., 2/13/20
Farrell, James T. (novelist); Chicago **(1904–1979)**
Farrell, Mike (actor); St. Paul, Minn., 2/6/39
Farrell, Suzanne (Roberta Sue Ficker) (ballerina); Cincinnati, 8/16/45
Farrow, Mia (actress); Los Angeles, 2/9/46
Fasanella, Ralph (painter); New York City, 9/2/14
Fassbinder, Rainer Werner (film, stage director); Bad Wörishofen, (Germany **(1946–1982)**
Fast, Howard (novelist); New York City, 11/11/14
Faubus, Orval E(ugene) (governor of Arkansas); Combs, Ark. **(1910–1994)**
Faulkner, William (novelist); New Albany, Miss. **(1897–1962)**
Fauré, Gabriel Urbain (composer); Pamiers, France **(1845–1924)**
Fawcett, Farrah (Mary Farrah Leni Fawcett) (actress); Corpus Christi, Tex., 2/2/47
Faye, Alice (Ann Leppert) (actress); New York City, 5/5/12
Feiffer, Jules (cartoonist); New York City, 1/26/29
Feininger, Lyonel (painter); New York City **(1871–1956)**
Feldman, Marty (actor, screenwriter, director); London **(1938–1982)**
Feldon, Barbara (actress); Pittsburgh, 3/12/41
Feliciano, José (singer); Larez, Puerto Rico, 9/10/45
Felker, Clay S. (editor, publisher); St. Louis, 10/2/25?
Fell, Norman (actor); Philadelphia, 3/24/23
Fellini, Federico (film director); Rimini, Italy **(1920–1993)**
Fender, Freddie (Baldemar Huerta) (singer); San Benito, Tex., 1937
Ferber, Edna (novelist); Kalamazoo, Mich. **(1885–1968)**
Ferguson, Maynard (jazz trumpeter); Verdun, Quebec, Canada, 5/4/28
Ferlinghetti, Lawrence (poet, writer, translator); Yonkers, N.Y., 3/24/19
Fermi, Enrico (atomic physicist); Rome **(1901–1954)**
Fernandel (Fernand Joseph Desire Contandin) (actor); Marseilles, France **(1903–1971)**
Ferraro, Geraldine Anne (political figure); New York City, 8/26/35
Ferrer, José (actor, director); Santurce, Puerto Rico **(1912–1992)**
Ferrer, Mel (actor); Elberon, N.J., 8/25/17
Fetchit, Stepin (Lincoln Theodore Perry) (comedian); Key West, Fla. **(1902–1985)**
Fiedler, Arthur (conductor); Boston **(1894–1979)**
Field, Eugene (poet); St. Louis **(1850–1895)**
Field, Marshall (merchant); nr. Conway, Mass. **(1834–1906)**
Field, Sally (actress); Pasadena, Calif., 11/6/46
Fielding, Henry (novelist); nr. Glastonbury, England **(1707–1754)**
Fields, Gracie (comedienne); Rochdale, England **(1898–1979)**
Fields, Totie (comedienne); Hartford, Conn. **(1931–1978)**
Fields, W. C. (William Claude Dukenfield) (comedian); Philadelphia **(1880–1946)**
Fiennes, Ralph (actor); Suffolk, England, 12/22/62
Fierstein, Harvey (Forbes) (playwright, actor); Brooklyn, 6/6/54
Filene, Edward A. (merchant); **(1860–1937)**
Finch, Peter (actor); Kensington, England **(1916–1977)**
Finney, Albert (actor); Salford, England, 5/9/36
Firkusny, Rudolf (pianist); Napajedla, former Czechoslovakia **(1912–1994)**
Fischer-Dieskau, Dietrich (baritone); Berlin, 5/28/25
Fishburne, Laurence (actor); Augusta, Ga., 7/30/61
Fisher, Carrie (actress); Los Angeles, 10/21/56
Fisher, Eddie (Edwin) (singer); Philadelphia, 8/10/28
Fitzgerald, Barry (William Joseph Shields) (actor); Dublin **(1888–1961)**
Fitzgerald, Ella (singer); Newport News, Va. **(1918–1996)**
Fitzgerald, F. Scott (Francis Scott Key) (novelist); St. Paul, Minn. **(1896–1940)**
Fitzgerald, Geraldine (actress); Dublin, 11/24/14
Fitzgerald, Pegeen (radio broadcaster); Norcatur, Kan. **(1910–1989)**
Flack, Roberta (singer); Black Mountain, N.C., 2/10/40
Flagstad, Kirsten (Wagnerian soprano); Hamar, Norway **(1895–1962)**
Flatt, Lester Raymond (bluegrass musician); Overton County, Tenn. **(1914–1979)**
Flaubert, Gustave (novelist); Rouen, France **(1821–1880)**
Fleming, Sir Alexander (bacteriologist); Lochfield, Scotland **(1881–1955)**
Fleming, Rhonda (Marilyn Louis) (actress); Los Angeles, 8/10/23
Fletcher, John (dramatist); Rye, Sussex, England **(1579–1625)**
Flynn, Errol (actor); Hobart, Tasmania **(1909–1959)**
Fodor, Eugene (violinist); Turkey Creek, Colo., 3/5/50
Fokine, Michel (dancer, choreographer); St. Petersburg, Russia **(1880–1942)**
Fonda, Henry (actor); Grand Island, Neb. **(1905–1982)**
Fonda, Jane (actress); New York City, 12/21/37

Fonda, Peter (actor); New York City, 2/23/39
Fontaine, Frank (singer, comedian); Cambridge, Mass. **(1920–1979)**
Fontaine, Joan (Joan de Havilland) (actress); Tokyo, 10/22/17
Fontanne, Lynn (actress); London **(1887–1983)**
Fonteyn, Dame Margot (Margaret Hookham) (ballerina); Reigate, England **(1919–1991)**
Foote, Shelby (historian); Greenville, Miss., 11/17/16
Forbes, Malcolm S(tevenson) (publisher, sportsman); Brooklyn, N.Y. **(1919–1990)**
Ford, Glenn (Gwyllyn Ford) (actor); Quebec, 5/1/16
Ford, Harrison (actor); Chicago, 7/13/42
Ford, Henry, (industrialist); Greenfield, Mich. **(1863–1947)**
Ford, John (film director); Cape Elizabeth, Me. **(1895–1973)**
Ford, Tennessee Ernie (Ernie Jennings Ford) (singer); Bristol, Tenn. **(1919–1991)**
Forrester, Maureen (contralto); Montreal, 7/25/30
Forsythe, John (actor); Penn's Grove, N.J., 1/29/18
Fosdick, Harry Emerson (clergyman); Buffalo, N.Y. **(1878–1968)**
Fosse, Bob (Robert Louis) (choreographer, director); Chicago **(1927–1987)**
Foster, Jodie (Alicia Christian Foster) (actress, director, producer); Los Angeles, 11/19/62
Foster, Stephen Collins (composer); nr. Pittsburgh **(1826–1864)**
Fox, Michael J. (actor, producer); Edmonton, Alta., Canada, 6/9/61
Foxx, Redd (John Elroy Sanford) (actor, comedian); St. Louis **(1922–1991)**
Foy, Eddie, Jr. (dancer, actor); New Rochelle, N.Y. **(1905–1983)**
Fracci, Carla (ballerina); Milan, Italy, 8/20/36
Fragonard, Jean Honoré (painter); Grasse, France **(1732–1806)**
Frampton, Peter (rock musician); Beckenham, England, 4/20/50
France, Anatole (Jacques Anatole François Thibault) (author); Paris **(1844–1924)**
Francescatti, Zino (violinist); Marseilles, France **(1902–1991)**
Franciosa, Anthony (Anthony Papaleo) (actor); New York City, 10/25/28
Francis, Anne (actress); Ossining, N.Y., 7/16/30
Francis, Arlene (Arlene Francis Kazanjian) (actress); Boston, 10/20/08
Francis, Connie (Concetta Franconero) (singer); Newark, N.J., 12/12/38
Francis, Genie (actress); Englewood, N.J., 5/26/62
Francis of Assisi, Saint (Giovanni Francesco Barnardone) (founder of Franciscans); Assisi, Italy **(1182–1226)**
Franck, César Auguste (composer); Liège (Belgium) **(1822–1890)**
Franco Bahamonde, Francisco (Chief of State); El Ferrol, Spain **(1892–1975)**
Frankenthaler, Helen (artist); New York City, 12/12/28
Franklin, Aretha (singer); Memphis, Tenn., 3/25/42
Franklin, Benjamin (statesman, scientist); Boston **(1706–1790)**
Franklin, Bonnie (actress); Santa Monica, Calif., 1/6/44
Franklin, John Hope (historian); Rentiesville, Okla., 1/2/15
Frann, Mary (actress); St. Louis, Mo., 2/27/43
Franz, Dennis (Dennis Schlachta) (actor); Chicago, 10/28/44
Frazer, Sir James George (anthropologist); Glasgow, Scotland **(1854–1941)**
Freeman, Morgan (actor); Memphis, Tenn., 6/1/37
Freud, Sigmund (psychoanalyst); Moravia, Czech Repubic **(1856–1939)**
Frey, Glenn (musician); Detroit, Mich., 11/6/48
Frick, Henry Clay (industrialist); Westmoreland Co., Pa. **(1849–1919)**
Friedan, Betty (Betty Naomi Goldstein) (feminist); Peoria, Ill., 2/4/21
Fromm, Erich (psychoanalyst); Frankfurt-am-Main, Germany **(1900–1980)**
Frost, David (TV entertainer); Tenterden, England, 4/7/39
Frost, Robert Lee (poet); San Francisco **(1874–1963)**
Fry, Christopher (playwright); Bristol, England, 12/18/07
Fugard, Athol (playwright); Middleburg, South Africa, 6/11/32
Fulbright, J. William (politician); Sumner, Mo. **(1905–1995)**
Fuller, Charles (playwright); Philadelphia, 3/5/39
Fuller, R(ichard) Buckminster (Jr.) (architect, educator); Milton, Mass. **(1895–1983)**
Fulton, Robert (inventor); Lancaster County, Pa. **(1765–1815)**
Funicello, Annette (actress); Utica, N.Y., 10/22/42
Funt, Allen (TV producer); Brooklyn, N.Y., 9/16/14

G

Gabin, Jean (actor); Paris **(1904–1976)**
Gable, (William) Clark (actor); Cadiz, Ohio **(1901–1960)**
Gabo, Naum (sculptor); Briansk, Russia **(1890–1977)**
Gabor, Eva (actress); Budapest **(1920–1995)**
Gabor, Zsa Zsa (Sari) (actress); Budapest, 2/6/17
Gabrieli, Giovanni (composer); Venice **(c.1557–1612)**
Gaddis, William (novelist); New York City, 1922
Gainsborough, Thomas (painter); Sudbury, Suffolk, England **(1727–1788)**

Galbraith, John Kenneth (economist); Iona Station, Ontario, Canada, 10/15/08
Galilei, Galileo (astronomer, physicist); Pisa, Italy **(1564–1642)**
Gallico, Paul (novelist); New York City **(1897–1976)**
Gallup, George H. (poll taker); Jefferson, Iowa **(1901–1984)**
Galsworthy, John (novelist, dramatist); Coombe, England **(1867–1933)**
Galway, James (flutist); Belfast, Northern Ireland, 12/8/39
Gambling, John A. (radio broadcaster); New York City, 1930
Gandhi, Indira (Indira Nehru) (Prime Minister); Allahabad, India **(1917–1984)**
Gandhi, Mohandas Karamchand (called Mahatma Gandhi) (Hindu leader); Porbandar, India **(1869–1948)**
Gannett, Frank E. (editor, publisher) **(1876–1957)**
Garagiola, Joe (Joseph Henry) (sportscaster); St. Louis, 2/12/26
Garbo, Greta (Greta Gustafsson) (actress); Stockholm **(1905–1990)**
Garcia, Jerry (rock musician); San Francisco **(1942–1995)**
Garcia Lorca, Frederico (poet, dramatist); Fuente Vaqueros, Spain **(1898–1936)**
Garden, Mary (soprano); Aberdeen, Scotland **(1874–1967)**
Gardenia, Vincent (actor); Naples, Italy **(1922–1992)**
Gardner, Ava (actress); Smithfield, N.C. **(1922–1990)**
Gardner, Erle Stanley (novelist); Malden, Mass. **(1889–1970)**
Garfield, John (Jules Garfinkle) (actor); New York City **(1913–1952)**
Garfunkel, Art (Arthur) (singer); Newark, N.J., 11/5/41
Garibaldi, Giuseppe (Italian nationalist leader); Nice, France **(1807–1882)**
Garland, Judy (Frances Gumm) (actress, singer); Grand Rapids, Minn. **(1922–1969)**
Garner, Erroll (jazz pianist); Pittsburgh **(1921–1977)**
Garner, James (James Bumgarner) (actor); Norman, Okla., 4/7/28
Garner, Peggy Ann (actress); Canton, Ohio **(1932–1984)**
Garr, Teri (actress); Lakewood, Ohio, 12/11/49
Garrison, William Lloyd (abolitionist); Newburyport, Mass. **(1805–1879)**
Garroway, Dave (TV host); Schenectady, N.Y. **(1913–1982)**
Garson, Greer (actress); County Down, Northern Ireland **(1903–1996)**
Garvey, Marcus Moziah (black nationalist leader); Jamaica **(1887–1940)**
Gassman, Vittorio (film actor, director); Genoa, Italy, 9/1/22
Gates, Bill (William Henry III) (software pioneer); Seattle, Wash., 10/28/55
Gates, Henry Louis, Jr. (scholar); Keyser, W. Va., 9/16/50
Gaudí, Antonio (architect); Reus, Spain **(1852–1926)**
Gauguin, Eugène Henri Paul (painter); Paris **(1848–1903)**
Gautama Buddha (Prince Siddhartha) (philosopher); Kapilavastu (India) **(c. 563–c. 483 B.C.E.)**
Gavin, John (actor, diplomat); Los Angeles, 4/8/35
Gaye, Marvin (singer); Washington, D.C. **(1939–1984)**
Gayle, Crystal (Brenda Gayle Webb) (singer); Paintsville, Ky., 1/9/51
Gaynor, Janet (actress); Philadelphia **(1906–1984)**
Gaynor, Mitzi (Francesca Mitzi Marlene de Czanyi von Gerber) (actress); Chicago, 9/4/31
Gazzara, Ben (Biago Anthony Gazzara) (actor); New York City, 8/28/30
Gedda, Nicolai (tenor); Stockholm, Sweden, 7/11/25
Geddes, Barbara Bel (actress); New York City, 10/31/22
Genet, Jean (playwright); Paris **(1910–1986)**
Genghis Khan (Temujin) (conqueror); nr. Lake Baikal, Russia **(1162–1227)**
Gentry, Bobbie (Roberta Streeter) (singer); Chickasaw Co., Miss., 7/27/44
George, David Lloyd (statesman); Manchester, England **(1863–1945)**
George, Henry (economist, reformer); Philadelphia **(1839–1897)**
Gere, Richard (actor); Philadelphia, 8/29/49
Gericault, Jean Louis (painter); Rouen, France **(1791–1824)**
Geronimo (Goyathlay) (Apache chieftain); Arizona **(1829–1909)**
Gershwin, George (composer); Brooklyn, N.Y. **(1898–1937)**
Gershwin, Ira (lyricist); New York City **(1896–1983)**
Getty, J. Paul (oil executive); Minneapolis **(1892–1976)**
Getz, Stan (saxophonist); Philadelphia **(1927–1991)**
Ghiberti, Lorenzo (goldsmith, sculptor); Florence **(1378–1455)**
Ghostley, Alice (actress); Eve, Mo., 8/14/26
Giacometti, Alberto (sculptor); Switzerland **(1901–1966)**
Giannini, Giancarlo (actor); La Spezia, Italy, 8/1/42
Gibbon, Edward (historian); Putney, England **(1737–1794)**
Gibson, Charles Dana (illustrator); Roxbury, Mass. **(1867–1944)**
Gibson, Henry (actor, comedian); Germantown, Pa., 9/21/35
Gibson, Mel (actor, director, producer); Peekskill, N.Y., 1/3/56
Gide, André (author); Paris **(1869–1951)**
Gielgud, Sir John (actor); London, 4/14/04
Gifford, Kathie Lee Epstein (talk show host); Paris, 8/16/53
Gilbert, Melissa (actress); Los Angeles, 5/8/64
Gilbert, Sir William Schwenck (librettist); London **(1836–1911)**
Gilels, Emil (concert pianist); Odessa, Ukraine **(1916–1985)**
Gillespie, Dizzy (John Birks Gillespie) (jazz trumpeter); Cheraw, S.C. **(1917–1993)**
Gilligan, Carol (Friedman) (psychologist); New York City, 11/28/36
Gimbel, Bernard F. (merchant); Vincennes, Ind. **(1885–1966)**

Gingold, Hermione (actress, comedienne); London **(1897–1987)**
Gingrich, Newt (politician); Harrisburg, Pa., 6/17/43
Ginsberg, Allen (poet); Newark, N.J. **(1926–1997)**
Giordano, Luca (painter); Naples, Italy **(1632–1705)**
Giorgione (painter); Castelfranco,(Italy) **(c.1477–1510)**
Giotto di Bondone (painter); Vespignamo (Italy) **(c.1266–1337)**
Giovanni, Nikki (poet); Knoxville, Tenn., 6/7/43
Giroud, Françoise (French government official); Geneva, 9/21/16
Gish, Dorothy (actress); Massillon, Ohio **(1898–1968)**
Gish, Lillian (Lillian de Guiche) (actress); Springfield, Ohio **(1893–1993)**
Givenchy, Hubert (fashion designer); Beauvais, France, 2/21/27
Gladstone, William Ewart (statesman); Liverpool, England **(1809–1898)**
Glaser, Paul Michael (actor, director); Cambridge, Mass., 3/25/43
Glass, Philip (composer); Baltimore, 1/31/37
Gleason, Jackie (comedian); Brooklyn, N.Y. **(1916–1987)**
Gless, Sharon (actress); Los Angeles, 5/31/43
Glover, Danny (actor); San Francisco, 7/22/47
Gluck, Christoph Willibald (composer); Erasbach(Germany) **(1714–1787)**
Gobel, George (comedian); Chicago **(1920–1991)**
Godard, Jean Luc (film director); Paris, 12/3/30
Goddard, Paulette (Marion Levy) (actress); Great Neck, N.Y. **(1911–1990)**
Goddard, Robert Hutchings (father of modern rocketry); Worcester, Mass. **(1882–1945)**
Godfrey, Arthur (entertainer); New York City **(1903–1983)**
Goebbels, Joseph Paul (Nazi leader); Rheydt, Germany **(1897–1945)**
Goering, Hermann (Nazi leader); Rosenheim, Germany **(1893–1946)**
Goethals, George Washington (engineer); Brooklyn, N.Y. **(1858–1928)**
Goethe, Johann Wolfgang von (poet, playwright, novelist); Frankfurt-am-Main, Germany **(1749–1832)**
Gogol, Nikolai Vasilievich (novelist); nr. Mirgorod, Ukraine **(1809–1852)**
Goldberg, Rube (cartoonist); San Francisco **(1883–1970)**
Goldberg, Whoopi (Caryn Johnson) (actress); New York City, 11/13/49
Goldblum, Jeff (actor); Pittsburgh, 10/22/52
Golden, Harry (Harry Goldhurst) (author); New York City **(1902–1981)**
Goldman, Emma (anarchist); Kovno, Lithuania **(1869–1940)**
Goldsmith, Oliver (dramatist, poet); County Longford, Ireland **(1728–1774)**
Goldwyn, Samuel (Samuel Goldfish) (film producer); Warsaw **(1882–1974)**
Gompers, Samuel (labor leader); London **(1850–1924)**
Goodall, Jane (Baroness van Lawick-Goodall) (ethologist); London, 4/3/34
Goodman, Benny (clarinetist); Chicago **(1909–1986)**
Goodwin, Doris (Helen) Kearns (historian); Rockville Center, N.Y., 1/4/43
Goodyear, Charles (inventor); New Haven, Conn. **(1800–1860)**
Gorbachev, Mikhail Sergeyevich (Soviet leader); Privolnoye, (Russia), 3/2/31
Gordimer, Nadine (novelist, short-story writer); Springs, South Africa, 12/20/23
Gordon, Dexter (jazz musician); Los Angeles **(1923–1990)**
Gordon, Ruth (actress); Wollaston, Mass. **(1896–1985)**
Gordy, Berry, Jr. (record company executive); Detroit, Mich., 11/28/29
Goren, Charles H. (bridge expert); Philadelphia **(1901–1991)**
Gorey, Edward (St. John) (illustrator, author); Chicago, 2/22/25
Gorki, Maxim (Alexei Maximovich Peshkov) (author); Nizhni Novgorod, Russia **(1868–1936)**
Gorky, Arshile (painter); Armenia **(1904–1948)**
Gormé, Eydie (singer); Bronx, N.Y., 8/16/32
Gorshin, Frank (actor); Pittsburgh, 4/5/34
Gossett, Louis, Jr. (actor); Brooklyn, N.Y., 5/27/36
Gottschalk, Louis Moreau (pianist, composer); New Orleans, La. **(1829–1869)**
Gould, Chester (cartoonist); Pawnee, Okla. **(1900–1985)**
Gould, Elliott (Elliott Goldstein) (actor); Brooklyn, N.Y., 8/29/38
Gould, Glenn (concert pianist); Toronto **(1932–1982)**
Gould, Morton (composer); Richmond Hill, Queens, N.Y. **(1913–1996)**
Gould, Stephen Jay (paleontologist, science writer); New York City, 9/10/41
Goulet, Robert (singer); Lawrence, Mass., 11/26/33
Gounod, Charles François (composer); Paris **(1818–1893)**
Goya y Lucientes, Francisco José de (painter); Fuendetodos, Spain **(1746–1828)**
Grable, Betty (actress); St. Louis **(1916–1973)**
Grace, Princess of Monaco (Grace Kelly) (ex-actress); Philadelphia **(1929–1982)**
Graham, Bill (Wolfgang Grajonca) (rock impresario); Berlin **(1930–1991)**
Graham, Billy (William F.) (evangelist); Charlotte, N.C., 11/7/18
Graham, Katharine Meyer (newspaper publisher); New York City, 6/16/17
Graham, Martha (choreographer); Pittsburgh **(1894–1991)**
Grahame, Gloria (Gloria Hallwood) (actress); Los Angeles **(1929–1981)**

Grainger, Percy Aldridge (pianist, composer); Melbourne, Australia **(1882–1961)**
Gramm, Donald (Grambach) (bass-baritone); Milwaukee **(1927–1983)**
Grammer, Kelsey (actor); St. Thomas, V.I., 2/21/55
Granger, Stewart (James Stewart) (actor); London **(1913–1993)**
Grant, Cary (Alexander Archibald Leach) (actor); Bristol, England **(1904–1986)**
Grant, Lee (Lyova Haskell Rosenthal) (actress); New York City, 10/31/30
Grass, Günter (novelist); Danzig, (Poland), 10/16/27
Graves, Nancy (Stevenson) (artist); Pittsfield, Mass. **(1940–1996)**
Graves, Peter (Peter Arness) (actor); Minneapolis, 3/18/26
Graves, Robert (writer); London **(1895–1985)**
Gray, Linda (actress); Santa Monica, Calif., 9/12/40
Gray, Thomas (poet); London **(1716–1771)**
Greco, José (dancer); Montorio nei Frentani, Italy, 12/23/18
Greeley, Horace (journalist, politician); Amherst, N.H. **(1811–1872)**
Green, Adolph (actor, lyricist); New York City, 12/2/15
Green, Al (singer); Forrest City, Ark., 4/13/46
Greene, Graham (novelist); Berkhamsted, England **(1904–1991)**
Greene, Lorne (actor); Ottawa **(1915–1987)**
Greene, Shecky (comedian, actor); Chicago, 4/8/25
Greenstreet, Sydney (actor); Sandwich, England **(1879–1954)**
Greer, Germaine (feminist); Melbourne, 1/29/39
Gregory, Cynthia (ballerina); Los Angeles, 7/8/46
Gregory, Dick (comedian); St. Louis, 1932
Gregory, Lady (Isabella) Augusta (playwright); Roxborough, Ireland **(1852–1932)**
Greuze, Jean-Baptiste (painter); Tournus, France **(1725–1805)**
Grey, Joel (Joel Katz) (actor); Cleveland, 4/11/32
Grey, Zane (author); Zanesville, Ohio **(1875–1939)**
Grieg, Edvard Hagerup (composer); Bergen, Norway **(1843–1907)**
Griffin, Merv (TV host, producer); San Mateo, Calif., 7/6/25
Griffith, Andy (actor); Mount Airy, N.C., 6/1/26
Griffith, David Lewelyn Wark (film producer); La Grange, Ky. **(1875–1948)**
Griffith, Melanie (actress); New York City, 8/9/57
Grigorovich, Yuri (choreographer); Leningrad, 1/1/27
Grimes, Tammy (actress); Lynn, Mass., 1/30/34
Grimm, Jacob (author of fairy tales); Hanau (Germany) **(1785–1863)**
Grimm, Wilhelm (author of fairy tales); Hanau (Germany) **(1786–1859)**
Gris, Juan (José Victoriano González) (painter); Madrid **(1887–1927)**
Grisham, John (attorney, author); Jonesboro, Ark., 2/8/55
Grodin, Charles (actor); Pittsburgh, 4/21/35
Gromyko, Andrei A. (diplomat); Starye Gromyki, Russia **(1909–1989)**
Gropius, Walter (architect); Berlin **(1883–1969)**
Gropper, William (painter, illustrator); New York City **(1897–1977)**
Gross, Michael (actor); Chicago, 6/21/47
Grosz, George (painter); Germany **(1893–1959)**
Grünewald, Matthias (Mathis Gothart Nithart) (painter); Würzburg, Germany **(c.1470–1528)**
Guggenheim, Meyer (capitalist); Langnau, Switzerland **(1828–1905)**
Guillaume, Robert (actor); St. Louis, Mo., 11/30/27
Guinness, Sir Alec (actor); London, 4/2/14
Guitry, Sacha (Alexandre) (actor, film director); St. Petersburg, Russia **(1885–1957)**
Gumbel, Bryant Charles (TV newscaster); New Orleans, 9/29/48
Gunther, John (author); Chicago **(1901–1970)**
Gutenberg, Johannes (printer); Mainz (Germany) **(c. 1397–1468)**
Guthrie, Arlo (singer); New York City, 7/10/47
Guthrie, Woody (folk singer, composer); Okemah, Okla. **(1912–1967)**
Gwenn, Edmund (actor); London **(1875–1959)**
Gwynne, Fred (actor); New York City **(1926–1993)**

H

Hackett, Bobby (trumpeter); Providence, R.I. **(1915–1976)**
Hackett, Buddy (Leonard Hacker) (comedian, actor); Brooklyn, N.Y., 8/31/24
Hackman, Gene (actor); San Bernardino, Calif., 1/30/31
Hagen, Uta (actress); Göttingen, Germany, 6/12/19
Haggard, Merle (songwriter); Bakersfield, Calif., 4/6/37
Hagman, Larry (Larry Hageman) (actor); Weatherford, Tex., 9/21/31
Haig, Alexander Meigs, Jr. (ex-Secretary of State, ex-general); Bala-Cynwyd, Pa., 12/2/24
Haile Selassie (Ras Tafari Makonnen) (ex-Emperor); Ethiopia **(1892–1975)**
Hailey, Arthur (novelist); Luton, England, 4/5/20
Halberstam, David (journalist); New York City, 4/10/34
Hale, Alan (actor, director); Washington, D.C. **(1892–1950)**
Hale, Barbara (actress); DeKalb, Ill., 4/18/21
Hale, Edward Everett (clergyman, author); Boston **(1822–1909)**
Hale, Nathan (American Revolutionary officer); Coventry, Conn. **(1755–1776)**
Halevi, Judah (Jewish poet); Toledo, Spain **(1085–1140)**

Haley, Alex (writer); Ithaca, N.Y. **(1921–1992)**
Haley, Jack (actor); Boston **(1899–1979)**
Hall, Arsenio (comedian, talk show host); Cleveland, Ohio, 2/12/58
Hall, Donald (Andrew, Jr.) (poet); New Haven, Conn., 9/20/28
Hall, Huntz (actor); New York City, 8/15/19
Hall, Monty (TV personality); Winnipeg, Canada, 8/25/23
Halley, Edmund (astronomer); London **(1656–1742)**
Hals, Frans (painter); Antwerp(Netherlands) **(c. 1580–1666)**
Halsey, William Frederick, Jr. (naval officer); Elizabeth, N.J. **(1882–1959)**
Hamel, Veronica (actress); Philadelphia, 11/20/43
Hamill, Pete (journalist); Brooklyn, N.Y., 6/24/35
Hamilton, Alexander (statesman); Nevis, British West Indies **(1755–1804)**
Hamilton, Alice (physician, reformer); New York City **(1869–1970)**
Hamilton, Edith (scholar); Dresden, Germany **(1867–1963)**
Hamilton, George (actor); Memphis, Tenn., 8/12/39
Hamilton, Margaret (actress); Cleveland **(1902–1985)**
Hamlin, Harry (actor); Pasadena, Calif., 10/30/51
Hamlisch, Marvin (composer, pianist); New York City, 6/2/44
Hammarskjöld, Dag (U.N. Secretary-General); Jönköping, Sweden **(1905–1961)**
Hammerstein, Oscar, II (librettist, stage producer); New York City **(1895–1960)**
Hampton, Lionel (vibraharpist, band leader); Birmingham, Ala., 4/12/13
Hamsun, Knut (Knut Pedersen) (novelist); Lom, Norway **(1859–1952)**
Hancock, Herbie (jazz musician); Chicago, 4/12/40
Hancock, John (statesman); Braintree, Mass. **(1737–1793)**
Hand, Learned (jurist); Albany, N.Y. **(1872–1961)**
Handel, George Frederick (Georg Friedrich Händel) (composer); Halle (Germany) **(1685–1759)**
Handy, William Christopher (blues composer); Florence, Ala. **(1873–1958)**
Hanks, Tom (actor, director, writer); Concord, Calif., 7/9/56
Hannah, Daryl (actress); Chicago, 12/19/60
Hannibal (Carthaginian general); North Africa **(247–182 B.C.E.)**
Hansberry, Lorraine (playwright); Chicago **(1930–1965)**
Hanson, Howard (conductor); Wahoo, Neb. **(1896–1981)**
Harburg, E. Y. "Yip" (songwriter); New York City **(1896–1981)**
Hardwicke, Sir Cedric (actor); Stourbridge, England **(1893–1964)**
Hardy, Oliver (comedian); Atlanta **(1892–1957)**
Hardy, Thomas (novelist); Dorsetshire, England **(1840–1928)**
Harkness, Edward S. (business executive); Cleveland **(1874–1940)**
Harlow, Jean (Harlean Carpentier) (actress); Kansas City, Mo. **(1911–1937)**
Harnick, Sheldon (lyricist); Chicago, 4/30/24
Harper, Valerie (actress); Suffern, N.Y., 8/22/40
Harrell, Lynn (cellist); New York City, 1/30/44
Harrelson, Woody (actor); Midland, Tex., 7/23/61
Harriman, W. (William) Averell (ex-Governor of New York); New York City **(1891–1986)**
Harrington, Pat., Jr. (actor, comedian); New York City, 8/13/29
Harris, Barbara (Sandra Markowitz) (actress); Evanston, Ill., 7/25/35
Harris, Emmylou (singer); Birmingham, Ala., 4/2/47
Harris, Julie (actress); Grosse Pointe Park, Mich., 12/2/25
Harris, Phil (actor, band leader); Linton, Ind. **(1906–1995)**
Harris, Richard (actor); Limerick, Ireland, 10/1/33
Harris, Rosemary (actress); Ashby, England, 9/19/30
Harris, Roy (composer); Lincoln County, Okla. **(1898–1979)**
Harrison, George (singer, songwriter); Liverpool, England, 2/25/43
Harrison, Gregory (actor); Avalon, Catalina Island, Calif., 5/31/50
Harrison, Sir Rex (Reginald Carey) (actor); Huyton, England **(1908–1990)**
Hart, Lorenz (lyricist); New York **(1895–1943)**
Hart, Mary (Mary Johanna Harum) (host); Sioux Falls, S.D., 11/8/51
Hart, Moss (playwright); New York City **(1904–1961)**
Hart, William S. (actor); Newburgh, N.Y. **(1862–1946)**
Harte, Bret (Francis Brett Harte) (author); Albany, N.Y. **(1836–1902)**
Hartford, Huntington (George Huntington Hartford II) (A&P. heir); New York City, 4/18/11
Hartford, John (singer, banjoist); New York City, 12/30/37
Hartley, Mariette (actress); New York City, 6/21/40
Hartman, David Downs (TV newscaster); Pawtucket, R.I., 5/19/35
Hartman Black, Lisa (actress); Houston, Tex., 6/1/56
Harvey, Laurence (Larushka Skikne) (actor); Joniskis, Lithuania **(1928–1973)**
Harvey, William (physician); Folkestone, England **(1578–1657)**
Hasselhoff, David (actor, producer); Baltimore, Md., 7/17/52
Hatcher, Teri (actress); Sunnyvale, Calif., 12/8/64
Havel, Vaclav (political leader, dramatist, poet); Prague, 10/5/36
Havoc, June (June Hovick) (actress); Seattle, 11/8/16
Hawking, Stephen (physicist, astronomer); Oxford, England, 1/8/42
Hawkins, Coleman (jazz musician); St. Joseph, Mo. **(1904–1969)**
Hawkins, Jack (actor); London **(1910–1973)**
Hawn, Goldie (actress, producer); Washington, D.C., 11/21/45
Haworth, Jill (actress); Sussex, England, 1945

Hawthorne, Nathaniel (novelist); Salem, Mass. **(1804–1864)**
Hay, John Milton (statesman); Salem, Ind. **(1838–1905)**
Hayakawa, Sessue (actor); Honshu, Japan **(1890–1973)**
Hayden, Melissa (ballerina); Toronto, 4/25/23
Hayden, Sterling (Sterling Relyea Walter) (actor, writer); Montclair, N.J. **(1916–1986)**
Haydn, Franz Joseph (composer); Rohrau (Austria) **(1732–1809)**
Hayes, Helen (Helen Hayes Brown) (actress); Washington, D.C. **(1900–1993)**
Hayes, Isaac (composer); Covington, Tenn., 8/20/42
Hayes, Peter Lind (comedian, singer); San Francisco, 6/25/15
Hayward, Leland (producer); Nebraska City, Neb. **(1902–1971)**
Hayward, Susan (Edythe Marrener) (actress); Brooklyn, N.Y. **(1919–1975)**
Hayworth, Rita (Margarita Cansino) (actress); New York City **(1918–1987)**
Head, Edith (costume designer); Los Angeles **(1907–1981)**
Heaney, Seamus (poet); Londonderry, Northern Ireland, 4/13/39
Hearst, William Randolph (publisher); San Francisco **(1863–1951)**
Hearst, William Randolph, Jr. (publisher); New York City **(1908–1993)**
Heatherton, Joey (actress); Rockville Centre, N.Y., 9/14/44
Hecht, Ben (author); New York City **(1894–1964)**
Heckart, Eileen (actress); Columbus, Ohio, 3/29/19
Heflin, Van (Emmet Evan Heflin) (actor); Walters, Okla. **(1910–1971)**
Hefner, Hugh (publisher); Chicago, 4/9/26
Hegel, Georg Wilhelm Friedrich (philosopher); Stuttgart (Germany) **(1770–1831)**
Heidegger, Martin (existentialist philosopher); Messkirch, Germany **(1889–1976)**
Heifetz, Jascha (concert violinist); Vilna, Russia **(1901–1987)**
Heine, Heinrich (Harry) (poet); Düsseldorf, Germany **(1797–1856)**
Heinemann, Gustav (ex-President of Germany); Schweim, Germany **(1899–1976)**
Heisenberg, Werner Karl (physicist); Würzburg, Germany **(1901–1976)**
Held, Anna (comedienne); Paris, France **(1873?–1918)**
Heller, Joseph (novelist); Brooklyn, N.Y., 5/1/23
Hellman, Lillian (playwright); New Orleans **(1905–1984)**
Helmond, Katherine (actress); Galveston, Tex., 7/5/34
Helms, Jesse (politician); Monroe, N.C., 10/18/21
Helmsley, Leona (business executive); New York City, c.1920
Hemingway, Ernest Miller (novelist); Oak Park, Ill. **(1899–1961)**
Hemingway, Margaux (actress); Portland, Ore. **(1955–1996)**
Hemmings, David (actor); Guilford, England, 11/2/41
Henderson, Florence (actress); Dale, Ind., 2/14/34
Henderson, Skitch (Lyle Russell Cedric) (conductor, pianist); Birmingham, England?, 1/27/18
Hendrix, Jimi (James Marshall Hendrix) (guitarist); Seattle **(1942–1970)**
Henley, Beth (playwright-actress); Jackson, Miss., 5/8/52
Henley, Don (musician); Linden, Tex., 7/22/47
Henner, Marilu (actress); Chicago, 4/6/52
Henning, Doug (magician, actor); Winnipeg, Canada, 1947?
Henreid, Paul (actor); Trieste **(1908–1992)**
Henri, Robert (painter); Cincinnati **(1865–1926)**
Henry VIII (King of England); Greenwich, England **(1491–1547)**
Henry, O. (William Sydney Porter) (story writer); Greensboro, N.C. **(1862–1910)**
Henry, Patrick (statesman); Hanover County, Va. **(1736–1799)**
Henson, Jim (puppeteer); Greenville, Miss. **(1936–1990)**
Hepburn, Audrey (actress); Brussels, Belgium **(1929–1993)**
Hepburn, Katharine (actress); Hartford, Conn., 5/12/07
Hepplewhite, George (furniture designer); England **(?–1786)**
Hepworth, Barbara (sculptor); Wakefield, England **(1903–1975)**
Herschel, William (Frederich Wilhelm) (astronomer); Hanover, Germany **(1738–1822)**
Herbert, George (poet); Montgomery Castle, Wales **(1593–1633)**
Herbert, Victor (composer); Dublin **(1859–1924)**
Herblock (Herbert L. Block) (political cartoonist); Chicago, 10/13/09
Herman, Pee-wee (Paul Reubens) (comedian); Peekskill, N.Y., 1952
Herman, Woody (Woodrow Charles) (band leader); Milwaukee **(1913–1987)**
Herod (called Herod the Great) (King of Judea) **(73 –4 B.C.E.)**
Herodotus (historian); Halicarnassus, Asia Minor (Turkey) **(c. 484–425 B.C.E.)**
Herrick, Robert (poet); London **(1591–1674)**
Herschel, William (Frederich Wilhelm) (astronomer); Hannover, Germany **(1738–1822)**
Hershey, Barbara (Barbara Herzstein) (actress); Hollywood, Calif., 2/5/48
Hesburgh, Theodore M. (educator); Syracuse, N.Y., 5/2/17
Hesseman, Howard (actor); Salem, Ore., 2/27/40
Heston, Charlton (actor); Evanston, Ill., 10/4/24
Heyerdahl, Thor (ethnologist, explorer); Larvik, Norway, 10/6/14
Hill, Anita (lawyer, professor); Lone Tree, Okla., 7/30/56
Hill, Benny (comedian); Southampton, England **(1925–1992)**
Hillary, Sir Edmund (mountain climber); New Zealand, 7/20/19
Hiller, Wendy (actress); Bramhall, England, 8/15/12

Hillerman, John (actor); Denison, Tex., 12/20/32
Hilton, Conrad (hotelier); San Antonio, N.M. **(1887–1979)**
Hindemith, Paul (composer); Hanau, Germany **(1895–1963)**
Hindenburg, Paul von (Paul Ludwig Hans Anton von Hindenburg und Beneckendorff) (German field marshall, president); Poznan (Poland) **(1847–1934)**
Hines, Earl "Fatha" (jazz pianist); Duquesne, Pa. **(1905–1983)**
Hines, Gregory (dancer, actor); New York City, 2/14/46
Hines, Jerome (Jerome Heinz) (basso); Los Angeles, 11/8/21
Hingle, Pat (actor); Denver, 7/19/24
Hippocrates (physician); Cos, Greece **(c. 460–c. 377 B.C.E.)**
Hirohito (Emperor); Tokyo **(1901–1989)**
Hiroshige, Ando (painter); Edo (Tokyo) **(1797–1858)**
Hirsch, Judd (actor); New York City, 3/15/35
Hirschfeld, Al (Albert) (cartoonist); St. Louis, 6/21/03
Hirschhorn, Joseph Herman (financier, speculator, art collector); Mitau, Latvia **(1899–1981)**
Hirt, Al (trumpeter); New Orleans, 11/7/22
Hiss, Alger (public official); Baltimore **(1904–1996)**
Hitchcock, Alfred J. (film director); London **(1899–1980)**
Hitler, Adolf (German dictator); Braunau, Austria **(1889–1945)**
Hitzig, William Maxwell (physician); Austria, 12/15/04
Hobbes, Thomas (philosopher); Westport, England **(1588–1679)**
Hobson, Laura Z. (Laura K. Zametkin) (novelist); New York City **(1900–1986)**
Ho Chi Minh, (Nguyen That Tranh) (Vietnamese nationalist leader); Kim Lien (Vietnam) **(1890–1969)**
Hockney, David (artist); Bradford, England, 7/9/37
Hoffa, James R(iddle) (labor leader); Brazil, Ind. **(1913–1975?; presumed murdered.)**
Hoffman, Dustin (actor, director); Los Angeles, 8/8/37
Hofmann, Hans (painter); Germany **(1880–1966)**
Hofstadter, Richard (historian); Buffalo, N.Y. **(1916–1970)**
Hogan, Paul (actor); Lightning Ridge, NSW, Australia, 10/8/39
Hogarth, William (painter, engraver); London **(1697–1764)**
Hokusai, Katauhika (artist); Yedo, Japan **(1760–1849)**
Holbein, Hans (the Elder) (painter); Augsburg (Germany) **(c. 1465–1524)**
Holbein, Hans (the Younger) (painter); Augsburg (Germany) **(c. 1497–1543)**
Holbrook, Hal (actor); Cleveland, 2/17/25
Holden, William (William Franklin Beedle, Jr.) (actor); O'Fallon, Ill. **(1918–1981)**
Holder, Geoffrey (dancer); Port-of-Spain, Trinidad, 8/1/30
Holiday, Billie (Eleanora Fagan) (jazz-blues singer); Baltimore **(1915–1959)**
Holliday, Judy (Judith Tuvim) (comedienne); New York City **(1922–1965)**
Holliman, Earl (actor); Delhi, La., 9/11/28
Holloway, Sterling (actor); Cedartown, Ga. **(1905–1992)**
Holly, Buddy (singer); Lubbock, Tex. **(1936–1959)**
Holm, Celeste (actress); New York City, 4/29/19
Holmes, Oliver Wendell (jurist); Boston **(1841–1935)**
Holt, Tim (actor); Beverly Hills, Calif. **(1918–1973)**
Home, Lord (Alexander Frederick Douglas-Home) (diplomat); London, 7/2/03
Homer, Winslow (painter); Boston, Mass. **(1836–1910)**
Homer (Greek poet) fl.850 B.C.E.
Homolka, Oscar (actor); Vienna **(1898–1978)**
Honegger, Arthur (composer); Le Havre, France **(1892–1955)**
Hook, Sidney (philosopher); New York City **(1902–1989)**
Hooker, John Lee (blues guitarist, singer, songwriter); Clarksdale, Miss., 8/22/20
Hoover, J. Edgar (FBI director); Washington, D.C. **(1895–1972)**
Hope, Bob (Leslie Townes Hope) (comedian); London, 5/29/03
Hopkins, Sir Anthony (actor); Port Talbot, Wales, 12/31/37
Hopkins, Gerald Manley (poet); Stratford, England **(1844–1899)**
Hopkins, Johns (financier); Anne Arundel County, Md. **(1795–1873)**
Hopper, Dennis (actor); Dodge City, Kan., 5/17/36
Hopper, Edward (painter); Nyack, N.Y. **(1882–1967)**
Horace (Quintus Horatius Flaccus) (poet); Venosa (Italy) **(65–8 B.C.E.)**
Horne, Lena (singer); Brooklyn, N.Y., 6/30/17
Horne, Marilyn (mezzo-soprano); Bradford, Pa., 1/16/34
Horowitz, Vladimir (pianist); Kiev, Ukraine **(1903–1989)**
Horsley, Lee (actor); Muleshoe, Tex., 5/15/55
Horton, Edward Everett (comedian); Brooklyn, N.Y. **(1887–1970)**
Hoskins, Bob (actor); Bury St. Edmunds, England, 10/26/42
Houdini, Harry (Ehrich Weiss) (magician); Appleton, Wis. **(1874–1926)**
Houseman, John (Jacques Haussmann) (producer, director, actor); Bucharest **(1902–1988)**
Housman, A(lfred) E(dward) (poet); Fockburg, England **(1859–1936)**
Houston, Charles Hamilton (civil rights lawyer); Washington, D.C. **(1895–1950)**
Houston, Samuel (political leader); Rockbridge County, Va. **(1793–1863)**
Houston, Whitney (singer); Newark, N.J., 8/9/63

Howard, Ken (actor); El Centro, Calif., 3/28/44
Howard, Leslie (Leslie Stainer) (actor); London **(1893–1943)**
Howard, Ron (actor, producer, director); Duncan, Okla., 3/1/54
Howard, Trevor (actor); Kent, England **(1916–1988)**
Howe, Elias (inventor); Spencer, Mass. **(1819–1867)**
Howe, Irving (literary critic); New York City **(1920–1993)**
Howe, Julia Ward (poet, reformer); New York City **(1819–1910)**
Hudson, Henry (English navigator) **(fl. 1607–1611)**
Hudson, Rock (born Roy Scherer, Jr.; took Roy Fitzgerald as legal name) (actor); Winnetka, Ill. **(1925–1985)**
Huggins, Nathan Irvin (historian); Chicago **(1927–1989)**
Hughes, Barnard (actor); Bedford Hills, N.Y., 7/16/15
Hughes, Charles Evans (jurist); Glens Falls, N.Y. **(1862–1948)**
Hughes, Howard (industrialist, film producer); Houston **(1905–1976)**
Hughes, Langston (poet); Joplin, Mo. **(1902–1967)**
Hugo, Victor Marie (author); Besançon, France **(1802–1885)**
Hulce, Tom (actor); Detroit, Mich., 12/6/53
Hume, David (philosopher); Edinburgh, Scotland **(1711–1776)**
Humperdinck, Engelbert (composer); Siegburg (Germany) **(1854–1921)**
Humperdinck, Engelbert (Arnold Dorsey) (singer); Madras, India, 5/2/36
Hunt, Helen (actress); Los Angeles, 6/15/63
Hunt, Marsha (actress); Chicago, 10/17/17
Hunter, Holly (actress); Atlanta, Ga., 3/20/58
Hunter, Kim (Janet Cole) (actress); Detroit, Mich., 11/12/22
Hunter, Tab (Arthur Andrew Gelien) (actor); New York City, 7/11/31
Hunter-Gault, Charlayne (activist, broadcast journalist); Due West, S.C., 2/27/42
Huntley, Chet (TV newscaster); Cardwell, Mont. **(1911–1974)**
Hurok, Sol (Solomon) (impresario); Pogar, Russia **(1884–1974)**
Hurst, Fannie (novelist); Hamilton, Ohio **(1889–1968)**
Hurston, Zora Neale (author); Eatonville, Fla. **(1901–1960)**
Hurt, John (actor); Shirebrook, England, 1/22/40
Hurt, William (actor); Washington, D.C., 3/20/50
Hus, Jan (Bohemian religious reformer); Husinetz, nr. Budweis (Czech Republic) **(c.1369–1415)**
Husing, Ted (sportscaster); New York City **(1901–1962)**
Hussein I (King); Jordan, 11/14/35
Hussein, Saddam (al-Tikriti) (Iraqi President); Tikrit, Iraq, 4/28/37
Huston, Anjelica (actress); Los Angeles, 7/8/51
Huston, John (actor, director, writer); Nevada, Mo. **(1906–1987)**
Huston, Walter (Walter Houghston) (actor); Toronto **(1884–1950)**
Hutchins, Robert M. (educator); Brooklyn, N.Y. **(1899–1977)**
Hutton, Barbara (Woolworth heiress); New York City **(1912–1979)**
Hutton, Betty (Betty Thornburg) (actress); Battle Creek, Mich., 2/26/21
Hutton, Lauren (actress, model); Charleston, S.C., 11/17/43
Hutton, Timothy (actor); Los Angeles, 8/16/60
Huxley, Aldous (author); Godalming, England **(1894–1963)**
Huxley, Sir Julian S. (biologist, author); London **(1887–1975)**
Huxley, Thomas Henry (biologist); Ealing, England **(1825–1895)**
Hyde Pierce, David (actor); Saratoga Springs, N.Y., 4/3/59

I

Iacocca, Lee (Lido Anthony) (business executive); Allentown, Pa., 10/15/24
Ian, Janis (singer); New York City, 5/7/51
Ibsen, Henrik (dramatist); Skien, Norway **(1828–1906)**
Inge, William (playwright); Independence, Kan. **(1913–1973)**
Ingres, Jean Auguste Dominique (painter); Montauban, France **(1780–1867)**
Inness, George (painter); nr. Newburgh, N.Y. **(1825–1894)**
Ionesco, Eugene (playwright); Slatina, Romania **(1912–1994)**
Ireland, Jill (actress); London **(1936–1990)**
Ireland, John (actor); Vancouver, B.C., Canada **(1914–1992)**
Ireland, Patricia (feminist, social activist); Oak Park, Ill., 10/19/45
Irons, Jeremy (actor); Cowes, Isle of Wight, England, 9/19/48
Irving, Amy (actress); Palo Alto, Calif., 9/10/53
Irving, John (Winslow) (writer); Exeter, N.H., 3/2/42
Irving, Washington (author); New York City **(1783–1859)**
Isherwood, Christopher (novelist, playwright); nr. Dilsey and High Lane, England **(1904–1986)**
Iturbi, José (concert pianist); Valencia, Spain **(1895–1980)**
Ives, Burl (Icle Ivanhoe) (singer); Hunt, Ill. **(1909–1995)**
Ives, Charles E(dward) (composer); Danbury, Conn. **(1874–1954)**
Ivins, Molly (journalist); Monterey, Calif., 8/30/44

J

Jackson, Anne (actress); Millvale, Pa., 9/3/26
Jackson, Glenda (actress); Cheshire, England, 5/9/36
Jackson, Gordon (actor); Glasgow, Scotland **(1923–1990)**

Jackson, Janet (singer); Gary, Ind., 5/16/66
Jackson, Rev. Jesse (civil rights leader); Greenville, S.C., 10/8/41
Jackson, Kate (actress); Birmingham, Ala., 10/29/49
Jackson, Mahalia (gospel singer); New Orleans **(1911–1972)**
Jackson, Maynard (mayor of Atlanta); Dallas, Tex., 3/23/38
Jackson, Michael (singer); Gary, Ind., 8/29/58
Jackson, Thomas Jonathan ("Stonewall") (general); Clarksburg, Va. (now W. Va.) **(1824–1863)**
Jacobi, Derek (actor); Leytonstone, England, 10/22/38
Jacobi, Lou (actor); Toronto, 12/26/13
Jacobs, Jane (urbanologist); Scranton, Pa., 5/1/16
Jaffe, Sam (actor); New York City **(1891–1984)**
Jagger, Dean (actor); Lima, Ohio **(1903–1991)**
Jagger, Mick (Michael Phillip) (singer); Dartford, England, 7/26/43
James, Harry (trumpeter); Albany, Ga. **(1916–1983)**
James, Henry (novelist); New York City **(1843–1916)**
James, Jesse Woodson (outlaw); Clay County, Mo. **(1847–1882)**
James, William (psychologist); New York City **(1842–1910)**
Jameson, (Margaret) Storm (novelist); Whitby, England **(1897–1986)**
Janis, Byron (pianist); McKeesport, Pa., 3/24/28
Janis, Conrad (actor, musician); New York City, 2/11/28
Jannings, Emil (actor); Brooklyn, N.Y. **(1886–1950)**
Janssen, David (David Meyer) (actor); Naponee, Neb. **(1930–1980)**
Jaworkski, Leon (Watergate special prosecutor); Waco, Tex. **(1905–1982)**
Jay, John (statesman, jurist); New York City **(1745–1829)**
Jeanmaire, Renée (dancer); Paris, 4/29/24
Jemison, Mae C. (astronaut, physician); Decatur, Ala., 10/17/56
Jenner, Edward (physician); Berkeley, England **(1749–1823)**
Jennings, Peter (news anchor); Toronto, Ont., Canada, 7/29/38
Jennings, Waylon (singer); Littlefield, Tex., 6/15/37
Jessel, George (entertainer); New York City **(1898–1981)**
Jessup, Philip C. (diplomat); New York City **(1897–1986)**
Jillian, Ann (actress); Cambridge, Mass., 1/29/51
Joan of Arc (Jeanne d'Arc) (saint, patriot); Domremy-la-Pucelle, France **(1412–1431)**
Jobs, Steven Paul (computer industry pioneer); San Francisco, 1955
Joel, Billy (singer); New York City, 5/9/49
Joffrey, Robert (Abdullah Jaffa Bey Khan) (choreographer); Seattle **(1930–1988)**
John, Elton (Reginald Kenneth Dwight) (singer, pianist); Pinner, England, 3/25/47
Johns, Jasper (painter, sculptor); Augusta, Ga., 5/15/30
Johnson, Don (actor); Flatt Creek, Mo., 12/15/49
Johnson, James Weldon (author, educator); Jacksonville, Fla. **(1871–1938)**
Johnson, Philip Cortalyou (architect); Cleveland, Ohio, 7/8/06
Johnson, Samuel (lexicographer, author); Lichfield, England **(1709–1784)**
Johnson, Van (actor); Newport, R.I., 8/20/16
Johnson, Virginia (human sexuality expert); Springfield, Mo., 2/11/25
Joliot-Curie, Frédéric (physicist); Paris **(1900–1958)**
Joliot-Curie, Irène (Irène Curie) (physicist); France **(1897–1956)**
Jolliet, Louis (Louis Joliet) (explorer); Beaupré, Canada **(1645–1700)**
Jolson, Al (Asa Yoelson) (actor, singer); St. Petersburg, Russia **(1886–1950)**
Jones, Allan (singer, actor); Old Forge, Pa. **(1908–1992)**
Jones, Buck (Charles Frederick Gebhart) (actor); Vincennes, Ind. **(1889–1942)**
Jones, Carolyn (singer, actress); Amarillo, Tex. **(1933–1983)**
Jones, Dean (actor); Morgan County, Ala., 1/25/35
Jones, George (singer); Saratoga, Tex., 9/12/31
Jones, Inigo (architect); London **(1573–1652)**
Jones, James (novelist); Robinson, Ill. **(1921–1977)**
Jones, James Earl (actor); Arkabutla, Miss., 1/17/31
Jones, Jennifer (Phyllis Isley) (actress); Tulsa, Okla., 3/2/19
Jones, John Paul (John Paul) (naval officer); Scotland **(1747–1792)**
Jones, Quincy (composer); Chicago, 3/14/33
Jones, Shirley (singer, actress); Smithtown, Pa., 3/31/34
Jones, Spike (host, orchestra leader); Long Beach, Calif. **(1911–1965)**
Jones, Tom (Thomas Jones Woodward) (singer); Pontypridd, Wales, 6/7/40
Jones, Tommy Lee (actor); San Saba, Tex., 9/15/46
Jong, Erica (writer); New York City, 3/26/42
Jonson, Ben (Benjamin) (poet, dramatist); Westminster, England **(1572–1637)**
Joplin, Janis (singer); Port Arthur, Tex. **(1943–1970)**
Joplin, Scott (ragtime pianist, composer); Texarkansas, Tex. **(1868–1917)**
Jordan, Barbara (U.S. Representative); Houston, Tex. **(1936–1996)**
Jordan, James Edward (radio actor-Fibber McGee); Peoria, Ill. **(1896–1988)**
Jordan, Marian (radio actress-Molly of Fibber McGee and Molly); Peoria, Ill. **(1898–1961)**
Joseph, (Chief Joseph) (Nez Perce Indian leader); eastern Ore. **(1841–1904)**

Josquin des Prés (usually known as Josquin) (composer); Conde-sur-L'Escaut?, Hainaut (Belgium) **(c.1445–1521)**
Jourdan, Louis (Louis Gendre) (actor); Marseilles, France, 6/19/19
Joyce, James (novelist); Dublin **(1882–1941)**
Juárez, Benito Pablo (statesman); Guelatao, Mexico **(1806–1872)**
Julia, Raul (Raúl Rafael Carlos Julia y Arcelay) (actor); San Juan, Puerto Rico **(1940–1994)**
Jung, Carl Gustav (psychoanalyst); Basel, Switzerland **(1875–1961)**
Jurado, Katy (Maria Christina Jurado Garcia) (actress); Guadalajara, Mexico, 1/16/24

K

Kabalevsky, Dmitri (composer); St. Petersburg, Russia **(1904–1987)**
Kafka, Franz (author); Prague **(1883–1924)**
Kádár, János (Communist Party leader); Hungary **(1912–1989)**
Kahn, Gus (songwriter); Coblenz, Germany **(1886–1941)**
Kahn, Louis I. (architect); Oesel Island, Estonia **(1901–1974)**
Kahn, Madeline (actress); Boston, 9/29/42
Kandinsky, Wassily (painter); Moscow **(1866–1944)**
Kanin, Garson (playwright); Rochester, N.Y., 11/24/12
Kant, Immanuel (philosopher); Königsberg (Kaliningrad, Russia) **(1724–1804)**
Kantor, MacKinlay (novelist); Webster City, Iowa **(1904–1977)**
Kaplan, Justin (writer, editor); New York City, 9/5/25
Karan, Donna (fashion designer); Forest Hills, N.Y., 10/2/48
Karloff, Boris (William Henry Pratt) (actor); London **(1887–1969)**
Kasem, Casey (disc jockey); Detroit, Mich., 4/27/32
Katt, William (actor); Los Angeles, 2/16/50
Kaufman, George S. (playwright); Pittsburgh **(1889–1961)**
Kavner, Julie (actress); Los Angeles, 9/7/51
Kaye, Danny (David Daniel Kominski) (comedian); Brooklyn, N.Y. **(1913–1987)**
Kaye, Sammy (band leader); Cleveland **(1910–1987)**
Kazan, Elia (director); Constantinople, Turkey, 9/7/09
Kazan, Lainie (Levine) (singer); New York City, 5/15/40
Kazantzakis, Nikos (writer); Herakleion, Crete **(1883–1957)**
Keach, Stacy (actor); Savannah, Ga., 6/2/41
Kean, Edmund (actor); London **(1787–1833)**
Keaton, Buster (Joseph Frank Keaton) (comedian); Piqua, Kan. **(1896–1966)**
Keaton, Diane (actress); Los Angeles, 1/5/46
Keaton, Michael (Michael Douglas) (actor); Robinson Township, Pa., 9/9/51
Keats, John (poet); London **(1795–1821)**
Keel, Howard (singer, actor); Gillespie, Ill., 4/13/19
Keeler, Ruby (Lehy Keeler) (actress, dancer); Halifax, Nova Scotia, Canada **(1910–1993)**
Kefauver, Estes (legislator); Madisonville, Tenn **(1903–1963)**
Keitel, Harvey (actor); Brooklyn, N.Y., 5/13/39
Keith, Brian (actor); Bayonne, N.J. **(1921–1997)**
Keller, Helen Adams (author, educator); Tuscumbia, Ala. **(1880–1968)**
Kellerman, Sally (actress); Long Beach, Calif., 6/2/38
Kelley, DeForest (actor); Atlanta, Ga., 1/20/20
Kelly, Emmett (clown); Sedan, Kan. **(1898–1979)**
Kelly, Gene (dancer, actor); Pittsburgh **(1912–1996)**
Kelly, Patsy (actress, comedienne); Brooklyn, N.Y. **(1910–1981)**
Kelly, Walt (cartoonist); Philadelphia **(1913–1973)**
Kemal Ataturk (Mustafa Kemal) (Turkish soldier, statesman); Salonika (Greece) **(1881–1938)**
Kempis, Thomas à (mystic); Kempis, Prussia (Germany) **(1380–1471)**
Kennan, George F. (diplomat); Milwaukee, 2/16/04
Kennedy, Arthur (actor); Worcester, Mass. **(1914–1990)**
Kennedy, George (actor); New York City, 2/18/25
Kennedy, John F., Jr. (publisher); Washington, D.C., 11/25/60
Kennedy, Joseph P. (financier); Boston **(1888–1969)**
Kennedy, Robert Francis (legislator); Brookline, Mass. **(1925–1968)**
Kennedy, Rose Fitzgerald (President's mother); Boston **(1890–1995)**
Kent, Allegra (ballerina); Santa Monica, Calif., 8/11/38
Kent, Rockwell (painter); Tarrytown Heights, N.Y. **(1882–1971)**
Kenton, Stan (Stanley Newcomb) (jazz musician); Wichita, Kan. **(1912–1979)**
Kepler, Johannes (astronomer); Weil (Germany) **(1571–1630)**
Kercheval, Ken (actor); Wolcottville, Ind., 7/15/35
Kerensky, Alexander Fedorovich (statesman); Simbirsk, Russia **(1881–1970)**
Kern, Jerome David (composer); New York City **(1885–1945)**
Kerns, Joanna (actress); San Francisco, 2/12/53
Kerr, Deborah (actress); Helensburgh, Scotland, 9/30/21
Kettering, Charles F. (engineer, inventor); nr. Loudonville, Ohio **(1876–1958)**
Key, Francis Scott (lawyer, author of national anthem); Frederick (Carroll) County, Md. **(1779–1843)**
Keyes, Frances Parkinson (novelist); Charlottesville, Va **(1885–1970)**

Keynes (John Maynard Keynes) (economist); Cambridge, England **(1883–1946)**
Khachaturian, Aram (composer); Tiflis, Russia **(1903–1978)**
Khomeini, Ayatollah Ruhollah (Islamic religious leader); Iran **(1900–1989)**
Khrushchev, Nikita S. (Soviet leader); Kalinovka, nr. Kursk, Ukraine **(1894–1971)**
Kidd, Michael (choreographer); Brooklyn, N.Y., 8/12/19
Kidd, William (called Captain Kidd) (pirate); Greenock, Scotland **(c. 1645–1701)**
Kidder, Margot (actress); Yellowknife, N.W.T., Canada, 10/17/48
Kidman, Nicole (actress); Honolulu, 6/20/67
Kiepura, Jan (tenor); Sosnowiec, Poland **(1904?–1966)**
Kieran, John (writer); New York City **(1892–1981)**
Kierkegaard, Sören Aalys (philosopher); Copenhagen **(1813–1855)**
Kiesinger, Kurt Georg (diplomat); Ebingen, Germany **(1904–1988)**
Kiley, Richard (actor, singer); Chicago, 3/31/22
Kilmer, Alfred Joyce (poet); New Brunswick, N.J. **(1886–1918)**
King, Alan (Irwin Alan Kniberg) (entertainer); Brooklyn, N.Y., 12/26/27
King, B.B. (Riley King) (guitarist); Itta Bena, Miss., 9/16/25
King, Carole (singer, songwriter); Brooklyn, N.Y., 2/9/41
King, Coretta Scott (civil rights leader); Marion, Ala., 4/27/27
King, Larry (TV host); New York City, 11/19/33
King, Martin Luther, Jr. (civil rights leader); Atlanta **(1929–1968)**
King, Stephen (writer); Portland,Maine, 9/21/47
Kingsley, Ben (Krishna Bhanji) (actor); Snainton, England, 12/31/43
Kingsley, Sidney (Sidney Kirschner) (playwright); New York City **(1906–1995)**
Kingsolver, Barbara (writer); Annapolis, Md., 4/8/55
Kingston, Maxine Hong (novelist); Stockton, Calif., 10/27/40
Kinsey, Alfred Charles (human sexuality expert); Hoboken, N.J. **(1894–1956)**
Kinski, Nastassja (Nastassja Nakszynski) (actress); West Berlin, 1/24/61
Kipling, Rudyard (author); Bombay **(1865–1936)**
Kipnis, Alexander (basso); Ukraine **(1891–1978)**
Kirby, George (comedian); Chicago **(1923–1995)**
Kirchner, Ernst Ludwig (painter); Aschaffenburg, Germany **(1880–1938)**
Kirk, Grayson (educator); Jeffersonville, Ohio, 10/12/03
Kirkland, Gelsey (ballerina); Bethlehem, Pa., 12/29/52
Kirkpatrick, Jeane Jordan (educator-public affairs); Duncan, Okla., 11/19/26
Kirkpatrick, Ralph (harpsichordist); Leominster, Mass. **(1911–1984)**
Kirstein, Lincoln (dance, theater executive); Rochester, N.Y. **(1907–1996)**
Kirsten, Dorothy (soprano); Montclair, N.J. **(1910–1992)**
Kissinger, Henry (Heinz Alfred Kissinger) (ex-Secretary of State); Furth, Germany, 5/27/23
Kitt, Eartha (singer); North, S.C., 1/26/28
Klee, Paul (painter); Münchenbuchsee, nr. Bern, Switzerland **(1879–1940)**
Klein, Calvin (fashion designer); Bronx, N.Y., 11/19/42
Klein, Robert (comedian); New York City, 2/8/42
Kleist, Henrich von (poet); Frankfurt an der Oder (Germany) **(1777–1811)**
Klemperer, Otto (conductor); Breslau (Poland) **(1885–1973)**
Klemperer, Werner (actor); Cologne, Germany, 3/22/20
Klimt, Gustav (painter); Vienna **(1862–1918)**
Kline, Kevin (actor); St. Louis, Mo., 10/24/47
Klugman, Jack (actor); Philadelphia, 4/27/22
Knight, Gladys (singer); Atlanta, 5/28/44
Knight, Ted (Tadeus Wladyslaw Konopka) (actor); Terryville, Conn. **(1923–1986)**
Knight, John S. (publisher); Bluefield, W. Va. **(1894–1981)**
Knopf, Alfred A. (publisher); New York City **(1892–1984)**
Knotts, Don (actor); Morgantown, W.Va., 7/21/24
Knox, John (religious reformer); Haddington, East Lothian, Scotland **(1505–1572)**
Koch, Robert (physician); Klausthal (Germany) **(1843–1910)**
Koestler, Arthur (novelist); Budapest **(1905–1983)**
Kokoschka, Oskar (painter); Póchlam Austria **(1886–1980)**
Kollwitz, Käthe (graphic artist, sculptor); Königsberg, (Russia) **(1867–1945)**
Koop, C. Everett (ex-Surgeon General); Brooklyn, N.Y., 10/14/16
Kooper, Al (singer, pianist); Brooklyn, N.Y., 2/5/44
Kopell, Bernie (actor); New York City, 6/21/33
Koppel, Ted (broadcast journalist); Lancashire, England, 2/8/40
Korman, Harvey (actor); Chicago, 2/15/27
Kosciusko, Thaddeus (Tadeusz Andrzej Bonawentura Kosciuszko) (military officer; Grand Duchy of Lithuania **(1746–1817)**
Kossuth, Lajos (patriot); Monok, Hungary **(1802–1894)**
Kostelanetz, André (orchestra conductor); St. Petersburg, Russia **(1901–1980)**
Kosygin, Aleksei N. (Premier); St. Petersburg, Russia **(1904–1980)**

Koussevitzky, Serge (Sergei) Alexandrovitch (orchestra conductor); Vishni Volochek, Tver, Russia **(1874–1951)**
Kovacs, Ernie (comedian); Trenton, N.J. **(1919–1962)**
Kramer, Stanley E. (film producer, director); New York City, 9/29/13
Kràus, Lili (pianist); Budapest **(1905–1986)**
Kreisler, Fritz (violinist, composer); Vienna **(1875–1962)**
Kresge, S. S. (merchant); Bald Mount, Pa. **(1867–1966)**
Krips, Josef (orchestra conductor); Vienna **(1902–1974)**
Kristofferson, Kris (singer); Brownsville, Tex., 6/22/36
Krupa, Gene (drummer); Chicago **(1909–1973)**
Krupp, Alfred (munitions magnate); Essen, Germany **(1812–1887)**
Kubelik, Rafael (conductor); Bychory, former Czechoslovakia **(1914–1996)**
Kublai Khan (Mongol conqueror) **(1216–1294)**
Kubrick, Stanley (producer, director); New York City, 7/26/28
Kudrow, Lisa (actress); Encino, Calif., 7/30/63
Kuralt, Charles (TV journalist); Wilmington, N.C. **(1934–1997)**
Kurosawa, Akira (film director); Tokyo, 3/23/10
Kurtz, Efrem (conductor); St. Petersburg, Russia **(1900–1995)**
Kurtz, Swoosie (actress); Omaha, Neb., 9/6/44

L

LaBelle, Patti (singer, actress); Philadelphia, 5/24/44
Ladd, Alan (actor); Hot Springs, Ark. **(1913–1964)**
Ladd, Cheryl (Cheryl Stoppelmoor) (actress); Huron, S.D., 7/12/51
Ladd, Diane (actress); Meridian, Miss., 11/29/32
Lafayette, Marquis de (Marie Joseph Paul Yves Roch Gilbert du Motier) (military officer); Auvergne, France **(1757–1834)**
Lafitte, Jean (pirate); Bayonne? France **(1780–1826)**
La Follette, Robert Marin (politician); Primrose, Wis. **(1855–1925)**
La Fontaine, Jean de (poet); Château-Thierry, France **(1621–1695)**
La Guardia, Fiorello Henry (Mayor of New York); New York City **(1882–1947)**
Lahr, Bert (Irving Lahrheim) (comedian); New York City **(1895–1967)**
Lahti, Christine (actress, director); Birmingham, Mich., 4/4/50
Laine, Frankie (Frank Paul LoVecchio) (singer); Chicago, 3/30/13
Laird, Melvin (ex-Secretary of Defense); Omaha, Neb., 9/1/22
Lake, Veronica (actress); Brooklyn, N.Y. **(1919–1973)**
Lamarck, Chevalier de (Jean Baptiste Pierre Antoine de Monet) (naturalist); Bazantin, France **(1744–1829)**
Lamarr, Hedy (Hedwig Kiesler) (actress); Vienna, 11/9/13
Lamas, Fernando (actor); Buenos Aires **(1915–1982)**
Lamas, Lorenzo (actor); Los Angeles, 1/20/58
Lamb, Charles (Elia) (essayist); London **(1775–1834)**
L'Amour, Louis (author); Jamestown, N.D. **(1908–1988)**
Lamour, Dorothy (Dorothy Kaumeyer) (actress); New Orleans **(1914–1996)**
Lancaster, Burt (actor); New York City **(1913–1994)**
Lanchester, Elsa (Elsa Sullivan) (actress); London **(1902–1986)**
Landau, Martin (actor); Brooklyn, N.Y., 6/20/31
Landers, Ann (columnist); Sioux City, Iowa, 7/4/18
Landon, Michael (Eugene Maurice Orowitz) (actor, director, producer); Forest Hills, Queens, N.Y. **(1936–1991)**
Lane, Abbe (singer); New York City, 1933
Lang, Fritz (film director); Vienna **(1890–1976)**
Lang, Paul Henry (music critic); Budapest **(1901–1991)**
Lange, Hope (actress); Redding Ridge, Conn., 11/28/33
Lange, Jessica (actress); Cloquet, Minn., 4/20/49
Langella, Frank (actor); Bayonne, N.J., 1/1/40
Langford, Frances (singer); Lakeland, Fla., 4/4/13
Langmuir, Irving (chemist); Brooklyn, N.Y. **(1881–1957)**
Langtry, Lillie (Emily Le Breton) (actress); Island of Jersey **(1852–1929)**
Lansbury, Angela (actress, producer); London, 10/16/25
Lansing, Robert (Robert Howell Brown) (actor); San Diego, Calif. **(1928–1994)**
Lanza, Mario (Alfred Arnold Cocozza) (singer, actor); Philadelphia **(1921–1959)**
Lao-Tzu (Li Erh) (philosopher); Honan Province, China **(c. 604–531 B.C.E.)**
Lardner, Ring (Ringgold Wilmar Lardner) (story writer); Niles, Mich. **(1885–1933)**
La Rouchefoucauld, Francois duc de (author); Paris **(1613–1680)**
Larroquette, John (actor); New Orleans, 11/25/47
Larson, Gary (cartoonist); Tacoma, Wash., 8/14/50
La Salle, Eriq (actor); Hartford, Conn., 7/23/62
La Salle, Sieur de (Robert Cavelier) (explorer); Rouen, France **(1643–1687)**
Lasch, Christopher (historian, social critic); Omaha, Neb. **(1932–1994)**
Lasser, Louise (actress); New York City, 4/11/39
La Tour, Georges de (painter); Vic-sur-Seille, France **(1593–1652)**
Lauder, Sir Harry (Harry MacLennan) (singer); Portobello, Scotland **(1870–1950)**
Laughton, Charles (actor); Scarborough, England **(1899–1962)**
Lauper, Cyndi (singer); New York City, 6/20/53

Laurel, Stan (Arthur Jefferson) (comedian); Ulverston, England **(1890–1965)**

Laurents, Arthur (playwright); New York City, 7/14/18

Laurie, Piper (Rosetta Jacobs) (actress); Detroit, Mich., 1/22/32

Lavin, Linda (actress); Portland, Me., 10/15/37

Lavoisier, Antoine-Laurent (chemist); Paris **(1743–1794)**

Lawford, Peter (actor); London **(1923–1984)**

Lawrence, David Herbert (novelist); Nottingham, England **(1885–1930)**

Lawrence, Gertrude (Gertrud Klasen) (actress); London **(1900–1952)**

Lawrence, Jacob (painter); Atlantic City, N.J., 9/7/17

Lawrence, Sharon (actress); Charlotte, N.C., 6/29/62

Lawrence, Steve (Sidney Leibowitz) (singer); Brooklyn, N.Y., 7/8/35

Lawrence of Arabia (Thomas Edward Lawrence, later changed to Shaw) (author, soldier); Tremadoc, Wales **(1888–1935)**

Lawrence, Vicki (actress); Inglewood, Calif., 3/26/49

Leach, Penelope (Balchin) (child psychologist, writer); London, 11/19/37

Leach, Robin (host, producer); London, 8/29/41

Leachman, Cloris (actress); Des Moines, Iowa, 4/30/26

Leadbelly, (Huddie Ledbetter) (blues singer, guitarist); Mooringsport, La. **(1885–1949)**

Leakey, Louis Seymour Bazett (anthropologist); Kabete, Kenya **(1903–1972)**

Leakey, Richard (paleoanthropologist, wildlife conservationist); Kenya, 12/19/44

Lean, David (film director); Croydon, England **(1908–1991)**

Lear, Edward (nonsense poet); London **(1812–1888)**

Lear, Evelyn (Shulman) (soprano); Brooklyn, N.Y., 1/8/29?

Lear, Norman (TV producer); New Haven, Conn., 7/27/22

Learned, Michael (actress); Washington, D.C., 4/9/39

Leary, Timothy (psychologist, LSD advocate); Springfield, Mass. **(1920–1996)**

Le Blanc, Matt (actor); Newton, Mass., 7/25/67

le Carré, John (David John Moore Cornwell) (novelist); Poole, England, 10/19/31

Le Corbusier (Charles Edouard Jeanneret) (architect); La Chaux-de-Fonds, Switzerland **(1887–1965)**

Lee, Christopher (actor); London, 5/27/22

Lee, Gypsy Rose (Rose Louise Hovick) (entertainer); Seattle **(1914–1970)**

Lee, Manfred B. (pseudonym Ellery Queen) (novelist); Brooklyn, N.Y. **(1905–1971)**

Lee, Michele (actress, singer); Los Angeles, 6/24/42

Lee, Peggy (Norma Engstrom) (singer); Jamestown, N.D., 5/26/20

Lee, Robert Edward (Confederate general); Stratford Estate, Va. **(1807–1870)**

Lee, Spike (Shelton Jackson Lee) (actor, director, writer, producer); Atlanta, 3/20/57

Leeuwenhoek, Anton van (zoologist); Delft (Netherlands) **(1632–1723)**

Le Gallienne, Eva (actress); London **(1899–1991)**

Lehár Franz (composer); Komárom (Hungary) **(1870–1948)**

Lehman, Herbert H. (Governor, Senator); New York City **(1878–1963)**

Lehmann, Lotte (soprano); Perleberg (Germany) **(1888–1976)**

Lehrer, Jim (TV newscaster); Wichita, Kan., 5/19/34

Leibniz, Gottfried W. von (scientist); Leipzig (Germany) **(1646–1716)**

Leibovitz, Annie (photographer); Westbury, Conn., 10/2/49

Leigh, Janet (Jeanetta Morrison) (actress); Merced, Calif., 7/6/27

Leigh, Jennifer Jason (Jennifer Morrow) (actress); Los Angeles, Calif., 2/5/62

Leigh, Vivien (Vivien Mary Hartley) (actress); Darjeeling, India **(1913–1967)**

Leinsdorf, Erich (conductor); Vienna **(1912–1993)**

Lemmon, Jack (actor); Boston, 2/8/25

Lenin, Vladimir (Vladimir Ilich Ulyanov) (Soviet leader); Simbirsk, Russia **(1870–1924)**

Lennon, John (singer, songwriter); Liverpool, England **(1940–1980)**

Leno, Jay (comedian, T.V. host); New Rochelle, N.Y., 4/28/50

Lenya, Lotte (Karoline Blamauer) (singer, actress); Vienna, Austria **(1898–1981)**

Leonard, Sheldon (actor, producer); New York City **(1907–1997)**

Lerner, Alan Jay (lyricist); New York City **(1918–1986)**

Lerner, Max (columnist); Minsk, Russia **(1902–1992)**

Le Roy, Mervyn (film producer); San Francisco **(1900–1987)**

Lessing, Doris (novelist); Kermanshah, Iran, 10/22/19

Letterman, David (TV host, producer); Indianapolis, 4/12/47

Levant, Oscar (pianist); Pittsburgh **(1906–1972)**

Levene, Sam (actor); New York City **(1905–1980)**

Levenson, Sam (humorist); New York City **(1911–1980)**

Levi, Carlo (novelist); Turin, Italy **(1902–1975)**

Levine, James (music director, Metropolitan Opera); Cincinnati, 6/23/43

Levine, Joseph E. (film producer); Boston **(1905–1987)**

Lewis, C(live) S(taples) (author); Belfast, Northern Ireland **(1898–1963)**

Lewis, Jerry (Joseph Levitch) (comedian, film director); Newark, N.J., 3/16/26

Lewis, Jerry Lee (singer); Ferriday, La., 9/29/35

Lewis, John Llewellyn (labor leader); Lucas, Iowa **(1880–1969)**

Lewis, Meriwether (explorer); Albemarle Co., Va. **(1774–1809)**

Lewis, (Percy) Wyndham (artist, writer); Bay of Fundi, Maine (at sea) **(1884–1957)**

Lewis, Shari (Shari Hurwitz) (puppeteer); New York City, 1/17/34

Lewis, Sinclair (novelist); Sauk Centre, Minn. **(1885–1951)**

Ley, Willy (science writer); Berlin **(1906–1969)**

Liberace (Wladziu Liberace) (pianist); West Allis, Wis. **(1919–1987)**

Lichtenstein, Roy (painter); New York City **(1923–1997)**

Lie, Trygve Halvdan (first U.N. Secretary-General); Oslo **(1896–1968)**

Light, Judith (actress); Trenton, N.J., 2/9/49

Lightfoot, Gordon (singer, songwriter); Orillia, Ontario, Canada, 11/17/38

Lillie, Beatrice (Lady Peel) (actress, comedienne); Toronto **(1898–1989)**

Limbaugh, Rush (political commentator); Cape Girardeau, Mo., 1/12/51

Lin, Maya (architect, sculptor); Athens, Ohio, 10/5/59

Lin Yutang (author); Changchow, China **(1895–1976)**

Lind, Jenny (Johanna Maria Lind) (soprano); Stockholm **(1820–1887)**

Lindbergh, Anne Morrow (author); Englewood, N.J., 6/22/06

Lindbergh, Charles A. (aviator); Detroit, Mich. **(1902–1974)**

Linden, Hal (Harold Lipshitz) (actor); New York City, 3/20/31

Lindsay, Howard (playwright); Waterford, N.Y. **(1889–1968)**

Lindstrom, Pia (TV newscaster); Stockholm, 11/?/38

Linkletter, Art (radio-TV personality); Moose Jaw, Saskatchewan, Canada, 7/17/12

Linnaeus, Carolus (Carl von Linné) (botanist); Råshult, Sweden **(1707–1778)**

Lipchitz, Jacques (sculptor); Druskieniki, Latvia **(1891–1973)**

Lippi, Fra Filippo (painter); Florence **(1406–1469)**

Lippmann, Walter (columnist, author, political analyst); New York City **(1889–1974)**

Lister, (Joseph Lister) (surgeon); Upton, England **(1827–1912)**

Liszt, Franz (composer, pianist); Raiding(Hungary) **(1811–1886)**

Lithgow, John (actor); Rochester, N.Y., 6/6/45

Little, Cleavon (actor, comedian); Chickasha, Okla. **(1939–1992)**

Little, Rich (impressionist); Ottawa, 11/26/38

Livingstone, David (missionary, explorer); Lanarkshire, Scotland **(1813–1873)**

Livingstone, Mary (Sadye Marks) (comedienne); Seattle **(1909–1983)**

Llewellyn, Richard (novelist); St. David's, Wales **(1906–1983)**

Lloyd, Harold (comedian); Burchard, Neb. **(1894–1971)**

Lloyd George, David (Earl of Dwyfor) (statesman); Manchester, England **(1863–1945)**

Lloyd Webber, Andrew (composer); London, England, 3/22/48

Locke, Alain L. (philosopher); Philadelphia **(1886–1954)**

Locke, John (philosopher); Somersetshire, England **(1632–1704)**

Lockhart, June (actress); New York City, 6/25/25

Lockwood, Margaret (actress); Karachi (Pakistan) **(1916–1990)**

Lodge, Henry Cabot (legislator); Boston **(1850–1924)**

Lodge, Henry Cabot, Jr. (diplomat); Nahant, Mass. **(1902–1985)**

Loesser, Frank (composer); New York City **(1910–1969)**

Loewe, Frederick (composer); Vienna **(1901–1988)**

Logan, Joshua (director, producer); Texarkana, Tex. **(1908–1988)**

Lollobrigida, Gina (Luigina Lollobrigida) (actress); Subiaco, Italy, 7/4/27

Lombard, Carole (Carol Jane Peters) (actress); Ft. Wayne, Ind. **(1908–1942)**

Lombardo, Guy (band leader); London, Ontario, Canada **(1902–1977)**

London, George (baritone); Montreal **(1920–1985)**

London, Jack (John Griffith London) (novelist); San Francisco **(1876–1916)**

Long, Huey Pierce (politician); Winnfield, La. **(1893–1935)**

Long, Shelley (actress); Fort Wayne, Ind., 8/23/49

Longfellow, Henry Wadsworth (poet); Portland, Me. **(1807–1882)**

Longworth, Alice Roosevelt (social figure); New York City **(1884–1980)**

Loos, Anita (novelist); Sissons, Calif. **(1888–1981)**

Lopez, Trini (singer); Dallas, Tex., 5/15/37

Lopez, Vincent (band leader); Brooklyn, N.Y. **(1895–1975)**

Lord, Jack (John Joseph Ryan) (actor); New York City, 12/30/30

Loren, Sophia (Sofia Scicolone) (actress); Rome, 9/20/34

Lorenz, Konrad (ethologist); Vienna **(1903–1989)**

Lorre, Peter (Laszlo Löewenstein) (actor); Rosenberg, former Czechoslovakia **(1904–1964)**

Loudon, Dorothy (actress, singer); Boston, 9/17/33

Louis XIV (King of France); St.-Germain-en-Laye, France **(1638–1715)**

Louise, Tina (actress); New York City, 2/11/37

Love, Susan (surgeon, oncologist, activist); Long Branch, N.J., 2/9/48

Lovecraft, Howard Phillips (author); Providence, R.I. **(1890–1937)**

Lowell, Amy (poet); Brookline, Mass. **(1874–1925)**

Lowell, James Russell (poet); Cambridge, Mass. **(1819–1891)**

Lowell, Robert (poet); Boston **(1917–1977)**

Loy, Myrna (Myrna Williams) (actress); nr. Helena, Mont. **(1905–1993)**

Loyola, St. Ignatius of (Iñigo de Oñez y Loyola) (founder of Jesuits); Gúipuzcoa Province, Spain **(1491–1556)**

Lubitsch, Ernst (film director); Berlin **(1892–1947)**

Lucas, George (film director); Modesto, Calif., 5/14/44

Lucci, Susan (actress); Scarsdale, N.Y., 12/23/48

Luce, Clare Boothe (playwright, former Ambassador); New York City **(1903–1987)**

Luce, Henry Robinson (editor, publisher); Tengchow, China **(1898–1967)**

Ludlum, Robert (author); New York City, 5/25/27

Lugosi, Bela (Bela Lugosi Blasko) (actor); Logos, Hungary **(1888–1956)**

Lully, Jean Baptiste (French composer); Florence **(1639–1687)**

Lumet, Sidney (director); Philadelphia, 6/25/24

Lunden, Joan (TV host); Fair Oaks, Calif., 9/19/50

Lunt, Alfred (actor); Milwaukee **(1892–1977)**

Lupino, Ida (actress, director); London **(1918–1995)**

LuPone, Patti (actress, singer); Northport, N.Y., 4/21/49

Luther, Martin (religious reformer); Eisleben (East Germany) **(1483–1546)**

Lynde, Paul (comedian); Mt. Vernon, Ohio **(1926–1982)**

Lynn, Loretta (singer); Butcher's Hollow, Ky., 4/14/35

M

Ma, Yo-Yo (cellist); Paris, 10/7/55

Maazel, Lorin (conductor); Neuilly, France, 3/5/30

MacArthur, Charles (playwright); Scranton, Pa. **(1895–1956)**

MacArthur, Douglas (five-star general); Little Rock Barracks, Ark. **(1880–1964)**

MacArthur, James (actor); Los Angeles, 12/8/37

Macaulay, Thomas Babington (author); Rothley Temple, England **(1800–1859)**

MacDermot, Galt (composer); Montreal, 12/19/28

MacDonald, James Ramsay (statesman); Lossiemouth, Scotland **(1866–1937)**

MacDonald, Jeanette (actress, soprano); Philadelphia **(1907–1965)**

Macdonald, Ross (Kenneth Millar) (mystery writer); Los Gatos, Calif. **(1915–1983)**

MacDowell, Edward Alexander (composer); New York City **(1861–1908)**

Macfadden, Bernarr (physical culturist); nr. Mill Spring, Mo. **(1868–1955)**

MacGraw, Ali (actress); New York City, 4/1/39

Machaut, Guillaume de (composer); Marchault, France **(1300–1377)**

Machiavelli, Niccolò (political philosopher); Florence(Italy) **(1469–1527)**

Mack, Ted (TV personality); Greeley, Colo. **(1904–1976)**

Mackie, Bob (designer); Monterey Park, Calif., 3/24/40

MacLaine, Shirley (Shirley MacLean Beatty) (actress); Richmond, Va., 4/24/34

MacLeish, Archibald (poet); Glencoe, Ill. **(1892–1982)**

Macmillan, Harold (ex-Prime Minister); London **(1894–1986)**

MacMurray, Fred (actor); Kankakee, Ill. **(1908–1991)**

MacNeil, Cornell (baritone); Minneapolis, 1925

MacNeil, Robert (TV newscaster); Montreal, Que., Canada, 1/19/31

MacRae, Gordon (singer); East Orange, N.J. **(1921–1986)**

MacRae, Sheila (comedienne); London, 9/24/24

Madison, Guy (Robert Moseley) (actor); Bakersfield, Calif. **(1922–1996)**

Madonna (Madonna Louise Ciccone) (singer, actress); Bay City, Mich., 8/16/58

Maeterlinck, Count Maurice (author); Ghent, Belgium **(1862–1949)**

Magellan, Ferdinand (Fernando de Magalhaes) (navigator); Sabrosa, Portugal **(c. 1480–1521)**

Magliozzi, Ray (host of "Car Talk" on NPR); Cambridge, Mass., 3/30/49

Magliozzi, Tom (host of "Car Talk" on NPR); Cambridge, Mass., 6/28/37

Magnani, Anna (actress); Rome **(1908–1973)**

Magritte, René (painter); Belgium **(1898–1967)**

Magsaysay, Ramón (statesman); Iba, Luzon, Philippines **(1907–1957)**

Mahan, Alfred Thayer (naval historian); West Point, N.Y. **(1840–1914)**

Mahler, Gustav (composer, conductor); Kalischt (Czechoslovakia) **(1860–1911)**

Mahoney, John (actor); Manchester, England, 6/20/40

Mailer, Norman (novelist); Long Branch, N.J., 1/31/23

Mailloi, Aristide (sculptor); Banyuls-sur-Mer, Rousillion, France **(1861–1944)**

Maimonides, Moses (Jewish philosopher); Cordoba, Spain **(1135–1204)**

Main, Marjorie (Mary Tomlinson Krebs) (actress); Acton, Ind. **(1890–1975)**

Mainbocher (Main Rousseau Bocher) (fashion designer); Chicago **(1891–1976)**

Majors, Lee (actor); Wyandotte, Mich., 4/23/40

Makarova, Natalia (ballerina); Leningrad, 11/21/40

Makeba, Miriam (singer); Johannesburg, South Africa, 3/4/32

Malamud, Bernard (novelist); Brooklyn, N.Y. **(1914–1986)**

Malcolm X, (Malcolm Little; el Hajj Ma lik el-Shabazz) (Black nationalist, religious leader); Omaha, Neb. **(1925–1965)**

Malden, Karl (Mladen Sekulovich) (actor); Chicago, 3/22/13

Malkovich, John (actor); Christopher, Ill., 12/9/53

Mallarmé, Stephane (poet, essayist); Paris **(1842–1898)**

Malle, Louis (director); Thumeries, France **(1932–1995)**

Malone, Dorothy (actress); Chicago, 1/30/25

Malraux, André (author); Paris **(1901–1976)**

Malthus, Thomas Robert (economist); nr. Dorking, England **(1766–1834)**

Mamet, David (playwright); Chicago, 11/30/47

Manchester, Melissa (singer); Bronx, N.Y., 2/15/51

Manchester, William (writer); Attleboro, Mass., 4/1/22

Mancini, Henry (composer, conductor); Cleveland **(1924–1994)**

Mandela, Nelson (Rolihlahla) (South African political activist); Umtata, Transkei, 6/11/18

Mandela, Winnie (Nomzamo) (South African political activist); Pondoland district of the Transkei, 1936?

Mandrell, Barbara (singer); Houston, 12/25/48

Manet, Edouard (painter); Paris **(1832–1883)**

Mangano, Silvana (actress); Rome **(1930–1989)**

Mangione, Chuck (hornist, pianist, composer); Rochester, N.Y., 11/29/40

Manilow, Barry (singer); Brooklyn, N.Y., 6/17/46

Mankiewicz, Frank F. (columnist); New York City, 5/16/24

Mankiewicz, Joseph L. (film writer, director); Wilkes-Barre, Pa. **(1909–1993)**

Mann, Horace (educator); Franklin, Mass. **(1796–1859)**

Mann, Thomas (novelist); Lübeck, Germany **(1875–1955)**

Mannes, Marya (writer); New York City, 11/14/04

Mansfield, Jayne (Jayne Palmer) (actress); Bryn Mawr, Pa. **(1932–1967)**

Mansfield, Katherine (story writer); Wellington, New Zealand **(1888–1923)**

Mantegna, Andrea (painter); Isola di Carturo, Italy **(1431–1506)**

Mantovani, Annunzio (conductor); Venice **(1905–1980)**

Mao Zedong (Tse-tung) (Chinese leader); Shao Shan, China **(1893–1976)**

Mapplethorpe, Robert (photographer); Floral Park, Queens, N.Y. **(1946–1989)**

Marat, Jean Paul (French revolutionist); Boudry, Neuchâtei, Switzerland **(1743–1793)**

Marceau, Marcel (mime); Strasbourg, France, 3/22/23

March, Fredric (Frederick Bickel) (actor); Racine, Wis. **(1897–1975)**

Marchand, Nancy (actress); Buffalo, N.Y., 6/19/28

Marconi, Guglielmo (inventor); Bologna, Italy **(1874–1937)**

Marcus Aurelius (Marcus Annius Verus) (Roman emperor); Rome **(121–180)**

Marcuse, Herbert (philosopher); Berlin **(1898–1979)**

Margaret Rose (Princess); Glamis Castle, Angus, Scotland, 8/21/30

Margrethe II (Queen); Copenhagen, 4/16/40

Margulies, Julianna (actress); Spring Valley, N.Y., 6/8/65

Marie Antoinette (Josephe Jeanne Marie Antoinette) (Queen of France); Vienna **(1755–1793)**

Marisol (Escobar) (Venezuelan-American sculptor); Paris, 1930

Markham, Edwin (poet); Oregon City, Ore. **(1852–1940)**

Markova, Dame Alicia (Lilian Alice Marks) (ballerina); London, 12/1/10

Marley, Bob (reggae singer, songwriter); Kingston, Jamaica **(1945–1981)**

Marlowe, Christopher (dramatist); Canterbury, England **(1564–1593)**

Marquand, J(ohn) P(hillips) (novelist); Wilmington, Del. **(1893–1960)**

Marquette, Jacques (missionary, explorer); Laon, France **(1637–1675)**

Marriner, Neville (conductor); Lincoln, England, 4/15/24

Marsalis, Wynton (musician); New Orleans, La., 10/18/61

Marsh, Jean (actress); Stoke Newington, England, 7/1/34

Marshall, E.G. (actor); Owatonna, Minn., 6/18/10

Marshall, George Catlett (general); Uniontown, Pa. **(1880–1959)**

Marshall, John (jurist); nr. Germantown, Va. **(1755–1835)**

Marshall, Penny (actress, director, producer); New York City, 10/15/42

Marshall, Thurgood (U.S. Supreme Court justice); Baltimore, Md. **(1908–1993)**

Martin, Dean (Dino Crocetti) (singer, actor); Steubenville, Ohio **(1917–1995)**

Martin, Mary (singer, actress); Weatherford, Tex. **(1913–1990)**

Martin, Steve (actor, writer, producer); Waco, Tex., 8/14/45

Martin, Tony (Alvin Morris) (singer); San Francisco, 12/25/13

Martinelli, Giovanni (tenor); Montagnana, Italy **(1885–1969)**

Martins, Peter (dancer, choreographer); Copenhagen, 10/27/45

Marvell, Andrew (poet); Winestead, England **(1621–1678)**

Marvin, Lee (actor); New York City **(1924–1987)**

Marx, Chico (Leonard) (comedian); New York City **(1891–1961)**

Marx, Groucho (Julius) (comedian); New York City **(1890–1977)**

Marx, Harpo (Arthur) (comedian); New York City **(1893–1964)**

Marx, Karl (Socialist writer); Treves (Germany) **(1818–1883)**

Marx, Zeppo (Herbert) (comedian); New York City **(1901–1979)**

Mary Stuart (Queen of Scotland); Linlithgow, Scotland **(1542–1587)**

Masaccio, (Tommaso di Giovanni di Simone Cassai) (painter); San Giovanni Valdarno, Tuscany **(1401–c.1428)**

Masaryk, Jan Garrigue (statesman); Prague (Czech Republic) **(1886–1948)**

Masaryk, Thomas Garrigue (statesman); Hodonin, Moravia **(1850–1937)**

Masefield, John (poet); Ledbury, England **(1878–1967)**
Masekela, Hugh (trumpeter); Wilbank, South Africa, 4/4/39
Mason, Jackie (Jacob Moshe Maza) (comedian); Sheboygan, Wis., 6/9/31
Mason, James (actor); Huddersfield, England **(1909–1984)**
Mason, Marsha (actress); St. Louis, Mo., 4/3/42
Massenet, Jules Emile Frédéric (composer); Montaud, France **(1842–1912)**
Massey, Raymond (actor); Toronto **(1896–1983)**
Massine, Léonide (choreographer); Moscow **(1895–1979)**
Masters, Edgar Lee (poet); Garnett, Kan. **(1869–1950)**
Masters, William (human sexuality expert); Cleveland, 12/27/15
Mastroianni, Marcello (actor); Fontana Liri, Italy **(1924–1996)**
Mather, Cotton (clergyman); Boston **(1663–1728)**
Mathis, Johnny (singer); San Francisco, 9/30/35
Matisse, Henri (painter); Le Cateau, France **(1869–1954)**
Matthau, Walter (Walter Matuschanskayasky) (actor); New York City, 10/1/20
Mature, Victor (actor); Louisville, Ky., 1/19/16
Maugham, W(illiam) Somerset (author); Paris **(1874–1965)**
Mauldin, Bill (political cartoonist); Mountain Park, N.M., 10/29/21
Maupassant, Henri René Albert Guy de (story writer); Normandy, France **(1850–1893)**
Maurois, André (Emile Herzog) (author); Elbauf, France **(1885–1967)**
Maximilian (Ferdinand Maximilian Joseph) (Emperor of Mexico); Vienna **(1832–1867)**
Maxwell, James Clerk (physicist); Edinburgh, Scotland **(1831–1879)**
Maxwell, (Ian) Robert (publisher); Selo Slatina, Czechoslavakia **(1923–1991)**
May, Elaine (Elaine Berlin) (entertainer, writer); Philadelphia, 4/21/32
May, Rollo (psychologist); Ada, Ohio **(1909–1994)**
Mayall, John (singer, songwriter); Manchester, England, 11/29/33
Mayer, Louis B. (movie executive); Minsk, Russia **(1885–1957)**
Mayo, Charles H. (surgeon); Rochester, Minn. **(1865–1939)**
Mayo, Charles W. (surgeon); Rochester, Minn. **(1898–1968)**
Mayo, Virginia (Jones) (actress); St. Louis, 11/30/20
Mayo, William J. (surgeon); Le Sueur, Minn. **(1861–1939)**
Mayron, Melanie (actress); Philadelphia, 10/20/52
Mazzini, Giuseppe (patriot); Genoa **(1805–1872)**
McBride, Patricia (ballerina); Teaneck, N.J., 8/23/42
McCallum, David (actor); Glasgow, Scotland, 9/19/33
McCambridge, Mercedes (actress); Joliet, Ill., 3/17/18
McCarthy, Eugene J. (ex-Senator); Watkins, Minn., 3/29/16
McCarthy, Joseph Raymond (Senator); Grand Chute, Wis. **(1908–1957)**
McCarthy, Kevin (actor); Seattle, 2/15/14
McCarthy, Mary (novelist); Seattle **(1912–1989)**
McCartney, Paul (singer, songwriter); Liverpool, England, 6/18/42
McClanahan, Rue (actress); Healdton, Okla., 2/21/35
McClellan, George Brinton (general); Philadelphia **(1826–1885)**
McClintock, Barbara (geneticist); Hartford, Conn. **(1902–1992)**
McCloy, John J. (lawyer, banker); Philadelphia **(1895–1989)**
McClure, Doug (actor); Glendale, Calif. **(1938–1995)**
McCormack, John (tenor); Athlone, Ireland **(1884–1945)**
McCormack, John W. (ex-Speaker of House); Boston **(1891–1980)**
McCormick, Cyrus Hall (inventor); Rockbridge County, Va. **(1809–1884)**
McCracken, James (dramatic tenor); Gary, Ind. **(1926–1988)**
McCrea, Joel (actor); Los Angeles **(1905–1990)**
McCullers, Carson (novelist); Columbus, Ga. **(1917–1967)**
McDaniel, Hattie (actress); Wichita, Kan. **(1895–1952)**
McDowall, Roddy (actor); London, 9/17/28
McDowell, Malcolm (actor); Leeds, England, 6/19/43
McFarland, Spanky (George Emmett) (actor); Fort Worth, Tex. **(1928–1993)**
McGavin, Darren (actor); San Joaquin, Calif., 5/7/22
McGinley, Phyllis (poet, writer); Ontario, Ore. **(1905–1978)**
McGoohan, Patrick (actor); Astoria, Queens N.Y., 1928
McGovern, Maureen (singer); Youngstown, Ohio, 7/27/49
McGuire, Dorothy (actress); Omaha, Neb., 6/14/19
McKellen, Ian (actor); Burnley, England, 5/25/39
McKenna, Siobhan (actress); Belfast, Northern Ireland **(1923–1986)**
McKuen, Rod (singer, composer); Oakland, Calif., 4/29/33
McLaglen, Victor (actor); Tunbridge Wells, Kent, England **(1886–1959)**
McLaughlin, John (guitarist); Yorkshire, England, 1942
McLean, Don (singer, songwriter); New Rochelle, N.Y., 10/2/45
McLuhan, Marshall (Herbert Marshall) (communications writer); Edmonton, Canada **(1911–1980)**
McMahon, Ed (TV personality); Detroit, Mich., 3/6/23
McMurtry, Larry (novelist); Wichita Falls, Tex., 6/3/36
McQueen, Butterfly (Thelma) (actress); Tampa, Fla. **(1911–1995)**
McQueen, Steve (Terence Stephen McQueen) (actor); Indianapolis **(1930–1980)**
McRaney, Gerald (actor); Collins, Miss., 8/19/47
Mead, Margaret (anthropologist); Philadelphia **(1901–1978)**
Meadows, Audrey (actress); Wu Chang, China **(1924–1996)**

Meadows, Jayne (actress); Wu Chang, China, 9/27/26
Meaney, Colm (actor); Dublin, Ireland, 5/30/53
Meany, George (labor leader); New York City **(1894–1980)**
Meara, Anne (actress); New York City, 9/20/29
Medici, Lorenzo de' (called Lorenzo the Magnificent) (Florentine ruler); Florence (Italy) **(1449–1492)**
Meek, Donald (actor); Glasgow, Scotland **(1880–1946)**
Meeker, Ralph (Ralph Rathgeber) (actor); Minneapolis **(1920–1988)**
Mehta, Zubin (conductor); Bombay, 4/29/36
Meir, Golda (Golda Myerson, nee Mabovitz) (ex-Premier of Israel); Kiev, Ukraine **(1898–1978)**
Melanie (Melanie Safka) (singer, songwriter); New York City, 2/3/47
Melba, Dame Nellie (Helen Porter Mitchell) (soprano); nr. Melbourne **(1861–1931)**
Melchior, Lauritz (Lebrecht Hommel) (heroic tenor); Copenhagen **(1890–1973)**
Mellon, Andrew William (financier); Pittsburgh **(1855–1937)**
Melville, Herman (novelist); New York City **(1819–1891)**
Mencken, Henry Louis (writer); Baltimore **(1880–1956)**
Mendel, Gregor Johann (geneticist); Heinzendorf, Austrian Silesia **(1822–1884)**
Mendeleyev, Dmitri Ivanovich (chemist); Tobolsk, Russia **(1834–1907)**
Mendelssohn-Bartholdy, Jakob Ludwig Felix (composer); Hamburg **(1809–1847)**
Mendès-France, Pierre (ex-Premier); Paris **(1905–1982)**
Mengele, Josef (Nazi, "Angel of Death"); Günzberg, Germany **(1911–1979)**
Menjou, Adolphe (actor); Pittsburgh **(1890–1963)**
Mennin, Peter (Peter Mennini) (composer); Erie, Pa. **(1923–1983)**
Menninger, William C. (psychiatrist); Topeka, Kan. **(1899–1966)**
Menotti, Gian Carlo (composer); Cadegliano, Italy, 7/7/11
Menuhin, Yehudi (violinist, conductor); New York City, 4/22/16
Menzies, Robert Gordon (ex-Prime Minister); Jeparit, Australia **(1894–1978)**
Mercer, Johnny (songwriter); Savannah, Ga. **(1909–1976)**
Mercer, Mabel (singer); Burton-on-Trent, England **(1900–1984)**
Mercer, Marian (actress, singer); Akron, Ohio, 11/26/35
Merchant, Ismail (Ismail Noormohamed Abdul Rehman) (film producer); Bombay, India, 12/25/36
Mercouri, Melina (actress); Athens **(1925–1994)**
Meredith, Burgess (actor); Cleveland **(1908–1997)**
Merman, Ethel (Ethel Zimmerman) (singer, actress); Astoria, Queens, N.Y. **(1909–1984)**
Merrick, David (David Margulois) (stage producer); St. Louis, 11/27/12
Merrill, Dina (actress); New York City, 12/9/25
Merrill, Gary (actor); Hartford, Conn. **(1915–1990)**
Merrill, Robert (baritone); Brooklyn, N.Y., 6/4/19
Merton, Thomas (clergyman, writer); France **(1915–1968)**
Mesmer, Franz Anton (physician); Itzmang, nr. Constance (Germany) **(1733–1815)**
Mesta, Perle (social figure); Sturgis, Mich. **(1889–1975)**
Metacom, (King Philip) (Wampanoag Indian sachem); (southeastern Mass.) **(1640–1676)**
Metternich, Prince Klemens Wenzel Nepomuk Lothar von (statesman); Coblenz(Germany) **(1773–1859)**
Mfume, Kweisi (Frizzell Gray) (politician, NAACP leader); Baltimore, Md., 10/24/48
Michelangelo Buonarroti (painter, sculptor, architect); Caprese (Italy) **(1475–1564)**
Michener, James A. (novelist); New York City, 2/3/07
Mickiewicz, Adam (Polish poet); Zozie, Belorussia (Belarus) **(1798–1855)**
Midler, Bette (singer, actress, producer); Honolulu, 12/1/45
Mielziner, Jo (stage designer); Paris **(1901–1976)**
Mies van der Rohe, Ludwig (architect, designer); Aachen, Germany **(1886–1969)**
Mikoyan, Anastas I. (diplomat); Sanain, Armenia **(1895–1978)**
Miles, Sarah (actress); Essex, England, 12/31/43
Miles, Sylvia (actress); New York City, 9/9/32
Miles, Vera (Vera Ralston) (actress); nr. Boise City, Okla., 8/23/30
Milhaud, Darius (composer); Aix-en-Provence, France **(1892–1974)**
Mill, John Stuart (philosopher); London **(1806–1873)**
Milland, Ray (Reginald Truscott-Jones) (actor); Neath, Wales **(1907–1986)**
Millay, Edna St. Vincent (poet); Rockland, Me. **(1892–1950)**
Miller, Ann (Lucille Ann Collier) (dancer, actress); Cherino, Tex., 4/12/23
Miller, Arthur (playwright); New York City, 10/17/15
Miller, Glenn (band leader); Clarinda, Iowa **(1904–1944)**
Miller, Henry (novelist); New York City **(1891–1980)**
Miller, Jason (John Miller) (playwright, actor); New York City, 4/22/39
Miller, Mitch (Mitchell) (musician); Rochester, N.Y., 7/4/11
Miller, Roger (singer); Fort Worth **(1936–1992)**
Millet, Jean François (painter); Gruchy, France **(1814–1875)**
Millett, Kate (feminist); St. Paul, 9/14/34
Millikan, Robert A. (physicist); Morrison, Ill. **(1869–1953)**
Mills, Donna (actress); Chicago, 12/11/41

Mills, Hayley (actress); London, 4/18/46
Mills, John (actor); Felixstowe, England, 2/22/08
Mills, Juliet (actress); London, 11/21/41
Milne, A(lan) A(lexander) (author); London **(1882–1956)**
Milner, Martin (actor); Detroit, Mich., 12/28/31
Milnes, Sherrill (baritone); Downers Grove, Ill., 1/10/35
Milstein, Nathan (concert violinist); Odessa (Ukraine) **(1904–1992)**
Milton, John (poet); London **(1608–1674)**
Mimieux, Yvette (actress); Hollywood, Calif., 1/8/41
Mineo, Sal (actor); New York City **(1939–1976)**
Mingus, Charles (jazz composer); Nogales, Ariz. **(1922–1979)**
Minnelli, Liza (singer, actress); Hollywood, Calif., 3/12/46
Minnelli, Vincente (film director); Chicago **(1913–1986)**
Minuit, Peter (Governor of New Amsterdam); Wesel (Germany) **(1580–1638)**
Miranda, Carmen (Maria do Carmo da Cunha) (singer, dancer); Lisbon **(1913–1955)**
Miró, Joan (painter); Barcelona **(1893–1983)**
Mirren, Helen (Ilynea Lydia Mironoff) (actress); London, 7/26/45
Mitchell, Cameron (actor); Dallastown, Pa. **(1918–1994)**
Mitchell, John N. (former Attorney General); Detroit, Mich. **(1913–1988)**
Mitchell, Joni (Roberta Joan Anderson) (singer, songwriter); Ft. Macleod, Canada, 11/7/43
Mitchell, Margaret (novelist); Atlanta **(1900–1949)**
Mitchell, Maria (astronomer); Nantucket, Mass. **(1818–1889)**
Mitchell, Thomas (actor); Elizabeth, N.J. **(1892–1962)**
Mitchum, Robert (actor); Bridgeport, Conn. **(1917–1997)**
Mitropoulos, Dimitri (orchestra conductor); Athens **(1896–1960)**
Mitterand, François (Maurice) (ex-prime minister of France); Jarnac, France **(1916–1996)**
Mix, Tom (actor); Mix Run, Pa. **(1880–1940)**
Modigliani, Amedeo (painter); Leghorn, Italy **(1884–1920)**
Moffo, Anna (soprano); Wayne, Pa., 6/27/34
Mohammed (prophet); Mecca (Saudi Arabia) **(570–632)**
Molière (Jean Baptiste Poquelin) (dramatist); Paris **(1622–1673)**
Moll, Richard (actor); Pasadena, Calif., 1/13/43?
Molnar, Ferenc (dramatist); Budapest **(1878–1952)**
Molotov, Vyacheslav M. (V. M. Skryabin) (diplomat); Kukarka, Russia **(1890–1986)**
Mondrian, Piet (painter); Amersfoort, Netherlands **(1872–1944)**
Monet, Claude (painter); Paris **(1840–1926)**
Monk, Meredith (choreographer, composer, performing artist); Lima, Peru, 11/20/42
Monk, Thelonious (pianist); Rocky Mount, N.C. **(1918–1982)**
Monroe, Marilyn (Norma Jean Mortenson or Baker) (actress); Los Angeles **(1926–1962)**
Monroe, Vaughn (Wilton) (band leader); Akron, Ohio **(1912–1973)**
Monsarrat, Nicholas (novelist); Liverpool, England **(1910–1979)**
Montaigne, Michel Eyquem de (essayist); nr. Bordeaux, France **(1533–1592)**
Montalban, Ricardo (actor); Mexico City, 11/25/20
Montand, Yves (Yvo Montand Livi) (actor, singer); Monsummano, Italy **(1921–1991)**
Montesquieu, Charles-Louis de Secondat, baron de La Brède and de, (philosopher); nr. Bordeaux, France **(1689–1755)**
Montessori, Maria (physician, educator); Chiaravalle, Italy **(1870–1952)**
Monteux, Pierre (conductor); Paris **(1875–1964)**
Monteverdi, Claudio (composer); Cremona Italy **(1567–1643)**
Montez, Maria (actress); Dominican Republican **(1918–1951)**
Montezuma II (Aztec emperor); Mexico **(1466–1520)**
Montgomery, Elizabeth (actress); Hollywood, Calif. **(1938–1995)**
Montgomery, Robert (Henry, Jr.) (actor); Beacon, N.Y. **(1904–1981)**
Montgomery of Alamein, 1st Viscount of Hindhead (Sir Bernard Law Montgomery) (military leader); London **(1887–1976)**
Montoya, Carlos (guitarist); Madrid **(1903–1993)**
Moore, Clement Clarke (author); New York City **(1779–1863)**
Moore, Demi (actress); Roswell, N.M., 11/11/62
Moore, Dudley (actor, writer, musician); Dagenham, England, 4/19/35
Moore, Garry (Thomas Garrison Morfit) (TV personality); Baltimore **(1915–1993)**
Moore, Grace (soprano); Jellico, Tenn. **(1901–1947)**
Moore, Henry (sculptor); Castleford, England **(1898–1986)**
Moore, Marianne (poet); Kirkwood, Mo. **(1887–1972)**
Moore, Mary Tyler (actress); Brooklyn, N.Y., 12/29/37
Moore, Melba (Beatrice) (singer, actress); New York City, 10/27/45
Moore, Roger (actor); London, 10/14/27
Moore, Thomas (poet); Dublin **(1779–1852)**
Moore, Victor (actor); Hammonton, N.J. **(1876–1962)**
Moorehead, Agnes (actress); Clinton, Mass. **(1906–1974)**
More, Henry (philosopher); Grantham, England **(1614–1687)**
More, Sir Thomas (statesman, author); London **(1478–1535)**
Moreau, Jeanne (actress); Paris, 1/23/28
Moreno, Rita (Rosita Dolores Alverio) (actress); Humacao, Puerto Rico, 12/11/31
Morgan, Frank (actor); New York City **(1890–1949)**
Morgan, Harry (actor); Detroit, Mich., 4/10/15

Morgan, Helen (Helen Riggins) (actress, singer); Danville, Ohio **(1900–1941)**
Morgan, Henry (comedian); New York City **(1915–1994)**
Morgan, John Pierpont (financier); Hartford, Conn. **(1837–1913)**
Moriarty, Michael (actor); Detroit, Mich., 4/5/41
Morini, Erica (concert violinist); Vienna **(1904–1995)**
Morison, Samuel Eliot (historian); Boston **(1887–1976)**
Morley, Christopher Darlington (novelist); Haverford, Pa. **(1890–1957)**
Morley, Robert (actor); Semley, England **(1908–1992)**
Morris, Chester (actor); New York City **(1901–1970)**
Morris, Mark (choreographer); Seattle, Wash., 8/29/56
Morris, William (poet, craftsman); Walthamstow, England **(1834–1896)**
Morrison, Jim (James Douglas Morrison) (singer, songwriter); Melbourne, Fla. **(1943–1971)**
Morrison, Toni (Chloe Anthony Wofford) (novelist); Lorain, Ohio, 2/18/31
Morrison, Van (singer); Belfast, Northern Ireland, 8/31/45
Morse, Marston (mathematician); Waterville, Me. **(1892–1977)**
Morse, Robert (actor); Newton, Mass., 5/18/31
Morse, Samuel Finley Breese (painter, inventor); Charlestown, Mass. **(1791–1872)**
Morton, Jelly Roll (Ferdinand Joseph La Menthe) (jazz composer); New Orleans, La. **(1890–1941)**
Mosley-Braun, Carol (U.S. Senator); Chicago, 8/16/47
Moses, Grandma (Mrs. Anna Mary Robertson Moses) (painter); Greenwich, N.Y. **(1860–1961)**
Moses, Robert (urban planner); New Haven, Conn. **(1888–1981)**
Mostel, Zero (Samuel Joel Mostel) (actor); Brooklyn, N.Y. **(1915–1977)**
Motherwell, Robert (artist, "action" painter); Aberdeen, Wash. **(1915–1991)**
Mott, Lucretia (Coffin) (feminist, reformer); Nantucket, Mass. **(1793–1880)**
Moussorgsky, Modest Petrovich (composer); Karev, Russia **(1839–1881)**
Moyers, Bill D. (Billy Don) (journalist); Hugo, Okla., 6/5/34
Moynihan, Daniel Patrick (New York Senator); Tulsa, Okla., 3/16/27
Mozart, Wolfgang Amadeus (Johannes Chrysostomus Wolfgangus Theophilus Mozart) (composer); Salzburg (Austria) **(1756–1791)**
Mudd, Roger (TV newscaster); Washington, D.C., 2/9/28
Muggeridge, Malcolm (Thomas) (writer); Croydon, England **(1903–1990)**
Muhammad, (founder of Islam); Mecca (Saudi Arabia) **(c.570–632)**
Muhammad, Elijah (Elijah Poole) (religious leader); Sandersville, Ga. **(1897–1975)**
Mulgrew, Kate (actress); Dubuque, Iowa, 4/29/55
Mulhare, Edward (actor); Ireland **(1923–1997)**
Mumford, Lewis (cultural historian, city planner); Flushing, Queens, N.Y. **(1895–1990)**
Munch, Edvard (painter); Löten, Norway **(1863–1944)**
Munchhausen, Karl Friedrick Hieronymus, baron von (anecdotist); Hanover, Germany **(1720–1797)**
Muni, Paul (Muni Weisenfreund) (actor); Lemburg, (Ukraine) **(1895–1967)**
Muñoz Marin, Luis (ex-governor of Puerto Rico); San Juan, P.R. **(1898–1980)**
Munsel, Patrice (soprano); Spokane, Wash., 5/14/25
Murdoch, Iris (novelist); Dublin, 7/15/19
Murdoch, Rupert (publisher); Melbourne, 3/11/31
Murillo, Bartolomé Esteban (painter); Seville, Spain **(1617–1682)**
Murphy, Audie (actor, war hero); Kingston, Tex. **(1924–1971)**
Murphy, Eddie (actor, comedian); Brooklyn, N.Y., 4/3/61
Murphy, George (actor, dancer, ex-Senator); New Haven, Conn. **(1902–1992)**
Murray, Arthur (dance teacher); New York City **(1895–1991)**
Murray, Bill (actor, comedian); Wilmette, Ill., 9/21/50
Murray, Kathryn (dance teacher); Jersey City, N.J., 1906
Murrow, Edward R. (commentator, government official); Greensboro, N.C. **(1908–1965)**
Musil, Robert (novelist); Klagenfurt, Austria **(1880–1942)**
Muskie, Edmund (political figure); Rumford, Me. **(1914–1996)**
Mussolini, Benito (Italian dictator); Dovia, Forli, Italy **(1883–1945)**
Muti, Riccardo (orchestra conductor); Naples, Italy, 7/28/41
Mutter, Anne-Sophie (violinist); Rheinfelden, Germany, 6/29/63
Myerson, Bess (consumer advocate); Bronx, N.Y., 7/16/24
Myrdal, Gunnar (sociologist, economist); Gustaf Parish, Sweden **(1898–1987)**

N

Nabokov, Vladimir (novelist); St. Petersburg, Russia **(1899–1977)**
Nabors, Jim (actor, singer); Sylacauga, Ala., 6/12/32
Nader, Ralph (consumer advocate); Winsted, Conn., 2/27/34
Nagel, Conrad (actor); Keokuk, Iowa **(1897–1970)**
Naish, J. Carrol (actor); New York City **(1900–1973)**
Naldi, Nita (Anita Donna Dooley) (actress); New York City **(1899–1961)**
Nash, Graham (singer); Blackpool, England, 1942

Nash, Ogden (poet); Rye, N.Y. **(1902–1971)**
Nasser, Gamal Abdel (statesman); Beni Mor, Egypt **(1918–1970)**
Nast, Thomas (cartoonist); Landau (Germany) **(1840–1902)**
Nation, Carry Amelia (temperance leader); Garrard County, Ky. **(1846–1911)**
Natwick, Mildred (actress); Baltimore **(1905–1994)**
Nazimova, Alla (actress); Yalta, Crimea, Russia **(1879–1945)**
Neagle, Anna (Marjorie Robertson) (actress); London **(1908–1986)**
Neal, Patricia (actress); Packard, Ky., 1/20/26
Neeson, Liam (William John) (actor); Ballymena, Northern Ireland, 6/7/52
Neff, Hildegarde (actress); Ulm, Germany, 12/28/25
Negri, Pola (Apolina Mathias-Chalupec) (actress); Bromberg (Poland) **(1899–1987)**
Nehru, Jawaharlal (first Prime Minister of India); Allahabad, India **(1889–1964)**
Neill, Sam (Nigel Neill) (actor); Ulster, Northern Ireland, 9/14/47
Nelligan, Kate (actress); London, Ont., Canada, 3/16/51
Nelson, Barry (Neilsen) (actor); San Francisco, 4/16/20
Nelson, David (actor); New York City, 10/24/36
Nelson, Harriet Hilliard (Peggy Lou Snyder) (actress); Des Moines, Iowa **(1909–1994)**
Nelson, Ozzie (Oswald) (actor); Jersey City, N.J. **(1907–1975)**
Nelson, Ricky (Eric) (singer, actor); Teaneck, N.J. **(1940–1985)**
Nelson, Viscount Horatio (naval officer); Burnham Thorpe, England **(1758–1805)**
Nelson, Willie (singer); Waco, Tex., 4/30/33
Nenni, Pietro (Socialist leader); Faenza, Italy **(1891–1980)**
Nero (Nero Claudius Caesar Drusus Germanicus) (Roman emperor); Antium, (Italy) **(37–68)**
Nero, Peter (pianist); New York City, 5/22/34
Netanyahu, Benjamin (Binyamin) (Israeli Prime Minister); Tel Aviv, Israel, 10/21/49
Nevelson, Louise (sculptor); Kiev, Russia **(1899–1988)**
Newhart, Bob (actor); Chicago, 9/5/29
Newhouse, Samuel I. (publisher); New York City **(1895–1979)**
Newley, Anthony (actor, songwriter); London, 9/24/31
Newman, Edwin (news commentator); New York City, 1/25/19
Newman, John Henry (prelate); London **(1801–1890)**
Newman, Paul (actor, director); Cleveland, 1/26/25
Newman, Randy (singer); Los Angeles, 11/28/43
Newton, Huey (black activist); New Orleans **(1942–1989)**
Newton, Sir Isaac (mathematician, scientist); nr. Grantham, England **(1642–1727)**
Newton, Wayne (singer); Norfolk, Va., 4/3/42
Newton-John, Olivia (singer); Cambridge, England, 9/26/48
Nichols, Mike (Michael Peschkowsky) (stage and film director); Berlin, 11/6/31
Nicholson, Jack (actor, director, writer); Neptune, N.J., 4/22/37
Nietzsche, Friedrich Wilhelm (philosopher); nr. Lützen Saxony (Germany) **(1844–1900)**
Nightingale, Florence (nurse); Florence, Italy **(1820–1910)**
Nijinsky, Vaslav (ballet dancer); Warsaw **(1890–1950)**
Nilsson, Birgit (soprano); West Karup, Sweden, 5/17/23
Nilsson, Harry (singer, songwriter); Brooklyn, N.Y. **(1941–1994)**
Nimitz, Chester W. (naval officer); Fredericksburg, Tex. **(1885–1966)**
Nimoy, Leonard (actor, director, writer, producer); Boston, 3/26/31
Nin, Ánais (author, diarist); Neuilly, France **(1903–1977)**
Niven, David (actor); Kirriemuir, Scotland **(1910–1983)**
Nizer, Louis (lawyer, author); London **(1902–1994)**
Nobel, Alfred Bernhard (industrialist); Stockholm **(1833–1896)**
Noguchi, Isamu (sculptor); Los Angeles **(1904–1988)**
Nolan, Lloyd (actor); San Francisco **(1902–1985)**
Nolte, Nick (actor); Omaha, Neb., 2/8/40
Norell, Norman (Norman Levinson) (fashion designer); Noblesville, Ind. **(1900–1972)**
Norman, Jessye (soprano); Augusta, Ga., 9/15/45
Norman, Marsha (Marsha Williams) (playwright); Louisville, Ky., 9/21/47
Normand, Mabel (actress); Boston **(1894–1930)**
Norstad, Gen. Lauris (ex-commander of NATO forces); Minneapolis **(1907–1988)**
North, John Ringling (circus director); Baraboo, Wis. **(1903–1985)**
North, Oliver (ex-military officer); San Antonio, Tex., 10/7/43
North, Sheree (actress); Los Angeles, 1/17/33
Norton, Eleanor Holmes (New York City government official, lawyer); Washington, D.C., 6/13/37
Nostradamus (Michel de Notredame) (astrologer); St. Rémy, France **(1503–1566)**
Novaes, Guiomar (pianist); São João de Boa Vista, Brazil **(1895–1979)**
Novak, Kim (Marilyn Novak) (actress); Chicago, 2/13/33
Novarro, Ramon (Ramon Samaniegoes) (actor); Durango, Mexico **(1899–1968)**
Novello, Ivor (actor, playwright, composer); Cardiff, Wales **(1893–1951)**
Nugent, Elliott (actor, director); Dover, Ohio **(1899–1980)**
Nureyev, Rudolf (ballet dancer); Siberia **(1938–1993)**
Nyro, Laura (singer, songwriter); Bronx, N.Y. **(1947–1997)**

O

Oakie, Jack (actor); Sedalia, Mo. **(1903–1978)**
Oakley, Annie (Phoebe Anne Oakley Mozee) (markswoman); Darke County, Ohio **(1860–1926)**
Oates, Joyce Carol (novelist); Lockport, N.Y., 6/16/38
Oberon, Merle (Estelle Merle O'Brien Thompson) (actress); Calcutta, India **(1911–1979)**
Oberth, Hermann (rocketry and space flight pioneer); Hermannstadt, Romania **(1894–1989)**
O'Brian, Hugh (Hugh J. Krampe) (actor); Rochester, N.Y., 4/19/30
O'Brien, Conan (TV personality); Brookline, Mass., 4/18/63
O'Brien, Edmond (actor); New York City **(1915–1985)**
O'Brien, Margaret (Angela Maxine O'Brien) (actress); San Diego, Calif., 1/15/37
O'Brien, Pat (William Joseph O'Brien, Jr.) (actor); Milwaukee **(1899–1983)**
O'Casey, Sean (playwright); Dublin **(1881–1964)**
Ochs, Adolph Simon (publisher); Cincinnati **(1858–1935)**
O'Connor, Carroll (actor); New York City, 8/2/24
Odets, Clifford (playwright); Philadelphia **(1906–1963)**
Odetta (Odetta Holmes) (folk singer, actress); Birmingham, Ala., 12/31/30
O'Donnell, Rosie (actress, talk show host); Commack, N.Y., 3/21/62
Offenbach, Jacques (composer); Cologne, Germany **(1819–1880)**
O'Hara, John (novelist); Pottsville, Pa. **(1905–1970)**
O'Hara, Maureen (Maureen FitzSimons) (actress); Dublin, 8/17/21
Ohlsson, Garrick (pianist); Bronxville, N.Y., 4/3/48
Ohrbach, Jerry (actor, singer); Bronx, N.Y., 10/20/35
Oistrakh, David (concert violinist); Odessa, Russia **(1908–1974)**
O'Keeffe, Georgia (painter); Sun Prairie, Wis. **(1887–1986)**
Oland, Warner (actor); Umea, Sweden **(1880–1938)**
Oldenburg, Claes (painter); Stockholm, Sweden, 1/28/29
Oliphant, Patrick B. (editorial cartoonist); Adelaide, Australia, 7/24/35
Oliver, Edna May (actress); Malden, Mass. **(1883–1942)**
Olivier, Sir Laurence (actor); Dorking, England **(1907–1989)**
Olmos, Edward James (actor); East Los Angeles, 2/24/47
Olmsted, Frederick Law (landscape architect); Hartford, Conn. **(1822–1903)**
Olsen, Ole (John Sigvard Olsen) (comedian); Peru, Ind. **(1892–1963)**
Omar Khayyam (poet, astronomer); Nishapur (Iran) (died c. 1123)
Onassis, Aristotle (shipping executive); Smyrna, Turkey **(1906–1975)**
Onassis, Christina (shipping executive); New York City **(1950–1988)**
Onassis, Jacqueline Kennedy (Jacqueline Bouvier) (First Lady); Southampton, N.Y. **(1929–1994)**
O'Neal, Ryan (Patrick) (actor); Los Angeles, 4/20/41
O'Neal, Tatum (actress); Los Angeles, 11/5/63
O'Neill, Eugene Gladstone (playwright); New York City **(1888–1953)**
O'Neill, Jennifer (actress); Rio de Janeiro, 2/20/49
Oppenheimer, J. Robert (nuclear physicist); New York City **(1904–1967)**
Orff, Carl (composer); Munich, Germany **(1895–1982)**
Orlando, Tony (Michael Anthony Orlando Cassavitis) (singer); New York City, 4/3/44
Ormandy, Eugene (conductor); Budapest **(1899–1985)**
Ormond, Julia (actress); Epsom, Surrey, U.K., 1/4/65
Orozco, José Clemente (painter); Zapotlán, Jalisco, Mexico **(1883–1949)**
Orwell, George (Eric Arthur Blair) (British author); Motihari, India **(1903–1950)**
Osborn, Paul (playwright); Evansville, Ind. **(1901–1988)**
Osborne, John (playwright); London **(1929–1994)**
Osler, Sir William (physician); Bondhead, Ontario, Canada **(1849–1919)**
Osmond, Donny (singer, actor); Ogden, Utah, 12/9/57
Osmond, Marie (Olive Marie) (singer, actress); Ogden, Utah, 10/13/59
O'Sullivan, Maureen (actress); County Roscommon, Ireland, 5/17/11
Oswald, Lee Harvey (presumed assassin); New Orleans **(1939–1963)**
Otis, Elisha (inventor); Halifax, Vt. **(1811–1861)**
O'Toole, Peter (actor); Connemara, Ireland, 8/2/33
Ovid (Publius Ovidius Naso) (poet); Sulmona (Italy) **(43 B.C.E.–C.E. 17)**
Owens, Buck (Alvis Edgar Owens) (singer); Sherman, Tex., 8/12/29
Ozawa, Seiji (orchestra conductor); Fentian (Shenyan), Manchuria, 7/1/35

P

Paar, Jack (TV personality); Canton, Ohio, 5/1/18
Pacino, Al (Alfred) (actor); New York City, 4/25/40
Packard, Vance (author); Granville Summit, Pa. **(1914–1996)**
Paderewski, Ignace Jan (pianist, statesman); Kurylowka, Russian Podolia **(1860–1941)**
Paganini, Nicolò (violinist); Genoa (Italy) **(1782–1840)**
Page, Geraldine (actress); Kirksville, Mo. **(1924–1987)**

Page, Patti (Clara Ann Fowler) (singer, entertainer); Claremore, Okla., 11/8/27

Pagels, Elaine Hiesey (religious scholar); Palo Alto, Calif., 2/13/43

Paglia, Camille (writer, social critic); Endicott, N.Y., 4/2/47

Paine, Thomas (political philosopher); Thetford, England **(1737–1809)**

Palance, Jack (Walter Palanuik) (actor); Lattimer, Pa., 2/18/20

Palestrina, Giovanni Pierluigi da (composer); Palestrina, Italy **(1526–1594)**

Paley, William S. (broadcasting executive); Chicago **(1901–1990)**

Palladio, Andrea (architect); Padua or Vicenza (Italy) **(1508–1580)**

Palmerston, Henry John Templeton (3rd Viscount) (statesman); Broadlands, England **(1784–1865)**

Paltrow, Gwyneth (actress); Los Angeles, 9/28/73

Papanicolaou, George N. (physician); Coumi, Greece **(1883–1962)**

Papas, Irene (Lelekou) (actress); Chiliomodian, Greece, 3/9/26

Papp, Joseph (Joseph Papirofsky) (stage producer, director); Brooklyn, N.Y. **(1921–1991)**

Paracelaus, Philippus (Aureolus Theophrastus Bombastus von Hohenheim) (physican); Einsiedeln, Switzerland **(1493–1541)**

Park, Chung Hee (President of South Korea); Sangmo-ri, Korea **(1917–1979)**

Parker, Charlie "Bird" (jazz musician); Kansas City, Kan. **(1920–1955)**

Parker, Dorothy (Dorothy Rothschild) (author); West End, N.J. **(1893–1967)**

Parker, Fess (actor); Fort Worth, Tex., 8/16/25

Parker, Suzy (model, actress); San Antonio, 10/28/33

Parkinson, C(yril) Northcote (historian); Durham, England **(1909–1993)**

Parkman, Francis (historian); Boston **(1823–1893)**

Parks, Bert (Bert Jacobson) (entertainer); Atlanta **(1914–1992)**

Parks, Gordon (film director); Ft. Scott, Kan., 11/30/12

Parks, Rosa (civil rights activist); Tuskegee, Ala., 2/4/13

Parnell, Charles Stewart (statesman); Avondale, Ireland **(1846–1891)**

Parnis, Mollie (Mollie Parnis Livingston) (fashion designer); New York City **(1905?–1992)**

Parsons, Estelle (actress); Marblehead, Mass., 11/20/27

Parton, Dolly (singer); Locust Ridge, Tenn., 1/19/46

Pascal, Blaise (philosopher); Clermont, France **(1623–1662)**

Pasternak, Boris Leonidovich (author); Moscow **(1890–1960)**

Pasternak, Joseph (film producer); Silagy-Somlyo, Romania **(1901–1991)**

Pasteur, Louis (chemist); Dôle, France **(1822–1895)**

Pastor, Tony (Antonio) (actor, theater manager); New York City **(1837–1908)**

Pater, Walter (Horatio) (writer); London **(1839–1894)**

Patinkin, Mandy (Mandel) (actor, singer); Chicago, 11/30/52

Paton, Alan (author); Pietermaritzburg, South Africa **(1903–1988)**

Patti, Adelina (soprano); Madrid **(1843–1919)**

Patton, George Smith, Jr. (general); San Gabriel, Calif. **(1885–1945)**

Paul, Alice (feminist, woman suffragist); Moorestown, N.J. **(1885–1977)**

Paul, Les (Lester William Polfus) (guitarist); Waukesha, Wis., 6/9/15

Paul VI (Giovanni Battista Montini) (Pope); Concesio, nr. Brescia, Italy **(1897–1978)**

Pauley, Jane (TV newscaster); Indianapolis, 10/31/50

Pauling, Linus Carl (chemist); Portland, Ore. **(1901–1994)**

Pavarotti, Luciano (tenor); Modena, Italy, 10/12/35

Pavlov, Ivan Petrovich (physiologist); Ryazan district, Russia **(1849–1936)**

Pavlova, Anna (ballerina); St. Petersburg, Russia **(1885–1931)**

Peale, Norman Vincent (clergyman); Bowersville, Ohio **(1898–1993)**

Pearl, Minnie (Sarah Ophelia Colley Cannon) (comedienne, singer); Centerville, Tenn., 10/25/12

Pears, Peter (tenor); Farnham, England **(1910–1986)**

Pearson, Drew (Andrew Russel Pearson) (columnist); Evanston. Ill. **(1897–1969)**

Pearson, Lester B. (statesman); Toronto **(1897–1972)**

Peary, Robert Edwin (explorer); Cresson, Pa. **(1856–1920)**

Peck, Gregory (actor); La Jolla, Calif., 4/5/16

Peckinpah, Sam (film director); Fresno, Calif. **(1925–1984)**

Peerce, Jan (tenor); New York City **(1904–1984)**

Pegler, (James) Westbrook (columnist); Minneapolis **(1894–1969)**

Pei, I(eoh) M(ing) (architect); Canton, China, 4/26/17

Penn, Arthur (director); Philadelphia, 9/27/22

Penn, Sean (actor, filmmaker); Los Angeles, 8/17/60

Penn, William (American colonist); London **(1644–1718)**

Penney, James C. (merchant); Hamilton, Mo. **(1875–1971)**

Peppard, George (actor); Detroit, Mich. **(1929–1994)**

Pepys, Samuel (diarist); Bampton, England **(1633–1703)**

Perelman, S(idney) J(oseph) (writer); Brooklyn, N.Y. **(1904–1979)**

Pergolesi, Giovanni Battista (composer); Jesi, Italy **(1710–1736)**

Pericles (statesman); Athens (died 429 B.C.E.)

Perkins, Anthony (actor); New York City **(1932–1992)**

Perkins, Frances (social reformer); Boston **(1882–1965)**

Perlman, Itzhak (violinist); Tel Aviv, Israel, 8/31/45

Perlman, Rhea (actress); Brooklyn, N.Y., 3/31/48

Perón, Isabel (María Estela Martínez Cartas) (former chief of state); La Rioja, Argentina, 2/4/31

Perón, Juan D. (statesman); nr. Lobos, Argentina **(1895–1974)**

Perón, Maria Eva Duarte de (political leader); Los Toldos, Argentina **(1919–1952)**

Perot, H. Ross (business executive); Texarkana, Tex., 6/27/30

Perrine, Valerie (actress, dancer); Galveston, Tex., 9/3/43

Perry, Matthew (actor); Williamstown, Mass., 8/19/69

Pershing, John Joseph (general); Linn County, Mo. **(1860–1948)**

Pestalozzi, Johann (educator); Zurich, Switzerland **(1746–1827)**

Peters, Bernadette (Bernadette Lazzara) (actress); New York City, 2/28/48

Peters, Brock (actor, singer); New York City, 7/2/27

Peters, Jean (actress); Canton, Ohio, 10/15/26

Peters, Roberta (Roberta Peterman) (soprano); New York City, 5/4/30

Petit, Roland (choreographer, dancer); Villemombe, France, 1924

Petrarch (Francesco Petrarca) (poet); Arezzo (Italy) **(1304–1374)**

Pfeiffer, Michelle (actress); Santa Ana, Calif., 4/29/58

Philbin, Regis (talk show host); New York City, 8/25/33

Philip (Philip Mountbatten) (Duke of Edinburgh); Corfu, Greece, 6/10/21

Piaf, Edith (Edith Gassion) (singer); Paris **(1916–1963)**

Piatigorsky, Gregor (cellist); Ekaterinoslav, Russia **(1903–1976)**

Piazza, Marguerite (soprano); New Orleans, 5/6/26

Picasso, Pablo (painter, sculptor); Málaga, Spain **(1881–1973)**

Pickett, Wilson (singer); Prattville, Ala., 3/18/41

Pickford, Mary (Gladys Mary Smith) (actress); Toronto **(1893–1979)**

Picon, Molly (actress); New York City **(1898–1992)**

Pidgeon, Walter (actor); East St. John, New Brunswick, Canada **(1898–1984)**

Pinter, Harold (playwright); London, 10/10/30

Pinza, Ezio (basso); Rome **(1892–1957)**

Pirandello, Luigi (dramatist, novelist); nr. Girgenti, Italy **(1867–1936)**

Piranesi, Giambattista (artist); Mestre, Italy **(1720–1778)**

Pissaro, Camille Jacob (painter); St. Thomas (U.S. Virgin Islands) **(1830–1903)**

Piston, Walter (composer); Rockland, Me. **(1894–1976)**

Pitman, Sir [Isaac] James (educator, publisher); Bath, England, 8/14/01

Pitt, Brad (actor); Shawnee, Okla., 12/18/64

Pitt, William ("Younger Pitt") (statesman); nr. Bromley, England **(1759–1806)**

Pitts, ZaSu (actress); Parsons, Kan. **(1898–1963)**

Pius XII (Eugenio Pacelli) (Pope); Rome **(1876–1958)**

Pizarro, Francisco (explorer); Trujillo, Spain **(c. 1476–1541)**

Planck, Max (physicist); Kiel, Germany **(1858–1947)**

Plath, Sylvia (poet); Boston **(1932–1963)**

Plato (Aristocies) (philosopher); Athens **(c. 427–347 B.C.E.)**

Pleasence, Donald (actor); Worksop, England **(1919–1995)**

Pleshette, Suzanne (actress); New York City, 1/31/37

Plimpton, George (author); New York City, 3/18/27

Plisetskaya, Maya (ballerina); Moscow, 11/20/25

Plowright, Joan (actress); Brigg, England, 10/28/29

Plummer, Christopher (actor); Toronto, 12/13/29

Plutarch (biographer); Chaeronea (Greece) **(c. 46–c. 120)**

Pocahontas (Matoaka) (American Indian princess); (Virginia) **(c. 1595–1617)**

Podhoretz, Norman (author); Brooklyn, N.Y., 1/16/30

Poe, Edgar Allan (poet, story writer); Boston, Mass. **(1809–1849)**

Poitier, Sidney (actor, director); Miami, Fla., 2/20/27

Polanski, Roman (director); Paris, 8/18/33

Pollard, Michael J. (actor); Passaic, N.J., 5/30/39

Pollock, Jackson (painter); Cody, Wyo. **(1912–1956)**

Polo, Marco (traveler); Venice **(c. 1254–1324)**

Pol Pot, (Cambodian dictator); Kompong Thom, Cambodia, 5/19/28

Pompadour, Mme. de (Jeanne Antoinette Poisson) (courtesan); Versailles **(1721–1764)**

Pompey (Gnaeus Pompeius Magnus) (general); Rome **(106–48 B.C.E.)**

Ponce de León, Juan (explorer); Servas, Spain **(c. 1460–1521)**

Pons, Lily (coloratura soprano); Cannes, France **(1904–1976)**

Ponselle, Rosa (soprano); Meriden, Conn. **(1897–1981)**

Ponti, Carlo (director; Milan, Italy, 12/11/13

Pontormo, Jacopo da (painter); Pontormo, Italy **(1492–1557)**

Pope, Alexander (poet); London **(1688–1744)**

Porter, Cole (songwriter); Peru, Ind. **(1891–1964)**

Porter, Katherine Anne (novelist); Indian Creek, Tex. **(1891–1980)**

Post, Wiley (aviator); Grand Plain, Tex. **(1900–1935)**

Poston, Tom (actor); Columbus, Ohio, 10/17/27

Potëmkin, Grigori Aleksandrovich, Prince (statesman); Khizovo (Khizov, Belarus) **(1739–1791)**

Potok, Chaim (author); New York City, 2/17/29

Potter, (Helen) Beatrix (author, illustrator); South Kensington, Middlesex, England **(1866–1943)**

Poulenc, Francis (composer); Paris **(1899–1963)**

Pound, Ezra (poet); Hailey, Idaho **(1885–1972)**

Poussin, Nicolas (painter); Villers, France **(1594–1665)**

Powell, Adam Clayton, Jr. (Congressman); New Haven, Conn. **(1908–1972)**

Powell, Colin L. (retired general); New York City, 4/5/37

Powell, Dick (actor); Mt. View, Ark. **(1904–1963)**

Powell, Eleanor (actress, tap dancer); Springfield, Mass. **(1912–1982)**
Powell, Jane (Suzanne Burce) (actress, singer); Portland, Ore., 4/1/29
Powell, William (actor); Pittsburgh **(1892–1984)**
Power, Tyrone (actor); Cincinnati, Ohio **(1914–1958)**
Powers, Stephanie (Taffy Paul) (actress); Hollywood, Calif., 11/12/42
Praxiteles (sculptor); Athens **(c.370–c.330 B.C.E.)**
Preminger, Otto (director, producer); Vienna **(1906–1986)**
Prentiss, Paula (Paula Ragusa) (actress); San Antonio, 3/4/39
Presley, Elvis (singer, actor); Tupelo, Miss. **(1935–1977)**
Presley, Priscilla (actress); Brooklyn, N.Y., 5/24/45
Preston, Robert (Robert Preston Meservey) (actor); Newton Highlands, Mass **(1918–1987)**
Previn, André (conductor); Berlin, 4/6/29
Previn, Dory (singer); Rahway, N.J., 10/22/29?
Price, Leontyne (Mary) (soprano); Laurel, Miss., 2/10/27
Price, Ray (country music artist); Perryville, Tex., 1/12/26
Price, Vincent (actor); St. Louis **(1911–1993)**
Pride, Charley (singer); Sledge, Miss., 3/18/38?
Priestley, J. B. (John B.) (author); Bradford, England **(1894–1984)**
Priestley, Joseph (chemist); nr. Leeds, England **(1733–1804)**
Primrose, William (violist); Glasgow, Scotland **(1904–1982)**
Prince (Prince Roger Nelson) (singer); Minneapolis, 6/7/58
Prince, Harold (stage producer); New York City, 1/30/28
Principal, Victoria (actress); Fukuoka, Japan, 1/3/45?
Prinze, Freddie (actor); New York City **(1954–1977)**
Pritchett, V(ictor) S(awdon) (literary critic); Ipswich, England **(1900–1997)**
Procter, William (scientist); Cincinnati **(1872–1951)**
Prokofiev, Sergei Sergeevich (composer); St. Petersburg, Russia **(1891–1953)**
Proulx, E. Annie (novelist); Norwich, Conn., 8/22/35
Proust, Marcel (novelist); Paris **(1871–1922)**
Provine, Dorothy (actress); Deadwood, S. Dak., 1/20/37
Prowse, Juliet (actress); Bombay **(1936–1996)**
Pryor, Richard (comedian); Peoria, Ill., 12/1/40
Ptolemy (Claudius Ptolemaeus) (astronomer, geographer); Ptolemais Hermii, (Egypt), fl. 2nd cent.
Pucci, Emilio (Marchese di Barsento) (fashion designer); Naples, Italy **(1914–1992)**
Puccini, Giacomo (composer); Lucca, Italy **(1858–1924)**
Puente, Tito (band leader); New York City, 4/20/23
Pulaski, Casimir (military officer); Podolia, Poland **(1748–1779)**
Pulitzer, Joseph (publisher); Makó (Hungary) **(1847–1911)**
Pullman, George (inventor); Brockton, N.Y. **(1831–1897)**
Purcell, Henry (composer); London **(1658–1695)**
Pusey, Nathan M. (educator); Council Bluffs, Iowa, 4/4/07
Pushkin, Alexander Sergeevich (poet, dramatist); Moscow **(1799–1837)**
Puzo, Mario (novelist); New York City, 10/15/21
Pyle, Ernest Taylor (journalist); Dana, Ind. **(1900–1945)**
Pythagoras (mathematician, philosopher); Samos (Greece) **(c. 582–c. 507B.C.E.)**

Q

Qaddafi, Muammar al- (Libyan leader); Libya, 1942
Quaid, Dennis (actor); Houston, Tex., 4/9/54
Quaid, Randy, (actor); Houston, Tex., 10/1/50
Quayle, Anthony (actor); Ainsdale, England **(1913–1989)**
Queen, Ellery: pen name of the late Frederic Dannay and the late Manfred B. Lee
Queler, Eve (conductor); New York City, 1/1/36
Quennell, Sir Peter Courtney (biographer); Bromley, England **(1905–1993)**
Quindlen, Anna (writer); Philadelphia, 7/8/53
Quinn, Anthony (actor); Chihuahua, Mexico, 4/21/16

R

Rabe, David (playwright); Dubuque, Iowa, 3/10/40
Rabelais, François (satirist); nr. Chinon, France **(c. 1490–1553)**
Rabi, I(sidor) I(saac) (physicist); Rymanow (Poland) **(1898–1988)**
Rabin, Yitzhak (former Israeli Prime Minister); Jerusalem **(1922–1995)**
Rachmaninoff, Sergei Wassilievitch (pianist, composer); Oneg Estate, Novgorod, Russia **(1873–1943)**
Racine, Jean Baptiste (dramatist); La Ferté-Milon, France **(1639–1699)**
Radner, Gilda (comedienne); Detroit, Mich. **(1946–1989)**
Raft, George (actor); New York City **(1895–1980)**
Rainier III (Prince); Monaco, 5/31/23
Rains, Claude (actor); London **(1889–1967)**
Raitt, Bonnie (singer); Burbank, Calif., 11/8/49
Raitt, John (actor, singer); Santa Ana, Calif., 1/19/17
Raleigh, Sir Walter (courtier, navigator); London **(1552?–1618)**
Rambeau, Marjorie (actress); San Francisco **(1889–1970)**
Rameau, Jean-Philippe (composer); Dijon, France **(1683–1764)**

Rampal, Jean-Pierre (Louis) (flutist); Marseilles, France, 7/1/22
Rand, Ayn (novelist, philosopher); St. Petersburg, Russia **(1905–1982)**
Randall, Tony (Leonard Rosenberg) (actor); Tulsa, Okla., 2/26/20
Randolph, A(sa) Philip (labor leader); Crescent City, Fla. **(1889–1979)**
Rankin, Jeannette (pacifist); Missoula, Mont. **(1880–1973)**
Raphael (Raffaello Santi) (painter, architect); Urbino (Italy) **(1483–1520)**
Rasputin, Grigori Efimovich (monk); Tobolsk Province, Russia **(1872–1916)**
Rathbone, Basil (actor); Johannesburg, South Africa **(1892–1967)**
Rather, Dan (TV newscaster); Wharton, Tex., 10/31/31
Rattigan, Terence (playwright); London **(1911–1977)**
Rauschenberg, Robert (painter); Port Arthur, Tex., 10/22/25
Ravel, Maurice Joseph (composer); Ciboure, France **(1875–1937)**
Ray, Aldo (DaRe) (actor); Pen Argyl, Pa. **(1926–1991)**
Ray, Gene Anthony (actor, dancer); Harlem, N.Y., 5/24/63
Ray, Man (painter); Philadelphia **(1890–1976)**
Ray, Satyajat (film director); Calcutta **(1921–1992)**
Raye, Martha (Margie Yvonne Reed) (comedienne, actress); Butte, Mont. **(1916–1994)**
Reasoner, Harry (TV commentator); Dakota City, Iowa **(1923–1991)**
Redding, Otis (singer); Dawson, Ga. **(1941–1967)**
Reddy, Helen (singer); Melbourne, 10/25/41
Redford, Robert (Charles Robert Redford, Jr.) (actor); Santa Monica, Calif., 8/18/37
Redgrave, Lynn (actress); London, 3/8/43
Redgrave, Sir Michael (actor); Bristol, England **(1908–1985)**
Redgrave, Vanessa (actress); London, 1/30/37
Redon, Odilon (artist); Bordeaux, France **(1840–1916)**
Reed, Donna (actress); Denison, Iowa **(1921–1986)**
Reed, Rex (critic); Ft. Worth, 10/2/40
Reed, Walter (army surgeon); Belroi, Va. **(1851–1902)**
Reese, Della (Deloreese Patricia Early) (singer, actress); Detroit, Mich., 7/6/32
Reeve, Christopher (actor, activist); New York City, 9/25/52
Reeves, Jim (singer); Panola County, Tex. **(1923–1964)**
Reich, Robert (Clinton Cabinet Member); Scranton, Pa., 6/24/46
Reich, Steve (composer); New York City, 10/3/36
Reid, Wallace (actor); St. Louis **(1891–1923)**
Reiner, Carl (actor); New York City, 3/20/22
Reiner, Fritz (conductor); Budapest **(1888–1963)**
Reiner, Robert (actor, director, writer, producer); Bronx, N.Y., 3/6/45
Reinhardt, Max (Max Goldmann) (theater producer); nr. Vienna **(1873–1943)**
Reiser, Paul (actor, producer); New York City, 3/30/57
Remarque, Erich Maria (novelist); Osnabrük, Germany **(1898–1970)**
Rembrandt (Rembrandt Harmensz van Rijn) (painter); Leyden, (Netherlands) **(1605–1669)**
Remick, Lee (Ann) (actress); Boston **(1935–1991)**
Rennert, Günther (opera director, producer); Essen, Germany, 4/1/11
Rennie, Michael (actor); Bradford, England **(1909–1971)**
Reno, Janet (U.S. Attorney General); Miami, Fla., 7/21/38
Renoir, Jean (film director, writer); Paris **(1894–1979)**
Renoir, Pierre Auguste (painter); Limoges, France **(1841–1919)**
Resnais, Alain (film director); Vannes, France, 6/3/22
Resnik, Regina (mezzo-soprano); New York City, 8/30/22
Respighi, Ottorino (composer); Bologna, Italy **(1879–1936)**
Reston, James (journalist); Clydebank, Scotland **(1909–1995)**
Reuther, Walter (labor leader); Wheeling, W. Va. **(1907–1970)**
Revere, Paul (silversmith, hero of famous ride); Boston **(1735–1818)**
Revson, Charles (business executive); Boston **(1906–1975)**
Reynolds, Burt (actor, director, producer); Lansing, Mich., 2/11/36
Reynolds, Debbie (Marie Frances Reynolds) (actress); El Paso, 4/1/32
Reynolds, Sir Joshua (painter); nr. Plymouth, England **(1723–1792)**
Reynolds, Marjorie (Goodspeed) (actress); Buhl, Idaho, 8/12/21
Rhodes, Cecil John (South African statesman); Bishop Stortford, England **(1853–1902)**
Rice, Anne (novelist); New Orleans, 10/14/41
Rice, Elmer (playwright); New York City **(1892–1967)**
Rice, Grantland (sports writer); Murfreesboro, Tenn. **(1880–1954)**
Rich, Buddy (Bernard) (drummer); Brooklyn, N.Y. **(1917–1987)**
Rich, Charlie (singer); Colt, Ark., 12/14/32
Richard I the Lion-hearted (King of England); Oxford, England **(1157–1199)**
Richards, Ann (Dorothy Ann Willis) (ex-governor of Texas); Lakeview, Tex., 9/1/33
Richards, Keith (rock singer); Dartford, England, 12/18/43
Richardson, Elliot L. (ex-Cabinet member); Boston, 7/20/20
Richardson, Sir Ralph (actor); Cheltenham, England **(1902–1983)**
Richardson, Tony (director); Shipley, England **(1928–1991)**
Richelieu, Duc de (Armand Jean du Plessis) (cardinal); Paris **(1585–1642)**
Richie, Lionel (singer, songwriter); Tuskegee, Ala., 1949?
Richter, Charles Francis (seismologist); Hamilton, Canada **(1900–1985)**
Richter, Sviatosiav (pianist); Zhitomir, Ukraine, 3/20/14
Rickenbacker, Edward V. (aviator); Columbus, Ohio **(1890–1973)**
Rickles, Don (comedian); New York City, 5/8/26

Rickover, Vice Admiral Hyman G. (atomic energy expert); Russia **(1900–1986)**

Riddle, Nelson (composer); Hackensack, N.J. **(1921–1985)**

Ride, Sally K(risten) (astronaut, astrophysicist); Encino, Calif., 5/26/51

Ridgway, General Matthew B. (ex-Army Chief of Staff); Ft. Monroe, Va. **(1895–1993)**

Riemenschneider, Tilman (sculptor); Osterode, Germany **(c.1460–1531)**

Rigg, Diana (actress); Doncaster, England, 7/20/38

Riley, James Whitcomb (poet); Greenfield, Ind. **(1849–1916)**

Rilke, Rainer Maria (poet); Prague **(1875–1926)**

Rimbaud, (Jean Nicolas) Arthur (poet); Charleville, France **(1854–1891)**

Rimsky-Korsakov, Nikolai Andreevich (composer); Tikhvin, Russia **(1844–1908)**

Rinehart, Mary (née Roberts) (novelist); Pittsburgh **(1876–1958)**

Ritchard, Cyril (actor, director); Sydney, Australia **(1898–1977)**

Ritter, John (Jonathan) (actor); Burbank, Calif., 9/17/48

Ritter, Tex (Woodward Maurice Ritter) (singer); Panola County, Tex. **(1905–1973)**

Ritter, Thelma (actress); Brooklyn, N.Y. **(1905–1969)**

Rivera, Chita (Dolores Conchita Figuero del Rivero) (dancer, actress, singer); Washington, D.C., 1/23/33

Rivera, Diego (painter); Guanajuato, Mexico **(1886–1957)**

Rivera, Geraldo (Miguel) (TV host); New York City, 7/3/43

Rivers, Joan (comedienne); Brooklyn, N.Y., 6/8/33

Rivers, Larry (Yitzroch Loiza Grossberg) (painter); New York City, 8/17/23

Roach, Hal (film producer); Elmira, N.Y. **(1892–1992)**

Robards, Jason, Jr. (actor); Chicago, 7/26/22

Robards, Jason, Sr. (actor); Hillsdale, Mich. **(1892–1963)**

Robbins, Harold (Harold Rubin) (novelist); New York City, 5/21/16

Robbins, Jerome (Jerome Rabinowitz) (choreographer); New York City, 10/11/18

Robbins, Marty (singer); Glendale, Ariz. **(1925–1982)**

Robbins, Tim (Timothy Francis) (actor, director); West Covina, Calif., 10/16/58

Roberts, Cokie (Mary Martha Corinne Morrison Claiborne Boggs) (broadcast journalist); New Orleans, 12/27/43

Roberts, Eric (actor); Biloxi, Miss., 4/18/56

Roberts, Julia (actress); Smyrna, Ga., 10/28/67

Roberts, Oral (Granville) (evangelist, publisher); nr. Ada, Okla., 1/24/18

Robertson, Cliff (actor); La Jolla, Calif., 9/9/25

Robertson, Dale (Dayle) (actor); Oklahoma City, 7/14/23

Robeson, Paul (singer, actor); Princeton, N.J. **(1898–1976)**

Robespierre, Maximilien François Marie Isidore de (French Revolutionist); Arras, France **(1758–1794)**

Robinson, Bill "Bojangles" (Luther) (dancer); Richmond, Va. **(1878–1949)**

Robinson, Edward G. (Emanuel Goldenberg) (actor); Bucharest **(1893–1973)**

Robinson, Edwin Arlington (poet); Head Tide, Me. **(1869–1935)**

Robinson, Smokey (singer, songwriter); Detroit, Mich., 2/19/40

Rochester (Eddie Anderson) (actor); Oakland, Calif. **(1905–1977)**

Rockefeller, David (banker); New York City, 6/12/15

Rockefeller, John Davison (business executive); Richford, N.Y. **(1839–1937)**

Rockefeller, John Davison, Jr. (industrialist); Cleveland **(1874–1960)**

Rockefeller, John D., 3rd (philanthropist); New York City **(1906–1978)**

Rockefeller, Laurance S. (conservationist); New York City, 5/26/10

Rockwell, Norman (painter, illustrator); New York City **(1894–1978)**

Rodgers, Jimmie (singer); Meridian, Miss. **(1897–1933)**

Rodgers, Richard (composer); New York City **(1902–1979)**

Rodin, François Auguste René (sculptor); Paris **(1840–1917)**

Rodzinski, Artur (conductor); Spalato, Dalmatia **(1894–1958)**

Roeg, Nicolas (film director); London, 8/15/28

Roentgen, Wilhelm Konrad (physicist); Lennep, Prussia **(1845–1923)**

Roethke, Theodore (poet); Saginaw, Mich. **(1908–1963)**

Rogers, Buddy (Charles) (actor); Olathe, Kan., 8/13/04

Rogers, Carl (psychologist); Oak Park, Ill. **(1902–1987)**

Rogers, Fred (TV producer, host); Latrobe, Pa., 3/20/28

Rogers, Ginger (Virginia McMath) (dancer, actress); Independence, Mo. **(1911–1995)**

Rogers, Kenny (singer); Houston, 8/21/38

Rogers, Roy (Leonard Slye) (actor); Cincinnati, 11/5/12

Rogers, Wayne (actor); Birmingham, Ala., 4/7/33

Rogers, Will (William Penn Adair Rogers) (humorist); Oologah, Okla. **(1879–1935)**

Rogers, William P. (ex-Secretary of State); Norfolk, N.Y., 6/23/13

Roland, Gilbert (actor); Juarez, Mexico **(1905–1994)**

Rolland, Romain (author); Clamecy, France **(1866–1944)**

Rollins, Sonny (saxophonist); New York City, 9/7/30

Romberg, Sigmund (composer); Szeged (Hungary) **(1887–1951)**

Rome, Harold (composer); Hartford, Conn. **(1908–1993)**

Romero, Cesar (actor); New York City **(1907–1994)**

Romney, George W. (automobile executive, governor); Chihuahua, Mexico **(1907–1995)**

Romulo, Carlos P. (diplomat, educator); Manila **(1899–1985)**

Ronsard, Pierre de (poet); La Possonnière nr. Couture (Couture-sur-Loir, France) **(1524–1585)**

Ronstadt, Linda (singer); Tucson, Ariz., 7/30/46

Rooney, Andy (TV personality); Albany, N.Y., 1/14/19

Rooney, Mickey (Joe Yule, Jr.) (actor); Brooklyn, N.Y., 9/23/20

Roosevelt, Anna Eleanor (reformer, humanitarian); New York City **(1884–1962)**

Rorem, Ned (composer); Richmond, Ind., 10/23/23

Rose, Billy (showman); New York City **(1899–1966)**

Rose, Leonard (concert cellist); Washington, D.C. **(1918–1984)**

Roseanne, (Roseanne Barr) (actress); Salt Lake City, 11/3/52

Rosenberg, Ethel (spy); New York City **(1915–1953)**

Rosenberg, Julius (spy); New York City **(1918–1953)**

Ross, Betsy (Betsey Griscom) (flagmaker); Philadelphia **(1752–1836)**

Ross, Diana (singer); Detroit, Mich., 3/26/44

Ross, Katharine (actress); Hollywood, Calif., 1/29/43

Rossellini, Isabella (model, actress); Rome, Italy, 6/18/52

Rossellini, Roberto (film director); Rome **(1906–1977)**

Rossetti, Christina Georgina (poet); London **(1830–1894)**

Rossetti, Dante Gabriel (painter, poet); London **(1828–1882)**

Rossini, Gioacchino Antonio (composer); Pesaro, Italy **(1792–1868)**

Rostand, Edmond (dramatist); Marseilles, France **(1868–1918)**

Rostow, Walt Whitman (economist); New York City, 10/7/16

Rostropovich, Mstislav (cellist, conductor); Baku, (Azerbaijan), 3/27/27

Roth, Henry (writer); Tysmenica (Ukraine) **(1906–1995)**

Roth, Philip (novelist); Newark, N.J., 3/19/33

Rothko, Mark (Marcus Rothkovich) (painter); Russia **(1903–1970)**

Rouault, Georges (painter); Paris **(1871–1958)**

Roundtree, Richard (actor); New Rochelle, N.Y., 9/7/42

Rousseau, Henri (painter); Laval, France **(1844–1910)**

Rousseau, Jean Jacques (philosopher); Geneva **(1712–1778)**

Rovere, Richard H. (journalist); Jersey City, N.J., 5/5/15

Rowan, Carl Thomas (journalist); Ravenscroft, Tenn., 8/11/25

Rowan, Dan (comedian); Beggs, Okla. **(1922–1987)**

Rowlands, Gena (actress); Cambria, Wis., 6/19/30

Rubens, Sir Peter Paul (painter); Siegen(Germany) **(1577–1640)**

Rubinstein, Arthur (concert pianist); Lódz(Poland) **(1887–1982)**

Rubinstein, Helena (cosmetics executive); Krakow(Poland) **(1882?–1965)**

Rubinstein, John (actor, composer); Los Angeles, 12/8/46

Rudel, Julius (conductor); Vienna, 3/6/21

Ruffo, Titta (baritone); Italy **(1878–1953)**

Runyon, (Alfred) Damon (journalist); Manhattan, Kan. **(1884–1945)**

Rushdie, (Ahmed) Salman (novelist); Bombay, India, 6/19/47

Rusk, Dean (ex-Sec. of State); Cherokee County, Ga. **(1909–1994)**

Ruskin, John (art critic); London **(1819–1900)**

Russell, Lord Bertrand (Arthur William) (mathematician, philosopher); Trelleck, Wales **(1872–1970)**

Russell, Jane (actress); Bemidji, Minn., 6/21/21

Russell, Ken (film director); Southhampton, England, 4/3/27

Russell, Leon (pianist, singer); Lawton, Okla., 4/2/41

Russell, Lillian (Helen Louise Leonard) (soprano); Clinton, Iowa **(1861–1922)**

Russell, Mark (satirist); Buffalo, N.Y., 8/23/32

Russell, Nipsy (comedian); Atlanta, 10/13/24

Russell, Rosalind (actress); Waterbury, Conn. **(1912–1976)**

Russell, Theresa (Theresa Paup) (actress); San Diego, Calif., 3/20/57

Rustin, Bayard (civil rights leader); West Chester, Pa. **(1910–1987)**

Rutherford, Dame Margaret (actress); London **(1892–1972)**

Ryan, Robert (actor); Chicago **(1909–1973)**

Rydell, Bobby (Robert Ridarelli) (singer); Philadelphia, 4/26/42

Ryder, Winona (Winona Horowitz) (actress); Winona, Minn., 10/29/71

Rysanek, Leonie (dramatic soprano); Vienna, 11/14/28

S

Saarinen, Eero (architect); Finland **(1910–1961)**

Sabin, Albert B. (polio researcher); Bialystok (Poland) **(1906–1993)**

Sabu (Dastagir) (actor); Karapur, India **(1924–1963)**

Sacagawea, (Shoshone Indian guide); Lemhi River valley, (Id.) **(c. 1786–1812)**

Sachs, Jeffrey D. (economist, educator); Michigan, 1954

Sadat, Anwar el- (President); Egypt **(1918–1981)**

Sade, Marquis de (Donatien Alphonse François, Comte de Sade) (libertine, writer); Paris **(1740–1814)**

Safer, Morley (TV newscaster); Toronto, 11/8/31

Sagan, Carl (Edward) (astronomer, astrophysicist); New York City **(1934–1996)**

Sagan, Françoise (novelist); Cajarc, France, 6/21/35

Sahl, Mort (Morton Lyon Sahl) (comedian); Montreal, 5/11/27

Saint, Eva Marie (actress); Newark, N.J., 7/4/24

Sainte-Marie, Buffy (Beverly) (folk singer); Craven, Saskatchewan, Canada, 2/20/41

Saint-Gaudens, Augustus (sculptor); Dublin **(1848–1907)**

Saint-Laurent, Yves (Henri Donat Mathieu) (fashion designer); Oran, Algeria, 8/1/36
Saint-Saens, Charles Camille (composer); Paris **(1835–1921)**
Sakharov, Andrei Dmitriyevich (nuclear physicist, peace activist); Russia **(1921–1989)**
Sales, Soupy (Milton Hines) (television entertainer); Franklinton, N.C., 1/6/26
Salinger, J(erome) D(avid) (novelist); New York City, 1/1/19
Salisbury, Harrison E. (journalist); Minneapolis **(1908–1993)**
Salk, Jonas (polio researcher); New York City **(1914–1995)**
Salk, Lee (psychologist); New York City **(1926–1992)**
Salomon, Haym (American Revolution financier); Leszno, Poland **(1740–1785)**
Sand, George (Amandine Lucille Aurore Dudevant, née Dupin) (novelist); Paris **(1804–1876)**
Sandburg, Carl (poet, biographer); Galesburg, Ill. **(1878–1967)**
Sanders, George (actor); St. Petersburg, Russia **(1906–1972)**
Sands, Tommy (singer); Chicago, 8/27/37
Sanger, Margaret (birth control advocate); Corning, N.Y. **(1883–1966)**
Santayana, George (philosopher); Madrid **(1863–1952)**
Sappho (poet); Lesbos (Greece), fl. 6th cent. B.C.E.
Sarandon, Susan (Susan Tomaling) (actress); New York City, 10/4/46
Sargent, John Singer (painter); Florence, Italy **(1856–1925)**
Sarnoff, David (radio executive); Minsk, (Belarus) **(1891–1971)**
Saroyan, William (novelist); Fresno, Calif. **(1908–1981)**
Sarrazin, Michael (actor); Quebec, 5/22/40
Sarto, Andrea del (Andrea Domenico d'Agnolo di Francesco) (painter); Florence (Italy) **(1486–1531)**
Sartre, Jean-Paul (existentialist writer); Paris **(1905–1980)**
Sassoon, Vidal (hair stylist); London, 1/17/28
Satie, Erik (Alfred Leslie) (composer); Paris **(1866–1925)**
Saul (King of Israel) fl. 11th cent. B.C.E.
Savalas, Telly (Aristoteles) (actor); Garden City, N.Y. **(1924–1994)**
Savonarola, Girolamo (religious reformer); Ferrara, Italy **(1452–1498)**
Sawyer, Diane (broadcast journalist); Glasgow, Ky., 12/22/45
Sayão, Bidú (soprano); Rio de Janeiro, 5/11/02
Scaasi, Arnold (Arnold Isaacs) (fashion designer); Montreal,
Scarlatti, Alessandro (composer); Palermo, Italy **(1659–1725)**
Scarlatti, Domenico (composer); Naples, Italy **(1685–1757)**
Scavullo, Francesco (photographer); Staten Island, N.Y., 1/16/29
Schama, Simon (historian); London, 2/13/45
Schapiro, Meyer (Meir) (art historian); Siauliai, Lithuania **(1904–1996)**
Schary, Dore (producer, writer); Newark, N.J. **(1905–1980)**
Schell, Maximilian (actor); Vienna, 12/8/30
Schiaparelli, Elsa (fashion designer); Rome **(1890–1973)**
Schiff, Dorothy (newspaper publisher); New York City **(1903–1989)**
Schiller, Johann Christoph Friedrich von (dramatist, poet); Marbach-(Germany) **(1759–1805)**
Schipa, Tito (tenor); Lecce, Italy **(1890–1965)**
Schippers, Thomas (conductor); Kalamazoo, Mich. **(1930–1977)**
Schlegel, Friedrich von (philosopher); Hannover, Germany **(1772–1829)**
Schlesinger, Arthur M., Jr. (historian); Columbus, Ohio, 10/15/17
Schnabel, Artur (pianist, composer); Lipnik, Austria **(1882–1951)**
Schneider, Romy (Rose-Marie Albach) (actress); Vienna **(1938–1982)**
Schoenberg, Arnold (composer); Vienna **(1874–1951)**
Schomberg, Arthur (bibliophile, antiquarian); San Juan, P.R. **(1874–1938)**
Schopenhauer, Arthur (philosopher); Danzig (Poland) **(1788–1860)**
Schubert, Franz Peter (composer); Vienna **(1797–1828)**
Schulberg, Budd (novelist); New York City, 3/27/14
Schulz, Charles M. (cartoonist); Minneapolis, 11/26/22
Schuman, Robert (statesman); Luxembourg **(1886–1963)**
Schuman, William (composer); New York City **(1910–1992)**
Schumann, Robert Alexander (composer); Zwickau (Germany) **(1810–1856)**
Schumann-Heink, Ernestine (contralto); nr. Prague **(1861–1936)**
Schwartz, Arthur (songwriter); Brooklyn, N.Y. **(1900–1984)**
Schwarzenegger, Arnold (bodybuilder, actor); Graz, Austria, 7/30/47
Schwarzkopf, Elisabeth (soprano); Jarotschin, Poznán, (Poland), 12/9/15
Schwarzkopf, H. Norman (retired general); Trenton, N.J., 8/22/34
Schweitzer, Albert (humanitarian); Kaysersburg, Upper Alsace **(1875–1965)**
Schwimmer, David (actor); New York City, 11/12/66
Scofield, Paul (actor); Hurstpierpoint, England, 1/21/22
Scorsese, Martin (actor, writer, director, producer); Flushing, N.Y., 11/17/42
Scott, George C. (actor); Wise, Va., 10/18/27
Scott, Hazel (singer, pianist); Port of Spain, Trinidad **(1920–1981)**
Scott, Lizabeth (Emma Matso) (actress); Scranton, Pa., 1923
Scott, Randolph (Randolph Crane) (actor); Orange County, Va **(1898–1987)**
Scott, Robert Falcon (explorer); Devonport, England **(1868–1912)**
Scott, Sir Walter (novelist); Edinburgh, Scotland **(1771–1832)**
Scott, Zachary (actor); Austin, Tex. **(1914–1965)**

Scotto, Renata (operatic soprano); Savona, Italy, 2/?/36?
Scruggs, Earl Eugene (bluegrass musician); Cleveland County, N.C., 1/6/24
Seattle, (Chief Seattle) (Suquamish Indian leader); Blake Island (Wash.) **(c.1786–1866)**
Sebastian, John (composer); New York City, 3/17/44
Seberg, Jean (actress); Marshalltown, Iowa **(1938–1979)**
Sedaka, Neil (singer); Brooklyn, N.Y., 3/13/39
Seeger, Pete (folk singer); New York City, 5/3/19
Segal, Erich (novelist); Brooklyn, N.Y., 6/16/37
Segal, George (actor); New York City, 2/13/36
Segovia, Andrés (guitarist); Linares, Spain **(1893–1987)**
Seinfeld, Jerry (comedian); Brooklyn, N.Y., 4/29/54
Selleck, Tom (actor); Detroit, Mich., 1/29/45
Sellars, Peter (theater director); Pittsburgh, 1958?
Sellers, Peter (actor); Southsea, England **(1925–1980)**
Selznick, David O. (producer); Pittsburgh **(1902–1965)**
Sendak, Maurice (Bernard) (children's book author, illustrator); Brooklyn, N.Y., 6/10/28
Sennett, Mack (Michael Sinnott) (film producer); Richmond, Quebec, Canada **(1880–1960)**
Sequoyah, (Cherokee linguist); Taskigi, Tenn. **(c.1770–1843)**
Serkin, Peter (pianist); New York City, 7/24/47
Serkin, Rudolf (pianist); Eger (Czech Republic) **(1903–1991)**
Serling, Rod (writer, TV host); Syracuse, N.Y. **(1924–1975)**
Sessions, Roger (composer); Brooklyn, N.Y. **(1896–1985)**
Seurat, Georges (painter); Paris **(1859–1891)**
Seuss, Dr. (Theodor Seuss Geisel) (author, illustrator); Springfield, Mass. **(1904–1991)**
Sevareid, Eric (TV commentator); Velva, N.D. **(1912–1991)**
Severinsen, Doc (Carl) (band leader); Arlington, Ore., 7/7/27
Sexton, Anne (poet); Newton, Mass. **(1928–1974)**
Seymour, Jane (actress); Wimbledon, England, 2/15/51
Shaffer, Peter (playwright); Liverpool, England, 5/15/26
Shaham, Gil (violinist); Urbana, Ill., 1971
Shahn, Ben(jamin) (painter); Kaunas, Lithuania **(1898–1969)**
Shakespeare, William (dramatist); Stratford on Avon, England **(1564–1616)**
Shandling, Garry (comedian, actor, producer); Chicago, Ill., 11/29/49
Shange, Ntozake (Paulette Williams) (poet, playwright); Trenton, N.J., 10/18/48
Shankar, Ravi (sitar player); Benares, India, 4/7/20
Sharif, Omar (Michael Shalhoub) (actor); Alexandria, Egypt, 4/10/32
Shatner, William (actor); Montreal, 3/22/31
Shaw, Artie (Arthur Arshawsky) (band leader); New York City, 5/23/10
Shaw, George Bernard (dramatist); Dublin **(1856–1950)**
Shaw, Irwin (novelist); Brooklyn, N.Y. **(1913–1984)**
Shaw, Robert (actor); Lancashire, England **(1927–1978)**
Shaw, Robert (chorale conductor); Red Bluff, Calif., 4/30/16
Shawn, Ted (Edwin Myers Shawn) (dancer, choreographer); Kansas City, Mo. **(1891–1972)**
Shearer, Moira (ballerina); Dunfermline, Scotland, 1/17/26
Shearer, Norma (actress); Montreal **(1900–1983)**
Shearing, George (pianist); London, 8/13/20
Sheen, Fulton J. (Peter Sheen) (Roman Catholic bishop); El Paso, Ill. **(1895–1979)**
Sheen, Martin (Ramon Estevez) (actor); Dayton, Ohio, 8/3/40
Shelley, Mary Wollstonecraft Godwin (writer); London **(1797–1851)**
Shelley, Percy Bysshe (poet); nr. Horsham, England **(1792–1822)**
Shepard, Sam (playwright); Ft. Sheridan, Ill., 11/5/43
Shepherd, Cybill (actress); Memphis, Tenn., 2/18/50
Sheraton, Thomas (furniture designer); Stockton-on-Tees, England **(1751–1806)**
Sheridan, Ann (actress); Denton, Tex. **(1915–1967)**
Sheridan, Philip (army officer); Albany, N.Y. **(1831–1888)**
Sheridan, Richard Brinsley (dramatist); Dublin **(1751–1816)**
Sherman, William Tecumseh (army officer); Lancaster, Ohio **(1820–1891)**
Sherwood, Robert Emmet (playwright); New Rochelle, N.Y. **(1896–1955)**
Shevardnadze, Eduard Amvrosiyevich (State Council Chairman, Georgia); Mamati, (Georgia), 1/25/28
Shields, Brooke (actress); New York City, 5/31/65
Shire, Talia (Coppola) (actress); Lake Success, N.Y., 4/25/46
Shirer, William L. (journalist, historian); Chicago **(1904–1993)**
Sholokhov, Mikhail (novelist); Veshenskaya, Russia **(1905–1984)**
Shore, Dinah (Frances Rose Shore) (singer); Winchester,Tenn. **(1917–1994)**
Short, Bobby (Robert Waltrip Short) (singer, pianist); Danville, Ill., 9/15/24
Shostakovich, Dmitri (composer); St. Petersburg, Russia **(1906–1975)**
Shriner, Herb (humorist, TV host); Toledo, Ohio **(1918–1970)**
Shriver, Maria (TV co-host); Chicago, 11/6/55
Shriver, Sargent (Robert Sargent Shriver, Jr.) (business executive); Westminster, Md., 11/9/15
Shulman, Max (novelist); St. Paul **(1919–1988)**

Sibelius, Jean (Johann Julius Christian Sibelius) (composer); Tavaste-hus (Finland) **(1865–1957)**
Sidney, Sir Philip (poet); Penshurst, England **(1554–1586)**
Sidney, Sylvia (actress); New York City, 8/8/10
Siepi, Cesare (basso); Milan, Italy, 2/10/23
Signoret, Simone (Simone Kaminker) (actress); Wiesbaden, Germany **(1921–1985)**
Sihanouk, Norodom (King of Cambodia); Cambodia, 10/31/22
Sikorsky, Igor I. (inventor); Kiev, Ukraine **(1889–1972)**
Sills, Beverly (Belle Silverman) (soprano, opera director); Brooklyn, N.Y., 5/25/29
Sills, Milton (actor); Chicago **(1882–1930)**
Silone, Ignazio (Secondo Tranquilli) (novelist); Pescina del Marsi, Italy **(1900–1978)**
Silverman, Fred (broadcasting executive); New York City, 9/13/37
Silver, Ron (actor); New York City, 7/2/46
Silvers, Phil (Philip Silversmith) (comedian); Brooklyn, N.Y. **(1912–1985)**
Sim, Alastair (actor); Edinburgh, Scotland **(1900–1976)**
Simenon, Georges (Georges Sim) (mystery writer); Liège, Belgium **(1903–1989)**
Simmons, Jean (actress); Crouch Hill, London, 1/31/29
Simon, Carly (singer, songwriter); New York City, 6/25/45
Simon, Neil (playwright); Bronx, N.Y., 7/4/27
Simon, Norton (business executive); Portland, Ore. **(1907–1993)**
Simon, Paul (singer, songwriter); Newark, N.J., 11/5/42
Simon, Simone (actress); Marseilles, France, 4/23/14
Simone, Nina (Eunice Kathleen Waymoa) (singer, pianist); Tryon, N.C., 2/21/33
Sinatra, Frank (Francis Albert) (singer, actor); Hoboken, N.J., 12/12/15
Sinclair, Upton Beall (novelist); Baltimore **(1878–1968)**
Singer, Isaac Bashevis (novelist); Radzymin (Poland) **(1904–1991)**
Singleton, John (writer, director); Los Angeles, 1/6/68
Sinise, Gary (actor, director); Chicago, 3/17/55
Siqueiros, David (painter); Chihuahua, Mexico **(1896–1974)**
Sisley, Alfred (painter); Paris **(1839–1899)**
Sitting Bull (Prairie Sioux Indian Chief); on Grand River, S.D. **(c. 1835–1890)**
Skelton, Red (Richard) (comedian); Vincennes, Ind. **(1913–1997)**
Skinner, B(urrhus) F(rederic) (psychologist); Susquehanna, Pa. **(1904–1990)**
Skinner, Otis (actor); Cambridge, Mass. **(1858–1942)**
Slatkin, Leonard (conductor); Los Angeles, 9/1/44
Sloan, Alfred P., Jr. (industrialist); New Haven, Conn. **(1875–1965)**
Sloan, John (painter); Lock Haven, Pa. **(1871–1951)**
Smetana, Bedrich (composer); Litomysl (Czech Republic) **(1824–1884)**
Smith, Adam (economist); Kirkaldy, Scotland **(1723–1790)**
Smith, Alexis (actress); Penticon, Canada **(1921–1993)**
Smith, Alfred Emanuel (politician); New York City **(1873–1944)**
Smith, Bessie (blues singer); Chattanooga, Tenn. **(1894–1937)**
Smith, Sir C. Aubrey (actor); London **(1863–1948)**
Smith, David (sculptor); Decatur, Ind. **(1906–1965)**
Smith, Harry (TV co-anchor); Hammond, Ind., 8/21/51
Smith, Howard K. (TV commentator); Ferriday, La., 5/12/14
Smith, Jaclyn (actress); Houston, 10/26/47
Smith, John (American colonist); Willoughby, Lincolnshire, England **(1580–1631)**
Smith, Joseph (religious leader); Sharon, Vt. **(1805–1844)**
Smith, Kate (Kathryn) (singer); Greenville, Va. **(1909–1986)**
Smith, Dame Maggie (actress); Ilford, England, 12/28/34
Smith, Patti Lee (singer, songwriter); Chicago, 12/30/46
Smith, Red (Walter) (sports columnist); Green Bay, Wis. **(1905–1982)**
Smits, Jimmy (actor); New York City, 7/9/58
Smollet, Tobias (novelist); Dalquhum, Scotland **(1721–1771)**
Smothers, Dick (Richard) (comedian); New York City, 11/20/39
Smothers, Tom (Thomas) (comedian); New York City, 2/2/37
Snow, Lord (Charles Percy) (author); Leicester, England **(1905–1980)**
Snowdon (Earl of (Anthony Armstrong-Jones)) (photographer); London, 3/7/30
Snyder, Tom (TV personality); Milwaukee, 5/12/36
Socrates (philosopher); Athens **(469–399 b.c.e.)**
Solomon (King of Israel); Jerusalem, fl. 950b.c.e.
Solon (lawgiver); Salamis (Greece) **(c. 630–559 b.c.e.)**
Solti, Sir Georg (conductor); Budapest, 10/21/12
Solzhenitsyn, Aleksandr (novelist); Kislovodsk, Russia, 12/11/18
Somers, Suzanne (Suzanne Mahoney) (actress); San Bruno, Calif., 10/16/46
Somes, Michael (ballet dancer); Horsley, England **(1917–1994)**
Sommer, Elke (Elke Schletz) (actress); Berlin, 11/5/42
Sondheim, Stephen (composer); New York City, 3/22/30
Sontag, Susan (author, film director); New York City, 1/28/33
Sophocles (dramatist); nr. Athens **(c. 496–406 b.c.e.)**
Sothern, Ann (Harriette Lake) (actress); Valley City, N.D., 1/22/09
Soul, David (David Solberg) (actor); Chicago, 8/28/43
Sousa, John Philip (composer); Washington, D.C. **(1854–1932)**
Soyer, Raphael (painter); Borisoglebsk, Russia **(1899–1987)**

Spaak, Paul-Henri (statesman); Brussels **(1899–1972)**
Spacek, Sissy (Mary Elizabeth) (actress); Quitman, Tex., 12/25/49
Spacey, Kevin (actor); South Orange, N.J., 7/26/59
Spark, Muriel (novelist); Edinburgh, Scotland, 2/1/18
Spector, Phil (rock producer); Bronx, N.Y., 12/25/40
Spencer, Herbert (philosopher); Derby, England **(1820–1903)**
Spender, Stephen (poet); nr. London **(1909–1995)**
Spengler, Oswald (philosopher); Blankenburg (Germany) **(1880–1936)**
Spenser, Edmund (poet); London **(1552?–1599)**
Spewack, Bella (playwright); Hungary **(1899–1990)**
Spiegel, Sam (producer); Jaroslaw (Poland) **(1901–1985)**
Spielberg, Steven (director, producer, writer, actor); Cincinnati, 12/18/47
Spillane, Mickey (Frank Spillane) (mystery writer); Brooklyn, N.Y., 3/9/18
Spinoza, Baruch (philosopher); Amsterdam (Netherlands) **(1632–1677)**
Spitalny, Phil (orchestra leader) **(1890–1970)**
Spivak, Lawrence (TV producer); Brooklyn, N.Y. **(1900–1994)**
Spock, Benjamin (pediatrician); New Haven, Conn., 5/2/03
Springsteen, Bruce (singer, songwriter); Freehold, N.J., 9/23/49
Sproul, Robert G. (educator); San Francisco **(1891–1975)**
Squanto (Wampanoag Indian emissary); Patuxet (Plymouth Bay, Mass.) **(c.1590–1622)**
St. Denis, Ruth (dancer, choreographer); Newark, N.J. **(1878–1968)**
St. James, Susan (Susan Miller) (actress); Los Angeles, 8/14/46
St. John, Jill (actress); Los Angeles, 8/19/40
St. Johns, Adela Rogers (journalist, author); Los Angeles **(1894–1988)**
Stack, Robert (actor); Los Angeles, 1/13/19
Stafford, Jo (singer); Coalinga, Calif., 11/12/18
Stahl, Lesley (broadcast journalist); Lynn, Mass., 12/16/41
Stalin, Joseph Vissarionovich (Iosif V. Dzhugashvili) (Soviet leader); nr. Tiflis (Georgia) **(1879–1953)**
Stallone, Sylvester (actor, writer, director); New York City, 7/6/46
Stamp, Terrence (actor); London, 1938
Stander, Lionel (actor); New York City **(1908–1994)**
Stanislavski (Konstantin Sergeevich Alekseev) (stage producer); Moscow **(1863–1938)**
Stanley, Sir Henry Morton (John Rowlands) (explorer); Denbigh, Wales **(1841–1904)**
Stanley, Kim (Patricia Reid) (actress); Tularosa, N.M., 2/11/25
Stans, Maurice H. (ex-Secretary of Commerce); Shakope, Minn., 3/22/08
Stanton, Elizabeth Cady (woman suffragist); Johnstown, N.Y. **(1815–1902)**
Stanton, Frank (broadcasting executive); Muskegon, Mich., 3/20/08
Stanwyck, Barbara (Ruby Stevens) (actress); Brooklyn, N.Y. **(1907–1990)**
Stapleton, Jean (Jeanne Murray) (actress); New York City, 1/19/23
Stapleton, Maureen (actress); Troy, N.Y., 6/21/25
Starker, János (cellist); Budapest, 7/5/26
Starr, Kay (Starks) (singer); Dougherty, Okla., 7/21/22
Starr, Ringo (Richard Starkey) (singer, songwriter); Liverpool, England, 7/7/40
Stassen, Harold E. (ex-government official); West St. Paul, Minn., 4/13/07
Steber, Eleanor (soprano); Wheeling, W. Va., 7/17/16
Steegmuller, Francis (biographer); New Haven, Conn. **(1906–1994)**
Steele, Tommy (singer); London, 12/17/36
Stegner, Wallace (Earle) (novelist, critic); Lake Mills, Iowa **(1909–1993)**
Steichen, Edward Jean (photographer, artist); Luxembourg **(1879–1973)**
Steiger, Rod (Rodney) (actor); Westhampton, N.Y., 4/14/25
Stein, Gertrude (author); Allegheny, Pa. **(1874–1946)**
Steinbeck, John Ernst (novelist); Salinas, Calif. **(1902–1968)**
Steinberg, David (comedian); Winnipeg, Manitoba, Canada, 8/19/42
Steinberg, William (conductor); Cologne, Germany **(1899–1978)**
Steinem, Gloria (feminist, publisher); Toledo, Ohio, 3/25/34
Steinmetz, Charles (electrical engineer); Breslau (Poland) **(1865–1923)**
Stendhal (Marie Henri Beyle) (novelist); Grenoble, France **(1783–1842)**
Stern, Isaac (concert violinist); Kreminiecz, Russia, 7/21/20
Sterne, Laurence (novelist); Clonmel, Ireland **(1713–1768)**
Stevens, Cat (Steven Georgiou) (singer, songwriter); London, 7/21/47
Stevens, Connie (Concetta Ingolia) (singer); Brooklyn, N.Y., 8/8/38
Stevens, George (film director); Oakland, Calif. **(1905–1975)**
Stevens, Risë (mezzo-soprano); New York City, 6/11/13
Stevens, Wallace (poet); Reading, Pa. **(1879–1955)**
Stevenson, Adlai Ewing (statesman); Los Angeles **(1900–1965)**
Stevenson, McLean (actor); Bloomington, Ill. **(1929–1996)**
Stevenson, Parker (actor); Philadelphia, 6/4/52
Stevenson, Robert Louis Balfour (novelist, poet); Edinburgh, Scotland **(1850–1894)**
Stewart, James (actor); Indiana, Pa. **(1908–1997)**
Stewart, Martha (entrepreneurial homemaker); Nutley, N.J., 8/3/41
Stewart, Patrick (actor); Mirfield, England, 7/13/49
Stewart, Rod (Roderick David) (singer); London, 1/10/45
Stieglitz, Alfred (photographer); Hoboken, N.J. **(1864–1946)**

Stiers, David Ogden (actor); Peoria, Ill., 10/31/42
Stiller, Jerry (actor); Brooklyn, N.Y., 6/8/29
Stills, Stephen (singer, songwriter); Dallas, 1/3/45
Sting (Gordon Matthew Sumner) (singer, composer); Wallsend, England, 10/2/51
Stipe, Michael (singer); Decatur, Ga., 1/4/60
Stockwell, Dean (actor); North Hollywood, Calif., 3/5/36
Stokes, Carl (TV newscaster); Cleveland, 6/21/27
Stokowski, Leopold (conductor); London **(1882–1977)**
Stone, Edward Durell (architect); Fayetteville, Ark. **(1902–1978)**
Stone, I(sidor) F(einstein) (journalist); Philadelphia **(1907–1989)**
Stone, Irving (Irving Tennenbaum) (novelist); San Francisco **(1903–1989)**
Stone, Lucy (woman suffragist); nr. West Brookfield, Mass. **(1818–1893)**
Stone, Oliver (director, writer, producer); New York City, 9/15/46
Stone, Robert (novelist); Brooklyn, N.Y., 8/21/37
Stone, Sharon (actress); Meadville, Pa., 3/10/58
Stone, Sly (Sylvester) (rock musician) 1944
Stooges, The Three (comedy team)
Stoppard, Tom (Thomas Straussler) (playwright); Zlin, (Slovakia), 7/3/37
Stout, Rex (mystery writer); Noblesville, Ind. **(1886–1975)**
Stowe, Harriet Elizabeth Beecher (novelist); Litchfield, Conn. **(1811–1896)**
Strachey, (Giles) Lytton (biographer); London **(1880–1932)**
Stradivari, Antonio (violinmaker); Cremona (Italy) **(1644–1737)**
Straight, Beatrice (actress); Old Westbury, N.Y., 8/2/18
Strasberg, Lee (stage director); Budanov, Austria **(1901–1982)**
Strasberg, Susan (actress); New York City, 5/22/38
Stratas, Teresa (soprano); Toronto, Ont., Canada, 5/26/38
Straus, Oskar (composer); Vienna **(1870–1954)**
Strauss, Johann (composer); Vienna **(1825–1899)**
Strauss, Lewis L. (naval officer, scientist); Charleston, W. Va. **(1896–1974)**
Strauss, Peter (actor); New York City, 2/20/47
Strauss, Richard (composer); Munich, Germany **(1864–1949)**
Stravinsky, Igor (composer); Orlenbaum, Russia **(1882–1971)**
Streep, Meryl (Mary Louise) (actress); Summit, N.J., 6/22/49
Streisand, Barbra (singer, actress, director, producer, writer); Brooklyn, N.Y., 4/24/42
Strindberg, (Johan) August (dramatist); Stockholm **(1849–1912)**
Stritch, Elaine (actress); Detroit, Mich., 2/2/25
Struthers, Sally Ann (actress); Portland, Ore., 7/28/48
Stuart, Gilbert Charles (painter); Rhode Island **(1755–1828)**
Stuart, James Ewell Brown (known as Jeb) (Confederate army officer); Patrick County, Va. **(1833–1864)**
Sturges, Preston (director, screenwriter, playwright); Chicago **(1898–1959)**
Stuyvesant, Peter (Governor of New Amsterdam); West Friesland (Netherlands) **(1592–1672)**
Styne, Jule (Julius Kerwin Stein) (songwriter); London **(1905–1994)**
Styron, William (William Clark Styron, Jr.) (novelist); Newport News, Va., 6/11/25
Suharto, (President of Indonesia); Sedaju-Godean, Java, 2/20/21
Sukarno, (Indonesian leader); Surabaja, Java **(1901–1970)**
Sullavan, Margaret Brooke (actress); Norfolk, Va. **(1911–1960)**
Sullivan, Sir Arthur Seymour (composer); London **(1842–1900)**
Sullivan, Barry (Patrick Barry) (actor); New York City **(1912–1994)**
Sullivan, Ed (columnist, TV personality); New York City **(1901–1974)**
Sullivan, Frank (Francis John) (humorist); Saratoga Springs, N.Y. **(1892–1976)**
Sullivan, Louis Henry (architect); Boston **(1856–1924)**
Sulzberger, Arthur Ochs (newspaper publisher); New York City, 2/5/26
Sumac, Yma (singer); Ichocan, Peru, 9/10/27
Summer, Donna (La Donna Andrea Gaines) (singer); Boston, 12/31/48
Sun Ra (Herman "Sunny" Blount) (jazz composer); Birmingham, Ala. **(1914?–1993)**
Sun Tzu (writer, military strategist); China **(fl. c.500–320 b.c.e.)**
Sun Yat-sen (statesman); nr. Macao **(1866–1925)**
Susann, Jacqueline (novelist); Philadelphia **(1918–1974)**
Susskind, David (TV producer); New York City **(1920–1987)**
Sutherland, Donald (actor); St. John, N.B., Canada, 7/17/34
Sutherland, Joan (soprano); Sydney, Australia, 11/7/26
Suzuki, Pat (actress); Cressey, Calif., 1931
Swados, Elizabeth (composer, playwright); Buffalo, N.Y., 2/5/51
Swanson, Gloria (Gloria May Josephine Svensson) (actress); Chicago **(1899–1983)**
Swarthout, Gladys (soprano); Deepwater, Mo. **(1904–1969)**
Swayze, John Cameron (news commentator); Wichita, Kan. **(1906–1995)**
Swayze, Patrick (actor, dancer); Houston, Tex., 8/18/54
Swendenborg, Emanuel (scientist, philosopher, mystic); Stockholm **(1688–1772)**
Swift, Jonathan (satirist); Dublin **(1667–1745)**
Swinburne, Algernon Charles (poet); London **(1837–1909)**

Swit, Loretta (actress); Passaic, N.J., 11/4/37
Swope, Herbert Bayard (journalist); St. Louis **(1882–1958)**
Sydow, von, Max (Carl Adolf von Sydow) (actor); Lund, Sweden, 4/10/29
Symons, Arthur (poet, critic); Milford Haven, Wales **(1865–1945)**
Synge, John Millington (dramatist); nr. Dublin **(1871–1909)**
Szilard, Leo (physicist); Budapest **(1898–1964)**

T

Taft, Robert Alphonso (legislator); Cincinnati **(1889–1953)**
Tagore, Sir Rabindranath (poet); Calcutta **(1861–1941)**
Tallchief, Maria (ballerina); Fairfax, Okla., 1/24/25
Talleyrand-Pèrigord, Charles Maurice de (statesman); Paris **(1754–1838)**
Talmadge, Norma (actress); Niagara Falls, N.Y. **(1897–1957)**
Talvela, Martti (basso); Hiitola, Finalnd **(1935–1989)**
Tamerlane (Timur) (Mongol conqueror); nr. Samarkand (Turkestan) **(c. 1336–1405)**
Tamiroff, Akim (actor); Baku (Azerbaijan) **(1899–1972)**
Tan, Amy (novelist); Oakland, Calif., 2/19/52
Tandy, Jessica (actress); London **(1909–1994)**
Tarbell, Ida Minerva (author, biographer); Erie Co., Pa. **(1857–1944)**
Tarkington, (Newton) Booth (novelist); Indianapolis **(1869–1946)**
Tate, Allen (John Orley) (poet, critic); Winchester, Ky. **(1899–1979)**
Tate, Sharon (actress); Dallas **(1943–1969)**
Tati, Jacques (Jacques Tatischeff) (actor); Pecq, France **(1908–1982)**
Taylor, Deems (composer); New York City **(1885–1966)**
Taylor, Elizabeth (actress); London, 2/27/32
Taylor, Harold (educator); Toronto, 9/28/14
Taylor, James (singer, songwriter); Boston, 3/12/48
Taylor, Laurette (Laurette Cooney) (actress); New York City **(1884–1946)**
Taylor, Gen. Maxwell D. (former Army Chief of Staff); Keytesville, Mo **(1901–1987)**
Taylor, Paul (choreographer); Wilkinsburg, Pa., 7/29/30
Taylor, Robert (Spangler Arlington Brugh) (actor); Filley, Neb. **(1911–1969)**
Tchaikovsky, Peter (Pëtr) Ilich (composer); Votkinsk, Russia **(1840–1893)**
Teasdale, Sara (poet); St. Louis **(1884–1933)**
Tebaldi, Renata (lyric soprano); Pesaro, Italy, 1/2/22
Tecumseh (Shawnee Indian chief); nr. Springfield, Ohio **(1768–1813)**
Te Kanawa, Kiri (soprano); Gisborne, New Zealand, 3/6/44
Telemann, Georg Philipp (composer); Magdeburg (Germany) **(1681–1767)**
Teller, Edward (atomic physicist); Budapest, 1/15/08
Templeton, Alec Andrew (pianist, composer); Cardiff, Wales **(1910–1963)**
Tennille, Toni (singer); Montgomery, Ala., 5/8/43
Tennyson, Alfred (1st Baron Tennyson) (poet); Somersby, England **(1809–1892)**
Tenskwatawa (Shawnee prophet); Old Piqua, Ohio **(c. 1770–c. 1835)**
Terhune, Albert Payson (novelist, journalist); Newark, N.J. **(1872–1942)**
Terkel, Studs (writer, interviewer); New York City, 5/16/12
Terry, Ellen Alicia (actress); Coventry, England **(1848–1928)**
Terry-Thomas (Thomas Terry Hoar Stevens) (actor); London **(1911–1990)**
Tesla, Nikola (electrical engineer, inventor); Smiljan (Croatia) **(1856–1943)**
Thackeray, William Makepeace (novelist); Calcutta **(1811–1863)**
Thalberg, Irving G. (producer); Brooklyn, N.Y. **(1899–1936)**
Thant, U (U.N. statesman); Pantanaw (Burma) **(1909–1974)**
Tharp, Twyla (dancer, choreographer); Portland, Ind., 7/1/42
Thatcher, Margaret (former Prime Minister); Grantham, England, 10/13/25
Thebom, Blanche (mezzo-soprano); Monessen, Pa., 9/19/19
Theodorakis, Mikis (composer); Chios, Greece, 7/29/25
Thicke, Alan (actor, composer); Kirland Lake, Ont., Canada, 3/1/47
Thieu, Nguyen Van (ex-President of South Vietnam); Trithuy (Vietnam), 4/5/23
Thomas, Danny (Amos Jacobs) (entertainer, TV producer); Deerfield, Mich. **(1912–1991)**
Thomas, Dylan Marials (poet); Carmarthenshire, Wales **(1914–1953)**
Thomas, Lowell (explorer, commentator); Woodington, Ohio **(1892–1981)**
Thomas, Marlo (actress); Detroit, Mich., 11/21/43
Thomas, Michael Tilson (conductor); Hollywood, Calif., 12/21/44
Thomas, Norman Mattoon (Socialist leader); Marion, Ohio **(1884–1968)**
Thomas, Philip Michael (actor); Columbus, Ohio, 5/26/49
Thomas, Richard (actor); New York City, 6/13/51
Thompson, Dorothy (writer); Lancaster, N.Y. **(1894–1961)**
Thompson, Emma (actress); London, 4/15/59
Thompson, Hunter (Stockton) (writer); Louisville, Ky., 7/18/39
Thompson, Sada (actress); Des Moines, Iowa, 9/27/29

Thomson, Virgil (Garnett) (composer); Kansas City, Mo. **(1896–1989)**
Thoreau, Henry David (naturalist, author); Concord, Mass. **(1817–1862)**
Thorndike, Dame Sybil (actress); Gainsborough, England **(1882–1976)**
Thurber, James Grover (author, cartoonist); Columbus, Ohio **(1894–1961)**
Thurmond, (John) Strom (U.S. Senator); Edgefield, S.C., 12/5/02
Tibbett, Lawrence (baritone); Bakersfield, Calif. **(1896–1960)**
Tiberius Caesar Augustus (Roman emperor); Capri **(42 B.C.E.–37 C.E.)**
Tiegs, Cheryl (model, actress); Minnesota, 9/25/47
Tierney, Gene (actress); Brooklyn, N.Y. **(1920–1991)**
Tillich, Paul (philosopher, theologian); Starzeddel, Germany **(1886–1965)**
Tillstrom, Burr (puppeteer); Chicago **(1917–1985)**
Tintoretto, Il (Jacopo Robusti) (painter); Venice **(1518–1594)**
Tiny Tim (Herbert Khaury) (entertainer); New York City **(1925–1996)**
Tiomkin, Dmitri (composer); St. Petersburg, Russia **(1894–1979)**
Titian (Tiziano Vecelli) (painter); Pieve di Cadore (Italy) **(1477–1576)**
Tito (Josip Broz or Brozovich) (President of Yugoslavia); Croatia (former Yugoslavia) **(1892–1980)**
Tocqueville, Alexis de (writer); Verneuil, France **(1805–1859)**
Todd, Michael (producer); Minneapolis, Minn. **(1907–1958)**
Todd, Richard (actor); Dublin, 6/11/19
Todd, Thelma (actress); Lawrence, Mass. **(1905–1935)**
Tolkien, J(ohn) R(onald) R(euel) (fantasy writer); Bloemfontein, South Africa **(1892–1973)**
Tolstoi, Count Leo (Lev) Nikolaevich (novelist); Tula Province, Russia **(1828–1910)**
Tomlin, Lily (actress, comedienne); Detroit, Mich., 9/1/39
Tone, Franchot (actor); Niagara Falls, N.Y. **(1905–1968)**
Tormé, Mel (Melvin) (singer); Chicago, 9/13/25
Torn, Rip (Elmore Torn, Jr.) (actor, director); Temple, Tex., 2/6/31
Torquemada, Tomásde (Spanish Inquisitor); Valladolid, Spain **(1420–1498)**
Toscanini, Arturo (orchestra conductor); Parma, Italy **(1867–1957)**
Totenberg, Nina (broadcast journalist); New York City, 1/14/44
Toulouse-Lautrec (Henri Marie Raymond de Toulouse-Lautrec Monfa) (painter); Albi, France **(1864–1901)**
Toynbee, Arnold J. (historian); London **(1889–1975)**
Tracy, Spencer (actor); Milwaukee **(1900–1967)**
Traubel, Helen (Wagnerian soprano); St. Louis **(1903–1972)**
Travanti, Daniel J. (actor); Kenosha, Wis., 3/7/40
Travolta, John (actor); Englewood, N.J., 2/18/54
Treacher, Arthur (actor); Brighton, England **(1894–1975)**
Tree, Sir Herbert Beerbolm (actor, manager); London **(1853–1917)**
Trevor, Claire (Wemlinger) (actress); New York City, 3/9/09
Trigère, Pauline (fashion designer); Paris, 11/4/12
Trilling, Diana (writer); New York City **(1905–1996)**
Trilling, Lionel (author, educator); New York City **(1905–1975)**
Trollope, Anthony (novelist); London **(1815–1882)**
Trotsky, Leon (Lev Davidovich Bronstein) (statesman); Elisavetgrad, Russia **(1879–1940)**
Troyanos, Tatiana (mezzo-soprano); New York City **(1938–1993)**
Trudeau, Garry (cartoonist); New York City, 1948
Trudeau, Pierre Elliott (former Prime Minister); Montreal, 10/18/19
Truffaut, François (film director); Paris **(1932–1984)**
Trujillo y Molina, Rafael Leonidas (Dominican Republic dictator); San Cristóbal, Dominican Republic **(1891–1961)**
Truman, Margaret (author); Independence, Mo., 2/17/24
Trump, Donald (business executive); New York City, 6/14/46
Truth, Sojourner (Isabella) (preacher, abolitionist); Ulster Co., N.Y. **(c. 1797–1883)**
Tryon, Thomas (actor, novelist); Hartford, Conn. **(1926–1991)**
Tsiolkovsky, Konstantin E. (father of cosmonautics); Izhevskoye, Russia **(1857–1935)**
Tubman, Harriet (Araminta) (abolitionist); Dorchester Co., Md. **(c. 1820–1913)**
Tuchman, Barbara (Wertheim) (historian, author); New York City **(1912–1989)**
Tucker, Forrest (actor); Plainfield, Ind. **(1919–1986)**
Tucker, Richard (tenor); New York City **(1914–1975)**
Tucker, Sophie (Sophia Kalish) (singer); Russia **(1884–1966)**
Tudor, Antony (choreographer); London **(1909–1987)**
Tune, Tommy (dancer, choreographer); Wichita Falls, Tex., 2/28/39
Turgenev, Ivan Sergeevich (novelist); Orel, Russia **(1818–1883)**
Turner, Ike (singer); Clarksdale, Miss., 11/5/31
Turner, Janine (actress); Lincoln, Neb., 12/6/62
Turner, Joseph M.W. (painter); London **(1775–1851)**
Turner, Kathleen (actress); Springfield, Mo., 6/19/54
Turner, Lana (Julia Jean Mildred Frances Turner) (actress); Wallace, Idaho **(1920–1995)**
Turner, Nat (civil rights leader); Southampton County, Va. **(1800–1831)**
Turner, Ted (business executive); Cincinnati, 11/19/38
Turner, Tina (Annie Mae Bullock) (singer); Nut Bush, Tenn., 11/26/39
Turpin, Ben (comedian); New Orleans **(1874–1940)**

Twain, Mark (Samuel Langhorne Clemens) (author); Florida, Mo. **(1835–1910)**
Tweed, William Marcy (politician); New York City **(1823–1878)**
Twiggy (Leslie Hornby) (model); London, 9/19/49
Twining, Gen. Nathan F. (former Air Force Chief of Staff); Monroe, Wis. **(1897–1982)**
Twitty, Conway (Harold Lloyd Jenkins) (singer, guitarist); Friars Point, Miss. **(1933–1993)**
Tyson, Cicely (actress); New York City, 12/19/33

U

Uccello, Paolo (painter); Florence **(1397–1475)**
Udall, Stewart L. (ex-Secretary of the Interior); St. Johns, Ariz., 1/31/20
Uggams, Leslie (singer, actress); New York City, 5/25/43
Ulanova, Galina (ballerina); St. Petersburg, Russia, 1/10/10
Ullman, Tracey (actress, singer); Slough, England, 12/30/59
Ullmann, Liv (actress); Tokyo, 12/16/39
Untermeyer, Louis (anthologist, poet); New York City **(1885–1977)**
Updike, John (novelist); Shillington, Pa., 3/18/32
Urey, Harold C. (physicist); Walkerton, Ind. **(1893–1981)**
Uris, Leon (novelist); Baltimore, 8/3/24
Ustinov, Peter (actor, producer); London, 4/16/21
Utrillo, Maurice (painter); Paris **(1883–1955)**

V

Vaccaro, Brenda (actress); Brooklyn, N.Y., 11/18/39
Vadim, Roger (Roger Vadim Plemiannikov) (film director); Paris, 1/26/28
Valentine, Karen (actress); Santa Rosa, Calif., 5/25/47
Valentino, Rudolph (Rodolpho d'Antonguolla) (actor); Castellaneta, Italy **(1895–1926)**
Valentino (Valentino Garavani) (fashion designer); nr. Milan, Italy, 5/11/32
Valéry, Paul (Ambroise Toussaint Jules) (poet, critic); Sète, France **(1871–1945)**
Vallee, Rudy (Hubert Prior Rudy Vallée) (band leader, singer); Island Pond, Vt. **(1901–1986)**
Valli, Frankie (Frank Castellaccio) (singer); Newark, N.J., 5/3/37
Van Allen, James Alfred (space physicist); Mt. Pleasant, Iowa, 9/7/14
Van Buren, Abigail (Mrs. Morton Phillips) (columnist); Sioux City, Iowa, 7/4/18
Vance, Vivian (actress); Cherryvale, Kan. **(1912–1979)**
Vanderbilt, Alfred G. (sportsman); London, 9/22/12
Vanderbilt, Cornelius (financier); Port Richmond, N.Y. **(1794–1877)**
Vanderbilt, Gloria (fashion designer); New York City, 2/20/24
Van Doren, Carl (writer, educator); Hope, Ill. **(1885–1950)**
Van Doren, Mamie (actress); Rowena, S.D., 2/6/33
Van Dyke, Dick (actor); West Plains, Mo., 12/13/25
Vandyke (or Van Dyck), Sir Anthony (painter); Antwerp (Belgium) **(1599–1641)**
Van Eyck, Jan (painter); Maeseyck (Belgium) **(c.1390–1441)**
Van Fleet, Jo (actress); Oakland, Calif. **(1915–1996)**
van Gogh, Vincent (painter); Groot Zundert, Brabant (Belgium) **(1853–1890)**
Van Hamel, Martine (ballerina); Brussels, 11/16/45
Van Heusen, Jimmy (Edward Chester Babcock) (songwriter); Syracuse, N.Y. **(1913–1990)**
Van Patten, Dick (actor); Richmond Hill, N.Y., 12/9/28
Van Peebles, Melvin (playwright); Chicago, 9/21/32
Vasari, Giorgio (art historian); Arezzo, Italy **(1511–1574)**
Vaughan, Sarah (singer); Newark, N.J. **(1924–1990)**
Vaughan Williams, Ralph (composer); Down Ampney, England **(1872–1958)**
Vaughn, Robert (actor); New York City, 11/22/32
Veblen, Thorstein (economist, social critic); Cato Township, Wis. **(1857–1929)**
Veidt, Conrad (actor); Potsdam, Germany **(1893–1943)**
Velázquez, Diego Rodriguez de Silva y (painter); Seville, Spain **(1599–1660)**
Venturi, Robert (Charles) (architect); Philadelphia, 6/25/25
Verdi, Giuseppe (composer); Roncole (Italy) **(1813–1901)**
Verdon, Gwen (actress); Culver City, Calif., 1/13/25
Vereen, Ben (actor, singer); Miami, Fla., 10/10/46
Verlaine, Paul (poet); Metz, France **(1844–1896)**
Vermeer, Jan (or Jan van der Meer van Delft) (painter); Delft (Netherlands) **(1632–1675)**
Verne, Jules (author); Nantes, France **(1828–1905)**
Veronese, Paolo (Paolo Cagliari) (painter); Verona **(1528–1588)**
Verrazano, Giovanni da (navigator); Florence (Italy) **(c. 1485–1528)**
Verrett, Shirley (mezzo-soprano); New Orleans, 5/31/33
Vesalius, Andreas (anatomist); Brussels, Belgium **(1515–1564)**

Vespucci, Amerigo (navigator); Florence (Italy) **(1454–1512)**
Vickers, Jon (tenor); Prince Albert, Sask, Canada, 10/29/26
Vico, Giovanni Battista (philosopher); Naples, Italy **(1668–1744)**
Victoria (Queen of England); London **(1819–1901)**
Vidal, Gore (novelist); West Point, N.Y., 10/3/25
Vidor, King (film director, producer); Galveston, Tex. **(1895–1982)**
Vigoda, Abe (actor); New York City, 2/24/21
Villa, Pancho (Doroteo Arango) (revolutionary); Hacienda de Rio Grande, San Juan del Rio, Mexico **(1877–1923)**
Villella, Edward (ballet dancer); Bayside, Queens, N.Y., 10/1/36
Villon, François (François de Montcorbier) (poet); Paris **(1431–1463)**
Vinton, Bobby (singer); Canonsburg, Pa., 4/16/35
Virgil(or Vergil) (Publius Vergilius Maro) (poet); nr. Mantua (Italy) **(70–19 B.C.E.)**
Vishnevskaya, Galina (soprano); St. Petersburg (Russia), 10/25/26
Vivaldi, Antonio (composer); Venice **(1678–1741)**
Vlaminck, Maurice de (painter); Paris **(1876–1958)**
Voight, Jon (actor); Yonkers, N.Y., 12/29/38
Volta, Alessandro (scientist); Como, Italy **(1745–1827)**
Voltaire (François Marie Arouet) (author); Paris **(1694–1778)**
von Aroldingen, Karin (Karin Awny Hannelore Reinbold von Aroedingen and Eltzinger) (ballet dancer); Greiz (Germany), 7/9/41
von Braun, Wernher (rocket scientist); Wirsitz, Germany **(1912–1977)**
von Furstenberg, Betsy (Elizabeth Caroline Maria Agatha Felicitas Therese von Furstenberg-Hedringen) (actress); Nelheim-Heusen, Germany, 8/16/35
von Fürstenberg, Diane (Diane Simone Michelle Halfin) (fashion designer); Brussels, 12/31/46
von Hindenburg, Paul (statesman); Posen (Poland) **(1847–1934)**
von Karajan, Herbert (conductor); Salzburg (Austria) **(1908–1989)**
Vonnegut, Kurt, Jr. (novelist); Indianapolis, 11/11/22
Von Stade, Frederica (mezzo-soprano); Somerville, N.J., 1945
Von Stroheim, Erich Oswald Hans Carl Maria von Nordenwall (actor, director); Vienna **(1885–1957)**
Von Zell, Harry (announcer); Indianapolis, Ind. **(1906–1981)**
Vreeland, Diana (Diana Da Iziel) (fashion journalist, museum consultant); Paris **(1903?–1989)**

W

Wagner, Lindsay (actress); Los Angeles, 6/22/49
Wagner, Robert (actor); Detroit, Mich., 2/10/30
Wagner, Robert F. (ex-Mayor of New York City); New York City **(1910–1991)**
Wagner, Wilhelm Richard (composer); Leipzig (Germany) **(1813–1883)**
Waits, Tom (blues singer); Pomona, Calif., 12/7/49
Waldheim, Kurt (ex-U.N. Secretary-General); St. Andrae-Wörden, Austria, 12/21/18
Walesa, Lech (Polish labor leader and ex-president); Popowo, Poland, 9/29/43
Walker, Alice (novelist, poet); Eatonon, Ga., 2/9/44
Walker, Nancy (Ann Myrtle Swoyer) (actress, comedienne); Philadelphia **(1922–1992)**
Walker, Robert (actor); Salt Lake City **(1918–1951)**
Walker, T-Bone (blues singer); Linden, Tex., 5/28/10
Wallace, DeWitt (publisher); St. Paul **(1889–1981)**
Wallace, George C. (ex-govenor); Clio, Ala., 8/25/19
Wallace, Irving (novelist); Chicago **(1916–1990)**
Wallace, Mike (Myron Wallace) (TV interviewer, commentator); Brookline, Mass., 5/9/18
Wallach, Eli (actor); Brooklyn, N.Y., 12/7/15
Wallenberg, Raoul (diplomat, humanitarian); Stockholm, Sweden **(1912–1947)**
Wallenstein, Alfred (conductor); Chicago **(1898–1983)**
Waller, Thomas "Fats" (pianist); New York City **(1904–1943)**
Wallis, Hal (film producer); Chicago **(1899–1986)**
Walpole, Horace (statesman, novelist); London **(1717–1797)**
Waltari, Mika (novelist); Helsinki, Finland **(1903–1979)**
Walter, Bruno (Bruno Walter Schlesinger) (orchestra conductor); Berlin **(1876–1962)**
Walters, Barbara (TV commentator); Boston, 9/25/31
Walton, Izaak (author); Stafford, England **(1593–1683)**
Wambaugh, Joseph (author, screenwriter); East Pittsburgh, 1/22/37
Wanamaker, John (merchant); Philadelphia **(1838–1922)**
Wanamaker, Sam (actor, director); Chicago **(1919–1993)**
Ward, Barbara (economist); York, England **(1914–1981)**
Warhol, Andy (Warhola) (artist); McKeesport, Pa. **(1928–1987)**
Waring, Fred (band leader); Tyrone, Pa. **(1900–1984)**
Warner, H. B. (Henry Bryan Warner Lickford) (actor); London **(1876–1958)**
Warren, Lesley Ann (actress); New York City, 8/16/46
Warren, Robert Penn (novelist); Guthrie, Ky. **(1905–1989)**
Warrick, Ruth (actress); St. Joseph, Mo., 6/29/15
Warwick, Dionne (singer); East Orange, N.J., 12/12/41

Washington, Booker Taliaferro (educator); Franklin County, Va. **(1856–1915)**
Washington, Denzel (actor); Mt. Vernon, N.Y., 12/28/54
Washington, Harold (ex-mayor of Chicago); Chicago **(1922–1987)**
Waters, Ethel (actress, singer); Chester, Pa. **(1896–1977)**
Waters, Muddy (McKinley Morganfield) (singer, guitarist); Rolling Fork, Miss. **(1915–1983)**
Waterston, Sam (actor); Cambridge, Mass., 11/15/40
Watson, Thomas John (industrialist); Campbell, N.Y. **(1874–1956)**
Watt, James (inventor); Greenock, Scotland **(1736–1819)**
Watteau, Jean-Antoine (painter); Valanciennes, France **(1684–1721)**
Wattleton, Faye (family planning advocate); St. Louis, Mo., 7/8/43
Watts, André (concert pianist); Nuremberg, Germany, 6/20/46
Waugh, Alec (Alexander Raban Waugh) (novelist); London **(1898–1981)**
Waugh, Evelyn (novelist); London **(1903–1966)**
Wayne, Anthony (military officer); Waynesboro (family farm), nr. Paoli, Pa. **(1745–1796)**
Wayne, David (David McMeekan) (actor); Traverse City, Mich. **(1914–1995)**
Wayne, John (Marion Michael Morrison) (actor); Winterset, Iowa **(1907–1979)**
Weaver, Dennis (actor); Joplin, Mo., 6/4/25
Weaver, Fritz (actor); Pittsburgh, 1/19/26
Weaver, Sigourney (actress); New York City, 10/8/49
Webb, Clifton (Webb Parmelee Hollenbeck) (actor); Indianapolis **(1893–1966)**
Webb, Jack (actor, producer); Santa Monica, Calif. **(1920–1982)**
Weber, Karl Maria Friedrich Ernst von (composer); nr. Lübeck (Germany) **(1786–1826)**
Webster, Daniel (statesman); Salisbury, N.H. **(1782–1852)**
Webster, Margaret (producer, director, actress); New York City **(1905–1973)**
Webster, Noah (lexicographer); West Hartford, Conn. **(1758–1843)**
Weill, Kurt (composer); Dessau, (Germany) **(1900–1950)**
Weir, Peter (director); Sydney, Australia, 8/21/44
Weizmann, Chaim (statesman); Grodno Province, Russia **(1874–1952)**
Welch, Raquel (Raquel Tejada) (actress); Chicago, 9/5/40
Weld, Tuesday (Susan) (actress); New York City, 8/27/43
Welk, Lawrence (band leader); Strasburg, N.D. **(1903–1992)**
Welles, Orson (actor, director, producer); Kenosha, Wis. **(1915–1985)**
Wellington, Duke of (Arthur Wellesley) (statesman); Ireland **(1769–1852)**
Wells, H(erbert) G(eorge) (author); Bromley, England **(1866–1946)**
Wells, Ida Bell (Barnett) (journalist); Holly Springs, Miss. **(1862–1931)**
Welty, Eudora (novelist); Jackson, Miss., 4/13/09
Wenner, Jann (publisher); New York City, 1/7/46
Werfel, Franz (novelist); Prague **(1890–1945)**
Werner, Oskar (Josef Schliessmayer) (actor, director); Vienna **(1922–1984)**
Wertheimer, Linda (radio journalist); Carlsbad, N.M., 3/19/43
Wertmueller, Lina (Arcanguela Felice Assunta W. von Elgg) (director); Rome, 8/14/28
Wesley, John (religious leader); Epworth Rectory, Lincolnshire, England **(1703–1791)**
West, Benjamin (painter); Springfield, Pa. **(1738–1820)**
West, Dame Rebecca (Cicily Fairfield) (novelist); County Kerry, Ireland **(1892–1983)**
West, Jessamyn (novelist); nr. North Vernon, Ind. **(1902–1984)**
West, Mae (actress); Brooklyn, N.Y. **(1893–1980)**
West, Nathanael (Nathan Weinstein) (novelist); New York City **(1902–1940)**
Westheimer, Ruth (Karola Ruth Siegel) (human sexuality expert); Frankfurt, Germany, 1928
Westinghouse, George (inventor); Central Bridge, N.Y. **(1846–1914)**
Westmoreland, William Childs (ex-Army Chief of Staff); Saxon, S.C., 3/26/14
Weyden, Roger van der (painter); Tournai (Belgium) **(c.1400–1464)**
Wharton, Edith Newbold (née Jones) (novelist); New York City **(1862–1937)**
Wheatley, Phyllis (poet); Senegal **(c. 1753–1784)**
Wheeler, Bert (Albert Jerome Wheeler) (comedian); Paterson, N.J. **(1895–1968)**
Whistler, James Abbott McNeill (painter, etcher); Lowell, Mass. **(1834–1903)**
Whitaker, Forest (actor); Longview, Tex., 7/15/61
White, Betty (actress); Oak Park, Ill., 1/17/22
White, Edmund (writer); Cincinnati, Ohio, 1/13/40
White, E(lwyn) B(rooks) (author); Mt. Vernon, N.Y. **(1899–1985)**
White, Pearl (actress); Green Ridge, Mo. **(1889–1938)**
White, Stanford (architect); New York City **(1853–1906)**
White, Theodore H. (historian); Boston **(1915–1986)**
White, Vanna (TV personality); Conway, S.C., 2/18/57
White, William Allen (journalist); Emporia, Kan. **(1868–1944)**
Whitehead, Alfred North (mathematician, philosopher); Isle of Thanet, England **(1861–1947)**

Whiteman, Paul (band leader); Denver **(1891–1967)**
Whiting, Margaret (singer, actress); Detroit, Mich., 7/22/24
Whitman, Walt (Walter) (poet); West Hills, N.Y. **(1819–1892)**
Whitmore, James (actor); White Plains, N.Y., 10/1/21
Whitney, Cornelius Vanderbilt (sportsman); New York City, 2/20/1899
Whitney, Eli (inventor); Westboro, Mass. **(1765–1825)**
Whitney, John Hay (publisher); Ellsworth, Me. **(1904–1982)**
Whittier, John Greenleaf (poet); Haverhill, Mass. **(1807–1892)**
Wideman, John Edgar (writer); Washington, D.C., 6/14/41
Widmark, Richard (actor); Sunrise, Minn., 12/26/14
Wiesel, Elie (Eliezer) (author); Signet, Romania, 9/30/28
Wiesenthal, Simon (Nazi hunter); Buchach (Ukraine), 12/31/08
Wilde, Cornel (film actor, producer); New York City **(1915–1989)**
Wilde, Oscar Fingal O'Flahertie Wills (author); Dublin **(1854–1900)**
Wilder, Billy (film producer, director); Vienna, 6/22/06
Wilder, Gene (Jerome Silberman) (actor, writer, director, producer); Milwaukee, 6/11/35
Wilder, Thornton (author); Madison, Wis. **(1897–1975)**
Wilding, Michael (actor); Westcliff, England **(1912–1979)**
Wilkins, Roy (civil rights leader); St. Louis **(1901–1981)**
Williams, Andy (singer); Wall Lake, Iowa, 12/3/30
Williams, Billy Dee (actor); New York City, 4/6/37
Williams, Cindy (actress); Van Nuys, Calif., 8/22/47
Williams, Edward Bennett (lawyer); Hartford, Conn. **(1920–1988)**
Williams, Emlyn (actor, playwright); Mostyn, Wales **(1905–1987)**
Williams, Esther (actress); Los Angeles, 8/8/23
Williams, Gluyas (cartoonist); San Francisco **(1888–1982)**
Williams, Hank, Sr. (Hiram King Williams) (singer); Georgiana, Ala. **(1923–1953)**
Williams, Joe (singer); Cordele, Ga., 12/12/18
Williams, John T. (composer, conductor); Queens, N.Y., 2/8/32
Williams, Paul (singer, composer, actor); Omaha, Neb., 9/19/40
Williams, Robin (actor, producer); Chicago, 7/21/52
Williams, Roger (clergyman); London **(1603?–1683)**
Williams, Tennessee (Thomas L. Williams) (playwright); Columbus, Miss. **(1911–1983)**
Williams, William Carlos (physician, poet); Rutherford, N.J. **(1883–1963)**
Williamson, Nicol (actor); Hamilton, Scotland, 9/14/38
Willkie, Wendell Lewis (lawyer); Elwood, Ind. **(1892–1944)**
Willis, Bruce (actor); Germany, 3/19/55
Willson, Meredith (composer); Mason City, Iowa **(1902–1984)**
Wilson, August (poet, writer, playwright); Pittsburgh, 1945
Wilson, Don (radio and TV announcer); Lincoln, Neb. **(1900–1982)**
Wilson, Dooley (actor, musician); Tyler, Tex. **(1894–1953)**
Wilson, Edmund (literary critic, author); Red Bank, N.J. **(1895–1972)**
Wilson, Flip (Clerow) (comedian); Jersey City, N.J., 12/8/33
Wilson, Harold (ex-Prime Minister); Huddersfield, England **(1916–1995)**
Wilson, Nancy (singer); Chillicothe, Ohio, 2/20/37
Wilson, Sloan (novelist); Norwalk, Conn., 5/8/20
Winchell, Walter (columnist); New York City **(1897–1972)**
Windsor, Duchess of (Bessie Wallis Warfield) Blue Ridge Summit, Pa. **(1896–1986)**
Windsor, Duke of (formerly King Edward VIII of England); Richmond Park, England **(1894–1972)**
Winfrey, Oprah (TV host, actress, producer); Kosciusko, Miss., 1/29/54
Winger, Debra (Mary Debra) (actress); Cleveland, Ohio, 5/17/55
Winkler, Henry (actor, director, producer); New York City, 10/30/45
Winningham, Mare (actress); Phoenix, Ariz., 5/16/59
Winter, Johnny (guitarist); Leland, Miss., 2/23/44
Winters, Jonathan (comedian); Dayton, Ohio, 11/11/25
Winters, Shelley (Shirley Schrift) (actress); East St. Louis, Ill., 8/18/22
Winthrop, John (first Governor, Massachusetts Bay Colony); Suffolk, England **(1588–1649)**
Wise, Stephen Samuel (rabbi); Budapest **(1874–1949)**
Withers, Jane (actress); Atlanta, 4/12/26
Wittgenstein, Ludwig (Josef Johann) (philosopher); Vienna **(1889–1951)**
Wodehouse, P(elham) G(renville) (novelist); Guildford, England **(1881–1975)**
Wolfe, Thomas Clayton (novelist); Asheville, N.C. **(1900–1938)**
Wolfe, Tom (journalist); Richmond, Va., 3/2/31
Wolff, Tobias (author); Birmingham, Ala., 6/19/45
Wolsey, Thomas (prelate, statesman); Ipswich, England **(c. 1475–1530)**
Wonder, Stevie (Steveland Judkins, later Steveland Morris) (singer; songwriter); Saginaw, Mich., 5/13/50
Wong, Anna May (Lu Tsong Wong) (actress); Los Angeles **(1907–1961)**
Wood, Grant (painter); Anamosa, Iowa **(1892–1942)**
Wood, Natalie (Natasha Gurdin) (actress); San Francisco **(1938–1981)**
Woodhouse, Barbara (Blackburn) (dog trainer, author, TV personality); Rathfarnham, Ireland **(1910–1988)**

Woodruff, Judy (broadcast journalist); Tulsa, Okla., 11/20/46
Woodson, Carter G. (historian); New Canton, Va. **(1875–1950)**
Woodward, Edward (actor); Croydon, England, 6/1/30
Woodward, Joanne (actress); Thomasville, Ga., 2/27/30
Woolf, Adeline Virginia (née Stephens) (novelist); London **(1882–1941)**
Woollcott, Alexander (author, critic); Phalanx, N.J. **(1887–1943)**
Woolley, Monty (Edgar Montillion Woolley) (actor); New York City **(1888–1963)**
Woolworth, Frank (merchant); Rodman, N.Y. **(1852–1919)**
Wopat, Tom (actor); Lodi, Wis., 9/9/50
Wordsworth, William (poet); Cockermouth, England **(1770–1850)**
Wouk, Herman (novelist); New York City, 5/27/15
Wovoka, (Jack Wilson) (Paiute Indian religious leader); (western Nev.) **(c.1858–1932)**
Wray, Fay (actress); Alberta, Canada, 9/14/07
Wren, Sir Christopher (architect); East Knoyle, England **(1632–1723)**
Wright, Frank Lloyd (architect); Richland Center, Wis. **(1869–1959)**
Wright, Martha (singer); Seattle, Wash., 3/23/26
Wright, Orville (inventor); Dayton, Ohio **(1871–1948)**
Wright, Richard (novelist); nr. Natchez, Miss. **(1908–1960)**
Wright, Wilbur (inventor); Millville, Ind. **(1867–1912)**
Wyatt, Jane (actress); Campgaw, N.J., 8/12/12
Wycliffe, John (church reformer); Hipswell, England **(1320–1384)**
Wyeth, Andrew (painter); Chadds Ford, Pa., 7/12/17
Wyle, Noah (actor); Hollywood, Calif., 6/4/71
Wyler, William (director); Mulhouse (France) **(1902–1981)**
Wyman, Jane (Sarah Jane Fulks) (actress); St. Joseph, Mo., 1/4/14
Wynette, Tammy (Wynette Pugh) (singer); Tupelo, Miss., 5/5/42
Wynn, Ed (Isaiah Edwin Leopold) (comedian); Philadelphia **(1886–1966)**
Wynn, Keenan (actor); New York City **(1916–1986)**

X

Xavier, St. Francis (Jesuit missionary); Pamplona, Navarre (Spain) **(1506–1552)**
Xenophon (soldier, historian, essayist); Athens, Greece **(c. 435–c. 355 B.C.E.)**
Xerxes, the Great (king); Persian Empire **(c. 519–465 B.C.E.)**

Y

Yeats, William Butler (poet); nr. Dublin **(1865–1939)**
Yevtushenko, Yevgeny (poet); Zima (Russia), 7/18/33
York, Michael (actor); Fulmer, England, 3/27/42
York, Susannah (Fletcher) (actress); London, 1/9/42
Yorty, Samuel W. (ex-Mayor of Los Angeles); Lincoln, Neb., 10/1/09
Yothers, Tina (actress); Whittier, Calif., 5/5/73
Young, Alan (actor); North Shield, England, 11/19/19
Young, Andrew (civil rights leader); New Orleans, 3/12/32
Young, Brigham (religious leader); Whitingham, Vt. **(1801–1877)**
Young, Gig (Byron Barr) (actor); St. Cloud, Minn. **(1917–1978)**
Young, Loretta (Gretchen Young) (actress); Salt Lake City, 1/6/13
Young, Neil (singer, songwriter); Toronto, 11/12/45
Young, Robert (actor); Chicago, 2/22/07
Youngman, Henny (comedian); Whitechapel, London, England, 3/16/06

Z

Zanuck, Darryl F. (producer); Wahoo, Neb. **(1902–1979)**
Zappa, Frank (Francis Vincent Zappa, Jr.) (singer, songwriter); Baltimore **(1940–1993)**
Zeffirelli, Franco (director); Florence, Italy, 2/12/23
Zenger, John Peter (printer, journalist); (Germany) **(1697–1746)**
Zhou Enlai (Premier); Hualyin, China **(1898–1976)**
Ziegfeld, Florenz (theatrical producer); Chicago **(1869–1932)**
Zimbalist, Efrem (concert violinist); Rostov-on-Don, Russia **(1889–1985)**
Zimbalist, Efrem, Jr. (actor); New York City, 11/30/23
Zimbalist, Stephanie (actress); New York City, 10/8/56
Zola, Emile (novelist); Paris **(1840–1902)**
Zoroaster (religious leader); Persian Empire **(c. 628–c. 551 B.C.E.)**
Zukerman, Pinchas (violinist); Tel Aviv, Israel, 7/16/48
Zukor, Adolph (movie executive); Risce, Hungary **(1873–1976)**
Zurbarán, Francisco de (painter); Fuentes de Cantos, Spain **(1598–1664)**
Zweig, Stefan (author); Vienna **(1881–1942)**
Zwingli, Huldrych (humanist); Wildaus, Switzerland **(1484–1531)**

Awards

Nobel Prizes

The Nobel prizes are awarded under the will of Alfred Bernhard Nobel, Swedish chemist and engineer, who died in 1896. The interest of the fund is divided annually among the persons who have made the most outstanding contributions in the fields of physics, chemistry, and physiology or medicine, who have produced the most distinguished literary work of an idealist tendency, and who have contributed most toward world peace.

In 1968, a Nobel Prize of economic sciences was established by Riksbank, the Swedish bank, in celebration of its 300th anniversary. The prize was awarded for the first time in 1969.

The prizes for physics and chemistry are awarded by the Swedish Academy of Science in Stockholm, the one for physiology or medicine by the Caroline Medical Institute in Stockholm, that for literature by the Academy in Stockholm, and that for peace by a committee of five elected by the Norwegian Storting. The distribution of prizes was begun on December 10, 1901, the anniversary of Nobel's death. The amount of each prize varies with the income from the fund and currently is about $190,000. No Nobel prizes were awarded for 1940, 1941, and 1942; prizes for literature were not awarded for 1914, 1918, and 1943. *(See* October 1997 Current Events for 1997 winners.)

PEACE

1901 Henri Dunant (Switzerland); Frederick Passy (France)
1902 Elie Ducommun and Albert Gobat (Switzerland)
1903 Sir William R. Cremer (U.K.)
1904 Institut de Droit International (Belgium)
1905 Bertha von Suttner (Austria)
1906 Theodore Roosevelt (U.S.)
1907 Ernesto T. Moneta (Italy) and Louis Renault (France)
1908 Klas P. Arnoldson (Sweden) and Frederik Bajer (Denmark)
1909 Auguste M. F. Beernaert (Belgium) and Baron Paul H. B. B. d'Estournelles de Constant de Rebecque (France)
1910 Bureau International Permanent de la Paix (Switzerland)
1911 Tobias M. C. Asser (Holland) and Alfred H. Fried (Austria)
1912 Elihu Root (U.S.)
1913 Henri La Fontaine (Belgium)
1915 No award
1916 No award
1917 International Red Cross
1919 Woodrow Wilson (U.S.)
1920 Léon Bourgeois (France)
1921 Karl H. Branting (Sweden) and Christian L. Lange (Norway)
1922 Fridtjof Nansen (Norway)
1923 No award
1924 No award
1925 Sir Austen Chamberlain (U.K.) and Charles G. Dawes (U.S.)
1926 Aristide Briand (France) and Gustav Stresemann (Germany)
1927 Ferdinand Buisson (France) and Ludwig Quidde (Germany)
1928 No award
1929 Frank B. Kellogg (U.S.)
1930 Lars O. J. Söderblom (Sweden)
1931 Jane Addams and Nicholas M. Butler (U.S.)
1932 No award
1933 Sir Norman Angell (U.K.)
1934 Arthur Henderson (U.K.)
1935 Karl von Ossietzky (Germany)
1936 Carlos de S. Lamas (Argentina)
1937 Lord Cecil of Chelwood (U.K.)
1938 Office International Nansen pour les Réfugiés (Switzerland)

1939 No award
1944 International Red Cross
1945 Cordell Hull (U.S.)
1946 Emily G. Balch and John R. Mott (U.S.)
1947 American Friends Service Committee (U.S.) and British Society of Friends' Service Council (U.K.)
1948 No award
1949 Lord John Boyd Orr (Scotland)
1950 Ralph J. Bunche (U.S.)
1951 Léon Jouhaux (France)
1952 Albert Schweitzer (French Equatorial Africa)
1953 George C. Marshall (U.S.)
1954 Office of U.N. High Commissioner for Refugees
1955 No award
1956 No award
1957 Lester B. Pearson (Canada)
1958 Rev. Dominique Georges Henri Pire (Belgium)
1959 Philip John Noel-Baker (U.K.)
1960 Albert John Luthuli (South Africa)
1961 Dag Hammarskjöld (Sweden)
1962 Linus Pauling (U.S.)
1963 Intl. Comm. of Red Cross; League of Red Cross Societies (both Geneva)
1964 Rev. Dr. Martin Luther King, Jr. (U.S.)
1965 UNICEF (United Nations Children's Fund)
1966 No award
1967 No award
1968 René Cassin (France)
1969 International Labour Organization
1970 Norman E. Borlaug (U.S.)
1971 Willy Brandt (West Germany)
1972 No award
1973 Henry A. Kissinger (U.S.); Le Duc Tho (North Vietnam)[1]
1974 Eisaku Sato (Japan); Sean MacBride (Ireland)
1975 Andrei D. Sakharov (U.S.S.R.)
1976 Mairead Corrigan and Betty Williams (both Northern Ireland)
1977 Amnesty International
1978 Menachem Begin (Israel) and Anwar el-Sadat (Egypt)
1979 Mother Teresa of Calcutta (India)
1980 Adolfo Pérez Esquivel (Argentina)
1981 Office of the United Nations High Commissioner for Refugees
1982 Alva Myrdal (Sweden) and Alfonso García Robles (Mexico)
1983 Lech Walesa (Poland)
1984 Bishop Desmond Tutu (South Africa)

1985	International Physicians for the Prevention of Nuclear War
1986	Elie Wiesel (U.S.)
1987	Oscar Arias Sánchez (Costa Rica)
1988	U.N. Peacekeeping Forces
1989	Dalai Lama (Tibet)
1990	Mikhail S. Gorbachev (U.S.S.R.)
1991	Daw Aung San Suu Kyi (Burma)
1992	Rigoberta Menchú (Guatemala)
1993	F.W. de Klerk and Nelson Mandela (both South Africa)
1994	Yasir Arafat (Palestine) and Yitzhak Rabin (Israel)
1995	Joseph Rotblat and Pugwash Conference on Science and World Affairs (U.K.)
1996	Carlos Filipe Ximenes Belo and José Ramos-Horta (East Timor)

1. Le Duc Tho refused prize, charging that peace had not yet been really established in South Vietnam.

LITERATURE

1901	René F. A. Sully Prudhomme (France)
1902	Theodor Mommsen (Germany)
1903	Björnstjerne Björnson (Norway)
1904	Frédéric Mistral (France) and José Echegaray (Spain)
1905	Henryk Sienkiewicz (Poland)
1906	Giosuè Carducci (Italy)
1907	Rudyard Kipling (U.K.)
1908	Rudolf Eucken (Germany)
1909	Selma Lagerlöf (Sweden)
1910	Paul von Heyse (Germany)
1911	Maurice Maeterlinck (Belgium)
1912	Gerhart Hauptmann (Germany)
1913	Rabindranath Tagore (India)
1915	Romain Rolland (France)
1916	Verner von Heidenstam (Sweden)
1917	Karl Gjellerup (Denmark) and Henrik Pontoppidan (Denmark)
1919	Carl Spitteler (Switzerland)
1920	Knut Hamsun (Norway)
1921	Anatole France (France)
1922	Jacinto Benavente (Spain)
1923	William B. Yeats (Ireland)
1924	Wladyslaw Reymont (Poland)
1925	George Bernard Shaw (Ireland)
1926	Grazia Deledda (Italy)
1927	Henri Bergson (France)
1928	Sigrid Undset (Norway)
1929	Thomas Mann (Germany)
1930	Sinclair Lewis (U.S.)
1931	Erik A. Karlfeldt (Sweden)
1932	John Galsworthy (U.K.)
1933	Ivan G. Bunin (Russia)
1934	Luigi Pirandello (Italy)
1935	No award
1936	Eugene O'Neill (U.S.)
1937	Roger Martin du Gard (France)
1938	Pearl S. Buck (U.S.)
1939	Frans Eemil Sillanpää (Finland)
1944	Johannes V. Jensen (Denmark)
1945	Gabriela Mistral (Chile)
1946	Hermann Hesse (Switzerland)
1947	André Gide (France)
1948	Thomas Stearns Eliot (U.K.)
1949	William Faulkner (U.S.)
1950	Bertrand Russell (U.K.)
1951	Pär Lagerkvist (Sweden)
1952	François Mauriac (France)
1953	Sir Winston Churchill (U.K.)
1954	Ernest Hemingway (U.S.)
1955	Halldór Kiljan Laxness (Iceland)
1956	Juan Ramón Jiménez (Spain)

1957	Albert Camus (France)
1958	Boris Pasternak (U.S.S.R.) (declined)
1959	Salvatore Quasimodo (Italy)
1960	St-John Perse (Alexis St.-Léger Léger) (France)
1961	Ivo Andric (Yugoslavia)
1962	John Steinbeck (U.S.)
1963	Giorgios Seferis (Seferiades) (Greece)
1964	Jean-Paul Sartre (France) (declined)
1965	Mikhail Sholokhov (U.S.S.R.)
1966	Shmuel Yosef Agnon (Israel) and Nelly Sachs (Sweden)
1967	Miguel Angel Asturias (Guatemala)
1968	Yasunari Kawabata (Japan)
1969	Samuel Beckett (Ireland)
1970	Aleksandr Solzhenitsyn (U.S.S.R.)
1971	Pablo Neruda (Chile)
1972	Heinrich Böll (Germany)
1973	Patrick White (Australia)
1974	Eyvind Johnson and Harry Martinson (both Sweden)
1975	Eugenio Montale (Italy)
1976	Saul Bellow (U.S.)
1977	Vicente Aleixandre (Spain)
1978	Isaac Bashevis Singer (U.S.)
1979	Odysseus Elytis (Greece)
1980	Czeslaw Milosz (U.S.)
1981	Elias Canetti (Bulgaria)
1982	Gabriel García Márquez (Colombia)
1983	William Golding (U.K.)
1984	Jaroslav Seifert (Czechoslovakia)
1985	Claude Simon (France)
1986	Wole Soyinka (Nigeria)
1987	Joseph Brodsky (U.S.)
1988	Naguib Mahfouz (Egypt)
1989	Camilo José Cela (Spain)
1990	Octavio Paz (Mexico)
1991	Nadine Gordimer (South Africa)
1992	Derek Walcott (Trinidad)
1993	Toni Morrison (U.S.)
1994	Kenzaburo Oe (Japan)
1995	Seamus Heaney (Ireland)
1996	Wislawa Szymborska (Poland)

PHYSICS

1901	Wilhelm K. Roentgen (Germany), for discovery of Roentgen rays
1902	Hendrik A. Lorentz and Pieter Zeeman (Netherlands), for work on influence of magnetism upon radiation
1903	A. Henri Becquerel (France), for work on spontaneous radioactivity; and Pierre and Marie Curie (France), for study of radiation
1904	John Strutt (Lord Rayleigh) (U.K.), for discovery of argon in investigating gas density
1905	Philipp Lenard (Germany), for work with cathode rays
1906	Sir Joseph Thomson (U.K.), for investigations on passage of electricity through gases
1907	Albert A. Michelson (U.S.), for spectroscopic and metrologic investigations
1908	Gabriel Lippmann (France), for method of reproducing colors by photography
1909	Guglielmo Marconi (Italy) and Ferdinand Braun (Germany), for development of wireless
1910	Johannes D. van der Waals (Netherlands), for work with the equation of state for gases and liquids
1911	Wilhelm Wien (Germany), for his laws governing the radiation of heat
1912	Gustaf Dalén (Sweden), for discovery of automatic regulators used in lighting lighthouses and light buoys

1913 Heike Kamerlingh-Onnes (Netherlands), for work leading to production of liquid helium
1914 Max von Laue (Germany), for discovery of diffraction of Roentgen rays passing through crystals
1915 Sir William Bragg and William L. Bragg (U.K.), for analysis of crystal structure by X rays
1916 No award
1917 Charles G. Barkla (U.K.), for discovery of Roentgen radiation of the elements
1918 Max Planck (Germany), discoveries in connection with quantum theory
1919 Johannes Stark (Germany), discovery of Doppler effect in Canal rays and decomposition of spectrum lines by electric fields
1920 Charles E. Guillaume (Switzerland), for discoveries of anomalies in nickel steel alloys
1921 Albert Einstein (Germany), for discovery of the law of the photoelectric effect
1922 Niels Bohr (Denmark), for investigation of structure of atoms and radiations emanating from them
1923 Robert A. Millikan (U.S.), for work on elementary charge of electricity and photoelectric phenomena
1924 Karl M. G. Siegbahn (Sweden), for investigations in X-ray spectroscopy
1925 James Franck and Gustav Hertz (Germany), for discovery of laws governing impact of electrons upon atoms
1926 Jean B. Perrin (France), for work on discontinuous structure of matter and discovery of the equilibrium of sedimentation
1927 Arthur H. Compton (U.S.), for discovery of Compton phenomenon; and Charles T. R. Wilson (U.K.), for method of perceiving paths taken by electrically charged particles
1928 In 1929, the 1928 prize was awarded to Sir Owen Richardson (U.K.), for work on the phenomenon of thermionics and discovery of the Richardson Law
1929 Prince Louis Victor de Broglie (France), for discovery of the wave character of electrons
1930 Sir Chandrasekhara Raman (India), for work on diffusion of light and discovery of the Raman effect
1931 No award
1932 In 1933, the prize for 1932 was awarded to Werner Heisenberg (Germany), for creation of the quantum mechanics
1933 Erwin Schrödinger (Austria) and Paul A. M. Dirac (U.K.), for discovery of new fertile forms of the atomic theory
1934 No award
1935 James Chadwick (U.K.), for discovery of the neutron
1936 Victor F. Hess (Austria), for discovery of cosmic radiation; and Carl D. Anderson (U.S.), for discovery of the positron
1937 Clinton J. Davisson (U.S.) and George P. Thomson (U.K.), for discovery of diffraction of electrons by crystals
1938 Enrico Fermi (Italy), for identification of new radioactivity elements and discovery of nuclear reactions effected by slow neutrons
1939 Ernest Orlando Lawrence (U.S.), for development of the cyclotron
1943 Otto Stern (U.S.), for detection of magnetic momentum of protons
1944 Isidor Isaac Rabi (U.S.), for work on magnetic movements of atomic particles
1945 Wolfgang Pauli (Austria), for work on atomic fissions
1946 Percy Williams Bridgman (U.S.), for studies and inventions in high-pressure physics
1947 Sir Edward Appleton (U.K.), for discovery of layer which reflects radio short waves in the ionosphere
1948 Patrick M. S. Blackett (U.K.), for improvement on Wilson chamber and discoveries in cosmic radiation
1949 Hideki Yukawa (Japan), for mathematical prediction, in 1935, of the meson
1950 Cecil Frank Powell (U.K.), for method of photographic study of atom nucleus, and for discoveries about mesons
1951 Sir John Douglas Cockcroft (U.K.) and Ernest T. S. Walton (Ireland), for work in 1932 on transmutation of atomic nuclei
1952 Edward Mills Purcell and Felix Bloch (U.S.), for work in measurement of magnetic fields in atomic nuclei
1953 Fritz Zernike (Netherlands), for development of "phase contrast" microscope
1954 Max Born (U.K.), for work in quantum mechanics; and Walther Bothe (Germany), for work in cosmic radiation
1955 Polykarp Kusch and Willis E. Lamb, Jr. (U.S.), for atomic measurements
1956 William Shockley, Walter H. Brattain, and John Bardeen (all U.S.), for developing electronic transistor
1957 Tsung Dao Lee and Chen Ning Yang (China), for disproving principle of conservation of parity
1958 Pavel A. Cherenkov, Ilya M. Frank, and Igor E. Tamm (all U.S.S.R.), for work resulting in development of cosmic-ray counter
1959 Emilio Segre and Owen Chamberlain (both U.S.), for demonstrating the existence of the anti-proton
1960 Donald A. Glaser (U.S.), for invention of "bubble chamber" to study subatomic particles
1961 Robert Hofstadter (U.S.), for determination of shape and size of atomic nucleus; Rudolf Mössbauer (Germany), for method of producing and measuring recoil-free gamma rays
1962 Lev D. Landau (U.S.S.R.), for his theories about condensed matter
1963 Eugene Paul Wigner, Maria Goeppert Mayer (both U.S.), and J. Hans D. Jensen (Germany), for research on structure of atom and its nucleus
1964 Charles Hard Townes (U.S.), Nikolai G. Basov and Aleksandr M. Prochorov (both U.S.S.R.), for developing maser and laser principle of producing high-intensity radiation
1965 Richard P. Feynman, Julian S. Schwinger (both U.S.), and Shinichiro Tomonaga (Japan), for research in quantum electrodynamics
1966 Alfred Kastler (France), for work on energy levels inside atom
1967 Hans A. Bethe (U.S.), for work on energy production of stars
1968 Luis Walter Alvarez (U.S.), for study of subatomic particles
1969 Murray Gell-Mann (U.S.), for study of subatomic particles
1970 Hannes Alfvén (Sweden), for theories in plasma physics; and Louis Néel (France), for discoveries in antiferromagnetism and ferrimagnetism
1971 Dennis Gabor (U.K.), for invention of holographic method of three-dimensional imagery
1972 John Bardeen, Leon N. Cooper, and John Robert Schrieffer (all U.S.), for theory of superconductivity, where electrical resistance in certain metals vanishes above absolute zero temperature

1973 Ivar Giaever (U.S.), Leo Esaki (Japan), and Brian D. Josephson (U.K.), for theories that have advanced and expanded the field of miniature electronics

1974 Antony Hewish (U.K.), for discovery of pulsars; Martin Ryle (U.K.), for using radiotelescopes to probe outer space with high degree of precision

1975 James Rainwater (U.S.) and Ben Mottelson and Aage N. Bohr (both Denmark), for showing that the atomic nucleus is asymmetrical

1976 Burton Richter and Samuel C. C. Ting (both U.S.), for discovery of subatomic particles known as J and psi

1977 Philip W. Anderson and John H. Van Vleck (both U.S.), and Nevill F. Mott (U.K.), for work underlying computer memories and electronic devices

1978 Arno A. Penzias and Robert W. Wilson (both U.S.), for work in cosmic microwave radiation; Piotr L. Kapitsa (U.S.S.R.), for basic inventions and discoveries in low-temperature physics

1979 Steven Weinberg, Sheldon L. Glashow (both U.S.), and Abdus Salam (Pakistan), for developing theory that electromagnetism and the "weak" force, which causes radioactive decay in some atomic nuclei, are facets of the same phenomenon

1980 James W. Cronin and Val L. Fitch (both U.S.), for work concerning the asymmetry of subatomic particles

1981 Nicolaas Bloembergen, Arthur L. Schawlow (both U.S.), and Kai M. Siegbahn (Sweden), for developing technologies with lasers and other devices to probe the secrets of complex forms of matter

1982 Kenneth G. Wilson (U.S.), for analysis of changes in matter under pressure and temperature

1983 Subrahmanyam Chandrasekhar and William A. Fowler (both U.S.), for complementary research on processes involved in the evolution of stars

1984 Carlo Rubbia (Italy) and Simon van der Meer (Netherlands), for their role in discovering three subatomic particles, a step toward developing a single theory to account for all natural forces

1985 Klaus von Klitzing (Germany), for developing an exact way of measuring electrical conductivity

1986 Ernst Ruska, Gerd Binnig (both Germany), and Heinrich Rohrer (Switzerland) for work on microscopes

1987 K. Alex Müller (Switzerland) and J. Georg Bednorz (Germany), for their discovery of high-temperature superconductors

1988 Leon M. Lederman, Melvin Schwartz, and Jack Steinberger (all U.S.), for research that improved the understanding of elementary particles and forces

1989 Norman F. Ramsey (U.S.), for work leading to development of the atomic clock, and Hans G. Dehmelt (U.S.) and Wolfgang Paul (Germany) for developing methods to isolate atoms and subatomic particles

1990 Richard E. Taylor (Canada), Jerome I. Friedman and Dr. Henry W. Kendall (both U.S.), for their "breakthrough in our understanding of matter" which confirmed the reality of quarks

1991 Pierre-Gilles de Gennes (France), for his discoveries about the ordering of molecules in substances ranging from "super" glue to an exotic form of liquid helium

1992 George Charpak (France), for his inventions of particle detectors

1993 Joseph H. Taylor and Russell A. Hulse (both U.S.), for their discovery of a binary pulsar

1994 Clifford G. Shull (U.S.) and Bertram N. Brockhouse (Canada), for adapting beams of neutrons as probes to explore the atomic structure of matter

1995 Martin L. Perl and Frederick Reines (both U.S.), for their discoveries of "two of nature's most remarkable subatomic particles"—the tau and the neutrino

1996 David M. Lee, Robert C. Richardson, and Douglas D. Osheroff (all U.S.), for their discovery of superfluity in helium-3

CHEMISTRY

1901 Jacobus H. van't Hoff (Netherlands), for laws of chemical dynamics and osmotic pressure in solutions

1902 Emil Fischer (Germany), for experiments in sugar and purin groups of substances

1903 Svante A. Arrhenius (Sweden), for his electrolytic theory of dissociation

1904 Sir William Ramsay (U.K.), for discovery and determination of place of inert gaseous elements in air

1905 Adolf von Baeyer (Germany), for work on organic dyes and hydroaromatic combinations

1906 Henri Moissan (France), for isolation of fluorine, and introduction of electric furnace

1907 Eduard Buchner (Germany), discovery of cell-less fermentation and investigations in biological chemistry

1908 Sir Ernest Rutherford (U.K.), for investigations into disintegration of elements

1909 Wilhelm Ostwald (Germany), for work on catalysis and investigations into chemical equilibrium and reaction rates

1910 Otto Wallach (Germany), for work in the field of alicyclic compounds

1911 Marie Curie (France), for discovery of elements radium and polonium

1912 Victor Grignard (France), for reagent discovered by him; and Paul Sabatier (France), for methods of hydrogenating organic compounds

1913 Alfred Werner (Switzerland), for linking up atoms within the molecule

1914 Theodore W. Richards (U.S.), for determining atomic weight of many chemical elements

1915 Richard Willstätter (Germany), for research into coloring matter of plants, especially chlorophyll

1916 No award

1917 No award

1918 Fritz Haber (Germany), for synthetic production of ammonia

1919 No award

1920 Walther Nernst (Germany), for work in thermochemistry

1921 Frederick Soddy (U.K.), for investigations into origin and nature of isotopes

1922 Francis W. Aston (U.K.), for discovery of isotopes in nonradioactive elements and for discovery of the whole number rule

1923 Fritz Pregl (Austria), for method of microanalysis of organic substances discovered by him

1924 No award

1925 In 1926, the 1925 prize was awarded to Richard Zsigmondy (Germany), for work on the heterogeneous nature of colloid solutions

1926 Theodor Svedberg (Sweden), for work on disperse systems

1927 In 1928, the 1927 prize was awarded to Heinrich Wieland (Germany), for investigations of bile acids and kindred substances

1928 Adolf Windaus (Germany), for investigations on constitution of the sterols and their connection with vitamins

1929 Sir Arthur Harden (U.K.) and Hans K. A. S. von Euler-Chelpin (Sweden), for research of fermentation of sugars

1930 Hans Fischer (Germany), for work on coloring matter of blood and leaves and for his synthesis of hemin

1931 Karl Bosch and Friedrich Bergius (both Germany), for invention and development of chemical high-pressure methods

1932 Irving Langmuir (U.S.), for work in realm of surface chemistry

1933 No award

1934 Harold C. Urey (U.S.), for discovery of heavy hydrogen

1935 Frédéric and Irène Joliot-Curie (both France), for synthesis of new radioactive elements

1936 Peter J. W. Debye (Netherlands), for investigations on dipole moments and diffraction of X rays and electrons in gases

1937 Walter N. Haworth (U.K.), for research on carbohydrates and Vitamin C; and Paul Karrer (Switzerland), for work on carotenoids, flavins, and Vitamins A and B

1938 Richard Kuhn (Germany), for carotinoid study and vitamin research (declined)

1939 Adolf Butenandt (Germany), for work on sexual hormones (declined the prize); and Leopold Ruzicka (Switzerland), for work with polymethylenes

1943 Georg Hevesy De Heves (Hungary), for work on use of isotopes as indicators

1944 Otto Hahn (Germany), for work on atomic fission

1945 Artturi Illmari Virtanen (Finland), for research in the field of conservation of fodder

1946 James B. Sumner (U.S.), for crystallizing enzymes; John H. Northrop and Wendell M. Stanley (both U.S.), for preparing enzymes and virus proteins in pure form

1947 Sir Robert Robinson (U.K.), for research in plant substances

1948 Arne Tiselius (Sweden), for biochemical discoveries and isolation of mouse paralysis virus

1949 William Francis Giauque (U.S.), for research in thermodynamics, especially effects of low temperature

1950 Otto Diels and Kurt Alder (both Germany), for discovery of diene synthesis enabling scientists to study structure of organic matter

1951 Glenn T. Seaborg and Edwin H. McMillan (both U.S.), for discovery of plutonium

1952 Archer John Porter Martin and Richard Laurence Millington Synge (both U.K.), for development of partition chromatography

1953 Hermann Staudinger (Germany), for research in giant molecules

1954 Linus C. Pauling (U.S.), for study of forces holding together protein and other molecules

1955 Vincent du Vigneaud (U.S.), for work on pituitary hormones

1956 Sir Cyril Hinshelwood (U.K.) and Nikolai N. Semenov (U.S.S.R.), for parallel research on chemical reaction kinetics

1957 Sir Alexander Todd (U.K.), for research with chemical compounds that are factors in heredity

1958 Frederick Sanger (U.K.), for determining molecular structure of insulin

1959 Jaroslav Heyrovsky (Czechoslovakia), for development of polarography, an electrochemical method of analysis

1960 Willard F. Libby (U.S.), for "atomic time clock" to measure age of objects by measuring their radioactivity

1961 Melvin Calvin (U.S.), for establishing chemical steps during photosynthesis

1962 Max F. Perutz and John C. Kendrew (U.K.), for mapping protein molecules with X-rays

1963 Carl Ziegler (Germany) and Giulio Natta (Italy), for work in uniting simple hydrocarbons into large molecule substances

1964 Dorothy Mary Crowfoot Hodgkin (U.K.), for determining structure of compounds needed in combatting pernicious anemia

1965 Robert B. Woodward (U.S.), for work in synthesizing complicated organic compounds

1966 Robert Sanderson Mulliken (U.S.), for research on bond holding atoms together in molecule

1967 Manfred Eigen (Germany), Ronald G. W. Norrish, and George Porter (both U.K.), for work in high-speed chemical reactions

1968 Lars Onsager (U.S.), for development of system of equations in thermodynamics

1969 Derek H. R. Barton (U.K.) and Odd Hassel (Norway), for study of organic molecules

1970 Luis F. Leloir (Argentina), for discovery of sugar nucleotides and their role in biosynthesis of carbohydrates

1971 Gerhard Herzberg (Canada), for contributions to knowledge of electronic structure and geometry of molecules, particularly free radicals

1972 Christian Boehmer Anfinsen, Stanford Moore, and William Howard Stein (all U.S.), for pioneering studies in enzymes

1973 Ernst Otto Fischer (W. Germany) and Geoffrey Wilkinson (U.K.), for work that could solve problem of automobile exhaust pollution

1974 Paul J. Flory (U.S.), for developing analytic methods to study properties and molecular structure of long-chain molecules

1975 John W. Cornforth (Australia) and Vladimir Prelog (Switzerland), for research on structure of biological molecules such as antibiotics and cholesterol

1976 William N. Lipscomb, Jr. (U.S.), for work on the structure and bonding mechanisms of boranes

1977 Ilya Prigogine (Belgium), for contributions to nonequilibrium thermodynamics, particularly the theory of dissipative structures

1978 Peter Mitchell (U.K.), for contributions to the understanding of biological energy transfer

1979 Herbert C. Brown (U.S.) and Georg Wittig (West Germany), for developing a group of substances that facilitate very difficult chemical reactions

1980 Paul Berg and Walter Gilbert (both U.S.), and Frederick Sanger (U.K.), for developing methods to map the structure and function of DNA, the substance that controls the activity of the cell

1981 Roald Hoffmann (U.S.) and Kenichi Fukui (Japan), for applying quantum-mechanics theories to predict the course of chemical reactions

1982 Aaron Klug (U.K.), for research in the detailed structures of viruses and components of life

1983 Henry Taube (U.S.), for research on how electrons transfer between molecules in chemical reactions

1984 R. Bruce Merrifield (U.S.), for research that revolutionized the study of proteins

1985 Herbert A. Hauptman and Jerome Karle (both U.S.), for their outstanding achievements in the development of direct methods for the determination of crystal structures

1986 Dudley R. Herschback, Yuan T. Lee (both U.S.), and John C. Polanyi (Canada) for their work on "reaction dynamics"

1987 Donald J. Cram and Charles J. Pedersen (both U.S.), and Jean-Marie Lehn (France), for wideranging research that has included the creation of artificial molecules that can mimic vital chemical reactions of the processes of life

1988 Johann Deisenhofer, Robert Huber, and Hartmut Michel (all West Germany), for unraveling the structure of proteins that play a crucial role in photosynthesis

1989 Thomas R. Cech and Sidney Altman (both U.S.), for their discovery, independently, that RNA could actively aid chemical reactions in the cells

1990 Elias James Corey (U.S.), for developing new ways to synthesize complex molecules ordinarily found in nature

1991 Richard R. Ernst (Switzerland), for refinements he developed in nuclear magnetic resonance spectroscopy

1992 Rudolph A. Marcus (U.S.), for his mathematical analysis of how the overall energy in a system of interacting molecules changes and induces an electron to jump from one molecule to another

1993 Kary B. Mullis (U.S.), and Michael Smith (Canada) for their contributions to the science of genetics

1994 George A. Olah (U.S.), University of Southern California in Los Angeles, for research that opened new ways to break apart and rebuild compounds of carbon and hydrogen

1995 F. Sherwood Rowland and Mario Molina (U.S.) and Paul Crutzen (The Netherlands), for their pioneering work in explaining the chemical processes that deplete the earth's ozone shield

1996 Richard E. Smalley, Robert F. Curl, Jr. (both U.S.), and Harold W. Kroto (U.K.), for discovery of a new class of carbon molecule

PHYSIOLOGY OR MEDICINE

1901 Emil A. von Behring (Germany), for work on serum therapy against diphtheria

1902 Sir Ronald Ross (U.K.), for work on malaria

1903 Niels R. Finsen (Denmark), for his treatment of lupus vulgaris with concentrated light rays

1904 Ivan P. Pavlov (U.S.S.R.), for work on the physiology of digestion

1905 Robert Koch (Germany), for work on tuberculosis

1906 Camillo Golgi (Italy) and Santiago Ramón y Cajal (Spain), for work on structure of the nervous system

1907 Charles L. A. Laveran (France), for work with protozoa in the generation of disease

1908 Paul Ehrlich (Germany) and Elie Metchnikoff (U.S.S.R.), for work on immunity

1909 Theodor Kocher (Switzerland), for work on the thyroid gland

1910 Albrecht Kossel (Germany), for achievements in the chemistry of the cell

1911 Allvar Gullstrand (Sweden), for work on the dioptrics of the eye

1912 Alexis Carrel (France), for work on vascular ligature and grafting of blood vessels and organs

1913 Charles Richet (France), for work on anaphylaxy

1914 Robert Bárány (Austria), for work on physiology and pathology of the vestibular system

1915-1918 No award

1919 Jules Bordet (Belgium), for discoveries in connection with immunity

1920 August Krogh (Denmark), for discovery of regulation of capillaries' motor mechanism

1921 No award

1922 In 1923, the 1922 prize was shared by Archibald V. Hill (U.K.), for discovery relating to heat-production in muscles; and Otto Meyerhof (Germany), for correlation between consumption of oxygen and production of lactic acid in muscles

1923 Sir Frederick Banting (Canada) and John J. R. Macleod (Scotland), for discovery of insulin

1924 Willem Einthoven (Netherlands), for discovery of the mechanism of the electrocardiogram

1925 No award

1926 Johannes Fibiger (Denmark), for discovery of the Spiroptera carcinoma

1927 Julius Wagner-Jauregg (Austria), for use of malaria inoculation in treatment of dementia paralytica

1928 Charles Nicolle (France), for work on typhus exanthematicus

1929 Christiaan Eijkman (Netherlands), for discovery of the antineuritic vitamins; and Sir Frederick Hopkins (U.K.), for discovery of growth-promoting vitamins

1930 Karl Landsteiner (U.S.), for discovery of human blood groups

1931 Otto H. Warburg (Germany), for discovery of the character and mode of action of the respiratory ferment

1932 Sir Charles Sherrington (U.K.) and Edgar D. Adrian (U.S.), for discoveries of the function of the neuron

1933 Thomas H. Morgan (U.S.), for discoveries on hereditary function of the chromosomes

1934 George H. Whipple, George R. Minot, and William P. Murphy (U.S.), for discovery of liver therapy against anemias

1935 Hans Spemann (Germany), for discovery of the organizer-effect in embryonic development

1936 Sir Henry Dale (U.K.) and Otto Loewi (Germany), for discoveries on chemical transmission of nerve impulses

1937 Albert Szent-Györgyi von Nagyrapolt (Hungary), for discoveries on biological combustion

1938 Corneille Heymans (Belgium), for determining importance of sinus and aorta mechanisms in the regulation of respiration

1939 Gerhard Domagk (Germany), for antibacterial effect of prontocilate

1943 Henrik Dam (Denmark) and Edward A. Doisy (U.S.), for analysis of Vitamin K

1944 Joseph Erlanger and Herbert Spencer Gasser (both U.S.), for work on functions of the nerve threads

1945 Sir Alexander Fleming, Ernst Boris Chain, and Sir Howard Florey (all U.K.), for discovery of penicillin

1946 Herman J. Muller (U.S.), for hereditary effects of X-rays on genes

1947 Carl F. and Gerty T. Cori (U.S.), for work on animal starch metabolism; Bernardo A. Houssay (Argentina), for study of pituitary

1948 Paul Mueller (Switzerland), for discovery of insect-killing properties of DDT

1949 Walter Rudolf Hess (Switzerland), for research on brain control of body; and Antonio Caetano de Abreu Freire Egas Moniz (Portugal), for development of brain operation

1950 Philip S. Hench, Edward C. Kendall (both U.S.), and Tadeus Reichstein (Switzerland), for discoveries about hormones of adrenal cortex

1951 Max Theiler (South Africa), for development of

anti-yellow-fever vaccine

1952 Selman A. Waksman (U.S.), for co-discovery of streptomycin

1953 Fritz A. Lipmann (Germany-U.S.) and Hans Adolph Krebs (Germany-U.K.), for studies of living cells

1954 John F. Enders, Thomas H. Weller, and Frederick C. Robbins (all U.S.), for work with cultivation of polio virus

1955 Hugo Theorell (Sweden), for work on oxidation enzymes

1956 Dickinson W. Richards, Jr., André F. Cournand (both U.S.), and Werner Forssmann (Germany), for new techniques in treating heart disease

1957 Daniel Bovet (Italy), for development of drugs to relieve allergies and relax muscles during surgery

1958 Joshua Lederberg (U.S.), for work with genetic mechanisms; George W. Beadle and Edward L. Tatum (both U.S.), for discovering how genes transmit hereditary characteristics

1959 Severo Ochoa and Arthur Kornberg (both U.S.), for discoveries related to compounds within chromosomes, which play a vital role in heredity

1960 Sir Macfarlane Burnet (Australia) and Peter Brian Medawar (U.K.), for discovery of acquired immunological tolerance

1961 Georg von Bekesy (U.S.), for discoveries about physical mechanisms of stimulation within cochlea

1962 James D. Watson (U.S.), Maurice H. F. Wilkins, and Francis H. C. Crick (both U.K.), for determining structure of deoxyribonucleic acid (DNA)

1963 Alan Lloyd Hodgkin, Andrew Fielding Huxley (both U.K.), and Sir John Carew Eccles (Australia), for research on nerve cells

1964 Konrad E. Bloch (U.S.) and Feodor Lynen (Germany), for research on mechanism and regulation of cholesterol and fatty acid metabolism

1965 François Jacob, André Lwoff, and Jacques Monod (all France), for study of regulatory activities in body cells

1966 Charles Brenton Huggins (U.S.), for studies in hormone treatment of cancer of prostate; Francis Peyton Rous (U.S.), for discovery of tumor-producing viruses

1967 Haldan K. Hartline, George Wald, and Ragnar Granit (all U.S.), for work on human eye

1968 Robert W. Holley, Har Gobind Khorana, and Marshall W. Nirenberg (all U.S.), for studies of genetic code

1969 Max Delbruck, Alfred D. Hershey, and Salvador E. Luria (all U.S.), for study of mechanism of virus infection in living cells

1970 Julius Axelrod (U.S.), Ulf S. von Euler (Sweden), and Sir Bernard Katz (U.K.), for studies of how nerve impulses are transmitted within the body

1971 Earl W. Sutherland, Jr. (U.S.), for research on how hormones work

1972 Gerald M. Edelman (U.S.), and Rodney R. Porter (U.K.), for research on the chemical structure and nature of antibodies

1973 Karl von Frisch and Konrad Lorenz (Austria), and Nikolaas Tinbergen (Netherlands), for their studies of individual and social behavior patterns

1974 George E. Palade and Christian de Duve (both U.S.) and Albert Claude (Belgium), for contributions to understanding inner workings of living cells

1975 David Baltimore, Howard M. Temin, and Renato Dulbecco (all U.S.), for work in interaction between tumor viruses and genetic material of the cell

1976 Baruch S. Blumberg and D. Carleton Gajdusek (both U.S.), for discoveries concerning new mechanisms for the origin and dissemination of infectious diseases

1977 Rosalyn S. Yalow, Roger C. L. Guillemin, and Andrew V. Schally (all U.S.), for research in role of hormones in chemistry of the body

1978 Daniel Nathans and Hamilton Smith (both U.S.) and Werner Arber (Switzerland), for discovery of restriction enzymes and their application to problems of molecular genetics

1979 Allan McLeod Cormack (U.S.) and Godfrey Newbold Hounsfield (U.K.), for developing computed axial tomography (CAT scan) X-ray technique

1980 Baruj Benacerraf and George D. Snell (both U.S.), and Jean Dausset (France), for discoveries that explain how the structure of cells relates to organ transplants and diseases

1981 Roger W. Sperry and David H. Hubel (both U.S.), and Torsten N. Wiesel (Sweden), for studies vital to understanding the organization and functioning of the brain

1982 Sune Bergstrom and Bengt Samuelsson (both Sweden), and John R. Vane (U.K.), for research in prostaglandins, a hormonelike substance involved in a wide range of illnesses

1983 Barbara McClintock (U.S.), for her discovery of mobile genes in the chromosomes of a plant that change the future generations of plants they produce

1984 Cesar Milstein (U.K./Argentina) Georges J.F. Kohler (West Germany), and Niels K. Jerne (U.K./Denmark) for their work in immunology

1985 Michael S. Brown and Joseph L. Goldstein (both U.S.), for their work which has drastically widened our understanding of the cholesterol metabolism and increased our possibilities to prevent and treat atherosclerosis and heart attacks

1986 Rita Levi-Montalcini (dual U.S./Italy) and Stanley Cohen (U.S.) for their contributions to the understanding of substances that influence cell growth

1987 Susumu Tonegawa (Japan), for his discoveries of how the body can suddenly marshal its immunological defenses against millions of different disease agents that it has never encountered before

1988 Gertrude B. Elion, George H. Hitchings (both U.S.), and Sir James Black (U.K.), for their discoveries of important principles for drug treatment

1989 J. Michael Bishop and Harold E. Varmus (both U.S.), for their unifying theory of cancer development

1990 Joseph E. Murray and E. Donnall Thomas (both U.S.), for their pioneering work in transplants

1991 Erwin Neher and Bert Sakmann (both Germany), for their research, particularly for the development of a technique called patch clamp

1992 Edmond H. Fischer and Edwin G. Krebs (both U.S.), for their discovery of a regulatory mechanism affecting almost all cells

1993 Phillip A. Sharp (U.S.) and Richard J. Roberts (U.K.), for their independent discovery in 1977 of "split genes"

1994 Alfred G. Gilman and Martin Rodbell (both U.S.), for discovery of G-proteins that help cells respond to outside signals

1995 Edward B. Lewis and Eric F. Wieschaus (both

U.S.) and Christiane Nüsslein-Volhard (Germany), for studies of the fruit fly that will help explain congenital malformations in humans
1996 Peter C. Doherty (Australia) and Rolf M. Zinkernagel (Switzerland), for discoveries about how the immune system recognizes virus-infected cells

ECONOMIC SCIENCE

1969 Ragnar Frisch (Norway) and Jan Tinbergen (Netherlands), for work in econometrics (application of mathematics and statistical methods to economic theories and problems)
1970 Paul A. Samuelson (U.S.), for efforts to raise the level of scientific analysis in economic theory
1971 Simon Kuznets (U.S.), for developing concept of using a country's gross national product to determine its economic growth
1972 Kenneth J. Arrow (U.S.) and Sir John R. Hicks (U.K.), for theories that help to assess business risk and government economic and welfare policies
1973 Wassily Leontief (U.S.), for devising the input-output technique to determine how different sectors of an economy interact
1974 Gunnar Myrdal (Sweden) and Friedrich A. von Hayek (U.K.), for pioneering analysis of the interdependence of economic, social and institutional phenomena
1975 Leonid V. Kantorovich (U.S.S.R.) and Tjalling C. Koopmans (U.S.), for work on the theory of optimum allocation of resources
1976 Milton Friedman (U.S.), for work in consumption analysis and monetary history and theory, and for demonstration of complexity of stabilization policy
1977 Bertil Ohlin (Sweden) and James E. Meade (U.K.), for contributions to theory of international trade and international capital movements
1978 Herbert A. Simon (U.S.), for research into the decision-making process within economic organizations
1979 Sir Arthur Lewis (U.K.) and Theodore Schultz (U.S.), for work on economic problems of developing nations
1980 Lawrence R. Klein (U.S.), for developing models for forecasting economic trends and shaping policies to deal with them
1981 James Tobin (U.S.), for analyses of financial markets and their influence on spending and saving by families and businesses
1982 George J. Stigler (U.S.), for work on government regulation in the economy and the functioning of industry
1983 Gerard Debreu (U.S.), in recognition of his work on the basic economic problem of how prices operate to balance what producers supply with what buyers want
1984 Sir Richard Stone (U.K.), for his work to develop the systems widely used to measure the performance of national economics
1985 Franco Modigliani (U.S.), for his pioneering work in analyzing the behavior of household savers and the functioning of financial markets
1986 James M. Buchanan (U.S.), for his development of new methods for analyzing economic and political decision-making
1987 Robert M. Solow (U.S.), for seminal contributions to the theory of economic growth
1988 Maurice Allais (France), for his pioneering development of theories to better understand market behavior and the efficient use of resources
1989 Trygve Haavelmo (Norway), for his pioneering work in methods for testing economic theories
1990 Harry M. Markowitz, William F. Sharpe, and Merton H. Miller (all U.S.), whose work provided new tools for weighing the risks and rewards of different investments and for valuing corporate stocks and bonds
1991 Ronald Coase (U.S.), for his pioneering work in how property rights and the cost of doing business affect the economy
1992 Gary S. Becker (U.S.), for "having extended the domain of economic theory to aspects of human behavior which had previously been dealt with—if at all—by other social science disciplines"
1993 Robert W. Fogel and Douglass C. North (both U.S.), for their work in economic history
1994 John F. Nash and John C. Harsanyi (both U.S.), and Reinhard Selten (Germany), for their pioneering work in game theory
1995 Robert E. Lucas, Jr. (U.S.), who has had the greatest influence on macroeconomic research since 1970
1996 James A. Mirrlees (U.K.) and William Vickrey (U.S.), for "their fundamental contributions to the economic theory of incentives"

Motion Picture Academy Awards (Oscars)

1928
Picture: *Wings*, Paramount
Director: Frank Borzage, *Seventh Heaven;* Lewis Milestone, *Two Arabian Nights*
Actress: Janet Gaynor, *Seventh Heaven, Street Angel, Sunrise*
Actor: Emil Jannings, *The Way of All Flesh, The Last Command*

1929
Picture: *The Broadway Melody*, MGM
Director: Frank Lloyd, *The Divine Lady*
Actress: Mary Pickford, *Coquette*
Actor: Warner Baxter, *In Old Arizona*

1930
Picture: *All Quiet on the Western Front*, Universal
Director: Lewis Milestone, *All Quiet on the Western Front*
Actress: Norma Shearer, *The Divorcee*
Actor: George Arliss, *Disraeli*

1931
Picture: *Cimarron;* RKO Radio
Director: Norman Taurog, *Skippy*

1928
Actress: Marie Dressler, *Min and Bill*
Actor: Lionel Barrymore, *A Free Soul*

1932
Picture: *Grand Hotel*, MGM
Director: Frank Borzage, *Bad Girl*
Actress: Helen Hayes, *The Sin of Madelon Claudet*
Actor: Fredric March, *Dr. Jekyll and Mr. Hyde,* and Wallace Beery, *The Champ*

1933
Picture: *Cavalcade*, Fox
Director: Frank Lloyd, *Cavalcade*
Actress: Katharine Hepburn, *Morning Glory*
Actor: Charles Laughton, *The Private Life of Henry VIII*

1934
Picture: *It Happened One Night*, Columbia
Director: Frank Capra, *It Happened One Night*
Actress: Claudette Colbert, *It Happened One Night*
Actor: Clark Gable, *It Happened One Night*

1935

Picture: *Mutiny on the Bounty*, MGM
Director: John Ford, *The Informer*
Actress: Bette Davis, *Dangerous*
Actor: Victor McLaglen, *The Informer*

1936

Picture: *The Great Ziegfeld*, MGM
Director: Frank Capra, *Mr. Deeds Goes to Town*
Actress: Luise Rainer, *The Great Ziegfeld*
Actor: Paul Muni, *The Story of Louis Pasteur*
Supporting Actress: Gale Sondergaard, *Anthony Adverse*
Supporting Actor: Walter Brennan, *Come and Get It*

1937

Picture: *The Life of Emile Zola*, Warner Bros.
Director: Leo McCarey, *The Awful Truth*
Actress: Luise Rainer, *The Good Earth*
Actor: Spencer Tracy, *Captains Courageous*
Supporting Actress: Alice Brady, *In Old Chicago*
Supporting Actor: Joseph Schildkraut, *The Life of Emile Zola*

1938

Picture: *You Can't Take It with You*, Columbia
Director: Frank Capra, *You Can't Take It with You*
Actress: Bette Davis, *Jezebel*
Actor: Spencer Tracy, *Boys Town*
Supporting Actress: Fay Bainter, *Jezebel*
Supporting Actor: Walter Brennan, *Kentucky*

1939

Picture: *Gone with the Wind*, Selznick MGM
Director: Victor Fleming, *Gone with the Wind*
Actress: Vivien Leigh, *Gone with the Wind*
Actor: Robert Donat, *Goodbye, Mr. Chips*
Supporting Actress: Hattie McDaniel, *Gone with the Wind*
Supporting Actor: Thomas Mitchell, *Stagecoach*

1940

Picture: *Rebecca*, Selznick-United Artists
Director: John Ford, *The Grapes of Wrath*
Actress: Ginger Rogers, *Kitty Foyle*
Actor: James Stewart, *The Philadelphia Story*
Supporting Actress: Jane Darwell, *The Grapes of Wrath*
Supporting Actor: Walter Brennan, *The Westerner*

1941

Picture: *How Green Was My Valley*, 20th Century-Fox
Director: John Ford, *How Green Was My Valley*
Actress: Joan Fontaine, *Suspicion*
Actor: Gary Cooper, *Sergeant York*
Supporting Actress: Mary Astor, *The Great Lie*
Supporting Actor: Donald Crisp, *How Green Was My Valley*

1942

Picture: *Mrs. Miniver*, MGM
Director: William Wyler, *Mrs. Miniver*
Actress: Greer Garson, *Mrs. Miniver*
Actor: James Cagney, *Yankee Doodle Dandy*
Supporting Actress: Teresa Wright, *Mrs. Miniver*
Supporting Actor: Van Heflin, *Johnny Eager*

1943

Picture: *Casablanca*, Warner Bros.
Director: Michael Curtiz, *Casablanca*
Actress: Jennifer Jones, *The Song of Bernadette*
Actor: Paul Lukas, *Watch on the Rhine*
Supporting Actress: Katina Paxinou, *For Whom the Bell Tolls*
Supporting Actor: Charles Coburn, *The More the Merrier*

1944

Picture: *Going My Way*, Paramount
Director: Leo McCarey, *Going My Way*
Actress: Ingrid Bergman, *Gaslight*
Actor: Bing Crosby, *Going My Way*
Supporting Actress: Ethel Barrymore, *None But the Lonely Heart*
Supporting Actor: Barry Fitzgerald, *Going My Way*

1945

Picture: *The Lost Weekend*, Paramount
Director: Billy Wilder, *The Lost Weekend*
Actress: Joan Crawford, *Mildred Pierce*
Actor: Ray Milland, *The Lost Weekend*

Supporting Actress: Anne Revere, *National Velvet*
Supporting Actor: James Dunn, *A Tree Grows in Brooklyn*

1946

Picture: *The Best Years of Our Lives*, Goldwyn-RKO Radio
Director: William Wyler, *The Best Years of Our Lives*
Actress: Olivia de Havilland, *To Each His Own*
Actor: Fredric March, *The Best Years of Our Lives*
Supporting Actress: Anne Baxter, *The Razor's Edge*
Supporting Actor: Harold Russell, *The Best Years of Our Lives*

1947

Picture: *Gentleman's Agreement*, 20th Century-Fox
Director: Elia Kazan, *Gentleman's Agreement*
Actress: Loretta Young, *The Farmer's Daughter*
Actor: Ronald Colman, *A Double Life*
Supporting Actress: Celeste Holm, *Gentleman's Agreement*
Supporting Actor: Edmund Gwenn, *Miracle on 34th Street*

1948

Picture: *Hamlet*, Rank-Two Cities-UI
Director: John Huston, *Treasure of Sierra Madre*
Actress: Jane Wyman, *Johnny Belinda*
Actor: Laurence Olivier, *Hamlet*
Supporting Actress: Claire Trevor, *Key Largo*
Supporting Actor: Walter Huston, *Treasure of Sierra Madre*

1949

Picture: *All the King's Men*, Rossen-Columbia
Director: Joseph L. Mankiewicz, *A Letter to Three Wives*
Actress: Olivia de Havilland, *The Heiress*
Actor: Broderick Crawford, *All the King's Men*
Supporting Actress: Mercedes McCambridge, *All the King's Men*
Supporting Actor: Dean Jagger, *Twelve O'Clock High*

1950

Picture: *All About Eve*, 20th Century-Fox
Director: Joseph L. Mankiewicz, *All About Eve*
Actress: Judy Holliday, *Born Yesterday*
Actor: José Ferrer, *Cyrano de Bergerac*
Supporting Actress: Josephine Hull, *Harvey*
Supporting Actor: George Sanders, *All About Eve*

1951

Picture: *An American in Paris*, MGM
Director: George Stevens, *A Place in the Sun*
Actress: Vivien Leigh, *A Streetcar Named Desire*
Actor: Humphrey Bogart, *The African Queen*
Supporting Actress: Kim Hunter, *A Streetcar Named Desire*
Supporting Actor: Karl Malden, *A Streetcar Named Desire*

1952

Picture: *The Greatest Show on Earth*, DeMille-Paramount
Director: John Ford, *The Quiet Man*
Actress: Shirley Booth, *Come Back, Little Sheba*
Actor: Gary Cooper, *High Noon*
Supporting Actress: Gloria Grahame, *The Bad and the Beautiful*
Supporting Actor: Anthony Quinn, *Viva Zapata!*

1953

Picture: *From Here to Eternity*, Columbia
Director: Fred Zinnemann, *From Here to Eternity*
Actress: Audrey Hepburn, *Roman Holiday*
Actor: William Holden, *Stalag 17*
Supporting Actress: Donna Reed, *From Here to Eternity*
Supporting Actor: Frank Sinatra, *From Here to Eternity*

1954

Picture: *On the Waterfront*, Horizon-American Corp., Columbia
Director: Elia Kazan, *On the Waterfront*
Actress: Grace Kelly, *The Country Girl*
Actor: Marlon Brando, *On the Waterfront*
Supporting Actress: Eva Marie Saint, *On the Waterfront*
Supporting Actor: Edmond O'Brien, *The Barefoot Contessa*

1955

Picture: *Marty*, Hecht and Lancaster, United Artists
Director: Delbert Mann, *Marty*
Actress: Anna Magnani, *The Rose Tattoo*
Actor: Ernest Borgnine, *Marty*
Supporting Actress: Jo Van Fleet, *East of Eden*
Supporting Actor: Jack Lemmon, *Mister Roberts*

1956

Picture: *Around the World in 80 Days*, Michael Todd Co., Inc.-United Artists
Director: George Stevens, *Giant*
Actress: Ingrid Bergman, *Anastasia*
Actor: Yul Brynner, *The King and I*
Supporting Actress: Dorothy Malone, *Written on the Wind*
Supporting Actor: Anthony Quinn, *Lust for Life*

1957

Picture: *The Bridge on the River Kwai*, Horizon Picture, Columbia
Director: David Lean, *The Bridge on the River Kwai*
Actress: Joanne Woodward, *The Three Faces of Eve*
Actor: Alec Guinness, *The Bridge on the River Kwai*
Supporting Actress: Miyoshi Umeki, *Sayonara*
Supporting Actor: Red Buttons, *Sayonara*

1958

Picture: *Gigi*, Arthur Freed Productions, Inc., MGM
Director: Vincente Minnelli, *Gigi*
Actress: Susan Hayward, *I Want to Live!*
Actor: David Niven, *Separate Tables*
Supporting Actress: Wendy Hiller, *Separate Tables*
Supporting Actor: Burl Ives, *The Big Country*

1959

Picture: *BenHur*, MGM
Director: William Wyler, *BenHur*
Actress: Simone Signoret, *Room at the Top*
Actor: Charlton Heston, *BenHur*
Supporting Actress: Shelley Winters, *The Diary of Anne Frank*
Supporting Actor: Hugh Griffith, *BenHur*

1960

Picture: *The Apartment*, Mirisch Co., Inc., United Artists
Director: Billy Wilder, *The Apartment*
Actress: Elizabeth Taylor, *Butterfield 8*
Actor: Burt Lancaster, *Elmer Gantry*
Supporting Actress: Shirley Jones, *Elmer Gantry*
Supporting Actor: Peter Ustinov, *Spartacus*

1961

Picture: *West Side Story*, Mirisch Pictures, Inc., and B and P Enterprises, Inc., United Artists
Director: Robert Wise and Jerome Robbins, *West Side Story*
Actress: Sophia Loren, *Two Women*
Actor: Maximillian Schell, *Judgment at Nuremberg*
Supporting Actress: Rita Moreno, *West Side Story*
Supporting Actor: George Chakiris, *West Side Story*

1962

Picture: *Lawrence of Arabia*, Horizon Pictures, Ltd.-Columbia
Director: David Lean, *Lawrence of Arabia*
Actress: Anne Bancroft, *The Miracle Worker*
Actor: Gregory Peck, *To Kill a Mockingbird*
Supporting Actress: Patty Duke, *The Miracle Worker*
Supporting Actor: Ed Begley, *Sweet Bird of Youth*

1963

Picture: *Tom Jones*, A Woodfall Production, United Artists-Lopert Pictures
Director: Tony Richardson, *Tom Jones*
Actress: Patricia Neal, *Hud*
Actor: Sidney Poitier, *Lilies of the Field*
Supporting Actress: Margaret Rutherford, *The V.I.P.s*
Supporting Actor: Melvyn Douglas, *Hud*

1964

Picture: *My Fair Lady*, Warner Bros.
Director: George Cukor, *My Fair Lady*
Actress: Julie Andrews, *Mary Poppins*
Actor: Rex Harrison, *My Fair Lady*
Supporting Actress: Lila Kedrova, *Zorba the Greek*
Supporting Actor: Peter Ustinov, *Topkapi*

1965

Picture: *The Sound of Music*, Argyle Enterprises Production, 20th Century-Fox
Director: Robert Wise, *The Sound of Music*
Actress: Julie Christie, *Darling*
Actor: Lee Marvin, *Cat Ballou*
Supporting Actress: Shelley Winters, *A Patch of Blue*
Supporting Actor: Martin Balsam, *A Thousand Clowns*

1966

Picture: *A Man for All Seasons*, Highland Films, Ltd., Production, Columbia
Director: Fred Zinnemann, *A Man for All Seasons*
Actress: Elizabeth Taylor, *Who's Afraid of Virginia Woolf?*
Actor: Paul Scofield, *A Man for All Seasons*
Supporting Actress: Sandy Dennis, *Who's Afraid of Virginia Woolf?*
Supporting Actor: Walter Matthau, *The Fortune Cookie*

1967

Picture: *In the Heat of the Night*, Mirisch Corp. Productions, United Artists
Director: Mike Nichols, *The Graduate*
Actress: Katharine Hepburn, *Guess Who's Coming to Dinner*
Actor: Rod Steiger, *In the Heat of the Night*
Supporting Actress: Estelle Parsons, *Bonnie and Clyde*
Supporting Actor: George Kennedy, *Cool Hand Luke*

1968

Picture: *Oliver!*, Columbia Pictures
Director: Sir Carol Reed, *Oliver!*
Actress: Katharine Hepburn, *The Lion in Winter* and Barbra Streisand, *Funny Girl*
Actor: Cliff Robertson, *Charly*
Supporting Actress: Ruth Gordon, *Rosemary's Baby*
Supporting Actor: Jack Albertson, *The Subject Was Roses*

1969

Picture: *Midnight Cowboy*, Jerome Hellman-John Schlesinger Production, United Artists
Director: John Schlesinger, *Midnight Cowboy*
Actress: Maggie Smith, *The Prime of Miss Jean Brodie*
Actor: John Wayne, *True Grit*
Supporting Actress: Goldie Hawn, *Cactus Flower*
Supporting Actor: Gig Young, *They Shoot Horses Don't They?*

1970

Picture: *Patton*, Frank McCarthy-Franklin J. Schaffner Production, 20th Century-Fox
Director: Franklin J. Schaffner, *Patton*
Actress: Glenda Jackson, *Women in Love*
Actor: George C. Scott, *Patton*
Supporting Actress: Helen Hayes, *Airport*
Supporting Actor: John Mills, *Ryan's Daughter*

1971

Picture: *The French Connection*, D'Antoni Productions, 20th Century-Fox
Director: William Friedkin, *The French Connection*
Actress: Jane Fonda, *Klute*
Actor: Gene Hackman, *The French Connection*
Supporting Actress: Cloris Leachman, *The Last Picture Show*
Supporting Actor: Ben Johnson, *The Last Picture Show*

1972

Picture: *The Godfather*, Albert S. Ruddy Production, Paramount
Director: Bob Fosse, *Cabaret*
Actress: Liza Minnelli, *Cabaret*
Actor: Marlon Brando, *The Godfather*
Supporting Actress: Eileen Heckart, *Butterflies Are Free*
Supporting Actor: Joel Gray, *Cabaret*

1973

Picture: *The Sting*, Universal-Bill-Phillips-George Roy Hill Production, Universal
Director: George Roy Hill, *The Sting*
Actress: Glenda Jackson, *A Touch of Class*
Actor: Jack Lemmon, *Save the Tiger*
Supporting Actress: Tatum O'Neal, *Paper Moon*
Supporting Actor: John Houseman, *The Paper Chase*

1974

Picture: *The Godfather, Part II*, Coppola Co. Production, Paramount
Director: Francis Ford Coppola, *The Godfather, Part II*
Actress: Ellen Burstyn, *Alice Doesn't Live Here Anymore*
Actor: Art Carney, *Harry and Tonto*
Supporting Actress: Ingrid Bergman, *Murder on the Orient Express*
Supporting Actor: Robert De Niro, *The Godfather, Part II*

1975

Picture: *One Flew Over the Cuckoo's Nest,* Fantasy Films Production, United Artists
Director: Milos Forman, *One Flew Over the Cuckoo's Nest*
Actress: Louise Fletcher, *One Flew Over the Cuckoo's Nest*
Actor: Jack Nicholson, *One Flew Over the Cuckoo's Nest*
Supporting Actress: Lee Grant, *Shampoo*
Supporting Actor: George Burns, *The Sunshine Boys*

1976

Picture: *Rocky,* Robert Chartoff-Irwin Winkler Production, United Artists
Director: John G. Avildsen, *Rocky*
Actress: Faye Dunaway, *Network*
Actor: Peter Finch, *Network*
Supporting Actress: Beatrice Straight, *Network*
Supporting Actor: Jason Robards, *All the President's Men*

1977

Picture: *Annie Hall,* Jack Rollins-Charles H. Joffe Production, United Artists
Director: Woody Allen, *Annie Hall*
Actress: Diane Keaton, *Annie Hall*
Actor: Richard Dreyfuss, *The Goodbye Girl*
Supporting Actress: Vanessa Redgrave, *Julia*
Supporting Actor: Jason Robards, *Julia*

1978

Picture: *The Deer Hunter,* Michael Cimino Film Production, Universal
Director: Michael Cimino, *The Deer Hunter*
Actress: Jane Fonda, *Coming Home*
Actor: Jon Voight, *Coming Home*
Supporting Actress: Maggie Smith, *California Suite*
Supporting Actor: Christopher Walken, *The Deer Hunter*

1979

Picture: *Kramer vs. Kramer,* Stanley Jaffe Production, Columbia Pictures
Director: Robert Benton, *Kramer vs. Kramer*
Actress: Sally Field, *Norma Rae*
Actor: Dustin Hoffman, *Kramer vs. Kramer*
Supporting Actress: Meryl Streep, *Kramer vs. Kramer*
Supporting Actor: Melvyn Douglas, *Being There*

1980

Picture: *Ordinary People,* Wildwood Enterprises Production, Paramount
Director: Robert Redford, *Ordinary People*
Actress: Sissy Spacek, *Coal Miner's Daughter*
Actor: Robert De Niro, *Raging Bull*
Supporting Actress: Mary Steenburgen, *Melvin and Howard*
Supporting Actor: Timothy Hutton, *Ordinary People*

1981

Picture: *Chariots of Fire,* Enigma Productions, Ladd Company/ Warner Bros.
Director: Warren Beatty, *Reds*
Actress: Katharine Hepburn, *On Golden Pond*
Actor: Henry Fonda, *On Golden Pond*
Supporting Actress: Maureen Stapleton, *Reds*
Supporting Actor: John Gielgud, *Arthur*

1982

Picture: *Gandhi,* Indo-British Films Production/Columbia
Director: Richard Attenborough, *Gandhi*
Actress: Meryl Streep, *Sophie's Choice*
Actor: Ben Kingsley, *Gandhi*
Supporting Actress: Jessica Lange, *Tootsie*
Supporting Actor: Louis Gossett, Jr., *An Officer and a Gentleman*

1983

Picture: *Terms of Endearment,* Paramount
Director: James L. Brooks, *Terms of Endearment*
Actress: Shirley MacLaine, *Terms of Endearment*
Actor: Robert Duvall, *Tender Mercies*
Supporting Actress: Linda Hunt, *The Year of Living Dangerously*
Supporting Actor: Jack Nicholson, *Terms of Endearment*

1984

Picture: *Amadeus,* Orion Pictures
Director: Milos Forman, *Amadeus*
Actress: Sally Field, *Places in the Heart*

Actor: F. Murray Abraham, *Amadeus*
Supporting Actress: Dame Peggy Ashcroft, *A Passage to India*
Supporting Actor: Haing S. Ngor, *The Killing Fields*

1985

Picture: *Out of Africa,* Universal
Director: Sydney Pollack, *Out of Africa*
Actress: Geraldine Page, *The Trip to Bountiful*
Actor: William Hurt, *Kiss of the Spider Woman*
Supporting Actress: Anjelica Huston, *Prizzi's Honor*
Supporting Actor: Don Ameche, *Cocoon*

1986

Picture: *Platoon,* Orion Pictures
Director: Oliver Stone, *Platoon*
Actress: Marlee Matlin, *Children of a Lesser God*
Actor: Paul Newman, *The Color of Money*
Supporting Actress: Dianne Wiest, *Hannah and Her Sisters*
Supporting Actor: Michael Caine, *Hannah and Her Sisters*

1987

Picture: *The Last Emperor,* Columbia Pictures
Director: Bernardo Bertolucci, *The Last Emperor*
Actress: Cher, *Moonstruck*
Actor: Michael Douglas, *Wall Street*
Supporting Actress: Olympia Dukakis, *Moonstruck*
Supporting Actor: Sean Connery, *The Untouchables*

1988

Picture: *Rain Man,* United Artists
Director: Barry Levinson, *Rain Man*
Actress: Jodie Foster, *The Accused*
Actor: Dustin Hoffman, *Rain Man*
Supporting Actress: Geena Davis, *The Accidental Tourist*
Supporting Actor: Kevin Kline: *A Fish Called Wanda*

1989

Picture: *Driving Miss Daisy,* Warner Brothers
Director: Oliver Stone, *Born on the Fourth of July*
Actress: Jessica Tandy, *Driving Miss Daisy*
Actor: Daniel Day-Lewis, *My Left Foot*
Supporting Actress: Brenda Fricker, *My Left Foot*
Supporting Actor: Denzel Washington, *Glory*

1990

Picture: *Dances With Wolves,* Orion
Director: Kevin Costner, *Dances With Wolves*
Actress: Kathy Bates, *Misery*
Actor: Jeremy Irons, *Reversal of Fortune*
Supporting Actress: Whoopi Goldberg, *Ghost*
Supporting Actor: Joe Pesci, *Goodfellas*

1991

Picture: *The Silence of the Lambs,* Orion
Director: Jonathan Demme, *The Silence of the Lambs*
Actress: Jodie Foster, *The Silence of the Lambs*
Actor: Anthony Hopkins, *The Silence of the Lambs*
Supporting Actress: Mercedes Ruehl, *The Fisher King*
Supporting Actor: Jack Palance, *City Slickers*

1992

Picture: *Unforgiven,* Warner Brothers
Director: Clint Eastwood, *Unforgiven*
Actress: Emma Thompson, *Howards End*
Actor: Al Pacino, *Scent of a Woman*
Supporting Actress: Marisa Tomei, *My Cousin Vinny*
Supporting Actor: Gene Hackman, *Unforgiven*

1993

Picture: *Schindler's List,* Universal
Director: Steven Spielberg, *Schindler's List*
Actress: Holly Hunter, *The Piano*
Actor: Tom Hanks, *Philadelphia*
Supporting Actress: Anna Paquin, *The Piano*
Supporting Actor: Tommy Lee Jones, *The Fugitive*

1994

Picture: *Forrest Gump,* Paramount
Director: Robert Zemeckis, *Forrest Gump*
Actress: Jessica Lange, *Blue Sky*
Actor: Tom Hanks, *Forrest Gump*
Supporting Actress: Dianne Wiest, *Bullets Over Broadway*
Supporting Actor: Martin Landau, *Ed Wood*

1995	1996
Picture: *Braveheart,* Paramount	**Picture:** *The English Patient,* Miramax
Director: Mel Gibson, *Braveheart*	**Director:** Anthony Minghella, *The English Patient*
Actress: Susan Sarandon, *Dead Man Walking*	**Actress:** Frances McDormand, *Fargo*
Actor: Nicolas Cage, *Leaving Las Vegas*	**Actor:** Geoffrey Rush, *Shine*
Supporting Actress: Mira Sorvino, *Mighty Aphrodite*	**Supporting Actress:** Juliette Binoche, *The English Patient*
Supporting Actor: Kevin Spacey, *The Usual Suspects*	**Supporting Actor:** Cuba Gooding, Jr., *Jerry Maguire*

Other Academy Awards for 1996

Art Direction: Stuart Craig, *The English Patient*
Cinematography: John Seale, *The English Patient*
Costume Design: Ann Roth, *The English Patient*
Directing: Anthony Minghella, *The English Patient*
Documentary (feature): Leon Gast and David Sonenberg, *When We Were Kings;* **(short subject):** Jessica Yu, *Breathing Lessons: The Life and Work of Mark O'Brien*
Editing: Walter Murch, *The English Patient*
Foreign-language film: *Kolya,,* Czech Republic
Makeup: Rick Baker and David Leroy Anderson, *The Nutty Professor*
Music (original musical or comedy score): Rachel Portman, *Emma;* **(original dramatic score):** Gabriel Yared, *The English Patient;* **(original song):** Andrew Lloyd Weber (music) and Tim Rice (lyrics), "You Must Love Me", *Evita*

Screenplay, Original: Ethan Coen and Joel Coen, *Fargo*
Screenplay, Adapted: Billy Bob Thornton, *Sling Blade*
Short subject (live action): David Frankel and Barry Jossen, *Dear Diary;* **(animated):** Tyron Montgomery and Thomas Stellmach, *Quest*
Sound: Walter Murch, Mark Berger, David Parker, and Chris Newman, *The English Patient*
Sound effects editing: Bruce Stambler, *The Ghost and the Darkness*
Visual effects: Volker Engel, Douglas Smith, Clay Pinney, and Joseph Viskocil, *Independence Day*
Gordon E. Sawyer Award: Donald C. Rogers, for his contribution to motion picture sound technology

Pulitzer Prize Awards

(For years not listed, no award was made.)

Source: Columbia University.

PULITZER PRIZES IN JOURNALISM

Meritorious Public Service

1918 *New York Times;* also special award to Minna Lewinson and Henry Beetle Hough
1919 *Milwaukee Journal*
1921 *Boston Post*
1922 *New York World*
1923 *Memphis Commercial Appeal*
1924 *New York World*
1926 *Columbus (Ga.) Enquirer Sun*
1927 *Canton (Ohio) Daily News*
1928 *Indianapolis Times*
1929 *New York Evening World*
1931 *Atlanta Constitution*
1932 *Indianapolis News*
1933 *New York World-Telegram*
1934 *Medford (Ore.) Mail Tribune*
1935 *Sacramento Bee*
1936 *Cedar Rapids (Iowa) Gazette*
1937 *St. Louis Post-Dispatch*
1938 *Bismarck (N.D.) Tribune*
1939 *Miami Daily News*
1940 *Waterbury (Conn.) Republican* and *American*
1941 *St. Louis Post-Dispatch*
1942 *Los Angeles Times*
1943 *Omaha World-Herald*
1944 *New York Times*
1945 *Detroit Free Press*
1946 *Scranton (Pa.) Times*
1947 *Baltimore Sun*
1948 *St. Louis Post-Dispatch*
1949 *(Lincoln) Nebraska State Journal*
1950 *Chicago Daily News;* and *St. Louis Post-Dispatch*
1951 *Miami Herald;* and *Brooklyn Eagle*
1952 *St. Louis Post-Dispatch*
1953 *Whiteville (N.C.) News Reporter;* and *Tabor City (N.C.) Tribune*
1954 *Newsday (Garden City, L.I.)*
1955 *Columbus (Ga.) Ledger* and *Sunday Ledger-Enquirer*
1956 *Watsonville (Calif.) Register-Pajaronian*
1957 *Chicago Daily News*
1958 *(Little Rock) Arkansas Gazette*
1959 *Utica (N.Y.) Observer Dispatch* and *Utica Daily Press*
1960 *Los Angeles Times*
1961 *Amarillo (Tex.) Globe-Times*
1962 *Panama City (Fla.) News-Herald*
1963 *Chicago Daily News*
1964 *St. Petersburg (Fla.) Times*
1965 *Hutchinson (Kan.) News*
1966 *Boston Globe*
1967 *Louisville Courier-Journal* and *Milwaukee Journal*
1968 *Riverside (Calif.) Press-Enterprise*
1969 *Los Angeles Times*
1970 *Newsday (Garden City, L.I.)*
1971 *Winston-Salem (N.C.) Journal and Sentinel*
1972 *New York Times*
1973 *Washington Post*
1974 *Newsday (Garden City, L.I.)*
1975 *Boston Globe*
1976 *Anchorage (Alaska) Daily News*
1977 *Lufkin (Tex.) News*
1978 *Philadelphia Inquirer*
1979 *Point Reyes (Calif.) Light*
1980 *Gannett News Service*
1981 *Charlotte (N.C.) Observer*
1982 *Detroit News*
1983 *Jackson (Miss.) Clarion-Ledger*
1984 *Los Angeles Times*
1985 *The Fort Worth Star-Telegram*
1986 *Denver Post*
1987 *Pittsburgh Press,* reporting by Andrew Schneider and Matthew Brelis
1988 *Charlotte (N.C.) Observer*
1989 *Anchorage Daily News*
1990 *Philadelphia Inquirer* and *Washington (N.C.) Daily News*
1991 *Des Moines Register,* reporting by Jane Schorer
1992 *Sacramento Bee* for "The Sierra in Peril" series by Tom Knudson
1993 *Miami Herald*
1994 *The Akron (Ohio) Beacon Journal*

1995 *The Virgin Islands Daily News*
1996 *The News and Observer* (Raleigh, N.C.)
1997 *The Times-Picayune* (New Orleans, La.)

Editorial

1917 *New York Tribune*
1918 *Louisville Courier-Journal*
1920 Harvey E. Newbranch *(Omaha Evening World-Herald)*
1922 Frank M. O'Brien *(New York Herald)*
1923 William Allen White *(Emporia* [Kan.] *Gazette)*
1924 *Boston Herald* (Frank Buxton); special prize: Frank I. Cobb *(New York World)*
1925 *Charleston* (S.C.) *News and Courier*
1926 *New York Times* (Edward M. Kingsbury)
1927 *Boston Herald* (F. Lauriston Bullard)
1928 Grover Cleveland Hall *(Montgomery* [Ala.] *Advertiser)*
1929 Louis Isaac Jaffe *(Norfolk Virginian-Pilot)*
1931 Charles S. Ryckman *(Fremont* [Neb.] *Tribune)*
1933 *Kansas City* (Mo.) *Star*
1934 E. P. Chase *(Atlantic* [Iowa] *News Telegraph)*
1936 Felix Morley *(Washington Post)*; George B. Parker (Scripps-Howard Newspapers)
1937 John W. Owens *(Baltimore Sun)*
1938 W. W. Waymack *(Des Moines Register and Tribune)*
1939 Ronald G. Callvert *(Portland Oregonian)*
1940 Bart Howard *(St. Louis Post-Dispatch)*
1941 Reuben Maury *(New York Daily News)*
1942 Geoffrey Parsons *(New York Herald Tribune)*
1943 Forrest W. Seymour *(Des Moines Register and Tribune)*
1944 *Kansas City* (Mo.) *Star* (Henry J. Haskell)
1945 George W. Potter *(Providence* [R.I.] *Journal-Bulletin)*
1946 Hodding Carter ([Greenville, Miss.] *Delta Democrat-Times)*
1947 William H. Grimes *(Wall Street Journal)*
1948 Virginius Dabney *(Richmond Times-Dispatch)*
1949 John H. Crider *(Boston Herald)*; Herbert Elliston *(Washington Post)*
1950 Carl M. Saunders *(Jackson* [Mich.] *Citizen Patriot)*
1951 William H. Fitzpatrick *(New Orleans States)*
1952 Louis LaCoss *(St. Louis Globe-Democrat)*
1953 Vermont C. Royster *(Wall Street Journal)*
1954 *Boston Herald* (Don Murray)
1955 *Detroit Free Press* (Royce Howes)
1956 Lauren K. Soth *(Des Moines Register and Tribune)*
1957 Buford Boone *(Tuscaloosa* [Ala.] *News)*
1958 Harry S. Ashmore *(Arkansas Gazette)*
1959 Ralph McGill *(Atlanta Constitution)*
1960 Lenoir Chambers *(Virginian-Pilot)*
1961 William J. Dorvillier *(San Juan* [P.R.] *Star)*
1962 Thomas M. Storke *(Santa Barbara* [Calif.] *News-Press)*
1963 Ira B. Harkey, Jr. *(Pascagoula* [Miss.] *Chronicle)*
1964 Hazel Brannon Smith *(Lexington* [Miss.] *Advertiser)*
1965 John R. Harrison *(Gainesville* [Fla.] *Daily Sun)*
1966 Robert Lasch *(St. Louis Post-Dispatch)*
1967 Eugene Patterson *(Atlanta Constitution)*
1968 John S. Knight (Knight Newspapers)
1969 Paul Greenberg *(Pine Bluff* [Ark.] *Commercial)*
1970 Phillip L. Geyelin *(Washington Post)*
1971 Horance G. Davis, Jr. *(Gainesville* [Fla.] *Sun)*
1972 John Strohmeyer *(Bethlehem* [Pa.] *Globe Times)*
1973 Roger Bourne Linscott *(Berkshire Eagle* [Pittsfield, Mass.])
1974 F. Gilman Spencer *(Trenton* [N.J.] *Trentonian)*

1975 John Daniell Maurice *(Charleston* [W. Va.] *Daily Mail)*
1976 Philip P. Kerby *(Los Angeles Times)*
1977 Warren L. Lerude, Foster Church and Norman F. Cardoza *(Reno* [Nev.] *Gazette* and *Nevada State Journal)*
1978 Meg Greenfield *(Washington Post)*
1979 Edwin M. Yoder, Jr. *(Washington Star)*
1980 Robert L. Bartley *(Wall Street Journal)*
1981 Not awarded
1982 Jack Rosenthal *(New York Times)*
1983 *Miami Herald*
1984 Albert Scardino *(Georgia Gazette)*
1985 Richard Aregood *(Philadelphia Daily News)*
1986 Jack Fuller *(Chicago Tribune)*
1987 Jonathan Freedman *(San Diego Tribune)*
1988 Jane E. Healy *(Orlando Sentinel)*
1989 Lois Wille *(Chicago Tribune)*
1990 Thomas J. Hylton *(Pottstown* [Pa.] *Mercury)*
1991 Ron Casey, Harold Jackson, and Joey Kennedy *(Birmingham* [Ala.] *News)*
1992 Maria Henson *(Lexington* [Ky.] *Herald-Leader)*
1994 R. Bruce Dold *(Chicago Tribune)*
1995 Jeffrey Good *(St. Petersburg* [Fla.] *Times)*
1996 Robert B. Semple, Jr. *(New York Times)*
1997 Michael Gartner*(Daily Tribune [Ames,Iowa])*

Correspondence

1929 Paul Scott Mowrer *(Chicago Daily News)*
1930 Leland Stowe *(New York Herald Tribune)*
1931 H. R. Knickerbocker *(Philadelphia Public Ledger* and *New York Evening Post)*
1932 Walter Duranty *(New York Times)*; Charles G. Ross *(St. Louis Post-Dispatch)*
1933 Edgar Ansel Mowrer *(Chicago Daily News)*
1934 Frederick T. Birchall *(New York Times)*
1935 Arthur Krock *(New York Times)*
1936 Wilfred C. Barber *(Chicago Tribune)*
1937 Anne O'Hare McCormick *(New York Times)*
1938 Arthur Krock *(New York Times)*
1939 Louis P. Lochner (Associated Press)
1940 Otto D. Tolischus *(New York Times)*
1941 Group award[1]
1942 Carlos P. Romulo *(Philippines Herald)*
1943 Hanson W. Baldwin *(New York Times)*
1944 Ernie Pyle (Scripps-Howard Newspaper Alliance)
1945 Harold V. (Hal) Boyle (Associated Press)
1946 Arnaldo Cortesi *(New York Times)*
1947 Brooks Atkinson *(New York Times)*
1948 Discontinued

1. For the public services and the individual achievements of American news reporters in the war zones.

Editorial Cartooning

1922 Rollin Kirby *(New York World)*
1924 Jay Norwood Darling *(New York Tribune)*
1925 Rollin Kirby *(New York World)*
1926 D. R. Fitzpatrick *(St. Louis Post-Dispatch)*
1927 Nelson Harding *(Brooklyn Eagle)*
1928 Nelson Harding *(Brooklyn Eagle)*
1929 Rollin Kirby *(New York World)*
1930 Charles R. Macauley *(Brooklyn Eagle)*
1931 Edmund Duffy *(Baltimore Sun)*
1932 John T. McCutcheon *(Chicago Tribune)*
1933 H. M. Talburt *(Washington Daily News)*
1934 Edmund Duffy *(Baltimore Sun)*
1935 Ross A. Lewis *(Milwaukee Journal)*
1937 C. D. Batchelor *(New York Daily News)*
1938 Vaughn Shoemaker *(Chicago Daily News)*
1939 Charles G. Werner *(Daily Oklahoman* [Oklahoma City])
1940 Edmund Duffy *(Baltimore Sun)*
1941 Jacob Burck *(Chicago Times)*
1942 Herbert L. Block (NEA Service)

1943 Jay Norwood Darling *(New York Herald Tribune)*
1944 Clifford K. Berryman *(Washington Evening Star)*
1945 Bill Mauldin (United Features Syndicate)
1946 Bruce Alexander Russell *(Los Angeles Times)*
1947 Vaughn Shoemaker *(Chicago Daily News)*
1948 Reuben L. Goldberg *(New York Sun)*
1949 Lute Pease *(Newark Evening News)*
1950 James T. Berryman *(Washington Evening Star)*
1951 Reg (Reginald W.) Manning *(Arizona Republic* [Phoenix])
1952 Fred L. Packer *(New York Mirror)*
1953 Edward D. Kuekes *(Cleveland Plain Dealer)*
1954 Herbert L. Block *(Washington Post* and *Times-Herald)*
1955 Daniel R. Fitzpatrick *(St. Louis Post-Dispatch)*
1956 Robert York *(Louisville Times)*
1957 Tom Little *(Nashville Tennessean)*
1958 Bruce M. Shanks *(Buffalo Evening News)*
1959 Bill Mauldin *(St. Louis Post-Dispatch)*
1961 Carey Orr *(Chicago Tribune)*
1962 Edmund S. Valtman *(Hartford Times)*
1963 Frank Miller *(Des Moines Register)*
1964 Paul Conrad (formerly of *Denver Post*, later on *Los Angeles Times)*
1966 Don Wright *(Miami News)*
1967 Patrick B. Oliphant *(Denver Post)*
1968 Eugene Gray Payne *(Charlotte* [N.C.] *Observer)*
1969 John Fischetti *(Chicago Daily News)*
1970 Thomas F. Darcy *(Newsday* [Garden City, L.I.])
1971 Paul Conrad *(Los Angeles Times)*
1972 Jeffrey K. MacNelly *(Richmond* [Va.] *News Leader)*
1974 Paul Szep *(Boston Globe)*
1975 Garry Trudeau (Universal Press Syndicate)
1976 Tony Auth *(Philadelphia Inquirer)*
1977 Paul Szep *(Boston Globe)*
1978 Jeffrey K. MacNelly *(Richmond* [Va.] *News Leader)*
1979 Herbert L. Block *(Washington Post)*
1980 Don Wright *(Miami News)*
1981 Mike Peters *(Dayton* [Ohio] *Daily News)*
1982 Ben Sargent *(Austin* [Tex.] *American-Statesman)*
1983 Richard Locher *(Chicago Tribune)*
1984 Paul Conrad *(Los Angeles Times)*
1985 Jeff MacNelly *(Chicago Tribune)*
1986 Jules Feiffer *(Village Voice)*
1987 Berke Breathed *(Washington Post* Writers Group)
1988 Doug Marlette *(Atlanta Constitution* and *Charlotte* [N.C.] *Observer)*
1989 Jack Higgins *(Chicago Sun-Times)*
1990 Tom Toles *(Buffalo News)*
1991 Jim Borgman *(Cincinnati Inquirer)*
1992 Signe Wilkinson, *(Philadelphia Daily News)*
1993 Stephen R. Benson, *(Arizona Republic)*
1994 Michael P. Ramirez *(The Commercial Appeal,* Memphis)
1995 Mike Luckovich *(The Atlanta Constitution)*
1996 Jim Morin *(The Miami Herald)*
1997 Walt Handelsman*(The Times-Picayune)*

News Photography

1942 Milton Brooks *(Detroit News)*
1943 Frank Noel (Associated Press)
1944 Frank Filan (Associated Press); Earle L. Bunker *(Omaha World-Herald)*
1945 Joe Rosenthal (Associated Press)
1947 Arnold Hardy
1948 Frank Cushing *(Boston Traveler)*
1949 Nat Fein *(New York Herald Tribune)*
1950 Bill Crouch *(Oakland Tribune)*
1951 Max Desfor (Associated Press)
1952 John Robinson and Don Ultang *(Des Moines Register & Tribune)*
1953 William M. Gallagher *(Flint* [Mich.] *Journal)*
1954 Mrs. Walter M. Schau
1955 John L. Gaunt, Jr. *(Los Angeles Times)*
1956 *New York Daily News*
1957 Harry A. Trask *(Boston Traveler)*
1958 William C. Beall *(Washington Daily News)*
1959 William Seaman *(Minneapolis Star)*
1960 Andrew Lopez (United Press International)
1961 Yasushi Nagao (Mainichi Newspapers, Tokyo)
1962 Paul Vathis (Harrisburg [Pa.] bureau of Associated Press)
1963 Hector Rondon *(La Republica,* Caracas, Venezuela)
1964 Robert H. Jackson *(Dallas Times Herald)*
1965 Horst Faas (Associated Press)
1966 Kyoichi Sawada (United Press International)
1967 Jack R. Thornell (Associated Press)
1968 News: Rocco Morabito *(Jacksonville* [Fla.] *Journal);* features: Toshio Sakai (United Press International)
1969 Spot news: Edward T. Adams (Associated Press); features: Moneta Sleet, Jr.
1970 Spot news: Steve Starr (Associated Press); features: Dallas Kinney *(Palm Beach Post)*
1971 Spot news: John Paul Filo *(Valley Daily News* and *Daily Dispatch* [Tarentum and New Kensington, Pa.]); features: Jack Dykinga *(Chicago Sun-Times)* .
1972 Spot news: Horst Faas and Michel Laurent (Associated Press); features: Dave Kennerly (United Press International)
1973 Spot news: Huynh Cong Ut *(Associated Press);* features: Brian Lanker *(Topeka Capital-Journal)*
1974 Spot news: Anthony K. Roberts (Associated Press); features: Slava Veder (Associated Press)
1975 Spot news: Gerald H. Gay *(Seattle Times);* features: Matthew Lewis *(Washington Post)*
1976 Spot news: Stanley J. Forman *(Boston Herald-American);* features: photographic staff of *Louisville Courier-Journal* and *Times*
1977 Spot news: Neal Ulevich (Associated Press) and Stanley J. Forman *(Boston Herald-American);* features: Robin Hood *(Chattanooga News-Free Press)*
1978 Spot news: John Blair, freelance, Evansville, Ind.; features: J. Ross Baughman (Associated Press)
1979 Spot news: Thomas J. Kelly, 3rd *(Pottstown* [Pa.] *Mercury);* features: photographic staff of *Boston Herald-American*
1980 Features: Erwin H. Hagler *(Dallas Times Herald)*
1981 Spot news: Larry C. Price *(Fort Worth Star-Telegram);* features: Taro M. Yamasaki *(Detroit Free Press)*
1982 Spot news: Ron Edmonds (Associated Press); features: John H. White *(Chicago Sun-Times)*
1983 Spot news: Bill Foley (Associated Press); features: James B. Dickman *(Dallas Times Herald)*
1984 Spot news: Stan Grossfeld *(Boston Globe);* features: Anthony Suau *(Denver Post)*
1985 Spot news: photographic staff of *Register,* Santa Ana, Calif.; features: Stan Grossfeld *(Boston Globe)*
1986 Spot news: Michel duCille and Carol Guzy *(Miami Herald);* features: Tom Gralish *(Philadelphia Inquirer)*
1987 Spot news: Kim Komenich *(San Francisco Examiner);* features: David Peterson *(Des Moines Register)*
1988 Spot news: Scott Shaw *(Odessa* [Texas] *American);* features: Michel duCille *(Miami Herald)*

1989 Spot news: Ron Olshwanger *(St. Louis Post-Dispatch);* features: Manny Crisostomo *(Detroit Free Press)*
1990 Spot news: *Oakland Tribune;* features: David C. Turnley *(Detroit Free Press)*
1991 Spot news: Greg Marinovich (Associated Press); features: William Snyder *(Dallas Morning News)*
1992 Spot news: Associated Press staff; features: John Kaplan *(Herald* [Monterey, Calif.] and *Pittsburgh Post-Gazette)*
1993 Spot news: William Snyder and Ken Geiger *(Dallas Morning News);* features: Associated Press
1994 Spot news: Paul Watson *(Toronto Star);* features: Kevin Carter, freelancer for *New York Times*
1995 Spot news: Carol Guzy *(Washington Post);* features: Associated Press Staff
1996 Spot news: Charles Porter IV, freelance photographer for Associated Press; features: Stephanie Walsh, freelance photographer for Newhouse News Service
1997 Spot news: Annie Wells (*The Press Democrat* [Santa Rosa, Calif.]); features: Alexander Zemlianichenko (Associated Press)

National Telegraphic Reporting
1942 Louis Stark *(New York Times)*
1944 Dewey L. Fleming *(Baltimore Sun)*
1945 James Reston *(New York Times)*
1946 Edward A. Harris *(St. Louis Post-Dispatch)*
1947 Edward T. Folliard *(Washington Post)*

National Reporting
1948 Bert Andrews *(New York Herald Tribune);* Nat S. Finney *(Minneapolis Tribune)*
1949 C. P. Trussell *(New York Times)*
1950 Edwin O. Guthman *(Seattle Times)*
1952 Anthony Leviero *(New York Times)*
1953 Don Whitehead (Associated Press)
1954 Richard Wilson (Cowles Newspapers)
1955 Anthony Lewis *(Washington Daily News)*
1956 Charles L. Bartlett *(Chattanooga Times)*
1957 James Reston *(New York Times)*
1958 Relman Morin (Associated Press) and Clark Mollenhoff *(Des Moines Register & Tribune)*
1959 Howard Van Smith *(Miami News)*
1960 Vance Trimble (Scripps-Howard Newspaper Alliance)
1961 Edward R. Cony *(Wall Street Journal)*
1962 Nathan G. Caldwell and Gene S. Graham *(Nashville Tennessean)*
1963 Anthony Lewis *(New York Times)*
1964 Merriman Smith (United Press International)
1965 Louis M. Kohlmeier *(Wall Street Journal)*
1966 Haynes Johnson *(Washington Evening Star)*
1967 Stanley Penn and Monroe Karmin *(Wall Street Journal)*
1968 Howard James *(Christian Science Monitor);* Nathan K. (Nick) Kotz *(Des Moines Register* and *Minneapolis Tribune)*
1969 Robert Cahn *(Christian Science Monitor)*
1970 William J. Eaton *(Chicago Daily News)*
1971 Lucinda Franks and Thomas Powers (United Press International)
1972 Jack Anderson *(United Feature Syndicate)*
1973 Robert Boyd and Clark Hoyt *(Knight Newspapers)*
1974 Jack White *(Providence* [R.I.] *Journal-Bulletin);* and James R. Polk *(Washington Star-News)*
1975 Donald L. Barlett and James B. Steele *(Philadelphia Inquirer)*
1976 James Risser *(Des Moines Register)*

1977 Walter Mears (Associated Press)
1978 Gaylord D. Shaw *(Los Angeles Times)*
1979 James Risser *(Des Moines Register)*
1980 Bette Swenson Orsini and Charles Stafford *(St. Petersburg Times)*
1981 John M. Crewdson *(New York Times)*
1982 Rick Atkinson *(Kansas City* [Mo.] *Times)*
1983 *Boston Globe*
1984 John N. Wilford *(New York Times)*
1985 Thomas J. Knudson *(Des Moines Register)*
1986 Craig Flournoy and George Rodrigue *(Dallas Morning News)* and Arthur Howe *(Philadelphia Inquirer)*
1987 *Miami Herald,* staff; *New York Times,* staff
1988 Tim Weiner *(Philadelphia Inquirer)*
1989 Donald L. Barlett and James B. Steele *(Philadelphia Inquirer)*
1990 Ross Anderson, Bill Dietrich, Mary Ann Gwinn, and Eric Nalder *(Seattle Times)*
1991 Marjie Lundstrom and Rochelle Sharpe (Gannett News Service)
1992 Jeff Taylor and Mike McGraw *(Kansas City Star)*
1993 David Marannis *(Washington Post)*
1994 Eileen Welsome *(Albuquerque* (N.M.) *Tribune)*
1995 Tony Horwitz *(Wall Street Journal)*
1996 Alix M. Freedman *(Wall Street Journal)*
1997 Staff of the *Wall Street Journal*

International Telegraphic Reporting
1942 Laurence Edmund Allen (Associated Press)
1943 Ira Wolfert (North American Newspaper Alliance, Inc.)
1944 Daniel De Luce (Associated Press)
1945 Mark S. Watson *(Baltimore Sun)*
1946 Homer W. Bigart *(New York Herald Tribune)*
1947 Eddy Gilmore (Associated Press)

International Reporting
1948 Paul W. Ward *(Baltimore Sun)*
1949 Price Day *(Baltimore Sun)*
1950 Edmund Stevens *(Christian Science Monitor)*
1951 Keyes Beech and Fred Sparks *(Chicago Daily News);* Homer Bigart and Marguerite Higgins *(New York Herald Tribune);* Relman Morin and Don Whitehead (Associated Press)
1952 John M. Hightower (Associated Press)
1953 Austin C. Wehrwein *(Milwaukee Journal)*
1954 Jim G. Lucas (Scripps-Howard Newspapers)
1955 Harrison E. Salisbury *(New York Times)*
1956 William Randolph Hearst, Jr. and Frank Conniff (Hearst Newspapers) and Kingsbury Smith (INS)
1957 Russell Jones (United Press)
1958 *New York Times*
1959 Joseph Martin and Philip Santora *(New York Daily News)*
1960 A. M. Rosenthal *(New York Times)*
1961 Lynn Heinzerling (Associated Press)
1962 Walter Lippmann (New York Herald Tribune Syndicate)
1963 Hal Hendrix *(Miami News)*
1964 Malcolm W. Browne (Associated Press) and David Halberstam *(New York Times)*
1965 J. A. Livingston *(Philadelphia Bulletin)*
1966 Peter Arnett (Associated Press)
1967 R. John Hughes *(Christian Science Monitor)*
1968 Alfred Friendly *(Washington Post)*
1969 William Tuohy *(Los Angeles Times)*
1970 Seymour M. Hersh (Dispatch News Service)
1971 Jimmie Lee Hoagland *(Washington Post)*
1972 Peter R. Kann *(Wall Street Journal)*
1973 Max Frankel *(New York Times)*
1974 Hedrick Smith *(New York Times)*

1975	William Mullen and Ovie Carter *(Chicago Tribune)*
1976	Sydney H. Schanberg *(New York Times)*
1978	Henry Kamm *(New York Times)*
1979	Richard Ben Cramer *(Philadelphia Inquirer)*
1980	Joel Brinkley and Jay Mather *(Louisville Courier-Journal)*
1981	Shirley Christian *(Miami Herald)*
1982	John Darnton *(New York Times)*
1983	Thomas L. Friedman *(New York Times)*
1984	Karen E. House *(Wall Street Journal)*
1985	Josh Friedman, Dennis Bell, and Ozier Muhammad *(Newsday)*
1986	Lewis M. Simons, Pete Carey, and Katherine Ellison *(San Jose Mercury News)*
1987	Michael Parks *(Los Angeles Times)*
1988	Thomas L. Friedman *(New York Times)*
1989	Bill Keller *(New York Times);* Glenn Frankel *(Washington Post)*
1990	Nicholas D. Kristof and Sheryl WuDunn *(New York Times)*
1991	Caryle Murphy *(Washington Post)* and Serge Schmemann *(New York Times)*
1992	Patrick J. Sloyan *(Newsday)*
1993	John F. Burns *(New York Times)* and Roy Gutman *(Newsday)*
1994	*Dallas Morning News,* team
1995	Mark Fritz *(Associated Press)*
1996	David Rohde *(Christian Science Monitor)*
1997	John F. Burns *(New York Times)*

Reporting

1917	Herbert B. Swope *(New York World)*
1918	Harold A. Littledale *(New York Evening Post)*
1920	John J. Leary, Jr. *(New York World)*
1921	Louis Seibold *(New York World)*
1922	Kirke L. Simpson (Associated Press)
1923	Alva Johnston *(New York Times)*
1924	Magner White *(San Diego Sun)*
1925	James W. Mulroy and Alvin H. Goldstein *(Chicago Daily News)*
1926	William Burke Miller *(Louisville Courier-Journal)*
1927	John T. Rogers *(St. Louis Post-Dispatch)*
1929	Paul Y. Anderson *(St. Louis Post-Dispatch)*
1930	Russell D. Owen *(New York Times);* special award: W. O. Dapping *(Auburn* [N.Y.] *Citizen)*
1931	A. B. MacDonald *(Kansas City* [Mo.] *Star)*
1932	W. C. Richards, D. D. Martin, J. S. Pooler, F. D. Webb, J. N. W. Sloan (all of *Detroit Free Press)*
1933	Francis A. Jamieson (Associated Press)
1934	Royce Brier *(San Francisco Chronicle)*
1935	William H. Taylor *(New York Herald Tribune)*
1936	Lauren D. Lyman *(New York Times)*
1937	John J. O'Neill *(New York Herald Tribune);* William Leonard Laurence *(New York Times);* Howard W. Blakeslee (Associated Press); Gobind Behari Lal (Universal Service); David Dietz (Scripps-Howard Newspapers)
1938	Raymond Sprigle *(Pittsburg Post-Gazette)*
1939	Thomas L. Stokes *(New York World-Telegram)*
1940	S. Burton Heath *(New York World-Telegram)*
1941	Westbrook Pegler *(New York World-Telegram)*
1942	Stanton Delaplane *(San Francisco Chronicle)*
1943	George Weller *(Chicago Daily News)*
1944	Paul Schoenstein and associates *(New York Journal-American)*
1945	Jack S. McDowell *(San Francisco Call-Bulletin)*
1946	William Leonard Laurence *(New York Times)*
1947	Frederick Woltman *(New York World-Telegram)*
1948	George E. Goodwin *(Atlanta Journal)*
1949	Malcolm Johnson *(New York Sun)*
1950	Meyer Berger *(New York Times)*
1951	Edward S. Montgomery *(San Francisco Examiner)*

1952	George de Carvalho *(San Francisco Chronicle)*
1953	Editorial staff *(Providence Journal and Evening Bulletin);*[1] Edward J. Mowery *(New York World-Telegram and Sun)*[2]
1954	*Vicksburg* (Miss.) *Sunday Post-Herald;*[1] Alvin Scott McCoy *(Kansas City* [Mo.] *Star)*[2]
1955	Mrs. Caro Brown *(Alice* [Tex.] *Daily Echo);*[1] Roland Kenneth Towery *(Cuero* [Tex.] *Record)*[2]
1956	Lee Hills *(Detroit Free Press);*[1] Arthur Daley *(New York Times)*[2]
1957	*Salt Lake Tribune;*[1] Wallace Turner and William Lambert *(Portland Oregonian)*[2]
1958	*Fargo* [N.D.] *Forum;*[1] George Beveridge *(Washington* [D.C.] *Evening Star)*[2]
1959	Mary Lou Werner *(Washington* [D.C.] *Evening Star);*[1] John Harold Brislin *(Scranton* [Pa.] *Tribune & Scrantonian)*[2]
1960	Jack Nelson *(Atlanta Constitution);*[1] Miriam Ottenberg *(Washington Evening Star)*[2]
1961	Sanche de Gramont *(New York Herald Tribune);*[1] Edgar May *(Buffalo Evening News)*[2]
1962	Robert D. Mullins *(Deseret News,* Salt Lake City);[1] George Bliss *(Chicago Tribune)*[2]
1963	Sylvan Fox, Anthony Shannon, and William Longgood *(New York World-Telegram and Sun);*[1] Oscar Griffin, Jr. (former editor of *Pecos* [Tex.] *Independent and Enterprise,* now on staff of *Houston Chronicle)*[2]

1. Reporting under pressure of edition deadlines. 2. Reporting not under pressure of edition deadlines.

General Local Reporting

1964	Norman C. Miller *(Wall Street Journal)*
1965	Melvin H. Ruder *(Hungry Horse News,* Columbia Falls, Mont.)
1966	Staff of *Los Angeles Times*
1967	Robert V. Cox *(Chambersburg* [Pa.] *Public Opinion)*
1968	Staff of *Detroit Free Press*
1969	John Fetterman *(Louisville Times* and *Courier-Journal)*
1970	Thomas Fitzpatrick *(Chicago Sun-Times)*
1971	Staff of *Akron* (Ohio) *Beacon*
1972	Richard Cooper and John Machacek *(Rochester* [N.Y.] *Times-Union)*
1973	*Chicago Tribune*
1974	Arthur M. Petacque and Hugh F. Hough *(Chicago Sun-Times)*
1975	*Xenia* (Ohio) *Daily Gazette*
1976	Gene Miller *(Miami Herald)*
1977	Margo Huston *(Milwaukee Journal)*
1978	Richard Whitt *(Louisville Courier-Journal)*
1979	Staff of *San Diego* (Calif.) *Evening Tribune*
1980	Staff of *Philadelphia Inquirer*
1981	*Longview* (Wash.) *Daily News*
1982	*Kansas City* (Mo.) *Star* and *Kansas City* (Mo.) *Times*
1983	*Fort Wayne* (Ind.) *News-Sentinel*
1984	*Newsday*

General News Reporting

1985	Thomas Turcol *(Virginian-Pilot and Ledger-Star)*
1986	Edna Buchanan *(Miami Herald)*
1987	*Akron Beacon Journal,* staff
1988	*Alabama Journal* (Montgomery), staff, *Lawrence* (Mass.) *Eagle-Tribune,* staff
1989	*Louisville Courier-Journal* staff
1990	*San Jose* (Calif.) *Mercury News*

Spot News Reporting

1991	*Miami Herald* staff
1992	*New York Newsday* staff
1993	*Los Angeles Times* staff
1994	*New York Times* staff
1995	*Los Angeles Times* staff

1996	Robert D. McFadden *(New York Times)*
1997	*Newsday* staff (Long Island, N.Y.)

Special Local Reporting

1964	James V. Magee, Albert V. Gaudiosi, and Frederick A. Meyer *(Philadelphia Bulletin)*
1965	Gene Goltz *(Houston Post)*
1966	John A. Frasca *(Tampa Tribune)*
1967	Gene Miller *(Miami Herald)*
1968	J. Anthony Lukas *(New York Times)*
1969	Albert L. Delugach and Denny Walsh *(St. Louis Globe-Democrat)*
1970	Harold Eugene Martin *(Montgomery Advertiser)*
1971	William Hugh Jones *(Chicago Tribune)*
1972	Timothy Leland, Gerard N. O'Neill, Stephen A. Kurkjian, and Ann DeSantis *(Boston Globe)*
1973	Sun Newspapers of Omaha, Neb.
1974	William Sherman *(New York Daily News)*
1975	*Indianapolis Star*
1976	*Chicago Tribune*
1977	Acel Moore and Wendell Rawls, Jr. *(Philadelphia Inquirer)*
1978	Anthony R. Dolan *(Stamford [Conn.] Advocate)*
1979	Gilbert M. Gaul and Elliot G. Jaspin *(Pottsville [Pa.] Republican)*
1980	Nils J. Bruzelius, Alexander B. Hawes, Jr., Stephen A. Kurkjian, Robert M. Porterfield, and Joan Vennochi *(Boston Globe)*
1981	Clark Hallas and Robert B. Lowe (*Arizona Daily Star*, Tucson)
1982	Paul Henderson *(Seattle Times)*
1983	Loretta Tofani *(Washington Post)*
1984	*Boston Globe*

Investigative Reporting

1985	Lucy Morgan and Jack Reed *(St. Petersburg [Fla.] Times)* and William K. Marimow *(Philadelphia Inquirer)*
1986	Jeffrey A. Marx and Michael M. York *(Lexington [Ky.] Herald Leader)*
1987	Daniel R. Biddle, H.G. Bissinger, and Fredric N. Tulsky *(Philadelphia Inquirer)*
1988	Dean Baquet, William C. Gaines, and Ann Marie Lipinski *(Chicago Tribune)*
1989	Bill Dedman *(Atlanta Journal and Constitution)*
1990	Lou Kilzer and Chris Ison *(Minneapolis-St. Paul Star Tribune)*
1991	Joseph T. Hallinan and Susan M. Headden *(Indianapolis Star)*
1992	Lorraine Adams and Dan Malone *(Dallas Morning News)*
1993	Jeff Brazil and Steve Berry *(Orlando [Fla.] Sentinel)*
1994	*Providence* (R.I.) *Journal-Bulletin* staff
1995	Stephanie Saul and Brian Donovan *(Newsday)*
1996	*Orange County Register* staff (Santa Ana, Calif.)
1997	Eric Nalder, Deborah Nelson, and Alex Tizon *(Seattle Times)*

Feature Writing

1979	Jon D. Franklin *(Baltimore Evening Sun)*
1980	Madeleine Blais *(Miami Herald)*
1981	Teresa Carpenter *(Village Voice,* New York)
1982	Saul Pett (Associated Press)
1983	Nan Robertson *(New York Times)*
1984	Peter M. Rinearson *(Seattle Times)*
1985	Alice Steinbach *(Baltimore Sun)*
1986	John Camp *(St. Paul Pioneer Press and Dispatch)*
1987	Steve Twomey *(Philadelphia Inquirer)*
1988	Jacqui Banaszynski *(St. Paul Pioneer Press Dispatch)*
1989	David Zucchino *(Philadelphia Inquirer)*
1990	Dave Curtin *(Colorado Springs Gazette Telegraph)*

1991	Sheryl James *(St. Petersburg [Fla.] Times)*
1992	Howell Raines *(New York Times)*
1993	George Lardner, Jr. *(Washington Post)*
1994	Isabel Wilkerson *(New York Times)*
1995	Ron Suskind *(Wall Street Journal)*
1996	Rick Bragg *(New York Times)*
1997	Lisa Pollak *(Baltimore Sun)*

Commentary

1970	Marquis W. Childs *(St. Louis Post-Dispatch)*
1971	William A. Caldwell *(Record* [Hackensack, N.J.])
1972	Mike Royko *(Chicago Daily News)*
1973	David S. Broder *(Washington Post)*
1974	Edwin A. Roberts, Jr. *(National Observer)*
1975	Mary McGrory *(Washington Star)*
1976	Walter W. (Red) Smith *(New York Times)*
1977	George F. Will *(Washington Post* Writers Group)
1978	William Safire *(New York Times)*
1979	Russell Baker *(New York Times)*
1980	Ellen H. Goodman *(Boston Globe)*
1981	Dave Anderson *(New York Times)*
1982	Art Buchwald (*Los Angeles Times* Syndicate)
1983	Claude Sitton *(Raleigh* [N.C.] *News & Observer)*
1984	Vermont Royster *(Wall Street Journal)*
1985	Murray Kempton *(Newsday)*
1986	Jimmy Breslin *(New York Daily News)*
1987	Charles Krauthammer *(Washington Post* Writers Group)
1988	Dave Barry *(Miami Herald)*
1989	Clarence Page *(Chicago Tribune)*
1990	Jim Murray *(Los Angeles Times)*
1991	Jim Hoagland *(Washington Post)*
1992	Anna Quindlen *(New York Times)*
1993	Liz Balmaseda *(Miami Herald)*
1994	William Raspberry *(Washington Post)*
1995	Jim Dwyer *(New York Newsday)*
1996	E.R. Shipp *(New York Daily News)*
1997	Eileen McNamara *(Boston Globe)*

Criticism

1970	Ada Louise Huxtable *(New York Times)*
1971	Harold C. Schonberg *(New York Times)*
1972	Frank Peters, Jr. *(St. Louis Post-Dispatch)*
1973	Ronald Powers *(Chicago Sun-Times)*
1974	Emily Genauer *(Newsday* Syndicate)
1975	Roger Ebert *(Chicago Sun-Times)*
1976	Alan M. Kriegsman *(Washington Post)*
1977	William McPherson *(Washington Post)*
1978	Walter Kerr *(New York Times)*
1979	Paul Gapp *(Chicago Tribune)*
1980	William A. Henry, 3rd *(Boston Globe)*
1981	Jonathan Yardley *(Washington Star)*
1982	Martin Bernheimer *(Los Angeles Times)*
1983	Manuela Hoelterhoff *(Wall Street Journal)*
1984	Paul Goldberger *(New York Times)*
1985	Howard Rosenberg *(Los Angeles Times)*
1986	Donal Henahan *(New York Times)*
1987	Richard Eder *(Los Angeles Times)*
1988	Tom Shales *(Washington Post)*
1989	Michael Skube *(News and Observer* [Raleigh, N.C.])
1990	Allan Temko *(San Francisco Chronicle)*
1991	David Shaw *(Los Angeles Times)*
1993	Michael Dirda *(Washington Post)*
1994	Lloyd Schwartz *(The Boston Phoenix)*
1995	Margo Jefferson *(New York Times)*
1996	Robert Campbell *(Boston Globe)*
1997	Tim Page *(Washington Post)*

Explanatory Journalism

1985	Jon Franklin *(Baltimore Evening Sun)*
1986	*New York Times*
1987	Jeff Lyon and Peter Gorner *(Chicago Tribune)*
1988	Daniel Hertzberg and James B. Stewart *(Wall Street Journal)*

1989	David Hanners, William Snyder, and Karen Blessen (Dallas Morning News)
1990	David A. Vise and Coll (Washington Post)
1991	Susan C. Faludi (Wall Street Journal)
1992	Robert S. Capers and Eric Lipton (Hartford Courant)
1993	Mike Toner (Atlanta Journal-Constitution)
1994	Ronald Kotulak (Chicago Tribune)
1995	Leon Dash and Lucian Perkins (Washington Post)
1996	Laurie Garrett (Newsday [Long Island, N.Y.])
1997	Michael Vitez, Ron Cortes, and April Saul (Philadelphia Inquirer)

Specialized Reporting

1985	Randall Savage and Jackie Crosby (Macon [Ga.] Telegraph and News)
1986	Andrew Schneider and Mary Pat Flaherty (Pittsburgh Press)
1987	Alex S. Jones (New York Times)
1988	Walt Bogdanich (Wall Street Journal)
1989	Edward Humes (Orange County Register)
1990	Tamar Stieber (Albuquerque (N.M.) Journal)

Beat Reporting

1991	Natalie Angier (New York Times)
1992	Deborah Blum (Sacramento Bee)
1993	Paul Ingrassia and Joseph B. White, (Wall Street Journal)
1994	Eric Freedman and Jim Mitzelfeld (Detroit News)
1995	David M. Shribman (Boston Globe)
1996	Bob Keeler (Newsday [Long Island, N.Y.])
1997	Byron Acohido (Seattle Times)

Special Citations

1938	Edmonton [Alberta] Journal, special bronze plaque for editorial leadership in defense of freedom of press in Province of Alberta
1941	New York Times, for the public educational value of its foreign news report
1944	Byron Price, Director of the Office of Censorship, for the creation and administration of the newspaper and radio codes; Mrs. William Allen White, for her husband's interest and services during the past seven years as a member of the Advisory Board of the Graduate School of Journalism, Columbia University; Richard Rodgers and Oscar Hammerstein II, for their musical Oklahoma!
1945	The cartographers of the American press, for their war maps
1947	(Pulitzer centennial year.) Columbia University and the Graduate School of Journalism, for their efforts to maintain and advance the high standards governing the Pulitzer Prize awards. The St. Louis Post-Dispatch, for its unswerving adherence to the public and professional ideals of its founder and its leadership in American journalism
1948	Dr. Frank D. Fackenthal, for his interest and service
1951	Cyrus L. Sulzberger (New York Times), for his exclusive interview with Archbishop Stepinac in a Yugoslav prison
1952	Kansas City Star, for coverage of 1951 floods; Max Kase (New York Journal-American), for exposures of bribery in college basketball
1953	New York Times, for its 17-year publication of "News of the Week in Review"; and Lester Markel, its founder
1957	Kenneth Roberts, for his historical novels
1958	Walter Lippmann (New York Herald Tribune), for his "wisdom, perception and high sense of responsibility" in his commentary on national and international affairs

1960	Garrett Mattingly, for The Armada
1961	American Heritage Picture History of the Civil War, as distinguished example of American book publishing
1964	Gannett Newspapers, Rochester, N.Y.
1973	James Thomas Flexner, for his biography George Washington
1974	Roger Sessions, for his "life's work in music"
1976	John Hohenberg, for "services for 22 years as administrator of the Pulitzer Prizes"; Scott Joplin, for his contributions to American music
1977	Alex Haley, for his novel, Roots
1978	E.B. White of New Yorker magazine and Richard L. Strout of Christian Science Monitor
1982	Milton Babbitt, "for his life's work as a distinguished and seminal American composer"
1984	Theodor Seuss Geisel (Dr. Seuss), for "books full of playful rhymes, nonsense words and strange illustrations"
1985	William H. Schuman, for "more than a half century of contribution to American music as a composer and educational leader"
1987	Joseph Pulitzer Jr., "for extraordinary services to American journalism and letters during his 31 years as chairman of the Pulitzer Prize Board and for his accomplishments as an editor and publisher"
1996	Herb Caen (San Francisco Chronicle), "for his extraordinary and continuing contribution as a voice and conscience of the city"

PULITZER PRIZES IN LETTERS

Fiction[1]

1918	His Family. Ernest Poole
1919	The Magnificent Ambersons. Booth Tarkington
1921	The Age of Innocence. Edith Wharton
1922	Alice Adams. Booth Tarkington
1923	One of Ours. Willa Cather
1924	The Able McLaughlins. Margaret Wilson
1925	So Big. Edna Ferber
1926	Arrowsmith. Sinclair Lewis
1927	Early Autumn. Louis Bromfield
1928	The Bridge of San Luis Rey. Thornton Wilder
1929	Scarlet Sister Mary. Julia Peterkin
1930	Laughing Boy. Oliver La Farge
1931	Years of Grace. Margaret Ayer Barnes
1932	The Good Earth. Pearl S. Buck
1933	The Store. T. S. Stribling
1934	Lamb in His Bosom. Caroline Miller
1935	Now in November. Josephine Winslow Johnson
1936	Honey in the Horn. Harold L. Davis
1937	Gone With the Wind. Margaret Mitchell
1938	The Late George Apley. John Phillips Marquand
1939	The Yearling. Marjorie Kinnan Rawlings
1940	The Grapes of Wrath. John Steinbeck
1942	In This Our Life. Ellen Glasgow
1943	Dragon's Teeth. Upton Sinclair
1944	Journey in the Dark. Martin Flavin
1945	A Bell for Adano. John Hersey
1947	All the King's Men. Robert Penn Warren
1948	Tales of the South Pacific. James A. Michener
1949	Guard of Honor. James Gould Cozzens
1950	The Way West. A. B. Guthrie, Jr.
1951	The Town. Conrad Richter
1952	The Caine Mutiny. Herman Wouk
1953	The Old Man and the Sea. Ernest Hemingway
1955	A Fable. William Faulkner
1956	Andersonville. MacKinlay Kantor
1958	A Death in the Family. James Agee
1959	The Travels of Jaimie McPheeters. Robert Lewis Taylor

1960	*Advise and Consent.* Allen Drury
1961	*To Kill a Mockingbird.* Harper Lee
1962	*The Edge of Sadness.* Edwin O'Connor
1963	*The Reivers.* William Faulkner
1965	*The Keepers of the House.* Shirley Ann Grau
1966	*Collected Stories of Katherine Anne Porter.* Katherine Anne Porter
1967	*The Fixer.* Bernard Malamud
1968	*The Confessions of Nat Turner.* William Styron
1969	*House Made of Dawn.* N. Scott Momaday
1970	*Collected Stories.* Jean Stafford
1972	*Angle of Repose.* Wallace Stegner
1973	*The Optimist's Daughter.* Eudora Welty
1975	*The Killer Angels.* Michael Shaara
1976	*Humboldt's Gift.* Saul Bellow
1978	*Elbow Room.* James Alan McPherson
1979	*The Stories of John Cheever.* John Cheever
1980	*The Executioner's Song.* Norman Mailer
1981	*A Confederacy of Dunces.* John Kennedy Toole
1982	*Rabbit Is Rich.* John Updike
1983	*The Color Purple.* Alice Walker
1984	*Ironweed.* William Kennedy
1985	*Foreign Affairs.* Alison Lurie
1986	*Lonesome Dove.* Larry McMurtry
1987	*A Summons to Memphis.* Peter Taylor
1988	*Beloved.* Toni Morrison
1989	*Breathing Lessons.* Anne Tyler
1990	*The Mambo Kings Play Songs of Love.* Oscar Hijuelos
1991	*Rabbit at Rest.* John Updike
1992	*A Thousand Acres.* Jane Smiley
1993	*A Good Scent From a Strange Mountain.* Robert Olen Butler
1994	*The Shipping News.* E. Annie Proulx
1995	*The Stone Diaries.* Carol Shields
1996	*Independence Day.* Richard Ford
1996	*Martin Dressler: The Tale of an American Dreamer.* Steven Millhauser

1. Before 1948, award was for novels only.

Drama

1918	*Why Marry?* Jesse Lynch Williams
1920	*Beyond the Horizon.* Eugene O'Neill
1921	*Miss Lulu Bett.* Zona Gale
1922	*Anna Christie.* Eugene O'Neill
1923	*Icebound.* Owen Davis
1924	*Hell-Bent Fer Heaven.* Hatcher Hughes
1925	*They Knew What They Wanted.* Sidney Howard
1926	*Craig's Wife.* George Kelly
1927	*In Abraham's Bosom.* Paul Green
1928	*Strange Interlude.* Eugene O'Neill
1929	*Street Scene.* Elmer L. Rice
1930	*The Green Pastures.* Marc Connelly
1931	*Alison's House.* Susan Glaspell
1932	*Of Thee I Sing.* George S. Kaufman, Morrie Ryskind, and Ira Gershwin
1933	*Both Your Houses.* Maxwell Anderson
1934	*Men in White.* Sidney Kingsley
1935	*The Old Maid.* Zöe Akins
1936	*Idiot's Delight.* Robert E. Sherwood
1937	*You Can't Take It With You.* Moss Hart and George S. Kaufman
1938	*Our Town.* Thornton Wilder
1939	*Abe Lincoln in Illinois.* Robert E. Sherwood
1940	*The Time of Your Life.* William Saroyan
1941	*There Shall Be No Night.* Robert E. Sherwood
1943	*The Skin of Our Teeth.* Thornton Wilder
1945	*Harvey.* Mary Chase
1946	*State of the Union.* Russel Crouse and Howard Lindsay
1948	*A Streetcar Named Desire.* Tennessee Williams
1949	*Death of a Salesman.* Arthur Miller
1950	*South Pacific.* Richard Rodgers, Oscar Hammerstein II, and Joshua Logan

1952	*The Shrike.* Joseph Kramm
1953	*Picnic.* William Inge
1954	*The Teahouse of the August Moon.* John Patrick
1955	*Cat on a Hot Tin Roof.* Tennessee Williams
1956	*The Diary of Anne Frank.* Frances Goodrich and Albert Hackett
1957	*Long Day's Journey Into Night.* Eugene O'Neill
1958	*Look Homeward, Angel.* Ketti Frings
1959	*J.B.* Archibald MacLeish
1960	*Fiorello!* George Abbott, Jerome Weidman, Jerry Bock, and Sheldon Harnick
1961	*All the Way Home.* Tad Mosel
1962	*How to Succeed in Business Without Really Trying.* Frank Loesser and Abe Burrows
1965	*The Subject Was Roses.* Frank D. Gilroy
1967	*A Delicate Balance.* Edward Albee
1969	*The Great White Hope.* Howard Sackler
1970	*No Place to Be Somebody.* Charles Gordone
1971	*The Effect of Gamma Rays on Man-in-the-Moon Marigolds.* Paul Zindel
1973	*That Championship Season.* Jason Miller
1975	*Seascape.* Edward Albee
1976	*A Chorus Line.* Conceived by Michael Bennett
1977	*The Shadow Box.* Michael Cristofer
1978	*The Gin Game.* Donald L. Coburn
1979	*Buried Child.* Sam Shepard
1980	*Talley's Folly.* Lanford Wilson
1981	*Crimes of the Heart.* Beth Henley
1982	*A Soldier's Play.* Charles Fuller
1983	*'Night, Mother.* Marsha Norman
1984	*Glengarry Glen Ross.* David Mamet
1985	*Sunday in the Park with George.* Stephen Sondheim and James Lapine
1987	*Fences.* August Wilson
1988	*Driving Miss Daisy.* Alfred Uhry
1989	*The Heidi Chronicles.* Wendy Wasserstein
1990	*The Piano Lesson.* August Wilson
1991	*Lost in Yonkers.* Neil Simon
1992	*The Kentucky Cycle.* Robert Schenkkan
1993	*Angels in America: Millennium Approaches.* Tony Kushner
1994	*Three Tall Women.* Edward Albee
1995	*The Young Man from Atlanta.* Horton Foote
1996	*Rent.* Jonathan Larson
1997	Not awarded

(For years not listed, no award was made.)

History of United States

1917	*With Americans of Past and Present Days.* J. J. Jusserand, Ambassador of France to United States
1918	*A History of the Civil War, 1861-1865.* James Ford Rhodes
1920	*The War With Mexico.* Justin H. Smith
1921	*The Victory at Sea.* William Sowden Sims in collaboration with Burton J. Hendrick
1922	*The Founding of New England.* James Truslow Adams
1923	*The Supreme Court in United States History.* Charles Warren
1924	*The American Revolution—A Constitutional Interpretation.* Charles Howard McIlwain
1925	*A History of the American Frontier.* Frederic L. Paxson
1926	*The History of the United States.* Edward Channing
1927	*Pinckney's Treaty.* Samuel Flagg Bemis
1928	*Main Currents in American Thought.* Vernon Louis Parrington
1929	*The Organization and Administration of the Union Army, 1861-1865.* Fred Albert Shannon
1930	*The War of Independence.* Claude H. Van Tyne
1931	*The Coming of the War: 1914.* Bernadotte E. Schmitt

1932 *My Experiences in the World War.* John J. Pershing

1933 *The Significance of Sections in American History.* Frederick J. Turner

1934 *The People's Choice.* Herbert Agar

1935 *The Colonial Period of American History.* Charles McLean Andrews

1936 *The Constitutional History of the United States.* Andrew C. McLaughlin

1937 *The Flowering of New England.* Van Wyck Brooks

1938 *The Road to Reunion, 1865-1900.* Paul Herman Buck

1939 *A History of American Magazines.* Frank Luther Mott

1940 *Abraham Lincoln: The War Years.* Carl Sandburg

1941 *The Atlantic Migration, 1607-1860.* Marcus Lee Hansen

1942 *Reveille in Washington.* Margaret Leech

1943 *Paul Revere and the World He Lived In.* Esther Forbes

1944 *The Growth of American Thought.* Merle Curti

1945 *Unfinished Business.* Stephen Bonsal

1946 *The Age of Jackson.* Arthur M. Schlesinger, Jr.

1947 *Scientists Against Time.* James Phinney Baxter, 3rd

1948 *Across the Wide Missouri.* Bernard DeVoto

1949 *The Disruption of American Democracy.* Roy Franklin Nichols

1950 *Art and Life in America.* Oliver W. Larkin

1951 *The Old Northwest, Pioneer Period 1815-1840.* R. Carlyle Buley

1952 *The Uprooted.* Oscar Handlin

1953 *The Era of Good Feelings.* George Dangerfield

1954 *A Stillness at Appomattox.* Bruce Catton

1955 *Great River: The Rio Grande in North American History.* Paul Horgan

1956 *The Age of Reform.* Richard Hofstadter

1957 *Russia Leaves the War: Soviet-American Relations, 1917-1920.* George F. Kennan

1958 *Banks and Politics in America: From the Revolution to the Civil War.* Bray Hammond

1959 *The Republican Era: 1869-1901.* Leonard D. White, assisted by Jean Schneider

1960 *In the Days of McKinley.* Margaret Leech

1961 *Between War and Peace: The Potsdam Conference.* Herbert Feis

1962 *The Triumphant Empire, Thunder-Clouds Gather in the West.* Lawrence H. Gipson

1963 *Washington, Village and Capital, 1800-1878.* Constance McLaughlin Green

1964 *Puritan Village: The Formation of a New England Town.* Sumner Chilton Powell

1965 *The Greenback Era.* Irwin Unger

1966 *Life of the Mind in America.* Perry Miller

1967 *Exploration and Empire: The Explorer and Scientist in the Winning of the American West.* William H. Goetzmann

1968 *The Ideological Origins of the American Revolution.* Bernard Bailyn

1969 *Origins of the Fifth Amendment.* Leonard W. Levy

1970 *Present at the Creation: My Years in the State Department.* Dean Acheson

1971 *Roosevelt: The Soldier of Freedom.* James McGregor Burns

1972 *Neither Black Nor White. Slavery and Race Relations in Brazil and the United States.* Carl N. Degler

1973 *People of Paradox: An Inquiry Concerning the Origin of American Civilization.* Michael Kammen

1974 *The Americans: The Democratic Experience,*
Vol. 3. Daniel J. Boorstin

1975 *Jefferson and His Time.* Dumas Malone

1976 *Lamy of Santa Fe.* Paul Horgan

1977 *The Impending Crisis: 1841-1861.* David M. Potter (posth)

1978 *The Invisible Hand: The Managerial Revolution in American Business.* Alfred D. Chandler, Jr.

1979 *The Dred Scott Case: Its Significance in Law and Politics.* Don E. Fehrenbacher

1980 *Been in the Storm So Long.* Leon F. Litwack

1981 *American Education: The National Experience; 1783-1876.* Lawrence A. Cremin

1982 *Mary Chesnut's Civil War.* C. Vann Woodward, editor

1983 *The Transformation of Virginia, 1740-1790.* Rhys L. Isaac

1985 *The Prophets of Regulation.* Thomas K. McCraw

1986 *. . . the Heavens and the Earth: A Political History of the Space Age.* Walter A. McDougall

1987 *Voyagers to the West: A Passage in the Peopling of America on the Eve of the Revolution.* Bernard Bailyn

1988 *The Launching of Modern American Science 1846-1876.* Robert V. Bruce

1989 *Parting the Waters,* Taylor Branch; *Battle Cry of Freedom.* James M. McPherson

1990 *In Our Image: America's Empire in the Philippines.* Stanley Karnow

1991 *A Midwife's Tale: The Life of Martha Ballard, Based on Her Diary 1785-1812.* Laurel Thatcher Ulrich

1992 *The Fate of Liberty: Abraham Lincoln and Civil Liberties.* Mark E. Neely, Jr.

1993 *The Radicalism of the American Revolution.* Gordon S. Wood

1995 *No Ordinary Time: Franklin and Eleanor Roosevelt: The Home Front in World War II.* Doris Kearns Goodwin

1996 *William Cooper's Town: Power and Persuasion on the Frontier of the Early American Republic.* Alan Taylor

1997 *Original Meanings: Politics and Ideas in the Making of the Constitution.* Jack N. Rakove

Biography or Autobiography

1917 *Julia Ward Howe.* Laura E. Richards and Maude Howe Elliott, assisted by Florence Howe Hall

1918 *Benjamin Franklin, Self-Revealed.* William Cabell Bruce

1919 *The Education of Henry Adams.* Henry Adams

1920 *The Life of John Marshall.* Albert J. Beveridge

1921 *The Americanization of Edward Bok.* Edward Bok

1922 *A Daughter of the Middle Border.* Hamlin Garland

1923 *The Life and Letters of Walter H. Page,* Burton J. Hendrick

1924 *From Immigrant to Inventor.* Michael Idvorsky Pupin

1925 *Barrett Wendell and His Letters.* M. A. DeWolfe Howe

1926 *The Life of Sir William Osler.* Harvey Cushing

1927 *Whitman.* Emory Holloway

1928 *The American Orchestra and Theodore Thomas.* Charles Edward Russell

1929 *The Training of an American. The Earlier Life and Letters of Walter H. Page.* Burton J. Hendrick

1930 *The Raven.* Marquis James

1931 *Charles W. Eliot.* Henry James

1932 *Theodore Roosevelt.* Henry F. Pringle

1933 *Grover Cleveland.* Allan Nevins

1934 *John Hay.* Tyler Dennett
1935 *R. E. Lee.* Douglas S. Freeman
1936 *The Thought and Character of William James.* Ralph Barton Perry
1937 *Hamilton Fish.* Allan Nevins
1938 *Pedlar's Progress.* Odell Shepard; *Andrew Jackson.* Marquis James
1939 *Benjamin Franklin.* Carl Van Doren
1940 *Woodrow Wilson. Life and Letters,* Vols. VII and VIII. Ray Stannard Baker
1941 *Jonathan Edwards.* Ola E. Winslow
1942 *Crusader in Crinoline.* Forrest Wilson
1943 *Admiral of the Ocean Sea.* Samuel Eliot Morison
1944 *The American Leonardo: The Life of Samuel F. B. Morse.* Carleton Mabee
1945 *George Bancroft: Brahmin Rebel.* Russel Blaine Nye
1946 *Son of the Wilderness.* Linnie Marsh Wolfe
1947 *The Autobiography of William Allen White*
1948 *Forgotten First Citizen: John Bigelow.* Margaret Clapp
1949 *Roosevelt and Hopkins.* Robert E. Sherwood
1950 *John Quincy Adams and the Foundations of American Foreign Policy.* Samuel Flagg Bemis
1951 *John C. Calhoun: American Portrait.* Margaret Louise Coit
1952 *Charles Evans Hughes.* Merlo J. Pusey
1953 *Edmund Pendleton, 1721-1803.* David J. Mays
1954 *The Spirit of St. Louis.* Charles A. Lindbergh
1955 *The Taft Story.* William S. White
1956 *Benjamin Henry Latrobe.* Talbot F. Hamlin
1957 *Profiles in Courage.* John F. Kennedy
1958 *George Washington.* Douglas Southall Freeman (Vols. 1-6) and John Alexander Carroll and Mary Wells Ashworth (Vol. 7)
1959 *Woodrow Wilson, American Prophet.* Arthur Walworth
1960 *John Paul Jones.* Samuel Eliot Morison
1961 *Charles Sumner and the Coming of the Civil War.* David Donald
1963 *Henry James: Vol. II, The Conquest of London, 1870-1881; Vol. III, The Middle Years, 1881-1895.* Leon Edel
1964 *John Keats.* Walter Jackson Bate
1965 *Henry Adams* (3 Vols.). Ernest Samuels
1966 *A Thousand Days.* Arthur M. Schlesinger, Jr.
1967 *Mr. Clemens and Mark Twain.* Justin Kaplan
1968 *Memoirs, 1925-1950.* George F. Kennan
1969 *The Man From New York.* B. L. Reid
1970 *Huey Long.* T. Harry Williams
1971 *Robert Frost: The Years of Triumph, 1915-1938.* Lawrence Thompson
1972 *Eleanor and Franklin: The Story of Their Relationship Based on Eleanor Roosevelt's Private Papers.* Joseph P. Lash
1973 *Luce and His Empire.* W. A. Swanberg
1974 *O'Neill, Son and Artist.* Louis Sheaffer
1975 *The Power Broker: Robert Moses and the Fall of New York.* Robert A. Caro
1976 *Edith Wharton: A Biography.* Richard W. B. Lewis
1977 *A Prince of Our Disorder.* John E. Mack
1978 *Samuel Johnson.* Walter Jackson Bate
1979 *Days of Sorrow and Pain: Leo Baeck and the Berlin Jews.* Leonard Baker
1980 *The Rise of Theodore Roosevelt.* Edmund Morris
1981 *Peter the Great.* Robert K. Massie
1982 *Grant: A Biography.* William S. McFeely
1983 *Growing Up.* Russell Baker
1984 *Booker T. Washington.* Louis R. Harlan
1985 *The Life and Times of Cotton Mather.* Kenneth Silverman

1986 *Louise Bogan: A Portrait,* Elizabeth Frank
1987 *Bearing the Cross: Martin Luther King Jr. and the Southern Christian Leadership Conference.* David J. Garrow
1988 *Look Homeward: A Life of Thomas Wolfe.* David Herbert Donald
1989 *Oscar Wilde.* Richard Ellmann
1990 *Machiavelli in Hell.* Sebastian de Grazia
1991 *Jackson Pollock: An American Saga.* Steven Naifeh and Gregory White Smith
1992 *Fortunate Son: The Healing of a Vietnam Vet.* Lewis B. Puller, Jr.
1993 *Truman.* David McCullough
1994 *W.E.B. DuBois: Biography of a Race, 1868-1919.* David Levering Lewis
1995 *Harriet Beecher Stowe: A Life.* Joan D. Hedrick
1996 *God: A Biography.* Jack Miles
1997 *Angela's Ashes: A Memoir.* Frank McCourt

Poetry[1]

1918 *Love Songs.* Sara Teasdale
1919 *Old Road to Paradise.* Margaret Widdemer; *Corn Huskers.* Carl Sandburg
1922 *Collected Poems.* Edwin Arlington Robinson
1923 *The Ballad of the Harp-Weaver; A Few Figs from Thistles;* eight sonnets in *American Poetry, 1922, A Miscellany.* Edna St. Vincent Millay
1924 *New Hampshire: A Poem With Notes and Grace Notes.* Robert Frost
1925 *The Man Who Died Twice.* Edwin Arlington Robinson
1926 *What's O'Clock.* Amy Lowell
1927 *Fiddler's Farewell.* Leonora Speyer
1928 *Tristram.* Edwin Arlington Robinson
1929 *John Brown's Body.* Stephen Vincent Benét
1930 *Selected Poems.* Conrad Aiken
1931 *Collected Poems.* Robert Frost
1932 *The Flowering Stone.* George Dillon
1933 *Conquistador.* Archibald MacLeish
1934 *Collected Verse.* Robert Hillyer
1935 *Bright Ambush.* Audrey Wurdemann
1936 *Strange Holiness.* Robert P. T. Coffin
1937 *A Further Range.* Robert Frost
1938 *Cold Morning Sky.* Marya Zaturenska
1939 *Selected Poems.* John Gould Fletcher
1940 *Collected Poems.* Mark Van Doren
1941 *Sunderland Capture.* Leonard Bacon
1942 *The Dust Which Is God.* William Rose Benét
1943 *A Witness Tree.* Robert Frost
1944 *Western Star.* Stephen Vincent Benét
1945 *V-Letter and Other Poems.* Karl Shapiro
1947 *Lord Weary's Castle.* Robert Lowell
1948 *The Age of Anxiety.* W. H. Auden
1949 *Terror and Decorum.* Peter Viereck
1950 *Annie Allen.* Gwendolyn Brooks
1951 *Complete Poems.* Carl Sandburg
1952 *Collected Poems.* Marianne Moore
1953 *Collected Poems, 1917-1952.* Archibald MacLeish
1954 *The Waking.* Theodore Roethke
1955 *Collected Poems.* Wallace Stevens
1956 *Poems—North & South.* Elizabeth Bishop
1957 *Things of This World.* Richard Wilbur
1958 *Promises: Poems, 1954-1956.* Robert Penn Warren
1959 *Selected Poems, 1928-1958.* Stanley Kunitz
1960 *Heart's Needle.* William Snodgrass
1961 *Times Three: Selected Verse From Three Decades.* Phyllis McGinley
1962 *Poems.* Alan Dugan
1963 *Pictures From Breughel.* William Carlos Williams
1964 *At the End of the Open Road.* Louis Simpson
1965 *77 Dream Songs.* John Berryman

1966	*Selected Poems.* Richard Eberhart
1967	*Live or Die.* Anne Sexton
1968	*The Hard Hours.* Anthony Hecht
1969	*Of Being Numerous.* George Oppen
1970	*Untitled Subjects.* Richard Howard
1971	*The Carrier of Ladders.* William S. Merwin
1972	*Collected Poems.* James Wright
1973	*Up Country.* Maxine Winokur Kumin
1974	*The Dolphin.* Robert Lowell
1975	*Turtle Island.* Gary Snyder
1976	*Self-Portrait in a Convex Mirror.* John Ashbery
1977	*Divine Comedies.* James Merrill
1978	*Collected Poems.* Howard Nemerov
1979	*Now and Then: Poems, 1976-1978.* Robert Penn Warren.
1980	*Selected Poems.* Donald Rodney Justice
1981	*The Morning of the Poem.* James Schuyler
1982	*The Collected Poems.* Sylvia Plath
1983	*Selected Poems.* Galway Kinnell
1984	*American Primitive.* Mary Oliver
1985	*Yin.* Carolyn Kizer
1986	*The Flying Change.* Henry Taylor
1987	*Thomas and Beulah.* Rita Dove
1988	*Partial Accounts: New and Selected Poems.* William Meredith
1989	*New and Collected Poems.* Richard Wilbur
1990	*The World Doesn't End.* Charles Simic
1991	*Near Changes.* Mona Van Duyn
1992	*Selected Poems.* James Tate
1993	*The Wild Iris.* Louise Gluck
1994	*Neon Vernacular.* Yusef Komunyakaa
1995	*Simple Truth.* Philip Levine
1996	*The Dream of the Unified Field.* Jorie Graham
1997	*Alive Together: New and Selected Poems.* Lisel Mueller

1. The poetry prize was established in 1922. The 1918 and 1919 awards were made from gifts provided by the Poetry Society.

General Nonfiction

1962	*The Making of the President, 1960.* Theodore H. White
1963	*The Guns of August.* Barbara W. Tuchman
1964	*Anti-Intellectualism in American Life.* Richard Hofstadter
1965	*O Strange New World.* Howard Mumford Jones
1966	*Wandering Through Winter.* Edwin Way Teale
1967	*The Problem of Slavery in Western Culture.* David Brion Davis
1968	*Rousseau and Revolution.* Will and Ariel Durant
1969	*So Human an Animal.* Rene Jules Dubos; *The Armies of the Night.* Norman Mailer
1970	*Gandhi's Truth.* Erik H. Erikson
1971	*The Rising Sun.* John Toland
1972	*Stilwell and the American Experience in China, 1911-1945.* Barbara W. Tuchman
1973	*Fire in the Lake: The Vietnamese and the Americans in Vietnam.* Frances FitzGerald; and *Children of Crisis* (Vols. 1 and 2). Robert M. Coles
1974	*The Denial of Death.* Ernest Becker
1975	*Pilgrim at Tinker Creek.* Annie Dillard
1976	*Why Survive? Being Old in America.* Robert N. Butler
1977	*Beautiful Swimmers: Watermen, Crabs and the Chesapeake Bay.* William W. Warner
1978	*The Dragons of Eden.* Carl Sagan
1979	*On Human Nature.* Edward O. Wilson
1980	*Gödel, Escher, Bach: An Eternal Golden Braid.* Douglas R. Hofstadter
1981	*Fin-de-Siecle Vienna: Politics and Culture.* Carl E. Schorske
1982	*The Soul of a New Machine.* Tracy Kidder

1983	*Is There No Place on Earth for Me?* Susan Sheehan
1984	*Social Transformation of American Medicine.* Paul Starr
1985	*The Good War: An Oral History of World War II.* Studs Terkel
1986	*Move Your Shadow: South Africa, Black and White.* Joseph Lelyveld; *Common Ground: A Turbulent Decade in the Lives of Three American Families.* J. Anthony Lukas
1987	*Arab and Jew: Wounded Spirits in a Promised Land.* David K. Shipler
1988	*The Making of the Atomic Bomb.* Richard Rhodes
1989	*A Bright Shining Lie.* Neil Sheehan
1990	*And Their Children After Them.* Dale Maharidge and Michael Williamson
1991	*The Ants.* Bert Holldobler and Edward O. Wilson
1992	*The Prize: The Epic Quest for Oil, Money and Power.* Daniel Yergin
1993	*Lincoln at Gettysburg: The Words That Remade America.* Garry Wills
1994	*Lenin's Tomb: The Last Days of the Soviet Empire.* David Remick
1995	*The Beak of the Finch: A Story of Evolution in Our Time.* Jonathan Weiner
1996	*The Haunted Land: Facing Europe's Ghosts After Communism.* Tina Rosenberg
1997	*Ashes to Ashes: America's Hundred-Year Cigarette War, the Public Health, and the Unabashed Triumph of Philip Morris.* Richard Kluger

Pulitzer Prizes in Music

1943	*Secular Cantata No. 2, A Free Song.* William Schuman
1944	*Symphony No. 4 (Op. 34).* Howard Hanson
1945	*Appalachian Spring.* Aaron Copland
1946	*The Canticle of the Sun.* Leo Sowerby
1947	*Symphony No. 3.* Charles Ives
1948	*Symphony No. 3.* Walter Piston
1949	*Louisiana Story* music. Virgil Thomson
1950	*The Consul.* Gian Carlo Menotti
1951	Music for opera *Giants in the Earth.* Douglas Stuart Moore
1952	*Symphony Concertante.* Gail Kubik
1954	*Concerto for Two Pianos and Orchestra.* Quincy Porter
1955	*The Saint of Bleecker Street.* Gian Carlo Menotti
1956	*Symphony No. 3.* Ernst Toch
1957	*Meditations on Ecclesiastes.* Norman Dello Joio
1958	*Vanessa.* Samuel Barber
1959	*Concerto for Piano and Orchestra.* John La Montaine
1960	*Second String Quartet.* Elliott Carter
1961	*Symphony No. 7.* Walter Piston
1962	*The Crucible.* Robert Ward
1963	*Piano Concerto No. 1.* Samuel Barber
1966	*Variations for Orchestra.* Leslie Bassett
1967	*Quartet No. 3.* Leon Kirchner
1968	*Echoes of Time and the River.* George Crumb
1969	*String Quartet No. 3.* Karel Husa
1970	*Time's Encomium.* Charles Wuorinen
1971	*Synchronisms No. 6 for Piano and Electronic Sound.* Mario Davidovsky
1972	*Windows.* Jacob Druckman
1973	*String Quartet No. 3.* Elliott Carter
1974	*Notturno.* Donald Martino
1975	*From the Diary of Virginia Woolf.* Dominick Argento
1976	*Air Music.* Ned Rorem

1977	*Visions of Terror and Wonder.* Richard Wernick		*Orchestra.* Mel Powell
1978	*Déjà Vu for Percussion Quartet and Orchestra.* Michael Colgrass	1991	*Symphony.* Shulamit Ran
		1992	*The Face of the Night, The Heart of the Dark.* Wayne Peterson
1979	*Aftertones of Infinity.* Joseph Schwantner		
1980	*In Memory of a Summer Day.* David Del Tredici	1993	*Trombone Concerto.* Christopher Rouse
1981	Not awarded	1994	*Of Reminiscences and Reflections.* Gunther Schuller
1982	*Concerto for Orchestra.* Roger Sessions		
1983	*Three Movements for Orchestra.* Ellen T. Zwilich	1995	*Stringmusic.* Morton Gould
1984	*Canti del Sole.* Bernard Rands	1996	*Lilacs.* George Walker
1985	*Symphony RiverRun.* Stephen Albert	1997	*Blood on the Field.* Wynton Marsalis
1986	*Wind Quintet IV.* George Perle		
1987	*The Flight Into Egypt.* John Harbison		
1988	*12 New Etudes for Piano.* William Bolcom		**Special Award**
1989	*Whispers Out of Time.* Roger Reynolds		
1990	*Duplicates: A Concerto for Two Pianos and*	1992	*Maus.* Art Spiegelman

National Society of Film Critics Awards, 1996

Best Picture: *Breaking the Waves*
Best Actor: Eddie Murphy, *The Nutty Professor*
Best Actress: Emily Watson, *Breaking the Waves*
Best Supporting Actor: Martin Donovan., *The Portrait of a Lady*
Best Supporting Actress: Barbara Hershey, *The Portrait of a Lady*
Best Director: Lars von Trier, *Breaking the Waves*

Best Screenplay: Albert Brooks and Monica Johnson, *Mother*
Best Cinematography: Robby Muller, *Breaking the Waves*
Best Foreign Film: *La Cérémonie*
Best Documentary: *When We Were Kings*
James Katz and Robert Harris received a special citation for their restoration of Alfred Hitchcock's *Vertigo*

New York Drama Critics' Circle Awards

1935-36
Winterset, Maxwell Anderson
1936-37
High Tor, Maxwell Anderson
1937-38
Of Mice and Men, John Steinbeck
Shadow and Substance, Paul Vincent Carroll[1]
1938-39
(No award) The White Steed, Paul Vincent Carroll[1]
1939-40
The Time of Your Life, William Saroyan
1940-41
Watch on the Rhine, Lillian Hellman
The Corn Is Green, Emlyn Williams[1]
1941-42
(No award) Blithe Spirit, Noel Coward[1]
1942-43
The Patriots, Sidney Kingsley
1943-44
(No award) Jacobowsky and the Colonel. Franz Werfel and S. N. Behrman[1]
1944-45
The Glass Menagerie, Tennessee Williams
1945-46
(No award) Carousel, Richard Rodgers and Oscar Hammerstein II[2]
1946-47
All My Sons, Arthur Miller
No Exit, Jean-Paul Sartre[1]
Brigadoon, Alan Jay Lerner and Frederick Loewe[2]
1947-48
A Streetcar Named Desire, Tennessee Williams
The Winslow Boy, Terence Rattigan[1]
1948-49
Death of a Salesman, Arthur Miller
The Madwoman of Chaillot, Jean Giraudoux and Maurice Valency[1]
South Pacific, Richard Rodgers, Oscar Hammerstein II, and Joshua Logan[2]
1949-50
The Member of the Wedding, Carson McCullers
The Cocktail Party, T. S. Eliot[1]
The Consul, Gian Carlo Menotti[2]
1950-51
Darkness at Noon, Sidney Kingsley[3]
The Lady's Not for Burning, Christopher Fry[1]
Guys and Dolls, Abe Burrows, Jo Swerling, and Frank Loesser[2]
1951-52
I Am a Camera, John Van Druten[4]
Venus Observed, Christopher Fry[1]

Pal Joey, Richard Rodgers, Lorenz Hart, and John O'Hara[2]
Don Juan in Hell, George B. Shaw[5]
1952-53
Picnic, William Inge The Love of Four Colonels, by Peter Ustinov[1]
Wonderful Town, Joseph Fields, Jerome Chodorov, Betty Comden, Adolph Green, and Leonard Bernstein[2]
1953-54
The Teahouse of the August Moon, John Patrick
Ondine, Jean Giraudoux[1]
The Golden Apple, John Latouche and Jerome Moross[2]
1954-55
Cat on a Hot Tin Roof, Tennessee Williams
Witness for the Prosecution, Agatha Christie[1]
The Saint of Bleecker Street, Gian Carlo Menotti[2]
1955-56
The Diary of Anne Frank, Frances Goodrich and Albert Hackett
Tiger at the Gates, Jean Giraudoux and Christopher Fry[1]
My Fair Lady, Frederick Loewe and Alan Jay Lerner[2]
1956-57
Long Day's Journey Into Night, Eugene O'Neill
Waltz of the Toreadors, Jean Anouilh[1]
The Most Happy Fella, Frank Loesser[2][6]
1957-58
Look Homeward, Angel, Ketti Frings[7]
Look Back in Anger, John Osborne[1]
The Music Man, Meredith Willson[2]
1958-59
A Raisin in the Sun, Lorraine Hansberry
The Visit, Friedrich Duerrenmatt-Maurice Valency[1]
La Plume de ma Tante, Robert Dhery and Gerard Calvi[2]
1959-60
Toys in the Attic, Lillian Hellman
Five Finger Exercise, Peter Shaffer[1]
Fiorello, Jerome Weidman, George Abbott, Jerry Bock, and Sheldon Harnick[2]
1960-61
All the Way Home, Tad Mosel[3]
A Taste of Honey, Shelagh Delaney[1]
Carnival, Michael Stewart[2]
1961-62
The Night of the Iguana, Tennessee Williams
A Man for All Seasons, Robert Bolt[1]
How to Succeed in Business Without Really Trying, Abe Burrows, Jack Weinstock, Willie Gilbert, and Frank Loesser[2][9]
1962-63
Who's Afraid of Virginia Woolf?, Edward Albee
Beyond the Fringe, Alan Bennett, Peter Cook, Jonathan Miller, and Dudley Moore[10]
1963-64
Luther, John Osborne

Hello, Dolly, Michael Stewart and Jerry Herman[2] [11]
The Trojan Women, Euripides[10] [12]
1964-65
The Subject Was Roses, Frank D. Gilroy
Fiddler on the Roof, Joseph Stein, Jerry Bock, and Sheldon Harnick[2] [13]
1965-66
The Persecution and Assassination of Marat as Performed by the Inmates of the Asylum of Charenton Under the Direction of the Marquis de Sade, Peter Weiss
The Man of La Mancha, Dale Wasserman, Mitch Leigh, and Joe Darion
1966-67
The Homecoming, Harold Pinter
Cabaret, Joe Masteroff, John Kander, and Fred Ebb[2] [14]
1967-68
Rosencrantz and Guildenstern Are Dead, Tom Stoppard
Your Own Thing, Donald Driver, Hal Hester, and Danny Apolinar[2]
1968-69
The Great White Hope, Howard Sackler
1776, Sherman Edwards and Peter Stone[2]
1969-70
Borstal Boy, Frank McMahon[15]
The Effect of Gamma Rays on Man-in-the-Moon Marigolds, Paul Zindel[16]
Company, George Furth and Stephen Sondheim[2]
1970-71
Home, David Storey
The House of Blue Leaves, John Guare[16]
Follies, James Goldman and Stephen Sondheim[2]
1971-72
That Championship Season, Jason Miller
Two Gentlemen of Verona, adapted by John Guare and Mel Shapiro[2]
The Screens, Jean Genet[1]
1972-73
The Changing Room, David Storey
The Hot I Baltimore, by Lanford Wilson[16]
A Little Night Music, Hugh Wheeler and Stephen Sondheim[2]
1973-74
The Contractors, David Storey
Short Eyes, Miguel Piñero[16]
Candide, Leonard Bernstein, Hugh Wheeler, and Richard Wilbur[2]
1974-75
Equus, Peter Shaffer
The Taking of Miss Janie, Ed Bullins[16]
A Chorus Line, James Kirkwood and Nicholas Dante[2]
1975-76
Travesties, Tom Stoppard
Streamers, David Rabe[16]
Pacific Overtures, Stephen Sondheim, John Weidman, and Hugh Wheeler[2]
1976-77
Otherwise Engaged, Simon Gray
American Buffalo, David Mamet[16]
Annie, Thomas Meehan, Charles Strouse, and Martin Charnin[2]
1977-78
Da, Hugh Leonard
Ain't Misbehavin', conceived by Richard Maltby, Jr.[2]
1978-79
The Elephant Man, Bernard Pomerance
Sweeney Todd, Hugh Wheeler and Stephen Sondheim[2]
1979-80
Talley's Folly, Lanford Wilson *Evita*,[2] Andrew Lloyd Webber and Tim Rice
Betrayal, Harold Pinter[1]
1980-81
A Lesson From Aloes, Athol Fugard
Crimes of the Heart, Beth Henley[16]
1981-82
The Life and Adventures of Nicholas Nickleby, adapted by David Edgar
A Soldier's Play, Charles Fuller[16]
1982-83
Brighton Beach Memoirs, Neil Simon
Plenty, David Hare[1]
Little Shop of Horrors, Alan Menken and Howard Ashman[2] [17]
1983-84

The Real Thing, Tom Stoppard
Glengarry Glen Ross, David Mamet[16]
Sunday in the Park with George, Stephen W Sondheim and James Lapine[2]
1984-85
Ma Rainey's Black Bottom, August Wilson
(No award for best musical or foreign play)
1985-86
Lie of the Mind, Sam Shepard
Benefactors, Michael Frayn[1]
The Search for Signs of Intelligent Life in the Universe, Lily Tomlin and Jane Wagner[10]
(No award for best musical)
1986-87
Fences, August Wilson
Les Liaisons Dangereuses, Christopher Hampton[1]
Les Miserables, Claude-Michel Schonberg and Alain Boublil[2]
1987-88
Joe Turner's Come and Gone, August Wilson
The Road to Mecca, Athol Fugard[1]
Into the Woods, Stephen Sondheim and James Lapine[2]
1988-89
The Heidi Chronicles, Wendy Wasserstein
Aristocrats, Brian Friel[1]
Largely New York, Bill Irwin[10]
(No award for best musical)
1989-90
The Piano Lesson, August Wilson
Privates on Parade, Peter Nichols[1]
City of Angels, Larry Gelbart, Cy Coleman, and David Zippel[2]
1990-91
Six Degrees of Separation, John Guare
Our Country's Good, Timberlake Wertenbaker[1]
The Will Rogers Follies, Cy Coleman, Peter Stone, Betty Comden, and Adolph Green[2]
Eileen Atkins, A Room of One's Own [10]
1991-92
Dancing at Lughnasa, Brian Friel
Two Trains Running, August Wilson[16]
(No award for best musical)
1992-93
Angels in America: Millenium Approaches, Tony Kushner
Someone Who'll Watch Over Me, Frank McGuinness[1]
Kiss of the Spider Woman, John Kander, Fred Ebb and Terrence McNally[2]
1993-94
Three Tall Women, Edward Albee
Twilight: Los Angeles, 1992, Anna Deavere Smith, writer/actress, a special award "for unique contribution to theatrical form."
(No award for best foreign play or best musical)
1994-95
Arcadia, Tom Stoppard
Love! Valour! Compassion!, Terrence McNally
Signature Theater Company for outstanding achievement.
(No award for best musical or best foreign play)
1995-96
Seven Guitars, August Wilson
Rent, Jonathan Larson[2]
Molly Sweeney, Brian Friel[1]
1996–97
How I Learned to Drive, by Paula Vogel
Violet, by Brian Crowley; based on the book *The Ugliest Pilgrim*, by Doris Bets
Skylight, David Hare
To the cast and creative team of *Chicago* for their distinguished contribution to the Broadway season.

1. Citation for best foreign play. 2. Citation for best musical. 3. Based on a novel by Arthur Koestler. 4. Based on Christopher Isherwood's *Berlin Stories*. 5. For "distinguished and original contribution to the theater." 6. Based on Sidney Howard's *They Knew What They Wanted*. 7. Based on a novel by Thomas Wolfe. 8. Based on James Agee's *A Death in the Family*. 9. Based on a book by Shepherd Mead. 10. Special citation. 11. Based on Thornton Wilder's *The Matchmaker*. 12. Translated by Edith Hamilton. 13. Based on Sholem Aleichem's Tevye stories, translated by Arnold Perl. 14. Based on John Van Druten's *I Am a Camera*, which won the award for best play in 1951-52. 15. Based on Brendan Behan's autobiography. 16. Citation for best American play. 17. Based on a story by Roger Corman.

1997 Obie Award Winners

Best Play: Naomi Wallace, *One Flea Spare*
Best Production: *Peter and Wendy*
Playwriting: Eve Ensler, *The Vagina Monologues;* David Henry Hwang, *Golden Child;* Paula Vogel, *How I Learned to Drive;* Lanford Wilson, *Sympathetic Magic*
Direction: Mark Brokaw, *How I Learned to Drive*
Performance: Andre Braugher, *Henry V;* Tsai Chin, *Golden Child;* Jennifer Dundas, *Good As New;* David Greenspan, *The Boys in the Band;* Karen Kandel, *Peter and Wendy;* Albert Macklin, *June Moon;* David Morse, *How I Learned to Drive;* Mary Louise Parker, *How I Learned to Drive;* Sharon Scruggs,

The Trojan Women; Ray Anthony Thomas, *Volunteer Man;* Ching Valdes-Aran, *Flipzoids*
Design: Derek McLane, sustained excellence of set design; Shirley Prendergast, sustained excellence of lighting design; Catherine Zuber, sustained excellence of costume design
Special Citations: Joanne Camp, sustained excellence of performance; Arthur French, sustained excellence of performance; Roger Guenveur Smith and Mark Anthony Thompson, *A Huey P. Newton Story;* Howard Crabtree and the creators of *When Pigs Fly;* James Hatch and Camille Billops; Dona Ann McAdams; *Tap Dogs;* Jeanine Tesori, music for *Violet*

Tony (Antoinette Perry) Awards, 1997

Play: *The Last Night of Ballyhoo*
Musical: *Titanic*
Revival — Play: *A Doll's House*
Revival — Musical: *Chicago*
Actor — Play: Christopher Plummer, *Barrymore*
Actress — Play: Janet McTeer, *A Doll's House:*
Actor — Musical: James Naughton, *Chicago*
Actress — Musical: Bebe Neuwirth, *Chicago*
Featured Actor — Play: Owen Teale, *A Doll's House*
Featured Actress — Play: Lynne Thigpen, *An American Daughter*
Featured Actor — Musical: Chuck Cooper, *The Life*

Featured Actress — Musical: Lillias White, *The Life*
Director — Play: Anthony Page, *A Doll's House*
Director — Musical: Walter Bobbie, *Chicago*
Book — Musical: *Titanic*
Score — Musical: *Titanic*
Orchestration: Jonathan Tunick, *Titanic*
Scenic Designer: Stewart Laing, *Titanic*
Costume Designer: Judith Dolan, *Candide*
Choreographer: Ann Reinking, *Chicago*
Lighting Designer: Ken Billington, *Chicago*
Regional Theater: Berkeley Repertory Theater
Lifetime Achievement: Bernard B. Jacobs

1997 National Magazine Awards

General Excellence: *I.D.* (circulation less than 100,000); *Wired* (circulation 100,000 to 400,000); *Outside* (circulation 400,000 to 1,000,000); *Vanity Fair* (circulation more than 1,000,000)
Personal Service: *Glamour*
Special Interests: *Smithsonian*
Reporting: *Outside*
Essays and Criticism: *The New Yorker*

Feature Writing: *Sports Illustrated*
Public Interest: *Fortune*
Design: *I.D.*
Fiction: *The New Yorker*
Single-Topic Issue: *Scientific American*
Photography: *National Geographic*
General Excellence in New Media: *Money*

Major Grammy Awards for Recording in 1997

Source: National Academy of Recording Arts and Sciences.

Record: "Change the World," Eric Clapton; Kenneth "Babyface" Edmonds, producer
Album: *Falling Into You,* Celine Dion
Song: "Change the World," Gordon Kennedy, Wayne Kirkpatrick and Tommy Sims, songwriters
New Artist: LeAnn Rimes
Male Pop Vocal: "Change the World," Eric Clapton
Female Pop Vocal: "Unbreak My Heart," Toni Braxton
Pop Duo or Group: "Free As a Bird," The Beatles
Pop Collaboration With Vocals: "When I Fall in Love," Natalie Cole with Nat King Cole
Pop Instrumental: "The Sinister Minister," Béla Fleck and the Flecktones
Pop Album: *Falling Into You,* Celine Dion
Traditional Pop Vocal: *Here's to the Ladies,* Tony Bennett
Female Rock Vocal: "If It Makes You Happy," Sheryl Crow
Male Rock Vocal: "Where It's At," Beck
Rock Performance by a Duo or Group With Vocal: "So Much to Say," Dave Matthews Band
Hard Rock: "Bullet With Butterfly Wings," Smashing Pumpkins
Metal: "Tire Me," Rage Against the Machine
Rock Instrumental: "SRV Shuffle," Jimmie Vaughan, Eric Clapton, Bonnie Raitt, Robert Cray, B.B. King, Buddy Guy, Dr. John and Art Neville
Rock Song: "Give Me One Reason," Tracy Chapman, songwriter
Rock Album: *Sheryl Crow,* Sheryl Crow
Alternative Music: *Odelay,* Beck
Female R&B Vocal: "You're Makin' Me High," Toni Braxton
Male R&B Vocal: "Your Secret Love," Luther Vandross
R&B by a Duo or Group: "Killing Me Softly With His Song," Fugees
R&B Song: "Exhale (Shoop, Shoop)," Kenneth "Babyface" Edmonds, songwriter
R&B Album: *Words,* The Tony Rich Project

Rap Solo: "Hey Lover," LL Cool J
Rap Duo or Group: "Tha Crossroads," Bone Thugs-n-Harmony
Rap Album: *The Score,* Fugees; Lauryn Hill, Prakazrel "Pras" & Wyclef, producers
Female Country Vocal: "Blue," LeAnn Rimes
Male Country Vocal: "Worlds Apart," Vince Gill
Country Duo or Group: "My Maria," Brooks & Dunn
Country Instrumental: "Jam Man," Chet Atkins
Country Song: "Blue," Bill Mack, songwriter
Country Album: *The Road to Ensenada,* Lyle Lovett; Billy Williams and Lyle Lovett, producers
Bluegrass Album: *True Life Blues: The Songs of Bill Monroe,* various artists
New Age Album: *The Memory of Trees,* Enya
Contemporary Jazz: *High Life,* Wayne Shorter
Jazz Vocal: *New Moon Daughter,* Cassandra Wilson
Jazz Instrumental Solo: "Cabin Fever," Michael Brecker
Jazz Instrumental, Individual or Group: *Tales From The Hudson,* Michael Brecker
Large Jazz Ensemble: *Live at Manchester Craftmen's Guild,* Count Basie Orchestra (with The New York Voices); Grover Mitchell, conductor
Latin Jazz: *Portraits of Cuba,* Paquito D'Rivera
Rock Gospel Album: *Jesus Freak,* DC Talk
Pop/Contemporary Gospel Album: *Tribute—The Songs of Andrae Crouch,* various artists; Norman Miller and Neal Joseph, producers
Southern Gospel, Country Gospel or Bluegrass Gospel Album: *I Love to Tell the Story—25 Timeless Hymns,* Andy Griffith
Traditional Soul Gospel Album: *Face to Face,* Cissy Houston
Contemporary Soul Gospel Album: *Whatcha Lookin' 4,* Kirk Franklin and the Family
Gospel Album by a Choir or Chorus: *Just A Word,* Shirley

Caesar's Outreach Convention Choir
Latin Pop: *Enrique Iglesias,* Enrique Iglesias
Tropical Latin: *La Rosa de los Vientos,* Ruben Blades
Mexican-American/Tejano Music: *Un Millon de Rosas,* La Mafia
Traditional Blues Album: *Deep in the Blues,* James Cotton
Contemporary Blues Album: *Just Like You,* Keb' Mo'
Traditional Folk Album: *Pete,* Pete Seeger
Contemporary Folk Album: *The Ghost of Tom Joad,* Bruce Springsteen
Reggae Album: *Hall of Fame—A Tribute to Bob Marley's 50th Anniversary,* Bunny Wailer
World Music Album: *Santiago,* The Chieftains
Polka Album: *Polka! All Night Long,* Jimmy Sturr
Musical Album for Children: *Dedicated to the One I Love,* Linda Ronstadt; George Massenburg and Linda Ronstadt, producers
Spoken Word Album for Children: *Stellaluna,* David Holt; Virginia Callaway, Steven Heller and David Holt, producers
Spoken Word or Non-Musical Album: *It Takes a Village,* Hillary Rodham Clinton
Spoken Comedy Album: *Rush Limbaugh Is a Big Fat Idiot,* Al Franken
Musical Show Album: *Riverdance,* various artists; Bill Whelan, producer, composer and lyricist
Instrumental Composition: "Manhattan (Island of Lights and Love)," Herbie Hancock and Jean Hancock, composers
Instrumental Composition for a Motion Picture or for Television: *Independence Day,* David Arnold, composer
Song Written Specifically for a Motion Picture or for Television: "Because You Loved Me" (From *Up Close and Personal*), Diane Warren, songwriter
Instrumental Arrangement: "An American Symphony (Mr. Holland's Opus)," Michael Kamen, arranger
Instrumental Arrangement With Accompanying Vocal(s): "When I Fall in Love," Alan Broadbent, David Foster and

Gordon Jenkins, arrangers
Producer of the Year Kenneth "Babyface" Edmonds
Classical Engineered Recording: *Copland: Dance Symphony; Short Symphony; Organ Symphony, Etc.,* William Hoekstra and Lawrence Rock, engineers
Classical Producer of the Year: Joanna Nickrenz
Classical Album: *Corigliano: Of Rage and Remembrance (Symphony No. 1, etc.),* Leonard Slatkin, conductor; Joanna Nickrenz, producer; various artists
Orchestral: *Prokofiev: Romeo and Juliet (Scenes From the Ballet),* Michael Tilson Thomas, conductor
Opera Recording: *Britten: Peter Grimes,* Richard Hickox, conductor; Philip Langridge, Alan Opie and Janice Watson, principal soloists; Brian Couzens, producer
Choral: "Walton: Belshazzar's Feast," Andrew Litton, conductor; Neville Creed and David Hill, chorus masters
Instrumental Soloist(s) Performance (With Orchestra): *Bartok: The Three Piano Concertos,* Yefim Bronfman, piano
Instrumental Soloist Performance (Without Orchestra): *The Romantic Master (Works of Saint-Saens; Handel, etc.),* Earl Wild, piano
Chamber Music: "Corigliano: String Quartet, etc.," Cleveland Quartet
Small Ensemble Performance (With or Without Conductor): "Boulez:...Explosante-Fixe....," Pierre Boulez, conductor
Classical Vocal: *Opera Arias (Works of Mozart, Wagner, Borodin, etc.),* Bryn Terfel, bass baritone
Classical Contemporary Composition: "Corigliano: String Quartet," John Corigliano, composer
Music Video, Short Form: "Free as A Bird," The Beatles; Joe Pytka, video director
Music Video, Long Form: *The Beatles Anthology,* The Beatles; Geoff Wonfor, video director; Chips Chipperfield, video producer

George Foster Peabody Awards for Broadcasting, 1996

Radio

Radio Smithsonian, presented on Public Radio International: *Black Radio: Telling It Like it Was*
Sound Portraits Productions Inc. for National Public Radio: *Remorse: The 14 Stories of Eric Morse*
WBEZ-FM Chicago: *This American Life*
The American Association for the Advancement of Science, Washington, D.C.: *Kinetic City Super Crew*
Personal Award: Peter Gzowski

Television

WCVB-TV Boston: *Who's Guarding the Guardians*
BBC News, London: *BBC News, London: Newsnight-Afghanistan*
WNBC-TV New York: *Passport to Kill.*
Center for New American Media, Midnight Films, and WETA-TV, Washington, presented on PBS: *Vote for Me: Politics in America*
Home Box Office, Telling Pictures, Channel 4 (U.K.), ZDF-Arte (Germany/France): *The Celluloid Closet*
Frontline/WGBH-TV Boston, Long Bow Group, Inc., and the Independent Television Service: *Frontline: The Gate of Heavenly Peace*
Home Box Office, Creative Thinking International, Ltd: *Paradise Lost: The Child Murders of Robin Hood Hills*
KOMO-TV, Seattle: for Local Programming Excellence, as demonstrated by *War on Children,* and *Earth Agenda: River of Bears, The Return of the Eagle,* and *Lolita: Spirit in the Water*
Frontline/WGBH-TV and Helen Whitney Productions: *Frontline: The Choice '96*
NOVA/WGBH-TV Boston and SVT1-Swedish Television, Bo G

Erikson Productions and Wanngard AB: *Nova: Odyssey of Life*
BBC, London, and WGBH-TV Boston: *People's Century*
Frontline/WGBH-TV Boston, Long Bow Group, Inc., and the Independent Television Service: *The American Experience: The Battle Over Citizen Kane*
KCET Los Angeles and BBC, London in association with The Imperial War Museum: *The Great War and Shaping of the 20th Century*
Turner Original Productions, Survivors of the Shoah Visual History Foundation: *Survivors of the Holocaust*
Ten Thirteen Productions, Twentieth Television in association with Fox Broadcasting Company: *The X-Files*
HBO Sports, New York: *The Journey of the African-American Athlete*
NBC, Wolf Films, in association with Universal Television: *Law and Order*
BBC, London, and A&E Television Networks, New York: *Pride and Prejudice*
Fox, Gracie Films, in association with Twentieth Television: *The Simpsons*
ABC, Steven Bocho Productions: *NYPD Blue*
BBC, London, and WGBH-TV Boston: *Mobil Masterpiece Theater: House of Cards, To Play the King,* and *The Final Cut*
Home Box Office, New York: *How Do You Spell God*
Carlton Television for Channel 4, London: *Wise Up*
ABC, Tomlin, and WagnerTheatricalz, in association with Kurtz & Friends: *Edith Ann's Christmas*
WCCO-TV, Minneapolis: *One to One: Mentoring*
Personal Award: *Bud Greenspan*

Alfred I. du Pont-Columbia University Broadcast News Awards

(For work broadcast between July 1, 1995, and June 30, 1996)
The Alfred I. duPont Awards, administered by Columbia University, recognize excellence in television and radio broadcasting. The awards were announced January 16, 1997.

Gold Baton
Yugoslavia: Death of a Nation (Brian Lapping Associates; BBC and the Discovery Channel)
Silver Batons
Television Awards: *Nightline:* "The State vs. Simpson: The Verdict", "Journey of a Country Doctor" and "Town Meeting: Thou Shalt Not Kill" (ABC); *60 Minutes:* "Punishing Saddam" and "Too Good to Be True" (CBS); *Dateline:* "Class Photo" (NBC); *Frontline:* "Shtetl" (PBS); *Nova:* "Plague Fighters" (PBS)
Major Market Television: WFAA, Dallas, Texas, and Robert Riggs for an investigative report into suspicious payments and commissions between a member of the Dallas Independent School Board and the insurance agent who provided the schools' many insurance and pension policies

Medium Market Television: No award
Small Market Television: KREM-TV, Spokane, Washington, and Tom Grant for investigating a rash of indictments on charges of sexual abuse in the rural area of Wenatchee, Washington
Independent Television Productions: Kirk Simon and Karen Goodman, *Buckminster Fuller: Thinking Out Loud* (PBS)
Cable Television: HBO for its commitment to serious long-form programming as exemplified by *High on Crack Street: Lost Lives in Lowell* and *The Celluloid Closet*
Radio Awards: NPR for Anne Garrels's coverage of the former Soviet Union; Norman Corwin and Mary Beth Kirchner, *Fifty Years After 14 August (NPR);* Radio Smithsonian, *Black Radio: Telling It Like It Was (PRI)*

TV Daytime Emmy Awards, 1997

Outstanding Drama: *General Hospital* (ABC)
Lead Actor in a Drama Series: Justin Deas, *Guiding Light* (CBS)
Lead Actress in a Drama Series: Jess Walton, *The Young and the Restless* (CBS)
Supporting Actor in a Drama Series: Ian Buchanan, *The Bold and the Beautiful* (CBS)
Supporting Actress in a Drama Series: Michelle Stafford, *The Young and the Restless* (CBS)
Younger Actor in a Drama Series: Kevin Mambo, *Guiding Light* (CBS)

Younger Actress in a Drama Series: Sarah Brown, *General Hospital* (ABC)
Outstanding Children's Series: *Reading Rainbow* (PBS)
Outstanding Children's Special: *Elmo Saves Christmas* (PBS)
Outstanding Children's Animated Program: *Animaniacs* (WB)
Outstanding Game Show: *The Price Is Right* (CBS)
Outstanding Game-Show Host: Pat Sajak, *Wheel of Fortune* (syndicated)
Outstanding Talk Show: *The Oprah Winfrey Show*
Outstanding Talk-Show Host: Rosie O'Donnell, *The Rosie O'Donnell Show* (syndicated)

National Book Awards, 1996

Established by Association of American Publishers
(American Book Awards 1980-86. Reverted to original name in 1987.)

Fiction: *Ship Fever and Other Stories*, Andrea Barrett (Norton)
Nonfiction: *An American Requiem: God, My Father and the War That Came Between Us*, James Carroll (Houghton Mifflin)

Poetry: *Scrambled Eggs and Whiskey: Poems 1991-1995*, Hayden Carruth (Copper Canyon Press)

National Book Critics Circle Awards, 1997

Fiction: *Women in Their Beds*, Gina Berriault (Counterpoint)
General Nonfiction: *Bad Land: An American Romance*, Jonathan Raban (Pantheon)
Biography or Autobiography: *Angela's Ashes*, Frank McCourt (Scribner)

Poetry: *Sun Under Wood*, Robert Hass (Ecco Press)
Criticism: *Finding a Form*, William Gass (Knopf)

Newbery, Caldecott, and Other American Library Association Awards for Children's Books, 1997

(For books published in 1996)

1997 Newbery Medal and Honor Books
The Newbery Medal is awarded annually by the American Library Association for the most distinguished contribution to American literature for children.
Newbery Medal for Best Book: *The View From Saturday*, E. L. Konigsburg (Jean Karl/Atheneum)
Newbery Honor Books: *A Girl Named Disaster*, Nancy Farmer (Richard Jackson/Orchard Books); *Moorchild*, Eloise McGraw (Margaret K. McElderry/Simon & Schuster); *The Thief*, Megan Whalen Turner (Greenwillow); *Belle Prater's Boy*, Ruth White (Farrar, Straus & Giroux)
1997 Caldecott Medal and Honor Books
The Caldecott Medal is awarded annually by the American Library Association for the most distinguished American picture book for children.
Caldecott Medal for Best Picture Book: *Golem*, illustrated and

written by David Wisniewski (Clarion/Houghton Mifflin)
Caldecott Honor Books: *Hush! A Thai Lullaby*, illustrated by Holly Meade, written by Minfong Ho (Orchard Books); *Starry Messenger*, illustrated and written by Peter Sis (Frances Foster Books/Farrar, Straus & Giroux); *The Paperboy*, Dav Pilkey (Richard Jackson/Orchard Books); *The Graphic Alphabet*, David Pelletier (Orchard Books)
The Coretta Scott King Award: (author): *SLAM!*, Walter Dean Myers (Scholastic Press); **(illustrator):** *Minty: A Story of Young Harriet Tubman*, Jerry Pinkney (Dial)
The Mildred L. Batchelder Award, for the publisher of the most outstanding book originally published in a foreign language: Farrar Straus Giroux, publisher of *The Friends*, Kazumi Yumoto, translated from the Japanese by Cathy Hirano
Margaret A. Edwards Award for Outstanding Literature for Young Adults: Gary Paulsen, a lifetime achievement award

Winners of Bollingen Prize in Poetry

($5,000 award[1] is given biennially. It is administered by Yale University and the Bollingen Foundation.

1949	Ezra Pound	1967	Robert Penn Warren
1950	Wallace Stevens	1969	John Berryman and Karl Shapiro
1951	John Crowe Ransom	1971	Richard Wilbur and Mona Van Duyn
1952	Marianne Moore	1973	James Merrill
1953	Archibald MacLeish and William Carlos Williams	1975	Archie Randolph Ammons
1954	W. H. Auden	1977	David Ignatow
1955	Léonie Adams and Louise Bogan	1979	W. S. Merwin
1956	Conrad Aiken	1981	Howard Nemerov and May Swenson
1957	Allen Tate	1983	Anthony Hecht and John Hollander
1958	E.E. Cummings	1985	John Ashbery and Fred Chappell
1959	Theodore Roethke	1987	Stanley Kunitz
1960	Delmore Schwartz	1989	Edgar Bowers
1961	Yvor Winters	1991	Laura Riding Jackson and Donald Justice
1962	John Hall Wheelock and Richard Eberhart	1993	Mark Strand
1963	Robert Frost	1995	Kenneth Koch
1965	Horace Gregory	1997	Gary Snyder

1. Beginning 1989 award increased to $10,000. It now stands at $25,000.

Kingsley Tufts Poetry Prize

$50,000 award given to a poet for a book published in the previous year. Established 1992, it is administered by the Claremont (California) Graduate School.

1993	Susan Mitchell, *Rapture*	1996	Deborah Digges, *Rough Music*
1994	Yusef Komunyakaa, *Neon Vernacular*	1997	Campbell McGrath
1995	Thomas Lux, *Split Horizon*		

Poets Laureate of the United States

Robert Penn Warren	1986-1987	Mona Van Duyn	1992-1993
Richard Wilbur	1987-1988	Rita Dove	1993-1995
Howard Nemerov	1988-1990	Robert Hass	1995-1997
Mark Strand	1990-1991	Robert Pinsky	1997-
Joseph Brodsky	1991-1992		

NOTE: The post was established in 1985. Appointment is for a one-year term, but is renewable.

Poets Laureate of England

Edmund Spenser	1591-1599	Laurence Eusden	1718-1730	Alfred Austin	1896-1913
Samuel Daniel	1599-1619	Colley Cibber	1730-1757	Robert Bridges	1913-1930
Ben Jonson	1619-1637	William Whitehead	1757-1785	John Masefield	1930-1967
William Davenant	1638-1668	Thomas Warton	1785-1790	C. Day Lewis	1967-1972
John Dryden[1]	1670-1689	Henry James Pye	1790-1813	Sir John Betjeman	1972-1984
Thomas Shadwell	1689-1692	Robert Southey	1813-1843	Ted Hughes	1984-
Nahum Tate	1692-1715	William Wordsworth	1843-1850		
Nicholas Rowe	1715-1718	Alfred Lord Tennyson	1850-1892		

1. First to bear the title officially. *Source: Encyclopaedia Britannica.*

1997 MacArthur Foundation Awards

Luis Alfaro, 35, performance artist, playwright, and poet; Los Angeles, Calif.

Lee Breuer, 60, playwright; New York, N.Y.

Vija Celmins, 58, painter and printmaker; New York, N.Y.

Eric L. Charnov, 49, theoretical biologist; Summit Park, Utah.

Elouise Cobell, 51, Native American advocate; Blackfeet Indian Reservation, Montana.

Peter Galison, 42, science historian; Cambridge, Mass.

Mark Harrington, 37, AIDS activist; New York, N.Y.

Eva Harris, 31, biologist; San Francisco, Calif.

Michael Kremer, 32, development economist; Cambridge, Mass.

Russell S. Lande, 45, biologist; Eugene, Ore.

Kerry James Marshall, 41, painter; Chicago, Ill.

Nancy A. Moran, 42, evolutionary biologist; Tucson, Ariz.

Han Ong, 29, playwright; New York, N.Y.

Kathleen A. Ross, 56, college president; Toppenish, Wash.

Pamela Samuelson, 48, lawyer; Berkeley, Calif.

Susan A. Stewart, 45, cultural and literary critic; Philadelphia, Pa.

Elizabeth Streb, 47, dancer and choreographer; New York, N.Y.

Trimpin, 45, musician and sculptor; Seattle, Wash.

Loic J.D. Wacquant, 36, sociologist; Berkeley, Calif.

Kara Elizabeth Walker, 27, artist; Providence, R.I.

Davis Foster Wallace, 35, writer; Bloomington, Ill.

Andrew J. Wiles, 44, mathematician; Princeton, N.J.

Brackette F. Williams, 46, anthropologist; Tucson, Ariz.

Presidential Medal of Freedom

The nation's highest civilian award, the Presidential Medal of Freedom, was established in 1963 by President John F. Kennedy to continue and expand presidential recognition of meritorious service which, since 1945, had been granted as the Medal of Freedom.

Awarded by President Clinton

1993*	Arthur Ashe, Jr. (athlete, tennis)
1993	William J. Brennan, Jr. (jurist)
1993	Marjory Stoneman Douglas (conservationist)
1993	J. William Fulbright (public servant)
1993*	Thurgood Marshall (jurist)
1993	General Colin L. Powell [1] (soldier)
1993*	Joseph L. Raugh, Jr. (civil rights and labor activist)
1993	Martha Raye (entertainer)
1993	John Minor Wisdom (public servant)
1994	Herbert Block (cartoonist)
1994*	Cesar Chavez (labor leader)
1994	Arthur Flemming (government servant)
1994	James Grant (Executive Director, UNICEF)
1994	Dorothy Height (civil rights leader)
1994	Barbara Jordan (public servant)
1994	Lane Kirkland (labor leader)
1994	Robert H. Michel (public servant)
1994	R. Sargent Shriver (government servant)
1995	Peggy Charren (children's television advocate)
1995	William Thaddeus Coleman, Jr. (public servant and civil rights advocate)
1995	Joan Ganz Cooney (children's television advocate)
1995	John Hope Franklin (historian)
1995	A. Leon Higginbotham, Jr. (jurist and civil rights advocate)

1995	Frank M. Johnson, Jr. (jurist)
1995	C. Everett Koop (public health worker)
1995	Gaylord A. Nelson (public servant and conservationist)
1995	Walter P. Reuther (labor leader)
1995	James W. Rouse (urban planner)
1995*	William C. Velasquez (voting rights advocate)
1995	Lew R. Wasserman (media executive)
1996	James Scott Brady (gun control advocate)
1996	Joseph Cardinal Bernadin (Catholic leader)
1996	Millard D. Fuller (founder, Habitat for Humanity)
1996	David Alan Hamburg (physician and children's advocate)
1996	John H. Johnson (founder, *Ebony* and *Jet*)
1996	Eugene M. Lang (founder, "I Have a Dream" Foundation)
1996	Jan Nowak-Jezioranski (WWII Polish resistence fighter)
1996	Antonia Pantoja (Puerto Rican educational and economic advocate)
1996	Rosa Parks (civil rights leader)
1996	Ginetta Sagan (advocate for political prisoners)
1996	Morris Udall (public servant)
1997	Robert Dole (public servant)
1997	William J. Perry (soldier)

1. With Distinction. NOTE: An asterisk following a year denotes a posthumous award.

Enrico Fermi Award

Named in honor of Enrico Fermi, the atomic pioneer, the $100,000 award is given in recognition of "exceptional and altogether outstanding" scientific and technical achievement in atomic energy. Awarded by the President, it is the U.S. government's oldest science and technology award.

1954	Enrico Fermi
1956	John von Neumann
1957	Ernest O. Lawrence
1958	Eugene P. Wigner
1959	Glenn T. Seaborg
1961	Hans A. Bethe
1962	Edward Teller
1963	J. Robert Oppenheimer
1964	Hyman G. Rickover
1966	Otto Hahn, Lise Meitner, and Fritz Strassman
1968	John A. Wheeler
1969	Walter H. Zinn
1970	Norris E. Bradbury
1971	Shields Warren and Stafford L. Warren
1972	Manson Benedict
1976	William L. Russell
1978	Harold M. Agnew and Wolfgang K.H. Panofsky
1980	Alvin M. Weinberg and Rudolf E. Peirls
1981	W. Bennett Lewis

1982	Herbert Anderson and Seth Neddermeyer
1983	Alexander Hollaender and John Lawrence
1984	Robert R. Wilson and Georges Vendryès
1985	Norman C. Rasmussen and Marshall N. Rosenblath
1986	Ernest D. Courant and M. Stanley Livingston
1987	Luis W. Alvarez and Gerald F. Tape
1988	Richard B. Setlow and Victor F. Weisskopf
1989	Award not given
1990	George A. Cowan and Robley D. Evans
1991	Award not given
1992	Leon M. Lederman, Harold Brown, and John S. Foster, Jr.
1993	Freeman J. Dyson and Liane B. Russell
1994	Award not given
1995	Ugo Fano and Martin Kamen
1996	Richard Garwin, Mortimer Elkind, and H. Rodney Withers

Fields Medal Winners

Awarded since 1936 by the International Congress of Mathematicians in Toronto to recognize outstanding mathematics achievement.

1990	Vladimir Drinfeld (Phys. Inst. Kharkov), Vaughan Jones (University of California, Berkeley), Shigefumi Mori (University of Kyoto), and Edward Witten (Institute for Advanced Study, Princeton)
1994	Pierre-Louis Lions (Université de Paris-Dauphine), Jean-Christophe Yoccoz (Université de Paris-Sud), Jean Bourgain (Institute for Advanced Study, Princeton), and Efim Zelmanov (University of Wisconsin)

Recipients of Kennedy Center Honors

1978 Marian Anderson (contralto), Fred Astaire (dancer-actor), Richard Rodgers (Broadway composer), Arthur Rubinstein (pianist), George Balanchine (choreographer).

1979 Ella Fitzgerald (jazz singer), Henry Fonda (actor), Martha Graham (choreographer), Tennessee Williams (playwright), Aaron Copland (composer).

1980 James Cagney (actor), Leonard Bernstein (composer-conductor), Agnes de Mille (choreographer), Lynn Fontanne (actress), Leontyne Price (soprano).

1981 Count Basie (jazz composer-pianist), Cary Grant (actor), Helen Hayes (actress), Jerome Robbins (choreographer), Rudolf Serkin (pianist).

1982 George Abbott (Broadway producer), Lillian Gish (actress), Benny Goodman (jazz clarinetist), Gene Kelly (dancer-actor), Eugene Ormandy (conductor).

1983 Katherine Dunham (dancer-choreographer), Elia Kazan (director-author), James Stewart (actor), Virgil Thomson (music critic-composer), Frank Sinatra (singer).

1984 Lena Horne (singer), Danny Kaye (comedian-actor), Gian Carlo Menotti (composer), Arthur Miller (playwright), Isaac Stern (violinist).

1985 Merce Cunningham (dancer-choreographer), Irene Dunne (actress), Bob Hope (comedian), Alan Jay Lerner (lyricist-playwright), Frederick Loewe (composer), Beverly Sills (soprano).

1986 Lucille Ball (comedienne), Ray Charles (musician), Yehudi Menuhin (violinist), Antony Tudor (choreographer), Hume Cronyn and Jessica Tandy (husband-and-wife acting team).

1987 Perry Como (singer), Bette Davis (actress), Sammy Davis Jr. (entertainer), Nathan Milstein (violinist), Alwin Nikolais (choreographer).

1988 Alvin Ailey (choreographer), George Burns (comedian-actor), Myrna Loy (actress), Alexander Schneider (violinist), Roger L. Stevens (theatrical producer and the Kennedy Center's founding chairman).

1989 Harry Belafonte (singer-actor), Claudette Colbert (actress), Alexandra Danilova (ballerina), Mary Martin (actress), William Schuman (composer)

1990 Dizzy Gillespie (jazz trumpeter), Katharine Hepburn (actress), Risë Stevens (mezzo-soprano), Jule Styne (composer), Billy Wilder (director)

1991 Roy Acuff (country songwriter and singer), Betty Comden and Adolph Green (co-authors of books and lyrics of musicals), the brothers Fayard and Harold Nicholas (dancers), Gregory Peck (actor), Robert Shaw (choral director).

1992 Lionel Hampton (jazz musician), Paul Newman (actor), Joanne Woodward (actress), Ginger Rogers (dancer-actress), Mstislav Rostropovich (cellist-conductor), Paul Taylor (choreographer).

1993 Johnny Carson (talk show host), Arthur Mitchell (dancer and choreographer), Georg Solti (conductor), Stephen Sondheim (composer and lyricist), Marion Williams (gospel singer).

1994 Kirk Douglas (actor), Aretha Franklin (singer), Morton Gould (composer), Harold Prince (producer and director), Pete Seeger (folk singer).

1995 Jacques D'Amboise (choreographer), Marilyn Horne (mezzo soprano), B.B. King (blues singer), Sidney Poitier (actor), Neil Simon (playwright).

1996 Edward Albee (playwright), Benny Carter (jazz musician), Johnny Cash (musician), Jack Lemmon (actor), Maria Tallchief (ballerina).

The Spingarn Medal

The Spingarn Medal is awarded annually by the National Association for the Advancement of Colored People (NAACP) for outstanding achievement by a black American.

1915	Ernest E. Judd	1944	Charles Drew	1971	Leon Howard Sullivan
1916	Charles Young	1945	Paul Robeson	1972	Gordon Parks
1917	Harry T. Burleigh	1946	Thurgood Marshall	1973	Wilson C. Riles
1918	William Stanley Braithwaite	1947	Percy Julian	1974	Damon Keith
1919	Archibald H. Grimke	1948	Channing H. Tobias	1975	Hank Aaron
1920	W.E.B. Du Bois	1949	Ralph J. Bunche	1976	Alvin Ailey
1921	Charles S. Gilpin	1950	Charles Hamilton Houston	1977	Alex Haley
1922	Mary B. Talbert	1951	Mabel Keaton Staupers	1978	Andrew Young
1923	George Washington Carver	1952	Harry T. Moore	1979	Rosa L. Parks
1924	Roland Hayes	1953	Paul R. Williams	1980	Rayford W. Logan
1925	James Weldon Johnson	1954	Theodore K. Lawless	1981	Coleman Young
1926	Carter G. Woodson	1955	Carl Murphy	1982	Benjamin E. Mays
1927	Anthony Overton	1956	Jackie Robinson	1983	Lena Horne
1928	Chalres W. Chesnutt	1957	Martin Luther King, Jr.	1984	Tom Bradley
1929	Mordecai Wyatt Johnson	1958	Daisy Bates and the Little Rock Nine	1985	Bill Cosby
1930	Henry A. Hunt			1986	Benjamin L. Hooks
1931	Richard Berry Harrison	1959	Edward Kennedy (Duke) Ellington	1987	Percy Ellis Sutton
1932	Robert Russa Moton			1988	Frederick Douglass Patterson
1933	Max Yergan	1960	Langston Hughes		
1934	William T.B. Williams	1961	Kenneth B. Clark	1989	Jesse Jackson
1935	Mary McLeod Bethune	1962	Robert C. Weaver	1990	L. Douglas Wilder
1936	John Hope	1963	Medgar Evers	1991	Colin T. Powell
1937	Walter White	1964	Roy Wilkins	1992	Barbara Jordan
1938	No award	1965	Leontyne Price	1993	Dorothy Irene Height
1939	Marian Anderson	1966	John H. Johnson	1994	Maya Angelou
1940	Louis T. Wright	1967	Edward W. Brooke III	1995	John Hope Franklin
1941	Richard Wright	1968	Sammy Davis, Jr.	1996	A. Leon Higginbotham, Jr.
1942	A. Philip Randolph	1969	Clarence M. Mitchell, Jr.	1997	Carl Rowan
1943	William H. Hastie	1970	Jacob Lawrence		

Entertainment & Culture

U.S. Symphony Orchestras and Their Music Directors

(With expenses over $1,050,000)

American Composers Orchestra: Dennis Russell Davies
American Symphony Orchestra: Leon Botstein
Atlanta Symphony: Yoel Levi
Austin Symphony: Sung Kwak
Baltimore Symphony: David Zinman
Baton Rouge Symphony: James Paul
Boston Symphony: Seiji Ozawa
Brooklyn Philharmonic: Robert Spano
Buffalo Philharmonic: Maximiano Valdes
Cedar Rapids Symphony: Christian Tiemeyer
Charleston Symphony: David Stahl
Charlotte Symphony: Peter McCoppin
Chattanooga Symphony & Opera Assn.: Robert Bernhardt
Chicago Symphony: Daniel Barenboim
Cincinnati Symphony: Jesus Lopez-Cobos
Cleveland Orchestra: Christoph von Dohnanyi
Colorado Springs Symphony: Yaacov Bergman[5]
Colorado Symphony (Denver): Marin Alsop
Columbus Symphony: Alessandro Siciliani
Dallas Symphony: Andrew Litton
Dayton Philharmonic: Neal Gittleman
Delaware Symphony: Stephen Gunzenhauser
Detroit Symphony: Neeme Jarvi
Florida Orchestra: Jahja Ling
Florida Philharmonic Orchestra: James Judd
Florida Symphonic Pops: Dr. Crafton Beck[3]
Florida West Coast Symphony Orchestra: Paul C. Wolfe[3]
Fort Wayne Philharmonic: Edvard Tchivzhel
Fort Worth Symphony: John Giordano
Grand Rapids Symphony: Catherine Comet
Grant Park Symphony (Chicago): Hugh Wolff[2]
Hartford Symphony: Michael Lankester
Honolulu Symphony Society: Donald Johanos
Houston Symphony: Christopher Eschenbach
Hudson Valley Philharmonic (Poughkeepsie): Randall Craig Fleischer
Indianapolis Symphony: Raymond Leppard
Jacksonville Symphony: Roger Nierenberg
Kansas City Symphony: William McGlaughlin
Knoxville Symphony: Kirk Trevor
Long Beach Symphony: JoAnn Falletta
Long Island Philharmonic: David Lockington
Los Angeles Chamber Orchestra: Christof Perick[2]
Los Angeles Philharmonic: Esa-Pekka Salonen
Louisville Orchestra: Max Bragado-Darman[4]
Memphis Symphony: Alan Balter
Milwaukee Symphony Orchestra: Andreas Delfs[5]
Minnesota Orchestra: Eiji Oue

Mississippi Symphony: Colman Pearce
Music of the Baroque: Thomas S. Wikman
Naples Philharmonic: Christopher Seaman
Nashville Symphony: Kenneth D. Schermerhorn
National Symphony (D.C.): Leonard Slatkin[5]
New Haven Symphony: Michael Palmer
New Jersey Symphony: Zdenek Macal[1]
New Mexico Symphony: David Lockington
New West Symphony: Boris Brott[3]
New World Symphony (Fla.): Michael Tilson Thomas[1]
New York Chamber Symphony of the 92nd St. Y: Gerard Schwarz
New York Philharmonic: Kurt Masur
New York Pops: Skitch Henderson
North Carolina Symphony: Gerhardt Zimmermann
Ohio Chamber Orchestra: David Lockington
Oklahoma City Philharmonic: Joel A. Levine
Omaha Symphony: Victor Yampolsky[1]
Oregon Symphony: James DePreist
Pacific Symphony (Calif.): Carl St. Clair
Philadelphia Orchestra: Wolfgang Sawallisch
Philharmonia Baroque Orchestra: Nicholas McGegan
Phoenix Symphony: James Sedares
Pittsburgh Symphony Orchestra: Mariss Jansons[5]
Portland Symphony: Toshiyuki Shimada
Puerto Rico Symphony: Eugene Kohn[6]
Rhode Island Philharmonic: Larry Rachleff
Richmond Symphony: George Manahan
Rochester Philharmonic: Robert Bernhardt[2]
St. Louis Symphony: Hans Vonk
St. Paul Chamber Orchestra: Hugh Wolff
San Antonio Symphony: Christopher Wilkins
San Francisco Symphony: Michael Tilson Thomas
San Jose Symphony: Leonid Grin
Santa Barbara Symphony Orchestra: Gisele Ben-Dor
Savannah Symphony: Philp B. Greenberg
Seattle Symphony: Gerard Schwarz
Shreveport Symphony: Dennis Simons
Spokane Symphony: Fabio Mechetti
Springfield Symphony (Mass.): Mark Russell Smith
Syracuse Symphony: Fabio Mechetti
Toledo Symphony: Andrew Massey
Tucson Symphony: George Hanson
Tulsa Philharmonic: Bernard Rubenstein
Utah Symphony: Joseph Silverstein
Virginia Symphony: JoAnn Falletta
West Virginia Symphony: Thomas B. Conlin[1]
Wichita Symphony: Zuohuang Chen
Winston-Salem Symphony Assn.: Peter J. Perret

1. Artistic Director. 2. Principal conductor. 3. Conductor. 4. Artistic Adviser. 5. Music Director Designate. 6. Music conductor. 7. Resident conductor. *Source:* American Symphony Orchestra League.

U.S. Opera Companies

(Budgets $2,000,000 and over)

American Musical Theatre of San Jose (Calif.), Dianna Schuster, Art. Dir.

Arizona Opera Company (Tucson), Glynn Ross, Gen. Dir.

Aspen Opera Theater Center (Colo.), Robert Harth, Pres. & CEO

Atlanta Opera, The (Ga.), William Fred Scott, Art. Dir.

Austin Lyric Opera (Tex.), Joseph McClain, Gen. Dir.

Baltimore Opera Company (Md.), Michael Harrison, Gen. Dir.

Boston Lyric Opera Company (Mass.), Janice Mancini Del Sesto, Gen. Dir.

Central City Opera House Association (Colo.), Daniel R. Rule, Gen. Mgr.

Cincinnati Opera Association (Ohio), James de Blasis, Art. Dir.

Civic Light Opera (Pittsburgh), Charles Gray, Exec. Dir.

Cleveland Opera (Ohio), David Bamberger, Gen. Dir.

Dallas Opera, The (Tex.), Plato S. Karayanis, Gen. Dir.

Florentine Opera Company (Milwaukee), Dennis W. Hanthorn, Gen. Dir.

Florida Grand Opera (Miami), Robert M. Heuer, Gen. Mgr. & CEO.

Gimmerglass Opera (Cooperstown, N.Y.), Paul Kellogg, Art. Dir.

Goodspeed Opera House (East Haddam, Conn.), Michael Price, Exec. Dir.

Hawaii Opera Theatre (Honolulu), J. Mario Ramos, Gen. & Art. Dir.

Houston Grand Opera Association (Tex.), R. David Gockley, Gen. Dir.

Kentucky Opera (Louisville), Thomson Smillie, Gen. Dir.

Long Beach Civic Light Opera (Calif.), J. Phillip Keene III, Exec. Dir.

Los Angeles Music Center Opera (Calif.), Peter Hemmings, Gen. Dir.

Lyric Opera of Chicago (Ill.), Ardis Krainik, Gen. Dir.

Lyric Opera of Kansas City (Mo.), Russell Patterson, Gen. Art. Dir.

Metro Lyric Opera (Allenhurst, N.J.), Era M. Tognoli, Gen. & Art. Dir.

Metropolitan Opera Association, (N.Y.), James Levine, Art. Dir.

Michigan Opera Theatre (Detroit), David DiChiera, Gen. Dir.

Minnesota Opera, The (Minneapolis), Kevin Smith, Pres.& Gen. Dir.

New York City Opera (N.Y.), Paul Kellogg, Gen. Dir.

New York City Opera National Company (N.Y.), Clifford Kellab, Tour Coord.

Ohio Light Opera (Wooster), James Stuart, Art. Dir.

Opera Colorado (Denver), Nathaniel Merrill, Pres.& Gen. Dir.

Opera Company of Philadelphia (Pa.), Robert B. Driver, Gen. Dir.

Opera Pacific (Irvine, Calif.), David DiChiera, Gen. Dir.

Opera Theater Center (Aspen), Robert Hirth, President & CEO.

Opera Theatre of St. Louis (Mo.), Charles MacKay, Gen. Dir.

Orlando Opera Company Inc. (Fla.), Robert Swedberg, Gen. Dir.

Palm Beach Opera Inc. (Fla.), Herbert P. Benn, Gen. Dir.

Pittsburgh Opera, Inc. (Pa.), Tito Capobianco, Gen. Dir.

Portland Opera Association (Ore.), Robert Bailey, Gen. Dir.

San Diego Civic Light Opera Association (Calif.), Leon Drew, Gen. Mgr.

San Diego Opera (Calif.), Ian D. Campbell, Gen. Dir.

San Francisco Opera (Calif.), Lotfi Mansouri, Gen. Dir.

San Francisco Opera Center (Calif.), Christopher Hahn, Dir.

Santa Barbara Civic Light Opera (Calif.), Paul Iannacone, Exec. Prod.

Santa Fe Opera (N.M.), John Crosby, Gen. Dir.

Sarasota Opera Association (Fla.), Deane Carroll Allyn, Exec. Dir.

Seattle Opera Association (Wash.), Speight Jenkins, Gen. Dir.

Virginia Opera (Norfolk), Peter Mark, Gen. Dir.

Utah Opera Company (Salt Lake City), Anne Ewers, Gen. Dir.

Washington Opera, The (D.C.), Placido Domingo, Art. Dir. Designate

Source: Musical America International Directory of the Performing Arts, 1996 edition.

U.S. Dance Companies

(Budgets $2,500,000 and over)

Alvin Ailey American Dance Theatre (1958): Barbara Hauptman, Exec. Dir.

American Ballet Theatre (1940): Kevin McKenzie, Art. Dir.

Atlanta Ballet Company (1929): Mary Bear Haden, Exec. Dir.

Ballet Florida (1986): Charles Surber, Exec. Dir.

BalletMet Columbus (1978): David Nixon, Art. Dir.

Ballet West (1968[1]): John Hart, Art. Dir.

Boston Ballet (1964): Bruce Marks, Art. Dir.

Cincinnati Ballet (1955): Peter Anastos, Art. Dir.

Cleveland San Jose Ballet (1976): Dennis Nahat, Art. Dir.

Colorado Ballet (1961): Martin Fredmann, Art. Dir.

Merce Cunningham Dance Company (1952): Merce Cunningham, Art. Dir.

Dance Theater of Harlem (1968): Arthur Mitchell, Art. Dir.

Feld Ballet New York (1974): Eliot Feld, Dir.

Martha Graham Dance Company (1927): Ron Protas, Art. Dir.

Houston Ballet (1968): Ben Stevenson, Art. Dir.

Joffrey Ballet of Chicago (1954): Gerald Arpino, Art. Dir.

Los Angeles Ballet (1995[2]): Andrew Deneau, Gen. Dir.

Miami City Ballet (1986): Edward Villella, Art. Dir.

Milwaukee Ballet (1970): Lillian R. Boese, Exec. Dir.

New York City Ballet (1948): Peter Martins, Ballet-Master-in-Chief

Ocheami-Afrikan Dance Company (1978): Kofe Anang, Art. Dir.

Pacific Northwest Ballet (1972): Kent Stowell and Francia Russell, Art. Dirs.

Pittsburgh Ballet Theater (1970): Patricia Wilde, Art. Dir.

San Francisco Ballet (1933): Helgi Tomasson, Art. Dir.

Paul Taylor Dance Company (1954): Paul Taylor, Dir.

Streb/Ringside (1985): Elizabeth Streb, Art. Dir.

Note: Year founded appears in parentheses after name. 1. Prior company founded 1963, name changed to Ballet West in 1968. 2. Originally founded 1954, survived several reincarnations, the most recent of which was begun in 1995. *Source:* Musical America International Directory of the Performing Arts, 1996 edition.

Bestselling Books, 1996

Source: Publishers Weekly

Hardcover Fiction

1. *The Celestine Prophecy*, James Redfield
2. *Primary Colors*, Anonymous
3. *The Horse Whisperer*, Nicholas Evans
4. *The Tenth Insight*, James Redfield
5. *The Runaway Jury*, John Grisham
6. *How Stella Got Her Groove Back*, Terry McMillan
7. *Executive Orders*, Tom Clancy
8. *Absolute Power*, David Balducci
9. *Moonlight Becomes You*, Mary Higgins Clark
10. *Gods and Generals*, Jeff Shaara
10. *The Deep End of the Ocean*, Jacquelyn Mitchard

Hardcover Nonfiction

1. *Men Are from Mars, Women Are from Venus*, John Gray
2. *The Zone*, Barry Sears with Bill Lawren
3. *The Seven Spiritual Laws of Success*, Deepak Chopra
4. *Simple Abundance*, Sarah Ban Breathnach
5. *Emotional Intelligence*, Daniel Goleman
6. *Midnight in the Garden of Good and Evil*, John Berendt
7. *Undaunted Courage*, Stephen E. Ambrose
8. *The Dilbert Principle*, Scott Adams
9. *Rush Limbaugh Is a Big Fat Idiot*, Al Franken
10. *In Contempt*, Christopher A. Darden with Jess Walter

Trade Paperbacks

1. *Chicken Soup for the Soul*, Jack Canfield and Mark Hansen, eds.
2. *Snow Falling on Cedars*, David Guterson
3. *Reviving Ophelia*, Mary Pipher
4. *Seven Habits of Highly Effective People*, Stephen R. Covey
5. *How the Irish Saved Civilization*, Thomas Cahill
6. *What to Expect When You're Expecting*, A. Eisenberg, H. Murkoff, and S. Hathaway
7. *Dr. Atkins' New Diet Revolution*, Dr. Robert C. Atkins
8. *Ten Stupid Things Women Do to Mess Up Their Lives*, Laura Schlessinger
9. *The Liars' Club*, Mary Karr
10. *A 3rd Serving of Chicken Soup for the Soul*, Jack Canfield and Mark Hansen, eds.

Mass Market Paperbacks

1. *The Rainmaker*, John Grisham
2. *The Two Dead Girls (Green Mile #1)*, Stephen King
3. *Beach Music*, Pat Conroy
4. *The Mouse on the Mile (Green Mile #2)*, Stephen King
5. *Sleepers*, Lorenzo Carcaterra
6. *The Lost World*, Michael Crichton

All-Time Children's Bestselling Books

From the date of publication (in parentheses) through the end of 1995.

Source: Publishers Weekly

Hardcovers

1. *The Poky Little Puppy*, Janette Sebring Lowrey (1942)
2. *The Tale of Peter Rabbit*, Beatrix Potter (1902)
3. *Tootle*, Gertrude Crampton (1945)
4. *Saggy Baggy Elephant*, Kathryn and Byron Jackson (1955)
5. *Scuffy the Tugboat*, Gertrude Crampton (1955)
6. *Pat the Bunny*, Dorothy Kunhardt (1940)
7. *Green Eggs and Ham*, Dr. Seuss (1960)
8. *The Cat in the Hat*, Dr. Seuss (1957)
9. *The Littlest Angel*, Charles Tazewell (1946)
10. *One Fish, Two Fish, Red Fish, Blue Fish*, Dr. Seuss (1960)

Paperbacks

1. *Charlotte's Web*, E.B. White, illus. by Garth Williams (1974)
2. *The Outsiders*, S.E. Hinton (1968)
3. *Tales of a Fourth Grade Nothing*, Judy Blume (1976)
4. *Shane*, Jack Schaeffer (1983)
5. *Are You There, God? It's Me, Margaret*, Judy Blume (1972)
6. *Where the Red Fern Grows*, Wilson Rawls (1974)
7. *A Wrinkle in Time*, Madeleine L'Engle (1973)
8. *Island of the Blue Dolphins*, Scott O'Dell (1971)
9. *Little House on the Prairie*, Laura Ingalls Wilder, illus. by Garth Williams (1971)
10. *Little House in the Big Woods*, Laura Ingalls Wilder, illus. by Garth Williams (1971)

Newbery Medal Winners

1922–1997

1922	*The Story of Mankind*, Hendrick Willem Van Loon	1933	*Young Fu of the Upper Yangtze*, Elizabeth Lewis
1923	*The Voyages of Dr. Doolittle*, Hugh A. Lofting	1934	*Invincible Louisa*, Cornelia Meigs
1924	*The Dark Frigate*, Charles Boardman Hawes	1935	*Dobry*, Monica Shannon
1925	*Tales from Silver Lands*, Charles Joseph Finger	1936	*Caddie Woodlawn*, Carol Ryrie Brink
1926	*Shen of the Sea*, Arthur Bowie Chrisman	1937	*Roller Skates*, Ruth Sawyer
1927	*Smoky, the Cowhorse*, Will James	1938	*The White Stag*, Kate Seredy
1928	*Gay-neck, the Story of a Pigeon*, Mukerji Dhan Gopal	1939	*Thimble Summer*, Elizabeth Enright
1929	*The Trumpeter of Krakow*, Eric P. Kelly	1940	*Daniel Boone*, James Henry Daugherty
1930	*Hitty, Her First Hundred Years*, Rachel Field	1941	*Call it Courage*, Armstrong Sperry
1931	*The Cat Who Went to Heaven*, Elizabeth Jane Coatsworth	1942	*The Matchlock Gun*, Walter Dumax Edmonds
1932	*Waterless Mountain*, Laura Adams Armer	1943	*Adam of the Road*, Elizabeth Janet
		1944	*Johnny Tremaine*, Esther Forbes
		1945	*Rabbit Hill*, Robert Lawson

1946 *Strawberry Girl*, Lois Lenski
1947 *Miss Hickory*, Carolyn Sherwin Bailey
1948 *The Twenty-One Balloons*, William Pene Du Bois
1949 *King of the Wind*, Marguerite Henry
1950 *The Door in the Wall*, Marguerite De Angeli
1951 *Amos Fortune, Free Man*, Elizabeth Yates
1952 *Ginger Pye*, Eleanor Estes
1953 *Secret of the Andes*, Ann Nolan Clark
1954 *. . . and Now Miguel*, Joseph Krumgold
1955 *The Wheel on the School*, Meindert DeJong
1956 *Carry On, Mr. Bowditch*, Jean Lee Latham
1957 *Miracles on Maple Hill*, Virginia Eggertsen Sorensen
1958 *Rifles for Watie*, Harold Keith
1959 *The Witch of Blackbird Pond*, Elizabeth George Speare
1960 *Onion John*, Joseph Krumgold
1961 *Island of the Blue Dolphin*, Scott O'Dell
1962 *The Bronze Bow*, Elizabeth George Speare
1963 *A Wrinkle in Time*, Madeleine L'Engle
1964 *It's Like This, Cat*, Emily Neville
1965 *Shadow of a Bull*, Maia Wojciechowska
1966 *I, Juan de Pareja*, Elizabeth Borton de Trevino
1967 *Up a Road Slowly*, Irene Hunt
1968 *From the Mixed Up Files of Mrs. Basil E. Frankweiler*
1969 *The High King*, Lloyd Alexander
1970 *Sounder*, William H. Armstrong
1971 *Summer of the Swans*, Betsy Cromer Byars

1972 *Mrs. Frisby and the Rats of NIMH*, Robert C. O'Brien
1973 *Julie of the Wolves*, Jean Craighead George
1974 *The Slave Dancer*, Paula Fox
1975 *M.C. Higgins, the Great*, Virginia Hamilton
1976 *The Grey King*, Susan Cooper
1977 *Roll of Thunder, Hear My Cry*, Mildred D. Taylor
1978 *Bridge to Terabithia*, Katherine Paterson
1979 *The Westing Game*, Ellen Raskin
1980 *A Gathering of Days: A New England Girl's Journal, 1830–32*, Joan W. Blos
1981 *Jackob Have I Loved*, Katherine Paterson
1982 *A Visit to William Blake's Inn: Poems for Innocent and Experienced Travelers*, Nancy Willard
1983 *Dicey's Song*, Cynthia Voigt
1984 *Dear Mr. Henshaw*, Beverly Cleary
1985 *The Hero and the Crown*, Robin McKinley
1986 *Sarah, Plain and Tall*, Patricia MacLachlan
1987 *The Whipping Boy*, Sid Fleischman
1988 *Lincoln: A Photobiography*, Russell Freedman
1989 *Joyful Noise: Poems for Two Voices*, Paul Fleischman
1990 *Number the Stars*, Lois Lowry
1991 *Maniac Magee: a Novel*, Jerry Spinelli
1992 *Shiloh*, Phyllis Reynolds
1993 *Missing May*, Cynthia Rylant
1994 *The Giver*, Lois Lowry
1995 *Walk Two Moons*, Sharon Creech
1996 *The Midwife's Apprentice*, Karen Cushman
1997 *The View from Saturday*, E.L. Konigsburg

Caldecott Medal Winners

1938–1997

1938 *Animals of the Bible, a Picture Book*, text selected by Helen Dean Fish, illustrated by Dorothy P. Lathrop
1939 *Mei Li*, written and illustrated by Thomas Handforth
1940 *Abraham Lincoln*, written and illustrated by Ingrid and Edgar Parin d'Aulaire
1941 *They Were Strong and Good*, written and illustrated by Robert Larson
1942 *Make Way for Ducklings*, written and illustrated by Robert McCloskey
1943 *The Little House*, written and illustrated by Virginia Lee Burton
1944 *Many Moons*, written by James Thurber, illustrated by Louis Slobodkin
1945 *Prayer for a Child*, written by Elizabeth Orton Jones
1946 *The Rooster Crows*
1947 *The Little Island*, written by Maud Fuller Petersham, illustrated by Maud and Miska Petersham
1948 *White Snow, Bright Snow*, written by Alvin Tresselt, illustrated by Roger Duvoisin
1949 *The Big Snow*, written and illustrated by Berta and Elmer Hader
1950 *Song of the Swallows*, written and illustrated by Leo Politi
1951 *The Egg Tree*, written and illustrated by Katherine Milhouse
1952 *Finders Keepers*, written by William Lipkind, illustrated by Nicolas Mordivinoff
1953 *The Biggest Bear*, written and illustrated by Lynd Ward
1954 *Madeline's Rescue*, written and illustrated by Ludwig Bemelmans
1955 *Cinderella, or The Little Glass Slipper*, translated and illustrated by Marcia Brown
1956 *Frog Went A-Courtin'*, retold by John Langstaff,

illustrated by Feodor Rojankovsky
1957 *A Tree is Nice*, written by Janice May Udry, illustrated by Marc Simont
1958 *Time of Wonder*, written and illustrated by Robert McCloskey
1959 *Chanticleer and the Fox*, adapted and illustrated by Barbara Cooney
1960 *Nine Days to Christmas*, written by Marie Hall Ets and Aurora Labastida, illustrated by Marie Hall Ets
1961 *Baboushka and the Three Kings*, written by Ruth Robbins, illustrated by Nicolas Sidjakov
1962 *Once a Mouse*, retold and illustrated by Marcia Brown
1963 *The Snowy Day*, written and illustrated by Ezra Jack Keats
1964 *Where the Wild Things Are*, written and illustrated by Maurice Sendak
1965 *May I Bring a Friend*, written by Beatrice Schenk De Reniers, illustrated by Beni Montresor
1966 *Always Room for One More*, written by Sorche Nic Leodhas, illustrated by Nonny Hogrogian
1967 *Sam, Bangs and Moonshine*, written and illustrated by Evaline Ness
1968 *Drummer Hoff*, written by Barbara Emberley, illustrated by Ed Emberley
1969 *The Fool of the World and The Flying Ship*, retold by Arthur Ransome, illustrated by Uri Shulevitz
1970 *Sylvester and the Magic Pebble*, written and illustrated by William Steig
1971 *A Story, A Story: An African Tale*, retold and illustrated by Gail E. Haley
1972 *One Fine Day*, written and illustrated by Nonny Hogrogian
1973 *The Funny Little Woman*, retold by Arlene Mosel, illustrated by Blair Lent

1974 *Duffy and the Devil*, retold by Harve Zemach, illustrated by Margo Zemach

1975 *Arrow to the Sun: A Pueblo Indian Tale*, adapted and illustrated by Gerald H. McDermott

1976 *Why Mosquitos Buzz in People's Ears (An African Tale)*, retold by Verna Aardema, illustrated by Leo and Diane Dillon

1977 *Ashanti to Zulu: African Traditions*, written by Margaret Musgrove, illustrated by Leo and Diane Dillon

1978 *Noah's Ark*, written and illustrated by Peter Spier

1979 *The Girl Who Loved Wild Horses*, written and illustrated by Paul Goble

1980 *Ox-Cart Man*, written by Donald Hall, illustrated by Barbara Cooney

1981 *Fables*, written and illustrated by Arnold Lobel

1982 *Jumanji*, written and illustrated by Chris Van Allsburg

1983 *Shadow*, translated and illustrated by Marcia Brown

1984 *The Glorious Flight Across the Channel with Louise Bleriot*, written and illustrated by Alice and Martin Provensen

1985 *St. George and the Dragon*, retold by Margaret Hodges, illustrated by Trini Shart Hyman

1986 *The Polar Express*, written and illustrated by Chris Van Allsburg

1987 *Hey Al*, written by Arthur Yorinks, illustrated by Richard Egielski

1988 *Owl Moon*, written by Jane Yolen, illustrated by John Schoenherr

1989 *Song and Dance Man*, written by Karen Ackerman, illustrated by Stephen Gammell

1990 *Lon Po Po: A Red-Riding Hood Story from China*, translated and illustrated by Ed Young

1991 *Black & White*, written and illustrated by David Macaulay

1992 *Tuesday*, written and illustrated by David Wiesner

1993 *Mirette on the High Wire*, written and illustrated by Emily Arnold McCully

1994 *Grandfather's Journey*, written and illustrated by Allen Say

1995 *Smoky Night*, written by Eve Bunting, illustrated by David Diaz

1996 *Officer Buckle and Gloria*, written and illustrated by Peggy Rathmann

1997 *Golem*, written and illustrated by David Wisniewski

Major City Public Libraries

City (branches)	Volumes	Circulation	Budget (in millions)	City (branches)	Volumes	Circulation	Budget (in millions)
Akron-Summit County, Ohio (17)	1,087,517	3,571,966	$16.7	Knoxville, Tenn. (16)	719,956	1,966,233	5.6
				Lincoln, Neb. (7)	606,024	2,028,000	4.9
Albuquerque, N.M. (15)	1,534,121	2,913,328	8.1	Long Beach, Calif. (11)	1,093,155	2,459,131	10.9
Annapolis, Md. (15)	1,310,359	5,002,677	11.9	Los Angeles County (88)	6,945,639[7]	15,300,000	57.9
Atlanta-Fulton County (31)	1,960,000	2,704,000	19.5	Louisville, Ky. (16)	1,033,008[2]	3,104,300	11.7
Austin, Tex. (19)	1,450,046	2,433,992	11.6	Madison, Wis. (8)	756,680	2,555,233	7.4
Baltimore (29)	2,600,000	1,518,524	22.8	Memphis, Tenn. (21)	1,720,046	3,737,834	14.2
Baton Rouge, La. (9)	1,100,603	2,465,857	14.2	Miami-Dade County, Fla. (31)	3,983,968	10,667,327	34.8
Birmingham, Ala. (19)	1,039,000	1,701,817	10.5	Milwaukee (12)	2,447,499	3,024,239	19.2
Boston (25)	6,581,736	3,500,000	30.1	Minneapolis (14)	2,114,887	2,651,753	16.9
Buffalo-Erie County, N.Y. (53)	3,600,000[1]	8,827,234	25.0	Nashville-Davidson County, Tenn. (18)	700,171[7]	2,072,921	10.3
Charleston-Kanawna County, W.Va. (8)	612,435	1,040,000	4.8	Newark, N.J. (11)	1,400,000	1,400,000	9.4
Charlotte, N.C. (22)	1,430,257	5,646,750	17.4	New Orleans (15)	953,867	1,116,525	6.3
Chicago (81)	6,465,991[2]	7,839,041	69.2	New York City:			
Cincinnati (41)	4,585,127	12,564,004	42.6	New York Public Library			
Cleveland (27)	3,479,931[5]	5,525,663	41.0	Branches (82)	11,466,261	11,194,409	104.0
Columbus Metropolitan, Ohio (21)	2,384,752	11,862,449	34.1	Research	41,452,558	—	94.0
				Brooklyn Public Library (60)	6,495,084	10,078,269	55.0
Dallas (22)	2,722,736	4,077,655	17.6	Queens Borough Public Library (62)	8,640,540	15,280,937	58.6
Dayton-Montgomery County, Ohio (20)	1,633,332	6,206,420	16.0				
Denver (21)	4,223,938	7,477,619	23.7	Norfolk, Va. (11)	970,112	383,844	3.8
Des Moines, Iowa (5)	611,105	1,370,947	4.5	Oklahoma City-County (12)	871,657	4,168,000	11.8
Detroit (24)	2,746,571	1,594,963	26.5	Omaha, Neb. (9)	728,235	2,289,858	8.9[8]
D.C. (27)	2,163,321[2]	1,803,599	19.7	Philadelphia (52)	7,983,088	6,530,277	38.8
El Paso (10)	1,277,003[3]	1,731,820	6.6[4]	Phoenix, Ariz. (12)	1,764,965	5,686,766	17.5
Erie, Pa. (6)	425,593	1,634,880	3.5	Pittsburgh (20)	2,004,299	3,029,038	18.0
Evansville-Vanderburgh Ind. (7)	803,380	1,432,278	6.2	Portland-Multnomah County, Ore. (14)	1,435,637	7,757,882	24.1
Fairfax County, Va. (19)	2,100,000	9,400,000	19.7	Providence, R.I. (9)	1,004,746	708,405	5.0
Fort Wayne-Allen County, Ind. (14)	3,231,808[5]	4,208,205	15.0	Richmond, Va. (10)	814,723	814,752	3.7
				Rochester, N.Y. (10)	2,000,000	1,582,730	10.6
Fort Worth (10)	2,029,363	4,388,337	7.9	Sacramento, Calif. (23)	1,343,224	3,587,042	16.5
Grand Rapids, Mich. (5)	976,640	1,084,540	6.2	St. Louis (15)	4,895,532	2,196,246	16.5
Greenville City-County, S.C. (11)	957,846	1,891,781	8.5	St. Paul (12)	1,050,555[9]	2,400,918	7.8
Hawaii State Public Library System (49)[6]	3,517,989[2]	7,374,583	20.8	St. Petersburg, Fla. (6)	448,938	1,107,342	3.2
				Salt Lake County, Utah (16)	1,552,750	6,017,265	15.2
				San Antonio (18)	1,681,040	3,450,299	15.9
Houston (34)	4,385,879	5,906,886	27.1	San Diego, Calif. (33)	2,465,162	6,370,488	22.6[11]
Independence, Mo. (29)	2,475,762	6,431,129	20.3	San Francisco, Calif. (26)	2,124,162[7]	4,345,072	36.3
Indianapolis-Marion County (21)	1,714,960	8,275,441	26.5	San Jose, Calif. (18)	1,434,351[10]	5,000,199	31.3
Jackson-Hinds County, Miss. (15)	583,324	820,523	2.9	Seattle (22)	2,414,767[10]	4,580,780	24.5
				Springfield, Mass. (8)	758,092	852,494	5.0
Jacksonville, Fla. (18)	2,687,980	3,693,283	14.3	Tampa, Fla. (17)	2,163,613	3,436,618	15.3
Kansas City, Mo. (9)	2,009,420	2,275,774	12.8	Tucson, Ariz. (19)	1,146,000	4,900,000	13.6

City (branches)	Volumes	Circulation	Budget (in millions)	City (branches)	Volumes	Circulation	Budget (in millions)
Tulsa City-County, Okla. (21)	1,040,574	3,719,407	10.2	Worcester, Mass. (2)	628,820	630,206	3.1
Wichita, Kan. (12)	970,882	1,821,287	4.7	Youngstown-Mahoning County, Ohio (22)	670,880	1,857,432	9.0
*Winston-Salem-Forsyth County, N.C. (9)	400,000	2,100,000	6.0				

1. Includes books and audio material. 2. Book collection only. 3. Includes books, periodicals, records, films, government documents (collection weeded). 4. Budget includes both general and bonded funds. 5. Includes government documents, bound periodicals, bound series. 6. State-wide system. 7. Includes books and audiovisual materials; excludes microforms. 8. Includes benefits, indirect costs, and county funding. 9. Includes books, audiovisual materials, government documents, and musical scores. 10. Includes all library materials. 11. Includes local funds, grants, and capital improvements. *Did not reply to questionnaire with updated information.

Longest Broadway Runs

Show	Dates*	Performances	Show	Dates*	Performances
1. Cats	10/82–present	6,138	14. Man of La Mancha	11/65–6/71	2,329
2. A Chorus Line	10/75–4/90	6,137	15. Abie's Irish Rose	5/22–10/27	2,327
3. Oh, Calcutta!	9/76–8/89	5,962	16. Oklahoma!	3/43–5/48	2,212
4. Les Misérables	3/87–present	4,231	17. Miss Saigon	4/91–present	2,150
5. Phantom of the Opera	1/88–present	3,923	18. Pippin	10/72–6/77	1,944
6. 42nd Street	8/80–1/89	3,485	19. South Pacific	4/49–1/54	1,925
7. Grease	2/72–4/80	3,388	20. Magic Show	5/74–12/78	1,920
8. Fiddler on the Roof	9/64–7/72	3,242	21. Gemini	5/77–9/81	1,819
9. Life With Father	11/39–7/47	3,224	22. Deathtrap	2/78–6/82	1,793
10. Tobacco Road	12/33–5/41	3,182	23. Harvey	11/44–1/49	1,775
11. Hello, Dolly!	1/64–12/70	2,844	24. Dancin'	3/78–6/82	1,774
12. My Fair Lady	3/56–9/62	2,717	25. La Cage Aux Folles	6/83–11/87	1,761
13. Annie	4/77–1/83	2,377			

*as of 6/19/97 Source: League of American Theatres and Producers

Glossary of Art Movements

Abstract Expressionism. American art movement of the 1940s that emphasized form and color within a nonrepresentational framework. Jackson Pollock initiated the revolutionary technique of splattering the paint directly on canvas to achieve the subconscious interpretation of the artist's inner vision of reality.

Art Deco. A 1920s style characterized by setbacks, zigzag forms, and the use of chrome and plastic ornamentation. New York's Chrysler Building is an architectural example of the style.

Art Nouveau. An 1890s style in architecture, graphic arts, and interior decoration characterized by writhing forms, curving lines, and asymmetrical organization. Some critics regard the style as the first stage of modern architecture.

Ashcan School. A group of New York realist artists, formed in 1908, who abandoned decorous subject matter and portrayed the more common as well as the sordid aspects of city life.

Assemblage (Collage). Forms of modern sculpture and painting utilizing readymades, found objects, and pasted fragments to form an abstract composition. Louise Nevelson's boxlike enclosures, each with its own composition of assembled objects, illustrate the style in sculpture. Pablo Picasso developed the technique of cutting and pasting natural or manufactured materials to a painted or unpainted surface.

Barbizon School (Landscape Painting). A group of painters who, around the middle of the 19th century, reacted against classical landscape and advocated a direct study of nature. They were influenced by English and Dutch landscape masters. Theodore Rousseau, one of the principal figures of the group, led the fight for outdoor painting. In this respect, the school was a forerunner of Impressionism.

Baroque. European art and architecture of the 17th and 18th centuries. Giovanni Bernini, a major exponent of the style, believed in the union of the arts of architecture, painting, and sculpture to overwhelm the spectator with ornate and highly dramatized themes. Although the style originated in Rome as the instrument of the Church, it spread throughout Europe in such monumental creations as the Palace of Versailles.

Beaux Arts. Elaborate and formal architectural style characterized by symmetry and an abundance of sculptured ornamentation. New York's old Custom House at Bowling Green is an example of the style.

Black or African-American Art. The work of American artists of African descent produced in various styles characterized by a mood of protest and a search for identity and historical roots.

Classicism. A form of art derived from the study of Greek and Roman styles characterized by harmony, balance, and serenity. In contrast, the Romantic Movement gave free rein to the artist's imagination and to the love of the exotic.

Constructivism. A form of sculpture using wood, metal, glass, and modern industrial materials expressing the technological society. The mobiles of Alexander Calder are examples of the movement.

Cubism. Early 20th-century French movement marked by a revolutionary departure from representational art. Pablo Picasso and Georges Bracque penetrated the surface of objects, stressing basic abstract geometric forms that presented the object from many angles simultaneously.

Dada. A product of the turbulent and cynical post-World War I period, this anti-art movement extolled the irrational, the absurd, the nihilistic, and the nonsensical. The reproduction of Mona Lisa adorned with a mustache is a famous example. The movement is regarded as a precursor of Surrealism. Some critics regard HAPPENINGS as a recent development of Dada. This movement incorporates environment and spectators as active and important ingredients in the production of random events.

Expressionism. A 20th-century European art movement that stresses the expression of emotion and the inner vision of the artist rather than the exact representation of nature. Distorted lines and shapes and exaggerated colors are used for emotional impact. Vincent Van Gogh is regarded as the precursor of this movement.

Fauvism. The name "wild beasts" was given to the group of early 20th-century French painters because their work was characterized by distortion and violent colors. Henri Matisse and Georges Rouault were leaders of this group.

Futurism. This early 20th-century movement originating in Italy glorified the machine age and attempted to represent machines and figures in motion. The aesthetics of Futurism affirmed the beauty of technological society.

Genre. This French word meaning "type" now refers to paintings that depict scenes of everyday life without any attempt at idealization. Genre paintings can be found in all ages, but the Dutch productions of peasant and tavern scenes are typical.

Impressionism. Late 19th-century French school dedicated to defining transitory visual impressions painted directly from nature, with light and color of primary importance. If the atmosphere changed, a totally different picture would emerge. It was not the object or event that counted but the visual impression as caught at a certain time of day under a certain light. Claude Monet and Camille Pissarro were leaders of the movement.

Mannerism. A mid-16th-century movement, Italian in origin, although El Greco was a major practitioner of the style. The human figure, distorted and elongated, was the most frequent subject.

Neoclassicism. An 18th-century reaction to the excesses of Baroque and Rococo, this European art movement tried to recreate the art of Greece and Rome

by imitating the ancient classics both in style and subject matter.

Neoimpressionism. A school of painting associated with George Seurat and his followers in late 19th-century France that sought to make Impressionism more precise and formal. They employed a technique of juxtaposing dots of primary colors to achieve brighter secondary colors, with the mixture left to the eye to complete (pointillism).

Op Art. The 1960s movement known as Optical Painting is characterized by geometrical forms that create an optical illusion in which the eye is required to blend the colors at a certain distance.

Pop Art. In this return to representational art, the artist returns to the world of tangible objects in a reaction against abstraction. Materials are drawn from the everyday world of popular culture—comic strips, canned goods, and science fiction.

Realism. A development in mid-19th-century France lead by Gustave Courbet. Its aim was to depict the customs, ideas, and appearances of the time using scenes from everyday life.

Rococo. A French style of interior decoration developed during the reign of Louis XV consisting mainly of asymmetrical arrangements of curves in paneling, porcelain, and gold and silver objects. The characteristics of ornate curves, prettiness, and gaiety can also be found in the painting and sculpture of the period.

Surrealism. A further development of Collage, Cubism, and Dada, this 20th-century movement stresses the weird, the fantastic, and the dreamworld of the subconscious.

Symbolism. As part of a general European movement in the latter part of the 19th century, it was closely allied with Symbolism in literature. It marked a turning away from painting by observation to transforming fact into a symbol of inner experience. Gauguin was an early practitioner.

Top 10 Classical Albums, 1996

1. *Immortal Beloved,* Soundtrack (Sony Classical)
2. *Chant II,* Benedictine Monks of Santo Domingo De Silos (Angel)
3. *Chant,* Benedictine Monks of Santo Domingo De Silos (Angel)
4. *The 3 Tenors in Concert 1994,* Carreras, Domingo, Pavarotti (Mehta) (Atlantic)
5. *In Concert,* Carreras, Domingo, Pavarotti (Mehta) (London)
6. *A Portrait,* Cecilia Bartoli (London)
7. *In Gabriel's Garden,* Wynton Marsalis (Sony Classical)
8. *Adagio,* Berlin Philharmonic (Karajan) (DG)
9. *The Choir,* Anthony Way/Stanislas Syrewicz (London)
10. *Paper Music,* Saint Paul Chamber Orchestra (McFerrin) (Sony Classical)

Source: © 1996 BPI Communications Inc. Used with permission from *Billboard*/SoundScan/BDS

Best of 1996

Top Single: "Macarena," Los Del Río
Top Album: *Jagged Little Pill,* Alanis Morissette
Top Female Singles Artist: Mariah Carey
Top Male Singles Artist: LL Cool J
Top Singles Group: Los Del Río
New Pop Artist: The Tony Rich Project
Top Country Artist: George Strait
Top R&B Artist: R. Kelly
Top Adult Contemporary Artist: Mariah Carey
Top Jazz Artist: Tony Bennett
Top Classical Artist: Benedictine Monks of Santo Domingo De Silos

Source: © 1996 BPI Communications Inc. Used with permission from *Billboard*/SoundScan/BDS

Top 10 Country Singles, 1996

1. "My Maria," Brooks & Dunn (Arista)
2. "Blue Clear Sky," George Strait (MCA)
3. "Time Marches On," Tracy Lawrence (Atlantic)
4. "Daddy's Money," Ricochet (Columbia)
5. "She Never Lets It Go To Her Heart," Tim McGraw (Curb)
6. "Living In a Moment," Ty Herndon (Epic)
7. "No One Needs to Know," Shania Twain (Mercury Nashville)
8. "You Can Feel Bad," Patty Loveless (Epic)
9. "Hypnotize the Moon," Clay Walker (Giant)
10. "No News," Lonestar (BNA)

Source: © 1996 BPI Communications Inc. Used with permission from *Billboard*/SoundScan/BDS

Top 10 Pop Albums, 1996

1. *Jagged Little Pill* Alanis Morrisette (Maverick/ Reprise)
2. *Daydream* Mariah Carey (Columbia)
3. *Falling Into You* Celine Dion (550 Music)
4. *Waiting to Exhale* Soundtrack (Arista)
5. *The Score* Fugees (Ruffhouse)
6. *The Woman in Me* Shania Twain (Mercury Nashville)
7. *Fresh Horses* Garth Brooks (Capitol Nashville)
8. *Anthology I* The Beatles (Apple)
9. *Cracked Rear View* Hootie & The Blowfish (Atlantic)
10. *Mellon Collie and the Infinite Sadness* The Smashing Pumpkins (Virgin)

Source: © 1996 BPI Communications Inc. Used with permission from *Billboard*/SoundScan/BDS

Top 10 Pop Singles, 1996

1. "Macarena (Bayside Boys Mix)," Los Del Río (RCA)
2. "One Sweet Day," Mariah Carey & Boyz II Men (Columbia)
3. "Because You Loved Me," (from *Up Close and Personal*) Celine Dion (550 Music)
4. "Nobody Knows," The Tony Rich Project (LaFace)
5. "Always Be My Baby," Mariah Carey (Columbia)
6. "Give Me One Reason," Tracy Chapman (Elektra)
7. "Tha Crossroads," Bone Thugs-N-Harmony (Ruthless)
8. "I Love You Always Forever," Donna Lewis (Atlantic)
9. "You're Makin' Me High/Let It Flow," Toni Braxton (LaFace)
10. "Twisted," Keith Sweat (Elektra)

Source: © 1996 BPI Communications Inc. Used with permission from *Billboard*/SoundScan/BDS

Top 10 R&B Singles, 1996

1. "You're Makin' Me High/Let it Flow," Toni Braxton (LaFace)
2. "All the Things (Your Man Won't Do)," (from *Don't Be a Menace*) Joe (Island)
3. "Tha Crossroads," Bone Thugs-N-Harmony (Ruthless)
4. "Down Low (Nobody Has to Know)," R. Kelly featuring Ronald Isley (Jive)
5. "Twisted," Keith Sweat (Elektra)
6. "How Do U Want It/California Love," 2Pac (featuring KC & JoJo) (Death Row)

Dollar Value of Recordings[1]

(in millions, net after returns)

	1986	1990	1994	1995	1996
CD	930.1	3,451.6	8,464.5	9,377.4	9,934.7
CD single	n.a.	6.0	56.1	110.9	184.1
Cassette	2,499.5	3,472.4	2,976.4	2,303.6	1,905.3
Cassette single	n.a.	257.9	274.9	236.3	189.3
LP/EP	983.0	86.5	17.8	25.1	36.8
Vinyl single	228.1	94.4	47.2	46.7	47.5
Music video	n.a.	172.3	231.1	220.3	236.1

1. List price value. *Source:* Recording Industry Association of America, Inc.

7. "Only You," 112 featuring the Notorious B.I.G. (Bad Boy)
8. "Sittin' Up In My Room," from *Waiting to Exhale*) Brandy (Arista)
9. "Before You Walk Out of My Life/Like This and Like That," Monica (Rowdy)
10. "Touch Me Tease Me," (from *The Nutty Professor*) Case featuring Foxxy Brown (Spoiled Rotten/Def Jam)

Source: © 1996 BPI Communications Inc. Used with permission from *Billboard*/SoundScan/BDS

Top 15 Concert Grosses of 1996

Amusement Business annually ranks domestic and international concert grosses and touring acts.

1. **Eagles,** $7,588,236; 86,000; Tokyo Dome, Japan
2. **Eagles, Kenny Wayne Shepherd,** $4,621,697; 99,924; Wembley Stadium, London
3. **Eagles,** $4,313,724; 40,000; Yokohama Arena, Japan
4. **The Who, Joan Osborne (7/16-18), Me'shell Ndege'ocello (7/20-22),** $4,064,720; 85,810; Madison Square Garden, New York, N.Y.
5. **The Clifford Ball: Phish,** $3,310,245; 135,267; Plattsburgh Air Force Base, N.Y.
6. **Kiss, D-Generation (7/25), CIV (7/26), 311 (7/27), The Nixons (7/28),** $3,267,670; 58,820; Madison Square Garden, New York, N.Y.
7. **Eagles, Kenny Wayne Shepherd,** $3,210,196; 72,000; RDS Stadium, Dublin, Ireland
8. **Tina Turner,** $2,722,500; 74,250; Flanders Expo, Ghent, Belgium
9. **Eagles,** $2,647,059; 30,000; Koshien Stadium, Osaka, Japan
10. **Tibetan Freedom Concert: Beastie Boys (6/15)/Red Hot Chili Peppers (6/16), Smashing Pumpkins, John Lee Hooker, Pavement (6/15), Bjork, Yoko Ono/IMA, Sonic Youth, Fugees (6/16) and others,** $2,617,420; 100,000; Polo Fields, Golden Gate Park, San Francisco, Calif.
11. **Eagles, Melissa Etheridge,** $2,461,528; 39,981; Flinders Park, Melbourne, Australia
12. **Eagles,** $2,333,510; 40,000; Aloha Stadium, Honolulu, Hawaii
13. **Eagles, Melissa Etheridge,** $2,317,875; 40,000; Cricket Ground, Sydney, Australia
14. **Eagles,** $2,294,118; 30,000; Fukuoka Dome, Japan
15. **Tina Turner,** $2,227,500; 60,750; Flanders Expo, Ghent, Belgium

Source: © 1996 BPI Communications Inc. Used with permission from *Amusement Business.*

Top 10 Video Sales, 1996

1. *Babe,* (Uni Dist. Corp.)
2. *Apollo 13,* (Uni Dist. Corp.)
3. *Pulp Fiction,* (Buena Vista Home Video)
4. *Playboy: The Best of Jenny McCarthy,* (Uni Dist. Corp.)
5. *The Aristocats,* (Buena Vista Home Video)
6. *Batman Forever,* (Warner Home Video)
7. *Jumanji,* (Columbia TriStar Home Video)
8. *Pocahontas,* (Buena Vista Home Video)
9. *Cinderella,* (Buena Vista Home Video)
10. *Heavy Metal,* (Columbia TriStar Home Video)

Source: © 1996 BPI Communications Inc. Used with permission from *Billboard*/SoundScan/BDS

The Rock and Roll Hall of Fame

1986
Chuck Berry
James Brown
Ray Charles
Sam Cooke
Fats Domino
The Everly Brothers
Buddy Holly
Jerry Lee Lewis
Elvis Presley
Little Richard
Nonperformers
Alan Freed
Sam Phillips
Early Influences
Robert Johnson
Jimmie Rodgers
Jimmy Yancey
Lifetime Achievement
John Hammond
1987
The Coasters
Eddie Cochran
Bo Diddley
Aretha Franklin
Marvin Gaye
Bill Haley
B.B. King
Clyde McPhatter
Ricky Nelson
Roy Orbison
Carl Perkins
Smokey Robinson
Joe Turner
Muddy Waters
Jackie Wilson
Nonperformers
Leonard Chess
Ahmet Ertegun
Jerry Leiber and Mike Stoller
Jerry Wexler
Early Influences
Louis Jordan

T-Bone Walker
Hank Williams
1988
Beach Boys
The Beatles
The Drifters
Bob Dylan
The Supremes
Nonperformer
Berry Gordy, Jr.
Early Influences
Woody Guthrie
Leadbelly
Les Paul
1990
Hank Ballard
Bobby Darin
The Four Seasons
The Four Tops
The Kinks
The Platters
Simon and Garfunkel
The Who
Nonperformers
Gerry Goffin and Carole King
Brian Holland, Eddie Holland
and Lamont Dozier
Early Influences
Louis Armstrong
Charlie Christian
Ma Rainey
1991
LaVern Baker
The Byrds
John Lee Hooker
The Impressions
Wilson Pickett
Jimmy Reed
Ike and Tina Turner
Nonperformers
Dave Bartholomew
Ralph Bass

Early Influence
Howlin' Wolf
Lifetime Achievement
Nesuhi Ertegun
1992
Bobby "Blue" Bland
Booker T. and the MG's
Johnny Cash
Jimi Hendrix Experience
The Isley Brothers
Sam and Dave
The Yardbirds
Nonperformers
Leo Fender
Bill Graham
Doc Pomus
Early Influences
Elmore James
Professor Longhair
1993
Ruth Brown
Cream
Creedence Clearwater Revival
The Doors
Etta James
Frankie Lymon and the Teenagers
Van Morrison
Sly and the Family Stone
Nonperformers
Dick Clark
Milt Gabler
Early Influence
Dinah Washington
1994
The Animals
The Band
Duane Eddy
The Grateful Dead
Elton John
John Lennon
Bob Marley

Rod Stewart
Nonperformer
Johnny Otis
Early Influence
Willie Dixon
1995
The Allman Brothers Band
Al Green
Janis Joplin
Led Zeppelin
Martha and the Vandellas
Neil Young
Frank Zappa
Nonperformer
Paul Ackerman
Early Influence
The Orioles
1996
David Bowie
Jefferson Airplane
Gladys Knight and the Pips
Little Willie John
Pink Floyd
Shirelles
Velvet Underground
Nonperformer
Tom Donahue
Early Influence
Pete Seeger
1997
The Bee Gees
Buffalo Springfield
Crosby, Stills and Nash
The Jackson Five
Joni Mitchell
Parliament-Funkadelic
The (Young) Rascals
Nonperformer
Syd Nathan
Early Influence
Mahalia Jackson
Bill Monroe

Top 10 Music Videos, 1996

1. *The Woman in Me,* Shania Twain (PolyGram Video)
2. *The Compleat Beatles,* The Beatles (Warner Home Video)
3. *Pulse,* Pink Floyd (Sony Music Video)
4. *Live From Austin, Texas,* Stevie Ray Vaughan & Double Trouble (Sony Music Video)
5. *Our First Video,* Mary-Kate & Ashley Olsen (WarnerVision Entertainment)
6. *Live At Madison Square Garden,* Mariah Carey (Sony Music Video)
7. *Live at the Acropolis,* Yanni (BMG Video)
8. *Video Greatest Hits-History,* Michael Jackson (Sony Music Video)
9. *The Beatles Anthology,* The Beatles (Turner Home Entertainment)
10. *Unplugged,* Kiss (PolyGram Video)

Source: © 1996 BPI Communications Inc. Used with permission from *Billboard*/SoundScan/BDS

Top 10 Kid Videos, 1996

1. *Cinderella,* (Buena Vista Home Video)
2. *The Lion King,* (Buena Vista Home Video)
3. *Pocahontas,* (Buena Vista Home Video)
4. *The Aristocats,* (Buena Vista Home Video)

5. *The Land Before Time III,* (Uni Dist. Corp.)
6. *Schoolhouse Rock: Grammar Rock,* (Paramount Home Video)
7. *The Many Adventures of Winnie the Pooh,* (Buena Vista Home Video)
8. *Balto,* (Uni Dist. Corp.)
9. *Mary-Kate & Ashley's Sleepover Party,* (WarnerVision Entertainment)
10. *Wallace and Gromit: A Grand Day Out,* (FoxVideo)

Source: © 1996 BPI Communications Inc. Used with permission from *Billboard*/SoundScan/BDS

Top 10 Video Rentals, 1996

1. *Braveheart,* (Paramount Home Video)
2. *The Usual Suspects,* (PolyGram Video)
3. *Seven,* (Turner Home Entertainment)
4. *Heat,* (Warner Home Video)
5. *12 Monkeys,* (Uni Dist. Corp.)
6. *Get Shorty,* (MGM/UA Home Video)
7. *Crimson Tide,* (Buena Vista Home Video)
8. *Casino,* (Uni Dist. Corp.)
9. *Executive Decision,* (Warner Home Video)
10. *The Net,* (Columbia TriStar Home Video)

Source: © 1996 BPI Communications Inc. Used with permission from *Billboard*/SoundScan/BDS

Billboard Top 10 Health and Fitness Videos

1. *The Grind Workout: Fitness With Flava,* (Sony Music Video)
2. *The Grind Workout Hip Hop Aerobics,* (Sony Music Video)
3. *The Firm: 5 Day Abs,* (BMG Video)
4. *The Firm: Low Impact Aerobics,* (BMG Video)
5. *Yoga Journal's Yoga Practice for Beginners,* (Healing Arts)
6. *The Firm: Body Sculpting Basics,* (BMG Video)
7. *The Firm: Not-So-Tough Aerobics,* (BMG Video)
8. *The Firm: Upper Body,* (BMG Video)
9. *Claudia Schiffer: Perfectly Fit Abs,* (FoxVideo CBS/Fox)
10. *Your Personal Best With Elle MacPherson,* (Buena Vista Home Video)

Source: © 1996 BPI Communications Inc. Used with permission from *Billboard*/SoundScan/BDS

Top 15 Regularly Scheduled Network Programs, 1996–97[1]

Rank	Program name (network)	Total percent of TV households
1.	E.R. (NBC)	21.2
2.	Seinfeld (NBC)	20.5
3.	Suddenly Susan (NBC)	17.0
4.	Friends (NBC)	16.8
4.	Naked Truth (NBC)	16.8
6.	Fired Up (NBC)	16.5
7.	NFL Monday Night Football (ABC)	16.2
8.	Single Guy (NBC)	14.1
9.	Home Improvement (ABC)	14.0
10.	Touched By An Angel (CBS)	13.6
11.	60 Minutes (CBS)	13.3
12.	20/20 (ABC)	12.8
13.	NYPD Blue (ABC)	12.5
14.	CBS Sunday Movie (CBS)	12.1
15.	Prime Time Live (ABC)	11.9

1. Sept. 16, 1996–May 21, 1997. *Source:* Nielsen Media Research. Copyright 1997, Nielsen Media Research.

Top 15 Syndicated TV Programs 1996–97 Season

Rank	Program	Rating (% U.S.)[1]
1.	Wheel of Fortune	11.8
2.	Home Improvement	9.7
2.	Jeopardy	9.7
4.	Oprah Winfrey Show	8.2
5.	Seinfeld	7.8
6.	National Geographic on Assignment	7.6
7.	Buena Vista I	7.4
8.	ESPN NFL—Regular Season	6.6
9.	Simpsons	6.5
10.	Entertainment Tonight	6.2
11.	MMN Home Team Baseball	6.1
11.	Portfolio XV	6.1
11.	WCW Wrestling	6.1
14.	Century 16	6.0
15.	Xena	5.7

1. Sept. 16, 1996–May 21, 1997. *Source:* Nielsen Syndication Service National TV Ratings. Copyright 1997, Nielsen Media Research.

Top Specials 1996–97[1]

Rank	Program name (network) [first telecast]	Rating (% of TV households)
1.	Academy Awards (ABC) [3/24/97]	27.4
2.	The Lion King (ABC) [11/03/96]	15.2
3.	CMA Awards (CBS) [10/2/96]	14.9
4.	Barbara Walters Special (ABC) [12/6/96]	14.3
5.	Golden Globe Awards (NBC) [1/19/97]	13.4

1. Sept. 16, 1996–May 21, 1997. *Source:* Nielsen Media Research. Copyright 1997, Nielsen Media Research.

Top Sports Shows 1996–97[1]

Rank	Program name (network)	Description	Rating (% of TV households)
1.	Super Bowl XXXI (Fox)	New England vs. Green Bay	43.3
2.	Fox Super Bowl XXX Kickoff (Fox)	New England vs. Green Bay	33.8
3.	Fox NFC Championship (Fox)	Carolina at Green Bay	30.1
4.	Fox Super Bowl Post Game (Fox)	New England vs. Green Bay	29.8
5.	AFC Championship Game (NBC)	Jacksonville at New England	28.5
6.	Fox NFC Playoff (Fox)	Dallas at Carolina	27.6
7.	NFL Playoff Game (NBC)	Pittsburgh at New England	21.2
8.	Fox World Series Game #5 (Fox)	N.Y. Yankees at Atlanta	20.0
9.	NFL Playoff Game (NBC)	Jacksonville at Denver	19.6
10.	Fox World Series Game #6 (Fox)	Atlanta at N.Y. Yankees	19.1

1. Sept. 16, 1996–May 21, 1997. *Source:* Nielsen Media Research. Copyright 1997, Nielsen Media Research.

Top Rated Movies 1996–97[1]

Rank	Program name (network)	Rating (% of TV households)	Rank	Program name (network)	Rating (% of TV households)
1.	Schindler's List (NBC)	20.9	13.	Forrest Gump (ABC)	14.5
2.	Asteroid, Pt. 1 (NBC)	19.9	13.	Mario Puzo's The Last Don, Pt. 2 (CBS)	14.5
3.	Asteroid, Pt. 2 (NBC)	19.0	15.	To Dance With Olivia (CBS)	14.3
4.	Mario Puzo's The Last Don, Pt. 1 (CBS)	17.8	16.	Old Man (CBS)	14.2
5.	The Odyssey, Pt. 1 (NBC)	17.3	16.	Jurassic Park (NBC)	14.2
6.	The Odyssey, Pt. 2 (NBC)	16.7	18.	The Bachelor's Baby (CBS)	14.1
7.	Pandora's Clock, Pt. 1 (NBC)	16.1	18.	The Fugitive (NBC)	14.1
8.	Pandora's Clock, Pt. 2 (NBC)	15.6	20.	Journey of the Heart (CBS)	13.5
9.	Mario Puzo's The Last Don, Pt. 3 (CBS)	15.3	21.	She Cried No (NBC)	13.4
10.	Rose Hill (CBS)	15.1	22.	Walton's Easter (CBS)	13.3
11.	A Match Made in Heaven (CBS)	14.8	23.	True Women, Pt. 1 (CBS)	13.2
12.	Mrs. Santa Claus (CBS)	14.7	24.	Sweet Dreams (NBC)	13.0
			25.	A few Good Men (NBC)	12.8

1. Sept. 16, 1995–May 25, 1997. *Source:* Nielsen Media Research. Copyright 1997, Nielsen Media Research.

Hours of TV Usage Per Week by Household Income

	Under $30,000	$30,000+	$40,000+	$50,000+	$60,000+
Nov. 1993	53 h 35 min	50 h 34 min	50 h 24 min (includes $50,000+)		47 h 13 min
Nov. 1994	53 h 46 min	52 h 05 min	50 h 04 min (includes $50,000+)		46 h 42 min
Nov. 1995	52 h 25 min	51 h 44 min	48 h 53 min		46 h 02 min
Nov. 1996	55 h 26 min	49 h 43 min	49 h 03 min	48 h 23 min	47 h 32 min

Source: Nielsen Media Research. Copyright 1997, Nielsen Media Research.

Television Set Ownership

(January 1997)

Households with	Number	Percent
Color TV sets	82,350,000	85
B&W only	490,000	1
2 or more sets	71,780,000	73
One set	25,220,000	27.0
Cable	65,090,730	67.2
Total TV households	**97,000,000**	**97.3**

Source: Nielsen Media Research. Copyright 1997, Nielsen Media Research.

Persons Viewing Prime Time[1]

(in millions)

	Total persons
Monday	95.3
Tuesday	94.9
Wednesday	93.2
Thursday	93.7
Friday	80.9
Saturday	78.9
Sunday	91.6
Total average	**89.9**

1. Average minute audiences May 1997. NOTE: Prime time is 8–11:00 p.m. (EST) except Sun. 7–11:00 p.m. *Source:* Nielsen Media Research. Copyright 1997, Nielsen Media Research.

Source of Household Viewing—Prime Time

Pay Cable, Basic Cable, and Non-Cable Households

(Monday–Sunday, 8–11:00 p.m.)

	Nov. 1996			Nov. 1995			Nov. 1994			Nov. 1993		
	Pay cable	Basic cable	Non-cable	Pay cable	Basic cable	Non-cable	Pay cable	Basic cable	Non-cable	Pay cable	Basic cable	Non-cable
% TV Usage	67.6	60.2	54.9	67.2	60.9	54.4	67.0	61.2	58.1	68.7	61.3	57.2
Pay Cable	8.2	—	—	9.2	—	—	9.3	—	—	9.2	—	—
Cable-originated programming	27.0	24.2	—	25.9	23.6	—	22.1	20.5	—	21.0	20.2	—
Other-on-air stations	7.0	6.2	9.2	6.9	5.4	9.3	7.2	7.8	12.7	7.2	7.1	11.4
Network affiliated stations	37.6	35.3	42.2	38.1	37.5	44.3	41.6	40.7	50.6	44.4	40.7	50.3
Network share	56	59	77	57	62	81	62	67	87	65	66	88

Source: Nielsen Media Research, NTI Cable Status Report. Copyright 1997, Nielsen Media Research.

Average Hours of Household TV Usage

(i hours and minutes per day)

	Yearly average	February	July
1985–86	7 h 10 min	7 h 48 min	6 h 37 min
1986–87	7 h 05 min	7 h 35 min	6 h 32 min
1987–88	6 h 59 min	7 h 38 min	6 h 31 min
1988–89	7 h 02 min	7 h 32 min	6 h 27 min
1989–90	6 h 55 min	7 h 16 min	6 h 24 min
1990–91	6 h 56 min	7 h 30 min	6 h 26 min
1991–92	7 h 04 min	7 h 32 min	6 h 39 min
1992–93	7 h 09 min	7 h 41 min	6 h 47 min
1993–94	7 h 15 min	7 h 51 min	6 h 53 min
1994–95	7 h 02 min	7 h 39 min	6 h 46 min
1995–96	7 h 17 min	n.a.	n.a.

NOTE: n.a. = not available. *Source:* Nielsen Media Research. Copyright 1997, Nielsen Media Research.

Weekly TV Viewing by Age

(in hours and minutes)

	Time per week		
	Nov. 1996	Nov. 1995	Nov. 1994
Women 18–24 years old	24 h 32 min	24 h 52 min	26 h 23 min
Women 25–54	30 h 44 min	31 h 45 min	30 h 55 min
Women 55 and over	41 h 50 min	42 h 20 min	41 h 11 min
Men 18–24	20 h 20 min	21 h 20 min	22 h 41 min
Men 25–54	28 h 4 min	28 h 23 min	27 h 13 min
Men 55 and over	37 h 8 min	37 h 58 min	38 h 38 min
Female Teens	18 h 19 min	19 h 59 min	20 h 20 min
Male Teens	19 h 59 min	20 h 38 min	21 h 59 min
Children 6–11	19 h 59 min	21 h 40 min	21 h 30 min
Children 2–5	23 h 21 min	24 h 52 min	24 h 42 min

Source: Nielsen Media Research. Copyright 1997, Nielsen Media Research.

Audience Composition by Selected Program Type[1]

(Average Minute Audience)

	General drama	Suspense and mystery drama	Situation comedy	Informational[2] 6–7:00 p.m.	Feature films	All regular network programs 7–11:00 p.m.
Women (18 and over)	6,280,000	6,550,000	5,790,000	5,790,000	7,130,000	6,610,000
Men (18 and over)	4,170,160	4,160,000	3,940,000	4,380,000	4,380,000	4,750,000
Teens (12–17)	720,000	33,000	1,010,000	230,000	890,000	840,000
Children (2–11)	900,000	740,000	1,360,000	430,000	990,000	1,080,000
Total persons (2+)	12,070,000	11,770,000	12,100,000	10,830,000	13,390,000	13,290,000

1. All figures are estimated for November 1996. 2. Multiweekly viewing. *Source:* Nielsen Media Research. Copyright 1997, Nielsen Media Research.

1996 Broadcast Film Critics Association Awards

The Broadcast Film Critics Association, formed in 1995, includes 84 television, radio, and online movie critics.

Best Picture *Fargo*
Best Actor Geoffrey Rush, *Shine*
Best Actress Frances McDormand, *Fargo*
Best Supporting Actor Cuba Gooding, Jr., *Jerry Maguire*
Best Supporting Actress Joan Allen, *The Crucible*
Best Director Anthony Minghella, *The English Patient*
Best Screenplay Anthony Minghella, *The English Patient*
Best Foreign Film *Ridicule*
Best Documentary *When We Were Kings*
Best Family Film *Fly Away Home*
Breakout Artist Renee Zellweger, *Jerry Maguire*
Child Performance Jonathan Lipnicki, *Jerry Maguire*

1996 Golden Globe Awards

The 54th Annual Golden Globe Awards, honoring excellence in film and television, were presented January 19, 1997 at Los Angeles's Beverly Hilton. Here are the movie awards.

Best Drama *The English Patient*
Best Actor in a Drama Geoffrey Rush, *Shine*
Best Actress in a Drama Brenda Blethyn, *Secrets and Lies*
Best Musical or Comedy *Evita*
Best Actor in a Musical or Comedy Tom Cruise, *Jerry Maguire*
Best Actress in a Musical or Comedy Madonna, *Evita*
Best Supporting Actor Edward Norton, *Primal Fear*
Best Supporting Actress Lauren Bacall, *The Mirror Has Two Faces*
Best Director Milos Forman, *The People vs. Larry Flynt*
Best Screenplay Scott Alexander and Larry Karaszewski, *The People vs. Larry Flynt*
Best Original Score Gabriel Yared, *The English Patient*
Best Original Song "You Must Love Me," *Evita*
Best Foreign Film *Kolya* (Czech Republic)

1996 New York Film Critics Circle Awards

Best Picture *Fargo*
Best Actor Geoffrey Rush, *Shine*
Best Actress Emily Watson, *Breaking the Waves*
Best Supporting Actor Harry Belafonte, *Kansas City*
Best Supporting Actress Courtney Love, *The People vs. Larry Flynt*
Best Director Lars von Trier, *Breaking the Waves*
Best Screenplay Albert Brooks and Monica Johnson, *Mother*
Best Cinematographer Robby Müller, *Breaking the Waves* and *Dead Man*
Best Foreign Film *The White Balloon*
Best Documentary *When We Were Kings*
Most Distinguished Reissue *Vertigo*

1996 Los Angeles Film Critics Association Awards

Best Picture *Secrets and Lies*
Best Actor Geoffrey Rush, *Shine*
Best Actress Brenda Blethyn, *Secrets and Lies*
Best Supporting Actor Edward Norton, *The People vs. Larry Flynt, Everyone Says I Love You,* and *Primal Fear*
Best Supporting Actress Barbara Hershey, *The Portrait of a Lady*
Best Director Mike Leigh, *Secrets and Lies*
Best Screenplay Joel and Ethan Coen, *Fargo*
Best Foreign Film *La Cérémonie*
Best Documentary *When We Were Kings*

1996 Boston Society of Film Critics Awards

Best Picture *Trainspotting*
Best Actor Geoffrey Rush, *Shine*
Best Actress Brenda Blethyn, *Secrets and Lies*
Best Supporting Actor Edward Norton, *The People vs. Larry Flynt, Everyone Says I Love You,* and *Primal Fear*
Best Supporting Actress Courtney Love, *The People vs. Larry Flynt*
Best Director Mike Leigh, *Secrets and Lies*
Best Screenplay Stanley Tucci and Joseph Tropiano, *Big Night*
Best Foreign Film *Ma Saison Préférée*
Best Documentary *Anne Frank Remembered*

Movie Revenues

	All-Time Box Office Grosses[1]	
1.	*Star Wars* (20th Century-Fox, 1977)	$460,987,469
2.	*E.T.* (Universal, 1982)	399,804,539
3.	*Jurassic Park* (Universal, 1993)	356,839,725
4.	*Forrest Gump* (Paramount, 1994)	329,690,974
5.	*The Lion King* (Buena Vista, 1994)	312,855,561
6.	*Return of the Jedi* (20th Century-Fox, 1983)	309,161,884
7.	*Independence Day* (20th Century-Fox, 1996)	306,169,255
8.	*The Empire Strikes Back* (20th Century-Fox, 1980)	290,268,568
9.	*Home Alone* (20th Century-Fox, 1990)	285,016,000
10.	*Jaws* (Universal, 1975)	260,000,000
11.	*Batman* (Warner Brothers, 1989)	251,188,924
12.	*Raiders of the Lost Ark* (Paramount, 1981)	242,374,454
13.	*Twister* (Warner Brothers, 1996)	241,708.908
14.	*Beverly Hills Cop* (Paramount, 1984)	234,760,478
15.	*Ghostbusters* (Columbia, 1984)	220,858,490
16.	*Mrs.Doubtfire* (20th Century-Fox, 1993)	219,194,773
17.	*The Lost World: Jurassic Park* (Universal, 1997)	218,334,199
18.	*Ghost* (Paramount, 1990)	217,631,306
19.	*Aladdin* (Buena Vista, 1992)	217,350,219
20.	*Back to the Future* (Universal, 1985)	210,609,762
21.	*Terminator 2* (TriStar, 1991)	204,446,562
22.	*Indiana Jones and the Last Crusade* (Paramount, 1989)	197,171,806
23.	*Gone With the Wind* (MGM/United Artists/TEC, 1939)	193,597,756
24.	*Toy Story* (Buena Vista, 1995)	191,773,049
25.	*Snow White* (RKO, Buena Vista, 1937)	184,925,486

	Top 25 Movies of 1996	
1.	*Independence Day* (Twentieth Century Fox)	$306,167,040
2.	*Twister* (Warner Bros.)	241,721,524
3.	*Mission: Impossible* (Paramount)	180,981,866
4.	*The Rock* (Buena Vista/Hollywood)	134,069,511
5.	*Ransom* (Buena Vista/Touchstone)	129,137,746
6.	*The Nutty Professor* (Universal)	128,814,019
7.	*The Birdcage* (MGM/UA)	124,060,553
8.	*101 Dalmatians* (live action; Buena Vista/Disney)	121,788,625
9.	*A Time to Kill* (Warner Bros.)	108,766,007
10.	*First Wives Club* (Paramount)	104,625,028
11.	*Phenomenon* (Buena Vista/Touchstone)	104,535,318
12.	*Eraser* (Warner Bros.)	101,295,562
13.	*The Hunchback of Notre Dame* (Buena Vista/Disney)	100,117,603
14.	*Star Trek: First Contact* (Paramount)	89,128,389
15.	*Space Jam* (Warner Bros.)	85,422,365
16.	*Jerry Maguire* (Sony/Tri-Star)	83,006,355
17.	*Broken Arrow* (Twentieth Century Fox)	70,770,147
18.	*The Cable Guy* (Sony/Columbia)	60,240,295
19.	*Courage Under Fire* (Twentieth Century Fox)	59,031,057
20.	*Jack* (Buena Vista/Hollywood)	58,554,258
21.	*Jingle All the Way* (Twentieth Century Fox)	57,194,776
22.	*Executive Decision* (Warner Bros.)	56,679,192
23.	*Primal Fear* (Paramount)	56,116,183
24.	*Beavis and Butt-Head Do America* (Paramount)	54,149,743
25.	*Tin Cup* (Warner Bros.)	53,888,896

1. As of July 9, 1997. Including reissues. *Source:* Exhibitor Relations Co. Inc.

All-Time Top Emmy Winners and Nominees

Most Emmys Won By Individuals

Dwight Hemion	16	Steven Bochco	9
Buz Kohan	13	Carl Reiner	8
Jan Scott	11	Mary Tyler Moore	8
Ian Fraser	11	Dinah Shore	8
Don Mischer	11		

Most Emmys Won By a Male Performer

Ed Asner	7	Dick Van Dyke	5
Art Carney	6	Hal Holbrook	5
Alan Alda	5	Carroll O'Connor	5
Peter Falk	5	Harvey Korman	4
Don Knotts	5	John Larroquette	4
Laurence Olivier	5		

Most Nominations for a Program

Cheers	117
*M*A*S*H*	109
Hill Street Blues	98

Most Emmys Won By a Series

The Mary Tyler Moore Show	29	*Hill Street Blues*	26
Cheers	27	*The Carol Burnett Show*	25

Most Nominations for an Individual

Dwight Hemion	42	Don Mischer	28
George Stevens, Jr.	31	Steven Bochco	28
Jan Scott	29	Buz Kohan	27
Alan Alda	28	George Schaefer	25

Most Emmys Won By a Female Performer

Dinah Shore	8	Valerie Harper	4
Mary Tyler Moore	8	Michael Learned	4
Cloris Leachman	5	Tyne Daly	4
Lily Tomlin	5	Rhea Perlman	4
Carol Burnett	5	Candice Bergen	4
Tracey Ullman	5		

Other Top Emmy Winners

Most Emmys Won By a	Record holder	Number of Emmys
Miniseries	*Roots*	9
Movie of the Week	*Eleanor and Franklin*	11
Network in a Single Year	CBS in 1973–1974	44
Series in Its First Season	*Hill Street Blues*	8
Series in a Single Season	*Hill Steet Blues* (1980–1981)	8
Best Drama Series	*Hill Street Blues*	4
	L.A. Law	
Best Comedy Series	*The Dick Van Dyke Show*	4
	All in the Family	
	Cheers	

Source: Academy of Television Arts and Sciences.

For 1997 Emmy winners, *see* September Current Events, and for past Emmy winners, *see* Awards.

Television Hall of Fame

Each year, the Academy of Television Arts and Sciences inducts up to seven people or programs to the Television Hall of Fame. Here are the past inductees honored for their outstanding and lasting contribution to television.

1984
Lucille Ball
Milton Berle
Paddy Chayefsky
Norman Lear
Edward R. Murrow
William S. Paley
David Sarnoff

1985
Carol Burnett
Sid Caesar
Walter Cronkite
Joyce Hall
Rod Serling
Ed Sullivan
Sylvester (Pat) Weaver

1986
Steve Allen
Fred Coe
Walt Disney
Jackie Gleason
Mary Tyler Moore
Frank Stanton
Burr Tillstrom

1987
Johnny Carson
Jacques-Yves Cousteau
Leonard Goldenson
Jim Henson
Bob Hope
Ernie Kovacs
Eric Sevareid

1988
Jack Benny
George Burns and Gracie Allen
Chet Huntley and David Brinkley
Red Skelton
David Susskind
David Wolper

1989
Roone Arledge
Fred Astaire
Perry Como
Joan Ganz Cooney
Don Hewitt
Carroll O'Connor
Barbara Walters

1990
Desi Arnaz
Leonard Bernstein
James Garner
I Love Lucy
Danny Thomas
Mike Wallace

1991
Bill Cosby
Andy Griffith
Ted Koppel
Sheldon Leonard
Dinah Shore
Ted Turner

1992
Dick Clark
John Chancellor
Phil Donahue
Mark Goodson
Bob Newhart
Agnes Nixon
Jack Webb

1993
Alan Alda
Howard Cosell
Barry Diller
Fred Friendly
Bill Hanna and Joseph Barbera
Oprah Winfrey

1994
Michael Landon
Richard Levinson and William Link
Jim McKay
Bill Moyers
Dick Van Dyke
Betty White

1995*
Ed Asner
Angela Lansbury
Aaron Spelling
Lew Wasserman
Marcy Carsey
Tom Werner
Charles Kuralt
Steven Bochco

*These are the newest members to the Television Hall of Fame, inducted at an October 5, 1996 ceremony at Walt Disney Resorts near Orlando, Florida.

Miss America Winners

1921	Margaret Gorman, Washington, D.C.	1965	Vonda Kay Van Dyke, Phoenix, Ariz.
1922-23	Mary Campbell, Columbus, Ohio	1966	Deborah Irene Bryant, Overland Park, Kan.
1924	Ruth Malcolmson, Philadelphia, Pa.	1967	Jane Anne Jayroe, Laverne, Okla.
1925	Fay Lamphier, Oakland, Calif.	1968	Debra Dene Barnes, Moran, Kan.
1926	Norma Smallwood, Tulsa, Okla.	1969	Judith Anne Ford, Belvidere, Ill.
1927	Lois Delaner, Joliet, Ill.	1970	Pamela Anne Eldred, Birmingham, Mich.
1933	Marion Bergeron, West Haven, Conn.	1971	Phyllis Ann George, Denton, Texas
1935	Henrietta Leaver, Pittsburgh, Pa.	1972	Laurie Lea Schaefer, Columbus, Ohio
1936	Rose Coyle, Philadelphia, Pa.	1973	Terry Anne Meeuwsen, DePere, Wis.
1937	Bette Cooper, Bertrand Island, N.J.	1974	Rebecca Ann King, Denver, Colo.
1938	Marilyn Meseke, Marion, Ohio	1975	Shirley Cothran, Fort Worth, Texas
1939	Patricia Donnelly, Detroit, Mich.	1976	Tawney Elaine Godin, Yonkers, N.Y.
1940	Frances Marie Burke, Philadelphia, Pa.	1977	Dorothy Kathleen Benham, Edina, Minn.
1941	Rosemary LaPlanche, Los Angeles, Calif.	1978	Susan Perkins, Columbus, Ohio
1942	JoCaroll Dennison, Tyler, Texas	1979	Kylene Baker, Galax, Va.
1943	Jean Bartel, Los Angeles, Calif.	1980	Cheryl Prewitt, Ackerman, Miss.
1944	Venus Ramey, Washington, D.C.	1981	Susan Powell, Elk City, Okla.
1945	Bess Myerson, New York, N.Y.	1982	Elizabeth Ward, Russellville, Ark.
1946	Marilyn Buford, Los Angeles, Calif.	1983	Debra Maffett, Anaheim, Calif.
1947	Barbara Walker, Memphis, Tenn.	1984	Vanessa Williams, Milwood, N.Y.[1]
1948	BeBe Shopp, Hopkins, Minn.	1984	Suzette Charles, Mays Landing, N.J.
1949	Jacque Mercer, Litchfield, Ariz.	1985	Sharlene Wells, Salt Lake City, Utah
1951	Yolande Betbeze, Mobile, Ala.	1986	Susan Akin, Meridian, Miss.
1952	Coleen Kay Hutchins, Salt Lake City, Utah	1987	Kellye Cash, Memphis, Tenn.
1953	Neva Jane Langley, Macon, Ga.	1988	Kaye Lani Rae Rafko, Monroe, Mich.
1954	Evelyn Margaret Ay, Ephrata, Pa.	1989	Gretchen Elizabeth Carlson, Anoka, Minn.
1955	Lee Meriwether, San Francisco, Calif.	1990	Debbye Turner, Mexico, Mo.
1956	Sharon Ritchie, Denver, Colo.	1991	Marjorie Judith Vincent, Oak Park, Ill.
1957	Marian McKnight, Manning, S.C.	1992	Carolyn Suzanne Sapp, Honolulu, Hawaii
1958	Marilyn Van Derbur, Denver, Colo.	1993	Leanza Cornett, Jacksonville, Fla.
1959	Mary Ann Mobley, Brandon, Miss.	1994	Kimberly Clarice Aiken, Columbia, S.C.
1960	Lynda Lee Mead, Natchez, Miss.	1995	Heather Whitestone, Birmingham, Ala.
1961	Nancy Fleming, Montague, Mich.	1996	Shawntel Smith, Muldrow, Okla.
1962	Maria Fletcher, Asheville, N.C.	1997	Tara Dawn Holland, Overland Park, Kan.
1963	Jacquelyn Mayer, Sandusky, Ohio	1998	Katherine Shindle, Evanston, Ill.
1964	Donna Axum, El Dorado, Ark.		1. Resigned July 23, 1984.

Top 100 Daily Newspapers in the United States

By Circulation, as of September 30, 1996

Newspapers	Circulation	Newspapers	Circulation
Wall Street Journal	1,783,532	Atlanta Constitution	308,301
Arlington (Va.) USA Today	1,591,629	Baltimore Sun	304,412
New York Times	1,071,120	Milwaukee Journal Sentinel	287,673
Los Angeles Times	1,029,073	San Jose Mercury News	285,735
Washington Post	789,198	Boston Herald	284,794
New York Daily News	734,277	Kansas City (Mo.) Star	279,305
Chicago Tribune	680,535	Sacramento Bee	276,758
Long Island (N.Y.) Newsday	564,754	Orlando Sentinel	262,802
Houston Chronicle	545,348	Buffalo News	262,045
Chicago Sun-Times	496,030	New Orleans Times-Picayune	259,577
San Francisco Chronicle	486,977	Tampa Tribune	255,142
Dallas Morning News	478,181	Fort Lauderdale Sun-Sentinel	255,050
Boston Globe	471,024	Columbus (Ohio) Dispatch	253,549
New York Post	429,642	Pittsburgh Post-Gazette	240,992
Philadelphia Inquirer	427,175	Detroit News	237,917
Newark (N.J.) Star-Ledger	405,869	Charlotte (N.C.) Observer	236,050
Minneapolis Star Tribune	393,740	Louisville (Ky.) Courier-Journal	232,539
Cleveland Plain Dealer	386,256	Indianapolis Star	230,095
Phoenix Arizona Republic	382,122	Omaha World-Herald	227,721
San Diego Union-Tribune	372,081	Seattle Times	226,287
Detroit Free Press	363,385	Los Angeles Investor's Business Daily	222,972
Miami Herald	361,279	Fort Worth Star-Telegram	221,860
Orange County (Calif.) Register	353,812	San Antonio Express-News	215,593
St. Petersburg (Fla.) Times	340,878	Hartford (Conn.) Courant	208,844
Portland Oregonian	338,586	Richmond (Va.) Times-Dispatch	208,632
Denver Post	334,436	Cincinnati Enquirer	205,233
St. Louis Post-Dispatch	321,461	Oklahoma City Daily Oklahoman	203,705
Denver Rocky Mountain News	316,910	St. Paul (Minn.) Pioneer Press	203,601

Newspapers	Circulation	Newspapers	Circulation
Norfolk Virginian-Pilot	201,683	Nashville Tennessean	146,788
Los Angeles Daily News	200,655	Rochester (N.Y.) Democrat and Chronicle	142,572
Seattle Post-Intelligencer	198,385	Grand Rapids Press	139,978
Jacksonville Times-Union	187,207	Allentown Morning Call	130,317
Austin American-Statesman	181,272	Arlington Heights (Ill.) Daily Herald	129,202
West Palm Beach (Fla.) Palm Beach Post	175,003	Tacoma News Tribune	128,432
Philadelphia Daily News	174,595	Salt Lake City Tribune	127,978
Little Rock Democrat-Gazette	172,223	Wilmington News Journal	125,637
Providence (R.I.) Journal	171,824	Columbia (S.C.) State	122,053
Memphis Commercial Appeal	170,952	Spokane Spokesman-Review	118,555
Des Moines Register	169,898	Atlanta Journal	118,260
Birmingham News	167,865	Knoxville News-Sentinel	115,636
Riverside (Calif.) Press-Enterprise	160,004	Albuquerque Journal	113,253
Tulsa World	158,610	Worcester (Mass.) Telegram & Gazette	112,976
Dayton Daily News	158,295	San Francisco Examiner	112,382
Neptune Asbury Park (N.J.) Press	156,473	Lexington (Ky.) Herald-Leader	111,623
Fresno (Calif.) Bee	152,591	Sarasota Herald-Tribune	110,179
Raleigh News & Observer	150,951	Charleston Post & Courier	108,162
Bergen County (N.J.) Record	150,122	Roanoke (Va.) Times	106,902
Akron Beacon Journal	148,914	Jackson (Miss.) Clarion-Ledger	105,571
Las Vegas Review-Journal	147,927	Colorado Springs Gazette	103,553
Toledo Blade	147,365	Honolulu Advertiser	103,522

Top 100 Daily Newspapers in the World According to 1996 Circulation

Newspaper	Circulation	Newspaper	Circulation
Yomiuri Shimbun (Japan)	14,485,393	Nishi Nippon Shimbun (Japan)	1,128,345
Asahi Shimbun (Japan)	12,660,066	Tokyo Shimbun (Japan)	1,128,345
Sichuan Ribao (China)	8,000,000	Hochi Shimbun (Japan)	1,079,500
Guangming Ribao (China)	6,000,000	New York Times (United States)	1,071,120
Mainichi Shimbun (Japan)	5,865,571	Tokyo Sports (Japan)	1,055,600
O Diario (Portugal)	5,666,915	Yediut Ahranot (Israel)	1,050,000
Bild (Germany)	5,567,100	Daily Telegraph (England)	1,040,316
News of The World (England)	4,607,189	Los Angeles Times (United States)	1,029,073
Chunichi Shimbun (Japan)	4,323,142	Neue Kronenzeitung (Austria)	1,000,480
Nihon Keizai Shimbun (Japan)	4,176,095	Jiefang Ribao (China)	1,000,000
Sun (England)	4,057,668	Nanfang Ribao (China)	1,000,000
Renmin Ribao (China)	3,000,000	Nongmin Ribao (China)	1,000,000
Sankei Shimbun (Japan)	2,876,351	Zhongguo Qingnian (China)	1,000,000
Chosun Ilbo (South Korea)	2,505,700	Al Akhbar (Egypt)	980,000
Gongren Ribao (China)	2,500,000	Nikkan Sports (Japan)	964,959
Daily Mirror (England)	2,484,238	Seoul Shinmun (South Korea)	900,000
Dong-A Ilbo (South Korea)	2,150,000	Xin Hua Ribao (China)	900,000
The People (England)	2,064,439	Kyoto Shimbun (Japan)	826,235
Daily Mail (England)	2,049,100	Chugoku Shimbun (Japan)	823,289
Al Ahram (Egypt)	2,000,000	Jang (Pakistan)	820,000
Hokkaido Shimbun (Japan)	1,975,949	Times of India (India)	813,300
Eleftherotypia (Greece)	1,858,316	Hubei Ribao (China)	800,000
Wall Street Journal (United States)	1,783,532	Ouest-France (France)	790,133
Kerala Kaumudi (India)	1,720,000	Washington Post (United States)	789,198
Wen Hui Bao Daily (China)	1,700,000	Kobe Shimbun (Japan)	775,359
Xin Min Wan Bao (China)	1,625,789	Holos Ukrainy (Ukraine)	768,000
USA Today (United States)	1,591,629	De Telegraf (Netherlands)	751,400
Sports Nippon (Japan)	1,560,204	Dziennik Zachodni (Poland)	750,000
Joong-Ang Daily News (South Korea)	1,550,000	New York Daily News (United States)	734,277
Economic Daily (China)	1,500,000	Daily Record (Scotland)	732,840
Kyung-Hyang Daily News (South Korea)	1,478,000	Zero Hora (Brazil)	727,188
Shizuoka Shimbun (Japan)	1,428,488	Diario dos Campos (Brazil)	725,000
NRZ (Germany)	1,332,800	Il Corriere della Sera (Italy)	723,471
West Deutche Allgemeine (Germany)	1,313,400	Sabah (Turkey)	722,950
United Daily News (Taiwan)	1,300,000	Jornal da Tarde (Brazil)	709,793
China Times (Taiwan)	1,270,000	Clarin Daily (Argentina)	700,000
Daily Express (England)	1,257,880	Pusan Ilbo (South Korea)	700,000
O Estado de Sao Paulo (Brazil)	1,230,160	Thai Rath (Thailand)	700,000
Jang Daily (Pakistan)	1,200,000	Zhejiang Ribao (China)	700,000
Jang Lahore (Pakistan)	1,200,000	Diario Insular (Portugal)	684,143
Akhbar El Yom/Al Akhbar (Egypt)	1,159,339	Chicago Tribune (United States)	680,535
Hankook Ilbo (South Korea)	1,156,000	Granma (Cuba)	675,000

Newspaper	Circulation	Newspaper	Circulation
The Times (England)	669,640	Sun Herald (Australia)	603,746
The Daily Star (England)	668,964	La Gazzetta dello Sport (Italy)	603,606
Al Goumhouryia (Egypt)	650,000	Central Daily News (Taiwan)	600,000
Guanxi Ribao (China)	650,000	Fujian Ribao (China)	600,000
Kahoku Shimpo (Japan)	642,554	Herald Sun (Australia)	600,000
Malayala Manorama (India)	630,068	Hurriyet (Pakistan)	600,000
La Nacion (Argentina)	630,000	Lioning Ribao (China)	600,000
Hurriyet (Turkey)	615,579	Oriental Daily News (Hong Kong)	600,000

Top 100 Consumer Magazines

Rank	Magazine	Circulation	Rank	Magazine	Circulation
1.	NRTA/AARP Bulletin	20,567,352	51.	First for Women	1,331,399
2.	Modern Maturity	20,528,786	52.	Teen	1,327,893
3.	Reader's Digest	15,072,260	53.	Rolling Stone	1,298,631
4.	TV Guide	13,013,938	54.	Golf Magazine	1,292,980
5.	National Geographic Magazine	9,025,003	55.	Entertainment Weekly	1,280,230
6.	Better Homes & Gardens	7,605,325	56.	Boys' Life	1,267,283
7.	Family Circle	5,239,074	57.	Consumers Digest	1,259,422
8.	Good Housekeeping	4,951,240	58.	The Elks Magazine	1,250,475
9.	Ladies' Home Journal	4,544,416	59.	Discover	1,228,111
10.	Woman's Day	4,317,604	60.	New Woman	1,222,143
11.	McCall's	4,290,216	61.	Mademoiselle	1,206,054
12.	Time	4,102,168	62.	Bon Appetit	1,197,505
13.	People Weekly	3,449,852	63.	Vogue	1,190,018
14.	Prevention	3,311,244	64.	Self	1,159,305
15.	Playboy	3,236,517	65.	PC Magazine	1,151,473
16.	Newsweek	3,194,769	66.	Kiplinger's Personal Finance	1,148,760
17.	Sports Illustrated	3,173,639	67.	Car and Driver	1,122,047
18.	Redbook	2,926,702	68.	Vanity Fair	1,115,760
19.	The American Legion Magazine	2,777,351	69.	The American Hunter	1,114,553
20.	Home & Away	2,719,931	70.	Scholastic Parent & Child	1,095,681
21.	Avenues	2,549,695	71.	PC World	1,091,987
22.	Southern Living	2,490,542	72.	The Family Handyman	1,089,755
23.	Cosmopolitan	2,486,393	73.	US	1,083,639
24.	National Enquirer	2,480,349	74.	Endless Vacation	1,083,582
25.	Seventeen	2,442,090	75.	Scouting	1,062,843
26.	Motorland	2,376,974	76.	Parenting Magazine	1,060,360
27.	U.S. News & World Report	2,260,857	77.	Country Home	1,043,599
28.	Star	2,220,711	78.	Sesame Street Magazine	1,032,627
29.	NEA Today	2,168,447	79.	AAA Going Places	1,029,054
30.	YM	2,153,815	80.	Home	1,017,227
31.	Glamour	2,115,488	81.	Motor Trend	1,013,326
32.	Smithsonian	2,095,819	82.	PC/Computing	1,005,213
33.	Martha Stewart Living	2,025,182	83.	Penthouse	1,005,006
34.	Money	1,993,119	84.	Essence	1,000,208
35.	V.F.W. Magazine	1,980,947	85.	Travel & Leisure	990,115
36.	Ebony	1,803,566	86.	Disney Adventures	977,349
37.	Popular Science	1,793,192	87.	Weight Watchers Magazine	976,063
38.	Field & Stream	1,750,180	88.	In Style	950,680
39.	Parents	1,737,249	89.	Health	943,543
40.	Country Living	1,647,925	90.	Victoria	943,125
41.	Life	1,601,069	91.	Shape	931,893
42.	American Rifleman	1,545,242	92.	American Homestyle & Gardening	930,155
43.	Golf Digest	1,515,829	93.	Jet	925,308
44.	Woman's World	1,504,067	94.	Elle	924,242
45.	Soap Opera Digest	1,468,333	95.	Globe	905,338
46.	Sunset	1,431,549	96.	Country America	902,122
47.	Popular Mechanics	1,428,356	97.	Today's Homeowner	901,266
48.	Cooking Light	1,379,055	98.	Business Week (North America)	893,771
49.	Men's Health	1,373,817	99.	House Beautiful	886,323
50.	Outdoor Life	1,353,061	100.	Gourmet	880,744

Average paid circulation for the six months ending Dec. 31, 1996. *Source:* Publishers Information Bureau

U.S. States

States and Territories

Data for state populations are the latest available from the U.S. Census Bureau. NOTE: Persons of Hispanic origin can be of any race. Largest cities include incorporated places only, as defined by the U.S. Census Bureau. They do not include adjacent or suburban areas. For secession and readmission dates of the former Confederate states, *see* the Confederate States of America.

For lists of Governors, Senators, and Representatives, *see* the Governors of the Fifty States, the Senate, and the House of Representatives.

ALABAMA

Capital: Montgomery
Governor: Fob James, Jr., R (to Jan. 1999)
Lieut. Governor: Don Siegelman, D (to Jan. 1999)
Secy. of State: Jim Bennett, R (to Jan. 1999)
Treasurer: Lucy Baxley, D (to Jan. 1999)
Atty. General: Jeff Sessions, R (to Jan. 1999)
Auditor: Pat Duncan, D (to Jan. 1999)
Organized as territory: March 3, 1817
Entered Union (rank): Dec. 14, 1819 (22)
Present constitution adopted: 1901
Motto: *Audemus jura nostra defendere* (We dare defend our rights)
State symbols: flower, Camellia (1959); **bird,** Yellowhammer (1927); **song,** "Alabama" (1931); **tree,** Southern pine (longleaf) (1949); **salt water fish,** Tarpon (1955); **fresh water fish,** Largemouth bass (1975); **horse,** Racking horse (1975); **mineral,** Hematite (1967); **rock,** Marble (1969); **game bird,** Wild turkey (1980); **dance,** Square dance (1981); **nut,** Pecan (1982); **fossil,** species *Basilosaurus Cetoides* (1984); **butterfly,** Eastern Tiger Swallowtail (1989); **insect,** Monarch butterfly (1989); **reptile,** Alabama red-bellied turtle (1990); **gemstone,** Star Blue Quartz (1990); **shell,** Scaphella junonia johnstoneae (1990).
Nickname: Yellowhammer State
Origin of name: May come from Choctaw meaning "thicket-clearers" or "vegetation-gatherers"
10 largest cities (1994): Birmingham, 264,527; Mobile, 204,490; Montgomery, 195,471; Huntsville, 160,325; Tuscaloosa, 79,797; Dothan, 55,792; Decatur, 52,465; Gadsden, 46,550; Hoover, 41,964; Florence, 36,770
Land area (rank): 50,750 sq mi. (131,443 sq km) (28)
Geographic center: In Chilton Co., 12 mi. SW of Clanton
Number of counties: 67
Largest county (area): Baldwin (1,590 sq mi.)
Largest county (1995 pop. est.): Jefferson, 657,827
State forests: 21 (48,000 ac.)
State parks: 22 (45,614 ac.)
1995 resident population est.: 4,252,982
1990 census population (rank): 4,040,587 (22). **Male:** 1,936,162; **Female:** 2,104,425. **White:** 2,975,797 (73.6%); **Black:** 1,020,705 (25.3%); **American Indian, Eskimo, or Aleut:** 16,506 (0.4%); **Asian or Pacific Islander:** 21,797 (0.5%); **Other race:** 5,782 (0.1%); **Hispanic:** 24,629 (0.6%). **1990 percent population under 18:** 26.2; **65 and over:** 12.9; **median age:** 33.0.

Spanish explorers are believed to have arrived at Mobile Bay in 1519, and the territory was visited in 1540 by the explorer Hernando de Soto. The first permanent European settlement in Alabama was founded by the French at Fort Louis de la Mobile in 1702. The British gained control of the area in 1763 by the Treaty of Paris, but had to cede almost all the Alabama region to the U.S. after the American Revolution. The Confederacy was founded at Montgomery in February 1861 and, for a time, the city was the Confederate capital.

During the last part of the 19th century, the economy of the state slowly improved. At Tuskegee Institute, founded in 1881 by Booker T. Washington, Dr. George Washington Carver carried out his famous agricultural research.

In the 1950s and '60s, Alabama was the site of such landmark civil-rights actions as the bus boycott in Montgomery (1955–56) and the "Freedom March" from Selma to Montgomery (1965).

Today paper, chemicals, rubber and plastics, apparel and textiles, and primary metals comprise the leading industries of Alabama. Continuing as a major manufacturer of coal, iron, and steel, Birmingham is also noted for its world-renowned medical center, especially for heart surgery. The state ranks high in the production of poultry, soybeans, milk, vegetables, livestock, wheat, cattle, cotton, peanuts, fruits, hogs, and corn.

Points of interest include the Helen Keller birthplace "Ivy Green" at Tuscumbia, the Space and Rocket Center at Huntsville, the White House of the Confederacy, the restored state Capitol, the Civil Rights Memorial, and Shakespeare Festival Theater Complex in Montgomery, the Civil Rights Institute in Birmingham, the Russell Cave near Bridgeport, and Bellingrath Gardens at Theodore, the U.S.S. Alabama at Mobile, Mound State Monument near Tuscaloosa, and the Gulf Coast area.

Famous natives and residents: Hank Aaron, baseball player; Ralph Abernathy, civil rights activist; Tallulah Bankhead, actress; Hugo L. Black, jurist; George Washington Carver, educator, agricultural chemist; Nat "King" Cole, entertainer; Marva Collins, educator; Kenneth Gibson, first black mayor of major eastern city (Newark); Lionel Hampton, jazz musician; W.C. Handy, composer; Kate Jackson, actress; Helen Keller, author and educator; Coretta Scott King, civil rights leader; Harper Lee, writer; Joe Louis, boxer; Willie Mays, baseball player; Jim Nabors, actor; Jesse Owens, athlete; Rosa Parks, civil rights activist; Wayne Rogers, actor; Tuscaloosa, Choctaw chief; George Wallace, ex-governor; William Weatherford (Red Eagle), Creek leader; Heather Whitestone, Miss America (1995).

ALASKA

Capital: Juneau
Governor: Tony Knowles, D (to Dec. 1998)
Lieut. Governor: Fran Ulmer, D (to Dec. 1998)
Commissioner of Administration: Mark Boyer
Atty. General: Bruce M. Bothelho, D
Organized as territory: 1912

Entered Union (rank): Jan. 3, 1959 (49)
Constitution ratified: April 24, 1956
Motto: North to the Future
State symbols: flower, Forget-me-not (1949); **tree,** Sitka spruce (1962); **bird,** Willow ptarmigan (1955); **fish,** King salmon (1962); **song,** "Alaska's Flag" (1955); **gem,** Jade (1968); **marine mammal,** Bowhead Whale (1983); **fossil,** Woolly Mammoth (1986); **mineral,** Gold (1968); **sport,** Dog Mushing (1972)
Nickname: The state is commonly called "The Last Frontier" or "Land of the Midnight Sun"
Origin of name: Corruption of Aleut word meaning "great land" or "that which the sea breaks against"
10 Largest cities: Anchorage, 253,649; Fairbanks, 34,321; Juneau, 28,758; Ketchikan, 8,781; Sitka, 8,780; Kodiak, 7,144; Kenai, 6,889; Bethel, 5,274; Wasilla, 5,119; Valdez, 4,400
Land area (rank): 570,374 sq mi. (1,477,267 sq km) (1)
Geographic center: 60 mi. NW of Mt. McKinley
Number of boroughs: 16
Largest borough (1995 pop. est.): Anchorage, 251,335
State forests: None
State parks: 5; 59 waysides and areas (3.3 million ac.)
1995 resident population est.: 603,617
1990 resident census population (rank): 550,043 (49). **Male:** 289,867; **Female:** 260,176. **White:** 415,492 (75.5%); **Black:** 22,451 (4.1%); **American Indian, Eskimo, or Aleut:** 85,698 (15.6%); **Asian or Pacific Islander:** 19,728 (3.6%); **Other race:** 6,675 (1.2%); **Hispanic:** 17,803 (3.2%). **1990 percent population under 18:** 31.3; **65 and over:** 4.1; **median age:** 29.4

Vitus Bering, a Dane working for the Russians, and Alexei Chirikov discovered the Alaskan mainland and the Aleutian Islands in 1741. The tremendous land mass of Alaska—equal to one fifth of the continental U.S.—was unexplored in 1867 when Secretary of State William Seward arranged for its purchase from the Russians for $7,200,000. The transfer of the territory took place on Oct. 18, 1867. Despite a price of about two cents an acre, the purchase was widely ridiculed as "Seward's Folly." The first official census (1880) reported a total of 33,426 Alaskans, all but 430 being of aboriginal stock. The Gold Rush of 1898 resulted in a mass influx of more than 30,000 people. Since then, Alaska has contributed billions of dollars' worth of products to the U.S. economy.

In 1968, a large oil and gas reservoir near Prudhoe Bay on the Arctic Coast was found. The Prudhoe Bay reservoir, with an estimated recoverable 10 billion barrels of oil and 27 trillion cubic feet of gas, is twice as large as any other oil field in North America. The Trans-Alaska pipeline was completed in 1977 at a cost of $7.7 billion. On June 20, oil started flowing through the 800-mile-long pipeline from Prudhoe Bay to the port of Valdez.

Other industries important to Alaska's economy are fisheries, wood and wood products, and furs, and tourism.

Denali National Park and Mendenhall Glacier in North Tongass National Forest are of interest, as is the large totem pole collection at Sitka National Historical Park. The Katmai National Park includes the "Valley of Ten Thousand Smokes," an area of active volcanoes.

Famous natives and residents: Clarence L. Andrews, author; Aleksandr Baranov, first governor of Russian America; Margaret Elizabeth Bell, author; Benny Benson, designed state flag at age 13; Vitus Bering, explorer; Charles E. Bunnell, educator; Susan Butcher, sled-dog racer; William A. Egan, first state governor; Carl Ben Eielson, pioneer pilot; Henry E. Gruennig, political leader; B. Frank Heintzleman, territorial governor; Walter J. Hickel, ex-governor; Sheldon Jackson, educator and missionary; Joe Juneau, prospector; Austin Lathrop, industrialist; Sydney Lawrence, painter; Ray Mala, actor; Virgil F. Partch, cartoonist; Joe Redington, Sr., sled-dog musher and promoter; Peter Trinble Rowe, first Episcopal bishop; Ivan Popov-Veniaminov (St. Innocent), Russian Orthodox missionary; Ferdinand Wrangel, educator; Samuel Hall Young, founder of first American church.

ARIZONA

Capital: Phoenix
Governor: Fife Symington, R (to Jan. 1999)
Secy. of State: Jane D. Hull, R (to Jan. 1999)
Atty. General: Grant Woods, R (to Jan. 1999[1])
State Treasurer: Tony West, R (to Jan. 1999)
Organized as territory: Feb. 24, 1863
Entered Union (rank): Feb. 14, 1912 (48)
Present constitution adopted: 1911
Motto: *Ditat Deus* (God enriches)
State symbols: flower: Flower of saguaro cactus (1931); **bird:** Cactus wren (1931); **colors:** Blue and old gold (1915); **song:** "Arizona March Song" (1919); **tree:** Palo Verde (1954); **neckwear,** Bolo tie (1973); **fossil,** Petrified wood (1988); **gemstone,** Turquoise (1974); **animals, mammal,** Ringtail; **reptile,** Arizona Ridge-nosed rattlesnake; **fish,** Arizona trout; **amphibian,** Arizona tree frog (1986)
Nickname: Grand Canyon State
Origin of name: From the Indian "Arizonac," meaning "little spring" or "young spring"
10 largest cities (1996 est. population): Phoenix, 1,180,740; Tucson, 449,635; Mesa, 343,710; Glendale, 186,695; Scottsdale, 178,525; Tempe, 156,000; Chandler, 141,735; Peoria, 78,310; Yuma, 63,150; Flagstaff, 55,885
Land area (rank): 114,000 sq mi. (296,400 sq km) (6)
Geographic center: In Yavapai Co., 55 mi. ESE of Prescott
Number of counties: 15
Largest county (1990 census): Maricopa, 2,122,101; (1996 est.: 2,634,625)
State forests: None
State parks: 24
1996 resident population est.: 4,462,300
1990 resident census population (rank): 3,665,228 (24). **Male:** 1,810,691; **Female:** 1,854,537. **White:** 2,963,186 (80.8%); **Black:** 110,524 (3.0%); **American Indian, Eskimo, or Aleut:** 203,527 (5.6%); **Asian or Pacific Islander:** 55,206 (1.5%); **Other race:** 332,785 (9.1%); **Hispanic:** 688,338 (18.8%). **1990 percent population under 18:** 26.8; **65 and over:** 13.1; **median age:** 32.2

1. Ran unopposed.

Marcos de Niza, a Spanish Franciscan friar, was the first European to explore Arizona. He entered the area in 1539 in search of the mythical Seven Cities of Gold. Although he was followed a year later by another gold seeker, Francisco Vásquez de Coronado, most of the early settlement was for missionary purposes. In 1775 the Spanish established Fort Tucson. In 1848, after the Mexican War, most of the Arizona territory became part of the U.S., and the southern portion of the territory was added by the Gadsden Purchase in 1853.

In 1973 one of the world's most massive dams, the New Cornelia Tailings, was completed near Ajo.

Arizona history is rich in legends of America's Old West. It was here that the great Indian chiefs Geronimo and Cochise led their people against the frontiersmen. Tombstone, Ariz., was the site of the West's most famous shoot-out—the gunfight at the O.K. Corral. Today, Arizona has one of the largest U.S. Indian populations; more than 14 tribes are represented on 20 reservations.

Manufacturing has become Arizona's most important industry. Principal products include electrical, communications, and aeronautical items. The state produces over half the country's copper. Agriculture is also important to the state's economy.

State attractions include the Grand Canyon, the Petrified Forest, and the Painted Desert. Hoover Dam, Lake Mead, Fort Apache, and the reconstructed London Bridge at Lake Havasu City are of particular interest.

Famous natives and residents: Apache Kid, Indian outlaw; Erma Bombeck, humorist, writer; Lynda Carter, actress; Cesar Chavez, labor leader; Cochise, Apache chief; Alice Cooper, singer, songwriter; Max Ernst, painter; Geronimo (Goyathlay), Apache chief; Barry Goldwater, politician; Zane Grey, novelist; Carl Trumbull Hayden, politician; George W. P. Hunt, first state governor; Bill Keane, cartoonist; Eusebio Kino, missionary; Percival Lowell, astronomer; Frank Luke, Jr., WWI fighter ace; Charles Mingus, jazz musician, composer; Carlos Montezuma, doctor and Indian spokesman; Sandra Day O'Connor, jurist; William O'Neill, frontier sheriff; Alexander M. Patch, general; William H. Pickering, astronomer; Linda Ronstadt, singer; Paolo Soleri, architect; Clyde W. Tombaugh, astronomer; Tanya Tucker, singer; Stewart Udall, ex-Secretary of the Interior; Pauline Weaver, frontier person; Frank Lloyd Wright, architect.

ARKANSAS

Capital: Little Rock
Governor: Mike Huckabee, R (to Jan. 1999)
Lieut. Governor: Winthrop Rockefeller, R (to 1998)
Secy. of State: Sharon Priest, D (to Jan. 1998)
Atty. General: Winston Bryant, D (to Jan. 1998)
Auditor of State: Gus Wingfield, D (to Jan. 1998)
Treasurer of State: Jimmie Lou Fisher Lumpkin, D (to Jan. 1998)
Land Commissioner: Charles Daniels, D (to Jan. 1998)
Organized as territory: March 2, 1819
Entered Union (rank): June 15, 1836 (25)
Present constitution adopted: 1874
Motto: *Regnat populus* (The people rule)
State symbols: flower, Apple Blossom (1901); **tree,** Pine (1939); **bird,** Mockingbird (1929); **insect,** Honeybee (1973); **song,** "Arkansas" (1963)
Nickname: Land of Opportunity
Origin of name: From the Quapaw Indians
10 largest cities (1994): Little Rock, 178,136; Fort Smith, 74,480; North Little Rock, 62,197; Pine Bluff, 57,971; Jonesboro, 50,209; Fayetteville, 49,219; Springdale, 36,553; Hot Springs, 35,644; Conway, 33,946; Rogers, 30,462
Land area (rank): 52,075 sq mi. (134,875 sq km) (27)
Geographic center: In Pulaski Co., 12 mi. NW of Little Rock
Number of counties: 75
Largest county (1995 pop. est.): Pulaski, 352,240
State forests: None
State parks: 44
1995 resident population est.: 2,483,769
1990 resident population (rank): 2,350,725 (33). **Male:** 1,133,076; **Female:** 1,217,649. **White:** 1,944,744 (82.7%); **Black:** 373,912 (15.9%); **American Indian, Eskimo, or Aleut:** 12,773 (0.5%); **Asian or Pacific Islander:** 12,530 (0.5%); **Other race:** 6,766 (0.3%); **Hispanic:** 19,876 (0.8%). **1990 percent population under 18:** 26.4; **65 and over:** 14.9; **median age:** 33.8.

Hernando de Soto, in 1541, was among the early European explorers to visit the territory. It was a Frenchman, Henri de Tonti, who in 1686 founded the first permanent white settlement—the Arkansas Post. In 1803 the area was acquired by the U.S. as part of the Louisiana Purchase.

Food products are the state's largest employing sector, with lumber and wood products a close second. Arkansas is also a leader in the production of cotton, rice, and soybeans. It also has the country's only active diamond mine; located near Murfreesboro, it is operated as a tourist attraction.

Hot Springs National Park, and Buffalo National River in the Ozarks are major state attractions.

Blanchard Springs Caverns, the Arkansas Territorial Restoration at Little Rock, and the Arkansas Folk Center in Mountain View are of interest.

Famous natives and residents: G.M. "Broncho Billy" Anderson, actor; Maya Angelou, author, poet; Katharine Susan Anthony, author; Helen Gurley Brown, author; Glen Campbell, singer; Hattie Caraway, first elected woman senator; Johnny Cash, singer; Eldridge Cleaver, Black activist; William Jefferson Clinton, 42nd President; Dizzy Dean, baseball player; Orval Faubus, ex-governor; John Gould Fletcher, writer; James W. Fulbright, ex-senator; John H. Johnson, publisher; Alan Ladd, actor; Douglas MacArthur, 5-star general; John Paul McConnell, U.S. Air Force officer; Ben Murphy, actor; Frank Pace, Jr., public official; Ben Piazza, actor; Albert Pike, pioneer teacher, lawyer; Dick Powell, actor; Opie P. Read, writer; Jenny D. Rice-Meyrowitz, painter; Brehon Burke Somervell, World Wars I and II U.S. Army officer; Mary Steenburgen, actress; Edward Durrell Stone, architect; Sam Walton, Wal-Mart founder; William C. Warfield, concert singer, actor.

CALIFORNIA

Capital: Sacramento
Governor: Pete Wilson, R (to Jan. 1999)
Lieut. Governor: Gray Davis, D (to Jan. 1999)
Secy. of State: Bill Jones, R (to Jan. 1999)
Controller: Cathleen Connell, D (to Jan. 1999)
Atty. General: Dan Lungren, R (to Jan. 1999)
Treasurer: Matt Fong, R (to Jan. 1999)
Supt. of Public Instruction: David Meaney
Entered Union (rank): Sept. 9, 1850 (31)
Present constitution adopted: 1879
Motto: *Eureka* (I have found it)
State symbols: flower, Golden poppy (1903); **tree,** California redwoods (*Sequoia sempervirens & Sequoia gigantea*) (1937 % 1953); **bird,** California valley quail (1931); **animal,** California grizzly bear (1953); **fish,** California golden trout (1947); **colors,** Blue and gold (1951); **song,** "I Love You, California" (1951)
Nickname: Golden State
Origin of name: From a book, *Las Sergas de Esplandián,* by Garcia Ordóñez de Montalvo, c. 1500
10 largest cities (1994): Los Angeles, 3,448,613; San Diego, 1,151,977; San Jose, 816,884; San Francisco, 734,676; Long Beach, 433,852; Fresno, 386,551; Sacramento, 373,964; Oakland, 366,926; Santa Ana, 290,827; Anaheim, 282,133
Land area (rank): 155,973 sq mi. (403,970 sq km) (3)
Geographic center: In Madera Co., 35 mi. NE of Madera
Number of counties: 58
Largest county (1995 pop. est.): Los Angeles, 9,138,789
State forests: 8 (70,283 ac.)
State parks and beaches: 180 (723,000 ac.)
1995 resident population est.: 31,589,153
1990 resident population (rank): 29,760,021 (1). **Male:** 14,897,627; **Female:** 14,862,394. **White:** 20,524,327 (69.9%); **Black:** 2,208,801 (7.4%); **American Indian, Eskimo, or Aleut:** 242,164 (0.8%); **Asian or Pacific Islander,** 2,845,659 (9.6%); **Other race:** 3,939,070 (13.2%); **Hispanic:** 7,687,938 (25.8%). **1990 percent population under 18:** 26.0; **65 and over:** 10.5; **median age:** 31.5.

Although California was sighted by Spanish navigator Juan Rodríguez Cabrillo in 1542, its first Spanish mission (at San Diego) was not established until 1769. California became a U.S. Territory in 1847 when Mexico surrendered it to John C. Frémont. On Jan. 24, 1848, James W. Marshall discovered gold at Sutter's Mill, starting the California Gold Rush and bringing settlers to the state in large numbers.

In 1964, the U.S. Census Bureau estimated that California had become the most populous state, surpassing New York. California also leads the country in personal income and consumer expenditures.

Leading industries include manufacturing (transportation equipment, machinery, and electronic equipment), agriculture, biotechnology, and tourism. Principal natural resources include timber, petroleum, cement, and natural gas.

More immigrants settle in California than any other state—more than one-third of the nation's total in 1994. Asian-Pacific Islanders led the influx.

Death Valley, in the southeast, is 282 feet below sea level, the lowest point in the nation; and Mt. Whitney (14,491 ft.) is the highest point in the contiguous 48 states. Lassen Peak is one of two active U.S. volcanoes outside of Alaska and Hawaii; its last eruptions were recorded in 1917. The General Sherman Tree in Sequoia National Park is estimated to be about 3,500 years old and a stand of bristlecone pine trees in the White Mountains may be over 4,000 years old.

Other points of interest include Yosemite National Park, Disneyland, Hollywood, the Golden Gate bridge, San Simeon State Park, and Point Reyes National Seashore.

Famous natives and residents: Gertrude Atherton, author; David Belasco, playwright and producer; Shirley Temple Black, actress, ambassador; Dave Brubeck, musician; Luther Burbank, horticulturalist; Julia Child, chef; Joe DiMaggio, baseball player; James H. Doolittle, Air Force general; Isadora Duncan, dancer; John Frémont, explorer; Robert Frost, poet; Henry George, economist; Richard "Pancho" Gonzales, tennis player; George E. Hale, astronomer; Bret Harte, writer; William Randolph Hearst, publisher; Sidney Howard, playwright; Collis Potter Huntington, financier; Helen Hunt Jackson, writer; Robinson Jeffers, poet; Anthony M. Kennedy, jurist; Jack London, author; James W. Marshall, first discovered gold; Aimee Semple McPherson, evangelist; Marilyn Monroe, actress; John Muir, naturalist; Richard M. Nixon, President; Isamu Noguchi, sculptor; Frank Norris, novelist; Kathleen Norris, novelist; George S. Patton, Jr., general; Robert Redford, actor; Sally K. Ride, astronaut; William Saroyan, author; Junípero Serra, missionary; Upton Sinclair, novelist; Leland Stanford, railroad magnate; Lincoln Steffens, journalist, author; John Steinbeck, author; Adlai Stevenson, statesman; Johann Sutter, pioneer; Michael Tilson Thomas, conductor; Earl Warren, jurist.

COLORADO

Capital: Denver
Governor: Roy Romer, D (to Jan. 1999)
Lieut. Governor: Gail Schoettler, D (to Jan. 1999)
Secy. of State: Vikki Buckley, R (to Jan 1999)
Treasurer: Bill Owens, R (to Jan. 1999)
Controller: Cliff Hall, R (appointed)
Atty. General: Gale Norton, R (to Jan. 1999)
Organized as territory: Feb. 28, 1861
Entered Union (rank): Aug. 1, 1876 (38)
Present constitution adopted: 1876
Motto: *Nil sine Numine* (Nothing without Providence)
State symbols: flower, Rocky Mountain columbine (1899); **tree,** Colorado blue spruce (1939); **bird,** Lark bunting (1931); **animal,** Rocky Mountain bighorn sheep (1961); **gemstone,** Aquamarine (1971); **colors,** Blue and white (1911); **song,** "Where the

Columbines Grow" (1915); **fossil,** Stegosaurus (1991)
Nickname: Centennial State
Origin of name: From the Spanish, "ruddy" or "red"
10 largest cities (1994): Denver, 493,559; Colorado Springs, 316,480; Aurora, 250,717; Lakewood, 126,031; Pueblo, 100,471; Fort Collins, 98,954; Arvada, 95,446; Westminster, 87,045; Boulder, 85,613; Greeley, 64,189
Land area (rank): 103,730 sq mi. (268,660 sq km) (8)
Geographic center: In Park Co., 30 mi. NW of Pikes Peak
Number of counties: 63
Largest county (1995 pop. est.): Denver, 494,462
State forests: 1 (71,000 ac.)
State parks: 44
1995 resident population est.: 3,746,585
1990 resident census population (rank): 3,294,394 (26). **Male:** 1,631,295; **Female:** 1,663,099. **White:** 2,095,474 (88.2%); **Black:** 133,146 (4.0%); **American Indian, Eskimo, or Aleut,** 27,776 (0.8%); **Asian or Pacific Islander,** 59,862 (1.8%); **Other race:** 168,136 (5.1%); **Hispanic:** 424,302 (12.9%). **1990 percent population under 18:** 26.1; **65 and over:** 10.0; **median age:** 32.5

First visited by Spanish explorers in the 1500s, the territory was claimed for Spain by Juan de Ulibarri in 1706. The U.S. obtained eastern Colorado as part of the Louisiana Purchase in 1803, the central portion in 1845 with the admission of Texas as a state, and the western part in 1848 as a result of the Mexican War.

Colorado has the highest mean elevation of any state, with more than 1,000 Rocky Mountain peaks over 10,000 feet high and 54 towering above 14,000 feet. Pikes Peak, the most famous of these mountains, was discovered by U.S. Army Lieut. Zebulon M. Pike in 1806.

Once primarily a mining and agricultural state, Colorado's economy is now driven by the service-producing industries, which provide jobs for approximately 82.4 percent of the state's non-farm work force. Tourism expenditures in the state total approximately 6 billion dollars annually. Tourist expenditures on the ski industry account for 1.8 billion dollars annually, approximately a third of the total tourist expenditures. The main tourist attractions in the state include Rocky Mountain National Park, Curecanti National Recreation Area, Mesa Verde National Park, the Great Sand Dunes and Dinosaur National Monuments, Colorado National Monument, and the Black Canyon of the Gunnison National Monument.

The two primary facets of Colorado's manufacturing industry are food and kindred products, and printing and publishing.

The mining industry, which includes oil and gas, coal, and metal mining, was important to Colorado's economy, but it now employs only 1.2 percent of the state's workforce. Denver is home to companies that control half of the nation's gold production. The farm industry, which is primarily concentrated in livestock, is also an important element of the state's economy. The primary crops in Colorado are corn, hay, and wheat.

Famous natives and residents: William E. Barrett, writer; William Bent, fur trader and pioneer; Charles F. Brannan, lawyer and public official; M. Scott Carpenter, astronaut; Lon Chaney, actor; Mary Coyle Chase, playwright; Jack Dempsey, boxer; Ralph Edwards, entertainer; John Evans, physician, educator; Douglas Fairbanks, actor; John Thomas Fante, writer; Eugene Fodor, violinist; Gene Fowler, writer; Erick Hawkins, choreographer; Homer Lea, soldier, writer; Ted Mack, TV host; Jaye P. Morgan, singer; Peg Murray, actress; Ouray, Ute Indian chief; Anne Parrish, writer; Barbara Rush, actress; Horace A. Tabor, silver king, Lieut.-Governor; Lowell Thomas, commentator and author; Dalton Trumbo, screenwriter, novelist; Byron R. White, jurist; Paul Whiteman, conductor; Don Wilson, announcer.

CONNECTICUT

Capital: Hartford
Governor: John G. Rowland, R (to Jan. 1999)
Lieut. Governor: M. Jodi Rell, R (to Jan. 1999)
Secy. of State: Miles S. Rapoport, D (to Jan. 1999)
Comptroller: Nancy Wyman, D (to Jan. 1999)
Treasurer: Christopher B. Burnham, R (to Jan. 1999)
Atty. General: Richard Blumenthal, D (to Jan. 1999)
Entered Union (rank): Jan. 9, 1788 (5)
Present constitution adopted: Dec. 30, 1965
Motto: *Qui transtulit sustinet* (He who transplanted still sustains)
State symbols: flower, Mountain Laurel (1907); **tree,** White Oak (1947); **animal,** Sperm Whale (1975); **bird,** American Robin (1943); **hero,** Nathan Hale (1985); **heroine,** Prudence Crandall (1995); **insect,** Praying Mantis (1977); **mineral,** Garnet (1977); **song,** "Yankee Doodle" (1978); **ship,** USS Nautilus (SSN571) (1983); **shellfish,** Eastern Oyster (1989); **fossil,** Eubrontes Giganteus (1991)
Official designation: *Constitution State* (1959)
Nickname: Nutmeg State
Origin of name: From an Indian word (Quinnehtukqut) meaning "beside the long tidal river"
10 largest cities (1994): Bridgeport, 132,919; Hartford, 124,196; New Haven, 119,604; Stamford, 107,199; Waterbury, 103,523; Norwalk, 78,710; New Britain, 69,887; Danbury, 64,675; Bristol, 60,647; Meriden, 56,928
Land area (rank): 4,845 sq mi. (12,550 sq km) (48)
Geographic center: In Hartford Co., at East Berlin
Number of counties: 8
Largest county (1995 pop. est.): Hartford 835,589
State forests: 30 (144,768 ac.)
State parks: 90 (31,729 ac.)
1995 resident population est.: 3,274,662
1990 resident population (rank): 3,287,116 (27). **Male:** 1,592,873; **Female:** 1,694,243. **White:** 2,859,353 (87.0%); **Black:** 274,269 (8.3%); **American Indian, Eskimo, or Aleut:** 6,654 (0.2%); **Asian or Pacific Islander:** 50,698 (1.5%); **Other race:** 96,142 (2.9%); **Hispanic:** 213,116 (6.5%). **1990 percent population under 18:** 22.8; **65 and over:** 13.6; **median age:** 34.4.

1. A Connecticut Party.

The Dutch navigator, Adriaen Block, was the first European of record to explore the area, sailing up the Connecticut River in 1614. In 1633, Dutch colonists built a fort and trading post near present-day Hartford, but soon lost control to English Puritans migrating south from the Massachusetts Bay Colony.

English settlements, established in the 1630s at Windsor, Wethersfield, and Hartford, united in 1639 to form the Connecticut Colony and adopted the *Fundamental Orders*.

The colony's royal charter of 1662 was exceptionally liberal. When Gov. Edmund Andros tried to seize it in 1687, it was hidden in the Hartford Oak, commemorated in Charter Oak Place.

Connecticut played a prominent role in the Revolutionary War, serving as the Continental Army's major supplier. Sometimes called the "Arsenal of the Nation," the state became one of the most industrialized in the nation.

Today, Connecticut factories produce weapons, sewing machines, jet engines, helicopters, motors, hardware and tools, cutlery, clocks, locks, ball bearings, silverware, and submarines. Hartford, which has the oldest U.S. newspaper still being published—the *Hartford Courant,* established 1764—is the insurance capital of the nation.

Poultry, fruit, and dairy products account for the largest portion of farm income, and Connecticut's shade-grown tobacco is acknowledged to be the state's most valuable crop per acre.

Connecticut is a popular resort area with its 250-mile Long Island Sound shoreline and many inland lakes. Among the major points of interest are Yale University's Gallery of Fine Arts and Peabody Museum. Other famous museums include the P.T. Barnum, Winchester Gun, and American Clock and Watch. The town of Mystic features a recreated 19th-century New England seaport and the Mystic Marinelife Aquarium.

Famous natives and residents: Dean Acheson, statesman; Ethan Allan, American Revolutionary soldier; Benedict Arnold, American Revolutionary general; Wadsworth Atheneum;, P.T. Barnum, showman; Henry Ward Beecher, clergyman; John Brown, abolitionist; Oliver Ellsworth, jurist; Eileen Farrell, soprano; Charles Goodyear, inventor; Nathan Hale, American Revolutionary officer; Dorothy Hamill, ice skater; Katharine Hepburn, actress; Charles Ives, composer; Edwin H. Land, inventor; John Pierpont Morgan, financier; Frederick Law Olmsted, landscape planner; Rosa Ponselle, soprano; Adam Clayton Powell, Jr., congressman; Benjamin Spock, pediatrician; Harriet Beecher Stowe, author; Morris R. Waite, jurist; Noah Webster, lexicographer.

DELAWARE

Capital: Dover
Governor: Thomas R. Carper, D (to Jan. 2001)
Lieut. Governor: Ruth Ann Minner, D (to Jan. 2001)
Secy. of State: Edward J. Freel, D (Pleasure of Governor)
State Treasurer: Janet C. Rzewnicki, R (to Jan. 2001)
Atty. General: M. Jane Brady, R (to Jan. 2001)
Entered Union (rank): Dec. 7, 1787 (1)
Present constitution adopted: 1897
Motto: Liberty and independence
State symbols: colors, Colonial blue and buff; **flower,** Peach blossom (1895); **tree,** American holly (1939); **bird,** Blue Hen chicken (1939); **insect,** Ladybug (1974); **fish,** Weakfish, *Cynoscion regalis* (1981); **song,** "Our Delaware"
Nicknames: Diamond State; First State; Small Wonder
Origin of name: From Delaware River and Bay; named in turn for Sir Thomas West, Lord De La War
10 Largest cities (1994): Wilmington, 72,799; Dover, 28,876; Newark, 27,386; Milford, 6,680; Seaford, 6,254; Smyrna, 5,700; Elsmere, 5,540; New Castle 5,131; Georgetown, 4,196; Middletown, 4,129
Land area (rank): 1,982 sq mi. (5,153 sq km) (49)
Geographic center: In Kent Co., 11 mi. S of Dover
Number of counties: 3
Largest county (1995 pop. est.): New Castle, 467,889
State forests: 3 (9,353 ac.)
State parks: 13
1996 resident population est.: 725,000
1990 resident census population (rank): 666,168 (46). **Male:** 322,968; **Female:** 343,200. **White:** 535,094 (80.3%); **Black:** 112,460 (16.9%); **American Indian, Eskimo, or Aleut:** 2,019 (0.3%); **Asian or Pacific Islander:** 9,057 (1.4%); **Other race:** 7,538 (1.1%); **Hispanic:** 15,820 (2.4%). **1990 percent population under 18:** 24.5; **65 and over:** 12.1; **median age:** 32.9.

Henry Hudson, sailing under the Dutch flag, is credited with Delaware's discovery in 1609. The following year, Capt. Samuel Argall of Virginia named Delaware for his colony's governor, Thomas West, Baron De La Warr. An attempted Dutch settlement failed in 1631. Swedish colonization began at Fort Christina (now Wilmington) in 1638, but New Sweden fell to Dutch forces led by New Netherlands' Gov. Peter Stuyvesant in 1655.

England took over the area in 1664 and it was transferred to William Penn as the southern Three Counties in 1682. Semiautonomous after 1704, Delaware fought as a separate state in the American Revolution and became the first state to ratify the constitution in 1787.

During the Civil War, although a slave state, Delaware did not secede from the Union.

In 1802, Éleuthère Irénée du Pont established a gunpowder mill near Wilmington that laid the foundation for Delaware's huge chemical industry. Delaware's manufactured products now also include vulcanized fiber, textiles, paper, medical supplies, metal products, machinery, machine tools, and automobiles.

Delaware also grows a great variety of fruits and vegetables and is a U.S. pioneer in the food-canning industry. Corn, soybeans, potatoes, and hay are important crops. Delaware's broiler chicken farms supply the big Eastern markets, fishing and dairy products are other important industries.

Points of interest include the Fort Christina Monument, Hagley Museum, Holy Trinity Church (erected in 1698, the oldest Protestant church in the United States still in use), and Winterthur Museum, in and near Wilmington; central New Castle, an almost unchanged late 18th-century capital; and the Delaware Museum of Natural History.

Popular recreation areas include Cape Henlopen, Delaware Seashore, Trapp Pond State Park, and Rehoboth Beach.

Famous natives and residents: Richard Allen, founder of African Methodist Episcopal Church; Valerie Bertinelli, actress; Robert Montgomery Bird, playwright and novelist; Henry S. Canby, editor and author; Annie Jump Cannon, astronomer; Elizabeth Margaret Chandler, author; Felix Darley, artist; John Dickinson, statesman; E.I. du Pont, industrialist; Oliver Evans, inventor; Thomas Garrett, abolitionist; Henry Heimlich, surgeon, inventor; Wilham Julius "Judy" Johnson, basketball player; J.P. Marquand, novelist; Howard Pyle, artist and author; George Read, jurist, signer of Declaration of Independence; Jay Saunders Redding, educator and author; Caesar Rodney, patriot, signer of Declaration of Independence; Frank Stephens, sculptor; Estelle Taylor, actress; George Alfred Townsend, journalist and author.

DISTRICT OF COLUMBIA

See Washington, D.C. listing in U.S. Cities.

FLORIDA

Capital: Tallahassee
Governor: Lawton Chiles, D (to Jan. 1999)
Lieut. Governor: Buddy McKay, D (to Jan. 1999)
Secy. of State: Sandra B. Mortham, R (to Jan. 1999)
Comptroller: Bob Milligan, R (to Jan. 1999)
Commissioner of Agriculture: Bob Crawford, D (to Jan. 1999)
Atty. General: Bob Butterworth, D (to Jan. 1999)
Organized as territory: March 30, 1822
Entered Union (rank): March 3, 1845 (27)
Present constitution adopted: 1969
Motto: In God we trust (1868)
State symbols: flower, Orange blossom (1909); **bird,** Mockingbird (1927); **song,** "Suwannee River" (1935)
Nickname: Sunshine State (1970)
Origin of name: From the Spanish, meaning "feast of flowers" (Easter)
10 largest cities (1995 pop. est.): Jacksonville (CC[1]), 635,230; Miami, 358,648; Tampa, 280,015; St. Petersburg, 240,318; Hialeah, 188,008; Orlando, 164,674; Fort Lauderdale, 149,238; Tallahassee, 124,773; Hollywood, 121,720; Clearwater, 98,784
Land area (rank): 53,997 sq mi. (139,852 sq km) (26)
Geographic center: In Hernando Co., 12 mi. NNW of Brooksville

Number of counties: 67
Largest county (1996 pop. est.): Dade, 2,013,821
State forests: 35 (550,000 ac.)
State parks: 147 (456,972 ac.)
1996 resident population est.: 14,411,536
1990 resident census population (rank): 12,937,926 (4). **Male:** 6,261,719; **Female:** 6,676,207. **White:** 10,749,285 (83.1%); **Black:** 1,759,534 (13.6%); **American Indian, Eskimo, or Aleut:** 36,335 (0.3%); **Asian or Pacific Islander:** 154,302 (1.2%); **Other race:** 238,470 (1.8%); **Hispanic:** 1,574,143 (12.2%). **1990 percent population under 18:** 22.2; **65 and over:** 18.3; **median age:** 36.4.

1. Consolidated City (Coextensive with Duval County).

In 1513, Ponce De Leon, seeking the mythical "Fountain of Youth," discovered and named Florida, claiming it for Spain. Later, Florida would be held at different times by Spain and England until Spain finally sold it to the United States in 1819. (Incidentally, France established a colony named Fort Caroline in 1564 in the state that was to become Florida.)

Florida's early 19th-century history as a U.S. territory was marked by wars with the Seminole Indians that did not end until 1842, although a treaty was actually never signed.

One of the nation's fastest-growing states, Florida's population has gone from 2.8 million in 1950 to more than 12.9 million in 1990.

Florida's economy rests on a solid base of tourism (in 1992 the state entertained more than 40.5 million visitors from all over the world), manufacturing, agriculture, and international trade.

In recent years, oranges, grapefruit and tomatoes lead Florida's crop list, followed by vegetables, potatoes, melons, strawberries, sugar cane, dairy products, cattle and calves, and forest products.

Major tourist attractions are Miami Beach, Palm Beach, St. Augustine (founded in 1565, thus the oldest permanent city in the U.S.), Daytona Beach, and Fort Lauderdale on the East Coast. West Coast resorts include Sarasota, Tampa, Key West and St. Petersburg. The Orlando area, where Disney World is located on a 27,000-acre site, is Florida's most popular tourist destination.

Also drawing many visitors are the NASA Kennedy Space Center's Spaceport USA, located in the town of Kennedy Space Center, Everglades National Park, and the Epcot Center.

Famous natives and residents: Julian "Cannonball" Adderley, jazz saxophonist; Pat Boone, singer; Fernando Bujones, ballet dancer; Steve Carlton, baseball player; Fay Dunaway, actress; Stepin Fetchit (Lincoln Theodore Perry), comedian; Lue Gim Gong, horticulturist; Dwight Gooden, baseball player; Zora Neale Hurston, writer; Daniel James, four-star general; James Weldon Johnson, author and educator; Frances Langford, singer; Little Richard, singer; Butterfly McQueen, actress; Jim Morrison, singer; Osceola, Seminole Indian leader; Sidney Poitier, actor; A. Philip Randolph, labor leader; Marjorie Kinnan Rawlings, author; Burt Reynolds, actor; Charles and John Ringling, circus entrepreneurs; Joseph W. Stilwell, army general; Norman E. Thargard, astronaut; Clarence Thomas, jurist; Ben Vereen, actor.

GEORGIA

Capital: Atlanta
Governor: Zell Miller, D (to Jan. 1999)
Lieut. Governor: Pierre Howard, D (to Jan. 1999)
Secy. of State: Lewis A. Massey, D (to Jan. 1999)
Insurance Commissioner: John Oxendine, D (to Jan. 1999)
Atty. General: Michael J. Bowers, R (to Jan. 1999)
Entered Union (rank): Jan. 2, 1788 (4)

Present constitution adopted: 1977
Motto: Wisdom, justice, and moderation
State symbols: flower, Cherokee rose (1916); **tree,** Live oak (1937); **bird,** Brown thrasher (1935); **song,** "Georgia on My Mind" (1922)
Nicknames: Peach State, Empire State of the South
Origin of name: In honor of George II of England
10 largest cities (1994): Atlanta, 396,052; Columbus[1], 186,470; Savannah, 140,597; Macon, 109,191; Athens-Clarke County, 89,181; Albany, 81,062; Roswell, 54,908; Marietta, 50,290; Warner Robins, 47,694; Valdosta, 44,787
Land area (rank): 57,919 sq mi. (150,010 sq km) (21)
Geographic center: In Twiggs Co., 18 mi. SE of Macon
Number of counties: 159
Largest county (1995 pop. est.): Fulton, 700,689
State forests: 25,258,000 ac. (67% of total state area)
State parks: 53 (42,600 ac.)
1995 resident population est.: 7,200,882
1990 resident census population (rank): 6,478,216 (11). **Male:** 3,144,503; **Female:** 3,333,713. **White:** 4,600,148 (71.0%); **Black:** 1,746,565 (27.0%); **American Indian, Eskimo, or Aleut:** 13,348 (0.2%); **Asian or Pacific Islander:** 75,781 (1.2%); **Other race:** 42,374 (0.7%); **Hispanic:** 108,922 (1.7%). **1990 percent population under 18:** 26.7; **65 and over:** 10.1; **median age:** 31.6.

1. Consolidated City (Coextensive with Muscogee County).

Hernando de Soto, the Spanish explorer, first traveled parts of Georgia in 1540. British claims later conflicted with those of Spain. After obtaining a royal charter, Gen. James Oglethorpe established the first permanent settlement in Georgia in 1733 as a refuge for English debtors. In 1742, Oglethorpe defeated Spanish invaders in the Battle of Bloody Marsh.

A Confederate stronghold, Georgia was the scene of extensive military action during the Civil War. Union General William T. Sherman burned Atlanta and destroyed a 60-mile wide path to the coast where he captured Savannah in 1864.

The largest state east of the Mississippi, Georgia is typical of the changing South with an ever-increasing industrial development. Atlanta, largest city in the state, is the communications and transportation center for the Southeast and the area's chief distributor of goods.

Georgia leads the nation in the production of paper and board, tufted textile products, and processed chicken. Other major manufactured products are transportation equipment, food products, apparel, and chemicals.

Important agricultural products are corn, cotton, tobacco, soybeans, eggs, and peaches. Georgia produces twice as many peanuts as the next leading state. From its vast stands of pine come more than half the world's resins and turpentine and 74.4 percent of the U.S. supply. Georgia is also a leader in the production of marble, kaolin, barite, and bauxite.

Principal tourist attractions in Georgia include the Okefenokee National Wildlife Refuge, Andersonville Prison Park and National Cemetery, Chickamauga and Chattanooga National Military Park, the Little White House at Warm Springs where Pres. Franklin D. Roosevelt died in 1945, Sea Island, the enormous Confederate Memorial at Stone Mountain, Kennesaw Mountain National Battlefield Park, and Cumberland Island National Seashore.

Famous natives and residents: Conrad Aiken, poet; James Bowie, soldier; James Brown, singer; Jim Brown, actor and athlete; Erskine Caldwell, writer; James E. Carter, ex-President; Ray Charles, singer; Lucius D. Clay, banker, ex-general; Ty Cobb, baseball player; Ossie Davis, actor & writer; James Dickey, poet; Mattiwilda Dobbs, soprano; Melvyn Douglas, actor; Rebecca Latimer Felton, first appointed woman U.S. senator; Roosevelt Grier, entertainer and ex-athlete; Oliver Hardy, comedian; Joel Chandler Harris, journalist and author; Larry Holmes, boxer; Miriam Hopkins, actress; Harry James, trumpeter; Jasper Johns, painter and sculptor; Stacy Keach, actor; DeForest Kelley, actor; Martin Luther King, Jr., civil rights leader; Gladys Knight, singer; Joseph R. Lamar, jurist; Juliette Gordon Low, U.S. Girl Scouts founder; Carson McCullers, novelist; Johnny Mercer, songwriter; Margaret Mitchell, novelist; Elijah Muhammad, religious leader; Jessye Norman, soprano; Otis Redding, singer; Burt Reynolds, actor; Jackie Robinson, baseball player; Dean Rusk, ex-Secretary of State; Nipsey Russell, comedian; Alice Walker, author; Joanne Woodward, actress.

HAWAII

Capital: Honolulu (on Oahu)
Governor: Benjamin Cayetano, D (to Dec. 1998)
Lieut. Governor: Mazie Hirono, D
Comptroller: Sam Callejo
Atty. General: Margery Bronster
Organized as territory: 1900
Entered Union (rank): Aug. 21, 1959 (50)
Motto: Ua Mau Ke Ea O Ka Aina I Ka Pono (The life of the land is perpetuated in righteousness)
State symbols: flower, Hibiscus (yellow) (1988); **song,** "Hawaii Ponoi" (1967); **bird,** Nene (hawaiian goose) (1957); **tree,** Kukui (Candlenut) (1959)
Nickname: Aloha State (1959)
Origin of name: Uncertain. The islands may have been named by Hawaii Loa, their traditional discoverer. Or they may have been named after Hawaii or Hawaiki, the traditional home of the Polynesians.
10 largest cities[1] (1994): Honolulu, 377,059; Hilo, 37,808; Kailua, 36,818; Kaneohe, 35,448; Waipahu, 31,435; Pearl City, 30,993; Waimalu, 29,967; Mililani Town, 29,359; Schofield Barracks, 19,597; Wahiawa, 17,386
Land area (rank): 6,423.4 sq mi. (16,636.5 sq km) (47)
Geographic center: Between islands of Hawaii and Maui
Number of counties: 4 plus one non-functioning county (Kalawao)
Largest county (1995 pop. est.): Honolulu, 877,198
State parks and historic sites: 70
1995 resident population est.: 1,186,815
1990 resident census population (rank): 1,108,229 (40). **Male:** 563,891; **Female:** 544,338. **White:** 369,616 (33.4%); **Black:** 27,195 (2.5%); **American Indian, Eskimo, or Aleut:** 5,099 (0.5%); **Asian or Pacific Islander:** 685,236 (61.8%); **Other race:** 21,083 (1.9%); **Hispanic:** 81,390 (7.3%). **1990 percent population under 18:** 25.3; **65 and over:** 11.3; **median age:** 32.6

1. Census Designated Place. There are no political boundaries to Honolulu or any other place, but statistical boundaries are assigned under state law.

First settled by Polynesians sailing from other Pacific islands between C.E. 300 and 600, Hawaii was visited in 1778 by British Captain James Cook who called the group the Sandwich Islands.

Hawaii was a native kingdom throughout most of the 19th century when the expansion of the vital sugar industry (pineapple came after 1898) meant increasing U.S. business and political involvement. In 1893, Queen Liliuokalani was deposed and a year later the Republic of Hawaii was established with Sanford B. Dole as president. Then, following its annexation in 1898, Hawaii became a U.S. Territory in 1900.

The Japanese attack on the naval base at Pearl Harbor on Dec. 7, 1941, was directly responsible for U.S. entry into World War II.

Hawaii, 2,397 miles west-southwest of San Francisco, is a 1,523-mile chain of islets and eight main islands—Hawaii, Kahoolawe, Maui, Lanai, Molokai, Oahu, Kauai, and Niihau. The Northwestern Hawaiian Islands, other than Midway, are administratively part of Hawaii.

The temperature is mild and Hawaii's soil is fertile for tropical fruits and vegetables. Cane sugar and pineapple are the chief products. Hawaii also grows coffee, bananas and nuts. The tourist business is Hawaii's largest source of outside income.

Hawaii's highest peak is Mauna Kea (13,796 ft.). Mauna Loa (13,679 ft.) is the largest volcanic mountain in the world in cubic content.

Among the major points of interest are Hawaii Volcanoes National Park (Hawaii), Haleakala National Park (Maui), Puuhonua o Honaunau National Historical Park (Hawaii), Polynesian Cultural Center (Oahu), the U.S.S. *Arizona* Memorial at Pearl Harbor, and Iolani Palace (the only royal palace in the U.S.), Bishop Museum, and Waikiki Beach (all in Honolulu).

Famous natives and residents: Salevaa Antinoe (Konishiki), sumo wrestler; George Ariyoshi, first Japanese-American elected governor; Hiram Bingham, missionary; Charles R. Bishop, banker and philanthropist; Tia Carrere, singer, actress; Samuel N. Castle, missionary, founder of Castle & Cooke Ltd. with Amos S. Cooke, missionary and educator; Father Damien, leper colony worker; Sanford B. Dole, territorial governor; Jean Erdman, dancer, choreographer; Hiram L. Fong, first Chinese-American senator; Don Ho, entertainer; Daniel K. Inouye, senator; Gerrit P. Judd, advisor of Hawaiian king; Keahumanu, female chief; Duke Paoa Kahanamoku, Olympic swimming champion; Kamehameha I, first Hawaiian king; Kamehameha V, last of the dynasty; George Parsons Lathrop, journalist and poet; Liliuokalani, queen, last Hawaiian monarch; Bette Midler, singer; Ellison Onizuka, astronaut; Kawaipuna Prejean, Hawaiian activist, proponent of Hawaiian sovereignty; Chad Rowan, Yokozuna, sumo wrestler; Harold Sakata, actor; Carolyn Suzanne Sapp, 1991 Miss America; James Shigeta, actor; Claus Spreckels, developer of Hawaiian sugar industry; Don Stroud, actor.

IDAHO

Capital: Boise
Governor: Philip E. Batt, R (to Jan. 1999)
Lieut. Governor: C.L. "Butch" Otter, R (to Jan. 1999)
Secy. of State: Pete T. Cenarrusa, R (to Jan. 1999)
State Auditor: J.D. Williams, D (to Jan. 1999)
Atty. General: Alan G. Lance, R (to Jan. 1999)
Treasurer: Lydia Justice Edwards, R (to Jan. 1999)
Organized as territory: March 3, 1863
Entered Union (rank): July 3, 1890 (43)
Present constitution adopted: 1890
Motto: *Esto perpetua* (It is forever)
State symbols: flower, Syringa (1931); **tree,** White pine (1935); **bird,** Mountain bluebird (1931); **horse,** Appaloosa (1975); **gem,** Star garnet (1967); **song,** "Here We Have Idaho"; **folk dance,** Square Dance; **fish,** Cutthroat trout (1990); **fossil,** Hagerman horse fossil (1988)
Nicknames: Gem State; Spud State; Panhandle State
Origin of name: Unknown. Though popularly believed to be an Indian word, it is an invented name whose meaning is unknown.
10 largest cities (1994): Boise, 145,987; Idaho Falls, 49,928; Pocatello, 49,634; Nampa, 35,333; Twin Falls, 31,568; Lewiston, 30,097; Coeur d'Alene, 28,457; Caldwell, 23,970; Moscow, 18,909; Meridian, 14,566
Land area (rank): 82,751 sq mi. (214,325 sq km) (11)
Geographic center: In Custer Co., at Custer, SW of Challis
Number of counties: 44, plus small part of Yellowstone National Park

Largest county (1995 est.): Ada, 251,831
State forests: 881,000 ac.
State parks: 22 (44,177 ac.)
1995 resident population est.: 1,163,261
1990 resident census population, sex, (rank): 1,006,749 (42). **Male:** 500,956; **Female:** 505,793. **White:** 950,451 (94.4%); **Black:** 3,370 (0.3%); **American Indian, Eskimo, or Aleut:** 13,780 (1.4%); **Asian or Pacific Islander:** 9,365 (0.9%); **Other race:** 29,783 (3.0%); **Hispanic:** 52,927 (5.3%). **1990 percent population under 18:** 30.6; **65 and over:** 12.0; **median age:** 31.5.

After its acquisition by the U.S. as part of the Louisiana Purchase in 1803, the region was explored by Meriwether Lewis and William Clark in 1805–06. Northwest boundary disputes with Great Britain were settled by the Oregon Treaty in 1846 and the first permanent U.S. settlement in Idaho was established by the Mormons at Franklin in 1860.

After gold was discovered on Orofino Creek in 1860, prospectors swarmed into the territory, but left little more than a number of ghost towns.

In the 1870s, growing white occupation of Indian lands led to a series of battles between U.S. forces and the Nez Percé, Bannock, and Sheepeater tribes.

Mining, lumbering, and irrigation farming have been important for years. Idaho produces more than one fifth of all the silver mined in the U.S. It also ranks high among the states in antimony, lead, cobalt, garnet, phosphate rock, vanadium, zinc, mercury, and gold.

Idaho's most impressive growth began when World War II military needs made processing agricultural products a big industry, particularly the dehydrating and freezing of potatoes. The state produces about one fourth of the nation's potato crop, as well as wheat, apples, corn, barley, sugar beets, and hops.

With the growth of winter sports, tourism now outranks mining in dollar revenue. Idaho's many streams and lakes provide fishing, camping, and boating sites. The nation's largest elk herds draw hunters from all over the world and the famed Sun Valley resort attracts thousands of visitors to its swimming and skiing facilities.

Other points of interest are the Craters of the Moon National Monument; Nez Percé National Historic Park, which includes many sites visited by Lewis and Clark; and the State Historical Museum in Boise.

Famous natives and residents: Joe Albertson, grocery chain founder; Cecil Andrus, ex-governor; T.H. Bell, educator; Ezra Taft Benson, Eisenhower's Secretary of Agriculture, pres. LDS church, marketing specialist; William E. Borah, ex-senator; Gutzon Borglum, Mt. Rushmore sculptor; Carol R. Brink, author; Frank F. Church, ex-senator; Fred Dubois, senator; Vardis Fisher, novelist; Lawrence H. Gipson, historian; Ernest Hemingway, author; Mariel Hemingway, actress; Chief Joseph, Nez Percé chief; Harmon Killebrew, baseball player; Jerry Kramer, football player, author; Ezra Pound, poet; Sacagawea, Shoshonean guide; J.R. Simplot, industrialist; Robert E. Smylie, political leader; Henry Spalding, missionary; Frank Steunenberg, ex-governor; Picabo Street, skier; David Tompson, founded first trading post; Lana Turner, actress.

ILLINOIS

Capital: Springfield
Governor: Jim Edgar, R (to Jan. 1999)
Lieut. Governor: Bob Kustra, R (to Jan. 1999)
Atty. General: Jim Ryan, R (to Jan. 1999)
Secy. of State: George H. Ryan, R (to Jan. 1999)
Comptroller: Loleta Didrickson, R (to Jan. 1999)
Treasurer: Judith Barr Topinka, R (to Jan. 1999)
Organized as territory: Feb. 3, 1809
Entered Union (rank): Dec. 3, 1818 (21)

Present constitution adopted: 1970
Motto: State sovereignty, national union
State symbols: flower, Violet (1908); **tree,** White oak (1973); **bird,** Cardinal (1929); **animal,** White-tailed deer (1982); **fish,** Bluegill (1987); **insect,** Monarch butterfly (1975); **song,** "Illinois" (1925); **mineral,** Fluorite (1965)
Nickname: Prairie State
Origin of name: Unknown. It is an invented name whose meaning, if any, is unknown
10 largest cities (1994): Chicago, 2,731,743; Rockford, 143,263; Peoria, 112,878; Aurora, 112,313; Springfield, 105,938; Naperville, 101,163; Elgin, 85,339; Decatur, 83,105; Joliet, 79,492; Arlington Heights Village, 77,438
Land area (rank): 55,593 sq mi. (143,987 sq km) (24)
Geographic center: In Logan County 28 mi. NE of Springfield
Number of counties: 102
Largest county (1995 pop. est.): Cook, 5,136,877
Public use areas: 187 (275,000 ac.), incl. state parks, memorials, forests and conservation areas
1995 resident population est.: 11,829,940
1990 resident census population (rank): 11,430,602 (6). **Male:** 5,552,233; **Female:** 5,878,369. **White:** 8,952,978 (78.3%); **Black:** 1,694,273 (14.8%); **American Indian, Eskimo, or Aleut:** 21,836 (0.2%); **Asian or Pacific Islander:** 285,311 (2.5%); **Other race:** 476,204 (4.2%); **Hispanic:** 904,446 (7.9%). **1990 percent population under 18:** 25.8; **65 and over:** 12.6; **median age:** 32.8.

French explorers Marquette and Joliet, in 1673, were the first Europeans of record to visit the region. In 1699 French settlers established the first permanent settlement at Cahokia, near present-day East St. Louis.

Great Britain obtained the region at the end of the French and Indian War in 1763. The area figured prominently in frontier struggles during the Revolutionary War and in Indian wars during the early 19th century.

Significant episodes in the state's early history include the growing migration of Eastern settlers following the opening of the Erie Canal in 1825; the Black Hawk War, which virtually ended the Indian troubles in the area; and the rise of Abraham Lincoln from farm laborer to President.

Today, Illinois stands high in manufacturing, coal mining, agriculture, and oil production. The sprawling Chicago district (including a slice of Indiana) is a great iron and steel producer, meat packer, grain exchange, and railroad center. Chicago is also famous as a Great Lakes port.

Illinois ranks third in the nation in export of agricultural products, first in corn and soybeans, and third in hog production. An important dairy state, Illinois is also a leader in corn, oats, wheat, barley, rye, truck vegetables, and the nursery products.

The state manufactures a great variety of industrial and consumer products: railroad cars, clothing, furniture, tractors, liquor, watches, and farm implements are just some of the items made in its factories and plants.

Central Illinois is noted for shrines and memorials associated with the life of Abraham Lincoln. In Springfield are the Lincoln Home, the Lincoln Tomb, and the restored Old State Capitol. Other points of interest are the home of Mormon leader Joseph Smith in Nauvoo and, in Chicago: the Art Institute, Field Museum, Museum of Science and Industry, Shedd Aquarium, Adler Planetarium, Merchandise Mart, and Chicago Portage National Historic Site.

Famous natives and residents: Franklin Pierce Adams, author; Jane Addams, social worker; Mary Astor, actress; Jack Benny, comedian; Black Hawk, Sauk Indian chief; Harry A. Blackmun, jurist; Ray Bradbury, author; William Jennings Bryan, orator and politician; Edgar Rice Burroughs, novelist; Gower Champion, choreographer; John Chancellor, TV commentator; Raymond Chandler, writer; Jimmy Connors, tennis champion; James Gould Cozzens, novelist; Richard J. Daley, ex-mayor of Chicago; Miles Davis, musician; Peter DeVries, novelist; Walt Disney, film animator and producer; John Dos Passos, author; James T. Farrell, novelist; Betty Friedan, feminist; Benny Goodman, musician; John Gunther, author; Ernest Hemingway, author; Charlton Heston, actor; Wild Bill Hickok, scout; William Holden, actor; Rock Hudson, actor; Burl Ives, singer; James Jones, novelist; John Jones, civil rights leader; Quincy Jones, composer; Keokuk (Watchful Fox), chief of the Sac and Fox Indians; Walter Kerr, drama critic; Archibald MacLeish, poet; David Mamet, playwright; Robert A. Millikan, physicist; Sherrill Milnes, baritone; Bill Murray, actor; Bob Newhart, actor, comedian; William S. Paley, broadcasting executive; Drew Pearson, columnist; Richard Pryor, comedian, actor; Ronald Reagan, ex-President; Carl Sandburg, poet; Sam Shepard, playwright; William L. Shirer, author and historian; John Paul Stevens, jurist; McLean Stevenson, actor; Preston Sturges, director; Gloria Swanson, actress; Carl Van Doren, writer and educator; Melvin Van Peebles, playwright; Irving Wallace, novelist; Alfred Wallenstein, conductor; Raquel Welch, actress; Florenz Ziegfield, theatrical producer.

INDIANA

Capital: Indianapolis
Governor: Frank O'Bannon, D (to Jan. 2001)
Lieut. Governor: Joseph E. Kernan, D (to Jan. 2001)
Secy. of State: Sue Anne Gilroy, R (to Feb. 1999)
Treasurer: Joyce Brinkman, R (to Feb. 1999)
Atty. General: Jeffrey A. Modisett, D (to Jan. 2001)
Auditor: Morris Wooden, R (to Dec. 1998)
Organized as territory: May 7, 1800
Entered Union (rank): Dec. 11, 1816 (19)
Present constitution adopted: 1851
Motto: The Crossroads of America
State symbols: flower, Peony (1957); **tree,** Tulip tree (1931); **bird,** Cardinal (1933); **song,** "On the Banks of the Wabash, Far Away" (1913); **river,** Wabash
Official language: English
Nickname: Hoosier State
Origin of name: Meaning "land of Indians"
10 largest cities (1994): Indianapolis, 752,279; Fort Wayne, 183,359; Evansville, 129,452; Gary, 114,256; South Bend, 105,092; Hammond, 82,837; Muncie, 71,407; Bloomington, 62,560; Anderson, 60,846; Terre Haute, 60,200
Land area (rank): 35,870 sq mi. (92,904 sq km) (38)
Geographic center: In Boone Co., 14 mi. NNW of Indianapolis
Number of Counties: 92
Largest county (1995 pop. est.): Marion, 817,604
State parks: 20 (56,871 ac.)
State historic sites: 17 (1,188 ac.)
1996 resident population est.: 5,840,528
1990 census population (rank): 5,544,159 (14). **Male:** 2,688,281; **Female:** 2,855,878. **White:** 5,020,700 (90.6%); **Black:** 432,092 (7.8%); **American Indian, Eskimo, or Aleut:** 12,720 (0.2%); **Asian or Pacific Islander:** 37,617 (0.7%); **Other race:** 41,030 (0.7%); **Hispanic:** 98,788 (1.8%). **1990 percent population under 18:** 26.3; **65 and over:** 12.6; **median age:** 32.8.

First explored for France by La Salle in 1679–80, the region figured importantly in the Franco-British struggle for North America that culminated with British victory in 1763.

George Rogers Clark led American forces against the British in the area during the Revolutionary War and, prior to becoming a state, Indiana was the scene of frequent Indian uprisings until the victory of Gen. William Henry Harrison at Tippecanoe in 1811.

Indiana's 41-mile Lake Michigan waterfront—one of the world's great industrial centers—turns out iron, steel, and oil products. Products include automobile parts and accessories, mobile homes and recreational vehicles, truck and bus bodies, aircraft engines, farm machinery, and fabricated structural steel. Phonograph records, wood office furniture, and pharmaceuticals are also manufactured.

The state is a leader in agriculture with corn the principal crop. Hogs, soybeans, wheat, oats, rye, tomatoes, onions, and poultry also contribute heavily to Indiana's agricultural output. Much of the building limestone used in the U.S. is quarried in Indiana, which is also a large producer of coal.

Wyandotte Cave, one of the largest in the U.S., is located in Crawford County in southern Indiana, and West Baden and French Lick are well known for their mineral springs. Other attractions include Indiana Dunes National Lakeshore, Indianapolis Motor Speedway, Lincoln Boyhood National Memorial, and the George Rogers Clark National Historical Park.

Famous natives and residents: George Ade, humorist; Leon Ames, actor; Anne Baxter, actress; Albert J. Beveridge, political leader; Larry Bird, basketball player; Bill Blass, fashion designer; Frank Borman, astronaut; Hoagy Carmichael, songwriter; James Dean, actor; Eugene V. Debs, Socialist leader; Lloyd C. Douglas, author; Theodore Dreiser, writer; Bernard F. Gimbel, merchant; Virgil Grissom, astronaut; Phil Harris, actor and band leader; John Milton Hay, statesman; James R. Hoffa, labor leader; Michael Jackson, singer; Buck Jones, actor; Alfred C. Kinsey, zoologist; David Letterman, TV host, comedian; Eli Lilly, pharmaceuticals manufacturer; Carole Lombard, actress; Shelley Long, actress; Marjorie Main, actress; James McCracken, tenor; Joaquin Miller, poet; Paul Osborn, playwright; Cole Porter, songwriter; Gene Stratton Porter, naturalist and author; Ernest Taylor Pyle, journalist; J. Danforth Quayle, ex-vice president; James Whitcomb Riley, poet; Knute Rockne, football coach; Ned Rorem, composer; Red Skelton, comedian; Rex Stout, mystery writer; Booth Tarkington, author; Twyla Tharp, dancer and choreographer; Forrest Tucker, actor; Harold C. Urey, physicist; Kurt Vonnegut, Jr., author; Dan Wakefield, author; Robert Wise, director; Jessamyn West, novelist; Wendell Willkie, lawyer; Wilbur Wright, inventor.

IOWA

Capital: Des Moines
Governor: Terry E. Branstad, R (to Jan. 1999)
Lieut. Governor: Joy Corning, R (to Jan. 1999)
Secy. of State: Paul Pate, R (to Jan. 1999)
Treasurer: Michael L. Fitzgerald, D (to Jan. 1999)
Atty. General: Tom Miller, D (to Jan. 1999)
Organized as territory: June 12, 1838
Entered Union (rank): Dec. 28, 1846 (29)
Present constitution adopted: 1857
Motto: Our liberties we prize and our rights we will maintain
State symbols: flower, Wild rose (1897); **bird,** Eastern goldfinch (1933); **colors,** Red, white, and blue (in state flag); **song,** "Song of Iowa"
Nickname: Hawkeye State
Origin of name: Probably from an Indian word meaning "this is the place," or "The Beautiful Land"
10 largest cities (1994): Des Moines, 193,965; Cedar Rapids, 113,438; Davenport, 96,964; Sioux City, 82,735; Waterloo, 66,537; Iowa City, 60,655; Dubuque, 59,084; Council Bluffs, 54,850; Ames, 46,562; West Des Moines, 37,243
Land area (rank): 55,875 sq mi. (144,716 sq km) (23)
Geographic center: In Story Co., 5 mi. NE of Ames
Number of counties: 99
Largest county (1996 pop. est.): Polk, 354,150
State forests: 5 (28,000 ac.)
State parks: 84 (49,237)

1996 resident population est.: 2,852,000
1990 resident census population (rank): 2,776,755 (30). **Male:** 1,344,802; **Female:** 1,431,953. **White:** 2,683,090 (96.6%); **Black:** 48,090 (1.7%); **American Indian, Eskimo, or Aleut:** 7,349 (0.3%); **Asian or Pacific Islander:** 25,476 (0.9%); **Other race:** 12,750 (0.5%); **Hispanic:** 32,647 (1.2%). **1990 percent population under 18:** 25.9; **65 and over:** 15.3; **median age:** 34.0

The first Europeans to visit the area were the French explorers, Father Jacques Marquette and Louis Joliet in 1673. The U.S. obtained control of the area in 1803 as part of the Louisiana Purchase.

During the first half of the 19th century, there was heavy fighting between white settlers and Indians. Lands were taken from the Indians after the Black Hawk War in 1832 and again in 1836 and 1837.

When Iowa became a state in 1846, its capital was Iowa City; the more centrally located Des Moines became the new capital in 1857. At that time, the state's present boundaries were also drawn.

Although Iowa produces a tenth of the nation's food supply, the value of Iowa's manufactured products is twice that of its agriculture. Major industries are food and associated products, non-electrical machinery, electrical equipment, printing and publishing, and fabricated products.

Iowa stands in a class by itself as an agricultural state. Its farms sell over $10 billion worth of crops and livestock annually. Iowa leads the nation in all corn, soybeans, livestock, and hog marketings, with about 25% of the pork supply and 6% of the grain-fed cattle. Iowa's forests produce hardwood lumber, particularly walnut, and its mineral products include cement, limestone, sand, gravel, gypsum, and coal.

Tourist attractions include the Herbert Hoover birthplace and library near West Branch; the Amana Colonies; Fort Dodge Historical Museum, Fort, and Stockade; the Iowa State Fair at Des Moines in August; and the Effigy Mounds National Monument at Marquette, a prehistoric Indian burial site.

Famous natives and residents: Bix Beiderbecke, jazz musician; Norman Borlang, plant pathologist and geneticist, Nobel Peace Prize winner; William "Buffalo Bill" F. Cody, scout; Johnny Carson, TV entertainer; Gardner Cowles, Jr., publisher; Simon Estes, bass-baritone; William Frawley, actor; George H. Gallup, poll taker; Susan Glaspell, writer; Herbert Hoover, President; MacKinlay Kantor, novelist; Charles A. Kettering, inventor; Ann Landers, columnist; Cloris Leachman, actress; John L. Lewis, labor leader; Glenn L. Martin, aviator, manufacturer; Elsa Maxwell, writer; Frederick L. Maytag, inventor and manufacturer; Glenn Miller, bandleader; Harriet Nelson, actress; Nathan M. Pusey, educator; David Rabe, playwright; Harry Reasoner, TV commentator; Donna Reed, actress; Lillian Russell, soprano; Robert Schiller, evangelist; Wallace Stegner, novelist and critic; Billy Sunday, evangelist; James A. Van Allen, space physicist; Abigail Van Buren, columnist; Henry A. Wallace, statesman and vice president; John Wayne, actor; Andy Williams, singer; Meredith Willson, composer; Grant Wood, painter.

KANSAS

Capital: Topeka
Governor: Bill Graves, R (to Jan. 1999)
Lieut. Governor: Gary Sherrer, R (to Jan. 1999)
Secy. of State: Ron Thornburgh, R (to Jan. 1999)
Treasurer: Sally Thompson, D (to Jan. 1999)
Atty. General: Carla Stovall, R (to Jan. 1999)
Commission of Insurance: Kathleen Sebelius, D (to Jan. 1999)
Organized as territory: May 30, 1854
Entered Union (rank): Jan. 29, 1861 (34)
Present constitution adopted: 1859

Motto: *Ad astra per aspera* (To the stars through difficulties)

State symbols: flower, Sunflower (1903); **tree,** Cottonwood (1937); **bird,** Western meadowlark (1937); **animal,** Buffalo (1955); **song,** "Home on Range" (1947)

Nicknames: Sunflower State; Jayhawk State

Origin of name: From a Sioux word meaning "people of the south wind"

10 largest cities (1994): Wichita, 310,236; Kansas City, 142,630; Overland Park, 125,225; Topeka, 120,646; Olathe, 72,455; Lawrence, 71,721; Salina, 44,167; Leavenworth, 42,250; Shawnee, 40,471; Hutchinson, 39,770

Land area (rank): 81,823 sq mi. (211,922 sq km) (13)

Geographic center: In Barton Co., 15 mi. NE of Great Bend

Number of counties: 105

Largest county (1995 pop. est.): Sedgwick, 419,333

State parks: 22 (14,394 ac.)

1995 resident population est.: 2,565,328

1990 resident census population (rank): 2,477,574 (32). **Male:** 1,214,645; **Female:** 1,262,929. **White:** 2,231,986 (90.1%); **Black:** 143,076 (5.8%); **American Indian, Eskimo, or Aleut:** 21,965 (0.9%); **Asian or Pacific Islander:** 31,750 (1.3%); **Other race:** 48,797 (2.0%); **Hispanic:** 93,670 (3.8%). **1990 percent population under 18:** 26.7; **65 and over:** 13.8; **median age:** 32.9.

Spanish explorer Francisco de Coronado, in 1541, is considered the first European to have traveled this region. La Salle's extensive land claims for France (1682) included present-day Kansas. Ceded to Spain by France in 1763, the territory reverted back to France in 1800 and was sold to the U.S. as part of the Louisiana Purchase in 1803.

Lewis and Clark, Zebulon Pike, and Stephen H. Long explored the region between 1803 and 1819. The first permanent settlements in Kansas were outposts—Fort Leavenworth (1827), Fort Scott (1842), and Fort Riley (1853)—established to protect travelers along the Santa Fe and Oregon Trails.

Just before the Civil War, the conflict between the pro- and anti-slavery forces earned the region the grim title "Bleeding Kansas."

Today, wheat fields, oil well derricks, herds of cattle, and grain storage elevators are chief features of the Kansas landscape. A leading wheat-growing state, Kansas also raises corn, sorghums, oats, barley, soy beans, and potatoes. Kansas stands high in petroleum production and mines zinc, coal, salt, and lead. It is also the nation's leading producer of helium.

Wichita is one of the nation's leading aircraft manufacturing centers, ranking first in production of private aircraft. Kansas City is an important transportation, milling, and meat-packing center.

Points of interest include the Kansas Museum of History at Topeka, the Eisenhower boyhood home and the new Eisenhower Memorial Museum and Presidential Library at Abilene, John Brown's cabin at Osawatomie, recreated Front Street in Dodge City, Fort Larned (once the most important military post on the Santa Fe Trail), and Fort Leavenworth and Fort Riley.

Famous natives and residents: Roscoe "Fatty" Arbuckle, actor; Clarence D. Batchelor, political cartoonist; Gwendolyn Brooks, poet; Walter P. Chrysler, auto manufacturer; Clark M. Clifford, ex-Secretary of Defense; John Steuart Curry, painter; Amelia Earhart, aviator; Milton S. Eisenhower, educator; Gary Hart, politician; William Inge, playwright; Walter Johnson, baseball pitcher; Osa L. Johnson, documentary film producer; Buster Keaton, comedian; Emmett Kelly, clown; Stan Kenton, jazz musician; James Lehrer, broadcast journalist; Edgar Lee Masters, poet; Mary McCarthy, actress; Hattie McDaniel, actress; William C. Menninger, psychiatrist; Gordon Parks, film director; Zasu Pitts, actress; Samuel Ramey, opera singer; Charles Robinson, statesman and first governor; Charles (Buddy) Rogers, actor; Damon Runyon, journalist; Eugene W. Smith, photojournalist; Milburn Stone, actor; John Cameron Swayze, news commentator; William Allen White, journalist; Charles E. Whittaker, jurist; Jess Willard, boxer.

KENTUCKY

Capital: Frankfort

Governor: Paul E. Patton, D (to Dec. 1999)

Lieut. Governor: Stephen L. Henry, D (to Dec. 1999)

Secy. of State: John Y. Brown III, D (to Dec. 1999)

State Treasurer: Ed Hatchett, D (to Dec. 1999)

State Auditor: John Kennedy Hamilton, D (to Dec. 1999)

Atty. General: A.B. Chandler III, D (to Dec. 1999)

Entered Union (rank): June 1, 1792 (15)

Present constitution adopted: 1891

Motto: United we stand, divided we fall

State symbols: tree, Tulip poplar (1994); **flower,** Goldenrod; **bird,** Kentucky cardinal; **song,** "My Old Kentucky Home"

Nickname: Bluegrass State

Origin of name: From an Iroquoian word "Ken-tah-ten" meaning "land of tomorrow"

10 largest cities (1994): Louisville, 270,308; Lexington-Fay 237,612; Owensboro, 53,645; Bowling Green, 45,451; Covington, 41,830; Hopkinsville, 32,283; Frankfort, 28,708; Henderson, 26,862; Paducah, 26,749; Jeffersontown, 24,314

Land area (rank): 39,732 sq mi. (102,907 sq km) (36)

Geographic center: In Marion Co., 3 mi. NNW of Lebanon

Number of counties: 120

Largest county (1995 pop. est.): Jefferson, 672,918

State forests: 9 (44,173 ac.)

State parks: 43 (40,574 ac.)

1995 resident population est.: 3,860,219

1990 resident census population (rank): 3,685,296 (23). **Male:** 1,785,235; **Female:** 1,900,061. **White:** 3,391,832 (92.0%); **Black:** 262,907 (7.1%); **American Indian, Eskimo, or Aleut:** 5,769 (0.2%); **Asian or Pacific Islander:** 17,812 (0.5%); **Other race:** 6,976 (0.2%); **Hispanic:** 21,984 (0.6%). **1990 percent population below age 18:** 25.9; **65 and over:** 12.7; **median age:** 33.0.

Kentucky was the first region west of the Allegheny Mountains settled by American pioneers. James Harrod established the first permanent settlement at Harrodsburg in 1774; the following year Daniel Boone, who had explored the area in 1767, blazed the Wilderness Trail and founded Boonesboro.

Politically, the Kentucky region was originally part of Virginia, but early statehood was gained in 1792.

During the Civil War, as a slaveholding state with a considerable abolitionist population, Kentucky was caught in the middle of the conflict, supplying both Union and Confederate forces with thousands of troops.

In recent years, manufacturing has shown important gains particularly in automotive assembly and parts manufacturing. Kentucky also prides itself on producing some of the nation's best tobacco, horses, and whiskey. Corn, soybeans, wheat, fruit, hogs, cattle, and dairy farming are among the agricultural items produced.

Among the manufactured items produced in the state are motor vehicles, furniture, aluminum ware, brooms, apparel, lumber products, machinery, textiles, and iron and steel products. Kentucky also produces significant amounts of petroleum, natural gas, fluorspar, clay, and stone. However, coal accounts for 90% of the total mineral income.

Louisville, the largest city, famed for the Kentucky Derby at Churchill Downs, is also the location of a large state university, whiskey distilleries, and cigarette factories. The Bluegrass country around Lexington is the home of some of the world's finest race horses. Other attractions are Mammoth Cave, the George S. Patton, Jr., Military Museum at Fort Knox, and Old Fort Harrod State Park.

Famous natives and residents: John Adair, pioneer and political leader; Muhammad Ali, boxer; Alben W. Barkley, ex-vice president; Louis D. Brandeis, jurist; John Mason Brown, critic; Kit Carson, scout; Champ Clark, politician; Rosemary Clooney, singer; Irvin S. Cobb, humorist; Jefferson Davis, president of Confederacy; Irene Dunne, actress; Crystal Gayle, singer; David W. Griffith, film producer; John M. Harlan, jurist; Elizabeth Hardwick, writer; Casey Jones, celebrated locomotive engineer; Abraham Lincoln, ex-President; Loretta Lynn, singer; Carry Amelia Nation, temperance leader; Patrician Neal, actress; George Reeves, actor; Wiley B. Rutledge, jurist; Diane Sawyer, broadcast journalist; Phil Simms, football player; Adlai Stevenson, ex-vice president; Allen Tate, poet and critic; Hunter Thompson, writer; Frederick M. Vinson, jurist; Robert Penn Warren, novelist.

LOUISIANA

Capital: Baton Rouge
Governor: Murphy J. "Mike" Foster, R (to Jan. 2000)
Lieut. Governor: Kathleen Blanco, D (to Jan. 2000)
Secy. of State: W. Fox McKeithen, R (to Jan. 2000)
Treasurer: Ken Duncan, D (to Jan. 2000)
Atty. General: Richard P. Ieyoub, D (to Jan. 2000)
Organized as territory: March 26, 1804
Entered Union (rank): April 30, 1812 (18)
Present constitution adopted: 1974
Motto: Union, justice, and confidence
State symbols: flower, Magnolia (1900); **tree,** Bald cypress (1963); **bird,** Pelican (1958); **songs,** "Give Me Louisiana" and "You Are My Sunshine"
Nicknames: Pelican State; Sportsman's Paradise; Creole State; Sugar State
Origin of name: In honor of Louis XIV of France
10 largest cities (1994): New Orleans, 484,149; Baton Rouge, 227,482; Shreveport, 196,982; Lafayette, 102,281; Kenner, 72,691; Lake Charles, 72,424; Monroe, 57,049; Bossier City, 54,419; Alexandria, 45,982; New Iberia, 33,658
Land area (rank): 43,566 sq mi. (112,836 sq km) (33)
Geographic center: In Avoyelles Parish, 3 mi. SE of Marksville
Number of parishes (counties): 64
Largest parish (1995 pop. est.): Orleans, 481,913
State forests: 1 (8,000 ac.)
State parks: 30 (13,932 ac.)
1995 resident population est.: 4,342,334
1990 resident census population (rank): 4,219,973 (21). **Male:** 2,031,386; **Female:** 2,188,587. **White:** 2,839,138 (67.3%); **Black:** 1,299,281 (30.8%); **American Indian, Eskimo, or Aleut:** 18,541 (0.4%); **Asian or Pacific Islander:** 41,099 (1.0%); **Other race:** 21,914 (0.5%); **Hispanic:** 93,044 (2.2%). **1990 percent population under 18:** 29.1; **65 and over:** 11.1; **median age:** 31.0.

Louisiana has a rich, colorful historical background. Early Spanish explorers were Piñeda, 1519; Cabeza de Vaca, 1528; and de Soto in 1541. La Salle reached the mouth of the Mississippi and claimed all the land drained by it and its tributaries for Louis XIV of France in 1682.

Louisiana became a French crown colony in 1731, was ceded to Spain in 1763, returned to France in 1800, and sold by Napoleon to the U.S. as part of the Louisiana Purchase (with large territories to the north and northwest) in 1803.

In 1815, Gen. Andrew Jackson's troops defeated a larger British army in the Battle of New Orleans, neither

side aware that the treaty ending the War of 1812 had been signed.

As to total value of its mineral output, Louisiana is a leader in natural gas, salt, petroleum, and sulfur production. Much of the oil and sulfur comes from offshore deposits. The state also produces large crops of sweet potatoes, rice, sugar cane, pecans, soybeans, corn, and cotton.

Leading manufactures include chemicals, processed food, petroleum and coal products, paper, lumber and wood products, transportation equipment, and apparel.

Louisiana marshes supply most of the nation's muskrat fur as well as that of opossum, raccoon, mink, and otter, and large numbers of game birds.

Major points of interest include New Orleans with its French Quarter and Superdome, plantation homes near Natchitoches and New Iberia, Cajun country in the Mississippi delta region, Chalmette National Historical Park, and the state capital at Baton Rouge.

Famous natives and residents: Louis Armstrong, musician; Geoffrey Beene, fashion designer; Truman Capote, writer; Kitty Carlisle, singer and actress; Van Cliburn, concert pianist; Michael De Bakey, heart surgeon; Fats Domino, musician; Louis Moreau Gottschalk, pianist, composer; Bryant Gumbel, TV newscaster; Lillian Hellman, playwright; Al Hirt, trumpeter; Mahalia Jackson, gospel singer; Jean Laffite, privateer; Dorothy Lamour, actress; John A. Lejeune, Marine Corps general; Elmore Leonard, author; Jerry Lee Lewis, singer; Huey P. Long, politician; Wynton Marsalis, musician; Jelly Roll Morton, jazz musician and composer; Huey Newton, black activist; Marguerite Piazza, soprano; Paul Prudhomme, chef; Howard K. Smith, TV commentator; Ben Turpin, comedian; Ray Walston, actor; Edward Douglas White, jurist.

MAINE

Capital: Augusta
Governor: Angus S. King, Jr., I (to Jan. 1999)
Secy. of State: Dan A. Gwadosky, D (to Jan. 1999)
Controller: Carol Whitney, R (to Jan. 1999)
Atty. General: Andrew Ketterer, D (to Jan. 1999)
Entered Union (rank): March 15, 1820 (23)
Present constitution adopted: 1820
Motto: *Dirigo* (I lead)
State symbols: flower, White pine cone and tassel (1895); **tree,** White pine tree (1945); **bird,** Chickadee (1927); **fish,** Landlocked salmon (1969); **mineral,** Tourmaline (1971); **song,** "State of Maine Song" (1937); **animal,** Moose (1979); **cat,** Maine Coon Cat (1985); **fossil,** Pertica quadrifaria (1985); **insect,** Honeybee (1975)
Nickname: Pine Tree State
Origin of name: First used to distinguish the mainland from the offshore islands. It has been considered a compliment to Henrietta Maria, Queen of Charles I of England. She was said to have owned the province of Mayne in France.
10 largest cities (1994): Portland, 61,982; Lewiston, 37,385; Bangor, 33,004; Auburn, 23,364; South Portland, 22,596; Biddeford, 20,416; Augusta, 19,770; Waterville, 16,233; Westbrook, 15,737; Saco, 15,386
Largest town (1990 census): Brunswick, 20,906
Land area (rank): 30,865 sq mi. (79,939 sq km) (39)
Geographic center: In Piscataquis Co., 18 mi. N of Dover-Foxcroft
Number of counties: 16
Largest county (1995 pop. est.): Cumberland, 248,526
State forests: 1 (21,000 ac.)
State parks: 26 (247,627 ac.)
State historic sites: 18 (403 ac.)
1995 resident population est.: 1,241,382

1990 resident census population (rank): 1,227,928 (38). **Male:** 597,850; **Female:** 630,078. **White:** 1,208,360 (98.4%); **Black:** 5,138 (0.4%); **American Indian, Eskimo, or Aleut:** 5,998 (0.5%); **Asian or Pacific Islander:** 6,683: (0.5%); **Other race:** 1,749 (0.1%); **Hispanic:** 6,829 (0.6%).

John Cabot and his son, Sebastian, are believed to have visited the Maine coast in 1498. However, the first permanent English settlements were not established until more than a century later, in 1623.

The first naval action of the Revolutionary War occurred in 1775 when colonials captured the British sloop *Margaretta* off Machias on the Maine coast. In that same year, the British burned Falmouth (now Portland).

Long governed by Massachusetts, Maine became the 23rd state as part of the Missouri Compromise in 1820.

Maine produces 98% of the nation's low-bush blueberries. Farm income is also derived from apples, potatoes, dairy products, and vegetables, with poultry and eggs the largest items.

The state is one of the world's largest pulp-paper producers. It ranks second in boot-and-shoe manufacturing. With almost 89% of its area forested, Maine turns out wood products from boats to toothpicks.

Maine leads the world in the production of the familiar flat tins of sardines, producing more than 75 million of them annually. Lobstermen normally catch 51% of the nation's total of lobsters. The 1995 catch was 36.5 million pounds, the second largest lobster catch in history.

A scenic seacoast, beaches, lakes, mountains, and resorts make Maine a popular vacationland. There are more than 2,500 lakes and 5,000 streams, plus 26 state parks, to attract hunters, fishermen, skiers, and campers.

Major points of interest are: Bar Harbor, Allagash National Wilderness Waterway, the Wadsworth-Longfellow House in Portland, Roosevelt Campobello International Park, and the St. Croix Island National Monument.

Famous natives and residents: F. Lee Bailey, defense attorney; Charles F. Browne (Artemus Ward), humorist; Cyrus Curtis, publisher; Dorothea Dix, civil rights reformer; John Ford, film director; Melville Fuller, jurist; Marsden Hartley, painter; Henry Wadsworth Longfellow, poet; Sarah Orne Jewett, author; Stephen King, writer; Linda Lavin, actress; Edna St. Vincent Millay, poet; Marston Morse, mathematician; Frank Munsey, publisher; Walter Piston, composer; George Putnam, publisher; Kenneth Roberts, historical novelist; Edwin Arlington Robinson, poet; Margaret Chase Smith, politician; Samantha Smith, peacemaker, actress; John Hay Whitney, publisher.

MARYLAND

Capital: Annapolis
Governor: Parris N. Glendening, D (to Jan. 1999)
Lieut. Gov.: Kathleen Kennedy Townsend, D (to Jan. 1999)
Secy. of State: John T. Willis, D (to Jan. 1999)
Comptroller of the Treasury: Louis L. Goldstein, D (to Jan. 1999)
Treasurer: Lucille Maurer, D (to Jan. 1999)
Atty. General: J. Joseph Curran, Jr., D (to Jan. 1999)
Entered Union (rank): April 28, 1788 (7)
Present constitution adopted: 1867
Motto: *Fatti maschii, parole femine* (Manly deeds, womanly words)
State symbols: bird, Baltimore oriole (1947); **boat,** Skipjack (1985); **crustacean,** Maryland Blue Crab (1989); **dog,** Chesapeake Bay retriever (1964); **flower,** Black-eyed susan (1918); **tree,** White oak (1941); **fish,** Rockfish (1965); **folk dance,** Square dancing (1994); **fossil shell,** Ecphora gardnerae

gardnerae (Wilson) (1994); **insect,** Baltimore checkerspot butterfly (1973); **song,** "Maryland! My Maryland!" (1939); **sport,** Jousting (1962)
Nicknames: Free State; Old Line State
Origin of name: In honor of Henrietta Maria (Queen of Charles I of England)
10 largest cities (1994): Baltimore, 702,979; Rockville, 47,078; Frederick, 46,630; Gaithersburg, 43,259; Bowie, 39,345; Hagerstown, 38,510; Annapolis, 35,169; Cumberland, 23,901; Salisbury, 22,204; Laurel, 21,567
Land area (rank): 9,775 sq mi. (25,316 sq km) (42)
Geographic center: In Prince Georges Co., 4½ mi. NW of Davidsonville
Number of counties: 23, and 1 independent city
Largest county (1995 pop. est.): Montgomery, 809,569
State forests: 13 (132,944 ac.)
State parks: 47 (87,670 ac.)
1995 resident population est.: 5,042,438
1990 resident census population (rank): 4,781,468 (19). **Male:** 2,318,671; **Female:** 2,462,797. **White:** 3,393,964 (71.0%); **Black:** 1,189,899 (24.9%); **American Indian, Eskimo, or Aleut:** 12,972 (0.3%); **Asian or Pacific Islander:** 139,719 (2.9%); **Other race:** 44,914 (0.9%); **Hispanic:** 125,102 (2.6%).
1990 percent population under 18: 24.3; **65 and over:** 10.8; **median age:** 33.0

Maryland was inhabited by Indians as early as circa 10,000 B.C.E., and permanent Indian villages were established by circa C.E. 1000.

In 1608, Capt. John Smith explored Chesapeake Bay. Charles I granted a royal charter for Maryland to Cecil Calvert, Lord Baltimore, in 1632, and English settlers, many of whom were Roman Catholic, landed on St. Clement's (now Blakistone) Island in 1634. Religious freedom, granted all Christians in the Toleration Act passed by the Maryland assembly in 1649, was ended by a Puritan revolt, 1654–58.

From 1763 to 1767, Charles Mason and Jeremiah Dixon surveyed Maryland's northern boundary line with Pennsylvania. In 1791, Maryland ceded land to form the District of Columbia.

In 1814, when the British unsuccessfully tried to capture Baltimore, the bombardment of Fort McHenry inspired Francis Scott Key to write *The Star Spangled Banner*.

The Baltimore clipper ship trade developed during the 19th century. During the Civil War, Maryland remained a Union state even while the battles of South Mountain (1862), Antietam (1862), and Monocacy (1864) were fought on her soil.

In 1904, the Great Fire of Baltimore occurred. In 1937, the City of Greenbelt, a New Deal model community, was chartered.

Maryland's Eastern Shore and Western Shore embrace the Chesapeake Bay, and the many estuaries and rivers create one of the longest waterfronts of any state. The Bay produces more seafood—oysters, crabs, clams, fin fish—than any comparable body of water. Important agricultural products, in order of cash value, are greenhouse and nursery products, chickens, dairy products, soy beans, corn, eggs, vegetables, melons and wheat. Maryland is a leader in vegetable canning. Stone, coal, sand, gravel, cement, and clay are the chief mineral products.

Manufacturing industries produce food and kindred products, instruments, chemicals, printing and publishing, transportation equipment, and primary metals. Baltimore, home of The Johns Hopkins University and Hospital, ranks as the nation's second port in foreign tonnage. Annapolis, site of the U.S. Naval Academy, has one of the earliest state houses (1772–79) still in regular use by a State government.

Among the popular attractions in Maryland are the Fort McHenry National Monument; Harpers Ferry and Chesapeake and Ohio Canal National Historic Parks; Antietam National Battlefield; National Aquarium, USS *Constellation*, and Maryland Science Center at Baltimore's Inner Harbor; Historic St. Mary's City; Jefferson Patterson Historical Park and Museum at St. Leonard; U.S. Naval Academy in Annapolis; Goddard Space Flight Center at Greenbelt; Assateague Island National Park Seashore; Ocean City beach resort; and Catoctin Mountain, Fort Frederick, and Piscataway parks.

Famous natives and residents: Benjamin Banneker, almanacker, mathematician-astronomer; John Barth, writer; Eubie Blake, musician; John Wilkes Booth, actor, Lincoln assassin; Francis X. Bushman, actor; James M. Cain, writer; Samuel Chase, jurist; Frederick Douglass, abolitionist; John Hurst Fletcher, Methodist bishop and educator; Christopher Gist, frontiersman; Philip Glass, composer; Matthew Henson, reached North Pole with Peary; Billie Holiday, jazz-blues singer; Johns Hopkins, financier; Reverdy Johnson, lawyer and statesman; Thomas Johnson, political leader; Francis Scott Key, laywer, author of National Anthem; Thurgood Marshall, jurist; H.L. Mencken, writer; Hezekiah Niles, journalist; Charles Wilson Peale, painter; Frank Perdue, farmer, businessman; James R. Randall, journalist, wrote state song; Babe Ruth, baseball player; Upton Sinclair, novelist; Roger B. Taney, jurist; George Alfred Townsend (Gath), journalist; Harriet Tubman, abolitionist; Leon Uris, novelist; Frank Zappa, singer.

MASSACHUSETTS

Capital: Boston
Governor: A. Paul Cellucci, R (to Jan. 1999)
Secy. of the Commonwealth: William F. Galvin, D (to Jan. 1999)
Treasurer & Receiver-General: Joseph D. Malone, R (to Jan. 1999)
Auditor of the Commonwealth: A. Joseph DeNucci, D (to Jan. 1999)
Atty. General: L. Scott Harshbarger, D (to Jan. 1999)
Present constitution drafted: 1780 (oldest U.S. state constitution in effect today)
Entered Union (rank): Feb. 6, 1788 (6)
Motto: *Ense petit placidam sub libertate quietem* (By the sword we seek peace, but peace only under liberty)
State symbols: flower, Mayflower (1918); **tree,** American elm (1941); **bird,** Chickadee (1941); **song,** "All Hail to Massachusetts" (1966); **beverage,** Cranberry juice (1970); **insect,** Ladybug (1974); **muffin,** Corn muffin; **dessert,** Boston cream pie
Nicknames: Bay State; Old Colony State
Origin of name: From two Indian words meaning "Great mountain place"
10 largest cities (1994): Boston, 547,725; Worcester, 165,387; Springfield, 149,164; Cambridge, 99,890; Lowell, 96,054; New Bedford, 94,623; Fall River, 89,425; Brockton, 87,411; Newton, 85,358; Quincy, 84,040
Land area (rank): 7,838 sq mi. (20,300 sq km) (45)
Geographic center: In Worcester Co., in S part of city of Worcester
Number of counties: 14
Largest county (1995 pop. est.): Middlesex, 1,408,450
State forests and parks: 129 (242,000 ac.)[1]
1995 resident population est.: 6,073,550
1990 resident census population (rank): 6,016,425 (13). **Male:** 2,888,745; **Female:** 3,127,680. **White:** 5,405,374 (89.8%); **Black:** 300,130 (5.0%); **American Indian, Eskimo, or Aleut:** 12,241 (0.2%); **Asian**

or Pacific Islander: 143,392 (2.4%); **Other race:** 155,288 (2.6%); **Hispanic:** 287,549 (4.8%). **1990 percent population under 18:** 22.5; **65 and over:** 13.6; **median age:** 33.6.

1. The Metropolitan District Commission, an agency of the Commonwealth serving municipalities in the Boston area, has about 14,000 acres of parkways and reservations under its jurisdiction.

Massachusetts has played a significant role in American history since the Pilgrims, seeking religious freedom, founded Plymouth Colony in 1620.

As one of the most important of the 13 colonies, Massachusetts became a leader in resisting British oppression. In 1773, the Boston Tea Party protested unjust taxation. The Minute Men started the American Revolution by battling British troops at Lexington and Concord on April 19, 1775.

During the 19th century, Massachusetts was famous for the vigorous intellectual activity of famous writers and educators and for its expanding commercial fishing, shipping, and manufacturing interests.

Massachusetts pioneered in the manufacture of textiles and shoes. Today, these industries have been replaced in importance by activity in the electronics and communications equipment fields.

The state's cranberry crop is the nation's largest. Also important are dairy and poultry products, nursery and greenhouse produce, vegetables, and fruit.

Tourism has become an important factor in the economy of the state because of its numerous recreational areas and historical landmarks.

Cape Cod has summer theaters, water sports, and an artists' colony at Provincetown. Tanglewood, in the Berkshires, features the summer concerts of the Boston Symphony.

Among the many other points of interest are Old Sturbridge Village in Sturbridge in central Massachusetts, Minute Man National Historical Park between Lexington and Concord, and, in Boston: Old North Church, Old State House, Faneuil Hall, the USS *Constitution* and the John F. Kennedy Library and Museum.

Famous natives and residents: John Adams, ex-president; John Quincy Adams, ex-president; Samuel Adams, patriot; Horatio Alger, novelist; Susan B. Anthony, woman suffragist; Clara Barton, American Red Cross founder; Leonard Bernstein, conductor; George Bush, ex-president; William Cullen Bryan, poet and editor; Luther Burbank, horticulturalist; John Cheever, novelist; John Singleton Copley, painter; E.E. Cummings, poet; Jacques d'Amboise, ballet dancer; Bette Davis, actress; Cecil B. DeMille, film director; Emily Dickinson, poet; Ralph Waldo Emerson, philosopher and poet; Geraldine Farrar, soprano, actress; Benjamin Franklin, statesman and scientist; Buckminster Fuller, architect and educator; Robert Goddard, father of modern rocketry; John Hancock, statesman; Nathaniel Hawthorne, novelist; Oliver Wendell Holmes, jurist; Winslow Homer, painter; Elias Howe, inventor; John F. Kennedy, ex-president; Amy Lowell, poet; James Russell Lowell, poet; Robert Lowell, poet; Horace Mann, educator; Cotton Mather, clergyman; Samuel F.B. Morse, painter and inventor; Edgar Allan Poe, writer; Paul Revere, silversmith, hero of ride; Dr. Seuss (Theodore Geisel), author and illustrator; David Souter, jurist; Lucy Stone, woman suffragist; Louis Henry Sullivan, architect; Henry David Thoreau, author; Barbara Walters, TV commentator; James McNeill Whistler, painter; Eli Whitney, inventor; John Greenleaf Whittier, poet.

MICHIGAN

Capital: Lansing
Governor: John M. Engler, R (to Jan. 1999)
Lieut. Governor: Connie Binsfeld, R (to Jan. 1999)
Secy. of State: Candace S. Miller, R (to Jan. 1999)
Atty. General: Frank J. Kelley, D (to Jan. 1999)
Organized as territory: Jan. 11, 1805

Entered Union (rank): Jan. 26, 1837 (26)
Present constitution adopted: April 1, 1963, (effective Jan. 1, 1964)
Motto: *Si quaeris peninsulam amoenam circumspice* (If you seek a pleasant peninsula, look around you)
State symbols: flower, Apple blossom (1897); **bird,** Robin (1931); **fishes,** Trout (1965), Brook trout (1988); **gem,** Isle Royal Greenstone (Chlorastrolite) (1972); **stone,** Petoskey Stone (1965); **tree,** White pine (1955); **soil,** Kalkaska Soil series (1990); **reptile,** Painted turtle (1996); **flag,** "Blue charged with the arms of the state" (1911)
Nickname: Wolverine State
Origin of name: From Indian word "Michigana" meaning "great or large lake"
10 largest cities (1994): Detroit, 992,038; Grand Rapids, 190,395; Warren, 142,625; Flint, 138,164; Lansing, 119,590; Sterling Heights, 119,505; Ann Arbor, 108,817; Livonia, 100,415; Dearborn, 86,187; Westland, 85,221
Land area (rank): 56,809.2 sq mi. (151,086 sq km) (22)
Geographic center: In Wexford Co., 5 mi. NNW of Cadillac
Number of counties: 83
Largest county (1995 pop. est.): Wayne, 2,055,500
State parks and recreation areas: 82 (250,000 ac.)
1995 resident population est.: 9,549,353
1990 resident census population (rank): 9,295,297 (8). **Male:** 4,512,781; **Female:** 4,787,516. **White:** 7,756,086 (83.4%); **Black:** 1,291,706 (13.9%); **American Indian, Eskimo, or Aleut:** 55,638 (0.6%); **Asian or Pacific Islander:** 104,983 (1.1%); **Other race:** 86,884 (0.9%); **Hispanic:** 201,596 (2.2%). **1990 percent population under 18:** 26.5; **65 and over:** 11.9; **median age:** 32.6.

Indian tribes were living in the Michigan region when the first European, Étienne Brulé of France, arrived in 1618. Other French explorers, including Marquette, Joliet, and La Salle, followed, and the first permanent settlement was established in 1668 at Sault Ste. Marie. France was ousted from the territory by Great Britain in 1763, following the French and Indian War.

After the Revolutionary War, the U.S. acquired most of the region, which remained the scene of constant conflict between the British and U.S. forces and their respective Indian allies through the War of 1812.

Bordering on four of the five Great Lakes, Michigan is divided into Upper and Lower Peninsulas by the Straits of Mackinac, which link Lakes Michigan and Huron. The two parts of the state are connected by the Mackinac Bridge, one of the world's longest suspension bridges. To the north, connecting Lakes Superior and Huron are the busy Sault Ste. Marie Canals.

While Michigan ranks first among the states in production of motor vehicles and parts, it is also a leader in many other manufacturing and processing lines including prepared cereals, machine tools, airplane parts, refrigerators, hardware, steel springs, and furniture.

The state produces important amounts of iron, copper, iodine, gypsum, bromine, salt, lime, gravel, and cement. Michigan's farms grow apples, cherries, beans, pears, grapes, potatoes, and sugar beets. Michigan's forests contribute significantly to the state's economy. Forest-based industries (wood product industry, tourism, and recreation) support nearly 180,000 jobs and contribute over $18 billion to the state economy. With 10,083 inland lakes and 3,288 miles of Great Lakes' shoreline, Michigan is a prime area for both commercial and sport fishing.

Points of interest are the automobile plants in Dearborn, Detroit, Flint, Lansing, and Pontiac; Mackinac Island; Pictured Rocks and Sleeping Bear Dunes National Lakeshores, Greenfield Village in Dearborn; and the many summer resorts along both the inland and Great Lakes.

Famous natives and residents: Nelsen Algren, novelist; Ralph J. Bunche, statesman, Ellen Burstyn, actress; Bruce Catton, historian; Roger Chaffee, astronaut; Francis Ford Coppola, film director; Thomas E. Dewey, politician; Edna Ferber, novelist; Henry Ford, industrialist; Ali Haji-Sheikh, football player; Julie Harris, actress; Earvin "Magic" Johnson, basketball player; Ring Lardner, story writer; Charles A. Lindbergh, aviator; Madonna, singer; Dick Martin, comedian; Terry McMillan, author; John N. Mitchell, former Attorney General; Gilda Radner, comedienne; Della Reese, singer; Jason Robards, Sr., actor; Diana Ross, singer; Thomas Schippers, conductor; Potter Stewart, jurist; Danny Thomas, entertainer; Margaret Whiting, singer; Stevie Wonder, singer.

MINNESOTA

Capital: St. Paul
Governor: Arne Carlson, R (to Jan. 1999)
Lieut. Governor: Joanne Benson, R (to Jan. 1999)
Secy. of State: Joan Anderson Growe, D (to Jan. 1999)
State Auditor: Judi Dutcher, R (to Jan. 1999)
Atty. General: Hubert H. Humphrey III, D (to Jan. 1999)
State Treasurer: Michael McGrath, D (to Jan. 1999)
Organized as territory: March 3, 1849
Entered Union (rank): May 11, 1858 (32)
Present constitution adopted: 1858
Motto: L'Étoile du Nord (The North Star)
State symbols: flower, Showy lady slipper (1902); **tree,** Red (or Norway) pine (1953); **bird,** Common loon (also called Great Northern Diver) (1961); **song,** "Hail Minnesota" (1945); **fish,** Walleye (1965); **mushroom,** Morel (1984)
Nicknames: North Star State; Gopher State; Land of 10,000 Lakes
Origin of name: From a Dakota Indian word meaning "sky-tinted water"
10 largest cities (1994): Minneapolis, 354,590; St. Paul, 262,071; Bloomington, 85,185; Duluth, 83,990; Rochester, 75,769; Coon Rapids, 62,364; Plymouth, 60,143; Brooklyn Park, 58,786; Eagan, 56,992; Burnsville, 55,081
Land area (rank): 79,617 sq mi. (206,207 sq km) (14)
Geographic center: In Crow Wing Co., 10 mi. SW of Brainerd
Number of counties: 87
Largest county (1995 pop. est.): Hennepin, 1,053,467
State forests: 56 (3,200,000+ ac.)
State parks: 66 (226,000 ac.)
1995 resident population est.: 4,609,548
1990 resident census population (rank): 4,375,099 (20). **Male:** 2,145,183; **Female:** 2,229,916. **White:** 4,130,395 (94.4%); **Black:** 94,944 (2.2%); **American Indian, Eskimo, or Aleut:** 49,909 (1.1%); **Asian or Pacific Islander:** 77,886 (1.8%); **Other race:** 21,965 (0.5%); **Hispanic:** 53,884 (1.2%). **1990 percent population under 18:** 26.7; **65 and over:** 12.5; **median age:** 32.5.

Following the visits of several French explorers, fur traders, and missionaries, including Marquette and Joliet and La Salle, the region was claimed for Louis XIV by Daniel Greysolon, Sieur Duluth, in 1679.

The U.S. acquired eastern Minnesota from Great Britain after the Revolutionary War and 20 years later bought the western part from France in the Louisiana Purchase of 1803. Much of the region was explored by U.S. Army Lt. Zebulon M. Pike before the northern strip of Minnesota bordering Canada was ceded by Britain in 1818.

The state is rich in natural resources. A few square miles of land in the north in the Mesabi, Cuyuna, and Vermillion ranges, produce more than 75% of the nation's iron ore. The state's farms rank high in yields of corn, wheat, rye, alfalfa, and sugar beets. Other leading farm products include butter, eggs, milk, potatoes, green peas, barley, soy beans, oats, and livestock.

Minnesota's factory production includes nonelectrical machinery, fabricated metals, flour-mill products, plastics, electronic computers, scientific instruments, and processed foods. It is also one of the nation's leaders in the printing and paper products industries.

Minneapolis is the trade center of the Northwest; and the headquarters of the world's largest super computer and grain distributor. St. Paul is the nation's biggest publisher of calendars and law books. These "twin cities" are the nation's third largest trucking center. Duluth has the nation's largest inland harbor and now handles a significant amount of foreign trade. Rochester is the home of the Mayo Clinic, an internationally famous medical center.

Today, tourism is a major revenue producer in Minnesota, with arts, fishing, hunting, water sports, and winter sports bringing in millions of visitors each year.

Among the most popular attractions are the St. Paul Winter Carnival; the Tyrone Guthrie Theatre, the Institute of Arts, Walker Art Center, and Minnehaha Park, in Minneapolis; Boundary Waters Canoe Area; Voyageurs National Park; North Shore Drive; and the Minnesota Zoological Gardens and the state's more than 10,000 lakes.

Famous natives and residents: LaVerne, Maxene, and Patti Andrews, singers; Warren E. Burger, jurist; William E. Colby, ex-director of CIA; William Demarest, actor; William O. Douglas, jurist; Bob Dylan, singer and composer; F. Scott Fitzgerald, novelist; Judy Garland, singer and actress; J. Paul Getty, oil executive; Cass Gilbert, architect; Duane Hanson, sculptor; Hubert H. Humphrey, senator and vice president; Jessica Lange, actress; Sinclair Lewis, novelist; Cornell MacNeil, baritone; Roger Maris, baseball player; E.G. Marshall, actor; Charles H. Mayo, surgeon; William J. Mayo, surgeon; Eugene J. McCarthy, ex-senator; Kate Millett, feminist; Gen. Lauris Norstad, ex-commander of NATO forces; Westbrook Pegler, columnist; John Sargent Pillsbury, flour milling; Marion Ross, actress; Jane Russell, actress; Harrison E. Salisbury, journalist; Charles M. Schulz, cartoonist; Max Shulman, novelist; Maurice H. Stans, ex-secretary of commerce; Harold E. Stassen, ex-government official; Michael Todd, producer; Frederick Weyerhaeuser, lumbering; Gig Young, actor.

MISSISSIPPI

Capital: Jackson
Governor: Kirk Fordice, R (to Jan. 2000)
Lieut. Governor: Ronnie Musgrove, D (to Jan. 2000)
Secy. of State: Eric Clark, D (to Jan. 2000)
Treasurer: Marshall Bennett, D (to Jan. 2000)
Auditor: Phil Bryant, R (to Jan. 2000)
Atty. General: Mike Moore, D (to Jan. 2000)
Agriculture and Commerce Commissioner: Lester Spell, D (to Jan. 2000)
Insurance commissioner: George Dale, D (to Jan. 2000)
Organized as Territory: April 7, 1798
Entered Union (rank): Dec. 10, 1817 (20)
Present constitution adopted: 1890
Motto: *Virtute et armis* (By valor and arms)
State symbols: flower, Flower or bloom of the magnolia or evergreen magnolia (1952); **wildflower,** Coreopsis (1991); **tree,** Magnolia (1938); **bird,** Mockingbird (1944); **song,** "Go, Mississippi" (1962); **stone,** Petrified wood (1976); **fish,** Largemouth or black bass (1974); **insect,** Honeybee (1980); **shell,**

Oyster shell (1974); **water mammal,** Bottlenosed dolphin or porpoise (1974); **fossil,** Prehistoric whale (1981); **land mammal,** White-tailed deer (1974), Red fox (1997); **waterfowl,** Wood duck (1974); **beverage,** Milk (1984); **butterfly,** Spicebush Swallowtail (1991); **dance,** Square dance (1995)
Nickname: Magnolia State
Origin of name: From an Indian word meaning "Father of Waters"
10 largest cities (1994): Jackson, 193,097; Biloxi, 47,832; Hattiesburg, 47,692; Greenville, 44,394; Gulfport, 43,023; Meridian, 42,608; Tupelo, 32,987; Pascagoula, 29,043; Vicksburg, 28,122; Columbus, 26,849
Land area (rank): 46,914 sq mi. (121,506 sq km) (31)
Geographic center: In Leake Co., 9 mi. WNW of Carthage
Number of counties: 82
Largest county (1995 pop. est.): Hinds, 251,031
State forests: 1 (1,760 ac.)
State parks: 27 (16,763 ac.)
1995 resident population est.: 2,697,243
1990 resident census population (rank): 2,573,216 (31). **Male:** 1,230,617; **Female:** 1,342,599. **White:** 1,633,461 (63.5%); **Black:** 915,057 (35.6%); **American Indian, Eskimo, or Aleut:** 8,525 (0.3%); **Asian or Pacific Islander:** 13,016 (0.5%); **Other race:** 3,157 (0.1%); **Hispanic:** 15,931 (0.6%). **1990 percent population under 18:** 29.0; **65 and over:** 12.5; **median age:** 31.2.

First explored for Spain by Hernando de Soto who discovered the Mississippi River in 1540, the region was later claimed by France. In 1699, a French group under Sieur d'Iberville established the first permanent settlement near present-day Ocean Springs.

Great Britain took over the area in 1763 after the French and Indian War, ceding it to the U.S. in 1783 after the Revolution. Spain did not relinquish its claims until 1798, and in 1810 the U.S. annexed West Florida from Spain, including what is now southern Mississippi.

For a little more than one hundred years, from shortly after the state's founding through the Great Depression, cotton was the undisputed king of Mississippi's largely agrarian economy. Over the last half-century, however, Mississippi has progressively deepened its commitment to diversification by balancing agricultural output with increased industrial activity.

Today, agriculture continues as a major segment of the state's economy. While the most acreage is devoted to soybeans, cotton is the largest cash crop—Mississippi remains third in the nation in cotton production. The state's farmlands yield important harvests of corn, peanuts, pecans, rice, sugar cane, sweet potatoes, soybeans and food grains as well as poultry, eggs, meat animals, dairy products, feed crops and horticultural crops. Mississippi remains the world's leading producer of pond-raised catfish. Mississippi boasts 100,000 of the 140,000 total acres nationwide of catfish ponds.

The state abounds in historical landmarks and is the home of the Vicksburg National Military Park. Other National Park Service areas are Brices Cross Roads National Battlefield Site, Tupelo National Battlefield, and part of Natchez Trace National Parkway. Pre-Civil War mansions are the special pride of Natchez, Oxford, Columbus, Vicksburg, and Jackson.

Famous natives and residents: Red Barber, sportscaster; Jimmy Buffet, singer, songwriter; Craig Claiborne, columnist and restaurant critic; Bo Diddley, guitarist; Charles Evers, civil rights leader; Medgar Evers, civil rights leader; William Faulkner, novelist; Shelby Foote, historian; Richard Ford, novelist; John Grisham, novelist; Barry Hannah, novelist; Beth Henley, playwright and actress; Jim Henson, puppeteer; James Earl Jones, actor; B.B. King, guitarist; Mary Ann Mobley, actress; Willie Morris, writer;

Elvis Presley, singer and actor; Leontyne Price, soprano; William Raspberry, columnist; Jerry Rice, football player; Jimmie Rodgers, singer; Sela Ward, actress; Muddy Waters, singer and guitarist; Eudora Welty, novelist; Tennessee Williams, playwright; Oprah Winfrey, talk show host and actress; Richard Wright, novelist; Tammy Wynette, country music star; Zig Ziglar, speaker, author.

MISSOURI

Capital: Jefferson City
Governor: Mel Carnahan, D (to Jan. 2001)
Lieut. Governor: Roger Wilson, D (to Jan. 2001)
Secy. of State: Rebecca ("Bekki") McDowell Cook, D (to Jan. 2001)
Auditor: Margaret Kelly, R (to Jan. 1999)
Treasurer: Bob Holden, D (to Jan. 2001)
Atty. General: Jeremiah "Jay" W. Nixon, D (to Jan. 2001)
Organized as territory: June 4, 1812
Entered Union (rank): Aug. 10, 1821 (24)
Present constitution adopted: 1945
Motto: *Salus populi suprema lex esto* (The welfare of the people shall be the supreme law)
State symbols: floral emblem, Hawthorn (1923); **bird,** Bluebird (1927); **song,** "Missouri Waltz" (1949); **fossil,** Crinoid (1989); **musical instrument,** Fiddle (1987); **rock,** Mozarkite (1967); **mineral,** Galena (1967); **insect,** Honeybee (1985); **tree,** Flowering dogwood (1955); **tree nut,** Eastern black walnut (1990); **animal,** Mule (1995); **dance,** Square dance (1995); **Missouri Day,** third Wednesday in October (1915)
Nickname: Show-me State
Origin of name: Named after a tribe called Missouri Indians. "Missouri" means "town of the large canoes."
10 largest cities (1994): Kansas City, 443,878; St. Louis, 368,215; Springfield, 149,727; Independence, 111,669; Columbia, 74,072; St. Joseph, 71,711; St. Charles, 56,339; Florissant, 51,398; Lee's Summit, 47,029; St. Peter's, 46,408
Land area (rank): 68,898 sq mi. (178,446 sq km) (18)
Geographic center: In Miller Co., 20 mi. SW of Jefferson City
Number of counties: 114, plus 1 independent city
Largest county (1995 pop. est.): St. Louis, 1,007,834
Conservation areas[1]: 518 (704,311 ac.)
Conservation accesses: 240 (10,619 ac.)
State parks and historic sites: 79 (134,496 ac.)
1995 resident population est.: 5,323,523
1990 resident census population (rank): 5,117,073 (15). **Male:** 2,464,315; **Female:** 2,652,758. **White:** 4,486,228 (87.7%); **Black:** 548,208 (10.7%); **American Indian, Eskimo, or Aleut:** 19,835 (0.4%); **Asian or Pacific Islander:** 41,277 (0.8%); **Other race:** 21,525 (0.4%); **Hispanic:** 61,702 (1.2%). **1990 percent population under 18:** 25.7; **65 and over:** 14.0; **median age:** 33.5.

1. Includes wildlife areas, natural history areas, state forests, and tower sites.

De Soto visited the Missouri area in 1541. France's claim to the entire region was based on La Salle's travels in 1682. French fur traders established Ste. Genevieve in 1735 and St. Louis was first settled in 1764.

The U.S. gained Missouri from France as part of the Louisiana Purchase in 1803, and the territory was admitted as a state following the Missouri Compromise of 1820. Throughout the pre-Civil War period and during the war, Missourians were sharply divided in their opinions about slavery and in their allegiances, supplying both Union and Confederate forces with troops. However, the state itself remained in the Union.

Historically, Missouri played a leading role as a gateway to the West, St. Joseph being the eastern starting point of the Pony Express, while the much-traveled Santa Fe and Oregon Trails began in Independence. Now a popular vacationland, Missouri has 11 major lakes and numerous fishing streams, springs, and caves. Bagnell Dam, across the Osage River in the Ozarks, completed in 1931, created one of the largest man-made lakes in the world, covering 65,000 acres of surface area.

Missouri's economy relies on a diversified industrial base. Service industries provide more income and jobs than any other segment, and include a growing tourism and travel sector. Wholesale and retail trade, manufacturing and agriculture also play significant roles in the state's economy. Missouri is a leading producer of transportation equipment (including automobile manufacturing and auto parts), beer and beverages, and defense and aerospace technology. Food processing is the state's fastest-growing industry, well-suited to the state's blend of agricultural, natural, energy and transportation resources. Missouri mines also produce 90% of the nation's principal (non-recycled) lead supply.

Missouri's largest corporate employers include McDonnell-Douglas, Wal-Mart, Trans World Airlines and Southwestern Bell. The state's top agricultural products include: grain, sorghum, hay, corn, soybeans, wheat, oats, barley, tobacco and rice. A well-established grape and wine program brings together aspects of agriculture, manufacturing and tourism to support a vibrant vintner industry.

Tourism draws hundreds of thousands of visitors to a number of Missouri points of interest: the country-music shows of Branson; Bass Pro Shops national headquarters (Springfield); the Gateway Arch at the Jefferson National Expansion (St. Loius); Mark Twain's boyhood home and cave (Hannibal); the Harry S Truman home and library (Independence); the scenic beauty of the Ozark National Scenic Riverways; and the Pony Express and Jesse James museums (St. Joseph). The state's different lakes regions also attract fishermen and sun-seekers from throughout the Midwest.

Famous natives and residents: Robert Altman, film director; Burt Bacharach, songwriter; Josephine Baker, singer and dancer; Wallace Beery, actor; Robert Russell Bennett, composer; Yogi Berra, baseball player; Thomas Hart Benton, painter; Susan Elizabeth Blow, educator; Bill Bradley, basketball player and ex-N.J. senator; Omar N. Bradley, 5-star general; Grace Bumbry, soprano; William Burroughs, writer; Sarah Caldwell, opera director and conductor; Martha Jane Canary (Calamity Jane), frontierswoman; George Washington Carver, scientist; Walter Cronkhite, TV newscaster; Robert Cummings, actor; Jane Darwell, actress; Walt Disney, artist; Jeanne Eagels, actress; T.S. Eliot, poet; Eugene Field, poet; Redd Foxx, actor and comedian; Betty Grable, actress; Dick Gregory, comic and activist; Jean Harlow, actress; George Hearn, actor; Al Hirschfeld, artist; Edwin Hubble, astronomer; Langston Hughes, poet; John Huston, film director; Jesse James, outlaw; Scott Joplin, composer; Bernarr MacFadden, physical culturist; Mary Margaret McBride, TV hostess; Marianne Moore, poet; Geraldine Page, actress; James C. Penney, merchant; Marlin Perkins, TV host, zoo director; John Joseph Pershing, general; Vincent Price, actor; Joseph Pulitzer, journalist; Doris Roberts, actress; Ginger Rogers, dancer and actress; Sacajawea, Indian guide for Lewis and Clark; Ted Shawn, dancer and choreographer; Casey Stengel, baseball player; Gladys Swarthout, soprano; Sara Teasdale, poet; Virgil Thomson, composer; Harry S Truman, ex-president; Mark Twain, author; Dick Van Dyke, actor; Ruth Warrick, actress; Dennis Weaver, actor; Pearl White, actress; Mary Wickes, actress; Laura Ingalls Wilder, author; Roy Wilkins, civil rights leader.

MONTANA

Capital: Helena
Governor: Marc Racicot, R (to Jan. 2001)
Lieut. Governor: Dennis R. Rehberg, R (to Jan. 2001)
Secy. of State: Mike Cooney, D (to Jan. 2001)
Auditor: Mark O'Keefe, D (to Jan. 2001)
Atty. General: Joe Mazurek, D (to Jan. 2001)
Organized as territory: May 26, 1864
Entered Union (rank): Nov. 8, 1889 (41)
Present constitution adopted: 1972
Motto: Oro y plata (Gold and silver)
State symbols: flower, Bitterroot (1895); **tree,** Ponderosa pine (1949); **stones,** Sapphire and agate (1969); **bird,** Western meadowlark (1981); **song,** "Montana" (1945)
Nickname: Treasure State
Origin of name: Chosen from Latin dictionary by J. M. Ashley. It is a Latinized Spanish word meaning "mountainous."
10 largest cities (1994): Billings, 86,578; Great Falls, 58,202; Missoula, 45,364; Butte-Silver Bow[1], 34,190; Helena, 26,339; Bozeman, 25,067; Kalispell, 13,214; Anaconda-Deer Lodge County, 10,229; Havre, 10,059; Miles City, 8,745
Land area (rank): 145,556 sq mi. (376,991 sq km) (4)
Geographic center: In Fergus Co., 12 mi. W of Lewistown
Number of counties: 56, plus small part of Yellowstone National Park
Largest county (1995 pop. est.): Yellowstone, 124,655
State forests: 7 (214,000 ac.)
State parks and recreation areas: 110 (18,273 ac.)
1995 resident population est.: 870,281
1990 resident census population (rank): 799,065 (44). **Male:** 395,769; **Female:** 403,296. **White:** 741,111 (92.7%); **Black:** 2,381 (0.3%); **American Indian, Eskimo, or Aleut:** 47,679 (6.0%); **Asian or Pacific Islander:** 4,259 (0.5%); **Other race:** 3,635 (0.5%); **Hispanic:** 12,174 (1.5%). **1990 percent population under 18:** 27.8; **65 and over:** 13.3; **median age:** 33.8.

1. Consolidated City.

First explored for France by François and Louis-Joseph Verendrye in the early 1740s, much of the region was acquired by the U.S. from France as part of the Louisiana Purchase in 1803. Before western Montana was obtained from Great Britain in the Oregon Treaty of 1846, American trading posts and forts had been established in the territory.

The major Indian wars (1867–1877) included the famous 1876 Battle of the Little Big Horn, better known as "Custer's Last Stand," in which Cheyennes and Sioux defeated George A. Custer and more than 200 of his men in southeastern Montana.

Much of Montana's early history was concerned with mining with copper, lead, zinc, silver, coal, and oil as principal products.

Butte is the center of the area that once supplied half of the U.S. copper.

Fields of grain cover much of Montana's plains; it ranks high among the states in wheat and barley, with rye, oats, flaxseed, sugar beets, and potatoes other important crops. Sheep and cattle raising make significant contributions to the economy.

Tourist attractions include hunting, fishing, skiing, and dude ranching. Glacier National Park, on the Continental Divide, is a scenic and vacation wonderland with 60 glaciers, 200 lakes, and many streams with good trout fishing.

Other major points of interest include the Custer Battlefield National Monument, Virginia City, Yellowstone National Park, Museum of the Plains Indians at Browning, and the Fort Union Trading Post and Grant-Kohr's Ranch National Historic Sites.

Famous natives and residents: Dorothy Baker, author; Dirk Benedict, actor; W.A. (Tony) Boyle, labor union official; Gary Cooper, actor; John Cowan, prospector and founder of Last Chance Gulch (now Helena); Alfred Bertram Guthrie, Pulitzer Prize-winning author; Chet Huntley, TV newscaster; Will James, writer and artist; Dorothy Johnson, author; Evel Knievel, daredevil motorcyclist; Myrna Loy, actress; David Lynch, filmmaker; Mike Mansfield, ex-senator; George Montgomery, actor; Jeannette Rankin, first woman elected to Congress; Martha Raye, actress; Charles M. Russell, Old West painter; Michael Smuin, choreographer; Lester C. Thurow, economist, educator.

NEBRASKA

Capital: Lincoln
Governor: Ben Nelson, D (to Jan. 1999)
Lieut. Governor: Kim Robak, D (to Jan. 1999)
Secy. of State: Scott Moore, R (to Jan. 1999)
Atty. General: Don Stenberg, R (to Jan. 1999)
Auditor: John Breslow, R (to Jan. 1999)
Treasurer: David Heineman, R (to Jan. 1999)
Organized as territory: May 30, 1854
Entered Union (rank): March 1, 1867 (37)
Present constitution adopted: Oct. 12, 1875 (extensively amended 1919–20)
Motto: Equality before the law
State symbols: flower, Goldenrod (1895); **tree,** Cottonwood (1972); **bird,** Western meadowlark (1929); **insect,** Honeybee (1975); **gemstone,** Blue agate (1967); **rock,** Prairie agate (1967); **fossil,** Mammoth (1967); **song,** "Beautiful Nebraska" (1967); **soil,** Typic Arguistolls, Holdrege Series (1979); **mammal,** Whitetail deer (1981); **grass,** Little Bluestem (1969)
Nicknames: Cornhusker State (1945); Beef State
Origin of name: From an Oto Indian word meaning "flat water"
10 largest cities (1994): Omaha, 345,033; Lincoln, 203,076; Bellevue, 41,274; Grand Island, 41,147; Kearney, 26,216; Fremont, 23,755; North Platte, 23,171; Hastings, 22,956; Norfolk, 22,435; Columbus, 20,514
Land area (rank): 76,644 sq mi. (198,508 sq km) (15)
Geographic center: In Custer Co., 10 mi. NW of Broken Bow
Number of counties: 93
Largest county (1995 pop. est.): Douglas, 434,147
State forests: None
State parks: 86 areas, historical and recreational; 8 major areas
1995 resident population est.: 1,637,112
1990 resident census population (rank): 1,578,417 (36). **Male:** 769,439; **Female:** 808,946. **White:** 1,480,558 (93.8%); **Black:** 57,404 (3.6%); **American Indian, Eskimo, or Aleut:** 12,410 (0.8%); **Asian or Pacific Islander:** 12,422 (0.8%); **Other race:** 15,591 (1.0%); **Hispanic:** 36,969 (2.3%). **1990 percent population under 18:** 27.2; **65 and over:** 14.1; **median age:** 33.0.

French fur traders first visited Nebraska in the early 1700s. Part of the Louisiana Purchase in 1803, Nebraska was explored by Lewis and Clark in 1804–06.

Robert Stuart pioneered the Oregon Trail across Nebraska in 1812–13 and the first permanent white settlement was established at Bellevue in 1823. Western Nebraska was acquired by treaty following the Mexican War in 1848. The Union Pacific began its transcontinental railroad at Omaha in 1865. In 1937, Nebraska became the only state in the Union to have a unicameral (one-house) legislature. Members are elected to it without party designation.

Nebraska is a leading grain-producer with bumper crops of grain sorghum, corn, and wheat. More varieties of grass, valuable for forage, grow in this state than in any other in the nation.

The state's sizable cattle and hog industries make Dakota City and Lexington among the nation's largest meat-packing centers.

Manufacturing has become diversified in Nebraska, strengthening the state's economic base. Firms making electronic components, auto accessories, pharmaceuticals, and mobile homes have joined such older industries as clothing, farm machinery, chemicals, and transportation equipment. Oil was discovered in 1939 and natural gas in 1949.

Among the principal attractions are Agate Fossil Beds, Homestead, and Scotts Bluff National Monuments; Chimney Rock National Historic Site; a recreated pioneer village at Minden; SAC Museum at Bellevue; the Stuhr Museum of the Prairie Pioneer with 57 original 19th-century buildings near Grand Island; the Sheldon Memorial Art Gallery at the University of Nebraska and the State Capitol in Lincoln; and the Lied Center for the Performing Arts located on the University of Nebraska campus in Lincoln; the Henry Doorly Zoo in Omaha; and the University of Nebraska State Museum in Lincoln.

Famous natives and residents: Grace Abbott, social worker; Bess Streeter Aldrich, author; Grover Cleveland Alexander, Hall of Fame pitcher; Fred Astaire, dancer and actor; Max Baer, boxer; Bil Baird, puppeteer; George Beadle, geneticist; Marlon Brando, actor; William Jennings Bryan, three-time U.S. presidential candidate; Warren Buffett, investor, one of world's richest men; Johnny Carson, host of "Tonight Show"; Willa Cather, author; Dick Cavett, TV entertainer; Richard B. Cheney, ex-secretary ofd Defense; Montgomery Clift, actor; James Coburn, actor; William "Buffalo Bill" Cody, showman of the West; Sandy Dennis, actress; Mignon Eberhart, author; Harold "Doc" Edgerton, inventor of stop-action strobe photography; Ruth Etting, singer, actress; Fr. Edward J. Flanagan, founder of Boys Town; Henry Fonda, actor; Gerald Ford, ex-president; Bob Gibson, baseball player; Hoot Gibson, actor; Howard Hanson, conductor; Leland Hayward, producer; Robert Henri, painter; David Janssen, actor; Susette La Flesche, Omaha Indian artist; Francis La Flesche, ethnologist; Melvin Laird, politician, ex-secretary of defense; Frank W. Leahy, football coach; Harold Lloyd, actor; Malcolm X, civil rights advocate; Irish McCalla, actress; Dorothy McGuire, actress; Julius Sterling Morton, politician, journalist, originated Arbor Day; John G. Neihardt, epic poet; Nick Nolte, actor; George W. Norris, U.S. Senator, unicameralism advocate; Nathan Pound, dean of Harvard Law School, botanist; Red Cloud, Indian rights advocate; Mari Sandoz, author; Standing Bear, Indian rights advocate; Inga Swenson, actress; Robert Taylor, actor; Paul Williams, singer, composer, actor; Julie Wilson, singer and actress; Daryl F. Zanuck, film producer.

NEVADA

Capital: Carson City
Governor: Robert J. Miller, D (to Jan. 1999)
Lieut. Governor: Lonnie L. Hammargren, R (to Jan. 1999)
Secy. of State: Dean Heller, R (to Jan. 1999)
Treasurer: Bob Seale, R (to Jan. 1999)
Controller: Darrel R. Daines, R (to Jan. 1999)
Atty. General: Frankie Sue Del Papa, D (to Jan. 1999)
Organized as territory: March 2, 1861
Entered Union (rank): Oct. 31, 1864 (36)
Present constitution adopted: 1864
Motto: All for Our Country
State symbols: flower, Sagebrush (1959); **trees,** Single-leaf pinon (1953) and Bristlecone pine (1987); **bird,** Mountain bluebird (1967); **animal,** Desert bighorn sheep (1973); **colors,** Silver and blue (1983);

song, "Home Means Nevada" (1933); **rock,** Sandstone (1987); **precious gemstone,** Virgin Valley Black Fire Opal (1987); **semiprecious gemstone,** Nevada Turquoise (1987); **grass,** Indian Ricegrass (1977); **metal,** Silver (1977); **fossil,** Ichthyosaur (1977); **fish,** Lahontan Cutthroat Trout (1981); **reptile,** Desert tortoise (1989); **state artifact,** Tule duck decoy (1995)
Nicknames: Sagebrush State; Silver State; Battle Born State
Origin of name: Spanish: "snowcapped"
10 largest cities (1994): Las Vegas, 327,878; Reno, 145,029; Henderson, 101,997; North Las Vegas, 64,536; Sparks, 60,238; Carson City, 45,117; Elko, 18,583; Boulder City, 13,092; Fallon, 7,404; Winnemucca, 7,089
Land area (rank): 109,806 sq mi. (284,397 sq km) (7)
Geographic center: In Lander Co., 26 mi. SE of Austin
Number of counties: 16, plus 1 independent city
Largest county (1995 pop. est.): Clark, 992,593
State forests: None
State parks: 20 (150,000 ac., including leased lands)
1995 resident population est.: 1,530,108
1990 resident census population (rank): 1,201,833 (39). **Male:** 611,880; **Female:** 589,953. **White:** 1,012,695 (84.3%); **Black:** 78,771 (6.6%); **American Indian, Eskimo, or Aleut:** 19,637 (1.6%); **Asian or Pacific Islander:** 38,127 (3.2%); **Other race:** 52,603 (4.4%); **Hispanic:** 124,419 (10.4%). **1990 percent population under 18:** 24.7; **65 and over:** 10.6; **median age:** 33.3.

Trappers and traders, including Jedediah Smith, and Peter Skene Ogden, entered the Nevada area in the 1820s. In 1843–45, John C. Fremont and Kit Carson explored the Great Basin and Sierra Nevada.

In 1848 following the Mexican War, the U.S. obtained the region and the first permanent settlement was a Mormon trading post near present-day Genoa.

The driest state in the nation with an average annual rainfall of only about 7 inches, much of Nevada is uninhabited, sagebrush-covered desert. The wettest part of state receives about 40 inches of precipitation per year, while driest spot has less than four inches per year.

Nevada was made famous by the discovery of the fabulous Comstock Lode in 1859 and its mines have produced large quantities of gold, silver, copper, lead, zinc, mercury, barite, and tungsten. Oil was discovered in 1954. Gold now far exceeds all other minerals in value of production.

In 1931, the state created two industries, divorce and gambling. For many years, Reno and Las Vegas were the "divorce capitals of the nation." More liberal divorce laws in many states have ended this distinction, but Nevada is the gambling and entertainment capital of the U.S. State gambling taxes account for 40.1% of general fund tax revenues. Although Nevada leads the nation in per capita gambling revenue, it ranks only fourth in total gambling revenue.

Near Las Vegas, on the Colorado River, stands Hoover Dam, which impounds the waters of Lake Mead, one of the world's largest artificial lakes.

The state's agricultural crop consists mainly of hay, alfalfa seed, barley, wheat, and potatoes.

Nevada manufactures gaming equipment; lawn and garden irrigation devices; titanium products; seismic and machinery monitoring devices; and specialty printing.

Major resort areas flourish in Lake Tahoe, Reno, and Las Vegas. Recreation areas include those at Pyramid Lake, Lake Tahoe, and Lake Mead and Lake Mohave, both in Lake Mead National Recreation Area. Among the other attractions are Hoover Dam, Virginia City, and Great Basin National Park (includes Lehman Caves).

Famous natives and residents: Eva Adams, ex-director of U.S. Mint; Andre Agassi, tennis player; Raymond T. Baker, ex-director of U.S. Mint; Helen Delich Bentley, government official, newspaperwoman; Robert Caples, painter; Walter Van Tilburg Clark, writer; Henry Comstock, prospector of "Comstock Lode" fame; Abby Dalton, actress; Michele Greene, actress; Sarah Winnemucca Hopkins, Paiute interpreter and peacemaker, author; Jack Kramer, tennis player; Paul Laxalt, politician; William Lear, aviation inventor; Robert C. Lynch, surgeon; John W. Mackay, benefactor, one of Big Four of Comstock Lode; Emma Nevada, opera singer; Thelma "Pat" Nixon, First Lady; James W. Nye, territory governor, ex-senator; Lute Pease, cartoonist, Pulitzer Prize winner; Edna Purviance, actress; Patty Sheehan, golfer; Jack Wilson, Paiute Indian prophet; George Wingfield, mining millionaire.

NEW HAMPSHIRE

Capital: Concord
Governor: Jeanne Shaheen, D (to Jan. 1999)
Treasurer: Georgie A. Thomas, R (to Dec. 1996)
Secy. of State: William M. Gardner, D (to Dec. 1996)
Commissioner: Patrick Duffy
Atty. General: Jeffrey R. Howard, R (to Mar. 1997)
Entered Union (rank): June 21, 1788 (9)
Present constitution adopted: 1784
Motto: Live free or die
State symbols: flower, Purple lilac (1919); **tree,** White birch (1947); **bird,** Purple finch (1957); **songs,** "Old New Hampshire" (1949) and "New Hampshire, My New Hampshire" (1963)
Nickname: Granite State
Origin of name: From the English county of Hampshire
10 largest cities (1994): Manchester, 96,640; Nashua, 79,631; Concord, 36,198; Rochester, 27,023; Dover, 24,891; Keene, 21,916; Portsmouth, 19,594; Laconia, 14,581; Claremont, 13,310; Lebanon, 12,466
Land area (rank): 8,969 sq mi. (23,231 sq km) (44)
Geographic center: In Belknap Co., 3 mi. E of Ashland
Number of counties: 10
Largest county (1995 pop. est.): Hillsborough, 349,572
State forests & parks: 210 (156,398 ac.)
1995 resident population est.: 1,148,253
1990 resident census population (rank): 1,109,252 (41). **Male:** 543,544; **Female:** 565,708. **White:** 1,087,433 (98.0%); **Black:** 7,198 (0.6%); **American Indian, Eskimo, or Aleut:** 2,134 (0.2%); **Asian or Pacific Islander:** 9,343 (0.8%); **Other race:** 3,144 (0.3%); **Hispanic:** 11,333 (1.0%). **1990 percent population under 18:** 25.1; **65 and over:** 11.3; **median age:** 32.8.

Under an English land grant, Capt. John Smith sent settlers to establish a fishing colony at the mouth of the Piscataqua River, near present-day Rye and Dover, in 1623. Capt. John Mason, who participated in the founding of Portsmouth in 1630, gave New Hampshire its name.

After a 38-year period of union with Massachusetts, New Hampshire was made a separate royal colony in 1679. As leaders in the revolutionary cause, New Hampshire delegates received the honor of being the first to vote for the Declaration of Independence on July 4, 1776. New Hampshire is the only state that ever played host at the formal conclusion of a foreign war when, in 1905, Portsmouth was the scene of the treaty ending the Russo-Japanese War.

Abundant water power early turned New Hampshire into an industrial state and manufacturing is the principal source of income in the state. The most important industrial products are electrical and other machinery, textiles, pulp and paper products, and stone and clay products.

Dairy and poultry farming and growing fruit, truck vegetables, corn, potatoes, and hay are the major agricultural pursuits.

Tourism, because of New Hampshire's scenic and recreational resources, now brings over $3.5 billion into the state annually.

Vacation attractions include Lake Winnipesaukee, largest of 1,300 lakes and ponds; the 724,000-acre White Mountain National Forest; Daniel Webster's birthplace near Franklin; Strawbery Banke, restored building of the original settlement at Portsmouth; and the famous "Old Man of the Mountain" granite head profile, the state's official emblem, at Franconia.

Famous natives and residents: Sherman Adams, ex-governor and presidential advisor; Salmon P. Chase, jurist; Charles Anderson Dana, editor; Mary Baker Eddy, founder of Christian Science Church; Dustin Farnum, actor; Thomas Green Fessenden, journalist and satirical poet; Daniel Chester French, sculptor; Horace Greeley, journalist and politician; Sarah J. Hale, editor; John Irving, writer; Benjamin F. Keith, theater entrepreneur; Jackson Hall Kelly, promoter of Oregon settlement; John Langdon, political leader; Sharon Christa McAuliffe, teacher and astronaut; Franklin Pierce, ex-president; Augustus Saint-Gaudens, sculptor; Alan Shepard, astronaut; Harlan F. Stone, jurist; Daniel Webster, statesman; Henry Wilson, politician and ex-vice president; Noah Worcester, clergyman and pacifist.

NEW JERSEY

Capital: Trenton
Governor: Christine Todd Whitman, R (to Jan. 1998)
Secy. of State: Lonna R. Hooks, R (to Jan. 1998)
Treasurer: Bryan W. Clymer, R (to Jan. 1998)
Atty. General: Peter Verniero, R (to Jan. 1998)
Chief Justice: Deborah T. Poritz, R (to Jan. 1998)
Entered Union (rank): Dec. 18, 1787 (3)
Present constitution adopted: 1947
Motto: Liberty and prosperity
State symbols: flower, Purple violet (1913); **bird,** Eastern goldfinch (1935); **insect,** Honeybee (1974); **tree,** Red oak (1950); **animal,** Horse (1977); **colors,** Buff and blue (1965); **folk dance,** Square dance; **dinosaur,** Hadrosaurus Foulkii; **fish,** Brook trout; **shell,** Knobbed whelk
Nickname: Garden State
Origin of name: From the Channel Isle of Jersey
10 largest cities (1994)[1]: Newark, 258,751; Jersey City, 226,022; Paterson, 138,290; Elizabeth, 106,298; Trenton, 84,441; Camden, 82,866; Clifton, 74,002; East Orange, 72,847; Bayonne, 62,270; Union City, 56,308
Land area (rank): 7,419 sq mi. (19,215 sq km) (46)
Geographic center: In Mercer Co., 5 mi. SE of Trenton
Number of counties: 21
Largest county (1995 pop. est.): Bergen, 845,189
State forests: 11
State parks: 35 (67,111 ac.)
1996 resident population est.: 7,987,933
1990 resident census population (rank): 7,730,188 (9). **Male:** 3,735,685; **Female:** 3,994,503. **White:** 6,130,465 (79.3%); **Black:** 1,036,825 (13.4%); **American Indian, Eskimo, or Aleut:** 14,970 (0.2%); **Asian or Pacific Islander:** 272,521 (3.5%); **Other race:** 275,407 (3.6%); **Hispanic:** 739,861 (9.6%). **1990 percent population under 18:** 23.3; **65 and over:** 13.4; **median age:** 34.5.

New Jersey's early colonial history was involved with that of New York (New Netherlands), of which it was a part. One year after the Dutch surrender to England in 1664, New Jersey was organized as an English colony under Gov. Philip Carteret.

In 1676 the colony was divided between Carteret and a company of English Quakers who had obtained the rights belonging to John, Lord Berkeley. New Jersey became a united, crown colony in 1702, administered by the royal governor of New York. Finally, in 1738, New Jersey was separated from New York under its own royal governor, Lewis Morris.

Because of its key location between New York City and Philadelphia, New Jersey saw much fighting during the American Revolution.

Today, New Jersey, an area of wide industrial diversification, is known as the Crossroads of the East. Products from over 15,000 factories can be delivered overnight to almost 60 million people, representing 12 states and the District of Columbia. The greatest single industry is chemicals and New Jersey is one of the foremost research centers in the world. Many large oil refineries are located in northern New Jersey and other important manufactures are pharmaceuticals, instruments, machinery, electrical goods, and apparel.

Of the total land area, 36% is forested (1992). Farmland is declining. In 1995 there were about 9,000 farms, with over 850,000 acres under harvest. The state ranks high in production of almost all garden vegetables. Tomatoes, asparagus, corn, and blueberries are important crops, and poultry and dairy farming make significant contributions to the state's economy.

Tourism is the second largest industry in New Jersey. The state has numerous resort areas on 127 miles of Atlantic coastline. In 1977, New Jersey voters approved legislation allowing legalized casino gambling in Atlantic City. Points of interest include the Delaware Water Gap, the Edison National Historic Site in West Orange, Princeton University, Liberty State Park, Jersey City, and the N.J. State Aquarium in Camden (opened 1992).

Famous natives and residents: Bud Abbott, comedian; Charles Addams, cartoonist; Edwin Aldrin, astronaut; Count Basie, band leader; Joan Bennett, actress; Jon Bon Jovi, musician; William J. Brennan, jurist; Aaron Burr, political leader; James Fenimore Cooper, novelist; Lou Costello, comedian; Stephen Crane, writer; Helen Gahagan Douglas, ex-Representative; Allen Ginsberg, poet; William Frederick Halsey, Jr., admiral; Alfred Joyce Kilmer, poet; Ernie Kovacs, comedian; Jerry Lewis, comedian, film director; Anne Morrow Lindbergh, author; Norman Mailer, novelist; Patricia McBride, ballerina; Richard Nixon, ex-president; Dorothy Parker, author; Joe Piscopo, comedian, actor; Paul Robeson, singer and actor; Philip Roth, novelist; Ruth St. Denis, dancer and choreographer; Antonin Scalia, jurist; H. Norman Schwarzkopf, general; Frank Sinatra, singer and actor; Bruce Springsteen, musician; Alfred Stieglitz, photographer; Albert Payson Terhune, journalist and novelist; Sarah Vaughan, singer; William Carlos Williams, physician and poet; Edmund Wilson, literary critic and author.

NEW MEXICO

Capital: Santa Fe
Governor: Gary Johnson, R (to Jan. 1999)
Lieut. Governor: Walter Bradley, R (to Jan. 1998)
Secy. of State: Stephanie Gonzales, D (to Jan. 1998)
Atty. General: Tom Udall, D (to Jan. 1998)
State Auditor: Robert E. Vigil, D (to Jan. 1998)
State Treasurer: Michael A. Montoya, D (to Jan. 1998)
Commissioner of Public Lands: Ray Powell, D (to Jan. 1998)
Organized as territory: Sept. 9, 1850
Entered Union (rank): Jan. 6, 1912 (47)
Present constitution adopted: 1911
Motto: *Crescit eundo* (It grows as it goes)
State symbols: flower, Yucca (1927); **tree,** Pinon (1949); **animal,** Black bear (1963); **bird,** Roadrunner (1949); **fish,** Cutthroat trout (1955); **vegetables,**

Chili and frijol (1965); **gem,** Turquoise (1967); **colors,** Red and yellow of old Spain (1925); **song,** "O Fair New Mexico" (1917); **Spanish language song,** "Asi Es Nuevo Méjico" (1971); **poem,** A Nuevo México (1991); **grass,** Blue gramma; **fossil,** Coelophysis; **cookie,** Bizcochito (1989); **insect,** Tarantula hawk wasp (1989)
Nicknames: Land of Enchantment; Sunshine State
Origin of name: From the country of Mexico
10 largest cities (1994): Albuquerque, 411,944; Las Cruces, 71,043; Santa Fe, 62,514; Roswell, 47,395; Rio Rancho, 41,492; Farmington, 38,169; Clovis, 36,091; Hobbs, 29,712; Alamogordo, 29,628; Carlsbad, 26,974
Land area (rank): 121,365 sq mi. (314,334 sq km) (5)
Geographic center: In Torrance Co., 12 mi. SSW of Willard
Number of counties: 33
Largest county (1995 pop. est.): Bernalillo, 522,328
State-owned forested land: 933,000 ac.
State parks: 29 (105,012 ac.)
1995 resident population est.: 1,685,401
1990 resident census population (rank): 1,515,069 (37). **Male:** 745,253; **Female:** 769,816. **White:** 1,146,028 (75.6%); **Black:** 30,210 (2.0%); **American Indian, Eskimo, or Aleut:** 134,355 (8.9%); **Asian or Pacific Islander:** 14,124 (0.9%); **Other race:** 190,352 (12.6%); **Hispanic:** 579,224 (38.2%). **1990 percent population under 18:** 29.5; **65 and over:** 10.8; **median age:** 31.3.

Francisco Vásquez de Coronado, Spanish explorer searching for gold, traveled the region that became New Mexico in 1540–42. In 1598 the first Spanish settlement was established on the Rio Grande River by Juan de Onate and in 1610 Santa Fe was founded and made the capital of New Mexico.

The U.S. acquired most of New Mexico in 1848, as a result of the Mexican War, and the remainder in the 1853 Gadsden Purchase. Union troops captured the territory from the Confederates during the Civil War. With the surrender of Geronimo in 1886, the Apache Wars and most of the Indian troubles in the area were ended.

Since 1945, New Mexico has been a leader in energy research and development with extensive experiments conducted at Los Alamos Scientific Laboratory and Sandia Laboratories in the nuclear, solar, and geothermal areas.

Minerals are the state's richest natural resource and New Mexico is one of the U.S. leaders in output of uranium and potassium salts. Petroleum, natural gas, copper, gold, silver, zinc, lead, and molybdenum also contribute heavily to the state's income.

The principal manufacturing industries include food products, chemicals, transportation equipment, lumber, electrical machinery, and stone-clay-glass products. More than two thirds of New Mexico's farm income comes from livestock products, especially sheep. Cotton, pecans, and sorghum are the most important field crops. Corn, peanuts, beans, onions, chile, and lettuce are also grown.

Tourist attractions in New Mexico include the Carlsbad Caverns National Park, Inscription Rock at El Morro National Monument, the ruins at Fort Union, Billy the Kid mementos at Lincoln, the White Sands and Gila Cliff Dwellings National Monuments, and the Chaco Culture National Historical Park.

Famous natives and residents: Kathy Baker, actress; Judy Blume, author; Ernest L. Blumenshein, artist; William "Billy the Kid" Bonney, outlaw; Richard Bradford, author; Ralph Bunche, Nobel Peace Prize winner; Bruce Cabot, actor; Glen Campbell, singer; Kit Carson, Army scout and trapper; Dennis Chavez, ex-senator; John Chisum, cattle king; Mangus Coloradas, Apache leader; Edward Condon, physicist; Bill Daily, actor; John Denver, singer; Bo Diddley, blues guitarist; Patrick Garrett, lawman; Greer Garson, actress; Sid Gutierrez, astronaut; William Hanna, animator; Neil Patrick Harris, actor; Carl Hatch, ex-senator; Tony Hillerman, author; Conrad Hilton, hotel executive; Dennis Hopper, actor; Peter Hurd, artist; Preston Jones, playwright, actor; Ralph Kiner, baseball player, sportscaster; Nancy Lopez, golfer; Maria Martínez, San Ildefonso Pueblo potter; Demi Moore, actress; Jim Morrison, singer, songwriter; Bill Mauldin, political cartoonist; Popé, San Juan Pueblo medicine man, leader; Georgia O'Keeffe, painter; Harrison Schmitt, astronaut, U.S. representative; Kim Stanley, actress; Slim Summerville, actor; Clyde Tombaugh, astronomer; Al Unser, Bobby Unser, auto racers; Victorio, Apache chief; Linda Wertheimer, NPR correspondent; Kathy Whitworth, golfer.

NEW YORK

Capital: Albany
Governor: George Pataki, R (to Jan. 1999)
Lieut. Governor: Elizabeth McCaughey, R (to Jan. 1999)
Secy. of State: Alexander Treadwell, R (to Jan. 1999)
Comptroller: Carl McCall, D (to Jan. 1999)
Atty. General: Dennis Vacco, R (to Jan. 1999)
Entered Union (rank): July 26, 1788 (11)
Present constitution adopted: 1777 (last revised 1938)
Motto: *Excelsior* (Ever upward)
State symbols: animal, Beaver (1975); **fish,** Brook trout (1975); **gem,** Garnet (1969); **flower,** Rose (1955); **tree,** Sugar maple (1956); **bird,** Bluebird (1970); **insect,** Ladybug (1989); **song,** "I Love New York" (1980)
Nickname: Empire State
Origin of name: In honor of the English Duke of York
10 largest cities (1994): New York, 7,333,253; Buffalo, 312,965; Rochester, 231,170; Yonkers, 183,490; Syracuse, 159,895; Albany, 104,828; New Rochelle, 66,764; Mount Vernon, 65,862; Schenectady, 64,274; Utica, 64,095
Land area (rank): 47,224 sq mi. (122,310 sq km) (30)
Geographic center: In Madison Co., 12 mi. S of Oneida and 26 mi. SW of Utica
Number of counties: 62
Largest county (1995 pop. est.): Kings, 2,244,021
State forest preserves: Adirondacks, 2,500,000 ac., Catskills, 250,000 ac.
State parks: 150 (250,000 ac.)
1996 resident population est.: 18,184,000
1990 resident census population (rank): 17,990,455 (2). **Male:** 8,625,673; **Female:** 9,364,782. **White:** 13,385,255 (74.4%); **Black:** 2,859,055 (15.9%); **American Indian, Eskimo, or Aleut:** 62,651 (0.3%); **Asian or Pacific Islander:** 693,760 (3.9%); **Other race:** 989,734 (5.5%); **Hispanic:** 2,214,026 (12.3%). **1990 percent population under 18:** 23.7; **65 and over:** 13.1; **median age:** 33.9,.

Giovanni da Verrazano, Italian-born navigator sailing for France, discovered New York Bay in 1524. Henry Hudson, an Englishman employed by the Dutch, reached the bay and sailed up the river now bearing his name in 1609, the same year that northern New York was explored and claimed for France by Samuel de Champlain.

In 1624 the first permanent Dutch settlement was established at Fort Orange (now Albany); one year later Peter Minuit is said to have purchased Manhattan Island from the Indians for trinkets worth about $24 and founded the Dutch colony of New Amsterdam (now New York City), which was surrendered to the English in 1664.

For a short time, New York City was the U.S. capital and George Washington was inaugurated there as first President on April 30, 1789.

New York's extremely rapid commercial growth may be partly attributed to Governor De Witt Clinton, who pushed through the construction of the Erie Canal (Buffalo to Albany), which was opened in 1825. Today, the 559-mile Governor Thomas E. Dewey Thruway connects New York City with Buffalo and with Connecticut, Massachusetts, and Pennsylvania express highways. Two toll-free superhighways, the Adirondack Northway (linking Albany with the Canadian border) and the North-South-Expressway (crossing central New York from the Pennsylvania border to the Thousand Islands) have been opened.

New York, with the great metropolis of New York City, is the spectacular nerve center of the nation. It is a leader in manufacturing, foreign trade, commercial and financial transactions, book and magazine publishing, and theatrical production.

New York City is not only a national but an international leader. A leading seaport, its John F. Kennedy International Airport is one of the busiest airports in the world. It is the largest manufacturing center in the country and its apparel industry is the city's largest manufacturing employer, with printing and publishing second.

Nearly all the rest of the state's manufacturing is done on Long Island, along the Hudson River north to Albany and through the Mohawk Valley, Central New York, and Southern Tier regions to Buffalo. The St. Lawrence seaway and power projects have opened the North Country to industrial expansion and have given the state a second seacoast.

The state ranks third in the nation in manufacturing with 1,057,100 employees in 1991. The principal industries are apparel, printing and publishing, leather products, instruments and electronic equipment.

The convention and tourist business is one of the state's most important sources of income.

New York farms are famous for raising cattle and calves, producing corn for grain, poultry, and the raising of vegetables and fruits. The state is a leading wine producer.

Among the major points of interest are Castle Clinton, Fort Stanwix, and Statue of Liberty National Monuments; Niagara Falls; U.S. Military Academy at West Point; National Historic Sites that include homes of Franklin D. Roosevelt at Hyde Park and Theodore Roosevelt in Oyster Bay and New York City; National Memorials, including Grant's Tomb and Federal Hall in New York City; Fort Ticonderoga; the Baseball Hall of Fame in Cooperstown; and the United Nations, skyscrapers, museums, theaters, and parks in New York City.

Famous natives and residents: Kareem Abdul-Jabbar, basketball player; Lucille Ball, actress; Humphrey Bogart, actor; James Cagney, actor; Maria Callas, soprano; Benjamin N. Cardozo, jurist; Paddy Chayefsky, playwright; Peter Cooper, industrialist and philanthropist; Aaron Copland, composer; Sammy Davis, Jr., actor and singer; Agnes de Mille, choreographer; Eamon De Valera, ex-president of Ireland; George Eastman, inventor; Millard Fillmore, ex-president; Lou Gehrig, baseball player; George Gershwin, composer; Learned Hand, jurist; Edward Hopper, painter; Julia Ward Howe, poet and reformer; Charles Evans Hughes, jurist; Washington Irving, author; Henry James, novelist; John Jay, jurist; Michael Jordan, basketball player; Jerome Kern, composer; Rockwell Kent, painter; Vince Lombardi, football coach; Chico, Groucho, Harpo, Zeppo Marx, comedians; Herman Melville, author; Ethel Merman, singer and actress; Ogden Nash, poet; Eugene O'Neill, playwright; Red Jacket, Seneca chief; John D. Rockefeller, industrialist; Norman Rockwell, painter and illustrator; Mickey Rooney, actor; Anna Eleanor Roosevelt, reformer and humanitarian; Franklin D. Roosevelt, ex-president; Theodore Roosevelt, ex-president; Jonas Salk, polio researcher; Margaret Sanger, birth control leader; Barbara Stanwyck, actress; Risë Stevens, mezzo-soprano; Richard Tucker, tenor; Martin Van Buren, ex-president; Mae West, actress; Walt Whitman, poet; Edith Wharton, novelist.

NORTH CAROLINA

Capital: Raleigh
Governor: James B. Hunt, Jr., D (to Jan. 2001)
Lieut. Governor: Dennis A. Wicker, D (to Jan. 2001)
Secy. of State: Elaine F. Marshall, D (to Jan. 2001)
Treasurer: Harlan E. Boyles, D (to Jan. 2001)
Auditor: Ralph Campbell, D (to Jan. 2001)
Atty. General: Michael Easley, D (to Jan. 2001)
Entered Union (rank): Nov. 21, 1789 (12)
Present constitution adopted: 1971
Motto: *Esse quam videri* (To be rather than to seem)
State symbols: flower, Dogwood (1941); **tree,** Pine (1963); **bird,** Cardinal (1943); **mammal,** Gray squirrel (1969); **insect,** Honeybee (1973); **reptile,** Eastern box turtle (1979); **gemstone,** Emerald (1973); **shell,** Scotch bonnet (1965); **historic boat,** Shad Boat (1987); **beverage,** Milk (1987); **rock,** Granite (1979); **dog,** Plott Hound (1989); **song,** "The Old North State" (1927); **colors,** Red and blue (1945)
Nickname: Tar Heel State
Origin of name: In honor of Charles I of England
10 largest cities (1994): Charlotte, 437,797; Raleigh, 236,707; Greensboro, 196,167; Winston-Salem, 155,128; Durham, 143,439; Fayetteville, 83,999; Jacksonville, 79,494; High Point, 72,208; Asheville, 64,261; Wilmington, 62,651
Land area (rank): 48,718 sq mi. (126,180 sq km) (29)
Geographic center: In Chatham Co., 10 mi. NW of Sanford
Number of counties: 100
Largest county (1995 pop. est.): Mecklenburg, 579,473
State forests: 1
State parks: 30 (125,000 ac.)
1995 resident population est.: 7,195,138
1990 resident census population (rank): 6,628,637 (10). **Male:** 3,214,290; **Female:** 3,414,347. **White:** 5,008,491 (75.6%); **Black:** 1,456,323 (22.0%); **American Indian, Eskimo, or Aleut:** 80,155 (1.2%); **Asian or Pacific Islander:** 52,166 (0.8%); **Other race:** 31,502 (0.5%); **Hispanic:** 76,726 (1.2%). **1990 percent population under 18:** 24.2; **65 and over:** 12.1; **median age:** 33.1.

English colonists, sent by Sir Walter Raleigh, unsuccessfully attempted to settle Roanoke Island in 1585 and 1587. Virginia Dare, born there in 1587, was the first child of English parentage born in America.

In 1653 the first permanent settlements were established by English colonists from Virginia near the Roanoke and Chowan Rivers.

The region was established as an English proprietary colony in 1663–65 and its early history was the scene of Culpepper's Rebellion (1677), the Quaker-led Cary Rebellion of 1708, the Tuscarora Indian War in 1711–13, and many pirate raids.

During the American Revolution, there was relatively little fighting within the state, but many North Carolinians saw action elsewhere. Despite considerable pro-Union, anti-slavery sentiment, North Carolina joined the Confederacy.

North Carolina is the nation's largest furniture, tobacco, brick, and textile producer. It holds second place in the Southeast in population and first place in the value of its industrial and agricultural production. This production is highly diversified, with metalworking, chemicals, and paper constituting enormous industries. Tobacco, corn, cotton, hay, peanuts, and truck and vegetable crops are of major importance. It is the country's leading producer of mica and lithium.

Tourism is also important, with travelers and vacationers spending more than $1 billion annually in North Carolina. Sports include year-round golfing, skiing at mountain resorts, both fresh and salt water fishing, and hunting.

Among the major attractions are the Great Smoky Mountains, the Blue Ridge National Parkway, the Cape Hatteras and Cape Lookout National Seashores, the Wright Brothers National Memorial at Kitty Hawk, Guilford Courthouse and Moores Creek National Military Parks, Carl Sandburg's home near Hendersonville, and the Old Salem Restoration in Winston-Salem.

Famous natives and residents: David Brinkley, TV newscaster; Howard Cosell, sportscaster; Virginia Dare, first person born in America to English parents; James B. Duke, industrialist; Roberta Flack, singer; Ava Gardner, actress; Richard Gatling, inventor; Billy Graham, evangelist; Kathryn Grayson, singer and actress; Jesse Helms, politician; O. Henry, story writer; Barbara Howar, broadcaster, writer; Andrew Johnson, ex-president; Charles Kuralt, TV journalist; Sugar Ray Leonard, boxer; Dolley Madison, ex-first lady; Ronni Milsap, country music singer; Theolonious Monk, pianist; Alfred Moore, jurist; Edward R. Murrow, commentator and government official; Walter Hines Page, journalist and ambassador; Floyd Patterson, boxer; Richard Petty, auto racer; James K. Polk, ex-president; Soupy Sales, comedian; Earl Scruggs, bluegrass musician; Randy Travis, musician; John Scott Trotter, orchestra leader; Thomas Wolfe, novelist.

NORTH DAKOTA

Capital: Bismarck
Governor: Edward T. Schafer, R (to 2000)
Lieut. Governor: Rosemarie Myrdal, R (to Dec. 15, 2000)
Secy. of State: Alvin A. Jaeger, R (to Dec. 31, 2000)
Auditor: Robert R. Peterson, R (to Dec. 31, 2000)
State Treasurer: Kathi Gilmore, D (to Dec. 31, 2000)
Atty. General: Heidi Heitkamp, D (to Dec. 31, 2000)
Organized as territory: March 2, 1861
Entered Union (rank): Nov. 2, 1889 (39)
Present constitution adopted: 1889
Motto: Liberty and union, now and forever: one and inseparable
State symbols: tree, American elm (1947); **bird,** Western meadowlark (1947); **song,** "North Dakota Hymn" (1947); **fish,** Northern Pike (1969); **grass,** Western wheatgrass (1977); **fossil,** Teredo petrified wood (1967); **beverage,** Milk (1983); **state march,** Spirit of the Land (1975); **flower,** Wild prairie rose (1907); **state language,** English (1987); **honorary equine,** Nokota horse (1993); **state dance,** Square dance (1995)
Nickname: Sioux State; Flickertail State, Peace Garden State
Origin of name: From the Sioux tribe, meaning "allies"
10 largest cities (1994): Fargo, 79,715; Bismarck, 52,592; Grand Forks, 50,168; Minot, 35,352; Dickinson, 16,190; Mandan, 15,827; Jamestown, 15,365; West Fargo, 13,771; Williston, 12,749; Wahpeton, 9,207
Land area (rank): 68,994 sq mi. (178,695 sq km) (17)
Geographic center: In Sheridan Co., 5 mi. SW of McClusky
Number of counties: 53
Largest county (1995 pop. est.): Cass, 111,440
State forests: None
State parks: 14 (14,922.6 ac.)
1995 resident population est.: 641,367
1990 resident census population (rank): 638,800 (47). **Male:** 318,201; **Female:** 320,599. **White:** 604,142 (94.6%); **Black:** 3,524 (0.6%); **American Indian, Eskimo, or Aleut:** 25,917 (4.1%); **Asian or Pacific Islander:** 3,462 (0.5%); **Other race:** 1,755 (0.3%); **Hispanic:** 4,665 (0.7%). **1990 percent population under 18:** 27.5; **65 and over:** 14.3; **median age:** 32.4.

North Dakota was explored in 1738–40 by French Canadians led by La Verendrye. In 1803, the U.S. acquired most of North Dakota from France in the Louisiana Purchase. Lewis and Clark explored the region in 1804–06 and the first settlements were made at Pembina in 1812 by Scottish and Irish families while this area was still in dispute between the U.S. and Great Britain.

In 1818, the U.S. obtained the northeastern part of North Dakota by treaty with Great Britain and took possession of Pembina in 1823.

North Dakota is the most rural of all the states, with farms covering more than 90% of the land. North Dakota ranks first in the Nation's production of spring and durum wheat, and the state's coal and oil reserves are plentiful.

Other agricultural products include barley, rye, sunflowers, dry edible beans, honey, oats, flaxseed, sugar beets, and hay; beef cattle, sheep, and hogs.

Recently, manufacturing industries have grown, especially food processing and farm equipment. The state also produces natural gas, lignite, salt, clay, sand, and gravel.

The Garrison Dam on the Missouri River provides extensive irrigation and produces 400,000 kilowatts of electricity for the Missouri Basin areas.

Known for its waterfowl, grouse, and deer hunting and bass, trout, and northern pike fishing, North Dakota has 20 state parks and recreation areas. Points of interest include the International Peace Garden near Dunseith, Fort Union Trading Post National Historic Site, the State Capitol at Bismarck, the Badlands, Theodore Roosevelt National Park, and Fort Lincoln, now a state park, from which Gen. George Custer set out on his last campaign in 1876.

Famous natives and residents: Lynn Anderson, singer; Maxwell Anderson, playwright; Dr. Robert H. Bahmer, U.S. archivist; Elizabeth Bodine, humanitarian; Dr. Anne Carlsen, educator; Ronald N. Davies, jurist; Angie Dickinson, actress; Ivan Dmitre, artist; Phyllis Frelich, actress; Bertin C. Gamble, founder of Gamble-Skogmo; William H. Gass, writer, philosopher; Rev. Richard C. Halverson, U.S. Senate chaplain; Phil D. Jackson, basketball player, coach; Dr. Leon O. Jacobson, researcher, educator; Harold K. Johnson, ex-army general; David C. Jones, U.S. Army general; Louis L'Amour, author; Peggy Lee, singer; William Lemke, ex-representative; Roger Maris, baseball player; Marquis de Mores, cattleman, established Medora; Gerald P. Nye, ex-senator; Casper Oimoen, skier; Arthur Peterson, radio and TV actor; Cliff (Fido) Purpur, hockey player, coach; James Rosenquist, painter; Harold Schaffer, founder of Gold Seal Co.; Eric Sevareid, TV commentator; Ann Sothern, actress; Dorothy Stickney, actress; Edward K. Thompson, Life magazine editor; Era Bell Thompson, Ebony magazine editor; Tommy Tucker, band leader; Lawrence Welk, band leader; Larry Woiwode, writer.

OHIO

Capital: Columbus
Governor: George V. Voinovich, R (to Jan. 1999)
Lieut. Governor: Nancy Putnam-Hollister, R (to Jan. 1999)
Secy. of State: Bob Taft, R (to Jan. 1999)
Auditor: Jim Petro, R (to Jan. 1999)
Treasurer: J. Kenneth Blackwell, R (to Jan. 1999)
Atty. General: Betty D. Montgomery, R (to Jan. 1999)
Entered Union (rank): March 1, 1803 (17)
Present constitution adopted: 1851
Motto: With God, all things are possible
State symbols: flower, Scarlet carnation (1904); **tree,** Buckeye (1953); **bird,** Cardinal (1933); **insect,** Ladybug (1975); **gemstone,** Flint (1965); **song,** "Beautiful Ohio" (1969); **drink,** Tomato juice (1965)
Nickname: Buckeye State

Origin of name: From an Iroquoian word meaning "great river"
10 largest cities (1994): Columbus, 635,913; Cleveland, 492,901; Cincinnati, 358,170; Toledo, 322,550; Akron, 221,886; Dayton, 178,540; Youngstown, 91,775; Parma, 85,792; Canton, 84,188; Lorain, 70,919
Land area (rank): 40,953 sq mi. (106,067 sq km) (35)
Geographic center: In Delaware Co., 25 mi. NNE of Columbus
Number of counties: 88
Largest county (1995 pop. est.): Cuyahoga, 1,398,169
State forests: 19 (172,744 ac.)
State parks: 71 (198,027 ac.)
1996 resident population est.: 11,172,782
1990 resident census population (rank): 10,847,115 (7). **Male:** 5,226,340; **Female:** 5,620,775. **White:** 9,521,756 (87.8%); **Black:** 1,154,826 (10.6%); **American Indian, Eskimo, or Aleut:** 20,358 (0.2%); **Asian or Pacific Islander:** 91,179 (0.8%); **Other race:** 58,996 (0.5%); **Hispanic:** 139,696 (1.3%). **1990 percent population under 18:** 25.8; **65 and over:** 13.0; **median age:** 33.3.

First explored for France by La Salle in 1669, the Ohio region became British property after the French and Indian War. Ohio was acquired by the U.S. after the Revolutionary War in 1783 and, in 1788, the first permanent settlement was established at Marietta, capital of the Northwest Territory.

The 1790s saw severe fighting with the Indians in Ohio; a major battle was won by Maj. Gen. Anthony Wayne at Fallen Timbers in 1794. In the War of 1812, Commodore Oliver H. Perry defeated the British in the Battle of Lake Erie on Sept. 10, 1813.

Ohio is one of the nation's industrial leaders, ranking third in the value of manufactured products. Important manufacturing centers are located in or near Ohio's major cities. Akron is known for rubber; Canton for roller bearings; Cincinnati for jet engines and machine tools; Cleveland for auto assembly and parts, refining, and steel; Dayton for office machines, refrigeration, and heating and auto equipment; Youngstown and Steubenville for steel; and Toledo for glass and auto parts.

The state's thousands of factories almost overshadow its importance in agriculture and mining. Its fertile soil produces soybeans, corn, oats, grapes, and clover. More than half of Ohio's farm receipts come from dairy farming and sheep and hog raising. Ohio is the top state in lime production and among the leaders in coal, clay, salt, sand, and gravel. Petroleum, gypsum, cement, and natural gas are also important.

Tourism is a valuable revenue producer, bringing in $8.5 billion in 1992, and ranking 10th among the 50 states. Attractions include the Indian burial grounds at Mound City Group National Monument, Perry's Victory International Peace Memorial, the Pro Football Hall of Fame at Canton, and the homes of Presidents Grant, Taft, Hayes, Harding, and Garfield.

Famous natives and residents: Neil Armstrong, astronaut; Kathleen Battle, soprano; George Bellows, painter and lithographer; Ambrose Bierce, journalist; Erma Bombeck, columnist; Bill Boyd (Hopalong Cassidy), actor; Milton Caniff, cartoonist; Hart Crane, poet; George Armstrong Custer, army officer; Dorothy Dandridge, actress; Doris Day, singer and actress; Clarence Darrow, lawyer; Ruby Dee, actress; Rita Dove, ex-U.S. Poet Laureate; Hugh Downs, TV broadcaster; Thomas A. Edison, inventor; Clark Gable, actor; James A. Garfield, ex-president; Lillian Gish, actress; John Glenn, astronaut and senator; Ulysses S. Grant, ex-president; Warren G. Harding, ex-president; Rutherford Hayes, ex-president; Benjamin Harrison, ex-president; William Dean Howells, novelist and critic; Zane Grey, author; Robert Henri, painter; Kenisaw Mountain Landis, first baseball commissioner; Dean

Martin, singer and actor; William McKinley, ex-president; Paul Newman, actor; Jack Nicklaus, golfer; Annie Oakley, markswoman; Norman Vincent Peale, clergyman; Tyrone Power, actor; Judith Resnik, astronaut; Eddie Rickenbacker, aviator; Arthur M. Schlesinger, Jr., historian; William Tecumseh Sherman, army general; Gloria Steinem, feminist; William H. Taft, ex-president; Tecumseh, Shawnee Indian chief; Lowell Thomas, explorer and commentator; James Thurber, author and cartoonist; Orville Wright, inventor; Cy Young, baseball player.

OKLAHOMA

Capital: Oklahoma City
Governor: Frank Keating, R (to Jan. 1999)
Lieut. Governor: Mary Fallin, R (to Jan. 1999)
Secy. of State: Tom Cole, R (to Jan. 1999)
Treasurer: Robert Butkin, D (to Jan. 1999)
Atty. General: Drew Edmondson, D (to Jan. 1999)
Organized as territory: May 2, 1890
Entered Union (rank): Nov. 16, 1907 (46)
Present constitution adopted: 1907
Motto: *Labor omnia vincit* (Labor conquers all things)
State symbols: flower, Mistletoe (1893); **tree,** Redbud (1937); **bird,** Scissor-tailed flycatcher (1951); **animal,** Bison (1972); **reptile,** Mountain boomer lizard (1969); **stone,** Rose Rock (barite rose) (1968); **colors,** Green and white (1915); **song,** "Oklahoma" (1953); **beverage,** Milk; **butterfly,** Black swallowtail; **fish,** White or Sand bass; **folk dance,** Square dance; **furbearer,** Raccoon; **game animal,** White-tailed deer; **grass,** Indiangrass; **insect,** Honeybee; **musical instrument,** Fiddle; **poem,** "Howdy Folks," David Randolph Milsten; **tree,** Redbud; **waltz,** "Oklahoma Wind"; **wildflower,** Indian blanket
Nickname: Sooner State
Origin of name: From two Choctaw Indian words meaning "red people"
10 largest cities (1994): Oklahoma City, 463,201; Tulsa, 374,851; Norman, 87,290; Lawton, 86,078; Broken Arrow, 65,679; Edmond, 61,224; Midwest City, 53,473; Enid, 45,851; Moore, 42,593; Muskogee, 39,299
Land area (rank): 68,679 sq mi. (177,877 sq km) (19)
Geographic center: In Oklahoma Co., 8 mi. N of Oklahoma City
Number of counties: 77
Largest county (1995 pop. est.): Oklahoma, 625,337
State forests: None
State parks: 36 (57,487 ac.)
1996 resident population est.: 3,300,900
1990 resident census population (rank): 3,145,585 (28). **Male:** 1,530,819; **Female:** 1,614,766. **White:** 2,583,512 (82.1%); **Black:** 233,801 (7.4%); **American Indian, Eskimo, or Aleut:** 252,420 (8.0%); **Asian or Pacific Islander:** 33,563 (1.1%); **Other race:** 42,289 (1.3%); **Hispanic:** 86,160 (2.7%). **1990 percent population under 18:** 26.6; **65 and over:** 13.5; **median age:** 33.2.

Francisco Vásquez de Coronado first explored the region for Spain in 1541. The U.S. acquired most of Oklahoma in 1803 in the Louisiana Purchase from France; the Western Panhandle region became U.S. territory with the annexation of Texas in 1845.

Set aside as Indian Territory in 1834, the region was divided into Indian Territory and Oklahoma Territory on May 2, 1890. The two were combined to make a new state, Oklahoma, on Nov. 16, 1907.

On April 22, 1889, the first day homesteading was permitted, 50,000 people swarmed into the area. Those who tried to beat the noon starting gun were called "Sooners," hence the state's nickname.

Oil made Oklahoma a rich state, but natural gas production has now surpassed it. Oil refining, meat packing, food processing, and machinery manufacturing (especially construction and oil equipment) are important industries.

Other minerals produced in Oklahoma include helium, gypsum, zinc, cement, coal, copper, and silver.

Oklahoma's rich plains produce bumper yields of wheat, as well as large crops of sorghum, hay, cotton, and peanuts. More than half of Oklahoma's annual farm receipts are contributed by livestock products, including cattle, dairy products, and broilers.

Tourist attractions include the National Cowboy Hall of Fame in Oklahoma City, the Will Rogers Memorial in Claremore, the Cherokee Cultural Center with a restored Cherokee village, the restored Fort Gibson Stockade near Muskogee, and the Lake Texoma recreation area, Pari-Mutual horse racing at Remington Park in Oklahoma City, and Blue Ribbon Downs in Sallisaw.

Famous natives and residents: Johnny Bench, baseball player; John Berryman, poet; Garth Brooks, singer; Iron Eyes Cody, Cherokee actor; L. Gordon Cooper, astronaut; Ralph Ellison, writer; James Garner, actor; Owen K. Garriott, astronaut; Vince Gill, singer; Chester Gould, cartoonist; Woody Guthrie, singer and composer; Roy Harris, composer; Paul Harvey, broadcaster; Van Heflin, actor; Ron Howard, actor and director; Ben Johnson, actor; Jennifer Jones, actress; Jeane Kirkpatrick, educator and public affairs spokesperson; Shannon Lucid, astronaut; Wilma P. Mankiller, Principal Chief of Cherokee Nation of Oklahoma; Mickey Mantle, baseball player; Reba McEntire, singer; Shannon Miller, Olympic gymnast; Bill Moyers, journalist; Daniel Patrick Moynihan, N.Y. Senator; Patti Page, singer; Mary Kay Place, actress and writer; Tony Randall, actor; Oral Roberts, evangelist; Dale Robertson, actor; Will Rogers, humorist; Dan Rowan, comedian; Thomas P. Stafford, astronaut; Maria Tallchief, ballerina; Jim Thorpe, athlete; Alfre Woodard, actress.

OREGON

Capital: Salem
Governor: John A. Kitzhaber, D (to Jan. 1999)
Secy. of State: Phil Keisling, D (to Jan. 1999)
Treasurer: James A. Hill, D (to Jan. 1999)
Atty. General: Theodore R. Kulongoski, D (to Jan. 1999)
Organized as territory: Aug. 14, 1848
Entered Union (rank): Feb. 14, 1859 (33)
Present constitution adopted: 1859
Motto: *Alis volat Propriis* (She flies with her own wings) (1987)
State symbols: flower, Oregon grape (1899); **tree,** Douglas fir (1939); **animal,** Beaver (1969); **bird,** Western meadowlark (1927); **fish,** Chinook salmon (1961); **rock,** Thunderegg (1965); **colors,** Navy blue and gold (1959); **song,** "Oregon, My Oregon" (1927); **insect,** Swallowtail butterfly (1979); **dance,** Square dance (1997); **nut,** Hazelnut (1989); **gemstone** Sunstone (1987)
Nickname: Beaver State
Poet Laureate: William E. Stafford (1974) [deceased]
Origin of name: Unknown. However, it is generally accepted that the name, first used by Jonathan Carver in 1778, was taken from the writings of Maj. Robert Rogers, an English army officer.
10 largest cities (1994 pop. est.): Portland, 450,777; Eugene, 118,122; Salem, 115,912; Gresham, 78,594; Beaverton, 59,367; Medford, 52,611; Springfield, 47,797; Corvallis, 46,244; Hillsboro, 44,470; Tigard, 35,509
Land area (rank): 96,003 sq mi. (248,647 sq km) (10)
Geographic center: In Crook Co., 25 mi. SSE of Prineville
Number of counties: 36
Largest county (1995 pop. est.): Multnomah, 614,104
State forests: 820,000 ac.

State parks: 240 (93,330 ac.)
1995 resident population est.: 3,140,585
1990 resident census population (rank): 2,842,321 (29). **Male:** 1,397,073; **Female:** 1,445,248. **White:** 2,636,787 (92.8%); **Black:** 46,178 (1.6%); **American Indian, Eskimo, or Aleut:** 38,496 (1.4%); **Asian or Pacific Islander:** 69,269 (2.4%); **Other race:** 51,591 (1.8%); **Hispanic:** 112,707 (4.0%). **1990 percent population under 18:** 25.5; **65 and over:** 13.8; **median age:** 34.5.

Spanish and English sailors are believed to have sighted the Oregon coast in the 1500s and 1600s. Capt. James Cook, seeking the Northwest Passage, charted some of the coastline in 1778. In 1792, Capt. Robert Gray, in the *Columbia*, discovered the river named after his ship and claimed the area for the U.S.

In 1805 the Lewis and Clark expedition explored the area and John Jacob Astor's fur depot, Astoria, was founded in 1811. Disputes for control of Oregon between American settlers and the Hudson Bay Company were finally resolved in the 1846 Oregon Treaty in which Great Britain gave up claims to the region.

Oregon has a $3.3 billion lumber and wood products industry, and an $859 million paper and allied manufacturing industry. Its salmon-fishing industry is one of the world's largest.

In agriculture, the state leads in growing peppermint, cover seed crops, blackberries, boysenberries, loganberries, black raspberries, and hazelnuts. It is second in raising hops, raspberries, sweet cherries, prunes, snap beans and onions. Oregon has the only nickel smelter in the United States.

With the low-cost electric power provided by Bonneville Dam, McNary Dam, and other dams in the Pacific Northwest, Oregon has developed steadily as a manufacturing state. Leading manufactures are lumber and plywood, metalwork, machinery, aluminum, chemicals, paper, food packing, and electronic equipment.

Crater Lake National Park, Mount Hood, and Bonneville Dam on the Columbia are major tourist attractions. Oregon Dunes National Recreation Area has been established near Florence. Other points of interest include the Oregon Caves National Monument, Cape Perpetua in Siuslaw National Forest, Columbia River Gorge between The Dalles and Troutdale, Hells Canyon, Newberry Volcanic National Monument, and John Day Fossil Beds National Monument.

Famous natives and residents: James Beard, food expert; Raymond Carver, writer, poet; Homer C. Davenport, political cartoonist; David Douglas, botanist; Abigail Scott Duniway, women's suffrage advocate; John E. Frohnmeyer, ex-chairman National Endowment of the Arts; Robert Gray, sea captain, discoverer of Columbia River; Matt Groening, cartoonist; Mark Hatfield, senator; Donald P. Hodel, ex-secretary of the Interior; Chief Joseph, Nez Percé chief; Dave Kingman, baseball player; Ursula LeGuin, writer; Edwin Markham, poet; Phyllis McGinley, author; Linus Pauling, chemist; Jane Powell, actress and singer; John Reed, poet and author; Harvey W. Scott,˙ editor; Doc Severinsen, band leader; Norton Simon, business executive; Paul M. Simon, Illinois senator; William E. Stafford, poet; Sally Struthers, actress.

PENNSYLVANIA

Capital: Harrisburg
Governor: Tom Ridge, R (to Jan. 1999)
Lieut. Governor: Mark Schweiker, R (to Jan. 1999)
Secy. of the Commonwealth: Yvette Kane, R (at the pleasure of the governor)
Auditor General: Robert P. Casey, Jr., D (to Jan. 2001)
Atty. General: D. Michael Fisher, R (to Jan. 2001)
Entered Union (rank): Dec. 12, 1787 (2)

Present constitution adopted: 1968
Motto: Virtue, liberty, and independence
State symbols: flower, Mountain laurel (1933); **tree,** Hemlock (1931); **bird,** Ruffed grouse (1931); **dog,** Great Dane (1965); **colors,** Blue and gold (1907); **song,** "Pennsylvania" (1990)
Nickname: Keystone State
Origin of name: In honor of Adm. Sir. William Penn, father of William Penn. It means "Penn's Woodland."
10 largest cities (1994): Philadelphia, 1,524,249; Pittsburgh, 358,883; Erie, 108,398; Allentown, 105,339; Reading, 78,246; Scranton, 77,964; Bethlehem, 72,821; Lancaster, 57,721; Harrisburg, 54,238; Altoona, 52,531
Land area (rank): 44,820 sq mi. (116,083 sq km) (32)
Geographic center: In Centre Co., 2½ mi. SW of Bellefonte
Number of counties: 67
Largest county (1995 pop. est.): Philadelphia, 1,498,971
State forests: 1,991,526 ac.
State parks: 114 (277,164.18 ac.)
1995 resident population est.: 12,071,842
1990 resident census population (rank): 11,881,643 (5). **Male:** 5,694,265; **Female:** 6,187,378. **White:** 10,520,201 (88.5%); **Black:** 1,089,795 (9.2%); **American Indian, Eskimo, or Aleut:** 14,733 (0.1%); **Asian or Pacific Islander:** 137,438 (1.2%); **Other race:** 119,476 (1.0%); **Hispanic:** 232,262 (2.0%). **1990 percent population under 18:** 23.5; **65 and over:** 15.4; **median age:** 35.

Rich in historic lore, Pennsylvania territory was disputed in the early 1600s among the Dutch, the Swedes, and the English. England acquired the region in 1664 with the capture of New York and in 1681 Pennsylvania was granted to William Penn, a Quaker, by King Charles II.

Philadelphia was the seat of the federal government almost continuously from 1776 to 1800; there the Declaration of Independence was signed in 1776 and the U.S. Constitution drawn up in 1787. Valley Forge, of Revolutionary War fame, and Gettysburg, the turning-point of the Civil War, are both in Pennsylvania. The Liberty Bell is located in a glass pavilion across from Independence Hall in Philadelphia.

With the decline of the coal, steel and railroad industries, Pennsylvania's industry has diversified, though the state still leads the country in the production of specialty steel. Pennsylvania is a leader in the production of chemicals, food, and electrical machinery and produces 10% of the nation's cement. Also important are brick and tiles, glass, limestone, and slate. Data processing is also increasingly important.

Pennsylvania's nine million agricultural acres (6 million acres for crops and pasture, 3 million acres in farm woodlands) produce a wide variety of crops and its 55,535 farms are the backbone of the state's economy. Leading products are milk, poultry and eggs, a variety of fruits, sweet corn, potatoes, mushrooms, cheese, beans, hay, maple syrup, and even Christmas trees.

Pennsylvania has the largest rural population in the nation. The state's farmers sell more than $3.3 billion in crops and livestock annually and agribusiness and food-related industries account for another $35 billion in economic activity annually.

Tourists now spend approximately $6 billion in Pennsylvania annually. Among the chief attractions: the Gettysburg National Military Park, Valley Forge National Historical Park, Independence National Historical Park in Philadelphia, the Pennsylvania Dutch region, the Eisenhower farm near Gettysburg, and the Delaware Water Gap National Recreation Area.

Famous natives and residents: Louisa May Alcott, novelist; Marian Anderson, contralto; Maxwell Anderson, dramatist; Samuel Barber, composer; John Barrymore, actor; Donald Barthelme, author; Stephen Vincent Benet, poet and story writer; Daniel Boone, frontiersman; Ed Bradley, TV anchorman; James Buchanan, ex-president; Alexander Calder, sculptor; Rachel Carson, biologist and author; Mary Cassatt, painter; Henry Steele Commager, historian; Bill Cosby, actor; Stuart Davis, painter; Jimmy & Tommy Dorsey, band leaders; W.C. Fields, comedian; Stephen Foster, composer; Robert Fulton, inventor; Grace, Princess of Monaco; Martha Graham, choreographer; Alexander Haig, ex-Secretary of State; Marilyn Horne, mezzo-soprano; Lee Iacocca, auto executive; Reggie Jackson, baseball player; Gene Kelly, dancer and actor; Gelsey Kirkland, ballerina; S.S. Kresge, merchant; Mario Lanza, actor and singer; George C. Marshall, 5-star general; George McClellan, ex-general; Margaret Mead, anthropologist; Andrew Mellon, financier; Tom Mix, actor; Arnold Palmer, golfer; Robert E. Peary, explorer; Man Ray, painter; Mary Roberts Rinehart, novelist; Betsy Ross, flagmaker; B.F. Skinner, psychologist; John Sloan, painter; Gertrude Stein, author; James Stewart, actor; John Updike, novelist; Honus Wagner, baseball player; Fred Waring, band leader; Ethel Waters, singer and actress; Anthony Wayne, military officer; August Wilson, poet, writer, and playwright; Duchess of Windsor (Wallis Warfield);, Andrew Wyeth, painter.

RHODE ISLAND

Capital: Providence
Governor: Lincoln Almond, R (to Jan. 1999)
Lieut. Governor: Bernard Jackvony, D (to Jan. 1999)
Secy. of State: Jim Langevin, D (to Jan. 1999)
Atty. General: Jeffery B. Pine, D (to Jan. 1999)
General Treasurer: Nancy J. Mayer, D (to Jan. 1999)
Entered Union (rank): May 29, 1790 (13)
Present constitution adopted: 1843
Motto: Hope
State symbols: flower, Violet (unofficial) (1968); **tree,** Red maple (official) (1964); **bird,** Rhode Island Red (official) (1954); **shell,** Quahog (official); **mineral,** Bowenite; **stone,** Cumberlandite; **colors,** Blue, white, and gold (in state flag); **song,** "Rhode Island" (1946)
Nickname: The Ocean State
Origin of name: From the Greek Island of Rhodes
10 largest cities (1994): Providence, 150,639; Warwick, 86,006; Cranston, 77,323; Pawtucket, 69,002; East Providence, 50,059; Woonsocket, 40,752; Newport, 24,214; Central Falls, 15,210
Land area (rank): 1,045 sq mi. (2,706 sq km) (50)
Geographic center: In Kent Co., 1 mi. SSW of Compton
Number of counties: 5
Largest county (1995 pop. est.): Providence, 580,015
State forests: 11 (20,900 ac.)
State parks: 17 (8,200 ac.)
1995 resident population est.: 999,794
1990 resident census population (rank): 1,003,464 (43). **Male:** 481,496; **Female:** 521,968. **White:** 917,375 (91.4%); **Black:** 38,861 (3.9%); **American Indian, Eskimo, or Aleut:** 4,071 (0.4%); **Asian or Pacific Islander:** 18,325 (1.8%); **Other race:** 24,832 (2.5%); **Hispanic:** 45,752 (4.6%). **1990 percent population under 18:** 22.5; **65 and over:** 15.0; **median age:** 34.

From its beginnings, Rhode Island has been distinguished by its support for freedom of conscience and action, started by Roger Williams, who was exiled by the Massachusetts Bay Colony Puritans in 1636, and was the founder of the present state capital, Providence. Williams was followed by other religious exiles who founded Pocasset, now Portsmouth, in 1638 and Newport in 1639.

Rhode Island's rebellious, authority-defying nature was further demonstrated by the burnings of the British revenue cutters *Liberty* and *Gaspee* prior to the Revolution, by its early declaration of independence from Great Britain in May 1776, its refusal to participate actively in the War of 1812, and by Dorr's Rebellion of 1842, which protested property requirements for voting.

Rhode Island, smallest of the fifty states, is densely populated and highly industrialized. It is a primary center for jewelry manufacturing in the United States. Electronics, metal, plastic products, and boat and ship construction are other important industries. Nonmanufacturing employment includes research in health, medicine, and the ocean environment. Providence is a wholesale distribution center for New England.

Two of New England's fishing ports are at Galilee and Newport. Rural areas of the state support small-scale farming including grapes for local wineries, turf grass and nursery stock.

Tourism is one of Rhode Island's largest industries, generating over a billion dollars a year in revenue.

Newport became famous as the summer capital of society in the mid-19th century. Touro Synagogue (1763) is the oldest in the U.S. Other points of interest include the Roger Williams National Memorial in Providence, Samuel Slater's Mill in Pawtucket, the General Nathanael Greene Homestead in Coventry and Block Island.

Famous natives and residents: Harry Anderson, actor; George M. Cohan, actor and dramatist; Eddie Dowling, actor and stage producer; Nelson Eddy, baritone and actor; Ann Smith Franklin, printer and almanac publisher; Charles Gorham, silversmith; Spalding Gray, writer, performance artist; Bobby Hackett, trumpeter; David Hartman, TV newscaster; Ruth Hussey, actress; Anne Hutchinson, religious leader; Thomas H. Ince, film producer; Wilbur John, Quaker leader; Van Johnson, actor; Clarence King, first director of the U.S. Geological Survey; Galway Kinnell, poet; Oliver LaFarge, writer; Irving R. Levine, news correspondent; H.P. Lovecraft, author; Ida Lewis, lighthouse keeper; John McLaughlin, political commentator, broadcaster; Dana C. Munro, educator and historian; Matthew C. Perry, naval officer; Oliver Hazard Perry, naval officer; King Philip (Metacomet), Indian leader; Gilbert Stuart, painter; Sarah Helen (Power) Whitman, poet; Jemima Wilkinson, religious leader; Roger Williams, clergyman and founder of Rhode Island; Leonard Woodcock, labor union official.

SOUTH CAROLINA

Capital: Columbia
Governor: David M. Beasley, R (to Jan. 1999)
Lieut. Governor: Robert L. Peeler, R (to Jan. 1999)
Secy. of State: Jim Miles, R (to Jan. 1999)
Comptroller General: Earle E. Morris, Jr., D (to Jan. 1999)
Atty. General: Charles M. Condon, R (to Jan. 1999)
Entered Union (rank): May 23, 1788 (8).
Present constitution adopted: 1895
Mottoes: *Animis opibusque parati* (Prepared in mind and resources) and *Dum spiro spero* (While I breathe, I hope)
State symbols: flower, Carolina yellow jessamine (1924); **tree,** Palmetto tree (1939); **bird,** Carolina wren (1948); **song,** "Carolina" (1911)
Nickname: Palmetto State
Origin of name: In honor of Charles I of England
10 largest cities (1994): Columbia, 104,101; Charleston, 76,854; North Charleston, 67,720; Greenville, 59,808; Rock Hill, 47,006; Spartanburg, 45,721; Sumter, 42,773; Mount Pleasant, 34,425; Florence, 32,387; Anderson, 29,722
Land area (rank): 30,111 sq mi. (77,988 sq km) (40)
Geographic center: In Richland Co., 13 mi. SE of Columbia
Number of counties: 46

Largest county (1995 pop. est.): Greenville, 339,908
State forests: 4 (124,052 ac.)
State parks: 50 (61,726 ac.)
1995 resident population est.: 3,673,287
1990 resident census population (rank): 3,486,703 (25). **Male:** 1,688,510; **Female:** 1,798,193. **White:** 2,406,974 (69.0%); **Black:** 1,039,884 (29.8%); **American Indian, Eskimo, or Aleut:** 8,246 (0.2%); **Asian or Pacific Islander:** 22,382 (0.6%); **Other race:** 9,217 (0.3%); **Hispanic:** 30,551 (0.9%) **1990 percent population under 18:** 26.4; **65 and over:** 11.4; **median age:** 32.0

Following exploration of the coast in 1521 by De Gordillo, the Spanish tried unsuccessfully to establish a colony near present-day Georgetown in 1526 and the French also failed to colonize Parris Island near Fort Royal in 1562.

The first English settlement was made in 1670 at Albemarle Point on the Ashley River, but poor conditions drove the settlers to the site of Charleston (originally called Charles Town). South Carolina, officially separated from North Carolina in 1729, was the scene of extensive military action during the Revolution and again during the Civil War. The Civil War began in 1861 as South Carolina troops fired on federal Fort Sumter in Charleston Harbor and the state was the first to secede from the Union.

Once primarily agricultural, South Carolina has built so many large textile and other mills that today its factories produce eight times the output of its farms in cash value. Charleston makes asbestos, wood, pulp, and steel products; chemicals, machinery, and apparel are also important.

Farms have become fewer but larger in recent years. South Carolina grows more peaches than any other state except California; it ranks fifth in overall tobacco production. Other farm products include cotton, peanuts, sweet potatoes, soybeans, corn, and oats. Poultry and dairy products are also important revenue producers.

Points of interest include Fort Sumter National Monument, Fort Moultrie, Fort Johnson, and aircraft carrier USS *Yorktown* in Charleston Harbor; the Middleton, Magnolia, and Cypress Gardens in Charleston; Cowpens National Battlefield; and the Hilton Head resorts.

Famous natives and residents: Bernard Baruch, statesman; Mary McLeod Bethune, educator; James F. Byrnes, senator, jurist, Secretary of State; John C. Calhoun, statesman; Mark Clark, general; Joe Frazier, prize fighter; Althea Gibson, tennis champion; Dizzy Gillespie, jazz trumpeter; DuBose Heyward, poet, playwright, novelist; Andrew Jackson, ex-president; Jesse Jackson, civil rights leader; Eartha Kitt, singer; Francis Marion "Swamp Fox," Revolutionary general; Ronald McNair, astronaut; John Rutledge, jurist; Strom Thurmond, politician; Charles Townes, physicist; William Westmoreland, ex-Army Chief of Staff; Vanna White, TV personality.

SOUTH DAKOTA

Capital: Pierre
Governor: William J. Janklow, R (to Jan. 1999)
Lieut. Governor: Carole Hillard, R (to Jan. 1999)
Atty. General: Mark Barnett, R (to Jan. 1999)
Secy. of State: Joyce Hazeltine, R (to Jan. 1999)
State Auditor: Vern Larson, R (to Jan. 1999)
State Treasurer: Richard Butler, D (to Jan. 1999)
Organized as territory: March 2, 1861
Entered Union (rank): Nov. 2, 1889 (40)
Present constitution adopted: 1889
Motto: Under God the people rule
State symbols: flower, American pasqueflower (1903); **grass,** Western wheat grass (1970); **soil,** Houdek

(1990); **tree,** Black Hills spruce (1947); **bird,** Ring-necked pheasant (1943); **insect,** Honeybee (1978); **animal,** Coyote (1949); **mineral stone,** Rose quartz (1966); **gemstone,** Fairburn agate (1966); **colors,** Blue and gold (in state flag); **song,** "Hail! South Dakota" (1943); **fish,** Walleye (1982); **musical instrument,** Fiddle (1989); **soil,** Houdek soil (1990)
Nicknames: Mount Rushmore State; Coyote State
Origin of name: From the Sioux tribe, meaning "allies"
10 largest cities (1994): Sioux Falls, 109,174; Rapid City, 57,609; Aberdeen, 25,091; Watertown, 19,279; Brookings, 17,241; Mitchell, 13,931; Yankton, 13,605; Pierre, 13,588; Huron, 12,494; Vermillion, 10,378
Land area (rank): 75,898 sq mi. (196,575 sq km) (16)
Geographic center: In Hughes Co., 8 mi. NE of Pierre
Number of counties: 67 (64 county governments)
Largest county (1995 pop. est.): Minnehaha, 135,641
State forests: None[1]
State parks: 13 plus 39 recreational areas (87,269 ac.)[2]
1995 resident population est.: 729,034
1990 resident census population (rank): 696,004 (45). **Male:** 342,498; **Female:** 353,506. **White:** 637,515 (91.6%); **Black:** 3,258 (0.5%); **American Indian, Eskimo, or Aleut:** 50,575 (7.3%); **Asian or Pacific Islander:** 3,123 (0.4%); **Other race:** 1,533 (0.2%); **Hispanic:** 5,252 (0.8%). **1990 percent population under 18:** 28.5; **65 and over:** 14.7; **median age:** 32.5.

1. No designated state forests; about 13,000 ac. of state land is forestland. 2. Acreage includes 39 recreation areas and 80 roadside parks, in addition to 12 state parks.

Exploration of this area began in 1743 when Louis-Joseph and François Verendrye came from France in search of a route to the Pacific.

The U.S. acquired the region as part of the Louisiana Purchase in 1803 and it was explored by Lewis and Clark in 1804–06. Fort Pierre, the first permanent settlement, was established in 1817 and, in 1831, the first Missouri River steamboat reached the fort.

Settlement of South Dakota did not begin in earnest until the arrival of the railroad in 1873 and the discovery of gold in the Black Hills the following year.

South Dakota's economy in recent years has benefited from an expanding and diversifying industrial base. Agriculture is a cultural and economic mainstay, but it no longer leads the state in employment or share of gross state product. Durable goods manufacturing and private services have evolved as the drivers of the economy. Tourism is also a booming industry in the state.

Agriculture is the state's leading industry. South Dakota leads the nation in the production of oats and ranks second among the states in the production of rye, flaxseed, and sunflower seed.

South Dakota is the nation's second leading producer of gold and the Homestake Mine is the richest in the U.S. Other minerals produced include berylium, bentonite, granite, silver, petroleum, and uranium.

The Black Hills are the highest mountains east of the Rockies. Mt. Rushmore, in this group, is famous for the likenesses of Washington, Jefferson, Lincoln, and Theodore Roosevelt, which were carved in granite by Gutzon Borglum. A memorial to Crazy Horse is also being carved in granite near Custer.

Other tourist attractions include the Badlands; the World's Only Corn Palace in Mitchell; and the city of Deadwood where Wild Bill Hickok was killed in 1876 and where gambling was recently legalized to truly recapture the city's Old West flavor.

Famous natives and residents: Sparky Anderson, baseball manager; Gertrude Bonnin (Zitkala-Sa), Sioux writer and pan-Indian activist; Tom Brokaw, TV newscaster; Robert Casey, writer; Myron Floren, accordionist; Joseph J. Foss,

WW II Marine fighter ace; Mary Hart, host; Crazy Horse, Oglala chief; Oscar Howe, Sioux artist; Hubert H. Humphrey, ex-vice president; Cheryl Ladd, actress; Ernest Orlando Lawrence, physicist; Russell Means, American Indian activist; George McGovern, politician; Arthur C. Mellette, first governor; Dorothy Provine, actress; Rain-in-the-Face, Hunkpapa Sioux chief; Red Cloud, chief of the Oglala Sioux; Ben Reifel, Brulé Sioux Congressman; Ole Edvart Rölvaag, writer; Sitting Bull, Chief of Hunkpappa Sioux; Norm Van Brocklin, football player; Mamie Van Doren, actress.

TENNESSEE

Capital: Nashville
Governor: Don Sundquist, R (to Jan. 1999)
Lieut. Governor: John S. Wilder, D (to Jan. 1997)
Secy. of State: Riley C. Darnell, D (to Jan. 1997)
Atty. General: John Knox Walkup, D (to Aug. 1998)
State Treasurer: Steve Adams, D (to Jan. 1997)
Entered Union (rank): June 1, 1796 (16)
Present constitution adopted: 1870; amended 1953, 1960, 1966, 1972, 1978
Motto: Agriculture and Commerce (1987)
Slogan: "Tennessee—America at its best!" (1965)
State symbols: flower, Iris (1933); **tree,** Tulip poplar (1947); **bird,** Mockingbird (1933); **horse,** Tennessee walking horse; **animal,** Raccoon (1971); **wild flower,** Passion flower (1973); **songs,** "Tennessee Waltz" (1965); My Homeland, Tennessee (1925); When It's Iris Time in Tennessee (1935); My Tennessee (1955); Rocky Top (1982); Tennessee (1992)
Nickname: Volunteer State
Origin of name: Of Cherokee origin; the exact meaning is unknown
10 largest cities (1994): Memphis, 614,289; Nashville-Davidson (CC[1]), 504,505; Knoxville, 169,311; Chattanooga, 152,259; Clarksville, 92,116; Murfreesboro, 56,194; Jackson, 52,343; Johnson City, 51,573; Kingsport, 38,476; Hendersonville, 36,625
Land area (rank): 41,220 sq mi. (106,759 sq km) (34)
Geographic center: In Rutherford Co., 5 mi. NE of Murfreesboro
Number of counties: 95
Largest county (1995 pop. est.): Shelby, 865,058
State forests: 13 (155,000 ac.)
State parks: 50 (133,000 ac.)
1995 resident population est.: 5,256,051
1990 resident census population (rank): 4,877,185 (17). **Male:** 2,348,928; **Female:** 2,528,257. **White:** 4,048,068 (83.0%); **Black:** 778,035 (16.0%); **American Indian, Eskimo, or Aleut:** 10,039 (0.2%); **Asian or Pacific Islander:** 31,839 (0.7%); **Other race:** 9,204 (0.2%); **Hispanic:** 32,741 (0.7%). **1990 percent population under 18:** 24.9; **65 and over:** 12.7; **median age:** 33.6.

1. Consolidated City.

First visited by the Spanish explorer de Soto in 1540, the Tennessee area would later be claimed by both France and England as a result of the 1670s and 1680s explorations of Marquette and Joliet, La Salle, and the Englishman James Needham and Gabriel Arthur.

Great Britain obtained the region following the French and Indian War in 1763 and it was rapidly occupied by settlers moving in from Virginia and the Carolinas.

During 1784–87, the settlers formed the "state" of Franklin, which was disbanded when the region was allowed to send representatives to the North Carolina legislature. In 1790 Congress organized the territory south of the Ohio River and Tennessee joined the Union in 1796.

Although Tennessee joined the Confederacy during the Civil War, there was much pro-Union sentiment in the state, which was the scene of extensive military action.

The state is now predominantly industrial; the majority of its population lives in urban areas. Among the most important products are chemicals, textiles, apparel, electrical machinery, furniture, and leather goods. Other lines include food processing, lumber, primary metals, and metal products. The state is known as the U.S. hardwood-flooring center and ranks first in the production of marble, zinc, pyrite, and ball clay.

Tennessee is one of the leading tobacco-producing states in the nation; its farming income is derived from livestock and dairy products, as well as corn, cotton, and soybeans.

With six other states, Tennessee shares the extensive federal reservoir developments on the Tennessee and Cumberland River systems. The Tennessee Valley Authority operates a number of dams and reservoirs in the state.

Among the major points of interest: the Andrew Johnson National Historic Site at Greenville, American Museum of Atomic Energy at Oak Ridge, Great Smoky Mountains National Park, The Hermitage (home of Andrew Jackson near Nashville), Rock City Gardens near Chattanooga, and three National Military Parks.

Famous natives and residents: James Agee, writer; Eddy Arnold, singer; Chet Atkins, guitarist; Julian Bond, Georgia legislator; Davy Crockett, frontiersman; David G. Farragut, first American admiral; Lester Flatt, bluegrass musician; Tennessee Ernie Ford, singer; Abe Fortas, jurist; Aretha Franklin, singer; Nikki Giovanni, poet; Al Gore, Jr., vice president; Red Grooms, artist; Isaac Hayes, composer; Benjamin L. Hooks, civil rights activist; Cordell Hull, ex-Sec. of State; Andrew Jackson, ex-president; Andrew Johnson, ex-president; Estes Kefauver, legislator; Anita Kerr, singer; Grace Moore, soprano; Dolly Parton, singer; Minnie Pearl, singer and comedienne; James K. Polk, president; Grantland Rice, sportswriter; Carl Rowan, journalist; Wilma Rudolph, sprinter; Sequoia, Cherokee scholar and educator; Cybil Shepherd, actress; Dinah Shore, actress, singer; Tina Turner, singer; Alvin York, World War I hero.

TEXAS

Capital: Austin
Governor: George W. Bush, R (to Jan. 1999)
Lieut. Governor: Bob Bullock, D (to Jan. 1999)
Secy. of State: Tony Garza, R (Apptd. by Gov.)
Comptroller: John Sharp, D (to Jan. 1999)
Atty. General: Dan Morales, D (to Jan. 1999)
Entered Union (rank): Dec. 29, 1845 (28)
Present constitution adopted: 1876
Motto: Friendship
State symbols: flower, Bluebonnet (1901); **tree,** Pecan (1919); **bird,** Mockingbird (1927); **song,** "Texas, Our Texas" (1929); **fish,** Guadalupe bass (1989); **seashell,** Lightning whelk (1987); **dish,** Chili (1977); **folk dance,** Square dance (1991); **fruit,** Texas Red grapefruit (1993); **gem,** Texas blue topaz (1969); **gemstone cut,** Lone Star Cut (1977); **grass,** Sideoats grass (1971); **reptile,** Horned lizard (1993); **stone,** Petrified palmwood (1969); **plant,** Prickly pear cactus; **insect,** Monarch butterfly; **pepper,** Jalapeño pepper; **mammal,** Longhorn; **small mammal,** Armadillo; **flying mammal,** Mexican free-tailed bat
Nickname: Lone Star State
Origin of name: From an Indian word meaning "friends"
10 largest cities (1994): Houston, 1,702,086; Dallas, 1,022,830; San Antonio, 998,905; El Paso, 579,307; Austin, 514,013; Fort Worth, 451,814; Arlington, 286,922; Corpus Christi, 275,419; Lubbock, 194,467; Garland, 194,218
Land area (rank): 261,914 sq mi. (678,358 sq km) (2)

Geographic center: In McCulloch Co., 15 mi. NE of Brady
Number of counties: 254
Largest county (1995 pop. est.): Harris, 3,076,867
State forests: 5 (7,609 ac.)
State parks: 218 (206 developed)
1995 resident population est.: 18,723,991
1990 resident census population (rank): 16,986,510 (3). **Male:** 8,365,963; **Female:** 8,620,547. **White:** 12,774,762 (75.2%); **Black:** 2,021,632 (11.9%); **American Indian, Eskimo, or Aleut:** 65,877 (0.4%); **Asian or Pacific Islander:** 319,459 (1.9%); **Other race:** 1,804,780 (10.6%); **Hispanic:** 4,339,905 (25.5%). **1990 percent population under 18:** 28.5; **65 and over:** 10.1; **median age:** 30.8.

Spanish explorers, including Cabeza de Vaca and Coronado, were the first to visit the region in the 16th and 17th centuries, settling at Ysleta near El Paso in 1682. In 1685, La Salle established a short-lived French colony at Matagorda Bay.

Americans, led by Stephen F. Austin, began to settle along the Brazos River in 1821 when Texas was controlled by Mexico, recently independent from Spain. In 1836, following a brief war between the American settlers in Texas and the Mexican government, the Independent Republic of Texas was proclaimed with Sam Houston as president. This war was famous for the battles of the Alamo and San Jacinto.

After Texas became the 28th U.S. state in 1845, border disputes led to the Mexican War of 1846–48.

Today, Texas, second only to Alaska in land area, leads all other states in such categories as oil, cattle, sheep, and cotton. Possessing enormous natural resources, Texas is a major agricultural state and an industrial giant.

Sulfur, salt, helium, asphalt, graphite, bromine, natural gas, cement, and clays give Texas first place in mineral production. Chemicals, oil refining, food processing, machinery, and transportation equipment are among the major Texas manufacturing industries.

Texas ranches and farms produce beef cattle, poultry, rice, pecans, peanuts, sorghum, and an extensive variety of fruits and vegetables.

Millions of tourists spend well over $20.6 billion annually visiting more than 70 state parks, recreation areas, and points of interest such as the Gulf Coast resort area, the Lyndon B. Johnson Space Center in Houston, the Alamo in San Antonio, the state capital in Austin, and the Big Bend and Guadalupe Mountains National Parks.

Famous natives and residents: Alvin Ailey, choreographer; Mary Kay Ash, cosmetics entrepreneur; Steven Fuller Austin, founding father of Texas; Gene Autry, singer and actor; Carol Burnett, comedienne; Cyd Charisse, actress and dancer; Denton A. Cooley, heart surgeon; Joan Crawford, actress; Dwight David Eisenhower, ex-president, general; A.J. Foyt, auto racer; Ben Hogan, golfer; Howard Hughes, industrialist and film producer; Jack Johnson, boxer; Lyndon B. Johnson, ex-president; George Jones, singer; Tommy Lee Jones, actor; Scott Joplin, composer; Trini Lopez, singer; Mary Martin, singer and actress; Spanky McFarland, actor; Audie Murphy, actor and war hero; Chester Nimitz, admiral; Sandra Day O'Connor, jurist; Buck Owens, singer; Katherine Anne Porter, novelist; Wiley Post, aviator; Dan Rather, TV newscaster; Robert Rauschenberg, painter; Tex Ritter, singer; Rip Torn, actor and director; Tommy Tune, dancer and choreographer; Dooley Wilson, actor and musician; Babe Didrikson Zaharias, athlete, golfer.

UTAH

Capital: Salt Lake City
Governor: Mike O. Leavitt, R (to Jan. 2001)
Lieut. Governor: Olene Walker, R (to Jan. 1997)

Atty. General: Jan Graham, D (to Jan. 1997)
Organized as territory: Sept. 9, 1850
Entered Union (rank): Jan. 4, 1896 (45)
Present constitution adopted: 1896
Motto: Industry
State symbols: flower, Sego lily (1911); **tree,** Blue spruce (1933); **bird,** California gull (1955); **emblem,** Beehive (1959); **song,** "Utah, We Love Thee" (1953); **gem,** Topaz; **animal,** Rocky Mountain Elk (1971); **fish,** Rainbow trout (1971); **insect,** Honeybee (1983); **grass,** Indian rice grass (1990); **fossil,** Allosaurus (1988); **cooking pot,** Dutch oven (1997); **fish,** Bonneville cutthroat trout (1997); **fruit,** Cherry (1997); **mineral,** Copper; **rock,** Coal (1991)
Nickname: Beehive State
Origin of name: From the Ute tribe, meaning "people of the mountains"
10 largest cities (1994): Salt Lake City, 171,849; West Valley City, 94,663; Provo, 88,519; Sandy, 85,406; Orem, 74,402; Ogden, 67,763; West Jordan, 49,979; Layton, 49,200; St. George, 38,950; Bountiful, 37,076
Land area (rank): 82,168 sq mi. (212,816 sq km) (12)
Geographic center: In Sanpete Co., 3 mi. N. of Manti
Number of counties: 29
Largest county (1995 pop. est.): Salt Lake, 808,383
National parks: 5
National monuments: 6
State parks/forests: 45 (64,097 ac.)
1995 resident population est.: 1,951,408
1990 resident census population (rank): 1,722,850 (35). **Male:** 855,759; **Female:** 867,091. **White:** 1,615,845 (93.8%); **Black:** 11,576 (0.7%); **American Indian, Eskimo, or Aleut:** 24,283 (1.4%); **Asian or Pacific Islander:** 33,371 (1.9%); **Other race:** 37,775 (2.2%); **Hispanic:** 84,597 (4.9%). **1990 percent population under 18:** 36.4; **65 and over:** 8.7; **median age:** 26.2.

The region was first explored for Spain by Franciscan friars, Escalante and Dominguez in 1776. In 1824 the famous American frontiersman Jim Bridger discovered the Great Salt Lake.

Fleeing the religious persecution encountered in eastern and middle-western states, the Mormons reached the Great Salt Lake in 1847 and began to build Salt Lake City. The U.S. acquired the Utah region in the treaty ending the Mexican War in 1848 and the first transcontinental railroad was completed with the driving of a golden spike at Promontory Summit in 1869.

Mormon difficulties with the federal government about polygamy did not end until the Mormon Church renounced the practice in 1890, six years before Utah became a state.

Rich in natural resources, Utah has long been a leading producer of copper, gold, silver, lead, zinc, and molybdenum. Oil has also become a major product. Utah shares rich oil shale deposits with Colorado and Wyoming. Utah also has large deposits of low sulphur coal.

Ranked eighth among the states in number of sheep in 1989, Utah also produces large crops of alfalfa, winter wheat, and beans.

Utah's traditional industries of agriculture and mining are complemented by increased tourism business and growing aerospace, biomedical, and computer-related businesses. Utah is home to computer software giant Novell.

Utah is a great vacationland with 11,000 miles of fishing streams and 147,000 acres of lakes and reservoirs. Among the many tourist attractions are Arches, Bryce Canyon, Canyonlands, Capitol Reef, and Zion National Parks; Dinosaur, Natural Bridges, and Rainbow Bridge National Monuments; the Mormon Tabernacle in Salt Lake City; and Monument Valley. Salt Lake City will be the site of the 2002 Winter Olympics.

Famous natives and residents: Maude Adams, actress; Roseanne, actress; Frank Borzage, film director and producer; John M. Browning, inventor; Butch Cassidy, outlaw; Laraine Day, actress; Bernard De Voto, writer; Avard Fairbanks, sculptor; Philo Farnsworth, television pioneer; Jake Garn, senator; John Gilbert, actor; J. Willard Marriott, restaurant and hotel chain founder; Peter Skene Ogden, fur trader, trapper; Merlin Olsen, football player; Donny Osmond, Marie Osmond, singers; Ivy Baker Priest, ex-U.S. treasurer; Lee Greene Richards, painter; Leroy Robertson, composer; Brent Scowcroft, business executive, consultant; Reed Smoot, first Morman elected to U.S. Senate; Mack Swain, actor; Everett Thorpe, painter; Robert Walker, actor; James Woods, actor; Brigham Young, territory governor and religious leader; Loretta Young, actress.

VERMONT

Capital: Montpelier
Governor: Howard B. Dean, D (to Jan. 1999)
Lieut. Governor: Douglas A. Racine, D (to Jan. 1999)
Secy. of State: James F. Milne, R (to Jan. 1999)
Treasurer: James H. Douglas, R (to Jan. 1999)
Auditor of Accounts: Edward S. Flanagan, D (to Jan. 1997)
Atty. General: William Sorrell, D (to Jan. 1999)
Entered Union (rank): March 4, 1791 (14)
Present constitution adopted: 1793
Motto: Vermont, Freedom, and Unity
State symbols: flower, Red clover (1894); **tree,** Sugar maple (1949); **bird,** Hermit thrush (1941); **animal,** Morgan horse (1961); **insect,** Honeybee (1978); **song,** "Hail, Vermont!" (1938)
Nickname: Green Mountain State
Origin of name: From the French "vert mont," meaning "green mountain"
10 largest cities (1994): Burlington, 38,306; Rutland, 17,489; South Burlington, 13,170; Barre, 9,466; Essex Junction, 8,702; Montpelier, 8,042; St. Albans, 7,650; Winooski, 6,219; Newport, 4,354; Bellows Falls, 3,357
Land area (rank): 9,249 sq mi. (23,956 sq km) (43)
Geographic center: In Washington Co., 3 mi. E of Roxbury
Number of counties: 14
Largest county (1995 pop. est.): Chittenden, 139,041
State forests: 34 (113,953 ac.)
State parks: 45 (31,325 ac.)
1995 resident population est.: 584,771
1990 resident census population (rank): 562,758 (48). **Male:** 275,492; **Female:** 287,266. **White:** 555,088 (98.6%); **Black:** 1,951 (0.3%); **American Indian, Eskimo, or Aleut:** 1,696 (0.3%); **Asian or Pacific Islander:** 3,215 (0.6%); **Other race:** 808 (0.1%); **Hispanic:** 3,661 (0.7%). **1990 percent population under 18:** 25.4; **65 and over:** 11.8; **median age:** 33.0.

The Vermont region was explored and claimed for France by Samuel de Champlain in 1609 and the first French settlement was established at Fort Ste. Anne in 1666. The first English settlers moved into the area in 1724 and built Fort Drummer on the site of present-day Brattleboro. England gained control of the area in 1763 after the French and Indian War.

First organized to drive settlers from New York out of Vermont, the Green Mountain Boys, led by Ethan Allen, won fame by capturing Fort Ticonderoga from the British on May 10, 1775, in the early days of the Revolutionary War.

In 1777 Vermont adopted its first constitution abolishing slavery and providing for universal male suffrage without property qualifications. In 1791 Vermont became the fourteenth state to join the Union.

Vermont leads the nation in the production of monument granite, marble, and maple syrup. It is also a leader in the production of talc.

Vermont's rugged, rocky terrain discourages extensive agricultural farming, but is well suited to raising fruit trees, and to dairy farming. Vermont has the highest proportion of dairy cows to humans in the nation.

Principal industrial products include electrical equipment, fabricated metal products, printing and publishing, and paper and allied products.

Tourism is a major industry in Vermont. Vermont's many famous ski areas include Stowe, Killington, Mt. Snow, Bromley, Jay Peak, and Sugarbush. Hunting and fishing also attract many visitors to Vermont each year. Among the many points of interest are the Green Mountain National Forest, Bennington Battle Monument, the Calvin Coolidge Homestead at Plymouth, and the Marble Exhibit in Proctor.

Famous natives and residents: Chester A. Arthur, ex-president; Orson Bean, actor; Calvin Coolidge, ex-president; George Dewey, admiral; John Dewey, philosopher and educator; Stephen A. Douglas, politician; James Fisk, financial speculator; Wilbur Fisk, clergyman and educator; Richard Morris Hunt, architect; William Morris Hunt, painter; Elisha Otis, inventor; Moses Pendleton, choreographer; Joseph Smith, religious leader; Ernest Thompson, actor, writer; Rudy Vallee, singer and band leader; Henry Wells, pioneer entrepreneur (Wells Fargo & Co.); Brigham Young, religious leader.

VIRGINIA

Capital: Richmond
Governor: George Allen, R (to Jan. 1998)
Lieut. Governor: Donald S. Beyer, Jr., D (to Jan. 1998)
Secy. of the Commonwealth: Betsy Davis Beamer (apptd. by governor)
Comptroller: William E. Landsidle (apptd. by governor)
Atty. General: James S. Gilmore, III, R (to Jan. 1998)
Entered Union (rank): June 25, 1788 (10)
Present constitution adopted: 1970
Motto: *Sic semper tyrannis* (Thus always to tyrants)
State symbols: flower, American dogwood (1918); **bird,** Cardinal (1950); **dog,** American foxhound (1966); **shell,** Oyster shell (1974); **song,** "Carry Me Back to Old Virginia" (1940)
Nicknames: The Old Dominion; Mother of Presidents
Origin of name: In honor of Elizabeth "Virgin Queen" of England
10 largest cities (1994): Virginia Beach, 430,295; Norfolk, 241,426; Richmond, 201,108; Chesapeake, 180,577; Newport News, 179,127; Arlington CDP, 174,503; Hampton, 139,628; Alexandria, 112,879; Portsmouth, 103,464; Roanoke, 96,643
Land area (rank): 39,598 sq mi. (102,558 sq km) (37)
Geographic center: In Buckingham Co., 5 mi. SW of Buckingham
Number of counties: 95, plus 40 independent cities
Largest county (1995 pop. est.): Fairfax, 887,205
State forests: 11 (50,636 ac.)
State parks and recreational parks: 28 (63,000 ac.)[1]
1996 resident population est.: 6,675,000
1990 resident census population (rank): 6,187,358 (12). **Male:** 3,033,974; **Female:** 3,153,384. **White:** 4,791,739 (77.4%); **Black:** 1,162,994 (18.8%); **American Indian, Eskimo, or Aleut:** 15,282 (0.2%); **Asian or Pacific Islander:** 159,053 (2.6%); **Other race:** 58,290 (0.9%); **Hispanic:** 160,288 (2.6%). **1990 percent population under 18:** 24.3; **65 and over:** 10.7; **median age:** 32.6.

1. Does not include portion of Breaks Interstate Park (Va.-Ky., 1,200 ac.) which lies in Virginia.

The history of America is closely tied to that of Virginia, particularly in the Colonial period. Jamestown, founded in 1607, was the first permanent English settlement in North America and slavery was introduced there in 1619. The surrenders ending both the American Revolution (Yorktown) and the Civil War (Appomattox) occurred in Virginia. The state is called the "Mother of Presidents" because eight chief executives of the United States were born there.

Today, Virginia has a large number of diversified manufacturing industries including transportation equipment, textiles, food processing and printing. Other important lines are electronic and other electric equipment, chemicals, apparel, lumber and wood products, furniture, and industrial machinery and equipment.

Agriculture remains an important sector in the Virginia economy and the state ranks among the top 10 in the U.S. in tomatoes, tobacco, peanuts, summer potatoes, turkeys, apples, broilers, and sweet potatoes. Other crops include corn, vegetables, and barley. Famous for Smithfield hams, Virginia also has a large dairy industry.

Coal mining accounts for roughly 75% of Virginia's mineral output, and lime, kyanite, and stone are also mined.

Points of interest include Mt. Vernon and other places associated with George Washington; Monticello, home of Thomas Jefferson; Stratford, home of the Lees; Richmond, capital of the Confederacy and of Virginia; and Williamsburg, the restored Colonial capital.

The Chesapeake Bay Bridge-Tunnel spans the mouth of Chesapeake Bay, connecting Cape Charles with Norfolk. Consisting of a series of low trestles, two bridges and two mile-long tunnels, the complex is 18 miles (29 km) long. It was opened in 1964.

Other attractions are the Shenandoah National Park, Fredericksburg and Spotsylvania National Military Park, the Booker T. Washington birthplace near Roanoke, Arlington House (the Robert E. Lee Memorial), the Skyline Drive, and the Blue Ridge National Parkway.

Famous natives and residents: Richard Arlen, actor; Arthur Ashe, tennis player; Pearl Bailey, singer; Russell Baker, columnist; Warren Beatty, actor; George Bingham, painter; Richard E. Byrd, polar explorer; Willa Cather, novelist; Roy Clark, country music artist; William Clark, explorer; Henry Clay, statesman; Joseph Cotten, actor; Ella Fitzgerald, singer; William H. Harrison, ex-president; Patrick Henry, statesman; Sam Houston, political leader; Thomas Jefferson, ex-president; Robert E. Lee, Confederate general; Meriwether Lewis, explorer; Shirley MacLaine, actress; James Madison, ex-president; John Marshall, jurist; Cyrus McCormick, inventor; James Monroe, ex-president; Opechancanough, Powhatan leader; John Payne, actor; Walter Reed, army surgeon; Matthew Ridgway, ex-Army Chief of Staff; Bill "Bojangles" Robinson, dancer; George C. Scott, actor; Sam Snead, golfer; James "Jeb" Stuart, Confederate army officer; Zachary Taylor, ex-president; Nat Turner, civil rights leader; John Tyler, ex-president; Booker T. Washington, educator; George Washington, first president; Woodrow Wilson, ex-president; Tom Wolfe, journalist.

WASHINGTON

Capital: Olympia
Governor: Gary Locke, D (to 2001)
Lieut. Governor: Joel Pritchard, R (to 1997)
Secy. of State: Ralph Munro, R (to 1997)
State Treasurer: Daniel K. Grimm, D (to 1997)
Atty. General: Christine Gregoire, D (to 1997)
Organized as territory: March 2, 1853
Entered Union (rank): Nov. 11, 1889 (42)
Present constitution adopted: 1889
Motto: Al-Ki (Indian word meaning "by and by")

State symbols: flower, Coast Rhododendron (1949); **tree,** Western hemlock (1947); **bird,** Willow goldfinch (1951); **fish,** Steelhead trout (1969); **gem,** Petrified wood (1975); **colors,** Green and gold (1925); **song,** "Washington, My Home" (1959); **folk song,** "Roll On Columbia, Roll On" (1987); **dance,** Square dance (1979)
Nicknames: Evergreen State; Chinook State
Origin of name: In honor of George Washington
10 largest cities (1994): Seattle, 520,947; Spokane, 192,781; Tacoma, 183,060; Bellevue, 84,239; Everett, 76,685; Federal Way, 72,802; Yakima, 61,976; Bellingham, 57,119; Vancouver, 51,847; Kennewick, 48,100
Land area (rank): 66,582 sq mi. (172,447 sq km) (20)
Geographic center: In Chelan Co., 10 mi. WSW of Wenatchee
Number of counties: 39
Largest county (1995 pop. est.): King, 1,595,243
State forest lands: 1,922,880 ac.
State parks: 215 (231,861 ac.)[1]
1995 resident population est.: 5,430,940
1990 resident census population (rank): 4,866,692 (18). **Male:** 2,413,747; **Female:** 2,452,945. **White:** 4,308,937 (88.5%); **Black:** 149,801 (3.1%); **American Indian, Eskimo, or Aleut:** 81,483 (1.7%); **Other race:** 115,513 (2.4%); **Hispanic:** 214,570 (4.4%). **1990 percent population under 18:** 25.9; **65 and over:** 11.8; **median age:** 33.1.

1. Parks and undeveloped areas administered by State Parks and Recreation Commission. Dept. of Wildlife administers wildlife and recreation areas totaling 428,989.5 acres.

As part of the vast Oregon Country, Washington territory was visited by Spanish, American, and British explorers—Bruno Heceta for Spain in 1775, the American Capt. Robert Gray in 1792, and Capt. George Vancouver for Britain in 1792–94. Lewis and Clark explored the Columbia River region and coastal areas for the U.S. in 1805–06.

Rival American and British settlers and conflicting territorial claims threatened war in the early 1840s. However, in 1846 the Oregon Treaty set the boundary at the 49th parallel and war was averted.

Washington is a leading lumber producer. Its rugged surface is rich in stands of Douglas fir, hemlock, ponderosa and white pine, spruce, larch, and cedar. The state holds first place in apples, lentils, dry edible peas, hops, pears, red raspberries, spearmint oil, and sweet cherries, and ranks high in apricots, asparagus, grapes, peppermint oil, and potatoes. Livestock and livestock products make important contributions to total farm revenue and the commercial fishing catch of salmon, halibut, and bottomfish makes a significant contribution to the state's economy.

Manufacturing industries in Washington include aircraft and missiles, shipbuilding and other transportation equipment, lumber, food processing, metals and metal products, chemicals, and machinery.

The Columbia River contains one third of the potential water power in the U.S., harnessed by such dams as the Grand Coulee, one of the greatest power producers in the world. Washington has over 1,000 dams built for a variety of purposes including irrigation, power, flood control, and water storage. Its abundance of electrical power makes Washington one of the nation's major producers of refined aluminum.

Among the major points of interest: Mt. Rainier, Olympic, and North Cascades. In 1980, Mount St. Helens, a peak in the Cascade Range in Southwestern Washington erupted on May 18th. Also of interest are National Parks; Whitman Mission and Fort Vancouver National Historic Sites; and the Pacific Science Center and Space Needle in Seattle.

Famous natives and residents: Bob Barker, TV host; Dyan Cannon, actress; Carol Channing, actress; Judy Collins, singer; Bing Crosby, singer, actor; Bob Crosby, musician; Merce Cunningham, choreographer; Howard Duff, actor; Frances Farmer, actress; Bill Gates, software executive; Jimi Hendrix, guitarist; Frank Herbert, writer; Robert Joffrey, choreographer; Gypsy Rose Lee, entertainer; Hank Ketcham, cartoonist; Mary McCarthy, novelist; Guthrie McClintic, theatrical producer and director; John McIntire, actor; Robert Motherwell, artist; Patrice Munsel, soprano; Ella Raines, actress; Jimmy Rogers, singer; Francis Scobee, astronaut; Seattle, Dwamish, Suquamish chief; Jeff Smith, TV cook; Smohalla, Indian prophet and chief; Adam West, actor; Martha Wright, singer; Audrey Wurdemann, poet.

WEST VIRGINIA

Capital: Charleston
Governor: Cecil H. Underwood, R (to Jan. 2001)
Secy. of State: Ken Heckler, D (to Jan. 1997)
State Auditor: Glen Gainer (to Jan. 1997)
Atty. General: Darrell McGraw, D (to Jan. 1997)
Entered Union (rank): June 20, 1863 (35)
Present constitution adopted: 1872
Motto: *Montani semper liberi* (Mountaineers are always free)
State symbols: flower, Rhododendron (1903); **tree,** Sugar maple (1949); **bird,** Cardinal (1949); **animal,** Black bear (1973); **colors,** Blue and gold (official) (1863); **songs,** "West Virginia, My Home Sweet Home," "The West Virginia Hills," and "This Is My West Virginia" (adopted by Legislature in 1947, 1961, and 1963 as official state songs)
Nickname: Mountain State
Origin of name: In honor of Elizabeth "Virgin Queen" of England
10 largest cities (1994): Charleston, 56,553; Huntington, 53,789; Wheeling, 33,969; Parkersburg, 33,102; Morgantown, 26,517; Weirton, 21,482; Fairmont, 20,627; Beckley, 18,453; Clarksburg, 17,678; Martinsburg, 14,921
Land area (rank): 24,087 sq mi. (62,384 sq km) (41)
Geographic center: In Braxton Co., 4 mi. E of Sutton
Number of counties: 55
Largest county (1995 pop. est.): Kanawha, 206,195
State forests: 9 (79,502 ac.)
State parks: 35 (74,508 ac.)
1995 resident population est.: 1,828,140
1990 resident census population (rank): 1,793,477 (34). **Male:** 861,536; **Female:** 931,941. **White:** 1,725,523 (96.2%); **Black:** 56,295 (3.1%); **American Indian, Eskimo, or Aleut:** 2,458 (0.1%); **Asian or Pacific Islander:** 7,459 (0.4%); **Other race:** 1,742 (0.1%); **Hispanic:** 8,489 (0.5%). **1990 percent population under 18:** 24.7; **65 and over:** 15.0; **median age:** 35.4.

West Virginia's early history from 1609 until 1863 is largely shared with Virginia, of which it was a part until Virginia seceded from the Union in 1861. Then the delegates of 40 western counties formed their own government, which was granted statehood in 1863.

First permanent settlement dates from 1731 when Morgan Morgan founded Mill Creek. In 1742 coal was discovered on the Coal River, an event that would be of great significance in determining West Virginia's future.

The state usually ranks 3rd in total coal production with about 15% of the U.S. total. It also is a leader in steel, glass, aluminum, and chemical manufactures; natural gas, oil, quarry products, and hardwood lumber.

Major cash farm products are poultry and eggs, dairy products, apples, and feed crops. Nearly 75% of West Virginia is covered with forests.

Tourism is increasingly popular in mountainous West Virginia and visitors spent $2.475 billion in 1990. More than a million acres have been set aside in 35 state parks and recreation areas and in 9 state forests, and national forests.

Major points of interest include Harpers Ferry and New River Gorge National River, The Greenbrier and Berkeley Springs resorts, the scenic railroad at Cass, and the historic homes in the Eastern Panhandle.

Famous natives and residents: George Brett, baseball player; Pearl S. Buck, author; Phyllis Curtin, soprano; Martin R. Delany, first Black Army major; Billy Dixon, frontiersman and scout; Joanne Dru, actress; Thomas "Stonewall" Jackson, Confederate general; John S. Knight, publisher; Don Knotts, actor; Peter Marshall, TV host; Kathy Mattea, country music superstar; Whitney D. Morrow, banker and diplomat; Mary Lou Retton, gymnast; Walter Reuther, labor leader; Eleanor Steber, soprano; Lewis L. Strauss, naval officer and scientist; Cyrus Vance, government official; William Lyne Wilson, legislator and university president; Chuck Yeager, test pilot and Air Force general.

WISCONSIN

Capital: Madison
Governor: Tommy G. Thompson, R (to Jan. 1999)
Lieut. Governor: Scott McCallum, R (to Jan. 1999)
Secy. of State: Douglas J. La Follette, D (to Jan. 1999)
State Treasurer: Jack C. Voight, R (to Jan. 1999)
Atty. General: James E. Doyle, D (to Jan. 1999)
Superintendent of Public Instruction: John Benson Nonpartisan (to July 1997)
Organized as territory: July 4, 1836
Entered Union (rank): May 29, 1848 (30)
Present constitution adopted: 1848
Motto: Forward
State symbols: flower, Wood violet (1949); **tree,** Sugar maple (1949); **grain,** corn (1990); **bird,** Robin (1949); **animal,** Badger; **wild life animal,** White-tailed deer (1957); **domestic animal,** Dairy cow (1971); **insect,** Honeybee (1977); **fish,** Musky (Muskellunge) (1955); **song,** "On Wisconsin"; **mineral,** Galena (1971); **rock,** Red Granite (1971); **symbol of peace:** Mourning Dove (1971); **soil,** Antigo Silt Loam (1983); **fossil,** Trilobite (1985); **dog,** American Water Spaniel (1986); **beverage,** Milk (1988); **dance,** Polka (1994)
Nickname: Badger State
Origin of name: French corruption of an Indian word whose meaning is disputed
10 largest cities (1994): Milwaukee, 617,044; Madison, 194,586; Green Bay, 102,708; Racine, 86,014; Kenosha, 85,122; Appleton, 69,594; West Allis, 61,259; Waukesha, 60,138; Eau Claire, 58,476; Janesville, 56,862
Land area (rank): 54,314 sq mi. (140,673 sq km) (25)
Geographic center: In Wood Co., 9 mi. SE of Marshfield
Number of counties: 72
Largest county (1995 pop. est.): Milwaukee, 931,242
State forests: 9 (476,004 ac.)
State parks & scenic trails: 45 parks, 14 trails (66,185 ac.)
1996 resident population est.: 5,142,999
1990 resident census population (rank): 4,891,769 (16). **Male:** 2,392,935; **Female:** 2,498,834. **White:** 4,512,523 (92.2%); **Black:** 244,539 (5.0%); **American Indian, Eskimo, or Aleut:** 39,387 (0.8%); **Asian or Pacific Islander:** 53,583 (1.1%); **Other race:** 41,737 (0.9%); **Hispanic:** 93,194 (1.9%). **1980 percent population under 18:** 26.4; **65 and over:** 13.3; **median age:** 32.9.

The Wisconsin region was first explored for France by Jean Nicolet, who landed at Green Bay in 1634. In 1660 a French trading post and Roman Catholic mission were established near present-day Ashland.

Great Britain obtained the region in settlement of the French and Indian War in 1763; the U.S. acquired it in 1783 after the Revolutionary War. However, Great Britain retained actual control until after the War of 1812. The region was successively governed as part of the territories of Indiana, Illinois, and Michigan between 1800 and 1836, when it became a separate territory.

Wisconsin is a leading state in milk and cheese production. In 1995 the state ranked first in the number of milk cows (1,475,000) and produced 30% of the nation's total output of cheese. Other important farm products are peas, beans, beets, corn, potatoes, oats, hay, and cranberries.

The chief industrial products of the state are automobiles, machinery, furniture, paper, beer, and processed foods. Wisconsin ranks second among the 47 paper-producing states.

Wisconsin is a pioneer in social legislation, providing pensions for the blind (1907), aid to dependent children (1913), and old-age assistance (1925). In labor legislation, the state was the first to enact an unemployment compensation law (1932) and the first in which a workman's compensation law actually took effect. Wisconsin had the first state-wide primary-election law and the first successful income-tax law. In April 1984, Wisconsin became the first state to adopt the Uniform Marital Property Act. The act took effect on January 1, 1986.

The state has over 14,000 lakes, of which Winnebago is the largest. Water sports, ice-boating, and fishing are popular, as are skiing and hunting. Public parks and forests take up one seventh of the land, with 45 state parks, 9 state forests, 14 state trails, 3 recreational areas, and 2 national forests.

Among the many points of interest are the Apostle Islands National Lakeshore; Ice Age National Scientific Reserve; the Circus World Museum at Baraboo; the Wolf, St. Croix, and Lower St. Croix national scenic riverways; and the Wisconsin Dells.

Famous natives and residents: Don Ameche, actor; Ray Chapman Andrews, naturalist and explorer; Walter Annenberg, media tycoon and philanthropist; Carrie Catt, woman suffragist; John R. Commons, economist; Tyne Daly, actress; August Derleth, author; Jeanne Dixon, seer; Zona Gale, novelist; Eric Heiden, skater; Woody Herman, band leader; Hildegarde, singer; Harry Houdini, magician; Hans V. Kaltenborne, journalist; Pee Wee King, singer; George F. Kennan, diplomat; Robert La Follette, politician; William D. Leahy, Fleet Admiral; Liberace, pianist; Charles Litel, actor; Allen Ludden, TV host; Alfred Lunt, actor; Frederic March, actor; Jackie Mason, comedian; John Ringling North, circus director; Pat O'Brien, actor; Georgia O'Keeffe, painter; Charlotte Rae, actress; William H. Rehnquist, jurist; Gena Rowlands, actress; Tom Snyder, newscaster; Spencer Tracy, actor; Thorstein Veblen, economist; Orson Welles, actor and producer; Thornton Wilder, author; Charles Winninger, actor; Frank Lloyd Wright, architect.

WYOMING

Capital: Cheyenne
Governor: Jim Geringer, R (to Jan. 1999)
Secy. of State: Diana Ohman, R (to Jan. 1999)
Auditor: Dave Ferrari, R (to Jan. 1999)
Supt. of Public Instruction: Judy Catchpole, R (to Jan. 1999)
Treasurer: Stanford S. Smith, R (to Jan. 1999)
Atty. General: Bill Hill, R (apptd. by Governor)
Organized as territory: May 19, 1869
Entered Union (rank): July 10, 1890 (44)
Present constitution adopted: 1890

Motto: Equal rights (1955)
State symbols: flower, Indian paintbrush (1917); **tree,** Cottonwood (1947); **bird,** Meadowlark (1927); **gemstone,** Jade (1967); **insignia,** Bucking horse (unofficial); **song,** "Wyoming" (1955)
Nickname: Equality State
Origin of name: From the Delaware Indian word, meaning "mountains and valleys alternating"; the same as the Wyoming Valley in Pennsylvania
10 largest cities (1994): Cheyenne, 53,559; Casper, 49,192; Laramie, 27,223; Rock Springs, 20,144; Gillette, 18,761; Sheridan, 14,798; Green River, 13,433; Evanston, 11,992; Riverton, 10,060; Rawlins, 9,239
Land area (rank): 97,105 sq mi. (251,501 sq km) (9)
Geographic center: In Fremont Co., 58 mi. ENE of Lander
Number of counties: 23, plus Yellowstone National Park
Largest county (1995 pop. est.): Laramie, 78,444
State forests: None
State parks and historic sites: 23 (58,498 ac.)
1996 resident population est.: 488,190
1990 resident census population (rank): 453,588 (50). **Male:** 227,007; **Female:** 226,581. **White:** 427,061 (94.2%); **Black:** 3,606 (0.8%); **American Indian, Eskimo, or Aleut,** 9,479 (2.1%); **Asian or Pacific Islander:** 2.806 (0.6%); **Other race:** 10,636 (2.3%); **Hispanic:** 25,751 (5.7%). **1990 percent population under 18:** 29.9; **65 and over:** 10.4; **median age:** 32.0.

The U.S. acquired the land comprising Wyoming from France as part of the Louisiana Purchase in 1803. John Colter, a fur-trapper, is the first white man known to have entered present Wyoming. In 1807 he explored the Yellowstone area and brought back news of its geysers and hot springs.

Robert Stuart pioneered the Oregon Trail across Wyoming in 1812–13 and, in 1834, Fort Laramie, the first permanent trading post in Wyoming, was built. Western Wyoming was obtained by the U.S. in the 1846 Oregon Treaty with Great Britain and as a result of the treaty ending the Mexican War in 1848.

When the Wyoming Territory was organized in 1869 Wyoming women became the first in the nation to obtain the right to vote. In 1925 Mrs. Nellie Tayloe Ross was elected first woman governor in the United States.

Wyoming's towering mountains and vast plains provide spectacular scenery, grazing lands for sheep and cattle, and rich mineral deposits.

Mining, particularly oil and natural gas, is the most important industry. Wyoming has the world's largest sodium carbonate (natrona) deposits and has the nation's second largest uranium deposits.

Wyoming ranks second among the states in wool production. In January 1995, it ranked third in sheep and lambs, exceeded only by Texas and California; it also had 1,410,000 cattle. Principal crops include wheat, oats, sugar beets, corn, potatoes, barley, and alfalfa.

Second in mean elevation to Colorado, Wyoming has many attractions for the tourist trade, notably Yellowstone National Park. Cheyenne is famous for its annual "Frontier Days" celebration. Flaming Gorge, the Fort Laramie National Historic Site, and Devils Tower and Fossil Butte National Monuments are other National points of interest.

Famous natives and residents: James Bridger, trapper, guide, storyteller; Dick Cheney, ex-Secretary of Defense; Buffalo Bill Cody;, John Colter, trader and first white man to enter Wyoming; June E. Downey, educator; Thomas Fitzpatrick, mountain man and guide; Curt Gowdy, sportscaster; Tom Horn, detective; Isabel Jewell, actress; Velma Linford, writer; Esther Morris, first woman judge;

Ted Olson, writer; John "Portugee" Phillips, frontiersman; Jackson Pollock, painter; Nellie Tayloe Ross, first woman elected governor of a state; Alan K. Simpson, senator; Jedediah S. Smith, mountain man and first American to reach California from the East; Alan Swallow, publisher, author; Willis Van Devanter, Supreme Court justice; Francis E. Warren, first state governor; Chief Washakie, chief of the Shoshone; James G. Watt, ex-Secretary of the Interior.

U.S. Territories and Outlying Areas

PUERTO RICO

(Commonwealth of Puerto Rico)
Governor: Pedro Rosselló, New Progressive Party (to 2001)
Capital: San Juan
Land area: 3,459 sq mi. (8,959 sq km)
Song: "La Borinqueña"
1996 est. population: 3,819,023
Languages: Spanish and English
Literacy rate: 90%
Labor force (1996): 1,267,000; 25% services, 23% government, 20% commerce, 15% manufacturing, 6% communications and transportation, 5% construction, 3% agriculture, 3% other.
Ethnic divisions: Almost entirely Hispanic.
10 largest municipalities (1990 census): San Juan, 437,745; Bayamón, 220,262; Ponce, 187,749; Carolina, 177,806; Caguas, 133,447; Mayagüez, 100,371; Arecibo, 93,385; Guaynabo, 92,886; Toa Baja, 89,454; Trujillo Alto, 61,120
Gross product (FY 1996): $30.3 billion; per capita $8,119; real growth rate 1.4%
Land use: 13% cropland, 41% meadows and pastures, 20% forest and woodland, 26% other.
Environment: Subtropical marine climate; high central mountain range circled by coastal plains; abundant agricultural production and foliage fostered by natural irrigation in all regions except relatively arid south coast.

The Commonwealth of Puerto Rico is located in the Caribbean Sea, about 1,000 miles east southeast of Miami, Florida. A possession of the United States, it consists of the island of Puerto Rico—smallest of the Greater Antilles, measuring about 100 miles from east to west and 35 miles across—plus the adjacent islets of Vieques, Culebra and Mona.

Discovered by Christopher Columbus in 1493, Puerto Rico subsequently became the only New World colony of Spain that never waged a war for independence. Despite this lack of animosity toward Madrid, however, Puerto Ricans warmly welcomed invading United States troops during the Spanish-American War of 1898. Since then, Puerto Rico has remained an unincorporated U.S. territory. Its people were granted American citizenship in 1917; were permitted to elect their own governor, beginning in 1948; and now fully administer their internal affairs under a constitution approved by the U.S. Congress in 1952.

From 1940 to 1968, Puerto Rican politics was dominated by a party advocating voluntary association with the U.S. Since then, a party favoring U.S. statehood has won five of eight gubernatorial elections—including the last two.

Puerto Rican voters have twice had the opportunity to express themselves directly on political status alternatives. In 1967, the outcome was commonwealth 60%; statehood 39%; independence 1%. In 1993, commonwealth dropped to 48.6%; statehood rose to 46.3%; independence polled 4.4%; and 0.6% of the ballots were blank or spoiled.

Under the commonwealth formula, residents of Puerto Rico lack voting representation in Congress and the right to participate in Presidential elections. Also, funding caps limit their access to several key Federal programs. As U.S. citizens, Puerto Ricans are subject to military service and most Federal laws. Residents of the Commonwealth pay no Federal income tax on locally-generated earnings, but Puerto Rico government income tax rates are set at a level that closely parallels Federal-plus-state levies on the mainland.

Puerto Rico is a major hub of Caribbean commerce, finance, tourism, and communications. San Juan is one of the world's busiest cruise ship ports, and Puerto Rico hosts hundreds of modern manufacturing facilities. Its population's standard of living is among the highest in the hemisphere.

Famous natives and residents: Aida Alvarez, administrator of the U.S. Small Business Administration; Deborah Carthy-Deu, Miss Universe 1985; José Cabranes, U.S. appeals court judge; Pablo Casals, cellist; Roberto Clemente, baseball player; Angel Cordero, jockey; Justino Diaz, opera singer; Beatriz "Gigi" Fernández, U.S. Olympic tennis gold medalist; Luis Ferré, political leader, philanthropist; José Ferrer, actor; José Luis González, writer; Juan González, baseball player; Gabriel Guerra-Mondragón, U.S. Ambassador to Chile; Raúl Juliá, actor; Javier López, baseball player; Jennifer López, actress; Marisol Malaret, Miss Universe 1970; Jacobo Morales, filmmaker; Rita Moreno, actress; Luis Muñoz-Marín, political leader; Antonia Novello, ex-Surgeon General; Miguel Piñero, dramatist; Tito Puente, Latin jazz artist; Chita Rivera, actress; Juan "Chi Chi" Rodríguez, golfer; José Serrano, (D-NY), member of Congress; Dayanara Torres, Miss Universe 1993; Juan Torruella, chief judge of U.S. First Circuit Court of Appeals Bernie Williams, baseball player.

GUAM

(Territory of Guam)
Governor: Carl T.C. Gutierrez (Nov. 1994)
Capital: Agaña; population (1990) 1,139
Land area: 212 sq mi. (549 sq km)
1996 est. population: 156,974; Average annual rate of natural increase: 2.04%; Birth rate: 24.2/1,000; infant mortality rate: 15.17/1,000; density per sq mi.: 751
1996 est. net migration: 3 migrants per 1,000 population
Ethnic divisions: Chamorro, 47%; Filipino, 25%; Caucasian, 10%; Chinese, Japanese, Korean, and other, 18%
Language: English and Chamorro, most residents bilingual; Japanese also widely spoken
Literacy rate: 99%
Labor force (1994): 66,460; 30.6% government, 69.4% private
Gross national product (1994 est.): $3 billion, per capita $20,000; inflation, 11% (1993); unemployment, 7.3% (Dec. 1994) **Industries:** U.S. military, tourism, transshipment services, concrete products, printing and publishing, food processing, textiles.

Guam is the largest and southernmost island in the Marianas Archipelago. After the Spanish-American War of 1898, Spain ceded Guam to the United States. From 1899 to 1949, the U.S. Navy administered Guam, except for 1941–1944 when Japanese forces seized and occupied the island. Guam was liberated by American military forces in the summer of 1944.

Today Guam is an unincorporated, organized territory of the United States. It is "unincorporated" because not all of the provisions of the U.S. constitution apply to the territory. It is an "organized" territory because the Congress provided the territory with an Organic Act in 1950 which organized the government much as a constitution would. The people of Guam have been citizens since 1950. They have been represented in the U.S. Congress since 1973 by a non-voting delegate, but do not participate in presidential elections.

Guam's government has three branches: executive, legislative, and judicial. The executive branch includes a governor and lieutenant governor elected by the pople to four-year terms, and various governmental departments and agencies. The legislative branch is a 21–member unicameral legislature whose members are elected every two years. The judicial system includes a territorial court, the Guam Superior Court, and a U.S. Federal District Court.

Guam's economy is based on two main sources of revenue: tourism and U.S. military spending (U.S. Naval and Air Force bases on Guam). Federal expenditures (FY94): $1,048 million; $457 million for wages and salaries and $295 million for purchases in the local economy. Due to the relocation of some U.S. defense missions to Guam from the Republic of the Philippines, defense spending is expected to remain high—at the half-billion dollars a year level. Guam's sophisticated business service envionment is attracting regional distribution centers of foreign and domestic companies. Today, more than 300 U.S. foreign sales corporations have set up offices in Guam.

The tourist industry has grown rapidly over the past 20 years. Visitors numbered about 1,361,830 in 1995. About 60% of the labor force works in the private sector and the rest for government.

U.S. VIRGIN ISLANDS

(Virgin Islands of the United States)

Governor: Dr. Roy L. Schneider (Jan. 1995)
Capital: Charlotte Amalie (on St. Thomas), population 1990: 12,331
1990 population: 101,809 (St. Croix, 50,139; St. Thomas, 48,166; St. John, 3,504)
Population (est. 1996): 97,120; average annual rate of natural increase: 1.24; birth rate: 17.57/1,000; infant mortality rate: 12.5/1,000; density per sq mi.: 735.8
Land area: 140 sq mi (363 sq km): St. Croix, 84 sq. mi. (218 sq km), St. Thomas, 32 sq mi (83 sq km), St. John, 20 sq mi. (52 sq km)
Ethnic divisions: West Indian, 74% (45% born in the Virgin Islands and 29% born elsewhere in the West Indies), U.S. mainland, 13%; Puerto Rican, 5%; other, 8%; black, 80%, white, 15%, other, 5%; 14% of Hispanic origin.
Language: English (official), but Spanish and various dialects are widely spoken.
Literacy rate: 90%
Labor force (1992): 48,620
Gross domestic product (1989): $1.34 billion, per capita $11,052
Aid: Western (non-U.S.) countries, official development assistance and other official flows, and bilateral commitments (1970–1989): $42 million.

The Virgin Islands, consisting of nine main islands and some 75 islets, were discovered by Columbus in 1493. Since 1666, England has held six of the main islands; the other three (St. Croix, St. Thomas, and St. John), as well as about 50 of the islets, were eventually acquired by Denmark, which named them the Danish West Indies. In 1917, these islands were purchased by the U.S. from Denmark for $25 million.

Congress granted U.S. citizenship to Virgin Islanders in 1927; and, in 1931, administration was transferred from the Navy to the Department of the Interior. Universal suffrage was given in 1936 to all persons who could read and write the English language. The Governor was elected by popular vote for the first time in 1970; previously he had been appointed by the President of the U.S. A unicameral 15-person legislature serves the Virgin Islands, and Congressional legislation gave the islands a non-voting Representative in Congress.

The "Constitution" of the Virgin Islands is the Revised Organic Act of 1954 in which the U.S. Congress defines the three branches of the territorial government, i.e., the Executive Branch, the Legislative Branch, and the Judicial Branch. Residents of the islands substantially enjoy the same rights as those enjoyed by mainlanders with one important exception: citizens of the U.S. Virgin Islands who are residents may not vote in presidential elections.

Tourism is the primary economic activity, accounting for more than 70% of the GDP and 70% of employment. Tourist expenditures are estimated to be over $791.5 million annually. In 1992, 1,963,800 tourists arrived in the Virgin Islands; about two-thirds were day visitors on cruise ships. The Virgin Islands economy has a diversified blend of heavy and light manufacturing industries, including a major oil refinery, alumina production, a rum distillery, watch assembly plants, pharmaceutical, garment-making, and sensitive-instrument assembly operations. All goods made in the Virgin Islands qualify for duty-free entry into the United States.

AMERICAN SAMOA

(Territory of American Samoa)

Governor: A.P. Lutali
Lieut. Governor: Tauese Pita Sunia
Capital: Pago Pago, population 1990: 3,519
Population (July 1993 est.): 53,139; average rate of natural increase: 3.9%; birth rate 37/1,000; infant mortality rate: 19/1,000; density per sq mi.: 300.2
Ethnic divisions: Samoan (Polynesian), 89%; Caucasian, 2%; Tongan, 4%; other, 6%
Language: Samoan (closely related to Hawaiian and other Polynesian languages) and English; most people are bilingual
Literacy rate: 99%
Labor force: 14,400
Land area: 77 sq mi (199 sq km)
Gross domestic product (1991): $128 million; per capita, $2,600; real growth rate: n.a.; inflation: 7%
Aid (1991): $21.0 million in operational funds and $1,227,000 in construction for capital-improvement projects from the U.S. Department of Interior.

American Samoa, a group of five volcanic islands and two coral atolls located some 2,600 miles south of Hawaii in the South Pacific Ocean, is an unincorporated, unorganized territory of the U.S., administered by the Department of the Interior.

Around 1000 B.C.E. Proto-polynesians established themselves in what is now American Samoa, and their descendants are one of the few remaining societies of Polynesians. American Samoa has been a territory of the United States since April 17, 1900, when the High Chiefs of Tutuila signed the Deeds of Cession for the islands of Tutuila and Aunu'u. In 1904 the High Chiefs also ceded the Manu'a islands of Ta'u, Ofu, Olosega, and Rose to the U.S. In 1929 Congress ratified the 1900 and 1904 deeds.

Until World War II the United States operated a coaling station and naval base in Pago Pago. In 1940 the port of Pago Pago became an advanced training and staging area for the U.S. Marine Corps in response to actions of the Japanese Empire. The people of American Samoa are U.S. nationals, and many have become naturalized American citizens.

Since World War II, American Samoa has developed a modern, self-governing political system. The government is divided into three branches: executive, legislative, and judicial. American Samoans elect a governor, lieutenant governor, and legislature. The legislature (Fono) consists of two houses: the Senate, selected by village chiefs (matai) for four-year terms, and the House of Representatives, elected by the general population for two-year terms. The Secretary of the Interior appoints the Chief Justice and the Associate Justice of the High Court of American Samoa. In 1981, American Samoa sent its first non-voting representative to the U.S. Congress.

Economic activity is strongly linked to the U.S., with which American Samoa does 80-90% of its foreign trade. Tuna fishing and tuna processing plants are the backbone of the private sector, with canned tuna the primary export ($300 million annually). The tuna canneries and the government are by far the two largest employers, each employing about 4,000 people. Other economic activities include a slowly developing tourist industry. Transfers from the U.S. government add substantially to American Samoa's economic well-being.

BAKER, HOWLAND, AND JARVIS ISLANDS

These Pacific islands, claimed by the United States in the 19th century, were placed under the control of the Department of the Interior by President Franklin D. Roosevelt on until May 13, 1936.

The three islands have a tropical climate with scant rainfall, constant wind, and a burning sun.

Baker Island is a saucer-shaped atoll with an area of approximately one square mile. It is about 1,650 miles from Hawaii.

Howland Island, 36 miles to the northwest, is approximately one and a half miles long and half a mile wide. It is a low-lying, nearly level, sandy, coral island surrounded by a narrow fringing reef.

Howland Island is related to the tragic disappearance of Amelia Earhart and Fred J. Noonan during the round-the-world flight in 1937. They left New Guinea on July 2, 1937, for Howland, but were never seen again.

Jarvis Island is several hundred miles to the east and is approximately one and one quarter miles long by one mile wide. It is a sandy coral island surrounded by a a narrow fringing reef.

Baker, Howland, and Jarvis have been uninhabited since 1942. In 1974, these islands became part of the National Wildlife Refuge System, administered by the U.S. Fish & Wildlife Service, Department of the Interior.

JOHNSTON ATOLL

Population (est. July 1995): 327
Land area: 1.08 sq. mi. (2.8 sq km); density
per sq mi.: 302.7

Johnston is a coral atoll about 700 miles southwest of Hawaii. It consists of four small islands—Johnston Island, Sand Island, Hikina Island, and Akau Island—which lie on a reef about 9 miles long in a northeast-southwest direction.

The atoll was discovered by Capt. Charles James Johnston of *H.M.S. Cornwallis* in 1807. In 1858 it was claimed by Hawaii, and later became a U.S. possession.

Johnston Atoll is a Naval Defensive Sea Area and Airspace Reservation and is closed to the public. The airspace entry control has been suspended but is subject to immediate reinstatement without notice. The administration of Johnston Atoll is under the jurisdiction of the Defense Nuclear Agency, Commander, Johnston Atoll (FCDNA), APO San Francisco, Calif. 96305.

The Atoll is managed cooperatively by the Defense Nuclear Agency and the Fish and Wildlife Service of the U.S. Department of the Interior as part of the National Wildlife Refuge system. In the early 1990s, a facility was opened to destroy U.S. chemical weapons.

KINGMAN REEF

Kingman Reef, located about 1,000 miles south of Hawaii, was discovered by Capt. E. Fanning in 1798, but named for Capt. W. E. Kingman, who rediscovered it in 1853. The reef, drying only on its northeast, east and southeast edges, is of atoll character. The reef is triangular in shape, with its apex northward; it is about 9.5 miles long, east and west, and 5 miles wide, north and south, within the 100-fathom curve. The island is uninhabited.

A United States possession, Kingman Reef is a Naval Defensive Sea Area and Airspace Reservation, and is closed to the public. The Airspace Entry Control has been suspended, but is subject to immediate reinstatement without notice. No vessel, except those authorized by the Secretary of the Navy, shall be navigated in the area within the 3-mile limit.

MIDWAY ISLANDS

Midway Islands, lying about 1,150 miles west-northwest of Hawaii, were discovered by Captain N. C. Brooks of the Hawaiian bark *Gambia* on July 5, 1859, in the name of the United States. The atoll was formally declared a U.S. possession in 1867, and in 1903 Theodore Roosevelt made it a naval reservation. The island was renamed "Midway" by the U.S. Navy in recognition of its geographic location on the route between California and Japan. Air traffic across the Pacific increased the island's importance in the mid-1930s, the San Francisco-Manilla mail route included a regular stop on Midway. Its military importance was soon recognized, and the Navy began building an air and submarine base there in 1940. The Battle of Midway, which took place from June 3-6, 1942, and featured aircraft based on carriers, was considered a turning point in World War II. After the war, the strategic importance of the island declined; the Midway stop for commercial air traffic was eliminated in 1950, and the air base closed in 1992.

Midway Islands consist of a circular atoll, 6 miles in diameter, and enclosing two islands. Eastern Island, on its southeast side, is triangular in shape, and about 1.2 miles long. Sand Island on its south side, is about 2.25 miles long in a northeast-southwest direction.

A National Wildlife Refuge was set up on Midway under an agreement with the Fish and Wildlife Service of the U.S. Dept. of the Interior, to protect the island's diverse and abundant wildlife..

The Midway Islands are within a Naval Defensive Sea Area. The Navy Department maintains an installation and has jurisdiction over the atoll. Permission to enter the Naval Defensive Sea Area must be obtained in advance from the Commander Third Fleet (N31), Pearl Harbor, Hawaii 96860.

Midway has no indigenous population. It is currently populated with 453 U.S. military personnel (July 1995 est.).

WAKE ISLAND

Total area: 2.5 sq mi. (6.5 sq km)
Comparative size: about 11 times the size of The Mall in Washington, D.C.
Population (1995 est.): no indigenous inhabitants; 302 U.S. military personnel and civilian contractors.
Economy: The economic activity is limited to providing services to U.S. military personnel and contractors on the island. All food and manufactured goods must be imported.

Wake Island, about halfway between Midway and Guam, is an atoll comprising the three islets of Wilkes, Peale, and Wake. They were discovered by the British in 1796 and annexed by the U.S. in 1899. The entire area comprises 3 square miles and has no indigenous population. In 1938, Pan American Airways established a seaplane base and Wake Island was used as a commercial base for several years. On Dec. 8, 1941, it was attacked by the Japanese, who finally took possession on Dec. 23. It was surrendered by the Japanese on Sept. 4, 1945.

The President, acting pursuant to the Hawaii Omnibus Act, assigned responsibility for Wake to the Secretary of the Interior in 1962. The Department of Transportation exercised civil administration of Wake through an agreement with the Department of the Interior until June 1972, at which time the Department of the Air Force assumed responsibility for the Territory.

The government of Wake Island has been administered by the U.S. Army and Strategic Defense Command since Oct. 1, 1994.

MARIANA ISLANDS

(The Commonwealth of The Northern Mariana Islands, or CNMI)
Governor: Frolian C. Tenorio (Jan. 1994)
Total area: 184.17 sq mi. (477 sq km)
Population (est. 1996): 52,284; growth rate: 3.04%; birth rate: 33/1,000; infant mortality: 37.96/1,000; density per sq mi.: 284. Most people in CNMI live on Saipan, which is also the seat of government; Rota and Tinian are also inhabited. About half the population consists of U.S. citizens and the other half consists of temporary alien workers.
Language: English is the official language, but Chamorro and Carolinian are the spoken local tongues. Japanese is also spoken in many of the hotels and shops, reflecting a heavy tourism industry.
Literacy rate: 96%
Economy: The government of the CNMI benefits substantially from U.S. financial assistance. Gross national product (1994 est.): $524 million; exports (mostly garments to the U.S.) $514 million, 1996; imports $587 million.

The Mariana Islands, east of the Philippines and south of Japan, include the islands of Rota, Saipan, Tinian, Pagan, Guguan, Agrihan, and Aguijan. They were ruled successively by Spain, Germany, and Japan before they became a U.N. Trusteeship after World War II. The Commonwealth of the Northern Mariana Islands (CNMI) became part of the United States pursuant to P.L. 94-241 as of November 3, 1986.

Tourism is the leading employer, affecting about 50% of the work force. Seventy-five percent of the tourists are Japanese.

Agricultural products are coconuts, fruits, cattle, and vegetables.

Minor Islands

NAVASSA ISLAND

Total area: 2 sq mi. (5.2 sq km)
Comparative size: About nine times the size of The Mall in Washington, D.C.

Navassa Island is located in the Caribbean Sea, 99.4 miles (160 km) south of the U.S. Naval Base at Guantanamo, Cuba, between Cuba, Haiti, and Jamaica. It is an unincorporated territory of the United States, administered by the Office of Insular Affairs within the U.S. Interior Department. Visitors require permission from the Office of Insular Affairs to land on the island, . The U.S. is responsible for its defense.

In the 19th century, the island's guano deposits were mined. The workers on this desolate island were badly treated, and once mutinied, killing their supervisors.

The island's terrain consists of a raised coral and limestone plateau, flat to undulating, and ringed by vertical cliffs, 30 to 50 feet (9 to 15 meters) high.

Navassa is uninhabited except by transient Haitian fisherman. The island is also claimed by Haiti.

PALMYRA ATOLL

Total area: 4.6 sq mi. (11.9 sq km)
Comparative size: About 20 times the size of The Mall in Washington, D.C.

Palmyra Atoll is an incorporated territory of the U.S., privately owned, but administered by the Office of Insular Affairs, U.S. Department of the Interior. The U.S. is responsible for its defense.

It is located in the North Pacific Ocean, 994 miles (1,600) kilometers sout-southwest of Honolulu, almost halfway between Hawaii and American Samoa. It was used as a military baase by the U.S. during World War II, but was not attacked. The Atoll consists of about 50 islets covered with dense vegetation, coconut trees, and balsa-like trees almost 100 feet (30 meters) high. Palmyra Atoll is uninhabited.

Tabulated Data on State Governments

State	Governor		Legislature[1]					Highest Court[2]		
	Term, years	Annual salary	Membership U[3]	L[4]	Term, U[3]	years L[4]	Salaries of members[5]	Members	Term, years	Annual salary
Alabama	4[10]	$ 87,643	35	105	4	4	$ 10 per diem	9	6	$115,695[6]
Alaska	4	81,648	20	40	4	2	24,012[20] per annum	5	3[8]	99,996[6]
Arizona	4	75,000	30	60	2	2	15,000 per annum	5	6	108,800[6]
Arkansas	4	60,000	35	100	4	2	12,500 per annum	7	8	95,216[6]
California	4	114,000	40	80	2	37	72,500 per annum	7	12	127,276[6]
Colorado	4	70,000	35	65	4	2	17,500 per annum	7	10	91,000[6]
Connecticut	4	78,000	36	151	2	2	16,760 per annum	7	8	113,042[6]
Delaware	4[9]	95,000	21	41	4	2	27,500 per annum	5	12	117,800[6]
Florida	4[10]	107,961	40	120	4[10]	2[27]	24,912 per annum	7	6	137,314
Georgia[10]	4	107,197	56	180	2	2	11,348 per annum	7	6	119,529
Hawaii	4	94,780	25	51	4	2	32,000 per year	5	10	93,780[6]
Idaho	4	85,000	35	70	2	2	12,360[20] per annum	5	6	79,183[6]
Illinois	4	110,537	59	118	4-2	2	42,265 per annum	7	10	112,124
Indiana	4[10]	77,200	50	100	4	2	11,600 per annum	5	2[8]	81,000
Iowa	4	98,200	50	100	4	2	20,120 per annum	9	8	100,600[6]
Kansas	4	80,355	40	125	4	2	138 per diem[18]	7	6	82,005[6]
Kentucky	4[7]	93,904	38	100	4	2	110 per diem[24]	7	8	94,095[6]
Louisiana	4	95,000	39	105	4	4	16,800 per annum	7	10	85,000
Maine	4	70,000	35	151	2	2	18,000 per biennium	7	7	80,392
Maryland	4[10]	120,000	47	141	4	4	29,700 per annum	7	10	107,300[6]
Massachusetts	4	90,000	40	160	2	2	46,410 per annum	7	(13)	95,880[6]
Michigan	4	121,166	38	110	4	2	50,629 per annum	7	8	118,758
Minnesota	4	114,000	67	134	4[14]	2	27,979 per annum	7	6	83,494
Mississippi	4	83,160	52	122	4	4	10,000 per session	9	8	90,800[6]
Missouri	4[9]	104,246	34	163	4[25]	2	26,803 per annum	7	12	105,717[6]
Montana	4	59,310	50	100	4	2	55 per diem	7	8	68,874
Nebraska	4[10]	65,000	49[11]	—	4[11]	—	12,000 per annum	7	6	94,893
Nevada	4	90,000	21	42	4	2	7,800 per biennium	5	6	107,600
New Hampshire	2	86,235	24	(12)	2	2	200 per biennium	5	(13)	95,628[6]
New Jersey	4[10]	130,000[28]	40	80	4[14]	2	35,000 per annum	7	7[15]	128,800[6]
New Mexico	4[10]	90,000	42	70	4	2	104 per diem	5	8	77,250[6]
New York	4	130,000	61	150	2	2	57,500 per annum	7	14	125,000[6]
North Carolina	4[10]	91,938	50	120	2	2	13,026 per annum	7	8	89,532[6]
North Dakota	4	73,176	49	98	4	2	111 per diem[19]	5	10	79,771[6]
Ohio	4	115,752	33	99	4	2	42,427 per annum	7	6	101,150[6]
Oklahoma	4	70,000	48	101	4	2	32,000 per annum	(17)	6	94,000[6]
Oregon	4[10]	80,000	30	60	4	2	1,092 per month	7	6	83,700
Pennsylvania	4[10]	125,000	50	203	4	2	47,000 per annum	7	10	119,750[6]
Rhode Island	4	69,900	50	100	2	2	10,000 per annum	5	(16)	104,403
South Carolina	4	106,078	46	124	4	2	10,400 per annum	5	10	92,986[6]
South Dakota	4[10]	85,357	35	70	4	2	8,000 per biennium	5	3[21]	78,763[6]
Tennessee	4	85,000	33	99	4	2	16,500 per annum	5	8	101,820
Texas	4	99,122	31	150	4	2	7,200 per annum	9	6	94,686[6]
Utah	4	85,200	29	75	4	2	100 per diem	5	3[20]	98,500[6]
Vermont	2	96,661	30	150	2	2	510[22] per week	5	6	83,072[6]
Virginia	4[7]	110,000	40	100	4	2	17,640[23] per annum	7	12	112,044[6]
Washington	4[26]	121,000	49	98	4[27]	2	25,900 per annum	9	6	107,200
West Virginia	4[10]	72,000	34	100	4	2	15,000 per annum	5	12	72,000
Wisconsin	4	102,882	33	99	4	2	39,211 per annum	7	6	100,690[6]
Wyoming	4	95,000	30	60	4	2	125 per diem	5	8	85,000

1. Known as *General Assembly* in Ark., Colo., Conn., Del., Ga., Ill., Iowa, Ind., Ky., Md., Mo., N.C., Ohio, Pa., R.I., S.C., Tenn., Vt., Va.; *Legislative Assembly* in N.D., Ore.; *General Court* in Mass., N.H.; *Legislature* in other states. Meets biennially in Calif., Ky., Maine, Mont., Nev., N.J., N.D., Ore., Pa., Texas. Wyoming Legislature has regular general session on odd numbered years and a budget session on even numbered years. Arkansas General Assembly meets every other year for 60 days in odd numbered years. Ohio General Assembly meets when deemed necessary. Legislative bodies meet annually in other states. 2. Known as *Court of Appeals* in Md., N.Y.; *Supreme Court of Virginia* in Va.; *Supreme Judicial Court* in Maine, Mass.; *Supreme Court* in other states. 3. Upper house: *Senate* in all states except Neb., which has a single-house legislative body, "the Legislature." 4. Lower house: *Assembly* in Calif., Nev., N.Y., Wis.; *House of Delegates* in Md., Va., W.Va.; *General Assembly* in N.J.; *House of Representatives* in other states. 5. Base salary. Does not include additional payments for expenses, mileage, special sessions, etc., or additional per diem payments. 6. Chief Justice receives a higher salary. 7. Cannot succeed himself. 8. Initial term; thereafter elected popularly for 10-year term. 9. May serve only 2 terms, consecutive or otherwise. 10. May not serve 3rd consecutive term. 11. Unicameral legislature. 12. Constitutional number: 375-400. 13. Until 70 years old. 14. Every 10 years (the year after census) term is only for 2 years. 15. 2nd term receive tenure, mandatory retirement at 70. 16. Term of good behavior. 17. Nine members in Supreme Court, highest in civil cases; five in Court of Criminal Appeals. 18. When in session, plus $600/mo. when not in session. 19. When in session, plus $250 per month

when not in session. 20. Leaders receive a higher salary. 21. Subsequent terms, 8 years. 22. To limit of $13,000 per biennium; $100 per diem for Special Session. 23. Upper house receives higher salary. 24. When in session, plus $950 a month when not in session. 25. Legislators may serve only eight years in each house, 16 combined. 26. No person is eligible who would have served during eight of the previous 14 years. 27. Have term limitations. 28. Legislated salary; salary received is $85,000. NOTE: Salaries are rounded to nearest dollar. *Source: Information Please* questionnaires to the states.

Land and Water Area of States, 1990

(in square miles)

State	Rank (total area)	Land[1] area	Water[2] area	Total area	State	Rank (total area)	Land[1] area	Water[2] area	Total area
Alabama	30	50,750.23	1,672.71	52,422.94	Nebraska	16	76,877.73	480.67	77,358.40
Alaska	1	570,373.55	86,050.59	656,424.14	Nevada	7	109,805.89	761.02	110,566.91
Arizona	6	113,642.26	364.00	114,006.26	New Hampshire	46	8,969.36	381.57	9,350.93
Arkansas	29	52,075.29	1,107.07	53,182.36	New Jersey	47	7,418.84	1,303.11	8,721.95
California	3	155,973.09	7,734.06	163,707.15	New Mexico	5	121,364.54	233.69	123,598.23
Colorado	8	103,729.54	370.78	104,100.32	New York	27	47,223.85	7,250.71	54,474.56
Connecticut	48	4,845.39	698.26	5,543.65	North Carolina	28	48,718.08	5,103.27	53,821.35
Delaware	49	1,954.62	534.76	2,489.38	North Dakota	19	68,994.24	1,709.59	70,703.83
Dist. of Columbia	—	61.41	6.95	68.36	Ohio	34	40,952.59	3,874.94	44,827.53
Florida	22	53,997.08	11,761.00	65,758.08	Oklahoma	20	68,678.57	1,224.33	69,902.90
Georgia	24	57,918.73	1,522.49	59,441.22	Oregon	9	96,002.58	2,383.17	98,385.75
Hawaii	43	6,423.34	4,508.24	10,931.58	Pennsylvania	33	44,819.61	1,238.63	46,058.24
Idaho	14	82,750.93	822.84	83,573.77	Rhode Island	50	1,044.98	500.12	1,545.10
Illinois	25	55,593.29	2,324.55	57,917.84	South Carolina	40	30,111.12	1,895.99	32,007.11
Indiana	38	35,870.18	549.91	36,420.09	South Dakota	17	75,897.74	1,223.72	77,121.46
Iowa	26	55,874.90	400.64	56,275.54	Tennessee	36	41,219.52	926.49	42,146.01
Kansas	15	81,823.02	458.98	82,282.00	Texas	2	261,914.26	6,686.70	268,600.96
Kentucky	37	39,732.31	678.93	40,411.24	Utah	13	82,168.15	2,735.97	84,904.12
Louisiana	31	43,566.03	8,277.44	51,843.47	Vermont	45	9,249.33	365.67	9,615.00
Maine	39	30,864.55	4,522.78	35,387.33	Virginia	35	39,597.79	3,171.09	42,768.88
Maryland	42	9,774.65	2,632.80	12,407.45	Washington	18	66,581.95	4,720.70	71,302.65
Massachusetts	44	7,837.98	2,716.81	10,554.79	West Virginia	41	24,086.55	144.89	24,231.44
Michigan	11	56,809.18	40,001.04	96,810.22	Wisconsin	23	54,313.71	11,189.50	65,503.21
Minnesota	12	79,616.66	7,326.05	86,942.71	Wyoming	10	97,104.55	713.56	97,818.11
Mississippi	32	46,913.64	1,519.95	48,433.59	**U.S. Total**		**3,536,341.73**	**251,083.35**	**3,787,425.08**
Missouri	21	68,898.01	810.80	69,708.81					
Montana	4	145,556.34	1,489.82	147,046.16					

1. Dry land and land temporarily or partially covered by water, such as marshland, swamps, etc.; streams and canals under one-eighth statute mile wide; and lakes, reservoirs, and ponds under 40 acres. 2. Permanent inland water surface, such as lakes, reservoirs, and ponds having an area of 40 acres or more; streams, sloughs, estuaries, and canals one-eighth statute mile or more in width; deeply indented embayments and sounds, and other coastal waters behind or sheltered by headlands or islands separated by less than 1 nautical mile of water, and islands under 40 acres in area. Excludes areas of oceans, bays, sounds, etc. lying within U.S. jurisdiction but not defined as inland water. *Source:* Department of Commerce, Bureau of the Census.

Regional Variations in Suicide Rates, 1990–1994

A recent study by the Centers for Disease Control reports distinct regional variations in the suicide rate in the United States, but fails to elucidate the cause for this difference. The study tracked deaths by suicide in the U.S. from 1990–1994, then manipulated the data to determine whether certain demographic characteristics might explain the reason for the higher suicide rate in the South and the lower rate in the Northeast. Experts in suicide studies are well aware that certain sub-populations (e.g., the elderly, males, non-Hispanic whites, Native Americans) exhibit higher suicide rates than the population at large. Theoretically, regions of the country with higher concentrations of these demographics would be more likely to have higher suicide rates. To test this hypothesis, the researchers controlled the data for certain demographic variables, but, surprisingly, the regional differences persist. For now, their cause remains a mystery.

Rate of Suicide in the United States, 1990–1994

Region/State	Number of suicides	Region/State	Number of suicides
Northeast		Florida	10,413
Connecticut	1,553	Georgia	4,275
Maine	838	Kentucky	2,572
Massachusetts	2,530	Louisiana	2,727
New Hampshire	697	Maryland	2,433
New Jersey	2,729	Mississippi	1,589
New York	7,551	North Carolina	4,319
Pennsylvania	6,976	Oklahoma	2,248
Rhode Island	454	South Carolina	2,278
Vermont	406	Tennessee	3,298
Total	**23,734**	Texas	11,316
Midwest		Virginia	4,008
Illinois	5,717	West Virginia	1,226
Indiana	3,575	**Total**	**57,509**
Iowa	1,598	**West**	
Kansas	1,546	Alaska	451
Michigan	5,403	Arizona	3,495
Minnesota	2,562	California	18,734
Missouri	3,448	Colorado	2,936
Nebraska	958	Hawaii	619
North Dakota	371	Idaho	915
Ohio	5,875	Montana	794
South Dakota	479	Nevada	1,606
Wisconsin	2,960	New Mexico	1,459
Total	**34,492**	Oregon	2,367
South		Utah	1,357
Alabama	2,659	Washington	3,512
Arkansas	1,550	Wyoming	464
Delaware	421	**Total**	**38,709**
District of Columbia	177	**Total**	**154,444**

Source: U.S. Department of Health and Human Services, Centers for Disease Control, *Morbidity and Mortality Weekly Report,* Aug. 29, 1997.

Rate of Suicide in the United States, 1990–94

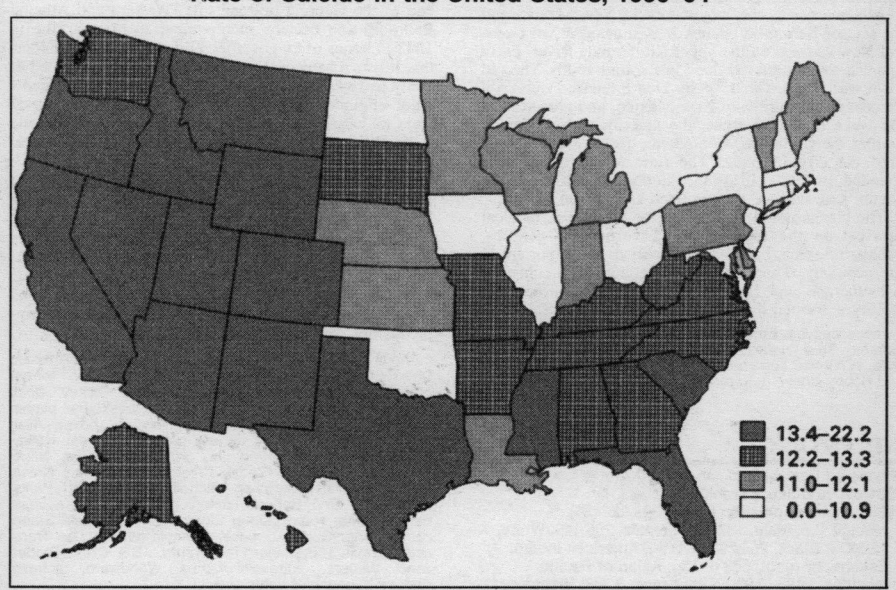

13.4–22.2
12.2–13.3
11.0–12.1
0.0–10.9

NOTE: Per 100,000 population. Adjusted to the age, sex, and race/ethnicity distribution of the 1980 U.S. population.

U.S. Cities

50 Largest Cities of the United States

(According to 1994 Census data)

Data supplied by Bureau of the Census and by the cities in response to *Information Please* questionnaires. Ranking of 50 largest cities based on July 1, 1994 census estimates. Per capita personal income data is given for the Metropolitan Statistical Area (MSA), the Primary Metropolitan Statistical Area (PMSA), or the Consolidated Metropolitan Statistical Area (CMSA), as noted, and is for 1992, unless otherwise noted. Average daily temperature data is from *County and City Data Book*. NOTE: Persons of Hispanic origin may be of any race.

ALBUQUERQUE, N.M.

Mayor: Martin J. Chavez
1994 est. population (rank): 411,994 (36)
1990 census population (rank): 384,619 (38); **% change,** 7.1; **Male,** 186,584; **Female,** 198,152; **White,** 301,010; **Black,** 11,484 (3.0%); **American Indian, Eskimo, or Aleut,** 11,708 (3.0%); **Asian or Pacific Islander,** 6,660 (1.7%); **Other race,** 53.874; **Hispanic origin,** 132,706 (34.5%). **1990 population under 18:** 25.0%; **65 and over:** 11.1%; **median age:** 32.5.
Land area: 163 sq mi. (422 sq km); **Alt.:** 4,958 ft.
Avg. daily temp.: Jan., 34.8° F; July, 78.8° F
Churches: 211; **City-owned parks:** 189; **Radio stations:** 43 (AM, 17; FM, 26); **Television stations:** 11
Civilian Labor Force: 224,003; **Unemployed:** 10,305, **Percent:** 4.6; **Per capita personal income (MSA) 1992:** $17,758
Chamber of Commerce: Greater Albuquerque Chamber of Commerce, 401 2nd St., N.W., Albuquerque, N.M. 87102. Albuquerque Hispanic Chamber of Commerce, 202 Central Ave., S.E., Albuquerque, N.M. 87102

Albuquerque is the largest city in New Mexico and the seat of Bernalillo county. It is situated in west central New Mexico on the upper Rio Grande River. Early Spanish settlers arrived there in the mid-1600s. The old town was founded in 1706 by Don Francisco Cuervo y Valdés, the Governor of New Mexico, and named after the Duke of Albuquerque, the viceroy of New Spain. During the Civil War, Confederate forces briefly occupied the city in 1862. The new town section was founded in 1880. In 1883, Albuquerque became the county seat and was incorporated as a city in 1891.

The city is noted as a center for health and medical services in the region, and government agencies, nuclear research, banking, and tourism are important to the economy. There is a growing high-tech center in Albuquerque and Intel Corp.'s largest manufacturing facility is located there.

Famous natives: Erna Fergusson, author; Annabeth Gish, actress; Fred Haney, baseball player, executive; Ernie Pyle, WWII war correspondent; Slim Summerville, actor; Al and Bobby Unser, auto racers.

ATLANTA, GA.[1]

Mayor: Bill Campbell (to Jan. 1998)
1994 est. population (rank): 396,052 (37)[2]
1990 census population (rank): 393,929 (36); **% change,** 0.5; **Male,** 187,877; **Female,** 206,140; **White,** 122,327; **Black,** 264,262 (67.1%); **American Indian, Eskimo, or Aleut,** 563 (0.1%); **Asian or Pacific Islander,** 3,498 (0.9%); **Other race,** 3,367; **Hispanic origin,** 7,525 (1.9%). **1990 population under 18:** 24.1%; **65 and over:** 11.3%; **median age:** 31.5.
City land area: 136 sq mi. (352.2 sq km); **Alt.:** Highest, 1,050 ft.; lowest, 940 ft.
Avg. daily temp.: Jan., 41.9° F; July, 78.6° F
Churches: 1,500; **City-owned parks:** 277 (3,178 ac.); **Radio stations:** AM, 7; FM, 20; **Television stations:** 8 commercial; 2 PBS
Civilian Labor Force (1996): 1,976,970; **Unemployed:** 75,260, **Percent:** 3.8; **Per capita personal income (MSA) 1996:** $23,567
Chamber of Commerce: Metro Atlanta Chamber of Commerce, 235 International Blvd., Atlanta, Ga. 30303

1. Information is gathered on the 20-county MSA 2. 1996 est. population: 3,505,970 (metro area).

Atlanta, the largest city and capital of Georgia, is the seat of Fulton county. It is situated in the northwest part of the state at the base of the Blue Ridge Mountains near the Chattahoochee River. The first European settler was Hardy Ivy who built a cabin there in 1833.

The town was founded as Terminus in 1837 as the end of the Georgia railroad line (Western and Atlantic Railroad) and became incorporated as Marthasville in 1843 in honor of ex-governor Lumpkin's daughter Martha. It was renamed Atlanta in 1845 and incorporated as a city in 1847. Its name was suggested by the railroad's chief engineer, J. Edgar Thomson, and was derived from its location at the end of the Georgia and Atlantic railroad line. The city later became the capital of Georgia in 1868.

During the Civil War, the city was burned and almost completely destroyed by General W.T. Sherman in November 1864. It was quickly rebuilt after the war and it grew rapidly due to the expansion of the railroads in the southwest. Atlanta's diverse economy is led by the service, communications, retail trade, manufacturing, and finance and insurance industries. The convention business is also important, and the 1996 Summer Olympic Games were held there.

Famous natives: Hank Aaron, baseball player; Arrested Development, recording artists; Jimmy Carter, former president; Ray Charles, singer; James Dickey, poet; Mattivilda Dobbs, soprano; Walt Frazier, basketball player; Oliver Hardy, comedian; Evander Holyfield, boxer; Allan Jackson, singer; Bobby Jones, golfer; DeForest Kelley, actor; Martin Luther King, Jr., civil rights leader, Nobel Peace Prize winner; Gladys Knight, singer; Kriss Kross, recording artists; Margaret Mitchell, novelist; Bert Parks, entertainer; Eric Roberts, actor; Julia Roberts, actress; Ferroll Sams, author; Doug Stone, singer; Pamela Stone, comedienne; Gwen Torrence, Olympic athlete; Lee Tracy, actor; Travis Tritt, singer; Ted Turner, TBS, CNN founder; Jane Withers, actress; Joanne Woodward, actress; Andrew Young, civil rights activist.

AUSTIN, TEX.

Mayor: Kirk Watson (to May 2000)
1994 est. population (rank): 514,013 (23)[1]
1990 census population (rank): 465,648 (27); **% change,** 10.4; **Male,** 232,473; **Female,** 233,149; **White,** 328,542; **Black,** 57,868 (12.4%); **American Indian, Eskimo, or Aleut:,** 1,756 (0.4%); **Asian or Pacific Islander,** 14,141 (3.0%); **Other race,** 63,315; **Hispanic origin,** 106,868 (23.0%). **1990 population under 18:** 23.1%; **65 and over:** 7.4%; **median age:** 28.9
Land area: 116 sq mi. (300 sq km); **Alt.:** From 425 ft. to over 1000 ft. elevation
Avg. daily temp.: Jan., 49.1° F; July, 84.7° F
Churches: 353 churches, representing 45 denominations; **City-owned parks and playgrounds:** 169 (11,800 ac.); **Radio stations:** AM, 6; FM, 12; **Television stations:** 3 commercial; 1 PBS; 1 independent
Civilian Labor Force (1995): 616,300; **Unemployed:** 20,338, **Percent:** 3.3; **Per capita personal income:** $18,770, Austin-San Marcos (MSA)
Chamber of Commerce: Greater Austin Chamber of Commerce, P.O. Box 1967, Austin, Tex. 78767

1. 1997 est. population 561,045.

Austin, the capital and seat of Travis county, is the fifth largest city in Texas. It is situated in the south central part of the state on the Colorado River. The site was called Waterloo in 1838 and in 1839 was incorporated as a city and chosen to become the capital of the independent Republic of Texas. Waterloo was renamed Austin in honor of Stephen F. Austin, the founder of the Texas Republic. It became the permanent capital of the state of Texas in 1870.

Austin's growth was spurred by several developments after the Civil War—the railroads reached the city in the 1870s; it was crossed by the important Chisholm cattle trail, and it became the seat of the state university in 1883.

Austin has a growing commercial and diversified manufacturing sector. Civilian government employment is 28% of the labor force and is important to the economy. As home to the University of Texas, Austin is a major research and development, and nationally recognized high-technology center. The city has a new convention center downtown.

Famous natives: Don Baylor, baseball player, manager; Earl Campbell, football player; Liz Carpenter, author; Dabney Coleman, actor; Ben Crenshaw, golfer; Michael Dell, founder Dell Computer Corp.; Tobe Hooper, film director; Lady Bird Johnson, former First Lady; Tom Kite, golfer; James Michener, author; Willie Nelson, musician; Amado Pena, artist; Darrell Royal, legendary UT football coach; Zachary Scott, actor; Jerry Jeff Walker, musician; Dalhart Windberg, artist.

BALTIMORE, MD.

Mayor: Kurt L. Schmoke (to Dec. 1999)
1994 est. population (rank): 702,979 (14)
1990 census population (rank): 736,014 (12); **% change,** -4.5; **Male,** 343,513; **Female,** 392,501; **White,** 287,753; **Black,** 435,768 (59.2%); **American Indian, Eskimo, or Aleut,** 2,555 (0.3%); **Asian or Pacific Islander,** 7,942 (1.1%); **Other race,** 1,996; **Hispanic origin,** 7,602 (1.0%). **1990 population under 18:** 24.4%; **65 and over:** 13.7%; **Median age:** 32.6
Land area: 80.3 sq mi. (208 sq km); **Alt.:** Highest, 490 ft.; lowest, sea level
Avg. daily temp.: Jan., 35.5° F; July, 79.9° F
Churches: Roman Catholic, 72; Jewish, 50; Protestant and others, 344; **City-owned parks:** 347 park areas and tracts (6,314 ac.); **Radio stations:** AM, 10; FM, 11; **Television stations:** 7 (including Home Shopping Network)

Civilian Labor Force: 333,043; **Unemployed:** 35,531, **Percent:** 10.7; **Per capita personal income (PMSA) 1992:** $22,412
Chamber of Commerce: Greater Baltimore Committee, 111 S. Calvert St., Ste. 1500, Baltimore, Md. 21202

Baltimore is the largest city in Maryland and is situated in the northern part of the state on the Patapsco River estuary, an arm of Chesapeake Bay. The city is independent and is in no county.

The site was settled in the early 17th century and founded as a town in 1729. The town was named after Lord Baltimore, the founder of Maryland, and was incorporated as a city in 1797. It has an excellent harbor and has been a principal port since the 18th century. Baltimore was a pioneer ship-building center and the Baltimore clipper was one of the best sailing ships of its day and was used extensively in world trade. It ranks today as the nation's second port in foreign tonnage.

Baltimore's economy is focused on manufacturing, in steel, heavy and light industries, ship construction, and scientific research and development.

Famous natives: Larry Adler, musician; John Astin, actor; Eubie Blake, pianist; Francis X. Bushman, actor; Charlie Chase, actor; Hans Conried, actor; Mildred Dunnock, actress; "Mama" Cass Elliot, singer; Barry Farber, broadcaster; Paul Ford, actor; Philip Glass, composer; Billy Holiday, singer; Barry Levinson, director; H.L. Mencken, writer; Babe Ruth, baseball player; Upton Sinclair, novelist; Leon Uris, novelist; Frank Zappa, musician.

BOSTON, MASS.

Mayor: Thomas Menino (to Dec. 1997)
1994 est. population (rank): 547,725 (21)
1990 census population (rank): 574,283 (20); **% change,** -4.6; **Male,** 275,972; **Female,** 298,311; **White,** 360,875; **Black,** 146,945 (25.6%); **American Indian, Eskimo, or Aleut,** 1,884 (0.3%); **Asian or Pacific Islander,** 30,388 (5.3%); **Other race,** 34,191; **Hispanic origin,** 61,955 (10.8%). **1990 population under 18:** 19.1%; **65 and over:** 11.5%; **median age:** 30.3
Land area: 47.2 sq mi. (122 sq km); **Alt.:** Highest, 330 ft.; lowest, sea level
Avg. daily temp.: Jan., 29.6° F; July, 73.5° F
Churches: Protestant, 187; Roman Catholic, 72; Jewish, 28; others, 100; **City-owned parks, playgrounds, etc.:** 2,276.36 ac.; **Radio stations:** AM, 9; FM, 12; **Television stations:** 10
Civilian Labor Force (1995): 284,448; **Unemployed:** 14,036, **Percent:** 4.9; **Per capita personal income (NECMA) 1992:** $24,109[1]
Chamber of Commerce: Boston Chamber of Commerce, 600 Atlantic Ave., Boston, Mass. 02210

1. Boston-Lawrence-Salem-Lowell-Brockton NECMA.

Boston is the capital and seat of Suffolk county and the largest city in Massachusetts. It is located in the eastern part of the state at the head of Boston Bay. It was incorporated as a city in 1822. No city in the U.S. is richer in historical associations than Boston, and no city has retained more of its original buildings as memorials to America's past.

Puritans from England settled at Boston in 1630, only ten years after the Pilgrims had landed at Plymouth in 1620. They named their new town Boston, after the former home of many of the Pilgrims in Lincolnshire, England. Fourteen years later, the pioneer Bostonians set aside the first public park in the U.S.—the Boston Common. The following year, 1635, they opened the first free public school in America. Today, the Boston metropolitan area is home to 68 colleges and universities.

Boston is a major industrial, financial, and educational hub and has one of the finest ports in the world.

The port of Boston ships more than $8.5 billion worth of goods each year.

Although the city's banking and financial services, insurance, and real estate sectors declined in the early 90's, other industries continue to grow, especially in the health care field. Boston has 25 medical research institutions, more than any other U.S. city, and its health care industry is growing at a rate of about 3% a year. The city's unique cultural and historic heritage makes it a center of tourism and its hotel industry ranks first in the nation in occupancy. Boston's other businesses are in high-technology, biotechnology, software, and electronics.

Famous natives: Samuel Adams, patriot; John Singleton Copley, painter; Ralph Waldo Emerson, philosopher and poet; Arthur Fiedler, conductor; Benjamin Franklin;, statesmen, scientist; Edward Everett Hale, clergyman, author; Oliver Wendell Holmes, jurist; Winslow Homer, painter; Joseph P. and Rose Fitzgerald Kennedy;, Jack Lemmon, actor; Robert Lowell, poet; Edgar Allan Poe, writer; Paul Revere, patriot, silversmith; John L. Sullivan, boxer; Barbara Walters, TV journalist.

CHARLOTTE, N.C.

Mayor: Pat McCrory (to Nov. 1999)
1994 est. population: 437,797 (32)[1]
1990 census population (rank): 395,934 (35); **% change,** 10.6; **Male,** 188,088; **Female,** 207,846; **White,** 259,760; **Black,** 125,827 (31.8%); **American Indian, Eskimo, or Aleut:** 1,425 (0.4%); **Asian or Pacific Islander:** 7,211 (1.8%); **Other race,** 1,711; **Hispanic origin,** 5,571 (1.4%). **1990 population under 18:** 24.2%; **65 and over:** 9.8%; **median age:** 32.1.
Land area: 214 sq mi. (544.2 sq km); **Alt.:** 765 ft.
Avg. daily temp.: Jan., 40.5° F; July, 78.5° F
Churches: Protestant, over 400; Roman Catholic, 8; Jewish, 3; Greek Orthodox, 1; **City-owned parks and parkways:** 130; **Radio stations:** AM, 10; FM, 17; **Television stations:** 4 commercial; 2 PBS
Civilian Labor Force (1996): 340,950; **Unemployed:** 10,150, **Percent:** 3.0; **Per capita personal income (MSA) 1996:** $15,291[2]
Chamber of Commerce: Charlotte Chamber, P.O. Box 32785, Charlotte, N.C., 28232

1.1997 est. population: 470,553. 2. Charlotte–Gastonia Rock Hill, N.C.–S.C.

Charlotte, North Carolina's largest city and seat of Mecklenburg county, is located in the southern part of the state near the South Carolina border. It was named for King George III of England's wife, Charlotte Sophia of Mecklenburg-Strelitz.

Settled about 1750, Charlotte was incorporated as a city in 1768 and made the county seat in 1774. Charlotte was a leading Confederate city during the Civil War and was the last meeting place of the full Confederate cabinet.

From 1800 to 1848, Charlotte was the center of U.S. gold production and a branch of the U.S. mint operated from there from 1837 to 1913.

The city has a highly diversified economy and is a foremost center for distribution, retailing, technology, and manufacturing. It is the second largest banking center in the U.S. It is the seat of the University of North Carolina at Charlotte.

Famous natives: Romare Bearden, artist; Richard G. Darman, government official; Billy Graham, evangelist; Charles Gwathmey, architect; Hamilton Jordan, government official; Donald Schollander, swimmer; Randolph Scott, actor.

CHICAGO, ILL.

Mayor: Richard M. Daley (to April 1999)
1994 est. population (rank): 2,731,743 (3)
1990 census population (rank): 2,783,726 (3); **% change,** –1.9; **Male,** 1,334,705; **Female,** 1,449,021; **White,** 1,263,524; **Black,** 1,087,711 (39.1%); **American Indian, Eskimo, or Aleut,** 7,064 (0.3%); **Asian or Pacific Islander,** 104,118 (3.7%); **Other race,** 321,309; **Hispanic origin,** 545,852 (19.6%). **1990 population under 18:** 26.0%; **65 and over:** 11.9%; **median age:** 31.3.
Land area: 228.469 sq mi. (592 sq km); **Alt.:** Highest, 672 ft.; lowest, 578.5 ft.
Avg. daily temp. (1996): Jan., 23.4° F; July, 69.9° F
Churches: Protestant, 850; Roman Catholic, 252; Jewish, 51; **City-owned parks:** 552; **Radio stations (1995):** AM, 20; FM, 31; **Television stations:** 14
Civilian Labor Force (PMSA 1996): 4,120,400; **Unemploye** 194,400, **Percent:** 4.7; **Per capita personal income (PMSA) 1994:** $25,865
Chamber of Commerce: Chicagoland Chamber of Commerce, 200 N. LaSalle, Chicago, Ill. 60601

Chicago is the largest city in Illinois and the seat of Cook county. Built directly on a lake front, it stretches for 22 miles along the southwestern shore of Lake Michigan.

The first white men known to have visited Chicago were Joliet and Father Marquette in 1673. The first permanent white settler in the area was John Kinzie, sometimes called the father of Chicago, who took over a trading post in 1796 that had been established 1791 by Jean Baptiste Point Sable, a French-speaking black fur trapper. Fort Dearborn, a blockhouse and stockade, was built in 1804, but was evacuated in 1812, with more than half of its garrison massacred at what is now the foot of 18th Street. Not until 1830 was the town laid out. The name Chicago is thought to come from the Algonquian Indian word Chicagou meaning "strong" or "powerful." Some early Frenchmen believed the name was derived from the Algonquian word for "onion place" because wild onions grew there.

Forty-one years later it was destroyed in the great Chicago fire of 1871. Chicago was incorporated as a village in 1833 and as a city in 1837.

Chicago is a major Great Lakes port and the commercial, financial, industrial, and cultural center of the Midwest. The manufacturing industries dominate the wholesale and retail trade, and trade in agricultural commodities is important to the economy. The Chicago Mercantile Exchange is the largest in the world.

Famous natives: Jack Benny, comedian; Edgar Rice Burroughs, author; Raymond Chandler, author; Hillary Rodham Clinton, lawyer, First Lady; Michael Crichton, author; Walt Disney, filmmaker; John Dos Passos, author; Bobby Fischer, chess player; Bob Fosse, choreographer, director; Benny Goodman, clarinetist; Dorothy Hamill, figure skater; Quincy Jones, composer; Gene Krupa, drummer; Dorothy Malone, actress; David Mamet, playwright; Bob Newhart, comedian; Kim Novak, actress; Donald O'Connor, actor; William L. Shirer, journalist, historian; Preston Sturges, film director; Gloria Swanson, actress; Melvin Van Peebles, playwright; Alfred Wallenstein, conductor; Robin Williams, comedian, actor; Robert Young, actor.

CINCINNATI, OHIO

Mayor: Roxanne Qualls (to Nov. 1997)
City Manager: John F. Shirey
1994 est. population (rank): 358,170 (46)
1990 census population (rank): 364,114 (45); **% change,** –1.6; **Male,** 169,305; **Female,** 194,735; **White,** 220,285; **Black,** 138,1312 (37.9%); **American Indian, Eskimo, or Aleut,** 660 (0.2%); **Asian or Pacific Islander,** 4,030

(1.1%); **Other race,** 933; **Hispanic origin,** 2,386 (0.7%). **1990 population under 18:** 25.1%; **65 and over:** 13.9%; **median age:** 30.9.

Land area: 78.1 sq mi. (202 sq km); **Alt.:** Highest, 960 ft.; lowest, 441 ft.

Avg. daily temp.: Jan., 30.3° F; July, 76.1° F

Churches: 850; **City-owned parks:** 96 (4,345 ac.); **Radio stations:** AM, 10; FM, 15 (Greater Cincinnati); **Television stations:** 8

Civilian Labor Force: 188,161; **Unemployed:** 14,318, **Percent:** 7.6; **Per capita personal income (PMSA) 1992:** $20,517[1]

Chamber of Commerce: Cincinnati Chamber of Commerce, 441 Vine St. Suite 300, Cincinnati, Ohio 45202

1. Ohio–Ky.–Ind.

Cincinnati is the third largest city in Ohio and the seat of Hamilton county. It is located on the Ohio River.

Cincinnati began as part of the Miami Purchase of 1788. The first settlement, Columbia, was begun by Benjamin Stites that same year. The town of Losantiville was founded in 1788 on a plateau above the Ohio River by Mathias Denman, Robert Patterson, and Israel Ludlow. Its strategic location in the Western Territory led to the building of Ft. Washington, the most ambitious military establishment in the territory. The community of Losantiville that grew up around the fort was renamed Cincinnati in 1790 by Gen. Arthur St. Clair, Commander of Ft. Washington and first governor of the Northwest Territory, after the Revolutionary officers' Society of the Cincinnati, founded by George Washington. It was incorporated as a village in 1802 and chartered as a city in 1819.

The city began to flourish as a commercial hub with the arrival of the first steamboat in 1811, the completion of the Miami and Erie Canal in 1827, and the coming of the first railroad in 1843.

Cincinnati is a port of entry and more than 46 million tons pass through each year. The city has a diverse economy and is a major center for manufacturing, wholesaling, and retailing, as well as insurance and finance companies and health services. Prominent manufacturing groups include: transportation equipment, which includes aircraft engines and auto parts; food and kindred products; metal working; general industrial machinery; chemicals; fabricated metal products; printing and publishing.

Famous natives: Eddie Arcaro, jockey; Theda Bara, actress; Doris Day, actress; Jim Dine, painter; Suzanne Farrell, ballerina; Robert Henri, painter; James Levine, music director; Adolph Ochs, publisher; Tyrone Power, actor; William Procter, scientist; Roy Rogers, actor; Pete Rose, baseball player; Steven Spielberg, filmmaker; Roger Staubach, football player; Robert A. Taft, legislator; William Howard Taft, ex-president.

CLEVELAND, OHIO

Mayor: Michael R. White (to Dec. 1997)
1994 est. population (rank): 492,901 (26)
1990 census population (rank): 505,616 (23); **% change,** –2.5; **Male,** 237,211; **Female,** 268,405; **White,** 250,234; **Black,** 235,405 (46.6%); **American Indian, Eskimo, or Aleut,** 1,562 (0.3%); **Asian or Pacific Islander,** 5,115 (1.0%); **Other race,** 13,300; **Hispanic origin,** 23,197 (4.6%). **1990 population under 18:** 26.9%; **65 and over:** 14.0%; **median age:** 31.9.

Land area: 79 sq mi. (205 sq km); **Alt.:** Highest, 1048 ft.; lowest, 573 ft.

Avg. daily temp.: Jan., 25.5° F; July, 71.6° F

Churches: [1] Protestant, 980; Roman Catholic, 187; Jewish, 31; Eastern Orthodox, 22; **City-owned parks:** 41 (1,930 ac.); **Radio stations:** AM, 15; FM, 17; **Television stations:** 7

Civilian Labor Force: 209,700; **Unemployed:** 19,900,

Percent: 9.7; **Per capita personal income (PMSA) 1992:** $21,533[1]

Chamber of Commerce: Greater Cleveland Growth Association, 200 Tower City Center, Cleveland, Ohio 44113

1. Cleveland–Lorain–Elyria.

Cleveland is the second largest city in Ohio and the seat of Cuyahoga county. It is located in the northeastern part of the state on Lake Erie. In the Colonial era, the Cleveland area was known as the Connecticut Western Reserve, part of a land grant made to Connecticut by King Charles II in 1662. The city was founded in 1796 by Gen. Moses Cleaveland, who was the head surveyor of the Connecticut Land Company. This company had bought three million acres in what is now northern Ohio. A permanent settlement was founded in 1799, named after the General, and the spelling was shortened to Cleveland. The city was incorporated in 1836.

Cleveland's industrial growth was stimulated by the opening of the Ohio and Erie Canals in 1832 and, later, the advent of the Civil War with the corresponding demand for machinery, railroad equipment, ships, and other items.

The port of Cleveland is the largest overseas general cargo port on Lake Erie. Greater Cleveland has long been famous as a diversified durable goods manufacturing area. Following the national trend, Cleveland has been shifting to a more services-based economy. Greater Cleveland is a world corporate center for leading national and multinational companies in industries ranging from transportation, insurance, retailing, and utilities, to commercial banking and finance.

Famous natives: Jim Backus, actor; Dorothy Dandridge, actress; Ruby Dee, actress; Phil Donahue, talk show host; Joel Grey, actor; Arsenio Hall, talk show host; Margaret Hamilton, actress; Philip Johnson, architect; Henry Mancini, composer; Burgess Meredith, actor; Paul Newman, actor; Carl Stokes, judge.

COLUMBUS, OHIO

Mayor: Gregory S. Lashutka (to Nov. 1999)
1994 est. population (rank): 635,913 (16)
1990 census population (rank): 632,945 (16); **% change,** 0.5; **Male,** 305,574; **Female,** 327,336; **White,** 471,025; **Black,** 142,748 (22.6%); **American Indian, Eskimo, or Aleut,** 1,469 (0.2%); **Asian or Pacific Islander,** 14,993 (2.4%); **Other race,** 2,675; **Hispanic origin,** 6,741 (1.1%). **1990 population under 18:** 23.7%; **65 and over:** 9.2%; **median age:** 29.4.

Land area: 203.269 sq mi. (526.47 sq km); **Alt.:** Highest, 902 ft.; lowest, 702 ft.

Avg. daily temp.: Jan., 27.1° F; July, 73.8° F

Churches: Protestant, 436; Roman Catholic, 62; Jewish, 5; Other, 8; **City-owned parks:** 203 (12,891 ac.); **Radio stations:** AM, 10; FM, 16; **Television stations:** 9 commercial, 3 PBS

Civilian Labor Force (1995): 554,733; **Unemployed:** 18,233, **Percent:** 3.3; **Per capita personal income:** $13,151

Chamber of Commerce: Columbus Area Chamber of Commerce, P.O. Box 1527, Columbus, Ohio 43216

Columbus, the largest city in Ohio, is the state capital and seat of Franklin county and is located in central Ohio on the Scioto River.

The first structures near downtown Columbus were earthen mounds constructed by Indian tribes known as the Mound Builders. The Indians lived alone in Central Ohio until the 1700s when the first explorers entered the Midwest. The first permanent settlement was founded by a surveyor from Kentucky, Lucas Sullivant, in 1797 and was named Franklinton. The site was laid out as the state capital in 1812 and named to honor Christopher

Columbus and became the capital in 1816. Columbus was chartered as a city in 1834 and annexed Franklinton in 1870. The city's growth was stimulated by the development of transportation facilities—a feeder to the Ohio Canal completed in 1832, the National Road in 1833, and the arrival of the railroad in 1850.

Columbus is a port of entry and a major industrial, commercial, manufacturing, and cultural center. It is the seat of Ohio State University. The city has enjoyed steady growth over the years due to its economic diversity—there is no single activity that dominates the economy.

Famous natives: Warner Baxter, actor; George Bellows, painter; Michael Feinstein, singer, pianist; Eileen Heckart, actress; Jack Nicklaus, golfer; Tom Poston, actor; Eddie Rickenbacker, aviator; Arthur M. Schlesinger, historian; James Thurber, writer; Nancy Wilson, singer.

DALLAS, TEX.

Mayor: Ron Kirk (to 1999)
City Manager: John Ware (apptd. Nov. 1993)
1994 est. population (rank): 1,022,830 (8)
1990 census population (rank): 1,007,618 (8); **% change,** 1.5; **Male,** 495,141; **Female,** 511,736; **White,** 556,760; **Black,** 296,994 (29.5%); **American Indian, Eskimo, or Aleut,** 4,792 (0.5%); **Asian or Pacific Islander,** 21,952 (2.2%); **Other race,** 126,379; **Hispanic origin,** 210,240 (20.9%). **1990 population under 18:** 25.0%; **65 and over:** 9.7%; **median age:** 30.6.
Land area: 378 sq mi. (979 sq km); **Alt.:** Highest, 750 ft.; lowest, 375 ft.
Avg. daily temp.: Jan., 45.0° F; July, 86.3° F
Churches: 1,974 (in Dallas Co.); **City-owned parks:** 296 (47,025 ac.); **Radio stations:** AM, 19; FM, 30; **Television stations:** 10 commercial, 1 PBS
Civilian Labor Force: 570,661; **Unemployed:** 50,526, **Percent:** 8.9; **Per capita personal income (PMSA) 1992:** $22,424
Chamber of Commerce: Dallas Chamber of Commerce, 1201 Elm, Dallas, Tex. 75270

Dallas is the second largest city in Texas and is the seat of Dallas county. It is situated 185 miles northeast of Austin on the Trinity River near the junction of its three forks. It was first settled by Tennessee lawyer John Neely Bryan as a trading post on the Trinity River in 1841. Many historians believe that John Neely Bryan named the city after George Mifflin Dallas, vice president under James K. Polk but there is no official agreement on this. It was incorporated as a town in 1856 and a city in 1871. The city developed as a cotton market in the 1870s and became the chief cotton producing region of Texas.

The economy is highly diversified and the city is the leading commercial, marketing, and industrial center of the southwest. The insurance business is important, and the service sector has experienced rapid growth. Dallas is also a popular tourist and convention city.

Famous natives: Tex Avery, animator, director; Robby Benson, actor; Ernie Banks, baseball player; Bebe Daniels, actress; Linda Darnell, actress; Lee Elder, golfer; Morgan Fairchild, actress; Trini Lopez, singer; Aaron Spelling, producer; Stephen Stills, singer; Sharon Tate, actress; Lee Trevino, golfer.

DENVER, COLO.

Mayor: Wellington Webb (to July 1999)
1994 est. population (rank): 493,559 (25)
1990 census population, sex, & (rank): 467,610 (26); **% change,** 5.5; **Male,** 227,517; **Female,** 240,093; **White,** 337,198; **Black,** 60,046 (12.8%); **American Indian,**

Eskimo, or Aleut, 5,381 (1.2%); **Asian or Pacific Islander,** 11,005 (2.4%); **Other race,** 53,980; **Hispanic origin,** 107,382 (23.0%); **1990 population under 18:** 22.0%; **65 and over:** 13.9%; **median age:** 33.9
Land area: 154.63 sq mi. (400.5 sq km); **Alt.:** Highest, 5,494 ft.; lowest, 5,140 ft.
Avg. daily temp.: Jan., 29.5° F; July, 73.3° F
Churches:[1] Protestant, 859; Roman Catholic, 60; Jewish, 13; **City-owned parks:** 205 (4,166 ac.); **City-owned mountain parks:** 40 (13,600 ac.); **Radio stations:** AM, 23; FM, 20[1]; **Television stations:** 17[1]
Civilian Labor Force: 245,495[2]; **Unemployed:** 17,527[2]; **Percent:** 7.1[2]; **Per capita personal income (PMSA) 1992:** $22,930
Chamber of Commerce: Greater Denver Chamber of Commerce, 1445 Market Street, Denver, Colo. 80202

1. Metropolitan area. 2. Denver City/County.

Denver is the largest city and capital of Colorado and the seat of Denver county. It lies at the foot of the Rocky Mountains and is situated at the junction of the South Platte River and Cherry Creek. The city was born in 1858 when gold was discovered in the sands of Cherry Creek and it began as a tough village of cabins, shacks, and tents. It was incorporated as a city in 1861 and became the territorial capital in 1867. The city is named for James W. Denver, governor of the Kansas Territory which included part of Colorado. The city prospered from the famous gold and silver mines of the 1870s and the 1880s.

Denver International Airport, the first major new airport to be opened in the U.S. in 21 years, opened to passenger traffic on Feb. 28, 1995, at a cost of $4.9 billion. At 53 square miles, it is the largest airport in North America.

Denver is an important cultural, industrial, transportation, tourist, and marketing center. It is also a regional center for many federal government agencies and a leader in the development of western energy resources.

Denver's fastest growing industries include contract construction, real estate, retail trade, and the federal government.

Famous natives: Tim Allen, comedian, actor; Ward Bond, actor; Douglas Fairbanks, Sr., actor; John Hart, newsman; Pat Hingle, actor; Ted Mack, TV host; Barbara Rush, actress; Alan K. Simpson, senator; Paul Whiteman, bandleader; Don Wilson, announcer.

DETROIT, MICH.

Mayor: Dennis W. Archer
1994 est. population (rank): 992,038 (10)
1990 census population (rank): 1,027,974 (7); **% change,** −3.5; **Male,** 476,814; **Female,** 551,160; **White,** 222,316; **Black,** 777,916 (75.7%); **American Indian, Eskimo, or Aleut,** 3,655 (0.4%); **Asian or Pacific Islander,** 8,461 (0.8%); **Other race,** 15,626; **Hispanic origin,** 28,473 (2.8%). **1990 population under 18:** 29.4%; **65 and over:** 12.2%; **median age:** 30.8.
Land area: 143 sq mi. (370 sq km); **Alt.:** Highest, 685 ft.; lowest, 574 ft.
Avg. daily temp.: Jan., 23.4° F; July, 71.9° F
Churches:[1] Protestant, 1,165; Roman Catholic, 89; Jewish, 2; **City-owned parks:** 56 parks (3,843 ac.); 393 sites (5,838 ac.); **Radio stations:** AM, 27; FM, 30 (includes 3 in Windsor, Ont.); **Television stations:** 8[2] (includes 1 in Windsor, Ont.)
Civilian Labor Force (1996): 387,425; **Unemployed:** 33,650, **Percent:** 8.7; **Per capita personal income:** $21,000
Chamber of Commerce: Greater Detroit Chamber of Commerce, 622 W. Lafayette, Detroit, Mich. 48226

1. Six-county metropolitan area. 2. Within four counties of Metro Detroit.

Detroit, the largest city in Michigan, is situated in the southeastern part of the state on the Detroit River. It is the seat of Wayne county. Detroit was incorporated as a city in 1815 and reincorporated in 1824.

Detroit is the oldest city of any size west of the seaboard colonies, having been founded by Antoine de la Mothe Cadillac on July 24, 1701, more than a century before Chicago was founded. The French were the first settlers and they gave the city its name from their word meaning "straight," referring to the 27-mile-long Detroit River which connects Lake Erie and Lake St. Clair. The river forms part of the international boundary, and marks the only point where Canada lies directly south of U.S. territory.

Because of its strategic location, Detroit was fought over by the French, the British, and the Indians. It was the headquarters for the British forces in the Northwest during the American Revolutionary War.

The first steam vessel, the *Walk-in-the-Water*, made its appearance on the Great Lakes in 1818, and Detroit was the western terminus for most of its voyages from Buffalo. Its link to all the important cities on the Great Lakes made it a major exporting port.

Detroit is one of the largest manufacturing cities in the U.S. and is the center of the automobile manufacturing industry, which has experienced a decline to foreign competition in the past decade. The health and medical care sector is important to the economy, and employment in the finance, insurance, and real estate industries has inched up in the Detroit metropolitan area since 1991.

Famous natives: Ralph Bunche, statesman; Francis Ford Coppola, director; Charles Lindbergh, aviator; Madonna, singer; John Mitchell, ex-U.S. Attorney General; George Peppard, actor; Gilda Radner, comedian; Della Reese, singer; Sugar Ray Robinson, boxer; Diana Ross, singer; Tom Selleck, actor; Margaret Whiting, singer.

Grande river near a site west of the present downtown El Paso which he called "El Paso del Rio del Norte," meaning the crossing of the river—the first use of the name "El Paso." In 1659, the mission of Nuestra Senora de Guadalupe was founded on a site that is present-day downtown Ciudad Juárez; the mission is still in use today. In 1682, Spanish colonists from Mexico founded the settlement of Ysleta within the site of the present-day city. However, it wasn't until 1827 that the first permanent settlement at El Paso was established by Juan María Ponce de León. The city's real growth started with the arrival of the Southern Pacific Railroad in 1881. El Paso was incorporated as a city in 1873.

In 1888, Mexico changed the name of Paso del Norte to Ciudad Juárez in honor of Benito Juárez. Later in 1967, the United States agreed to cede a long disputed part of El Paso to Mexico due to changes in the course of the Rio Grande which forms the international boundary between the two countries. El Paso and its sister city of Ciudad Juárez across the U.S./Mexico border are inexorably joined by culture and economy. El Paso and Juárez make up the largest international metroplex in the world.

El Paso is an important port of entry to the U.S. from Mexico. The apparel industry plays a major role in the El Paso area. The high technology, medical device manufacturing, plastics, refining, automotive, food processing, and defense-related industries are important to the economy. El Paso's service sector has experienced the healthiest growth since 1983. El Paso is also a major tourist resort.

Famous natives: Manuel Acosta, artist; Don Bluth, animation director; Vicki Carr, singer; Sam Donaldson, newsman; Judith Ivey, actress; Guy Kibbee, actor; Sandra Day O'Connor, Supreme Court justice; Debbie Reynolds, actress; Irene Ryan, actress.

EL PASO, TEX.

Mayor: Carlos Ramirez
1994 est. population (rank): 579,307 (19)[1]
1990 census population, sex, & (rank): 515,342 (22); **% change,** 12.4; **Male,** 247,163; **Female,** 268,179; **White,** 396,122; **Black,** 17,708 (3.4%); **American Indian, Eskimo, or Aleut,** 2,239 (0.4%); **Asian or Pacific Islander,** 5,956 (1.2%); **Other race,** 93,317; **Hispanic origin,** 355,169 (69.0%). **1990 population under 18:** 31.9%; **65 and over:** 8.7%; **median age:** 28.7
Land area: 247.4 sq mi. (641 sq km); **Alt.:** 4,000 ft.
Avg. daily temp.: Jan., 44.2° F; July, 82.5° F
Churches: Protestant, 320; Roman Catholic, 39; Jewish, 3; others, 20; **City-owned parks:** 116[2] (1,180 ac.); **Radio Stations:** AM, 18; FM, 17; **Television stations:** 6
Civilian Labor Force (1995): 285,100; **Unemployed:** 31,100, **Percent:** 10.9; **Per capita personal income:** $12,790
Chamber of Commerce: El Paso Chamber of Commerce and El Paso Hispanic Chamber of Commerce, 10 Civic Center Plaza, El Paso, Tex. 79944

1. 1997 est. population: 596,804. 2. Includes 109 developed and 7 undeveloped parks.

El Paso, the fourth largest city in Texas and the seat of El Paso county, is located in the far western part of the state on the north bank of the Rio Grande River, opposite the Mexican city of Ciudad Juárez on the south bank.

In 1581, Spanish explorers came through the Pass of the North to test the missionary and mining possibilities of New Mexico. The area had been inhabited for centuries by various Indian groups. On April 30, 1598, Juan de Onate took formal possession of the area for King Philip II of Spain and subsequently crossed the Rio

FORT WORTH, TEX.

Mayor: Kenneth Barr (to May 1999)
City Manager: Bob Terrell
1994 est. population (rank): 451,814 (29) [1]
1990 census population (rank): 447,619 (28); **% change,** 0.9; **Male,** 220,268; **Female,** 227,351; **White,** 285,549; **Black,** 98,532 (22.0%); **American Indian, Eskimo, or Aleut,** 1,914 (0.4%); **Asian or Pacific Islander,** 8,910 (2.0%); **Other race,** 52,714; **Hispanic origin,** 87,345 (19.5%). **1990 population under 18:** 26.6%; **65 and over:** 11.2%; **median age:** 30.3.
Land area: 296.36 sq mi. (768 sq km); **Alt.:** Highest, 780 ft.; lowest, 520 ft.
Avg. daily temp.: Jan., 44.2° F; July, 82.5° F
Churches: 941, representing 72 denominations; **City-owned parks:** 195 (6,321 ac. plus 3,500 ac. in Nature Center); **Radio stations:** AM, 5; FM, 20; **Television stations:** 15 (9 local)
Civilian Labor Force (1996): 244,188; **Unemployed:** 13,758, **Percent:** 5.63; **Per capita personal income (MSA) 1992:** $20,250[2]
Chamber of Commerce: Fort Worth Chamber of Commerce, 777 Taylor Street, Suite 900, Fort Worth, Tex. 76102

1. 1997 est. population: 484,500. 2. Fort Worth–Arlington.

Fort Worth, seat of Tarrant county, is situated in the north central part of Texas on the Trinity River.

The city was founded by Major Ripley Arnold in 1849 as a military outpost on the Trinity River to protect settlers moving westward from frequent Indian attacks. It was named after Gen. William J. Worth, the commander of the Texas army. Fort Worth was incorporated in 1873. Its growth was stimulated in the 1870s by the proximity to the Chisholm cattle trail. It prospered as a meat packing and shipping center when the Texas and Pacific Railway arrived in 1876, and later experienced a new boom when oil was discovered nearby in 1917. The establishment of military installations in the area during both world wars also spurred the economy.

Ft. Worth has traditionally been a diverse center of manufacturing and is not dependent on the oil or financial sectors. The city's industries range from clothing and food products to jet fighters, helicopters, computers, pharmaceuticals, and plastics. Ft. Worth is a national leader in aviation products, electronic equipment, and refrigeration equipment. It is home to a multitude of major corporate headquarters, office, and distribution centers.

Famous natives: Robert Bass, financier; Kate Capshaw, actress; Sandra Heynie, golfer; Patricia Highsmith, writer; Spanky McFarland, actor; R. Bruce Merrifield, Nobelist in chemistry; Roger Miller, singer; Fess Parker, actor; Rex Reed, critic; Johnny Rutherford, auto racer; Liz Smith, columnist.

FRESNO, CALIF.

Mayor: Jim Patterson (to May 2000)
City Manager: Jeffrey M. Reid
1994 est. population (rank): 386,551 (38)[1]
1990 census population (rank): 354,091 (47); **% change,** 9.2; **Male,** 172,241; **Female,** 181,961; **White,** 209,604; **Black,** 29,409 (8.3%); **American Indian, Eskimo, or Aleut,** 3,729 (1.1%); **Asian or Pacific Islander,** 44,358 (12.5%); **Other race,** 67,102; **Hispanic origin,** 105,787 (29.9%). **1990 population under 18:** 31.7%; **65 and over:** 10.1%; **median age:** 28.4.
Land area: 99.38 sq mi. (257.39 sq km); **Alt.:** 328 ft.
Avg. daily temp.: Jan., 45.5° F; July, 81.0° F
Churches: 450 (approximate); **City-owned parks:** 38 (690 ac.); **Radio stations:** AM 11[2]; FM 13[2]; Bilingual 1; **Television stations:** 8[2]
Civilian Labor Force: 174,496; **Unemployed:** 22,708, **Percent:** 13.0; **Per capita personal income (MSA) 1992:** $16,376
Chamber of Commerce: Fresno County and City Chamber of Commerce, P.O. Box 1469, 2331 Fresno St., Fresno, Calif. 93716

1. 1996 est. population: 402,000. 2. Metropolitan area.

Fresno is located in central California, 184 miles southeast of San Francisco and 222 miles northwest of Los Angeles. It is the seat of Fresno county. Fresno was incorporated as a city in 1885.

Fresno began as a station for the Central Pacific Railroad in 1872 and was made the seat of Fresno county in 1874. The city's name is Spanish for the ash trees that the early explorers found in the area.

Fresno is the world capital of the agri-business with 250 different crops produced by 7,500 farmers on 1.9 million irrigated acres, worth $3 billion a year. Fresno county's top five crops are grapes, cotton, tomatoes, cattle and calves, and turkeys. The city is also a trade, financial, media, and commercial center. Its diverse industries include agricultural chemicals, farm equipment, canned fruit and vegetables, clothing, computer software, electric wire, pumps, glass, and plastic products.

Famous natives: Mike Connors, actor; Maynard Dixon, painter; Bruce Furniss, swimmer; Jon Hall, actor; Daryle Lamonica, football player; Sam Peckinpah, director; William Saroyan, novelist; Tom Seaver, baseball player.

HONOLULU, HAWAII

Mayor: Jeremy Harris (to Jan. 2001)
1994 est. population (rank): 385,881 (39)
1990 census population (rank): 377,059 (39)[1]; **% change,** 2.3; **Male,** 186,371; **Female,** 190,688; **White,** 104,038 (27.6%); **Black,** 7,371 (1.95%); **American Indian, Eskimo, or Aleut,** 1,197 (0.3%); **Asian or Pacific Islander,** 259,629 (68.9%); **Other race,** 4,824 (1.3%); **Hispanic origin,** 18,017 (4.8%). **1990 population under 18:** 19.8%; **65 and over:** 15.5%; **median age:** n.a.
Land area: 89 sq mi. (230 sq km); **Alt.:** Highest, 4,025 ft.; lowest, sea level
Avg. daily temp.: Jan., 72.6° F; July, 81° F
Churches: Roman Catholic, 39; Buddhist, 51; Jewish, 2; Protestant and others, 402; **City-owned parks:** 6,146 ac.; **Radio stations:** AM, 18; FM, 13; **Television stations:** 9
Civilian Labor Force (1996 avg.): 428,900[2]; **Unemployed:** 20,950[2], **Percent:** 4.9[2]; **Per capita personal income (1994):** $25,328
Chamber of Commerce: Chamber of Commerce of Hawaii, 1132 Bishop St., Suite 200, Honolulu, Hawaii 96813

1. Census Designated Place; the census bureau does not include the entire city and county in its census of Honolulu. If it did, the 1990 census and rank would be 836,231 (12). 2. City and county.

Honolulu is the capital (on Oahu) and largest city in Hawaii. It is also the seat of Honolulu county. The city and county of Honolulu include the entire island of Oahu, the major island of the state of Hawaii. It is situated in the central Pacific Ocean 2,397 miles westsouthwest of San Francisco. Honolulu's name means "sheltered harbor" and derives from the native words hono meaning "a bay" and lulu meaning "sheltered."

Honolulu's early history was one of turbulence and conflict. One of the last areas on the globe to be explored and exploited by Europeans (it was first visited by British Captain James Cook in 1778), Hawaii was subject to strong pressures from many forces, including American missionaries who arrived in 1820, and opportunistic whalers. These whalers were among those who built Honolulu originally, bringing trade, commerce, and prosperity that led to expansion into the sugar and pineapple industries.

As early as 1814, Russia tried to move in and Russian soldiers built a bastion at the harbor's edge. The British flag was raised in 1843 and French forces occupied Honolulu in 1849. Each time control was given back to the independent kingdom without bloodshed. In 1898, a group of Americans completed a project attempted at intervals during the previous 65 years—annexation to the United States. Honolulu was incorporated as a city in 1907.

Honolulu was bombed by Japan in a surprise attack on the unprepared U.S. naval base at Pearl Harbor on Dec. 7, 1941. This action forced the United States to enter World War II and "Remember Pearl Harbor," became a famous American wartime slogan.

Hawaiian statehood in 1959 and the viability of commercial air travel to the island brought boom times to Honolulu. Tourism is the city's principal industry, followed by federal defense expenditures and agricultural exports (chiefly pineapples).

Famous natives: Hiram Bingham, explorer; Jean Erdman, dancer, choreographer; Hiram Fong, senator; Daniel Inouye, senator; Duke Kahanamoku, surfer, Olympian swimmer; Bette Midler, actress, singer; Kelly Preston, actress; Louise Morgan Sill, author; Don Stroud, actor; Merlin D. Tuttle, biologist, wildlife photographer.

HOUSTON, TEX.

Mayor: Robert C. Lanier (to Dec. 1997)
1994 est. population (rank): 1,702,086 (4)
1990 census population (rank): 1,630,864 (4); **% change,** 4.4; **Male,** 809,048; **Female,** 821,505; **White,**

859,069; **Black,** 457,990 (28.1%); **American Indian, Eskimo, or Aleut,** 4,126 (0.3%); **Asian or Pacific Islander,** 67,113 (4.1%); **Other race,** 242,255; **Hispanic origin,** 450,483 (27.6%). **1990 population under 18:** 26.7%; **65 and over:** 8.3%; **median age:** 30.4.
Land area: 594.03 sq mi. (1,521 sq km); **Alt.:** Highest, 120 ft.; lowest, sea level
Avg. daily temp.: Jan., 51.4° F; July, 83.1° F
Churches: 1,750[2]; **City-owned parks:** 307 (32,598 ac.); **Radio stations:** AM, 22; FM, 32[1]; **Television stations:** 13 commercial, 1 PBS
Civilian Labor Force: 979,931; **Unemployed:** 65,315, **Percent:** 6.7; **Per capita personal income (PMSA) 1992:** $21,737
Chamber of Commerce: Greater Houston Partnership, 1200 Smith, Suite 700, Houston, Tex. 77002

1. Includes annexations since 1970. 2. Harris County.

Houston, the largest city in Texas and seat of Harris county, is located in the southeastern part of the state near the Gulf of Mexico.

Sam Houston was the commander-in-chief of the Texas troops who fought a successful war of rebellion against the domination by Mexico, which had been in possession of Texas. On April 21, 1836, Houston's men won a decisive victory in which the Mexican dictator, Gen. Santa Anna, was taken prisoner and forced to sign the treaty that launched the Republic of Texas. In September, a constitution was ratified, and Houston was elected president. The Texas Republic was recognized by the U.S. and by the major European powers. The present city of Houston was incorporated in 1837 and named after Sam Houston; it was the Republic's first capital.

The port of Houston is a leader in the U.S. in foreign tonnage handled. The city is a major business, financial, science, and technology center. Houston is outstanding in oil and natural gas production and is the energy capital of the world. It is the home of one of the largest medical facilities in the world—the Texas Medical Center—and the focus of the aerospace industry. The Lyndon B. Johnson Space Center is the nation's headquarters for manned spaceflight.

Famous natives: Debbie Allen, choreographer; Lance Alworth, football player; Denton Cooley, heart surgeon; Jim Demaret, golfer; Allen Drury, novelist; Shelly Duvall, actress; A.J. Foyt, auto racer; Howard Hughes, industrialist; Barbara C. Jordan, educator, lawyer, politician; Barbara Mandrell, singer; Annette O'Toole, actress; Dennis and Randy Quaid, actors; Kenny Rogers, singer; Patrick Swayze, actor, dancer.

INDIANAPOLIS, IND.

Mayor: Stephen Goldsmith (to Dec. 31, 1999)
1994 est. population (rank): 752,279 (12)
1990 census population (rank)[2]: 731,311 (13); **% change,** 2.9; **Male,** 352,309; **Female,** 389,643; **White,** 564,447; **Black,** 166,031 (22.4%); **American Indian, Eskimo, or Aleut,** 1,580 (0.2%); **Asian or Pacific Islander,** 6,943 (0.9%); **Other race,** 2,951; **Hispanic origin,** 7,790 (1.0%). **1990 population under 18:** 25.6%; **65 and over:** 11.5%; **median age:** 31.8.
Land area: 352 sq mi. (912 sq km); **Alt.:** Highest, 840 ft.; lowest, 700 ft.
Avg. daily temp.: Jan., 26.0 F; July, 75.1° F
Churches: 1,200[1]; **City-owned parks:** 130 (9,375 ac.); **Radio stations:** AM, 8[3]; FM, 17[3]; **Television stations:** 7[1]
Civilian Labor Force: 441,780[1] **Unemployed:** 20,820[1], **Percent:** 4.7[1]; **Per capita personal income (MSA) 1992:** $20,992
Chamber of Commerce: Indianapolis Chamber of Commerce, 320 N. Meridian St., Indianapolis, Ind. 46204

1. Marion County. 2. Consolidated city. 3. Metropolitan area.

Indianapolis, the largest city in Indiana and seat of Marion county, is located in the central part of the state on the West Fork of the White River. Its name derives from combining "Indiana" with "polis," the Greek word for city.

Indianapolis was settled in 1820 and, in 1825, its site was chosen as the state capital and it was incorporated as a city in 1832 and reincorporated in 1838. The city's growth began when the railroad reached it in 1847. Toward the end of the 19th century, the discovery of nearby natural gas and the start of the automobile industry hastened its industrial expansion. On Jan. 1, 1970, Indianapolis merged with the surrounding Marion county.

Indianapolis is an important center of a rich agricultural region and a major grain and livestock market. It is also a focal point of commerce, transportation, and manufacturing for the region. Some leading industries are electronics, pharmaceuticals, and food processing. The financial sector, and service and insurance industries are growing rapidly.

Indianapolis is the site of the world-famous 500-mile automobile race and the Indiana State Fair.

Famous natives: Monte Blue, actor; David Letterman, TV host; Steve McQueen, actor; Jane Pauley, TV newscaster; Booth Tarkington, author; Kurt Vonnegut, Jr., author; Harry Von Zell, announcer; Clifton Webb, actor.

JACKSONVILLE, FLA.

Mayor: John Delaney (to June 30, 1999)
1994 est. population (rank): 665,070 (15)
1990 census population (rank)[1]: 635,230 (15); **% change,** 4.7; **Male,** 328,737; **Female,** 344,234; **White,** 489,604; **Black,** 163,902 (24.4%); **American Indian, Eskimo, or Aleut,** 1,904 (0.3%); **Asian or Pacific Islander,** 12,940 (1.9%); **Other race,** 4,621; **Hispanic origin,** 17,333 (2.6%). **1990 population under 18:** 25.9%; **65 and over:** 10.7%; **median age:** 31.5.
Land area: 759.6 sq mi. (1,967 sq km); **Alt.:** Highest, 71 ft.; lowest, sea level
Avg. daily temp.: Jan., 53.2° F; July, 81.3° F
Churches: Protestant, 794; Roman Catholic, 21; Jewish, 5; others, 22; **City-owned parks and playgrounds:** 138 (1,522 ac.); **Radio stations:** AM, 14; FM, 16; **Television stations:** 6 commercial, 1 PBS, 1 religious
Civilian Labor Force: 328,211; **Unemployed:** 24,051, **Percent:** 7.3; **Per capita personal income (MSA) 1992:** $19,146
Chamber of Commerce: Jacksonville Area Chamber of Commerce, Jacksonville, Fla. 32202

1. Consolidated city.

Jacksonville, Florida's largest city, is located in Duval county in the northeast corner of Florida on the banks of the St. Johns River and adjacent to the Atlantic Ocean. It is the largest metropolitan area in northeast Florida and southeast Georgia.

Starting in the 16th century, French, Spanish, and English explorers and colonists were attracted to the region by the St. Johns River. The site was settled by Lewis Hogans in 1816. Jacksonville was laid out in 1822 and was named after Gen. Andrew Jackson, the first military governor of Florida. It was incorporated as a city in 1832.

During the Civil War, much of the city was destroyed by Union forces who occupied Jacksonville four times. The city was rebuilt and, following the development of its harbor and the railroads, fast became the transportation hub and leading industrial city in Florida by the 1880s. In 1968, Jacksonville annexed Duval county.

Jacksonville is the transportation hub and distribution focal point in the state. The strength of the city's economy lies in its broad diversification. The area's economy is balanced among distribution, financial services, biomedical, consumer goods, information services, manufacturing, and other industries. Jacksonville has the largest deepwater port in the South Atlantic and is the leading port in the U.S. for automobile imports.

Famous natives: Mae Axton, songwriter; Pat Boone, singer; Judy Canova, comedian; Harold Carmichael, football player; Merion C. Cooper, producer, director; Billy Daniels, vocalist, Storm Davis, athlete; Bob Hayes, athlete; Wanda Hendrix, actress; James Weldon Johnson, author, educator; John Rosamond Johnson, musician, composer; Mark McCumber, pro golfer; Ray Mercer, boxer; Charles "Hoss" Singleton, songwriter; Bill Terry, Baseball Hall of Fame; Donnie Van Zant, rock musician; Ronnie Van Zant, rock musician; Leeroy Yarbrough, auto racer.

KANSAS CITY, MO.

Mayor: Emanuel Cleaver II (to April 1999)
City Manager: Larry J. Brown (apptd. Nov. 1993)
1994 est. population (rank): 443,878 (31)
1990 census population (rank): 434,829 (31); **%
change:** 2.1; **Male,** 206,965; **Female,** 228,181; **White,** 290,572; **Black,** 128,768 (29.6%); **American Indian, Eskimo, or Aleut,** 2,144 (0.5%); **Asian or Pacific Islander,** 5,239 (1.2%); **Other race,** 8,423; **Hispanic origin,** 17,017 (3.9%). **1990 population under 18:** 24.8%; **65 and over:** 12.9%; **median age:** 32.8.
Land area: 317 sq mi. (821 sq km); **Alt.:** Highest, 1,014 ft.; lowest, 722 ft.
Avg. daily temp.: Jan., 28.4° F; July, 80.9 F
Churches: 1,100 churches of all denominations[1]; **City-owned parks and playgrounds:** 189 (10,647 ac.); **Radio stations:** AM, 14; FM, 19[1]; **Television stations:** 7[1]
Civilian Labor Force: 239,600; **Unemployed:** 15,400, **Percent:** 6.4; **Per capita personal income (MSA) 1992:** $20,948[2]
Chamber of Commerce: Chamber of Commerce of Greater Kansas City, 911 Main St., Kansas City, Mo. 64105

1. Metropolitan area. 2. Kansas City, Mo.–Kan.

Kansas City is the largest city in Missouri. It is located in the western part of the state, at the junction of the Missouri and Kansas Rivers. Kansas City is located in Jackson, Clay, Platte, and Cass counties.

In 1821, the year Missouri entered the Union, French trader François Chouteau came from St. Louis to establish a trading post on the site of the present city to take advantage of the growing fur trade with the Kansa, Osage, Wyandotte, and other tribes. In 1833, a settlement was laid out by John Calvin McCoy and developed, called the town of Westport Landing. The community became the Town of Kansas and was incorporated as a city in 1850 and renamed Kansas City in 1889. The city's name reflects its Native American heritage—its site was within the territory of the Kansa or Kaw Indians.

The city grew rapidly in the mid-1880s as the starting point for gold prospectors and settlers heading westward. The coming of the Missouri-Pacific railroad in 1865 and the spanning of the Missouri River by the Hannibal Bridge in 1869 also contributed to the city's growth, and it prospered as a center for the nation's cattle business.

The Kansas City metropolitan area once known primarily for agriculture and manufacturing, has expanded its economic base to include strong growth in areas of telecommunications, banking and finance, and the service industry. A transportation hub since the 1800s, the area enjoys a national and regional prominence as a distribution and manufacturing center. Kansas City ranks nationally as first in greeting card publishing, frozen food storage and distribution, and first in hard winter

wheat marketing, second in wheat flour production, and third in auto and truck assembly. The area is one of ten federal regional centers and employs over 25,000 in local, state, and federal government. The city is also a regional center for health care, employing over 55,000 in this industry.

Famous natives: Robert Altman, director; Edward Asner, actor; Burt Bacharach, composer; Noah and Wallace Beery, actors; Robert Russell Bennett, composer; Jeanne Eagels, actress; Jean Harlow, actress; Ted Shawn, dancer, choreographer; Casey Stengel, baseball player; Virgil Thompson, composer; Tom Watson, golfer.

LAS VEGAS, NEV.

Mayor: Jan Jones
1994 est. population (rank): 327,878 (49)[1]
1990 census population (rank): 258,204 (63); **% change:** 27.0; **Male,** 130,981; **Female,** 127,314; **White,** 202,549 (78.4%); **Black,** 29,529 (11.4%); **American Indian, Eskimo, or Aleut,** 2,282 (0.9%); **Asian or Pacific Islander,** 9,325 (3.6%); **Other race,** 14,610; **Hispanic origin,** 32,369 (12.5%); **1990 population under 18:** 25.0%; **65 and over:** 10.3%; **median age:** 32.5.
Land area: 83.3 sq mi. (1,215.7 sq km); **elevation: 1,174 ft.**
Max., Min. daily temp.: Jan., 34–57° F; July, 76–106° F
Churches: over 500 churches and synagogues; **Radio stations:** AM 12; FM 21 **Television stations:** 7
Civilian Labor Force: (1990 census): 131,001; **Unemploye** 19,043, **Percent:** 4.9; **Per capita personal income (MSA) 1992:** $19,994
Chamber of Commerce: 711 East Desert Inn Road, Las Vegas, Nev. 89109-2797

1. 1995 est. population: 371,809.

Las Vegas, seat of Clark County in southeastern Nevada, is the largest city in the state and one of the fastest growing cities in the United States. Between April 1990 and July 1994, the Las Vegas metropolitan area population increased by 26%, growing from 852,646 to 1,076,267.

The area was discovered by Spanish explorers in 1829. The site of Las Vegas ("The Meadows" in Spanish) was originally a watering place for travelers on their way to southern California. It was first settled by Mormons in 1855, who were attracted by its artesian springs. They abandoned their settlement two years later in 1857 and the U.S. Army established Fort Baker there in 1864. In 1867, Las Vegas was detached from the Arizona Territory and joined Nevada.

The town was established in 1905 and started to grow with the arrival of San Pedro, Los Angeles, and Salt Lake Railroad in 1905. However, its growth did not really begin until shortly after 1931, when the Nevada legislature legalized gambling in an effort to lift the state from the Great Depression. The construction of nearby Hoover Dam economically aided the area as well.

The Las Vegas that we know today basically began after World War II when the idea of large hotels along the brand new "Strip" was developed.

Las Vegas is the Marriage Capital of America. There are 50 wedding chapels in the city. Tourism and the convention industry are the city's major source of income. In addition, manufacturing, government, warehousing, and trucking are major sources of employment. Many high-technology companies are also located there. Three of the reasons for that are the city's proximity to sophisticated military technology centers like Nellis Air Force Base, the top-secret Nuclear Testing Grounds, and the College of Engineering at the University of Nevada, Las Vegas.

Las Vegas has a favorable business climate: taxes are relatively low, and there are neither city nor state income taxes. This is because gambling and sales taxes, paid by tourists, have allowed the city and state governments to avoid personal and corporate income taxes.

Popular nearby tourist attractions are Hoover Dam and Lake Mead (largest man-made lake in U.S.), Lake Mojave, the Mt. Charleston Recreation Area, Red Rock Canyon, and the Death Valley National Monument.

Famous natives: Andre Agassi, tennis player; Clara Bow, actress; Howard Hughes, industrialist and film producer; B.B. King, blues singer, guitarist; Jack Kramer, tennis player; Phyllis McGuire, singer; Benjamin Siegel, hotel-casino promoter; Orson Welles, actor, producer; Joe Williams, jazz singer.

LONG BEACH, CALIF.

Mayor: Beverly O'Neill (to April 1998)
City Manager: James C. Hankla
1994 est. population (rank): 433,852 (34)[1]
1990 census population (rank): 429,321 (32); **% change,** 1.1; **Male,** 216,685; **Female,** 212,748; **1996 est. population breakdown: White,** 168,074 (39.3%); **Black,** 63,376 (14.8%); **American Indian, Eskimo, or Aleut,** 2,322 (0.5%); **Asian or Pacific Islander,** 66,767 (15.6%); **Hispanic origin,** 125,269 (29.3%). **1990 population under 18:** 25.5%; **65 and over:** 10.8%; **median age:** 30.0.
Land area: 49.8 sq mi. (129 sq km); **Alt.:** Highest, 170 ft.; lowest, sea level
Avg. daily temp.: Jan., 55.2° F; July, 72.8° F
Churches: 236; **City-owned parks:** 64 (2,000 ac.); **Radio stations:** AM, 2; FM, 2; **Television stations:** 8 (metro area)
Civilian Labor Force: 205,390; **Unemployed:** 14,810, **Percent:** 7.2; **Per capita personal income (PMSA) 1992:** $21,434[2]
Chamber of Commerce: Long Beach Area Chamber of Commerce, One World Trade Center, Suite 350, Long Beach, Calif. 90831-0350

1. 1996 est. population: 425,807 (32). 2. Los Angeles–Long Beach MSA.

Long Beach is the fifth largest city in California and is situated on San Pedro Bay, south of Los Angeles, in Los Angeles county.

The town was laid out and settled in 1881 by developer W.E. Willmore who sold lots in the site as a seaside resort community called Willmore City. It was renamed Long Beach for its 8½-mi. beach in 1884. The city was incorporated in 1888 and reincorporated in 1897.

Long Beach is a major industrial port. The services and manufacturing industries together account for over 30% of the local economy. Retail trade and government are the next largest sectors, accounting for an additional 30% of employment. Tourism is also important to the economy. Minor industries include transportation, communication and utilities, wholesale trade, finance, insurance, and real estate. Long Beach's economy has been adversely affected by cutbacks in the defense and aircraft production industries.

Famous natives: Jack Anderson, journalist; Jennifer Bartlett, artist; Barbara Britton, actress; Nicholas Cage, actor; Spike Jones, orchestra leader; Sally Kellerman, actress; Billie Jean King, tennis player; Martha Rae Watson, track; Heather Watts, dancer.

LOS ANGELES, CALIF.

Mayor: Richard Riordan (to June 2001)
1994 est. population (rank): 3,448,613 (2)
1990 census population (rank): 3,485,557 (2); **% change,** –1.1; **Male,** 1,750,055; **Female,** 1,735,343;
White, 1,841,182; **Black,** 487,674 (14.0%); **American Indian, Eskimo, or Aleut,** 16,379 (0.5%); **Asian or Pacific Islander,** 341,807 (9.8%); **Other race,** 798,356; **Hispanic origin,** 1,391,411 (39.9%). **1990 population under 18:** 24.8%; **65 and over:** 10.0%; **median age:** 30.7.
Land area: 467.4 sq mi. (1,210.57 sq km); **Alt.:** Highest, 5,081 ft.; lowest, sea level
Avg. daily temp.: Jan., 57.2° F; July, 74.1° F
Churches: 2,000 of all denominations; **City-owned parks:** 355 (15,357 ac.); **Radio stations:** AM, 35; FM, 53; **Television stations:** 19
Civilian Labor Force: 1,827,505; **Unemployed:** 198,626, **Percent:** 10.9; **Per capita personal income (PMSA) 1992:** $21,434[1]
Chamber of Commerce: Los Angeles Chamber of Commerce, 404 S. Bixel St., Los Angeles, Calif. 90017

1. Los Angeles–Long Beach.

Los Angeles is the largest city in California and the second largest urban area in the nation. It is located in the southern part of the state on the Pacific Ocean. It is the seat of Los Angeles county. Geographically, it extends more than 40 miles from the mountains to the sea.

The Spanish explorer, Gaspar de Portolá visited the site in 1769. On Sept. 4, 1781, the Mexican Provincial Governor, Filipe de Neve, founded "El Pueblo de Nuestra Señora la Reina de Los Angeles"—meaning "The Village of Our Lady, the Queen of the Angels." The pueblo became the capital of the Mexican province, Alta California, and it was the last place to surrender to the U.S. at the time of the American occupation in 1847. By the Treaty of Guadalupe Hidalgo in 1848, Mexico ceded California to the United States and Los Angeles was incorporated as a city in 1850.

The city's phenomenal growth was brought about primarily by its equable climate, which attracted people and industry from all parts of the nation; the development of its citrus-fruit industry; the discovery of oil in the area during the early 1890s; the development of its man-made harbor—its port is one of the busiest in the U.S.; and the growth of the motion picture industry in the early 20th century. Today, Hollywood is a suburb of Los Angeles.

Los Angeles is a major hub of shipping, manufacturing, industry, and finance, and is world renowned in the entertainment and communications fields. It is a favorite vacation destination and attracts millions of tourists to the area each year from all over the world.

Los Angeles county is the nation's largest manufacturing center, surpassing Chicago, New York, and Detroit. The ports of Los Angeles and Long Beach are second only to New York as the largest customs district in the United States.

Major employers in the Los Angeles Five-County area are in the business and management sector. Growth in the key wholesale industries—apparel and textiles, furniture, jewelry, and toys—and the boom in industrial trade have been forecast for the region in the nineties. Other important sectors are health services and international trade and investment. The aerospace and technology industries have declined due to defense cutbacks but are still expected to be a viable part of the region's economy.

Famous natives: Busby Berkeley, choreographer, director; Marge Champion, dancer, choreographer; Jackie Coogan, actor; Jackie Cooper, actor; Linda Fratianne, figure skater; Jodie Foster, actress, director; John Gavin, actor, diplomat; Pancho Gonzalez, tennis player; Cynthia Gregory, ballerina; Jerome Hines, basso; Dustin Hoffman, actor; Theodore Harold Maiman, laser inventor; Marilyn Monroe, actress; Isamu Noguchi, sculptor; Leonard Slotkin, conductor; Duke Snider, baseball player; Adlai E. Stevenson, statesman; Madeleine Stowe, actress; Darryl Strawberry, baseball player.

MEMPHIS, TENN.

Mayor: W.W. Herenton (to Dec. 1999)
1994 est. population (rank): 614,289 (18)
1990 census population (rank): 618,652 (18); **% change,** –0.7; **Male,** 285,010; **Female,** 325,327; **White,** 268,600; **Black,** 334,737 (54.8%); **American Indian, Eskimo, or Aleut,** 960 (0.2%); **Asian or Pacific Islander,** 4,805 (0.8%); **Other race,** 1,235; **Hispanic origin,** 4,455 (0.7%). **1990 population under 18:** 26.9%; **65 and over:** 12.2%; **median age:** 31.5.
Land area: 277 sq mi. (702 sq km); **Alt.:** Highest, 417 ft.
Avg. daily temp.: Jan., 39.6° G; July, 82.1° F
Churches: 2000+; **Parks and playgrounds:** 230 (13,291 ac.); **Radio stations:** AM, 14; FM, 15; **Television stations:** 6
Civilian Labor Force: 292,819; **Unemployed:** 25,640, **Percent:** 8.8; **Per capita personal income (MSA) 1992:** $19,517
Chamber of Commerce: Memphis Area Chamber of Commerce, P.O. Box 224, Memphis, Tenn. 38103

Memphis, the largest city in Tennessee and the seat of Shelby county, is located in the southwestern corner of the state, on the Mississippi River.

The first settlers of Memphis were the Chickasaw Indians, who had a village named Chisca there on the bluffs overlooking the Mississippi River. Hernando de Soto, in 1541, is said to have had his first glimpse of the Mississippi from the site of Memphis; and in the next century, Joliet and Marquette stopped there to trade with the Indians. The French explorer Sieur de La Salle tried to claim the region for France in 1682 and built Fort Prudhomme there. The area was ceded to the United States by the Chickasaw Indians in 1818. Memphis was officially established in 1819 by three enterprising businessmen from Nashville, James Winchester, John Overton, and future president Andrew Jackson. Jackson named it after the ancient Egyptian city because of its Nilelike site on the Mississippi River. Memphis was incorporated as a city in 1826 and became an important Mississippi River port.

During the Civil War, Memphis was a Confederate military center. In 1862, Federal forces won a gunboat battle on the river at Memphis and General Sherman was enabled to take the city.

Memphis's population was devastated by several yellow-fever epidemics during the 1870s and the city did not recover its prosperity until the end of the 19th century.

Memphis is one of the country's largest inland ports and is known as "America's Distribution Center" serving the northeast, southeast, and southwest regions of the country. Memphis is a leader in agribusiness, cultivating soybeans, rice, grain sorghum, winter wheat, corn, and livestock raising. The city is the world's largest trading center for spot cotton, handling over 40% of the nation's spot cotton crops annually. It is the largest hardwood lumber trading and processing center in the world and is estimated to be the nation's third largest total food processor.

Health care and related activities such as medical education and biomedical research is Memphis's largest industry, bringing over $2.5 billion a year to the local economy. Also important are high tech communications.

Famous natives: Kathy Bates, actress; Dixie Carter, actress; Rosalind Cash, singer; Aretha Franklin, singer; Morgan Freeman, actor; Al Green, singer; George Hamilton, actor; Anfernee "Penny" Hardaway, basketball player; Isaac Hayes, singer; Hal Holbrook, actor; Benjamin Hooks, organization official; B.B. King, singer; Hal Needham, director; Charlie Rich, singer; Cybill Shepherd, actress; Robert Siodmak, director Fred Smith, business executive; Rufus Thomas, singer; Kemmons Wilson, business executive.

MIAMI, FLA.

Mayor: Joe Carollo (to Nov. 1997)
City manager: Edward Marquez (apptd. Nov. 1996)
1994 est. population (rank): 373,024 (42)
1990 census population (rank): 358,648 (46); **% change,** 4.0; **Male,** 173,223; **Female,** 185,325; **White,** 235,358; **Black,** 98,207 (27.4%); **American Indian, Eskimo, or Aleut,** 545 (0.2%); **Asian or Pacific Islander,** 2,272 (0.6%); **Other race,** 22,166; **Hispanic origin,** 223,964 (62.5%). **1990 population under 18:** 23.0%; **65 and over,** 16.6%; **median age,** 36.0.
Land area: 34.3 sq mi. (89 sq km); **Water area:** 19.5 sq mi.; **Alt.:** Average, 12 ft.
Avg. daily temp.: Jan., 67.1° F; July, 82.4° F
Churches (Dade County): Protestant, 850; Roman Catholic, 61; Jewish, 64; **City-owned parks (Miami):** 109; **Radio stations (Dade County):** 29; **Television stations (Dade County):** 9 TV, 1 Cable
Civilian Labor Force: 181,684; **Unemployed:** 21,348, **Percent:** 11.8; **Per capita personal income (PMSA) 1992:** $17,124
Chamber of Commerce: Greater Miami Chamber of Commerce, 1601 Biscayne Blvd., Miami, Fla. 33132

Miami, the second largest city in Florida and seat of Dade County, is located in the southeastern part of the state, on Biscayne Bay.

The area was once the home of the Tequesta Indians until they were nearly wiped out by European diseases and warfare brought on by two centuries of Spanish control of Florida. Miami was founded in 1870 near the site of Ft. Dallas built in 1835 during the Seminole Indian wars. The city's name is probably derived from "Mayaimi," the Indian word for "big water."

Miami is the only U.S. city to have been conceived by a woman. Julia Tuttle, a Clevelander, arrived there in 1891 and bought several hundred acres on the bank of the Miami River. She convinced New York financier Henry M. Flagler of the area's vast potential and persuaded him to extend his Florida East Coast Railroad to Miami in 1896, the year the city was incorporated. Flagler dredged Miami harbor, built the renowned Royal Palm Hotel, which opened Jan. 1, 1897, and promoted the area as a winter playground. Tourists flocked there and, by 1910, the city was a thriving recreational area. Miami survived the collapse of a land speculation boom in the 1920s, and severe hurricanes in 1926 and 1935, and continued to grow in the aftermath of these disasters.

Miami experienced one of its most monumental population boosts during the 1960s when about 260,000 Cuban refugees arrived on its shore seeking freedom. They made a great impact on Miami, now a bilingual metropolis, and spurred economic growth.

Miami is an international banking and finance center and the city has the greatest concentration of international and Edge Act banks[1] in North America, which constitute a major employment base. Greater Miami[2] has a highly diversified economy with over 170 multinational Miami-based companies, a bevy of Fortune 500 companies, and a rapidly growing manufacturing and distribution center. Miami ranks number one in Florida for total manufacturing income, employment, and number of manufacturing establishments. Greater Miami is the nation's leader in biomedical technology and the health care sector is a major industry. It is also part of an area known as the Computer Coast of Florida, and its growing technologies include computers, electrical engineering, and plastics manufacturing.

Miami is one of the world's leading year-round resort centers with tourism contributing over 60% of the area's economy. The city is a major transportation hub and the port of Miami is the world's largest cruise port and a major seaport for cargo. The famous island resort of

Miami Beach, incorporated in 1915, is part of Greater Miami and is connected to Miami by four causeways.
1. Edge Act banks may make only foreign loans and accept foreign deposits. 2. Greater Miami is made up of 27 municipalities of which the City of Miami is the largest.

Famous natives: Fernando Bujones, dancer; Steve Carlton, baseball player; Debbie Harry, singer; Dick Howser, baseball player and manager; Sidney Poitier, actor; Janet Reno, Attorney General of the U.S.; Ben Vereen, actor; Ellen Zwilich, composer.

MILWAUKEE, WIS.

Mayor: John O. Norquist (to April 2000)
1994 est. population (rank): 617,044 (17)[1]
1990 census population (rank): 628,088 (17); **%
change,** –1.8; **Male,** 296,837; **Female,** 331,251; **White,**
398,033; **Black,** 191,255 (30.5%); **American Indian,
Eskimo, or Aleut,** 5,858 (0.9%); **Asian or Pacific
Islander,** 11,817 (1.9%); **Other race,** 21,125; **Hispanic
origin,** 39,409 (6.3%). **1990 population under 18:**
27.4%; **65 and over:** 12.4%; **median age:** 30.3.
Land area: 95.8 sq mi. (248 sq km); **Alt.:** 580.60 ft.
Avg. daily temp.: Jan., 18.7° F; July, 70.5° F
Churches: 411; **County-owned parks:** 14,785 ac.; **Radio
stations:** AM, 9; FM, 18; **Television stations:** 11
Civilian Labor Force (1995): 296,700; **Unemployed:**
14,900, **Percent:** 5.0; **Per capita personal income
(PMSA) 1993:** $22,786
Chamber of Commerce: Metropolitan Milwaukee Association of Commerce, 828 N. Broadway, Milwaukee, Wis. 53202; Milwaukee Minority Chamber of Commerce, 2821 N. 4th St., Milwaukee, Wis. 53212; Hispanic Chamber of Commerce, 1125 W. National Ave., Milwaukee, Wis. 53204

1. 1996 est. population: 620,609.
Milwaukee, the largest city in Wisconsin and seat of Milwaukee county, is located in the southeastern part of the state on Lake Michigan.
French missionaries visited the site of Milwaukee in the seventeenth century, but it was not until 1795 that Jacques Vieau established a fur-trading post there. The first permanent white settler, Vieau's son-in-law, Solomon Juneau, an agent of the American Fur Company, made his home there in 1818. The settlement merged with several neighboring villages in 1838 to form Milwaukee, and the city was incorporated in 1846. Its name is derived from an Algonquian Indian word Milo-aki meaning "beautiful land." A large wave of German immigrants arrived after 1848 and contributed greatly to the city's political, economic, and cultural development.
Milwaukee is one of the great industrial centers in the country and one of the largest Great Lakes ports. Currently, port commerce runs over 3.3 million tons per year.
Its economy was forged by heavy industries but is now diversified. Manufacturing remains strong and Milwaukee manufacturers are national leaders in lithographic commercial printing and the production of medical diagnostic instruments, small gasoline engines, malt beverages, iron and steel forgings, mining and construction machinery, robotics, speed changers and drives, and electronic controls. Milwaukee's high-tech manufacturing community is the ninth-largest among the nation's 31 major metropolitan areas. Once known as a "beer town," less than one percent of Milwaukee's workforce is involved in beer production. However, beer still plays an important role and almost 11% of the nation's malt beverage is produced there.
Tourism is important to the economy and about 5 million people visit Milwaukee every year.

Famous natives: Donald Gramm, bass-baritone; Woody Herman, band leader; Al Jarreau, singer; George F. Kennan, diplomat; Alfred Lunt, actor; Douglas MacArthur, army general; Pat O'Brien, actor; Tom Snyder, TV personality; Speech, member of rap group, "Arrested Development;" Spencer Tracy, actor; Gene Wilder, actor; Jerry and David Zucker, film producers.

MINNEAPOLIS, MINN.

Mayor: Sharon Sayles-Belton (to Jan. 1998)
1994 est. population (rank): 354,590 (47)
1990 census population (rank): 368,383 (42); **%
change,** –3.7; **Male,** 178,671; **Female,** 189,712; **White,**
288,967; **Black,** 47,948 (13.0%); **American Indian,
Eskimo, or Aleut,** 12,335 (3.3%); **Asian or Pacific
Islander,** 15,723 (4.3%); **Other race,** 3,410; **Hispanic
origin,** 7,900 (2.1%). **1990 population under 18:**
20.6%; **65 and over:** 13.0%; **median age:** 31.7
Land area: 58.7 sq mi. (143 sq km); **Alt.:** Highest, 945 ft.;
lowest, 695 ft.
Avg. daily temp.: Jan., 11.2° F; July, 73.1° F
Churches: 419; **City-owned parks:** 153; **Radio stations:**
AM, FM, 15 (metro area); **Television stations:** 6
(metro area)
Civilian Labor Force: 204,477; **Unemployed:** 9,905,
Percent: 4.8; **Per capita personal income (MSA)
1992:** $23,284[1]
Chamber of Commerce: Greater Minneapolis Chamber of Commerce, Young Quinlan Building, 81 S. Ninth Street, Suite 200, Minneapolis, Minn. 55402-3223

1. Minneapolis–St. Paul Minn.–Wis.
Minneapolis, the largest city in Minnesota and seat of Hennepin county, is located in the southeast central part of the state on the Mississippi River. It is adjacent to its "twin city" of St. Paul. The Minneapolis-St. Paul Standard Metropolitan Statistical Area is the 15th largest in the United States.
In 1680, Father Louis Hennepin visited the future site of Minneapolis and gave the Falls of St. Anthony their name. Lieutenant Zebulon Pike made a treaty with the Sioux Indians in 1805–06 by which they ceded to the whites land including the Falls of St. Anthony and the site of Minneapolis. Fort Snelling was built in 1819–20 and, in 1823, the government built a lumber and flour mill. Flour milling became the major industry of early Minneapolis and made the city the milling capital of the world. The town of St. Anthony was established on the east bank of the Mississippi in 1848 and the town of Minneapolis grew up on the opposite bank of the river. The name Minneapolis is a combination of the Dakota Sioux word "minna" for water and the Greek word "polis" for city. Minneapolis was incorporated as a city in 1867 and, in 1872, the city of St. Anthony (chartered in 1860) was annexed to it. After the spread of the railroads in the 1870s, Minneapolis became the gateway to the Northern Great Plains.
Minneapolis is a center of industry and commerce serving a large agricultural region. During the 20th century, manufacturing, food processing, milling, computers, health services, and graphic arts developed as Minneapolis's major industries. Sixteen Fortune 500 industrial and 17 Fortune service companies are headquartered there. The city is the home of the world's largest cash grain market and is the headquarters of the Ninth Federal Reserve Bank.

Famous natives: La Verne, Maxene, Patti Andrews, singers; James Arness, actor; Lew Ayres, actor; Patty Berg, golfer; Virginia Bruce, actress; J. Paul Getty, oil executive; Peter Graves, actor; George Roy Hill, director; Cornell MacNeil, baritone; Ralph Meeker, actor; Westbrook Pegler, columnist; Prince, singer; Harrison Salisbury, journalist; Charles Schulz, cartoonist; Anne Tyler, writer; Bud Wilkinson, football player; David Winfield, baseball player.

NASHVILLE-DAVIDSON, TENN.

Mayor: Philip N. Bredesen
1994 est. population (rank): 504,505 (24)[1]
1990 census population (rank)[2]: 488,366 (25); **% change,** 3.3; **Male,** 242,492; **Female,** 268,292; **White,** 381,740; **Black,** 119,273 (23.4%); **American Indian, Eskimo, or Aleut,** 1,162 (0.2%); **Asian or Pacific Islander,** 7,081 (1.4%); **Other race,** 1,528; **Hispanic origin,** 4,775 (0.9%). **1990 population under 18:** 22.8%; **65 and over:** 11.6%; **median age:** 32.6.
Land area: 533 sq mi. (1,380 sq km); **Altitude:** Highest, 1,100 ft.; lowest, approx. 400 ft.
Avg. daily temp.: Jan., 36.7° F; July, 76.6° F
Churches: Protestant, 781; Roman Catholic, 18; Jewish, 3; **City-owned parks:** 76 (6,650 ac.); **Radio stations:** AM, 15; FM, 19; **Television stations:** 11
Civilian Labor Force (1997): 313,636; **Unemployed:** 9,225, **Percent:** 2.9; **Per capita personal income (1995):** $23,655
Chamber of Commerce: Nashville Area Chamber of Commerce, 161 Fourth Ave. North, Nashville, Tenn. 37219

1. 1997 est. population: 536,650. 2. Consolidated city.

The consolidated city of Nashville-Davidson is the capital and second largest city in Tennessee and is located in the north central part of the state on the Cumberland River. It is the seat of Davidson county.

During the winter of 1779–80, James Robertson and John Donelson founded a settlement at Big Salt Lick by the Cumberland River at the present site of the city. They built forts on both sides of the river naming one of them Fort Nashborough in honor of Francis Nash, a Revolutionary War general. In 1784, the town was named Nashville and was incorporated as a city in 1806.

Nashville became the capital of Tennessee in 1843 and was the seat of Davidson county until 1963 when it merged with the county to become Nashville-Davidson.

Nashville's best known industries are recording, publishing, and the distribution of music, especially country music. The city is a port of entry and an important industrial and commercial center serving the Upper South. Its diverse economy includes automobiles, apparel, publishing, insurance, and banking. Health care services is the largest industry. Nashville is the home of several religious organizations and is a major tourist attraction and convention center.

Famous natives: Gregg Allman, singer; Rita Coolidge, singer; Al Gore, vice president; Red Grooms, artist; Barbara Howar, hostess, writer; Minnie Pearl, comedienne; Annie Potts, actress; Paula Robeson, flutist; Dinah Shore, actress, singer.

NEW ORLEANS, LA.

Mayor: Marc H. Morial
1994 est. population (rank): 484,149 (27)
1990 census population (rank): 496,938 (24); **% change,** −2.6; **Male,** 230,883; **Female,** 266,055; **White,** 173,554; **Black,** 307,728 (61.9%); **American Indian, Eskimo, or Aleut,** 759 (0.2%); **Asian or Pacific Islander,** 9,678 (1.9%); **Other race,** 5,219; **Hispanic origin,** 17,238 (3.5%). **1990 population under 18:** 27.5%; **65 and over,** 13.0%; **median age,** 31.6.
Land area: 199.4 sq mi. (516 sq km); **Alt.:** Highest, 15 ft.; lowest, −4 ft.
Avg. daily temp.: Jan., 52.4° F; July, 77° F
Churches: 712; **City-owned parks:** 165 (299 ac.); **Radio stations:** AM, 12; FM, 14; **Television stations:** 7
Civilian Labor Force: 205,610[1]; **Unemployed:** 15,055[1], **Percent:** 7.3[1]; **Per capita personal income (MSA)** 1992: $18,087
Chamber of Commerce: The Chamber/New Orleans and

the River Region, 301 Camp Street, New Orleans, La. 70130

1. New Orleans City/Orleans Parish.

New Orleans, the largest city in Louisiana and seat of Orleans Parish, is located in the southeastern part of the state, between the Mississippi River and Lake Ponchartrain.

One of the few cities of the nation that has been under three flags, New Orleans has belonged to Spain, France, and the U.S. The French founded it in 1718 and named it in honor of the Duke of Orleans. In 1762, France ceded the city and the territory to Spain. On 1800, the territory was returned to France, but government authorities did not take over until 1803, only 20 days before the region became part of the U.S. in the Louisiana Purchase.

New Orleans is famous for its French Quarter, which attracts both tourists and gourmets. The Mardi Gras—a week of carnival held in New Orleans before the beginning of Lent—is the most spectacular festival in the U.S., and is a popular tourist attraction.

New Orleans is one of the world's greatest international ports, one of the largest in the nation, and a major focus of the city's economy. New Orleans is home to the corporate offices of oil companies with major offshore operations in the Gulf of Mexico, as well as the distribution and service centers of offshore equipment suppliers and fabricators. The manufacturing industry is a significant part of the economy, with petroleum, petrochemical, shipbuilding, and aerospace industries all playing a role. The New Orleans region also functions as a mining, processing, and transportation center for other minerals, principally sulfur. Service industries are playing a larger role, with health care and telecommunications leading the way. The information services sector is one of the fastest-growing, and the New Orleans region is widely regarded as a leading center of medicine and health care in the South.

Tourism has grown rapidly in recent years and New Orleans hosts more than seven million visitors annually.

Famous natives: Louis Armstrong, musician; Truman Capote, author; Fats Domino, musician; Louis Gottschalk, pianist, composer; Bryant Gumbel, TV personality; Lillian Hellman, playwright, author; Al Hirt, musician; Mahalia Jackson, singer; Dorothy Lamour, actress; Wynton Marsalis, musician; Huey Newton, activist; Marguerite Piazza, soprano; Rusty Staub, baseball player; Ben Turpin, comedian; Shirley Verrett, mezzo-soprano; Carl Weathers, actor; Del Williams, football player.

NEW YORK, N.Y.

Mayor: Rudolph W. Guiliani (to Dec. 1997)
Borough Presidents: Bronx, Fernando Ferrer; Brooklyn, Howard Golden; Manhattan, Ruth W. Messinger; Queens, Claire Shulman; Staten Island, Guy V. Molinari
1994 est. population (rank): 7,333,253 (1)
1990 census population (rank): 7,322,564 (1)[1]; **% change,** 0.1; **Male,** 3,437,687; **Female,** 3,884,877; **White,** 3,827,088; **Black,** 2,102,512 (28.7%); **American Indian, Eskimo, or Aleut,** 27,531 (0.4%); **Asian or Pacific Islander,** 512,719 (7.0%); **Other race,** 852,714; **Hispanic origin,** 1,783,511 (24.4%).[1] **1990 population under 18:** 23.0%; **65 and over:** 13.0%; **median age:** 33.7.
Land area: 321.8 sq mi. (826.68 sq km) (Queens, 112.1; Brooklyn, 81.8; Staten Island, 60.2; Bronx, 44.0; Manhattan, 23.7); **Alt.:** Highest, 410 ft.; lowest, sea level
Avg. daily temp.: Jan., 31.8° F; July, 76.7° F
Churches: Protestant, 1,766; Jewish, 1,256; Roman Catholic, 437; Orthodox, 66; **City-owned parks:** 1,701 (27,118 ac.); **Radio stations:** AM, 13; FM, 18; **Television stations:** 6 commercial, 1 public
Civilian Labor Force: 3,311,000; **Unemployed:** 359,000,

Percent: 10.8; **Per capita personal income (PMSA) 1992:** $27,039

Chamber of Commerce: New York Chamber of Commerce and Industry, One Battery Park Plaza, New York, N.Y. 10004

1. Race breakdown figures according to N.Y.C. Dept. of City Planning: White, non-Hispanic, 3,163,125; Black, non-Hispanic, 1,847,049; American Indian, Eskimo and Aleut, non-Hispanic, 17,871; Asian and Pacific Islander, non-Hispanic, 489,157; Hispanic, 1,783,511.

New York City is the largest city in the United States. It is located in the southern part of New York State, at the mouth of the Hudson River (also known as North River as it passes Manhattan Island).

In 1609, Henry Hudson, who worked for the Dutch East India Company, sailed up the river that now bears his name and went as far as Albany. Five years later, a permanent settlement was established at what is now New York, but it was originally called New Amsterdam by the Dutch governors. One of them, Peter Minuit, was said to have bought Manhattan Island from the Indians for $24 worth of beads, buttons, and trinkets. In 1664, Great Britain's Duke of York sent a fleet which quietly seized the settlement from the Dutch, without bloodshed, and rechristened the colony in honor of the Duke.

Control of New York passed to the young U.S. at the end of the Revolutionary War, and George Washington was inaugurated President in New York's old City Hall. Congress met in New York from 1785 to 1790.

In 1898, when Greater New York was chartered, the city expanded to include the following five boroughs which are also counties in New York State: Manhattan (New York county); Brooklyn (Kings county); Bronx (Bronx county); Queens (Queens county); and Staten Island (Richmond county).

There is a growing effort among Staten Island residents to separate from Greater New York and become an independent city of Staten Island.

The Big Apple is the most populous city in the United States, a major world capital, and a world leader in finance, the arts, and communications. The city is also the center of advertising, fashion, publishing, and radio broadcasting in the United States. New York has many museums, art galleries, and educational institutions. The port of New York is one of the finest in the world. The city is the home of the United Nations and is headquarters for some of the world's largest corporations.

Famous natives: Kareem Abdul-Jabbar, basketball player; Woody Allen, actor, director; Robert Anderson, playwright; Martina Arroyo, soprano; Jean Arthur, actress; Lauren Bacall, actress; James Baldwin, novelist; Harry Belafonte, singer, actor; Humphrey Bogart, actor; James Cagney, actor; Maria Callas, soprano; Paddy Chayefsky, playwright; Aaron Copland, composer; Sammy Davis, Jr., singer, actor; Agnes de Mille, choreographer; Robert De Niro, actor; Eamon De Valera, ex-president of Ireland; Gertrude Elion, Nobel Prize in medicine; Lou Gehrig, baseball player; George Gershwin, composer; Ira Gershwin, lyricist; Jackie Gleason, actor; Hank Greenberg, baseball player; Rita Hayworth, actress; Lena Horne, singer; Julia Ward Howe, poet, reformer; Washington Irving, author; Henry James, novelist; John Jay, statesman, jurist; Michael Jordan, basketball player; Jerome Kern, composer; Sandy Koufax, baseball player; Michael Landon, actor; Roy Lichtenstein, painter; Vince Lombardi, football player, coach; Chico, Groucho, Harpo, Zeppo Marx, comedians; Herman Melville, novelist; Yehudi Menuhin, violinist; Ethel Merman, singer, actress; James Michener, novelist; Arthur Miller, playwright; Eugene O'Neill, playwright; J. Robert Oppenheimer, nuclear physicist; Al Pacino, actor; Jan Peerce, tenor; Roberta Peters, soprano; Elmer Rice, playwright; Jerome Robbins, choreographer; Norman Rockwell, painter, illustrator; Eleanor Roosevelt, reformer, humanitarian; Theodore Roosevelt, ex-president; Jonas Salk, polio researcher; Beverly Sills, soprano; Neil Simon, playwright; Risë Stevens, mezzo-soprano; Barbra Streisand, singer, actress; Ed Sullivan, TV personality; Fats Waller, pianist; Mae West, actress; Edith Wharton, novelist; Rosalyn Yalow, Nobel Prize in medicine.

OAKLAND, CALIF.

Mayor: Elihu Mason Harris (to Jan. 1998)
City Manager (interim): Kofi Bonner
1994 est. population (rank): 366,926 (44)[1]
1990 census population (rank): 372,242 (39); **% change,** −1.4; **Male,** 178,824; **Female,** 193,418; **White,** 120,849; **Black,** 163,335 (43.9%); **American Indian, Eskimo, or Aleut,** 2,371 (0.6%); **Asian or Pacific Islander,** 54,931 (14.8%); **Other race,** 30,756; **Hispanic origin,** 51,711 (13.9%). **1990 population under 18,** 24.9%; **65 and over,** 12.0%; **median age:** 32.7.
Land area: 53.9 sq mi. (140 sq km); **Alt.:** Highest, 1,700 ft.; lowest, sea level
Avg. daily temp.: Jan., 49.0° F; July, 63.7° F
Churches: 374, representing over 78 denominations in the City; over 500 churches in Alameda County; **City-owned parks:** 2,196 ac.; **Radio stations:** AM, 1; **Television stations:** 1 commercial
Civilian Labor Force: 180,624; **Unemployed:** 18,148, **Percent:** 10.0; **Per capita personal income (PMSA) 1992:** $24,359
Chamber of Commerce: Oakland Chamber of Commerce, 475 Fourteenth St., Oakland, Calif. 94612-1903

1. 1997 est. population: 386,100

Oakland is located in the west central part of California on the east side of San Francisco Bay. It is the seat of Alameda county.

Don Luis Peralta first settled the site of Oakland in 1820 when he established the Rancho San Antonio. The gold rush of 1849 attracted more people to the area and the city's population continued to grow after a ferry service to San Francisco was started in 1851. Oakland was incorporated as a town in 1852 and as a city in 1854. It was named after the numerous oak trees found in the area. Oakland became the western terminus of the Central Pacific Railroad in 1869 and the seat of Alameda county in 1873.

During the latter part of the 19th century and also in 1910, additional territory was annexed to Oakland and the city assumed its present size. In 1906, thousands of people fled to Oakland in the aftermath of the San Francisco earthquake and settled there permanently, furthering the city's growth. Oakland's economic development continued to rise with the opening of the San Francisco-Oakland Bay Bridge in 1936.

Oakland is a major center of culture and commerce. It is an important container shipping port and the terminus of three transcontinental railroads. Oakland's industries include shipbuilding, food processing, chemicals, pharmaceuticals, electrical and high technology manufacturing. Oakland is also a leading importer of foreign cars. The city is the headquarters of many national and international corporations.

Famous natives: Buster Crabbe, actor; Frederick Cottrell, inventor; Dennis Eckersley, athlete; Hammer, singer, dancer, songwriter; Rod McKuen, singer, composer; Russ Meyer, producer, director; Eddie (Anderson) Rochester, actor; George Stevens, director; Amy Tan, writer; Jo Van Fleet, actress.

OKLAHOMA CITY, OKLA.

Mayor: Ron Norick (to April 1998)
City Manager: Don Bown
1994 est. population (rank): 463,201 (28)
1990 census population (rank): 444,724 (29); **% change,** 4.2; **Male,** 214,466; **Female,** 230,253; **White,** 332,539; **Black,** 71,064 (16.0%); **American Indian,**

Eskimo, or Aleut, 18,794 (4.2%); **Asian or Pacific Islander,** 10,491 (2.4%); **Other race,** 11,831; **Hispanic origin,** 22,033 (5.0%). **1990 population under 18:** 26.0%; **65 and over:** 11.9%; **median age:** 32.4.
Land area: 608.2 sq mi. (1,575 sq km); **Alt.:** Highest, 1,320 ft.; lowest, 1,140 ft.
Avg. daily temp.: Jan., 35.9° F; July, 82.1° F
Churches: Roman Catholic, 25; Jewish, 2; Protestant and others, 741; **City-owned parks:** 138 (3,944 ac.);
Television stations: 8; **Radio stations:** AM, 10; FM, 14
Civilian Labor Force: 325,050; **Unemployed:** 11,040, **Percent:** 3.4; **Per capita personal income (MSA) 1994:** $19,031
Chamber of Commerce: Greater Oklahoma City Chamber of Commerce, 123 Park Ave., Oklahoma City, Okla. 73102

Oklahoma City, the state capital and seat of Oklahoma county, is the largest city in Oklahoma. It is located in the central part of the state on the North Canadian River.

Oklahoma City sprang into being almost overnight. On April 22, 1889, the government threw open the territory for settlement, and there was a classic rush across the line to stake claims. Within a short time, a sprawling tent city sprang up near the Santa Fe railroad railroad tracks and Oklahoma City was a bustling town of 10,000. The city was incorporated in 1890 and replaced Guthrie as the state capital in 1910. Oil was discovered in the city in 1928 and petroleum production became a mainstay of the city's economy.

Oklahoma City is the wholesale and distributing center for the state, and the city's stockyards are the largest stocker and feeder cattle market in the world. Following the decline of the energy sector, Oklahoma City is fostering a private entrepreneurial environment and a more diversified economy. Within the service sector, health services are projected to grow, followed by retail trade and business services. Aerospace, distribution, and telecommunications have been targeted for business attraction. Nearby Tinker Air Force Base, one of the world's largest air depots, is a major city employer.

Famous natives: Johnny Bench, baseball; Lon Chaney, Jr., actor; Ralph Ellison, writer; Kay Francis, actress; Dale Robertson, actor; Ted Shackleford, actor; Pamela Tiffin, actress Vince Gill, country singer.

OMAHA, NEB.

Mayor: Hal Daub (to 2001)
1994 est. population (rank): 345,033 (48)
1990 census population (rank): 335,719 (48); **% change,** 2.8; **Male,** 160,392; **Female,** 175,403; **White,** 281,603; **Black,** 43,989 (13.1%); **American Indian, Eskimo, or Aleut,** 2,274 (0.7%); **Asian or Pacific Islander,** 3,412 (1.0%); **Other race,** 4,517; **Hispanic origin,** 10,288 (3.1%). **1990 population under 18:** 25.4%; **65 and over:** 12.9%; **median age:** 32.2.
Land area: 112 sq mi. (290 sq km); **Alt.:** Highest, 1,270 ft.
Avg. daily temp.: Jan., 20.2° F; July, 77.7° F
Churches: Protestant, 246; Roman Catholic, 44; Jewish, 4; **City-owned parks:** 164 (over 7,400 ac.); **Radio stations:** AM, 7; FM, 13; **Television stations:** 4
Civilian Labor Force: 177,387; **Unemployed:** 8,298, **Percent:** 4.7; **Per capita personal income (MSA) 1992:** $20,242[1]
Chamber of Commerce: Omaha Chamber of Commerce, 1301 Harney St., Omaha, Neb. 68102

1. Omaha, Neb.–Iowa.
Omaha, the largest city in Nebraska and the seat of Douglas county, is located in the eastern part of the state on the west bank of the Missouri River opposite Council Bluffs, Iowa.

The area was visited by the Lewis and Clark expedition in 1804, and the U.S. Army built Ft. Atkinson nearby in 1819. Pierre Cabanne established a fur-trading post at the site in 1825. The first Mormon migrants wintered there in 1846–47 on their way to Utah. The city grew rapidly as the most northerly supply point for overland wagons to the Far West.

The city was officially founded in 1854 after the Nebraska Territory was opened for settlement. It was named for the Omaha Indians living nearby, whose tribal name means "those who go upstream or against the current." Omaha was incorporated as a city in 1857 and was the capital of the Nebraska Territory from 1855 to 1867. The city continued to thrive as a point of entry and a major transportation center when the Union Pacific trans-continental railroad arrived in 1869.

Omaha is a major market for food processing, telecommunications, and insurance. Other important industries include electrical equipment, finance, as well as printing and publishing.

Famous natives: Fred Astaire, dancer, actor; Max Baer, boxer; Ronald Boone, former NBA professional; Robert Boozer, former NBA professional; Marlon Brando, actor; Montgomery Clift, actor; Gerald Ford, ex-president; Bob Gibson, baseball; Swoosie Kurtz, actress; Melvin Laird, ex-Secretary of Defense; Dorothy McGuire, actress; Nick Nolte, actor; Gale Sayers, football; Malcolm X, political activist; Paul Williams, singer, composer.

PHILADELPHIA, PA.

Mayor: Edward G. Rendell (to Jan. 2000)
1994 est. population (rank): 1,524,249 (5)
1990 census population (rank): 1,585,577 (5); **% change,** –3.9; **Male,** 737,763; **Female,** 847,814; **White,** 848,586; **Black,** 631,936 (39.9%); **American Indian, Eskimo, or Aleut,** 3,454 (0.2%); **Asian or Pacific Islander,** 43,522 (2.7%); **Other race,** 58,079; **Hispanic origin,** 89,193 (5.6%). **1990 population under 18:** 23.9%; **65 and over:** 15.2%; **median age:** 33.2.
Land area: 136 sq mi. (352 sq km); **Alt.:** Highest, 440 ft.; lowest, sea level
Avg. daily temp.: Jan., 31.2° F; July, 76.5° F
Churches: Roman Catholic, 133; Jewish, 55; Protestant and others, 830; **City-owned parks:** 630 (10,252 ac.); **Radio stations:** AM, 40[1]; FM, 43[1]; **Television stations:** 14[1]
Civilian Labor Force (1997 est.): 652,126[1]; **Unemployed:** 41,085[1], **Percent:** 8.8[2]; **Per capita personal income (PMSA) 1994:** $25,220[1]
Chamber of Commerce: Philadelphia Chamber of Commerce, 1234 Market Street, Suite 1800, Philadelphia, Pa. 19107

1. Philadelphia City/County.
Philadelphia, the largest city in Pennsylvania and seat of Philadelphia county (coterminous), is located in the southeastern part of the state at the junction of the Schuylkill and Delaware Rivers.

Philadelphia, the "City of Brotherly Love," was settled in 1681 by Capt. William Markham, who, with a small band of colonists, was sent out by his cousin, William Penn. Penn arrived the following year.

In the period before the American Revolution, the city outstripped all others in the colonies in education, arts, science, industry, and commerce. In 1774–76, the First and Second Continental Congresses met in Philadelphia; and, from 1781–83, the city was the capital of the U.S. under the Articles of Confederation. In 1790, it became the nation's capital under the Constitution and remained so until the seat of the federal government moved to Washington in 1800.

Within a half-century of the founding of the nation at Independence Hall, Philadelphia had emerged as the "world's greatest workshop." The steam locomotives and hat factories of the 19th century have been replaced by diverse manufacturing specialties such as chemicals (including pharmaceuticals), medical devices, transportation equipment, and printing and publishing. In the services sector, Philadelphia is a major net "exporter" in subsectors such as health services, insurance carriers, legal services, and architecture and engineering services.

The city abounds in landmarks of early American history, including Independence Hall and the Liberty Bell.

Famous natives: Marian Anderson, contralto; Frankie Avalon, singer, actor; John, Lionel, and Ethel Barrymore, actors; Edmund Bacon, city planner; Kevin Bacon, actor; Boyz II Men, R&B group Mary Cassatt, artist; Wilt Chamberlain, basketball player; Chubby Checker, singer; Bill Cosby, actor; Stuart Davis, painter; Thomas Eakins, painter, sculptor; Fabian, singer; W.C. Fields, comedian; Benjamin Franklin, inventor, statesman; Frank Furness, architect; Stan Getz, saxophonist; Grace (Kelly), Princess of Monaco; Walt Kelly, cartoonist; Jack Klugman, actor; Patti LaBelle, singer; Mario Lanza, singer, actor; George McClellan, general; Margaret Mead, anthropologist; Edgar Allen Poe, author; Anna Quindlen, writer, Pulitzer Prize winner; Man Ray, painter; Betsy Ross, flagmaker; Bobby Rydell, singer; Will Smith, actor; Jacqueline Susann, novelist; Robert Venturi, architect.

PHOENIX, ARIZ.

Mayor: Skip Rimsza (to Oct. 1999)
City Manager: Frank Fairbanks (appt. May 1990)
1994 est. population (rank): 1,048,949 (7)[1]
1990 census population (rank): 984,309 (9); **% change,** 6.6; **Male,** 487,589; **Female,** 495,814; **White,** 803,332; **Black,** 51,053 (5.2%); **American Indian, Eskimo, or Aleut,** 18,225 (1.9%); **Asian or Pacific Islander,** 16,303 (1.7%); **Other race,** 94,490; **Hispanic origin,** 197,103 (20.0%). **1990 population under 18:** 27.2%; **65 and over,** 9.7%; **median age,** 31.1.
Land area: 469.3 sq mi. (1,215.5 sq km); **Alt.:** Highest, 2,740 ft.; lowest, 1,017 ft.
Avg. daily temp.: Jan., 53.6° F; July, 93.5° F
City-owned parks: 200 (30,412 ac.); **Radio stations:** AM, 20; FM, 20; **Television stations:** 9 commercial; 1 PBS
Civilian Labor Force: 1,482,000; **Unemployed:** 51,200, **Percent:** 3.3; **Per capita personal income (MSA)** 1992: $19,018
Chamber of Commerce: Phoenix Chamber of Commerce, 201 N. Central, Phoenix, Ariz. 85073

1. 1997 est. population: 1,187,944.

Phoenix, the capital of Arizona and seat of Maricopa county, is the largest city in the state. It is located in the center of Arizona on the Salt River.

The prehistoric Hohokam Indians first settled the area about 300 B.C.E. and dug a system of extensive irrigation canals for farming. The Indian culture mysteriously broke up in the 1400s. The site was permanently resettled again by Jack Swilling and "Lord Darrell" Duppa about 1867. Because the city was founded on the ruins of the ancient civilization, it was named Phoenix after the legendary Phoenix bird that could regenerate itself. The irrigation canals were restored for farming, and ranching and prospecting began in the surrounding area. The city quickly grew as an important trading center.

Phoenix was incorporated as a city in 1881 and was made the territorial capital in 1889. It became the state capital when Arizona was admitted to the Union in 1912.

Phoenix is a center of agriculture and commerce. Major industries include government, agricultural products, aerospace technology, electronics, air-conditioning, leather goods, and Indian arts and crafts. The city of Phoenix is renowned as a leader in local government management and received the 1993 Bertelsmann Foundation award for the best managed city in the world.

Famous natives: Lynda Carter, actress; Joan Ganz Cooney, TV executive; Alice Cooper, musician; Arthur A. Fletcher, government official; Barry Goldwater, politician; Stevie Nicks, musician; Charles S. Robb, politician; Mare Winningham, actress.

PITTSBURGH, PA.

Mayor: Tom Murphy (to Jan. 1998)
1994 est. population (rank): 358,883 (45)
1990 census population (rank): 369,879 (40); **% change,** –3.0; **Male,** 171,722; **Female,** 198,157; **White,** 266,791; **Black,** 95,362 (25.8%); **American Indian, Eskimo, or Aleut,** 671 (0.2%); **Asian or Pacific Islander,** 5,937 (1.6%); **Other race,** 1,118; **Hispanic origin,** 3,468 (0.9%). **1990 population under 18:** 19.8%; **65 and over,** 17.9%; **median age:** 34.6.
Land area: 55.5 sq mi. (144 sq km); **Alt.:** Highest, 1,240 ft.; lowest, 715 ft.
Avg. daily temp.: Jan., 26.7° F; July, 72.0° F
Churches: Protestant, 348; Roman Catholic, 86; Jewish, 28; Orthodox, 26; **City-owned parks and playgrounds:** 270 (2,572 ac.); **Radio stations:** AM, 12; FM, 20; **Television stations:** 11
Civilian Labor Force: 164,100; **Unemployed:** 8,700, **Percent:** 5.3; **Per capita personal income (MSA)** 1992: $24,957
Chamber of Commerce: The Chamber of Commerce of Greater Pittsburgh, 3 Gateway Center, Pittsburgh, Pa. 15222

Pittsburgh, the second largest city in Pennsylvania and seat of Allegheny county, is located in the southwestern part of the state at the junction where the Allegheny and Monongahela Rivers join to form the Ohio River.

Some of the first inhabitants of the area were the Shawnee, Seneca, Delaware, and Iroquois Indians who had left the area by 1754. That year a detachment of troops from Virginia put a fort on the site of present Pittsburgh (Ft. Prince George) considering it a strategic spot. Following the original Virginia settlers, the French seized the spot and named it Ft. Duquesne; and, in 1758, the British took it away from the French. The British built a new fort and named it after the British Prime Minister, William Pitt. A town developed around the fort and was incorporated as the City of Pittsburgh in 1816.

By the late 1800s, Pittsburgh had become a world leader in iron and steelmaking, and it remained so for nearly a century. In the early 1980s, the country's domestic steel industry collapsed causing major upheavals in Pittsburgh's manufacturing sector.

The Pittsburgh region underwent a successful diversified economic transition, shifting from heavy industries to light manufacturing, advanced technologies such as industrial automation, advanced materials, software engineering and biomedical technology, medicine, education, finance, and corporate services. Pittsburgh is a national leader in health care services and is the world's leading center for organ transplantation. The city is a hub of international business and was ranked eighth by Fortune 500 as a major corporate headquarters center.

Pittsburgh is also a major U.S. transportation center and is one of the nation's largest inland ports in terms of tonnage.

Famous natives: Rachel Carson, ecologist; Henry Steele Commager, historian; Bill Cullen, radio and TV entertainer; John Davidson, singer, actor; Billy Eckstine, singer; Erroll Garner, jazz pianist; Scott Glenn, actor; Martha Graham, dancer, choreographer; George S. Kaufman, playwright; Michael Keaton, actor; Gene Kelly, actor, dancer; Oscar Levant, pianist; Andrew Mellon, financier; Adolphe Menjou, actor; William Powell, actor; Mary Roberts Rinehart, novelist; Peter Sellars, theater director; David O. Selznick, producer; Joseph Wambaugh, novelist; Andy Warhol, artist; August Wilson, playwright.

PORTLAND, ORE.

Mayor: Vera Katz (to Jan. 1997)
1994 est. population (rank).: 450,777 (30)
1990 census population (rank): 438,802 (30); **% change,** 2.7; **Male,** 211,914; **Female,** 225,405; **White,** 370,135; **Black,** 33,530 (7.7%); **American Indian, Eskimo, or Aleut,** 5,399 (1.2%); **Asian or Pacific Islander,** 23,185 (5.3%); **Other race,** 5,070; **Hispanic origin,** 13,874 (3.2%). **1990 population under 18:** 21.9%; **65 and over,** 14.6%; **median age:** 34.5.
Land area: 137.8 sq mi. (357 sq km); **Alt.:** Highest, 1073 ft.; lowest, sea level
Avg. daily temp.: Jan., 38.9° F; July, 67.7° F
Churches: Protestant, 450; Roman Catholic, 48; Jewish, 9; Buddhist, 6; other, 190; **City-owned parks:** 200 (over 9,400 ac.); **Radio stations:** AM: 14, FM: 14; **Television stations:** 5 commercial, 1 public
Civilian Labor Force: 248,724; **Unemployed:** 18,372, **Percent:** 7.4; **Per capita personal income (PMSA) 1992:** $20,681
Chamber of Commerce: Portland Chamber of Commerce, 221 NW 2nd Ave., Portland, Ore. 97209

Portland, the largest city in Oregon and seat of Multnomah county, is located in the northwestern part of the state on the Willamette River.

Lewis and Clark camped at the site of Portland in 1805 on their expedition across the continent. Portland was founded in 1845 and was almost called Boston after the city in Massachusetts. Its two founders, Amos Lovejoy from Massachusetts and Francis Pettygrove from Maine, flipped a coin to decide the name of the new town. Pettygrove won the toss and named the place Portland after his hometown in Maine. Portland was incorporated as a city in 1851.

Portland's growth was stimulated during the 1850s as a supply base for the California gold rush, the development of its salmon and lumber industries, and by the arrival of the railroad in 1883. The city continued to grow during 1879 to 1900 as a supply point for the Alaska gold rush and as the site of the Lewis and Clark Centennial Exposition in 1905.

The port of Portland leads the west in grain exports and is among the top five auto import centers in the United States. The port ranks third in overall volume behind Los Angeles and Long Beach.

Portland has a diverse economy with a broad base of manufacturing, distribution, wholesale and retail trade, regional government, and business services. Major manufacturing industries include machinery, electronics, metals, transportation equipment, and lumber and wood products. High technology is a thriving part of Portland's economy with over 500 high tech companies located in the metropolitan area. Tourism is also important to Portland's economy.

Famous natives: James Beard, food expert; Pietro Belluschi, architect; Richard Fosbury, high jumper; Matt Groening, cartoonist; Margaux Hemingway, actress; Phil Knight, founder of Nike; Terrance Knox, actor; Jeff Lorber, jazz musician; Linus Pauling, chemist; Jane Powell, singer, actress; Ahmad Rashad, football player, sportscaster; Susan Ruttan, actress; Pat Schroeder, congressperson; Doc Severinson, band leader; Norton Simon, business executive; Sally Ann Struthers, actress; Gus Van Sant, film director; Lindsay Wagner, actress; Mitch Williams, baseball pitcher.

SACRAMENTO, CALIF.

Mayor: Joe Serna, Jr. (to March 2000)
1994 est. population (rank): 373,964 (41)[1]
1990 census population (rank): 369,365 (42); **% change,** 1.2; **Male,** 178,737; **Female,** 190,628; **White,** 221,963; **Black,** 56,521 (15.3%); **American Indian, Eskimo, or Aleut,** 4,561 (1.2%); **Asian or Pacific Islander,** 55,426 (15.0%); **Other race,** 30,894; **Hispanic origin,** 60,007 (16.2%). **1990 population under 18:** 26.2%; **65 and over,** 12.1%; **median age:** 31.8.
Land area: 98 sq mi. (254 sq km);
Avg. daily temp.: Jan., 47.1° F; July, 76.6° F
City park & recreational facilities: 134+ (1,427+ ac.); **Television stations:** 7
Civilian Labor Force: 185,283 (1994); **Unemployed:** 16,418, **Percent:** 7.7; **Per capita personal income (PMSA) 1992:** $20,398
Chamber of Commerce: Sacramento Chamber of Commerce, 917 7th St., Sacramento, Calif. 95814; West Sacramento Chamber of Commerce, 834-C Jefferson Blvd., Sacramento, Calif. 95691

1. 1995 est. population: 396,032.

Sacramento is the capital and seventh largest city in California and is the seat of Sacramento county. It is located in the north central part of the state at the confluence of the Sacramento and American Rivers.

In 1839, German-born Swiss citizen John Augustus Sutter obtained a grant from the Mexican governor to establish a colony for fellow Swiss emigrants on a large tract of land in the vicinity which he named New Helvetia (New Switzerland) and established Fort Sutter there as a trading post.

After gold was discovered on Sutter's property in 1848, the settlement rapidly expanded as the prominent supply point for gold prospectors coming from the East. Sacramento was laid out in 1848 and named after the principal river in California which ran beside it. The river's name in Spanish honors the Holy Sacrament. It became incorporated as a city in 1849 and was made the state capital in 1854. Sacramento was the terminus of the first railroad in 1856 and the western terminus of the Pony Express in 1860.

The city has always been a hub of river transportation and is a major deep-water port connected to the Pacific Ocean. Sacramento's economy is highly diversified and, along with state government and military installations, its industries include aerospace, high technology, furniture, chemicals, pharmaceuticals, meat packing, and food processing of crops from the Central Valley.

The defense sector of the economy declined and Mather Air Force Base and the Army Depot were closed in 1995.

Famous natives: Joan Didion, author; Mark Goodson, TV producer; Tom Hanks, actor; Henry Hathaway, director; Anthony M. Kennedy, Supreme Court justice; Molly Ringwald, actress.

ST. LOUIS, MO.

Mayor: Clarence Harmon (to April 2001)
1994 est. population (rank): 368,215 (43)
1990 census population (rank): 396,685 (34); **% change,** –7.2; **Male,** 180,680; **Female,** 216,005; **White,** 202,085; **Black,** 188,408 (47.5%); **American Indian, Eskimo, or Aleut,** 950 (0.2%); **Asian or Pacific Islander,** 3,733 (0.9%); **Other race,** 1,509; **Hispanic origin,** 5,124 (1.3%). **1990 population under 18:** 25.2%; **65 and over:** 16.6%; **median age:** 32.8.
Land area: 61.4 sq mi. (159 sq km); **Alt.:** Highest, 616 ft.; lowest, 413 ft.
Avg. daily temp.: Jan., 28.8° F; July, 78.9° F
Churches: 900[1]; **City-owned parks:** 89 (2,639 ac.); **Radio stations:** AM, 21; FM 27[1]; **Television stations:** 6 commercial; 1 PBS
Civilian Labor Force: 179,278; **Unemployed:** 14,379, **Percent:** 8.0; **Per capita personal income (MSA) 1992:** $22,700[2]
Chamber of Commerce: St. Louis Regional Commerce and Growth Association, 100 S. Fourth St., Ste. 500, St. Louis, Mo. 63102

1. Metropolitan area. 2. St. Louis, Mo.–Ill.

St. Louis, the second largest city in Missouri, is located in the east central part of the state on the Mississippi River. The city is independent and is not part of any county.

St. Louis was founded by the French in 1764 when Auguste Chouteau established a fur-trading post and Pierre Laclède Liguest, a New Orleans merchant, founded a town in February 1764 at the present site. They named it after King Louis XV of France and his patron saint, Louis IX. From 1770 to 1803, St. Louis was a Spanish possession and retroceded to France in 1803 in accordance with the Treaty of San Ildefonso (1800), only to be acquired by the U.S. as part of the Louisiana purchase that year.

The town was incorporated in 1809. From 1812 to 1821, St. Louis was the capital of the Missouri Territory and was incorporated as a city in 1822.

John Jacob Astor opened the Western branch of the American Fur Company in 1819 and the city prospered during the early part of the 19th century as a center for the transportation of the fur trade. St. Louis's commercial growth continued as a major transportation hub with the development of steamboat traffic and the later expansion of the railroads in the 1850s. The world-famous Louisiana Purchase Exposition was held here in 1904.

Manufacturing is important to the city's economy, and its highly developed industries include automobiles, aircraft and space technology, metal fabrication, beer, steelmaking, chemicals, food processing, and storage and distribution.

The giant stainless steel Gateway Arch, 630 feet high, standing on the banks of the Mississippi symbolizes St. Louis as the Gateway to the West.

Famous natives: Josephine Baker, singer; Yogi Berra, baseball player; Grace Bumbry, mezzo-soprano; Morris Carnovsky, actor; T.S. Eliot, poet; Eugene Field, poet; Redd Foxx, comedian; Joe Garagiola, baseball player; John Goodman, actor; Betty Grable, actress; Dick Gregory, comedian; Al Hirschfeld, cartoonist; Kevin Kline, actor; David Merrick, producer; Vincent Price, actor; Judy Rankin, golfer; Leon Spinks, boxer; Herbert Bayard Swope, journalist; Sara Teasdale, poet; Helen Traubel, soprano; Roy Wilkins, civil rights leader.

SAN ANTONIO, TEX.

Mayor: Howard Peak
City Manager: Alexander E. Briseno (apptd. April 27, 1990)
1994 est. population (rank): 998,905 (9)[1]
1990 census population (rank): 935,393 (10); **% change,** 6.8; **Male,** 450,695; **Female,** 485,238; **White,** 676,082; **Black,** 65,884 (7.0%); **American Indian, Eskimo, or Aleut,** 3,303 (0.4%); **Asian or Pacific Islander,** 10,703 (1.1%); **Other race,** 179,961; **Hispanic origin,** 520,282 (55.6%). **1990 population under 18:** 29.0%; **65 and over:** 10.5%; **median age:** 29.8.
Land area: 360 sq mi. (933.4 sq km); **Alt.:** 700 ft.
Avg. daily temp.: Jan., 51.2° F; July, 86.1° F
City-owned parks: 6,717 ac.; **Radio stations:** AM, 20; FM, 22; **Television stations:** 9
Civilian Labor Force: 695,110; **Unemployed:** 32,177, **Percent:** 4.6; **Per capita personal income (MSA)** 1992: $17,282
Chamber of Commerce: Greater San Antonio Chamber of Commerce, P.O. Box 1628, 602 E. Commerce, San Antonio, Tex. 78296

1. 1997 est. population: 1,115,600.

San Antonio, the third largest city in Texas and seat of Bexar county, is located in the south central part of the state, on the San Antonio River.

The site of San Antonio was first visited in 1691 by a Franciscan friar on the feast day of St. Anthony and was named San Antonio de Padua in his honor. San Antonio was permanently settled on May 1, 1718, when the Spanish governor of Coahuila and Texas, Martin de Alarcón, founded the presidio (a fort) of San Antonio de Bejar (Bexar) and the mission of San Antonio de Valero (later called the Alamo[1]) on the site of a Coahuiltecan Indian village. San Antonio remained almost continuously under Spanish rule until 1812 when Mexico won its independence from Spain.

During the outbreak of the Texas revolution (1835) against the tyranny of Mexican dictator General Santa Anna, San Antonio was captured by a small band of rebels who occupied the fortified mission of the Alamo in December 1835. The historic battle of the Alamo was fought there (Feb. 24 to March 6, 1836) and its 183 besieged defenders were massacred by Santa Anna's troops. Their heroism aroused the anger and fighting spirit of Texans to shout their famous battle cry "Remember the Alamo!" and defeat the Mexicans six weeks later (April 21, 1836) at the battle of San Jacinto. Texas became an independent republic in 1836 and San Antonio was incorporated as a city on Jan. 5, 1837.

After the Civil War, San Antonio prospered as a major shipping point for cattle with the arrival of the railroad in 1877. The city has been an important military center since World War II and is the home to five of the largest military installations in the nation, including Fort Sam Houston constructed in 1876. San Antonio is a leading livestock center and one of the largest produce exchange markets. The city's industries are highly diversified and tourism is important to the economy.

1. Spanish for the cottonwood tree.

Famous natives: Carol Burnett, comedienne; Cody Carlson, football player; Henry G. Cisneros, Secretary HUD; Joan Crawford, actress; Cito Gaston, baseball manager; Ann Harding, actress; Jesse James Leija, boxer; Emilio Navaira, Tejano music singer; Oliver North, military officer, government official; Suzy Parker, model, actress; Paula Prentiss, actress; Kyle Rote, football player; David R. Scott, astronaut; John Silber, university president; Patsy Torres, Tejano music singer; Edward H. White, astronaut.

SAN DIEGO, CALIF.

Mayor: Susan Golding
City Manager: Jack McGrory (apptd. April 1991)
1994 est. population (rank): 1,151,977 (6)[1]
1990 census population (rank): 1,110,623 (6); **% change,** 3.7; **Male,** 566,464; **Female,** 544,085; **White,** 745,406; **Black,** 104,261 (9.4%); **American Indian, Eskimo, or Aleut,** 6,800 (0.6%); **Asian or Pacific Islander,** 130,945 (11.8%); **Other race,** 123,137; **Hispanic origin,** 229,519 (20.7%). **1990 population under 18:** 23.1%; **65 and over:** 10.2%; **median age:** 30.5.
Land area: 330.7 sq miles (857 sq km); **Alt.:** Highest, 1,591 ft.; lowest, sea level
Avg. daily temp.: Jan., 56.8° F; July, 70.3° F
Churches: Roman Catholic, 39; Jewish, 9; Protestant, 334; Eastern Orthodox, 8; other, 18; **City park and recreation facilities:** 164 (17,207 ac.); **Radio stations:** AM, 8; FM, 18; **Television stations:** 9
Civilian Labor Force: 548,687; **Unemployed:** 41,301, **Percent:** 7.5; **Per capita personal income (MSA)** 1992: $20,384
Chamber of Commerce: San Diego Chamber of Commerce, 402 West Broadway, Suite 1000, San Diego, Calif. 92101

1. 1995 est. population: 1,197,676.

San Diego is the second largest city in California. It is located in the southwestern part of the state, on San Diego Bay.

Portuguese navigator Juan Rodríguez Cabrillo claimed the bay in 1542 for Spain. The site was named San Miguel by Cabrillo. On Nov. 12, 1602, Don Sebastian de Viscaíno came ashore with his party on the day of St. Didacus (San Diego in Spanish) and celebrated a mass in the saint's honor. By coincidence, Viscaíno's flagship was named *San Diego*. He renamed the place San Diego after the 15th century saint.

In 1769, Franciscan Father Junípero Serra established the first California mission there—San Diego del Alcala. In 1822, Mexico won control of the town after it declared its independence from Spain. In 1846, during the Mexican War, San Diego was seized by the United States and incorporated into a city in 1850 after California joined the Union that same year.

Today, San Diego's excellent natural harbor is a busy commercial port and a hub of U.S. naval operations. However, the naval training center at San Diego is slated to be closed due to defense cutbacks. Other leading industries are electronics, aerospace and missiles, medical and scientific research, oceanography, and agriculture. Its magnificent climate and proximity to Mexico have made tourism a significant part of the city's economy.

Famous natives: Billy Casper, golfer; Florence Chadwick, swimmer; Dennis Conner, yacht racer; Ted Danson, actor; Robert Duvall, actor; Nanette Fabray, actress; Robert Lansing, actor; Margaret O'Brien, actress; Carol Vaness, soprano; Ted Williams, baseball player; Mickey Wright, golfer.

SAN FRANCISCO, CALIF.

Mayor: Willie L. Brown, Jr. (to Jan. 2000)
1994 est. population (rank): 734,676 (13)
1990 census population (rank): 723,959 (14); **% change,** 1.5; **Male,** 362,497; **Female,** 361,462; **White,** 387,783; **Black,** 79,039 (10.9%); **American Indian, Eskimo, or Aleut,** 3,456 (0.5%); **Asian or Pacific Islander,** 210,876 (29.1%); **Other race,** 42,805; **Hispanic origin,** 100,717 (13.9%). **1990 population under 18:** 16.1%; **65 and over:** 14.6%; **median age:** 35.8.
Land area: 46.1 sq mi. (120 sq km); **Alt.:** Highest, 925 ft.; lowest, sea level
Avg. daily temp.: Jan., 48.5° F; July, 62.2° F
Churches: 540 of all denominations; **City-owned parks and squares:** 225; **Radio stations:** 29; **Television stations:** 10
Civilian Labor Force (1995): 398,000[1]; **Unemployed (S.F. residents):** 26,000[1], **Percent:** 6.4[1]; **Per capita personal income (PMSA) 1992:** $31,262[2]
Chamber of Commerce: Greater San Francisco Chamber of Commerce, 465 California St., San Francisco, Calif. 94104

1. San Francisco City/County.

San Francisco, the fourth largest city in California, is coextensive with San Francisco county. It is located in the northern part of the state between the Pacific Ocean and San Francisco Bay. A narrow arm of land embraces San Francisco Bay, the largest land-locked harbor in the world, and shelters it from the Pacific Ocean. On this arm of land is San Francisco, a city on hills, almost surrounded by water.

A Franciscan father who was sailing with Sebastián Rodríguez Cermeño named the bay San Francisco on Nov. 7, 1595. In 1776, the Spaniards established a presidio, or military post, and a Franciscan mission on the end of the beautiful peninsula. In the following year, a little town called Yerba Buena, Spanish for "Good Herb," because mint grew in abundance, was founded around the mission.

In 1846, during the Mexican War, Yerba Buena was taken over by the United States. It was renamed San Francisco in 1847 and became incorporated as a city in 1850.

When gold was discovered in California in 1848, the city's population jumped to 10,000, and it experienced turbulent years until order was established by Vigilance Committees, first in 1851, and again in 1856. Then followed a period of more orderly growth and the foundations of the great commerce and industry of today were laid.

In 1906, San Francisco experienced the nation's worst earthquake which, together with the fire that followed, practically destroyed the city. The city was quickly rebuilt and grew rapidly as a leading transportation, industrial, and cultural center. In the 19th century, the American explorer and soldier, John C. Frémont, known as The Pathfinder, named the entrance to the bay, the Golden Gate, and the famous bright orange Golden Gate Bridge was dedicated in May 1937.

Not just where the city meets the bay, but a vital part of the economic and cultural fabric of northern California, the port of San Francisco covers 7½ miles of waterfront as diverse and changing as the city itself. The port is home to a broad range of commercial, maritime, and public activities including ship repair, passenger cruising, ferry and excursion boats, commercial and sport fishing, and public parks. Its major shipping terminals serve shipping lines from around the world. The port also manages over 23 million sq. ft. of commercial real estate including office, retail, industrial, parking, and warehouse facilities. Fisherman's Wharf, Alcatraz, Hyde St. Pier, and Pier 39 all make the port of San Francisco one of the world's leading visitor destinations.

San Francisco inspires entrepreneurs to start their own businesses, and small businesses have a very important place in the economy. More than 80% of the city's 33,800 businesses have fewer than 15 employees. The high-tech industries of electronics and biotechnology are well represented throughout the Bay Area. With nearly 30% of the worldwide biotechnology labor force, and 360 biotech firms, the Bay Area has been appropriately called "Bionic Bay." Tourism is one of San Francisco's largest industries and the largest employer of city residents. Nearly 13.4 million persons visit San Francisco each year and annual visitor spending is $231 million, providing 66,400 jobs.

The military has played an important role in the San Francisco and the Bay Area's economy, but its impact will decline due to defense cutbacks.

San Francisco is also the banking and financial center of the West and is home to a Federal Reserve Bank and a United States Mint. More than 60 foreign banks maintain offices there.

Famous natives: Gracie Allen, comedienne; Luis Walter Alvarez, Nobel Prize in physics; David Belasco, dramatist, producer; Mel Blanc, actor, voice specialist; Rosemary Casals, tennis player; Isadora Duncan, dancer; Clint Eastwood, actor; Robert Frost, poet; Rube Goldberg, cartoonist; William Randolph Hearst, publisher; Bruce Lee, actor; Mervyn LeRoy, director; Jack London, novelist; Johnny Mathis, singer; Lloyd Nolan, actor; O.J. Simpson, football player; Robert G. Sproul, educator; Irving Stone, novelist; Natalie Wood, actress.

SAN JOSE, CALIF.

Mayor: Susan Hammer (to Dec. 31, 1998)
City Manager: Regina V.K. Williams (apptd. Nov. 1994)
1994 population (est): 816,884 (11)[1]
1990 census population (rank): 782,224 (11); **% change,** 4.4; **Male,** 397,709; **Female,** 384,539; **White,** 491,280; **Black,** 36,790 (4.7%); **American Indian, Eskimo, or Aleut,** 5,416 (0.7%); **Asian or Pacific Islander,** 152,815 (19.5%); **Other race,** 95,947; **Hispanic origin,** 208,388 (26.6%). **1990 population under 18:** 26.7%; **65 and over:** 7.2%; **median age:** 30.4.
Land area: 180.8 sq mi. (468.27 sq km); **Alt.:** Highest, 4,372 ft.; lowest, sea level
Avg. daily temp.: Jan., 49.5° F; July, 68.8° F

Churches: 403; **City-owned parks and playgrounds:** 152 (3,136 ac.); **Radio stations:** 14; **Television stations:** 4

Civilian Labor Force: 420,686; **Unemployed:** 33,484, **Percent:** 8.0; **Per capita personal income (PMSA) 1992:** $25,924[1]

Chamber of Commerce: San Jose Chamber of Commerce, One Paseo de San Antonio, San Jose, Calif. 95113

1. 1997 est. population: 873,300

San Jose, the third largest city in California and seat of Santa Clara county, is located in the northern part of the state in the Santa Clara Valley near San Francisco Bay, 50 miles south of downtown San Francisco.

San Jose was founded on Nov. 29, 1777, by Spanish colonizers who named the settlement Pueblo de San José de Guadalupe in honor of Saint Joseph and after the Guadalupe River on which the pueblo (town) was situated. The town was the first city to be established in California.

After California became a U.S. territory in 1847, San Jose became the first state capital from December 1849 to 1852 and was incorporated as a city in 1850. The city developed commercially as a supply base for gold prospectors and, when the railroad connected it with San Francisco in 1864, it became the distribution point for agricultural products from the Santa Clara Valley.

Today, the city continues to be the distribution and food-processing center for the surrounding rich agricultural region producing seasonal fruits and grapes. More than 50 wineries grace the Valley.

Computers are big business here and San Jose is the capital of Silicon Valley (Santa Clara), the nation's center of high technology where more than 3,000 high tech companies are located. Silicon Valley is also one of the world's leading centers for medical treatment and research. Heart transplants, gene splicing, and transportable baby incubators were developed there.

San Jose has healthy retail, transportation, and tourism industries as well, and is the primary center for real estate and industrial development in the area.

Famous natives: "Fatty" Arbuckle, actor; Chuck Berry, singer, guitarist; Cesar Chavez, labor leader; Peggy Fleming, figure skater; Farley Granger, actor; Edmund Lowe, actor; Jim Plunkett, football player.

SEATTLE, WASH.

Mayor: Norman B. Rice (to Dec. 31, 1997)

1994 est. population (rank): 520,947 (22)

1990 census population (rank): 516,259 (21); **% change,** 0.9; **Male,** 252,042; **Female,** 264,217; **White,** 388,858 (75.3%); **Black,** 51,948 (10.1%); **American Indian, Eskimo, or Aleut,** 7,326 (1.4%); **Asian or Pacific Islander,** 60,819 (11.8%); **Other race,** 7,308 (1.4%); **Hispanic origin,** 18,349 (3.6%). **1990 population under 18:** 16.5%; **65 and over:** 15.2%; **median age:** 34.9.

Land area: 144.6 sq mi. (375 sq km); **Alt.:** Highest, 521 ft.; lowest, sea level

Avg. daily temp.: Jan., 39.6° F; July, 67.8° F

Churches: Roman Catholic, 35; Jewish, 13; Protestant, 491; others, 19; **City-owned parks, playgrounds, etc.:** 397 (6,000+ ac.); **Radio stations:** AM, 20; FM, 24; **Television stations:** 7

Civilian Labor Force (1996): (3 counties) 1,147,263; **Unemployed:** 57,363, **Percent:** 5.0 **Per capita personal income:** $29,564

Chamber of Commerce: Greater Seattle Chamber of Commerce, 1301 5th Ave., Suite 2400, Seattle, Wash. 98101-2603

Seattle is the largest city in Washington and the seat of King county. A city of steep hills, Seattle lies in western Washington between two bodies of water—Puget Sound on the west and Lake Washington on the east. Its fine landlocked harbor has made Seattle one of the major ports in the United States.

Seattle was first settled by five pioneer families from Illinois at Alki Point at the south end of Elliott Bay in 1851. They moved in 1852 to the eastern shore of the bay and laid out a town in 1853. It was named Seattle after a friendly Suquamish Indian Chief (Seattle is only an approximation of his name).

Seattle successfully withstood an Indian attack in 1856 and was incorporated as a city in 1869. A disastrous fire almost destroyed the entire business district in 1889. When the Great Northern Railway arrived in 1893, the city became a major rail terminus and it grew rapidly. It was a boom town during the Alaska gold rush of 1897 and continued to prosper as a major Pacific port of entry with the opening of the Panama Canal in 1914.

Seattle is the region's commercial and transportation hub and the center of manufacturing, trade, and finance. Its important diversified industries include aircraft, lumber and forest products, fishing, high technology, food processing, boat building, machinery, fabricated metals, chemicals, pharmaceuticals, and apparel.

Famous natives: Chester Carlson, Xerox inventor; Carol Channing, actress; Judy Collins, singer; Fred Couples, golfer; Gail Devers, athlete; Frances Farmer, actress; William Gates, Microsoft founder; June Havoc, actress; Jimi Hendrix, guitarist; Robert Joffrey, choreographer; Gypsy Rose Lee, entertainer; Mary Livingstone, comedienne; Kevin McCarthy, actor; Mary McCarthy, novelist; Jeff Smith, food expert; Martha Wright, singer.

TOLEDO, OHIO

Mayor: Carlton Finkbeiner (to Jan. 1998)

1994 est. population (rank): 322,550 (50)

1990 census population (rank): 332,943 (49); **% change,** –3.1; **Male,** 157,941; **Female,** 175,002; **White,** 256,239; **Black,** 65,598 (19.7%); **Americn Indian, Eskimo, or Aleut,** 920 (0.3%); **Asian or Pacific Islander,** 3,487 (1.0%); **Other race,** 6,699; **Hispanic origin,** 13,207 (4.0%). **1990 population under 18:** 26.2%; **65 and over:** 13.6%; **median age:** 31.7.

Land area: 84.2 sq mi. (218 sq km); **Alt.:** 630 ft.

Avg. daily temp.: Jan., 22.5° F; July, 72.1° F

Churches: Protestant, 301; Roman Catholic, 55; Jewish, 4; others, 98; **City-owned parks and playgrounds:** 134 (2,650.90 ac.); **Radio stations:** AM, 8; FM, 8; **Television stations:** 6

Civilian Labor Force (1996): 158,200; **Unemployed:** 9,400, **Percent:** 6.0; **Per capita personal income (MSA) 1994:** $21,233

Chamber of Commerce: Toledo Area Chamber of Commerce, 300 Madison Ave., Ste. 200, Toledo, Ohio 43604

Toledo, the fourth largest city in Ohio and seat of Lucas county, is located in the northwestern part of the state on the Maumee River at Lake Erie.

The first European to visit the area was the French explorer Étienne Brulé in 1615. The first white settlement in the area was at Fort Industry built by Gen. "Mad Anthony" Wayne in 1794, after he defeated the Indians at the Battle of Fallen Timbers fought nearby. The village of Port Lawrence was established next to the fort in 1817 and the village of Vistula was established nearby in 1832. The two villages were united in 1833 and named Toledo after the city in Spain. They became incorporated as a city in 1837.

Both Michigan and Ohio claimed the Toledo area, which at the time was part of Michigan Territory. The bloodless dispute (Toledo War of 1835) was settled by Congress when it awarded the city to Ohio. In return, Michigan received the Upper Peninsula and admission to the Union.

The city developed as a transportation center with the arrival of the railroad in 1836 and the opening of canals in the 1840s. It continued to prosper with the development of the Ohio coalfields, the tapping of gas and oil deposits, and the establishment of the glassworks by Edward Libbey in 1888.

Toledo is a leading commercial and manufacturing center and a major Great Lakes port. Total annual tonnage through the Port of Toledo ranges from 10 to 15 million tons and includes three distinct types of cargo: coal and iron ore, grain, and a wide range of general cargoes.

Toledo is the home of numerous major corporate headquarters and has 13 financial institutions in the area. Major diversified manufacturing industries include Jeeps, glass and plastic containers, fiberglass, automotive components, petroleum refining, coal products, and natural gas distribution. Other important industries are printing and publishing, food products, furniture, and fabricated metal products.

Famous natives: Cliff Arquette, actor; Anita Baker, singer; Teresa Brewer, singer; Jamie Farr, actor; Otto Kruger, actor; Herb Shriner, humorist; Gloria Steinem, feminist; Art Tatum, jazz pianist.

TUCSON, ARIZ.

Mayor: George Miller (to Dec. 1999)
1994 est. population (rank): 434,726 (33)[1]
1990 census population (rank): 408,754 (33); **% change,** 6.4; **Male,** 197,319; **Female,** 208,071; **White,** 305,055; **Black,** 17,366 (4.3%); **American Indian, Eskimo, or Aleut,** 6,464 (1.6%); **Asian or Pacific Islander,** 8,901 (2.2%); **Other race,** 67,604; **Hispanic origin,** 118,595 (29.3%). **1990 population under 18:** 24.5%; **65 and over:** 12.6%; **median age:** 30.6.
Land area: 162 sq mi. (419 sq km); **Alt.:** 2,400 ft.
Avg. daily temp.: Jan., 51.1° F; July, 86.2° F
Churches: Protestant, 340; Roman Catholic, 42; other, 150; **City-owned parks and parkways:** (25,349 ac.); **Radio stations:** AM, 15; FM, 17; **Television stations:** 3 commercial; 1 educational; 3 other
Civilian Labor Force (1996): 373,600; **Unemployed:** 12,100, **Percent:** 3.4; **Per capita personal income (1996):** $20,100
Chamber of Commerce: Tucson Metropolitan Chamber of Commerce, P.O. Box 991, Tucson, Ariz. 85702

1. 1997 est. population: 452,298.

Tucson is the second largest city in Arizona and the seat of Pima county. It is located in the southeastern part of the state on the Santa Cruz River.

The site was originally settled by the prehistoric Hohokam Indians (300 B.C.E.–C.E. 1400s). The first Europeans to visit the area were Spanish missionaries in the 17th century. In 1700, the Jesuit missionary explorer Father Eusebio Fancisco Kino founded the mission of San Xavier del Bac close by the Papago Indian village of Stjukshon (later called Tucson). Stjukshon is an Indian word meaning "village of the dark spring at the foot of the mountain." The Papago Indians are descendants of the ancient Hohakam peoples.

In 1776, Spanish colonists from Mexico constructed a presidio (fort) at Tucson as protection against the hostile Apache Indians and also established the mission of San Jose de Tucson nearby. Tucson remained a military outpost under Spanish rule and later Mexican control until the area was sold to the United States as part of the Gadsden Purchase in 1853. Tucson was the capital of the Arizona Territory from 1867 to 1877. It was incorporated as a city in 1877. The town grew rapidly when the Southern Pacific Railroad arrived in 1880 and silver and copper deposits were discovered nearby.

Tucson is a popular vacation and health resort due to its sunny, mild, and dry climate and unique desert location. Tourism is important to the city's economy. Major industries include aerospace and missile production, high technology, optics, biotechnology, environmental technology, software, and electronics. Tucson is also the commercial center for the surrounding area's agriculture and mining industries.

Famous natives: Rose E. Bird, jurist; Dennis De Concini, senator; Barbara Eden, actress; Linda Ronstadt, singer.

TULSA, OKLA.

Mayor: M. Susan Savage (to May 1998)
1994 est. population (rank): 374,851 (40)
1990 census population (rank): 367,302 (44); **% change,** 2.1; **Male,** 175,538; **Female,** 191,764; **White,** 291,444; **Black,** 49,825 (13.6%); **American Indian, Eskimo, or Aleut,** 17,091 (4.7%); **Asian or Pacific Islander,** 5,133 (1.4%); **Other race,** 3,809; **Hispanic origin,** 9,564 (2.6%). **1990 population under 18:** 24.4%; **65 and over:** 12.7%; **median age:** 33.1.
Land area: 191.5 sq mi. (497.1 sq km); **Alt.:** 674 ft.
Avg. daily temp.: Jan., 35.2°F; July, 83.2°F
Churches: Protestant, 593; Roman Catholic, 32; Jewish, 2; others, 4; **City parks and playgrounds:** 121 (6,050 ac.); **Radio stations:** AM, 9; FM, 21; **Television stations:** 7 commercial; 1 PBS; 1 cable
Civilian Labor Force (1995): 381,400; **Unemployed:** 14,493, **Percent:** 3.8; **Per capita personal income (1995):** $20,419
Chamber of Commerce: Metropolitan Tulsa Chamber of Commerce, 616 S. Boston, Tulsa, Okla. 74119

Tulsa, the second largest city in Oklahoma and seat of Tulsa county, is located in the northeastern part of the state on the Arkansas River.

Tulsa was settled in the 1830s by Creek Indians from Alabama who were forcibly sent to the area (then part of Indian Territory) under the Indian Removal Act of 1830. Creek medicine-men planted ashes from their old home at the new site and the Creeks named their new village "Tulsy" meaning old town in memory of their former home in Tallassee, Alabama. In time, the village became the town of Tulsa.

The coming of the first railroad in 1882 attracted white settlers to Tulsa and the town developed into a cattle shipping center. When enormous oil deposits were discovered at nearby Red Fork in 1901 and at Glenn Pool in 1905, the city experienced rapid growth as a center of a booming petroleum industry. Tulsa was incorporated as a city in 1898 and chartered in 1908.

Tulsa is the center of the state's petroleum industry and has a diversified economy. Important industries include aerospace, chemicals, computer parts, automobile glass, fabricated metals, and industrial machinery. The city became a major inland port when the Tulsa Port of Catoosa opened in 1971. It is the national headquarters of the U.S. Junior Chamber of Commerce (Jaycees).

Famous natives: Garth Brooks, singer; Blake Edwards, director; Paul Harvey, commentator; Jennifer Jones, actress; Henry R. Kravis, investment banker; Daniel Patrick Moynihan, senator; Tony Randall, actor; Alfre Woodard, actress; Judy Woodruff, journalist.

VIRGINIA BEACH, VA.

Mayor: Meyera E. Obendorf (to June 2000)
1994 est. population (rank): 430,295 (35)
1990 census population (rank): 393,089 (37); **% change,** 9.5; **Male,** 199,571; **Female,** 193,498; **White,** 316,408; **Black,** 54,671 (13.9%); **American Indian, Eskimo, or Aleut,** 1,384 (0.4%); **Asian or Pacific**

Islander, 17,025 (4.3%); **Other race,** 3,581; **Hispanic origin,** 12,137 (3.1%); **1990 population under 18:** 28.0%; **65 and over:** 5.9%; **median age:** 28.9.
Land area: 258.7 sq mi. (670 sq km); **Alt.:** 12 ft.
Avg. daily temp.: Jan., 39.9° F; July, 78.4° F
Churches: Protestant, 159; Catholic, 8; Jewish, 4; **City-owned parks:** 182 (1,748 ac.); **Radio stations:** AM 18, FM 26; **Television stations:** 4 commercial, 1 PBS, 1 cable
Civilian Labor Force: 194,579; **Unemployed:** 11,541, **Percent:** 5.9; **Per capita personal income (MSA) 1992:** $18,077[1]
Chamber of Commerce: Hampton Roads Chamber of Commerce, 4512 Virginia Beach Blvd., Virginia Beach, Va., 23456

1. Norfolk–Virginia Beach–Newport News.

Virginia Beach, the largest city in Virginia, is located in the southeasternmost portion of the state on the Atlantic coastline. It is independent and is not part of any county.

The first English settlers to set foot in America landed at Cape Henry at the tip of Virginia Beach on April 29, 1607. They were led by John Smith on his way to establishing Jamestown. The first permanent settlement within the city limits was made at Lynnhaven Bay in 1621. Cape Henry became an important port for British merchant ships calling on America, and it was here that the French Fleet led by Admiral Comte de Grasse blockaded the British Fleet during the American Revolution.

Virginia Beach gained its reputation as a famous vacation resort in the 19th century, following the building of a railroad connecting its oceanfront with Norfolk and the construction of its first hotel in 1883. Virginia Beach was incorporated as a town in 1906 and as a city in 1952. In 1963, Princess Anne County and Virginia Beach merged and gave the present city an area of 310 square miles of oceanfront.

Tourism is the mainstay of the economy and 2.5 million people visit Virginia Beach overnight each year. Virginia Beach's economy is supported by four nearby military bases and diverse industries, including agriculture (165 farms), computer software, engineering, and technical services.

Famous natives and residents: V.C. Andrews, novelist; Raymond Brian Buckland, occult writer; Edgar Cayce, psychic; Ann Woodruff Compton, news correspondent; D.J. Dozier, football and baseball player; George Eastman, inventor; Scott McKenzie, singer; Juice Newton, singer; Kenneth S. Reightler, Jr., astronaut; Pat Robertson, evangelist; Grace Sherwood, accused witch; Henry Walke, naval officer in Mexican and Civil Wars; Pernell "Sweet Pea" Whitaker, boxer; Skip Wilkins, wheelchair athlete.

WASHINGTON, D.C.

Created municipal corporation: Feb. 21, 1871
Mayor: Marion Barry (to Jan. 1999)
Motto: *Justitia omnibus* (Justice to all)
Flower: American beauty rose; **Tree:** Scarlet oak
1994 est. population: 578,014 (20)
1990 census population (rank): 606,900 (19); **% change,** –6.6; **Male,** 282,970; **Female,** 323,930; **White,** 179,667; **Black,** 399,604 (65.8%); **American Indian, Eskimo, or Aleut,** 1,466 (0.2%); **Asian or Pacific Islander,** 11,214 (1.8%); **Other race,** 14,949; **Hispanic origin,** 32,710 (5.4%)
Land area: 68.25 sq mi. (177 sq km); **Alt.:** Highest, 420 ft.; lowest, sea level

Avg. daily temp.: Jan., 35.2° F; July, 78.9° F
Churches: Protestant, 610; Roman Catholic, 132; Jewish, 9; **City parks:** 753 (7,725 ac.); **Radio stations:** AM, 9; FM, 38; **Television stations:** 19
Civilian Labor Force: 276,000; **Unemployed:** 23,000, **Percent:** 8.4; **Per capita personal income (PMSA) 1992:** $26,817[1]
Board of Trade: Greater Washington Board of Trade, 1129 20th Street, N.W., Washington, D.C. 20036
Chamber of Commerce: D.C. Chamber of Commerce, 1319 F St., NW, Washington, D.C. 20004

1. Washington, D.C.–Md.-Va.–W.Va.

The District of Columbia—identical with the City of Washington—is the capital of the United States and the first carefully planned capital in the world. It is located between Virginia and Maryland on the Potomac River. The district is named after Columbus.

D.C. history began in 1790 when Congress directed selection of a new capital site, 100 miles square, along the Potomac. When the site was determined, it included 30.75 square miles on the Virginia side of the river. In 1846, however, Congress returned that area to Virginia, leaving the 68.25 square miles ceded by Maryland in 1788. The seat of government was transferred from Philadelphia to Washington on Dec. 1, 1800, and President John Adams became the first resident in the White House.

The city was planned and partly laid out by Major Pierre Charles L'Enfant, a French engineer. This work was perfected and completed by Major Andrew Ellicott and Benjamin Banneker, a freeborn black man, who was an astronomer and mathematician. In 1814, during the War of 1812, a British force fired the capital including the White House.

Until Nov. 3, 1967, the District of Columbia was administered by three commissioners appointed by the president. On that day, a government consisting of a mayor-commissioner and a 9-member Council, all appointed by the president with the approval of the Senate, took office. On May 7, 1974, the citizens of the District of Columbia approved a Home Rule Charter, giving them an elected mayor and 13-member council—their first elected municipal government in more than a century. The District also has one nonvoting member in the House of Representatives and an elected Board of Education.

On Aug. 22, 1978, Congress passed a proposed constitutional amendment to give Washington, D.C. voting representation in the Congress. The amendment had to be ratified by at least 28 state legislatures within seven years to become effective. As of 1985 it died.

A petition asking for the District's admission to the Union as the 51st state was filed in Congress on September 9, 1983. The District is continuing this drive for statehood.

The federal government and tourism are the mainstays of the city's economy, and many unions, business, professional and nonprofit organizations are headquartered there.

Famous natives: Edward Albee, playwright; Billie Burke, comedienne; Ina Claire, actress; John Foster Dulles, statesman; Duke Ellington, musician; Jane Greer, actress; Goldie Hawn, actress; Helen Hayes, actress; J. Edgar Hoover, ex-director F.B.I.; William Hurt, actor; Noor al-Hussein, Queen of Jordan; Michael Learned, actress; Roger Mudd, newscaster; Eleanor Holmes Norton, government official; Chita Rivera, dancer, actress; Leonard Rose, cellist; John Philip Sousa, composer; Frances Sternhagen, actress.

Top 50 Cities in the U.S. by Estimated 1994 Population and Rank

City and state	April 1, 1990 (census)	July 1, 1994 (estimate)	Change, 1990–94 Number	Change, 1990–94 Percent	City Rank Population 1990	City Rank Population 1994	Percent change 1990–94
New York, N.Y.	7,322,564	7,333,253	10,689	0.1	1	1	149
Los Angeles, Calif.	3,485,557	3,448,613	−36,944	−1.1	2	2	170
Chicago, Ill.	2,783,726	2,731,743	−51,983	−1.9	3	3	179
Houston, Tex.	1,630,864	1,702,086	71,222	4.4	4	4	82
Philadelphia, Pa.	1,585,577	1,524,249	−61,328	−3.9	5	5	194
San Diego, Calif.	1,110,623	1,151,977	41,354	3.7	6	6	93
Phoenix, Ariz.	984,309	1,048,949	64,640	6.6	9	7	60
Dallas, Tex.	1,007,618	1,022,830	15,212	1.5	8	8	127
San Antonio, Tex.	935,393	998,905	63,512	6.8	10	9	55
Detroit, Mich.	1,027,974	992,038	−35,936	−3.5	7	10	191
San Jose, Calif.	782,224	816,884	34,660	4.4	11	11	81
Indianapolis (remainder), Ind.[1]	731,311	752,279	20,968	2.9	13	12	101
San Francisco, Calif.	723,959	734,676	10,717	1.5	14	13	128
Baltimore, Md.	736,014	702,979	−33,035	−4.5	12	14	195
Jacksonville (remainder), Fla.[1]	635,230	665,070	29,840	4.7	15	15	77
Columbus, Ohio	632,945	635,913	2,968	0.5	16	16	143
Milwaukee, Wis.	628,088	617,044	−11,044	−1.8	17	17	176
Memphis, Tenn.	618,652	614,289	−4,363	−0.7	18	18	162
El Paso, Tex.	515,342	579,307	63,965	12.4	22	19	22
Washington, D.C.	606,900	567,094	−39,806	−6.6	19	20	205
Boston, Mass.	574,283	547,725	−26,558	−4.6	20	21	196
Seattle, Wash.	516,259	520,947	4,688	0.9	21	22	135
Austin, Tex.	465,648	514,013	48,365	10.4	27	23	30
Nashville-Davidson (remainder), Tenn.[1]	488,366	504,505	16,139	3.3	25	24	97
Denver, Co.	467,610	493,559	25,949	5.5	26	25	68
Cleveland, Ohio	505,616	492,901	−12,715	−2.5	23	26	185
New Orleans, La.	496,938	484,149	−12,789	−2.6	24	27	186
Oklahoma City, Okla.	444,724	463,201	18,477	4.2	29	28	89
Fort Worth, Tex.	447,619	451,814	4,195	0.9	28	29	134
Portland, Ore.	438,802	450,777	11,975	2.7	30	30	104
Kansas City, Mo.	434,829	443,878	−9,049	−2.1	31	31	115
Charlotte, N.C.	395,934	437,797	41,863	10.6	35	32	28
Tucson, Ariz.	408,754	434,726	25,972	6.4	33	33	63
Long Beach, Calif.	429,321	433,852	4,531	1.1	32	34	133
Virginia, Beach, Va.	393,089	430,295	37,206	9.5	37	35	33
Albuquerque, N.M.	384,619	411,994	27,375	7.1	38	26	50
Atlanta, Ga.	393,929	396,052	2,123	0.5	36	37	140
Fresno, Calif.	354,091	386,551	32,460	9.2	47	38	37
Honolulu CDP, Hawaii[2]	377,059	385,881	8,822	2.3	39	39	109
Tulsa, Okla.	367,302	374,851	7,549	2.1	44	40	116
Sacramento, Calif.	369,365	373,964	4,599	1.2	42	41	131
Miami, Fla.	358,648	373,024	14,376	4.0	46	42	90
St. Louis, Mo.	396,685	368,215	−28,470	−7.2	34	43	206
Oakland, Calif.	372,242	366,926	−5,316	−1.4	40	44	173
Pittsburgh, Pa.	369,879	358,883	−10,996	−3.0	41	45	188
Cincinnati, Ohio	364,114	358,170	−5,944	−1.6	45	46	175
Minneapolis, Minn.	368,383	354,590	−13,793	−3.7	43	47	193
Omaha, Neb.	335,719	345,033	9,314	2.8	48	48	102
Las Vegas, Nev.	258,204	327,878	69,674	27.0	63	49	4
Toledo, Ohio	332,943	322,550	−10,393	−3.1	49	50	189

1. The term "remainder" following a city name indicates that it is part of a consolidated city-county government and that the populations of other incorporated places in the county have been excluded from the population totals shown here. 2. Honolulu CDP (census designated place) is not incorporated as a city but is recognized for census purposes as a large urban place. Honolulu CDP is coextensive with Honolulu Judicial District within the City and County of Honolulu. NOTE: These estimates are consistent with the population as enumerated in the 1990 census, and have not been adjusted for census coverage errors. *Source:* U.S. Bureau of the Census.

Tabulated Data on City Governments

City	Mayor		City manager's salary[1,2]	Council or Commission			
	Term, years	Salary[1]		Name	Members	Term, years	Salary[1,3]
Albuquerque, N.M.	4	$ 73,500	—	Council	9	4	$ 7,028
Atlanta	4	100,000	—	Council	18	4	22,000
Austin, Tex.	3	35,000	$125,000	Council	7	3	30,000
Baltimore	4	95,000	—	Council	19	4	37,000
Boston	4	110,000	—	Council	13	2	54,500
Charlotte, N.C.	2	25,000	128,621	Council	11	2	12,000
Chicago	4	170,000	—	Council	50	4	75,000
Cincinnati	2	50,121	143,085	Council	9	2	46,621
Cleveland	4	101,286	—	Council	21	4	47,751
Columbus, Ohio	4	98,000	—	Council	7	4	25,000
Dallas	2	50[5]	179,001	Council	15	2	50[5]
Denver	4	97,812	—	Council	13	4	43,000
Detroit	4	143,000	—	Council	9	4	66,000
El Paso	2	25,000	—	Council	8[6]	2	15,000
Fort Worth	2	75[5]	131,258	Council	8	2	75[5]
Fresno, Calif.	4	99,000	120,000	Council	8[6]	4	28,800
Honolulu	4	100,000	95,000[4]	Council	9	4	38,500
Houston	6	133,005	—	Council	14	2	36,614
Indianapolis	4	83,211	—	Council	29	4	14,705
Jacksonville, Fla.	2	110,000	105,000[7]	Council	19	4	24,000
Kansas City, Mo.	4	59,400	132,500	Council	13[6]	4	26,400
Las Vegas	4	75,800	112,499	Council	4	4	33,480
Long Beach, Calif.	4	88,228	173,500	Council	9	4	22,057
Los Angeles	4[13]	127,491	182,094[4]	Council	15	4	98,070
Memphis, Tenn.	4	110,000	98,000[4]	Council	13	4	20,100
Miami, Fla.	4	5,000	170,000	Commission	5	4	5,000
Milwaukee	4	112,362	—	Council	17	4	52,528
Minneapolis	4	73,486	95,888	Council	13	4	54,578
Nashville, Tenn.	4	75,000	8,900[8]	Council	40	4	6,900
New Orleans	4	90,000	57,900	Council	7	4	42,500
New York	4	165,000	138,000[8]	Council	51	4	70,500
Oakland, Calif.	4	97,740	147,090[14]	Council	9[6]	4	47,880[12,13]
Oklahoma City	4	2,000	100,000	Council	8	4	20[9]
Omaha, Neb.	4	84,148	—	Council	7	4	24,537
Philadelphia	4	110,000	95,000[7]	Council	17	4	65,000
Phoenix, Ariz.	4	37,500	143,500	Council	9[6]	4	35,000
Pittsburgh	4	81,222	—	Council	9	4	46,312
Portland, Ore.	4	83,416	—	Council	4	4	70,261
Sacramento	4	1,652[11]	124,963	Council	9	4	1,251[11]
St. Louis	4	71,266	—	Board of Alderman	29	4	18,500
San Antonio	2	3,000[10]	115,000	Council	11[6]	2	20[5]
San Diego, Calif.	4	65,300	132,792	Council	8	4	49,000
San Francisco	4	140,862	127,081	Bd. of Supvrs.	11	4	23,924
San Jose, Calif.	4	87,550	158,000	Council	10	4	58,240
Seattle	4	115,654	—	Council	9	4	73,377
Toledo, Ohio	4	75,000	—	Council	12	4	18,500
Tucson, Ariz.	4	36,000	127,000	Council	7[6]	4	18,000
Tulsa, Okla.	4	70,000	—	Council	9	2	12,000
Virginia Beach, Va.	4	20,000	125,000	Council	11	4	18,000
Washington, D.C.	4	90,705	115,700	Council	13	4	71,885

1. Annual salary unless otherwise indicated; does not include additional payments for expenses, special sessions, etc. 2. City Manager's term is indefinite and at will of Council (or Mayor). 3. In some cities, leaders receive a higher salary. 4. Appointed by Mayor, approved by Council. 5. Per Council meeting. 6. Including Mayor. 7. Appointed by Mayor; not subject to Council confirmation. 8. No City Manager; salary is for Deputy or Vice Mayor. 9. Per Council meeting; not to exceed 5 meetings a month. 10. Plus Council pay. 11. Per month. 12. Council also serves as the Redevelopment Agency for which there is additional compensation. 13. At mayor's request; limited to 2 terms. 14. Denotes average based on range. *Source: Information Please* questionnaires to the cities.

U.S. Telephone Area Codes and Time Zones[1]

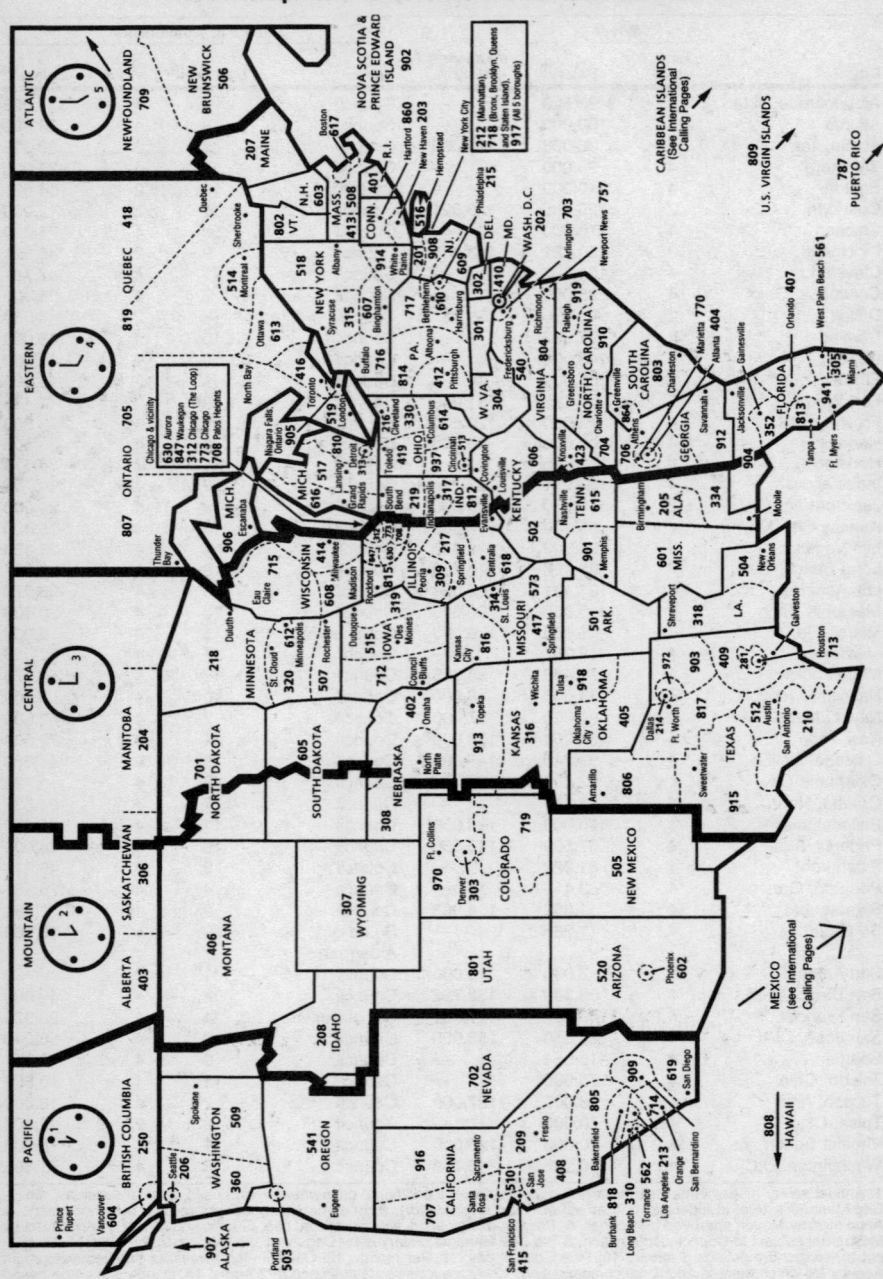

1. Does not include most recent area codes in eastern Massachusetts, 781 and 981, effective September 1997.

U.S. Cities with Population Over 50,000

ZIP codes provided below indicate the primary ZIP code for each city; please consult a ZIP code directory to find the appropriate ZIP code for a particular address. NOTE: Census Designated Place (CDP)—A statistical area comprising a densely settled concentration of population that is not incorporated but which resembles an incorporated place in that local people can identify it with a name.

City	ZIP code	1994 pop. est.	1994 rank
Alabama			
Birmingham	35203	264,527	61
Decatur	35601	52,465	514
Dothan	36302	55,792	470
Huntsville	35813	160,325	113
Mobile	36601	204,490	76
Montgomery	36119	195,471	81
Tuscaloosa	35401	79,797	290
Alaska			
Anchorage	99501	253,649	63
Arkansas			
Fort Smith	72917	74,480	319
Jonesboro	72401	50,209	548
Little Rock	72231	178,136	102
North Little Rock	72114	62,197	402
Pine Bluff	71601	57,971	441
Arizona			
Chandler	85225	119,227	159
Flagstaff	86004	50,708	540
Gilbert town	85234	51,074	535
Glendale	85301	168,439	108
Mesa	85201	313,649	52
Peoria	85345	70,139	348
Phoenix	85026	1,048,949	7
Scottsdale	85251	152,439	117
Tempe	85282	144,289	129
Tucson	85726	434,726	33
Yuma	85364	67,185	364
California			
Alameda	94501	78,672	302
Alhambra	91715	84,411	269
Anaheim	92803	282,133	58
Antioch	94509	73,019	326
Apple Valley town	92307	51,994	522
Arcadia	91006	50,654	541
Bakersfield	93380	191,060	89
Baldwin Park	91706	72,763	333
Bellflower	90706	66,667	368
Berkeley	94704	99,830	213
Buena Park	90622	72,671	334
Burbank	91505	99,665	214
Camarillo	93010	56,734	458
Carlsbad	92008	65,461	377
Carson	90745	90,025	240
Cerritos	90703	54,786	486
Chino	91710	64,781	380
Chula Vista	92010	149,255	122
Clovis	93612	60,281	419
Compton	90221	96,477	222
Concord	94520	111,889	177
Corona	91720	92,898	233
Costa Mesa	92628	98,427	216
Daly City	94015	94,036	232
Diamond Bar	91765	58,828	434
Downey	90241	99,889	211
El Cajon	92020	92,658	234
El Monte	91731	104,661	196
Encinitas	92024	57,029	453
Escondido	92025	116,349	165
Fairfield	94533	83,776	276
Fontana	92335	103,737	198
Fountain Valley	92708	55,467	476
Fremont	94537	183,575	93
Fresno	93706	386,551	38
Fullerton	92634	116,863	163
Garden Grove	92642	147,958	124
Gardena	90247	53,479	501
Glendale	92109	178,481	101
Newark		258,751	64
Glendora	91740	51,957	523
Hawthorne	90250	75,329	314
Hayward	94544	115,590	167

City	ZIP code	1994 pop. est.	1994 rank
Hesperia	92345	59,131	430
Huntington Beach	92647	189,220	91
Huntington Park	90255	55,712	471
Inglewood	90311	110,085	181
Irvine	92713	125,624	148
La Habra	90631	53,664	496
La Mesa	90241	54,316	491
Laguna Niguel	92654	56,681	460
Lake Forest		59,894	425
Lakewood	90714	79,416	297
Lancaster	93534	119,186	160
Livermore	94550	63,362	393
Lodi	95240	52,423	515
Long Beach	90809	433,852	34
Los Angeles	90052	3,448,613	2
Lynwood	90262	64,809	379
Merced	95340	60,348	418
Milpitas	95035	55,927	469
Mission Viejo	92690	83,813	275
Modesto	95350	176,357	104
Montebello	90640	61,519	407
Monterey Park	91754	57,921	442
Moreno Valley	92388	139,311	137
Mountain View	94041	65,812	375
Napa	94558	63,444	392
National City	92050	57,538	446
Newport Beach	92658	70,668	344
Norwalk	90650	100,744	207
Oakland	94615	366,926	44
Oceanside	92054	146,229	125
Ontario	91761	134,825	141
Orange	92613	116,785	164
Oxnard	93030	145,863	127
Palmdale	93550	103,423	201
Palo Alto	94303	56,925	456
Paramount	90723	52,209	517
Pasadena	91109	134,170	142
Pico Rivera	90660	62,566	397
Pittsburg	94565	52,036	519
Pleasanton	94566	57,682	444
Pomona	91768	143,870	130
Rancho Cucamonga	91739	114,799	169
Redding	96049	72,906	327
Redlands	92373	64,526	384
Redondo Beach	92077	64,236	387
Redwood City	94063	67,786	358
Rialto	92376	83,519	277
Richmond	94802	87,944	245
Riverside	92517	241,644	66
Rosemead	91770	52,024	520
Roseville	95678	53,019	506
Sacramento	95813	373,964	41
Salinas	93907	119,814	154
San Bernardino	92403	181,718	97
San Buenaventura (Ventura)	93001	96,769	219
San Diego	92199	1,151,977	6
San Francisco	94188	734,676	13
San Jose	95101	816,884	11
San Leandro	94577	69,490	351
San Mateo	94402	87,836	246
Santa Ana	92799	290,827	55
Santa Barbara	93102	85,626	258
Santa Clara	95050	94,562	230
Santa Clarita	91380	123,676	152
Santa Maria	93454	65,932	373
Santa Monica	90406	87,047	250
Santa Rosa	95402	116,962	162
Santee	92071	55,222	478
Simi Valley	93065	106,949	189
South Gate	90280	91,907	237
South San Francisco	94080	56,576	461
Stockton	95213	222,633	74

City	ZIP code	1994 pop. est.	1994 rank
Sunnyvale	94086	119,584	157
Thousand Oaks	91359	110,981	180
Torrance	90510	138,219	139
Tustin	92681	58,480	437
Union City	94587	55,383	477
Upland	91786	61,827	406
Vacaville	95687	83,008	279
Vallejo	94590	111,484	179
Victorville	92392	50,123	550
Visalia	93277	85,073	266
Vista	92083	79,816	288
Walnut Creek	94596	62,030	403
West Covina	91790	103,298	202
Westminster	92684	79,751	292
Whittier	90605	79,813	289
Yorba Linda	92686	61,497	408
Colorado			
Arvada	80001	95,446	225
Aurora	80010	250,717	65
Boulder	80302	85,613	259
Colorado Springs	80910	316,480	51
Denver	80201	493,559	25
Fort Collins	80521	98,954	215
Greeley	80631	64,189	388
Lakewood	80215	126,031	147
Longmont	80501	56,264	465
Pueblo	81003	100,471	208
Thornton	80229	63,079	395
Westminster	80030	87,045	251
Connecticut			
Bridgeport	06602	132,919	144
Bristol	06010	60,647	415
Danbury	06810	64,675	381
Hartford	06101	124,196	151
Meriden	06450	56,928	455
New Britain	06050	69,887	349
New Haven	06511	119,604	155
Norwalk	06856	78,710	301
Stamford	06910	107,199	188
Waterbury	06701	103,523	199
West Haven	06616	52,848	509
District of Columbia			
Washington	20066	578,014	20
Delaware			
Wilmington	19850	72,799	332
Florida			
Boca Raton	33431	66,422	371
Boynton Beach	33436	51,230	532
Cape Coral	33990	84,968	267
Clearwater	34618	99,838	212
Coral Springs	33075	92,612	235
Davie town	33329	57,156	448
Daytona Beach	32114	64,644	382
Delray Beach	33444	51,026	536
Fort Lauderdale	33310	162,842	112
Fort Myers	33907	50,489	543
Gainesville	32602	87,806	247
Hialeah	33010	194,120	85
Hollywood	33022	124,992	150
Jacksonville (remainder)	32203	665,070	15
Lakeland	33805	71,255	341
Largo	34640	67,721	361
Lauderhill	33152	52,023	521
Melbourne	32901	68,024	357
Miami	33152	373,024	42
Miami Beach	33119	90,153	239
North Miami	33261	53,504	500
Ocala	32678	53,225	504
Orlando	32862	176,948	103
Palm Bay	32901	75,139	315
Pembroke Pines	33084	81,498	285
Pensacola	32501	60,025	424
Plantation	33318	74,748	318
Pompano Beach	33060	75,719	312
Port St. Lucie	34985	70,399	346
Sarasota	34230	54,411	489
St. Petersburg	33730	238,585	68
Sunrise	33322	75,038	316
Tallahassee	32301	133,718	143

City	ZIP code	1994 pop. est.	1994 rank
Tampa	33630	285,523	57
West Palm Beach	33406	75,456	313
Georgia			
Albany	31706	81,062	286
Athens-Clarke County (remainder)	30601	89,181	242
Atlanta	30304	396,052	37
Columbus (remainder)	31908	186,470	92
Macon	31201	109,191	183
Marietta	30060	50,290	547
Roswell	30075	54,908	483
Savannah	31402	140,597	135
Hawaii			
Honolulu CDP	96820	385,881	39
Idaho			
Boise City	83708	145,987	126
Illinois			
Arlington Heights village	60005	77,438	307
Aurora	60505	112,313	176
Bloomington	61701	55,570	473
Champaign	61820	66,888	365
Chicago	60607	2,731,743	3
Cicero town	60650	74,823	317
Decatur	62523	83,105	278
Des Plaines	60018	52,896	508
Downers Grove village	60515	50,622	542
Elgin	60120	85,339	262
Evanston	60201	73,433	324
Joliet	60436	79,492	296
Mount Prospect village	60056	53,605	498
Naperville	60540	101,163	206
Oak Lawn village	60455	56,690	459
Oak Park village	60301	54,385	490
Peoria	61601	112,878	175
Rockford	61125	143,263	132
Schaumburg village	60194	73,521	323
Skokie village	60077	58,980	433
Springfield	62703	105,938	191
Waukegan	60085	67,751	360
Wheaton	60187	54,298	492
Indiana			
Anderson	46011	60,846	411
Bloomington	47408	62,560	398
Evansville	47708	129,452	145
Fort Wayne	46802	183,359	95
Gary	46401	114,256	170
Hammond	46320	82,837	282
Indianapolis (remainder)	46206	752,279	12
Muncie	47302	71,407	340
South Bend	46624	105,092	194
Terre Haute	47808	60,200	421
Iowa			
Cedar Rapids	52401	113,438	172
Council Bluffs	51501	54,850	484
Davenport	52802	96,964	218
Des Moines	50318	193,965	86
Dubuque	52001	59,084	432
Iowa City	52240	60,655	414
Sioux City	51101	82,735	283
Waterloo	50703	66,537	369
Kansas			
Kansas City	66106	142,630	133
Lawrence	66044	71,721	338
Olathe	66061	72,455	335
Overland Park	66204	125,225	149
Topeka	66603	120,646	153
Wichita	67276	310,236	54
Kentucky			
Lexington-Fayette	40511	237,612	69
Louisville	40231	270,308	60
Owensboro	42301	53,645	497
Louisiana			
Baton Rouge	70821	227,482	72
Bossier City	71111	54,419	488
Kenner	70062	72,891	328
Lafayette	70501	102,281	204
Lake Charles	70601	72,424	336
Monroe	71203	57,049	452
New Orleans	70113	484,149	27
Shreveport	71102	196,982	79

City	ZIP code	1994 pop. est.	1994 rank
Maine			
Portland	04101	61,982	404
Maryland			
Baltimore	21233	702,979	14
Massachusetts			
Boston	02205	547,725	21
Brockton	02402	87,411	248
Cambridge	02139	99,890	210
Chicopee	01020	55,024	481
Fall River	02720	89,425	241
Haverhill	01830	52,962	507
Lawrence	01842	63,117	394
Lowell	01853	96,054	224
Lynn	01901	78,312	304
Malden	02148	51,803	526
Medford	02155	55,671	472
New Bedford	02740	94,623	229
Newton	02164	85,358	261
Quincy	02369	84,040	272
Somerville	02143	68,940	354
Springfield	01101	149,164	123
Taunton	02780	51,624	527
Waltham	02154	54,791	485
Worcester	01613	165,387	109
Michigan			
Ann Arbor	48103	108,817	186
Battle Creek	49016	55,053	480
Dearborn	48120	86,187	253
Dearborn Heights	48127	58,288	439
Detroit	48283	992,038	10
East Lansing	48823	50,322	546
Farmington Hills	48333	79,144	298
Flint	48502	138,164	140
Grand Rapids	49501	190,395	90
Kalamazoo	49423	81,644	284
Lansing	48924	119,590	156
Livonia	48150	100,415	209
Pontiac	48343	66,708	367
Rochester Hills	48309	66,267	372
Roseville	48066	51,592	528
Royal Oak	48068	68,431	356
Saginaw	48605	70,607	345
Southfield	48037	79,789	291
St. Clair Shores	48080	63,834	390
Sterling Heights	48311	119,505	158
Taylor	48180	68,541	355
Troy	48099	79,029	299
Warren	48090	142,625	134
Westland	48185	85,221	263
Wyoming	49509	63,688	391
Minnesota			
Bloomington	55431	85,185	264
Brooklyn Park	55429	58,786	436
Burnsville	55337	55,081	479
Coon Rapids	55433	62,364	400
Duluth	55806	83,990	274
Eagan	55121	56,992	454
Minneapolis	55401	354,590	47
Minnetonka	55345	50,778	539
Plymouth	55441	60,143	422
Rochester	55901	75,769	311
St. Cloud	56301	50,785	538
St. Paul	55101	262,071	62
Mississippi			
Jackson	39205	193,097	87
Missouri			
Columbia	65201	74,072	321
Florissant	63033	51,398	531
Independence	64050	111,669	178
Kansas City	64108	443,878	31
Springfield	65801	149,727	121
St. Charles	63301	56,339	463
St. Joseph	64501	71,711	339
St. Louis	63155	368,215	43
Montana			
Billings	59101	86,578	252
Great Falls	59401	58,202	440
Nebraska			
Lincoln	68501	203,076	77

City	ZIP code	1994 pop. est.	1994 rank
Omaha	68108	345,033	48
Nevada			
Henderson	89015	101,997	205
Las Vegas	89199	327,878	49
North Las Vegas	89030	64,536	383
Reno	89510	145,029	128
Sparks	89431	60,238	420
New Hampshire			
Manchester	03103	96,640	221
Nashua	03060	79,631	294
New Jersey			
Bayonne	7002	62,270	401
Camden	8101	82,866	280
Clifton	7015	74,002	322
East Orange	7019	72,847	329
Elizabeth	7207	106,298	190
Jersey City	7303	226,022	73
Passaic	7055	56,042	468
Paterson	7510	138,290	138
Trenton	8650	84,441	268
Union City	7087	56,308	464
Vineland	8360	54,673	487
New Mexico			
Albuquerque	87101	411,994	36
Las Cruces	88001	71,043	342
Santa Fe	87501	62,514	399
New York			
Albany	12288	104,828	195
Binghamton	13902	51,144	533
Buffalo	14240	312,965	53
Mount Vernon	10551	65,862	374
New Rochelle	10802	66,764	366
New York	10199	7,333,253	1
Niagara Falls	14302	60,517	417
Rochester	14692	231,170	71
Schenectady	12305	64,274	385
Syracuse	13220	159,895	114
Troy	12180	52,606	511
Utica	13504	64,095	389
Yonkers	10702	183,490	94
North Carolina			
Asheville	28810	64,261	386
Cary town	27511	60,775	412
Charlotte	28228	437,797	32
Durham	27701	143,439	131
Fayetteville	28302	83,999	273
Gastonia	28052	59,093	431
Greensboro	27420	196,167	80
High Point	27260	72,208	337
Jacksonville	28540	79,494	295
Raleigh	27611	236,707	70
Rocky Mount	27801	51,941	524
Wilmington	28402	62,651	396
Winston-Salem	27102	155,128	116
North Dakota			
Bismarck	58501	52,592	512
Fargo	58102	79,715	293
Grand Forks	58201	50,168	549
Ohio			
Akron	44309	221,886	75
Canton	44711	84,188	271
Cincinnati	45234	358,170	46
Cleveland	44101	492,901	26
Cleveland Heights	44118	51,477	530
Columbus	43216	635,913	16
Dayton	45401	178,540	100
Elyria	44035	57,119	449
Euclid	44117	53,251	503
Hamilton	45011	64,912	378
Kettering	45429	59,357	428
Lakewood	44107	57,063	451
Lorain	44052	70,919	343
Mansfield	44901	53,192	505
Mentor	44060	50,058	552
Parma	44129	85,792	257
Springfield	45501	70,388	347
Toledo	43601	322,550	50
Warren	44481	50,343	545
Youngstown	44501	91,775	238

City	ZIP code	1994 pop. est.	1994 rank
Oklahoma			
Broken Arrow	74012	65,679	376
Edmond	73034	61,224	410
Lawton	73501	86,078	254
Midwest City	73125	53,473	502
Norman	73069	87,290	249
Oklahoma City	73125	463,201	28
Tulsa	74103	374,851	40
Oregon			
Beaverton	97005	59,367	427
Eugene	97401	118,122	161
Gresham	97030	78,594	303
Medford	97501	52,611	510
Portland	97208	450,777	30
Salem	97301	115,912	166
Pennsylvania			
Allentown	18101	105,339	193
Altoona	16601	52,531	513
Bethlehem	18016	72,821	330
Erie	16515	108,398	187
Harrisburg	17107	54,238	493
Lancaster	17604	57,721	443
Philadelphia	19104	1,524,249	5
Pittsburgh	15290	358,883	45
Reading	19612	78,246	305
Scranton	18505	77,964	306
Rhode Island			
Cranston	02920	77,323	308
East Providence	02914	50,059	551
Pawtucket	02860	69,002	353
Providence	02904	150,639	119
Warwick	02886	86,006	256
South Carolina			
Charleston	29423	76,854	309
Columbia	29292	104,101	197
Greenville	29602	59,808	426
North Charleston	29406	67,720	362
South Dakota			
Rapid City	57701	57,609	445
Sioux Falls	57101	109,174	184
Tennessee			
Chattanooga	37421	152,259	118
Clarksville	37040	92,116	236
Jackson	38301	52,343	516
Johnson City	37601	51,573	529
Knoxville	37950	169,311	107
Memphis	38101	614,289	18
Murfreesboro	37130	56,194	467
Nashville-Davidson (remainder)	37229	504,505	24
Texas			
Abilene	79604	110,034	182
Amarillo	79120	165,036	110
Arlington	76010	286,922	56
Austin	78710	514,013	23
Baytown	77520	67,454	363
Beaumont	77707	115,022	168
Brownsville	78520	112,904	173
Bryan	77801	60,756	413
Carrollton	75006	94,261	231
College Station	77840	57,273	447
Corpus Christi	78469	275,419	59
Dallas	75260	1,022,830	8
Denton	76201	69,210	352
El Paso	79910	579,307	19
Fort Worth	76161	451,814	29
Galveston	77550	59,224	429
Garland	75040	194,218	84
Grand Prairie	75051	108,908	185
Harlingen	78550	55,522	474
Houston	77201	1,702,086	4
Irving	75015	164,917	111
Killeen	76541	82,856	281
Laredo	78041	149,914	120
Lewisville	75067	51,143	534
Longview	75602	73,265	325
Lubbock	79402	194,467	83
McAllen	78501	95,299	226
Mesquite	75149	113,631	171
Midland	79711	96,163	223
North Richland Hills	76182	55,471	475
Odessa	79761	94,763	227
Pasadena	77501	129,292	146
Plano	75075	157,394	115
Port Arthur	77640	58,795	435
Richardson	75080	78,989	300
San Angelo	76902	88,726	243
San Antonio	78284	998,905	9
Temple	76501	52,087	518
Tyler	75712	80,194	287
Victoria	77901	60,584	416
Waco	76702	105,892	192
Wichita Falls	76307	97,766	217
Utah			
Ogden	84401	67,763	359
Orem	84057	74,402	320
Provo	84601	88,519	244
Salt Lake City	84199	171,849	106
Sandy	84070	85,406	260
West Valley City	84199	94,663	228
Virginia			
Alexandria	22313	112,879	174
Arlington CDP	22210	174,603	105
Chesapeake	23320	180,577	98
Danville	24541	54,227	494
Hampton	23670	139,628	136
Lynchburg	24506	66,491	370
Newport News	23607	179,127	99
Norfolk	23501	241,426	67
Portsmouth	23707	103,464	200
Richmond	23232	201,108	78
Roanoke	24022	96,643	220
Suffolk	23434	54,922	482
Virginia Beach	23450	430,295	35
Washington			
Bellevue	98009	84,239	270
Bellingham	98225	57,119	450
Everett	98201	76,685	310
Federal Way	98063	72,802	331
Seattle	98109	520,947	22
Spokane	99210	192,781	88
Tacoma	98413	183,060	96
Vancouver	98661	51,847	525
Yakima	98903	61,976	405
West Virginia			
Charleston	25301	56,553	462
Huntington	25704	53,789	495
Wisconsin			
Appleton	54911	69,594	350
Eau Claire	54703	58,476	438
Green Bay	54303	102,708	203
Janesville	53545	56,862	457
Kenosha	53140	85,122	265
La Crosse	54601	50,877	537
Madison	53714	194,586	82
Milwaukee	53203	617,044	17
Oshkosh	54901	56,229	466
Racine	53403	86,014	255
Sheboygan	53081	50,368	544
Waukesha	53186	60,138	423
West Allis	53214	61,259	409
Wyoming			
Cheyenne	82001	53,559	499

U.S. Statistics

Profile of the United States

This profile was created by the editors of *Information Please* from many data sources. Most figures are approximate. For additional details about the United States, please refer to the appropriate sections of the *Information Please Almanac*. NOTE: figures given are latest available at press time.

Geography

Number of states: 50
Land area (1990): 3,536,341. Share of world land area (1990): 6.2%
Northernmost point: Point Barrow, Alaska
Easternmost point: West Quoddy Head, Maine
Southernmost point: Ka Lae (South Cape), Hawaii
Westernmost point: Cape Wrangell, Alaska[1]
Geographic center: in Butte County, S.D. (44' 58' N. lat., 103' 46' W. long.)
1. The extreme points are measured from the geographic center of the United States (incl. Alaska and Hawaii), west of Castle Rock, S.D. 44° 58' N. lat., 103° 46' W. long. If measured from the prime meridian in Greenwich, England, Cape Wrangell, Alaska, would be the easternmost point.

Population

Total[1] (1997): 267,368,000
Center of population (1990): 9.7 miles northwest of Steelville in Crawford County, Missouri.
Males (1997): 130,897,000
Females (1997): 136,470,000
White (1997): 221,103,000 (82% of pop.)
Black (1997): 33,889,000 (12.7% of pop.)
Hispanic origin (can be of any race) (1997): 29,156,000 (10.9% of pop.)
American Indian, Eskimo, Aleut (1997): 2,319,000 (0.9% of pop.)
Asian and Pacific Islanders (1997): 10,056,000 (3.8% of pop.)
Median age (1997): 34.9
Baby boomers (1992): 77,000,000
Rural population (1990): 66,964,000
Metropolitan population (1990): 192,725,741
Families (March 1996): 39,594,000
Average family size (March 1996): 3.26
Home ownership (1995): 64.7% of pop.
Married (March 1996): 53,567,000
Never Married (1995): 30,286,000
Divorced (1995) 7,383,000
Unmarried couples (1995): 3,661,000
Single parents (1995): female, 12,514,000; male, 3,513,000
Widowed (1995): 2,284,000
1. Resident population of the U.S. plus Armed Forces overseas.

Vital Statistics

Births (1996): 3,899,000 (14.7 per 1,000)
Deaths (1996): 2,311,000 (8.7 per 1,000)
Marriages (1996): 2,344,000 (8.8 per 1,000)
Divorces (1996): 1,150,000 (4.3 per 1,000)
Infant mortality rate (1996): 7.2 per 1,000
Legal abortions (1992): 1,528,930
Life expectancy (1995): Total U.S., both sexes, 75.8; total men, 72.5; total women, 78.9; white men, 73.4; white women, 79.6; black men, 65.2; black women, 73.9.

Civilian Labor Force

All (1996): 133,900,000 (5.4% are unemployed)
Males (1996): 72,100,000 (5.4% are unemployed)
Females (1996): 61,800,000 (5.4% are unemployed)
Work at home (telecommuters, est. 1993): 7.6 million
Farms (1995): 2,073,320; total acres (1995 preliminary): 972,253,000. Farm population (1994): 5,024,000; percent of civilian population, 1.8%.

Income and Credit

Gross Domestic Product (1996): $7,580.0 billion
Federal budget (est. 1997): total receipts, $1,505.4 billion; total outlays, $1,631.0 billion; total deficit, $125.6 billion
Personal income per capita (1996): $24,294
Median family income (1995): $49,687
Individual shareholders (1992): 51,300,000
Number below poverty level (1995): white, 24,400,000; black, 9,900,000; Hispanic, 8,600,000

Education

Public elementary pupils, Grades 1–8 (1995): 28,383,000
Public secondary pupils, Grades 9–12 (1995): 13,751,000
Private elementary pupils, Grades 1–8 (1995): 3,430,000
Private secondary pupils, Grades 9–12 (1995): 1,213,000
College enrollment, public (1995): 11,371,000
College enrollment, private (1995): 3,342,000
College graduates (1995–96): 1,195,000
Money spent on public elementary and secondary education (1994–95): $260,142,000
Projected public school teachers (1994): 2,550,000; elementary, 1,536,000; secondary, 1,014,000; private elementary and secondary school teachers (1994): 370,000
Average salary for public school teachers (1995): $37,436

Conveniences

Radio stations (July 1997): AM, 4,987 and FM, 4,932
Television stations (July 1997): 1,092; cable, est. 9,000
Registered automobiles (est. 1995): 134,981,000
Newspaper circulation (1995): 58,193,391
Cable TV subscribers (1997): 65,090,730
Total TV households (1997): 97,000,000
TV Homes with VCRs (est. 1997): 74%
Households with computers (1997): 31.9% of pop.

Crime

Total arrests (est. 1995): 10,362,736; Under 18 years, 2,084,428; Males, 8,245,284; Females, 2,117,452; Under 18, 503,582
Child neglect and abuse cases (1993): 1,936,242
Prisoners under sentence of death (1994): 2,890
Law enforcement officers killed (1994): 146
Total murder victims (1995): 20,043
Households touched by crime (1995): 13,867,143 (–0.9% change from '94)
Violent crime (1995): 1,798,785 (–3.2% change from '94)
Theft (1995): 2,594,995 (–4.3% change from '94)

Demographic State of the Nation: 1997

Source: U.S. Bureau of the Census, Current Population Reports, Series P23-193, March 1997.

Only 7 of 10 Children Live with 2 Parents

The proportion of children under 18 years living with two parents[1] declined from 85 percent in 1970 to 69 percent in 1995. The proportion living with one parent grew from 12 percent to 27 percent. Rising divorce rates and the delaying of first marriages among adults are two of the major factors contributing to the growing proportion of children in one-parent living arrangements.

A child in a single-parent living arrangement in 1995 was nearly as likely to be living with a parent who had never married (35 percent) as with a parent who was divorced (38 percent). Another 23 percent of these children lived with a parent who was separated or living apart from his or her spouse for some other reason, and 4 percent of them lived with a widowed parent.

White children are less likely to be living with one parent than are black children or children of Hispanic origin. The proportions living with one parent in 1995 were 21 percent for white children, 56 percent for black children, and 33 percent for Hispanic children.

Educational Attainment Levels Continue to Rise

In March 1995, 82 percent of all adults ages 25 and over had completed at least high school and 23 percent had earned a bachelor's degree or more. Both figures are the highest ever recorded in the United States. The rise in educational attainment for the general adult population is driven principally by the replacement of older, less-educated people by younger people who have completed substantially more education. For example, in 1995, 87 percent of persons 25 to 34 years old had completed high school, compared with 57 percent of persons ages 75 and over.

Overall, post-secondary attainment levels are higher for men than for women. While there was no statistical difference in 1995 between men and women ages 25 and over in terms of high school completion (both 82 percent), 46 percent of women and 50 percent of men had completed some college or more. Twenty-six percent of men had obtained a bachelor's degree, compared with only 20 percent of women.

There are also sizable differences in high school completion rates among whites, blacks, and persons of Hispanic origin ages 25 and over. Among whites, 83 percent have at least a high school degree, compared with 74 percent for blacks, and 53 percent for persons of Hispanic origin.

However, the gap between the educational attainment of the white and black populations ages 25 to 29 has narrowed. While the proportion of persons with at least a high school degree remained relatively unchanged for the younger white population (87 percent) during the last decade, the proportion of blacks in the same age category with a high school degree increased from 81 percent in 1985 to 87 percent in 1995.

Nearly 1 in 11 Americans Are Foreign Born[2]

The estimated 23 million foreign-born persons in 1995 represented 8.8 percent of the U.S. population (nearly 1 in 11). While this is substantially larger than the 4.8 percent foreign born in 1970, a much greater proportion of the U.S. population was foreign born during the early part of this century. The percent foreign born declined from a high of 14.7 percent in 1910 to a low of 4.8 in 1970, and then increased steadily (although there was no significant change from 1994 to 1995).

Among the foreign born in 1995, 68.0 percent were white, 7.2 percent were black, and 18.4 percent were Asian and Pacific Islander. Nearly half (46.4 percent) of all foreign-born persons were of Hispanic origin.

More than one-quarter (6.7 million) of the total foreign-born population in 1995 were born in Mexico. The Philippines was the second largest country of origin, with 1 million persons born there. Over half a million foreign-born persons came from each of the following countries: Canada, China, Cuba, the Dominican Republic, El Salvador, Jamaica, Korea, Germany, Great Britain, and Poland.

California had the largest foreign-born population in 1995, over 7.7 million persons, or one-quarter of all California residents. New York ranked second in the number of foreign born with 3.0 million. Other states with large numbers of foreign born include Texas (2.1 million), Florida (2.0 million), New Jersey (1.1 million), and Illinois (1.0 million).[3]

Households Experienced Overall Increase in Income

From 1994 to 1995, real median household income[4] increased by 2.7 percent, from $33,178 to $34,076. Even though income remains below its 1989 prerecessionary peak of $35,421 (in 1995 dollars), the gap is narrowing. In 1994, real median household income was 6.3 percent below the 1989 level; in 1995, it was 3.8 percent below the 1989 level. Moreover, selected groups have returned to their 1989 median income levels. Households in the Midwest, black households, family households maintained by a woman with no husband present, and households maintained by persons 55 to 64 years old all had incomes in 1995 comparable to their 1989 incomes.

Historically, the long-term trend among households has been toward increasing income inequality. However, from 1994 to 1995, the amount of inequality in the distribution of income remained unchanged.

---

1. These parents may be the child's biological, step, or adoptive parents.

2. Natives are persons born in the United States, Puerto Rico, or an insular area of the United States such as Guam or the U.S. Virgin Islands, and persons who were born in a foreign country but who had at least one parent who was a U.S. citizen. All other persons are foreign born.
3. The differences in number of foreign born between Texas and Florida and between New Jersey and Illinois are not significant.
4. All changes in real income and real earnings refer to comparisons after adjusting for inflation. The income data in this section are based on money income from regularly received sources before taxes and exclude capital gains and the value of noncash benefits, such as employment-based health insurance or food stamps.

Although the percentages of both men and women who worked year round, full time increased from 1994 to 1995, neither gender experienced an increase in real earnings. In fact, the real median earnings of women working year round, full time declined from $22,834 in 1994 to $22,497 in 1995—a 1.5 percent drop after adjusting for inflation. In 1995, the median earnings of men was $31,496. The female-to-male earnings ratio for year-round, full-time workers in 1995 was 0.71, not statistically different from the all-time high ratio of 0.72 reached in 1990.

Significant Drop in Poverty Level

In 1995, the number of people below the official government poverty level was 36.4 million, representing 13.8 percent of the nation's population—both significantly lower than the corresponding 1994 figures of 38.1 million poor and a poverty rate of 14.5 percent. However, the 1995 poverty rate is still higher than the 1989 rate of 13.1 percent, the most recent low point achieved during the economic expansion of November 1982 to July 1990.

Children under 18 continue to represent a very large segment of the poor (40 percent) even though they make up only about one-fourth of the total population. Children under age 6 have been particularly vulnerable—in 1995, the overall poverty rate for these children was 23.7 percent.

40 Million Without Health Insurance

Throughout the entire 1995 calendar year, an estimated 41 million people in the United States (15.4 percent of the population) were without health insurance (unchanged from the previous year). Most people (70.3 percent) were covered by a private insurance plan for some or all of 1995. Most private insurance was employment-based, in that it was obtained through a current or former employer or union. The remaining insured people had government coverage, including Medicare (13.1 percent), Medicaid (12.1 percent), and military health care (3.5 percent). Many people are covered by more than one plan.

Despite the existence of programs such as Medicaid and Medicare, 30.2 percent of the poor (11 million) had no health insurance of any kind in 1995. This percentage—which was double the rate for all people—was unchanged from the previous year. Poor people comprised 27.1 percent of all uninsured people. Medicaid was the most widespread type of coverage among the poor, covering 46.4 percent of them at some time during 1995.

Homeownership Rate Was at Highest Level Since 1983

In 1995, 65 percent of occupied housing units were lived in by their owners. This is the highest homeownership rate since 1983, and 0.7 percentage points above the 1994 rate. Married-couple families were much more likely to own their own homes than were other types of family or nonfamily households—80 percent in 1995, compared with 55 percent for families maintained by men and 45 percent for families maintained by women.

In 1995, 51 percent of one-person households owned their own homes. The homeownership rate was 44 percent for men living alone and 55 percent for women living alone.

There were 113 million housing units in the United States in 1995, of which 65 million were owner occupied, 35 million were renter occupied, and 13 million were vacant. □

Population

Colonial Population Estimates (in round numbers)

Year	Population	Year	Population
1610	350	1700	250,900
1620	2,300	1710	331,700
1630	4,600	1720	466,200
1640	26,600	1730	629,400
1650	50,400	1740	905,600
1660	75,100	1750	1,170,800
1670	111,900	1760	1,593,600
1680	151,500	1770	2,148,100
1690	210,400	1780	2,780,400

Covers years before the establishment of the U.S. Census in 1790. *See* following page for National Census figures, 1790 to 1990.

Total Population

Area	1990	1980	1970
50 states of U.S.	248,709,873	226,545,805	203,302,031
48 conterminous	247,051,601	225,179,263	202,229,535
Alaska	550,043	401,851	302,583
Hawaii	1,108,229	964,691	769,913
American Samoa	46,773	32,297	27,159
Canal Zone	(1)	(1)	44,198
Corn Islands	—	—	(2)
Guam	133,152	105,979	84,996
Johnston Atoll	n.a.	327	1,007
Midway	(3)	453	2,220
Puerto Rico	3,522,037	3,196,520	2,712,033
Swan Islands	n.a.	n.a.	22
Trust Ter. of Pac. Is.	15,122[5]	132,929[4]	90,940
Virgin Is. of U.S.	101,809	96,569	62,468
Wake Island	(3)	302	1,647
Population abroad	922,819	995,546	1,737,836
Armed forces	910,611	515,408	1,057,776
Total	**253,451,585**	**231,106,727**	**208,066,557**

1. Reverted to Panama. 2. Returned to Nicaragua April 25, 1971. 3. No indigenous population. 4. Includes Northern Mariana Islands. 5. Palau only Trust Territory remaining. NOTE: n.a. = not available. *Source:* Department of Commerce, Bureau of the Census.

National Censuses[1]

Year	Resident population[2]	Land area, sq mi.	Pop. per sq m
1790	3,929,214	864,746	4.5
1800	5,308,483	864,746	6.1
1810	7,239,881	1,681,828	4.3
1820	9,638,453	1,749,462	5.5
1830	12,866,020	1,749,462	7.4
1840	17,069,453	1,749,462	9.8
1850	23,191,876	2,940,042	7.9
1860	31,443,321	2,969,640	10.6
1870	39,818,449	2,969,640	13.4
1880	50,155,783	2,969,640	16.9
1890	62,947,714	2,969,640	21.2
1900	75,994,575	2,969,834	25.6
1910	91,972,266	2,969,565	31.0
1920	105,710,620	2,969,451	35.6
1930	122,775,046	2,977,128	41.2
1940	131,669,275	2,977,128	44.2
1950	150,697,361	2,974,726	50.7
1960	179,323,175	3,540,911	50.6
1970	203,302,031	3,540,023	57.4
1980	226,545,805	3,539,289	64.0
1990	248,709,873	3,536,278	70.3

1. Beginning with 1960, figures include Alaska and Hawaii. 2. Excludes armed forces overseas. *Source:* Department (Commerce, Bureau of the Census.

Population Distribution by Age, Race, Nativity, and Sex

			Age				Race and Nativity				
								White[1]			
Year	Total	Under 5	5-19	20-44	45-64	65 and over	Total	Native born	Foreign born	Black	Othe races
Percent Distribution											
1860[2]	100.0	15.4	35.8	35.7	10.4	2.7	85.6	72.6	13.0	14.1	0.3
1870[2]	100.0	14.3	35.4	35.4	11.9	3.0	87.1	72.9	14.2	12.7	0.2
1880[2]	100.0	13.8	34.3	35.9	12.6	3.4	86.5	73.4	13.1	13.1	0.3
1890[3]	100.0	12.2	33.9	36.9	13.1	3.9	87.5	73.0	14.5	11.9	0.3
1900	100.0	12.1	32.3	37.7	13.7	4.1	87.9	74.5	13.4	11.6	0.5
1910	100.0	11.6	30.4	39.0	14.6	4.3	88.9	74.4	14.5	10.7	0.4
1920	100.0	10.9	29.8	38.4	16.1	4.7	89.7	76.7	13.0	9.9	0.4
1930	100.0	9.3	29.5	38.3	17.4	5.4	89.8	78.4	11.4	9.7	0.5
1940	100.0	8.0	26.4	38.9	19.8	6.8	89.8	81.1	8.7	9.8	0.4
1950	100.0	10.7	23.2	37.6	20.3	8.1	89.5	82.8	6.7	10.0	0.5
1960	100.0	11.3	27.1	32.2	20.1	9.2	88.6	83.4	5.2	10.5	0.9
1970[2]	100.0	8.4	29.5	31.7	20.6	9.8	87.6	83.4	4.3	11.1	1.4
1980	100.0	7.2	24.8	37.1	19.6	11.3	83.1	n.a.	n.a.	11.7	5.2
1990	100.0	7.6	21.3	40.1	18.6	12.5	83.9	n.a.	n.a.	12.3	3.8
Males per 100 Females											
1860[2]	104.7	102.4	101.2	107.9	111.5	98.3	105.3	103.7	115.1	99.6	260.8
1870[2]	102.2	102.9	101.2	99.2	114.5	100.5	102.8	100.6	115.3	96.2	400.7
1880[2]	103.6	103.0	101.3	104.0	110.2	101.4	104.0	102.1	115.9	97.8	362.2
1890[3]	105.0	103.6	101.4	107.3	108.3	104.2	105.4	102.9	118.7	99.5	165.2
1900	104.4	102.1	100.9	105.8	110.7	102.0	104.9	102.8	117.4	98.6	185.2
1910	106.0	102.5	101.3	108.1	114.4	101.1	106.6	102.7	129.2	98.9	185.6
1920	104.0	102.5	100.8	102.8	115.2	101.3	104.4	101.7	121.7	99.2	156.6
1930	102.5	103.0	101.4	100.5	109.1	100.5	102.9	101.1	115.8	97.0	150.6
1940	100.7	103.2	102.0	98.1	105.2	95.5	101.2	100.1	111.1	95.0	140.5
1950	98.6	103.9	102.5	96.2	100.1	89.6	99.0	98.8	102.0	93.7	129.7
1960	97.1	103.4	102.7	95.6	95.7	82.8	97.4	97.6	94.2	93.3	109.7
1970[2]	94.8	104.0	103.3	95.1	91.6	72.1	95.3	95.9	83.8	90.8	100.2
1980	94.5	104.7	104.0	98.1	90.7	67.6	94.8	n.a.	n.a.	89.6	100.3
1990	95.1	104.8	105.0	99.8	92.5	67.2	95.9	n.a.	n.a.	89.8	96.5

1. The 1980 and 1990 census data for white and other races categories are not directly comparable to those shown for the preceding years because of the changes in the way some persons reported their race, as well as changes in procedure relating to racial classification. 2. Excludes persons for whom age is not available. 3. Excludes persons enumerated in the Indian Territory and on Indian reservations. NOTES: Data exclude Armed Forces overseas. Beginning in 1960, include Alaska and Hawaii. n.a. = not available. *Source:* Department of Commerce, Bureau of the Census.

Ratio of Males to Females, by Age Group, 1950 to 1995

(Number of males per 100 females. Total resident population)

Age	1950 (Apr. 1)	1960 (Apr. 1)	1970 (Apr. 1)	1980 (Apr. 1)	1990[1] (Apr. 1)	1995 (July 1)
All ages	98.6	97.1	94.8	94.5	95.1	95.4
Under 14 years	103.7	103.4	103.9	104.6	104.9	104.9
14 to 24 years	98.2	98.7	98.7	101.9	104.6	104.4
25 to 44 years	96.4	95.7	95.5	97.4	98.9	99.2
45 to 64 years	100.1	95.7	91.6	90.7	92.5	93.5
65 years and over	89.6	82.8	72.1	67.6	67.2	69.0

Source: U.S. Bureau of the Census, *U.S. Census of Population: 1950*, vol. II, part 1; *1960*, vol. I, part 1; *1970*, vol. 1, part Current Population Reports, P25-1095 and P25-1130; Population Paper Listings PPL-41; and unpublished data.

Population by State

State	1990	Percent change, 1980-90	Pop. per sq mi., 1990	Pop. rank, 1990	1980	1950	1900	1790
Alabama	4,040,587	+3.8	79.6	22	3,893,888	3,061,743	1,828,697	—
Alaska	550,403	+36.9	1.0	49	401,851	128,643	63,592	—
Arizona	3,665,228	+34.8	32.3	24	2,718,215	749,587	122,931	—
Arkansas	2,350,725	+2.8	45.1	33	2,286,435	1,909,511	1,311,564	—
California	29,760,021	+25.7	190.4	1	23,667,902	10,586,223	1,485,053	—
Colorado	3,294,394	+14.0	31.8	26	2,889,964	1,325,089	539,700	—
Connecticut	3,287,116	+5.8	674.7	27	3,107,576	2,007,280	908,420	237,946
Delaware	666,168	+12.1	344.8	46	594,338	318,085	184,735	59,096
D.C.	606,900	-4.9	—	—	638,333	802,178	278,718	—
Florida	12,937,926	+32.7	238.9	4	9,746,324	2,771,305	528,542	—
Georgia	6,478,216	+18.6	109.9	11	5,463,105	3,444,578	2,216,331	82,548
Hawaii	1,108,229	+14.9	172.5	41	964,691	499,794	154,001	—
Idaho	1,006,749	+6.7	12.2	42	943,935	588,637	161,772	—
Illinois	11,430,602	0.0	205.4	6	11,426,518	8,712,176	4,821,550	—.
Indiana	5,544,159	+1.0	154.2	14	5,490,224	3,934,224	2,516,462	—
Iowa	2,776,755	-4.7	49.6	30	2,913,808	2,621,073	2,231,853	—
Kansas	2,477,574	+4.8	30.3	32	2,363,679	1,905,299	1,470,495	—
Kentucky	3,685,296	+0.7	92.9	23	3,660,777	2,944,806	2,147,174	73,677
Louisiana	4,219,973	+0.3	94.8	21	4,205,900	2,683,516	1,381,625	—
Maine	1,227,928	+9.2	39.6	38	1,124,660	913,774	694,466	96,540
Maryland	4,781,468	+13.4	486.0	19	4,216,975	2,343,001	1,188,044	319,728
Massachusetts	6,016,425	+4.9	768.9	13	5,737,037	4,690,514	2,805,346	378,787
Michigan	9,295,297	+0.4	163.2	8	9,262,078	6,371,766	2,420,982	—
Minnesota	4,375,099	+7.3	55.0	20	4,075,970	2,982,483	1,751,394	—
Mississippi	2,573,216	+2.1	54.5	31	2,520,638	2,178,914	1,551,270	—
Missouri	5,117,073	+4.1	74.2	15	4,916,686	3,954,653	3,106,665	—
Montana	799,065	+1.6	5.5	44	786,690	591,024	243,329	—
Nebraska	1,578,385	+0.5	20.6	36	1,569,825	1,325,510	1,066,300	—
Nevada	1,201,833	+50.1	10.9	39	800,493	160,083	42,335	—
New Hampshire	1,109,252	+20.5	123.3	40	920,610	533,242	411,588	141,885
New Jersey	7,730,188	+5.0	1,035.1	9	7,364,823	4,835,329	1,883,669	184,139
New Mexico	1,515,069	+16.3	12.5	37	1,302,894	681,187	195,310	—
New York	17,990,455	+2.5	379.7	2	17,558,072	14,830,192	7,268,894	340,120
North Carolina	6,628,637	+12.7	135.7	10	5,881,766	4,061,929	1,893,810	393,751
North Dakota	638,800	-2.1	9.0	47	652,717	619,636	319,146	—
Ohio	10,847,115	+0.5	264.5	7	10,797,630	7,946,627	4,157,545	—
Oklahoma	3,145,585	+4.0	45.8	28	3,025,290	2,233,351	790,391[1]	—
Oregon	2,842,321	+7.9	29.5	29	2,633,105	1,521,341	413,536	—
Pennsylvania	11,881,643	+0.1	264.7	5	11,863,895	10,498,012	6,302,115	434,373
Rhode Island	1,003,464	+5.9	951.1	43	947,154	791,896	428,556	68,825
South Carolina	3,486,703	+11.7	115.4	25	3,121,820	2,117,027	1,340,316	249,073
South Dakota	696,004	+0.8	9.1	45	690,768	652,740	401,570	—
Tennessee	4,877,185	+6.2	118.5	17	4,591,120	3,291,718	2,020,616	35,691
Texas	16,986,510	+19.4	64.8	3	14,229,191	7,711,194	3,048,710	—
Utah	1,722,850	+17.9	20.9	35	1,461,037	688,862	276,749	—
Vermont	562,758	+10.0	60.7	48	511,456	377,747	343,641	85,425
Virginia	6,187,358	+15.7	155.8	12	5,346,818	3,318,680	1,854,184	747,610[2]
Washington	4,866,692	+17.8	73.1	18	4,132,156	2,378,963	518,103	—
West Virginia	1,793,477	-8.0	73.8	34	1,949,644	2,005,552	958,800	—
Wisconsin	4,891,769	+4.0	89.9	16	4,705,767	3,434,575	2,069,042	—
Wyoming	453,588	-3.4	4.7	50	469,557	290,529	92,531	—
Total U.S.	248,709,873	+9.8	—	—	226,545,805	151,325,798	76,212,168	3,929,214

Includes population of Indian Territory: 1900, 392,960. 2. Until 1863, Virginia included what is now West Virginia. *Source:* Department of Commerce, Bureau of the Census.

Estimated 1992 Population of Metro Areas Over One Million

Metropolitan statistical area (MSA) Consolidated metropolitan statistical area (CMSA)	July 1, 1992	Metropolitan statistical area (MSA) Consolidated metropolitan statistical area (CMSA)	July 1, 1992
New York-Northern New Jersey-Long Island, NY-NJ-CT-PA CMSA	19,670,175	Tampa-St. Petersburg-Clearwater, FL MSA	2,107,271
		Denver-Boulder-Greeley, CO CMSA	2,089,321
Los Angeles-Riverside-Orange County, CA CMSA	15,047,772	Portland-Salem, OR-WA CMSA	1,896,895
		Cincinnati-Hamilton, OH-KY-IN CMSA	1,865,002
Chicago-Gary-Kenosha, IL-IN-WI CMSA	8,410,402	Milwaukee-Racine, WI CMSA	1,629,420
Washington-Baltimore, DC-MD-VA-WV CMSA	6,919,572	Kansas City, MO-KS MSA	1,616,930
		Sacramento-Yolo, CA CMSA	1,563,374
San Francisco-Oakland-San Jose, CA CMSA	6,409,891	Norfolk-Virginia Beach-Newport News, VA-NC MSA	1,496,672
Philadelphia-Wilmington-Atlantic City, PA-NJ-DE-MD CMSA	5,938,528	Indianapolis, IN MSA	1,424,050
Boston-Worcester-Lawrence, MA-NH-ME-CT CMSA	5,438,815	Columbus, OH MSA	1,394,067
		San Antonio, TX MSA	1,378,619
Detroit-Ann Arbor-Flint, MI CMSA	5,245,906	Orlando, FL MSA	1,304,700
Dallas-Fort Worth, TX CMSA	4,214,532	New Orleans, LA MSA	1,302,697
Houston-Galveston-Brazoria, TX CMSA	3,962,365	Charlotte-Gastonia-Rock Hill, NC-SC MSA	1,212,393
Miami-Fort Lauderdale, FL CMSA	3,309,246	Buffalo-Niagara Falls, NY MSA	1,193,901
Atlanta, GA MSA	3,142,857	Hartford, CT MSA	1,155,725
Seattle-Tacoma-Bremerton, WA CMSA	3,131,392	Providence-Fall River-Warwick, RI-MA MSA	1,131,133
Cleveland-Akron, OH CMSA	2,890,402	Salt Lake City-Ogden, UT MSA	1,128,121
Minneapolis-St. Paul, MN-WI MSA	2,617,973	Rochester, NY MSA	1,081,244
San Diego, CA MSA	2,601,055	Greensboro-Winston-Salem-High Point, NC MSA	1,078,377
St. Louis, MO-IL MSA	2,518,528		
Pittsburgh, PA MSA	2,406,452	Memphis, TN-AR-MS MSA	1,033,813
Phoenix-Mesa, AZ MSA	2,330,353	Nashville, TN MSA	1,023,315

NOTE: These estimates are consistent with the population as enumerated in the 1990 census, and have not been adjusted for census coverage errors. *Source:* U.S. Bureau of the Census. Areas defined by the Office of Management and Budget as of June 30, 1993.

Getting to Work in the City

Travel-to-work characteristics for the 15 largest cities by population in the United States: 1990

City of residence	Total workers 16 years and over	Means of transportation (%)				Average travel time to work (min.)
		Drove alone	Carpool	Public transit	Other Means[1]	
New York, NY	3,183,088	24.0%	8.5%	53.4%	14.0%	36.5
Los Angeles, CA	1,629,096	65.2	15.4	10.5	8.9	26.5
Chicago, IL	1,181,677	46.3	14.8	29.7	9.2	31.5
Houston, TX	772,957	71.7	15.5	6.5	6.3	24.7
Philadelphia, PA	640,577	44.7	13.2	28.7	13.5	27.4
San Diego, CA	560,913	70.7	12.8	4.2	12.2	20.4
Detroit, MI	325,054	67.8	16.1	10.7	5.3	24.7
Dallas, TX	500,566	72.5	15.2	6.7	5.7	24.0
Phoenix, AZ	473,966	73.7	15.1	3.3	7.9	23.0
San Antonio, TX	395,551	73.4	15.5	4.9	6.2	21.7
San Jose, CA	400,932	76.9	14.6	3.5	5.1	25.5
Indianapolis, IN	362,777	78.0	13.4	3.3	5.2	20.8
Baltimore, MD	307,679	50.9	16.8	22.0	10.2	26.0
San Francisco, CA	382,309	38.5	11.5	33.5	16.5	26.9
Jacksonville, FL	312,958	75.5	14.2	2.7	7.6	21.6

1. Includes commuting by motorcycle, bicycle, walking, and all other means. Also includes those who worked at home
NOTE: May not add due to rounding. *Source:* U.S. Census Bureau, Department of Commerce.

Resident Population of the United States:
Estimates, by Sex, Race, and Hispanic Origin, with Median Age, 1997

(Numbers in thousands)

	Total population	% of population	Median age	Male population	Female population
All races	267,368	100.0	34.9	130,897	136,470
White	221,103	82.7	36.0	108,793	112,310
Black	33,889	12.7	29.7	16,091	17,798
American Indian, Eskimo, and Aleut	2,319	0.9	27.2	1,151	1,168
Asian and Pacific Islander	10,056	3.8	31.0	4,862	5,194
Hispanic origin (of any race)	29,156	10.9	26.5	14,987	14,169

Source: U.S. Bureau of the Census, web: www.census.gov.

Resident Population of the United States:
Estimates, by Age and Sex, 1997

	Both sexes	Male	Female
Population, all ages	267,368,000	130,897,000	136,470,000
Median age	34.9	33.8	36.1
Five-year age groups			
Under 5 years	19,058,000	9,753,000	9,305,000
5 to 9 years	19,719,000	10,094,000	9,625,000
10 to 14 years	19,046,000	9,760,000	9,286,000
15 to 19 years	19,040,000	9,813,000	9,227,000
20 to 24 years	17,484,000	8,969,000	8,515,000
25 to 29 years	18,902,000	9,488,000	9,413,000
30 to 34 years	20,803,000	10,370,000	10,433,000
35 to 39 years	22,662,000	11,307,000	11,355,000
40 to 44 years	21,326,000	10,573,000	10,753,000
45 to 49 years	18,449,000	9,065,000	9,384,000
50 to 54 years	15,117,000	7,361,000	7,756,000
55 to 59 years	11,677,000	5,608,000	6,069,000
60 to 64 years	10,042,000	4,739,000	5,303,000
65 to 69 years	9,776,000	4,466,000	5,310,000
70 to 74 years	8,728,000	3,803,000	4,925,000
75 to 79 years	7,047,000	2,908,000	4,139,000
80 to 84 years	4,635,000	1,710,000	2,925,000
85 to 89 years	2,449,000	765,000	1,683,000
90 to 94 years	1,055,000	271,000	784,000
95 to 99 years	296,000	63,000	233,000
100 years and over	58,000	10,000	47,000
Special age categories			
18 years and over	197,966,000	95,316,000	102,649,000
65 years and over	34,044,000	13,998,000	20,046,000

Preference for Racial or Ethnic Terminology,
Census Bureau Survey, May 1995

Preferred Term	Percent	Preferred Term	Percent
Hispanic		**Black**	
Hispanic	57.88%	Black	44.15%
Latino	11.74	African-American	28.07
Of Spanish origin	12.34	Afro-American	12.12
Some other term	7.85	Negro	3.28
No preference	10.18	Colored	1.09
White		Some other term	2.19
White	61.66%	No preference	9.11
Caucasian	16.53	**American Indian**	
European-American	2.35	American Indian	49.76%
Anglo	.96	Alaska Native	3.51
Some other term	1.97	Native American	37.35
No preference	16.53	Some other term	3.66
		No preference	5.72

Immigrants to U.S. by Country of Origin

Figures are totals, not annual averages, and were tabulated as follows: 1820–67, alien passengers arrived; 1868–91 and 1895–97, immigrant aliens arrived; 1892-94 and 1898 to present, immigrant aliens admitted. From 1989 totals include legalized immigrants. (Data before 1906 relate to country whence alien came; 1906–80, to country of last permanent residence; 1981 to present data based on country of birth.)

Countries	1996	1820-1996	1981-90	1971-80	1961-70	1951-60	1941-50	1820-1940
Europe:	4,007	12,230	479	329	98	59	85	2,040
Albania[1]								
Austria[2]	554	2,664,728	4,636	9,478	20,621	67,106	24,860	2,534,617
Belgium	651	212,894	5,706	5,329	9,192	18,575	12,189	158,205
Bulgaria[3]	2,066	78,029	2,342	1,188	619	104	375	65,856
Former Czechoslovakia[1]	1,389	156,848	11,500	6,023	3,273	918	8,347	120,013
Denmark	608	374,287	5,380	4,439	9,201	10,984	5,393	335,025
Estonia[1]	280	2,254	137	91	163	185	212	506
Finland[1]	602	40,315	3,265	2,868	4,192	4,925	2,503	19,593
France	3,079	795,259	23,124	25,069	45,237	51,121	38,809	594,998
Germany[2]	6,748	7,105,301	70,111	74,414	190,796	477,765	226,578	6,021,951
Greece	1,452	704,679	29,130	92,369	85,969	47,608	8,973	430,608
Hungary[2]	1,183	167,871	9,764	6,550	5,401	36,637	3,469	1,609,158
Ireland	1,731	4,780,891	32,823	11,490	32,966	48,362	14,789	4,580,557
Italy	2,501	5,353,213	32,894	129,368	214,111	185,491	57,661	4,719,223
Latvia[1]	736	6,603	359	207	510	352	361	1,192
Lithuania[1]	1,080	7,967	482	248	562	242	683	2,201
Luxembourg[1]	32	3,284	234	307	556	684	820	565
Netherlands	1,423	382,109	11,958	10,492	30,606	52,277	14,860	253,759
Norway[4]	354	756,448	3,901	3,941	15,484	22,935	10,100	697,095
Poland[5]	8,481	743,376	97,390	37,234	53,539	9,985	7,571	414,755
Portugal	3,766	518,753	40,020	101,710	76,065	19,588	7,423	256,044
Romania[6]	5,198	246,657	39,963	12,393	2,531	1,039	1,076	156,945
Spain	1,591	289,611	15,698	39,141	44,659	7,894	2,898	170,123
Sweden[4]	1,098	1,398,578	10,211	6,531	17,116	21,697	10,665	1,325,208
Switzerland	677	362,792	7,076	8,235	18,453	17,675	10,547	295,680
United Kingdom	13,657	5,197,150	142,123	137,374	213,822	202,824	139,306	4,266,561
Former U.S.S.R.[7]	2,588	3,749,777	84,081	38,961	2,465	671	571	3,343,361
Former Yugoslavia[3]	2,011	158,540	19,182	30,540	20,381	8,225	1,576	56,787
Other Europe	3,605	65,875	2,661	4,049	4,904	9,799	3,447	36,060
Total Europe	147,581	36,410,452	705,630	800,368	1,123,492	1,325,727	621,147	32,468,776
Asia:	25,106	1,232,740	388,686	124,326	34,764	9,657	16,709	382,173
China[8]								
India	44,859	703,339	261,841	164,134	27,189	1,973	1,761	9,873
Israel	3,126	152,473	36,353	37,713	29,602	25,476	476	—
Japan[9]	6,011	498,333	43,248	49,775	39,988	46,250	1,555	277,591
Turkey	3,657	425,601	20,843	13,399	10,142	3,519	798	361,236
Other Asia	207,413	5,010,282	2,042,025	1,198,831	285,957	66,374	15,729	44,053
Total Asia[10]	268,248	8,000,844	2,066,455	1,588,178	427,642	153,249	37,028	1,074,926
America:	15,825	4,348,541	119,204	169,939	413,310	377,952	171,718	3,005,728
Canada and Newfoundland[11]								
Central America	44,289	1,153,217	458,753	134,640	101,330	44,751	21,665	49,154
Mexico[12]	163,572	5,246,392	1,653,250	640,294	453,937	299,811	60,589	778,255
South America	61,769	1,588,408	455,977	295,741	257,954	91,628	21,831	121,302
West Indies	116,801	3,372,716	892,392	741,126	470,213	123,091	49,725	446,971
Other America[12]	51	117,574	1,352	995	19,630	59,711	29,276	56
Total America	340,540	15,945,081	3,580,928	1,982,735	1,716,374	996,944	354,804	4,401,466
Africa	52,889	561,569	192,212	80,779	28,954	14,092	7,367	26,060
Australia and New Zealand	2,750	160,870	20,169	23,788	19,562	11,506	13,805	54,437
Pacific Islands[13]	-	63,034	21,041	17,454	5,560	1,470	746	11,089
Countries not specified[14]	5	272,254	196	12	93	12,491	142	253,689
Total all countries	605,793	61,207,884	7,338,062	4,493,314	3,321,677	2,515,479	1,035,039	38,290,443

1. Countries established since beginning of World War I are included with countries to which they belonged. 2. Data for Austria-Hungary not reported until 1861. Austria and Hungary recorded separately after 1905, Austria included with Germany 1938–45. 3. Bulgaria, Serbia, Montenegro first reported in 1899. Bulgaria reported separately since 1920. In 1920, separate enumeration for Kingdom of Serbs, Croats, Slovenes; since 1922, recorded as Yugoslavia. 4. Norway included with Sweden 1820–68. 5. Included with Austria-Hungary, Germany, and Russia 1899–1919. 6. No record of immigration until 1880. 7. From 1931–63, the U.S.S.R. was broken down into European U.S.S.R. and Asian U.S.S.R. Since 1964, total U.S.S.R. has been reported in Europe. 8. Beginning in 1957, China includes Taiwan. 9. No record of immigration until 1861. 10. From 1934, Asia included Philippines; before 1934, recorded in separate tables as insular travel. 11. Includes all British North American possessions, 1820–98. 12. No record of immigration, 1886–93. 13. Included with "Countries not specified" prior to 1925. 14. Includes 32,897 persons returning in 1906 to their homes in U.S. NOTE: Data are latest available. *Source:* Department of Justice, Immigration and Naturalization Service.

The Foreign Born Population in the United States: 1990 and 1980

25 Largest Places of Birth

1990 Rank	Place of Birth	Number	Percent	1980 Rank	Place of Birth	Number	Percent
	United States	19,767,316	100.0		United States	14,079,906	100.0
1	Mexico	4,298,014	21.7	1	Mexico	2,199,221	15.6
2	Philippines	912,674	4.6	2	Germany	849,384	6.0
3	Canada	744,830	3.8	3	Canada	842,859	6.0
4	Cuba	736,971	3.7	4	Italy	831,922	5.9
5	Germany	711,929	3.6	5	United Kingdom	669,149	4.8
6	United Kingdom	640,145	3.2	6	Cuba	607,814	4.3
7	Italy	580,592	2.9	7	Philippines	501,440	3.6
8	Korea	568,397	2.9	8	Poland	418,128	3.0
9	Vietnam	543,262	2.7	9	Soviet Union	406,022	2.9
10	China	529,837	2.7	10	Korea	289,885	2.1
11	El Salvador	465,433	2.4	11	China	286,120	2.0
12	India	450,406	2.3	12	Vietnam	231,120	1.6
13	Poland	388,328	2.0	13	Japan	221,794	1.6
14	Dominican Republic	347,858	1.8	14	Portugal	211,614	1.5
15	Jamaica	334,140	1.7	15	Greece	210,998	1.5
16	Soviet Union	333,725	1.7	16	India	206,087	1.5
17	Japan	290,128	1.5	17	Ireland	197,817	1.4
18	Colombia	286,124	1.4	18	Jamaica	196,811	1.4
19	Taiwan	244,102	1.2	19	Dominican Republic	169,147	1.2
20	Guatemala	225,739	1.1	20	Yugoslavia	152,967	1.1
21	Haiti	225,393	1.1	21	Austria	145,607	1.0
22	Iran	210,941	1.1	22	Hungary	144,368	1.0
23	Portugal	210,122	1.1	23	Colombia	143,508	1.0
24	Greece	177,398	0.9	24	Iran	121,505	0.9
25	Laos	171,577	0.9	25	France	120,215	0.9

Source: U.S. Bureau of the Census, 1993.

Non-English Language Speaking Americans, 1990

Top 50 languages spoken at home, ranked for persons five years old and over

Language	1990 Population 5 years and over	1980 Population 3 years and over	Percent change
U.S. population	230,445,777	216,384,403	6.5
Total, non-English speaking	31,844,979	23,711,574	34.3
Spanish	17,339,172	11,549,333	50.1
French	1,702,176	1,572,275	8.3
German	1,547,099	1,606,743	−3.7
Italian	1,308,648	1,633,279	−19.9
Chinese	1,249,213	631,737	97.7
Tagalog[1]	843,251	451,962	86.6
Polish	723,483	826,150	−12.4
Korean	626,478	275,712	127.2
Vietnamese	507,069	203,268	149.5
Portuguese	429,860	361,101	19.0
Japanese	427,657	342,205	25.0
Greek	388,260	410,462	−5.4
Arabic	355,150	225,597	57.4
Hindi and related	331,484	129,968	155.1
Russian	241,798	174,623	38.5
Yiddish	213,064	320,380	−33.5
Thai	206,266	89,052	131.6
Persian	201,865	109,293	84.7
French Creole	187,658	24,885	654.1
Armenian	149,694	102,301	46.3
Navaho	148,530	123,169	20.6
Hungarian	147,902	180,083	−17.9
Hebrew	144,292	99,166	45.4
Dutch	142,684	146,429	−2.6
Mon-Khmer[2]	127,441	16,417	676.3
Gujarathi[3]	102,418	36,865	177.8
Ukrainian	96,568	122,300	−21.0

Language	1990 Population 5 years and over	1980 Population 3 years and over	Percent change
Czech	92,485	123,059	−24.8
Pennsylvania Dutch	83,525	68,202	22.5
Miao[4]	81,877	16,189	405.8
Norwegian	80,723	113,227	−28.7
Slovak	80,388	87,941	—8.6
Swedish	77,511	100,886	−23.2
Serbocroatian	70,964	83,216	−14.7
Kru[5]	65,848	24,506	168.7
Rumanian	65,265	32,502	100.8
Lithuanian	55,781	73,234	−23.8
Finnish	54,350	69,386	−21.7
Panjabi	50,005	19,298	159.1
Formosan	46,044	13,661	237.0
Croatian	45,206	42,479	6.4
Turkish	41,876	27,459	52.5

NOTE: The data for 1980 in this table are for the population 3 years old and over; for 1990 they are for persons 5 years and over. 1. Filipino language of Manila and adjacent provinces. 2. Language spoken in southeast Asia, mostly in Cambodia. 3. Language of Gujarat region of western India. 4. Language of Hmong people of mountainous regions of southern China and adjacent areas of Vietnam, Laos, and Thailand. 5. Language spoken in Western Africa, chiefly in Liberia. *Source:* Census data published April 1993.

Immigrants Admitted as Permanent Residents Under Refugee Acts, by Country of Birth: 1971 to 1994

Covers immigrants who were allowed to enter the United States under 1953 Refugee Relief Act and later acts; Hungarian parolees under July 1958 Act; refugee-escapee parolees under July 1960 Act; conditional entries by refugees under Oct. 1965 Act; Cuban parolees under Nov. 1966 Act; beginning 1978, Indochina refugees under Act of Oct. 1977; beginning 1980, refugee-parolees under the Act of Oct. 1978, and asylees under the Act of March 1980; and beginning 1981 refugees under the Act of March 1980.

Country of birth	1971–80 total	1981–90 total	1991–93 total	1994
Total	**539,447**	**1,013,620**	**383,459**	**121,434**
Europe[1]	71,858	155,512	158,862	54,978
Albania	395	353	1,812	733
Bulgaria	1,238	1,197	1,176	138
Czechoslovakia	3,646	8,204	1,097	41
Greece	478	1,408	194	65
Hungary	4,358	4,942	1,126	37
Poland	5,882	33,889	6,448	334
Romania	6,812	29,798	12,901	1,199
Soviet Union, former[2]	31,309	72,306	130,955	50,756
Azerbaijan	n.a.	n.a.	n.a.	2,668
Belarus	n.a.	n.a.	n.a.	5,156
Moldova	n.a.	n.a.	n.a.	2,154
Russia	n.a.	n.a.	n.a.	10,359
Ukraine	n.a.	n.a.	n.a.	19,366
Uzbekistan	n.a.	n.a.	n.a.	3,211
Spain	5,317	736	183	55
Yugoslavia	11,297	324	201	506
Asia[1]	210,683	712,092	154,967	45,768
Afghanistan	542	22,946	6,415	1,665
Cambodia	7,739	114,064	5,053	557
China[3]	13,760	7,928	2,673	774
Hong Kong	3,468	1,916	358	82
Iran	364	46,773	15,483	2,186
Iraq	6,851	7,540	2,414	4,400
Laos	21,690	142,964	23,700	4,482
Philippines	216	3,403	592	103
Syria	1,336	2,145	463	34
Thailand	1,241	30,259	11,375	3,076
Turkey	1,193	1,896	204	156
Vietnam	150,266	324,453	83,947	27,318
North America[1]	252,633	121,840	53,205	14,204
Cuba	251,514	113,367	29,475	11,998
El Salvador	45	1,383	2,803	275
Nicaragua	36	5,590	18,793	6
South Amreica[1]	1,244	1,976	1,223	383
Africa[1]	2,991	22,149	15,155	6,078
Egypt	1,473	426	105	37
Ethiopia	1,307	18,542	10,532	2,530
Other	38	51	47	23

n.a. = Not available. 1. Includes other countries, not shown separately. 2. Includes other republics and unknown republics, not shown separately. 3. Includes Taiwan. *Source:* U.S. Immigration and Naturalization Service, *Statistical Yearbook,* annual; and releases.

Persons Below Poverty Level

Race and Hispanic Origin, Age, and Region, 1995

	Number	Percent		Number	Percent
Total[1]	36,425	13.8%	45 to 54 years	2,470	7.8%
White	24,423	11.2	55 to 59 years	1,163	10.3
Black	9,872	29.3	60 to 64 years	996	10.2
Asian and Pacific Islander	1,411	14.6	65 years and over	3,318	10.5
Hispanic origin[2]	8,574	30.3	Northeast	6,445	12.5
Under 18 years	14,665	20.8	Midwest	6,785	11.0
18 to 24 years	4,553	18.3	South	14,458	15.7
25 to 34 years	5,196	12.7	West	8,736	14.9
35 to 44 years	4,064	9.4			

1. Includes races not shown separately. 2. Persons of Hispanic origin may be of any race. *Source:* "Income, Poverty, and Valuation of Noncash Benefits" *Current Population Reports,* U.S. Bureau of the Census, web: www.census.gov.

Weighted Average Poverty Thresholds for Families of Specified Size, 1960–1995

Calendar year	Individual	2 persons	Families of 3 persons or more				
			3 persons	4 persons	5 persons	6 persons	7 persons or more
1960	$1,490	$1,924	$ 2,359	$ 3,022	$ 3,560	$ 4,002	$ 4,921
1965	1,582	2,048	2,514	3,223	3,797	4,264	5,248
1970	1,954	2,525	3,099	3,968	4,680	5,260	6,468
1975	2,724	3,506	4,293	5,500	6,499	7,316	9,022
1980	4,190	5,363	6,565	8,414	9,966	11,269	13,955
1985	5,469	6,998	8,573	10,989	13,007	14,696	16,656
1990	6,652	8,509	10,419	13,359	15,792	17,839	20,241
1995	7,763	9,933	12,158	15,569	18,408	20,804	23,552

Source: U.S. Bureau of the Census, web: www.census.gov.

Marital Status and Household Characteristics

Marriages and Divorces, 1900–1996

Year	Marriage		Divorce[1]	
	Number	Rate[2]	Number	Rate[2]
1900	709,000	9.3	55,751	0.7
1910	948,166	10.3	83,045	0.9
1920	1,274,476	12.0	170,505	1.6
1930	1,126,856	9.2	195,961	1.6
1940	1,595,879	12.1	264,000	2.0
1950	1,667,231	11.1	385,144	2.6
1960	1,523,000	8.5	393,000	2.2
1965	1,800,000	9.3	479,000	2.5
1970	2,158,802	10.6	708,000	3.5
1975	2,152,662	10.1	1,036,000	4.9
1980	2,406,708	10.6	1,182,000	5.2
1982	2,495,000	10.8	1,180,000	5.1
1983	2,444,000	10.5	1,179,000	5.0
1984	2,487,000	10.5	1,155,000	4.9
1985	2,425,000	10.2	1,187,000	5.0
1986	2,400,000	10.0	1,159,000	4.8
1987	2,421,000	9.9	1,157,000	4.8
1988	2,389,000	9.7	1,183,000	4.8
1989	2,404,000	9.7	1,163,000	4.7
1990	2,448,000	9.8	1,175,000	4.7
1991	2,371,000	9.4	1,187,000	4.7
1992	2,362,000	9.2	1,215,000	4.8
1993	2,334,000	9.0	1,187,000	4.6
1994	2,362,000	9.1	1,191,000	4.6
1995	2,336,000	8.9	1,169,000	4.4
1996	2,344,000	8.8	1,150,000	4.3

1. Includes annulments. 2. Per 1,000 population. Divorce rates for 1941-46 are based on population including armed forces overseas. Marriage rates are based on population excluding armed forces overseas. NOTE: Marriage and divorce figures for most years include some estimated data. Alaska is included beginning 1959, Hawaii beginning 1960. *Source:* Department of Health and Human Services, National Center for Health Statistics, web: www.dhhs.gov.

Marital Status of the Population

Years	Married	Never married	Widowed	Divorced
Males				
All races				
1995	57,750,000	30,286,000	2,284,000	7,383,000
1990	55,833,000	27,505,000	2,333,000	6,283,000
1980	51,813,000	24,227,000	1,977,000	3,930,000
1970	47,109,000	19,832,000	2,051,000	1,567,000
1960*	41,781,000	15,274,000	2,112,000	1,106,000
1950*	36,866,000	14,400,000	2,264,000	1,071,000
White				
1995	50,658,000	23,667,000	1,921,000	6,321,000
1990	49,542,000	22,078,000	1,930,000	5,359,000
1980	46,721,000	20,174,000	1,642,000	3,351,000
1970	42,732,000	17,080,000	1,722,000	1,333,000
1960*	38,042,000	13,286,000	1,816,000	986,000
1950*	33,451,000	12,892,000	1,986,000	972,000
Black				
1995	4,632,000	5,031,000	310,000	852,000
1990	4,489,000	4,319,000	338,000	802,000
1980	4,053,000	3,410,000	308,000	521,000
1970	3,949,000	2,468,000	307,000	212,000
1960*	3,739,000	1,988,000	296,000	120,000
1950*	3,415,000	1,508,000	278,000	99,000
Females				
All races				
1995	58,984,000	24,693,000	11,082,000	10,270,000
1990	56,797,000	22,718,000	11,477,000	8,845,000
1980	52,965,000	20,226,000	10,758,000	5,966,000
1970	48,148,000	17,167,000	9,734,000	2,717,000
1960*	42,583,000	12,252,000	8,064,000	1,708,000
1950*	37,577,000	11,418,000	6,734,000	1,373,000
White				
1995	51,390,000	18,250,000	9,399,000	8,445,000
1990	49,986,000	17,438,000	9,800,000	7,284,000
1980	47,277,000	16,318,000	9,296,000	4,990,000
1970	43,286,000	14,703,000	8,559,000	2,340,000
1960*	38,545,000	10,796,000	7,099,000	1,420,000
1950*	34,042,000	10,241,000	5,902,000	1,219,000
Black				
1995	4,942,000	5,250,000	1,380,000	1,525,000
1990	4,813,000	4,416,000	1,392,000	1,344,000
1980	4,508,000	3,401,000	1,319,000	880,000
1970	4,384,000	2,248,000	1,120,000	355,000
1960*	4,038,000	1,456,000	965,000	288,000
1950*	3,534,000	1,178,000	832,000	154,000

*1950 and 1960 data are for the population 14 years old and over. Nonwhite data is shown for black for these years. *Source:* U.S. Bureau of the Census, *Current Population Reports*, Series P20–484, "Marital Status and Living Arrangements: March 1994," web: www.census.gov.

Americans Become More Charitable

According to the *Chronicle of Philanthropy*, Americans gave $23.5 billion to charity in 1995, up 5 percent from the previous year. The top 400 charities included 138 colleges and universities, 21 human service groups, 24 religious organizations, 34 international groups, and 21 health charities.

The top ten charities for 1995 were:

(1) Salvation Army
(2) American Red Cross
(3) Catholic Charities
(4) American Cancer Society
(5) Second Harvest

(6) United Jewish Appeal
(7) Harvard University
(8) Boys and Girls Clubs of America
(9) YWCA of the USA
(10) American Heart Association

Percent of Population Never Married

Age group	All races 1995	All races 1980	All races 1970	White 1995	White 1980	White 1970	Black 1995	Black 1980	Black 1970
Males:	80.7	68.8	54.6	79.1	67.0	54.5	90.5	79.3	56.1
20 to 24									
25 to 29	51.0	33.1	19.1	48.6	31.4	17.8	65.0	44.2	28.4
30 to 34	28.2	15.9	9.4	25.4	14.2	9.2	40.0	30.0	9.2
35 to 39	20.3	7.8	7.2	18.2	6.6	6.1	35.1	18.5	15.8
40 to 44	14.0	7.1	6.3	12.5	6.7	5.7	25.1	10.8	11.2
45 to 54	8.1	6.1	7.5	7.1	5.6	7.1	17.6	11.7	10.4
55 to 64	5.0	5.3	7.8	4.3	5.2	7.6	12.7	5.9	9.1
65 and over	4.2	4.9	7.5	3.9	4.8	7.4	6.7	5.5	5.7
Females:	66.7	50.2	35.8	63.7	47.2	34.6	83.9	68.5	43.5
20 to 24									
25 to 29	35.3	20.9	10.5	30.8	18.3	9.2	68.6	37.2	18.8
30 to 34	19.0	9.5	6.2	15.7	8.1	5.5	40.1	19.0	10.8
35 to 39	12.6	6.2	5.4	9.7	5.2	4.6	30.6	12.2	12.1
40 to 44	8.7	4.8	4.9	6.7	4.3	4.8	21.8	9.0	6.9
45 to 54	8.1	4.7	4.9	5.1	4.4	4.9	14.2	7.7	4.4
55 to 64	4.3	4.5	6.8	3.8	4.4	7.0	9.3	5.7	4.7
65 and over	4.2	5.9	7.7	4.0	6.1	8.0	6.3	4.5	4.2

Source: U.S. Bureau of the Census, web: www.census.gov.

Persons Living Alone, by Sex and Age

(numbers in thousands)

Sex and Age[1]	1995 Number	1995 Percent	1994 Number	1994 Percent	1990 Number	1990 Percent	1980 Number	1980 Percent	1970 Number	1970 Percent
BOTH SEXES										
15 to 24 years	1,196	5.0	1,126	4.8	1,210	5.3	1,726	9.4	556	5.1
25 to 44 years	7,316	29.6	7,235	30.6	7,110	30.9	4,729	25.8	1,604	14.8
45 to 64 years	6,377	26.0	5,967	25.3	5,502	23.9	4,514	24.7	3,622	33.4
65 years and over	9,844	39.8	9,285	39.3	9,176	39.9	7,328	40.1	5,071	46.7
Total, 15 years and over	24,732	100.0	23,613	100.0	22,999	100.0	18,296	100.0	10,851	100.0
MALE										
15 to 24 years	623	3.0	570	6.0	674	7.4	947	13.6	274	2.5
25 to 44 years	4,476	44.1	4,359	46.2	4,231	46.8	2,920	41.9	933	8.6
45 to 64 years	2,787	11.0	2,473	26.2	2,203	24.3	1,613	23.2	1,152	10.6
65 years and over	2,254	22.2	2,037	21.6	1,942	21.5	1,486	21.3	1,174	10.8
Total, 15 years and over	10,140	100.0	9,439	100.0	9,049	100.0	6,966	100.0	3,532	100.0
FEMALE										
15 to 24 years	572	2.0	557	3.9	536	3.8	779	6.9	282	2.6
25 to 44 years	2,839	19.5	2,872	20.3	2,881	20.7	1,809	16.0	671	6.2
45 to 64 years	3,589	15.0	3,493	24.6	3,300	23.7	2,901	25.6	2,470	22.8
65 years and over	7,591	52.0	7,248	51.1	7,233	51.8	5,842	51.6	3,897	35.9
Total, 15 years and over	14,592	100.0	14,171	100.0	13,950	100.0	11,330	100.0	7,319	100.0

1. Prior to 1980, data are for persons 14 years and older. NOTE: Details may not add because of rounding. *Source:* U.S. Bureau of the Census, web: www.census.gov.

Characteristics of Unmarried-Couple Households, 1995

(numbers in thousands)

Characteristics	Number	Percent	Characteristics	Number	Percent
Unmarried-couple households	3,668	100.0	Presence of children:		
			No children under 15 years	2,349	64.0
Age of householders:			Some children under 15 years	1,319	36.0
Under 25 years	742	20.2			
25-44 years	2,188	59.7	Sex of householders:		
45-64 years	558	15.2	Male	2,076	56.6
65 years and over	180	4.9	Female	1,593	43.4

Source: U.S. Bureau of the Census, web: www.census.gov.

Households, Families, and Married Couples

	Households		Families		Married couples
Date	Number	Average population per household	Number	Average population per family	Number
June 1890	12,690,000	4.93	—	—	
April 1930	29,905,000	4.11	—	—	25,174,000
April 1940	34,949,000	3.67	32,166,000	3.76	28,517,000
March 1950	43,554,000	3.37	39,303,000	3.54	36,091,000
April 1955	47,874,000	3.33	41,951,000	3.59	37,556,000
March 1960[1]	52,799,000	3.33	45,111,000	3.67	40,200,000
March 1965	57,436,000	3.29	47,956,000	3.70	42,478,000
March 1970	63,401,000	3.14	51,586,000	3.58	45,373,000
March 1975	71,120,000	2.94	55,712,000	3.42	47,547,000
March 1980	80,776,000	2.76	59,550,000	3.29	49,714,000
March 1985	86,789,000	2.69	62,706,000	3.23	51,114,000
March 1990	93,347,000	2.63	66,090,000	3.17	53,256,000
March 1995	98,990,000	2.65	69,305,000	3.19	54,944,000
March 1996	99,627,000	2.65	69,594,000	3.26	53,567,000

1. First year in which figures for Alaska and Hawaii are included. *Source:* U.S. Bureau of the Census, web: www.census.gov.

Singles in the United States

The ratio of unmarried men per 100 unmarried women in U.S. Metro Areas, 1990

Highest Ratio Men to Women

Rank	Metro Area	Ratio
1	Jacksonville, N.C. MSA	223.64
2	Killeen–Temple, Tex. MSA	122.75
3	Fayetteville, N.C. MSA	117.66
4	Brazoria, Tex. PMSA	116.71
5	Lawton, Okla. MSA	115.63
6	State College, Pa. MSA	112.98
7	Clarksville–Hopkinsville, Tenn.–Ky. MSA	112.71
8	Anchorage, Alaska MSA	112.45
9	Salinas–Seaside–Monterey, Calif. MSA	112.01
10	Bryan–College Station, Tex. MSA	111.40
11	Bremerton, Wash. MSA	108.30
12	San Diego, Calif. MSA	105.33
13	Honolulu, Hawaii MSA	105.22
14	Las Vegas, Nev. MSA	104.65
15	Yuma, Ariz. MSA	104.64
16	Grand Forks, N.D. MSA	104.19
17	San Jose, Calif. PMSA	103.63
18	Reno, Nev. MSA	103.52
19	Lafayette–West Lafayette, Ind. MSA	102.01
20	Fort Walton Beach, Fla. MSA	101.70
21	Vallejo–Fairfield–Napa, Calif. PMSA	101.68
22	Lake County, Ill. PMSA	101.56
23	Champaign–Urbana–Rantoul, Ill. MSA	101.33
24	Jackson, Miss. MSA	101.24
25	Colorado Springs, Colo. MSA	99.42

NOTE: Unmarried includes never-married, widowed, and divorced persons, 15 years or older. Metro Areas as defined June 30, 1990. The presence of a military base, college or university, etc. in a metropolitan area may have a significant impact on the size of the ratio. MSA—Metropolitan Statistical Area. CMSA—Consolidated Metropolitan Statistical Area. PMSA—Primary Metropolitan Statistical Area. *Source:* U.S. Bureau of the Census, web: www.census.gov.

Lowest Ratio Men to Women

Rank	Metro Area	Ratio
1	Sarasota, Fla. MSA	65.57
2	Bradenton, Fla. MSA	68.41
3	Altoona, Pa. MSA	69.42
4	Springfield, Ill. MSA	69.63
5	Jacksonville, Tenn. MSA	69.72
6	Gadsden, Ala. MSA	69.86
7	Wheeling, W.Va.–Ohio MSA	70.48
8	Charleston, W.Va. MSA	70.65
9	St. Joseph, Mo. MSA	70.93
10	Lynchburg, Va. MSA	71.04
11	Roanoke, Va. MSA	71.09
12	Asheville, N.C. MSA	71.14
13	Shreveport, La. MSA	71.54
14	Birmingham, Ala. MSA	71.63
15	Danville, Va. MSA	71.72
16	Pittsburgh, Pa. PMSA	72.04
17	Monroe, La. MSA	72.06
18	Owensboro, Ky. MSA	72.14
19	Pittsburgh–Beaver Valley, Pa. CMSA	72.16
20	Florence, Ala. MSA	72.20
21	Sherman–Denison, Tex. MSA	72.27
22	Florence, S.C. MSA	72.32
23	Huntington–Ashland, W.Va.–Ky.–Ohio MSA	72.67
24	Cumberland, Md.–W.Va. MSA	72.73
25	Steubenville–Weirton, Ohio–W.Va. MSA	72.87

NOTE: Unmarried includes never-married, widowed, and divorced persons, 15 years or older. Metro Areas as defined June 30, 1990. The presence of a military base, college or university, etc. in a metropolitan area may have a significant impact on the size of the ratio. MSA—Metropolitan Statistical Area. CMSA—Consolidated Metropolitan Statistical Area. PMSA—Primary Metropolitan Statistical Area. *Source:* U.S. Bureau of the Census, web: www.census.gov.

Families Maintained by Women, with No Husband Present

(numbers in thousands)

	1995		1990		1980		1970		1960	
	Number	Percent	Number	Percent	Number	Percent	Number	Percent	Number	Percent
Age of women:										
Under 35 years	4,089	33.5	3,699	34.0	3,015	34.6	1,364	24.4	796	17.7
35 to 44 years	3,502	28.7	2,929	26.9	1,916	22.0	1,074	19.2	940	20.9
45 to 64 years	3,094	25.3	2,790	25.6	2,514	28.9	2,021	36.1	1,731	38.5
65 years and over	1,536	12.6	1,471	13.5	1,260	14.5	1,131	20.2	1,027	22.9
Median age	40.4	—	40.7	—	41.7	—	48.5	—	50.1	—
Presence of children:										
No own children under 18 years	4,606	37.7	4,290	39.4	3,260	37.4	2,665	47.7	2,397	53.3
With own children under 18 years	7,615	62.3	6,599	60.6	5,445	62.6	2,926	52.3	2,097	46.7
Total own children under 18 years	13,419	—	11,378	—	10,204	—	6,694	—	4,674	—
Average per family	1.10	—	1.04	—	1.17	—	1.20	—	1.04	—
Average per family with children	1.76	—	1.72	—	1.87	—	2.29	—	2.24	—
Race:										
White	8,031	65.7	7,306	67.1	6,052	69.5	4,165	74.5	3,547	78.9
Black[1]	3,716	30.4	3,275	30.1	2,495	28.7	1,382	24.7	947	21.1
Other	473	3.9	309	2.8	158	1.8	44	0.8	n.a.	n.a.
Marital status:										
Married, husband absent	2,160	17.7	1,947	17.9	1,769	20.3	1,326	23.7	1,099	24.5
Widowed	2,283	18.7	2,536	23.3	2,570	29.5	2,396	42.9	2,325	51.7
Divorced	4,537	37.1	3,949	36.3	3,008	34.6	1,259	22.5	694	15.4
Never married	3,240	26.5	2,457	22.6	1,359	15.6	610	10.9	376	8.4
Total	**12,220**	**100.0**	**10,890**	**100.0**	**8,705**	**100.0**	**5,591**	**100.0**	**4,494**	**100.0**

1. Includes other races in 1960. NOTE: n.a. = not available. (—) as shown in this table, means "not applicable." *Source:* U.S. Bureau of the Census, web: www.census.gov.

Median Age at First Marriage

Year	Males	Females	Year	Males	Females	Year	Males	Females
1890	26.1	22.0	1940	24.3	21.5	1990	26.1	23.9
1900	25.9	21.9	1950	22.8	20.3	1993	26.5	24.5
1910	25.1	21.6	1960	22.8	20.3	1994	26.7	24.5
1920	24.6	21.2	1970	23.2	20.8	1995	26.9	24.5
1930	24.3	21.3	1980	24.7	22.0			

Source: U.S. Bureau of the Census, web: www.census.gov.

Use of Credit Cards by Families: 1989 and 1992

General purpose credit cards include Mastercard, Visa, Optima, and Discover cards. All dollar figures are given in constant 1992 dollars based on consumer price index data as published by U.S. Bureau of Labor Statistics. Families include one-person units.

Family income	Percent having a general purpose credit card	Median new charges on last month's bills	Median balance[1]	Percent of cardholding families who—		
				Almost always pay off the balance	Sometimes pay off the balance	Hardly ever pay off the balance
1989, total	56.4	$200	$1,100	52.0	21.8	26.1
1992, total	63.3	200	1,000	54.5	19.1	26.4
Less than $10,000	25.9	100	800	57.4	12.2	30.4
$10,000 to $24,999	52.3	100	900	49.5	21.3	29.1
$25,000 to $49,999	73.1	200	1,200	47.0	21.2	31.7
$50,000 to $99,999	88.5	300	1,500	58.7	18.6	22.8
$100,000 and more	91.2	500	3,000	75.2	14.3	10.5

1. Among families having a balance. *Source:* Board of Governors of the Federal Reserve System, *Statistical Abstract of the U.S., 1996*, web: www.census.gov/stat_abstract/.

Selected Family Characteristics

Characteristics[1]	1995 Number (000s)	1995 Median income	Characteristics[1]	1995 Number (000s)	1995 Median income
ALL RACES			Male householder, no wife present	2,712	35,129
All households	99,627	$34,076	Female householder, no husband present	8,284	24,431
Age of householder					
Under 65 years	78,141	39,148	Number of earners		
15 to 24 years	5,282	20,979	No earners	17,964	14,267
25 to 34 years	19,225	34,701	1 earner	27,639	29,175
35 to 44 years	23,226	43,465	2 earners or more	38,907	53,990
45 to 54 years	18,008	48,058	2 earners	30,701	50,910
55 to 64 years	12,401	38,077	3 earners	6,058	64,311
65 years and over	21,486	19,096	4 earners or more	2,149	75,092
65 to 74 years	11,908	23,031			
75 years and over	9,578	15,342	Size of household		
			1 person	21,194	17,512
Region			2 persons	28,615	36,939
Northeast	19,695	36,111	3 persons	13,873	44,997
Midwest	23,707	35,839	4 persons	12,659	51,611
South	35,143	30,942	5 persons	5,350	49,073
West	21,082	35,979	6 persons	1,856	47,249
			7 persons or more	965	41,109
Type of household					
Family households	69,594	41,224	**BLACK**		
Married-couple family	53,567	47,129	All households	11,577	22,393
Male householder, no wife present	3,513	33,534	Age of householder		
Female householder, no husband present	12,514	21,348	Under 65 years	9,799	24,545
			15 to 24 years	774	12,825
Number of earners			25 to 34 years	2,633	21,871
No earners	21,281	13,102	35 to 44 years	2,889	28,097
1 earner	33,538	27,567	45 to 54 years	2,118	30,120
2 earners or more	44,809	52,813	55 to 64 years	1,385	21,842
2 earners	35,320	50,000	65 years and over	1,777	13,246
3 earners	6,982	63,191	65 to 74 years	1,064	15,925
4 earners or more	2,507	74,243	75 years and over	713	9,886
Size of household			Region		
1 person	24,900	17,063	Northeast	2,165	21,947
2 persons	32,526	35,700	Midwest	2,153	22,027
3 persons	16,724	42,244	South	6,163	22,567
4 persons	15,118	49,531	West	1,096	23,416
5 persons	6,631	45,710			
6 persons	2,357	44,263	Type of household		
7 persons or more	1,372	39,013	Family households	8,055	26,838
WHITE			Married-couple family	3,713	41,362
All households	84,511	35,766	Male householder, no wife present	573	27,071
Age of householder			Female householder, no husband present	3,769	15,589
Under 65 years	65,186	41,481			
15 to 24 years	4,254	22,203	Number of earners		
25 to 34 years	15,730	36,912	No earners	2,764	7,651
35 to 44 years	19,373	45,924	1 earner	4,678	20,268
45 to 54 years	15,214	50,607	2 earners or more	4,135	42,341
55 to 64 years	10,614	40,150	2 earners	3,310	40,357
65 years and over	19,326	19,590	3 earners	624	48,737
65 to 74 years	10,583	23,816	4 earners or more	201	67,415
75 years and over	8,743	15,807			
			Size of household		
Region			1 person	3,055	13,229
Northeast	16,959	37,772	2 persons	3,034	24,133
Midwest	21,095	37,220	3 persons	2,197	25,578
South	28,297	32,917	4 persons	1,715	32,086
West	18,160	36,390	5 persons	919	27,630
			6 persons	366	28,028
Type of household			7 persons or more	291	28,908
Family households	58,869	43,265			
Married-couple family	47,873	47,608			

Characteristics[1]	1995 Number (000s)	1995 Median income
HISPANIC ORIGIN OF HOUSEHOLDER[2]		
All households	7,939	22,860
Age of householder		
Under 65 years	7,041	24,399
15 to 24 years	749	16,854
25 to 34 years	2,195	23,187
35 to 44 years	2,109	26,492
45 to 54 years	1,181	29,441
55 to 64 years	808	22,859
65 years and over	898	13,513
65 to 74 years	609	14,561
75 years and over	289	12,277
Region		
Northeast	1,368	19,936
Midwest	535	27,777
South	2,725	21,907
West	3,311	24,368
Type of household		
Family households	6,287	25,491

Characteristics[1]	1995 Number (000s)	1995 Median income
Married-couple family	4,247	30,195
Male householder, no wife present	436	25,053
Female householder, no husband present	1,604	14,755
Number of earners		
No earners	1,363	7,486
1 earner	2,923	18,062
2 earners or more	3,654	36,963
2 earners	2,712	34,170
3 earners	651	43,709
4 earners or more	290	56,612
Size of household		
1 person	1,260	11,074
2 persons	1,788	22,127
3 persons	1,528	22,977
4 persons	1,508	27,903
5 persons	964	26,701
6 persons	523	29,114
7 persons or more	368	30,180

1. Household data as of March 1995. 2. Persons of Hispanic origin may be of any race. NOTE: Data are the latest available. *Source:* U.S. Bureau of the Census, *Current Population Reports*, web: www.census.gov.

Births

Live Births and Birth Rates, by Year

Year	Births[1]	Rate[2]	Year	Births[1]	Rate[2]	Year	Births[1]	Rate[2]
1910	2,777,000	30.1	1961[3]	4,268,326	23.3	1979	3,494,398	15.9
1915	2,965,000	29.5	1962[3]	4,167,362	22.4	1980	3,612,258	15.9
1920	2,950,000	27.7	1963[3]	4,098,020	21.7	1982	3,680,537	15.9
1925	2,909,000	25.1	1964[3]	4,027,490	21.0	1983	3,638,933	15.5
1930	2,618,000	21.3	1965[3]	3,760,358	19.4	1984	3,669,141	15.5
1935	2,377,000	18.7	1966[3]	3,606,274	18.4	1985	3,760,561	15.8
1940	2,559,000	19.4	1967[4]	3,520,959	17.8	1986	3,731,000	15.5
1945	2,858,000	20.4	1968[3]	3,501,564	17.5	1987	3,829,000	15.7
1950	3,632,000	24.1	1969[3]	3,600,206	17.8	1988	3,913,000	15.9
1952[3]	3,913,000	25.1	1970[3]	3,731,386	18.4	1989	4,021,000	16.2
1953[3]	3,965,000	25.1	1971[3]	3,555,970	17.2	1990	4,179,000	16.7
1954[3]	4,078,000	25.3	1972	3,258,411	15.6	1991	4,111,000	16.2
1955	4,104,000	25.0	1973	3,136,965	14.9	1992	4,084,000	16.0
1956[3]	4,218,000	25.2	1974	3,159,958	14.9	1993	4,039,000	15.7
1957[3]	4,308,000	25.3	1975	3,144,198	14.8	1994	3,979,000	15.3
1958[3]	4,255,000	24.5	1976	3,167,788	14.8	1995	3,892,000	14.8
1959[3]	4,295,000	24.3	1977	3,326,632	15.4	1996	3,899,000	14.7
1960[3]	4,257,850	23.7	1978	3,333,279	15.3			

1. Figures through 1959 include adjustment for under-registration; beginning 1960, figures represent number registered. For comparison, the 1959 registered count was 4,245,000. 2. Rates are per 1,000 population estimated as of July 1 for each year except 1940, 1950, 1960, 1970, and 1980, which are as of April 1, the census date; for 1942–46 based on population including armed forces overseas. 3. Based on 50% sample of births. 4. Based on a 20 to 50% sample of births. NOTE: Alaska is included beginning 1959; Hawaii beginning 1960. Since 1972, based on 100% of births in selected states and on 50% sample in all other states. *Sources:* Department of Health and Human Services, National Center for Health Statistics, web: www.dhhs.gov.

Live Births by Age and Race of Mother

Year[1]/race	Total	Under 15	15-19	20-24	25-29	30-34	35-39	40-44	45+
					Age of Mother				
1940	2,558,647	3,865	332,667	799,537	693,268	431,468	222,015	68,269	7,558
1945	2,858,449	4,028	298,868	832,746	785,299	554,906	296,852	78,853	6,897
1950	3,631,512	5,413	432,911	1,155,167	1,041,360	610,816	302,780	77,743	5,322
1955	4,014,112	6,181	493,770	1,290,939	1,133,155	732,540	352,320	89,777	5,430
1960	4,257,850	6,780	586,966	1,426,912	1,092,816	687,722	359,908	91,564	5,182
1965	3,760,358	7,768	590,894	1,337,350	925,732	529,376	282,908	81,716	4,614
1970	3,731,386	11,752	644,708	1,418,874	994,904	427,806	180,244	49,952	3,146
1975	3,144,198	12,642	582,238	1,093,676	936,786	375,500	115,409	26,319	1,628
1980	3,612,258	10,169	552,161	1,226,200	1,108,291	550,354	140,793	23,090	1,200
1985	3,760,561	10,220	467,485	1,141,320	1,201,350	696,354	214,336	28,334	1,162
1990	4,158,212	11,657	521,826	1,093,730	1,277,108	886,063	317,583	48,607	1,638
1995	3,899,589	12,242	499,873	965,547	1,063,539	904,666	383,745	67,250	2,727
White	3,098,885	5,854	349,635	743,123	873,022	754,662	316,166	54,232	2,191
Black	603,139	5,927	133,694	183,435	133,535	96,084	42,507	7,702	255
American Indian[2]	37,278	203	7,764	11,969	8,571	5,777	2,488	493	13
Asian or Pacific Islander	160,287	258	8,780	27,020	48,411	48,143	22,584	4,823	268

1. Data for 1940–55 are adjusted for under-registration. Beginning 1960, only registered births are shown. Data for 1960–70 based on a 50% sample of births. For 1972–84, based on 100% of births in selected states and on 50% sample in all other states. Beginning 1989, births are tabulated by race of mother; previously based on race of child. 2. Includes births to Aleuts and Eskimos. NOTE: Data refer only to births occurring within the U.S. *Source:* Department of Health and Human Services, National Center for Health Statistics, web: www.dhhs.gov.

Births to Unmarried Women (in thousands, except as indicated)

Age and race	1993	1990	1985	1980	1975	1970	1965	1960	1950
By age of mother:									
Under 15 years	11.5	10.7	9.4	9.0	11.0	9.5	6.1	4.6	3.2
15-19 years	357.4	350.0	270.9	262.8	222.5	190.4	123.1	87.1	56.0
20-24 years	438.5	403.9	300.4	237.3	134.0	126.7	90.7	68.0	43.1
25-29 years	233.8	230.0	152.0	99.6	50.2	40.6	36.8	32.1	20.9
30-34 years	132.3	118.2	67.3	41.0	19.8	19.1	19.6	18.9	10.8
35-39 years	55.6	44.1	24.0	13.2	8.1	9.4	11.4	10.6	6.0
40 years and over	11.1	8.5	4.1	2.9	2.3	3.0	3.7	3.0	1.7
By race:[1]									
White	742.1	669.7	433.0	320.1	186.4	175.1	123.7	82.5	53.5
Black	452.5	495.7	395.2	345.7	261.6	223.6	167.5	141.8	88.1
Total of above births	1,194.6	1,165.4	828.2	665.8	447.9	398.7	291.2	224.3	141.6
Percent of all births[2]	31.0	28.0	22.0	18.4	14.2	10.7	7.7	5.3	3.9
Rate[3]	45.3	43.8	32.8	29.4	24.8	26.4	23.4	21.8	14.1

1. For 1988 and prior years births were tabulated by race of child. Beginning 1989, births are tabulated by race of mother. 2. Through 1955, based on data adjusted for under-registration; thereafter, registered births. 3. Rate per 1,000 unmarried (never married, widowed, and divorced) women, 15–44 years old. NOTE: Data are latest available. *Source:* Department of Health and Human Services, National Center for Health Statistics, web: www.dhhs.gov.

Live Births by Sex and Sex Ratio

Year	Total[1, 2] Male	Female	Males per 1,000 females	White Male	Female	Males per 1,000 females	Black Male	Female	Males per 1,000 females
1985	1,927,983	1,832,578	1,052	1,536,646	1,454,727	1,056	308,575	299,618	1,030
1986	1,924,868	1,831,679	1,051	1,523,914	1,446,525	1,053	315,788	305,433	1,034
1987	1,951,153	1,858,241	1,050	1,535,517	1,456,971	1,054	325,259	316,308	1,028
1988	2,002,424	1,907,086	1,050	1,562,675	1,483,487	1,053	341,441	330,535	1,033
1989	2,069,490	1,971,468	1,050	1,606,757	1,525,234	1,053	360,131	349,264	1,031
1990	2,129,495	2,028,717	1,050	1,654,928	1,570,415	1,054	367,455	357,121	1,029
1991	2,101,518	2,009,389	1,046	1,659,077	1,582,196	1,049	346,455	336,147	1,031
1992	2,082,097	1,982,917	1,050	1,641,811	1,559,867	1,053	342,726	330,907	1,036
1993	2,048,861	1,951,379	1,050	1,616,332	1,533,501	1,054	333,984	324,891	1,028
1994	2,022,589	1,930,178	1,048	1,599,803	1,521,401	1,051	322,554	313,837	1,028
1995	1,996,355	1,930,234	1,049	1,588,427	1,510,458	1,052	308,115	297,024	1,031

1. Excludes births to nonresidents of U.S. 2. Includes races other than white and black. *Source:* Department of Health and Human Services, National Center for Health Statistics, web: www.dhhs.gov.

Live Births and Birth Rates by State

State	1995 number	1995 rate	1993[1] number	1993[1] rate	State	1995 number	1995 rate	1993[1] number	1993[1] rate
Alabama	60,329	14.2	61,706	14.8	Montana	11,142	12.8	11,365	13.5
Alaska	10,244	17.0	11,073	18.5	Nebraska	23,243	14.2	23,224	14.4
Arizona	72,463	17.2	69,056	17.5	Nevada	25,056	16.4	22,403	16.2
Arkansas	35,175	14.2	34,289	14.1	New Hampshire	14,665	12.8	15,436	13.7
California	552,045	17.5	585,324	18.8	New Jersey	114,828	14.5	117,686	15.0
Colorado	54,332	14.5	54,022	15.2	New Mexico	26,920	16.0	27,852	17.2
Connecticut	44,334	13.5	46,700	14.2	New York	271,369	15.0	282,392	15.6
Delaware	10,266	14.3	10,568	15.1	North Carolina	101,592	14.1	101,357	14.6
D.C.	9,014	16.3	10,629	18.4	North Dakota	8,476	13.2	8,690	13.6
Florida	188,723	13.3	192,537	14.0	Ohio	154,064	13.8	158,793	14.4
Georgia	112,282	15.6	110,622	16.0	Oklahoma	45,672	13.9	46,243	14.3
Hawaii	18,595	15.7	19,593	16.8	Oregon	42,811	13.6	41,576	13.7
Idaho	18,035	15.5	17,440	15.8	Pennsylvania	151,850	12.6	160,762	13.4
Illinois	185,812	15.7	190,788	16.3	Rhode Island	12,776	12.9	13,976	14.0
Indiana	82,835	14.3	83,949	14.7	South Carolina	50,926	13.9	53,835	14.8
Iowa	36,810	13.0	37,826	13.4	South Dakota	10,475	14.4	10,719	15.0
Kansas	37,201	14.5	37,406	14.8	Tennessee	73,173	13.9	73,017	14.3
Kentucky	52,377	13.6	53,000	14.0	Texas	322,753	17.2	322,071	17.9
Louisiana	65,641	15.1	69,402	16.2	Utah	39,577	20.3	37,127	20.0
Maine	13,896	11.2	15,065	12.2	Vermont	6,783	11.6	7,457	13.0
Maryland	72,396	14.4	74,988	15.1	Virginia	92,578	14.0	94,944	14.7
Massachusetts	81,648	13.4	84,668	14.1	Washington	77,228	14.2	78,645	15.0
Michigan	134,642	14.1	139,855	14.8	West Virginia	21,162	11.6	21,792	12.0
Minnesota	63,263	13.7	64,648	14.3	Wisconsin	67,479	13.2	69,767	13.8
Mississippi	41,344	15.3	42,149	16.0	Wyoming	6,261	13.0	6,555	14.0
Missouri	73,028	13.7	75,253	14.4	**Total**	3,899,589	14.8	4,000,240	15.5

1. Revised. NOTE: Data by place of residence. Rates are per 1,000 population. *Source:* Department of Health and Human Services, National Center for Health Statistics, web: www.dhhs.gov.

Selected Characteristics of Births, by Race of Mother, 1995

Characteristic	All races	White	Black	American Indian[1]	Asian or Pacific Islander
Percentage of mothers who:					
Had prenatal care beginning in the first trimester	81.3	83.6	70.4	66.7	79.9
Had late or no prenatal care	4.2	3.5	7.6	9.5	4.3
Were tobacco users[2]	13.9	15.0	10.6	20.9	3.4
Were alcohol users[3]	1.5	1.4	2.3	4.3	0.4
Gained less than 16 lbs[4]	10.7	9.5	16.6	14.8	9.6
Had Caesarean births	20.8	20.8	21.8	18.1	18.7
Percentage of infants who:					
Were born prior to 37 full weeks	11.0	9.7	17.7	12.4	9.9
Weighed less than 1,500 grams (3 lb 4 oz.)	1.3	1.1	3.0	1.1	0.9
Weighed less than 2,500 grams (5 lb 8 oz.)	7.3	6.2	13.1	6.6	6.9
Weighed 4,000 grams (8 lb 4 oz.) or more	10.3	11.5	5.3	12.5	6.0
Had 5-minute Apgar scores of less than 7[5]	1.4	1.2	2.5	1.4	1.0

1. Includes births to Aleuts and Eskimos. 2. Excludes data for Calif., Ind., N.Y. (but includes N.Y.C.), and S.D., which did not report tobacco use on birth certificate. 3. Excludes data for Calif. and S.D., which did not report alcohol use on birth certificate. 4. Excludes data for Calif., which did not report weight gain on birth certificate. 5. Excludes data for Calif. and Tex., which did not report Apgar scores on birth certificate. Apgar scores are derived from evaluations of five major signs at one minute and five minutes after birth. Each sign is given a score of 0–2 for a total of ten possible points; scores of 7–10 are considered normal, 4–7 may require resuscitative measures, and 0–3 require immediate resuscitation. The signs and scores (0-1-2) are as follows: Activity or muscle tone (absent—arms and legs flexed—active movement); Pulse (absent—below 100 bpm—above 100 bpm); Grimace or reflex irritability (no response—grimace—sneeze, cough, pulls away); Appearance or skin color (blue-gray, pale all over—normal, except for extremities—normal over entire body); Respiration (absent—slow, irregular—good, crying). *Source:* U.S. Department of Health and Human Services, web: www.dhhs.gov.

Women Who Have Had a Child in the Last Year, by Age: 1980 to 1994

Age of Mother	Total births per 1,000 women			First births per 1,000 women		
	1980	1990	1994	1980	1990	1994
Total	71.1	67.0	64.7	28.5	26.4	27.4
15 to 29 years old[1]	103.7	90.8	85.6	48.6	43.2	46.3
15 to 19 years old	n.a.	39.8	45.2	n.a.	30.1	36.3
20 to 24 years old[2]	96.6	113.4	100.7	n.a.	51.8	58.4
25 to 29 years old	114.8	112.1	107.7	n.a.	46.2	43.9
30 to 44 years old	35.4	44.7	46.6	6.3	10.6	11.0
30 to 34 years old	60.0	80.4	90.4	n.a.	21.9	23.0
35 to 39 years old	26.9	37.3	36.0	n.a.	6.5	7.3
40 to 44 years old	9.9	8.6	9.6	n.a.	1.2	1.8

1. For 1980–88, 18 to 29 years old. 2. For 1980–88, 18 to 24 years old. n.a. = not available. *Source:* U.S. Bureau of the Census, *Current Population Reports*, web: www.census.gov.

Contraceptive Use by Women, 15 to 44 Years Old: 1990

Contraceptive status and method	Race			Marital status		
	White	Black	Hispanic	Never married	Currently married	Formerly married
All women (numbers in 1,000)	**42,968**	**7,510**	**5,500**	**20,788**	**30,561**	**7,033**
Percent distribution						
Surgically sterile	31.2%	31.4%	23.9%	5.7%	43.9%	42.3%
Pill	17.3	16.7	16.4	21.7	14.5	12.8
IUD	0.8	0.8	1.0	0.4	1.0	1.4
Diaphragm	1.8	1.0	0.8	0.3	2.9	0.5
Condom	10.3	11.4	8.9	13.0	9.9	5.6
Periodic abstinence	1.6	0.7	1.9	0.8	2.4	0.4
Withdrawal	0.6	0.4	0.4	0.7	0.5	0.1
Other methods[1]	2.2	2.8	2.3	1.6	2.1	5.0

1. Douche, suppository, and less frequently used methods. *Source:* U.S. National Center for Health Statistics, *Advance Data from Vital and Health Statistics*, No. 182, web: www.dhhs.gov.

Mortality
Fifteen Leading Causes of Death in the U.S., 1995

			Age-adjusted death rate					
			Rates per 100,000 population		Percent change		Ratio	
Rank	Cause of death	Percent of total deaths	Death rate	1995	1994 to 1995	1979 to 1995	Male to female	Black to white
	All causes	100.0	880.0	503.9	−0.7	−12.7	1.7	1.6
1	Diseases of the heart	31.9	280.7	138.3	−1.5	−30.7	1.8	1.5
2	Malignant neoplasms (cancer)	23.3	204.9	129.9	−1.2	−0.7	1.4	1.4
3	Cerebrovascular diseases (stroke)	6.8	60.1	26.7	0.8	−35.8	1.2	1.8
4	Chronic obstructive pulmonary diseases and allied conditions	4.5	39.2	20.8	−1.0	42.5	1.5	0.8
5	Accidents and adverse effects	4.0	35.5	30.5	0.7	−28.9	2.5	1.3
	Motor vehicle accidents	1.9	16.5	16.3	1.2	−29.7	2.3	1.0
	All other accidents and adverse effects	2.2	19.0	14.2	0	−27.6	2.9	1.5
6	Pneumonia and influenza	3.6	31.6	12.9	−0.8	15.2	1.6	1.4
7	Diabetes mellitus	2.6	22.6	13.3	3.1	35.7	1.2	2.4
8	Human immunodeficiency virus infection (AIDS)	1.9	16.4	15.6	1.3	n.a.	5.0	4.7
9	Suicide	1.4	11.9	11.2	0	−4.3	4.5	0.6
10	Chronic liver disease and cirrhosis	1.1	9.6	7.6	−3.8	−36.7	2.4	1.3
11	Nephritis, nephrotic syndrome, and nephrosis	1.0	9.0	4.3	0	0	1.5	2.8
12	Homicide and legal intervention	1.0	8.7	9.4	−8.7	−7.8	3.7	6.1
13	Septicemia	0.9	8.0	4.1	2.5	78.3	1.2	2.7
14	Alzheimer's disease	0.9	7.8	2.7	8.0	1,250.0	1.0	0.7
15	Atherosclerosis	0.7	6.4	2.3	0	−59.6	1.4	1.0
	All other causes	14.5	127.6	—	—	—	—	—

Source: U.S. National Center for Health Statistics, *Monthly Vital Statistics Report*, 1997, web: www.dhhs.gov.

Number of Deaths and Death Rates from Selected Types of Cancer, 1995

(Rates per 100,000 population)

Cause of death	Both sexes		Male		Female	
	Number	Rate	Number	Rate	Number	Rate
Cancer (malignant neoplasms)[1]	538,455	204.9	281,611	219.5	256,844	191.0
Esophagous	10,969	4.2	8,333	6.5	2,636	2.0
Stomach	13,645	5.2	8,010	6.2	5,635	4.2
Colon, rectum, rectosigmoid junction, and anus	57,333	21.8	28,261	22.0	29,072	21.6
Pancreas	26,766	10.2	12,826	10.0	13,940	10.4
Trachea, bronchus, and lung	151,200	57.5	91,856	71.6	59,344	44.1
Skin	6,907	2.6	4,297	3.3	2,610	1.9
Cervix	4,503	1.7	—	—	4,503	3.3
Uterus	6,237	2.4	—	—	6,237	4.6
Ovary	13,342	5.1	—	—	13,342	9.9
Prostate	34,475	13.1	34,475	26.9	—	—
Bladder	11,084	4.2	7,521	5.9	3,563	2.7
Kidney and other and unspecified urinary organs	11,555	4.4	6,894	5.4	4,661	3.5
Brain and other and unspecified parts of nervous system	12,063	4.6	6,537	5.1	5,526	4.1
Hodgkin's disease	1,431	0.5	799	0.6	632	0.5
Malignant lymphoma other than Hodgkin's disease	22,522	8.6	11.694	9.1	10,828	8.1

1. Includes figures from all types of cancer, including those not shown. *Source:* U.S. National Center for Health Statistics, *Monthly Vital Statistics Report,* 1997, web: www.dhhs.gov.

Cumulative AIDS Deaths in the United States Through 1996

Race/ethnicity and age at death[1]	Females, cumulative total	Males, cumulative total	Cumulative total	Race/ethnicity and age at death[1]	Females, cumulative total	Males, cumulative total	Cumulative total
White, not Hispanic				**Asian/Pacific Islander**			
Under 15	376	508	884	Under 15	13	18	31
15–24	413	2,359	2,772	15–24	5	31	36
25–34	3,791	49,441	53,232	25–34	64	617	681
35–44	3,699	69,572	73,271	35–44	79	930	1,009
45–54	1,409	30,737	32,146	45–54	44	449	493
55 or older	1,457	13,010	14,467	55 or older	36	188	224
All ages	11,173	165,841	177,014	All ages	243	2,234	2,477
Black, not Hispanic				**American/Indian/Alaska Native**			
Under 15	1,210	1,198	2,408	Under 15	8	10	18
15–24	1,104	2,150	3,254	15–24	3	22	25
25–34	9,106	28,206	37,312	25–34	48	291	339
35–44	10,481	39,152	49,633	35–44	39	280	319
45–54	3,183	15,542	18,725	45–54	13	89	102
55 or older	1,486	6,547	8,033	55 or older	7	35	42
All ages	26,613	92,925	119,538	All ages	118	730	848
Hispanic				**All racial/ethnic groups**			
Under 15	500	553	1,053	Under 15	2,111	2,288	4,399
15–24	413	1,185	1,598	15–24	1,939	5,752	7,691
25–34	3,671	17,449	21,120	25–34	16,684	96,069	112,753
35–44	3,614	21,156	24,770	35–44	17,922	131,200	149,122
45–54	1,218	8,163	9,381	45–54	5,871	55,021	60,892
55 or older	581	3,285	3,866	55 or older	3,569	23,083	26,652
All ages	10,013	51,843	61,856	All ages	48,186	313,818	362,004

1. Data tabulated under "all ages" include 495 persons whose age at death is unknown. Data tabulated under "all racial/ethnic groups" include 271 persons whose race/ethnicity is unknown. *Source:* Centers for Disease Control *HIV/AIDS Surveillance Report,* Vol. 8, No. 2.

Accident Rates, 1995

Class of accident		One every	Class of accident		One every
All accidents	Deaths	6 minutes	Workers off-job	Deaths	13 minute
	Injuries	2 seconds		Injuries	5 second
Motor-vehicle	Deaths	12 minutes	Home	Deaths	20 minute
	Injuries	14 seconds		Injuries	4 second
Work	Deaths	99 minutes	Public non-motor-	Deaths	26 minute
	Injuries	9 seconds	vehicle	Injuries	5 second

NOTE: Data are latest available. *Source:* National Safety Council.

Improper Driving as Factor in Accidents

	Fatal accidents		Injury accidents		All accidents	
Kind of improper driving	1995	1994	1995	1994	1995	1994
Improper driving	**68.1%**	**63.7**	**73.5%**	**65.7**	**75.5%**	**67.2**
Speed too fast or unsafe	19.8	19.5	13.9	11.2	14.0	11.9
Right of way	15.2	15.1	25.5	24.1	22.9	21.3
Failed to yield	*10.2*	*9.1*	*18.1*	*15.0*	*17.0*	*14.5*
Passed stop sign	*2.2*	*2.6*	*2.4*	*3.1*	*1.9*	*2.5*
Disregarded signal	*3.0*	*3.4*	*5.0*	*6.0*	*4.0*	*4.5*
Drove left of center	9.1	9.4	2.4	2.5	2.2	2.3
Improper overtaking	1.5	1.6	1.3	1.2	1.5	1.4
Made improper turn	2.3	2.6	2.8	2.9	4.2	4.1
Followed too closely	0.5	0.5	7.0	5.9	7.2	5.6
Other improper driving	19.7	15.0	20.7	17.9	23.6	20.6
No improper driving stated	**31.9**	**36.3**	**26.5**	**34.3**	**24.5**	**32.8**
Total	**100.0%**	**100.0%**	**100.0%**	**100.0%**	**100.0%**	**100.0**

NOTE: Figures are latest available. *Source:* Motor-vehicle reports from 11 (1993) and 17 (1994) state traffic authorities to National Safety Council.

Motor-Vehicle Deaths by Type of Accident

Year	Pedes-trians	Other motor vehicles	Railroad trains	Pedal-cycles[1]	Animal-drawn vehicle, animal, or streetcars	Fixed objects[1]	Deaths from non-collision accidents[1]	Total deaths[2]
					Deaths from collisions with—			
1980	9,700	23,000	739	1,200	100	3,700	14,700	53,172
1985	8,300	19,900	500	1,100	100	2,800	12,900	45,600
1990	7,400	19,400	600	1,000	100	12,900	4,900	46,300
1995	6,300	19,400	500	900	100	12,300	4,400	43,900

1. Estimates for 1990 and later are not comparable to earlier years. 2. Totals do not equal sums of various types because totals are estimated. NOTE: Figures are latest available. *Source:* National Safety Council.

Accidental Deaths by Principal Types

Year	Motor vehicle	Falls	Drown-ing[1]	Fire burns[2]	Suffocation by ingested object	Fire-arms	Poison (solid, liquid)	Poison by gas
1987	48,700	11,300	5,300	4,800	3,200	1,400	4,400	1,000
1988	49,000	12,000	5,000	5,000	3,600	1,400	5,300	1,000
1989	46,900	12,400	4,600	4,400	3,900	1,600	5,600	900
1990	46,300	12,400	5,200	4,300	3,200	1,400	5,700	800
1991	43,500	12,200	4,600	4,200	2,900	1,400	5,600	800
1992	40,300	12,400	4,300	4,000	2,700	1,400	5,200	700
1993	42,000	13,500	4,800	4,000	2,900	1,600	6,500	700
1994	43,000	13,300	4,000	4,200	3,000	1,500	8,000	700
1995	43,900	12,600	4,500	4,100	2,800	1,400	10,000	600

1. Includes drowning in water transport accidents. 2. Includes burns by fire and deaths resulting from conflagration regardless of nature of injury. NOTE: Figures are latest available. *Source:* National Safety Council.

Deaths, by State

State	1996 number	State	1996 number	State	1996 number
Alabama	42,668	Louisiana	40,460	Oklahoma	33,224
Alaska	2,562	Maine	11,035	Oregon	28,293
Arizona	39,005	Maryland	41,965	Pennsylvania	129,463
Arkansas	25,666	Massachusetts	55,328	Rhode Island	9,574
California	232,266	Michigan	83,972	South Carolina	34,603
Colorado	25,853	Minnesota	36,804	South Dakota	6,314
Connecticut	29,183	Mississippi	26,756	Tennessee	49,934
Delaware	6,443	Missouri	53,697	Texas	136,593
Dist. of Col.	6,317	Montana	7,710	Utah	11,077
Florida	153,746	Nebraska	15,472	Vermont	4,885
Georgia	58,802	Nevada	12,897	Virginia	52,847
Hawaii	7,861	New Hampshire	9,114	Washington	39,493
Idaho	8,685	New Jersey	71,895	West Virginia	19,106
Illinois	106,355	New Mexico	12,325	Wisconsin	45,047
Indiana	54,321	New York	162,875	Wyoming	3,610
Iowa	26,315	North Carolina	66,357	**Total**	**2,311,157**
Kansas	23,868	North Dakota	5,753		
Kentucky	37,550	Ohio	105,213		

Source: U.S. National Center for Health Statistics, *Monthly Vital Statistics Report,* 1997, web: www.dhhs.gov.

U.S. Annual Death Rates

Year	Rate	Year	Rate	Year	Deaths	Rate
1900	17.2	1948	9.9	1972	1,963,944	9.4
1905	15.9	1949	9.7	1973	1,973,003	9.3
1910	14.7	1950	9.6	1974	1,934,388	9.1
1915	13.2	1951	9.7	1975	1,892,879	8.8
1920	13.0	1952	9.6	1976	1,909,440	8.8
1925	11.7	1953	9.6	1977	1,899,597	8.6
1930	11.3	1954	9.2	1978	1,927,788	8.7
1931	11.1	1955	9.3	1979	1,913,841	8.5
1932	10.9	1956	9.4	1980	1,989,841	8.7
1933	10.7	1957	9.6	1982	1,974,797	8.5
1934	11.1	1958	9.5	1983	2,019,201	8.6
1935	10.9	1959	9.4	1984	2,039,369	8.6
1936	11.6	1960	9.5	1985	2,086,440	8.7
1937	11.3	1962	9.5	1986	2,099,000	8.7
1938	10.6	1963	9.6	1987	2,127,000	8.7
1939	10.6	1964	9.4	1988	2,171,000	8.8
1940	10.8	1965	9.4	1989	2,155,000	8.7
1941	10.5	1966	9.5	1990	2,162,000	8.6
1942	10.3	1967	9.4	1991	2,165,000	8.5
1943	10.9	1968	9.7	1992	2,177,000	8.5
1944	10.6	1969	9.5	1993	2,268,000	8.8
1945	10.6	1970[1]	9.5	1994	2,286,000[2]	8.8
1946	10.0	1971	9.3	1995	2,309,000	8.8
1947	10.1			1996	2,311,000	8.7

1. First year for which deaths of nonresidents are excluded. 2. Provisional. NOTE: Includes only deaths occurring within the registration states. Beginning with 1933, area includes entire U.S.; with 1959 includes Alaska, and with 1960 includes Hawaii. Excludes fetal deaths. Rates per 1,000 population residing in area, as of April 1 for 1940, 1950, 1960, 1970, and 1980, and estimated as of July 1 for all other years. *Sources:* Department of Health and Human Services, National Center for Health Statistics, web: www.dhhs.gov.

Death Rates, by Age, 1995

(Rates per 100,000 population in specified group.)

	Both sexes	Male	Female		Both sexes	Male	Female
All ages[1]	888.0	914.1	847.3	40–44 years	275.9	378.3	175.9
Under 1 year[2]	768.8	843.8	690.1	45–49 years	376.1	497.8	258.9
1–4 years	40.6	44.8	36.2	50–54 years	567.7	729.6	414.7
5–9 years	19.7	22.5	16.7	55–59 years	871.8	1,106.7	655.3
10–14 years	25.5	31.0	19.6	60–64 years	1,382.3	1,765.3	1,042.0
15–19 years	83.5	119.5	45.7	65–69 years	2,058.3	2,650.2	1,566.4
20–24 years	107.1	161.9	50.6	70–74 years	3,131.4	4,029.6	2,441.6
25–29 years	119.3	173.9	64.5	75–79 years	4,722.4	6,042.2	3,815.9
30–34 years	160.3	231.6	89.5	80–84 years	7,542.1	9,633.6	6,363.0
35–39 years	208.9	292.1	126.6	85 years and over	15,469.5	17,978.9	14,492.4

1. Figures for age not stated are included in All ages but not distributed among age groups. 2. Death rates for "Under 1 year" (based on population estimates) differ from infant mortality rates (based on live births). *Source:* U.S. National Center for Health Statistics, *Monthly Vital Statistics Report,* 1997, web: www.dhhs.gov.

Expectation of Life
Expectation of Life by Sex, 1850–1995

	Age								
Calendar period	0	10	20	30	40	50	60	70	80
WHITE MALES									
1850[1]	38.3	48.0	40.1	34.0	27.9	21.6	15.6	10.2	5.9
1890[1]	42.50	48.45	40.66	34.05	27.37	20.72	14.73	9.35	5.40
1900–1902[2]	48.23	50.59	42.19	34.88	27.74	20.76	14.35	9.03	5.10
1909–1911[2]	50.23	51.32	42.71	34.87	27.43	20.39	13.98	8.83	5.09
1919–1921[3]	56.34	54.15	45.60	37.65	29.86	22.22	15.25	9.51	5.47
1929–1931	59.12	54.96	46.02	37.54	29.22	21.51	14.72	9.20	5.26
1939–1941	62.81	57.03	47.76	38.80	30.03	21.96	15.05	9.42	5.38
1949–1951	66.31	58.98	49.52	40.29	31.17	22.83	15.76	10.07	5.88
1959–1961[5]	67.55	59.78	50.25	40.98	31.73	23.22	16.01	10.29	5.89
1969–1971[6]	67.94	59.69	50.22	41.07	31.87	23.34	16.07	10.38	6.18
1979–1981	70.82	61.98	52.45	43.31	34.04	25.26	17.56	11.35	6.76
1990	72.7	63.5	54.0	44.7	35.6	26.7	18.7	12.1	7.1
1993	73.1	63.8	54.2	44.9	35.9	27.0	18.9	12.3	7.1
1995	73.4	64.1	54.5	45.2	36.1	27.3	19.3	12.5	7.2
WHITE FEMALES									
1850[1]	40.5	47.2	40.2	35.4	29.8	23.5	17.0	11.3	6.4
1890[1]	44.46	49.62	42.03	35.36	28.76	22.09	15.70	10.15	5.75
1900–1902[2]	51.08	52.15	43.77	36.42	29.17	21.89	15.23	9.59	5.50
1909–1911[2]	53.62	53.57	44.88	36.96	29.26	21.74	14.92	9.38	5.35
1919–1921[3]	58.53	55.17	46.46	38.72	30.94	23.12	15.93	9.94	5.70
1929–1931	62.67	57.65	48.52	39.99	31.52	23.41	16.05	9.98	5.63
1939–1941	67.29	60.85	51.38	42.21	33.25	24.72	17.00	10.50	5.88
1949–1951	72.03	64.26	54.56	45.00	35.64	26.76	18.64	11.68	6.59
1959–1961[5]	74.19	66.05	56.29	46.63	37.13	28.08	19.69	12.38	6.67
1969–1971[6]	75.49	66.97	57.24	47.60	38.12	29.11	20.79	13.37	7.59
1979–1981	78.22	69.21	59.44	49.76	40.16	30.96	22.45	14.89	8.65
1990	79.4	70.1	60.3	50.6	41.0	31.6	23.0	15.4	9.0
1993	79.5	70.1	60.3	50.6	41.0	31.7	23.0	15.3	8.9
1995	79.6	70.2	60.4	50.6	41.0	31.7	23.0	15.4	8.9
ALL OTHER MALES[4]									
1900–1902[2]	32.54	41.90	35.11	29.25	23.12	17.34	12.62	8.33	5.12
1909–1911[2]	34.05	40.65	33.46	27.33	21.57	16.21	11.67	8.00	5.53
1919–1921[3]	47.14	45.99	38.36	32.51	26.53	20.47	14.74	9.58	5.83
1929–1931	47.55	44.27	35.95	29.45	23.36	17.92	13.15	8.78	5.42
1939–1941	52.33	48.54	39.74	32.25	25.23	19.18	14.38	10.06	6.46
1949–1951	58.91	52.96	43.73	35.31	27.29	20.25	14.91	10.74	7.07
1959–1961[5]	61.48	55.19	45.78	37.05	28.72	21.28	15.29	10.81	6.87
1969–1971[6]	60.98	53.67	44.37	36.20	28.29	21.24	15.35	10.68	7.57
1979–1981	65.63	57.40	47.87	39.13	30.64	22.92	16.54	11.36	7.22
1990	67.0	58.5	49.0	40.3	31.9	23.9	17.0	11.4	7.0
1993	67.3	58.6	49.2	40.6	32.2	24.3	17.3	11.5	6.9
1995	67.9	59.1	49.6	40.8	32.4	24.6	17.6	11.7	7.0

Calendar period	Age								
	0	10	20	30	40	50	60	70	80
ALL OTHER FEMALES[4]									
1900–1902[2]	35.04	43.02	36.89	30.70	24.37	18.67	13.60	9.62	6.48
1909–1911[2]	37.67	42.84	36.14	29.61	23.34	17.65	12.78	9.22	6.05
1919–1921[3]	46.92	44.54	37.15	31.48	25.60	19.76	14.69	10.25	6.58
1929–1931	49.51	45.33	37.22	30.67	24.30	18.60	14.22	10.38	6.90
1939–1941	55.51	50.83	42.14	34.52	27.31	21.04	16.14	11.81	8.00
1949–1951	62.70	56.17	46.77	38.02	29.82	22.67	16.95	12.29	8.15
1959–1961[5]	66.47	59.72	50.07	40.83	32.16	24.31	17.83	12.46	7.66
1969–1971[6]	69.05	61.49	51.85	42.61	33.87	25.97	19.02	13.30	9.01
1979–1981	74.00	65.64	55.88	46.39	37.16	28.59	20.49	14.44	9.17
1990	75.2	66.6	56.8	47.3	38.1	29.2	21.3	14.5	8.8
1993	75.5	66.7	56.9	47.4	38.2	29.5	21.4	14.5	8.7
1995	75.7	66.8	57.0	47.5	38.3	29.6	21.5	14.5	8.7

1. Massachusetts only; white and nonwhite combined, the latter being about 1% of the total. 2. Original Death Registration States. 3. Death Registration States of 1920. 4. Data for periods 1900-1902 to 1929-1931 relate to blacks only. 5. Alaska and Hawaii included beginning in 1959. 6. Deaths of nonresidents of the United States excluded starting in 1970. *Sources:* Department of Health and Human Services, National Center for Health Statistics, web: www.dhhs.gov.

Life Expectancy at Birth by Race and Sex: United States, 1940–1995

Year	All races			White			Black		
	Both sexes	Male	Female	Both sexes	Male	Female	Both sexes	Male	Female
1995	75.8	72.5	78.9	76.5	73.4	79.6	69.6	65.2	73.9
1994	75.7	72.4	79.0	76.5	73.3	79.6	69.5	64.9	73.9
1993	75.5	72.2	78.8	76.3	73.1	79.5	69.2	64.6	73.7
1992	75.8	72.3	79.1	76.5	73.2	79.8	69.6	65.0	73.9
1991	75.5	72.0	78.9	76.3	72.9	79.6	69.3	64.6	73.8
1990	75.4	71.8	78.8	76.1	72.7	79.4	69.1	64.5	73.6
1989	75.1	71.7	78.5	75.9	72.5	79.2	68.8	64.3	73.3
1988	74.9	71.4	78.3	75.6	72.2	78.9	68.9	64.4	73.2
1987	74.9	71.4	78.3	75.6	72.1	78.9	69.1	64.7	73.4
1986	74.7	71.2	78.2	75.4	71.9	78.8	69.1	64.8	73.4
1985	74.7	71.1	78.2	75.3	71.8	78.7	69.3	65.0	73.4
1984	74.7	71.1	78.2	75.3	71.8	78.7	69.5	65.3	73.6
1983	74.6	71.0	78.1	75.2	71.6	78.7	69.4	65.2	73.5
1982	74.5	70.8	78.1	75.1	71.5	78.7	69.4	65.1	73.6
1981	74.1	70.4	77.8	74.8	71.1	78.4	68.9	64.5	73.2
1980	73.7	70.0	77.4	74.4	70.7	78.1	68.1	63.8	72.5
1979	73.9	70.0	77.8	74.6	70.8	78.4	68.5	64.0	72.9
1978	73.5	69.6	77.3	74.1	70.4	78.0	68.1	63.7	72.4
1977	73.3	69.5	77.2	74.0	70.2	77.9	67.7	63.4	72.0
1976	72.9	69.1	76.8	73.6	69.9	77.5	67.2	62.9	71.6
1975	72.6	68.8	76.6	73.4	69.5	77.3	66.8	62.4	71.3
1974	72.0	68.2	75.9	72.8	69.0	76.7	66.0	61.7	70.3
1973	71.4	67.6	75.3	72.2	68.5	76.1	65.0	60.9	69.3
1972[1]	71.2	67.4	75.1	72.0	68.3	75.9	64.7	60.4	69.1
1971	71.1	67.4	75.0	72.0	68.3	75.8	64.6	60.5	68.9
1970	70.8	67.1	74.7	71.7	68.0	75.6	64.1	60.0	68.3
1960	69.7	66.6	73.1	70.6	67.4	74.1	—	—	—
1950	68.2	65.6	71.1	69.1	66.5	72.2	—	—	—
1940	62.9	60.8	65.2	64.2	62.1	66.6	—	—	—

— Data not available. 1. Deaths based on a 50-percent sample. *Source:* U.S. National Center for Health Statistics, *Monthly Vital Statistics Report*, web: www.dhhs.gov.

Homeownership Rates, by Age of Householder: 1985 to 1995

(in percent)

Age	1985	1986	1987	1988	1989	1990	1991	1992	1993[1]	1994	1995
Total	63.9%	63.8 %	64.0%	63.8%	63.9%	63.9%	64.1%	64.1%	64.0%	64.0%	64.7%
Less than 25 years old	17.2	17.2.	16.0	15.8	16.6	15.7	15.3	14.9	14.8	14.9	15.9
25 to 29 years old	37.7	36.7	36.4	35.9	35.3	35.2	33.8	33.6	33.6	34.1	34.4
30 to 34 years old	54.0	53.6	53.5	53.2	53.2	51.8	51.2	50.5	50.8	50.6	53.1
35 to 39 years old	65.4	64.8	64.1	63.6	63.4	63.0	62.2	61.4	61.8	61.2	62.1
40 to 44 years old	71.4	70.5	70.8	70.7	70.2	69.8	69.5	69.1	68.6	68.2	68.6
45 to 49 years old	74.3	74.1	74.6	74.4	74.1	73.9	73.7	74.2	73.7	73.8	73.7
50 to 54 years old	77.5	78.1	77.8	77.1	77.2	76.8	76.1	76.2	77.2	76.8	77.0

Age	1985	1986	1987	1988	1989	1990	1991	1992	1993[1]	1994	1995
55 to 59 years old	79.2	80.0	80.0	79.3	79.1	78.8	79.5	79.3	78.9	78.4	78.8
60 to 64 years old	79.9	79.8	80.4	79.8	80.1	79.8	80.5	81.2	80.9	80.1	80.3
65 to 69 years old	79.5	79.4	79.5	80.0	80.0	80.0	81.4	80.8	80.7	80.6	81.0
70 to 74 years old	76.8	77.2	77.7	77.7	77.8	78.4	78.8	79.0	79.9	80.1	80.9
75 years old and over	69.8	70.0	70.8	70.8	71.2	72.3	73.1	73.3	73.4	73.5	74.6

1. Based on 1990 census controls. *Source:* U.S. Bureau of the Census, *Current Housing Reports*, web: www.census.gov.

Mental Health: Lifetime Prevalence of Psychiatric Disorders, 1990–92

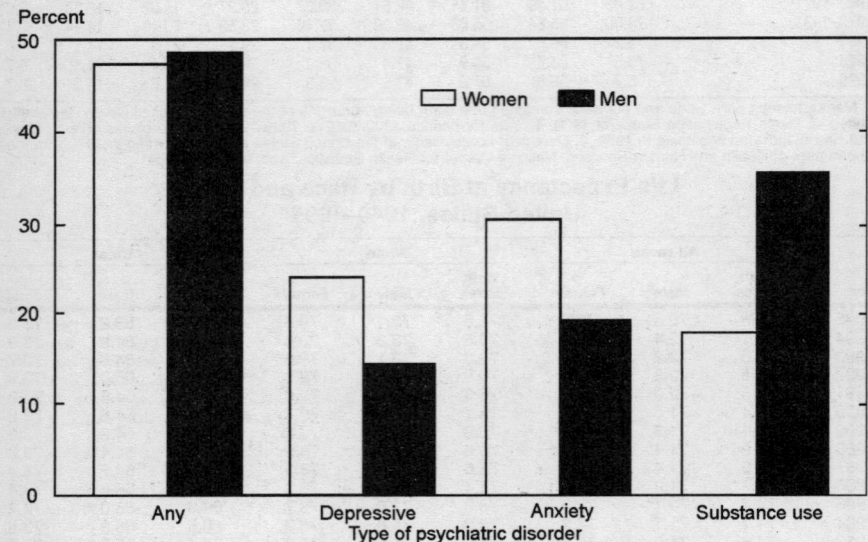

NOTES: Persons 15–54 years are represented. The presence of a psychiatric disorder did not have to be formally diagnosed for persons to be included as having had a disorder. The category "Any Disorder" includes disorders not included in the specific types shown. *Source:* University of Michigan, Institute for Social Research/Survey Research Center, National Comorbidity Survey.

Participation in Various Leisure Activities: 1992

	Adult population (mil.)	Attendance at—			Participation in—				
		Movies	Sports events	Amuse-ment park	Exercise program	Playing sports	Outdoor activities[1]	Home improvement/ repair	Gardening
Total	185.8	59%	37%	50%	60%	39%	34%	48%	55%
Sex: Male	89.0	60	44	51	61	50	39	53	46
Female	96.8	59	30	50	59	29	29	42	62
Race: White	158.8	60	38	51	61	40	37	50	57
Black	21.1	54	32	45	51	32	10	32	39
Other	5.9	62	20	46	51	38	28	31	42
Age: 18 to 24 years old	24.1	82	51	68	67	59	43	33	31
25 to 34 years old	42.4	70	47	68	67	52	41	47	51
35 to 44 years old	39.8	68	43	58	62	44	42	58	57
45 to 54 years old	27.7	58	35	44	62	34	36	57	64
55 to 64 years old	21.2	40	23	30	56	21	21	53	63
65 to 74 years old	18.3	34	20	29	50	18	21	42	63
75 to 96 years old	12.3	19	7	14	34	7	5	20	55
Education: Grade school	14.3	16	9	24	24	10	11	24	44
Some high school	18.6	35	19	35	39	18	21	34	50
High school graduate	69.4	54	33	51	55	34	31	47	53
Some college	39.2	21	45	59	71	49	42	53	55
College graduate	26.2	77	51	58	75	55	42	52	61
Graduate school	18.1	81	51	54	79	57	51	65	65

1. Camping, hiking, canoeing. *Source:* U.S. National Endowment for the Arts, *Arts Participation in America: 1982 to 1992.*

Law Enforcement & Crime

Church Arson

Although there have been incidents of arson at houses of worship in the past, they had been viewed as isolated incidents by local authorities. But in 1996 it became clear that church arson was a national crime trend in the United States. There had been a particularly sharp increase in fires set to African-American churches in the South—of the 429 arsons reported since January 1995, 162 involved black churches, more than three-quarters of which were located in the South. In response to this disturbing phenomenon, President Clinton established the National Church Arson Task Force in 1996, which has conducted the largest number of arson investigations in history and is currently the country's major ongoing civil rights investigation.

Hundreds of churches, religious schools, and synagogues were burned, congregations left temporarily homeless, rural wooden churches completely destroyed, 100-year-old Bibles ruined, and tens of millions of dollars in damages sustained. The church arsons reopened the wound of racism and religious intolerance in the national psyche. Although few Americans would argue that this wound had only recently begun to heal, many believe racism had at least become a more subtle form of bigotry rather than the primitive and brutal hatred associated with earlier decades.

There is, however, no evidence to support the theory of a nationwide conspiracy, as some have suggested. Only a few of the fires have been linked to each other, and these have been confined to a small geographic area. While there have been a handful of cases in which members and former members of hate groups have been convicted of these arsons, most were not committed by members of organized hate groups. An examination of the Task Force's finding reveals wide range of motives and a full spectrum of victims as well as victimizers, defying formulaic explanations of the arsons.

Of the 199 persons arrested, 160 are white, 34 are black, and 5 are Hispanic. Eighty-three people arrested were juveniles. Of the 123 suspects arrested at African-American churches, 55 are white, 25 are African American and one is Hispanic. Five of the white suspects were arrested for arsons at both African-American and non-African-American churches. Known motives range from blatant racism and religious hatred to financial profit, burglary, and personal revenge.

Thousands of Americans have donated time and money to help rebuild the burned churches. Habitat for Humanity, one of the volunteer groups, estimates that more than 15,000 individuals have helped in the rebuilding process. Twenty-five houses of worship have been rebuilt and 65 more are currently being constructed. While the arsons are an appalling setback for civil rights, the untold Americans that have responded augurs well for the future of American religious and racial tolerance.

Convictions for Arson Against Houses of Worship

Source: National Church Arson Task Force, Bureau of Tobacco and Firearms

The National Church Arson Task Force has conducted 429 investigations between January 1, 1995 and May 1997, arrested 199 suspects, and convicted 110 defendants in connection with fires at 78 houses of worship. Hundreds of additional investigations are in progress. Below is a listing of the 78 churches where there have been convictions, and a brief profile of the crime and the perpetrator.

ALABAMA

Faith Whole Truth Holiness Church (Pennington). October 31, 1995, black church: burned and vandalized by two white males, 15 and 20.

New Liberty Baptist Church (Tyler). Feb. 28, 1996, black church: burned by white male (20) volunteer firefighter because he was angry that he was not allowed to preach at the church.

ARIZONA

Our Lady of Guadalupe Chapel and Union Baptist Church (Yuma). Sept. 30, 1996 and Oct. 1, 1996, a Hispanic and a black church, respectively: burned by white male (25) who set the fires to cover up evidence of burglaries. Our Lady of Guadalupe was completely destroyed.

CALIFORNIA

Trinity Presbyterian Church (Spring Valley). March 18, 1996, interracial church: burned by a white male (28).

DELAWARE

Saint Andrews Presbyterian (Newark). March 25, 1996, white church: burned by four white males (12 to 14) to cover up stealing cake and soda.

FLORIDA

First Born Church of the Living God (Tallahassee). May 6, 1997, black church: burglarized and burned by black male (20).

Jacksonville Jewish Center (Jacksonville). Feb. 22, 1997: pipe bomb planted by white male (32).

Trinity United Methodist (Saint Petersburg). Oct. 24, 1996, interracial church: burned by a black male (18) who threw a Molotov cocktail at its exterior. The fire occurred during the civil disturbances over the police shooting of an black man.

ILLINOIS

First Presbyterian Church (Libertyville). Oct. 1, 1996, white church: burned and swastikas spray-painted on it walls by four white males (14 to 16).

IOWA

Saint Boniface (Westphalia). July 7, 1996, white church: burned by two white males (10 and 12). The carpeting was spoiled by defecation, a car nearby was burglarized and it also received minor burn damage.

Hickory Grove Community Church (Ottumwa). Sept. 2, 1996, white church: burned by white male (46).

KENTUCKY

Methodist Church of Christ (Nicholasville). June 28, 1996, three white males (16 to 17) burglarized this white church and then attempted to set the church on fire. One of the juveniles also made a satanic drawing on the wall.

Mount Zion Baptist Church (Somerset). March 9, 1996, white church: burned by white male (28) who was a volunteer fire fighter.

Saint Therese Catholic Church (Louisville). May 1, 1996, white church: burned by four white males (15 to 18).

LOUISIANA

Assembly of God (Westwego). April 15, 1995, white church: burned by a white male.

Saint Genevieve Catholic Church (Thibodeaux). Feb. 18, 1997, interracial church: burned by two white males (14).

Saint Peter's Catholic Church and Pine Prairie First Baptist Church (Pine Prairie). March 1, 1996, and Feb. 23, 1997, white churches: burned by white male juvenile (12).

New Birth Missionary Baptist Church (Lake Charles). Dec. 10, 1996, black church: burned by two black male juveniles (12 and 13).

MAINE

Saint Anne's Catholic Church (Lisbon). July 6, 1996, white church: two minor explosive devices were set off in the parking lot by a white male (22).

MARYLAND

Thawley's Chapel (Hillsboro). Sept. 2, 1996, white church: burned by two white males (13 and 19).

John Watters Meeting House (Bel Air). March 21, 1996, white church: burned and vandalized by four males, three white and one black.

MICHIGAN

Cass Community United Methodist Church (Detroit). Aug. 25, 1996, white church: a sofa and chair in the courtyard were set on fire by a black male (20).

MINNESOTA

Brooklyn Park Evangelical Free Church (Brooklyn Park). Aug. 15, 1996, white church: vandalized and burned by white juvenile (15). Investigators found a drawing of a five-point star and the words "Satan lives" on one of the church walls. The church had been providing counseling to people involved in satanic worship. The juvenile indicated that he felt left out of the youth group that met the previous night and committed the vandalism to get even.

Grace Lutheran (Westbrook). June 20, 1996, white church: burned by two white juveniles, 10 and 12. Both stated that they got the idea to burn the church from watching television.

MISSISSIPPI

Lynch Chapel United Methodist (Clinton). Nov. 1, 1995, black church: burned by black male (19), who lived next door to the church.

Mallalieu Methodist Church (Meridian). Dec. 11, 1996, black church: burned by three white juveniles (14, 15, and 16), who also defaced the communion altar, doors, and wall of the church with racial epithets.

Elbethel Baptist Church (Satartia). March 30, 1996, black church: burned by white male (37).

MISSOURI

Shilo Baptist Church (Kansas City) and Ozark Primitive Baptist (Webster County). May 5, 1996, white churches: burned by two white males (29 and 31).

Amity Freewill Baptist Church (Niangua). Dec. 30, 1996, white church: burned by two white males (18 and 19). The entire church was destroyed.

Greers Chapel Baptist Church (Sikeston). Sept. 13, 1996, black church: burned by three white males (18 to 19). The church was completely destroyed.

New Bethel Church (Anderson). Oct. 16, 1996, white church: burned by white male (27).

NEVADA

Church of Christ (Henderson). Sept. 19, 1996, black church: burned by a white male (23). Witnesses stated that he attempted to burglarize the church and failed. After the failed burglary, he stated he would burn the church because its members were black.

NEW YORK

Temple Beth El (Rockaway), Temple Derech Emuch (Rockaway), and Yeshiva of Belle (Belle Harbor). Jan. 13, 1995, April 30, 1995, and May 6, 1995, respectively: synagogues: burned by white male (41). The defendant had asked various organizations for money, and when they began refusing him he burned their buildings.

NORTH CAROLINA

Mount Tabor Baptist Church (Cerro Gordo). May 23, 1996, black church: burned by two black males (32 and 22).

Matthews-Murkland Presbyterian Church (Charlotte). June 6, 1996, black church: burned by white female (13) with satanic and racist beliefs.

Pleasant Ridge United Church of Christ (Greensboro). June 28, 1996, white church: burned by white male (19).

Ohovah A.M.E. (Orrum). Jan. 6, 1996, black church: burglarized, vandalized, and burned by white male (29).

Pleasant Hill Baptist Church (Lumberton). May 24, 1996, black church: burned by white volunteer fireman (17).

Beulah Land Baptist Church (Roaring River). July 1, 1996, black church: burned by white male (40).

Saint James African Methodist Episcopal Zion Church (Maysville). June 30, 1996, black church: burned by white male (19).

OHIO

Ebeneezer Full Gospel Missionary Baptist Church (Canton). June 18, 1996, black church: a chair was set on fire inside the church by two white males: (44 and 22).

OREGON

Immanuel Free Methodist Church (Portland). June 20, 1996, interracial church: burned by black male (21), who threw two mason jar gasoline fire bombs through a church window.

PENNSYLVANIA

First United Methodist Church (Middle District). November 4, 1996, white church: burned by white male (27).

SOUTH CAROLINA

Life Christian Assembly (North Charleston). June 17, 1996, interracial church: the shed behind the church was burned by two white juveniles (9 and 10).

Mount Zion A.M.E. Church (Greeleyville) and Macedonia Baptist Church (Manning). June 20 and 21, 1995, respectively; black church: burned by four white ex-members of the Ku Klux Klan (23, 24, 51, and 52).

Rice Chapel (Buffalo). May 8, 1994, black church: burned by male volunteer fire fighter (22; race not specified).

New Saint Paul Apostolic Church (Florence). June 11, 1996, black church: burned by three white juveniles (10, 11, and 12).

Johns Island Church (Johns Island). July 16, 1996, black church: burned by the black pastor (51) of the church. The building was still under construction at the time of the arson.

Spring Hill A.M.E. Church (Dillon). Aug. 1, 1996, black church: burned by two white males (17). The church was totally destroyed.

TENNESSEE

Canaan A.M.E. Church (Maury County) and Friendship Missionary Baptist Church (Maury County). Jan. 29, 1995, black churches: firebombed by three white males (33, 35, and 43).

Church of the Nativity (Bartlett). June 29, 1996, white church: burned by white pastor (46).

Saint Mary's Episcopal School, Holy Communion School, Shady Grove Presbyterian, Colonial Park United Methodist Church, Emmanuel United Methodist, Calvary Baptist Church (all Memphis). Occurring between Oct. 16, 1995, and April 20, 1996, respectively, all six white churches: burned by white male (26).

Church of God of Prophecy (Dyersburg). July 22, 1996, white church: burned by black male (20).

TEXAS

Victory Baptist Church (Denison). June 5, 1995, black church: burned by white male (26).

Audubon Park Baptist Church/ New Revelation Mission (Garland). July 11, 1996, interracial church: burned by white male (33).

Real Rock Church (Houston). Feb. 2, 1996, black church: burned by black male (10).

Church of the Living God (Greenville). June 10, 1996, black church: burned by black male (18).

Macedonia Baptist Church (Bristol). March 22, 1997, black church: burned by two white males (22 and 25).

UTAH

Templo Casa De Oracion (Salt Lake). March 28, 1996, white church: burned by white female (32).

VIRGINIA

Green Run Baptist Church (Virginia Beach). June 18, 1996, interracial church: burned by two white males (13 and 16).

First Baptist Church of Centralia (Chesterfield). April 16, 1996, black church: burned by two white females (16 and 20) and white male (20).

Bethany Baptist Church (Portsmouth). Aug. 14, 1995, white church: burned by white male (34).

WASHINGTON

Naval Air Station Chapel (Whidbey Island-Oak Harbor). Jan. 21, 1996, interracial church: burned by black male (23). □

Summary of Hate Crime Statistics, 1995

	Number of incidents	Number of offenses	Number of victims	Number of known offenders
Bias Motivation				
Race:	4,831	6,170	6,438	5,751
Anti-White	1,226	1,511	1,554	2,032
Anti-Black	2,988	3,805	3,945	3,099
Anti-American Indian/Alaskan Native	41	59	59	38
Anti-Asian/Pacific Islander	355	484	496	380
Anti-Multi-Racial Group	221	311	384	202
Ethnicity/National Origin:	814	1,022	1,044	958
Anti-Hispanic	516	680	698	685
Anti-Other Ethnicity/National Origin	298	342	346	273
Religion:	1,277	1,414	1,617	437
Anti-Jewish	1,058	1,145	1,236	350
Anti-Catholic	31	35	53	8
Anti-Protestant	36	47	65	12
Anti-Islamic	29	39	41	26
Anti-Other Religious Group	102	122	196	36
Anti-Multi-Religious Group	20	25	25	4
Anti-Atheism/Agnosticism/etc.	1	1	1	1
Sexual Orientation:	1,019	1,266	1,347	1,273
Anti-Male Homosexual	735	915	937	1,031
Anti-Female Homosexual	146	189	191	131
Anti-Homosexual	103	125	182	80
Anti-Heterosexual	17	19	19	13
Anti-Bisexual	18	18	18	18
Multiple Bias	6	23	23	14
Total	7,947	9,895	10,4679	8,433

Source: U.S. Department of Justice, *Uniform Crime Reports.*

Crime Index by State, 1995

State	Crime index total	Rate per 100,000 inhab- itants	Violent crime	Property crime	Murder and non-neg- ligent man- slaughter	State	Crime index total	Rate per 100,000 inhab- itants	Violent crime	Property crime	Murder and non-neg- ligent man- slaughter
Ala.	206,188	4,848.1	26,894	179,294	475	Mont.[2]	46,153	5,304.9	1,484	44,669	26
Alas.	34,753	5,753.8	4,656	30,097	55	Neb.	74,393	4,544.5	6,253	68,140	48
Ariz.	346,450	8,213.6	30,095	316,355	439	Nev.	100,664	6,579.3	14,461	86,203	163
Ark.	116,521	4,690.9	13,741	102,780	259	N.H.	30,484	2,655.4	1,314	29,170	21
Calif.	1,841,984	5,831.1	305,154	1,536,830	3,531	N.J.	373,708	4,703.7	47,652	326,056	409
Colo.	202,199	5,396.3	16,494	185,705	216	N.M.	108,312	6,428.0	13,804	94,508	148
Conn.	147,481	4,503.2	13,293	134,188	150	N.Y.	827,025	4,560.1	152,683	674,342	1,550
Del.	36,988	5,158.7	5,198	31,790	25	N.C.	405,764	5,639.5	46,508	359,256	677
D.C.[1]	67,441	12,173.5	14,744	52,697	360	N.D.	18,373	2,866.3	556	17,817	6
Fla.	1,090,999	7,701.5	151,711	939,288	1,037	Ohio	491,223	4,405.2	53,799	437,424	600
Ga.	432,322	6,003.6	47,317	385,005	683	Okla.	183,463	5,596.8	21,770	161,693	400
Hi.	85,447	7,198.6	3,509	81,938	56	Ore.	206,173	6,563.9	16,408	189,765	129
Idaho	51,189	4,401.5	3,745	47,444	48	Pa.	406,209	3,364.9	51,586	354,623	755
Ill.[2]	645,408	5,455.7	117,836	527,572	1,221	P.R.[3]	106,088	n.a.	22,450	83,638	864
Ind.	268,768	4,631.5	30,451	238,317	466	R.I.	42,021	4,244.5	3,643	38,378	33
Iowa	116,575	4,101.9	10,071	106,504	51	S.C.	222,723	6,063.8	36,067	186,656	292
Kan.[2]	125,350	4,886.9	10,792	114,558	159	S.D.	22,312	3,060.6	1,513	20,799	13
Ky.	129,377	3,351.7	14,079	115,298	276	Tenn.	281,864	5,362.7	40,549	241,315	557
La.	289,873	6,676.0	43,741	246,132	740	Tex.	1,064,336	5,684.3	124,303	940,033	1,693
Me.	40,763	3,284.7	1,631	39,132	25	Utah	118,832	6,090.8	6,415	112,417	76
Md.	317,382	6,294.8	49,757	267,625	596	Vt.	20,087	3,433.7	692	19,395	13
Mass.	263,710	4,341.6	41,739	221,971	217	Va.	264,005	3,989.2	23,921	240,084	503
Mich.	494,903	5,182.8	65,680	429,223	808	Wash.	340,513	6,269.8	26,300	314,213	275
Minn.	207,327	4,497.3	16,416	190,911	182	W.Va.	44,935	2,458.2	3,842	41,093	89
Miss.	121,755	4,514.5	13,560	108,195	348	Wis.	199,064	3,885.7	14,399	184,665	219
Mo.	272,617	5,120.5	35,339	237,278	469	Wyo.	20,737	4,320.2	1,220	19,517	10

NOTE: The Crime Index is composed of the violent and property crime categories. In 1995, 13% of the Index offenses reported to law enforcement agencies were violent crimes and 87% were property crimes. Violent crimes are murder, forcible rape, robbery, and aggravated assault. Property crimes are burglary, larceny-theft, and auto-theft. Data are not included for the property crime of arson. 1. Includes offenses reported by the Zoological Police. 2. Complete data were not available for the states of Illinois, Kansas, and Montana; therefore it was necessary that their crime counts be estimated. 3. n.a. = not available. The 1996 Bureau of Census population for Puerto Rico was not available; therefore no rates per 100,000 inhabitants are provided. *Source: F.B.I. Uniform Crime Reports for the United States, 1996.*

Crime Rates for Selected Large Cities: 1994

(Offenses known to the police per 100,000 population.)

City ranked by population size, 1994[1]	Violent crime				Property crime		
	Murder	Forcible rape	Robbery	Aggravated assault	Burglary	Larceny-theft	Motor vehicle theft
New York, NY	21.3	36.3	988.8	814.5	1,204.6	2,859.9	1,300.7
Los Angeles, CA	23.8	43.8	868.0	1,123.4	1,226.2	3,120.5	1,434.3
Chicago, IL	33.1	(2)	1,210.5	1,440.9	1,563.6	4,323.4	1,427.9
Houston, TX	21.3	53.0	567.7	665.5	1,451.5	3,239.2	1,287.2
Philadelphia, PA	25.9	46.2	814.2	436.2	903.9	2,588.3	1,620.0
San Diego, CA	9.7	34.5	329.0	704.8	1,102.8	3,012.0	1,371.8
Phoenix, AZ	21.5	40.7	320.7	697.6	1,983.7	5,063.9	1,920.3
Dallas, TX	27.8	90.1	666.0	805.2	1,680.7	4,542.1	1,664.9
Detroit, MI	52.9	109.2	1,249.4	1,275.8	2,167.3	4,170.2	2,892.4
San Antonio, TX	19.4	56.5	278.1	293.1	1,642.4	5,491.5	987.7
Honolulu, HI	4.0	30.2	120.1	132.7	1,137.5	4,831.7	650.3
San Jose, CA	4.0	46.0	136.0	539.5	714.3	2,390.1	554.6
Las Vegas, NV	14.0	76.3	505.6	655.6	1,548.9	3,900.1	1,027.8
San Francisco, CA	12.3	39.4	893.2	516.5	1,086.2	4,547.0	1,247.2
Baltimore, MD	43.4	86.2	1,525.3	1,179.4	2,150.6	5,736.4	1,830.8
Jacksonville, FL	15.5	94.5	499.7	910.2	2,089.2	5,023.9	990.7
Columbus, OH	15.4	104.8	555.5	367.8	2,019.9	4,596.1	1,037.3
Milwaukee, WI	22.1	68.2	638.9	314.4	1,345.7	4,060.8	1,699.6
Memphis, TN	25.3	110.6	793.6	638.6	2,503.4	3,834.7	1,863.7
Washington, DC	70.0	43.7	1,107.2	1,441.8	1,760.9	5,205.8	1,448.6
El Paso, TX	7.8	41.2	192.2	708.8	756.7	4,762.2	690.7
Boston, MA	15.3	81.4	762.5	1,056.4	1,221.3	4,378.3	2,019.0
Seattle, WA	12.8	58.9	469.4	669.1	1,515.2	6,803.7	1,188.9
Charlotte, NC	16.5	66.4	514.7	1,129.2	1,958.9	5,400.8	599.5
Nashville-Davidson, TN	14.0	97.4	508.7	1,178.2	1,600.2	5,520.6	1,145.8
Austin, TX	7.2	48.7	301.4	277.7	1,377.2	5,160.1	768.7
Denver, CO	15.8	71.6	335.4	498.0	1,518.1	3,272.1	1,222.1
Cleveland, OH	26.1	148.0	775.1	580.6	1,581.7	2,554.4	1,790.3
New Orleans, LA	85.8	88.3	976.1	736.7	2,037.3	4,431.3	1,734.2
Fort Worth, TX	27.9	87.4	503.7	658.7	1,756.3	5,020.7	1,134.5
Portland, OR	10.8	86.4	506.2	1,298.7	1,727.8	6,125.0	2,060.8
Oklahoma City, OK	14.1	118.4	379.0	891.4	2,233.2	7,308.3	1,060.3
Long Beach, CA	17.9	37.4	767.3	594.1	1,453.0	3,057.0	1,603.6
Tucson, AZ	8.4	65.5	229.3	802.9	1,632.3	7,976.6	1,539.9
Kansas City, MO	32.3	111.6	848.8	1,442.5	2,723.4	5,718.4	1,674.4
Virginia Beach, VA	7.7	33.9	142.5	86.8	759.8	3,713.9	221.3
Atlanta, GA	46.4	102.6	1,299.4	2,122.5	2,951.3	7,511.6	2,084.6
St. Louis, MO	63.5	77.9	1,543.1	2,066.1	3,207.2	7,105.9	2,286.9
Sacramento, CA	15.9	44.7	588.5	557.2	2,073.7	4,775.4	2,271.1
Fresno, CA	22.0	50.2	734.3	813.5	2,001.5	4,871.2	3,548.4
Tulsa, OK	11.0	77.6	280.6	846.3	1,715.8	3,289.0	1,180.4
Miami, FL	30.5	58.2	1,537.2	1,787.7	2,967.8	8,064.9	2,730.7
Oakland, CA	36.9	85.1	1,021.1	1,050.8	1,850.4	4,688.0	1,900.7
Minneapolis, MN	16.7	155.9	928.7	806.3	2,387.6	5,738.1	1,133.7
Pittsburgh, PA	17.4	70.8	669.8	355.7	1,176.1	3,409.7	1,449.3
Cincinnati, OH	10.4	104.1	580.7	627.9	1,640.5	4,577.2	472.0
Toledo, OH	12.1	107.3	523.0	462.1	1,985.6	4,849.5	1,191.0
Buffalo, NY	27.7	86.3	1,007.8	1,002.3	2,247.2	3,774.6	1,406.2
Wichita, KS	13.3	70.7	334.8	323.4	2,053.2	5,328.9	1,083.9
Mesa, AZ	5.4	38.0	129.0	576.9	1,582.8	4,863.4	1,100.3
Colorado Springs, CO	4.5	73.0	128.5	275.5	971.7	4,865.1	349.2
Tampa, FL	21.0	101.1	1,146.4	2,214.1	2,964.1	7,297.5	3,736.8
Santa Ana, CA	25.3	27.3	604.4	393.8	836.8	2,864.0	1,271.6
Arlington, TX	6.3	50.2	228.1	567.4	1,210.1	4,325.1	865.9
Anaheim, CA	8.6	32.3	406.2	500.9	1,175.6	3,201.7	1,229.4
Corpus Christi, TX	4.7	64.3	177.7	609.7	1,534.2	6,939.8	487.2
Louisville, KY	18.8	51.4	473.0	461.4	1,593.5	2,945.3	887.1
St. Paul, MN	10.6	98.1	318.0	568.9	1,485.7	3,881.0	738.8
Newark, NJ	35.4	76.4	2,130.8	1,598.0	2,375.4	4,118.8	3,492.3
Birmingham, AL	49.8	100.7	730.7	1,563.6	2,392.4	6,009.7	1,344.8
Norfolk, VA	23.5	60.4	460.3	371.9	1,199.8	4,823.1	696.1
Anchorage, AK	8.7	78.1	287.4	602.8	897.2	4,619.0	863.7

1. Crime data are not available for Indianapolis, IN and Albuquerque, NM in 1994. 2. The rate for forcible rape is not shown because the forcible rape figures were not in accordance with national Uniform Crime Reporting guidelines. *Source: Statistical Abstract of the United States, 1996.*

Arrests by Race, 1995

Offense charged	White	Black	American Indian or Alaskan Native	Asian or Pacific Islander	Offense charged	White	Black	American Indian or Alaskan Native	Asian or Pacific Islander
		Percent distribution[1]					Percent distribution[1]		
Total	**66.8%**	**30.9%**	**1.1%**	**1.1%**	Sex offenses, except forcible rape and prostitution	75.0	22.6	1.1	1.3
Murder[2]	43.4	54.4	.8	1.4					
Forcible rape	55.6	42.4	1.0	1.1	Drug abuse violation	62.1	36.9	.5	.6
Robbery	38.7	59.5	.5	1.3	Gambling	53.3	41.3	.5	4.9
Aggravated assault	59.6	38.4	.9	1.1	Offenses against family and children	65.2	32.2	1.0	1.7
Burglary	67.0	31.0	.9	1.1					
Larceny—theft	64.8	32.4	1.1	1.6	Driving under the influence	86.4	10.9	1.5	1.2
Motor vehicle theft	58.5	38.3	1.2	2.0					
Arson	74.2	23.7	1.0	1.0	Liquor laws	79.6	17.3	2.4	.7
Other assaults	63.0	34.7	1.2	1.1	Drunkenness	80.8	16.4	2.4	.4
Forgery and counterfeiting	65.0	33.1	.6	1.4	Disorderly conduct	62.9	35.1	1.3	.6
Fraud	64.0	34.7	.5	.8	Vagrancy	52.4	45.0	2.3	.4
Embezzlement	64.9	33.1	.6	1.4	All other offenses except traffic	63.1	34.7	1.0	1.1
Stolen property—buying, receiving, possessing	58.6	39.4	.7	1.2	Suspicion	51.9	47.5	.4	.2
Vandalism	73.4	23.9	1.4	1.3	Curfew and loitering law violations	75.8	21.3	1.3	1.6
Weapons—carrying, possessing, etc.	59.4	38.8	.7	1.2					
Prostitution and commercialized vice	60.9	36.8	.5	1.7	Runaways	76.9	19.0	.9	3.2

1. Because of rounding, the percentages may not add up to total. 2. Includes non-negligent manslaughter. *Source: Uniform Crime Reports, 1995.*

Total Arrest Trends by Sex, 1986 and 1995

Offense	Male			Female		
	1986	1995	Percent change	1986	1995	Percent change
Total	**7,334,777**	**8,245,284**	**+12.4**	**1,535,932**	**2,117,452**	**+37.9**
Murder[1]	12,572	13,927	+10.8	1,725	1,457	−15.5
Forcible rape	26,016	23,809	−8.5	268	297	+10.8
Robbery	104,871	116,741	+11.3	8,800	12,068	+37.1
Aggravated assault	225,720	328,476	+45.5	34,731	70,938	+104.2
Burglary	297,599	236,495	−20.5	26,403	29,868	+13.1
Larceny—theft	687,289	704,565	+2.5	301,636	351,580	+16.6
Motor vehicle theft	104,886	119,175	+13.6	11,012	18,058	+64.0
Arson	10,918	11,413	+4.5	1,780	2,156	+21.1
Other assaults	413,578	710,249	+71.7	74,427	173,621	+133.3
Forgery and counterfeiting	42,281	53,878	+27.4	21,724	30,190	+39.0
Fraud	193,934	175,491	+25.4	105,845	120,093	+13.5
Embezzlement	5,498	6,105	+11.0	3,359	4,727	+40.7
Stolen property—buying, receiving, possessing	86,569	98,682	+14.0	11,142	16,300	+46.3
Vandalism	157,051	180,511	+14.9	18,538	28,194	+52.1
Weapons—carrying, possessing, etc.	131,980	157,036	+19.0	10,508	13,299	+26.6
Prostitution and commercialized vice	31,959	29,576	−7.5	59,805	45,068	−24.6
Sex offenses, except forcible rape and prostitution	66,795	60,672	−9.2	5,722	5,346	−6.6
Drug abuse violations	545,008	872,834	+60.2	91,813	175,485	+91.1
Gambling	20,125	12,357	−38.6	4,196	2,296	−45.3
Offenses against family and children	33,064	66,351	+100.7	5,991	18,286	+205.2
Driving under the influence	1,076,712	784,253	−27.2	139,271	132,914	−4.6
Liquor laws	310,759	321,160	+3.3	61,773	73,461	+18.9
Drunkenness	603,473	431,851	−28.4	58,470	57,534	−1.6
Disorderly conduct	382,094	381,093	−.3	88,267	105,980	+20.1
Vagrancy	27,556	15,760	−42.8	3,708	3,822	+3.1
All other offenses, except traffic	1,697,711	2,185,462	+28.7	303,907	491,970	+61.9
Curfew and loitering law violations	44,288	72,649	+64.0	14,642	30,787	+110.3
Runaways	48,471	74,713	+54.1	66,469	101,657	+52.9

1. Includes non-negligent manslaughter. *Source:* Department of Justice, Federal Bureau of Investigation, *Uniform Crime Reports for the United States, 1995.*

Total Arrests Under Age 21, 1995

	Number of Arrests	Percent		Number of Arrests	Percent
Total, under 21	11,416,346	100.0%	17	488,032	4.3%
Total, under 18	2,084,428	18.3%	18	513,215	4.5%
Total, under 15	711,348	6.2%	19	477,964	4.2%
15	416,617	3.6%	20	440,740	3.9%
16	468,431	4.1%	21	402,812	3.5%

NOTE: Based on reports furnished to the FBI by 9,498 agencies covering a 1995 estimated population of 196,440,000. *Source:* Department of Justice, Federal Bureau of Investigation, *Uniform Crime Reports for the United States, 1995.*

Murder Victims by Weapons Used

		Weapons used or cause of death						
		Guns						
Year	Murder victims, total	Total	Percent	Cutting or stabbing	Blunt object[1]	Strangulation, hands, fists, feet, or pushing	Arson[2]	All other[3]
1965	8,773	5,015	57.2%	2,021	505	894	226	112
1970	13,649	9,039	66.2	2,424	604	1,031	353	198
1975	18,642	12,061	64.7	3,245	1,001	1,646	193	496
1980	21,860	13,650	62.0	4,212	1,094	1,666	291	947
1985	17,545	10,296	58.7	3,694	972	1,491	243	849
1989	18,954	11,832	62.4	3,458	1,128	1,416	234	886
1990	20,045	12,847	64.1	3,503	1,075	1,424	287	909
1991	21,676	14,373	66.3	3,430	1,099	1,529	195	847
1992	22,716	15,489	68.2	3,296	1,040	1,445	203	1,043
1993	23,180	16,136	69.6	2,967	1,022	1,482	217	1,168
1994	22,084	15,463	70.0	2,802	912	1,452	196	1,079
1995	20,043	13,673	68.2	2,538	904	1,414	166	960

1. Refers to club, hammer, etc. 2. Before 1973, includes drowning. 3. Includes poison, explosives, unknown, drowning, asphyxiation, narcotics, other means, and weapons not stated. *Source:* Department of Justice, Federal Bureau of Investigation, *Uniform Crime Reports for the United States, 1995.*

Criminal Victimization Experienced in the United States in 1994

	Number in millions	Rates per 1,000[1]	Percent of measured crime	Percent of this crime reported to police
All crimes	42.4	—	100%	36%
Violent crime	10.9	51	26%	42%
Simple assault	6.6	31	16%	36%
Aggravated assault	2.5	12	6%	52%
Robbery	1.3	6	3%	55%
Rape/Sexual assault	.4	2	*	32%
Personal theft[2]	.5	2	1%	33%
Property crime	31.0	308	73%	34%
Property thefts	23.8	236	56%	27%
Household burglary	5.5	54	13%	50%
Motor vehicle theft	1.8	18	4%	78%

1. Per 1,000 persons age 12 or older, or per 1,000 households. 2. Includes pocket picking and purse snatching. — Not applicable. *Less than .1%

- In 1994 for every 1,000 persons age 12 or older, there occurred:
  —2 rapes or attempted rapes
  —3 assaults with serious injury
  —4 robberies with property taken.
- The violent crime rate has been essentially unchanged since 1992, following a slight increase between 1985 and 1991. Property crime continued a 15-year decline.
- The young, blacks, and males were most vulnerable to violent crime:
  —1 in 9 persons age 12 to 15, compared to 1 in 196 age 65 or more
  —1 in 16 blacks, compared to 1 in 20 whites
  —1 in 17 males, compared to 1 in 24 females

- Compared to those households with annual incomes of $15,000 or more, persons in households with incomes of less than $15,000 were:
  —3 times more likely to be raped or sexually assaulted
  —2 times more likely to be robbed
  —1½ times more likely to be a victim of an aggravated assault.
- Almost two-thirds of victims of completed rapes did not report the crime to the police.
- Two-thirds of victims of rape or sexual assault knew their assailants.
- A third of robbery victims were injured as a result of the incident.

Source: Criminal Victimization in the United States, 1995, Bureau of Justice Statistics.

Federal Prosecutions of Public Corruption: 1980 to 1994

(Prosecution of persons who have corrupted public office in violation of Federal Criminal Statutes.)

Prosecution status	1994	1993	1992	1991	1990	1989	1988	1985	1980
Total:[1] Indicted	1,165	1,371	1,189	1,452	1,176	1,348	1,274	1,157	727
Convicted	969	1,362	1,081	1,194	1,084	1,149	1,067	997	602
Awaiting trial	332	403	380	346	300	375	288	256	213
Federal officials: Indicted	571	627	624	803	615	695	629	563	123
Convicted	488	595	532	665	583	610	529	470	131
Awaiting trial	124	133	139	149	103	126	86	90	16
State officials: Indicted	99	113	84	115	96	71	66	79	72
Convicted	97	133	92	77	79	54	69	66	51
Awaiting trial	17	39	24	42	28	18	14	20	28
Local officials: Indicted	248	309	232	242	257	269	276	248	247
Convicted	202	272	211	180	225	201	229	221	168
Awaiting trial	96	132	91	88	98	122	79	49	82

1. Includes individuals who are neither public officials nor employees, but who were involved with public officials or employees in violating the law, now shown separately. NOTE: Figures are latest available. Source: U.S. Department of Justice, Report to Congress on the Activities and Operations of the Public Integrity Section, annual, from Statistical Abstract of the United States 1996.

Characteristics of the Prison Population, 1997

Characteristic	Number	Percent	Characteristic	Number	Percent
Gender			1–3 years	11,122	14%
Male	92,116	93%	3–5 years	11,470	14%
Female	7,059	7%	5–10 years	19,875	25%
Inmates by race			10–15 years	17,676	22%
White	56,200	57%	15–20 years	7,781	10%
Black	39,836	40%	20+ years	8,934	11%
Asian	1,658	1.6%	Life	2,375	3%
Native American	1,481	1.5%	**Type of offense**		
Ethnicity			Drug offenses	52,956	60.2%
Hispanic	27,230	27%	Robbery	8,414	9.6%
Non-Hispanic	71,945	72%	Firearms, explosives, arson	7,950	9.0%
Citizenship			Extortion, fraud, bribery	4,962	5.6%
United States	72,541	74%	Property offenses	5,194	5.9%
Mexico	8,609	9%	Violent offenses	2,270	2.6%
Colombia	4,334	4%	Immigration	2,988	3.4%
Cuba	2,759	3%	Continuing criminal enterprise	667	0.8%
Other/Unknown	11,024	11%	White collar	644	0.7%
Average inmate age	37		Courts or corrections	560	0.6%
Sentence imposed			National security	74	0.1%
Under 1 year	1,625	2%	Miscellaneous	1,339	1.5%

Source: Federal Bureau of Prisons.

Law Enforcement Officers Killed or Assaulted: 1980 to 1994

(Covers officers killed feloniously and accidentally in line of duty; includes federal officers. 1988 excludes Florida and Kentucky.)

	1994	1993	1992	1991	1990	1989	1988	1987	1980
Northeast	18	12	16	16	13	23	17	24	31
Midwest	29	27	15	26	20	22	18	31	23
South	50	57	68	55	68	68	77	51	72
West	30	22	23	17	23	23	39	40	32
Puerto Rico	6	11	7	8	8	8	—	1	6
Outlying areas, foreign countries	5	—	—	1	—	1	4	—	1
Total killed	**138**	**129**	**129**	**123**	**132**	**145**	**155**	**147**	**165**
Assaults									
Population (1,000)[1]	260,431	210,658	217,997	191,397	199,065	189,641	186,418	190,025	182,288
Number of—									
Agencies	10,626	9,809	10,682	9,263	9,483	9,213	8,866	8,957	9,235
Police officers	480,343	454,105	460,430	405,069	412,314	380,232	369,743	378,977	345,554
Firearm	3,168	4,002	4,455	3,532	3,662	3,154	2,759	2,789	3,295
Knife or cutting instrument	1,513	1,574	2,095	1,493	1,641	1,379	1,367	1,561	1,653
Other dangerous weapon	7,210	7,551	8,604	7,014	7,390	5,778	5,573	5,685	5,415
Hands, fists, feet, etc.	53,021	53,848	66,098	50,813	59,101	51,861	49,053	53,807	47,484
Total assaulted	**64,912**	**66,975**	**81,252**	**62,852**	**71,794**	**62,172**	**58,752**	**63,842**	**57,847**

1. Represents the number of persons covered by agencies shown. NOTE: Data are latest available. Source: Statistical Abstract of the United States, 1996.

Prisoners Under Sentence of Death[1]

Characteristic	1980	1990	1994	Characteristic	1980	1990	1994
White	418	1,368	1,645	Marital status:			
Black and other	270	978	1,245	Never married	268	998	1,320
Under 20 years	11	8	19	Married	229	632	707
20 to 24 years	173	168	231	Divorced[2]	217	726	863
25 to 34 years	334	1,110	1,088	Time elapsed since sentencing:			
35 to 54 years	186	1,006	1,449	Less than 12 months	185	231	280
55 years and over	10	64	103	12 to 47 months	389	753	755
Years of schooling completed:				48 to 71 months	102	438	379
7 years or less	68	178	186	72 months and over	38	934	1,476
8 years	74	186	198	Legal status at arrest:			
9 to 11 years	204	775	930	Not under sentence	384	1,345	1,662
12 years	162	729	939	Parole or probation[3]	115	578	800
More than 12 years	43	209	255	Prison or escaped	45	128	103
Unknown	163	279	382	Unknown	170	305	325
				Total	**688**	**2,346**	**2,890**

1. For 1980 and 1990 revisions to the total number of prisoners were not carried to the characteristics except for race. 2. Includes widows, widowers, and unknown. 3. Includes persons on mandatory conditional release, work release, leave, AWOL, or bail. NOTE: As of Dec. 31. Excludes prisoners under sentence of death confined in local correctional systems pending appeal or who had not been committed to prison. *Source:* U.S. Bureau of Justice Statistics, *Capital Punishment,* annual, from *Statistical Abstract of the United States, 1996.*

Methods of Execution[1]

State	Minimum age	Method	State	Minimum age	Method
Alabama	16	Electrocution	New Jersey	18	Lethal injection
Alaska	—	No death penalty	New Mexico	18	Lethal injection
Arizona [1]	none	Lethal injection or gas	New York	19	Lethal injection
Arkansas[2]	14	Lethal injection or electrocution	North Carolina	17	Lethal gas or injection
			North Dakota	—	No death penalty
California[3]	18	Lethal gas or injection	Ohio	18	Electrocution or lethal injection
Colorado	18	Lethal injection			
Connecticut	18	Lethal injection	Oklahoma[8]	16	Lethal injection, electrocution, or firing squad
Delaware[4]	16	Lethal injection or hanging			
D.C.	—	No death penalty	Oregon	18	Lethal injection
Florida	16	Electrocution	Pennsylvania	none	Lethal injection
Georgia	17	Electrocution	Rhode Island	—	No death penalty
Hawaii	—	No death penalty	South Carolina	none	Electrocution or lethal injection
Idaho	none	Lethal injection or firing squad			
			South Dakota	none	Lethal injection
Illinois	18	Lethal injection	Tennessee	18	Electrocution
Indiana	16	Lethal injection	Texas	17	Lethal injection
Iowa	—	No death penalty	Utah	none	Firing squad or lethal injection
Kansas	18	Lethal injection			
Kentucky	16	Electrocution	Vermont	—	No death penalty
Louisiana	none	Lethal injection	Virginia	14	Electrocution or lethal injection
Maine	—	No death penalty			
Maryland[5]	18	Lethal injection or gas	Washington	18	Hanging or lethal injection
Massachusetts	—	No death penalty	West Virginia	—	No death penalty
Michigan	—	No death penalty	Wisconsin	—	No death penalty
Minnesota	—	No death penalty	Wyoming[9]	16	Lethal injection or gas
Mississippi[6]	16	Lethal injection or gas	U.S. (Fed. Govt.)[10]	18	Lethal injection
Missouri	16	Lethal injection or gas	American Samoa	—	No death penalty
Montana	none	Hanging or lethal injection	Guam	—	No death penalty
Nebraska	18	Electrocution	Puerto Rico	—	No death penalty
Nevada	16	Lethal injection	Virgin Islands	—	No death penalty
New Hampshire[7]	17	Lethal injection or hanging			

1. Arizona authorizes lethal injection for persons sentenced after 11/15/92; those sentenced before that date may select lethal injection or lethal gas. 2. Arkansas authorizes lethal injection for persons committing a capital offense after 7/4/83; those who committed the offense before that date may select lethal injection or electrocution. 3. Use of lethal gas is currently prohibited in California pending a legal challenge in Federal court. 4. Delaware authorizes lethal injection for those whose capital offense occurred after 6/13/86; those who committed the offense before that date may select lethal injection or hanging. 5. Maryland authorizes lethal injection for all inmates, as of 3/25/94. One inmate, convicted prior to that date, has selected lethal gas for method of execution. 6. Mississippi authorizes lethal injection for those convicted after 7/1/84 and lethal gas for those convicted earlier. 7. New Hampshire authorizes hanging only if lethal injection cannot be given. 8. Oklahoma authorizes electrocution if lethal injection is ever held to be unconstitutional and firing squad if both lethal injection and electrocution are held unconstitutional. 9. Wyoming authorizes lethal gas if lethal injection is ever held to be unconstitutional. 10. The method of execution of Federal prisoners is lethal injection, pursuant to 28 CFR, Part 26. For offenses under the Violent Crime Control and Law Enforcement Act of 1994, the method is that of the state in which the conviction took place, pursuant to 18 USC 3596. *Source: Capital Punishment, 1995.*

Motor Vehicle Laws, 1996

State	Age for license		Age for driver's license[1]			Driver's license duration	Fee	Annual safety inspection required
	Motor-cycle	Moped	Regular	Learner's	Restrictive			
Alabama	14	14	16	15[5]	14[11]	4 yrs.	$20.00	no[15]
Alaska	16	14	16	14	14[6, 11]	5	15.00	no[15]
Arizona	16	16	18	15 7 mo.[5, 6]	16[6]	Until 60	10/25.00	no[16, 18]
Arkansas	16	10[10]	16	14-16[5]	14[6 9]	4	14.00	yes
California	18[19]	16[19]	18	15[4, 7, 8]	16[4]	4	12.00	no[18]
Colorado	16	16	21	15 6 mo.[6, 9]	15 1/4[6, 8, 9]	5	15.00	no[18]
Connecticut	16	16	16[4]	16[4]		4	28.50/43.50	no
Delaware	18[19]	16	18	15 10 mo.[4]	16[4, 6]	5	12.50	yes
D. C.	16	16	18	(5, 7)	16[6]	4	20.00	yes[21]
Florida	15	15	16	15[5]	15[6]	4 or 6	20.00	no[18]
Georgia	16	15	16	15	16[6]	4	15.00	no[18]
Hawaii	15	15	18	15[5, 7]	15[6]	4[12]	6/12.00	yes
Idaho	16[19]	16[19]	17	15[4, 5, 7]	15[3, 4]	4	20.50	no
Illinois	18	16[19]	18	(5)	16[4, 6]	4 or 5	10.00	no[18]
Indiana	16	15	18	16[7, 8]	16 1 mo.[4, 6]	4[13]	6.00	no[18]
Iowa	16[19]	14	14	14	14[4, 6]	4[2]	8/16.00	no[15]
Kansas	14	14	16	(5)	14	4	8/14.00	no[15]
Kentucky	16	16	18	(5)	16[6]	4	10.00	no
Louisiana	15	15	14[27]	14[6]	17[3]	4	18.00	yes[21]
Maine	16[4]	15[4]	17	15[4, 7]	16[4]	6	30.00	yes
Maryland	18[19]	16	18[28]	15 9 mo.[5, 9]	16[4, 6]	5	30.00	no[18, 20]
Massachusetts	17	16	17	(5)	16 1/2[3 4, 6]	5	33.75	yes[21]
Michigan	18[19]	15	18	15[4, 6, 7]	16[4, 6]	2 or 4	6/12.00	no[31]
Minnesota	18[22]	15	18	(5)	16[4]	4	18.50/37.50	no[15]
Mississippi	15	15	16	(5)		4[29]	20.00	yes
Missouri	15.5[4]	16	16	15 1/2[23]	15 1/2[23]	3	7.50	yes[18]
Montana	15[4]	15[4]	18	(5)	15[4, 6]	8[30]	16.00/32.00	no
Nebraska	16	16	16	15[7]	14	4	15.00	no
Nevada	16	15.5	16	15 1/2[5, 6, 9]	14[3, 6]	4	15.50/20.50	no[18]
New Hampshire	18[19]	16[4]	18		16[4]	4	32.00	yes[21]
New Jersey	17	15	17		16	4	16/17.50	yes
New Mexico	16	13	16	15[4]	14[9]	4	13.00	no
New York	17	15	17[4]	16	16[6]	4	22.25	yes
North Carolina	18	16	18	15[4, 6, 9]	16	5	10.00	yes
North Dakota	16	14	16	(5)	14[4, 6]	4	10.00	no[15]
Ohio	18	14	18	16[5, 6]	14[11]	4	10.75	no[18]
Oklahoma	16		16	(8)	15 1/2[4]	4	18.00	yes
Oregon	16[19]	16	16	15[6, 9]	14	4	26.25	no[15]
Pennsylvania	16	16	16	16[6, 7]	16[6]	4	27.00	yes
Rhode Island	16	16	16	(5)	16[4]	5	30.00	yes
South Carolina	16	14	16	15[9]	15	5	12.50	yes
South Dakota	16	14	16	14[7]	14[3]	5	8.00	no
Tennessee	16	14	16	15[7]	14	5	19.50	no
Texas	18[19]	15	16[4]	15	15[4, 7]	4	16.00	yes
Utah	16	16	16[4, 6]	16	15 9 mo.[8, 9]	5	15/20.00	yes
Vermont	18	16	18	15[5, 9]	16[7]	2 or 4	12/20.00	yes
Virginia	18[19]	16	18	15[5, 6, 7]	16[4, 6]	4	12.00	yes
Washington	18[19]	16	18	15[8]	16[4]	4	14.00	no[14]
West Virginia	18[19]	16	18	15[9]	16	4	10.50	yes
Wisconsin	18[19]	16	18	15 1/2[5]	16[4, 6]	4	15.00	no[31]
Wyoming	18	15[22]	16	15[6, 7]	15[6, 7]	4	20.00	yes

1. Full driving privileges at age given in "Regular" column. A license restricted or qualified in some manner may be obtained at age given in "Restricted" column. 2. 2 years if under 18 or over 70. 3. Hours of operation restricted. 4. Must have completed approved driver education course. 5. Learner's permit required. 6. Guardian's or parental consent required. 7. Driver with learner's permit must be accompanied by locally licensed operator 18 years or older. 8. Must be enrolled in driver education course. 9. Driver with learner's permit must be accompanied by locally licensed operator 21 years or older. 10. Up to 50 cc. 11. Restricted to mopeds. 12. 2 years if 15-24 or over 65. 13. 3 years if over 75. 14. Individual inspection upon reasonable grounds. 15. State troopers are authorized to inspect at their discretion. 16. Arizona emission inspection fee $5.40. 17. Annual emissions test in some counties. 18. Annual emissions test. 19. 18; 16 if approved driver training course completed. 20. All used vehicles upon resale or transfer. 21. Required on out-of-state or salvaged vehicles. Emissions tested in some counties. 22. May obtain instruction permit with motorcycle endorsement. 23. Driver with learner's permit must be accompanied by licensed parent of guardian. 24. Emission test every two years in Bernalillo County. 25. Biennial emission inspection in the Portland metro area and Rogue Valley. 26. Emission test required in some areas. 27. All first-time new licensees must complete state-approved pre-licensing course. 28. All new drivers must complete 3-hour alcohol-awareness program. 29. 1 year if under 18. 30. 4 years if under 21 or over 75. 31. Some counties have an additional 1 to 2.75 county tax. NOTES: A driver's license is required in every state. All states have an *implied consent* Chemical Test Law for alcohol. *Source:* Reprinted with permission of the American Automobile Association, Heathrow, Fla.

Education

Trying to Turn Around Their Schools, Americans Focus on Role of Parents

Americans look at the failure of their schools and see in them the failure of the family. They think about what will set the schools right, and they don't hesitate to give an answer: parents.

Parents, straightening out their unruly children. Parents, holding the family together. Parents, setting a good example.

Americans want better teachers, smaller classes, and smarter school computers, and they say academic standards could use toughening. But what has led to the failure of public schools, and what will turn them around, they say in a *Wall Street Journal*/NBC News poll, is getting parents involved with schools, and holding them responsible for their children.

Their "intuitions are correct," says Fred Morrison, a psychologist at Loyola University in Chicago. Kids who start school not knowing the things parents are supposed to teach—following instructions, the alphabet, colors and numbers—never catch up. Their future is "set in stone," he says. Their school performance "stays the same because whatever their parents are doing stays the same."

The irony is that parents insist they are involved with their children's schools—that it's everyone else who isn't. Most of those surveyed said they read aloud to their children, help them with homework, attend parent-teacher conferences.

But ask the kids, and there's a different perception. When the National Commission on Children talked a few years ago to youngsters ages 10 to 13, 72 percent said they wished they could talk to their parents more about homework. And when the Department of Education asked fourth-graders about their television habits, 43 percent said they watched four or more hours a day. That doesn't leave a lot of time for reading with dad.

"Almost no one is able to concede failure" on the main responsibilities of parenthood, says pollster Thomas Riehle of Peter Hart Research. "They know it's important, and it's just unthinkable" to admit they may have been too busy to help with algebra.

Researchers say one of the surest predictors of a child's achievement is how involved parents are. Three factors that parents can control—student absenteeism, books in the home, and TV time—explain 90 percent of the difference in eight-grade math scores across the country, research published by the Department of Education shows.

Americans surveyed in the *Wall Street Journal* poll were firm: parents, not schools, should be responsible for discipline, for teaching manners and sportsmanship, for after-school care, for making sure their children do their homework.

Yet today, schools are asked to assume more and more parental duties: drug and AIDS education, values lessons, before- and after-school services, nutrition and now, conflict resolution.

Eleven Detroit schools that took part in a pilot conflict-resolution program found it saved them $100,000 in teacher salaries, administrative time, and suspension rooms. Truancy and violence were reduced. But it also supplanted one academic class period a week.

Parents are also clear about what the schools should—and shouldn't—do. They aren't much interested in experimental teaching methods. Or a longer school day—even though most mothers of school-age children hold outside jobs. Nor do they think more homework is the answer.

Marshall Smith, the deputy secretary of education, doubts that Americans really distrust school innovation. They know the workplace is changing, and that education has to change too, he says, adding: "I think they're open to changes, as long as those changes are focused on the basics."

What Americans told pollsters is that to improve schools, start with the teachers. The National Commission on Teaching and America's Future calls teacher training and performance "a national shame." One quarter of high-school teachers aren't trained in the subjects they're teaching. A third of all high-school math teachers don't have even a minor in mathematics. Only 18 states require their new teachers to take a technology course.

With public-school enrollments rising and one-fifth of all teachers approaching retirement age, two million new teachers must be hired over the next decade, the Department of Education estimates. And yet, the indifference of students and administrators alike often leads to demoralization: almost a third of each new crop of teachers leave within three years.

Poll respondents are strongly behind annual competency tests for teachers, and they want them to teach basic skills using tried-and-true teaching methods. Far fewer support paying rewards to the best teachers, indicating indifference to the President's plan to single out 100,000 of the best and certify them as master teachers.

Where human teachers leave off, Americans want computers to take over, a sentiment they share with the President. The Clinton administration wants to spend $2 billion over the next five years connecting public schools to the Internet.

There's no evidence that the Internet will improve schools. "Right now, we're taking it on faith," says Penelope Engel of Educational Testing Service. But 71 percent of those surveyed share that faith, viewing better technology as a plus.

Nearly as many, 70 percent, advocate smaller classes. In the biggest test of the notion that kids learn better in small classes, California is offering its schools an extra $650 per student—$971 million—to cut class size to 20 in the lowest grades. The idea has proved so popular that the governor recently added $95 million for portable schoolrooms to house the new classes.

But while computers and smaller classes are big-ticket items in a school-district budget—and while 70 percent of Americans say they'd be willing to pay higher taxes for education—they also say money isn't the problem, or the solution. It's the family, they say. And they say it resoundingly. □

Family Reading

	Percentage of 3- to 5-year-olds[1] who were read to daily by a family member				Percentage of 3- to 5-year-olds[1] who were read to daily by a family member		
	1993	1995	1996		1993	1995	1996
Overall	53%	58%	57%	One or no parent	46	49	46
Gender				**Mother's education[3]**			
Male	51	57	56	Less than high school	37	40	37
Female	54	59	57	High school/GED	48	48	49
Race and Hispanic origin[2]				Vocational/technical or some college	57	64	62
White, non-Hispanic	59	65	64				
Black, non-Hispanic	39	43	44	College graduate	71	76	77
Hispanic	37	38	39	**Mother's employment status[3]**			
Poverty status							
Above poverty threshold	56	62	61	35 hours or more per week	52	55	54
At or below poverty threshold	44	48	46	Less than 35 hours per week	56	63	59
Family type							
Two parents	55	61	61	Not in labor force	55	60	59

1. Estimates based on children who have yet to enter kindergarten. 2. Persons of Hispanic origin may be of any race. 3. Children without mothers in the home are not included. *Source:* U.S. Department of Education, National Center for Education Statistics.

Trends in Enrollments for Foreign Language Studies

Change in Enrollments from 1990 to 1995

Russian	−44.6%
German	−27.8%
French	−24.6%
Italian	−11.9%
Latin	−8.1%
Japanese	−2.2%
Ancient Greek	−0.8%
Hebrew	1.0%
Portuguese	5.2%
Spanish	13.5%
Arabic	27.9%
Chinese	35.8%

Foreign Language Study Trends

Data from a recent Modern Language Association study indicate that students on America's college campuses are shifting their attention away from Russia and toward China. Enrollment in Russian language classes dropped nearly 45 percent between 1990 and 1995, while that in Chinese classes increased by nearly 36 percent. The percentage changes don't tell the whole story, however, since Russian and Chinese comprise but a small number of the enrollees. The study of modern languages continues to be dominated by Spanish, French, and German, in that order. Though some 67,000 fewer students enrolled in French classes in 1995 than in 1990, this number was still more than double that of German, the third most popular language. Spanish continues to lead in languages studied, however, and an increase of more than 72,000 students pushed Spanish enrollments to nearly three times those of French in 1995.

Foreign Language Enrollment by Language, 1990–1995

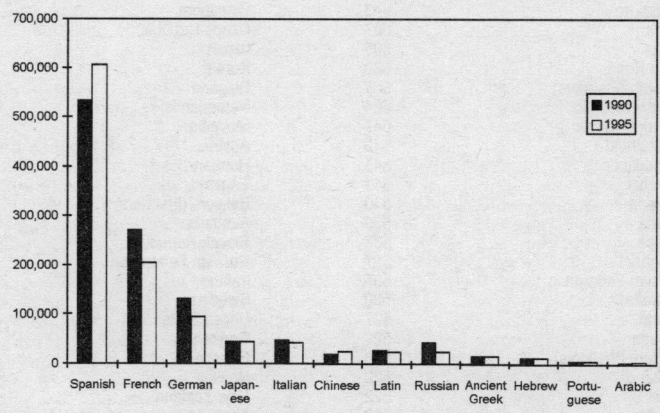

Source: Foreign Language Enrollments in United States Institutions of Higher Education, Fall 1995, Modern Language Association

Computer Use in Schools, 1984–85 and 1993–94

Level	1984–85				1993–94			
	Total schools	Percent with PCs	Number of PCs[1]	Students per PC	Total schools	Percent with PCs	Number of PCs[1]	Students per PC
Public Schools	81,100	85.1	569,825	63.5	83,435	98.6	4,079,260	10.8
Elementary	50,967	82.2	215,393	79.3	50,033	98.7	1,863,499	12.1
Middle/Jr. High	9,791	93.1	100,331	61.2	12,181	99.6	717,298	11.1
Senior High	15,152	94.6	228,726	51.5	14,322	99.5	1,237,086	9.0
K–12/other	5,190	70.3	25,375	45.8	6,899	86.8	261,377	9.6
Catholic Schools	9,463	63.4	28,427	73.5	8,345	97.9	197,944	13.0
Elementary	7,831	56.4	15,863	85.1	6,940	97.9	137,275	14.0
Middle/Jr. High	1,481	87.0	12,147	57.8	1,255	97.9	56,443	10.7
K–12/other	151	46.4	417	n.a.	150	96.2	4,226	10.4
Other Private Schools	14,946	46.4	33,731	40.5	13,983	85.7	193,362	11.9
Elementary	8,226	45.1	13,400	42.7	7,118	85.9	77,363	13.2
Middle/Jr. High	950	82.7	6,266	40.1	1,039	86.3	26,339	8.1
K–12/other	5,770	42.4	14,065	n.a.	5,826	85.1	89,666	11.8
Total	105,509	77.7	631,983	62.7	105,763	97.5	4,470,572	11.0

n.a. = not available 1. Includes estimates for schools not reporting number of PCs. *Source:* Statistical Abstract of the United States, 1996

Funding for Public Elementary and Secondary Education, 1986–87 to 1994–95

(In thousands except percent)

School year	Total	Federal	State	Local[1]	% Federal	% State	% Local[1]
1986–87	158,523,693	10,146,013	78,830,437	69,547,243	6.4	49.7	43.9
1987–88	169,561,974	10,716,687	84,004,415	74,840,873	6.3	49.5	44.1
1988–89	191,210,310	11,872,419	91,158,363	88,179,529	6.2	47.4	46.1
1989–90	207,752,932	12,700,784	98,238,633	96,813,516	6.1	47.3	46.6
1990–91	223,340,537	13,776,066	105,324,533	104,239,939	6.2	47.2	46.7
1991–92	234,588,732	15,493,330	108,783,449	110,311,953	6.6	46.4	47.0
1992–93	248,496,276	17,267,351	113,396,992	117,831,933	6.9	45.6	47.4
1993–94[2]	247,626,000	17,261,000	113,403,000	116,961,000	7.0	45.8	47.2
1994–95	260,142,000	18,336,000	117,462,000	124,344,000	7.0	45.2	47.8

1. Includes a relatively small amount from nongovernmental sources (gifts, tuition, and transportation fees from patrons). 2. Revised from previously published figures. *Source:* U.S. Department of Education, Digest of Education Statistics 1996.

Mathematics and Science Achievement Around the World

	Eighth Grade* Achievement in Mathematics		Eighth Grade* Achievement in Science	
Rank	Country	Average Achievement	Country	Average Achievement
1	Singapore	643	Singapore	607
2	Korea	607	Czech Republic	574
3	Japan	605	Japan	571
4	Hong Kong	588	Korea	565
5	Belgium (Flanders)	565	Bulgaria	565
6	Czech Republic	564	Netherlands	560
7	Slovak Republic	547	Slovenia	560
8	Switzerland	545	Austria	558
9	Netherlands	541	Hungary	554
10	Slovenia	541	England	552
11	Bulgaria	540	Belgium (Flanders)	550
12	Austria	539	Australia	545
13	France	538	Slovak Republic	544
14	Hungary	537	Russian Federation	538
15	Russian Federation	535	Ireland	538
16	Australia	530	Sweden	535
17	Ireland	527	United States	534
18	Canada	527	Germany	531
19	Belgium (Wallonia)	526	Canada	531
20	Thailand	522	Norway	527
21	Israel	522	New Zealand	525
22	Sweden	519	Thailand	525
23	Germany	509	Israel	524
24	New Zealand	508	Hong Kong	522

	Eighth Grade* Achievement in Mathematics			Eighth Grade* Achievement in Science	
Rank	Country	Average Achievement		Country	Average Achievement
25	England	506		Switzerland	522
26	Norway	503		Scotland	517
27	Denmark	502		Spain	517
28	United States	500		France	498
29	Scotland	498		Greece	497
30	Latvia (LSS)	493		Iceland	494
31	Spain	487		Romania	486
32	Iceland	487		Latvia (LSS)	485
33	Greece	484		Portugal	480
34	Romania	482		Denmark	478
35	Lithuania	477		Lithuania	476
36	Cyprus	474		Belgium (Wallonia)	471
37	Portugal	454		Iran, Islamic Rep.	470
38	Iran, Islamic Rep.	428		Cyprus	463
39	Kuwait	392		Kuwait	430
40	Colombia	385		Colombia	411
41	South Africa	354		South Africa	326

* Eighth grade in most countries. Latvia is annotated LSS for Latvian Speaking Schools only. *Source:* IEA Third International Mathematics and Science Study (TIMSS), Boston College, 1994–95.

High School and College Graduates

School Year	High School			College[1]		
	Men	Women	Total	Men	Women	Total
1900	38,075	56,808	94,883	22,173	5,237	27,410
1910	63,676	92,753	156,429	28,762	8,437	37,199
1920	123,684	187,582	311,266	31,980	16,642	48,622
1929–30	300,376	366,528	666,904	73,615	48,869	122,484
1939–40	578,718	642,757	1,221,475	109,546	76,954	186,500
1949–50	570,700	629,000	1,199,700	328,841	103,217	432,058
1959–60	898,000	966,000	1,864,000	254,063	138,377	392,440
1969–70	1,433,000	1,463,000	2,896,000	484,174	343,060	827,234
1974–75	1,541,000	1,599,000	3,140,000	533,797	425,052	978,849
1978–79	1,531,800	1,602,400	3,134,200	529,996	460,242	990,238
1979–80	1,500,000	1,558,000	3,058,000	526,327	473,221	999,548
1980–81	1,483,000	1,537,000	3,020,000	470,000	465,000	935,000
1981–82	1,474,000	1,527,000	3,001,000	473,000	480,000	953,000
1982–83	1,437,000	1,451,000	2,888,000	479,140	490,370	969,510
1983–84	n.a.	n.a.	2,767,000	482,319	491,990	974,309
1984–85	n.a.	n.a.	2,677,000	482,528	496,949	979,477
1985–86	n.a.	n.a.	2,643,000	485,923	501,900	987,823
1986–87	n.a.	n.a.	2,694,000	480,854	510,485	991,339
1987–88	n.a.	n.a.	2,773,000	477,203	517,626	994,829
1988–89	n.a.	n.a.	2,727,000	483,346	535,409	1,018,755
1989–90	n.a.	n.a.	2,588,000	491,696	559,648	1,051,344
1990–91	n.a.	n.a.	2,503,000	504,045	590,493	1,094,538
1991–92	n.a.	n.a.	2,482,000	520,811	615,742	1,136,553
1992–93	n.a.	n.a.	2,490,000	532,881	632,297	1,165,178
1993–94	n.a.	n.a.	2,479,000	532,422[2]	636,853[2]	1,169,275[2]
1994–95	n.a.	n.a.	2,552,000[2,3]	535,000[4]	657,000[4]	1,192,000[4]
1995–96	n.a.	n.a.	2,572,000[2,3]	533,000[4]	663,000[4]	1,195,000[4]

1. Bachelors's degrees. Includes first-professional degrees for years 1900–1960. 2. Revised from previously published data. 3. Public high school graduates based on state estimates. 4. Projected. n.a. = not available. NOTE: Includes graduates from public and private schools. Beginning in 1959–60, figures include Alaska and Hawaii. Because of rounding, details may not add to totals. Most recent data available. *Source:* Department of Education, National Center for Education Statistics.

School Enrollment by Grade, Control, and Race

(in thousands)

Grade level and type of control	White Oct. 1995[3]	White Oct. 1990[3]	White Oct. 1980[4]	Black Oct. 1995[3]	Black Oct. 1990[3]	Black Oct. 1980[4]	All races[1] Oct. 1995[3]	All races[1] Oct. 1990[3]	All races[1] Oct. 1980[4]
Nursery school: Public	1,435	896	432	478	283	180	2,012	1,212	633
Private	2,117	1,961	1,205	185	148	115	2,387	2,188	1,354
Kindergarten: Public	2,440	2,609	2,172	563	574	440	3,174	3,322	2,690
Private	592	472	423	89	62	50	704	567	486
Grades 1–8: Public	22,009	20,997	19,743	4,845	4,431	4,058	28,383	26,615	24,398
Private	2,953	2,359	2,768	339	199	202	3,430	2,676	3,051
Grades 9–12: Public	10,575	9,429	12,056[2]	2,370	1,937	2,200[2]	13,751	11,911	14,556[2]
Private	1,043	810	—	111	65	—	1,213	906	—
College: Public	9,311	9,049	8,875[2]	1,352	1,120	1,007[2]	11,371	10,754	10,180[2]
Private	2,712	2,439	—	420	274	—	3,342	2,869	—
Total: Public	45,770	42,954	—	9,608	8,344	—	58,691	53,823	—
Private	9,416	8,041	—	1,144	748	—	11,077	9,204	—
Grand Total	**55,186**	**50,995**	**47,673**	**10,752**	**9,092**	**8,251**	**69,768**	**63,027**	**57,348**

1. Includes persons of Hispanic origin. 2. Total public and private. Breakdown not available. 3. Estimates controlled to 1990 census base. 4. Estimates controlled to 1970 census base. Source: Department of Commerce, Bureau of the Census.

Major U.S. College and University Libraries, 1996

Top 50 based on number of volumes in library

Academic Institution	Volumes	Microforms	Academic Institution	Volumes	Microforms
Harvard	13,369,855	7,953,568	Iowa	3,751,596	5,819,830
Yale	9,758,341	5,240,110	U. of Pittsburgh	3,730,778	3,651,950
U. of Illinois, Urbana	8,840,326	4,577,775	Pennsylvania State	3,724,916	3,355,549
U. of California, Berkeley	8,462,123	5,675,702	Rutgers	3,567,690	5,149,326
U. of Texas	7,329,663	5,295,504	New York	3,508,001	4,001,184
U. of Michigan	6,874,648	5,566,940	U. of Kansas	3,450,463	2,983,680
Columbia	6,792,274	5,124,800	U. of Georgia	3,392,238	5,507,430
U. of California, Los Angeles	6,772,851	5,815,667	U. of Southern California	3,344,620	5,588,965
Stanford	6,746,550	4,843,443	U. of Florida	3,258,300	6,026,299
U. of Chicago	5,982,101	2,308,586	Arizona State	3,175,896	6,484,688
Cornell	5,952,217	6,980,459	Johns Hopkins	3,172,679	3,585,880
Indiana	5,790,384	3,743,511	Washington U.-St. Louis	3,164,136	2,809,952
U. of Wisconsin	5,737,834	4,392,043	Suny-Buffalo	2,991,288	4,740,453
U. of Washington	5,601,263	6,432,950	Wayne State	2,960,222	3,417,154
Princeton	5,405,087	3,892,428	South Carolina	2,933,864	4,281,147
U. of Minnesota	5,376,090	5,242,524	Rochester	2,922,335	4,102,438
Alberta	5,085,060	3,637,355	U. of Hawaii	2,888,498	5,657,508
Ohio State	4,977,610	4,196,464	Louisiana State	2,878,866	4,995,722
North Carolina	4,674,502	4,044,679	U. of California, Davis	2,871,796	3,689,558
Duke	4,534,208	3,314,158	Brown	2,810,163	1,561,108
U. of Pennsylvania	4,437,523	2,999,180	Missouri	2,768,911	6,365,210
U. of Arizona	4,343,130	5,309,084	U. of Massachusetts	2,762,244	2,193,812
U. of Virginia	4,276,435	4,569,358	Syracuse	2,692,147	3,621,095
Michigan State	4,047,477	5,101,191	U. of Colorado	2,672,243	5,569,400
Northwestern	3,840,439	3,284,677	U. of Kentucky	2,633,632	5,593,370

1. Includes reels of microfilm and number of microcards, microprint sheets, and microfiches. Source: Association of Research Libraries.

College and University Endowments, 1995–96

(top 75 in millions of dollars)

Institution	Endowment (market value)	Voluntary support	Expenditures	Institution	Endowment (market value)	Voluntary support	Expenditures
Harvard Univ.	9,058.9	309.4	1,521.0	Northwestern Univ.	2,062.6	107.8	750.5
Yale Univ.	4,860.0	172.2	896.4	Cornell Univ.	1,853.1	219.7	n.a.
Princeton Univ.	4,566.8	117.4	354.5	William Marsh Rice Univ.	1,850.3	50.8	n.a.
Stanford Univ.	3,932.0	312.9	958.0	Univ. of Chicago	1,676.0	127.0	748.8
Columbia Univ.	2,558.1	163.9	1,209.3	Univ. of Michigan	1,665.9	121.6	1,383.5
Massachusetts Inst. of Tech.	2,493.6	132.5	839.6	Mayo Foundation	1,227.6	194.0	245.2
				Univ. of Notre Dame	1,227.3	75.6	267.7
Washington Univ.	2,344.6	84.4	n.a.	Vanderbilt Univ.	1,112.0	62.2	522.3
Texas A&M Univ.	2,208.0	110.1	814.3	Univ. of Calif.–Berkeley	1,103.5	141.8	889.7
Univ. of Pennsylvania	2,109.0	153.1	966.0	Dartmouth Col.	1,082.9	90.9	279.5

Institution	Endowment (market value)	Voluntary support	Expenditures	Institution	Endowment (market value)	Voluntary support	Expenditures
Univ. of Southern California	1,022.3	128.6	911.0	Washington and Lee Univ.	532.8	30.3	55.0
Duke Univ.	1,008.9	181.3	677.6	Indiana Univ.	532.3	131.1	1,068.5
Case Western Reserve Univ.	995.7	75.1	317.4	Macalester Col.	525.8	5.0	49.4
Johns Hopkins Univ.	982.6	125.9	1500.2	Carnegie-Mellon Univ.	524.3	48.2	358.0
Univ. of Minnesota	954.9	140.5	1,265.8	Univ. of Delaware	521.2	23.6	327.1
Univ. of Texas–Austin	831.7	81.1	811.2	Univ. of Pittsburgh	518.4	41.6	648.1
California Inst. of Tech.	827.7	62.2	324.5	Pomona Col.	495.4	19.4	53.7
Univ. of Virginia	823.3	104.4	545.6	Univ. of Tulsa	477.0	15.7	78.0
Univ. of Rochester	811.5	41.8	324.0	Univ. of Kansas	475.4	52.3	288.2
New York Univ.	809.1	91.0	1,115.9	Wake Forest Univ.	474.9	39.7	387.3
Brown Univ.	803.8	72.2	262.2	George Washington Univ.	469.7	28.9	392.9
Purdue Univ.	713.3	61.0	712.0	Amherst Col.	455.3	26.8	61.4
Rockefeller Univ.	709.1	31.9	105.6	St. Louis Univ.	449.0	18.5	205.5
Univ. of Calif.–Los Angeles	708.0	139.8	1,237.4	Georgetown Univ.	446.5	54.0	467.6
Ohio State Univ.	649.6	124.1	985.0	Berea Col.	445.8	18.1	34.9
Swarthmore Col.	624.0	15.7	59.6	Boston Univ.	443.7	44.0	797.5
Univ. of Cincinnati	621.3	35.4	515.5	Univ. of Illinois	440.4	118.2	1,673.5
Princeton Theol. Sem.	608.8	2.9	29.1	Lehigh Univ.	438.1	36.6	166.1
Wellesley Col.	605.5	27.3	101.5	Pennsylvania State Univ.	426.6	83.2	1,121.7
Texas Christian Univ.	602.7	20.0	97.6	Middlebury Col.	423.4	11.2	81.2
Boston Col.	600.3	24.2	265.6	Georgia Inst. of Tech.	421.8	45.3	405.2
Univ. of N.C.–Chapel Hill	596.8	94.6	742.2	Univ. of Calif.–San Francisco	419.2	126.3	725.0
Smith Col.	583.2	26.5	102.8	Trinity Univ.	412.5	8.7	49.0
Grinnell Col.	571.5	11.1	44.3	Univ. of Iowa	410.0	85.2	624.3
Southern Methodist Univ.	562.8	20.6	165.2	Vassar Col.	403.3	25.9	76.0
Williams Col.	561.1	28.1	70.9	Univ. of Tennessee	401.0	55.8	769.7
Univ. of Richmond	550.2	58.7	75.3	Tulane Univ. of Louisiana	397.6	31.5	346.6
Univ. of Wisconsin–Madison	539.0	186.7	1,052.7	Univ. of Washington	395.2	154.6	1,014.0

Source: Council for Aid to Education.

Average Monthly Earnings by Field of Degree, Spring 1993

Field of Degree	Mean earnings	Field of Degree	Mean earnings
Medicine/dentistry	$5,049	Police science/law enforcement	2,178
Law	4,353	Biology	2,118
Economics	3,330	Social science	1,970
Engineering	3,117	Religion/theology	1,963
Agriculture/forestry	2,973	Nursing/pharmacy/technical health	1,889
Mathematics/statistics	2,583	Education	1,884
Business/management	2,426	Liberal arts/humanities	1,733
Physical/earth sciences	2,357	Vocational/technical studies	1,713
English/journalism	2,331	Home economics	1,165
Psychology	2,236	**Overall**	**$2,339**

Source: Census Bureau, Current Population Reports, December 1995.

Mean Earnings by Educational Attainment, Sex, and Race, March 1996

Educational attainment	Total, both sexes	Total, male	Total, female	White, both sexes	Black, both sexes	Hispanic, both sexes
Overall	$26,792	$33,251	$19,414	$27,556	$20,537	$18,262
Doctorate	64,550	71,016	47,733	64,608	(B)	(B)
Professional	85,322	101,730	47,959	85,229	(B)	(B)
Master's	47,609	58,302	34,911	48,029	38,294	36,633
Bachelor's	36,980	46,111	26,841	37,711	29,666	30,602
Associate	27,780	33,881	22,429	28,137	26,818	23,406
Some college, no degree	22,392	28,458	16,152	22,898	20,275	18,903
High school graduate	21,431	26,333	15,970	22,154	17,072	18,333
Not a high school graduate	14,013	16,745	9,790	14,234	12,956	13,068

B = Basis is fewer than 200,000 people. *Source:* Census Bureau, Current Population Survey, March 1996 Update.

Accredited U.S. Senior Colleges and Universities

Source: The information below comes to us from *The Princeton Review's Complete Book of Accredited Colleges, 1998 Edition.*

Schools are listed alphabetically within each state and are accredited four-year institutions offering at least a Bachelor's degree. Tuition, room, and board listed are average annual figures (including fees) subject to fluctuation, usually covering two semesters, two out of three trimesters, or three out of four quarters, depending on the school calendar. For further information, write to the Registrar of the school concerned.

| Institution Name; City, State Zip (Control) | Students | Percent | | Tuition | | Room and board |
		Women	Accepted	In-State	Out-of-State	
ALABAMA						
Alabama A&M University; Normal, Ala. 35762 (Pub)	3,852	52	66	$ 1,932	$ 3,864	$2,678
Alabama State University; Montgomery, Ala. 36101 (Pub)	4,456	56	68	$ 1,500	$ 3,000	$2,700
Athens State College; Athens, Ala. 35611 (Pub)	1,271	62	100	$ 1,884	$ 3,510	$ 825
Auburn University; Auburn University, Ala. 36849 (Pub)	5,645	61	92	$ 2,130	$ 6,390	$4,727
Auburn University-Montgomery; Montgomery, Ala. 36124-4023 (Pub)	18,396	48	89	$ 2,355	$ 7,065	$1,695
Birmingham-Southern College; Birmingham, Ala. 35254 (P)	1,409	57	95	$13,100	$13,100	$5,370
Faulkner University; Montgomery, Ala. 36109 (P)	1,945	56	64	$ 6,560	$ 6,560	$3,700
Huntingdon College; Montgomery, Ala. 36106 (P)	647	60	72	$ 9,710	$ 9,710	$4,810
Jacksonville State University; Jacksonville, Ala. 36265 (Pub)	6,548	55	93	$ 1,940	$ 2,910	$2,870
Judson College (Ala.); Marion, Ala. 36756 (P)	233	100	82	$ 6,130	$ 6,130	$3,700
Miles College; Birmingham, Ala. 35208 (P)	1,234	52	100	$ 4,000	$ 4,000	$2,750
Oakwood College; Huntsville, Ala. 35896 (P)	1,666	59	82	$ 6,639	$ 6,639	$3,999
Samford University; Birmingham, Ala. 35229 (P)	2,571	60	88	$ 9,432	$ 9,432	$4,196
Spring Hill College; Mobile, Ala. 36608 (P)	1,161	56	90	$12,420	$12,420	$4,960
Stillman College; Tuscaloosa, Ala. 35403 (P)	842	67	77	$ 5,200	$ 5,200	$3,100
Talladega College; Talladega, Ala. 35160 (P)	642	65	38	$ 5,666	$ 5,666	$2,964
Troy State University; Troy, Ala. 36082 (Pub)	5,382	56	73	$ 2,055	$ 4,110	$3,630
Troy State University at Dothan; Dothan, Ala. 36304 (Pub)	5,126	62	78	$ 2,100	$ 4,200	
Troy State University at Montgomery; Montgomery, Ala. 36103 (Pub)	2,816	59	94	$ 1,980	$ 3,960	
Tuskegee University; Tuskegee, Ala. 36088 (P)	2,969	54	65	$ 8,662	$ 8,662	$4,432
University of Alabama; Tuscaloosa, Ala. 35487 (Pub)	10,692	56	88	$ 2,400	$ 4,800	$3,680
University of Alabama-Birmingham; Birmingham, Ala. 35294 (Pub)	5,230	49	77	$ 2,698	$ 5,656	$5,490
University of Alabama-Huntsville; Huntsville, Ala. 35899 (Pub)	14,195	51	78	$ 2,470	$ 6,268	$3,645
University of Mobile; Mobile, Ala. 36663 (P)	1,943	62	82	$ 6,840	$ 6,840	$4,080
University of Montevallo; Montevallo, Ala. 35115 (Pub)	2,702	68	75	$ 2,640	$ 5,280	$3,142
University of North Alabama; Florence, Ala. 35632 (Pub)	4,698	57	76	$ 1,902	$ 3,804	$2,840
University of South Alabama; Mobile, Ala. 36688 (Pub)	10,159	55	93	$ 2,184	$ 4,368	$2,940
University of West Alabama; Livingston, Ala. 35470 (Pub)	1,838	53	76	$ 1,920	$ 1,920	$2,205
ALASKA						
Alaska Pacific University; Anchorage, Alaska 99508 (P)	286	65	88	$ 7,920	$ 7,920	$4,300
Sheldon Jackson College; Sitka, Alaska 99835 (P)	223	51	100	$ 9,000	$ 9,000	$4,800
University of Alaska-Anchorage; Anchorage, Alaska 99508 (Pub)	16,746	56	81	$ 1,035	$ 3,105	$6,310
University of Alaska-Fairbanks; Fairbanks, Alaska 99775 (Pub)	7,393	59	79	$ 2,160	$ 6,480	$3,690
University of Alaska-Southeast; Juneau, Alaska 99801 (Pub)	2,782	55	88	$ 1,680	$ 5,554	$5,044
ARIZONA						
Arizona State University; Tempe, Ariz. 85287-0112 (Pub)	31,859	50	78	$ 2,009	$ 8,377	$4,287
Embry-Riddle Aeronautical University (Ariz.); Prescott, Ariz. 86301 (P)	1,435	16	84	$ 8,610	$ 8,610	$4,080
Grand Canyon University; Phoenix, Ariz. 85017 (P)	1,972	62	87	$ 8,670	$ 8,670	$3,750
Northern Arizona University; Flagstaff, Ariz. 86011 (Pub)	14,250	54	83	$ 2,060	$ 7,826	$3,400
Prescott College; Prescott, Ariz. 86301 (P)	718	63	74	$11,000	$11,000	
University of Arizona; Tucson, Ariz. 85721 (Pub)	26,468	51	74	$ 1,940	$ 8,308	$4,190
Western International University; Phoenix, Ariz. 85021 (P)	840	43	18	$ 3,960	$ 3,960	
ARKANSAS						
Arkansas State University; State University, Ark. 72467 (Pub)	8,762	55	73	$ 2,000	$ 5,090	$2,840
Arkansas Tech University; Russellville, Ark. 72801 (Pub)	4,541	53	90	$ 2,016	$ 4,032	$2,896
Harding University; Searcy, Ark. 72149 (P)	3,464	53	63	$ 5,775	$ 5,775	$3,802

Institution Name; City, State Zip (Control)	Students	Percent		Tuition		Room and board
		Women	Accepted	In-State	Out-of-State	
Henderson State University; Arkadelphia, Ark. 71999 (Pub)	3,252	55	94	$ 1,980	$ 3,960	$2,856
Hendrix College; Conway, Ark. 72032 (P)	982	55	90	$ 9,790	$ 9,790	$3,807
John Brown University; Siloam Springs, Ark. 72761 (P)	1,295	54	68	$ 9,120	$ 9,120	$4,390
Lyon College; Batesville, Ark. 72503 (P)	539	57	51	$ 9,870	$ 9,870	$4,418
Ouachita Baptist University; Arkadelphia, Ark. 71998 (P)	1,604	52	77	$ 7,550	$ 7,550	$2,970
Philander Smith College; Little Rock, Ark. 72203 (P)	925	63	54	$ 3,288	$ 3,288	$2,630
Southern Arkansas University-Magnolia; Magnolia, Ark. 71753-5000 (Pub)	2,279	56	98	$ 1,898	$ 2,906	$2,530
University of Arkansas; Fayetteville, Ark. 72701 (Pub)	8,559	59	74	$ 2,538	$ 6,008	$3,687
University of Arkansas-Little Rock; Little Rock, Ark. 72204 (Pub)	2,200	56	68	$ 2,130	$ 4,522	$2,435
University of Arkansas-Monticello; Monticello, Ark. 71656 (Pub)	3,425	59	98	$ 1,680	$ 3,888	$2,510
University of Arkansas-Pine Bluff; Pine Bluff, Ark. 71601 (Pub)	11,844	46	88	$ 1,944	$ 5,136	$3,480
University of Central Arkansas; Conway, Ark. 72035 (Pub)	7,952	60	93	$ 2,392	$ 4,364	$2,800
University of the Ozarks; Clarksville, Ark. 72830 (P)	573	55	96	$ 7,000	$ 7,000	$3,400
Williams Baptist College; Walnut Ridge, Ark. 72476 (P)	564	55	79	$ 4,800	$ 4,800	$2,722
CALIFORNIA						
Art Center College of Design; Pasadena, Calif. 91103 (P)	1,383	36	54	$16,200	$16,200	
Azusa Pacific University; Azusa, Calif. 91702 (P)	2,475	60	88	$13,550	$13,550	$4,482
Biola University; La Mirada, Calif. 90639 (P)	1,926	59	83	$14,286	$14,286	$4,851
Brooks Institute of Photography; Santa Barbara, Calif. 93108 (P)	324	40	89	$14,100	$14,100	
California Baptist College; Riverside, Calif. 92504 (P)	1,446	57	91	$ 8,190	$ 8,190	$4,594
California College of Arts and Crafts; San Francisco, Calif. 94107 (P)	1,056	57	69	$14,950	$14,950	$4,696
California Institute of Technology; Pasadena, Calif. 91125 (P)	893	26	25	$18,000	$18,000	$5,478
California Institute of the Arts; Valencia, Calif. 91355 (P)	709	36	39	$17,250	$17,250	$5,450
California Lutheran University; Thousand Oaks, Calif. 91360 (P)	1,859	52	76	$14,350	$14,350	$5,640
California Polytechnic State University-San Luis Obispo; San Luis Obispo, Calif. 93407 (Pub)	15,947	43	55	$ 2,075	$ 5,904	$5,553
California State Polytechnic University-Pomona; Pomona, Calif. 91768 (Pub)	14,874	42	60	$ 1,893	$ 7,797	$5,850
California State University-Bakersfield; Bakersfield, Calif. 93311 (Pub)	4,189	63	68	$ 1,947	$ 9,320	$4,070
California State University-Chico; Chico, Calif. 95929 (Pub)	12,298	51	83	$ 2,046	$ 9,426	$4,981
California State University-Dominguez Hills; Carson, Calif. 90747 (Pub)	7,085	64	76	$ 911	$ 8,783	$2,598
California State University-Fresno; Fresno, Calif. 93740 (Pub)	14,100	55	71	$ 1,822	$ 8,818	$4,498
California State University-Fullerton; Fullerton, Calif. 92634 (Pub)	18,828	57	84	$ 1,920	$ 9,792	$3,792
California State University-Hayward; Hayward, Calif. 94542 (Pub)	9,778	62	80	$ 1,800	$ 9,180	$6,991
California State University-Long Beach; Long Beach, Calif. 90840 (Pub)	21,094	55	83	$ 1,816	$ 9,196	$5,100
California State University-Los Angeles; Los Angeles, Calif. 90032 (Pub)	13,995	59	53	$ 1,788	$ 9,168	$2,915
California State University-Northridge; Northridge, Calif. 91330 (Pub)	21,720	55	82	$ 1,970	$ 7,820	$5,071
California State University-Sacramento; Sacramento, Calif. 95819 (Pub)	18,713	54	68	$ 1,950	$ 9,330	$4,825
California State University-San Bernardino; San Bernardino, Calif. 92407 (Pub)	11,007	59	70	$ 1,869	$ 7,773	$4,380
California State University-San Marcos; San Marcos, Calif. 92096-0001 (Pub)	1,284	66	79	$ 1,700	$ 5,904	
California State University-Stanislaus; Turlock, Calif. 95382 (Pub)	6,100	61	60	$ 1,915	$ 8,803	$5,220
Chapman University; Orange, Calif. 92866 (Pub)	2,299	56	76	$17,990	$17,990	$6,454
Christian Heritage College; El Cajon, Calif. 92019-1157 (P)	555	54	75	$ 9,670	$ 9,670	$4,326
Claremont McKenna College; Claremont, Calif. 91711 (P)	952	43	29	$18,320	$18,320	$6,460
Cogswell Polytechnical Institute; Sunnyvale, Calif. 94089 (P)	458	10	95	$ 7,320	$ 7,320	$3,200
College of Notre Dame (Calif.); Belmont, Calif. 94002 (P)	973	71	77	$11,000	$14,400	$6,400
Concordia University (Calif.); Irvine, Calif. 92612-3299 (P)	771	67	62	$12,250	$12,250	$4,920
Dominican College of San Rafael; San Rafael, Calif. 94901-2298 (P)	1,025	79	81	$15,524	$15,524	$6,968
Fresno Pacific University; Fresno, Calif. 93702 (P)	816	65	75	$11,100	$11,100	$4,100

Institution Name; City, State Zip (Control)	Students	Percent		Tuition		Room and board
		Women	Accepted	In-State	Out-of-State	
Golden Gate University; San Francisco, Calif. 94105 (P)	1,853	57	86	$ 7,800	$ 7,800	
Harvey Mudd College; Claremont, Calif. 91711 (P)	643	25	46	$18,960	$18,960	$7,197
Holy Names College; Oakland, Calif. 94619 (P)	600	68	70	$13,150	$13,150	$5,522
Humboldt State University; Arcata, Calif. 95521 (Pub)	6,315	50	76	$ 1,958	$ 7,862	$4,934
John F. Kennedy University; Orinda, Calif. 94563 (P)	40	79		$ 7,056	$ 7,056	
LaSierra University; Riverside, Calif. 92515 (P)	1,385	52	76	$13,320	$13,320	$3,990
Loma Linda University; Loma Linda, Calif. 92350 (Pub)	1,249	69		$13,650	$13,650	$1,890
Loyola Marymount University; Los Angeles, Calif. 90045 (P)	4,164	57	66	$15,440	$15,440	$6,492
Menlo College; Atherton, Calif. 94027 (P)	516	39	79	$15,980	$15,980	$6,500
Mills College; Oakland, Calif. 94613 (P)	850	100	84	$15,260	$15,260	$6,480
Monterey Institute of International Studies; Monterey, Calif. 93940 (P)	36	60	57	$16,200	$16,200	
Mount Saint Mary's College (Calif.); Los Angeles, Calif. 90049 (P)	1,609	94	62	$14,050	$14,050	$5,800
National University; San Diego, Calif. 92108 (P)	3,894	52	100	$ 6,600	$ 6,600	
New College of California; San Francisco, Calif. 94102 (P)	900	64	90	$ 7,880	$ 7,880	
Occidental College; Los Angeles, Calif. 90041 (P)	1,721	52	73	$18,900	$18,900	$5,660
Otis College of Art & Design; Los Angeles, Calif. 90045 (P)	691	58	70	$14,900	$14,900	$4,490
Pacific Christian College; Fullerton, Calif. 92631 (P)	702	50	90	$ 8,200	$ 8,200	$3,584
Pacific Union College; Angwin, Calif. 94508 (P)	1,455	53	67	$12,960	$12,960	$4,050
Patten College; Oakland, Calif. 94601 (P)	627	41	91	$ 6,672	$ 6,672	$2,300
Pepperdine University; Malibu, Calif. 90263 (P)	2,816	58	51	$21,100	$21,100	$6,980
Pitzer College; Claremont, Calif. 91711 (P)	869	48	76	$20,088	$20,088	$6,694
Point Loma Nazarene College; San Diego, Calif. 92106 (P)	2,051	61	91	$10,880	$10,880	$4,480
Pomona College; Claremont, Calif. 91711 (P)	1,428	49	34	$20,500	$20,500	$8,180
Saint John's Seminary; Camarillo, Calif. 93012 (P)	66	0	82	$ 6,420	$ 6,420	$2,500
Saint Mary's College (Calif.); Moraga, Calif. 94575 (P)	2,153	54	83	$15,880	$15,880	$7,109
Samuel Merritt College; Oakland, Calif. 94609 (P)	309	90	67	$13,865	$13,865	$4,410
San Diego State University; San Diego, Calif. 92182 (Pub)	29,331	55	82	$ 1,902	$ 5,904	$4,700
San Francisco Art Institute; San Francisco, Calif. 94133 (P)	441	48	70	$17,400	$17,400	
San Francisco Conservatory of Music; San Francisco, Calif. 94122 (P)	156	53	67	$16,300	$16,300	
San Francisco State University; San Francisco, Calif. 94132 (Pub)	19,102	57	72	$ 1,982	$ 9,362	$5,225
San Jose State University; San Jose, Calif. 95192 (Pub)	20,993	51	77	$ 2,017	$ 7,921	$5,786
Santa Clara University; Santa Clara, Calif. 95053 (P)	4,230	53	66	$16,455	$16,455	$7,026
Scripps College; Claremont, Calif. 91711 (P)	700	100	77	$19,480	$19,480	$7,750
Simpson College; Redding, Calif. 96003 (P)	844	58	71	$ 7,600	$ 7,600	$3,800
Sonoma State University; Rohnert Park, Calif. 94928 (Pub)	5,868	60	83	$ 2,130	$ 8,034	$5,455
Southern California College; Costa Mesa, Calif. 92626 (P)	1,084	57	86	$11,320	$11,320	$4,860
Stanford University; Stanford, Calif. 94305 (P)	6,550	50	16	$20,490	$20,490	$7,340
The Master's College; Santa Clara, Calif. 91321-1200 (P)	767	54	78	$11,980	$11,980	$4,986
Thomas Aquinas College; Santa Paula, Calif. 93060 (P)	223	43	81	$13,900	$13,900	$5,300
United States International University; San Diego, Calif. 92131 (Pub)	366	55	78	$10,800	$10,800	$4,530
University of California-Berkeley; Berkeley, Calif. 94720-5800 (Pub)	21,358	49	36	$ 4,354	$12,748	$7,226
University of California-Davis; Davis, Calif. 95616 (Pub)	16,699	53	73	$ 4,174	$11,873	$5,283
University of California-Irvine; Irvine, Calif. 92717 (Pub)	13,390	53	71	$ 4,064	$ 8,984	$6,322
University of California-Los Angeles; Los Angeles, Calif. 90024 (Pub)	23,914	52	39	$ 4,050	$13,034	$6,490
University of California-Riverside; Riverside, Calif. 92521 (Pub)	7,433	50	78	$ 4,112	$12,506	$5,705
University of California-San Diego; La Jolla, Calif. 92093-0337 (Pub)	14,623	50	50	$ 4,198	$ 8,984	$6,836
University of California-Santa Barbara; Santa Barbara, Calif. 93106 (Pub)	16,281	53	78	$ 4,098	$12,492	$6,131
University of California-Santa Cruz; Santa Cruz, Calif. 95064 (Pub)	8,629	60	83	$ 4,136	$12,530	$6,429
University of Judaism; Los Angeles, Calif. 90077 (P)	101	60	81	$13,910	$13,910	$7,290
University of LaVerne; La Verne, Calif. 91750 (P)	2,953	57	74	$12,900	$12,900	$5,050
University of Redlands; Redlands, Calif. 92373-0999 (P)	1,318	55	84	$18,300	$18,300	$7,096
University of San Diego; San Diego, Calif. 92110 (P)	3,915	55	81	$14,860	$14,860	$6,500
University of San Francisco; San Francisco, Calif. 94117 (P)	4,570	62	77	$14,920	$14,920	$6,934
University of Southern California; Los Angeles, Calif. 90089 (P)	13,716	48	72	$19,516	$19,516	$6,714
University of the Pacific; Stockton, Calif. 95211 (P)	2,758	56	85	$18,260	$18,260	$5,526

Institution Name; City, State Zip (Control)	Students	Percent		Tuition		Room and board
		Women	Accepted	In-State	Out-of-State	
West Coast University; Los Angeles, Calif. 90020-1765 (P)	500	40		$10,200	$10,200	
Westmont College; Santa Barbara, Calif. 93108 (P)	1,320	60	86	$17,486	$17,486	$6,048
Whittier College; Whittier, Calif. 90608 (P)	1,301	55	70	$18,624	$18,624	$6,230
Woodbury University; Burbank, Calif. 91510 (P)	948	54	79	$13,275	$13,275	$5,685
COLORADO						
Adams State College; Alamosa, Colo. 81102 (Pub)	2,176	57	86	$ 1,452	$ 5,244	$4,040
Colorado Christian University; Lakewood, Colo. 80226 (P)	1,625	58	85	$ 9,360	$ 9,360	$4,560
Colorado College; Colorado Springs, Colo. 80903 (P)	1,921	53	58	$19,980	$19,980	$5,100
Colorado School of Mines; Golden, Colo. 80401 (Pub)	2,400	25	80	$ 4,494	$13,980	$4,730
Colorado State University; Fort Collins, Colo. 80523 (Pub)	18,451	51	77	$ 2,258	$ 9,480	$4,716
Colorado Technical University; Colorado Springs, Colo. 80907 (P)	1,232	21	92	$ 6,075	$ 6,075	
Fort Lewis College; Durango, Colo. 81301 (Pub)	4,109	47	73	$ 1,594	$ 7,424	$4,000
Mesa State College; Grand Junction, Colo. 81502-2647 (Pub)	4,724	56	87	$ 1,986	$ 6,106	$4,538
Metropolitan State College of Denver; Denver, Colo. 80217 (Pub)	17,624	56	83	$ 1,445	$ 5,914	
Regis University; Denver, Colo. 80221-1099 (P)	1,160	56	77	$14,900	$14,900	$6,100
United States Air Force Academy; Colorado Springs, Colo. 80840 (Pub)	4,308	16	18	$ —	$ —	
University of Colorado, Boulder; Boulder, Colo. 80309 (Pub)	20,006	47	80	$ 2,790	$14,463	$4,370
University of Colorado, Colorado Springs; Colorado Springs, Colo. 80933 (Pub)	4,159	57	76	$ 2,118	$ 8,438	$5,400
University of Colorado-Denver; Denver, Colo. 80217 (Pub)	6,533	52	84	$ 1,916	$10,064	$5,782
University of Denver; Denver, Colo. 80208 (P)	2,951	52	78	$17,532	$17,532	$5,538
University of Northern Colorado; Greeley, Colo. 80639 (Pub)	8,594	59	79	$ 1,914	$ 8,416	$4,270
University of Southern Colorado; Pueblo, Colo. 81001 (Pub)	4,056	53	85	$ 2,171	$ 7,988	$4,508
Western State College of Colorado; Gunnison, Colo. 81231 (Pub)	2,536	41	86	$ 1,440	$ 6,418	$4,649
CONNECTICUT						
Albertus Magnus College; New Haven, Conn. 06511 (P)	1,225	65	47	$13,104	$13,104	$6,136
Central Connecticut State University; New Britain, Conn. 06050 (Pub)	9,151	50	67	$ 2,062	$ 6,674	$5,300
Connecticut College; New London, Conn. 06320 (P)	1,870	56	43	$28,475	$28,475	
Eastern Connecticut State University; Willimantic, Conn. 06226 (Pub)	4,222	53	80	$ 3,771	$ 9,105	$4,756
Fairfield University; Fairfield, Conn. 06430 (P)	3,100	52	71	$17,900	$17,900	$7,024
Quinnipiac College; Hamden, Conn. 06518 (P)	4,134	60	60	$13,440	$13,440	$6,750
Sacred Heart University; Fairfield, Conn. 06432 (P)	3,843	55	85	$12,212	$12,212	$6,380
Saint Joseph College; West Hartford, Conn. 06117 (P)	1,200	99	87	$13,800	$13,800	$5,300
Southern Connecticut State University; New Haven, Conn. 06515 (Pub)	7,568	55	72	$ 2,062	$ 6,674	$5,566
Teikyo Post University; Waterbury, Conn. 06723-2540 (P)	1,550	66	83	$12,000	$12,000	$5,600
Trinity College (Conn.); Hartford, Conn. 06016 (P)	2,004	50	46	$20,650	$20,650	$6,120
United States Coast Guard Academy; New London, Conn. 06320 (Pub)	807	27	11	$ 3,000	$ 3,000	
University of Bridgeport; Bridgeport, Conn. 06601 (P)	1,001	53	83	$13,000	$13,000	$6,810
University of Connecticut; Storrs, Conn. 06269 (Pub)	11,336	50	67	$ 5,242	$13,760	$5,462
University of Hartford; West Hartford, Conn. 06117 (P)	5,354	48	82	$16,380	$16,380	$6,890
University of New Haven; West Haven, Conn. 06516 (P)	3,004	37	84	$11,190	$11,190	$3,000
Wesleyan University; Middletown, Conn. 06457 (P)	2,741	53	32	$21,910	$21,910	$6,030
Western Connecticut State University; Danbury, Conn. 06810 (Pub)	4,679	51	61	$ 2,012	$ 6,510	$4,496
Yale University; New Haven, Conn. 06520 (P)	5,401	49	18	$23,100	$23,100	$6,850
DELAWARE						
Delaware State University; Dover, Del. 19901 (Pub)	2,695	56	69	$ 2,636	$ 6,236	$4,704
Goldey-Beacom College; Wilmington, Del. 19808 (P)	1,480	66	82	$ 7,080	$ 7,080	$3,290
University of Delaware; Newark, Del. 19716 (P)	14,829	58	66	$ 3,990	$11,250	$4,590
Wesley College; Dover, Del. 19901 (P)	1,325	52	85	$10,879	$10,879	$4,674
Wilmington College (Del.); New Castle, Del. 19720 (P)	583	62	100	$ 4,392	$ 4,392	
DISTRICT OF COLUMBIA						
American University; Washington, D.C. 20016 (P)	5,433	59	79	$18,300	$18,300	$7,350
Corcoran School of Art; Washington, D.C. 20006 (P)	280	60	53	$10,980	$10,980	$4,000
Gallaudet University; Washington, D.C. 20002 (P)	1,302	53	62	$ 5,100	$ 5,100	$5,700
George Washington University; Washington, D.C. 20052 (P)	6,581	55	58	$19,065	$19,065	$6,910
Georgetown University; Washington, D.C. 20057 (Pub)	6,338	52	23	$21,216	$21,216	$8,091
Howard University; Washington, D.C. 20059 (P)	5,906	62	60	$ 8,580	$ 8,580	$5,056
Mount Vernon College; Washington, D.C. 20007 (P)	341	99	47	$15,430	$15,430	$7,340
Southeastern University; Washington, D.C. 20024 (P)	301	58	90	$ 4,980	$ 4,980	

Institution Name; City, State Zip (Control)	Students	Percent		Tuition		Room and board
		Women	Accepted	In-State	Out-of-State	
The Catholic University of America; Washington, D.C. 20064 (P)	2,380	53	67	$16,500	$16,500	$7,036
Trinity College (D.C.); Washington, D.C. 20017-1094 (P)	417	100	85	$12,830	$12,830	$6,670
University of the District of Columbia; Washington, D.C. 20008 (Pub)	10,004	56		$ 1,008	$ 4,032	
FLORIDA						
Barry University; Miami Shores, Fla. 33161 (P)	5,756	62	77	$12,790	$12,790	$5,680
Bethune-Cookman College; Daytona Beach, Fla. 32114 (P)	2,335	58	84	$ 6,780	$ 6,780	$3,874
Clearwater Christian College; Clearwater, Fla. 34619-9997 (P)	518	53	85	$ 6,500	$ 6,500	$3,400
Eckerd College; St. Petersburg, Fla. 33711 (P)	1,466	56	83	$16,950	$16,950	$4,660
Embry-Riddle Aeronautical University (Fla.); Daytona Beach, Fla. 32114 (P)	3,930	14	84	$ 8,610	$ 8,610	$3,640
Flagler College; St. Augustine, Fla. 32085 (P)	1,496	62	58	$ 5,760	$ 5,760	$3,580
Florida A&M University; Tallahassee, Fla. 32307 (Pub)	9,877	58	60	$ 1,981	$ 7,898	$3,281
Florida Atlantic University; Boca Raton, Fla. 33431 (Pub)	15,995	59	74	$ 2,080	$ 7,850	$4,680
Florida Institute of Technology; Melbourne, Fla. 32901 (P)	1,885	31	86	$15,060	$15,060	$4,392
Florida International University; Miami, Fla. 33199 (Pub)	20,337	56	64	$ 1,790	$ 6,695	$4,380
Florida Memorial College; Miami, Fla. 33054 (P)	1,488	63		$ 4,920	$ 4,920	$3,236
Florida Southern College; Lakeland, Fla. 33801 (P)	1,714	58	74	$ 9,260	$ 9,260	$5,300
Florida State University; Tallahassee, Fla. 32306 (Pub)	23,051	55	73	$ 1,882	$ 7,127	$4,472
Jacksonville University; Jacksonville, Fla. 32211 (P)	2,019	55	71	$12,000	$12,000	$4,750
Lynn University; Boca Raton, Fla. 33431 (P)	1,450	48	80	$15,450	$15,450	$6,250
New College of the University of South Florida; Sarasota, Fla. 34243-2197 (Pub)	596	54	59	$ 2,167	$ 8,461	$4,018
Nova Southeastern University; Fort Lauderdale, Fla. 33314 (P)	3,902	65	77	$ 9,750	$ 9,750	$5,250
Palm Beach Atlantic College; West Palm Beach, Fla. 33416 (P)	1,543	59	80	$ 9,300	$ 9,300	$3,990
Ringling School of Art & Design; Sarasota, Fla. 34234 (P)	819	35	58	$13,050	$13,050	$6,692
Rollins College; Winter Park, Fla. 32789 (P)	1,413	55	71	$19,450	$19,450	$6,340
Saint John Vianney College Seminary; Miami, Fla. 33165 (P)	44		100	$ 6,400	$ 6,400	$4,000
Saint Leo College; Saint Leo, Fla. 33574 (P)	902	60	68	$ 9,900	$ 9,900	$5,140
Saint Thomas University; Miami, Fla. 33054 (P)	2,326	53	68	$11,400	$11,400	$4,000
Southeastern College of Assemblies of God; Lakeland, Fla. 33801-6099 (P)	1,090	48	64	$ 4,640	$ 4,640	$3,274
Stetson University; DeLand, Fla. 32720 (P)	1,851	57	86	$14,100	$14,100	$5,090
University of Central Florida; Orlando, Fla. 32816 (Pub)	21,831	52	69	$ 1,829	$ 7,074	$3,610
University of Florida; Gainesville, Fla. 32611 (Pub)	30,008	48	59	$ 1,793	$ 7,038	$4,500
University of Miami; Coral Gables, Fla. 33124-4616 (Pub)	8,377	53	57	$18,220	$18,220	$7,102
University of North Florida; Jacksonville, Fla. 32224 (Pub)	8,662	58	70	$ 1,748	$ 6,650	$3,640
University of South Florida; Tampa, Fla. 33620 (Pub)	24,313	58	67	$ 1,960	$ 7,200	$4,598
University of Tampa; Tampa, Fla. 33606-1490 (P)	2,157	58	82	$13,420	$13,420	$4,630
University of West Florida; Pensacola, Fla. 32514 (Pub)	5,684	58	86	$ 1,819	$ 7,064	$2,032
Warner Southern College; Lake Wales, Fla. 33853 (P)	601	61	56	$ 7,200	$ 7,200	$3,816
Webber College; Babson Park, Fla. 33827 (P)	438	44	96	$ 6,790	$ 6,790	$3,200
GEORGIA						
Agnes Scott College; Decatur, Ga. 30030 (P)	661	100	82	$14,825	$14,825	$6,230
Albany State College; Albany, Ga. 31705 (Pub)	2,356	65	70	$ 1,584	$ 5,463	$3,180
Armstrong State College; Savannah, Ga. 31419 (Pub)	5,042	68	82	$ 1,836	$ 5,715	$3,921
Augusta College; Augusta, Ga. 30904 (Pub)	4,711	61	79	$ 2,400	$ 7,572	
Berry College; Rome, Ga. 30149-5031 (P)	1,855	61	82	$ 9,678	$ 9,678	$4,660
Brenau University; Gainesville, Ga. 30501 (P)	1,423	97	74	$10,350	$10,350	$6,330
Brewton-Parker College; Mount Vernon, Ga. 30445 (P)	1,682	54	70	$ 5,265	$ 5,265	$2,565
Clark Atlanta University; Atlanta, Ga. 30314 (P)	4,391	70	70	$ 9,148	$ 9,148	$5,600
Columbus State University; Columbus, Ga. 31907 (Pub)	4,766	62	73	$ 1,941	$ 6,402	$3,825
Covenant College; Lookout Mountain, Ga. 30750 (P)	711	54	79	$12,550	$12,550	$4,120
Emory University; Atlanta, Ga. 30322 (P)	5,736	53	44	$20,870	$20,870	$6,800
Fort Valley State College; Fort Valley, Ga. 31030 (Pub)	2,124	59		$ 1,833	$ 4,677	$ 975
Georgia College; Milledgeville, Ga. 31061 (Pub)	4,384	64	97	$ 1,921	$ 5,800	$3,345
Georgia Institute of Technology; Atlanta, Ga. 30332 (Pub)	9,469	28	56	$ 2,901	$ 9,621	$5,700
Georgia Southern University; Statesboro, Ga. 30460 (Pub)	12,594	45	70	$ 2,055	$ 5,934	$3,696
Georgia Southwestern College; Americus, Ga. 31709 (Pub)	2,071	63	75	$ 2,067	$ 5,946	$3,033
Georgia State University; Atlanta, Ga. 30303 (Pub)	16,786	59	98	$ 2,385	$ 8,640	$3,600
Kennesaw State College; Marietta, Ga. 30061 (Pub)	10,994	59	86	$ 1,246	$ 3,832	
LaGrange College; LaGrange, Ga. 30240 (P)	963	59	79	$ 9,486	$ 9,486	$4,185
Mercer University; Macon, Ga. 31207 (P)	4,203	56	88	$13,896	$13,896	$4,740

Institution Name; City, State Zip (Control)	Students	Percent		Tuition		Room and board
		Women	Accepted	In-State	Out-of-State	
Morehouse College; Atlanta, Ga. 30314 (P)	3,005	0	68	$ 7,700	$ 7,700	$5,976
Morris Brown College; Atlanta, Ga. 30314 (P)	1,891	58	66	$ 7,244	$ 7,244	$4,750
North Georgia College; Dahlonega, Ga. 30597 (Pub)	2,784	63	66	$ 1,584	$ 5,427	$3,157
Oglethorpe University; Atlanta, Ga. 30319 (P)	776	60	81	$15,820	$15,820	$4,990
Paine College; Augusta, Ga. 30910 (P)	915	64	63	$ 6,220	$ 6,220	$3,020
Piedmont College; Demorest, Ga. 30535 (P)	891	63	67	$ 6,360	$ 6,360	$3,850
Savannah College of Art & Design; Savannah, Ga. 31402 (P)	2,672	42	73	$12,600	$12,600	$6,200
Savannah State University; Savannah, Ga. 31404 (Pub)	2,822	56	66	$ 2,130	$ 6,009	$2,970
Shorter College; Rome, Ga. 30165-4298 (P)	202	62	83	$ 7,750	$ 7,750	$4,050
Southern College of Technology; Marietta, Ga. 30060 (Pub)	3,296	17	74	$ 1,851	$ 5,730	$3,600
Southern Polytechnic State University; Marietta, Ga. 30060 (Pub)	3,464	16		$ 1,851	$ 5,730	$3,600
Spelman College; Atlanta, Ga. 30314 (P)	1,899	100	54	$ 8,150	$ 8,150	$6,130
State University of West Georgia; Carrollton, Ga. 30118 (Pub)	6,189	61	65	$ 1,989	$ 5,868	$3,225
The Atlanta College of Art; Atlanta, Ga. 30309 (P)	3,096	47	86	$11,150	$11,150	$3,550
Toccoa Falls College; Toccoa Falls, Ga. 30598 (P)	892	54	69	$ 6,970	$ 6,970	$3,708
University of Georgia; Athens, Ga. 30602 (P)	22,301	54	56	$ 2,694	$ 7,875	$4,045
Valdosta State University; Valdosta, Ga. 31698 (Pub)	8,465	59	73	$ 2,139	$ 6,600	$3,929
Wesleyan College; Macon, Ga. 31210 (P)	448	100	84	$13,200	$13,200	$5,100
West Georgia College; Carrollton, Ga. 30118 (Pub)	6,189	60	65	$ 1,989	$ 5,868	$3,225
HAWAII						
Brigham Young University-Hawaii Campus; Laie Oahu, Hawaii 96762 (P)	2,287	62	59	$ 1,900	$ 1,900	$3,500
Chaminade University of Honolulu; Honolulu, Hawaii 96816 (P)	1,920	54	84	$10,800	$10,800	$5,300
Hawaii Pacific University; Honolulu, Hawaii 96813 (P)	7,158	49	77	$ 7,500	$ 7,500	$7,400
University of Hawaii-Manoa; Honolulu, Hawaii 96822 (Pub)	12,524	55	64	$ 2,304	$ 7,752	$4,437
University of Hawaii-Hilo; Hilo, Hawaii 96720-4091 (Pub)	2,723	61	64	$ 1,272	$ 6,888	$4,810
IDAHO						
Albertson College; Caldwell, Idaho 83605 (P)	620	53	86	$15,100	$15,100	$3,675
Boise State University; Boise, Idaho 83725 (Pub)	6,552	58	89	$ 1,964	$ 7,310	$3,370
Idaho State University; Pocatello, Idaho 83209 (Pub)	9,011	53	85	$ 1,726	$ 5,674	$3,220
Lewis-Clark State College; Lewiston, Idaho 83501 (Pub)	2,978	59	99	$ 1,868	$ 6,830	$3,130
Northwest Nazarene College; Nampa, Idaho 83686 (P)	1,118	56	41	$11,340	$11,340	$3,270
University of Idaho; Moscow, Idaho 83844-4140 (Pub)	7,107	43	92	$ 1,942	$ 7,742	$3,680
ILLINOIS						
Augustana College (Ill.); Rock Island, Ill. 61201 (P)	2,214	59	76	$14,598	$14,598	$4,449
Aurora University; Aurora, Ill. 60506 (P)	1,270	60	80	$10,800	$10,800	$4,134
Barat College; Lake Forest, Ill. 60045 (P)	719	68	73	$12,570	$12,570	$4,966
Benedictine University; Lisle, Ill. 60532 (P)	1,741	52	86	$11,640	$11,640	$4,618
Blackburn College; Carlinville, Ill. 62626 (P)	448	46	74	$ 6,850	$ 6,850	$2,700
Bradley University; Peoria, Ill. 61625 (P)	4,935	52	89	$12,610	$12,610	$4,690
Chicago State University; Chicago, Ill. 60628 (Pub)	7,237	70	43	$ 2,336	$ 6,272	$5,000
College of Saint Francis; Joliet, Ill. 60435 (P)	1,324	53	70	$11,950	$11,950	$4,740
Columbia College (Ill.); Chicago, Ill. 60605-1996 (P)	5,355	48	90	$ 8,030	$ 8,030	$4,456
Concordia University (Ill.); River Forest, Ill. 60305-1499 (P)	1,245	68	81	$10,752	$10,752	$4,623
DePaul University; Chicago, Ill. 60604 (P)	9,788	57	78	$12,750	$12,750	$5,500
Dominican University; River Forest, Ill. 60305 (P)	875	74	80	$12,850	$12,850	$4,880
Eastern Illinois University; Charleston, Ill. 61920 (Pub)	10,106	58	74	$ 2,052	$ 6,156	$3,434
Elmhurst College; Elmhurst, Ill. 60126 (P)	2,775	65	69	$10,976	$10,976	$4,660
Eureka College; Eureka, Ill. 61530 (P)	502	49	80	$13,066	$13,066	$4,142
Greenville College; Greenville, Ill. 62246-0159 (P)	900	53	71	$12,576	$12,576	$4,750
Illinois College; Jacksonville, Ill. 62650 (P)	905	55	88	$ 9,500	$ 9,500	$4,200
Illinois Institute of Technology; Chicago, Ill. 60616 (P)	1,959	23	67	$15,840	$15,840	$4,620
Illinois State University; Normal, Ill. 61790 (Pub)	16,773	57	78	$ 2,952	$ 8,856	$3,840
Illinois Wesleyan University; Bloomington, Ill. 61702 (P)	1,911	51	61	$16,300	$16,300	$4,424
Judson College; Elgin, Ill. 60123 (P)	933	55	77	$10,380	$10,380	$4,780
Kendall College; Evanston, Ill. 60201 (P)	500	45		$ 8,931	$ 8,931	$4,998
Knox College; Galesburg, Ill. 61401 (P)	1,140	54	82	$17,571	$17,571	$4,662
Lake Forest College; Lake Forest, Ill. 60045 (P)	1,150	51	78	$19,600	$19,600	$4,500
Lewis University; Romeoville, Ill. 60441 (P)	3,148	56	85	$10,016	$10,016	$4,400
Loyola University of Chicago; Chicago, Ill. 60611 (P)	7,669	63	86	$14,400	$14,400	$6,210
MacMurray College; Jacksonville, Ill. 62650 (P)	669	57	76	$11,400	$11,400	$4,130
McKendree College; Lebanon, Ill. 62254 (P)	1,787	61	91	$ 9,750	$ 9,750	$4,050
Millikin University; Decatur, Ill. 62522 (P)	1,930	57	85	$13,290	$13,290	$4,828
Monmouth College (Ill.); Monmouth, Ill. 61462 (P)	837	57	78	$13,965	$13,965	$4,275
National-Louis University; Evanston, Ill. 60201 (P)	3,076	72	76	$12,150	$12,150	$5,256
North Central College; Naperville, Ill. 60566 (P)	2,177	55	83	$13,725	$13,725	$4,950
North Park College; Chicago, Ill. 60625 (P)	1,437	59	80	$13,990	$13,990	$4,780
Northeastern Illinois University; Chicago, Ill. 60625 (Pub)	7,403	60	69	$ 2,352	$ 6,432	
Northern Illinois University; DeKalb, Ill. 60115 (Pub)	16,423	54	74	$ 3,036	$ 9,106	$3,600

Institution Name; City, State Zip (Control)	Students	Percent		Tuition		Room and board
		Women	Accepted	In-State	Out-of-State	
Northwestern University; Evanston, Ill. 60204 (P)	7,609	51	32	$18,108	$18,108	$6,054
Olivet Nazarene University; Bourbonnais, Ill. 60901 (P)	1,700	55	82	$10,696	$10,696	$4,560
Principia College; Elsah, Ill. 62028 (P)	533	55	93	$13,206	$13,206	$5,586
Quincy University; Quincy, Ill. 62301 (P)	1,050	51	71	$12,080	$12,080	$4,420
Rockford College; Rockford, Ill. 61108 (P)	1,066	64	75	$14,750	$14,750	$4,500
Roosevelt University; Chicago, Ill. 60605 (P)	4,279	59	75	$10,830	$10,830	$5,500
Saint Xavier University; Chicago, Ill. 60655 (P)	2,378	73	82	$12,450	$12,450	$5,184
School of the Art Institute of Chicago; Chicago, Ill. 60603 (P)	1,430	57	76	$17,160	$17,160	$5,150
Southern Illinois University-Carbondale; Carbondale, Ill. 62901 (Pub)	18,712	41	72	$ 2,550	$ 7,650	$3,489
Southern Illinois University-Edwardsville; Edwardsville, Ill. 62026 (Pub)	8,610	57	85	$ 1,928	$ 5,784	$3,238
Trinity Christian College; Palos Heights, Ill. 60463 (P)	619	63	94	$11,250	$11,250	$4,435
Trinity International University; Deerfield, Ill. 60015 (P)	769	49	93	$11,700	$11,700	$4,560
University of Chicago; Chicago, Ill. 60637 (P)	3,515	46	58	$22,086	$22,086	$7,604
University of Illinois-Chicago; Chicago, Ill. 60680 (Pub)	16,190	54	61	$ 2,870	$ 8,610	$5,528
University of Illinois-Urbana-Champaign; Urbana, Ill. 61801 (Pub)	26,738	46	70	$ 3,150	$ 8,580	$4,560
Vandercook College of Music; Chicago, Ill. 60616 (P)	65	40	85	$ 9,400	$ 9,400	$4,800
Western Illinois University; Macomb, Ill. 61455 (Pub)	9,644	51	69	$ 2,040	$ 6,120	$3,613
Wheaton College (Ill.); Wheaton, Ill. 60187 (P)	2,315	51	52			$4,550
INDIANA						
Anderson College; Anderson, Ind. 46012 (P)	2,097	55	77	$11,840	$11,840	$3,980
Ball State University; Muncie, Ind. 47306 (Pub)	16,558	53	89	$ 3,188	$ 8,448	$3,952
Butler University; Indianapolis, Ind. 46208 (P)	3,165	60	85	$15,570	$15,570	$5,300
Calumet College of Saint Joseph; Whiting, Ind. 46394 (P)	1,125	69	71	$ 5,460	$ 5,460	
DePauw University; Greencastle, Ind. 46135 (P)	2,147	55	81	$15,955	$15,955	$5,400
Earlham College; Richmond, Ind. 47374 (P)	1,005	57	83	$17,898	$17,898	$4,412
Franklin College; Franklin, Ind. 46131 (P)	908	51	86	$12,210	$12,210	$4,000
Goshen College; Goshen, Ind. 46526 (P)	1,014	56	87	$11,450	$11,450	$4,000
Grace College and Seminary; Winona Lake, Ind. 46590 (P)	645	59	72	$ 9,820	$ 9,820	$4,282
Hanover College; Hanover, Ind. 47243 (P)	1,051	52	71	$ 9,750	$ 9,750	$4,550
Huntington College; Huntington, Ind. 46750 (P)	700	53	87	$11,700	$11,700	$4,570
Indiana Institute of Technology; Fort Wayne, Ind. 46803 (P)	1,380	35	65	$10,850	$10,850	$4,300
Indiana State University; Terre Haute, Ind. 47809 (Pub)	9,490	52	88	$ 1,598	$ 3,196	$4,143
Indiana University-Bloomington; Bloomington, Ind. 47405 (Pub)	27,480	55	83	$ 3,326	$10,890	$4,220
Indiana University-Kokomo; Kokomo, Ind. 46904 (Pub)	3,209	68	99	$ 2,612	$ 6,773	
Indiana University-Purdue Univ. Fort Wayne; Fort Wayne, Ind. 46805 (Pub)	9,889	57	99	$ 2,700	$ 6,420	
Indiana University-Purdue Univ. Indianapolis; Indianapolis, Ind. 46202 (Pub)	19,950	60	88	$ 3,065	$ 9,405	$3,100
Indiana University-South Bend; South Bend, Ind. 46634 (Pub)	6,102	62	78	$ 2,763	$ 7,561	
Indiana University East; Richmond, Ind. 47374 (Pub)	2,302	68	100	$ 2,611	$ 6,773	
Indiana University Northwest; Gary, Ind. 46408 (Pub)	4,620	67	53	$ 2,611	$ 6,772	
Indiana University Southeast; New Albany, Ind. 47150 (Pub)	4,854	62	99	$ 2,715	$ 7,044	
Indiana Wesleyan University; Marion, Ind. 46953 (P)	1,947	62	72	$10,260	$10,260	$4,042
Manchester College; North Manchester, Ind. 46962 (P)	1,030	48	80	$12,070	$12,070	$4,330
Marian College; Indianapolis, Ind. 46222 (P)	1,352	66	56	$11,440	$11,440	$4,212
Oakland City University; Oakland City, Ind. 47660 (P)	1,030	46	96	$ 7,800	$ 7,800	$3,146
Purdue University-Calumet; Hammond, Ind. 46323 (Pub)	8,345	51	85	$ 2,436	$ 6,132	$5,345
Purdue University-West Lafayette; West Lafayette, Ind. 47907 (Pub)	26,401	42	90	$ 3,210	$10,640	$4,520
Rose-Hulman Institute of Technology; Terre Haute, Ind. 47803 (P)	1,500	12	63	$16,900	$16,900	$5,000
Saint Francis College (Ind.); Fort Wayne, Ind. 46808 (P)	954	73	81	$10,710	$10,710	$4,270
Saint Joseph's College (Ind.); Rensselaer, Ind. 47978 (P)	876	54	85	$12,260	$12,260	$4,780
Saint Mary-of-the-Woods College; St. Mary-of-the-Wood, Ind. 47876 (P)	1,204	100	86	$11,940	$11,940	$4,570
Saint Mary's College (Ind.); Notre Dame, Ind. 46556 (P)	1,527	100	82	$14,170	$14,170	$4,966
Taylor University; Upland, Ind. 46989 (P)	1,866	54	61	$12,560	$12,560	$4,220
Tri-State University; Angola, Ind. 46703 (P)	1,146	28	85	$10,749	$10,749	$4,644
University of Evansville; Evansville, Ind. 47722 (P)	3,085	56	91	$13,600	$13,600	$4,520
University of Indianapolis; Indianapolis, Ind. 46227 (P)	2,906	60	89	$12,350	$12,350	$4,330
University of Notre Dame; Notre Dame, Ind. 46556 (P)	7,857	45	40	$20,000	$20,000	$4,850
University of Southern Indiana; Evansville, Ind. 47712 (Pub)	7,324	57	99	$ 2,400	$ 5,888	$1,920
Valparaiso University; Valparaiso, Ind. 46383 (P)	2,754	56	86	$14,560	$14,560	$3,930
Wabash College; Crawfordsville, Ind. 47933 (P)	824	0	69	$15,400	$15,400	$4,780
IOWA						
Briar Cliff College; Sioux City, Iowa 51104 (P)	1,116	68	85	$11,280	$11,280	$4,017

Institution Name; City, State Zip (Control)	Students	Percent		Tuition		Room and board
		Women	Accepted	In-State	Out-of-State	
Buena Vista University; Storm Lake, Iowa 50588 (P)	2,473	62	91	$14,848	$14,848	$4,375
Central College; Pella, Iowa 50219 (P)	1,236	57	86	$12,152	$12,152	$3,808
Clarke College; Dubuque, Iowa 52001 (P)	1,050	66	82	$11,730	$11,730	$4,480
Coe College; Cedar Rapids, Iowa 52402 (P)	1,202	54	90	$16,170	$16,170	$4,570
Cornell College; Mount Vernon, Iowa 52314 (P)	1,105	60	88	$17,080	$17,080	$4,670
Dordt College; Sioux Center, Iowa 51250 (P)	1,269	50	91	$11,300	$11,300	$3,030
Drake University; Des Moines, Iowa 50311 (P)	3,630	59	93	$14,380	$14,380	$4,920
Graceland College; Lamoni, Iowa 50140 (P)	1,061	51	59	$10,750	$10,750	$3,500
Grand View College; Des Moines, Iowa 50316 (P)	1,478	63	88	$10,400	$10,900	$3,620
Grinnell College; Grinnell, Iowa 50112 (P)	1,314	55	73	$17,142	$17,142	$5,152
Iowa State University; Ames, Iowa 50011 (Pub)	18,235	43	90	$ 2,470	$ 8,284	$3,508
Iowa Wesleyan College; Mount Pleasant, Iowa 52641 (P)	794	62	83	$11,640	$11,640	$3,920
Loras College; Dubuque, Iowa 52004 (P)	1,736	52	81	$11,800	$11,800	$4,000
Luther College; Decorah, Iowa 52101 (P)	2,409	60	93	$15,630	$15,630	$3,700
Maharishi International University; Fairfield, Iowa 52557 (P)	813	43	99	$14,670	$14,670	$4,960
Marycrest International University; Davenport, Iowa 52804 (P)	905	60	63	$11,226	$11,226	$4,462
Morningside College; Sioux City, Iowa 51106 (P)	1,178	57	94	$11,060	$11,060	$4,070
Mount Mercy College; Cedar Rapids, Iowa 52402 (P)	1,131	70	87	$11,370	$11,370	$3,800
Mount Saint Clare College; Clinton, Iowa 52732 (P)	515	65	86	$10,900	$10,900	$3,870
Northwestern College (Iowa); Orange City, Iowa 51041 (P)	1,161	57	95	$10,850	$10,850	$3,250
Saint Ambrose University; Davenport, Iowa 52803 (P)	1,735	55	85	$11,740	$11,740	$4,420
Simpson College (Iowa); Indianola, Iowa 50125 (P)	1,802	56	84	$12,975	$12,975	$4,290
University of Dubuque; Dubuque, Iowa 52001 (P)	672	45	85	$12,150	$12,150	$4,340
University of Iowa; Iowa City, Iowa 52242 (Pub)	18,586	54	86	$ 2,566	$ 9,422	$3,825
University of Northern Iowa; Cedar Falls, Iowa 50614 (Pub)	11,405	57	84	$ 2,470	$ 6,688	$3,272
Upper Iowa University; Fayette, Iowa 52142 (P)	640	20	74	$ 9,750	$ 9,750	$3,770
Wartburg College; Waverly, Iowa 50677 (P)	1,467	57	85	$12,870	$12,870	$3,860
Westmar University; Le Mars, Iowa 51031 (P)	757	30	76	$10,480	$10,480	$4,620
William Penn College; Oskaloosa, Iowa 52577 (P)	737	46	79	$11,000	$11,000	$3,490
KANSAS						
Baker University; Baldwin City, Kans. 66006 (P)	1,424	51	79	$ 9,600	$ 9,600	$4,300
Benedictine College; Atchison, Kans. 66002 (P)	925	46	99	$11,100	$11,100	$4,460
Bethany College (Kans.); Lindsborg, Kans. 67456-1897 (P)	698	48	65	$10,540	$10,540	$3,335
Bethel College (Kans.); North Newton, Kans. 67117 (P)	618	58	89	$10,290	$10,290	$4,200
Emporia State University; Emporia, Kans. 66801 (Pub)	4,495	61	100	$ 1,406	$ 5,516	$3,345
Fort Hays State University; Hays, Kans. 67601 (Pub)	4,346	53	98	$ 1,787	$ 5,459	$2,496
Friends University; Wichita, Kans. 67213 (P)	1,968	56	61	$10,015	$10,015	$3,250
Kansas Newman College; Wichita, Kans. 67213 (P)	1,857	69	35	$ 9,000	$ 9,000	$3,626
Kansas State University; Manhattan, Kans. 66506 (Pub)	16,935	46	69	$ 2,400	$ 8,400	$3,500
Kansas Wesleyan University; Salina, Kans. 67401 (P)	675	63	72	$ 9,120	$ 9,120	$3,500
McPherson College; McPherson, Kans. 67460 (P)	426	47		$ 9,250	$ 9,250	$4,840
Mid America Nazarene University; Olathe, Kans. 66062 (P)	1,266	55	100	$ 8,790	$ 8,790	$4,496
Ottawa University; Ottawa, Kans. 66067 (P)	575	49	67	$ 8,350	$ 8,350	$3,620
Pittsburg State University; Pittsburg, Kans. 66762 (Pub)	6,426	49	93	$ 2,016	$ 6,280	$3,316
Saint Mary College; Leavenworth, Kans. 66048 (P)	839	72	96	$ 9,750	$ 9,750	$4,950
Southwestern College; Winfield, Kans. 67156 (P)	635	53	96	$ 8,650	$ 8,650	$3,796
Sterling College; Sterling, Kans. 67579 (P)	475	51	69	$10,076	$10,076	$3,884
Tabor College; Hillsboro, Kans. 67063 (P)	500	50	62	$10,360	$10,360	$4,000
University of Kansas; Lawrence, Kans. 66045 (Pub)	16,659	51	62	$ 1,965	$ 8,269	$3,736
Washburn University; Topeka, Kans. 66621 (Pub)	5,400	59	96	$ 3,050	$ 6,690	$3,410
Wichita State University; Wichita, Kans. 67260 (Pub)	10,536	57	76	$ 1,665	$ 7,195	$3,639
KENTUCKY						
Alice Lloyd College; Pippa Passes, Ky. 41844 (P)	511	52	69	$ 6,360	$ 4,000	$2,480
Asbury College; Wilmore, Ky. 40390 (P)	1,167	58	82	$11,234	$11,234	$3,150
Bellarmine College; Louisville, Ky. 40205 (P)	1,282	58	88	$10,850	$10,850	$3,580
Berea College; Berea, Ky. 40404 (P)	1,524	55	31	$ —	$ —	$3,168
Brescia College; Owensboro, Ky. 42301 (P)	716	30	84	$ 8,400	$ 8,400	$3,456
Campbellsville University; Campbellsville, Ky. 42718-2799 (P)	1,492	53	66	$ 7,200	$ 7,200	$3,610
Centre College; Danville, Ky. 40422 (P)	980	49	82	$13,000	$13,000	$4,600
Cumberland College; Williamsburg, Ky. 40769 (P)	1,517	52	64	$ 8,430	$ 8,430	$3,776
Eastern Kentucky University; Richmond, Ky. 40475 (Pub)	14,558	56	95	$ 1,970	$ 5,450	$3,396
Georgetown College; Georgetown, Ky. 40324 (P)	1,175	57	90	$ 9,540	$ 9,640	$4,050
Kentucky State University; Frankfort, Ky. 40601 (P)	2,280	56	63	$ 1,740	$ 5,220	$3,088
Kentucky Wesleyan College; Owensboro, Ky. 42302 (P)	714	56	80	$ 9,220	$ 9,220	$4,500
Lindsey Wilson College; Columbia, Ky. 42728 (P)	1,006	51	79	$ 7,008	$ 7,008	$3,550
Morehead State University; Morehead, Ky. 40351 (Pub)	6,823	57	89	$ 2,090	$ 5,570	$2,400
Murray State University; Murray, Ky. 42071-0009 (Pub)	7,120	55	66	$ 1,740	$ 5,220	$3,220

Institution Name; City, State Zip (Control)	Students	Percent		Tuition		Room and board
		Women	Accepted	In-State	Out-of-State	
Northern Kentucky University; Highland Heights, Ky. 41099 (Pub)	10,245	58	100	$ 2,020	$ 5,500	$3,164
Pikeville College; Pikeville, Ky. 41501 (P)	824	69	100	$ 6,500	$ 6,500	$3,050
Spalding University; Louisville, Ky. 40203 (P)	1,055	79	84	$ 9,000	$ 9,000	$2,650
Thomas More College; Crestview Hills, Ky. 41017 (P)	1,237	53	77	$10,970	$10,970	$4,500
Transylvania University; Lexington, Ky. 40508 (P)	918	54	91	$12,150	$12,150	$4,810
University of Kentucky; Lexington, Ky. 40506 (Pub)	17,036	50	78	$ 2,676	$ 7,356	$3,200
University of Louisville; Louisville, Ky. 40292 (Pub)	16,089	52	65	$ 2,570	$ 7,250	$4,480
Western Kentucky University; Bowling Green, Ky. 42101 (Pub)	12,618	55	97	$ 1,740	$ 5,220	$3,110
LOUISIANA						
Centenary College of Louisiana; Shreveport, La. 71134 (P)	734	57	83	$11,050	$11,050	$3,900
Dillard University; New Orleans, La. 70122 (P)	1,584	78	90	$ 8,000	$ 8,000	$4,250
Grambling State University; Grambling, La. 71245 (Pub)	6,828	58	76	$ 4,728	$ 6,374	$2,612
Louisiana College; Pineville, La. 71359 (P)	1,003	59	81	$ 4,488	$ 4,488	$1,529
Louisiana State University-Baton Rouge; Baton Rouge, La. 70803 (Pub)	21,413	50	81	$ 2,687	$ 5,987	$3,570
Louisiana State University-Shreveport; Shreveport, La. 71115 (Pub)	3,354	70	99	$ 2,080	$ 5,010	$2,000
Louisiana Tech University; Ruston, La. 71272 (Pub)	7,882	50	98	$ 2,352	$ 4,347	$2,805
Loyola University New Orleans; New Orleans, La. 70118 (P)	2,595	60	86	$12,948	$12,948	$5,850
McNeese State University; Lake Charles, La. 70609 (Pub)	7,316	59	99	$ 2,012	$ 5,542	$2,310
Nicholls State University; Thibodaux, La. 70310 (Pub)	6,355	59	92	$ 2,017	$ 2,592	$2,700
Northeast Louisiana University; Monroe, La. 71209 (Pub)	10,214	59	96	$ 1,644	$ 4,044	$2,108
Northwestern State University of Louisiana; Natchitoches, La. 71497 (Pub)	8,303	64	100	$ 2,067	$ 4,507	$2,216
Our Lady of Holy Cross College; New Orleans, La. 70114 (P)	1,350	76	99	$ 4,400	$ 4,400	
Southeastern Louisiana University; Hammond, La. 70402 (Pub)	13,121	59	86	$ 2,040	$ 4,272	$2,320
Southern University-Baton Rouge; Baton Rouge, La. 70813 (Pub)	7,976	57		$ 2,028	$ 4,808	$2,952
Southern University of New Orleans; New Orleans, La. 70126 (Pub)				$ 1,662	$ 3,432	
Tulane University; New Orleans, La. 70118-5680 (P)	6,402	50	78	$19,700		$6,314
University of New Orleans; New Orleans, La. 70148 (Pub)	11,689	56	89	$ 2,362	$ 5,154	$3,386
University of Southwestern Louisiana; Lafayette, La. 70504 (Pub)	15,281	57	99	$ 1,885	$ 5,485	$2,250
Xavier University of Louisiana; New Orleans, La. 70125 (P)	2,956	71	88	$ 7,700	$ 7,700	$4,700
MAINE						
Bates College; Lewiston, Maine 04240 (P)	1,672	51	36	$28,650	$28,650	
Bowdoin College; Brunswick, Maine 04011-8441 (P)	1,581	51	29	$22,460	$22,460	$6,115
Colby College; Waterville, Maine 04901 (P)	1,764	52	31	$29,190	$29,190	$5,650
College of the Atlantic; Bar Harbor, Maine 04609 (P)	250	70	69	$16,991	$16,991	$4,975
Husson College; Bangor, Maine 04401 (P)	1,717	62	87	$ 8,700	$ 8,700	$4,740
Maine College of Art; Portland, Maine 04101 (P)	283	53	88	$14,850	$14,850	$6,060
Maine Maritime Academy; Castine, Maine 04420 (Pub)	615	12	78	$ 4,100	$ 7,340	$4,895
Saint Joseph's College (Maine); Windham, Maine 04062-1198 (P)	744	64	80	$11,270	$11,270	$5,650
Thomas College; Waterville, Maine 04901 (P)	712	62	96	$10,200	$10,200	$4,950
Unity College; Unity, Maine 04988 (Pub)	512	40	89	$10,330	$10,330	$5,050
University of Maine; Orono, Maine 04469 (Pub)	2,272	69	74	$ 3,060	$ 7,470	$4,842
University of Maine-Farmington; Farmington, Maine 04938 (Pub)	767	61	96	$ 2,820	$ 6,870	$4,142
University of Maine-Fort Kent; Fort Kent, Maine 04743 (Pub)	915	60	83	$ 2,940	$ 7,200	$3,600
University of Maine-Machias; Machias, Maine 04654 (Pub)	1,403	60	80	$ 2,256	$ 5,496	$4,075
University of Maine-Presque Isle; Presque Isle, Maine 04769 (Pub)	9,161	46	77	$ 3,570	$10,110	$3,704
University of New England; Biddeford, Maine 04005 (P)	1,402	69	71	$13,575	$13,575	$5,595
University of Southern Maine; Gorham, Maine 04038 (Pub)	8,055	59	98	$ 3,330	$ 9,420	$4,554
Westbrook College; Portland, Maine 04103 (P)	1,000	70	66	$11,650	$11,650	$4,900
MARYLAND						
Bowie State University; Bowie, Md. 20715 (Pub)	2,960	61	34	$ 2,814	$ 5,542	$4,075
Capitol College; Laurel, Md. 20708 (P)	609	15	91	$ 9,192	$ 9,192	$2,952
College of Notre Dame of Maryland; Baltimore, Md. 21210 (P)	2,650	100	83	$11,740	$11,740	$5,845
Columbia Union College; Takoma Park, Md. 20912 (P)	1,172	60	79	$10,950	$10,950	$3,990
Coppin State College; Baltimore, Md. 21216 (Pub)	2,931	64	55	$ 2,867	$ 6,872	$5,050
Frostburg State University; Frostburg, Md. 21532 (Pub)	4,852	49	85	$ 3,280	$ 6,990	$4,770
Goucher College; Baltimore, Md. 21204 (P)	1,020	71	87	$18,400	$18,400	$6,800

Institution Name; City, State Zip (Control)	Students	Percent		Tuition		Room and board
		Women	Accepted	In-State	Out-of-State	
Hood College; Frederick, Md. 21701 (P)	1,034	94	84	$16,418	$16,418	$6,792
Johns Hopkins University; Baltimore, Md. 21218 (P)	3,623	38	40	$21,700	$21,700	$7,355
Loyola College (Md.); Baltimore, Md. 21210 (P)	3,205	55	71	$15,200	$15,200	$6,720
Maryland Institute, College of Art; Baltimore, Md. 21217 (P)	903	53	63	$16,750	$16,750	$5,540
Morgan State University; Baltimore, Md. 21239 (Pub)	5,356	59	47	$ 2,364	$ 6,526	$4,990
Mount Saint Mary's College (Md.); Emmitsburg, Md. 21727 (P)	1,476	53	78	$15,450	$15,450	$6,450
Saint John's College (Md.); Annapolis, Md. 21404 (P)	438	48	86	$20,980	$20,980	$6,010
Saint Mary's College of Maryland; St. Mary's City, Md. 20686 (Pub)	1,444	57	58	$ 5,000	$ 8,550	$5,220
Salisbury State University; Salisbury, Md. 21801 (Pub)	5,294	57	48	$ 2,746	$ 6,498	$5,240
Towson State University; Towson, Md. 21252-0001 (Pub)	13,063	59	69	$ 3,080	$ 8,158	$5,044
United States Naval Academy; Annapolis, Md. 21402 (Pub)	4,040	16	18	$ —	$ —	$ —
University of Baltimore; Baltimore, Md. 21201 (Pub)	1,966	53	92	$ 3,804	$ 9,300	
University of Maryland, College Park; College Park, Md. 20742 (Pub)	24,529	48	61	$ 4,460	$10,589	$5,807
University of Maryland-Baltimore County; Baltimore, Md. 21228 (Pub)	8,808	50	61	$ 4,150	$ 8,742	$5,025
University of Maryland-Eastern Shore; Princess Anne, Md. 21853 (Pub)	2,862	58	75	$ 3,240	$ 7,776	$4,330
Villa Julie College; Stevenson, Md. 21153 (P)	1,844	82	81	$ 8,510	$ 8,510	$3,090
Washington College; Chestertown, Md. 21620 (P)	1,006	57	84	$17,800	$17,800	$5,740
Western Maryland College; Westminster, Md. 21157 (P)	1,382	54	83	$16,125	$16,125	$5,365
MASSACHUSETTS						
American International College; Springfield, Mass. 01109 (P)	1,426	52	77	$ 9,750	$ 9,750	$5,310
Amherst College; Amherst, Mass. 01002 (P)	1,607	47	19	$22,680	$22,680	$6,000
Anna Maria College; Paxton, Mass. 01612 (P)	411	61	84	$11,600	$11,600	$5,256
Assumption College; Worcester, Mass. 01615 (P)	2,177	60	72	$14,700	$14,700	$6,020
Atlantic Union College; South Lancaster, Mass. 01561 (P)	1,193	52	94	$11,000	$11,000	$3,600
Babson College; Babson Park, Mass. 02157 (P)	1,627	63	48	$18,940	$18,940	$7,800
Bentley College; Waltham, Mass. 02154 (P)	3,116	42	66	$16,400	$16,400	$6,810
Berklee College of Music; Boston, Mass. 02215 (P)	2,850	20	75	$14,150	$14,150	$7,650
Boston College; Chestnut Hill, Mass. 02167 (P)	8,958	53	41	$19,770	$19,770	$7,770
Boston Conservatory; Boston, Mass. 02215 (P)	318	70	45	$14,300	$14,300	$6,800
Boston University; Boston, Mass. 02215 (P)	14,892	57	53	$21,970	$21,970	$7,570
Bradford College; Haverhill, Mass. 01835-7393 (P)	588	62	78	$15,380	$15,380	$6,590
Brandeis University; Waltham, Mass. 02254 (P)	2,968	54	53	$21,440	$21,440	$6,910
Bridgewater State College; Bridgewater, Mass. 02325 (Pub)	6,932	57	69	$ 1,338	$ 5,726	$4,313
Clark University; Worcester, Mass. 01610 (P)	1,840	58	79	$20,500	$20,500	$4,250
College of the Holy Cross; Worcester, Mass. 01610 (P)	2,656	53	44	$19,700	$19,700	$6,750
Curry College; Milton, Mass. 02186 (P)	1,442	51	81	$15,250	$15,250	$5,815
Eastern Nazarene College; Quincy, Mass. 02170 (P)	709	57	78	$10,110	$10,110	$3,750
Elms College; Chicopee, Mass. 01013 (P)	961	100	93	$12,950	$12,950	$5,000
Emerson College; Boston, Mass. 02116 (P)	2,340	56	67	$17,376	$17,376	$8,250
Emmanuel College (Mass.B516); Boston, Mass. 02115 (P)	1,376	86	84	$14,212	$14,212	$6,785
Fitchburg State College; Fitchburg, Mass. 01420 (Pub)	4,239	58	59	$ 1,338	$ 5,726	$4,110
Framingham State College; Framingham, Mass. 01701 (Pub)	4,296	65	73	$ 1,270	$ 5,950	$3,943
Gordon College; Wenham, Mass. 01984 (P)	1,224	63	85	$14,520	$14,520	$4,840
Hampshire College; Amherst, Mass. 01002 (P)	1,068	56	70	$23,480	$23,480	$6,225
Harvard and Radcliffe Colleges; Cambridge, Mass. 02138 (P)	7,098	44	11	$19,770	$19,770	$6,995
Hellenic College; Brookline, Mass. 02146 (P)	64	29	77	$ 7,400	$ 7,400	$5,600
Lesley College; Cambridge, Mass. 02138 (P)	508	100	75	$13,700	$13,700	$6,440
Massachusetts College of Art; Boston, Mass. 02115 (Pub)	2,057	59	54	$ 1,320	$ 6,900	$6,400
Massachusetts College of Pharmacy & Allied Health; Boston, Mass. 02215 (P)	1,235	61	66	$12,400	$12,400	$7,250
Massachusetts Institute of Technology; Cambridge, Mass. 02139 (P)	4,429	39	25	$23,100	$23,100	$6,550
Massachusetts Maritime Academy; Buzzards Bay, Mass. 02532 (Pub)	750	10	67	$ 1,390	$ 6,634	$3,800
Merrimack College; North Andover, Mass. 01845 (P)	2,000	50	79	$14,530	$14,530	$7,000
Mount Holyoke College; South Hadley, Mass. 01075 (P)	1,889	100	65	$22,200	$22,200	$6,525
New England Conservatory of Music; Boston, Mass. 02115 (P)	371	53	51	$17,900	$17,900	$8,375
Nichols College; Dudley, Mass. 01571 (P)	1,247	35	86	$10,744	$10,744	$6,200
North Adams State College; North Adams, Mass. 01247 (Pub)	1,516	51	68	$ 1,338	$ 5,726	$4,340
Northeastern University; Boston, Mass. 02115 (P)	11,387	47	74	$16,320	$16,320	$8,265
Pine Manor College; Chestnut Hill, Mass. 02167 (P)	370	100	78	$16,000	$16,000	$6,900
Regis College; Weston, Mass. 02193 (P)	1,206	100	91	$15,250	$15,250	$6,900

Institution Name; City, State Zip (Control)	Students	Percent		Tuition		Room and board
		Women	Accepted	In-State	Out-of-State	
Salem State College; Salem, Mass. 01970 (Pub)	8,607	57		$ 3,198	$ 7,332	$3,689
School of the Museum of Fine Arts; Boston, Mass. 02115 (P)	522	61	77	$13,995	$13,995	
Simmons College; Boston, Mass. 02115 (P)	1,377	100	69	$17,472	$17,472	$7,228
Simon's Rock College of Bard; Great Barrington, Mass. 01230 (P)	334	56	39	$19,250	$19,250	$6,100
Smith College; Northampton, Mass. 01063 (P)	2,593	100	52	$21,360	$21,360	$7,250
Springfield College; Springfield, Mass. 01109 (P)	2,046	51	55	$12,830	$12,830	$5,800
Stonehill College; North Easton, Mass. 02357 (P)	2,776	57	54	$13,720	$13,720	$6,660
Suffolk University; Boston, Mass. 02108 (P)	3,070	56	72	$12,840	$12,840	$8,350
Tufts University; Medford, Mass. 02155 (P)	4,539	53	31	$22,230	$22,230	$6,838
University of Massachusetts-Amherst; Amherst, Mass. 01003 (Pub)	19,467	48	74	$ 2,004	$ 8,952	$4,520
University of Massachusetts-Boston; Boston, Mass. 02125-3393 (Pub)	8,918	56	66	$ 2,004	$ 8,842	
University of Massachusetts-Dartmouth; North Dartmouth, Mass. 02747-2300 (Pub)	4,846	50	67	$ 4,151	$10,733	$6,752
University of Massachusetts-Lowell; Lowell, Mass. 01854 (Pub)	6,087	40	80	$ 4,422	$10,069	$4,677
Wellesley College; Wellesley, Mass. 02181 (P)	2,197	100	40	$20,554	$20,554	$6,416
Wentworth Institute of Technology; Boston, Mass. 02115 (P)	2,149	14	73	$11,500	$11,500	$6,200
Western New England College; Springfield, Mass. 01119 (P)	2,902	37	70	$10,580	$10,580	$6,120
Westfield State College; Westfield, Mass. 01086 (Pub)	4,137	50	63	$ 1,270	$ 5,440	$4,441
Wheaton College (Mass.); Norton, Mass. 02766 (P)	1,350	66	75	$20,620	$20,620	$6,470
Wheelock College; Boston, Mass. 02215 (P)	682	96	78	$15,520	$15,520	$6,000
Williams College; Williamstown, Mass. 01267 (P)	1,992	49	24	$21,759	$21,759	$6,140
Worcester Polytechnic Institute; Worcester, Mass. 01609 (P)	2,597	21	82	$18,910	$18,910	$6,240
Worcester State College; Worcester, Mass. 01602 (Pub)	5,067	58	67	$ 1,338	$ 5,726	$4,050
MICHIGAN						
Adrian College; Adrian, Mich. 49221 (P)	1,049	49	89	$12,730	$12,730	$4,120
Albion College; Albion, Mich. 49224 (P)	1,580	51	92	$16,160	$16,160	$4,890
Alma College; Alma, Mich. 48801 (P)	1,423	55	90	$14,100	$14,100	$5,052
Andrews University; Berrien Springs, Mich. 49104 (P)	1,853	55	34	$10,896	$10,896	$3,360
Aquinas College; Grand Rapids, Mich. 49506-1799 (P)	1,825	64	92	$12,910	$12,910	$4,324
Calvin College; Grand Rapids, Mich. 49546 (P)	3,993	55	96	$12,225	$12,225	$4,340
Center for Creative Studies; Detroit, Mich. 48202 (P)	921	40	76	$13,620	$13,620	$5,500
Central Michigan University; Mount Pleasant, Mich. 48859 (Pub)	14,640	57	77	$ 3,443	$ 8,191	$4,176
Cleary College; Ypsilanti, Mich. 48197 (P)	644	68	60	$ 7,488	$ 7,488	
Detroit College of Business; Dearborn, Mich. 48126 (P)	5,527	78	100	$ 8,036	$ 8,036	
Eastern Michigan University; Ypsilanti, Mich. 48197 (Pub)	17,982	58	74	$ 3,430	$ 8,088	$4,400
Ferris State University; Big Rapids, Mich. 49307 (Pub)	9,192	44	97	$ 3,812	$ 7,732	$4,792
GMI Engineering and Management Institute; Flint, Mich. 48504 (P)	2,430	19	74	$13,576	$13,576	$3,776
Grand Rapids Baptist College; Grand Rapids, Mich. 49505 (P)	1,082	55	89	$ 7,050	$ 7,050	$4,082
Grand Valley State University; Allendale, Mich. 49401 (Pub)	11,734	60	85	$ 2,866	$ 6,650	$4,380
Hillsdale College; Hillsdale, Mich. 49242 (P)	1,197	50	81	$12,110	$12,110	$5,180
Hope College; Holland, Mich. 49422 (P)	2,825	57	91	$14,878	$14,878	$4,696
Kalamazoo College; Kalamazoo, Mich. 49006 (P)	1,302	58	94	$17,214	$17,214	$5,421
Kendall College of Art and Design; Grand Rapids, Mich. 49503 (P)	527	54	62	$10,500	$10,500	
Lake Superior State University; Sault Sainte Marie, Mich. 49783 (Pub)	3,264	47	94	$ 3,642	$ 7,158	$4,646
Lawrence Technological University; Southfield, Mich. 48075 (P)	3,310	24	80	$ 8,160	$ 8,160	$3,276
Madonna University; Livonia, Mich. 48150 (P)	4,029	76	81	$ 5,670	$ 5,670	$5,986
Marygrove College; Detroit, Mich. 48221 (P)	1,087	85	52	$ 9,190	$ 9,190	$ —
Michigan State University; East Lansing, Mich. 48824 (Pub)	32,318	52	81	$ 4,102	$11,167	$3,942
Michigan Technological University; Houghton, Mich. 49931 (Pub)	5,541	25	94	$ 3,822	$ 9,105	$4,284
Northern Michigan University; Marquette, Mich. 49855 (Pub)	7,144	52	92	$ 1,492	$ 5,264	$4,141
Northwood University; Midland, Mich. 48640 (P)	1,386	37	49	$10,350	$10,350	$4,734
Oakland University; Rochester, Mich. 48309 (Pub)	10,423	63	84	$ 3,448	$10,160	$4,250
Olivet College; Olivet, Mich. 49076 (P)	824	56	83	$12,160	$12,160	$3,920
Saginaw Valley State University; University Center, Mich. 48710 (Pub)	6,385	60	92	$ 2,993	$ 6,261	$4,140
Saint Mary's College (Mich.); Orchard Lake, Mich. 48033 (P)	350	57	52	$ 6,300	$ 6,300	$4,500
Siena Heights College; Adrian, Mich. 49221 (P)	993	55	94	$ 9,970	$ 9,970	$4,220
Spring Arbor College; Spring Arbor, Mich. 49283 (P)	1,916	57	99	$10,280	$10,280	$4,070
University of Detroit Mercy; Detroit, Mich. 48219 (P)	4,484	55	77	$12,216	$12,216	$4,560

| Institution Name; City, State Zip (Control) | Students | Percent | | Tuition | | Room and board |
		Women	Accepted	In-State	Out-of-State	
University of Michigan-Ann Arbor; Ann Arbor, Mich. 48109-1316 (Pub)	23,515	49	68	$ 5,820	$18,450	$5,340
University of Michigan-Dearborn; Dearborn, Mich. 48128 (Pub)	6,744	55	77	$ 2,928	$10,650	
University of Michigan-Flint; Flint, Mich. 48502 (Pub)	5,984	62	83	$ 3,309	$ 9,823	
Wayne State University; Detroit, Mich. 48202 (Pub)	19,248	57	81	$ 3,150	$ 7,020	$3,271
Western Michigan University; Kalamazoo, Mich. 49008 (Pub)	19,803	55	82	$ 3,332	$ 7,795	$4,257
William Tyndale College; Farmington Hills, Mich. 48331 (P)	512	52	81	$ 6,000	$ 6,000	$2,730
MINNESOTA						
Augsburg College; Minneapolis, Minn. 55454 (P)	1,501	54	82	$13,850	$13,850	$4,986
Bemidji State University; Bemidji, Minn. 56601 (Pub)	4,587	52	68	$ 2,520	$ 5,630	$3,369
Bethel College (Minn.); Saint Paul, Minn. 55112 (P)	2,039	60	81	$13,840	$13,840	$4,950
Carleton College; Northfield, Minn. 55057 (P)	1,942	50	50	$20,988	$20,988	$4,290
College of Saint Benedict; Saint Joseph, Minn. 56374 (P)	1,958	100	92	$14,620	$14,620	$4,706
Concordia College (Minn.); St. Paul, Minn. 55104-5494 (P)	1,027	58	68	$11,355	$11,355	$4,200
Crown College; St. Bonifacius, Minn. 55375 (P)	618	54	98	$ 8,340	$ 8,340	$3,920
Gustavus Adolphus College; St. Peter, Minn. 56082 (P)	2,362	54	81	$15,940	$15,940	$4,010
Hamline University; Saint Paul, Minn. 55104 (P)	1,655	57	84	$14,182	$14,182	$4,536
Macalester College; St. Paul, Minn. 55105 (P)	1,715	56	55	$17,580	$17,580	$5,275
Mankato State University; Mankato, Minn. 56002 (Pub)	11,441	51	87	$ 2,518	$ 5,626	$2,965
Martin Luther College; New Ulm, Minn. 56073 (P)	817	47	86	$ 3,990	$ 3,990	$2,205
Minneapolis College of Art & Design; Minneapolis, Minn. 55404 (P)	541	44	83	$13,870	$13,870	$3,600
Moorhead State University; Moorhead, Minn. 56563 (Pub)	5,917	61	90	$ 2,355	$ 5,307	$2,958
Northwestern College (Minn.); St. Paul, Minn. 55113 (P)	1,538	59	75	$12,750	$12,750	
Saint Cloud State University; Saint Cloud, Minn. 56301 (Pub)	13,260	51	86	$ 2,897	$ 5,847	$3,027
Saint John's University (Minn.); Collegeville, Minn. 56321 (P)	1,687	0	87	$14,620	$14,620	$4,574
Saint Mary's University of Minnesota; Winona, Minn. 55987 (P)	1,400	52	88	$11,700	$11,700	$3,900
Southwest State University; Marshall, Minn. 56258 (Pub)	2,362	56	73	$ 2,496	$ 5,624	$2,957
St. Olaf College; Northfield, Minn. 55057 (P)	2,854	59	81	$16,500	$16,500	$4,020
The College of Saint Catherine; Saint Paul, Minn. 55105 (P)	2,198	100	90	$12,960	$12,960	$4,282
The College of Saint Scholastica; Duluth, Minn. 55811 (P)	1,474	74	92	$13,056	$13,056	$3,807
University of Minnesota; Minneapolis, Minn. 55455 (Pub)	930	58	100	$ 3,640		$4,056
University of Minnesota-Crookston; Crookston, Minn. 56716 (Pub)	7,100	47	85	$ 3,850	$11,004	$3,492
University of Minnesota-Duluth; Duluth, Minn. 55812 (Pub)	1,970	57	84	$ 4,404	$12,020	$3,912
University of Minnesota-Morris; Morris, Minn. 56267 (Pub)	19,689	51	55	$ 4,090	$10,787	$3,714
University of Saint Thomas (Minn.); St. Paul, Minn. 55105 (P)	5,066	52	91	$13,728	$13,728	$4,559
Winona State University; Winona, Minn. 55987 (Pub)	6,500	57	65	$ 2,600	$ 5,800	$3,200
MISSISSIPPI						
Alcorn State University; Lorman, Miss. 39096 (Pub)	2,555	61	36	$ 2,389	$ 4,891	$2,229
Belhaven College; Jackson, Miss. 39202 (P)	1,083	60	77	$ 8,390	$ 8,390	$3,190
Delta State University; Cleveland, Miss. 38733 (Pub)	3,344	59	97	$ 2,294	$ 4,888	$2,300
Jackson State University; Jackson, Miss. 39217 (Pub)	5,250	56	55	$ 2,380	$ 2,594	$3,288
Millsaps College; Jackson, Miss. 39210 (P)	1,252	52	78	$12,948	$12,948	$5,176
Mississippi College; Clinton, Miss. 39058 (P)	2,333	57	83	$ 7,200	$ 7,200	$1,720
Mississippi State University; Mississippi State, Miss. 39762 (Pub)	11,548	42	83	$ 1,996	$ 4,816	$4,100
Mississippi University for Women; Columbus, Miss. 39701 (Pub)	3,023	82	76	$ 2,284	$ 4,786	$2,557
Mississippi Valley State University; Itta Bena, Miss. 38941 (Pub)	2,169	58	25	$ 2,278	$ 4,780	$2,300
Rust College; Holly Springs, Miss. 38635 (P)	937	63	44	$ 4,725	$ 4,725	$2,275
Tougaloo College; Tougaloo, Miss. 39174 (P)	982	69	50	$ 5,712	$ 5,712	$2,696
University of Mississippi; University, Miss. 38677 (Pub)	8,384	52	78	$ 2,631	$ 5,451	$3,186
University of Southern Mississippi; Hattiesburg, Miss. 39406 (Pub)	10,647	57	72	$ 2,590	$ 5,410	$2,490
William Carey College; Hattiesburg, Miss. 39401 (P)	1,762	68	52	$ 4,950	$ 4,950	$2,520
MISSOURI						
Avila College; Kansas City, Mo. 64145 (P)	1,063	74	91	$10,100	$10,100	$4,150
Central Methodist College; Fayette, Mo. 65248 (P)	1,152	57	90	$ 9,570	$ 9,570	$3,770
Central Missouri State University; Warrensburg, Mo. 64093 (Pub)	8,934	53	77	$ 2,640	$ 5,280	$3,962
College of the Ozarks; Point Lookout, Mo. 65726 (P)	1,525	53	14			$2,200
Columbia College (Mo.); Columbia, Mo. 65216 (P)	6,719	57	99	$ 8,974	$ 8,974	$4,024

Institution Name; City, State Zip (Control)	Students	Percent Women	Accepted	Tuition In-State	Out-of-State	Room and board
Culver-Stockton College; Canton, Mo. 63435 (P)	1,031	66	84	$ 8,800	$ 8,800	$4,000
Drury College; Springfield, Mo. 65802 (P)	1,371	47	93	$ 9,500	$ 9,500	$3,856
Evangel College; Springfield, Mo. 65802 (P)	1,574	56	87	$ 7,700	$ 7,700	$3,440
Fontbonne College; Saint Louis, Mo. 63105 (P)	1,294	74	84	$10,000	$10,000	$4,400
Hannibal-LaGrange College; Hannibal, Mo. 63401 (P)	882	64	70	$ 6,880	$ 6,880	$2,740
Harris-Stowe State College; Saint Louis, Mo. 63103 (Pub)	1,723	65	66	$ 2,070	$ 4,078	
Kansas City Art Institute; Kansas City, Mo. 64111 (P)	598	44	70	$16,320	$16,320	$4,694
Lincoln University (Mo); Jefferson City, Mo. 65102 (Pub)	3,306	53	90	$ 2,016	$ 4,032	$2,676
Lindenwood College; Saint Charles, Mo. 63301 (P)	2,891	55	55	$ 9,950	$ 9,950	$5,000
Maryville University of Saint Louis; Saint Louis, Mo. 63141-7299 (P)	2,706	71	81	$10,850	$10,850	$5,000
Missouri Baptist College; Saint Louis, Mo. 63141 (P)	2,373	56	75	$ 7,710	$ 7,710	$3,770
Missouri Southern State College; Joplin, Mo. 64801 (Pub)	5,258	54	97	$ 1,960	$ 3,920	$1,585
Missouri Valley College; Marshall, Mo. 65340 (P)	1,214	38	82	$ 9,700	$ 9,700	$5,000
Missouri Western State College; Saint Joseph, Mo. 64507 (Pub)	5,109	62	100	$ 2,406	$ 4,422	$3,098
Northwest Missouri State University; Maryville, Mo. 64468 (Pub)	5,179	55	84	$ 2,415	$ 4,207	$3,690
Park College; Parkville, Mo. 64152 (P)	1,059	63	74	$ 4,100	$ 4,100	$4,220
Rockhurst College; Kansas City, Mo. 64110-2561 (P)	2,157	56	91	$11,000	$11,000	$4,350
Saint Louis College of Pharmacy; Saint Louis, Mo. 63110 (P)	793	62	87	$11,000	$11,000	$4,850
Saint Louis University; Saint Louis, Mo. 63103 (P)	9,476	52	76	$13,900	$13,900	$5,110
Southeast Missouri State University; Cape Girardeau, Mo. 63701 (Pub)	7,799	58	90	$ 2,705	$ 5,015	$3,800
Southwest Baptist University; Bolivar, Mo. 65613 (P)	2,498	65	66	$ 7,708	$ 7,708	$2,623
Southwest Missouri State University; Springfield, Mo. 65804 (Pub)	18,811	54	94	$ 2,670	$ 5,340	$3,340
Stephens College; Columbia, Mo. 65215 (P)	925	95	88	$14,830	$14,830	$5,540
Truman State University; Kirksville, Mo. 63501 (Pub)	6,033	57	72	$ 3,256	$ 5,736	$3,992
University of Missouri-Columbia; Columbia, Mo. 65211 (Pub)	15,651	52	90	$ 3,630	$10,851	$4,172
University of Missouri-Kansas City; Kansas City, Mo. 64110 (Pub)	5,632	53	62	$ 3,330	$ 6,624	$3,875
University of Missouri-Rolla; Rolla, Mo. 65401 (Pub)	4,342	24	97	$ 4,388	$11,334	$4,220
University of Missouri-Saint Louis; St. Louis, Mo. 63121 (Pub)	9,498	58	81	$ 3,688	$ 9,643	$4,845
Washington University in Saint Louis; Saint Louis, Mo. 63130-4899 (P)	5,033	49	51	$21,000	$21,000	$6,593
Webster University; Saint Louis, Mo. 63119 (P)	4,202	64	69	$10,292	$10,292	$4,850
Westminster College (Mo.); Fulton, Mo. 65251 (P)	662	40	89	$11,700	$11,700	$4,330
William Jewell College; Liberty, Mo. 64068 (P)	1,172	60	87	$11,130	$11,130	$3,220
William Woods University; Fulton, Mo. 65251 (P)	971	95	83	$11,850	$11,850	$5,000
MONTANA						
Carroll College (Mont.); Helena, Mont. 59625 (P)	1,352	63	94	$11,316	$11,316	$4,384
Montana State University-Billings; Billings, Mont. 59101 (Pub)	4,006	63	100	$ 2,388	$ 6,559	$4,050
Montana State University-Bozeman; Bozeman, Mont. 59717 (Pub)	10,432	44	75	$ 2,677	$ 9,776	$4,236
Montana State University-Northern; Havre, Mont. 59501 (Pub)	1,509	52	100	$ 2,349	$ 6,661	$3,490
Montana Tech of the University of Montana; Butte, Mont. 59701 (Pub)	1,886	36	83	$ 2,365	$ 6,769	$3,560
Rocky Mountain College; Billings, Mont. 59102 (P)	937	53	99	$ 9,994	$ 9,994	$4,992
University of Great Falls; Great Falls, Mont. 59405 (P)	1,237	68	100	$ 6,900	$ 6,900	$1,320
University of Montana; Missoula, Mont. 59812 (Pub)	9,854	51	83	$ 2,766	$ 7,468	$4,162
Western Montana College; Dillon, Mont. 59725 (Pub)	1,115	44	95	$ 2,400	$ 6,600	$3,800
NEBRASKA						
Chadron State College; Chadron, Nebr. 69337 (Pub)	2,615	54	100	$ 1,650	$ 3,300	$2,926
Clarkson College; Omaha, Nebr. 68131 (P)	426	90	39	$ 7,570	$ 7,570	$1,850
College of Saint Mary; Omaha, Nebr. 68124 (P)	1,069	99	81	$10,996	$10,996	$4,080
Concordia College (Nebr.); Seward, Nebr. 68434 (P)	949	56	84	$10,150	$10,150	$3,540
Creighton University; Omaha, Nebr. 68178 (P)	3,679	59	92	$11,746	$11,746	$4,726
Dana College; Blair, Nebr. 68008 (P)	614	54	91	$10,500	$10,500	$3,780
Doane College; Crete, Nebr. 68333 (P)	1,476	53	90	$10,680	$10,680	$3,390
Hastings College; Hastings, Nebr. 68902 (P)	1,075	53	74	$10,290	$10,290	$3,594
Midland Lutheran College; Fremont, Nebr. 68025 (P)	1,062	55	89	$12,300	$12,300	$3,260
Nebraska Wesleyan University; Lincoln, Nebr. 68504 (P)	1,561	57	99	$10,284	$10,284	$3,520
Peru State College; Peru, Nebr. 68421 (Pub)	2,058	55	75	$ 1,650	$ 330	$2,966
Union College; Lincoln, Nebr. 68506 (P)	553	55	90	$ 9,550	$ 9,550	$3,120
University of Nebraska-Kearney; Kearney, Nebr. 68849 (Pub)	7,141	53	96	$ 1,823	$ 3,413	$2,888
University of Nebraska-Lincoln; Lincoln, Nebr. 68588 (Pub)	18,954	46	83	$ 2,250	$ 6,120	$3,525
University of Nebraska-Omaha; Omaha, Nebr. 68182 (Pub)	12,078	53	96	$ 1,796	$ 4,847	
Wayne State College; Wayne, Nebr. 68787 (Pub)	3,212	57	99	$ 1,650	$ 3,300	$2,870

Institution Name; City, State Zip (Control)	Students	Percent		Tuition		Room and board
		Women	Accepted	In-State	Out-of-State	
NEVADA						
Deep Springs College; Dyer, Nev. 89010 (P)	25	0	8	$ —	$ —	$ —
Sierra Nevada College; Incline Village, Nev. 89450 (P)	500	40	97	$10,200	$10,200	$5,200
University of Nevada-Las Vegas; Las Vegas, Nev. 89154 (Pub)	15,663	53	85	$ 1,995	$ 7,430	$5,300
University of Nevada-Reno; Reno, Nev. 89557 (Pub)	9,150	51	86	$ 1,920	$ 7,020	$2,195
NEW HAMPSHIRE						
Colby-Sawyer College; New London, N.H. 03257 (P)	675	62	81	$15,530	$15,530	$5,950
Daniel Webster College; Nashua, N.H. 03063 (P)	536	30	81	$14,280	$14,280	$5,650
Dartmouth College; Hanover, N.H. 03755 (P)	4,285	48	20	$21,951	$21,951	$6,282
Franklin Pierce College; Rindge, N.H. 03461 (P)	1,327	48	75	$14,850	$14,850	$4,930
Keene State College; Keene, N.H. 03435 (Pub)	732	58	76	$ 2,850	$ 8,510	$4,508
New England College; Henniker, N.H. 03242 (P)	978	43	86	$15,784	$15,784	$5,920
New Hampshire College; Manchester, N.H. 03106 (P)	3,975	45	81	$12,400	$12,400	$5,756
Notre Dame College; Manchester, N.H. 03104 (P)	750	73	90	$11,440	$11,440	$5,295
Plymouth State College; Plymouth, N.H. 03264 (Pub)	4,015	50	86	$ 2,850	$ 8,510	$4,394
Rivier College; Nashua, N.H. 03060 (P)	1,728	84	78	$12,300	$12,300	$5,380
Saint Anselm College; Manchester, N.H. 03102 (P)	1,928	57	84	$14,550	$14,550	$5,710
University of New Hampshire; Durham, N.H. 03824 (Pub)	10,649	56	77	$ 4,020	$12,990	$4,354
NEW JERSEY						
Bloomfield College; Bloomfield, N.J. 07003 (P)	1,929	69	50	$ 9,100	$ 9,100	$4,650
Caldwell College; Caldwell, N.J. 07006 (P)	1,646	62	67	$10,800	$10,800	$5,300
Centenary College; Hackettstown, N.J. 07840 (P)	920	74	83	$11,900	$11,900	$5,800
College of Saint Elizabeth; Morristown, N.J. 07960 (P)	1,385	92	83	$11,400	$11,400	$5,400
Drew University; Madison, N.J. 07940 (P)	1,475	58	74	$19,872	$19,872	$5,972
Fairleigh Dickinson University; Rutherford, N.J. 07070 (P)	7,010	52	65	$12,600	$12,600	$5,864
Felician College; Lodi, N.J. 07644 (P)	978	85	73	$ 8,550	$ 8,550	
Georgian Court College; Lakewood, N.J. 08701 (P)	1,667	95	94	$10,332	$10,332	$4,500
Jersey City State College; Jersey City, N.J. 07305 (Pub)	6,213	56	49	$ 3,528	$ 4,998	$5,000
Kean College of New Jersey; Union, N.J. 07083 (Pub)	9,879	63		$ 3,367	$ 4,684	$4,970
Livingstone College/Hood Theological Seminary; New Brunswick, N.J. 08903 (P)	3,032	39	60	$ 6,090	$ 6,090	$3,450
Monmouth University (N.J.); W. Long Branch, N.J. 07764-1898 (P)	3,875	57	85	$13,270	$13,270	$6,623
Montclair State University; Upper Montclair, N.J. 07043 (Pub)	9,203	60	46	$ 3,466	$ 4,906	$5,334
New Jersey Institute of Technology; Newark, N.J. 07102 (Pub)	5,007	19	67	$ 4,638	$ 8,982	$5,630
Princeton University; Princeton, N.J. 08544 (P)	4,601	46	13	$22,000	$22,000	$6,325
Ramapo College of New Jersey; Mahwah, N.J. 07430 (Pub)	4,532	54	50	$ 3,752	$ 5,496	$5,426
Richard Stockton College of New Jersey; Pomona, N.J. 08240 (Pub)	5,979	56	48	$ 2,624	$ 4,224	$4,626
Rider University; Lawrenceville, N.J. 08648 (P)	3,633	60	85	$14,400	$14,400	$6,030
Rowan College of New Jersey; Glassboro, N.J. 08028 (Pub)	7,933	56	43	$ 2,210	$ 4,110	$4,715
Rutgers University-Camden College of Arts & Sciences; Camden, N.J. 08102 (Pub)	2,223	60	57	$ 4,262	$ 8,676	$5,134
Rutgers University-College of Engineering; New Brunswick, N.J. 08903-2101 (Pub)	2,156	20	72	$ 4,732	$ 9,626	$5,134
Rutgers University-College of Nursing; Newark, N.J. 07102 (Pub)	370	90	26	$ 4,262	$ 8,676	$5,134
Rutgers University-College of Pharmacy; New Brunswick, N.J. 08903-2101 (Pub)	899	62	39	$ 4,732	$ 9,626	$5,134
Rutgers University-Cook College; New Brunswick, N.J. 08903-2101 (Pub)	3,160	50	61	$ 4,732	$ 9,626	$5,134
Rutgers University-Douglass College; New Brunswick, N.J. 08903-2101 (Pub)	2,965	100	71	$ 4,262	$ 8,676	$5,134
Rutgers University-Livingston College; New Brunswick, N.J. 08903-2101 (Pub)	3,032	39	61	$ 4,262	$ 8,676	$5,134
Rutgers University-Mason Gross School of the Arts; New Brunswick, N.J. 08903-2101 (Pub)	499	54	23	$ 4,262	$ 8,676	$5,134
Rutgers University-Newark College of Arts & Sciences; Newark, N.J. 07102 (Pub)	3,684	53	52	$ 4,262	$ 8,676	$5,134
Rutgers University-Rutgers College; New Brunswick, N.J. 08903-2101 (Pub)	10,317	51	52	$ 4,262	$ 8,676	$5,134
Saint Peter's College; Jersey City, N.J. 07306 (P)	3,437	53	83	$11,228	$11,228	$5,530
Seton Hall University; South Orange, N.J. 07079 (P)	4,096	52	80	$12,300	$12,300	$6,796
Stevens Institute of Technology; Hoboken, N.J. 07030 (P)	1,363	22	70	$18,300	$18,300	$6,400
The College of New Jersey; Ewing, N.J. 08628-0718 (Pub)	5,744	60	45	$ 3,465	$ 6,051	$5,750
Thomas Edison State College; Trenton, N.J. 08608 (Pub)	8,575	41	100	$ 495	$ 880	
Westminster Choir College of Rider University; Princeton, N.J. 08540 (P)	280	57	22	$15,120	$15,120	$6,610
William Paterson College of New Jersey; Wayne, N.J. 07470 (Pub)	7,654	59	47	$ 3,380	$ 5,360	$4,960

Institution Name; City, State Zip (Control)	Students	Percent		Tuition		Room and board
		Women	Accepted	In-State	Out-of-State	
NEW MEXICO						
College of Santa Fe; Santa Fe, N.M. 87505 (P)	1,556	57	79	$11,796	$11,796	$4,400
College of the Southwest; Hobbs, N.M. 88240 (P)	538	73	43	$ 4,290	$ 4,290	$3,414
Eastern New Mexico University; Portales, N.M. 88130 (Pub)	3,296	56	99	$ 1,518	$ 5,586	$1,300
New Mexico Highlands University; Las Vegas, N.M. 87701 (Pub)	2,054	52	94	$ 1,560	$ 6,204	$3,100
New Mexico Institute of Mining & Technology; Socorro, N.M. 87801 (Pub)	1,217	31	77	$ 1,450	$ 5,988	$3,308
New Mexico State University; Las Cruces, N.M. 88003 (Pub)	11,872	52	80	$ 2,196	$ 7,152	$3,180
Saint John's College (N.M.); Santa Fe, N.M. 87501 (P)	385	45	81	$18,520	$18,520	$6,005
University of New Mexico; Albuquerque, N.M. 87131 (Pub)	15,726	56	74	$ 1,987	$ 7,442	$4,176
Western New Mexico University; Silver City, N.M. 88061 (Pub)	2,081	62	100	$ 1,394	$ 4,652	$2,260
NEW YORK						
Adelphi University; Garden City, N.Y. 11530 (P)	2,787	66	71	$12,800	$12,800	$6,450
Albany College of Pharmacy; Albany, N.Y. 12208 (P)	695	59	76	$10,000	$10,000	$4,800
Alfred University; Alfred, N.Y. 14802 (P)	2,014	49	84	$18,498	$18,498	$6,407
Audrey Cohen College; New York, N.Y. 10013 (P)	1,017	70	69	$ 8,800	$ 8,800	
Bard College; Annandale-on-Hudson, N.Y. 12504 (P)	1,072	52	54	$21,700	$21,700	$6,812
Barnard College; New York, N.Y. 10027 (P)	2,219	100	46	$20,324	$20,324	$8,374
Binghamton University; Binghamton, N.Y. 13902 (P)	9,349	53	42	$ 3,400	$ 8,300	$4,814
Boricua College; New York, N.Y. 10032 (P)	1,072	78	31	$ 6,100	$ 6,100	
Canisius College; Buffalo, N.Y. 14208 (P)	3,275	47	84	$12,600	$12,600	$5,825
City University of New York-Baruch College; New York, N.Y. 10010 (Pub)	12,730	57	57	$ 3,200	$ 6,800	
City University of New York-Brooklyn College; Brooklyn, N.Y. 11210 (Pub)	11,478	58	83	$ 3,200	$ 6,800	
City University of New York-City College; New York, N.Y. 10031 (Pub)	9,616	51	60	$ 3,200	$ 6,800	
City University of New York-College of Staten Island; Staten Island, N.Y. 10314 (Pub)	10,704	58	100	$ 3,200	$ 6,800	$ —
City University of New York-Hunter College; New York, N.Y. 10021 (Pub)	14,602	71	54	$ 3,200	$ 6,800	$1,840
City University of New York-John Jay College of Criminal Justice; New York, N.Y. 10019 (Pub)	9,790	56	54	$ 2,450	$ 5,050	
City University of New York-Lehman College; Bronx, N.Y. 10468 (Pub)	7,698	72	51	$ 3,200	$ 6,800	
City University of New York-Medgar Evers College; Brooklyn, N.Y. 11225 (Pub)	5,402		100	$ 3,200	$ 6,800	
City University of New York-Queens College; Flushing, N.Y. 11367 (Pub)	13,442	61	61	$ 3,200	$ 6,800	
City University of New York-York College; Jamaica, N.Y. 11451 (Pub)	6,869	68	100	$ 3,200	$ 6,800	
Clarkson University; Potsdam, N.Y. 13699 (P)	2,356	25	86	$17,893	$17,893	$6,486
Colgate University; Hamilton, N.Y. 13346 (P)	2,849	52	37	$22,610	$22,610	$6,110
College of Aeronautics; Flushing, N.Y. 11371 (P)	956	5	96	$ 7,650	$ 7,650	$3,924
College of Insurance; New York, N.Y. 10007 (P)	575	52	58	$12,730	$12,730	$8,200
College of Mount Saint Vincent; Riverdale, N.Y. 10471 (P)	1,262	82	68	$13,000	$13,000	$6,240
College of New Rochelle; New Rochelle, N.Y. 10801 (P)	1,121	98	88	$11,000	$11,000	$5,700
Columbia University; New York, N.Y. 10027 (P)	3,570	49	50	$20,882	$20,882	$7,162
Concordia College (N.Y.); Bronxville, N.Y. 10708 (P)	496	56	75	$11,400	$11,400	$5,310
Cooper Union; New York, N.Y. 10003 (P)	844	35	16	$ 8,300	$ 8,300	$8,415
Cornell University; Ithaca, N.Y. 14850 (P)	13,512	47	33	$21,914	$21,914	$7,110
Daemen College; Amherst, N.Y. 14226 (P)	1,791	70	75	$ 9,950	$ 9,950	$5,200
Dominican College of Blauvelt; Orangeburg, N.Y. 10962 (P)	1,781	71	75	$ 9,750	$ 9,750	$6,000
Dowling College; Long Island, N.Y. 11769 (P)	3,666	59	93	$10,980	$10,980	$3,350
D'Youville College; Buffalo, N.Y. 14201 (P)	1,377	75	53	$ 9,510	$ 9,510	$4,600
Eastman School of Music; Rochester, N.Y. 14604-2599 (P)	491	53	32	$18,700	$18,700	$7,160
Elmira College; Elmira, N.Y. 14901 (P)	1,566	60	76	$17,550	$17,550	$5,880
Eugene Lang College; New York, N.Y. 10011 (P)	369	66	70	$18,120	$18,120	$8,555
Fashion Institute of Technology; New York, N.Y. 10001 (P)	8,430	79	50	$ 2,585	$ 6,200	$4,820
Fordham University; New York, N.Y. 10458 (P)	4,474	57	70	$16,800	$16,800	$7,800
Hamilton College; Clinton, N.Y. 13323 (P)	1,684	47	44	$22,700	$22,700	$5,560
Hartwick College; Oneonta, N.Y. 13820 (P)	1,490	53	93	$20,480	$20,480	$5,570
Hobart and William Smith Colleges; Geneva, N.Y. 14456 (P)	1,785	52	76	$21,927	$21,927	$6,564
Hofstra University; Hempstead, N.Y. 11549 (P)	8,431	53	88	$12,240	$12,240	$6,450
Houghton College; Houghton, N.Y. 14744 (P)	1,389	64	77	$12,344	$12,344	$4,238
Iona College; New Rochelle, N.Y. 10801 (P)	2,500	51	72	$13,100	$13,100	$7,200
Ithaca College; Ithaca, N.Y. 14850-7020 (P)	5,460	54	73	$16,130	$16,130	$6,990
Juilliard School; New York, N.Y. 10023 (P)	490	52	11	$14,400	$14,400	$6,500
Keuka College; Keuka Park, N.Y. 14478 (P)	938	71	84	$11,040	$11,040	$5,524

| Institution Name; City, State Zip (Control) | Students | Percent | | Tuition | | Room and board |
		Women	Accepted	In-State	Out-of-State	
Laboratory Institute of Merchandising; New York, N.Y. 10022 (P)	184	97	70	$11,300	$11,300	
LeMoyne College; Syracuse, N.Y. 13214 (P)	1,768	58	80	$13,120	$13,120	$5,680
Long Island University-Brooklyn; Brooklyn, N.Y. 11201 (P)	4,193	66	59	$11,680	$11,680	$5,800
Long Island University-C.W. Post; Brookville, N.Y. 11548 (P)	4,670	55	76	$13,120	$13,120	$5,880
Long Island University-Southampton; Southampton, N.Y. 11968 (P)	1,273	58	85	$13,050	$13,050	$6,530
Manhattan College; Riverdale, N.Y. 10471 (P)	2,602	50	69	$13,800	$13,800	$7,150
Manhattan School of Music; New York, N.Y. 10027 (P)	441	53	44	$15,800	$15,800	$9,000
Manhattanville College; Purchase, N.Y. 10577 (P)	906	65	73	$16,120	$16,120	$7,680
Mannes College of Music; New York, N.Y. 10024 (P)	106	50	18	$14,580	$14,580	$6,000
Marist College; Poughkeepsie, N.Y. 12601 (P)	3,935	57	64	$11,400	$11,400	$6,300
Marymount College; Tarrytown, N.Y. 10591 (P)	947	94	84	$12,500	$12,500	$7,200
Marymount Manhattan College; New York, N.Y. 10021 (P)	2,014	77	79	$11,990	$11,990	$5,500
Medaille College; Buffalo, N.Y. 14214 (P)	914	74	67	$ 9,750	$ 4,400	$ 800
Mercy College; Dobbs Ferry, N.Y. 10522 (P)	5,868	58	90	$ 7,200	$ 7,200	$7,400
Molloy College; Rockville Centre, N.Y. 11571-5002 (P)	1,981	81		$ 9,600	$ 9,600	
Mount Saint Mary College; Newburgh, N.Y. 12550 (P)	1,599	68	59	$ 9,870	$ 9,870	$5,250
Nazareth College of Rochester; Rochester, N.Y. 14618-3790 (P)	1,763	76	79	$11,926	$11,926	$5,690
New York Institute of Technology; Old Westbury, N.Y. 11568 (P)	6,737	30	78	$ 9,300	$ 9,300	$6,220
New York University; New York, N.Y. 10011 (P)	14,177	58	44	$21,730	$21,730	$8,170
Niagara University; Niagara University, N.Y. 14109 (P)	2,291	62	81	$12,390	$12,390	$ 658
Nyack College; Nyack, N.Y. 10960 (P)	1,011	55	72	$ 9,660	$ 9,660	$4,420
Pace University; New York, N.Y. 10038 (P)	6,070	62	57	$12,710	$12,710	$5,340
Pace University; White Plains, N.Y. 10603 (P)	7,901	62	99	$12,710	$12,710	$5,340
Parsons School of Design; New York, N.Y. 10011 (P)	1,910	69	49	$18,200	$17,100	$8,028
Polytechnic University; Brooklyn, N.Y. 11201 (P)	1,588	14	81	$17,890	$17,890	$4,240
Pratt Institute; Brooklyn, N.Y. 11205 (P)	2,115	44	45	$16,801	$16,801	$7,754
Rensselaer Polytechnic Institute; Troy, N.Y. 12180 (P)	4,137	25	82	$19,075	$19,075	$6,377
Roberts Wesleyan College; Rochester, N.Y. 14624 (P)	1,134	64	89	$11,412	$11,412	$4,056
Rochester Institute of Technology; Rochester, N.Y. 14623 (P)	8,125	34	77	$16,083	$16,083	$6,417
Russell Sage College; Troy, N.Y. 12180 (P)	1,038	100	96	$13,950	$13,950	$5,670
Saint Bonaventure University; St. Bonaventure, N.Y. 14778 (P)	1,839	52	90	$11,919	$11,919	$5,326
Saint Francis College (N.Y.); Brooklyn Heights, N.Y. 11201 (P)	2,257	57	84	$ 6,930	$ 6,930	
Saint John Fisher College; Rochester, N.Y. 14618 (P)	2,000	55	78	$12,300	$12,300	$5,870
Saint John's University (N.Y.); Jamaica, N.Y. 11439 (P)	14,091	55	87	$10,950	$10,950	
Saint Joseph's College (Brooklyn); Brooklyn, N.Y. 11205 (P)	1,381	76	59	$ 7,794	$ 7,794	
Saint Lawrence University; Canton, N.Y. 13617 (P)	1,965	50	66	$20,410	$20,410	$6,110
Saint Thomas Aquinas College; Sparkill, N.Y. 10976 (P)	2,101	61	77	$10,500	$10,500	$6,700
Sarah Lawrence College; Bronxville, N.Y. 10708 (P)	1,072	74	54	$22,530	$22,530	$6,902
School of Visual Arts; New York, N.Y. 10010 (P)	4,857	41	70	$12,400	$12,400	$4,800
Siena College; Loudonville, N.Y. 12211 (P)	3,188	54	76	$11,840	$11,840	$5,435
Skidmore College; Saratoga Springs, N.Y. 12866 (P)	2,189	60	66	$20,670	$20,670	$6,110
State University of New York-Albany; Albany, N.Y. 12222 (Pub)	9,622	48	59	$ 3,400	$ 8,300	$5,241
State University of New York-Buffalo; Buffalo, N.Y. 14260 (Pub)	15,571	45	71	$ 3,400	$ 8,300	$5,800
State University of New York-Stony Brook; Stony Brook, N.Y. 11794 (Pub)	11,267	51	58	$ 3,400	$ 8,300	$5,594
State University of New York College-Brockport; Brockport, N.Y. 14420 (Pub)	7,229	53	55	$ 3,400	$ 8,300	$4,780
State University of New York College-Buffalo; Buffalo, N.Y. 14222 (Pub)	9,421	57	60	$ 3,400	$ 8,300	$4,220
State University of New York College-Cortland; Cortland, N.Y. 13045 (Pub)	5,357	55	52	$ 3,400	$ 8,300	$5,140
State University of New York College-Fredonia; Fredonia, N.Y. 14063 (Pub)	4,350	56	64	$ 3,400	$ 8,300	$4,550
State University of New York College-Geneseo; Geneseo, N.Y. 14454 (Pub)	5,252	64	56	$ 3,400	$ 8,300	$4,490
State University of New York College-New Paltz; New Paltz, N.Y. 12561 (Pub)	6,009	62	43	$ 3,400	$ 8,300	$4,980
State University of New York College-Old Westbury; Old Westbury, N.Y. 11568 (Pub)	3,790	57		$ 3,400	$ 8,300	$4,616
State University of New York College-Oneonta; Oneonta, N.Y. 13820 (Pub)	5,319	59	75	$ 3,400	$ 8,300	$5,658
State University of New York College-Oswego; Oswego, N.Y. 13126 (Pub)	7,345	51		$ 3,400	$ 8,300	$5,728
State University of New York College-Plattsburgh; Plattsburgh, N.Y. 12901 (Pub)	5,331	57	69	$ 3,400	$ 8,300	$4,250
State University of New York College-Potsdam; Potsdam, N.Y. 13676 (Pub)	3,581	59	84	$ 3,400	$ 8,300	$4,900

Institution Name; City, State Zip (Control)	Students	Percent		Tuition		Room and board
		Women	Accepted	In-State	Out-of-State	
State University of New York College-Purchase; Purchase, N.Y. 10577 (Pub)	3,111	58	54	$ 3,400	$ 8,300	$5,096
State University of New York Empire State College; Saratoga Springs, N.Y. 12866 (Pub)	6,778	51	95	$ 3,400	$ 8,300	
State University of New York Maritime College; Bronx, N.Y. 10465 (Pub)	636	10	66	$ 3,400	$ 8,300	$5,500
Syracuse University; Syracuse, N.Y. 13244 (P)	10,180	52	65	$17,550	$17,550	$7,760
The College of Saint Rose; Albany, N.Y. 12203 (P)	2,535	73	75	$11,024	$11,024	$5,646
The Jewish Theological Seminary of America; New York, N.Y. 10027 (P)	138	55	80	$ 7,190	$ 7,190	$6,650
Touro College; New York, N.Y. 10001 (P)	6,812	68	64	$ 8,500	$ 8,500	$4,500
Union College (N.Y.); Schenectady, N.Y. 12308 (P)	2,044	47	55	$21,945	$21,945	$6,330
United States Merchant Marine Academy; Kings Point, N.Y. 11024 (Pub)	950	12	58	$ —	$ —	
United States Military Academy; West Point, N.Y. 10996 (Pub)	4,016	13	12	$ —	$ —	
University of Rochester; Rochester, N.Y. 14627 (P)	4,727	51	52	$20,540	$20,540	$7,160
Utica College of Syracuse University; Utica, N.Y. 13502 (P)	1,748	63	85	$14,116	$14,116	$5,380
Vassar College; Poughkeepsie, N.Y. 12601 (P)	2,245	60	48	$21,150	$21,150	$6,310
Wadhams Hall Seminary College; Ogdensburg, N.Y. 13669 (P)	28	14	82	$ 4,490	$ 4,490	$4,200
Wagner College; Staten Island, N.Y. 10301 (P)	1,615	58	71	$15,300	$15,300	$5,800
Webb Institute; Glen Cove, N.Y. 11542 (P)	85	15	48			$5,800
Wells College; Aurora, N.Y. 13026 (P)	400	100	87	$17,100	$17,100	$5,900
Yeshiva University; New York, N.Y. 10033 (P)	1,990	43		$12,100	$12,100	$4,080
NORTH CAROLINA						
Appalachian State University; Boone, N.C. 28608 (Pub)	10,878	52	61	$ 1,793	$ 8,947	$2,840
Barton College; Wilson, N.C. 27893 (P)	1,295	65	97	$ 8,926	$ 8,926	$4,198
Belmont Abbey College; Belmont, N.C. 28012 (P)	831	56	87	$ 9,920	$ 9,920	$5,346
Bennett College; Greensboro, N.C. 27401 (P)	664	100	70	$ 5,600	$ 5,600	$3,095
Campbell University; Buies Creek, N.C. 27506 (P)	4,623	56	60	$ 9,350	$ 9,350	$3,550
Catawba College; Salisbury, N.C. 28144 (P)	1,101	51	84	$11,352	$11,352	$4,500
Davidson College; Davidson, N.C. 28036 (P)	1,613	49	36	$20,595	$20,595	$5,918
Duke University; Durham, N.C. 27708 (P)	6,272	49	30	$29,520	$29,250	$6,605
East Carolina University; Greenville, N.C. 27858 (Pub)	14,409	58	77	$ 874	$ 8,028	$3,480
Elizabeth City State College; Elizabeth City, N.C. 27909 (Pub)	1,773	62	79	$ 628	$ 6,360	$3,163
Elon College; Elon College, N.C. 27244 (P)	3,427	57	70	$10,477	$10,477	$4,170
Fayetteville State University; Fayetteville, N.C. 28301 (Pub)	3,249	64	93	$ 876	$ 8,028	$3,150
Gardner-Webb University; Boiling Springs, N.C. 28017 (P)	2,763	58	84	$ 9,620	$ 4,630	$4,470
Greensboro College; Greensboro, N.C. 27401 (P)	1,023	61	75	$ 9,350	$ 9,350	$4,040
Guilford College; Greensboro, N.C. 27410 (P)	1,071	51	85	$14,180	$14,180	$5,270
High Point University; High Point, N.C. 27262 (P)	2,411	60	84	$ 8,860	$ 8,860	$4,820
Johnson C. Smith University; Charlotte, N.C. 28216 (P)	1,283	59	61	$ 7,473	$ 7,473	$3,253
Lees-McRae College; Banner Elk, N.C. 28604 (P)	453	43	78	$ 8,998	$ 8,998	$3,276
Lenoir-Rhyne College; Hickory, N.C. 28603 (P)	1,474	63	86	$12,036	$12,036	$4,400
Mars Hill College; Mars Hill, N.C. 28754 (P)	1,300	51	87	$ 8,350	$ 8,350	$3,800
Meredith College; Raleigh, N.C. 27607 (P)	2,336	100	88	$ 7,420	$ 7,420	$3,570
Methodist College; Fayetteville, N.C. 28311 (P)	1,293	47	71	$11,250	$11,250	$4,400
Montreat College; Montreat, N.C. 28757 (P)	678	50	83	$ 9,656	$ 9,656	$3,752
North Carolina A&T State University; Greensboro, N.C. 27411 (Pub)	6,598	50	65	$ 1,668	$ 8,818	$3,430
North Carolina Central University; Durham, N.C. 27707 (Pub)	4,339	62	69	$ 1,748	$ 8,028	$3,240
North Carolina School of the Arts; Winston-Salem, N.C. 27117 (Pub)	656	39	36	$ 1,359	$ 9,570	$3,970
North Carolina State University; Raleigh, N.C. 27695 (Pub)	19,026	40	74	$ 2,200	$10,732	$4,350
North Carolina Wesleyan College; Rocky Mount, N.C. 27804 (Pub)	81	50	82	$ 6,600	$ 6,600	$4,500
Pembroke State University; Pembroke, N.C. 28372 (Pub)	2,690	60	91	$ 1,467	$ 8,620	$2,856
Pfeiffer College; Misenheimer, N.C. 28109 (P)	847	51	81	$ 9,816	$ 9,816	$4,000
Queens College; Charlotte, N.C. 28274 (P)	1,110	79	76	$12,310	$12,310	$5,380
Saint Andrews Presbyterian College; Laurinburg, N.C. 28352 (P)	662	54	84	$12,015	$12,015	$5,300
Saint Augustine's College; Raleigh, N.C. 27610 (P)	1,584	54	39	$ 4,100	$ 4,100	$3,600
Salem College; Winston-Salem, N.C. 27108 (P)	814	97	87	$12,200	$12,200	$7,320
Shaw University; Raleigh, N.C. 27601 (P)	2,432	58	75	$ 5,716	$ 5,716	$3,476
University of North Carolina-Asheville; Asheville, N.C. 28804 (Pub)	2,194	56	60	$ 1,774	$ 8,090	$3,627
University of North Carolina-Chapel Hill; Chapel Hill, N.C. 27599 (Pub)	15,363	59	37	$ 2,161	$10,693	$4,500
University of North Carolina-Charlotte; Charlotte, N.C. 28223-0001 (Pub)	12,220	52	72	$ 1,716	$ 8,870	$3,386
University of North Carolina-Greensboro; Greensboro, N.C. 27412 (Pub)	9,694	66	80	$ 1,016	$ 9,584	$3,940

| Institution Name; City, State Zip (Control) | Students | Percent | | Tuition | | Room and board |
		Women	Accepted	In-State	Out-of-State	
University of North Carolina-Wilmington; Wilmington, N.C. 28403 (Pub)	7,980	59	63	$ 840	$ 7,682	$3,910
Wake Forest University; Winston-Salem, N.C. 27109 (P)	3,771	50	42	$18,500	$18,500	$5,100
Warren Wilson College; Asheville, N.C. 28815 (P)	620	58	86	$12,250	$12,250	$4,000
Western Carolina University; Cullowhee, N.C. 28723 (Pub)	5,674	51	85	$ 874	$ 8,028	$2,674
Wingate University;. Wingate, N.C. 28174 (P)	1,200	48	79	$10,650	$10,650	$3,850
Winston-Salem State University; Winston-Salem, N.C. 27110 (Pub)	2,781	64	79	$ 1,446	$ 7,486	$3,265
NORTH DAKOTA						
Dickinson State University; Dickinson, N.D. 58601 (Pub)	1,591	56	100	$ 1,680	$ 4,486	$2,478
Jamestown College; Jamestown, N.D. 58405 (P)	1,094	53	96	$ 8,420	$ 8,420	$3,080
Mayville State University; Mayville, N.D. 58257 (Pub)	756	50	100	$ 1,680	$ 4,486	$2,835
Minot State University; Minot, N.D. 58707 (Pub)	3,483	63	99	$ 2,044	$ 5,018	$2,049
North Dakota State University; Fargo, N.D. 58105 (Pub)	8,664	43	81	$ 2,236	$ 5,970	$3,135
University of Mary; Bismarck, N.D. 58504 (P)	1,867	62	90	$ 7,230	$ 7,230	$2,890
University of North Dakota; Grand Forks, N.D. 58202 (Pub)	9,351	49	73	$ 2,677	$ 6,411	$3,117
Valley City State University; Valley City, N.D. 58072 (Pub)	1,121	48	94	$ 1,680	$ 4,486	$2,770
OHIO						
Antioch College; Yellow Springs, Ohio 45387 (P)	735	63	74	$16,322	$16,322	$3,796
Ashland University; Ashland, Ohio 44805 (P)	2,591	57	80	$12,600	$12,600	$5,001
Baldwin-Wallace College; Berea, Ohio 44017 (P)	4,105	59	84	$13,275	$13,275	$4,881
Bluffton College; Bluffton, Ohio 45817 (P)	1,065	53	88	$11,250	$11,250	$4,641
Bowling Green State University; Bowling Green, Ohio 43403 (Pub)	14,912	57	83	$ 4,190	$ 8,930	$3,914
Capital University; Columbus, Ohio 43209 (P)	2,769	64	83	$14,760	$14,760	$4,200
Case Western Reserve University; Cleveland, Ohio 44106 (P)	3,679	42	79	$17,100	$17,100	$4,860
Cedarville College; Cedarville, Ohio 45314 (P)	2,509	54	87	$ 8,448	$ 8,448	$4,716
Central State University; Wilberforce, Ohio 45384 (Pub)	1,954	49	66	$ 3,318	$ 7,293	$6,660
Cleveland Institute of Art; Cleveland, Ohio 44106 (P)	513	46	81	$12,376	$12,376	$4,650
Cleveland Institute of Music; Cleveland, Ohio 44106 (P)	226	50	48	$16,365	$16,365	$5,220
Cleveland State University; Cleveland, Ohio 44115 (Pub)	11,660	52	98	$ 2,222	$ 4,444	$2,784
College of Mount Saint Joseph; Cincinnati, Ohio 45233 (P)	1,383	68	80	$11,300	$11,300	$4,730
College of Wooster; Wooster, Ohio 44691 (P)	1,700	51	89	$18,380	$18,380	$4,850
Columbus College of Art and Design; Columbus, Ohio 43215 (P)	1,494	43	63	$11,280	$11,280	$5,700
Defiance College; Defiance, Ohio 43512 (P)	875	47	80	$12,950	$12,950	$3,780
Denison University; Granville, Ohio 43023 (P)	1,910	51	82	$19,310	$19,310	$5,370
Franciscan University of Steubenville; Steubenville, Ohio 43952 (P)	1,521	59	88	$11,080	$11,080	$4,730
Franklin University; Columbus, Ohio 43215 (P)	4,005	33	100	$ 5,152	$ 5,152	
Heidelberg College; Tiffin, Ohio 44883 (P)	1,124	45	89	$14,606	$14,606	$4,674
Hiram College; Hiram, Ohio 44234 (P)	858	53	87	$16,224	$16,224	$5,254
John Carroll University; University Heights, Ohio 44118 (P)	3,519	52	89	$13,883	$13,883	$5,662
Kent State University; Kent, Ohio 44242 (Pub)	15,982	60	88	$ 4,288	$ 7,768	$4,030
Kenyon College; Gambier, Ohio 43022 (P)	1,547	53	67	$21,370	$21,370	$3,820
Lake Erie College; Painesville, Ohio 44077 (P)	512	31	80	$13,750	$13,750	$4,940
Lourdes College; Sylvania, Ohio 43560 (P)	1,547	82	86	$ 8,100	$ 8,100	
Malone College; Canton, Ohio 44709 (P)	1,894	59	88	$11,130	$11,130	$4,600
Marietta College; Marietta, Ohio 45750 (P)	1,061	46	68	$15,950	$15,950	$4,586
Miami University; Oxford, Ohio 45056 (P)	13,640	55	72	$ 4,210	$ 9,966	$4,440
Mount Union College; Alliance, Ohio 44601 (P)	1,407	49		$13,130	$13,130	$3,760
Mount Vernon Nazarene College; Mount Vernon, Ohio 43050 (P)	1,470	57	94	$ 9,430	$ 9,430	$3,843
Muskingum College; New Concord, Ohio 43762 (P)	1,201	49	82	$ 9,850	$ 9,850	$4,280
Notre Dame College of Ohio; South Euclid, Ohio 44121 (P)	611	100	90	$11,000	$11,000	$4,095
Oberlin College; Oberlin, Ohio 44074 (P)	2,842	58	65	$21,425	$21,425	$6,174
Ohio Dominican College; Columbus, Ohio 43219 (P)	1,883	66	92	$ 9,350	$ 9,350	$4,720
Ohio Northern University; Ada, Ohio 45810 (P)	2,560	49	90	$18,870	$18,870	$4,680
Ohio State University-Columbus; Columbus, Ohio 43210 (Pub)	35,486	47	85	$ 3,468	$10,335	$4,907
Ohio State University-Lima; Lima, Ohio 45804 (Pub)	1,281	59	56	$ 3,345	$10,212	
Ohio State University-Newark; Newark, Ohio 43055 (Pub)	1,522	61	54	$ 3,345	$10,212	$2,800
Ohio University; Athens, Ohio 45701 (Pub)	16,075	53	73	$ 4,275	$ 8,994	$4,548
Ohio Wesleyan University; Delaware, Ohio 43015 (P)	1,835	51	85	$19,140	$19,140	$6,180
Otterbein College; Westerville, Ohio 43081 (P)	2,488	62	86	$14,358	$14,358	$4,569
Pontifical College Josephinum; Columbus, Ohio 43235 (P)	42	7	100	$ 6,420	$ 6,420	$2,320

Institution Name; City, State Zip (Control)	Students	Percent Women	Percent Accepted	Tuition In-State	Tuition Out-of-State	Room and board
Shawnee State University; Portsmouth, Ohio 45662 (Pub)	3,505	62	100	$ 2,976	$ 5,151	$3,813
The Union Institute; Cincinnati, Ohio 45206 (P)	767	61	73	$ 5,472	$ 5,472	
Tiffin University; Tiffin, Ohio 44883 (P)	1,150	50	85	$ 8,700	$ 8,700	$4,200
University of Akron; Akron, Ohio 44325 (P)	22,755	52	100	$ 3,486	$ 8,686	$4,062
University of Cincinnati; Cincinnati, Ohio 45221 (Pub)	21,272	48	85	$ 3,918	$ 9,805	$4,881
University of Dayton; Dayton, Ohio 45469 (P)	5,899	51	90	$13,690	$13,690	$4,500
University of Findlay; Findlay, Ohio 45840 (P)	3,155	47	78	$13,000	$13,000	$5,210
University of Rio Grande; Rio Grande, Ohio 45674 (P)	1,971	58	93	$ 2,784	$ 7,362	$4,386
University of Toledo; Toledo, Ohio 43606 (Pub)	18,187	52	97	$ 3,778	$ 9,063	$4,092
Urbana University; Urbana, Ohio 43078-2091 (P)	1,179	49	79	$ 9,336	$ 9,336	$4,350
Ursuline College; Pepper Pike, Ohio 44124 (P)	1,153	95	84	$10,710	$10,710	$4,330
Walsh University; North Canton, Ohio 44720 (P)	1,261	54	53	$ 9,900	$ 9,900	$4,760
Wilberforce University; Wilberforce, Ohio 45384 (P)	775	65	25	$ 7,290	$ 7,290	$4,100
Wilmington College (Ohio); Wilmington, Ohio 45177 (P)	1,973	50	84	$12,300	$12,300	$4,590
Wittenberg University; Springfield, Ohio 45501 (P)	2,000	54	88	$19,140	$19,140	$4,860
Wright State University; Dayton, Ohio 45435 (Pub)	11,843	53	90	$ 3,600	$ 7,200	$4,180
Xavier University (Ohio); Cincinnati, Ohio 45207 (P)	3,956	54	95	$12,950	$12,950	$5,480
Youngstown State University; Youngstown, Ohio 44555 (P)	11,554	53	79	$ 3,366	$ 7,002	$4,200
OKLAHOMA						
Bartlesville Wesleyan College; Bartlesville, Okla. 74006 (P)	571	65	75	$ 7,860	$ 7,860	$3,400
Cameron University; Lawton, Okla. 73505 (Pub)	5,009	51	94	$ 1,790	$ 4,235	$2,530
East Central University; Ada, Okla. 74820 (Pub)	3,786	58	95	$ 1,491	$ 3,553	$2,068
Langston University; Langston, Okla. 73050 (Pub)	3,864	57	62	$ 1,857	$ 2,352	$2,580
Northeastern State University; Tahlequah, Okla. 74464 (Pub)	7,075	50	91	$ 1,620	$ 3,945	$3,170
Northwestern Oklahoma State University; Alva, Okla. 73717 (Pub)	1,501	54	90	$ 1,818	$ 3,818	$2,316
Oklahoma Baptist University; Shawnee, Okla. 74801 (P)	2,412	59	95	$ 6,500	$ 6,500	$3,110
Oklahoma Christian University of Science and Arts; Oklahoma City, Okla. 73136 (P)	1,534	47	91	$ 7,600	$ 7,600	$3,840
Oklahoma City University; Oklahoma City, Okla. 73106 (P)	2,421	55	82	$ 8,050	$ 8,050	$3,990
Oklahoma Panhandle State University; Goodwell, Okla. 73939 (Pub)	1,366	53	100	$ 1,290	$ 3,765	$1,870
Oklahoma State University; Stillwater, Okla. 74078 (Pub)	14,124	46	86	$ 2,148	$ 5,838	$3,988
Oral Roberts University; Tulsa, Okla. 74171 (P)	2,788	57	61	$ 9,392	$ 9,392	$4,452
Phillips University; Enid, Okla. 73701 (P)	525	49	85	$ 6,300	$ 6,300	$3,904
Southeastern Oklahoma State University; Durant, Okla. 74701 (Pub)	3,401	54	84	$ 1,305	$ 3,630	$2,348
Southern Nazarene University; Bethany, Okla. 73008 (P)	1,536	55	100	$ 7,860	$ 7,860	$3,978
Southwestern College of Christian Ministries; Bethany, Okla. 73008 (P)	160	55	84	$ 3,139	$ 3,139	$2,270
Southwestern Oklahoma State University; Weatherford, Okla. 73096 (Pub)	4,423	56	99	$ 1,305	$ 3,630	$2,160
University of Central Oklahoma; Edmond, Okla. 73034 (Pub)	11,603	57	94	$ 1,716	$ 3,495	$2,431
University of Oklahoma; Norman, Okla. 73019 (Pub)	13,250	46	88	$ 2,178	$ 5,868	$3,904
University of Science & Arts of Oklahoma; Chickasha, Okla. 73018 (Pub)	1,523	65	91	$ 1,725	$ 4,208	$1,980
University of Tulsa; Tulsa, Okla. 74104 (P)	2,945	54	83	$12,850	$12,850	$4,252
OREGON						
Blue Mountain College; Pendleton, Ore. 97801 (P)				$ 3,960	$ 3,960	$2,240
Eastern Oregon State College; La Grande, Ore. 97850 (Pub)	2,168	53	61	$ 3,162	$ 3,162	$3,900
George Fox University; Newberg, Ore. 97132 (P)	1,314	61	87	$14,300	$14,300	$6,920
Lewis & Clark College; Portland, Ore. 97219-7899 (P)	1,868	56	66	$18,530	$18,530	$5,770
Linfield College; McMinnville, Ore. 97128 (P)	2,654	55	88	$14,976	$14,976	$4,642
Oregon Institute of Technology; Klamath Falls, Ore. 97601 (Pub)	2,339	42	76	$ 3,330	$10,557	$4,045
Oregon State University; Corvallis, Ore. 97331 (Pub)	11,430	43		$ 3,432	$10,420	$4,587
Pacific Northwest College of Art; Portland, Ore. 97205 (P)	280	56	78	$10,072	$10,072	$4,670
Pacific University; Forest Grove, Ore. 97116 (P)	1,061	60	85	$15,368	$15,368	$4,514
Portland State University; Portland, Ore. 97207 (Pub)	10,796	52	86	$ 3,060	$ 9,108	$5,385
Reed College; Portland, Ore. 97202 (P)	1,248	53	76	$22,180	$22,180	$6,200
Southern Oregon State College; Ashland, Ore. 97520 (Pub)	4,097	53	77	$ 3,045	$ 9,063	$4,010
University of Oregon; Eugene, Ore. 97403 (Pub)	13,874	52	90	$ 3,646	$12,014	$4,646
University of Portland; Portland, Ore. 97203 (P)	2,078	53	92	$15,420	$15,420	$4,710
Warner Pacific College; Portland, Ore. 97215 (P)	594	62	87	$ 9,500	$ 9,500	$3,750
Western Baptist College; Salem, Ore. 97301 (P)	720	58	91	$10,490	$10,490	$4,550
Western Oregon University; Monmouth, Ore. 97361 (Pub)	3,791	58	56	$ 3,096	$ 9,108	$3,829
Willamette University; Salem, Ore. 97301 (P)	1,727	57	74	$20,200	$20,200	$5,280

Institution Name; City, State Zip (Control)	Students	Percent		Tuition		Room and board
		Women	Accepted	In-State	Out-of-State	
PENNSYLVANIA						
Albright College; Reading, Pa. 19612 (P)	1,366	51	85	$17,195	$17,195	$5,180
Allegheny College; Meadville, Pa. 16335 (P)	1,846	54	71	$18,720	$18,720	$4,670
Allentown College of Saint Francis de Sales; Center Valley, Pa. 18034 (P)	1,716	54	81	$10,990	$10,990	$5,260
Alvernia College; Reading, Pa. 19607 (P)	1,265	61	77	$10,250	$10,250	$5,000
Beaver College; Glenside, Pa. 19038 (P)	1,637	73	75	$15,560	$15,560	$6,520
Bloomsburg University of Pennsylvania; Bloomsburg, Pa. 17815 (Pub)	6,395	62	68	$ 4,162	$ 9,360	$3,090
Bryn Mawr College; Bryn Mawr, Pa. 19010-2899 (P)	1,205	100	58	$20,210	$20,210	$7,370
Bucknell University; Lewisburg, Pa. 17837 (P)	3,340	50	49	$21,080	$21,080	$5,200
Cabrini College; Radnor, Pa. 19087 (P)	1,719	68	88	$11,660	$11,660	$6,700
California University of Pennsylvania; California, Pa. 15419 (Pub)	4,779	53	83	$ 3,468	$ 8,824	$4,008
Carlow College; Pittsburgh, Pa. 15213 (P)	2,085	92	79	$10,730	$10,730	$4,692
Carnegie Mellon University; Pittsburgh, Pa. 15213 (P)	4,823	32	47	$20,275	$20,275	$6,225
Cedar Crest College; Allentown, Pa. 18104 (P)	1,669	94	77	$15,210	$15,210	$5,525
Chatham College; Pittsburgh, Pa. 15232 (P)	477	100	87	$14,460	$14,460	$5,548
Chestnut Hill College; Philadelphia, Pa. 19118-2693 (P)	754	100	83	$14,450	$14,450	$6,220
Cheyney University of Pennsylvania; Cheyney, Pa. 19319 (Pub)	1,076	51	71	$ 2,954	$ 7,352	$4,804
Clarion University of Pennsylvania; Clarion, Pa. 16214 (Pub)	5,249	60	89	$ 3,362	$ 8,566	$3,160
College Misericordia; Dallas, Pa. 18612 (P)	1,590	75	61	$13,120	$13,120	$6,150
Delaware Valley College; Doylestown, Pa. 18901 (P)	2,095	50	75	$13,700	$13,700	$5,476
Dickinson College; Carlisle, Pa. 17013 (P)	1,743	54	83	$20,260	$20,260	$5,560
Drexel University; Philadelphia, Pa. 19104 (P)	6,805	32	78	$13,680	$13,680	$6,718
Duquesne University; Pittsburgh, Pa. 15282 (P)	5,751	57	65	$13,396	$13,396	$5,803
East Stroudsburg University of Pennsylvania; East Stroudsburg, Pa. 18301 (Pub)	4,564	56	67	$ 3,368	$ 8,566	$3,626
Eastern College; St. Davids, Pa. 19087 (P)	1,594	66	48	$12,700	$ 1,270	$5,440
Edinboro University of Pennsylvania; Edinboro, Pa. 16444 (Pub)	6,035	60	78	$ 3,368	$ 8,566	$3,616
Elizabethtown College; Elizabethtown, Pa. 17022 (P)	1,677	68	74	$16,230	$16,230	$4,900
Franklin & Marshall College; Lancaster, Pa. 17604 (P)	1,807	48	59	$22,664	$22,664	$4,906
Gannon University; Erie, Pa. 16541 (P)	2,826	56	76	$11,980	$11,980	$4,860
Geneva College; Beaver Falls, Pa. 15010 (P)	1,656	52	84	$11,250	$11,250	$4,750
Gettysburg College; Gettysburg, Pa. 17325 (P)	2,025	52	66	$21,522	$21,522	$4,760
Grove City College; Grove City, Pa. 16127 (P)	2,310	49	48	$ 6,576	$ 6,576	$3,816
Gwynedd-Mercy College; Gwynedd Valley, Pa. 19437 (P)	1,502	80	55	$12,280	$12,280	$5,800
Haverford College; Haverford, Pa. 19041 (P)	1,137	52	35	$21,534	$21,534	$7,070
Holy Family College; Philadelphia, Pa. 19114 (P)	2,162	76	78	$10,300	$10,300	
Immaculata College; Immaculata, Pa. 19345 (P)	1,626	88	91	$11,900	$11,900	$5,855
Indiana University of Pennsylvania; Indiana, Pa. 15705 (Pub)	12,144	55	63	$ 3,368	$ 8,566	$3,332
Juniata College; Huntingdon, Pa. 16652 (P)	1,038	52	85	$16,480	$16,480	$4,700
King's College (Pa.); Wilkes-Barre, Pa. 18711 (P)	2,151	51	74	$12,400	$12,400	$5,780
Kutztown University of Pennsylvania; Kutztown, Pa. 19530 (Pub)	6,925	58	73	$ 3,368	$ 8,566	$3,500
Lafayette College; Easton, Pa. 18042 (P)	2,026	46	63	$21,120	$21,120	$6,560
LaRoche College; Pittsburgh, Pa. 15237 (P)	1,340	67	91	$ 9,712	$ 9,712	$5,198
LaSalle University; Philadelphia, Pa. 19141 (P)	3,810	54	80	$14,470	$14,470	$6,180
Lebanon Valley College; Annville, Pa. 17003 (P)	1,634	53	75	$14,960	$14,960	$4,945
Lehigh University; Bethlehem, Pa. 18015 (P)	4,232	38	54	$20,500	$20,500	$5,830
Lincoln University (Pa.); Lincoln University, Pa. 19352 (Pub)	1,211	58	63	$ 8,181	$ 8,181	$3,215
Lock Haven University of Pennsylvania; Lock Haven, Pa. 17745 (Pub)	3,440	55	70	$ 3,368	$ 8,566	$3,784
Lycoming College; Williamsport, Pa. 17701 (P)	1,488	56	75	$15,400	$15,400	$4,500
Mansfield University of Pennsylvania; Mansfield, Pa. 16933 (Pub)	2,684	56	77	$ 3,224	$ 8,198	$3,438
Marywood University; Scranton, Pa. 18509 (P)	1,758	75	76	$12,640	$12,640	$5,200
Mercyhurst College; Erie, Pa. 16546 (P)	2,635	52	77	$10,920	$10,920	$4,500
Messiah College; Grantham, Pa. 17027 (P)	2,517	60	85	$11,800	$11,800	$5,400
Millersville University of Pennsylvania; Millersville, Pa. 17551 (Pub)	6,746	59	55	$ 3,368	$ 8,566	$4,300
Moore College of Art & Design; Philadelphia, Pa. 19103 (P)	370	100	62	$15,000	$15,000	$6,000
Moravian College; Bethlehem, Pa. 18018 (P)	1,724	52	77	$17,140	$17,140	$5,785
Muhlenberg College; Allentown, Pa. 18104 (P)	2,117	53	67	$18,660	$18,660	$5,025
Neumann College; Aston, Pa. 19014 (P)	1,126	77	79	$11,700	$11,700	
Pennsylvania State University-Behrend College; Erie, Pa. 16563 (Pub)	2,941	37	74	$ 5,434	$11,774	$4,176
Pennsylvania State University-University Park; University Park, Pa. 16802 (Pub)	31,009	45	49	$ 5,250	$11,746	$4,176
Philadelphia College of Bible; Langhorne, Pa. 19047 (P)	926	51	60	$ 8,290	$ 8,290	$4,630
Philadelphia College of Pharmacy and Science; Philadelphia, Pa. 19104-4495 (P)	2,030	62	68	$12,930	$12,930	$5,500

Institution Name; City, State Zip (Control)	Students	Percent		Tuition		Room and board
		Women	Accepted	In-State	Out-of-State	
Philadelphia College of Textiles and Science; Philadelphia, Pa. 19144 (P)	2,706	61	81	$12,716	$12,716	$ 5,874
Point Park College; Pittsburgh, Pa. 15222 (P)	2,221	52	86	$10,460	$10,460	$ 5,072
Robert Morris College; Moon Township, Pa. 15108-1189 (P)	3,998	51	97	$ 7,350	$ 7,350	$ 4,744
Rosemont College; Rosemont, Pa. 19010 (P)	736	100	67	$12,960	$12,960	$ 6,500
Saint Francis College (Pa.); Loretto, Pa. 15940 (P)	1,211	54	71	$11,680	$11,680	$ 5,350
Saint Joseph's University; Philadelphia, Pa. 19131 (P)	4,077	55	69	$15,915	$15,915	$ 6,780
Saint Vincent College; Latrobe, Pa. 15650 (P)	1,215	50	85	$12,400	$12,400	$ 4,410
Seton Hill College; Greensburg, Pa. 15601 (P)	899	94	92	$12,210	$12,210	$ 4,570
Shippensburg University of Pennsylvania; Shippensburg, Pa. 17257 (Pub)	5,657	54	70	$ 3,368	$ 8,566	$ 3,700
Slippery Rock University of Pennsylvania; Slippery Rock, Pa. 16057 (Pub)	6,452	57	79	$ 3,368	$ 8,566	$ 3,552
Susquehanna University; Selinsgrove, Pa. 17870 (P)	1,573	52	76	$18,350	$18,350	$ 5,230
Swarthmore College; Swarthmore, Pa. 19081 (P)	1,435	54	30	$21,792	$21,792	$ 7,500
Temple University; Philadelphia, Pa. 19122 (Pub)	16,982	56	63	$ 5,628	$10,510	$ 5,712
Thiel College; Greenville, Pa. 16125 (P)	980	55	84	$12,420	$12,420	$ 5,090
University of Pennsylvania; Philadelphia, Pa. 19104 (P)	14,520	47	30	$18,964	$18,964	$ 7,500
University of Pittsburgh; Pittsburgh, Pa. 15260 (Pub)	1,381	51	84	$ 5,416	$11,776	$ 4,964
University of Pittsburgh-Bradford; Bradford, Pa. 16701 (Pub)	1,263	62	91	$ 5,416	$11,776	$ 4,450
University of Pittsburgh-Greensburg; Greensburg, Pa. 15601 (Pub)	3,143	51	86	$ 5,416	$11,776	$ 3,970
University of Pittsburgh-Johnstown; Johnstown, Pa. 15904 (Pub)	12,757	52	67	$ 5,416	$11,776	$ 4,770
University of Scranton; Scranton, Pa. 18510 (P)	3,173	55	67	$14,800	$14,800	$ 6,074
University of the Arts; Philadelphia, Pa. 19102 (P)	1,183	53	81	$13,850	$13,850	$ 3,980
Ursinus College; Collegeville, Pa. 19426 (P)	1,196	53	81	$17,170	$17,170	$ 5,690
Villanova University; Villanova, Pa. 19085 (P)	6,000	50	65	$18,600	$18,600	$ 7,000
Washington & Jefferson College; Washington, Pa. 15301 (P)	1,256	48	86	$17,190	$17,190	$ 4,205
Waynesburg College; Waynesburg, Pa. 15370 (P)	1,281	51	78	$ 9,800	$ 9,800	$ 4,050
West Chester University of Pennsylvania; West Chester, Pa. 19383 (Pub)	9,388	60	61	$ 3,368	$ 8,566	$ 4,312
Westminster College (Pa.); New Wilmington, Pa. 16172 (P)	1,473	59	88	$14,650	$14,650	$ 4,280
Widener University; Chester, Pa. 19013 (P)	3,968	47	87	$14,380	$14,380	$ 6,200
Wilkes University; Wilkes-Barre, Pa. 18766 (P)	2,425	45	78	$11,150	$11,150	$ 5,130
Wilson College; Chambersburg, Pa. 17201 (P)	283	100	93	$12,600	$12,600	$ 5,805
York College of Pennsylvania; York, Pa. 17405 (P)	4,858	57	71	$ 5,800	$ 5,800	$ 4,390
RHODE ISLAND						
Brown University; Providence, R.I. 02912 (P)	5,992	52	22	$21,592	$21,592	$ 6,538
Bryant College; Smithfield, R.I. 02917 (P)	3,102	42	83	$13,900	$13,900	$ 6,700
Providence College; Providence, R.I. 02918 (P)	3,653	58	71	$16,350	$16,350	$ 6,919
Rhode Island College; Providence, R.I. 02908 (Pub)	7,149	65	74	$ 2,969	$ 7,489	$ 5,283
Rhode Island School of Design; Providence, R.I. 02903 (P)	1,860	56	43	$18,450	$18,450	$ 6,618
Roger Williams University; Bristol, R.I. 02809 (P)	3,364	46	92	$14,520	$14,520	$ 7,000
Salve Regina University; Newport, R.I. 02840 (P)	1,463	66	88	$15,450	$15,450	$ 7,100
University of Rhode Island; Kingston, R.I. 02881 (Pub)	11,350	55	81	$ 3,154	$10,846	$ 5,500
SOUTH CAROLINA						
Benedict College; Columbia, S.C. 29204 (P)	1,422	59		$ 6,304	$ 6,304	$ 3,620
Charleston Southern University; Charleston, S.C. 29423 (P)	2,128	56	68	$ 8,724	$ 8,724	$ 3,360
Clemson University; Clemson, S.C. 29634-5124 (Pub)	12,520	45	78	$ 3,195	$ 8,503	$ 3,888
Coastal Carolina University; Conway, S.C. 29528-6054 (P)	4,304	57	77	$ 2,910	$ 7,840	$ 2,810
Coker College; Hartsville, S.C. 29550 (P)	942	66	70	$12,392	$12,392	$ 4,551
College of Charleston; Charleston, S.C. 29424 (Pub)	9,006	62	73	$ 3,190	$ 6,380	$ 3,850
Columbia College (S.C.); Columbia, S.C. 29203 (P)	1,100	100	81	$11,535	$11,535	$ 4,160
Converse College; Spartanburg, S.C. 29302 (P)	730	100	92	$13,800	$13,800	$ 4,025
Erskine College; Due West, S.C. 29639 (P)	523	58	86	$12,996	$12,996	$ 4,760
Francis Marion University; Florence, S.C. 29501 (Pub)	3,294	55	75	$ 3,130	$ 6,260	$ 3,310
Furman University; Greenville, S.C. 29613 (P)	2,461	55	80	$16,256	$16,256	$ 4,449
Lander University; Greenwood, S.C. 29649 (Pub)	2,536	65	89	$ 3,600	$ 5,832	$ 3,340
Limestone College; Gaffney, S.C. 29340 (P)	366	48	76	$ 8,200	$ 8,200	$ 3,700
Morris College; Sumter, S.C. 29150 (P)	911	64	87	$ 4,990	$ 4,990	$ 2,691
Newberry College; Newberry, S.C. 29108 (P)	648	50	89	$11,330	$11,330	$ 2,950
Presbyterian College; Clinton, S.C. 29325 (P)	1,153	50	81	$13,125	$13,125	$ 4,034
South Carolina State University; Orangeburg, S.C. 29117 (Pub)	4,911	57	59	$ 2,400	$ 4,880	$ 2,856
Southern Wesleyan University; Central, S.C. 29630 (Pub)	1,214	58	42	$ 9,416	$ 9,416	$ 3,380
The Citadel; Charleston, S.C. 29409 (Pub)	1,967	1	86	$ 6,860	$10,854	$10,170
University of South Carolina-Aiken; Aiken, S.C. 29801 (Pub)	2,976	65	73	$ 2,848	$ 6,910	$ 3,412
University of South Carolina-Columbia; Columbia, S.C. 29208 (Pub)	15,747	54	78	$ 3,380	$ 8,575	$ 3,690

Institution Name; City, State Zip (Control)	Students	Percent		Tuition		Room and board
		Women	Accepted	In-State	Out-of-State	
University of South Carolina-Spartanburg; Spartanburg, S.C. 29303 (Pub)	3,285	63	61	$ 2,848	$ 6,910	$3,350
Voorhees College; Denmark, S.C. 29042 (P)	810	58	82	$ 4,784	$ 4,784	$2,706
Winthrop University; Rock Hill, S.C. 29733 (Pub)	4,182	68	87	$ 3,818	$ 6,860	$3,662
Wofford College; Spartanburg, S.C. 29303 (P)	1,066	46	84	$14,675	$14,675	$4,185
SOUTH DAKOTA						
Augustana College (S.D.); Sioux Falls, S.D. 57197 (P)	1,637	66	92	$12,968	$12,968	$3,772
Black Hills State University; Spearfish, S.D. 57799 (Pub)	3,997	58	100	$ 1,646	$ 4,840	$2,537
Dakota State University; Madison, S.D. 57042 (Pub)	1,437	53	91	$ 2,858	$ 6,050	$2,676
Dakota Wesleyan University; Mitchell, S.D. 57301 (P)	710	62	83	$ 8,475	$ 8,475	$3,210
Huron University; Huron, S.D. 57350 (P)	404	47	70	$ 7,878	$ 7,878	$3,470
Mount Marty College; Yankton, S.D. 57078 (P)	895		92	$ 8,388	$ 8,388	$3,644
National College; Rapid City, S.D. 57709 (P)	506	56	99	$ 7,920	$ 7,920	$3,270
Northern State University; Abardeen, S.D. 57401 (Pub)	2,871	57	97	$ 1,646	$ 4,840	$2,340
Oglala Lakota College; Kyle, S.D. 57752 (Pub)				$ 1,200	$ 1,200	
Presentation College; Aberdeen, S.D. 57401 (P)	422	79	100	$ 7,090	$ 7,090	$3,046
Sinte Gleska University; Rosebud, S.D. 57570 (P)	653	70	59	$ 1,660	$ 1,660	
South Dakota School of Mines & Technology; Rapid City, S.D. 57701 (Pub)	2,225	26	75	$ 1,696	$ 5,376	$2,860
South Dakota State University; Brookings, S.D. 57007 (Pub)	7,356	48	93	$ 1,696	$ 5,376	$2,344
University of Sioux Falls; Sioux Falls, S.D. 57105 (P)	829	56	96	$10,750	$10,750	$3,600
University of South Dakota; Vermillion, S.D. 57069 (Pub)	5,858	56	98	$ 1,696	$ 5,376	$2,647
TENNESSEE						
Austin Peay State University; Clarksville, Tenn. 37044 (Pub)	7,556	61	89	$ 1,714	$ 6,050	$2,870
Belmont University; Nashville, Tenn. 37212 (P)	2,553	59	77	$ 9,250	$ 9,250	$3,980
Bryan College; Dayton, Tenn. 37321 (P)	455	57	64	$ 9,400	$ 9,400	$3,950
Carson-Newman College; Jefferson City, Tenn. 37760 (P)	2,060	58	86	$ 9,500	$ 9,500	$3,670
Christian Brothers University; Memphis, Tenn. 38104 (P)	1,454	50	84	$10,700	$10,700	$3,650
Cumberland University; Lebanon, Tenn. 37087-3554 (P)	712	49	93	$ 7,990	$ 7,990	$1,595
East Tennessee State University; Johnson City, Tenn. 37614 (Pub)	9,160	58	84	$ 1,928	$ 6,264	$3,000
Fisk University; Nashville, Tenn. 37208 (P)	812	70	78	$ 7,500	$ 7,500	$4,304
Freed-Hardeman University; Henderson, Tenn. 38340 (P)	1,216	53	68	$ 6,208	$ 6,208	$3,790
Johnson Bible College; Knoxville, Tenn. 37998 (P)	388	47	99	$ 4,300	$ 4,300	$3,200
King College; Bristol, Tenn. 37620 (P)	537	58	70	$ 9,560	$ 9,560	$3,444
Knoxville College; Knoxville, Tenn. 37921 (P)	1,177	35	25	$ 9,482	$ 9,482	$3,450
Lambuth University; Jackson, Tenn. 38301 (P)	1,036	55	65	$ 5,650	$ 5,650	$3,750
Lane College; Jackson, Tenn. 38301 (P)	768	50	58	$ 5,400	$ 5,400	$3,600
LeMoyne-Owen College; Memphis, Tenn. 38126 (P)	1,090	60	87	$ 6,300	$ 6,300	$4,000
Lincoln Memorial University; Harrogate, Tenn. 37752 (P)	1,541	63	78	$ 6,800	$ 6,800	$3,160
Lipscomb University; Nashville, Tenn. 37204 (P)	2,457	55	89	$ 8,430	$ 8,430	$3,910
Maryville College; Maryville, Tenn. 37801 (P)	928	53	75	$13,030	$13,030	$4,500
Memphis College of Art; Memphis, Tenn. 38104 (P)	216	46	85	$10,250	$10,250	$4,275
Middle Tennessee State University; Murfreesboro, Tenn. 37132 (Pub)	15,890	55	69	$ 1,714	$ 6,050	$2,558
Milligan College; Milligan College, Tenn. 37682 (P)	796	60	86	$ 9,200	$ 9,200	$3,440
Rhodes College; Memphis, Tenn. 38112 (P)	1,419	55	75	$16,392	$16,392	$5,110
Southern College of Seventh-Day Adventists; Collegedale, Tenn. 37315 (P)	1,625	56	98	$ 9,156	$ 9,156	$3,782
Tennessee State University; Nashville, Tenn. 37209 (Pub)	7,013	62	50	$ 1,916	$ 6,252	$3,380
Tennessee Technological University; Cookeville, Tenn. 38505 (Pub)	7,007	47	89	$ 1,890	$ 6,226	$3,100
Tennessee Wesleyan College; Athens, Tenn. 37371-0040 (P)	738	63	84	$ 6,500	$ 6,500	$3,870
The University of Memphis; Memphis, Tenn. 38152 (Pub)	15,485	57	70	$ 2,112	$ 6,448	$2,470
Trevecca Nazarene College; Nashville, Tenn. 37210 (P)	1,114	56	100	$ 8,064	$ 8,064	$3,890
Tusculum College; Greeneville, Tenn. 37743 (P)	1,042	56	76	$10,900	$10,900	$3,700
Union University; Jackson, Tenn. 38305 (P)	1,832	65	80	$ 7,680	$ 7,680	$3,005
University of Tennessee-Chattanooga; Chattanooga, Tenn. 37403 (Pub)	7,021	56	53	$ 2,064	$ 6,400	$4,547
University of Tennessee-Knoxville; Knoxville, Tenn. 37996 (Pub)	18,825	51	75	$ 2,200	$ 6,556	$3,620
University of Tennessee-Martin; Martin, Tenn. 38238 (Pub)	5,368	57	56	$ 1,924	$ 6,260	$3,444
University of the South; Sewanee, Tenn. 37383 (P)	1,266	50	66	$16,790	$16,790	$4,460
Vanderbilt University; Nashville, Tenn. 37203-1727 (P)	5,807	48	60	$20,900	$20,900	$7,430
TEXAS						
Abilene Christian University; Abilene, Tex. 79699 (P)	3,754	52	48	$ 922	$ 922	$3,810
Angelo State University; San Angelo, Tex. 76909 (Pub)	5,702	53	71	$ 1,904	$ 8,324	$3,784

Institution Name; City, State Zip (Control)	Students	Percent		Tuition		Room and board
		Women	Accepted	In-State	Out-of-State	
Austin College; Sherman, Tex. 75090-4440 (P)	1,124	55	79	$13,435	$13,435	$5,174
Baylor University; Waco, Tex. 76798-7008 (P)	10,500	56	88	$ 8,070	$ 8,070	$4,254
Concordia Lutheran College; Austin, Tex. 78705 (P)	706	57	96	$ 8,100	$ 8,100	$4,200
Dallas Baptist University; Dallas, Tex. 75211 (P)	2,661	59	88	$ 5,952	$ 5,952	$3,378
East Texas Baptist University; Marshall, Tex. 75670 (P)	1,248	60	73	$ 5,940	$ 5,940	$4,260
East Texas State University; Commerce, Tex. 75429 (Pub)	5,347	57	67	$ 1,854	$ 1,854	$3,600
Hardin-Simmons University; Abilene, Tex. 79698 (P)	1,872	50	88	$ 6,900	$ 6,900	$4,780
Houston Baptist University; Houston, Tex. 77074 (P)	1,610	63	76	$ 7,800	$ 7,800	$3,489
Howard Payne University; Brownwood, Tex. 76801 (P)	1,468	49	90	$ 5,490	$ 5,490	$3,450
Huston-Tillotson College; Austin, Tex. 78702 (P)	701	55	87	$ 5,160	$ 5,160	$4,253
Jarvis Christian College; Hawkins, Tex. 75765 (P)	557	54	90	$ 6,694	$ 6,694	$3,485
Lamar University; Beaumont, Tex. 77710 (Pub)	9,496	53	82	$ 864	$ 4,752	$3,040
Lee College; Cleveland, Tex. 37320-3450 (P)	2,657	53		$ 5,496	$ 5,496	$3,700
LeTourneau University; Longview, Tex. 75607 (P)	1,842	35	50	$10,090	$10,090	$4,630
Lubbock Christian University; Lubbock, Tex. 79407 (P)	1,035	56	96	$ 7,750	$ 7,750	$4,916
McMurry University; Abilene, Tex. 79697 (P)	1,384	55	70	$ 7,200	$ 7,200	$3,767
Midwestern State University; Wichita Falls, Tex. 76308 (P)	4,954	55	77	$ 768	$ 5,904	$3,470
Our Lady of the Lake University; San Antonio, Tex. 78207 (P)	2,365	77	74	$ 9,540	$ 9,540	$3,984
Prairie View A&M University; Prairie View, Tex. 77446 (Pub)	4,968	52	90	$ 2,057	$ 8,477	$1,882
Rice University; Houston, Tex. 77251 (P)	2,633	41	25	$ 9,950	$ 9,950	$5,725
Saint Edward's University; Austin, Tex. 78704 (P)	2,546	60	77	$10,730	$10,730	$4,700
Saint Mary's University; San Antonio, Tex. 78228 (P)	2,560	55	87	$ 9,934	$ 9,934	$3,773
Sam Houston State University; Huntsville, Tex. 77341 (Pub)	11,096	55	84	$ 768	$ 5,904	$3,198
Schreiner College; Kerrville, Tex. 78028 (P)	675	56	80	$ 9,735	$ 9,735	$6,380
Southern Methodist University; Dallas, Tex. 75275 (P)	5,362	54	90	$14,186	$14,186	$5,268
Southwest Texas State University; San Marcos, Tex. 78666 (Pub)	17,677	54	68	$ 960	$ 7,380	$3,787
Southwestern Adventist University; Keene, Tex. 76059 (P)		58	100	$ 8,400	$ 8,400	$4,084
Southwestern University; Georgetown, Tex. 78626 (P)	1,183	58	79	$14,000	$14,000	$5,269
Stephen F. Austin State University; Nacogdoches, Tex. 75962 (Pub)	10,116	56	71	$ 960	$ 6,660	$3,992
Sul Ross State University; Alpine, Tex. 79832 (Pub)	1,818	46	99	$ 960	$ 7,380	$3,300
Tarleton State University; Stephenville, Tex. 76402 (Pub)	5,551	50	74	$ 960	$ 7,380	$3,226
Texas A&M University-College Station; College Station, Tex. 77843 (Pub)	34,298	46	69	$ 1,020	$ 7,440	$4,560
Texas A&M University-Galveston; Galveston, Tex. 77553 (Pub)	1,203	46	84	$ 2,194	$ 8,614	$3,254
Texas Christian University; Fort Worth, Tex. 76129 (P)	5,810	59	74	$ 9,900	$ 9,900	$3,860
Texas College; Tyler, Tex. 75702 (P)				$ 4,800	$ 4,800	$2,630
Texas Lutheran College; Seguin, Tex. 78155 (P)	1,324	60		$ 9,450	$ 9,450	$3,612
Texas Southern University; Houston, Tex. 77004 (Pub)	8,832	70		$ 576	$ 4,428	$1,700
Texas Tech University; Lubbock, Tex. 79409 (Pub)	20,420	46	81	$ 1,020	$ 7,440	$4,200
Texas Wesleyan University; Fort Worth, Tex. 76105 (P)	1,871	65	79	$ 7,550	$ 7,550	$3,484
Texas Woman's University; Denton, Tex. 76204 (Pub)	5,752	95		$ 1,342	$ 4,774	$2,992
Trinity University; San Antonio, Tex. 78212 (P)	2,251	51	79	$13,500	$13,500	$5,545
University of Central Texas; Killeen, Tex. 76540-1416 (P)	701	55		$ 4,680	$ 4,680	$3,158
University of Dallas; Irving, Tex. 75062 (P)	1,088	63	89	$12,920	$12,920	$4,918
University of Houston; Houston, Tex. 77204-2161 (Pub)	21,522	54	100	$ 960	$ 7,380	
University of Houston-Downtown; Houston, Tex. 77002 (Pub)	21,522	52	62	$ 816	$ 5,904	$4,405
University of Mary Hardin-Baylor; Belton, Tex. 76513 (P)	2,010	69	71	$ 5,850	$ 5,850	$3,136
University of North Texas; Denton, Tex. 76203 (Pub)	19,181	51	76	$ 768	$ 5,904	$3,766
University of Saint Thomas (Tex.); Houston, Tex. 77006 (P)	1,403	66	83	$ 9,840	$ 9,840	$4,180
University of Texas-Pan American; Edinburg, Tex. 78539 (Pub)	11,627	58	100	$ 991	$ 3,486	$1,241
University of Texas-Arlington; Arlington, Tex. 76019 (Pub)	16,579	50	88	$ 1,859	$ 6,995	$2,000
University of Texas-Austin; Austin, Tex. 78712 (Pub)	35,789	49	61	$ 2,842	$ 8,406	$4,260
University of Texas-Brownsville; Brownsville, Tex. 78520-4991 (Pub.)	2,081	63	95	$ 1,024	$ 7,872	
University of Texas-Dallas; Richardson, Tex. 75083-0688 (Pub)	5,293	50	74	$ 960	$ 7,380	$5,255
University of Texas-El Paso; El Paso, Tex. 79968 (Pub)	13,159	54	79	$ 839	$ 3,407	$1,600
University of Texas-Permian Basin; Odessa, Tex. 79762 (Pub)	1,219	64	74	$ 960	$ 7,380	$1,580
University of Texas-San Antonio; San Antonio, Tex. 78249 (Pub)	15,437	52	43	$ 1,754	$ 6,362	$4,674
University of Texas-Tyler; Tyler, Tex. 75701 (Pub)	2,468	65	86	$ 788	$ 5,904	
University of the Incarnate Word; San Antonio, Tex. 78209 (P)	2,241	70	80	$10,600	$10,600	$4,467
Wayland Baptist University; Plainview, Tex. 79072 (P)	3,328	40	99	$ 5,850	$ 5,850	$3,219

Institution Name; City, State Zip (Control)	Students	Percent		Tuition		Room and board
		Women	Accepted	In-State	Out-of-State	
West Texas A&M University; Canyon, Tex. 79016 (Pub)	5,329	55	92	$ 816	$ 5,952	$2,846
Wiley College; Marshall, Tex. 75670 (P)	463	50	97	$ 3,960	$ 3,960	$3,138
UTAH						
Brigham Young University; Provo, Utah 84602 (P)	26,553	52	77	$ 2,530	$ 2,530	$3,930
Southern Utah University; Cedar City, Utah 84720 (Pub)	5,426	56	91	$ 1,386	$ 5,238	$2,070
University of Utah; Salt Lake City, Utah 84112 (Pub)	21,966	45	91	$ 1,725	$ 6,066	$4,195
Utah State University; Logan, Utah 84322 (Pub)	16,703	51	99	$ 1,701	$ 5,979	$3,579
Weber State University; Ogden, Utah 84408 (Pub)	13,692	53	100	$ 1,518	$ 5,313	$3,270
Westminster College of Salt Lake City; Salt Lake City, Utah 84105 (P)	1,473	66	89	$10,200	$10,200	$4,358
VERMONT						
Bennington College; Bennington, Vt. 05201 (P)	289	66	71	$26,400	$26,400	
Burlington College; Burlington, Vt. 05401 (P)	160	60	100	$ 6,600	$ 6,600	
Castleton State College; Castleton, Vt. 05735 (Pub)	1,867	54	87	$ 3,620	$ 8,380	$4,936
College of Saint Joseph in Vermont; Rutland, Vt. 05701 (P)	478	66	93	$ 8,300	$ 8,300	$4,850
Goddard College; Plainfield, Vt. 05667 (P)	257	59	87	$15,056	$15,056	$4,660
Green Mountain College; Poultney, Vt. 05764 (P)	585	51	85	$14,360	$14,360	$3,190
Johnson State College; Johnson, Vt. 05656 (Pub)	1,569	47	78	$ 3,780	$ 8,760	$5,086
Lyndon State College; Lyndonville, Vt. 05851 (Pub)	1,145	45	88	$ 3,432	$ 7,944	$4,854
Marlboro College; Marlboro, Vt. 05344 (P)	280	54	72	$19,100	$19,100	$6,400
Middlebury College; Middlebury, Vt. 05753 (P)	2,120	50	29	$29,340	$29,340	
Norwich University; Northfield, Vt. 05663 (P)	1,500	30	94	$14,634	$14,634	$5,536
Saint Michael's College; Colchester, Vt. 05439 (P)	1,989	55	62	$14,640	$14,640	$6,375
Southern Vermont College; Bennington, Vt. 05201 (P)	697	58	72	$ 8,370	$ 8,370	$4,304
Trinity College of Vermont; Burlington, Vt. 05401 (P)	889	94	94	$12,120	$12,120	$6,012
University of Vermont; Burlington, Vt. 05401 (Pub)	7,375	54	75	$ 6,732	$16,824	$4,706
VIRGINIA						
Averett College; Danville, Va. 24541 (P)	1,611	57	86	$11,450	$11,450	$4,150
Bluefield College; Bluefield, Va. 24605 (P)	756	53	91	$ 8,770	$ 8,770	$4,610
Bridgewater College; Bridgewater, Va. 22812 (P)	1,033	56	83	$13,270	$13,270	$5,630
Christopher Newport University; Newport News, Va. 23606 (Pub)	4,565	61	82	$ 3,426	$ 8,100	$4,650
Clinch Valley College of the U. of Virginia; Wise, Va. 24293 (Pub)	1,387	59	48	$ 3,258	$ 7,782	$4,158
Eastern Mennonite University; Harrisonburg, Va. 22801 (Pub)	1,023	61	92	$12,000	$12,000	$4,500
Emory and Henry College; Emory, Va. 24327 (P)	833	49	86	$10,938	$10,938	$4,800
Ferrum College; Ferrum, Va. 24088 (P)	1,075	42	74	$10,750	$10,750	$4,850
George Mason University; Fairfax, Va. 22030 (Pub)	13,331	55	69	$ 4,242	$11,952	$5,080
Hampden-Sydney College; Hampden-Sydney, Va. 23943 (P)	956	0	84	$14,909	$14,909	$5,557
Hampton University; Hampton, Va. 23668 (P)	5,155	60	52	$ 8,198	$ 8,198	$3,878
Hollins College; Roanoke, Va. 24020 (P)	844	100	81	$14,560	$14,560	$5,975
James Madison University; Harrisonburg, Va. 22807 (Pub)	11,643	55	63	$ 4,104	$ 8,580	$4,884
Liberty University; Lynchburg, Va. 24506 (P)	3,603	49	73	$ 7,680	$ 7,680	$4,800
Longwood College; Farmville, Va. 23909 (Pub)	2,960	67	76	$ 4,416	$ 9,888	$4,360
Lynchburg College; Lynchburg, Va. 24501 (P)	1,413	64	86	$14,720	$14,720	$4,400
Mary Baldwin College; Staunton, Va. 24402 (P)	1,160	98	86	$13,200	$13,200	$7,000
Mary Washington College; Fredericksburg, Va. 22401 (Pub)	3,499	65	55	$ 3,556	$ 8,516	$5,080
Marymount University; Arlington, Va. 22207 (P)	1,940	76	74	$12,400	$12,400	$5,810
Norfolk State University; Norfolk, Va. 23504 (Pub)	7,252	61	95	$ 2,865	$ 6,492	$4,096
Old Dominion University; Norfolk, Va. 23529 (Pub)	8,346	53	81	$ 3,990	$10,350	$4,540
Radford University; Radford, Va. 24142 (Pub)	8,527	59	80	$ 3,146	$ 7,720	$4,312
Randolph-Macon College; Ashland, Va. 23005 (P)	1,101	48	80	$15,865	$15,865	$4,175
Randolph-Macon Woman's College; Lynchburg, Va. 24503 (P)	698	100	89	$15,880	$15,880	$6,720
Roanoke College; Salem, Va. 24153 (P)	1,694	59	83	$14,750	$14,750	$4,850
Saint Paul's College; Lawrenceville, Va. 23868 (P)	666	57	72	$ 5,256	$ 5,256	$3,834
Shenandoah University; Winchester, Va. 22601 (P)	1,261	66	81	$14,400	$14,400	$5,050
Sweet Briar College; Sweet Briar, Va. 24595 (P)	734	100	91	$15,420	$15,420	$6,510
The College of William and Mary; Williamsburg, Va. 23187-8795 (P)	5,357	58	42	$ 5,032	$15,404	$4,586
University of Richmond; Richmond, Va. 23173 (P)	2,945	49	50	$17,570	$17,570	$3,755
University of Virginia; Charlottesville, Va. 22906 (Pub)	12,211	52	33	$ 4,786	$15,030	$4,279
Virginia Commonwealth University; Richmond, Va. 23284 (Pub)	14,610	59	82	$ 3,125	$11,382	$4,487
Virginia Intermont College; Bristol, Va. 24201 (P)	451	68	80	$10,450	$10,450	$4,700
Virginia Military Institute; Lexington, Va. 24450 (Pub)	1,218	0	78	$ 3,655	$10,680	$3,695
Virginia State University; Petersburg, Va. 23806 (Pub)	3,053	58	78	$ 1,951	$ 6,430	$4,910
Virginia Tech; Blacksburg, Va. 24061 (Pub)	21,099	41	81	$ 3,500	$10,152	$3,250
Virginia Wesleyan College; Norfolk/Virginia Beach, Va. 23502 (P)	1,568	67	88	$13,400	$13,400	$5,550
Washington and Lee University; Lexington, Va. 24450 (P)	1,645	41	31	$16,040	$16,040	$5,303

Institution Name; City, State Zip (Control)	Students	Percent		Tuition		Room and board
		Women	Accepted	In-State	Out-of-State	
WASHINGTON						
Central Washington University; Ellensburg, Wash. 98926 (Pub)	7,837	52	76	$ 2,526	$ 8,961	$4,400
Cornish College of the Arts; Seattle, Wash. 98102 (P)	650	56	79	$11,540	$11,540	
Eastern Washington University; Cheney, Wash. 99004 (Pub)	6,326	58	90	$ 2,430	$ 8,616	$4,293
Gonzaga University; Spokane, Wash. 99258 (P)	3,008	53	81	$14,900	$14,900	$4,950
Northwest College; Kirkland, Wash. 98083 (P)	802	54	98	$ 8,415	$ 8,415	$3,990
Pacific Lutheran University; Tacoma, Wash. 98447 (P)	3,087	60	96	$14,560	$14,560	$4,690
Saint Martin's College; Lacey, Wash. 98503 (P)	1,061	56	88	$12,610	$12,610	$4,590
Seattle Pacific University; Seattle, Wash. 98119 (P)	2,506	64	91	$14,130	$14,130	$5,418
Seattle University; Seattle, Wash. 98122 (P)	3,272	58	66	$14,805	$14,805	$5,493
The Evergreen State College; Olympia, Wash. 98505 (Pub)	3,498	57	88	$ 2,346	$ 8,295	$4,470
University of Puget Sound; Tacoma, Wash. 98416 (P)	2,768	59	82	$18,790	$18,790	$4,920
University of Washington; Seattle, Wash. 98195 (Pub)	24,592	50	69	$ 3,138	$ 9,753	$4,455
Walla Walla College; College Place, Wash. 99324 (P)	1,667	49		$11,916	$11,916	$3,387
Washington State University; Pullman, Wash. 99164 (Pub)	16,686	50	89	$ 3,142	$ 9,758	$4,150
Western Washington University; Bellingham, Wash. 98225 (Pub)	10,252	59	83	$ 2,613	$ 8,796	$4,478
Whitman College; Walla Walla, Wash. 99362 (P)	1,349	54	54	$19,580	$19,580	$5,640
Whitworth College; Spokane, Wash. 99251 (P)	1,577	59	85	$13,620	$13,620	$4,900
WEST VIRGINIA						
Alderson-Broaddus College; Philippi, W.V. 26416 (P)	709	58	61	$12,115	$12,115	$4,165
Bethany College (W.V.); Bethany, W.V. 26032 (P)	730	46	76	$15,750	$15,750	$5,390
Bluefield State College; Bluefield, W.V. 24701 (Pub)	2,700	55	64	$ 2,044	$ 4,968	
Concord College; Athens, W.V. 24712 (P)	2,357	59	93	$ 2,218	$ 4,798	$3,468
Davis & Elkins College; Elkins, W.V. 26241 (P)	732	60	91	$10,580	$10,580	$4,890
Fairmont State College; Fairmont, W.V. 26554 (Pub)	6,555	51	99	$ 2,040	$ 4,840	$3,600
Glenville State College; Glenville, W.V. 26351 (Pub)	2,179	56	100	$ 1,956	$ 4,560	$3,560
Marshall University; Huntington, W.V. 25755 (Pub)	8,778	55	90	$ 2,116	$ 5,878	$4,240
Salem-Teikyo University; Salem, W.V. 26426 (P)	738	35	76	$11,658	$11,658	$3,952
Shepherd College; Shepherdstown, W.V. 25443 (Pub)	3,845	60	50	$ 2,228	$ 5,348	$4,139
University of Charleston; Charleston, W.V. 25304 (P)	1,424	70	79	$11,600	$11,600	
West Liberty State College; West Liberty, W.V. 26074 (Pub)	2,412	55	95	$ 2,020	$ 5,460	$3,100
West Virginia Institute of Technology; Montgomery, W.V. 25136 (Pub)	2,460	34	100	$ 2,298	$ 5,760	$3,660
West Virginia State College; Institute, W.V. 25112 (Pub)	4,530	55	99	$ 2,116	$ 5,158	$4,950
West Virginia University; Morgantown, W.V. 26506-6009 (Pub)	14,897	47	89	$ 2,336	$ 7,356	$4,832
West Virginia Wesleyan College; Buckhannon, W.V. 26201 (P)	1,531	55	85	$14,975	$14,975	$3,915
Wheeling Jesuit University; Wheeling, W.V. 26003 (P)	1,296	59	88	$13,000	$13,000	$4,870
WISCONSIN						
Alverno College; Milwaukee, Wis. 53234 (P)	2,191	100	65	$ 9,672	$ 9,672	$4,040
Beloit College; Beloit, Wis. 53511 (P)	1,270	57	70	$18,850	$18,850	$4,140
Cardinal Stritch College; Milwaukee, Wis. 53217 (P)	2,764	62	78	$ 8,960	$ 8,960	$3,880
Carroll College (Wis.); Waukesha, Wis. 53186 (P)	1,542	66	87	$13,190	$13,190	$4,130
Carthage College; Kenosha, Wis. 53140 (P)	2,164	52	90	$14,600	$14,600	$4,195
Concordia University (Wis.); Mequon, Wis. 53097 (P)	4,022	59	73	$10,700	$10,700	$3,700
Edgewood College; Madison, Wis. 53711 (P)	1,500	73	80	$ 9,000	$ 9,000	$3,800
Lakeland College; Sheboygan, Wis. 53082 (P)	3,300	55	87	$10,820	$10,820	$4,220
Lawrence University; Appleton, Wis. 54912-0599 (P)	1,146	52	58	$19,494	$19,494	$4,425
Marian College of Fond Du Lac; Fond du Lac, Wis. 54935 (P)	1,856	67	90	$10,560	$10,560	$3,800
Marquette University; Milwaukee, Wis. 53201 (P)	7,462	53	86	$14,710	$14,710	$5,350
Milwaukee Institute of Art and Design; Milwaukee, Wis. 53202 (P)	518	42	74	$13,700	$13,700	$6,035
Milwaukee School of Engineering; Milwaukee, Wis. 53202 (P)	2,537	16	91	$13,305	$13,305	$3,615
Mount Mary College; Milwaukee, Wis. 53222 (P)	1,287		85	$10,740	$10,740	$3,750
Mount Senario College; Ladysmith, Wis. 54848 (P)	1,048	31	68	$ 9,500	$ 9,500	$3,400
Northland College; Ashland, Wis. 54806 (P)	787	53	94	$11,380	$11,380	$4,060
Ripon College; Ripon, Wis. 54971 (P)	734	57	88	$16,780	$16,780	$4,400
Saint Norbert College; De Pere, Wis. 54115 (P)	1,975	59	89	$14,434	$14,434	$5,120
Silver Lake College; Manitowoc, Wis. 54220 (P)	822	70	92	$ 9,630	$ 9,630	$4,090
University of Wisconsin-Eau Claire; Eau Claire, Wis. 54701 (Pub)	10,023	60	85	$ 2,574	$ 8,038	$2,904
University of Wisconsin-Green Bay; Green Bay, Wis. 54311 (Pub)	5,530	62	89	$ 2,540	$ 7,830	$2,950
University of Wisconsin-LaCrosse; LaCrosse, Wis. 54601 (Pub)	8,435	56	81	$ 2,570	$ 7,740	$2,800
University of Wisconsin-Madison; Madison, Wis. 53706 (Pub)	26,910	51	69	$ 2,881	$ 9,636	$3,829
University of Wisconsin-Milwaukee; Milwaukee, Wis. 53201 (Pub)	17,032	52	81	$ 3,102	$ 9,965	$4,040
University of Wisconsin-Parkside; Kenosha, Wis. 53141 (Pub)	3,879	58	93	$ 2,114	$ 6,562	$3,200

| Institution Name; City, State Zip (Control) | Students | Percent | | Tuition | | Room and board |
		Women	Accepted	In-State	Out-of-State	
University of Wisconsin-Platteville; Platteville, Wis. 53818 (Pub)	4,665	35	83	$ 2,319	$ 8,216	$2,914
University of Wisconsin-River Falls; River Falls, Wis. 54022 (Pub)	4,975	58	80	$ 2,445	$ 7,580	$2,776
University of Wisconsin-Stevens Point; Stevens Point, Wis. 54481 (Pub)	8,024	53	77	$ 2,650	$ 8,400	$3,260
University of Wisconsin-Stout; Menomonie, Wis. 54751 (Pub)	6,709	48	94	$ 2,619	$ 8,083	$2,922
University of Wisconsin-Superior; Superior, Wis. 54880 (Pub)	2,314	51	83	$ 2,463	$ 7,927	$3,148
University of Wisconsin-Whitewater; Whitewater, Wis. 53190 (Pub)	9,157	54	84	$ 2,560	$ 7,920	$2,700
University of Wisconsin Oshkosh; Oshkosh, Wis. 54901 (Pub)	8,751	57	49	$ 2,550	$ 8,320	$2,658
Viterbo College; La Crosse, Wis. 54601 (P)	1,639	70	90	$10,880	$10,880	$4,050
Wisconsin Lutheran College; Milwaukee, Wis. 53226 (P)	364	59	95	$10,900	$10,900	$4,100
WYOMING						
University of Wyoming; Laramie, Wyo. 82071 (Pub)	8,820	52	97	$ 2,326	$ 7,414	$4,245

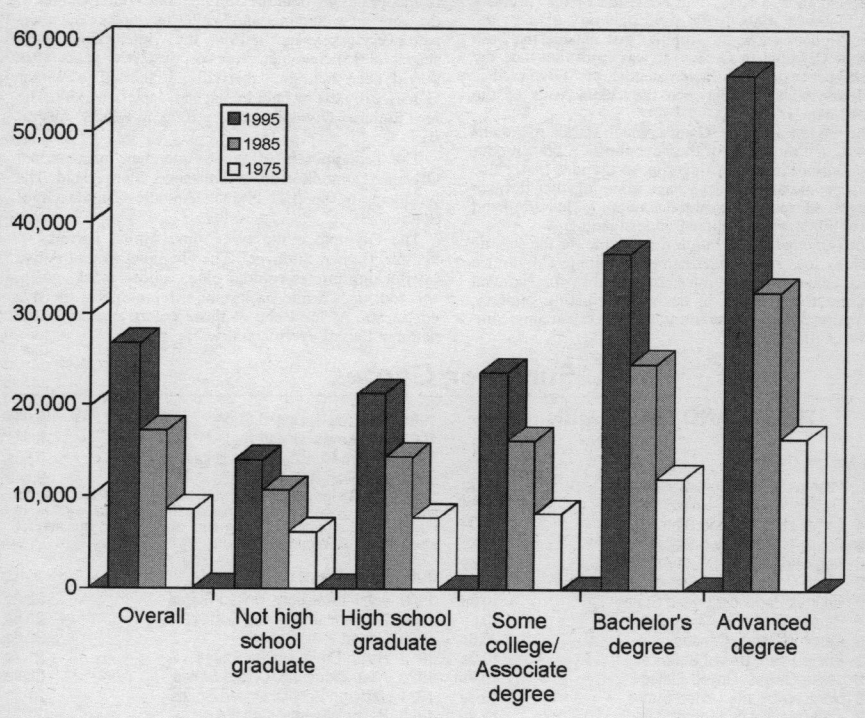

Mean Earnings of Workers 18 Years and Over by Educational Attainment, 1975 to 1995

Source: Census Bureau, Current Population Survey

Sports

The Olympic Games

1896	Athens	1948	St. Moritz (W)	1976	Montreal (S)
1900	Paris	1948	London (S)	1980	Lake Placid (W)
1904	St. Louis	1952	Oslo (W)	1980	Moscow (S)
1906	Athens	1952	Helsinki (S)	1984	Sarajevo, Yugoslavia (W)
1908	London	1956	Cortina d'Ampezzo, Italy (W)	1984	Los Angeles (S)
1912	Stockholm	1956	Melbourne (S)	1988	Calgary, Alberta (W)
1920	Antwerp	1960	Squaw Valley, Calif. (W)	1988	Seoul, South Korea (S)
1924	Chamonix (W)	1960	Rome (S)	1992	Albertville, France (W)
1924	Paris (S)	1964	Innsbruck, Austria (W)	1992	Barcelona, Spain (S)
1928	St. Moritz (W)	1964	Tokyo (S)	1994	Lillehammer, Norway (W)
1928	Amsterdam (S)	1968	Grenoble, France (W)	1996	Atlanta, Ga. (S)
1932	Lake Placid (W)	1968	Mexico City (S)	1998	Nagano, Japan (W)
1932	Los Angeles (S)	1972	Sapporo, Japan (W)	2000	Sydney, Australia (S)
1936	Garmisch-Partenkirchen (W)	1972	Munich (S)	2002	Salt Lake City (W)
1936	Berlin (S)	1976	Innsbruck, Austria (W)	2004	Athens (S)

(W)—Site of Winter Games. (S)—Site of Summer Games

The first Olympic Games of which there is record were held in 776 B.C.E., and consisted of one event, a great foot race of about 200 yards held on a plain by the River Alpheus (now the Ruphia) just outside the little town of Olympia in Greece. It was from that date the Greeks began to keep their calendar by "Olympiads," the four-year spans between the celebrations of the famous games.

The modern Olympic Games, which started in Athens in 1896, are the result of the devotion of a French educator, Baron Pierre de Coubertin, to the idea that, since young people and athletics have gone together through the ages, education and athletics might go hand-in-hand toward a better international understanding.

The principal organization responsible for the staging of the Games is the International Olympic Committee (IOC). Other important roles are played by the National Olympic Committees in each participating country, international sports federations, and the organizing committee of the host city.

Beginning in 1994, the IOC decided to change the format of having both the Summer and Winter Games in the same year. Summer and Winter Olympics now alternate every two years. In 1994, the Winter Games were staged in Lillehammer, Norway, just two years after they'd been held in Albertville, France. The Winter Games will next be held in Nagano, Japan, in 1998. The next Summer Olympics will be 2000 in Sydney, Australia.

The headquarters of the 89-member International Olympic Committee are in Lausanne, Switzerland. The president of the IOC is Juan Antonio Samaranch of Spain.

The Olympic motto is "Citius, Altius, Fortius,"— "Faster, Higher, Stronger." The Olympic symbol is five interlocking circles colored blue, yellow, black, green, and red, on a white background, representing the five continents. At least one of those colors appears in the national flag of every country.

Summer Games

TRACK AND FIELD–MEN

100-Meter Dash

1896	Thomas Burke, United States	12.0s
1900	Francis W. Jarvis, United States	10.8s
1904	Archie Hahn, United States	11.0s
1906	Archie Hahn, United States	11.2s
1908	Reginald Walker, South Africa	10.8s
1912	Ralph Craig, United States	10.8s
1920	Charles Paddock, United States	10.8s
1924	Harold Abrahams, Great Britain	10.6s
1928	Percy Williams, Canada	10.8s
1932	Eddie Tolan, United States	10.3s
1936	Jesse Owens, United States	10.3s[1]
1948	Harrison Dillard, United States	10.3s
1952	Lindy Remigino, United States	10.4s
1956	Bobby Morrow, United States	10.5s
1960	Armin Hary, Germany	10.2s
1964	Robert Hayes, United States	10.0s
1968	James Hines, United States	9.9s
1972	Valery Borzow, U.S.S.R.	10.14s
1976	Hasely Crawford, Trinidad and Tobago	10.06s
1980	Allan Wells, Britain	10.25s

1984	Carl Lewis, United States	9.99s
1988	Carl Lewis, United States	9.92s[2]
1992	Linford Christie, Great Britain	9.96s
1996	Donovan Bailey, Canada	9.84s[3]

1. Wind assisted. 2. Lewis was awarded the gold medal when Ben Johnson of Canada, the original winner in 09.79s, was stripped of the medal after testing positive for steroid use. 3. World record.

200-Meter Dash

1900	John Tewksbury, United States	22.2s
1904	Archie Hahn, United States	21.6s
1908	Robert Kerr, Canada	22.6s
1912	Ralph Craig, United States	21.7s
1920	Allan Woodring, United States	22.0s
1924	Jackson Scholz, United States	21.6s
1928	Percy Williams, Canada	21.8s
1932	Eddie Tolan, United States	21.2s
1936	Jesse Owens, United States	20.7s
1948	Melvin E. Patton, United States	21.1s
1952	Andrew Stanfield, United States	20.7s
1956	Bobby Morrow, United States	20.6s
1960	Livio Berruti, Italy	20.5s
1964	Henry Carr, United States	20.3s

1968	Tommie Smith, United States	19.8s
1972	Vallery Borzov, U.S.S.R.	20.0s
1976	Don Quarrie, Jamaica	20.23s
1980	Pietro Mennea, Italy	20.19s
1984	Carl Lewis, United States	19.80s
1988	Joe DeLoach, United States	19.75s
1992	Mike Marsh, United States	20.01s
1996	Michael Johnson, United States	19.32s[1]

1. World record.

400-Meter Dash

1896	Thomas Burke, United States	54.2s
1900	Maxwell Long, United States	49.4s
1904	Harry Hillman, United States	49.2s
1906	Paul Pilgrim, United States	53.2s
1908	Wyndham Halswelle, Great Britain (walkover)	50.0s
1912	Charles Reidpath, United States	48.2s
1920	Bevil Rudd, South Africa	49.6s
1924	Eric Liddell, Great Britain	47.6s
1928	Ray Barbuti, United States	47.8s
1932	William Carr, United States	46.2s
1936	Archie Williams, United States	46.5s
1948	Arthur Wint, Jamaica, B.W.I.	46.2s
1952	George Rhoden, Jamaica, B.W.I.	45.9s
1956	Charles Jenkins, United States	46.7s
1960	Otis Davis, United States	44.9s
1964	Mike Larrabee, United States	45.1s
1968	Lee Evans, United States	43.8s
1972	Vincent Matthews, United States	44.66s
1976	Alberto Juantorena, Cuba	44.26s
1980	Viktor Markin, U.S.S.R.	44.60s
1984	Alonzo Babers, United States	44.27s
1988	Steve Lewis, United States	43.87s
1992	Quincy Watts, United States	43.50s
1996	Michael Johnson, United States	43.49s

800-Meter Run

1896	Edwin Flack, Australia	2m11.0s
1900	Alfred Tysoe, Great Britain	2m1.4s
1904	James Lightbody, United States	1m56.0s
1906	Paul Pilgrim, United States	2m1.2s
1908	Mel Sheppard, United states	1m52.8s
1912	Ted Meredith, United States	1m51.9s
1920	Albert Hill, Great Britain	1m53.4s
1924	Douglas Lowe, Great Britain	1m52.4s
1928	Douglas Lowe, Great Britain	1m51.8s
1932	Thomas Hampson, Great Britain	1m49.8s
1936	John Woodruff, United States	1m52.9s
1948	Malvin Whitfield, United States	1m49.2s
1952	Malvin Whitfield, United States	1m49.2s
1956	Tom Courtney, United States	1m47.7s
1960	Peter Snell, New Zealand	1m46.3s
1964	Peter Snell, New Zealand	1m45.1s
1968	Ralph Doubell, Australia	1m44.3s
1972	David Wottle, United States	1m45.9s
1976	Alberto Juantorena, Cuba	1m43.5s
1980	Steve Ovett, Britain	1m45.4s
1984	Joaquin Cruz, Brazil	1m43.0s
1988	Paul Ereng, Kenya	1m43.45s
1992	William Tanui, Kenya	1m43.66s
1996	Vebjoern Rodal, Norway	1m42.58s

1,500-Meter Run

1896	Edwin Flack, Australia	4m33.2s
1900	Charles Bennett, Great Britain	4m6.0s
1904	James Lightbody, United States	4m5.4s
1906	James Lightbody, United States	4m12.0s
1908	Mel Sheppard, United States	4m3.4s
1912	Arnold Jackson, Great Britain	3m56.8s
1920	Albert Hill, Great Britain	4m1.8s
1924	Paavo Nurmi, Finland	3m53.6s
1928	Harry Larva, Finland	3m53.2s
1932	Luigi Becali, Italy	3m51.2s

1936	Jack Lovelock, New Zealand	3m47.8s
1948	Henri Eriksson, Sweden	3m49.8s
1952	Joseph Barthel, Luxembourg	3m45.2s
1956	Ron Delany, Ireland	3m41.2s
1960	Herb Elliott, Australia	3m35.6s
1964	Peter Snell, New Zealand	3m38.1s
1968	Kipchoge Keino, Kenya	3m34.9s
1972	Pekka Vasala, Finland	3m36.3s
1976	John Walker, New Zealand	3m39.17s
1980	Sebastian Coe, Britain	3m38.4s
1984	Sebastian Coe, Britain	3m32.53s
1988	Peter Rono, Kenya	3m35.96s
1992	Fermin Cacho Ruiz, Spain	3m40.12s
1996	Noureddine Morceli, Algeria	3m35.78s

5,000-Meter Run

1912	Hannes Kolehmainen, Finland	14m36.6s
1920	Joseph Guillemot, France	14m55.6s
1024	Paavo Nurmi, Finland	14m31.2s
1928	Willie Ritola, Finland	14m38.0s
1932	Lauri Lehtinen, Finland	14m30.0s
1936	Gunnar Hockert, Finland	14m22.2s
1948	Gaston Reiff, Belgium	14m17.6s
1952	Emil Zatopek, Czechoslovakia	14m6.6s
1956	Vladimir Kuts, U.S.S.R.	13m39.6s
1960	Murray Halberg, New Zealand	13m43.4s
1964	Bob Schul, United States	13m48.8s
1968	Mohamed Gammoudi, Tunisia	14m.05s
1972	Lasse Viren, Finland	13m26.4s
1976	Lasse Viren, Finland	13m24.76s
1980	Miruts Yifter, Ethiopia	13m21.0s
1984	Saud Aouita, Morocco	13m5.59s
1988	John Ngugi, Kenya	13m11.70s
1992	Dieter Baumann, Germany	13m12.52s
1996	Venuste Niyongabo, Burundi	13m07.96s

10,000-Meter Run

1912	Hannes Kolehmainen, Finland	31m20.8s
1920	Paavo Nurmi, Finland	31m45.8s
1924	Willie Ritola, Finland	30m23.2s
1928	Paavo Nurmi, Finland	30m18.8s
1932	Janusz Kusocinski, Poland	30m11.4s
1936	Ilmari Salminen, Finland	30m15.4s
1948	Emil Zatopek, Czechoslovakia	29m59.6s
1952	Emil Zatopek, Czechoslovakia	29m17.0s
1956	Vladimir Kuts, U.S.S.R.	28m45.6s
1960	Peter Bolotnikov, U.S.S.R.	28m32.2s
1964	Billy Mills, United States	28m24.4s
1968	Nartali Temu, Kenya	29m27.4s
1972	Lasse Viren, Finland	27m38.4s
1976	Lasse Viren, Finland	27m40.38s
1980	Miruts Yifter, Ethiopia	27m42.7s
1984	Alberto Cova, Italy	27m47.5s
1988	Mly Brahim Boutaib, Morocco	27m21.46s
1992	Khalid Skah, Morocco	27m47.70s
1996	Haile Gebrselassie, Ethiopia	27m07.34s

Marathon

1896	Spiridon Loues, Greece	2h58m50.0s
1900	Michel Teato, France	2h59m45.0s
1904	Thomas Hicks, United States	3h28m53.0s
1906	William J. Sherring, Canada	2h51m23.65s
1908	John J. Hayes, United States	2h55m18.4s
1912	Kenneth McArthur, South Africa	2h36m54.8s
1920	Hannes Kolehmainen, Finland	2h32m35.8s
1924	Albin Stenroos, Finland	2h41m22.6s
1928	A.B. El Quafi, France	2h32m57.0s
1932	Juan Zabala, Argentina	2h31m36.0s
1936	Kitei Son, Japan	2h29m19.2s
1948	Delfo Cabrera, Argentina	2h34m51.6s
1952	Emil Zatopek, Czechoslovakia	2h23m3.2s
1956	Alain Mimoun, France	2h25m0.0s
1960	Abebe Bikila, Ethiopia	2h15m16.2s

1964	Abebe Bikila, Ethiopia	2h12m11.2s
1968	Mamo Wold, Ethiopia	2h20m26.4s
1972	Frank Shorter, United States	2h12m19.8s
1976	Walter Cierpinski, East Germany	2h09m55.0s
1980	Walter Cierpinski, East Germany	2h11m3.0s
1984	Carlos Lopes, Portugal	2h9m21.0s
1988	Gelindo Bordin, Italy	2hr10m47.0s
1992	Hwang Young-Cho, South Korea	2h13m23.0s
1996	Josia Thugwane, South Africa	2h12m36.0s

110-Meter Hurdles

1896	Thomas Curtis, United States	17.6s
1900	Alvin Kraenzlein, United States	15.4s
1904	Frederick Schule, United States	16.0s
1906	R.G. Leavitt, United States	16.2s
1908	Forrest Smithson, United States	15.0s
1912	Frederick Kelly, United States	15.1s
1920	Earl Thomson, Canada	14.8s
1924	Daniel Kinsey, United States	15.0s
1928	Sydney Atkinson, South Africa	14.8s
1932	George Saling, United States	14.6s
1936	Forrest Towns, United States	14.2s
1948	William Porter, United States	13.9s
1952	Harrison Dillard, United States	13.7s
1956	Lee Calhoun, United States	13.5s
1960	Lee Calhoun, United States	13.8s
1964	Hayes Jones, United States	13.6s
1968	Willie Davenport, United States	13.3s
1972	Rodney Milburn, United States	13.24s
1976	Guy Drut, France	13.30s
1980	Thomas Munkett, East Germany	13.20s
1984	Roger Kingdom, United States	13.20s
1988	Roger Kingdom, United States	12.98s
1992	Mark McCoy, Canada	13.12s
1996	Allen Johnson, United States	12.95s

200-Meter Hurdles

1900	Alvin Kraenzlein, United States	25.4s
1904	Harry Hillman, United States	24.6s

400-Meter Hurdles

1900	John Tewksbury, United States	57.6s
1904	Harry Hillman, United States	53.0s
1908	Charles Bacon, United States	55.0s
1920	Frank Loomis, United States	54.0s
1924	F. Morgan Taylor, United States	52.6s
1928	Lord David Burghley, Great Britain	53.4s
1932	Robert Tisdall, Ireland	51.8s[1]
1936	Glenn Hardin, United States	52.4s
1948	Roy Cochran, United States	51.1s
1952	Charles Moore, United States	50.8s
1956	Glenn Davis, United States	50.1s
1960	Glenn Davis, United States	49.3s
1964	Rex Cawley, United States	49.6s
1968	David Hemery, Great Britain	48.1s
1972	John Akii-Bua, Uganda	47.8s
1976	Edwin Moses, United States	47.64s
1980	Volker Beck, East Germany	48.70s
1984	Edwin Moses, United States	47.75s
1988	Andre Phillips, United States	47.19s
1992	Kevin Young, United States	46.78s
1996	Derrick Adkins, United States	47.54s

1. Record not allowed.

2,500-Meter Steeplechase

1900	George Orton, United States	7m34.0s
1904	James Lightbody, United States	7m39.6s

3,000-Meter Steeplechase

1920	Percy Hodge, Great Britain	10m0.4s
1924	Willie Ritola, Finland	9m33.6s
1928	Toivo Loukola, Finland	9m21.8s
1932	Volmari Iso-Hollo, Finland	10m33.4s[1]
1936	Volmari Iso-Hollo, Finland	9m03.8s

1948	Thure Sjoestrand, Sweden	9m04.6s
1952	Horace Ashenfelter, United States	8m45.4s
1956	Chris Brasher, Great Britain	8m41.2s
1960	Zdzislaw Krzyskowiak, Poland	8m34.2s
1964	Gaston Roelants, Belgium	8m30.8s
1968	Amos Biwott, Kenya	8m51.0s
1972	Kipchoge Keino, Kenya	8m23.6s
1976	Anders Gardervd, Sweden	8m08.02s
1980	Bronislaw Malinowski, Poland	8m09.7s
1984	Julius Korir, Kenya	8m11.8s
1988	Julius Karluki, Kenya	8m05.51s
1992	Matthew Birir, Kenya	8m08.84s
1996	Joseph Keter, Kenya	8m07.12s

1. About 3,450 meters-extra lap by error.

10,000-Meter Walk

1912	George Goulding, Canada	46m28.4s
1920	Ugo Frigerio, Italy	48m6.2s
1924	Ugo Frigerio, Italy	47m49.0s
1948	John Mikaelsson, Sweden	45m13.2s
1952	John Mikaelsson, Sweden	45m2.8s

20,000-Meter Walk

1956	Leonid Spirin, U.S.S.R.	1h31m27.4s
1960	Vladimir Golubnichy, U.S.S.R.	1h34m7.2s
1964	Ken Mathews, Great Britain	1h29m34.0s
1968	Vladimir Golubnichy, U.S.S.R.	1h33m58.4s
1972	Peter Frenkel, East Germany	1h26m42.4s
1976	Daniel Bautista, Mexico	1h24m40.6s
1980	Maurizio Damiliano, Italy	1h23m35.5s
1984	Ernesto Conto, Mexico	1m23.13.0s
1988	Jozef Pribilinec, Czechoslovakia	1h19m57.0s
1992	Daniel Plaza, Spain	1h21m45.0s
1996	Jefferson Perez, Ecuador	1h20m7.0s

50,000-Meter Walk

1932	Thomas W. Green, Great Britain	4h50m10.0s
1936	Harold Whitlock, Great Britain	4h30m41.1s
1948	John Ljunggren, Sweden	4h41m52.0s
1952	Giuseppe Dordoni, Italy	4h28m7.8s
1956	Norman Read, New Zealand	4h30m42.8s
1960	Donald Thompson, Great Britain	4h25m30.0s
1964	Abdon Pamich, Italy	4h11m12.4s
1968	Christoph Hohne, East Germany	4h20m13.6s
1972	Bern Kannernberg, West Germany	3h56m11.6s
1980	Hartwig Guader, East Germany	3h49m24.0s
1984	Raul Gonzalez, Mexico	3hr37m26.6s
1988	Viacheslau Ivanenko, U.S.S.R.	3h438m29.0s
1992	Andrei Perlov, Unified Team[1]	3h50m13.0s
1996	Robert Korzeniowski, Poland	3h43m30.0s

1. Former Soviet Union team.

400-Meter Relay (4x100)

1912	Great Britain	42.4s
1920	United States	42.2s
1924	United States	41.0s
1928	United States	41.0s
1932	United States	40.0s
1936	United States	39.8s
1948	United States	40.6s
1952	United States	40.1s
1956	United States	39.5s
1960	Germany	39.5s
1964	United States	39.0s
1968	United States	38.2s
1972	United States	38.19s
1976	United States	38.33s
1980	U.S.S.R.	38.26s
1984	United States	37.83s
1988	U.S.S.R.	38.19s
1992	United States	37.40s[1]
1996	Canada	37.69s

1. World record.

1,600-Meter Relay (4x400)

1912	United States	3m16.6s
1920	Great Britain	3m22.2s
1924	United States	3m16.0s
1928	United States	3m14.2s
1932	United States	3m8.2s
1936	Great Britain	3m9.0s
1948	United States	3m10.4s
1952	Jamaica, B.W.I.	3m3.9s
1956	United States	3m4.8s
1960	United States	3m2.2s
1964	United States	3m0.7s
1968	United States	2m56.1s
1972	Kenya	2m59.8s
1976	United States	2m58.65s
1980	U.S.S.R.	3m01.1s
1984	United States	2m57.91s
1988	United States	2m56.16s
1992	United States	2m55.74s[1]
1996	United States	2m55.99s

1. World record.

Team Race

		Pts
1900	Great Britain (5,000 meters)	26
1904	United States (4 miles)	27
1908	Great Britain (3 miles)	6
1912	United States (3,000 meters)	9
1920	United States (3,000 meters)	10
1924	Finland (3,000 meters)	9

Standing High Jump

1900	Ray Ewry, United States	5 ft 5 in.
1904	Ray Ewry, United States	4 ft. 11 in.
1906	Ray Ewry, United States	5 ft 1⅝ in.
1908	Ray Ewry, United States	5 ft 2 in.
1912	Platt Adams, United States	5 ft 4⅛ in.

Running High Jump

1896	Ellery Clark, United States	5 ft 11¼ in.
1900	Irving Baxter, United States	6 ft 2¾ in.
1904	Samuel Jones, United States	5 ft 11 in.
1906	Con Leahy, Ireland	5 ft 9⅞ in.
1908	Harry Porter, United States	6 ft 3 in.
1912	Alma Richards, United States	6 ft 4 in.
1920	Richmond Landon, United States	6 ft 4¼ in.
1924	Harold Osborn, United States	6 ft 5 15/16 in.
1928	Robert W. King, United States	6 ft 4⅜ in.
1932	Duncan McNaughton, Canada	6 ft 5⅝ in.
1936	Cornelius Johnson, United States	6 ft 7 15/16 in.
1948	John Winter, Australia	6 ft 6 in.
1952	Walter David, United States	6 ft 8 15/16 in.
1956	Charles Damas, United States	6 ft 11¼ in.
1960	Robert Shavlakadze, U.S.S.R.	7 ft 1 in.
1964	Valeri Brumel, U.S.S.R.	7 ft 1¾ in.
1968	Dick Fosbury, United States	7 ft 4¼ in.
1972	Yuri Tarmak, U.S.S.R.	7 ft 3¾ in.
1976	Jacek Wszola, Poland	(2.25m) 7 ft 4½ in.
1980	Gerd Wessig, East Germany	7 ft 8¾ in.
1984	Dietmar Mogenburg, West Germany	7 ft 8½ in.
1988	Guennadi Avdeenko, U.S.S.R.	7 ft ½ in.
1992	Javier Sotomayer, Cuba	7 ft 8½ in.
1996	Charles Austin, United States	7 ft 10 in.

Long Jump

1896	Ellery Clark, United States	20 ft 9¾ in.
1900	Alvin Kraenzlein, United States	23 ft 6⅞ in.
1904	Myer Prinstein, United States	24 ft 1 in.
1906	Myer Prinstein, United States	23 ft 7½ in.
1908	Frank Irons, United States	24 ft 6½ in.
1912	Albert Gutterson, United States	24 ft 11¼ in.
1920	William Petterssen, Sweden	23 ft 5½ in.
1924	DeHart Hubbard, United States	24 ft 5⅛ in.
1928	Edward B. Hamm, United States	25 ft 4¾ in.
1932	Edward Gordon, United States	25 ft ¾ in.
1936	Jesse Owens, United States	26 ft 5 5/16 in.
1948	Willie Steele, United States	25 ft 8 in.
1952	Jerome Biffle, United States	24 ft 10 in.
1956	Gregory Bell, United States	25 ft 8¼ in.
1960	Ralph Boston, United States	26 ft 7¾ in.
1964	Lynn Davies, Great Britain	26 ft 5¾ in.
1968	Bob Beamon, United States	29 ft 2½ in.
1972	Randy Williams, United States	27 ft ½ in.
1976	Arnie Robinson, United States	(8.35m) 24 ft 7¾ in.
1980	Lutz Dombrowski, E. Germany	28 ft ¼ in.
1984	Carl Lewis, United States	28 ft ¼ in.
1988	Carl Lewis, United States	28 ft 7¼ in.
1992	Carl Lewis, United States	28 ft 5½ in.
1996	Carl Lewis, United States	27 ft 10¾ in.

Triple Jump

1896	James B. Connolly, United States	45 ft
1900	Myer Prinstein, United States	47 ft 4¼ in.
1904	Myer Prinstein, United States	47 ft
1906	P.G. O'Connor, Ireland	46 ft 2 in.
1908	Timothy Ahearne, Great Britain	48 ft 1¼ in.
1912	Gustaf Lindblom, Sweden	48 ft 5⅛ in.
1920	Vilho Tuulos, Finland	47 ft 6⅞ in.
1924	Archie Winter, Australia	50 ft 11⅛ in.
1928	Mikio Oda, Japan	49 ft 10 13/16 in.
1932	Chuhei Nambu, Japan	51 ft 7 in.
1936	Naoto Tajima, Japan	52 ft 5⅞ in.
1948	Arne Ahman, Sweden	50 ft 6¼ in.
1952	Adhemar da Silva, Brazil	53 ft 2½ in.
1956	Adhemar da Silva, Brazil	53 ft 7½ in.
1960	Jozef Schmidt, Poland	55 ft 1¾ in.
1964	Jozef Schmidt, Poland	55 ft 3¼ in.
1968	Viktor Saneyev, U.S.S.R.	57 ft ¾ in.
1972	Viktor Saneyev, U.S.S.R.	56 ft 11 in.
1976	Viktor Saneyev, U.S.S.R.	(17.29m) 56 ft 8¾ in.
1980	Jaak Uudmae, U.S.S.R.	56 ft 11⅛ in.
1984	Al Joyner, United States	56 ft 7½ in.
1988	Hristo Markov, Bulgaria	57 ft 9¼ in.
1992	Mike Conley, United States	59 ft 7½ in.
1996	Kenny Harrison, United States	59 ft 4¼ in.

Pole Vault

1896	William Hoyt, United States	10 ft 9¾ in.
1900	Irving Baxter, United States	10 ft 9⅞ in.
1904	Charles Dvorak, United States	11 ft 6 in.
1906	Fernand Gouder, France	11 ft 6 in.
1908	Alfred Gilbert, United States, and Edward Cook, United States (tie)	12 ft 2 in.
1912	Harry Babcock, United States	12 ft 11½ in.
1920	Frank Foss, United States	13 ft 5 9/16 in.
1924	Lee Barnes, United States	12 ft 11½ in.
1928	Sabin W. Carr, United States	13 ft 9⅜ in.
1932	William Miller, United States	14 ft 1⅞ in.
1936	Earle Meadows, United States	14 ft 3¼ in.
1948	Guinn Smith, United States	14 ft ¼ in.
1952	Robert Richards, United States	14 ft 11⅛ in.
1956	Robert Richards, United States	14 ft 11½ in.
1960	Don Bragg, United States	15 ft 5⅛ in.
1964	Fred Hansen, United States	16 ft 8¾ in.
1968	Bob Seagren, United States	17 ft 8½ in.
1972	Wolfgang Nordwig, East Germany	18 ft ½ in.
1976	Tadeusz Slusarski, Poland	(5.50m) 18 ft ½ in.
1980	Wladyslaw Kozakiewics, Poland	18 ft 11½ in.
1984	Pierre Quinon, France	18 ft 10¼ in.
1988	Sergei Bubka, U.S.S.R.	18 ft 4¼ in.
1992	Maxim Tarassov, Unified Team[1]	19 ft 0¼ in.
1996	Jean Galfione, France	19 ft 5¼ in.

1. Former Soviet Union team.

16-lb Shot-Put

1896	Robert Garrett, United States	36 ft 9¾ in.
1900	Richard Sheldon, United States	46 ft 3⅛ in.

1904	Ralph Rose, United States	48 ft 7 in.
1906	Martin Sheridan, United States	40 ft 4⅘ in.
1908	Ralph Rose, United States	46 ft 7½ in.
1912	Pat McDonald, United States	50 ft 4 in.
1920	Ville Porhola, Finland	48 ft 7⅛ in.
1924	Clarence Houser, United States	49 ft 2½ in.
1928	John Kuck, United States	52 ft 11 11/16 in.
1932	Leo Sexton, United States	52 ft 6 3/16 in.
1936	Hans Woellke, Germany	53 ft 1¾ in.
1948	Wilbur Thompson, United States	56 ft 2 in.
1952	Parry O'Brien, United States	57 ft 1½ in.
1956	Parry O'Brien, United States	60 ft 11 in.
1960	Bill Nied¾ in.	
1964	Dallas Long, United States 66 ft 8¼ in.	
1968	Randy Matson, United States	67 ft 4¾ in.
1972	Wladyslaw Komar, Poland	69 ft 6 in.
1976	Udo Beyer, East Germany	(21.05m) 69 ft ¾ in.
1980	Vladmir Klselyov, U.S.S.R.	70 ft ½ in.
1984	Alessandro Andrei, Italy	69 ft 9 in.
1988	Uhf Timmerman, East Germany	73 ft 8¾ in.
1992	Michael Stulze, United States	71 ft 2½ in.
1996	Randy Barnes, United States	70 ft 11¼ in.

Discus Throw

1896	Robert Garrett, United States	95 ft 7½ in.
1900	Rudolf Bauer, Hungary	118 ft 2⅞ in.
1904	Martin Sheridan, United States	128 ft 10½ in.
1906	Martin Sheridan, United States	136 ft ⅓ in.
1908	Martin Sheridan, United States	134 ft 2 in.
1912	Armas Taipale, Finland	145 ft 9/16 in.
1920	Elmer Niklander, Finland	146 ft 7 in.
1924	Clarence Houser, United States	151 ft 5¼ in.
1928	Clarence Houser, United States	155 ft 2⅖ in.
1932	John Anderson, United States	162 ft 4⅞ in.
1936	Ken Carpenter, United States	165 ft 7⅜ in.
1948	Adolfo Consolini, Italy	173 ft 2 in.
1952	Simeon Iness, United States	180 ft 6½ in.
1956	Al Oerter, United States	184 ft 10½ in.
1960	Al Oerter, United States	194 ft 2 in.
1964	Al Oerter, United States	200 ft 1½ in.
1968	Al Oerter, United States	212 ft 6 in.
1972	Ludvik Danek, Czechoslovakia	211 ft 3 in.
1976	Mac Wilkins, United States	(67.5m) 221 ft 5 in.
1980	Viktor Rashchupkin, U.S.S.R.	218 ft 8 in.
1984	Rolf Dannenberg, West Germany	218 ft 6 in.
1988	Jurgen Schult, East Germany	225 ft 9¼ in.
1992	Romas Ubartas, Lithuania	213 ft 7¾ in.
1996	Lars Riedel, Germany	227 ft 8 in.

Javelin Throw

1906	Eric Lemming, Sweden	175 ft 6 in.
1908	Eric Lemming, Sweden	179 ft 10½ in.
1912	Eric Lemming, Sweden	198 ft 11¼ in.
1920	Jonni Myyra, Finland	215 ft 9¾ in.
1924	Jonni Myyra, Finland	206 ft 6¾ in.
1928	Eric Lundquist, Sweden	218 ft 6⅛ in.
1932	Matti Jarvinen, Finland	238 ft 7 in.
1936	Gerhard Stoeck, Germany	235 ft 8 5/16 in.
1948	Kaj Rautavaara, Finland	228 ft 10½ in.
1952	Cy Young, United States	242 ft¾ in.
1956	Egil Danielsen, Norway	281 ft 2¼ in.
1960	Viktor Tsibuelnko, U.S.S.R.	277 ft 8⅜ in.
1964	Pauli Nevala, Finland	271 ft 2¼ in.
1968	Janis Lusis, U.S.S.R.	295 ft 7 in.
1972	Klaus Wolfermann, West Germany	296 ft 10 in.
1976	Miklos Nemeth, Hungary	(94.58m) 310 ft 4 in.
1980	Dainis Kula, U.S.S.R.	299 ft 2⅜ in.
1984	Arto Haerkoenen, Finland	284 ft 8 in.
1988	Tapio Korjus, Finland	276 ft 6 in.
1992	Jan Zelezny, Czechoslovakia	294 ft 2 in.
1996	Jan Zelezny, Czech Republic	289 ft 3 in.

16-lb Hammer Throw

1900	John Flanagan, United States	167 ft 4 in.
1904	John Flanagan, United States	168 ft 1 in.
1908	John Flanagan, United States	170 ft 4¼ in.
1912	Matt McGrath, United States	179 ft 7⅛ in.
1920	Pat Ryan, United States	173 ft 5⅝ in.
1924	Fred Tootell, United States	174 ft 10¼ in.
1928	Patrick O'Callaghan, Ireland	168 ft 7½ in.
1932	Patrick O'Callaghan, Ireland	176 ft 11⅛ in.
1936	Karl Hein, Germany	185 ft 4 in.
1948	Imre Nemeth, Hungary	183 ft 11½ in.
1952	Jozsef Csermak, Hungary	197 ft 11 9/16 in.
1956	Harold Connolly, United States	207 ft 2¾ in.
1960	Vasily Rudenkov, U.S.S.R.	220 ft 1⅝ in.
1964	Romuald Klim, U.S.S.R.	228 ft 9½ in.
1968	Gyula Zsivotzky, Hungary	240 ft 8 in.
1972	Anatoly Bondarchuk, U.S.S.R.	247 ft 8½ in.
1976	Yuri Sedykh, U.S.S.R.	(77.52m) 254 ft 4 in.
1980	Yuri Sedykh, U.S.S.R.	(81.80m) 268 ft 4½ in.
1984	Juha Tiainen, Finland	256 ft 2 in.
1988	Sergei Litvinov, U.S.S.R.	278 ft 2½ in.
1992	Andrey Abduvaliyev, Unified Team[1]	270 ft 9½ in.
1996	Balasz Kiss, Hungary	266 ft 6 in.

1. Former Soviet Union team.

Decathlon

1912	Jim Thorpe, United States	—
	Hugo Wieslander, Sweden	—
1920	Helge Lovland, Norway	6,804.35 pts.
1924	Harold Osborn, United States	7,710.775 pts.
1928	Paavo Yrjola, Finland	8,053.29 pts.
1932	James Bausch, United States	8,462.23 pts.
1936	Glenn Morris, United States	7,900 pts.[1]
1948	Robert B. Mathias, United States	7,139 pts.
1952	Robert B. Mathias, United States	7,887 pts.
1956	Milton Campbell, United States	7,937 pts.
1960	Rafer Johnson, United States	8,392 pts.
1964	Willi Holdorf, Germany	7,887 pts.[1]
1968	Bill Toomey, United States	8,193 pts.
1972	Nikolai Avilov, U.S.S.R.	8,454 pts.
1976	Bruce Jenner, United States	8,618 pts.
1980	Daley Thompson, Britain	8,495 pts.
1984	Daley Thompson, Britain	8,797 pts.
1988	Christian Schenk, East Germany	8,488 pts.
1992	Robert Zmelik, Czechoslovakia	8,611 pts.
1996	Dan O'Brien, United States	8,824 pts.

1. Point system revised.

TRACK AND FIELD–WOMEN

100-Meter Dash

1928	Elizabeth Robinson, United States	12.2s
1932	Stella Walsh, Poland	11.9s
1936	Helen Stephens, United States	11.5s
1948	Fanny Blankers-Koen, Netherlands	11.9s
1952	Marjorie Jackson, Australia	11.5s
1956	Betty Cuthbert, Australia	11.5s
1960	Wilma Rudolph, United States	11.0s
1964	Wyomia Tyus, United States	11.4s
1968	Wyomia Tyus, United States	11.0s
1972	Renate Stecher, East Germany	11.07s
1976	Annegret Richter, West Germany	11.08s
1980	Lyudmila Kondratyeva, U.S.S.R.	11.06s
1984	Evelyn Ashford, United States	10.97s
1988	Florence Griffith-Joyner, United States	10.54s
1992	Gail Devers, United States	10.82s
1996	Gail Devers, United States	10.94s

200-Meter Dash

1948	Fanny Blankers-Koen, Netherlands	24.4s
1952	Marjorie Jackson, Australia	23.7s
1956	Betty Cuthbert, Australia	23.4s
1960	Wilma Rudolph, United States	24.0s

1964	Edith McGuire, United States	23.0s
1968	Irena Szewinska, Poland	22.5s
1972	Renate Stecher, East Germany	22.4s
1976	Baerbel Eckert, East Germany	22.37s
1980	Barbara Wockel, East Germany	22.03s
1984	Valerie Brisco-Hooks, United States	21.81s
1988	Florence Griffith-Joyner, United States	21.34s
1992	Gwen Torrence, United States	21.81s
1996	Marie-Jose Perec, France	22.12s

400-Meter Dash

1964	Betty Cuthbert, Australia	52.0s
1968	Colette Besson, France	52.0s
1972	Monika Zehrt, East Germany	51.08s
1976	Irena Szewinska, Poland	49.29s
1980	Marita Koch, East Germany	48.88s
1984	Valerie Brisco-Hooks, United States	48.83s
1988	Olga Bryzguina, U.S.S.R.	48.65s
1992	Marie Jose-Perec, France	48.83s
1996	Marie Jose-Perec, France	48.25s

800-Meter Run

1928	Lina Radke, Germany	2m16.8s
1960	Ljudmila Shevcova, U.S.S.R.	2m4.3s
1964	Ann Packer, Great Britain	2m1.1s
1968	Madeline Manning, United States	2m0.9s
1972	Hildegard Falck, West Germany	1m58.6s
1976	Tatiana Kazankina, U.S.S.R.	1m54.94s
1980	Nadezhda Olizarenko, U.S.S.R.	1m53.5s
1984	Doina Melinte, Romania	1m57.60s
1988	Sigrun Wodars, East Germany	1m56.10s
1992	Ellen Van Langen, Netherlands	1m55.54s
1993	Svetlana Masterkova, Russia	1m57.73s

1,500-Meter Run

1972	Ludmila Bragina, U.S.S.R.	4m01.4s
1976	Tatiana Kazankina, U.S.S.R.	4m05.48s
1980	Tatiana Kazankina, U.S.S.R.	3m56.6s
1984	Gabriella Dorio, Italy	4m03.25s
1988	Paula Ivan, Romania	3m53.96s
1992	Hassiba Boulmerka, Algeria	3m55.30s
1996	Svetlana Masterkova, Russia	4m00.83s

5,000-Meter Run

1996	Wang, Jun-Xia, China	14m59.88s

10,000-Meter Run

1992	Derartu Tulu, Ethiopia	31m6.02s
1996	Fernanda Ribeiro, Portugal	31m01.63s

80-Meter Hurdles

1932	Mildred Didrikson, United States	11.7s
1936	Trebisonda Valla, Italy	11.7s
1948	Fanny Blankers-Koen, Netherlands	11.2s
1952	Shirley S. de la Hunty, Australia	10.9s
1956	Shirley S. de la Hunty, Australia	10.7s
1960	Irina Press, U.S.S.R.	10.8s
1964	Karin Balzer, Germany	10.5s[1]
1968	Maureen Caird, Australia	10.3s

1. Wind assisted.

100-Meter Hurdles

1972	Annelie Ehrhardt, East Germany	12.59s
1976	Johanna Schaller, East Germany	12.77s
1980	Vera Komisova, U.S.S.R.	12.56s
1984	Benita Fitzgerald-Brown, United States	12.84s
1988	Jordanka Donkova, Bulgaria	12.38s
1992	Paraskevi Patoulidou, Greece	12.64s
1996	Ludmila Engquist, Sweden	12.58s

400-Meter Hurdles

1984	Nawai El Moutawakel, Morocco	54.61s
1988	Debra Flintoff-King, Australia	53.17s
1992	Sally Gunnell, Great Britain	53.23s
1996	Deon Hemmings, Jamaica	52.82s

400-Meter Relay

1928	Canada	48.4s
1932	United States	47.0s
1936	United States	46.9s
1948	Netherlands	47.5s
1952	United States	45.9s
1956	Australia	44.5s
1960	United States	44.5s
1964	Poland	43.6s
1968	United States	42.8s
1972	West Germany	42.81s
1976	East Germany	42.55s
1980	East Germany	41.60s
1984	United States	41.65s
1988	United States	41.98s
1992	United States	42.11s
1996	United States	41.95s

1,600-Meter Relay

1972	East Germany	3m23s
1976	East Germany	3m19.23s
1980	U.S.S.R.	3m20.2s
1984	United States	3m18.29s
1988	U.S.S.R.	3m15.18s
1992	Unified Team[1]	3m20.20s
1996	United States	3m20.91s

1. Former Soviet Union team.

10,000-Meter Walk

1992	ChenYue-Ling, China	44m32s
1996	Yelena Nikolayeva, Russia	41m49s

Marathon

1984	Joan Benoit, United States	2h24m52s
1988	Rose Mota, Portugal	2h25m40s
1992	Valentina Yegorova, Unified Team	2h32m41s
1996	Fatuma Roba, Ethiopia	2h26m05s

Running High Jump

1928	Ethel Catherwood, Canada	5 ft 3 in.
1932	Jean Shiley, United States	5 ft 5¼ in.
1936	Ibolya Csak, Hungary	5 ft 3 in.
1948	Alice Coachman, United States	5 ft 6⅛ in.
1952	Ester Brand, South Africa	5 ft 5¾ in.
1956	Mildred McDaniel, United States	5 ft 9¼ in.
1960	Iolanda Balas, Romania	6 ft ¾ in.
1964	Iolanda Balas, U.S.S.R.	6 ft 2¾ in.
1968	Miloslava Rezkova, Czechoslovakia	5 ft 11¾ in.
1972	Ulrike Meyfarth, West Germany	6 ft 3⅝ in.
1976	Rosemarie Ackerman, E. Germany	(1.93m) 6 ft 4 in.
1980	Sara Simeoni, Italy	6 ft 5½ in.
1984	Ulrike Meyfarth, West Germany	6 ft 7½ in.
1988	Louise Ritter, United States	6 ft 8 in.
1992	Heike Henkel, Germany	6 ft 7½ in.
1996	Stefka Kostadinova, Bulgaria	6 ft 8¾ in.

Long Jump

1948	Olga Gyarmati, Hungary	18 ft 8¼ in.
1952	Yvette Williams, New Zealand	20 ft 5¾ in.
1956	Elzbieta Krzesinska, Poland	20 ft 9¾ in.
1960	Vera Krepkina, U.S.S.R.	20 ft 10¾ in.
1964	Mary Rand, Great Britain	22 ft 2 in.
1968	Viorica Ciscopoleanu, Romania	22 ft 4½ in.
1972	Heidemarie Rosendahl, West Germany	22 ft 3 in.
1976	Angela Voigt, East Germany	(6.72m) 22 ft ½ in.
1980	Tatiana Kolpakova, U.S.S.R.	23 ft 2 in.
1984	Anisoara Stanciu, Romania	22 ft 10 in.
1988	Jackie Joyner-Kersee, United States	24 ft 3½ in.
1992	Heike Drechsler, Germany	23 ft 5¼ in.
1996	Chioma Ajunwa, Nigeria	23 ft 4½ in.

Triple Jump

1996	Inessa Kravets, Ukraine	50 ft 3½ in.

Shot-Put

1948	Micheline Ostermeyer, France	45 ft 1½ in.

1952	Galina Zybina, U.S.S.R.	50 ft 1½ in.
1956	Tamara Tishkyevich, U.S.S.R.	54 ft 5 in.
1960	Tamara Press, U.S.S.R.	56 ft 9⅞ in.
1964	Tamara Press, U.S.S.R.	59 ft 6 in.
1968	Margitta Gummel, East Germany	64 ft 4 in.
1972	Nadezhda Chizhova, U.S.S.R.	69 ft
1976	Ivanka Christova, Bulgaria	(21.16m) 69 ft 5 in.
1980	Ilona Sluplanek, East Germany	73 ft 6 in.
1984	Claudia Losch, West Germany	67 ft 2¼ in.
1988	Natalya Lisovskaya, U.S.S.R.	72 ft 11½ in.
1992	Svetlana Kriveleva, Unified Team[1]	69 ft 1¼ in.
1996	Astrid Kumbernuss, Germany	67 ft 5½ in.

1. Former Soviet Union team.

Discus Throw

1928	Helena Konopacka, Poland	129 ft 11⅞ in.
1932	Lillian Copeland, United States	133 ft 2 in.
1936	Gisela Mauermayer, Germany	156 ft 3³⁄₁₆ in.
1948	Micheline Ostermeyer, France	137 ft 6½ in.
1956	Olga Fikotova, Czechoslovakia	176 ft 1½ in.
1960	Nina Ponomareva, U.S.S.R.	180 ft 8¼ in.
1964	Tamara Press, U.S.S.R.	187 ft 10¾ in.
1968	Lia Manoliu, Romania	191 ft 2½ in.
1972	Faina Melnik, U.S.S.R.	218 ft 7 in.
1976	Evelin Schlaak, East Germany	(69.00m) 226 ft 4 in.
1980	Evelin Jahl, East Germany	229 ft 6½ in.
1984	Ria Stalman, Netherlands	214 ft 5 in.
1988	Martina Hellmann, East Germany	237 ft 2¼ in.
1992	Maritza Marten, Cuba	229 ft 10¼ in.
1996	Ilke Wyludda, Germany	228 ft 6½ in.

Javelin Throw

1932	Mildred Didrikson, United States	143 ft 4 in.
1936	Tilly Fleischer, Germany	148 ft 2¾ in.
1948	Herma Bauma, Austria	149 ft 6 in.
1952	Dana Zatopek, Czechoslovakia	165 ft 7 in.
1956	Inessa Janzeme, U.S.S.R.	176 ft 8 in.
1960	Elvira Ozolina, U.S.S.R.	183 ft 8 in.
1964	Mihaela Penes, Romania	198 ft 7½ in.
1968	Angela Nemeth, Hungary	198 ft
1972	Ruth Fuchs, East Germany	209 ft 7 in.
1976	Ruth Fuchs, East Germany	(65.94m) 216 ft 4 in.
1980	Maria Colon, Cuba	224 ft 5 in.
1984	Tessa Sanderson, Britain	228 ft 2 in.
1988	Petra Felke, East Germany	245 ft
1992	Silke Renke, Germany	224 ft 2½ in.
1996	Heli Rantanen, Finland	222 ft 11 in.

Pentathlon

1964	Irina Press, U.S.S.R.	5,246 pts.
1968	Ingrid Becker, West Germany	5,098 pts.
1972	Mary Peters, Britain	4,801 pts.
1976	Siegrun Siegl, East Germany	4,745 pts.
1980	Nadyeszhda Tkachenko, U.S.S.R.	5,083 pts.
1984	Daniele Masala, Italy	5,469 pts.
1988	Jackie Joyner-Kersee, United States	7,291 pts.

Heptathlon

1992	Jackie Joyner-Kersee, United States	7,044 pts.
1996	Ghada Shouaa, Syria	6,780 pts.

SWIMMING—MEN

50 Meter Freestyle

1988	Matt Biondi, United States	22.14s
1992	Alexander Popov, Unified Team[1]	21.91s
1996	Alexander Popov, Russia	22.13s

1. Former Soviet Union team.

100 Meter Freestyle

1896	Alfred Hajos, Hungary	1m22.2s
1904	Zoltan de Halmay, Hungary	1m2.8s[1]
1906	Charles Daniels, United States	1m13.0s
1908	Charles Daniels, United States	1m5.6s
1912	Duke P. Kahanamoku, United States	1m3.4s

1920	Duke P. Kahanamoku, United States	1m1.4s
1924	John Weissmuller, United States	59.0s
1928	John Weissmuller, United States	58.6s
1932	Yasuji Miyazaki, Japan	58.2s
1936	Ferenc Csik, Hungary	57.6s
1948	Walter Ris, United States	57.3s
1952	Clarke Scholes, United States	57.4s
1956	Jon Henricks, Australia	55.4s
1960	John Devitt, Australia	55.2s
1964	Don Schollander, United States	53.4s
1968	Michael Wenden, Australia	52.2s
1972	Mark Spitz, United States	51.22s
1976	Jim Montgomery, United States	49.99s
1980	Jorg Woithe, East Germany	50.40s
1984	Rowdy Gaines, United States	49.80s
1988	Matt Biondi, United States	48.63s
1992	Alexander Popov, Unified Team[2]	49.02s
1996	Alexander Popov, Russia	48.74s

1. 100 yards. 2. Former Soviet Union team.

200-Meter Freestyle

1900	Frederick Lane, Australia	2m25.2s
1904	Charles Daniels, United States	2m44.2s[1]
1968	Michael Wenden, Australia	1m55.2s
1972	Mark Spitz, United States	1m52.78s
1976	Bruce Furniss, United States	1m50.29s
1980	Sergei Kopiliakov, U.S.S.R.	4m49.81s
1984	Michael Gross, West Germany	1m47.44s
1988	Duncan Armstrong, Australia	1m47.25s
1992	Evgueni Sadovyi, Unified Team[2]	1m46.70s
1996	Danyon Loader, New Zealand	1m47.63s

1. 220 yards 2. Former Soviet Union team.

400-Meter Freestyle

1896	Paul Neumann, Austria	8m12.6s[1]
1904	Charles Daniels, United States	6m16.2s[2]
1906	Otto Sheff, Austria	6m23.8s
1908	Henry Taylor, Great Britain	5m36.8s
1912	George Hodgson, Canada	5m24.4s
1920	Norman Ross, United States	5m26.8s
1926	John Weissmuller, United States	5m4.2s
1928	Albert Zorilla, Argentina	5m1.6s
1932	Clarence Crabbe, United States	4m48.4s
1936	Jack Medica, United States	4m44.5s
1948	William Smith, United States	4m41.0s
1952	Jean Boiteux, France	4m30.7s
1956	Murray Rose, Australia	4m27.3s
1960	Murray Rose, Australia	4m18.3s
1964	Don Schollander, United States	4m12.2s
1968	Mike Burton, United States	4m9.0s
1972	Bradford Cooper, Australia	4m00.27s[3]
1976	Brian Goodell, United States	3m51.93s
1980	Vladimir Salnikov, U.S.S.R.	3m51.31s
1984	George DiCarlo, United States	3m51.23s
1988	Uwe Dassier, East Germany	3m46.95s
1992	Evgueni Sadovyi, Unified Team	3m45.00s[4]
1996	Danyon Loader, New Zealand	3m47.97s

1. 500 meters. 2. 440 yards. 3. Rich DeMont, United States, won but was disqualified following day for medical reasons. 4. World record.

1,500 Meter Freestyle

1904	Emil Rausch, Germany	27m18.2s[1]
1906	Henry Taylor, Great Britain	28m28.0s[2]
1908	Henry Taylor, Great Britain	22m48.4s
1912	George Hodgson, Canada	22m0.0s
1920	Norman Ross, United States	22m23.2s
1924	Andrew Charlton, Australia	20m6.6s
1928	Arne Borg, Sweden	19m51.8s
1932	Kusuo Kitamura, Japan	19m12.4s
1936	Noboru Terada, Japan	19m13.7s
1948	James McLane, United States	19m18.5s
1952	Ford Konno, United States	18m30.0s

1956	Murray Rose, Australia	17m58.9s
1960	Jon Konrads, Australia	17m19.6s
1964	Robert Windle, Australia	17m1.7s
1968	Michael Burton, United States	16m38.9s
1972	Michael Burton, United States	15m52.58s
1976	Brian Goodell, United States	15m02.4s
1980	Vladimir Salnikov, U.S.S.R.	14m58.27s
1984	Michael O'Brien, United States	15m05.2s
1988	Vladimir Salnikov, U.S.S.R.	15m00.4s
1992	Kieren Perkins, Australia	14m43.48s
1996	Kieren Perkins, Australia	14m56.4s

1. One mile. 2. 1,600 meters

100-Meter Backstroke

1904	Walter Brack, Germany	1m16.8s[1]
1908	Arno Bieberstein, Germany	1m24.6s
1912	Harry Hebner, United States	1m21.2s
1920	Warren Kealoha, United States	1m15.2s
1924	Warren Kealoha, United States	1m13.2s
1928	George Kojac, United States	1m8.2s
1932	Masaji Kiyokawa, Japan	1m8.6s
1936	Adolph Kiefer, United States	1m5.9s
1948	Allen Stack, United States	1m6.4s
1952	Yoshinobu Oyakawa, United States	1m5.4s
1956	David Thiele, Australia	1m2.2s
1960	David Thiele, Australia	1m1.9s
1968	Roland Matthes, East Germany	58.7s
1972	Roland Matthes, East Germany	56.58s
1976	John Naber, United States	55.49s
1980	Bengt Baron, Sweden	56.53s
1984	Rick Carey, United States	55.79s
1988	Daichi Suzuki, Japan	55.05s
1992	Mark Tewksbury, Canada	53.98s
1996	Jeff Rouse, United States	54.10s

1. 100 yards

200-Meter Backstroke

1900	Ernst Hoppenberg, Germany	2m47.0s
1964	Jed Graef, United States	2m10.3s
1968	Roland Matthes, East Germany	2m9.6s
1972	Roland Matthes, East Germany	2m2.82s
1976	John Naber, United States	1m59.19s
1980	Sandor Wladar, Hungary	2:01.93s
1984	Rick Carey, United States	2m00.23s
1988	Igor Polianski, U.S.S.R.	1m59.37s
1992	Martin Lopez Zubero, Spain	1m58.47s
1996	Brad Bridgewater, United States	1m58.54s

100-Meter Breaststroke

1968	Donald McKenzie, United States	1m7.7s
1972	Nobutaka Taguchi, Japan	1m4.94s
1976	John Hencken, United States	1m03.11s
1980	Duncan Goodhew, Britain	1m03.34s
1984	Steve Lindquist, United States	1m01.65s
1988	Adrian Moorhouse, Great Britain	1m02.04s
1992	Nelson Diebel, United States	1m01.50s
1996	Fred Deburghgraeve, Belgium	1m00.60s[1]

1. World record.

200-Meter Breaststroke

1908	Frederick Holman, Great Britain	3m9.2s
1912	Walter Bathe, Germany	3m1.8s
1920	Haken Malmroth, Sweden	3m4.4s
1924	Robert Skelton, United States	2m56.6s
1928	Yoshiyuki Tsuruta, Japan	2m48.8s
1932	Yoshiyuki Tsuruta, Japan	2m45.4s
1936	Tetsuo Hamuro, Japan	2m41.5s
1948	Joseph Verdeur, United States	2m39.3s
1952	John Davies, Australia	2m34.4s
1956	Masaura Furukawa, Japan	2m34.7s
1960	Bill Muliken, United States	2m37.4s
1964	Ian O'Brien, Australia	2m27.8s
1968	Felipe Munoz, Mexico	2m28.7s

1972	John Hencken, United States	2m21.55s
1976	David Willkie, Britain	2m15.11s
1980	Robertas Zulpa, U.S.S.R.	2m15.85s
1984	Victor Davis, Canada	2m13.34s
1988	Jozef Szabo, Hungary	2m13.52s
1992	Mike Barrowman, United States	2m10.16s
1996	Norbert Rozsa, Hungary	2m12.57s

100-Meter Butterfly

1968	Douglas Russell, United States	55.9s
1972	Mark Spitz, United States	54.27s
1976	Matt Vogel, United States	54.35s
1980	Par Arvidsson, Sweden	54.92s
1984	Michael Gross, West Germany	53.08s
1988	Anthony Nesty, Surinam	53.0s
1992	Pablo Morales, United States	53.32s
1996	Denis Pankratov, Russia	52.27s[1]

1. World record.

200-Meter Butterfly

1956	Bill Yorzyk, United States	2m19.3s
1960	Mike Troy, United States	2m12.8s
1964	Kevin Berry, Australia	2m6.6s
1968	Carl Robie, United States	2m8.7s
1972	Mark Spitz, United States	2m00.7s
1976	Mike Bruner, United States	1m59.23s
1980	Sergei Fesenko, U.S.S.R.	1m59.76s
1984	Jon Sieben, Australia	1m57.0s
1988	Michael Gross, East Germany	1m56.94s
1992	Mel Stewart, United States	1m56.26s
1996	Denis Pankratov, Russia	1m56.51s

200-Meter Individual Medley

1968	Charles Hickcox, United States	2m12s
1972	Gunnar Larsson, Sweden	2m7.17s
1988	Tamas Darnyi, Hungary	2m0.17s
1992	Tamas Darnyi, Hungary	2m0.76s
1996	Attila Czene, Hungary	1m59.91s

400-Meter Individual Medley

1964	Dick Roth, United States	4m45.4s
1968	Charles Hickox, United States	4m48.4s
1972	Gunnar Larsson, Sweden	4m31.98s
1976	Rod Strachan, United States	4m23.68s
1980	Aleksandr Sidorenko, U.S.S.R.	4m22.8s
1984	Alex Baumann, Canada	4m17.41s
1988	Tamas Darnyi, Hungary	4m14.75s
1992	Tamas Darnyi, Hungary	4m14.23s
1996	Tom Dolan, United States	4m14.90s

400-Meter Freestyle Relay

1964	United States	3m32.2s
1968	United States	3m31.7s
1972	United States	3m26.42s
1988	United States	3m16.52s
1992	United States	3m16.74s
1996	United States	3m15.41s

800-Meter Freestyle Relay

1908	Great Britain	10m55.6s
1912	Australia	10m11.2s
1920	United States	10m4.4s
1924	United States	9m53.4s
1928	United States	9m36.2s
1932	Japan	8m58.4s
1936	Japan	8m51.5s
1948	United States	8m46.1s
1952	United States	8m31.1s
1956	Australia	8m23.6s
1960	United States	8m10.2s
1964	United States	7m52.1s
1968	United States	7m52.3s
1972	United States	7m35.78s
1976	United States	7m23.22s
1980	U.S.S.R.	7m23.50s

1984	United States	7m16.59s
1988	United States	7m12.51s
1992	Unified Team[1]	7m11.95s
1996	United States	7m14.84s

1. Former Soviet Union team.

400-Meter Medley Relay

1960	United States	4m5.4s
1964	United States	3m58.4s
1968	United States	3m54.9s
1972	United States	3m48.16s
1976	United States	3m42.22s
1980	Australia	3m45.70s
1984	United States	3m39.30s
1988	United States	3m36.93s
1992	United States	3m36.93s
1996	United States	3m34.84s[1]

1. World record.

Springboard Dive

		Points
1908	Albert Zuerner, Germany	85.50
1912	Paul Guenther, Germany	79.23
1920	Louis Kuehn, United States	675.00
1924	Albert White, United States	696.4
1928	Pete Desjardins, United States	185.04
1932	Michael Galitzen, United States	161.38
1936	Richard Degener, United States	163.57
1948	Bruce Harlan, United States	163.64
1952	David Browning, United States	205.59
1956	Robert Clotworthy, United States	159.56
1960	Gary Tobian, United States	170.00
1964	Ken Sitzberger, United States	159.90
1968	Bernard Wrightson, United States	170.15
1972	Vladimir Vasin, U.S.S.R.	594.09
1976	Phil Boggs, United States	619.05
1980	Alexsandr Portnov, U.S.S.R.	905.02
1984	Greg Louganis, United States	754.41
1988	Greg Louganis, United States	730.80
1992	Mark Lenzi, United States	676.53
1996	Xiong Ni, China	701.46

Platform Dive

		Points
1904	G.E. Sheldon, United States	12.75
1906	Gottlob Walz, Germany	156.00
1908	Hialmar Johansson, Sweden	83.75
1912	Erik Adlerz, Sweden	73.94
1920	Clarence Pinkston, United States	100.67
1924	Albert White, United States	487.30
1928	Pete Desjardins, United States	98.74
1932	Harold Smith, United States	124.80
1936	Marshall Wayne, United States	113.58
1948	Samuel Lee, United States	130.05
1952	Samuel Lee, United States	156.28
1956	Joaquin Capilla, Mexico	152.44
1960	Bob Webster, United States	165.56
1964	Bob Webster, United States	148.58
1968	Klaus Dibiasi, Italy	164.18
1972	Klaus Dibiasi, Italy	504.12
1976	Klaus Dibiasi, Italy	600.51
1980	Falk Hoffman, E. Germany	835.65
1984	Greg Louganis, United States	710.91
1988	Greg Louganis, United States	638.61
1992	Sun, Shu-Wei, China	677.31
1996	Dmitri Saoutine, Russia	692.34

SWIMMING–WOMEN

50-Meter Freestyle

1988	Kristin Otto, East Germany	25.49s
1992	Yang, Wen-Yi, China	24.79s
1996	Amy Van Dyken, United States	24.87s

100-Meter Freestyle

1912	Fanny Durack, Australia	1m22.2s
1920	Ethelda Bleibtrey, United States	1m13.6s
1924	Ethel Lackie, United States	1m12.4s
1928	Albina Osipowich, United States	1m11.0s
1932	Helene Madison, United States	1m6.8s
1936	Hendrika Mastenbroek, Netherlands	1m5.9s
1948	Greta Andersen, Denmark	1m6.3s
1952	Katalin Szoke, Hungary	1m6.8s
1956	Dawn Fraser, Australia	1m2.0s
1960	Dawn Fraser, Australia	1m1.2s
1964	Dawn Fraser, Australia	59.5s
1968	Marge Jan Henne, United States	1m0.0s
1972	Sandra Neilson, United States	58.59s
1976	Kornelia Ender, East Germany	55.65s
1980	Barbara Krause, East Germany	54.79s
1984	Carrie Steinseifer, United States	55.92s
1988	Kristin Otto, East Germany	54.93s
1992	Zhuang Yong, China	54.64s
1996	Le Jingyi, China	54.5s

200-Meter Freestyle

1968	Debbie Meyer, United States	2m10.5s
1972	Shane Gould, Australia	2m3.56s
1976	Kornelia Ender, East Germany	1m59.26s
1980	Barbara Krause, East Germany	1m58.33s
1984	Mary Wayle, United States	1m59.23s
1988	Heike Friedrich, East Germany	1m57.65s
1992	Nicole Haislett, United States	1m57.90s
1996	Claudia Poll, Costa Rica	1m58.16s

400-Meter Freestyle

1920	Ethelda Bleibtrey, United States	4m34.0s[1]
1924	Martha Norelius, United States	6m2.2s
1928	Martha Norelius, United States	5m42.8s
1932	Helene Madison, United States	5m28.5s
1936	Hendrika Mastenbroek, Netherlands	5m26.4s
1948	Ann Curtis, United States	5m17.8s
1952	Valerie Gyenge, Hungary	5m12.1s
1956	Lorraine Crapp, Australia	4m54.6s
1960	Chris von Saltza, United States	4m50.6s
1964	Ginny Duenkel, United States	4m43.3s
1968	Debbie Meyer, United States	4m31.8s
1972	Shane Gould, Australia	4m19.04s
1976	Petra Thumer, East Germany	4m09.89s
1980	Ines Diers, East Germany	4m08.76s
1984	Tiffany Cohen, United States	4m07.10s
1988	Janet Evans, United States	4m03.85s
1992	Dagmar Hase, Germany	4m07.18s
1996	Michelle Smith, Ireland	4m07.25s

1. 300 meters.

800-Meter Freestyle

1968	Debbie Meyer, United States	9m24.0s
1972	Keena Rothhammer, United States	8m53.68s
1976	Petra Thumer, East Germany	8m37.14s
1980	Michelle Ford, Australia	8m28.90s
1984	Tiffany Cohen, United States	8m24.95s
1988	Janet Evans, United States	8m20.20s
1992	Janet Evans, Unites States	8m25.52s
1996	Brooke Bennett, Unites States	8m27.89s

100-Meter Backstroke

1924	Sybil Bauer, United States	1m23.2s
1928	Marie Braun, Netherlands	1m22.0s
1932	Eleanor Holm, United States	1m19.4s
1936	Dina Senff, Netherlands	1m18.9s
1948	Karen Harup, Denmark	1m14.4s
1952	Joan Harrison, South Africa	1m14.3s
1956	Judy Grinham, Great Britain	1m12.9s
1960	Lynn Burke, United States	1m9.3s
1964	Cathy Ferguson, United States	1m7.7s
1968	Kaye Hall, United States	1m6.2s
1972	Melissa Belote, United States	1m5.78s
1976	Ulrike Richter, East Germany	1m1.83s
1980	Rica Reinisch, East Germany	1m0.86s

1984	Theresa Andrews, United States	1m2.55s
1988	Kristin Otto, East Germany	1m0.89s
1992	Krisztina Egerszegi, Hungary	1m0.68s
1996	Beth Botsford, United States	1m1.19s

200-Meter Backstroke

1968	Pokey Watson-United States	2m24.8s
1972	Melissa Belote, United States	2m19.19s
1976	Ulrike Richter, East Germany	2m13.43s
1980	Rica Reinisch, East Germany	2m11.77s
1984	Jolanda DeRover, Netherlands	2m12.38s
1988	Krisztina Egerszegi, Hungary	2m09.29s
1992	Krisztina Egerszegi, Hungary	2m07.06s
1996	Krisztina Egerszegi, Hungary	2m07.83s

100-Meter Breaststroke

1968	Djurdjica Bjedov, Yugoslavia	1m15.8s
1972	Catherine Carr, United States	1m13.58s
1976	Hannelore Anke, East Germany	1m11.16s
1980	Ute Geweniger, East Germany	1m10.22s
1984	Petra Van Staveren, Netherlands	1m09.88s
1988	Tainia Dangalakova, Bulgaria	1m07.95s
1992	Elena Roudkovskaia, Unified Team	1m08.00s
1996	Penny Heyns, South Africa	1m07.73s

200-Meter Breaststroke

1924	Lucy Morton, Great Britain	3m33.2s
1928	Hilde Schrader, Germany	3m12.6s
1932	Clare Dennis, Australia	3m6.3s
1936	Hideko Maehata, Japan	3m3.6s
1948	Nel van Vliet, Netherlands	2m57.2s
1952	Eva Szekely, Hungary	2m51.7s
1956	Ursala Happe, Germany	2m53.1s
1960	Anita Lonsbrough, Great Britain	2m49.5s
1964	Galina Prozumenschikova, U.S.S.R.	2m46.4s
1968	Sharon Wichman, United States	2m44.4s
1972	Beverly Whitfield, Australia	2m41.71s
1976	Marina Koshevaia, U.S.S.R.	2m33.35s
1980	Lina Kachushite, U.S.S.R.	2m29.54s
1984	Anne Ottenbrite, Canada	2m30.38s
1988	Silke Hoerner, East Germany	2m26.71s
1992	Kyoko Iwasaki, Japan	2m26.65s
1996	Penny Heyns, South Africa	2m25.41s

100-Meter Butterfly

1956	Shelley Mann, United States	1m11.0s
1960	Carolyn Schuler, United States	1m9.5s
1964	Sharon Stouder, United States	1m4.7s
1968	Lynn McClements, Australia	1m5.5s
1972	Mayumi Aoki, Japan	1m3.34s
1976	Kornelia Ender, East Germany	1m00.13s
1980	Caren Metschuck, East Germany	1m00.42s
1984	Mary Meagher, United States	59.26s
1988	Kristin Otto, East Germany	59.0s
1992	Qian Hong, China	58.62s
1996	Amy Van Dyken, United States	59.13s

200-Meter Butterfly

1968	Ada Kok, Netherlands	2m24.7s
1972	Karen Moe, United States	2m15.57s
1976	Andrea Pollack, East Germany	2m11.41s
1980	Ines Geissler, East Germany	2m10.44s
1984	Mary Meagher, United States	2m06.90s
1988	Kathleen Nord, East Germany	2m9.51s
1992	Summer Sanders, United States	2m06.67s
1996	Susan O'Neill, Australia	2m07.76s

200-Meter Individual Medley

1968	Claudia Kolb, United States	2m24.7s
1972	Shane Gould, Australia	2m23.07s
1984	Tracy Caulkins, United States	2m12.64s
1988	Daniela Hunger, East Germany	2m12.59s
1992	Lin Lee, China	2m11.55s[1]
1996	Michelle Smith, Ireland	2m13.93s

1. World record.

400-Meter Individual Medley

1964	Donna de Varona, United States	5m18.7s
1968	Claudia Kolk, United States	5m8.5s
1972	Gail Neall, Australia	5m2.97s
1976	Ulrike Tauber, East Germany	4m42.77s
1980	Petra Schneider, East Germany	4m36.29s
1984	Tracy Caulkins, United States	4m39.21s
1988	Janet Evans, United States	4m37.76s
1992	Krisztina Egerszegi, Hungary	4m36.54s
1996	Michelle Smith, Ireland	4m39.18s

400-Meter Freestyle Relay

1912	Great Britain	5m52.8s
1920	United States	5m11.6s
1924	United States	4m58.8s
1928	United States	4m47.6s
1932	United States	4m38.0s
1936	Netherlands	4m36.0s
1948	United States	4m29.2s
1952	Hungary	4m24.4s
1956	Australia	4m17.1s
1960	United States	4m8.9s
1964	United States	4m3.8s
1968	United States	4m2.5s
1972	United States	3m55.19s
1976	United States	3m44.82s
1980	East Germany	3m42.71s
1984	United States	3m44.43s
1988	East Germany	3m40.63s
1992	United States	3m39.46s
1996	United States	3m39.29s

800-Meter Freestyle Relay

1996	United States	7m59.87s

400-Meter Medley Relay

1960	United States	4m41.1s
1964	United States	4m33.9s
1968	United States	4m28.3s
1972	United States	4m20.75s
1976	East Germany	4m07.95s
1980	East Germany	4m06.67s
1984	United States	4m08.34s
1988	East Germany	4m03.74s
1992	United States	4m02.54s[1]
1996	United States	4m02.88s

1. World record.

Springboard Dive

		Points
1920	Aileen Riggin, United States	539.90
1924	Elizabeth Becker, United States	474.50
1928	Helen Meany, United States	78.62
1932	Georgia Coleman, United States	87.52
1936	Marjorie Gestring, United States	89.27
1948	Victoria M. Draves, United States	108.74
1952	Patricia McCormick, United States	147.30
1956	Patricia McCormick, United States	142.36
1960	Ingrid Kramer, Germany	155.81
1964	Ingrid Kramer Engel, Germany	145.00
1968	Sue Gossick, United States	150.77
1972	Micki King, United States	450.03
1976	Jennifer Chandler, United States	506.19
1980	Irina Kalinina, U.S.S.R.	725.91
1984	Sylvie Bernier, Canada	530.70
1988	Gao Min, China	580.23
1992	Gao Min, China	572.40
1996	Fu Ming-Xia, China	547.68

Platform Dive

	Points
1912 Greta Johansson, Sweden	39.90
1920 Stefani Fryland, Denmark	34.60
1924 Caroline Smith, United States	166.00
1928 Elizabeth B. Pinkston, United States	31.60
1932 Dorothy Poynton, United States	40.26
1936 Dorothy Poynton Hill, United States	33.92
1948 Victoria M. Draves, United States	68.87
1952 Patricia McCormick, United States	79.37
1956 Patricia McCormick, United States	84.85
1960 Ingrid Kramer, Germany	91.28
1964 Lesley Bush, United States	99.80
1968 Milena Duchkova, Czechoslovakia	109.59
1972 Ulrika Knape, Sweden	390.00
1976 Elena Vaytsekhovskaia, U.S.S.R.	406.59
1980 Martina Jaschke, East Germany	596.25
1984 Zhou Ji-Hong, China	435.51
1988 Xu Yan-Mei, China	445.20
1992 Fu Ming-Xia, China	461.43
1996 Fu Ming-Xia, China	521.58

BASKETBALL–MEN

1904	United States	1972	U.S.S.R.
1936	United States	1976	United States
1948	United States	1980	Yugoslavia
1952	United States	1984	United States
1956	United States	1988	U.S.S.R.
1960	United States	1992	United States
1964	United States	1996	United States
1968	United States		

BASKETBALL–WOMEN

1976	U.S.S.R.	1988	United States
1980	U.S.S.R.	1992	Unified Team[1]
1984	United States	1996	United States

1. Former Soviet Union team.

DISTRIBUTION OF MEDALS—1996 SUMMER GAMES

Country	Gold	Silver	Bronze	Total	Country	Gold	Silver	Bronze	Total
United States	44	32	25	101	Ethiopia	2	0	1	3
Germany	20	18	27	65	Algeria	2	0	1	3
Russia	26	21	16	63	Iran	1	1	1	3
China	16	22	12	50	Slovakia	1	1	1	3
Australia	9	9	23	41	Argentina	0	2	1	3
France	15	7	15	37	Austria	0	1	2	3
Italy	13	10	12	35	Armenia	1	1	0	2
South Korea	7	15	5	27	Croatia	1	1	0	2
Cuba	9	8	8	25	Portugal	1	0	1	2
Ukraine	9	2	12	23	Thailand	1	0	1	2
Canada	3	11	8	22	Namibia	0	2	0	2
Hungary	7	4	10	21	Slovenia	0	2	0	2
Romania	4	7	9	20	Malaysia	0	1	1	2
Netherlands	4	5	10	19	Moldova	0	1	1	2
Poland	7	5	5	17	Uzbekistan	0	1	1	2
Spain	5	6	6	17	Georgia	0	0	2	2
Britain	1	8	7	16	Morocco	0	0	2	2
Bulgaria	3	7	5	15	Trinidad & Tobago	0	0	2	2
Belarus	1	6	8	15	Burundi	1	0	0	1
Brazil	3	2	10	15	Costa Rica	1	0	0	1
Japan	3	6	5	14	Ecuador	1	0	0	1
Czech Republic	4	3	4	11	Hong Kong	1	0	0	1
Kazakhstan	3	4	4	11	Syria	1	0	0	1
Greece	4	4	0	8	Azerbaijan	0	1	0	1
Sweden	2	4	2	8	Bahamas	0	1	0	1
Kenya	1	4	3	8	Latvia	0	1	0	1
Switzerland	4	3	0	7	Philippines	0	1	0	1
Norway	2	2	3	7	Taiwan	0	1	0	1
Denmark	4	1	1	6	Tonga	0	1	0	1
Turkey	4	1	1	6	Zambia	0	1	0	1
New Zealand	3	2	1	6	India	0	0	1	1
Belgium	2	2	2	6	Israel	0	0	1	1
Nigeria	2	1	3	6	Lithuania	0	0	1	1
Jamaica	1	3	2	6	Mexico	0	0	1	1
South Africa	3	1	1	5	Mongolia	0	0	1	1
North Korea	2	1	2	5	Mozambique	0	0	1	1
Ireland	3	0	1	4	Puerto Rico	0	0	1	1
Finland	1	2	1	4	Tunisia	0	0	1	1
Indonesia	1	1	2	4	Uganda	0	0	1	1
Yugoslavia	1	1	2	4					

BOXING

(U.S. winners only)
(U.S. boycotted Olympics in 1980)

Flyweight-112 pounds (51 kilograms)

1904	George Finnegan	1952	Nate Brooks
1920	Frank De Genaro	1976	Leo Randolph
1924	Fidel La Barba	1984	Steve McCrory

Bantamweight-119 (54 kg)

| 1904 | O.L. Kirk | 1988 | Kennedy McKinney |

Featherweight-126 pounds (57 kg)

| 1904 | O.L. Kirk | 1984 | Meldrick Taylor |
| 1924 | Jackie Fields | | |

Lightweight-132 pounds (60 kg)

1904	H.J. Spanger	1976	Howard Davis
1920	Samuel Mosberg	1984	Pernell Whitaker
1968	Ronnie Harris	1992	Oscar De La Hoya

Light Welterweight-140 pounds (63.5 kg)

| 1952 | Charles Adkins | 1976 | Ray Leonard |
| 1972 | Ray Seales | 1984 | Jerry Page |

Welterweight-148 pounds (67 kg)

| 1904 | Al Young | 1984 | Mark Breland |
| 1932 | Edward Flynn | | |

Light Middleweight-157 pounds (71 kg)

| 1960 | Wilbert McClure | 1996 | David Reid |
| 1984 | Frank Tate | | |

Middleweight-165 pounds (75 kg)

1904	Charles Mayer	1960	Eddie Cook
1932	Carmen Barth	1976	Michael Spinks
1952	Floyd Patterson		

Light Heavyweight-179 pounds (81 kg)

1920	Edward Eagan	1960	Cassius Clay
1952	Norvel Lee	1976	Leon Spinks
1956	James Boyd	1988	Andrew Maynard

Heavyweight-201 pounds

1904	Sam Berger	1968	George Foreman
1952	Edward Sanders	1984	Henry Tilman
1956	Pete Rademacher	1988	Ray Mercer
1964	Joe Frazier		

Super Heavyweight (unlimited)

| 1984 | Tyrell Biggs |

Other 1996 Summer Olympic Games Champions

Archery
Women's individual—Kim Kyung Wook, South Korea
Women's team—South Korea
Men's individual—Justin Huish, United States
Men's team—United States

Badminton
Men's singles—Poul-Erik Hoyer-Larsen, Denmark
Men's doubles—Indonesia (Rexy Mainaky, Ricky Subagja)
Women's singles—Bang Soo-Hyun, South Korea
Women's doubles—China (Ge Fei, Gu Jun)
Mixed doubles—South Korea (Gil Young-Ahl, Kim Dong-Moon)

Baseball
Men—Cuba

Beach Volleyball
Women—Jackie Silva/Sandra Pires, Brazil
Men—Karch Kiraly/Kent Steffes, United States

Canoe-Kayak—Men
Canoe single slalom—Michal Martikan, Slovakia
Canoe slalom pairs—France
Kayak slalom singles—Oliver Fix, Germany
Canoe singles 500m—Martin Doktor, Czech Republic
Canoe singles 1,000m—Martin Doktor, Czech Republic
Canoe pairs 500m—Csaba Horvath/Gyorgy Kolonics, Hungary
Canoe pairs 1,000m—Andreas Dittmer/Gunar Kirchbach, Germany
Kayak singles 500m—Antonio Rossi, Italy
Kayak singles 1,000m—Knut Holmann, Norway
Kayak pairs 500m—Kay Bluhm/Torsten Gutsche, Germany
Kayak pairs 1,000m—Antonio Rossi/Daniele Scarpa, Italy
Kayak fours 1,000m—Germany

Kayak—Women
Single slalom—Stepnka Hilgertova, Czech Republic
500m singles—Rita Koban, Hungary
500m pairs—Agneta Andersson/Susanne Gunnarsson, Sweden
500m pairs—Germany

Cycling—Men
Individual road race—Pascal Richard, Switzerland
1 km time trial—Florian Rousseau, France
Individual pursuit—Andrea Collinelli, Italy
Individual spring—Jens Fiedler, Germany
Individual point race—Silvio Martinello, Italy
Team pursuit—France
Cross country—Bart Jan Brentjens, Netherlands
Individual time trial—Miguel Indurain, Spain

Cycling—Women
Individual road race—Jeannie Longo-Ciprelli, France
Track sprint—Felicia Ballanger, France
Individual pursuit—Antonella Bellutti, Italy
Point race—Nathalie Lancien, France
Cross country—Paola Pezzo, Italy
Individual time trial—Zulfiya Zabirova, Russia

Equestrian
Three-day team event—Australia
Individual three-day—Blyth Tait, New Zealand

Team dressage—Germany
Individual dressage—Isabell Werth, Germany
Team jumping—Germany
Show jumping—Ulrich Kirchhoff, Germany

Fencing—Men
Individual epee—Aleksandr Beketov, Russia
Individual sabre—Stanislav Pozydnakov, Russia
Individual foil—Alessandro Puccini, Italy
Team epee—Italy
Team sabre—Russia
Team foil—Russia

Fencing—Women
Individual epee—Laura Flessel, France
Individual foil—Laura Badea, Romania
Team epee—France
Team foil—Italy

Field Hockey
Women—Australia
Men—Netherlands

Gymnastics—Men
Team—Russia
All-around—Li Xiao-Shuang, China
Floor exercise—Ioannis Melissanidis, Greece
Vault—Alexei Nemov, Russia
Parallel bars—Rustram Sharipov, Ukraine
High bar—Andreas Wecker, Germany
Pommel horse—Li Dong-Hua, Switzerland
Rings—Yuri Chechi, Italy

Gymnastics—Women
Team—United States
All-around—Lilia Podkopayeva, Ukraine
Balance beam—Shannon Miller, United States
Floor exercise—Lilia Podkopayeva, Ukraine
Uneven bars—Svetlana Chorkina, Russia
Vault—Simona Amanar, Romania

Judo—Men
Extra-lightweight—Tadahiro Nomura, Japan
Half-lightweight—Udo Quellmalz, Germany
Lightweight—Kenzo Nakamura, Japan
Half-middleweight—Djamel Bouras, France
Middleweight—Jeon Ki Young, South Korea
Light-heavyweight—Pawel Nastula, Poland
Heavyweight—David Douillet, France

Judo—Women
Extra-lightweight—Sun Kye, North Korea
Half-lightweight—Marie-Claire Restoux, France
Lightweight—Driulis Gonzalez, Cuba
Half-middleweight—Yuko Emoto, Japan
Middleweight—Cho Min Sun, South Korea

Light-heavyweight—Ulla Werbrouck, Belgium
Heavyweight—Sun Fu-Ming, China

Modern Pentathlon
Individual—Aleksandr Parygin, Kazakhstan

Rhythmic Gymnastics
Team—Spain
Individual—Ekaterina Serebryanskaya, Ukraine

Rowing—Men
Coxless pairs—Great Britain
Coxless four—Australia
Single sculls—Xeno Müller, Switzerland
Double sculls—Italy
Lightweight double sculls—Switzerland
Eight—Netherlands
Quadruple sculls—Germany
Lightweight coxless four—Denmark

Rowing—Women
Coxless pairs—Australia
Single sculls—Yekaterina Khodotovich, Belarus
Double sculls—Canada
Eight—Romania
Quadruple sculls—Germany
Lightweight double sculls—Romania

Shooting—Women
10m air rifle—Renata Mauer, Poland
10m air pistol—Olga Klochneva, Russia
Double trap—Kim Rhode, United States
Rifle three position—Aleksandra Ivosev, Yugoslavia
24m sport pistol—Li Dui-Hong, China

Shooting—Men
10m air pistol—Roberto Di Donna, Italy
Trap—Michael Diamond, Australia
Air rifle—Artem Khadzhibekov, Russia
50m free pistol—Boris Kokorev, Russia
Double trap—Russell Mark, Australia
25m rapid fire pistol—Ralf Schumann, Germany
50m rifle prone—Christian Klees, Germany
Running game target—Yank Ling, China
50m free rifle 3-position—Jean-Pierre Amat, France
Skeet shooting—Ennio Falco, Italy

Soccer
Women—United States
Men—Nigeria

Softball
United States

Synchronized Swimming
Team—United States

Table Tennis
Women's singles—Deng Ya-Ping, China
Women's doubles—China (Deng Ya-Ping, Qiao Hong)
Men's singles—Liu, Guo-Liang, China
Men's doubles—China (Kong Ling-Hui, Liu Guo-Liang)

Team Handball
Women—Denmark
Men—Croatia

Tennis
Men's singles—Andre Agassi, United States
Men's doubles—Todd Woodbridge and Mark Woodforde, Australia
Women's singles—Lindsay Davenport, United States
Women's doubles—Gigi Fernandez and Mary Jo Fernandez, United States

Volleyball
Women—Cuba
Men—Netherlands

Water Polo
Spain

Weightlifting
119 lb—Halil Mutlu, Turkey
130 lb—Tang Ling-Shen, China
141 lb—Naim Suleymanoglu, Turkey
154 lb—Zhan Xu-Gang, China
161.5 lb—Pablo Lara, Cuba
183 lb—Pyrros Dias, Greece
200.5 lb—Aleksey Petrov, Russia
218 lb—Akakide Kakiashvilis, Greece
238 lb—Timur Taimazov, Ukraine
238+ lb—Andre Chemerkin, Russia

Wrestling—Greco-Roman
105.5 lb—Sim Kwon-Ho, South Korea
114.5 lb—Armen Nazaryan, Armenia
125.5 lb—Yuri Melnichenko, Kazakhstan
136.5 lb—Wlodzimierz Zwadzki, Poland
149.5 lb—Ryszard Wolny, Poland
163 lb—Feliberto Ascuy Aquilera, Cuba
180.5 lb—Hamza Yerlikiya, Turkey
198 lb—Vyacheslav Oleynyk, Ukraine
220 lb—Andrzej Wronski, Poland
286 lb—Aleksandr Karelin, Russia

Wrestling—Freestyle
105.5 lb—Kim Il, North Korea
114.5 lb—Valentin Jordanov, Bulgaria
125.5 lb—Kendall Cross, United States
136.5 lb—Tom Brands, United States
149.5 lb—Vadim Bogiev, Russia
163 lb—Bouvaisa Satiev, Russia
180.5 lb—Khadzhimurad Magomedov, Russia
198.5 lb—Rsaul Khadem, Iran
220 lb—Kurt Angle, United States
286 lb—Mahmut Demir, Turkey

Yachting
Men's Mistral—Nikolaos Kaklamanakis, Greece
Men's 470—Ukraine
Men's Finn—Mateusz Kusznierewicz, Poland
Women's Mistral—Lee Lai-Shan, Hong Kong
Women's Europe—Kristine Rough, Denmark
Women's 470—Spain
Open Laser—Robert Scheidt, Brazil
Open Tornado—Spain
Open Soling—Germany
Open Star—Brazil

Winter Games

FIGURE SKATING–MEN

1908	Ulrich Salchow, Sweden
1920	Gillis Grafstrom, Sweden
1924	Gillis Grafstrom, Sweden
1928	Gillis Grafstrom, Sweden
1932	Karl Schaefer, Austria
1936	Karl Schaefer, Austria
1948	Richard Button, United States
1952	Richard Button, United States
1956	Hayes Alan Jenkins, United States
1960	David Jenkins, United States
1964	Manfred Schnelldorfer, Germany
1968	Wolfgang Schwartz, Austria
1972	Ondrej Nepela, Czechoslovakia
1976	John Curry, Great Britain
1980	Robin Cousins, Great Britain
1984	Scott Hamilton, United States
1988	Brian Boitano, United States
1992	Viktor Petrenko, Unified Team*
1994	Alexei Urmanov, Russia

*Former Soviet Union team.

FIGURE SKATING–WOMEN

1908	Madge Syers, Britain
1920	Magda Julin-Maurey, Sweden
1924	Herma Szabo-Planck, Austria
1928	Sonja Henie, Norway
1932	Sonja Henie, Norway
1936	Sonja Henle, Norway
1948	Barbara Ann Scott, Canada
1952	Jeannette Altwegg, Great Britain
1956	Tenley Albright, United States
1960	Carol Heiss, United States
1964	Sjoukje Dijkstra, Netherlands
1968	Peggy Fleming, United States
1972	Beatrix Schuba, Austria
1976	Dorothy Hamill, United States
1980	Anett Poetzsch, East Germany
1984	Katarina Witt, East Germany
1988	Katarina Witt, East Germany
1992	Kristi Yamaguchi, United States
1994	Oksana Baiul, Ukraine

SPEED SKATING–MEN

(U.S. winners only)

500 Meters

1924	Charles Jewtraw	44.0
1932	John A. Shea	43.4
1952	Kenneth Henry	43.2
1964	Terrence McDermott	40.1
1980	Eric Heiden	38.03

1,000 Meters

1976	Peter Mueller	1:19.32
1980	Eric Heiden	1:15.18
1994	Dan Jansen	1:12.43[1]

1,500 Meters

1932	John A. Shea	2:57.5
1980	Eric Heiden	1:55.44

5,000 Meters

1932	Irving Jaffee	9:40.8
1980	Eric Heiden	7:02.29

10,000 Meters

1932	Irving Jaffee	19:13.6
1980	Eric Heiden	14:28.13

1. World record.

SPEED SKATING–WOMEN

(U.S. winners only)

500 Meters

1972	Anne Henning	43.33
1976	Sheila Young	42.76
1988	Bonnie Blair	39.10
1992	Bonnie Blair	40.33
1994	Bonnie Blair	39.25

1,000 Meters

1992	Bonnie Blair	1:21.90
1994	Bonnie Blair	1:18.74

1,500 Meters

1972	Dianne Holum	2:20.85

SKIING, ALPINE–MEN

Downhill

1948	Henri Oreiller, France	2m55.0s
1952	Zeno Colo, Italy	2m30.8s
1956	Anton Sailer, Austria	2m52.2s
1960	Jean Vuarnet, France	2m06.2s
1964	Egon Zimmermann, Austria	2m18.16s
1968	Jean-Claude Killy, France	1m59.85s
1972	Bernhard Russi, Switzerland	1m51.43s
1976	Franz Klammer, Austria	1m45.72s
1980	Leonhard Stock, Austria	1m45.50s
1984	Bill Johnson, United States	1m45.59s
1988	Pirmin Zurbriggen, Switzerland	1m59.63s
1992	Patrick Ortlieb, Austria	1m50.37s
1994	Tommy Moe, United States	1m45.75s

Slalom

1948	Edi Reinalter, Switzerland	2m10.3s
1952	Othmar Schneider, Austria	2m00.0s
1956	Anton Sailer, Austria	194.7 pts.
1960	Ernst Hinterseer, Austria	2m08.9s
1964	Josef Stiegler, Austria	2m10.13
1968	Jean-Claude Killy, France	1m39.73s
1972	Francisco Fernandez Ochoa, Spain	1m49.27s
1976	Piero Gros, Italy	2m03.29s
1980	Integmar Stenmark, Sweden	1m44.26s
1984	Phil Mahre, United States	1m39.41s
1988	Alberto Tomba, Italy	1m39.47s
1992	Finn Christian, Norway	1m44.39s
1994	Thomas Stangassinger, Austria	2m2.02s

Giant Slalom

1952	Stein Eriksen, Norway	2m25.0s
1956	Anton Sailer, Austria	3m00.1s
1960	Roger Staub, Switzerland	1m48.3s
1964	François Bonlieu, France	1m46.71s
1968	Jean-Claude Killy, France	3m29.28s
1972	Gustavo Thoeni, Italy	3m09.52s
1976	Heini Hemmi, Switzerland	3m26.97s
1980	Ingemar Stenmark, Sweden	2m40.74s
1984	Max Julen, Switzerland	1m20.54s
1988	Alberto Tomba, Italy	2m06.37s
1992	Alberto Tomba, Italy	2m06.98s
1994	Markus Wasmeier, Germany	2m52.46s

SKIING, ALPINE–WOMEN

Downhill

1948	Hedi Schlunegger, Switzerland	2m28.3s
1952	Trude Jochum-Beiser, Austria	1m47.1s
1956	Madeleine Berthod, Switzerland	1m40.1s
1960	Heidi Biebl, Germany	1m37.6s
1964	Christi Haas, Austria	1m55.39s
1968	Olga Pall, Austria	1m40.87s
1972	Marie-Therese Nadig, Switzerland	1m36.68s

1976 Rosi Mittermeier, West Germany	1m46.16s
1980 Annemarie Proell Moser, Austria	1m37.52s
1984 Michela Figini, Switzerland	1m13.36s
1988 Marina Kiehl, West Germany	1m25.86s
1992 Kerrin Lee-Gartner, Canada	1m52.55s
1994 Katja Seizinger, Germany	1m35.93s

Slalom

1948 Gretchen Fraser, United States	1m57.2s
1952 Andrea Mead Lawrence, United States	2m10.6s
1956 Renee Colliard, Switzerland	112.3 pts.
1960 Anne Heggtveigt, Canada	1m49.6s
1964 Christine Goitschel, France	1m29.86s
1968 Marielle Goitschel, France	1m25.86s
1972 Barbara Cochran, United States	1m31.24s
1976 Rosi Mittermeier, West Germany	1m30.54s
1980 Hanni Wenzel, Liechtenstein	1m25.09s
1984 Paoletta Magoni, Italy	1m36.47s
1988 Vreni Schneider, Switzerland	1m36.69s
1992 Petra Kronberger, Austria	1m32.68s
1994 Vreni Schneider, Switzerland	1m56.01s

Giant Slalom

1952 Andrea M. Lawrence, United States	2m06.8s
1956 Ossi Reichert, Germany	1m56.5s
1960 Yvonne Ruegg, Switzerland	1m39.9s
1964 Marielle Goitschel, France	1m52.24s
1968 Nancy Greene, Canada	1m51.97s
1972 Marie-Therese Nadig, Switzerland	1m29.90s
1976 Kathy Kreiner, Canada	1m29.13s
1980 Hanni Wenzel, Liechtenstein	2m41.66s
1984 Debbie Armstrong, United States	2m20.98s
1988 Vreni Schneider, Switzerland	2m06.49s
1992 Pernilla Wiberg, Sweden	2m12.74s
1994 Deborah Compagnoni, Italy	2m30.97s

1994 UNITED STATES MEDALISTS

Figure Skating
Women—SILVER—Nancy Kerrigan, Stoneham, Mass.

Alpine Skiing
Men's Downhill—GOLD—Tommy Moe, Palmer, Alaska.
Men's Super Giant Slalom—SILVER—Tommy Moe, Palmer, Alaska.
Women's Downhill—SILVER—Picabo Street, Sun Valley, Idaho.
Women's Super Giant Slalom—GOLD—Diann Roffe-Steinrotter, Potsdam, N.Y.

Freestyle Skiing
Women's Moguls—SILVER—Liz McIntyre, Winter Park, Colo.

Speedskating
Women's 500 meters—GOLD—Bonnie Blair, Milwaukee, Wis.
Women's 1,000 meters—GOLD—Bonnie Blair, Milwaukee, Wis.
Men's 1,000 meters—GOLD—Dan Jansen, Greenfield, Wis.

Short Track Speedskating
Women's 3,000 meter relay—BRONZE—United States (Karen Cashman, Quincy, Mass.; Amy Peterson, Maplewood, Minn.; Cathy Turner, Hilton, N.Y.; Nicole Ziegelmayer, Milwaukee, Wis.)
Women's 500 meters—GOLD—Cathy Turner, Hilton, N.Y.—BRONZE—Amy Peterson, Maplewood, Minn.
Men's 5,000 meter relay—SILVER—United States (Randy Bartz, Milwaukee, Wis.; John Coyle, Milwaukee, Wis.; Eric Flaim, Hyde Park, Mass.; Andy Gabel, Northbrook, Ill.)

DISTRIBUTION OF MEDALS 1994 WINTER OLYMPIC GAMES

(Lillehammer, Norway)

	Gold	Silver	Bronze	Total
Norway	10	11	5	26
Germany	9	7	8	24
Russia	11	8	4	23
Italy	7	5	8	20
United States	6	5	2	13
Canada	3	6	4	13
Austria	3	3	4	10
Switzerland	2	4	2	8
South Korea	4	1	1	6
Finland	0	1	5	6
Japan	1	2	2	5
France	0	1	4	5
Netherlands	0	1	3	4
Sweden	2	1	0	3
Kazakhstan	1	2	0	3
China	0	1	2	3
Slovenia	0	0	3	3
Ukraine	1	0	1	2
Belarus	0	2	0	2
Britain	0	0	2	2
Uzbekistan	1	0	0	1
Australia	0	0	1	1

ICE HOCKEY

1920	Canada	1968	U.S.S.R.
1924	Canada	1972	U.S.S.R.
1928	Canada	1976	U.S.S.R.
1932	Canada	1980	United States
1936	Great Britain	1984	U.S.S.R.
1948	Canada	1988	U.S.S.R.
1952	Canada	1992	Unified Team[*]
1956	U.S.S.R.	1994	Sweden
1960	United States	*Former Soviet Union
1964	U.S.S.R.	team.	

FINAL 1994 OLYMPIC HOCKEY STANDINGS

Group A	W	L	T	GF	GA
Finland	5	0	0	25	4
Germany	3	2	0	11	14
Czech Republic	3	2	0	16	11
Russia	3	2	0	20	14
Austria	1	4	0	13	28
Norway	0	5	0	5	19

Group B	W	L	T	GF	GA
Slovakia	3	0	2	26	14
Canada	3	1	1	17	11
Sweden	3	1	1	23	13
United States	1	1	3	21	17
Italy	1	4	0	15	31
France	0	4	1	11	30

Championship
Sweden 3, Canada 2 (Shootout)
Bronze Medal
Finland 4, Russia 0
Fifth Place
Czech Republic 7, Slovakia 1
Seventh Place
Germany 4, United States 3

Other 1994 Winter Olympic Games Champions

Biathlon
Men's 10-kilometer—Sergei Tchepikov, Russia
Men's 20-kilometer—Sergei Tarasov, Russia
Men's 4 × 7.5 kilometer relay—Germany
Women's 7.5 kilometer—Myriam Bedard, Canada
Women's 15-kilometers—Myriam Bedard, Canada
Women's 4 × 7.5 kilometer relay—Russia

Bobsledding
2-man—Switzerland I
4-man—Germany II

Figure Skating
Men's singles—Alexei Urmanov, Russia
Women's singles—Oksana Baiul, Ukraine
Pairs—Ekaterina Gordeeva and Sergei Grinkov, Russia
Ice dancing—Oksana Gritschuk and Evgeni Platov, Russia

Speed Skating-Men
500m—Aleksandr Golubev, Russia
1,000m—Dan Jansen, United States
1,500m—Johann Olav Koss, Norway
5,000m—Johann Olav Koss, Norway
10,000m—Johann Olav Koss, Norway

Speed Skating-Women
500m—Bonnie Blair, United States
1,000m—Bonnie Blair, United States

1,500m—Emese Hunyady, Austria
3,000m—Svetlana Bazhanova, Russia
5,000m—Claudia Pechstein, Germany

Luge
Men's singles—Georg Hackl, Germany
Men's doubles—Kurt Brugger and Wilfried Huber, Italy
Women's singles—Gerda Weissensteiner, Italy

Skiing, Nordic-Men
Combined team—Japan
Combined—Fred Borre Lundberg, Norway
90-meter jump—Espen Bredesen, Norway
120-meter jump—Jens Weissflog, Germany
Team 120-meter jump—Germany
10-kilometer classical—Bjorn Dahlie, Norway
15-kilometer free pursuit—Bjorn Dahlie, Norway
30-kilometer freestyle—Thomas Alsgaard, Norway
50-kilometer classical—Vladimir Smirnov, Kazakhstan
4 × 10 kilometer relay—Italy

Skiing, Nordic-Women
5-kilometer classical—Lyubov Egorova, Russia
10-kilometer free pursuit—Lyubov Egorova, Russia
15-kilometer freestyle—Manuela Di Centa, Italy
30-kilometer classical—Manuela Di Centa, Italy
4 × 5 kilometer relay—Russia

United States Best-Ever 13 Medals at 1994 Winter Olympics

The names Nancy Kerrigan and Tonya Harding dominated the 1994 Winter Olympics in Lillehammer, Norway. While Kerrigan won a silver medal and Harding none at all, the pre-Olympics attack on Kerrigan's knee, in which associates of Harding and even Harding herself were implicated, kept the spotlight on figure skating as soap opera rather than sport.

The on-ice big name for the United States, as it won a Winter Games record 13 medals, was Bonnie Blair of Milwaukee, Wis. Blair won gold in both the 500-meter and 1,000-meter speed skating races, giving her a career total of five gold medals. That's one more than any American woman had ever won, winter or summer. With one gold medal at Calgary in 1988, two at

Albertville in 1992, and two at Lillehammer, Blair passed diver Pat McCormack, swimmer Janet Evans, and sprinter Evelyn Ashford.

The U.S. won a surprising four medals in Alpine skiing, two by Tommy Moe of Palmer, Alaska, and one each by Diann Roffe-Steinrotter and Picabo Street.

The most emotional moment of the 1994 Winter Games for the American team came when Dan Jansen, in his final attempt, finally took the long-awaited gold medal in the 1,000-meter speedskating event. He not only won it, but did so in world record time.

Norway won the medals race with 26, two ahead of Germany with 24. Russia was third with 23, and Italy a surprising fourth with 20.

Iditarod

25TH IDITAROD TRAIL SLED DOG RACE—1997

(Alaska, March 1–11, 1997)

The annual 1,159-mile race stretches from Anchorage to Nome, Alaska. Begun in 1973, the course follows an old frozen river route and is named after a deserted mining town along the way. The Iditarod also commemorates a famous midwinter emergency mission to get medical supplies to Nome during a 1925 diphtheria epidemic. Men and women mushers compete together.

Course: Anchorage to Nome.

1997 Champion—

Martin Buser, a 38-year-old Swiss-born musher, won the 25th annual Iditarod Trail Sled Dog Race on March 11. Buser, who also won the race in 1992 and 1994, reached Nome and the finish line of the 1,161-mile course in 9 days, 8 hours, and 31 minutes. The Iditarod began March 1 in Anchorage. In even-numbered years, the trail follows the 1,151-mile long Northern Route, while odd-numbered years it takes the slightly different

1,161-mile Southern Route. The 25th anniversary running was marred by the deaths of four dogs, including one dog in the team of Joe Redington, the founder of the race. Buser, who finished the race with ten of his original 16 dogs, took home $50,000 and a new pickup. Doug Swingley, the 1995 champion, placed second, about two hours behind Buser.

Winning times since 1980:
1980, Joe May, 14 days-7 hours-11 minutes; 1981, Rick Swenson, 12-8-45; 1982, Rick Swenson, 16-4-40; 1983, Rick Mackey, 12-14-10; 1984, Dean Osmar, 12-15-7; 1985, Libby Riddles, 18-00-20; 1986, Susan Butcher, 11-15-6; 1987, Susan Butcher, 11-2-5; 1988, Susan Butcher, 11-11-41; 1989, Joe Runyan, 11-5-24; 1990, Susan Butcher, 11-1-34; 1991, Rick Swenson, 12-16-34; 1992, Martin Buser, 10-19-17; 1993, Jeff King, 10-15-38; 1994, Martin Buser, 10-13-2; 1995, Doug Swingly, 9-2-42; 1996, Jeff King, 9-5-43; 1997, Martin Buser, 9-8-31.

Football

The pastime of kicking around a ball goes back beyond the limits of recorded history. Ancient savage tribes played football of a primitive kind. There was a ball-kicking game played by Athenians, Spartans, and Corinthians 2500 years ago, which the Greeks called *Episkuros*. The Romans had a somewhat similar game called *Harpastum* and are supposed to have carried the game with them when they invaded the British Isles in the First Century, B.C.

Undoubtedly the game known in the United States as Football traces directly to the English game of Rugby, though the modifications have been many. Informal football was played on college lawns well over a century ago, and an annual Freshman-Sophomore series of "scrimmages" began at Yale in 1840. The first formal intercollegiate football game was the Princeton-Rutgers contest at New Brunswick, N.J. on Nov. 6, 1869, with Rutgers winning by 6 goals to 4.

In those days, games were played with 25, 20, 15, or 11 men on a side. In 1880, there was a convention at which Walter Camp of Yale persuaded the delegates to agree to a rule calling for 11 players on a side.

The first professional game was played in 1895 at Latrobe, Pa. The National Football League was founded in 1921. The All-American Conference went into action in 1946. At the end of the 1949 season the two circuits merged, retaining the name of the older league. In 1960, the American Football League began operations. In 1970, the leagues merged. The United States Football League played its first season in 1983, from March to July. It suspended spring operation after the 1985 season, and planned a 1986 move to fall, but suspended operations again.

In 1991, another effort at spring football was launched, but this time it had the backing of the National Football League. The World League of American Football debuted in March 1991 with ten teams. Three of them were in Europe. The other seven were in North America, including the Montreal Machine in Canada. With television contracts signed with ABC and USA Cable Network, the league seemed to be on sound footing from the beginning. But after just two seasons, it was suspended. The league returned in 1995, but only with six teams in Europe.

College Football

NATIONAL COLLEGE FOOTBALL CHAMPIONS

The "National Collegiate A.A. Football Guide" recognizes as unofficial national champion the team selected each year by press association polls. The Associated Press poll (of writers) does not agree with the United Press International poll (of coaches); the guide lists both teams selected.

1937	Pittsburgh	1951	Tennessee	1963	Texas	1974	Oklahoma and So. California
1938	Texas Christian	1952	Mich. State	1964	Alabama		
1939	Texas A & M	1953	Maryland	1965	Alabama and Mich. State	1975	Oklahoma
1940	Minnesota	1954	Ohio State and U.C.L.A.			1976	Pittsburgh
1941	Minnesota			1966	Notre Dame	1977	Notre Dame
1942	Ohio State	1955	Oklahoma	1967	So. California	1978	Alabama and So. California
1943	Notre Dame	1956	Oklahoma	1968	Ohio State		
1944	Army	1957	Auburn and Ohio State	1969	Texas	1979	Alabama
1945	Army			1970	Texas and Nebraska	1980	Georgia
1946	Notre Dame	1958	Louisiana State			1981	Clemson
1947	Notre Dame	1959	Syracuse	1971	Nebraska	1982	Penn State
1948	Michigan	1960	Minnesota	1972	So. California	1983	Miami
1949	Notre Dame	1961	Alabama	1973	Notre Dame and U. of Ala.	1984	Brigham Young
1950	Oklahoma	1962	So. California			1985	Oklahoma

1986	Penn State
1987	Miami
1988	Notre Dame
1989	Miami
1990	Colorado and Georgia Tech
1991	Miami and Washington
1992	Alabama
1993	Florida State
1994	Nebraska
1995	Nebraska
1996	Univ. of Florida

RECORD OF ANNUAL MAJOR COLLEGE FOOTBALL BOWL GAMES

Rose Bowl

(At Pasadena, Calif.)

1902	Michigan 49, Stanford 0
1916	Washington State 14, Brown 0
1917	Oregon 14, Pennsylvania 0
1918	Mare Island Marines 19, Camp Lewis 7
1919	Great Lakes 17, Mare Island Marines 0
1920	Harvard 7, Oregon 6
1921	California 28, Ohio State 0
1922	Washington and Jefferson 0, California 0
1923	So. California 14, Penn State 3
1924	Navy 14, Washington 14
1925	Notre Dame 27, Stanford 10
1926	Alabama 20, Washington 19
1927	Alabama 7, Stanford 7
1928	Stanford 7, Pittsburgh 6
1929	Georgia Tech 8, California 7
1930	So. California 47, Pittsburgh 14

1931	Alabama 24, Wash. State 0
1932	So. California 21, Tulane 12
1933	So. California 35, Pittsburgh 0
1934	Columbia 7, Stanford 0
1935	Alabama 29, Stanford 13
1936	Stanford 7, So. Methodist 0
1937	Pittsburgh 21, Washington 0
1938	California 13, Alabama 0
1939	So. California 7, Duke 3
1940	So. California 14, Tennessee 0
1941	Stanford 21, Nebraska 13
1942	Oregon State 20, Duke 16[1]
1943	Georgia 9, U.C.L.A. 0
1944	So. California 29, Washington 0
1945	So. California 25, Tennessee 0
1946	Alabama 34, So. California 14
1947	Illinois 45, U.C.L.A. 14
1948	Michigan 49, So. California 0
1949	Northwestern 20, California 14
1950	Ohio State 17, California 14
1951	Michigan 14, California 6

1952	Illinois 40, Stanford 7
1953	So. California 7, Wisconsin 0
1954	Michigan State 28, U.C.L.A. 20
1955	Ohio State 20, So. California 7
1956	Michigan State 17, U.C.L.A. 14
1957	Iowa 35, Oregon State 19
1958	Ohio State 10, Oregon 7
1959	Iowa 38, California 12
1960	Washington 44, Wisconsin 8
1961	Washington 17, Minnesota 7
1962	Minnesota 21, U.C.L.A. 3
1963	So. California 42, Wisconsin 37
1964	Illinois 17, Washington 7
1965	Michigan 34, Oregon State 7
1966	U.C.L.A. 14, Michigan State 12
1967	Purdue 14, So. California 13
1968	So. California 14, Indiana 3
1969	Ohio State 27, So. California 16
1970	So. California 10, Michigan 3
1971	Stanford 27, Ohio State 17
1972	Stanford 13, Michigan 12

1973	So. California 42, Ohio State 17
1974	Ohio State 42, So. California 21
1975	So. California 18, Ohio State 17
1976	U.C.L.A. 23, Ohio State 10
1977	So. California 14, Michigan 6
1978	Washington 27, Michigan 20
1979	So. California 17, Michigan 10
1980	So. California 17, Ohio State 16
1981	Michigan 23, Washington 6
1982	Washington 28, Iowa 0
1983	U.C.L.A. 24, Michigan 14
1984	U.C.L.A. 45, Illinois 9
1985	USC 20, Ohio St. 17
1986	U.C.L.A. 45, Iowa 28
1987	Arizona State 22, Michigan 15
1988	Michigan State 20, USC 17
1989	Michigan 22, So. California 14
1990	USC 17, Michigan 10
1991	Washington 46, Iowa 34
1992	Washington 34, Michigan 14
1993	Michigan 38, Washington 31
1994	Wisconsin 21, UCLA 16
1995	Penn State 38, Oregon 20
1996	South Carolina 41, Northwestern 32
1997	Ohio State 20, Arizona State 17

1. Played at Durham, N.C.

Orange Bowl
(At Miami)

1933	Miami (Fla.) 7, Manhattan 0
1934	Duquesne 33, Miami (Fla.) 7
1935	Bucknell 26, Miami (Fla.) 0
1936	Catholic 20, Mississippi 19
1937	Duquesne 13, Mississippi State 12
1938	Auburn 6, Michigan State 0
1939	Tennessee 17, Oklahoma 0
1940	Georgia Tech 21, Missouri 7
1941	Mississippi State 14, Georgetown 7
1942	Georgia 40, Texas Christian 26
1943	Alabama 37, Boston College 21
1944	Louisiana State 19, Texas A & M 14
1945	Tulsa 26, Georgia Tech 12
1946	Miami (Fla.) 13, Holy Cross 6
1947	Rice 8, Tennessee 0
1948	Georgia Tech 20, Kansas 14
1949	Texas 41, Georgia 28
1950	Santa Clara 21, Kentucky 13
1951	Clemson 15, Miami (Fla.) 14
1952	Georgia Tech 17, Baylor 14
1953	Alabama 61, Syracuse 6
1954	Oklahoma 7, Maryland 0
1955	Duke 34, Nebraska 7
1956	Oklahoma 20, Maryland 6
1957	Colorado 27, Clemson 21
1958	Oklahoma 48, Duke 21
1959	Oklahoma 21, Syracuse 6
1960	Georgia 14, Missouri 0
1961	Missouri 21, Navy 14
1962	Louisiana State 25, Colorado 7
1963	Alabama 17, Oklahoma 0
1964	Nebraska 13, Auburn 7
1965	Texas 21, Alabama 17
1966	Alabama 39, Nebraska 28
1967	Florida 27, Georgia Tech 12
1968	Oklahoma 26, Tennessee 24
1969	Penn State 15, Kansas 14
1970	Penn State 10, Missouri 3
1971	Nebraska 17, Louisiana State 12
1972	Nebraska 38, Alabama 6

1973	Nebraska 40, Notre Dame 6
1974	Penn State 16, Louisiana State 9
1975	Notre Dame 13, Alabama 11
1976	Oklahoma 14, Michigan 6
1977	Ohio State 27, Colorado 10
1978	Arkansas 31, Oklahoma 6
1979	Oklahoma 31, Nebraska 24
1980	Oklahoma 24, Florida State 7
1981	Oklahoma 18, Florida State 17
1982	Clemson 22, Nebraska 15
1983	Nebraska 21, Louisiana State 20
1984	Miami 31, Nebraska 30
1985	Washington 28, Oklahoma 17
1986	Oklahoma 25, Penn St. 10
1987	Oklahoma 42, Arkansas 8
1988	Miami 20, Oklahoma 14
1989	Miami 23, Nebraska 3
1990	Notre Dame 21, Colorado 6
1991	Colorado 10, Notre Dame 9
1992	Miami 22, Nebraska 0
1993	Florida State 27, Nebraska 14
1994	Florida State 18, Nebraska 16
1995	Nebraska 24, Miami 17
1996	Florida State 31, Notre Dame 26
1997	Nebraska 41, Virginia Tech 21

Sugar Bowl
(At New Orleans)

1935	Tulane 20, Temple 14
1936	Texas Christian 3, Louisiana State 2
1937	Santa Clara 21, Louisiana State 14
1938	Santa Clara 6, Louisiana State 0
1939	Texas Christian 15, Carnegie Tech 7
1940	Texas A & M 14, Tulane 13
1941	Boston College 19, Tennessee 13
1942	Fordham 2, Missouri 0
1943	Tennessee 14, Tulsa 7
1944	Georgia Tech 20, Tulsa 18
1945	Duke 29, Alabama 26
1946	Oklahoma A & M 33, St. Mary's (Calif.) 13
1947	Georgia 20, North Carolina 10
1948	Texas 27, Alabama 7
1949	Oklahoma 14, North Carolina 6
1950	Oklahoma 35, Louisiana State 0
1951	Kentucky 13, Oklahoma 7
1952	Maryland 28, Tennessee 13
1953	Georgia Tech 24, Mississippi 7
1954	Georgia Tech 42, West Virginia 19
1955	Navy 21, Mississippi 0
1956	Georgia Tech 7, Pittsburgh 0
1957	Baylor 13, Tennessee 7
1958	Mississippi 39, Texas 9
1959	Louisiana State 7, Clemson 0
1960	Mississippi 21, Louisiana State 0
1961	Mississippi 14, Rice 6
1962	Alabama 10, Arkansas 3
1963	Mississippi 17, Arkansas 13
1964	Alabama 12, Mississippi 7
1965	Louisiana State 13, Syracuse 10
1966	Missouri 20, Florida 18
1967	Alabama 34, Nebraska 7

1968	Louisiana State 20, Wyoming 13
1969	Arkansas 16, Georgia 2
1970	Mississippi 27, Arkansas 22
1971	Tennessee 34, Air Force Academy 13
1972	Oklahoma 40, Auburn 22
1973	Oklahoma 14, Penn State 0
1974	Notre Dame 24, Alabama 23
1975	Nebraska 13, Florida 10
1976	Alabama 13, Penn State 6
1977	Pittsburgh 27, Georgia 3
1978	Alabama 35, Ohio State 6
1979	Alabama 14, Penn State 7
1980	Alabama 24, Arkansas 9
1981	Georgia 17, Notre Dame 10
1982	Pittsburgh 24, Georgia 20
1983	Penn State 27, Georgia 23
1984	Auburn 9, Michigan 7
1985	Nebraska 28, LSU 10
1986	Tennessee 35, Miami, Fla. 7
1987	Nebraska 30, Louisiana State 15
1988	Syracuse 16, Auburn 16 (tie)
1989	Florida State 13, Auburn 7
1990	Miami 33, Alabama 25
1991	Tennessee 23, Virginia 22
1992	Notre Dame 39, Florida 28
1993	Alabama 34, Miami 13
1994	Florida 41, West Virginia 7
1995	Florida State 23, Florida 17
1996	Virginia Tech 28, Texas 10
1997	Florida 52, Florida State 20

Cotton Bowl
(At Dallas)

1937	Texas Christian 16, Marquette 6
1938	Rice 28, Colorado 14
1939	St. Mary's (Calif.) 20, Texas Tech. 13
1940	Clemson 6, Boston College 3
1941	Texas A & M 13, Fordham 12
1942	Alabama 29, Texas A & M 21
1943	Texas 14, Georgia Tech 7
1944	Randolph Field 7, Texas 7
1945	Oklahoma A & M 34, Texas Christian 0
1946	Texas 40, Missouri 27
1947	Louisiana State 0, Arkansas 0
1948	So. Methodist 13, Penn State 13
1949	So. Methodist 21, Oregon 13
1950	Rice 27, North Carolina 13
1951	Tennessee 20, Texas 14
1952	Kentucky 20, Texas Christian 7
1953	Texas 16, Tennessee 0
1954	Rice 28, Alabama 6
1955	Georgia Tech 14, Arkansas 6
1956	Mississippi 14, Texas Christian 13
1957	Texas Christian 28, Syracuse 27
1958	Navy 20, Rice 7
1959	Air Force 0, Texas Christian 0
1960	Syracuse 23, Texas 14
1961	Duke 7, Arkansas 6
1962	Texas 12, Mississippi 7
1963	Louisiana State 13, Texas 0
1964	Texas 28, Navy 6
1965	Arkansas 10, Nebraska 7
1966	Louisiana State 14, Arkansas 7
1967	Georgia 24, So. Methodist 9
1968	Texas A & M 20, Alabama 16
1969	Texas 36, Tennessee 13

1970 Texas 21, Notre Dame 17	1996 Colorado 38, Oregon 6	1974 Texas Tech 28, Tennessee 19
1971 Notre Dame 24, Texas 11	1997 Brigham Young 19, Kansas State 15	1975 Auburn 27, Texas 3
1972 Penn State 30, Texas 6		1976 Maryland 13, Florida 0
1973 Texas 17, Alabama 13	**Gator Bowl**	1977 Notre Dame 20, Penn State 9
1974 Nebraska 19, Texas 3	(At Jacksonville, Fla.)	1978 Pittsburgh 34, Clemson 3
1975 Penn State 41, Baylor 20	1953 Florida 14, Tulsa 13	1979 Clemson 17, Ohio State 15
1976 Arkansas 31, Georgia 10	1954 Texas Tech 35, Auburn 13	1980 North Carolina 17, Michigan 15
1977 Houston 30, Maryland 21	1955 Auburn 33, Baylor 13	1981 Pittsburgh 37, South Carolina 9
1978 Notre Dame 38, Texas 10	1956 Vanderbilt 25, Auburn 13	1982 North Carolina 31, Arkansas 27
1979 Notre Dame 35, Houston 34	1957 Georgia Tech 21, Pittsburgh 14	1983 Florida State 31, West Virginia 12
1980 Houston 17, Nebraska 14	1958 Tennessee 3, Texas A & M 0	1984 Florida 14, Iowa 6
1981 Alabama 30, Baylor 2	1959 Mississippi 7, Florida 3	1985 Oklahoma St. 21, South Carolina 14
1982 Texas 14, Alabama 12	1960 Arkansas 14, Georgia Tech 7	1986 Florida State 34, Oklahoma State 23
1983 Southern Methodist 7, Pittsburgh 3	1961 Florida 13, Baylor 12	1987 Clemson 27, Stanford 21
1984 Georgia 10, Texas 9	1962 Penn State 30, Georgia Tech 15	1988 LSU 30, South Carolina 13
1985 Boston College 45, Houston 28	1963 Florida 17, Penn State 7	1989 Georgia 34, Michigan St. 27
1986 Texas A & M 36, Auburn 16	1964 No. Carolina 35, Air Force 0	1990 Clemson 27, West Virginia 7
1987 Ohio State 28, Texas A&M 12	1965 Florida State 36, Oklahoma 19	1991 Michigan 35, Mississippi 3
1988 Texas A & M 35, Notre Dame 10	1966 Georgia Tech 31, Texas Tech 21	1992 Oklahoma 38, Virginia 14
1989 UCLA 17, Arkansas 3	1967 Tennessee 18, Syracuse 12	1993 Florida 27, No. Carolina St. 10
1990 Tennessee 31, Arkansas 27	1968 Penn State 17, Florida State 17 (tie)	1994 Alabama 24, No. Carolina 10
1991 Miami 46, Texas 3	1969 Missouri 35, Alabama 10	1995 Tennessee 45, Virginia Tech 23
1992 Florida State 10, Texas A&M 2	1970 Florida 14, Tennessee 13	1996 Syracuse 41, Clemson 0
1993 Notre Dame 28, Texas A&M 3	1971 Auburn 35, Mississippi 28	1997 North Carolina 20, West Virginia 13
1994 Notre Dame 24, Texas A&M 21	1972 Georgia 7, North Carolina 3	
1995 Southern California 55, Texas Tech 14	1973 Auburn 24, Colorado 3	

RESULTS OF OTHER 1996 SEASON BOWL GAMES

Alamo (San Antonio, Texas, Dec. 29, 1996)—Iowa 27, Texas Tech 0

Aloha (Honolulu, Hawaii, Dec. 25, 1996)—Navy 42, California 38

Carquest Classic (Miami, Fla., Dec. 27, 1996)—Miami 31, Virginia 21

Citrus (Orlando, Fla., Jan. 1, 1997)—Tennessee 48, Northwestern 28

Copper (Tucson, Ariz., Dec. 27, 1996)—Wisconsin 38, Utah 10

Fiesta (Tempe, Ariz., Jan. 1, 1997)—Penn State 38, Texas 15

Heritage (Atlanta, Ga., Dec. 31, 1996)—Howard 27, Southern 24

Holiday (San Diego, Calif., Dec. 30, 1996)—Colorado 33, Washington 21

Independence (Shreveport, La., Dec. 31, 1996)—Auburn 32, Army 29

Las Vegas (Las Vegas, Nev., Dec. 19, 1996)—Nevada 18, Ball State 15

Liberty (Memphis, Tenn., Dec. 27, 1996)—Syracuse 30, Houston 17

Outback (Tampa, Fla., Jan. 1, 1997)—Alabama 17, Michigan 14

Peach (Atlanta, Ga., Dec. 28, 1996)—Louisiana State 10, Clemson 7

Sun (El Paso, Texas, Dec. 31, 1996)—Stanford 38, Michigan State 0

HEISMAN MEMORIAL TROPHY WINNERS

The Heisman Memorial Trophy is presented annually by the Downtown Athletic Club of New York City to the nation's outstanding college football player, as determined by a poll of sportswriters and sportscasters.

1935 Jay Berwanger, Chicago	1957 John Crow, Texas A & M	1978 Billy Sims, Oklahoma
1936 Larry Kelley, Yale	1958 Pete Dawkins, Army	1979 Charles White, Southern California
1937 Clinton Frank, Yale	1959 Billy Cannon, Louisiana State	
1938 Davey O'Brien, Texas Christian	1960 Joe Bellino, Navy	1980 George Rogers, South Carolina
1939 Nile Kinnick, Iowa	1961 Ernie Davis, Syracuse	1981 Marcus Allen, Southern California
1940 Tom Harmon, Michigan	1962 Terry Baker, Oregon State	
1941 Bruce Smith, Minnesota	1963 Roger Staubach, Navy	1982 Hershel Walker, Georgia
1942 Frank Sinkwich, Georgia	1964 John Huarte, Notre Dame	1983 Mike Rozier, Nebraska
1943 Angelo Bertelli, Notre Dame	1965 Mike Garrett, Southern California	1984 Doug Flutie, Boston College
1944 Leslie Horvath, Ohio State		1985 Bo Jackson, Auburn
1945 Felix Blanchard, Army	1966 Steve Spurrier, Florida	1986 Vinnie Testeverde, Miami
1946 Glenn Davis, Army	1967 Gary Beban, U.C.L.A.	1987 Tim Brown, Notre Dame
1947 Johnny Lujack, Notre Dame	1968 O.J. Simpson, Southern California	1988 Barry Sanders, Oklahoma State
1948 Doak Walker, So. Methodist		1989 Andre Ware, Houston
1949 Leon Hart, Notre Dame	1969 Steve Owens, Oklahoma	1990 Ty Detmer, Brigham Young
1950 Vic Janowicz, Ohio State	1970 Jim Plunkett, Stanford	1991 Desmond Howard, Michigan
1951 Dick Kazmaier, Princeton	1971 Pat Sullivan, Auburn	1992 Gino Torretta, Miami
1952 Billy Vessels, Oklahoma	1972 Johnny Rodgers, Nebraska	1993 Charlie Ward, Florida State
1953 Johnny Lattner, Notre Dame	1973 John Cappelletti, Penn State	1994 Rashaan Salaam, Colorado
1954 Alan Ameche, Wisconsin	1974-75 Archie Griffin, Ohio State	1995 Eddie George, Ohio State
1955 Howard Cassady, Ohio State	1976 Tony Dorsett, Pittsburgh	1996 Danny Wuerffel, Florida
1956 Paul Hornung, Notre Dame	1977 Earl Campbell, Texas	

1996 N.C.A.A. CHAMPIONSHIP PLAYOFFS

DIVISION I-AA

Quarterfinals
(Dec. 7, 1996)
Montana 44, East Tennessee
   State 14
Troy State 31, Murray State 3
Marshall 54, Furman 0
Northern Iowa 38, William & Mary 35
Semifinals
(Dec. 14, 1996)
Montana 70, Troy State 7
Marshall 31, Northern Iowa 14
Championship
(Dec. 21, 1996)
Marshall 49, Montana 29

DIVISION II

Quarterfinals
(Nov. 30, 1996)
Clarion State, Pa 23, Ferris State 21
Northern Colorado 27, Northwest Mis-
   souri
   State 26
Carson-Newman, Tenn. 24, Valdosta
   State, Ga. 19
UC Davis 26, Central Oklahoma 7
Semifinals
(Dec. 7, 1996)
Northern Colorado 19, Clarion, Pa. 18
Carson-Newman, Tenn. 29, UC Davis 26
Championship
(Dec. 14, 1996)
Northern Colorado 23, Carson-Newman,
   Tenn. 14

DIVISION III

Quarterfinals
(Nov. 30, 1996)
Mount Union, Ohio 49, Illinois Wesleyan
   14
Lycoming, Pa. 31, Albright, Pa.13
Rowan, N.J. 7, College of New Jersey 3
Wisconsin-LaCross 37, St. John's, Minn.
   30
Semifinals
(Dec. 7, 1996)
Rowan, N.J. 33, Lycoming, Pa. 14
Mount Union, Ohio 39, Wisconsin-
   LaCrosse 21
Championship
(Dec. 14, 1996)
Mount Union, Ohio 56, Rowan, N.J. 24

1996 NATIONAL ASSOCIATION OF INTERCOLLEGIATE ATHLETICS CHAMPIONSHIPS

DIVISION I

Semifinals
(Nov. 23, 1996)
Southwestern Oklahoma State 17, Northwestern Oklahoma
   State 7
Montana Tech 49, Carroll College, Mont. 28
Championship
(Dec. 7, 1996)
Southwestern Oklahoma State 33, Montana Tech 31

DIVISION II

Semifinals
(Dec. 14, 1996)
Western Washington 28, Findlay, Ohio 21
Sioux Falls, S.D. 28, Evangel, Mo. 22
Championship
(Dec. 21, 1996)
Sioux Falls, S.D. 47, Western Washington 25

COLLEGE FOOTBALL HALL OF FAME

(P.O. Box 11146, South Bend, Indiana)

(Date given is player's last year of competition)

Players

Abell, Earl—Colgate, 1915
Agase, Alex—Purdue/Illinois, 1946
Agganis, Harry—Boston Univ., 1952
Albert, Frank—Stanford, 1941
Aldrich, Chas. (Ki)—T.C.U., 1938
Aldrich, Malcolm—Yale, 1921
Alexander, Joseph—Syracuse, 1920
Alworth, Lance—Arkansas, 1961
Ameche, Alan (Horse)—Wisconsin, 1954
Amling, Warren—Ohio State, 1946
Anderson, Dick—Colorado, 1967
Anderson, Donny—Texas Tech, 1965
Anderson, H. (Hunk)—Notre Dame, 1921
Atkins, Doug—Tennessee, 1952
Babich, Bob—Miami-Ohio, 1968
Bacon, C. Everett—Wesleyan, 1912
Bagnell, Francis (Reds)—Penn, 1950
Baker, Hobart (Hobey)—Princeton, 1913
Baker, John—So. Calif., 1931
Baker, Terry—Oregon State, 1962
Ballin, Harold—Princeton, 1914
Banonis, Vince—Detroit, 1941
Barnes, Stanley—So. California, 1921
Barrett, Charles—Cornell, 1915
Baston, Bert—Minnesota, 1916
Battles, Cliff—W. Va. Wesleyan, 1931
Baugh, Sammy—Texas Christian U., 1936
Vaughan, Maxie—Georgia Tech, 1959
Bausch, James—Kansas, 1930
Beagle, Ron—Navy, 1955
Beban, Gary—UCLA, 1967
Bechtol, Hub—Texas Tech, 1946
Beck, Ray—Georgia Tech, 1951
Beckett, John—Oregon, 1913
Bednarik, Chuck—Pennsylvania 1948
Behm, Forrest—Nebraska, 1940
Bell, Bobby—Minnesota, 1962
Bellino, Joe—Navy, 1960
Below, Marty—Wisconsin, 1923
Benbrook, A.—Michigan, 1911
Bertelli, A.—Notre Dame, 1943
Berry, Charlie—Lafayette, 1924

Berwanger, John (Jay)—Chicago, 1935
Bettencourt, Larry—St. Mary's, 1927
Biletnikoff, Fred—Florida State, 1964
Blanchard, Felix (Doc)—Army, 1946
Bock, Ed—Iowa State, 1938
Bomar, Lynn—Vanderbilt, 1924
Bomeisler, Doug (Bo)—Yale, 1913
Booth, Albie-Yale, 1931
Borries, Fred—Navy, 1934
Bosely, Bruce—West Virginia, 1955
Bosseler, Don—Miami, Fla., 1956
Bottari, Vic—California, 1939
Boynton, Ben—Williams, 1920
Bozis, Al—Georgetown, 1941
Bradshaw, Terry—Louisiana Tech, 1969
Brewer, Charles—Harvard, 1895
Bright, John—Drake, 1951
Brodie, John—Stanford, 1956
Brooke, George—Pennsylvania, 1895
Brown, Bob—Nebraska, 1963
Brown, George—Navy, San Diego St., 1947
Brown, Gordon—Yale, 1900
Brown, Jim—Syracuse, 1956
Brown, John, Jr.—Navy, 1913
Brown, Johnny Mack—Alabama, 1925
Brown, Raymond (Tay)—So. Calif., 1932
Buchanan, Buck—Grambling State, 1962
Bunker, Paul—Army, 1902
Burford, Chris—Stanford, 1959
Burton, Ron—Northwestern, 1956
Butkus, Dick—Illinois, 1964
Butler, Robert—Wisconsin, 1912
Cafego, George—Tennessee, 1939
Cagle, Chris—SW La./Army, 1929
Cain, John—Alabama, 1932
Cameron, Eddie—Wash. & Lee, 1924
Campbell, David C.—Harvard, 1901
Campbell, Earl—Texas, 1977
Cannon, Billy—L.S.U., 1959
Cannon, Jack—Notre Dame, 1929
Cappelletti, John—Penn State, 1973
Carideo, Frank—Notre Dame, 1930
Caroline, J.C.—Illinois, 1954
Carney, Charles—Illinois, 1921

Carpenter, Bill—Army, 1959
Carpenter, C. Hunter—VPI, 1905
Carroll, Charles—Washington, 1928
Casanova, Tommy—Louisiana State, 1971
Casey, Edward L.—Harvard, 1919
Cassady, Howard—Ohio State, 1955
Chamberlain, Guy—Nebraska, 1915
Chapman, Sam—Cal.-Berkeley, 1938
Chappuis, Bob—Michigan, 1947
Christman, Paul—Missouri, 1940
Cichy, Joe—North Dakota State, 1970
Clark, Earl (Dutch)—Colo. College, 1929
Cleary, Paul—USC, 1947
Clevenger, Zora—Indiana, 1903
Cloud, Jack—William & Mary, 1948
Cochran, Gary—Princeton, 1895
Cody, Josh—Vanderbilt, 1920
Coleman, Don—Mich. State, 1951
Conerly, Chuck—Mississippi, 1947
Connor, George—Notre Dame, 1947
Corbin, W.—Yale, 1888
Corbus, William—Stanford, 1933
Cowan, Hector—Princeton, 1889
Coy, Edward H. (Tad)—Yale, 1909
Crawford, Fred—Duke, 1933
Crow, John D.—Texas A&M, 1957
Crowley, James—Notre Dame, 1924
Csonka, Larry—Syracuse, 1967
Cutter, Slade—Navy, 1934
Czarobski, Ziggie—Notre Dame, 1947
Dale, Carroll—Virginia Tech, 1959
Dalrymple, Gerald—Tulane, 1931
Daniell, James—Ohio State, 1941
Dalton, John—Navy, 1912
Daly, Charles—Harvard/Army, 1902
Daniell, Averell—Pittsburgh, 1936
Davies, Tom—Pittsburgh, 1921
Davis, Ernest—Syracuse, 1961
Davis, Glenn—Army, 1946
Davis, Robert T.—Georgia Tech, 1947
Dawkins, Pete—Army, 1958
Delaney, Joe—Northwestern State, 1980
DeLong, Steve—Tennessee, 1964
Den Herder, Vern—Central (Iowa), 1970

De Rogatis, Al—Duke, 1940
DesJardien, Paul—Chicago 1914
Devino, Aubrey—Iowa, 1921
DeWitt, John—Princeton, 1903
Dial, Buddy—Rice, 1958
Ditka, Mike—Pittsburgh, 1960
Dobbs, Glenn—Tulsa, 1942
Dodd, Bobby—Tennessee, 1930
Donan, Holland—Princeton, 1950
Donchess, Joseph—Pittsburgh, 1929
Dorsett, Tony—Pittsburgh, 1976
Dougherty, Nathan—Tennessee, 1909
Drahos, Nick—Cornell, 1940
Driscoll, Paddy—Northwestern, 1917
Drury, Morley—So. California, 1927
Dryer, Fred—San Diego State, 1968
Dudek, Joe—Plymouth State, 1985
Dudley, William (Bill)—Virginia, 1941
Duncan, Randy—Iowa, 1958
Easley, Ken—UCLA, 1980
Eckersall, Walter—Chicago, 1906
Edwards, Turk—Washington State, 1931
Edwards, William—Princeton, 1900
Eichenlaub, R.—Notre Dame, 1913
Eisenhauer, Steve—Navy, 1953
Elking, Larry—Baylor, 1964
Elliott, Chalmers—Purdue, 1944 & Mich.,
  1947
Elliott, Pete—Michigan, 1948
Elmendorf, Dave—Texas A&M, 1970
Evans, Ray—Kansas, 1947
Exendine, Albert—Carlisle, 1908
Falaschi, Nello—Santa Clara, 1934
Fears, Tom—Santa Clara/UCLA, 1947
Feathers, Beattie—Tennessee, 1933
Fenimore, Robert—Oklahoma State, 1947
Fenton, G.E. (Doc)—La. State U., 1910
Ferguson, Bob—Ohio State, 1961
Ferraro, John—So. California, 1944
Fesler, Wesley—Ohio State, 1930
Fincher, Bill—Georgia Tech, 1920
Fischer, Bill—Notre Dame, 1948
Fish, Hamilton—Harvard, 1909
Fisher, Robert—Harvard, 1911
Flowers, Abe—Georgia Tech, 1920
Flowers, Charlie—Mississippi, 1959
Fortmann, Daniel—Colgate, 1935
Francis, Sam—Nebraska, 1936
Franco, Edmund (Ed)—Fordham, 1937
Frank, Clint—Yale, 1937
Franz, Rodney—California, 1949
Frederickson, Tucker—Auburn, 1964
Friedman, Benny—Michigan, 1926
Gabriel, Roman—North Carolina St., 1961
Gain, Bob—Kentucky, 1950
Galiffa, Arnold—Army, 1949
Gallarneau, Hugh—Stanford, 1941
Garbisch, Edgar—Army, 1924
Garrett, Mike—USC, 1965
Gelbert, Charles—Pennsylvania, 1896
Geyer, Forest—Oklahoma, 1915
Gibbs, Jake—Mississippi, 1960
Giel, Paul—Minnesota, 1953
Gifford, Frank—So. California, 1951
Gilbert, Walter—Auburn, 1936
Gilmer, Harry—Alabama, 1947
Gipp, George—Notre Dame, 1920
Gladchuk, Chet—Boston College, 1940
Glass, Bill—Baylor, 1956
Glover, Rich—Nebraska, 1972
Goldberg, Marshall—Pittsburgh, 1938
Goodreault, Gene—Boston College, 1940
Gordon, Walter—California, 1918
Governale, Paul—Columbia, 1942
Grabowski, Jim—Illinois, 1965
Graham, Otto—Northwestern, 1943
Grange, Harold (Red)—Illinois, 1925
Grayson, Roberty—Stanford, 1935
Green, Hugh—Pittsburgh, 1980
Green, Joe—North Texas State, 1968
Griese, Bob—Purdue, 1966
Griffin, Archie—Ohio State, 1975
Grinnell, William—Tufts, 1934
Groom, Jerry—Notre Dame, 1950
Gulick, Merel—Hobart, 1929
Guyon, Joe—Georgia Tech, 1919

Hadl, John—Kansas, 1961
Hale, Edwin—Mississippi Col, 1921
Hall, Parker—Mississippi, 1938
Ham, Jack—Penn State, 1970
Hamilton, Robert (Bones)—Stanford, 1935
Hamilton, Tom—Navy, 1925
Hanson, Vic—Syracuse, 1926
Harder, Pat—Wisconsin, 1942
Hardwick, H. (Tack)—Harvard, 1914
Hare, T. Truxton—Pennsylvania, 1900
Harley, Chick—Ohio State, 1919
Harmon, Tom—Michigan, 1940
Harpster, Howard—Carnegie Tech, 1928
Hart, Edward J. Princeton, 1911
Hart, Leon—Notre Dame, 1949
Hartman, Bill—Georgia, 1937
Hawkins, Frank—Nevada, 1980
Hazel, Homer—Rutgers, 1924
Healey, Ed—Dartmouth, 1916
Heffelfiner, W. (Pudge)—Yale, 1891
Hein, Mel—Washington State, 1930
Heinrich, Don—Washington, 1952
Hendricks, Ted—Miami, 1968
Henry, Wilbur—Wash. & Jefferson, 1919
Herschberger, Clarence—Chicago, 1899
Herwig, Robert—California, 1937
Heston, Willie—Michigan, 1904
Hickman, Herman—Tennessee, 1931
Hickok, William—Yale, 1895
Hill, Dan—Duke, 1938
Hillebrand, A.R. (Doc)—Princeton, 1900
Hinkey, Frank—Yale, 1894
Hinkle, Carl—Vanderbilt, 1937
Hinkle, Clark—Bucknell, 1932
Hirsch, Elroy—Wis./Mich., 1943
Hitchcock, James—Auburn, 1932
Hoffman, Frank—Notre Dame, 1931
Hogan, James J.—Yale, 1904
Holland, Jerome (Brud)—Cornell, 1938
Holleder, Don—Army, 1955
Hollenbeck, William—Penn., 1908
Holovak, Michael—Boston College, 1942
Holt, Pierce—Angelo State, 1980
Holub, E.J.—Texas Tech, 1960
Hornung, Paul—Notre Dame, 1956
Horrell, Edwin—California, 1924
Horvath, Les—Ohio State, 1944
Howe Arthur—Yale, 1911
Howell, Millard (Dixie)—Alabama, 1934
Hubbard, Cal—Centenary, 1926
Hubbard, John—Amherst, 1906
Hubert, Allison—Alabama, 1925
Huff, Robert Lee (Sam)—W. Va., 1955
Humble, Weldon G.—Rice, 1946
Hunley, Ricky—Arizona, 1983
Hunt, Joel—Texas A&M, 1927
Huntington, Ellery—Colgate, 1914
Hutson, Don—Alabama, 1934
Ingram, James—Navy, 1906
Isbell, Cecil—Purdue, 1937
Jablonsky, Harvey—Wash. U./Army, 1933
Janowicz, Vic—Ohio State, 1951
Jenkins, Darold—Missouri, 1941
Jensen, Jack—Cal-Berkeley, 1948
Joesting, Herbert—Minnesota, 1927
Johnson, Billy—Widener, 1973
Johnson, Gary—Grambling State, 1974
Johnson, James—Carlisle, 1903
Johnson, Robert—Tennessee, 1967
Johnson, Ron—Michigan, 1968
Jones, Calvin—Iowa, 1955
Jones, Gormer—Ohio State, 1935
Jordan, Lee Roy—Alabama, 1962
Juhan, Frank—Univ. of South, 1910
Justice, Charlie—North Carolina, 1949
Kaer, Mort—So. California, 1926
Karras, Alex—Iowa, 1957
Kavanaugh, Kenneth—La. State U., 1939
Kaw, Edgar—Cornell, 1922
Kazmaier, Richard—Princeton, 1951
Keck, James—Princeton, 1921
Kelley, Larry—Yale, 1936
Kelly, William—Montana, 1926
Kenna, Ed—Syracuse, 1906
Kern, George—Boston College, 1941
Ketcham, Henry—Yale, 1913

Keyes, Leroy—Purdue, 1968
Killinger, William—Penn State, 1922
Kimbrough, John—Texas A&M, 1940
Kinard, Frank—Mississippi, 1937
King, Philip—Princeton, 1893
Kinnick, Nile—Iowa, 1939
Kipke, Harry—Michigan, 1923
Kirkpatrick, John Reed—Yale, 1910
Kitzmiller, John—Oregon, 1929
Koch, Barton—Baylor, 1931
Kitner, Malcolm—Texas, 1942
Kramer, Ron—Michigan, 1956
Kroll, Alex—Rutgers, 1961
Krueger, Charlie—Texas A&M, 1957
Kwalick, Ted—Penn State, 1968
Lach, Steve—Duke, 1941
Lane, Myles—Dartmouth, 1927
Lattner, Joseph J.—Notre Dame, 1953
Lauricella, Hank—Tennessee, 1952
Lautenschlaeger—Tulane, 1925
Layden, Elmer—Notre Dame, 1924
Layne, Bobby—Texas, 1947
Lea, Langdon—Princeton, 1895
LeBaron, Eddie—Univ. of Pacific, 1949
Leech, James—Va. Mil. Inst., 1920
Lester, Darrell—Texas Christian, 1935
Lilly, Bob—Texas Christian, 1960
Little, Floyd—Syracuse, 1966
Lio, Augie—Georgetown, 1940
Locke, Gordon—Iowa, 1922
Lomax, Neil—Portland (Ore.) State, 1980
Lourie, Don—Princeton, 1921
Lucas, Richard—Penn State, 1959
Luckman, Sid—Columbia, 1938
Lujack, John—Notre Dame, 1947
Lund, J.L. (Pug)—Minnesota, 1934
Lynch, Jim—Notre Dame, 1966
MacAfee, Ken—Notre Dame, 1977
Macomber, Bart—Illinois, 1915
MacLeod, Robert—Dartmouth, 1938
Maegle, Dick—Rice, 1954
Mahan, Edward W.—Harvard, 1915
Majors, John—Tennessee, 1956
Mallory, William—Yale, 1893
Mancha, Vaughn—Alabama, 1947
Mann, Gerald—So. Methodist, 1927
Manning, Archie—Mississippi, 1970
Manske, Edgar—Northwestern, 1933
Marinaro, Ed—Cornell, 1971
Markov, Vic—Washington, 1937
Marshall, Robert—Minnesota, 1907
Martin, Jim—Notre Dame, 1949
Matson, Ollie—San Fran. U., 1952
Matthews, Ray—Texas Christ. U., 1928
Maulbetsch, John—Michigan, 1914
Mauthe, J.L. (Pete)—Penn State, 1912
Maxwell, Robert—Chi./Swarthmore, 1906
McAfee, George—Duke, 1939
McClung, Thomas L.—Yale, 1891
McColl, William F.—Stanford, 1951
McCormick, James B.—Princeton, 1907
McDonald, Tom—Oklahoma, 1956
McDowall, Jack—No. Car. State, 1927
McElhenny, Hugh—Washington, 1951
McEver, Gene—Tennessee, 1931
McEwan, John—Minn./Army, 1916
McFadden, J.B.—Clemson, 1939
McFadin, Bud—Texas, 1950
McGee, Mike—Duke, 1959
McGinley, Edward—Pennsylvania, 1924
McGovern, J.—Minnesota, 1910
McGraw, Thurman—Colorado State, 1949
McGriff, Tyrone—Florida A&M, 1979
McKeever, Mike—USC, 1960
McLaren, George—Pittsburgh, 1918
McMillan, Dan—U.S.C./Calif., 1922
McMillin, A.N. (Bo)—Centre, 1921
McWhorter, Robert—Georgia, 1913
Mercer, Leroy—Pennsylvania, 1912
Meredith, Don—Southern Methodist, 1959
Merritt, Frank—Army, 1943
Metzger, Bert—Notre Dame, 1930
Meyland, Wayne—Nebraska, 1967
Michaels, Lou—Kentucky, 1957
Michels, John—Tennessee, 1952
Mickal, Abe—La. State U., 1935

Miller, Creighton—Notre Dame, 1943
Miller, Don—Notre Dame, 1925
Miller, Edgar (Rip)—Notre Dame, 1924
Miller, Eugene—Penn State, 1913
Miller, Fred—Notre Dame, 1928
Millner, Wayne—Notre Dame, 1935
Milstead, Century—Wabash, Yale, 1923
Minds, John—Pennsylvania, 1897
Minisi, Anthony—Navy, Pennsylvania, 1947
Modzelewski, Dick—Maryland, 1952
Moffatt, Alex—Princeton, 1884
Molinski, Ed—Tennessee, 1940
Montgomery, Cliff—Columbia, 1933
Montgomery, Wilbert—Abilene Christian, 1976
Moomaw, Donn—U.C.L.A., 1952
Morley, William—Columbia, 1903
Morris, George—Georgia Tech, 1952
Morris, Larry—Georgia Tech., 1954
Morton, Craig—California, 1964
Morton, William—Dartmouth, 1931
Moscrip, Monk—Stanford, 1935
Muller, Harold (Brick)—Calif., 1922
Nagurski, Bronko—Minnesota, 1929
Nevers, Ernie—Stanford, 1925
Newell, Marshall—Harvard, 1893
Newman, Harry—Michigan, 1932
Newsome, Ozzie—Alabama, 1977
Nielsen, Gifford—Brigham Young, 1976
Nobis, Tommy—Texas, 1965
Nomellini, Leo—Minnesota, 1949
Oberland, Andrew—Dartmouth, 1925
O'Brien, Davey—Texas Christ. U., 1938
O'Brien, Ken—UC-Davis, 1982
O'Dea, Pat-Wisconsin, 1899
Odell, Robert—Pennsylvania, 1943
O'Hearn, J.—Cornell, 1915
Olds, Robin—Army, 1942
Oliphant, Elmer—Purdue/Army, 1917
Olsen, Merlin—Utah State, 1961
Onkotz, Dennis—Penn State, 1969
Oosterbaan, Ben—Michigan, 1927
O'Rourke, Charles—Boston College, 1940
Orsi, John—Colgate, 1931
Osgood, W.D.—Cornell/Penn, 1895
Osmanski, William—Holy Cross, 1938
Owen, George—Harvard, 1922
Owens, Jim—Oklahoma, 1949
Owens, Steve—Oklahoma, 1969
Page, Alan—Notre Dame, 1966
Pardee, Jack—Texas A&M, 1956
Parilli, Vito (Babe)—Kentucky, 1951
Parker, Clarence (Ace)—Duke, 1936
Parker, Jackie—Miss. State, 1953
Parker, James—Ohio State, 1956
Payton, Walter—Jackson State, 1974
Pazzetti, V.J.—Wes./Lehigh, 1912
Peabody, Endicott—Harvard, 1941
Peck, Robert—Pittsburgh, 1916
Pellegrini, Bob—Maryland, 1955
Pennock, Stanley B.—Harvard, 1914
Pfann, George—Cornell, 1923
Phillips, H.D.—U. of South, 1904
Phillips, Loyd—Arkansas, 1966
Pingel, John—Michigan State, 1938
Pihos, Pete—Indiana, 1945
Pinckert, Ernie—So. California, 1931
Plunkett, Jim—Stanford, 1970
Poe, Arthur—Princeton, 1899
Pollard, Fritz—Brown, 1916
Poole, Barney—Miss./Army, 1947
Powell, Marvin—Southern California, 1976
Pregulman, Merv—Michigan, 1943
Price, Eddie—Tulane, 1949
Pund, Henry—Georgia Tech, 1928
Ramsey, Gerrard—Wm. & Mary, 1942
Reasons, Gary—Northwestern State (La.), 1983
Redman, Rick—Washington, 1964
Reeds, Claude—Oklahoma, 1913
Reid, Mike—Penn St., 1970
Reid, Steve—Northwestern, 1936
Reid, William—Harvard, 1900
Reifsnyder, Bob—Navy, 1958
Renfro, Mel—Oregon, 1963
Rentner, Ernest—Northwestern, 1932

Reynolds, Robert—Nebraska, 1952
Reynolds, Robert—Stanford, 1935
Richter, Les—California, 1951
Richter, Pat—Wisconsin, 1962
Riley, John—Northwestern, 1931
Rimington, Dave—Nebraska, 1982
Rinehart, Charles—Lafayette, 1897
Roberts, J.D.—Oklahoma, 1953
Robeson, Paul—Rutgers, 1918
Robinson, Dave—Penn State, 1962
Robinson, Jerry—UCLA, 1978
Rodgers, Ira—West Virginia, 1919
Rogers, Edward L.—Minnesota, 1903
Rogers, George—South Carolina, 1980
Romig, Joe—Colorado, 1961
Rosenberg, Aaron—So. California, 1934
Rote, Kyle—So. Methodist, 1950
Routt, Joe—Texas A&M, 1937
Salmon, Louis—Notre Dame, 1904
Sauer, George—Nebraska, 1933
Savitsky, George—Pennsylvania, 1947
Saxon, Jimmy—Texas, 1961
Sayers Gale—Kansas, 1964
Scarbath, Jack—Maryland, 1952
Scarlett, Hunter—Pennsylvania, 1909
Schloredt, Bob—Washington, 1960
Schoonover, Wear—Arkansas, 1929
Schreiner, Dave—Wisconsin, 1942
Schultz, Adolf (Germany)—Mich., 1908
Schwab, Frank—Lafayette, 1922
Schwartz, Marchmont—Notre Dame, 1931
Schwegler, Paul—Washington, 1931
Scott, Clyde—Arkansas, 1949
Scott, Richard—Navy, 1947
Scott, Tom—Virginia, 1953
Seibels, Henry—Sewanee, 1899
Sellers, Ron—Florida State, 1968
Selmon, Lee Roy—Oklahoma, 1975
Shakespeare, Bill—Notre Dame, 1935
Shelton, Murray—Cornell, 1915
Shevlin, Tom—Yale, 1905
Shively, Bernie—Illinois, 1926
Simons, Claude—Tulane, 1934
Sims, Billy—Oklahoma, 1979
Simpson, O.J.—So. Calif., 1968
Singletary, Mike—Baylor, 1977-1980
Sington, Fred—Alabama, 1930
Sinkwich, Frank—Georgia, 1942
Sitko, Emil—Notre Dame, 1949
Skladany, Joe—Pittsburgh, 1933
Slater, F.F. (Duke)—Iowa, 1921
Smith, Bruce—Minnesota, 1941
Smith, Bubba—Michigan State, 1966
Smith, Ernie—So. California, 1932
Smith, Harry—So. California, 1939
Smith, Jim Ray—Baylor, 1954
Smith, John (Clipper)—Notre Dame, 1927
Smith, Riley—Alabama, 1935
Smith, Vernon—Georgia, 1931
Snow, Neil—Michigan, 1901
Sparlis, Al—U.C.L.A., 1945
Spears, Clarence W.—Dartmouth, 1915
Spears, W.D.—Vanderbilt, 1927
Sprackling, William—Brown, 1911
Sprague, M. (Bud)—Texas/Army, 1928
Spurrier, Steve—Florida, 1966
Stafford, Harrison—Texas, 1932
Stagg, Amos Alonzo—Yale, 1889
Starcevich, Max—Washington, 1936
Staubach, Roger—Navy, 1963
Steffen, Walter—Chicago, 1908
Steffy, Joe—Army, 1947
Stein, Herbert—Pittsburgh, 1921
Steuber, Robert—Missouri, 1943
Stevens, Mal—Yale, 1923
Stevenson, Vincent—Pennsylvania, 1905
Stillwagon, Jim—Ohio State, 1970
Stinchcomb, Gaylord—Ohio State, 1920
Strom, Brock—Air Force, 1959
Strong, Ken—New York Univ., 1928
Strupper, George—Georgia Tech, 1917
Stuhldreher, Harry—Notre Dame, 1924
Stydahar, Joe—West Virginia, 1935
Suffridge, Robert—Tennessee, 1940
Suhey, Steve—Pennsylvania State, 1947
Sullivan, Pat—Auburn, 1971

Sundstrom, Frank—Cornell, 1923
Swann, Lynn—USC, 1973
Swanson, Clarence—Nebraska, 1921
Swiacki, Bill—Holy Cross/Colombia, 1947
Swink, Jim—Texas Christian, 1956
Taliafarro, George—Indiana, 1948
Tarkenton, Fran—Georgia, 1960
Tavener, John—Indiana, 1944
Taylor, Bruce—Boston Univ., 1969
Taylor, Charles—Stanford, 1942
Thomas, Aurelius—Ohio St., 1957
Thompson, Joe—Pittsburgh, 1907
Thomsen, Lynn—Austana, 1986
Thorne, Samuel B.—Yale, 1906
Thorpe, Jim—Carlisle, 1912
Ticknor, Ben—Harvard, 1930
Tigert, John—Vanderbilt, 1904
Tinsley, Gaynell—La. State U., 1936
Tipton, Eric—Duke, 1938
Tonnemaker, Clayton—Minnesota, 1949
Torrey, Robert—Pennsylvania, 1906
Travis, Ed Tarkio—Missouri, 1920
Trippi, Charles—Georgia, 1946
Tryon, J. Edward—Colgate, 1925
Tubbs, Jerry—Oklahoma, 1956
Utay, Joe—Texas A&M, 1907
Van Brocklin, Norm—Oregon, 1948
Van Sickel, Dale—Florida, 1929
Van Surdam, Henderson—Wesleyan, 1905
Very, Dexter—Penn State, 1912
Vessels, Billy—Oklahoma, 1952
Vick, Ernie—Michigan, 1921
Wagner, Huber—Pittsburgh, 1913
Walker, Doak—So. Methodist, 1949
Wallace, Bill—Rice, 1935
Walsh, Adam—Notre Dame, 1924
Warburton, I. (Cotton)—So. Calif., 1934
Ward, Robert (Bob)—Maryland, 1951
Warner, William—Cornell, 1903
Washington, Ken—U.C.L.A., 1939
Weatherall, Jim—Oklahoma, 1951
Webster, George—Michigan St., 1966
Wedemeyer, Herman J.—St. Mary's, 1947
Weekes, Harold—Columbia, 1902
Weiner, Art—North Carolina, 1949
Weir, Ed—Nebraska, 1925
Welch, Gus—Carlisle, 1914
Weller, John—Princeton, 1935
Wendell, Percy—Harvard, 1913
West, D. Belford—Colgate, 1919
Westfall, Bob—Michigan, 1941
Weyand, Alex—Army, 1915
Wharton, Charles—Pennsylvania, 1896
Wheeler, Arthur—Princeton, 1894
White, Byron (Whizzer)—Colorado, 1937
White, Charles—USC, 1979
White, Danny—Arizona State, 1973
White, Randy—Maryland, 1974
Whitmire, Don—Alabama/Navy, 1944
Wickhorst, Frank—Navy, 1926
Widseth, Ed—Minnesota, 1936
Wildung, Richard—Minnesota, 1942
Williams, Bob—Notre Dame, 1950
Williams, James—Rice, 1949
Willis, William—Ohio State, 1945
Wilson, George—Washington, 1925
Wilson, George—Lafayette, 1928
Wilson, Harry—Penn State/Army, 1923
Wilson, Marc—BYU, 1979
Wistert, Albert A.—Michigan, 1942
Wistert, Al—Michigan, 1942
Wistert, Frank (Whitey)—Mich., 1933
Wood, Barry—Harvard, 1931
Wojciechowicz, Alex—Fordham, 1936
Wyant, Andrew—Bucknell/Chicago, 1894
Wyatt, Bowden—Tennessee, 1938
Wyckoff, Clint—Cornell, 1896
Yarr, Tom—Notre Dame, 1931
Yary, Ron—USC, 1968
Yoder, Lloyd—Carnegie Tech, 1926
Young, Claude (Buddy)—Illinois, 1946
Young, Harry—Wash. & Lee, 1916
Young, Walter—Oklahoma, 1938
Youngblood, Jack—Florida, 1970
Youngblood, Jim—Tennessee, 1972
Zarnas, Gus—Ohio State, 1937

Coaches

Bill Alexander	Gil Dobie	Morley Jennings	Clarence Munn	Schwartzwalder
Dr. Ed Anderson	Bobby Dodd	Howard Jones	Frank Murray	Clark Shaughnessy
Ike Armstrong	Michael Donohue	L. (Biff) Jones	William Murray	Buck Shaw
Earl Banks	Vince Dooley	Thomas (Tad) Jones	Ed (Hooks) Mylin	Edgar Sherman
Harry Baujan	Gus Dorais	Ralph (Shug) Jordan	Earle (Greasy) Neale	Andrew L. Smith
Matty Bell	Bill Edwards	Andy Kerr	Jess Neely	Carl Snavely
Hugo Bezdek	Charles (Rip) Engle	Frank Kush	David Nelson	Amos A. Stagg
Dana X. Bible	Don Faurot	Frank Leahy	Robert Neyland	Gilbert Steinke
Bernie Bierman	Jake Gaither	George E. Little	Homer Norton	Jock Sutherland
Bob Blackman	Sid Gillman	Lou Little	Frank (Buck) O'Neill	James Tatum
Earl (Red) Blaik	Ernest Godfrey	El (Slip) Madigan	Bennie Owen	Frank W. Thomas
Frank Broyles	Ray Graves	Dave Maurer	Ara Parseghian	Lee Tressell
Paul "Bear" Bryant	Andy Gustafson	Charley McClendon	Doyt Perry	Thad Vann
Harold Burry	Jack Harding	Herbert McCracken	James Phalea	John H. Vaught
Jim Butterfield	Edward K. Hall	Daniel McGugin	Tommy Prothro	Wallace Wade
James "Wally" Butts	Richard Harlow	John McKay	John Ralston	Lynn Waldorf
Charles W. Caldwell	Jesse Harper	Allyn McKeen	E.N. Robinson	Glenn (Pop) Warner
Walter Camp	Percy Haughton	DeOrmond (Tuss)	Knute Rockne	E.E. (Tad) Wieman
Len Casanova	Woody Hayes	McLaughry	E.L. (Dick) Romney	John W. Wilce
Frank Cavanaugh	John W. Heisman	John Merritt	William W. Roper	Bud Wilkinson
Richard Colman	R.A. (Bob) Higgins	L.R. (Dutch) Meyer	Darrell Royal	Henry L. Williams
Fritz Crisler	Paul Hoernemann	Bernie Moore	Henry (Red) Sanders	George W. Woodruff
Duffy Daugherty	Orin E. Hollingberry	Scrappy Moore	George F. Sanford	Warren Woodson
Bob Devaney	Frank Howard	Jack Mollenkopf	Bo Schembechler	Bowden Wyatt
Dan Devine	William Ingram	Ray Morrison	Francis A. Schmidt	Fielding H. Yost
	Don James	George A. Munger	Floyd (Ben)	Robert Zuppke

Professional Football

NATIONAL FOOTBALL LEAGUE FINAL STANDINGS 1996

AMERICAN FOOTBALL CONFERENCE

Eastern Division

	W	L	T	Pct	Pts	Op
New England Patriots[1]	11	5	0	.688	418	313
Buffalo Bills[2]	10	6	0	.625	319	266
Indianapolis Colts[2]	9	7	0	.563	317	334
Miami Dolphins	8	8	0	.500	339	325
New York Jets	1	15	0	.063	279	454

Central Division

	W	L	T	Pct	Pts	Op
Pittsburgh Steelers[1]	10	6	0	.625	344	257
Jacksonville Jaguars[2]	9	7	0	.563	325	335
Cincinnati Bengals	8	8	0	.500	372	369
Houston Oilers	8	8	0	.500	345	319
Baltimore Ravens	4	12	0	.250	371	441

Western Division

	W	L	T	Pct	Pts	Op
Denver Broncos[1]	13	3	0	.813	391	275
Kansas City Chiefs	9	7	0	.563	297	300
San Diego Chargers	8	8	0	.500	310	376
Oakland Raiders	7	9	0	.438	340	293
Seattle Seahawks	7	9	0	.438	317	376

1. Division champion. 2. Wild card qualifier for playoffs.
Playoffs: Jacksonville 30, Buffalo 27; Pittsburgh 42, Indianapolis 14; Jacksonville 30, Denver 27; New England 28, Pittsburgh 3; New England 20, Jacksonville 6.

NATIONAL FOOTBALL CONFERENCE

Eastern Division

	W	L	T	Pct	Pts	Op
Dallas Cowboys[1]	10	6	0	.625	286	259
Philadelphia Eagles[2]	10	6	0	.625	363	341
Washington Redskins	9	7	0	.563	364	312
Arizona Cardinals	7	9	0	.438	300	397
New York Giants	6	10	0	.375	242	297

Central Division

	W	L	T	Pct	Pts	Op
Green Bay Packers[1]	13	3	0	.813	456	210
Minnesota Vikings[2]	9	7	0	.563	298	315
Chicago Bears	7	9	0	.438	283	305
Tampa Bay Buccaneers	6	10	0	.375	221	293
Detroit Lions	5	11	0	.313	302	368

Western Division

	W	L	T	Pct	Pts	Op
Carolina Panthers[1]	12	4	0	.750	367	218
San Francisco 49ers[2]	12	4	0	.750	398	257
St. Louis Rams	6	10	0	.375	303	409
Atlanta Falcons	3	13	0	.231	309	461
New Orleans Saints	3	13	0	.231	229	339

1. Division champion. 2. Wild card qualifier for playoffs.
Playoffs: Dallas 40, Minnesota 15; San Francisco 14, Philadelphia 0; Green Bay 35, San Francisco 14; Carolina 26, Dallas 17; Green Bay 30, Carolina 13.

LEAGUE CHAMPIONSHIP—SUPER BOWL XXXI

(January 26, 1997, Louisiana Superdome, New Orleans, La. Attendance: 72,301, no shows: 0. Time: 3:21)

Scoring

	1st Q	2nd Q	3rd Q	4th Q	Final
New England Patriots	14	0	7	0	21
Green Bay Packers	10	17	8	0	35

First Quarter: Green Bay (11:28)—A. Rison 54 yd. pass from B. Favre. Green Bay (8:42)—C. Jacke 37 yd. Field Goal. New England (6:35)—K. Byars 1 yd. pass from D. Bledsoe. New England (2:33)—B. Coates 4 yd. pass from D. Bledsoe.
Second Quarter: Green Bay (14:04)—A. Freeman 81 yd. pass from B. Favre. Green Bay (8:15)—C. Jacke 31 yd. Field Goal. Green Bay (1:11)—B. Favre 2 yd. run.
Third Quarter: New England (3:27)—C. Martin 18 yd. run. Green Bay (3:10)—D. Howard 99 yd. kickoff return.

Fourth Quarter: No score.

Statistics of the Game

	Patriots	Packers
First Downs	16	16
Rushes—Yards	13-43	36-115
Passing Yards	214	208
Return Yards	30	114
Att—Comp—Int	48-25-4	27-14-0
Fumbles—Lost	0-0	0-0
Penalties—Yards	2-22	3-41
FG Made—Att	0-0	2-3
Time of Possession	25:45	34:15

INDIVIDUAL STATISTICS

Rushing: GREEN BAY: D. Levens 14–61, E. Bennett 17–40, B. Favre 4–12, W. Henderson 1–2. NEW ENGLAND: C. Martin 11–42, D. Bledsoe 1–1, D. Meggett 1–0.

Passing: GREEN BAY: B. Favre 27–14. NEW ENGLAND: D. Bledsoe 48–25.

Receiving: GREEN BAY: A. Freeman 3–105, D. Levens 3–23, A. Rison 2–77, W. Henderson 2–14, M. Chmura 2–13, K. Jackson 1–10, E. Bennett 1–4. NEW ENGLAND: B. Coates 6–67, T. Glenn 4–62, K. Byars 4–42, S. Jefferson 3–34, C. Martin 3–28, D. Meggett 3–8, V. Brisby 2–12.

SUPER BOWLS I-XXX

Game	Date	Winner	Loser	Site	Attendance
XXXI	Jan. 26, 1997	Green Bay (NFC) 35	New England (AFC) 21	Superdome, New Orleans, La.	72,301
XXX	Jan. 28, 1996	Dallas (NFC) 27	Pittsburgh (AFC) 17	Sun Devil Stadium, Tempe, Ariz.	76,347
XXIX	Jan. 29, 1995	San Francisco (NFC) 49	San Diego (AFC) 26	Joe Robbie Stadium, Miami, Fla.	74,107
XXVIII	Jan. 30, 1994	Dallas (NFC) 30	Buffalo (AFC) 13	Georgia Dome, Atlanta, Ga.	72,817
XXVII	Jan. 31, 1993	Dallas (NFC) 52	Buffalo (AFC) 17	Rose Bowl, Pasadena, Calif.	98,374
XXVI	Jan. 26, 1992	Washington (NFC) 37	Buffalo (AFC) 24	Metrodome, Minneapolis, Minn.	63,130
XXV	Jan. 27, 1991	Giants (NFC) 20	Buffalo (AFC) 19	Tampa Stadium, Tampa, Fla.	73,813
XXIV	Jan. 28, 1990	San Francisco (NFC) 55	Denver (AFC) 10	Superdome, New Orleans	72,919
XXIII	Jan. 22, 1989	San Francisco (NFC) 20	Cincinnati (AFC) 16	Joe Robbie Stadium, Miami, Fla.	75,179
XXII	Jan. 31, 1988	Washington (NFC) 42	Denver (AFC) 10	Jack Murphy Stadium, San Diego, Calif.	73,302
XXI	Jan. 25, 1987	Giants (NFC) 39	Denver (AFC) 20	Rose Bowl, Pasadena, Calif.	101,063
XX	Jan. 26, 1986	Chicago (NFC) 46	New England (AFC) 10	Superdome, New Orleans	73,818
XIX	Jan. 20, 1985	San Francisco (NFC) 38	Miami (AFC) 16	Stanford Stadium, Palo Alto, Calif.	84,059
XVIII	Jan. 22, 1984	Los Angeles Raiders (AFC) 38	Washington (NFC) 9	Tampa Stadium, Tampa, Fla	72,920
XVII	Jan. 30, 1983	Washington (NFC) 27	Miami (AFC) 17	Rose Bowl, Pasadena, Calif.	103,667
XVI	Jan. 24, 1982	San Francisco (NFC) 26	Cincinnati (AFC) 21	Silverdome, Pontiac, Mich.	81,270
XV	Jan. 25, 1981	Oakland (AFC) 27	Philadelphia (NFC) 10	Superdome, New Orleans	75,500
XIV	Jan. 20, 1980	Pittsburgh (AFC) 31	Los Angeles (NFC) 19	Rose Bowl, Pasadena	103,985
XIII	Jan. 21, 1979	Pittsburgh (AFC) 35	Dallas (NFC) 31	Orange Bowl, Miami	79,484
XII	Jan. 15, 1978	Dallas (NFC) 27	Denver (AFC) 10	Superdome, New Orleans	75,583
XI	Jan. 9, 1977	Oakland (AFC) 32	Minnesota (NFC) 14	Rose Bowl, Pasadena	103,424
X	Jan. 18, 1976	Pittsburgh (AFC) 21	Dallas (NFC) 17	Orange Bowl, Miami	80,187
IX	Jan. 12, 1975	Pittsburgh (AFC) 16	Minnesota (NFC) 6	Tulane Stadium, New Orleans	80,997
VIII	Jan. 13, 1974	Miami (AFC) 24	Minnesota (NFC) 7	Rice Stadium, Houston	71,882
VII	Jan. 14, 1973	Miami (AFC) 14	Washington (NFC) 7	Memorial Coliseum, Los Angeles	90,182
VI	Jan. 16, 1972	Dallas (NFC) 24	Miami (AFC) 3	Tulane Stadium, New Orleans	81,591
V	Jan. 17, 1971	Baltimore (AFC) 16	Dallas (NFC) 13	Orange Bowl, Miami	79,204
IV	Jan. 11, 1970	Kansas City (AFL) 23	Minnesota (NFL) 7	Tulane Stadium, New Orleans	80,562
III	Jan. 12, 1969	New York (AFL) 16	Baltimore (NFL) 7	Orange Bowl, Miami	75,389
II	Jan. 14, 1968	Green Bay (NFL) 33	Oakland (AFL) 14	Orange Bowl, Miami	75,546
I	Jan. 15, 1967	Green Bay (NFL) 35	Kansas City (AFL) 10	Memorial Coliseum, Los Angeles	61,946

NOTE: Super Bowls I to IV were played before the American Football League and National Football League merged into the NFL, which was divided into two conferences, the NFC and AFC.

NATIONAL LEAGUE CHAMPIONS

Year	Champion	(W-L-T)	Year	Champion	(W-L-T)	Year	Champion	(W-L-T)
1921	Chicago Bears (Staley's)	(10-1-1)	1925	Chicago Cardinals	(11-2-1)	1928	Providence Steamrollers	(8-1-2)
1922	Canton Bulldogs	(10-0-2)	1926	Frankford Yellow Jackets	(14-1-1)	1929	Green Bay Packers	(12-0-1)
1923	Canton Bulldogs	(11-0-1)				1930	Green Bay Packers	(10-3-1)
1924	Cleveland Indians	(7-1-1)	1927	New York Giants	(11-1-1)	1931	Green Bay Packers	(12-2-0)
						1932	Chicago Bears	(7-1-6)

Year	Eastern Conference winners (W-L-T)	Western Conference winners (W-L-T)	League champion playoff results
1933	New York Giants (11-3-0)	Chicago Bears (10-2-1)	Chicago Bears 23, New York 21
1934	New York Giants (8-5-0)	Chicago Bears (13-0-0)	New York 30, Chicago Bears 13
1935	New York Giants (9-3-0)	Detroit Lions (7-3-2)	Detroit 26, New York 7
1936	Boston Redskins (7-5-0)	Green Bay Packers (10-1-1)	Green Bay 21, Boston 6
1937	Washington Redskins (8-3-0)	Chicago Bears (9-1-1)	Washington 28, Chicago Bears 21
1938	New York Giants (8-2-1)	Green Bay Packers (8-3-0)	New York 23, Green Bay 17
1939	New York Giants (9-1-1)	Green Bay Packers (9-2-0)	Green Bay 27, New York 0
1940	Washington Redskins (9-2-0)	Chicago Bears (8-3-0)	Chicago Bears 73, Washington 0
1941	New York Giants (8-3-0)	Chicago Bears (10-1-1)[2]	Chicago Bears 37, New York 9
1942	Washington Redskins (10-1-1)	Chicago Bears (11-0-0)	Washington 14, Chicago Bears 6
1943	Washington Redskins (6-3-1)[2]	Chicago Bears (8-1-1)	Chicago Bears 41, Washington 21
1944	New York Giants (8-1-1)	Green Bay Packers (8-2-0)	Green Bay 14, New York 7
1945	Washington Redskins (8-2-0)	Cleveland Rams (9-1-0)	Cleveland 15, Washington 14
1946	New York Giants (7-3-1)	Chicago Bears (8-2-1)	Chicago Bears 24, New York 14
1947	Philadelphia Eagles (8-4-0)[2]	Chicago Cardinals (9-3-0)	Chicago Cardinals 28, Philadelphia 21
1948	Philadelphia Eagles (9-2-1)	Chicago Cardinals (11-1-0)	Philadelphia 7, Chicago Cardinals 0
1949	Philadelphia Eagles (11-1-0)	Los Angeles Rams (8-2-2)	Philadelphia 14, Los Angeles 0

Year	Eastern Conference winners (W-L-T)	Western Conference winners (W-L-T)	League champion playoff results
1950[1]	Cleveland Browns (10-2-0)[2]	Los Angeles Rams (9-3-0)[2]	Cleveland 30, Los Angeles 28
1951[1]	Cleveland Browns (11-1-0)	Los Angeles Rams (8-4-0)	Los Angeles 24, Cleveland 17
1952[1]	Cleveland Browns (8-4-0)	Detroit Lions (9-3-0)[2]	Detroit 17, Cleveland 7
1953	Cleveland Browns (11-1-0)	Detroit Lions (10-2-0)	Detroit 17, Cleveland 16
1954	Cleveland Browns (9-3-0)	Detroit Lions (9-2-1)	Cleveland 56, Detroit 10
1955	Cleveland Browns (9-2-1)	Los Angeles Rams (8-3-1)	Cleveland 38, Los Angeles 14
1956	New York Giants (8-3-1)	Chicago Bears (9-2-1)	New York 47, Chicago Bears 7
1957	Cleveland Browns (9-2-1)	Detroit Lions (8-4-0)[2]	Detroit 59, Cleveland 14
1958	New York Giants (9-3-0)[2]	Baltimore Colts (9-3-0)	Baltimore 23, New York 17[3]
1959	New York Giants (10-2-0)	Baltimore Colts (9-3-0)	Baltimore 31, New York 16
1960	Philadelphia Eagles (10-2-0)	Green Bay Packers (8-4-0)	Philadelphia 17, Green Bay 13
1961	New York Giants (10-3-1)	Green Bay Packers (11-3-0)	Green Bay 37, New York 0
1962	New York Giants (12-2-0)	Green Bay Packers (13-1-0)	Green Bay 16, New York 7
1963	New York Giants (11-3-0)	Chicago Bears (11-1-2)	Chicago 14, New York 10
1964	Cleveland Browns (10-3-1)	Baltimore Colts (12-2-0)	Cleveland 27, Baltimore 0
1965	Cleveland Browns (11-3-0)	Green Bay Packers (11-3-1)[2]	Green Bay 23, Cleveland 12
1966	Dallas Cowboys (10-3-1)	Green Bay Packers (12-2-0)	Green Bay 34, Dallas 27
1967	Dallas Cowboys (9-5-0)[2]	Green Bay Packers (9-4-1)[2]	Green Bay 21, Dallas 17
1968	Cleveland Browns (10-4-0)[2]	Baltimore Colts (13-1-0)[2]	Baltimore 34, Cleveland 0
1969	Cleveland Browns (10-3-1)[2]	Minnesota Vikings (12-2-0)[2]	Minnesota 27, Cleveland 7

1. League was divided into American and National Conferences, 1950-52 and again in 1970, when leagues merged. 2. Won divisional playoff. 3. Won at 8:15 of sudden death overtime period.

NATIONAL CONFERENCE CHAMPIONS

Year	Eastern Division	Central Division	Western Division	Champion
1970	Dallas Cowboys (10-4-0)	Minnesota Vikings (12-2-0)	San Francisco 49ers (10-3-1)	Dallas
1971	Dallas Cowboys (11-3-0)	Minnesota Vikings (11-3-0)	San Francisco 49ers (9-5-0)	Dallas
1972	Washington Redskins (11-3-0)	Green Bay Packers (10-4-0)	San Francisco 49ers (8-5-1)	Washington
1973	Dallas Cowboys (10-4-0)	Minnesota Vikings (12-2-0)	Los Angeles Rams (12-2-0)	Minnesota
1974	St. Louis Cardinals (10-4-0)	Minnesota Vikings (10-4-0)	Los Angeles Rams (10-4-0)	Minnesota
1975	St. Louis Cardinals (11-3-0)	Minnesota Vikings (12-2-0)	Los Angeles Rams (12-2-0)	Dallas
1976	Dallas Cowboys (11-3-0)	Minnesota Vikings (11-2-1)	Los Angeles Rams (10-3-1)	Minnesota
1977	Dallas Cowboys (12-2-0)	Minnesota Vikings (9-5-0)	Los Angeles Rams (10-4-0)	Dallas
1978	Dallas Cowboys (12-4-0)	Minnesota Vikings (8-7-1)	Los Angeles Rams (12-4-0)	Dallas
1979	Dallas Cowboys (11-5-0)	Tampa Bay Buccaneers (10-6-0)	Los Angeles Rams (9-7-0)	Los Angeles
1980	Philadelphia Eagles (12-4-0)	Minnesota Vikings (9-7-0)	Atlanta Falcons (12-4-0)	Philadelphia
1981	Dallas Cowboys (12-4-0)	Tampa Bay Buccaneers (9-7-0)	San Francisco 49ers (13-3-0)	San Francisco
1982*				
1983	Washington Redskins (14-2-0)	Detroit Lions (8-8-0)	San Francisco 49ers (10-6-0)	Washington
1984	Washington Redskins (11-5-0)	Chicago Bears (10-6-0)	San Francisco 49ers (15-1-0)	San Francisco
1985	Dallas Cowboys (10-6-0)	Chicago Bears (15-1-0)	Los Angeles Rams (11-5-0)	Chicago
1986	New York Giants (14-2-0)	Chicago Bears (14-2-0)	San Francisco 49ers (10-5-1)	New York
1987	Washington Redskins (11-4-0)	Chicago Bears (11-4-0)	San Francisco 49ers (13-2-0)	Washington
1988	Philadelphia Eagles (10-6-0)	Chicago Bears (12-4-0)	San Francisco 49ers (10-6-0)	San Francisco
1989	New York Giants (12-4-0)	Minnesota Vikings (10-6-0)	San Francisco 49ers (14-2-0)	San Francisco
1990	New York Giants (13-3-0)	Chicago Bears (11-5-0)	San Francisco 49ers (14-2-0)	New York
1991	Washington (14-2-0)	Detroit Lions (12-4-0)	New Orleans Saints (11-5-0)	Washington
1992	Dallas Cowboys (13-3-0)	Minnesota Vikings (11-5-0)	San Francisco 49ers (14-2-0)	Dallas
1993	Dallas Cowboys (12-4-0)	Detroit Lions (10-6-0)	San Francisco 49ers (10-6-0)	Dallas
1994	Dallas Cowboys (12-4-0)	Minnesota Vikings (10-6-0)	San Francisco 49ers (13-3-0)	San Francisco
1995	Dallas Cowboys (12-4-0)	Green Bay Packers (11-5-0)	San Francisco 49ers (11-5-0)	Dallas
1996	Dallas Cowboys (10-6-0)	Green Bay Packers (13-3-0)	Carolina Panthers (12-4-0)	Green Bay

*Schedule reduced to 9 games from usual 16, with no standings kept in Eastern, Central, and Western Divisions, because of 57-day player strike. Washington Redskins won conference title and also had best regular-season record (8-1-0).

AMERICAN LEAGUE CHAMPIONS

Year	Eastern Division (W-L-T)	Western Division (W-L-T)	League champion, playoff results
1960	Houston Oilers (10-4-0)	Los Angeles Chargers (10-4-0)	Houston 24, Los Angeles 16
1961	Houston Oilers (10-3-1)	San Diego Chargers (12-2-0)	Houston 10, San Diego 3
1962	Houston Oilers (11-3-0)	Dallas Texans (11-3-0)	Dallas 20, Houston 17[1]
1963	Boston Patriots (8-6-1)[2]	San Diego Chargers (11-3-0)	San Diego 51, Boston 10
1964	Buffalo Bills (12-2-0)	San Diego Chargers (8-5-1)	Buffalo 20, San Diego 7
1965	Buffalo Bills (10-3-1)	San Diego Chargers (9-2-3)	Buffalo 23, San Diego 0
1966	Buffalo Bills (9-4-1)	Kansas City Chiefs (11-2-1)	Kansas City 31, Buffalo 7
1967	Houston Oilers (9-4-1)	Oakland Raiders (13-1-0)	Oakland 40, Houston 7
1968	New York Jets (11-3-0)	Oakland Raiders (12-2-0)[2]	New York 27, Oakland 23
1969	New York Jets (10-4-0)	Oakland Raiders (12-1-1)	Kansas City 17, Oakland 7[3]

1. Won at 2:45 of second sudden death overtime period. 2. Won divisional playoff. 3. Kansas City defeated New York, 13-6, and Oakland defeated Houston, 56-7, in interdivisional playoffs.

AMERICAN CONFERENCE CHAMPIONS

Year	Eastern Division	Central Division	Western Division	Champion
1970	Baltimore Colts (11-2-1)	Cincinnati Bengals (8-6-0)	Oakland Raiders (8-4-2)	Baltimore
1971	Miami Dolphins (10-3-1)	Cleveland Browns (9-5-0)	Kansas City Chiefs (10-3-1)	Miami
1972	Miami Dolphins (14-0-0)	Pittsburgh Steelers (11-3-0)	Oakland Raiders (10-3-1)	Miami
1973	Miami Dolphins (12-2-0)	Cincinnati Bengals (10-4-0)	Oakland Raiders (9-4-1)	Miami
1974	Miami Dolphins (11-3-0)	Pittsburgh Steelers (10-3-1)	Oakland Raiders (12-2-0)	Pittsburgh
1975	Baltimore Colts (10-4-0)	Pittsburgh Steelers (12-2-0)	Oakland Raiders (12-2-0)	Pittsburgh
1976	Baltimore Colts (11-3-0)	Pittsburgh Steelers (10-4-0)	Oakland Raiders (13-1-0)	Oakland
1977	Baltimore Colts (10-4-0)	Pittsburgh Steelers (9-5-0)	Denver Broncos (12-2-0)	Denver
1978	New England Patriots (11-5-0)	Pittsburgh Steelers (14-2-0)	Denver Broncos (10-6-0)	Pittsburgh
1979	Miami Dolphins (10-6-0)	Pittsburgh Steelers (12-4-0)	San Diego Chargers (12-4-0)	Pittsburgh
1980	Buffalo Bills (11-5-0)	Cleveland Browns (11-5-0)	San Diego Chargers (11-5-0)	Oakland
1981	Miami Dolphins (11-4-1)	Cincinnati Bengals (12-4-0)	San Diego Chargers (10-6-0)	Cincinnati
1982*	Miami Dolphins won the conference title, but the Los Angeles Raiders had best regular-season record (8-1-0).			
1983	Miami Dolphins (12-4-0)	Pittsburgh Steelers (10-6-0)	Los Angeles Raiders (12-4-0)	Los Angeles
1984	Miami Dolphins (14-2-0)	Pittsburgh Steelers (9-7-0)	Denver Broncos (13-3-0)	Miami
1985	Miami Dolphins (12-4-0)	Cleveland Browns (8-8)	Los Angeles Raiders (12-4-0)	New England
1986	New England Patriots (11-5-0)	Cleveland Browns (12-4-0)	Denver Broncos (11-5-0)	Denver
1987	Indianapolis Colts (9-6-0)	Cleveland Browns (10-5-0)	Denver Broncos (10-4-1)	Denver
1988	Buffalo Bills (12-4-0)	Cincinnati Bengals (12-4-0)	Seattle Seahawks (9-7-0)	Cincinnati
1989	Buffalo Bills (9-7-0)	Cleveland Browns (9-6-1)	Denver Broncos (11-5-0)	Denver
1990	Buffalo Bills (13-3-0)	Cincinnati Bengals (9-7-0)	Los Angeles Raiders (12-4-0)	Buffalo
1991	Buffalo Bills (13-3-0)	Houston Oilers (11-5-0)	Denver Broncos (12-4-0)	Buffalo
1992	Miami Dolphins (11-5-0)	Pittsburgh Steelers (11-5-0)	San Diego Chargers (11-5-0)	Buffalo
1993	Buffalo Bills (12-4-0)	Houston Oilers (12-4-0)	Kansas City Chiefs (11-5-0)	Buffalo
1994	Miami Dolphins (10-6-0)	Pittsburgh Steelers (12-4-0)	San Diego Chargers (11-5-0)	San Diego
1995	Buffalo Bills (10-6-0)	Pittsburgh Steelers (11-5-0)	Kansas City Chiefs (13-3-0)	Pittsburgh
1996	New England Patriots (11-5-0)	Pittsburgh Steelers (10-6-0)	Denver Broncos (13-3-0)	New England

*Schedule reduced to 9 games from usual 16, with no standings kept in Eastern, Central, and Western Divisions, because of 57-day player strike.

PRO FOOTBALL HALL OF FAME

(National Football Museum, Canton, Ohio)

Teams named are those with which player is best identified; figures in parentheses indicate number of playing seasons.

Adderley, Herb, defensive back, Packers, Cowboys (12)	1961–72
Alworth, Lance, wide receiver, Chargers, Cowboys (12)	1962–72
Atkins, Doug, defensive end, Browns, Bears, Saints (17)	1953–69
Badgro, Morris, end, N.Y. Yankees, Giants, Bklyn. Dodgers (8)	1927, 1930–36
Barney, Lem, defensive back, Lions (11)	1967–78
Battles, Cliff, back, Redskins (6)	1932–37
Baugh, Sammy, quarterback, Redskins (16)	1936–52
Bednarik, Chuck, center-lineback, Eagles (14)	1949–62
Bell, Bert, NFL founder, Eagles and Steelers, NFL Commissioner	1946–59
Bell, Bobby, linebacker, Chiefs (12)	1963–74
Berry, Raymond, end, Colts (13)	1955–67
Bidwell, Charles W., owner, Chicago Cardinals	1933–47
Biletnikoff, Fred, wide receiver, Raiders (14)	1965–1978
Blanda, George, quarterback-kicker, Bears, Oilers, Raiders (27)	1949–75
Blount, Mel, cornerback, Pittsburgh Steelers (14)	1970–83
Bradshaw, Terry, quarterback, Pittsburgh Steelers (14)	1970–83
Brown, Jim, fullback, Browns (9)	1957–65
Brown, Paul E., coach, Browns (1946–62), Bengals (1968–75)	1946–75
Brown, Roosevelt, tackle, Giants (13)	1953–65
Brown, Willie, cornerback, Broncos, Raiders (16)	1963–78
Buchanan, Buck, tackle, Chiefs (11)	1963–73
Butkus, Dick, linebacker, Bears (9)	1965–73
Campbell, Earl, running back, Oilers, Saints (8)	1978–85
Canadeo, Tony, back, Packers (11)	1941–52
Carr, Joe, NFL president (18)	1921–39
Chamberlin, Guy, end, 4 teams (9)	1919–27
Christiansen, Jack, defensive back, Lions (8)	1951–58
Clark, Earl (Dutch), quarterback, Spartans, Lions (7)	1931–38
Connor, George, tackle, linebacker, Bears (8)	1948–55
Conzelman, Jimmy, quarterback, 5 teams (10), owner	1921–48
Creekmur, Lou, offensive tackle/guard, Lions (10)	1950–59
Csonka, Larry, back, Dolphins, Giants (11)	1968–79

Davis, Al, owner, Raiders, coach, general manager	1963–present
Davis, Willie, defensive end, Packers (10)	1960–69
Dawson, Len, quarterback, Steelers, Browns, Texans, Chiefs (19)	1957–75
Dierdorf, Dan, tackle/center, Cardinals (13)	1971–83
Ditka, Mike, tight end, Bears, Eagles, Cowboys (12)	1961–72
Donovan, Art, defensive tackle, Colts (12)	1950–61
Dorsett, Tony, running back, Cowboys, Broncos (12)	1977–88
Driscoll, John (Paddy), quarterback, Cards, Bears (11)	1919–29
Dudley, Bill, back, Steelers, Lions, Redskins (9)	1942–53
Edwards, Albert Glen (Turk), tackle, Redskins (9)	1932–40
Ewbank, Weeb, coach, Colts, Jets (20)	1954–73
Fears, Tom, end, Rams (9); coach, Saints	1948-56
Finks, Jim, administrator/general manager, Vikings, Bears, Saints	1964–93
Flaherty, Ray, end, Yankees, Giants (9); coach, Redskins, Yankees (14)	1928–49
Ford, Len, end, def. end, Browns, Packers (11)	1948–58
Fouts, Dan, quarterback, Chargers (15)	1973–87
Fortmann, Daniel J., guard, Bears (8)	1936–43
Gatski, Frank, offensive lineman, Browns (12)	1946–57
George, Bill, linebacker, Bears, Rams (15)	1952–66
Gibbs, Joe, coach, Redskins (11)	1981–92
Gifford, Frank, back, Giants (12)	1952–64
Gillman, Sid, coach, Rams, Chargers, Oilers (18)	1955–70, 73–74
Graham, Otto, quarterback, Browns (10)	1946–55
Grange, Harold (Red), back, Bears, Yankees (9)	1925–34
Grant, Bud, coach, Vikings (18)	1967–85
Greene, Joe, defensive tackle, Steelrs (13)	1968–81
Gregg, Forrest, tackle, Packers (15)	1956–71
Griese, Bob, quarterback, Dolphins (14)	1967–80
Groza, Lou, place-kicker, tackle, Browns (21)	1946–67
Guyon, Joe, back, 6 teams (8)	1919–27
Halas, George, NFL founder, owner and coach, Staleys and Bears, end (11)	1919–27
Ham, Jack, linebacker, Steelers (13)	1970–82

N.F.L. INDIVIDUAL LIFETIME, SEASON, AND GAME RECORDS

(American Football League records were incorporated into NFL records after merger of the leagues)

Players listed in boldface were active during the 1996 season. The All-American Football Conference (AAFC) existed from 1946 to 1949. The 49ers, Browns, and Colts merged with the NFL in 1949.

All-Time Leading Touchdown Scorers
(Through 1996)

		Yrs	Rush	Rec	Ret	Total
1	**Jerry Rice**	12	10	154	1	165
2	**Marcus Allen**	15	112	21	1	134
3	Jim Brown	9	106	20	0	126
4	Walter Payton	13	110	15	0	125
5	John Riggins	14	104	12	0	116
6	**Emmitt Smith**	7	108	7	0	115
7	Lenny Moore	12	63	48	2	113
8	Don Hutson	11	3	99	3	105
9	Steve Largent	14	1	100	0	101
	Franco Harris	13	91	9	0	100
11	Eric Dickerson	11	90	6	0	96
12	Jim Taylor	10	83	10	0	93
13	Tony Dorsett	12	77	13	1	91
	Bobby Mitchell	11	18	65	8	91
	Barry Sanders	8	84	7	0	91

All-Time Leading Receivers
(Through 1996)

		Yrs	No	Yards	Avg	TD
1	**Jerry Rice**	12	1050	16,377	15.6	154
2	**Art Monk**	16	940	12,721	13.5	68
3	Steve Largent	14	819	13,089	16.0	100
4	**Henry Ellard**	14	775	13,177	17.0	61
5	**Andre Reed**	12	766	10,884	14.2	75
6	James Lofton	16	764	14,004	18.3	75
7	Charlie Joiner	18	750	12,146	16.2	65
8	**Gary Clark**	11	699	10,856	15.5	65
9	**Cris Carter**	10	667	8,367	12.5	76
10	Ozzie Newsome	13	662	7,980	12.1	47
11	**Irving Fryar**	13	650	10,111	15.6	69
12	Charley Taylor	13	649	9,110	14.0	79
13	Drew Hill	15	634	9,831	15.5	60
14	Don Maynard	15	633	11,834	18.7	88
15	Raymond Berry	13	631	9,275	14.7	68

All-Time Leading Passers
(Minimum 1,500 attempts. Through 1996)

		Yrs	Att	Cmp	Cmp%	Yards	Avg Gain	TD	Int	Rating
1	**Steve Young**	12	3192	2059	64.5	25,479	7.98	174	85	96.2
2	Joe Montana	15	5391	3409	63.2	40,551	7.52	273	139	92.3
3	**Brett Favre**	6	2693	1667	61.9	18,724	6.95	147	79	88.6
4	**Dan Marino**	14	6904	4134	59.9	51,636	7.48	369	209	88.3
5	**Jim Kelly**	11	4779	2874	60.1	35,467	7.42	237	175	84.4
6	Roger Staubach	11	2958	1685	57.0	22,700	7.67	153	109	83.4
7	**Troy Aikman**	8	3178	2000	62.9	22,733	7.15	110	98	83.0
8	Neil Lomax	8	3153	1817	57.6	22,771	7.22	136	90	82.7
9	Sonny Jurgensen	18	4262	2433	57.1	32,224	7.56	255	189	82.63
10	Len Dawson	19	3741	2136	57.1	28,711	7.67	239	183	82.56
11	Ken Anderson	16	4475	2654	59.3	32,838	7.34	197	160	81.86
12	**Bernie Kosar**	12	3365	1994	59.3	23,301	6.92	124	87	81.83
13	**Jeff Hostetler**	11	2194	1278	58.2	15,531	7.10	89	61	81.80
14	Danny White	13	2950	1761	59.7	21,959	7.44	155	132	81.7
15	**Dave Krieg**	17	5288	3092	58.5	37,946	7.18	261	199	81.5

Note: The NFL does not recognize records from the All-American Football Conference (1946-49). If it did, **Otto Graham** would rank 5th (after Favre) with the following stats: 10 Yrs; 2,626 Att; 1,464 Comp; 55.8 Comp Pct; 23,584 Yards; 8.98 Avg Gain; 174 TD; 6.6 TD Pct; 135 Int; 5.1 Int Pct; and 86.6 Rating Pts.

All-Time Leading Scorers
(Through 1996)

		Yrs	TD	FG	PAT	Total
1	George Blanda	26	9	335	943	2002
2	Jan Stenerud	19	0	373	580	1699
3	**Nick Lowery**	17	0	380	555	1695
4	**Gary Anderson**	15	0	351	483	1536
5	**Morten Andersen**	15	0	351	463	1516
6	Eddie Murray	16	0	325	498	1473
7	Pat Leahy	18	0	304	558	1470
8	Jim Turner	16	1	304	521	1439
	Norm Johnson	15	0	297	548	1439
10	Matt Bahr	17	0	300	522	1422
11	Mark Moseley	16	0	300	482	1382
12	Jim Bakken	17	0	282	534	1380
13	Fred Cox	15	0	282	519	1365
14	Lou Groza	17	1	234	641	1349
15	Jim Breech	14	0	243	517	1246

All-Time Leading Rushers
(Through 1996)

		Yrs	Car	Yards	Avg	TD
1	Walter Payton	13	3838	16,726	4.4	110
2	Eric Dickerson	11	2996	13,259	4.4	90
3	Tony Dorsett	12	2936	12,739	4.3	77
4	Jim Brown	9	2359	12,312	5.2	106
5	Franco Harris	13	2949	12,120	4.1	91
6	**Marcus Allen**	15	2898	11,738	4.1	112
7	**Barry Sanders**	8	2384	11,725	4.9	84
8	John Riggins	14	2916	11,352	3.9	104
9	O.J. Simpson	11	2404	11,236	4.7	61
10	**Thurman Thomas**	9	2566	10,762	4.2	62
11	Ottis Anderson	14	2562	10,273	4.0	81
12	**Emmitt Smith**	7	2334	10,160	4.4	108
13	Earl Campbell	8	2187	9,407	4.3	74
14	Jim Taylor	10	1941	8,597	4.4	83
15	Joe Perry	14	1737	8,378	4.8	53

Scoring

Most points scored, lifetime—2,002, George Blanda, Chicago Bears, 1949-58; Baltimore, 1950; Houston, 1960-66; Oakland, 1967-75 (9tds, 943 pat, 335 fgs).

Most points, season—176, Paul Hornung, Green Bay, 1960 (15 td, 41 pat, 15 fg).

Most points, game—40, Ernie Nevers, Chicago Cardinals, 1929 (6 td, 4 pat).

Most touchdowns, lifetime—165, Jerry Rice, San Francisco, 1985–96.

Most touchdowns, season—25, Emmitt Smith, Dallas, 1995.

Most points after touchdown, lifetime—943, George Blanda, Chicago Bears, 1949–58; Baltimore, 1950; Houston, 1960–66; Oakland, 1967–75.

Most points after touchdown, game—9, Pat Harder, Cardinals vs. N.Y. Giants, 1948; Bob Waterfield, Los Angeles vs. Baltimore, 1950; Charlie Gogolak, Washington vs. N.Y. Giants, 1966.

Most field goals, lifetime—380, Nick Lowery, New England, 1978; Kansas City Chiefs, 1980–93; N.Y. Jets, 1994–96.

Most field goals, season—37, John Kasay, Carolina, 1996.

Most field goals, game—7, Jim Bakken, St. Louis, 1967; and Rick Karlis, Minnesota, 1989.

Longest field goal—63 yards, Tom Dempsey, New Orleans, 1970.

Rushing

Most yards gained, lifetime—16,726, Walter Payton, Chicago Bears, 1975–1987.

Most yards gained, season—2,105, Eric Dickerson, Los Angeles, 1984.

Most yards gained, game—275, Walter Payton, Chicago, 1977.

Most touchdowns, lifetime—110, Walter Payton, Chicago, 1975–1987.

Most touchdowns, season—25, Emmitt Smith, Dallas, 1995.

Most touchdowns, game—6, Ernie Nevers, Chicago Cardinals, 1929.

Longest run from scrimmage—99 yards, Tony Dorsett, Dallas, Jan. 3, 1983.

Receiving

Most pass receptions, lifetime—1,050, Jerry Rice, San Francisco, 1985–1996.

Most pass receptions, season—123, Herman Moore, Detroit, 1995.

Most pass receptions, game—18, Tom Fears, Los Angeles, 1950.

Most yards gained, pass receptions, lifetime—16,377, Jerry Rice, San Francisco, 1985–1996.

Most yards gained receptions, season—1,848, Jerry Rice, San Francisco, 1995.

Most yards gained receptions, game—336, Willie Anderson, Los Angeles Rams, Nov. 26, 1989 vs. New Orleans.

Most touchdown receptions, lifetime—154, Jerry Rice, San Francisco, 1985–1996.

Most touchdown pass receptions, season—22, Jerry Rice, San Francisco 49ers, 1987.

Most touchdown pass receptions, game—5, Bob Shaw, Chicago Cards, 1950; Kellen Winslow, San Diego Chargers, 1981; Jerry Rice, San Francisco 49ers, 1990.

Interceptions

Most pass interceptions, lifetime—277, George Blanda, 1949–1975.

Most pass interceptions, season—14, Richard (Night Train) Lane, Los Angeles, 1952.

Most pass interceptions, game—4, by 17 players.

Longest pass interception return—104 yards, James Willis, Philadelphia vs. Dallas, Nov. 3, 1996.

Kicking

Highest average punting, lifetime—45.16 yards, Sammy Baugh, Washington, 1937–52.

Longest punt return—103 yards, Robert Bailey, L.A. Rams, 1994.

Longest kick-off return—106 yards, Roy Green, St. Louis, 1979; Al Carmichael, Green Bay, 1956; Noland Smith, Kansas City, 1967.

Passing

Most touchdown passes, season—48, Dan Marino, Miami, 1984.

Most touchdown passes, game—7, Sid Luckman, Chicago Bears, 1943; Adrian Burk, Philadelphia, 1954; George Blanda, Houston, 1961; Y.A. Tittle, New York Giants, 1963; Joe Kapp, Minnesota, 1969.

Longest pass completion—99 yards, Frank Filchock (to Andy Farkas), Washington, 1939; George Izo (to Bob Mitchell), Washington, 1963; Karl Sweetan (to Pat Studstill), Detroit, 1966; Sonny Jurgensen (to Gerry Allen), Washington, 1968; Jim Plunkett (to Cliff Branch) L.A. Raiders, 1985; Ron Jaworksi (to Mike Quick), Philadelphia, 1985; Stan Humphries (to Tony Martin), San Diego, 1994; Brett Favre (to Robert Brooks), Green Bay, 1995.

Most passes completed, lifetime—4,134, Dan Marino, Miami, 1983–96.

Most passes completed, season—404, Warren Moon, 1991.

Most passes completed, game—45, Drew Bledsoe, New England, 1994.

Most touchdown passes, lifetime—369, Dan Marino, Miami, 1983–96.

Most yards gained, lifetime—51,636, Dan Marino, Miami, 1983–96.

Most yards gained, season—5,084, Dan Marino, Miami, 1984.

Most yards gained, game—554, Norm Van Brocklin, Los Angeles, 1951.

Sports Personalities

A name in parentheses is the original name or form of name. Localities are places of birth. Dates of birth appear as month/day/year. **Boldface** years in parentheses are dates of **(birth-death)**.

Information has been gathered from many sources, including the individuals themselves. However, the *Information Please Almanac* cannot guarantee the accuracy of every individual item.

Aaron, Hank (Henry) (baseball); Mobile, Ala., 2/5/34
Abbott, Jim (baseball); Flint, Mich., 9/19/67
Abdul-Jabbar, Kareem (Lewis Ferdinand Alcindor, Jr.) (basketball); New York City, 4/16/47
Adderly, Herbert A. (football); Philadelphia, 6/8/39
Affleck, Francis (auto racing) **(1951–1985)**
Agassi, Andre (tennis); Las Vegas, Nev., 4/29/70
Aikman, Troy (football); Henryetta, Okla., 11/21/66
Ali, Muhammad (Cassius Clay) (boxing); Louisville, Ky., 1/18/42
Allen, Dick (Richard Anthony) (baseball); Wampum, Pa., 3/8/42

Allen, George (football) **(1918–1990)**
Allison, Bobby (Robert Arthur) (auto racing); Hueytown, Ala., 12/3/37
Allison, Davey (auto racing); Hueytown, Ala. **(1961–1993)**
Alston, Walter (baseball); Venice, Ohio **(1911–1984)**
Alworth, Lance (football); Houston, 8/3/40
Ameche, Alan (football); Houston, Tex. **(1933–1988)**
Anderson, Ken (football); Batavia, Ill., 2/15/49
Anderson, Sparky (George) (baseball); Bridgewater, S.D., 2/22/34
Andretti, Mario (auto racing); Montona, Trieste, Italy, 2/28/40
Anthony, Earl (bowling); Kent, Wash., 4/27/38

Appling, Luke (baseball); High Point, N.C **(1907–1990)**
Arcaro, Eddie (George Edward) (jockey); Cincinnati, 2/19/16
Ashe, Arthur (tennis); Richmond, Va. **(1943–1993)**
Ashford, Evelyn (track & field); Shreveport, La., 4/15/57
Austin, Tracy (tennis); Rolling Hills, Calif., 12/2/62
Averill, Earl (baseball); Everett, Wash. **(1915–1983)**
Babashoff, Shirley (swimming); Whittier, Calif., 1/31/57
Baer, Max (boxing); Omaha, Neb. **(1909–1959)**
Bagwell, Jeff (baseball); Boston, Mass., 5/17/68
Bailey, Donovan (track); Canada, 12/16/67
Banks, Ernie (baseball); Dallas, 1/31/31
Bannister, Roger (runner); Harrow, England, 3/24/29
Barkley, Charles (basketball); Leeds, Ala., 2/20/63
Barry, Rick (Richard) (basketball); Elizabeth, N.J., 3/28/44
Bauer, Hank (Henry) (baseball); East St. Louis, Ill., 7/31/22
Baugh, Sammy (football); Temple, Tex., 3/17/14
Bayi, Filbert (runner); Karratu, Tanganyika, 6/23/53
Baylor, Elgin (basketball); Washington, D.C., 9/16/34
Beamon, Bob (long jumper); New York City, 8/2/46
Becker, Boris (tennis); Leiman, W. Germany, 11/22/67
Bee, Clair (basketball); Cleveland, Ohio **(1896–1983)**
Beliveau, Jean (hockey); Three Rivers, Quebec, Canada, 8/31/31
Belle, Albert (baseball); Shreveport, La., 8/25/66
Beman, Deane (golf); Washington, D.C., 4/22/38
Bench, Johnny (Johnny Lee) (baseball); Oklahoma City, 12/7/47
Berg, Patty (Patricia Jane) (golf); Minneapolis, 2/13/18
Berra, Yogi (Lawrence) (baseball); St. Louis, 5/12/25
Biletnikoff, Frederick (football); Erie, Pa., 2/23/43
Bing, Dave (basketball); Washington, D.C., 11/24/43
Bird, Larry (basketball); French Lick, Ind., 12/7/56
Blaik, Earl H. (football); Detroit **(1897–1989)**
Blanda, George Frederick (football); Youngwood, Pa., 9/17/27
Bledsoe, Drew (football); Walla Walla, Wash., 2/14/72
Blue, Vida (baseball); Mansfield, La., 7/28/49
Bodine, Brett (auto racing); Chemung, N.Y., 1/11/59
Bodine, Geoff (auto racing); Chemung, N.Y., 4/18/49
Boggs, Wade (baseball); Omaha, Neb., 6/15/58
Bonds, Barry (baseball); Riverside, Calif., 7/24/64
Borg, Björn (tennis); Stockholm, 6/6/56
Boros, Julius (golf); Fairfield, Conn. **(1920–1994)**
Bossy, Mike (hockey); Montreal, 1/22/57
Boston, Ralph (long jumper); Laurel, Miss., 5/9/39
Bourque, Ray (hockey); Montreal, Que., 12/28/60
Bradley, Bill (William Warren) (basketball); Crystal City, Mo., 7/28/43
Bradley, Pat (golf); Westford, Mass., 3/24/51
Bradshaw, Terry (football); Shreveport, La., 9/2/48
Brathwaite, Chris (track); Eugene, Ore. **(1948–1984)**
Breedlove, Craig (Norman) (speed driving); Los Angeles, 3/23/38
Brett, George (baseball); Glendale, W. Va., 5/15/53
Brock, Louis Clark (baseball); El Dorado, Ark., 6/18/39
Brown, Jimmy (football); St. Simon Island, Ga., 2/17/36
Brumel, Valeri (high jumper); Tolbuzino, Siberia, 4/14/42
Bryant, Paul "Bear" (football); Tuscaloosa, Ala. **(1913–1983)**
Bryant, Rosalyn Evette (track); Chicago, 1/7/56
Burton, Michael (swimming); Des Moines, Iowa, 7/3/47
Butkus, Dick (Richard Marvin) (football); Chicago, 12/9/42
Calipari, John (basketball); Moon, Pa., 2/10/59
Campanella, Roy (baseball); Homestead, Pa. **(1921–1993)**
Campbell, Earl (football); Tyler, Tex., 3/29/55
Canseco, Jose (baseball); Havana, Cuba, 7/2/64
Caponi, Donna Maria (golf); Detroit, 1/29/45
Cappelletti, Gino (football); Keewatin, Minn., 3/26/34
Carew, Rod (Rodney Cline) (baseball); Gatun, Panama, 10/1/45
Carlos, John (sprinter); New York City, 6/5/45
Carlton, Steven Norman (baseball); Miami, Fla., 12/22/44
Carner, Joanne Gunderson, Mrs. Don (golf); Kirkland, Wash., 3/4/39
Casals, Rosemary (tennis); San Francisco, 9/16/48
Casper, Billy (golf); San Diego, Calif., 6/24/31
Caulkins, Tracy (swimming); Winona, Minn., 1/11/63
Cauthen, Steve (jockey); Covington, Ky., 5/1/60
Chamberlain, Wilt (Wilton) (basketball); Philadelphia, 8/21/36
Chandler, A.B. (Happy) (baseball); Louisville, Ky. **(1899–1991)**
Chandler, Spud (baseball); Commerce, Ga. **(1907–1990)**
Chapot, Frank (equestrian); Camden, N.J., 2/24/34
Chinaglia, Giorgio (soccer); Carrara, Italy, 1/24/47
Clarke, Bobby (Robert Earle) (hockey); Flin Flon, Manitoba, Canada, 8/13/49
Clemens, Roger (baseball); Dayton, Ohio, 8/4/62
Clemente, Roberto Walker (baseball); Carolina, Puerto Rico **(1934–1972)**
Cobb, Ty (Tyrus Raymond) (baseball); Narrows, Ga. **(1886–1961)**
Cochran, Barbara Ann (skiing); Claremont, N.H., 1/14/51
Cochran, Marilyn (skiing); Burlington, Vt., 2/7/50
Cochran, Robert (skiing); Claremont, N.H., 12/11/51
Coe, Sebastian Newbold (track); London, England, 9/29/56
Coffey, Paul (hockey); Weston, Ont., 6/1/61

Colavito, Rocky (Rocco Domenico) (baseball); New York City, 8/10/33
Coleman, Derrick (basketball); Mobile, Ala., 6/21/67
Comaneci, Nadia (gymnast); Onesti, Romania, 11/12/61
Conigliaro, Tony (baseball); Revere, Mass. **(1945–1990)**
Connors, Jimmy (James Scott) (tennis); East St. Louis, Ill., 9/2/52
Cordero, Angel (jockey); Santurce, Puerto Rico, 5/8/42
Cosell, Howard (broadcaster); Winston-Salem, N.C. **(1918–1995)**
Courier, Jim (tennis); Sanford, Fla., 8/17/70
Cournoyer, Yvan Serge (hockey); Drummondville, Quebec, Canada, 11/22/43
Court, Margaret Smith (tennis); Albury, New South Wales, Australia, 7/16/42
Cousy, Bob (basketball); New York City, 8/9/28
Crabbe, Buster (swimming); Scottsdale, Ariz. **(1908–1983)**
Crenshaw, Ben (golf); Austin, Tex., 1/11/52
Cronin, Joe (baseball executive); San Francisco **(1906–1984)**
Cruyff, Johan (soccer); Amsterdam, Netherlands, 4/25/47
Csonka, Larry (Lawrence Richard) (football); Stow, Ohio, 12/25/46
Dancer, Stanley (harness racing); New Egypt, N.J., 7/25/27
Dantley, Adrian (basketball); Washington, D.C., 2/28/56
Dark, Alvin (baseball); Comanche, Okla., 1/7/22
Davenport, Willie (track); Troy, Ala., 6/6/43
Dawson, Andre (baseball); Miami, Fla., 7/10/54
Dawson, Leonard Ray (football); Alliance, Ohio, 6/20/35
Dean, Dizzy (Jay Hanna) (baseball); Lucas, Ark. **(1911–1974)**
DeBusschere, Dave (basketball); Detroit, 10/16/40
Delvecchio, Alex Peter (hockey); Fort William, Ontario, Canada, 12/4/31
Demaret, Jim (golf); Houston **(1910–1983)**
Dempsey, Jack (William H.) (boxing); Manassa, Colo. **(1895–1983)**
DeVicenzo, Roberto (golf); Buenos Aires, 4/14/23
Dibbs, Edward George (tennis); Brooklyn, New York, 2/23/51
Dietz, James W. (rowing); New York, N.Y., 1/12/49
DiMaggio, Joe (baseball); Martinez, Calif., 11/25/14
Dionne, Marcel (hockey); Drummondville, Quebec, Canada, 8/3/51
Dominguín, Luis Miguel (matador); Madrid, 12/9/26
Dorsett, Tony (football); Rochester, Pa., 4/7/54
Dryden, Kenneth (hockey); Hamilton, Ontario, Canada, 8/4/47
Drysdale, Don (baseball); Van Nuys, Calif. **(1936–1993)**
Duran, Roberto (boxing); Panama City, 6/16/51
Durocher, Leo (baseball); West Springfield, Mass. **(1906–1991)**
Durr, Francois (tennis); Algiers, Algeria, 12/25/42
Eckersley, Dennis (baseball); Oakland, Calif., 10/3/54
El Cordobés, (Manuel Benitez Pérez) (matador); Palma del Rio, Córdoba, Spain, 5/4/36(?)
Elder, Lee (golf); Dallas, 7/14/34
Elway, John (football); Port Angeles, Wash., 6/28/60
Emerson, Roy (tennis); Kingsway, Australia, 11/3/36
Ender, Kornelia (swimming); Plauen, East Germany, 10/25/58
Erving, "Dr. J" (Julius) (basketball); Roosevelt, N.Y., 2/22/50
Esposito, Phil (Philip Anthony) (hockey); Sault Ste. Marie, Ontario, Canada, 2/20/42
Evans, Lee (runner); Mandena, Calif., 2/25/47
Everett, Chris (Christine Marie) (tennis); Fort Lauderdale, Fla., 12/21/54
Ewbank, Weeb (football); Richmond, Ind., 5/6/07
Ewing, Patrick (basketball); Kingston, Jamaica, 8/5/62
Feller, Robert (Bobby) (baseball); Van Meter, Iowa, 11/3/18
Feuerbach, Allan Dean (track); Preston, Iowa, 1/12/48
Finley, Charles O. (sportsman); Ensley, Ala. **(1918–1996)**
Fischer, Bobby (chess); Chicago, 3/9/43
Fitzsimmons, Bob (Robert Prometheus) (boxing); Cornwall, England **(1862–1917)**
Fleming, Peggy Gale (ice skating); San Jose, Calif., 7/27/48
Ford, Whitey (Edward) (baseball); New York City, 10/21/28
Foreman, George (boxing); Marshall, Tex., 1/10/49
Fosbury, Richard (high jumper); Portland, Ore., 3/6/47
Fox, Nellie (Jacob Nelson) (baseball); St. Thomas, Pa. **(1927–1975)**
Foxx, James Emory (baseball); Sudlersville, Md. **(1907–1967)**
Foyt, A. J. (auto racing); Houston, 1/16/35
Fratianne, Linda (figure skating); Los Angeles, 8/2/60
Frazier, Joe (boxing); Beauford, S.C., 1/17/44
Frazier, Walt (basketball); Atlanta, 3/29/45
Frick, Ford C. (baseball); Wawaka, Ind. **(1894–1978)**
Furillo, Carl (baseball); Stony Creek Mills, Pa. **(1922–1989)**
Furniss, Bruce (swimming); Fresno, Calif., 5/27/57
Gable, Dan (wrestling); Waterloo, Iowa, 10/25/45
Gabriel, Roman (football); Wilmington, N.C., 8/5/40
Gallagher, Michael Donald (skiing); Yonkers, N.Y., 10/3/41
Garvey, Steve (baseball); Tampa, Fla., 12/22/48
Gehrig, Lou (Henry Louis) (baseball); New York City **(1903–1941)**
Gehringer, Charlie (baseball); Fowlerville, Mich. **(1903–1993)**
Geoffrion, "Boom Boom" (Bernie) (hockey); Montreal, 2/14/31
Gerulaitis, Vitas (tennis); Brooklyn, N.Y. **(1954–1994)**
Gervin, George (basketball); Long Beach, Calif., 4/27/52
Giacomin, Ed (hockey); Sudbury, Ontario, Canada, 6/6/39
Giamatti, A. Bartlett (baseball); South Hadley, Mass. **(1938–1989)**

Gibson, Bob (baseball); Omaha, Neb., 11/9/35
Gifford, Frank (football); Santa Monica, Calif., 8/16/30
Gilbert, Rod (Rodrique) (hockey); Montreal, 7/1/41
Giles, Warren (baseball executive); Tiskilwa, Ill. (1896–1979)
Gilmore, Artis (basketball); Chipley, Fla., 9/21/49
Glance, Harvey (track); Phenix City, Ala., 3/28/57
Gonzalez, Pancho (tennis); Los Angeles (1928–1995)
Goodell, Brian Stuart (swimming); Stockton, Calif., 4/2/59
Gooden, Dwight (baseball); Tampa, Fla., 11/16/64
Goodrich, Gail (basketball); Los Angeles, 4/23/43
Goolagong, Cawley, Evonne (tennis); Griffith, Australia, 7/31/51
Gordon, Jeff (auto racing); Vallejo, Calif., 8/4/71
Gossage, "Goose" (Rich) (baseball); Colorado Springs, Colo., 4/5/51
Gottfried, Brian (tennis); Baltimore, Md., 1/27/52
Graf, Steffi (tennis); Mannheim, W. Germany, 6/14/69
Graham, David (golf); Windson, Australia, 5/23/46
Graham, Otto Everett (football); Waukegan, Ill., 12/6/21
Grange, Red (Harold) (football); Forksville, Pa. (1904–1991)
Green, Hubert (golf); Birmingham, Ala., 12/28/46
Greene, Charles E. (sprinter); Pine Bluff, Ark., 3/21/45
Greene, "Mean" (Joe (football); Temple, Tex., 9/24/46
Gretzky, Wayne (hockey); Brantford, Ont., 1/26/61
Griese, Bob (Robert Allen) (football); Evansville, Ind., 2/3/45
Griffey, Ken, Jr. (baseball); Donora, Pa., 11/21/69
Groebli, "Mr. Frick" (Werner) (ice skating); Basil, Switzerland, 4/21/15
Grove, Lefty (Robert Moses) (baseball); Lonaconing, Md. (1900–1975)
Groza, Lou (football); Martins Ferry Ohio, 1/25/24
Guidry, Ronald Ames (baseball); Lafayette, La., 8/28/50
Gwynn, Tony (baseball); Los Angeles, Calif., 5/9/60
Halas, George (football); Chicago (1895–1983)
Hall, Gary (swimming); Fayetteville, N.C., 8/7/51
Hamill, Dorothy (figure skating); Chicago, 1956(?)
Hamilton, Scott (figure skating); Bowling Green, Ohio, 8/28/58
Hammond, Kathy (runner); Sacramento, Calif., 11/2/51
Hardaway, Anfernee (basketball); Memphis, Tenn., 7/18/72
Harris, Franco (football); Ft. Dix, N.J., 3/7/50
Hartack, William, Jr. (jockey); Colver, Pa., 12/9/32
Hasek, Dominik (hockey); Pardubice, Czechoslovakia, 1/29/65
Haughton, William (harness racing); Gloversville, N.Y. (1923–1986)
Havlicek, John (basketball); Martins Ferry, Ohio, 4/8/40
Hayes, Elvin (basketball); Rayville, La., 11/17/45
Hayes, Woody (football); Upper Arlington, Ohio (1913–1987)
Haynie, Sandra (golf); Fort Worth, 6/4/43
Heiden, Eric (speed skating); Madison, Wis., 6/14/58
Hencken, John (swimming); Culver City, Calif., 5/29/54
Henderson, Rickey (baseball); Chicago, 12/25/58
Henie, Sonja (ice skater); Oslo (1912–1969)
Herman, Floyd Caves (Babe) (baseball); Buffalo, N.Y. (1903–1987)
Hernandez, Keith (baseball); San Francisco, 10/20/53
Hershiser, Orel (baseball); Buffalo, N.Y., 9/16/58
Hickcox, Charles (swimming); Phoenix, Ariz., 2/6/47
Hines, James (sprinter); Dumas, Ark., 9/10/46
Hodges, Gil (baseball); Princeton, Ind. (1924–1972)
Hogan, Ben (golf); Dublin, Tex. (1912–1997)
Holmes, Larry (boxing); Cuthert, Ga., 11/3/49
Hornsby, Rogers (baseball); Winters, Tex. (1896–1963)
Hornung, Paul (football); Louisville, Ky., 12/23/35
Houk, Ralph (baseball); Lawrence, Kan., 8/9/19
Howard, Elston (baseball); St. Louis (1929–1980)
Howe, Gordon (hockey); Floral, Sask., Canada, 3/31/28
Howell, Jim Lee (football); Lonoke, Ark. (1914–1995)
Howser, Dick (baseball); Miami, Fla. (1937–1987)
Hubbell, Carl (baseball); Carthage, Mo. (1903–1988)
Huff, Sam (Robert Lee) (football); Morgantown, W. Va., 10/4/34
Hull, Bobby (hockey); Point Anne, Ontario, Canada, 1/3/39
Hunter, "Catfish" (Jim) (baseball); Hertford, N.C., 4/8/46
Huntley, Joni (track); McMinnville, Ore., 8/4/56
Hutson, Donald (football); Pine Bluff, Ark., 1/31/13
Insko, Del (harness racing); Amboy, Minn., 7/10/31
Irwin, Hale (golf); Joplin, Mo., 6/3/45
Jackson, Reggie (baseball); Wyncote, Pa., 5/18/46
Jagr, Jaromir (hockey); Kladno, Czechoslovakia, 2/15/72
Jeffries, James J. (boxing); Carroll, Ohio (1875–1953)
Jenkins, Ferguson Arthur (baseball); Chatham, Ontario, Canada, 12/13/43
Jenner, (W.) Bruce (track); Mt. Kisco, N.Y., 10/28/49
Jezek, Linda (swimming); Palo Alto, Calif., 3/10/60
Johnson, "Magic" (Earvin) (basketball); E. Lansing, Mich., 8/14/59
Johnson, Anthony (rowing); Washington, D.C., 11/16/40
Johnson, Jack (John Arthur) (boxing); Galveston, Tex. (1876–1946)
Johnson, Jimmy (football); Port Arthur, Tex., 8/14/43
Johnson, Rafer (decathlon); Hillsboro, Tex., 8/18/35
Johnson, Randy (baseball); Walnut Creek, Calif., 9/10/63
Johnson, Wilham Julius (Judy) (baseball); Wilmington, Del. (1899–1989)
Jones, Deacon (David) (football); Eatonville, Fla., 12/9/38

Jordan, Michael (basketball); Brooklyn, N.Y., 2/17/63
Joyner, Florence Griffith (sprinter); Mojave Desert, Calif., 12/21/59
Joyner-Kersee, Jackie (track); East St. Louis, Ill., 3/3/62
Juantoreno, Alberto (track); Santiago, Cuba, 12/3/51
Jurgensen, Sonny (football); Wilmington, N.C., 8/23/34
Justice, Dave (baseball); Cincinnati, Ohio, 4/14/66
Kaat, Jim (baseball); Zeeland, Mich., 11/7/38
Kaline, Al (Albert) (baseball); Baltimore, 12/19/34
Keino, Kipchoge (runner); Kapchemoiymo, Kenya, 1/17/40
Kelly, Leroy (football); Philadelphia, 5/20/42
Kelly, Red (Leonard Patrick) (hockey); Simcoe, Ontario, Canada, 7/9/27
Killebrew, Harmon (baseball); Payette, Idaho, 6/29/36
Killy, Jean-Claude (skiing); Saint-Cloud, France, 8/30/43
Kilmer, Bill (William Orland) (football); Topeka, Kan., 9/5/39
King, Bille Jean (Bille Jean Moffitt) (tennis); Long Beach, Calif., 11/22/43
Kinsella, John (swimming); Oak Park, Ill., 8/26/52
Kluszeewski, Ted (baseball); Argo, Ill. (1924–1988)
Kodes, Jan (tennis); Prague, 3/1/46
Kolb, Claudia (swimming); Hayward, Calif., 12/19/49
Korbut, Olga (gymnast); Grodno, Byelorussia, U.S.S.R., 5/16/55
Koufax, Sandy (Sanford) (baseball); Brooklyn, N.Y., 12/30/35
Kramer, Jack (tennis); Las Vegas, Nev., 8/1/21
Kramer, Jerry (football); Jordan, Mont., 1/23/36
Kuenn, Harvey (baseball); West Allis, Wis. (1930–1988)
Kuhn, Bowie Kent (baseball); Takoma Park, Md., 10/28/26
Lafleur, Guy Damien (hockey); Thurson, Quebec, Canada, 8/20/51
Laird, Ronald (walker); Louisville, Ky., 5/31/35
Lamonica, Daryle (football); Fresno, Calif., 7/17/41
Landis, Kenesaw Mountain (1st baseball commissioner); Millville, Ohio (1866–1944)
Landry, Tom (football); Mission, Tex., 9/11/24
Landy, John (runner); Australia, 4/4/30
Larrieu, Francie (track); Palo Alto, Calif., 11/28/52
La Russa, Tony (baseball); Tampa, Fla., 10/4/44
Lasorda, Tom (baseball); Norristown, Pa., 9/22/27
Laver, Rod (tennis); Rockhampton, Australia, 8/9/38
Layne, Bobby (football); Lubbock, Texas (1927–1986)
Leetch, Brian (hockey); Corpus Christi, Tex., 3/3/68
Lemieux, Mario (hockey); Montreal, Quebec, Canada, 10/5/65
Lendl, Ivan (tennis); Prague, 3/7/60
Leonard, Benny (Benjamin Leiner) (boxing); New York City (1896–1947)
Leonard, Sugar Ray (boxing); Wilmington, N.C., 5/17/56
Lewis, Carl (track); Willingboro, N.J., 7/1/61
Lindros, Eric (hockey); London, Ont., 2/28/73
Liquori, Marty (runner); Montclair, N.J., 9/11/49
Little, Lou (football); Leominster, Mass. (1893–1979)
Littler, Gene (golf); La Jolla, Calif., 7/21/30
Lobo, Rebecca (basketball); Southwick, Mass., 10/6/73
Lombardi, Vince (football); Brooklyn, N.Y. (1913–1970)
Longden, Johnny (horse racing); Wakefield, England, 2/14/07
Lopat, Eddie (baseball); New York, N.Y. (1918–1992)
Lopez, Al (baseball); Tampa, Fla., 8/20/08
Lopez, Nancy (golf); Torrance, Calif., 1/6/57
Louis, Joe (Joe Louis Barrow) (boxing); Lafayette, Ala. (1914–1981)
Lukas, D. Wayne (horses); Antigo, Wis., 9/2/35
Lynn, Frederic Michael (baseball); Chicago, Ill., 2/3/52
Lynn, Janet (figure skating); Rockford, Ill., 4/6/53
Mack, Connie (Cornelius Alexander McGillicuddy) (baseball executive); East Brookfield, Mass. (1862–1956)
Mackey, John (football); New York City, 9/24/41
Maddux, Greg (baseball); San Angelo, Texas, 4/15/67
Mahovlich, Frank (Francis William) (hockey); Timmins, Ontario, Canada, 1/10/38
Mahre, Phil (skiing); White Pass, Wash., 5/10/57
Malone, Karl (basketball); Summerfield, La., 7/24/63
Malone, Moses (basketball); Petersburg, Va., 3/23/55
Mandlikova, Hana (tennis); Prague, Czechoslovakia, 2/62
Mann, Carol (golf); Buffalo, N.Y., 2/3/41
Manning, Madeline (runner); Cleveland, 1/11/48
Mantle, Mickey Charles (baseball); Spavinaw, Okla. (1931–1995)
Maravich, "Pistol Pete" (Peter Aliquippa, Pa. (1948–1988)
Marble, Alice (tennis); Palm Springs, Calif. (1913–1990)
Marciano, Rocky (boxing); Brockton, Mass. (1923–1969)
Marichal, Juan (baseball); Laguna Verde, Montecristi, Dominican Republic, 10/20/37
Marino, Dan (football); Pittsburgh, Pa., 9/15/61
Maris, Roger (baseball); Hibbing, Minn. (1934–1985)
Martin, Billy (Alfred Manuel) (baseball); Berkeley, Calif. (1928–1989)
Martin, Christy (boxing); Mullers, W.Va.,
Martin, Rick (Richard Lionel) (hockey); Verdun, Quebec, Canada, 7/26/51
Mathews, Ed (Edwin) (baseball); Texarkana, Tex., 10/13/31
Mattingly, Don (baseball); Evansville, Ind., 4/20/61
Matson, Randy (shot putter); Kilgore, Tex., 3/5/45

Mays, Willie (baseball); Westfield, Ala., 5/6/31
McAdoo, Bob (basketball); Greensboro, N.C., 9/25/51
McCarthy, Joe (Joseph Vincent) (baseball); Philadelphia **(1887–1978)**
McCovey, Willie Lee (baseball); Mobile, Ala., 1/10/38
McDonald, Lanny (hockey); Hanna, Alberta, Canada, 2/16/53
McDowell, Jack (baseball); Van Nuys, Calif., 1/16/66
McEnroe, John Patrick, Jr. (tennis); Wiesbaden, Germany, 2/16/59
McGraw, John Joseph (baseball); Truxton, N.Y. **(1873–1934)**
McGwire, Mark (baseball); Pomona, Calif., 10/1/63
McLain, Dennis (baseball); Chicago, 3/24/44
McMillan, Kathy Laverne (track); Raeford, N.C., 11/7/57
Merrill, Janice (track); New London, Conn., 6/18/62
Messier, Mark (hockey); Edmonton, Alberta, Canada, 1/18/61
Meyer, Deborah (swimming); Haddonfield, N.J., 8/14/52
Meyers, Anne (basketball); San Diego, Calif., 3/26/55
Middlecoff, Cary (golf); Halls, Tenn., 1/6/21
Mikita, Stan (hockey); Sokolce, Czechoslovakia, 5/20/40
Milburn, Rodney, Jr. (hurdler); Opelousas, La., 5/18/50
Miller, Cheryl (basketball); Riverside, Calif., 1/3/64
Miller, Johnny (golf); San Francisco, 4/29/47
Miller, Reggie (basketball); Riverside, Calif., 8/24/65
Montana, Joe (football); New Eagle, Pa., 6/11/56
Montgomery, Jim (swimming); Madison, Wis., 1/24/55
Moody, Helen Willis (tennis); Centerville, Calif., 10/6/06
Moore, Archie (boxing); Benoit, Miss., 12/13/16
Morgan, Joe Leonard (baseball); Bonham, Tex., 9/19/43
Morrall, Earl (football); Muskegon, Mich., 5/17/34
Morton, Craig L. (football); Flint, Mich., 2/5/43
Mosconi, Willie (pocket billiards); Philadelphia **(1913–1993)**
Moses, Edward Corley (track); Dayton, Ohio, 8/31/58
Mungo, Van Lingo (baseball); Pageland, S.C. **(1911–1985)**
Munson, Thurman (baseball); Akron, Ohio **(1947–1979)**
Murphy, Calvin (basketball); Norwalk, Conn., 5/9/48
Murray, Eddie (baseball); Los Angeles, Calif., 2/24/56
Musial, Stan (baseball); Donora, Pa., 11/21/20
Myers, Linda (archery); York, Pa., 6/19/47
Naber, John (swimming); Evanston, Ill., 1/20/56
Namath, Joe (Joseph William) (football); Beaver Falls, Pa., 5/31/43
Nastase, Ilie (tennis); Bucharest, 7/19/46
Navratilova, Martina (tennis); Prague, 10/18/56
Nehemiah, Renaldo (track); Newark, N.J., 3/24/59
Nelson, Cindy (skiing); Lutsen, Minn., 8/19/55
Newcombe, John (tennis); Sydney, Australia, 5/23/43
Niekro, Phil (baseball); Lansing, Ohio, 4/1/39
Nicklaus, Jack (golf); Columbus, Ohio, 1/21/40
Norman, Gregory (golf); Mount Isa, Australia, 2/10/55
Oerter, Al (discus thrower); New York City, 9/19/36
Olajuwon, Hakeem (basketball); Lagos, Nigeria, 1/21/63
Oldfield, Barney (racing driver); Fulton County, Ohio **(1878–1946)**
Oliva, Tony (Pedro) (baseball); Pinar Del Rio, Cuba, 7/20/40
Olsen, Merlin Jay (football); Logan, Utah, 9/15/40
O'Malley, Walter (baseball executive); New York City **(1903–1979)**
O'Neal, Shaquille (basketball); Newark, N.J., 3/6/72
Orantes, Manuel (tennis); Granada, Spain, 2/6/49
Orr, Bobby (hockey); Parry Sound, Ontario, Canada, 3/20/48
Ovett, Steve (track); Brighton, England, 10/9/55
Owens, Jesse (track); Decatur, Ala. **(1914–1980)**
Paige, Satchell (Leroy) (baseball); Mobile, Ala. **(1906–1982)**
Palmer, Arnold (golf); Latrobe, Pa., 9/10/29
Palmer, James Alvin (baseball); New York City, 10/15/45
Parent, Bernard Marcel (hockey); Montreal, 4/3/45
Park, Brad (Douglas Bradford) (hockey); Toronto, Ontario, Canada, 7/6/48
Parseghian, Ara (football); Akron, Ohio, 5/21/23
Pasarell, Charles (tennis); San Juan, Puerto Rico, 2/12/44
Patterson, Floyd (boxing); Waco, N.C., 1/4/35
Peete, Calvin (golf); Detroit, Mich., 7/18/43
Pelé (Edson Arantes do Nascimento) (soccer); Tres Coracoes, Brazil, 10/23/40
Perry, Gaylord (baseball); Williamston, N.C., 9/15/38
Perry, Jim (baseball); Williamston, N.C., 10/30/36
Petrovic, Drazen (basketball); Yugoslavia **(1965–1993)**
Pettit, Bob (basketball); Baton Rouge, La., 12/12/32
Petty, Richard Lee (auto racing); Randleman, N.C., 7/2/37
Pincay, Laffit, Jr. (jockey); Panama City, Panama, 12/29/46
Plager, Barclay (ice hockey); Kirkland Lake, Ontario **(1941–1988)**
Plante, Jacques (hockey); Sahwinigan Falls, Quebec, Canada, 1/17/29
Player, Gary (golf); Johannesburg, South Africa, 11/1/35
Plunkett, Jim (football); San Jose, Calif., 12/5/47
Potvin, Denis Charles (hockey); Hull, Quebec, Canada, 10/29/53
Powell, Boog (John) (baseball); Lakeland, Fla., 8/17/41
Powell, Mike (track); Philadelphia, 11/10/63
Prefontaine, Steve Roland (runner); Coos Bay, Ore. **(1951–1975)**
Prince, Bob (baseball announcer); Pittsburgh **(1917–1985)**
Proell, Annemarie Moser (Alpine skier); Kleinarl, Austria, 3/27/53
Ralston, Dennis (tennis); Bakersfield, Calif., 7/27/42

Rankin, Judy Torluemke (golf); St. Louis, Mo., 2/18/45
Raschi, Vic (baseball); West Springfield, Mass. **(1919–1988)**
Ratelle, Jean (Joseph Gilbert Yvon Jean) (hockey); St. Jean, Quebec, Canada, 10/29/53
Rawls, Betsy (Elizabeth Earle) (golf); Spartanburg, S.C., 5/4/28
Reed, Willis (basketball); Hico, La., 6/25/42
Reese, Pee Wee (Harold) (baseball); Ekron, Ky., 7/23/19
Resch, Glenn "Chico" (hockey); Moose Jaw, Saskatchewan, Canada, 7/10/48
Rice, Jerry (football); Crawford, Miss., 10/13/62
Richard, Maurice (hockey); Montreal, 8/14/24
Riessen, Martin (tennis); Hinsdale, Ill., 12/4/41
Rigney, William (baseball); Alameda, Calif., 1/29/18
Ripken, Cal, Jr. (baseball); Havre de Grace, Md., 8/24/60
Rizzuto, Phil (baseball); New York City, 9/25/18
Robertson, Oscar (basketball); Charlotte, Tenn., 11/24/38
Robinson, Arnie (track); San Diego, Calif., 4/7/48
Robinson, Brooks (baseball); Little Rock, Ark., 5/18/37
Robinson, Dave (basketball); Key West, Fla., 8/6/65
Robinson, Frank (baseball); Beaumont, Tex., 8/31/35
Robinson, Jackie (baseball); Cairo, Ga. **(1919–1972)**
Robinson, Larry Clark (hockey); Marvelville, Ontario, Canada, 6/2/51
Robinson, "Sugar" Ray (boxing); Detroit **(1920–1989)**
Rockne, Knute Kenneth (football); Voss, Norway **(1888–1931)**
Rockwell, Martha (skiing); Providence, R.I., 4/26/44
Rono, Harry (track); Kiptaragon, Kenya, 2/12/52
Rooney, Art (football); Pittsburgh, Pa. **(1901–1988)**
Rose, Pete (Peter Edward) (baseball); Cincinnati, 4/14/42
Rosenbloom, Maxie (boxing); New York City **(1904–1976)**
Rosewall, Ken (tennis); Sydney, Australia, 11/2/34
Rote, Kyle (football); San Antonio, 10/27/28
Roush, Edd (baseball); Oakland City, Ind. **(1893–1988)**
Rozelle, Pete (Alvin Ray) (commissioner of National Football League); South Gate, Calif. **(1926–1996)**
Rudolph, Wilma Glodean (sprinter); St. Bethlehem, Tenn. **(1940–1994)**
Russell, Bill (basketball); Monroe, La., 2/12/34
Ruth, Babe (George Herman Ruth) (baseball); Baltimore **(1895–1948)**
Rutherford, Johnny (auto racing); Fort Worth, 3/12/38
Ryan, Nolan (Lynn Nolan, Jr.) (baseball); Refugio, Tex., 1/31/47
Ryon, Luann (archery); Long Beach, Calif., 1/13/53
Ryun, Jim (runner); Wichita, Kan., 4/29/47
Salazar, Alberto (track); Havana, 8/7/58
Sampras, Pete (tennis); Washington, D.C., 8/12/71
Samuels, Howard (horse racing soccer); New York City **(1920–1984)**
Sanders, Barry (football); Wichita, Kan., 7/16/68
Sanders, Deion (baseball/football); Ft. Myers, Fla., 8/9/67
Santana, Manuel (Manuel Santana Martinez) (tennis); Chamartin, Spain, 5/10/38
Sayers, Gale (football); Wichita, Kan., 5/30/43
Schmidt, Mike (baseball); Dayton, Ohio, 9/27/49
Schoendienst, Red (Albert) (baseball); Germantown, Ill., 2/2/23
Schollander, Donald (swimming); Charlotte, N.C., 4/30/46
Seagren, Bob (Robert Lloyd) (pole vaulter); Pomona, Calif., 10/17/46
Seau, Junior (football); Oceanside, Calif., 1/19/69
Seaver, Tom (baseball); Fresno, Calif., 11/17/44
Seidler, Maren (track); Brooklyn, N.Y., 6/11/62
Selke, Frank (ice hockey); Canada **(1893–1985)**
Sewell, Joe (baseball); Titus, Ala. **(1898–1990)**
Shepherd, Lee (auto racing) **(1945–1985)**
Shero, Fred (hockey); Camden, N.J. **(1945–1990)**
Shoemaker, Willie (jockey); Fabens, Tex., 8/19/31
Shore, Eddie (ice hockey); Saskatchewan, Canada **(1902–1985)**
Shorter, Frank (runner); Munich, Germany, 10/31/47
Shriver, Pam (tennis); Baltimore, 7/4/62
Shula, Don (Donald Francis) (football); Grand River, Ohio, 1/4/30
Silvester, Jay (discus thrower); Tremonton, Utah, 2/27/37
Simpson, O.J. (Orenthal James) (football); San Francisco, 7/9/47
Sims, Billy (football); St. Louis, 9/18/55
Smith, Bubba (Charles Aaron) (football); Orange, Tex., 2/28/45
Smith, Emmitt (football); Escambia, Fla., 5/15/69
Smith, Ozzie (baseball); Mobile, Ala., 12/26/54
Smith, Ronnie Ray (sprinter); Los Angeles, 3/28/49
Smith, Stanley Roger (tennis); Pasadena, Calif., 12/14/46
Smith, Tommie (sprinter); Clarksville, Tex., 6/5/44
Smoke, Marcia Jones (canoeing); Oklahoma City, 7/18/41
Snead, Sam (golf); Hot Springs, Va., 5/27/12
Sneva, Tom (auto racing); Spokane, Wash., 6/1/48
Snider, Duke (Edwin) (baseball); Los Angeles, 9/19/26
Solomon, Harold (tennis); Washington, D.C., 9/17/52
Spahn, Warren (baseball); Buffalo, N.Y., 4/23/21
Speaker, Tristram (baseball); Hubbard City, Tex. **(1888–1958)**
Spencer, Brian (ice hockey); Fort St. James, British Columbia **(1949–1988)**
Spinks, Leon (boxing); St. Louis, 7/11/53
Spitz, Mark (swimming); Modesto, Calif., 2/10/50
Stabler, Kenneth (football); Foley, Ala., 12/25/45

Stagg, Amos Alonzo (football); West Orange, N.J. (1862–1965)
Stargell, Willie (Wilver Dornell) (baseball); Earlsboro, Okla., 3/6/41
Starr, Bart (football); Montgomery, Ala., 1/9/34
Staub, "Rusty" (Daniel) (baseball); New Orleans, 4/4/44
Staubach, Roger (football); Cincinnati, 2/5/42
Steinkraus, William C. (equestrian); Cleveland, 10/12/25
Stenerud, Jan (football); Fetsund, Norway, 11/26/42
Stengel, Casey (Charles Dillon) (baseball); Kansas City, Mo. (1891–1975)
Stenmark, Ingemar (Alpine skier); Tarnaby, Sweden, 3/18/56
Stevens, Scott (hockey); Completon, New Brunswick, 5/4/66
Stockton, Richard LaClede (tennis); New York City, 2/18/51
Stones, Dwight Edwin (track); Los Angeles, 12/6/53
Strawberry, Darryl (baseball); Los Angeles, 3/12/62
Sullivan, John Lawrence (boxing); Boston (1858–1918)
Summitt, Pat (basketball); Henrietta, Tenn., 6/14/52
Sutton, Don (Donald Howard) (baseball); Clio, Ala., 4/2/45
Swann, Lynn (football); Alcoa, Tenn., 3/7/52
Tanner, Leonard Roscoe III (tennis); Chattanooga, Tenn., 10/15/51
Tarkenton, Fran (Francis) (football); Richmond, Va., 2/3/40
Tebbetts, Birdie (George R.) (baseball); Nashua, N.H., 11/10/14
Theismann, Joe (football); New Brunswick, N.J., 9/9/46
Thomas, Frank (baseball); Columbus, Ga., 5/27/68
Thomas, Isiah (basketball); Chicago, Ill., 4/30/61
Thomas, Thurman (football); Houston, Texas, 5/16/66
Thompson, David (basketball); Shelby, N.C., 7/13/54
Thorpe, Jim (James Francis) (all-around athlete); nr. Prague, Okla. (1888–1953)
Tilden, William Tatem II (tennis); Philadelphia (1893–1953)
Tittle, Y. A. (Yelberton Abraham) (football); Marshall, Tex., 10/24/26
Toomey, William (decathlon); Philadelphia, 1/10/39
Trevino, Lee (golf); Dallas, 12/1/39
Trottier, Bryan (hockey); Val Marie, Sask., Canada, 7/17/56
Tunney, Gene (James J.) (boxing); New York City (1898–1978)
Tyus, Wyomia (runner); Griffin, Ga., 8/29/45
Ueberroth, Peter (baseball); Evanston, Ill., 9/2/37
Unitas, John (football); Pittsburgh, 5/7/33
Unser, Al (auto racing); Albuquerque, N. Mex., 5/29/39
Unser, Bobby (auto racing); Albuquerque, N. Mex., 2/20/34
Valenzuela, Fernando (baseball); Sonora, Mexico, 11/1/60
Valvano, Jim (basketball); New York, N.Y. (1946–1993)
Van Brocklin, Norm (football); Eagle Butte, S. Dak. (1926–1983)
Vaughn, Mo (baseball); Norwalk, Conn., 12/15/67
Vilas, Guillermo (tennis); Mar del Plata, Argentina, 8/17/52

Viola, Frank (baseball); Hempstead, N.Y., 4/19/60
Viren, Lasse (track); Myrskyla, Finland, 7/12/49
Vitale, Dick (basketball); E. Rutherford, N.J., 6/9/39
Wade, Virginia (tennis); Bournemouth, England, 7/10/45
Wagner, Honus (John Peter Honus) (baseball); Carnegie, Pa. (1867–1955)
Waitz, Grete (Andersen) (running); Oslo, Norway, 10/1/53
Walcott, Jersey Joe (Arnold Cream) (boxing); Merchantville, N.J. (1914–1994)
Wallace, Rusty (auto racing); St. Louis, Mo., 8/14/56
Walsh, Adam (football) (1902–1985)
Walton, Bill (basketball); La Mesa, Calif., 11/5/52
Waterfield, Bob (football); Burbank, Calif (1921–1983)
Watson, Martha Rae (track); Long Beach, Calif., 8/19/46
Watson, Tom (golf); Kansas City, Mo., 9/4/49
Weaver, Earl (baseball); St. Louis, 8/14/30
Weiskopf, Tom (golf); Massillon, Ohio, 11/9/42
Weiss, George (baseball executive); New Haven, Conn. (1895–1972)
Weissmuller, Johnny (swimmer and actor); Windber, Pa. (1904–1984)
West, Jerry (basketball); Cheylan, W. Va., 5/28/38
White, Reggie (football); Chattanooga, Tenn., 12/19/61
White, Willye B. (long jumper); Money, Miss., 1/1/36
Whitworth, Kathy (golf); Monahans, Tex., 9/27/39
Wilkens, Mac Maurice (track); Eugene, Ore., 11/15/50
Wilkins, Lennie (basketball) 11/25/37
Wilkinson, Bud (football); Minneapolis, 4/23/16
Williams, Dick (baseball); St. Louis, 5/7/29
Williams, Ted (baseball); San Diego, Calif., 8/30/18
Wills, Maury (baseball); Washington, D.C., 10/2/32
Winfield, Dave (baseball); St. Paul, Minn., 10/3/51
Wohlhuter, Richard C. (runner); Geneva, Ill., 12/23/45
Wood, "Smokey" (Joseph) (baseball); Kansas City, Mo. (1890–1985)
Woodhead, Cynthia (swimming); Riverside, Calif., 2/7/64
Woods, Tiger (Eldrick) (golf); Long Beach, Calif.,, 12/30/75
Wottle, David James (runner); Canton, Ohio, 8/7/50
Wright, Mickey (Mary Kathryn) (golf); San Diego, Calif., 2/14/35
Yarborough, Cale (William Caleb) (auto racing); Timmonsville, S.C., 3/27/39
Yarbrough, Leeroy (auto racing); Jacksonville, Fla. (1938–1984)
Yastrzemski, Carl (baseball); Southampton, N.Y., 8/22/39
Young, Cy (Denton True) (baseball); Gilmore, Ohio (1867–1955)
Young, Sheila (speed skater, bicycle racer); Detroit, 10/14/50
Young, Steve (football); Salt Lake City, Utah, 10/11/61
Zaharias, Babe Didrikson (golf); Port Arthur, Tex. (1913–1956)

Weightlifting

U.S. WEIGHTLIFTING FEDERATION

MEN'S NATIONAL CHAMPIONSHIPS

(April 25–27, 1997, Blaine, Minn.)

	Snatch	C&J[1]	Total[2]
54 kg—Shelton Gilyard	85.0	110.0	195.0
59 kg—Brian Okada	95.0	120.0	215.0
64 kg—Bryan Jacob	120.0	145.0	265.0
70 kg—Oscar Chaplin III	132.5	165.0	297.5
76 kg—Tim McRae	150.0	180.0	330.0
83 kg—Kevin Dittler	132.5	160.0	292.5
91 kg—David Conragan	132.5	167.5	300.0
99 kg—Tom Gough	165.0	210.0	375.0
108 kg—Wes Barnett	165.0	210.0	375.0
108+ kg—Shane Hamman	165.0	197.5	362.5

1. Clean and jerk. 2. All results in kilograms.

WOMEN'S NATIONAL CHAMPIONSHIPS

(April 25–27, 1997, Blaine, Minn.)

	Snatch	C&J[1]	Total[2]
46 kg—Andrea Lyons	57.5	80.0	137.5
50 kg—Tara Nott	65.0	90.0	155.0
54 kg—Melanie Pritchard	72.5	95.0	167.5
59 kg—Christina Wilson	82.5	100.0	182.5
64 kg—Lee Rentmeester	95.0	112.5	207.5
70 kg—Cara Heads	77.5	105.0	182.5
76 kg—Khadijah Hunter	90.5	105.0	195.5
83 kg—Vikki Scaffe	87.5	100.0	187.5
83+ kg—Decia Stenzel	97.5	110.0	207.5

1. Clean and jerk. 2. All results in kilograms.

Basketball

Basketball may be the one sport whose exact origin is definitely known. In the winter of 1891–92, Dr. James Naismith, an instructor in the Y.M.C.A. Training College (now Springfield College) at Springfield, Mass., deliberately invented the game of basketball in order to provide indoor exercise and competition for the students between the closing of the football season and the opening of the baseball season. He affixed peach baskets overhead on the walls at opposite ends of the gymnasium and organized teams to play his new game in which the purpose was to toss an association (soccer) ball into one basket and prevent the opponents from tossing the ball into the other basket. The game is fundamentally the same today, though there have been improvements in equipment and some changes in rules.

Because Dr. Naismith had eighteen available players when he invented the game, the first rule was: "There shall be nine players on each side." Later the number of players became optional, depending upon the size of the available court, but the five-player standard was adopted when the game spread over the country. United States soldiers brought basketball to Europe in World War I, and it soon became a world-wide sport.

College Basketball

NATIONAL COLLEGIATE A.A. CHAMPIONS

1939 Oregon	1953 Indiana	1967–73 U.C.L.A.	1987 Indiana
1940 Indiana	1954 La Salle	1974 No. Carolina State	1988 Kansas
1941 Wisconsin	1955 San Francisco	1975 U.C.L.A.	1989 Michigan
1942 Stanford	1956 San Francisco	1976 Indiana	1990 Nevada-Las Vegas
1943 Wyoming	1957 North Carolina	1977 Marquette	1991 Duke
1944 Utah	1958 Kentucky	1978 Kentucky	1992 Duke
1945 Oklahoma A & M	1959 California	1979 Michigan State	1993 North Carolina
1946 Oklahoma A & M	1960 Ohio State	1980 Louisville	1994 Arkansas
1947 Holy Cross	1961 Cincinnati	1981 Indiana	1995 U.C.L.A.
1948 Kentucky	1962 Cincinnati	1982 North Carolina	1996 Kentucky
1949 Kentucky	1963 Loyola (Chicago)	1983 North Carolina State	1997 Arizona
1950 C.C.N.Y.	1964 U.C.L.A.	1984 Georgetown	
1951 Kentucky	1965 U.C.L.A.	1985 Villanova	
1952 Kansas	1966 Texas Western	1986 Louisville	

NATIONAL INVITATION TOURNAMENT (NIT) CHAMPIONS

1939 Long Island U.	1955 Duquesne	1970 Marquette	1985 U.C.L.A.
1940 Colorado	1956 Louisville	1971 North Carolina	1986 Ohio State
1941 Long Island U.	1957 Bradley	1972 Maryland	1987 So. Mississippi
1942 West Virginia	1958 Xavier (Cincinnati)	1973 Virginia Tech	1988 Connecticut
1943–44 St. John's (N.Y.C.)	1959 St. John's (N.Y.C.)	1974 Purdue	1989 St. John's
1945 DePaul	1960 Bradley	1975 Princeton	1990 Vanderbilt
1946 Kentucky	1961 Providence	1976 Kentucky	1991 Stanford
1947 Utah	1962 Dayton	1977 St. Bonaventure	1992 Virginia
1948 St. Louis	1963 Providence	1978 Texas	1993 Minnesota
1949 San Francisco	1964 Bradley	1979 Indiana	1994 Villanova
1950 C.C.N.Y.	1965 St. John's (N.Y.C.)	1980 Virginia	1995 Virginia Tech
1951 Brigham Young	1966 Brigham Young	1981 Tulsa	1996 Nebraska
1952 La Salle	1967 So. Illinois	1982 Bradley	1997 Michigan
1953 Seton Hall	1968 Dayton	1983 Fresno State	
1954 Holy Cross	1969 Temple	1984 Michigan	

N.C.A.A. MAJOR COLLEGE INDIVIDUAL SCORING RECORDS

Single Season Averages

Player, Team	Year	G	FG	FT	Pts	Avg
Pete Maravich, Louisiana State	1969–70	31	522[1]	337	1,381[1]	44.5[1]
Pete Maravich	1968–69	26	433	282	1,148	44.2
Pete Maravich	1967–68	26	432	274	1,138	43.8
Frank Selvy, Furman	1953–54	29	427	355[1]	1,209	41.7
Johnny Neumann, Mississippi	1970–71	23	366	191	923	40.1
Freeman Williams, Portland State	1976–77	26	417	176	1,010	38.8
Billy McGill, Utah	1961–62	26	394	221	1,009	38.8
Calvin Murphy, Niagara	1967–68	24	337	242	9,16	38.2
Austin Carr, Notre Dame	1969–70	29	444	218	1,106	38.1

1. Record.

N.C.A.A. CAREER SCORING TOTALS

Division I

Player, Team	Last year	G	FG	FT	Pts	Avg
Pete Maravich, Louisiana State	1970	83	1,387[1]	893[1]	3,667[1]	44.2[1]
Austin Carr, Notre Dame	1971	74	1,017	526	2,560	34.6
Oscar Robertson, Cincinnati	1960	88	1,052	869	2,973	33.8
Calvin Murphy, Niagara	1970	77	947	654	2,548	33.1
Dwight Lamar[2]	1973	57	768	326	1,862	32.7
Frank Selvy, Furman	1954	78	922	694	2,538	32.5
Rick Mount, Purdue	1970	72	910	503	2,323	32.3
Darrel Floyd, Furman	1956	71	868	545	2,281	32.1
Nick Werkman, Seton Hall	1964	71	812	649	2,273	32.0

1. Record. 2. Also played two seasons in college division.

Division II

Player, Team	Last year	G	FG	FT	Pts	Avg
Travis Grant, Kentucky State	1972	121	1,760[1]	525	4,045[1]	33.4[1]
John Rinka, Kenyon	1970	99	1,261	729	3,251	32.8
Florindo Vieira, Quinnipiac	1957	69	761	741	2,263	32.8
Willie Shaw, Lane	1964	76	960	459	2,379	31.3
Mike Davis, Virginia Union	1969	89	1,014	730	2,758	31.0
Henry Logan, Western Carolina	1968	107	1,263	764	3,290	30.7
Willie Scott, Alabama State	1969	103	1,277	601	3,155	30.6
Gregg Northington, Alabama State	1972	75	894	403	2,191	29.2
Bob Hopkins, Grambling	1956	126	1,403	953	3,759	29.8

1. Record.

TOP SINGLE-GAME SCORING MARKS

Player, Team (Opponent)	Yr	Pts	Player, Team (Opponent)	Yr	Pts
Selvy, Furman (Newberry)	1954	100[1]	Maravich, LSU (Alabama)	1970	69
Arizin, Villanova (Phi. NAMC)	1949	85	Murphy, Niagara (Syracuse)	1969	68
Williams, Portland State (Rocky Mtn.)	1978	81	Floyd, Furman (Morehead)	1955	67
Mlkvy, Temple (Wilkes)	1951	73	Maravich, LSU (Tulane)	1969	66
Bradshaw, U.S. International (Loyola-CA)	1991	72	Handlan, W & L (Furman)	1951	66
Williams, Portland State (So. Oregon)	1977	71	Roberts, Oral Roberts (N.C. A&T)	1977	66

1. Record.

MEN'S N.C.A.A. BASKETBALL CHAMPIONSHIPS—1997

Division I

First Round—East
Texas 71, Wisconsin 58
Coppin State 78, South Carolina 65
New Mexico 59, Old Dominion 55
Louisville 65, Massachusetts 57
California 55, Princeton 52
Villanova 101, Long Island 91
North Carolina 82, Fairfield 74
Colorado 80, Indiana 62

First Round—Southeast
Chattanooga 73, Georgia 70
Illinois 90, USC 77
Providence 81, Marquette 59
Duke 71, Murray St. 68
Kansas 78, Jackson State 64
Purdue 83, Rhode Island 76 (OT)
Coll. of Charleston 77, Maryland 66
Arizona 65, South Alabama 57

First Round—Midwest
Clemson 68, Miami (Ohio) 56
Tulsa 81, Boston Univ. 52
Temple 62, Mississippi 40
Minnesota 78, S.W. Texas St. 46
Cincinnati 86, Butler 69
Iowa State 69, Illinois State 57
Xavier 80, Vanderbilt 66
UCLA 109, Charleston South. 75

First Round—West
UNC–Charlotte 79, Georgetown 67
Utah 75, Navy 61
Wake Forest 68, St. Mary's 46

Stanford 80, Oklahoma 67
Boston Coll. 73, Valparaiso 66
St. Joseph's 75, Pacific 65
Kentucky 92, Montana 54
Iowa 73, Virginia 60

Second Round—East
Louisville 64, New Mexico 63
Texas 82, Coppin State 81
North Carolina 73, Colorado 56
California 75, Villanova 68

Second Round—Southeast
Providence 98, Duke 87
Chattanooga 75, Illinois 63
Kansas 75, Purdue 61
Arizoza 73, Coll. of Charleston 69

Second Round—Midwest
Clemson 65, Tulsa 59
Minnesota 76, Temple 57
Iowa State 67, Cincinnati 66
UCLA 96, Xavier 83

Second Round—West
Utah 77, UNC–Charlotte 58
Stanford 72, Wake Forest 66
St. Joseph's 81, Boston College 77
Kentucky 75, Iowa 69

Third Round—East
Louisville 78, Texas 63
North Carolina 63, California 57

Third Round—Southeast
Arizona 85, Kansas 82
Providence 71, Chattanooga 65

Third Round—Midwest
Minnesota 90, Clemson 84 (2OT)
UCLA 74, Iowa St. 73 (OT)

Third Round—West
Utah 82, Stanford 77 (OT)
Kentucky 83, St. Joseph's 68

Regional Finals
East—North Carolina 97, Louisville 74
Southeast—Arizona 96, Providence 92 (OT)
Midwest—Minnesota 80, UCLA 72
West—Kentucky 72, Utah 59

National Semifinals
March 29, 1997, RCA Dome, Indianapolis.
Arizona 66, North Carolina 58
Kentucky 78, Minnesota 69

National Final
March 31, 1997, RCA Dome, Indianapolis.
Arizona 84, Kentucky 79

Division II

Semifinals
California State–Bakersfield 81, Salem–Teikyo 68
Northern Kentucky 79, Lynn 58

Championship
California State–Bakersfield 57, Northern Kentucky 56

WOMEN'S N.C.A.A. CHAMPIONSHIPS—1997

Division I
First Round—East
North Carolina 78, Harvard 53
Michigan State 75, Portland 70
George Washington 61, Northwestern 46
Tulane 72, UC–Santa Barbara 69
Notre Dame 93, Memphis 62
Texas 66, S.W. Texas State 38
St. Joseph's 70, Kansas State 52
Alabama 94, St. Francis 50
First Round—Midwest
Connecticut 103, Lehigh 35
Iowa 56, North Carolina State 50
Duke 71, DePaul 56
Illinois 79, Drake 62
Oregon 80, San Diego State 68
Tennessee 91, Grambling 54
Stephen F. Austin 79, Toledo 66
Colorado 69, Marshall 49
First Round—Mideast
Old Dominion 102, Liberty 52
Purdue 74, Maryland 48
Marquette 70, Clemson 66
LSU 88, Maine 79
USC 68, San Francisco 55
Florida 92, Florida International 68
Auburn 65, Louisville 65
L.A. Tech 94, St. Peter's 50
First Round—West
Stanford 111, Howard 59
Texas TEch 47, Montana 45
Utah 66, Iowa State 57

Virginia 96, Troy State 74
Vanderbilt 74, Washington 62
Kansas 81, Detroit 67
Arizona 76, W. Kentucky 54
Georgia 91, E. Kentucky 55
Second Round—East
North Carolina 81, Michigan State 71
George Washington 81, Tulane 67
Notre Dame 86, Texas 83
St. Joseph's 52, Alabama 61
Second Round—Midwest
Connecticut 72, Iowa 53
Illinois 85, Duke 67
Tennessee 76, Oregon 59
Colorado 66, Stephen F. Austin 57
Second Round—Mideast
Old Dominion 69, Purdue 65
LSU 71, Marquette 58
Florida 92, USC 78
L.A. Tech 74, Auburn 48
Second Round—West
Stanford 67, Texas Tech 45
Virginia 65, Utah 46
Vanderbilt 51, Kansas 44
Georgia 80, Arizona 74
Third Round—East
George Washington 55, North Carolina 46
Notre Dame 87, Alabama 71
Third Round—Midwest
Connecticut 78, Illinois 71
Tennessee 75, Colorado 67

Third Round—Mideast
Old Dominion 62, LSU 49
Florida 71, L.A. Tech 57
Third Round—West
Stanford 91, Virginia 69
Georgia 66, Vanderbilt 52
Regional Finals
East—Notre Dame 62, George Washington 52
Midwest—Tennessee 91, Connecticut 81
Mideast—Old Dominion 53, Florida 51
West—Stanford 82, Georgia 47
National Semifinals
March 28, 1997, Cincinnati, Ohio
Tennessee 80, Notre Dame 66
Old Dominion 83, Stanford 82
National Championship
March 30, 1997, Cincinnati, Ohio
Tennessee 68, Old Dominion 59

Division II
Semifinals
Southern Indiana 70, UC–Davis 62
North Dakota 70, Bentley 48
Championship
North Dakota 94, Southern Indiana 78

Division III
Semifinals
New York Univ. 84, Scranton 72
Wis.–Eau Claire 77, Capital 63
Championship
New York Univ. 72, Wis.–Eau Claire 70

LEADING N.C.A.A. MEN—1996–97

Scoring

	FG%	3FG/Att	FT%	Pts	Avg
Charles Jones, LIU-Brooklyn	.451	109/303	.634	903	30.1
Ed Gray, California	.461	38/126	.790	644	24.8
Adonal Foyle, Colgate	.565	1/7	.487	682	24.4
Raymond Tutt, UC-Santa Barbara	.515	55/118	.800	649	24.0
Antonio Daniels, Bowling Green	.547	45/104	.777	767	24.0
Donnie Carr, La Salle	.350	99/289	.768	646	23.9
Olivier Saint Jean, San Jose St.	.492	26/71	.730	619	23.8
James Cotton, Long Beach St	.439	63/171	.833	634	23.5
Roderick Blakney, S. Carolina St.	.428	61/101	.738	655	23.4
Cory Carr, Texas Tech.	.427	94/249	.792	646	23.1

Rebounding

	Gm	No	Avg
Tim Duncan, Wake Forest	31	457	14.7
Adonal Foyle, Colgate	28	368	13.1
Lorenzo Coleman, Tennessee Tech.	28	333	11.9
Tony Battie, Texas Tech.	28	329	11.8
Muntrelle Dobbins, Arkansas-LR	28	320	11.4
Eric Taylor, St. Francis-PA	27	306	11.3
Kory Billups, Chicago St.	27	304	11.3
Nate Huffman, Central Mich.	26	287	11.0
Greg Smith, Delaware	31	342	11.0
H. L. Coleman, Wyoming	28	303	10.8

Assists

	Gm	No	Avg
Kenny Mitchell, Dartmouth	26	203	7.8
Brevin Knight, Stanford	30	234	7.8
Kareem Gilbert, Tennessee St.	25	191	7.6
Jamar Nesbit, Illinois St.	30	219	7.3
Chad Peckinpaugh, Eastern Ill.	27	196	7.3
Anthony Johnson, Charleston (S.C.)	32	229	7.2
Chad Townsend, Murray St.	30	212	7.1
Ed Cota, North Carolina	34	234	6.9
Ali Ton, Davidson	28	190	6.8
Antonio Daniels, Bowling Green	32	216	6.8

LEADING N.C.A.A. WOMEN—1996–97

Scoring

	Gm	Pts	Avg
Cindy Blodgett, Maine	30	810	27.0
Kim Williams, DePaul	29	727	25.1
Sheila Danker, New Hampshire	28	683	24.4
Amy Kieckbusch, Morehead St.	28	670	23.9
Vita Redding, Brown	26	618	23.8
Alicia Thompson, Texas Tech.	29	686	23.7
Korie Hlede, Duquesne	28	634	22.6
Tina Thompson, USC	29	653	22.5
Kisa Bradley, Oral Roberts	26	580	22.3
Diane Seng, Tennessee Tech.	29	644	22.2

Rebounding

	Gm	No	Avg
Etoila Mitchell, Georgia St.	25	330	13.2
Angie Iverson, Minnesota	28	344	12.3
Melanie Halker, Siena	28	341	12.2
Mfon Udoka, DePaul	28	339	12.1
Karen Johnson, Delaware St.	28	327	11.7
Kathy Caldwell, New Hampshire	28	321	11.5
Pam Durkin, Rider	27	307	11.4
Amber Hall, Washington	22	244	11.1
Angie Potthoff, Penn St.	27	299	11.1
Dana Wynne, Seton Hall	27	295	10.9

Assists

	Gm	No	Avg
Tamika Matlock, Michigan St.	30	229	7.6
Alli Bills, Utah	28	213	7.6
Jade Hyett, Washington St.	27	205	7.6
Ticha Penicheiro, Old Dominion	36	271	7.5
Kelley Westhoff, Northern Iowa	25	180	7.2
Gina Graziani, Miami-Fla.	29	198	6.8
Katy Winski, Loyola-Ill.	26	177	6.8
Tredena Robinson, Troy St.	30	204	6.8
Heather Fiore, Canisius	27	182	6.7
Nicki Taggart, Marquette	31	206	6.6

OTHER TOURNAMENTS—1996–1997

MEN
NIT—Michigan 82, Florida State 72
NAIA Div. I—Life, Ga. 73, Oklahoma Baptist 64
NAIA Div. II—Bethel, Ind. 95, Siena Heights, Mich. 94

WOMEN
NAIA Div. I—Southern Nazarene (Okla.) 78, Union (Tenn.), 73Life, Ga. 73, Oklahoma Baptist 64
NAIA Div. II—NW Nazarene (Idaho) 64, Black Hills St. (S.D.) 46

Professional Basketball

NATIONAL BASKETBALL ASSOCIATION CHAMPIONS

Source: National Basketball Association.

The National Basketball Association was originally the Basketball Association of America. It took its current name in 1949 when it merged with the National Basketball League.

Season	Eastern Conference (W-L)	Western Conference (W-L)	Playoff Champions[1]
1946–47	Washington Capitols (49-11)	Chicago Stags (39-22)	Philadelphia Warriors
1947–48	Philadelphia Warriors (27-21)	St. Louis Bombers (29-19)	Baltimore Bullets
1948–49	Washington Capitols (38-22)	Rochester Royals (45-15)	Minneapolis Lakers
1949–50	Syracuse Nationals (51-13)	Indianapolis Olympians (39-25)	Minneapolis Lakers
1950–51	Philadelphia Warriors (40-26)	Minneapolis Lakers (44-24)	Rochester Royals
1951–52	Syracuse Nationals (40-26)	Rochester Royals (41-25)	Minneapolis Lakers
1952–53	New York Knickerbockers (47-23)	Minneapolis Lakers (48-22)	Minneapolis Lakers
1953–54	New York Knickerbockers (44-28)	Minneapolis Lakers (46-26)	Minneapolis Lakers
1954–55	Syracuse Nationals (43-29)	Ft. Wayne Pistons (43-29)	Syracuse Nationals
1955–56	Philadelphia Warriors (45-27)	Ft. Wayne Pistons (37-35)	Philadelphia Warriors
1956–57	Boston Celtics (44-28)	St. Louis Hawks (38-34)	Boston Celtics
1957–58	Boston Celtics (48-23)	St. Louis Hawks (41-31)	St. Louis Hawks
1958–59	Boston Celtics (52-20)	St. Louis Hawks (49-23)	Boston Celtics
1959–60	Boston Celtics (59-16)	St. Louis Hawks (46-29)	Boston Celtics
1960–61	Boston Celtics (57-22)	St. Louis Hawks (51-28)	Boston Celtics
1961–62	Boston Celtics (60-20)	Los Angeles Lakers (54-26)	Boston Celtics
1962–63	Boston Celtics (58-22)	Los Angeles Lakers (53-27)	Boston Celtics
1963–64	Boston Celtics (59-21)	San Francisco Warriors (48-32)	Boston Celtics
1964–65	Boston Celtics (62-18)	Los Angeles Lakers (49-31)	Boston Celtics
1965–66	Philadelphia 76ers (55-25)	Los Angeles Lakers (45-35)	Boston Celtics
1966–67	Philadelphia 76ers (68-13)	San Francisco Warriors (44-37)	Philadelphia 76ers
1967–68	Philadelphia 76ers (62-20)	St. Louis Hawks (56-26)	Boston Celtics
1968–69	Baltimore Bullets (57-25)	Los Angeles Lakers (55-27)	Boston Celtics
1969–70	New York Knickerbockers (60-22)	Atlanta Hawks (48-34)	New York Knicks
1970–71	Baltimore Bullets (42-40)	Milwaukee Bucks (66-16)	Milwaukee Bucks
1971–72	New York Knickerbockers (48-34)	Los Angeles Lakers (69-13)	Los Angeles Lakers
1972–73	New York Knickerbockers (57-25)	Los Angeles Lakers (60-22)	New York Knicks
1973–74	Boston Celtics (56-26)	Milwaukee Bucks (59-23)	Boston Celtics
1974–75	Washington Bullets (60-22)	Golden State Warriors (48-34)	Golden State Warriors
1975–76	Boston Celtics (54-28)	Phoenix Suns (42-40)	Boston Celtics
1976–77	Philadelphia 76ers (50-32)	Portland Trail Blazers (49-33)	Portland Trail Blazers
1977–78	Washington Bullets (44-38)	Seattle Super Sonics (47-35)	Washington Bullets
1978–79	Washington Bullets (54-28)	Seattle Super Sonics (52-30)	Seattle Super Sonics
1979–80	Philadelphia 76ers (59-23)	Los Angeles Lakers (60-22)	Los Angeles Lakers
1980–81	Boston Celtics (62-20)	Houston Rockets (40-42)	Boston Celtics
1981–82	Philadelphia 76ers (58-24)	Los Angeles Lakers (57-25)	Los Angeles Lakers
1982–83	Philadelphia 76ers (65-17)	Los Angeles Lakers (58-24)	Philadelphia 76ers
1983–84	Boston Celtics (56-26)	Los Angeles Lakers (58-24)	Boston Celtics
1984–85	Boston Celtics (63-19)	Los Angeles Lakers (62-20)	Los Angeles Lakers
1985–86	Boston Celtics (67-15)	Houston Rockets (51-31)	Boston Celtics
1986–87	Boston Celtics (59-23)	Los Angeles Lakers (65-17)	Los Angeles Lakers
1987–88	Detroit Pistons (54-28)	Los Angeles Lakers (62-20)	Los Angeles Lakers
1988–89	Detroit Pistons (63-18)	Los Angeles Lakers (57-25)	Detroit Pistons
1989–90	Detroit Pistons (59-23)	Portland Trail Blazers (59-23)	Detroit Pistons
1990–91	Chicago Bulls (61-21)	Los Angeles Lakers (58-24)	Chicago Bulls
1991–92	Chicago Bulls (67-15)	Portland Trail Blazers (57-25)	Chicago Bulls
1992–93	Chicago Bulls (57-25)	Phoenix Suns (62-20)	Chicago Bulls
1993–94	New York Knicks (57-25)	Houston Rockets (58-24)	Houston Rockets
1994–95	Orlando Magic (57-25)	Houston Rockets (47-35)	Houston Rockets
1995–96	Chicago Bulls (72-10)	Seattle SuperSonics (64-18)	Chicago Bulls
1996–97	Chicago Bulls (69-13)	Utah Jazz (64-18)	Chicago Bulls

1. Playoffs may involve teams other than conference winners.

INDIVIDUAL N.B.A. SCORING CHAMPIONS

Season	Player, Team	G	FG	FT	Pts	Avg
1953–54	Neil Johnston, Philadelphia Warriors	72	591	577	1,759	24.4
1954–55	Neil Johnston, Philadelphia Warriors	72	521	589	1,631	22.7
1955–56	Bob Pettit, St. Louis Hawks	72	646	557	1,849	25.7
1956–57	Paul Arizin, Philadelphia Warriors	71	613	591	1,817	25.6
1957–58	George Yardley, Detroit Pistons	72	673	655	2,001	27.8
1958–59	Bob Pettit, St. Louis Hawks	72	719	667	2,105	29.2
1959–60	Wilt Chamberlain, Philadelphia Warriors	72	1,065	577	2,707	37.6
1960–61	Wilt Chamberlain, Philadelphia Warriors	79	1,251	531	3,033	38.4
1961–62	Wilt Chamberlain, Philadelphia Warriors	80	1,597	835	40,29	50.4
1962–63	Wilt Chamberlain, San Francisco Warriors	80	1,463	660	3,586	44.8
1963–64	Wilt Chamberlain, San Francisco Warriors	80	1,204	540	2,948	36.9
1964–65	Wilt Chamberlain, San Francisco Warriors-Phila. 76ers	73	1,063	408	2,534	34.7
1965–66	Wilt Chamberlain, Philadelphia 76ers	79	1,074	501	2,649	33.5
1966–67	Rick Barry, San Francisco Warriors	78	1,011	753	2,775	35.6
1967–68	Dave Bing, Detroit Pistons	79	835	472	2,142	27.1
1968–69	Elvin Hayes, San Diego Rockets	82	930	467	2,327	28.4
1969–70	Jerry West, Los Angeles Lakers	74	831	647	2,309	31.2
1970–71	Lew Alcindor,[1] Milwaukee Bucks	82	1,063	470	2,596	31.7
1971–72	Kareem Abdul-Jabbar, Milwaukee Bucks	81	1,159	504	2,822	34.8
1972–73	Nate Archibald, Kansas City-Omaha Kings	80	1,028	663	2,719	34.0
1973–74	Bob McAdoo, Buffalo Braves	74	901	459	2,261	30.8
1974–75	Bob McAdoo, Buffalo Braves	82	1,095	641	2,831	34.5
1975–76	Bob McAdoo, Buffalo Braves	78	934	559	2,427	31.1
1976–77	Pete Maravich, New Orleans Jazz	73	886	501	2,273	31.1
1977–78	George Gervin, San Antonio Spurs	82	864	504	2,232	27.2
1978–79	George Gervin, San Antonio Spurs	80	947	471	2,365	29.6
1979–80	George Gervin, San Antonio Spurs	78	1,024	505	2,585	33.1
1980–81	Adrian Dantley, Utah Jazz	80	909	632	2,452	30.7
1981–82	George Gervin, San Antonio Spurs	79	993	555	2,551	32.3
1982–83	Alex English, Denver Nuggets	82	959	406	2,326	28.4
1983–84	Adrian Dantley, Utah Jazz	79	802	813	2,418	30.6
1984–85	Bernard King, New York Knicks	55	691	426	1,809	32.9
1985–86	Dominique Wilkins, Atlanta Hawks	78	888	527	2,366	30.3
1986–87	Michael Jordan, Chicago Bulls[2]	82	1,098	833	3,041	37.1
1987–88	Michael Jordan, Chicago Bulls[3]	82	1,069	723	2,868	35.0
1988–89	Michael Jordan, Chicago Bulls[4]	81	966	674	2,633	32.5
1989–90	Michael Jordan, Chicago Bulls[5]	82	1,034	593	2,753	33.6
1990–91	Michael Jordan, Chicago Bulls[6]	82	990	571	2,580	31.5
1991–92	Michael Jordan, Chicago Bulls[7]	80	943	491	2,404	30.1
1992–93	Michael Jordan, Chicago Bulls[8]	78	992	476	2,541	32.6
1993–94	David Robinson, San Antonio Spurs[9]	80	840	693	2,383	29.8
1994–95	Shaquille O'Neal, Orlando Magic[10]	79	930	455	2,315	29.3
1995–96	Michael Jordan, Chicago Bulls[11]	82	916	548	2,491	30.4
1996–97	Michael Jordan Chicago Bulls[11]	82	920	480	2,431	29.6

1. (Kareem Abdul-Jabbar). 2. Also had 12 3-point field goals. 3. Also had 7 3-point field goals. 4. Also had 27 3-point field goals. 5. Also had 92 3-point field goals. 6. Also had 29 3-point-field goals. 7. Attempted 27 3-pt field goals in 1991–92. 8. Also had 81 3-pt field goals in 1992–93. 9. Also had 10 3-pt field goals in 1993–94. 10. O'Neal scored no 3-pt field goals in 1994–95. 11. Also had 111 3-pt field goals in 1995–96 and 1996–97

N.B.A. MOST VALUABLE PLAYERS

1956	Bob Pettit
1957	Bob Cousy
1958	Bill Russell
1959	Bob Pettit
1960	Wilt Chamberlain
1961–63	Bill Russell
1964	Oscar Robertson
1965	Bill Russell
1966–68	Wilt Chamberlain
1969	Wes Unseld
1970	Willis Reed
1971–72	Lew Alcindor (Kareem Abdul-Jabbar)
1973	Dave Cowens
1974	Kareem Abdul-Jabbar, Milwaukee
1975	Bob McAdoo, Buffalo
1976–77	Kareem Abdul-Jabbar, Los Angeles
1978	Bill Walton, Portland
1979	Moses Malone, Houston
1980	Kareem Abdul-Jabbar, Los Angeles
1981	Julius Erving, Philadelphia
1982	Moses Malone, Houston
1983	Moses Malone, Philadelphia
1984	Larry Bird, Boston
1985	Larry Bird, Boston
1986	Larry Bird, Boston
1987	Earvin Johnson, Los Angeles
1988	Michael Jordan, Chicago
1989	Earvin Johnson, Los Angeles
1990	Earvin Johnson, Los Angeles
1991	Michael Jordan, Chicago
1992	Michael Jordan, Chicago
1993	Charles Barkley, Phoenix
1994	Hakeem Olajuwon, Houston
1995	David Robinson, San Antonio
1996	Michael Jordan, Chicago
1997	Karl Malone, Utah

N.B.A. LIFETIME LEADERS

(Through 1996–97 season)

NBA and ABA records combined

Most Games Played

Robert Parish	1,611	Paul Silas	1,254
Kareem Abdul-Jabbar	1,560	Alex English	1,193
Moses Malone	1,455	James Edwards	1,168
Elvin Hayes	1,303	Tree Rollins	1,156
John Havlicek	1,270	Hal Greer	1,122
Buck Williams[1]	1,266		

Free Throws

	FT	Att	Pct
Moses Malone	8,531	11,090	.769
Oscar Robertson	7,694	9,185	.838
Jerry West	7,160	8,801	.814
Dolph Schayes	6,979	8,273	.844
Adrian Dantley	6,832	8,351	.818
Kareem Abdul-Jabbar	6,712	9,304	.721
Karl Malone[1]	6,505	8,983	.724
Michael Jordan[1]	6,233	7,394	.843
Bob Pettit	6,182	8,119	.761
Wilt Chamberlain	6,057	11,862	.511

Blocked Shots

Hakeem Olajuwon[1]	3,363	Robert Parish	2,361
Kareem Abdul-Jabbar	3,189	Manute Bol	2,087
Mark Eaton	3,064	George Johnson	2,082
Tree Rollins	2,542	Larry Nance	2,027
Patrick Ewing[1]	2,516	David Robinson[1]	2,012

Field Goals

	FG	Att	Pct
Kareem Abdul-Jabbar	15,837	28,307	.559
Wilt Chamberlain	12,681	23,497	.540
Elvin Hayes	10,976	24,272	.452
Alex English	10,659	21,036	.507
John Havlicek	10,513	23,930	.439
Michael Jordan[1]	10,077	19,793	.509
Dominique Wilkins[1]	9,913	21,457	.462
Robert Parish	9,614	17,914	.537
Karl Malone[1]	9,510	18,032	.527
Oscar Robertson	9,508	19,620	.485

1. Still active going into 1997–98 season.

Scoring Average

Minimum of 400 games or 10,000 points.

	Gm	Pts	Avg
Michael Jordan[1]	848	26,920	31.7
Wilt Chamberlain	1,045	31,419	30.1
Elgin Baylor	846	23,149	27.4
Jerry West	932	25,192	27.0
Bob Pettit	792	20,880	26.4
George Gervin	791	20,708	26.2
Karl Malone[1]	980	25,592	26.1
Oscar Robertson	1,040	26,710	25.7
David Robinson[1]	563	14,366	25.5
Dominique Wilkins[1]	1,047	26,454	25.3

Steals

John Stockton[1]	2,531	Isiah Thomas	1,861
Maurice Cheeks	2,310	Derek Harper[1]	1,861
Michael Jordan[1]	2,165	Hakeem Olajuwon[1]	1,811
Alvin Robertson	2,112		
Clyde Drexler[1]	2,081	Magic Johnson	1,724
		Scottie Pippen[1]	1,692

Rebounds

Wilt Chamberlain	23,924	Robert Parish	14,715
Bill Russell	21,620	Nate Thurmond	14,464
Kareem Abdul-Jabbar	17,440	Walt Bellamy	14,241
Elvin Hayes	16,279	Wes Unseld	13,769
Moses Malone	16,212	Jerry Lucas	12,942

Assists

John Stockton[1]	12,156	Len Wilkens	7,211
Magic Johnson	10,141	Bob Cousy	6,955
Oscar Robertson	9,887	Guy Rodgers	6,917
Isiah Thomas	9,061	Mark Jackson[1]	6,813
Maurice Cheeks	7,392	Nate Archibald	6,476

Points

Kareem Abdul-Jabbar	38,387	Oscar Robertson	26,710
Wilt Chamberlain	31,419	Dominique Wilkins[1]	26,534
Moses Malone	27,409	John Havlicek	26,395
Elvin Hayes	27,313	Alex English	25,613
Michael Jordan[1]	26,920	Karl Malone[1]	25,592

N.B.A. INDIVIDUAL RECORDS

(Through 1996–97 season)

Most points, game—100, Wilt Chamberlain, Philadelphia, 1962

Most points, quarter—33, George Gervin, San Antonio, 1978

Most points, half—59, Wilt Chamberlain, Philadelphia, 1962

Most free throws, game—28, Wilt Chamberlain, Philadelphia, 1962; 28, Adrian Dantley, Utah, 1984

Most free throws, quarter—14, Rick Barry, San Francisco, 1966

Most free throws, half—20, Michael Jordan, Chicago, 1992

Most field goals, game—36, Wilt Chamberlain, Philadelphia, 1962

Most consecutive gield goals, game—18, Wilt Chamberlain, San Francisco, 1963; Philadelphia, 1967

Most assists, game—30, Scott Skiles, Orlando vs. Denver, 1990

Most rebounds, game—55, Wilt Chamberlain, Philadelphia vs. Boston, 1960

Most 3-pt. field goals, game—11, Dennis Scott, Orlando vs. Atlanta, 1996

N.B.A. TEAM RECORDS

Most points, game—186, Detroit at Denver, 3 overtimes, 1983
Most points, quarter—58, Buffalo at. Boston, 1972
Most points, half—107, Phoenix vs. Denver, 1990
Most points, overtime period—22, Detroit vs. Cleveland, 1973
Most field goals, game—74, Detroit, 1983
Most field goals, quarter—24, Phoenix, 1990
Most field goals, half—43, Phoenix, 1990
Most assists, game—53, Milwaukee, 1978
Most rebounds, game—109, Boston, 1960
Most points, both teams, game—370 (Detroit 186, Denver 184) 3 overtimes, Denver, December 13, 1983

Most points, both teams, quarter—99 (San Antonio 53, Denver 46), 1984
Most points, both teams, half—174 (Phoenix 107, Denver 67), 1990
Longest winning streak—33, Los Angeles, 1971–72
Longest losing streak—24, Cleveland, Mar.–Nov. 1982
Longest winning streak at home—44, Chicago, Mar. 1995–April 1996
Most games won, season—72, Chicago, 1995–96
Most games lost, season—73, Philadelphia, 1972–73
Highest average points per game—126.5, Denver, 1981–82

NATIONAL BASKETBALL ASSOCIATION FINAL STANDINGS—1996–97

EASTERN CONFERENCE

Atlantic Division

	W	L	Pct	GB
*Miami	61	21	.744	—
†New York	57	25	.695	4
†Orlando	45	37	.549	16
†Washington	44	38	.537	17
New Jersey	26	56	.317	35
Philadelphia	22	60	.268	39
Boston	15	67	.183	46

Central Division

	W	L	Pct	GB
*Chicago	69	13	.841	—
†Atlanta	56	26	.683	13
†Charlotte	54	28	.659	15
†Detroit	54	28	.659	15
Cleveland	42	40	.512	27
Indiana	39	43	.476	30
Milwaukee	33	49	.402	36
Toronto	30	52	.366	39

*Division champion. †Playoff qualifier.

WESTERN CONFERENCE

Midwest Division

	W	L	Pct	GB
*Utah	64	18	.780	—
†Houston	57	25	.695	7
†Minnesota	40	42	.488	24
Dallas	24	58	.293	40
Denver	21	61	.256	43
San Antonio	20	62	.244	44
Vancouver	14	68	.171	50

	W	L	Pct	GB
*Seattle	57	25	.695	—
†L.A. Lakers	56	26	.683	1
†Portland	49	33	.598	8
†Phoenix	40	42	.488	17
†L.A. Clippers	36	46	.439	21
Sacramento	34	48	.415	23
Golden State	30	52	.366	27

N.B.A. PLAYOFFS—1997

EASTERN CONFERENCE

First Round
(Best of 5)
Chicago defeated Washington, 3 games to 0
Miami defeated Orlando, 3 games to 2
New York defeated Charlotte, 3 games to 0
Atlanta defeated Detroit, 3 games to 2

Second Round
(Best of 7)
Chicago defeated Atlanta, 4 games to 1
Miami defeated New York, 4 games to 3

Conference Finals
(Best of 7)
Chicago defeated Miami, 4 games to 1
May 20—CHICAGO 84, Miami 77
May 22—CHICAGO 75, Miami 68
May 24—Chicago 98, MIAMI 74
May 26—MIAMI 87, Chicago 80
May 28—CHICAGO 100, Miami 87

WESTERN CONFERENCE

First Round
(Best of 5)
Utah defeated Los Angeles, 3 games to 0
Seattle defeated Phoenix, 3 games to 2

NOTE: All caps denotes home team

Houston defeated Minnesota, 3 games to 0
Los Angeles defeated Portland, 3 games to 1

Second Round
(Best of 7)
Utah defeated Los Angeles, 4 games to 1
Houston defeated Seattle, 4 games to 3

Conference Finals
(Best of 7)
Utah defeated Houston, 4 games to 2
May 19—UTAH 101, Houston 86
May 21—UTAH 104, Houston 92
May 23—HOUSTON 118, Utah 100
May 25—HOUSTON 95, Utah 92
May 27—UTAH 96, Houston 91
May 29—Utah 103, HOUSTON 100

CHAMPIONSHIP

Chicago Bulls defeated Utah Jazz, 4 games to 2
June 1—CHICAGO 84, Utah 82
June 4—CHICAGO 97, Utah 85
June 6—UTAH 104, Chicago 93
June 8—UTAH 78, Chicago 73
June 11—Chicago 90, UTAH 88
June 13—CHICAGO 90, Utah 86

LEADING SCORERS—1996–1997

Minimum of 49 games played or 1,344 points scored

	Gm	Pts	Avg
Michael Jordan, Chicago	82	2,431	29.6
Karl Malone, Utah	82	2,249	27.4
Glen Rice, Charlotte	79	2,115	26.8
Mitch Richmond, Sacramento	81	2,095	25.9
Latrell Sprewell, Golden State	80	1,938	24.2
Allen Iverson, Philadelphia	76	1,787	23.5
Hakeem Olajuwon, Houston	78	1,810	23.2
Patrick Ewing, New York	78	1,751	22.4
Kendall Gill, New Jersey	82	1,789	21.8
Gary Payton, Seattle	82	1,785	21.8
Reggie Miller, Indianapolis	81	1,751	21.6
Grant Hill, Detroit	80	1,710	21.4
Glenn Robinson, Milwaukee	80	1,689	21.1
Vin Baker, Milwaukee	78	1,637	21.0
Jerry Stackhouse, Philadelphia	81	1,679	20.7

STEALS LEADERS—1996–1997

Minimum of 49 games played or 120 steals

	Gm	Stl	Avg
Mookie Blaylock, Atlanta	78	212	2.72
Doug Christie, Toronto	81	201	2.48
Gary Payton, Seattle	82	197	2.40
Eddie Jones, L.A. Lakers	80	189	2.36
Rick Fox, Boston	76	167	2.20
David Wesley, Boston	74	162	2.19
Allen Iverson, Philadelphia	76	157	2.07
John Stockton, Utah	82	166	2.02
Greg Anthony, Vancouver	65	129	1.98
Kenny Anderson, Portland	82	162	1.98

ASSISTS LEADERS—1996–1997

Minimum of 49 games played or 384 assists

	Gm	Ast	Avg
Mark Jackson, Indianapolis	82	935	11.4
John Stockton, Utah	82	860	10.5
Kevin Johnson, Phoenix	70	653	9.3
Jason Kidd, Phoenix	55	496	9.0
Rod Strickland, Portland	82	727	8.9
Damon Stoudamire, Toronto	81	709	8.8
Tim Hardaway, Miami	81	695	8.6
Nick Van Exel, L.A. Lakers	79	672	8.5
Robert Pack, Dallas	54	452	8.4
Stephon Marbury, Minneapolis	67	522	7.8
Allen Iverson, Philadelphia	76	567	7.5
Grant Hill, Detroit	80	583	7.3
David Wesley, Boston	74	537	7.3
Mugsy Bogues, Charlotte	65	469	7.2

BLOCKED-SHOTS LEADERS—1996–1997

Minimum of 49 games played or 96 block shots

	Gm	Blk	Avg
Shawn Bradley, Dallas	73	248	3.40
Dikembe Mutombo, Atlanta	80	264	3.30
Shaquille O'Neal, L.A. Lakers	51	147	2.88
Alonzo Mourning, Miami	66	189	2.86
Ervin Johnson, Denver	82	227	2.77
Patrick Ewing, New York	78	189	2.42
Vlade Divac, Charlotte	81	180	2.22
Hakeem Olajuwon, Houston	78	173	2.22
Kevin Garnett, Minneapolis	77	163	2.12
Marcus Camby, Toronto	63	130	2.06

FIELD GOAL PERCENTAGE LEADERS—1996–1997

Minimum of 288 field goals made

	Gm	FG	Att	Pct
Gheorghe Muresan, Washington	73	327	541	.604
Tyrone Hill, Cleveland	74	357	595	.600
Rasheed Wallace, Portland	62	380	681	.558
Shaquille O'Neal, L.A. Lakers	51	552	991	.557
Chris Mullin, Golden State	79	438	792	.553
Karl Malone, Utah	82	864	1571	.550
John Stockton, Utah	82	416	759	.548
Dallase Davis, Indianapolis	80	370	688	.538
Danny Manning, Phoenix	77	426	795	.536
Gary Trent, Portland	82	361	674	.536

FREE-THROW PERCENTAGE LEADERS—1996–1997

Minimum of 120 free throws made

	Gm	FT	Att	Pct
Mark Price, Golden State	70	155	171	.906
Terrell Brandon, Cleveland	78	268	297	.902
Jeff Hornacek, Utah	82	293	326	.899
Ricky Pierce, Charlotte	60	139	155	.897
Mario Elie, Houston	78	207	231	.896
Reggie Miller, Indianapolis	81	418	475	.880
Malik Sealy, L.A. Clippers	80	254	290	.876
Hersey Hawkins, Seattle	82	258	295	.875
Darrick Martin, L.A. Clippers	82	218	250	.872
Glen Rice, Charlotte	79	464	535	.867
Joe Dumars, Detroit	79	222	256	.867

REBOUND LEADERS—1996–1997

Minimum of 49 games played or 768 rebounds

	Gm	Reb	Avg
Dennis Rodman, Chicago	55	883	16.1
Dikembe Mutombo, Denver	80	929	11.6
Anthony Mason, Charlotte	73	829	11.4
Ervin Johnson, Denver	82	913	11.1
Patrick Ewing, New York	78	834	10.7
Chris Webber, Washington	72	743	10.3
Vin Baker, Milwaukee	78	804	10.3
Loy Vaught, L.A. Clippers	82	817	10.0
Shawn Kemp, Seattle	81	807	10.0
Tyrone Hill, Cleveland	74	736	9.9
Karl Malone, Utah	82	809	9.9
Charles Oakley, New York	80	781	9.8
Dale Davis, Indianapolis	80	772	9.7
Michael Smith, Sacramento	81	769	9.5
Rony Seikaly, Orlando	74	701	9.5

3-POINT FIELD GOAL PERCENT LEADERS—1996–1997

Minimum of 82 3-point field goals made

	Gm	3FG	Att	Pct
Steve Kerr, Chicago	82	110	237	.464
Kevin Johnson, Phoenix	70	89	202	.441
Joe Dumars, Detroit	79	166	384	.432
Mitch Richmond, Sacramento	81	204	477	.428
Reggie Miller, Indianapolis	81	229	536	.427
Dell Curry, Charlotte	68	126	296	.426
Terry Mills, Detroit	79	175	415	.422
Mario Elie, Houston	78	120	286	.420
Voshon Lenard, Miami	73	183	442	.414

Women's Professional Basketball

AMERICAN BASKETBALL LEAGUE

Eastern Conference

	W	L	Pct	GB
*Columbus	31	9	.775	—
†Richmond	21	19	.525	10
Atlanta	18	22	.450	13
New England	16	24	.400	15

Western Conference

	W	L	Pct	GB
*Colorado	25	15	.625	—
†San Jose	18	22	.450	7
Seattle	17	23	.425	8
Portland	14	26	.350	11

NOTE: Conference champions (*) and playoff qualifiers (†) are noted. GB refers to Games Behind leader.

ABL PLAYOFFS

Semifinals

Date	Result
Feb. 23	at Richmond 80, Colorado 77
Feb. 25	Richmond 82, at Colorado 68
	Richmond wins series, 2–0
Feb. 23	Columbus 94, at San Jose 69
Feb. 25	at Columbus 81, San Jose 69
	Columbus wins series, 2–0

Finals (Best of 5)

Columbus wins series, 3 games to 2

Date	Winner	Home Court
Mar. 2	Columbus, 90–89	at Columbus
Mar. 4	Richmond, 75–62	at Columbus
Mar. 8	Richmond, 72–67	at Richmond
Mar. 9	Columbus, 95–84	at Richmond
Mar. 11	Columbus, 77–64	at Columbus

ABL ANNUAL AWARDS

Most Valuable Player: Nikki McCray, Columbus
New Pro Award: Crystal Robinson, Colorado

Defensive Player of the Year: Debbie Black, Colorado
Coach of the Year: Brian Agler, Columbus

WOMEN'S NATIONAL BASKETBALL ASSOCIATION

Eastern Conference

	W	L	Pct	GB
*Houston	18	10	.643	—
†New York	17	11	.607	1
†Charlotte	15	13	.536	3
Cleveland	15	13	.536	3

Western Conference

	W	L	Pct	GB
*Phoenix	16	12	.571	—
Los Angeles	14	14	.500	2
Sacramento	10	18	.357	6
Utah	7	21	.250	9

NOTE: Conference champions (*) and playoff qualifiers (†) are noted. GB refers to Games Behind leader.

Semifinals
Single-game elimination

Date	Result
Aug. 28	at Houston 70, Charlotte 54

(Leading Scorer: Cynthia Cooper, Houston, 31 pts.)

Date	Result
Aug. 28	New York 59, at Phoenix 41

(Leading Scorer: Rebecca Lobo, New York, 16 pts.)

Championship Game

Date	Result
Aug. 30	at Houston 65, New York 51

(Leading Scorer: Cynthia Cooper, Houston, 25 pts.)

WNBA ANNUAL AWARDS

Most Valuable Player: Cynthia Cooper, Houstonston
Defensive Player of the Year: Teresa Weatherspoon, New York

Sportsmanship Award: Haixia Zheng, Los Angeles
Coach of the Year: Van Chancellor, Houston

LEADING SCORERS—1997

	Gm	Pts	Avg
Cynthia Cooper, Houston	28	621	22.2
Ruthie Bolton-Holifield, Sacramento	23	447	19.4
Lisa Leslie, Los Angeles	28	445	15.9
Wendy Palmer, Utah	28	443	15.8
Jennifer Gillom, Phoenix	28	440	15.7

STEALS LEADERS—1997

	Gm	Steals	Avg
Teresa Weatherspoon, New York	28	83	3.0
Michele Timms, Phoenix	27	71	2.6
Kim Perrot, Houston	28	69	2.5
Umeki Webb, Phoenix	28	68	2.4
Ruthie Bolton-Holifield, Sacramento	23	54	2.4

Hockey

Ice hockey, by birth and upbringing a Canadian game, is an offshoot of field hockey. Some historians say that the first ice hockey game was played in Montreal in December 1879 between two teams composed almost exclusively of McGill University students, but others assert that earlier hockey games took place in Kingston, Ontario, or Halifax, Nova Scotia. In the Montreal game of 1879, there were fifteen players on a side, who used an assortment of crude sticks to keep the puck in motion. Early rules allowed nine men on a side, but the number was reduced to seven in 1886 and later to six.

The first governing body of the sport was the Amateur Hockey Association of Canada, organized in 1887. In the winter of 1894–95, a group of college students from the United States visited Canada and saw hockey played. They became enthused over the game and introduced it as a winter sport when they returned home. The first professional league was the International Hockey League, which operated in northern Michigan in 1904–06.

Until 1910, professionals and amateurs were allowed to play together on "mixed teams," but this arrangement ended with the formation of the first "big league," the National Hockey Association, in eastern Canada in 1910. The Pacific Coast League was organized in 1911 for western Canadian hockey. The league included Seattle and later other American cities. The National Hockey League replaced the National Hockey Association in 1917. Boston, in 1924, was the first American city to join that circuit. The league expanded to include western cities in 1967. The Stanley Cup was competed for by "mixed teams" from 1894 to 1910, thereafter by professionals. It was awarded to the winner of the NHL playoffs from 1926–67 and now to the league champion. The World Hockey Association was organized in October 1972 and was dissolved after the 1978–79 season when the NHL absorbed four of the teams.

The National Hockey League Players Association staged a 10-day strike near the end of the 1991–92 season, the first strike in the league's 75-year history.

STANLEY CUP WINNERS

Emblematic of World Professional Championship; N.H.L. Championship after 1967

1894 Montreal A.A.A.	1926 Montreal Maroons	1962–64 Toronto Maple Leafs
1895 Montreal Victorias	1927 Ottawa Senators	1965–66 Montreal Canadiens
1896 Winnipeg Victorias	1928 N.Y. Rangers	1967 Toronto Maple Leafs
1897–99 Montreal Victorias	1929 Boston Bruins	1968–69 Montreal Canadiens
1900 Montreal Shamrocks	1930–31 Montreal Canadiens	1970 Boston Bruins
1901 Winnipeg Victorias	1932 Toronto Maple Leafs	1971 Montreal Canadiens
1902 Montreal A.A.A.	1933 N.Y. Rangers	1972 Boston Bruins
1903–05 Ottawa Silver Seven	1934 Chicago Black Hawks	1973 Montreal Canadiens
1906 Montreal Wanderers	1935 Montreal Maroons	1974–75 Philadelphia Flyers
1907 Kenora Thistles[1]	1936–37 Detroit Red Wings	1976–79 Montreal Canadiens
1907 Mont. Wanderers[2]	1938 Chicago Red Hawks	1980–83 New York Islanders
1908 Montreal Wanderers	1939 Boston Bruins	1984 Edmonton Oilers
1909 Ottawa Senators	1940 N.Y. Rangers	1985 Edmonton Oilers
1910 Montreal Wanderers	1941 Boston Bruins	1986 Montreal Canadiens
1911 Ottawa Senators	1942 Toronto Maple Leafs	1987 Edmonton Oilers
1912–13 Quebec Bulldogs	1943 Detroit Red Wings	1988 Edmonton Oilers
1914 Toronto	1944 Montreal Canadiens	1989 Calgary Flames
1915 Vancouver Millionaries	1945 Toronto Maple Leafs	1990 Edmonton Oilers
1916 Montreal Canadiens	1946 Montreal Canadiens	1991 Pittsburgh Penguins
1917 Seattle Metropolitans	1947–49 Toronto Maple Leafs	1992 Pittsburgh Penguins
1918 Toronto Arenas	1950 Detroit Red Wings	1993 Montreal Canadiens
1919 No champion	1951 Toronto Maple Leafs	1994 N.Y. Rangers
1920–21 Ottawa Senators	1952 Detroit Red Wings	1995 N.J. Devils
1922 Toronto St. Patricks	1953 Montreal Canadiens	1996 Colorado Avalanche
1923 Ottawa Senators	1954–55 Detroit Red Wings	1997 Detroit Red Wings
1924 Montreal Canadiens	1956–60 Montreal Canadiens	1. January. 2. March.
1925 Victoria Cougars	1961 Chicago Black Hawks	

N.H.L. CHAMPIONS

Wales Trophy

1939 Boston	1963 Toronto	1976–79 Montreal	1994 N.Y. Rangers
1940 Boston	1964 Montreal	1980 Buffalo	1995 Quebec
1941 Boston	1965 Detroit	1981 Montreal	1996 Florida
1942 New York	1966 Montreal	1982 New York Islanders	1997 Philadelphia
1943 Detroit	1967 Chicago	1983 New York Islanders	
1944–47 Montreal	**Eastern Division**	1984 New York Islanders	1. Prior to 1994 was the
1948 Toronto	1968–69 Montreal	1985 Philadelphia	Wales Conference.
1948–55 Detroit	1970 Chicago	1986 Montreal	
1956 Montreal	1971 Boston	1987 Philadelphia	**CAMPBELL BOWL**
1957 Detroit	1972 Boston	1988 Boston	**Western Division**
1958–62 Montreal	1973 Montreal	1989 Montreal	1968 Philadelphia
	1974 Boston	1990 Boston	1969 St. Louis
	Eastern Conference[1]	1991 Pittsburgh	1970 St. Louis
	1975 Buffalo	1992 Pittsburgh	1971–73 Chicago
		1993 Montreal	1974 Philadelphia

Western Conference[2]

1975	Philadelphia	
1976–77	Philadelphia	
1978–79	N.Y. Islanders	
1980	Philadelphia	
1981	New York Islanders	

1982	Edmonton
1983	Edmonton
1984	Edmonton
1985	Edmonton
1986	Calgary
1987	Edmonton

1988	Edmonton
1989	Calgary
1990	Edmonton
1991	Minnesota
1992	Chicago
1993	Los Angeles

1994	Detroit
1995	Detroit
1996	Colorado
1997	Detroit

2. Prior to 1994 was the Campbell Conference.

NATIONAL HOCKEY LEAGUE YEARLY TROPHY WINNERS

The Hart Trophy—Most Valuable Player

1924	Frank Nighbor, Ottawa
1925	Billy Burch, Hamilton
1926	Nels Stewart, Montreal Maroons
1927	Herb Gardiner, Montreal Canadiens
1928	Howie Morenz, Montreal Canadiens
1929	Roy Worters, N.Y. Americans
1930	Nels Stewart, Montreal Maroons
1931–32	Howie Morenz, Montreal Canadiens
1933	Eddie Shore, Boston
1934	Aurel Joliat, Montreal Canadiens
1935–36	Eddie Shore, Boston
1937	Babe Siebert, Montreal Canadiens
1938	Eddie Shore, Boston
1939	Toe Blake, Montreal Canadiens
1940	Eddie Goodfellow, Detroit
1941	Bill Cowley, Boston
1942	Tom Anderson, N.Y. Americans
1943	Bill Cowley, Boston
1944	Babe Pratt, Toronto
1945	Elmer Lach, Montreal Canadiens
1946	Max Bentley, Chicago
1947	Maurice Richard, Montreal Canadiens
1948	Buddy O'Connor, N.Y. Rangers
1949	Sid Abel, Detroit
1950	Chuck Rayner, N.Y. Rangers
1951	Milt Schmidt, Boston
1952–53	Gordon Howe, Detroit
1954	Al Rollins, Chicago
1955	Ted Kennedy, Toronto
1956	Jean Belveau, Montreal Canadiens
1957–58	Gordon Howe, Detroit
1959	Andy Bathgate, N.Y. Rangers
1960	Gordon Howe, Detroit
1961	Bernie Geoffrion, Montreal Canadiens
1962	Jacques Plante, Montreal Canadiens
1963	Gordon Howe, Detroit
1964	Jean Beliveau, Montreal Canadiens
1965–66	Bobby Hull, Chicago
1967–68	Stan Mikita, Chicago
1969	Phil Esposito, Boston
1970–72	Bobby Orr, Boston
1973	Bobby Clarke, Philadelphia
1974	Phil Esposito, Boston
1975–76	Bobby Clarke, Philadelphia
1977–78	Guy Lafleur, Montreal
1979	Bryan Trottier, N.Y. Islanders
1980	Wayne Gretzky, Edmonton
1981	Wayne Gretzky, Edmonton
1982	Wayne Gretzky, Edmonton
1983	Wayne Gretzky, Edmonton
1984	Wayne Gretzky, Edmonton
1985	Wayne Gretzky, Edmonton
1986	Wayne Gretzky, Edmonton
1987	Wayne Gretzky, Edmonton
1988	Mario Lemieux, Pittsburgh
1989	Wayne Gretzky, Los Angeles
1990	Mark Messier, Edmonton
1991	Brett Hull, St. Louis
1992	Mark Messier, N.Y. Rangers
1993	Mario Lemieux, Pittsburgh
1994	Sergei Fedorov, Detroit
1995	Eric Lindros, Philadelphia
1996	Mario Lemieux, Pittsburgh
1997	Dominik Hasek, Buffalo

Vezina Trophy—Leading Goalkeeper

1956–60	Jacques Plante, Montreal
1961	Johnny Bower, Toronto
1962	Jacques Plante, Montreal
1963	Glenn Hall, Chicago
1964	Charlie Hodge, Montreal
1965	Terry Sawchuk—Johnny Bower, Toronto
1966	Lorne Worsley—Charlie Hodge, Montreal
1967	Glen Hall—Denis DeJordy, Chicago
1968	Lorne Worsley—Rogatien Vachon, Montreal
1969	Glen Hall—Jacques Plante, St. Louis
1970	Tony Esposito, Chicago
1971	Ed Giacomin—Gilles Villemure, New York
1972	Tony Esposito—Gary Smith, Chicago
1973	Ken Dryden, Montreal
1974	Bernie Parent, Philadelphia and Tony Esposito, Chicago
1975	Bernie Parent, Philadelphia
1976	Ken Dryden, Montreal
1977–79	Ken Dryden—Michel Larocque, Montreal
1980	Bob Sauve—Don Edwards, Buffalo
1981	Richard Sevigny, Denis Herron and Michel Larocque, Montreal
1982	Billy Smith, New York Islanders
1983	Pete Peeters, Boston
1984	Tom Barrasso, Buffalo
1985	Pelle Lindbergh, Philadelphia
1986	John Vanbiesbrouck, New York Rangers
1987	Ron Hextall, Philadelphia
1988	Grant Fuhr, Edmonton
1989	Patrick Roy, Montreal
1990	Patrick Roy, Montreal
1991	Ed Belfour, Chicago
1992	Patrick Roy, Montreal
1993	Ed Belfour, Chicago
1994	Dominik Hasek, Buffalo
1995	Dominik Hasek, Buffalo
1996	Jim Carey, Washington
1997	Dominik Hasek, Buffalo

James Norris Trophy—Defenseman

1954	Red Kelly, Detroit
1955–58	Doug Harvey, Montreal
1959	Tom Johnson, Montreal
1960–62	Doug Harvey, Montreal; New York (62)
1963–65	Pierre Pilote, Chicago
1966	Jacques Laperriere, Montreal
1967	Harry Howell, New York
1968–75	Bobby Orr, Boston
1976	Denis Potvin, N.Y. Islanders
1977	Larry Robinson, Montreal
1978–79	Denis Potvin, N.Y. Islanders
1980	Larry Robinson, Montreal
1981	Randy Carlyle, Pittsburgh
1982	Doug Wilson, Chicago
1983–84	Rod Langway, Washington
1985	Paul Coffey, Edmonton
1986	Paul Coffey, Edmonton
1987	Ray Bourque, Boston
1988	Ray Bourque, Boston
1989	Chris Chelios, Montreal
1990	Ray Bourque, Boston
1991	Ray Bourque, Boston
1992	Brian Leetch, N.Y. Rangers
1993	Chris Chelios, Chicago
1994	Ray Bourque, Boston
1995	Paul Coffey, Detroit
1996	Chris Chelios, Chicago
1997	Bryan Leetch, N.Y. Rangers

Lady Byng Trophy—Sportsmanship

1960	Don McKenney, Boston
1961	Red Kelly, Detroit
1962–63	Dave Keon, Toronto
1964	Ken Wharram, Chicago
1965	Bobby Hull, Chicago
1966	Alex Delvecchio, Detroit
1967–68	Stan Mikita, Chicago
1969	Alex Delvecchio, Detroit
1970	Phil Goyette, St. Louis
1971	John Bucyk, Boston
1972	Jean Ratelle, New York
1973	Gil Perrault, Buffalo
1974	John Bucyk, Boston
1975	Marcel Dionne, Detroit
1976	Jean Ratelle, N.Y. Rangers-Boston
1977	Marcel Dionne, Los Angeles
1978	Butch Goring, Los Angeles
1979	Bob MacMillan, Atlanta
1980	Wayne Gretzky, Edmonton
1981	Rick Kehoe, Pittsburgh
1982	Rick Middleton, Boston
1983–84	Mike Bossy, N.Y. Islanders
1985	Jari Kurri, Edmonton
1986	Mike Bossy, N.Y. Islanders
1987	Joe Mullen, Calgary

1988 Mats Naslund, Montreal	1978 Mike Bossy, N.Y. Islanders	1960 Bobby Hull, Chicago
1989 Joe Mullen, Calgary	1979 Bobby Smith, Minnesota	1961 Bernie Geoffrion, Montreal
1990 Brett Hull, St. Louis	1980 Ray Bourque, Boston	1962 Bobby Hull, Chicago
1991 Wayne Gretzky, Los Angeles	1981 Peter Stastny, Quebec	1963 Gordie Howe, Detroit
1992 Wayne Gretzky, Los Angeles	1982 Dale Hawerchuk, Winnipeg	1964–65 Stan Mikita, Chicago
1993 Pierre Turgeon, N.Y. Islanders	1983 Steve Larmer, Chicago	1966 Bobby Hull, Chicago
1994 Wayne Gretzky, Los Angeles	1984 Tom Barrasso, Buffalo	1967–68 Stan Mikita, Chicago
1995 Ron Francis, Pittsburgh	1985 Mario Lemieux, Pittsburgh	1969 Phil Esposito, Boston
1996–97 Paul Kariya, Anaheim	1986 Gary Suter, Calgary	1970 Bobby Orr, Boston

Calder Trophy—Rookie

	1987 Luc Robitaille, Los Angeles	1971–74 Phil Esposito, Boston
1962 Bobby Rousseau, Montreal	1988 Joe Nievwendyk, Calgary	1975 Bobby Orr, Boston
1963 Kent Douglas, Toronto	1989 Brian Leetch, N.Y. Rangers	1976–78 Guy Lafleur, Montreal
1964 Jacques Laperriere, Montreal	1990 Sergei Makarov, Calgary	1979 Bryan Trottier, N.Y. Islanders
1965 Roger Crozier, Detroit	1991 Ed Belfour, Chicago	1980 Marcel Dionne, Los Angeles
1966 Brit Selby, Toronto	1992 Pavel Bure, Vancouver	1981–87 Wayne Gretzky, Edmonton
1967 Bobby Orr, Boston	1993 Teemu Selanne, Winnipeg	1988 Mario Lemieux, Pittsburgh
1968 Derek Sanderson, Boston	1994 Martin Brodeur, New Jersey	1989 Mario Lemieux, Pittsburgh
1969 Danny Grant, Minnesota	1995 Peter Forsberg, Quebec	1990 Wayne Gretzky, Los Angeles
1970 Tony Esposito, Chicago	1996 Daniel Alfredsson, Ottawa	1991 Wayne Gretzky, Los Angeles
1971 Gilbert Perrault, Buffalo	1997 Bryan Berard, N.Y. Islanders	1992 Mario Lemieux, Pittsburgh
1972 Ken Dryden, Montreal		1993 Mario Lemieux, Pittsburgh
1973 Steve Vickers, N.Y Rangers	**Art Ross Trophy—Leading**	1994 Wayne Gretzky, Los Angeles
1974 Denis Potvin, N.Y. Islanders	**scorer**	1995 Jaromir Jagr, Pittsburgh
1975 Eric Vail, Atlanta	1955 Bernie Geoffrion, Montreal	1996–97 Mario Lemieux, Pittsburgh
1976 Bryan Trottier, N.Y. Islanders	1956 Jean Beliveau, Montreal	
1977 Willi Plett, Atlanta	1957 Gordie Howe, Detroit	
	1958–59 Dickie Moore, Montreal	

STANLEY CUP PLAYOFFS—1997

EASTERN CONFERENCE

New Jersey Devils defeated Montreal Canadiens, 4 games to 1

Buffalo Sabares defeated Ottawa Senators, 4 games to 3

Philadelphia Flyers defeated Pittsburgh Penguins, 4 games to 1

New York Rangers defeaeted Florida Panthers, 4 games to 1

Semifinals

New York Rangers defeated New Jersey Devils, 4 games to 1

Philadelphia Flyers defeated Buffalo Sabres, 4 games to 1

Finals

Philadelphia Flyers defeated New York Rangers, 4 games to 1

May 16—PHILADELPHIA 3, New York 1
May 18—New York 5, PHILADELPHIA 4
May 20—Philadelphia 6, NEW YORK 3
May 23—PHILADELPHIA 4, New York 2

NOTE: Homes teams are in capitals.

WESTERN CONFERENCE

Quarterfinals

Edmonton Oilers defeated Dallas Stars, 4 games to 3

Colorado Avalanche defeated Chicago Blackhawks, 4 games to 2

Detroit Red Wings defeated St. Louis Blues, 4 games to 2

Anaheim Mighty Ducks defeated Phoenix Coyotes, 4 games to 3

Semifinals

Colorado Avalanche defeated Edmonton Oilers, 4 games to 1

Detroit Red Wings defeated Anaheim Mighty Ducks, 4 games to 0

Finals

Detroit Red Wings defeated Colorado Avalanche, 4 games to 2

May 15—COLORADO 2, Detroit 1
May 17—Detroit 4, COLORADO 2
May 19—DETROIT 2, Colorado 1
May 22—DETROIT 6, Colorado 0
May 24—COLORADO 6, Detroit 0
May 26—DETROIT 3, Colorado 1

STANLEY CUP CHAMPIONSHIP FINALS

Detroit Red Wings defeated Philadelphia Flyers, 4 games to 0

May 31—Detroit 4, PHILADELPHIA 2
June 3—Detroit 4, PHILADELPHIA 2
June 5—DETROIT 6, Philadelphia 1
June 7—DETROIT 2, Philadelphia 1

Conn Smythe Award for most valuable player in the play-offs: Mike Vernon, Detroit Red Wings.

OTHER N.H.L. AWARDS—1997

Frank Selke Trophy (top defensive forward)—Michael Peca, Buffalo

King Clancy Trophy (Humanitarian community involvement)—Trevor Linden, Vancouver

Jack Adams Trophy (Coach of the Year)—Ted Nolan, Buffalo

Bill Masterson Trophy (Sportsmanship)—Tony Granato, San Jose

NATIONAL HOCKEY LEAGUE FINAL STANDINGS OF THE CLUBS—1996–97

EASTERN CONFERENCE
Northeast Division

	W	L	T	Pts	GF	GA
[1]Buffalo	40	30	12	92	237	208
[2]Pittsburgh	38	36	8	84	285	280
[2]Ottawa	31	36	15	77	226	234
[2]Montreal	31	36	15	77	249	276
Hartford	32	39	11	75	226	256
Boston	26	47	9	61	234	300

Atlantic Division

	W	L	T	Pts	GF	GA
[1]New Jersey	45	23	14	104	231	182
[2]Philadelphia	45	24	13	103	274	217
[2]Florida	35	28	19	89	221	201
[2]NY Rangers	38	34	10	86	258	231
Washington	33	40	9	75	214	231
Tampa Bay	32	40	10	74	217	247
NY Islanders	29	41	12	70	240	250

1. Division champion. 2. Playoff qualifier.

WESTERN CONFERENCE
Central Division

	W	L	T	Pts	GF	GA
[1]Dallas	48	26	8	104	252	198
[2]Detroit	38	26	18	94	253	197
[2]Phoenix	38	37	7	83	240	243
[2]St. Louis	36	35	11	83	236	239
[2]Chicago	34	35	13	81	223	210
Toronto	30	44	8	68	230	273

Pacific Division

	W	L	T	Pts	GF	GA
[1]Colorado	49	24	9	107	277	205
[2]Anaheim	36	33	13	85	245	233
[2]Edmonton	36	37	9	81	252	247
Vancouver	35	40	7	77	257	273
Calgary	32	41	9	73	214	239
Los Angeles	28	43	11	67	214	268
San Jose	27	47	8	62	211	278

N.H.L. LEADING SCORERS—1996–97

	GP	G	A	Pts
Mario Lemieux, Pittsburgh	76	50	72	122
Teemu Selanne, Anaheim	78	51	58	109
Paul Kariya, Anaheim	69	44	55	99
John LeClair, Philadelphia	82	50	47	97
Wayne Gretzky, NY Rangers	82	25	72	97
Jaromir Jagr, Pittsburgh	63	47	48	95
Mats Sundin, Toronto	82	41	53	94
Zigmund Palffy, NY Islanders	80	48	42	90
Ron Francis, Pittsburgh	81	27	63	90
Brendan Shanahan, Hart-Det	81	47	41	88

N.H.L. LEADING GOALTENDERS— 1996–97

	Gm	Min	GAA	Record
Martin Brodeur, New Jersey	67	3,838	1.88	37–14–13
Andy Moog, Dallas	48	2,738	2.15	28–13–5
Jeff Hackett, Chicago	41	2,473	2.16	19–18–4
Dominik Hasek, Buffalo	67	4,037	2.27	37–20–10
John Vanbiesbrouck, Florida	57	3,347	2.29	27–19–10
Chris Osgood, Detroit	47	2,769	2.30	23–13–9
Patrick Roy, Colorado	62	3,698	2.32	38–15–7
Mark Fitzpatrick, Florida	30	1,680	2.36	8–9–9
Mike Vernon, Detroit	33	1,952	2.43	13–11–8
Garth Snow, Philadelphia	35	1,884	2.52	14–8–8

N.H.L. CAREER SCORING LEADERS

(Through 1996–97 season)

		Yrs	Gm	G	A	Pts
1	**Wayne Gretzky**	18	1,335	862	1843	2705
2	Gordie Howe	26	1,767	801	1049	1850
3	Marcel Dionne	18	1,348	731	1040	1771
4	Phil Esposito	18	1,282	717	873	1590
5	**Mark Messier**	18	1,272	575	977	1552
6	**Mario Lemieux**	12	745	613	881	1494
7	Stan Mikita	22	1,394	541	926	1467
8	**Paul Coffey**	17	1,211	381	1063	1444
9	Bryan Trottier	18	1,279	524	901	1425
10	**Dale Hawerchuk**	16	1,188	518	891	1409
11	**Jari Kurri**	16	1,181	596	780	1376
12	John Bucyk	23	1,540	556	813	1369
13	**Ray Bourque**	18	1,290	362	1001	1363
14	Guy Lafleur	17	1,126	560	793	1353
15	**Ron Francis**	16	1,166	403	944	1347
16	**Steve Yzerman**	14	1,023	539	801	1340
17	**Denis Savard**	17	1,196	473	865	1338
18	Gilbert Perreault	17	1,191	512	814	1326
19	**Mike Gartner**	18	1,372	696	612	1308
20	Alex Delvecchio	24	1,549	456	825	1281

Players active during 1996–97 season in **bold** type.

Chess

WORLD CHAMPIONS

Both the International Chess Federation (FIDE) and the breakaway Professional Chess Association (PCA) were to stage world championship matches in 1995. Azerbaijan's Garry Kasparov, 31, who was FIDE world champion until he quit to join the PCA, became the PCA's first world champion in 1993. He defended his title in the fall against Viswanathan Anand, 24, of India. Kasparov's old rival, Anatoly Karpov, who reclaimed the FIDE title in 1993, will also defend.

1894–	Emanuel Lasker, Germany
1921	
1921–27	Jose R. Capablanca, Cuba
1927–35	Alexander A. Alekhine, U.S.S.R.
1935–37	Dr. Max Euwe, Netherlands
1937–46	Alexander A. Alekhine, U.S.S.R.[1]
1948–57	Mikhail Botvinnik, U.S.S.R.
1957–58	Vassily Smyslov, U.S.S.R.
1958–60	Mikhail Botvinnik, U.S.S.R.
1960–61	Mikhail Tal, U.S.S.R.
1961–63	Mikhail Botvinnik, U.S.S.R.
1963–68	Tigran Petrosian, U.S.S.R.
1969–71	Boris Spassky, U.S.S.R.
1972–74	Bobby Fischer, Los Angeles
1975	Bobby Fischer[2], Anatoly Karpov, U.S.S.R.
1976–85	Anatoly Karpov, U.S.S.R.[3]
1985–	Garry Kasparov, Russia[4]
1993–	Anatoly Karpov[5]

1. Alekhine, a French citizen, died while champion. 2. Relinquished title. 3. In 1978, Karpov defeated Viktor Korchnoi 6 games to 5. 4. PCA world champion after 1993. 5. FIDE world champion.

UNITED STATES CHAMPIONS

1909–36	Frank J. Marshall, New York
1936–44	Samuel Reshevsky, New York[1]
1944–46	Arnold S. Denker, New York
1946	Samuel Reshevsky, Boston
1948	Herman Steiner, Los Angeles
1951–52	Larry Evans, New York
1954–57	Arthur Bisguier, New York
1958–61	Bobby Fischer, Brooklyn, N.Y.
1962	Larry Evans, New York
1963–67	Bobby Fischer, New York
1968	Larry Evans, New York
1969–71	Samuel Reshevsky, Spring Valley, N.Y.
1972	Robert Byrne, Ossining, N.Y.
1973	Lubomir Kavelek, Washington; John Grefe, San Francisco
1974–77	Walter Browne, Berkeley, Calif.
1978–79	Lubomir Kavalek, New York
1980	Tie, Walter Browne, Berkeley, Calif. Larry Christiansen, Modesto, Calif. Larry Evans, Reno, Nev.
1981–82[2]	Tie, Walter Browne, Berkeley, Calif. Yasser Seirawan, Seattle, Wash.
1983	Tie, Walter Browne, Berkeley, Calif.

	Larry Christiansen, Los Angeles, Calif., Roman Dzindzichashvili, Corona, N.Y.
1984–85	Lev Alburt, New York City
1986	Yasser Seirawan, Seattle, Wash.
1987	Tie—Nick Defirmian, San Francisco, and Joel Benjamin, Brooklyn, N.Y.
1988	Michael Wilder, Princeton, N.J.
1989	Tie, Stuart Rachels, Birmingham, Ala. Yasser Seirawan, Seattle, Wash. Roman Dzindzichashvili, New York, N.Y.
1990–91	Lev Alburt, New York, N.Y.
1992	Gata Kamsky, Brooklyn, N.Y. Patrick Wolff, Somerville, Mass.
1993	Alexander Shabalov, Pittsburgh, Pa. and Alex Yermolinski, Edison, N.J.
1994	Boris Gulko, Fairlawn, N.J.
1995	Patrick Wolff, Somerville, Mass.
1996	Alex Yurmolinsky, Cleveland, Ohio
1997	Esther Epstein, Mass. (women) Joel Benjamin, N.Y. (men)

1. In 1942, Isaac I. Kashdan of New York was co-champion for a while because of a tie with Reshevsky in that year's tournament. Reshevsky won the play-off. 2. Championship not contested in 1982.

Bowling

The game of bowling in the United States is an indoor development of the more ancient outdoor game that survives as lawn bowling. The outdoor game is prehistoric in origin and probably goes back to Primitive Man and round stones that were rolled at some target. It is believed that a game something like nine-pins was popular among the Dutch, Swiss and Germans as long ago as A.D. 1200 at which time the game was played outdoors with an alley consisting of a single plank 12 to 18 inches wide along which was rolled a ball toward three rows of three pins each placed at the far end of the alley. When the first indoor alleys were built and how the game was modified from time to time are matters of dispute.

It is supposed that the early settlers of New Amsterdam (New York City) being Dutch, they brought their two bowling games with them. About a century ago the game of nine-pins was flourishing in the United States but so corrupted by gambling on matches that it was barred by law in New York and Connecticut. Since the law specifically barred "nine-pins," it was eventually evaded by adding another pin and thus legally making it a new game.

Various organizations were formed to make rules for bowling and supervise competition in the United States but none was successful until the American Bowling Congress, organized Sept. 9, 1895, became the ruling body.

AMERICAN BOWLING CONGRESS CHAMPIONS

Year	Singles	All-events	Year	Singles	All-events
1959	Ed Lubanski	Ed Lubanski	1980	Mike Eaton	Steve Fehr
1960	Paul Kulbaga	Vince Lucci	1981	Rob Vital	Rod Toft
1961	Lyle Spooner	Luke Karen	1982	Bruce Bohm	Rich Wonders
1962	Andy Renaldo	Billy Young	1983	Rick Kendrick	Tony Cariello
1963	Fred Delello	Bus Owalt	1984	Bob Antczak and Neal Young (tie)	Bob Goike
1964	Jim Stefanich	Les Zikes, Jr.			
1965	Ken Roeth	Tom Hathaway	1985	Glen Harbison	Barry Asher
1966	Don Chapman	John Wilcox	1986	Jess Mackey	Ed Marazka
1967	Frank Perry	Gary Lewis	1987	Terry Taylor	Ryan Schafer
1968	Wayne Kowalski	Vince Mazzanti	1988	Steve Hutkowski	Rick Steelsmith
1969	Greg Campbell	Eddie Jackson	1989	Paul Tetreault	George Hall
1970	Jake Yoder	Mike Berlin	1990	Bob Hochrein	Mike Neumann
1971	Al Cohn	Al Cohn	1991	Ed Deines	Tom Howery
1972	Bill Pointer	Mac Lowry	1992	Bob Youker and Gary Blatchford (tie)	Mike Tucker
1973	Ed Thompson	Ron Woolet			
1974	Gene Krause	Bob Hart	1993	Dan Bock	Jeff Nimke
1975	Jim Setser	Bobby Meadows	1994	John Weltzien	Thomas Holt
1976	Mike Putzer	Jim Lindquist	1995	Matt Surina	Jeff Kwiatkowski
1977	Frank Gadaleto	Bud Debenham	1996	Donald Scudder, Jr.	Scott Kurtz
1978	Rich Mersek	Chris Cobus	1997	John Socha	Jeff Richgels
1979	Rick Peters	Bob Basacchi			

PROFESSIONAL BOWLERS ASSOCIATION

National Championship Tournament

1960	Don Carter	1970	Mike McGrath	1980	Johnny Petraglia	1990	Jim Pencak
1961	Dave Soutar	1971	Mike Lemongello	1981	Earl Anthony	1991	Mike Miller
1962	Carmen Salvino	1972	Johnny Guenther	1982	Earl Anthony	1992	Eric Forkel
1963	Billy Hardwick	1973	Earl Anthony	1983	Earl Anthony	1993	Ron Palombi
1964	Bob Strampe	1974	Earl Anthony	1984	Bob Chamberlain	1994	David Traber
1965	Dave Davis	1975	Earl Anthony	1985	Mike Aulby	1995	Scott Alexander
1966	Wayne Zahn	1976	Paul Colwell	1986	Tom Crites	1996	Butch Soper
1967	Dave Davis	1977	Tommy Hudson	1987	Randy Pedersen	1997	Rich Steelsmith
1968	Wayne Zahn	1978	Warren Nelson	1988	Brian Voss		
1969	Mike McGrath	1979	Mike Aulby	1989	Pete Weber		

BOWLING PROPRIETORS' ASSOCIATION OF AMERICA—MEN

United States Open[1]

1971	Mike Lemongello	1978	Nelson Burton, Jr.	1985	Marshall Holman	1992	Robert Lawrence
1972	Don Johnson	1979	Joe Berardi	1986	Steve Cook	1993	Del Ballard, Jr.
1973	Mike McGrath	1980	Steve Martin	1987	Del Ballard	1994	Justin Hromek
1974	Larry Laub	1981	Marshall Holman	1988	Pete Weber	1995	Dave Husted
1975	Steve Neff	1982	Dave Husted	1989	Mike Aulby	1996	Dave Husted
1976	Paul Moser	1983	Gary Dickinson	1990	Ron Palumbi, Jr.		
1977	Johnny Petraglia	1984	Mark Roth	1991	Pete Weber		

1. Replaced All-Star tournament and is rolled as part of B.P.A. tour. NOTE: There was no 1997 tournament.

WOMEN'S INTERNATIONAL BOWLING CONGRESS CHAMPIONS

Year	Singles	All-events	Year	Singles	All-events
1959	Mae Bolt	Pat McBride	1981	Virginia Norton	Virginia Norton
1960	Marge McDaniels	Judy Roberts	1982	Gracie Freeman	Aleta Rzepecki
1961	Elaine Newton	Evelyn Teal	1983	Aleta Rzepecki	Virginia Norton
1962	Martha Hoffman	Flossie Argent	1984	Freida Gates	Shinobu Saitoh
1963	Dot Wilkinson	Helen Shablis	1985	Polly Schwarzel	Aleta Sill
1964	Jean Havlish	Jean Havlish	1986	Dana Stewart	Robin Romeo
1965	Doris Rudell	Donna Zimmer-man			and Maria Lewis (tie)
1966	Gloria Bouvia	Kate Helbig	1987	Regi Junak	Leanne Barrette
1967	Gloria Paeth	Carol Miller	1988	Michelle Meyer-Welty	Lisa Wagner
1968	Norma Parks	Susie Reichley	1989	Lorraine Anderson	Nancy Fehn
1969	Joan Bender	Helen Duval	1990	Dana Miller-Mackie and Paula Carter	Carol Norman
1970	Dorothy Fothergill	Dorothy Fothergill			
1971	Mary Scruggs	Lorrie Nichols	1991	Debbie Kuhn	Debbie Kuhn
1972	D. D. Jacobson	Mildred Mar-torella	1992	Patty Ann	Mitsuko Tokimoto
			1993	Karen Collurs and Kari Murph (tie)	Bertha Blackshur and Sharon Davis (tie)
1973	Bobby Buffaloe	Toni Calvery			
1974	Shirley Garms	Judy C. Soutar	1994	Vicki Fifield	Wendy Macpherson-Papanos
1975	Barbara Leicht	Virginia Norton			
1976	Bev Shonk	Betty Morris			
1977	Akiko Yamaga	Akiko Yamaga	1995	Beth Owen	Beth Owen
1978	Mae Bolt	Annese Kelly	1996	Cindy Berlanga	Lorrie Nichols
1979	Betty Morris	Betty Morris	1997	Jean Schmidt	Kendra Cameron
1980	Betty Morris	Cheryl Robinson			

BOWLING PROPRIETORS' ASSOCIATION OF AMERICA—WOMEN

United States Open

1971	Paula Carter	1978	Donna Adamek	1985	Pat Mercatanti	1992	Tish Johnson
1972	Lorrie Nichols	1979	Diana Silva	1986	Wendy MacPherson	1993	Dede Davidson
1973	Mildred Martorella	1980	Pat Costello (Calif.)	1987	Carol Nurman	1994	Aleta Sill
1974	Pat Costello (Calif.)	1981	Donna Adamek	1988	Lisa Wagner	1995	Tish Johnson
1975	Paula Carter	1982	Shinobu Saitoh	1989	Robin Romeo	1996	Liz Johnson
1976	Patty Costello (Pa.)	1983	Dana Miller	1990	Dana Miller-Mackie		
1977	Betty Morris	1984	Karen Ellingsworth	1991	Anne Marie Duggan		

NOTE: There was no 1997 tournament.

WIBC QUEENS TOURNAMENT CHAMPIONS

1961 Janet Harman	1971 Mildred Martorella	1981 Katsuko Sugimoto	1991 Dede Davidson
1962 Dorothy Wilkinson	1972 Dorothy Fothergill	1982 Katsuko Sugimoto	1992 Cindy Coburn-Carroll
1963 Irene Monterosso	1973 Dorothy Fothergill	1983 Aleta Rzepecki	1993 Jan Schmidt
1964 D.D. Jacobson	1974 Judy Soutar	1984 Kazue Inahashi	1994 Anne Marie Duggan
1965 Betty Kuczynski	1975 Cindy Powell	1985 Aleta Sill	1995 Sandy Postma
1966 Judy Lee	1976 Pamela Buckner	1986 Cora Fiebig	1996 Lisa Wagner
1967 Mildred Martorella	1977 Dana Stewart	1987 Cathy Almeida	1997 Sandra-Jo Shiery-Odom
1968 Phyllis Massey	1978 Loa Boxberger	1988 Wendy McPherson	
1969 Ann Feigel	1979 Donna Adamek	1989 Carol Gianotti	
1970 Mildred Martorella	1980 Donna Adamek	1990 Patty Ann	

PROFESSIONAL BOWLERS ASSOCIATION CHAMPIONSHIP—1997

(Toledo, Ohio, Mar. 21, 1997)

Winner—Rick Steelsmith defeated Brian Voss, 218–190 in title match.
2. Brian Voss, Atlanta, Ga.
3. Wayne Webb, Peoria, Ill.
4. Norm Duke, Clermont, Fla.
5. Tim Criss, Bel Air, Md.

WOMEN'S INTERNATIONAL BOWLING CONGRESS TOURNAMENT—1997

(Mar. 1–July 14, 1997, Reno, Nev.)

Singles— Jan Schmidt, Rochelle, Ill.	765
Doubles— Jennifer Klekamp, Cincinnati, Ohio and Regina Snodgrass, Versailles, Ind.	1,345
All Events— Kendra Cameron, Gambrilis, Md.	2,039
Team— Contour Power Grips, Vallejo, Calif. and Here 4 Beer, Glendale, Ariz.	3,017

AMERICAN BOWLING CONGRESS TOURNAMENT—1997

(Feb. 8–June 7, 1997, Huntsville, Ala.)

Regular Division

Singles— John Socha, New Berlin, Wis.	847
Doubles— Rob Steuber and Paul Zuehlke, Oshkosh, Wis.	1,464
All Events— Jeff Richgels, Oregon, Wis.	2,241
Team— Dan Ottman Enterprises, Troy, Mich.	3,379

Booster Division

Team— Pinsetter Lanes #1, West Point, Miss.	2,883

AMERICAN BOWLING CONGRESS MASTERS TOURNAMENT—1997

(April 29–May 3, 1997, Huntsville, Ala.)

Jason Queen, Decatur, Ill., defeated Erik Forkel, Tuscon, Ariz. 248–194 in final match.

Skiing

HISTORY OF SKIING IN THE UNITED STATES

Skis were devised for utility, to aid those who had to travel over snow. The Norwegians, Swedes, Lapps, and other inhabitants of northern lands used skis for many centuries before skiing became a sport. Emigrants from these countries brought skis to the United States with them. The first skier of record in the United States was a mailman by the name of "Snowshoe" Thompson, born and raised in Telemarken, Norway, who came to the United States and, beginning in 1850, used skis through 20 successive winters in carrying mail from Northern California to Carson Valley, Idaho.

Ski clubs sprang up over 100 years ago where there were Norwegian and Swedish settlers in Wisconsin and Minnesota and ski contests were held in that territory in 1886. On Feb. 21, 1904, at Ishpenning, Mich., a small group of skiers organized the National Ski Association. In 1961 it was renamed the United States Ski Association.

ALPINE WORLD CUP OVERALL WINNERS

Year	Men	Women	Team
967	Jean-Claude Killy, France	Nancy Greene, Canada	France
1968	Jean-Claude Killy, France	Nancy Greene, Canada	France
1969	Karl Schranz, Austria	Gertrude Gabl, Austria	Austria
1970	Karl Schranz, Austria	Michel Jacot, France	France
1971	Gustavo Thoeni, Italy	Annemarie Proell, Austria	France
1972	Gustavo Thoeni, Italy	Annemarie Proell, Austria	France
1973	Gustavo Thoeni, Italy	Annemarie Proell Moser, Austria	Austria
1974	Piero Gros, Italy	Annemarie Proell Moser, Austria	Austria
1975	Gustavo Thoeni, Italy	Annemarie Proell Moser, Austria	Austria
1976	Ingemar Stenmark, Sweden	Rosi Mittermaier, West Germany	Austria
1977	Ingemar Stenmark, Sweden	Lise-Marie Morerod, Switzerland	Austria
1978	Ingemar Stenmark, Sweden	Hanni Wenzel, Liechtenstein	Austria
1979	Peter Luescher, Switzerland	Annemarie Proell Moser, Austria	Austria
1980	Andreas Wenzel, Liechtenstein	Hanni Wenzel, Liechtenstein	Liechtenstein
1981	Phil Mahre, United States	Marie-Theres Nadig, Switzerland	Switzerland
1982	Phil Mahre, United States	Erika Hess, Switzerland	Austria
1983	Phil Mahre, United States	Tamara McKinney, United States	Switzerland
1984	Pirmin Zurbriggen, Switzerland	Erika Hess, Switzerland	Switzerland
1985	Marc Girardelli, Luxembourg	Michela Figini, Switzerland	Switzerland

Year	Men	Women	Team
1986	Marc Girardelli, Luxembourg	Maria Walliser, Switzerland	Switzerland
1987	Pirmin Zubriggen, Switzerland	Maria Walliser, Switzerland	Switzerland
1988	Pirmin Zubriggen, Switzerland	Michela Figini, Switzerland	Switzerland
1989	Marc Girardelli, Luxembourg	Vreni Schneider, Switzerland	Switzerland
1990	Pirmin Zubriggen, Switzerland	Petra Kronberger, Austria	Austria
1991	Marc Girardelli, Luxembourg	Petra Kronberger, Austria	Austria
1992	Paul Accola, Switzerland	Petra Kronberger, Austria	Switzerland
1993	Marc Girardelli, Luxembourg	Anita Wachter, Austria	Austria
1994	Kjetil Andre Aamodt, Norway	Anita Wachter, Austria	Austria
1995	Alberto Tomba, Italy	Vreni Schneider, Switzerland	Austria
1996	Lasse Kjus, Norway	Katja Seizinger, Germany	Austria
1997	Luc Alphand, France	Pernilla Wiberg, Sweden	Austria

1997 UNITED STATES ALPINE CHAMPIONSHIPS

Women's Slalom
1. Kristina Koznick, U.S.A.
2. Carrie Sheinberg, U.S.A.
3. Katerina Tichy, Czech Republic
4. Alex Shaffer, U.S.A.
5. Edda Mutter, Germany

Women's Giant Slalom
1. Deborah Compagnoni, Italy
2. Katja Seizinger, Germany
3. Karin Roten, Switzerland
4. Isolde Kostner, Italy
5. Pernilla Wiberg, Sweden

Women's Downhill
1. Hilary Lindh, U.S.A.
2. Megan Gerety, U.S.A.
3. Katie Monahan, U.S.A.
4. Kirsten Clark, U.S.A.
5. Shana Switzer, U.S.A.

Women's Combined
1. Carrie Sheinberg, U.S.A.
2. Kirsten Clark, U.S.A.
3. Liz Skibiski, U.S.A.

Men's Slalom
1. Martin Tichy, Czech Republic
2. Casey Puckett, U.S.A., and Uros Pavlovcic, Slovenia (tie)
4. Chip Knight, U.S.A.
5. Matt Grosjean, U.S.A.

Men's Giant Slalom
1. Sacha Gros, U.S.A.
2. Uros Pavlovcic, Slovenia
3. Dane Spencer, U.S.A.
4. Chris Puckett, U.S.A.
5. Thomas Vonn, U.S.A.

Men's Downhill
1. Tommy Moe, U.S.A.
2. AJ Kitt, U.S.A.
3. Chris Puckett, U.S.A.
4. Chad Fleischer, U.S.A.
5. Mike Makar, U.S.A.

Men's Combined
1. Chris Puckett, U.S.A.
2. Sacha Gros, U.S.A.
3. Casey Puckett, U.S.A.

1997 ALPINE WORLD CUP CHAMPIONS

Men	Pts
Overall— Luc Alphand, France	1,130
Downhill— Luc Alphand, France	779
Super G— Luc Alphand, France	351
Giant Slalom— Michael Von Gruenigen, Switzerland	660
Slalom— Thomas Sykora, Austria	695

Women	Pts
Overall— Pernilla Wiberg, Sweden	1,960
Downhill— Renate Götschl, Austria	483
Super G— Hilda Gerg, Germany	490
Giant Slalom— Deborah Compagnoni, Italy	560
Slalom— Lara Magoni, Italy	770

1997 NATIONS CUP STANDINGS

Overall

1.	Austria	10,436	2. Italy	2,930
2.	Italy	6,138	3. Switzerland	2,308
3.	Switzerland	5,381	4. France	1,984
4.	France	4,395		
5.	Germany	n.a.		

Men
1. Austria 3,081

Women

1.	Austria	7,355
2.	Italy	3,208
3.	Switzerland	3,073
4.	France	2,411

1997 WORLD CUP SKI JUMPING

1. Primoz Peterka, Slovakia — 1,402
2. Dieter Thoma, Germany — 1,208
3. Kazuyoshi Funaki, Japan — 1,018
4. Takanobu Okabe, Japan — 941
5. Hiroya Saitoh, Japan — 923

UNITED STATES SKI JUMPING CHAMPIONSHIPS—1997

(Jan. 20–21, 1997, Lake Placid, N.Y.)
Large Hill (120 meters)—Randy Weber, Steamboat Springs, Colo.
Normal Hill (90 meters)—Randy Weber, Steamboat Springs, Colo.

1997 CROSS COUNTRY WORLD CUP

Women
1. Elena Valebe, Russia — 940
2. Stefania Belmondo, Italy — 909
3. Katerina Neumannova, Czech Republic — 525
4. Nina Gavriljuk, Russia — 518
5. Olga Danilova, Russia — 414

Men
1. Björn Daehlie, Norway — 845
2. Mika Myllyla, Finland — 580
3. Fulvio Valbusa, Italy — 523
4. Erling Jevne, Norway — 480
5. Silvio Fauner, Italy — 447

1997 FREESTYLE SKIING WORLD CUP

Women

Acro-Ski—Elena Batalova, Russia
Moguls—Tatjana Mittermayer, Germany
Aerials—Veronica Brenner, Canada

Men

Acro-Ski—Fabrice Becker, France
Moguls—Jean-Luc Brassard, Canada
Aerials—Nicolas Fontaine, Canada

JAMES E. SULLIVAN MEMORIAL AWARD WINNERS
(Amateur Athlete of Year Chosen in Amateur Athletic Union Poll)

1930	Robert Tyre Jones, Jr.	Golf
1931	Bernard E. Berlinger	Track and field
1932	James A. Bausch	Track and field
1933	Glenn Cunningham	Track and field
1934	William R. Bonthron	Track and field
1935	W. Lawson Little, Jr.	Golf
1936	Glenn Morris	Track and field
1937	J. Donald Budge	Tennis
1938	Donald R. Lash	Track and field
1939	Joseph W. Burk	Rowing
1940	J. Gregory Rice	Track and field
1941	Leslie MacMitchell	Track and field
1942	Cornelius Warmerdam	Track and field
1943	Gilbert L. Dodds	Track and field
1944	Ann Curtis	Swimming
1945	Felix (Doc) Blanchard	Football
1946	Y. Arnold Tucker	Football
1947	John B. Kelly, Jr.	Rowing
1948	Robert B. Mathias	Track and field
1949	Richard T. Button	Figure skating
1950	Fred Wilt	Track and field
1951	Robert E. Richards	Track and field
1952	Horace Ashenfelter	Track and field
1953	Major Sammy Lee	Diving
1954	Malvin Whitfield	Track and field
1955	Harrison Dillard	Track and field
1956	Patricia McCormick	Diving
1957	Bobby Jo Morrow	Track and Field
1958	Glenn Davis	Track and field
1959	Parry O'Brien	Track and field
1960	Rafer Johnson	Track and field
1961	Wilma Rudolph Ward	Track and field
1962	Jim Beatty	Track and field
1963	John Pennel	Track and field
1964	Don Schollander	Swimming
1965	Bill Bradley	Basketball
1966	Jim Ryun	Track and field
1967	Randy Matson	Track and field
1968	Debbie Meyer	Swimming
1969	Bill Toomey	Decathlon
1970	John Kinsella	Swimming
1971	Mark Spitz	Swimming
1972	Frank Shorter	Marathon
1973	Bill Walton	Basketball
1974	Rick Wohlhuter	Track
1975	Tim Shaw	Swimming
1976	Bruce Jenner	Track and field
1977	John Naber	Swimming
1978	Tracy Caulkins	Swimming
1979	Kurt Thomas	Gymnastics
1980	Eric Heiden	Speed skating
1981	Carl Lewis	Track and field
1982	Mary Decker Tabb	Track and field
1983	Edwin Moses	Track and field
1984	Greg Louganis	Diving
1985	Joan Benoit-Samuelson	Marathon
1986	Jackie Joyner-Kersee	Heptathlon
1987	Jim Abbott	Baseball
1988	Florence Griffith-Joyner	Track and field
1989	Janet Evans	Swimming
1990	John Smith	Wrestling
1991	Mike Powell	Track and field
1992	Bonnie Blair	Speed skating
1993	Charles Ward	Football/basketball
1994	Dan Jansen	Speed skating
1995	Bruce Baumgartner	Wrestling
1996	Michael Johnson	Track and field

Speed Skating

U.S. OUTDOOR CHAMPIONS (LONG TRACK)

Men

1959–60	Ken Bartholomew
1961	Ed Rudolph
1962	Floyd Bedbury
1963	Tom Gray
1964	Neil Blatchford
1965–66	Rich Wurster
1967	Mike Passarella
1968–70	Peter Cefalu
1971	Jack Walters
1972	Barth Levy
1973	Mike Woods
1974	Leigh Barczewski, Mike Passarella
1975	Rich Wurster
1976	John Wurster
1977	Jim Chapin
1978	Bill Heinkel
1979	Erik Henriksen
1980	Greg Oly
1981	Tom Grannes
1982	Greg Oly
1983–84	Michael Ralston
1985	Andy Gabel
1986	Eric Klein
1987	Dave Paulicic
1988	Patrick Wentland
1989	Matt Trimble
1990	Andy Zak
1991	Pat Seltsam
1992	Mike Jansen
1993	Brian Smith
1994	K.C. Boutiette
1995	David Tamburrino
1996	K.C. Boutiette

Women

1960	Mary Novak
1961	Jean Ashworth
1962	Jean Omelenchuk
1963	Jean Ashworth
1964	Diane White
1965	Jean Omelenchuk
1966	Diane White
1967	Jean Ashworth
1968	Helen Lutsch
1969	Sally Blatchford
1970–71	Sheila Young
1972	Ruth Moore, Nancy Thorne
1973	Nancy Class
1974	Kris Garbe
1975	Nancy Swider
1976	Connie Carpenter
1977	Liz Crowe
1978	Paula Class, Betsy Davis
1979	Gretchen Byrnes
1980	Shari Miller
1981–82	Lisa Merrifield
1983–84	Janet Hainstock
1985	Betsy Davis
1986	Deb Perkins
1987	Laura Zuckerman
1988	Elise Brinich
1989	Liza Merrifield
1990	Jane Eickhoff
1991	Liza Dennehy
1992	Hilary Mills
1993	Chantal Bailey
1994–96	Moira D'Andrea

WORLD SPEED SKATING RECORDS (LONG TRACK)

Distance	Time	Skater	Place	Year
Men				
500m	0:35.76	Dan Jansen, United States	Calgary, Canada	1994
1,000m	1:12.37	Yasunori Miyabe, Japan	Calgary, Canada	1994
1,500m	1:50.05	Neal Marshall, Canada	Calgary, Canada	1997
3,000m	3:56.16	Thomas Blos, Netherlands	Calgary, Canada	1992
5,000m	6:34.96	Johann Olav Koss, Norway	Lillehammer, Norway	1994
10,000m	13:30.55	Johann Olav Koss, Norway	Lillehammer, Norway	1994
Women				
500m	0:38.69	Bonnie Blair, United States	Calgary, Canada	1995
1,000m	1:17.65	Christa Rothenburger, Germany	Calgary, Canada	1988
1,500m	1:59.30	Karin Kania, Germany	Medeo, U.S.S.R.	1986
3,000m	4:09.32	Gunda Niemann, Germany	Calgary, Canada	1994
5,000m	7:03:26	Gunda Niemann, Germany	Calgary, Canada	1994

U.S. SPRINT CHAMPIONSHIPS—1997

Men	Time
500m—Casey FitzRandolph	36.60
1,000m—Casey FitzRandolph	1:13.30
Overall standings:	Points
1. Casey FitzRandolph	147.010
2. Cory Carpenter	149.220
3. David Cruikshank	150.415
Women	Time
500m—Becky Sundstrom	41.02
1,000m—Becky Sundstrom	1:21.25
Overall standings:	Points
1. Becky Sundstrom	163.010
2. Moira D'Andrea	164.660
3. Tama Sundstrom	167.080

1997 WORLD CUP CHAMPIONS

Men

500 meters	Hiroyasu Shimizu, Japan
1,000 meters	Manabu Horii, Japan
1,500 meters	Rintje Ritsma, Netherlands
5,000 meters	Rintje Ritsma, Netherlands
Women	
500 meters	Ruihong Xue, China
1,000 meters	Franziska Schenk, Germany
1,500 meters	Gunda Niemann, Germany
3,000 meters	Ronny de Jong, Netherlands

U.S. SHORT TRACK CHAMPIONSHIPS—1997

(March 7–9, 1997, Walpole, Mass.)

Women	Time
500m—Erin Porter	0:47.96
1,000m—Caroline Hallisey	1:41.05
1,500m—Julie Goskowicz	2:37.08
3,000m—Erin Porter	5:53.03

Overall Ranking: 1. Erin Porter, 2. Julie Goskowicz, 3. Caroline Hallisey

Men	Time
500m—Andy Gabel	0:44.19
1,000m—Daniel Weinstein	1:37.03
1,500m—Apolo Anton Ohno	2:22.02
3,000m—Rusty Smith	5:21.01

Overall Ranking: 1. Apolo Anton Ohno, 2. Andy Gabel, 3. Rusty Smith

WORLD CHAMPIONSHIPS—1997

(Feb. 14–16, 1997, Nagano, Japan)

Men		Women	
500 meters	Kyou-Hyuk Lee, South Korea	500 meters	Annamarie Thomas, Netherlands
1,500 meters	Ids Postma, Netherlands	1,500 meters	Gunda Niemann, Germany
5,000 meters	Bart Veldkamp, Netherlands	3,000 meters	Gunda Niemann, Germany
10,000 meters	Bart Veldkamp, Netherlands	5,000 meters	Gunda Niemann, Germany
All-around	Ids Postma, Netherlands	All-around	Gunda Niemann, Germany

Figure Skating

WORLD CHAMPIONS

Men

1960	Alain Giletti, France
1961	No competition
1962	Donald Jackson, Canada
1963	Don McPherson, Canada
1964	Manfred Schnelldorfer, West Germany
1965	Alain Calmat, France
1966–68	Emmerich Danzer, Austria
1969–70	Tim Wood, United States
1971–73	Ondrej Nepela, Czechoslovakia
1974	Jan Hoffman, East Germany
1975	Sergei Volkov, U.S.S.R.
1976	John Curry, Britain
1977	Vladimir Kovalev, U.S.S.R.
1978	Charles Tickner, United States
1979	Vladimir Kovalev, U.S.S.R.
1980	Jan Hoffman, East Germany
1981–84	Scott Hamilton, United States
1985	Alexandr Fadeev, U.S.S.R.
1986	Brian Boitano, United States
1987	Brian Orser, Canada
1988	Brian Boitano, United States
1989–91	Kurt Browning, Canada
1992	Viktor Petrenko, Unified Team
1993	Kurt Browning, Canada
1994	Elvis Stojko, Canada
1995	Elvis Stojko, Canada
1996	Todd Eldredge, United States
1997	Elvis Stojko, Canada

Women
1956–60 Carol Heiss, United States
1961 No competition
1962–64 Sjoukje Dijkstra, Netherlands
1965 Petra Burka, Canada
1966–68 Peggy Fleming, United States
1969–70 Gabriele Seyfert, East Germany
1971–72 Beatrix Schuba, Austria
1973 Karen Magnusson, Canada
1974 Christine Errath, East Germany
1975 Dianne de Leeuw, Netherlands

1976 Dorothy Hamill, United States
1977 Linda Fratianne, United States
1978 Anett Poetzsch, East Germany
1979 Linda Fratianne, United States
1980 Anett Poetzsch, East Germany
1981 Denise Beillmann, Switzerland
1982 Elaine Zayak, United States
1983 Rosalynn Sumners, United States

1984–85 Katarina Witt, East Germany
1986 Debi Thomas, United States
1987–88 Katarina Witt, East Germany
1989 Midori Ito, Japan
1990 Jill Trenary, United States
1991–92 Kristi Yamaguchi, United States
1993 Oksana Baiul, Ukraine
1994 Yuka Sato, Japan
1995 Chen Lu, China
1996 Michelle Kwan, United States
1997 Tara Lipinski, United States

U.S. CHAMPIONS

Men
1946–52 Richard Button
1953–56 Hayes Jenkins
1957–60 David Jenkins
1961 Bradley Lord
1962 Monty Hoyt
1963 Tommy Liz
1964 Scott Allen
1965 Gary Visconti
1966 Scott Allen
1967 Gary Visconti
1968–70 Tim Wood
1971 John M. Petkevich
1972 Ken Shelley
1973–75 Gordon McKellen
1976 Terry Kubicka
1977–80 Charles Tickner
1981–84 Scott Hamilton

1985–88 Brian Boitano
1989 Christopher Bowman
1990–91 Todd Eldredge
1992 Christopher Bowman
1993–94 Scott Davis
1995 Todd Eldredge
1996 Rudy Galindo
1997 Todd Eldridge
Women
1943–48 Gretchen Merrill
1949–50 Yvonne Sherman
1951 Sonya Klopfer
1952–56 Tenley Albright
1957–60 Carol Heiss
1961 Laurence Owen
1962 Barbara Roles Pursley
1963 Lorraine Hanlon
1964–68 Peggy Fleming

1969–73 Janet Lynn
1974–76 Dorothy Hamill
1977–80 Linda Fratianne
1981 Elaine Zayak
1982–84 Rosalynn Sumners
1985 Tiffany Chin
1986 Debi Thomas
1987 Jill Trenary
1988 Debi Thomas
1989–90 Jill Trenary
1991 Tonya Harding
1992 Kristi Yamaguchi
1993 Nancy Kerrigan
1994 Tonya Harding
1995 Nicole Bobek
1996 Michelle Kwan
1997 Tara Lipinski

1997 WORLD CHAMPIONSHIPS
Men's singles
Gold: Elvis Stojko, Canada
Silver: Todd Eldredge, Unites States
Bronze: Alexei Yagudin, Russia
Women's singles
Gold: Tara Lipinski, United States
Silver: Michelle Kwan, United States
Bronze: Nicole Bobek, United States
Pairs
Gold: Mandy Wotzel and Ingo Steuer, Germany
Silver: Marina Eltsova and Andrei Bushkov, Russia
Bronze: Jenni Meno and Todd Sand, Unites States
Dance
Gold: Oksana Gritschuk and Evgeny Platov, Russia
Silver: Anjelica Krylova and Oleg Ovsiannikov, Russia
Bronze: Oksana Kazakova and Artur Dmitriev, Russia

1997 UNITED STATES CHAMPIONSHIPS

Senior men—Todd Eldridge, Chatham, Mass.
Senior women—Tara Lipinski, Philadelphia, Pa.
Senior pairs—Kyoko Ina, Guttenberg, N.J., and Jason Dungjen, Goshen, N.Y.
Senior dance—Elizabeth Punsalan, Syracuse, N.Y., and Jerod Swallo, Ann Arbor, Mich.

Swimming

WORLD RECORDS—MEN

(Through September 19, 1997)

Distance	Record	Holder	Country	Date
Freestyle				
50 meters	0:21.81	Tom Jager	United States	March 24, 1990
100 meters	0:48.21	Alexander Popov	Russia	June 18, 1994
200 meters	1:46.69	Georgio Lamberti	Italy	Aug. 15, 1989
400 meters	3:43.80	Kieren Perkins	Australia	Sept. 9, 1994
800 meters	7:46.00	Kieren Perkins	Australia	Aug. 24, 1994
1,500 meters	14:41.66	Kieren Perkins	Australia	Aug. 24, 1994

Distance	Record	Holder	Country	Date
Backstroke				
100 meters	53.86	Jeff Rouse	United States	July 31, 1992
200 meters	1:56.57	Martin Zubero	Spain	Nov. 23, 1991
Breaststroke				
100 meters	1:00.60	Fred de Burghgraeve	Belgium	July 20, 1996
200 meters	2:10.16	Mike Barrowman	United States	July 29, 1992
Butterfly				
100 meters	0:52.27	Denis Pankrat	Russia	June 24, 1996
200 meters	1:55.22	Denis Pankratov	Russia	June 14, 1995
Individual Medley				
200 meters	1:58.16	Jani Sievinen	Finland	Sept. 11, 1994
400 meters	4:12.30	Tom Dolan	United States	Sept. 6, 1994
Medley Relay				
400 meters	3:34.84	United States	Olympic Team	July 26, 1996
Freestyle Relay				
400 meters	3:15.11	United States	Pan Pacific Team	Aug. 12, 1995
800 meters	7:11.95	Unified Team	Former Soviet Union	July 27, 1992

Approved by the International Swimming Federation (F.I.N.A.) (F.I.N.A. discontinued acceptance of records in yards in 1968)
Source: United States Swim Team.

WORLD RECORDS—WOMEN

(Through September 19, 1997)

Distance	Record	Holder	Country	Date
Freestyle				
50 meters	0:24.51	Jingyi Le	China	Sept. 11, 1994
100 meters	0:54.01	Jingyi Le	China	Sept. 5, 1994
200 meters	1:56.78	Franziska van Almsick	Germany	Sept. 6, 1994
400 meters	4:03.85	Janet Evans	United States	Sept. 22, 1988
800 meters	8:16.22	Janet Evans	United States	Aug. 20, 1989
1,500 meters	15:52.10	Janet Evans	United States	March 26, 1988
Backstroke				
100 meters	1:00.16	Chijong He	China	Sept. 10, 1994
200 meters	2:06.62	Kristina Egerszegi	Hungary	Aug. 26, 1991
Breaststroke				
100 meters	1:07.02	Penny Heyns	South Africa	July 21, 1996
200 meters	2:24.76	Rebecca Brown	Australia	March 16, 1994
Butterfly				
100 meters	0:57.93	Mary T. Meagher	United States	Aug. 16, 1981
200 meters	2:05.96	Mary T. Meagher	United States	Aug. 13, 1981
Individual Medley				
200 meters	2:11.65	Lin Li	China	July 30, 1992
400 meters	4:36.10	Petra Schneider	East Germany	Aug. 1, 1982
Medley Relay				
400 meters	4:01.67	China	National Team	Sept. 10, 1994
Freestyle Relay				
400 meters	3:37.91	China	National Team	Sept. 7, 1994
800 meters	7:55.47	East Germany	National Team	Aug. 18, 1987

Approved by the International Swimming Federation (F.I.N.A.) (F.I.N.A. discontinued acceptance of records in yards in 1968)
Source: United States Swim Team.

AMERICAN SWIMMING RECORDS

(As of September 19, 1997)

Distance	Holder	Record	Date
MEN			
Freestyle			
50 meters	Tom Jager	0:21.81	March 24, 1990
100 meters	Matt Biondi	0:48.42	August 10, 1988
200 meters	Matt Biondi	1:47.72	August 15, 1989
400 meters	Matt Cetlinski	3:48.06	August 11, 1988
800 meters	Sean Killion	7:52.45	July 27, 1987
1,500 meters	George DiCarlo	15:01.51	June 30, 1984
Backstroke			
100 meters	Jeff Rouse	0:53.86	July 31, 1992
200 meters	Tripp Schwenk	1:58.33	August 1, 1995
Breaststroke			
100 meters	Jeremey Linn	1:00.77	July 20, 1996
200 meters	Mike Barrowman	2:10.16	July 29, 1992
Butterfly			
100 meters	Pablo Morales	0:52.84	June 23, 1986
200 meters	Melvin Stewart	1:55.69	January 12, 1991
Individual Medley			
200 meters	David Wharton	2:00.11	August 20, 1989
400 meters	Tom Dolan	4:12.30	September 6, 1994
Medley Relay			
400 meters	U.S. Olympic Team	3:34.84	July 26, 1996
Freestyle Relay			
400 meters	U.S. Pan Pacific Team	3:15.11	August 12, 1995
800 meters	U.S. National Team	7:12.51	September 21, 1988

Distance	Holder	Record	Date
WOMEN			
Freestyle			
50 meters	Amy Van Dyken	0:24.87	July 26, 1996
100 meters	Jenny Thompson	0:54.48	March 1, 1992
200 meters	Nicole Haislett	1:57.55	March 27, 1992
400 meters	Janet Evans	4:03.85	September 22, 1988
800 meters	Janet Evans	8:16.22	August 20, 1989
1,500 meters	Janet Evans	15:52.10	March 26, 1988
Backstroke			
100 meters	Lea Loveless	1:00.82	July 30, 1992
200 meters	Betsy Mitchell	2:08.60	June 27, 1986
Breaststroke			
100 meters	Amanda Beard	1:08.09	July 21, 1996
200 meters	Anita Nall	2:25.35	March 3, 1992
Butterfly			
100 meters	Mary T. Meagher	0:57.93	August 16, 1981
200 meters	Mary T. Meagher	2:05.96	August 13, 1981
Individual Medley			
200 meters	Summer Sanders	2:11.91	July 30, 1992
400 meters	Summer Sanders	4:37.58	July 26, 1992
Medley Relay			
400 meters	U.S. National Team	4:02.54	July 30, 1992
Freestyle Relay			
400 meters	U.S. National Team	3:39.46	July 28, 1992
800 meters	U.S. National Team	8:02.12	August 17, 1986

N.C.A.A. SWIMMING AND DIVING CHAMPIONSHIPS—1997

Women

(March 20–22, 1997, University of Minnesota, Twin Cities)

50-yard freestyle—Catherine Fox, Stanford	0:22.01
100-yard freestyle—Martina Moravcova, Southern Methodist	0:48.18
200-yard freestyle—Martina Moravcova, Southern Methodist	1:43.08
500-yard freestyle—Lindsay Benko, Southern California	4:44.93
1,650-yard freestyle—Trina Jackson, Arizona	15:59.82
100-yard backstroke—Catherine Fox, Stanford	0:53.23
200-yard backstroke—Lindsay Benko, Southern California	1:54.42
100-yard breaststroke—Gretchen Hegner, Minnesota	1:00.32
200-yard breaststroke—Kristin Quance, U.S.C.	2:09.62
100-yard butterfly—Mimi Bowen, Auburn	0:52.05
200-yard butterfly—Lia Oberstar, Southern Methodist	1:56.76
200-yard individual medley—Martina Moravcova, Southern Methodist	1:55.81
400-yard individual medley—Kristine Quance, Southern California	4:06.54
200-yard medley relay—Auburn	1:39.57
400-yard medley relay—Southern Methodist	3:39.06
200-yard freestyle relay—Arizona	1:29.56
400-yard freestyle relay—Stanford	3:16.72
800-yard freestyle relay—Southern Methodist	7:09.92
1-meter springboard dive—Vera Ilyina, Texas	455.90
3-meter springboard dive—Vera Ilyina, Texas	587.80
10-meter platform dive—Laura Wilkinson, Texas	606.10

Team standings:
1. Southern California, 406.0
2. Stanford, 395.0
3. Southern Methodist, 353.5

Men

(March 27–30, 1997, University of Minnesota, Twin Cities)

50-yard freestyle—Brett Hawke, Auburn	0:19.19
100-yard freestyle—Lars Frolander, Southern Methodist	0:42.89
200-yard freestyle—John Piersma, Michigan	1:34.88
500-yard freestyle—John Piersma, Michigan	4:15.79
1650-yard freestyle—Ryk Neethling, Arizona	14:43.44
100-yard backstroke—Neil Walker, Texas	0:45.25
200-yard backstroke—Lenny Krayzelburg, Southern California	1:41.10
100-yard breaststroke—Jeremy Linn, Tennessee	0:52.32
200-yard breaststroke—Jeremy Linn, Tennessee	1:55.27
100-yard butterfly—Lars Frolander, Southern Methodist	0:46.28
200-yard butterfly—Stephen Parry, Florida State	1:44.28
200-yard individual medley—Kris Babylon, Georgia	1:45.19
400-yard individual medley—Tom Wilkens, Stanford	3:45.59
200-yard freestyle relay—Auburn	1:17.54
400-yard freestyle relay—Auburn	1:25.40
800-yard freestyle relay—Michigan	6:23.51
200-yard medley relay—Auburn	1:25.40
1-meter springboard dive—Rio Ramirez, Miami, Fla.	610.05
3-meter springboard dive—Tyce Routson, Miami, Fla.	643.10
10-meter platform dive—Tyce Routson, Miami, Fla.	811.80

Team standings:
1. Auburn, 496.5
2. Stanford, 340.0
3. Georgia, 297.0

PHILLIPS 66 NATIONAL SWIMMING CHAMPIONSHIPS—1997

Men

50-meter freestyle—Bill Pilczuk, Auburn Aquatics	0:22.45
100-meter freestyle—Scott Tucker, West Florida	0:49.68
200-meter freestyle—Josh Davis, Athletes in Action	1:49.00
400-meter freestyle—Chad Carvin, Hillenbrand Aqua	3:50.13
800-meter freestyle—Timothy Siciliano, North Coast	8:02.83
1500-meter freestyle—Chad Carvin, Hillenbrand Aqua	15:15.63
100-meter backstroke—Lenny Krayzelburg, Trojan Swim Club	0:54.69
200-meter backstroke—Lenny Krayzelburg, Trojan Swim Club	2:58.04
100-meter backstroke—Kurt Grote, Santa Clara Swim	1:01.45
200-meter breaststroke—Kurt Grote, Santa Clara Swim	2:12.35
100-meter butterfly—Neil Walker, Verona Aquatic	0:53.06
200-meter butterfly—Tom Malchow, Club Wolverine	1:58.37
200-meter individual medley—Tom Dolan, Curl-Burke Swim	2:01.18
400-meter individual medley—Tom Dolan, Curl-Burke Swim	4:17.13
4 x 100 medley relay—Santa Clara "A" Men	3:42.52
4 x 100 free relay—Santa Clara "A" Men	3:24.28
4 x 200 free relay—Club Wolverine "A"	7:30.71

Women

50-meter freestyle—Amy Van Dyken, Greenwood Athletics	0:25.10
100-meter freestyle—Jenny Thompson, Stanford Swimming	0:54.96
200-meter freestyle—Cristina Teuscher, Badger Swim Club	2:01.00
400-meter freestyle—Brooke Bennett, BSTC Blue Wave	4:11.34
800-meter freestyle—Brooke Bennett, BSTC Blue Wave	8:28.79
1,500-meter freestyle—Brooke Bennett, BSTC Blue Wave	16:10.93
100-meter backstroke—Lea Maurer, Badger Swim Club	1:01.53
200-meter backstroke—Amanda Adkins, Greater Columbus	2:12.62
100-meter backstroke—Kristy Kowal, Athens Bulldogs	1:08.80
200-meter breaststroke—Jenna Street, Bolles Sharks	2:28.97
100-meter butterfly—Misty Hyman, Arizona Desert Fox	0:59.49
200-meter butterfly—Misty Hyman, Arizona Desert Fox	2:09.08
200-meter individual medley—Kristine Quance, Trojan Swim Club	2:13.55
400-meter individual medley—Kristine Quance, Trojan Swim Club	4:39.67
4 x 100 medley relay—Trojan Swim Club	4:14.59
4 x 200 free relay—Bolles "A" Women	8:18.70

NATIONAL DIVING CHAMPIONSHIPS—1997

(Aug. 12–16, 1997, Southern Methodist University, Dallas, Texas)

MEN	Points	WOMEN	Points
Synchronized platform—John Kiani and Hank Richardson, Woodlands Diving Team	299.82	Synchronized 3-meter—Kathy Pesek and Tracy Bonner, Tennessee Diving	260.94
Synchronized 3-meter—P.J. Bogard, Minnesota Diving Club, and Kent Ferguson, Mustangs in the Sun	319.02	Synchronized platform—Kristin Link, Mustangs in the Sun, and Lindsay Long, Cincinnati Stingrays	247.44
Platform—David Pichler, Atlantic Diving Team	632.70	3-meter—Laura Wilkinson, Woodlands Diving Team	536.73
3-meter—Troy Dumais, Trojan Dive Club	666.36	1-meter—Erica Sorgi, Mission Viejo Nadadores	284.79
1-meter—Troy Dumais, Trojan Dive Club	399.33	Platform—Laura Wilkinson,m Woodlands Diving Team	503.49

Boxing

Whether it be called pugilism, prize fighting or boxing, there is no tracing "the Sweet Science" to any definite source. Tales of rivals exchanging blows for fun, fame or money go back to earliest recorded history and classical legend. There was a mixture of boxing and wrestling called the "pancratium" in the ancient Olympic Games and in such contests the rivals belabored one another with hands fortified with heavy leather wrappings that were sometimes studded with metal. More than one Olympic competitor lost his life at this brutal exercise.

There was little law or order in pugilism until Jack Broughton, one of the early champions of England, drew up a set of rules for the game in 1743. Broughton, called "the father of English boxing," also is credited with having invented boxing gloves. However, these gloves—or "mufflers" as they were called—were used only in teaching "the manly art of self-defense" or in training bouts. All professional championship fights were contested with "bare knuckles" until 1892, when John L. Sullivan lost the heavyweight championship of the world to James J. Corbett in New Orleans in a bout in which both contestants wore regulation gloves.

The Broughton rules were superseded by the London Prize Ring Rules of 1838. The 8th Marquis of Queensberry, with the help of John G. Chambers, put forward the "Queensberry Rules" in 1866, a code that called for gloved contests. Amateurs took quickly to the Queensberry Rules, the professionals slowly.

HISTORY OF WORLD HEAVYWEIGHT CHAMPIONSHIP FIGHTS

(Bouts in which a new champion was crowned)

Date	Where held	Winner, weight, age	Loser, weight, age	Rounds
Sept. 7, 1892	New Orleans, La.	James J. Corbett, 178 (26)	John L. Sullivan, 212 (33)	21
March 17, 1897	Carson City, Nev.	Bob Fitzsimmons, 167 (34)	James J. Corbett, 183 (30)	KO 14
June 9, 1899	Coney Island, N.Y.	James J. Jeffries, 206 (24)[1]	Bob Fitzsimmons, 167 (37)	KO 11
Feb. 23, 1906	Los Angeles	Tommy Burns, 180 (24)[2]	Marvin Hart, 188 (29)	20
Dec. 26, 1908	Sydney, N.S.W.	Jack Johnson, 196 (30)	Tommy Burns, 176 (27)	KO 14
April 5, 1915	Havana, Cuba	Jess Willard, 230 (33)	Jack Johnson, 205½ (37)	KO 26
July 4, 1919	Toledo, Ohio	Jack Dempsey, 187 (24)	Jess Willard, 245 (37)	KO 3
Sept. 23, 1926	Philadelphia	Gene Tunney, 189 (28)[3]	Jack Dempsey, 190 (31)	10
June 12, 1930	New York	Max Schmeling, 188 (24)	Jack Sharkey, 197 (27)	WF 4
June 21, 1932	Long Island City	Jack Sharkey, 205 (29)	Max Schmeling, 188 (26)	15
June 29, 1933	Long Island City	Primo Carnera, 260½ (26)	Jack Sharkey, 201 (30)	KO 6
June 14, 1934	Long Island City	Max Baer, 209½ (25)	Primo Carnera, 263¼ (27)	KO 11
June 13, 1935	Long Island City	Jim Braddock, 193¾ (29)	Max Baer, 209½ (26)	15
June 22, 1937	Chicago	Joe Louis, 197¼ (23)	Jim Braddock, 197 (31)	KO 8
June 22, 1949	Chicago	Ezzard Charles, 181¾ (27)[4]	Joe Walcott, 195½ (35)	15
Sept. 27, 1950	New York	Ezzard Charles, 184½ (29)[5]	Joe Louis, 218 (36)	15
July 18, 1951	Pittsburgh	Joe Walcott, 194 (37)	Ezzard Charles, 182 (30)	KO 7
Sept. 23, 1952	Philadelphia	Rocky Marciano, 184 (29)[6]	Joe Walcott, 196 (38)	KO13
Nov. 30, 1956	Chicago	Floyd Patterson, 182¼ (21)	Archie Moore, 187¾ (42)	KO 5
June 26, 1959	New York	Ingemar Johansson, 196 (26)	Floyd Patterson, 182 (24)	KO 3
June 20, 1960	New York	Floyd Patterson, 190 (25)	Ingemar Johansson, 194¾ (27)	KO 5
Sept. 25, 1962	Chicago	Sonny Liston, 214 (28)	Floyd Patterson, 189 (27)	KO 1
Feb. 25, 1964	Miami Beach, Fla.	Cassius Clay, 210 (22)[7]	Sonny Liston, 218 (30)	KO 7
March 4, 1968	New York	Joe Frazier, 204½ (24)[8]	Buster Mathis, 243½ (23)	KO 11
April 27, 1968	Oakland, Calif.	Jimmy Ellis, 197 (28)[9]	Jerry Quarry, 195 (22)	15
Feb. 16, 1970	New York	Joe Frazier, 205 (26)[10]	Jimmy Ellis, 201 (29)	KO 5
Jan. 22, 1973	Kingston, Jamaica	George Foreman, 217½ (24)	Joe Frazier, 214 (29)	KO 2
Oct. 30, 1974	Kinshasa, Zaire	Muhammad Ali, 216½ (32)	George Foreman, 220 (26)	KO 8
Feb. 15, 1978	Las Vegas, Nev.	Leon Spinks, 197 (25)	Muhammad Ali, 224½ (36)	15
June 9, 1978	Las Vegas, Nev.	Larry Holmes, 212 (28)[11]	Ken Norton, 220 (32)	15
Sept. 15, 1978	New Orleans	Muhammad Ali, 221 (36)[12]	Leon Spinks, 201 (25)	15

Date	Where held	Winner, weight, age	Loser, weight, age	Rounds
Oct. 20, 1979	Pretoria, S. Africa	John Tate, 240 (24)[13]	Gerrie Coetzee, 222 (24)	15
March 31, 1980	Knoxville, Tenn.	Mike Weaver, 207½ (27)	John Tate, 232 (25)	KO 15
Dec. 10, 1982	Las Vegas, Nev.	Michael Dokes, 216 (24)	Mike Weaver, 209½ (30)	KO 1
Sept. 23, 1983	Richfield, Ohio	Gerrie Coetzee, 215 (28)	Michael Dokes, 217 (25)	KO 10
March 9, 1984	Las Vegas, Nev.	Tim Witherspoon, 220½ (26)[14]	Greg Page, 239½ (25)	12
Aug. 31, 1984	Las Vegas, Nev.	Pinklon Thomas, 216 (26)	Tim Witherspoon, 217 (26)	12
Nov. 9, 1984	Las Vegas, Nev.	Larry Holmes, 221½ (35)[15]	James Smith 227 (31)	KO 12
Dec. 1, 1984	Sun City, S. Africa	Greg Page, 236 (25)[16]	Gerry Coetzee, 217 (29)	KO 8
April 29, 1985	Buffalo, N.Y.	Tony Tubbs, 229 (26)[16]	Greg Page, 239½ (26)	15
Sept. 21,1985	Las Vegas, Nev.	Michael Spinks, 200 (29)	Larry Holmes, 221 (35)	15
Jan. 17, 1986	Atlanta, Ga.	Tim Witherspoon, 227 (28)	Tony Tubbs, 229 (27)	15
Nov. 23, 1986	Las Vegas, Nev.	Mike Tyson, 217 (20)[17]	Trevor Berbick, 220 (29)	KO 2
Dec. 12, 1986	New York, N.Y.	James Smith, 230 (33)[16]	Tim Witherspoon, 218 (29)	KO 1
March 7, 1987	Las Vegas, Nev.	Mike Tyson, 217 (20)[16]	James Smith, 230 (33)	12
Feb. 10, 1990	Tokyo	James "Buster" Douglas,[18] 231½ (29)	Mike Tyson (220) (23)	KO 10
Oct. 25, 1990	Las Vegas, Nev.	Evander Holyfield, 208 (28)	James "Buster" Douglas, 246 (30)	KO 3
Nov. 13, 1992	Las Vegas, Nev.	Riddick Bowe,[19] 235 (25)	Evander Holyfield, 205 (30)	12
Nov. 6, 1993	Las Vegas, Nev.	Evander Holyfield, 217 (30)	Riddick Bowe, 246 (26)	12
April 22, 1994	Las Vegas, Nev.	Michael Moorer, 214 (26)	Evander Holyfield,[20] 214 (31)	12
Sept 24, 1994	London, England	Oliver McCall,[21] 228 (29)	Lennox Lewis, 238	2
Nov. 5, 1994	Las Vegas, Nev.	George Foreman,[22] 250 (45)	Michael Moorer, 222 (26)	10
April 8, 1995	Las Vegas, Nev.	Bruce Seldon,[23] 232 (28)	Tony Tucker 238 (36)	7
Dec.9, 1995	Stuttgart, Ger.	Frans Botha,[24] 227 (28)	Axel Schulz, 222 (27)	12
March 16, 1996	Las Vegas, Nev.	Mike Tyson,[25] 220 (29)	Frank Bruno, 247 (34)	3
June 22, 1996	Dortmund, Ger.	Michael Moore, 222 (28)	Axel Schulz, 222 (27)	12
Sept. 7, 1996	Las Vegas, Nev.	Mike Tyson, 219 (30)	Bruce Seldon, 229 (29)	1

1. Jeffries retired as champion in March 1905. He named Marvin Hart and Jack Root as leading contenders and agreed to referee their fight in Reno, Nev., on July 3, 1905, with the stipulation that he would term the winner the champion. Hart, 190 (28), knocked out Root, 171 (29), in the 12th round. 2. Burns claimed the title after defeating Hart. 3. Tunney retired as champion after defeating Tom Heeney on July 26, 1928. 4. After Louis announced his retirement as champion on March 1, 1949, Charles won recognition from the National Boxing Association as champion by defeating Walcott. 5. Charles gained undisputed recognition as champion by defeating Louis, who came out of retirement. 6. Retired as Champion April 27, 1956. 7. The World Boxing Association later withdrew its recognition of Clay as champion and declared the winner of a bout between Ernie Terrell and Eddie Machen would gain its version of the title. Terrell, 199 (25), won a 15-round decision from Machen, 192 (32), in Chicago on March 5, 1965. Clay, 212¼ (25) and Terrell, 212½ (27) met in Houston on Feb. 6, 1967, Clay winning a 15-round decision. 8. Winner recognized by New York, Massachusetts, Maine, Illinois, Texas and Pennsylvania to fill vacated title when Clay was stripped of championship for failing to accept U.S. Induction. 9. Bout was final of eight-man tournament to fill Clay's place and is recognized by World Boxing Association. 10. Bout settled controversy over title. 11. Holmes won World Boxing Council title after WBC had withdrawn recognition of Spinks, March 18, 1978, and awarded its title to Norton. WBC said Spinks had reneged on agreement to fight Norton. 12. Ali regained World Boxing Association championship. 13. Tate won WBA title after Ali retired and left it vacant. 14. Tim Witherspoon and Greg Page fought for the WBC heavyweight title vacated by Larry Holmes, who could not come to agreement on a deal to fight Page, the No. 1 contender. Holmes declared he would fight under the banner of the International Boxing Federation. Several dates were set and postponed for fights between Holmes and Gerry Coetzee, the WBA champ, the latest being Nov. 16, 1984. 15. First fight under banner of International Boxing Federation. 16. New WBC champion. 17. New WBC champion. 18. New undisputed champion. 19. The WBC stripped Bowe of its version of the title in December 1992 and named Lennox Lewis champion. 20. After the loss, Holyfield retired. 21. New WBC champion. Lennox Lewis had been named champion in 1992 and had won three title defenses before losing to McCall. 22. For combined WBA/IBF titles. Later WBA stripped Foreman of title for failing to fight no. 1 contender Tony Tucker. IBF also stripped Foreman on June 29, 1995. 23. New WBA champion. 24. Botha later tested positive for steroids and was stripped of the title. 25. New WBC champion. 26. New IBF champion.

OTHER WORLD BOXING TITLEHOLDERS

(Through Sept. 1, 1997)

Light Heavyweight

1903	Jack Root, George Gardner	1939	Melio Bettina	1974	John Conteh (WBA), Bob Foster (WBC)[1] [4]
1903–05	Bob Fitzsimmons	1939–41	Billy Conn[2]		
1905–12	Philadelphia Jack O'Brien[1]	1941	Anton Christoforidis (NBA)	1975–76	Victor Galindez (WBA), John Conteh (WBC)
1912–16	Jack Dillon	1941–48	Gus Lesnevich		
1916–20	Battling Levinsky	1948–50	Freddie Mills	1977	Victor Galindez (WBA), John Conteh (WBC),[2] Miguel Cuello (WBC)
1920–22	Georges Carpentier	1950–52	Joey Maxim		
1923	Battling Siki	1952–61	Archie Moore[3]		
1923–25	Mike McTigue	1961–63	Harold Johnson	1978	Victor Galindez (WBA), Mike Rossman (WBA), Miguel Cuello (WBC), Mate Parlov (WBC), Marvin Johnson (WBC)
1925–26	Paul Berlenbach	1963–65	Willie Pastrano		
1926–27	Jack Delaney[2]	1965–66	José Torres		
1927	Mike McTigue	1966–67	Dick Tiger		
1927–29	Tommy Loughran	1968	Dick Tiger, Bob Foster	1979	Mike Rossman (WBA), Victor Galindez (WBA), Marvin Johnson (WBC), Matthew (Franklin) Saad Muhammad (WBC)
1930	Jimmy Slattery	1969–70	Bob Foster		
1930–34	Maxie Rosenbloom	1971	Vicente Rondon (WBA), Bob Foster (WBC)		
1934–35	Bob Olin	1972–73	Bob Foster (WBA, WBC)		
1935–39	John Henry Lewis				

1980	Matthew Saad Muhammad (WBC), Marvin Johnson (WBA), Eddie (Gregory) Mustafa Muhammad (WBA)
1981	Matthew Saad Muhammad (WBC), Eddie Mustafa Muhammad (WBA), Michael Spinks (WBA) Dwight Braxton (WBC)
1982	Dwight Braxton (WBC), Michael Spinks (WBA)
1983	Michael Spinks (undisputed)
1984	Michael Spinks (undisputed)
1985	Michael Spinks (undisputed)[5]
1986	Marvin Johnson (WBA), Dennis Andries (WBC)
1987	Thomas Hearns (WBC), Virgil Hill (WBA), Bobby Czyz (IBF)
1988	Charles Williams (IBF), Virgil Hill (WBA), Donny LaLonde (WBC), Sugar Ray Leonard (WBC)
1989	Dennis Andries (WBC), Virgil Hill (WBA), Charles Williams (IBF), Jeff Harding (WBC)
1990	Virgil Hill (WBA), Charles Williams (IBF), Jeff Harding (WBC), Dennis Andries (WBC)
1991	Virgil Hall (WBA), Thomas Hearns (WBA), Dennis Andries (WBC), Charles Williams (IBF)
1992	Charlie Williams (IBF), James Waring (IBF), Jeff Harding (WBC)
1993	Virgil Hill (WBA), Jeff Harding (WBC), Henry Maske (IBF)
1994	Virgil Hill (WBA), Mike McCallum (WBC), Henry Maske (IBF)
1995	Virgil Hill (WBA), Fabio Tiozzo (WBC), Henry Maske (IBF)
1996–97	Virgil Hill (WBA), Fabio Tiozzo (WBC), Henry Maske (IBF)

1. Retired. 2. Abandoned title. 3. NBA withdrew recognition in 1961, New York Commission in 1962; recognized thereafter only by California and Europe. 4. WBC withdrew recognition. 5. Spinks relinquished title in 1985 to fight for heavyweight title.

Middleweight

1867–72	Tom Chandler
1872–81	George Rooke
1881–82	Mike Donovan[1]
1884–91	Jack (Nonpareil) Dempsey
1891–97	Bob Fitzsimmons[2]
1908	Stanley Ketchel, Billy Papke
1908–10	Stanley Ketchel[3]
1913	Frank Klaus
1913–14	George Chip
1914–17	Al McCoy
1917–20	Mike O'Dowd
1920–23	Johnny Wilson
1923–26	Harry Greb
1926	Tiger Flowers
1926–31	Mickey Walker[2]

1931–41	Gorilla Jones, Ben Jeby, Marcel Thil, Lou Brouillard, Vince Dundee, Teddy Yarosz, Babe Risko, Freddy Steele, Al Hostak, Solly Kreiger, Fred Apostoli, Cerferino Garcia, Ken Overlin, Billy Soose, Tony Zale[4]
1941–47	Tony Zale
1947–48	Rocky Graziano
1948	Tony Zale
1948–49	Marcel Cerdan
1949–51	Jake LaMotta
1952	Ray Robinson, Randy Turpin
1951–52	Ray Robinson[1]
1953–55	Carl Olson
1955–57	Ray Robinson[5]
1957	Gene Fullmer, Ray Robinson
1957–58	Carmen Basilio
1958–60	Ray Robinson[6]
1960–61	Paul Pender[7]
1959–62	Gene Fullmer (NBA)
1961–62	Terry Downes[1]
1962	Paul Pender[1]
1962–63	Dick Tiger
1963–65	Joey Giardello
1965–66	Dick Tiger
1966	Emile Griffith
1967	Nino Benvenuti, Emile Griffith
1968	Emile Griffith, Nino Benvenuti
1969	Nino Benvenuti
1970	Nino Benvenuti, Carlos Monzon
1971–73	Carlos Monzon
1974–75	Carlos Monzon (WBA), Rodrigo Valdez (WBC)
1976	Carlos Monzon (WBA, WBC), Rodrigo Valdez (WBC)
1977	Carlos Monzon (WBA, WBC),[1] Rodrigo Valdez (WBA, WBC)
1978	Rodrigo Valdez, Hugo Corro
1979	Hugo Corro, Vito Antuofermo
1980	Vito Antuofermo, Alan Minter, Marvin Hagler
1981	Marvin Hagler
1982–86	Marvelous Marvin Hagler (undisputed)
1987	Marvin Hagler (undisputed), Sugar Ray Leonard (undisputed)
1988	Sumbu Kalambay (WBA), Thomas Hearns (WBC), Iran Barkley (WBC), Frank Tate (IBF), Michael Nunn (IBF), James Kinchen (NABF)
1989	Michael Nunn (IBF), Mike McCallum (WBA), Iran Barkley (WBC), Roberto Duran (WBC)
1990	Michael McCallum (WBA), Michael Nunn (IBF), Iran Barkley (WBC)
1991	Michael Nunn (IBF), James Toney (IBF), Michael McCallum (WBA)
1992	James Toney (IBF), Julian Jackson (WBC), Reggie Johnson (WBA)

1993	Reggie Johnson (WBA), Gerald McClellan (WBA), Roy Jones (IBF)
1994	Julian Jackson (WBA), Gerald McClellan (WBA), Roy Jones (IBF)
1995	Jorge Castro (WBA), Julian Jackson (WBC), Bernard Hopkins (IBF)
1996	William Joppy (WBA), Keith Holmes (WBC), Bernard Hopkins (IBF)
1997	Shinji Takehara (WBA), Quincy Taylor (WBC), Bernard Hopkins (IBF)

1. Retired. 2. Abandoned title. 3. Died. 4. National Boxing Association and New York Commission disagreed on champions. Those listed were accepted by one or the other until Zale gained worldwide recognition. 5. Ended retirement in 1954. 6. NBA withdrew recognition. 7. Recognized by New York, Massachusetts, and Europe.

Welterweight

1892–94	Mysterious Billy Smith
1894–96	Tommy Ryan
1896	Kid McCoy[2]
1896–	
1900	Mysterious Billy Smith
1900	Rube Ferns
1900–01	Matty Matthews
1901	Ruby Ferns
1901–04	Joe Walcott
1904	Dixie Kid[2]
1904–06	Joe Walcott
1906–07	Honey Mellody
1907	Mike (Twin) Sullivan[2]
1915–19	Ted Lewis
1919–22	Jack Britton
1922–26	Mickey Walker
1926–27	Pete Latzo
1927–29	Joe Dundee
1929–30	Jackie Fields
1930	Young Jack Thompson
1930–31	Tommy Freeman
1931	Young Jack Thompson
1931–32	Lou Brouillard
1932–33	Jackie Fields
1933	Young Corbett 3rd
1933–34	Jimmy McLarnin, Barney Ross
1934–35	Jimmy McLarnin
1935–38	Barney Ross
1938–40	Henry Armstrong
1940–41	Fritzie Zivic
1941–46	Freddie Cochrane
1946	Marty Servo[1]
1946–51	Ray Robinson[2]
1951	Johnny Bratton (NBA)
1951–54	Kid Gavilan
1954–55	Johnny Saxton
1955	Tony DeMarco
1955–56	Carmen Basilio
1956	Johnny Saxton
1956–57	Carmen Basilio[2]
1958	Virgil Akins
1959–60	Don Jordan
1960–61	Benny (Kid) Paret
1961	Emile Griffith
1961–62	Benny (Kid) Paret
1962–63	Emile Griffith, Luis Rodriguez
1963–66	Emile Griffith[2]
1966–69	Curtis Cokes
1969	Curtis Cokes, José Napoles
1970	José Napoles, Billy Backus

1971	Billy Backus, José Napoles
1972–74	José Napoles
1975	José Napoles (WBA, WBC),[3] Angel Espada (WBA), John Stracey (WBC)
1976	Angel Espada (WBA), José Cuevas (WBA), John Stracey (WBC), Carlos Palomino
1977–78	José Cuevas (WBA), Carlos Palomino (WBC)
1979	José Cuevas (WBA), Carlos Palomino (WBC), Wilfredo Benitez (WBC)
1980	José Cuevas (WBA), Ray Leonard (WBC), Roberto Duran (WBC), Thomas Hearns (WBA)
1981	Ray Leonard (WBC), Thomas Hearns (WBA), Ray Leonard (WBC, WBA)
1982	Ray Leonard
1983–85	Donald Curry (WBA)
1983–85	Milton McCrory (WBC)
1985–86	Donald Curry (undisputed)
1987	Mark Breland (WBA), Marlon Starling (WBA), Lloyd Honeyghan (IBF)
1988	Marlon Starling (WBA), Tomas Molinares (WBA), Lloyd Honeyghan (WBC), Simon Brown (IBF)
1989	Mark Breland (WBA), Marlon Starling (WBC), Simon Brown (IBF)
1990	Mark Breland (WBA), Aaron Davis (WBA), Simon Brown (IBF), Marlon Starling (WBC), Maurice Blocker (WBC)
1991	Meldrick Taylor (WBA), Simon Brown (IBF, WBC)
1992	Meldrick Taylor (WBA), James "Buddy" McGirt (WBC), Maurice Blocker (IBF)
1993	Cristiano Espana (WBA), Pernell Whitaker (WBC), Felix Trinidad (IBF)
1994	Ike Quartey (WBA), Pernell Whitaker (WBC), Felix Trinidad (IBF)
1995	Ike Quartey (WBA), Pernell Whitaker (WBC), Felix Trinidad (IBF)
1996–97	Ike Quartey (WBA), Pernell Whitaker (WBC), Felix Trinidad (IBF)

1. Retired. 2. Abandoned title. 3. WBA withdrew recognition.

Lightweight

1869–99	Kid Lavigne
1899–	
1902	Frank Erne
1902–08	Joe Gans
1908–10	Battling Nelson
1910–12	Ad Wolgast
1912–14	Willie Ritchie
1914–17	Freddy Welsh
1917–25	Benny Leonard[1]
1925	Jimmy Goodrich
1925–26	Rocky Kansas
1926–30	Sammy Mandell
1930	Al Singer
1930–33	Tony Canzoneri
1933–35	Barney Ross[2]
1935–36	Tony Canzoneri
1936–38	Lou Ambers
1938–39	Henry Armstrong
1939–40	Lou Ambers
1940–41	Lew Jenkins
1941–42	Sammy Angott[1]
1943–47	Beau Jack (N.Y.), Bob Montgomery (N.Y.), Sammy Angott (NBA), Juan Zurita (NBA), Ike Williams (NBA)
1947–51	Ike Williams
1951–52	James Carter
1952	Lauro Salas
1952–54	James Carter
1954	Paddy DeMarco
1954–55	James Carter
1955–56	Wallace Smith
1956–62	Joe Brown
1962–65	Carlos Ortiz
1965	Ismael Laguna
1965–68	Carlos Ortiz
1968	Teo Cruz
1969	Teo Cruz, Mando Ramos
1970	Mando Ramos, Ismael Laguna, Ken Buchanan
1971	Ken Buchanan (WBA), Mando Ramos (WBC), Pedro Carrasco (WBC)
1972	Ken Buchanan (WBA), Roberto Duran (WBA), Pedro Carrasco (WBC), Mando Ramos (WBC), Chango Carmona (WBC), Rodolfo Gonzalez (WBC)
1973	Roberto Duran (WBA), Rodolfo Gonzalez (WBC)
1974	Roberto Duran (WBA), Rodolfo Gonzalez (WBC), Guts Ishimatsu (WBC)
1975	Roberto Duran (WBA), Guts Ishimatsu (WBC)
1976	Roberto Duran (WBA), Guts Ishimatsu (WBC), Esteban De Jesus (WBC)
1977	Roberto Duran (WBA), Esteban De Jesus (WBC)
1978	Roberto Duran (WBA, WBC)
1979	Roberto Duran,[2] Jim Watt (WBC), Ernesto Espana (WBA)
1980	Ernesto Espana (WBA), Hilmer Kenty (WBA), Jim Watt (WBC)
1981	Hilmer Kenty (WBA), Sean O'Grady (WBA), James Watt (WBA), Alexis Arguello (WBC), Arturo Frias (WBA)
1982	Arturo Frias (WBA), Ray Mancini (WBA), Alexis Arguello (WBC)
1983	Edwin Rosario (WBC), Ray Mancini (WBA)
1984	Edwin Rosario (WBC), Livingstone Bramble (WBA)
1985	Jose Luis Ramirez (WBC), Hector Camacho (WBC), Livingstone Bramble (WBA)
1986	Hector Camacho (WBC), Livingstone Bramble (WBA), Jim Paul (IBF)
1987	Edwin Rosario (WBA), Jose Luis Ramirez (WBC), Greg Haugen (IBF)
1988	Jose Luis Ramirez (WBC), Julio Cesar Chavez (WBA), Greg Haugen (IBF), Julius Cesar Chavez (WBC & WBA title unified)
1989	Pernell Whitaker (IBF, WBC), Edwin Rosario (WBA)
1990	Pernell Whitaker (IBF, WBC), Juan Nazario (WBA)
1991	Pernell Whitaker (IBF, WBA, WBC)
1992	Pernell Whitaker (IBF, WBA, WBC),[3] Joey Gamache (WBA).
1993	Dingaan Thobela (WBA), Angel Gonzalez (WBC), Freddie Pendleton (IBF)
1994	Orzubek Nazarov (WBA), Angel Gonzalez (WBC), Rafael Ruelas (IBF)
1995	Orzubek Nazarov (WBA), Angel Gonzalez (WBC), Oscar de la Hoya (IBF)
1996	Gusshie Nazarov (WBA), Jean Baptiste Mendy (WBC), Phillip Holiday (IBF)
1997	Orzubek Nazarov (WBA), Jean Baptiste Mendy (WBC), Philip Holiday (IBF)

1. Retired. 2. Abandoned title. 3. Moving up in weight class, so resigned titles.

Featherweight

1889	Dal Hawkins[1]
1890	Billy Murphy
1892–	
1900	George Dixon
1900–01	Terry McGovern
1901	Young Corbett[1]
1901–12	Abe Attell
1912–23	Johnny Kilbane
1923	Eugene Criqui
1923–25	Johnny Dundee[1]
1925–27	Louis (Kid) Kaplan[1]
1927–28	Benny Bass
1928	Tony Canzoneri
1928–29	Andre Routis
1929–32	Battling Battalino[1]
1932	Tommy Paul (NBA), Kid Chocolate (N.Y.)
1933–36	Freddie Miller
1936–37	Petey Sarron
1937–38	Henry Armstrong[1]
1938–40	Joey Archibald
1940–41	Harry Jefra, Joey Archibald
1941–42	Chalky Wright
1942–48	Willie Pep
1948–49	Sandy Saddler[2]
1949–50	Willie Pep
1950–57	Sandy Saddler
1957–59	Kid Bassey
1959–63	Davey Moore
1963–64	Sugar Ramos
1964–67	Vicente Saldivar[2]
1968	Howard Winstone, José Legra,[3] Paul Rojas (WBA), Sho Saijo (WBA)
1969	Sho Saijo (WBA), Johnny Famechon[3]
1970	Sho Saijo (WBA), Johnny Famechon,[3] Vicente Salvidar,[3] Kuniaki Shibata[3]

1971	Sho Saijo (WBA), Antonio Gomez (WBA), Kuniaki Shibata (WBC)
1972	Antonio Gomez (WBA), Ernesto Marcel (WBA), Kuniaki Shibata (WBC), Clemente Sanchez (WBC), José Legra (WBC)
1973	Ernesto Marcel (WBA), José Legra (WBC), Eder Jofre (WBC)
1974	Ernesto Marcel (WBA),[2] Ruben Olivares (WBA), Alexis Arguello (WBA), Eder Jofre (WBC), Bobby Chacon (WBC)
1975	Alexis Arguello (WBA), Bobby Chacon (WBC), Ruben Olivares (WBC), David Kotey (WBC)
1976	Alexis Arguello (WBA),[2] David Kotey (WBC), Danny Lopez (WBC)
1977	Rafael Ortega (WBA), Danny Lopez (WBC)
1978	Rafael Ortega (WBA), Cecilio Lastra (WBA), Eusebio Pedroza (WBA), Danny Lopez (WBC)
1979	Eusebio Pedroza (WBA), Danny Lopez (WBC)
1980	Eusebio Pedroza (WBA), Danny Lopez (WBC), Salvador Sanchez (WBC)
1981	Eusebio Pedroza (WBA), Salvador Sanchez (WBC)
1982	Eusebio Pedroza (WBA), Salvador Sanchez (WBC)[4]
1983	Juan Laporte (WBC), Eusebio Pedroza (WBA)
1984	Wilfred Gomez (WBC), Eusebio Pedroza (WBA)
1985	Eusebio Pedroza (WBA), Barry McGuigan (WBA), Azumah Nelson (WBC)
1986	Barry McGuigan (WBA), Stevie Cruz (WBA), Azumah Nelson (WBC)
1987	Azumah Nelson (WBC), Antonio Esparragoza (WBA)
1988	Calvin Grove (IBF), Jorge Paez (IBF), Antonio Esparragoza (WBA), Jeff Fenech (WBC)
1989	Jorge Paez (IBF), Antonio Esparragoza (WBA), Jeff Fenech (WBC)
1990	Marcos Villasana (WBC), Antonio Esparragoza (WBA), Jorge Paez (IBF)
1991	Park Young-Kyun (WBA), Troy Dorsey (IBF), Marcos Villagana (WBC)
1992	Paul Hodkinson (WBC), Manuel Medina (IBF), Yung Kyun Park (WBA)
1993	Yung-Kyun Park (WBA), Goyo Vargas (WBC), Tom Johnson (IBF)
1994	Eloy Rojas (WBA), Kevin Kelley (WBC), Tom Johnson (IBF)
1995	Eloy Rojas (WBA), Alejandro Gonzalez (WBC), Tom Johnson (IBF)

| 1996 | Wilfredo Vázquez (WBA), Luisto Espinosa (WBC), Tom Johnson (IBF) |
| 1997 | Elroy Rojas (WBA), Luisto Espinosa (WBC), Tom Johnson (IBF) |

1. Abandoned title. 2. Retired. 3. Recognized in Europe, Mexico, and Orient. 4. Killed in auto accident.

Bantamweight

1890–92	George Dixon[1]
1894–99	Jimmy Barry[2]
1899–	
1900	Terry McGovern[1]
1901	Harry Harris[1]
1902–03	Harry Forbes
1903–04	Frankie Neil
1904	Joe Bowker[1]
1905–07	Jimmy Walsh[1]
1910–14	Johnny Coulon
1914–17	Kid Williams
1917–20	Pete Herman
1920	Joe Lynch
1920–21	Joe Lynch, Pete Herman, Johnny Buff
1922	Johnny Buff, Joe Lynch
1923	Joe Lynch
1924	Joe Lynch, Abe Goldstein
1924	Abe Goldstein, Eddie "Cannonball" Martin
1925	Eddie "Cannonball" Martin, Charlie "Phil" Rosenberg[3]
1927–28	Bud Taylor (NBA)[1]
1929–34	Al Brown
1935	Al Brown, Baltazar Sangchili
1936	Baltazar Sangchili, Tony Marino, Sixto Escobar
1937	Sixto Escobar, Harry Jeffra
1938	Harry Jeffra, Sixto Escobar
1939–40	Sixto Escobar[2]
1940–42	Lou Salica
1942–46	Manuel Ortiz
1947	Manuel Ortiz, Harold Dade
1948–50	Manuel Ortiz
1950–52	Vic Toweel
1952–54	Jimmy Carruthers[2]
1954–55	Robert Cohen
1956	Robert Cohen, Mario D'Agata, Raul Macias (NBA)
1957	Mario D'Agata, Alphonse Halimi
1958–59	Alphonse Halimi
1959–60	Jose Becerra[2]
1960–61	Alphonse Halimi[4]
1961–62	Johnny Caldwell[4]
1961–65	Eder Jofre
1965–68	Masahika "Fighting" Harada
1968	Masahika "Fighting" Harada, Lionel Rose
1969	Lionel Rose, Ruben Olivares
1970	Ruben Olivares, Chucho Castillo
1971	Chucho Castillo, Ruben Olivares
1972	Ruben Olivares, Rafael Herrera, Enrique Pinder

1973	Enrique Pinder (WBA), Romeo Anaya (WBA), Arnold Taylor (WBA), Rodolfo Martinez (WBC), Rafael Herrera
1974	Arnold Taylor (WBA), Soo Hwan Hong (WBA), Rafael Herrera (WBC), Rodolfo Martinez (WBC)
1975	Soo Hwan Hong (WBA), Alfonso Zamora (WBA), Rodolfo Martinez (WBC)
1976	Alfonso Zamora (WBA), Rodolfo Martinez (WBC), Carlos Zarate (WBC)
1977	Alfonso Zamora (WBA), Jorge Lujan (WBA), Carlos Zarate (WBC)
1978	Jorge Lujan (WBA), Carlos Zarate (WBC)
1979	Jorge Lujan (WBA), Carlos Zarate (WBC), Lupe Pintor (WBC)
1980	Jorge Lujan (WBA), Lupe Pintor (WBC), Julian Solis (WBA), Jeff Chandler (WBA)
1981	Lupe Pintor (WBC), Jeff Chandler (WBA)
1982	Lupe Pintor (WBC), Jeff Chandler (WBA)
1983	Jeff Chandler (WBA), Albert Dauila (WBC)
1984	Richie Sandqual (WBA), Albert Dauila (WBC)
1985	Richard Sandoval (WBA), Daniel Zaragoza (WBC), Miguel Lora (WBC)
1986	Richard Sandoval (WBA), Bernardo Pinango (WBA), Jeff Fenech (IBF)
1987	Bernardo Pinango (WBA), Takuya Muguruma (WBA), Miguel Lora (WBC)
1988	Wilfred Vasquez (WBA), Jibaro Perez (WBC), Moon Sung-gil (WBA), Orlando Canizales (IBF)
1989	Jibaro Perez (WBC), Moon Sung-gil (WBA), Orlando Canizales (IBF), Kaokor Galaxy (WBA), Luis Espinosa (WBA)
1990	Orlando Canizales (IBF), Jibaro Perez (WBC), Luis Espinosa (WBA)
1991	Greg Richardson (WBC), Orlando Canizales (IBF), Luis Espinosa (WBA)
1992	Joichiro Tatsuyoshi (WBC), Victor Manuel Rabanales (WBC), Eddie Cook (WBA), Orlando Gonzales (IBF)
1993	Jorge Julio (WBA), Byun-Jong-il (WBC), Orlando Canizales (IBF)
1994	John Michael Johnson (WBA), Yasuei Yakushiji (WBC), Orlando Canizales (IBF)
1995	Daorun Chuwatang (WBA), Yasuei Yakushiji (WBC), Mbulelo Botile (IBF)
1996–97	Nana Konado (WBA), Wayne McCullough (WBC), Mbulelo Botile (IBF)

1. Abandoned title. 2. Retired. 3. Deprived of title for failing to make weight. 4. Recognized in Europe.

Flyweight

1916–23	Jimmy Wilde
1923–25	Pancho Villa[1]
1925	Frankie Genaro
1925–27	Fidel La Barba[2]
1927–31	Corporal Izzy Schwartz, Frankie Genaro, Emile (Spider) Pladner, Midget Wolgast, Young Perez[3]
1932–35	Jackie Brown
1935–38	Bennie Lynch[4]
1939	Peter Kane[4]
1943–47	Jackie Paterson[1]
1947–50	Rinty Monaghan[2]
1950	Terry Allen
1950–52	Dado Marino
1952–54	Yoshio Shirai
1954–60	Pascual Perez
1960–62	Pone Kingpetch
1962–63	Masahika (Fighting) Harada
1963–64	Hiroyuki Ebihara
1964–65	Pone Kingpetch
1965–66	Salvatore Burrini
1966	Walter McGown, Chartchai Chionoi
1966–68	Charchai Chionoi
1969	Bernabe Villacampa, Efran Torres (WBA)
1970	Bernabe Villacampa, Chartchai Chionoi, Erbito Salavarria, Berkrerk Chartvanchai (WBA), Masao Ohba (WBA)
1971	Masao Ohba (WBA), Erbito Salavarria (WBC)
1972	Masao Ohba (WBA), Erbito Salavarria (WBC), Betulio Gonzalez (WBC), Venice Borkorsor (WBC)
1973	Masao Ohba (WBA), Chartchai Chionoi (WBA), Venice Borkorsor (WBC), Betulio Gonzalez (WBC)
1974	Chartchai Chionoi (WBA), Susumu Hanagata (WBA), Betulio Gonzalez (WBC), Shoji Oguma (WBC)
1975	Susumu Hanagata (WBA), Erbito Salavarria (WBA), Shoji Oguma (WBC), Miguel Canto (WBC)
1976	Erbito Salavarria (WBA), Alfonso Lopez (WBA), Guty Espadas (WBA), Miguel Canto (WBC)
1977	Guty Espadas (WBA), Miguel Canto (WBC)
1978	Guty Espadas (WBA), Betulio Gonzalez (WBA), Miguel Canto (WBC)
1979	Betulio Gonzalez (WBA), Miguel Canto (WBC), Park Chan-Hee (WBC)
1980	Luis Ibarra (WBA), Kim Tae Shik (WBA), Park Chan-Hee (WBC), Shoji Oguma (WBC)
1983	Frank Cedeno (WBC), Santos Lacia (WBA)
1984	Koji Kobayashy (WBA), Gabriel Bernal (WBC), Santos Laciar (WBA)
1985	Sot Chitlada (WBC), Santos Laciar (WBA)
1986	Hilario Zapata (WBA), Julio Cesar-Chevez (WBC)
1987	Shin Hi Sop (IBF), Chang Ho Choi (IBF), Sot Chitlada (WBC)
1988	Sot Chitlada (WBC), Kim Young Kang (WBC), Duke McKenzie (IBF), Fidel Bassa (WBA)
1989	Kim Young-gang (WBC), Sot Chitlada (WBC), Lee Yol-woo (WBA), Duke McKenzie (IBF), Dave McAuley (IBF), Jesus Rojas (WBA)
1990	Sot Chitlada (WBC), Kim Bong-Jung (WBA), Lee Yul-woo (WBA), Dave McAuley (IBF), Leopard Tamakuma (WBA)
1991	Muangchai Kittasem (WBC), Kim-Young-Kang (WBC), Elvis Alvarez (WBA), Dave McAuley (IBF)
1992	Kim Young-Kang (WBA), Yuri Arbachakov (WBC), Rodolfo Blanco (IBF)
1993	David Griman (WBA), Yuri Arbachakov (WBC), P. Sitbangprachan (IBF)
1994	Saen Sor Ploenchit (WBA), Yuri Arbachakov (WBC), Humberto Gonzalez (IBF)
1995	Saen Sor Ploenchit (WBA), Yuri Arbachakov (WBC), Humberto Gonzalez (IBF)
1996	Saen Sor Ploenchit (WBA), Yuri Arbachakov (WBC), Mark Johnson (IBF)
1997	Saen Sor Pleonchit (WBA), Yuri Arbachakov (WBC), Vacant (IBF)

1. Died. 2. Retired. 3. Claimants to NBA and New York Commission titles. 4. Abandoned title.

Horse Racing

Ancient drawings on stone and bone prove that horse racing is at least 3000 years old, but Thoroughbred Racing is a modern development. Practically every thoroughbred in training today traces its registered ancestry back to one or more of three sires that arrived in England about 1728 from the Near East and became known, from the names of their owners, as the Byerly Turk, the Darley Arabian, and the Godolphin Arabian. The Jockey Club (English) was founded at Newmarket in 1750 or 1751 and became the custodian of the Stud Book as well as the court of last resort in deciding turf affairs.

Horse racing took place in this country before the Revolution, but the great lift to the breeding industry came with the importation in 1798, by Col. John Hoomes of Virginia, of Diomed, winner of the Epsom Derby of 1780. Diomed's lineal descendants included such famous stars of the American turf as American Eclipse and Lexington. From 1800 to the time of the Civil War there were race courses and breeding establishments plentifully scattered through Virginia, North Carolina, South Carolina, Tennessee, Kentucky, and Louisiana.

The oldest stake event in North America is the Queen's Plate, a Canadian fixture that was first run in the Province of Quebec in 1836. The oldest stake event in the United States is The Travers, which was first run at Saratoga in 1864. The gambling that goes with horse racing and trickery by jockeys, trainers, owners, and track officials caused attacks on the sport by reformers and a demand among horse racing enthusiasts for an honest and effective control of some kind, but nothing of lasting value to racing came of this until the formation in 1894 of The Jockey Club.

"TRIPLE CROWN" WINNERS IN THE UNITED STATES
(Kentucky Derby, Preakness and Belmont Stakes)

Year	Horse	Owner	Year	Horse	Owner
1919	Sir Barton	J. K. L. Ross	1946	Assault	Robert J. Kleberg
1930	Gallant Fox	William Woodward	1948	Citation	Warren Wright
1935	Omaha	William Woodward	1973	Secretariat	Meadow Stable
1937	War Admiral	Samuel D. Riddle	1977	Seattle Slew	Karen Taylor
1941	Whirlaway	Warren Wright	1978	Affirmed	Louis Wolfson
1943	Count Fleet	Mrs. John Hertz			

KENTUCKY DERBY

Churchill Downs; 3-year-olds; 1¼ miles.

Year	Winner	Jockey	Wt.	Win val.	Year	Winner	Jockey	Wt.	Win val.
1875	Aristides	O. Lewis	100	$2,850	1937	War Admiral	C. Kurtsinger	126	52,050
1876	Vagrant	R. Swim	97	2,950	1938	Lawrin	E. Arcaro	126	47,050
1877	Baden Baden	W. Walker	100	3,300	1939	Johnstown	J. Stout	126	46,350
1878	Day Star	J. Carter	100	4,050	1940	Gallahadion	C. Bierman	126	60,150
1879	Lord Murphy	C. Schauer	100	3,550	1941	Whirlaway	E. Arcaro	126	61,275
1880	Fonso	G. Lewis	105	3,800	1942	Shut Out	W. D. Wright	126	64,225
1881	Hindoo	J. McLaughlin	105	4,410	1943	Count Fleet	J. Longden	126	60,725
1882	Apollo	B. Hurd	102	4,560	1944	Pensive	C. McCreary	126	64,675
1883	Leonatus	W. Donohue	105	3,760	1945	Hoop Jr.	E. Arcaro	126	64,850
1884	Buchanan	I. Murphy	110	3,990	1946	Assault	W. Mehrtens	126	96,400
1885	Joe Cotton	E. Henderson	110	4,630	1947	Jet Pilot	E. Guerin	126	92,160
1886	Ben Ali	P. Duffy	118	4,890	1948	Citation	E. Arcaro	126	83,400
1887	Montrose	I. Lewis	118	4,200	1949	Ponde	S. Brooks	126	91,600
1888	Macbeth II	G. Covington	115	4,740	1950	Middleground	W. Boland	126	92,650
1889	Spokane	T. Kiley	118	4,970	1951	Count Turf	C. McCreary	126	98,050
1890	Riley	I. Murphy	118	5,460	1952	Hill Gail	E. Arcaro	126	96,300
1891	Kingman	I. Murphy	122	4,680	1953	Dark Star	H. Moreno	126	90,050
1892	Azra	A. Clayton	122	4,230	1954	Determine	R. York	126	102,050
1893	Lookout	E. Kunze	122	4,090	1955	Swaps	W. Shoemaker	126	108,400
1894	Chant	F. Goodale	122	4,020	1956	Needles	D. Erb	126	123,450
1895	Halma	J. Perkins	122	2,970	1957	Iron Liege	W. Hartack	126	107,950
1896	Ben Brush	W. Simms	117	4,850	1958	Tim Tam	I. Valenzuela	126	116,400
1897	Typhoon H	F. Garner	117	4,850	1959	Tomy Lee	W. Shoemaker	126	119,650
1898	Plaudit	W. Simms	117	4,850	1960	Venetian Way	W. Hartack	126	114,850
1899	Manuel	F. Taral	117	4,850	1961	Carry Back	J. Sellers	126	120,500
1900	Lieut. Gibson	J. Boland	117	4,850	1962	Decidedly	W. Hartack	126	119,650
1901	His Eminence	J. Winkfield	117	4,850	1963	Chateaugay	B. Baeza	126	108,900
1902	Alan-a-Dale	J. Winkfield	117	4,850	1964	Northern Dancer	W. Hartack	126	114,300
1903	Judge Himes	H. Booker	117	4,850	1965	Lucky Debonair	W. Shoemaker	126	112,000
1904	Elwood	F. Prior	117	4,850	1966	Kauai King	D. Brumfield	126	120,500
1905	Agile	J. Martin	122	4,850	1967	Proud Clarion	R. Ussery	126	119,700
1906	Sir Huon	R. Troxler	117	4,850	1968	Forward Pass[1]	I. Valenzuela	126	122,600
1907	Pink Star	A. Minder	117	4,850	1969	Majestic Prince	W. Hartack	126	113,200
1908	Stone Street	A. Pickens	117	4,850	1970	Dust Commander	M. Manganello	126	127,800
1909	Wintergreen	V. Powers	117	4,850	1971	Canonero II	G. Avila	126	145,500
1910	Donau	F. Herbert	117	4,850	1972	Riva Ridge	R. Turcotte	126	140,300
1911	Meridian	G. Archibald	117	4,850	1973	Secretariat	R. Turcotte	126	155,050
1912	Worth	C. H. Shilling	117	4,850	1974	Cannonade	A. Cordero, Jr.	126	274,000
1913	Donerail	R. Goose	117	5,475	1975	Foolish Pleasure	J. Vasquez	126	209,600
1914	Old Rosebud	J. McCabe	114	9,125	1976	Bold Forbes	A. Cordero, Jr.	126	165,200
1915	Regret	J. Notler	112	11,450	1977	Seattle Slew	J. Cruguet	126	214,700
1916	George Smith	J. Loftus	117	9,750	1978	Affirmed	S. Cauthen	126	186,900
1917	Omar Khayyam	C. Borel	117	16,600	1979	Spectacular Bid	R. Franklin	126	228,650
1918	Exterminator	W. Knapp	114	14,700	1980	Genuine Risk	J. Vasquez	126	250,550
1919	Sir Barton	J. Loftus	112½	20,825	1981	Pleasant Colony	J. Velasquez	126	317,200
1920	Paul Jones	T. Rice	126	30,375	1982	Gato del Sol	E. Delahoussaye	126	417,600
1921	Behave Yourself	C. Thompson	126	38,450	1983	Sunny's Halo	E. Delahoussaye	126	426,000
1922	Morvich	A. Johnson	126	46,775	1984	Swale	L. Pincay, Jr.	126	537,400
1923	Zev	E. Sande	126	53,600	1985	Spend a Buck	A. Cordero, Jr.	126	406,800
1924	Black Gold	J. D. Mooney	126	52,775	1986	Ferdinand	W. Shoemaker	126	609,400
1925	Flying Ebony	E. Sande	126	52,950	1987	Alysheba	C. McCarron	126	618,600
1926	Bubbling Over	A. Johnson	126	50,075	1988	Winning Colors	Gary Stevens	126	611,200
1927	Whiskery	L. McAtee	126	51,000	1989	Sunday Silence	Patrick Valenzuela	126	574,200
1928	Reigh Count	C. Lang	126	55,375					
1929	Clyde Van Dusen	L. McAtee	126	53,950	1990	Unbridled	Craig Perret	126	581,000
1930	Gallant Fox	E. Sande	126	50,725	1991	Strike the Gold	Chris Antley	126	655,800
1931	Twenty Grand	C. Kurtsinger	126	48,725	1992	Lil E. Tee	P. Day	126	724,800
1932	Burgoo King	E. James	126	52,350	1993	Sea Hero	Jerry Bailey	126	735,900
1933	Brokers Tip	D. Meade	126	48,925	1994	Go For Gin	Chris McCarron	126	628,800
1934	Cavalcade	M. Garner	126	28,175	1995	Thunder Gulch	Gary Stevens	126	707,400
1935	Omaha	W. Saunders	126	39,525	1996	Grindstone	Jerry Bailey	126	869,800
1936	Bold Venture	I. Hanford	126	37,725	1997	Silver Charm	Gary Stevens	126	700,000

1. Dancer's Image finished first but was disqualified after traces of drug were found in system.

PREAKNESS STAKES

Pimlico; 3-year-olds; 1³⁄₁₆ miles; first race 1873.

Year	Winner	Jockey	Wt.	Win val.	Year	Winner	Jockey	Wt.	Win val.
1919	Sir Barton	J. Loftus	126	$24,500	1964	Northern Dancer	W. Hartack	126	$124,200
1930	Gallant Fox	E. Sande	126	51,925	1965	Tom Rolfe	R. Turcotte	126	128,100
1931	Mate	G. Ellis	126	48,225	1966	Kauai King	D. Brumfield	126	129,000
1932	Burgoo King	E. James	126	50,375	1967	Damascus	W. Shoemaker	126	141,500
1933	Head Play	C. Kurtsinger	126	26,850	1968	Forward Pass	I. Valenzuela	126	142,700
1934	High Quest	R. Jones	126	25,175	1969	Majestic Prince	W. Hartack	126	129,500
1935	Omaha	W. Saunders	126	25,325	1970	Personality	E. Belmonte	126	151,300
1936	Bold Venture	G. Woolf	126	27,325	1971	Canonero II	G. Avila	126	137,400
1937	War Admiral	C. Kurtsinger	126	45,600	1972	Bee Bee Bee	E. Nelson	126	135,300
1938	Dauber	M. Peters	126	51,875	1973	Secretariat	R. Turcotte	126	129,900
1939	Challedon	G. Seabo	126	53,710	1974	Little Current	M. Rivera	126	156,000
1940	Bimelech	F.A. Smith	126	53,230	1975	Master Derby	D. McHargue	126	158,100
1941	Whirlaway	E. Arcaro	126	49,365	1976	Elocutionist	J. Lively	126	129,700
1942	Alsab	B. James	126	58,175	1977	Seattle Slew	J. Cruguet	126	138,600
1943	Count Fleet	J. Longden	126	43,190	1978	Affirmed	S. Cauthen	126	136,200
1944	Pensive	C. McCreary	126	60,075	1979	Spectacular Bid	R. Franklin	126	165,300
1945	Polynesian	W.D. Wright	126	66,170	1980	Codex	A. Cordero	126	180,600
1946	Assault	W. Mehrtens	126	96,620	1981	Pleasant Colony	J. Velasquez	126	270,800
1947	Faultless	D. Dodson	126	98,005	1982	Aloma's Ruler	J. Kaenel	126	209,900
1948	Citation	E. Arcaro	126	91,870	1983	Deputed Testimony	D. Miller	126	251,200
1949	Capot	T. Atkinson	126	79,985					
1950	Hill Prince	E. Arcaro	126	56,115	1984	Gate Dancer	A. Cordero	126	243,600
1951	Bold	E. Arcaro	126	83,110	1985	Tank's Prospect	Pat Day	126	423,200
1952	Blue Man	C. McCreary	126	86,135	1986	Snow Chief	A. Solis	126	411,900
1953	Native Dancer	E. Guerin	126	65,200	1987	Alysheba	C. McCarron	126	421,100
1954	Hasty Road	J. Adams	126	91,600	1988	Risen Star	E. Delahoussaye	126	413,700
1955	Nashua	E. Arcaro	126	67,550	1989	Sunday Silence	P. Valenzuela	126	438,230
1956	Fabius	W. Hartack	126	84,250	1990	Summer Squall	Pat Day	126	445,900
1957	Bold Ruler	E. Arcaro	126	65,250	1991	Hansel	Jerry Bailey	126	432,770
1958	Tim Tam	I. Valenzuela	126	97,900	1992	Pine Bluff	C. McCarron	126	484,120
1959	Royal Orbit	W. Harmatz	126	136,200	1993	Prairie Bayou	Mike Smith	126	471,835
1960	Bally Ache	R. Ussery	126	121,000	1994	Tabasco Cat	Pat Day	126	447,720
1961	Carry Back	J. Sellers	126	126,200	1995	Timber Country	Pat Day	126	446,810
1962	Greek Money	J. Rotz	126	135,800	1996	Louis Quatorze	Pat Day	126	458,120
1963	Candy Spots	W. Shoemaker	126	127,500	1997	Silver Charm	Gary Stevens	126	488,150

BELMONT STAKES

Belmont Park; 3-year-olds; 1½ miles.

Run at Jerome Park 1867 to 1890; at Morris Park 1890–94; at Belmont Park 1905–62; at Aqueduct 1963–67. Distance 1⅝ miles prior to 1874; reduced to 1½ miles, 1874; reduced to 1¼ miles, 1890; reduced to 1⅛ miles, 1893; increased to 1¼ miles, 1895; increased to 1⅜ miles, 1896; reduced to 1¼ miles in 1904; increased to 1½ miles, 1926.

Year	Winner	Jockey	Wt.	Win val.	Year	Winner	Jockey	Wt.	Win val.
1919	Sir Barton	J. Loftus	126	$11,950	1949	Capot	T. Atkinson	126	$60,900
1930	Gallant Fox	E. Sande	126	66,040	1950	Middleground	W. Boland	126	61,350
1931	Twenty Grand	C. Kurtsinger	126	58,770	1951	Counterpoint	D. Gorman	126	82,000
1932	Faireno	T. Malley	126	55,120	1952	One Count	E. Arcaro	126	82,400
1933	Hurryoff	M. Garner	126	49,490	1953	Native Dancer	E. Guerin	126	82,500
1934	Peace Chance	W.D. Wright	126	43,410	1954	High Gun	E. Guerin	126	89,000
1935	Omaha	W. Saunders	126	35,480	1955	Nashua	E. Arcaro	126	83,700
1936	Granville	J. Stout	126	29,800	1956	Needles	D. Erb	126	83,600
1937	War Admiral	C. Kurtsinger	126	38,020	1957	Gallant Man	W. Shoemaker	126	77,300
1938	Pasteurized	J. Stout	126	34,530	1958	Cavan	P. Anderson	126	73,440
1939	Johnstown	J. Stout	126	37,020	1959	Sword Dancer	W. Shoemaker	126	93,525
1940	Bimelech	F.A. Smith	126	35,030	1960	Celtic Ash	W. Hartack	126	96,785
1941	Whirlaway	E. Arcaro	126	39,770	1961	Sherluck	B. Baeza	126	104,900
1942	Shut Out	E. Arcaro	126	44,520	1962	Jaipur	W. Shoemaker	126	109,550
1943	Count Fleet	J. Longden	126	35,340	1963	Chateaugay	B. Baeza	126	101,700
1944	Bounding Home	G.L. Smith	126	55,000	1964	Quadrangle	M. Ycaza	126	110,850
1945	Pavot	E. Arcaro	126	56,675	1965	Hail to All	J. Sellers	126	104,150
1946	Assault	W. Mehrtens	126	75,400	1966	Amberoid	W. Boland	126	117,700
1947	Phalanx	R. Donoso	126	78,900	1967	Damascus	W. Shoemaker	126	104,950
1948	Citation	E. Arcaro	126	77,700					

Year	Winner	Jockey	Wt.	Win val.
1968	Stage Door Johnny	H. Gustines	126	$117,700
1969	Arts and Letters	B. Baeza	126	104,050
1970	High Echelon	J. Rotz	126	115,000
1971	Pass Catcher	R. Blum	126	97,710
1972	Riva Ridge	R. Turcotte	126	93,540
1973	Secretariat	R. Turcotte	126	90,120
1974	Little Current	M. Rivera	126	101,970
1975	Avatar	W. Shoemaker	126	116,160
1976	Bold Forbes	A. Cordero, Jr.	126	117,000
1977	Seattle Slew	J. Cruguet	126	109,080
1978	Affirmed	S. Cauthen	126	110,580
1979	Coastal	R. Hernandez	126	161,400
1980	Temperence Hill	E. Maple	126	176,220
1981	Summing	G. Martens	126	170,580
1982	Conquistador Cielo	L. Pincay, Jr.	126	159,720
1983	Caveat	L. Pincay, Jr.	126	215,100
1984	Swale	L. Pincay, Jr.	126	310,020
1985	Creme Fraiche	Eddie Maple	126	307,740
1986	Danzig Connection	C. McCarron	126	338,640
1987	Bet Twice	C. Perret	126	329,160
1988	Risen Star	E. Delahoussaye	126	303,720
1989	Easy Goer	P. Day	126	413,520
1990	Go And Go	Michael Kinane	126	411,600
1991	Hansel	Jerry Bailey	126	417,480
1992	A.P. Indy	E. Delahoussaye	126	458,880
1993	Colonial Affair	Julie Krone	126	444,450
1994	Tabasco Cat	Pat Day	126	392,280
1995	Thunder Gulch	Gary Stevens	126	415,440
1996	Editor's Note	R. Douglas	126	437,880
1997	Touch Gold	C. McCarron	126	432,600

TRIPLE CROWN RACES—1997

Kentucky Derby (Churchill Downs, Louisville, Ky., May 3, 1997). Gross purse: $1,000,000. Distance: 1¼ miles. Order of finish: 1. Silver Charm (Stevens), mutual returns: $10.00, $4.80, $4.20. 2. Captain Bodgit (Solis), $4.80, $3.80. 3. Free House (Flores), $5.80. 4. Pulpit (Sellers). 5. Crypto Star (Day). 6. Phantom On Tour (Bailey). 7. Jack Flash (Perret). 8. Hello [Ire] (Smith). 9. Concerto (Marquez, Jr.). 10. Celtic Warrior (Torres). 11. Crimson Classic (Albarado). 12. Shammy Davis (Martinez). 13. Deeds Not Words (Nakatani). Winner's purse: $700,000. Margin of victory: head. Time of race: 2:02 ⅖.

Preakness Stakes (Pimlico, Baltimore Md., May 17, 1997). Gross purse: $751,000. Distance: 1 ¹³⁄₁₆ miles. Order of finish: 1. Silver Charm (Stevens), mutuel returns: $8.20, $4.00, $2.60. 2. Free House (Desormeaux), $3.60, $2.20. 3. Captain Bodgit (Solis), $2.40. 4. Touch Gold (McCarron). 5. Frisk Me Now (King). 6. Concerto (Smith). 7. Hoxie (Santos). 8. Wild Tempest (Bravo). 9. Cryp Too (Lopez). 10. Jack At The Bank (McCauley). Winner's purse: $488,150. Margin of victory: head. Time of race: 1:54 ⅖.

Belmont Stakes (Belmont Park, Belmont N.Y., June 7, 1997). Gross purse: $721,000. Distance: 1½ miles. Order of finish: 1. Touch Gold (McCarron), mutuel returns: $7.30, $3.30, $2.60. 2. Silver Charm (Stevens), $3.00, $2.40. 3. Free House (Desormeaux), $2.70. 4. Crypto Star (Day). 5. Irish Silence (Velazquez). 6. Wild Rush (Bailey). 7. Mr. Energizer (Ortega). Winner's purse: $432,600. Margin of victory: 1¾ length. Time of race: 2:28 ⅘.

ECLIPSE AWARDS—1996

(Presented Feb. 4, 1997)

Horse of the Year	Cigar
4-year-old and up colt, horse, or gelding	Cigar
3-year-old colt or gelding	Skip Away
3-year-old filly	Yanks Music
4-year-old and up filly or mare	Jewel Princess
Jockey	Jerry Bailey
Trainer	William Mott
Breeder	Farnsworth Farms
Owner	Allen Paulson
Apprentice jockey	Neil Poznansky
2-year old colt or gelding	Boston Harbor
2-year-old filly	Storm Song
Sprinter	Lit De Justice
Male turf horse	Singspiel
Female turf horse	Wandesta
Steeplechase	Correggio

(Based on vote by the Thoroughbred Racing Associations, the *Daily Racing Form*, and the National Turf Writers Association.)

Track and Field

WORLD RECORDS—MEN

(Through Sept. 20, 1997)

Recognized by the International Athletic Federation.
The I.A.A.F. decided late in 1976 not to recognize records in yards except for the one-mile run.
The I.A.A.F. also requires automatic timing for all records for races of 400 meters or less.

Event	Record	Holder	Home Country	Where Made	Date
Running					
100 m	0:09.84	Donovan Bailey	Canada	Atlanta, Ga.	July 27, 1996
200 m	0:19.32	Michael Johnson	United States	Atlanta, Ga.	Aug. 1, 1996
400 m	0:43.29	Butch Reynolds	United States	Indianapolis, Ind.	Aug. 17, 1988
800 m	1:41.11	Wilson Kipketer	Denmark	Köln, Germany	Aug. 24, 1997
1,000 m	2:12.18	Sebastian Coe	England	Oslo, Norway	July 11, 1981
1,500 m	3:27.37	Noureddine Morceli	Algeria	Nice, France	July 12, 1995
1 mile	3:44.39	Noureddine Morceli	Algeria	Rieti, Italy	Sept. 5, 1993
2,000 m	4:47.88	Noureddine Morceli	Algeria	Paris	July 3, 1995
3,000 m	7:20.67	Daniel Komen	Kenya	Rieti, Italy	Sept. 1, 1996
3,000 m steeplechase	7:55.72	Bernard Barmasai	Kenya	Köln, Germany	Aug. 24, 1997

Event	Record	Holder	Home Country	Where Made	Date
5,000 m	12:39.74	Daniel Komen	Kenya	Brussels, Belgium	Aug. 22, 1997
10,000 m	26:27.85	Paul Tergat	Kenya	Brussels, Belgium	Aug. 22, 1997
25,000 m	1:13:55.80	Toshihiko Seko	Japan	Christchurch, N.Z.	March 22, 1981
30,000 m	1:29:18.80	Toshihiko Seko	Japan	Christchurch, N.Z.	March 22, 1981
20,000 m	56:55.60	Arturo Barrios	Mexico	La Fleche, France	March 30, 1991
1 hour	21,101 m	Arturo Barrios	Mexico	La Fleche, France	March 30, 1991
Marathon	2:06.50	Belayneh Densimo	Ethiopia	Rotterdam	April 17, 1988
Walking					
20,000 m	1:17:25.50	Bernardo Segura	Mexico	Fana, Norway	May 7, 1994
2 hours	29,572 m	Maurizio Damilano	Italy	Cuneo, Italy	Oct. 3, 1992
30,000 m	2:01:44	Maurizio Damilano	Italy	Cuneo, Italy	Oct. 3, 1992
50,000 m	3:40:57.9	Thierry Toutain	France	Héricourt	Sept. 29, 1996
Hurdles					
110 m	0:12.91	Colin Jackson	Great Britain	Stuttgart, Germany	Aug. 20, 1993
400 m	0:46.78	Kevin Young	United States	Barcelona, Spain	Aug. 6, 1992
Relay Races					
400 m (4 × 100)	0:37.40	United States		Stuttgart, Germany	Aug. 21, 1993
800 m (4 × 200)	1:18.68	Santa Monica T.C.	United States	Walnut, Calif.	April 17, 1994
1,600 m (4 × 400)	2:54.29	United States		Stuttgart, Germany	Aug. 21 1993
3,200 m (4 × 800)	7:03.89	National Team[1]	Britain	London	Aug. 30, 1982
Field Events					
High Jump	2.45 m	Javier Sotomayor	Cuba	Salamanca, Spain	July 27, 1993
Long jump	8.95 m	Mike Powell	United States	Yokyo, Japan	Aug. 30, 1991
Triple Jump	18.29 m	Jonathan Edwards	Great Britain	Gothenburg, Sweden	Aug. 7, 1995
Pole vault	6.14 m	Sergey Bubka	Ukraine	Sestriere, Italy	July 31, 1994
Shot-put	23.12 m	Randy Barnes	United States	Los Angeles	May 20, 1990
Discus throw	74.08 m	Juergen Schult	East Germany	Neubrandenburg, E. Germany	June 6, 1986
Hammer throw	86.74 m	Yuriy Syedikh	U.S.S.R.	Stuttgart, Germany	Aug. 30, 1986
Javelin throw	98.48 m	Jan Zelezny	Czech Republic	Jena, Germany	May 25, 1996
Decathlon	8,891 pts.	Dan O'Brien	United States	Talence, France	Sept. 4–5, 1992

1. National Team: Peter Elliot, Garry Cook, Steve Cram, Sebastian Coe

WORLD RECORDS—WOMEN

(Through Sept. 20, 1997)

Event	Record	Holder	Home Country	Where Made	Date
Running					
100 m	0:10.49	Florence Griffith-Joyner	United States	Indianapolis, Ind.	July 16, 1988
200 m	0:21.56	Florence Griffith-Joyner	United States	Seoul, South Korea	Oct. 1, 1988
400 m	0:47.60	Martina Koch	East Germany	Canberra, Australia	Oct. 6, 1985
800 m	1:53.28	Jarmila Kratochvilova	Czechoslovakia	Munich, W. Ger.	July 26, 1983
1000 m	2:28.98	Svetlana Masterkova	Russia	Brussels, Belgium	Aug. 23, 1996
1,500 m	3:50.46	Qu Yunxia	China	Beijing, China	Sept. 11, 1993
1 mile	4:12.56	Svetlana Masterkova	Russia	Zurich, Switzerland	Aug. 14, 1996
3,000 m	8:06.11	Wang Junxia	China	Beijing, China	Sept. 13, 1993
5,000 m	14:36.45	Fernanda Ribeiro	Portugal	Hechtel, Belgium	July 22, 1995
10,000 m	29:31.78	Wang Junxia	China	Beijing, China	Sept. 8, 1993
20,000 m	1:06:48.80	Izumi Maki	Japan	Amagasaki, Japan	Sept. 19, 1993
25,000 m	1:29:29.20	Karolina Szabo	Hungary	Budapest, Hungary	April 22, 1988
30,000 m	1:47:05.60	Karolina Szabo	Hungary	Budapest, Hungary	April 22, 1988
Marathon	2:21:06.0	Ingrid Kristiansen	Norway	London	April 21, 1985
Walking					
5,000 m	20:13.26	Kerry Saxby-Junna	Australia	Hobart, Australia	Feb. 25, 1996
10,000 m	41:37.90	Gao Hongmiao	China	Beijing, China	April 7, 1994
Hurdles					
100-m hurdles	0:12.21	Yordanka Kondova	Bulgaria	Stara Zagora, Bulgaria	Aug. 20, 1988
400 m	0:52.61	Kim Batten	United States	Gothenburg, Sweden	Aug. 11, 1995
Relay Races					
400 m (4 × 100)	0:41.53	East Germany	E. Germany	Berlin, E. Ger.	July 31, 1983
800 m (4 × 200)	1:28.15	East Germany	E. Germany	Jena, E. Ger.	Aug. 9, 1980
1,600 m (4 × 400)	3:15.18	Soviet Union	U.S.S.R.	Seoul, South Korea	Oct. 1, 1988
3,200 m (4 × 800)	7:52.3	U.S.S.R.	U.S.S.R.	Podolsk, U.S.S.R.	Aug. 16, 1976
Field Events					
High jump	2.09 m	Stefka Kostadinova	Bulgaria	Rome	Aug. 30, 1987

Event	Record	Holder	Home Country	Where Made	Date
Pole Vault	4:55 m	Emma George	Australia	Melbourne, Australia	Feb. 20, 1997
Long jump	7.52 m	Galina Chistyakova	U.S.S.R.	Leningrad	June 11, 1988
Triple jump	15.50 m	Ana Biryukova	Russia	Stuttgart, Germany	Aug. 21, 1993
Shot-put	22.63 m	Natalya Lisovskaya	U.S.S.R.	Moscow	June 7, 1987
Discus throw	76.80 m	Gabriele Reinsch	East Germany	Neubrandenburg, E. Ger.	July 9, 1988
Hammer	73.10 m	Olga Kuzenkova	Russia	Munich, Germany	June 22, 1997
Javelin throw	80.00 m	Petra Felke	East Germany	Potsdam	Sept. 9, 1988
Heptathlon	7,291 pts	Jackie Joyner-Kersee	United States	Seoul, South Korea	Sept. 24, 1988

AMERICAN RECORDS—MEN

(Through Sept. 20, 1997)

Event	Record	Holder	Where Made	Date
Running				
100 m	0:09.85	Leroy Burrell	Lausanne, Switzerland	July 6, 1994
200 m	0:19.32	Michael Johnson	Atlanta, Ga.	Aug. 1, 1996
400 m	0:43.29	Butch Reynolds	Indianapolis, Ind.	Aug. 17, 1988
800 m	1:42.60	Johnny Gray	Koblenz, W. Ger.	Aug. 29, 1985
1,000 m	2:13.90	Richard Wohlhuter	Oslo, Norway	July 30, 1974
1,500 m	3:29.77	Sydney Maree	Cologne, W. Ger.	Aug. 25, 1985
1 mile	3:47.69	Steve Scott	Oslo, Norway	July 7, 1982
2,000 m	4:54.71	Steve Scott	Ingelheim, W. Ger.	Aug. 31, 1982
3,000 m	7:31.69	Bob Kennedy	Brussels, Belgium	Aug. 23, 1996
5,000 m	12:58.21	Bob Kennedy	Zurich, Switzerland	Aug. 14, 1996
10,000 m	27:20.56	Mark Nenow	Brussels	Sept. 5, 1986
20,000 m	58:15.00	Bill Rodgers	Boston, Mass.	Aug. 9, 1977
25,000 m	1:14:11.80	Bill Rodgers	Saratoga, Cal.	Feb. 21, 1979
30,000 m	1:31:49.00	Bill Rodgers	Saratoga, Cal.	Feb. 21, 1979
1 hour	12 mi., 1,351 yds	Bill Rodgers	Boston, Mass.	Aug. 9, 1977
3,000-m steeplechase	8:09.17	Henry Marsh	Koblenz, W. Ger.	Aug. 29, 1985
Hurdles				
110 m	0:12.92	Roger Kingdom	Berlin	Aug. 16, 1989
		Allen Johnson	Brussels, Belgium	Aug. 23, 1996
400 m	0:46.78	Kevin Young	Barcelona	Aug. 6, 1992
Relay Races				
400 m (4 × 100)	0:37.40	USA National Team	Stuttgart, Germany	Aug. 21, 1993
800 m (4 × 200)	1:18.68	Santa Monica T.C.	Walnut, Calif.	April 17, 1994
1,600 m (4 × 400)	2:54.29	USA National Team	Stuttgart, Germany	Aug. 22, 1993
3,200 m (4 × 800)	7:06.50	Santa Monica T.C.	Walnut, Calif.	Apr. 26, 1986
Field Events				
High jump	7 ft. 10½ in.	Charles Austin	Zurich	Aug. 7, 1991
Long jump	29 ft. 4½ in.	Mike Powell	Tokyo, Japan	Aug. 30, 1991
Triple jump	59 ft. 4 in.	Kenny Harrison	Atlanta, Ga.	July 27, 1996
Pole vault	19 ft. 7½ in.	Lawrence Johnson	Knoxville, Tenn.	May 25, 1996
Shot-put	75 ft. 10¼ in.	Randy Barnes	Los Angeles	May 20, 1990
Discus throw	237 ft. 4 in.	Ben Plucknett	Stockholm, Swe.	July 7, 1981
Javelin throw	285 ft. 10 in.	Tom Pukstys	Jena	May 25, 1997
Hammer throw	270 ft. 9 in.	Lance Deal	Milan, Italy	July 9, 1996
Decathlon	8,891 pts	Dan O'Brien	Talence, France	Sept. 4–5, 1992

AMERICAN RECORDS—WOMEN

(Through Sept. 20, 1997)

Event	Record	Holder	Where Made	Date
Running				
100 m	0:10.49	Florence Griffith-Joyner	Indianapolis, Ind.	July 16, 1988
200 m	0:21.56	Florence Griffith-Joyner	Seoul, South Korea	Oct. 1, 1988
400 m	0:48.83	Valerie Brisco-Hooks	Los Angeles, Cal.	Aug. 6, 1984
800 m	1:56.78	Jearl Miles-Clark	Brussels, Belgium	Aug. 22, 1997
1,500 m	3:57.12	Mary Decker Slaney	Stockholm, Swe.	July 26, 1983
1,000 m	2:34.8	Mary Decker Slaney	Eugene, Ore.	July 4, 1985
1 mile	4:16.71	Mary Decker Slaney	Zurich	Aug. 21, 1985
3,000 m	8:29.69	Mary Decker Slaney	Cologne	Aug. 25, 1985
5,000 m	14:56.04	Amy Rudolph	Stockholm, Sweden	July 8, 1996
10,000 m	31:28.92	Francie L. Smith	Austin, Texas	April 4, 1991
Hurdles				
100 m hurdles	0:12.46	Gail Devers	Stuttgart, Germany	Aug. 20, 1993
400 m hurdles	0:52.61	Kim Batten	Gothenburg, Sweden	Aug. 11, 1995
Relay Races				
400 m (4 × 100)	41.47	U.S.A. National Team	Athens, Greece	Aug. 9, 1997
800 m (4 × 200)	1:30.20	Nike International	Philadelphia, Pa.	Apr. 26, 1997
1,600 m (4 × 400)	3:15.51	U.S. Olympic Team	Seoul, South Korea	Oct. 1, 1988

Event	Record	Holder	Where Made	Date
Field Events				
Pole vault	14 ft. 7¼ in.	Stacy Dragila	Modesto, Calif.	May 10, 1997
High jump	6 ft. 8 in.	Louise Ritter	Austin, Tex.	July 9, 1988
Long jump	24 ft. 7 in.	Jackie Joyner-Kersee	New York, N.Y.	May 22, 1994
Triple jump	47 ft. 3½ in.	Sheila Hudson	Stockholm, Sweden	July 8, 1996
Shot-put	66 ft. 2½ in.	Ramon Pagel	San Diego, Calif.	June 25, 1988
Discus throw	216 ft. 10 in.	Carol Cady	San Jose, Calif.	May 31, 1986
Hammer throw	210 ft. 8 in.	Dawn Ellerbe	Walnut, Calif.	April 19, 1997
Javelin throw	227 ft. 5 in.	Kate Schmidt	Furth, W. Ger.	Sept. 10, 1977
Heptathlon	7,291 pts	Jackie Joyner-Kersee	Seoul, South Korea	Sept. 23–24, 1988

HISTORY OF THE RECORD FOR THE MILE RUN

Source: USA Track & Field

Time	Athlete	Country	Year	Location
4:36.5	Richard Webster	England	1865	England
4:29.0	William Chinnery	England	1868	England
4:28.8	Walter Gibbs	England	1868	England
4:26.0	Walter Slade	England	1874	England
4:24.5	Walter Slade	England	1875	London
4:23.2	Walter George	England	1880	London
4:21.4	Walter George	England	1882	London
4:18.4	Walter George	England	1884	Birmingham, England
4:18.2	Fred Bacon	Scotland	1894	Edinburgh, Scotland
4:17.0	Fred Bacon	Scotland	1895	London
4:15.6	Thomas Conneff	United States	1895	Travers Island, N.Y.
4:15.4	John Paul Jones	United States	1911	Cambridge, Mass.
4:14.4	John Paul Jones	United States	1913	Cambridge, Mass.
4:12.6	Norman Taber	United States	1915	Cambridge, Mass.
4:10.4	Paavo Nurmi	Finland	1923	Stockholm
4:09.2	Jules Ladoumegue	France	1931	Paris
4:07.6	Jack Lovelock	New Zealand	1933	Princeton, N.J.
4:06.8	Glenn Cunningham	United States	1934	Princeton, N.J.
4:06.4	Sydney Wooderson	England	1937	London
4:06.2	Gundar Hägg	Sweden	1942	Goteborg, Sweden
4:06.2	Arne Andersson	Sweden	1942	Stockholm
4:04.6	Gunder Hägg	Sweden	1942	Stockholm
4:02.6	Arne Andersson	Sweden	1943	Goteborg, Sweden
4:01.6	Arne Andersson	Sweden	1944	Malmo, Sweden
4:01.4	Gunder Hägg	Sweden	1945	Malmo, Sweden
3:59.4	Roger Bannister	England	1954	Oxford, England
3:58.0	John Landy	Australia	1954	Turku, Finland
3:57.2	Derek Ibbotson	England	1957	London
3:54.5	Herb Elliott	Australia	1958	Dublin
3:54.4	Peter Snell	New Zealand	1962	Wanganui, N.Z.
3:54.1	Peter Snell	New Zealand	1964	Auckland, N.Z.
3:53.6	Michel Jazy	France	1965	Rennes, France
3:51.3	Jim Ryun	United States	1966	Berkeley, Calif.
3:51.1	Jim Ryun	United States	1967	Bakersfield, Calif.
3:51.0	Filbert Bayi	Tanzania	1975	Kingston, Jamaica
3:49.4	John Walker	New Zealand	1975	Goteborg, Sweden
3:49.0	Sebastian Coe	England	1979	Oslo
3:48.8	Steve Ovett	England	1980	Oslo
3:48.53	Sebastian Coe	England	1981	Zurich, Switzerland
3:48.40	Steve Ovett	England	1981	Koblenz, W. Ger.
3:47.33	Sebastian Coe	England	1981	Brussels
3:46.31	Steve Cram	England	1985	Oslo
3:44.39	Noureddine Morceli	Algeria	1993	Rieti, Italy

TOP TEN WORLD'S FASTEST OUTDOOR MILES

Source: USA Track & Field

Time	Athlete	Country	Date	Location
3:44.39	Nouraddine Morceli	Algeria	Sept. 5, 1993	Rieti, Italy
3:46.31	Steve Cram	England	July 27, 1985	Oslo
3:47.33	Sebastian Coe	England	Aug. 28, 1981	Brussels
3:47.69	Steve Scott	United States	July 7, 1982	Oslo
3:47.79	Jose Gonzalez	Spain	July 27, 1985	Oslo

Time	Athlete	Country	Date	Location
3:48.40	Steve Ovett	England	Aug. 26, 1981	Koblenz, W. Ger.
3:48.53	Sebastian Coe	England	Aug. 19, 1981	Zurich
3:48.53	Steve Scott	United States	June 26, 1982	Oslo
3:48.8	Steve Ovett	England	July 1, 1980	Oslo
3:48.83	Sydney Maree	United States	Sept. 9, 1981	Rieti, Italy

NOTE: Professional marks not included.

TOP TEN WORLD'S FASTEST INDOOR MILES

Source: USA Track & Field

Time	Athlete	Country	Date	Location
3:48.45	Hicham El Guerrouj	Morocco	1997	
3:49.78	Eamonn Coghlan	Ireland	Feb. 27, 1983	East Rutherford, N.J.
3:50.6	Eamonn Coghlan	Ireland	Feb. 20, 1981	San Diego
3:50.7	Noureddine Morceli	Algeria	Feb. 20, 1993	Birmingham, England
3:50.94	Marcus O'Sullivan	Ireland	Feb. 13, 1988	East Rutherford, N.J.
3:51.2	Ray Flynn[1]	Ireland	Feb. 27, 1983	East Rutherford, N.J.
3:51.66	Marcus O'Sullivan	Ireland	Feb. 10, 1989	East Rutherford, N.J.
3:51.8	Steve Scott[1]	United States	Feb. 20, 1981	San Diego
3:52.28	Steve Scott[2]	United States	Feb. 27, 1983	East Rutherford, N.J.
3:52.30	Frank O'Mara	Ireland	Feb. 1986	New York

1. Finished second. 2. Finished third.

IAAF WORLD CHAMPIONSHIPS—1997

(Athens, Greece, Aug. 3–10, 1997)

Men's Events

100m—Maurice Green, United States	09.86
200m—Ato Boldon, Trinidad	20.04
400m—Michael Johnson, United States	44.12
1,500m—Hicham El Guerrouj, Morocco	3:35.83
5,000m—Daniel Komen, Kenya	13:07.38
Marathon—Abel Anton, Spain	2:13.16
400m hurdles—Stephane Diagana, France	47.70
3,000m steeplechase—Wilson Boit Kipketer, Kenya	8:05.84
High jump—Javier Sotomayor, Cuba	7 ft. 9¼ in.
Pole vault—Sergey Bubka, Ukraine	19 ft. 8½ in.
Shot put—John Godina, United States	70 ft. 4¼ in.

Decathlon—Tomas Dvorak, Czech Republic   8,837 pts.

Women's Events

100m—Marion Jones, United States	10.83
200m—Zhanna Pintusevich, Ukraine	22.32
800m—Ana Fidelia Quirot, Cuba	1:57.14
1,500m—Carla Sacramento, Portugal	4:04.24
5,000m—Gabriela Szabo, Romania	14:57.68
Marathon—Hiromi Suzuki, Japan	2:29.48
4x100m relay—United States	41.47
400m hurdles—Nezha Bidouane, Morocco	52.97
High jump—Hanne Haugland, Norway	6 ft. 6¼ in.
Shot put—Astrid Kumbernuss, Germany	67 ft. 11½ in.
Javelin—Trine Hattestad, Norway	225 ft. 8 in.
Heptathlon—Sabine Braun, Germany	6,739 pts.

1996–97 NCAA DIVISION 1 INDIVIDUAL CHAMPIONS

WOMEN'S EVENTS

100m—Sevatheda Fynes, Michigan State	11.04
200m—Sevatheda Fynes, Michigan State	22.61
400m—LaTarsha Stroman, Louisiana State	50.60
800m—Dana Riley, Texas	2:02.89
1,500m—Becki Wells, Florida	4:12.84
3,000m—Kathy Butler, Wisconsin	9:01.23
5000m—Amy Skieresz, Arizona	15:46.76
10,000m—Amy Skieresz, Arizona	33:14.22
100m hurdles—Astia Walker, Louisiana State	12.85
400m hurdles—Ryan Tolbert, Vanderbilt	54.54
4 x 100m relay—Louisiana State	43.17
4 x 400m relay—Texas	3:28.43
High jump—Kajsa Bergqvist, Southern Methodist	6 ft. 4 in.
Long jump—Trecia Smith, Pittsburgh	21 ft. 10 in.
Triple jump—Suzette Lee, Louisiana State	45 ft. 8 in.
Shot put—Tressa Thompson, Nebraska	60 ft. 8½ in.
Discus—Seilala Sua, U.C.L.A.	200 ft. 6 in.
Javelin—Windy Dean, Southern Methodist	191 ft. 2 in.
Hammer—Dawn Ellerbe, South Carolina	207 ft. 4 in.
Heptathlon—Tiffany Lott, Brigham Young	6,211 pts.

MEN'S EVENTS

100m—Obadele Thompson, Texas-El Paso	10.13
200m—Obadele Thompson, Texas-El Paso	20.03
400m—Roxbert Martin, Oklahoma	44.77
800m—Bryan Woodward, Georgetown	1:46.45
1,500m—Seneca Lassiter, Arkansas	3:40.22
5,000m—Mebrahtom Keflezighi, U.C.L.A.	13:44.17
10,000m—Mebrahtom Keflezighi, U.C.L.A.	28:51.18
110m hurdles—Reggie Torrian, Wisconsin	13.39
400m hurdles—Joey Woody, N. Iowa	48.59
3000m steeplechase—Pascal Dobert, Wisconsin	8:31.68
4 x 100m relay—Texas A & M	38.80
4 x 400m relay—Oklahoma	3:01.25
High jump—Ivan Wagner, Texas	7 ft. 6½ in.
Pole vault—Clark Humphreys, Auburn	18 ft. 4½ in.
Long jump—Robert Howard, Arkansas	26 ft. 11¼ in.
Triple jump—Robert Howard, Arkansas	55 ft. 6½ in.
Shot put—Adam Nelson, Dartmouth	64 ft. 4½ in.
Discus—Jason Tunks, Southern Methodist	195 ft. 11 in.
Javelin—Mats Nilsson, Alabama	245 ft. 9 in.
Hammer—Bengt Johansson, Southern Calif.	230 ft. 1 in.
Decathlon—James Dunkleberger, Wisconsin	7,924 pts.

Gymnastics

WORLD CHAMPIONSHIPS—1997

(Lausanne, Switzerland, Finals: Sept. 5–7, 1997)

Men	Pts
Floor exercise—1. Nemov, Russia	9.625
2. Karbanenko, Russia	9.550
3. Li Xiaopeng, China	9.537
Pommel horse—1. Belenki, Germany	9.700
2. Poujade, France	9.700
3. Pae, North Korea	9.700
Still rings—1. Chechi, Italy	9.775
2. Csollany, Hungary	9.687
3. Ivankov, Belarus	9.662
Vault—1. Fedorchenko, Kazakhstan	9.581
2. Krukov, Russia	9.556
3. Ianculescu, Romania	9.437
Parallel bars—1. Zhang, China	9.775
2. Li Xiaopeng, China	9.737
3. Tsukahara, Japan	9.562
High bar—1. Tanskanen, Finland	9.700
2. Carballo, Spain	9.675
3. Beresch, Ukraine	9.625
All-around—1. Ivan Ivankov, Belarus	56.887
2. Alexei Bondarenko, Russia	56.061
3. Naoya Tsukahara, Japan	56.023

Women	Pts
Vault—1. Amanar, Romania	9.712
2. Zhou, China	9.606
3. Gogean, Romania	9.600
Uneven bars—1. Khorkina, Russia	9.875
2. Meng Fei, China	9.800
3. Bi Wenjing, China	9.787
Balance beam—1. Gogean, Romania	9.800
2. Khorkina, Russia	9.787
3. Kui, China	9.787
Floor—1. Gogean, Romania	9.800
2. Khorkina, Russia	9.800
3. Produnova, Russia	9.775
All-around—1. Svetlana Khorkina, Russia	38.636
2. Simona Amanar, Romania	38.587
3. Elena Produnova, Russia	38.549

NATIONAL CHAMPIONSHIPS—1997

(Denver, Colo., Finals Aug. 13–14, 1997)

Men	Pts
Floor exercise—1. Jason Gatson	9.15
2. John Macready	9.00
3. Jay Thornton	8.90
Pommel horse—1. John Roethlisberger	9.30
2. Sanjuan Jones	9.05
3. Ken Schiess	9.05
Rings—1. Blaine Wilson	9.15
2. Chris Camiscioli	8.85
3. John Roethlisberger	8.75
Vault—1. Blaine Wilson	9.65
2. Michael Dutka	9.50
3. Jason Gatson	9.45
Parallel bars—1. Blaine Wilson	9.55
2. Jim Foody	9.45
3. Jason Gatson	9.30
High bar—1. Douglas Stibel	9.35
2. John Roethlisberger	9.15
3. John Macready	9.00
All-around—1. Blaine Wilson	54.550
2. Jason Gatson	52.850
3. John Macready	52.700

Women (Listed with club affiliation)	Pts
Vault—1. Vanessa Atler	9.513
2. Kristin Maloney	9.450
3. Jeanette Antolin	9.363
Uneven bars—1. Kristy Powell	9.550
2. Mary Beth Arnold	9.400
3. Jamie Dantzscher	9.325
Balance beam—1. Kendall Beck	9.425
2. Raegan Tomasek	9.400
3. Kaitie Dyson	9.375
Floor exercise—1. Lindsay Wing	9.700
2. Dominique Moceanu	9.600
3. Kristen Maloney	9.500
All-around—1. Vanessa Atler	37.188
2. Kristy Powell	37.088
3. Kristin Maloney	36.875

Tennis

Lawn tennis is a comparatively modern modification of the ancient game of court tennis. Major Walter Clopton Wingfield thought that something like court tennis might be played outdoors on lawns, and in December, 1873, at Nantclwyd, Wales, he introduced his new game under the name of *Sphairistike* at a lawn party. The game was a success and spread rapidly, but the name was a total failure and almost immediately disappeared when all the players and spectators began to refer to the new game as "lawn tennis." In the early part of 1874, a young lady named Mary Ewing Outerbridge returned from Bermuda to New York, bringing with her the implements and necessary equipment of the new game, which she had obtained from a British Army supply store in Bermuda. Miss Outerbridge and friends played the first game of lawn tennis in the United States on the grounds of the Staten Island Cricket and Baseball Club in the spring of 1874.

For a few years, the new game went along in haphazard fashion until about 1880, when standard measurements for the court and standard equipment within defi-nite limits became the rule. In 1881, the U.S. Lawn Tennis Association (whose name was changed in 1975 to U.S. Tennis Association) was formed and conducted the first national championship at Newport, R.I. The international matches for the Davis Cup began with a series between the British and United States players on the courts of the Longwood Cricket Club, Chestnut Hill, Mass., in 1900, with the home players winning.

Professional tennis, which got its start in 1926 when the French star Suzanne Lenglen was paid $50,000 for a tour, received full recognition in 1968. Staid old Wimbledon, the London home of what are considered the world championships, let the pros compete. This decision ended a long controversy over open tennis and changed the format of the competition. The United States championships were also opened to the pros and the site of the event, long held at Forest Hills, N.Y., was shifted to the National Tennis Center in Flushing Meadows, N.Y., in 1978. Pro tours for men and women became worldwide in play that continued throughout the year.

DAVIS CUP CHAMPIONSHIPS

No matches in 1901, 1910, 1915–18, and 1940–45.

1900	United States 3, British Isles 0	1935	Great Britain 5, United States 0	1970	United States 5, West Ger-
1902	United States 3, British Isles 2	1936	Great Britain 3, Australia 2		many 0
1903	British Isles 4, United States 1	1937	United States 4, Great Britain 1	1971	United States 3, Romania 2
1904	British Isles 5, Belgium 0	1938	United States 3, Australia 2	1972	United States 3, Romania 2
1905	British Isles 5, United States 0	1939	Australia 3, United States 2	1973	Australia 5, United States 0
1906	British Isles 5, United States 0	1946	United States 5, Australia 0	1974	South Africa (Default by India)
1907	Australasia 3, British Isles 2	1947	United States 4, Australia 1	1975	Sweden 3, Czechoslovakia 2
1908	Australasia 3, United States 2	1948	United States 5, Australia 0	1976	Italy 4, Chile 1
1909	Australasia 5, United States 0	1949	United States 4, Australia 1	1977	Australia 3, Italy 1
1911	Australasia 5, United States 0	1950	Australia 4, United States 1	1978	United States 4, Britain 1
1912	British Isles 3, Australasia 2	1951	Australia 3, United States 2	1979	United States 5, Italy 0
1913	United States 3, British Isles 2	1952	Australia 4, United States 1	1980	Czechoslovakia 3, Italy 2
1914	Australasia 3, United States 2	1953	Australia 3, United States 2	1981	United States 3, Argentina 1
1919	Australasia 4, British Isles 1	1954	United States 3, Australia 2	1982	United States 3, France 0
1920	United States 5, Australasia 0	1955	Australia 5, United States 0	1983	Australia 3, Sweden 2
1921	United States 5, Japan 0	1956	Australia 5, United States 0	1984	Sweden 4, United States 1
1922	United States 4, Australasia 1	1957	Australia 3, United States 2	1985	Sweden 3, West Germany 2
1923	United States 4, Australasia 1	1958	United States 3, Australia 2	1986	Australia 3, Sweden 2
1924	United States 5, Australasia 0	1959	Australia 3, United States 2	1987	Sweden 5, Austria 0
1925	United States 5, France 0	1960	Australia 4, Italy 1	1988	West Germany 4, Sweden 1
1926	United States 4, France 1	1961	Australia 5, Italy 0	1989	West Germany 3, Sweden 2
1927	France 3, United States 2	1962	Australia 5, Mexico 0	1990	United States 3, Australia 2
1928	France 4, United States 1	1963	United States 3, Australia 2	1991	France 3, United States 1
1929	France 3, United States 2	1964	Australia 3, United States 2	1992	United States 3, Switzerland 1
1930	France 4, United States 1	1965	Australia 4, Spain 1	1993	Germany 4, Australia 1
1931	France 3, Great Britain 2	1966	Australia 4, India 1	1994	Sweden 4, Russia 1
1932	France 3, United States 2	1967	Australia 4, Spain 1	1995	United States 3, Russia 1
1933	Great Britain 3, France 2	1968	United States 4, Australia 1	1996	France 3, Sweden 2
1934	Great Britain 4, United States 1	1969	United States 5, Romania 0		

FEDERATION CUP CHAMPIONSHIPS

World team competition for women conducted by International Lawn Tennis Federation.

1963	United States 2, Australia 1	1976	United States 2, Australia 1	1986	United States 3,
1964	Australia 2, United States 1	1977	United States 2, Australia 1		Czechoslovakia 0
1965	Australia 2, United States 1	1978	United States 2, Australia 1	1987	West Germany 2, United States 1
1966	United States 3, West Germany 0	1979	United States 3, Australia 0	1988	Czechoslovakia 2, Soviet Union 1
1967	United States 2, Britain 0	1980	United States 3, Australia 0	1989	United States 3, Spain 0
1968	Australia 3, Netherlands 0	1981	United States 3, Britain 0	1990	United States 2, Soviet Union 1
1969	United States 2, Australia 1	1982	United States 3, West Germany 0	1991	Spain 2, United States 1
1970	Australia 3, West Germany 0	1983	Czechoslovakia 2, West	1992	Germany 2, Spain 1
1971	Australia 3, Britain 0		Germany 1	1993	Spain 3, Australia 0
1972	South Africa 2, Britain 1	1984	Czechoslovakia 2, Australia 1	1994	Spain 3, United States 0
1973	Australia 3, South Africa 0	1985	Czechoslovakia 2, United	1995	Spain 3, United States 2
1974	Australia 2, United States 1		States 1	1996	United States 5, Spain 0
1975	Czechoslovakia 3, Australia 0				

U.S. CHAMPIONS

Singles—Men

NATIONAL		1916	R. N. William II	1943	Joseph Hunt	1965	Manuel Santana
1881–87	Richard D. Sears	1917–18	R. Lindley Murray[2]	1944–45	Frank Parker	1966	Fred Stolle
1888–89	Henry Slocum, Jr.	1919	William Johnston	1946–47	Jack Kramer	1967	John Newcombe
1890–92	Oliver S. Campbell	1920–25	Bill Tilden	1948–49	Richard Gonzales	1968	Arthur Ashe
1893–94	Robert D. Wrenn	1926–27	Jean Rene Lacoste	1950	Arthur Larsen	1969	Rod Laver
1895	Fred H. Hovey	1928	Henri Cochet	1951–52	Frank Sedgman	**OPEN**	
1896–97	Robert D. Wrenn	1929	Bill Tilden	1953	Tony Trabert	1968	Arthur Ashe
1898–1900	Malcolm Whitman	1930	John H. Doeg	1954	Vic Seixas	1969	Rod Laver
1901–02	William A. Larned	1931–32	Ellsworth Vines	1955	Tony Trabert	1970	Ken Rosewall
1903	Hugh L. Doherty	1933–34	Fred J. Perry	1956	Ken Rosewall	1971	Stan Smith
1904	Holcombe Ward	1935	Wilmer L. Allison	1957	Mal Anderson	1972	Ilie Nastase
1905	Beals C. Wright	1936	Fred J. Perry	1958	Ashley Cooper	1973	John Newcombe
1906	William J. Clothier	1937–38	Don Budge	1959–60	Neale Fraser	1974	Jimmy Connors
1907–11	William A. Larned	1939	Robert L. Riggs	1961	Roy Emerson	1975	Manuel Orantes
1912–13	Maurice McLough-	1940	Donald McNeill	1962	Rod Laver	1976	Jimmy Connors
	lin[1]	1941	Robert L. Riggs	1963	Rafael Osuna	1977	Guillermo Vilas
1914	R. N. Williams II	1942	Fred Schroeder	1964	Roy Emerson	1978	Jimmy Connors
1915	William Johnston						

1979	John McEnroe	1984	John McEnroe	1990	Pete Sampras	1994	Andre Agassi
1980–81	John McEnroe	1985–87	Ivan Lendl	1991	Stefan Edberg	1995	Pete Sampras
1982	Jimmy Connors	1988	Mats Wilander	1992	Stefan Edberg	1996	Pete Sampras
1983	Jimmy Connors	1989	Boris Becker	1993	Pete Sampras	1997	Patrick Rafter

1. Challenge Round Abandoned in 1912. 2. Patriotic Tournament in 1917.

Singles—Women

NATIONAL							
1887	Ellen F. Hansel	1909–11	Hazel V. Hotchkiss	1947	Louise Brough	1974	Billie Jean King
1888–89	Bertha Townsend	1912–14	Mary K. Browne	1948–50	Margaret Osborne duPont	1975–78	Chris Evert
1890	Ellen C. Roosevelt	1915–18	Molla Bjurstedt			1979	Tracy Austin
1891–92	Mabel E. Cahill	1919	Hazel Hotchkiss	1951–53	Maureen Connolly	1980	Chris Evert-Lloyd
1893	Aline M. Terry	1920–22	Molla Bjurstedt Mallory	1954–55	Doris Hart	1981	Tracy Austin
1894	Helen R. Helwig			1956	Shirley Fry	1982	Chris Evert-Lloyd
1895	Juliette P. Atkinson	1923–25	Helen N. Wills	1957–58	Althea Gibson	1983–84	Martina Navratilova
1896	Elisabeth H. Moore	1926	Molla B. Mallory	1959	Maria Bueno	1985	Hana Mandlikova
1897–98	Juliette P. Atkinson	1927–29	Helen N. Wills	1960–61	Darlene Hard	1986–87	Martina Navratilova
1899	Marion Jones	1930	Betty Nuthall	1962	Margaret Smith	1988	Steffi Graf
1900	Myrtle McAteer	1931	Helen Wills Moody	1963–64	Maria Bueno	1989	Steffi Graf
1901	Elisabeth H. Moore	1932–35	Helen Jacobs	1965	Margaret Smith	1990	Grabriela Sabatini
1902	Marion Jones	1936	Alice Marble	1966	Maria Bueno	1991	Monica Seles
1903	Elisabeth H. Moore	1937	Anita Lizana	1967	Billie Jean King	1992	Monica Seles
1904	May Sutton	1938–40	Alice Marble	1968–69	Margaret Smith Court[1]	1993	Steffi Graf
1905	Elisabeth H. Moore	1941	Sarah Palfrey Cooke	**OPEN**		1994	Arantxa Sanchez Vicario
1906	Helen Homans			1968	Virginia Wade	1995	Steffi Graf
1907	Evelyn Sears	1942–44	Pauline Betz	1969–70	Margaret Court	1996	Steffi Graf
1908	Maud Bargar-Wallach	1945	Sarah Cooke	1971–72	Billie Jean King	1997	Martina Hingis
		1946	Pauline Betz	1973	Margaret Court		

1. With the inaugural of the Open Tournament in 1968, the United States Lawn Tennis Association held a championship at Longwood, Chestnut Hill, Mass. which barred contract professionals in 1968 and 1969.

Doubles—Men

NATIONAL					
1920	Bill Johnston-C. J. Griffin	1951	Frank Sedgman-Ken McGregor	1976	Marty Riessen-Tom Okker
1921–22	Bill Tilden-Vincent Richards	1952	Vic Seixas-Mervyn Rose	1977	Frew McMillan-Bob Hewitt
1923	Bill Tilden-B. I. C. Norton	1953	Mervyn Rose-Rex Hartwig	1978	Bob Lutz-Stan Smith
1924	H. O. Kinsey-R. G. Kinsey	1954	Vic Seixas-Tony Trabert	1979	John McEnroe-Peter Fleming
1925–26	Vincent Richards-R. N. Williams II	1955	Kosei Kamo-Atsushi Miyagi	1980	Stan Smith-Bob Lutz
1927	Bill Tilden-Frank Hunter	1956	Lewis Hoad-Ken Rosewall	1981	John McEnroe-Peter Fleming
1928	G. M. Lott, Jr.-V. Hennessy	1957	Ashley Cooper-Neale Fraser	1982	Kevin Curren-Steve Denton
1929–30	G. M. Lott, Jr.-J. H. Doeg	1958	Ham Richardson-Alex Olmedo	1983	John McEnroe-Peter Fleming
1931	W. L. Allison-John Van Ryn	1959–60	Neale Fraser-Roy Emerson	1984	John Fitzgerald-Tomas Smid
1932	E. H. Vines, Jr.-Keith Gledh	1961	Chuck McKinley-Dennis Ralston	1985	Ken Flach-Robert Seguso
1933–34	G. M. Lott, Jr.-L. R. Stoefen	1962	Rafael Osuna-Antonio Palafox	1986	Andres Gomez-Slobodan Zivojinovic
1935	W. L. Allison-John Van Ryn	1963–64	Chuck McKinley-Dennis Ralston	1987	Stefan Edberg-Anders Jarryd
1936	Don Budge-Gene Mako	1965–66	Fred Stolle-Roy Emerson	1988	Sergio Casal-Emilio Sanchez
1937	G. von Cramm-H. Henkel	1967	John Newcombe-Tony Roche	1989	John McEnroe-Mark Woodforde
1938	Don Budge-Gene Mako	1968	Stan Smith-Bob Lutz[1]	1990	Pieter Aldrich-Danie Visser
1939	A. K. Quist-J. E. Bromwich	1969	Richard Crealy-Allan Stone[1]	1991	John Fitzgerald-Anders Jarryd
1940–41	Jack Kramer-F. R. Schroeder	**OPEN**		1992	Jim Grabb-Richey Reneberg
1942	Gardnar Mulloy-Bill Talbert	1968	Stan Smith-Bob Lutz	1993	Ken Flach-Rick Leach
1943	Jack Kramer-Frank Parker	1969	Fred Stolle-Ken Rosewall	1994	Jacco Hingh-Paul Haarhuis
1944	Don McNeill-Bob Falkenburg	1970	Nikki Pilic-Fred Barthes	1995	Todd Woodbridge-Mark Woodforde
1945	Gardnar Mulloy-Bill Talbert	1971	John Newcombe-Roger Taylor	1996	Todd Woodbridge-Mark Woodforde
1946	Gardnar Mulloy-Bill Talbert	1972	Cliff Drysdale-Roger Taylor	1997	Yevgeny Kafelnikov-Daniel Vacek
1947	Jack Kramer-Fred Schroeder	1973	John Newcombe-Owen Davidson		
1948	Gardnar Mulloy-Bill Talbert	1974	Bob Lutz-Stan Smith		
1949	John Bromwich-William Sidwell	1975	Jimmy Connors-Ilie Nastase		
1950	John Bromwich-Frank Sedgman				

1. With the inaugural of the Open Tournament in 1968, the United States Lawn Tennis Association held a national championship at Longwood, Chestnut Hill, Mass. which barred contract professionals in 1968 and 1969.

Doubles—Women

NATIONAL		
1924	G. W. Wightman–Helen Wills	
1925	Mary K. Browne–Helen Wills	
1926	Elizabeth Ryan–Eleanor Goss	
1927	L. A. Godfree–Ermyntrude Harvey	
1928	Hazel Hotchkiss Wightman–Helen Wills	
1929	Phoebe Watson–L. R. C. Michell	
1930	Betty Nuthall–Sarah Palfrey	
1931	Betty Nuthall–E. B. Wittingstall	
1932	Helen Jacobs–Sarah Palfrey	
1933	Betty Nuthall–Freda James	
1934	Helen Jacobs–Sarah Palfrey	
1935	Helen Jacobs–Sarah Palfrey Fabyan	
1936	Marjorie G. Van Ryn–Carolin Babcock	
1937–40	Sarah Palfrey Fabyan–Alice Marble	
1941	Sarah Palfrey Cooke–Margaret Osborne	
1942–47	A. Louise Brough–Margaret Osborne	
1948–50	A. Louise Brough–Margaret O. duPont	
1951–54	Doris Hart–Shirley Fry	
1955–57	A. Louise Brough–Margaret O. duPont	
1958–59	Darlene Hard–Jeanne Arth	
1960	Darlene Hard–Maria Bueno	

1961	Darlene Hard–Lesley Turner	
1962	Darlene Hard–Maria Bueno	
1963	Margaret Smith–Robyn Ebbern	
1964	Karen Hantze Susman–Billie Jean Moffitt	
1965	Nancy Richey–Carole Caldwell Graebner	
1966	Nancy Richey–Maria Bueno	
1967	Billie Jean King–Rosemary Casals	
1968	Margaret Court–Maria Bueno[1]	
1969	Margaret Court–Virginia Wade[1]	
OPEN		
1968	Maria Bueno–Margaret Court	
1969	Darlene Hard–Francoise Durr	
1970	Margaret Court–Judy Dalton	
1971	Rosemary Casals–Judy Dalton	
1972	Francoise Durr–Betty Stove	
1973	Margaret Court–Virginia Wade	
1974	Billie Jean King–Rosemary Casals	
1975	Margaret Court–Virginia Wade	
1976	Linky Boshoff–Ilana Kloss	
1977	Martina Navratilova–Betty Stove	

1978	Billie Jean King–Martina Navratilova	
1979	Betty Stove–Wendy Turnbull	
1980	Billie Jean King–Martina Navratilova	
1981	Kathy Jordan–Anne Smith	
1982	Rosemary Casals–Wendy Turnbull	
1983–84	Martina Navratilova–Pam Shriver	
1985	Claudia Khode-Kilsch–Helena Sukova	
1986–87	Martina Navratilova–Pam Shriver	
1988	Gigi Fernandez–Robin White	
1989	Hana Mandlikova–Martina Navratilova	
1990	Gigi Fernandez–Martina Navratilova	
1991	Pam Shriver–Natalia Zvereva	
1992	Gigi Fernandez–Natalia Zvereva	
1993	Arantxa Sanchez Vicario–Helena Sukova	
1994	Jana Novotna–Arantxa Sanchez Vicario	
1995	Gigi Fernandez–Natasha Zvereva	
1996	Gigi Fernandez–Natasha Zvereva	
1997	Lindsay Davenport–Jana Novotna	

1. With the inaugural of the Open Tournament in 1968, the United States Lawn Tennis Association held a national championship at Longwood, Chestnut Hill, Mass. which barred contract professionals in 1968 and 1969.

UNITED STATES CHAMPIONS—1997

United States Open
(Flushing Meadow, N.Y., Aug. 25–Sept. 7, 1997)
Men's singles—Patrick Rafter defeated Greg Rusedski, 6–3, 6–2, 4–6, 7–5.
Women's singles—Martina Hingis defeated Venus Williams, 6–0, 6–4.
Men's doubles—Yevgeny Kaflnikov and David Vacek

defeated Jonas Bjorkman and Niklas Kluti, 7–6, (10–8), 6–3.
Women's doubles—Lindsay Davenport and Jana Novotna defeated Gigi Fernandez and Natasha Zvereva, 6–3, 6–4.
Mixed doubles—Manon Bollegraf and Rick Leach defeated Mercedes Paz and Pablo Albano, 3–6, 7–5, 7–6, (7–3).

BRITISH (WIMBLEDON) CHAMPIONS

(Amateur from inception in 1877 through 1967)

SINGLES—MEN

1908–09	Arthur Gore	1933	J. H. Crawford	1959	Alex Olmedo	1983–84	John McEnroe
1910–13	A. F. Wilding	1934–36	Fred Perry	1960	Neale Fraser	1985–86	Boris Becker
1914	N. E. Brookes	1937–38	Don Budge	1961–62	Rod Laver	1987	Pat Cash
1919	G. L. Patterson	1939	Robert L. Riggs	1963	Chuck McKinley	1988	Stefan Edberg
1920–21	Bill Tilden	1946	Yvon Petra	1964–65	Roy Emerson	1989	Boris Becker
1922	G. L. Patterson	1947	Jack Kramer	1966	Manuel Santana	1990	Stefan Edberg
1923	William Johnston	1948	R. Falkenburg	1967	John Newcombe	1991	Michael Stich
1924	Jean Borotra	1949	Fred Schroeder	1968–69	Rod Laver	1992	Andre Agassi
1925	Rene Lacoste	1950	Budge Patty	1970–71	John Newcombe	1993	Peter Sampras
1926	Jean Borotra	1951	Richard Savitt	1972	Stan Smith	1994	Pete Sampras
1927	Henri Cochet	1952	Frank Sedgman	1973	Jan Kodes	1995	Pete Sampras
1928	Rene Lacoste	1953	Vic Seixas	1974	Jimmy Connors	1996	Richard Krajicek
1929	Jean Cochet	1954	Jaroslav Drobny	1975	Arthur Ashe	1997	Pete Sampras
1930	Bill Tilden	1955	Tony Trabert	1976–80	Bjorn Borg		
1931	S. B. Wood	1956–57	Lewis Hoad	1981	John McEnroe		
1932	Ellsworth Vines	1958	Ashley Cooper	1982	Jimmy Connors		

SINGLES—WOMEN

1919–23	Lenglen	1939	Alice Marble	1964	Maria Bueno	1980	Evonne Goolagong
1924	Kathleen McKane	1946	Pauline M. Betz	1965	Margaret Smith		Cawley
1925	Lenglen	1947	Margaret Osborne	1966–67	Billie Jean King	1981	Chris Evert-Lloyd
1926	Godfree	1948–50	A. Louise Brough	1968	Billie Jean King	1982–87	Martina Navratilova
1927–29	Helen Wills	1951	Doris Hart	1969	Ann Jones	1988–89	Steffi Graf
1930	Helen Wills Moody	1952–54	Maureen Connolly	1970	Margaret Court	1990	Martina Navratilova
1931	Frl. C. Aussen	1955	A. Louise Brough	1971	Evonne Goolagong	1991	Steffi Graf
1932–33	Helen Wills Moody	1956	Shirley Fry	1972–73	Billie Jean King	1992	Steffi Graf
1934	D. E. Round	1957–58	Althea Gibson	1974	Chris Evert	1993	Steffi Graf
1935	Helen Wills Moody	1959–60	Maria Bueno	1975	Billie Jean King	1994	Conchita Martinez
1936	Helen Jacobs	1961	Angela Mortimer	1976	Chris Evert	1995	Steffi Graf
1937	D. E. Round	1962	Karen Susman	1977	Virginia Wade	1996	Steffi Graf
1938	Helen Wills Moody	1963	Margaret Smith	1978–79	Martina Navratilova	1997	Martina Hingis

DOUBLES—MEN

1953	K. Rosewall–L. Hoad	1968–70	John Newcombe–Tony Roche	1982	Paul McNamee–Peter McNamara
1954	R. Hartwig–M. Rose	1971	Rod Laver–Roy Emerson	1983–84	John McEnroe–Peter Fleming
1955	R. Hartwig–L. Hoad	1972	Bob Hewitt–Frew McMillan		
1956	L. Hoad–K. Rosewall	1973	Jimmy Connors–Ilie Nastase	1985	Heinz Gunthardt–Balazs Taroczy
1957	Gardnar Mulloy–Budge Patty	1974	John Newcombe–Tony Roche	1986	Joakim Nystrom–Mats Wilander
1958	Sven Davidson–Ulf Schmidt				
1959	Roy Emerson–Neale Fraser	1975	Vitas Gerulaitis–Sandy Mayer	1987	Ken Flach–Robert Seguso
1960	Dennis Ralston–Rafael Osuna	1976	Brian Gottfried–Raul Ramirez	1988	Ken Flach–Robert Seguso
1961	Roy Emerson–Neale Fraser	1977	Ross Case–Geoff Masters	1989	John Fitzgerald–Anders Jarryd
1962	Fred Stolle–Bob Hewitt	1978	Fred McMillan–Bob Hewitt		
1963	Rafael Osuna–Antonio Palafox	1979	Peter Fleming–John McEnroe	1990	Rick Leach–Jim Pugh
1964	Fred Stolle–Bob Hewitt	1980	Peter McNamara–Paul McNamee	1991	Anders Jarryd–John Fitzgerald
1965	John Newcombe–Tony Roche	1981	John McEnroe–Peter Fleming	1992	John McEnroe–Michael Stich
1966	John Newcombe–Ken Fletcher			1993–97	Todd Woodbridge–Mark Woodforde
1967	Bob Hewitt–Frew McMillan				

DOUBLES—WOMEN

1956	Althea Gibson–Angela Buxton	1973	Billie Jean King–Rosemary Casals	1987	Claudia Khode-Kilsch–Helena Sukova
1957	Althea Gibson–Darlene Hard	1974	Evonne Goolagong–Peggy Michel	1988	Steffi Graf–Gabriela Sabatini
1958	Althea Gibson–Maria Bueno	1975	Ann Kiyomura–Kazuko Sawamatsu	1989	Jana Novotna–Helena Sukova
1959	Darlene Hard–Jeanne Arth				
1960	Darlene Hard–Maria Bueno	1976	Chris Evert–Martina Navratilova	1990	Jana Novotna–Helena Sukova
1961	Karen Hantze–Billie Jean Moffitt	1977	Helen Cawley–JoAnne Russell	1991	Pam Shriver–Natalia Zvereva
1962	Karen Hantze Susman–Billie Jean Moffitt	1978	Wendy Turnbull–Kerry Reid	1992	Gigi Fernandez–Natalia Zvereva
1963	Darlene Hard–Maria Bueno	1979	Billie Jean King–Martina Navratilova	1993	Gigi Fernandez–Natalia Zvereva
1964	Margaret Smith–Les Turnerley	1980	Kathy Jordan–Anne Smith	1994	Gigi Fernandez–Natalia Zvereva
1965	Billie Jean Moffitt–Maria Bueno	1981	Martina Navratilova–Pam Shriver	1995	Jana Novotna–Arantxa Sanchez Vicario
1966	Nancy Richey–Maria Bueno	1982–84	Pam Shriver–Martina Navratilova	1996	Martina Hingis–Helena Sukova
1967–68	Billie Jean King–Rosemary Casals	1985	Kathy Jordan–Elizabeth Smylie	1997	Gigi Fernandez–Natasha Zvereva
1969	Margaret Court–Judy Tegart	1986	Pam Shriver–Martina Navratilova		
1970–71	Billie Jean King–Rosemary Casals				
1972	Billie Jean King–Betty Stove				

OTHER 1997 CHAMPIONS

Wimbledon Open

(Wimbledon, England, June 23–July 6, 1997)
Men's singles—Pete Sampras defeated Cedric Pioline, 6–4, 6–2, 6–4.
Women's singles—Martina Hingis defeated Jana Novotna, 2–6, 6–3, 6–3.
Men's doubles—Todd Woodbridge and Mark Woodforde defeated Jacco Eltingh and Paul Haarhuis, 7–6 (7–4), 7–6 (9–7), 5–7, 6–3.

Women's doubles—Gigi Fernandez and Natasha Zvereva defeated Nicole Arendt and Manon Bollegraf, 7–6 (7–4), 6–4.
Mixed doubles—Cyril Suk and Helena Sukova defeated Andrei Olhovskiy and Larisa Neiland, 4–6, 6–3, 6–4.

French Open

(Paris, May 26–June 8, 1997)
Men's singles—Gustavo Kuerten defeated Sergi Bruguera, 6–3, 6–4, 6–2.

Women's singles—Iva Majoli defeated Martina Hingis, 6–4, 6–2.

Men's doubles—Yevgeny Kafalnikov and Daniel Vacek defeated Todd Woodbridge and Mark Woodforde, 7–6 (14–12), 4–6, 6–3.

Women's doubles—Gigi Fernandez and Natasha Zvereva defeated Mary Joe Fernandez and Lisa Raymond, 6–2, 6–3.

Mixed doubles—Rika Hiraki and Mahesh Bhupathi defeated Lisa Raymond and Patrick Galbraith, 6–4, 6–1.

Australian Open

(Melbourne, Australia, Jan. 13–26, 1997

Men's singles—Pete Sampras defeated Carlos Moya, 6–2, 6–3, 6–3.

Women's singles—Martina Hingis defeated Mary Pierce, 6–2, 6–2.

Men's doubles—Todd Woodbridge and Mark Woodforde defeated Sebastien Lareau and Alex O'Brien, 4–6, 7–5, 7–5, 6–3.

Women's doubles—Martina Hingis and Natasha Zvereva defeated Lindsay Davenport and Lisa Raymond, 6–2, 6–2.

Mixed doubles—Manon Bollegraf and Rick Leach defeated Larisa Neiland and John De Jager, 6–3, 6–7 (5–7), 7–5.

MEN'S MONEY WINNERS—1997

(Through Sept. 14, 1997)

1.	Pete Sampras, United States	$1,905,078
2.	Patrick Rafter, Australia	1,432,084
3.	Michael Chang, United States	1,327,720
4.	Yevgeny Kafelnikov, Russia	1,171,392
5.	Gustavo Kuerten, Brazil	1,155,213
6.	Alex Corretja, Spain	1,089,272
7.	Thomas Muster, Austria	1,084,190
8.	Todd Woodbridge, Australia	1,077,318
9.	Marcelo Rios, Chile	1,034,855
10.	Jonas Bjorkman, Sweden	965,130
11.	Sergi Bruguera, Spain	958,808
12.	Felix Mantilla, Spain	934,483
13.	Mark Woodforde, Australia	921,697
14.	Goran Ivanisevic, Croatia	848,797
15.	Albert Costa, Spain	846,084
16.	Carlos Moya, Spain	779,390
17.	Richard Krajicek, Netherlands	745,364
18.	Mark Philippoussis, Australia	743,481
19.	Andrei Medvedev, Ukraine	704,578
20.	Greg Rusedski, England	696,473

WOMEN'S MONEY WINNERS—1997

(Through Sept. 7, 1997)

1.	Martina Hingis, Switzerland	$3,096,311
2.	Lindsay Davenport, United States	1,133,106
3.	Iva Majoli, Croatia	1,129,087
4.	Jana Novotna, Czech Republic	875,340
5.	Monica Seles, United States	771,705
6.	Mary Joe Fernandez, United States	695,997
7.	Arantxa Sanchez Vicario, Spain	681,392
8.	Natasha Zvereva, Bulgaria	676,778
9.	Mary Pierce, France	670,689
10.	Amanda Coetzer, South Africa	569,924
11.	Irina Spirlea, Romania	550,798
12.	Gigi Fernandez, United States	443,082
13.	Conchita Martinez, Spain	427,479
14.	Venus Williams, United States	426,861
15.	Sandrine Testud, France	371,858
16.	Ruxandra Dragomir, Romania	357,747
17.	Manon Bollegraf, Netherlands	347,179
18.	Nicole Arendt, United States	336,452
19.	Lisa Raymond, United States	336,110
20.	Anke Huber, Germany	334,100

Rowing

Rowing goes back so far in history that there is no possibility of tracing it to any particular aboriginal source. The oldest rowing race still on the calendar is the "Doggett's Coat and Badge" contest among professional watermen of the Thames (England) that began in 1715. The first Oxford-Cambridge race was held at Henley in 1829. Competitive rowing in the United States began with matches between boats rowed by professional oarsmen of the New York waterfront. They were oarsmen who rowed the small boats that plied as ferries from Manhattan Island to Brooklyn and return, or who rowed salesmen down the harbor to meet ships arriving from Europe. Since the first salesman to meet an incoming ship had some advantage over his rivals, there was keen competition in the bidding for fast boats and the best oarsmen. This gave rise to match races.

Amateur boat clubs sprang up in the United States between 1820 and 1830 and seven students of Yale joined together to purchase a four-oared lap-streak gig in 1843. The first Harvard-Yale race was held Aug. 3, 1852, on Lake Winnepesaukee, N.H. The first time an American college crew went abroad was in 1869 when Harvard challenged Oxford and was defeated on the Thames. There were early college rowing races on Lake Quinsigamond, near Worcester, Mass., and on Saratoga Lake, N.Y., but the Intercollegiate Rowing Association in 1895 settled on the Hudson, at Poughkeepsie, as the setting for the annual "Poughkeepsie Regatta." In 1950 the I.R.A. shifted its classic to Marietta, Ohio, and in 1952 it was moved to Syracuse, N.Y. The National Association of Amateur Oarsmen, organized in 1872, has conducted annual championship regattas since that time.

INTERCOLLEGIATE ROWING ASSOCIATION REGATTA

(Varsity Eight-Oared Shells)

Rowed at 4 miles, Poughkeepsie, N.Y., 1895–97, 1899–1916, 1925–32, 1934–41. Rowed at 3 miles, Saratoga, N.Y., 1898; Poughkeepsie, 1921–24, 1947–49; Syracuse, N.Y., 1952–1963, 1965–67. Rowed at 2,000 meters, Syracuse, N.Y., 1964 and from 1968 on. Rowed at 2 miles, Ithaca, N.Y., 1920; Marietta, Ohio, 1950–51. Suspended 1917–19, 1933, 1942–46.

Year	Time	First	Second	Year	Time	First	Second
1895	21:25	Columbia	Cornell	1899	20:04	Pennsylvania	Wisconsin
1896	19:59	Cornell	Harvard	1900	19:44 ⅗	Pennsylvania	Wisconsin
1897	20:47 ⅘	Cornell	Columbia	1901	18:53 ⅕	Cornell	Columbia
1898	15:51 ½	Pennsylvania	Cornell	1902	19:03 ⅗	Cornell	Wisconsin

Year	Time	First	Second	Year	Time	First	Second
1903	18:57	Cornell	Georgetown	1955	15:49.9	Cornell	Pennsylvania
1904	20:22 ⅗	Syracuse	Cornell	1956	16:22.4	Cornell	Navy
1905	20:29	Cornell	Syracuse	1957	15:26.6	Cornell	Pennsylvania
1906	19:36 ⅘	Cornell	Pennsylvania	1958	17:12.1	Cornell	Navy
1907	20:02 ⅖	Cornell	Columbia	1959	18:01.7	Wisconsin	Syracuse
1908	19:24 ⅕	Syracuse	Columbia	1960	15:57	California	Navy
1909	19:02	Cornell	Columbia	1961	16:49.2	California	Cornell
1910	20:42 ⅕	Cornell	Pennsylvania	1962	17:02.9	Cornell	Washington
1911	20:10 ⅘	Cornell	Columbia	1963	17:24	Cornell	Navy
1912	19:31 ⅗	Cornell	Wisconsin	1964	6:31.1	California	Washington
1913	19:28 ⅗	Syracuse	Cornell	1965	16:51.3	Navy	Cornell
1914	19:37 ⅘	Columbia	Pennsylvania	1966	16:03.4	Wisconsin	Navy
1915	19:36 ⅘	Cornell	Stanford	1967	16:13.9	Pennsylvania	Wisconsin
1916	20:15 ⅖	Syracuse	Cornell	1968	6:15.6	Pennsylvania	Washington
1920	11:02 ⅗	Syracuse	Cornell	1969	6:30.4	Pennsylvania	Dartmouth
1921	14:07	Navy	California	1970	6:39.3	Washington	Wisconsin
1922	13:33 ⅗	Navy	Washington	1971	6:06	Cornell	Washington
1923	14:03 ⅕	Washington	Navy	1972	6:22.6	Pennsylvania	Brown
1924	15:02	Washington	Wisconsin	1973	6:21	Wisconsin	Brown
1925	19:24 ⅘	Navy	Washington	1974	6:33	Wisconsin	M.I.T.
1926	19:28 ⅗	Washington	Navy	1975	6:08.2	Wisconsin	M.I.T.
1927	20:57	Columbia	Washington	1976	6:31	California	Princeton
1928	18:35 ⅘	California	Columbia	1977	6:32.4	Cornell	Pennsylvania
1929	22:58	Columbia	Washington	1978	6:39.5	Syracuse	Brown
1930	21:42	Cornell	Syracuse	1979	6:26.4	Brown	Wisconsin
1931	18:54 ⅕	Navy	Cornell	1980	6:46	Navy	Northeastern
1932	19:55	California	Cornell	1981	5:57.3	Cornell	Navy
1934	19:44	California	Washington	1982	5:57.5	Cornell	Princeton
1935	18:52	California	Cornell	1983	6:14.4	Brown	Navy
1936	19:09 ⅗	Washington	California	1984	5:54.7	Navy	Pennsylvania
1937	18:33 ⅗	Washington	Navy	1985	5:49.9	Princeton	Brown
1938	18:19	Navy	California	1986	5:50.2	Brown	Pennsylvania
1939	18:12 ⅗	California	Washington	1987	6:02.9	Brown	Wisconsin
1940	22:42	Washington	Cornell	1988	6:14.0	Northeastern	Brown
1941	18:53 ⅗⁄₁₀	Washington	California	1989	5:56.0	Penn	Wisconsin
				1990	5:55.5	Wisconsin	Pennsylvania
1947	13:59 ⅕	Navy	Cornell	1991	6:05.2	Northeastern	Pennsylvania
1948	14:06 ⅖	Washington	California	1992	6:10.5	Dartmouth	Harvard
1949	14:42 ⅗	California	Washington	1993	5:59.1	Brown	Pennsylvania
1950	8:07.5	Washington	California	1994	5:54.4	Brown	Princeton
1951	7:50.5	Wisconsin	Washington	1995	5:31.3[2]	Brown	Navy
1952	15:08.1	Navy	Princeton	1996	5:29.6[2]	Princeton	Washington
1953	15:29.6	Navy	Cornell	1997	5:51.0	Washington	Brown
1954	16:04.4	Navy[1]	Cornell			1. Disqualified. 2. New course record.	

Harness Racing

Oliver Wendell Holmes, the famous Autocrat of the Breakfast Table, wrote that the running horse was a gambling toy but the trotting horse was useful and, furthermore, "horse-racing is not a republican institution; horse-trotting is." Oliver Wendell Holmes was a born-and-bred New Englander, and New England was the nursery of the harness racing sport in America. Pacers and trotters were matters of local pride and prejudice in Colonial New England, and, shortly after the Revolution, the Messenger and Justin Morgan strains produced many winners in harness racing "matches" along the turnpikes of New York, Connecticut, Rhode Island, Massachusetts, Vermont, and New Hampshire.

There was English thoroughbred blood in Messenger and Justin Morgan, and, many years later, it was blended in Rysdyk's Hambletonian, foaled in 1849. Hambletonian was not particularly fast under harness but his descendants have had almost a monopoly of prizes, titles, and records in the harness racing game. Hambletonian was purchased as a foal with its dam for a total of $124 by William Rysdyk of Goshen, N.Y., and made a modest fortune for the purchaser.

Trotters and pacers often were raced under saddle in the old days, and, in fact, the custom still survives in some places in Europe. Dexter, the great trotter that lowered the mile record from 2:19 ¾ to 2:17 ¼ in 1867, was said to handle just as well under saddle as when pulling a sulky. But as sulkies were lightened in weight and improved in design, trotting under saddle became less common and finally faded out in this country.

WORLD RECORDS

Established in a race or against time at one mile.

(Through Sept. 25, 1997)

Source: United States Trotting Association

Pacing on Mile Track

Div.	Horse	Driver	Track	Date	Time
2C	The Big Dog	Joe S. Anderson	Woodbine	8/17/96	1:51.3
	Gothic Dream	John D. Campbell	Woodbine	8/31/96	1:51.3
2F	Miss Easy	John D. Campbell	Lexington, Ky.	9/25/90	1:51.2
2G	Hot Chilli Pepper	Andy Ray Miller	Springfield, Ill.	8/15/96	1:52.2
	Wrestling Matt	John D. Campbell	Woodbine	8/30/96	1:52.2
3C	Jenna's Beach Boy	William R. Fahy	Lexington, Ky.	9/30/95	1:48.4
3F	Shady Daisy	Michel La Chance	Lexington, Ky.	10/4/91	1:51.0
	Ellamony	Jack G. Moiseyev	Meadowlands	8/12/93	1:51.0
	Immortality	John D. Campbell	Lexington, Ky.	10/7/93	1:51.0
3G	Gee Gee Digger	Howard G. Parker	Meadowlands	8/10/96	1:49.3
4H	Jenna's Beach Boy	William R. Fahy	Meadowlands	6/22/96	1:47.3
4M	Sweetgeorgiabrown	Mark J. Kesmodel	Meadowlands	8/9/96	1:50.1
4G	Staying Together	William A. O'Donnell	Meadowlands	6/19/93	1:48.2
5+H	Riyadh	William Roy Gale	Woodbine	8/17/96	1:48.4
5+M	Ellamony	Ronald W. Waples	Meadowlands	6/23/95	1:50.3
5"G	Armbro Maestro	Mark J. Kermodel	Meadowlands	6/15/96	1:49.2
	Darth Raider	James A. Morrill, Jr.	Meadowlands	7/6/96	1:49.2

Trotting on a Mile Track

Div.	Horse	Driver	Track	Date	Time
2C	Mack Lobell	John D. Campbell	Lexington, Ky.	10/3/86	1:55.3
2F	CR Kay Suzie	Carl E. Allen	Meadowlands	8/3/94	1:55.1
2G	I'm Impeccable	David A. Rankin	Lexington, Ky.	9/28/89	1:57.2
	Harmony Oaks Royal	Andy Ray Miller	Springfield, Ill.	8/12/95	1:57.2
3C	Mack Lobell	John D. Campbell	Springfield, Ill.	8/21/87	1:52.1
3F	Continental Victory	Michel La Chance	Meadowlands	8/3/96	1:52.1
3G	Champion On Ice	David R. Magee	Springfield, Ill.	8/12/94	1:53.2
4H	Pine Chip	John D. Campbell	Meadowlands	8/6/94	1:52.4
4M	Beat The Wheel	Catello R. Manzi	Meadowlands	7/8/94	1:51.4
4G	Champion On Ice	David R. Magee	Springfield, Ill.	8/12/95	1:53.1
5+H	Wesgate Crown	Catello R. Manzi	Meadowlands	7/27/96	1:52.3
5+M	Beat The Wheel	Catello R. Manzi	Meadowlands	7/6/95	1:53.3
5+G	Oaklea Count	Ronald W. Waples	Meadowlands	8/3/96	1:52.1

HISTORY OF TRADITIONAL HARNESS RACING STAKES

THE HAMBLETONIAN

Year	Winner	Driver	Best time	Total purse
1967	Speedy Streak	Del Cameron	2:00	$122,650
1968	Nevele Pride	Stanley Dancer	1:59 ⅖	116,190
1969	Lindy's Pride	Howard Beissinger	1:57 ⅗	124,910
1970	Timothy T.	John Simpson, Jr.	1:58 ⅖[1]	143,630
1971	Speedy Crown	Howard Beissinger	1:57 ⅖	129,770
1972	Super Bowl	Stanley Dancer	1:56 ⅖	119,090
1973	Flirth	Ralph Baldwin	1:57 ⅕	144,710
1974	Christopher T	Billy Haughton	1:58 ⅗	160,150
1975	Bonefish	Stanley Dancer	1:59[2]	232,192
1976	Steve Lobell	Billy Haughton	1:56 ⅖	263,524
1977	Green Speed	Billy Haughton	1:55 ⅗	284,131
1978	Speedy Somolli	Howard Beissinger	1:55[3]	241,280
1979	Legend Hanover	George Sholty	1:56 ⅕	300,000
1980	Burgomeister	Billy Haughton	1:56 ⅗	293,570
1981	Shiaway St. Pat	Ray Remmen	2:01 ⅛[4]	838,000
1982	Speed Bowl	Tommy Haughton	1:56 ⅘	875,750
1983	Duenna	Stanley Dancer	1:57 ⅖	1,000,000
1984	Historic Free	Ben Webster	1:56 ⅖	1,219,000
1985	Prakas	Bill O'Donnell	1:54 ⅗	1,272,000
1986	Nuclear Kosmos	Ulf Thoresen	1:56	1,172,082
1987	Mack Lobell	John Campbell	1:53 ⅗	1,046,300
1988	Armbro Goal	John Campbell	1:54 ⅗	1,156,800
1989	Park Avenue Joe	Ron Wayples	1:55 ⅗	1,131,000
1990	Embassy Lobell	Michel Lachance	1:56 ⅕	1,346,000

Year	Winner	Driver	Best time	Total purse
1991	Giant Victory	Jack Moiseyev	1:54 4/5	1,238,000
1992	Alf Palema	Mickey McNichol	1:56 3/5	1,288,000
1993	American Winner	Ron Pierce	1:53 1/5	1,200,000
1994	Victory Dream	Michel Lachance	1:53 4/5	1,200,000
1995	Tagliabue	John Campbell	1:54 3/5	1,200,000
1996	Continentalvictory	Michel La Chance	1:52 4/5	1,200,000
1997	Malabar Man	Malvern Burroughs	1:55	1,000,000

Three-year-old trotters. One mile. Guy McKinney won first race at Syracuse in 1926; held at Goshen, N.Y., 1930–1942, 1944–1956; at Yonkers, N.Y., 1943; at Du Quoin, Ill., 1957–1980. Since 1981, the race has been held at The Meadowlands in East Rutherford, N.J. 1. By Formal Notice. 2. By Yankee Bambino. 3. By Speedy Somolli and Florida Pro. 4. By Super Juan.

LITTLE BROWN JUG

Year	Winner	Driver	Best time	Total purse
1967	Best of All	Jim Hackett	1:59[1]	$84,778
1968	Rum Customer	Billy Haughton	1:59 3/5	104,226
1969	Laverne Hanover	Billy Haughton	2:00 2/5	109,731
1970	Most Happy Fella	Stanley Dancer	1:57 1/5	100,110
1971	Nansemond	Herve Filion	1:57 2/5	102,994
1972	Strike Out	Keith Waples	1:56 3/5	104,916
1973	Melvin's Woe	Joe O'Brien	1:57 3/5	120,000
1974	Ambro Omaha	Billy Haughton	1:57	132,630
1975	Seatrain	Ben Webster	1:57[2]	147,813
1976	Keystone Ore	Stanley Dancer	1:56 4/5[3]	153,799
1977	Governor Skipper	John Chapman	1:56 1/5	150,000
1978	Happy Escort	William Popfinger	1:55 2/5[4]	186,760
1979	Hot Hitter	Herve Filion	1:55 3/5	226,455
1980	Niatross	Clint Galbraith	1:54 4/5	207,361
1981	Fan Hanover	Glen Garnsey	1:56[5]	243,799
1982	Merger	John Campbell	1:56 3/5	328,900
1983	Ralph Hanover	Ron Waples	1:55 3/5	358,800
1984	Colt 46	Norman Boring	1:53 3/5	366,717
1985	Nihilator	Bill O'Donnell	1:52 1/5	350,730
1986	Barberry Spur	Bill O'Donnell	1:52 4/5	407,684
1987	Jaguar Spur	Richard Stillings	1:55 3/5	412,330
1988	B.J. Scoot	Michel Lachance	1:52 3/5	486,050
1989	Goalie Jeff	Michel Lachance	1:54 1/5	500,200
1990	Beach Towel	Ray Remmen	1:53 3/5	253,049
1991	Precious Bunny	Jack Moiseyev	1:54 1/5	575,150
1992	Fake Left	Ron Waples	1:54 2/5	556,210
1993	Life Sign	John Campbell	1:52	465,500
1994	Magical Mike	Michel LaChance	1:52 3/5	512,830
1995	Nick's Fantasy	John Campbell	1:51 2/5	543,670
1996	Armbro Operative	Michel La Chance	1:52 3/5	542,220
1997	Western Dreamer	Michel La Chance	1:51 1/5	605,210

Three-year-old pacers. One Mile. Raced at Delaware County Fair Grounds, Delaware, Ohio. 1. By Nardin's Byrd. 2. By Albert's Star. 3. By Armbro Ranger. 4. By Falcon Almahurst. 5. By Seahawk Hanover.

HARNESS HORSE OF THE YEAR

Year	Winner	Year	Winner	Year	Winner
1959	Bye Bye Byrd, Pacer	1975	Savoir, Trotter	1987–88	Mack Lobell
1960–61	Adios Butler, Pacer	1976	Keystone Ore, Pacer	1989	Matt's Scooter
1962	Su Mac Lad, Trotter	1977	Green Speed, Trotter	1990	Beach Towel
1963	Speedy Scot, Trotter	1978	Abercrombie, Pacer	1991	Precious Bunny
1964–66	Bret Hanover, Pacer	1979–80	Niatross, Pacer	1992	Artsplace
1967–69	Nevele Pride, Trotter	1981	Fan Hanover, Pacer	1993	Staying Together
1970	Fresh Yankee, Trotter	1982–83	Cam Fella, Pacer	1994	Cam's Card Shark
1971–72	Albatross, Pacer	1984	Fancy Crown, Trotter	1995	CR Kay Suzie
1973	Sir Dalrae, Pacer	1985	Nihilator, Trotter	1996	Continentalvictory
1974	Delmonica Hanover, Trotter	1986	Forrest Skipper		

Chosen in poll conducted by United States Trotting Association in conjunction with the U.S. Harness Writers Assn.

Golf

It may be that golf originated in Holland—historians believe it did—but certainly Scotland fostered the game and is famous for it. In fact, in 1457 the Scottish Parliament, disturbed because football and golf had lured young Scots from the more soldierly exercise of archery, passed an ordinance that "futeball and golf be utterly cryit doun and nocht usit." James I and Charles I of the royal line of Stuarts were golf enthusiasts, whereby the game came to be known as "the royal and ancient game of golf."

The golf balls used in the early games were leather-covered and stuffed with feathers. Clubs of all kinds were fashioned by hand to suit individual players. The great step in spreading the game came with the change from the feather ball to the guttapercha ball about 1850. In 1860, formal competition began with the establishment of an annual tournament for the British Open championship. There are records of "golf clubs" in the

United States as far back as colonial days but no proof of actual play before John Reid and some friends laid out six holes on the Reid lawn in Yonkers, N.Y., in 1888 and played there with golf balls and clubs brought over from Scotland by Robert Lockhart. This group then formed the St. Andrews Golf Club of Yonkers, and golf was established in this country.

However, it remained a rather sedate and almost aristocratic pastime until a 20-year-old ex-caddy, Francis Ouimet of Boston, defeated two great British professionals, Harry Vardon and Ted Ray, in the United States Open championship at Brookline, Mass., in 1913. This feat put the game and Francis Ouimet on the front pages of the newspapers and stirred a wave of enthusiasm for the sport. The greatest feat so far in golf history is that of Robert Tyre Jones, Jr., of Atlanta, who won the British Open, the British Amateur, the U.S. Open, and the U.S. Amateur titles in one year, 1930.

THE MASTERS TOURNAMENT WINNERS

Augusta National Golf Club, Augusta, Ga.

Year	Winner	Score	Year	Winner	Score	Year	Winner	Score
1934	Horton Smith	284	1957	Doug Ford	283	1978	Gary Player	277
1935	Gene Sarazen[1]	282	1958	Arnold Palmer	284	1979	Fuzzy Zoeller[1]	280
1936	Horton Smith	285	1959	Art Wall, Jr.	284	1980	Severiano Ballesteros	275
1937	Byron Nelson	283	1960	Arnold Palmer	282	1981	Tom Watson	280
1938	Henry Picard	285	1961	Gary Player	280	1982	Craig Stadler[1]	284
1939	Ralph Guldahl	279	1962	Arnold Palmer[1]	280	1983	Severiano Ballesteros	280
1940	Jimmy Demaret	280	1963	Jack Nicklaus	286	1984	Ben Crenshaw	277
1941	Craig Wood	280	1964	Arnold Palmer	276	1985	Bernhard Langer	282
1942	Byron Nelson[1]	280	1965	Jack Nicklaus	271	1986	Jack Nicklaus	279
1943–45 No Tournaments			1966	Jack Nicklaus[1]	288	1987	Larry Mize[1]	285
1946	Herman Keiser	282	1967	Gay Brewer, Jr.	280	1988	Sandy Lyle	281
1947	Jimmy Demaret	281	1968	Bob Goalby	277	1989	Nick Faldo[1]	283
1948	Claude Harmon	279	1969	George Archer	281	1990	Nick Faldo	278
1949	Sam Snead	282	1970	Billy Casper[1]	279	1991	Ian Woosnam	277
1950	Jimmy Demaret	283	1971	Charles Coody	279	1992	Fred Couples	275
1951	Ben Hogan	280	1972	Jack Nicklaus	286	1993	Bernard Langer	277
1952	Sam Snead	286	1973	Tommy Aaron	283	1994	Jose Maria Olazabal	279
1953	Ben Hogan	274	1974	Gary Player	278	1995	Ben Crenshaw	274
1954	Sam Snead[1]	289	1975	Jack Nicklaus	276	1996	Nick Faldo	276
1955	Cary Middlecoff	279	1976	Ray Floyd	271	1997	Tiger Woods	270
1956	Jack Burke	289	1977	Tom Watson	276			

1. Winner in playoff.

U.S. OPEN CHAMPIONS

Year	Winner	Score	Where played	Year	Winner	Score	Where played
1895	Horace Rawlins	173	Newport	1913	Francis Ouimet[1] [2]	304	Brookline
1896	James Foulis	152	Shinnecock Hills	1914	Walter Hagen	290	Midlothian
1897	Joe Lloyd	162	Chicago	1915	Jerome D.	297	Baltusrol
1898[3]	Fred Herd	328	Myopia		Travers[2]		
1899	Willie Smith	315	Baltimore	1916	Charles Evans,	286	Minikahda
1900	Harry Vardon	313	Chicago		Jr.[2]		
1901	Willie Anderson[1]	331	Myopia	1917–18	No tournaments[4]		
1902	Laurie Auchterlonie	307	Garden City	1919	Walter Hagen[2]	301	Brae Burn
1903	Willie Anderson[1]	307	Baltusrol	1920	Edward Ray	295	Inverness
1904	Willie Anderson	303	Glen View	1921	Jim Barnes	289	Columbia
1905	Willie Anderson	314	Myopia	1922	Gene Sarazen	288	Skokie
1906	Alex Smith	295	Onwentsia	1923	R. T. Jones, Jr.[1] [2]	296	Inwood
1907	Alex Ross	302	Philadelphia	1924	Cyril Walker	297	Oakland Hills
1908	Fred McLeod[1]	322	Myopia	1925	Willie Macfarlane[1]	291	Worcester
1909	George Sargent	290	Englewood	1926	R. T. Jones, Jr.[2]	293	Scioto
1910	Alex Smith[1]	298	Philadelphia	1927	Tommy Armour[1]	301	Oakmont
1911	John McDermott[1]	307	Chicago	1928	Johnny Farrell[1]	294	Olympia Fields
1912	John McDermott	294	Buffalo	1929	R. T. Jones, Jr.[1] [2]	294	Winged Foot

Year	Winner	Score	Where played	Year	Winner	Score	Where played
1930	R. T. Jones, Jr.[2]	287	Interlachen	1968	Lee Trevino	275	Oak Hill
1931	Billy Burke[1]	292	Inverness	1969	Orville Moody	281	Champions G. C.
1932	Gene Sarazen	286	Fresh Meadow				
1933	John Goodman[2]	287	North Shore	1970	Tony Jacklin	281	Hazeltine
1934	Olin Dutra	293	Merion	1971	Lee Trevino[1]	280	Merion
1935	Sam Parks, Jr.	299	Oakmont	1972	Jack Nicklaus	290	Pebble Beach
1936	Tony Manero	282	Baltusrol	1973	Johnny Miller	279	Oakmont
1937	Ralph Guldahl	281	Oakland Hills	1974	Hale Irwin	287	Winged Foot
1938	Ralph Guldahl	284	Cherry Hills	1975	Lou Graham[1]	287	Medinah
1939	Byron Nelson[1]	284	Philadelphia	1976	Jerry Pate	277	Atlanta A.C.
1940	Lawson Little[1]	287	Canterbury	1977	Hubert Green	278	Southern Hills
1941	Craig Wood	284	Colonial	1978	Andy North	285	Cherry Hills
1942–45	No tournaments[5]			1979	Hale Irwin	284	Inverness
1946	Lloyd Mangrum[1]	284	Canterbury	1980	Jack Nicklaus	272	Baltusrol
1947	Lew Worsham[1]	282	St. Louis	1981	David Graham	273	Merion
1948	Ben Hogan	276	Riviera	1982	Tom Watson	282	Pebble Beach
1949	Cary Middlecoff	286	Medinah	1983	Larry Nelson	280	Oakmont
1950	Ben Hogan[1]	287	Merion	1984	Fuzzy Zoeller[1]	276	Winged Foot
1951	Ben Hogan	287	Oakland Hills	1985	Andy North	279	Oakland Hills
1952	Julius Boros	281	Northwood	1986	Ray Floyd	279	Shinnecock Hills
1953	Ben Hogan	283	Oakmont	1987	Scott Simpson	277	Olympic Golf Club
1954	Ed Furgol	284	Baltusrol				
1955	Jack Fleck[1]	287	Olympic	1988	Curtis Strange[1]	278	The Country Club
1956	Cary Middlecoff	281	Oak Hill				
1957	Dick Mayer[1]	298	Inverness	1989	Curtis Strange	278	Oak Hill Country Club
1958	Tommy Bolt	283	Southern Hills				
1959	Bill Casper, Jr.	282	Winged Foot	1990	Hale Irwin[1]	280	Medinah C.C.
1960	Arnold Palmer	280	Cherry Hills	1991	Payne Stewart[1]	282	Hazeltine
1961	Gene Littler	281	Oakland Hills	1992	Tom Kite	285	Pebble Beach
1962	Jack Nicklaus[1]	283	Oakmont	1993	Lee Janzen	272	Baltusrol
1963	Julius Boros[1]	293	Country Club	1994	Ernie Els	279	Oakmont
1964	Ken Venturi	278	Congressional	1995	Corey Pavin	280	Shinnecock Hills
1965	Gary Player[1]	282	Bellerive	1996	Steve Jones	278	Oakland Hills
1966	Bill Casper[1]	278	Olympic	1997	Ernie Els	276	Congressional C.C.
1967	Jack Nicklaus	275	Baltusrol				

1. Winner in playoff. 2. Amateur. 3. In 1898, competition was extended to 72 holes. 4. In 1917, Jock Hutchison, with a 292, won an Open Patriotic Tournament for the benefit of the American Red Cross at Whitemarsh Valley Country Club. 5. In 1942, Ben Hogan, with a 271 won a Hale American National Open Tournament for the benefit of the Navy Relief Society and USO at Ridgemoor Country Club.

U.S. AMATEUR CHAMPIONS

Year	Winner	Year	Winner	Year	Winner	Year	Winner
1895	Charles B. Macdonald	1924–25	R. T. Jones, Jr.	1954	Arnold Palmer	1978	John Cook
1896–97	H. J. Whigham	1926	George Von Elm	1955–56	Harvie Ward	1979	Mark O'Meara
1898	Findlay S. Douglas	1927–28	R. T. Jones, Jr.	1957	Hillman Robbins	1980	Hal Sutton
1899	H. M. Harriman	1929	H. R. Johnston	1958	Charles Coe	1981	Nathaniel Crosby
1900–01	Walter J. Travis	1930	R. T. Jones, Jr.	1959	Jack Nicklaus	1982	Jay Sigel
1902	Louis N. James	1931	Francis Ouimet	1960	Deane Beman	1983	Jay Sigel
1903	Walter J. Travis	1932	Ross Somerville	1961	Jack Nicklaus	1984	Scott Verplank
1904–05	H. Chandler Egan	1933	G. T. Dunlap, Jr.	1962	Labron Harris, Jr.	1985	Sam Randolph
1906	Eben M. Byers	1934–35	Lawson Little	1963	Deane Beman	1986	Buddy Alexander
1907–08	Jerome D. Travers	1936	John W. Fischer	1964	Bill Campbell	1987	Bill Mayfair
1909	Robert A. Gardner	1937	John Goodman	1965[2]	Robert Murphy, Jr.	1988	Eric Meeks
1910	W. C. Fownes, Jr.	1938	Willie Turnesa	1966	Gary Cowan[1]	1989	Chris Patton
1911	Harold H. Hilton	1939	Marvin H. Ward	1967	Bob Dickson	1990	Phil Mickelson
1912–13	Jerome D. Travers	1940	R. D. Chapman	1968	Bruce Fleisher	1991	Mitch Voges
1914	Francis Ouimet	1941	Marvin H. Ward	1969	Steven Melnyk	1992	Justin Leonard
1915	Robert A. Gardner	1946	Ted Bishop	1970	Lanny Wadkins	1993	John Harris
1916	Charles Evans, Jr.	1947	Robert Riegel	1971	Gary Cowan	1994	Tiger Woods
1919	S. D. Herron	1948	Willie Turnesa	1972	Vinny Giles 3d	1995	Tiger Woods
1920	Charles Evans, Jr.	1949	Charles Coe	1973[3]	Craig Stadler	1996	Tiger Woods
1921	Jesse P. Guilford	1950	Sam Urzetta	1974	Jerry Pate	1997	Matthew Kuchar
1922	Jess W. Sweetser	1951	Billy Maxwell	1975	Fred Ridley		
1923	Max R. Marston	1952	Jack Westland	1976	Bill Sander		
		1953	Gene Littler	1977	John Fought		

1. Winner in playoff. 2. Tourney switched to medal play through 1972. 3. Return to match play.

U.S. P.G.A. CHAMPIONS

1916	Jim Barnes	1944	Bob Hamilton	1963	Jack Nicklaus	1982	Ray Floyd
1919	Jim Barnes	1945	Byron Nelson	1964	Bobby Nichols	1983	Hal Sutton
1920	Jock Hutchison	1946	Ben Hogan	1965	Dave Marr	1984	Lee Trevino
1921	Walter Hagen	1947	Jim Ferrier	1966	Al Geiberger	1985	Hubert Green
1922–23	Gene Sarazen	1948	Ben Hogan	1967	Don January[1]	1986	Bob Tway
1924–27	Walter Hagen	1949	Sam Snead	1968	Julius Boros	1987	Larry Nelson
1928–29	Leo Diegel	1950	Chandler Harper	1969	Ray Floyd	1988	Jeff Sluman
1930	Tommy Armour	1951	Sam Snead	1970	Dave Stockton	1989	Payne Stewart
1931	Tom Creavy	1952	Jim Turnesa	1971	Jack Nicklaus	1990	Mac Grady
1932	Olin Dutra	1953	Walter Burkemo	1972	Gary Player	1991	John Daly
1933	Gene Sarazen	1954	Chick Harbert	1973	Jack Nicklaus	1992	Nick Price
1934	Paul Runyan	1955	Doug Ford	1974	Lee Trevino	1993	Paul Azinger[1]
1935	Johnny Revolta	1956	Jack Burke, Jr.	1975	Jack Nicklaus	1994	Nick Price
1936–37	Denny Shute	1957	Lionel Hebert	1976	Dave Stockton	1995	Steve Elkington
1938	Paul Runyan	1958[2]	Dow Finsterwald	1977	Lanny Wadkins[1]	1996	Mark Brooks
1939	Henry Picard	1959	Bob Rosburg	1978	John Mahaffey	1997	Davis Love III
1940	Byron Nelson	1960	Jay Hebert	1979	David Graham[1]		
1941	Victor Ghezzi	1961	Jerry Barber[1]	1980	Jack Nicklaus		
1942	Sam Snead	1962	Gary Player	1981	Larry Nelson		

1. Winner in playoff. 2. Switched to medal play.

U.S. WOMEN'S AMATEUR CHAMPIONS

1916	Alexa Stirling	1941	Mrs. Frank Newell	1963	Anne Quast Welts	1981	Juli Inkster
1919–20	Alexa Stirling	1946	Mildred Zaharias	1964	Barbara McIntire	1982	Juli Inkster
1921	Marion Hollins	1947	Louise Suggs	1965	Jean Ashley	1983	Joanne Pacillo
1922	Glenna Collett	1948	Grace Lenczyk	1966	JoAnne Gunderson	1984	Deb Richard
1923	Edith Cummings	1949	Mrs. D. G. Porter	1967	Lou Dill	1985	Michiko Hattori
1924	Dorothy Campbell	1950	Beverly Hanson	1968	JoAnne G. Carner	1986	Kay Cockerill
	Hurd	1951	Dorothy Kirby	1969	Catherine LaCoste	1987	Kay Cockerill
1925	Glenna Collett	1952	Jacqueline Pung	1970	Martha Wilkinson	1988	Pearl Sinn
1926	Helen Stetson	1953	Mary Lena Faulk	1971	Laura Baugh	1989	Vicki Goetze
1927	Mrs. M. B. Horn	1954	Barbara Romack	1972	Mary Ann Budke	1990	Pat Hurst
1928–30	Glenna Collett	1955	Patricia Lesser	1973	Carol Semple	1991	Amy Fruhwirth
1931	Helen Hicks	1956	Marlene Stewart	1974	Cynthia Hill	1992	Vicki Goetze
1932–34	Virginia Van Wie	1957	JoAnne Gunderson	1975	Beth Daniel	1993	Jill McGill
1935	Glenna Collett Vare	1958	Anne Quast	1976	Donna Horton	1994	Wendy Ward
1936	Pamela Barton	1959	Barbara McIntire	1977	Beth Daniel	1995	Kelli Kuehne
1937	Mrs. J. A. Page, Jr.	1960	JoAnne Gunderson	1978	Cathy Sherk	1996	Kelli Kuehne
1938	Patty Berg	1961	Anne Quast Decker	1979	Carolyn Hill	1997	Silvia Cavalleri
1939–40	Betty Jameson	1962	JoAnne Gunderson	1980	Juli Inkster		

U.S. WOMEN'S OPEN CHAMPIONS

Year	Winner	Score	Year	Winner	Score	Year	Winner	Score
1946	Patty Berg (match play)	—	1963	Mary Mills	289	1981	Pat Bradley	279
			1964	Mickey Wright[1]	290	1982	Janet Alex	283
1947	Betty Jameson	295	1965	Carol Mann	290	1983	Jan Stephenson	290
1948	Mildred D. Zaharias	300	1966	Sandra Spuzich	297	1984	Hollis Stacy	290
1949	Louise Suggs	291	1967	Catherine LaCoste[2]	294	1985	Kathy Baker	280
1950	Mildred D. Zaharias	291	1968	Susie Berning	289	1986	Jane Geddes[1]	287
1951	Betsy Rawls	293	1969	Donna Caponi	294	1987	Laura Davies[1]	285
1952	Louise Suggs	284	1970	Donna Caponi	287	1988	Liselotte Neumann	277
1953	Betsy Rawls[1]	302	1971	JoAnne Carner	288	1989	Betsy King	278
1954	Mildred D. Zaharias	291	1972	Susie Berning	299	1990	Betsy King	284
1955	Fay Crocker	299	1973	Susie Berning	290	1991	Meg Mallon	283
1956	Katherine Cornelius[1]	302	1974	Sandra Haynie	295	1992	Patty Sheehan	280
1957	Betsy Rawls	299	1975	Sandra Palmer	295	1993	Lauri Merten	280
1958	Mickey Wright	290	1976	JoAnne Carner[1]	292	1994	Patty Sheehan	277
1959	Mickey Wright	287	1977	Hollis Stacy	292	1995	Annika Sorenstam	278
1960	Betsy Rawls	291	1978	Hollis Stacy	289	1996	Annika Sorenstam	272
1961	Mickey Wright	293	1979	Jerilyn Britz	284	1997	Alison Nicholas	274
1962	Murle Lindstrom	301	1980	Amy Alcott	280			

1. Winner in playoff. 2. Amateur.

BRITISH OPEN CHAMPIONS

(First tournament, held in 1860, was won by Willie Park, Sr.)

Year	Winner	Score	Year	Winner	Score	Year	Winner	Score
1920	George Duncan	303	1950	Bobby Locke	279	1974	Gary Player	282
1921	Jock Hutchison[1]	296	1951	Max Faulkner	285	1975	Tom Watson[1]	279
1922	Walter Hagen	300	1952	Bobby Locke	287	1976	Johnny Miller	279
1923	A. G. Havers	295	1953	Ben Hogan	282	1977	Tom Watson	268
1924	Walter Hagen	301	1954	Peter Thomson	283	1978	Jack Nicklaus	281
1925	Jim Barnes	300	1955	Peter Thomson	281	1979	Severiano Ballesteros	283
1926	R. T. Jones, Jr.	291	1956	Peter Thomson	286	1980	Tom Watson	271
1927	R. T. Jones, Jr.	285	1957	Bobby Locke	279	1981	Bill Rogers	276
1928	Walter Hagen	292	1958	Peter Thomson[1]	278	1982	Tom Watson	284
1929	Walter Hagen	292	1959	Gary Player	284	1983	Tom Watson	275
1930	R. T. Jones, Jr.	291	1960	Kel Nagle	278	1984	Severiano Ballesteros	276
1931	Tommy Armour	296	1961	Arnold Palmer	284	1985	Sandy Lyle	282
1932	Gene Sarazen	283	1962	Arnold Palmer	276	1986	Greg Norman	280
1933	Denny Shute1	292	1963	Bob Charles[1]	277	1987	Nick Faldo	279
1934	Henry Cotton	283	1964	Tony Lema	279	1988	Seve Ballesteros	273
1935	A. Perry	283	1965	Peter Thomson	285	1989	Mark Calcavecchia	275
1936	A. H. Padgham	287	1966	Jack Nicklaus	282	1990	Nick Faldo	270
1937	Henry Cotton	290	1967	Roberto de Vicenzo	278	1991	Ian Baker-Finch	272
1938	R. A. Whitcombe	295	1968	Gary Player	289	1992	Nick Faldo	272
1939	R. Burton	290	1969	Tony Jacklin	280	1993	Greg Norman	267
1940	Sam Snead	290	1970	Jack Nicklaus[1]	283	1994	Nick Price	268
1947	Fred Daly	294	1971	Lee Trevino	278	1995	John Daly	282
1948	Henry Cotton	283	1972	Lee Trevino	278	1996	Tom Lehman	271
1949	Bobby Locke[1]	283	1973	Tom Weiskopf	276	1997	Justin Leonard	272

OTHER 1996 PGA TOUR WINNERS

(Through Sept. 19, 1997)

Mercedes Championships—Tiger Woods	$216,000
Phoenix Open—Steve Jones	270,000
AT&T Pebble Beach National Pro-Am—Mark O'Meara	342,000
Buick Invitational of California—Mark O'Meara	270,000
United Airlines Hawaiian Open—Paul Stankowski	216,000
Tucson Chrysler Classic—Jeff Sluman	234,000
Nissan Open—Nick Faldo	252,000
Doral-Ryder Open—Steve Elkington	324,000
Honda Classic—Stuart Appleby	270,000
The Players Championship—Steve Elkington	630,000
MCI Classic—Nick Price	270,000
Shell Houston Open—Phil Blackmar	288,000
BellSouth Classic—Scott McCarron	270,000
Byron Nelson Classic—Tiger Woods	324,000
Memorial Tournament—Vijay Singh	342,000
Kemper Open—Justin Leonard	270,000
Buick Classic—Ernie Els	270,000
FedEx St. Jude Classic—Greg Norman	270,000
Motorola Western Open—Tiger Woods	360,000
Sprint International—Phil Mickelson	306,000
NEC World Series of Golf—Greg Norman	396,000

OTHER 1997 LPGA TOUR WINNERS

(Through Sept. 19, 1997)

Chrysler-Plymouth Tournament of Champions— Annika Sörenstam	$115,000
Cup Noodles Hawaiian Ladies Open—Annika Sörenstam	97,500
Alpine Australian Ladies Masters—Gail Graham	97,500
Welch's/Circle K Championship—Donna Andrews	75,000
Nabisco Dinah Shore—Betsy King	135,000
Sprint Titleholders Championship—Tammie Green	180,000
Sara Lee Classic—Terry-Jo Myers	101,250
McDonald's LPGA Championship—Chris Johnson	180,000
LPGA Corning Classic—Rosie Jones	97,500
Oldsmobile Classic—Pat Hurst	90,000
The Edina Realty Classic—Danielle Ammac- capane	90,000
Rochester International—Penny Hammel	90,000
ShopRite LPGA Classic—Michelle McGann	135,000
Jamie Farr Kroger Classic—Kelly Robbins	105,000
du Maurier Ltd. Classic—Colleen Walker	180,000
Friendly's Classic—Deb Richard	82,500
Weetabix Women's British Open—Karrie Webb	136,125
Star Bank LPGA Classic—Colleen Walker	82,500
Safeway LPGA Golf Championship—Chris Johnson	82,500
SAFECO Classic—Karrie Webb	82,500

Auto Racing

INDIANAPOLIS 500

Year	Winner	Car	Time	mph	Second place
1911	Ray Harroun	Marmon	6:42:08	74.59	Ralph Mulford
1912	Joe Dawson	National	6:21:06	78.72	Teddy Tetzloff
1913	Jules Goux	Peugeot	6:35:05	75.93	Spencer Wishart
1914	René Thomas	Delage	6:03:45	82.47	Arthur Duray
1915	Ralph DePalma	Mercedes	5:33:55.51	89.84	Dario Resta

Year	Winner	Car	Time	mph	Second place
1916[1]	Dario Resta	Peugeot	3:34:17	84.00	Wilbur D'Alene
1919	Howard Wilcox	Peugeot	5:40:42.87	88.05	Eddie Hearne
1920	Gaston Chevrolet	Monroe	5:38:32	88.62	René Thomas
1921	Tommy Milton	Frontenac	5:34:44.65	89.62	Roscoe Sarles
1922	Jimmy Murphy	Murphy Special	5:17:30.79	94.48	Harry Hartz
1923	Tommy Milton	H. C. S. Special	5:29.50.17	90.95	Harry Hartz
1924	L. L. Corum-Joe Boyer	Dusenberg Special	5:05:23.51	98.23	Earl Cooper
1925	Peter DePaolo	Dusenberg Special	4:56:39.45	101.13	Dave Lewis
1926[2]	Frank Lockhart	Miller Special	4:10:14.95	95.904	Harry Hartz
1927	George Souders	Dusenberg Special	5:07:33.08	97.54	Earl DeVore
1928	Louis Meyer	Miller Special	5:01:33.75	99.48	Lou Moore
1929	Ray Keech	Simplex Special	5:07:25.42	97.58	Louis Meyer
1930	Billy Arnold	Miller-Hartz Special	4:58:39.72	100.448	Shorty Cantlon
1931	Louis Schneider	Bowes Special	5:10:27.93	96.629	Fred Frame
1932	Fred Frame	Miller-Hartz Special	4:48:03.79	104.144	Howard Wilcox
1933	Louis Meyer	Tydol Special	4:48:00.75	104.162	Wilbur Shaw
1934	Bill Cummings	Boyle Products Special	4:46:05.20	104.863	Mauri Rose
1935	Kelly Petillo	Gilmore Special	4:42:22.71	106.240	Wilbur Shaw
1936	Louis Meyer	Ring Free Special	4:35:03.39	109.069	Ted Horn
1937	Wilbur Shaw	Shaw-Gilmore Special	4:24:07.80	113.580	Ralph Hepburn
1938	Floyd Roberts	Burd Piston Ring Special	4:15:58.40	117.200	Wilbur Shaw
1939	Wilbur Shaw	Boyle Special	4:20:47.39	115.035	Jimmy Snyder
1940	Wilbur Shaw	Boyle Special	4:22:31.17	114.277	Rex Mays
1941	Floyd Davis-Mauri Rose	Noc-Out Hose Clamp Special	4:20:36.24	115.117	Rex Mays
1946	George Robson	Thorne Engineering Special	4:21:26.71	114.820	Jimmy Jackson
1947	Mauri Rose	Blue Crown Special	4:17:52.17	116.338	Bill Holland
1948	Mauri Rose	Blue Crown Special	4:10:23.33	119.814	Bill Holland
1949	Bill Holland	Blue Crown Special	4:07:15.97	121.327	Johnny Parsons
1950[3]	Johnnie Parsons	Wynn's Friction Proof Special	2:46:55.97	124.002	Bill Holland
1951	Lee Wallard	Belanger Special	3:57:38.05	126.244	Mike Nazaruk
1952	Troy Ruttman	Agajanian Special	3:52:41.88	128.922	Jim Rathmann
1953	Bill Vukovich	Fuel Injection Special	3:53:01.69	128.740	Art Cross
1954	Bill Vukovich	Fuel Injection Special	3:49:17.27	130.840	Jim Bryan
1955	Bob Sweikert	John Zink Special	3:53:59.13	128.209	Tony Bettenhausen
1956	Pat Flaherty	John Zink Special	3:53:28.84	128.490	Sam Hanks
1957	Sam Hanks	Belond Exhaust Special	3:41:14.25	135.601	Jim Rathmann
1958	Jimmy Bryan	Belond A-P Special	3:44:13.80	133.791	George Amick
1959	Rodger Ward	Leader Card 500 Roadster	3:40:49.20	135.857	Jim Rathmann
1960	Jim Rathmann	Ken-Paul Special	3:36:11.36	138.767	Rodger Ward
1961	A. J. Foyt	Bowes Special	3:35:37.49	139.130	Eddie Sachs
1962	Rodger Ward	Leader Card Special	3:33:50.33	140.293	Len Sutton
1963	Parnelli Jones	Agajanian Special	3:29:35.40	143.137	Jim Clark
1964	A. J. Foyt	Sheraton-Thompson Spl.	3:23:35.83	147.350	Rodger Ward
1965	Jim Clark	Lotus-Ford	3:19:05.34	150.686	Parnelli Jones
1966	Graham Hill	Red Ball Lola-Ford	3:27:52.53	144.317	Jim Clark
1967[4]	A. J. Foyt	Sheraton-Thompson Coyote-Ford	3:18:24.22	151.207	Al Unser
1968	Bobby Unser	Rislone Eagle-Offenhauser	3:16:13.76	152.882	Dan Gurney
1969	Mario Andretti	STP Hawk-Ford	3:11:14.71	156.867	Dan Gurney
1970	Al Unser	Johnny Lightning P. J. Colt-Ford	3:12:37.04	155.749	Mark Donohue
1971	Al Unser	Johnny Lightning P. J. Colt-Ford	3:10:11.56	157.735	Peter Revson
1972	Mark Donohue	Sunoco McLaren-Offenhauser	3:04:05.54	162.962	Al Unser
1973[5]	Gordon Johncock	STP Eagle-Offenhauser	2:05:26.59	159.036	Bill Vukovich, Jr.
1974	Johnny Rutherford	McLaren-Offenhauser	3:09:10.06	158.589	Bobby Unser
1975[6]	Bobby Unser	Jorgensen Eagle-Offenhauser	2:54:55.08	149.213	Johnny Rutherford
1976[7]	Johnny Rutherford	Hy-gain McLaren-Offenhauser	1:42:52.48	148.725	A. J. Foyt
1977	A. J. Foyt	Gilmore Coyote-Foyt	3:05:57.16	161.331	Tom Sneva
1978	Al Unser	1st Nat'l City Lola-Cosworth	3:05:54.99	161.363	Tom Sneva
1979	Rick Mears	Gould Penske-Cosworth	3:08:27.97	158.899	A. J. Foyt
1980	Johnny Rutherford	Pennzoil Chaparral-Cosworth	3:29:59.56	142.862	Tom Sneva
1981[8]	Bobby Unser	Norton Penske-Cosworth	3:35:41.78	139.029	Mario Andretti
1982	Gordon Johncock	STP Wildcat-Cosworth	3:05:09.14	162.029	Rick Mears
1983	Tom Sneva	Texaco Star March-Cosworth	3:05:03.06	162.117	Al Unser
1984	Rick Mears	Pennzoil March-Cosworth	3:03:21.00	162.962	Roberto Guerrero
1985	Danny Sullivan	Miller March-Cosworth	3:16:06.069	152.982	Mario Andretti
1986	Bobby Rahal	Budweiser March-Cosworth	2:55:43.48	170.722	Kevin Cogan
1987	Al Unser, Sr.	Cummins March-Cosworth	3:04:59.147	162.175	Roberto Guerrero
1988	Rick Mears	Pennzoil Penske P.C.17-Chevrolet	3:27:10.204	144.809	Emerson Fittipaldi
1989	Emerson Fittipaldi	Marlboro Penske-Cosworth	2:59:01.04	167.581	Al Unser, Jr.
1990	Arie Luyendyk	Domino's Pizza Lola-Cosworth	2:41:18.248	185.987	Bobby Rahal

Year	Winner	Car	Time	mph	Second place
1991	Rick Mears	Marlboro Penske-Cosworth	2:50:01.018	176.460	Michael Andretti
1992	Al Unser, Jr.	Valvoline-Chevrolet	3:43.05.148	134.477	Scott Goodyear
1993	Emerson Fittipaldi	Penske-Chevrolet	3:10:49.860	157.207	Arie Luyendyk
1994	Al Unser, Jr.	Penske-Mercedes	3:06:29.006	160.872	Jacques Villeneuve
1995	Jacques Villeneuve	Reynard-Ford	3:15:17.561	156.616	Christian Fittipaldi
1996	Buddy Lazier	Reynard-Ford	3:22:45.753	147.956	Davy Jones
1997	Arie Luyendyk	G Force-Aurora	3:25:43.388	145.827	Scott Goodyear

1. 300 miles. 2. Race ended at 400 miles because of rain. 3. Race ended at 345 miles because of rain. 4. Race, postponed after 18 laps because of rain on May 30, was finished on May 31. 5. Race postponed May 28 and 29 was cut to 332.5 miles because of rain, May 30. 6. Race ended at 435 miles because of rain. 7. Race ended at 255 miles because of rain. 8. Andretti was awarded the victory the day after the race after Bobby Unser, whose car finished first, was penalized one lap and dropped from first place to second for passing other cars illegally under a yellow caution flag. Unser appealed the decision to the U.S. Auto Club and was upheld. A panel ruled the penalty was too severe and instead fined Unser $40,000, but restored the victory to him.

U.S. 500

The U.S. 500 was started in 1996 by IndyCar, after Indianapolis 500 race officials joined forced with IndyCar's upstart rivals the Indy Racing League. A disagreement over the number of automatic qualifiers that would be given to IRL drivers spurred IndyCar to stage a Memorial Day race of its own to go head-to-head with the Indy 500. In 1997 the race was held on July 27.

Year	Winner	Car	Time	mph	Second place
1996	Jimmy Vasser	Reynard-Honda	3:11:48	156.403	Mauricio Gugelmin
1997	Alex Zanardi	Reynard-Honda	2:59:35.58	167.044	Mark Blundell

NATIONAL ASSOCIATION FOR STOCK CAR AUTO RACING WINSTON CUP CHAMPIONS

Year	Winner	Year	Winner	Year	Winner	Year	Winner
1949	Red Byron	1961	Ned Jarrett	1974–75	Richard Petty	1987	Dale Earnhardt
1950	Bill Rexford	1962–63	Joe Weatherly	1976–78	Cale Yarborough	1988	Bill Elliott
1951	Herb Thomas	1964	Richard Petty	1979	Richard Petty	1989	Rusty Wallace
1952	Tim Flock	1965	Ned Jarrett	1980	Dale Earnhardt	1990	Dale Earnhardt
1953	Herb Thomas	1966	David Pearson	1981	Darrell Waltrip	1991	Dale Earnhardt
1954	Lee Petty	1967	Richard Petty	1982	Darrell Waltrip	1992	Alan Kulwicki[1]
1955	Tim Flock	1968–69	David Pearson	1983	Bobby Allison	1993	Dale Earnhardt
1956–57	Buck Baker	1970	Bobby Isaac	1984	Terry Labonte	1994	Dale Earnhardt
1958–59	Lee Petty	1971–72	Richard Petty	1985	Darrell Waltrip	1995	Jeff Gordon
1960	Rex White	1973	Benny Parsons	1986	Dale Earnhardt	1996	Terry Labonte

1. Kulwicki was killed in a plane crash in April 1993.

INDYCAR NATIONAL CHAMPIONS

Year	Winner	Year	Winner	Year	Winner	Year	Winner
1910	Ray Harroun	1931	Louis Schneider	1958	Tony Betten-hausen	1980	Johnny Ruther-ford
1911	Ralph Mulford	1932	Bob Carey	1959	Rodger Ward	1981–82	Rick Mears
1912	Ralph DePalma	1933	Louis Meyer	1960–61	A. J. Foyt	1983	Al Unser
1913	Earl Cooper	1934	Bill Cummings	1962	Rodger Ward	1984	Mario Andretti
1914	Ralph DePalma	1935	Kelly Petillo	1963–64	A. J. Foyt	1985	Al Unser
1915	Earl Cooper	1936	Mauri Rose	1965–66	Mario Andretti	1986–87	Bobby Rahal
1916	Dario Resta	1937	Wilbur Shaw	1967	A. J. Foyt	1988	Danny Sullivan
1917	Earl Cooper	1938	Floyd Roberts	1968	Bobby Unser	1989	Emerson Fittipaldi
1918	Ralph Mulford	1939	Wilbur Shaw	1969	Mario Andretti		
1919	Howard Wilcox	1940–41	Rex Mays	1970	Al Unser	1990	Al Unser, Jr.
1920	Gaston Chevrolet	1946–48	Ted Horn	1971–72	Joe Leonard	1991	Michael Andretti
1921	Tommy Milton	1949	Johnnie Parsons	1973	Roger McCluskey	1992	Bobby Rahal
1922	James Murphy	1950	Henry Banks	1974	Bobby Unser	1993	Nigel Mansell
1923	Eddie Hearne	1951	Tony Betten-hausen	1975	A. J. Foyt	1994	Al Unser, Jr.
1924	James Murphy			1976	Gordon Johncock	1995	Jacques Ville-neuve
1925	Peter DePaolo	1952	Chuck Stevenson	1977–78	Tom Sneva		
1926	Harry Hartz	1953	Sam Hanks	1979	Rick Mears (CART), A.J. Foyt (USAC)[1]	1996	Jimmy Vasser
1927	Peter DePaolo	1954	Jimmy Bryan				
1928–29	Louis Meyer	1955	Bob Sweikert				
1930	Billy Arnold	1956–57	Jimmy Bryan				

1. Two separate series were held in 1979. NOTE: There have been three sanctioning bodies for the series: the Automobile Association of America (1909–1955), the U.S. Auto Club (1956–1979), and the Championship Auto Racing Team (CART), 1979–present.

1996 INDYCAR POINTS LEADERS

1. Jimmy Vasser	154	4. Al Unser, Jr.	125	7. Bobby Rahal	102	10. Scott Pruett	82
2. Michael Andretti	132	5. Christian Fittipaldi	110	8. Bryan Herta	86		
3. Alex Zanardi	132	6. Gil de Ferran	104	9. Greg Moore	84		

1996 NASCAR LEADING POINT WINNERS

Driver	Pts	Winnings	Driver	Pts	Winnings
1. Terry Labonte	4,657	$4,030,648	11. Bobby Labonte	3,590	$1,475,196
2. Jeff Gordon	4,620	3,428,485	12. Ken Schrader	3,540	1,089,603
3. Dale Jarrett	4,568	2,985,418	13. Jeff Burton	3,538	884,303
4. Dale Earnhardt	4,327	2,285,926	14. Michael Waltrip	3,535	1,182,811
5. Mark Martin	4,278	1,887,396	15. Jimmy Spencer	3,476	1,090,876
6. Ricky Rudd	3,845	1,503,025	16. Ted Musgrave	3,466	961,512
7. Rusty Wallace	3,717	1,665,315	17. Geoff Bodine	3,218	1,031,762
8. Sterling Marlin	3,682	1,588,425	18. Rick Mast	3,190	924,559
9. Bobby Hamilton	3,639	1,151,235	19. Morgan Shepherd	3,133	719,059
10. Ernie Irvan	3,632	1,686,313	20. Ricky Craven	3,078	941,959

WORLD GRAND PRIX DRIVER CHAMPIONS

1950	Giuseppe Farina, Italy, Alfa Romeo	1974	Emerson Fittipaldi, Brazil, McLaren-Ford
1951	Juan Fangio, Argentina, Alfa Romeo	1975	Niki Lauda, Austria, Ferrari
1952	Alberto Ascari, Italy, Ferrari	1976	James Hunt, Britain, McLaren-Ford
1953	Alberto Ascari, Italy, Ferrari	1977	Niki Lauda, Austria, Ferrari
1954	Juan Fangio, Argentina, Maserati, Mercedes-Benz	1978	Mario Andretti, United States, Lotus
1955	Juan Fangio, Argentina, Mercedes-Benz	1979	Jody Scheckter, South Africa, Ferrari
1956	Juan Fangio, Argentina, Lancia-Ferrari	1980	Alan Jones, Australia, Williams-Ford
1957	Juan Fangio, Argentina, Masserati	1981	Nelson Piquet, Brazil, Brabham-Ford
1958	Mike Hawthorn, England, Ferrari	1982	Kiki Rosberg, Finland, Williams-Ford
1959	Jack Brabham, Australia, Cooper	1983	Nelson Piquet, Brazil. Brabham-BMW
1960	Jack Brabham, Australia, Cooper	1984	Nikki Lauda, Austria, McLaren-Porsche
1961	Phil Hill, United States, Ferrari	1985	Alain Prost, France, McLaren-Porsche
1962	Graham Hill, England, BRM	1986	Alain Prost, France, McLaren-Porsche
1963	Jim Clark, Scotland, Lotus-Ford	1987	Nelson Piquet, Brazil, Williams-Honda
1964	John Surtees, England, Ferrari	1988	Aryton Senna, Brazil, McLaren-Honda
1965	Jim Clark, Scotland, Lotus-Ford	1989	Alain Prost, France, McLaren-Honda
1966	Jack Brabham, Australia, Brabham-Repco	1990	Ayrton Senna, Brazil, McLaren-Honda
1967	Denis Hulme, New Zealand, Brabham-Repco	1991	Aryton Senna, Brazil, McLaren-Honda
1968	Graham Hill, England, Lotus-Ford	1992	Nigel Mansell, Britain, Williams-Renault
1969	Jackie Stewart, Scotland, Matra-Ford	1993	Alain Prost
1970	Jochen Rindt, Austria, Lotus-Ford	1994	William Schumacher, Germany, Benetton
1971	Jackie Stewart, Scotland, Tyrrell-Ford	1995	William Schumacher, Germany, Benetton Renault
1972	Emerson Fittipaldi, Brazil, Lotus-Ford	1996	Damon Hill, Britain, Williams
1973	Jackie Stewart, Scotland, Tyrrell-Ford		

Yachting

AMERICA'S CUP RECORD

First race in 1851 around Isle of Wight, Cowes, England. First defense and all others through 1920 held 30 miles off New York Bay. Races since 1930 held 30 miles off Newport, R.I. Conducted as one race only in 1851 and 1870; best four-of-seven basis, 1871; best two-of-three, 1876–1887; best three-of-five, 1893–1901; best four-of-seven, since 1930. Figures in parentheses indicate number of races won.

Year	Winner and owner	Loser and owner
1851	AMERICA (1), John C. Stevens, U.S.	AURORA, T. Le Marchant, England[1]
1870	MAGIC (1), Franklin Osgood, U.S.	CAMBRIA, James Ashbury, England[2]
1871	COLUMBIA (2), Franklin Osgood, U.S.[3] SAPPHO (2), William P. Douglas, U.S.	LIVONIA (1), James Ashbury, England
1876	MADELEINE (2), John S. Dickerson, U.S.	COUNTESS OF DUFFERIN, Chas. Gifford, Canada
1881	MISCHIEF (2), J. R. Busk, U.S.	ATALANTA, Alexander Cuthbert, Canada
1885	PURITAN (2), J. M. Forbes-Gen. Charles Paine, U.S.	GENESTA, Sir Richard Sutton, England
1886	MAYFLOWER (2), Gen. Charles Paine, U.S.	GALATEA, Lt. William Henn, England
1887	VOLUNTEER (2), Gen. Charles Paine, U.S.	THISTLE, James Bell et al., Scotland
1893	VIGILANT (3), C. Oliver Iselin et al., U.S.	VALKYRIE II, Lord Dunraven, England
1895	DEFENDER (3), C. O. Iselin–W. K. Vanderbilt–E. D. Morgan, U.S.	VALKYRIE III, Lord Dunraven–Lord Lonsdale–Lord Wolverton, England
1899	COLUMBIA (3), J. P. Morgan–C. O. Iselin, U.S.	SHAMROCK I, Sir Thomas Lipton, Ireland
1901	COLUMBIA (3), Edwin D. Morgan, U.S.	SHAMROCK II, Sir Thomas Lipton, Ireland

Year	Winner and owner	Loser and owner
1903	RELIANCE (3), Cornelius Vanderbilt et al., U.S.	SHAMROCK III, Sir Thomas Lipton, Ireland
1920	RESOLUTE (3), Henry Walters et al., U.S.	SHAMROCK IV (2), Sir Thomas Lipton, Ireland
1930	ENTERPRISE (4), Harold S. Vanderbilt et al., U.S.	SHAMROCK V, Sir Thomas Lipton, Ireland
1934	RAINBOW (4), Harold S. Vanderbilt, U.S.	ENDEAVOUR (2), T. O. M. Sopwith, England
1937	RANGER (4), Harold S. Vanderbilt, U.S.	ENDEAVOUR II, T. O. M. Sopwith, England
1958	COLUMBIA (4), Henry Sears et al., U.S.	SCEPTRE, Hugh Goodson et al., England
1962	WEATHERLY (4), Henry D. Mercer et al., U.S.	GRETEL (1), Sir Frank Packer et al., Australia
1964	CONSTELLATION (4), New York Y.C. Syndicate, U.S.	SOVEREIGN (0), J. Anthony Bowden, England
1967	INTREPID (4), New York Y.C. Syndicate, U.S.	DAME PATTIE (0), Sydney (Aust.) Syndicate
1970	INTREPID (4), New York Y.C. Syndicate, U.S.	GRETEL II (1), Sydney (Aust.) Syndicate
1974	COURAGEOUS (4), New York, N.Y. Syndicate, U.S.	SOUTHERN CROSS (0), Sydney (Aust.) Syndicate
1977	COURAGEOUS (4), New York, N.Y. Syndicate, U.S.	AUSTRALIA (0), Sun City (Aust.) Syndicate
1980	FREEDOM (4), New York, N.Y. Syndicate, U.S.	AUSTRALIA (1), Alan Bond et al, Australia
1983	AUSTRALIA II (4), Alan Bond et al., Australia	LIBERTY, (3) New York, N.Y. Syndicate, U.S.
1987	STARS & STRIPES (4), Dennis Conner et al., United States	KOOKABURRA III (0), Iain Murray et al., Australia
1988[4]	STARS & STRIPES, Dennis Conner, et al., United States	NEW ZEALAND, Michael Fay, et al., New Zealand
1992	AMERICA 3, Bill Koch, et al., United States	IL MORO DI VENEZIA, Paul Cayard, et al., Italy
1995	BLACK MAGIC, Peter Blake, et al., New Zealand	YOUNG AMERICA, Dennis Conner, et al., United States

1. Fourteen British yachts started against America; Aurora finished second. 2. Cambria sailed against 23 U.S. yachts and finished tenth. 3. Columbia was disabled in the third race, after winning the first two; Sappho substituted and won the fourth and fifth. 4. Shortly after Dennis Conner and his 60-foot, twin-hulled catamaran easily defeated the challenge of the New Zealand, a 133-foot, single-hulled yacht in the waters off San Diego in early September 1988, a New York State Supreme Court judge ruled that the Americans did not live up to the America's Cup Deed of Gift, which means competing boats must be similar. The judge ruled that the Americans had an unfair advantage over the monohulled ship, and awarded the Cup to New Zealand. However, an Appeal awarded the Cup to the United States.

Little League

LITTLE LEAGUE WORLD SERIES CHAMPIONS

Year	Champion	Runner-up	Score	Year	Champion	Runner-up	Score
1947	Williamsport, Pa.	Lock Haven, Pa.	16–7	1974	Kao Hsiung, Taiwan	El Cajon, Calif.	7–2
1948	Lock Haven, Pa.	St. Petersburg, Fla.	6–5	1975	Lakewood, N.J.	Tampa, Fla.	4–3
1949	Hammontown, N.J.	Pensacola, Fla.	5–0	1976	Tokyo, Japan	Campbell, Calif.	10–3
1950	Houston, Tex.	Bridgeport, Conn.	2–1	1977	Kao Hsiung, Taiwan	El Cajon, Calif.	7–2
1951	Stamford, Conn.	Austin, Tex.	3–0	1978	Pin-Tung, Taiwan	Danville, Calif.	11–1
1952	Norwalk, Conn.	Monongahela, Pa.	4–3	1979	Hsien, Taiwan	Campbell, Calif.	2–1
1953	Birmingham, Ala.	Schenectady, N.Y.	1–0	1980	Hua Lian, Taiwan	Tampa, Fla.	4–3
1954	Schenectady, N.Y.	Colton, Calif.	7–5	1981	Tai-Chung, Taiwan	Tampa, Fla.	4–2
1955	Morrisville, Pa.	Merchantville, N.J.	4–3	1982	Kirkland, Wash.	Hsien, Taiwan	6–0
1956	Roswell, N.M.	Merchantville, N.J.	3–1	1983	Marietta, Ga.	Barahona, D. Rep.	3–1
1957	Monterrey, Mex.	LaMesa, Calif.	4–0	1984	Seoul, S. Korea	Altamonte Springs, Fla.	6–2
1958	Monterrey, Mex.	Kankakee, Ill.	10–1	1985	Seoul, S. Korea	Mexicali, Mex.	7–1
1959	Hamtramck, Mich.	Auburn, Calif.	12–0	1986	Tianan Park, Taiwan	Tucson, Ariz.	12–0
1960	Levittown, Pa.	Ft. Worth, Tex.	5–0	1987	Hua Lian, Taiwan	Irvine, Calif.	21–1
1961	El Cajon, Calif.	El Campo, Tex.	4–2	1988	Tai-Chung, Taiwan	Pearl City, Haw.	10–0
1962	San Jose, Calif.	Kankakee, Ill.	3–0	1989	Trumbull, Conn.	Kaohsiung, Taiwan	5–2
1963	Granada Hills, Calif.	Stratford, Conn.	2–1	1990	Taipei, Taiwan	Shippensburg, Pa.	9–0
1964	Staten Island, N.Y.	Monterrey, Mex.	4–0	1991	Tai-Chung, Taiwan	San Ramon Valley, Calif.	11–0
1965	Windsor Locks, Conn.	Stoney Creek, Can.	3–1				
1966	Houston, Tex.	W. New York, N.J.	8–2	1992*	Long Beach, Calif.	Zamboanga, Phil.	6–0
1967	West Tokyo, Japan	Chicago, Ill.	4–1	1993	Long Beach, Calif.	David Chiriqui, Pan.	3–2
1968	Osaka, Japan	Richmond, Va.	1–0	1994	Maracaibo, Venezuela	Northridge, Calif.	4–3
1969	Taipei, Taiwan	Santa Clara, Calif.	5–0	1995	Tainan, Taiwan	Spring, Texas	17–3
1970	Wayne, N.J.	Campbell, Calif.	2–0	1996	Kao-Hsuing City, Taipei	Cranston, R.I.	13–3
1971	Tainan, Taiwan	Gary, Ind.	12–3	1997	Guadalupe, Mexico	South Mission Viejo, Calif.	5–4
1972	Taipei, Taiwan	Hammond, Ind.	6–0				
1973	Tainan City, Taiwan	Tucson, Ariz.	12–0				

* Long Beach declared a 6–0 winner after the international tournament committee determined that Zamboanga City had used players that were not within its city limits.

Baseball

The popular tradition that baseball was invented by Abner Doubleday at Cooperstown, N.Y., in 1839 has been enshrined in the Hall of Fame and National Museum of Baseball erected in that town, but research has proved that a game called "Base Ball" was played in this country and England before 1839. The first team baseball as we know it was played at the Elysian Fields, Hoboken, N.J., on June 19, 1846, between the Knickerbockers and the New York Nine. The next fifty years saw a gradual growth of baseball and an improvement of equipment and playing skill.

Historians have it that the first pitcher to throw a curve was William A. (Candy) Cummings in 1867. The Cincinnati Red Stockings were the first all-professional team, and in 1869 they played 64 games without a loss. The standard ball of the same size and weight, still the rule, was adopted in 1872. The first catcher's mask was worn in 1875. The National League was organized in 1876. The first chest protector was worn in 1885. The three-strike rule was put on the books in 1887, and the four-ball ticket to first base was instituted in 1889. The pitching distance was lengthened to 60 feet 6 inches in 1893, and the rules have been modified only slightly since that time.

The American League, under the vigorous leadership of B. B. Johnson, became a major league in 1901. Judge Kenesaw Mountain Landis, by action of the two major leagues, became Commissioner of Baseball in 1921. Peter Ueberroth bacame baseball's fifth commissioner and took office Oct. 1, 1984.

Ueberroth did not seek a new term in 1989 and was succeeded by Bart Giamatti who died suddenly on Sept. 1, 1989. Francis T. Vincent, Jr., replaced him on Sept. 13, 1989.

Vincent, under pressure from owners to relinquish some of his powers, resigned in late 1992. Bud Selig, principal owner of the Milwaukee Brewers, headed a baseball executive committee that ruled baseball during the search for a new commissioner that extended late into 1993. The search was put on hold pending resolution of baseball's labor situation. No progress had been made through late 1995.

MAJOR LEAGUE ALL-STAR GAME

Year	Date	Winning league and manager	Runs	Losing league and manager	Runs	Winning pitcher	Losing pitcher	Site	Paid attendance
1933	July 6	A.L. (Mack)	4	N.L. (McGraw)	2	Gomez	Hallahan	Chicago A.L.	47,595
1934	July 10	A.L. (Cronin)	9	N.L. (Terry)	7	Harder	Mungo	New York N.L.	48,363
1935	July 8	A.L. (Cochrane)	4	N.L. (Frisch)	1	Gomez	Walker	Cleveland A.L.	69,831
1936	July 7	N.L. (Grimm)	4	A.L. (McCarthy)	3	J. Dean	Grove	Boston N.L.	25,556
1937	July 7	A.L. (McCarthy)	8	N.L. (Terry)	3	Gomez	J. Dean	Washington A.L.	31,391
1938	July 6	N.L. (Terry)	4	A.L. (McCarthy)	1	Vander Meer	Gomez	Cincinnati N.L.	27,067
1939	July 11	A.L. (McCarthy)	3	N.L. (Hartnett)	1	Bridges	Lee	New York A.L.	62,892
1940	July 9	N.L. (McKechnie)	4	A.L. (Cronin)	0	Derringer	Ruffing	St. Louis N.L.	32,373
1941	July 8	A.L. (Baker)	7	N.L. (McKechnie)	5	E. Smith	Passeau	Detroit A.L.	54,674
1942	July 6	A.L. (McCarthy)	3	N.L. (Durocher)	1	Chandler	Cooper	New York N.L.	34,178
1943	July 13[1]	A.L. (McCarthy)	5	N.L. (Southworth)	3	Leonard	Cooper	Philadelphia A.L.	31,938
1944	July 11[1]	N.L. (Southworth)	7	A.L. (McCarthy)	1	Raffensberger	Hughson	Pittsburgh N.L.	29,589
1946	July 9	A.L. (O'Neill)	12	N.L. (Grimm)	0	Feller	Passeau	Boston A.L.	34,906
1947	July 8	A.L. (Cronin)	2	N.L. (Dyer)	1	Shea	Sain	Chicago N.L.	41,123
1948	July 13	A.L. (Harris)	5	N.L. (Durocher)	2	Raschi	Schmitz	St. Louis A.L.	34,009
1949	July 12	A.L. (Boudreau)	11	N.L. (Southworth)	7	Trucks	Newcombe	Brooklyn N.L.	32,577
1950	July 11	N.L. (Shotton)	4	A.L. (Stengel)	3[3]	Blackwell	Gray	Chicago A.L.	46,127
1951	July 10	N.L. (Sawyer)	8	A.L. (Stengel)	3	Maglie	Lopat	Detroit A.L.	52,075
1952	July 8	N.L. (Durocher)	3	A.L. (Stengel)	2[4]	Rush	Lemon	Philadelphia A.L.	32,785
1953	July 14	N.L. (Dressen)	5	A.L. (Stengel)	1	Spahn	Reynolds	Cincinnati N.L.	30,846
1954	July 13	A.L. (Stengel)	11	N.L. (Alston)	9	Stone	Conley	Cleveland A.L.	68,751
1955	July 12	N.L. (Durocher)	6	A.L. (Lopez)	5[5]	Conley	Sullivan	Milwaukee N.L.	45,643
1956	July 10	N.L. (Alston)	7	A.L. (Stengel)	3	Friend	Pierce	Washington A.L.	28,843
1957	July 9	A.L. (Stengel)	6	N.L. (Alston)	5	Bunning	Simmons	St. Louis N.L.	30,693
1958	July 8	A.L. (Stengel)	4	N.L. (Haney)	3	Wynn	Friend	Baltimore A.L.	48,829
1959[2]	July 7	N.L. (Haney)	5	A.L. (Stengel)	4	Antonelli	Ford	Pittsburgh N.L.	35,277
	Aug. 3	A.L. (Stengel)	5	N.L. (Haney)	3	Walker	Drysdale	Los Angeles N.L.	55,105
1960[2]	July 11	N.L. (Alston)	5	A.L. (Lopez)	3	Friend	Monbouquette	Kansas City A.L.	30,619
	July 13	N.L. (Alston)	6	A.L. (Lopez)	0	Law	Ford	New York A.L.	38,362
1961[2]	July 11	N.L. (Murtaugh)	5	A.L. (Richards)	4[6]	Miller	Wilhelm	San Francisco N.L.	44,115
	July 31	N.L. (Murtaugh)	1	A.L. (Richards)	1[7]	—	—	Boston A.L.	31,851
1962[2]	July 10	N.L. (Hutchinson)	3	A.L. (Houk)	1	Marichal	Pascual	Washington A.L.	45,480
	July 30	A.L. (Houk)	9	N.L. (Hutchinson)	4	Herbert	Mahaffey	Chicago N.I..	38,359
1963	July 9	N.L. (Dark)	5	A.L. (Houk)	3	Jackson	Bunning	Cleveland A.L.	44,160
1964	July 7	N.L. (Alston)	7	A.L. (Lopez)	4	Marichal	Radatz	New York N.L.	50,850
1965	July 13	N.L. (March)	6	A.L. (Lopez)	5	Koufax	McDowell	Minnesota A.L.	46,706
1966	July 12	N.L. (Alston)	2	A.L. (Mele)	1[6]	Perry	Rickert	St. Louis N.L.	49,926
1967	July 11	N.L. (Alston)	2	A.L. (Bauer)	1[8]	Drysdale	Hunter	Anaheim A.L.	46,309
1968	July 9	N.L. (Schoendienst)	1	A.L. (Williams)	0	Drysdale	Tiant	Houston A.L.	48,321
1969	July 23	N.L. (Schoendienst)	9	A.L. (M. Smith)	3	Carlton	Stottlemyre	Washington A.L.	45,259
1970	July 14	N.L. (Hodges)	5	A.L. (Weaver)	4	Osteen	Wright	Cincinnati N.L.	51,838
1971	July 13	N.L. (Weaver)	6	N.L. (Anderson)	4	Blue	Ellis	Detroit A.L.	53,559
1972	July 25	N.L. (Murtaugh)	4	A.L. (Weaver)	3[6]	McGraw	McNally	Atlanta N.L.	53,107
1973	July 24[1]	N.L. (Anderson)	7	A.L. (Williams)	1	Wise	Blyleven	Kansas City A.L.	40,849

Year	Date	Winning league and manager	Runs	Losing league and manager	Runs	Winning pitcher	Losing pitcher	Site	Paid attendance
1974	July 23[1]	N.L. (Berra)	7	A.L. (Williams)	2	Brett	Tiant	Pittsburgh N.L.	50,706
1975	July 15[1]	N.L. (Alston)	6	A.L. (Dark)	3	Matlack	Hunter	Milwaukee A.L.	51,540
1976	July 13	N.L. (Anderson)	7	A.L. (D. Johnson)	1	R. Jones	Fidrych	Philadelphia N.L.	63,974
1977	July 19[1]	N.L. (Anderson)	7	A.L. (Martin)	5	Sutton	Palmer	New York A.L.	56,683
1978	July 11[1]	N.L. (Lasorda)	7	A.L. (Martin)	3	Sutter	Gossage	San Diego N.L.	51,549
1979	July 17[1]	N.L. (Lasorda)	7	A.L. (Lemon)	6	Sutter	Kern	Seattle A.L.	58,905
1980	July 8[1]	N.L. (Tanner)	4	A.L. (Weaver)	2	Reuss	John	Los Angeles N.L.	56,088
1981	Aug. 9[1]	N.L. (Green)	5	A.L. (Frey)	4	Blue	Fingers	Cleveland* A.L.	72,086
1982	July 13[1]	N.L. (Lasorda)	4	A.L. (Martin)	1	Rogers	Eckersley	Montreal N.L.	59,057
1983	July 6[1]	A.L. (Kuenn)	13	N.L. (Herzog)	3	Steib	Soto	Chicago A.L.	43,801
1984	July 11[1]	N.L. (Owens)	3	A.L. (Altobelli)	1	Leg	Steib	San Francisco, N.L.	57,756
1985	July 16[1]	N.L. (Williams)	6	A.L. (Anderson)	1	Hoyt	Morris	Minneapolis, A.L.	54,960
1986	July 15[1]	N.L. (Howser)	3	N.L. (Herzog)	2	Clemens	Gooden	Houston, N.L.	45,774
1987	July 14[1]	N.L. (Johnson)	2	N.L. (McNamara)	0	Smith	Howell	Oakland, A.L.	49,671
1988	July 12[1]	A.L. (Kelly)	2	N.L. (Herzog)	1	Viola	Gooden	Cincinnati, N.L	55,837
1989	July 11[1]	A.L. (LaRussa)	5	N.L. (Lasorda)	3	Ryan	Smoltz	California, A.L.	64,036
1990	July 10[1]	A.L. (LaRussa)	2	N.L. (Craig)	0	Saberhagen	Brantley	Chicago, N.L.	39,071
1991	July 9[1]	A.L. (LaRussa)	4	N.L. (Piniella)	2	Key	Martinez	Toronto, A.L.	52,383
1992	July 14	A.L. (Kelly)	13	N.L. (Cox)	6	Brown	Glavine	San Diego, N.L.	59,372
1993	July 13	A.L. (Gaston)	9	N.L. (Cox)	3	McDowell	Burkett	Baltimore, A.L.	48,147
1994	July 12	N.L. (Fregosi)	8	A.L. (Gaston)	7	Jones	Bere	Pittsburgh, N.L.	59,568
1995	July 11	N.L. (Alou)	3	A.L. (Showalter)	2	Slocumb	Rogers	Texas, A.L.	50,920
1996	July 9	N.L. (Cox)	6	A.L. (Hargrove)	0	Smoltz	Nagy	Philadelphia, N.L.	62,670
1997	July 8	A.L. (Torre)	3	N.L. (Cox)	1	Johnson	Maddux	Cleveland, A.L.	44,916

1. Night game. 2. Two games. 3. Fourteen innings. 4. Five innings, rain. 5. Twelve innings. 6. Ten innings. 7. Called because of rain after nine innings. 8. Fifteen innings. * Game was originally scheduled for July 14, but was put off because of players' strike. NOTE: No game in 1945.

NATIONAL BASEBALL HALL OF FAME

Cooperstown, N.Y.

Fielders

Member	Active years	Member	Active years	Member	Active years
Aaron, Henry (Hank)	1954–1976	Comiskey, Charles	1882–1894	Hornsby, Rogers	1915–1937
Anson, Adrian (Cap)	1876–1897	Combs, Earle	1924–1935	Irvin, Monford (Monte)[1]	1939–1956
Aparicio, Luis	1956–1973	Connor, Roger	1880–1897	Jackson, Reggie	1967–1987
Appling, Lucius (Luke)	1930–1950	Crawford, Samuel	1899–1917	Jackson, Travis	1922–1936
Ashburh, Richie	1948–1962	Cronin, Joseph	1926–1945	Jennings, Hugh	1891–1918
Averill, H. Earl	1929–1941	Cuyler, Hazen (Kiki)	1921–1938	Johnson, William (Judy)[1]	1921–1937
Baker, J. Frank (Home Run)	1908–1922	Dandridge, Ray[1]	1933–1953	Kaline, Albert W.	1953–1974
		Delahanty, Edward	1888–1903	Keeler, William (Wee Willie)	1892–1910
Bancroft, David	1915–1930	Dickey, William	1928–1946		
Banks, Ernest	1953–1971	Dihigo, Martin[1]	1923–1945	Kell, George	1943–1957
Beckley, Jacob	1888–1907	DiMaggio, Joseph	1936–1951	Kelley, Joseph	1891–1908
Bell, James (Cool Papa)[1]	1920–1947	Doerr, Bobby	1937–1951	Kelly, George	1915–1932
Bench, John	1967–1983	Duffy, Hugh	1888–1906	Kelly, Michael (King)	1878–1893
Berra, Lawrence (Yogi)	1946–1965	Ewing, William	1880–1897	Killebrew, Harmon	1954–1975
Bottomley, James	1922–1937	Eyers, John	1902–1919	Kiner, Ralph	1946–1955
Boudreau, Louis	1938–1952	Ferrell, Rick	1929–1947	Klein, Charles H. (Chuck)	1928–1944
Bresnahan, Roger	1897–1915	Flick, Elmer	1898–1910	Lajoie, Napoleon	1896–1916
Brock, Lou	1961–1980	Fox, Nellie	1947–1965	Lazzeri, Tony	1926–1939
Brouthers, Dennis	1879–1896	Foxx, James	1925–1945	Leonard, Walter (Buck)[1]	1933–1955
Burkett, Jesse	1890–1905	Frisch, Frank	1919–1937	Lindstrom, Frederick	1924–1936
Campanella, Roy	1948–1957	Gehrig, H. Louis (Lou)	1923–1939	Lloyd, John Henry[1]	1905–1931
Carew, Rod	1967–1985	Gehringer, Charles	1924–1942	Lombardi, Ernie	1932–1947
Carey, Max	1910–1929	Gibson, Josh[1]	1929–1946	Mantle, Mickey	1951–1968
Chance, Frank	1898–1914	Goslin, Leon (Goose)	1921–1938	Manush, Henry (Heinie)	1923–1939
Charleston, Oscar[1]	1915–1954	Greenberg, Henry (Hank)	1933–1947	Maranville, Walter (Rabbit)	1912–1935
Clarke, Fred	1894–1915	Hafey, Charles (Chick)	1924–1937	Matthews, Edwin	1952–1968
Clemente, Roberto	1955–1972	Hamilton, William	1888–1901	Mays, Willie	1951–1973
Cobb, Tyrus	1905–1928	Hartnett, Charles (Gabby)	1922–1941	McCarthy, Thomas	1884–1896
Cochrane, Gordon (Mickey)	1925–1937	Heilmann, Harry	1914–1932	McGraw, John J.	1891–1906
		Herman, William	1931–1947	McCovey, Willie	1959–1980
Collins, Edward	1906–1930	Hooper, Harry	1909–1925	Medwick, Joseph (Ducky)	1932–1948
Collins, James	1895–1908				

Member	Active years	Member	Active years	Member	Active years
Mize, John (The Big Cat)	1936–1953	Schalk, Raymond	1912–1929	Vaughan, Arky	1932–1948
Morgan, Joe	1963–1984	Schoendienst, Red	1945–1963	Wagner, John (Honus)	1897–1917
Musial, Stanley	1941–1963	Schmidt, Mike	1973–1989	Wallace, Roderick (Bobby)	1894–1918
O'Rourke, James	1876–1894	Sewell, Joseph	1920–1933	Waner, Lloyd	1927–1945
Ott, Melvin	1926–1947	Simmons, Al	1924–1944	Waner, Paul	1926–1945
Reese, Harold (Pee Wee)	1940–1958	Sisler, George	1915–1930	Ward, John (Monte)	1878–1894
Rice, Edgar (Sam)	1915–1934	Slaughter, Enos	1938–1959	Wells, Willie	1924–1949
Rizzuto, Phil	1941–1956	Snider, Edwin D. (Duke)	1947–1964	Wheat, Zachariah	1909–1927
Robinson, Brooks	1955–1977	Speaker, Tristram	1907–1928	Williams, Billy	1959–1976
Robinson, Frank	1956–1976	Stargell, Willie	1962–1982	Williams, Theodore	1939–1960
Robinson, Jack	1947–1956	Terry, William	1923–1936	Wilson, Lewis R. (Hack)	1923–1934
Robinson, Wilbert	1886–1902	Thompson, Samuel	1885–1906	Yastrzemski, Carl	1961–1983
Roush, Edd	1913–1931	Tinker, Joseph	1902–1916	Youngs, Ross (Pep)	1917–1926
Ruth, Babe	1914–1935	Traynor, Harold (Pie)	1920–1937		

1. Negro League player selected by special committee.

Pitchers

Alexander, Grover	1911–1930	Griffith, Clark	1891–1914	Paige, Leroy (Satchel)[1]	1926–1965
Bender, Charles (Chief)	1903–1925	Grimes, Burleigh	1916–1934	Palmer, Jim	1965–1984
Brown, Mordecai (3-Finger)	1903–1916	Grove, Robert (Lefty)	1925–1941	Pennock, Herbert	1912–1934
		Haines, Jesse	1918–1937	Perry, Gaylord	1962–1983
Bunning, Jim	1955–1971	Hoyt, Waite	1918–1938	Plank, Edward	1901–1917
Carlton, Steve	1965–1988	Hubbell, Carl	1928–1943	Radbourn, Charles (Hoss)	1880–1891
Chesbro, John	1899–1909	Hunter, Jim (Catfish)	1965–1979	Rixey, Eppa	1912–1933
Clarkson, John	1882–1894	Jenkins, Ferguson	1965–1983	Roberts, Robert (Robin)	1948–1966
Coveleski, Stanley	1912–1928	Johnson, Walter	1907–1927	Ruffing, Charles (Red)	1924–1947
Day, Leon[1]	1935–1955	Joss, Adrian	1902–1910	Rusie, Amos	1889–1901
Dean, Jerome (Dizzy)	1930–1947	Keefe, Timothy	1880–1893	Seaver, Tom	1967–1986
Drysdale, Don	1956–1969	Koufax, Sanford (Sandy)	1955–1966	Spahn, Warren	1942–1965
Faber, Urban (Red)	1914–1933	Lemon, Robert	1946–1958	Vance, Arthur (Dazzy)	1915–1935
Feller, Robert	1936–1956	Lyons, Theodore	1923–1946	Waddell, Rube	1897–1910
Fingers, Rollie	1968–1985	Marichal, Juan	1960–1975	Walsh, Edward	1904–1917
Ford, Edward (Whitey)	1950–1967	Marquard, Richard (Rube)	1908–1924	Welch, Michael (Mickey)	1880–1892
Foster, Andrew (Rube)	1897–1926	Mathewson, Christopher	1900–1916	Wilhelm, Hoyt	1952–1972
Foster, Bill	1923–1937	McGinnity, Joseph	1899–1908	Willis, Vic	1898–1910
Galvin, James (Pud)	1876–1892	Newhouser, Hal	1939–1955	Wynn, Early	1939–1963
Gibson, Bob	1959–1975	Nichols, Charles (Kid)	1890–1906	Young, Denton (Cy)	1890–1911
Gomez, Vernon (Lefty)	1930–1943	Niekro, Phil	1959–1987		

1. Negro League player selected by special committee.

Officials and Others

Alston, Walter[1]
Barlick, Al[4]
Barrow, Edward[1,2]
Bulkeley, Morgan G.[2]
Cartwright, Alexander[2]
Chadwick, Henry[3]
Chandler, A.B.[6]
Comiskey, Charles[1]
Conlan, John[2]
Connolly, Thomas[4]
Cummings, William A.[5]

Durocher, Leo[1]
Evans, William G.[4,2]
Foster, Rube[2]
Frick, Ford C.[6,2]
Giles, Warren C.[2]
Hanlon, Ned[2]
Harridge, William[2]
Harris, Stanley R.[7]
Hubbard, R. Calvin[4]
Huggins, Miller J.[1]

Hulbert, William[2]
Johnson, B. Bancroft[2]
Klem, William[4]
Landis, Kenesaw M.[6]
Lasorda, Tommy[1]
Lopez, Alfonso R.[7]
Mack, Connie[1,2]
MacPhail, Leland S.[2]
McCarthy, Joseph V.[1]
McGowan, Bill[4]

McKechnie, William B.[1]
Rickey, W. Branch[1,2]
Spalding, Albert G.[4]
Stengel, Charles D.[7]
Veeck, Bill[2]
Weaver, Earl[1]
Weiss, George M.[2]
Wright, George[5]
Wright, Harry[5,1]
Yawkey, Thomas[2]

1. Manager. 2. Executive. 3. Writer-statistician. 4. Umpire. 5. Early player. 6. Commissioner. 7. Player-manager.

BASEBALL'S PERFECTLY PITCHED GAMES[1]

(no opposing runner reached base)

Lee Richmond—Worcester vs. Cleveland (NL) June 12, 1880	(1–0)	Charles Robertson—Chicago vs. Detroit (AL) April 30, 1922	(2–0)
John M. Ward—Providence vs. Buffalo (NL) June 17, 1880	(5–0)	Don Larsen[3]—New York (AL) vs. Brooklyn (NL) Oct. 8, 1956	(2–0)
Cy Young—Boston vs. Philadelphia (AL) May 5, 1904	(3–0)	Jim Bunning—Philadelphia vs. New York (NL) June 21, 1964	(6–0)
Addie Joss—Cleveland vs. Chicago (AL) Oct. 2, 1908	(1–0)	Sandy Koufax—Los Angeles vs. Chicago (NL) Sept. 9, 1965	(1–0)
Ernest Shore[2]—Boston vs. Washington (AL) June 23, 1917	(4–0)	Jim Hunter—Oakland vs. Minnesota (AL) May 8, 1968	(4–0)

Len Barker—Cleveland vs. Toronto (AL) May 15, 1981 (3–0)

Mike Witt—California vs. Texas (AL) Sept. 30, 1984 (1–0)

Tom Browning—Cincinnati vs. Los Angeles (NL) Sept. 16, 1988 (1–0)

Dennis Martinez—Montreal vs. Los Angeles (NL) July 28, 1991 (2–0)

Kenny Rogers—Texas vs. California (AL) July 28, 1994 (4–0)

1. Harvey Haddix, of Pittsburgh, pitched 12 perfect innings against Milwaukee (NL), May 26, 1959 but lost game in 13th on error and hit. 2. Shore, relief pitcher for Babe Ruth who walked first batter before being ejected by umpire, retired 26 batters who faced him and baserunner was out stealing. 3. World Series.

LIFETIME BATTING, PITCHING, AND BASE-RUNNING RECORDS

(Records Through 1996)

Hits (3,000 or more)

Pete Rose	4,256
Ty Cobb	4,189
Henry Aaron	3,771
Stan Musial	3,630
Tris Speaker	3,514
Carl Yastrzemski	3,419
Honus Wagner	3,415
Eddie Collins	3,312
Willie Mays	3,283
Nap Lajoie	3,242
Eddie Murray	3,218
George Brett	3,154
Paul Waner	3,152
Robin Yount	3,142
Dave Winfield	3,110
Rod Carew	3,053
Lou Brock	3,023
Paul Molitor	3,014
Al Kaline	3,007
Roberto Clemente	3,000

Earned Run Average (Minimum 1,500 innings pitched)

Ed Walsh	1.82
Addie Joss	1.88
Mordecai Brown	2.06
John Ward	2.10
Christy Mathewson	2.13
Rube Waddell	2.16
Walter Johnson	2.17
Orval Overall	2.23
Tommy Bond	2.25
Ed Reulbach	2.28
Will White	2.28
Jim Scott	2.30
Ed Plank	2.35
Larry Corcoran	2.36
Ed Cicotte	2.38
Ed Killian	2.38
George McQuillan	2.38
Doc White	2.38
Nap Rucker	2.42
Terry Larkin	2.43
Jim McCormick	2.43
Jeff Tesreau	2.43

Runs Scored

Ty Cobb	2,246
Hank Aaron	2,174
Babe Ruth	2,174
Pete Rose	2,165

Willie Mays	2,062
Cap Anson	1,996
Stan Musial	1,949
Lou Gehrig	1,888
Tris Speaker	1,882
Mel Ott	1,859
Frank Robinson	1,829
Rickey Henderson	1,829
Eddie Collins	1,821
Carl Yastrzemski	1,816
Ted Williams	1,798
Charlie Gehringer	1,774
Jimmie Foxx	1,751
Honus Wagner	1,736
Jim O'Rourke	1,729
Jesse Burkett	1,720
Willie Keeler	1,719
Billy Hamilton	1,690
Bid McPhee	1,678
Mickey Mantle	1,677
Dave Winfield	1,669
Joe Morgan	1,650
Paul Molitor	1,644

Strikeouts, Pitching

Nolan Ryan	5,714
Steve Carlton	4,136
Bert Blyleven	3,701
Tom Seaver	3,640
Don Sutton	3,574
Gaylord Perry	3,534
Walter Johnson	3,509
Phil Niekro	3,342
Ferguson Jenkins	3,192
Bob Gibson	3,117
Jim Bunning	2,855
Mickey Lolich	2,832
Cy Young	2,803
Frank Tanana	2,773
Roger Clemens	2,590
Warren Spahn	2,583
Bob Feller	2,581
Tim Keefe	2,560
Jerry Koosman	2,556
Christy Mathewson	2,502

Home Runs (350 or More)

Hank Aaron	755
Babe Ruth	714
Willie Mays	660
Frank Robinson	586

Harmon Killebrew	573
Reggie Jackson	563
Mike Schmidt	548
Mickey Mantle	536
Jimmie Foxx	534
Willie McCovey	521
Ted Williams	521
Eddie Mathews	512
Ernie Banks	512
Mel Ott	511
Eddie Murray	501
Lou Gehrig	493
Stan Musial	475
Willie Stargell	475
Dave Winfield	465
Carl Yastrzemski	452
Dave Kingman	442
Andre Dawson	438
Billy Williams	426
Darrell Evans	414
Duke Snider	407
Al Kaline	399
Dale Murphy	398
Graig Nettles	390
Johnny Bench	389
Dwight Evans	385
Frank Howard	382
Jim Rice	382
Tony Perez	379
Orlando Cepeda	379
Norm Cash	377
Carlton Fisk	376
Rocky Colavito	374
Gil Hodges	370
Ralph Kiner	369
Joe DiMaggio	361
Johnny Mize	359
Yogi Berra	358
Joe Carter	357
Lee May	354
Cal Ripken	353

Shutouts

Walter Johnson	110
Grover Alexander	90
Christy Mathewson	79
Cy Young	76
Ed Plank	69
Warren Spahn	63
Nolan Ryan	61
Tom Seaver	61
Bert Blyleven	60

Don Sutton	58
Pud Galvin	57
Ed Walsh	57
Bob Gibson	56
Mordecai Brown	55
Steve Carlton	55
Jim Palmer	53
Gaylord Perry	53
Juan Marichal	52

Strikeouts, Batting

Reggie Jackson	2,597
Willie Stargell	1,936
Mike Schmidt	1,883
Tony Perez	1,867
Dave Kingman	1,816
Bobby Bonds	1,757
Dale Murphy	1,748
Lou Brock	1,730
Mickey Mantle	1,710
Harmon Killebrew	1,699
Dwight Evans	1,697
Dave Winfield	1,686
Lee May	1,570
Dick Allen	1,556
Willie McCovey	1,550
Dave Parker	1,537
Frank Robinson	1,532
Lance Parrish	1,527
Willie Mays	1,526

Walks

Babe Ruth	2,056
Ted Williams	2,019
Joe Morgan	1,865
Carl Yastrzemski	1,845
Mickey Mantle	1,733
Mel Ott	1,708
Rickey Henderson	1,675
Eddie Yost	1,614
Darrell Evans	1,605
Stan Musial	1,599
Pete Rose	1,566
Harmon Killebrew	1,559
Lou Gehrig	1,508
Mike Schmidt	1,507
Eddie Collins	1,499
Willie Mays	1,464
Jimmie Foxx	1,452
Eddie Mathews	1,444
Frank Robinson	1,420
Hank Aaron	1,402

RECORD OF WORLD SERIES GAMES

(Through 1996)

Figures in parentheses for winning pitchers (WP) and losing pitchers (LP) indicate the game number in the series.

1903—Boston A.L. 5 (Jimmy Collins); Pittsburgh N.L. 3 (Fred Clarke). WP—Bos.: Dinneen (2, 6, 8), Young (5, 7); Pitts.: Phillippe (1, 3, 4). LP—Bos.: Young (1), Hughes (3), Dinneen (4); Pitts.: Leever (2, 6), Kennedy (5), Phillippe (7, 8).

1904—No series.

1905—New York N.L. 4 (John J. McGraw); Philadelphia A.L. 1 (Connie Mack). WP—N.Y.: Mathewson (1, 3, 5); McGinnity (4); Phila.: Bender (2). LP—N.Y.: McGinnity (2); Phila.: Plank (1, 4), Coakley (3), Bender (5).

1906—Chicago A.L. 4 (Fielder Jones); Chicago N.L. 2 (Frank Chance). WP—Chi.: A.L.: Altrock (1), Walsh (3, 5), White (6); N.L.: Reulbach (2), Brown (4). LP—Chi.: A.L.: White (2), Altrock. (4); Chi.: N.L.: Brown (1, 6), Pfeister (3, 5).

1907—Chicago N.L. 4 (Frank Chance); Detroit A.L. 0 (Hugh Jennings. First game tied 3–3, 12 innings. WP—Pfeister (2), Reulbach (3), Overall (4), Brown (5). LP—Mullin (2, 5), Siever (3), Donovan (4).

1908—Chicago N.L. 4 (Frank Chance); Detroit A.L. 1 (Hugh Jennings). WP—Chi.: Brown (1, 4), Overall (2, 5); Det.: Mullin (3). LP—Chi.: Pfeister (3); Det.: Summers (1, 4), Donovan (2, 5).

1909—Pittsburgh N.L. 4 (Fred Clarke); Detroit A.L. 3 (Hugh Jennings). WP—Pitts.: Adams (1, 5, 7), Maddox (3); Det.: Donovan (2), Mullin (4, 6). LP—Pitts.: Camnitz (2), Leifield (4), Willis (6); Det.: Mullin (1), Summers (3, 5), Donovan (7).

1910—Philadelphia A.L. 4 (Connie Mack); Chicago N.L. 1 (Frank Chance). WP—Phila.: Bender (1), Coombs (2, 3, 5); Chi.: Brown (4). LP—Phila.: Bender (4); Chi.: Overall (1), Brown (2, 5), McIntyre (3).

1911—Philadelphia A.L. 4 (Connie Mack); New York N.L. 2 (John J. McGraw). WP—Phila.: Plank (2), Coombs (3), Bender (4, 6); N.Y.: Mathewson (1), Crandall (5). LP—Phila.: Bender (1), Plank (5); N.Y.: Marquard (2), Mathewson (3, 4), Ames (6).

1912—Boston A.L. 4 (J. Garland Stahl); New York N.L. 3 (John J. McGraw). Second game tied, 6–6, 11 innings. WP—Bos.: Wood (1, 4, 8), Bedient (5); N.Y.: Marquard (3, 6), Tesreau (7). LP—Bos.: O'Brien (2), Wood (7); N.Y.: Tesreau (1, 4), Mathewson (5, 8).

1913—Philadelphia A.L. 4 (Connie Mack); New York N.L. 1 (John J. McGraw). WP—Phila.: Bender (1, 4), Bush (2), Plank (5); N.Y.: Mathewson (2); LP—Phila.: Plank (2); N.Y.: Marquard (1), Tesreau (3), Demaree (4), Mathewson (5).

1914—Boston N.L. 4 (George Stallings); Philadelphia A.L. 0 (Connie Mack). WP—Rudolph (1, 4), James (2, 3). LP—Bender (1), Plank (2), Bush (3), Shawkey (4).

1915—Boston A.L. 4 (Bill Carrigan); Philadelphia N.L. 1 (Pat Moran). WP—Bos.: Foster (2, 5), Leonard (3), Shore (4); Phila.: Alexander (1). LP—Bos.: Shore (1); Phila.: Mayer (2), Alexander (3), Chalmers (4), Rixey (5).

1916—Boston A.L. 4 (Bill Carrigan); Brooklyn N.L. 1 (Wilbert Robinson). WP—Bos.: Shore (1, 5), Ruth (2), Leonard (4); Bklyn.: Coombs (3). LP—Bos.: Mays (3); Bklyn.: Marquard (1, 4), Smith (2), Pfeffer (5).

1917—Chicago A.L. 4 (Clarence Rowland); New York N.L. 2 (John J. McGraw). WP—Chi.: Cicotte (1), Faber (2, 5, 6); N.Y.: Benton (3), Schupp (4). LP—Chi.: Cicotte (3), Faber (4); N.Y.: Sallee (1, 5), Anderson (2), Benton (6).

1918—Boston A.L. 4 (Ed Barrow); Chicago N.L. 2 (Fred Mitchell). WP—Bos.: Ruth (1, 4), Mays (3, 6); Chi.: Tyler (2), Vaughn (5). LP—Bos.: Bush (2), Jones (5); Chi.: Vaughn (1, 3), Douglas (4), Tyler (6).

1919—Cincinnati N.L. 5 (Pat Moran); Chicago A.L. 3 (William Gleason). WP—Cin.: Ruether (1), Sallee (2), Ring (4), Eller (5, 8); Chi.: Kerr (3, 6), Cicotte (7). LP—Cin.: Fisher (3), Ring (6), Sallee (7); Chi.: Cicotte (1, 4), Williams (2, 5, 8).

1920—Cleveland A.L. 5 (Tris Speaker); Brooklyn N.L. 2 (Wilbert Robinson). WP—Cleve.: Coveleski (1, 4, 7), Bagby (5), Mails (6); Bklyn.: Grimes (2), Smith (3). LP—Cleve.: Bagby (2), Caldwell (3). Bklyn.: Marquard (1), Cadore (4), Grimes (5, 7), Smith (6).

1921—New York N.L. 5 (John J. McGraw); New York A.L. 3 (Miller Huggins). WP—N.Y. N.L.: Barnes (3, 6), Douglas (4, 7), Nehf (8); N.Y. A.L.: Mays (1), Hoyt (2, 5). LP—N.Y. N.L.: Nehf (2, 5), Douglas (1, 7). N.Y. A.L.: Quinn (3), Mays (4, 7), Shawkey (6), Hoyt (8).

1922—New York N.L. 4 (John J. McGraw); New York A.L. 0 (Miller Huggins). Second game tied 3–3, 10 innings. WP—Ryan (1), Scott (3), McQuillan (4), Nehf (5); LP—Bush (1, 5), Hoyt (3), Mays (4).

1923—New York A.L. 4 (Miller Huggins); New York N.L. 2 (John J. McGraw). WP—N.Y. A.L.: Pennock (2, 6), Shawkey (4), Bush (5); N.Y. N.L.: Ryan (1), Nehf (3). LP—N.Y. A.L.: Bush (1), Jones (2), Scott (5), Bentley (5), Nehf (6).

1924—Washington A.L. 4 (Bucky Harris); New York N.L. 3 (John J. McGraw). WP—Wash.: Zachary (2, 6), Mogridge (4), Johnson (7); N.Y.: Nehf (1), McQuillan (3), Bentley (5). LP—Wash.: Johnson (1, 5), Marberry (3); N.Y.: Bentley (2, 7), Barnes (4), Nehf (6).

1925—Pittsburgh N.L. 4 (Bill McKechnie); Washington A.L. 3 (Bucky Harris). WP—Pitts.: Aldridge (2, 5), Kremer (6, 7); Wash.: Johnson (1, 4), Ferguson (3). LP—Pitts.: Meadows (1), Kremer (3), Yde (4); Wash.: Coveleski (2, 5), Ferguson (6), Johnson (7).

1926—St. Louis N.L. 4 (Rogers Hornsby); New York A.L. 3 (Miller Huggins). WP—St. L.: Alexander (2, 6), Haines (3, 7); N.Y.: Pennock (1, 5), Hoyt (4). LP—St. L.: Sherdel (1, 5), Reinhart (4); N.Y.: Shocker (2), Ruether (3), Shawkey (6), Hoyt (7).

1927—New York A.L. 4 (Miller Huggins); Pittsburgh N.L. 0 (Donie Bush). WP—Hoyt (1), Pipgras (2), Pennock (3), Moore (4). LP—Kremer (1), Aldridge (2), Meadows (3), Miljus (4).

1928—New York A.L. 4 (Miller Huggins); St. Louis N.L. 0 (Bill McKechnie). WP—Hoyt (1, 4), Pipgras (2), Zachary (3). LP—Sherdel (1, 4), Alexander (2), Haines (3).

1929—Philadelphia A.L. 4 (Connie Mack); Chicago N.L. 1 (Joe McCarthy). WP—Phila.: Ehmke (1), Earnshaw (2), Rommel (4), Walberg (5); Chi.: Bush (3). LP—Phila.: Earnshaw (3) Chi.: Root (1), Malone (2, 5), Blake (4).

1930—Philadelphia A.L. 4 (Connie Mack); St. Louis N.L. 2 (Gabby Street). WP—Phila.: Grove (1, 5), Earnshaw (2, 6); St. L.: Hallahan (3), Haines (4). LP—Phila.: Walberg (3), Grove (4); St. L.: Grimes (1, 5), Rhem (2), Hallahan (6).

1931—St. Louis N.L. 4 (Gabby Street); Philadelphia A.L. 3 (Connie Mack). WP—St. L.: Hallahan (2, 5), Grimes (3, 7); Phila.: Grove (1, 6), Earnshaw (4). LP—St. L.: Derringer (1, 6), Johnson (4); Phila.: Earnshaw (2, 7), Grove (3), Hoyt (5).

1932—New York A.L. (Joe McCarthy); Chicago N.L. 0 (Charles Grimm). WP—Ruffing (1), Gomez (2), Pipgras (3), Moore (4). LP—Bush (1), Warneke (3), Root (3), May (4).

1933—New York N.L. 4 (Bill Terry); Washington A.L. 1 (Joe Cronin). WP—N.Y.: Hubbell (1, 4), Schumacher (2), Luque (5); Wash.: Whitehill (3). LP—N.Y.: Fitzsimmons (3); Wash.: Stewart (1), Crowder (2), Weaver (4), Russell (5).

1934—St. Louis N.L. 4 (Frank Frisch); Detroit A.L. 3 (Mickey Cochrane). WP—St. L.: J. Dean (1, 7), P. Dean (3, 6); Det.: Rowe (2), Auker (4), Bridges (5). LP—St. L.: W. Walker (2, 4), J. Dean (5); Det.: Crowder (1), Bridges (3), Rowe (6), Auker (7).

1935—Detroit A.L. 4 (Mickey Cochrane); Chicago N.L. 2 (Charles Grimm). WP—Det.: Bridges (2, 6), Rowe (3), Crowder (4); Chi.: Warneke (1, 5); LP—Det.: Rowe (1, 5), Chi.: Root (2), French (3, 6), Carleton (4).

1936—New York A.L. 4 (Joe McCarthy); New York N.L. 2 (Bill Terry). WP—N.Y. A.L.: Gomez (2, 6), Hadley (3), Pearson (4); N.Y. N.L.: Hubbell (1), Schumacher (5); LP—N.Y. A.L.: Ruffing (1), Malone (5); N.Y. N.L.: Schumacher (2), Fitzsimmons (3, 6), Hubbell (4).

1937—New York A.L. 4 (Joe McCarthy); New York N.L. 1 (Bill Terry). WP—N.Y. A.L.: Gomez (1, 5), Ruffing (2), Pearson (3); N.Y. N.L.: Hubbell (4). LP—N.Y. A.L.: Hadley (4); N.Y. N.L.: Hubbell (1), Melton (2, 5), Schumacher (3).

1938—New York A.L. 4 (Joe McCarthy); Chicago N.L. 0 (Gabby Hartnett). WP—Ruffing (1, 4), Gomez (2), Pearson (3) LP—Lee (1, 4), Dean (2), Bryant (3).

1939—New York A.L. 4 (Joe McCarthy); Cincinnati N.L. 0 (Bill McKechnie). WP—Ruffing (1), Pearson (2), Hadley (3), Murphy (4). LP—Derringer (1), Walters (2, 4), Thompson (3).

1940—Cincinnati N.L. 4 (Bill McKechnie); Detroit A.L. 3 (Del Baker). WP—Cin.: Walters (2, 6), Derringer (4, 7); Det.: Newsom (1, 5), Bridges (3). LP—Cin.: Derringer (1), Turner (3), Thompson (5); Det.: Rowe (2, 6), Trout (4), Newsom (7).

1941—New York A.L. 4 (Joe McCarthy); Brooklyn N.L. 1 (Leo Durocher). WP—N.Y.: Ruffing (1), Russo (3), Murphy (4), Bonham (5); Bklyn: Wyatt (2). LP—N.Y.: Chandler (2); Bklyn: Davis (1), Casey (3, 4), Wyatt (5).

1942—St. Louis N.L. 4 (Billy Southworth); New York A.L. 1 (Joe McCarthy). WP—St. L.: Beazley (2, 5), White (3), Lanier (4); N.Y.: Ruffing (1). LP—St. L.: Cooper (1); N.Y.: Bonham (2), Chandler (3), Donald (4), Ruffing (5).

1943—New York A.L. 4 (Joe McCarthy); St. Louis N.L. 1 (Billy Southworth). WP—N.Y.: Chandler (1, 5), Borowy (3), Russo (4); St. L.: Cooper (2). LP—N.Y.: Bonham (2); St. L.: Lanier (1), Brazle (3), Brecheen (4), Cooper (5).

1944—St. Louis N.L. 4 (Billy Southworth); St. Louis A.L. 2 (Luke Sewell). WP—St. L. N.L.: Donnelly (2), Brecheen (4), Cooper (5), Lanier (6); St. L. A.L.: Galehouse (1), Kramer (3). LP—St. L. N.L.: Cooper (1), Wilks (3); St. L. A.L.: Muncrief (2), Jakucki (4), Galehouse (5), Potter (6).

1945—Detroit A.L. 4 (Steve O'Neill); Chicago N.L. 3 (Charles Grimm). WP—Det.: Trucks (2), Trout (4), Newhouser (5, 7); Chi.: Borowy (1, 6), Passeau (3). LP—Det.: Newhouser (1), Overmire (3), Trout (6); Chi.: Wyse (2), Prim (4), Borowy (5, 7).

1946—St. Louis N.L. 4 (Eddie Dyer); Boston A.L. 3 (Joe Cronin). WP—St. L.: Brecheen (2, 6, 7), Munger (4); Bos.: Johnson (1), Ferriss (3), Dobson (5). LP—St. L.: Pollet (1), Dickson (3), Brazle (5); Bos.: Harris (2, 6), Hughson (4), Klinger (7).

1947—New York A.L. 4 (Bucky Harris); Brooklyn N.L. 3 (Burt Shotton). WP—N.Y.: Shea (1, 5), Reynolds (2), Page (7); Bklyn.: Casey (3, 4), Branca (6). LP—N.Y.: Newsom (3), Bevens (4), Page (6); Bklyn.: Branca (1), Lombardi (2), Barney (5), Gregg (7).

1948—Cleveland A.L. 4 (Lou Boudreau); Boston N.L. 2 (Billy Southworth). WP—Cleve.: Lemon (2, 6), Bearden (3), Gromek (4); Bos.: Sain (1), Spahn (5). LP—Cleve.: Feller (1, 5); Bos.: Spahn (2), Bickford (3), Sain (4), Voiselle (6).

1949—New York A.L. 4 (Casey Stengel); Brooklyn N.L. 1 (Burt Shotton). WP—N.Y.: Reynolds (1), Page (3), Lopat (4), Raschi (5); Bklyn.: Roe (2). LP—N.Y.: Raschi (2); Bklyn.: Newcombe (1, 4), Branca (3), Barney (5).

1950—New York A.L. 4 (Casey Stengel); Philadelphia N.L. 0 (Eddie Sawyer). WP—Raschi (1), Reynolds (2), Ferrick

(3), Ford (4). LP—Konstanty (1), Roberts (2), Meyer (3), Miller (4).

1951—New York A.L. 4 (Casey Stengel); New York N.L. 2 (Leo Durocher). WP—N.Y. A.L.: Lopat (2, 5), Reynolds (4), Raschi (6); N.Y. N.L.: Koslo (1), Hearn (3). LP—N.Y. A.L.: Reynolds (1), Raschi (3); N.Y. N.L.: Jansen (2, 5), Maglie (4), Koslo (6).

1952—New York A.L. 4 (Casey Stengel); Brooklyn N.L. 3 (Chuck Dressen). WP—N.Y.: Raschi (2, 6), Reynolds (4, 7); Bklyn.: Black (1), Roe (3), Erskine (5). LP—N.Y.: Reynolds (1), Lopat (3), Sain (5); Bklyn.: Erskine (2), Black (4, 7), Loes (6).

1953—New York A.L. 4 (Casey Stengel); Brooklyn N.L. 2 (Chuck Dressen). WP—N.Y.: Sain (1), Lopat (2), McDonald (5), Reynolds (6); Bklyn.: Erskine (3), Loes (4). LP—N.Y.: Raschi (3), Ford (4); Bklyn.: Labine (1, 6), Roe (2), Podres (5).

1954—New York N.L. 4 (Leo Durocher); Cleveland A.L. 0 (Al Lopez). WP—Grissom (1), Antonelli (2), Gomez (3), Liddie (4). LP—Lemon (1, 4), Wynn (2), Garcia (3).

1955—Brooklyn N.L. 4 (Walter Alston); New York A.L. 3 (Casey Stengel). WP—Bklyn.: Podres (3, 7), Labine (4), Craig (5); N.Y.: Ford (1, 6), Byrne (2). LP—Bklyn.: Newcombe (1), Loes (2), Spooner (6); N.Y.: Turley (3), Larsen (4), Grim (5), Byrne (7).

1956—New York A.L. 4 (Casey Stengel); Brooklyn N.L. 3 (Walter Alston). WP—N.Y.: Ford (3), Sturdivant (4), Larsen (5), Kucks (7); Bklyn.: Maglie (1), Bessent (2), Labine (6). LP—N.Y.: Ford (1), Morgan (2), Turley (6); Bklyn.: Craig (3), Erskine (4), Maglie (5), Newcombe (7).

1957—Milwaukee N.L. 4 (Fred Haney); New York A.L. 3 (Casey Stengel). WP—Mil.: Burdette (2, 5, 7), Spahn (4); N.Y.: Ford (1), Larsen (3), Turley (6). LP—Mil.: Spahn (1), Buhl (3), Johnson (6); N.Y.: Shantz (2), Grim (4), Ford (5), Larsen (7).

1958—New York A.L. 4 (Casey Stengel); Milwaukee N.L. 3 (Fred Haney). WP—N.Y.: Larsen (3), Turley (5, 7), Duren (6); Mil.: Spahn (1, 4), Burdette (2). LP—N.Y.: Duren (1), Turley (2), Ford (4); Mil.: Rush (3), Burdette (5, 7), Spahn (6).

1959—Los Angeles N.L. 4 (Walter Alston); Chicago A.L. 2 (Al Lopez). WP—L.A.: Podres (2), Drysdale (3), Sherry (4, 6); Chi.: Wynn (1), Shaw (5). LP—L.A.: Craig (1), Koufax (5); Chi.: Shaw (2), Donovan (3), Staley (4), Wynn (6).

1960—Pittsburgh N.L. 4 (Danny Murtaugh); New York A.L. 3 (Casey Stengel). WP—Pitts.: Law (1, 4), Haddix (5, 7); N.Y.: Turley (2), Ford (3, 6). LP—Pitts.: Friend (2, 6), Mizell (3); N.Y.: Ditmar (1, 5), Terry (4, 7).

1961—New York A.L. 4 (Ralph Houk); Cincinnati N.L. 1 (Fred Hutchinson). WP—N.Y.: Ford (1, 4), Arroyo (3), Daley (5); Cin.: Jay (2). LP—N.Y.: Terry (2); Cin.: O'Toole (1, 4), Purkey (3), Jay (5).

1962—New York A.L. 4 (Ralph Houk); San Francisco N.L. 3 (Al Dark). WP—N.Y.: Ford (1), Stafford (3), Terry (5, 7); S.F. Sanford (2), Larsen (4), Pierce (6). LP—N.Y.: Terry (2), Coates (4), Ford (6); S.F.: O'Dell (1), Pierce (3), Sanford (5, 7).

1963—Los Angeles N.L. 4 (Walter Alston); New York A.L. 0 (Ralph Houk). WP—Koufax (1, 4), Podres (2), Drysdale (3). LP—Ford (1, 4), Downing (2), Bouton (3).

1964—St. Louis N.L. 4 (Johnny Keane); New York A.L. 3 (Yogi Berra). WP—St. L.: Sadecki (1), Craig (4), Gibson (5, 7); N.Y.: Stottlemyre (2), Bouton (3, 6). LP—St. L.: Gibson (2), Schultz (3), Simmons (6); N.Y.: Ford (1), Downing (4), Mikkelsen (5), Stottlemyre (7).

1965—Los Angeles N.L. 4 (Walter Alston); Minnesota A.L. 3 (Sam Mele). WP—L.A.: Osteen (3), Drysdale (4), Koufax (5, 7); Minn.: Grant (1, 6), Kaat (2). LP—L.A.: Drysdale (1), Koufax (2), Osteen (6); Minn.: Pascual (3), Grant (4), Kaat (5, 7).

1966—Baltimore A.L. 4 (Hank Bauer); Los Angeles N.L. 0 (Walter Alston). WP—Drabowsky (1), Palmer (2), Bunker

(3), McNally (4). LP—Drysdale (1, 4), Koufax (2), Osteen (3).

1967—St. Louis N.L. 4 (Red Schoendienst); Boston A.L. 3 (Dick Williams). WP—St. L.: Gibson (1, 4, 7), Briles (3); Bos.: Lonborg (2, 5); Wyatt (6). LP—St. L.: Hughes (2), Carlton (5), Lamabe (6); Bos.: Santiago (1, 4), Bell (3), Lonborg (7).

1968—Detroit A.L. 4 (Mayo Smith); St. Louis N.L. 3 (Red Schoendienst). WP—Det.: Lolich (2, 5, 7), McLain (6); St. L.: Gibson (1, 4), Washburn (3). LP—Det.: McLain (1, 4), Wilson (3); St. L.: Briles (2), Hoerner (5), Washburn (6), Gibson (7).

1969—New York N.L. 4 (Gil Hodges); Baltimore A.L. 1 (Earl Weaver). WP—N.Y.: Koosman (2, 5), Gentry (3), Seaver (4); Balt.: Cuellar (1). LP—N.Y.: Seaver (1); Balt.: McNally (2), Palmer (3), Hall (4), Watt (5).

1970—Baltimore A.L. 4 (Earl Weaver); Cincinnati N.L. 1 (Sparky Anderson) 1. WP—Balt.: Palmer (1), Phoebus (2), McNally (3), Cuellar (5); Cin.: Carroll (4). LP—Cin.: Nolan (1), Wilcox (3), Cloninger (3), Merritt (5); Balt.: Watt (4).

1971—Pittsburgh N.L. 4 (Danny Murtaugh); Baltimore A.L. 3 (Earl Weaver). WP—Pitts.: Blass (3, 7), Kison (4), Briles (5); Balt.: McNally (1, 6), Palmer (2). LP—Pitts.: Ellis (1), R. Johnson (2), Miller (6); Balt.: Cuellar (3, 7), Watt (4) McNally (5).

1972—Oakland A.L. 4 (Dick Williams); Cincinnati N.L. (Sparky Anderson) 3. WP—Oakland: Holtzman (1), Hunter (2, 7), Fingers (4); Cincinnati: Billingham (3), Grimsley (5, 6). LP—Oakland: Odom (3), Fingers (5), Blue (6); Cincinnati: Nolan (1), Grimsley (2), Carroll (4), Borbon (7).

1973—Oakland A.L. 4 (Dick Williams): New York N.L. 3 (Yogi Berra). WP—Oakland: Holtzman (1, 7), Lindblad (3), Hunter (6). New York: McGraw (2), Matlack (4), Koosman (5). LP—Oakland: Fingers (4), Holtzman (4), Blue (5). New York: Matlack (1, 7) Parker (3), Seaver (6).

1974—Oakland A.L. 4 (Al Dark); Los Angeles N.L. 1 (Walter Alston). WP—Oakland: Fingers (1, 4), Hunter (3), Holtzman (4), Odom (5). Los Angeles: Sutton (2). LP—Oakland: Blue (2), Los Angeles: Messersmith (1, 4), Downing (3), Marshall (5).

1975—Cincinnati N.L. 4 (Sparky Anderson); Boston A.L. 3 (Darrell Johnson). WP—Cincinnati: Eastwick (2, 3), Gullett (5), Carroll (7); Boston: Tiant (1, 4), Wise (6). LP—Cincinnati: Gullett (1), Norman (4), Darcy (6); Boston: Drago (3), Willoughby (3), Cleveland (5), Burton (7).

1976—Cincinnati N.L. 4 (Sparky Anderson); New York A.L. 0 (Billy Martin). WP—Gullett (1), Billingham (2), Zachry (3), Nolan (4). LP—Alexander (1), Hunter (2), Ellis (3), Figueroa (4).

1977—New York A.L. 4 (Billy Martin); Los Angeles N.L. 2 (Tom Lasorda). WP—New York: Lyle (1), Torrez (3, 6), Guidry (4); Los Angeles: Hooton (2), Sutton (5). LP—New York: Hunter (2), Gullett (5); Los Angeles: Rhoden (1), John (3), Rau (4), Hooton (6).

1978—New York A.L. 4 (Bob Lemon), Los Angeles N.L. 2 (Tom Lasorda); WP—New York: Guidry (3), Gossage (4); Beattie (5), Hunter (6); Los Angeles: John (1), Hooton (2). LP—New York: Figueroa (1), Hunter (4); Los Angeles: Sutton (3, 6), Welch (4), Hooton (5).

1979—Pittsburgh N.L. 4 (Chuck Tanner), Baltimore A.L. 3 (Earl Weaver); WP—Pittsburgh: D. Robinson (2), Blyleven (5), Candelaria (6), Jackson (7); Baltimore: Flanagan (1), McGregor (3), Stoddard (4). LP—Pittsburgh: Kison (1), Candelaria (3), Tekulve (4); Baltimore: Stanhouse (2), Flanagan (5), Palmer (6), McGregor (7).

1980—Philadelphia N.L. 4 (Dallas Green), Kansas City A.L. 2 (Jim Frey); WP—Philadelphia: Walk (1), Carlton (2), McGraw (5), Carlton (6); Kansas City: Quisenberry (3), Leonard (4). LP—Philadelphia: McGraw (3), Christenson (4); Kansas City: Leonard (1), Quisenberry (2), Quisenberry (5), Gale (6).

1981—Los Angeles N.L. 4 (Tom Lasorda), New York A.L. 2 (Bob Lemon); WP—Los Angeles: Valenzuela (3), Howe (4), Reuss (5), Hooton (6); New York: Guidry (1), John (2). LP—Los Angeles: Reuss (1), Hooton (2); New York: Frazier (3), Frazier (4), Guidry (5), Frazier (6).

1982—St. Louis N.L. 4 (Whitey Herzog), Milwaukee A.L. 3 (Harvey Kuenn); WP—St. Louis: Sutter (2), Andujar (3), Stuper (6), Andujar (7). Milwaukee: Caldwell (1), Slaton (4), Caldwell (5). LP—St. Louis: Forsch (1), Bair (4), Forsch (5). Milwaukee: McClure (2), Vuckovich (3), Sutton (6), McClure (7).

1983—Baltimore A.L. 4 (Joe Altobelli), Philadelphia N.L. 1 (Paul Owens); WP—Baltimore: Boddicker (2), Palmer (3), Davis (4), McGregor (5). Philadelphia: Denny (1).

1984—Detroit A.L. 4 (Sparky Anderson), San Diego N.L. 1 (Dick Williams); WP—Det.: Morris (1, 4), Wilcox (3), Lopez (5), San Diego: Hawkins (2). LP—Det.: Petry (2), San Diego: Thurmond (1), Lollar (3), Show (4), Hawkins (5).

1985—Kansas City A.L. 4 (Dick Howser), St. Louis N.L. 3 (Whitey Herzog); WP—KC: Saberhagen (3,7) Quisenberry (6), Jackson (5). St. Louis: Tudor (1,4) Dayley (2). LP—KC: Jackson (1), Leibrandt (2), Black (4); St. Louis: Andujar (3), Forsch (5), Worrell (6), Tudor (7).

1986—New York N.L. 4 (Dave Johnson); Boston A.L. (John McNamara) 3 WP—N.Y.—Ojeda (3), Darling (4), Aguilera (6), McDowell (7), Bos: Hurst (1), (5), Crawford (2). LP—N.Y. Darling (1), Gooden (2, 5).

1987—Minnesota, A.L. 4 (Tom Kelly); St. Louis N.L. (Whitey Herzog) 3. WP—Minn. Viola (1, 7), Blyleven (2), Schatzeder (6), St. Louis: Tudor (3), Forsch (4), Cox (5). LP—Minn. Berenguer (3), Viola (4), Blyleven (5); St. Louis: Magrane (1), Cox (2, 7), Tudor (6).

1988—Los Angeles N.L. 4 (Tommy Lasorda); Oakland A.L. (Tony LaRussa) 1. WP—Los Angeles: Hershiser (2, 5), Pena (1), Belcher (3); Oakland: Honeycutt (3). LP—Los Angeles: Howell (3); Oakland: Davis (2, 5), Eckersley (1), Stewart (4).

1989—Oakland, A.L. 4 (Tony LaRussa); San Francisco N.L. 0 (Roger Craig). WP—Oakland: Dave Stewart (1, 3), Mike Moore (2, 4). LP—San Francisco: Scott Garrelts (1, 3), Don Robinson (2), Rick Reuschel (2).

1990—Cincinnati N.L. 4 (Lou Piniella); Oakland A.L. 0 (Tony LaRussa). WP—Cincinnati: Jose Rijo (1, 4), Rob Dibble (2), Tom Browning (3). LP—Oakland: Dave Stewart (1, 4), Dennis Eckersley (2), Mike Moore (3).

1991—Minnesota, A.L. 4 (Tom Kelly); Atlanta, N.L. 3 (Bobby Cox). WP—Minnesota: Morris (1,7), Tapani (2), Aguilera (6). Atlanta: Clancy (3), Stanton (2), Glavine (5). LP—Minnesota: Aguilera (3), Gurhtie (4), Tapani (5). Atlanta: Leibrandt (1, 6), Glavine (2), Pena (7).

1992—Toronto, A.L. 4 (Cito Gaston); Atlanta, N.L. 2 (Bobby Cox). WP—Toronto: Ward (2, 3), Key (4, 6). Atlanta: Glavine (1), Smoltz (5). LP—Toronto: Morris (1, 5). Atlanta: Leibrandt (2), Reardon (2), Avery (3), Glavine (4).

1993—Toronto, A.L. 4 (Cito Gaston); Philadelphia, N.L. 2 (Jim Fregosi). WP—Toronto: Leiter (1), Hentgen (3), Castillo (4), Ward (6). Philadelphia: Mullholland (2), Schilling (5). LP—Toronto: Stewart (2), Guzman (3). Philadelphia: Schilling (1), Jackson (3), Williams (4, 6).

1994—World Series cancelled due to players' strike.

1995—Atlanta, N.L. 4 (Bobby Cox); Cleveland, A.L. 2 (Mike Hargrove). WP—Atlanta: Maddux (1), Glavine (2,6), Avery (4). Cleveland: Mesa (3), Hershiser (5). LP—Atlanta: Pena (3), Maddux (5). Cleveland: Hershiser (1), Martinez (2), Hill (4), Poole (6).

1996—New York, A.L. 4 (Joe Torre); Atlanta, N.L. 2 (Bobby Cox). WP—New York: Cone (3), Lloyd (4), Pettitte (5), Key (6). Atlanta: Smoltz (3), Maddux (2). LP—New York: Pettitte (1), Key (2). Atlanta: Glavine (3), Avery (4), Smoltz (5), Maddux (6).

WORLD SERIES CLUB STANDING

(Through 1996)

	Series	Won	Lost	Pct.		Series	Won	Lost	Pct.
Toronto (A)	2	2	0	1.000	Detroit (A)	9	4	5	.444
Pittsburgh (N)	7	5	2	.714	New York (N-Giants)	14	5	9	.357
New York (A)	34	23	11	.676	Washington (A)	3	1	2	.333
Oakland (A)	6	4	2	.667	Philadelphia (N)	5	1	4	.200
Cleveland (A)	4	2	2	.500	Chicago (N)	10	2	8	.200
Minnesota (A)	3	2	1	.667	Brooklyn (N)	9	1	8	.111
New York (N-Mets)	3	2	1	.667	St. Louis (A)	1	0	1	.000
Philadelphia (A)	8	5	3	.625	San Francisco (N)	2	0	2	.000
St. Louis (N)	15	9	6	.600	Milwaukee (A)	1	0	1	.000
Boston (A)	9	5	4	.556	San Diego (N)	1	0	1	.000
Los Angeles (N)	9	5	4	.556	Atlanta (N)	4	1	3	.250
Cincinnati (N)	9	5	4	.556					
Milwaukee (N)	2	1	1	.500	**Recapitulation**				
Boston (N)	2	1	1	.500					
Chicago (A)	4	2	2	.500					Won
Baltimore (A)	6	3	3	.500	American League				53
Kansas City (A)	2	1	1	.500	National League				37

LIFETIME WORLD SERIES RECORDS

(Through 1996)

Most hits—71, Yogi Berra, New York A.L., 1947, 1949–53, 1955–58, 1960–63.

Most runs—42, Mickey Mantle, New York A.L., 1951–53, 1955–58, 1960–64.

Most runs batted in—40, Mickey Mantle, New York A.L., 1951–53, 1955–58, 1960–64.

Most home runs—18, Mickey Mantle, New York A.L., 1951–53, 1955–58, 1960–64.

Most bases on balls—43, Mickey Mantle, New York A.L., 1951–53, 1955–58, 1960–64.

Most strikeouts—54, Mickey Mantle, New York A.L., 1951–53, 1955–58, 1960–64.

Most stolen bases—14, Eddie Collins, Philadelphia A.L. 1910–11, 13–14; Chicago A.L., 1917, 1919. Lou Brock, St. Louis N.L., 1964, 67–68.

Most victories, pitcher—10, Whitey Ford, New York A.L., 1950, 1953, 1955–58, 1960–64.

Most times member of winning team—10, Yogi Berra, New York A.L., 1947, 1949–53, 1956, 1961–62.

Most victories, no defeats—6, Vernon Gomez, New York A.L., 1932, 1936(2), 1937(2), 1938.

Most shutouts—4, Christy Mathewson, New York N.L., 1905 (3), 1913.

Most innings pitched—146, Whitey Ford, New York A.L., 1950, 1953, 1955–58, 1960–1964

Most consecutive scoreless innings—33⅔, Whitey Ford, New York A.L., 1960 (18), 1961 (14), 1962 (1⅔).

Most strikeouts by pitcher—94, Whitey Ford, New York A.L., 1950, 1953, 1955–58, 1960–64.

SINGLE GAME AND SINGLE SERIES RECORDS

(Through 1996)

Most hits game—5, Paul Molitor, Milwaukee A.L., first game vs. St. Louis, N.L., 1982.

Most 4-hit games, series—2, Robin Yount, Milwaukee A.L., first and fifth games vs. St. Louis N.L., 1982.

Most hits inning—2, held by many players.

Most hits series—13 (7 games) Bobby Richardson, New York A.L., 1964; Lou Brock, St. Louis N.L., 1968; 12 (6 games) Billy Martin, New York A.L., 1953; 12 (8 games) Buck Herzog, New York N.L., 1912; Joe Jackson, Chicago A.L., 1919; 10 (4 games) Babe Ruth, New York A.L., 1928; 9 (5 games) held by 8 players.

Most home runs, series—5 (6 games) Reggie Jackson, New York A.L., 1977; 4 (7 games) Babe Ruth, New York A.L., 1926; Duke Snider, Brooklyn N.L., 1952, 1955; Hank Bauer, New York A.L., 1958; Gene Tenace, Oakland A.L., 1972; 4 (4 games) Lou Gehrig, New York A.L., 1928; 3 (6 games) Babe Ruth, New York A.L., 1923; Ted Kluszewski, Chicago A.L., 1959; 3 (5 games) Donn Clendenon, New York Mets N.L., 1969.

Most home runs, game—3, Babe Ruth, New York A.L., 1926 and 1928; Reggie Jackson, New York A.L., 1977.

Most strikeouts, series—12 (6 games) Willie Wilson, Kansas City A.L., 1980; 11 (7 games) Ed Mathews, Milwaukee N.L., 1958; Wayne Garrett, New York N.L., 1973; 10 (8 games) George Kelly, New York N.L., 1921; 9 (6 games) Jim Bottomley, St. Louis N.L., 1930; 9 (5 games) Carmelo Martinez, San Diego, N.L., 1984; Duke Snider, Brooklyn N.L., 1949; 7 (4 games) Bob Muesel, New York A.L., 1927.

Most stolen bases, game—3, Honus Wagner, Pittsburgh N.L., 1909; Willie Davis, Los Angeles N.L., 1965; Lou Brock, St. Louis N.L., 1967 and 1968.

Most strikeouts by pitcher, game—17, Bob Gibson, St. Louis N.L. 1968.

Most strikeouts by pitcher in succession—6, Horace Eller, Cincinnati N.L., 1919; Moe Drabowsky, Baltimore A.L., 1966.

Most strikeouts by pitcher, series—35 (7 games) Bob Gibson, St. Louis N.L., 1968; 28 (8 games) Bill Dinneen, Boston A.L., 1903; 23 (4 games) Sandy Koufax, Los Angeles, 1963; 20 (6 games) Chief Bender, Philadelphia A.L., 1911; 18 (5 games) Christy Mathewson, New York N.L., 1905.

Most bases on balls, series—11 (7 games) Babe Ruth, New York A.L., 1926; Gene Tenace, Oakland A.L., 1973; 9 (6 games) Willie Randolph, New York A.L., 1981; 7 (5 games) James Sheckard, Chicago N.L., 1910; Mickey Cochrane, Philadelphia N.L., 1929; Joe Gordon, New York A.L., 1941; 7 (4 games) Hank Thompson, New York N.L., 1954.

Most consecutive scoreless innings one series—27, Christy Mathewson, New York N.L., 1905.

AMERICAN LEAGUE HOME RUN CHAMPIONS

Year	Player, team	No.	Year	Player, team	No.	Year	Player, team	No.
1901	Nap Lajoie, Phila.	13	1935	Jimmy Foxx, Phila., and	36	1969	Harmon Killebrew, Minn.	49
1902	Ralph Seybold, Phila.	16		Hank Greenberg, Det.		1970	Frank Howard, Wash.	44
1903	Buck Freeman, Bost.	13	1936	Lou Gehrig, N.Y.	49	1971	Bill Melton, Chicago	33
1904	Harry Davis, Phila.	10	1937	Joe DiMaggio, N.Y.	46	1972	Dick Allen, Chicago	37
1905	Harry Davis, Phila.	8	1938	Hank Greenberg, Det.	58	1973	Reggie Jackson, Oak.	32
1906	Harry Davis, Phila.	12	1939	Jimmy Foxx, Bost.	35	1974	Dick Allen, Chicago	32
1907	Harry Davis, Phila.	8	1940	Hank Greenberg, Det.	41	1975	Reggie Jackson, Oak., and	36
1908	Sam Crawford, Det.	7	1941	Ted Williams, Bost.	37		George Scott, Mil.	
1909	Ty Cobb, Det.	9	1942	Ted Williams, Bost.	36	1976	Graig Nettles, N.Y.	32
1910	J. Garland Stahl, Bost.	10	1943	Rudy York, Det.	34	1977	Jim Rice, Boston	39
1911	Franklin Baker, Phila.	9	1944	Nick Etten, N.Y.	22	1978	Jim Rice, Boston	46
1912	Franklin Baker, Phila.	10	1945	Vern Stephens, St. L.	24	1979	Gorman Thomas, Milwaukee	45
1913	Franklin Baker, Phila.	12	1946	Hank Greenberg, Det.	44	1980	Reggie Jackson, N.Y., and	41
1914	Franklin Baker, Phila., and	8	1947	Ted Williams, Bost.	32		Ben Oglivie, Mil.	
	Sam Crawford, Det.		1948	Joe DiMaggio, N.Y.	39	1981*	Tony Armas, Oak.,	22
1915	Robert Roth, Chi.-Cleve.	7	1949	Ted Williams, Bost.	43		Dwight Evans, Bost.,	
1916	Wally Pipp, N.Y.	12	1950	Al Rosen, Cleve.	37		Bobby Grich, Calif., and	
1917	Wally Pipp, N.Y.	9	1951	Gus Zernial, Chi.-Phila.	33		Eddie Murray, Balt. (tie)	
1918	Babe Ruth, Bost., and	11	1952	Larry Doby, Cleve.	32	1982	Gorman Thomas, Mil., and	39
	Clarence Walker, Phila.		1953	Al Rosen, Cleve.	43		Reggie Jackson, Calif.	
1919	Babe Ruth, Bost.	29	1954	Larry Doby, Cleve.	32	1983	Jim Rice, Boston	39
1920	Babe Ruth, N.Y.	54	1955	Mickey Mantle, N.Y.	37	1984	Tony Armas, Boston	43
1921	Babe Ruth, N.Y.	59	1956	Mickey Mantle, N.Y.	52	1985	Darrell Evans, Detroit	40
1922	Ken Williams, St. L.	39	1957	Roy Sievers, Wash.	42	1986	Jesse Barfield, Toronto	40
1923	Babe Ruth, N.Y.	41	1958	Mickey Mantle, N.Y.	42	1987	Mark McGwire, Oakland	49
1924	Babe Ruth, N.Y.	46	1959	Rocky Colavito, Cleve., and	42	1988	Jose Canseco, Oakland	42
1925	Bob Meusel, N.Y.	33		Harmon Killebrew, Wash.		1989	Fred McGriff, Toronto	36
1926	Babe Ruth, N.Y.	47	1960	Mickey Mantle, N.Y.	40	1990	Cecil Fielder, Detroit	51
1927	Babe Ruth, N.Y.	60	1961	Roger Maris, N.Y.	61	1991	Jose Canseco, Oakland and	44
1928	Babe Ruth, N.Y.	54	1962	Harmon Killebrew, Minn.	48		Cecil Fielder, Detroit (tie)	
1929	Babe Ruth, N.Y.	46	1963	Harmon Killebrew, Minn.	45	1992	Juan Gonzalez, Texas	43
1930	Babe Ruth, N.Y.	49	1964	Harmon Killebrew, Minn.	49	1993	Juan Gonzalez, Texas	46
1931	Lou Gehrig, N.Y., and	46	1965	Tony Conigliaro, Bost.	32	1994[1]	Ken Griffey, Jr., Seattle	40
	Babe Ruth, N.Y.		1966	Frank Robinson, Balt.	49	1995	Albert Belle, Cleveland	50
1932	Jimmy Foxx, Phila.	58	1967	Carl Yastrzemski, Bost., and	44	1996	Mark McGwire, Oakland	52
1933	Jimmy Foxx, Phila.	48		Harmon Killebrew, Minn.		1997	Ken Griffey, Jr., Seattle	56
1934	Lou Gehrig, N.Y.	49	1968	Frank Howard, Wash.	44			

* Split season because of player strike. 1. Season ended on August 12 because of a players' strike.

AMERICAN LEAGUE BATTING CHAMPIONS

Year	Player, team	Avg	Year	Player, team	Avg	Year	Player, team	Avg
1901	Nap Lajoie, Phila.	.422	1927	Harry Heilmann, Det.	.398	1953	Mickey Vernon, Wash.	.337
1902	Ed Delahanty, Wash.	.376	1928	Goose Goslin, Wash.	.379	1954	Bobby Avila, Cleve.	.341
1903	Nap Lajoie, Cleve.	.355	1929	Lew Fonseca, Cleve.	.369	1955	Al Kaline, Det.	.340
1904	Nap Lajoie, Cleve.	.381	1930	Al Simmons, Phila.	.381	1956	Mickey Mantle, N.Y.	.353
1905	Elmer Flick, Cleve.	.306	1931	Al Simmons, Phila.	.390	1957	Ted Williams, Bost.	.388
1906	George Stone, St. L.	.358	1932	Dale Alexander, Det.-Bost.	.367	1958	Ted Williams, Bost.	.328
1907	Ty Cobb, Det.	.350	1933	Jimmy Foxx, Phila.	.356	1959	Harvey Kuenn, Det.	.353
1908	Ty Cobb, Det.	.324	1934	Lou Gehrig, N.Y.	.363	1960	Pete Runnels, Bost.	.320
1909	Ty Cobb, Det.	.377	1935	Buddy Myer, Wash.	.349	1961	Norman Cash, Det.	.361
1910	Ty Cobb, Det.	.385	1936	Luke Appling, Chi.	.388	1962	Pete Runnels, Bost.	.326
1911	Ty Cobb, Det.	.420	1937	Charley Gehringer, Det.	.371	1963	Carl Yastrzemski, Bost.	.321
1912	Ty Cobb, Det.	.410	1938	Jimmy Foxx, Bost.	.349	1964	Tony Oliva, Minn.	.323
1913	Ty Cobb, Det.	.390	1939	Joe DiMaggio, N.Y.	.381	1965	Tony Oliva, Minn.	.321
1914	Ty Cobb, Det.	.368	1940	Joe DiMaggio, N.Y.	.352	1966	Frank Robinson, Balt.	.316
1915	Ty Cobb, Det.	.369	1941	Ted Williams, Bost.	.406	1967	Carl Yastrzemski, Bost.	.326
1916	Tris Speaker, Cleve.	.386	1942	Ted Williams, Bost.	.356	1968	Carl Yastrzemski, Bost.	.301
1917	Ty Cobb, Det.	.383	1943	Luke Appling, Chi.	.328	1969	Rod Carew, Minn.	.332
1918	Ty Cobb, Det.	.382	1944	Lou Boudreau, Cleve.	.327	1970	Alex Johnson, Calif.	.329
1919	Ty Cobb, Det.	.384	1945	George Sternweiss, N.Y.	.309	1971	Tony Oliva, Minn.	.337
1920	George Sisler, St. L.	.407	1946	Mickey Vernon, Wash.	.353	1972	Rod Carew, Minn.	.318
1921	Harry Heilmann, Det.	.394	1947	Ted Williams, Bost.	.343	1973	Rod Carew, Minn.	.350
1922	George Sisler, St. L.	.420	1948	Ted Williams, Bost.	.369	1974	Rod Carew, Minn.	.364
1923	Harry Heilmann, Det.	.403	1949	George Kell, Det.	.343	1975	Rod Carew, Minn.	.359
1924	Babe Ruth, N.Y.	.378	1950	Billy Goodman, Bost.	.354	1976	George Brett, Kansas City	.333
1925	Harry Heilmann, Det.	.393	1951	Ferris Fain, Phila.	.344	1977	Rod Carew, Minn.	.388
1926	Heinie Manush, Det.	.378	1952	Ferris Fain, Phila.	.327	1978	Rod Carew, Minn.	.333

Year	Player, team	Avg	Year	Player, team	Avg	Year	Player, team	Avg
1979	Fred Lynn, Boston	.333	1986	Wade Boggs, Boston	.357	1993	John Olerud, Toronto	.363
1980	George Brett, Kansas City	.390	1987	Wade Boggs, Boston	.363	1994[1]	Paul O'Neill, New York	.359
1981*	Carney Lansford, Bost.	.336	1988	Wade Boggs, Boston	.366	1995	Edgar Martinez, Seattle	.356
1982	Willie Wilson, Kansas City	.332	1989	Kirby Puckett, Minnesota	.339	1996	Alex Rodriguez, Seattle	.358
1983	Wade Boggs, Boston	.361	1990	George Brett, Kansas City	.328	1997	Frank Thomas, Chicago	.347
1984	Don Mattingly, New York	.343	1991	Julio Franco, Texas	.341			
1985	Wade Boggs, Boston	.368	1992	Edgar Martinez, Seattle	.343			

* Split season because of player strike. 1. Season ended on August 12 because of a players' strike.

NATIONAL LEAGUE HOME RUN CHAMPIONS

Year	Player, team	No.	Year	Player, team	No.	Year	Player, team	No.
1876	George Hall, Phila. Athletics	5	1917	Davis Robertson, N.Y., and	12	1957	Henry Aaron, Mil.	44
1877	George Shaffer, Louisville	3		Cliff Cravath, Phila.		1958	Ernie Banks, Chi.	47
1878	Paul Hines, Providence	4	1918	Cliff Cravath, Phila.	8	1959	Ed Mathews, Mil.	46
1879	Charles Jones, Bost.	9	1919	Cliff Cravath, Phila.	12	1960	Ernie Banks, Chi.	41
1880	James O'Rourke, Bost., and	6	1920	Cy Williams, Phila.	15	1961	Orlando Cepeda, San Fran.	46
	Harry Stovey, Worcester		1921	George Kelly, N.Y.	23	1962	Willie Mays, San Fran.	49
1881	Dan Brouthers, Buffalo	8	1922	Rogers Hornsby, St. L.	42	1963	Henry Aaron, Mil., and	44
1882	George Wood, Det.	7	1923	Cy Williams, Phila.	41		Willie McCovey, San Fran.	
1883	William Ewing, N.Y.	10	1924	Jacques Fournier, Bkln.	27	1964	Willie Mays, San Fran.	47
1884	Ed Williamson, Chi.	27	1925	Rogers Hornsby, St. L.	39	1965	Willie Mays, San Fran.	52
1885	Abner Dalrymple, Chi.	11	1926	Hack Wilson, Chi.	21	1966	Henry Aaron, Atlanta	44
1886	Arthur Richardson, Det.	11	1927	Hack Wilson, Chi., and	30	1967	Henry Aaron, Atlanta	39
1887	Roger Connor, N.Y., and	17		Cy Williams, Phila.		1968	Willie McCovey, San Fran.	36
	Wm. O'Brien, Wash.		1928	Hack Wilson, Chi., and	31	1969	Willie McCovey, San Fran.	45
1888	Roger Connor, N.Y.	14		Jim Bottomley, St. L.		1970	Johnny Bench, Cin.	45
1889	Sam Thompson, Phila.	20	1929	Chuck Klein, Phila.	43	1971	Willie Stargell, Pitts.	48
1890	Tom Burns, Bklyn, and	13	1930	Hack Wilson, Chi.	56	1972	Johnny Bench, Cin.	40
	Mike Tiernan, N.Y.		1931	Chuck Klein, Phila.	31	1973	Willie Stargell, Pitts.	44
1891	Harry Stovey, Bost., and	16	1932	Chuck Klein, Phila., and	38	1974	Mike Schmidt, Phila.	36
	Mike Tiernan, N.Y.			Mel Ott, N.Y.		1975	Mike Schmidt, Phila.	38
1892	Jim Holliday, Cin.	13	1933	Chuck Klein, Phila.	28	1976	Mike Schmidt, Phila.	38
1893	Ed Delahanty, Phila.	19	1934	Mel Ott, N.Y., and	35	1977	George Foster, Cin.	52
1894	Hugh Duffy, Bost., and	18		Rip Collins, St. L.		1978	George Foster, Cin.	40
	Robert Lowe, Bost.		1935	Wally Berger, Bost.	34	1979	Dave Kingman, Chicago	48
1895	Bill Joyce, Wash.	17	1936	Mel Ott, N.Y.	33	1980	Mike Schmidt, Phila.	48
1896	Ed Delahanty, Phila., and	13	1937	Mel Ott, N.Y., and	31	1981*	Mike Schmidt, Phila.	31
	Sam Thompson, Phila.			Joe Medwick, St. L.		1982	Dave Kingman, N.Y.	37
1897	Nap Lajoie, Phila.	10	1938	Mel Ott, N.Y.	36	1983	Mike Schmidt, Phila.	40
1898	James Colins, Bost.	14	1939	John Mize, St. L.	28	1984	Mike Schmidt, Phila. and	36
1899	John Freeman, Wash.	25	1940	John Mize, St. L.	43		Dale Murphy, Atlanta	
1900	Herman Long, Bost.	12	1941	Dolph Camilli, Bklyn.	34	1985	Dale Murphy, Atlanta	37
1901	Sam Crawford, Con.	16	1942	Mel Ott, N.Y.	30	1986	Mike Schmidt, Phila.	37
1902	Tom Leach, Pitts.	6	1943	Bill Nicholson, Chi.	29	1987	Andre Dawson, Chicago	49
1903	James Sheckard, Bklyn.	9	1944	Bill Nicholson, Chi.	33	1988	Darryl Strawberry, N.Y.	39
1904	Harry Lumley, Bklyn.	9	1945	Tommy Holmes, Bost.	28	1989	Kevin Mitchell, San Fran-	47
1905	Fred Odwell, Cin.	9	1946	Ralph Kiner, Pitts.	23		cisco	
1906	Tim Jordan, Bklyn	12	1947	Ralph Kiner, Pitts., and	51	1990	Ryne Sandberg, Chicago	40
1907	David Brain, Bost.	10		John Mize, N.Y.		1991	Howard Johnson, N.Y.	38
1908	Tim Jordan, Bklyn.	12	1948	Ralph Kiner, Pitts., and	40	1992	Fred McGriff, San Diego	35
1909	John Murray, N.Y.	7		John Mize, N.Y.		1993	Barry Bonds, San Francisco	46
1910	Fred Beck, Bost., and	10	1949	Ralph Kiner, Pitts.	54	1994[1]	Matt Williams, San Francisco	43
	Frank Schulte, Chi.		1950	Ralph Kiner, Pitts.	47	1995	Dante Bichette, Colorado	40
1911	Frank Schulte, Chi.	21	1951	Ralph Kiner, Pitts.	42	1996	Andreas Galarraga, Colo-	40
1912	Henry Zimmerman, Chi.	14	1952	Ralph Kiner, Pitts., and	37		rado	
1913	Cliff Cravath, Phila.	19		Hank Sauer, Chi.		1997	Larry Walker, Colorado	49
1914	Cliff Cravath, Phila.	19	1953	Ed Mathews, Mil.	47			
1915	Cliff Cravath, Phila.	24	1954	Ted Kluszewski, Cin.	49			
1916	Davis Robertson, N.Y., and	12	1955	Willie Mays, N.Y.	51			
	Fred Williams, Chi.		1956	Duke Snider, Bklyn.	43			

* Split season because of player strike. 1. Season ended on August 12 because of a players' strike.

NATIONAL LEAGUE BATTING CHAMPIONS

Year	Player, team	Avg	Year	Player, team	Avg	Year	Player, team	Avg
1876	Roscoe Barnes, Chicago	.404	1879	Cap Anson, Chicago	.407	1882	Dan Brouthers, Buffalo	.367
1877	Jim White, Boston	.385	1880	George Gore, Chicago	.365	1883	Dan Brouthers, Buffalo	.371
1878	Abner Dalrymple, Mil.	.356	1881	Cap Anson, Chicago	.399	1884	James O'Rourke, Buffalo	.350

Year	Player, team	Avg	Year	Player, team	Avg	Year	Player, team	Avg
1885	Roger Connor, N. Y.	.371	1922	Rogers Hornsby, St. Louis	.401	1960	Dick Groat, Pittsburgh	.325
1886	King Kelly, Chicago	.388	1923	Rogers Hornsby, St. Louis	.384	1961	Roberto Clemente, Pitts.	.351
1887	Cap Anson, Chicago	.421	1924	Rogers Hornsby, St. Louis	.424	1962	Tommy Davis, L. A.	.346
1888	Cap Anson, Chicago	.343	1925	Rogers Hornsby, St. Louis	.403	1963	Tommy Davis, L. A.	.326
1889	Dan Brouthers, Boston	.373	1926	Gene Hargrave, Cincinnati	.353	1964	Roberto Clemente, Pitts.	.339
1890	John Glasscock, N. Y.	.336	1927	Paul Waner, Pittsburgh	.380	1965	Roberto Clemente, Pitts.	.329
1891	William Hamilton, Phila.	.338	1928	Rogers Hornsby, Boston	.387	1966	Matty Alou, Pittsburgh	.342
1892	Dan Brouthers, Bklyn., and Clarence Childs, Cleve.	.335	1929	Lefty O'Doul, Phila.	.398	1967	Roberto Clemente, Pitts.	.357
			1930	Bill Terry, N.Y.	.401	1968	Pete Rose, Cincinnati	.335
1893	Hugh Duffy, Boston	.378	1931	Chick Hafey, St. Louis	.349	1969	Pete Rose, Cincinnati	.348
1894	Hugh Duffy, Boston	.438	1932	Lefty O'Doul, Brooklyn	.368	1970	Rico Carty, Atlanta	.366
1895	Jesse Burkett, Cleveland	.423	1933	Chuck Klein, Phila.	.368	1971	Joe Torre, St. Louis	.363
1896	Jesse Burkett, Cleveland	.410	1934	Paul Waner, Pittsburgh	.362	1972	Billy Williams, Chicago	.333
1897	Willie Keeler, Baltimore	.432	1935	Arky Vaughan, Pittsburgh	.385	1973	Pete Rose, Cincinnati	.338
1898	Willie Keeler, Baltimore	.379	1936	Paul Waner, Pittsburgh	.373	1974	Ralph Garr, Atlanta	.353
1899	Ed Delahanty, Phila.	.408	1937	Joe Medwick, St. Louis	.374	1975	Bill Madlock, Chicago	.354
1900	Honus Wagner, Pittsburgh	.381	1938	Ernie Lombardi, Cin.	.342	1976	Bill Madlock, Chicago	.339
1901	Jesse Burkett, St. Louis	.382	1939	John Mize, St. Louis	.349	1977	Dave Parker, Pittsburgh	.338
1902	Clarence Beaumont, Pitts.	.357	1940	Debs Garms, Pittsburgh	.355	1978	Dave Parker, Pittsburgh	.334
1903	Honus Wagner, Pittsburgh	.355	1941	Pete Reiser, Brooklyn	.343	1979	Keith Hernandez, St. Louis	.344
1904	Honus Wagner, Pittsburgh	.349	1942	Ernie Lombardi, Boston	.330	1980	Bill Buckner, Chicago	.324
1905	Cy Seymour, Cincinnati	.377	1943	Stan Musial, St. Louis	.357	1981*	Bill Madlock, Pittsburgh	.341
1906	Honus Wagner, Pittsburgh	.339	1944	Dixie Walker, Brooklyn	.357	1982	Al Oliver, Montreal	.331
1907	Honus Wagner, Pittsburgh	.350	1945	Phil Cavarretta, Chicago	.355	1983	Bill Madlock, Pittsburgh	.323
1908	Honus Wagner, Pittsburgh	.354	1946	Stan Musial, St. Louis	.365	1984	Tony Gwynn, San Diego	.351
1909	Honus Wagner, Pittsburgh	.339	1947	Harry Walker, St. L.-Phila.	.363	1985	Willie McGee, St. Louis	.353
1910	Sherwood Magee, Phila.	.331	1948	Stan Musial, St. Louis	.376	1986	Tim Raines, Montreal	.334
1911	Honus Wagner, Pittsburgh	.334	1949	Jackie Robinson, Brooklyn	.342	1987	Tony Gwynn, San Diego	.370
1912	Henry Zimmerman, Chicago	.372	1950	Stan Musial, St. Louis	.346	1988	Tony Gwynn, San Diego	.313
1913	Jake Daubert, Brooklyn	.350	1951	Stan Musial, St. Louis	.355	1989	Tony Gwynn, San Diego	.336
1914	Jake Daubert, Brooklyn	.329	1952	Stan Musial, St. Louis	.336	1990	Willie McGee, St. Louis	.335
1915	Larry Doyle, New York	.320	1953	Carl Furillo, Brooklyn	.344	1991	Terry Pendleton, Atlanta	.319
1916	Hal Chase, Cincinnati	.339	1954	Willie Mays, N. Y.	.345	1992	Gary Sheffield, San Diego	.330
1917	Edd Roush, Cincinnati	.341	1955	Richie Ashburn, Phila.	.338	1993	Andres Galarraga, Colorado	.370
1918	Zack Wheat, Brooklyn	.335	1956	Henry Aaron, Mil.	.328	1994¹	Tony Gwynn, San Diego	.394
1919	Edd Roush, Cincinnati	.321	1957	Stan Musial, St. Louis	.351	1995	Tony Gwynn, San Diego	.368
1920	Rogers Hornsby, St. Louis	.370	1958	Richie Ashburn, Phila.	.350	1996	Ellis Burks, Colorado	.344
1921	Rogers Hornsby, St. Louis	.397	1959	Henry Aaron, Mil.	.355	1997	Tony Gwynn, San Diego	.372

* Split season because of player strike. 1. Season ended on August 12 because of a players' strike.

AMERICAN LEAGUE PENNANT WINNERS

Year	Club	Manager	Won	Lost	Pct	Year	Club	Manager	Won	Lost	Pct
1901	Chicago	Clark C. Griffith	83	53	.610	1927¹	New York	Miller J. Huggins	110	44	.714
1902	Philadelphia	Connie Mack	83	53	.610	1928¹	New York	Miller J. Huggins	101	53	.656
1903¹	Boston	Jimmy Collins	91	47	.659	1929¹	Philadelphia	Connie Mack	104	46	.693
1904²	Boston	Jimmy Collins	95	59	.617	1930¹	Philadelphia	Connie Mack	102	52	.662
1905	Philadelphia	Connie Mack	92	56	.622	1931	Philadelphia	Connie Mack	107	45	.704
1906¹	Chicago	Fielder A. Jones	93	58	.616	1932¹	New York	Joseph V. McCarthy	107	47	.695
1907	Detroit	Hugh A. Jennings	92	58	.613	1933	Washington	Joseph E. Cronin	99	53	.651
1908	Detroit	Hugh A. Jennings	90	63	.588	1934	Detroit	Gordon Cochrane	101	53	.656
1909	Detroit	Hugh A. Jennings	98	54	.645	1935¹	Detroit	Gordon Cochrane	93	58	.616
1910¹	Philadelphia	Connie Mack	102	48	.680	1936¹	New York	Joseph V. McCarthy	102	51	.667
1911¹	Philadelphia	Connie Mack	101	50	.669	1937¹	New York	Joseph V. McCarthy	102	52	.662
1912¹	Boston	J. Garland Stahl	105	47	.691	1938¹	New York	Joseph V. McCarthy	99	53	.651
1913¹	Philadelphia	Connie Mack	96	57	.627	1939¹	New York	Joseph V. McCarthy	106	45	.702
1914	Philadelphia	Connie Mack	99	53	.651	1940	Detroit	Delmar D. Baker	90	64	.584
1915¹	Boston	William F. Carrigan	101	50	.669	1941¹	New York	Joseph V. McCarthy	101	53	.656
1916¹	Boston	William F. Carrigan	91	63	.591	1942	New York	Joseph V. McCarthy	103	51	.669
1917¹	Chicago	Clarence H. Rowland	100	54	.649	1943¹	New York	Joseph V. McCarthy	98	56	.636
1918¹	Boston	Ed Barrow	75	51	.595	1944	St. Louis	Luke Sewell	89	65	.578
1919	Chicago	William Gleason	88	52	.629	1945¹	Detroit	Steve O'Neill	88	65	.575
1920¹	Cleveland	Tris Speaker	98	56	.636	1946	Boston	Joseph E. Cronin	104	50	.675
1921	New York	Miller J. Huggins	98	55	.641	1947¹	New York	Stanley R. Harris	97	57	.630
1922	New York	Miller J. Huggins	94	60	.610	1948¹	Cleveland	Lou Boudreau	97	58	.626
1923¹	New York	Miller J. Huggins	98	54	.645	1949¹	New York	Casey Stengel	97	57	.630
1924¹	Washington	Stanley R. Harris	92	62	.597	1950¹	New York	Casey Stengel	98	56	.636
1925	Washington	Stanley R. Harris	96	55	.636	1951¹	New York	Casey Stengel	98	56	.636
1926	New York	Miller J. Huggins	91	63	.591	1952¹	New York	Casey Stengel	95	59	.617

Year	Club	Manager	Won	Lost	Pct
1953[1]	New York	Casey Stengel	99	52	.656
1954	Cleveland	Al Lopez	111	43	.721
1955	New York	Casey Stengel	96	58	.623
1956[1]	New York	Casey Stengel	97	57	.630
1957	New York	Casey Stengel	98	56	.636
1958[1]	New York	Casey Stengel	92	62	.597
1959	Chicago	Al Lopez	94	60	.610
1960	New York	Casey Stengel	97	57	.630
1961[1]	New York	Ralph Houk	109	53	.673
1962[1]	New York	Ralph Houk	96	66	.593
1963	New York	Ralph Houk	104	57	.646
1964	New York	Yogi Berra	99	63	.611
1965	Minnesota	Sam Mele	102	60	.630
1966[1]	Baltimore	Hank Bauer	97	63	.606
1967	Boston	Dick Williams	92	70	.568
1968[1]	Detroit	Mayo Smith	103	59	.636
1969	Baltimore[3]	Earl Weaver	109	53	.673
1970[1]	Baltimore[3]	Earl Weaver	108	54	.667
1971	Baltimore[4]	Earl Weaver	101	57	.639
1972[1]	Oakland[5]	Dick Williams	93	62	.600
1973[1]	Oakland[6]	Dick Williams	94	68	.580
1974[1]	Oakland[6]	Alvin Dark	90	72	.556
1975	Boston[4]	Darrell Johnson	95	65	.594
1976	New York[7]	Billy Martin	97	62	.610
1977[1]	New York[7]	Billy Martin	100	62	.617

Year	Club	Manager	Won	Lost	Pct
1978[1]	New York[7]	Billy Martin and Bob Lemon	100	63	.613
1979	Baltimore[8]	Earl Weaver	102	57	.642
1980	Kansas City[9]	Jim Frey	97	65	.599
1981	New York[10]	Gene Michael-Bob Lemon	59	48	.551*
1982	Milwaukee[11]	Harvey Kuenn	95	67	.586
1983[1]	Baltimore[12]	Joe Altobelli	98	64	.605
1984[1]	Detroit[13]	Sparky Anderson	104	58	.642
1985[1]	Kansas City[14]	Dick Howser	91	71	.562
1986	Boston[11]	John McNamara	95	66	.590
1987	Minnesota[15]	Tom Kelly	85	77	.525
1988	Oakland[16]	Tony LaRussa	104	58	.642
1989	Oakland[17]	Tony LaRussa	99	63	.611
1990	Oakland[18]	Tony LaRussa	103	59	.636
1991	Minnesota[19]	Tom Kelly	95	67	.586
1992	Toronto[10]	Cito Gaston	96	66	.593
1993	Toronto[12]	Cito Gaston	95	67	.586
1994	Strike ended season Aug. 11. No playoffs, no pennant winner.				
1995	Cleveland[20]	Mike Hargrove	100	44	.694
1996	New York[21]	Joe Torre	92	70	.568
1997	Cleveland[6]	Mike Hargrove	86	75	.534

* Split season because of player strike. 1. World Series winner. 2. No World Series. 3. Defeated Minnesota, Western Division winner, in playoff. 4. Defeated Oakland, Western Division Leader, in playoff. 5. Defeated Detroit, Eastern Division winner, inplayoff. 6. Defeated Baltimore, Eastern Division winner, in playoff. 7. Defeated Kansas City, Western Division winner, in playoff. 8. Defeated California, Western Division winner, in playoff. 9. Defeated New York, Eastern Division winner, in playoff. 10. Defeated Oakland, Western Division winner, in playoff. 11. Defeated California, Western Division winner, in playoff. 12. Defeated Chicago, Western Division winner, in playoff. 13. Defeated Kansas City, Western Division winner, in playoff. 14. Defeated Toronto, Eastern Division winner, in playoff. 15. Defeated Detroit, Eastern winner, in playoff. 16. Defeated Boston, Eastern division winner, in playoffs. 17. Defeated Toronto, Eastern Division winner, in playoffs. 18. Defeated Boston, Eastern Division winner, in playoffs. 19. Defeated Toronto, Eastern Division winner, in playoffs. 20. Defeated Seattle Mariners, Western Division winner, in playoffs. 21. Defeated Baltimore Orioles, Eastern Division wild-card team, in playoffs.

NATIONAL LEAGUE PENNANT WINNERS

Year	Club	Manager	Won	Lost	Pct
1876	Chicago	Albert G. Spalding	52	14	.788
1877	Boston	Harry Wright	31	17	.646
1878	Boston	Harry Wright	41	19	.683
1879	Providence	George Wright	55	23	.705
1880	Chicago	Adrian C. Anson	67	17	.798
1881	Chicago	Adrian C. Anson	56	28	.667
1882	Chicago	Adrian C. Anson	55	29	.655
1883	Boston	John F. Morrill	63	35	.643
1884	Providence	Frank C. Bancroft	84	28	.750
1885	Chicago	Adrian C. Anson	87	25	.777
1886	Chicago	Adrian C. Anson	90	34	.726
1887	Detroit	W. H. Watkins	79	45	.637
1888	New York	James J. Mutrie	84	47	.641
1889	New York	James J. Mutrie	83	43	.659
1890	Brooklyn	Wm. H. McGunnigle	86	43	.667
1891	Boston	Frank G. Selee	87	51	.630
1892	Boston	Frank G. Selee	102	48	.680
1893	Boston	Frank G. Selee	86	44	.662
1894	Baltimore	Edward H. Hanlon	89	39	.695
1895	Baltimore	Edward H. Hanlon	87	43	.669
1896	Baltimore	Edward H. Hanlon	90	39	.698
1897	Boston	Frank G. Selee	93	39	.705
1898	Boston	Frank G. Selee	102	47	.685
1899	Brooklyn	Edward H. Hanlon	88	42	.677
1900	Brooklyn	Edward H. Hanlon	82	54	.603
1901	Pittsburgh	Fred C. Clarke	90	49	.647
1902	Pittsburgh	Fred C. Clarke	103	36	.741
1903	Pittsburgh	Fred C. Clarke	91	49	.650
1904	New York[2]	John J. McGraw	106	47	.693
1905	New York[1]	John J. McGraw	105	48	.686
1906	Chicago	Frank L. Chance	116	36	.763

Year	Club	Manager	Won	Lost	Pct
1907	Chicago[1]	Frank L. Chance	107	45	.704
1908	Chicago[1]	Frank L. Chance	99	55	.643
1909	Pittsburgh[1]	Fred C. Clarke	110	42	.724
1910	Chicago	Frank L. Chance	104	50	.675
1911	New York	John J. McGraw	99	54	.647
1912	New York	John J. McGraw	103	48	.682
1913	New York	John J. McGraw	101	51	.664
1914	Boston[1]	George T. Stallings	94	59	.614
1915	Philadelphia	Patrick J. Moran	90	62	.592
1916	Brooklyn	Wilbert Robinson	94	60	.610
1917	New York	John J. McGraw	98	56	.636
1918	Chicago	Fred L. Mitchell	84	45	.651
1919	Cincinnati[1]	Patrick J. Moran	96	44	.686
1920	Brooklyn	Wilbert Robinson	93	61	.604
1921	New York[1]	John J. McGraw	94	59	.614
1922	New York[1]	John J. McGraw	93	61	.604
1923	New York	John J. McGraw	95	58	.621
1924	New York	John J. McGraw	93	60	.608
1925	Pittsburgh[1]	Wm. B. McKechnie	95	58	.621
1926	St. Louis[1]	Rogers Hornsby	89	65	.578
1927	Pittsburgh	Donie Bush	94	60	.610
1928	St. Louis	Wm. B. McKechnie	95	59	.617
1929	Chicago	Joseph V. McCarthy	98	54	.645
1930	St. Louis	Gabby Street	92	62	.597
1931	St. Louis[1]	Gabby Street	101	53	.656
1932	Chicago	Charles J. Grimm	90	64	.584
1933	New York[1]	William H. Terry	91	61	.599
1934	St. Louis[1]	Frank F. Frisch	95	58	.621
1935	Chicago	Charles J. Grimm	100	54	.649
1936	New York	William H. Terry	92	62	.597
1937	New York	William H. Terry	95	57	.625

Year	Club	Manager	Won	Lost	Pct
1938	Chicago	Gabby Hartnett	89	63	.586
1939	Cincinnati	Wm. B. McKechnie	97	57	.630
1940	Cincinnati[1]	Wm. B. McKechnie	100	53	.654
1941	Brooklyn	Leo E. Durocher	100	54	.649
1942	St. Louis[1]	Wm. H. Southworth	106	48	.688
1943	St. Louis[1]	Wm. H. Southworth	105	49	.682
1944	St. Louis[1]	Wm. H. Southworth	105	49	.682
1945	Chicago	Charles J. Grimm	98	56	.636
1946	St. Louis[1]	Edwin H. Dyer	98	58	.628
1947	Brooklyn	Burton E. Shotton	94	60	.610
1948	Boston	Wm. H. Southworth	91	62	.595
1949	Brooklyn	Burton E. Shotton	97	57	.630
1950	Philadelphia	Edwin M. Sawyer	91	63	.591
1951	New York	Leo E. Durocher	98	59	.624
1952	Brooklyn	Charles W. Dressen	96	57	.630
1953	Brooklyn	Charles W. Dressen	105	49	.682
1954	New York[1]	Leo E. Durocher	97	57	.630
1955	Brooklyn[1]	Walter Alston	98	55	.641
1956	Brooklyn	Walter Alston	93	61	.604
1957	Milwaukee1	Fred Haney	95	59	.617
1958	Milwaukee	Fred Haney	92	62	.597
1959	Los Angeles[1]	Walter Alston	88	68	.564
1960	Pittsburgh[1]	Danny Murtaugh	95	59	.617
1961	Cincinnati	Fred Hutchinson	93	61	.604
1962	San Francisco	Alvin Dark	103	62	.624
1963	Los Angeles[1]	Walter Alston	99	63	.611
1964	St. Louis[1]	Johnny Keane	93	69	.574
1965	Los Angeles[1]	Walter Alston	97	65	.599
1966	Los Angeles	Walter Alston	95	67	.586
1967	St. Louis[1]	Red Schoendienst	101	60	.627
1968	St. Louis	Red Schoendienst	97	65	.599
1969	New York[1 3]	Gil Hodges	100	62	.617
1970	Cincinnati[4]	Sparky Anderson	102	60	.630
1971	Pittsburgh[1 5]	Danny Murtaugh	97	65	.599
1972	Cincinnati[4]	Sparky Anderson	95	59	.617
1973	New York[6]	Yogi Berra	82	79	.509
1974	Los Angeles[4]	Walter Alston	102	60	.630
1975	Cincinnati[1 4]	Sparky Anderson	108	54	.667
1976	Cincinnati[7 1]	Sparky Anderson	102	60	.630
1977	Los Angeles[7]	Tom Lasorda	98	64	.605
1978	Los Angeles[7]	Tom Lasorda	95	67	.586
1979[1]	Pittsburgh[6]	Chuck Tanner	98	64	.605
1980[1]	Philadelphia[8]	Dallas Green	91	71	.562
1981	Los Angeles[1 9]	Tom Lasorda	63	47	.573*
1982[1]	St. Louis[3]	Whitey Herzog	92	70	.568
1983	Philadelphia[11]	Paul Owens	90	72	.556
1984	San Diego[12]	Dick Williams	92	70	.568
1985	St. Louis[1 5]	Whitey Herzog	101	61	.623
1986	New York[8]	Dave Johnson	108	54	.667
1987	St. Louis[5]	Whitey Herzog	95	67	.586
1988	Los Angeles[10]	Tom Lasorda	94	67	.584
1989	San Francisco[12]	Roger Craig	92	70	.568
1990	Cincinnati[4]	Lou Piniella	91	71	.562
1991	Atlanta[4]	Bobby Cox	94	68	.580
1992	Atlanta[4]	Bobby Cox	98	64	.605
1993	Philadelphia[3]	Jim Fregosi	97	65	.599
1994	Strike ended season Aug. 11. No playoffs, no pennant winner.				
1995	Atlanta[13]	Bobby Cox	90	54	.625
1996	Atlanta[14]	Bobby Cox	96	66	.593
1997	Florida[15]	Jim Leyland	92	70	.568

* Split season because of player strike. 1. World Series winner. 2. No World Series. 3. Defeated Atlanta, Western Division winner, in playoff. 4. Defeated Pittsburgh, Eastern Division winner, in playoff. 5. Defeated San Francisco, Western Division winner, in playoff. 6. Defeated Cincinnati, Western Division winner, in playoff. 7. Defeated Philadelphia, Eastern Division winner, in playoff. 8. Defeated Houston, Western Division winner, in playoff. 9. Defeated Montreal, Eastern Division winner, in playoff. 10. Defeated New York, Eastern Division winner, in playoff. 11. Defeated Los Angeles, Western Division winner, in playoff. 12. Defeated Chicago, Eastern Division champion, in playoff. 13. Defeated Cincinnati, Central Division winner, in playoff. 14. Defeated St. Louis, Central Division winner, in playoff. 15. Eastern Division wildcard Florida defeated Atlanta, Eastern Division winner, in playoff.

MOST VALUABLE PLAYERS

(Baseball Writers Association selections)

American League

1931	Lefty Grove, Philadelphia
1932–33	Jimmy Foxx, Philadelphia
1934	Mickey Cochrane, Detroit
1935	Hank Greenberg, Detroit
1936	Lou Gehrig, New York
1937	Charlie Gehringer, Detroit
1938	Jimmy Foxx, Boston
1939	Joe DiMaggio, New York
1940	Hank Greenberg, Detroit
1941	Joe DiMaggio, New York
1942	Joe Gordon, New York
1943	Spurgeon Chandler, New York
1944–45	Hal Newhouser, Detroit
1946	Ted Williams, Boston
1947	Joe DiMaggio, New York
1948	Lou Boudreau, Cleveland
1949	Ted Williams, Boston
1950	Phil Rizzuto, New York
1951	Yogi Berra, New York
1952	Bobby Shantz, Philadelphia
1953	Al Rosen, Cleveland
1954–55	Yogi Berra, New York
1956–57	Mickey Mantle, New York
1958	Jackie Jensen, Boston
1959	Nellie Fox, Chicago
1960–61	Roger Maris, New York
1962	Mickey Mantle, New York
1963	Elston Howard, New York
1964	Brooks Robinson, Baltimore
1965	Zoilo Versalles, Minnesota
1966	Frank Robinson, Baltimore
1967	Carl Yastrzemski, Boston
1968	Dennis McLain, Detroit
1969	Harmon Killebrew, Minnesota
1970	John (Boog) Powell, Baltimore
1971	Vida Blue, Oakland
1972	Dick Allen, Chicago
1973	Reggie Jackson, Oakland
1974	Jeff Burroughs, Texas
1975	Fred Lynn, Boston
1976	Thurman Munson, New York
1977	Rod Carew, Minnesota
1978	Jim Rice, Boston
1979	Don Baylor, California
1980	George Brett, Kansas City
1981	Rollie Fingers, Milwaukee
1982	Robin Yount, Milwaukee
1983	Cal Ripken, Jr., Baltimore
1984	Willie Hernandez, Detroit
1985	Don Mattingly, New York
1986	Roger Clemens, Boston
1987	George Bell, Toronto
1988	Jose Canseco, Oakland
1989	Robin Yount, Milwaukee
1990	Rickey Henderson, Oakland
1991	Cal Ripken, Jr., Baltimore
1992	Dennis Eckersley, Oakland
1993	Frank Thomas, Chicago
1994	Frank Thomas, Chicago
1995	Mo Vaughn, Boston
1996	Juan Gonzales, Texas

National League

1931	Frank Frisch, St. Louis
1932	Chuck Klein, Philadelphia
1933	Carl Hubbell, New York
1934	Dizzy Dean, St. Louis
1935	Gabby Hartnett, Chicago
1936	Carl Hubbell, New York

1937	Joe Medwick, St. Louis	1958–59	Ernie Banks, Chicago	1979	Willie Stargell, Pittsburgh
1938	Ernie Lombardi, Cincinnati	1960	Dick Groat, Pittsburgh	1979	Keith Hernandez, St. Louis
1939	Bucky Walters, Cincinnati	1961	Frank Robinson, Cincinnati	1980	Mike Schmidt, Philadelphia
1940	Frank McCormick, Cincinnati	1962	Maury Wills, Los Angeles	1981	Mike Schmidt, Philadelphia
1941	Dolph Camilli, Brooklyn	1963	Sandy Koufax, Los Angeles	1982	Dale Murphy, Atlanta
1942	Mort Cooper, St. Louis	1964	Ken Boyer, St. Louis	1983	Dale Murphy, Atlanta
1943	Stan Musial, St. Louis	1965	Willie Mays, San Francisco	1984	Ryne Sandberg, Chicago
1944	Marty Marion, St. Louis	1966	Roberto Clemente, Pittsburgh	1985	Willie McGee, St. Louis
1945	Phil Cavarretta, Chicago			1986	Mike Schmidt, Philadelphia
1946	Stan Musial, St. Louis	1967	Orlando Cepeda, St. Louis	1987	Andre Dawson, Chicago
1947	Bob Elliott, Boston	1968	Bob Gibson, St. Louis	1988	Kirk Gibson, Los Angeles
1948	Stan Musial, St. Louis	1969	Willie McCovey, San Francisco	1989	Kevin Mitchell, San Francisco
1949	Jackie Robinson, Brooklyn				
1950	Jim Konstanty, Philadelphia	1970	Johnny Bench, Cincinnati	1990	Barry Bonds, Pittsburgh
1951	Roy Campanella, Brooklyn	1971	Joe Torre, St. Louis	1991	Terry Pendleton, Atlanta
1952	Hank Sauer, Chicago	1972	Johnny Bench, Cincinnati	1992	Barry Bonds, Pittsburgh
1953	Roy Campanella, Brooklyn	1973	Pete Rose, Cincinnati	1993	Barry Bonds, Pittsburgh
1954	Willie Mays, New York	1974	Steve Garvey, Los Angeles	1994	Jeff Baswell, Houston
1955	Roy Campanella, Brooklyn	1975–76	Joe Morgan, Cincinnati	1995	Barry Larkin, Cincinnati
1956	Don Newcombe, Brooklyn	1977	George Foster, Cincinnati	1996	Ken Caminiti, San Diego
1957	Henry Aaron, Milwaukee	1978	Dave Parker, Pittsburgh		

CY YOUNG AWARD

1956	Don Newcombe, Brooklyn N.L.	1974	Catfish Hunter, Oakland A.L.; Mike Marshall, Los Angeles N.L.	1987	Roger Clemens, Boston, A.L.; Steve Bedrosian, Philadelphia, N.L.
1957	Warren Spahn, Milwaukee N.L.	1975	Jim Palmer, Baltimore A.L.; Tom Seaver, New York N.L.	1988	Frank Viola, Minnesota, A.L.; Orel Hershiser, Los Angeles, N.L.
1958	Bob Turley, New York A.L.				
1959	Early Wynn, Chicago A.L.	1976	Jim Palmer, Baltimore A.L.; Randy Jones, San Diego N.L.		
1960	Vernon Law, Pittsburgh, N.L	1977	Sparky Lyle, N.Y., A.L.; Steve Carlton, Philadelphia N.L.	1989	Bret Saberhagen, Kansas, A.L.; Mark Davis, San Diego, N.L.
1961	Whitey Ford, New York A.L.				
1962	Don Drysdale, Los Angeles N.L.	1978	Ron Guidry, N.Y., A.L.; Gaylord Perry, San Diego N.L.	1990	Bob Welch, Oakland, A.L.; Doug Drabek, Pittsburgh, N.L.
1963	Sandy Koufax, Los Angeles N.L.				
1964	Dean Chance, Los Angeles A.L.	1979	Mike Flanagan, Baltimore, A.L.; Bruce Sutter, Chicago, N.L.	1991	Roger Clemens, Boston, A.L.; Tom Glavine, Atlanta, N.L.
1965	Sandy Koufax, Los Angeles N.L.				
1966	Sandy Koufax, Los Angeles N.L.	1980	Steve Stone, Baltimore, A.L.; Steve Carlton, Philadelphia, N.L.	1992	Dennis Eckersley, Oakland, A.L.; Greg Maddux, Atlant, N.L.
1967	Jim Lonborg, Boston A.L.; Mike McCormick, San Francisco N.L.	1981	Rollie Fingers, Milwaukee, A.L.; Fernando Valenzuela, Los Angeles, N.L.	1993	Jack McDowell, Chicago, A.L.; Greg Maddux, Atalanta, N.L.
1968	Dennis McLain, Detroit A.L.; Bob Gibson, St. Louis N.L.	1982	Pete Vuckovich, Milwaukee, A.L.; Steve Carlton, Philadelphia, N.L.	1994	David Cone, Kansas, A.L.; Greg Maddux, Atlanta, N.L.
1969	Mike Cuellar, Baltimore A.L. and Dennis McLain, Detroit A.L. (tied); Tom Seaver, N.Y. N.L.	1983	LaMarr Hoyt, Chicago, A.L.; John Denny, Philadelphia, N.L.	1995	Randy Johnson, Seattle, A.L.; Greg Maddux, Atlanta, N.L.
1970	Jim Perry, Minnesota A.L; Bob Gibson, St. Louis N.L.	1984	Willie Hernandez, Detroit, A.L.; Rick Sutcliffe, Chicago, N.L.	1996	Pat Hentgen, Toronto, A.L.; John Smoltz, Atlanta, N.L.
1971	Vida Blue, Oakland A.L.; Ferguson Jenkins, Chicago N.L.	1985	Bret Saberhagen, A.L.; Dwight Gooden, N.L.		
1972	Gaylord Perry, Cleveland A.L.; Steve Carlton, Phila. N.L.	1986	Roger Clemens, Boston, A.L.; Mike Scott, Houston, N.L.		
1973	Jim Palmer, Baltimore A.L.; Tom Seaver, New York N.L.				

MAJOR LEAGUE ALL-TIME PITCHING RECORDS

(Through 1996)

Most Games Won—511, Cy Young, Cleveland N.L., 1890–98, St. Louis N.L., 1899–1900, Boston A.L., 1901–08, Cleveland A.L., 1909–11, Boston N.L., 1911.

Most Games Won, Season—59, Hoss Radbourne, Providence N.L., 1884. (Since 1900—41, Jack Chesbro, New York A.L., 1904.)

Most Consecutive Games Won—24, Carl Hubbell, New York N.L., 1936 (16) and 1937 (8).

Most Consecutive Games Won, Season—19, Tim Keefe, New York N.L., 1888; Rube Marquard, New York N.L., 1912.

Most Years Won 20 or More Games—16, Cy Young, Cleveland N.L., 1891–98, St. Louis N.L., 1899–1900, Boston A.L., 1901–04, 1907–08.

Most Shutouts—113, Walter Johnson, Wash. A.L., 1907–27.

Most Shutouts, Season—16, Grover Alexander, Philadelphia N.L., 1916.

Most Consecutive Shutouts—6, Don Drysdale, Los Angeles, N.L., 1968.

Most Consecutive Scoreless Innings—59, Orel Hershiser, Los Angeles Dodgers, 1988.

Most Strikeouts—5,714, Nolan Ryan, New York N.L., California A.L., Houston N.L., 1968–1988 Texas, 1989–93.

Most Strikeouts, Season—513, Matthew Kilroy, Baltimore A.A., 1886. (Since 1900—383, Nolan Ryan, California, A.L., 1973.)

Most Strikeouts, Game—21, Tom Cheney, Washington A.L., 1962, 16 innings. Nine innings: 20, Roger Clemens, Boston, A.L., 1986; 19, Charles McSweeney, Providence N.L., 1884; Hugh Dailey, Chicago U.A., 1884. (Since 1900—19, Steve Carlton, St. Louis N.L. vs.

New York, Sept. 15, 1969; Tom Seaver, New York N.L. vs. San Diego, April 22, 1970; Nolan Ryan, California A.L. vs. Boston, Aug. 12, 1974; David Cone, New York N.L. vs. Philadelphia, Oct. 6, 1991.)

Most Consecutive Strikeouts—10, Tom Seaver, New York N.L. vs. San Diego, April 22, 1970.

Most Games, Season—106, Mike Marshall, Los Angeles, N.L., 1974.

Most Complete Games, Season—75, William White, Cincinnati N.L., 1879. (Since 1900—48, Jack Chesbro, New York A.L., 1904.)

MAJOR LEAGUE LIFETIME RECORDS

(Through 1996)

Wins
*Indicates left-handed pitcher.

		Yrs	GS	W	L	Pct
1	Cy Young	22	815	511	316	.618
2	Walter Johnson	21	666	416	279	.599
3	Christy Mathewson	17	551	373	188	.665
	Grover Alexander	20	598	373	208	.642
5	Warren Spahn*	21	665	363	245	.597
6	Kid Nichols	15	561	361	208	.634
	Pud Galvin	14	682	361	308	.540
8	Tim Keefe	14	594	342	225	.603
9	Steve Carlton*	24	709	329	244	.574
10	Eddie Plank*	17	527	327	193	.629
11	John Clarkson	12	518	326	177	.648
12	Don Sutton	23	756	324	256	.559
13	Nolan Ryan	27	773	324	292	.526
14	Phil Niekro	24	716	318	274	.537
15	Gaylord Perry	22	690	314	265	.542
16	Old Hoss Radbourn	12	503	311	194	.616
	Tom Seaver	20	647	311	205	.603
18	Mickey Welch	13	549	308	209	.596
19	Lefty Grove*	17	456	300	141	.680
	Early Wynn	23	612	300	244	.551
21	Tommy John*	26	700	288	231	.555
22	Bert Blyleven	22	685	287	250	.534
23	Robin Roberts	19	609	286	245	.539
24	Tony Mullane	13	505	285	220	.564
25	Ferguson Jenkins	19	594	284	226	.557
26	Jim Kaat*	25	625	283	237	.544
27	Red Ruffing	22	536	273	225	.548
28	Burleigh Grimes	19	495	270	212	.560
29	Jim Palmer	19	521	268	152	.638
30	Bob Feller	18	484	266	162	.621

Pitchers Active in 1996
(150 or more lifetime victories)

		Yrs	GS	W	L	Pct
1	Dennis Martinez	21	547	240	182	.569
2	Dennis Eckersley	22	361	192	165	.538
3	Roger Clemens	13	382	192	111	.634
4	Frank Viola*	15	420	176	150	.540
5	Mark Langston*	13	397	172	145	.543
6	Fernando Valenzuela*	16	406	171	141	.548
7	Dwight Gooden	12	334	168	92	.646
8	Greg Maddux	11	332	165	104	.613
9	Orel Hershiser	14	362	165	117	.585
10	Jimmy Key*	13	344	164	104	.612

Leading Batters, by Batting Average
*Indicates left-handed hitter.

		Yrs	AB	H	Avg
1	Ty Cobb*	24	11,429	4191	.367
2	Rogers Hornsby	23	8,137	2930	.358
3	Joe Jackson*	13	4,981	1774	.356
4	Ed Delahanty	16	7,509	2597	.346
5	Tris Speaker*	22	10,197	3514	.345
6	Ted Williams*	19	7,706	2654	.344
7	Billy Hamilton*	14	6,284	2163	.344
8	Willie Keeler*	19	8,585	2947	.343
9	Dan Brouthers*	19	6,711	2296	.342
10	Babe Ruth*	22	8,399	2873	.342
11	Harry Heilmann	17	7,787	2660	.342
12	Pete Browning	13	4,820	1646	.341
13	Bill Terry*	14	6,428	2193	.341
14	George Sisler*	15	8,267	2812	.340
15	Lou Gehrig*	17	8,001	2721	.340
16	Jesse Burkett*	16	8,413	2853	.339
17	Nap Lajoie	21	9,592	3244	.338
18	Tony Gwynn*	15	7,595	2560	.337
19	Riggs Stephenson	14	4,508	1515	.336
20	Al Simmons	20	8,761	2927	.334
21	Wade Boggs*	15	8,100	2697	.333
22	Paul Waner*	20	9,459	3152	.333
23	Eddie Collins*	25	9,951	3313	.333
24	Stan Musial*	22	10,972	3630	.331
25	Sam Thompson*	14	6,005	1986	.331

Players Active in 1996
(600 or more lifetime hits)

		Yrs	AB	H	Avg
1	Tony Gwynn*	15	7,595	2,560	.337
2	Wade Boggs*	15	8,100	2,697	.333
3	Frank Thomas	7	3,291	1,077	.327
4	Edgar Martinez	10	3,276	1,031	.315
5	Kenny Lofton*	6	2,821	883	.313
6	Mark Grace*	9	4,903	1,514	.309
7	Hal Morris*	9	2,922	902	.309
8	Paul Molitor	19	9,795	3,014	.308
9	Jeff Bagwell	6	3,091	950	.307
10	Mike Piazza	5	2,002	653	.307
11	Chuck Knoblauch	6	3,328	1,019	.306
12	Mike Greenwell*	12	4,623	1,400	.303
13	Julio Franco	14	6,813	2,061	.303

MAJOR LEAGUE INDIVIDUAL ALL-TIME RECORDS

(Through 1996)

Highest Batting Average, Season—.442, James O'Neill, St. Louis, A.A., 1887; .438, Hugh Duffy, Boston, N.L., 1894 (Since 1900—.424, Rogers Hornsby, St. Louis, N.L., 1924; .422, Nap Lajoie, Phil., A.L., 1901)

Most Times at Bat—14,053, Pete Rose, Cincinnati, N.L., 1963–78; Philadelphia, N.L., 1979–83; Montreal, N.L., 1984; Cincinnati, N.L., 1984–86.

Most Years Batted .300 or Better—23, Ty Cobb, Detroit A.L., 1906–26, Philadelphia A.L., 1927–28.

Most Hits—4,256, Pete Rose, Cincinnati 1963–79, Philadelphia 1980–83, Montreal 1984, Cincinnati 1984–86.

Most Hits, Season—257, George Sisler, St. Louis A.L., 1920.

Most Hits, Game (9 innings)—7, Wilbert Robinson, Baltimore N.L., 6 singles, 1 double, 1892. Rennie Stennett, Pittsburgh N.L., 4 singles, 2 doubles, 1 triple, 1975.

Most Hits, Game (extra innings)—9, John Burnett, Cleveland A.L., 18 innings, 7 singles, 2 doubles, 1932.

Most Hits in Succession—12, Mike Higgins, Boston A.L., in four games, 1938; Walt Dropo, Detroit A.L., in three games, 1952.

Most Consecutive Games Batted Safely—56, Joe DiMaggio, New York A.L., 1941.

Most Runs—2,245, Ty Cobb, Detroit A.L., 1905–26, Philadelphia A.L., 1927–28.

Most Runs, Season—196, William Hamilton, Philadelphia N.L., 1894. (Since 1900—177, Babe Ruth, New York A.L., 1921.)

Most Runs, Game—7, Guy Hecker, Louisville A.A., 1886. (Since 1900—6, by Mel Ott, New York N.L., 1934, 1944; Johnny Pesky, Boston A.L., 1946; Frank Torre, Milwaukee N.L., 1957.)

Most Runs Batted in—2,297, Henry Aaron, Milwaukee N.L., 1954–1965; Atlanta N.L., 1966–74; Milwaukee A.L., 1975–76.

Most Runs Batted in, Season—190, Hack Wilson, Chicago N.L., 1930.

Most Runs Batted In, Game—12, Jim Bottomley, St. Louis N.L., 1924, and Mark Whiten, St. Louis N.L., 1993.

Most Home Runs—755, Henry Aaron, Milwaukee N.L., 1954–1965; Atlanta N.L., 1966–74; Milwaukee A.L., 1975–76.

Most Home Runs, Season—61, Roger Maris, New York A.L., 1961 (162–game season); 60, Babe Ruth, New York A.L., 1927 (154-game season)

Most Home Runs with Bases Filled—23, Lou Gehrig, New York A.L., 1927–39.

Most 2-Base Hits—793, Tris Speaker, Boston A.L., 1907–15, Cleveland A.L., 1916–26, Washington A.L., 1927, Philadelphia A.L., 1928.

Most 2-Base Hits, Season—67, Earl Webb, Boston A.L., 1931.

Most 2-base Hits, Game—4, by many.

Most 3-Base Hits—312, Sam Crawford, Cincinnati N.L., 1899–1902, Detroit A.L., 1903–17.

Most 3-Base Hits, Season—36, Owen Wilson, Pittsburgh N.L., 1912.

Most 3-Base Hits, Game—4, George Strief, Philadelphia A.A., 1885; William Joyce, New York N.L., 1897. (Since 1900—3, by many.)

Most Games Played—3,562, Pete Rose, Cincinnati N.L., Philadelphia N.L., Montreal N.L., 1964–86.

Most Consecutive Games Played—2,543, Cal Ripken, Jr., Baltimore Orioles, A.L., 1981–

Most Bases on Balls—2,056, Babe Ruth, Boston A.L., 1914–19; New York A.L., 1920–34, Boston N.L., 1935.

Most Bases on Balls, Season—170, Babe Ruth, New York A.L., 1923.

Most Bases on Balls, Game—6, Jimmy Foxx, Boston A.L., 1938.

Most Strikeouts, Season—189, Bobby Bonds, San Francisco N.L., 1970.

Most Strikeouts, Game (9 innings)—5, by many.

Most Strikeouts, Game (extra innings)—6, Carl Weilman, St. Louis A.L., 15 innings, 1913; Don Hoak, Chicago N.L., 17 innings, 1956; Fred Reichardt, California A.L., 17, innings, 1966; Billy Cowan, California A.L., 20, 1971; Cecil Cooper, Boston A.L., 15, 1974.

Most Pinch-hits, Lifetime—150, Manny Mota, S.F., 1962; Pitt., 1963–68; Montreal, 1969; L.A., 1969–80, N.L.

Most Pinch-hits, Season—25, Jose Morales, Montreal N.L., 1976.

Most Consecutive Pinch-hits—9, Dave Philley, Phil., N.L., 1958 (8), 1959 (1).

Most Pinch-hit Home Runs, Lifetime—18, Gerald Lynch, Pitt.-Cin. N.L., 1957–66.

Most Pinch-hit Home Runs, Season—6, Johnny Frederick, Brooklyn, N.L., 1932.

Most Stolen Bases, Lifetime—1,186, Rickey Henderson, 1979–84 Oakland, 1985–89 New York (A.L.), 1989–95 Oakland, 1996 San Diego, 1997 Anaheim

Most Stolen Bases, Season—156, Harry Stovey, Phil., A.A., 1888. Since 1900: 130, Rickey Henderson, Oak., A.L., 1982; 118, Lou Brock, St. Louis, N.L., 1974.

Most Stolen Bases, Game—7, George Gore, Chicago N.L. 1881; William Hamilton, Philadelphia N.L. 1894. (Since 1900—6, Eddie Collins, Philadelphia A.L., 1912.) and Otis Nixon, Atlanta N.L., 1991.

Most Time Stealing Home, Lifetime—35, Ty Cobb, Detroit-Phil. A.L., 1905–28.

ROOKIE OF THE YEAR

(Baseball Writers Association selections)

American League

1949 Roy Sievers, St. Louis	1966 Tommy Agee, Chicago	1982 Cal Ripken, Jr., Baltimore
1950 Walt Dropo, Boston	1967 Rod Carew, Minnesota	1983 Ron Kittle, Chicago
1951 Gil McDougald, New York	1968 Stan Bahnsen, New York	1984 Alvin Davis, Seattle
1952 Harry Byrd, Philadelphia	1969 Lou Piniella, Kansas City	1985 Ozzie Guillen, Chicago
1953 Harvey Kuenn, Detroit	1970 Thurman Munson, New York	1986 Jose Canseco, Oakland
1954 Bob Grim, New York	1971 Chris Chambliss, Cleveland	1987 Mark McGwire, Oakland
1955 Herb Score, Cleveland	1972 Carlton Fisk, Boston	1988 Walter Weiss, Oakland
1956 Luis Aparicio, Chicago	1973 Alonzo Bumbry, Baltimore	1989 Gregg Olson, Baltimore
1957 Tony Kubek, New York	1974 Mike Hargrove, Texas	1990 Sandy Alomar Jr., Cleveland
1958 Albie Pearson, Washington	1975 Fred Lynn, Boston	1991 Chuck Knoblauch, Minnesota
1959 Bob Allison, Washington	1976 Mark Fidrych, Detroit	1992 Pat Listach, Milwaukee
1960 Ron Hansen, Baltimore	1977 Eddie Murray, Baltimore	1993 Tim Salmon, California
1961 Don Schwall, Boston	1978 Lou Whitaker, Detroit	1994 Bob Hamelin, Kansas City
1962 Tom Tresh, New York	1979 Alfredo Griffin, Toronto	1995 Marty Cordova, Minnesota
1963 Gary Peters, Chicago	1979 John Castino, Minnesota	1996 Derek Jeter, New York
1964 Tony Oliva, Minnesota	1980 Joe Charboneau, Cleveland	
1965 Curt Blefary, Baltimore	1981 Dave Righetti, New York	

National League

1949	Don Newcombe, Brooklyn	1966	Tommy Helms, Cincinnati	1982	Steve Sax, Los Angeles
1950	Sam Jethroe, Boston	1967	Tom Seaver, New York	1983	Darryl Strawberry, New York
1951	Willie Mays, New York	1968	Johnny Bench, Cincinnati	1984	Dwight Gooden, New York
1952	Joe Black, Brooklyn	1969	Ted Sizemore, Los Angeles	1985	Vince Coleman, St. Louis
1953	Jim Gilliam, Brooklyn	1970	Carl Morton, Montreal	1986	Todd Worrell, St. Louis
1954	Wally Moon, St. Louis	1971	Earl Williams, Atlanta	1987	Benito Santiago, San Diego
1955	Bill Virdon, St. Louis	1972	Jon Matlack, New York	1988	Chris Sabo, Cincinnati
1956	Frank Robinson, Cincinnati	1973	Gary Matthews, San Francisco	1989	Jerome Walton, Chicago
1957	Jack Sanford, Philadelphia	1974	Bake McBride, St. Louis	1990	Dave Justice, Atlanta
1958	Orlando Cepeda, San Francisco	1975	John Montefusco, San Francisco	1991	Jeff Baguell, Houston
1959	Willie McCovey, San Francisco	1976	Pat Zachry, Cincinnati	1992	Eric Karros, Los Angeles
1960	Frank Howard, Los Angeles	1976	Bruce Metzger, San Diego	1993	Mike Piazza, Los Angeles
1961	Billy Williams, Chicago	1977	Andre Dawson, Montreal	1994	Raul Mondesi, Los Angeles
1962	Ken Hubbs, Chicago	1978	Bob Horner, Atlanta	1995	Hideo Nomo, Los Angeles
1963	Pete Rose, Cincinnati	1979	Rick Sutcliffe, Los Angeles	1996	Todd Hollandsworth, Los Angeles
1964	Richie Allen, Philadelphia	1980	Steve Howe, Los Angeles		
1965	Jim Lefebvre, Los Angeles	1981	Fernando Valenzuela, Los Angeles		

MOST HOME RUNS IN ONE SEASON

(45 or More)

HR	Player/Team	Year	HR	Player/Team	Year
61	Roger Maris, New York (AL)	1961	48	Harmon Killebrew, Minnesota (AL)	1962
60	Babe Ruth, New York (AL)	1927	48	Willie Stargell, Pittsburgh (NL)	1971
59	Babe Ruth, New York (AL)	1921	48	Dave Kingman, Chicago (NL)	1979
58	Jimmy Foxx, Philadelphia (AL)	1932	48	Mike Schmidt, Philadelphia (NL)	1980
58	Hank Greenberg, Detroit (AL)	1938	48	Albert Belle, Cleveland (AL)	1996
56	Hack Wilson, Chicago (NL)	1930	47	Babe Ruth, New York (AL)	1926
56	Ken Griffey, Jr., Seattle (AL)	1997	47	Ralph Kiner, Pittsburgh (NL)	1950
54	Babe Ruth, New York (AL)	1920	47	Ed Mathews, Milwaukee (NL)	1953
54	Babe Ruth, New York (AL)	1928	47	Ernie Banks, Chicago (NL)	1958
54	Ralph Kiner, Pittsburgh (NL)	1949	47	Willie Mays, San Francisco (NL)	1964
54	Mickey Mantle, New York (AL)	1961	47	Henry Aaron, Atlanta (NL)	1971
52	Mickey Mantle, New York (AL)	1956	47	Reggie Jackson, Oakland (AL)	1969
52	Willie Mays, San Francisco (NL)	1965	47	George Bell, Toronto (AL)	1987
52	George Foster, Cincinnati (NL)	1977	47	Kevin Mitchell, San Francisco (NL)	1989
52	Mark McGwire, Oakland (AL)	1996	47	Andres Galarraga, Colorado (NL)	1996
51	Ralph Kiner, Pittsburgh (NL)	1947	47	Juan Gonzalez, Texas (AL)	1996
51	John Mize, New York (NL)	1947	46	Babe Ruth, New York (AL)	1924
51	Willie Mays, New York (NL)	1955	46	Babe Ruth, New York, (AL)	1929
51	Cecil Fielder (AL)	1990	46	Babe Ruth, New York (AL)	1931
50	Jimmy Foxx, Boston (AL)	1938	46	Lou Gehrig, New York (AL)	1931
50	Albert Belle, Cleveland (AL)	1995	46	Joe DiMaggio, New York (AL)	1937
50	Brady Anderson, Baltimore (AL)	1996	46	Ed Mathews, Milwaukee (NL)	1959
49	Babe Ruth, New York (AL)	1930	46	Orlando Cepeda, San Francisco (NL)	1961
49	Lou Gehrig, New York (AL)	1934			
49	Lou Gehrig, New York (AL)	1936	46	Jim Rice, Boston (AL)	1978
49	Ted Kluszewski, Cincinnati (NL)	1954	46	Juan Gonzalez, Texas (AL)	1993
49	Willie Mays, San Francisco (NL)	1962	46	Barry Bonds, San Francisco (NL)	1993
49	Harmon Killebrew, Minnesota (AL)	1964	45	Harmon Killebrew, Minnesota (AL)	1963
49	Frank Robinson, Baltimore (AL)	1966	45	Willie McCovey, San Francisco (NL)	1969
49	Harmon Killebrew, Minnesota (AL)	1969			
49	Mark McGwire, Oakland (AL)	1987	45	Johnny Bench, Cincinnati (NL)	1970
49	Andre Dawson, Chicago (NL)	1987	45	Gorman Thomas, Milwaukee (AL)	1979
49	Ken Griffey, Jr., Seattle (AL)	1996	45	Henry Aaron, Milwaukee (NL)	1962
49	Larry Walker, Colorado (NL)	1997	45	Ken Griffey, Jr., Seattle (AL)	1993
48	Jimmy Foxx, Philadelphia (AL)	1933			

MAJOR LEAGUE BASEBALL—1997

AMERICAN LEAGUE FINAL STANDINGS—1997

EASTERN DIVISION

Team	W	L	Pct	GB
Baltimore Orioles	98	64	.605	—
New York Yankees	96	66	.583	2
Detroit Tigers	79	83	.488	19
Boston Red Sox	78	84	.481	20
Toronto Blue Jays	76	86	.3469	22

CENTRAL DIVISION

Team	W	L	Pct	GB
Cleveland Indians	86	75	.534	—
Chicago White Sox	80	81	.497	6
Milwaukee Brewers	78	83	.484	8
Minnesota Twins	68	94	.420	18½
Kansas City Royals	67	94	.416	19

WESTERN DIVISION

Team	W	L	Pct	GB
Seattle Mariners	90	72	.556	—
Anaheim Angels	84	78	.519	6
Texas Rangers	77	85	.475	13
Oakland Athletics	65	97	.401	25

AMERICAN LEAGUE LEADERS—1997

Batting—Frank Thomas, Chicago	.346
Runs—Ken Griffey, Jr., Seattle	125
Hits—Nomar Garciaparra, Boston	209
Runs batted in—Ken Griffey, Jr., Seattle	147
Triples—Nomar Garciaparra, Boston	11
Doubles—John Valentin, Boston	47
Home runs—Ken Griffey, Jr., Seattle	56
Stolen bases—Brian L. Hunter, Detroit	74
Walks—Jay Buhner, Seattle	119
Slugging percentage—Ken Griffey, Jr., Seattle	.646
Strikeouts—Melvin Nieves, Detroit	157

A.L. Pitching

Victories—Roger Clemens, Toronto	21
Earned run average—Roger Clemens, Toronto	2.05
Strikeouts—Roger Clemens, Toronto	292
Shutouts—Roger Clemens, Pat Hentgen, Toronto	3
Complete games—Roger Clemens, Toronto	9
Saves—Randy Myers, Baltimore	45
Innings pitched—Roger Clemens, Pat Hentgen, Toronto	264

American League Divisional Series

Cleveland Indians defeat New York Yankees, 3 games to 2
Sept. 30—NEW YORK 8, Cleveland 6
Oct. 2—Cleveland 7, NEW YORK 5
Oct. 4—New York 6, CLEVELAND 1
Oct. 5—CLEVELAND 3, New York 1
Oct. 6—CLEVELAND 4, New York 3

Baltimore Orioles defeat Seattle Mariners, 3 games to 1
Oct. 1—Baltimore 9, SEATTLE 3
Oct. 2—Baltimore 9, SEATTLE 3
Oct. 4—Seattle 4, BALTIMORE 2
Oct. 5—BALTIMORE 3, Seattle 1

(HOME TEAM IN CAPS.)

NATIONAL LEAGUE FINAL STANDINGS—1997

EASTERN DIVISION

Team	W	L	Pct	GB
Atlanta Braves	101	61	.623	—
Florida Marlins	92	70	.568	9
New York Mets	88	74	.543	13
Montreal Expos	78	84	.481	23
Philadelphia Phillies	68	94	.420	33

CENTRAL DIVISION

Team	W	L	Pct	GB
Houston Astros	84	78	.519	—
Pittsburgh Pirates	79	83	.488	5
Cincinnati Reds	76	86	.469	8
St. Louis Cardinals	73	89	.451	11
Chicago Cubs	68	94	.420	16

WESTERN DIVISION

Team	W	L	Pct	GB
San Francisco Giants	90	72	.556	—
Los Angeles Dodgers	88	74	.543	2
Colorado Rockies	83	79	.512	7
San Diego Padres	76	86	.469	14

NATIONAL LEAGUE LEADERS—1997

Batting—Tony Gwynn, San Diego	.372
Runs—Craig Biggio, Houston	146
Hits—Tony Gwynn, San Diego	220
Runs batted in—Andres Galarraga, Colorado	140
Triples—Delino Deshields, St.Louis	14
Doubles—Mark Grudzielanek, Montreal	54
Home runs—Larry Walker, Colorado	49
Stolen bases—Tony Womack, Pittsburgh	60
Walks—Barry Bonds, San Francisco	145
Slugging percentage—Larry Walker, Colorado	.720
Strikeouts—Sammy Sosa, Chicago	174

N.L. Pitching

Victories—Denny Neagle, Atlanta	20
Earned run average—Pedro J. Martinez, Montreal	1.90
Strikeouts—Curt Schilling, Philadelphia	319
Shutouts—Carlos Perez, Montreal	5
Complete games—Pedro J. Martinez, Montreal	13
Saves—Jeff Shaw, Cincinnati	42
Innings pitched—John Smoltz, Atlanta	256

National League Divisional Series

Atlanta Braves defeat Houston Astros, 3 games to 0
Sept. 30—ATLANTA 2, Houston 1
Oct. 1—ATLANTA 13, Houston 3
Oct. 3—Atlanta 4, HOUSTON 1

Florida Marlins defeat San Francisco Giants, 3 games to 0
Sept. 30—FLORIDA 2, San Francisco 1
Oct. 1—FLORIDA 7, San Francisco 6
Oct. 3—Florida 6, SAN FRANCISCO 2

(HOME TEAM IN CAPS.)

AMERICAN LEAGUE AVERAGES—1997

Team Batting

	Avg	AB	R	H	HR	RBI
Boston	.291	5,779	850	1,683	185	810
New York	.287	5,710	891	1,636	161	846
Cleveland	.286	5,556	868	1,589	220	810
Seattle	.280	5,614	925	1,574	264	890
Texas	.274	5,653	807	1,548	187	773
Chicago	.273	5,491	779	1,498	158	740
Anaheim	.272	5,628	829	1,531	161	775

	Avg	AB	R	H	HR	RBI
Minnesota	.270	5,634	772	1,522	132	730
Baltimore	.268	5,584	812	1,498	196	780
Kansas City	.264	5,599	747	1,478	158	711
Milwaukee	.260	5,444	681	1,415	135	643
Oakland	.260	5,589	763	1,451	197	714
Detroit	.258	5,481	784	1,415	176	743
Toronto	.244	5,473	655	1,333	147	627

Individual Batting
(Based on 300 plate appearances.)

	Avg	AB	R	H	HR	RBI
Frank Thomas, Chicago	.347	530	110	184	35	125
Edgar Martinez, Seattle	.330	542	104	179	28	108
David Justice, Cleveland	.329	495	84	163	33	101
Bernie Williams, New York	.328	509	107	167	21	100
Manny Ramirez, Cleveland	.328	561	99	184	26	88
Paul O'Neill, New York	.324	553	89	179	21	117
Rusty Greer, Texas	.321	601	112	193	26	87
Reggie Jefferson, Boston	.319	489	74	156	13	67
Mo Vaughn, Boston	.315	527	91	166	35	96
Ivan Rodriguez, Texas	.313	597	98	187	20	77
Troy O'Leary, Boston	.309	499	65	154	15	80
John Valentin, Boston	.306	575	95	176	18	77
Nomar Garciaparra, Boston	.306	684	122	209	30	98
Paul Molitor, Minnesota	.305	538	63	164	10	89
Ken Griffey, Jr., Seattle	.304	608	125	185	56	147
Garret Anderson, Anaheim	.303	624	76	189	8	92
Harold Baines, Baltimore	.301	452	55	136	16	67
Alex Rodriguez, Seattle	.300	587	100	176	23	84
Joey Cora, Seattle	.300	574	105	172	11	54
Darin Erstad, Anaheim	.299	539	99	161	16	77
Bob Higginson, Detroit	.299	546	94	163	27	101

Individual Pitching
(Based on 3 decisions.)

	W	L	ERA	IP	H	BB	SO
Roger Clemens, Toronto	21	7	2.05	264.0	204	68	292
Randy Johnson, Seattle	20	4	2.28	213.0	147	77	291
David Cone, New York	12	6	2.82	195.0	155	86	222
Andy Pettitte, New York	18	7	2.88	240.1	233	65	166
Justin Thompson, Detroit	15	11	3.02	223.1	188	66	151
Mike Mussina, Baltimore	15	8	3.20	224.2	197	54	218
Kevin Appier, Kansas City	9	13	3.40	235.2	215	74	196
Jimmy Key, Baltimore	16	10	3.43	212.1	210	82	141
Jeff Fassero, Seattle	16	9	3.61	234.1	226	84	189
Pat Hentgen, Toronto	15	10	3.68	264.0	252	71	160
Scott Erickson, Baltimore	16	7	3.69	221.2	218	61	131
Tom Gordon	6	10	3.74	182.2	155	78	159
Jamie Moyer, Seattle	17	5	3.86	188.2	187	43	113
Brad Radke, Minnesota	20	10	3.87	239.2	238	48	174
Scott Kamieniecki, Baltimore	10	6	4.01	179.1	179	67	109
Willie Blair, Detroit	16	8	4.17	175.0	186	46	90
Darren Oliver, Texas	13	12	4.20	201.1	213	82	104
David Wells, New York	16	10	4.21	218.0	239	45	156
Bob Tewksbury, Minnesota	8	13	4.22	168.2	200	31	92
Chuck Finley, Anaheim	13	6	4.23	164.0	152	65	155

Team Pitching

	W	ERA	SHO	SV	HR	BB	SO
New York	96	3.84	10	51	144	532	1,165
Baltimore	98	3.91	10	59	164	563	1,139
Toronto	76	3.92	16	35	167	497	1,150
Milwaukee	78	4.24	8	44	177	541	1,012
Anaheim	84	4.52	5	39	202	605	1,050
Detroit	79	4.56	8	42	178	552	982
Texas	77	4.69	9	33	169	541	925
Kansas City	67	4.71	5	29	186	531	961
Cleveland	86	4.73	3	39	181	575	1,036
Chicago	80	4.74	7	52	175	575	961
Seattle	91	4.79	8	38	192	598	1,207
Boston	78	4.88	4	40	149	610	987
Minnesota	68	5.02	4	30	187	495	908
Oakland	65	5.49	1	38	197	642	953

NATIONAL LEAGUE AVERAGES—1997

Team Batting

	Avg	AB	R	H	HR	RBI
Colorado	.288	5,603	923	1,611	239	869
San Diego	.271	5,609	795	1,519	152	761
Atlanta	.270	5,528	791	1,490	174	755
Los Angeles	.268	5,544	742	1,488	174	706
Chicago	.263	5,489	687	1,444	127	642
New York	.262	5,524	777	1,448	153	741
Pittsburgh	.262	5,507	724	1,441	129	686
Florida	.259	5,439	740	1,410	136	703
Houston	.259	5,502	777	1,427	133	720
Montreal	.258	5,526	691	1,423	172	659
San Francisco	.258	5,480	784	1,414	172	746
Philadelphia	.255	5,443	668	1,390	116	622
St. Louis	.255	5,524	689	1,409	144	653
Cincinnati	.253	5,484	651	1,386	142	612

Individual Batting
(Based on 300 plate appearances.)

	Avg	AB	R	H	HR	RBI
Tony Gwynn, San Diego	.372	592	97	220	17	119
Larry Walker, Colorado	.366	568	143	208	49	130
Mike Piazza, Los Angeles	.362	556	104	201	40	124
Kenny Lofton, Atlanta	.333	493	90	164	5	48
Wally Joyner, San Diego	.327	455	59	149	13	83
Mark Grace, Chicago	.319	555	87	177	13	78
Andres Galarraga, Colorado	.318	600	120	191	41	140
Edgardo Alfonzo, New York	.315	518	84	163	10	72
Raul Mondesi, Los Angeles	.310	616	95	191	30	87
Craig Biggio, Houston	.309	619	146	191	22	81
Dante Bichette, Colorado	.308	561	81	173	26	118
Jeff Blauser, Atlanta	.308	519	90	160	17	70
David Segui, Montreal	.307	459	75	141	21	68
Vinny Castilla, Colorado	.304	612	94	186	40	113
Shawon Dunston, Pittsburgh	.300	490	71	147	14	57
Doug Glanville, Chicago	.300	474	79	142	4	35
Bobby Bonilla, Florida	.297	562	77	167	17	96
Chipper Jones, Atlanta	.295	597	100	176	21	111
Delino Deshields, St. Louis	.295	572	92	169	11	58
Ray Lankford, St. Louis	.295	465	94	137	31	98
Mickey Morandini, Philadelphia	.295	553	83	163	1	39

Individual Pitching
(Based on 10 decisions.)

	W	L	ERA	IP	H	BB	SO
Pedro J. Martinez, Montreal	17	8	1.90	241.1	158	67	305
Greg Maddux, Atlanta	19	4	2.20	232.2	200	20	177
Darryl Kile, Houston	19	7	2.57	255.2	208	94	205
Ismael Valdes, Los Angeles	10	11	2.65	196.2	171	47	140
Kevin Brown, Florida	16	8	2.69	237.1	214	66	205
Rick Reed, New York	13	9	2.89	208.1	186	31	113
Tom Glavine, Atlanta	14	7	2.96	240.0	197	79	152
Curt Schilling, Philadelphia	17	11	2.97	254.1	208	58	319
Denny Neagle, Atlanta	20	5	2.97	233.1	204	49	172
John Smoltz, Atlanta	15	12	3.02	256.0	234	63	241

	W	L	ERA	IP	H	BB	SO
Andy Benes, St. Louis	10	7	3.10	177.0	149	61	175
Shawn Estes, San Francisco	19	5	3.18	201.0	162	100	181
Matt Morris, St. Louis	12	9	3.19	217.0	208	69	149
Chan Ho Park, Los Angeles	14	8	3.38	192.0	149	70	166
Kirk Rueter, San Franciso	13	6	3.45	190.2	194	52	115
Chris Holt, Houston	8	12	3.52	209.2	211	61	95
Alex Fernandez, Florida	17	12	3.59	220.2	193	69	183
Bobby Jones, New York	15	9	3.63	193.1	177	63	125
Francisco Cordova, Pittsburgh	11	8	3.63	178.2	175	49	121
Mark Clark, Chicago	14	8	3.82	205.0	213	59	123

Team Pitching

	W	ERA	SHO	SV	HR	BB	SO
Atlanta	101	3.18	17	37	111	450	1,196
Los Angeles	88	3.63	6	45	163	546	1,232
Houston	84	3.67	12	37	134	511	1,138
Florida	92	3.83	10	39	131	639	1,188
St. Louis	73	3.90	3	39	124	535	1,133
New York	88	3.95	8	49	160	504	982
Montreal	78	4.14	14	37	149	557	1,138
Pittsburgh	79	4.28	8	41	143	560	1,080
Cincinnati	76	4.42	8	49	173	558	1,159
San Francisco	90	4.42	9	45	160	579	1,041
Chicago	68	4.44	4	37	185	590	1,072
Philadelphia	68	4.87	7	35	171	616	1,209
San Diego	76	4.99	2	43	172	596	1,059
Colorado	83	5.25	5	38	196	566	870

AMERICAN LEAGUE CHAMPIONSHIP SERIES—1997

Cleveland Indians win series, 4 games to 2

1st Game, at Baltimore, Oct. 8, 1997

Cleveland	000	000	000	—	0	4	1
Baltimore	102	000	00x	—	3	6	1

Pitchers—Cleveland: Ogea, Brian Anderson. Baltimore: Erickson, Myers. Winner: Erickson. Loser: Ogea. Attendance: 49,029.

2nd Game, at Baltimore, Oct. 9, 1997

Cleveland	200	000	030	—	5	6	3
Baltimore	020	002	000	—	4	8	1

Pitchers—Cleveland: Nagy, Morman, Juden, Assenmacher, Jackson, Mesa. Baltimore: Key, Kamieniecki, Benitez, Mills. Winner: Assenmacher. Loser: Benitez. Attendance: 49,131.

3rd Game, at Cleveland, Oct. 11, 1997

Baltimore	000	000	001	000	1	8	1
Cleveland	000	000	100	001	2	6	0

Pitchers—Baltimore: Mussina, Benitez, Orosco, Mills, Rhodes, Myers. Cleveland: Hershiser, Assenmacher, Jackson, Mesa, Juden, Morman, Plunk. Winner: Plunk. Loser: Myers. Attendance: 45,047.

4th Game, at Cleveland, Oct. 12, 1997

Baltimore	014	000	101	—	7	12	2
Cleveland	020	140	001	—	8	13	0

Pitchers—Baltimore: Erickson, Rhodes, Mills, Orosco, Benitez. Cleveland: Wright, Brian Anderson, Juden, Assenmacher, Jackson, Mesa. Winner: Mesa. Loser: Mills. Attendance: 45,081.

5th Game, at Cleveland, Oct. 13, 1997

Baltimore	002	000	002	—	4	10	1
Cleveland	000	000	002	—	2	8	1

Pitchers—Baltimore: Kamieniecki, Key, Myers. Cleveland: Ogea, Assenmacher, Jackson. Winner: Kamieniecki. Loser: Ogea. Attendance: 45,068.

6th Game, at Baltimore, Oct. 15, 1997

Cleveland	000	000	000	01	1	3	0
Baltimore	000	000	000	00	0	10	0

Pitchers—Cleveland: Nagy, Assenmacher, Jackson, Brian Anderson, Mesa. Baltimore: Mussina, Myers, Benitez. Winner: Brian Anderson. Loser: Benitez. Attendance: 49,075.

NATIONAL LEAGUE CHAMPIONSHIP SERIES—1997

Florida Marlins win series, 4 games to 2

1st Game, at Atlanta, Oct. 7, 1997

Florida	302	000	000	—	5	6	0
Atlanta	101	001	000	—	3	5	2

Pitchers—Florida: Brown, Cook, Powell, Nen. Atlanta: Maddux, Neagle. Winner: Brown. Loser: Maddux. Attendance: 49,244.

2nd Game, at Atlanta, Oct. 8, 1997

Florida	000	000	010	—	1	3	1
Atlanta	302	000	20x	—	7	13	0

Pitchers—Florida: Fernandez, Leiter, Heredia, Vosberg. Atlanta: Glavine, Cather, Wohlers. Winner: Glavine. Loser: Fernandez. Attendance: 48,933.

3rd Game, at Florida, Oct. 10, 1997

Atlanta	000	101	000	—	2	6	1
Florida	000	104	00x	—	5	8	1

Pitchers—Atlanta: Smoltz, Cather, Ligtenberg. Florida: Saunders, Hernandez, Cook, Nen. Winner: Hernandez. Loser: Smoltz. Attendance: 53,857.

4th Game, at Florida, Oct. 11, 1997

Atlanta	101	020	000	—	4	11	0
Florida	000	000	000	—	0	4	0

Pitchers—Atlanta: Neagle. Florida: Leiter, Heredia, Vosberg. Winner: Neagle. Loser: Leiter. Attendance: 54,890.

5th Game, at Florida, Oct. 12, 1997

Atlanta	010	000	000	—	1	3	0
Florida	100	000	10x	—	2	5	0

Pitchers—Atlanta: Maddux, Cather. Florida: Hernandez. Winner: Hernandez. Loser: Maddux. Attendance: 51,892.

6th Game, at Atlanta, Oct. 14, 1997

Florida	400	003	000	—	7	10	1
Atlanta	120	000	001	—	4	11	1

Pitchers—Florida: Brown. Atlanta: Glavine, Cather, Ligtenberg, Embree. Winner: Brown. Loser: Glavine. Attendance: 50,446.

WORLD SERIES—1997

Florida Marlins win series, 4 games to 3

1st Game—Florida, Oct. 18
Florida 7, Cleveland 4

CLEVELAND (AL)	AB	R	H	RBI	FLORIDA (NL)	AB	R	H	RBI
Roberts 2b	4	1	2	0	White cf	4	0	0	0
Vizquel ss	4	0	0	0	Renteria ss	4	0	0	1
Ramirez rf	3	1	1	1	Sheffield rf	2	1	0	0
Justice lf	4	0	2	1	Bonilla 3b	3	2	2	0
Williams 3b	5	0	1	0	Daulton 1b	2	1	1	0
Thome 1b	5	1	1	0	Conine 1b	2	0	1	1
Alomar c	5	0	1	0	Alou lf	3	1	1	3
Grissom cf	3	1	2	0	Johnson c	3	1	1	1
Hershiser p	2	0	0	0	Counsell 2b	3	1	1	0
Juden p	0	0	0	0	Hernandez p	2	0	0	0
Branson ph	1	0	0	0	Cook p	0	0	0	0
Plunk p	0	0	0	0	Powell p	0	0	0	0
Gile ph	1	0	1	1	Cangelosi ph	1	0	0	0
Assenmacher p	0	0	0	0	Nen p	0	0	0	0
Totals	**37**	**4**	**11**	**4**	**Totals**	**29**	**7**	**7**	**6**

Cleveland	100	011	010	—	4	11	0
Florida	001	420	00x	—	7	7	1

E—Sheffield. LOB—Cleveland 12, Florida 6. 2B—Roberts 2, Grissom, Giles, Counsel. HR—Ramirez (1) off Hernandez, Thome (1) off Hernandez, Alou (1) off Hershiser, Johnson (1) off Hershiser. S—Vizquel, Hernandez. GIDP—Conine. DP—Cleveland 1 (Roberts, Vizquel and Thome).

	IP	H	R	ER	BB	SO	HR	ERA
Cleveland								
Hershiser (L 0–1)	4⅓	6	7	7	4	2	2	14.54
Juden	⅔	0	0	0	2	0	0	0.00
Plunk	2	1	0	0	1	1	0	0.00
Assenmacher	1	0	0	0	0	2	0	0.00
Florida								
Hernandez (W 1–0)	5⅔	8	3	3	2	5	2	4.76
Cook	1⅔	0	0	0	1	2	0	0.00
Powell	⅔	1	1	1	2	1	0	13.50
Nen (S 1)	1	2	0	0	2	0	0	0.00

WP—Juden. Umpires—Home, Montague (NL); First, Ford (AL); Second, West (NL); Third, Kosc (AL); Left, Marsh (NL); Right, Kaiser (AL). T—3:19. Att.—67,245.

2nd Game—Florida, Oct. 19
Cleveland 6, Florida 1

CLEVELAND (AL)	AB	R	H	RBI	FLORIDA (NL)	AB	R	H	RBI
Roberts 2b	3	0	1	2	White cf	5	0	2	0
Fernandez ph-2b	2	0	2	0	Renteria ss	4	1	2	0
Vizquel ss	4	1	2	0	Sheffield rf	2	0	1	0
Ramirez rf	5	0	0	0	Bonilla 3b	4	0	0	0
Justice lf	3	0	1	1	Conine 1b	3	0	1	1
Williams 3b	4	2	2	0	Daulton ph-1b	1	0	0	0
Thome 1b	4	0	1	0	Alou lf	4	0	2	0
Alomar c	4	2	2	2	Johnson c	3	0	0	0
Grissom cf	4	1	3	1	Zaun ph	1	0	0	0
Ogea p	2	0	0	0	Counsell 2b	3	0	0	0
Jackson p	1	0	0	0	Brown p	2	0	0	0
Mesa p	0	0	0	0	Heredia p	0	0	0	0
					Eisenreich ph	1	0	0	0
					Alfonseca p	0	0	0	0
					Floyd ph	1	0	0	0
Totals	**36**	**6**	**14**	**6**	**Totals**	**34**	**1**	**8**	**1**

Cleveland	100	032	000	—	6	14	0
Florida	100	000	000	—	1	8	0

LOB—Cleveland 6, Florida 9. 2B—Vizquel, Fernandez, Renteria, Alou 2, White. HR—Alomar (1) off Brown. CS—Justice. S—Ogea. GIDP—Alomar, Ramirez 2, Sheffield. DP—Cleveland 1 (Williams, Roberts and Thome);

Florida 3 (Bonilla, Counsell and Conine), (Counsell, Renteria and Conine), Bonilla, Counsell and Daulton).

	IP	H	R	ER	BB	SO	HR	ERA
Cleveland								
Ogea (W 1–0)	6⅔	7	1	1	1	4	0	1.35
Jackson	1⅓	1	0	0	0	1	0	0.00
Mesa	1	0	0	0	1	1	0	0.00
Florida								
Brown (L 0–1)	6	10	6	6	2	4	1	9.00
Heredia	1	1	0	0	0	1	0	0.00
Alfonseca	2	3	0	0	0	0	0	0.00

HBP—by Ogea (Sheffield). Umpires—Home, Ford (AL); First, West (NL); Second, Kosc (AL); Third, Marsh (NL); Left, Kaiser (AL); Right, Montague (NL). T—2:48. Att.—67,025.

3rd Game—Cleveland, Oct. 21
Florida 14, Cleveland 11

FLORIDA (NL)	AB	R	H	RBI	CLEVELAND (AL)	AB	R	H	RBI
White cf	5	0	1	0	Roberts lf	5	1	1	2
Renteria ss	4	2	2	1	Vizquel ss	4	0	0	1
Sheffield rf	5	2	3	5	Ramirez rf	5	0	1	1
Bonilla 3b	5	1	1	2	Justice lf	3	2	0	0
Daulton 1b	4	3	2	1	Williams 3b	5	0	1	1
Conine 1b	0	0	0	0	Alomar c	3	2	2	1
Alou lf	5	0	0	0	Giles ph	0	1	0	0
Eisenreich dh	3	1	2	2	Thome 1b	4	3	2	2
Abbott ph-dh	1	0	0	0	Fernandez 2b	4	0	1	1
Floyd ph-dh	0	1	0	0	Grissom cf	3	2	2	1
Johnson c	5	2	3	0					
Counsell 2b	5	2	2	1					
Totals	**42**	**14**	**16**	**12**	**Totals**	**36**	**11**	**10**	**10**

Florida	101	102	207	—	14	16	3
Cleveland	200	320	004	—	11	10	3

E—Leiter, Bonilla 2, Grissom, Thome, Fernandez. LOB—Florida 9, Cleveland 9. 2B—Sheffield, Roberts. HR—Sheffield (1) off Nagy, Daulton (1) off Nagy, Eisenreich (1) off Nagy, Thome (2) off Leiter. SF—Fernandez. S—Roberts. GIDP—Bonilla, Sheffield, Grissom. DP—Florida 1 (Counsell, Renteria and Daulton); Cleveland 2 (Thome, Vizquel and Nagy), (Vizquel, Fernandez and Thome).

	IP	H	R	ER	BB	SO	HR	ERA
Florida								
Leiter	4⅔	6	7	4	6	3	1	7.71
Heredia	2⅓	0	0	0	1	0	0	0.00
Cook (W 1–0)	1	1	0	0	0	1	0	0.00
Nen	1	3	4	4	2	1	0	18.00
Cleveland								
Nagy	6	6	5	5	4	5	3	7.50
Anderson	⅓	1	1	1	0	0	0	27.00
Jackson	⅔	2	1	1	1	0	0	4.50
Assenmacher	3	0	0	0	1	0	0	0.00
Plunk (L 0–1)	⅔	2	4	3	2	1	0	10.12
Morman	⅓	0	2	0	1	1	0	0.00
Mesa	⅓	2	1	1	0	0	0	6.75

WP—Mesa. IBB—off Jackson (Daulton), off Plunk (Floyd). Umpires—Home, West (NL); First, Kosc (AL); Second, Marsh (NL); Third, Kaiser (AL); Left, Montague (NL); Right, Ford (AL). T—4:12. Att.—44,880.

4th Game—Cleveland, Oct. 22
Cleveland 10, Florida 3

FLORIDA (NL)	AB	R	H	RBI	CLEVELAND (AL)	AB	R	H	RBI
White cf	4	0	0	0	Roberts lf	4	0	1	0
Renteria ss	4	0	1	0	Giles lf	1	0	1	1
Sheffield rf	3	0	0	0	Vizquel ss	5	2	2	0

FLORIDA (NL) — CLEVELAND (AL)

Florida (NL)	AB	R	H	RBI	Cleveland (AL)	AB	R	H	RBI
Bonilla 3b	4	0	0	0	Ramirez rf	4	2	1	2
Daulton 1b	3	2	2	0	Justice dh	3	2	1	0
Alou lf	3	1	1	2	Williams 3b	3	3	3	2
Eisenreich dh	2	0	2	1	Alomar c	5	0	3	3
Arias ph	1	0	0	0	Thome 1b	4	0	1	0
Johnson c	4	0	0	0	Fernandez 2b	5	1	2	1
Counsell 2b	2	0	0	0	Grissom cf	4	0	0	0
Abbott ph	1	0	0	0					
Totals	31	3	6	3	Totals	38	10	15	9

Florida   000 102 000 — 3 6 2
Cleveland   303 001 12x — 10 15 0

E—Saunders, Renteria. LOB—Florida 6, Cleveland 10. 2B—Daulton, Alomar, Roberts. HR—Alou (2) off Wright, Ramirez (2) off Saunders, Williams (1) off Powell. SB—Counsell (1), Vizquel (1). CS—Giles. GIDP—Bonilla. DP—Cleveland 2 (Fernandez, Vizquel and Thome), (Thome).

	IP	H	R	ER	BB	SO	HR	ERA
Florida								
Saunders (L 0–1)	2	7	6	6	3	2	1	27.00
Alfonseca	3	3	0	0	0	4	0	0.00
Vosberg	2	3	2	2	2	1	0	9.00
Powell	1	2	2	2	1	0	1	16.20
Cleveland								
Wright (W 1–0)	6	5	3	3	5	5	1	4.50
Anderson (S 1)	3	1	0	0	2	2	0	2.70

WP—Wright. Umpires—Home, Kosc (AL); First, Marsh (NL); Second, Kaiser (AL); Third, Montague (NL); Left, Ford (AL); Right, West (NL). T—3:15. Att—44,877.

5th Game—Cleveland, Oct. 23
Florida 8, Cleveland 7

Florida (NL)	AB	R	H	RBI	Cleveland (AL)	AB	R	H	RBI
White cf	4	0	2	2	Roberts 2b	3	1	0	0
Renteria ss	5	0	2	0	Vizquel ss	4	1	1	0
Sheffield rf	5	1	2	0	Ramirez rf	5	0	1	0
Bonilla 3b	4	1	1	0	Justice dh	5	0	1	2
Arias pr-3b	0	1	0	0	Williams 3b	3	2	1	0
Daulton dh	5	1	2	0	Thome1b	4	2	2	1
Alou lf	5	2	3	4	Alomar c	5	1	2	4
Conine 1b	5	1	1	0	Giles lf	1	0	0	0
Johnson c	5	1	3	2	Grissom cf	4	0	1	0
Counsell 2b	2	0	0	0					
Totals	40	8	15	8	Totals	34	7	9	7

Florida   020 004 011 — 8 15 2
Cleveland   013 000 003 — 7 9 0

E—Hernandez, Counsell. LOB—Florida 9, Cleveland 9. 2B—White 2, Daulton, Bonilla. 3B—Thome. HR—Alomar (2) off Hernandez, Alou (3) off Hershiser. SB—Alou (1), Daulton (1). S—Vizquel. GIDP—Bonilla, Alomar, Justice. DP—Florida 2 (Renteria, Counsell and Conine), (Hernandez, Renteria and Conine); Cleveland 1 (Roberts, Vizquel and Thome).

	IP	H	R	ER	BB	SO	HR	ERA
Florida								
Hernandez (W 2–0)	8	7	6	5	8	2	1	5.27
Nen (S 2)	1	2	1	0	0	1	0	12.00
Cleveland								
Hershiser (L 0–2)	5⅔	9	6	6	2	3	1	11.70
Morman	0	0	0	0	1	0	0	0.00
Plunk	⅓	0	0	0	1	1	0	9.00
Juden	1⅓	2	1	1	0	0	0	4.50
Assenmacher	⅔	1	0	0	1	1	0	0.00
Mesa	1	3	1	1	0	1	0	7.71

Morman pitched to 1 batter in the 6th. Hernandez pitched to 2 batters in the 9th. Umpires—Home, Marsh (NL); First, Kaiser (AL); Second, Montague (NL); Third, Ford (AL); Left, West (NL); Right, Kosc (AL). T—3:39. Att—44,888.

6th Game—Florida, Oct. 25
Cleveland 4, Florida 1

Cleveland (AL)	AB	R	H	RBI	Florida (NL)	AB	R	H	RBI
Roberts 2b	3	0	1	0	White cf	5	0	3	0
Fernandez ph-2b	1	0	1	0	Renteria ss	5	0	0	0
Vizquel ss	4	1	1	0	Sheffield rf	3	0	0	0
Ramirez rf	1	0	0	2	Bonilla 3b	4	0	0	0
Justice lf	4	0	0	0	Conine 1b	2	0	0	0
Williams 3b	4	1	2	0	Eisenreich ph-1b	1	0	0	0
Thome 1b	3	1	0	0	Alou lf	3	1	1	0
Alomar c	3	0	0	0	Johnson c	4	0	2	0
Grissom cf	3	0	0	0	Counsell 2b	4	0	1	0
Ogea p	2	1	2	2	Brown p	1	0	0	0
Jackson p	1	0	0	0	Daulton ph	0	0	0	1
Assenmacher p	0	0	0	0	Heredia p	0	0	0	0
Seitzer ph	1	0	0	0	Cangelosi ph	1	0	1	0
Mesa p	0	0	0	0	Powell p	0	0	0	0
					Vosberg p	0	0	0	0
					Floyd ph	1	0	0	0
Totals	30	4	7	4	Totals	34	1	8	1

Cleveland   021 010 000 — 4 7 0
Florida   000 010 000 — 1 8 0

LOB—Cleveland 5, Florida 11. 2B—Vizquel, Ogea, Williams. 3B—White. SB—Vizquel 2 (3), White (1). CS—Roberts. SF—Ramirez 2, Daulton. GIDP—Roberts. DP—Florida 1 (Counsell, Renteria and Conine).

	IP	H	R	ER	BB	SO	HR	ERA
Cleveland								
Ogea (W 2–0)	5	4	1	1	2	1	0	1.54
Jackson	2	2	0	0	2	2	0	2.25
Assenmacher	1	1	0	0	0	1	0	0.00
Mesa (S 1)	1	1	0	0	0	1	0	5.40
Florida								
Brown (L 0–2)	5	4	4	4	3	2	0	8.18
Heredia	2	0	0	0	0	4	0	0.00
Powell	1	2	0	0	0	1	0	10.12
Vosberg	1	0	0	0	1	1	0	6.00

Ogea pitched to 1 batter in the 6th. Powell pitched to 1 batter in the 9th. IBB—off Vosberg (Alomar). Umpires—Home, Kaiser (AL); First, Montague (NL); Second, Ford (AL); Third, West (NL); Left, Kosc (AL); Right, Marsh (NL). T—3:15. Att—67,498.

7th Game—Florida, Oct. 26
Florida 3, Cleveland 2

Cleveland (AL)	AB	R	H	RBI	Florida (NL)	AB	R	H	RBI
Vizquel ss	5	0	1	0	White cf	6	0	0	0
Fernandez 2b	5	0	2	2	Renteria ss	5	0	3	1
Ramirez rf	3	0	0	0	Sheffield rf	4	0	1	0
Justice lf	5	0	0	0	Daulton 1b	3	0	0	0
Williams 3b	2	0	0	0	Conine ph-1b	1	0	0	0
Alomar c	5	0	1	0	Nen p	0	0	0	0
Thome 1b	4	1	1	0	Cangelosi ph	1	0	0	0
Grissom cf	4	1	1	1	Powell p	0	0	0	0
Wright p	2	0	0	0	Alou lf	5	1	1	0
Assenmacher p	0	0	0	0	Bonilla 3b	5	1	2	1
Jackson p	0	0	0	0	Johnson c	4	0	1	0
Anderson p	0	0	0	0	Zaun pr-c	1	0	0	0
Giles ph	1	0	0	0	Counsell 2b	3	1	0	1
Mesa p	0	0	0	0	Leiter p	0	0	0	0
Nagy p	0	0	0	0	Cook p	0	0	0	0
					Floyd ph	0	0	0	0
					Abbott ph	1	0	0	0
					Alfonseca p	0	0	0	0
					Heredia p	0	0	0	0
					Eisenreich 1b	1	0	0	0
Totals	36	2	6	2	Totals	40	3	8	3

	IP	H	R	ER	BB	SO	HR	ERA

Cleveland 002 000 000 00— 2 6 2
Florida   000 000 101 01— 3 8 0

Two out when winning run scored. E—Ramirez, Fernandez. LOB—Cleveland 8, Florida 12. 2B—Renteria. HR—Bonilla (1) off Wright. SB—Vizquel 2 (5). S—Wright. SF—Counsell. GIDP—Thome 2, Daulton. DP—Cleveland 1 (Fernandez, Vizquel and Thome); Florida 2 (Daulton, Renteria and Daulton), (Counsell, Renteria and Eisenreich).

	IP	H	R	ER	BB	SO	HR	ERA
Cleveland								
Wright	6⅓	2	1	1	5	7	1	2.92
Assenmacher	⅔	0	0	0	0	1	0	0.00
Jackson	⅔	0	0	0	0	1	0	1.93
Anderson	⅓	0	0	0	0	0	0	2.45
Mesa	1⅔	4	1	1	0	2	0	5.40

	IP	H	R	ER	BB	SO	HR	ERA
Nagy (L 0–1)	1	2	1	0	1	0	0	6.43
Florida								
Leiter	6	4	2	2	4	7	0	5.06
Cook	1	0	0	0	0	2	0	0.00
Alfonseca	1⅓	0	0	0	1	1	0	0.00
Heredia	0	1	0	0	0	0	0	0.00
Nen	1⅔	1	0	0	0	3	0	7.71
Powell (W 1–0)	1	0	0	0	1	0	0	7.36

Heredia pitched to 1 batter in the 9th. IBB—off Leiter (Ramirez), off Nagy (Eisenreich). Umpires—Home, Montague (NL); First, Ford (AL); Second, West (NL); Third, Kosc (AL); Left, Marsh (NL); Right, Kaiser (AL). T—4:11. Att.—67,204.

Series MVP—Livan Hernandez.

Soccer

The early history of the sport is uncertain. A form of the game in which a leather ball was dribbled was played in China as early as the 4th century B.C. The Romans played a variation of soccer which eventually spread throughout Europe. British schools and universities played soccer (known as football) during the 1800s, however, each school used different sets of rules and the number of players varied. This difficulty was corrected on Oct. 26, 1863, when the Football Association (FA) was formed in London for the purpose of unifying the rules of the game.

The Federation of International Football Associations (FIFA) was created in 1913 as a world governing body to coordinate all of the national associations in the world. The FIFA held the first World Cup Championship tournament in 1930 in Montevideo, Uruguay. Today, soccer is the world's most popular sport.

WORLD CUP

1930	Uruguay	1950	Uruguay	1970	Brazil
1934	Italy	1954	West Germany	1974	West Germany
1938	Italy	1958	Brazil	1978	Argentina
1942	No competition	1962	Brazil	1982	Italy
1946	No competition	1966	England	1986	Argentina
				1990	West Germany
				1994	Brazil

WORLD CUP—1994

FINAL GROUP STANDINGS

	W	L	T	GF	GA	Pts
Group A						
x-Romania	2	1	0	5	5	6
x-Switzerland	1	1	1	5	4	4
x-United States	1	1	1	3	3	4
y-Colombia	1	2	0	4	5	3
Group B						
x-Brazil	2	0	1	6	1	7
x-Sweden	1	0	2	6	4	5
y-Russia	1	2	0	7	6	3
y-Cameroon	0	2	1	3	11	1
Group C						
x-Germany	2	0	1	5	3	7
x-Spain	1	0	2	6	4	5
y-South Korea	0	1	2	4	5	2
y-Bolivia	0	2	1	1	4	1
Group D						
x-Nigeria	2	1	0	6	2	6
x-Bulgaria	2	1	0	6	3	6
x-Argentina	2	1	0	6	3	6
y-Greece	0	3	0	0	10	0
Group E						
x-Mexico	1	1	1	3	3	4
x-Ireland	1	1	1	2	2	4
x-Italy	1	1	1	2	2	4
y-Norway	1	1	1	1	1	4
Group F						
x-Netherlands	2	1	0	4	3	6
x-Saudi Arabia	2	1	0	4	3	6
x-Belgium	2	1	0	2	1	6
y-Morocco	0	3	0	2	4	0

x-Advance to next round. y-Eliminated.

CHAMPIONSHIP

Italy 0, Brazil 0 (Brazil won 3–2 in shootout)

WORLD CUP

All-Time Top 10

		Tourneys	Total Games	Record (W-L-T)	Total Pts
1.	Brazil	14	66	44–11–11	99
2.	West Germany	12	68	39–14–15	93
3.	Italy	12	54	31–11–12	74
4.	Argentina	10	48	24–15–9	57
5.	England	9	41	18–11–12	48
6.	Uruguay	9	37	15–14–8	38
7.	Soviet Union	7	31	15–10–6	36
8.	France	9	34	15–14–5	35
9.	Yugoslavia	8	33	14–12–7	35
10.	Hungary	9	32	15–14–3	33
	Spain	8	32	13–12–7	33

MAJOR LEAGUE SOCCER 1997 FINAL STANDINGS

Conference champions (*) and playoff qualifiers (+) are noted. SOW refers to shootout wins. Teams receive three points for a win but just one point for a shootout win. The GF and GA columns refer to Goals For and Goals Against in regulation play. All caps denotes home team.

EASTERN CONFERENCE

	W	L	SOW	Pts	GF	GA
*Washington	21	11	4	55	70	53
+Tampa Bay	17	15	3	45	55	60
+Columbus	15	17	3	39	42	41
+New England	15	17	4	37	40	53
New York/New Jersey	13	19	2	35	43	53

Eastern Conference Semifinals

(Best of 3)

Columbus defeats Tampa Bay, 2 games to 0
Oct. 5—Columbus 2, TAMPA BAY 1
Oct. 8—COLUMBUS 2, Tampa Bay 0

Washington D.C. defeats New England, 2 games to 0
Oct. 5—New England 1, WASHINGTON D.C. 4
Oct. 8—Washington D.C. 2, NEW ENGLAND 1

Eastern Conference Finals

(Best of 3)

Washington wins series, advances to MLS Cup
Oct. 12—WASHINGTON D.C. 3, Columbus 2
Oct. 15—Washington D.C. 1, COLUMBUS 0

WESTERN CONFERENCE

	W	L	SOW	Pts	GF	GA
*Kansas City	21	11	7	49	57	51
+Los Angeles	16	16	2	44	55	44
+Dallas	16	16	3	42	55	49
+Colorado	14	18	2	38	50	59
San Jose	12	20	3	30	55	59

Western Conference Semifinals

(Best of 3)

Colorado defeats Kansas City, 2 games to 0
Oct. 4—Colorado 3, KANSAS CITY 0
Oct. 8—COLORADO 3, Kansas City 2

Dallas defeats Los Angeles, 2 games to 0
Oct. 5—Dallas 1, LOS ANGELES 0
Oct. 8—DALLAS 3, Los Angeles 0

Western Conference Finals

(Best of 3)

Colorado wins series, advances to MLS Cup
Oct. 12—Colorado 1, DALLAS 0
Oct. 15—COLORADO 2, Dallas 1

MLS CUP

Oct. 26, RFK Stadium, Washington, D.C.

Washington, D.C. 2, Colorado 1

	1st	2nd	Total
Colorado	0	1	1
Washington, D.C.	1	1	2

First half—Washington goal scored by Jaime Moreno, 37th minute.

Second half—Second Washington goal scored by Tony Sanneh, 68th minute. Colorado goal scored by Adrian Paz, 75th minute.

1997 REGULAR SEASON

LEADING SCORERS

	Gm	G	A	Pts
Preki, Kansas City	27	12	17	41
Jaime Moreno, Washington	20	16	8	40
Raul Diaz Arce, Washington	22	15	6	36
Ronald Cerritos, San Jose	22	12	10	34
Giovanni Savarese, N.Y./N.J.	29	14	4	32

GOAL-SCORING

	G	Pts
Jaime Moreno, Washington	20	16
Raul Diaz Arce, Washington	22	15
Giovanni Savarese, N.Y./N.J.	29	14

ASSISTS

	Gm	No
Carlos Valderrama, Tampa Bay	20	19
Preki, Kansas City	27	17
Chris Henderson, Colorado	30	14
Eddie Lewis, San Jose	29	13

LEADING GOALKEEPERS

	Gm	Min	Shots	Svs	GAA	W–L
B. Friedel, Columbus	29	2,609	168	131	1.21	14–15
W. Zenga, New England	22	1,980	110	79	1.27	15–7
J. Campos, Los Angeles	19	1,584	85	60	1.31	12–5
M. Hahnemann, Colorado	25	2,157	144	111	1.54	13–11
M. Ammann, Kansas City	29	2,597	157	110	1.56	21–8

SHOTS

	Gm	Shots
Robert Warzycha, Columbus	31	92
Preki, Kansas City	27	83
Harut Karapetyan, Los Angeles	30	76
Jeff Baicher, San Jose	32	74
Alberto Naveda, New England	29	71

SHOOTOUT GOALS

	Gm	No
Mark Chung, Kansas City	32	7
Imad Baba, New England	29	6
Preki, Kansas City	27	5
Pete Marino, Columbus	28	5

GAME-WINNING ASSISTS

	Gm	GWA
Mauricio Cienfuegos, Los Angeles	22	6
Carlos Valderrama, Tampa Bay	20	5
Preki, Kansas City	27	4
Chris Armas, Los Angeles	28	4
Steve Ralston, Tampa Bay	29	4

SHOT PERCENTAGE

	Gm	SOG	Shots	Shot %
Gerell Elliott, Dallas	28	34	45	75.6%
Jaime Moreno, Washington	20	48	66	72.7
Pete Marino, Columbus	28	28	40	70.0
Raul Diaz Arce, Washington	22	47	68	69.1
Vitalis Takawira, Kansas City	28	32	47	68.1

Taxes

History of the Income Tax in the United States

Source: Ernst & Young LLP

The nation had few taxes in its early history. From 1791 to 1802, the United States Government was supported by internal taxes on distilled spirits, carriages, refined sugar, tobacco and snuff, property sold at auction, corporate bonds, and slaves. The high cost of the War of 1812 brought about the nation's first sales taxes on gold, silverware, jewelry, and watches. In 1817, however, Congress did away with all internal taxes, relying on tariffs on imported goods to provide sufficient funds for running the Government.

In 1862, in order to support the Civil War effort, Congress enacted the nation's first income tax law. It was a forerunner of our modern income tax in that it was based on the principles of graduated, or progressive, taxation and of withholding income at the source. During the Civil War, a person earning from $600 to $10,000 per year paid tax at the rate of 3%. Those with incomes of more than $10,000 paid taxes at a higher rate. Additional sales and excise taxes were added, and an "inheritance" tax also made its debut. In 1866, internal revenue collections reached their highest point in the nation's 90-year history—more than $310 million, an amount not reached again until 1911.

The Act of 1862 established the office of Commissioner of Internal Revenue. The Commissioner was given the power to assess, levy, and collect taxes, and the right to enforce the tax laws through seizure of property and income and through prosecution. His powers and authority remain very much the same today.

In 1868, Congress again focused its taxation efforts on tobacco and distilled spirits and eliminated the income tax in 1872. It had a short-lived revival in 1894 and 1895. In the latter year, the U.S. Supreme Court decided that the income tax was unconstitutional because it was not apportioned among the states in conformity with the Constitution.

In 1913, the 16th Amendment to the Constitution made the income tax a permanent fixture in the U.S. tax system. The amendment gave Congress legal authority to tax income and resulted in a revenue law that taxed incomes of both individuals and corporations. In fiscal year 1918, annual internal revenue collections for the first time passed the billion-dollar mark, rising to $5.4 billion by 1920. With the advent of World War II, employment increased, as did tax collections—to $7.3 billion. The withholding tax on wages was introduced in 1943 and was instrumental in increasing the number of taxpayers to 60 million and tax collections to $43 billion by 1945.

In 1981, Congress enacted the largest tax cut in U.S. history, approximately $750 billion over six years. The tax reduction, however, was partially offset by two tax acts, in 1982 and 1984, which attempted to raise approximately $265 billion.

On Oct. 22, 1986, President Reagan signed into law The Tax Reform Act of 1986, one of the most far-reaching reforms of the United States tax system since the adoption of the income tax. In an attempt to remain revenue neutral, the Act called for a $120 billion increase in business taxation and a corresponding decrease in individual taxation over a five-year period.

Following what seemed to be a yearly tradition of new tax acts which began in 1986, the Revenue Reconciliation Act of 1990 was signed into law on November 5, 1990. As with the '87, '88, and '89 acts, the 1990 act, while providing a number of substantive provisions, was small in comparison with the 1986 act. The emphasis of the 1990 act was increased taxes on the wealthy.

On August 10, 1993, President Clinton signed the Revenue Reconciliation Act of 1993 into law. The Act's purpose was to reduce by approximately $496 billion the Federal deficit that would otherwise accumulate in fiscal years 1994 through 1998. Approximately $241 billion of the deficit reduction will be accomplished through tax increases.

On August 5, 1997, President Clinton signed the Taxpayer Relief Act of 1997. The Act included $152 billion in tax cuts. The bills provisions include a cut in capital gains tax for individuals, a $500 per child tax credit, estate tax relief, tax incentives for education and a host of revenue-raising and tax-simplification provisions.

In recent years, the tax system has come under increased scrutiny leading to proposals for tax reform. Many policy makers in Washington have advocated some form of flat tax, a value added tax, or a retail sales tax—or a combination of these. Because any new tax law would have to be considered and passed by the Presidential administration and both branches of Congress before a transition would take place, it is unlikely that a radically changed tax system would become fully effective prior to the year 2000.

Internal Revenue Service

The Internal Revenue Service (IRS), a bureau of the U.S. Treasury Department, is the federal agency charged with the administration of the tax laws passed by Congress. The IRS functions through a national office in Washington, 4 regional offices, 63 district offices, and 10 service centers.

Operations involving most taxpayers are carried out in the district offices and service centers. District offices are organized into Resources Management, Examination, Collection, Taxpayer Service, Employee Plans and Exempt Organizations, and Criminal Investigation. All tax returns are filed with the service centers, where the IRS computer operations are located.

IRS service centers are processing an ever increasing number of returns and documents. Prior to 1987, all tax return processing was performed by hand. This process

Internal Revenue Service

	1996	1995	1994	1993	1992	1970
U.S. population (in thousands)	266,109	263,730	261,698	259,015	256,219	204,878
Number of IRS employees	102,082	112,023	110,665	113,352	116,673	68,683
Cost to govt. of collecting $100 in taxes	$0.49	$0.55	$0.58	$0.60	$0.58	$0.45
Tax per capita	$5,586.00	$5,216.44	$4,878.00	$4,543.33	$4,374.38	$955.31
Collections by principal sources (in thousands of dollars)						
Total IRS collections	$1,486,546,674	$1,375,731,835	$1,276,466,776	$1,176,685,625	$1,120,799,558	$195,722,096
Income and profits taxes						
Individual	$745,313,276	$675,779,337	$619,819,153	$585,774,159	$557,723,156	$103,651,585
Corporation	$189,054,791	$174,422,173	$154,204,684	$131,547,509	$117,950,796	$35,036,983
Employment taxes	$492,365,178	$465,405,305	$443,831,352	$411,510,516	$400,080,904	$37,449,188
Estate and gift taxes	$17,591,817	$15,144,394	$15,606,793	$12,890,965	$11,479,116	$3,680,076
Alcohol taxes	NOTE 2	NOTE 2	NOTE 2	NOTE 2	NOTE 2	$4,746,382
Tobacco taxes	NOTE 2	NOTE 2	NOTE 2	NOTE 2	NOTE 2	$2,094,212
Manufacturers' excise taxes	NOTE 1	NOTE 1	NOTE 1	NOTE 1	NOTE 1	6,683,061
All other taxes	$42,221,611	$44,980,627	$43,004,794	$34,962,476	$33,565,587	$2,380,609

NOTE: For fiscal year ending September 30th. NOTE 1: Manufacturers' excise taxes are included in the "All other taxes" amount. NOTE 2: Alcohol and tobacco tax collections are now collected and reported by the Bureau of Alcohol, Tobacco, and Firearms. *Source:* IRS 1996 Annual Report.

was time consuming and costly. In an attempt to improve the speed and efficiency of the manual processing procedure, the IRS began testing an electronic return filing system beginning with the filing of 1985 returns.

The two most significant results of the test were that refunds for the electronically-filed returns were issued more quickly and the tax processing error rate was significantly lower when compared to paper returns.

Electronic filing of individual income tax returns with refunds became an operational program in selected areas for the 1987 processing year. In 1994 13,510,000 individual returns were filed electronically, compared to 11,143,000 in 1995, and 14,977,123 in 1996.

In addition to expanding the program for the electronic filing of individual returns, the IRS has also implemented programs for the electronic filing of partnership, fiduciary, and employee benefit plan returns.

Auditing Tax Returns

Most taxpayers' contacts with the IRS arise through the auditing of their tax returns. The Service has been empowered by Congress to inquire about all persons who may be liable for any tax and to obtain for review the books and/or records pertinent to those taxpayers' returns. A wide-ranging audit operation is carried out in the 63 district offices by 16,078 revenue agents and 2,831 tax auditors.

Selecting Individual Returns for Audit

The primary method used by the IRS in selecting returns for audits is a computer program that measures the probability of tax error in each return. The higher the score, the greater the tax change potential. Other returns are selected for examination on the basis of claims for refund, multi-year audits, related return audits, and other audits initiated by the IRS as a result of informants' information, special compliance programs, and the information document matching program.

In 1996, the IRS recommended additional tax and penalties on 1,941,546 individual returns, totaling $7.6 billion.

The Appeals Process

The IRS attempts to resolve tax disputes through an administrative appeals system. Taxpayers who, after audit of their tax returns, disagree with a proposed change in their tax liabilities are entitled to an independent review of their cases. Taxpayers are able to seek an immediate, informal appeal with the Appeals Office. If, however, the dispute arises from a field audit and the amount in question exceeds $10,000, a taxpayer must submit a written protest. Alternatively, the taxpayer can wait for the examiner's report and then request consideration by the Appeals Office and file a protest if necessary. Taxpayers may represent themselves or be represented by an attorney, accountant, or any other advisor authorized to practice before the IRS. Taxpayers can forego their right to the above process and await receipt of a deficiency notice. At this juncture, taxpayers can either (1) not pay the deficiency and petition the Tax Court by a required deadline or (2) pay the deficiency and file a claim for refund with the District Director's office. If the claim is not allowed, a suit for refund may be brought either in the District Court or the Claims Court within a specified period.

Federal Individual Income Tax

The Federal individual income tax is levied on the worldwide income of U.S. citizens and resident aliens and on certain types of U.S. source income of nonresidents. For a non-itemizer, "tax table income" is adjusted gross income less $2,650 for each personal exemption and the standard deduction. If a taxpayer itemizes, tax table income is adjusted gross income minus total itemized deductions and personal exemptions. In addition, individuals may also be subject to the alternative minimum tax.

Tax Brackets—1997 Taxable Income

Joint return	Single taxpayer	Rate
$0–$41,200	$0–$24,650	15.0%
41,201–99,600	24,651–59,750	28.0%
99,601–151,750	59,751–124,650	31.0%[2]
151,751–271,050	124,651–271,050	36.0%[2]
271,051 and up[1]	271,051 and up[1]	39.6%[2]

1. The deduction for personal exemptions is phased out as the taxpayer's gross income exceeds $176,950 for a joint return and $117,950 for single taxpayers. 2. The tax rate is effectively increased because total otherwise allowable itemized deductions are reduced by 3% of the taxpayer's adjusted gross income in excess of $117,950.

Who Must File a Return[1]

You must file a return if you are:	and your gross income is at least:
Single (legally separated, divorced, or married living apart from spouse with dependent child)	$6,800
Head of household	$8,700
Married, filing jointly, living together at end of year (or at date of death of spouse)	$12,200
Married, filing separate return, or married but not living together at end of year over age 65	$2,650

1. In 1997.

Adjusted Gross Income

Gross income consists of wages and salaries, unemployment compensation, tips and gratuities, interest, dividends, annuities, rents and royalties, up to 85% of Social Security benefits if the recipient's income exceeds a base amount, and certain other types of income. Among the items excluded from gross income, and thus not subject to tax, are public assistance benefits and interest on exempt securities (mostly state and local bonds).

Adjusted gross income is determined by subtracting from gross income: alimony paid, penalties on early withdrawal of savings, payments to an I.R.A. (reduced proportionately based upon adjusted gross income levels if taxpayer is an active participant in an employer maintained retirement plan), payments to a Keogh retirement plan, and self-employed health insurance payments and moving expenses.

Itemized Deductions

Taxpayers may itemize deductions or take the standard deduction. The standard deduction amounts for 1996 are as follows: Married filing jointly and surviving spouses, $6,900; Heads of household, $6,050; Single, $4,150; and Married filing separate returns, $3,450.

Taxpayers who are age 65 or over or are blind are entitled to an additional standard deduction of $1,000 for single taxpayers and $800 for a married taxpayer.

In itemizing deductions, the following are major items that may be deducted in 1996: state and local income and property taxes, charitable contributions, employee moving expenses, medical expenses (exceeding 7.5% of adjusted gross income), casualty losses (only the amount over the $100 floor which exceeds 10% of adjusted gross income), mortgage interest, and miscellaneous deductions (deductible only to the extent by which cumulatively they exceed 2% of adjusted gross income).

Personal Exemptions

Personal exemptions are available to the taxpayer for himself, his spouse, and his dependents. The 1996 amount is $2,650 for each individual. No exemption is allowed to a taxpayer who can be claimed as a dependent on another taxpayer's return.

Credits

Taxpayers can reduce their income tax liability by claiming the benefit of certain tax credits. Each dollar of tax credit offsets a dollar of tax liability. The following are a few of the available tax credits:

Certain low-income households may claim an Earned Income Credit. The maximum Earned Income Credit is $332 for taxpayers with no qualifying children, $2,210 for taxpayers with one qualifying child and $3,656 for taxpayers with two or more qualifying children. This maximum credit will be reduced if earned income or adjusted gross income exceeds $11,930, or $5,430 for taxpayers with no qualifying children. For families with one qualifying child, the credit will be zero if earned income or adjusted gross income exceeds $25,760; for families with two or more qualifying children, the credit will be zero if income exceeds $29,290, and for families with no qualifying children, the credit will be zero if income exceeds $9,770. The earned income credit is a refundable credit.

A credit for Child and Dependent Care Expenses is available for amounts paid to care for a child or other dependent so that the taxpayer can work. The credit is between 20% and 30% (depending on adjusted gross income) of up to $2,400 of employment-related expenses for one qualifying child or dependent and up to $4,800 of expenses for two or more qualifying individuals.

The elderly and those under 65 who are retired under total disability may be entitled to a credit of up to $750 (if single) or $1,125 (if married and filing jointly). No credit is available if the taxpayer is single and has adjusted gross income of $17,500 or more. Similarly, the credit is unavailable to a married couple filing jointly if their adjusted gross income exceeds $25,000.

Federal Income Tax Comparisons

Taxes at Selected Rate Brackets After Standard Deductions and Personal Exemptions[1]

Adjusted gross income	Single return listing no dependents					Joint return listing two dependents				
	1997	1996	1995	1994	1975	1997	1996	1995	1994	1975
$10,000	$ 493	$ 518	$ 540	$ 563	$ 1,506	$ –3,500	$ –3,556	$–3,110[2]	$–2,527[2]	$ 829
20,000	1,980	2,018	2,040	2,063	4,153	975	–1,324	–773	–358	2,860
30,000	3,480	3,518	3,573	3,693	8,018	2,475	1,965	2,018	2,078	5,804
40,000	6,092	6,246	6,373	6,493	12,765	3,975	3,465	3,518	3,578	9,668
50,000	8,892	9,046	9,173	9,293	18,360	5,475	4,965	5,018	5,078	14,260

1. For comparison purposes, tax rate schedules were used. 2. Refund based on a basic earned income credit for families with dependent children.

State Taxes on Individuals

State	Sales/use tax (percent)[1]	Income tax (percent)[2]	State	Sales/use tax (percent)[1]	Income tax (percent)[2]
Alabama	4.0	2.0 – 5.0	Nebraska	5.0	2.62 – 6.99
Alaska	none	none	Nevada	6.5	none
Arizona	5.0	3.0 – 5.6	New Hampshire	none	none[4]
Arkansas	4.625	1.0 – 7.0	New Jersey	6.0	1.4 – 6.37
California	6.0	1.0 – 9.3	New Mexico	5.0	1.7 – 8.5
Colorado	3.0	5.0	New York	4.0	4.0 – 6.85
Connecticut	6.0	3.0 – 4.5	North Carolina	4.0	6.0 – 7.75
Delaware	none	0.0 – 6.9	North Dakota	5.0	2.67 – 12.0
Florida	6.0	none	Ohio	5.0	0.693 – 7.004
Georgia	4.0	1.0 – 6.0	Oklahoma	4.5	0.5 – 7.0
Hawaii	4.0	2.0 – 10.0	Oregon	none	5.0 – 9.0
Idaho	5.0	2.0 – 8.2	Pennsylvania	6.0	2.8
Illinois	6.25	3.0	Rhode Island	7.0	27.5[5]
Indiana	5.0	3.4	South Carolina	5.0	2.5 – 7.0
Iowa	5.0	0.4 – 9.98	South Dakota	4.0	none
Kansas	4.9	4.4 – 7.75	Tennessee	6.0	none[4]
Kentucky	6.0	2.0 – 6.0	Texas	6.25	none
Louisiana	4.0	2.0 – 6.1	Utah	4.75	2.3 – 7.0
Maine	6.0	2.0 – 8.5	Vermont	5.0	25[5]
Maryland	5.0	2.0 – 5.0	Virginia	3.5	2.0 – 5.75
Massachusetts	5.0	5.95 – 12.0 [3]	Washington	6.5	none
Michigan	6.0	4.4	West Virginia	6.0	3.0 – 6.5
Minnesota	6.5	6.0 – 8.5	Wisconsin	5.0	4.9 – 6.93
Mississippi	7.0	3.0 – 5.0	Wyoming	4.0	none
Missouri	4.225	1.5 – 6.0	Washington, D.C.	5.75	6.0 – 9.5
Montana	none	2.0 – 11.0			

1. Local and county taxes, if any, are additional. 2. Tax rate for individuals; unless otherwise noted, range denotes progressive structure; higher income pays higher rate. 3. Higher rate applies to interest and dividend income. 4. Income tax limited to dividends and interest income only. *Source:* The Federation of Tax Administrators, sso.org/fta/ind_inc.html, and *Information Please Almanac* questionnaires to the states.

Federal Corporation Taxes

Corporations are taxed under a graduated tax rate structure. If a corporation has taxable income in excess of $100,000, the amount of tax shall be increased by the lesser of five percent of such excess or $11,750. When a corporation has taxable income in excess of $15,000,000 the amount of tax shall be increased by an additional amount equal to the lesser of three percent of such excess or $100,000.

If the corporation qualifies, it may elect to be an S corporation. If it makes this election, the corporation will not (with certain exceptions) pay corporate tax on its income. Its income is instead passed through and taxed to its shareholders. There are several requirements a corporation must meet to qualify as an S corporation, including having 75 or fewer shareholders and having only one class of stock.

Tax Brackets—1997

Taxable income	Tax rate
$0–$50,000	15%
$50,001–$75,000	25%
$75,001–$100,000	34%
$100,001–$335,000	39%
$335,001–$10,000,000	34%
$10m–$15m	35%
$15m–$18.3m	38%
$18.3m and up	35%

State Corporation Income and Franchise Taxes

All states except Texas, Nevada, South Dakota, Washington, and Wyoming impose a tax on corporation net income. The majority of states impose the tax at flat rates ranging from 2.3% to approximately 10.75%. Several states have adopted a graduated basis of rates for corporations.

Nearly all states follow the federal law in defining net income. However, many states provide for varying exclusions and adjustments.

A state is empowered to tax all of the net income of its domestic corporations. With regard to non-resident corporations, however, it may only tax the net income on business carried on within its boundaries. Corporations are, therefore, required to apportion their incomes among the states where they do business, and pay a tax to each of these states. Nearly all states provide an apportionment to their domestic corporations, too, in order that they not be unduly burdened. Several states tax unincorporated businesses separately.

Federal Estate and Gift Taxes

A Federal Estate Tax Return must generally be filed for the estate of every U.S. citizen or resident whose gross estate, adjusted taxable gifts, and specific exemption exceed $600,000. An estate tax return must also generally be filed for the estate of a non-resident, if the value of his gross estate in the U.S. is more than $60,000 at the date of death. The estate tax return is due nine months after the date of death of the decedent, but a reasonable extension of time to file may be obtained for good reason.

Under the unified federal estate and gift tax structure, individuals who made taxable gifts during the calendar year are required to file a gift tax return by April 15 of the following year.

A unified credit of $192,800 is available to offset both estate and gift taxes. Any part of the credit used to offset gift taxes is not available to offset estate taxes. As a result, although they are still taxable as gifts, lifetime transfers no longer cushion the impact of progressive estate tax rates. Lifetime transfers and transfers made at death are combined for estate tax rate purposes.

Gift taxes are computed by applying the uniform rate schedule to lifetime taxable transfers (after deducting the unified credit) and subtracting the taxes payable for prior taxable periods. In general, estate taxes are computed by applying the uniform rate schedule to cumulative transfers and subtracting the gift taxes paid. An appropriate adjustment is made for taxes on lifetime transfers—such as certain gifts within three years of death—in a decedent's estate.

Among the deductions allowed in computing the amount of the estate subject to tax are funeral expenditures, administrative costs, claims and bequests to religious, charitable, and fraternal organizations or government welfare agencies, and state inheritance taxes. For transfers made after 1981 during life or death, there is an unlimited marital deduction.

An annual gift tax exclusion is provided that permits tax-free gifts to each donee of $10,000 for each year. A husband and wife who agree to treat gifts to third persons as joint gifts can exclude up to $20,000 a year to each donee. An unlimited exclusion for medical expenses and school tuition paid for the benefit of any donee is also available.

Federal Taxes Collected and Spent, by State

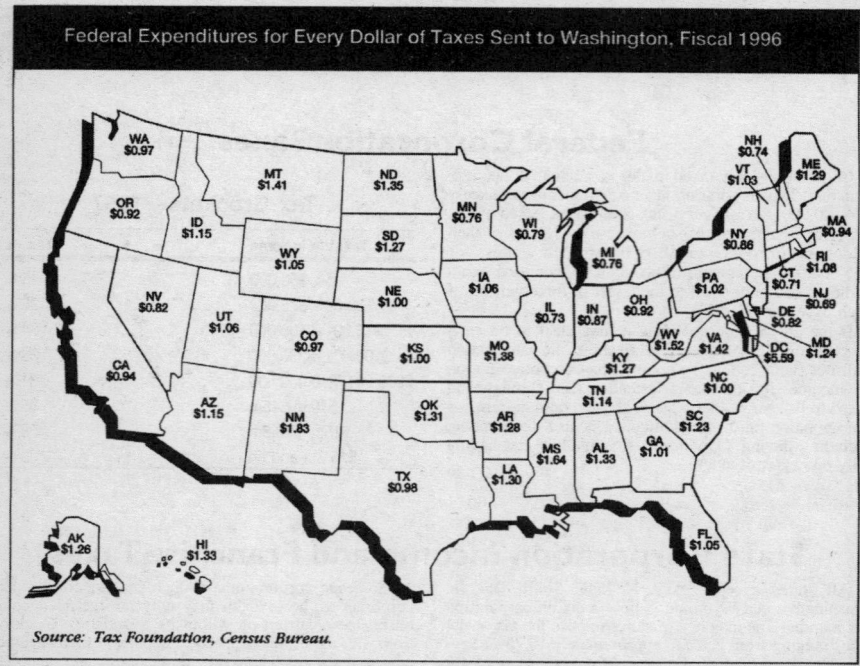

Federal Expenditures for Every Dollar of Taxes Sent to Washington, Fiscal 1996

Source: *Tax Foundation, Census Bureau.*

Current Events

Wrap-Up of International Events

Africa

Africa has been experiencing one of its most violent periods since the Colonial era, with fighting taking place in the Democratic Republic of Congo, the Congo Republic, Rwanda, Burundi, Nigeria, Sierra Leone, Liberia, Cameroon, Central African Republic, Angola, Somalia, and Sudan. At the center of Africa's unrest during 1997 was Zaire.

Mobutu Sese Seko, Zaire's flamboyant dictator for 32 years, was overthrown in May, ending one of the world's most corrupt and megalomaniacal regimes. The last of the CIA-nurtured Cold War despots, Mobutu deftly courted France and the U.S., which used Zaire as a launching pad for covert operations against bordering countries, particularly Marxist Angola. Mobutu's disastrous policies drove his country to economic collapse while he siphoned off millions of dollars for himself. Laurent Kabila and his long-standing but little-known guerrilla movement launched a seven-month campaign that ousted Mobutu and renamed the country the Democratic Republic of Congo, its name before Mobutu changed it to Zaire in 1971.

Mobutu's downfall began in October 1996, when he planned to banish the Zairian Tutsi who had lived for centuries in eastern Zaire. Neighboring Rwanda's Tutsi-led government came to their aid, as did other rebel groups, one of which was led by Kabila. After conquering eastern Zaire, Kabila earned the support of a host of Mobutu's enemies, including Uganda, Burundi, Tanzania, Zambia, Zimbabwe, and Angola. His troops swept through the country, encountering little resistance. Mobutu fled in exile to Morocco on May 16, where he died of cancer in September.

Elation over Mobutu's downfall faded as Kabila's own autocratic style emerged. He stymied U.N. human rights investigations and continued to depend on foreign troops for border skirmishes rather than establish a strong national army. Many Congolese dismissed him as a puppet ruler who allowed his country to be overrun by outsiders. These foreign armies, many of whom were pro-Tutsi, exacerbated ethnic tensions. Kabila's shaky grip on the country worried many of his neighbors, who had hoped a unified Congo would stabilize the entire region.

Ethnic violence continued unabated in neighboring countries. Following Kabila's takeover of Zaire, Rwanda relapsed into civil war, with Rwandan Hutu mounting a guerrilla war against the Tutsi-dominated army along the Congolese-Rwandan border. In Burundi, where a Tutsi-led military coup in July 1996 ignited civil war, Hutu rebels on the Congolese and Tanzanian borders renewed their attempts to topple the government. In Uganda, guerrillas with bases in the Democratic Republic of Congo became intent on the downfall of President Yoweri Museveni, denouncing him as pro-Tutsi. The Democratic Republic of Congo's western neighbor, the Congo Republic, resurfaced from a four-month civil war (June 5–Oct. 15) with the former Marxist dictator Denis Sassou-Nguesso at its helm. Buttressed by military aid from Angola, he overthrew President Pascal Lissouba, the country's first democratically elected president.

The continent's two oases of hope continue to be Uganda and South Africa. South Africa's Truth and Reconciliation Commission, which promises amnesty to those who confess their crimes under the Apartheid system, grapples with its enlightened but painful process of national recovery. Uganda's Yoweri Museveni has transformed the ruins of Idi Amin and Milton Obote's Uganda into an economic miracle. He and Nelson Mandela serve as the charismatic mentors to other African countries, preaching a philosophy of self-sufficiency and anti-corruption.

Asia

In Cambodia, the Khmer Rouge stronghold in the western jungles splintered in 1997, with factions warring against each other or defecting. The Khmer Rouge provoked the already fierce rivalry between co-prime ministers Prince Norodom Ranariddh and Hun Sen, both of whom courted Khmer Rouge factions in an effort to shore up their power. In early July, Hun Sen took advantage of the charged political atmosphere to depose Ranariddh, officially the First Prime Minister and the country's only popularly elected leader. Hun Sen later brutally cleaned house by executing more than 40 political opponents. Skirmishes between Ranariddh's forces and Hun Sen's troops continued through the fall. Meanwhile, King Norodom Sihanouk, a beloved but ineffectual figurehead, was unable to broker peace between Hun Sen and his son, Prince Ranariddh.

Shortly after the July coup, the Khmer Rouge tried their notorious leader, Pol Pot, who had not been seen by the West in more than two decades, and sentenced him to lifetime house arrest in a trial broadcast from a Khmer Rouge camp in the jungle. Why the Khmer Rouge chose that time to stage the trial is unclear, beyond the apparent wish to distance themselves from Pol Pot and garner the good graces of the international community. But much of the world felt this home-style justice to be inadequate; as one of history's most monstrous despots, Pol Pot warranted an international tribunal for his crimes against humanity.

Hong Kong was returned to Chinese sovereignty on July 1, 1997, when Britain's lease on the New Territories expired. The chief executive under the new government, Tung Chee Hwa, formulated a policy based upon the concept of "one country, two systems," thus preserving Hong Kong as a vibrant capitalist enclave. Its status as a free port and its social, economic, and judicial systems were to remain unchanged for 50 years. The international community anxiously eyed the Chinese takeover for signs of its commitment to uphold the region's free-market economy.

Terrorism: Peru and Algeria

In Peru, Tupac Amaru rebels took approximately 600 people hostage at the residence of the Japanese ambassador in Lima during a reception on December 17, 1996. President Alberto Fujimoro refused to bargain with the rebels, who demanded the release of jailed comrades. After four months of negotiations and the rebels' gradual release of most of the hostages, Peruvian soldiers stormed the embassy, rescuing all but one of the remaining 70 hostages, and killing all 14 rebels.

In Algeria, the undeclared civil war that has claimed more than 60,000 lives since 1992 escalated in its brutality and senselessness. Islamic extremists, who had originally focused their attacks on government officials and then shifted to intellectuals and journalists, most recently abandoned political motivations entirely by targeting defenseless villagers in mass slaughters as savage as they have been random. The government has been markedly ineffectual in stemming the violence, and there is some evidence that the army has looked the other way. Algeria has refused international mediation, and the outside world remains in the dark about much of what occurs within its borders.

Peace Negotiations: The Middle East and Northern Ireland

Israeli-Palestinian peace negotiations in 1997 were repeatedly undermined by both sides. Although the Hebron accord was signed in January, calling for the withdrawal of Israeli troops from the city, the construction of new Jewish settlements on the West Bank in March profoundly upset progress toward peace. Terrorism erupted after a brief one-year absence, with radical Hamas suicide bombers claiming the lives of more than 20 Israeli civilians and wounding hundreds in bombings in March, July, and September. Targeting a crowded Tel Aviv café and a busy Jerusalem marketplace among other places and indiscriminately killing men, women, and children, the new attacks again forced Israelis to live under the mortal threat of terrorism. Israeli Prime Minister Benjamin Netanyahu, accusing Palestinian Authority President Yasser Arafat of lax security, retaliated with draconian sanctions against Palestinians working in Israel, including the withholding of millions of dollars in tax revenue, a blatant violation of the Oslo accords. Netanyahu's commitment to peace also appeared disingenuous when he persisted in authorizing right-wing Israelis to build new settlements in mostly Arab East Jerusalem, demonstrating that while he professed to pursue a land settlement with Palestinians, he was in fact engaging in hawkish expansionism. Arafat, meanwhile, seemed unwilling or unable to curb the violence. With some contending that peace was impossible in the face of Palestinian terrorism and others maintaining that terrorism was the by-product of stalled peace talks, there was little hope of moving forward.

Adding to the tensions, two Mossad agents, from Israel's legendary secret service, botched an assassination attempt on Hamas's political leader in Jordan on September 25, an act that simultaneously exhibited Israel's own violent tactics and alienated Jordan, Israel's sole Arab friend. In exchange for the captured Mossad agents, Netanyahu freed a number of Palestinian prisoners, including Sheik Ahmed Yassin, Hamas's spiritual leader. Yassin and Arafat are long-time rivals and ideological opposites, and it is thus uncertain how this new mix of leaders will affect the peace negotiations.

Northern Ireland has made a significant step in the direction of stemming sectarian violence. The first formal peace talks began on October 6 with representatives of eight major Northern Irish political parties participating, a feat that in itself required three years of negotiations. Two smaller Protestant parties, including Ian Paisley's Democratic Unionists, boycotted the talks. For the first time, Sinn Fein won two seats in the British Parliament, which went to Sinn Fein President Gerry Adams and second-in-command Martin McGuinness. Although the election strengthened the IRA's political legitimacy, it was their resumption of the 17-month cease-fire, which had collapsed in February 1996, that gained the IRA a place at the negotiating table.

Europe

Eighteen years of Conservative rule ended in May when Tony Blair and the Labour Party triumphed in the British elections. Blair has been compared to Bill Clinton for his youthful, telegenic personality and centrist views. He has embarked upon constitutional reform aimed at decentralizing the U.K.; Scotland and Wales have elected this fall to form their own parliaments. Blair's controversial meeting in October with Sinn Fein's political leader, Gerry Adams, was the first meeting in 76 years between a British Prime Minister and a Sinn Fein leader. It infuriated numerous factions but was a symbolic gesture in support of the nascent peace talks in Northern Ireland.

Difficulties continue in smoothing out the single currency issue. Midyear meetings in Amsterdam confirmed the schedule for the so-called euro to be rolled out in 1999, but only countries that can meet the strict economic conditions will be permitted to participate. Both France and Germany will need to implement tough austerity measures to rein in budget deficits to less than 3% of gross national product, the level required to join the common currency. At the center of the debate is the philosophy of the euro: will it be rooted in Germany's emphasis on monetary stability or in France's drive to cut the ranks of Europe's 18 million unemployed? France's socialist government faced domestic pressure to increase capital expenditures in order to reduce the unemployment rate, rather than reduce spending to meet the targets mandated by the euro. Italy's government narrowly survived a crisis brought about by a debate on its budget, which had been dramatically cut to improve Italy's chances of joining the euro in 1999.

The Balkans

Bosnia's long-delayed municipal elections finally succeeded in taking place, but little else has improved in this ravaged nation. The terms of the December 1995 Dayton Peace accord have largely been ignored by Bosnian Serbs, with the former president, Radovan Karadzic, still controlling the Serbian enclave with impunity, under the noses of NATO forces. Many indicted war criminals, including Karadzic, remain at large, and few of the refugees have been repatriated. Biljana Plavsic, the current Bosnian Serb president, is supported by the West; but given her history as a hardline nationalist, her commitment to a united Bosnia is at best tenuous and opportunistic. NATO forces have exhibited more decisiveness than in the past, closing in on some war criminals and seizing four television stations broadcasting inflammatory Serb propaganda. By the next night, however, Serbs had regained control of the stations. Despite NATO's pledge in October to remain in Bosnia beyond the 1998 mandate, the force remains mired in its chronic ambivalence, unable to decide whether to jump into the fray or stand by and hope its presence is enough to spawn peace.

Albania's experiment with democratic reform and a free-market economy went disastrously awry, plunging the entire country into anarchy in March 1997. Large numbers of citizens in the poorest, and, until recently, most isolated country in Europe invested in shady, get-rich-quick pyramid schemes. When five of these schemes collapsed in the beginning of the year, robbing Albanians of an estimated $1.2 billion in savings, their rage turned against the government, which appeared to have sanctioned the nationwide swindle. Rioting broke out, the country's fragile infrastructure collapsed, and gangsters and rebels overran the country, resulting in more than 1,500 deaths. A multinational protection force eventually restored order and set up the elections that formally ousted President Sali Berisha. Thirty-six countries and international organizations have united to assist in Albania's reconstruction. —*BB* □

Wrap-up of National Events

Political posturing and partisan nit-picking took center stage against a stable backdrop of a strong and growing economy. The only high-profile evidence of the bipartisan cooperation President Clinton called for in his second inaugural address was the passage of a balanced-budget agreement. But this legislation required fewer than the usual compromises by each party, since windfall tax revenues generated by the strong economy meant fewer pet projects needed to be cut.

The budget battle had its share of casualties, though. The budget bill that passed the Congress emerged from the White House a few items lighter, as Clinton took this opportunity to exercise the line-item veto for the first time. The criteria Clinton used for his veto included the number of people affected by the item, whether it was good public policy, and whether it was part of the deal originally struck with Congress. He vetoed three tax breaks: one would have reimbursed New York State $200 million in Medicaid fees, vetoed since other states were not receiving the same subsidy; the second was a capital gains cut for sugar beet processing plants (its principal beneficiary would have been a large contributor to the Republican party whose taxes would have been significantly reduced); the third would have reduced the taxes on financial institutions that relocate funds in overseas banks. Critics within House Speaker Newt Gingrich's office claimed the vetos were more politics than policy, but Clinton defended his choices as being in the interests of the nation at large. In October, Clinton used the veto again to cancel 38 items in a military construction bill, saving $287 million.

Other important legislation was needlessly delayed by political squabbling between the parties. A bill to send financial aid to victims of the Red River flood in the northern Plains was held up for weeks when House Republicans tacked on two unrelated clauses about government shut-downs and methods to be used in conducting the 2000 census. Clinton vowed to veto the bill unless the provisions were removed, but Republicans would not back down. The bill eventually landed on the Oval Office desk and was promptly vetoed. When polls showed that the public was blaming Republicans for delaying the disaster relief, the $8.6 billion bill was resubmitted minus the provisions, and was signed.

Ongoing Investigations

At the end of 1996, House Speaker Newt Gingrich had been under investigation for possible ethics violations in using tax-exempt money for political purposes. A House sub-committee found him guilty of providing inaccurate and misleading information to investigators, and fined him an unprecedented $300,000. In a show of party unity, former senator Bob Dole offered to lend Gingrich the money as a personal loan. The arrangement was praised by some as an improvement over earlier plans to pay the fine out of campaign contributions, while others criticized the plan as a violation of ethics rules, which prohibit lawmakers from accepting loans from any source other than banks and financial institutions.

Eager to turn attention from their own embattled party, Republicans began calling for a full-scale investigation into alleged campaign financing irregularities by Democrats in the 1996 election. Senior Democratic officials allegedly pressured Clinton and Vice President Al Gore to raise funds for the re-election bid. Republicans objected to Gore's placing phone calls requesting donations from his office in the White House, and to Clinton's apparent use of White House perks to compensate significant donors. Early morning coffee with the Presi-

dent, or an overnight stay in the Lincoln bedroom were the most frequently cited *quid-pro-quos* for large donations to the Democratic National Committee (DNC). Democratic efforts to expand the investigation to include Republican fundraising practices were largely unsuccessful, as were Republican attempts to convince Attorney General Janet Reno to appoint a special prosecutor to investigate the Democrats.

Further allegations centered on the role of contributions from non-U.S. citizens, particularly in China, and the possibility that the Chinese were buying political influence with their illegal contributions. Current rules stipulate that only U.S. citizens are eligible to contribute to political campaigns and parties; the investigation showed a string of donations by Chinese companies and individuals, often filtered through intermediaries on their way into the coffers of the DNC or the Republican National Committee (RNC). Both parties returned significant portions of the donations they received in 1996 because they were either unable to verify the source of the donation, or because the source was improper.

The other facet of the investigation focused on how the funds were raised. Both National Committees are eligible for "soft-money" donations that are not subject to the dollar-amount limitations placed on donations to a particular candidate. The rules stipulate, however, that these donations cannot be solicited or received on the grounds of the White House. By September the Senate committee investigating fundraising irregularities had turned its gaze to the activities of Vice President Gore. Reno in September called for a review of Gore's phone calls, the first step in appointing an independent council investigation. Later in September, Reno also called for a review of all White House phone records, possibly leading to an independent council investigation of Clinton, as well.

The fervent interest in uncovering alleged violations of campaign finance rules was not evident outside the beltway, however. The Congressional investigations were largely ignored by the American public, who seemed to feel that the tactics used in the 1996 election were symptomatic of the need for finance reform rather than cause for a partisan witch hunt. Cynics and critics of the investigations charged that the investigations would not alter the outcome of the election, and were therefore a waste of taxpayer dollars. Ironically, Republicans stymied Clinton's efforts at reforming campaign financing in his first term, and Majority Leader Trent Lott met the call for reform in 1997 with procedural maneuvers to cut short the debate and prevent passage of reform legislation.

Investigations into Clinton's Washington activities were mirrored by those into alleged wrongdoing in his life in Arkansas. A sexual harassment suit brought against President Clinton for alleged actions while he was Governor of Arkansas had been long delayed through a series of legal tactics. The Supreme Court ruled in May, however, that the lawsuit brought by Paula Jones could proceed, overruling Clinton's claims that a sitting President should not be distracted by such suits while in office. The Whitewater investigation also continued throughout the year. Billing records from the Rose law firm, where Mrs. Clinton was a partner, mysteriously reappeared just days before Mrs. Clinton was to testify before a grand jury in January. This was the first time a First Lady had been called to testify before a federal grand jury, but that was just the beginning of the focus on Mrs. Clinton. Legal notes summarizing conversations between Mrs. Clinton and attorneys were subpoenaed as well, and turned over after months of legal wrangling alleging violation of attorney-client privilege. The notes ultimately contained nothing incriminating.

Sexual Harassment

Politicians weren't the only subjects of investigations in 1997. A series of sexual harassment, sexual misconduct, and sexual discrimination complaints in various branches of the armed forces erupted, resulting in numerous investigations and courts martial. In November 1996, several female recruits at the Army's Aberdeen Proving Ground complained of sexual harassment by drill instructors. The Army instituted a hot line that soldiers could use to anonymously report incidents of sexual discrimination, harassment, or assault. Those accused were removed from their posts pending investigation into the charges. By the time the line was 9 days old, it had logged over 4,000 calls, leading to more than 550 investigations. There were 12 indictments at Aberdeen alone. Staff Sergeant Delmar Simpson was convicted in May of rape and sexual misconduct, and sentenced to 25 years in military prison.

A cloud of sexual misconduct also loomed over the nomination process to fill the impending vacancy of Chairman of the Joint Chiefs of Staff. The top candidate, Gen. Joseph Ralston, admitted to having had an extra-marital affair a decade prior to his nomination. Normally the topic would not have been raised in the context of such a nomination process, but the Air Force had dismissed its only female B-52 pilot, Lt. Kelly Flinn, only weeks before for what amounted to adultery charges. Ignoring Ralston's admission would have been tantamount to sexual discrimination since they would be selectively enforcing the military's code of conduct, which prohibits adultery. The committee was spared the high-profile decision when Ralston withdrew his name.

In September, an army investigator ruled that Sgt. Major of the Army Gene McKinney, the top-ranking enlisted soldier, should be court martialed on 22 counts of sexual misconduct. The counts stem from allegations by six women who had worked with McKinney.

A long-delayed report on sexual harassment in the military finally came out in September. Sexual harassment and discrimination in the army is "commonplace," according to the report, regardless of the victim's race, rank, or gender. Sexual assault, however, is rare. The Army pledged to add an extra week to its basic training to focus on gender issues, and to make clear its "zero tolerance" for sexual discrimination.

Political Infighting

In mid-summer, no longer content with fighting across the aisle, Republicans began taking aim at their own members. In late July, a group of dissidents decided to hold a no-confidence vote to oust the party leader Newt Gingrich from his post as House Speaker. The handling of the disaster-aid bill was cited as an example of the Speaker's inability to lead the party. The coup was aborted, however, and Tom Delay, Republican majority whip, and Bill Paxon, former chairman of the Republican National Committee, resigned their party positions and apologized to party members.

In a separate incident, Senate Foreign Relations Committee chairman Jesse Helms (R-N.C.) refused to hold confirmation hearings for fellow-Republican Gov. William Weld of Massachusetts, Clinton's nominee for ambassador to Mexico. Helms claimed that Weld was too soft on drugs, which would prove troublesome in an ambassadorial role for a country with an acknowledged drug problem. Weld did not go quietly into that dark night, however, and took his case to the media, stirring controversy and ill-will before conceding defeat.

Affirmative Action Setbacks

One of the most hotly debated topics of the year was that of affirmative action. A ballot initiative in California, Proposition 209, gave a resounding mandate to efforts to roll back the affirmative action policies put in place over the past 30 years to redress discrimination against women and minorities. The California law, approved by voters in November 1996 (54–46%) and based on policies instituted at the University of California a year before, prohibits admissions and hiring policies from using race, gender, or ethnicity as factors in choosing candidates.

The effect of the policy was evident in the first year in which it affected admissions; at Boalt Hall Law School at Berkeley, admissions of black students dropped by 80% and Hispanic students by 50%. Civil rights groups petitioned Supreme Court Justice Sandra Day O'Connor, who handles emergency requests from California, to block enforcement of the new law, which was to go into effect in August. Regardless of whether O'Connor chooses to act on the emergency request, the Supreme Court will hear a number of formal challenges to the law during its 1997–98 session, which begins in October.

The affirmative action debate took place as the President vowed to make improved relations between the races a top priority in his second term. He convened an advisory committee on race relations, and has promised to act on their recommendations, which are expected in mid-1998. The races are particularly divided in their opinions of the progress made in race relations. According to a June 1997 Gallup poll, 79% of whites believe that African-Americans have an equal chance of getting a job as whites, while only 46% of blacks agree. One unfortunate area of agreement also emerged from the poll: 44% of both groups believe that whites are highly prejudiced. The good news is that 62% of both groups consider themselves to hold little or no prejudices; clearly there is work to be done on this front.

Welfare Reform

A year after the historic legislation was signed into law, the national welfare rolls have dropped by 1.5 million people to the lowest numbers in 27 years. Most of those who have left have been able to find jobs in the expanding economy, but experts warn that further reductions won't come so easily. Those who have already left the rolls were the most "employable" recipients; those who remain are more likely to be "unemployable" due to drug addiction, or physical or mental handicaps. Furthermore, although the economy is providing new jobs, there are fewer middle-income jobs available so "workfare" recipients are most likely to find lower-paying jobs.

The news for these new additions to the labor pool gets worse. Republican efforts to exempt welfare-to-work employees from the $5.15 minimum wage further exacerbates the wage problem and inflames the debate over whether welfare reform is actually helping anyone. While Republicans claim a reduced wage for welfare recipients will make them more attractive to potential employers, Democrats claim that welfare recipients are entitled to the same "living wage" as other Americans. The "working poor" are becoming ever-more apparent in the increased demands on food banks. Second Harvest, the nation's second-largest food bank, reports increased demands for food at half of its 183 centers. The government accounted for 13.5% of publicly distributed food in 1997, down from 22.2% in 1991. Private sources say the additional strain on their reserves cannot sustain the growing need as welfare reform requires people to take work—any work—even if it doesn't pay enough to put food on the table. —*TMV* □

What Happened in 1996–97

Highlights of the important events of the year from November 1996 to October 1997, organized month by month, in three categories for easy reference. For the year's major Supreme Court decisions, *see* Major Decisions of the U.S. Supreme Court, 1997. Countries of the World covers specific international events, country by country.

November 1996

World

Zaire–Rwanda Warfare Erupts (Nov. 1): Two African countries trade artillery barrages. Fighting drives another half-million Hutu refugees from United Nations camps in Zaire. **(Nov. 15):** Hundreds of thousands of Rwandan refugees stream homeward from eastern Zaire after Zairian rebels rout ethnic Hutu militias that had prevented the refugees from returning home.

U.S. Entrepreneur Slain in Moscow (Nov. 4.): Paul E. Tatum, 39, shot dead in downtown area. He had been involved in dispute over control of a major hotel.

Pakistan's Prime Minister Arrested (Nov. 5): Government of Benazir Bhutto dismissed by President on charges of corruption, abuse of power, intimidation of judiciary, and law and order breakdown.

Muslim Exiles Storm Village in Bosnia (Nov. 11): Fighting erupts as several hundred battle Serbs in attempt to reclaim homes that Muslims formerly occupied. **(Nov. 12):** Fierce fighting between Serbs and Muslims rages for second day. Russian troops withdraw.

Canada Proposes Aid Force for Zaire (Nov. 12): Volunteers to lead move to bring food and protection to more than a million refugees displaced by fighting. **(Nov. 19):** Clinton administration pleased by relatively peaceful homecoming of refugees. Agrees to send at most 800 troops to help distribute relief aid as part of Canadian-led mission.

U.S. to Keep Troops in Bosnia (Nov. 15): Clinton, in change of policy, says thousands will remain to protect fragile peace. He says "rebuilding the fabric of Bosnia's economic and political life is taking longer than anticipated."

Pope and Fidel Castro Meet at Vatican (Nov. 19): Pontiff accepts invitation from Cuban leader to visit Cuba. Meeting is crucial turning point in relations of Roman Catholic Church and Communist regime.

Yeltsin Orders Troops Withdrawn from Chechnya (Nov. 23): Moscow loses face-saving military presence in break-away region. Chechnya plans elections in January.

Serbian Demonstrators Jeer President (Nov. 25): More than 100,000 demand removal of Slobodan Milosevic for invalidating opposition election victories.

Asian-Pacific Economic Conference Held (Nov. 26): President Clinton persuades 17 other leaders to endorse efforts to virtually eliminate tariffs on computers and other information technology by year 2000.

First Verdict by War Crimes Panel (Nov. 29): Hague tribunal sentences former Bosnian Serb soldier to ten years in prison for role in massacre of unarmed civilian men by army execution squad.

Diplomats Approve Zaire Aid Mission (Nov. 29): Fourteen nations represented at Ottawa. Formal approval given to mission that could airlift food to refugees in eastern Zaire. Extent of emergency need uncertain.

Nation

U.S. Eases Rules on Medical Research (Nov. 1): F.D.A., for first time, adopts regulations to permit enrollment of some patients in study without their consent. Careful restrictions applied.

F.B.I. Quits Saudi Blast Inquiry (Nov. 1): Director charges lack of cooperation by Saudi Arabian officials and calls back agents sent to investigate bombing in June that killed 19 American airmen at quarters.

Clinton Shakes Up Government (Nov. 6): Following election victory, he accepts resignations of some top Cabinet officers, including Secretary of State Warren Christopher and Leon Panetta, Chief of Staff.

Two Charged with Rape at Army Base (Nov. 7): Officer and drill instructor accused of assaulting female privates at Maryland training center. More than two dozen women complain of sexual harassment. **(Nov. 17):** The Army's sexual harassment hotline has received more than 4,000 calls, about 550 of which will be investigated further.

House Democrats Re-Elect Leaders (Nov. 18): Representative Richard A. Gephardt, minority leader, stresses bipartisan cooperation and says "we remain ready to compromise" with Republicans.

C.I.A. Official Charged with Espionage (Nov. 18): Harold J. Nicholson arraigned after accusation that he betrayed U.S. secrets to Russia for money.

U.S. to Relax Air Bag Standards (Nov. 21): Transportation Department moves to meet rising public anxiety over danger to children and small adults.

F.D.A. Commissioner Resigns (Nov. 25): Dr. David A. Kessler leaves for personal reasons after six years. Fought to regulate tobacco, worked for standard nutrition labeling, and speeded drug approval process.

Business/Science/Society

New Contract Averts G.M. Strike (Nov. 2): U.A.W. and auto company reach three-year agreement designed to keep current employment and cut labor costs.

Cyclone Kills More Than 1,000 in India (Nov. 9): At least another thousand are missing and presumed dead as storm devastates more than 800 southeastern villages in path. Some 500,000 homeless. Refugee camps set up.

Air Collision in India Kills 349 (Nov. 12): All passengers and crew perish in crash of Saudi Arabian Airlines Boeing 747 and Kazak Airlines Ilyushin 76 near New Delhi Airport. No survivors found.

Texaco Settles Discrimination Lawsuit (Nov. 15): Agrees to pay more than $140 million, a record for racial discrimination cases. Settlement follows disclosure of tape recording of executives planning to destroy documents and disparaging minority groups.

Oldest Space Shuttle Orbits on Mission (Nov. 19): Columbia, 15 years old, blasts off at Cape Canaveral, Fla., with five-member crew. The 16-day mission will deploy, then retrieve, two scientific satellites and test techniques for building space station.

Hijacked Plane Crashes in Indian Ocean (Nov. 23): Ethiopian Airlines Boeing 767 plunges into sea off Comoro Islands with 175 passengers and crew aboard after running out of fuel. Death toll is 127, 2 of the 3 Ethiopian hijackers survive.

O. J. Simpson Shaky on Witness Stand (Nov. 25): On second day of testimony at civil trial in wrongful death suit, he says he cannot recall events at time of the killing of former wife and her friend.

U.S. Judge Blocks California Preference Plan (Nov. 27): Holds up enforcement of Proposition 209, approved by voters, prohibiting consideration of race and gender preference in state-run affirmative action programs.

December 1996

World

Czech President Undergoes Surgery (Dec. 2): Vaclav Havel, 60, operated upon for lung cancer. He led peaceful overthrow of Communist rulers in 1989.

Russian Coal Miners Strike (Dec. 3): Hundreds of thousands walk out to win back pay, in arrears for months. At least 180 mines across nation crippled.

South African Court Approves Constitution (Dec. 4): Accepts post-apartheid basic law renouncing racism and guaranteeing equal rights for all peoples.

Serbian Court Upholds Vote Annulment (Dec. 8): Affirms President Slobodan Milosevic in canceling local election results that had given control of the capital to the opposition. Increased demonstrations result.

Iraq Gets Right to Sell Oil (Dec. 9): U.N. permits marketing in limited quantities to raise funds for food, medicine, and other civilian needs. Sales had been prohibited since invasion of Kuwait. **(Dec. 10):** Iraq begins pumping oil after six years.

NATO Expands into Eastern Europe (Dec. 11): Moves to expand alliance to include former Communist nations. In gesture to Russia, NATO offers to negotiate special charter and increase military cooperation.

Israel Restores Funds for Settlements (Dec. 13): Cabinet votes large subsidies for West Bank despite warnings of confrontation with Palestinians and fears of politicians on both sides of peril to peace process.

Ghanaian Named U.N. Secretary General (Dec. 13): Security Council picks Kofi Annan, 58, to succeed Boutros Boutros-Ghali. Choice follows long confrontation between United States and France. **(Dec. 17):** General Assembly elects him formally.

I.M.F. Resumes Payments to Russia (Dec. 15): International Monetary Fund to continue disbursing $10.1 billion loan. Action represents qualified endorsement of Moscow's economic policies.

More than 100,000 Refugees Return to Rwanda (Dec. 16): Ordered to leave from Tanzania, where they had lived for nearly three years. Most are Hutus who had fled homes in 1994.

Six Red Cross Workers Slain in Chechnya (Dec. 17): Five women, four of them nurses, and a construction worker are shot in their sleep in hospital compound. Attack called worst in 133-year history of Red Cross.

Peru Guerrillas Seize 490 Hostages (Dec. 18): Capture high-ranking diplomats in raid on party at residence of Japanese ambassador. Threaten to kill captives unless government agrees to release imprisoned comrades in Túpac Amaru rebel group. **(Dec. 23):** Rebels release 225 hostages in a Christmas gesture. **(Dec. 28):** Rebels release another 20 hostages; 83 still held.

Thousands March in Belgrade Protest (Dec. 26): On 37th day of demonstrations, opposition forces continue objection to rule of President Slobodan Milosevic and Serbia's economic devastation. Crowds defy President's stepped-up pressure to stay off streets.

Guatemala Armistice Ends 36-Year Civil War (Dec. 29): Government and leftist guerrillas halt struggle in which more than 100,000 perished.

Train Bombing Kills Scores in India (Dec. 30): Two bombs explode under tracks just after crowded passenger train leaves Kokrajhar station. Police blame explosion, which killed 18 and injured 60, on separatist Bodo rebels.

Nation

Clinton Fills Top Security Posts (Dec. 5): Appoints Madeleine K. Albright, 59, chief U.N. delegate, to be first female Secretary of State. Names William S. Cohen, 56, moderate Maine Republican retiring from Senate, as Secretary of Defense. President also chooses his National Security Adviser, Anthony Lake, to be Director of Central Intelligence. Samuel R. Berger, Mr. Lake's deputy, will succeed him.

Regulation of Wetlands Tightened (Dec. 10): Administration to phase out expedited permit procedure that allowed developers to drain tens of thousands of acres that absorb floods and protect wildlife.

Air Force Clears General in Saudi Bombing (Dec. 11): Finds Brig. Gen. Terryl J. Schwalier took reasonable steps to protect against terrorist bombing in June 1996, in which 19 Americans were killed and 500 wounded.

Clinton Fills Economic Posts (Dec. 13): President names William M. Daley to be Secretary of Commerce; Charlene Barshefsky, Trade Representative, and Gene Sperling, to National Economic Council. He also appoints Bill Richardson Chief Delegate to United Nations.

Clinton Legal Fund Rejects Donations (Dec. 16): Returns or refuses to accept $639,000 after private investigators fail to verify sources of money. Fund set up to help pay Clintons' Whitewater bills.

President Completes Cabinet (Dec. 20): Seeks increased racial and ethnic diversity. Following named: Frederico F. Peña, Secretary of Energy; Rodney Slater, replacing Peña as Secretary of Transportation; Alexis Herman, Secretary of Labor; Andrew M. Cuomo, Secretary of Housing and Urban Development. Mr. Peña is Hispanic; Mr. Slater and Ms. Herman are black; Mr. Cuomo is white.

Gingrich Apologizes for Ethics Violations (Dec. 21): House subcommittee finds Speaker used tax-exempt money for political purposes and provided "inaccurate, incomplete, and unreliable information" about role of political action committee in college course he taught. Gingrich apologizes to the House.

Business/Science/Society

U.S. Spacecraft Launched Toward Mars (Dec. 4): Unmanned Mars *Pathfinder* scheduled to land on July 4, 1997, to deliver a remotely controlled roving vehicle.

Longest Space Shuttle Flight Ends (Dec. 7): *Columbia* and its five astronauts land at Cape Canaveral, Fla., after record of nearly 18 days in orbit. Science mission had been marred by jammed hatch.

Freighter Crashes New Orleans Shopping Mall (Dec. 14): Hundreds flee and 116 are injured as massive *Bright Field* loses power and much of steering ability. Pilot's maneuver averted worse river front catastrophe.

Two Huge Aerospace Companies to Merge (Dec. 15): Boeing Company announces plans to acquire McDonnell Douglas Corporation in $13.3 billion deal, tenth-largest in U.S. history and largest ever in aerospace industry.

U.S. Judge Rejects Breast Implant Evidence (Dec. 18): Rules in Oregon case that link to disease is not scientifically valid. He dismisses claims by 70 women.

TV Industry Offers New Rating System (Dec. 19): Executives propose labeling shows as suitable or unsuitable for children because of sexual or violent content.

O. J. Simpson Granted Custody of Two Children (Dec. 20): Los Angeles judge restores them to former football star despite accusations that he is responsible for deaths of their mother and her friend.

January 1997

World

Two Sentenced to Death in Rwanda Massacre (Jan. 3): Court condemns Hutu men in first attempt to punish those responsible for half a million killings in 1994.

Serbia Rejects Appeals to Honor Vote (Jan. 3): Milosevic government refuses to reinstate opposition victories in key cities. Despite call by European organization, President stiffens stand against tens of thousands of demonstrators.

Joint Government Meets in Bosnia (Jan. 3): Leaders of former opponents pledge peaceful future. Unified government paves way for reconstruction.

Marchers Paralyze Belgrade (Jan. 5): Tens of thousands of anti-government demonstrators defy police ban on marches. Weeks-long street marches protest Socialists' annulling of opposition election victories.

Gunmen Kill Senior Mexican Drug Prosecutor (Jan. 5): Assassinate Odín Gutiérrez Rico, who investigated several prominent drug-related killings.

Israel Gives Up Most of West Bank City (Jan. 12): Finally breaks deadlock with Palestinians over withdrawal from part of Hebron. (Jan. 16): After bitter disputes, Israel's coalition cabinet votes, 11–7, to approve Hebron accord, and Parliament quickly agrees. (Jan. 17): Palestinian forces claim control of most of Hebron, which Israelis had occupied for 30 years.

Mexico Repays Loan Ahead of Time (Jan. 15): President reports return of $12.5 billion borrowed to avert financial collapse two years previously.

New Bulgarian President Sworn In (Jan. 19): Petar Stoyanov, calls for new parliamentary elections, a major demand of huge crowds of street demonstrators.

Dozens Dead in Algerian Violence (Jan. 20): Car bomb outside Algiers café kills more than 30 and injures many. Hours earlier, Islamic militants massacred 36 villagers south of capital, decapitating some.

Chechnya Elects New President (Jan. 27): Voters in rebelling Russian region choose Aslan Maskhadov, 49, army chief of staff in victorious battle for independence. Foreign and Russian observers report election to have been fair and democratic.

Clergy Lead Belgrade Marchers (Jan. 27): After ten weeks of demonstrations against government policies, more than 100,000 march through Serbian capital in largest religious procession since World War II. Orthodox Patriarch Pavle is at head of marchers.

Get-Rich Schemes Fail in Albania (Jan. 28): Violent demonstrations protest collapse of pyramid investment schemes. Government promises to help pay back losses.

U.S. Reports Human Rights Flaws (Jan. 29): Administration finds worsened conditions in China, Nigeria, Cuba, and Burma (Myanmar). Record of Russia and other former Soviet states is found to be mixed.

Benazir Bhutto Rebuffed in Pakistan (Jan. 29): Former Prime Minister loses reelection chance when high court rules her ousted government was corrupt.

Nation

Panel Considers Social Security Changes (Jan. 6): Advisory group suggests nation consider investing part of system's revenues in stock market to insure solvency of the retirement program.

Newt Gingrich Reelected as House Speaker (Jan. 7): Narrowly wins in vote despite nine Republican defections over his admission of ethics violations.

Pentagon Criticized on Investigation of Gulf War Illness (Jan. 7): Special White House panel finds no proof that exposure to chemical weapons was cause but calls for further study of malady afflicting veterans, citing Pentagon's research as inadequate.

U.S. Shuttle Joins Russian Space Station (Jan. 12): *Atlantis* craft launched at Cape Canaveral, Fla., with crew of six. (Jan. 14): *Atlantis* docks flawlessly with space station *Mir*. They begin five days of joint operations. U.S. astronaut John E. Blaha prepares to return home after four months on Russian craft. Dr. Jerry L. Linenger, a physician, leaving *Atlantis* to replace Blaha.

Medals of Honor Awarded Black Veterans (Jan. 13): Seven World War II heroes finally granted citation denied previously because of race. The only living survivor of the seven, Joseph Vernon Baker, attends White House ceremony.

Gingrich Found Guilty of Ethics Violations (Jan. 17): House ethics subcommittee concludes speaker used tax-exempt funds for his politically related college course and supplied Congress with false information. Finds pattern of "disregard and lack of respect for the standards of conduct" that should be upheld by a congressman. (Jan. 21): House reprimands Gingrich. Votes penalty, 395–28, and fines him $300,000, the most severe sanction ever imposed upon a Speaker.

President Clinton Starts Second Term (Jan. 20): In inaugural address as 42nd President, he calls for racial unity and urges Republican Congress to avoid partisanship and join in his mission.

F.B.I. Laboratory Found Defective (Jan. 28): Justice Department reveals defects in operation. F.B.I. orders personnel shakeup and general overhauling. (Jan. 30): Inquiry also uncovers complaints about handling of evidence in Oklahoma City bombing case.

Business/Science/Society

Death Toll Above 200 in Europe Cold Wave (Jan. 3): Deepest freeze in decade grips continent.

Floods Cause Wide Damage in West (Jan. 5): Thousands homeless. Northern California especially hard hit. Storms blamed for many deaths in northwest.

Plane Crash Kills 29 Near Detroit (Jan. 9): Commuter turboprop craft plunges to ground in snowstorm on approach to Detroit Metropolitan Airport.

VW to Pay $100 Million in Espionage Suit (Jan. 9): Agrees to reimburse General Motors to settle lawsuit alleging theft of trade secrets by Volkswagen.

Two Women Quit the Citadel (Jan. 12): Kim Messer and Jeanie Mentavlos drop out as cadets, citing weeks of what they consider abuse by student superiors. Two other women remain in corps of 1,700.

Two Bombs Damage Atlanta Abortion Clinic (Jan. 16): None hurt in first explosion. Second injures six, including investigators and news reporters.

Bill Cosby's Son Slain (Jan. 16): Ennis Cosby, 27, graduate student, shot on Los Angeles freeway ramp in apparent robbery attempt as he changed flat tire. Ennis was only son of popular television star.

ABC Assessed $5.5 Million in Penalty (Jan. 22): Federal jury in Greensboro, N.C., awards punitive damages to Food Lion supermarket chain from network and two employees for news techniques using hidden cameras and undercover reporters.

Freeze Damages Florida Crops (Jan. 23): Worst in seven years causes possible $250 million loss in state.

Supermarket Chain Settles Bias Suit (Jan. 24): Publix agrees to pay $81.5 million for accusation that it discriminated against 100,000 women employees.

U.S. Economy Found to Be Strong (Jan. 31): Government reports vigorous 4.7 percent growth in final quarter of 1996, fueled by increase in exports. One measure finds inflation to be lowest in 30 years.

February 1997

World

Colombia Curbs TV News Broadcasts (Feb. 1): Congress gives commission broad powers to remove programs on basis of content. Some see retaliation for shows linking drug dealers and prominent politicians.

Three Nations Agree to Freeze Nazis' Gold Loot (Feb. 3): U.S., U.K., and France consider using $68 million in gold bars as possible core of fund to compensate victims of Nazis' holocaust. **(Feb. 5): Three Swiss banks plan fund for Nazis' victims.** Under pressure from American Jewish groups, they agree to setup $70 million initial amount as "humanitarian fund for the victims of the Holocaust."

Benazir Bhutto Loses in Pakistan's Election (Feb. 4): Ousted Prime Minister suffers sharp rebuff from Pakistan Muslim League, led by Nawaz Sharif, 47, industrialist, nation's leader from 1990 to 1993.

Two Israeli Copters Collide; 73 Killed (Feb. 4): All aboard perish in midair crash of craft ferrying soldiers to South Lebanon in worst military air disaster in Israel's history. Cause uncertain.

Serbian President Accepts Voting Results (Feb. 4): After 77 days of Belgrade street protests, Slobodan Milosevic reverses decision and restores opposition victories in local elections.

Ecuadorean Crisis Ends Peacefully (Feb. 9): Under agreement with Congress, Mrs. Rosalia Arteaga, 40, will serve as Interim President, first woman in post.

Europe Delays Challenge to U.S. on Havana Trade (Feb. 12): Officials seek compromise by asking World Trade Organization to postpone action against American sanctions on companies doing business with Cuba.

68 Nations Widen Telecommunications Markets (Feb. 15): Geneva conference endorses landmark agreement to grant access to all rivals. Action commits governments to unlock state telephone monopolies.

Deng Xiaoping Dead at 92 (Feb. 19): Chinese leader was one of top Communist revolutionaries and an architect of economic modernizations that transformed most populous nation. Dies of Parkinson's disease. **(Feb. 25):** Final eulogy to Deng delivered by President Jiang Zemin, who pledges he will continue Deng's policies.

Albright Meets Yeltsin (Feb. 21): But U.S. Secretary of State finds Russians cool to expansion of NATO despite her assurances of friendship.

Opposition Controls Belgrade Council (Feb. 21): Coalition attains a major goal in its campaign to unseat President Slobodan Milosevic.

Jewish Housing in East Jerusalem Planned (Feb. 26): Israeli Government approves large development, provoking Arab and international denunciation.

U.S. Certifies Mexico as Ally in War on Drugs (Feb. 28): Clinton acts after Mexican government makes commitments sought by American law enforcement agencies.

Nation

Army's Top Soldier Accused in Sex Case (Feb. 3): Gene C. McKinney, Sergeant Major of the Army, charged by 22-year veteran with assaulting her in Hawaii. Later McKinney quits Army panel reviewing policies against sexual harassment. **(Feb. 10):** Under Congressional pressure, Army suspends McKinney.

President Gives State of Union Message (Feb. 4): Clinton, in second-term address, sounds "call to action" for nation. Says federal government can help improve education, modernize technology, and provide health care. G.O.P. speaker stresses racial amity.

Clinton Offers $1.69 Trillion Budget (Feb. 6): President says it would cut taxes on the middle class, increase spending on education and health care, and result in an end to federal deficits by 2002. Republican leaders in Congress cool to proposals.

Term Limits Drive Defeated in Congress (Feb. 12): House vote, 217–211, falls short of two-thirds required for a constitutional amendment, dooming campaign for limitation, at least during 105th Congress.

Whitewater Counsel Changes Mind (Feb. 17): Kenneth W. Starr says he plans to resign to become a law dean at Pepperdine University in California. **(Feb. 21):** After wide criticism from staff and prominent Republicans, he announces he will not resign until his investigation is completed.

Virginia Legislature Retires State Song (Feb. 17): Votes, 100–0, to repeal "Carry Me Back to Old Virginia." Song under criticism for glorifying slavery.

Clinton Approved Reward for Top Donors (Feb. 25): Memo reveals President's approval of plan for Democratic Party to offer meals, coffee, outings, and stays in Lincoln Bedroom as campaign incentives.

AIDS Deaths Decline Sharply (Feb. 25): U.S. health officials report casualty rate has fallen "substantially" since epidemic began in 1981.

Former F.B.I. Supervisor Admits Spying (Feb. 28): Earl Edwin Pitts, ex-supervisor for agency, pleads guilty in federal court to charges that for years he sold Russians classified information for $244,000.

Business/Science/Society

O. J. Simpson Found Liable in Civil Suit (Feb. 4): Jury in Santa Monica, Calif., rules former football star responsible in wrongful death lawsuit brought by families of victims, Nicole Brown Simpson and Ronald L. Goldman. Jury awards Goldman family $8.5 million in compensatory damages. **(Feb. 10):** Jury orders Simpson to pay $25 million in punitive damages to families of two victims.

Air Force Jets Fly Close to Airliners (Feb. 7): All flights in East Coast areas suspended after two encounters of National Guard planes and civilian craft within a week. **(Feb. 10):** After two more incidents, Air Force announces plan to re-educate pilots on encountering commercial planes.

Human Era in Americas Pushed Back (Feb. 10): Archeologists conclude after long debate that humans reached southern Chile 12,500 years ago. This is more than 1,000 years earlier than previously thought.

Stock Market Surges to New High (Feb. 13): Dow Jones industrial average passes 7,000 points for first time despite worries by Washington and Wall Street analysts that share prices are too high.

Astronauts Repair Hubble Telescope in Space (Feb. 15): Two of shuttle *Discovery's* crew install new targeting device fitted with special optics to correct Hubble's misshapen mirror. **(Feb. 18):** After 33 hours of space walks, astronauts complete tune-up and repair Hubble's blistered skin.

Cloning of Sheep Stirs Ethical Controversy (Feb. 23): Scottish scientist replaces genetic material to create duplicate animal. Team removes last practical barrier in reproductive technology. Moral issues involved debated widely across world.

Gunman Spreads Terror atop Empire State Building (Feb. 23): Palestinian, 69, kills tourist, wounds seven others and fatally shoots himself on 86th floor observation deck of 102-story New York landmark.

Du Pont Heir Convicted in Killing (Feb. 25): John E. du Pont, 58, found guilty of third-degree murder but mentally ill when he shot Olympic gold medalist David Schultz on grounds of country estate.

Vienna Philharmonic Admits Women Players (Feb. 27): In face of protests on overseas tour, including New York, members of venerable symphony vote to break 155-year-old tradition of exclusion.

Earthquakes Kill 150 in Iran and Pakistan (Feb. 28): Hundreds more injured. Death toll may rise.

March 1997

World

Albanian Cabinet Quits After Protests (March 1): President Sali Berisha announces resignation of Prime Minister Aleksander Meksi's government after talks do not end rioting over failed pyramid investment schemes.

Clinton Welcomes Yasir Arafat (March 3): With Palestinian leader at his side, President mildly rebukes Israeli government for decision to allow construction of thousands of homes for Jews in East Jerusalem, fearing damage to region's peace effort.

Swiss Plan Fund to Aid Holocaust Victims (March 5): Propose creation of $4.7 billion principal account, the interest from it would benefit survivors of Nazi oppression and other calamities.

Yeltsin Pledges to Speed Up Reforms (March 6): Russian President reassures nation of leadership after months of illness and seclusion. Promises to clean up government. **(March 7):** Yeltsin appoints as First Deputy Prime Minister Anatoly B. Chubais, 41, effective but unpopular aide. Chubais will control economy.

U.S. Vetoes U.N. Censure of Israel (March 7): Blocks Security Council resolution to criticize Israeli government for plan to build new Jewish settlement in Arab East Jerusalem. All 14 other nations back measure, calling proposal a threat to Mideast peace.

Nigerian Nobel Laureate Faces Treason Charge (March 12): Government accuses playwright Wole Soyinka and 11 other dissidents in bombings at army installations.

Jordanian Kills Seven Israeli Schoolgirls (March 13): Soldier wounds six others in group visiting shared area in Jordan Valley. He is seized after gun jammed.

State of Emergency in Albania (March 13): Government moves to exert control following collapse of pyramid investment schemes. Angry mobs loot military warehouses in southern city and engage in wide-scale looting of banks and shops. Many killed.

Major City in Zaire Falls to Rebels (March 15): Kisangani, last government-held city in eastern Zaire, taken after night of fighting. Capture poses threat to 31-year rule of President Mobutu.

Israel Begins East Jerusalem Housing Project (March 18): Soldiers guard site as bulldozers scrape ground for new Jewish neighborhood, center of crisis in Prime Minister Netanyahu's dealing with Palestinians.

Suicide Bomber Kills Four in Tel Aviv (March 21): Blast rips through crowded café, wounding dozens. Act is blow to Israeli–Palestinian peace.

Clinton and Yeltsin End Two-Day Summit Talks (March 21): At Helsinki summit, U.S. and Russian Presidents agree to differ on NATO expansion. Determine formally that Russia will negotiate partnership with Western alliance before members are added.

Fighting Rages 7th Day on West Bank (March 26): Palestinian youths battle Israeli soldiers as conflict spreads. Protesters burn U.S. and Israeli flags.

European Union Bars Turkey as Member (March 26): German Foreign Minister says nation does not qualify for place because of record on human rights.

Chinese Question Gore on Campaign Gifts (March 26): Vice President, during Beijing visit, assures Chinese that Washington inquiry on possible influence in 1996 election will not affect economic and diplomatic relationship during the investigation.

Millions Strike in Russian Protest (March 27): Workers demonstrate against government over privations endured since economic reforms were introduced.

Arafat's Police Control Arab Rioters (March 30): Keep tight grip on Palestinians on West Bank to prevent violence on annual day of protest.

Grenades Kill Many at Cambodian Rally (March 30): Scores injured in attack on hundreds attending opposition rally. New democracy regime shaken.

Nation

C.I.A. Official Pleads Guilty to Spying (March 3): Harold J. Nicholson, 46, in plea agreement, admits he had sold secrets to Russia when deputy station chief in Malaysia. Recently had trained C.I.A. recruits.

Balanced-Budget Amendment Defeated (March 4): By single vote, Senate dooms requirement for eighth time in 15 years. Backers blame political pressure.

Clinton Defends 1996 Fund-Raising Actions (March 7): President says he might have asked for contributions.

Senate Votes Broad Financing Inquiry (March 11): In policy change, unanimously approves wide investigation of White House and Congressional fund-raising.

Clinton Injured in Accidental Fall (March 14): Suffers torn tendon in right kneecap and undergoes surgery. Summit meeting with Russian President delayed.

Clinton Names Acting C.I.A. Chief to Head Agency (March 19): Nominates George J. Tenet, 44, as Director of Central Intelligence to end turmoil in Senate hearings over confirmation of original nominee, Anthony Lake.

House Votes Ban on Type of Abortion (March 20): For fourth time, moves to outlaw procedure that opponents call partial-birth abortion. Vote is 295–136, enough to override expected veto by President.

Federal Reserve Raises Interest Rate (March 25): Increase of quarter of a point to 5.5 percent is first in more than two years. Raise is warning of possible inflationary pressure on the economy.

Clinton Forms Panel for Health Care Study (March 26): Appoints 34-member panel to draft bill of rights for consumers and study need for federal regulation of private health insurance plans.

U.S. Expels Belarus Diplomat (March 26): Retaliates for "unwarranted and unjustified" ousting of American diplomat monitoring an anti-government march.

Business/Science/Society

Earthquake Toll Rises in Mideast (March 1): Deaths in Iran and Pakistan rise to more than 550. Villagers and relief workers fear total in thousands.

Tornadoes Wreak Havoc in Three States (March 2): At least 35 killed in Arkansas, Ohio, and Kentucky. Deadly storms spread wide devastation.

New Leader for Mother Teresa's Order (March 13): Sister Nirmala, Hindu convert to Roman Catholicism, elected to head Missionaries of Charity.

Suspect Charged with Cosby Killing (March 13): Mikhail Markhasev, 18, Russian immigrant, accused of slaying Ennis Cosby, son of Bill Cosby, TV star, on West Coast highway in apparent robbery attempt.

Tobacco Company Admits Addiction Peril (March 20): Liggett Group Inc. concedes that smoking can cause cancer, is addictive, and that the company targeted advertising to minors. Agrees to settle lawsuits brought by 22 states charging that industry hid health dangers.

Cellular Phone Privacy Breached (March 20): Team of computer security experts crack key part of electronic code devised to protect calls made with new digital generation of cellular telephones.

Cult Members Commit Mass Suicide (March 27): Thirty-nine men and women found dead at estate at Rancho Santa Fe, Calif. Victims belonged to obscure computer-related group. Videotapes told of intention.

Court Orders Simpson to Give up Belongings (March 27): Judge in civil case calls for surrender of golf clubs and trophies to help pay multi-million-dollar judgment that jury awarded family of slain Ronald L. Goldman.

April 1997

World

Old Enemy of Mobutu Elected in Zaire (April 1): Parliament, in move to mollify rebels, names Etienne Tshisekedi, opponent of President, as Prime Minister.

I.R.A. Threat Halts Big Race in Britain (April 5): But no bomb is found at Liverpool racetrack, where Grand National Steeplechase was scheduled. Police order 60,000 evacuated, including Princess Anne.

Zairian Troops Mutiny and Join Rebels (April 7): Government suffers setback as soldiers in second-largest city surrender to advancing foe. Thousands in capital hail commander of liberation forces.

India's Coalition Government Defeated (April 11): Loses parliamentary vote of confidence. General election possible as three parties contend for power.

Pope Visits Sarajevo (April 12): John Paul II arrives with message of reconciliation. Earlier police reported 23 land mines had been removed from motorcade route from airport and cathedral. **(April 13):** Pontiff celebrates mass within sight of graveyard full of Bosnian war victims.

Fire Kills 300 Pilgrims Outside Mecca (April 15): Sweeps through Saudi Arabia encampment where 2 million Muslims had met for one of Islam's holiest rituals.

Albanians Greet First Peace Force Troops (April 15): Vanguard of 6,000 soldiers from eight European countries under Italian command arrives a month after Balkan nation disintegrated into near-anarchy.

Netanyahu Avoids Charges in Scandal Inquiry (April 16): New political crisis erupts in Israel as police say Prime Minister may have traded support from coalition ally in return for plea bargain. **(April 20):** Prosecutors drop charges against Prime Minister because of insufficient evidence.

Prime Minister Named in India (April 19): Coalition government ends three-week crisis by choosing Inder K. Gujral. As two-time Foreign Minister, he won praise for improving India's relations with neighbors.

Thousands of Rwandan Refugees Trapped in Zaire (April 30): U.N. begins airlift to return to Rwanda victims of conflict as thousands more terrified refugees gather in camp near jungle town, uncertain of their fate. Many fear reprisals from Tutsi-led Government in Rwanda.

Nation

Court Upholds California's Preference Ban (April 8): U.S. Appeals bench affirms constitutionality. Rules voters had right to forbid use of racial and gender-based preferences in affirmative action programs.

C.I.A. Suggests Error on Iraqi Arms (April 9): Report indicates that intelligence errors may have led to demolition of ammunition bunker filled with chemical weapons that may have exposed thousands of U.S. troops to deadly nerve gas after Persian Gulf war.

Court Voids Line-Item Veto Law (April 10): Federal judge strikes down as unconstitutional new statute giving President power to cancel individual appropriations and tax benefits in legislation.

Court Upholds California Marijuana Law (April 11): U.S. judge in Los Angeles rules Clinton Administration cannot move to punish doctors who recommend drug for patients under new state statute.

Clinton Partner Gets Three-Year Sentence (April 14): U.S. judge imposes prison term on James B. McDougal, charged with illegally obtaining millions in federally backed loans. Whitewater inquiry is rejuvenated.

Reno Refuses Special Prosecutor (April 14): Attorney General rejects Republican demands, saying Justice Department career prosecutors are capable of handling investigation into financing of President Clinton's re-election campaign.

Loan from Dole to Pay Gingrich Fine (April 17): House Speaker announces he will borrow $300,000 as payment for penalty in ethics inquiry. Former Senator Bob Dole calls loan "investment" in G.O.P.'s future.

Whitewater Grand Jury's Life Extended (April 22): Federal judge in Arkansas grants request of special prosecutor after he reports discovery of evidence of obstruction of justice and needs more time.

Christian Coalition Leader Resigns (April 23): Ralph Reed quits as executive director to start consulting concern to elect Christian-oriented candidates around country. Reed built Coalition into one of the most powerful forces in Republican politics.

Senate Approves Chemical Weapons Treaty (April 24): Votes 74–26, for international convention to prohibit production, storage, and use of poison gas. Republican Leader Trent Lott rallied support.

Court Backs F.D.A. on Tobacco Oversight (April 25): U.S. judge in North Carolina rules agency can regulate tobacco as a drug. But he decides it lacks authority to control advertising aimed at youths.

Vigorous Economy Aids U.S. Budget (April 30): Has grown at fastest pace in nine years in first quarter. Administration predicts surge will help reduce deficit to $75 billion, lowest in 20 years.

Labor Secretary Confirmed after Impasse (April 30): Senate, 85–13, approves Alexis Herman after months of delay over her role in campaign fund-raising.

Business/Science/Society

Presbyterians Vote Homosexual Curb (April 1): Majority of regional bodies enact into law its policy against ordaining practicing homosexuals.

Russian Space Station Repaired (April 9): Fuel, fire extinguishers, and spare parts reach *Mir* space station so American and two Russians can cure overheating in primary system to purge carbon dioxide.

Black-Asian Golfer Sets Masters Record (April 13): Tiger Woods, 21, wins at Augusta, Ga., by a tournament-record 12 strokes. Score is 18-under-par.

Jackie Robinson Honored on Anniversary (April 15): Some 50,000 crowd New York's Shea Stadium to honor man who 50 years previously broke color barrier in major league baseball as first black player. His mother and daughter join President Clinton in tributes.

Top Tobacco Companies Seek Accord (April 16): Two largest concerns, R.J.R. Nabisco and Philip Morris, move to settle legal and political difficulties in talks on major concessions, including more than $250 billion to compensate states and individuals.

Woman, 63, Gives Birth to Baby Girl (April 23): Doctors believe she is oldest woman ever to bear a child.

Trial Begins in Oklahoma City Bombing (April 24): Timothy J. McVeigh faces federal court in Denver for charges of committing terrorist act that killed 168.

Missing A-10 Pilot Believed Dead (April 25): Air Force reports recovery of human remains at site in Colorado Rockies where wreckage of crashed Thunderbolt had been discovered. Flier, Capt. Craig Button, disappeared after veering away from training flight.

Thousands Flee North Dakota Flood (April 27): Waters of Red River recede after inundating area nearly a quarter the size of Lake Superior. Ninety percent of Grand Forks under water. Many of city's 50,000 residents face crushing damage to property.

Texas Militants Free Two Hostages (April 28): Officials give up jailed member of separatist group in exchange for releasing pair. Police face armed standoff.

Ex-Drill Sergeant Convicted in Rapes (April 29): Army jury at Aberdeen, Md., finds Staff Sgt. Delmar G. Simpson guilty of attacks on six women.

May 1997

World

Labor Party Victorious in British Election (May 2): Tony Blair leads historic sweep to end 18 years of Conservative rule. Oxford-educated lawyer, 43, had transformed party from Socialist tradition.

Britain Change Monetary Policy (May 6): New Labor government grants control of interest rates to London's Central Bank. Move heartens European leaders and financial executives, who had been skeptical.

U.N. Panel Convicts Bosnian Serb (May 7): War crimes tribunal concludes first trial by finding Dusan Tadic, 41, guilty of killing two policemen and persecuting and torturing many Muslim civilians in Bosnia.

U.S. Report Criticizes Swiss (May 7): Charges Swiss Government deliberately failed to respect a 1946 agreement to return hundreds of millions of dollars that Nazi Germany looted from European banks and Holocaust victims. U.S. faulted for lack of attention.

U.S. Recognizes Rebel Regime in Zaire (May 10): Accepts new name, Democratic Republic of Congo, and pledges help in building democratic government.

Pope Appeals for Peace in Middle East (May 10): On visit to Lebanon, John Paul II calls for reconciliation in all countries where Christians and Muslims live together. **(May 11):** Tens of thousands attend mass in Beirut.

Yeltsin Signs Chechnya Peace Treaty (May 12): President of Russia and Chechen leader describe accord as end of centuries-old conflict between Russia and rebellious region in Caucasus. Use of force barred.

Russia Accepts NATO Expansion (May 14): Reluctantly agrees to Washington's plan to include Moscow's former satellites in Central Europe. **(May 27):** Clinton and other NATO leaders join Russia's President Yeltsin in Paris in signing "Founding Act" for mutual cooperation and security.

President of Zaire Quits Post (May 16): Mobutu Sese Seko flees before rebels advance after 32 years of ruling Africa's third-largest country.

Rebel Chief Claims Zaire Presidency (May 17): As troops enter capital, Kinshasa, Laurent Kabila declares himself President of Democratic Republic of Congo. He suspends Zairian Constitution.

Russian Premier Cuts Budget 20 Percent (May 21): Reform government bids Parliament slash spending on military and state-subsidized industries.

Russia and Belarus to Form New Union (May 23): Leaders sign symbolic agreement at Kremlin ceremony.

Islamic Militants Gain in Afghanistan (May 24): Taliban movement nears completion of goal of reuniting nation under single government after nearly 20 years.

Moderate Candidate Elected in Iran (May 24): Mohammed Khatami wins presidency in landslide. Campaigned on platform of tolerance and social reform.

Russia and Ukraine Sign Friendship Treaty (May 28): Accord ending long dispute allows Russia to keep part of former Soviet fleet at Ukrainian port of Sevastopol. **(May 31):** Presidents sign compact to try to improve relations between Slavic states.

Foreigners Evacuated From Sierra Leone (May 30): U.S. Marines land in Freetown, capital. Rescue hundreds fleeing looting and violence after armed coup.

Ruling Party Victorious in Indonesia (May 30): Government consolidates hold in election after violent campaign.

Pope Returns to Poland for Visit (May 31): John Paul II says nation, expecting bid to join NATO, can play meaningful role in European affairs.

Nation

Budget-Balancing Agreement Reached (May 1): Clinton and G.O.P. leaders in Congress accept five-year plan after years of dispute. Accord helped by news that deficits are likely to be below estimates.

F.D.A. Approves Laser for Dental Work (May 7): Sanctions device that makes local anesthesia unnecessary for painless repairing of most cavities.

G.O.P. Returns Donations to Hong Kong (May 8): National Committee announces return of more than $100,000 to aviation services and real estate company. Party for first time admits illegal foreign donations.

U.S. Supplies 116 Big Guns to Sarajevo (May 9): Sends large artillery pieces to correct main weaknesses of army of Muslim–Croat Federation in Bosnia and to set stage for withdrawal of American forces.

Clinton Apologizes for Syphilis Experiment (May 16): President expresses government's regret for Tuskegee program in which black men were left untreated for years as part of government study.

Senate, 64–36, Votes Antiabortion Bill (May 20): For first time, measure would ban a specific procedure, "partial-birth." Clinton veto expected.

First Woman B-52 Pilot Leaves Air Force (May 22): Lieut. Kelly Flinn, 26, accepts general discharge to avoid court-martial on adultery and other charges.

Business/Science/Society

Parents Deny Role in Slaying of Daughter (May 1): At Boulder, Colo., news conference, Ramseys proclaim innocence in death of JonBenet Ramsey, 6, tiny beauty queen, center of national interest.

Armed Standoff in West Texas Ends (May 3): Leader of secessionist group and three others surrender and lay down weapons. Two others hunted after flight.

Tobacco Company Wins Florida Lawsuit (May 5): Jury declines to order R.J. Reynolds to pay damages to family of woman who died of lung cancer at 49 after smoking for 34 years. Negligence claim rejected.

Teachers Union Names New Head (May 6): Sandra Feldman elected by 940,000–member American Federation of Teachers.

Army Sergeant Sentenced in Rapes (May 6): Military court at Aberdeen, Md. base convicts Staff Sgt. Delmar G. Simpson of attacks on six trainees and sentences him to 25 years. Court orders him to be dishonorably discharged with loss of benefits.

Top Army Soldier Named in Sex Case (May 7): Gene C. McKinney, Sergeant Major of the Army, charged with misconduct and indecent assault involving four service women over nearly three years. He denies allegations.

I.B.M. Computer Wins Chess Match (May 11): Deep Blue causes a human world champion, Garry Kasparov, to quit after 19 moves in sixth and final game.

4,000 Reported Dead in East Iran Earthquake (May 12): Casualty figures differ as U.S. and others rally to aid victims. Damage estimated at $66.7 million.

Russia Resumes Funds for Space Station (May 15): U.S. space agency reports work has begun on crucial components for international joint project.

Jetliner Bombed in Construction Test (May 17): Old Boeing 747 blown up at British air base to test new hardening techniques to thwart bombs.

Death Toll Past 350 in Bangladesh Cyclone (May 19): Storm spreads wide damage in coastal region.

U.S.–Russian Linkup in Orbit Ends (May 21): Crew of space shuttle *Atlantis* prepares to undock from Russian *Mir* station after delivering a new oxygen generator and other repair equipment. Crew also delivers Dr. C. Michael Foale to replace Dr. Jerry M. Linenger as American on *Mir* team.

Death Toll Set at 30 in Texas Tornadoes (May 29): Wide central region devastated by half-dozen storms.

June 1997

World

French Vote for Leftists (June 1): In setback to President Chirac, Socialists and Communists gain allies. Vote is a mandate to reject economic austerity and press strong measures to reduce 12.8 percent unemployment rate.

Socialist Leader Named French Premier (June 2): President Chirac appoints Lionel Jospin in move to unite left and right in arresting economic decline.

Canadian Premier Keeps Office (June 3): Prime Minister Jean Chrétien wins second consecutive election. But his Liberal Party's strength in House of Commons falls to 155 seats, a bare majority.

Pope Concludes Visit to Native Poland (June 10): In farewell speech at airport, John Paul II again appeals for national unity and applauds Poles for meeting challenges of democratic transition. He calls on nation to uphold fundamental moral values.

Top U.N. Human Rights Official Named (June 12): Secretary General appoints Mary Robinson, who resigned her post as President of Ireland to promote civil rights worldwide. She is a barrister and an expert on human rights law.

Israeli Court Bars Trial of Netanyahu (June 15): Supreme tribunal upholds Attorney General's decision not to prosecute Prime Minister or Justice Minister on charges in influence-peddling case.

I.R.A. Killings Cancel Peace Talks (June 16): British government calls off negotiations after Irish faction slays two policemen in Northern Ireland.

European Union Bolsters Currency Merger (June 16): Rejects French challenge and agrees to "stability pact" that stresses tight government spending and renews commitment to create a common currency.

Canada Deports Saudi in 1996 Bombing (June 17): Hands over to U.S. suspect implicated in deaths of 19 Americans in Saudi Arabia after suspect agrees to cooperate with Justice Department investigators.

Pakistani Seized in C.I.A. Killings (June 17): Afghan tribal leaders and Pakistani officials aid in capture of fugitive sought in deaths of two officers outside agency's Virginia headquarters in 1993.

Swiss Join Security Pact (June 21): Agree to limited participation in NATO's Partners for Peace in first step away from traditional isolation.

"Summit of Eight" Ends Denver Session (June 22): With Russia as new partner, nations' leaders vote long list of proposals, including call for democracy in Hong Kong and new commitment to peace in Bosnia. Clinton, in break with Europeans, refuses to commit U.S. to specific reduction in "greenhouse gases."

Hong Kong Returns to Chinese Rule (June 30): Transfer of British colony begins with simple ceremony. **(July 1):** China resumes sovereignty, ending 150 years of British rule. In martial musical ceremony, Britain's Union Jack is lowered and Beijing's red banner is raised as prosperous capitalist territory is given over to communist control.

Islamic Rule Ends in Turkey (June 30): Mesut Yilmaz named Prime Minister after forming government he says will end year's experiment.

Ruling Party Defeated in Albania (June 30): President Sali Berisha concedes loss in election after five years in which nation was reduced to chaos.

Nation

Homicides Down 11 Percent in Nation (June 1): Overall violent crime fell 7 percent, F.B.I. reports.

Two-Star General Retires Because of Adultery (June 2): Maj. Gen. John Longhouser, commander of Army's Aberdeen Proving Ground, resigns rather than face possible charges of adultery.

Clinton Supports "Soft Money" Ban (June 5): Endorses move to have Federal Election Commission outlaw large unregulated donations to political parties.

Jobless Rate Lowest Since 1973 (June 6): Level in U.S. fell to 4.8 percent in May. Economy flourishing, with low unemployment and low rate of inflation.

Ethics Panel Urges Ban on Human Cloning (June 7): Study ordered by President Clinton calls for legislation to restrict practice as "morally unacceptable."

Clinton Vetoes Flood Relief Measure (June 9): Blocks $8.6 billion emergency aid bill because of unrelated provisions attached to it by Republicans. Each side blames the other as obstructionist, preventing critical flood relief aid to victims in 33 states. **(June 12):** G.O.P. capitulates on flood relief bill. Congress votes for measure after Republicans agree to delete and modify provisions opposed by President. Clinton signs revised version.

General Rejects Joint Chiefs Post (June 9): Air Force Gen. Joseph W. Ralston withdraws name from consideration after failing to convince Congress that he was worthy despite adulterous affair in 1980s.

U.S. Plans to Pay Dues Arrears to U.N. (June 10): Clinton and Senate Republicans and Democrats agree on plan to pay $819 million over next three years if U.N. reduces budget as well as U.S. share of payments.

Historic Tobacco Settlement Reached (June 20): Proposed agreement would change the way cigarettes are marketed, provide $368.5 billion to compensate states for treating tobacco-related illnesses, and alter legal, regulatory, and public health standards. Accord, subject to ratification, reached by state attorneys general, plaintiffs' lawyers, and industry representatives.

Senate Votes Rise in Medicare Cost for Wealthy (June 24): Also backs two-year increase in eligibility age.

Clinton Approves Tighter Pollution Limits (June 25): Orders stricter limits on deadly soot and choking smog. Offers states and cities substantial flexibility in choosing how to meet new goals.

Congress Votes Major Tax Cuts (June 26): House, 253–179, passes biggest reduction in 16 years despite Democratic charges that bill favors rich. Measure includes reductions in capital gains levy and provides tax breaks for education. **(June 27):** Senate, 80–18, approves modified measure with Democratic support.

Clinton Presents Tax Cut Program (June 30): Stresses education aid in $135 billion reduction over five years but leans toward Republican proposals.

Business/Science/Society

Theologians Back Study of Women's Ordination (June 7): Roman Catholic group challenges Vatican and calls for discussion of possibility of women as priests.

Jury Votes Death Penalty for McVeigh (June 13): Federal panel in Denver votes unanimously that Timothy J. McVeigh, 29, be executed for bombing of federal building in Oklahoma City that killed 168 persons and injured 850 others on April 19, 1995.

Southern Baptists Urge Disney Boycott (June 18): Convention votes action against entire Disney empire. Delegates protest pro-homosexual policies.

Killer in "Megan Case" Sentenced to Die (June 20): New Jersey court dooms Jesse K. Timmendequas, whose rape and murder of 7-year-old neighbor resulted in passage of "Megan's Law" to protect children from sex offenders by requiring that communities be notified of convicted sex offenders living in their midst.

Betty Shabazz, 61, Rights Activist, Dies of Burns (June 23): Widow of Malcolm X fatally injured in fire apparently set by troubled grandson, aged 12.

Russian Space Station Damaged in Collision (June 25): Unmanned space cargo vessel crashes into *Mir* during practice docking in most serious accident for a manned spacecraft. Much of power supply knocked out.

July 1997

World

Cambodia Faction Claims Victory (July 6): One of two prime ministers, Hun Sen, former Communist, ousted his rival co-prime minister, Prince Norodom Ramariddh. **(July 15):** At least 40 executed and hundreds arrested in widespread Cambodian purge against political opponents of Hun Sen.

Governing Party Defeated in Mexico (July 6): Voters sweepingly reject Institutional Revolutionary Party, which had controlled Parliament and the nation for seven years. However, President Ernesto Zedillo wins. Opposition had credited him with taking a major step toward consolidating Mexico's democracy.

NATO Invites Three Eastern Nations (July 8): Madrid conference votes to add Poland, Czech Republic, and Hungary, eight years after West won cold war. NATO leaders invite them to join alliance in time for its 50th anniversary in 1999. President Clinton calls action great day "for the cause of freedom."

NATO Troops Kill Serbian War-Crimes Suspect (July 10): Also seize another in shootout in northwestern Bosnia in first attempt to arrest suspects at large.

Bosnian Serb Sentenced for Atrocities (July 14): U.N. war-crimes tribunal metes 20-year prison term to Dusan Tadic, 41, for crimes against humanity in "ethnic cleansing" campaign against civilians.

I.R.A. Announces New Cease-Fire (July 19): Move by Irish Republican Army could lead to resumption of negotiations for peace in Northern Ireland.

Yeltsin Vetoes Bill to Restrict Religions (July 22): Rejects Parliament's measure to protect Orthodox Church from competition from other denominations.

Swiss Publish List of Bank Accounts (July 23): Reveal some 2,000 dormant ones from World War II era, including many Holocaust victims. List contains more than twice the number of such accounts banks had identified as recently as 1996. Worldwide publication is break with Swiss tradition of bank secrecy.

Terrorist Blast Kills Many in Jerusalem (July 30): Two men carrying bombs perish with at least 13 others in crowded market. More than 150 wounded, many seriously. Militant Islamic organization Hamas takes responsibility. Suicide bombing is worst since Israeli Premier Benjamin Netanyahu took office.

Israelis Threaten Crackdown in Arab Areas (July 31): Israelis reportedly send commandos into Palestinian zones and to decree punitive measures against Palestinian authorities in response to suicide bombing.

Nation

Inquiry Finds White House Aide Was Suicide (July 15): Whitewater independent counsel upholds findings that Vincent W. Foster, Jr. took his own life in 1993.

Clinton Picks Head of Joint Chiefs of Staff (July 16): Chooses Army Gen. Henry H. Shelton as nominee after months of search impeded by Pentagon's response to sexual misconduct of service officers.

Senate Panel Grants Immunity to Witnesses (July 23): Justice Department rebuffed by bipartisan action in investigation of campaign finance abuses.

Republican Ex-Chairman Defends Fund-Raising (July 24): Haley Barbour, countering Democrats, tells Senate inquiry that party did not accept illegal foreign campaign contributions while he was leader.

White House and G.O.P. Agree on Budget (July 28): Congressional Republicans and Clinton Administration agree on how to balance budget for first time in nearly three decades. They also agree on methods of cutting taxes for first time since 1981.

Congress Approves Major Fiscal Measures (July 31): House and Senate vote largest tax cuts since 1981, with reduction of $96 billion over five years, reducing capital gains and real estate levies. Senate, 85–15, passes bill to balance budget by 2002. Measure already approved by House, 346–85.

Business/Science/Society

Space Shuttle Accomplishes Research (July 1): Columbia orbits to complete gravity experiments cut short by power failure in April. **(July 17):** Columbia and crew of seven land at Cape Canaveral, Fla. Commander, Air Force Lieut. Col. James D. Halsell, Jr., reports successful completion of mission.

Mississippi Settles Tobacco Suit (July 3): Four major cigarette makers agree to pay state $3.4 billion over 25 years to resolve case over health-care costs associated with smoking.

Two Major Arms Producers Merge (July 3): Lockheed Martin Corporation announces it is buying Northrop Grumman Corporation for $9.3 billion.

U.S. Spacecraft Lands on Mars (July 4): *Pathfinder* makes perfect landing after seven-month journey and begins studies of planet's makeup and whether life could have existed. Carries moving vehicle *Sojourner* to collect data on surface of Mars.

Russia Sends Supplies to Crippled *Mir* (July 5): Spacecraft contains badly needed supplies to repair the space station, which was damaged in June.

Nevada Panel Suspends Mike Tyson's License (July 9): State commission revokes boxing license and fines him $3 million for biting Evander Holyfield's ear in heavyweight title fight on June 25.

O. J. Simpson Home Sold at Auction (July 14): Hawthorne Savings bank buys former football star's Los Angeles estate for $2,631,259 in foreclosure action.

***Mir* Commander Reports Illness (July 14):** Chief of Russian space station says he is experiencing heart irregularities. Repair mission faces delay.

Famed Fashion Designer Shot Dead (July 15): Gianni Versace, 50, slain as he opens gate of palatial South Beach home in Miami Beach, Fla. **(July 24):** Officials confirm Andrew P. Cunanan, 27, sought in killing of Versace and four other men, had killed himself.

Error Disables Russian Space Station (July 17): Astronaut mistakenly disconnects cable on *Mir*, cutting off guidance system that gathers solar energy.

Episcopal Leaders Vote Accord With Lutherans (July 18): Overwhelmingly approve pact to bring church into "full communion" with Evangelical Lutheran Church in America. Pooling of resources would result.

Deaf Mexicans Held in Forced Labor (July 19): New York City police discover two houses filled with men, women, and children immigrants compelled to work 18 hours a day selling trinkets in subways and airports.

Floods Devastate Central Europe (July 20 et seq.): About 100 dead in Poland and Czech Republic. Heavy rains swell rivers to flood levels from the Danube in Hungary and Austria to the Inn and the Salzach in Bavaria.

Carroll O'Connor Cleared in Slander Suit (July 25): Jury in Los Angeles rejects claim by drug supplier that TV star had slandered him by blaming him for causing death of O'Connor's son in drug-induced suicide.

Two Guilty in Bill Cosby Extortion (July 25): Autumn Jackson, 22, and two others convicted of trying to extort $40 million from TV star, whom she claimed was her father. She faces long prison term.

Roman Shipwrecks Found in Deep Sea (July 30): Scientists using once-secret nuclear submarine locate ancient hulls in Mediterranean off Sicily.

August 1997

World

Israel Steps Up Pressure on Palestinians (Aug. 1): Arrests dozens in wake of suicide bombing in crowded market. Delays drastic action against Palestinian leaders.

Guerrillas Rain Rockets on Northern Israel (Aug. 19): Islamic forces seek to avenge attack by militiamen aligned with Israel. No retaliation planned.

NATO Troops Raid Bosnian Serb Base (Aug. 20): Capture six police bases in Banja Luka, neutralizing power center held by Radovan Karadzic, Bosnian Serb leader wanted for trial on war crimes charges.

Pope Cheered on Paris Visit (Aug. 24): A million hear John Paul II officiate at open-air mass concluding six-day youth festival. Youths from 160 countries hear plea to build "civilization of love."

Former East German Leader Sentenced (Aug. 25): Berlin court metes six-year prison term to Egon Krenz, last hard-line Communist, charged with responsibility for deaths of hundreds trying to flee to West.

North Korean Envoy Defects to U.S. (Aug. 25): Chang Sung Gil, Ambassador to Egypt, is first top diplomat to abandon Communist state. **(Aug. 26):** U.S. announces it will grant defector political asylum. **(Aug. 28):** North Korea quits arms conference, leaves Washington talks on its export of missiles, in violent protest against U.S. asylum for diplomat.

National Party Chief Resigns in South Africa (Aug. 26): F. W. de Klerk, former president, retires from politics. He negotiated an end to apartheid but failed to make his party a multi-racial organization.

Israel Ends Blockade of Bethlehem (Aug. 27): Removes four-week military ban to end irritant in Israeli-Palestinian relations. Action follows several days of clashes with Palestinian youths.

Two G.I.s Hurt in Clash With Serbs (Aug. 28): Hundreds attack peacekeeping troops trying to seize control of police station in Brcko, Bosnia, from forces loyal to Radovan Karadzic, wartime Bosnian Serb leader.

Sinn Fein Invited to New Peace Talks (Aug. 29): Britain extends bid to Irish Republican Army representatives for first time since outbreak of sectarian violence in Northern Ireland 28 years previously.

Nation

Clinton Exercises Line-Item Veto (Aug. 11): Becomes first President to exercise new power by striking down two narrow tax breaks and provision to help New York State get more Medicaid money. Challenge on constitutional grounds appears likely.

Clinton Postpones Amtrak Strike (Aug. 21): Moves to delay for 60 days possible nationwide walkout, invoking Railway Labor Act. Emergency panel set up.

Former Agriculture Secretary Indicted (Aug. 27): Federal grand jury charges Mike Espy, 43, Cabinet member in 1993–94, with mail and wire fraud, taking illegal gratuities, witness tampering, and other offenses.

Business/Science/Society

Strike Cripples United Parcel Service (Aug. 3): Some 185,000 members of Teamsters Union walk out as union and shipping company fail to reach agreement on pension funds and use of part-time workers. Businesses and customers across nation inconvenienced. **(Aug. 18):** After 80 hours of intense negotiations, company and union announce tentative agreement to end 15-day strike. U.P.S. says it had feared bigger losses.

Plane Crash Kills 225 on Guam (Aug. 5): South Korean jet liner, Boeing 747-300, crashes in hill jungle. **(Aug. 8):** Evidence said to suggest pilot error.

Microsoft Pays Apple $150 Million (Aug. 6): Apple company announces financial and business partnership with its archrival, Microsoft Corporation.

Relief Craft Links to Russian Space Station (Aug. 7): Guidance system fails on spaceship carrying relief crew to repair the damaged *Mir.* However, space station crew manually guides relief craft to docking. **(Aug. 14):** Russian commander and flight engineer return to Earth after six months of highly publicized disasters.

Exploration of Mars a Success (Aug. 8): *Pathfinder* spacecraft has transmitted thousands of pictures in more than a month on planet. Its roving vehicle *Sojourner* has explored wide area of landing site.

Earliest Human Footprints Discovered (Aug. 14): Scientists report finding fossilized footprints of anatomically modern human in 117,000-year-old sandstone on shores of South African lagoon.

Timothy J. McVeigh Sentenced to Death (Aug. 14): Federal judge in Denver metes penalty decreed by jury in Oklahoma City bombing. Prisoner quotes cryptically from dissenting opinion by Supreme Court Justice Brandeis on powers of government.

Canadian Is World's Oldest Person (Aug. 14): Title given by *Guinness Book of World Records* to Marie-Louise Febronie Meilleur of Northern Ontario, aged 117.

Minority Contract Program Modified (Aug. 14): In major change, Administration moves to make it easier for white companies to qualify for government jobs.

Russian Space Station Suffers More Troubles (Aug. 18): The *Mir's* main computer fails during docking maneuver and sends station spinning out of control. Crew uses engines of *Mir's* space capsule to push wobbling station toward its orbit to align with sun and recharge batteries. **(Aug. 22):** Crew conducts six-hour mission to restore electrical cables cut off June 25 in docking crash with cargo ship.

Dow Chemical Loses Breast Implant Case (Aug. 18): Jury in Louisiana finds company deceived women by hiding information about health risks of silicone used in devices. Panel heard first class-action suit brought against a company involved in implant industry.

Lutherans Vote Ties With Others (Aug. 18): Evangelicals approve historic agreement for close cooperation with Presbyterian Church (U.S.A.), United Church of Christ, and Reformed Church in America. Lutheran leaders reject similar ties with Episcopal Church.

Valujet and F.A.A. Faulted in Crash (Aug. 19): National Transportation Safety Board holds Federal Aviation Administration and airline responsible for fire that caused 110 deaths in Everglades in 1995.

Teamsters' Election Ruled Invalid (Aug. 22): Federal official orders new ballot after overturning Ron Carey's 1996 election as president of International Brotherhood. U.S. election overseer finds Carey's campaign received illegal contributions.

Cigarette Makers Settle With Florida (Aug. 25): Agree to pay $11.3 billion in lawsuit related to smoking toll and to undertake wide public health moves. Pact will also affect similar cases in Mississippi.

Record Bank Merger Announced (Aug. 30): Nationsbank to acquire leading Florida franchise, Barnett Banks, for $15.5 billion in stock, a record in banking.

Princess Diana, 36, Killed in Car Crash (Aug. 31): Divorced wife of Britain's Prince Charles and glamorous good-will ambassador for AIDS and land-mine victims. Fatally injured with two others in Paris in accident involving car being pursued by photographers on motorcycles. **(Aug. 31):** Prince Charles brings Princess Diana's remains back from Paris. There is worldwide mourning.

September 1997

World

Three Suicide Bombers Kill Four in Jerusalem (Sept. 4): Explosions in crowded shopping promenade wound some 200 Israelis and tourists. New attack threatens Israeli-Palestine peace agreement.

NATO Troops Defuse Second Uprising in Bosnia (Sept. 9): Disarm dozens of Serb hardliners in Banja Luka in the midst of angry supporters of President Biljana Plavsic, a backer of Dayton peace accords.

Palestinians Arrest Islamic Militants (Sept. 9): Hold scores of members of Hamas movement after U.S. and Israeli protests against suicide bombings in Jerusalem. Sweeps are widest in more than a year.

Northern Ireland Peace Talks Resume (Sept. 9): Sinn Fein, political wing of Irish Republican Army, commits itself for first time to exclusively peaceful methods in attempt to achieve settlement.

Scots Vote for Separate Parliament (Sept. 11): Support legislature of their own for first time since 1707. Nation retains ties with British crown and leaders.

Swiss Plan First Payment to Holocaust Victims (Sept. 17): Nine months after agreement, plan to disburse up to $1,000 to each of 12,000 people in Eastern Europe.

Helicopter Crash Kills Envoy and 11 Aides in Bosnia (Sept. 17): Senior German diplomat among victims, including five Americans on election mission.

Welsh Vote for Own Elected Assembly (Sept. 18): Approve London's offer by extremely narrow margin.

Solidarity Leads in Polish Election (Sept. 21): Right-of-center coalition appears to have defeated government dominated by former Communists.

Sudden Attack Kills 85 in Algiers (Sept. 23): At least 67 wounded in unexplained massacre, second-worst in six years of undeclared civil war since army canceled possible election victory by Islamic Salvation Front.

New Israeli Housing on West Bank (Sept. 24): Over U.S. objections, Prime Minister Netanyahu pledges 300 new homes for settlers.

Israel Frees Hamas Founder (Sept. 30): Flies Islamic Militant leader to Jordan because of ill health.

Nation

Gore Target of Campaign Finance Inquiry (Sept. 3): Justice Department begins preliminary inquiry into allegations concerning fund solicitation.

Senate Repeals Tax Break for Tobacco (Sept. 10): In setback for industry, 95–3 vote removes $50 billion from tax reduction legislation.

Army's Leaders Faulted on Sex Abuse (Sept. 11): Panel reports investigation revealed widespread "harassment" crossing gender, rank, and race lines.

Memo Links Gore to Fund-Raising (Sept. 11): Top aide said to have listed "talking points" for Vice President to use at 1996 White House meeting.

Nation's Health Reported Improved (Sept. 11): Analysis finds increased longevity and record-low infant deaths.

Weld Drops Fight for Nomination (Sept. 15): Withdraws as candidate for envoy to Mexico after five-month opposition by Senator Jesse Helms, chairman of House Foreign Relations Committee.

Chairman of Joint Chiefs of Staff Named (Sept. 16): Gen. Henry H. Shelton confirmed by Senate to succeed Gen. John M. Shalikashvili.

I.R.S. Head Apologizes for Agents (Sept. 25): Acting commissioner tells Senate inquiry he regrets abuses of taxpayers and pledges immediate reforms.

Congress Votes $247.5 Billion Spending Bill (Sept. 25): House and Senate approved measure that will let President extend stay of U.S. troops in Bosnia.

Business/Science/Society

Arizona Governor Convicted on Fraud Charges (Sept. 3): Federal jury finds Fife Symington guilty in deals as commercial real estate developer.

Mother Teresa Dead at 87 (Sept. 5): Roman Catholic nun who won 1979 Nobel Peace Prize for work among the world's poorest is mourned by India and the world. Lived in Calcutta; founded order of Missionaries of charity. (**Sept. 13**): Mother Teresa buried after six-hour ceremonies with military escort and rifle salute.

Pageantry Marks Diana's Funeral (Sept. 6): Millions line streets to hear solemn service in Westminster Abbey. Crowds shower hearse with flowers when it carries Princess to burial site at ancestral home in Northamptonshire.

Hundreds Die as Haitian Ferry Sinks (Sept. 8): Overcrowded craft capsizes at Monthrouis.

Accord Reached in West Coast Transit Strike (Sept. 12): San Francisco officials and union reach tentative agreement to end Bay Area week-long traffic tie-up.

Two Diet Drugs Withdrawn (Sept. 15): Two makers heed request of F.D.A. New information reported to show some cases of heart valve damage from Pondimin and Redux, often used in combination with one another and known as fen-phen.

Three Plead Guilty in Teamster Election (Sept. 18): Aides to union's president admit illegal contributions to his re-election drive. They say scheme involved officials of the Democratic Party.

Wall Street Merger Announced (Sept. 24): Travelers Group to acquire powerful Salomon Brothers for $9 billion to rival major financial institutions.

Plane Crash on Sumatra Kills 234 (Sept. 26): All aboard Airbus A-300 perish as airliner hits hilly terrain 30 miles short of Medan, Indonesia, airport. Thick haze from widespread forest fires contributed to crash.

At Least Ten Dead in Italian Earthquakes (Sept. 26): Tremors shatter Basilica of St. Francis of Assisi, damaging 13th century frescoes in famous shrine.

U.S. Space Shuttle Docks With Mir (Sept. 27): Atlantis joins Russian station safely and brings new computer to replace ailing equipment. David A. Wolf, 41, a physician, replaces Michael Foale as U.S. crew member for four-month stay on space station.

Major Emmy Awards for TV, 1997

(Sept. 14, 1997)

Drama Series: *Law & Order* (NBC)
   Actress: Gillian Anderson, *The X-Files*
   Actor: Dennis Franz, *NYPD Blue*
   Supporting actress: Kim Delaney, *NYPD Blue*
   Supporting actor: Hector Elizondo, *Chicago Hope*
Comedy Series: *Frasier* (NBC)
   Actress: Helen Hunt, *Mad About You*
   Actor: John Lithgow, *3rd Rock From the Sun*
   Supporting actress: Kristen Johnson, *3rd Rock From the Sun*
   Supporting actor: Michael Richards, *Seinfeld*
Variety, Music or Comedy Series: *Tracey Takes On . . .* (HBO)
Variety, Music or Comedy Special: *Chris Rock: Bring the Pain* (HBO)
Miniseries or Special: *Prime Suspect 5: Errors of Judgment* (PBS)
   Actress: Alfre Woodard, *Miss Evers' Boys*
   Actor: Armand Assante, *Gotti*
   Supporting actress: Diana Rigg, *Rebecca*
   Supporting actor: Beau Bridges, *The Second Civil War*
Made for TV Movie: *Miss Evers' Boys* (HBO)
Individual Performance, Variety or Music Program: Bette Midler, *Bette Midler: Diva Las Vegas*

October 1997

World

U.S. Sends Carrier to Gulf (Oct. 3): The *Nimitz* is dispatched in a warning to Iran to halt air attacks on Iraq, a violation of the no-flight zone imposed at the end of the Persian Gulf War.

Assassination Attempt Embroils Israel (Oct. 6): Prime Minister criticized over failed attempt to kill the political leader of Hamas, an Islamic militant group. Netanyahu defends assassination attempt as "just" action against terrorism, but releases 20 prisoners, including Hamas founder Sheik Ahmed Yassin, in concessionary move that explained Israel's unexpected release of the leader on Sept. 30.

Ten Bosnian Croats Surrender for Trial (Oct. 6): One of most-wanted war-crimes suspects is among group who turn themselves in to international tribunal.

Germany Raises Interest Rates (Oct. 9): Central Bank alarms world economic centers with first increase in five years; European stock markets suffer.

Political Crisis Settled in Italy (Oct. 14): Prime Minister Romano Prodi and Communists reach accord on budget restrictions to meet strict financial requirements for joining common European currency.

Yeltsin Blocks No-Confidence Vote (Oct. 15): Threatens to call early elections if Parliament passes measure that could impede his economic reforms.

Coup in Congo (Oct. 16): Denis Sassou-Nguesso, the former military ruler, takes over the presidential palace and, with help from Angola, overthrows President Pascal Lissouba, the country's first democratically elected president.

Nation

Reno Clears Clinton on Campaign Funds (Oct. 3): Attorney General, in letter to Republicans, says she has found no evidence that President misused his office for raising money. In separate action, she extends review of Vice President Gore's telephone solicitations. The review may lead to the appointment of an independent counsel.

Campaign-Finance Bill Blocked (Oct. 7): Republican leader uses procedural tactics to stalemate bipartisan bill on campaign finance reform.

President Defends Fund-Raising Actions (Oct. 8): Clinton seeks to calm furor over belated disclosure of White House videotapes of meetings with donors. Current and future advisers present same story to Congress and federal grand jury.

NEA Chairman to Resign (Oct. 8): Citing Congressional hostility toward the National Endowment for the Arts, Jane Alexander confirms her plans to step down as chairman.

U.S. Brands 30 Groups as Terrorist Threats (Oct. 8): Outlaws contributions to these foreign organizations and makes it illegal for their members to enter the U.S.

Attorney General Defends Actions (Oct. 9): Janet Reno aggressively defends the Justice Department handling of investigation into campaign finances.

Clinton Exercises Line-Item Veto (Oct. 14): He rejects 13 projects worth $141 million from Defense Department budget, having cut 38 items totalling $287 million from a military construction bill on Oct. 7.

Business/Science/Society

Religious Revival Rally Held in Capital (Oct. 4): Promise Keepers, an all-male evangelical Christian organization, holds one of the largest meetings ever in Washington.

Fossil Auctioned for $8.36 Million (Oct. 4): Most complete remains of Tyrannosaurus rex ever found are sold to Field Museum of Natural History in Chicago using funds from McDonald's and Disney, who will both display casts of the fossil.

Rockefeller Foundation Names President (Oct. 6): Appoints Dr. Gordon Conway, British agricultural ecologist at University of Sussex, as 12th head. He is the first non-American to lead the $2.8 billion foundation, which pledged $107 million in gifts in 1996.

Shuttle Returns U.S. Astronaut From *Mir* (Oct. 6): *Atlantis* brings Dr. Michael Foale back to Earth after troublesome 4½ months on Russian space station. Weather delayed the landing for a day.

Brightest Star Ever Is Discovered (Oct. 8): Hubble Space Telescope reveals object that would fill all of our solar system within Earth's orbit.

At Least 141 Dead in Pacific Coast Hurricane (Oct. 9): Pauline ravages strip of Mexico's shoreline, setting off deadly floods and landslides in the tourist resort area of Acapulco.

Nonsmoker Class-Action Lawsuit Settled (Oct. 10): Cigarette companies agree to pay $300 million to study tobacco-related diseases, but admit no link between passive smoke and illness. Industry must also pay legal fees of the 60,000 former and current airline flight attendants and their survivors, who brought the suit.

Jet Car Sets Land Speed Record (Oct. 15): British team reaches average speed of 763.035 mph in a 10-ton car powered by jet engines.

NASA Launches Plutonium-Powered Probe (Oct. 15): Despite protests from anti-nuclear activists who were concerned about radiation poisoning if the rocket exploded on the launch pad, the launch goes smoothly. The probe will travel 2.2 billion miles over seven years to explore Saturn's moons.

Former Highest-Ranking Enlisted Man in Army Arraigned (Oct. 16): Sgt. Major Gene McKinney pleads innocent to 20 criminal counts of sexual misconduct.

1997 Nobel Prize Winners

Peace: International Campaign to Ban Landmines (founded 1992) and Jody Williams (U.S.) for their work to ban and remove antipersonnel landmines worldwide. The Committee lauded their success in developing a "process which in the space of a few years changed a ban on anti-personnel mines from a vision to a feasible reality."

Literature: Dario Fo (Italy) for his work as a satirical dramatist, director, and actor. "With a blend of laughter and gravity, he opens our eyes to abuses and injustices in society and also the wider historical perspective in which they can be placed," the Committee said.

Physics: Steven Chu, William B. Phillips (both U.S.), and Claude Cohen-Tannoudji (France) for developing a method to cool and trap atoms using light from lasers. The discovery could lead to more accurate atomic clocks for use in space navigation.

Chemistry: Paul D. Boyer (U.S.), Jens C. Skou (Denmark), and John E. Walker (U.K.) for their discoveries about a molecule that allows the human body to store and transfer energy between cells. Skou received half the prize money for his discovery of an enzyme that works with adenosine triphosphate (ATP) to regulate levels of potassium and sodium in cells. Boyer and Walker shared the other half for their discovery of the process that creates ATP.

Medicine: Stanley B. Prusiner (U.S.) for his discovery of a new type of germ, called prions, that causes degenerative brain disorders, including "mad cow" disease. Critics conceded the existence of prions, but not that they cause disease.

Economics: Robert C. Merton and Myron S. Scholes (both U.S.) for developing a formula that determines the value of stock options and other derivatives.

People in the News

Marv Albert, sportscaster who became the focus of a lurid media feeding frenzy when he went on trial on felony charges of forcible sodomy. He later pleaded guilty to misdemeanor assault charges.

Madeleine Albright, born in Prague, became the first woman Secretary of State. Her reputation as a straight-talk negotiator with a personal touch developed during her tenure as U.S. representative to the U.N.

Marshall Applewhite, leader of the Heaven's Gate cult whose members believed that a space ship, hiding behind comet Hale-Bopp, would deliver them to the next phase of their lives after they committed suicide. Applewhite and 38 followers consumed lethal doses of phenobarbital and vodka in March.

Vernon Baker, 77-year-old veteran, one of seven black soldiers who received the Congressional Medal of Honor in January 1997 for his role in World War II. Baker is the only one still alive.

Ennis Cosby, son of actor Bill Cosby, was killed on January 16 as he was changing a tire near a freeway in Los Angeles. An 18-year-old Ukranian immigrant, **Mikail Markhasev,** was arrested in mid-March and charged with the crime.

Andrew Cunanan was found dead in a Florida boat house after a killing spree that included Italian designer **Gianni Versace.**

Ellen DeGeneres ended speculation about the sexual orientation of her TV character in a "coming out" episode. DeGeneres had declared earlier that she, too, was gay and announced that actress **Anne Heche** was her lover.

John du Pont, heir to the chemical empire, was ordered to reimburse Delaware County $742,107 for the cost of convicting him in the murder of Olympic wrestler **David Schultz.** Du Pont was sentenced to 13 to 30 years, having been found guilty but mentally ill in February.

Linda Finch, San Antonio businesswoman, completed a journey to retrace the final flight path of Amelia Earhart, who disappeared in the south Pacific more than sixty years ago. She flew the same make and model plane as Earhart, a restored 1935 Lockheed Electra 10E.

Lt. Kelly Flinn, first female bomber pilot, was allowed to resign from the Air Force rather than face court martial on charges of disobeying orders, fraternizing with an enlisted officer, and adultery. The charges were criticized by many civilians as unfairly targeting women, while military personnel criticized the Air Force's leniency in allowing her an uncharacterized (i.e., neither honorable nor dishonorable) discharge.

Alberto Fujimoro, President of Peru, ordered a raid on Tupac Amaru guerillas in the Japanese embassy in April. They had been holding Japanese diplomats since they took over the embassy in December 1996. None of the 14 rebels survived the raid.

Martina Hingis, 16-year-old Swiss tennis player, won the Australian Open, becoming the youngest female to win a Grand Slam event in 110 years.

John Huang, Democratic fund raiser, was linked to more than $1 million in questionable contributions.

Autumn Jackson, age 22, was found guilty of attempting to extort $40 million from **Bill Cosby,** whom she alleges is her father. Cosby had paid the woman's mother approximately $40,000 per year for her care, but had denied paternity.

Laurent Kabila led his rebel army to take city after city in Zaire. Once in power, he changed the name of the country to Democratic Republic of Congo, postponed elections for at least two years, and cracked down on opposition demonstrations.

Joe Kennedy withdrew from the Massachusetts gubernatorial race in the wake of publicity surrounding his request for an annulment of his first marriage and accusations

that his younger brother **Michael Kennedy** had had sex with his teenage babysitter. Cousin **John Kennedy, Jr.,** called the pair "poster boys for bad behavior" in the September issue of his *George* magazine.

Jonathan Levin, inner-city school teacher and son of Time-Warner executive Gerald Levin, was tortured and murdered by a former student who decided to rob him when Levin's wealthy parentage came to light.

Tara Lipinski, 14, became the youngest ever to win the Ladies' U.S. National Figure Skating Championship title. At 4' 8" and 75 pounds, it seems the downsizing trend has extended from the board room to the ice rink.

Abner Louima, Haitian immigrant brutalized by the New York City police when he was arrested outside a Brooklyn nightclub. Officers **Thomas Wiese, Thomas Bruder, Justin Volpe,** and **Charles Schwarz** were accused of beating Louima, and Volpe is accused of sexually assaulting and torturing him.

Sir Paul McCartney was knighted by Queen Elizabeth II for his service to music. He dedicated his knighthood to fellow ex-Beatles, **Ringo Starr, George Harrison,** and the late **John Lennon.**

Timothy McVeigh and **Terry Nichols,** accused in the Oklahoma City bombing in 1995, underwent separate trials in Denver on the federal charges stemming from the deaths of 8 federal employees. McVeigh was convicted in his trial and sentenced to death. Both still face trial in Oklahoma for the other 163 deaths.

Chris Patten, last British Governor of Hong Kong, presided over ceremonies on June 30 returning the former colony to China.

Gen. Joseph Ralston, who had been the leading candidate to become Chairman of the Joint Chiefs of Staff, opted to withdraw his name from consideration following disclosure of an adulterous affair he had more than a decade ago. The publicity over the military's seemingly inconsistent treatment of adultery by men and women soldiers led to calls for reform of the entire military penal code.

JonBenet Ramsey, 6-year-old beauty queen, was found murdered in her parents' Boulder, Colorado, home Dec. 26, 1996. Her death and the subsequent murder investigation drew attention to "Little Miss" beauty pageants, focusing on the ethics of sexualizing the innocence of young girls.

Trevor Rees-Jones was the sole survivor of the car crash in Paris that killed **Princess Diana,** her companion, film producer **Dodi al-Fayed,** and the driver **Henri Paul.** Paul's blood alcohol content was triple the French legal limit.

Tung Chee-hwa, who took over as governor of Hong Kong on July 1, is a mixture of Eastern and Western influences. Though born in China, he was raised in Hong Kong, educated in Britain, and employed in the U.S.

Ted Turner announced plans to donate $1 billion to the United Nations for humanitarian (i.e., *not* administrative) programs in a move he hoped would encourage philanthropy in other wealthy individuals.

Mike Tyson bit off a piece of opponent **Evander Holyfield's** ear in a heavyweight boxing match, resulting in a revocation of Tyson's boxing license and a fine of $3 million, which is the maximum 10 percent-of-purse allowed under Nevada regulations.

Gov. William Weld of Massachusetts resigned to actively lobby for his nomination to be Ambassador to Mexico. Senate Foreign Relations Committee Chairman **Jesse Helms** vowed from the outset to block the nomination by refusing to hold hearings to discuss it. Weld regarded the rhetoric as a challenge, and took his case to the media in a five-month fight before ultimately conceding defeat.

Tiger Woods became the youngest golfer ever to win the Masters Tournament.

Deaths

(October 1996–October 1997)

Adler, Dr. Kurt Alfred, 92: psychotherapist who sought to put into practice new approach developed by his father, famed Viennese psychiatrist, Alfred Adler. May 28, 1997.

Anderson, Eugenie M., 87: first U.S. woman ambassador. Appointed envoy to Denmark by President Truman in 1949. March 31, 1997.

Auerbach, Dr. Oscar, 92: pathologist who found first evidence in lung tissue of link between cancer and cigarette smoking. Jan. 15, 1997.

Ayres, Lew, 88: film actor famed for role in *All Quiet on the Western Front* in 1930. Played title role in *Young Dr. Kildare.* Dec. 30, 1996.

Bell, Quentin, 86: British author, artist, critic, and biographer of his aunt, the novelist Virginia Woolf. Chronicler of Bloomsbury artistic group. Dec. 16, 1996.

Bernardin, Joseph Cardinal, 68: Roman Catholic Archbishop of Chicago. A moderate church leader influential in American Catholicism. Nov. 14, 1996.

Berry, Richard, 61: songwriter famous for the three-chord rock song "Louie, Louie" (1956), which became an icon of American popular music and has been recorded hundreds of times. Jan. 25, 1997.

Brennan, William J., Jr., 91: retired Supreme Court Justice known for liberal vision of the Constitution as a vehicle for social and political change. July 24, 1997.

Burroughs, William S., 83: writer of Beat Generation. Best known for his controversial novel, *Naked Lunch,* his eccentric, drug-soaked life, and for accidentally shooting his wife to death while playing "William Tell." Aug. 2, 1997.

Caesar, Irving, 101: famed Tin Pan Alley lyricist. Wrote words for such favorite songs as "Tea for Two" and "Is It True What They Say about Dixie?" Dec. 17, 1996.

Cooke, Jack Kent, 84: built empire in newspapers, cable television, and sports. Owned Los Angeles Lakers, Washington Redskins, and the Chrysler building in New York. April 6, 1997.

Cousteau, Jacques, 87: French oceanographer and explorer. His books, films, and TV programs covered four decades of underseas exploration. June 25, 1997.

Danilova, Alexandra, 93: internationally famous ballet star known for theatrical flair. She performed with Diaghilev's Ballets Russes and other legendary dance companies. July 13, 1997.

de Kooning, Willem, 92: native of Holland who became an innovator in American art. Epitomized movement known as Abstract Expressionism. March 19, 1997.

Deng Xiaoping, 92: former leader of the Chinese Communist Party and one of its founding revolutionaries, and since 1978, the architect of economic modernization. Feb. 19, 1997.

Denver, John, 53: singer, composer, and actor known for his gentle country/folk songs and environmental concerns. Oct. 12, 1997.

Diana, Princess of Wales, 36: divorced wife of Prince Charles, heir to British throne. Famed for campaign against land mines, support for AIDS sufferers, and other causes. One of the world's most glamorous and popular women. Aug. 31, 1997.

Dicke, Dr. Robert H., 80: scientist who conducted classic experiments in gravity and was early believer in Big Bang theory of creation of universe. March 5, 1997.

Dickey, James, 73: hard-drinking Southern poet best known for his novel and screenplay, *Deliverance.* Jan. 21, 1997.

Dorris, Michael, 52: novelist who wrote about American Indian subjects and nonfiction writer of a memoir, *The Broken Cord,* that addressed fetal alcohol syndrome and won the National Book Critics Circle Award. April 10 or 11, 1997.

Draper, Paul, 86: intellectual and witty tap dancer, an international star in 1930s and '40s. Known for stylish dancing to classical music. Sept. 20, 1996.

Edel, Leon, 80: biographer whose writing on Henry James won Pulitzer Prize and National Book Award. Sept. 5, 1997.

Flemming, Arthur S., 91: Secretary of Health, Education, and Welfare from 1958 to 1961, under President Eisenhower. Also held other high posts in government and education. Sept. 7, 1996.

Fosdick, Dorothy, 83: foreign policy expert who helped in creation of United Nations, the Marshall Plan, and NATO, in the 1940s. Feb. 5, 1997.

Frankl, Dr. Victor E., 92: Viennese psychiatrist who used prisoner-of-war experience to write work on human survival, *Man's Search for Meaning,* that opened new avenues for modern psychotherapy. Sept. 2, 1997.

Fuchs, Joseph, 97: American violinist and teacher acclaimed for his performances of old and new music. March 14, 1997.

Ginsberg, Allen, 70: poet of the Beat Generation whose poem "Howl" inspired the sexual revolution and became an anthem of the counterculture. April 5, 1997.

Graham, Rev. Robert A., 84: an American Jesuit priest, one of the foremost Roman Catholic authorities on Vatican's role in rescue of Jews in World War II. Feb. 10, 1997.

Graham, Robert Klark, 90: made fortune by developing shatterproof plastic eyeglass lenses. Later established sperm bank, whose first donors were Nobel Prize winners. Feb. 13, 1997.

Harriman, Pamela, 76: U.S. Ambassador to France and a leading figure in Democratic Party, helping rebuild it in 1980s. Also known for her numerous high-profile marriages and liaisons. Feb. 5, 1997.

Helmsley, Harry B., 87: billionaire New York real estate broker and investor. Jan. 4, 1997.

Herzog, Chaim, 78: Israeli statesman. Served as President from 1983 to 1993, chief delegate to United Nations from 1975 to 1978, as well as many other high-ranking positions. April 17, 1997.

Hiss, Alger, 92: diplomat and government lawyer convicted of perjury in espionage case that became a Cold War riddle. He played important role in founding of United Nations. Nov. 15, 1996.

Hogan, Ben, 84: famous golf champion noted for wide influence on the game. July 25, 1997.

Huggins, Dr. Charles B., 95: winner of Nobel Prize for discoveries that led to drug treatment for cancer and to modern treatment of prostate and breast cancer. Jan. 12, 1997.

Jacobs, Helen Hull, 88: women's tennis champion. Winner of United States national title four straight times, 1932–1935; Wimbledon singles in 1936. Mainstay for U.S. Wightman Cup team, 1927–39. June 2, 1997.

Jagan, Cheddi B., 78: prominent Caribbean political leader. Led Guyana to independence. March 6, 1997.

Khariton, Yuli B., 92: Russian physicist who oversaw development of first Soviet atomic bomb. Dec. 19, 1996.

Klebnikov, George, 73: pioneer of simultaneous language interpretation at Nuremberg trials. Helped introduce it at United Nations. Nov. 12, 1996.

Kuralt, Charles, 62: CBS prize-winning journalist who roamed country to interview the ordinary and the obscure, also a noted war correspondent during Vietnam War. July 4, 1997.

Lane, Burton, 84: Broadway and Hollywood composer. Wrote melodies for *Finian's Rainbow* and such favorite songs as "On a Clear Day You Can See Forever." Jan. 5, 1997.

Leakey, Mary, 83: matriarch of fossil-hunting family. Noted for discovery of bones, stone tools, and footprints of early humans. Dec. 9, 1996.

Lichtenstein, Roy, 73: master of Pop painting who drew inspiration from comic pages. Sept. 2, 1997.

Lukas, J. Anthony, 64: Author and reporter who won two Pulitzer Prizes for exploration of racial and social fault lines in modern society. His most famous work, *Common Ground,* explored desegregation in Boston. June 5, 1997.

Manley, Michael, 72: former prime minister of Jamaica, socialist-turned-freemarketer, who governed the country during its turbulent period of unrest and poverty in the 1980s. March 6, 1997.

Mastroianni, Marcello, 72: Italian actor with romantic charm as Latin lover. An international star and a favorite of Fellini, he was featured in such films as *La Dolce Vita* and *8½.* Dec. 19, 1996.

Meredith, Burgess, 89: versatile actor on stage, screen, and in television. Career spanned most of twentieth century. Sept. 9, 1997.

Michener, James A., 90: won the Pulitzer Prize for his first book, *Tales of the South Pacific,* and went on to fill bestseller lists with monumental historical-geographical sagas. Oct. 16, 1997.

Mitchum, Robert, 79: veteran Hollywood screen actor famed for "tough guy" roles as criminal and war hero. July 1, 1997.

Mobutu Sese Seko, 66: Grandiose dictator of Zaire. Last of Cold War rulers who grew rich in providing bulwark against Communism. Sept. 7, 1997.

Mother Teresa, 87: Roman Catholic nun who won 1979 Nobel Peace Prize for work among the poorest of the world's poor. Had lived in India for five decades. Founded Missionaries of Charity. Famed globally for compassionate, effective way of sponsoring projects to aid the indigent and ill, orphans, lepers, and the dying. Sept. 5, 1997.

Nyro, Laura, 49: singer-songwriter who was a pioneer of introspective 1960s folk music. April 8, 1997.

Okudzhava, Bulat S., 73: Russian poet whose works helped create important literature of dissent in Soviet Union in 1950s and '60s. June 12, 1997.

Packard, Vance, 82: journalist and social critic who warned against advertising excesses, social climbing, and planned obsolescence. Dec. 12, 1996.

Pritchett, V. S., 96: versatile British writer, famous for more than six decades for works in fiction, nonfiction, biography, and literary criticism. March 20, 1997.

Rand, Paul, 82: pioneer in graphic design. Made innovative visual identities for major American companies. Adapted European avant-garde art movements of 1920s to commercial use. Nov. 26, 1996.

Rey, Margaret E., 90: children's book writer who collaborated with her husband, H. A. Rey, on the "Curious George" books. Dec. 23, 1996.

Richter, Sviatoslav, 82: world-famous Russian pianist. Aug. 8, 1997.

Robbins, Harold, 81: best-selling author who specialized in steamy novels about the rich and famous. Oct. 14, 1997.

Rosten, Leo, 88: writer, scholar, and language expert, author of *The Joys of Yiddish* and other works celebrating Jewish language and culture. Feb. 19, 1997.

Rowse. A. L., 93: Flamboyant British Shakespearean scholar who identified the "Dark Lady" of Shakespeare's sonnets. Oct. 3, 1997.

Royko, Mike, 64: caustic Chicago columnist who wrote the best-selling biography of Mayor Richard J. Daley, *Boss.* April 29, 1997.

Rozelle, Pete, 70: commissioner who oversaw changes that made National Football League premier professional sports organization for past four decades. Dec. 6, 1996.

Sagan, Carl, 62: Pulitzer Prize-winning astronomer acclaimed by millions through books and television appearances. Famed for belief that life might exist elsewhere in universe. Dec. 20, 1996.

Sarnoff, Robert W., 78: succeeded father as chairman of RCA Corporation and guided it into news and other businesses. Feb. 23, 1997.

Shabazz, Betty, 61: widow of Malcolm X and rights activist for black Americans. June 23, 1997.

Skelton, Red (Richard), 84: radio and TV comedian who charmed audience with miming and gentle wit. Sept. 17, 1997.

Stewart, James, 89: star of 88 movies, portraying roles of decent, folksy Americans; hero of U.S. Air Force in World War II. July 2, 1997.

Stone, Jon, 65: Emmy Award-winning writer, producer, and director. Helped create *Sesame Street* and its favorite characters. March 30, 1997.

Sutherland, Brig. Gen. Edwin Van Valkenberg, 82: career Army officer and scholar. Fought Germans in World War II and later headed English Department at West Point. Jan. 6, 1997.

Tartikoff, Brandon, 48: one of most successful showmen in network television. Aug. 27, 1997.

Tiny Tim (Herbert Khaury), 66?: ukulele player and falsetto singer known for a single song, "Tiptoe through the Tulips With Me." Nov. 30, 1996.

Tsongas, Paul E., 55: former Massachusetts Senator. Only presidential candidate in 1992 Democratic campaign to offer painful but realistic solutions to economic problems. Jan. 18, 1997.

Versace, Gianni, 50: Italian fashion designer famed for daring and innovative clothes inspired by pop culture. July 15, 1997.

Weisgall, Hugo, 84: composer and teacher known for use of atonality in opera and other works. March 11, 1997.

Zinnemann, Fred, 89: director of films dealing with issues of moral courage, including Academy-Award winning *From Here to Eternity* and *A Man for All Seasons.* March 14, 1997.

At Information Please, we never stop gathering information. After all, it's our mission to be the authoritative one-volume reference source with answers to all your questions.

"But what about all those late-breaking events that have occurred since my last edition?" you ask. Well, now we've got the answer for that, too:

Announcing the

1998 Information Please® Almanac
Mid-Year Supplement

Yours **FREE!**

(You pay only shipping and handling.)

This exclusive update supplements the *1998 Information Please Almanac* and puts today's most recent facts at your fingertips. No other printed almanac offers anything like it, and because you are a valued Information Please reader, we're offering it to you FREE.

The 1998 update will provide the latest profiles and statistics on:

Current Events in the U.S. and around the world
People in the News
U.S. and World Demographics
Science and Technology
Sports
Entertainment

To order, please send your **Name,** Company (if applicable), **Street Address,** P.O. Box (if applicable), **City, State, ZIP Code,** E-mail (if applicable), and **Phone Number,** along with a check or money order for $3.95 for shipping and handling, to:

Information Please LLC
Attn. Mid-Year Supplement
31 St. James Avenue
Boston, MA 02116-4101

The world of information is constantly changing. We hope you will take advantage of this unprecedented FREE offer to update your *1998 Information Please Almanac* today.

information
please LLC

Please note: Orders must be received by August 31, 1998. Please print all information clearly; incomplete orders cannot be processed. Supplement will be issued in July 1998. Please allow 2–4 weeks for delivery. Offer good while supplies last.